KLINCK MEMORIAL LIBRARY
Concordia College
River Forest, IL 60305

WITHDRAWN

KLINCK MEMORIAL LIBRARY
Concordia College
River Forest, IL 60305

EARLIER PUBLICATIONS IN THIS SERIES

EDUCATIONAL, PSYCHOLOGICAL, AND PERSONALITY TESTS OF 1933 AND 1934

EDUCATIONAL, PSYCHOLOGICAL, AND PERSONALITY TESTS OF 1933, 1934, AND 1935

EDUCATIONAL, PSYCHOLOGICAL, AND PERSONALITY TESTS OF 1936

THE NINETEEN THIRTY-EIGHT MENTAL MEASUREMENTS YEARBOOK

THE NINETEEN FORTY MENTAL MEASUREMENTS YEARBOOK

THE THIRD MENTAL MEASUREMENTS YEARBOOK

THE FOURTH MENTAL MEASUREMENTS YEARBOOK

THE FIFTH MENTAL MEASUREMENTS YEARBOOK

TESTS IN PRINT

THE SIXTH MENTAL MEASUREMENTS YEARBOOK

READING TESTS AND REVIEWS

PERSONALITY TESTS AND REVIEWS

THE SEVENTH MENTAL MEASUREMENTS YEARBOOK

TESTS IN PRINT II

ENGLISH TESTS AND REVIEWS

FOREIGN LANGUAGE TESTS AND REVIEWS

INTELLIGENCE TESTS AND REVIEWS

MATHEMATICS TESTS AND REVIEWS

PERSONALITY TESTS AND REVIEWS II

READING TESTS AND REVIEWS II

SCIENCE TESTS AND REVIEWS

SOCIAL STUDIES TESTS AND REVIEWS

VOCATIONAL TESTS AND REVIEWS

THE EIGHTH MENTAL MEASUREMENTS YEARBOOK

TESTS IN PRINT III

ASSOCIATE EDITORS
Stephen N. Elliott (Assistant Director)
Joseph C. Witt

CHIEF EDITORIAL ASSOCIATE
Debra A. Funk

PRODUCTION AND SECRETARIAL
Linda R. Weber (Secretarial Specialist)
Evelyn K. Johnson (Clerical Assistant III)

TESTS
IN PRINT III

AN INDEX TO TESTS,
TEST REVIEWS, AND THE LITERATURE
ON SPECIFIC TESTS

Edited by

JAMES V. MITCHELL, JR.
Director, The Buros Institute of Mental Measurements

KLINCK MEMORIAL LIBRARY
Concordia College
River Forest, IL 60305

The Buros Institute of Mental Measurements
The University of Nebraska-Lincoln
Lincoln, Nebraska
1983
Distributed by The University of Nebraska Press

Copyright 1983 and published by the Buros Institute of Mental Measurements of
The University of Nebraska-Lincoln, 135 Bancroft Hall, The University of
Nebraska-Lincoln, Lincoln, Nebraska 68588-0348. No part of this publication may be
reproduced in any form nor may any of the contents be used in an informational storage,
retrieval, or transmission system without the prior written permission of the publisher.

ISBN 910674-52-3

To the memory of
OSCAR KRISEN BUROS

TABLE OF CONTENTS

	Page
MMY TEST REVIEWERS	xi
PREFACE	xxiii
INTRODUCTION	xxv
TESTS IN PRINT	1
INDEX OF TITLES	487
CLASSIFIED SUBJECT INDEX	521
PUBLISHERS DIRECTORY AND INDEX	567
INDEX OF NAMES	579

TEST REVIEWERS[1]

Ira E. Aaron, 6–8
Harold H. Abelson, 3
Murray Aborn, 4
Fred L. Adair, 8
Clifford R. Adams, 6
Elizabeth C. Adams, 4
Georgia S. Adams, 7–8
Mary Friend Adams, 8
C. J. Adcock, 5–7
Dorothy C. Adkins, 3–7
Dan L. Adler, 5
Janet G. Afflerbach, 5
Lois G. Afflerbach, 5
Frederick B. Agard, 3
J. Stanley Ahmann, 6–8
Mary D. Ainsworth, 5
Peter W. Airasian, 8
Lewis E. Albright, 6–8
Norma A. Albright, 2
John Charles Alderson, 8
Lawrence M. Aleamoni, 8
Henry A. Alker, 7–8
Robert M. Allen, 8
John C. Almack, 1–2
William D. Altus, 4
Jean D. Amberson, 4
Sueann Robinson Ambron, 8
Vera M. Amerson, 3
Anne Anastasi, 1–8
Nicholas Anastasiow, 7–8
Oliver F. Anderhalter, 4, 6–7
Charles V. Anderson, 8
Howard R. Anderson, 1–7
Irving H. Anderson, 1, 3

James M. Anderson, 3–4, 6
Kenneth E. Anderson, 4, 6
Robert P. Anderson, 8
Lawrence Andrus, 2
Harvey A. Andruss, 3
Edgar Anstey, 6
James A. Armentrout, 8
Christian O. Arndt, 2
Dwight L. Arnold, 4–5
Gwen F. Arnold, 4
Theodore A. Ashford, 3, 5
Lear Ashmore, 8
Alexander W. Astin, 6–7
Samuel D. Atkins, 1–2
Mary C. Austin, 6
Frederic L. Ayer, 3–4
George W. Ayer, 8
J. Douglas Ayers, 6–8
James C. Babcock, 2
Andrew R. Baggaley, 5–6
Leonard L. Baird, 7
Thomas S. Baldwin, 7–8
Benjamin Balinsky, 4–5
Rachel S. Ball, 2
Warren R. Baller, 4–5
Irol W. Balsley, 6
Charlotte E. K. Banks, 4–5
Nicholas W. Bankson, 8
Allan G. Barclay, 7
Walter Barnes, 1
W. Leslie Barnette, Jr., 8
A. S. Barr, 3
Rebecca C. Barr, 7–8
Richard S. Barrett, 6

Thomas C. Barrett, 6
Frank Barron, 5
W. L. Bashaw, 7
Alan R. Bass, 8
Robert H. Bauernfeind, 5–8
Brent Baxter, 3–5
Ernest Edward Bayles, 1
Nancy Bayley, 2–3, 5
Kenneth L. Bean, 5–6
Robert M. Bear, 3–4
Harold P. Bechtoldt, 4–7
Roland L. Beck, 2–3
Samuel J. Beck, 2, 5
Wesley C. Becker, 6
Ralph C. Bedell, 3, 5
H. R. Beech, 6
Fred S. Beers, 1
E. G. Begle, 7–8
Isaac I. Bejar, 8
John E. Bell, 4–6
Albert A. Bennett, 2–3
George K. Bennett, 3–7
Peter M. Bentler, 6–7
Arthur L. Benton, 3–4, 7
H. E. Benz, 2
Ralph F. Berdie, 3–7
Harry D. Berg, 3–8
Paul Conrad Berg, 7
Allen Berger, 7–8
Michael Berger, 8
Robert G. Bernreuter, 1–4
Emmett A. Betts, 6
William Betz, 1, 3
Charles L. Bickel, 2

[1] Numbers after names represent the *Mental Measurements Yearbooks* in which reviews appear.

Marion A. Bills, 3
Walter V. Bingham, 1
William C. Bingham, 6, 8
L. B. Birch, 6–7
Reign H. Bittner, 3–4
Harold H. Bixler, 3–4
Ake Bjerstedt, 5–6
Donald B. Black, 6–7
Hillel Black, 6
John D. Black, 5–6, 8
J. M. Blackburn, 2
James H. Blackhurst, 1
E. G. Blackstone, 3
C. B. Blakemore, 6
Emery P. Bliesmer, 6
Jack Block, 8
Paul J. Blommers, 3–6
Benjamin S. Bloom, 3–5, 7
Bruce M. Bloxom, 7–8
Milton L. Blum, 3–4
Jack L. Bodden, 7–8
Joan Bollenbacher, 5
Brian F. Bolton, 8
Guy L. Bond, 2
Ivan A. Booker, 1–4
Daniel R. Boone, 7–8
Edward S. Bordin, 3–5
Fred H. Borgen, 7–8
Harold Borko, 6–7
Walter C. Borman, 8
John R. Bormuth, 7
Morton Bortner, 6, 8
Thomas J. Bouchard, Jr., 7–8
John E. Bowers, 6
E. J. G. Bradford, 3–4
Francis F. Bradshaw, 1
James Braswell, 7–8
John R. Braun, 7–8
Arthur H. Brayfield, 4–6
W. C. Brenke, 3
Ann Brewington, 3
Ann Brickner, 7
Robert G. Bridgham, 7
M. Alan Brimer, 5–7
Stanley L. Brodsky, 8
Hubert E. Brogden, 3–4
Nelson Brooks, 1–6
M. Eustace Broom, 2
R. A. Brotemarkle, 3
Alfred S. Brown, 3
Andrew W. Brown, 2
Charles M. Brown, 6
Clara M. Brown, 1–2
Frederick G. Brown, 7–8
William A. Brownell, 1–5
Leo J. Brueckner, 1–4
James E. Bryan, 5–8
Miriam M. Bryan, 4, 6–8

N. Dale Bryant, 5–8
Aaron D. Buchanan, 8
William D. Buffington, 8
Robert L. Burch, 4
Kenneth E. Burchett, 8
Thomas C. Burgess, 6
Carolyn L. Burke, 7
R. Will Burnett, 4
Paul S. Burnham, 3
Donald G. Burns, 4
Emily T. Burr, 3
Alvin G. Burstein, 6–7
Cyril Burt, 3, 5
Nancy W. Burton, 7
Guy T. Buswell, 2
H. J. Butcher, 7
James N. Butcher, 8
Katharine G. Butler, 7–8
Dorcas Susan Butt, 8
Margaret C. Byrne, 7–8
Leonard S. Cahen, 7–8
G. P. Cahoon, 3–4
James R. Caldwell, 7
Kathryn Hoover Calfee, 8
Robert C. Calfee, 8
Leroy G. Callahan, 8
David P. Campbell, 6–8
Donald T. Campbell, 4–6
Dugal Campbell, 6
J. Arthur Campbell, 6, 8
Joel T. Campbell, 6–7
Vincent N. Campbell, 7
Kenneth A. Carlson, 8
Thorsten R. Carlson, 7–8
W. L. Carr, 2
David J. Carroll, 8
John B. Carroll, 4–8
L. Ray Carry, 7
Harold D. Carter, 1–4
Launor F. Carter, 4
W. H. Cartwright, 3
Frank P. Cassaretto, 5
Burton M. Castner, 2
Robert S. Cathcart, 5
Psyche Cattell, 1, 3
Raymond B. Cattell, 2
Courtney B. Cazden, 7–8
Stella Center, 1
Edward J. Cervenka, 8
Hester Chadderdon, 1–2, 4
Robert C. Challman, 4, 6–7
E. G. Chambers, 3–5
Laura H. Chapman, 8
Clinton I. Chase, 7–8
Henry Chauncey, 3, 6
Maurice Chazan, 7
Brad S. Chissom, 7–8
Edmund P. Churchill, 3

Ruth D. Churchill, 3, 5
Cherry Ann Clark, 5
D. F. Clark, 7
Gale W. Clark, 5
J. F. Clark, 5
John L. D. Clark, 7–8
John R. Clark, 2
Kenneth E. Clark, 4
Philip M. Clark, 8
Stanley Clark, 4–6
Willis W. Clark, 6
H. Harrison Clarke, 4
Glen U. Cleeton, 3
W. V. Clemans, 6
Dorothy M. Clendenen, 5–7
Victor B. Cline, 7
James R. Clopton, 8
Richard W. Coan, 6–8
Charles N. Cofer, 3–5
William E. Coffman, 3, 5–8
Bertram D. Cohen, 6, 8
Jacob Cohen, 6–8
John Cohen, 3
S. Alan Cohen, 7
Stephen L. Cohen, 8
Nancy S. Cole, 7–8
Roberta R. Collard, 7
Richard Colwell, 7–8
W. D. Commins, 1–4
Andrew L. Comrey, 5, 7–8
Clinton C. Conrad, 2
Herbert S. Conrad, 1–4
John Cook, 7–8
Walter W. Cook, 2–3, 5
William W. Cooley, 6
Clyde H. Coombs, 3
Stephen M. Corey, 1–2
Ethel L. Cornell, 1
Frank Costin, 8
William C. Cottle, 5
Stuart A. Courtis, 1, 4
Douglas Courtney, 3–4
John A. Cox, Jr., 5
Marion Monroe Cox, 1, 3
Richard C. Cox, 8
Rick Crandall, 8
A. Garr Cranney, 8
Charles J. Cranny, 8
Albert B. Crawford, 2
William R. Crawford, 6–7
William J. E. Crissy, 4
R. Lenox Criswell, 2
John O. Crites, 6–8
Lysle W. Croft, 3–4
Lee J. Cronbach, 3–8
Douglas P. Crowne, 6
William M. Cruickshank, 4
Thomas E. Culliton, Jr., 6

MMY TEST REVIEWERS

Edward E. Cureton, 1–2, 4
Louise W. Cureton, 4
Thomas K. Cureton, 3
William Curr, 5
Francis D. Curtis, 1–2
Peter A. Dahl, 8
W. Grant Dahlstrom, 4–6, 8
John T. Dailey, 4–5
Edgar Dale, 3
Reginald R. Dale, 5
Fred Damarin, 8
Richard H. Dana, 5–8
John C. Daniels, 5
John G. Darley, 1–2
Richard E. Darnell, 8
Jane Dass, 8
John H. Daugherty, 3
Charlotte Croon Davis, 3–6, 8
D. Russell Davis, 4–5
Edwin W. Davis, 3
Frederick B. Davis, 1–5, 7
Parker Davis, Jr., 3
Paul C. Davis, 6
Robert A. Davis, 3
Stanley E. Davis, 6
Helen C. Dawe, 3
Robyn M. Dawes, 8
Carolyn Dawson, 8
Lester W. Dearborn, 6
James Deese, 5
Frank P. DeLay, 2
Gabriel M. Della-Piana, 6
Vincent J. Dell'Orto, 8
Dennis J. Deloria, 7–8
Harold A. Delp, 4
Randy Demaline, 8
Robert G. Demaree, 4, 7–8
George D. Demos, 6
Evelyn Deno, 7
Susan K. Deri, 3
Clarence Derrick, 4–8
Mayhew Derryberry, 3
Lawrence G. Derthick, 5
Harry R. DeSilva, 2
M. Vere DeVault, 7
Edward F. deVillafranca, 8
Joseph C. Dewey, 1–2
Esther E. Diamond, 8
Louis M. DiCarlo, 6
Charles F. Dicken, 6
Gwendolen S. Dickson, 1, 3
Paul B. Diederich, 1–2, 7
John S. Diekhoff, 3–5
Robert L. Dipboye, 8
Richard F. Docter, 7
Robert H. Dolliver, 7–8
George Domino, 7–8
Thomas F. Donlon, 8

Jerome E. Doppelt, 4–8
Harl R. Douglass, 2–3
N. M. Downie, 6
John Downing, 8
Kenneth O. Doyle, Jr., 8
Vincent R. D'Oyley, 7
Raleigh M. Drake, 2–5
Richard M. Drake, 2–3
Ralph Mason Dreger, 8
Arnold Dresden, 1
Paul L. Dressel, 3–8
James Drever, 2
Philip H. Dreyer, 8
Laura A. Driscoll, 8
Robert C. Droege, 7
Priscilla A. Drum, 8
Philip H. DuBois, 3, 6–7
Gerald G. Duffy, 7
Lydia A. Duggins, 5
Stanley G. Dulsky, 2–3
Harold B. Dunkel, 2–6
Jack W. Dunlap, 1–3
James A. Dunn, 7
S. S. Dunn, 5–6
Marvin D. Dunnette, 6
Daniel R. Dupecher, 8
Walter N. Durost, 4–8
Ralph D. Dutch, 6–8
August Dvorak, 2
Beatrice J. Dvorak, 3
Carol Anne Dwyer, 8
Henry S. Dyer, 5–6
Robert Dykstra, 7–8
Norman Eagle 5, 7–8
Maurice J. Eash, 8
Howard Easley, 2
Robert L. Ebel, 4–8
Allen L. Edwards, 6
Bateman Edwards, 2
Reginald Edwards, 5
Byron R. Egeland, 8
Lee H. Ehman, 8
William J. Eichman, 6–8
Dorothy H. Eichorn, 5–8
Philip Eisenberg, 3
William Eller, 6
Warwick B. Elley, 8
M. H. Elliott, 3
Albert Ellis, 3–7
Lon L. Emerick, 8
W. G. Emmett, 3–4
Norman S. Endler, 8
Max D. Engelhart, 1–2, 4–6
Bertram Epstein, 4
Gerald L. Ericksen, 6–7
Lawrence W. Erickson, 6–8
Richard C. Erickson, 8
Emanuel E. Ericson, 2

Leonard D. Eron, 5–7
Anna S. Espenschade, 4–5
Barbara F. Esser, 6–7
Alvin C. Eurich, 1–2
Alexander Even, 7
Lorraine D. Eyde, 8
H. J. Eysenck, 3–8
Paul R. Farnsworth, 1–3, 5–6
Roger Farr, 7–8
Ray N. Faulkner, 1–2
Harold P. Fawcett, 2–5
Jay W. Fay, 1
Ethel M. Feagley, 3
Howard F. Fehr, 4
Elizabeth Fehrer, 3
Henry Feinberg, 1
Shirley C. Feldmann, 8
Leonard S. Feldt, 5–8
George A. Ferguson, 3–6
Leonard W. Ferguson, 6
Robert H. Ferrell, 5
C. E. Ficken, 2
James A. Field, Jr., 5
Gordon Fifer, 5
Nikola N. Filby, 8
Warren G. Findley, 2–8
Stefan R. Fink, 8
Seymour Fisher, 6
Wayne D. Fisher, 6
Joshua A. Fishman, 5
Donald W. Fiske, 5
James A. Fitzgerald, 5
Robert Fitzpatrick, 7–8
John C. Flanagan, 1, 3–4, 6
C. M. Fleming, 4
W. G. Fleming, 6
Charles D. Flory, 1, 3
John P. Foley, Jr., 5–7
Joseph J. Foley, 8
Mary O. Folsom, 7
Marie C. Fontana, 8
Thomas G. Foran, 1
Bertram R. Forer, 6
Frank J. Fornoff, 6, 8
Elaine Forsyth, 3
Robert A. Forsyth, 7–8
Tomlinson Fort, 2
Judson W. Foust, 2
Hanford M. Fowler, 4–5
Raymond D. Fowler, Jr., 7–8
Charles Fox, 2
Lynn H. Fox, 8
Austin C. Frank, 8
Thomas T. Frantz, 7–8
Elizabeth D. Fraser, 5–6
Wayne A. Frederick, 5
Norman Frederiksen, 3–8
Frank S. Freeman, 4–5

David Freides, 7–8
J. Joseph Freilinger, 8
John W. French, 3–8
Joseph L. French, 7
Robert L. French, 6
Sidney J. French, 3
Benno G. Fricke, 5–6
David A. Frisbie, 8
Clifford P. Froehlich, 4–5
Gustav J. Froehlich, 3–6
Benjamin Fruchter, 5
F. P. Frutchey, 1
Edward B. Fry, 6–8
Douglas H. Fryer, 3
Verne C. Fryklund, 2
Paul H. Furfey, 1
Edward J. Furst, 6–8
N. L. Gage, 4–5
Eugene L. Gaier, 5
Rosslyn Gaines, 7
Bessie Lee Gambrill, 2
Eric F. Gardner, 4–8
Sol L. Garfield, 7
Alan Garfinkel, 8
Edgar R. Garrett, 7
Henry E. Garrett, 1–5
Ann L. Gebhardt, 2
Karl W. Gehrkens, 2
Kenneth E. Gell, 2
J. Raymond Gerberich, 2–6
Joanne C. Gersten, 8
John J. Geyer, 7–8
Edwin E. Ghiselli, 3
Cecil A. Gibb, 5–7
H. H. Giles, 1–2
John W. Gittinger, 5
Gene V Glass, 7–8
James R. Glennon, 6
Goldine C. Gleser, 6–8
Marvin D. Glock, 5–7
Lewis R. Goldberg, 7–8
Stephen L. Golding, 8
Bert A. Goldman, 6–7
Leo Goldman, 6
Ronald Goldman, 8
Marcel L. Goldschmid, 7
Keith Goltry, 2
Elizabeth J. Goodacre, 7
Florence L. Goodenough, 2–3
Clarence J. Goodnight, 7
Leonard D. Goodstein, 6–8
William L. Goodwin, 8
Edwin Gordon, 7
Hans C. Gordon, 2–3
Leonard V. Gordon, 6–8
Harrison G. Gough, 4–8
Neil Gourlay, 5
C. Ray Graham, 8

Grace Graham, 1–2
William S. Gray, 1, 3–4
Russel F. Green, 6–7
Edward B. Greene, 3–5
Harry A. Greene, 2–3
Konrad Gries, 4–5
J. Jeffrey Grill, 8
Arnold B. Grobman, 7
Hulda Grobman, 7–8
Patrick Groff, 8
Norman E. Gronlund, 8
Richard E. Gross, 5–8
Foster E. Grossnickle, 1–4
William R. Grove, 3–4
Wilson H. Guertin, 5–6
Walter S. Guiler, 4
J. P. Guilford, 1–5
Robert M. Guion, 8
Arlen R. Gullickson, 7–8
R. Gulliford, 7
Harold Gulliksen, 1–2, 4
John Flagg Gummere, 2
John W. Gustad, 5
George M. Guthrie, 8
John T. Guthrie, 7–8
Malcolm D. Gynther, 7–8
Laura B. Hadley, 2
John H. Haefner, 5–6
Elizabeth Hagen, 5–7
Michio P. Hagiwara, 7–8
Milton E. Hahn, 3–4, 6
A. Ralph Hakstian, 7–8
Alfred E. Hall, 8
W. E. Hall, 3
Wallace B. Hall, 6
Raphael M. Haller, 7–8
Harvey Halpern, 8
Ronald K. Hambleton, 8
E. W. Hamilton, 6
Nelson G. Hanawalt, 3–5
C. H. Handschin, 2
Gerald S. Hanna, 8
Lavone A. Hanna, 2–3
Paul R. Hanna, 4
Jo–Ida C. Hansen, 8
Gary R. Hanson, 7
Lenore W. Harmon, 8
Robert A. Harper, 6–7
Thomas W. Harrell, 3
Philip L. Harriman, 4–6
Albert J. Harris, 3, 6–7
Chester W. Harris, 3–4
Dale B. Harris, 4–8
David P. Harris, 7–8
Jesse G. Harris, Jr., 6
Larry A. Harris, 7–8
Robert C. Harris, 7
Theodore L. Harris, 6

Mary T. Harrison, 7
Charles M. Harsh, 3–4
Ruth N. Hartley, 8
George W. Hartmann, 1, 4
Rodney T. Hartnett, 8
Louis D. Hartson, 1
Maurice L. Hartung, 1, 3
Glen Hass, 3
J. O. Hassler, 1–2
J. Thomas Hastings, 4–6, 8
Richard S. Hatch, 6
Starke R. Hathaway, 3
John T. Hatten, 8
G. E. Hawkins, 2
David G. Hawkridge, 7–8
Mary R. Haworth, 5–6
Edward N. Hay, 3–5
James R. Hayden, 5–6
Leslie M. Haynes, 4
Kenneth L. Heaton, 4
Earle R. Hedrick, 2
David K. Heenan, 5–6
Lloyd H. Heidgerd, 6
Louis M. Heil, 2
Alfred B. Heilbrun, Jr., 5–8
Alice W. Heim, 4–7
Harry Heller, 2
William H. Helme, 6
G. C. Helmstadter, 7
John K. Hemphill, 6–7
V. A. C. Henmon, 1
Edwin R. Henry, 4
William E. Henry, 4–5
William Hered, 6
David O. Herman, 6–8
Virgil E. Herrick, 4–5
A. N. Hieronymus, 5–7
E. H. C. Hildebrandt, 3
Walker H. Hill, 5
John R. Hills, 6–8
Philip Himelstein, 7
Elmer D. Hinckley, 4
C. B. Hindley, 6
Marshall S. Hiskey, 6–7
Jean Hoard, 2
James R. Hobson, 2–5
Emil H. Hoch, 8
Elton Hocking, 3–4
James O. Hodges, 8
Robert Hogan, 7–8
Thomas P. Hogan, 8
Dorothy E. Holberg, 3
Raymond H. Holden, 7
Warren S. Holmes, 2
Robert R. Holt, 4
Wayne H. Holtzman, 5, 7
Charles Holzwarth, 2
Charles H. Honzik, 4

Marjorie P. Honzik, 6–7
Albert B. Hood, 8
Joyce E. Hood, 8
Stephen B. Hood, 8
Florence E. Hooper, 3
Kenneth D. Hopkins 6–8
John L. Horn, 7
Thomas D. Horn, 7–8
John E. Horrocks, 5–6
Clark W. Horton, 2–5
Daniel L. Householder, 8
Carl I. Hovland, 3–5
Robert W. Howard, 2
Edgar Howarth, 8
Duncan Howie, 5
Monica M. Hoye, 3
Cyril J. Hoyt, 4–7
Kenneth B. Hoyt, 6
Carl J. Huberty, 7–8
Edith M. Huddleston, 4
Mildred H. Huebner, 7–8
Violet Hughes, 2
Doncaster G. Humm, 2
Lloyd G. Humphreys, 3–6
John D. Hundleby, 6
Stephen Hunka, 6
Albert L. Hunsicker, 4
E. Patricia Hunt, 2
Jane V. Hunt, 7–8
Thelma Hunt, 3
William A. Hunt, 3
George W. Hunter, 1–2
Archer W. Hurd, 1
Ludwig Immergluck, 3
Henry A. Imus, 3
Mario Iona, 8
Margaret Ives, 3
Edward F. Iwanicki, 8
Douglas N. Jackson, 7–8
Joseph F. Jackson, 2–3
Robert W. B. Jackson, 5
Richard M. Jaeger, 8
Alice N. Jameson, 3
Colleen B. Jamison, 7
Frank C. Jean, 1
John R. Jennings, 5
Arthur R. Jensen, 5–7
Carl F. Jesness, 7
Richard Jessor, 5
Frank B. Jex, 6
A. Pemberton Johnson, 5
Cecil D. Johnson, 5
Dale D. Johnson, 8
Laura B. Johnson, 2
Leland P. Johnson, 4
Marjorie S. Johnson, 8
Palmer O. Johnson, 1–5
Richard T. Johnson, 6–8

Richard W. Johnson, 8
Joseph A. Johnston, 7
Carleton C. Jones, 1–2
Clive Jones, 7
David Jones, 7
Dorothy L. Jones, 7
Edward S. Jones, 1–2
F. Nowell Jones, 3
H. Gwynne Jones, 6
Harold E. Jones, 1–4
Kenneth J. Jones, 6
Randall L. Jones, 8
Robert A. Jones, 5
Worth R. Jones, 5–6
A. M. Jordan, 2
Richard H. Jordan, 3
Helen L. Jorstad, 8
Ehud Jungwirth, 8
Clifford E. Jurgensen, 3–6
Joseph Justman, 5
Paul E. Kambly, 4
Harry W. Karn, 4
M. Ray Karnes, 4
Lawrence M. Kasdon, 7–8
Walter Kass, 5
Edward S. Katkin, 8
Walter Katkovsky, 6
Martin R. Katz, 5–8
Raymond A. Katzell, 3–8
Alan S. Kaufman, 8
Walter V. Kaulfers, 1–7
Michael J. Kavanagh, 8
T. J. Keating, 2
J. A. Keats, 5–6
Penelope Kegel–Flom, 8
Gertrude Keir, 4
Thomas Kellaghan, 8
Truman L. Kelley, 2
Theodore E. Kellogg, 4–5
E. Lowell Kelly, 3–7
William E. Kendall, 6
Katherine G. Keneally, 4
James E. Kennedy, 6–7
Douglas T. Kenny, 5
Grace H. Kent, 2–3
Barbara K. Keogh, 8
Robert E. Keohane, 2
Newell C. Kephart, 7
Willard A. Kerr, 3–4, 6–7
Gilbert C. Kettelkamp, 6
Thomas E. Kieren, 8
Jeremy Kilpatrick, 7–8
Elaine F. Kinder, 1
Glen D. King, 8
Joseph E. King, 3
Forrest A. Kingsbury, 2
Albert J. Kingston, 6–8
Lucien B. Kinney, 2, 4

John R. Kinzer, 3
Wayne K. Kirchner, 6
Barbara A. Kirk, 7
Philip M. Kitay, 6–7
Tom Kitwood, 8
Paul M. Kjeldergaard, 6
Seymour G. Klebanoff, 4
Benjamin Kleinmuntz, 6–8
Milton V. Kline, 6
Paul Kline, 7–8
William E. Kline, 7–8
Martin Kling, 7–8
Robert R. Knapp, 7
John F. Knutson, 7
Kate L. Kogan, 3–4
William S. Kogan, 4
David Kopel, 1–2
Abraham K. Korman, 8
Stephen M. Koziol, Jr., 8
David R. Krathwohl, 5
Charles J. Krauskopf, 7–8
Roy A. Kress, 7–8
A. C. Krey, 1
Philip H. Kriedt, 6
Russell P. Kropp, 5
Morris Krugman, 3–5
John D. Krumboltz, 6
Frederic Kuder, 2–3
F. Kuhlmann, 2
Dana G. Kurfman, 7–8
Albert K. Kurtz, 4–6, 8
W. C. Kvaraceus, 3–4
Lou LaBrant, 2
Eleanor M. Ladd, 8
Robert Lado, 7
Tom A. Lamke, 5
Elaine L. La Monica, 8
W. Elmer Lancaster 2,
Daniel Landis, 7
Herbert A. Landry, 2
Edward Landy, 5
Frank J. Landy, 8
Theos A. Langlie, 1
Charles R. Langmuir, 3–6
Gerald V. Lannholm, 3–5
Richard I. Lanyon, 7–8
Luis M. Laosa, 8
Glenda Lappan, 8
Peter A. Lappan, Jr., 6–8
William S. Larson, 2–6
Julian J. Lasky, 7
Robert L. Lathrop, 7
Allan L. LaVoie, 8
J. S. Lawes, 6–7
C. H. Lawshe, Jr., 3
Martha E. Layman, 4
Wilbur L. Layton, 4–8
Herbert Lederer, 8

Richard Ledgerwood, 1
J. Murray Lee, 1, 5
S. G. Lee, 6–7
D. Welty Lefever, 1–6
Paul R. Lehman, 7–8
Irvin J. Lehmann, 6–8
Roger T. Lennon, 4–5
Theodore, F. Lentz, 3
J. Paul Leonard, 2–3
Donald A. Leton, 7–8
Eugene E. Levitt, 6–8
Philip M. Levy, 6
Seymour Levy, 6
Roy D. Lewis, 5
Lester M. Libo, 7–8
John Liggett, 5–6
Paul M. Limbert, 1
E. F. Lindquist, 5
Mary Montgomery Lindquist, 8
C. Mauritz Lindvall, 7–8
W. Line, 2
James C. Lingoes, 6
James B. Lingwall, 8
Robert L. Linn, 8
Gary E. Lintereur, 8
William M. Littell, 7
Orrel E. Little, 3
Alice K. Liveright, 2
Aileene S. Lockhart, 7
Jane Loevinger, 4, 8
R. Duane Logue, 8
Paul R. Lohnes, 6–8
Walter F. W. Lohnes, 7
Paul S. Lomax, 3
John W. Lombard, 7–8
John A. Long, 3
Louis Long, 3
Andrew Longacre, 2
Frank M. Loos, 4
Peter G. Loret, 6
Irving Lorge, 2–3, 5
Margaret F. Lorimer, 6
Maurice Lorr, 5–8
C. M. Louttit, 1–4
Kenneth Lovell, 6–7
Ruth Lowes, 3
Ardie Lubin, 4
William H. Lucio, 6
William H. Lucow, 5
James Lumsden, 5, 8
Robert W. Lundin, 5–7
Clifford E. Lunneborg, 7–8
Patricia W. Lunneborg, 8
David T. Lykken, 6–8
Howard B. Lyman, 6–7
Hugh Lytton, 8
Henry S. Maas, 3
Charles C. McArthur, 7

John N. McCall, 7
Raymond J. McCall, 5
W. C. McCall, 2
William A. McCall, 2
James M. McCallister, 3
Boyd R. McCandless, 4, 6–7
James J. McCarthy, 7–8
James Leslie McCary, 8
Robert L. McCaul, 2–3
Clara J. McCauley, 2
R. W. McCulloch, 5
Constance M. McCullough, 2–3, 5, 7
S. P. McCutchen, 1–2
Arthur S. McDonald, 6
D. W. McElwain, 4–5
William C. McGaghie, 8
Christine H. McGuire, 5–8
Wilbert J. McKeachie, 8
Michael G. McKee, 7
Gordon N. Mackenzie, 3–4
Margaret G. McKim, 3–4
Arthur C. MacKinney, 6–8
Saunders Mac Lane, 6
Kenneth F. McLaughlin, 6
John McLeish, 4, 7
Jonathon C. McLendon, 6
John McLeod, 8
Douglas M. McNair, 7–8
Jeanette McPherrin, 2
John V. McQuitty, 3–4
Louis L. McQuitty, 4
Leija V. McReynolds, 8
Paul McReynolds, 7–8
George F. Madaus, 8
Faith Madden, 4
Thomas W. Mahan, Jr., 6
James Mainwaring, 5
Julius B. Maller, 1–2
George G. Mallinson, 6–8
Jacqueline V. Mallinson, 6–8
Berenice Mallory, 2
Dean R. Malsbary, 8
Milton M. Mandell, 4
Lester Mann, 7–8
M. Jacinta Mann, 5
John Manning, 5, 7
Winton H. Manning, 6
Herschel T. Manuel, 2–5
Melvin R. Marks, 6
Stanley S. Marzolf, 3
Bertram B. Masia, 6
Carolyn E. Massad, 8
Ross W. Matteson, 4
Francis N. Maxfield, 1–2
James Maxwell, 3–5
Samuel T. Mayo, 6–8
Arthur B. Mays, 2

Richard A. Meade, 5
Arthur W. Meadows, 5
I. G. Meddleton, 5
Albert E. Meder, Jr., 5
Paul E. Meehl, 3
Edwin I. Megargee, 7–8
Howard D. Mehlinger, 7–8
William A. Mehrens, 7–8
Manfred J. Meier, 7–8
Norman C. Meier, 2
William B. Meldrum, 1, 3
P. L. Mellenbruch, 5
Richard S. Melton, 6, 8
H. Meltzer, 3
Gerald A. Mendelsohn, 6
Robert J. Menges, 8
Ivan N. Mensh, 4
Gerald M. Meredith, 7
Philip R. Merrifield, 6
Jack C. Merwin, 6–8
William R. Merz, 8
Bernadine Meyer, 5
Donald L. Meyer, 6
John H. Meyer, 3
C. Edward Meyers, 8
Joan J. Michael, 7
William B. Michael, 4–8
William J. Micheels, 4–5
T. R. Miles, 5–6, 8
John E. Milholland, 5–8
Lovick C. Miller, 7–8
Jason Millman, 6–8
J. B. Miner, 2
J. H. Minnick, 2
Lorenz Misbach, 3
James V. Mitchell, Jr., 7–8
Ronald W. Mitchell, 7
Arthur Mittman, 6–8
Huberto Molina, 8
William G. Mollenkopf, 3–4, 8
Floyd V. Monaghan, 7
Eason Monroe, 3
Marion Monroe, 1, 3
Joseph E. Moore, 2–4, 6
Terence Moore, 6
Walter J. Moore, 7
G. A. V. Morgan, 5–7
Alice E. Moriarty, 7
John B. Morris, 5
Irving Morrissett, 8
Coleman Morrison, 6
Frances Crook Morrison, 5–6
Harriet B. Morrison, 1–2
Nathan Morrison, 3
Thomas F. Morrison, 2
H. T. Morse, 3
N. W. Morton, 1–2, 4
P. L. Morton, 2

Harold E. Moser, 5
Donald L. Mosher, 7–8
Charles I. Mosier, 2–3
C. Scott Moss, 6
Stephan J. Motowidlo, 8
Kate Hevner Mueller, 5
Ina V. S. Mullis, 8
Leo A. Munday, 7
Allyn M. Munger, 6
Joseph A. Murphy, 7–8
Wilbur F. Murra, 1–2
Elsie Murray, 4
James L. Mursell, 1–3
Bernard I. Murstein, 6–8
Charles T. Myers, 5, 8
Sheldon S. Myers, 6–7
Dean H. Nafziger, 8
Theodor F. Naumann, 6–7
Louis C. Nanassy, 5
Doris E. Nason, 8
Diana S. Natalicio, 8
Leo Nedelsky, 5–6
Charles O. Neidt, 5–6
Clarence H. Nelson, 3–8
Jack L. Nelson, 8
Charles Neuringer, 8
Theodore Newcomb, 2
Phyllis L. Newcomer, 8
T. Ernest Newland, 6–7
Bernard H. Newman, 7
Joseph Newman, 4
Kenneth R. Newton, 5
William H. Nibbelink, 8
Robert C. Nichols, 6, 8
John Nisbet, 5–7
Stanley D. Nisbet, 4–7
Anthony J. Nitko, 8
Victor H. Noll, 1–7
Claude E. Norcross, 4
Warren T. Norman, 5–7
Raymond C. Norris, 5
Robert D. North, 5–7
Paul A. Northrop, 1–2
Edward S. Noyes, 2–3
Jum C. Nunnally, 7
Thomas Oakland, 8
C. A. Oakley, 2–3
C. O. Oakley, 3
Thomas C. O'Brien, 7–8
Anna S. Ochoa, 8
Charles W. Odell, 1–3
Donald W. Oliver, 6
Mary Ellen Oliverio, 5, 7–8
Carl J. Olson, 7
Pedro T. Orata, 2
Jacob S. Orleans, 2–6
David B. Orr, 6–7
Agnes E. Osborne, 3

Alan Osborne, 7–8
R. T. Osborne, 7
Worth J. Osburn, 1–2, 4
Stuart Oskamp, 7–8
Alton O'Steen, 2
Jay L. Otis, 3–4
William A. Owens, 6, 8
C. Robert Pace, 3–8
Albert G. Packard, 3
Ellis Batten Page, 6–8
Orville Palmer, 5
Osmond E. Palmer, 5–7
Jean M. Palormo, 6
Josephine B. Pane, 7
Gino Parisi, 7
Anna Parsek, 2
A. Harry Passow, 4, 8
Donald G. Paterson, 2–4
Gerald R. Patterson, 5
Willard W. Patty, 4
Walter Pauk, 7
Jerome D. Pauker, 6–8
David A. Payne, 6–7
Robert W. Payne, 6–8
William G. Peacher, 4
P. David Pearson, 8
John Gray Peatman, 2
Elazar J. Pedhazur, 8
E. A. Peel, 4–5
Charles W. Pendleton, 8
John P. Penna, 8
L. S. Penrose, 3
William H. Perkins, 7
Kathleen N. Perret, 5
Charles C. Peters, 1
Donald R. Peterson, 6
Harold A. Peterson, 7–8
Rolf A. Peterson, 8
Shailer Peterson, 3
Roger P. Phelps, 7–8
Theodore G. Phillips, 5–7
Hale C. Pickett, 3
Douglas A. Pidgeon, 5–8
John Pierce-Jones, 5–6
Ellen V. Piers, 6
Myrtle L. Pignatelli, 2
Len Pikaart, 7–8
A. E. G. Pilliner, 5–8
Paul Pimsleur, 6
Rudolf Pintner, 1
Gus P. Plessas, 6–8
Lynnette B. Plumlee, 3, 5–7
Robert C. Pooley, 2–7
James M. Porter, Jr., 3
Lyman W. Porter, 6
Stanley D. Porteus, 2
Winifred L. Post, 4–5
Kenneth E. Poucher, 8

Norman T. Pratt, Jr., 1–2
Daniel A. Prescott, 1
Joan Preston, 7
Ralph C. Preston, 3–4
H. Vernon Price, 5
Jack Price, 7
Ray G. Price, 3, 6–7
Roy A. Price, 2–3
Hugh F. Priest, 7
M. L. Kellmer Pringle, 4–7
Glen W. Probst, 7
Barton B. Proger, 8
Earl V. Pullias, 2
Alan C. Purves, 7–8
Fred Pyrczak, 8
M. Y. Quereshi, 7–8
Albert I. Rabin, 4–5, 7
S. Rachman, 6
John A. Radcliffe, 5–6
John F. Randolph, 3
Earl F. Rankin, 7–8
Evelyn Raskin, 4
Alton L. Raygor, 6, 8
S. A. Rayner, 5
Homer B. C. Reed, Jr., 8
James C. Reed, 7–8
Edwin H. Reeder, 3–4
William R. Reevy, 6
Richard J. Reisboard, 8
Ralph M. Reitan, 6–7
Willard E. Reitz, 7
H. H. Remmers, 1, 3, 5
Maynard C. Reynolds, 5
Marvin Reznikoff, 7
James A. Rice, 8
Gilbert J. Rich, 3
James M. Richards, Jr., 7–8
Roger A. Richards, 5–8
T. W. Richards, 4
J. A. Richardson, 5
John S. Richardson, 4
M. W. Richardson, 1–2
S. C. Richardson, 5
James H. Ricks, Jr., 4–6, 8
Paul R. Rider, 2
C. Alan Riedesel, 6–8
William Rieman, III, 3–4
Edward G. Rietz, 5
Henry L. Rietz, 1
Seymour Rigrodsky, 7
C. Alan Riedesel, 8
Alice R. Rines, 8
Henry D. Rinsland, 1–4
Harry N. Rivlin, 4–5
James P. Rizzo, 6
A. Oscar H. Roberts, 7
Holland Roberts, 2–6
G. Edith Robinson, 7

H. Alan Robinson, 6-8
Helen M. Robinson, 4-7
Richard D. Robinson, 8
Alec Rodger, 2-4
David A. Rodgers, 7
Carl R. Rogers, 2
Cyril A. Rogers, 5
Frederick R. Rogers, 2
Virginia M. Rogers, 7
W. Todd Rogers, 7
Thomas A. Romberg, 7-8
Leonard G. Rorer, 7
Carl L. Rosen, 7-8
Ephraim Rosen, 4
Marvin Rosen, 8
John H. Rosenbach, 7-8
Robert L. Rosenbaum, 8
Paul C. Rosenbloom, 6
Nancy L. Roser, 8
Benjamin Rosner, 5-7
Jerome Rosner, 7
Alan O. Ross, 6
C. C. Ross, 2-3
Charles S. Ross, 4-5
Paul F. Ross, 6
Myron F. Rosskopf, 5
Harold F. Rothe, 4
John W. M. Rothney, 1, 3-7
Julian B. Rotter, 3
Harold L. Royer, 6
Arthur B. Royse, 5-6
Stanley I. Rubin, 6
Floyd L. Ruch, 3-4, 6
Giles M. Ruch, 2
C. H. Ruedisili, 3
Mabel E. Rugen, 3
Edward A. Rundquist, 3
David H. Russell, 2-4
Harry J. Russell, 2-3
Leo P. Ruth, 8
Roger A. Ruth, 7-8
David G. Ryans, 3-4, 6
Richard Rystrom, 7-8
Darrell L. Sabers, 8
Everett B. Sackett, 1, 6
H. Bradley Sagen, 6-7
Rachel Salisbury, 2
C. Sanders, 5
H. J. Sants, 6
Bert R. Sappenfield, 5-6
Irwin G. Sarason, 6
Theodore R. Sarbin, 4
Helen Sargent, 4
I. David Satlow, 5
George A. Satter, 3-4
Jerome M. Sattler, 8
Aulus W. Saunders, 2
David R. Saunders, 5

Jean-Guy Savard, 7
Gilbert Sax, 8
Douglas E. Scates, 1, 3, 5
William L. Schaaf, 4
Willis C. Schaefer, 4
Joyce Parr Schaie, 8
K. Warner Schaie, 8
Johann H. Schepers, 6
Alvin W. Schindler, 1-2, 4
Frank L. Schmidt, 8
Arnold E. Schneider, 3
Leroy H. Schnell, 2-3
Lyle F. Schoenfeldt, 7-8
William Schofield, 4-6
Fred J. Schonell, 2, 4-5
William B. Schrader, 4-6
H. E. Schrammel, 1
Robert L. Schreiner, 8
Herbert Schueler, 3-6
Douglas G. Schultz, 4, 6-7
Harold A. Schultz, 4, 6
Richard Schupbach, 8
Donald H. Schuster, 6-7
Richard E. Schutz, 6-8
Joseph J. Schwab, 3
Mariette Schwarz, 6
Dean M. Schweickhard, 2
Gladys C. Schwesinger, 4
Craig S. Scott, 8
Louise B. Scott, 5
May V. Seagoe, 4
Carl E. Seashore, 2
Harold G. Seashore, 3-6
Virginia Seavey, 3
William Seeman, 4
Stanley J. Segal, 6
David Segel, 1, 3-4
Esther F. Segner, 2
S. B. Sells, 5-7
R. B. Selover, 3
Boris Semeonoff, 6
Melvin I. Semmel, 7
Helen Shacter, 4
Laurance F. Shaffer, 3-6
Spencer Shank, 1
Stephen Sharp, 8
Marvin E. Shaw, 8
Carleton B. Shay, 7-8
Marion F. Shaycoft, 5-6
Eugene C. Sheeley, 7-8
William D. Sheldon, 4
Ralph L. Shelton, 7-8
Lorrie Shepard, 8
John C. Sherwood, 6-8
Benjamin Shimberg, 3-4, 6-7
Stanley L. Shinall, 8
Richard E. Shine, 7
Walter C. Shipley, 3

Sidney W. Shnayer, 8
Edwin S. Shneidman, 5
Edward J. Shoben, Jr., 4
J. Harlan Shores, 4
Louis Shores, 4
Lawrence D. Shriberg, 8
Evan D. Shull, 7
L. K. Shumaker, 7
Arthur B. Silverstein, 7-8
Verner M. Sims, 1, 3-5
Jacob O. Sines, 8
Harry Singer, 7-8
Edward R. Sipay, 7-8
Rodney W. Skager, 7
Edgar P. Slack, 3
Patrick Slater, 3
William Sloan, 4-5
C. Ebblewhite Smith, 2
Donald E. P. Smith, 5-6
Fred M. Smith, 7
Henry P. Smith, 4
I. Macfarlane Smith, 4-6
J. Philip Smith, 8
Jane E. Smith, 7
Kenneth J. Smith, 7-8
Lyman J. Smith, 7
Mary Lee Smith, 8
Nick L. Smith, 8
Nila Banton Smith, 4
Percival Smith, 2
William L. Smith, 8
Charles D. Smock, 7
Daniel W. Snader, 3
William U. Snyder, 3
Robert J. Solomon, 5-6
Ronald K. Sommers, 8
Anita Miller Sostek, 8
Larry Sowder, 8
George D. Spache, 3-7
Emma Spaney, 4-5
Geraldine Spaulding, 3, 5
C. Spearman, 2
Donald Spearritt, 5
Robert K. Speer, 2
Douglas Spencer, 2-3
Peter L. Spencer, 2
Charles D. Spielberger, 8
Herbert F. Spitzer, 3-4
Bernard Spolsky, 6
Otfried Spreen, 6
Robert F. Stahmann, 8
Robert E. Stake, 6
John M. Stalnaker, 1-2, 4-6
Roy W. Stanhope, 5
Julian C. Stanley, 4-6
Charles W. Stansfield, 8
Joel Stark, 7-8
E. P. Starke, 4

Anna S. Starr, 1
Russell G. Stauffer, 5–6
John E. Stecklein, 6
Leslie P. Steffe, 7–8
Harry L. Stein, 5–6
Jack M. Stein, 6–7
William Stephenson, 4–6
Naomi Stewart, 4–6
Charles A. Stickland, 4
Clarence R. Stone, 2
L. Joseph Stone, 4–5
Ruth M. Strang, 1–2, 5
Lawrence J. Stricker, 6, 8
Ruth Strickland, 5
Stanley R. Strong, 8
Charles R. Strother, 3–5
J. B. Stroud, 3
Hans H. Strupp, 7
Dewey B. Stuit, 3–4
George W. Sturrock, 5
Frederick H. Stutz, 3, 5
Alan R. Suess, 7–8
Richard M. Suinn, 7
W. L. Sumner, 4
Norman D. Sundberg, 5–8
Donald E. Super, 3–6, 8
J. P. Sutcliffe, 5
John Sutherland, 5–6
Marilyn N. Suydam, 7–8
Edward O. Swanson, 6
Richard A. Swanson, 7–8
Robert M. Swanson, 8
Robert S. Swanson, 8
Jon D. Swartz, 8
Clifford H. Swensen, Jr., 5
Percival M. Symonds, 2–5
Hilda Taba, 1–2, 4
Abraham J. Tannenbaum, 6
Earl S. Taulbee, 8
Calvin W. Taylor, 5
Erwin K. Taylor, 3–7
Howard R. Taylor, 3–4
Hugh Taylor, 7
Ronald N. Taylor, 8
Wallace W. Taylor, 2–3
Florence M. Teagarden, 2–5
Lorene Teegarden, 2
Auke Tellegen, 8
Mildred C. Templin, 4
Edward A. Tenney, 2
W. Wesley Tennyson, 5
James B. Tharp, 2, 4
Paul W. Thayer, 6, 8
Herbert A. Thelen, 3
William N. Thetford, 6
C. L. Thiele, 2–3
Charles S. Thomas, 1–2
Cleveland A. Thomas, 5

Albert S. Thompson, 1–2, 4–6
Anton Thompson, 4
John H. Thompson, 1
Richard A. Thompson, 8
Edith I. M. Thomson, 3
Godfrey H. Thomson, 2
Robert L. Thorndike, 2–8
Robert M. Thorndike, 8
Louis P. Thorpe, 3
Robert H. Thouless, 3
David V. Tiedeman, 4–8
Ernest W. Tiegs, 1–3
Joseph Tiffin, 1
James A. Till, 8
Murray H. Tillman, 8
Miles A. Tinker, 1–4
Carol K. Tittle, 7
Hazel M. Toliver, 3
Herbert A. Tonne, 1, 3, 5
Herbert A. Topps, 3
T. L. Torgerson, 3
Agatha Townsend, 3, 5–6
Marion R. Trabue, 1–2
Kenneth J. Travers, 7
Robert M. W. Travers, 3–5
Arthur E. Traxler, 1–7
Frances O. Triggs, 3
Harold C. Trimble, 6–8
Marie E. Trost, 2
Maurice E. Troyer, 3
R. M. Tryon, 1–2
Robert C. Tryon, 2
Bruce W. Tuckman, 8
J. Jaap Tuinman, 8
Simon H. Tulchin, 2–3
Mary E. Turnbull, 4–6
William W. Turnbull, 3–6
Clarence E. Turner, 2–6
Mervyn L. Turner, 5
Austin H. Turney, 1–2
Lawrence J. Turton, 7–8
F. T. Tyler, 3
Leona E. Tyler, 4–7
Ralph W. Tyler, 2–3, 5
Thomas A. Tyler, 8
C. C. Upshall, 3
Marguerite Uttley, 3
Curtis C. Vail, 1
Paolo Valesio, 7
Robert E. Valett, 7
Forrest L. Vance, 6–7
Henry Van Engen, 4
Byron H. Van Roekel, 5–7
Neil J. Van Steenberg, 4–5
William J. Valmont, 8
Gerald R. Van Hecke, 8
Byron H. Van Roekel, 8
Donald J. Veldman, 6–7

Frank R. Vellutino, 8
Magdalen D. Vernon, 5–6
Philip E. Vernon, 2, 4–8
Verna L. Vickery, 5
Roland Vinette, 3
Morris S. Viteles, 2–3
J. R. Jefferson Wadkins, 7–8
Guy W. Wagner, 1
John Wagner, 7
William W. Waite, 3–4
J. V. Waits, 3
David A. Walker, 7
Helen M. Walker, 1
W. D. Wall, 4
S. Rains Wallace, 4–5
Wimburn L. Wallace, 5–8
Norman E. Wallen, 6
James A. Walsh, 7–8
W. Bruce Walsh, 7
Edwin Wandt, 4, 7
Morey J. Wantman, 4–6
F. W. Warburton, 4–5
Charles F. Ward, 7
William C. Ward, 7–8
James L. Wardrop, 8
David M. Wark, 7
Charles F. Warnath, 6, 8
Neil D. Warren, 3, 5
Willard G. Warrington, 5–7
Ruth W. Washburn, 3
Alan T. Waterman, 2
Eugene A. Waters, 2
John G. Watkins, 6
Ralph K. Watkins, 2
Richard W. Watkins, 7–8
Goodwin Watson, 1–3
Robert I. Watson, 3
J. Fred Weaver, 5
Harold Webster, 5–6
William J. Webster, 7
David Wechsler, 2–3
Thaddeus E. Weckowicz, 8
Walter L. Wehner, 8
Charles C. Weidemann, 1–2
David P. Weikart, 7
Sheldon A. Weintraub, 7–8
David J. Weiss, 7–8
Henry Weitz, 3–8
Carolyn M. Welch, 3
Wayne W. Welch, 8
A. T. Welford, 4
Beth L. Wellman, 3
F. L. Wells, 1–3
Tim L. Wentling, 8
Joseph M. Wepman, 7
Emmy E. Werner, 6–7
Edgar B. Wesley, 1–4
Alexander G. Wesman, 4–7

Leonard J. West, 7–8
Bert W. Westbrook, 7–8
George Westby, 4–6
Alida S. Westman, 8
Frederick L. Westover, 4
Harry G. Wheat, 2
D. K. Wheeler, 5
Edward M. White, 8
Howard R. White, 4
Dean K. Whitla, 6
Carroll A. Whitmer, 2–3
Randolph H. Whitworth, 8
J. Lee Wiederholt, 8
Jerry S. Wiggins, 6–7
Katherine W. Wilcox, 3
S. S. Wilks, 1–2
Haydn S. Williams, 5
J. Robert Williams, 6
Edmund G. Williamson, 1–2
Warren W. Willingham, 6
Carl G. Willis, 7–8
Margaret Willis, 2
John M. Willits, 3, 5

Victor L. Willson, 8
J. Richard Wilmeth, 6
Guy M. Wilson, 1–3
James W. Wilson, 7
Herbert D. Wing, 4–6
Harris Winitz, 8
William L. Winnett, 7
George P. Winship, Jr., 6–7
R. Winterbourn, 5
Robert D. Wirt, 6–7
Emory E. Wiseman, 7
Stephen Wiseman, 3, 5
Ernest C. Witham, 2
J. Richard Wittenborn, 3–4
Paul A. Witty, 3
Richard M. Wolf, 8
Dael L. Wolfle, 1–2, 4
Leroy Wolins, 6
Frank B. Womer, 6–8
E. F. Wonderlic, 3
Hugh B. Wood, 2
Ray G. Wood, 3
Clifford Woody, 1, 3

D. A. Worcester, 2–4
Blaine R. Worthen, 7–8
F. Lynwood Wren, 3
C. Gilbert Wrenn, 1–2, 5
Robert L. Wright, 7
William J. Wright, 8
J. Wayne Wrightstone, 1–3, 5
Jack Wrigley, 5
Ll. Wynn Jones, 2
Kaoru Yamamoto, 8
Alfred Yates, 5
Aubrey J. Yates, 7
Albert H. Yee, 7
Dale Yoder, 4
James E. Ysseldyke, 8
William Yule, 8
Louis C. Zahner, 2–3, 5
O. L. Zangwill, 3
Sheldon Zedeck, 8
Edwin Ziegfeld, 2–4
Wayne S. Zimmerman, 6–7
Donald G. Zytowski, 7–8

TESTS IN PRINT III

PREFACE

The publication of *Tests in Print III* is both a sad and a significant milestone. It is sad because it marks the first publication in this series that was not edited by Oscar Krisen Buros, who passed away in 1978. It is significant because it represents a determination to continue the work of the founder and to insure contributions of like kind and importance in the future. For over 40 years Oscar Buros was the editor and publisher of *The Mental Measurements Yearbooks*, *Tests in Print*, and separate monographs covering specific areas of testing. *The Mental Measurements Yearbooks*, containing critical reviews by professionals of all commercially published tests in English, quickly achieved a reputation for integrity, scholarship, and professional responsibility. Under his leadership the *Yearbooks* and other Institute publications became an invaluable resource for test users throughout the world. They also became a prime force in stimulating increased awareness of the necessity for improvement in the construction, validation, and use of tests. As an unabashed crusader for better tests and the more effective use of tests, Oscar Buros made an immense impact on the field of testing that should be felt for some time to come.

A vehicle for insuring that continuing impact was established when Luella Buros, his wife and lifelong companion in Institute activities, took steps to relocate the Institute at The University of Nebraska–Lincoln. Support from University administrators and a welcome initial grant from The University of Nebraska Foundation provided fertile ground for the transplanting of an institute that had become an institution. It goes without saying that those of us who are part of the new Buros Institute staff are deeply committed to the Buros tradition and the furtherance of its historic objectives.

As its name implies, *Tests in Print III* is the third in a series that was first published in 1961. It is the twenty-fifth publication in the larger series, listed on an earlier page, that includes all of the *Tests in Print* volumes, *The Mental Measurements Yearbooks*, and the various monographs covering special areas of testing. Historical accounts of the *Tests in Print* series and the larger series including *The Mental Measurements Yearbooks* have been presented in the prefaces and introductions for *Tests in Print II* and *The Eighth Mental Measurements Yearbook*, and they will not be repeated here. However, since no volume in the larger series can be understood without reference to the overall purposes and organization of the series, a brief description of the series will be provided in the first part of the Introduction to follow.

A volume of this kind cannot be published without the combined effort and support of many people. The Editor extends his deepest gratitude to Luella Buros for her beneficent gifts and unfailing support of the new Buros Institute as it established its roots in a new location. The staff of the Institute, listed on an earlier page, deserves great credit for their very capable handling of the complicated and endless tasks that must be successfully accomplished to publish a work of this nature. We are also deeply indebted to our graduate students, who have uniformly provided excellent service in all manner of assignments. Since their names are not mentioned elsewhere, we extend our grateful thanks here to Leslie Carlson, Julie Christofferson, Judy Crosby, Gregory Finch, Patricia Halama, G. David Harris, Clark House, Sherral Miller, Christopher Milne, Audrey Muehe, John Olson, and Anthony Paolo. We are also most appreciative of the specialized help provided to us on many occasions by Curtis Hill of the university computing center.

Our gratitude is extended to our National Advisory Committee, consisting of Luella Buros, T. Anne Cleary, the late Robert Ebel, Roger Lennon, Ellis Page, Daniel Reschly, Lyle Schoenfeldt, Richard Snow, Julian Stanley, and Frank Womer, who were most resourceful and helpful in providing insights about our work and our relationship to the field. Gratitude is also extended to our Departmental Advisory Committee, who provided help and support for our publication efforts with *Tests in Print III* and also for the planning of our annual symposium and publications related thereto; this committee consists of Robert Brown, Roger Bruning, David Dixon, Terry Gutkin, Kenneth Orton, Wayne Piersel, Barbara Plake, and Royce Ronning. We thank also The University of Nebraska Foundation and its president, Mr. D. B. Varner, for fiscal and moral support that have been important to our development. Also important to our development have been administrators of The University of Nebraska–Lincoln and The University of Nebraska Press, whose support, consultation, and administrative assistance have been appreciated on many occasions. Acknowledgment should also be made of the role of Cecil Reynolds in initiating efforts to bring the Buros Institute to The University of Nebraska. And last but far from least is my wife, Margaret, with whom sharing and caring have always added a very special dimension to both work and life.

James V. Mitchell, Jr.

INTRODUCTION

Tests in Print III, the third volume of its kind, is the twenty-fifth publication of the Buros Institute of Mental Measurements. The twenty-five publications of the Buros Institute may be classified into three general categories:

1. *Mental Measurements Yearbooks*
2. separate monographs covering specific areas of testing (e.g., *Personality Tests and Reviews*, *Vocational Tests and Reviews*, etc.)
3. *Tests in Print*

The *Mental Measurements Yearbooks*, of which eight have been published, consist principally of descriptive listings, references, and critical reviews of commercially published tests in English. The separate monographs are collections of those listings, references, and critical reviews pertaining to a specific area that have appeared in all Institute volumes to date. *Tests in Print* consists of descriptive listings and references, without reviews, of commercially published tests that are in print and available for purchase or use. It also serves as a comprehensive index to the contents of the *Mental Measurements Yearbooks* published to date. Criteria for inclusion of a test in *TIP* and *MMY* are quite different. Criteria for inclusion of a test in *MMY* are that the test be either new or revised since the last volume published by the Institute, or that the test has generated 20 or more references since that last volume. The criterion for inclusion of a test in *TIP* is simply that the test is in print and available for purchase or use. The publications in the series are interlocking volumes with extensive cross-referencing requiring their coordinated use as a system.

It is in this context that *Tests in Print III*, the present and newest addition to the series, is now made available to the testing public. Descriptive and explanatory information about this newest publication is presented below.

TESTS IN PRINT III

The contents of *Tests in Print III* include: (a) a comprehensive bibliography of commercially available tests published as separates for use with English-speaking subjects; (b) comprehensive bibliographies, for specific tests, of references related to the construction, validity, or use of the tests in various settings; (c) a test title index that includes all in-print tests, out-of-print tests (cumulative back to *TIP II*), and occasional tests for which status information was unreported or unknown; (d) a classified subject index which also describes the population for which each test is intended and provides multiple classifications for tests where appropriate; (e) a publishers directory and index, including addresses and test listings by publisher; and (f) a name index which includes the names of all authors of tests, reviews, or references.

Tests in Print III also introduces some innovations in terms of organization, page headings, and pagination. The organization of the volume is encyclopedic in nature, with the tests being ordered alphabetically by title. Thus if the title of a test is known, the reader can locate the test immediately without having to consult the Index of Titles. The test classifications continue to appear in the Classified Subject Index, but the new organization permits some tests to be included in more than one classification, a feature which provides flexible classification faithful to reality and a Classified Subject Index of optimum use to the reader.

The page headings reflect the encyclopedic organization. The page heading of the left-hand page cites the number and title of the first test listed on that page, and the page heading of the right-hand page cites the number and title of the last test listed on that page. All numbers presented in the various indexes are test numbers, not page numbers. Page numbers, important only for the Table of Contents, are indicated at the bottom of each page.

TESTS

Tests in Print III contains 2672* test entries, 8.3 percent more than *TIP II* (1974) and 25.7 percent more than *TIP I* (1961). The in-print status of these tests was confirmed by direct correspondence with publishers. Seven hundred eighty-nine of these tests are new or revised since the publication of *The Eighth Mental Measurements Yearbook*. Table 1 presents the number of test entries included in each major classification of the Classified Subject Index. Two new categories, Developmental and Neuropsychological, have been added since the publication of *The Eighth Yearbook*, principally to reflect changes in the field. Addition of the number of tests in each classification exceeds

*Some changes had to be initiated after this volume went to press, but the total number of tests remains the same. After all tests were numbered, three test entries were inserted (1874A, 1993A, 2467A), and three were deleted. The deleted tests are indicated by the compound number assigned to the immediately preceding entry (16-7, 950-1, 1154-5).

the total number of tests in *TIP III*, since some tests are listed in more than one classification. Any classification system, of course, is to some degree dependent on human judgment. Yet broad comparisons between categories are often interesting and useful. It is interesting to note, for example, that once again the category of personality tests includes by far the greatest number of tests of any category in *TIP III*.

Table 1
Test Entries in *TIP III* by Major Classification

Classification	Number of Test Entries
Achievement Batteries	74
Developmental	87
English	199
Fine Arts	33
Foreign Language	104
Intelligence and Scholastic Aptitude	245
Mathematics	162
Miscellaneous	314
Multi-Aptitude Batteries	29
Neuropsychological	24
Personality	576
Reading	267
Science	78
Sensory-Motor	51
Social Studies	81
Speech and Hearing	84
Vocations	487

REVIEWS AND EXCERPTS

Tests in Print III serves as a master index of in-print tests that refers the reader to all the original test reviews and excerpted test reviews that appeared for these tests in all of the *Mental Measurements Yearbooks* to date. In addition, it refers readers to entries and reviews in earlier yearbooks for all tests which have gone out of print since *TIP II* or *The Eighth Yearbook*. Authors of reviews and excerpts are named following the test entries in cross references to the appropriate *MMY*. Although *TIP III* will serve a very useful function by providing a comprehensive bibliography of tests in print, the cross references to the critical reviews are also of great importance if tests are to be used wisely. Thus *TIP* and the *MMY's* are inseparable partners in the cause of promoting effective selection and use of tests.

A total of 1561 persons have contributed reviews to one or more *MMY's*. The number of reviewers per yearbook has increased from 133 in 1938 to 484 in 1978. Because of their important contributions to the *Mental Measurements Yearbooks*, a complete listing of *MMY* test reviewers is presented on page xi.

REFERENCES

This volume presents specific test bibliographies consisting of references in English on the construction, validity, and use of the tests included in the volume. There are 12,170 references listed. Since some references involved the use of more than one test, these references are multiple-listed under each of the tests in question. Earlier publications of the Buros Institute reported the huge growth in the amount of literature involving the use of commercially published tests, and that growth has continued unabated. It was partly to compensate for this unrestrained growth and also to keep publication costs under control that a decision was made not to include theses or dissertations in the specific test bibliographies of *TIP III*. Yet readers will continue to find specific test bibliographies of unusual completeness in this volume.

The references that are included in this volume represent a massive and continuous search effort through the professional journals by staff of the Buros Institute. Specific criteria for inclusion of a reference in an Institute publication are such that a test must have a role of some importance in the reference for it to be included. As has been traditional with Buros Institute publications, specific test bibliographies are first arranged chronologically and then alphabetically by author within year to facilitate orderly searching.

Table 2 shows the 50 tests in *TIP III* with the largest number of references that have been identified for specific tests since references were previously published in 1978 in *The Eighth Mental Measurements Yearbook*. Within the table the tests are also rank-ordered according to number of references. The Minnesota Multiphasic Personality Inventory continues to reign supreme as a generator of references, as it did for the *8th MMY* and as it has cumulatively throughout the history of Institute publications. A comparison of this table with Table 8 of the *8th MMY*, however, will reveal some waxing and waning of tests other than this continuing front-runner. The projective tests, for example, seem to be losing ground. A revision of a widely used instrument will often result in a surge of references and a change in rank. Yet there is also a relative consistency in the reference generation and ranking of some instruments that suggests a perpetuating allegiance to the instrument that some may regard as deserved and others as undeserved. In any event, the references for specific tests in *TIP III* can be extremely helpful in assessing the relative merit of tests and suggesting their most appropriate and effective uses. They are also of unquestionable value in research.

Table 2

Reference Frequencies for the Fifty Tests in *TIP III* Generating the Largest Number of References Since the *8th MMY*

Test (with rank)	Number of References
1. Minnesota Multiphasic Personality Inventory	748
2. Wechsler Intelligence Scale for Children-Revised	650
3. Wechsler Adult Intelligence Scale-Revised	577
4. Peabody Picture Vocabulary Test-Revised	302
5. State-Trait Anxiety Inventory	278
6. Wide Range Employability Sample Test	250
7. Eysenck Personality Inventory	245
8. Personality Research Form	205
9. Stanford-Binet Intelligence Scale, Third Revision	203
10. Progressive Matrices	200
11. California Psychological Inventory	195
12. Sixteen Personality Factor Questionnaire	182
13. [Bender-Gestalt Test]	158
14. Rorschach	155
15. College Board Scholastic Aptitude Test and Test of Standard Written English	152
16. Tennessee Self Concept Scale	120
17. Adjective Checklist	117
18. Multiple Affect Adjective Check List	108
19. Piers-Harris Children's Self Concept Scale (The Way I Feel About Myself)	107
20. Torrance Tests of Creative Thinking	107
21. Thematic Apperception Test	105
22. Bayley Scales of Infant Development	101

23. Metropolitan Achievement Tests, 5th Edition (1978)	99
24. Strong-Campbell Interest Inventory	99
25. Personal Orientation Inventory	98
26. Iowa Tests of Basic Skills, Forms 7 and 8	97
27. Wechsler Memory Scale	96
28. Embedded Figures Test	89
29. Group Embedded Figures Test	88
30. Profile of Mood States	84
31. Slosson Intelligence Test	82
32. Stanford Achievement Test: Mathematics Tests, 1973 Edition	80
33. Wechsler Preschool and Primary Scale of Intelligence	80
34. Kit of Factor Referenced Cognitive Tests	78
35. Gates-MacGinitie Reading Tests	77
36. ACT Assessment Program	76
37. Eysenck Personality Questionnaire	72
38. Metropolitan Readiness Test, 1976 Edition	72
39. Edwards Personal Preference Schedule	70
40. Present State Examination	70
41. Otis-Lennon School Ability Test	67
42. Peabody Individual Achievement Test	67
43. Shipley-Institute of Living Scale for Measuring Intellectual Impairment	64
44. McCarthy Scales of Children's Abilities	60
45. Comprehensive Tests of Basic Skills, [Forms U & V]	59
46. California Achievement Tests, Forms C and D	58
47. Developmental Test of Visual-Motor Integration	57
48. Harvard Group Scale of Hypnotic Susceptibility	57
49. AAMD Adaptive Behavior Scale for Children and Adults, 1974 Revision	55
50. Self Directed Search: A Guide to Educational and Vocational Planning	55

INDEXES

As mentioned earlier, *Tests in Print III* includes four indexes which should be invaluable to users of the volume: (1) an Index of Titles, (2) a Classified Subject Index, (3) a Publishers Directory and Index, and (4) an Index of Names. Additional comment on these indexes will be presented below.

Index of Titles. Since the organization of *TIP III* is encyclopedic in nature, with the tests being ordered alphabetically by title throughout the volume, the test title index does not have to be consulted to find a test for which the title is known. However, the title index has three features which make it useful beyond its function as a complete title listing. First, it includes cross-reference information that is useful for tests with superseded or alternative titles or tests which are commonly (and often inaccurately) known by multiple titles. Second, it groups some tests in relation to the overall program or series to which they pertain (e.g., the Advanced Placement Examinations, the ACS Examinations in chemistry). Third, it includes tests that have gone out of print since *TIP II* and the *8th MMY* and refers readers to their last entries or reviews in these previous volumes. To differentiate between in-print and out-of-print tests in the title index it is particularly important for readers to read carefully the instructions on the use of the test title index that precede the title listing. It is also important to keep firmly in mind that the numbers in this index, like all *TIP III* indexes, are *test numbers* and not page numbers.

Classified Subject Index. Referred to in earlier Institute publications as the Scanning Index, the Classified Subject Index is of great help to readers who seek a listing of tests in given subject areas. As reported earlier, the Classified Subject Index now provides for multiple listing of tests for which alternative classifications are possible, a feature which further extends the range of tests that are brought to the attention of a reader with particular subject interests. Each entry in this index also includes the population for which the test is considered appropriate by its author. The Classified Subject Index represents a very useful starting point for readers who know their area of interest but do not know how to further focus that interest in order to identify the best test or tests for their particular purposes.

Publishers Directory and Index. The Publishers Directory and Index includes the names and addresses of the publishers of all tests included in *TIP III* plus a listing of test entry numbers for each individual publisher. The total number of test publishers listed is 565. The index can be particularly useful in obtaining addresses for requesting specimen sets or catalogs after the referenced reviews in *The Mental Measurements Yearbooks* have been read and evaluated. It can also be useful when a reader knows the publisher of a certain test but is uncertain of the test name, or when a reader is interested in the range of tests published by a given publisher.

Index of Names. The Index of Names is an analytical index indicating authorship of a test, test review, excerpted review, or reference dealing with a specific test. As usual, all numbers in the index refer to test numbers and not page numbers. The reading of the instructions preceding the index is again essential. The listing of references involves two numbers, with the first number referring to the test number and the following number, in parentheses, referring to the reference number in the reference listing for that test (i.e., ref, 859(836) refers to reference 836 for test 859).

Forenames have been reduced to initials in accordance with common practice and to keep indexing costs under control. Since authors are not always consistent in the way they list their names on publications, two or more listings may refer to the same person. On the other hand, the use of initials instead of forenames increases the probability that the citations for two or more persons will be listed together. These ambiguities can be resolved in almost all cases by referring to the cited material, where authors' names are given exactly as reported in the article, book, or test.

HOW TO USE THIS BOOK

A reference book like *Tests in Print III* can be of far greater benefit to a reader if a little time is taken to become familiar with what it has to offer and how one might most effectively use it to obtain the information wanted. The first step in this process is to read the Introduction to *TIP III* in its entirety; the Introduction has been kept as brief and simple as possible to encourage such reading. The second step is to become familiar with the four indexes and particularly with the instructions preceding each index listing. The third step is to make actual use of the book by looking up needed information. This third step is simple enough if one keeps in mind the following possibilities:

1. If you know the title of the test, use the alphabetical page headings to go directly to the test entry.
2. If you don't know, can't find, or are unsure of the title of a test, consult the Index of Test Titles for possible variants of the name or consult the appropriate subject area of the Classified Subject Index for other possible leads or for similar or related tests in the same area. (Other uses for both of these indexes were described earlier.)
3. If you know the author of a test but not the title or publisher, consult the Index of Names and look up the author's titles until you find the test you want.
4. If you know the test publisher but not the title or author, consult the Publishers Directory and Index and look up the publisher's titles until you find the test you want.
5. Once you have found the test or tests you are looking for, read the descriptive entries for these tests carefully so that you can take advantage of the information provided. A description of the information provided in these test entries will be presented later in this section.
6. The test entries will often refer you to additional information or reviews appearing in the *Mental Measurements Yearbooks*. To maximize the usefulness of *TIP III* and your knowledge of the test(s) in question, it is essential that you actively seek out this information in these other volumes.
7. Once you have obtained all the available information on a test or tests from *TIP III* and companion volumes of the *Mental Measurements Yearbooks*, it is often a useful next step to order a specimen set of the materials wanted. The Publishers Directory and Index has the address information needed to obtain specimen sets or catalogs.

The descriptive entries for each test included in *TIP III*, although not as comprehensive as the *MMY* entries because of the number of tests involved, still contains a large amount of useful information. For each test an attempt has been made to present the following information in the order given:

a) TITLE. Test titles are printed in boldface type. Secondary or series titles are set off from main titles by a colon. Titles are always presented exactly as reported in the test materials. When the titles on the test booklet and manual differ, the title on the test booklet is given in boldface; the second title is generally given in italic type within the entry. Entry titles which differ from those reported in the test materials (generally because no definitive title is used) are enclosed in brackets. Stars (★) precede titles of tests which have not been listed before in any publication of The Buros Institute of Mental Measurements; asterisks (*) precede titles of tests which have been revised or supplemented since their last listing.

b) DESCRIPTION OF THE GROUPS FOR WHICH THE TEST IS INTENDED. The grade, chronological age, semester range, or employment category is usually given. "Grades 1.5–2.5, 2–3, 4–12, 13–17" means that there are four test booklets: a booklet for the middle of the first grade through the middle of the second grade, a booklet for the beginning of the second grade through the end of the third grade, a booklet for grades 4 through 12 inclusive, and a booklet for undergraduate and graduate students in colleges and universities. "First, second semester" means that there are two test booklets: one covering the work of the first semester, the other covering the work of the second semester. "1, 2 semesters" indicates that the second booklet covers the work of two semesters. "Ages 10-2 to 11-11" means ages 10 years 2 months to 11 years 11 months; and "grades 4–6 to 5–9" means the sixth month in the fourth grade through the ninth month in the fifth grade. Commas are used to separate levels. "High school and college" denotes a single test booklet for both levels; "High school, college" denotes two test booklets, one for high school and one for college.

c) DATE OF PUBLICATION. The inclusive range of publication dates for the various forms, accessories, and editions of a test is reported. When publication dates do not appear on the materials and the date has been secured through correspondence with the publisher, it is enclosed in brackets.

d) ACRONYM. When a test is often referred to by an acronym, the acronym is given in the test entry immediately following the publication date.

e) PART SCORES. The number of part scores is presented along with their titles or descriptions of what they are intended to represent.

f) SPECIAL COMMENTS. Some entries contain special notations, such as: "for research use only"; "revision of the *ABC Test* "; "tests administered monthly at centers throughout the United States"; "subtests available as separates"; and "verbal creativity." A statement such as "verbal creativity" is intended to further describe what the test claims to measure. Some of the test entries include factual statements which imply criticism of the test such as "1980 test identical with test copyrighted 1970" and "no manual."

g) AUTHOR. For most tests, all authors are reported. In the case of tests which appear in a new form each year, only authors of the most recent forms are listed. Names are reported exactly as printed on test booklets. Names of editors are generally not reported.

h) PUBLISHER. The name of the publisher or distributor is reported for each test. Foreign publishers are identified by listing the country in brackets immediately following the name of the publisher. The Publishers Directory and Index must be consulted for a publisher's address.

i) CLOSING ASTERISK. An asterisk following the publisher's name indicates that an entry was prepared from a firsthand examination of the test materials.

j) FOREIGN ADAPTATIONS. Revisions and adaptations of tests for foreign use are listed in parentheses following the description of the original edition.

k) SUBLISTINGS. Levels, editions, subtests, or parts of a test which are available in separate booklets are sometimes presented as sublistings with titles set in small capitals. Sub-sublistings are indented and titles are set in italic type.

l) CROSS REFERENCES. For tests which have been previously listed in a Buros Institute publication, a test entry includes—if relevant—a final paragraph containing a cross reference to the reviews, excerpts, and references for that test in those volumes. In the cross references, "8:1023" refers to test 1023 in *The Eighth Yearbook*, "T2:144" refers to test 144 in *Tests in Print II*, "7:637" refers to test 637 in *The Seventh Yearbook*, "P:262" refers to test 262 in *Personality Tests and Reviews I*, "2:1427" refers to test 1427 in *The 1940 Yearbook*, and "1:1110" refers to test 1110 in *The 1938 Yearbook*. In the case of batteries and programs, the paragraph also includes cross references—from the battery to the separately listed subtests and vice versa—to entries in this volume and to entries and reviews in earlier yearbooks. Test numbers not preceded by a colon refer to tests in this yearbook; for example, "see 45" refers to test 45 in this volume.

If a reader encounters something in a test description which is not understood, the descriptive material presented above can be referred to again and can often help to resolve the misunderstanding.

We regret to report that some publishers—a very small minority—are not willing to send us the complimentary materials we need for our work. Since we are a non-profit organization under grant from The University of Nebraska Foundation, we cannot afford to purchase these materials. Thus some tests—again a very small minority—may not appear in *TIP III* because of the rejection of our request for complimentary materials.

A reader using this volume as effectively as it can be used will find it a major source of important information impossible to find elsewhere. From such effective use can come substantive gains in the selection and interpretation of commercially published tests.

TESTS IN PRINT

[1]

AAHPER Cooperative Health Education Test. Grades 5–6, 7–9; 1971–72; Educational Testing Service; Addison-Wesley Publishing Co., Inc.*

REFERENCES

1. REDICAN, K. J., OLSEN, L. K., & MATHIS, R. M. A comparison of the cognitive effects of two prototype health education curriculums on selected elementary school children. *Journal of School Health*, 1979, 49, 340–342.

[2]

AAHPER Cooperative Physical Education Tests. Grades 4–6, 7–9, 10–12; 1970; Educational Testing Service; Addison-Wesley Publishing Co., Inc.*

See T2:911 (1 reference) and 7:593.

REFERENCES

1. See T2:911.
2. KOEING, C. R., JOHNSON, D. J., & GRAVES, M. Comparison of two methods of developing manipulative skills of children in upper elementary grades. *Perceptual & Motor Skills*, 1978, 47, 605–606.

[3]

AAHPER-Kennedy Foundation Special Fitness Test for the Mentally Retarded. Ages 8–18; 1968; adaptation of *AAHPER Youth Fitness Test*; 7 scores: flexed arm hang, sit-up, shuttle run, standing broad jump, 50-yard dash, softball throw, 300-yard run-walk; adaptation by G. Lawrence Rarick; American Alliance for Health, Physical Education, Recreation and Dance.*

For additional information, see 7:594 (2 references).

[4]

AAHPER Sport Skills Tests. Ages 10–18; 1965–69; 5 tests; Donald K. Brace (*a–d*) and Frank D. Sills (*e*); American Alliance for Health, Physical Education, Recreation and Dance.*

a) ARCHERY SKILLS TEST. 1967; 4 scores for boys, 3 scores for girls.
b) BASKETBALL SKILLS TEST. 1966; 9 scores.
c) FOOTBALL SKILLS TEST. Boys; 1965; 10 scores.
d) SOFTBALL SKILLS TEST. 1966; 8 scores.
e) VOLLEYBALL SKILLS TEST. 1969; 4 scores.

For additional information, see 7:595 (3 references).

REFERENCES

1–3. See 7:595.
4. HOPKINS, D. R. Factor analysis of selected basketball skill tests. *Research Quarterly*, 1977, 48, 535–540.
5. FORD, H. T., & PACKETT, J. R. Effects of prescribed weight–training and basketball programs on selected basketball skill test scores. *Perceptual & Motor Skills*, 1980, 50, 1151–1155.

[5]

AAHPER Youth Fitness Test. Grades 5–12; 1958–76; 6 scores: pull-up (boys), flexed-arm hang (girls), flexed-knee sit-up, shuttle run, standing broad jump, 50-yard dash, 600-yard run-walk (optional substitute for run-walk test: 1 mile or 9-minute run for ages 10–12, 1½ mile or 12-minute run for ages 13 and over); 1976 manual by Paul Hunsicker and Guy G. Reiff; American Alliance for Health, Physical Education, Recreation and Dance.*

For additional information, see 8:407 (15 references); see also T2:914 (22 references); for a review by Aileene S. Lockhart, see 7:596 (104 references); see also 6:715 (21 references).

REFERENCES

1–21. See 6:715.
22–126. See 7:596.
127–149. See T2:914.
150–164. See 8:407.
165. CURETON, K. J., BOILEAU, R. A., LOHMAN, T. G., & MISNER, J. E. Determinants of distance running performance in children: Analysis of a path model. *Research Quarterly*, 1977, 48, 270–279.
166. SLAUGHTER, M. H., LOHMAN, T. G., & MISNER, J. E. Relationship of somatotype and body composition to physical performance in 7- to 12-year-old boys. *Research Quarterly*, 1977, 48, 159–168.
167. THAXTON, A. B., ROTHSTEIN, A. L., & THAXTON, N. A. Comparative effectiveness of two methods of teaching physical education to elementary school girls. *Research Quarterly*, 1977, 48, 420–427.
168. CHRISTENSON, B. Computerizing the AAHPER Youth Fitness Test. *Journal of Physical Education & Recreation*, 1978, 49, 66.

169. PLOWMAN, S. A., & FALLS, H. B. AAHPER Youth Fitness Test revision: How fit? and for what? *Journal of Physical Education & Recreation*, 1978, 49, 22-24.
170. BEEDLE, B. Frequency of participation in sports and capacity for motor fitness: A trend analysis. *Perceptual & Motor Skills*, 1981, 52, 386.

[6]
AAMD Adaptive Behavior Scale for Children and Adults, 1974 Revision.

Mentally retarded and emotionally maladjusted ages 3-adults, grades 2-6; 1969-75; ABS; ratings in 21 or 24 areas: independent functioning, physical development, economic activity, language development, numbers and times domestic activity(*a* only), vocational activity, self-direction, responsibility, socialization, violent and destructive behavior, antisocial behavior, rebellious behavior, untrustworthy behavior, withdrawal, stereotyped behavior and odd mannerisms, inappropriate interpersonal manners, unacceptable vocal habits, unacceptable or eccentric habits, self-abusive behavior (*a* only), hyperactive tendencies, sexually aberrant behavior (*a* only), psychological disturbances, use of medications; 2 editions; Kazuo Nihira, Ray Foster, Max Shellhaas, and Henry Leland; American Association on Mental Deficiency.*

a) [STANDARD VERSION.] Ages 3-adult.
b) PUBLIC SCHOOL VERSION. Grades 2-6; manual by Nadine Lambert, Myra Windmiller, Linda Cole, and Richard Figueroa; distributed by Publishers Test Service.*

For additional information, a review by Morton Bortner, and an excerpted review by C. H. Ammons and R. B. Ammons, see 8:493 (25 references); see also T2:1092 (3 references); for reviews by Lovick C. Miller and Melvyn I. Semmel of an earlier edition, see 7:37 (9 references).

REFERENCES

1-9. See 7:37.
10-12. See T2:1092.
13-37. See 8:493.
38. COHEN, H., CONROY, J. W., FRAZER, D. W., SNELBECKER, G. E., & SPREAT, S. Behavioral effects of interinstitutional relocation of mentally retarded residents. *American Journal of Mental Deficiency*, 1977, 82, 12-18.
39. DUCKETT, J. Adaptive and maladaptive behavior of idiots savants. *American Journal of Mental Deficiency*, 1977, 82, 308-311.
40. EYMAN, R. K., & CALL, T. Maladaptive behavior and community placement of mentally retarded persons. *American Journal of Mental Deficiency*, 1977, 82, 137-144.
41. GRANT, G. W. B., & MOORES, B. Resident characteristics and staff behavior in two hospitals for mentally retarded adults. *American Journal of Mental Deficiency*, 1977, 82, 259-265.
42. LEE, D. Y. Evaluation of a group counseling program designed to enhance social adjustment of mentally retarded adults. *Journal of Counseling Psychology*, 1977, 24, 318-323.
43. MCDEVITT, S. C., MCDEVITT, S. C., & ROSEN, M. Adaptive Behavior Scale, Part II: A cautionary note and suggestions for revisions. *American Journal of Mental Deficiency*, 1977, 82, 210-212.
44. BACA, L., & CERVANTES, H. The assessment of minority students: Are adaptive behavior scales the answer? *Psychology in the Schools*, 1978, 15, 366-370.
45. CUNNINGHAM, T., & PRESNALL, D. Relationship between dimensions of adaptive behavior and sheltered workshop productivity. *American Journal of Mental Deficiency*, 1978, 82, 386-393.
46. HOLYROYD, J., & GOLDENBERG, I. The use of goal attainment scaling to evaluate a ward treatment program for disturbed children. *Journal of Clinical Psychology*, 1978, 34, 732-739.
47. MENDELSOHN, M., & ERDWINS, C. The Disruptive Behavior Scale: An objective assessment of unmanageable social behavior in adolescents. *Journal of Clinical Psychology*, 1978, 34, 426-428.
48. MILLHAM, J., CHILCUTT, J., & ATKINSON, B. L. Comparability of naturalistic and controlled observation assessment of adaptive behavior. *American Journal of Mental Deficiency*, 1978, 83, 52-59.
49. SINGER, J. H. Evaluating program placement in an institution for the mentally retarded: A multivariate approach. *Journal of Special Education*, 1978, 12, 133-142.

50. ALGOZZINE, R., WHORTON, J. E., & REID, W. R. Special class exit criteria: A modest beginning. *Journal of Special Education*, 1979, 13, 132-136.
51. BAILEY, B. S., & RICHMOND, B. O. Adaptive behavior of retarded, slow-learner, and average intelligence children. *Journal of School Psychology*, 1979, 17, 260-263.
52. BOYD, L. A., & CHISSON, B. S. Analysis of the AAMD Adaptive Behavior Scale: Public School Version. *Perceptual & Motor Skills*, 1979, 49, 595-600.
53. BURKHART, G., & SEIM, R. The effects of institutionalization on retardates social independence. *Journal of Mental Deficiency Research*, 1979, 23, 213-218.
54. GOLLY, K., & HOSCH, H. M. Adaptive Behavior Scale: Development as a diagnostic tool via discriminant analysis. *American Journal of Mental Deficiency*, 1979, 83, 518-523.
55. HEMMING, H., COOK, M., GILBERT, K. A., & LAVENDER, A. Gaze patterns of mentally retarded adults in two contrasting environments. *American Journal of Mental Deficiency*, 1979, 83, 561-565.
56. ISETT, R. D., & SPREAT, S. Test-retest and interrater reliability of the AAMD Adaptive Behavior Scale. *American Journal of Mental Deficiency*, 1979, 84, 93-95.
57. KNOBBE, T., MEIER, P., WENAR, C., & CORDERO, L. Psychological development of children who received intrauterine transfusions. *American Journal of Obstetrics & Gynecology*, 1979, 133, 877-879.
58. MALGADY, R. G., BARCHER, P. R., TOWNER, G., & DAVIS, J. Language factors in vocational evaluation of mentally retarded workers. *American Journal of Mental Deficiency*, 1979, 83, 432-438.
59. PANEK, P. E., WAGNER, E. E., & SUEN, H. Hand Test indices of violent and destructive behavior for institutionalized mental retardates. *Journal of Personality Assessment*, 1979, 43, 376-378.
60. ROSZKOWSKI, M. J., & WALLEN, A. Association of weight and overactivity in institutionalized mentally retarded adults. *Perceptual & Motor Skills*, 1979, 49, 241-242.
61. SPREAT, S. Informant scoring errors on the Adaptive Behavior Scale. *American Journal of Mental Deficiency*, 1979, 83, 411-414.
62. TAYLOR, R. L., WARREN, S. A., & SLOCUMB, P. R. Categorizing behavior in terms of severity: Considerations for part two of the Adaptive Behavior Scale. *American Journal of Mental Deficiency*, 1979, 83, 411-414.
63. VANCE, H. Sex differences on the WISC-R for retarded children and youth. *Psychology in the Schools*, 1979, 16, 27-31.
64. WEINSTOCK, A., WULKAN, P., COLON, C. J., COLEMAN, J., & GONCALVES, S. Stress inoculation and interinstitutional transfer of mentally retarded individuals. *American Journal of Mental Deficiency*, 1979, 83, 385-390.
65. WIMMER, D. An investigation of the cognitive content of career education for the mildly mentally retarded. *Education & Training of the Mentally Retarded*, 1979, 14, 42-49.
66. CARSRUD, A. L., CARSRUD, K. B., & DODD, B. G. Randomly monitored staff utilization of behavior modification techniques: Long-term effects on clients. *Journal of Consulting & Clinical Psychology*, 1980, 48, 704-710.
67. CLEMENTS, P. R., BOST, L. W., DUBOIS, Y. G., & TURPIN, W. B. Adaptive Behavior Scale Part Two: Relative severity of maladaptive behavior. *American Journal of Mental Deficiency*, 1980, 84, 465-469.
68. GIVENS, T. Scorer reliability on the AAMD Adaptive Behavior Scale, Public School Version, Part One. *Psychology in the Schools*, 1980, 17, 335-338.
69. HOLMES, C. B., & BATT, R. Is choking others really equivalent to stamping one's feet? An analysis of Adaptive Behavior Scale items. *Psychological Reports*, 1980, 46, 1277-1278.
70. KATZ-GARRIS, L., HADLEY, T. J., GARRIS, R. P., & BARNHILL, B. A factor analytic study of the Adaptive Behavior Scale. *Psychological Reports*, 1980, 47, 807-814.
71. KAY, S. R. Progressive figure drawings in the developmental assessment of mentally retarded psychotics. *Perceptual & Motor Skills*, 1980, 50, 583-590.
72. KING, T., & SOUCAR, E. An attempt to assess and predict adaptive behavior of institutionalized mentally retarded clients. *American Journal of Mental Deficiency*, 1980, 84, 406-410.
73. MARKS, H. E., & RODD-MARKS, J. On an attempt to assess and predict adaptive behavior of institutionalized mentally retarded clients. *American Journal of Mental Deficiency*, 1980, 85, 195.
74. MEALOR, D. J., & RICHMOND, B. O. Adaptive behavior: Teachers and parents disagree. *Exceptional Children*, 1980, 46, 386-389.
75. ROSZKOWSKI, M. J. Concurrent validity of the Adaptive Behavior Scale as assessed by the Vineland Social Maturity Scale. *American Journal of Mental Deficiency*, 1980, 85, 86-89.
76. ROSZKOWSKI, M. J., & BEAN, A. G. The Adaptive Behavior Scale (ABS) and IQ: How much unshared variance is there? *Psychology in the Schools*, 1980, 17, 452-459.
77. SCHEEL, V., & GALBRAITH, G. C. Adaptation to visual-motor rearrangement of mentally retarded individuals: Relationship to Adaptive Behavior Scale scores. *American Journal of Mental Deficiency*, 1980, 84, 627-632.

78. SPREAT, S. The Adaptive Behavior Scale: A study of criterion validity. *American Journal of Mental Deficiency*, 1980, 85, 61–68.
79. SUTTER, P., MAYEDA, T., CALL, T., YANAGI, G., & YEE, S. Comparisons of successful and unsuccessful community–placed mentally retarded persons. *American Journal of Mental Deficiency*, 1980, 85, 262–267.
80. WEBER, D. B., & EPSTEIN, H. R. Contrasting adaptive behavior ratings of male and female institutionalized residents across two settings. *American Journal of Mental Deficiency*, 1980, 84, 397–400.
81. WEBSTER, P. S. Occupational role development in the young adult with mild mental retardation. *American Journal of Occupational Therapy*, 1980, 34, 13–18.
82. ARNDT, S. A general measure of adaptive behavior. *American Journal of Mental Deficiency*, 1981, 85, 554–556.
83. ASATO, H., TWIGGS, D. G., & ELLISON, S. EMG biofeedback training for a mentally retarded individual with cerebral palsy. *Physical Therapy*, 1981, 61, 1447–1451.
84. CLEMENTS, P. R., DUBOIS, Y., BOST, L., & BRYAN, C. Adaptive Behavior Scale, Part Two: Predictive efficiency of severity and frequency scores. *American Journal of Mental Deficiency*, 1981, 85, 433–434.
85. EYMAN, R. K., BORTHWICK, S. A., & MILLER, C. Trends in maladaptive behavior of mentally retarded persons placed in community and institutional settings. *American Journal of Mental Deficiency*, 1981, 85, 473–477.
86. GULLY, K. J. Emotionally disturbed children: Their adaptive behaviors and development in residential treatment. *Child Study Journal*, 1981, 11, 91–97.
87. HEMMING, H., LAVENDER, T., & PILL, R. Quality of life of mentally retarded adults transferred from large institutions to new small units. *American Journal of Mental Deficiency*, 1981, 86, 157–169.
88. LAMBERT, N. M., & HARTSOUGH, C. S. Development of a simplified diagnostic scoring method for the school version of the Adaptive Behavior Scale. *American Journal of Mental Deficiency*, 1981, 86, 138–147.
89. MATSON, J. L. Use of independence training to teach shopping skills to mildly mentally retarded adults. *American Journal of Mental Deficiency*, 1981, 86, 178–183.
90. NIHIRA, K., MINK, I. T., & MEYERS, C. E. Relationship between home environment and school adjustment of TMR children. *American Journal of Mental Deficiency*, 1981, 86, 8–15.
91. SEARLS, E., ISETT, R., & BOWDERS, T. Examination of item weighting on the Adaptive Behavior Scale Part II. *Perceptual & Motor Skills*, 1981, 53, 654.
92. THIEL, G. W. Relationship of IQ, adaptive behavior, age, and environmental demand to community–placement success of mentally retarded adults. *American Journal of Mental Deficiency*, 1981, 86, 208–211.

[7]

The ABC Inventory to Determine Kindergarten and School Readiness. Entrants to kgn and grade 1; 1965; Normand Adair and George Blesch; Research Concepts.* (In-print status uncertain; no reply from publisher.)

See T2:1691 (2 references); for a review by David P. Weikart, see 7:739 (2 references).

REFERENCES

1–2. See 7:739.
3–4. See T2:1691.
5. RANDEL, M. A., FRY, M. A., & RALLS, E. M. Two readiness measures as predictors of first- and third-grade reading achievement. *Psychology in the Schools*, 1977, 14, 37–40.
6. SCHOOLER, D. L., & ANDERSON, R. L. Race differences on the Developmental Test of Visual–Motor Integration, the Slosson Intelligence Test, and the ABC Inventory. *Psychology in the Schools*, 1979, 16, 453–456.

[8]

Abortion Scale. Older adolescents and adults; 1972; attitudes toward abortion; Panos D. Bardis; the Author.*

For additional information, see 8:331 (1 reference).

[9]

*****Abstract Reasoning: Differential Aptitude Tests.** Grades 8–12 and adults; 1947–77; George K. Bennett, Harold G. Seashore, and Alexander G. Wesman; The Psychological Corporation.* For the complete battery entry, see 732.

For additional information regarding an earlier edition, see 8:185 (3 references); see also T2:333 (7 references).

For reviews of the complete battery, see 8:485 (2 reviews, 1 excerpt), 7:673 (1 review, 1 excerpt), 6:767 (2 reviews), 5:605 (2 reviews), 4:711 (3 reviews), and 3:620 (1 excerpt).

REFERENCES

1–7. See T2:333.
8–10. See 8:185.
11. EASTMAN, P. M., & BEHR, M. J. Interaction between structure of intellect factors and two methods of presenting concepts of logic. *Journal for Research in Mathematics Education*, 1977, 8, 379–381.
12. COHN, S. J. Cognitive characteristics of the top–scoring third of the 1976 talent search contestants. *Gifted Child Quarterly*, 1978, 22, 416–420.
13. ARNOLD, P., & WALTER, G. Communication and reasoning skills of deaf and hearing signers. *Perceptual & Motor Skills*, 1979, 49, 192–194.
14. DOBSON, K. S., & NEUFELD, R. W. J. Stress–related appraisals: A regression analysis. *Canadian Journal of Behavioural Science*, 1979, 11, 274–285.
15. PARASINIS, I., & LONG, G. L. Relationships among spatial skills, communication skills, and field independence in deaf students. *Perceptual & Motor Skills*, 1979, 49, 879–887.
16. SILVER, E. A. Student perceptions of relatedness among mathematical verbal problems. *Journal of Research in Mathematics Education*, 1979, 10, 195–210.
17. BECKER, B. J. Performance of a group of mathematically able youths on the mathematics usage and natural sciences reading tests of the American College Test Battery vs the Scholastic Aptitude Test. *Gifted Child Quarterly*, 1980, 24, 138–143.

[10]

AC Test of Creative Ability. Engineers and supervisors; 1953–60; 9 scores: quantity (3 scores), uniqueness (4 scores), quality, total; subtests yielding quantity scores may be administered alone for quantity scores only; Richard H. Harris (test), A. L. Simberg (test), and Measurement Research Division, Human Resources Center, University of Chicago (manual); the Center.*

See T2:2340 (23 references); for reviews by Samuel T. Mayo, Philip R. Merrifield, and Albert S. Thompson, see 6:1130 (1 reference).

REFERENCES

1. See 6:1130.
2–24. See T2:2340.
25. VOSS, H. G. The effect of experimentally induced activation on creativity. *Journal of Psychology*, 1977, 96, 3–9.

[11]

Academic Aptitude Test. Bantu pupils in Form V, first-year university; 1974–76; AAT; 10 scores: reasoning (non-verbal, verbal), vocabulary (English, Afrikaans), reading comprehension (English, Afrikaans), number comprehension, squares, spatial perception, mathematical ability; test by Rina Minnie, J. S. Gericke, F. W. Gericke, J. C. Chamberlain, and B. P. A. Strauss; Human Sciences Research Council [South Africa].*

For additional information, see 8:481.

[12]

Academic Aptitude Test: Non-Verbal Intelligence: Acorn National Aptitude Tests. Grades 7–16 and adults; 1943–57; 4 scores: spatial relations, physical relations, graphic relations, total; Andrew Kobal, J. Wayne Wrightstone, and Karl R. Kunze; Psychometric Affiliates.*

For additional information, see 5:303; for a review by William B. Schrader, see 4:274.

[13]

Academic Aptitude Test: Verbal Intelligence: Acorn National Aptitude Tests. Grades 7–16 and adults; 1943–52; 4 scores: general information, mental alertness, comprehension of relations, total; Andrew Kobal, J. Wayne Wrightstone, and Karl R. Kunze; Psychometric Affiliates.*

For additional information, see 5:304; for a review by William B. Schrader, see 4:275; for a review by Marion A. Bills, see 3:215.

[14]
Academic Freedom Survey. College students and faculty; 1954; 3 scores: student, faculty, total; Paul Slivnick and Academic Freedom Committee, Illinois Division, American Civil Liberties Union; Psychometric Affiliates.*

For additional information, see 5:531.

[15]
Academic Proficiency Battery. College entrants; 1969; APB; 5 scores: social sciences, commercial sciences, natural sciences, mathematical sciences, languages (either English or Afrikaans); F. A. Fouché, N. F. Alberts, and C. L. J. Minnaar (test); Human Sciences Research Council [South Africa].*

For additional information, see 7:1.

[16–7]
Academic Readiness Scale. First grade entrants; 1968; ARS; a similar rating scale, *End of First Grade Progress Scale*, "suitable for older children," is available without a manual; ratings by teachers in 14 areas: motor, perceptual-motor (2 scores), persistence, memory, attention, number recognition, counting, word recognition, vocabulary, interest in curriculum, social, humor, emotional; also includes form for recording opinions of teachers and parents regarding children being considered for retention or special class placement; 2 levels; Harold F. Burks; Arden Press.* (In-print status uncertain; no reply from publisher.)

For additional information and reviews by Dennis J. Deloria and Eleanor M. Ladd, see 8:795 (1 reference); see also T2:1693 (1 reference).

[18]
Academic-Technical Aptitude Tests. "Coloured pupils" in standards 6–8; 1970; ATA; the coordination and writing speed tests are taken from the *N. B. Aptitude Tests (Junior)*; 10 scores: verbal reasoning, non-verbal reasoning, computations, spatial perceptions (2-D), mechanical reasoning, language comprehension, spatial perception (3-D), comparison, coordination, writing speed; all test materials are in both English and Afrikaans except the Technical Report which is in Afrikaans; K. Owen (7 tests and manual) and C. P. Celliers (language comprehension test); Human Sciences Research Council [South Africa].*

[19]
A.C.E.R. Advanced Test B40. Ages 13 and over; 1940–66; formerly called *Adult Test (B40)*; Australian Council for Educational Research [Australia].*

See T2:323 (6 references) and 7:328 (4 references); for a review by C. Sanders, see 5:296 (3 references).

[20]
ACER Advanced Test N. Ages 15 and over; 1951–52; not available to government schools; Australian Council for Educational Research [Australia].*

For additional information and reviews by A. E. G. Pilliner and C. Sanders, see 5:307.

[21]
A.C.E.R. Advanced Tests AL and AQ. College and superior adults; 1953–73; 2 tests; D. Spearritt (manual); Australian Council for Educational Research [Australia].*
a) TEST AL. 1953–55; linguistic.
b) TEST AQ. 1953–73; quantitative; 1973 metric edition identical with test published 1954 except for 2 new and 4 revised items.

See T2:324 (3 references); for a review by Duncan Howie, see 5:295.

REFERENCES

1–3. See T2:324.
4. BYRNE, B., & SINCLAIR, J. Memory for tonal sequence and timbre: A correlation with familial handedness. *Neuropsychologia*, 1979, 17, 539–542.

[22]
***ACER and University of Melbourne Music Evaluation Kit.** Beginning of secondary school; 1976–79; MEK; criterion-referenced; 40 specific objectives in 7 areas: pitch discrimination (6 objectives), discrimination in the length of sounds (5), volume discrimination (10), tone colour discrimination (2), patterns recognition (6), identification of instruments and instrumental groups (5), knowledge of musical signs and symbols (6); Jennifer Bryce and Max Cooke; Australian Council for Educational Research [Australia].*

For additional information, see 8:89.

[23]
A.C.E.R. Arithmetic Tests: Standardized for Use in New Zealand. Ages 9–12; 1957; identical with corresponding parts of *A.C.E.R. Arithmetic Tests*; 4 tests: addition, multiplication, subtraction, division; manual by A. E. Fieldhouse; New Zealand Council for Educational Research [New Zealand].*

See T2:690 (1 reference) and 5:453.

[24]
★ACER Checklists for School Beginners. Age 5; 1974–77; ratings by parents and teachers in 5 areas: social development, emotional development, motor skills, memory and attention, language skills; (parent's checklist available in Arabic, Greek, Italian, Maltese, Serbo-Croatian, Spanish, and Turkish); Helga A. H. Rowe; Australian Council for Educational Research [Australia].*

[25]
★ACER Chemistry Test Item Collection: Year 12 (Chemtic). Grade 12; 1980–81; Australian Council for Educational Research [Australia].*

[26]
★ACER Class Achievement Test in Mathematics. Grades 4–5, 6–7; 1976–79; CATIM; "based upon an 'Australian-average' syllabus"; criterion-referenced; 4 item classification areas: knowledge, computation, application, understanding; Australian Council for Educational Research [Australia].*

[27]
★**ACER Early School Series.** 5–5$\frac{1}{2}$-year-old school beginners; 1981; ESS; criterion-referenced; estimation of cognitive development and maturity for early identification of children who may be at risk of developing learning disabilities; handbook entitled *Early Identification and Intervention*; 10 tests; Helga A. H. Rowe; Australian Council for Educational Research [Australia].*

a) TESTS OF AUDITORY ANALYSIS SKILLS. 2 tests.
 1) *Auditory Discrimination Test.* Includes same types of sound-contrasts used in the Wepman Test.
 2) *Recognition of Initial Consonant Sounds Test.*

b) CONCEPTUAL SKILLS TESTS. 2 tests.
 1) *Number Test.*
 2) *Figure Formation Test.* Provides rough indication of child's general intellectual maturity.

c) LANGUAGE SKILLS TESTS.
 1) *Tests of Syntax.* 5 tests.
  (*a*) Preposition Test.
  (*b*) Pronouns Test.
  (*c*) Verb Tense Test.
  (*d*) Negation Test.
  (*e*) Comprehension Test.
 2) *Word Knowledge Test.* Designed to identify children unable to comprehend a sample of English words which many Australian teachers would expect from 5-year-olds.

[28]
A.C.E.R. Higher Tests. Ages 13 and over; 1944–73; formerly called *A.C.E.R. General Ability Test: Advanced M*; 3 scores: linguistic, quantitative, total; 2 parts; D. Spearritt (original manual), M. L. Clark (revised manual), and B. Christeson (form W); Australian Council for Educational Research [Australia].*

a) FORMS ML AND WL [LINGUISTIC].
b) FORMS MQ AND WQ [QUANTITATIVE].

See T2:325 (1 reference) and 6:432 (1 reference); for a review by C. Sanders, see 5:297.

REFERENCES

1. See 6:432.
2. See T2:325.
3. BRAUN, N. J., & KNOCHE, M. Prediction of job performance using psychological appraisal testing: A validity study. *Australian Psychologist*, 1978, 13, 379–389.
4. POOLE, M. E. Identifying early school leaving. *Australian Journal of Education*, 1978, 22, 13–24.

[29]
A.C.E.R. Intermediate Test A. Ages 10–0 to 14–0; 1938–61; Australian Council for Educational Research [Australia].*

For additional information, see 6:433.

[30]
A.C.E.R. Intermediate Tests C and D. Ages 10–0 to 14–0; 1939–72; 2 tests, only 1 test currently available; Australian Council for Educational Research [Australia].*

a) TEST C. 1939–53; formerly called *A.C.E.R. General Test C.* Out of print.
b) TEST D. 1947–72; 1972 metric edition of test identical with test published 1947 except for 3 new and 5 revised items; not available to government schools; D. Spearritt (original manual) and M. L. Clark (revised manual).

See T2:327 (1 reference); for a review by James Lumsden, see 5:298 (2 references).

REFERENCES

1–2. See 5:298.
3. See T2:327.
4. POWER, C. N. Effects of student characteristics and level of teacher-student interaction on achievement and attitudes. *Contemporary Educational Psychology*, 1977, 2, 265–274.
5. DUNKIN, M. J., & DOENAU, S. J. A replication study of unique and joint contributions to variance in student achievement. *Journal of Educational Psychology*, 1980, 72, 394–403.
6. HOWELL, E. R., SMITH, G. A., & STANLEY, G. Reading disability and visual spatial frequency specific effects. *Australian Journal of Psychology*, 1981, 33, 97–102.

[31]
A.C.E.R. Junior Non-Verbal Test. Ages 8.5–12.0; 1949–53; manual by D. Spearritt; Australian Council for Educational Research [Australia].*

See T2:328 (3 references); for a review by D. A. Pidgeon, see 5:301 (1 reference).

REFERENCES

1. See 5:301.
2–4. See T2:328.
5. EVANS, G., GEORGEFF, M., & POOLE, M. E. Training in information selection for communication. *Australian Journal of Education*, 1980, 24, 137–154.

[32]
A.C.E.R. Junior Test A. Ages 8.5–12.0; 1946–58; formerly called *General Test T*; Australian Council for Educational Research [Australia].*

For additional information, see 6:434; for a review by R. Winterbourn, see 5:299.

[33]
★**ACER Listening Tests: 10-year-olds and 14-year-olds.** Ages 10, 14; 1981; 5 major subtests: comprehending words and statements, understanding instructions, comprehending passages, comprehending conversation, comprehending in different situations, plus 8 minor subtests and total; Faye Holzer; Australian Council for Educational Research [Australia].*

[34]
A.C.E.R. Lower Grades General Ability Scale, Second Edition. Ages 6–6 to 9–1; 1962–66; 5 scores: picture vocabulary, picture arrangement, picture analogies, picture series, total; M. L. Clark; Australian Council for Educational Research [Australia].*

See T2:330 (1 reference) and 7:329.

REFERENCES

1. See T2:330.
2. HENRY, J. A. Elementary school science experiences and reading achievement in six-year-old-children. *Genetic Psychology Monographs*, 1978, 98, 159–179.

[35]
★**ACER Mathematics Profile Series.** Grades 4–10; 1977–80; MAPS; 4 tests; Greg Cornish and Robin Wines; Australian Council for Educational Research [Australia].*

a) OPERATIONS TEST. Grades 4–10; 1978.
b) SPACE TEST. Grades 5–10; 1978.
c) MEASUREMENT TEST. Grades 7–10; 1979.
d) NUMBER TEST. Grades 7–10; 1980.

[36]
ACER Mathematics Tests: AM Series. Grades 4–6; 1969–79; 14 tests; Australian Council for Educational Research [Australia].

a) TEST AM 1: NUMERATION, COUNTING, AND NUMBER PATTERNS.
b) TEST AM 2: PLACE VALUE.
c) TEST AM 3: SETS.
d) TEST AM 4: WHOLE NUMBERS.
e) TEST AM 5: MONEY.
f) TEST AM 6: COMMON FRACTIONS.
g) TEST AM 7: DECIMAL FRACTIONS.
h) TEST AM 8: SPATIAL RELATIONS.
i) TEST AM 9: LENGTH.
j) TEST AM 10: AREA.
k) TEST AM 11: MASS AND WEIGHT.
l) TEST AM 12: CAPACITY AND VOLUME.
m) TEST AM 13: TIME.
n) TEST AM 14: GRAPHS.

REFERENCES

1. BECK, T. An Australian study of school environments. *Australian Journal of Education*, 1980, 24, 1–12.

[37]
A.C.E.R. Mechanical Comprehension Test. Ages 13.5 and over; 1942–53; Australian Council for Educational Research [Australia].*

For additional information and reviews by John R. Jennings and Hayden S. Williams, see 5:874 (2 references); for a review by D. W. McElwain, see 4:756.

REFERENCES

1–2. See 5:874.
3. BRAUN, N. J., & KNOCHE, M. Prediction of job performance using psychological appraisal testing: A validity study. *Australian Psychologist*, 1978, 13, 379–389.

[38]
A.C.E.R. Mechanical Reasoning Test. Ages 13–9 and over; 1951–62; abbreviated adaptation of *A.C.E.R. Mechanical Comprehension Test*; T. M. Whitford (revised manual) and Research and Guidance Branch, Queensland Department of Public Instruction (test); Australian Council for Educational Research [Australia]. (British norms supplement: 1978; Gill Nyfield; NFER-Nelson Publishing Co. [England].)*

See T2:2238 (3 references) and 6:1082; for reviews by John R. Jennings and Hayden S. Williams, see 5:875.

[39]
A.C.E.R. Number Test. Ages 13.5 and over; 1942–55; manual by D. Spearritt; Australian Council for Educational Research [Australia].*

See T2:691 (2 references) and 5:454; for a review by Leslie M. Haynes of the original edition, see 4:399.

[40]
★ACER Paragraph Reading Test. Grades 6–8; 1976–77; Australian Council for Educational Research [Australia].*

[41]
★ACER Physics Unit Tests: Diagnostic Aids. Grades 11–12; 1978–80; collection of 21 separate tests and 21 diagnostic aids corresponding to the tests; 21 tests: physical measurement, vectors, motion in one dimension, motion on a plane, dynamics, work and energy, linear momentum, oscillations, gravity and Kepler's laws, waves, light—reflection and refraction, light—interference diffraction and spectra, models of light, kinetic theory of gases, static charges, electric field and potential difference, current electricity, the magnetic field, induced EMF, atomic physics, quantum physics; Graeme Wilmot; Australian Council for Educational Research [Australia].*

[42]
ACER Primary Reading Survey Tests. Grades 1, 2, 3, 4, 5, 6; 1971–73; interim manuals prepared by G. P. Withers in collaboration with M. L. Clark, W. T. Renehan (manual A-D), and B. Rechter (manual A-D); Australian Council for Educational Research [Australia].*

a) LEVEL AA. Grade 1; 1972–73; word recognition.
b) LEVEL BB. Grade 2; 1972–73; 2 parts.
　1) *Part 1: Word Knowledge.*
　2) *Part 2: Comprehension.*
c) LEVEL A. Grade 3; 1971–72; 2 parts.
　1) *Part 1: Word Knowledge.*
　2) *Part 2: Comprehension.*
d) LEVEL B. Grade 4; 1971–72; 2 parts.
　1) *Part 1: Word Knowledge.*
　2) *Part 2: Comprehension.*
e) LEVEL C. Grade 5; 1971–72; 2 parts.
　1) *Part 1: Word Knowledge.*
　2) *Part 2: Comprehension.*
f) LEVEL D. Grade 6; 1971–73; 5 parts.
　1) *Part 1: Word Knowledge.*
　2) *Part 2: Comprehension.*
　3) *Part 1A: Word Discrimination.*
　4) *Part 1B: Word Formation.*
　5) *Part 1C: Dictionary Skills.*

For additional information, see 8:714.

REFERENCES

1. HENRY, J. A. Elementary school science experiences and reading achievement in six-year-old children. *Genetic Psychology Monographs*, 1978, 98, 159–179.
2. MARJORIBANKS, K. Ethnicity, school attitudes, intelligence and academic achievement. *International Journal of Psychology*, 1978, 13, 167–178.
3. ROSENTHAL, D., & MORRISON, S. On being a minority in the classroom: A study of the influence of ethnic mix on cognitive functioning and attitudes in working class children. *Australian Journal of Education*, 1978, 22, 144–160.
4. BECK, T. An Australian study of school environments. *Australian Journal of Education*, 1980, 24, 1–12.

[43]
ACER Short Clerical Test—Form C. Ages 13 and over; 1953–67; 2 scores: checking, arithmetic; Australian Council for Educational Research [Australia].*

For additional information, see 7:986.

[44]
A.C.E.R. Silent Reading Tests: Standardized for Use in New Zealand. Ages 9–12; 1955; 3 parts; tests identical with corresponding parts of Form B (Part 2) and Form C (Parts 1 and 3) of *A.C.E.R. Silent Reading Tests*; A. E. Fieldhouse (manual); New Zealand Council for Educational Research [New Zealand].*

a) PART 1, WORD KNOWLEDGE.
b) PART 2, SPEED OF READING.
c) PART 3, READING FOR MEANING.

See T2:1531 (2 references) and 5:618.

[45]
A.C.E.R. Speed and Accuracy Tests. Ages 13.5 and over; 1942–62; 2 scores: number checking, name checking; revised manual by T. M. Whitford; Australian Council for Educational Research [Australia].*

See T2:2118 (1 reference) and 6:1031 (2 references); for a review by D. W. McElwain of an earlier form, see 4:719.

REFERENCES

1-2. See 6:1031.
3. See T2:2118.
4. RICHARDSON, A. The meaning and measurement of memory imagery. *British Journal of Psychology*, 1977, 68, 29–43.
5. BRAUN, N. J., & KNOCHE, M. Prediction of job performance using psychological appraisal testing: A validity study. *Australian Psychologist*, 1978, 13, 379–389.

[46]
★**ACER Spelling Test Years 3–6.** School years 3, 4, 5, 6; 1976–81; ACER STY 3–6; Australian Council for Educational Research [Australia].*

[47]
ACER Test of Learning Ability. Grades 4, 6; 1976, c1971–76; TOLA; 4 scores: verbal comprehension, general reasoning, syllogistic reasoning, total; Australian Council for Educational Research [Australia].*

For additional information, see 8:174.

[48]
A.C.E.R. Word Knowledge Test—Adult Form B. Ages 18 and over; 1933–60; identical with part 1 of *A.C.E.R. Silent Reading Tests*, Form B for grades 3–8 except for directions; manual by T. M. Whitford; Australian Council for Educational Research [Australia].*

For additional information, see 6:327 (1 reference).

[49]
Achievement Test—Hebrew Language. Grades 5–7; 1973; Testing Bureau of the National Curriculum Research Institute; Jewish Education Service of North America, Inc.*

[50]
Achievement Test in Jewish History. Junior high school; 1962; 4 scores: informational background, terms and concepts, personalities, total; original forms by Leon H. Spotts; revision, manual, and technical report by Gerhard Lang; National Curriculum Research Institute; Jewish Education Service of North America, Inc.*

For additional information, see 6:749.

[51]
Achievement Test—Jewish Life and Observances. Grades 5–7; 1973; Testing Bureau of the National Curriculum Research Institute; Jewish Education Service of North America, Inc.*

[52]
Achievement Test—The State of Israel. "Pupils who have completed an organized course of study on the State of Israel"; 1973; Testing Bureau of the National Curriculum Research Institute; Jewish Education Service of North America, Inc.*

[53]
★**Achievement Tests: Grades 1–8.** Grades 1, 2, 3, 4, 5, 6, 7, 8; 1980; 4 scores: comprehension skills, vocabulary skills, language skills, study skills; Anne Groom; Macmillan Publishing Co., Inc.*

[54]
Achievement Tests in Nursing. Students in schools of registered nursing; 1952–71; tests administered at any time by individual schools; 14 tests; The Psychological Corporation.*

a) ANATOMY AND PHYSIOLOGY. 1953–68.
b) CANCER NURSING. 1967.
c) GENERAL CHEMISTRY. 1954–64.
d) ORGANIC AND INORGANIC CHEMISTRY. 1964.
e) COMMUNICABLE DISEASES. 1953–61.
f) MEDICAL NURSING. 1952–68.
g) MICROBIOLOGY. 1952–68.
h) NUTRITION AND DIET THERAPY. 1952–68.
i) OBSTETRICAL NURSING. 1952–68.
j) PEDIATRIC NURSING. 1952–68.
k) PHARMACOLOGY. 1952–68.
l) PSYCHIATRIC NURSING. 1952–71.
m) PSYCHOLOGY AND SOCIOLOGY. 1957–68.
n) SURGICAL NURSING. 1952–68.

For additional information, see 7:1112.

[55]
Achievement Tests in Practical Nursing. Practical nursing students; 1957–67; tests administered at any time by individual schools; The Psychological Corporation.*

For additional information, see 7:1113 (1 reference).

[56]
*****ACS Examination: Brief Course in Organic Chemistry.** 1 semester college; 1956–77; Examinations Committee, American Chemical Society.*

For additional information, see 7:821 (1 reference); for an excerpted review by LeRoy D. Johnson of an earlier form, see 6:905.

[57]
*****ACS Examination in Analytical Chemistry, Graduate Level.** Entering graduate students; 1961–81; Examinations Committee, American Chemical Society.*

See T2:1815 (1 reference), 7:822 (1 reference), and 6:899 (1 reference).

[58]
*****ACS Examination in Analytical Chemistry (Quantitative Analysis).** College; 1944–82; Examinations Committee, American Chemical Society.*

For additional information, see 7:836 (1 reference); see also 6:907 (1 reference); for an excerpted review by H. E. Wilcox of an earlier form, see 5:735; for reviews by William B. Meldrum and William Rieman III, see 3:563.

[59]
*****ACS Examination in Biochemistry.** College; 1947–82; Examinations Committee, American Chemical Society.*

For additional information, see 7:823 (1 reference); for an excerpted review by Wilhelm R. Frisell of an earlier form, see 6:898 (2 references).

[60]
ACS Examination in Brief Qualitative Analysis. College; 1961–77; Examinations Committee, American Chemical Society.
See T2:1818 (4 references) and 7:825; for an excerpted review by W. H. Waggoner of an earlier form, see 6:906 (4 references); see also 4:608 (2 references).

[61]
ACS Examination in General Chemistry. 1 year college; 1934–81; Examinations Committee, American Chemical Society.*
For additional information and a review by Frank J. Fornoff, see 8:837 (3 references); see also T2:1819 (1 reference) and 7:826 (5 references); for reviews by J. A. Campbell and William Hered and an excerpted review by S. L. Burson, Jr. of earlier forms, see 6:902 (3 references); for reviews by Frank P. Cassaretto and Palmer O. Johnson, see 5:732 (2 references); for a review by Kenneth E. Anderson, see 4:610 (1 reference); for reviews by Sidney J. French and Florence E. Hooper, see 3:557 (3 references); see also 2:1593 (5 references).

[62]
★ACS Examination in General Chemistry (Brief Test). 1 year college; 1981; Examinations Committee, American Chemical Society.

[63]
★ACS Examination in General-Organic-Biological Chemistry (for Allied Health Science Programs). 1979; 4 scores: general, organic, biological, total; each subtest has 2 parts and various combinations of subtests and parts may be administered to fit a particular course; Examinations Committee, American Chemical Society.*

[64]
ACS Examination in Inorganic Chemistry. College juniors and seniors and graduate students; 1961–81; Examinations Committee, American Chemical Society.*
For additional information, see 8:838 (2 references); see also T2:1820 (1 reference) and 7:827 (2 references); for a review by Frank J. Fornoff and an excerpted review by George B. Kauffman of an earlier form, see 6:903 (1 reference).

REFERENCES
1. See 6:903.
2–3. See 7:827.
4. See T2:1820.
5–6. See 8:838.
7. SIENKO, M. J. The ACS inorganic exam and its influence (?) on the inorganic curriculum. *Journal of Chemical Education*, 1980, 57, 765–766.

[65]
ACS Examination in Inorganic Chemistry, Graduate Level. Entering graduate students; 1965–81; Examinations Committee, American Chemical Society.
See T2:1821 (1 reference) and 7:828.

[66]
ACS Examination in Instrumental Determinations (Analysis). College juniors and seniors; 1966–81; Examinations Committee, American Chemical Society.
For additional information, see 7:830 (1 reference).

[67]
ACS Examination in Organic Chemistry. 1 year college; 1942–82; Examinations Committee, American Chemical Society.*
For additional information, see 8:840 (3 references); see also 7:831 (3 references) and 6:905 (4 references); for a review by Shailer Peterson of an earlier form, see 3:558.

[68]
ACS Examination in Organic Chemistry, Graduate Level. Entering graduate students; 1961–81; Examinations Committee, American Chemical Society.*
For additional information, see 8:841 (2 references); see also 7:832 (1 reference) and 6:900 (1 reference).

[69]
ACS Examination in Physical Chemistry. 1 year college; 1946–81; subtests cover thermodynamics, chemical dynamics, quantum chemistry, and may be administered separately or together; Examinations Committee, American Chemical Society.*
For additional information and a review by Gerald R. Van Hecke, see 8:842 (2 references); see also T2:1826 (2 references), 7:833 (2 references), and 6:904 (1 reference); for a review by Alfred S. Brown of an earlier form, see 3:559.

[70]
★ACS Examination in Physical Chemistry for the Life Sciences. 1 semester college; 1982; Examinations Committee, American Chemical Society.

[71]
ACS Examination in Physical Chemistry, Graduate Level. Entering graduate students; 1961–81; distribution restricted to graduate schools; Examinations Committee, American Chemical Society.*
For additional information and a review by Gerald R. Van Hecke, see 8:843 (1 reference); see also 7:834 (2 references) and 6:901 (1 reference).

[72]
★ACS Examination in Polymer Chemistry. College; 1982; Examinations Committee, American Chemical Society.

[73]
ACS Examination in Qualitative Analysis. College; 1939–69; Examinations Committee, American Chemical Society.*
For additional information, see 7:835; for an excerpted review by Richard E. Frank of an earlier form, see 6:906 (4 references); for a review by William Rieman III, see 4:608; for reviews by William B. Meldrum and William Rieman III, see 3:562.

[74]
ACS-NSTA Examination in High School Chemistry, [Advanced Level]. Advanced high school classes; 1963–82; sponsored jointly with the National Science Teachers Association; Examinations Committee, American Chemical Society.*
For additional information and reviews by Peter A. Dahl and John P. Penna, see 8:844 (1 reference); for a review by Irvin J. Lehmann of the 1970 and earlier

forms, see 7:838 (3 references); for reviews by Frank J. Fornoff and William Hered, see 6:909.

[75]
ACS-NSTA Examination in High School Chemistry, [Lower Level]. 1 year high school; 1957–81; sponsored jointly with the National Science Teachers Association; Examinations Committee, American Chemical Society.*
For additional information and a review by Edward F. DeVillafranca, see 8:845 (11 references); see also T2:1830 (3 references); for reviews by William R. Crawford and Irvin J. Lehmann of Form 1971 and earlier forms, see 7:837 (9 references); for reviews by Frank J. Fornoff and William Hered and excerpted reviews by Christine Jansing and Joseph Schmuckler, see 6:908 (5 references); for reviews by Edward G. Rietz and Willard G. Warrington, see 5:729.

[76]
ACT Assessment Program. Candidates for college entrance; 1959–82; ACT; formerly called *ACT Test Battery*; academic tests administered 5 times a year (February, April, June, October, December) at centers established by the publisher; special editions available for administration to the handicapped; American College Testing Program.*
a) ACADEMIC TESTS. 1959–82; 5 scores: English usage, mathematics usage, social studies reading, natural sciences reading, composite.
b) ACT INTEREST INVENTORY. 1973–82; 6 scores: science, creative arts, social service, business contact, business detail, technical.
c) STUDENT PROFILE SECTION. 1964–82; survey inventory of admissions/enrollment information, educational plans/interests/needs, special educational needs/interests/goals, college extracurricular plans, financial aid, background information, factors influencing college choice, high school educational information, high school extracurricular activities, out-of-class accomplishments, evaluation of high school experience, information about educational opportunities.
For additional information and a review by John R. Hills, see 8:469 (208 references); see also T2:1044 (97 references); for a review by Wimburn L. Wallace of an earlier program, see 7:330 (265 references); for reviews by Max D. Engelhart and Warren G. Findley and an excerpted review by David V. Tiedeman, see 6:1 (14 references).

REFERENCES

1–14. See 6:1.
15–279. See 7:330.
280–376. See T2:1044.
377–584. See 8:469.
585. AMEG COMMISSION ON SEX BIAS IN MEASUREMENT. A case history of change: A review of responses to the challenge of sex bias in career interest inventories. *Measurement & Evaluation in Guidance*, 1977, 10, 148–152.
586. BACON, M. L. Factors affecting retention and loss of associate-degree students in University of Kentucky community colleges. *Journal of Business Education*, 1977, 53, 45.
587. BORGERS, S. B., HENDRIX, J. C., & PRICE, G. E. Does counselor response to occupational choice indicate sex stereotyping? *Journal of the National Association of Women Deans & Counselors*, 1977, 41, 17–20.
588. HANSON, G. R., NOETH, R. J., & PREDIGER, D. J. Validity of diverse procedures for reporting interest scores: An analysis of longitudinal data. *Journal of Counseling Psychology*, 1977, 24, 487–493.
589. JOHNSON, D. C. The TOEFL and domestic students: Conclusively inappropriate. *Teachers of English to Speakers of Other Languages Quarterly*, 1977, 11, 79–86.
590. KIM, P. Y. Personal economic understanding and college business and economics courses. *Delta Pi Epsilon Journal*, 1977, 14, 22–35.
591. NORRIS, L., & COCHRAN, D. J. The SIGI prediction system: Predicting college grades with and without tests. *Measurement & Evaluation in Guidance*, 1977, 10, 134–140.
592. OHLSON, E. L., & MEIN, L. The difference in level of anxiety in undergraduate mathematics and nonmathematics majors. *Journal for Research in Mathematics Education*, 1977, 8, 48–56.
593. PEDRINI, B. C., & PEDRINI, D. T. Grade point evaluation of an experimental program for disadvantaged college freshmen. *College Student Journal*, 1977, 11, 318–325.
594. PEDRINI, B. C., & PEDRINI, D. T. Multivariate prediction of attrition/persistence for disadvantaged and control collegians. *College Student Journal*, 1977, 11, 239–242.
595. PREDIGER, D. J., & HANSON, G. R. Some consequences of using raw–score reports of vocational interests. *Journal of Educational Measurement*, 1977, 14, 323–333.
596. SANFORD, T. R. The test score decline: An overview. *High School Journal*, 1977, 60, 302–316.
597. THIBEAULT, R. J., ZETLER, A. G., & WILSON, A. P. The achievement of bus transported pupils. *Journal of Teaching & Learning*, 1977, 2, 17–22.
598. VOGEL, R. E., & HALINSKI, R. S. Success on the CLEP General Examinations as a function of ACT performance. *Measurement & Evaluation in Guidance*, 1977, 10, 44–47.
599. ZIMMERMAN, W. S., PARKS, H., & GRAY, K. The validity of traditional cognitive measures and of scales of the study attitudes and methods survey in the prediction of the academic success of educational opportunity program students. *Educational & Psychological Measurement*, 1977, 37, 465–470.
600. ALEAMONI, L. M., & OBOLER, L. ACT versus SAT in predicting first semester GPA. *Educational & Psychological Measurement*, 1978, 38, 393–399.
601. BOULANGER, F. D. Teacher training in science: The effects of three feedback modes on learning a science principle. *Science Education*, 1978, 62, 195–202.
602. BURKHART, B. R., GYNTHER, M. D., & CHRISTIAN, W. L. Psychological mindedness, intelligence, and item subtlety endorsement patterns on the MMPI. *Journal of Clinical Psychology*, 1978, 34, 76–79.
603. CARNEY, P., ISAKSON, R. L., & ELLSWORTH, R. An exploration of grade inflation and some related factors in higher education. *College & University*, 1978, 53, 217–230.
604. DOWNEY, R. G. Differences between entering freshmen from different size high schools. *Journal of College Student Personnel*, 1978, 19, 353–359.
605. FERGUSON, R., & MAXEY, E. J. Trends in the academic performance of high school and college students. *Journal of College Student Personnel*, 1978, 19, 505–511.
606. FERGUSON, R. L., & SCHMEISER, C. B. The Mathematics Usage Test of the ACT Assessment Program: An overview of its purpose, content, and use. *Mathematics Teacher*, 1978, 71, 182–191.
607. FOWLER, B., & KROLL, B. M. Verbal skills as factors in the passageless validation of reading comprehension tests. *Perceptual & Motor Skills*, 1978, 47, 335–338.
608. GORMAN, C. D., CLOVER, W. H., & DOHERTY, M. E. Can we learn anything about interviewing real people from "interviews" of paper people? Two studies of the external validity of a paradigm. *Organizational Behavior & Human Performance*, 1978, 22, 165–192.
609. KELLY, J. A., & WORELL, L. Personality characteristics, parent behaviors, and sex of subject in relation to cheating. *Journal of Research in Personality*, 1978, 12, 179–188.
610. MCDADE, C. E. Subsumption versus educational set: Implications for sequencing of instructional materials. *Journal of Educational Psychology*, 1978, 70, 137–141.
611. MENASCO, M. B., & CURRY, D. J. An assessment of the Role Construct Repertory Test. *Applied Psychological Measurement*, 1978, 2, 361–367.
612. PEDRINI, B. C., & PEDRINI, D. T. Evaluating experimental and control programs for attrition/persistence. *Journal of Educational Research*, 1978, 71, 234–237.
613. POWERS, S. M., & POWERS, W. A. Instructor–prepared notes and achievement in introductory psychology. *Journal of Experimental Education*, 1978, 46, 37–41.
614. PREDIGER, D. J., & HANSON, G. R. Must interest inventories provide males and females with divergent vocational guidance. *Measurement & Evaluation in Guidance*, 1978, 11, 88–98.
615. ROBINSON, J. A., & BENNIK, C. D. Field articulation and working memory. *Journal of Research in Personality*, 1978, 12, 439–449.
616. ROWAN, R. W. The predictive value of the ACT at Murray State University over a four–year college program. *Measurement & Evaluation in Guidance*, 1978, 11, 143–149.

617. RUSSO, T. J., & CHECKETTS, K. T. Three sets of ordered variables and their association to the American College Test scores. *Journal of Educational Research*, 1978, 71, 198–202.
618. STIGGINS, R. J., SCHMEISER, C. B., & FERGUSON, R. L. Validity of the ACT assessment as an indicator of reading ability. *Applied Psychological Measurement*, 1978, 2, 337–344.
619. WEAVER, W. T. Educators in supply and demand: Effects on quality. *School Review*, 1978, 86, 552–593.
620. WIKOFF, R. L., & KAFKA, G. F. Interrelationships between the choice of college major, the ACT and the Sixteen Personality Factor Questionnaire. *Journal of Educational Research*, 1978, 71, 320–324.
621. WILLIAMS, J. H., & MUEHL, S. Relations among student and teacher perceptions of behavior. *Journal of Negro Education*, 1978, 47, 328–336.
622. ZUCKERMAN, D. M. Retrospective study of interests and abilities that predict life goals and sex–role attitudes of college women. *Psychological Reports*, 1978, 43, 1151–1157.
623. AYERS, J. B., & QUALLS, G. S. Concurrent and predictive validity of the National Teachers Examinations. *Journal of Educational Research*, 1979, 73, 86–92.
624. BLIMLING, G. S., & HAMPLE, D. Structuring the peer environment in residence halls to increase academic performance in average–ability students. *Journal of College Student Personnel*, 1979, 20, 310–316.
625. BLIMLING, G. S., & PAULSEN, F. M. The Educational Developmental Group Enrichment (EDGE) program: A comprehensive model for student development in residence halls. *Journal of the National Association for Women Deans, Administrators & Counselors*, 1979, 42, 24–33.
626. BROWN, P. S. A discriminant analysis of ACT profile data differentiating enrollees and nonenrollees. *Journal of College Student Personnel*, 1979, 20, 209–216.
627. CREASER, J. W., & CARSELLO, C. J. Isolating factors related to paraprofessional effectiveness. *Journal of Counseling Psychology*, 1979, 26, 259–262.
628. DINIUS, S. H., & MCINTYRE, S. C. Development and utilization of a personality battery for accountants. *Psychological Reports*, 1979, 44, 43–53.
629. LAMB, R. R., & PREDIGER, D. J. Criterion–related validity of sex–restrictive and unisex interest scales: A comparison. *Journal of Vocational Behavior*, 1979, 15, 231–246.
630. LUNNEBORG, P. W. Service vs. technical interest–Biggest sex difference of all? *Vocational Guidance Quarterly*, 1979, 28, 146–153.
631. NAHINSKY, I. D., MORGAN, M. S., & OESCHGER, D. E. Cognitive strategies, field dependence, and the abstraction process. *Journal of Research in Personality*, 1979, 13, 490–504.
632. PREDIGER, D. J., & LAMB, R. R. The validity of sex–balanced and sex–restrictive vocational interest reports: A comparison. *Vocational Guidance Quarterly*, 1979, 28, 16–24.
633. SCHMECK, R. R., & GROVE, E. Academic achievement and individual differences in learning processes. *Applied Psychological Measurement*, 1979, 3, 43–49.
634. SPARACINO, J., & HANSELL, S. Physical attractiveness and academic performance: Beauty is not always talent. *Journal of Personality*, 1979, 47, 449–469.
635. THOMAS, B. Promoting creativity in nursing education. *Nursing Research*, 1979, 28, 115–119.
636. THOMAS, C. L. Relative effectiveness of high school grades for predicting college grades: Sex and ability level effects. *Journal of Negro Education*, 1979, 48, 6–13.
637. BECKER, B. J. Performance of a group of mathematically able youths on the mathematics usage and natural sciences reading tests of the American College Test Battery vs the Scholastic Aptitude Test. *Gifted Child Quarterly*, 1980, 24, 138–143.
638. BOOTH, S. B., SOMERVILL, J. W., & GILGEN, A. R. Relationships among locus of control, academic achievement, and perception of autokinetic movement. *Perceptual & Motor Skills*, 1980, 50, 1263–1267.
639. DIAMOND, E. E. The AMEG commission report on sex bias in achievement testing. *Measurement & Evaluation in Guidance*, 1980, 13, 135–147.
640. FOOTE, B. Determined– and undetermined–major students: How different are they? *Journal of College Student Personnel*, 1980, 21, 29–34.
641. FOWLER, B., & KROLL, B. M. Relationship of apprehension about writing to performance as measured by grades in a college course on composition. *Psychological Reports*, 1980, 46, 583–586.
642. LAMB, R. R., & PREDIGER, D. J. Construct validity of raw score and standard score reports of vocational interests. *Journal of Educational Measurement*, 1980, 17, 107–115.
643. LOYD, B. H., FORSYTH, R., & HOOVER, H. D. Relationship of elementary and secondary school achievement test scores to later academic success. *Educational & Psychological Measurement*, 1980, 40, 1117–1124.
644. SCOTT, T. B., & ANADON, M. A comparison of the vocational interest profiles of native American and Caucasian college–bound students. *Measurement & Evaluation in Guidance*, 1980, 13, 35–42.

645. SHAW, R., & BUNT, M. M. Behavior of college students when matched or mismatched for course structure. *Journal of Educational Research*, 1980, 73, 41–45.
646. SNOWMAN, J., LEITNER, D. W., SNYDER, V., & LOCKHART, L. A comparison of the predictive validities of selected academic tests of the American College Test (ACT) Assessment Program and the descriptive tests of language skills for college freshmen in a basic skills program. *Educational & Psychological Measurement*, 1980, 40, 1159–1166.
647. STOCK, W. A., & SCHMID, R. F. Creating an institutional perspective for evaluating the admission of minorities. *Journal of American Association of Collegiate Registrars*, 1980, 56, 76–82.
648. WHITELY, S. E. Modeling aptitude test validity from cognitive components. *Journal of Educational Psychology*, 1980, 72, 750–769.
649. BARTLUNG, H. C., & HOOD, A. An 11–year follow–up of measured interest and vocational choice. *Journal of Counseling Psychology*, 1981, 28, 27–35.
650. BETZ, N. E., & WOLFE, L. K. Comparison of the utility of two approaches to sex–balanced interest scales for college women. *Journal of Vocational Behavior*, 1981, 19, 61–77.
651. DALLAM, J. W., & DAWES, B. E. What follow–up studies tell about student retention. *College & University*, 1981, 56, 151–159.
652. FRANCO, J. N., & KACZMAREK, M. The ACT assessment as a predictor of college performance for Mexican Americans. *National Association of Women Deans, Administrators & Counselors Journal*, 1981, 45, 17–19.
653. HALPIN, G., HALPIN, G., & SCHAER, B. B. Relative effectiveness of the California Achievement Tests in comparison with the ACT Assessment, College Board Scholastic Aptitude Test, and high school grade point average in predicting college grade point average. *Educational & Psychological Measurement*, 1981, 41, 821–827.
654. MACKIN, R. K., & HANSEN, L. S. A theory–based career development course: A plant in the garden. *School Counselor*, 1981, 28, 325–334.
655. MALLOCH, D. C., & MICHAEL, W. B. Predicting student grade point average at a community college from Scholastic Aptitude Tests and from measures representing three constructs in Vroom's expectancy theory model of motivation. *Educational & Psychological Measurement*, 1981, 41, 1127–1135.
656. OVCHARCHYN, C. A., JOHNSON, H. H., & PETZEL, T. P. Type A behavior, academic aspirations, and academic success. *Journal of Personality*, 1981, 49, 248–256.
657. PLAKE, B. S., SMITH, E. P., & DAMSTEEGT, D. C. A validity investigation of the Achievement Anxiety Test. *Educational & Psychological Measurement*, 1981, 41, 1215–1222.
658. SCHAEFFER, R. H. Meaningful practice on the computer: Is it possible? *Foreign Language Annals*, 1981, 14, 133–137.
659. SLANEY, R. B., & RUSSELL, J. E. A. An investigation of different levels of agreement between expressed and inventoried vocational interests among college women. *Journal of Counseling Psychology*, 1981, 28, 221–228.
660. STINARD, T. A., & DOLPHIN, W. D. Which students benefit from self–paced mastery instruction and why. *Journal of Educational Psychology*, 1981, 73, 754–763.

[77]

*ACT Career Planning Program. Grades 8 through 10, grade 11 through adults; 1973–82; 2 levels; American College Testing Program.

a) LEVEL I. Grades 8 through 10; 1973–82; CPP Level I; 18 scores: 6 ability scores (reading skills, numerical skills, language usage, clerical skills, mechanical reasoning, space relations), 6 interest scores (social service, business contact, business detail, technical, science, creative arts), 6 experience scores (same as interest scores), plus items on background and career and educational plans.

b) LEVEL II. Grade 11 through adults; 1976–82; CPP Level II; 21 scores: 6 ability scores (same as in *a* above), 8 interest scores (business contact, business detail, trades, technology, science, health, creative arts, social service), 7 experience scores (same as interest scores, excluding health), plus math and English placement composites, estimated ACT composite, questions on background and plans, and 12 optional local items.

For additional information and an excerpted review by Charles C. Healy of an earlier edition, see 8:989 (16 references); see also T2:2101 (4 references).

REFERENCES

1-4. See T2:2101.
5-20. See 8:989.
21. HANSON, G. R., NOETH, R. J., & PREDIGER, D. J. Validity of diverse procedures for reporting interest scores: An analysis of longitudinal data. *Journal of Counseling Psychology*, 1977, 24, 487-493.
22. MEHRENS, W. A. Career Planning Program test review. *Measurement & Evaluation in Guidance*, 1977, 10, 185-189.

[78]

★**ACT Evaluation/Survey Service.** Junior high school students through adults; 1979-82; ESS; survey instruments and scoring/reporting services to assist educational institutions in collecting and using student survey information; series of 11 survey instruments: Adult Learner Needs Assessment, Alumni, Alumni (2-year College Form), Entering Student, Student Opinion, Student Opinion (2-year College Form), Postsecondary Plans, Withdrawing/Nonreturning Student (long form, short form), Student Needs Assessment, High School Student Opinion; American College Testing Program.

[79]

ACT Proficiency Examination Program. College and adults; 1964-82; PEP; for college accreditation of nontraditional study, advanced placement, or assessment of educational achievement; most tests administered 4 times annually (February, May, August, November) at centers established by the publisher; 47 tests (29 objective, 7 essay, 11 objective and essay); American College Testing Program.*

a) COLLEGE PROFICIENCY EXAMINATIONS. 1964-82; CPE; single subject examinations designed to enable people to earn college credits for "knowledge gained outside of the formal college classroom"; 17 tests: Adult Nursing, Afro-American History, American History, Anatomy and Physiology, Corrective and Remedial Instruction in Reading, Criminal Investigation, Earth Science, Educational Psychology, Freshman English, Fundamentals of Nursing, History of American Education, Introduction to Criminal Justice, Maternal and Child Nursing (2 tests: Associate Degree, Baccalaureate Degree), Psychiatric/Mental Health Nursing, Reading Instruction in the Elementary School, Shakespeare.

b) REGENTS EXTERNAL DEGREE EXAMINATIONS. 1973-82; REDE; area examinations designed primarily "to enable independent students with college-level knowledge to earn a degree without attending college"; 30 tests: Accounting (5 tests), Business Environment and Strategy, Commonalities in Nursing Care (2 tests), Differences in Nursing Care (3 tests), Finance (3 tests), Health Restoration (2 tests), Health Support (2 tests), Management of Human Resources (3 tests), Marketing (3 tests), Nursing Health Care, Occupational Strategy (Nursing), Operations Management (3 tests), Professional Strategies (Nursing).

For additional information, see 8:470.

[80]

ACT Proficiency Examination in Adult Nursing. Baccalaureate level nursing students; 1976-82; for college accreditation of nontraditional study, advanced placement, or assessment of educational achievement; test administered 6 times annually (February, March, May, June, October, November) at centers established by the publisher; developed by the New York State Education Department; American College Testing Program.*

For additional information, see 8:1108.

[81]

ACT Proficiency Examination in Afro-American History. College and adults; 1972-82; for college accreditation of nontraditional study, advanced placement, or assessment of educational achievement; test administered 3 times annually (February, May, November) at centers established by the publisher; developed by the New York State Education Department; American College Testing Program.*

For additional information, see 8:906.

[82]

ACT Proficiency Examination in American History. College level and adults; 1981-82; for college accreditation of nontraditional study, advanced placement, or assessment of educational achievement; test administered 3 times annually (February, May, November) at centers established by the publisher; objective and essay tests; developed by the New York State Education Department; American College Testing Program.

[83]

ACT Proficiency Examination in Anatomy and Physiology. College and adults (associate degree); 1975-82; for college accreditation of nontraditional study, advanced placement, or assessment of educational achievement; test administered 6 times annually (February, March, May, June, October, November) at centers established by the publisher; developed by the New York State Education Department; American College Testing Program.*

For additional information, see 8:857.

[84]

ACT Proficiency Examination in Business Environment and Strategy. College and adults; 1973-82; for college accreditation of nontraditional study, advanced placement, or assessment of educational achievement; test administered 4 times annually (February, May, June, November) at centers established by the publisher; developed by the University of the State of New York; American College Testing Program.*

For additional information, see 8:1065.

[85]

ACT Proficiency Examination in Corrective and Remedial Instruction in Reading. College and adults; 1975-82; for college accreditation of nontraditional study, advanced placement, or assessment of educational achievement; test administered 3 times annually (February, May, November) at centers established by the publisher; developed by the New York State Education Department; American College Testing Program.*

For additional information, see 8:715.

[86]

ACT Proficiency Examination in Criminal Investigation. College and adults; 1975-82; for college accreditation of nontraditional study, advanced placement, or assessment of educational achievement; test administered 3 times annually (February, May, November) at centers established by the publisher; developed by the New York State Education Department; American College Testing Program.*

For additional information, see 8:1090.

[87]
ACT Proficiency Examination in Earth Science. College and adults; 1966–82; for college accreditation of nontraditional study, advanced placement, or assessment of educational achievement; test administered 3 times annually (February, May, November) at centers established by the publisher; 2 parts: objective, essay; developed by the University of the State of New York; American College Testing Program.*
For additional information, see 8:858.

[88]
ACT Proficiency Examination in Educational Psychology. College and adults; 1964–82; for college accreditation of nontraditional study, advanced placement, or assessment of educational achievement; test administered 3 times annually (February, May, November) at centers established by the publisher; developed by the New York State Education Department; American College Testing Program.*
For additional information, see 8:458.

[89]
ACT Proficiency Examination in Freshman English. College and adults; 1964–82; for college accreditation of nontraditional study, advanced placement, or assessment of educational achievement; test administered 3 times annually (February, May, November) at centers established by the publisher; 2 parts: objective, essay; developed by the New York State Education Department; American College Testing Program.*
For additional information, see 8:38.

[90]
ACT Proficiency Examination in Fundamentals of Nursing. College and adults (associate degree); 1969–82; for college accreditation of nontraditional study, advanced placement, or assessment of educational achievement; test administered 6 times annually (February, March, May, June, October, November) at centers established by the publisher; developed by the New York State Education Department; American College Testing Program.*
For additional information, see 8:1109.

[91]
ACT Proficiency Examination in History of American Education. College and adults; 1965–82; for college accreditation of nontraditional study, advanced placement, or assessment of educational achievement; test administered 3 times annually (February, May, November) at centers established by the publisher; 2 parts: objective, essay; developed by the New York State Education Department; American College Testing Program.*
For additional information, see 8:360.

[92]
ACT Proficiency Examination in Introduction to Criminal Justice. College and adults; 1975–82; for college accreditation of nontraditional study, advanced placement, or assessment of educational achievement; test administered 3 times annually (February, May, November) at centers established by the publisher; developed by the New York State Education Department; American College Testing Program.*
For additional information, see 8:1091.

[93]
ACT Proficiency Examination in Nursing Health Care. College and adults (associate degree); 1973–82; for college accreditation of nontraditional study, advanced placement, or assessment of educational achievement; test administered 6 times annually (February, March, May, June, October, November) at centers established by the publisher; developed by the University of the State of New York; American College Testing Program.*
For additional information, see 8:1110.

[94]
ACT Proficiency Examination in Occupational Strategy, Nursing. College and adults (associate degree); 1973–82; for college accreditation of nontraditional study, advanced placement, or assessment of educational achievement; test administered 6 times annually (February, March, May, June, October, November) at centers established by the publisher; developed by the University of the State of New York; American College Testing Program.*
For additional information, see 8:1111.

[95]
ACT Proficiency Examination in Professional Strategies, Nursing. Baccalaureate level nursing students; 1979–82; for college accreditation of nontraditional study, advanced placement, or assessment of educational achievement; test administered 6 times annually (February, March, May June, October, November) at centers established by the publisher; developed by the University of the State of New York; American College Testing Program.

[96]
ACT Proficiency Examination in Psychiatric/Mental Health Nursing. Baccalaureate level nursing students; 1968–82; for college accreditation of nontraditional study, advanced placement, or assessment of educational achievement; test administered 6 times annually (February, March, May, June, October, November) at centers established by the publisher; developed by the New York State Education Department; American College Testing Progam.*
For additional information, see 8:1112.

[97]
ACT Proficiency Examination in Reading Instruction in the Elementary School. College and adults; 1973–82; for college accreditation of nontraditional study, advanced placement, or assessment of educational achievement; test administered 3 times annually (February, May, November) at centers established by the publisher; developed by the New York State Education Department; American College Testing Program.*
For additional information, see 8:716.

[98]
ACT Proficiency Examination in Shakespeare. College and adults; 1964–82; for college accreditation of nontraditional study, advanced placement, or assessment

of educational achievement; test administered 3 times annually (February, May, November) at centers established by the publisher; 2 parts: objective, essay; developed by the New York State Education Department; American College Testing Program.*

For additional information, see 8:63.

[99]
ACT Proficiency Examinations in Accounting. College and adults; 1973–82; for college accreditation of nontraditional study, advanced placement, or assessment of educational achievement; tests (except *a*) administered 2 times annually (May, November) at centers established by the publisher; 5 tests; developed by the University of the State of New York; American College Testing Program.*
a) LEVEL 1. 1973–82; test administered 4 times annually (February, May, June, November); objective test.
b) LEVEL 2. 1973–82; objective and essay tests.
c) LEVEL 3. 1974–82; 3 essay tests.
  1) *Area 1, Business Law and Federal Income Taxation.*
  2) *Area 2, Auditing and Cost Analysis.*
  3) *Area 3, Advanced Theory and Special Problems.*
For additional information, see 8:1063.

[100]
ACT Proficiency Examinations in Commonalities in Nursing Care, Areas I and II. College and adults (associate degree); 1973–82; for college accreditation of nontraditional study, advanced placement, or assessment of educational achievement; tests administered 6 times annually (February, March, May, June, October, November) at centers established by the publisher; 2 objective tests; developed by the University of the State of New York; American College Testing Program.*

For additional information, see 8:1113.

[101]
ACT Proficiency Examinations in Differences in Nursing Care, Areas I and II. College and adults (associate degree); 1974–82; for college accreditation of nontraditional study, advanced placement, or assessment of educational achievement; tests administered 6 times annually (February, March, May, June, October, November) at centers established by the publisher; 3 objective tests; developed by the University of the State of New York; American College Testing Program.*

For additional information, see 8:1114.

[102]
ACT Proficiency Examinations in Finance. College and adults; 1973–82; for college accreditation of nontraditional study, advanced placement, or assessment of educational achievement; tests (except *a*) administered 2 times annually (May, November) at centers established by the publisher; 3 tests; developed by the University of the State of New York; American College Testing Program.*
a) LEVEL 1. 1973–82; test administered 4 times annually (February, May, June, November); objective test.
b) LEVEL 2. 1973–82; objective and essay tests.
c) LEVEL 3. 1974–82; essay test.
For additional information, see 8:1066.

[103]
ACT Proficiency Examinations in Health Restoration, Areas I and II. Baccalaureate level nursing students; 1980–82; for college accreditation of nontraditional study, advanced placement, or assessment of educational achievement; tests administered 6 times annually (February, March, May, June, October, November) at centers established by the publisher; 2 tests; developed by the University of the State of New York; American College Testing Program.

[104]
ACT Proficiency Examinations in Health Support, Areas I and II. Baccalaureate level nursing students; 1979–82; for college accreditation of nontraditional study, advanced placement, or assessment of educational achievement; tests administered 6 times annually (February, March, May, June, October, November) at centers established by the publisher; 2 tests; developed by the University of the State of New York; American College Testing Program.

[105]
ACT Proficiency Examinations in Management of Human Resources. College and adults; 1973–82; for college accreditation of nontraditional study, advanced placement, or assessment of educational achievement; tests (except *a*) administered 2 times annually (May, November) at centers established by the publisher; 3 tests; developed by the University of the State of New York; American College Testing Program.*
a) LEVEL 1. 1973–82; test administered 4 times annually (February, May, June, November); objective test.
b) LEVEL 2. 1973–82; objective and essay tests.
c) LEVEL 3. 1974–82; essay test.
For additional information, see 8:1067.

[106]
ACT Proficiency Examinations in Marketing. College and adults; 1973–82; for college accreditation of nontraditional study, advanced placement, or assessment of educational achievement; tests (except *a*) administered 2 times annually (May, November) at centers established by the publisher; 3 tests; developed by the University of the State of New York; American College Testing Program.*
a) LEVEL 1. 1973–82; test administered 4 times annually (February, May, June, November); objective test.
b) LEVEL 2. 1973–82; objective and essay tests.
c) LEVEL 3. 1974–82; essay test.
For additional information, see 8:1068.

[107]
ACT Proficiency Examinations in Maternal and Child Nursing. College and adults; 1968–82; for college accreditation of nontraditional study, advanced placement, or assessment of educational achievement; tests administered 6 times annually (February, March, May, June, October, November) at centers established by the publisher; 2 tests; developed by the New York State Education Department; American College Testing Program.*
a) ASSOCIATE DEGREE. 1970–76.
b) BACCALAUREATE DEGREE. 1968–76.
For additional information, see 8:1115.

[108]
ACT Proficiency Examinations in Operations Management. College and adults; 1973–82; for college accreditation of nontraditional study, advanced placement, or assessment of educational achievement; tests (except *a*) administered 2 times annually (May, November) at centers established by the publisher; 3 tests; developed by the University of the State of New York; American College Testing Program.*
a) LEVEL 1. 1973–82; test administered 4 times annually (February, May, June, November); objective test.
b) LEVEL 2. 1973–82; objective and essay tests.
c) LEVEL 3. 1974–82; essay test.
For additional information, see 8:1069.

[109]
Action-Choice Tests for Competitive Sports Situations. High school and college; 1960; sportsmanship; Mary Jane Haskins and Betty Grant Hartman; Mary Jane Haskins.* (In-print status uncertain; no reply from publisher.)
For additional information, see 6:716 (2 references).

[110]
★**Activities For Assessing Classification Skills, Experimental Edition.** Ages 7–8 and slow learning children, 9–12 and advanced younger children; 1979; 4 scores: additive classification, class inclusion, cross-classification, matrices and intersections; Rachel Gal-Choppin; NFER-Nelson Publishing Co. [England].*

[111]
Adaptability Test. Job applicants; 1942–67; Joseph Tiffin and C. H. Lawshe; Science Research Associates, Inc.*
See T2:337 (3 references) and 7:333 (6 references); for a review by John M. Willits, see 5:305 (13 references); for reviews by Anne Anastasi and Marion A. Bills, see 3:216 (3 references).

REFERENCES
1–3. See 3:216.
4–16. See 5:305.
17–22. See 7:333.
23–25. See T2:337.
26. HORTON, R. L. Some relationships between personality and consumer decision making. *Journal of Marketing Research,* 1979, 16, 233–246.

[112]
★**Adaptive Functioning Index.** Ages 14 and over in rehabilitation or special education settings; 1971–78; AFI; ratings by staff; Nancy J. Marlett and E. Anne Hughson (program workbook and target workbook); Vocational and Rehabilitation Research Institute [Canada].*
a) SOCIAL EDUCATION TEST. 9 scores: reading, writing, communication, concept attainment, number concepts, time, money handling, community awareness, motor movements.
b) VOCATIONAL CHECK LIST. 12 scores: basic work habits (independence, making decisions, use and care of equipment and materials, taking direction), work skills (speed of movement, ability to follow instructions, competence, skill level), acceptance skills (appearance, attendance/punctuality, self-expression, relations with co-workers).

c) RESIDENTIAL CHECK LIST. 15 scores: personal routines (cleanliness, appearance and eating, room management, time management, health), community awareness (transportation, shopping, leisure, budgeting, cooking and home management), social maturity (communication, consideration, getting friends, keeping friends, handling problems).
d) ADAPTIVE FUNCTIONING OF THE DEPENDENT HANDICAPPED. Profoundly handicapped of all ages; checklist; 20 scores: nursing care (medications, body tone, medical care, observation for injury, feeding), physical development (head, legs, body, hands (or feet), movement), awareness (eye contact, contact with his world, contact with people, communication, contact with things), self help (feeding, eating, washing, dressing, toileting).

[113]
Addiction Research Center Inventory. Drug addicts; 1961–67; ARCI; test booklet title is *The ARC Inventory*; subjective effects of drugs and various dimensions of psychiatric disorders; 29 scales: carelessness, general drug, psychopathic deviate, alcohol withdrawal, opiate withdrawal, 7 empirical drug scales (alcohol, amphetamine, chlorpromazine, LSD, morphine, pentobarbital, pyraphexyl), 7 group pattern scales (alcohol, amphetamine, chlorpromazine, LSD, morphine, morphine-amphetamine, pentobarbital-chlorpromazine-alcohol), 10 factor scales (reactivity, efficiency, patience-impatience, sentimental, uncritical, immaturity, masculinity-femininity, inadequacy, impulsivity, neurotic sensitivity versus psychopathic toughness); Harris E. Hill, Charles A. Haertzen, and Richard E. Belleville; National Institute of Drug Abuse, Addiction Research Center (Attn. Charles A. Haertzen).*
See T2:1093 (8 references) and P:3 (15 references).

REFERENCES
1–15. See P:3.
16–23. See T2:1093.
24. HAERTZEN, C. A., MARTIN, W. R., HEWETT, B. B., & SANDQUIST, V. Measurement of psychopathy as a state. *Journal of Psychology,* 1978, 100, 201–204.
25. ANGRIST, B., & GERSHON, S. Variable attenuation of amphetamine effects by lithium. *American Journal of Psychiatry,* 1979, 136, 806–810.
26. VAN DYKE, C., JATLOW, P., UNGERER, J., BARASH, P., & BYCK, R. Cocaine and lidocaine have similar psychological effects after intranasal application. *Life Sciences,* 1979, 24, 271–274.
27. COWAN, J. D., KAY, D. C., NEIDERT, G. L., ROSS, F. E., & BELMORE, S. M. Defeated and joyless: Potential measures of change in drug abuser characteristics. *Journal of Nervous & Mental Disease,* 1980, 168, 391–399.

[114]
★**Additional Personality Factor Inventory—2.** College and adults; 1975–80; APF2; 10 scores: fear of being socially unacceptable, hope, general activity, anxiety-state, existential realization, involvement, unusuality, dislikes-annoyances, external control, rigidity; Edgar Howarth; the Author.*

[115]
Aden-Crosthwait Adolescent Psychology Achievement Test. College; 1963–70; Robert C. Aden and Charles Crosthwait; Psychometric Affiliates.*
For additional information, see 7:640 (1 reference).

[116]
*The Adjective Checklist. Grades 9–16 and adults; 1952–80; ACL; 37 scales: number of adjectives checked,

number of favorable adjectives checked, number of unfavorable adjectives checked, communality, achievement, dominance, endurance, order, intraception, nurturance, affiliation, heterosexuality, exhibition, autonomy, aggression, change, succorance, abasement, deference, counseling readiness, self-control, self-confidence, personal adjustment, ideal self, creative personality, military leadership, masculine attributes, feminine attributes, critical parent, nurturing parent, adults, free child, adapted child, high origence-low intellectence, high origence-high intellectence, low origence-low intellectence, low origence-high intellectence; (Spanish edition available); Harrison G. Gough and Alfred B. Heilbrun, Jr.; Consulting Psychologists Press, Inc.*

For additional information, see 8:495 (202 references); see also T2:1094 (85 references); for reviews by Leonard G. Rorer and Forrest L. Vance, see 7:38 (131 references); see also P:4 (102 references).

REFERENCES

1–102. See P:4.
103–233. See 7:38.
234–318. See T2:1094.
319–520. See 8:495.

521. ALBAUM, G. Birth order and creativity: Some further evidence. *Psychological Reports*, 1977, 40, 792–794.
522. ALBAUM, G., & BAKER, K. Cross-validation of a creativity scale for the Adjective Check List. *Educational & Psychological Measurement*, 1977, 37, 1057–1061.
523. ALKER, H. A., & OWEN, D. W. Biological, trait, and behavioral-sampling predictions of performance in a stressful life setting. *Journal of Personality & Social Psychology*, 1977, 35, 717–723.
524. BEDEIAN, A. G., & ZMUD, R. W. Some evidence relating to convergent validity of Form B of Coopersmith's Self-Esteem Inventory. *Psychological Reports*, 1977, 40, 725–726.
525. BOURNE, E. Can we describe an individual's personality? Agreement on stereotype versus individual attributes. *Journal of Personality & Social Psychology*, 1977, 35, 863–872.
526. CARTWRIGHT, L. K. Personality changes in a sample of women physicians. *Journal of Medical Education*, 1977, 52, 467–474.
527. CARTWRIGHT, R., BUTTERS, E., WEINSTEIN, M., & KROEKER, L. The effects of presleep stimuli of different sources and types on REM sleep. *Psychophysiology*, 1977, 14, 388–392.
528. CHEEK, F. E., & BAKER, J. C. Self-control training for inmates. *Psychological Reports*, 1977, 41, 559–568.
529. DOMINO, G. Transcendental meditation and creativity: An empirical investigation. *Journal of Applied Psychology*, 1977, 62, 358–362.
530. GOUGH, H. G., & HALL, W. B. A comparison of physicians who did or did not respond to a postal questionnaire. *Journal of Applied Psychology*, 1977, 62, 777–780.
531. GOUGH, H. G., & HALL, W. B. Number of children wanted and expected by American physicians. *Journal of Psychology*, 1977, 96, 45–53.
532. HEILBRUN, A. B., JR., & LANDAUER, S. P. Stereotypic and specific attributions of parental characteristics by late-adolescent siblings. *Child Development*, 1977, 48, 1748–1751.
533. HOLLANDSWORTH, J. G., JR., GALASS, J. P., & GAY, M. L. The Adult Self Expression Scale: Validation by the multitrait–multimethod procedure. *Journal of Clinical Psychology*, 1977, 33, 407–415.
534. LUBIN, B., HORNED, C. M., & KNAPP, R. R. Scores on Adjective Check List, Eysenck Personality Inventory, and Depression Adjective Check List for a male prison population. *Perceptual & Motor Skills*, 1977, 45, 567–570.
535. MARKUS, H. Self-schemata and processing information about the self. *Journal of Personality and Social Psychology*, 1977, 35, 63–78.
536. PARISH, T. S., & EADS, G. M. The Personal Attribute Inventory as a self-concept scale. *Educational & Psychological Measurement*, 1977, 37, 1063–1067.
537. PARISH, T. S., EADS, G. M., & ADAMS, D. E. The Personal Attribute Inventory as a self concept scale: A preliminary report. *Psychological Reports*, 1977, 41, 1141–1142.
538. PATRICK, A. W., & ZUCKERMAN, M. An application of the state-trait concept to the need for achievement. *Journal of Research in Personality*, 1977, 11, 459–465.
539. RAY, C. Psychological implications of mastectomy. *British Journal of Social & Clinical Psychology*, 1977, 16, 373–377.
540. SHIFFLER, N., LYNCH-SAUER, J., & NADELMAN, L. Relationship between self-concept and classroom behavior in two informal elementary classrooms. *Journal of Educational Psychology*, 1977, 69, 349–359.
541. SILVESTRI, R. Implosive therapy treatment of emotionally disturbed retardates. *Journal of Consulting & Clinical Psychology*, 1977, 45, 14–22.
542. VIDONI, D. O. Factor analytic scales of the Adjective Check List (ACL) replicated across samples: Implications for validity. *Educational & Psychological Measurement*, 1977, 37, 535–539.
543. WILLIAMS, J. E., & BEST, D. L. Sex stereotypes and trait favorability on the Adjective Check List. *Educational & Psychological Measurement*, 1977, 37, 101–110.
544. ZIMET, S. G., & ZIMET, C. N. Teachers view people: Sex–role stereotyping. *Psychological Reports*, 1977, 41, 583–591.
545. BEDEIAN, A. G., & ARMENAKIS, A. A. Relationships between age and Adjective Check List scales. *Psychological Reports*, 1978, 43, 821–822.
546. BEDEIAN, A. G., & TOULIATOS, J. Work–related motives and self-esteem in American women. *Journal of Psychology*, 1978, 99, 63–70.
547. BERNARD, L. C., & EPSTEIN, D. J. Sex role conformity in homosexual and heterosexual males. *Journal of Personality Assessment*, 1978, 42, 505–511.
548. DAVIS, G. A., & BULL, K. S. Strengthening affective components of creativity. *Journal of Educational Psychology*, 1978, 70, 833–836.
549. DIPBOYE, R. L., ZULTOWSKI, W. H., DEWHIRST, H. D., & ARVEY, R. D. Self-esteem as a moderator of the relationship between scientific interests and the job satisfaction of physicists and engineers. *Journal of Applied Psychology*, 1978, 63, 289–294.
550. DUTHIE, R. B., HOPE, L., & BARKER, D. G. Selected personality traits of marital artists as measured by The Adjective Check List. *Perceptual & Motor Skills*, 1978, 47, 71–76.
551. FORMAN, B. D., & FORMAN, S. G. Irrational beliefs and personality. *Journal of Personality Assessment*, 1978, 42, 613–620.
552. GOUGH, H. G., LAZZARI, R., & FIORAVANTI, M. Self versus ideal self: A comparison of five Adjective Check List indices. *Journal of Consulting & Clinical Psychology*, 1978, 46, 1085–1091.
553. GOUGH, H. G., LAZZARI, R., FIORAVANTI, M., & STRACCA, M. An Adjective Check List scale to predict military leadership. *Journal of Cross-Cultural Psychology*, 1978, 9, 381–400.
554. GREENBERG, R. P., & ZELDOW, P. B. Sex differences in preferences for an ideal therapist. *Journal of Personality Assessment*, 1978, 40, 474–478.
555. GREGORY, R. J., & MORRIS, L. M. Adjective correlates for women on the CPI scales: A replication. *Journal of Personality Assessment*, 1978, 42, 258–264.
556. HASTINGS, A. C. The Oakland poltergeist. *Journal of the American Society of Psychical Research*, 1978, 72, 233–256.
557. HEILBRUN, A. B., JR. An exploration of antecedents and attributes of androgynous and undifferentiated sex roles. *Journal of Genetic Psychology*, 1978, 132, 97–107.
558. HEILBRUN, A. B. Prediction of continuing client contact in a brief-treatment campus mental health agency. *Psychological Reports*, 1978, 42, 481–482.
559. HEILBRUN, A. B., JR. Projective and repressive styles of processing aversive information. *Journal of Consulting & Clinical Psychology*, 1978, 46, 156–164.
560. KAY, E. J., LYONS, A., NEWMAN, W., MANKIN, D., & LOEB, R. C. A longitudinal study of the personality correlates of marijuana use. *Journal of Consulting & Clinical Psychology*, 1978, 46, 470–477.
561. KELLY, J. A., FURMAN, W., & YOUNG, V. Problems associated with the typological measurement of sex roles and androgyny. *Journal of Consulting & Clinical Psychology*, 1978, 46, 1574–1576.
562. LAZZARI, R., FIORAVANTI, M., & GOUGH, H. G. A new scale for the Adjective Check List based on self vs. ideal-self discrepancies. *Journal of Clinical Psychology*, 1978, 34, 361–365.
563. LESTER, D., & ARCURI, A. F. Personality correlates of police discretion to enforce traffic laws. *Psychological Reports*, 1978, 43, 1166.
564. MILLER, S. H., O'REILLY, C. A., ROBERTS, K. H., & FOLKINS, C. H. Factor structure and scale reliabilities of the Adjective Check List. *Journal of Consulting & Clinical Psychology*, 1978, 46, 189–191.
565. MURRELL, M. E., LESTER, D., & ARCURI, A. F. Is the "police personality" unique to police officers? *Psychological Reports*, 1978, 43, 298.
566. NOWICKI, S., JR., & DUKE, M. P. Examination of counseling variables within a social learning framework. *Journal of Counseling Psychology*, 1978, 25, 1–7.
567. O'GRADY, K. E., JANDA, L. H., LANCASTER, D. W., & MIKULKA, P. J. Imaginative role-playing, need for achievement, and perceived outcome in relation to occupational status. *Journal of Research in Personality*, 1978, 12, 329–334.
568. PINE, M. A. Self–concept, informal education, reading achievement in grade one. *Reading Teacher*, 1978, 31, 412–417.
569. POLIT, D. F. Stereotypes relating to family-size status. *Journal of Marriage & the Family*, 1978, 40, 105–114.
570. SMALL, A. C., & BATLIS, N. C. Factor structure of Adjective Check List under different instructional sets. *Psychological Reports*, 1978, 43, 1111–1114.

571. STEER, R. A., GASTA, C., KOTZKER, E., & SCHUT, J. Need similarity in husbands and wives who are receiving methadone maintenance therapy. *Journal of Clinical Psychology*, 1978, 34, 558–561.

572. SUTKER, P. B., ALLAIN, A. N., SMITH, C. J., & COHEN, G. H. Addict descriptions of therapeutic community, multimodality, and methadone maintenance treatment clients and staff. *Journal of Consulting & Clinical Psychology*, 1978, 46, 508–517.

573. TARR, L. H. Developmental sex–role theory and sex–role attitudes in late adolescents. *Psychological Reports*, 1978, 42, 807–814.

574. WALDROP, R., APFELDORF, M., & HUNLEY, P. J. Orientation to authority in the domiciliary. *Psychological Reports*, 1978, 43, 1011–1018.

575. WALKER, J. T., & KRASNOFF, A. G. The horizontality principle in young men and women. *Perceptual & Motor Skills*, 1978, 46, 1055–1061.

576. WERNER, P. D. Personality and attitude–activism correspondence. *Journal of Personality & Social Psychology*, 1978, 36, 1375–1390.

577. WHITESEL, L. S. Personalities of women art students. *Studies in Art Education*, 1978, 20, 56–63.

578. WIGGINS, J. S., & HOLZMULLER, A. Psychological androgyny and interpersonal behavior. *Journal of Consulting & Clinical Psychology*, 1978, 46, 40–52.

579. ZUROFF, D. C., & SCHWARZ, J. C. Effects of transcendental meditation and muscle relaxation on trait anxiety, maladjustment, locus of control, and drug use. *Journal of Consulting & Clinical Psychology*, 1978, 46, 264–271.

580. ZUROFF, D. C., & SCHWARZ, J. C. An instrument for measuring the behavioral dimension of social anxiety. *Psychological Reports*, 1978, 42, 371–379.

581. BABAD, E. Y. Personality correlates of susceptibility to biasing information. *Journal of Personality & Social Psychology*, 1979, 37, 195–202.

582. BROOKS, F. R., & JOHNSON, R. W. Self-descriptive adjectives associated with a Jungian personality inventory. *Psychological Reports*, 1979, 44, 747–750.

583. DIPBOUYE, R. L., ZULTOWSKI, W. H. DEWHIRST, H. D., & ARVEY, R. D. Self–esteem as a moderator of performance–satisfaction relationships. *Journal of Vocational Behavior*, 1979, 15, 193–206.

584. FORMAN, B. D., & FORMAN, S. G. Irrational beliefs and psychological needs. *Journal of Personality Assessment*, 1979, 43, 633–637.

585. GOUGH, H. G. A creative personality scale for the Adjective Check List. *Journal of Personality & Social Psychology*, 1979, 37, 1398–1405.

586. GOUGH, H., FIORAVANTI, M., & LAZZARI, R. A cross-cultural unisex ideal self scale for the Adjective Check List. *Journal of Clinical Psychology*, 1979, 35, 314–319.

587. HEILBRUN, A. B., JR., & SCHWARTZ, H. L. Defensive style and performance on objective personality measures. *Journal of Personality Assessment*, 1979, 43, 517–525.

588. HORTON, R. L. Some relationships between personality and consumer decision making. *Journal of Marketing Research*, 1979, 16, 233–246.

589. IRONSON, G. H., & DAVIS, G. A. Faking high or low creativity scores on the Adjective Check List. *Journal of Creative Behavior*, 1979, 13, 139–145.

590. JONES, E. E., & ZOPPEL, C. L. Personality differences among blacks in Jamaica and the United States. *Journal of Cross–Cultural Psychology*, 1979, 10, 435–456.

591. KATZ, A. N., & POAG, J. R. Sex differences in instructions to "be creative" on divergent and non-divergent test scores. *Journal of Personality*, 1979, 47, 518–530.

592. LOEFFLER, D., & FIEDLER, L. Woman–a sense of identity: A counseling intervention to facilitate personal growth in women. *Journal of Counseling Psychology*, 1979, 26, 51–57.

593. MUCKLOW, B. M., & PHELAN, G. K. Lesbian and traditional mothers' responses to adult response to child behavior and self-concept. *Psychological Reports*, 1979, 44, 880–882.

594. NIELSEN, L. Characteristics of an ideal college. *Improving College & University Teaching*, 1979, 27, 163–167.

595. O'GRADY, K. E., FREDA, J. S., & MIKULKA, P. J. A comparison of the Adjective Check List, Bem Sex Role Inventory, and Personal Attributes Questionnaire masculinity and feminity subscales. *Multivariate Behavioral Research*, 1979, 14, 215–225.

596. ROBINSON, B. E. Men caring for the young: An androgynous perspective. *Family Coordinator*, 1979, 28, 553–560.

597. SCHAFER, R. B., & BRAITO, R. Self-concept and role performance evaluation among marriage partners. *Journal of Marriage & the Family*, 1979, 41, 801–810.

598. TESCH, F. E. Interpersonal proximity and impression formation: A partial examination of Hall's proxemic model. *Journal of Social Psychology*, 1979, 107, 43–55.

599. WILLIAMS, J. E., DAWS, J. T., BEST, D. L., TILQUIN, C., WESLEY, F., & BJERKE, T. Sex–trait stereotypes in France, Germany, and Norway. *Journal of Cross–Cultural Psychology*, 1979, 10, 133–156.

600. ZEITNER, R. M., & WEIGHT, D. G. The pupillometric response as a parameter of self-esteem. *Journal of Clinical Psychology*, 1979, 35, 176–183.

601. BAUCOM, D. H. Independent CPI masculinity and femininity scales: Psychological correlates and a sex-role typology. *Journal of Personality Assessment*, 1980, 44, 262–271.

602. BECK, M. D., & BECK, C. K. Multi-trait–multimethod validation of four personality measures with a high-school sample. *Educational & Psychological Measurement*, 1980, 40, 1005–1011.

603. BEDEIAN, A. G., ARMENAKIS, A. A., & CURRAN, S. M. Personality correlates of role stress. *Psychological Reports*, 1980, 46, 627–632.

604. BLAIR, M. C., & FRETZ, B. R. Interpersonal skills training for premedical students. *Journal of Counseling Psychology*, 1980, 27, 380–384.

605. CLABBY, J. F., JR. The Wit: A personality analysis. *Journal of Personality Assessment*, 1980, 44, 307–310.

606. CONSTANTINI, E., & CRAIK, K. H. Personality and politicians: California party leaders, 1960–1976. *Journal of Personality & Social Psychology*, 1980, 38, 641–661.

607. EDWARDS, J. R., & WILLIAMS, J. E. Sex-trait stereotypes among young children and young adults: Canadian findings and cross–national comparisons. *Canadian Journal of Behavioural Science*, 1980, 12, 210–220.

608. GRAYSON, P. Personality and satisfaction with their relationship by married and cohabiting couples. *Psychological Reports*, 1980, 47, 555–558.

609. HEILBRUN, A. B., JR., & SCHWARTZ, H. L. Self-esteem and self-reinforcement in men alcoholics. *Journal of Studies on Alcohol*, 1980, 41, 1134–1142.

610. HELSON, R. Challenger and upholder syndromes in critics. *Journal of Personality & Social Psychology*, 1980, 38, 825–838.

611. LEWIS, J., BENTLEY, C., & SAWYER, A. The relationship between selected personality traits and self–esteem among female nursing students. *Educational & Psychological Measurement*, 1980, 40, 259–260.

612. LI-REPAC, D. Cultural influences on clinical perception. A comparison between Caucasian and Chinese-American therapists. *Journal of Cross-Cultural Psychology*, 1980, 11, 327–342.

613. ROSE, G. S., & BEDNAR, R. L. Effects of positive and negative self-disclosure and feedback on early group development. *Journal of Counseling Psychology*, 1980, 27, 63–70.

614. SMALL, A. C., & TEAGNO, L. Identification and academic achievement in college females. *College Student Journal*, 1980, 14, 54–59.

615. SUTKER, P. B., & O'NEIL, P. M. Evaluation of a drug abuse education course for law enforcement and treatment specialists. *International Journal of the Addictions*, 1980, 15, 125–135.

616. TODT, E. H., & HOWELL, R. J. Vocal cues as indices of schizophrenia. *Journal of Speech & Hearing Research*, 1980, 23, 517–526.

617. WIENS, A. N., HARPER, R. G., & MATARAZZO, J. D. Personality correlates of nonverbal interview behavior. *Journal of Clinical Psychology*, 1980, 36, 205–215.

618. WILLIAMS, K. B., & WILLIAMS, J. E. The assessment of transactional analysis ego states via the Adjective Check List. *Journal of Personality Assessment*, 1980, 44, 120–129.

619. CHAMPOUX, J. E. An exploratory study of the role of job scope, need for achievement, and social status in the relationship between work and nonwork. *Sociology & Social Research*, 1981, 65, 153–176.

620. FIORAVANTI, M., GOUGH, H. G., & FRERE, L. J. English, French, and Italian Adjective Check Lists: A social desirability analysis. *Journal of Cross–Cultural Psychology*, 1981, 12, 462–472.

621. FOLKINS, C., WIESELBERG, N., & SPENSLEY, J. Discipline stereotyping and evaluative attitudes among community mental health center staff. *American Journal of Orthopsychiatry*, 1981, 51, 140–148.

622. GOUGH, H. G., & WEISS, D. S. A nontransformational test of intellectual competence. *Journal of Applied Psychology*, 1981, 66, 102–110.

623. HARRINGTON, D. M., & ANDERSEN, S. M. Creativity, masculinity, feminity and three models of psychological androgyny. *Journal of Personality & Social Psychology*, 1981, 41, 744–757.

624. HEILBRUN, A. B., JR. Gender differences in the functional linkage between androgyny, social cognition, and competence. *Journal of Personality & Social Psychology*, 1981, 41, 1106–1118.

625. JOHNSON, J. A. The "self-disclosure" and "self-presentation" views of item response dynamics and personality scale validity. *Journal of Personality & Social Psychology*, 1981, 40, 761–769.

626. LEVENTHAL, G., & MATTURO, M. Males' attitudes towards women: What they say and what they do. *Psychological Reports*, 1981, 48, 333–334.

627. MATTHEWS, K. A., BATSON, C. D., HORN, J., & ROSENMAN, R. H. "Principles in his nature which interest him in the fortune of others...": The heritability of empathic concern for others. *Journal of Personality*, 1981, 49, 237–247.

628. MILLARD, P. H., & SMITH, C. Personal belongings–A positive effect? *Gerontologist*, 1981, 21, 85–90.

629. MOSSHOLDER, K. W., DEWHIRST, H. D., & ARVEY, R. D. Vocational interest and personality differences between development and research personnel: A field study. *Journal of Vocational Behavior*, 1981, 19, 233–243.

630. MOTOWIDLO, S. J. Construct validity for a measure of generalized expectancy of task success. *Educational & Psychological Measurement*, 1981, 41, 963–972.

631. ROBINSON, J. A. Context effects in retrospective judgements of personal experiences. *Bulletin of the Psychonomic Society*, 1981, 17, 147–150.
632. ROGERS, T. R., FOREHAND, R., GRIEST, D. L., WELLS, K. C., & MCMAHON, R. J. Socioeconomic status: Effects on parent and child behaviors and treatment outcome of parent training. *Journal of Clinical Child Psychology*, 1981, 10, 98–101.
633. SEIF, B. Counselor religious orientation and student discrimination of counselor-offered therapeutic level. *Counseling & Values*, 1981, 26, 2–12.
634. TARRIER, N., & GOMES, L. F. Knowledge of sex–trait stereotypes: Effects of age, sex and social class on Brazilian children. *Journal of Cross-Cultural Psychology*, 1981, 12, 81–93.
635. URSANO, R. J. The Viet Nam era prisoner of war: Precaptivity personality and the development of psychiatric illness. *American Journal of Psychiatry*, 1981, 138, 315–318.
636. WEISS, D. S. The effects of systematic variations in information on judges' descriptions of personality. *Journal of Personality & Social Psychology*, 1981, 37, 2121–2136.
637. WEISS, D. S. A multigroup study of personality patterns in creativity. *Perceptual & Motor Skills*, 1981, 52, 735–746.

[117]
Adjustment and Adaptation Profiles. Children and adults in mental health, counseling, or medical service centers; 1974–81; measure the current adjustment of children or adults to life and to the community; 4 scales; Robert B. Ellsworth and Shanae L. Ellsworth; Consulting Psychologists Press, Inc.
a) CAAP SCALE (CHILD AND ADOLESCENT ADJUSTMENT PROFILE). Children and adolescents; 1977–78; 5 scores: peer relations, dependency, hostility, productivity, withdrawal.
b) PARS SCALE (PERSONAL ADJUSTMENT AND ROLE SKILLS). Adults; 1974–81; 8 scores: close relations, alienation, anxiety, confusion, alcohol-drug use, house activity, child relations, employment.
c) PAL-C SCALE (PROFILE OF ADAPTATION TO LIFE-CLINICAL). Adults; 1978–79; 7 scores: negative emotions, psychological well being, income management, physical symptoms, alcohol/drugs, close interpersonal relationships, child interpersonal.
d) PAL-H (PROFILE OF ADAPTATION TO LIFE-HOLISTIC). Adults; 1978–81; 7 scores same as in *c* above, plus 5 life style areas correlated with good adjustment: social activity, self activity, nutrition and exercise, personal growth, spiritual awareness.

For additional information and a review by William J. Eichman of an earlier edition of the PARS Scale, see 8:638 (6 references).

[118]
The Adjustment Inventory. Grades 9–16, adults; 1934–63; AI; 2 levels; Hugh M. Bell; Consulting Psychologists Press, Inc.*
a) REVISED (1962) STUDENT FORM. Grades 9–16; 1934–63; 6 scores: home, health, submissiveness, emotionality, hostility, masculinity.
b) ADULT FORM. Adults; 1938–39; 6 scores: home, occupational, health, social, emotional, total.

See T2:1095 (77 references) and P:5 (16 references); for a review by Forrest L. Vance and an excerpted review by Laurence Siegel, see 6:59 (11 references); see also 5:30 (26 references); for reviews by Nelson G. Hanawalt and Theodore R. Sarbin, see 4:28 (104 references); for reviews by Raymond B. Cattell, John G. Darley, C. M. Louttit, and Percival M. Symonds of the original Student Form, reviews by S. J. Beck, J. P. Guilford, and Doncaster G. Humm of the Adult Form, and an excerpted review by Ruth A. Pedersen, see 2:1200 (15 references); for a review by Austin H. Turney of the Student Form, see 1:912.

REFERENCES

1–15. See 2:1200.
16–119. See 4:28.
120–145. See 5:30.
146–156. See 6:59.
157–172. See P:5.
173–249. See T2:1095.
250. ZHEUTLIN, S., & GOLDSTEIN, S. G. The prediction of psychosocial adjustment subsequent to cardiac insult. *Journal of Clinical Psychology*, 1977, 33, 706–710.
251. ROGERS, S., & LEUNES, A. A psychometric and behavioral comparison of delinquents who were abused as children with their nonabused peers. *Journal of Clinical Psychology*, 1979, 35, 470–472.

[119]
Administrator Image Questionnaire. School administrators; 1968 (no date on test materials); AIQ; ratings by groups such as teachers, other administrators, or noncertified personnel "to provide educational administrators with confidential feedback designed to help them work more effectively with people"; 24 ratings: verbal fluency, consideration of others, attitude toward job, technical competence, achievement drive, supportiveness, flexibility, performance under stress, openness, encouragement of staff participation, ability to delegate responsibility, innovativeness, success in communicating expectations, fairness, maintenance of staff morale, sense of humor, decision-making ability, evaluating ability, managerial skill, awareness, self-control, leadership skill, appearance, average; scoring must be done by publisher; Educator Feedback Center, Western Michigan University; the Center.* (In-print status uncertain; no reply from publisher.)

For additional information and a review by Richard M. Jaeger and Craig S. Scott, see 8:362 (1 reference).

[120]
Adolescent Alienation Index. Ages 12–19; 1971; AAI; F. K. Heussenstamm; Monitor.*

For additional information and reviews by David Freides and Robert Hogan, see 8:496 (1 reference); see also T2:1096 (1 reference).

[121]
Adult Basic Learning Examination. Adults with achievement levels grades 1–4, 5–8, 9–12; 1967–74; ABLE; 6 scores: vocabulary, reading, spelling, arithmetic (computation, problem solving, total); 3 levels plus screening test; Bjorn Karlsen, Richard Madden, and Eric F. Gardner; The Psychological Corporation.*

For additional information, see 8:2 (4 references); see also T2:3 (3 references); for a review by A. N. Hieronymus and excerpted reviews by Edward B. Fry and James W. Hall of Levels 1 and 2, see 7:3.

REFERENCES

1–3. See T2:3.
4–7. See 8:2.
8. MALATESTA, C. Z., CIRCO, J., & SMITH, B. A discriminating, non-discriminatory test battery for a prison population. *Corrective & Social Psychiatry & Journal of Behavior Technology, Methods & Therapy*, 1977, 23, 15–17.
9. COLES, G. S., ROTH, L., & POLLACK, I. W. Literacy skills of long-term hospitalized mental patients. *Hospital & Community Psychiatry*, 1978, 29, 512–516.
10. LUCAS, W. A., & SPARTANBURG S. C. Testing the effectiveness of video, voice, and data feedback. *Journal of Communication*, 1978, 28, 168–179.

11. COLES, G. S., CIPOREN, F., KONIGSBERG, R., & COHEN, B. Educational therapy in a community mental health center. *Community Mental Health Journal*, 1980, 16, 79–89.
12. JAMES, J. F., GREGORY, D., JONES, R. K., & RUNDELL, O. H. Psychiatric morbidity in prisons. *Hospital & Community Psychiatry*, 1980, 31, 674–677.
13. HECTOR, J. H., & FRANDSEN, H. Calculator algorithms for fractions with community college students. *Journal for Research in Mathematics Education*, 1981, 12, 349–355.

[122]
★Adult Self Expression Scale. Adults; 1974–75; ASES; Melvin L. Gay, James G. Hollandsworth, Jr., and John P. Galassi; Adult Self Expression Scale.*

REFERENCES
1. GAY, M. L.; HOLLANDSWORTH, J. G., JR., & GALASSI, J. P. An assertiveness inventory for adults. *Journal of Counseling Psychology*, 1975, 22, 340–344.
2. HOLLANDSWORTH, J. G., JR., GALASSI, J. P., & GAY, M. L. The Adult Self Expression Scale: Validation using the multitrait–multimethod procedure. *Journal of Clinical Psychology*, 1977, 33, 407–415.

[123]
Advanced Mathematics (Including Trigonometry): Minnesota High School Achievement Examinations. High school; 1951–70; a new, revised, or previously inactive form issued each May; Achievement Examinations for Secondary Schools, High School Achievement Examinations, and Midwest High School Achievement Examinations have also been used as series titles; edited by V. L. Lohmann; American Guidance Service.*

For additional information concerning out of print and inactive forms, see 7:450 and 5:441; for reviews by Lynnette B. Plumlee and James P. Rizzo of Forms E (1962) and F (1963), see 6:593; for a review by Emma Spaney of Form A (1955), see 5:442.

[124]
Advanced Placement Examinations. High school students desiring credit for college level courses or admission to advanced courses; 1954–82; APE; available to secondary schools for annual administration on specified days in May; inactive forms are available to colleges for local administration in the *Testing Academic Achievement* program; 21 tests: American History, Biology, Chemistry, Composition and Literature, European History, French Language, French Literature, German Language, History of Art, Language and Composition, Latin (Catullus-Horace), Latin (Vergil), Mathematics (2 tests: Calculus AB, Calculus BC), Music Listening and Literature, Music Theory, Physics (2 tests: Physics B, Physics C), Spanish Language, Spanish Literature, Studio Art; program administered by The College Board and Educational Testing Service.*

For additional information and reviews by Paul L. Dressel and David A. Frisbie, see 8:471 (5 references); see also T2:1045 (4 references); for reviews by Warren G. Findley and Alexander G. Wesman of an earlier program, see 7:662 (3 references); see also 6:761 (5 references). For reviews of individual tests, see 8:112 (1 review), 8:113 (2 reviews), 8:126 (1 review), 8:153 (1 review), 8:846 (1 review), 8:862 (1 review), 6:893 (1 review), 6:1000 (1 review), 5:205 (1 review), 5:211 (1 review), 5:273 (1 review), 5:419 (1 review), 5:724 (1 review), 5:743 (1 review), 5:750 (1 review), and 5:812 (2 reviews).

REFERENCES
1–5. See 6:761.
6–8. See 7:662.
9–12. See T2:1045.
13–17. See 8:471.
18. DIAMOND, E. E. The AMEG commission report on sex bias in achievement testing. *Measurement & Evaluation in Guidance*, 1980, 13, 135–147.

[125]
Advanced Placement Examination in American History. High school students desiring credit for college level courses and admission to advanced courses; 1956–82; available to secondary schools for annual administration on specified days in May; an inactive form is available to colleges for local administration and scoring; program administered by The College Board and Educational Testing Service.*

For additional information, see 8:907; see also T2:1980 (1 reference); for a review by Harry D. Berg of an earlier form, see 6:1000 (1 reference); for reviews by James A. Field, Jr. and Christine McGuire, see 5:812. For reviews of the APE program, see 8:471 (2 reviews) and 7:662 (2 reviews).

[126]
Advanced Placement Examination in Biology. High school students desiring credit for college level courses and admission to advanced courses; 1956–82; available to secondary schools for annual administration on specified days in May; an inactive form is available to colleges for local administration and scoring; program administered by The College Board and Educational Testing Service.*

For additional information, see 8:831 (1 reference); see also 7:807 (1 reference); for a review by Clarence H. Nelson of earlier forms, see 6:893 (1 reference); for a review by Clark W. Horton, see 5:724. For reviews of the APE program, see 8:471 (2 reviews) and 7:662 (2 reviews).

[127]
Advanced Placement Examination in Chemistry. High school students desiring credit for college level courses and admission to advanced courses; 1954–82; available to secondary schools for annual administration on specified days in May; an inactive form is available to colleges for local administration and scoring; program administered by The College Board and Educational Testing Service.*

For additional information and a review by J. Arthur Campbell, see 8:846; see also T2:1832 (1 reference) and 6:915 (1 reference); for a review by Theo. A. Ashford of an earlier form, see 5:743. For reviews of the APE program, see 8:471 (2 reviews) and 7:662 (2 reviews).

[128]
*Advanced Placement Examination in English (Composition and Literature).** High school students desiring credit for college level courses and admission to advanced courses; 1956–82; available to secondary schools for annual administration on specified days in May; an inactive form is available to colleges for local administration and scoring; program administered by The College Board and Educational Testing Service.*

For additional information and a review by Ellis Batten Page of an earlier edition, see 8:39; see also T2:51 (2 references) and 7:184 (1 reference); for a review by Robert C. Pooley of an earlier form of the English Composition test, see 5:205; for a review by John S. Diekhoff of an earlier form of the literature test, see 5:211. For reviews of the APE program, see 8:471 (2 reviews) and 7:662 (2 reviews).

[129]
*Advanced Placement Examination in English (Language and Composition). High school students desiring credit for college level courses and admission to advanced courses; 1981–82; available to secondary schools for annual administration on specified days in May; an inactive form is available to colleges for local administration and scoring; program administered by The College Board and Educational Testing Service.

For additional information and a review by Ellis Batten Page of an earlier edition, see 8:39; see also T2:51 (2 references) and 7:184 (1 reference); for a review by Robert C. Pooley of an earlier form of the English Composition test, see 5:205. For reviews of the APE program, see 8:471 (2 reviews) and 7:662 (2 reviews).

[130]
Advanced Placement Examination in European History. High school students desiring credit for college level courses and admission to advanced courses; 1956–82; available to secondary schools for annual administration on specified days in May; an inactive form is available to colleges for local administration and scoring; program administered by The College Board and Educational Testing Service.*

For additional information, see 8:908 (1 reference); see also 6:1001 (2 references). For reviews of the APE program, see 8:471 (2 reviews) and 7:662 (2 reviews).

[131]
Advanced Placement Examination in French Language, Level 3. High school students desiring credit for college level courses and admission to advanced courses; 1971–82; available to secondary schools for annual administration on specified days in May; for a lower level test, see CLEP Subject Examination in College French, Levels 1 and 2; an inactive form is available to colleges for local administration and scoring; program administered by The College Board and Educational Testing Service.*

For additional information and a review by Michio Peter Hagiwara, see 8:112. For reviews of the APE program, see 8:471 (2 reviews).

REFERENCES

1. KURTZMAN, H. Comparative comprehension of interlanguage and target language. *Perceptual & Motor Skills*, 1978, 47, 1141–1142.

[132]
Advanced Placement Examination in French Literature, Level 3. High school students desiring credit for college level courses and admission to advanced courses; 1954–82; available to secondary schools for annual administration on specified days in May; for a lower level test, see CLEP Subject Examination in College French, Levels 1 and 2; an inactive form is available to colleges for local administration and scoring; program administered by The College Board and Educational Testing Service.*

For additional information and reviews by Michio Peter Hagiwara and Joseph A. Murphy, see 8:113 (3 references); see also 7:268 (1 reference) and 6:368 (3 references). For reviews of the APE program, see 8:471 (2 reviews) and 7:662 (2 reviews).

[133]
*Advanced Placement Examination in German Language, Level 3. High school students desiring credit for college level courses and admission to advanced courses; 1956–82; available to secondary schools for annual administration on specified days in May; for a lower level test, see CLEP Subject Examination in College German, Levels 1 and 2; an inactive form is available to colleges for local administration and scoring; program administered by The College Board and Educational Testing Service.

For reviews of the APE program, see 8:471 (2 reviews) and 7:662 (2 reviews).

[134]
*Advanced Placement Examination in History of Art. High school students desiring credit for college level courses and admission to advanced courses; 1972–82; an individual study may be substituted for an optional essay; available to secondary schools for annual administration on specified days in May; an inactive form is available to colleges for local administration and scoring; program administered by The College Board and Educational Testing Service.

For additional information concerning an earlier edition, see 8:83. For reviews of the APE program, see 8:471 (2 reviews).

[135]
*Advanced Placement Examination in Latin, Level 3 (Catullus-Horace). High school students desiring credit for college level courses and admission to advanced courses; 1980–82; available to secondary schools for annual administration on specified days in May; an inactive form is available to colleges for local administration and scoring; program administered by The College Board and Educational Testing Service.

For additional information concerning an earlier edition of the Classics examination, see 8:144 (3 references). For reviews of the APE program, see 8:471 (2 reviews) and 7:662 (2 reviews).

[136]
*Advanced Placement Examination in Latin, Level 3 (Vergil). High school students desiring credit for college level courses and admission to advanced courses; 1972–82; available to secondary schools for annual administration on specified days in May; an inactive form is available to colleges for local administration and scoring; program administered by The College Board and Educational Testing Service.

For additional information concerning an earlier edition of the Classics examination, see 8:144 (3 references). For reviews of the APE program, see 8:471 (2 reviews) and 7:662 (2 reviews).

[137]
*Advanced Placement Examination in Music Listening and Literature. High school students

desiring credit for college level courses and admission to advanced courses; 1978–82; available to secondary schools for annual administration on specified days in May; previous essay questions available; an inactive form is available to colleges for local administration and scoring; program administered by The College Board and Educational Testing Service.

For additional information concerning an earlier edition of the Music examination, see 8:90. For reviews of the APE program, see 8:471 (2 reviews).

[138]

*Advanced Placement Examination in Music Theory.** High school students desiring credit for college level courses and admission to advanced courses; 1978–82; available to secondary schools for annual administration on specified days in May; previous essay questions available; an inactive form is available to colleges for local administration and scoring; program administered by The College Board and Educational Testing Service.

For additional information concerning an earlier edition of the Music examination, see 8:90. For reviews of the APE program, see 8:471 (2 reviews).

[139]

*Advanced Placement Examination in Spanish Language, Level 3.** High school students desiring credit for college level courses and admission to advanced courses; 1976–82; available to secondary schools for annual administration on specified days in May; program administered by The College Board and Educational Testing Service.

For additional information and a review by George W. Ayer of an earlier edition, see 8:153 (1 reference); see also 7:313 (2 references) and 6:421 (1 reference). For reviews of the APE program, see 8:471 (2 reviews) and 7:662 (2 reviews).

REFERENCES

1. See 6:421.
2–3. See 7:313.
4. See 8:153.
5. LISKIN-GASPARRO, J. E., MODU, C. C., & SCHRAIBMAN, J. The validity of the multiple-choice component of the Advanced Placement Spanish Language Examination. *Hispania*, 1979, 62, 98–105.

[140]

*Advanced Placement Examination in Spanish Literature, Level 3.** High school students desiring credit for college level courses and admission to advanced courses; 1956–82; for a lower level test, see *CLEP Subject Examination in College Spanish, Levels 1 and 2*; available to secondary schools for annual administration on specified days in May; an inactive form is available to colleges for local administration and scoring; program administered by The College Board and Educational Testing Service.

For additional information and a review by George W. Ayer of an earlier edition, see 8:153 (1 reference); see also 7:313 (2 references) and 6:421 (1 reference). For reviews of the APE program, see 8:471 (2 reviews) and 7:662 (2 reviews).

[141]

*Advanced Placement Examination in Studio Art.** High school students desiring credit for college level courses and admission to advanced courses; 1972–82; candidate submits materials (original works, written commentary, slides) for evaluation of quality, concentration, and breadth; available to secondary schools for annual administration on specified days in May; program administered by The College Board and Educational Testing Service.

For additional information concerning an earlier edition, see 8:83. For reviews of the APE program, see 8:471 (2 reviews).

[142]

Advanced Placement Examinations in Mathematics. High school students desiring credit for college level courses and admission to advanced courses; 1954–82; available to secondary schools for annual administration on specified days in May; an inactive form is available to colleges for local administration and scoring; program administered by The College Board and Educational Testing Service.*

a) CALCULUS AB. Equivalent of 1 year of college elementary functions and calculus.
b) CALCULUS BC. Equivalent of 1 year college calculus.

For additional information, see 8:309 (1 reference); see also T2:742 (1 reference), 7:451 (2 references), and 6:570 (4 references); for a review by Paul L. Dressel of an earlier form, see 5:419. For reviews of the APE program, see 8:471 (2 reviews) and 7:662 (2 reviews).

[143]

Advanced Placement Examinations in Physics. High school students desiring credit for college level courses and admission to advanced courses; 1954–82; available to secondary schools for annual administration on specified days in May; 2 levels (candidate elects only one); an inactive form is available to colleges for local administration and scoring; program administered by The College Board and Educational Testing Service.*

a) PHYSICS B. Equivalent of 1 year terminal course in college physics.
b) PHYSICS C. Equivalent of 1 year nonterminal course in college physics; 1 or 2 scores: mechanics (part 1), electricity and magnetism (part 2); 2 parts in each test booklet (candidate elects either one or both parts).

For additional information and a review by Mario Iona, see 8:862 (3 references); see also 6:927 (2 references); for a review by Leo Nedelsky of an earlier form, see 5:750. For reviews of the APE program, see 8:471 (2 reviews) and 7:662 (2 reviews).

REFERENCES

1–2. See 6:927.
3–5. See 8:862.
6. IONA, M. The physics advanced placement exams: What should one know besides physics to pass? *Physics Teacher*, 1978, 16, 150–153.

[144]

Affect Scale. College; 1960–71; AS; 4 scores: myself, others, myself plus others, myself minus others; no manual; Ricardo Girona; the Author.* (In-print status uncertain; no reply from publisher.)

[145]

★**Affective Domain Descriptor Program.** Ages 6–18; 1978; ADD; "a useful tool in helping teach students an awareness of acceptable and unacceptable behaviors for the classroom"; based on monitoring positive behaviors rather than negative ones; 9 behavioral factors: attends to task, emotionally responsive, participates socially, emotional control, need for adult contact, ability to delay, socially non-aggressive, ethical behavior, cooperation, plus a daily average; Richard D. Goeman and Deirdre A. Hestand; B. L. Winch & Associates.*

[146]

★**Affective Perception Inventory.** Grades 1–3, 4–8, 9–12; 1979–80; API; ratings by self and others; 9 scales: academic self in 6 classroom disciplines (language arts, math, science, social studies, the arts, physical education), 3 role scales (self as a person, self as a student, self in a school environment); (Spanish, French, and Italian editions available); Anthony T. Soares and Louise M. Soares; SOARES Associates.*
a) FORM P-PRIMARY LEVEL. Grades 1–3.
b) FORM I-INTERMEDIATE LEVEL. Grades 4–8.
c) FORM A-ADVANCED LEVEL. Grades 9–12.

[147]

The African T.A.T. Urban African adults; 1960–61; no manual; J. C. de Ridder; Industrial Psychological Services [South Africa].* (In-print status uncertain; no reply from publisher.)
See T2:1444 (2 references), P:412 (1 reference), and 6:200 (1 reference).

[148]

★**AH1 Forms X and Y.** Ages 7–11 for classroom purposes and 5–11 for research; 1977; downward extension of AH_2/AH_3; perceptual reasoning; 5 scores: series, likes, analogies, differents, total; A. W. Heim, K. P. Watts, and V. Simmonds; NFER-Nelson Publishing Co. [England].*

[149]

*****AH2/AH3.** Ages 9 and over; 1974–78; 4 scores: verbal, numerical, perceptual, total; A. W. Heim, K. P. Watts, V. Simmonds, and Gill Nyfield (norms supplement); NFER-Nelson Publishing Co. [England].*
For additional information, see 8:175 (1 reference).

REFERENCES

1. See 8:175.
2. HEIM, A. W., UNWIN, S. M., & WATTS, K. P. An investigation into disordered adolescents by means of the Brook Reaction Test. *British Journal of Social & Clinical Psychology*, 1977, 16, 253–268.
3. SACKS, H. V., & EYSENCK, M. W. Convergence–divergence and the learning of concrete and abstract sentences. *British Journal of Psychology*, 1977, 68, 215–221.
4. SEDDON, G. M. The effects of chronological age on the relationship of academic achievement with extraversion and neuroticism: A follow-up study. *British Journal of Educational Psychology*, 1977, 47, 187–192.
5. HINDLEY, C. B., & OWEN, C. F. The extent of individual changes in IQ for ages between 6 months and 17 years, in a British longitudinal sample. *Journal of Child Psychology & Psychiatry & Allied Disciplines*, 1978, 19, 329–350.
6. MARJORIBANKS, K. Teacher perceptions of student behavior, social environment, and cognitive performance. *Journal of Genetic Psychology*, 1978, 133, 217–228.
7. METCALFE, R. J. A. Divergent thinking 'threshold effect' – IQ, age, or skill? *Journal of Experimental Education*, 1978, 47, 4–8.
8. SHADBOLT, D. R. Interactive relationships between measured personality and teaching strategy variables. *British Journal of Educational Psychology*, 1978, 48, 227–231.
9. GLOSSOP, J. A., APPELYARD, R., & ROBERTS, C. Achievement relative to a measure of general intelligence. *British Journal of Educational Psychology*, 1979, 49, 249–257.
10. HINDLEY, C. B., & OWEN, C. F. An analysis of individual patterns of DQ and IQ curves from 6 months to 17 years. *British Journal of Psychology*, 1979, 70, 273–293.
11. LLOYD-BOSTOCK, S. M. A. Convergent–divergent thinking and arts–science orientation. *British Journal of Psychology*, 1979, 70, 155–163.

12. MARJORIBANKS, K. Intelligence, social environment, and academic achievement: A regression surface analysis. *Journal of Experimental Education*, 1979, 47, 346–351.
13. MICHELL, L., & LAMBOURNE, R. D. An association between high intellectual ability and an imaginative and analytic approach to the discussion of open questions. *British Journal of Educational Psychology*, 1979, 49, 60–72.
14. MACLEAN, A. W., & MCGHIE, A. The AH4 group test of general intelligence in a Canadian high school sample. *Canadian Journal of Behavioural Science*, 1980, 12, 288–291.
15. WHITE, A. P., & ZAMMARELLI, J. E. Convergence principals: Information in the answer sets of some multiple-choice intelligence tests. *Applied Psychological Measurement*, 1981, 5, 21–27.

[150]

Ahr's Individual Development Survey. Grades kgn–1; 1970; AIDS; screening test completed by parent to identify possible learning or behavior problems; 3 major sections: the family, the child, the school; A. Edward Ahr; Priority Innovations, Inc.*

[151]

★**Alberta Essay Scales: Models.** High school English teachers; "a means for checking writing skills against standards prevailing in 1964"; Verner R. Nyberg and Adell M. Nyberg; University of Alberta [Canada].*

REFERENCES

1. NYBERG, V. R., & NYBERG, A. M. Reliability of the Alberta Essay Scales. *Alberta Journal of Educational Research*, 1980, 26, 64–67.

[152]

The Alcadd Test. Adults; 1949; identification of alcoholic addicts and individuals with alcoholic problems; 6 scores: regularity of drinking, preference for drinking over other activities, lack of controlled drinking, rationalization of drinking, excessive emotionality, total; Morse P. Manson; Western Psychological Services.*
See T2:1098 (1 reference) and P:7 (3 references); for a review by Dugal Campbell, see 6:60 (6 references); for reviews by Charles H. Honzik and Albert L. Hunsicker, see 4:30.

REFERENCES

1–6. See 6:60.
7–9. See P:7.
10. See T2:1098.
11. HILTON, M. R., & LOKARE, V. G. The evaluation of a questionnaire measuring severity of alcoholic dependence. *British Journal of Psychiatry*, 1978, 132, 42–48.
12. MOHS, R. C., TINKLENBERG, J. R., ROTH, W. T., & KOPELL, B. S. Showing of short-term memory scanning in alcoholics. *Journal of Studies on Alcohol*, 1978, 39, 1908–1915.
13. ORNSTEIN, P. The Alcadd Test as a predictor of post-hospital drinking behavior. *Psychological Reports*, 1978, 43, 611–617.

[153]

Algebra, Geometry and Trigonometry Test for Stds 9 and 10. Standards 9, 10; 1973; 2 overlapping levels in a single booklet; S. J. P. Kruger; Human Sciences Research Council [South Africa].*
For additional information, see 8:296.

[154]

Algebra Test for Engineering and Science: National Achievement Tests. College entrants; 1958–61; 2 scores: part 1, total; A. B. Lonski; Psychometric Affiliates.*
For additional information and a review by Peter A. Lappan, Jr., see 6:595.

[155]
[Aliferis-Stecklein Music Achievement Tests].
Music students; 1954–62, c1947–62; 2 levels; James Aliferis and John E. Stecklein (*b*); University of Minnesota Press.*

a) ALIFERIS MUSIC ACHIEVEMENT TEST: COLLEGE ENTRANCE LEVEL. Entering freshman music students; 1954, c1947–54; 4 scores: melody, harmony, rhythm, total.

b) ALIFERIS-STECKLEIN MUSIC ACHIEVEMENT TEST: COLLEGE MIDPOINT LEVEL. Music students at end of grade 14 or beginning of grade 15; 1962, c1952–62; subtitle is *A Measure of Auditory-Visual Discrimination*; 4 scores: melodic interval, chord, rhythm, total.

See T2:194 (5 references); for reviews by Paul R. Farnsworth and Herbert D. Wing of *b*, see 6:347 (5 references); for a review by Herbert D. Wing of *a*, see 5:243 (5 references).

[156]
★**Alphabet Mastery.** Second semester kindergarten to 2.5, second semester kindergarten and over; 1975; no scores, standards of mastery determined by examiner; Enid L. Huelsberg; Ann Arbor Publishers, Inc.*

a) LEVEL 1: MANUSCRIPT. Second semester kgn to 2.5.
b) LEVEL 2: CURSIVE. Second semester kgn and over.

[157]
Alternate Uses. Grades 6–16 and adults; 1960; revision of *Unusual Uses*; experimental form; spontaneous flexibility; no manual for Forms B, C; Paul R. Christensen, J. P. Guilford, Philip R. Merrifield, and Robert C. Wilson; Sheridan Psychological Services, Inc.*

For additional information, see 8:235 (32 references); see also T2:542 (94 references) and 6:542 (7 references).

REFERENCES

1–7. See 6:542.
8–101. See T2:542.
102–133. See 8:235.
134. DOMINO, G. Primary process thinking in dream reports as related to creative achievement. *Journal of Consulting & Clinical Psychology*, 1976, 44, 929–932.
135. POOLE, M. E. Social class–sex contrasts in patterns of cognitive style. *Australian Journal of Education*, 1977, 21, 233–255.
136. PRICE–WILLIAMS, D. R., & RAMIREZ, M., III. Divergent thinking, cultural differences, and bilingualism. *Journal of Social Psychology*, 1977, 103, 3–11.
137. SANDERS, S. J., TEDFORD, W. H., JR., & HARDY, B. W. Effects of musical stimuli on creativity. *Psychological Record*, 1977, 27, 463–471.
138. JONES, W. H., CHERNOVETZ, M. E. O., & HANSSON, R. O. The enigma of androgyny: Differential implications for males and females? *Journal of Consulting & Clinical Psychology*, 1978, 46, 298–313.
139. KIRTON, M. Have adaptors and innovators equal levels of creativity. *Psychological Reports*, 1978, 42, 695–698.
140. MANGAN, G. L. The relationship of mobility of inhibition to rate of inhibitory growth and measures of flexibility, extraversion, and neuroticism. *Journal of General Psychology*, 1978, 99, 271–279.
141. METCALFE, R. J. A. Divergent thinking "threshold effect"–IQ, age, or skill? *Journal of Experimental Education*, 1978, 47, 4–8.
142. POOLE, M. E. Exploration of relationship inherent in linguistic, cognitive and verbal processing domains. *Psychological Reports*, 1978, 43, 639–647.
143. DURIO, H. F. A factor analysis of response task constraint in measures of creative aptitude. *Gifted Child Quarterly*, 1979, 23, 829–836.
144. GUNDLACH, R. H., & GESELL, G. P. Extent of psychological differentiation and creativity. *Perceptual & Motor Skills*, 1979, 48, 319–333.
145. HOCEVAR, D. A comparison of statistical infrequency and subjective judgment as criteria in the measurement of originality. *Journal of Personality Assessment*, 1979, 43, 297–299.
146. HOCEVAR, D. Ideational fluency as a confounding factor in the measurement of originality. *Journal of Educational Psychology*, 1979, 71, 191–196.
147. HOCEVAR, D., & MICHAEL, W. B. The effects of scoring formulas on the discriminant validity of tests of divergent thinking. *Educational & Psychological Measurement*, 1979, 39, 917–921.
148. KATZ, A. N., & POAG, J. R. Sex differences in instructions to "be creative" on divergent and non–divergent test scores. *Journal of Personality*, 1979, 47, 518–530.
149. PATSIOKAS, A. T., CLUM, G. A., & LUSCOMB, R. L. Cognitive characteristics of suicide attempters. *Journal of Consulting & Clinical Psychology*, 1979, 47, 478–484.
150. RIDLEY, D. R., & BIRNEY, R. C. Long–term effects of training procedures on originality tests. *Journal of Educational Research*, 1979, 72, 128–131.
151. KEEFE, J. A., & MAGARO, P. A. Creativity and schizophrenia: An equivalence of cognitive processing. *Journal Of Abnormal Psychology*, 1980, 89, 390–398.
152. MANNING, C. M., GETTYS, C., NICEWANDER, A., FISHER, S., & MEHLE, T. Predicting individual differences in generation of hypotheses. *Psychological Reports*, 1980, 47, 1199–1214.
153. TAN–WILLMAN, C. Fostering creativity and its effect on moral reasoning of prospective teachers. *Journal of Creative Behavior*, 1980, 14, 258–263.
154. HARRINGTON, D. M., & ANDERSEN, S. M. Creativity, masculinity, feminity and three models of psychological androgyny. *Journal of Personality & Social Psychology*, 1981, 41, 744–757.

[158]
★**Ambiguous Word Language Dominance Test, Spanish/English.** Bilingual students ages 10 and over; 1978; AWLDT; Gary D. Keller; Publishers Test Service.*

[159]
American Government: IOX Objectives-Based Tests. Grades 10–12; 1973–74; criterion-referenced; 32 tests; series description by W. James Popham; tests developed under the direction of Barbara S. Cummings; Instructional Objectives Exchange.*

For additional information and reviews by Dana G. Kurfman and Jack L. Nelson, see 8:917.

[160]
*****American High School Mathematics Examinations.** High school students competing for individual and school awards; 1950–82; AHSME; test administered annually in March at participating secondary schools; (Spanish, Braille, and large-type editions available); sponsored jointly by the Mathematical Association of America, Society of Actuaries, Mu Alpha Theta, National Council of Teachers of Mathematics, and Casualty Actuarial Society; M.A.A. Committee on High School Contests.

For additional information and a review by Thomas P. Hogan, see 8:252 (1 reference); see also T2:598 (3 references).

[161]
American History: Junior High—Objective. 1, 2 semesters in grades 7–9; 1963–70; revision of *Objective Tests in American History—Jr. H.S.* by John Barrett; 12 tests; no manual; Perfection Form Co.* (In-print status uncertain; no reply from publisher.)

a) EXPLORATION AND COLONIZATION.
b) REVOLUTIONARY AMERICA.
c) FOUNDATION OF A STRONG GOVERNMENT.
d) THE DEVELOPMENT OF DEMOCRACY.
e) WESTWARD EXPANSION.
f) FIRST SEMESTER TEST.
g) DIVISION AND REUNION.
h) A MODERN AMERICA.
i) AMERICA BECOMES A WORLD POWER.
j) POST WORLD WAR II.

k) SECOND SEMESTER TEST.
l) FINAL TEST.

[162]
American History: Senior High—Objective. 1, 2 semesters high school; 1960–70; revision of *Objective Tests in American History* by Earl Bridgewater; 13 tests; no manual; Perfection Form Co.* (In-print status uncertain; no reply from publisher.)
a) THE HERITAGE OF COLONIAL AMERICA.
b) BACKGROUND OF THE REVOLUTIONARY WAR, THE REVOLUTIONARY WAR AND ESTABLISHING A NEW GOVERNMENT (1763–1789).
c) THE UNITED STATES CONSTITUTION.
d) WASHINGTON'S ADMINISTRATION THROUGH THE WAR OF 1812.
e) EXPANSION WESTWARD AND THE JACKSONIAN ERA (1815 THRU 1841).
f) EXPANSION, WAR AND RECONSTRUCTION (1841–1868).
g) FIRST SEMESTER EXAMINATION.
h) THE EMERGENCE OF MODERN AMERICA.
i) THE UNITED STATES BECOMES A WORLD POWER (SPANISH-AMERICAN WAR, WORLD WAR 1, AND SETTLEMENT 1896–1921).
j) PROSPERITY AND DEPRESSION (1920 THRU 1940).
k) WORLD LEADERSHIP (1940–PRESENT).
l) SECOND SEMESTER EXAMINATION.
m) FINAL EXAMINATION.
For additional information concerning the earlier tests, see 6:1006.

[163]
The American Home Scale. Grades 8–16; 1942; socioeconomic status; 5 scores: cultural, aesthetic, economic, miscellaneous, total; W. A. Kerr and H. H. Remmers; Psychometric Affiliates.*
See T2:1039 (5 references) and 5:596 (2 references); for reviews by Henry S. Maas and Verner M. Sims, see 3:417 (7 references).

[164]
American Institute of Certified Public Accountants Testing Programs. Grades 13–16 and accountants; 1946–72; 2 programs: College Accounting Testing Program (tests available at any time) and Professional Accounting Testing Program (tests available to accountant employers at any time and also administered at regional testing centers); 3 tests; Committee on Personnel Testing, American Institute of Certified Public Accountants; distributed by The Psychological Corporation.*
a) ORIENTATION TEST. 3 scores: verbal, quantitative, total.
b) ACHIEVEMENT TESTS: LEVELS 1 AND 2.
c) STRONG VOCATIONAL INTEREST BLANK FOR MEN. Scored for 34 scales and plotted on an accountant's profile.
See T2:2323 (7 references), 5:911 (6 references), and 4:787 (15 references).

[165]
American Literacy Test. Adults; 1962; vocabulary; John J. McCarty; Psychometric Affiliates.*
For additional information and a review by Victor H. Noll, see 6:328.

[166]
American Literature Anthology Tests. High school; 1959–70; revisions of the *Objective Tests in American Anthology* by Carl H. Larson and the *Alternate Objective Tests in American Anthology* by Dorothy A. Mason; 7 tests; no manual; Perfection Form Co.* (In-print status uncertain; no reply from publisher.)
a) COLONIAL TIMES AND MAKING OF A NATION.
b) FLOWERING OF THE EAST.
c) THE GENIUS OF NEW ENGLAND.
d) CIVIL WAR AND THE WESTWARD MOVEMENT.
e) GROWTH OF REALISM.
f) MODERN AMERICAN LITERATURE.
g) FINAL TEST.
For additional information concerning the earlier tests, see 7:223.

[167]
American Numerical Test. Adults in "that great middle and upper middle block of vocations which emphasize shop and white collar skills involving number competence"; 1962; John J. McCarty; Psychometric Affiliates.*
For additional information and reviews by Marvin D. Glock and Richard T. Johnson, see 6:604.

[168]
American School Achievement Tests: Arithmetic Readiness. Grades kgn–1; 1941–55; identical with the numbers subtest of the Primary Battery 1 of *American School Achievement Tests*; Robert V. Young, Willis E. Pratt, and Frank Gatto; PRO-ED.*
For additional information and a review by Harold E. Moser, see 5:455. For reviews of the complete battery, see 6:2 (2 reviews), 5:1 (2 reviews), 4:1 (1 review), and 3:1 (2 reviews).

[169]
American School Achievement Tests, Revised Edition. Grades 1, 2–3, 4–6, 7–9; 1941–75; ASAT; subtests in reading, arithmetic, and language and spelling available as separates (grades 2–9); partial batteries are available without social studies and science (grades 4–9); 4 levels; Willis E. Pratt, George A. W. Stouffer, Jr., and Joan R. Yanuzzi; PRO-ED.*
a) PRIMARY BATTERY 1. Grade 1; 5 scores: reading (word recognition, word meaning, average), numbers, total average.
b) PRIMARY BATTERY 2. Grades 2–3; 9 scores: reading (sentences and words, paragraphs, average), arithmetic (computation, problems, average), language, spelling, total average.
c) INTERMEDIATE BATTERY. Grades 4–6; 11 scores: reading (sentences and words, paragraphs, average), arithmetic (computation, problems, average), language, spelling, social studies, science, total average.
d) ADVANCED BATTERY. Grades 7–9; 11 scores: same as for intermediate battery.
For additional information, reviews by Edward J. Furst and George F. Madaus, and an excerpted review by Alan Krichev, see 8:4 (1 reference); see also T2:4 (1 reference); for reviews by Robert H. Bauernfeind and Frank B. Womer of an earlier edition, see 6:2; for reviews by J. Raymond Gerberich and Virgil E. Herrick, see 5:1; for a review by Ralph C. Preston of the original edition, see 4:1

(1 reference); for reviews by Walter W. Cook and Gordon N. Mackenzie (with Glen Hass), see 3:1. For reviews of subtests, see 8:40 (1 review), 8:302 (1 review), 8:717 (1 review), 5:174 (2 reviews), 5:455 (1 review), 5:456 (2 reviews), and 5:620 (2 reviews).

[170]
American School Achievement Tests: Part 4, Social Studies and Science. Grades 4–6, 7–9; 1941–63; 2 scores: social studies, science; Willis E. Pratt, Robert V. Young (manuals), and Clara E. Cockerille; PRO-ED.*

For additional information, see 6:963.

[171]
American School Achievement Tests: Part 1, Reading, Revised Edition. Grades 2–3, 4–6, 7–9; 1941–75; 3 scores: sentence and word meaning, paragraph meaning, average; Willis E. Pratt, George A. W. Stouffer, Jr., and Joan R. Yanuzzi; PRO-ED.*

For additional information and a review by Edward B. Fry, see 8:717 (1 reference); for reviews by Russell G. Stauffer and Agatha Townsend of an earlier edition, see 5:620. For reviews of the complete battery, see 8:4 (2 reviews, 1 excerpt), 6:2 (2 reviews), 5:1 (2 reviews), 4:1 (1 review), and 3:1 (2 reviews).

[172]
American School Achievement Tests: Part 3, Language and Spelling, Revised Edition. Grades 2–3, 4–6, 7–9; 1941–75; 2 scores: language, spelling; Willis E. Pratt, George A. W. Stouffer, Jr., and Joan R. Yanuzzi; PRO-ED.*

For additional information and a review by Alan C. Purves, see 8:40; see also 6:248 (1 reference); for reviews by M. A. Brimer and Clarence Derrick of an earlier edition, see 5:174. For reviews of the complete battery, see 8:4 (2 reviews, 1 excerpt), 6:2 (2 reviews), 5:1 (2 reviews), 4:1 (1 review), and 3:1 (2 reviews).

[173]
American School Achievement Tests: Part 2, Arithmetic, Revised Edition. Grades 2–3, 4–6, 7–9; 1941–75; 3 scores: computation, problems, average; Willis E. Pratt, George A. W. Stouffer, Jr., and Joan R. Yanuzzi; PRO-ED.*

For additional information and a review by Leslie P. Steffe, see 8:302; see also 6:605 (1 reference); for reviews by Joseph Justman and J. Fred Weaver of an earlier edition, see 5:456. For reviews of the complete battery, see 8:4 (2 reviews, 1 excerpt), 6:2 (2 reviews), 5:1 (2 reviews), 4:1 (1 review), and 3:1 (2 reviews).

[174]
American School Intelligence Test. Grades kgn–3, 4–6, 7–9, 10–12; 1961–63; ASIT; tests for grades 4–12 "developed from the *Illinois General Intelligence Scale*" ('20–26) for grades 3–8; Willis E. Pratt, M. R. Trabue, Rutherford B. Porter, and George A. W. Stouffer, Jr.; PRO-ED.*

For additional information and reviews by David A. Payne and Frank B. Womer, see 6:439 (1 reference).

[175]
American School Reading Readiness Test, Revised. First grade entrants; 1941–64; Willis E. Pratt, George W. Stouffer (1964 form), Robert V. Young (1941 and 1955 forms), and Carroll A. Whitmer (1941 and 1955 forms); Bobbs-Merrill Co., Inc.*

For additional information and reviews by Joan Bollenbacher and Helen M. Robinson, see 5:675 (3 references); for reviews by David H. Russell and Paul A. Witty, see 3:513.

[176]
American School Reading Tests. Grades 10–13; 1955; 3 scores: vocabulary, reading rate, comprehension; Willis E. Pratt and Stanley W. Lore; Bobbs-Merrill Co., Inc.*

For additional information and reviews by Henry S. Dyer and Donald E. P. Smith, see 5:621.

[177]
[American Transit Association Tests]. Transit operating personnel; 1941–51; 4 tests; Glen U. Cleeton, Merwyn A. Kraft, and Robert F. Royster; American Transit Association.* (In-print status uncertain; no reply from publisher.)

a) STANDARD EXAMINATION FOR TRANSIT EMPLOYEES. 1941–46; intelligence.
b) PERSONAL REACTION TEST FOR TRANSIT EMPLOYEES. 1943–46; personality.
c) THE PLACEMENT INTERVIEW FOR TRANSIT EMPLOYEES. 1946; 9 ratings (moral character, mental ability, motor ability, health, motivation, stability, maturity, sociability, manner and appearance) in 3 areas (work experience, schooling and childhood, personal history).
d) A STANDARDIZED ROAD TEST FOR BUS OPERATORS. 1951.

See T2:2469 (1 reference) and 5:912; for reviews by Harold G. Seashore, Morris S. Viteles, and J. V. Waits of *a–c*, see 3:696 (1 reference).

[178]
Analysis of Readiness Skills: Reading and Mathematics. Grades kgn–1; 1972, c1969–72; 5 scores: visual perception of letters, letter identification, mathematics (identification, counting), total; orally administered in English or Spanish; Mary C. Rodrigues, William H. Vogler, and James F. Wilson; Riverside Publishing Co.*

For additional information and reviews by John T. Guthrie and Charles T. Myers, see 8:796.

REFERENCES
1. KNOX, B. J., & GLOVER, J. A. A note on preschool experience effects on achievement, readiness, and creativity. *Journal of Genetic Psychology*, 1978, 132, 151–152.

[179]
Analysis of Relationships. Grades 12–16 and industry; 1960; manual subtitle is *A Test of Mental Ability*; Edwin E. Ghiselli; Consulting Psychologists Press, Inc.*

See T2:341 (1 reference); for reviews by Gustav J. Froehlich and Wimburn L. Wallace, see 6:440 (2 references).

[180]
Analytical Survey Test in Computational Arithmetic. Grades 7–12; 1930–57; H. C. Christofferson and W. S. Guiler; Bobbs-Merrill Co., Inc.*

See T2:696 (3 references); for a review by Emma Spaney, see 5:457.

[181]
★**Ann Arbor Learning Inventory.** Grades kgn–1, 2–4; 1977–78; Waneta B. Bullock and Barbara Meister; Ann Arbor Publishers, Inc.*
a) LEVEL KGN–1. Grades kgn–1; 1978.
b) LEVEL 2–4. Grades 2–4; 1977.

[182]
★**The ANSER System—Aggregate Neurobehavioral Student Health and Educational Review.** Ages 3–5, 6–11, 12+; 1980–81; series of questionnaires to be completed by parents, school personnel, and students; for use with children possessing learning and/or behavioral problems; no scores: parent questionnaire covers 11 areas (family history, possible pregnancy problems, newborn infant problems, health problems, functional problems, early development, early educational experience, skills and interests, activity-attention problems, associated behaviors, associated strengths), school questionnaire covers educational setting and program, special facilities available, results of previous testing and 3 checklists (performance area, activity-attention behavioral observations, associated behavioral observations); Melvin D. Levine; Educators Publishing Service, Inc.*
a) FORM 1. Ages 3–5; 2 questionnaires: parent, school.
b) FORM 2. Ages 6–11; 2 questionnaires: parent, school.
c) FORM 3. Ages 12+; 2 questionnaires: parent, school.
d) FORM 4. Ages 9+; self-administered student profile; no scores, 10 developmental areas: fine motor, gross motor, memory, attention, language, general efficiency, visual-spatial processing, sequencing, general academic performance, social interaction.

[183]
The Anton Brenner Developmental Gestalt Test of School Readiness. Ages 5–6; 1964; BGT; also called *Brenner Gestalt Test*; an optional rating scale provides 2 scores: achievement-ability, social-emotional; Anton Brenner; Western Psychological Services.*
For additional information and a review by Dennis J. Deloria, see 7:742 (8 references); see also 6:844a (8 references).

[184]
The Anxiety Scale for the Blind. Blind and partially sighted ages 13 and over; 1966–68; ASB; experimental form; Richard E. Hardy; American Foundation for the Blind.*
For additional information and an excerpted review by Barton B. Proger, see 8:498 (1 reference); see also T2:1100 (1 reference) and P:8 (3 references).

[185]
AO Sight Screener. Adults; 1945–56; targets are available for both readers and nonreaders of English letters and numbers; American Optical Corporation, Industrial Safety Division.*
See T2:1906 (8 references) and 5:770 (8 references); for reviews by Henry A. Imus and F. Nowell Jones, see 3:460 (7 references).

[186]
Application Interview Screening Form. Job applicants; 1965; 10 ratings by interviewer: work experience, previous education and training, job knowledge, intelligence, sociability, ambition, emotional stability, fluency, maturity, leadership capacity; Psychological Publications Press.* (In-print status uncertain; no reply from publisher.)
For additional information, see 7:1067.

[187]
The Applied Biological and Agribusiness Interest Inventory. Grade 8; 1965–71; revision of *Vocational Agriculture Interest Inventory*; 5 scores: animals, plants, mechanics, business, total; Robert W. Walker and Glenn Z. Stevens; Interstate Printers & Publishers, Inc.*
For additional information and a review by Ehud Jungwirth, see 8:990; for a review by David P. Campbell of the original edition, see 7:1038 (4 references).

[188]
APT Manual Dexterity Test. Automobile and truck mechanics and mechanics' helpers; 1960–63; Bentley Barnabas (supplement); Associated Personnel Technicians, Inc.*
For additional information, see 6:1076.

[189]
Aptitude Assessment Battery: Programming. Programmers and trainees; 1967–69; AABP; no manual; distribution restricted to employers of programmers, not available to school personnel; Jack M. Wolfe; Programming Specialists, Inc.* (In-print status uncertain; no reply from publisher.)
For additional information, see 7:1087 (1 reference).

[190]
Aptitude Tests for Occupations. Grades 9–13 and adults; 1951; 6 tests; Wesley S. Roeder and Herbert B. Graham; PRO-ED.*
a) PERSONAL-SOCIAL APTITUDE.
b) MECHANICAL APTITUDE.
c) GENERAL SALES APTITUDE.
d) CLERICAL ROUTINE APTITUDE.
e) COMPUTATIONAL APTITUDE.
f) SCIENTIFIC APTITUDE.
See T2:1066 (3 references); for a review by Lloyd G. Humphreys, see 5:891; for a review by Clifford P. Froehlich and an excerpted review by Laurance F. Shaffer, see 4:710.

[191]
Aptitude Tests for School Beginners. Grade 1 entrants; 1974–76; ASB; 7 or 8 scores: perception, spatial, reasoning, numerical, gestalt, co-ordination, memory, verbal comprehension (optional for Blacks, omitted for Indians); an abbreviated battery (reasoning, numerical, and gestalt subtests) may be administered to obtain total score only; 4 editions; D. J. Swart (manuals), T. M. Coetzee (manual for *a*), Margaretha Tredoux (manual for *b*), and N. M. Olivier (manual for *d*); Human Sciences Research Council [South Africa].*
a) ["BLACK EDITION."] 1974–75; verbal comprehension subtest; instructions in 7 African languages.
b) ["COLOURED EDITION."] 1974; verbal comprehension subtest; Afrikaans manual available.
c) ["INDIAN EDITION."] 1974–76.
d) ["WHITE EDITION."] 1974; verbal comprehension subtest; Afrikaans manual available.

For additional information, see 8:482.

[192]
Aptitudes Associates Test of Sales Aptitude: A Test for Measuring Knowledge of Basic Principles of Selling. Applicants for sales positions; 1947–60; Martin M. Bruce; Martin M. Bruce, Ph.D., Publishers.*

For additional information, see 6:1169 (6 references); for reviews by Milton E. Hahn and Donald G. Paterson, see 4:824.

[193]
A.P.U. Arithmetic Test. Ages 11–18; 1976; S. J. Closs and M. J. Hutchings; Hodder & Stoughton Educational [England].*

For additional information, see 8:301.

[194]
A.P.U. Vocabulary Test. Ages 11–17; 1976; S. J. Closs; Hodder & Stoughton Educational [England].*

For additional information, see 8:77.

[195]
Arithmetic Reasoning Test: [Personnel Research Institute Clerical Battery]. Clerical applicants and high school; 1948; Jay L. Otis and David J. Chesler; Psychological Research Services.*

For additional information, see 4:403. For reviews of the complete battery, see 4:729 (2 reviews).

REFERENCES

1. BOOTH, R. F., & NEWMAN, K. Social status and minority recruit performance in the navy: Some implications for affirmative action programs. *Sociological Quarterly*, 1977, 18, 564–573.
2. WEBSTER, E. G., BOOTH, R. F., GRAHAM, W. K., & ALF, E. F. A sex comparison of factors related to success in naval hospital corps school. *Personnel Psychology*, 1978, 31, 95–106.

[196]
Arithmetic Test (Fundamentals and Reasoning): Municipal Tests: National Achievement Tests. Grades 3–6, 6–8; 1938–56; subtest of *Municipal Battery*; Robert K. Speer and Samuel Smith; Psychometric Affiliates.*

For additional information, see 5:463; for reviews by Foster E. Grossnickle and Charles S. Ross, see 4:406. For reviews of the complete battery, see 5:18 (1 review), 4:20 (1 review), and 2:1191 (2 reviews).

[197]
Arithmetic Test: National Achievement Tests. Grades 3–8; 1936–61; 2 tests; no manual; Robert K. Speer and Samuel Smith; Psychometric Affiliates.*
a) FUNDAMENTALS. 1938–61; 4 scores: fundamentals-speed, number comparisons, fundamentals-skills, total.
b) REASONING. 1936–60; 5 scores: comparisons, problem analysis, finding problem key, problems, total.

For additional information, see 6:613; for reviews by R. L. Morton and Leroy E. Schnell, see 2:1449; for reviews by William A. Brownell and W. J. Osburn, see 1:889.

[198]
Arithmetic Tests EA2A and EA4. Ages 14.5 and over; 1947–72; subtest of *N.I.I.P. Engineering Apprentice Selection Test Battery*; arithmetic attainment; 2 tests; National Institute of Industrial Psychology; NFER-Nelson Publishing Co. [England].*
a) TEST EA2A. 1947–71; decimalized version of *Test EA2*; also referred to as *Engineering Arithmetic Test 2*; 1971 test identical with test copyrighted 1947 except for 1 revised item.
b) TEST EA4. 1972; metricated version of a; no manual.

For additional information concerning Test EA2, see 7:1096d.

[199]
Arithmetical Problems: Test A/68. Job applicants with at least 10 years of education; 1955–62; test in English and Afrikaans; no manual; National Institute for Personnel Research [South Africa].*

[200]
The Arizona Articulation Proficiency Scale: Revised. Mental ages 2–14 and over; 1963–70; AAPS; Janet Barker Fudala; Western Psychological Services.*

For additional information, reviews by Raphael M. Haller and Ronald K. Sommers, and an excerpted review by Barton B. Proger, see 8:954 (6 references); see also T2:2065 (2 references), 7:948 (2 references), and 6:307a (2 references).

REFERENCES

1–2. See 6:307a.
3–4. See 7:948.
5–6. See T2:2065.
7–12. See 8:954.
13. MULLEN, P. A., & WHITEHEAD, R. L. Stimulus picture identification in articulation testing. *Journal of Speech & Hearing Disorders*, 1977, 42, 113–118.
14. BLACHE, S., & O'BRIEN, M. A clinical prototype for auditory memory span. *Journal of Communication*, 1978, 11, 519–527.
15. DEPUTY, P. N., & HUTCHINSON, J. M. Some additional observations on the Arizona Articulation Proficiency Scale. *ASHA*, 1979, 21, 757. (Abstract)
16. SCHISSEL, R. J., & JAMES, L. B. A comparison of childrens performance on two tests of articulation. *Journal of Speech & Hearing Disorders*, 1979, 44, 363–372.
17. HULIT, L. M., HOWARD, M. R., & FOSTER, S. K. Effects of delay interval and pictorial cues on a sentence imitation task. *Perceptual & Motor Skills*, 1980, 51, 91–100.
18. KORNSE, D. D., MANNI, J. L., RUBENSTEIN, H., & GRAZIANI, L. J. Developmental apraxia of speech and manual dexterity. *Journal of Communication Disorders*, 1981, 14, 321–330.
19. SINGH, S., HAYDEN, M. E., & TOOMBS, M. S. The role of distinction features in articulation errors. *Journal of Speech & Hearing Disorders*, 1981, 46, 174–183.
20. TOOMBS, M. S., SINGH, S., & HAYDEN, M. E. Markedness of features in the articulatory substitutions of children. *Journal of Speech & Hearing Disorders*, 1981, 46, 184–191.

[201]
Arlin-Hills Attitude Surveys. Grades kgn–3, 4–6, 7–12; 1976; student attitudes; for measurement of groups, not individuals; 4 tests; Marshall Arlin; Psychologists and Educators, Inc.*
a) ATTITUDE TOWARD LANGUAGE ARTS.
b) ATTITUDE TOWARD LEARNING PROCESSES.
c) ATTITUDE TOWARD MATHEMATICS.
d) ATTITUDE TOWARD TEACHERS.

For additional information, see 8:499 (1 reference).

REFERENCES

1. See 8:499.

2. ARLIN, M., & ROTH, G. Pupils' use of time while reading comics and books. *American Educational Research Journal*, 1978, 15, 201–216.
3. ARLIN, M., & WHITLEY, T. W. Perceptions of self-managed learning opportunities and academic locus of control: A causal interpretation. *Journal of Educational Psychology*, 1978, 70, 988–992.

[202]

★Armed Services Vocational Aptitude Battery. High school (some seniors must be included); 1967–82; ASVAB; an aptitude battery designed for use both in high schools and to select and classify all enlistees at the Armed Forces Examining and Entrance Stations (AFEES) across the country; tests administered and scored without charge by Department of Defense personnel; copies of the ASVAB results for students in the 11th and 12th grade are furnished to the local recruiting stations of each of the armed services; 12 subtests: general information (GI), numerical operations (NO), attention to detail (AD), word knowledge (WK), arithmetic reasoning (AR), space perception (SP), mathematics knowledge (MK), electronics information (EI), mechanical comprehension (MC), general science (GS), shop information (SI), automotive information (AI), combinations of which produce 6 composite scores: verbal (WK+GS), math (AR+MK), perceptual speed (3AD+NO), mechanical (SP+MC), trade technical (AI+EI+SI), academic ability (WK+RC); US Military Enlistment Processing Command.*

For additional information and a review by David J. Weiss, see 8:483 (4 references); see also T2:1067 (1 reference).

REFERENCES

1. See T2:1067.
2–5. See 8:483.
6. KELSO, G. I., HOLLAND, J. L., & GOTTREDSON, G. D. The relation of self–reported competencies to aptitude test scores. *Journal of Vocational Behavior*, 1977, 10, 99–103.
7. MODJESKI, R. B., & MICHAEL, W. B. The relationship of the general educational performance index measure to other indicators of educational development in each of three samples from an United States Army population. *Educational & Psychological Measurement*, 1978, 38, 377–391.
8. VANDERPLOEG, A. J., & MUELLER, S. G. An examination of the Armed Services Vocational Aptitude Battery. *Measurement & Evaluation in Guidance*, 1978, 11, 70–77.
9. CRONBACH, L. J. The Armed Services Vocational Aptitude Battery-A test battery in transition. *Personnel & Guidance Journal*, 1979, 57, 232–237.
10. DIAMOND, E. E. The AMEG commission report on sex bias in achievement testing. *Measurement & Evaluation in Guidance*, 1980, 13, 135–147.
11. HOLDEN, C. Doubts mounting about all–volunteer force. *Science*, 1980, 209, 1095–1099.
12. DILLON, R. F., & WISHER, R. A. The predictive validity of eye movement indices for technical school qualifying test performance. *Applied Psychological Measurement*, 1981, 5, 43–49.
13. MORACCO, J., WILSON, D., & FLOYD, M. A comparison of the occupational aspirations of a select group of military men and women. *Vocational Guidance Quarterly*, 1981, 30, 149–156.

[203]

Art Vocabulary. Grades 6–12; 1969; AV; R. H. Silverman, R. Hoepfner, and M. Hendricks; Monitor.*

For additional information and reviews by Kenneth E. Burchett and Laura H. Chapman, see 8:84.

[204]

Arthur Point Scale of Performance Tests. Ages 4.5 or 5.5 to superior adults; 1925–47; 2 editions; Grace Arthur.*

a) FORM I. Ages 5.5 to superior adults; 1925–43; 10 tests: *Knox Cube Test (Arthur Revision), Seguin Form Board (Arthur Revision), Two-Figure Form Board, Casuist Form Board, Manikin Test, Feature Profile Test, Mare and Foal Formboard, Healy Pictorial Completion Test 1, Porteus Maze Test (1924 Series), The Block-Design Test (Arthur Modification)*; Stoelting Co.

b) REVISED FORM II. Ages 4.5 to superior adults; 1933–47; 5 tests: *Knox Cube Test (Arthur Revision), Seguin Form Board (Arthur Revision), Arthur Stencil Design Test I, Porteus Maze Test (Arthur Revision), Healy Pictorial Completion Test II*; The Psychological Corporation.

See T2:483 (21 references); for a review by William R. Grove, see 4:335 (12 references); for an excerpted review, see 3:271 (20 references); for reviews by Andrew W. Brown and Carroll A. Whitmer and an excerpted review by Donald Snedden, see 2:1379 (17 references).

[205]

★Assessing Reading Difficulties: A diagnostic and remedial approach. Children in primary school and over; 1980; 3 error scores: last sound different, middle sound different, first sound different; Lynette Bradley; Macmillan Education [England].*

[206]

★Assessment in Mathematics. Primary and lower secondary school children; 1980–81; criterion-referenced; 5 areas: number, measure, shape, probability and statistics, relations; R. W. Strong, Coordinator, Somerset Local Education Authority; Macmillan Education [England].*

[207]

★Assessment in Nursery Education. Ages 3–5; 1978; AINE; assessment by teacher's observation and performance tasks; assessment in 5 areas: social skills and social thinking, talking and listening, thinking and doing, manual and tool skills, physical skills; Margaret Bate and Marjorie Smith; NFER-Nelson Publishing Co. [England].*

[208]

★Assessment of Basic Competencies. Ages 3+–15 years; 1981; ABC; norm- and criterion-referenced; Jwalla P. Somwaru; Scholastic Testing Service, Inc.*

a) INFORMATION PROCESSING. 1 form in 3 booklets: observing skills, organizing skills, relating skills.

b) LANGUAGE. 1 form in 5 booklets: understanding words, comprehending expressions, producing expressions, reading, decoding.

c) MATHEMATICS. 1 form in 3 booklets: knowing number and operations, understanding concepts, solving problems.

[209]

★Assessment of Basic Competencies: Information Processing Module. Ages 3–15; 1981; norm- and criterion-referenced; 1 form in 3 booklets: observing skills, organizing skills, relating skills; Jwalla P. Somwaru; Scholastic Testing Service, Inc.* For the complete battery entry, see 208.

[210]

★Assessment of Basic Competencies: Language Module. Ages 3–15; 1981; norm- and criterion-referenced; 1 form in 5 booklets: understanding words, comprehending expressions, producing expressions, reading, decoding; Jwalla P. Somwaru; Scholastic Testing Service, Inc.* For the complete battery entry, see 208.

[211]
★Assessment of Basic Competencies: Mathematics Module. Ages 3–15; 1981; norm- and criterion-referenced; 1 form in 3 booklets: knowing number and operations, understanding concepts, solving problems; Jwalla P. Somwaru; Scholastic Testing Service, Inc.* For the complete battery entry, see 208.

[212]
Assessment of Children's Language Comprehension, 1973 Revision. Ages 3–7; 1969–74; ACLC; 4 scores: vocabulary, 2 critical elements, 3 critical elements, 4 critical elements; 2 editions; Rochana Foster, Jane J. Giddan, and Joel Stark; Consulting Psychologists Press, Inc.*
a) [INDIVIDUAL FORM.] 1969–74.
b) GROUP FORM. 1973; abbreviated version for preliminary screening.

For additional information and a review by James A. Till, see 8:452 (3 references).

REFERENCES

1–3. See 8:452.
4. RINGLER, N., TRAUSE, M. A., KLAUS, M., & KENNELL, J. The effects of extra postpartum contact and maternal speech patterns on children's IQs, speech, and language comprehension at five. *Child Development*, 1978, 49, 862–865.
5. BEADLE, K. R. Clinical interactions of verbal language, learning and behavior. *Journal of Clinical Child Psychology*, 1979, 8, 201–205.
6. ZWITMAN, D. H., & SONDERMAN, J. C. A syntax program designed to present base linguistic structures to language–disordered children. *Journal of Communication Disorders*, 1979, 12, 323–335.
7. FIELDS, T. A., & ASHMORE, L. L. Effect of elicitation variables on analysis of language samples for normal and language–disordered children. *Perceptual & Motor Skills*, 1980, 50, 911–919.
8. GEFFNER, D. S., & FREEMAN, L. R. Assessment of language comprehension of 6-year-old deaf children. *Journal of Communication Disorders*, 1980, 13, 455–470.
9. KLEECK, A. V., & CARPENTER, R. L. The effects of children's language comprehension level on adults' child–directed talk. *Journal of Speech & Hearing Research*, 1980, 23, 546–569.
10. TESKA, J. A., & STONEBURNER, R. L. The concept and practice of second–level screening. *Psychology in the Schools*, 1980, 17, 192–195.
11. CHAPMAN, D. L., & NATION, J. E. Patterns of language performance in educable mentally retarded children. *Journal of Communication Disorders*, 1981, 14, 245–254.

[213]
★Assessment of Coping Style. Grades kgn–8, 9–12; 1981; ACS; manual title is *Analysis of Coping Style*; revision of the *School Picture-Story Test*; 12 scores: 3 externalized (attack, avoidance, denial), 3 internalized (attack, avoidance, denial), for both authority and peer interaction sources; Herbert F. Boyd and G. Orville Johnson; Charles E. Merrill Publishing Co.*

[214]
★The Assessment of Phonological Processes. Ages 2–9; 1980; leads to the identification of patterns in child speech; 10 occurrence scores: syllable reduction, cluster reduction, prevocalic singleton omissions, postvocalic singleton omissions, stridency deletion, velar deviations, liquid deviations (2 scores), nasal deviations, glide deviations; Barbara Williams Hodson; Interstate Printers & Publishers, Inc.*

[215]
★Assessment of Qualitative and Structural Dimensions of Object Representations. Adolescents and adults (patients and normals); 1981; AQSDOR; subject's descriptions of significant figures (e.g., parents) rated by judges; ratings in 4 areas: personal qualities, degree of ambivalence in description, length of description, conceptual level; Sidney J. Blatt, Eve S. Chevron, Donald M. Quinlan, and Steven Wein; Sidney J. Blatt.*

[216]
★Assessment of Reading Growth. Grades 3, 7, 11; 1979–80; criterion-referenced tests of reading comprehension based on National Assessment of Educational Progress; 3 levels; Edward Fry; Jamestown Publishers.*
a) LEVEL 9. Grade 3; 1979; 2 scores: literal comprehension, inferential comprehension.
b) LEVEL 13. Grade 7; 1979; 2 scores: literal comprehension, inferential comprehension.
c) LEVEL 17. Grade 11; 1980; 3 scores: literal comprehension, inferential comprehension, total comprehension.

[217]
★Assessment of Skills in Computation. Junior high school; 1978–79; ASC; Los Angeles Unified School District; CTB/McGraw-Hill.*

[218]
Association Adjustment Inventory. Normal and institutionalized adults; 1959; AAI; adaptation of *Kent-Rosanoff Free Association Test*; 13 scores: juvenility, psychotic responses, depressed-optimistic, hysteric-nonhysteric, withdrawal-sociable, paranoid-naive, rigid-flexible, schizophrenic-objective, impulsive-restrained, sociopathic-empathetic, psychosomapathic-physical contentment, anxious-relaxed, total; Martin M. Bruce; Martin M. Bruce, Ph.D., Publishers.*

For additional information, see P:413; for reviews by W. Grant Dahlstrom and Bertram R. Forer and an excerpted review by Edward S. Bordin, see 6:201.

[219]
★Athlete's Affective Response Profile. High school and college and adult athletes; 1980–81; AARP; 24 scores: 4 scores (intensity, concentration, anxiety, physical readiness) for 6 different points in time (24 hours before, at breakfast, just before, after start, at peak, something wrong); E. E. Oetting and C. W. Cole (profile); Rocky Mountain Behavioral Science Institute, Inc.* (In-print status uncertain; no reply from publisher.)

[220]
Attitude to School Questionnaire. Grades kgn–2; 1976; ASQ; Guy P. Strickland, Ralph Hoepfner, and Stephen P. Klein; Monitor.*

For additional information, see 8:363.

REFERENCES

1. BRACKEN, B. A. Comparison of self–attitudes of gifted children and children in a nongifted normative group. *Psychological Reports*, 1980, 47, 715–718.

[221]
★Attitude Toward School. Elementary, secondary school students; 1977; "an IOX measureable objectives collection"; criterion-referenced; 2 levels; Instructional Objectives Exchange (School Sentiment Index), Elaine L. Lindheim, and Caren M. Gitlin; Instructional Objectives Exchange.*
a) ELEMENTARY LEVEL. Pre-reading and reading elementary students; 11 measures: School Sentiment Index, take your pick, let's pretend, classmates, lights/camera/ action,

my class, let's write a letter (pre-reading), short composition (reading), my classroom, magazine story, subject choice, television station.

b) SECONDARY LEVEL. Secondary students; 13 measures: School Sentiment Index, take your pick, imagine that, classmates, lights/camera/action, this class, short composition, this classroom, magazine survey, class activities checklist, preferred class activities, elective program, television station.

[222]

★**Attitude Toward School K-12.** Grades kgn–3, 4–6, 7–12; 1972; "an IOX measureable objectives collection"; criterion-referenced; utilizes direct self-report, inferential self-report, and observation; 3 levels; Instructional Objectives Exchange.*

a) PRIMARY. Grades kgn–3; 11 objectives: school sentiment (comprehensive, teacher, school subjects, social climate, peers, general), a picture choice, compliance with assigned tasks, school attendance, school conduct (compliance with school rules), school tardiness.

b) INTERMEDIATE. Grades 4–6; 15 objectives: school sentiment (same as in *a* above), subject area preference, imagine that, the story, looking back, the school play, compliance with assigned tasks, school attendance, school conduct (compliance with school rules), school tardiness.

c) SECONDARY. Grades 7–12; 16 objectives: school sentiment (same as in *a* above), subject area preference, what would happen, imagine that, take your pick, high school on T.V., class attendance, class tardiness, grade level completion, school conduct (same as in *b* above), unwillingness to transfer.

REFERENCES

1. McGee, R. Measuring affective behavior in physical education. *Journal of Physical Education & Recreation*, 1977, 48, 29–30.

[223]

★**Attitudes Related to Tolerance 9–12.** Grades 9–12; 1971; "an IOX measureable objectives collection"; criterion-referenced; utilizes direct self-report, indirect, and observation; 13 objectives: personal perspective (2 objectives), policy choice, group description scale, interaction attitude index, social reactions—specific populations (caucasian-negro), contemporary image, situation reaction, ethnic attitude, sociometric techniques, observation form, unobtrusive measures (2 objectives); Instructional Objectives Exchange.*

[224]

★**Attitudes Toward Mainstreaming Scale.** Adults; 1980; ATMS; no manual; Joan D. Berryman, W. R. Neal, Jr., and Charles Berryman; University of Georgia.*

REFERENCES

1. Berryman, J. D., & Neal, W. R., Jr. The cross validation of the Attitudes Toward Mainstreaming Scale. *Educational & Psychological Measurement*, 1980, 40, 469–474.
2. Berryman, J. D., Neal, W. R., Jr., & Robinson, J. E. The development of a scale to measure attitudes toward mainstreaming. *Journal of Educational Research*, 1980, 73, 199–203.
3. Berryman, J. D., & Berryman, C. *Use of the Attitudes Toward Mainstreaming Scale with Rural Georgia Teachers*. Paper presented at the Annual Meeting of the American Educational Research Association, Los Angeles, April 13, 1981. (ERIC Document Reproduction Service No. ED 201 420)

[225]

Attitudes Toward Parental Control of Children. Adults; 1936; Ralph M. Stogdill and Henry H. Goddard; Ralph M. Stogdill.* (In-print status uncertain; no reply from publisher.)

For additional information, see P:11; see also 2:1205 (2 references).

[226]

Auditory Discrimination Test. Ages 5–8; 1958–73; ADT; "ability to recognize the fine differences that exist between the phonemes used in English speech"; Joseph M. Wepman; Language Research Associates, Inc.*

For additional information, see 8:932 (74 references); see also T2:2028 (82 references); for a review by Louis M. DiCarlo of the original edition, see 6:940 (2 references).

REFERENCES

1–2. See 6:940.
3–84. See T2:2028.
85–158. See 8:932.
159. Bartolucci, G., & Pierce, S. J. A preliminary comparison of phonological development in autistic, normal, and mentally retarded subjects. *British Journal of Disorders of Communication*, 1977, 12, 137–147.
160. Hare, B. A. Perceptual deficits are not a cue to reading problems in second grade. *Reading Teacher*, 1977, 30, 624–628.
161. Lombard, T. J., & Harney, B. J. Auditory discrimination as a predictor of reading for bilingual Mexican–American migrant children. *Perceptual & Motor Skills*, 1977, 45, 479–484.
162. Parr, V. E. Auditory word discrimination in male children diagnosed as having minimal brain dysfunction. *Journal of Clinical Psychology*, 1977, 33, 1064–1069.
163. Margolis, H. Auditory perceptual test performance and the reflection–impulsivity dimension. *Journal of Learning Disabilities*, 1977, 10, 164–172.
164. Haggerty, R., & Stamm, J. S. Dichotic auditory fusion levels in children with learning disabilities. *Neuropsychologia*, 1978, 16, 349–360.
165. Koenke, K. A comparison of three auditory discrimination–perception tests. *Academic Therapy*, 1978, 14, 463–468.
166. Margolis, H., & Brannigan, G. G. Conceptual tempo as a parameter for predicting reading achievement. *Journal of Educational Research*, 1978, 71, 342–345.
167. Quorn, K. C., & Yore, L. D. Comparison studies of reading readiness program skills acquisition by different methods: Formal reading readiness program, informal reading readiness program, and a kindergarten science program. *Science Education*, 1978, 62, 459–465.
168. Satz, P., & Friel, J. Predictive validity of an abbreviated screening battery. *Journal of Learning Disabilities*, 1978, 11, 347–351.
169. Williams, F., & Oakland, T. A three-year auditory perception program for low–SES minority children. *Journal of Special Education*, 1978, 12, 331–344.
170. Belka, D. E., & Williams, H. G. Prediction of later cognitive behavior from early school perceptual–motor, perceptual, and cognitive performances. *Perceptual & Motor Skills*, 1979, 49, 131–141.
171. Klein, P. S., & Schwartz, A. A. Effects of training auditory sequential memory and attention on reading. *Journal of Special Education*, 1979, 13, 365–374.
172. Needleman, H. L., Gunnoe, C., Leviton, A., Reed, R., Peresie, H., Maher, C., & Barrett, P. Deficits in psychologic and classroom performance of children with elevated dentine lead levels. *New England Journal of Medicine*, 1979, 300, 689–695.
173. Sabatino, D. A. The definition and assessment of visual and auditory perception. *Journal of Clinical Child Psychology*, 1979, 8, 188–194.
174. Swanson, L. Auditory recall of conceptually, phonetically, and linguistically similar words by normal and learning–disabled children. *Journal of Special Education*, 1979, 13, 63–67.
175. Temple, I. G., Williams, H. G., & Bateman, N. J. A test battery to assess intrasensory and intersensory development of young children. *Perceptual & Motor Skills*, 1979, 48, 643–659.
176. White, M., Batini, P., Satz, P., & Friel, J. Predictive validity of a screening battery for children "at risk" for reading failure. *British Journal of Educational Psychology*, 1979, 49, 132–137.
177. Belka, D. E., & Williams, H. G. Canonical relationships among perceptual-motor, perceptual, and cognitive behaviors in children. *Research Quarterly for Exercise & Sport*, 1980, 51, 463–477.
178. Cohen, S., Evans, G. W., Krantz, D. S., & Stokols, D. Physiological, motivational, and cognitive effects of aircraft noise on children. *American Psychologist*, 1980, 35, 231–243.

179. COOK, J. E., NOLAN, G. A., & ZANOTTI, R. J. Treating auditory perception problems: The NIM helps. *Academic Therapy*, 1980, 15, 473–481.
180. MARGOLIS, H., LEONARD, H. S., BRANNIGAN, G. G., & HEVERLY, M. A. The validity of Form F of the Matching Familiar Figures Test with kindergarten children. *Journal of Experimental Child Psychology*, 1980, 29, 12–22.
181. PALMER, L. L. Auditory discrimination development through vestibulo–cochlear stimulation. *Academic Therapy*, 1980, 16, 53–68.
182. ZAGAR, R., ARBIT, J., & FRIEDLAND, J. Structure of a psychodiagnostic test battery for children. *Journal of Clinical Psychology*, 1980, 36, 313–318.
183. BOUNTRESS, N. G., & LADERBERG, C. M. A comparison of two tests of speech–sound discrimination. *Journal of Communication Disorders*, 1981, 14, 149–156.
184. COHEN, S., EVANS, G. W., KRANTZ, D. S., STOKOLS, D., & KELLY, S. Aircraft noise and children: Longitudinal and cross–sectional evidence on adaptation to noise abatement. *Journal of Personality & Social Psychology*, 1981, 40, 331–345.
185. LYON, R., REITTA, S., WATSON, B., PORCH, B., & RHODES, J. Selected linguistic and perceptual abilities of empirically derived subgroups of learning disabled readers. *Journal of School Psychology*, 1981, 19, 152–166.
186. MILLER, J. W., & MCKENNA, M. C. Disabled readers: Their intellectual and perceptual capacities at differing ages. *Perceptual & Motor Skills*, 1981, 52, 467–472.
187. RYCKMAN, D. B. Reading achievement, IQ, and simultaneous-successive processing among normal and learning–disabled children. *Alberta Journal of Educational Research*, 1981, 27, 74–83.
188. SEMEL, E. M., & WIIG, E. H. Semel Auditory Processing Program: Training effects among children with language–learning disabilities. *Journal of Learning Disabilities*, 1981, 14, 192–196.
189. STEIN, G. M., GIBBONS, R. D., & MELDMAN, M. J. Lateral eye movement and handedness as measures of functional brain asymmetry in learning disability. *Cortex*, 1981, 16, 223–229.

[227]

Auditory Memory Span Test. Ages 5–8; 1973; "ability to recall single syllable spoken words in progressively increasing series"; Joseph M. Wepman and Anne Morency; Language Research Associates, Inc.*

For additional information and a review by J. Joseph Freilinger, see 8:933 (2 references).

[228]

Auditory Pointing Test. Ages 5–10; 1974; "testing STM [short-term memory] of children with oral speech and language problems"; 4 scores: memory span, sequential memory, last item, total; Janet B. Fudala, Lu Vern H. Kunze, and John D. Ross; Academic Therapy Publications.*

For additional information and reviews by Stephen B. Hood and James B. Lingwall, see 8:421 (1 reference).

[229]

Auditory Sequential Memory Test. Ages 5–8; 1973; digit recall; Joseph M. Wepman and Anne Morency; Language Research Associates, Inc.*

For additional information and a review by J. Joseph Freilinger, see 8:934.

[230]

Auditory Tests. Grades 2 and over; 1951–56; also called *C.I.D. Auditory Tests*; 3 tests on 2 sets of records; Central Institute for the Deaf; Technisonic Studios, Inc.* (Availability uncertain; no reply from manufacturer.)
a) AUDITORY TESTS W-1 AND W-2: SPONDAIC WORD LISTS. Recorded adaptation of *Auditory Test No. 9* developed by Harvard University Psycho-Acoustic Laboratory; threshold for speech; 2 tests.
1) *Test W-1.* A "constant level" test in which sound intensity must be attenuated by examiner.

2) *Test W-2.* A "descending level" test in which sound intensity has been attenuated on the record in downward steps of 3 decibels.
b) AUDITORY TEST W-22: PHONETICALLY-BALANCED WORD LISTS. Words selected in part from lists developed by Harvard University Psycho-Acoustic Laboratory; discrimination for speech at levels above threshold.

See T2:2031 (30 references) and 6:941 (20 references).

REFERENCES

1–20. See 6:941.
21–50. See T2:2031.
51. REED, C. M., RUBIN, S. I., BRAIDA, L. D., & DURLACH, N. I. Analytic study of tadoma method: Discrimination ability of untrained observers. *Journal of Speech & Hearing Research*, 1978, 21, 625–637.
52. PUNCH, J. L., & PARKER, C. A. Pairwise listener preferences in hearing and evaluation. *Journal of Speech & Hearing Research*, 1981, 24, 366–374.

[231]

Austin Spanish Articulation Test. Ages 3–12; 1974; ASAT; scores in 4 areas: consonants, vowels, diphthongs, clusters; examiner must have "a working knowledge" of Spanish phonemes; Teaching Resources Corporation.*

For additional information, a review by Diana S. Natalicio, and an excerpted review by Tony L. Carvajal, see 8:154 (1 reference).

[232]

★**Australian Item Bank.** Grades 8–12; 1978; AIB; teaching and evaluation materials in multiple choice format; 3 item banks; Australian Council for Educational Research [Australia].*
a) MATHEMATICS ITEM BANK.
b) SCIENCE ITEM BANK.
c) SOCIAL SCIENCE ITEM BANK.

[233]

*****Australian Test for Advanced Music Studies.** Tertiary education entrance level; 1974–78; ATAMS; 3 tests; 4 scores: 3 scores listed below plus total; test by Doreen Bridges and Bernard Rechter with the assistance of Jennifer Knight; Australian Council for Educational Research [Australia].*
a) BOOK 1: TONAL AND RHYTHM MEMORY AND MUSICAL PERCEPTION.
b) BOOK 2: AURAL/VISUAL DISCRIMINATION, SCORE READING AND UNDERSTANDING OF NOTATION.
c) BOOK 3: COMPREHENSION AND APPLICATION OF LEARNED MUSIC MATERIAL.

For additional information and a review by Roger P. Phelps, see 8:91.

REFERENCES

1. BRIDGES, D. Developed perceptual-cognitive abilities in music as measured by the Australian Test for Advanced Music Studies (ATAMS). *Council for Research in Music Education. Bulletin*, 1979, 59, 8–12.

[234]

★**Autism Screening Instrument for Educational Planning, (First Edition).** Preschool and school aged severely handicapped and autistic; 1978–80; ASIEP; 5 subtest scores: autism behavior checklist, sample of vocal behavior, interaction assessment, educational assessment of functional skills, prognosis of learning rate; David A. Krug, Joel R. Arick, and Patricia J. Almond; ASIEP Education Co.*

[235]
Balthazar Scales of Adaptive Behavior. "Profoundly and severely mentally retarded adults and the younger less retarded"; 1971–76; BSAB; formerly called *Central Wisconsin Colony Scales of Adaptive Behavior;* 2 sections; Earl E. Balthazar; Consulting Psychologists Press, Inc.*

a) SECTION 1: THE SCALES OF FUNCTIONAL INDEPENDENCE. 1971–76; 8 ratings: eating (dependent feeding, finger foods, spoon usage, fork usage, drinking, total), dressing, toileting.

b) SECTION 2: SCALES OF SOCIAL ADAPTATION. 1973; 19 ratings grouped in 7 categories: unadaptive self-directed behaviors (5 ratings), unadaptive interpersonal behaviors (2 ratings), adaptive self-directed behaviors (1 rating), adaptive interpersonal behaviors (3 ratings), verbal communication (2 ratings), play activities (3 ratings), response to instructions (3 ratings), plus 9 checklist items of personal care and other behaviors.

For additional information, reviews by Robert M. Allen and C. Edward Meyers, and excerpted reviews by A. B. Silverstein and Barton B. Proger, see 8:500 (7 references); see also T2:1107 (2 references).

REFERENCES

1–2. See T2:1107.
3–9. See 8:500.
10. LATHEY, J. W. Assessing classroom environment and prioritizing goals for the severely retarded. *Exceptional Children*, 1978, 45, 190–195.
11. PHILLIPS, J. L., & BALTHAZAR, E. E. Some correlates of language deterioration in severely and profoundly retarded long term institutionalized residents. *American Journal of Mental Deficiency*, 1979, 83, 402–408.

[236]
Baltimore County French Test. 1 year high school; 1962; 2 scores: parts A, B; Baltimore County French Language Committee; Bobbs-Merrill Co., Inc.*

For additional information and reviews by Nelson Brooks and Mary E. Turnbull, see 6:364 (1 reference).

[237]
Baltimore County Spanish Test. 1 year high school; 1962; 2 scores: parts A, B; Baltimore County Spanish Language Committee; Bobbs-Merrill Co., Inc.*

For additional information and a review by Alan Garfinkel, see 8:155; for a review by Mariette Schwarz, see 6:418.

[238]
Barber Scales of Self-Regard for Preschool Children. Ages 2–5; 1975–76; ratings by parents, teachers, and others; 7 scales; John H. Peatling (except guide for parents), Lucie W. Barber, and the Research Staff; Union College Character Research Project.* (In-print status uncertain; no reply from publisher.)

a) SCALE 1, PURPOSEFUL LEARNING OF SKILLS.
b) SCALE 2, COMPLETING TASKS.
c) SCALE 3, COPING WITH FEARS.
d) SCALE 4, CHILDREN'S RESPONSES TO REQUESTS.
e) SCALE 5, DEALING WITH FRUSTRATIONS.
f) SCALE 6, SOCIALLY ACCEPTABLE BEHAVIOR.
g) SCALE 7, DEVELOPING IMAGINATION IN PLAY.

For additional information and reviews by Laura A. Driscoll and Sheldon A. Weintraub, see 8:501 (1 reference).

[239]
***The Barclay Classroom Assessment System.** Grades 3–6; 1971–81; formerly *The Barclay Classroom Climate Inventory* (BCCI); for the early detection of learning-related and socio-affective problems of child functioning in the classroom; teacher, peer, and self ratings in classes of 10 to 40 students; classroom and individual computer printout yields narrative statements on 9 factor scores (self vs. peer vs. teacher total ratings, self-competency, vocational awareness, reinforcers, attitude toward school, peer nominations, teacher expectations, relation of ratings to achievement estimates, suspected problems), plus 47 scores: 5 self-competency scores (artistic-intellectual, outdoor-mechanical, social-cooperative, enterprising, total), 7 group nomination scores (artistic-intellectual, outdoor-mechanical, social-cooperative, enterprising, total, reticence, disruptiveness), 9 vocational preference scales (outdoor-mechanical, intellectual-scientific, social, conventional, enterprising, arts, conservative, status, total), 12 teacher rating scales (personal adjustment positive, personal adjustment negative, social adjustment positive, social adjustment negative, work habits and attitudes positive, work habits and attitudes negative, total teacher rating positive, total teacher rating negative, 4 temperament scales (external-predictable, external-unpredictable, internal-predictable, internal-unpredictable)), 8 self-rated reinforcer scales (self-stimulating, esthetic, intellectual task-oriented, family-oriented, conventional, male peer group, female peer group, classroom climate index), and 6 factor scores (task-order achievement, control-predictability, reserved-internal, physical-activity, sociability-affiliation, enterprising-dominance); James R. Barclay; Western Psychological Services.*

For additional information and a review by Richard M. Wolf of the earlier edition, see 8:502 (10 references).

REFERENCES

1–10. See 8:502.
11. JERDONEK, C. Improving cognitive motivation through strategies of intervention. *Peabody Journal of Education*, 1978, 55, 136–144.
12. KEHLE, T. J., & GUIDUBALDI, J. Effect of EMR placement models on affective and social development. *Psychology in the Schools*, 1978, 15, 275–282.
13. STILWELL, W. E., & BARCLAY, J. R. Effects of affective education interventions in the elementary school. *Psychology in the Schools*, 1979, 16, 80–87.
14. BARCLAY, J. R., & WU, W. Classroom climates in Taiwanese and American elementary schools: A cross–cultural study. *Contemporary Educational Psychology*, 1980, 5, 65–82.
15. KEHLE, T. J., & GUIDUBALDI, J. Do too many cooks spoil the broth?: Evaluation of team placement and individual educational plans on enhancing the social competence of handicapped students. *Journal of Learning Disabilities*, 1980, 13, 26–30.

[240]
Barclay Early Childhood Skill Assessment Guide. Preschool–grade 1; 1973–76; BECSAG; checklist by teachers (self-concept section orally administered to child) plus ratings by parent; 4 scores: sensory-motor-perceptual, discrimination learning, self-concept, social skills; scoring must be done by publisher; Lisa K. Barclay and James R. Barclay; Educational Skills Development, Inc.*

For additional information and reviews by N. Dale Bryant and Frank R. Vellutino, see 8:423.

[241]
Barclay Learning Needs Assessment Inventory. Grades 6–12 and college; 1975–79; BLNAI; self-report learning problems checklist and ratings by peer, parent, teacher, or counselor; 7 scores: self-competency, group interaction, self-control, verbal skills, energy and persistence, cognitive-motivation, attitude; James R. Barclay; Educational Skills Development, Inc.

For additional information and a review by Rodney T. Hartnett of an earlier edition, see 8:503 (1 reference).

[242]
Barrett-Ryan English Test. Grades 7–13; 1926–61; E. R. Barrett, Teresa M. Ryan, M. W. Sanders (Forms 1, 2, 3), H. E. Schrammel (Forms 1948, 1954, manual), and E. R. Wood (manual); Bureau of Educational Measurements.*

See T2:54 (1 reference); for a review by Clarence Derrick, see 6:250 (2 references); for a review by J. Raymond Gerberich, see 5:175.

[243]
Barron-Welsh Art Scale: A Portion of the Welsh Figure Preference Test. Ages 6 and over; 1959–63, c1949–63; BWAS; a separate booklet printing of the art scale and revised art scale items from Welsh Figure Preference Test, Research Edition; George S. Welsh and Frank Barron (test); Consulting Psychologists Press, Inc.*

For additional information, see 8:504 (30 references); see also T2:1109 (23 references); for reviews by Leonard L. Baird and G. C. Helmstadter, see 7:41 (40 references); see also P:15 (20 references). For references to reviews of the Welsh Figure Preference Test, see T2:1437.

REFERENCES

1–20. See P:15.
21–60. See 7:41.
61–83. See T2:1109.
84–113. See 8:504.
114. ALPAUGH, P. K., & BIRREN, J. E. Variables affecting creative contributions across the adult life span. Human Development, 1977, 20, 240–248.
115. DOMINO, G. Transcendental meditation and creativity: An empirical investigation. Journal of Applied Psychology, 1977, 62, 358–362.
116. RIDLEY, D. R. Communicability and complexity as predictors of creativity: Validity of the Barron-Welsh Art Scale. Perceptual & Motor Skills, 1977, 45, 399–408.
117. RIDLEY, D. R. Preference for stimulus complexity and architectural creativity. Perceptual & Motor Skills, 1977, 45, 815–818.
118. RUMP, E. E. Study of Graves Design Judgment Test and Barron-Welsh Revised Art Scale. Perceptual & Motor Skills, 1977, 45, 843–847.
119. SANDERS, S. J., TEDFORD, W. H., JR., & HARDY, B. W. Effects of musical stimuli on creativity. Psychological Record, 1977, 27, 463–471.
120. CHEMTOB, C. M. Paradoxical complementarity in the esthetic preferences of the cerebral hemispheres: An exploratory study. Perceptual & Motor Skills, 1979, 48, 799–806.
121. TITTLER, B. I., ROLL, S., & PRASINOS, S. Effects of sharing a secret on subsequent level of openness. Psychological Reports, 1979, 45, 891–896.
122. CHAMBERS, J. A., BARRON, F., & SPRECHER, J. W. Identifying gifted Mexican-American students. Gifted Child Quarterly, 1980, 24, 123–128.
123. DUFFY, R. A. An analysis of aesthetic sensitivity and creativity with other variables in grades four, six, eight, and ten. Journal of Educational Research, 1980, 73, 26–30.
124. KEEFE, J. A., & MAGARO, P. A. Creativity and schizophrenia: An equivalence of cognitive processing. Journal of Abnormal Psychology, 1980, 89, 390–398.

[244]
★Barsch Learning Style Inventory. Grades 7–12 and college; 1980; manual title is Spelling Plus; 3 scores: visual preference, auditory preference, tactual preference; Jeffrey Barsch and Betty Creson (manual); Academic Therapy Publications.*

[245]
Basic Arithmetic Skill Evaluation. Grades 1, 2, 3, 4, 5, 6, 7–9; 1973–74; BASE; criterion-referenced; 16 to 40 basic skill scores (3 items per skill); 7 color-coded levels; no manual; Lola J. May and Vernon R. Hood; Educational Division, Readers Digest.*
a) [LEVEL 1.] Grade 1; 20 scores.
b) [LEVEL 2.] Grade 2; 16 scores.
c) [LEVEL 3.] Grade 3; 23 scores.
d) [LEVEL 4.] Grade 4; 16 scores.
e) [LEVEL 5.] Grade 5; 23 scores.
f) [LEVEL 6.] Grade 6; 21 scores.
g) BASE II [LEVEL 7]. Grades 7–9; 40 scores: whole numbers (13 scores), fractions (14 scores), decimals-percent-story problems (13 scores).

For additional information and a review by Jason Millman, see 8:303.

[246]
Basic Economics Test. Grades 4–6; 1980–81; BET; substantive revision of the Test of Elementary Economics; John F. Chizmar and Ronald S. Halinski; Joint Council on Economic Education.

For additional information and reviews by Mary Friend Adams and James O. Hodges of an earlier edition, see 8:901 (1 reference).

[247]
Basic Educational Skills Inventory. Grades kgn–6; 1972–73; BESI; criterion-referenced; subtests available as separates; 2 tests; Gary Adamson, Morris Shrago, and Glen Van Etten; B. L. Winch & Associates.*
a) READING. 2 levels.
1) Level A. 12 scores: memory for sentences, direction in space, same or different, naming the alphabet from memory, printing capital letters from memory, manuscript printing of dictated small letters, naming printed letters, matching letters, writing and naming capital cursive letters, naming cursive written letters, sight words, total.
2) Level B. 23 scores: rhyming sounds, initial consonants and vowels, final consonants, initial consonant blends and digraphs (2 scores), final consonant blends and digraphs, auditory blending of words, initial consonants, final consonants, initial vowels, medial vowels, printed vowels and consonants, printed letter blends and digraphs, beginning and ending word patterns, blending printed words, blending phonetic elements, double vowels and diphthongs, hard and soft sounds, prefixes, suffixes, prefixes—suffixes, syllabication, total.
b) MATH. 2 levels.
1) Level A. 11 scores: quantity, naming printed numbers, matching numbers, counting pictured objects, dot to dot, counting orally, writing numbers, number sequencing, ordinal and cardinal concepts, number words, total.
2) Level B. 21 scores: addition (facts, problems), subtraction (facts, problems), multiplication (facts, problems), division problems, fractions (6 scores),

decimals (4 scores), decimal-fraction-percent transformation, time, money, total.

For additional information and reviews by Georgia S. Adams and Peter W. Airasian, see 8:5; for reviews of subtests, see 8:253 (1 review) and 8:718 (1 review).

[248]

Basic Educational Skills Inventory: Math. Grades kgn–6; 1972–73; criterion-referenced; Gary Adamson, Morris Shrago, and Glen Van Etten; B. L. Winch & Associates.*

a) LEVEL A. 11 scores: quantity, naming printed numbers, matching numbers, counting pictured objects, dot to dot, counting orally, writing numbers, number sequencing, ordinal and cardinal concepts, number words, total.

b) LEVEL B. 21 scores: addition (facts, problems), subtraction (facts, problems), multiplication (facts, problems), division problems, fractions (6 scores), decimals (4 scores), decimal-fraction-percent transformation, time, money, total.

For additional information and a review by William H. Nibbelink, see 8:253. For reviews of the complete battery, see 8:5 (2 reviews).

[249]

Basic Educational Skills Inventory: Reading. Grades kgn–6; 1972–73; criterion-referenced; 2 levels; Gary Adamson, Morris Shrago, and Glen Van Etten; B. L. Winch & Associates.*

a) LEVEL A. 12 scores: memory for sentences, direction in space, same or different, naming the alphabet from memory, printing capital letters from memory, manuscript printing of dictated small letters, naming printed letters, matching letters, writing and naming capital cursive letters, naming cursive written letters, sight words, total.

b) LEVEL B. 23 scores: rhyming sounds, initial consonants and vowels, final consonants, initial consonant blends and digraphs (2 scores), final consonant blends and digraphs, auditory blending of words, initial consonants, final consonants, initial vowels, medial vowels, printed vowels and consonants, printed letter blends and digraphs, beginning and ending word patterns, blending printed words, blending phonetic elements, double vowels and diphthongs, hard and soft sounds, prefixes, suffixes, prefixes—suffixes, syllabification, total.

For additional information and a review by Priscilla A. Drum, see 8:718. For reviews of the complete battery, see 8:5 (2 reviews).

[250]

★**Basic Educational Skills Test.** Grades 1.5–5; 1979; BEST; for detecting children who are at risk academically; 3 tests: reading, writing, mathematics; Ruth C. Segel and Sandra H. Golding; Academic Therapy Publications.*

[251]

★**Basic Inventory of Natural Language.** Grades kgn–12; 1977–79; BINL; 3 scores: fluency, level of complexity, average sentence length; Charles H. Herbert; CHECpoint Systems, Inc.*

REFERENCES
1. SATTLER, J. M., AVILA, V., HOUSTON, W. B., & TONEY, D. H. Performance of bilingual Mexican–American children on Spanish and English versions of the Peabody Picture Vocabulary Test. *Journal of Consulting & Clinical Psychology*, 1980, 48, 782–784.

[252]

Basic Mathematics Tests. Ages 7–0 to 8–0, 8–0 to 9–0, 9–7 to 10–10, 10–0 to 12–6, 12–0 to 14–6; 1969–72; 5 levels; NFER-Nelson Publishing Co. [England].*

a) BASIC MATHEMATICS TEST A [ORAL]. Ages 7–0 to 8–0; 1971.
b) BASIC MATHEMATICS TEST B [ORAL]. Ages 8–0 to 9–0; 1971.
c) BASIC MATHEMATICS TEST C. Ages 9–7 to 10–10; 1970–72.
d) BASIC MATHEMATICS TEST DE. Ages 10–0 to 12–6; 1969–72.
e) BASIC MATHEMATICS TEST FG. Ages 12–0 to 14–6; 1969.

For additional information concerning *c–e*, see 7:452.

REFERENCES
1. YOUNGMAN, M. B. Six reactions to school transfer. *British Journal of Educational Psychology*, 1978, 48, 280–289.
2. TURNBULL, H., & DAVIDSON, G. A regional survey of attainment in reading and mathematics. *British Journal of Educational Psychology*, 1980, 50, 91.

[253]

★**Basic Number Diagnostic Test.** Ages 5–7; 1980; 13 scores: reciting numbers, naming numbers, copying over, copying underneath, writing numbers in sequence, writing numbers to dictation, counting bricks, selecting bricks, addition sums with objects, addition sums with numerals, subtraction sums with objects, subtraction sums with numerals, total; W. E. C. Gillham; Hodder & Stoughton Educational [England].*

[254]

★**Basic Number Screening Test.** Ages 7–12; 1976–80; W. E. C. Gillham and K. A. Hesse; Hodder & Stoughton Educational [England].*

[255]

★**Basic Reading Inventory, Second Edition.** Reading level grades kgn–8; 1978–81; BRI; 3 reading level scores (independent, instructional, frustration) for each of 3 subtests (word recognition in isolation, word recognition in context, comprehension); Jerry L. Johns; Kendall/Hunt Publishing Co.*

[256]

Basic School Skills Inventory. Ages 4–8; 1975–83; BSSI; observational ratings and performance test items; "both a norm-referenced and a criterion-referenced instrument"; 7 scores: daily living skills, writing, oral communication, reading readiness, number readiness, classroom behavior, total; Donald D. Hammill and James Leigh; PRO-ED.

For additional information and reviews by Byron R. Egeland and Lawrence M. Kasdon, see 8:424 (2 references).

[257]

A Basic Screening and Referral Form for Children With Suspected Learning and Behavioral Disabilities. Grades 1–12; 1972; teacher ratings in 8 areas: social-personal, conceptual-cognitive, language, perceptual-motor (visual-motor, visual, auditory), sensory-motor, gross-motor plus a pupil work sample; no manual; Robert E. Valett; Fearon Education.*

[258]
Basic Sight Word Test. Grades 1–2; 1942; Edward W. Dolch; Garrard Publishing Co.*
See T2:1657 (5 references).

[259]
★**Basic Skills Assessment.** Grades 7 and over; 1977–81; BSA; Educational Testing Service; Addison-Wesley Publishing Co., Inc.*
a) READING. 3 scores: literal comprehension, inference-evaluation, total.
b) A WRITER'S SKILLS. 5 scores: spelling, capitalization-punctuation, usage, logic-evaluation, total.
c) MATHEMATICS. 3 scores: computation, applications, total.
d) WRITING SAMPLE. A direct measure of writing.

[260]
★**Basic Skills Assessment: Mathematics.** Grades 7 and over; 1977–79; 3 scores: computation, applications, total; Educational Testing Service; Addison-Wesley Publishing Co., Inc.* For the complete battery entry, see 259.

[261]
★**Basic Skills Assessment: Reading.** Grades 7 and over; 1977–79; 3 scores: literal comprehension, inference-evaluation, total; Educational Testing Service; Addison-Wesley Publishing Co., Inc.* For the complete battery entry, see 259.

[262]
★**Basic Skills Assessment: A Writer's Skills.** Grades 7 and over; 1977–79; 5 scores: spelling, capitalization-punctuation, usage, logic-evaluation, total; Educational Testing Service; Addison-Wesley Publishing Co., Inc.* For the complete battery entry, see 259.

[263]
★**Basic Skills Assessment: Writing Sample.** Grades 7 and over; 1977; a direct measure of writing; Educational Testing Service; Addison-Wesley Publishing Co., Inc.* For the complete battery entry, see 259.

[264]
Basic Skills in Arithmetic Test. Grades 6–12; 1945; William L. Wrinkle, Juanita Sanders, and Elizabeth H. Kendel; Science Research Associates, Inc.*
See T2:704 (1 reference); for reviews by Jacob S. Orleans and F. Lynwood Wren, see 3:335.

REFERENCES
1. See T2:704.
2. ALDRIDGE, W. S. Effects of electronic calculators on achievement of middle school remedial mathematics students. *Business Education Forum*, 1977, 32, 35.

[265]
★**Basic Skills Inventory.** Grades kgn–1, 1–2, 2–3, 3–4, 4–5, 5–6, 7–8, 9–10, 11–12; 1980–82; BSI; "a set of ready-made general achievement assessment instruments designed to test common objectives or minimum competencies"; 3 subtests: reading, language arts, and mathematics which may be ordered singly or as combined booklets; 8 levels; Los Angeles County Superintendent of Schools Test Development Center; Intran Corporation.*
a) READING.
 1) *Grades K–1.* Scores from 3 major areas: phonetic analysis, vocabulary, comprehension.
 2) *Grades 1–2.* Scores from 5 major areas: phonetic analysis, structural analysis, vocabulary, comprehension, study skills.
 3) *Grades 2–3.* Scores from 5 areas: same as 2 above.
 4) *Grades 3–4.* Scores from 5 areas: same as 2 above.
 5) *Grades 5–6.* Scores from 5 areas: same as 2 above.
 6) *Grades 7–8.* Scores from 4 major areas: structural analysis, vocabulary, comprehension, study skills.
 7) *Grades 9–10.* Scores from 4 areas: same as 6 above.
 8) *Grades 11–12.* Scores from 4 areas: same as 6 above.
b) LANGUAGE ARTS.
 1) *Grades K–1.* Scores from 3 major areas: language analysis, conventions, expression/comprehension.
 2) *Grades 1–2.* Scores from 3 areas: same as 1 above.
 3) *Grades 2–3.* Scores from 3 areas: same as 1 above.
 4) *Grades 3–4.* Scores from 4 major areas: spelling, punctuation, sentence structure, verb usage.
 5) *Grades 5–6.* Scores from 4 areas: same as 4 above.
 6) *Grades 7–8.* Scores from 4 areas: same as 4 above.
 7) *Grades 9–10.* Scores from 4 areas: same as 4 above.
 8) *Grades 11–12.* Scores from 4 areas: same as 4 above.
c) MATHEMATICS.
 1) *Grades K–1.* Scores from 3 major areas: comprehension, computation, application.
 2) *Grades 1–2.* Scores from 3 areas: same as 1 above.
 3) *Grades 2–3.* Scores from 3 areas: same as 1 above.
 4) *Grades 3–4.* Scores from 4 major areas: basic operations, basic operations with decimals, basic operations with fractions, applications.
 5) *Grades 5–6.* Scores from 4 areas: same as 4 above.
 6) *Grades 7–8.* Scores from 4 areas: same as 4 above.
 7) *Grades 9–10.* Scores from 4 areas: same as 4 above plus comprehension of geometric formulas.
 8) *Grades 11–12.* Scores from 4 areas: same as 4 above plus application and comprehension of geometric formulas.

[266]
★**Basic Skills Inventory: Language Arts.** Grades kgn–1, 1–2, 2–3, 3–4, 5–6, 7–8, 9–10, 11–12; 1980–82; 8 levels; Los Angeles County Superintendent of Schools Test Development Center; Intran Corporation.* For the complete battery entry, see 265.
a) GRADES K–1. Scores from 3 major areas: language analysis, conventions, expression/comprehension.
b) GRADES 1–2. Scores from 3 areas: same as *a* above.
c) GRADES 2–3. Scores from 3 areas: same as *a* above.
d) GRADES 3–4. Scores from 4 major areas: spelling, punctuation, subject-verb agreement, sentence types.
e) GRADES 5–6. Scores from 4 areas: same as *d* above.
f) GRADES 7–8. Scores from 4 areas: same as *d* above.
g) GRADES 9–10. Scores from 4 areas: same as *d* above.
h) GRADES 11–12. Scores from 4 areas: same as *d* above.

[267]
★**Basic Skills Inventory: Mathematics.** Grades kgn–1, 1–2, 2–3, 3–4, 5–6, 7–8, 9–10, 11–12; 1980–82; 8 levels; Los Angeles County Superintendent of Schools Test Development Center; Intran Corporation.* For the complete battery entry, see 265.
a) GRADES K–1. Scores from 3 major areas: comprehension, computation, application.
b) GRADES 1–2. Scores from 3 areas: same as for *a* above.

c) GRADES 2-3. Scores from 3 areas: same as for *a* above.
d) GRADES 3-4. Scores from 4 major areas: basic operations, basic operations with decimals, basic operations with fractions, applications.
e) GRADES 5-6. Scores from 4 areas: same as *d* above.
f) GRADES 7-8. Scores from 4 areas: same as *d* above.
g) GRADES 9-10. Scores from 4 areas: same as *d* above, plus application and comprehension of geometric formulas.
h) GRADES 11-12. Scores from 4 areas: same as *d* above, plus application and comprehension of geometric formulas.

[268]

★**Basic Skills Inventory: Reading.** Grades kgn-1, 1-2, 2-3, 3-4, 5-6, 7-8, 9-10, 11-12; 1980-82; 8 levels; Los Angeles County Superintendent of Schools Test Development Center; Intran Corporation.* For the complete battery entry, see 265.
a) GRADES K-1. Scores from 3 major areas: phonetic analysis, vocabulary, comprehension.
b) GRADES 1-2. Scores from 5 major areas: phonetic analysis, structural analysis, vocabulary, comprehension, study skills.
c) GRADES 2-3. Scores from 5 areas: same as *b* above.
d) GRADES 3-4. Scores from 5 areas: same as *b* above.
e) GRADES 5-6. Scores from 5 areas: same as *b* above.
f) GRADES 7-8. Scores from 4 major areas: structural analysis, vocabulary, comprehension, study skills.
g) GRADES 9-10. Scores from 4 areas: same as *f* above.
h) GRADES 11-12. Scores from 4 areas: same as *f* above.

[269]

Basic Word Vocabulary Test. Grades 4 and over; 1975; BWVT; criterion-referenced; statistical data based on a prepublication form and "final" form which was later revised by replacing 90 distractors; original test by Harold J. Dupuy; Jamestown Publishers.*

For additional information and reviews by Kenneth D. Hopkins and Darrell L. Sabers, see 8:78.

REFERENCES

1. See 8:78.
2. WEINSTOCK, R. B. Anagram solving as influenced by solution word frequency, anagram transition probability, and subject's vocabulary level. *Bulletin of the Psychonomic Society*, 1979, 14, 375-378.

[270]

Bayley Scales of Infant Development. Ages 2-30 months; 1969; BSID; 2 scores: mental, motor, plus 30 behavior ratings; the mental and motor scales "draw heavily upon" the *California First-Year Mental Scale*, the *California Preschool Mental Scale*, and the *California Infant Scale of Motor Development*; Nancy Bayley; The Psychological Corporation.*

For additional information and a review by Fred Damarin, see 8:206 (28 references); see also T2:484 (11 references); for reviews by Roberta R. Collard and Raymond H. Holden, see 7:402 (20 references).

REFERENCES

1-20. See 7:402.
21-31. See T2:484.
32-59. See 8:206.
60. DuBose, R. F. Predictive value of infant intelligence scales with multiply handicapped children. *American Journal of Mental Deficiency*, 1977, 81, 388-390.
61. GOLDEN, M., MONTARE, A., & BRIDGER, W. Verbal control of delay behavior in two-year-old boys as a function of social class. *Child Development*, 1977, 48, 1107-1111.
62. GOODMAN, J. F. Medical diagnosis and intelligence levels in young mentally retarded children. A follow-up study. *Journal of Mental Deficiency Research*, 1977, 21, 205-212.
63. HASLAM, R. H. A., ALLEN, J. R., DORSEN, M. M., KANOFSKY, D. L., MELLITS, E. D., & NORRIS, D. A. The sequelae of group B B-hemolytic streptococcal meningitis in early infancy. *American Journal of Diseases of Children*, 1977, 131, 845-849.
64. HOROWITZ, F. D., ASHTON, J., CULP, R., GADDIS, E., LEVIN, S., & REICHMANN, B. The effects of obstetrical medication on the behavior of Israeli newborn infants and some comparisons with Uruguayan and American infants. *Child Development*, 1977, 48, 1607-1623.
65. HUNT, J. V., & RHODES, L. Mental development of preterm infants during the first year. *Child Development*, 1977, 48, 204-210.
66. JASON, L. Modifying parent-child interactions in a disadvantaged family. *Journal of Clinical Child Psychology*, 1977, 6, 38-40.
67. JOHNSON, D., & BRODY, N. Visual habituation, sensorimotor development, and tempo of play in one-year-old infants. *Child Development*, 1977, 48, 315-319.
68. LaVECK, B., & LaVECK, G. D. Sex differences in development among young children with Down's Syndrome. *Journal of Pediatrics*, 1977, 91, 767-769.
69. MIRANDA, S. B., HACK, M., FANTZ, R. L., FANAROFF, A. A., & KLAUS, M. H. Neonatal pattern vision: A predictor of future mental performance? *Journal of Pediatrics*, 1977, 91, 642-647.
70. RAMEY, C. T., & SMITH, B. J. Assessing the intellectual consequences of early intervention with high-risk infants. *American Journal of Mental Deficiency*, 1977, 81, 318-324.
71. SOSTEK, A. M., & ANDERS, T. F. Relationships among the Brazelton Neonatal Scale, Bayley Infant Scales, and early temperament. *Child Development*, 1977, 48, 320-323.
72. WEINTRAUB, M., & LEWIS, M. The determinants of children's responses to separation. *Monographs of the Society for Research in Child Development*, 1977, 42, 1-78.
73. WILLERMAN, L., & FIEDLER, M. R. Intellectually precocious preschool children: Early development and later intellectual accomplishments. *Journal of Genetic Psychology*, 1977, 131, 13-20.
74. WING, L., GOULD, J., YEATES, S. R., & BRIERLEY, L. M. Symbolic play in severely mentally retarded and in autistic children. *Journal of Child Psychology & Psychiatry & Allied Disciplines*, 1977, 18, 167-178.
75. APPELBAUM, A. S. Validity of the revised Denver Developmental Screening Test for referred and nonreferred samples. *Psychological Reports*, 1978, 43, 227-233.
76. COHEN, S. E. Maternal employment and mother-child interaction. *Merrill-Palmer Quarterly*, 1978, 24, 189-197.
77. DAVIDSON, P. W., WILLOUGHBY, R. H., O'TUAMA, L. A., SWISHER, C. N., & BENJAMINS, D. Neurological and intellectual sequelae of Reye's Syndrome. *American Journal of Mental Deficiency*, 1978, 82, 535-541.
78. DOLAN, A. B., & MATHENY, A. P., JR. A distinctive growth curve for a group of children with academic learning problems. *Journal of Learning Disabilities*, 1978, 11, 490-494.
79. EIDUSON, B. T., & ALEXANDER, J. W. The role of children in alternative family styles. *Journal of Social Issues*, 1978, 34, 149-167.
80. EIPPER, D. S., & AZEN, S. P. A comparison of two developmental instruments in evaluating children with Down's syndrome. *Physical Therapy*, 1978, 58, 1066-1069.
81. ESON, M. E., YEN, J. K., & BOURKE, R. S. Assessment of recovery from serious head injury. *Journal of Neurology, Neurosurgery & Psychiatry*, 1978, 41, 1036-1042.
82. FIELD, T. M., HALLOCK, N. F., DEMPSEY, J. R., & SHUMAN, H. H. Mothers' assessments of term and pre-term infants with respiratory distress syndrome. *Child Psychiatry & Human Development*, 1978, 9, 75-85.
83. FIELD, T., HALLOCK, N., TING, G., DEMPSEY, J., DABIRI, C., & SHUMAN, H. H. A first-year follow-up of high-risk infants: Formulating a cumulative risk index. *Child Development*, 1978, 49, 119-131.
84. GOLDSON, E., FITCH, M. J., WENDELL, T. A., & KNAPP, G. Child abuse. *American Journal of Diseases of Children*, 1978, 132, 790-793.
85. GOODMAN, J. F., & CAMERON, J. The meaning of IQ constancy in young retarded children. *Journal of Genetic Psychology*, 1978, 132, 109-119.
86. GREENBERG, D. B., WILSON, W. R., MOORE, J. M., & THOMPSON, G. Visual reinforcement audiometry (VRA) with young Down's Syndrome children. *Journal of Speech & Hearing Disorders*, 1978, 43, 448-458.
87. HASKETT, J., & HOLLAR, D. W. Sensory reinforcement and contingency awareness of profoundly retarded children. *American Journal of Mental Deficiency*, 1978, 83, 60-68.
88. HASKINS, R., RAMEY, C. T., STEDMAN, D. J., BLACHER-DIXON, J., & PIERCE, J. E. Effects of repeated assessment on standardized test

performance by infants. *American Journal of Mental Deficiency*, 1978, 83, 233-239.
89. MANS, L., CICCHETTI, D., & SROUFE, L. A. Mirror reactions of Down's Syndrome infants and toddlers: Cognitive underpinnings of self-recognition. *Child Development*, 1978, 49, 1247-1250.
90. MATAS, L., AREND, R. A., & SROUFE, L. A. Continuity of adaptation in the second year: The relationship between quality of attachment and later competence. *Child Development*, 1978, 49, 547-556.
91. MORRISON, D., & POTHIER, P. Effects of sensory-motor training on the language development of retarded preschoolers. *American Journal of Orthopsychiatry*, 1978, 48, 310-319.
92. OSKI, F. A., & HONIG, A. S. The effects of therapy on the developmental scores of iron-deficient infants. *Journal of Pediatrics*, 1978, 92, 21-25.
93. PAPE, K. E., BUNCIC, R. J., ASHBY, S., & FIRZHARDINGE, P. M. The status at two years of low-birth-weight infants born in 1974 with birth weights of less than 1,001 gm. *Journal of Pediatrics*, 1978, 92, 253-260.
94. POLLITT, E., GREENFIELD, D., & LEIBEL, R. Signifiance of Bayley Scale score changes following iron therapy. *Journal of Pediatrics*, 1978, 92, 177-178.
95. RAMEY, C. T., & CAMPBELL, F. A. Compensatory education for disadvantaged children. *School Review*, 1978, 87, 171-189.
96. SALLUSTRO, F., & ATWELL, C. W. Body rocking, head banging, and head rolling in normal children. *Journal of Pediatrics*, 1978, 93, 704-708.
97. SAMEROFF, A. J., KRAFCHUK, E. E., & BAKOW, H. A. Issues in grouping items from the Neonatal Behavioral Assessment Scale. *Monographs of the Society for Research in Child Development*, 1978, 43, 46-59.
98. STREISSGUTH, A. P., HERMAN, C. S., & SMITH, D. W. Intelligence, behavior, and dysmorphogenesis in the fetal alcohol syndrome: A report of 20 patients. *Journal of Pediatrics*, 1978, 92, 363-367.
99. SNYDER, L. S. Communicative and cognitive abilities and disabilities in the sensorimotor period. *Merrill-Palmer Quarterly*, 1978, 24, 161-180.
100. WALZER, S., WOLFF, P. H., BOWEN, D., SILBERT, A. R., BASHIR, A. S., GERALD, P. S., & RICHMOND, J. B. A method for the longitudinal study of behavioral development in infants and children: The early development of XXY children. *Journal of Child Psychology & Psychiatry & Allied Disciplines*, 1978, 19, 213-229.
101. ZESKIND, P. S., & RAMEY, C. T. Fetal malnutrition: An experimental study of its consequences on infant development in two care giving environments. *Child Development*, 1978, 49, 1155-1162.
102. BENNETT, F. C., SELLS, C. J., & BRAND, C. Influences on measured intelligence in Down's Syndrome. *American Journal of Diseases of Children*, 1979, 133, 700-703.
103. BLACK, L., STEINSCHNEIDER, A., & SHEEHE, P. R. Neonatal respiratory instability and infant development. *Child Development*, 1979, 50, 561-564.
104. BRADLEY, R. H., CALDWELL, B. M., & ELARDO, R. Home environment and cognitive development in the first 2 years: A cross-lagged panel analysis. *Developmental Psychology*, 1979, 15, 246-250.
105. BRUNNER, R. L., O'GRADY, D. J., PARTIN, J. C., PARTIN, J. S., & SCHUBERT, W. K. Neuropsychologic consequences of Reye Syndrome. *Journal of Pediatrics*, 1979, 95, 706-711.
106. CLARKE-STEWART, K. A., VANDER STOEP, L. P., & KILLIAN, G. A. Analysis and replication of mother-child relations at two years of age. *Child Development*, 1979, 50, 777-793.
107. CAMFIELD, C. S., CHAPLIN, S., DOYLE, A., SHAPIRO, S. H., CUMMINGS, C., & CAMFIELD, P. R. Side effects of phenobarbital in toddlers: Behavioral and cognitive aspects. *Journal of Pediatrics*, 1979, 95, 361-365.
108. COHEN, S. E., & BECKWITH, L. Preterm infant interaction with the caregiver in the first year of life and competence at age two. *Child Development*, 1979, 50, 767-776.
109. COMMEY, J. O. O., & FITZHARDINGE, P. M. Handicap in the preterm small-for-gestational age infant. *Journal of Pediatrics*, 1979, 94, 779-786.
110. FEIN, G. G., & APFEL, N. The development of play: Style, structure, and situations. *Genetic Psychology Monographs*, 1979, 99, 231-250.
111. GOLD, P. Suspected neurological impairment and cognitive abilities: A longitudinal study. *Psychological Reports*, 1979, 45, 215-218.
112. GOLD, P. Suspected neurological impairment (SNI) and cognitive abilities: A longitudinal study of selected skills and predictive accuracy. *Journal of Clinical Child Psychology*, 1979, 8, 35-38.
113. GOLD, P., & BERK, R. A. Prediction of the academic success of children with suspected neurological impairments. *Journal of Clinical Psychology*, 1979, 35, 505-509.
114. GUNN, P., BERRY, P., & ANDREWS, R. Vocalization and looking behaviour of Down's Syndrome infants. *British Journal of Psychology*, 1979, 70, 259-263.
115. JENNINGS, K. D., HARMON, R. J., MORGAN, G. A., GAITER, J. L., & YARROW, L. J. Exploratory play as an index of mastery motivation: Relationships to persistence, cognitive functioning, and environmental measures. *Developmental Psychology*, 1979, 15, 386-394.

116. JESUDASON, V., AMBUJADEVI, K. R., & BHOGLE, S. Determinants of motor and mental development during early childhood. *Indian Journal of Social Work*, 1979, 40, 27-40.
117. KLEIN, R. P., & DURFEE, J. T. Prediction of preschool social behavior from social-emotional development at one year. *Child Psychiatry & Human Development*, 1979, 9, 145-151.
118. MARCUS, B. B., RUTTLE, K., & VIETZE, P. M. Relationships among attachment behaviors during reunion at 13 and 32 months of age. *Psychological Reports*, 1979, 45, 59-62.
119. MERRITT, T. A., WHITE, C. L., JACOB, J., KURLINSKI, J., MARTIN, J., DISESSA, T. G., EDWARDS, D., FRIEDMAN, W. F., & GLUCK, L. Patient ductus arteriosus treated with ligation or indomethacin: A follow-up study. *Journal of Pediatrics*, 1979, 95, 588-594.
120. PUESCHEL, S. M., & BARSEL-BOWERS, G. A dominantly inherited congenital anomaly syndrome with blepharophimosis. *Journal of Pediatrics*, 1979, 95, 1010-1012.
121. RAMEY, C. T., FARRAN, D. C., & CAMPBELL, F. A. Predicting IQ from mother-infant interactions. *Child Development*, 1979, 50, 804-814.
122. RUBIN, R. A., & BALOW, B. Measures of infant development and socioeconomic status as predictors of later intelligence and school achievement. *Developmental Psychology*, 1979, 15, 225-227.
123. RUBIN, R. A., BALOW, B., & FISCH, R. O. Neonatal serum, biliruben levels related to cognitive development at ages 4 through 7 years. *Journal of Pediatrics*, 1979, 94, 601-604.
124. SIEGEL, L. S. Infant perceptual, cognitive, and motor behaviors as predictors of subsequent cognitive and language development. *Canadian Journal of Psychology*, 1979, 33, 382-395.
125. STEVENSON, M. B. Effects of infant sociability and the caretaking environment on infant cognitive performance. *Child Development*, 1979, 50, 340-349.
126. TARTAGLIA, J. F., EHRLICH, C. H., BUTTERFIELD, P., & KOOPS, B. Identification of specific language disability in hyaline membrane disease babies. *ASHA*, 1979, 21, 688. (Abstract)
127. WATERS, E., WIPPMAN, J., & SROUFE, L. A. Attachment, positive affect, and competence in the peer group: Two studies in construct validation. *Child Development*, 1979, 50, 821-829.
128. BAKEMAN, R., & BROWN, J. V. Early interaction: Consequences for social and mental development at three years. *Child Development*, 1980, 51, 437-447.
129. BERRY, P., GUNN P., & ANDREWS, R. Behavior of Down's Syndrome infants in a strange situation. *American Journal of Mental Deficiency*, 1980, 85, 213-218.
130. BRADLEY, R. H., & CALDWELL, B. M. The relation of home environment, cognitive competence, and IQ among males and females. *Child Development*, 1980, 51, 1140-1148.
131. BROWN, J. V., LaROSSA, M. M., AYLWARD, G. P., DAVIS, D. J., RUTHERFORD, P. K., & BAKEMAN, R. Nursery-based intervention with prematurely born babies and their mothers: Are there effects? *Journal of Pediatrics*, 1980, 97, 487-491.
132. CELEDON, J. M., CSASZAR, D., MIDDLETOWN, J., & DE ANDRACA, I. The effect of treatment on mental and psychomotor development of marasmic infants according to age of admission. *Journal of Mental Deficiency Research*, 1980, 24, 27-35.
133. CLARKE-STEWART, K. A., UMEH, B. J., SNOW, M. E., & PEDERSON, J. A. Development and prediction of children's sociability from 1 to 2 1/2 years. *Developmental Psychology*, 1980, 16, 290-302.
134. DANEMAN, D., & HOWARD, N. J. Neonatal thyrotoxicosis: Intellectual impairment and craniosynostosis in later years. *Journal of Pediatrics*, 1980, 97, 257-259.
135. FIELD, T. M., WIDMAYER, S. M., STRINGER, S., & IGNATOFF, E. Teenage, lower-class, black mothers and their preterm infants: An intervention and developmental follow-up. *Child Development*, 1980, 51, 426-436.
136. GRAY, S. W., & RUTTLE, K. The family-oriented home visiting program: A longitudinal study. *Genetic Psychology Monographs*, 1980, 102, 299-316.
137. HOCK, E. Working and nonworking mothers and their infants: A comparative study of maternal caregiving characteristics and infant social behavior. *Merrill-Palmer Quarterly*, 1980, 26, 79-101.
138. KILBRIDE, P. L. Sensorimotor behavior of Baganda and Samoa infants. *Journal of Cross-Cultural Psychology*, 1980, 11, 131-152.
139. KLEIN, R. P., & YARROW, L. J. Maternal behavior and sharing by toddlers. *Psychological Reports*, 1980, 46, 1057-1058.
140. LANGENDOERFER, S., HAVERKAMP, A. D., MURPHY, J., NOWICK, K. D., ORLEANS, M., PACOSA, F., & VAN DOORNINCK, W. Pediatric follow-up of a randomized controlled trial of intrapartum fetal monitoring techniques. *Journal of Pediatrics*, 1980, 97, 103-107.
141. LaVECK, B., HAMMOND, M. A., & LaVECK, G. D. Minor congenital anomalies and behavior in different home environments. *Journal of Pediatrics*, 1980, 96, 940-943.
142. METZL, M. N. Teaching parents a strategy for enhancing infant development. *Child Development*, 1980, 51, 583-586.

143. O'CONNOR, M. J. A comparison of preterm and full-term infants on auditory discrimination at four months and on Bayley Scales of Infant Development at eighteen months. *Child Development*, 1980, 51, 81–88.
144. WILCOX, B. M., STAFF, P., & ROMAINE, M. F. A comparison of individual with multiple assignment of caregivers to infants in day care. *Merrill–Palmer Quarterly*, 1980, 26, 53–62.
145. BRINKER, R. P., & GOLDBART, J. The problem of reliability in the study of early communication skills. *British Journal of Psychology*, 1981, 72, 27–41.
146. CULLEN, S. M., CRONK, C. E., PUESCHEL, S. M., SCHNELL, R. R., & REED, R. Social development and feeding milestones of young Down's Syndrome children. *American Journal of Mental Deficiency*, 1981, 85, 410–415.
147. GOLD, P. Suspected neurological impairment (SNI) and cognitive abilities: A longitudinal study of selected skills and predictive accuracy. *Journal of Clinical Child Psychology*, 1981, 8, 35–38.
148. GUNN, P., BERRY, P., & ANDREWS, R. J. The temperament of Down's syndrome infants: A research note. *Journal of Child Psychology & Psychiatry & Allied Disciplines*, 1981, 22, 189–194.
149. JOHNSON, D. L. The influence of an intensive parent education program on behavioral continuity of mothers and children. *Child Study Journal*, 1981, 11, 187–199.
150. LIVINGOOD, A. B., & BORENGASSER, M. A. Cerebral gigantism in infancy: Implications for psychological and social development. *Child Psychiatry & Human Development*, 1981, 12, 46–53.
151. LOILSON, G. S., DESMOND, M. M., & WAIT, R. B. Follow-up of methadone–treated and untreated narcotic–dependent women and their infants: Health, developmental, and social implications. *Journal of Pediatrics*, 1981, 98, 716–722.
152. Londerville, S., & Main, M. Security of attachment, compliance, and maternal training methods in the second year of life. *Developmental Psychology*, 1981, 17, 289–299.
153. MARCUS, J., AUERBACH, J., WILKINSON, L., & BURACK, C. M. Infants at risk for schizophrenia. *Archives of General Psychiatry*, 1981, 38, 703.
154. MARKESTAD, T., & FITZHARDINGE, P. M. Growth and development in children recovering from bronchopulmonary dysplasia. *Journal of Pediatrics*, 1981, 98, 597–602.
155. MOESCHLER, J. B., BENNETT, F. C., & CROMWELL, L. D. Use of the *CT* scan in the medical evaluation of the mentally retarded child. *Journal of Pediatrics*, 1981, 98, 63–65.
156. NAGLIERI, J. A. Extrapolated developmental indices for the Bayley Scales of Infant Development. *American Journal of Mental Deficiency*, 1981, 85, 548–550.
157. PROCOPIS, P. A mild form of Menkes steely hair syndrome. *Journal of Pediatrics*, 1981, 98, 97–99.
158. RAMEY, C. T., & BROWNLEE, J. R. Improving the identification of high–risk infants. *American Journal of Mental Deficiency*, 1981, 85, 504–511.
159. ROTHBERG, A. D., MAISELS, J., BAGNATO, S., MURPHY, J., GIFFORD, K., MCKINLEY, K., PALMER, E. A., & VANNUCCI, R. C. Outcome for survivors of mechanical ventilation weighing less than 1,250 gm at birth. *Journal of Pediatrics*, 1981, 98, 106–111.
160. SIEGEL, L. S. Infant tests as predictors of cognitive and language development at two years. *Child Development*, 1981, 52, 545–557.

[271]

★Behavior Analysis Forms for Clinical Intervention. Behavior therapy clients; 1977; BAFCI; 36 plans, questionnaires, scales, forms, schedules, and data forms in areas such as client history, motivation for change, reinforcement, and social performance; Joseph R. Cautela; Research Press.*

[272]

★Behavior Rating Instrument for Autistic and Other Atypical Children. Autistic and atypical children; 1977; BRIAAC; 9 scores: relationship to an adult, communication, drive for mastery, vocalization and expressive speech, sound and speech reception, social responsiveness, body movement, psychobiological development, total; Bertram A. Ruttenberg, Beth I. Kalish, Charles Wenar and Enid G. Wolf; Stoelting Co.*

REFERENCES

1. KATES, L., SCHEIN, J. D., & WOLF, E. G. Assessment of deaf blind children: A study of the use of the Behavior Rating Instrument for Autistic and Other Atypical Children. *Viewpoints in Teaching & Learning*, 1981, 57, 54–63.

[273]

★Behavior Rating Profile. Grades 1–12; 1978; BRP; ecological approach to behavioral assessment; 5 checklists: student rating scales (home, school, peer), teacher rating scale, parent rating scale, plus 1 sociogram score; Linda L. Brown and Donald D. Hammill; PRO-ED.*

REFERENCES

1. KRATOCHWILL, T. R., & SANCHEZ, D. Behavior Rating Profile: An ecological approach to behavioral assessment. *Journal of School Psychology*, 1981, 19, 283–288.

[274]

★Behavior Rating Scales. Grades kgn–8; 1970–75; ratings by teachers; no manual; Patricia B. Elmore and Donald L. Beggs; Patricia B. Elmore.*

[275]

Behavior Status Inventory. Psychiatric inpatients; 1969 (reprinted with 1971 copyright); BSI; ratings in 7 areas (personal appearance, manifest behavior, attitude, verbal behavior, social behavior, work or school behavior, cognitive behavior) and total patient asset score; no manual; William T. Martin; Psychologists and Educators, Inc.*

For additional information and a review by Alfred B. Heilbrun, Jr., see 8:505.

[276]

★Behavioral Academic Self-Esteem. Preschool–grade 8; 1982; BASE; ratings by teachers or parents; 6 scores: student initiative, social attention, success/failure, social attraction, self-confidence, total; Stanley Coopersmith and Ragnar Gilberts; Consulting Psychologists Press, Inc.*

[277]

Beltone Audiometers. Grades kgn and over; 1954–73; 6 models; Beltone Electronics Corporation.* (Availability uncertain; no reply from manufacturer.)

a) BELTONE PORTABLE AUDIOMETERS. 1955–67; 3 models (solid state), each available in portable (D) or desk-top (DW) styling.

1) *Models 9-D and 9-DW.* 1967; for air conduction screening and threshold testing in schools and industry.
2) *Models 10-D and 10-DW.* 1967; for use in schools, industry, clinics, and physicians' offices; for pure tone air and bone conduction testing with masking.
3) *Models 12-D and 12-DW.* 1967; for use by otologists and clinical audiologists; for pure tone (air and bone conduction) and speech testing.

b) BELTONE CLINICAL AUDIOMETERS. 1958–73; for pure tone (air and bone conduction) and live, recorded, and taped speech testing; 3 models.

1) *Model 200-C (AC operated).* 1973; for clinical and general diagnostic procedures.
2) *Clinical Research Audiometers.* 1969; for use by audiological scientists; 2 models (solid state): Models CR-4000, CR-5000 (similar to CR-4000 but with additional flexibility of signal routing between the 2 channels).

See T2:2032 (1 reference); concerning earlier models, see 6:943. For comments by Louis M. DiCarlo on screening audiometers in general and specific comments on an earlier Beltone portable model and three other portable audiometers, see 6:942.

REFERENCES

1. See T2:2032.
2. IGLEHART, V. R., CONNER, D., & SINNETTE, C. H. A comprehensive school health program in Harlem: A retrospective view. *Journal of School Health*, 1977, 47, 88–93.

[278]

★**Bem Sex–Role Inventory.** High school and college and adults; 1978–81; test is titled *Bem Inventory*; self-administered; 3 scores: femininity, masculinity, femininity-minus-masculinity difference; Sandra Lipsitz Bem; Consulting Psychologists Press, Inc.*

[279]

★**Bench Mark Measures.** Ungraded; 1977; developed primarily to be used in conjunction with the Alphabetic Phonics curriculum, but can also be useful as instruments to measure any student's general phonic knowledge; Aylett R. Cox; Educators Publishing Service, Inc.*

[280]

[**Bender-Gestalt Test**]. Ages 4 and over; 1938–77; the original Bender-Gestalt is listed as *a* below; the modifications listed as *b–h* consist primarily of alterations in administration procedure, new scoring systems, or expanded interpretive procedures, rather than changes in the test materials; *c* and *d* provide, in addition, for use of the materials as projective stimuli for associations.

a) VISUAL MOTOR GESTALT TEST. Ages 4 and over; 1938–46; VMGT; Lauretta Bender; American Orthopsychiatric Association, Inc.*

b) THE BENDER GESTALT TEST. Ages 4 and over; 1951; BGT; Gerald R. Pascal and Barbara J. Suttell; Grune & Stratton, Inc.*

c) * THE HUTT ADAPTATION OF THE BENDER-GESTALT TEST. Ages 7 and over; 1944–77; HABGT; Max L. Hutt; Grune & Stratton, Inc.*

d) THE BENDER VISUAL MOTOR GESTALT TEST FOR CHILDREN. Ages 4–12; 1962; utilizes same test cards as *a*; Aileen Clawson; Western Psychological Services.*

e) THE BENDER GESTALT TEST FOR YOUNG CHILDREN. Ages 5–10; 1963–75; a developmental scoring system; Elizabeth Munsterberg Koppitz; Grune & Stratton, Inc.*

f) ★ THE WATKINS BENDER-GESTALT SCORING SYSTEM. Ages 5–14; 1976; WBSS; Ernest O. Watkins; Academic Therapy Publications.*

g) THE TWO-COPY DRAWING FORM. Ages 4 and over; 1964; Western Psychological Services.*

h) THE CANTER BACKGROUND INTERFERENCE PROCEDURE FOR THE BENDER GESTALT TEST. Ages 4 and over; 1966–70; BIP; also called *BIP Bender Test*; Arthur Canter; Counselor Recordings and Tests.

For additional information, see 8:506 (253 references); see also T2:1447 (144 references); for a review by Philip M. Kitay, see 7:161 (192 references); see also P:415 (170 references); for a review by C. B. Blakemore and an excerpted review by Fred Y. Billingslea, see 6:203 (99 references); see also 5:172 (118 references); for reviews by Arthur L. Benton and Howard R. White, see 4:144 (34 references); see also 3:108 (8 references).

REFERENCES

1–8. See 3:108.
9–42. See 4:144.
43–160. See 5:172.
161–259. See 6:203.
260–429. See P:415.
430–621. See 7:161.
622–765. See T2:1447.
766–1018. See 8:506.
1019. BARKER, T. E., & BLACK, F. W. Klinefelter Syndrome in a military population. *Archives of General Psychiatry*, 1976, 33, 607–610.
1020. WHYTE, L. Prescriptive teaching: Changes in stage of logico-mathematical thinking and spatial development in a group of opportunity class children. *Alberta Journal of Educational Research*, 1976, 22, 34–43.
1021. AMANTE, D., VAN HOUTEN, V. W., GRIEVE, J. H., BADER, C. A., & MARGULES, P. H. Neuropsychological deficit, ethnicity, and socioeconomic status. *Journal of Consulting & Clinical Psychology*, 1977, 45, 524–535.
1022. BELL, A. E., ABRAHAMSON, D. S., & MCRAE, K. N. Reading retardation: A 12-year prospective study. *Journal of Pediatrics*, 1977, 91, 363–370.
1023. BRANCONNIER, R. J., & COLE, J. O. A memory assessment technique for use in geriatric psychopharmacology: Drug efficacy trial with naftidrofuryl. *Journal of the American Geriatrics Society*, 1977, 25, 186–188.
1024. BROWN, M. J. Comparison of the Developmental Test of Visual-Motor Integration and the Bender-Gestalt Test. *Perceptual & Motor Skills*, 1977, 45, 981–982.
1025. CASKEY, W. E., & LARSON, G. L. Two modes of administration of the Bender Visual-Motor Gestalt Test of kindergarten children. *Perceptual & Motor Skills*, 1977, 45, 1003–1006.
1026. EXNER, J. E., & MURRILLO, L. G. A long term follow-up of schizophrenics treated with regressive ECT. *Diseases of the Nervous System*, 1977, 38, 162–168.
1027. FESHBACH, S., ADELMAN, H., & FULLER, W. Prediction of reading and related academic problems. *Journal of Educational Psychology*, 1977, 69, 299–308.
1028. FISH, B. Neurobiologic antecedents of schizophrenia in children. *Archives of General Psychiatry*, 1977, 34, 1297–1313.
1029. FRIEDMAN, A. F., WAKEFIELD, J. A., JR., SASEK, J., & SCHROEDER, D. A new scoring system for the Spraings Multiple Choice Bender Gestalt test. *Journal of Clinical Psychology*, 1977, 33, 205–207.
1030. GOLDSTONE, S., LHARMAN, W. T., & NURNBERG, H. G. Temporal information processing by alcoholics. *Journal of Studies on Alcohol*, 1977, 38, 2009–2024.
1031. GREGORY, M. K. Emotional indicators on the Bender-Gestalt and the Devereux Child Behavior Rating Scale. *Psychology in the Schools*, 1977, 14, 433–437.
1032. HOFMAN, R. J., & MIELE, T. A. Design completion–time for seven-year-old children. *Perceptual & Motor Skills*, 1977, 45, 387–390.
1033. HUDGINS, A. L. Assessment of visual–motor disabilities in young children: Toward differential diagnosis. *Psychology in the Schools*, 1977, 14, 252–260.
1034. HUTT, M. L., & DATES, B. G. Reliabilities and interrelationships of two HABGT scales in a male delinquent population. *Journal of Personality Assessment*, 1977, 41, 353–357.
1035. HUTT, M. L., DATES, B. G., & REID, D. M. The predictive ability of HABGT scales for a male delinquent population. *Journal of Personality Assessment*, 1977, 41, 492–496.
1036. JEFFREY, H., SCOTT, J., CHANDLER, D., & DUGDALE, A. E. Deafness after bacterial meningitis. *Archives of Diseases in Childhood*, 1977, 52, 555–559.
1037. JOESTING, J. Correlations of scores on Bender Visual–Motor Gestalt Test and WISC–R. *Perceptual & Motor Skills*, 1977, 45, 980.
1038. KIMBALL, J. G. The Southern California Sensory Integration Tests and the Bender Gestalt: A correlational study. *American Journal of Occupational Therapy*, 1977, 31, 295–299.
1039. KOFF, E., BOYLE, P., & PUESCHEL, S. M. Perceptual motor functioning in children with phenylketonuria. *American Journal of Diseases of Children*, 1977, 131, 1084–1087.
1040. LERER, R. J., & LERER, M. P. Responses of adolescents with minimal brain dysfunction to methylphenidate. *Journal of Learning Disabilities*, 1977, 10, 223–228.
1041. LERER, R. J., LERER, M. P., & ARTNER, J. The effects of methylphenidate on the handwriting of children with minimal brain dysfunction. *Journal of Pediatrics*, 1977, 91, 127–132.
1042. LIFSHITZ, M. Person perception and social interaction of Jewish and Druze kindergartern children in Israel. *Annals of the New York Academy of Science*, 1977, 285, 338–354.
1043. LOCHER, P. J., & WORMS, P. F. Visual scanning strategies of neurologically impaired, perceptually impaired, and normal children viewing the Bender–Gestalt designs. *Psychology in the Schools*, 1977, 14, 147–157.
1044. LYLE, O. E., & GOTTESMAN, I. I. Premorbid psychometric indicators of the gene for Huntington's Disease. *Journal of Consulting & Clinical Psychology*, 1977, 45, 1011–1022.

1045. MARMORALE, A. M., & BROWN, F. Bender–Gestalt performance of Puerto Rican, White, and Negro children. *Journal of Clinical Psychology*, 1977, 33, 224–228.

1046. MCCORMICK, D. P. Pediatric evaluation of children with school problems. *American Journal of Diseases of Children*, 1977, 131, 318–322.

1047. MCDERMOTT, P. A. Measures of diagnostic data usage as discriminants among training and experience levels in school psychology. *Psychology in the Schools*, 1977, 14, 323–331.

1048. NEEL, A. F. Social and biological factors in child development. *Psychological Reports*, 1977, 40, 1143–1146.

1049. PRYZWANSKY, W. B. The use of the Developmental Test of Visual–Motor Integration as a group screening instrument. *Psychology in the Schools*, 1977, 14, 419–422.

1050. RAO, A. V., & NAMMALVAR, N. The course and outcome in depressive illness. *British Journal of Psychiatry*, 1977, 130, 392–396.

1051. RICHMOND, B. O., & ALIOTTI, N. C. Developmental skills of advantaged and disadvantaged children on perceptual tasks. *Psychology in the Schools*, 1977, 14, 461–466.

1052. RINGEL, S. P., CARROLL, J. E., & SCHOLD, S. C. The spectrum of mild X–linked recessive muscular dystrophy. *Archives of Neurology*, 1977, 34, 408–416.

1053. ROCHFORD, J., GRANT, I., & LaVIGNE, G. Medical students and drugs: Further neuropsychological and use pattern considerations. *International Journal of the Addictions*, 1977, 12, 1057–1065.

1054. ROE, K. V. Effect of economic level and impulsivity on the Bender–Gestalt performance of Greek children. *Perceptual & Motor Skills*, 1977, 45, 523–527.

1055. ROHN, R. D., SARLES, R. M., KENNY, T. J., REYNOLDS, B. J., & HEALD, F. P. Adolescents who attempt suicide. *Journal of Pediatrics*, 1977, 90, 636–638.

1056. RUDY, K. R. The Short Form Test of Academic Aptitude (SFTAA) as a determinant of minimal brain dysfunction in children. *Journal of General Psychology*, 1977, 96, 169–176.

1057. SOBOTKA, K. R., BLACK, F. W., HILL, S. D., & PORTER, R. J. Some psychological correlates of developmental dyslexia. *Journal of Learning Disabilities*, 1977, 10, 363–369.

1058. TAUB, H. B., GOLDSTEIN, K. M., & CAPUTO, D. V. Indices of neonatal prematurity as discriminators of development in middle childhood. *Child Development*, 1977, 48, 797–805.

1059. THOMSON, A. J., SEARLE, M., & RUSSELL, G. Quality of survival after severe birth asphyxia. *Archives of Diseases in Childhood*, 1977, 52, 620–626.

1060. WALLBROWN, J. D., WALLBROWN, F. H., & ENGIN, A. W. The validity of two clinical tests of visual–motor perception. *Journal of Clinical Psychology*, 1977, 33, 491–495.

1061. WEST, P., HILL, S. Y., & ROBINS, L. N. The Canter Backround Interference Procedure (BIP): Effects of demographic variables on diagnosis. *Journal of Clinical Psychology*, 1977, 33, 765–771.

1062. ANDERT, J. N., HUSTAK, T. L., & DINNING, W. D. Bender–Gestalt reproduction times for retarded adults. *Journal of Clinical Psychology*, 1978, 34, 927–929.

1063. ARBIT, J., & ZAGER, R. Psychometrics of a neuropsychological test battery. *Journal of Clinical Psychology*, 1978, 34, 460–465.

1064. ARNOLD, L. E., HUESTIS, R. D., WEMMER, D., & SMELTZER, D. J. Differential effect of amphetamine optical isomers on Bender Gestalt performance of the minimally brain dysfunctioned. *Journal of Learning Disabilities*, 1978, 11, 127–132.

1065. BHATARA, V., CLARK, D. L., & ARNOLD, L. E. Behavioral and nystagmus response of a hyperkinetic child to vestibular stimulation. *American Journal of Occupational Therapy*, 1978, 32, 311–316.

1066. BLACK, F. W., & STRUB, R. L. Digit repetition performance in patients with focal brain damage. *Cortex*, 1978, 14, 12–21.

1067. BOSAEUS, E. The relationship between psychological test results and EEG patterns in healthy children. *Scandinavian Journal of Psychology*, 1978, 19, 181–191.

1068. BOTWINICK, J., WEST, R., & STORANDT, M. Predicting death from behavioral test performance. *Journal of Gerontology*, 1978, 33, 755–762.

1069. BRANCONNIER, R. J., & COLE, J. O. The impairment index as a symptom–independent parameter of drug efficacy in geriatric psychopharmacology. *Journal of Gerontology*, 1978, 33, 217–223.

1070. BRANNIGAN, G. G., MARGOLIS, H., & BARONE, R. J. Bender Gestalt signs as indicants of conceptual impulsivity. *Journal of Personality Assessment*, 1978, 42, 233–236.

1071. CARTER, D. E., SPERO, A. J., & WALSH, J. A. A comparison of the Visual Aural Digit Span and the Bender Gestalt as discriminators of low achievement in the primary grades. *Psychology in the Schools*, 1978, 15, 194–198.

1072. COLLETTE–HARRIS, M., & MINKE, K. A. A behavioral experimental analysis of dyslexia. *Behaviour Research and Therapy*, 1978, 16, 291–295.

1073. DESMOND, M. M., FISHER, E. S., VORDERMAN, A. L., SCHAFFER, H. G., ANDREW, L. P., ZION, T. E., & CATLIN, F. I. The longitudinal course of congenital rubella encephalitis in nonretarded children. *Journal of Pediatrics*, 1978, 93, 584–591.

1074. DOR–SHAV, N. K. On the long–range effects of concentration camp internment on Nazi victims: 25 years later. *Journal of Consulting & Clinical Psychology*, 1978, 46, 1–11.

1075. GUPTA, R., CECI, S. J., & SLATER, A. M. Visual discrimination in good and poor readers. *Journal of Special Education*, 1978, 12, 409–416.

1076. HAUER, A. L., & ARMENTROUT, J. A. Failure of the Bender–Gestalt and Wechsler tests to differentiate children with and without seizure disorders. *Perceptual & Motor Skills*, 1978, 47, 199–202.

1077. HOLTZMAN, R. N. N., RUDEL, R. G., & GOLDENSOHN, E. S. Paroxysmal alexia. *Cortex*, 1978, 14, 592–603.

1078. KRYNICKI, V. E. Cerebral dysfunction in repetitively assaultive adolescents. *Journal of Nervous & Mental Disease*, 1978, 166, 59–67.

1079. LIFSHITZ, M. Bender–Gestalt Test and social interactions of kindergarten children: Effects of socialization practices. *Psychology in the Schools*, 1978, 15, 180–188.

1080. MCMANIS, D. L., FIGLEY, C., RICHERT, M., & FABRE, T. Memory–For–Designs, Bender–Gestalt, Trail Making Test, and WISC–R performance of retarded and adequate readers. *Perceptual & Motor Skills*, 1978, 46, 443–450.

1081. MENDHIRATTA, S. S., WIG, N. N., & VERMA, S. K. Some psychological correlates of long–term heavy cannabis users. *British Journal of Psychiatry*, 1978, 132, 482–486.

1082. MILLICHAP, J. G. Growth of hyperactive children treated with methylphenidate. *Journal of Learning Disabilities*, 1978, 11, 567–570.

1083. NEMEC, R. E. Effect of controlled background interference on test performance by right and left hemiplegics. *Journal of Consulting & Clinical Psychology*, 1978, 46, 294–297.

1084. NORTON, J. C. The Trail Making Test and Bender Background Interference Procedure as screening devices. *Journal of Clinical Psychology*, 1978, 34, 916–922.

1085. PAGE, R. D., & SCHAUB, L. H. EMG biofeedback applicability for differing personality types. *Journal of Clinical Psychology*, 1978, 34, 1014–1020.

1086. PARK, R. Performance on geometric figure copying tests as predictors of types of errors in decoding. *Reading Research Quarterly*, 1978–79, 14, 100–118.

1087. PETERSEN, C. R., & HART, D. H. Use of multiple discriminant function analysis in evaluation of a state–wide system for identification of educationally handicapped children. *Psychological Reports*, 1978, 43, 743–755.

1088. PRANDONI, J. R., & SWARTZ, C. P. Rorschach protocols for three diagnostic categories of adult offenders: Normative data. *Journal of Personality Assessment*, 1978, 42, 115–120.

1089. RASKIN, A., GERSHON, S., CROOK, T. H., SATHANANTHAN, G., & FERRIS, S. The effects of hyperbaric and normobaric oxygen on cognitive impairment in the elderly. *Archives of General Psychiatry*, 1978, 35, 50–56.

1090. RASKIN, L. M., BLOOM, A. S., KLEE, S. H., & REESE, A. The assessment of developmentally disabled children with the WISC–R, Binet, and other tests. *Journal of Clinical Psychology*, 1978, 34, 111–114.

1091. RUSSELL, H. L., & CARTER, J. L. Biofeedback training with children: Consultation, questions, applications and alternatives. *Journal of Clinical Child Psychology*, 1978, 7, 23–25.

1092. SHEALY, A. E. Comparison of two non–intellective scales of intelligence and their relationship to intellectual changes following surgery. *Psychological Reports*, 1978, 42, 51–56.

1093. SHEALY, A. E., & WALKER, D. R. Minnesota Multiphasic Personality Inventory prediction of intellectual changes following cardiac surgery. *Journal of Nervous & Mental Disease*, 1978, 166, 263–267.

1094. SPELLACY, F., & PETER, B. Dyscalculia and elements of the developmental Gerstmann Syndrome in school children. *Cortex*, 1978, 14, 197–206.

1095. STEDMAN, J. M., LAWLIS, G. F., CORTNER, R. H., & ACHTERBERG, G. Relationships between WISC–R factors, Wide–Range Achievement Test scores, and visual–motor maturation in children referred for psychological examination. *Journal of Consulting & Clinical Psychology*, 1978, 46, 869–872.

1096. WADE, T. C., BAKER, T. B., MORTON, T. L., & BAKER, L. J. The status of psychological testing in clinical psychology: Relationships between test use and professional activities and orientations. *Journal of Personality Assessment*, 1978, 42, 3–10.

1097. WAGNER, E. E., KLEIN, I., & WALTER, T. Differentiation of brain damage among low IQ subjects with three projective techniques. *Journal of Personality Assessment*, 1978, 42, 49–55.

1098. WEITHORN, C. J., & KAGEN, E. Interaction of language development and activity level on performance of first graders. *American Journal of Orthopsychiatry*, 1978, 48, 148–159.

1099. ABRAHAMSON, D. S., & BELL, A. E. Assessment of the school readiness section of the early detection inventory: Preschool prediction across situational factors. *Journal of School Psychology*, 1979, 17, 162–171.

1100. BELKA, D. E., & WILLIAMS, H. G. Prediction of later cognitive behavior from early school perceptual–motor, perceptual, and cognitive performances. *Perceptual & Motor Skills*, 1979, 49, 131–141.

1101. BELLEZA, T., RAPPAPORT, M., HOPKINS, H. K., & HALL, K. Visual scanning and matching dysfunction in brain-damaged patients with drawing impairment. *Cortex*, 1979, 15, 19–36.

1102. BLAHA, J., FAWAZ, N., & WALLBROWN, F. H. Information processing components of Koppitz Errors on the Bender Visual–Motor Gestalt Test. *Journal of Clinical Psychology*, 1979, 35, 784–790.

1103. BRUNNER, R. L., O'GRADY, D. J., PARTIN, J. C., PARTIN, J. S., & SCHUBERT, W. K. Neuropsychologic consequences of Reye syndrome. *Journal of Pediatrics*, 1979, 95, 706–711.

1104. CARR, A. C., GOLDSTEIN, E. G., HUNT, H. F., & KERNBERG, O. F. Psychological tests and borderline patients. *Journal of Personality Assessment*, 1979, 43, 582–590.

1105. DASTOOR, D. P., KLINGNER, A., MULLER, H. F., & KACHANOFF, R. A psychogeriatric assessment program. V. Three-year follow-up. *Journal of the American Geriatrics Society*, 1979, 27, 162–169.

1106. DINERO, T. E., DONAH, C. H., & LARSON, G. L. The Slingerland Screening Tests for Identifying Children with Specific Language Disability: Screening for learning disabilities in first grade. *Perceptual & Motor Skills*, 1979, 49, 971–978.

1107. FINEBERG, B. L., SOWARDS, S. K., & COCHRAN, G. M. Comparison of two tests of visual–motor skills. *Perceptual & Motor Skills*, 1979, 48, 156.

1108. HARKULICH, J. F., MARCHNER, T. J., & BROWN, E. B. Neurological, neuropsychological, and behavioral correlates of Klinefelter's Syndrome. *Journal of Nervous & Mental Disease*, 1979, 167, 359–363.

1109. HETRICK, E. W. Bender visual–motor abilities of slow learners. *Perceptual & Motor Skills*, 1979, 49, 31–34.

1110. HOLLAND, T. R., & WADSWORTH, H. M. Comparison and combination of recall and background interference procedures for the Bender–Gestalt Test with brain-damaged and schizophrenic patients. *Journal of Personality Assessment*, 1979, 43, 123–127.

1111. KAUFMAN, D., & KAUFMAN, P. Strategy training and remedial techniques. *Journal of Learning Disabilities*, 1979, 12, 416–419.

1112. KENNY, T. J., ROHN, R., SARLES, R. M., REYNOLDS, B. J., & HEALD, F. P. Visual–motor problems of adolescents who attempt suicide. *Perceptual & Motor Skills*, 1979, 48, 599–602.

1113. LANGHORNE, J. E., & LONEY, J. A four-fold model for subgrouping the hyperkinetic/MBD syndrome. *Child Psychiatry & Human Development*, 1979, 9, 153–159.

1114. MARTIN, J. D., BLAIR, G. E., GRAH, C. R., & SHOAFF, J. E. Correlation of the scores on Barron's Ego Strength scale with the scores on the Bender Gestalt Test. *Educational & Psychological Measurement*, 1979, 39, 187–191.

1115. McCARRON, L., & HORN, P. W. Haptic visual discrimination and intelligence. *Journal of Clinical Psychology*, 1979, 35, 117–120.

1116. MÜLLER, H. F., DASTOOR, D. P., KLINGNER, A., COLE, M., & BOILLAT, J. Amantadine in senile dementia: Electroencephalographic and clinical effects. *Journal of the American Geriatrics Society*, 1979, 27, 9–16.

1117. OAKLAND, T., & FEIGENBAUM, D. Multiple sources of test bias on the WISC-R and Bender–Gestalt Test. *Journal of Consulting and Clinical Psychology*, 1979, 47, 968–974.

1118. RIEDER, D. O., & NICHOLS, P. L. Offspring of schizophrenics III. *Archives of General Psychiatry*, 1979, 36, 665–674.

1119. SABATINO, D. A. The definition and assessment of visual and auditory perception. *Journal of Clinical Child Psychology*, 1979, 8, 188–194.

1120. SATTERFIELD, J. H., CANTWELL, D. P., & SATTERFIELD, B. T. Multimodality treatment. *Archives of General Psychiatry*, 1979, 36, 965–974.

1121. SCHNEIDER, M. A., & SPIVACK, G. An investigative study of the Bender–Gestalt: Clinical validation of its use with a reading disabled population. *Journal of Clinical Psychology*, 1979, 35, 346–351.

1122. SMITH, J. D., & WINNICK, R. H. Practice effects within a multiple-phase administration. *Perceptual & Motor Skills*, 1979, 48, 439–442.

1123. SMITH, S. M. Standardized tests used in correctional institutions. *Journal of Employment Counseling*, 1979, 16, 178–188.

1124. TEJANI, A., MAHADEVAN, R., DOBIAS, B., NANGIA, B. S., & VARMA, P. N. Total parenteral nutrition of the neonate–A long-term follow-up. *Journal of Pediatrics*, 1979, 94, 803–80.

1125. TERVOORT, B. T., & ANSINK, B. J. Cortical word deafness in a child: A case history. *Journal of Communication Disorders*, 1979, 12, 211–216.

1126. TOBACK, C., & RAJKUMAR, S. The emotional disturbance underlying alopecia areata, alopecia totalis, and trichotillomania. *Child Psychiatry & Human Development*, 1979, 10, 114–117.

1127. TRAHAN, D., & STRICKLIN, A. Bender Gestalt emotional indicators and acting-out behavior in young children. *Journal of Personality Assessment*, 1979, 43, 365–375.

1128. ZINKUS, P. W., & GOTTLIEB, M. I. Patterns of perceptual deficits in academically deficient juvenile delinquents. *Psychology in the Schools*, 1979, 16, 19–27.

1129. ASHMORE, R. J., & SNYDER, R. T. Relationship of visual and auditory short-term memory to later reading achievement. *Perceptual & Motor Skills*, 1980, 51, 15–18.

1130. AVIEZER, Y., & SIMPSON, S. Variability and instability in perceptual and reading functions of brain–injured children. *Journal of Learning Disabilities*, 1980, 13, 41–47.

1131. BASH, I. Y., & ALPERT, M. The determination of malingering. *Annals of the New York Academy of Science*, 1980, 347, 86–99.

1132. BATSHAW, M. L., ROAN, Y., JUNG, A. L., ROSENBERG, L. A., & BRUSILOW, S. W. Cerebral dysfunction in asymptomatic carriers of ornithine transcarbamylase deficiency. *New England Journal of Medicine*, 1980, 302, 482–485.

1133. BELKA, D. E., & WILLIAMS, H. G. Canonical relationships among perceptual–motor, perceptual, and cognitive behaviors in children. *Research Quarterly for Exercise & Sport*, 1980, 51, 463–477.

1134. BONHEUR, H., & ROSNER, R. Sex offenders: A descriptive analysis of cases studied at a forensic psychiatry clinic. *Journal of Forensic Sciences*, 1980, 25, 3–14.

1135. BOOK, R. M. Identification of educationally at-risk children during the kindergarten year: A four-year follow-up study of group test performance. *Psychology in the Schools*, 1980, 17, 153–158.

1136. BURCH, E. A., & POWELL, C. H. The psychiatric assessment of a Vietnamese refugee through art. *American Journal of Psychiatry*, 1980, 137, 236–237.

1137. CASKEY, W. E., JR., & LARSON, G. L. Scores on group and individually administered Bender–Gestalt Test and Otis–Lennon IQs of kindergarten children. *Perceptual & Motor Skills*, 1980, 50, 387–390.

1138. CHAVEZ, E. L., & GONZALES-SINGH, E. Hispanic assessment: A case study. *Professional Psychology*, 1980, 11, 163–168.

1139. CZEIZEL, A., LÁNYI-ENGLEMAYER, A., KLUJBER, L., MÉTNEKI, J., & TUSNÁDY, G. Etiological study of mental retardation in Budapest, Hungary. *American Journal of Mental Deficiency*, 1980, 85, 120–128.

1140. DE LA FUENTE, J. R., & ROSENBAUM, A. H. Neuroendocrine dysfunction and blood levels of tricyclic antidepressants. *American Journal of Psychiatry*, 1980, 137, 1260–1261.

1141. EICH, W. F. Use of brief intelligence tests administered in pediatric practice. *Psychological Reports*, 1980, 46, 551–554.

1142. EVANS, D., BOWIE, M. D., HANSEN, J. D. L., MOODIE, A. D., & VAN DER SPUY, H. I. J. Intellectual development and nutrition. *Journal of Pediatrics*, 1980, 97, 358–363.

1143. HENDLER, N., CIMINI, C., MA, T., & LONG, D. A comparison of cognitive impairment due to benzodiazepines and to narcotics. *American Journal of Psychiatry*, 1980, 137, 828–830.

1144. HILL, E. F. A comparison of three psychological testings of a transsexual. *Journal of Personality Assessment*, 1980, 44, 52–101.

1145. LACKS, P. B., & NEWPORT, K. A comparison of scoring systems and level of scorer experience on the Bender–Gestalt Test. *Journal of Personality Assessment*, 1980, 44, 351–357.

1146. NIELSEN, H. H. A longitudinal study of the psychological aspects of myelomeningocele. *Scandinavian Journal of Psychology*, 1980, 21, 45–54.

1147. POWELL, B. J., PENICK, E. C., & READ, M. R. Psychological adjustment and sex-role affiliation in an alcoholic population. *Journal of Clinical Psychology*, 1980, 36, 801–805.

1148. RICHARDS, J. S. Visual memory in left hemiplegia: A clinical evaluation of verbally mediated theories of visual memory. *Perceptual & Motor Skills*, 1980, 51, 13–14.

1149. ROGERS, D. L. Bender test recall in children: An unreliable test. *Perceptual & Motor Skills*, 1980, 50, 859–862.

1150. SCZECHOWICZ, E., & HINRICHSEN, J. J. Effects of instructional set on Bender recall performance of learning disabled and normal children. *Journal of Personality Assessment*, 1980, 44, 465–490.

1151. SNYDER, R. T., MASSONG, S. R., & ASHMORE, R. J. Relationship of Bender memory to achievement in arithmetic by first graders. *Perceptual & Motor Skills*, 1980, 51, 795–798.

1152. SOLWAY, K. S., HAYS, J. R., SCHREINER, D., & CANSLER, D. Clinical study of youths petitioned for certification as adults. *Psychological Reports*, 1980, 46, 1067–1073.

1153. SPIRITO, A. Scores on Bender–Gestalt and Developmental Test of Visual–Motor Integration of learning-disabled children. *Perceptual & Motor Skills*, 1980, 50, 1214.

1154. STEINKAMP, M. W. Relationships between environmental distractions and task performance of hyperactive and normal children. *Journal of Learning Disabilities*, 1980, 13, 209–214.

1155. TAMKIN, A. The Weigl Color-Form Sorting Test as an index of cortical function. *Journal of Clinical Psychology*, 1980, 36, 778–781.

1156. VINCENT, K. R. Semi-automated full battery. *Journal of Clinical Psychology*, 1980, 36, 437–446.

1157. WALLBROWN, F. H., & FREMONT, T. The stability of Koppitz scores on the Bender–Gestalt for reading disabled children. *Psychology in the Schools*, 1980, 17, 181–184.

1158. WHITEHOUSE, D., SHAH, U., & PALMER, F. B. Comparison of sustained-release and standard methylphenidate in the treatment of minimal brain dysfunction. *Journal of Clinical Psychiatry*, 1980, 41, 282–285.

1159. ANDERSON, B., & RALLIS, K. Relationship between Bender errors, emotional indicators and performance on Bender recall. *Perceptual & Motor Skills*, 1981, 53, 497-498.
1160. BRODER, P. K., DUNIVANT, N., SMITH, E. C., & SUTTON, L. P. Further observations on the link between learning disabilities and juvenile delinquency. *Journal of Educational Psychology*, 1981, 73, 838-850.
1161. DEAN, R. S., & KUNDERT, D. K. The effects of abstractiveness in mediation with learning-problem children. *Journal of Clinical Child Psychology*, 1981, 10, 173-175.
1162. DEAN, R. S., & KUNDERT, D. K. Intelligence and teachers' ratings as predictors of abstract and concrete learning. *Journal of School Psychology*, 1981, 19, 78-85.
1163. DEMERS, S. T., WRIGHT, D., & DAPPEN, L. Comparison of scores on two visual-motor tests for children referred for learning or adjustment difficulties. *Perceptual & Motor Skills*, 1981, 53, 863-867.
1164. DONNELLY, E. F., JESTE, D. V., & WYATT, R. J. Tardive dyskinesia and perceptual dysfunction. *Perceptual & Motor Skills*, 1981, 53, 689-690.
1165. FABIAN, M. S., PARSONS, O. A., & SILBERSTEIN, J. A. Impaired perceptual-cognitive functioning in women alcoholics: Cross-validated findings. *Journal of Studies on Alcohol*, 1981, 42, 217-229.
1166. GRAF, M. H., & HAMERSMA, R. J. Performance of three-year-old children on the Beery Visual-Motor Integration Test. *Perceptual & Motor Skills*, 1981, 53, 562.
1167. KERNBERG, O. F., GOLDSTEIN, E. G., CARR, A. C., HUNT, H. F., BAUER, S. F., & BLUMENTHAL, R. Diagnosing borderline personality: A pilot study using multiple diagnostic methods. *Journal of Nervous & Mental Disease*, 1981, 169, 225-231.
1168. KODMAN, F., JR. Perceptual motor learning with moderately retarded persons. *Perceptual & Motor Skills*, 1981, 53, 25-26.
1169. KOPPITZ, E. M. The Bender Gestalt and VADS test performance of learning disabled middle school pupils. *Journal of Learning Disabilities*, 1981, 14, 96-98.
1170. LAMBERT, N. M. The clinical validity of the process for assessment of effective student functioning. *Journal of School Psychology*, 1981, 19, 323-334.
1171. PONTIUS, A. Geometric figure-rotation task and face representation in dyslexia: Role of spatial relations and orientation. *Perceptual & Motor Skills*, 1981, 53, 607-614.
1172. PORTER, G. L., & BINDER, D. M. A pilot study of visual-motor developmental inter-test reliability: The Beery Developmental Test of Visual Motor Integration and the Bender Visual Motor Gestalt Test. *Journal of Learning Disabilities*, 1981, 14, 124-127.
1173. REICH, P., DESILVA, R. A., LOWN, B., & MURAWSKI, B. J. Acute psychological disturbances preceding life-threatening ventricular arrhythmias. *JAMA*, 1981, 246, 233-235.
1174. SILBERSTEIN, J. A., & PARSONS, O. A. Neuropsychological impairment in female alcoholics: Replication and extension. *Journal of Abnormal Psychology*, 1981, 90, 179-182.
1175. SNYDER, P. P., SNYDER, R. T., & MASSONG, S. F. The visual motor integration test: High interjudge reliability, high potential for diagnostic error. *Psychology in the Schools*, 1981, 18, 55-59.
1176. TOLOR, A., & BARBIERI, R. J. Different facets of sex anxiety. *Perceptual & Motor Skills*, 1981, 52, 546.
1177. WILLIAMS, A. J., WILLIAMS, M. A., WALKER, C. A., & BUSH, P. G. The Robin Anomalad (Pierre Robin Syndrome)-A follow up study. *Archives of Diseases in Childhood*, 1981, 56, 663-668.

[281]
The Bender-Purdue Reflex Test: For Signs of Symmetric Tonic Neck Reflex Immaturity.
Ages 6-12; 1976; child's posture as "he creeps on hands and knees, first forward, then backward, against manual resistance," as related to current or latent learning disabilities; Miriam L. Bender; Academic Therapy Publications.*

For additional information and a review by Richard E. Darnell, see 8:868.

[282]
Bennett Mechanical Comprehension Test.
Grades 9-12 and adults; 1940-70; BMCT; revision of *Tests of Mechanical Comprehension*, Forms AA, BB, W1; George K. Bennett and William A. Owens (Form CC); The Psychological Corporation. (British manual and norms supplement: 1973-78; Peter Saville (manual) and Gill Nyfield (norms supplement); NFER-Publishing Co. [England].)*

See T2:2239 (9 references); for reviews by Harold P. Bechtoldt and A. Oscar H. Roberts, and an excerpted review by Ronald K. Hambleton, see 7:1049 (22 references); see also 6:1094 (15 references) and 5:889 (46 references); for a review by N. W. Morton of earlier forms, see 4:766 (28 references); for reviews by Charles M. Harsh, Lloyd G. Humphreys, and George A. Satter, see 3:683 (19 references).

REFERENCES

1-19. See 3:683.
20-47. See 4:766.
48-93. See 5:889.
94-108. See 6:1094.
109-130. See 7:1049.
131-139. See T2:2239.
140. BELMONT, L. Birth order, intellectual competence, and psychiatric status. *Journal of Individual Psychology*, 1977, 33, 97-104.
141. BELMONT, L., WITTES, J., & STEIN, Z. Relation of birth order, family size and social class to psychological functions. *Perceptual & Motor Skills*, 1977, 45, 1107-1116.
142. DENISI, A. S., & SHAW, J. B. Investigation of the uses of self-reports of abilities. *Journal of Applied Psychology*, 1977, 62, 641-644.
143. MOUNT, M. K., MUCHINSKY, P. M., & HANSEN, L. M. The predictive validity of a work sample: A laboratory study. *Personnel Psychology*, 1977, 30, 637-645.
144. GOUGH, H. G., LAZZARI, R., FIORAVANTI, M., & STRACCA, M. An adjective checklist scale to predict military leadership. *Journal of Cross-Cultural Psychology*, 1978, 9, 381-400.
145. DORAN, R. L., & DIETRICH, M. C. Psychomotor abilities of science and nonscience high school students. *Journal of Research in Science Teaching*, 1980, 17, 495-502.
146. SCHMIDT, F. L., HUNTER, J. E., & CAPLAN, J. R. Validity generalization results for two job groups in the petroleum industry. *Journal of Applied Psychology*, 1981, 66, 261-273.

[283]
Benton Visual Retention Test, Revised Edition.
Ages 8 and over; 1946-74; BVRT; manual title is *Revised Visual Retention Test*; Arthur L. Benton; The Psychological Corporation.*

For additional information, see 8:236 (32 references); see also T2:543 (71 references) and 6:543 (22 references); for a review by Nelson G. Hanawalt, see 5:401 (5 references); for reviews by Ivan Norman Mensh, Joseph Newman, and William Schofield of the original edition, see 4:360 (3 references); for an excerpted review, see 3:297.

REFERENCES

1-3. See 4:360.
4-8. See 5:401.
9-30. See 6:543.
31-101. See T2:543.
102-133. See 8:236.
134. APRIL, R. S., & TSE, P. C. Crossed aphasia in a Chinese bilingual dextral. *Archives of Neurology*, 1977, 34, 766-770.
135. ARENBERG, D. The effects of auditory augmentation on visual retention for young and old adults. *Journal of Gerontology*, 1977, 32, 192-195.
136. BERGLUND, M., LEIJONQUIST, H., & HÖRLÉN, M. Prognostic significance and reversibility of cerebral dysfunction in alcoholics. *Journal of Studies on Alcohol*, 1977, 38, 1761-1770.
137. CHRISTODOULOU, G. N. The syndrome of Capgras. *British Journal of Psychiatry*, 1977, 130, 556-564.
138. GIAMBRA, L. M. A factor analytic study of daydreaming, imaginal process, and temperament: A replication on an adult male life-span sample. *Journal of Gerontology*, 1977, 32, 675-680.
139. KLJAJIĆ, I. Benton OCS and OES as actuarial indices of brain pathology. *Journal of Clinical Psychology*, 1977, 33, 792-794.
140. SPELLACY, F. Neuropsychological differences between violent and nonviolent adolescents. *Journal of Clinical Psychology*, 1977, 33, 966-969.
141. ARENBERG, D. Differences and changes with age in the Benton Visual Retention Test. *Journal of Gerontology*, 1978, 33, 534-540.
142. BERGLUND, M., & LEIJONQUIST, H. Prediction of cerebral dysfunction in alcoholics: A study of health insurance records. *Journal of Studies on Alcohol*, 1978, 39, 1968-1974.

143. BOSAEUS, E. The relationship between psychological test results and EEG patterns in healthy children. *Scandinavian Journal of Psychology*, 1978, 19, 181–191.
144. GUSTAFSON, L., & HAGBERG, B. Recovery in hydrocephalic dementia after shunt operation. *Journal of Neurology, Neurosurgery & Psychiatry*, 1978, 41, 940–947.
145. HOLTZMAN, R. N. N., RUDEL, R. G., & GOLDENSOHN, E. S. Paroxysmal alexia. *Cortex*, 1978, 14, 592–603.
146. KAPUR, M. A short screening battery of tests to detect organic brain dysfunction. *Journal of Clinical Psychology*, 1978, 34, 104–111.
147. SPELLACY, F. Neuropsychological discrimination between violent and non-violent men. *Journal of Clinical Psychology*, 1978, 34, 49–52.
148. WATSON, C. G., DAVIS, W. E., & GASSER, B. The separation of organics from depressives with ability- and personality-based tests. *Journal of Clinical Psychology*, 1978, 34, 393–397.
149. HAMILTON, M., STOCKER, M. J., & SPENCER, C. M. Post–ECT cognitive defect and elevation of blood pressure. *British Journal of Psychiatry*, 1979, 135, 77–78.
150. JEEVES, M. A., SIMPSON, D. A., & GEFFEN, G. Functional consequences of the transcallosal removal of intraventricular tumours. *Journal of Neurology, Neurosurgery, & Psychiatry*, 1979, 42, 134–142.
151. PENK, W. E., CHARLES, H. L., & VAN HOOSE, T. A. Psychological test comparison of day hospital and inpatient treatment. *Journal of Clinical Psychology*, 1979, 35, 837–839.
152. STONES, M. J. Rekitting the Wechsler Paired–Associate Task: The Waterford Index. *Journal of Clinical Psychology*, 1979, 35, 626–630.
153. WALKER, B. B., & SANDMAN, C. A. Influences of an analog of the neuropeptide ACTH 4–9 on mentally retarded adults. *American Journal of Mental Deficiency*, 1979, 83, 346–352.
154. BATSHAW, M. L., ROAN, Y., JUNG, A. L., ROSENBERG, L. A., & BRUSILOW, S. W. Cerebral dysfunction in asymptomatic carriers of ornithine transcarbamylase deficiency. *New England Journal of Medicine*, 1980, 302, 482–485.
155. BESSON, J. A. O. A diagnostic pointer to adult metachromatic leucodystrophy. *British Journal of Psychiatry*, 1980, 137, 186–187.
156. ECKARDT, M. J., RYBACK, R. S., & PAUTLER, C. P. Neuropsychological deficits in alcoholic men in their mid thirties. *American Journal of Psychiatry*, 1980, 137, 932–936.
157. GUTHRIE, A., & ELLIOT, W. A. The nature and reversibility of cerebral impairment in alcoholism: Treatment implications. *Journal of Studies on Alcohol*, 1980, 41, 147–155.
158. CAMPBELL, A. L., JR., BOGEN, J. E., & SMITH, A. Disorganization and reorganization due to cognitive and sensorimotor functions in cerebral commissurotomy: Compensatory roles of the forebrain commissures and cerebral hemispheres in man. *Brain*, 1981, 104, 493–511.
159. PENK, W. E., BROWN, A. S., ROBERTS, W. R., DOLAN, M. P., ATKINS, H. G., & ROBINOWITZ, R. Visual memory of black and white male heroin and nonheroin drug users. *Journal of Abnormal Psychology*, 1981, 90, 486–489.
160. PENK, W. E., BROWN, A. S., ROBERTS, W. R., DOLAN, M. P., ATKINS, H. G., & ROBINOWITZ, R. Visual memory of male Hispanic–American heroin addicts. *Journal of Consulting & Clinical Psychology*, 1981, 49, 771–772.

[284]

★**The Ber-Sil Spanish Test.** Ages 5–12, 13–17; 1972–77; Marjorie L. Beringer; Ber-Sil Co.*

a) ELEMENTARY LEVEL, 1976 REVISED EDITION. Ages 5–12; 5 scores: vocabulary, response to directions, writing, geometric figures, draw a boy or girl; (Cantonese, Mandarin, Korean, Persian, Ilokano, and Tagalog editions available).

b) SECONDARY LEVEL, EXPERIMENTAL EDITION. Ages 13–17; 4 scores: vocabulary, dictation of sentences, draw a boy or a girl, mathematics.

[285]

Berry-Talbott Language Test: Comprehension of Grammar. Ages 5–8; 1966; BTLT; experimental; "to *explore* the child's ability to make up and to use rules of grammar and syntax" using nonsense words; 8 scores: plural noun, past tense, third person singular, possessive singular-plural, derived adjective, adjective: comparative-superlative, diminutive-derived word, progressive-derived word; Mildred F. Berry and Ruth Talbott; Berry Language Tests.*

REFERENCES

1. VOGEL, S. A. Morphological ability in normal and dyslexic children. *Journal of Learning Disabilities*, 1977, 10, 35–43.
2. BRUMFIELD, S. M. Morphological performance by the deaf under two testing conditions. *ASHA*, 1978, 20, 817.

[286]

★**Bessell Measurement of Emotional Maturity Scales.** Ages 5–11; 1978; MEM; ratings by teachers; 63 measures of behavioral functioning in 4 component areas: awareness traits, relating traits, competence traits, integrity traits; Harold Bessell; Psych/Graphic Publishers.* (In-print status uncertain; no reply from publisher.)

[287]

Biblical Survey Test. College; 1961; 2 scores: New Testament, Old Testament; Edna SoRelle and Joseph V. West; distributed by Baylor University Press.*

[288]

★**Biemiller Test of Reading Processes.** Grades 2–6; 1981; BTORP; 5 scores: letters, story #1, word list #1, story #2, word list #2; Andrew Biemiller; Guidance Centre, University of Toronto [Canada].*

[289]

★**Bilingual Oral Language Test.** Grades 7–12; 1976–78; BOLT; designed to measure oral language skills in English or Spanish; verbal responses scored as correct or incorrect by comparing them to suggested scoring standards, and total correct is translated to one of five proficiency levels in English or Spanish; Sam Cohen, Roberto Cruz, and Raul Bravo; B.M.P. (Bilingual Media Productions), Inc.*

[290]

Bilingual Syntax Measure. Bilingual children grades kgn–2; 1973–76; BSM; second-language oral proficiency in English or Spanish; 2 editions (English, Spanish), both of which may be administered as an indicator of language dominance; scoring consists of assigning of child to one of five proficiency levels ranging from no speaking or comprehension of the language to proficient; Marina K. Burt, Heidi C. Dulay, and Eduardo Hernandez Ch.; The Psychological Corporation.*

For additional information, reviews by Isaac I. Bejar and C. Ray Graham, and an excerpted review by John W. Oller, Jr., see 8:156 (4 references).

REFERENCES

1–4. See 8:156.
5. TORONTO, A. S. Bilingual Syntax Measure. *ASHA*, 1978, 20, 580.
6. ARNOLD, M. R., ROSADO, J. W., JR., & PENFIELD, D. A. Language choice by bilingual Puerto Rican children on a picture labeling task. *Modern Language Journal*, 1979, 63, 349–354.
7. DI PIETRO, R. J. Filling the elementary curriculum with languages: What are the effects? *Modern Language Journal*, 1979, 63, 192–201.
8. WEBER–OLSEN, M. Three children's second language acquisition of English morphemes. *ASHA*, 1979, 21, 722. (Abstract)
9. SATTLER, J. M., AVILA, V., HOUSTON, W. B., & TONEY, D. H. Performance of bilingual Mexican–American children on Spanish and English versions of the Peabody Picture Vocabulary Test. *Journal of Consulting & Clinical Psychology*, 1980, 48, 782–784.

[291]

★**Bilingual Syntax Measure II.** Grades 3–12; 1978; BSM II; upward extension of the *Bilingual Syntax Measure*; second-language oral proficiency with respect to syntactic structures in English and Spanish; 2 editions (English, Spanish), both of which may be administered as an indicator of language dominance; scoring for each edition consists of assigning child to one of six proficiency levels ranging from no speaking of language to proficient; Marina K. Burt, Heidi C. Dulay, and Eduardo Hernandez Ch.; The Psychological Corporation.*

[292]
Bingham Button Test. Disadvantaged children ages 3–6; 1967; BBT; "knowledge and understanding of simple terms and relationships"; William J. Bingham; Bingham Button Test.*

For additional information and a review by Alan S. Kaufman, see 8:207.

[293]
Biology: Minnesota High School Achievement Examinations. High school; 1951–70; a new, revised, or previously inactive form issued each May; Achievement Examinations for Secondary Schools, High School Achievement Examinations, and Midwest High School Achievement Examinations have also been used as series titles for tests now out of print; edited by V. L. Lohmann; American Guidance Service.*

For additional information concerning out of print and inactive forms, see 7:811, 5:719, and 5:722; for a review by Barbara F. Esser of Form E (1962) and Form F (1963), see 6:890.

[294]
Bipolar Psychological Inventory. College and adults; 1971–72; BPI; 15 scores: defensiveness, psychic pain, depression, self degradation, dependence, unmotivated, social withdrawal, family discord, sexual immaturity (Form A), problem index (Form B), social deviancy, impulsiveness, hostility, insensitivity, invalid, lie; Robert J. Howell, I. Reed Payne, and Allan V. Roe; Diagnostic Specialists, Inc.*

For additional information, see 8:507 (11 references).

REFERENCES

1–11. See 8:507.
12. OLDROYD, R. J., & HOWELL, R. J. Personality, intellectual, and behavioral differences between Black, Chicano, & White prison inmates in the Utah State Prison. *Psychological Reports*, 1977, 41, 187–191.
13. DAWKINS, M. P., TERRY, J. A., & DAWKINS, M. P. Personality and life style factors in utilization of mental health services. *Psychological Reports*, 1980, 46, 383–386.
14. LEAK, G. K. Effects of highly structured versus nondirective group counseling approaches on personality and behavioral measures of adjustment in incarcerated felons. *Journal of Counseling Psychology*, 1980, 27, 520–523.
15. MCGUIRE, J. P., & LEAK, G. K. Prediction of self-disclosure from objective personality assessment techniques. *Journal of Clinical Psychology*, 1980, 36, 201–204.

[295]
★**Birth to Three Developmental Scale.** Birth to 3 years and older children suspected to fall below the 3-year age level developmentally; 1979; criterion-referenced; designed for early identification of developmental delay; 4 behavior categories divided into 6-month age intervals: oral language (comprehension, expression), problem solving, social/personal, motor; Tina E. Bangs and Susan Dodson; Teaching Resources Corporation.*

[296]
The BITCH Test (Black Intelligence Test of Cultural Homogeneity). Adolescents and adults; 1972; BITCH; a vocabulary test of Afro-American expressions used as an intelligence test for blacks and, when administered to whites, as "a measure of sensitivity and responsivity" to black experience; manual also uses the title *The Bitch-100: A Culture-Specific Test*; Robert L. Williams; Robert L. Williams & Associates, Inc.*

For additional information and reviews by Lee J. Cronbach and Charles J. Krauskopf, see 8:176 (8 references).

REFERENCES

1–8. See 8:176.
9. MATARAZZO, J. D., & WIENS, A. N. Black Intelligence Test of Cultural Homogeneity and Wechsler Adult Intelligence Scale scores of black and white police applicants. *Journal of Applied Psychology*, 1977, 62, 57–63.
10. YOUNG, A., & REARDEN, J. Black Intelligence Test of Cultural Homogeneity and Shipley–Institute of Living Scale scores for black Chicago youths. *Psychological Reports*, 1979, 45, 457–458.

[297]
Black History: A Test to Create Awareness and Arouse Interest. Teachers; 1974; no manual or directions for administration and scoring; Gregory C. Coffin, Elsie F. Harley, and Bessie M. L. Rhodes; Coffin Associates.* (In-print status uncertain; no reply from publisher.)

For additional information, see 8:909 (1 reference).

[298]
The Blacky Pictures: A Technique for the Exploration of Personality Dynamics. Ages 5 and over; 1950–67; BP; psychosexual development; Gerald S. Blum; scoring blanks by Earl S. Taulbee and David E. Stenmark; Psychodynamic Instruments.* (In-print status uncertain; no reply from publisher.)

See T2:1448 (47 references) and P:416 (39 references); for a review by Bert R. Sappenfield, see 6:204 (34 references); for a review by Kenneth R. Newton and an excerpted review by Samuel J. Beck, see 5:125 (38 references); for a review by Albert Ellis and excerpted reviews by M. M. Genn, Ephraim Rosen, and Laurance F. Shaffer, see 4:102 (7 references).

REFERENCES

1–7. See 4:102.
8–45. See 5:125.
46–79. See 6:204.
80–118. See P:416.
119–165. See T2:1448.
166. TOUHEY, J. C. Penis envy attitudes toward castration–like punishment of sexual aggression. *Journal of Research in Personality*, 1977, 11, 1–9.
167. PRINS, D., & BEAUDET, R. Defense preference and stutterers' speech disfluencies: Implications for the nature of the disorder. *Journal of Speech & Hearing Research*, 1980, 23, 757–768.
168. GERZI, S., & BERMAN, E. Emotional reactions of expectant fathers to their wives' first pregnancy. *British Journal of Medical Psychology*, 1981, 54, 259–265.

[299]
The Blind Learning Aptitude Test. Blind ages 6–20; 1971; BLAT; tactual discrimination test not employing Braille stimuli; T. Ernest Newland; University of Illinois Press.*

For additional information and reviews by Thomas S. Baldwin and Murray H. Tillman, see 8:320 (4 references).

[300]
★**Bloom Sentence Completion Survey.** Students ages 6–21, adults; 1974–75; BSCS; attitudes toward

important factors in everyday living; 8 scores: age-mates (students)/people (adults), physical self, family, psychological self, self-directedness, education (students)/work (adults), accomplishment, irritants; Wallace Bloom; Stoelting Co.*

[301]
Bobbs-Merrill Arithmetic Achievement Tests. Grades 1, 2, 3, 4, 5, 6, 7, 8–9; 1963; 3 scores: concepts and problems, computation, total; William E. Kline and Harry J. Baker; Bobbs-Merrill Co., Inc.*

For additional information and a review by C. Alan Riedesel, see 7:513.

[302]
Boehm Test of Basic Concepts. Grades kgn–2; 1967–71; a picture test based on concepts (e.g., below, more, last) "commonly found in preschool and primary instructional materials"; BTBC; (Spanish directions ('70) available); Ann E. Boehm; The Psychological Corporation.*

For additional information and an excerpted review by Theodore A. Dahl, see 8:178 (22 references); see also T2:344 (1 reference); for reviews by Boyd R. McCandless and Charles D. Smock, and excerpted reviews by Frank S. Freeman, George Lawlor, Victor H. Noll, and Barton B. Proger, see 7:335 (1 reference).

REFERENCES
1. See 7:335.
2. See T2:344.
3–24. See 8:178.
25. AULT, R. L., CROMER, C. C., & MITCHELL, C. The Boehm Test of Basic Concepts: A three-dimensional version. *Journal of Educational Research*, 1977, 70, 186–188.
26. CAMP, B. W. Verbal mediation in young aggressive boys. *Journal of Abnormal Psychology*, 1977, 86, 145–153.
27. CAMP, B. W., VAN DOORNINCK, W. J., ZIMET, S. G., & DAHLEM, N. W. Verbal abilities in young aggressive boys. *Journal of Educational Psychology*, 1977, 69, 129–135.
28. ERNHART, C. B., SPANER, S. D., & JORDON, T. E. Validity of selected preschool screening tests. *Contemporary Educational Psychology*, 1977, 2, 78–89.
29. LAMARRE, P. A. Paradigmatic–syntagmatic responses of bilingual students and reading comprehension. *National Reading Conference Yearbook*, 1977, 275–279.
30. CULATTA, B. The relationship between perceptual dysfunction and language disorders: A case report. *Journal of Communication Disorders*, 1978, 11, 51–63.
31. HARDMAN, M. L. A functional administrative teaching model for academic programming with the trainable mentally retarded. *Education & Training of the Mentally Retarded*, 1978, 13, 23–28.
32. HUTCHERSON, R. Correlating the Boehm and PPVT. *Academic Therapy*, 1978, 13, 285–288.
33. MOERS, F., & HARRIS, J. Instruction in basic concepts and first-grade achievement. *Psychology in the Schools*, 1978, 15, 84–86.
34. STEINBAUER, E., & HELLER, M. S. The Boehm Test of Basic Concepts as a predictor of academic achievement in grades 2 and 3. *Psychology in the Schools*, 1978, 15, 357–360.
35. BELKA, D. E., & WILLIAMS, H. G. Prediction of later cognitive behavior from early school perceptual–motor, perceptual, and cognitive performances. *Perceptual & Motor Skills*, 1979, 49, 131–141.
36. SEEFELDT, C. The effects of a program designed to increase young children's perception of texture. *Studies in Art Education*, 1979, 20, 40–44.
37. BELKA, D. E., & WILLIAMS, H. G. Canonical relationships among perceptual-motor, perceptual, and cognitive behaviors in children. *Research Quarterly for Exercise & Sport*, 1980, 51, 463–477.
38. CUMMINGS, J. A., & NELSON, R. B. Basic concepts in the oral directions of group achievement tests. *Journal of Educational Research*, 1980, 73, 259–261.
39. VANE, J. R., & MOTTA, R. W. Test response inconsistency in young children. *Journal of School Psychology*, 1980, 18, 25–33.

40. BRADLEY, M., & BRADBARD, M. R. Effects of allowing four–year–olds to manipulate teaching materials on their learning of space and quantity concepts. *Journal of General Psychology*, 1981, 104, 265–273.
41. BRENZA, B. A., KRICOS, P. B., & LASKY, E. Z. Comprehension and production of basic semantic concepts by older hearing–impaired children. *Journal of Speech & Hearing Research*, 1981, 24, 414–419.
42. PIERSEL, W. C., & REYNOLDS, C. R. Factorial validity of item classification of the Boehm Test of Basic Concepts (BTBC), Forms A and B. *Educational & Psychological Measurement*, 1981, 41, 579–583.

[303]
Bookkeeping: Minnesota High School Achievement Examinations. High school; 1951–70; a new, revised, or previously inactive form issued each May; Achievement Examinations for Secondary Schools, High School Achievement Examinations, and Midwest High School Achievement Examinations have also been used as series titles; edited by V. L. Lohmann; American Guidance Service.*

For additional information concerning out of print and inactive forms, see 7:553 and 5:502; for a review by Harold L. Royer of Form F (1963), see 6:35; for a review by I. David Satlow of Form A (1955) and Form B (1952), see 5:504.

[304]
Bookkeeping Test: National Business Entrance Tests. Grades 11–16 and adults; 1938–72; National Business Education Association.* (In-print status uncertain; no reply from publisher.)

For additional information and a review by Robert M. Swanson, see 8:322 (1 reference); for reviews by Harvey A. Andruss and Ray G. Price of an earlier form, see 3:368. For reviews of the complete battery, see 6:33 (1 review), 5:515 (3 reviews), and 3:396 (1 review).

[305]
★**The Booklet Category Test.** Adolescents and adults; 1979–81; BCT; booklet version of the *Halstead Category Test*; diagnosis of brain damage; Nick A. DeFilippis and Elizabeth McCampbell; Psychological Assessment Resources, Inc.*

[306]
Borman-Sanders Elementary Science Test. 1, 2 semesters in grades 5–8; 1964; BSEST; Ina M. Borman and M. W. Sanders; Bureau of Educational Measurements.*

For additional information and a review by Carl J. Olson, see 7:785.

[307]
Borromean Family Index. Adolescents and adults; 1975; attitudes and feelings about one's family; 2 scores: internal (forces that attract toward family), external (forces that pull away); 2 tests: for married persons, for single persons; Panos D. Bardis; the Author.*

For additional information, see 8:332 (1 reference).

[308]
Boston Diagnostic Aphasia Examination. Aphasic patients; 1972; BDAE; 44 scores: severity rating, fluency (articulation rating, phrase length, verbal agility), auditory comprehension (word discrimination, body part identification, commands, complex material), naming (responsive, confrontation, animal, body part), oral reading (word reading, oral sentence), repetition (words, high-probability sentences, low-probability sentences), paraphasia (neologis-

tic distortion, literal, verbal, extended), automatized speech (sequences, reciting), reading comprehension (symbol discrimination, word recognition, oral spelling, word picture matching, sentences and paragraphs), writing (mechanics, serial writing, primer-level dictation, written confrontation naming, spelling to dictation, sentences to dictation, narrative writing), music (singing, rhythm), parietal (drawing to command, stick memory, total fingers, right-left, arithmetic, clock setting, 3-dimensional blocks) plus 7 ratings: melodic line, phrase length, articulatory agility, grammatical form, paraphasia in running speech, word finding, auditory comprehension; Harold Goodglass with the collaboration of Edith Kaplan; Lea & Febiger.*

For additional information and reviews by Daniel R. Boone and Manfred J. Meier, see 8:955 (1 reference).

REFERENCES

1. See 8:955.
2. BENSON, D. F. The third alexia. *Archives of Neurology*, 1977, 34, 327–331.
3. BOLLER, F., VRTUNSKI, B., MACK, J. L., & KIM, Y. Neuropsychological correlates of hypertension. *Archives of Neurology*, 1977, 34, 701–705.
4. FARMER, A. Self-correctional strategies in the conversational speech of aphasic and nonphasic brain damaged adults. *Cortex*, 1977, 13, 327–334.
5. WIIG, E. H., LAPOINT, C., & SEMEL, E. M. Relationships among language processing and production abilities of learning disabled adolescents. *Journal of Learning Disabilities*, 1977, 10, 292–299.
6. CAINE, E. D., HUNT, R. D., WEINGARTNER, H., & EBERT, M. H. Huntington's Dementia. *Archives of General Psychiatry*, 1978, 35, 377–384.
7. PEASE, D. M., & GOODGLASS, H. The effects of cuing on picture naming in aphasia. *Cortex*, 1978, 14, 178–189.
8. DAMON, S. G., LESSER, R., & WOODS, R. T. Behavioural treatment of social difficulties with an aphasic woman and a dysarthric man. *British Journal of Disorders of Communication*, 1979, 14, 31–38.
9. GOODGLASS, H., & STUSS, D. T. Naming to picture versus description in three aphasic subgroups. *Cortex*, 1979, 15, 199–211.
10. LAUGHLIN, S. A., NAESER, M. A., & GORDON, W. P. Effects of three syllable durations using the melodic intonation therapy technique. *Journal of Speech & Hearing Research*, 1979, 22, 311–320.
11. NAESER, M. A., & HAYWARD, R. W. The resolving stroke and aphasia: A case study with computerized tomography. *Archives of Neurology*, 1979, 36, 233–235.
12. PEACH, R. K., & BAQUET, G. M. Localizing lesions and treatment measurements of aphasics by the SSW. *ASHA*, 1979, 21, 718. (Abstract)
13. SCHWARTZ, R., SHIPKIN, D., & CERMAK, L. S. Verbal and nonverbal memory abilities of adult brain damaged patients. *American Journal of Occupational Therapy*, 1979, 33, 79–83.
14. WAPNER, W., & GARDNER, H. A note on patterns of comprehension and recovery in global aphasia. *Journal of Speech & Hearing Research*, 1979, 22, 765–772.
15. ZURIF, E. B., CARAMAZZA, A., FOLDI, N. S., & GARDNER, H. Lexical semantics and memory for words in aphasia. *Journal of Speech & Hearing Research*, 1979, 22, 456–467.
16. CUMMINGS, J., HEBBEN, N. A., OBLER, L., & LEONARD, P. Nonaphasic misnaming and other neurobehavioral features of an unusual toxic encephalopathy: Case study. *Cortex*, 1980, 16, 315–323.
17. GLEASON, J. B., GOODGLASS, H., OBLER, L., GREEN, E., HYDE, M. R., & WEINTRAUB, S. Narrative strategies of aphasic and normal-speaking subjects. *Journal of Speech & Hearing Research*, 1980, 23, 370–382.
18. KERTESZ, A., & PHIPPS, J. The numerical taxonomy of acute and chronic aphasic syndromes. *Psychological Research*, 1980, 41, 179–198.
19. NAESER, M., & CHAN, S. W. C. Case study of a Chinese aphasic with the Boston Diagnostic Aphasia Exam. *Neuropsychologia*, 1980, 18, 389–410.
20. O'CONNELL, P. F., & O'CONNELL, E. J. Speech–language pathology services in a skilled nursing facility: A retrospective study. *Journal of Communication Disorders*, 1980, 13, 93–103.
21. BROWN, C. S., & CULLINAN, W. L. Word-retrieval difficulty and disfluent speech in adult anomic speakers. *Journal of Speech & Hearing Research*, 1981, 24, 358–365.
22. CROSSON, B., & WARREN, R. L. Dichotic ear preference for C–V–C words in Wernicke's and Broca's aphasia. *Cortex*, 1981, 17, 249–258.
23. DEUTSCH, S. E. Oral form identification as a measure of cortical sensory dysfunction in apraxia of speech and aphasia. *Journal of Communication Disorders*, 1981, 14, 65–73.
24. DRUMMOND, S. S., GALLAGHER, T. M., & MILLS, R. H. Word-retrieval in aphasia: An investigation of semantic complexity. *Cortex*, 1981, 17, 63–82.
25. FABER, R., & REICHSTEIN, M. B. Language dysfunction in schizophrenia. *British Journal of Psychiatry*, 1981, 139, 519–522.
26. GALLAHER, A. J. Syntactic versus semantic performances of agrammatic Broca's aphasics on tests of constituent–element-ordering. *Journal of Speech & Hearing Research*, 1981, 24, 217–223.
27. NANCE, A. L., & OCHSNER, G. J. Language modality performance patterns in aphasia. *Journal of Communication Disorders*, 1981, 14, 421–428.
28. PIERCE, R. S. Facilitating the comprehension of tense related sentences in aphasia. *Journal of Speech & Hearing Disorders*, 1981, 46, 364–368.
29. SHALLICE, T. Phonological agraphia and the lexical route in writing. *Brain*, 1981, 104, 413–429.

[309]

Botel Reading Inventory. Grades 1–4, 1–6, 1–12; 1961–70; BRI; 4 tests; 9 scores: frustrational, instructional (placement), and free reading grade score for each of tests *a*, *b*, and *d*; Morton Botel; Follett Publishing Co.*

a) WORD RECOGNITION TEST. Grades 1–4; 1961–70; oral reading fluency; 8 "graded" 20-word lists described as samples of reading materials at 8 levels (PP, P, 1^2, 2^1, 2^2, 3^1, 3^2, $4+$); 3 grade scores: frustration level (0–65%), instructional level (70–90%), free reading level (95–100%).

b) WORD OPPOSITES TEST. Grades 1–12; 1961–70; a vocabulary test described as "an estimate of reading comprehension"; 10 "graded" 10-word lists described as samples of reading materials at 10 levels (1, 2^1, 2^2, 3^1, 3^2, 4, 5, 6, 7–8, 9–12); 3 grade scores: frustration level (0–60%), instructional level (70–80%), free reading level (90–100%).

c) PHONICS MASTERY TEST. Grades 1–4; 1961–70; "knowledge of key word perception skills"; 3 levels of phonic skills, each level to be mastered 100% before going on to the next.

d) SPELLING PLACEMENT TEST. Grades 1–6; 1970; 5 "graded" 20-word lists described as samples from the author's *Spelling and Writing Patterns*, at 5 levels (1–2, 3, 4, 5, 6); 3 grade scores: frustration level (0–80%), instructional level (85–90%), independent level (95–100%).

See T2:1658 (2 references) and 7:727 (5 references); for reviews by Ira E. Aaron and Charles M. Brown, see 6:834.

REFERENCES

1–5. See 7:727.
6–7. See T2:1658.
8. WEST, E. M., & LAGOTIC, D. L. The accuracy of adult disabled readers' perceptions of their own reading difficulties. *National Reading Conference Yearbook*, 1979, 161–162.

[310]

Bradfield Classroom Interaction Analysis. Grades kgn–12; 1973; observer recordings of classroom interactions; 3 parts in 1 booklet, which may be used separately or in combination; Robert H. Bradfield and Jane Criner; Academic Therapy Publications.*

a) TEACHER STYLE SCALE. Teacher interaction in 6 categories and 3 modes, plus 3 ratings: warm-cold personality, structured-loose classroom environment, authoritarian-democratic attitude.

b) PUPIL/PUPIL/TEACHER INTERACTION SCALE. Interaction in 6 categories of any 4 children in classroom.

c) TEACHER ATTENTION AND PUPIL BEHAVIOR SCALE. 6 scores (positive teacher attention, negative teacher attention, child's nontask behavior, 3 rate per minute scores) for each of 4 children in classroom.

For additional information and a review by Georgia S. Adams, see 8:508.

[311]
Brazelton Neonatal Assessment Scale. Ages 3 days to 4 weeks; 1973; BNAS; also called *Brazelton Behavioral Assessment Scale*; 47 scores: 27 behavioral items, 20 elicited responses; T. Berry Brazelton and others; published by Spastics International Medical Publications; distributed by William Heinemann Medical Books [England].* (U.S. distributor: J. B. Lippincott Co.)* (U.S. in-print status uncertain; no reply from publisher.)

For additional information, a review by Anita Miller Sostek, and an excerpted review by Stephen Wolkind, see 8:208 (15 references).

REFERENCES

1–15. See 8:208.
16. CHANDLER, L., & ROE, M. D. Behavioral and neurological comparisons of neonates born to mothers of differing social environments. *Child Psychiatry & Human Development*, 1977, 8, 25–30.
17. HOROWITZ, F. D., ASHTON, J., CULP, R., GADDIS, E., LEVIN, S., & REICHMANN, B. The effects of obstetrical medication on the behavior of Israeli newborn infants and some comparisons with Uruguayan and American infants. *Child Development*, 1977, 48, 1607–1623.
18. OSOFSKY, J. D., & O'CONNELL, E. J. Patterning of newborn behavior in an urban population. *Child Development*, 1977, 48, 532–536.
19. SOSTEK, A. M., & ANDERS, T. F. Relationships among the Brazelton Neonatal Scale, Bayley Infant Scales, and early temperament. *Child Development*, 1977, 48, 320–323.
20. ALS, H. Assessing an assessment: Conceptual considerations, methodological issues, and a perspective on the future of the Neonatal Behavioral Assessment Scale. *Monographs of the Society for Research in Child Development*, 1978, 43, 14–28.
21. BONTA, B. W., GAGUARDI, J. V., WILLIAMS, V., & WARSHAW, J. B. Naloxone reversal of mild neuro behavioral depression in normal newborn infants after routine obstetric analgesia. *Journal of Pediatrics*, 1978, 94, 102–105.
22. BRAZELTON, T. B. Introduction: Organization and stability of newborn behavior: A commentary on the Brazelton Neonatal Behavior Assessment Scale. *Monographs of the Society for Research in Child Development*, 1978, 43, 1–13.
23. DE VRIES, M., & SUPER, C. M. Contextual influences on the Neonatal Behavioral Assessment Scale and implications for its cross-cultural use. *Monographs of the Society for Research in Child Development*, 1978, 43, 92–101.
24. FIELD, T. M., HALLOCK, N. F., DEMPSEY, J. R., & SHUMAN, H. H. Mothers' assessments of term and pre-term infants with respiratory distress syndrome. *Child Psychiatry & Human Development*, 1978, 9, 75–85.
25. FIELD, T., HALLOCK, N., TING, G., DEMPSEY, J., DABIRI, C., & SHUMAN, H. H. A first-year follow-up of high-risk infants: Formulating a cumulative risk index. *Child Development*, 1978, 49, 119–131.
26. HOROWITZ, F. D., SULLIVAN, J. W., & LINN, P. Stability and instability in the newborn infant: The quest for elusive threads. *Monographs of the Society for Research in Child Development*, 1978, 43, 29–45.
27. KAYE, K. Discriminating among normal infants by multivariate analysis of Brazelton scores: Lumping and smoothing. *Monographs of the Society for Research in Child Development*, 1978, 43, 60–80.
28. SAMEROFF, A. J. Summary and conclusions: The future of newborn assessment. *Monographs of the Society for Research in Child Development*, 1978, 43, 102–123.
29. SAMEROFF, A. J., KRAFCHUK, E. E., & BAKOW, H. A. Issues in grouping items from the Neonatal Behavioral Assessment Scale. *Monographs of the Society for Research in Child Development*, 1978, 43, 46–59.
30. STANDLEY, K., SOULE, A. B., COPANS, S. A., & KLEIN, R. P. Multidimensional sources of infant temperament. *Genetic Psychology Monographs*, 1978, 98, 203–231.
31. STRAUSS, M. E., & ROURKE, D. L. A multivariate analysis of the Neonatal Behavioral Assessment Scale in several samples. *Monographs of the Society for Research in Child Development*, 1978, 43, 81–91.
32. FIELD, T. M. Visual and cardiac responses to animate and inanimate faces by young term and preterm infants. *Child Development*, 1979, 50, 188–194.
33. BAKEMAN, R., & BROWN, J. V. Early interaction: Consequences for social and mental development at three years. *Child Development*, 1980, 51, 437–447.
34. BROWN, J. V., LaROSSA, M. M., AYLWARD, G. P., DAVIS, D. J., RUTHERFORD, P. K., & BAKEMAN, R. Nursery-based intervention with prematurely born babies and their mothers: Are there effects? *Journal of Pediatrics*, 1980, 97, 487–491.
35. FIELD, T. M., WIDMAYER, S. M., STRINGER, S., & IGNATOFF, E. Teenage, lower-class, black mothers and their preterm infants: An intervention and developmental follow-up. *Child Development*, 1980, 51, 426–436.
36. FRANKEL, D. G., ARBEL, T., & MENDROVSKI, L. Stability and distinctiveness in interaction of mother and neonate. *Psychological Reports*, 1980, 47, 1103–1108.
37. LANGENDOERFER, S., HAVERKAMP, A. D., MURPHY, J., NOWICK, K. D., ORLEANS, M., PACOSA, F., & VAN DOORNINCK, W. Pediatric follow-up of a randomized controlled trial of intrapartum fetal monitoring techniques. *Journal of Pediatrics*, 1980, 97, 103–107.
38. LAVECK, B., HAMMOND, M. A., & LAVECK, G. D. Minor congenital anomalies and behavior in different home environments. *Journal of Pediatrics*, 1980, 96, 940–943.
39. NELSON, N. M., ENKIN, M. W., SAIGAL, S., BENNETT, K., MILNER, R., & SACKETT, D. L. A randomized clinical trial of the Leboyer approach to childbirth. *New England Journal of Medicine*, 1980, 302, 655–660.
40. WATERS, E., VAUGHN, B. E., & EGELAND, B. R. Individual differences in infant–mother attachment relationships at age one: Antecedents in neonatal behavior in an urban, economically disadvantaged sample. *Child Development*, 1980, 51, 208–216.
41. WISE, S., & GROSSMAN, F. K. Adolescent mothers and their infants: Psychological factors in early attachment and interaction. *American Journal of Orthopsychiatry*, 1980, 50, 454–468.
42. ANDERSON, C. J. Enhancing reciprocity between mother and neonate. *Nursing Research*, 1981, 30, 89–93.
43. BOUKYDIS, C. F. Z. Adult perception of infant appearance: A review. *Child Psychiatry & Human Development*, 1981, 11, 241–254.
44. CROCKENBERG, S. B. Infant irritability, mother responsiveness, and social support influences on the security of infant–mother attachment. *Child Development*, 1981, 52, 857–865.
45. MARCUS, J., AUERBACH, J., WILKINSON, L., & BURACK, C. M. Infants at risk for schizophrenia. *Archives of General Psychiatry*, 1981, 38, 703.
46. MURRAY, A. D., DOLBY, R. M., NATION, R. L., & THOMAS, D. B. Effects of epidural anesthesia on newborns and their mothers. *Child Development*, 1981, 52, 71–82.

[312]
Breslich Algebra Survey Test. 1, 2 semesters high school; 1930–31; 7 scores: algebraic concepts, simplifying expressions, solving equations, deriving equations, formulas and graphs, factoring, total; E. R. Breslich; Bobbs-Merrill Co., Inc.*

For additional information and a review by John R. Clark, see 2:1435.

[313]
Brigance Diagnostic Inventory of Basic Skills. Grades kgn–6; 1976; IBS; criterion-referenced; 141 specific-objective tests in 4 areas: readiness, reading (word recognition, oral reading, word analysis, vocabulary), language arts (handwriting, grammar mechanics, spelling, reference skills), mathematics (grade level, numbers, operations, measurement, geometry); (Spanish edition available); Albert Brigance; Curriculum Associates, Inc.*

For additional information, see 8:6.

REFERENCES

1. WARTENBERG, H. Brigance Diagnostic Inventory of Basic Skills. *Reading Teacher*, 1978, 31, 833–834.

[314]
★**Brigance Diagnostic Inventory of Early Development.** Ages 0–7; 1978; IED; criterion-referenced; 98 skills tests in 6 areas: psychomotor (preambulatory motor skills, gross motor skills, fine motor skills), self-help, speech and language (pre-speech, speech and language skills), general knowledge and comprehension, early academic skills (readiness, basic reading skills, manuscript

writing, math); Albert Brigance; Curriculum Associates, Inc.*

[315]
★**Brigance Diagnostic Inventory of Essential Skills.** Grades 4–12; 1981; IES; criterion-referenced; 10 rating scales and 180 specific-objectives; tests in 4 areas: reading (word recognition grade placement, oral reading, reading comprehension, functional word recognition, word analysis), language arts (reference skills, schedules and graphs, writing, forms, spelling), mathematics (math grade placement, numbers, number facts, computations of whole numbers, fractions, decimals, percents, measurement, metrics, math vocabulary), life skills (health and safety, vocational, money and finance, travel and transportation, food and clothing, oral communication and telephone skills); Albert Brigance; Curriculum Associates, Inc.*

[316]
★**Brigance K & 1 Screen for Kindergarten and First Grade.** Grades kgn, 1; 1982; Albert H. Brigance; Curriculum Associates, Inc.*
a) KINDERGARTEN. Grade kgn; 13 scores: personal data response, color recognition, picture vocabulary, visual discrimination, visual-motor skills, gross motor skills, rote counting, identification of body parts, follows verbal directions, numeral comprehension, prints personal data, syntax and fluency, total.
b) FIRST GRADE. Grade 1; 14 scores: personal data response, color recognition, picture vocabulary, visual discrimination, visual-motor skills, draw a person (body image), rote counting, recites alphabet, numeral comprehension, recognition of lower case letters, auditory discrimination, prints personal data, numerals in sequence, total.

[317]
Bristol Achievement Tests. Ages 8–0 to 9–11, 9–0 to 10–11, 10–0 to 11–11, 11–0 to 12–11, 12–0 to 13–11; 1969; BAT; 3 tests available as separates; NFER-Nelson Publishing Co. [England].*
a) ENGLISH LANGUAGE. 6 scores: word meaning, paragraph meaning, sentence organisation, organisation of ideas, spelling and punctuation, total; Alan Brimer and Herbert Gross.
b) MATHEMATICS. 6 scores: number, reasoning, space, measurement, arithmetic laws and processes, total; Alan Brimer.
c) STUDY SKILLS. 6 scores: properties, structures, processes, explanations, interpretations, total; Alan Brimer, Margaret Fidler, Wynne Harlen, and John Taylor.

For additional information and reviews by G. A. V. Morgan and A. E. G. Pilliner, see 7:4. For a review of the English language subtest, see 7:185; the mathematics subtest, see 7:453; and the study skills subtest, see 7:776.

[318]
Bristol Achievement Tests: English Language. Ages 8–0 to 9–11, 9–0 to 10–11, 10–0 to 11–11, 11–0 to 12–11, 12–0 to 13–11; 1969; 6 scores: word meaning, paragraph meaning, sentence organisation, organisation of ideas, spelling and punctuation, total; Alan Brimer and Herbert Gross; NFER-Nelson Publishing Co. [England].*

For additional information and a review by Ralph D. Dutch, see 7:185. For reviews of the complete battery, see 7:4 (2 reviews).

[319]
Bristol Achievement Tests: Mathematics. Ages 8–9, 9–10, 10–11, 11–12, 12–13; 1969; 6 scores: number, reasoning, space, measurement, arithmetic laws and processes, total; Alan Brimer; NFER-Nelson Publishing Co. [England].*

For additional information and a review by Kenneth Lovell, see 7:453. For a review of the complete battery, see 7:4.

[320]
Bristol Achievement Tests: Study Skills. Ages 8–9, 9–10, 10–11, 11–12, 12–13; 1969; 6 scores: properties, structures, processes, explanations, interpretations, total; Alan Brimer, Margaret Fidler, Wynne Harlen, and John Taylor; NFER-Nelson Publishing Co. [England].*

For additional information and a review by Elizabeth J. Goodacre, see 7:776. For reviews of the complete battery, see 7:4 (2 reviews).

[321]
Bristol Social Adjustment Guides. Ages 5–15; 1956–66; BSAG; ratings by teachers and others; adjustment score and an optional delinquency prediction score for boys; 3 editions; D. H. Stott and E. G. Sykes (*a*, *b*); Hodder & Stoughton Educational [England].*
a) THE CHILD IN SCHOOL. 1956–66. (American edition: Ages 5–16; 1956–67; EdITS/Educational and Industrial Testing Service.*)
b) THE CHILD IN RESIDENTIAL CARE. 1956–66.
c) THE CHILD IN THE FAMILY. 1956–66.
d) DELINQUENCY PREDICTION INSTRUMENT. Boys ages 5–15; 1961–66; consists of a delinquency prediction key to be used with the diagnostic form for *The Child in School* scale and a teacher's questionnaire for preliminary identification of pupils to be rated on the scale.

See T2:1112 (17 references) and P:20 (6 references); for reviews by G. A. V. Morgan and M. L. Kellmer Pringle and excerpted reviews by R. G. Andry, Mary Engel, A. W. Heim, Read D. Tuddenham, and P. E. Vernon, see 6:68 (13 references).

REFERENCES

1–13. See 6:68.
14–19. See P:20.
20–36. See T2:1112.
37. GHODSIAN, M. Children's behaviour and the BSAG: Some theoretical and statistical considerations. *British Journal of Social & Clinical Psychology*, 1977, 16, 23–28.
38. STOTT, D. H., & WILSON, D. M. The adult criminal as juvenile. *British Journal of Criminology*, 1977, 17, 47–57.
39. HALE, R. L. A factor analytic study of the Bristol Social Adjustment Guides in a rural school population. *Psychological Reports*, 1978, 42, 215–218.
40. Stott, D. H. Association of motor impairment with various types of behavior disturbance. *Journal of Learning Disabilities*, 1978, 11, 147–154.
41. TEW, B. The 'cocktail party syndrome' in children with hydrocephalus and spina bifida. *British Journal of Disorders of Communication*, 1979, 14, 89–101.
42. WHITEHEAD, L. Sex differences in children's responses to family stress: A re–evaluation. *Journal of Child Psychology & Psychiatry & Allied Disciplines*, 1979, 20, 247–254.
43. GHODSIAN, M., FOGELMAN, K., LAMBEET, L., & TIBBENHAM, A. Changes in behaviour ratings of a national sample of children. *British Journal of Social & Clinical Psychology*, 1980, 19, 247–256.

[322] ★The British Ability Scales

44. HALE, R. L. Cluster analysis in school psychology: An example. *Journal of School Psychology*, 1981, 19, 51–56.
45. HALE, R. L., & ZUCKERMAN, C. Application of confirmatory factor analysis to verify the construct validity of the Behavior Problem Checklist and the Bristol Social Adjustment Guides. *Educational & Psychological Measurement*, 1981, 41, 843–850.

[322]

★**The British Ability Scales.** Ages 2.5–8, 5–17; 1977–79; BAS; each scale may be used independently; 24 scales; Colin D. Elliott, David J. Murray, and Lea S. Pearson; NFER-Nelson Publishing Co. [England].*
a) SPEED OF INFORMATION PROCESSING. Ages 8–17.
b) MATRICES. Ages 5–17.
c) FORMAL OPERATIONAL THINKING. Ages 8–17.
d) SIMILARITIES. Ages 5–17.
e) SOCIAL REASONING. Ages 5–17.
f) BLOCK DESIGN-LEVEL. Ages 4–17.
g) BLOCK DESIGN-POWER. Ages 4–17.
h) ROTATION OF LETTER-LIKE FORMS. Ages 8–14.
i) VISUALIZATION OF CUBES. Ages 8–17.
j) COPYING. Ages 4–8.
k) MATCHING LETTER-LIKE FORMS. Ages 5–9.
l) VERBAL-TACTILE MATCHING. Ages 2.5–8.
m) RECALL OF DESIGNS. Ages 5–17.
n) IMMEDIATE VISUAL RECALL. Ages 5–17.
o) DELAYED VISUAL RECALL. Ages 5–17.
p) RECALL OF DIGITS. Ages 2.5–17.
q) VISUAL RECOGNITION. Ages 2.5–8.
r) NAMING VOCABULARY. Ages 2.5–8.
s) WORD READING. Ages 5–14.
t) VERBAL COMPREHENSION. Ages 2.5–8.
u) WORD DEFINITIONS. Ages 5–17.
v) VERBAL FLUENCY. Ages 4–17.
w) BASIC ARITHMETIC. Ages 5–14.
x) EARLY NUMBER SKILLS. Ages 2.5–8.

[323]

Bruce Vocabulary Inventory. Business and industry; 1959–67; Martin M. Bruce; Martin M. Bruce, Ph.D., Publishers.*

For additional information and reviews by Fred H. Borgen and Robert Fitzpatrick, see 7:231.

[324]

*****Bruininks-Oseretsky Test of Motor Proficiency.** Ages 4–5 to 14–5; 1978; revised edition of *The Oseretsky Tests of Motor Proficiency*; 3 scores: gross motor composite, fine motor composite, battery composite; Robert H. Bruininks; American Guidance Service.*

See T2:1898 (15 references) for references of an earlier edition; for a review by Anna Espenschade, see 4:650 (10 references); for an excerpted review, see 3:472 (6 references).

REFERENCES
1–6. See 3:472.
7–16. See 4:650.
17–31. See T2:1898.
32. HACKER, B. Bruininks–Oseretsky Test of Motor Proficiency. *American Journal of Occupational Therapy*, 1979, 33, 120.
33. BEITEL, P. A., & MEAD, B. J. Bruininks–Oseretsky Test of Motor Proficiency: A viable measure for 3- to 5-year old children. *Perceptual & Motor Skills*, 1980, 51, 919–923.
34. CANTOR, S., TREVENEN, C., POSTUMA, R., DUECK, R., & FJELDSTED, B. Is childhood schizophrenia a cholinergic disease. *Archives of General Psychiatry*, 1980, 37, 658–667.

[325]

Buckingham Extension of the Ayres Spelling Scale. Grades 2–9; [1918?]; B. R. Buckingham; Bobbs-Merrill Co., Inc.*

See T2:146 (9 references).

[326]

Buffalo Reading Test for Speed and Comprehension. Grades 9–16; 1933–41; 3 scores: speed, comprehension, total; Mazie Earle Wagner and Daniel S. P. Schubert (1965 manual); Mazie Earle Wagner.*

See T2:1534 (1 reference); for reviews by Holland Roberts and William W. Turnbull, see 3:477.

[327]

Burks' Behavior Rating Scale for Organic Brain Dysfunction. Grades kgn–6; 1968; BBRS; ratings by teachers; 4 scores: vegetative-autonomic, perceptual-discriminative, social-emotional, total; Harold F. Burks; Arden Press.* (In-print status uncertain; no reply from publisher.)

For additional information and reviews by Robert M. Allen and James C. Reed, see 8:510 (1 reference).

[328]

Burks' Behavior Rating Scales. Preschool and kgn, grades 1–8; 1968–69; BBRS; experimental; ratings of problem children by teachers or parents in 18 or 20 areas: self blame, anxiety, withdrawal, dependency, ego strength, physical strength, coordination, intellectuality, academics (upper level), attention, impulse control, reality contact, sense of identity, suffering, anger control, sense of persecution, sexuality (upper level), aggressiveness, resistance, social conformity; Harold F. Burks; Arden Press.* (In-print status uncertain; no reply from publisher.)

See T2:1115 (1 reference) and 7:46 (2 references).

REFERENCES
1–2. See 7:46.
3. See T2:1115.
4. HARRIS, W. J., DRUMMOND, R. J., SCHULTZ, E. W., & KING, D. R. The factor structure of three teacher rating scales and a self-report inventory of children's source traits. *Journal of Learning Disabilities*, 1978, 11, 583–585.

[329]

★**Burt Word Reading Test, New Zealand Revision.** Ages 6–0 to 12–11 years; 1981; revision and New Zealand standardization of *The Burt Word Reading Test*; provides an estimate of word recognition skills for 110 words; original test by Cyril Burt; 1938 revision by P. E. Vernon; 1974 revision by Scottish Council for Research in Education; current revision by Alison Gilmore, Cedric Croft, and Neil Reid; New Zealand Council for Educational Research [New Zealand].*

[330]

The Burt Word Reading Test, 1974 Revision. Ages 5 and over; 1921–76; BWRT; revision of *The Burt (Rearranged) Word Reading Test*; pronunciation; original test by Cyril Burt; earlier revision by P. E. Vernon; current revision by Scottish Council for Research in Education; Hodder & Stoughton Educational [England].*

For additional information, see 8:783 (5 references); see also T2:1680 (7 references) and 7:738 (3 references).

REFERENCES

1-3. See 7:738.
4-10. See T2:1680.
11-15. See 8:783.
16. EISER, C., & LANSDOWN, R. Retrospective study of intellectual development in children treated for acute lymphoblastic leukaemia. *Archives of Diseases in Childhood,* 1977, 52, 525-529.
17. EISER, C. Intellectual abilities among survivors of childhood leukaemia as a function of CNS irradiation. *Archives of Diseases in Childhood,* 1978, 53, 391-395.
18. GUPTA, R., CECI, S. J., & SLATER, A. M. Visual discrimination in good and poor readers. *Journal of Special Education,* 1978, 12, 409-416.
19. EISER, C. Effects of chronic illness on intellectual development. *Archives of Diseases in Childhood,* 1980, 55, 766-770.

[331]
Business English Test: The Dailey Vocational Tests. Grades 8-12 and adults; 1964-65; BET; John T. Dailey and Kenneth B. Hoyt (manual); Riverside Publishing Co.*

For additional information, see 7:976c. For reviews of the complete battery, see 7:976 (2 reviews, 2 excerpts).

[332]
Business Fundamentals and General Information Test: National Business Entrance Tests. Grades 11-16 and adults; 1938-72; National Business Education Association.* (In-print status uncertain; no reply from publisher.)

For additional information and a review by Dean R. Malsbary, see 8:323 (1 reference); for reviews by Vera M. Amerson and C. C. Upshall of an earlier form, see 3:369. For reviews of the complete battery, see 6:33 (1 review), 5:515 (3 reviews), and 3:396 (1 review).

REFERENCES

1. See 8:323.
2. HOPKINS, C. R., & MCLEAN, G. N. Comparative effectiveness of three capstone office education courses using in-class measures. *Delta Pi Epsilon Journal,* 1978, 20, 12-22.

[333]
Business Judgment Test, Revised. Adults; 1953-69; BJT; Martin M. Bruce; Martin M. Bruce, Ph.D., Publishers.*

See T2:2275 (1 reference); for a review by Jerome E. Doppelt, and an excerpted review by Kenneth D. Orton, see 7:1059 (1 reference); see also 6:1101 (4 references); for a review by Edward B. Greene, see 5:893.

[334]
Business Test. Clerical workers; 1952-71; intelligence; Edward N. Hay; E. F. Wonderlic & Associates, Inc.*

For additional information and reviews by Louis C. Nanassy and James H. Ricks, Jr., see 5:311.

[335]
★**Buswell-John Diagnostic Test for Fundamental Processes in Arithmetic.** Pupils doing unsatisfactory work in arithmetic; no date on test materials; to discover how children work through arithmetic problems; no scores; G. T. Buswell and Lenore John; Bobbs-Merrill Co., Inc.*

[336]
The Butler Life Science Concept Test. Grades 1-6; 1965-69; LSCT; D. F. Butler; Psychometric Affiliates.*

For additional information and a review by Victor H. Noll, see 7:786.

[337]
Buttons: A Projective Test for Pre-Adolescent and Adolescent Boys and Girls. Grades 7-9; 1963; maladjustment; 3 scores: initial, content, total; Esther P. Rothman and Pearl H. Berkowitz; Western Psychological Services.*

For additional information and a review by Willard E. Reitz, see 7:162.

[338]
The Bzoch-League Receptive-Expressive Emergent Language Scale: For the Measurement of Language Skills in Infancy. Birth to age 3; 1970-71; also called *REEL Scale;* manual entitled *Assessing Language Skills in Infancy;* 3 scores: receptive, expressive, combined; Kenneth R. Bzoch and Richard League; Anhinga Press.*

For additional information and excerpted reviews by Alex Bannatyne, Dale L. Johnson, and Barton B. Proger, see 8:956 (5 references); see also T2:2067 (2 references).

REFERENCES

1-2. See T2:2067.
3-7. See 8:956.
8. HASLAM, R. H. A., ALLEN, J. R., DORSEN, M. M., KANOFSKY, D. L., MELLITS, E. D., & NORRIS, D. A. The sequelae of group B B-hemolytic streptococcal meningitis in early infancy. *American Journal of Diseases of Children,* 1977, 131, 845-849.
9. FOWLER, W., & SWENSON, A. The influence of early language stimulation on development: Four studies. *Genetic Psychology Monographs,* 1979, 100, 73-109.
10. TARTAGLIA, J. F., EHRLICH, C. H., BUTTERFIELD, P., & KOOPS, B. Identification of specific language disability in hyaline membrane disease babies. *ASHA,* 1979, 21, 688. (Abstract)
11. MELNICK, C. R., MICHALS, K. K., & MATALON, R. Linguistic development of children with phenylketonuria and normal intelligence. *Journal of Pediatrics,* 1981, 98, 269-272.

[339]
★**C-PAC: Clinical Probes of Articulation Consistency.** Ages 5 and over; 1981; C-PAC; 2 scores for consonant and vocalic R probes, vowel and diphthong probes have only a single word and sentence score; Wayne Secord and Roxie M. Ball (storytelling manual); Charles E. Merrill Publishing Co.*

[340]
C-R Opinionaire. Grades 11-16 and adults; 1935-46, c1935; CRO; conservatism-radicalism; Theodore F. Lentz; Character Research Association.*

See T2:1116 (7 references) and P:21 (3 references); for a review by George W. Hartmann, see 4:39 (5 references); for a review by Goodwin Watson, see 2:1212 (5 references); for a review by H. H. Remmers, see 1:899.

[341]
★**CAAP Scale.** Children and adolescents seen in mental health centers; 1977-78; also called *Child and Adolescent Adjustment Profile;* pre- and posttreatment ratings by

significant other; 5 scores: peer relations, dependency, hostility, productivity, withdrawal; Robert B. Ellsworth and Shanae L. Ellsworth (scale and manual); Consulting Psychologists Press, Inc.*

[342]
The CAHPER Fitness-Performance II Test. Ages 7–17, 18–44; 1966–80; 2 levels; Canadian Association for Health, Physical Education and Recreation [Canada].*

a) CHILDREN. Ages 7–17; 1966; 6 scores: speed sit up, standing broad jump, shuttle run, flexed arm hang, 50 yard run, 300 yard run.

b) ADULTS. Ages 18–44; 1971; 5 scores: speed sit up, standing broad jump, adipose tissue mensuration, grip strength, flexibility.

See T2:919 (2 references) and 7:599 (1 reference).

REFERENCES

1. See 7:599.
2–3. See T2:919.
4. SHEPHARED, R. J., LAVALLEE, H., JEGUIER, J. C., LaBARRE, R., VOLLE, M., & RAJIC, M. Season of birth and variations in stature, body mass, and performance. *Human Biology*, 1979, 51, 299–316.

[343]
Cain-Levine Social Competency Scale. Mentally retarded children age 5–13; 1963; CLSCS; rating scale based upon information obtained from parents; 5 scores: self-help, initiative, social skills, communication, total; Leo F. Cain, Samuel Levine, and Freeman F. Elzey; Consulting Psychologists Press, Inc.*

For additional information and a review by Marvin Rosen, see 8:512 (2 references); see also T2:1117 (5 references) and P:23 (3 references); for a review by Marshall S. Hiskey, see 6:69.

REFERENCES

1–3. See P:23.
4–8. See T2:1117.
9–10. See 8:512.
11. MEALOR, D. J., & RICHMOND, B. O. Adaptive behavior: Teachers and parents disagree. *Exceptional Children*, 1980, 46, 386–389.

[344]
***California Achievement Tests, Forms C and D.** Grades kgn–0 to kgn–9, kgn–6 to 1–9, 1–6 to 2–9, 2–6 to 3–9, 3–6 to 4–9, 4–6 to 5–9, 5–6 to 6–9, 6–6 to 7–9, 7–6 to 9–9, 9–6 to 12–9; 1957–78; CAT/C & D; 10 levels; CTB/McGraw-Hill.*

a) LEVEL 10. Grade kgn–0 to kgn–9; 10 scores: listening for information, letter forms, letter names, letter sounds, visual discrimination, sound matching, total, mathematics, alphabet skills, visual and auditory discrimination.

b) LEVEL 11. Grades kgn–6 to 1–9; 9 scores: phonic analysis, reading vocabulary, reading comprehension, total, language expression, mathematics computation, mathematics concepts and applications, total mathematics, total.

c) LEVEL 12. Grades 1–6 to 2–9; 13 scores: phonic analysis, structural analysis, reading vocabulary, reading comprehension, total, spelling, language mechanics, language expression, total language, mathematics computation, mathematics concepts and applications, total mathematics, total.

d) LEVEL 13. Grades 2–6 to 3–9; 13 scores: same as for *c*.

e) LEVEL 14. Grades 3–6 to 4–9; 12 scores: reading vocabulary, reading comprehension, total reading, spelling, language mechanics, language expression, total language, mathematics computation, mathematics concepts and applications, total mathematics, total, reference skills.

f) LEVEL 15. Grades 4–6 to 5–9; 12 scores: same as for *e*.
g) LEVEL 16. Grades 5–6 to 6–9; 12 scores: same as for *e*.
h) LEVEL 17. Grades 6–6 to 7–9; 12 scores: same as for *e*.
i) LEVEL 18. Grades 7–6 to 9–9; 12 scores: same as for *e*.
j) LEVEL 19. Grades 9–6 to 12–9; 12 scores: same as for *e*.

For additional information and reviews by Miriam M. Bryan and Frank Womer of the 1970 edition, see 8:10 (33 references); see also T2:7 (28 references) and 7:5 (32 references); for reviews by Jack C. Merwin and Robert D. North of the 1957 edition, see 6:3 (19 references); for a review by Charles O. Neidt, see 5:2 (10 references); for reviews by Warren G. Findley, Alvin W. Schindler, and J. Harlan Shores of the 1950 edition, see 4:2 (8 references); for a review by Paul A. Witty of the 1943 edition, see 3:15 (3 references); for reviews by C. W. Odell and Hugh B. Wood of an earlier edition, see 2:1193 (1 reference); for a review by D. Welty Lefever and an excerpted review by E. L. Abell, see 1:876. For reviews of subtests, see 8:45 (2 reviews), 8:257 (1 review), 8:719 (2 reviews), 6:251 (1 review), 5:177 (2 reviews), 5:468 (1 review), 4:151 (2 reviews), 4:411 (1 review), 4:530 (2 reviews, 1 excerpt), 2:1292 (2 reviews), 2:1459 (2 reviews), 2:1563 (1 review), 1:893 (1 review), and 1:1110 (2 reviews).

REFERENCES

1. See 2:1193.
2–4. See 3:15.
5–12. See 4:2.
13–22. See 5:2.
23–41. See 6:3.
42–73. See 7:5.
74–101. See T2:7.
102–134. See 8:10.
135. BALDWIN, A. Y. Tests can underpredict: A case study. *Phi Delta Kappan*, 1977, 58, 620–621.
136. CALLAWAY, A. B., MASON, G. E., & McDANIEL, H. Coordination of instruction in language arts. *Southern Journal of Educational Research*, 1977, 11, 81–90.
137. DIAMOND, J. J., AYRER, J., FISHMAN, R., & GREEN, P. Are inner city children test-wise? *Journal of Educational Measurement*, 1977, 14, 39–45.
138. HALL, G. E., & LOUCKS, S. F. A developmental model for determining whether the treatment is actually implemented. *American Educational Research Journal*, 1977, 14, 263–276.
139. HANEY, R., MICHAEL, W. B., & MARTOIS, J. The prediction of success of three ethnic samples on a state board certification examination for nurses from performance on academic course variables and on standardized achievement and study skills measures. *Educational & Psychological Measurement*, 1977, 37, 949–964.
140. KENT, R. N., & O'LEARY, K. D. Treatment of conduct problem children: BA and/or PhD therapists. *Behavior Therapy*, 1977, 8, 653–658.
141. KIESLING, H. Productivity of instructional time by mode of instruction for students at varying levels of reading skill. *Reading Research Quarterly*, 1977–78, 13, 554–582.
142. O'LEARY, S. G., & SCHNEIDER, M. R. Special class placement for conduct problem children. *Exceptional Children*, 1977, 44, 24–30.
143. O'REILLY, R. P., & STREETER, R. E. Report on the development and validation of a system for measuring literal comprehension in a multiple-choice cloze format: Preliminary factor analytic results. *Journal of Reading Behavior*, 1977, 9, 45–69.
144. RENTZ, R. R., & BASHAW, W. L. The National Reference Scale for Reading: An application of the Rasch model. *Journal of Educational Measurement*, 1977, 14, 161–179.
145. SLINDE, J. A., & LINN, R. L. Vertically equated tests: Fact or phantom? *Journal of Educational Measurement*, 1977, 14, 23–32.
146. SOLOMON, D., & KENDALL, A. J. Dimension of children's classroom behavior, as perceived by teachers. *American Educational Research Journal*, 1977, 14, 411–421.
147. STEWART, D. W., & MORRIS, L. Intelligence and academic achievement in a clinical adolescent population. *Psychology in the Schools*, 1977, 14, 513–518.

148. TOULIATOS, J., LINDHOLM, B. W., & RICH, A. Interaction of race with other variables on achievement in school. *Psychology in the Schools*, 1977, 14, 360–363.
149. WALLBROWN, J. D., WALLBROWN, F. H., & ENGIN, A. W. The prediction of first grade achievement with behavioral ratings taken during kindergarten. *Journal of Experimental Education*, 1977, 45, 16–20.
150. CARPENTER, D., & CARPENTER, S. The concurrent validity of the Larsen–Hammill Test of Written Spelling in relation to the California Achievement Test. *Educational & Psychological Measurement*, 1978, 38, 1201–1205.
151. COULSON, J. E. National evaluation of the Emergency School Aid Act (ESAA): A review of methodological issues. *Journal of Educational Statistics*, 1978, 3, 1–60.
152. FITZGERALD, T. P., & FITZGERALD, E. F. A cross cultural study of three measures of comprehension at the primary and intermediate levels. *Educational Research Quarterly*, 1978, 3, 84–92.
153. FLYNN, T. M., & FLYNN, L. A. Evaluation of the predictive ability of five screening measures administered during kindergarten. *Journal of Experimental Education*, 1978, 46, 65–70.
154. JENSEN, L. R. Diagnosis and evaluation of creativity, research and thinking skills of academically talented elementary students. *Gifted Child Quarterly*, 1978, 22, 98–110.
155. LLOYD, D. N. Prediction of school failure from third grade data. *Educational & Psychological Measurement*, 1978, 38, 1193–1200.
156. OAKLAND, T. Predictive validity of readiness tests for middle and lower socioeconomic status Anglo, Black, and Mexican American children. *Journal of Educational Psychology*, 1978, 70, 574–582.
157. RYAN, F. L. Selected non-cognitive variables and student achievement in a high-level questioning environment. *Journal of Experimental Education*, 1978, 47, 46–51.
158. SHASBY, G., & KINGSLEY, R. F. A study of behavior and body type in troubled youth. *Journal of School Health*, 1978, 48, 103–107.
159. STEWART, J. A new California Achievement Test (CAT) battery from CTB/McGraw-Hill. *Reading Teacher*, 1978, 31, 717.
160. TOULIATOS, J., LINDHOLM, B. W., & RICH, A. Influence of family background on scholastic achievement. *Journal of Experimental Education*, 1978, 46, 22–27.
161. WELLISCH, J. B., MACQUEEN, A. H., CARRIERE, R. A., & DUCK, G. A. School management and organization in successful schools. *Sociology of Education*, 1978, 51, 211–226.
162. WILLIAMS, F., & OAKLAND, T. A three-year auditory perception program for low–SES minority children. *Journal of Special Education*, 1978, 12, 331–344.
163. YEN, W. M. Measuring individual differences with an information-processing model. *Journal of Educational Psychology*, 1978, 70, 72–86.
164. ZEICHNER, K. M. Group membership in the elementary school classroom. *Journal of Educational Psychology*, 1978, 70, 554–564.
165. ADELMAN, H., TAYLOR, L., FULLER, W., & NELSON, P. Discrepancies among student, parent, and teacher ratings of the severity of a student's problems. *American Educational Research Journal*, 1979, 16, 38–41.
166. BECK, F. W., & GUEDRY, P. Reading phase of academic skills enhancement programs. *Journal of College Student Personnel*, 1979, 20, 276.
167. EMMER, E. T., EVERTSON, C. M., & BROPHY, J. E. Stability of teacher effects in junior high classrooms. *American Educational Research Journal*, 1979, 16, 71–75.
168. GAENSBAUER, T. J., & LAZERWITZ, J. L. Classification of military offenders. *Crime & Delinquency*, 1979, 25, 42–54.
169. HARRISON, B. T., & RAYBURN, W. G. Open admissions does not kill colleges. *Peabody Journal of Education*, 1979, 56, 144–153.
170. MACY, D. J., BAKER, J. A., & KOSINSKI, S. C. An empirical study of the Myklebust Learning Quotient. *Journal of Learning Disabilities*, 1979, 12, 93–96.
171. NUTTING, P. A., PRICE, T. B., & BATY, M. L. Non-health professionals and the school-age child: Early intervention for behavioral problems. *Journal of School Health*, 1979, 49, 73–78.
172. OLGUIN, L., & MICHAEL, W. B. The development and preliminary validation of the Olguin Diagnostic Test of Auditory Perception for Spanish language-oriented children. *Educational & Psychological Measurement*, 1979, 39, 985–999.
173. OLGUIN, L., & MICHAEL, W. B. The factorial validity of the Olguin Diagnostic Test of Auditory Perception for Spanish language-oriented children. *Educational & Psychological Measurement*, 1979, 39, 1005–1010.
174. SLINDE, J. A., & LINN, R. L. The Rasch model, objective measurement, equating, and robustness. *Applied Psychological Measurement*, 1979, 3, 437–452.
175. WALKER, L. Newfoundland dialect interference in fourth grade spelling. *Alberta Journal of Educational Research*, 1979, 25, 221–233.
176. WEINER, M., & ZIBRIN, M. Dissimilarities in grade-equivalent scores on different standardized tests of achievement: A threat to criterion-related validity. *Educational & Psychological Measurement*, 1979, 39, 923–928.
177. ALHEIDT, P. The effect of reading ability on Rorschach performance. *Journal of Personality Assessment*, 1980, 44, 3–10.
178. BRIDGEMAN, B. Generality of a 'fast' or 'slow' test-taking style across a variety of cognitive tasks. *Journal of Educational Measurement*, 1980, 17, 211–217.
179. CUMMINGS, J. A., & NELSON, R. B. Basic concepts in the oral directions of group achievement tests. *Journal of Educational Research*, 1980, 73, 259–261.
180. DIAMOND, E. E. The AMEG commission report on sex bias in achievement testing. *Measurement & Evaluation in Guidance*, 1980, 13, 135–147.
181. EVERTSON, C. M., ANDERSON, C. W., ANDERSON, L. M., & BROPHY, J. E. Relationships between classroom behaviors and student outcomes in junior high mathematics and English classes. *American Educational Research Journal*, 1980, 17, 43–60.
182. EVERTSON, C. M., EMMER, E. T., & BROPHY, J. T. Predictors of effective teaching in junior high mathematics classrooms. *Journal for Research in Mathematics Education*, 1980, 11, 167–178.
183. IWANICKI, E. F. A new generation of standardized achievement test batteries: A profile of their major features. *Journal of Educational Measurement*, 1980, 17, 155–162.
184. KNIFONG, J. D. Computational requirements of standardized word problem tests. *Journal for Research in Mathematics Education*, 1980, 11, 3–9.
185. MORGAN, M. Television viewing and reading: Does more equal better? *Journal of Communication*, 1980, 30, 159–165.
186. OAKLAND, T. An evaluation of the ABIC, pluralistic norms, and estimated learning potential. *Journal of School Psychology*, 1980, 18, 3–11.
187. SANDOVAL, J. Reliability and concurrent validity of Light's Retention Scale. *Psychology in the Schools*, 1980, 17, 442–445.
188. YEN, W. M. The extent, causes and importance of context effects on item parameters for two latent trait models. *Journal of Educational Measurement*, 1980, 17, 297–311.
189. HALPIN, G., HALPIN, G., & SCHAER, B. B. Relative effectiveness of the California Achievement Tests in comparison with the ACT Assessment, College Board Scholastic Aptitude Test, and high school grade point average in predicting college grade point average. *Educational & Psychological Measurement*, 1981, 41, 821–827.
190. NYBERG, V. R., & BLACKMORE, D. E. A longitudinal study of grade III achievement in Edmonton public schools. *Alberta Journal of Educational Research*, 1981, 27, 154–159.
191. PARIS, S. G., & MYERS, M., II. Comprehension monitoring, memory, and study strategies of good and poor readers. *Journal of Reading Behavior*, 1981, 13, 5–22.
192. PELLEGRINI, A. D., LONG, J. V., & HORWITZ, S. H. An empirical investigation of two variance estimation procedures for use with criterion-referenced tests. *Psychology in the Schools*, 1981, 18, 93–98.

[345]
*California Achievement Tests: Mathematics, Form C.** Grades 3–6 to 4–9, 4–6 to 5–9, 5–6 to 6–9, 6–6 to 7–9, 7–6 to 9–9, 9–6 to 12–9; 1973–80; 3 scores: computation, concepts and applications, total; 9 levels; CTB/McGraw-Hill.* For the complete battery entry, see 344.

For additional information and a review by E. G. Begle of the 1970 edition, see 8:257 (8 references); see also T2:603 (12 references) and 7:455 (25 references); for a review by Robert D. North of the 1957 edition, see 5:468; for a review by Robert L. Burch of an earlier edition of the tests for grades 1–9, see 4:411; for reviews by C. L. Thiele and Harry Grove Wheat, see 2:1459; for a review by William A. Brownell, see 1:893. For reviews of an earlier edition of the complete battery, see 8:10 (2 reviews), 6:3 (2 reviews), 5:2 (1 review), 4:2 (3 reviews), 3:15 (1 review), 2:1193 (2 reviews), and 1:876 (1 review, 1 excerpt).

REFERENCES

1–25. See 7:455.
26–37. See T2:603.
38–45. See 8:257.
46. OAKLAND, T., & FEIGENBAUM, D. Multiple sources of test bias on the WISC-R and Bender–Gestalt Test. *Journal of Consulting & Clinical Psychology*, 1979, 47, 968–974.

[346]
*California Achievement Tests: Reading, Forms C and D.** Grades 3–6 to 4–9, 4–6 to 5–9, 5–6 to 6–9, 6–6 to 7–9, 7–6 to 9–9, 9–6 to 12–9; 1973–80; 3 scores:

[347] California Achievement Tests: Spelling and Reference Skills, Form C

vocabulary, comprehension, total; 6 levels; CTB/-McGraw-Hill.* For the complete battery entry, see 344.

For additional information and reviews by John W. Lombard and Kenneth J. Smith of the 1970 edition, see 8:719 (26 references); see also T2:1536 (27 references), 7:683 (29 references), 6:784 (13 references) and 5:622 (5 references); for reviews by John C. Flanagan and James R. Hobson and an excerpted review by Laurance F. Shaffer of the 1950 edition, see 4:530; for a review by Frederick B. Davis, see 2:1563; for reviews by Ivan A. Booker and Joseph C. Dewey, see 1:1110. For reviews of an earlier edition of the complete battery, see 8:10 (2 reviews), 6:3 (2 reviews), 5:2 (1 review), 4:2 (3 reviews), 3:15 (1 review), 2:1193 (2 reviews), and 1:876 (1 review, 1 excerpt).

REFERENCES

1–5. See 5:622.
6–18. See 6:784.
19–47. See 7:683.
48–74. See T2:1536.
75–100. See 8:719.
101. HUSHAK, L. J. The role of schools in reducing the variance of cognitive skills. *Journal of Educational Research*, 1977, 70, 115–122.
102. MEDWAY, F. J., & BARON, R. M. Locus of control and tutor's instructional style as determinants of cross-age tutoring effectiveness. *Contemporary Educational Psychology*, 1977, 2, 298–310.
103. SHAFFER, G. L. An investigation of the relationships of selected components of readability and comprehension at the secondary school level. *National Reading Conference Yearbook*, 1977, 244–252.
104. WALTER, G. G. Relationship of word knowledge to word frequency in young adult deaf students. *Journal of Communication Disorders*, 1978, 11, 137–148.
105. OAKLAND, T., & FEIGENBAUM, D. Multiple sources of test bias on the WISC–R and Bender-Gestalt Test. *Journal of Consulting & Clinical Psychology*, 1979, 47, 968–974.
106. BRAVERMAN, B. B., EGELSTON-DODD, J., HERTZOG, M., QUINSLAND, L., & AUSTIN, A. The effect of training in the use of diacritical markings on the learning of medical terminology by young hearing-impaired adults. *Volta Review*, 1980, 82, 468–475.
107. SCHELL, L. M. California Achievement Tests: Reading (CAT, Forms C and D). *Journal of Reading*, 1980, 23, 624–628.

[347]
★California Achievement Tests: Spelling and Reference Skills, Form C. Grades 3–6 to 4–9, 4–6 to 5–9, 5–6 to 6–9, 6–6 to 7–9, 7–6 to 9–9, 9–6 to 12–9; 1973–80; 6 levels; CTB/McGraw-Hill. For the complete battery entry, see 344.

For additional information and reviews of the 1970 complete battery edition, see 8:10 (2 reviews).

[348]
★The California Child Q-Set. 1980; CCQ; for an upward extension see *The California Q-Set*; Q-sort ratings of children by teachers and counselors in 9 categories, ranging from extremely uncharacteristic to extremely characteristic; Jeanne Block and Jack Block; Consulting Psychologists Press, Inc.*

REFERENCES

1. BUS, D. M., BLOCK, J. H., & BLOCK, J. Preschool activity level: Personality correlates and developmental implications. *Child Development*, 1980, 51, 401–408.
2. BLOCK, J. H., BLOCK, J., & MORRISON, A. Parental agreement–disagreement on child-rearing orientations and gender-related personality correlates in children. *Child Development*, 1981, 52, 965–974.

[349]
The California Life Goals Evaluation Schedules. Ages 15 and over; 1966–69; CLGES; 10 scores: esteem, profit, fame, power, leadership, security, social service, interesting experiences, self-expression, independence; Milton E. Hahn; Western Psychological Services.*

See T2:1118 (2 references); for a review by Robert W. Lundin, see 7:47 (3 references).

REFERENCES

1–3. See 7:47.
4–5. See T2:1118.
6. MLOTT, S. R., & LIRA, F. T. Dogmatism, locus of control, and life goals in stable and unstable marriages. *Journal of Clinical Psychology*, 1977, 33, 142–146.
7. BAKER, W. G., III. Changes in life goals as related to success in a nursing leadership role. *Nursing Research*, 1979, 28, 234–236.

[350]
California Marriage Readiness Evaluation. Premarital counselees; 1965; CMRE; 12 scores: personality (character, emotional maturity, marriage readiness, total), preparation for marriage (family experiences, dealing with money, planning ability, total), interpersonal compatibility (marriage motivation, compatibility, total), total; Morse P. Manson; Western Psychological Services.*

For additional information and a review by Robert A. Harper, see 7:560.

[351]
California Occupational Preference System. High school and college; 1966–76; COPS; also called *COPSystem* and *COPSystem Inventory*; revision of *California Occupational Preference Survey*; 14 scores: consumer economics, outdoor, clerical, communication, and 2 scores (skilled, professional) for each of the following: science, technology, business, arts, service; Robert R. Knapp and Lila Knapp; EdITS/Educational and Industrial Testing Service.*

For additional information and reviews by Jo-Ida C. Hansen and Wilbur L. Layton, see 8:992 (1 reference); see also T2:2170 (2 references); for reviews by Jack L. Bodden and John W. French and an excerpted review by Robert H. Bauernfeind of the original edition, see 7:1012 (1 reference).

REFERENCES

1. See 7:1012.
2–3. See T2:2170.
4. See 8:992.
5. KNAPP, R. R., KNAPP, L., & BUTTAFUOCO, P. M. Interest changes and the classification of occupations. *Measurement & Evaluation in Guidance*, 1978, 11, 14–19.
6. KNAPP, R. R., KNAPP, L., & MICHAEL, W. B. The relationship of clustered interest measures and declared college major: Concurrent validity of the COP System Interest Inventory. *Educational & Psychological Measurement*, 1979, 39, 939–945.

[352]
California Phonics Survey. Grades 7–12 and college; 1956–63; CPS; shortened version of *Stanford Diagnostic Phonics Survey, Research Edition*; 9 error analysis scores for Form 1 (Form 2 yields total score only): long-short vowel confusion, other vowel confusion, consonants-confusion with blends and digraphs, consonant-vowel reversals, configuration, endings, negatives-opposites-sight words, rigidity, total; Grace M. Brown and Alice B. Cottrell; CTB/McGraw-Hill.*

See T2:1617 (1 reference); for a review by Constance M. McCullough, see 7:714 (1 reference); for a review by Thomas E. Culliton, Jr., see 6:820 (1 reference).

REFERENCES

1. See 6:820.
2. See 7:714.

3. See T2:1617.
4. EGRY, A. M. An analysis of phonic abilities found in high school shorthand teachers and students and of the phonetic patterns of correspondence of the most–used business words. *Business Education Forum*, 1977, 32, 40.
5. SMITH, B. D. Do we need differential diagnosis at the college level? No. *Journal of Reading*, 1977, 21, 62–66.
6. EGRY, A. M. An analysis of phonic abilities found in high school shorthand teachers and students and of the phonetic patterns of correspondence of the most–used business words. *Journal of Business Education*, 1978, 53, 231.

[353]
California Preschool Social Competency Scale.
Ages 2.5–5.5; 1969; CPSCS; ratings by teachers; Samuel Levine, Freeman F. Elzey, and Mary Lewis; Consulting Psychologists Press, Inc.*

For additional information, reviews by Hugh Lytton and Robert C. Calfee, and an excerpted review by Barton B. Proger, see 8:513 (2 references).

REFERENCES

1–2. See 8:513.
3. FLINT, D. L., HICK, T. L., HORAN, M. D., IRVINE, D. J., & KUKUK, S. E. Dimensionality of the California Preschool Social Competency Scale. *Applied Psychological Measurement*, 1980, 4, 203–212.

[354]
*California Psychological Inventory.
Ages 13 and over; 1956–75; CPI; 18 or 24 scores: dominance (Do), capacity for status (Cs), sociability (Sy), social presence (Sp), self-acceptance (Sa), sense of well-being (Wb), responsibility (Re), socialization (So), self-control (Sc), tolerance (To), good impression (Gi), communality (Cm), achievement via conformance (Ac), achievement via independence (Ai), intellectual efficiency (Ie), psychological-mindedness (Py), flexibility (Fx), femininity (Fe), 6 additional scores included when scored by the publisher (empathy, independence, managerial interests, work orientation, leadership, social maturity); (French, German, Italian, and Spanish editions available); Harrison G. Gough; Consulting Psychologists Press, Inc.*

For additional information and a review by Malcolm D. Gynther, see 8:514 (452 references); see also T2:1121 (166 references); for reviews by Lewis R. Goldberg and James A. Walsh and an excerpted review by John O. Crites, see 7:49 (370 references); see also P:27 (249 references); for a review by E. Lowell Kelly, see 6:71 (116 references); for reviews by Lee J. Cronbach and Robert L. Thorndike and an excerpted review by Laurance F. Shaffer, see 5:37 (33 references).

REFERENCES

1–33. See 5:37.
34–144. See 6:71.
145–393. See P:27.
394–764. See 7:49.
765–930. See T2:1121.
931–1382. See 8:514.
1383. ALKER, H. A., & OWEN, D. W. Biological, trait, and behavioral-sampling predictions of performance in a stressful life setting. *Journal of Personality & Social Psychology*, 1977, 35, 717–723.
1384. ARMENTROUT, J. A. Comparison of standard and short–form scores of Canadian adults on the California Psychological Inventory. *Perceptual & Motor Skills*, 1977, 45, 1088.
1385. AVERETT, M., & MCMANIS, D. L. Relationship between extraversion and assertiveness and related personality characteristics. *Psychological Reports*, 1977, 41, 1187–1193.
1386. BECKER, S. Personality correlates of the discrepancy between expressed and inventoried interest scores. *Measurement & Evaluation in Guidance*, 1977, 10, 24–30.
1387. BROWNE, J. A., & HOWARTH, E. A comprehensive factor analysis of personality questionnaire items: A test of twenty putative factor hypotheses. *Multivariate Behavioral Research*, 1977, 12, 399–427.
1388. BURGER, G. K., PICKETT, L., & GOLDMAN, M. Second order factors in the California Psychological Inventory. *Journal of Personality Assessment*, 1977, 41, 58–62.
1389. CADOW, B. The MMPI and CPI as measures of a prison treatment population. *FCI Research Reports*, 1977, 9, 1–12.
1390. CAMPBELL, J. B., & CHUN, K. Interinventory predictability and content overlap of the 16PF and the CPI. *Applied Psychological Measurement*, 1977, 1, 51–63.
1391. CARTWRIGHT, L. K. Personality changes in a sample of women physicians. *Journal of Medical Education*, 1977, 52, 467–474.
1392. COHEN, A., & FARLEY, F. H. The common–item problem in measurement: Effects on cross–cultural invariance of personality inventory structure. *Educational & Psychological Measurement*, 1977, 37, 757–760.
1393. GOEBEL, B., & HARRIS, E. Impact of sex-role values on cognitive performance. *Psychological Reports*, 1977, 41, 1251–1256.
1394. GOLDBERG, L. R. What if we administered the "wrong" inventory? The prediction of scores on the Personality Research Form scales from those on the California Psychological Inventory and vice versa. *Applied Psychological Measurement*, 1977, 1, 339–354.
1395. GOUGH, H. G., & HALL, W. B. A comparison of physicians who did or did not respond to a postal questionnaire. *Journal of Applied Psychology*, 1977, 62, 777–780.
1396. GOUGH, H. G., & HALL, W. B. Number of children wanted and expected by American physicians. *Journal of Psychology*, 1977, 96, 45–53.
1397. HASKELL, S. D., & HANDLER, L. Personality and background predictors of a young wife's desired family size. *Journal of Clinical Psychology*, 1977, 33, 755–759.
1398. HELMES, E., REED, P. L., & JACKSON, D. N. Desirability and frequency scale values and endorsement proportions for items of Personality Research Form–E. *Psychological Reports*, 1977, 41, 435–444.
1399. HELSON, R. The creative spectrum of authors of fantasy. *Journal of Personality*, 1977, 45, 310–326.
1400. HESKIN, K. J., BOLTON, N., BANISTER, P. A., & SMITH, F. V. Prisoners' personality: A factor analytically derived structure. *British Journal of Social & Clinical Psychology*, 1977, 16, 203–206.
1401. HIRSCHFELD, R. M. A., MATTHEWS, S. M., MOSHER, L. R., & MENN, A. Z. Being with madness: Personality characteristics of three treatment staffs. *Hospital & Community Psychiatry*, 1977, 28, 267–273.
1402. INA-OKA, H., & MATSUI, T. An extended use of the instrumentality theory of attitude for obtaining self-acceptance measures. *Journal of Applied Psychology*, 1977, 62, 124–126.
1403. JOESTING, J. Correlations among scales, What Kind of Person Are You and California Psychological Inventory. *Psychological Reports*, 1977, 40, 147–156.
1404. JUDD, L. L., HUBBARD, B., JANOWSKY, D. S., HUEY, L. Y., & ATTEWELL, P. A. The effect of lithium carbonate on affect, mood, & personality of normal subjects. *Archives of General Psychiatry*, 1977, 34, 346–351.
1405. KIRTON, M. Characteristics of high lie scorers. *Psychological Reports*, 1977, 40, 279–280.
1406. KIRTON, M. Relatedness of married couples' scores on "adorno" type tests. *Psychological Reports*, 1977, 40, 1013–1014.
1407. KIRTON, M. J. Ray's Balanced Dogmatism Scale re–examined. *British Journal of Social & Clinical Psychology*, 1977, 16, 97–98.
1408. NELSON, V. L., NIELSEN, E. C., & CHECKETTS, K. T. Interpersonal attitudes of suicidal individuals. *Psychological Reports*, 1977, 40, 983–989.
1409. NERVIANO, V. J., & WEITZEL, W. D. The 16PF and CPI: A comparison. *Journal of Clinical Psychology*, 1977, 33, 400–406.
1410. NEVO, B. Personality differences between Kibbutz born and city born adults. *Journal of Psychology*, 1977, 96, 303–308.
1411. PERRY, H. B. An analysis of the professional performance of physician's assistants. *Journal of Medical Education*, 1977, 52, 639–647.
1412. PETERSON, P. L. Interactive effects of student anxiety, achievement orientation, and teacher behavior on student achievement and attitude. *Journal of Educational Psychology*, 1977, 69, 779–792.
1413. PIPER, W. E., DEBBANE, E. G., & GARANT, J. Group psychotherapy outcome research: Problems and prospects of a first–year project. *International Journal of Group Psychotherapy*, 1977, 27, 321–341.
1414. PLAX, T. G., & ROSENFELD, L. B. Antecedents of change in attitudes of males and females. *Psychological Reports*, 1977, 41, 811–821.
1415. RAMANAIAH, N. V. Stylistic components of human judgment: The generality of individual differences. *Applied Psychological Measurement*, 1977, 1, 23–29.
1416. REYNOLDS, C. H., & NICHOLS, R. C. Factor scales of the CPI: Do they capture the valid variance? *Educational & Psychological Measurement*, 1977, 37, 907–915.
1417. ROSÉN, A. Conceptual system and personality: A multivariate study of system stage and personality correlates. *Journal of Research in Personality*, 1977, 11, 416–430.
1418. ROSÉN, A. On the dimensionality of the California Psychological Inventory. *Journal of Consulting & Clinical Psychology*, 1977, 45, 583–591.
1419. ROSENFELD, L. B., & PLAX, T. G. Clothing as communication. *Journal of Communication*, 1977, 27, 24–31.

1420. SELZER, M. L., VINOKUR, A., & WILSON, T. D. A psychosocial comparison of drunken drivers and alcoholics. *Journal of Studies on Alcohol*, 1977, 38, 1294–1312.

1421. SMALL, A. C., BILLER, H. B., GROSS, R. B., & PROCHASKA, J. O. Congruency of sex-role identification in normal and disturbed adolescent males. *Psychological Reports*, 1977, 41, 39–46.

1422. STANKOV, L. Some experiences with the F scale in Yugoslavia. *British Journal of Social & Clinical Psychology*, 1977, 16, 111–121.

1423. STROUP, A. L., & MANDERSCHEID, R. W. CPI and 16PF second-order factor congruence. *Journal of Clinical Psychology*, 1977, 33, 1023–1026.

1424. TYSON, G. A. Astrology or season of birth: A "split-sphere test." *Journal of Psychology*, 1977, 95, 285–287.

1425. VOLGER, R. E., WEISSBACH, T. A., COMPTON, J. V., & MARTIN, G. T. Integrated behavior change techniques for problem drinkers in the community. *Journal of Consulting & Clinical Psychology*, 1977, 45, 267–279.

1426. WECKOWICZ, T. E., COLLIER, G., & SPRENG, L. Field dependence, cognitive functions, personality traits, and social values in heavy cannabis users and nonuser controls. *Psychological Reports*, 1977, 41, 291–302.

1427. WEITZEL, W. D., NERVIANO, V. J., & HATCHER, R. W. Adolescent failure during secondary socialization: A study of army trainee casualties. *Journal of Psychiatric Research*, 1977, 13, 125–135.

1428. WIDOM, C. S. A methodology for studying noninstitutionalized psychopaths. *Journal of Consulting & Clinical Psychology*, 1977, 45, 674–683.

1429. ZARSKI, J. J., SWEENEY, T. J., & BARCIKOWSKI, R. S. Counseling effectiveness as a function of counselor social interest. *Journal of Counseling Psychology*, 1977, 24, 1–5.

1430. ABRAMS, D., & KING, G. D. An empirical investigation of the modeling of depression. *Psychological Reports*, 1978, 42, 823–832.

1431. AHLGREN, A., & WALBERG, H. J. Basic dimensions in characteristics of classroom groups. *Alberta Journal of Educational Research*, 1978, 24, 244–256.

1432. ALKER, H. A., & GAWIN, F. On the intrapsychic specificity of happiness. *Journal of Personality*, 1978, 46, 311–322.

1433. AMOS, S. P. Personality differences between established and less-established male and female creative artists. *Journal of Personality Assessment*, 1978, 42, 374–377.

1434. BECKMAN, L. J. Sex-role conflict in alcoholic women: Myth or reality. *Journal of Abnormal Psychology*, 1978, 87, 408–417.

1435. BORDEN, R. J., & FRANCIS, J. L. Who cares about ecology? Personality and sex differences in environmental concern. *Journal of Personality*, 1978, 46, 190–203.

1436. BREEN, L. J., PROCIUK, T. J., ENDLER, N. S., & OKADA, M. Person X situation interaction in personality prediction: Some specifics of the person factor. *Journal of Consulting & Clinical Psychology*, 1978, 46, 567–568.

1437. BURKHART, B. R., GYNTHER, M. D., & CHRISTIAN, W. L. Psychological mindedness, intelligence, and item subtlety endorsement patterns on the MMPI. *Journal of Clinical Psychology*, 1978, 34, 76–79.

1438. CROSS, D. T., BARCLAY, A., & BURGER, G. K. Differential effects of ethnic membership, sex, and occupation on the California Psychological Inventory. *Journal of Personality Assessment*, 1978, 42, 597–603.

1439. DALY, J. A. The assessment of social-communicative anxiety via self-reports: A comparison of measures. *Communication Monographs*, 1978, 45, 204–218.

1440. DIENER, E., & DEFOUR, D. Does television violence enhance program popularity? *Journal of Personality & Social Psychology*, 1978, 36, 333–341.

1441. DUCK, S. W., & CRAIG, G. Personality similarity and the development of friendship: A longitudinal study. *British Journal of Social & Clinical Psychology*, 1978, 17, 237–242.

1442. FISHER, S. Anxiety and sex role in body landmark functions. *Journal of Research in Personality*, 1978, 12, 87–99.

1443. FRANKLE, A. H. Sequential response shift rate: A correlate of human adaptivity measurable with existing personality inventories. *Journal of Psychology*, 1978, 98, 129–143.

1444. GOLDBERG, L. R. The reliability of reliability: The generality and correlates of intra-individual consistency in responses to structured personality inventories. *Applied Psychological Measurement*, 1978, 2, 269–291.

1445. GREGORY, R. J., & MORRIS, L. M. Adjective correlates for women on the CPI scales: A replication. *Journal of Personality Assessment*, 1978, 42, 258–264.

1446. HAERTZEN, C. A., MARTIN, W. R., HEWETT, B. B., & SANDQUIST, V. Measurement of psychopathy as a state. *Journal of Psychology*, 1978, 100, 201–204.

1447. HARE, R. D., FRAZELLE, J., & COX, D. N. Psychopathy and physiological responses to threat of an aversive stimulus. *Psychophysiology*, 1978, 15, 165–172.

1448. HASTINGS, A. C. The Oakland poltergeist. *Journal of the American Society of Psychical Research*, 1978, 72, 233–256.

1449. HEAPS, R. A. Relating physical and psychological fitness: A psychological point of view. *Journal of Sports Medicine & Physical Fitness*, 1978, 18, 399–408.

1450. HOGAN, J. C. Personological dynamics of leadership. *Journal of Research in Personality*, 1978, 12, 390–395.

1451. JOFFE, P. E., & BOST, B. A. Coping and defense in relation to accommodation among a sample of blind men. *Journal of Nervous & Mental Disease*, 1978, 166, 537–552.

1452. KAY, E. J., LYONS, A., NEWMAN, W., MANKIN, D., & LOEB, R. C. A longitudinal study of the personality correlates of marijuana use. *Journal of Consulting & Clinical Psychology*, 1978, 46, 470–477.

1453. KING, E. H. College mathematics: Open vs lecture. *Improving College & University Teaching*, 1978, 26, 50–51.

1454. KURTINES, W. M. A measure of autonomy. *Journal of Personality Assessment*, 1978, 42, 253–257.

1455. KURTINES, W. M., BALL, L. R., & WOOD, G. H. Personality characteristics of long-term recovered alcoholics: A comparative analysis. *Journal of Consulting & Clinical Psychology*, 1978, 46, 971–977.

1456. LIDBERG, L., LEVANDER, S. E., SCHALLING, D., & LIDBERG, Y. Necker cube reversals, arousal and psychopathy. *British Journal of Social & Clinical Psychology*, 1978, 17, 355–361.

1457. LYONS, A. W. Personality of high and low self-disclosers. *Journal of Humanistic Psychology*, 1978, 18, 83–85.

1458. MAYES, B., & KLUGH, H. E. Birthdate psychology: A look at some new data. *Journal of Psychology*, 1978, 99, 27–30.

1459. MCCLAIN, E. Feminists and nonfeminists: Contrasting profiles in independence and affiliation. *Psychological Reports*, 1978, 43, 435–441.

1460. MCCLAIN, E. W. Personality difference between intrinsically religious and nonreligious students: A factor analytic study. *Journal of Personality Assessment*, 1978, 42, 159–166.

1461. MIDDLETON, P. A test of Sarbin's self-role congruency theory within a role-playing therapy analogue situation. *Journal of Clinical Psychology*, 1978, 34, 505–511.

1462. MILLS, C. Is sex role related to intellectual abilities? *Gifted Child Quarterly*, 1978, 22, 536–538.

1463. MILLS, C., & HOGAN, R. A role theoretical interpretation of personality scale item responses. *Journal of Personality*, 1978, 46, 778–785.

1464. MORRIS, J. H., & SNYDER, R. A. Convergent validities of the Resultant Achievement Motivation Test and the Presatie Motivatie Test with Ac and Ai scales of the CPI. *Educational & Psychological Measurement*, 1978, 38, 1151–1155.

1465. NELL, V., & STRÜMPFER, D. J. W. The power motive, power, n and fear of weakness. *Journal of Personality Assessment*, 1978, 42, 56–62.

1466. OSTRAND, J., & CREASER, J. Development of counselor candidate dominance in three learning conditions. *Journal of Psychology*, 1978, 99, 199–202.

1467. PALLADINO, J. J., & DOMINO, G. Differences between counseling center clients and nonclients on three measures. *Journal of College Student Personnel*, 1978, 19, 497–501.

1468. PATTERSON, V., & HEILBRON, D. Therapist personality and treatment outcome: A test of the interaction hypothesis using the Campbell A–B scale. *Psychiatric Quarterly*, 1978, 50, 320–332.

1469. POTTS, C., PLANT, W. T., & SOUTHERN, M. L. Conventional sex differences in personality: Does sex or verbal ability level account for more variance. *Psychological Reports*, 1978, 43, 931–936.

1470. RABEN, C. S., SNYDER, R. A., HOFFMAN, R. G., & FARR, J. L. An examination of the construct validity and reliability of the Ghiselli Self-Description Inventory as a measure of self-esteem. *Applied Psychological Measurement*, 1978, 2, 73–81.

1471. ROESSLER, R., LESTER, J. W., BUTLER, W. T., RANKIN, B., & COLLINS, F. Cognitive and noncognitive variables in the prediction of preclinical performance. *Journal of Medical Education*, 1978, 53, 678–680.

1472. ROMINE, P. G., & CROWELL, O. Construct validity: Person-orientation and value-orientation scales of the California Psychological Inventory. *Psychological Reports*, 1978, 42, 317–318.

1473. SABINI, J. P., & SILVER, M. Objectifiability and calling rights into play: An empirical study. *Human Relations*, 1978, 31, 791–807.

1474. TSUJIMOTO, R. N., & NARDI, P. M. A comparison of Kohlberg's and Hogan's theories of moral development. *Social Psychology Quarterly*, 1978, 41, 235–245.

1475. WEINSTEIN, N. D. Individual differences in reactions to noise: A longitudinal study in a college dormitory. *Journal of Applied Psychology*, 1978, 63, 458–466.

1476. WERNER, P. D. Personality and attitude-activism correspondence. *Journal of Personality & Social Psychology*, 1978, 36, 1375–1390.

1477. BABL, J. D. Compensatory masculine responding as a function of sex role. *Journal of Consulting & Clinical Psychology*, 1979, 47, 252–257.

1478. BOHANNON, W. E., & MILLS, C. J. Psychometric properties and underlying assumptions of two measures of masculinity/femininity. *Psychological Reports*, 1979, 44, 431–450.

1479. BUBENZER, D. L., ZARSKI, J. J., & WALTER, D. A. Measuring social interest: A validation study. *Journal of Individual Psychology*, 1979, 35, 202–213.
1480. BUHRICH, N., & MCCONAGHY, N. Tests of gender feelings and behavior in homosexuality, transvestism, and transsexualism. *Journal of Clinical Psychology*, 1979, 35, 187–191.
1481. BURGER, G. K., & CROSS, D. T. Personality types as measured by the California Psychological Inventory. *Journal of Consulting & Clinical Psychology*, 1979, 47, 65–71.
1482. CARPENTER, J. C., & FREESE, J. J. Three aspects of self-disclosure as they relate to quality of adjustment. *Journal of Personality Assessment*, 1979, 43, 78–85.
1483. COHEN, A., & FARLEY, F. H. The common item in measurement: Effects on structure. *Multivariate Behavioral Research*, 1979, 14, 91–108.
1484. DIENER, E., & KERBER, K. W. Personality characteristics of American gun-owners. *Journal of Social Psychology*, 1979, 107, 227–238.
1485. FISHER, L., ROWLEY, P. T., & LIPKIN, M., JR. Predicting immediate outcome of genetic counseling following genetic screening. *Social Biology*, 1979, 26, 289–301.
1486. GENDREAU, P., GRANT, B. A., LEIPCIGER, M., & COLLINS, S. Norms and recidivism rates for the MMPI and selected experimental scales on a Canadian delinquent sample. *Canadian Journal of Behavioural Science*, 1979, 11, 21–31.
1487. GREENE, R. L., HARRIS, M. E., & MACON, R. S. Another look at personal validation. *Journal of Personality Assessment*, 1979, 43, 419–423.
1488. HARRIS, T. L., & BROWN, N. W. Congruent validity of the Rathus Assertiveness Schedule. *Educational & Psychological Measurement*, 1979, 39, 181–186.
1489. HARRIS, T. L., & SCHWAB, R. Personality characteristics of androgynous and sex-typed females. *Journal of Personality Assessment*, 1979, 43, 614–616.
1490. HEILBRUN, A. B., JR. Psychopathy and violent crime. *Journal of Consulting & Clinical Psychology*, 1979, 47, 509–516.
1491. HEILBRUN, A. B., JR., & SCHWARTZ, H. L. Defensive style and performance on objective personality measures. *Journal of Personality Assessment*, 1979, 43, 517–525.
1492. HERJANIC, B. M., BARREDO, V. H., HERJANIC, M., & TOMELLERI, C. J. Children of heroin addicts. *International Journal of the Addictions*, 1979, 14, 919–931.
1493. HONG, K. M., WIRT, R. D., YELLIN, A. M., & HOPWOOD, J. Psychological attributes, patterns of life change, and illness susceptibility. *Journal of Nervous & Mental Disease*, 1979, 167, 275–281.
1494. IRVINE, R. W. Structure of school, personality, and high school dropouts. *Journal of Negro Education*, 1979, 48, 67–72.
1495. JURKOVIC, G. J. Dimensions of moral character and drug use among rural high school students. *Journal of Clinical Psychology*, 1979, 35, 894–896.
1496. KAPLAN, S. L., ROSMAN, B. L., LIEBMAN, R., & HONIG, P. Predicting performance in a child psychiatry program for pediatric residents. *Journal of Medical Education*, 1979, 54, 42–50.
1497. MERZBACHER, C. F. A diet and exercise regimen: Its effect upon mental acuity and personality, a pilot study. *Perceptual & Motor Skills*, 1979, 48, 367–371.
1498. MOTOWIDLO, S. J. Development of a measure of generalized expectancy of task success. *Educational & Psychological Measurement*, 1979, 39, 69–80.
1499. OMIZO, M. M., WARD, R., & MICHAEL, W. B. Personality measures as predictors of success in a counselor education master's degree program. *Educational & Psychological Measurement*, 1979, 39, 947–953.
1500. PETERSON, P. L. Aptitude X treatment interaction effects of teacher structuring and student participation in college instruction. *Journal of Educational Psychology*, 1979, 71, 521–533.
1501. PLAX, T. G., & ROSENFELD, L. B. Receiver differences and the comprehension of spoken messages. *Journal of Experimental Education*, 1979, 48, 23–28.
1502. QUERY, W. T. Changes in scores on California Psychological Inventory among seminarians: What happened to the class of '68. *Psychological Reports*, 1979, 45, 129–130.
1503. REDFERING, D. L. Relationship between attitudes toward feminism and levels of dogmatism, achievement, and anxiety. *Journal of Psychology*, 1979, 101, 297–304.
1504. ROGERS, S., & LEUNES, A. A psychometric and behavioral comparison of delinquents who were abused as children with their non-abused peers. *Journal of Clinical Psychology*, 1979, 35, 470–472.
1505. SANFORD, J. Personality and paranormal experience: The relationship between social adjustment, extroversion, neuroticism, and the report of psychic phenomena. *Journal of Parapsychology*, 1979, 43, 54–55.
1506. SCHNEIER, C. E. Measuring cognitive complexity: Developing reliability, validity, and norm tables for a personality instrument. *Educational & Psychological Measurement*, 1979, 39, 599–612.
1507. SCISSONS, E. H. Profiles of ability: Characteristics of Canadian engineers. *Engineering Education*, 1979, 69, 822–836.
1508. SMITH, S. D., & SMITH, W. D. Teaching the poor: Its effect on student teacher self-concept. *Journal of Teacher Education*, 1979, 30, 45–49.
1509. STAMP, P. Girls and mathematics: Parental variables. *British Journal of Educational Psychology*, 1979, 49, 39–50.
1510. TAUB, J. M., & HAWKINS, D. R. Aspects of personality associated with irregular sleep habits in young adults. *Journal of Clinical Psychology*, 1979, 35, 296–304.
1511. VOGEL, P. A. Development of a measure for the study of peer self-help integrity groups. *Journal of Consulting & Clinical Psychology*, 1979, 47, 986–988.
1512. WAID, W. M., ORNE, M. T., & WILSON, S. K. Socialization, awareness, and the electrodermal response to deception and self-disclosure. *Journal of Abnormal Psychology*, 1979, 88, 663–666.
1513. WEBB, W. B. Are short and long sleepers different? *Psychological Reports*, 1979, 44, 259–264.
1514. WORMITH, J. S., & HASENPUSCH, B. Multidimensional measurement of delayed gratification preference with incarcerated offenders. *Journal of Clinical Psychology*, 1979, 35, 218–225.
1515. ALBERT R. S. Exceptionally gifted boys and their parents. *Gifted Child Quarterly*, 1980, 24, 174–179.
1516. ANTILL, J. K., & CUNNINGHAM, J. D. The relationship of masculinity, feminity, and androgyny to self-esteem. *Australian Journal of Psychology*, 1980, 32, 195–207.
1517. BAUCOM, D. H. Independent CPI masculinity and femininity scales: Psychological correlates and a sex-role typology. *Journal of Personality Assessment*, 1980, 44, 262–271.
1518. BECKMAN, L. J., DAY, T., BARDSLEY, P., & SEEMAN, A. Z. The personality characteristics and family backgrounds of women alcoholics. *International Journal of the Addictions*, 1980, 15, 147–154.
1519. BETZ, N. E., & BANDER, R. S. Relationship of MMPI Mf and CPI Fe scales to fourfold sex role classifications. *Journal of Personality & Social Psychology*, 1980, 39, 1245–1248.
1520. BIAGGIO, M. K. Anger arousal and personality characteristics. *Journal of Personality & Social Psychology*, 1980, 39, 352–356.
1521. BIANCHI, J. R., & BEAN, A. G. The prediction of voluntary withdrawals from college: An unsolved problem. *Journal of Experimental Education*, 1980, 49, 29–33.
1522. BURKE, R. J., & WEIR, T. Personality, value and behavioral correlates of the type A individual. *Psychological Reports*, 1980, 46, 171–181.
1523. BUSS, D. M., & CRAIK, K. H. The frequency concept of disposition: Dominance and prototypically dominant acts. *Journal of Personality*, 1980, 48, 379–392.
1524. DOMINO, G., & BOHN, S. A. Hypnagogic exploration: Sleep positions and personality. *Journal of Clinical Psychology*, 1980, 36, 760–762.
1525. ELLINGTON, J. E., MARSH, L. A., & CRITELLI, J. W. Personality characteristics of women with masculine names. *Journal of Social Psychology*, 1980, 111, 211–218.
1526. ELLIS, R. A., & LEITNER, D. W. Social desirability as a variable affecting responses on the California Psychological Inventory. *Psychological Reports*, 1980, 47, 1223–1226.
1527. ERDWINS, C. J., TYER, Z. E., & MELLINGER, J. C. Personality traits of mature women in student versus homemaker roles. *Journal of Psychology*, 1980, 105, 189–195.
1528. EREZ, M. Correlates of leadership style: Field-dependence and social intelligence versus social orientation. *Perceptual & Motor Skills*, 1980, 50, 231–238.
1529. FARLEY, F. H., & COHEN, A. Common items and reliability in personality measurement. *Journal of Research in Personality*, 1980, 14, 207–211.
1530. GREENE, R. L., BAUCOM, D. H., & MACON, R. S. Students' acceptance of high and low generalized personality interpretations. *Journal of Clinical Psychology*, 1980, 36, 166–170.
1531. HARMON, M. H. The Barron Ego Strength Scale: A study of personality correlates among normals. *Journal of Clinical Psychology*, 1980, 36, 433–436.
1532. HELSON, R. Challenger and upholder syndromes in critics. *Journal of Personality & Social Psychology*, 1980, 38, 825–838.
1533. HERBERT, T. T. An exploratory investigation into the nature of the part-time MBA student. *Human Relations*, 1980, 33, 279–295.
1534. KELSO, G. I., & TAYLOR, K. F. Psychologists as judges: A consensual validation of a personality typology. *Australian Journal of Psychology*, 1980, 32, 135–139.
1535. KENDALL, P. C., MOSES, J. A., JR., & FINCH, A. J., JR. Impulsivity and persistence in adult inpatient (impulse) offenders. *Journal of Clinical Psychology*, 1980, 36, 363–365.
1536. KENDALL, P. C., & WILCOX, L. E. Cognitive-behavioral treatment for impulsivity: Concrete versus conceptual training in non-self-controlled problem children. *Journal of Consulting & Clinical Psychology*, 1980, 48, 80–91.
1537. LEAK, G. K. Effects of highly structured versus nondirective group counseling approaches on personality and behavioral measures of

adjustment in incarcerated felons. *Journal of Counseling Psychology*, 1980, 27, 520-523.

1538. LI-REPAC, D. Cultural influences on clinical perception. A comparison between Caucasian and Chinese–American therapists. *Journal of Cross–Cultural Psychology*, 1980, 11, 327-342.

1539. MARTINEZ, R. L., & KIDD, A. H. Two personality characteristics in adult pet-owners and non-owners. *Psychological Reports*, 1980, 47, 318.

1540. McGUIRE, J. P., & LEAK, G. K. Prediction of self-disclosure from objective personality assessment techniques. *Journal of Clinical Psychology*, 1980, 36, 201-204.

1541. McKNIGHT, R. T. Prediction of hypnotizability from personality variables of the California Psychological Inventory: A multiple regression analysis. *Psychological Reports*, 1980, 47, 1319-1322.

1542. MILLS, C. J., & BOHANNON, W. E. Character structure and jury behavior: Conceptual and applied implications. *Journal of Personality & Social Psychology*, 1980, 38, 662-667.

1543. MILLS, C. J., & BOHANNON, W. E. Personality characteristics of effective state police officers. *Journal of Applied Psychology*, 1980, 65, 680-684.

1544. NELSON, J. G., ADAMS, D. R., FOSTER, S. F., & FARLEY, F. H. Socialization and empathy as predictors of moral judgment: Test of a model. *Counseling & Values*, 1980, 24, 264-271.

1545. O'CONNELL, A. N. Correlates of life style: Personality, role concept, attitudes, influences, and choices. *Human Relations*, 1980, 33, 589-601.

1546. PETERSON, P. L., JANICKI, T. C., & SWING, S. R. Aptitude–treatment interaction effects of three social studies teaching approaches. *American Educational Research Journal*, 1980, 17, 339-360.

1547. PFOUTS, J. H. Birth order, age-spacing, IQ differences, and family relations. *Journal of Marriage & the Family*, 1980, 42, 517-531.

1548. PLAX, T. G., & ROSENFELD, L. B. Individual differences in the credibility and attitude change relationship. *Journal of Social Psychology*, 1980, 111, 79-89.

1549. POLOVY, P. A study of moral development and personality relationships in adolescents and young adult Catholic students. *Journal of Clinical Psychology*, 1980, 36, 752-757.

1550. ROSS, H. G., & HARRIGAN, J. Small group learning climates and achievement styles. *Journal of Experimental Education*, 1980, 48, 307-315.

1551. SHUGER, D., & DEBOUT, J. Contrasts in Gestalt and analytic therapy. *Journal of Humanistic Psychology*, 1980, 20, 21-39.

1552. SLADE, P., & JENNER, F. A. Attitudes to female roles, aspects of menstruation and complaining of menstrual symptoms. *British Journal of Social & Clinical Psychology*, 1980, 19, 109-113.

1553. TERBORG, J. R., RICHARDSON, P., & PRITCHARD, R. D. Person-situation effects in the prediction of performance: An investigation of ability, self-esteem, and reward contingencies. *Journal of Applied Psychology*, 1980, 65, 574-583.

1554. TWA, R. J., & GREENE, M. Prediction of success in student teaching as a criterion for selection in teacher education programs. *Alberta Journal of Educational Research*, 1980, 26, 1-13.

1555. WATKINS, D., & ASTILLA, E. Intellective and non–intellective predictors of academic achievement at a Filipino university. *Educational & Psychological Measurement*, 1980, 40, 245-249.

1556. ZWEIGENHAFT, R. L., HAYES, K. N., & HAAGEN, C. H. The psychological impact of names. *Journal of Social Psychology*, 1980, 110, 203-210.

1557. ARON, A., ORME-JOHNSON, D., & BRUBAKER, P. The transcendental meditation program in the college curriculum: A 4-year longitudinal study of effects on cognitive and affective functioning. *College Student Journal*, 1981, 15, 140-146.

1558. ASSOR, A., ARONOFF, J., & MESSÉ, L. Attribute relevance as a moderator of the effects of motivation on impression formation. *Journal of Personality & Social Psychology*, 1981, 41, 789-796.

1559. BERNARD, L. C. The multidimensional aspects of masculinity–feminity. *Journal of Personality & Social Psychology*, 1981, 41, 797-802.

1560. BROOK, J. S., WHITMAN, M., & GORDON, A. S. Maternal and personality determinants of adolescent smoking behavior. *Journal of Genetic Psychology*, 1981, 139, 185-193.

1561. BUSS, D. M., & CRAIK, K. H. The act frequency analysis of interpersonal dispositions: Aloofness, gregariousness, dominance and submissiveness. *Journal of Personality*, 1981, 49, 175-192.

1562. CAMPAGNA, W. D., & O'TOOLE, J. J. A comparison of the personality profiles of Roman Catholic and male Protestant seminarians. *Counseling & Values*, 1981, 26, 62-67.

1563. FOSTER, P. J. Clinical discussion groups: Verbal participation and outcomes. *Journal of Medical Education*, 1981, 56, 831-838.

1564. GERMAN, S. C., & COTTLE, W. C. The use of the CPI to ascertain differences between more and less effective student paraprofessional helpers. *Journal of the National Association for Women Deans, Administrators, & Counselors*, 1981, 44, 11-16.

1565. GODDARD, R. C. Increase in assertiveness and actualization as a function of didactic training. *Journal of Counseling Psychology*, 1981, 28, 279-287.

1566. GOUGH, H. G., & WEISS, D. S. A nontransformational test of intellectual competence. *Journal of Applied Psychology*, 1981, 66, 102-110.

1567. JOHNSON, J. A. The "self–disclosure" and "self–presentation" views of item response dynamics and personality scale validity. *Journal of Personality & Social Psychology*, 1981, 40, 761-769.

1568. KAVANAGH, M. J., HURST, M. W., & ROSE, R. The relationship between job satisfaction and psychiatric health symptoms for air traffic controllers. *Personnel Psychology*, 1981, 34, 691-707.

1569. KLEIN, H. M., & WILLERMAN, L. Psychological masculinity and femininity and typical and maximal dominance expression in women. *Journal of Personality & Social Psychology*, 1981, 37, 2059-2070.

1570. LAUFER, W. S., JOHNSON, J. A., & HOGAN, R. Ego control and criminal behavior. *Journal of Personality & Social Psychology*, 1981, 41, 179-184.

1571. LORR, M., & BURGER, G. K. Personality types in data from California Psychological Inventory as defined by cluster analysis. *Psychological Reports*, 1981, 48, 115-118.

1572. MARTIN, J. D., BLAIR, G. E., & CASH, M. Correlation of the self–actualizing value subscale of the Personal Orientation Inventory with the self–acceptance, socialization, and self–control scales of the California Psychological Inventory. *Educational & Psychological Measurement*, 1981, 41, 589-593.

1573. MARTIN, J. D., BLAIR, G. E., SADOWSKI, C., & WHEELER, K. J. Intercorrelations among the Slosson Intelligence Test, the Shipley–Institute of Living Scale, and the Intellectual Efficiency Scale of the California Psychological Inventory. *Educational & Psychological Measurement*, 1981, 41, 595-598.

1574. MURRAY, S. G. Personality characteristics of adult women with low or high profiles on the SCII or SVIB occupational scales. *Journal of Applied Psychology*, 1981, 66, 422-430.

1575. PITARIU, H. Validation of the CPI feminity scale in Romania. *Journal of Cross–Cultural Psychology*, 1981, 12, 111-117.

1576. WEISS, D. S. A multigroup study of personality patterns in creativity. *Perceptual & Motor Skills*, 1981, 52, 735-746.

1577. ZUCKER, R. A., BATTISTICH, V. A., & LANGER, G. B. Sexual behavior, sex-role adaptation and drinking in young women. *Journal of Studies on Alcohol*, 1981, 42, 457-465.

[355]

[Re California Psychological Inventory.] Behaviordyne Psychodiagnostic Laboratory Service. A computerized scoring and interpreting service for qualified users of the CPI or the MMPI; 1969–76; formerly called *OPTIMUM Psychodiagnostic Consultation Service*; various types of interpretive reports are available: types 1 (for industrial psychologists and personnel counselors), 2 (for counselors and caseworkers), 3 (for correctional counselors), 5 (for physicians), 6 (standard report for psychiatrists and psychologists), 7 (detailed report for use before psychoanalysis or intensive psychotherapy), 7B (brief type 7 report); brief form of the other types of reports also available; additional options available with each type of report: self-report (separate printout of narrative second-person statements for presentation to client), penal option (inclusion of forensic statements, with reports 2, 6, 7, and 7B only), research option (inclusion of data on factor loadings and 166 clinical scales); although the reports may be based on either the CPI or the MMPI, publisher recommends that the CPI be used with types 1–3 reports and the MMPI with types 5–7 reports; no manual; original system by Joseph C. Finney, Charles Dwight Auvenshine, David Fulton Smith, and Donald E. Skeeters; Behaviordyne, Inc.*

For additional information, see 8:515 (1 reference). For reviews of the Behaviordyne service for the MMPI, see 8:619 (2 reviews) and 7:107 (1 review).

[356]

The California Q-Set. Adults; 1961–78; CQ-Set; for a downward extension see *The California Child Q-Set*; allows professionals and laymen to describe another's personality; ratings in 9 categories ranging from extremely uncharacteristic to extremely characteristic; Jack Block; Consulting Psychologists Press, Inc.*

For additional information and reviews by Allen L. Edwards and David T. Lykken and excerpted reviews by Samuel J. Beck and John E. Exner, Jr., see 6:72 (2 references); see also P:28 (1 reference).

REFERENCES

1–2. See 6:72.
3. See P:28.
4. BEM, D. J., & FUNDER, D. C. Predicting more of the people more of the time: Assessing the personality of situations. *Psychological Review*, 1978, 85, 485–501.

[357]

California Test of Personality. Grades kgn–3, 4–8, 7–10, 9–14, adults; 1939–53; CTP; 15 scores: self-reliance, sense of personal worth, sense of personal freedom, feeling of belonging, withdrawing tendencies, nervous symptoms, total personal adjustment, social standards, social skills, anti-social tendencies, family relations, school relations or occupation relations (adult level), community relations, total social adjustment, total adjustment; Louis P. Thorpe, Willis W. Clark, and Ernest W. Tiegs; CTB/McGraw-Hill.*

For additional information, see 8:516 (67 references); see also T2:1123 (196 references), P:29 (73 references), and 6:73 (49 references); for a review by Verner M. Sims, see 5:38 (93 references); for reviews by Laurance F. Shaffer and Douglas Spencer and an excerpted review by Earl R. Gabler of the original edition, see 3:26 (27 references); for reviews by Raymond B. Cattell, Percival M. Symonds, and P. E. Vernon and an excerpted review by Marion M. Lamb of the elementary and secondary levels, see 2:1213.

REFERENCES

1–24. See 3:26.
25–117. See 5:38.
118–166. See 6:73.
167–239. See P:29.
240–435. See T2:1123.
436–502. See 8:516.
503. BOWD, A. D. Field–dependence and performance on Piagetian invariance tasks: A cross–cultural comparison. *Journal of Genetic Psychology*, 1977, 130, 157–158.
504. FOSTER, G., & KEECH, V. Teacher reactions to the label of educable mentally retarded. *Education & Training of the Mentally Retarded*, 1977, 12, 307–311.
505. GALLUZZI, E. G., & ZUCKER, K. B. Level of adjustment and the self– and others–concepts. *Psychology in the Schools*, 1977, 14, 104–108.
506. GOLD, D., & ANDRES, D. Maternal employment and child development at three age levels. *Journal of Research & Development in Education*, 1977, 10, 20–29.
507. KERN, R. M., & HANKINS, G. Adlerian group counseling with contracted homework. *Elementary School Guidance & Counseling*, 1977, 11, 284–290.
508. LEBRON-RODRIGUEZ, D. E., & PASNAK, R. Induction of intellectual gains in blind children. *Journal of Experimental Child Psychology*, 1977, 24, 505–515.
509. LERNER, R. M., & LERNER, J. V. Effects of age, sex, and physical attractiveness on child–peer relations, academic performance, and elementary school adjustment. *Developmental Psychology*, 1977, 13, 585–590.
510. GIACOBBE, G. A., & GRAHAM, R. M. The responses of aggressive emotionally disturbed and normal boys to selected musical stimuli. *Journal of Music Therapy*, 1978, 15, 118–135.
511. GOLD, D., & ANDRES, D. Comparisons of adolescent children with employed and nonemployed mothers. *Merrill–Palmer Quarterly*, 1978, 24, 241–254.
512. GOLD, D., & ANDRES, D. Developmental comparisons between ten–year–old children with employed and nonemployed mothers. *Child Development*, 1978, 49, 75–84.
513. JOHNSON, R. A., & YARBOROUGH, B. H. The effects of marks on the development of academically talented elementary pupils. *Gifted Child Quarterly*, 1978, 22, 498–505.
514. SILVERMAN, E. M., & ZIMMER, C. Women who stutter: Personality and speech characteristics. *ASHA*, 1978, 20, 736. (Abstract)
515. YARBOROUGH, B. H., & JOHNSON, R. A. The relationship between intelligence levels and benefits from innovative, nongraded elementary schooling and traditional, graded schooling. *Educational Research Quarterly*, 1978, 3, 28–38.
516. DORETHY, R., & REEVES, D. Mental functioning, perceptual differentiation, personality, and achievement among art and non–art majors. *Studies in Art Education*, 1979, 20, 52–63.
517. EDMONDSON, R. J. Utilization of HDP and TA programs to enhance self esteem. *Elementary School Guidance & Counseling*, 1979, 13, 299–301.
518. HUDGINS, E. W. Examining the effectiveness of affective education. *Psychology in the Schools*, 1979, 16, 581–585.
519. GOLD, D., & ANDRES, D. Maternal employment and development of ten–year–old Canadian francophone children. *Canadian Journal of Behavioural Science*, 1980, 12, 233–240.
520. SHARKEY, C. T. Sense of personal worth, self–esteem, and anomia of child–abusing mothers and controls. *Journal of Clinical Psychology*, 1980, 36, 817–820.
521. YARBOROUGH, B. H., & JOHNSON, R. A. How meaningful are marks in promoting growth in reading? *Reading Teacher*, 1980, 33, 644–651.
522. YARBOROUGH, B. H., & JOHNSON, R. A. A six–year study of sex differences in intellectual functioning, reading/language arts achievement, and affective development. *Journal of Psychology*, 1980, 106, 55–61.
523. KLEIN, J. R., LITT, I. F., ROSENBERG, A., & UDALL, L. The effect of aspirin on dysmenorrhea in adolescents. *Journal of Pediatrics*, 1981, 98, 987–990.
524. LEHMAN, E. B., & ERDWINS, C. J. The social and emotional adjustment of young, intellectually–gifted program. *Gifted Child Quarterly*, 1981, 25, 134–137.

[358]

★**Callahan Anxiety Pictures.** Ages 5–13; 1978; CAP; Roger J. Callahan; Sunset Distributors.*

[359]

*****Camelot Behavioral Checklist.** Mentally retarded; 1974–77; CBC; ratings by parents, ward attendants and teachers; 11 scores: self help, physical development, home duties, vocational behaviors, economic behaviors, independent travel, numerical skills, communication skills, social behaviors, responsibility, total; Ray W. Foster; Camelot Behavioral Systems.*

For additional information, see 8:517.

[360]

★**Canadian Achievement Tests, Form A.** Grades 1.6–2.9, 2.6–3.9, 3.6–4.9, 4.6–5.9, 5.6–6.9, 6.6–7.9, 7.6–9.9, 9.6–12.9; 1981; CAT, Form A; criterion-referenced and norm-referenced; 8 overlapping levels; McGraw-Hill Ryerson Ltd. [Canada].*

a) LOCATOR TESTS. Grades 3–6, 6–12; 2 tests (reading comprehension, mathematics) for each level (Grades 3–6, 6–12) the total score of which determines placement at the appropriate level of the CAT, Form A.
b) LEVEL 12. Grades 1.6–2.9; 9 subtests in 4 areas: reading (phonic analysis, structural analysis, reading vocabulary, reading comprehension), spelling, language (mechanics, expression), mathematics (computation, concepts and applications).
c) LEVEL 13. Grades 2.6–3.9; subtests same as for *b* above.
d) LEVEL 14. Grades 3.6–4.9; 8 subtests in 5 areas: reading (vocabulary, comprehension), spelling, language (mechanics, expression), mathematics (computation, concepts and applications), reference skills.
e) LEVEL 15. Grades 4.6–5.9; subtests same as for *d* above.
f) LEVEL 16. Grades 5.6–6.9; subtests same as for *d* above.

g) LEVEL 17. Grades 6.6–7.9; subtests same as for *d* above.
h) LEVEL 18. Grades 7.6–9.9; subtests same as for *d* above.
i) LEVEL 19. Grades 9.6–12.9; subtests same as for *d* above.

[361]
Canadian Cognitive Abilities Test. Grades kgn–1, 2–3, 3–9; 1954–81; CCAT; original test by Robert L. Thorndike, Elizabeth Hagen, and Irving Lorge (*a*); adaptation by Edgar N. Wright; Nelson Canada [Canada].*

a) PRIMARY BATTERIES. Grades kgn–1, 2–3; 1954–81; adaptation of *Cognitive Abilities Test*; 2 levels.
  1) *Primary* 1. Grades kgn–1.
  2) *Primary* 2. Grades 2–3.

b) MULTI-LEVEL EDITION. Grades 3–9; 1954–81; 3 scores: verbal, quantitative, nonverbal.

For additional information, see 8:180 (2 references). For reference to reviews of the *Cognitive Abilities Test*, see 8:181.

REFERENCES
1–2. See 8:180.
3. KERSHNER, J. R. Cerebral dominance in disabled readers, good readers, and gifted children: Search for a valid model. *Child Development*, 1977, 48, 61–67.
4. BARIK, H. C., & SWAIN, M. Evaluation of a French immersion program: The Ottawa study through grade five. *Canadian Journal of Behavioural Science*, 1978, 10, 192–201.
5. BEHRENS, L. T., & VERNON, P. E. Personality correlates of over-achievement and under-achievement. *British Journal of Educational Psychology*, 1978, 48, 290–297.
6. CUMMINS, J., & DAS, J. P. Simultaneous and successive syntheses and linguistic processes. *International Journal of Psychology*, 1978, 13, 129–138.
7. LUKASEVICH, A., & GRAY, R. F. Open space, open education, and pupil performance. *Elementary School Journal*, 1978, 79, 108–114.

[362]
Canadian Lorge-Thorndike Intelligence Tests, Multi-Level Edition. Grades 3–9; 1954–67; CLTIT; adaptation of *Lorge-Thorndike Intelligence Tests*, Multi-Level Edition; 3 scores: verbal, non-verbal, composite; original test by Irving Lorge, Robert L. Thorndike, and Elizabeth Hagen; adaptation by Edgar N. Wright; Nelson Canada [Canada].*

For additional information, see 7:341.

REFERENCES
1. BANRETI-FUCHS, K. M. Attitudinal correlates of academic achievement in elementary school children. *British Journal of Educational Psychology*, 1978, 48, 176–185.
2. LUCE, S. R., & HOGE, R. D. Relations among teacher rankings, pupil-teacher interactions, and academic achievement: A test of the teacher expectancy hypothesis. *American Education Research Journal*, 1978, 15, 489–500.
3. BANNER, C. N. Child-rearing attitudes of mothers of under-, average-, and over-achieving children. *British Journal of Educational Psychology*, 1979, 49, 150–155.
4. CHAPMAN, J. W., & BOERSMA, F. J. Learning disabilities, locus of control, and mother attitudes. *Journal of Educational Psychology*, 1979, 71, 250–258.
5. SAKLOFSKE, D. H., & KELLY, I. W. The Quick Test: Its relationship with the Canadian Test of Basic Skills and the Canadian Lorge-Thorndike Intelligence Tests. *Psychological Reports*, 1980, 46, 802.
6. CHAPMAN, J. W., CULLEN, J. L., BOERSMA, F. J., & MAGUIRE, T. O. Affective variables and school achievement: A study of possible causal influences. *Canadian Journal of Behavioural Science*, 1981, 13, 181–192.

[363]
Canadian Tests of Basic Skills. Grades 1.7–2.5, 2.6–3.5, 3–8; 1955–81; CTBS; Canadian adaptation of *Iowa Tests of Basic Skills*; original test by E. F. Lindquist, A. N. Hieronymus, and others; adaptation by Ethel M. King; Nelson Canada [Canada].*

a) PRIMARY BATTERY: LEVELS 7–8. Grades 1.7–2.5, 2.6–3.5; 8 scores: vocabulary, word analysis, reading, spelling, mathematics (concepts, problems, total), composite.

b) MULTILEVEL EDITION: LEVELS 9–14. Grades 3–8; 15 scores: vocabulary, reading comprehension, language (spelling, capitalization, punctuation, usage, total), work-study skills (maps, graphs and tables, reference materials, total), mathematics skills (concepts, problem solving, total); 6 overlapping levels (grades 3, 4, 5, 6, 7, 8) in a single booklet.

For additional information, see 8:11 (1 reference); for a review by L. B. Birch of the earlier edition of *b*, see 7:6.

REFERENCES
1. See 8:11.
2. BARRON, R. W., & BARON, J. How children get meaning from printed words. *Child Development*, 1977, 48, 587–594.
3. BELL, A. E., ABRAHAMSON, D. S., & MCRAE, K. N. Reading retardation: A 12-year prospective study. *Journal of Pediatrics*, 1977, 91, 363–370.
4. GREER, R. N., & BLANK, S. S. Cognitive style, conceptual tempo and problem solving: Modification through programmed instruction. *American Educational Research Journal*, 1977, 14, 295–315.
5. BANRETI-FUCHS, K. M. Attitudinal correlates of academic achievement in elementary school children. *British Journal of Educational Psychology*, 1978, 48, 176–185.
6. BARIK, H. C., & SWAIN, M. Evaluation of a French immersion program: The Ottawa study through grade five. *Canadian Journal of Behavioural Science*, 1978, 10, 192–201.
7. GOLD, D., & ANDRES, D. Developmental comparisons between ten-year-old children with employed and nonemployed mothers. *Child Development*, 1978, 49, 75–84.
8. LUCE, S. R., & HOGE, R. D. Relations among teacher rankings, pupil-teacher interactions, and academic achievement: A test of the teacher expectancy hypothesis. *American Educational Research Journal*, 1978, 15, 489–500.
9. LUKASEVICH, A., & GRAY, R. F. Open space, open education, and pupil performance. *Elementary School Journal*, 1978, 79, 108–114.
10. BANNER, C. N. Child-rearing attitudes of mothers of under-, average-, and over-achieving children. *British Journal of Educational Psychology*, 1979, 49, 150–155.
11. BESSAI, F., & COZAC, C. Gains of fifth and sixth grade readers from in-school tutoring. *Reading Teacher*, 1980, 33, 567–570.
12. NEUFELD, J. S., & COZAC, E. A study of the self-concept of intellectually superior children. *Alberta Journal of Educational Research*, 1980, 26, 149–158.
13. SAKLOFSKE, D. H., & KELLY, I. W. The Quick Test: Its relationship with the Canadian Test of Basic Skills and the Canadian Lorge-Thorndike Intelligence Tests. *Psychological Reports*, 1980, 46, 802.
14. SHAPSON, S. M., WRIGHT, E. N., EASON, G., & FITZGERALD, J. An experimental study of the effects of class size. *American Educational Research Journal*, 1980, 17, 141–152.
15. FISK, R. A., & JANZEN, H. L. Identifying learning disabled students with a selected psychoeducational test battery. *Alberta Journal of Educational Research*, 1981, 27, 252–263.
16. TASCHOW, H. G. Innercity Canadian native and non-native pupils' achievement in reading, writing, and speaking. *Reading Teacher*, 1981, 34, 799–803.

[364]
★The Canfield Time Problems Inventory. Management and administrative personnel; 1980; TPRI; a measure of why individuals waste time; 4 scores: priorities, planning, delegation, self-discipline; Albert A. Canfield; Humanics Media.*

[365]
★CAP Achievement Series. Grades preschool–kgn.5, kgn.0–1.5, 1.0–2.5, 2.0–3.5, 3.0–4.5, 4.0–5.5, 5.0–6.5, 6.0–7.5, 7.0–9.5, 9.0–11.5, 11.0–12.9; 1980–82; 11 levels; John W. Wick and Jeffrey K. Smith; American Testronics.*
a) LEVEL 4. Grades preschool–kgn.5; 4 scores: reading, mathematics, language, total.
b) LEVEL 5. Grades kgn.0–1.5; 4 scores: same as for level 4.
c) LEVEL 6. Grades 1.0–2.5; 4 scores: same as for level 4.
d) LEVEL 7. Grades 2.0–3.5; 12 scores: word attack, reading (vocabulary, comprehension, total), mathematics (concepts, computation, total), language (spelling, capitalization and punctuation, grammar, total), basic skills total.
e) LEVEL 8. Grades 3.0–4.5; 13 scores: same as for level 7 plus problem solving included in mathematics.
f) LEVEL 9. Grades 4.0–5.5; 13 scores: reading (vocabulary, comprehension, total), mathematics (computation, concepts, problem solving, total), language (spelling, capitalization and punctuation, grammar, total), reference and study skills, basic skills total.
g) LEVEL 10. Grades 5.0–6.5; 13 scores: same as for level 9.
h) LEVEL 11. Grades 6.0–7.5; 13 scores: same as for level 9.
i) LEVEL 12. Grades 7.0–9.5; 13 scores: same as for level 9.
j) LEVEL 13. Grades 9.0–11.5; 8 scores: reading, mathematics, language, basic skills total, English, writing, social studies, science.
k) LEVEL 14. Grades 11.0–12.9; 8 scores: same as for level 13.

[366]
★Career Adaptive Behavior Inventory. Disabled students ages 5–15; 1980; CAB; ratings by parents, teachers, or other professionals in 10 major categories: academics, communication, interest, leisure time, motor, responsibility, self-concept, self-help, socialization, task performance; Thomas P. Lombardi; Special Child Publications.*

[367]
Career Assessment Inventory. "Individuals [grades 8 and over] seeking a career that does not generally require a four-year or advanced college degree"; 1975–82; CAI; vocational interests; 119 scores: 6 theme (realistic, investigative, artistic, social, enterprising, conventional), 22 basic interest (mechanical/fixing, electronics, carpentry, manual/skilled trades, agriculture, nature/outdoors, animal service, science, numbers, writing, performing/entertaining, arts/crafts, social service, teaching, child care, medical service, religious activities, business, sales, office practices, clerical/clerking, food service), 91 occupational (aircraft mechanic, auto mechanic, bus driver, camera repair technician, carpenter, conservation officer, dental laboratory technician, drafter, electrician, emergency medical technician, farmer/rancher, firefighter, forest ranger, hardware store manager, janitor/janitress, machinist, mail carrier, musical instrument repairperson, navy enlisted serviceperson, orthotist/prosthetist, painter, park ranger, pipefitter/plumber, police officer, printer, radio/TV repairperson, security guard, sheet metal worker, telephone repairperson, tool/die maker, truck driver, veterinary technician, chiropractor, computer programmer, dental hygienist, electronic technician, math-science teacher, medical laboratory technician, radiological technician, respiratory therapy technician, surveyor, advertising artist/writer, advertising executive, author/writer, counselor-chemical dependency, interior designer, legal assistant, librarian, musician, newspaper reporter, photographer, piano technician, athletic trainer, child care assistant, cosmetologist, elementary school teacher, licensed practical nurse, nurse aide, occupational therapy assistant, operating room technician, physical therapy assistant, registered nurse, barber/hairstylist, buyer/merchandiser, card/gift shop manager, caterer, florist, food service manager, hotel/motel manager, insurance agent, manufacturing representative, personnel manager, private investigator, purchasing agent, real estate agent, reservation agent, restaurant manager, travel agent, accountant, bank teller, bookkeeper, cafeteria worker, court reporter, data entry operator, dental assistant, executive housekeeper, medical assistant, pharmacy technician, secretary, teacher aide, waiter/waitress); Charles B. Johansson; NCS Interpretive Scoring Systems.
For additional information and reviews of an earlier edition by Jack L. Bodden and Paul R. Lohnes, see 8:993.

REFERENCES
1. WEISER, M. A., KLIMEK, R. J., & HODINKO, B. Career perspectives of male prison inmates in college courses. *Journal of Vocational Behavior*, 1981, 19, 36–41.

[368]
Career Awareness Inventory. Grades 4–8; 1974–75; CAI; LaVerna M. Fadale; Scholastic Testing Service, Inc.*
For additional information and reviews by Nancy S. Cole and Mary Lee Smith, see 8:994 (1 reference).

REFERENCES
1. See 8:994.
2. RICH, N. S. Occupational knowledge: To what extent is rural youth handicapped? *Vocational Guidance Quarterly*, 1978, 27, 320–325.
3. SINK, C. Career Awareness Inventory (CAI). *Measurement & Evaluation in Guidance*, 1980, 13, 120–122.

[369]
Career Counseling Personal Data Form. Vocational counselees; 1962; no manual; John B. Ahrens; Martin M. Bruce, Ph.D., Publishers.*
For additional information, see 6:1113.

[370]
★Career Decision Scale. Grades 9–12 and college; 1976–80; Samuel H. Osipow, Clarke G. Carney (scale), Jane Winer (scale), Barbara Yanico (scale), and Maryanne Koschier (scale); Marathon Consulting & Press.*

[371]
★Career Development Inventory [Consulting Psychologists Press, Inc.]. Grades 8–12, college; 1979–81; CDI; measures vocational maturity; 8 scores: career planning, career exploration, decision making, world-of-work information, knowledge of preferred occupational group, career development-attitudes, career development knowledge and skills, total; Donald E. Super, Albert S. Thompson, Richard H. Lindeman, Jean P. Jordaan, and Roger A. Myers; Consulting Psychologists Press, Inc.*

[372]

Career Development Inventory [Science Research Associates, Inc.]. Grades 9–10 and out-of-school youth and adults; 1974–75; CDI; 17 scores: an occupational-consideration rating (low, moderate, or high) for 3 educational levels of entry (early, delayed, late) in each of 6 occupational groupings (technical/mechanical/skilled, scientific/theoretical [no early entry level], artistic/literary/musical, social/personal service, persuasive/managerial, clerical/computational); Ester E. Diamond and G. Frederic Kuder (test, part 2); Science Research Associates, Inc.*

For additional information, reviews by William C. Bingham and James H. Ricks, Jr., and an excerpted review by Fred H. Borgen, see 8:995 (1 reference).

REFERENCES

1. See 8:995.
2. MORRISON, R. F. Career adaptivity: The effective adaptation of managers of changing role demands. *Journal of Applied Psychology*, 1977, 62, 549–558.
3. BORGEN, F. H. Review of the Career Development Program. *Measurement & Evaluation in Guidance*, 1978, 10, 244–247.
4. SCHENK, G. E., JOHNSTON, J. A., & JACOBSEN, K. The influence of a career group experience on the vocational maturity of college students. *Journal of Vocational Behavior*, 1979, 14, 284–296.
5. SUPER, D. E., & THOMPSON, A. S. A six-scale, two-factor measure of adolescent career or vocational maturity. *Vocational Guidance Quarterly*, 1979, 28, 6–15.
6. YOUNG, R. A. The effects of value confrontation and reinforcement counseling on the career planning attitudes and behavior of adolescent males. *Journal of Vocational Behavior*, 1979, 15, 1–11.
7. KUHLMAN-HARRISON, J., & NEELY, M. A. Discriminant validity of Career Development Inventory scales in grade 10 students. *Educational & Psychological Measurement*, 1980, 40, 475–478.
8. PEROVICH, G. M., & MIERZWA, J. A. Group facilitation of vocational maturity and self-esteem in college students. *Journal of College Student Personnel*, 1980, 21, 206–211.
9. SALTOUN, J. Fear of failure in career development. *Vocational Guidance Quarterly*, 1980, 29, 35–41.
10. JOHNSON, R. P., & RIKER, H. C. Retirement maturity: A valuable concept for preretirement counselors. *Personnel & Guidance Journal*, 1981, 59, 291–295.
11. NEELY, M. A., & JOHNSON, C. W. The relationship of performance on six scales of the Career Development Inventory to sex, father's education, and father's occupation. *Educational & Psychological Measurement*, 1981, 41, 917–921.

[373]

*****Career Guidance Inventory.** Grades 7–13 students interested in trades, services, and technologies; revision in examiner's manual only; 1972–79; CGI; 25 scores: 14 engineering related trades (carpentry and woodworking, masonry, mechanical repair, painting and decorating, plumbing and pipefitting, printing, tool and die making, sheet metal and welding, drafting and design, mechanical engineering, industrial production, civil and architectural engineering, electrical engineering, chemical and laboratory) and 11 nonengineering related services (environmental health, agriculture and forestry, business management, communications, data processing, sales, transportation services, protective services, medical laboratory, nursing, food service); James E. Oliver; Educational Guidance, Inc.*

For additional information and a review by Bert W. Westbrook, see 8:996.

[374]

Career Maturity Inventory. Grades 6–12; 1973; CMI; formerly called *Vocational Development Inventory*; 2 tests; John O. Crites; CTB/McGraw-Hill.*
a) ATTITUDE SCALE.
b) COMPETENCE TEST, RESEARCH EDITION. 5 scores: self-appraisal, occupational information, goal selection, planning, problem solving.

For additional information, reviews by Martin R. Katz and Donald G. Zytowski, and an excerpted review by Garth Sorenson, see 8:997 (152 references); see also T2:2103 (35 references).

REFERENCES

1–35. See T2:2103.
36–187. See 8:997.
188. HOLLAND, J. L., & HOLLAND, J. E. Vocational indecision: More evidence and speculation. *Journal of Counseling Psychology*, 1977, 24, 404–414.
189. KELSO, G. I. The relation of school grade to ages and stage in vocational development. *Journal of Vocational Behavior*, 1977, 10, 287–301.
190. MCGOWAN, A. S. Vocational maturity and anxiety among vocationally undecided and indecisive students. The effectiveness of Holland's Self-Directed Search. *Journal of Vocational Behavior*, 1977, 10, 196–204.
191. MOORE, T. L., & MCLEAN, J. E. A validation study of the Career Maturity Inventory Attitude Scale. *Measurement & Evaluation Guidance*, 1977, 10, 113–116.
192. NEELY, M. A., & HANNA, G. S. A study of the concurrent validity of the Career Maturity Inventory. *Educational & Psychological Measurement*, 1977, 37, 1087–1090.
193. OLIVER, L. W. Evaluating career counseling outcome for three modes of test interpretation. *Measurement & Evaluation in Guidance*, 1977, 10, 153–161.
194. OMVIG, C. P., & THOMAS, E. G. Relationship between career education, sex, and career maturity of sixth and eighth grade pupils. *Journal of Vocational Behavior*, 1977, 11, 322–331.
195. BAILEY, J. A., & PIERCE, K. A. The career concept scale: An assessment of career judgment. *Journal of Employment Counseling*, 1978, 15, 67–72.
196. BINGHAM, G. Career attitudes among boys with and without specific learning disabilities. *Exceptional Children*, 1978, 44, 341–342.
197. EGNER, J. R., & JACKSON, D. J. Effectiveness of a counseling intervention program for teaching career decision-making skills. *Journal of Counseling Psychology*, 1978, 25, 45–52.
198. GANSTER, D. C., & LOVELL, J. E. An evaluation of a career development seminar using Crite's Career Maturity Inventory. *Journal of Vocational Behavior*, 1978, 13, 172–180.
199. HANNA, G. S., & NEELY, M. A. Discriminant validity of Career Maturity Inventory scales in grade 9 students. *Educational & Psychological Measurement*, 1978, 38, 571–574.
200. HANNA, G. S., & NEELY, M. A. Reliability of the CMI attitude scale. *Measurement & Evaluation in Guidance*, 1978, 11, 114–116.
201. MILLER, M. F. Childhood experience antecedents of career maturity attitudes. *Vocational Guidance Quarterly*, 1978, 27, 137–143.
202. POWERS, R. J. Enhancement of former drug abusers' career development through structured group counseling. *Journal of Counseling Psychology*, 1978, 25, 585–587.
203. PUTNAM, B. A., HOSIE, T. W., & HANSEN, J. C. Sex differences in self-concept variables and vocational attitude maturity of adolescents. *Journal of Experimental Education*, 1978, 47, 23–27.
204. WOODCOCK, P. R., & HERMAN, A. Fostering career awareness in tenth-grade girls. *School Counselor*, 1978, 25, 256–264.
205. ADELSTEIN, D. M., & WEBSTER, D. W. Cross-sectional, longitudinal and composite longitudinal data on the Career Maturity Inventory attitude scale. *Journal of Vocational Behavior*, 1979, 14, 102–111.
206. CAREY, M. A., & WEBER, L. J. Evaluating an experience-based career education program. *Vocational Guidance Quarterly*, 1979, 27, 216–222.
207. LEACH, J. A. A comparative study between CETA, special needs, and office occupations students on attainment of occupational survival skills and career attitude maturity. *Journal of Industrial Teacher Education*, 1979, 16, 21–28.
208. MEIR, E. I., & SHIRAN, D. The occupational cylinder as a means for vocational maturity enhancement. *Journal of Vocational Behavior*, 1979, 14, 279–283.
209. SNODGRASS, G., & HEALY, C. C. Developing a replicable career decision-making counseling procedure. *Journal of Counseling Psychology*, 1979, 26, 210–216.

210. WINER, J. L., CESARI, J., & HAASE, R. F. Cognitive complexity and career maturity among college students. *Journal of Vocational Behavior*, 1979, 15, 186–192.
211. YATES, C., JOHNSON, N., & JOHNSON, J. Effects of the use of the vocational exploration group on career maturity. *Journal of Counseling Psychology*, 1979, 26, 368–370.
212. BINGHAM, G. Career maturity of learning disabled adolescents. *Psychology in the Schools*, 1980, 17, 135–139.
213. DILLARD, J. M., & PERRIN, D. W. Puerto Rican, Black, and Anglo adolescents' career aspirations, expectations, and maturity. *Vocational Guidance Quarterly*, 1980, 28, 313–321.
214. NEELY, M. A. Career Maturity Inventory interpretations for grade 9 boys and girls. *Vocational Guidance Quarterly*, 1980, 29, 113–123.
215. RUBINTON, N. Instruction in career decision making and decision-making styles. *Journal of Counseling Psychology*, 1980, 27, 581–588.
216. WARE, M. E. Antecedents of educational/career preferences and choices. *Journal of Vocational Behavior*, 1980, 16, 312–319.
217. WARE, M. E., & APPRICH, R. V. Variations in career cognition measures among groups of college women. *Measurement & Evaluation in Guidance*, 1980, 13, 179–183.
218. WARE, M. E., & POGGE, D. L. Concomitants of certainty in career-related choices. *Vocational Guidance Quarterly*, 1980, 28, 322–327.
219. WESTBROOK, B. W., CUTTS, C. C., MADISON, S. S., & ARCIA, M. A. The validity of the Crite's model of career maturity. *Journal of Vocational Behavior*, 1980, 16, 249–281.
220. DILLARD, J. M., & CAMPBELL, N. J. Influences of Puerto Rican, Black, and Anglo parents' career behavior on their adolescent children's career development. *Vocational Guidance Quarterly*, 1981, 30, 139–148.
221. GARDNER, D. C. Career maturity and locus of control: Important factors in career training. *College Student Journal*, 1981, 15, 239–246.
222. JEPSEN, D. A., & PREDIGER, D. J. Dimensions of adolescent career development. A multi-instrument analysis. *Journal of Vocational Behavior*, 1981, 19, 350–368.
223. JOHNSON, N., JOHNSON, J., & YATES, C. A 6-month follow-up on the effects of the vocational exploration group on career maturity. *Journal of Counseling Psychology*, 1981, 28, 70–71.
224. KARAYANNI, M. Career maturity of emotionally maladjusted high school students. *Vocational Guidance Quarterly*, 1981, 29, 213–220.
225. KAZANAS, H. C., & KRASKA, M. F. The meaning and value of work and occupational awareness of high school seniors. *Journal of Industrial Teacher Education*, 1981, 18, 23–31.
226. KIULIGHAN, D. M., JR., HAGESETH, J. A., TIPTON, R. M., & McGOVERN, T. V. Effects of matching treatment approaches and personality types in group vocational counseling. *Journal of Counseling Psychology*, 1981, 28, 315–320.
227. MACKIN, R. K., & HANSEN, L. S. A theory-based career development course: A plant in the garden. *School Counselor*, 1981, 28, 325–334.
228. REGEHR, C. N., & HERMAN, A. Developing the skills of career decision making and self-assessment in ninth-grade students. *School Counselor*, 1981, 28, 335–342.
229. SEWELL, T. E., PALMO, A. J., & MANNI, J. L. High school dropout, psychological, academic, and vocational factors. *Urban Education*, 1981, 16, 65–76.
230. SOMMERS, J. K. The effects of industrial arts upon the career maturity of selected seventh and eighth grade adolescents. *Journal of Industrial Teacher Education*, 1981, 18, 46–60.
231. STROHMER, D. C. Exploratory use of Crite's CMI-attitude scale with rehabilitation clients. *Rehabilitation Counseling Bulletin*, 1981, 24, 370–373.
232. WARE, M. E., & POGGE, D. L. The relationship between career preferences and words and images, career decision making skills and sex. *College Student Journal*, 1981, 15, 328–334.
233. WEISER, M. A., KLIMEK, R. J., & HODINKO, B. Career perspectives of male prison inmates in college courses. *Journal of Vocational Behavior*, 1981, 19, 36–41.
234. WIGGINS, J. D., & MOODY, A. A field-based comparison of four career-exploration approaches. *Vocational Guidance Quarterly*, 1981, 30, 15–20.
235. YONGUE, I. T., TODD, R. M., & BURTON, J. K. The effects of didactic classroom instruction versus field exposure on career maturity. *Journal of Vocational Behavior*, 1981, 19, 369–373.

[375]
★Career Skills Assessment Program. High school and college students; 1977–79; CSAP; experimental edition; 6 tests; Career Skills Assessment Program of The College Board.*
a) SELF EVALUATION AND DEVELOPMENT SKILLS. 1977–78; 5 scores: understanding individual differences, evaluating individual characteristics and test results, changing personal characteristics and behavior, locating and interpreting information about self, applying knowledge about self to career opportunities.
b) CAREER AWARENESS SKILLS. 1977; 4 scores: relating abilities/values/needs/and experience to career choices, locating/evaluating/and interpreting information for career choices, knowing facts about career opportunities, finding out about educational requirements for occupations.
c) CAREER DECISION-MAKING SKILLS. 1977; 7 scores: defining the problem, establishing an action plan, clarifying values, identifying alternatives, discovering probable outcomes, eliminating alternatives systematically, starting action.
d) EMPLOYMENT SEEKING SKILLS. 1977; 5 scores: anticipating job prospects, finding and interpreting facts and sources on available jobs, identifying appropriately written letters/resumes/and applications, describing appropriate appearance and behavior as one is interviewed and evaluated for a job, evaluating when a specific job fits a person's needs and interests.
e) WORK EFFECTIVENESS SKILLS. 1977–78; 7 scores: identifying employer and employee responsibilities, developing effective work habits, achieving effective working relationships with co-workers, managing work situations to achieve personal satisfaction, giving and receiving supervision effectively, advancing on the job, planning job changes.
f) PERSONAL ECONOMICS SKILLS. 1977; 7 scores: figuring your paycheck and income tax, understanding personal banking procedures, purchasing goods and services and paying bills, insuring yourself and your possessions, borrowing and using credit, understanding investment procedures, understanding basic economic ideas.

REFERENCES
1. WESTBROOK, B. W., & ROGERS, B. Career Skills Assessment Program. *Measurement & Evaluation in Guidance*, 1980, 13, 107–115.

[376]
Caring Relationship Inventory. Premarital and marital counselees; 1966–75; CRI; 7 scores: affection, friendship, eros, empathy, self-love, being love, deficiency love; Everett L. Shostrom; EdITS/Educational and Industrial Testing Services.*
For additional information and reviews by Donald L. Mosher and Robert F. Stahmann, see 8:333 (5 references); for a review by Albert Ellis, see 7:561; see also P:31 (1 reference).

[377]
★Carrow Auditory-Visual Abilities Test. Ages 4–10; 1981; CAVAT; 2 batteries; Elizabeth Carrow-Woolfolk; Teaching Resources Corporation.*
a) VISUAL ABILITIES BATTERY. 5 subtests: visual discrimination matching, visual discrimination memory, visual-motor copying, visual-motor memory, motor speed.
b) AUDITORY ABILITIES BATTERY. 9 subtests: picture memory, picture sequence selection, digits forward, digits backward, sentence repetition, word repetition, auditory blending, auditory discrimination in quiet, auditory discrimination in noise.

[378]
Carrow Elicited Language Inventory. Ages 3–7; 1974; CELI; 18 scores: grammar (articles, adjectives,

nouns, noun plurals, pronouns, verbs, negatives, contractions, adverbs, prepositions, demonstratives, conjunctions); type (substitutions, omissions, additions, transpositions, reversals), total; Elizabeth Carrow; Teaching Resources Corporation.*

For additional information and a review by Courtney B. Cazden, see 8:957 (3 references).

REFERENCES

1-3. See 8:957.
4. SOMMERS, R. K., & STARKEY, K. L. Dichotic verbal processing in Down's Syndrome children having qualitatively different speech and language skills. *American Journal of Mental Deficiency*, 1977, 82, 44-53.
5. CHAPMAN, D. L., & FRIEDMAN, D. Comparison of three expressive syntax measures with four year olds. *ASHA*, 1978, 20, 832.
6. GEERS, A. E., & MOOG, J. S. Syntactic maturity of spontaneous speech and elicited imitations of hearing–impaired children. *Journal of Speech & Hearing Disorders*, 1978, 43, 380-391.
7. MCDADE, H. L., & SIMPSON, M. A. The use of delayed imitation to test grammatical performance. *ASHA*, 1978, 20, 831.
8. RICKER, L. H., RITTERMAN, S. I., SILVA, S. S., & CARLSON, R. L. Comparative examination of language–delayed and language–normal children on CELI and NWLT. *ASHA*, 1978, 20, 820. (Abstract)
9. WILCOX, M. J., & LEONARD, L. B. Experimental acquisition of wh-questions in language-disordered children. *Journal of Speech & Hearing Research*, 1978, 21, 220-239.
10. HAYNES, W. O., & HAYNES, M. D. Pragmatics and elicited imitation: Children's performance on discursively related and discursively unrelated sentences. *Journal of Communication Disorders*, 1979, 12, 471-479.
11. HOWARD, M. R., HULIT, L. M., & FOSTER, S. Syntactic accuracy and semantic equivalency of nonverbatim imitation responses. *ASHA*, 1979, 21, 734. (Abstract)
12. ORCHIK, D. J., KRYGIER, K. M., RAGSDALE, R., & BROWN, J. B. Language performance in mild and moderate sensorineural hearing loss. *ASHA*, 21, 1979, 698. (Abstract)
13. SMITHEIMER, L. S., O'BRIEN, D. P., PETTAS, M., & CANTER, M. A. Syntactic development of learning–disabled children. *ASHA*, 1979, 21, 760. (Abstract)
14. FIELDS, T. A., & ASHMORE, L. L. Effect of elicitation variables on analysis of language samples for normal and language–disordered children. *Perceptual & Motor Skills*, 1980, 50, 911-919.
15. HULIT, L. M., HOWARD, M. R., & FOSTER, S. K. Effects of delay interval and pictorial cues on a sentence imitation task. *Perceptual & Motor Skills*, 1980, 51, 91-100.
16. SPARKS, S., & HUTCHINSON, B. Cri Du Chat: Report of a case. *Journal of Communication Disorders*, 1980, 13, 9-13.
17. ALLEN, D. V., BLISS, L. S., & TIMMONS, J. Language evaluation: Science or art? *Journal of Speech & Hearing Disorders*, 1981, 46, 66-68.
18. GUILFORD, A. M., SCHEUERLE, J., & SHONBURN, S. Aspects of language development in the gifted. *Gifted Child Quarterly*, 1981, 25, 159-163.
19. HOWELL, J., SKINNER, C., GRAY, M., & BROOMFIELD, S. A study of the comparative effectiveness of different language tests with two groups of children. *British Journal of Disorders of Communication*, 1981, 16, 31-42.
20. SEMEL, E. M., & WIIG, E. H. Semel Auditory Processing Program: Training effects among children with language–learning disabilities. *Journal of Learning Disabilities*, 1981, 14, 192-196.

[379]
★**Caso Test for Limited English Speaking Students.** Limited English-speaking students ages 8-12 living in an English-speaking setting; 1971-79; CTLESS; ratings in 3 areas: phonetics, comprehension, picture generating response; Adolph Caso; Kaso Industries, Inc.*

[380]
Cass-Sanders Psychology Test. High school and college; 1964; Dal H. Cass and M. W. Sanders; Bureau of Educational Measurements.*

For additional information, see 7:643.

[381]
Cattell Infant Intelligence Scale. Ages 3-30 months; 1940-60; downward extension of *Stanford-Binet Intelligence Scale, Second Revision*; Psyche Cattell; The Psychological Corporation.*

For additional information and a review by Fred Damarin, see 8:209 (7 references); see also T2:487 (27 references) and 6:515 (22 references); for reviews by Florence M. Teagarden and Beth L. Wellman and excerpted reviews by Rachel Stutsman Ball, C. M. Louttit, T. L. McCulloch, Norma V. Schneidemann, and Helen Speyer, see 3:281.

REFERENCES

1-22. See 6:515.
23-49. See T2:487.
50-56. See 8:209.
57. BEVERIDGE, M., & MITTLER, P. Feedback, language and listener performance in severely retarded children. *British Journal of Disorders of Communication*, 1977, 12, 149-157.
58. DUBOSE, R. F. Predictive value of infant intelligence scales with multiply handicapped children. *American Journal of Mental Deficiency*, 1977, 81, 388-390.
59. GAMER, E., GRUNEBAUM, H., COHLER, B. J., & GALLANT, D. H. Children at risk: Performance of three–year–olds and their mentally ill and well mothers on an interaction task. *Child Psychiatry & Human Development*, 1977, 8, 102-114.
60. HUNT, J. V., & RHODES, L. Mental development of preterm infants during the first year. *Child Development*, 1977, 48, 204-210.
61. SANCHEZ, O., MAMUNES, P., & YUNIS, J. J. Partial trisomy 20 (20q13) and partial trisomy 21 (21pter-21q21.3). *Journal of Medical Genetics*, 1977, 14, 459-462.
62. WISNIEWSKI, L., PURDY, G., HASSOLD, T., WILSON, C., BENTLEY, K., HACKEL, E., & HIGGINS, J. V. An interstitial deletion of chromosome 9 in a girl with multiple congenital anomalies. *Journal of Medical Genetics*, 1977, 14, 455-459.
63. BRITTAN, E. A study of object concept development in institutionalized and home–reared infants. *Journal of Psychology*, 1978, 100, 251-260.
64. DIEBOLD, M. H., CURTIS, W. S., & DUBOSE, R. F. Developmental scales versus observational measures for deaf–blind children. *Exceptional Children*, 1978, 44, 275-278.
65. DOYLE, A. B., & SOMERS, K. The effects of group and family day care on infant attachment behaviours. *Canadian Journal of Behavioural Science*, 1978, 10, 38-45.
66. OHWAKI, S., & STAYTON, S. E. The relation of length of institutionalization to the intellectual functioning of the profoundly retarded. *Child Development*, 1978, 49, 105-109.
67. LOU, H. C., SKOV, H., & PEDERSEN, H. Low cerebral blood flow: A risk factor in the neonate. *Journal of Pediatrics*, 1979, 95, 606-609.
68. SNELL, M. E. Higher functioning residents as language trainers of the mentally retarded. *Education & Training of the Mentally Retarded*, 1979, 14, 77-84.
69. CONNOLLY, B., MORGAN, S., RUSSELL, F. F., & RICHARDSON, B. Early intervention with Down syndrome children. *Physical Therapy*, 1980, 60, 1405-1408.
70. DWYER, J. T., MILLER, L. G., ARDUINO, N. L., ANDREW, E. M., DIETZ, W. H., JR., REED, J. C., & REED, H. B. C., JR. Mental age and IQ of predominantly vegetarian children. *Journal of the American Dietetic Association*, 1980, 76, 142-147.
71. ILMER, S., & DREWS, J. Differential analysis of selected prompts and neurological variables in motor assessment of moderately mentally retarded children. *American Journal of Mental Deficiency*, 1980, 84, 508-517.
72. KLEBANOFF, M. A., & NEFF, J. M. Familial dysautonomia associated with recurrent osteomyelitis in a non–Jewish girl. *Journal of Pediatrics*, 1980, 96, 75-77.
73. NIELSEN, H. H. A longitudinal study of the psychological aspects of myelomeningocele. *Scandinavian Journal of Psychology*, 1980, 21, 45-54.
74. SPARKS, S., & HUTCHINSON, B. Cri Du Chat: Report of a case. *Journal of Communication Disorders*, 1980, 13, 9-13.
75. PETERSON, P. L., JANICKI, T. C., & SWING, S. R. Ability x treatment interaction effects on children's learning in large–group and small–group approaches. *American Educational Research Journal*, 1981, 18, 453-473.

[382]
CGP Self-Scoring Placement Tests in English and Mathematics. Students entering postsecondary institutions with open-door policies; 1976, c1962-76; also called *Self-Scoring Placement Tests in English and Mathematics*; self-scoring edition of the achievement/placement tests in the *Comparative Guidance and Placement Program*

(CGP); 6 tests ('72); may be used independently or in combination with full or modified CGP Program; student usually takes 4 tests (reading, written English expression, and 2 mathematics tests in prescribed combinations depending on amount of algebra studied) but single tests may be administered; subtests available as separates; published by The College Board and Educational Testing Service.*

a) SELF-SCORING ENGLISH PLACEMENT TESTS. 2 tests.
  1) *Reading Placement Test.*
  2) *Written English Expression Placement Test.*

b) SELF-SCORING MATHEMATICS PLACEMENT TESTS. 4 tests usually administered in following pairs: computation and applied arithmetic for students with less than 1 year of high school algebra, computation and elementary algebra for students with 1 year, elementary algebra and advanced algebra for students with more than 1 year.
  1) *Computation Placement Test.*
  2) *Applied Arithmetic Placement Test.*
  3) *Elementary Algebra Placement Test.*
  4) *Intermediate Algebra Placement Test.*

For additional information and reviews by Ronald K. Hambleton and J. Thomas Hastings, see 8:7. For reviews of subtests, see 8:61 (1 review) and 8:289 (1 review); for reference to reviews of the CGP Program, see 8:475.

[383]
Change Agent Questionnaire. Adults, whose work primarily concerns changing behavior of others; 1969–73; CAQ; "underlying assumptions and practical strategies employed by agents of change as they seek to influence others"; 4 scores (philosophy, strategy, evaluation, total) for each of 5 styles of change: client-centered, charismatic, custodial, credibility, compliance; no manual; Jay Hall and Martha S. Williams; Teleometrics Int'l.*

For additional information, see 8:1105.

[384]
Chapin Social Insight Test. Ages 13 and over; 1967–68; CSIT; F. Stuart Chapin (test) and Harrison G. Gough (manual); Consulting Psychologists Press, Inc.*

For additional information and reviews by Richard I. Lanyon and David B. Orr, see 7:51; see also P:34 (3 references).

REFERENCES

1–3. See P:34.
4. ZEDECK, S., & KAFRY, D. Capturing rater policies for processing evaluation data. *Organizational Behavior & Human Performance*, 1977, 18, 269–294.
5. BERNARD, L. C., & EPSTEIN, D. J. Sex role conformity in homosexual and heterosexual males. *Journal of Personality Assessment*, 1978, 42, 505–511.
6. MILLS, C., & HOGAN, R. A role theoretical interpretation of personality scale item responses. *Journal of Personality*, 1978, 46, 778–785.
7. SADOWSKI, C. J. Social insight and evaluative reliability. *Perceptual & Motor Skills*, 1978, 47, 422.
8. BROCKNER, J. The effects of self-esteem, success–failure, and self-consciousness on task performance. *Journal of Personality & Social Psychology*, 1979, 37, 1732–1741.
9. SADOWSKI, C. J., & WOODWARD, H. R. Note on the reliability and scoring of the Chapin Social Insight Test. *Psychological Reports*, 1980, 47, 510.

[385]
★**Characteristics Scale.** Grades kgn–8; 1970–75; ratings by teachers; no manual; Patricia B. Elmore and Donald L. Beggs; Patricia B. Elmore.*

[386]
★**Chart of Initiative and Independence.** Mentally handicapped adults; 1980; CII; assessment of environmental opportunities available to clients and their current and potential use of those resources; ratings by staff; I. Macdonald and T. Couchman; NFER-Nelson Publishing Co. [England].*

[387]
Chatterji's Non-Language Preference Record. Ages 11–16; 1962; 10 scores: fine arts, literary, scientific, medical, agricultural, mechanical, crafts, outdoor, sports, household work; S. Chatterji; distributed by Manasayan [India].*

See T2:2173 (6 references) and 6:1050.

[388]
★**Checklist/Guide to Selecting a Small Computer.** Individuals selecting a small computer for a business; 1980; ratings of "essential" or "nice-to-have" characteristics in 10 areas: display features, keyboard features, printer features, controller features, software, word processing, service, training, miscellaneous, costs; Wilma E. Bennett; Pilot Books.*

[389]
Chemical Operators Selection Test, Revised Edition. Chemical operators and applicants; 1958–71; test by M. A. Storr, J. H. McPherson, P. A. Maschino, and R. G. Garner; manual by J. I. Wegener; Dow Chemical Co.* (In-print status uncertain; no reply from publisher.)

For additional information, see 7:1104; see also 6:1141 (1 reference).

[390]
Chemistry: Minnesota High School Achievement Examinations. High school; 1955–73; a new, revised, or previously inactive form issued each May; Achievement Examinations for Secondary Schools, High School Achievement Examinations, and Midwest High School Achievement Examinations have also been used as series titles; edited by V. L. Lohmann; American Guidance Service.*

For additional information concerning out of print and inactive forms, see 7:843, 6:912, and 5:738; for a review by Edward G. Rietz of Form A (1955) and Form B (1957), see 5:741.

[391]
★**Child Anxiety Scale.** Grades kgn–5; 1980; CAS; John S. Gillis; Institute for Personality and Ability Testing, Inc.*

[392]
The Child Behavior Rating Scale. Grades kgn–3; 1960–62; CBRS; ratings by teachers or parents; 6 adjustment scores: self, home, social, school, physical, total; Russell N. Cassel; Western Psychological Services.*

For additional information and a review by James A. Dunn, see 7:52; see also P:35 (1 reference).

REFERENCES

1. See P:35.
2. MORACCO, J., & KAZANDKIAN, A. Effectiveness of behavior counseling and consulting with non-western elementary school children. *Elementary School Guidance & Counseling*, 1977, 11, 244–251.

3. CRNIC, K. A. Maternal sensitivity to children in problem situations. *American Journal of Orthopsychiatry*, 1978, 48, 291–299.
4. SCOVERN, A. W., BUKSTEL, L. H., KILMANN, P. R., LAVAL, R. A., BUSEMEYER, J., & SMITH, V. Effects of parent counseling on the family system. *Journal of Counseling Psychology*, 1980, 27, 268–275.

[393]

★The CHILD Center Operational Assessment Tool. Regular or special classroom students; 1971–77; OAT; criterion-referenced; assesses and identifies children with special educational needs; The Child Center; the Author.*

a) READING/SPELLING TEST. 1971–77; both forms are to be used together; 3 areas: primary learning abilities, phonic encoding-decoding, structural analysis encoding-decoding.

b) MATH TEST. 1971.
  1) *Basic Concepts.* 4 areas: numeration, basic operations, place value, fractions.
  2) *Operational Skills.* 6 areas: addition and subtraction, multiplication, division, fractions, decimals, percents.

c) LANGUAGE TEST. 1971; 3 areas: memory and sequencing, auditory discrimination, similarities.

d) BEHAVIORAL QUESTIONNAIRE. 1971; ratings by teachers; 8 scores: learning, lability, coordination, self-esteem, concentration, inappropriate involuntary behavior, motor expression, school attitude.

[394]

★Child Development Center Q-Sort. Ages 1.5 to adult; 1968; CDCQ; manual title is *A Method for Assessing Personality Development for Follow-Up Evaluations of the Preschool Child*; sorting of personality characteristics by mental health workers, psychologists, psychiatrists, social workers, or specially trained teachers; Frances Fuchs Schachter, Allan Cooper (manual), and Rona Gordet (manual); Stoelting Co.*

REFERENCES

1. SCHACHTER, F. F., COOPER, A., & GORDET, R. A method for assessing personality development for follow-up evaluations of the preschool child. *Monographs of the Society for Research in Child Development*, 1968, 33, 1–55.

[395]

★Childrens Adaptive Behavior Scale. Ages 5–10; 1980; CABS; 6 scores: language development, independent functioning, family role performance, economic-vocational activity, socialization, total; Bert O. Richmond and Richard H. Kicklighter; Humanics Ltd.*

REFERENCES

1. RICHMOND, B. O., & HORN, W. R. Children's Adaptive Behavior Scale: A new measure of adaptive functioning. *Psychology in the Schools*, 1980, 17, 159–162.

[396]

Children's Apperception Test. Ages 3–10; 1949–74; CAT; 3 editions; Leopold Bellak, Sonya Sorel Bellak, Mary R. Haworth (checklist), and Marvin S. Hurvich (manual for *c*); C.P.S., Inc.*

a) CHILDREN'S APPERCEPTION TEST. 1949–74.

b) CHILDREN'S APPERCEPTION TEST—SUPPLEMENT. 1952–55; 10 pictures, one or more of which may be presented in addition to the regular CAT.

c) CHILDREN'S APPERCEPTION TEST (HUMAN FIGURES). 1965; designed to be "equivalent" to the regular CAT cards.

See T2:1451 (23 references) and P:419 (18 references); for reviews by Bernard I. Murstein and Robert D. Wirt, see 6:206 (19 references); for reviews by Douglas T. Kenny and Albert I. Rabin, see 5:126 (15 references); for reviews by John E. Bell and L. Joseph Stone and excerpted reviews by M. M. Genn, Herbert Herman, Robert R. Holt, Laurance F. Shaffer, and Adolf G. Woltmann, see 4:103 (2 references).

REFERENCES

1–2. See 4:103.
3–17. See 5:126.
18–36. See 6:206.
37–54. See P:419.
55–77. See T2:1451.
78. SCHROTH, M. L. The relationships between motives on the Children's Apperception Test. *Journal of Genetic Psychology*, 1979, 134, 219–224.

[397]

★Children's Depression Scale. Ages 9–16; 1978; CDS; card sort into 5 categories; 66 items in 2 areas: depressive (48 items), positive (18 items); 6 subscale scores: affective responsive, social problems, self-esteem, pre-occupation with own sickness and death, guilt, pleasure, plus 2 total scores: depressive, positive; Moshe Lang and Miriam Tisher; Australian Council for Educational Research [Australia].*

REFERENCES

1. HOLLAN, S. D. Children's Depression Scale. *Journal of Child Psychology & Psychiatry & Allied Disciplines*, 1980, 21, 371–372.

[398]

Children's Embedded Figures Test. Ages 5–12; 1963–71; CEFT; revision of the Goodenough-Eagle modification of the *Embedded Figures Test*; Stephen A. Karp, Norma Konstadt (test), and manual coauthors Herman A. Witkin, Philip K. Oltman, and Evelyn Raskin; Consulting Psychologists Press, Inc.*

For additional information, see 8:519 (53 references); see also T2:1127 (14 references); for a review by Sheldon A. Weintraub, see 7:53 (15 references); see also P:36 (7 references) and 6:746 (2 references).

REFERENCES

1–2. See 6:74b.
3–9. See P:36.
10–24. See 7:53.
25–38. See T2:1127.
39–91. See 8:519.
92. BOWD, A. D. Field–dependence and performance on Piagetian invariance tasks: A cross–cultural comparison. *Journal of Genetic Psychology*, 1977, 130, 157–158.
93. CAMPBELL, S. B., SCHLEIFER, M., WEISS, G., & PERLMAN, T. A two-year follow-up of hyperactive preschoolers. *American Journal of Orthopsychiatry*, 1977, 47, 149–162.
94. FINLEY, G. E., SOLLA, J., & COWAN, P. A. Field dependence-independence, egocentrism, and conservation in young children. *Journal of Genetic Psychology*, 1977, 131, 155–156.
95. KAGAN, S., ZAHN, G. L., & GEALY, J. Competition and school achievement among Anglo-American and Mexican–American children. *Journal of Educational Psychology*, 1977, 69, 432–441.
96. KNUDSON, K. H. M., & KAGAN, S. Visual perspective role-taking and field–independence among Anglo American and Mexican American children of two ages. *Journal of Genetic Psychology*, 1977, 131, 243–253.
97. SALOMON, G. Effects of encouraging Israeli mothers to co-observe "Sesame Street" with their five–year–olds. *Child Development*, 1977, 48, 1146–1151.
98. SHAPSON, S. M. Hypothesis testing and cognitive style in children. *Journal of Educational Psychology*, 1977, 69, 452–463.
99. TAYLOR, L. J. Sex and psychological differentiation. *Psychological Reports*, 1977, 41, 192–194.
100. THOMAS, J. R., & BENDER, P. R. A developmental explanation for children's motor behavior: A neo–Piagetian interpretation. *Journal of Motor Behavior*, 1977, 9, 81–93.

101. THORNELL, J. G. Individual differences in cognitive styles and the guidance variable in instruction. *Journal of Experimental Education*, 1977, 45, 9–12.
102. WAGNER, D. A. Ontogeny of the Ponzo Illusion: Effects of age, schooling, and environment. *International Journal of Psychology*, 1977, 12, 161–176.
103. BURIEL, R. Relationship of three field–dependence measures to the reading and math achievement of Anglo American and Mexican children. *Journal of Educational Psychology*, 1978, 70, 167–174.
104. CONNOR, J. M., SCHACKMAN, M., & SERBIN, L. A. Sex–related differences in response to practice on a visual–spatial test and generalization to a related test. *Child Development*, 1978, 49, 24–29.
105. CONNOR, J. M., SERBIN, L. A., & FREEMAN, M. Training visual–spatial ability in EMR children. *American Journal of Mental Deficiency*, 1978, 83, 116–121.
106. DINGES, N. G., & HOLLENBECK, A. R. Field dependence–independence in Navajo children. *International Journal of Psychology*, 1978, 13, 215–220.
107. GILDEMEISTER, J. E., & FRIEDMAN, P. Cognitive style and visual analysis in first graders of high and low verbal ability. *Perceptual & Motor Skills*, 1978, 47, 759–766.
108. JAHODA, G. Cross–cultural study of factors influencing orientation errors in the reproduction of Kohs–type figures. *British Journal of Psychology*, 1978, 69, 45–57.
109. LEE, A., FANT, H., LIFE, M. L., LIPE, L. O., & CARTER, J. A. Field independence and performance on ball–handling tasks. *Perceptual & Motor Skills*, 1978, 46, 439–442.
110. MOORE, S. F., & COLE, S. Cognitive self–mediation training with hyperkinetic children. *Bulletin of the Psychonomic Society*, 1978, 12, 18–20.
111. WEISZ, J. R., QUINLAN, D. M., O'NEILL, P., & O'NEILL, P. C. The Rorschach and structured tests of perception as indices of intellectual development in mentally retarded and nonretarded children. *Journal of Experimental Child Psychology*, 1978, 25, 326–336.
112. BRUININKS, V. L., & MAYER, J. H. Longitudinal study of cognitive abilities and academic achievement. *Perceptual & Motor Skills*, 1979, 48, 1011–1021.
113. COWARD, R. T., & LANGE, G. Recall and recall–organization behaviors of field–dependent and field–independent children. *Psychological Reports*, 1979, 44, 191–197.
114. HAREL, Z. Discriminating between survivors and nonsurvivors among working class aged living in the community. *Gerontologist*, 1979, 19, 83–89.
115. LAOSA, L. M., & DEAVILA, E. A. Development of cognitive styles among Chicanos in traditional and dualistic communities. *International Journal of Psychology*, 1979, 14, 91–98.
116. BAKER, A. M. The relationship between cognitive style and imitation in children. *Journal of Genetic Psychology*, 1980, 136, 303–304.
117. BLUMBERG, N. L. Effects of neonatal risk, maternal attitude, and cognitive style on early postpartum adjustment. *Journal of Abnormal Psychology*, 1980, 89, 139–150.
118. CROMACK, T. R., & STONE, M. K. Validation of a Group Embedded Figures Test for young children. *Perceptual & Motor Skills*, 1980, 51, 483–486.
119. LAOSA, L. M. Maternal teaching strategies and cognitive styles in Chicano families. *Journal of Educational Psychology*, 1980, 72, 45–54.
120. PIERCE, J. W. Field independence and imagery-assisted prose recall of children. *Journal of Educational Psychology*, 1980, 72, 200–203.
121. SARACHO, O. The relationship between the teachers' cognitive style and their perceptions of their students' academic achievements. *Educational Research Quarterly*, 1980, 5, 40–49.
122. SARACHO, O. N., & DAYTON, C. M. Relationship of teachers' cognitive styles to pupils' academic achievement gains. *Journal of Educational Psychology*, 1980, 72, 544–549.
123. SCOTT, N. A., & MOORE, W. A. Differences in locus of control orientation between normal and learning disabled boys. *Psychological Reports*, 1980, 46, 795–801.
124. VAIDYA, S., & CHANSKY, N. Cognitive development and cognitive style as factors in mathematics achievement. *Journal of Educational Psychology*, 1980, 72, 326–330.
125. RYCKMAN, D. B. Reading achievement, IQ, and simultaneous–successive processing among normal and learning–disabled children. *Alberta Journal of Educational Research*, 1981, 27, 74–83.

[399]
The Children's Hypnotic Susceptibility Scale.
Ages 5–12, 13–16; 1963, c1962; CHSS; downward extension of *Stanford Hypnotic Susceptibility Scale*, on which its content is based; Perry London; Consulting Psychologists Press, Inc.*

See T2:1128 (4 references) and P:37 (4 references); for reviews by C. Scott Moss and John G. Watkins and an excerpted review by Andre Weitzenhoffer, see 6:75 (2 references).

[400]
*Children's Personality Questionnaire, 1975 Edition.
Ages 8–12; 1959–79; CPQ; test booklet title is *What You Do and What You Think*; 14 scores: reserved vs. warmhearted (A), dull vs. bright (B), affected by feelings vs. emotionally stable (C), undemonstrative vs. excitable (D), obedient vs. assertive (E), sober vs. enthusiastic (F), disregards rules vs. conscientious (G), shy vs. venturesome (H), tough-minded vs. tender-minded (I), vigorous vs. circumspect individualism (J), forthright vs. shrewd (N), self-assured vs. apprehensive (O), uncontrolled vs. controlled (Q_3), relaxed vs. tense (Q_4); (German and Spanish editions (Forms A and B, '63) available); Rutherford B. Porter and Raymond B. Cattell; Institute for Personality and Ability Testing, Inc. (South African adaptation: Standards 1–2 [ages 8–9], 3–5/6 [ages 10–13]; 1973; adaptation by L. du Toit and E. M. Madge; Human Sciences Research Council [South Africa].)*

For additional information and a review by Harrison G. Gough, see 8:520 (46 references); see also T2:1129 (60 references) and P:38 (14 references); for reviews by Anne Anastasi, Wilbur L. Layton, and Robert D. Wirt of the 1963 edition, see 6:122 (2 references).

REFERENCES

1–2. See 6:122.
3–16. See P:38.
17–76. See T2:1129.
77–122. See 8:520.
123. BELL, A. E., ABRAHAMSON, D. S., & MCRAE, K. N. Reading retardation: A 12-year prospective study. *Journal of Pediatrics*, 1977, 91, 363–370.
124. MCINTIRE, W. G., & DRUMMOND, R. J. Multiple predictors of self-concept in children. *Psychology in the Schools*, 1977, 14, 295–298.
125. WILLIAMS, R. E. Programmed instruction for creativity. *Programmed Learning & Educational Technology*, 1977, 14, 50–64.
126. MARJORIBANKS, K. Personality and environmental correlates of cognitive performance and school related affective characteristics: A regression surface analysis. *Alberta Journal of Educational Research*, 1978, 24, 230–243.
127. BIRD, E. I. Multivariate personality analysis of two children's hockey teams. *Perceptual & Motor Skills*, 1979, 48, 967–973.
128. KILMANN, P. R., HENRY, S. E., SCARBRO, H., & LAUGHLIN, J. E. The impact of affective education on elementary school underachievers. *Psychology in the Schools*, 1979, 16, 217–223.
129. MARJORIBANKS, K. Family and school environmental correlates of intelligence, personality, and school related affective characteristics. *Genetic Psychology Monographs*, 1979, 99, 165–183.
130. BOLTON, B. Comments on "Comments on the reliability of a personality questionnaire used in physical education and sport research". *Psychological Reports*, 1980, 46, 1133–1134.
131. BURDSAL, C., & BUEL, C. L. A short term community based early stage intervention program for behavior problem youth. *Journal of Clinical Psychology*, 1980, 36, 226–241.
132. HUNT, D., & RANDHAWA, B. S. Personality factors and ability groups. *Perceptual & Motor Skills*, 1980, 50, 902.
133. KING, D. R., HARRIS, W. J., & DRUMMOND, R. J. Personality source traits of intermediate elementary students selected as emotionally handicapped and their nonhandicapped peers. *Psychology in the Schools*, 1980, 17, 168–173.
134. MARJORIBANKS, K. Person–school environment correlates of children's affective characteristics. *Journal of Educational Psychology*, 1980, 72, 583–591.
135. MINDINGALL, A., LIBB, J. W., & WELCH, M. Locus of control and personality functioning of learning disabled children. *Journal of Clinical Psychology*, 1980, 36, 137–141.
136. ZENDEL, I. H., & PIHL, R. O. Torque and learning and behavior problems in children. *Journal of Consulting & Clinical Psychology*, 1980, 48, 602–604.
137. COHEN, L. K. Personality trait differences between children with high and low others–concepts. *Contemporary Education*, 1981, 52, 112–117.

138. DuPlessis, J. M., & Lochner, L. M. The effects of group psychotherapy on the adjustment of four 12-year-old boys with learning and behavior problems. *Journal of Learning Disabilities*, 1981, 14, 209–212.

[401]

Christensen-Guilford Fluency Tests. Grades 7–16 and adults; 1957–73; 4 tests; Paul R. Christensen and J. P. Guilford; Sheridan Psychological Services, Inc.*
a) WORD FLUENCY.
b) IDEATIONAL FLUENCY I.
c) ASSOCIATIONAL FLUENCY I.
d) EXPRESSIONAL FLUENCY.

For additional information, see 8:237 (20 references); see also T2:546 (48 references); for a review by J. A. Keats and Albert S. Thompson, see 6:544 (4 references).

REFERENCES

1–4. See 6:544.
5–52. See T2:546.
53–72. See 8:237.
73. Cohen, D., Schaie, K. W., & Gribbin, K. The organization of spatial abilities in older men and women. *Journal of Gerontology*, 1977, 32, 578–585.
74. Judd, L. L., Hubbard, B., Janowsky, D. S., Huey, L. Y., & Takahashi, K. I. The effect of lithium carbonate on the cognitive functions of normal subjects. *Archives of General Psychiatry*, 1977, 34, 355–357.

[402]

Chriswell Structural Dexterity Test. Grades 7–9; 1953–63; manual title is *Structural Dexterity Test of Mechanical Ability*; M. Irving Chriswell; Vocational Guidance Service.* (In-print status uncertain; no reply from publisher.)

For additional information, see 6:1083 (1 reference); for a review by A. Pemberton Johnson, see 5:876.

[403]

Chronologial Age Computer. Ages 3–7 to 19–5; 1961–73; for determining CA's at month of testing from birthdate; new set of computing slides issued each September; B. A. Linsday; American Guidance Service.*

For additional information, see 6:660.

[404]

CIRCUS. Nursery school and kgn entrants, first grade entrants; 1974–76, c1972–76; a battery designed "to diagnose the instructional needs of individual children and to monitor and evaluate early education programs"; Educational Testing Service; Addison-Wesley Publishing Co., Inc.*
a) CIRCUS A. Nursery school and kgn entrants; 1974–76; 14 tests, 2 scales for teacher ratings of pupils, and a questionnaire for teacher ratings of the educational environment.
1) *Activities Inventory.* Ratings by teachers; 4 ratings (frequency, complexity, adult help, peer group structure) for each of 15 activities: physical-motor (4), academic (4), role playing-fantasy (4), music-art (3).
2) *CIRCUS Behavior Inventory.* 3 ratings by teachers: following procedures, enjoyment, talking.
3) *Copy What You See: Perceptual-Motor Coordination.*
4) *Do You Know?: General Information.*
5) *Educational Environment Questionnaire.* EEQ; ratings by teachers in 3 areas: class, school, teacher.
6) *Finding Letters and Numbers: Letter and Numeral Recognition and Discrimination.* 4 scores: capital letters, lower-case letters, numbers, total.
7) *How Much and How Many: Quantitative Concepts.* 4 scores: counting, relational terms, numerical concepts, total.
8) *How Words Sound: Auditory Discrimination.* 4 scores: consonants (initial, final), medial vowels, total.
9) *How Words Work: Aspects of Functional Language.* 4 scores: verb forms, prepositions/negation/conjunctions, syntax, total.
10) *Listen to the Story: Comprehension, Interpretation, and Recall of Oral Language.* 3 scores: comprehension, interpretation, total.
11) *Look-Alikes: Visual Discrimination.* 2 scores: total, complex matching.
12) *Make A Tree: Divergent Pictorial Production.* Construction of a tree using paper mosaics; 3 scores: appropriateness, unusualness, difference between 2 constructions.
13) *Noises: Discrimination of Real-World Sounds.*
14) *Say and Tell: Productive Language.* 11 scores: description (3 scores), functional language (5 scores), narration (3 scores).
15) *See and Remember: Visual and Associative Memory.*
16) *Think It Through: Problem Solving.* 4 scores: problem identification, classification, solution evaluation and time sequence, total.
17) *What Words Mean: Receptive Vocabulary.* 4 scores: nouns, verbs, modifiers, total.
b) CIRCUS B. First grade entrants; 1974–76; 12 tests, a scale for teacher rating of pupils, and a questionnaire for teacher ratings of the educational environment.
1) *Activities Inventory.* 1975–76; ratings by teachers; 4 ratings (frequency, complexity, structure preference, situation preference) for each of 9 activities: physical (2), language (2), number, science, classroom citizenship, music-art (2).
2) *Copy What You See: Perceptual Motor Coordination.* 1975–76.
3) *Do You Know?: General Information.* 1975–76.
4) *Educational Environment Questionnaire.* 1975–76; EEQ; ratings by teachers in 3 areas: class, school, teacher.
5) *Finding Letters and Numbers: Letter and Numeral Recognition and Discrimination.* 1974–76; details same as *a* 6.
6) *How Much and How Many: Quantitative Concepts.* 1975–76; 7 scores: counting, numerical concepts, adding and subtracting, subtotal, mathematical concepts, conservation, subtotal.
7) *Listen to the Story: Comprehension, Interpretation and Recall of Oral Language.* 1975–76; 4 scores: comprehension, interpretation, vocabulary, total.
8) *Look-Alikes: Visual Discrimination.* 1975–76.
9) *Make A Tree: Divergent Pictorial Production.* 1974–76; details same as *a* 12.
10) *Say and Tell: Productive Language.* 1975–76; 11 scores: description (2 scores), functional language (5 scores), narration (4 scores).
11) *See and Remember: Visual Memory.* 1975–76.
12) *Things I Like: Interests and Preferences.* 1976; 2 scores: verbal/nonverbal, group/individual.
13) *Think It Through: Problem Solving.* 1975–76; 3 scores: word problems, patterns, mazes.
14) *Word Puzzles.* 1976; 5 scores: sounds, consonants (beginning, ending), whole words, total.

For additional information, reviews by Sueann Robinson Ambron, William L. Goodwin, and excerpted reviews by James Raths and Lilian G. Katz, and Rochelle Selbert Mayer, see 8:7A (3 references).

REFERENCES

1-3. See 8:7A.
4. JURS, S. CIRCUS, Form A test review. *Personnel & Guidance Journal*, 1977, 56, 121-122.
5. MAYER, R. S. CIRCUS: Comprehensive program of assessment services for pre–primary children. *Journal of Educational Measurement*, 1977, 14, 65-72.
6. BOURDEAU, L., & RYAN, T. J. Teacher interaction with preschool children: Attitudes, contacts, and their effects. *Canadian Journal of Behavioural Science*, 1978, 10, 281-295.
7. DIAMOND, E. E. The AMEG commission report on sex bias in achievement testing. *Measurement & Evaluation in Guidance*, 1980, 13, 135-147.
8. SINGER, D. G., & SINGER, J. L. Television viewing and aggressive behavior in preschool children: A field study. *Annals of the New York Academy of Science*, 1980, 347, 289-303.

[405]

★**The Clarke Reading Self-Assessment Survey**. Grades 11-12 and college freshmen; 1978; SAS; self-administered, self-scored; 15 scores: reading (speed, comprehension, interpretation, total), organization of facts and ideas (word lists, concept, diagrams, paragraph parts, total), writing skills (word usage, sentence structure, writing mechanics-punctuation, research and writing, total), total; John H. Clarke and Simon Wittes; Academic Therapy Publications.*

[406]

Classification Test Battery. Illiterate and semi-literate applicants for unskilled and semiskilled mining jobs; 1970-71; CTB; replaces *General Adaptability Battery*; nonverbal reasoning and spatial ability; tests administered at centers established by firms employing the publisher's consultation and training services; 4 tests, 4 scores: 3 scores listed below (*b, c, d*), total; pre-test instructions in any of 9 African languages or in English, all test instructions presented by silent motion pictures; National Institute for Personnel Research [South Africa].*
a) COLOURED PEG BOARD. Unscored "buffer test."
b) PATTERN REPRODUCTION TEST.
c) CIRCLES TEST.
d) FORM SERIES TEST.

REFERENCES

1. ROSENTHAL, D., & MORRISON, S. On being a minority in the classroom: A study of the influence of ethnic mix on cognitive functioning and attitudes in working class children. *Australian Journal of Education*, 1978, 22, 144-160.

[407]

Classroom Atmosphere Questionnaire. Grades 4-9; 1971; CAQ; ratings of teacher by students; 2 scores: acceptance-understanding, problem solving skills; no manual; James K. Hoffmeister; Test Analysis and Development Corporation.*

For additional information and a review by Edward F. Iwanicki, see 8:366.

[408]

*****Classroom Environment Index**. Grades 7 through graduate school; 1971; CEI; previously listed under *Stern Environment Indexes*; 38 scores: 30 press scores (abasement-assurance, achievement, adaptability-defensiveness, affiliation, aggression-blame avoidance, change-sameness, conjunctivity-disjunctivity, counteraction, deference-restiveness, dominance-tolerance, ego achievement, emotionality-placidity, energy-passivity, exhibitionism-inferiority avoidance, fantasied achievement, harm avoidance-risk taking, humanities and social science, impulsiveness-deliberation, narcissism, nurturance, objectivity-projectivity, order-disorder, play-work, practicalness-impracticalness, reflectiveness, science, sensuality-puritanism, sexuality-prudishness, supplication-autonomy, understanding), 6 factor scores (humanistic-intellectual climate, group intellectual life, achievement standards, personal dignity, orderliness, science) based on combinations of the press scores, and 2 second-order factor scores (developmental press, control press); George G. Stern and William J. Walker; Evaluation Research Associates.*

See T2:1395 (38 references), 7:143 (59 references), P:256 (65 references), and 6:92 (19 references).

REFERENCES

1-19. See 6:92.
20-84. See P:256.
85-143. See 7:143.
144-181. See T2:1395.
182. PAYNE, R., & MANSFIELD, R. Correlates of individual perceptions of organizational climate. *Journal of Occupational Psychology*, 1978, 51, 209-218.

[409]

Classroom Environment Scale. Students and teachers in grades 7-12; 1974; CES; a part of *The Social Climate Scales* (2227); 9 scores: involvement, affiliation, teacher support, task orientation, competition, order and organization rule clarity, teacher control, innovation; Rudolf H. Moos and Edison J. Trickett; Consulting Psychologists Press, Inc.*

For additional information and reviews by Maurice J. Eash and C. Robert Pace, see 8:521 (3 references). For a review of *The Social Climate Scales*, see 8:681.

REFERENCES

1-3. See 8:521.
4. ELLISON, T. A., & TRICKETT, E. J. Environmental structure and the perceived similarity–satisfaction relationship: Traditional and alternative schools. *Journal of Personality*, 1978, 46, 57-71.
5. HEARN, J. C., & MOOS, R. H. Subject matter and classroom climate: A test of Holland's environmental propositions. *American Educational Research Journal*, 1978, 15, 111-124.
6. MOOS, R. H. A typology of junior high and high school classrooms. *American Educational Research Journal*, 1978, 15, 53-66.
7. MOOS, R. H., & MOOS, B. S. Classroom social climate and student absences and grades. *Journal of Educational Psychology*, 1978, 70, 263-269.
8. NIELSEN, H. D., & MOOS, R. H. Exploration and adjustment in high school classrooms: A study of person–environment fit. *Journal of Educational Research*, 1978, 72, 52-57.
9. TRICKETT, E. J. Toward a social–ecological conception of adolescent socialization: Normative data on contrasting types of public school classrooms. *Child Development*, 1978, 49, 408-414.
10. EVANS, G. W., & LOVEL, B. Design modification in an open–plan school. *Journal of Educational Psychology*, 1979, 71, 41-49.
11. SCHULTZ, R. A. Student importance ratings as an indicator of the structure of actual and ideal sociopsychological climates. *Journal of Educational Psychology*, 1979, 71, 827-839.
12. FRY, P. S., & COE, K. J. Interaction among dimensions of academic motivation and classroom social climate: A study of the perceptions of junior high and high school pupils. *British Journal of Educational Psychology*, 1980, 50, 33-42.

[410]

Cleary-Now Test of Perceptual-Motor Readiness. Grades kgn-1; 1973-74; "visual-perceptual readiness for reading"; Brian Cleary and Joseph Now; distributed by Stoelting Co.*

For additional information, see 8:869.

[411]
CLEP General Examinations. 1–2 years or equivalent; 1964–76; for college accreditation of nontraditional study, advanced placement or assessment of educational attainment; inactive forms available to colleges for local administration and scoring; program administered by The College Board and Educational Testing Service.*
a) COMPLETE BATTERY. 1964–76; tests administered monthly at centers throughout the United States; 5 tests, 13 scores as listed below.
  1) *Book 1.* 3 tests, 7 scores: English composition, natural sciences (biological, physical, total), mathematics (basic skills, content, total).
  2) *Book 2.* 2 tests, 6 scores: humanities (fine arts, literature, total), social sciences and history (social sciences, history, total).
b) SEPARATE TEST BOOKLETS. 1964–74; 6 tests.
  1) *English Composition and English Composition with Essay.*
  2) *Humanities.* 3 scores: fine arts, literature, total.
  3) *Mathematics.* 3 scores: basic skills, content, total.
  4) *Natural Sciences.* 3 scores: biological, physical, total.
  5) *Social Sciences and History.* 3 scores: social sciences, history, total.
For additional information and a review by Lawrence M. Aleamoni and John E. Milholland, see 8:8 (20 references); see also T2:10 (7 references).

REFERENCES

1–7. See T2:10.
8–27. See 8:8.
28. VOGEL, R. E., & HALINSKI, R. S. Success on the CLEP General Examinations as a function of ACT performance. *Measurement & Evaluation in Guidance*, 1977, 10, 44–47.

[412]
***CLEP General Examinations: English Composition and English Composition Test with Essay.** 1–2 years or equivalent; 1964–77; for college accreditation of nontraditional study, advanced placement, or assessment of educational attainment; *English Composition Test with Essay* administered in December only; both tests administered by The College Board and Educational Testing Service.*
For additional information, see 8:42 (4 references); see also T2:58 (1 reference).

REFERENCES

1. See T2:58.
2–5. See 8:42.
6. FAIGLEY, L., DALY, J. A., & WITTE, S. P. The role of writing apprehension in writing performance and competence. *Journal of Educational Research*, 1981, 75, 16–21.

[413]
CLEP General Examinations: Humanities. 1–2 years or equivalent; 1964–76; for college accreditation of nontraditional study, advanced placement, or assessment of educational attainment; 3 scores: fine arts, literature, total; program administered by The College Board and Educational Testing Service.*
For additional information and a review by Clarence Derrick, see 8:9 (1 reference).

[414]
CLEP General Examinations: Mathematics. 1–2 years or equivalent; 1964–76; for college accreditation of nontraditional study, advanced placement, or assessment of educational attainment; 3 scores: skills and concepts, content, total; program administered by The College Board and Educational Testing Service.*
For additional information and a review by William E. Kline, see 8:254 (1 reference).

[415]
CLEP General Examinations: Natural Sciences. 1–2 years or equivalent; 1964–76; for college accreditation of nontraditional study, advanced placement, or assessment of educational attainment; 3 scores: biological, physical, total; program administered by The College Board and Educational Testing Service.*
For additional information and a review by George G. Mallinson, see 8:824 (2 references).

[416]
CLEP General Examinations: Social Sciences and History. 1–2 years or equivalent; 1964–76; for college accreditation of nontraditional study, advanced placement, or assessment of educational attainment; 3 scores: social science, history, total; program administered by The College Board and Educational Testing Service.*
For additional information and a review by Richard E. Gross, see 8:886 (1 reference).

[417]
CLEP Subject Examination in Afro-American History. Persons entering college or already in college; 1973–76; for college accreditation of nontraditional study, advanced placement, or assessment of educational achievement; tests administered 10 months of the year at centers throughout the United States; program administered by The College Board and Educational Testing Service.*
For additional information, see 8:910. For reviews of the CLEP program, see 8:473 (3 reviews).

[418]
CLEP Subject Examination in American Government. Persons entering college or already in college; 1965–76; for college accreditation of nontraditional study, advanced placement, or assessment of educational achievement; tests administered 10 months of the year at centers throughout the United States; program administered by The College Board and Educational Testing Service.*
For additional information and a review by Howard D. Mehlinger, see 8:919. For reviews of the CLEP program, see 8:473 (3 reviews) and 7:664 (3 reviews).

[419]
★**CLEP Subject Examination in American History I: Early Colonizations to 1877.** Persons entering college or already in college; 1980; for college accreditation of nontraditional study, advanced placement, or assessment of educational achievement; tests administered 10 months of the year at centers throughout the United States; program administered by The College Board and Educational Testing Service.

[420]
★**CLEP Subject Examination in American History II: 1865 to the Present.** Persons entering college or already in college; 1980; for college accreditation of nontraditional study, advanced placement, or assessment of educational achievement; tests administered 10 months of the year at centers throughout the United States;

program administered by The College Board and Educational Testing Service.

[421]
CLEP Subject Examination in American Literature. Persons entering college or already in college; 1971–76; for college accreditation of nontraditional study, advanced placement, or assessment of educational achievement; tests administered 10 months of the year at centers throughout the United States; program administered by The College Board and Educational Testing Service.*

For additional information and a review by Leo P. Ruth, see 8:64. For reviews of the CLEP program, see 8:473 (3 reviews).

[422]
CLEP Subject Examination in Analysis and Interpretation of Literature. Persons entering college or already in college; 1964–76; for college accreditation of nontraditional study, advanced placement, or assessment of educational achievement; tests administered 10 months of the year at centers throughout the United States; program administered by The College Board and Educational Testing Service.*

For additional information and a review by John C. Sherwood, see 8:65 (1 reference). For reviews of the CLEP program, see 8:473 (3 reviews) and 7:664 (3 reviews).

[423]
CLEP Subject Examination in Anatomy, Physiology, Microbiology: North Carolina Nursing Equivalency Examinations. Persons entering college or already in college; 1974–76; for college accreditation of nontraditional study, advanced placement, or assessment of educational achievement; tests administered 10 months of the year at centers throughout the United States; program administered by The College Board and Educational Testing Service.*

For additional information, see 8:1116. For reviews of the CLEP program, see 8:473 (3 reviews).

[424]
CLEP Subject Examination in Behavioral Sciences for Nurses: North Carolina Nursing Equivalency Examinations. Persons entering college or already in college; 1974–76; for college accreditation of nontraditional study, advanced placement, or assessment of educational achievement; tests administered 10 months of the year at centers throughout the United States; program administered by The College Board and Educational Testing Service.*

For additional information, see 8:1117. For reviews of the CLEP program, see 8:473 (3 reviews).

[425]
CLEP Subject Examination in Calculus With Elementary Functions. Persons entering college or already in college; 1974–76; for college accreditation of nontraditional study, advanced placement, or assessment of educational achievement; tests administered 10 months of the year at centers throughout the United States; program administered by The College Board and Educational Testing Service.*

For additional information and a review by J. Philip Smith, see 8:255. For reviews of the CLEP program, see 8:473 (3 reviews).

[426]
CLEP Subject Examination in Clinical Chemistry. Medical technologists; 1972–76; for college accreditation of nontraditional study, advanced placement, or assessment of educational achievement; tests administered 10 months of the year at centers throughout the United States; program administered by The College Board and Educational Testing Service.*

For additional information, see 8:1097. For reviews of the CLEP program, see 8:473 (3 reviews).

[427]
CLEP Subject Examination in College Algebra. Persons entering college or already in college; 1968–76; for college accreditation of nontraditional study, advanced placement, or assessment of educational achievement; tests administered 10 months of the year at centers throughout the United States; program administered by The College Board and Educational Testing Service.*

For additional information and a review by J. Philip Smith, see 8:297. For reviews of the CLEP program, see 8:473 (3 reviews) and 7:664 (3 reviews).

[428]
***CLEP Subject Examination in College Algebra-Trigonometry.** Persons entering college or already in college; 1968–80; for college accreditation of nontraditional study, advanced placement, or assessment of educational achievement; tests administered 10 months of the year at centers throughout the United States; program administered by The College Board and Educational Testing Service.*

For additional information and a review by Peter A. Lappan, Jr., see 8:256 (1 reference); for a review by Carl G. Willis, see 7:454. For reviews of the CLEP program, see 8:473 (3 reviews) and 7:664 (3 reviews).

[429]
CLEP Subject Examination in College Composition. Persons entering college or already in college; 1965–76; for college accreditation of nontraditional study, advanced placement, or assessment of educational achievement; tests administered 10 months of the year at centers throughout the United States; program administered by The College Board and Educational Testing Service.*

For additional information and a review by Charlotte Croon Davis, see 8:43 (2 references); for a review by David P. Harris of Form NCT, see 7:186. For reviews of the CLEP program, see 8:473 (3 reviews) and 7:664 (3 reviews).

REFERENCES

1–2. See 8:43.
3. CHRISTENSEN, M. The College Level Examination Program's freshman English equivalency examinations. *Research in the Teaching of English*, 1977, 11, 186–192.

[430]
CLEP Subject Examination in College French, Levels 1 and 2. Persons entering college or already in college; 1975–76; for college accreditation of nontraditional study, advanced placement, or assessment of educational achievement; tests administered 10 months of

the year at centers throughout the United States; 3 scores: reading comprehension, listening comprehension, total; program administered by The College Board and Educational Testing Service.*

For additional information and a review by Michio Peter Hagiwara, see 8:115. For reviews of the CLEP program, see 8:473 (3 reviews).

[431]
CLEP Subject Examination in College German, Levels 1 and 2. Persons entering college or already in college; 1975–76; for college accreditation of nontraditional study, advanced placement, or assessment of educational achievement; tests administered 10 months of the year at centers throughout the United States; 3 scores: reading comprehension, listening comprehension, total; program administered by The College Board and Educational Testing Service.*

For additional information and reviews by Stefan R. Fink and Herbert Lederer, see 8:127. For reviews of the CLEP program, see 8:473 (3 reviews).

[432]
CLEP Subject Examination in College Spanish, Levels 1 and 2. Persons entering college or already in college; 1975–76; for college accreditation of nontraditional study, advanced placement, or assessment of educational achievement; tests administered 10 months of the year at centers throughout the United States; 3 scores: reading comprehension, listening comprehension, total; program administered by The College Board and Educational Testing Service.*

For additional information, see 8:157. For reviews of the CLEP program, see 8:473 (3 reviews).

[433]
CLEP Subject Examination in Computers and Data Processing. Persons entering college or already in college; 1968–76; for college accreditation of nontraditional study, advanced placement, or assessment of educational achievement; tests administered 10 months of the year at centers throughout the United States; program administered by The College Board and Educational Testing Service.*

For additional information, see 8:1076. For reviews of the CLEP program, see 8:473 (3 reviews) and 7:664 (3 reviews).

[434]
CLEP Subject Examination in Dental Materials: Dental Auxiliary Education. Dental hygienists and assistants; 1976–77; for college accreditation of nontraditional study, advanced placement, or assessment of educational achievement; tests administered 10 months of the year at centers throughout the United States; program administered by The College Board and Educational Testing Service.*

For additional information, see 8:1081. For reviews of the CLEP program, see 8:473 (3 reviews).

[435]
***CLEP Subject Examination in Educational Psychology.** Persons entering college or already in college; 1967–76; for college accreditation of nontraditional study, advanced placement, or assessment of educational achievement; tests administered 10 months of the year at centers throughout the United States; program administered by The College Board and Educational Testing Service.*

For additional information, see 8:459. For reviews of the CLEP program, see 8:473 (3 reviews) and 7:664 (3 reviews).

[436]
CLEP Subject Examination in Elementary Computer Programming-Fortran IV. Persons entering college or already in college; 1971–76; for college accreditation of nontraditional study, advanced placement, or assessment of educational achievement; tests administered 10 months of the year at centers throughout the United States; program administered by The College Board and Educational Testing Service.*

For additional information, see 8:1077. For reviews of the CLEP program, see 8:473 (3 reviews).

[437]
CLEP Subject Examination in English Literature. Persons entering college or already in college; 1970–76; for college accreditation of nontraditional study, advanced placement, or assessment of educational achievement; tests administered 10 months of the year at centers throughout the United States; program administered by The College Board and Educational Testing Service.*

For additional information and a review by Edward M. White, see 8:66. For reviews of the CLEP program, see 8:473 (3 reviews).

[438]
***CLEP Subject Examination in Freshman English.** Persons entering college or already in college; 1973–80; for college accreditation of nontraditional study, advanced placement, or assessment of educational achievement; tests administered 10 months of the year at centers throughout the United States; program administered by The College Board and Educational Testing Service.*

For additional information and a review by Leonard S. Feldt of an earlier edition, see 8:44 (1 reference). For reviews of the CLEP program, see 8:473 (3 reviews).

[439]
CLEP Subject Examination in Fundamentals of Nursing: North Carolina Nursing Equivalency Examinations. Persons entering college or already in college; 1974–76; for college accreditation of nontraditional study, advanced placement, or assessment of educational achievement; tests administered 10 months of the year at centers throughout the United States; program administered by The College Board and Educational Testing Service.*

For additional information and a review by Alice R. Rines, see 8:1118. For reviews of the CLEP program, see 8:473 (3 reviews).

[440]
***CLEP Subject Examination in General Biology.** Persons entering college or already in college; 1970–78; for college accreditation of nontraditional study, advanced placement, or assessment of educational achievement; tests administered 10 months of the year at centers

throughout the United States; program administered by The College Board and Educational Testing Service.*

For additional information and a review by Clarence H. Nelson, see 8:832. For reviews of the CLEP program, see 8:473 (3 reviews) and 7:664 (3 reviews).

[441]
CLEP Subject Examination in General Chemistry. Persons entering college or already in college; 1964–76; for college accreditation of nontraditional study, advanced placement, or assessment of educational achievement; tests administered 10 months of the year at centers throughout the United States; program administered by The College Board and Educational Testing Service.*

For additional information and a review by J. Arthur Campbell, see 8:847. For reviews of the CLEP program, see 8:473 (3 reviews) and 7:664 (3 reviews).

[442]
***CLEP Subject Examination in General Psychology.** Persons entering college or already in college; 1967–80; for college accreditation of nontraditional study, advanced placement, or assessment of educational achievement; tests administered 10 months of the year at centers throughout the United States; program administered by The College Board and Educational Testing Service.*

For additional information and a review by Alfred E. Hall of an earlier edition, see 8:460. For reviews of the CLEP program, see 8:473 (3 reviews) and 7:664 (3 reviews).

REFERENCES
1. HARGRETT, N. T., & CHAPMAN, D. W. Instructor assessment of a standardized proficiency test for course exemption. *Educational Research Quarterly*, 1978, 3, 31–38.
2. CHAPMAN, D. W., & HARGRETT, N. T. College exemption in psychology using CLEP: A reexamination. *Journal of College Student Personnel*, 1979, 20, 317–322.

[443]
CLEP Subject Examination in Head, Neck, and Oral Anatomy: Dental Auxiliary Education. Dental hygienists and assistants; 1976–77; for college accreditation of nontraditional study, advanced placement, or assessment of educational achievement; tests administered 10 months of the year at centers throughout the United States; program administered by The College Board and Educational Testing Service.*

For additional information, see 8:1082. For reviews of the CLEP program, see 8:473 (3 reviews).

[444]
CLEP Subject Examination in Hematology. Medical technologists; 1972–76; for college accreditation of nontraditional study, advanced placement, or assessment of educational achievement; tests administered 10 months of the year at centers throughout the United States; program administered by The College Board and Educational Testing Service.*

For additional information, see 8:1098. For reviews of the CLEP program, see 8:473 (3 reviews).

[445]
***CLEP Subject Examination in Human Growth and Development.** Persons entering college or already in college; 1969–76; for college accreditation of nontraditional study, advanced placement, or assessment of educational achievement; tests administered 10 months of the year at centers throughout the United States; program administered by The College Board and Educational Testing Service.*

For additional information, see 8:410. For reviews of the CLEP program, see 8:473 (3 reviews) and 7:664 (3 reviews).

[446]
CLEP Subject Examination in Immunohematology and Blood Banking. Medical technologists; 1972–76; for college accreditation of nontraditional study, advanced placement, or assessment of educational achievement; tests administered 10 months of the year at centers throughout the United States; program administered by The College Board and Educational Testing Service.*

For additional information, see 8:1099. For reviews of the CLEP program, see 8:473 (3 reviews).

[447]
CLEP Subject Examination in Introduction to Management. Persons entering college or already in college; 1969–76; for college accreditation of nontraditional study, advanced placement, or assessment of educational achievement; tests administered 10 months of the year at centers throughout the United States; program administered by The College Board and Educational Testing Service.*

For additional information, see 8:1070. For reviews of the CLEP program, see 8:473 (3 reviews) and 7:664 (3 reviews).

[448]
CLEP Subject Examination in Introductory Accounting. Persons entering college or already in college; 1970–76; for college accreditation of nontraditional study, advanced placement, or assessment of educational achievement; tests administered 10 months of the year at centers throughout the United States; program administered by The College Board and Educational Testing Service.*

For additional information, see 8:1064. For reviews of the CLEP program, see 8:473 (3 reviews) and 7:664 (3 reviews).

[449]
CLEP Subject Examination in Introductory Business Law. Persons entering college or already in college; 1970–76; for college accreditation of nontraditional study, advanced placement, or assessment of educational achievement; tests administered 10 months of the year at centers throughout the United States; program administered by The College Board and Educational Testing Service.*

For additional information, see 8:1071. For reviews of the CLEP program, see 8:473 (3 reviews) and 7:664 (3 reviews).

[450]
***CLEP Subject Examination in Introductory Macroeconomics.** Persons entering college or already in college; 1974–80; for college accreditation of nontraditional study, advanced placement, or assessment of educational achievement; tests administered 10 months of the year at centers throughout the United States; program

[451]
CLEP Subject Examination in Introductory Marketing. administered by The College Board and Educational Testing Service.

For additional information, see 8:894. For reviews of the CLEP program, see 8:473 (3 reviews).

[451]
CLEP Subject Examination in Introductory Marketing. Persons entering college or already in college; 1968–81; for college accreditation of nontraditional study, advanced placement, or assessment of educational achievement; tests administered 10 months of the year at centers throughout the United States; program administered by The College Board and Educational Testing Service.

For additional information, see 8:1072. For reviews of the CLEP program, see 8:473 (3 reviews) and 7:664 (3 reviews).

[452]
CLEP Subject Examination in Introductory Micro- and Macroeconomics. Persons entering college or already in college; 1975–81; for college accreditation of nontraditional study, advanced placement, or assessment of educational achievement; tests administered 10 months of the year at centers throughout the United States; program administered by The College Board and Educational Testing Service.

For additional information, see 8:895. For reviews of the CLEP program, see 8:473 (3 reviews).

[453]
CLEP Subject Examination in Introductory Microeconomics. Persons entering college or already in college; 1974–80; for college accreditation of nontraditional study, advanced placement, or assessment of educational achievement; tests administered 10 months of the year at centers throughout the United States; program administered by The College Board and Educational Testing Service.

For additional information, see 8:896. For reviews of the CLEP program, see 8:473 (3 reviews).

[454]
CLEP Subject Examination in Introductory Sociology. Persons entering college or already in college; 1965–76; for college accreditation of nontraditional study, advanced placement, or assessment of educational achievement; tests administered 10 months of the year at centers throughout the United States; program administered by The College Board and Educational Testing Service.*

For additional information, see 8:925. For reviews of the CLEP program, see 8:473 (3 reviews) and 7:664 (3 reviews).

[455]
CLEP Subject Examination in Medical-Surgical Nursing: North Carolina Nursing Equivalency Examinations. Persons entering college or already in college; 1974–76; for college accreditation of nontraditional study, advanced placement, or assessment of educational achievement; tests administered 10 months of the year at centers throughout the United States; program administered by The College Board and Educational Testing Service.*

For additional information and a review by Elaine L. La Monica, see 8:1119. For reviews of the CLEP program, see 8:473 (3 reviews).

[456]
CLEP Subject Examination in Microbiology. Medical technologists; 1972–76; for college accreditation of nontraditional study, advanced placement, or assessment of educational achievement; tests administered 10 months of the year at centers throughout the United States; program administered by The College Board and Educational Testing Service.*

For additional information, see 8:1100. For reviews of the CLEP program, see 8:473 (3 reviews).

[457]
CLEP Subject Examination in Money and Banking. Persons entering college or already in college; 1967–76; for college accreditation of nontraditional study, advanced placement, or assessment of educational achievement; tests administered 10 months of the year at centers throughout the United States; program administered by The College Board and Educational Testing Service.*

For additional information, see 8:1073. For reviews of the CLEP program, see 8:473 (3 reviews) and 7:664 (3 reviews).

[458]
CLEP Subject Examination in Oral Radiography: Dental Auxiliary Education. Dental hygienists and assistants; 1976–77; for college accreditation of nontraditional study, advanced placement, or assessment of educational achievement; tests administered 10 months of the year at centers throughout the United States; program administered by The College Board and Educational Testing Service.*

For additional information, see 8:1083. For reviews of the CLEP program, see 8:473 (3 reviews).

[459]
CLEP Subject Examination in Statistics. Persons entering college or already in college; 1967–76; for college accreditation of nontraditional study, advanced placement, or assessment of educational achievement; tests administered 10 months of the year at centers throughout the United States; program administered by The College Board and Educational Testing Service.*

For additional information, see 8:313. For reviews of the CLEP program, see 8:473 (3 reviews) and 7:664 (3 reviews).

[460]
CLEP Subject Examination in Tooth Morphology and Function: Dental Auxiliary Education. Dental hygienists and assistants; 1976–77; for college accreditation of nontraditional study, advanced placement, or assessment of educational achievement; tests administered 10 months of the year at centers throughout the United States; program administered by The College Board and Educational Testing Service.*

For additional information, see 8:1084. For reviews of the CLEP program, see 8:473 (3 reviews).

[461]
*CLEP Subject Examination in Trigonometry. Persons entering college or already in college; 1968–76;

for college accreditation of nontraditional study, advanced placement, or assessment of educational achievement; tests administered 10 months of the year at centers throughout the United States; program administered by The College Board and Educational Testing Service.*

For additional information, see 8:314. For reviews of the CLEP program, see 8:473 (3 reviews) and 7:664 (3 reviews).

[462]

★**CLEP Subject Examination in Western Civilization I: Ancient Near East to 1648.** Persons entering college or already in college; 1980; for college accreditation of nontraditional study, advanced placement, or assessment of educational achievement; tests administered 10 months of the year at centers throughout the United States; program administered by The College Board and Educational Testing Service.

[463]

★**CLEP Subject Examination in Western Civilization II: 1648 to the Present.** Persons entering college or already in college; 1980; for college accreditation of nontraditional study, advanced placement, or assessment of educational achievement; tests administered 10 months of the year at centers throughout the United States; program administered by The College Board and Educational Testing Service.

[464]

Clerical Aptitude Test: Acorn National Aptitude Tests. Grades 7–16 and adults; 1943–50; 4 scores: business practice, number checking, date-name-address checking, total; Andrew Kobal, J. Wayne Wrightstone, and Karl R. Kunze; Psychometric Affiliates.*

For additional information, see 5:847 (1 reference); for reviews by Marion A. Bills, Donald G. Paterson, Henry Weitz, and E. F. Wonderlic, see 3:623.

REFERENCES
1. See 5:847.
2. BELMONT, L., WITTES, J., & STEIN, Z. Relation of birth order, family size and social class to psychological functions. *Perceptual & Motor Skills*, 1977, 45, 1107–1116.
3. BOOTH, R. F., & NEWMAN, K. Social status and minority recruit performance in the navy: Some implications for affirmative action programs. *Sociological Quarterly*, 1977, 18, 564–573.

[465]

Clerical Skills Series. Clerical workers and applicants; 1966–69; CSS; 10 tests; Martin M. Bruce; Martin M. Bruce, Ph.D., Publishers.*
a) ALPHABETIZING-FILING. 1966.
b) ARITHMETIC. 1966–69.
c) CLERICAL SPEED AND ACCURACY. 1966.
d) CODING. 1966.
e) EYE-HAND ACCURACY. 1966.
f) GRAMMAR AND PUNCTUATION. 1966.
g) SPELLING. 1966–69.
h) SPELLING-VOCABULARY. 1966.
i) VOCABULARY. 1966.
j) WORD FLUENCY. 1966.

For additional information and a review by Robert Fitzpatrick, see 7:988.

[466]

*****Clerical Speed and Accuracy: Differential Aptitude Tests.** Grades 8–12 and adults; 1947–77; George K. Bennett, Harold G. Seashore, and Alexander G. Wesman; The Psychological Corporation.* For the complete battery entry, see 732.

For additional information regarding an earlier edition, see 8:324; see also T2:781 (2 references). For reviews of the complete battery, see 8:485 (2 reviews, 1 excerpt), 7:673 (1 review, 1 excerpt), 6:767 (2 reviews), 5:605 (2 reviews), 4:711 (3 reviews), and 3:620 (1 excerpt).

REFERENCES
1–2. See T2:781.
3. ARNOLD, P., & WALTER, G. Communication and reasoning skills of deaf and hearing signers. *Perceptual and Motor Skills*, 1979, 49, 192–194.

[467]

Clerical Tests. Applicants for clerical positions; 1951–66; 6 tests; no manual; Stevens, Thurow & Associates, Inc.*
a) INVENTORY J, ARITHMETICAL REASONING. 1966.
b) INVENTORY K, ARITHMETICAL PROFICIENCY. 1951–66.
c) INVENTORY M, INTERPRETATION OF TABULATED MATERIAL. 1951–66.
d) INVENTORY R, INTERPRETATION OF TABULATED MATERIAL. 1951–66.
e) INVENTORY S, ALPHABETICAL FILING. 1951–66.
f) INVENTORY Y, GRAMMAR. 1951–66.

For additional information, see 7:989.

[468]

Clerical Tests, Series N. Applicants for clerical positions not involving frequent use of typewriter or verbal skill; 1940–59; 5 scores: comparing names and numbers, copying names, copying numbers, addition and multiplication, mental ability; 5 tests and 1 application form; Stevens, Thurow & Associates, Inc.*
a) INVENTORY E, COMPARING NAMES AND NUMBERS.
b) INVENTORY F, COPYING NUMBERS.
c) INVENTORY G, ADDITION AND MULTIPLICATION.
d) INVENTORY H, COPYING NAMES.
e) INVENTORY NO. 2. Mental ability.
f) APPLICATION FOR POSITION.

For additional information, see 6:1036.

[469]

Clerical Tests, Series V. Applicants for typing and stenographic positions; 1940–59; 5 scores: grammar, spelling, vocabulary, typing (words per minute), mental ability; 5 tests and 1 application form; Stevens, Thurow & Associates, Inc.*
a) INVENTORY A, GRAMMAR.
b) INVENTORY B, SPELLING.
c) INVENTORY C, VOCABULARY.
d) TEST OF TYPEWRITING ABILITY.
e) INVENTORY NO. 2. Mental ability.
f) APPLICATION FOR POSITION.

For additional information, see 6:1037.

[470]

Clerical Worker Examination. Clerical workers;1962–63; test booklet title is *Clerical Worker*; 5 scores: clerical speed and accuracy, verbal ability, quantitative ability, total ability, total; McCann Associates.*

For additional information, see 6:1038.

[471]

★**Clifton Assessment Procedures for the Elderly.** Ages 60 and over; 1979–81; CAPE; assesses cognitive and behavioral competence of the elderly; 2 tests plus combination short version; 9 scores yielding a cognitive, behavioural, and overall dependency grade; A. H. Pattie and C. J. Gilleard; Hodder & Stoughton Educational [England].*

a) COGNITIVE ASSESSMENT SCALE. CAS; revision of *Clifton Assessment Schedule*; 4 scores: information/orientation, mental ability, psychomotor (adaptation of Gibson Spiral Maze), total.

b) BEHAVIOUR RATING SCALE. BRS; shortened version of *Stockton Geriatric Rating Scale*; 5 scores: physical disability, apathy, communication difficulties, social disturbance, total.

c) SURVEY VERSION. Short version of CAPE for quick assessment; consists of information/orientation scale of the CAS and the physical disability scale of the BRS.

REFERENCES

1. KLINE, P. Clifton Assessment Procedures for the Elderly (CAPE). *British Journal of Psychiatry*, 1980, 136, 199.

[472]

*****Clinical Analysis Questionnaire.** Ages 16 and over; 1970–80; CAQ; 37 scores (listed below): 28 primary factor scores and 9 second-order factor scores; Samuel E. Krug; Institute for Personality and Ability Testing, Inc.*

a) PART 1 (NORMAL PERSONALITY TRAITS). Shortened version of the *Sixteen Personality Factor Questionnaire*; the regular version of the 16PF may be substituted; 16 primary factor scores: warmth (A), intelligence (B), emotional stability (C), dominance (E), impulsivity (F), conformity (G), boldness (H), sensitivity (I), suspiciousness (L), imagination (M), shrewdness (N), insecurity (O), radicalism (Q_1), self-sufficiency (Q_2), self-discipline (Q_3), tension (Q_4), plus 5 second-order factor scores: extraversion (Ex), anxiety (Ax), tough poise (Ct), independence (In), superego strength (Se).

b) PART 2 (THE CLINICAL FACTORS). 12 primary factor scores: hypochondriasis (D_1), suicidal depression (D_2), agitation (D_3), anxious depression (D_4), low energy depression (D_5), guilt and resentment (D_6), boredom and withdrawal (D_7), paranoia (P_a), psychopathic deviation (Pp), schizophrenia (Sc), psychasthenia (As), psychological inadequacy (Ps), plus 4 second-order factor scores: socialization (So), depression (D), psychoticism (P), neuroticism (Ne).

For additional information and a review by Douglas McNair, see 8:522 (7 references); see also T2:1131 (1 reference) and 7:54 (1 reference).

REFERENCES

1. See 7:54.
2. See T2:1131.
3–9. See 8:522.
10. KRUG, S. E., & LAUGHLIN, J. E. Second-order factors among normal and pathological primary personality traits. *Journal of Consulting & Clinical Psychology*, 1977, 45, 575–582.
11. NICHOLS, M. P., & KNOPF, I. J. Refining computerized test interpretations: An in-depth approach. *Journal of Personality Assessment*, 1977, 41, 157–159.
12. SCHWARTZ, S., & BURDSAL, C. A factor–analytic examination of the relationship of personality variables to hypnotizability. *Journal of Clinical Psychology*, 1977, 33, 356–360.
13. COSTELLO, R. M., LAWLIS, F. G., MANDERS, K. R., & CELISTINO, J. F. Empirical derivation of a partial personality typology of alcoholics. *Journal of Studies on Alcohol*, 1978, 39, 1258–1266.
14. DONOVAN, D. M., O'LEARY, M. R., & WALKER, R. D. Validation of a subjective helplessness measure. *Journal of Personality Assessment*, 1979, 43, 461–467.
15. MULLANEY, J. A., & TRIPPETT, C. J. Alcohol dependence and phobias: Clinical description and relevance. *British Journal of Psychiatry*, 1979, 135, 565–573.
16. STAR, B., CLARK, C. G., GOETZ, K. M., & O'MALIA, L. Psychosocial aspects of wife battering. *Social Casework*, 1979, 8, 479–487.
17. JAMES, J. F., GREGORY, D., JONES, R. K., & RUNDELL, O. H. Psychiatric morbidity in prisons. *Hospital & Community Psychiatry*, 1980, 31, 674–677.
18. O'LEARY, M. R., CALSYN, D. A., & FAURIA, T. The Group Embedded Figures Test: A measure of cognitive style or cognitive impairment. *Journal of Personality Assessment*, 1980, 44, 532–537.
19. BABAD, E. Y., & INBAR, J. Performance and personality correlates of teacher's susceptibility to biasing information. *Journal of Personality & Social Psychology*, 1981, 40, 553–561.
20. O'LEARY, M. R., FAURIA, T., CALSYN, D. A., & FEHRENBACH, P. A. Cognitive style, personality traits, and treatment attrition among alcoholics. *International Journal of the Addictions*, 1981, 16, 1143–1148.

[473]

Clinical Behavior Check List and Rating Scale. Clinical clients; 1965; 10 ratings: cooperation, activity level, intelligence, disposition, persistence, sociability, emotional stability, attention, communicativeness, relaxation-tension; Psychological Research and Development Institute; Psychological Publications Press.* (In-print status uncertain; no reply from publisher.)

For additional information, see P:40.

[474]

★**Clinical Evaluation of Language Functions—Diagnostic Battery.** Grades kgn–12; 1980; CELF; measures language functions in areas of phonology, syntax, semantics, memory, and word finding and retrieval; 15 scores: word and sentence structure, word classes, linguistic concepts, relationships and ambiguities, oral directions, spoken paragraphs, word series, confrontation naming, word associations, model sentence, formulated sentences, processing speech sounds, producing speech sounds (blends, final, initial); Eleanor M. Semel and Elisabeth H. Wiig; Charles E. Merrill Publishing Co.*

[475]

★**Clinical Evaluation of Language Functions, Elementary and Advanced Screening Tests.** Grades kgn–5, 5–12; 1980; CELF; a screening measure of language processing and production abilities, developed and standardized with the *CELF-Diagnostic Battery*; Eleanor M. Semel and Elisabeth H. Wiig; Charles E. Merrill Publishing Co.*

a) ELEMENTARY LEVEL. Grades kgn–5; 3 scores: processing, production, total.

b) ADVANCED LEVEL. Grades 5–12; 3 scores: same as *a* above.

[476]

Clinical Experience Record for Nursing Students. Nursing students and nurses; 1960–75; CERNS; for recording by instructor of "critical incidents" (rated effective or ineffective) in 12 or 15 areas listed below; no scores; John C. Flanagan, Angeline C. Marchese, Grace Fivars, and Shirley A. Tuska (manual); Psychometric Techniques Associates.*

a) CLINICAL PERFORMANCE RECORD. 1960–75; 12 areas: planning and organizing and adapting nursing care, checking, meeting patient's adjustment and emotional needs, meeting patient's physical and medical needs, applying scientific principles to nursing care, observing and reporting and charting, adaptability to new or stressful situations, relations with co-workers and physicians and visitors, judgment regarding professional values, use of learning opportunities, acceptance of professional responsibility, personal appearance/conduct.

b) PERFORMANCE/PROGRESS RECORD—PSYCHIATRIC/-MENTALLY RETARDED PATIENT CARE. 1970; 15 areas: providing for comfort and hygiene and other physical needs, checking and observing, training the patient, controlling reluctant or undesirable behavior, recognizing and responding to emotional needs, preventing injury to patient, preventing injury to self or other staff members, coping with emergencies, using ingenuity, taking personal responsibility, maintaining ethical and moral behavior, contributing to effective ward management, interacting with families and visitors and the public, keeping records and reporting, supervising and assisting working patients.

For additional information, see 8:1120 (1 reference).

[477]

Closure Flexibility (Concealed Figures). Industrial employees; 1956–65; revision of *Gottschaldt Figures*; L. L. Thurstone (test), T. E. Jeffrey (test), and Manpower Research and Development Division, Human Resources Center, University of Chicago (manual); the Center.*

See T2:547 (9 references) and 7:435 (9 references); for a review by Leona E. Tyler, see 6:545 (4 references).

REFERENCES

1–4. See 6:545.
5–13. See 7:435.
14–22. See T2:547.
23. MANGAN, G. L. The relationship of mobility of inhibition to rate of inhibitory growth and measures of flexibility, extraversion, and neuroticism. *Journal of General Psychology*, 1978, 99, 271–279.
24. LAVRAKAS, P. J., & MAIER, R. A. Differences in human ability to judge veracity from the audio medium. *Journal of Research in Personality*, 1979, 13, 139–153.
25. TUTTLE, H. G., GUITART, J., & ZAMPOGNA, J. Effects of cultural presentations on attitudes of foreign language students. *Modern Language Journal*, 1979, 63, 177–182.
26. OTTESON, J. P. Stylistic and personality correlates of lateral eye movements: A factor analytic study. *Perceptual & Motor Skills*, 1980, 50, 995–1010.
27. GAYLE, G. M. H. Another look at personality motivation and second language learning in a bilingual context. *Alberta Journal of Educational Research*, 1981, 27, 145–153.

[478]

Closure Speed (Gestalt Completion). Industrial employees; 1956–66; formerly called *Gestalt Completion: A Test of Speed of Closure*; L. L. Thurstone (test), T. E. Jeffrey (test), and Norman J. Kantor (manual); Human Resources Center, University of Chicago.*

See T2:548 (1 reference) and 7:436 (2 references); for a review by Leona E. Tyler, see 6:546 (3 references).

REFERENCES

1–3. See 6:546.
4–5. See 7:436.
6. See T2:548.
7. LOO, R. Personality dimensions and reversible perspective in Embedded Figures Test. *Perceptual & Motor Skills*, 1978, 46, 1016–1018.
8. WEISZ, J. R., QUINLAN, D. M., O'NEILL, P., & O'NEILL, P. C. The Rorschach and structured tests of perception as indices of intellectual development in mentally retarded and nonretarded children. *Journal of Experimental Child Psychology*, 1978, 25, 326–336.

[479]

Cloze Procedure [Ebbinghaus Completion Method] as Applied to Reading. Invented in 1897 by Ebbinghaus, this historical testing procedure has been used to measure reading comprehension as well as intelligence, achievement in college courses, association, imagination, language ability, and "numerous other 'faculties' "; many different names were used to refer to the procedure and its modification, e.g., Ebbinghaus completion test, mutilated sentence (or text) test, combination/method, sentence (or story) completion, missing word test, conjectural test, incomplete sentences test, completion exercise, controlled completion test, and multiple-choice Ebbinghaus; in 1953, Taylor applied the technique (designating it the cloze procedure) to measuring the readability or difficulty of textual materials-the designation quickly caught on to include all missing-word techniques used to measure both reading comprehension and readability of textual material (the cloze procedure is unique in that in addition to measuring examinee responses as other tests do, it is sometimes used solely to measure the readability of the test material itself); a variety of names have since been used for cloze procedures, e.g., precloze, postcloze, multiple choice cloze, random cloze, and rational cloze.

For additional information and reviews by John Charles Alderson, Warwick B. Elley, and William L. Smith, see 8:720 (400 references).

REFERENCES

1–400. See 8:720.
401. DESILVA, W. P., & HEMSLEY, D. R. The influence of context on language perception in schizophrenia. *British Journal of Social & Clinical Psychology*, 1977, 16, 337–345.
402. BRATT, H. M. Hemisphere asymmetry in school age children. *School Science & Mathematics*, 1979, 79, 158–160.
403. MANSCHRECK, T. C., MAHER, B. A., RUCKLOS, M. E., & WHITE, M. T. The predictability of thought disordered speech in schizophrenic patients. *British Journal of Psychiatry*, 1979, 134, 595–601.
404. PAIGE, W. D. The effects of the level of readability and use of a glossary on the comprehension of technical material. *Journal of Industrial Teacher Education*, 1981, 18, 43–52.

[480]

★CLS: Classroom Learning Screening. Grades 1, 2, 3, 4, 5, 6; 1980; 2 derived scores (performance, learning) from each of 3 learning channels (see write, hear write, see say) in math, spelling, and reading; Carl H. Koenig and Harold P. Kunzelmann; Charles E. Merrill Publishing Co.*

[481]

★Cluster Analysis of Wechsler/WRAT. Ages 5 and over; 1979; manual title is *Meanings and Measures of Mental Tests*; provides cluster analyses of the *Wechsler Intelligence Scale for Children (WISC)* and the Revised form *(WISC-R)*, the *Wide Range Achievement Test (WRAT)*, and *Wechsler Adult Intelligence Scale (WAIS)*; Joseph F. Jastak and Sarah Jastak; Jastak Associates, Inc.*

[482]

Clymer-Barrett Prereading Battery. First grade entrants; 1966–69; CBPB; 4 scores: visual discrimination, auditory discrimination, visual-motor, total; short screening form consisting of 2 of the 6 subtests yields a single score; Theodore Clymer and Thomas C. Barrett; Chapman, Brook & Kent.*

See T2:1699 (2 references); for reviews by Roger Farr and Kenneth J. Smith, see 7:744 (2 references).

REFERENCES

1–2. See 7:744.

3-4. See T2:1699.
5. RICHEK, M. A. Readiness skills that predict initial word learning using 2 different methods of instruction. *Reading Research Quarterly,* 1977-1978, 13, 200-222.
6. OAKLAND, T. Predictive validity of readiness tests for middle and lower socioeconomic status Anglo, Black, and Mexican American children. *Journal of Educational Psychology,* 1978, 70, 574-582.
7. QUARN, K. C., & YORE, L. D. Comparison studies of reading readiness skills acquisition by different methods: Formal reading readiness program, informal reading readiness program, and a kindergarten science program. *Science Education,* 1978, 62, 459-465.
8. WILLIAMS, F., & OAKLAND, T. A three-year auditory perception program for low-SES minority children. *Journal of Special Education,* 1978, 12, 331-344.
9. SHEPARD, L. Construct and predictive validity of the California Entry Level Test. *Educational & Psychological Measurement,* 1979, 39, 867-877.

[483]
Cognitive Abilities Test. Grades kgn-1, 2-3, 3-12; 1954-74; CAT; Robert L. Thorndike, Elizabeth Hagan, and Irving Lorge (*a*); Riverside Publishing Co.*
a) PRIMARY BATTERIES. Grades kgn-1, 2-3; 1954-74; revision of Levels 1 and 2 of *Lorge-Thorndike Intelligence Tests.*
 1) *Primary 1.* Grades kgn-1.
 2) *Primary 2.* Grades 2-3.
b) MULTI-LEVEL EDITION. Grades 3-12; 1971-74; 3 scores: verbal, quantitative, nonverbal. (British adaptation of the Multi-Level Edition: Ages 8-18; 1973; NFER-Nelson Publishing Co. [England].)*
 1) *Verbal Battery.*
 2) *Quantitative Battery.*
 3) *Nonverbal Battery.*

For additional information and reviews by Kenneth D. Hopkins and Robert C. Nichols, see 8:181 (12 references); for reviews by Marcel L. Goldschmid and Carol K. Tittle and an excerpted review by Richard C. Cox of the primary batteries, see 7:343.

REFERENCES

1-12. See 8:181.
13. LEINHARDT, G. Program evaluation: An empirical study of individualized instruction. *American Educational Research Journal,* 1977, 14, 277-293.
14. LESIAK, J. The Gates-MacGinitie Readiness Skills Test and Illinois Test of Psycholinguistic Abilities as predictors of first grade reading. *Psychology in the Schools,* 1977, 14, 4-10.
15. MORAN, M. R., & BYRNE, M. C. Mastery of verb tense markers by normal and learning-disabled children. *Journal of Speech & Hearing Research,* 1977, 20, 529-542.
16. SEATON, H. W., & SMITH, S. D. The use of receptive and expressive language development activities for improving students' reading achievement. *National Reading Conference Yearbook,* 1977, 82-87.
17. WINNE, P. H. Aptitude-treatment interactions in an experiment on teacher effectiveness. *American Educational Research Journal,* 1977, 14, 389-409.
18. FENNEMA, E. H., & SHERMAN, J. A. Sex-related differences in mathematics achievement and related factors: A further study. *Journal for Research in Mathematics Education,* 1978, 9, 189-203.
19. GOOD, T. L., & BECKERMAN, T. M. An examination of teachers' effects on high, middle, and low aptitude students' performance on a standardized achievement test. *American Educational Research Journal,* 1978, 15, 477-482.
20. JOHNSON, R. A., & YARBOROUGH, B. H. The effects of marks on the development of academically talented elementary pupils. *Gifted Child Quarterly,* 1978, 22, 498-505.
21. LEWIS, J., & TODD, R. The relationship of cognitive abilities scores with social studies achievement. *Educational & Psychological Measurement,* 1978, 38, 463-464.
22. LONGSTRETH, L. E. Level I-level II abilities as they affect performance of three races in the college classroom. *Journal of Educational Psychology,* 1978, 70, 289-297.
23. STAYROOK, N. G., CORNO, L., & WINNE, P. H. Path analyses relating student perceptions of teacher behavior to student achievement. *Journal of Teacher Education,* 1978, 29, 51-56.
24. YARBOROUGH, B. H., & JOHNSON, R. A. The relationship between intelligence levels and benefits from innovative, nongraded elementary schooling and traditional, graded schooling. *Educational Research Quarterly,* 1978, 3, 28-38.
25. BOSSE, M. A. Do creative children behave differently? *Journal of Creative Behavior,* 1979, 13, 119-126.
26. CORNO, L. A hierarchical analysis of selected naturally occurring aptitude-treatment interactions in the third grade. *American Educational Research Journal,* 1979, 16, 391-409.
27. GEORGE, W. C. The talent-search concept: An identification strategy for the intellectually gifted. *Journal of Special Education,* 1979, 13, 221-237.
28. LEINHARDT, G., SEEWALD, A. M., & ENGEL, M. Learning what's taught: Sex differences in instruction. *Journal of Educational Psychology,* 1979, 71, 432-439.
29. MAYFIELD, B. Teacher perception of creativity, intelligence and achievement. *Gifted Child Quarterly,* 1979, 23, 812-817.
30. OLLENDICK, D. G. Parental locus of control and the assessment of children's personality characteristics. *Journal of Personality Assessment,* 1979, 43, 401-405.
31. SMITH, N. M. Allocation of time and achievement in elementary social studies. *Journal of Educational Research,* 1979, 72, 231-236.
32. ALHEIDT, P. The effect of reading ability on Rorschach performance. *Journal of Personality Assessment,* 1980, 44, 3-10.
33. CORNO, L. Individual and class level effects of a parent-assisted instruction in classroom memory support strategies. *Journal of Educational Psychology,* 1980, 72, 278-292.
34. KANOY, R. C., III, JOHNSON, B. W., & KANOY, K. W. Locus of control and self-concept in achieving and underachieving bright elementary students. *Psychology in the Schools,* 1980, 17, 395-399.
35. OKOH, N. Bilingualism and divergent thinking among Nigerian and Welsh school children. *Journal of Social Psychology,* 1980, 110, 163-170.
36. RUSS, S. W. Primary process integration on the Rorschach and achievement in children. *Journal of Personality Assessment,* 1980, 44, 338-344.
37. SHERMAN, J. Mathematics, spatial visualization, and related factors: Changes in girls and boys, grades 8-11. *Journal of Educational Psychology,* 1980, 72, 476-482.
38. SHERMAN, J. A. Predicting mathematics grades of high school girls and boys: A further study. *Contemporary Educational Psychology,* 1980, 5, 249-255.
39. WIDIGER, T. A., KNUDSON, R. M., & RORER, L. G. Convergent and discriminant validity of measures of cognitive styles and abilities. *Journal of Personality & Social Psychology,* 1980, 39, 116-129.
40. YARBOROUGH, B. H., & JOHNSON, R. A. How meaningful are marks in promoting growth in reading? *Reading Teacher,* 1980, 33, 644-651.
41. YARBOROUGH, B. H., & JOHNSON, R. A. A six-year study of sex differences in intellectual functioning, reading/language arts achievement, and affective development. *Journal of Psychology,* 1980, 106, 55-61.
42. SCHROTH, M. L. Type I and type II abilities in children and learning rate. *Journal of Genetic Psychology,* 1981, 138, 95-102.
43. SMEAD, V., & CHASE, C. I. Student expectations as they relate to achievement in eighth grade mathematics. *Journal of Educational Research,* 1981, 75, 115-120.
44. WHITELY, S. E., & SCHNEIDER, L. M. Information structure for geometric analogies: A test theory approach. *Applied Psychological Measurement,* 1981, 5, 383-397.

[484]
*****Cognitive Skills Assessment Battery, Second Edition.** Pre-kgn-kgn; 1974-81; CSAB; criterion-referenced; 98 item scores (49 consist of plus or minus) in 18 areas: basic information (4 scores), identification of body parts (4 scores), color identification (4 scores), shape identification (4 scores), symbol discrimination (10 scores), visual-auditory discrimination (6 scores), auditory discrimination (6 scores), number knowledge (10 scores), letter naming (2 scores), vocabulary (6 scores), information from pictures (4 scores), picture comprehension (4 scores), story comprehension (4 scores), multiple directions (4 scores), large muscle coordination (4 scores), visual-motor coordination (6 scores), memory (8 scores), response during assessment (8 scores); Ann E. Boehm and Barbara R. Slater; Teachers College Press.*

For additional information and reviews by Kathryn Hoover Calfee and Barbara K. Keogh, see 8:797.

REFERENCES
1. CLARK, C. M. Cognitive Skills Assessment Battery, 1974 edition. *Journal of School Psychology*, 1977, 15, 281–282.
2. CORDONI, B. K. Boehm & Slater/Cognitive Skills Assessment Battery. *Journal of Learning Disabilities*, 1978, 11, 671–672.

[485]
Coitometer. Older adolescents and adults; 1974; knowledge of the physical aspects of human coitus; no manual; Panos D. Bardis; the Author.*

For additional information, see 8:334.

[486]
College and University Environment Scales, Second Edition. College; 1962–69; CUES; an adaptation of the *College Characteristics Index*; students' conceptions of "the prevailing atmosphere or climate of the campus"; 7 scores: practicality, community, awareness, propriety, scholarship, campus morale, quality of teaching and faculty-student relationships; C. Robert Pace; Educational Testing Service.*

For additional information, see 8:523 (100 references); see also T2:1133 (69 references); for reviews by Paul L. Dressel and James V. Mitchell, Jr., see 7:56 (99 references); see also P:42 (40 references).

REFERENCES
1–40. See P:42.
41–139. See 7:56.
140–208. See T2:1133.
209–308. See 8:523.
309. CORAZZINI, J. G., & WILSON, S. Students, the environment and their interaction: Assessing student needs and planning for change. *Journal of the National Association of Women Deans & Counselors*, 1977, 40, 68–72.
310. KLIMEK, R. J., & HODINKO, B. A. Psychological climate of the multicampus community college: A campus amalgam? *Journal of College Student Personnel*, 1977, 18, 482–485.
311. VELA, J. E. A comparison of Chicano and Anglo perceptions of the university environment. *Journal of College Student Personnel*, 1977, 18, 462–466.
312. ANDERSON, R. E. A financial and environmental analysis of strategic policy changes at small private colleges. *Journal of Higher Education*, 1978, 49, 30–46.

[487]
College Board Achievement Test in American History and Social Studies. Candidates for college entrance; 1901–76; test administered 6 times annually (January, March, May, June, November, December) at centers established by the publisher; an inactive form, entitled *College Placement Test in American History and Social Studies*, is available for local administration and scoring; program administered by The College Board and Educational Testing Service.*

For additional information, see 8:887; see also T2:1939 (1 reference); for a review by Howard R. Anderson of earlier forms, see 6:966; for a review by Ralph W. Tyler, see 5:786 (3 references); for a review by Robert L. Thorndike, see 4:662 (6 references). For reviews of the testing program, see 6:760 (2 reviews).

[488]
College Board Achievement Test in Biology. Candidates for college entrance; 1915–76; test administered 6 times annually (January, March, May, June, November, December) at centers established by the publisher; an inactive form entitled *College Placement Test in Biology*, is available for local administration and scoring; program administered by The College Board and Educational Testing Service.*

For additional information, see 8:833 (1 reference); see also 7:813 (2 references) and 6:892 (3 references); for a review by Elizabeth Hagen of an earlier form, see 5:723; for a review by Clark W. Horton, see 4:600. For reviews of the testing program, see 6:760 (2 reviews).

[489]
College Board Achievement Test in Chemistry. Candidates for college entrance; 1901–76; test administered 6 times annually (January, March, May, June, November, December) at centers established by the publisher; inactive forms, entitled *College Placement Test in Chemistry*, are available for local administration and scoring; program administered by The College Board and Educational Testing Service.*

For additional information, see 8:848 and 7:844 (3 references); for a review by William Hered of earlier forms, see 6:914 (4 references); for a review by Max D. Engelhart, see 5:742 (2 references); for a review by Evelyn Raskin, see 4:617 (4 references). For reviews of the testing program, see 6:760 (2 reviews).

[490]
College Board Achievement Test in English Composition. Candidates for college entrance; 1943–76; test administered 6 times annually (January, March, May, June, November, December) at centers established by the publisher; inactive forms, entitled *College Placement Test in English Composition*, are available for local administration and scoring; program administered by The College Board and Educational Testing Service.*

For additional information and reviews by David P. Harris and Leo P. Ruth, see 8:46 (2 references); see also T2:64 (1 reference) and 7:188 (10 references); for reviews by Charlotte Croon Davis, Robert C. Pooley, and Holland Roberts of earlier forms, see 6:287 (6 references); see also 5:204 (14 references); for a review by Charlotte Croon Davis (with Frederick B. Davis), see 4:178 (6 references). For reviews of the testing program, see 6:760 (2 reviews).

[491]
College Board Achievement Test in European History and World Cultures. Candidates for college entrance; 1901–76; test administered 2 times annually (May, December) at centers established by the publisher; an inactive form, entitled *College Placement Test in European History and World Cultures*, is available for local administration and scoring; program administered by The College Board and Educational Testing Service.*

For additional information, see 8:888; for a review by David K. Heenan of earlier forms, see 6:967. For reviews of the testing program, see 6:760 (2 reviews).

[492]
College Board Achievement Test in French Reading. Candidates for college entrance with 2–4 years high school French; 1901–76; test administered 6 times annually (January, March, May, June, November, December) at centers established by the publisher; inactive

forms, entitled *College Placement Test in French Reading*, are available for local administration and scoring; program administered by The College Board and Educational Testing Service.*

For additional information and a review by Helen L. Jorstad, see 8:116; see also 6:366 (4 references) and 5:263 (2 references); for a review by Walter V. Kaulfers of earlier forms, see 4:237 (7 references). For reviews of the testing program, see 6:760 (2 reviews).

[493]
College Board Achievement Test in German Reading. Candidates for college entrance with 2–4 years high school German; 1901–76; test administered 6 times annually (January, March, May, June, November, December) at centers established by the publisher; inactive forms, entitled *College Placement Test in German Reading*, are available for local administration and scoring; program administered by The College Board and Educational Testing Service.*

For additional information and a review by Randall L. Jones, see 8:128; for a review by Gilbert C. Kettelkamp of earlier forms, see 6:383; for a review by Harold B. Dunkel, see 5:272 (3 references); for a review by Herbert Shueler, see 4:244 (3 references). For reviews of the testing program, see 6:760 (2 reviews).

[494]
College Board Achievement Test in Hebrew. Candidates for college entrance with 2–4 years high school Hebrew; 1961–76; test administered 2 times annually (May, December) at centers established by the publisher; an inactive form, entitled *College Placement Test in Hebrew Reading*, is available for local administration and scoring; program administered by The College Board and Educational Testing Service.*

For additional information, see 8:139. For reviews of the testing program, see 6:760 (2 reviews).

[495]
College Board Achievement Test in Latin. Candidates for college entrance with 2–4 years high school Latin; 1901–76; test administered 2 times annually (May, December) at centers established by the publisher; inactive forms, entitled *College Placement Test in Latin Reading*, are available for local administration and scoring; program administered by The College Board and Educational Testing Service.*

For additional information, see 8:145; for a review by Konrad Gries of an earlier form, see 5:280 (1 reference); for a review by Harold B. Dunkel, see 4:250 (2 references). For reviews of the testing program, see 6:760 (2 reviews).

[496]
College Board Achievement Test in Literature. Candidates for college entrance; 1968–76; test administered 6 times annually (January, March, May, June, November, December) at centers established by the publisher; an inactive form, entitled *College Placement Test in Literature*, is available for local administration and scoring; program administered by The College Board and Educational Testing Service.*

For additional information, see 8:67; see also 7:217 (2 references). For reviews of the testing program, see 6:760 (2 reviews).

[497]
College Board Achievement Test in Physics. Candidates for college entrance; 1901–76; test administered 6 times annually (January, March, May, June, November, December) at centers established by the publisher; inactive forms, entitled *College Placement Test in Physics*, are available for local administration and scoring; program administered by The College Board and Educational Testing Service.*

For additional information, see 8:863 (1 reference); see also 7:855 (2 references) and 6:926 (4 references); for a review by Theodore G. Phillips of an earlier form, see 5:749 (2 references); for a review by Palmer O. Johnson, see 4:633 (3 references). For reviews of the testing program, see 6:760 (2 reviews).

[498]
College Board Achievement Test in Spanish Reading. Candidates for college entrance with 2–4 years high school Spanish; 1902–76; test administered 6 times annually (January, March, May, June, November, December) at centers established by the publisher; inactive forms, entitled *College Placement Test in Spanish Reading*, are available for local administration and scoring; program administered by The College Board and Educational Testing Service.*

For additional information, see 8:158; see also 6:419 (1 reference), 5:287 (1 reference), and 4:259 (3 references). For reviews of the testing program, see 6:760 (2 reviews).

[499]
College Board Achievement Tests in Mathematics. Candidates for college entrance; 1901–1976; administered 6 times annually (January, March, May, June, November, December) at centers established by the publisher; inactive forms entitled *College Placement Test in Mathematics, Level 1 and Level 2* are available for local administration and scoring; 2 levels; program administered by The College Board and Educational Testing Service.*

For additional information and reviews by Jeremy Kilpatrick and Peter A. Lappan, Jr. of Level 1, see 8:258 (4 references); see also 7:456 (4 references). For additional information concerning Level 2, see 8:259 (1 reference); see also 7:457 (1 reference). For reviews of the testing program, see 6:760 (2 reviews).

[500]
College Board Admissions Testing Program. Candidates for college entrance; 1901–77; ATP; most tests administered 6 times annually (January, March, May, June, November, December) at centers established by the publisher; an optional questionnaire, *Student Descriptive Questionnaire*, provides background information to colleges; special administration arrangements available for the physically handicapped; Braille and large-type editions available for the visually handicapped; program administered by The College Board and Educational Testing Service.*

a) COLLEGE BOARD SCHOLASTIC APTITUDE TEST AND TEST OF STANDARD WRITTEN ENGLISH. 1926–77; SAT, TSWE.

b) COLLEGE BOARD ACHIEVEMENT TESTS. 1901–76; 14 tests: American History and Social Studies, Biology, Chemistry, English Composition, European History and World Cultures, French Reading, German Reading, Hebrew, Latin, Literature, Mathematics (2 levels), Physics, Spanish Reading; inactive forms are available for local administration and scoring in the *College Placement Tests* program.

For additional information, see 8:472 (6 references); see also T2:1048 (9 references) and 7:663 (16 references); for reviews by Benno G. Fricke and Dean K. Whitla of an earlier program, see 6:760 (12 references); see also 5:599 (3 references) and 4:526 (9 references). For reviews of individual tests, see 8:46 (2 reviews), 8:128 (1 review), 8:147 (1 review), 8:258 (2 reviews), 7:344 (2 reviews), 6:287 (3 reviews), 6:289 (1 review), 6:383 (1 review), 6:384 (2 reviews), 6:449 (2 reviews), 6:568 (1 review), 6:569 (1 review), 6:914 (1 review), 6:966 (1 review), 6:967 (1 review), 5:272 (1 review), 5:277 (1 review), 5:280 (1 review), 5:318 (1 review), 5:723 (1 review), 5:742 (1 review), 5:749 (1 review), 5:786 (1 review), 4:178 (1 review), 4:237 (1 review), 4:244 (1 review), 4:250 (1 review), 4:285 (1 review), 4:367 (1 review), 4:368 (1 review), 4:600 (1 review), 4:617 (1 review), 4:633 (1 review), and 4:662 (1 review).

REFERENCES

1–9. See 4:526.
10–12. See 5:599.
13–24. See 6:760.
25–40. See 7:663.
41–49. See T2:1048.
50–55. See 8:472.
56. DIAMOND, E. E. The AMEG commission report on sex bias in achievement testing. *Measurement & Evaluation in Guidance*, 1980, 13, 135–147.
57. ZAJONC, R. B., & BARGH, J. Birth order, family size, and decline of SAT scores. *American Psychologist*, 1980, 35, 662–668.
58. ALDERMAN, D. L. Students self-selection and test repetition. *Educational & Psychological Measurement*, 1981, 41, 1073–1081.

[501]
College Board Scholastic Aptitude Test and Test of Standard Written English. Candidates for college entrance; 1926–77; SAT, TSWE; test administered 6 times annually (January, March, May, June, November, December) at centers established by the publishers; 5 scores: 4 aptitude scores (reading comprehension, vocabulary, total verbal, mathematics), 1 achievement score (written English); the *Test of Standard Written English* is also available as a separate; program administered by The College Board and Educational Testing Service.*

For additional information, see 8:182 (217 references); see also T2:357 (148 references); for reviews by Philip H. DuBois and Wimburn L. Wallace of an earlier form, see 7:344 (298 references); for reviews by John E. Bowers and Wayne S. Zimmerman, see 6:449 (79 references); for a review by John T. Dailey, see 5:318 (20 references); for a review by Frederick B. Davis, see 4:285 (22 references). For reviews of the testing program, see 6:760 (2 reviews).

REFERENCES

1–22. See 4:285.
23–42. See 5:318.
43–121. See 6:449.
122–419. See 7:344.
420–567. See T2:357.
568–784. See 8:182.
785. BAILEY, R. L. The Test of Standard Written English: Another look. *Measurement & Evaluation in Guidance*, 1977, 10, 70–74.
786. BRELAND, H. M. Can multiple-choice tests measure writing skills? *College Board Review*, 1977, 103, 11–13, 32–33.
787. CHAPMAN, M. Father absence, stepfathers, and the cognitive performance of college students. *Child Development*, 1977, 48, 1155–1158.
788. DALTON, S., ANASTASIOW, M., & BRIGMAN, S. L. The relationship of underachievement and college attrition. *Journal of College Student Personnel*, 1977, 18, 501–505.
789. EDWARDS, R. C. Personal traits and "success" in schooling and work. *Educational & Psychological Measurement*, 1977, 37, 125–138.
790. FEDERMAN, E. J., & BAILEY, K. G. Extending the Similarities subtest of the WAIS for increased validity. *Journal of Clinical Psychology*, 1977, 33, 1055–1059.
791. HACKMAN, J. D., & JOHNSON, P. How well do freshmen write? Implications for placement and pedagogy. *College & University*, 1977, 53, 81–99.
792. HAIER, R. J. Moral reasoning and moral character: Relationships between the Kohlberg and the Hogan models. *Psychological Reports*, 1977, 40, 215–226.
793. HEATH, D. H. Academic predictors of adult maturity and competence. *Journal of Higher Education*, 1977, 48, 613–632.
794. JOHNSTON, J. D. Improving high school/college articulation for compensatory students through early basic skills evaluation. *National Reading Conference Yearbook*, 1977, 105–109.
795. JONES, C. O., ROWEN, M. R., & TAYLOR, H. E. An overview of the Mathematics Achievement Tests offered in the admissions testing program of the College Entrance Examination Board. *Mathematics Teacher*, 1977, 70, 197–208.
796. LORD, F. M. Optimal number of choices per item–A comparison of four approaches. *Journal of Educational Measurement*, 1977, 14, 33–38.
797. MAYER, R. E. Different rule systems for counting behavior acquired in meaningful and rote contexts of learning. *Journal of Educational Psychology*, 1977, 69, 537–546.
798. MAYER, R. E. Problem-solving performance with task overload: Effects of self-pacing and trait anxiety. *Bulletin of the Psychonomic Society*, 1977, 9, 283–286.
799. On further examination: The SAT score decline. *Science News*, 1977, 112, 148–149.
800. PENTECOSTE, J. C., & LOWE, W. F. The Quick Test as a predictive instrument for college success. *Psychological Reports*, 1977, 41, 759–762.
801. PLATNICK, D. M., & RICHARDS, L. G. Individual differences related to performance on two word-recognition tasks. *American Journal of Psychology*, 1977, 90, 133–144.
802. PRYOR, J. B., GIBBONS, F. X., WICKLUND, R. A., FAZIO, R. H., & HOOD, R. Self-focused attention and self-report validity. *Journal of Personality*, 1977, 45, 513–527.
803. SANFORD, T. R. The test score decline: An overview. *High School Journal*, 1977, 60, 302–316.
804. SIEGFRIED, J. J. Is teaching the best way to learn? An evaluation of benefits and costs to undergraduate student proctors in elementary economics. *Southern Economic Journal*, 1977, 43, 1394–1400.
805. SMITH, D. G. College classroom interactions and critical thinking. *Journal of Educational Psychology*, 1977, 69, 180–190.
806. STANLEY, J. C. The predictive value of the SAT for brilliant seventh- and eighth-graders. *College Board Review*, 1977–1978, 106, 31–37.
807. STOFFER, G. R., DAVIS, K. E., & BROWN, J. B., JR. The consequences of changing initial answers on objective tests: A stable effect and a stable misconception. *Journal of Educational Research*, 1977, 70, 272–277.
808. TURNER, R. G., & HIBBS, C. Vocational interest and personality correlates of differential abilities. *Psychological Reports*, 1977, 40, 727–730.
809. WERTS, C. E., ROCK, D. A., LINN, R. L., & JÖRESKOG, K. G. Validating psychometric assumptions within and between several populations. *Educational & Psychological Measurement*, 1977, 37, 863–872.
810. WITKIN, H. A., MOORE, C. A., OLTMAN, P. K., GOODENOUGH, D. R., FRIEDMAN, F., OWEN, D. R., & RASKIN, E. Role of the field-dependent and field-independent cognitive styles in academic evolution: A longitudinal study. *Journal of Educational Psychology*, 1977, 69, 197–211.
811. YOCH, K., & NOWICKI, S., JR. The role of reinforcement value in the prediction of academic achievement. *Journal of Genetic Psychology*, 1977, 130, 159–160.
812. ZIMMERMAN, W. S., PARKS, H., & GRAY, K. The validity of traditional cognitive measures and of scales of the Study Attitudes and

Methods Survey in the prediction of the academic success of educational opportunity program students. *Educational & Psychological Measurement,* 1977, 37, 465–470.

813. ALEAMONI, L. M., & OBOLER, L. ACT versus SAT in predicting first semester GPA. *Educational & Psychological Measurement,* 1978, 38, 393–399.

814. BAILEY, R. L. Principal components analysis of the old and the new: The SAT vs. the CSUC English Placement Test. *Measurement & Evaluation in Guidance,* 1978, 11, 162–168.

815. BATLIS, N. C. Job involvement as a predictor of academic performance. *Educational & Psychological Measurement,* 1978, 38, 1177–1180.

816. BLATCHLEY, M. E., HERZOG, P. M., & RUSSELL, J. D. Effects of self-study on achievement in a medical–surgical nursing course. *Nursing Outlook,* 1978, 26, 444–447.

817. BRASWELL, J. S. The College Board Scholastic Aptitude Test: An overview of the mathematical portion. *Mathematics Teacher,* 1978, 71, 168–180.

818. COHN, S. J. Cognitive characteristics of the top-scoring third of the 1976 talent search contestants. *Gifted Child Quarterly,* 1978, 22, 416–420.

819. COX, W. M. Spelling accuracy as a function of repression-sensitization. *British Journal of Educational Psychology,* 1978, 48, 84–85.

820. CRAWFORD, J. Interactions of learner characteristics with the difficulty level of the instruction. *Journal of Educational Psychology,* 1978, 70, 523–531.

821. DUDLEY, J. R. A remedial skills course for under–prepared college students. *Journal of Educational Research,* 1978, 71, 143–148.

822. FLEXER, R. J. Comparison of lecture and laboratory strategies in a mathematics course for prospective elementary teachers. *Journal for Research in Mathematics Education,* 1978, 9, 103–117.

823. GOUGH, H. G., LAZZARI, R., FIORAVANTI, M., & STRACCA, M. An Adjective Check List scale to predict military leadership. *Journal of Cross-Cultural Psychology,* 1978, 9, 381–400.

824. HARTMAN, W. T., & BELL, D. P. The predictive value of the Stanford University admissions rating system. *College & University,* 1978, 53, 280–290.

825. HOFFMAN, R. G. Variables affecting university student ratings of instructor behavior. *American Educational Research Journal,* 1978, 15, 287–299.

826. HOSSEINI, A. A. Preliminary report on the validity of the Scholastic Aptitude Test in Iran? *Psychological Reports,* 1978, 43, 99–102.

827. LANDERS, D. M., FELTZ, D. L., OBERMEIER, G. E., & BROUSE, T. R. Socialization via interscholastic athletics: Its effects on educational attainment. *Research Quarterly for Exercise & Sport,* 1978, 49, 475–483.

828. MAYER, R. E. Advance organizers that compensate for the organization of text. *Journal of Educational Psychology,* 1978, 70, 880–886.

829. MICHAEL, W. B., & SHAFFER, P. The comparative validity of the California State University and Colleges English Placement Test (CSUC-EPT) in the prediction of fall semester grade point average and English course grades of first-semester entering freshman. *Educational & Psychological Measurement,* 1978, 38, 985–1001.

830. MILLS, C. Is sex role related to intellectual abilities? *Gifted Child Quarterly,* 1978, 22, 536–538.

831. MYERS, L. B., & LEVY, G. W. Description and prediction of the intractable inmate. *Journal of Research in Crime & Delinquency,* 1978, 15, 214–228.

832. NIEMAN, L. L., & SMITH, W. F. Individualized instruction: Its effects upon achievement and interest in beginning college Spanish. *Modern Language Journal,* 1978, 62, 157–167.

833. OSTERLUND, B. L., & CHENEY, K. A holistic essay–reading composite as criterion for the validity of the Test of Standard Written English. *Measurement & Evaluation in Guidance,* 1978, 11, 155–158.

834. PANACKAL, A. A., & HEFT, C. S. Cloze technique and multiple choice technique: Reliability and validity. *Educational & Psychological Measurement,* 1978, 38, 917–932.

835. SABINE, G. Encouraging minority enrollments: Five institutions' efforts. *Intellect,* 1978, 106, 329–332.

836. SHARP, L. F., & CHASON, L. R. The use of moderator variables in predicting college student attrition. *Journal of College Student Personnel,* 1978, 19, 388–393.

837. SUBKOVIAK, M. J. Empirical investigation of procedures for estimating reliability for mastery tests. *Journal of Educational Measurement,* 1978, 15, 111–116.

838. TROUTMAN, J. G. Cognitive predictors of final grades in finite mathematics. *Educational & Psychological Measurement,* 1978, 38, 401–404.

839. TURNER, R. G. Effects of differential request procedures and self-consciousness on trait attributions. *Journal of Research in Personality,* 1978, 12, 431–438.

840. WEAVER, W. T. Educators in supply and demand: Effects on quality. *School Review,* 1978, 86, 552–593.

841. WERTS, C. E., ROCK, D. R., LINN, R. L., & JÖRESKOG, K. G. A general method of estimating the reliability of a composite. *Educational & Psychological Measurement,* 1978, 38, 933–938.

842. WILDMAN, R. C. Life change with college grades as a role-performance variable. *Social Psychology,* 1978, 41, 34–45.

843. WINTER, D. G., & McCLELLAND, D. C. Thematic analysis: An empirically derived measure of the effects of liberal arts education. *Journal of Educational Psychology,* 1978, 70, 8–16.

844. AUSTIN, J. D. High school calculus and first-quarter college calculus grades. *Journal for Research in Mathematics Education,* 1979, 10, 69–72.

845. BRELAND, H. M., & GAYNOR, J. C. A comparison of direct and indirect assessments of writing skill. *Journal of Educational Measurement,* 1979, 16, 119–128.

846. BROWN, S. E., & WHITE, A. J. Differences between actual and predicted grade point averages of black and white college students. *Perceptual & Motor Skills,* 1979, 48, 1140–1142.

847. BRUSH, D. H., & SCHOENFELDT, L. F. Interrelationships among interests, life–history, and educational criteria. *Applied Psychological Measurement,* 1979, 3, 165–175.

848. DECOSTER, D. A. The effects of residence hall room visitation upon academic achievement for college students. *Journal of College Student Personnel,* 1979, 20, 520–525.

849. DOEBLER, L. K., & FOREMAN, S. T. National Educational Development Tests as a predictor of College Entrance Examination Board Scholastic Aptitude Test scores. *Educational & Psychological Measurement,* 1979, 39, 909–911.

850. DOWNEY, R. G. Item–option weighting of achievement tests: Comparative study of methods. *Applied Psychological Measurement,* 1979, 3, 453–461.

851. GARNI, K. F. Attrition and graduation rate differences between commuter students admitted to an urban university in 1970 and 1974. *Journal of the American Association of Collegiate Registrars,* 1979, 54, 238–247.

852. GEORGE, W. C. The talent–search concept: An identification strategy for the intellectually gifted. *Journal of Special Education,* 1979, 13, 221–237.

853. GOODENOUGH, D. R., OLTMAN, P. K., FRIEDMAN, F., MOORE, C. A., WITKIN, H. A., OWEN, D., & RASKIN, E. Cognitive styles in the development of medical careers. *Journal of Vocational Behavior,* 1979, 14, 341–351.

854. GOTTHEIL, E., EXLINE, R. V., & WINKELMAYER, R. Judging emotions of normal and schizophrenic subjects. *American Journal of Psychiatry,* 1979, 136, 1049–1054.

855. HARRISON, B. T., & RAYBURN, W. G. Open admissions does not kill colleges. *Peabody Journal of Education,* 1979, 56, 144–153.

856. HEREFORD, S. M. The Keller plan within a conventional academic environment. An empirical 'meta–analytic' study. *Engineering Education,* 1979, 70, 250–260.

857. KINDER, D. R. "On further examination" of the SAT report. *Contemporary Education,* 1979, 50, 173–175.

858. KINTISCH, L. S. Classroom techniques for improving Scholastic Aptitude Test scores. *Journal of Reading,* 1979, 22, 416–419.

859. KUBEY, R. W. Radiation and decline of scholastic aptitude scores. *Psychological Reports,* 1979, 45, 862.

860. MA, L., & WOOSTER, R. A. The effect of unemployment on the college student's academic performance. *College Student Journal,* 1979, 13, 12–20.

861. MA, L., & WOOSTER, R. A. Marital status and academic performance in college. *College Student Journal,* 1979, 13, 106–111.

862. McDONALD, R. T., & GAWKOSKI, R. S. Predictive value of SAT scores and high school achievement for success in a college honors program. *Educational & Psychological Measurement,* 1979, 39, 411–414.

863. McLEOD, D. B., & ADAMS, V. M. The interaction of field independence with small–group instruction in mathematics. *Journal of Experimental Education,* 1979–1980, 48, 118–124.

864. MICHAEL, W. B., & SHAFFER, P. A comparison of the validity of the Test of Standard Written English (TSWE) and of the California State University and Colleges English Placement Test (CSUC-EPT) in the prediction of grades in a basic English composition course and of overall freshman year grade point average. *Educational & Psychological Measurement,* 1979, 39, 131–145.

865. MICHAEL, W. B., & SHAFFER, P. An evaluation of alternative measures for assessing language proficiency skills of junior level students in a school of communications and professional studies. *Educational & Psychological Measurement,* 1979, 39, 879–889.

866. NAHINSKY, I. D., MORGAN, M. S., & OESCHGER, D. E. Cognitive strategies field dependence, and the abstraction process. *Journal of Research in Personality,* 1979, 13, 490–504.

867. The nuclear radiation/SAT decline connection. *Phi Delta Kappan,* 1979, 61, 184–187.

868. OVERALL, J. U., & MARSH, H. W. Midterm feedback from students: Its relationship to instructional improvement and students' cognitive and affective outcomes. *Journal of Educational Psychology,* 1979, 71, 856–865.

869. PASCARELLA, E. P., & TERENZINI, P. T. Interaction effects in Spady's and Tinto's conceptual models of college dropout. *Sociology of Education*, 1979, 52, 197–210.

870. SANTA, C. M., & TRUSCOTT, R. B. A college reading program: The integration of reading, writing, speaking and thinking within the content areas. *College Student Journal*, 1979, 13, 391–397.

871. SMITH, G. M., & FOGG, C. P. Predicting college performance from a bivariate grid: Analysis and discussion of the grid's practical utility, accuracy, and multivariate logic. *Educational & Psychological Measurement*, 1979, 39, 843–857.

872. SMITH, R. J. Test coaching dispute lingers. *Science*, 1979, 205, 1114.

873. WASSERMAN, M. An evaluation of a compensatory introductory sociology section. *Journal of Experimental Education*, 1979, 47, 162–171.

874. WIDERSTROM, A. H., JENGELESKI, J. L., & CHANSKY, N. M. Predicting freshman GPA of law/justice students. *Educational & Psychological Measurement*, 1979, 39, 439–443.

875. WORMACK, L. Cognitive predictors of articulation in writing. *Perceptual & Motor Skills*, 1979, 48, 1151–1156.

876. ALDERMAN, D. L., & POWERS, D. E. The effects of special preparation on SAT–Verbal scores. *American Educational Research Journal*, 1980, 17, 239–251.

877. AUSTIN, J. D. When to allow student questions on homework. *Journal for Research in Mathematics Education*, 1980, 11, 71–75.

878. BECKER, B. J. Performance of a group of mathematically able youths on the mathematics usage and natural sciences reading tests of the American College Test Battery vs the Scholastic Aptitude Test. *Gifted Child Quarterly*, 1980, 24, 138–143.

879. BENBOW, C. P., & STANLEY, J. C. Intellectually talented students: Family profiles. *Gifted Child Quarterly*, 1980, 24, 119–122.

880. BENBOW, C. P., & STANLEY, J. C. Sex differences in mathematical ability: Fact or artifact? *Science*, 1980, 210, 1262–1264.

881. BIANCHI, J. R., & BEAN, A. G. The prediction of voluntary withdrawals from college: An unsolved problem. *Journal of Experimental Education*, 1980, 49, 29–33.

882. CIANFLONE, R., & ZULLO, T. G. The relationship of an early measure of intelligence to the ability to learn sight vocabulary words and to later reading achievement. *Educational & Psychological Measurement*, 1980 40, 1197–1200.

883. CRANDALL, J. E. Adler's concept of social interest: Theory, measurement, and implications for adjustment. *Journal of Personality & Social Psychology*, 1980, 39, 481–495.

884. DISPOTO, R. G. Affective changes associated with student teaching. *College Student Journal*, 1980, 14, 190–195.

885. Does coaching raise SAT scores? Two studies say yes, it does. *Phi Delta Kappan*, 1980, 62, 68–69.

886. ERWIN, T. D., & MILLIKAN, J. L. The relationship of the Nelson–Denny Reading Test to the Scholastic Aptitude Verbal Tests. *Measurement & Evaluation in Guidance*, 1980, 13, 169–171.

887. FOOTE, B. Determined– and undetermined–major students: How different are they? *Journal of College Student Personnel*, 1980, 21, 29–34.

888. FRAAS, J. W. The use of seven simulation games in a college economics course. *Journal of Experimental Education*, 1980, 48, 264–280.

889. GUSSETT, J. C. Achievement test scores and Scholastic Aptitude Test scores as predictors of College Level Examination Program scores. *Educational & Psychological Measurement*, 1980, 40, 213–218.

890. HAMMACK, F. M., & COOKSON, P. W. Colleges attended by graduates of elite secondary schools *Educational Forum*, 1980, 44, 483–490.

891. HOUSTON, L. N. Predicting academic achievement among specially admitted black female college students. *Educational & Psychological Measurement*, 1980, 40, 1189–1195.

892. JACKSON, R. The Scholastic Aptitude Test: A response to Slack and Porter's "critical appraisal." *Harvard Educational Review*, 1980, 50, 382–391.

893. KOLATA, G. B. Math and sex: Are girls born with less ability? *Science*, 1980, 210, 1234–1235.

894. MARSH, H. W., & OVERALL, J. U. Validity of students' evaluations of teaching effectiveness: Cognitive and affective criteria. *Journal of Educational Psychology*, 1980, 72, 468–475.

895. MAYER, R. E., & BROMAGE, B. K. Different recall protocols for technical texts due to advance organizers. *Journal of Educational Psychology*, 1980, 72, 209–225.

896. MCCARTHY, S. V. College women with differential linguistic-quantitative ability patterns: Performance on trail making tests. *Perceptual & Motor Skills*, 1980, 50, 1215–1218.

897. MCDUFFIE, T. E., JR., & BRUCE, M. H. Predicting achievement and success in an AT biology program. *Journal of Research in Science Teaching*, 1980, 17, 449–454.

898. MCGINN, P. V., VIERNSTEIN, M. C., & HOGAN, R. Fostering the intellectual development of verbally gifted adolescents. *Journal of Educational Psychology*, 1980, 72, 494–498.

899. MICHAEL, W. B., COOPER, T., SHAFFER, P., & WALLIS, E. A comparison of the reliability and validity of ratings of student performance on essay examinations by professors of English and by professors in other disciplines. *Educational & Psychological Measurement*, 1980, 40, 183–195.

900. NAIRN, A. Class in the guise of merit. *Educational Leadership*, 1980, 37, 651–653.

901. NEWLON, L. L., & GAITHER, G. H. Factors contributing to attrition: An analysis of program impact on persistence patterns. *College & University*, 1980, 55, 237–251.

902. PALLRAND, G. J., & MORETTI, V. Relationship of cognitive level to instructional patterns of high school seniors. *Journal of Research in Science Teaching*, 1980, 17, 185–190.

903. PANACKAL, A. A. Rigid and flexible course requirements and achievement in a college of education. *College Student Journal*, 1980, 14, 135–141.

904. PASCARELLA, E. T., & TERENZINI, P. T. Predicting freshman persistence and voluntary dropout decisions from a theoretical model. *Journal of Higher Education*, 1980, 51, 60–75.

905. PETERSON, J. M., & LANSKY, L. M. Success in architecture: Handedness and/or visual thinking. *Perceptual & Motor Skills*, 1980, 50, 1139–1143.

906. RAMIREZ, M. P., MAGRINA, A., & ALLEN, J. E. Initial development and validation of the academic self–concept scale. *Educational & Psychological Measurement*, 1980, 40, 1013–1016.

907. ROBINSON, M. A., & STRALEY, H. W. The effect of a teacher–aide experience on mathematics aptitude. *School Science & Mathematics*, 1980, 80, 245–250.

908. ROVEZZI-CARROLL, S., & THOMPSON, D. L. Forecasting college success for low–income students. *Journal of College Student Personnel*, 1980, 21, 340–343.

909. SLACK, W. V., & PORTER, D. The Scholastic Aptitude Test: A critical appraisal. *Harvard Educational Review*, 1980, 50, 154–175.

910. SLACK, W. V., & PORTER, D. Training, validity, and the issue of aptitude: A reply to Jackson. *Harvard Educational Review*, 1980, 50, 392–401.

911. VAILLANT, G. E., & MILOFSKY, E. Natural history of male psychological health: IX. Empirical evidence for Erikson's model of the life cycle. *American Journal of Psychiatry*, 1980, 137, 1348–1359.

912. WERTS, C. E., BRELAND, H. M., GRANDY, J., & ROCK, D. R. Using longitudinal data to estimate reliability in the presence of correlated measurement errors. *Educational & Psychological Measurement*, 1980, 40, 19–29.

913. WESTBROOK, B. W., CUTTS, C. C., MADISON, S. S., & ARCIA, M. A. The validity of the Crite's model of career maturity. *Journal of Vocational Behavior*, 1980, 16, 249–281.

914. WINSTON, R. B., JR., HUTSON, G. S., & MCCAFFREY, S. S. Environmental influences on fraternity academic achievement. *Journal of College Student Personnel*, 1980, 21, 449–455.

915. WORMACK, L. Sex differences in factorial dimension of verbal, logical, mathematical and visuospatial ability. *Perceptual & Motor Skills*, 1980, 50, 445–446.

916. WRIGHT, P., & KRIEWALL, M. A. State–of–mind effects on the accuracy with which utility functions predict marketplace choice. *Journal of Marketing Research*, 1980, 17, 277–293.

917. ZAJONC, R. B., & BARGH, J. Birth order, family size, and decline of SAT scores. *American Psychologist*, 1980, 35, 662–668.

918. ALDERMAN, D. L. Student self–selection and test repetition. *Educational & Psychological Measurement*, 1981, 41, 1073–1081.

919. ALEXANDER, K. L., PALLAS, A. M., & COOK, M. A. Measure for measure: On the use of endogenous ability data in school–process research. *American Sociological Review*, 1981, 46, 619–631.

920. ALICHNE, M. C., & BELLUCCI, J. T. Prediction of freshman students' success in a baccalaureate nursing program. *Nursing Research*, 1981, 30, 49–53.

921. BEJAR, I. I., & BLEW, E. O. Grade inflation and the validity of the Scholastic Aptitude Test. *American Educational Research Journal*, 1981, 18, 143–156.

922. DEBOER, G. E. The direct and indirect contributions of a series of intellective and non–intellective student attributes to the prediction of high school and college achievement: A path analytic mode. *Educational & Psychological Measurement*, 1981, 41, 487–494.

923. FAIGLEY, L., DALY, J. A., & WITTE, S. P. The role of writing apprehension in writing performance and competence. *Journal of Educational Research*, 1981, 75, 16–21.

924. GOLMON, M. E., & BERRY, C. A. Comparative predictive validity of the new MCAT using different admissions criteria. *Journal of Medical Education*, 1981, 56, 981–986.

925. HALPIN, G., HALPIN, G., & SCHAER, B. B. Relative effectiveness of the California Achievement Tests in comparison with the ACT Assessment, College Board Scholastic Aptitude Test, and high school grade point average in predicting college grade point average. *Educational & Psychological Measurement*, 1981, 41, 821–827.

926. HODGSON, J. W. Cognitive versus behavioral–interpersonal approaches to the group treatment of depressed college students. *Journal of Counseling Psychology*, 1981, 28, 243–249.

927. KRESS, G. C., JR., & DOGON, I. L. A correlational study of preadmission predictor variables and dental school performance. *Journal of Dental Education*, 1981, 45, 207–210.

928. MALLOCH, D. C., & MICHAEL, W. B. Predicting student grade point average at a community college from Scholastic Aptitude Tests and from measures representing three constructs in Vroom's expectancy theory model of motivation. *Educational & Psychological Measurement*, 1981, 41, 1127–1135.

929. MESSICK, S., & JUNGEBLUT, A. Time and method in coaching for the SAT. *Psychological Bulletin*, 1981, 89, 191–196.

930. MESTRE, J. P. Predicting academic achievement among bilingual Hispanic college technical students. *Educational & Psychological Measurement*, 1981, 41, 1255–1264.

931. PINES, S. F. A procedure for predicting underachievement in mathematics among female college students. *Educational & Psychological Measurement*, 1981, 41, 1137–1146.

932. SCHAEFFER, R. H. Meaningful practice on the computer: Is it possible? *Foreign Language Annals*, 1981, 14, 133–137.

933. SCHAFER, A. T., & GRAY, M. W. Sex and mathematics. *Science*, 1981, 211, 231.

934. STANLEY, J. C., & BENBOW, C. P. Using the SAT to find intellectually talented seventh graders. *College Board Review*, 1981–1982, 122, 3–7.

935. SUDDICK, D. E. The Test of Standard Written English and resulting placement patterns: A follow-up of performance of older upper-division and master level students. *Educational & Psychological Measurement*, 1981, 41, 599–601.

936. WILSON, D. G., & WAGNER, E. E. The Watson–Glaser Critical Thinking Appraisal as a predictor of performance in a critical thinking course. *Educational & Psychological Measurement*, 1981, 41, 1319–1322.

[502]
*College Characteristics Index. Grades 13–16; 1957–70; CCI; previously listed under *Stern Environment Indexes*; a short form is available; 49 scores: 30 press scores (abasement-assurance, achievement, adaptability-defensiveness, affiliation, aggression-blame avoidance, change-sameness, conjunctivity-disjunctivity, counteraction, deference-restiveness, dominance-tolerance, ego achievement, emotionality-placidity, energy-passivity, exhibitionism-inferiority avoidance, fantasied achievement, harm avoidance-risk taking, humanities and social science, impulsiveness-deliberation, narcissism, nurturance, objectivity-projectivity, order-disorder, play-work, practicalness-impracticalness, reflectiveness, science, sensuality-puritanism, sexuality-prudishness, supplication-autonomy, understanding), 11 factor scores (aspiration level, intellectual climate, student dignity, academic climate, academic achievement, self-expression, group life, academic organization, social form, play-work, vocational climate) based on combinations of the press scores, 3 second-order factor scores (intellectual climate, non-intellectual climate, impulse control), and 5 composite culture factor scores (expressive, intellectual, protective, vocational, collegiate) based on combinations of need scores with press scores; George G. Stern; Evaluation Research Associates.*

See T2:1395 (38 references); for reviews by Wilbur L. Layton and Rodney W. Skager, see 7:143 (59 references); see also P:256 (65 references) and 6:92 (19 references).

REFERENCES

1–19. See 6:92.
20–84. See P:256.
85–143. See 7:143.
144–181. See T2:1395.

182. PAYNE, R., & MANSFIELD, R. Correlates of individual perceptions of organizational climate. *Journal of Occupational Psychology*, 1978, 51, 209–218.

[503]
College English Placement Test. College entrants; 1969; CEPT; Oscar M. Haugh and James I. Brown; Riverside Publishing Co.*

For additional information and excerpted reviews by Ramon Veal (with W. Geiger Ellis), see 8:47 (2 references); see also T2:65 (2 references); for reviews by Clarence Derrick and Osmond E. Palmer, see 7:189.

REFERENCES

1–2. See T2:65.
3–4. See 8:47.
5. TWA, R. J., & GREENE, M. Prediction of success in student teaching as a criterion for selection in teacher education programs. *Alberta Journal of Educational Research*, 1980, 26, 1–13.

[504]
College English Test: National Achievement Tests. Grades 12–13; 1937–43; 7 scores: punctuation, capitalization, language usage, sentence structure, modifiers, miscellaneous principles, total; A. C. Jordan; Psychometric Affiliates.*

For additional information and a review by Osmond E. Palmer, see 5:178; for reviews by Constance M. McCullough and Robert W. Howard, see 2:1269.1.

[505]
The College Inventory of Academic Adjustment. College; 1949; CIAA; 7 scores: curricular adjustment, maturity of goals and level of aspiration, personal efficiency-planning and use of time, study skills and practices, mental health, personal relations, total; Henry Borow; Consulting Psychologists Press, Inc.*

See T2:1134 (5 references) and P:43 (8 references); for a review by Leonard D. Goodstein, see 6:77 (12 references); for reviews by Lysle W. Croft and Harrison G. Gough, see 4:34 (3 references).

[506]
College Level Examination Program. Persons entering college or already in college; 1964–81; CLEP; for college accreditation of nontraditional study, advanced placement, or assessment of educational achievement; tests administered 10 months of the year at centers throughout the United States; 2 series of examinations; program administered by The College Board and Educational Testing Service.

a) GENERAL EXAMINATIONS. 1964–77; 13 scores: English Composition, Natural Sciences (biological, physical, total), Mathematics (skills and concepts, content, total), Humanities (fine arts, literature, total), Social Sciences and History (social sciences, history, total).

b) SUBJECT EXAMINATIONS. 1964–81; 47 tests listed separately: Afro-American History, American Government, American History I, American History II, American Literature, Analysis and Interpretation of Literature, Anatomy/Physiology/Microbiology, Behavioral Sciences for Nurses, Calculus With Elementary Functions, Clinical Chemistry, College Algebra, College Algebra-Trigonometry, College Composition, College French, College German, College Spanish, Computers and Data Processing, Dental Materials, Educational Psychology, Elementary Computer Programming-Fortran IV, English Literature, Freshman English, Fundamentals of Nursing, General Biology, General Chemistry, General Psychology, Head/Neck and Oral Anatomy, Hematology, Human Growth and Development, Immunohematology and Blood Banking, Introduction to Management, Introductory Accounting, Introductory Business Law, Introductory Macroeconomics, Introductory Marketing, Introductory Micro- and Macroeconomics, Introductory Microeconomics, Introductory Sociology, Medical-Surgical Nursing, Microbiology, Money and Banking, Oral Radiography, Statistics, Tooth Morphology and Function, Trigonometry, Western Civilization I, Western Civilization II.

For additional information and reviews by Paul L. Dressel, David A. Frisbie, and Wimburn L. Wallace of an earlier program, see 8:473 (15 references); for reviews of the General Examinations, see 8:8 (2 reviews); for reviews of the separate Subject Examinations, see 8:43 (1 review), 8:44 (1 review), 8:64 (1 review), 8:65 (1 review), 8:66 (1 review), 8:255 (1 review), 8:256 (1 review), 8:297 (1 review), 8:365 (1 review), 8:460 (1 review), 8:832 (1 review), 8:847 (1 review), 8:911 (1 review), 8:919 (1 review), 8:1119 (1 review), and 8:1120 (1 review); see also T2:1050 (4 references); for reviews by Alexander W. Astin, Benjamin S. Bloom, and Warren G. Findley, see 7:664 (7 references).

REFERENCES

1–7. See 7:664.
8–11. See T2:1050.
12–26. See 8:473.
27. MARCO, G. L. Item characteristic curve solutions to three intractable testing problems. *Journal of Educational Measurement*, 1977, 14, 139–160.
28. SIEGFRIED, J. J. Is teaching the best way to learn? An evaluation of benefits and costs to undergraduate student proctors in elementary economics. *Southern Economic Journal*, 1977, 43, 1394–1400.
29. MCKENZIE, R. B. Is teaching the best way to learn?: Comment. *Southern Economic Journal*, 1978, 44, 994–997.
30. MUELLER, T. College Level Examination Program–College French–Levels 1 and 2. *Modern Language Journal*, 1978, 62, 282.
31. LOSAK, J. Are students who write the College Level Examination Program placed in academic jeopardy? *Journal of Higher Education*, 1979, 50, 22–29.
32. DIAMOND, E. E. The AMEG commission report on sex bias in achievement testing. *Measurement & Evaluation in Guidance*, 1980, 13, 135–147.
33. GUSSETT, J. C. Achievement test scores and Scholastic Aptitude Test scores as predictors of College Level Examination Program scores. *Educational & Psychological Measurement*, 1980, 40, 213–218.

[507]
College Placement Tests. Entering college freshmen; 1962–75; CPT; inactive forms of *College Board Achievement Tests* available for local administration and scoring; 25 tests: American History and Social Studies, Biology, Chemistry, English Composition, European History and World Cultures, French Listening Comprehension, French Reading, French Listening-Reading, German Listening Comprehension, German Listening-Reading, German Reading, Greek Reading, Hebrew Reading, Italian Listening-Reading, Italian Reading, Latin Reading, Literature, Mathematics (2 levels), Physics, Russian Listening-Reading, Russian Reading, Spanish Listening Comprehension, Spanish Listening-Reading, Spanish Reading; program administered by The College Board and Educational Testing Service.*

For additional information, see 8:474; for a review by John R. Hills, see 7:665.

REFERENCES

1. HALFF, N. F., & FRISBIE, D. A. College foreign language study related to high school foreign language study. *Modern Language Journal*, 1977, 61, 401–406.
2. GORDON, M. Predictive strategies in diagnostic tasks. *Nursing Research*, 1980, 29, 39–45.

[508]
College Placement Test in American History and Social Studies. Entering college freshmen; 1962–75; inactive form of *College Board Achievement Test in American History and Social Studies* available for local administration and scoring; program administered by The College Board and Educational Testing Service.*

For additonal information, see 8:889; for a review by Howard R. Anderson of an earlier form, see 6:966; for a review by Ralph W. Tyler, see 5:786; for a review by Robert L. Thorndike, see 4:662. For a review of the CPT program, see 7:665.

[509]
College Placement Test in Biology. Entering college freshmen; 1962–75, c1961–75; inactive form of *College Board Achievement Test in Biology* available for local administration and scoring; program administered by The College Board and Educational Testing Service.*

For additional information, see 8:834 (1 reference); for a review by Elizabeth Hagen of an earlier form, see 5:723; for a review by Clark W. Horton, see 4:600. For a review of the CPT program, see 7:665.

[510]
College Placement Test in Chemistry. Entering college freshman; 1962–75, c1956–75; inactive forms of *College Board Achievement Test in Chemistry* available for local administration and scoring; program administered by The College Board and Educational Testing Service.*

For additional information, see 8:849; for a review by William Hered of earlier forms, see 6:914; for a review by Max D. Engelhart, see 5:742; for a review by Evelyn Raskin, see 4:617. For a review of the CPT program, see 7:665.

[511]
College Placement Test in European History and World Cultures. Entering college freshmen; 1963–75; inactive form of *College Board Achievement Test in European History and World Cultures* available for local administration and scoring; program administered by The College Board and Educational Testing Service.*

For additional information, see 8:890. For a review by David K. Heenan of Form OPL (formerly LAC₁), see 6:967. For a review of the CPT program, see 7:665.

[512]
College Placement Test in French Listening Comprehension. Entering college freshmen; 1962–75, c1955–75; inactive forms of *College Board Achievement Test in French Listening Comprehension* available for local administration and scoring; program administered by The College Board and Educational Testing Service.*

For additional information see 8:117 (1 reference); see also 7:270 (1 reference). For a review of the CPT program, see 7:665.

[513]
College Placement Test in French Listening-Reading. Entering college freshmen; 1971–75; inactive forms of the discontinued *College Board Achievement Test in French Listening-Reading* available for local administration and scoring; 3 scores: listening, reading, total; program administered by The College Board and Educational Testing Service.*

For additional information, see 8:118.

[514]
College Placement Test in French Reading. Entering college freshmen; 1962–75, c1955–75; inactive form of *College Board Achievement Test in French Reading* available for local administration and scoring; program administered by The College Board and Educational Testing Service.*

For additional information, see 8:119 (1 reference); see also 7:271 (1 reference); for a review by Walter V. Kaulfers of earlier forms, see 4:237. For a review of the CPT program, see 7:665.

[515]
College Placement Test in German Listening Comprehension. Entering college freshmen; 1962–75, c1955–75; inactive forms of *College Board Achievement Test in German Listening Comprehension* available for local administration and scoring; program administered by The College Board and Educational Testing Service.*

For additional information, see 8:129 (1 reference); see also 7:284 (2 references); for reviews by Harold B. Dunkel and Herbert Schueler of earlier forms, see 6:384. For a review of the CPT program, see 7:665.

[516]
College Placement Test in German Listening-Reading. Entering college freshmen; 1971–75; inactive forms of the discontinued *College Board Archievement Test in German Listening-Reading* available for local administration and scoring; 3 scores: listening, reading, total; program administered by The College Board and Educational Testing Service.*

For additional information, see 8:130 (1 reference).

[517]
College Placement Test in German Reading. Entering college freshmen; 1962–75, c1957–75; inactive forms of *College Board Achievement Test in German Reading* available for local administration and scoring; program administered by The College Board and Educational Testing Service.*

For additional information, see 8:131; see also 7:285 (2 references); for a review by Gilbert C. Kettelkamp of earlier forms, see 6:383; for a review by Harold B. Dunkel, see 5:272; for a review by Herbert Schueler, see 4:244. For a review of the CPT program, see 7:665.

[518]
College Placement Test in Greek Reading. Entering college freshmen; 1962–75, c1957–75; inactive form of *College Board Achievement Test in Greek* available for local administration and scoring; program administered by The College Board and Educational Testing Service.*

For additional information, see 8:138; for a review by Konrad Gries of an earlier form, see 5:277. For a review of the CPT program, see 7:665.

[519]
College Placement Test in Hebrew Reading. Entering college freshmen; 1962–75, c1961–75; inactive form of *College Board Achievement Test in Hebrew* available for local administration and scoring; program administered by The College Board and Educational Testing Service.*

For additional information, see 8:140. For a review of the CPT program, see 7:665.

[520]
College Placement Test in Italian Listening-Reading. Entering college freshmen; 1971–75; inactive form of the discontinued *College Board Achievement Test in Italian Listening-Reading* available for local administration and scoring; 3 scores: listening, reading, total; program administered by The College Board and Educational Testing Service.*

For additional information, see 8:142.

[521]
College Placement Test in Italian Reading. Entering college freshmen; 1962–75, c1957–75; inactive form of *College Board Achievement Test in Italian Reading* available for local administration and scoring; program administered by The College Board and Educational Testing Service.*

For additional information, see 8:143; for a review by Paolo Valesio, see 7:300. For a review of the CPT program, see 7:665.

[522]
College Placement Test in Latin Reading. Entering college freshmen; 1962–75, c1955–72; inactive forms of *College Board Achievement Test in Latin* available for local administration and scoring; program administered by The College Board and Educational Testing Service.*

For additional information, see 8:146; for a review by Konrad Gries of an earlier form, see 5:280; for a review by Harold B. Dunkel, see 4:250. For a review of the CPT program, see 7:665.

[523]
College Placement Test in Literature. Entering college freshmen; 1968–75; inactive form of *College Board Achievement Test in Literature* available for local administration and scoring; program administered by The College Board and Educational Testing Service.*

For additional information, see 8:68. For a review of the CPT program, see 7:665.

[524]
College Placement Test in Physics. Entering college freshmen; 1962–75, c1954–75; inactive forms of *College Board Achievement Test in Physics* available for local administration and scoring; program administered by The College Board and Educational Testing Service.*

For additional information, see 8:864; for a review by Theodore G. Phillips of an earlier form, see 5:749; for a review by Palmer O. Johnson, see 4:633. For a review of the CPT program, see 7:665.

[525]
College Placement Test in Russian Listening-Reading. Entering college freshmen; 1971–75; inactive form of the discontinued *College Board Achievement Test in Russian Listening-Reading* available for local administration and scoring; 3 scores: listening, reading, total; program administered by The College Board and Educational Testing Service.*

For additional information, see 8:149.

[526]
College Placement Test in Russian Reading. Entering college freshmen; 1962–75; inactive forms of *College Board Achievement Test in Russian* available for local administration and scoring; program administered by The College Board and Educational Testing Service.*

For additional information, see 8:150. For a review of the CPT program, see 7:665.

[527]
College Placement Test in Spanish Listening Comprehension. Entering college freshmen; 1962–75, c1955–72; inactive form of *College Board Achievement Test in Spanish Listening Comprehension* available for local administration and scoring; program administered by The College Board and Educational Testing Service.*

For additional information, see 8:159 (1 reference); see also 7:315 (1 reference) and 6:422 (1 reference). For a review of the CPT program, see 7:665.

[528]
College Placement Test in Spanish Listening-Reading. Entering college freshmen; 1971–75; inactive forms of the discontinued *College Board Achievement Test in Spanish Listening-Reading* available for local administration and scoring; 3 scores: listening, reading, total; program administered by The College Board and Educational Testing Service.*

For additional information, see 8:160.

[529]
College Placement Test in Spanish Reading. Entering college freshmen; 1962–75, c1955–75; inactive forms of *College Board Achievement Test in Spanish Reading* available for local administration and scoring; program administered by The College Board and Educational Testing Service.*

For additional information, see 8:161 (1 reference); see also 7:316 (1 reference). For a review of the CPT program, see 7:665.

[530]
College Placement Tests in English Composition. Entering college freshmen; 1962–75, c1958–75; inactive form of *College Board Achievement Test in English Composition* available for local administration and scoring; 2 tests: 60-minute version, shortened version entitled *College Placement Test in English Composition*; program administered by The College Board and Educational Testing Service.*

For additional information, see 8:48 (20 references); for a review by John C. Sherwood, see 7:190 (3 references); for reviews by Charlotte Croon Davis, Robert C. Pooley, and Holland Roberts of earlier forms, see 6:287; for a review by Charlotte Croon Davis (with Frederick B. Davis), see 4:178. For a review of the CPT program, see 7:665.

[531]
College Placement Tests in Mathematics. Entering college freshmen; 1964–75; inactive forms of *College Board Achievement Test in Mathematics, Level 1 and Level 2* are available for local administration and scoring; 2 levels; program administered by The College Board and Educational Testing Service.*

For additional information, see 8:260 (Level 1) and 8:261 (Level 2). For a review of the CPT program, see 7:665.

[532]
★**College Student Experiences.** College; 1979–81; quality of effort students put into opportunities offered by the college environment; 4 areas: college activities, opinions about college, college environment, estimate of gains; C. Robert Pace; Higher Education Research Institute of the University of California, Los Angeles.*

[533]
*****Color-matching Aptitude Test, 1978 Edition.** Adults; 1944–78; 1978 test identical with 1964 test except for minor refinements; formerly called *Inter-Society Color Council Color Aptitude Test*; Color Test Evaluation Committee, Inter-Society Color Council; Federation of Societies for Coatings Technology.

See T2:1915 (11 references) and 5:779 (5 references).

[534]
Columbia Mental Maturity Scale, Third Edition. Ages 3–6 to 9–11; 1954–72; CMMS; Bessie B. Burgemeister, Lucille Hollander Blum, and Irving Lorge; The Psychological Corporation.*

For additional information, reviews by Byron R. Egeland and Alan S. Kaufman, and an excerpted review by Joseph M. Petrosko, see 8:210 (18 references); see also T2:489 (43 references); for reviews by Marshall S. Hiskey and T. Ernest Newland of the 1959 edition, see 6:517 (22 references); see also 5:402 (13 references).

REFERENCES

1–13. See 5:402.
14–35. See 6:517.
36–78. See T2:489.
79–96. See 8:210.
97. MARGOLIS, H. Auditory perceptual test performance and the reflection–impulsivity dimension. *Journal of Learning Disabilities*, 1977, 10, 164–172.
98. BOUNTRESS, N. Comprehension of pronominal reference by speakers of black English. *Journal of Speech & Hearing Research*, 1978, 21, 96–102.
99. LEVI, G., & MUSATTI, T. Phonemic synthesis in poor readers. *British Journal of Disorders of Communication*, 1978, 13, 65–74.
100. LUNDBERG, I., & TARNEUS, M. Nonreaders' awareness of the basic relationship between spoken and written words. *Journal of Experimental Child Psychology*, 1978, 25, 404–412.
101. MARGOLIS, H., & BRANNIGAN, G. G. Conceptual tempo as a parameter for predicting reading achievement. *Journal of Educational Research*, 1978, 71, 342–345.
102. PHILLIPS, B. L., PASEWARK, R. A., & TINDALL, R. C. Relationship among McCarthy Scales of Children's Abilities, WPPSI, and Columbia Mental Maturity Scale. *Psychology in the Schools*, 1978, 15, 352–356.
103. ROSEN, R. C., & LIGHTNER, E. S. Phenotypic malformations in association with maternal trimethadione therapy. *Journal of Pediatrics*, 1978, 92, 240–244.
104. MCMICHAEL, P. The hen or the egg? Which comes first–antisocial emotional disorders or reading disability. *British Journal of Educational Psychology*, 1979, 49, 226–238.
105. MARGOLIS, H., LEONARD, H. S., BRANNIGAN, G. G., & HEVERLY, M. A. The validity of form F of the Matching Familiar Figures Test with kindergarten children. *Journal of Experimental Child Psychology*, 1980, 29, 12–22.
106. MCMICHAEL, P. Reading difficulties, behavior, and social status. *Journal of Educational Psychology*, 1980, 72, 76–86.
107. SCHWAM, E. "MORE" is "LESS": Sign language comprehension in deaf and hearing children. *Journal of Experimental Child Psychology*, 1980, 29, 249–263.
108. ANWAR, F. Visual–motor localizations in normal and subnormal development. *British Journal of Psychology*, 1981, 72, 43–57.
109. ANWAR, F., & HERMELIN, B. Movement after-effects in normal development. *Psychological Research*, 1981, 43, 307–315.

110. HENDERSON, S. E., MORRIS, J., & FRITH, U. The motor deficit in Down's syndrome children: A problem of timing? *Journal of Child Psychology & Psychiatry & Allied Disciplines*, 1981, 22, 233–245.
111. WILLIAMS, A. J., WILLIAMS, M. A., WALKER, C. A., & BUSH, P. G. The Robin Anomalad (Pierre Robin Syndrome –A follow up study. *Archives of Diseases in Childhood*, 1981, 56, 663–668.

[535]
The Columbus: Picture Analysis of Growth Towards Maturity. Ages 5–20; 1969; M. J. Langeveld; S. Karger AG [Switzerland].*

For additional information and excerpted reviews by C. H. Ammons (with R. B. Ammons) and Steven G. Vandenberg, see 7:164 (1 reference).

[536]
Commerce Reading Comprehension Test. Grades 12–16 and adults; 1956–58; Irma T. Halfter and Raymond J. McCall; Department of Psychological Testing, DePaul University.* (In-print status uncertain; no reply from publisher.)

See T2:1538 (1 reference) and 5:624.

[537]
Commercial Tests. Standards 6–8; 1962; 6 scores: arithmetic (computations, problems), comparison, synonyms, alphabetizing, spelling and punctuation; Human Sciences Research Council [South Africa].*

For additional information, see 8:1034.

[538]
★The Communication Screen. Ages 2–10 to 3–9, 3–10 to 4–9, 4–10 to 5–9; 1981; preschool speech-language screening tool; performance rated as pass, suspect, or fail; Nancy Striffler and Sharon Willig; Communication Skill Builders, Inc.*

[539]
★Communication Sensitivity Inventory. Managers; 1970–78; CSI; 4 scores: feeling response, challenge response, more information response, recommendation response; W. J. Reddin and Ken Rowell; Organizational Tests Ltd. [Canada].*

[540]
Communicative Evaluation Chart From Infancy to Five Years. 1963–64; CEC; for "early detection of childhood communicative disabilites"; no manual; Ruth M. Anderson, Madeline Miles, and Patricia A. Matheny; Educators Publishing Service, Inc.*

For additional information, see 7:949.

[541]
★Community Living Observational System. Severely and profoundly mentally retarded persons living in group homes; 1977; CLOS; codings by a trained observer in 14 separate classes of behavioral events; Valerie Taylor and Daniel Close; Rehabilitation Research and Training Center in Mental Retardation.*

REFERENCES

1. CLOSE, D. W. Community living for severely and profoundly retarded adults: A group home study. *Education & Training of the Mentally Retarded*, 1977, 12, 256–262.

[542]
Community Oriented Programs Environment Scale. Patients and staff of community oriented psychiatric facilities; 1974; COPES; a part of *The Social Climate Scales* (2227); 10 scores: involvement, support, spontaneity, autonomy, practical orientation, personal problem orientation, anger and aggression, order and organization, program clarity, staff control; Rudolf H. Moos; Consulting Psychologists Press, Inc.*

For additional information and a review by Richard I. Lanyon, see 8:525 (17 references). For a review of *The Social Climate Scales*, see 8:681.

REFERENCES

1–17. See 8:525.
18. CRONKITE, R. C., & MOOS, R. H. Evaluating alcoholism treatment programs: An integrated approach. *Journal of Consulting & Clinical Psychology*, 1978, 46, 1105–1119.
19. MOOS, R. H., & BROMET, E. Relation of patient attributes to perceptions of the treatment environment. *Journal of Consulting & Clinical Psychology*, 1978, 46, 350–351.
20. O'DONNELL, J. M., COLLINS, J. L., & SCHULER, S. Psychosocial perceptions of the nursing home: A comparative analysis of staff, resident, and cross-generational perspectives. *Gerontologist*, 1978, 18, 267–271.
21. OIKAWA, K., DEONAUTH, J., & BREIDBART, S. Mental retardation and elevated serotonin levels in adults. *Life Sciences*, 1978, 23, 45–48.
22. FISCHER, J. The relationship between alcoholic patients' milieu perception and measures of their drinking during a brief follow-up period. *International Journal of the Addictions*, 1979, 14, 1151–1156.
23. HALL, S. M., BASS, A., HARGREAVES, W. A., & LOEB, P. Contingency management and information feedback in outpatient heroin detoxification. *Behavior Therapy*, 1979, 10, 443–451.

[543]
★Comparative Guidance and Placement Program. Entrants to postsecondary institutions; 1954–79; CGP; a battery of background, abilities, and interest measures which may be administered at any time by participating colleges; full program or modified program (excluding special abilities tests) may be administered; program administered by The College Board and Educational Testing Service.*

a) INTEREST AND BACKGROUND INVENTORIES. Questions are on battery answer sheet and may be completed earlier at home by the student to lessen administration time.
1) *Biographical Inventory.* Modification of the *Student Descriptive Questionnaire*; yields an academic motivation score.
2) *Comparative Interest Index.* Revision of *Academic Interest Measures*; 11 scores: mathematics, physical sciences, engineering technology, biology, health, home economics, secretarial, business, social sciences, fine arts, music.
b) ACHIEVEMENT/PLACEMENT TESTS. For a self-scoring edition (which may be used independently or with the full or modified program), see 382; 5 scores: reading, sentences, mathematics (part 1, part 2, total); student takes one of three 2-part mathematics tests: Test C (computation, applied arithmetic) for students with less than 1 year high school algebra, Test D (computation, elementary algebra) with 1 year, Test E (elementary algebra, intermediate algebra) with more than 1 year.
c) SPECIAL ABILITIES. 3 scores: year 2000 (ability to follow directions), mosaic comparisons (perceptual speed and accuracy), letter groups (inductive reasoning).

For a review by Norman Eagle of an earlier edition, see 8:475 (18 references); see also T2:1052 (8 references); for reviews by C. Robert Pace and H. Bradley Sagen of an earlier program, see 7:666.

REFERENCES

1–2. See 7:666.
3–10. See T2:1052.

11–28. See 8:475.

29. WEINER, M., & ZIBRIN, M. Dissimilarities in grade-equivalent scores on different standardized tests of achievement: A threat to criterion-related validity. *Educational & Psychological Measurement*, 1979, 39, 923–928.

30. BANKS, J. M. The complementary roles of selected cognitive and noncognitive factors in predicting persistence and performance in beginning Gregg shorthand at the community college level. *Journal of Business Education*, 1980, 56, 75–77.

31. DIAMOND, E. E. The AMEG commission report on sex bias in achievement testing. *Measurement & Evaluation in Guidance*, 1980, 13, 135–147.

[544]
Complex Figure Test. Ages 16 and over; 1970–73; CFT; brain damage; originally published in Dutch in 1970 as a revision of *Test de Copie d'une Figure Complexe* (1959) by André Rey; R. S. H. Visser; Swets Test Services [The Netherlands].* (U. S. Distributor: Swets North America, Inc.)

For additional information and an excerpted review by C. H. Ammons and R. B. Ammons, see 8:526 (1 reference).

[545]
Comprehension of Oral Language. Grades kgn–1; 1962–73; parallel editions in English and Spanish; Guidance Testing Associates.* (In-print status uncertain; no reply from publisher.)

[546]
Comprehension Test for College of Education Students. Training college students and applicants for admission; 1962; E. L. Black; distributed by NFER-Nelson Publishing Co. [England].*

For additional information, see 6:785.

[547]
Comprehensive Ability Battery. Ages 15 and over; 1975–77; CAB; 20 scores listed below; 4 test booklets; A. Ralph Hakstian and Raymond B. Cattell; Institute for Personality and Ability Testing, Inc.*

a) CAB–1. 4 scores: verbal ability, numerical ability, spatial ability, speed of closure.
b) CAB–2. 5 scores: perceptual speed and accuracy, inductive reasoning, flexibility of closure, rote memory, mechanical ability.
c) CAB–3/4. 5 scores: memory span, meaningful memory, spelling, auditory ability, esthetic judgment.
d) CAB–5. 6 scores: spontaneous flexibility, ideational fluency, word fluency, originality, aiming, representational drawing.

For additional information and reviews by John B. Carroll and Robert M. Thorndike, see 8:484 (3 references).

REFERENCES

1–3. See 8:484.
4. FRY, K. L., & THOMPSON, D. S. Comparison of selected measures of field dependence. *Perceptual & Motor Skills*, 1977, 45, 861–862.
5. HAKSTIAN, A. R., & BENNET, R. W. Validity studies using the Comprehensive Ability Battery (CAB): I. Academic achievement criteria. *Educational & Psychological Measurement*, 1977, 37, 425–437.
6. HAKSTIAN, A. R., & BENNET, R. W. Validity studies using the Comprehensive Ability Battery (CAB): II. Relationships with the DAT and GATB. *Educational & Psychological Measurement*, 1978, 38, 1003–1015.
7. HAKSTIAN, A. R., & CATTELL, R. B. Higher-stratum ability structures on a basis of twenty primary abilities. *Journal of Educational Psychology*, 1978, 70, 657–669.
8. HAKSTIAN, A. R., & GALE, C. A. Validity studies using the Comprehensive Ability Battery (CAB): III. Performance in conjunction with personality and motivational traits. *Educational & Psychological Measurement*, 1979, 39, 389–400.

[548]
Comprehensive Developmental Evaluation Chart. Developmental ages birth to 3 years; 1975; CDEC; ratings in 11 areas: reflexes, gross motor, manipulation, vision, feeding, receptive language, expressive language, cognitive/social, muscle tone, hips, hearing; Shirley Cliff, Diane Carr, Jennifer Gray, Carol Nymann, and Sandra Redding; El Paso Rehabilitation Center.*

For additional information, see 8:211.

[549]
A Comprehensive English Language Test for Speakers of English as a Second Language. Non-native speakers of English; 1970; CELT; 3 tests; David P. Harris and Leslie A. Palmer; McGraw-Hill Book Co., Inc.*
a) LISTENING.
b) STRUCTURE.
c) VOCABULARY.

For additional information and a review by John B. Carroll, see 7:260.

REFERENCES

1. NORTON, S. J., SCHULTZ, M. C., REED, C. M., BRAIDA, L. D., DURLACH, N. I., RABINOWITZ, W. M., & CHOMSKY, C. Analytic study of the Tadoma method: Background and preliminary results. *Journal of Speech & Hearing Research*, 1977, 20, 574–595.
2. MORAN, R. T. Keying results on the CELT-structure test to U.S. grade level instructional materials. *TESOL Quarterly*, 1978, 12, 139–143.
3. DOUGLAS, D., & YAMADA, J. The effect of knowledge on content of cloze scores. *TESOL Quarterly*, 1979, 13, 120–121.
4. HOSLEY, D., & MEREDITH, K. Inter- and intra-test correlates of the TOEFL. *TESOL Quarterly*, 1979, 13, 209–217.

[550]
Comprehensive Identification Process. Ages 2.5–5.5; 1975; CIP; screening program "to identify every child in a community who is eligible for a special preschool program or needs some kind of medical attention or therapy to function at full potential when he or she enters school"; 25 scores: 24 scores listed below plus final recommendations (scores consist of classification into 1 of 3 categories: pass, rescreen or refer to agency or program, complete evaluation recommended); R. Reid Zehrbach; Scholastic Testing Service, Inc.*

a) CIP CHILD INTERVIEWER'S RECORD FORM. 5 scores: hearing screening, vision screening, developmental (fine motor, cognitive-verbal, gross motor).
b) CIP SPEECH AND EXPRESSIVE LANGUAGE RECORD FORM. 5 scores: articulation, voice, fluency, expressive language, total; Joan Good Erickson.
c) CIP OBSERVATION OF BEHAVIOR FORM. 7 scores: hearing and receptive language, vision, physical/motor, speech and expressive language, social behavior (response, interaction), affective behavior.
d) CIP PARENT INTERVIEW FORM. History and ratings by parent; 7 scores: pregnancy/birth/hospitalization, walking/toilet training, hearing, vision, speech and expressive language, medical, social affect.

[551] *Comprehensive Tests of Basic Skills, [Forms U & V]

For additional information and reviews by Robert P. Anderson and Phyllis L. Newcomer, see 8:425 (1 reference).

[551]
Comprehensive Tests of Basic Skills, [Forms U & V]. Grades kgn–0 to kgn–9, kgn–6 to 1–6, 1–0 to 1–9, 1–6 to 2–9, 2–6 to 3–9, 3–6 to 4–9, 4–6 to 6–9, 6–6 to 8–9, 8–6 to 12–9; 1968–81; CTBS; previous edition (Forms S and T) still available; CTB/McGraw-Hill.

a) LEVEL A. Grades kgn–0 to kgn–9; 6 scores: reading (visual recognition, sound recognition, vocabulary, oral comprehension, total), mathematics concepts and applications.

b) LEVEL B. Grades kgn–6 to 1–6; 6 scores: reading (word attack, vocabulary, oral comprehension, total), language expression, mathematics concepts and applications.

c) LEVEL C. Grades 1–0 to 1–9; 8 scores: reading (word attack, vocabulary, reading comprehension, total), language expression, mathematics (mathematics computation, mathematics concepts and applications, total).

d) LEVEL D. Grades 1–6 to 2–9; 14 scores: reading (word attack, vocabulary, reading comprehension, total), language (language mechanics, language expression, total), mathematics (mathematics computation, mathematics concepts and applications, total), total, spelling, science, social studies.

e) LEVEL E. Grades 2–6 to 3–9; 14 scores: same as for d.

f) LEVEL F. Grades 3–6 to 4–9; 14 scores: reading (vocabulary, reading comprehension, total), language (language mechanics, language expression, total), mathematics (mathematics computation, mathematics concepts and applications, total), total, spelling, science, social studies, reference skills.

g) LEVEL G. Grades 4–6 to 6–9; 14 scores: same as for f.

h) LEVEL H. Grades 6–6 to 8–9; 14 scores: same as for f.

i) LEVEL J. Grades 8–6 to 12–9; 14 scores: same as for f.

For reviews by Warren G. Findley and Anthony J. Nitko of an earlier edition, see 8:12 (13 references); see also T2:11 (1 reference); for reviews by J. Stanley Ahmann and Frederick G. Brown and excerpted reviews by Brooke B. Collison and Peter A. Taylor (rejoinder by Verna White) of Forms Q and R, see 7:9. For reviews of subtests of earlier editions, see 8:721 (1 review), 8:825 (1 review), 7:685 (1 review), 7:514 (2 reviews), and 7:778 (1 review).

REFERENCES

1. See T2:11.
2–14. See 8:12.
15. BARRETT, D. E. Reflection–impulsivity as a predictor of children's academic achievement. *Child Development*, 1977, 48, 1443–1447.
16. KAGAN, S., ZAHN, G. L., & GEALY, J. Competition and school achievement among Anglo–American and Mexican-American children. *Journal of Educational Psychology*, 1977, 69, 432–441.
17. KATZ, L. Reading ability and single–letter orthographic redundancy. *Journal of Educational Psychology*, 1977, 69, 653–659.
18. MAY, R. J., ALEXANDER, D. G., & HOLCOMBE, B. M. The validity of seven easily obtainable economic and demographic predictors of achievement test performance. *Educational & Psychological Measurement*, 1977, 37, 1017–1022.
19. MULLER, D., CHAMBLISS, J., & WOOD, M. Relationships between area–specific measures of self–concept, self–esteem and academic achievement for junior high school students. *Perceptual & Motor Skills*, 1977, 45, 1117–1118.
20. PALMER, L. L. Characteristics of near–point and far–point binocular and monocular sighting in classroom and opthalmological populations. *Perceptual & Motor Skills*, 1977, 45, 707–711.
21. RENTZ, R. R., & BASHAW, W. L. The National Reference Scale for Reading: An application of the Rasch model. *Journal of Educational Measurement*, 1977, 14, 161–179.
22. SLINDE, J. A., & LINN, R. L. Vertically equated tests: Fact or phantom? *Journal of Educational Measurement*, 1977, 14, 23–32.
23. ZIMMERMAN, W. S., PARKS, H., & GRAY, K. The validity of traditional cognitive measures and of scales of the study attitudes and methods survey in the prediction of the academic success of educational opportunity program students. *Educational & Psychological Measurement*, 1977, 37, 465–470.
24. BERRY, S. Monitoring student achievement for accountability: The demonstration of a model. *Journal of Educational Research*, 1978, 71, 308–313.
25. CROW, T. A. Correlations among children's academic achievement, strength, motor skills, and self control. *Perceptual & Motor Skills*, 1978, 47, 86.
26. DAVID, J. L., & PELAVIN, S. H. Evaluating compensatory education: Over what period of time should achievement be measured? *Journal of Educational Measurement*, 1978, 15, 91–99.
27. GALL, M. D., WARD, B. A., BERLINER, D. C., CAHEN, L. S., WINNE, P. H., ELASHOFF, J. D., & STANTON, G. C. Effects of questioning techniques and recitation on student learning. *American Educational Research Journal*, 1978, 15, 175–199.
28. KAMM, K. A five-year study of the effects of a skill–centered approach to the teaching of reading. *Journal of Educational Research*, 1978, 72, 104–112.
29. MAY, R. J., JR., ALEXANDER, D. G., & HOLCOMBE, B. M. The validity of seven easily obtainable economic and demographic predictors of achievement test performance. *Educational & Psychological Measurement*, 1978, 38, 445–450.
30. MODJESKI, R. B., & MICHAEL, W. B. The relationship of the general educational performance index measure to other indicators of educational development in each of three samples from an United States Army population. *Educational & Psychological Measurement*, 1978, 38, 377–391.
31. MOORE, F. B., & PARR, G. D. Models of bilingual education: Comparisons of effectiveness. *Elementary School Journal*, 1978, 79, 93–97.
32. PORTER, A. C., SCHMIDT, W. H., FLODEN, R. E., & FREEMAN, D. J. Practical significance in program evaluation. *American Educational Research Journal*, 1978, 15, 529–539.
33. SCHROEDER, N. Failure to relate academic ability to the lateral eye–shift in elementary school children. *Perceptual & Motor Skills*, 1978, 47, 135–139.
34. YEN, W. M. Measuring individual differences with an information–processing model. *Journal of Educational Psychology*, 1978, 70, 72–86.
35. BARNES, J., FISHER, J., & PALMER, M. Family characteristics and intellectual growth: An examination by race. *Educational & Psychological Measurement*, 1979, 39, 625–636.
36. BECK, F. W., & GUEDRY, P. Reading phase of academic skills enhancement programs. *Journal of College Student Personnel*, 1979, 20, 276.
37. CAPPADONA, D. L., & KERZNER-LIPSKY, D. Prediction of school mathematical achievement from motivation, self–concept, teachers' ratings and ability measures. *School Science & Mathematics*, 1979, 79, 140–144.
38. CAREY, M. A., & WEBER, L. J. Evaluating an experience–based career education program. *Vocational Guidance Quarterly*, 1979, 27, 216–222.
39. CURTIS, C. J., MICHAEL, J. J., & MICHAEL, W. B. The predictive validity of the Developmental Test of Visual–Motor Integration under group and individual modes of administration relative to academic performance measures of second–grade pupils without identifiable major learning disabilities. *Educational & Psychological Measurement*, 1979, 39, 401–410.
40. FAVERO, J., DOMBROWER, J., MICHAEL, W. B., & DOMBROWER, E. The concurrent validity and factor structure of seventeen structure–of–intellect measures reflecting behavioral content. *Educational & Psychological Measurement*, 1979, 39, 1019–1034.
41. KILMANN, P. R., HENRY, S. E., SCARBRO, H., & LAUGHLIN, J. E. The impact of affective education on elementary school underachievers. *Psychology in the Schools*, 1979, 16, 217–223.
42. LARNED, D. T., & MULLER, D. Development of self-concept in grades one through nine. *Journal of Psychology*, 1979, 102, 143–155.
43. MACY, D. J., BAKER, J. A., & KOSINSKI, S. C. An empirical study of the Myklebust learning quotient. *Journal of Learning Disabilities*, 1979, 12, 93–96.
44. MAYFIELD, B. Teacher perception of creativity, intelligence and achievement. *Gifted Child Quarterly*, 1979, 23, 812–817.
45. SHEPARD, L. Construct and predictive validity of the California entry level test. *Educational & Psychological Measurement*, 1979, 39, 867–877.
46. SLINDE, J. A., & LINN, R. L. The Rasch model, objective measurement, equating, and robustness. *Applied Psychological Measurement*, 1979, 3, 437–452.

47. SMITH, J. K., & KRAJKOVICH, J. G. Validation of the Image of Science and Scientists Scale. *Educational & Psychological Measurement*, 1979, 39, 495–498.
48. ALGOZZINE, B., WHORTON, J., & SIDERS, J. The relationship between intelligence and achievement: A reconsideration based on restricted groups. *Journal for Special Educators*, 1980, 17, 57–63.
49. BLANCHARD, J. S. Preliminary investigation of transfer between single-word decoding ability and contextual reading comprehension by poor readers in grade six. *Perceptual & Motor Skills*, 1980, 51, 1271–1281.
50. BRASSELL, A., PETRY, S., & BROOKS, D. M. Ability grouping, mathematics achievement, and pupil attitudes toward mathematics. *Journal of Research in Mathematics Education*, 1980, 11, 22–28.
51. BURNS, R. B. Relation of aptitudes to learning at different points in time during instruction. *Journal of Educational Psychology*, 1980, 72, 785–795.
52. DAVIS, B. G., TRIMBLE, C. S., & VINCENT, D. R. Does age of entrance affect school achievement? *Elementary School Journal*, 1980, 80, 133–143.
53. GOSE, A., WOODEN, S., & MULLER, D. The relative potential of self–concept and intelligence as predictors of achievement. *Journal of Psychology*, 1980, 104, 279–281.
54. HUYNH, H., & SAUNDERS, J. C. Accuracy of two procedures for estimating reliability of mastery tests. *Journal of Educational Measurement*, 1980, 17, 351–358.
55. KLEIN, A. E. Redundancy in the Comprehensive Tests of Basic Skills. *Educational & Psychological Measurement*, 1980, 40, 1105–1110.
56. KNIFONG, J. D. Computational requirements of standardized word problem tests. *Journal for Research in Mathematics Education*, 1980, 11, 3–9.
57. LEHN, T., VLADOVIC, R., & MICHAEL, W. B. The short–term predictive validity of a standardized reading test and of scales reflecting six dimensions of academic self–concept relative to selected high school achievement criteria for four ethnic groups. *Educational & Psychological Measurement*, 1980, 40, 1017–1031.
58. MICHAEL, W. B., VLADOVIC, R., LEHN, T., & COOPER, T. Cognitive and affective factor dimensions in each of four high school samples of different ethnicity. *Educational & Psychological Measurement*, 1980, 40, 1043–1050.
59. OWINGS, R. A., PETERSEN, G. A., BRANSFORD, J. D., MORRIS, C. D., & STEIN, B. S. Spontaneous monitoring and regulation of learning: A comparison of successful and less successful fifth graders. *Journal of Educational Psychology*, 1980, 72, 250–256.
60. PECK, R., BLATTSTEIN, D., BLATTSTEIN, A., & FOX, R. Comparison of self, peer, and teacher ratings of student coping as predictors of achievement, self-esteem, and attitudes. *Journal of Teacher Education*, 1980, 31, 45–52.
61. SARACHO, O. The relationship between the teachers' cognitive style and their perceptions of their students' academic achievements. *Educational Research Quarterly*, 1980, 5, 40–49.
62. SARACHO, O. N., & DAYTON, C. M. Relationship of teachers' cognitive styles to pupils' academic achievement gains. *Journal of Educational Psychology*, 1980, 72, 544–549.
63. TORGESEN, J. K., & HOUCK, D. G. Processing deficiencies of learning–disabled children who perform poorly on the Digit Span Test. *Journal of Educational Psychology*, 1980, 72, 141–160.
64. WEST, J., SONSTEGARD, M., & HAGERMAN, H. A study of counseling and consulting in Appalachia. *Elementary School Guidance & Counseling*, 1980, 15, 5–13.
65. DUMBROWER, J., FAVERO, J., MICHAEL, W. B., & COOPER, T. L. An attempt to determine the construct validity of measures hypothesized to represent an orientation to right, left, or integrated hemispheric brain function for a sample of primary school children. *Educational & Psychological Measurement*, 1981, 41, 1175–1194.
66. KARWEIT, N., & SLAVIN, R. E. Measurement and modeling choices in studies of time and learning. *American Educational Research Journal*, 1981, 18, 143–156.
67. KATZ, R. B., SHANKWEILER, D., & LIBERMAN, I. Y. Memory for item order and phonetic recoding in the beginning reader. *Journal of Experimental Child Psychology*, 1981, 32, 474–484.
68. MAESTAS, L. C. Ethnicity and high school student achievement across rural and urban districts. *Educational Research Quarterly*, 1981, 6, 33–42.
69. PELLEGRINI, A. D., LONG, J. V., & HORWITZ, S. H. An empirical investigation of two variance estimation procedures for use with criterion-referenced tests. *Psychology in the Schools*, 1981, 18, 93–98.
70. TAYLOR, L. K., & MICHAEL, W. B. A correlational study of academic self–concept, intellectual achievement responsibility, social cognition, and reading. *Educational Research Quarterly*, 1981, 6, 13–23.
71. WAY, J. W. Achievement and self–concept in multiage classrooms. *Educational Research Quarterly*, 1981, 6, 69–75.
72. WOLF, F. M., & BLIXT, S. L. A cross–sectional cross lagged panel analysis of mathematics achievement and attitudes: Implications for the interpretation of the direction of predictive validity. *Educational & Psychological Measurement*, 1981, 41, 829–834.
73. YEN, W. M. Using simulation results to choose a latent trait model. *Applied Psychological Measurement*, 1981, 5, 245–262.

[552]

Comprehensive Tests of Basic Skills: Mathematics, [Forms U & V]. Grades kgn–6 to 1–6, 1–0 to 1–9, 1–6 to 2–9, 2–6 to 3–9, 3–6 to 4–9, 4–6 to 6–9, 6–6 to 8–9, 8–6 to 12–9; 1968–81; previous edition (Forms S and T) still available; 8 levels; CTB/McGraw-Hill. For the complete battery entry, see 551.

a) LEVEL B. Grades kgn–6 to 1–6.
b) LEVEL C. Grades 1–0 to 1–9; 3 scores: mathematics computation, mathematics concepts and applications, total.
c) LEVEL D. Grades 1–6 to 2–9; 3 scores: same as for *b* above.
d) LEVEL E. Grades 2–6 to 3–9; 3 scores: same as for *b* above.
e) LEVEL F. Grades 3–6 to 4–9; 3 scores: same as for *b* above.
f) LEVEL G. Grades 4–6 to 6–9; 3 scores: same as for *b* above.
g) LEVEL H. Grades 6–6 to 8–9; 3 scores: same as for *b* above.
h) LEVEL J. Grades 8–6 to 12–9; 3 scores: same as for *b* above.

See T2:707 (1 reference); for reviews by Jack Price and C. Alan Riedesel of an earlier edition, see 7:514. For reviews of an earlier edition of the complete battery, see 8:12 (2 reviews) and 7:9 (2 reviews, 3 excerpts).

REFERENCES

1. See T2:707.
2. CALISTE, E. R. Students' adjustment from open to structured schools. *Contemporary Education*, 1979, 50, 138–145.
3. KILMANN, P. R., HENRY, S. E., SCARBRO, H., & LAUGHLIN, J. E. The impact of affective education on school underachievers. *Psychology in the Schools*, 1979, 16, 217–223.
4. GANDARA, P., KEOGH, B. K., & YOSHIOKA–MAXWELL, B. Predicting academic performance of Anlgo and Mexican–American kindergarten children. *Psychology in the Schools*, 1980, 17, 174–177.
5. KARWEIT, N., & SLAVIN, R. E. Measurement and modeling choices in studies of time and learning. *American Educational Research Journal*, 1981, 18, 143–156.

[553]

Comprehensive Tests of Basic Skills: Reading, [Forms U & V]. Grades kgn–6 to 1–6, 1–0 to 1–9, 1–6 to 2–9, 2–6 to 3–9, 3–6 to 4–9, 4–6 to 6–9, 6–6 to 8–9, 8–6 to 12–9; 1968–81; previous edition (Forms S and T) still available; 4 scores: word attack, vocabulary, comprehension, total; 8 levels; CTB/McGraw-Hill. For the complete battery entry, see 551.

a) LEVEL B. Grades kgn–6 to 1–6.
b) LEVEL C. Grades 1–0 to 1–9.
c) LEVEL D. Grades 1–6 to 2–9.
d) LEVEL E. Grades 2–6 to 3–9.
e) LEVEL F. Grades 3–6 to 4–9.
f) LEVEL G. Grades 4–6 to 6–9.
g) LEVEL H. Grades 6–6 to 8–9.
h) LEVEL J. Grades 8–6 to 12–9.

For additional information and a review by Randy Demaline of an earlier edition, see 8:721 (9 references); see also T2:1542 (3 references); for a review by Earl F. Rankin of earlier forms, see 7:685. For reviews of an earlier edition of the complete battery, see 8:12 (2 reviews) and 7:9 (2 reviews, 3 excerpts).

REFERENCES

1–3. See T2:1542.
4–12. See 8:721.

13. HUSHAK, L. J. The role of schools in reducing the variance of cognitive skills. *Journal of Educational Research*, 1977, 70, 115–122.
14. DORVAL, B., WALLACH, L., & WALLACH, M. A. Field evaluation of a tutorial reading program emphasizing phoneme identification skills. *Reading Teacher*, 1978, 31, 784–790.
15. MICHAEL, W. B., SMITH, R. A., & MICHAEL, J. J. Further development and validation of a self-concept measure involving school-related activities. *Educational & Psychological Measurement*, 1978, 38, 527–535.
16. WALLBROWN, F. H., BROWN, D. H., & ENGIN, A. W. A factor analysis of reading attitudes along with measures of reading achievement and scholastic aptitude. *Psychology in the Schools*, 1978, 15, 160–165.
17. BORG, W. R. Teacher coverage of academic content and pupil achievement. *Journal of Educational Psychology*, 1979, 71, 635–645.
18. CALISTE, E. R. "Students" adjustment from open to structured schools. *Contemporary Education*, 1979, 50, 138–145.
19. KILMANN, P. R., HENRY, S. E., SCARBRO, H., & LAUGHLIN, J. E. The impact of affective education on elementary school underachievers. *Psychology in the Schools*, 1979, 16, 217–223.
20. SASSENRATH, J. M., PIERCE, L. C., & MADDUX, R. E. Functional color components used in reading instruction. *Psychology in the Schools*, 1979, 16, 132–136.
21. GANDARA, P., KEOGH, B. K., & YOSHIOKA-MAXWELL, B. Predicting academic performance of Anglo and Mexican-American kindergarten children. *Psychology in the Schools*, 1980, 17, 174–177.
22. LAMBERT, N. M., & URBANSKI, C. Behavioral profiles of children with different levels of achievement. *Journal of School Psychology*, 1980, 18, 58–66.
23. LEHN, T., VLADOVIC, R., & MICHAEL, W. B. The short term predictive validity of a standardized reading test and of scales reflecting six dimensions of academic self-concept relative to selected high school achievement criteria for four ethnic groups. *Journal of Educational & Psychological Measurement*, 1980, 40, 1017–1031.
24. MICHAEL, W. B., LEHN, T., VLADOVIC, R., & COOPER, T. Cognitive and affective factor dimensions in each of four high school samples of different ethnicity. *Journal of Educational & Psychological Measurement*, 1980, 40, 1043–1050.
25. LEINHARDT, G., ZIGMOND, N., & COOLEY, W. W. Reading instruction and its effects. *American Educational Research Journal*, 1981, 18, 343–361.

[554]

★Comprehensive Tests of Basic Skills: Science and Social Studies, [Third Edition]. Grades 1–6 to 2–9, 2–6 to 3–9, 3–6 to 4–9, 4–6 to 6–9, 6–6 to 8–9, 8–6 to 12–9; 1968–81; 6 levels; CTB/McGraw-Hill. For the complete battery entry, see 551.
a) LEVEL D. Grades 1–6 to 2–9.
b) LEVEL E. Grades 2–6 to 3–9.
c) LEVEL F. Grades 3–6 to 4–9.
d) LEVEL G. Grades 4–6 to 6–9.
e) LEVEL H. Grades 6–6 to 8–9.
f) LEVEL J. Grades 8–6 to 12–9.

For additional information and a review by Arlen R. Gullickson of an earlier edition of the science subtest, see 8:825. For reviews of an earlier edition of the complete battery, see 8:12 (2 reviews).

[555]

Computation Test A/67. Job applicants with at least 6 years of education; 1956–63; multiplication; National Institute for Personnel Research [South Africa].*

For additional information, see 6:618.

[556]

Computer Operator Aptitude Battery. Experienced operators and trainees; 1973–74; COAB; 4 scores: sequence recognition, format checking, logical thinking, total; A. Joanne Holloway; Science Research Associates, Inc.*

For additional information and reviews by Richard T. Johnson and Nick L. Smith, see 8:1078.

[557]

Computer Programmer Aptitude Battery. Applicants for training or employment in computer programmer and systems analysis fields; 1964–74; CPAB; 6 scores: verbal meaning, reasoning, letter series, number ability, diagramming, total; Jean Maier Palormo; Science Research Associates, Inc.* (British edition: 1964–71; standardization supplement by Peter Saville; NFER-Nelson Publishing Co. [England].)*

For additional information and a review by Nick L. Smith, see 8:1079 (3 references); see also T2:2334 (2 references); for reviews by Richard T. Johnson and Donald J. Veldman, see 7:1089 (2 references).

REFERENCES

1–2. See 7:1089.
3–4. See T2:2334.
5–7. See 8:1079.
8. SCHMIDT, F. L., GAST-ROSENBERG, I., & HUNTER, J. E. Validity generalization results for computer programmers. *Journal of Applied Psychology*, 1980, 65, 643–661.

[558]

Comrey Personality Scales. Ages 16 and over; 1970; CPS; 10 scores: trust vs. defensiveness (T), orderliness vs. lack of compulsion (O), social conformity vs. rebelliousness (C), activity vs. lack of energy (A), emotional stability vs. neuroticism (S), extraversion vs. introversion (E), masculinity vs. femininity (M), empathy vs. egocentrism (P), validity check (V), response bias (R); Andrew L. Comrey; EdITS/Educational and Industrial Testing Service.*

For additional information and a review by Edgar Howarth, see 8:527 (27 references); see also T2:1139 (4 references); for reviews by R. G. Demaree and M. Y. Quereshi, see 7:59 (20 references).

REFERENCES

1–20. See 7:59.
21–24. See T2:1139.
25–51. See 8:527.
52. ANCOLI, S., & GREEN, K. F. Authoritarianism, introspection, and alpha wave biofeedback training. *Psychophysiology*, 1977, 14, 40–43.
53. BROWNE, J. A., & HOWARTH, E. A comprehensive factor analysis of personality questionnaire items: A test of twenty putative factor hypotheses. *Multivariate Behavioral Research*, 1977, 12, 399–427.
54. CLIFF, N. Further study of cognitive processing models for inventory response. *Applied Psychological Measurement*, 1977, 1, 41–49.
55. GERSHEN, J. A., & MCCREARY, C. P. Comparing personality traits of male and female dental students: A study of two freshman classes. *Journal of Dental Education*, 1977, 41, 618–622.
56. LORR, M., O'CONNOR, J. P., & SEIFERT, R. F. A comparison of four personality inventories. *Journal of Personality Assessment*, 1977, 41, 520–526.
57. BARNETT, O. Nonprofessionals in the rehabilitation of mentally disordered sex offenders. *Community Mental Health Journal*, 1978, 14, 110–115.
58. COMREY, A. L., SAFI, A., & BACKER, T. E. Psychiatric screening with the Comrey Personality Scales. *Psychological Reports*, 1978, 42, 1127–1130.
59. COMREY, A. L., WONG, C., & BACKER, T. E. Further validation of the social conformity scale of the Comrey Personality Scales. *Psychological Reports*, 1978, 43, 165–166.
60. HOIBERG, A. Effects of participation in the physical conditioning platoon. *Journal of Clinical Psychology*, 1978, 34, 410–416.
61. HOIBERG, A, & PUGH, W. M. Predicting navy effectiveness: Expectations, motivation, personality, aptitude, and background variables. *Personnel Psychology*, 1978, 31, 841–852.
62. LEE, H. B., & COMREY, A. L. An empirical comparison of two minimum residual factor extraction methods. *Multivariate Behavioral Research*, 1978, 13, 497–507.
63. VANDENBERG, S. G., & PRICE, R. A. Replication of the factor structure of the Comrey Personality Scales. *Psychological Reports*, 1978, 42, 343–352.

64. WEBSTER, E. G., BOOTH, R. F., GRAHAM, W. K., & ALF, E. F. A sex comparison of factors related to success in naval hospital caps school. *Personnel Psychology*, 1978, 31, 95–106.
65. WILCOX, W. W., & WENGER, W. K. Reliability and stability of the Comrey Personality Scales in a clinical setting. *Journal of Clinical Psychology*, 1978, 34, 555–557.
66. KANNARKAT, J. P., & BAYTON, J. A. Validity of Adler's active–constructive, active–destructive, passive–constructive, and passive–destructive typology. *Journal of Research in Personality*, 1979, 13, 351–360.
67. LEE, H. B., & COMREY, A. L. Distortions in a commonly used factor analytic procedure. *Multivariate Behavioral Research*, 1979, 14, 301–321.
68. STEIBE, S. C., BOULET, D. B., & LEE, D. C. Trainee trait empathy, age, trainer functioning, client age and training time as discriminators of successful empathy training. *Canadian Counsellor*, 1979, 14, 41–46.
69. VAN TUINEN, M., & RAMARAIAH, N. V. A multimethod analysis of selected self–esteem measures. *Journal of Research in Personality*, 1979, 13, 16–24.
70. WOOD, D., DEL NUOVO, A., BUCKY, S. F., SCHEIN, S., & MICHALIK, M. Psychodrama with an alcohol abuser population. *Group Psychotherapy, Psychodrama & Sociometry*, 1979, 32, 75–88.
71. ANTILL, J. K., & CUNNINGHAM, J. D. The relationship of masculinity, feminity, and androgyny to self–esteem. *Australian Journal of Psychology*, 1980, 32, 195–207.
72. FRANCES, R. J., TIMM, S., & BUCKY, S. Studies of familial and nonfamilial alcoholism. *Archives of General Psychiatry*, 1980, 37, 564–566.
73. BOOTH, R. F. Factor stability of the Comrey Personality Scales. *Educational & Psychological Measurement*, 1981, 41, 309–314.

[559]

Concept Assessment Kit—Conservation. Ages 4–7; 1968; CAKC; 2 editions; Marcel L. Goldschmid and Peter M. Bentler; EdITS/Educational and Industrial Testing Service.*

a) FORMS A AND B. 13 scores: 2 scores (behavior, explanation) in each of 6 areas (2-dimensional space, number, substance, continuous quantity, weight, discontinuous quantity), total.

b) FORM C. 13 scores: 2 scores (behavior, explanation) in area (3 scores) and length (3 scores), total.

For additional information, see 8:238 (32 references); see also T2:549 (5 references); for a review by J. Douglas Ayers, and excerpted reviews by Rheta DeVries (with Lawrence Kohlberg), Vernon C. Hall (with Michael Mery), and Charles D. Smock, see 7:437 (5 references).

REFERENCES

1–5. See 7:437.
6–10. See T2:549.
11–42. See 8:238.
43. COUTTS, L. M., MASON, P., WATERMAN, L., KOBASIGAWA, A. The "Concept Assessment Kit–Conservation": Supplementary data. *Canadian Journal of Behavioural Science*, 1977, 9, 81–83.
44. PRAWAT, R. S., & JONES, H. A longitudinal study of language development in children at different levels of cognitive development. *Merrill–Palmer Quarterly*, 1977, 23, 115–120.
45. PRAWAT, R. S., & HANES, B. F. Sentence comprehension as a function of conservation, age, and IQ. *Child Study Journal*, 1977, 8, 43–53.
46. SOLLOD, R., & LAPIDUS, L. B. Concrete operational thinking, diagnosis, & psychopathology in hospitalized schizophrenics. *Journal of Abnormal Psychology*, 1977, 86, 199–202.
47. ANDERSON, D. R., & CLARK, A. T. Comparison of conservation training procedures. *Psychological Reports*, 1978, 43, 495–499.
48. HENRY, J. A. Elementary school science experiences and reading achievement in six-year-old children. *Genetic Psychology Monographs*, 1978, 98, 159–179.
49. LITROWNIK, A. J., FRANZINI, L. R., LIVINGSTON, M. K., & HARVEY, S. Developmental priority of identity conservation: Acceleration of identity and equivalence in normal and moderately retarded children. *Child Development*, 1978, 49, 201–208.
50. PRICKETT, J. Comparison of children's vocabulary comprehension with conservation ability. *ASHA*, 1978, 20, 822.
51. RUBIN, K. H., BROWN, I. D. R., & PRIDDLE, R. L. The relationships between measures of fluid, crystallized, and "Piagetian" intelligence in elementary–school–aged children. *Journal of Genetic Psychology*, 1978, 132, 29–36.
52. WALKER, A. A. A developmental sequence of skills leading to conservation. *Journal of Genetic Psychology*, 1978, 132, 313–314.

53. WHITE, E., ELSOM, B., & PRAWAT, R. Children's conceptions of death. *Child Development*, 1978, 49, 307–310.
54. BORYS, S. V., & SPITZ, H. H. Effect of peer interaction on the problem-solving behavior of mentally retarded youths. *American Journal of Mental Deficiency*, 1979, 84, 273–279.
55. BROWN, M. H., SKEEN, P., & OSBORN, D. K. Young children's perception of the reality of television. *Contemporary Education*, 1979, 50, 129–133.
56. JAMISON, W., & DANSKY, J. L. Identifying developmental prerequisites of cognitive acquisitions. *Child Development*, 1979, 50, 449–454.
57. SERAFINE, M. L. A measure of meter conservation in music, based on Piaget's theory. *Genetic Psychology Monographs*, 1979, 99, 185–229.
58. SILVERSTEIN, A. B., BROWNLEE, L., & LEGUTKI, G. Reliability of the Concept Assessment Kit–Conservation for educable mentally retarded children. *Psychology in the Schools*, 1980, 17, 4–6.
59. WASIK, B. H., DAY, B. D., & WASIK, J. L. Basic concepts and conservation skill training in kindergarten children. *Perceptual & Motor Skills*, 1980, 50, 71–80.

[560]

Concept Attainment Test. College and adults; 1959; CAT; J. M. Schepers; National Institute for Personnel Research [South Africa].*

[561]

★**Concept Formation: The Assessment and Remediation of Concept Deficit in the Young Child.** Ages 3–8; 1978; Elizabeth Tabaka-Juedes; Communication Skill Builders, Inc.*

[562]

Concept-Specific Anxiety Scale. College and adults; 1972; CAS; for research use only; anxiety elicited by locally determined stimuli; 3 scores: physiological response, mood, total; 2 versions: CAS I for use with printed verbal stimuli, CAS II for use with pictorial stimuli; C. W. Cole and E. R. Oetting; Rocky Mountain Behavioral Science Institute, Inc.* (In-print status uncertain; no reply from publisher.)

For additional information and a review by Edward S. Katkin, see 8:528 (4 references); see also T2:1141 (3 references).

REFERENCES

1–3. See T2:1141.
4–7. See 8:528.
8. HAWKINS, J. G., BRADLEY, R. W., & WHITE, G. W. Anxiety and the process of deciding about a major and vocation. *Journal of Counseling Psychology*, 1977, 24, 398–403.

[563]

Conceptual Systems Test. Grades 7 and over; 1971; CST; concreteness-abstractness; 6 scores: divine fate control, need for structure order, need to help people, need for people, interpersonal aggression, anomie; no manual; O. J. Harvey and James K. Hoffmeister; Test Analysis and Development Corporation.*

For additional information and a review by Andrew L. Comrey, see 8:529 (24 references); see also T2:1142 (5 references).

REFERENCES

1–5. See T2:1142.
6–29. See 8:529.
30. KAPLAN, M. N. An aptitude–treatment interaction study of student choice and completion in a PSI choice. *Engineering Education*, 1978, 69, 273–284.
31. WATSON, J. Conceptual systems of undergraduate nursing students as compared with university students at large and practicing nurses. *Nursing Research*, 1978, 27, 151–155.
32. PUTNAM, L. L. Preference for procedural order in task-oriented small groups. *Communication Monographs*, 1979, 46, 193–218.

[564]

Concise Word Reading Tests. Ages 7–12; 1969; R. J. Andrews; Teaching and Testing Resources [Australia].*

[565]

Conflict Management Survey. Adults; 1969–73; CMS; "manner in which individuals react to and attempt to manage differences between themselves and others"; 5 scores (personal orientation, interpersonal relationships, small group relationships, intergroup relationships, total) for each of 5 conflict management styles (based on varying degrees of concern for the relationship and concern for personal goals); no manual; Jay Hall; Teleometrics Int'l.*

For additional information and a review by Frank J. Landy, see 8:1173 (2 references).

[566]

Consequences. Grades 9–16 and adults; 1058; 2 scores: originality, ideational fluency; P. R. Christensen, P. R. Merrifield, and J. P. Guilford; Sheridan Psychological Services, Inc.*

For additional information, see 8:239 (23 references); see also T2:551 (71 references); for a review by Goldine C. Gleser of the 10-item test, see 6:547 (13 references).

REFERENCES

1–13. See 6:547.
14–84. See T2:551.
85–107. See 8:239.
108. BOWERS, P. Hypnosis and creativity: The search for the missing link. *Journal of Abnormal Psychology*, 1979, 88, 564–572.
109. HOCEVAR, D. Ideational fluency as a confounding factor in the measurement of originality. *Journal of Educational Psychology*, 1979, 71, 191–196.
110. HOCEVAR, D., & MICHAEL, W. B. The effects of scoring formulas on the discriminant validity of tests of divergent thinking. *Educational & Psychological Measurement*, 1979, 39, 917–921.

[567]

★**Content Inventories: English, Social Studies, Science.** Grades 4, 5, 6, 7, 8, 9, 10, 11, 12; 1979; CI; screening instrument to determine general reading and study skills; 3 reading levels: independent, instructional, frustration; Lana McWilliams and Thomas A. Rakes; Kendall/Hunt Publishing Co.*

[568]

★**Continuing Education Assessment Inventory.** Mentally retarded adolescents and adults; 1975–82; CEAI; criterion-referenced; designed for "mentally retarded individuals who have not as yet reached minimal development in vocational independence and/or adequate independence in personal and social skills"; ratings in seven areas: independence, leisure time, prevocational, self-care, mobility, communication, personal and social development; Gertrude A. Barber, Beth Lane, Shirley Johnson, and Alfred P. Riccomini; Barber Center Press, Inc.*

[569]

The Cooper-McGuire Diagnostic Word-Analysis Test. Grades 1–5 and over; 1970–72; criterion-referenced; 3 readiness-for-word-analysis goals (letter names and shapes, auditory discrimination of letter sounds and blending ability, visual discrimination of word forms), 2 phonic analysis goals (consonant sounds, vowel sounds), 4 structural analysis goals (root words and endings, compound words and contractions, prefixes and suffixes, syllables); 32 overlapping tests with 1 to 13 tests administered at a given reader level; J. Louis Cooper and Marion L. McGuire; Croft, Inc.*

For additional information and a review by John McLeod, see 8:750.

[570]

Cooperative English Tests. Grades 9–12, 13–14; 1940–65; CET; 6 scores: reading comprehension (vocabulary, level, speed, total), English expression, total; revision by Clarence Derrick, David P. Harris, and Biron Walker; Addison-Wesley Publishing Co., Inc.*

For additional information, see 8:49 (20 references); see also T2:69 (107 references); for reviews by Leonard S. Feldt and Margaret F. Lorimer, and an excerpted review by Laurence Siegel, see 6:256 (52 references); see also 5:179 (58 references) and 4:155 (53 references); for reviews by J. Paul Leonard, Edward S. Noyes, and Robert C. Pooley of an earlier edition, see 3:120 (29 references); see also 2:1276 (1 reference). For reviews of the expression subtest, see 6:258 (2 reviews); the reading subtest, see 6:806 (2 reviews); and an earlier edition of the reading subtest, see 3:497 (2 reviews).

REFERENCES

1–2. See 2:1276.
3–31. See 3:120.
32–84. See 4:155.
85–142. See 5:179.
143–194. See 6:256.
195–301. See T2:69.
302–321. See 8:49.
322. ROBERTS, A. D., GABLE, R. K., & OWEN, S. V. An evaluation of minicourse curricula in secondary social studies. *Journal of Experimental Education*, 1977, 46, 4–11.
323. DUDLEY, J. R. A remedial skills course for under-prepared college students. *Journal of Educational Research*, 1978, 71, 143–148.
324. KNIKER, C. R., & KACHEL, D. W. Measuring student values through projective techniques. *Counseling & Values*, 1978, 23, 33–40.
325. LAMBRECHT, J. J. First- and second-year shorthand achievement for Century 21, Forkner and Gregg shorthand. *Delta Pi Epsilon Journal*, 1978, 20, 12–26.
326. PANACKAL, A. A., & HEFT, C. S. Cloze technique and multiple choice technique: Reliability and validity. *Educational & Psychological Measurement*, 1978, 38, 917–932.
327. SHARF, R. S. Evaluation of a computer-based narrative interpretation of a test battery. *Measurement & Evaluation in Guidance*, 1978, 11, 50–53.
328. DOWNEY, R. G. Item-option weighting of achievement tests: Comparative study of methods. *Applied Psychological Measurement*, 1979, 3, 453–461.
329. LEONARDSON, G. R. The contribution of academic factors in predicting graduate school success. *College Student Journal*, 1979, 13, 21–24.

[571]

Cooperative English Tests: English Expression. Grades 9–12, 13–14; 1940–60; this subtest of the *Cooperative English Tests* is a revision of the subtests *Effectiveness of Expression* and *Mechanics of Expression* in earlier editions of the battery; revision by Clarence Derrick, David P. Harris, and Biron Walker; Addison-Wesley Publishing Co., Inc.*

For additional information and reviews by John C. Sherwood and John M. Stalnaker, see 6:258; for a review by Chester W. Harris of an earlier edition, see 4:155. For reviews of the complete battery, see 6:256 (2 reviews, 1 excerpt) and 3:120 (3 reviews).

[572]

★The Cooperative Institutional Research Program. College freshmen, transfer, and part-time students; 1980–81; CIRP; test entitled *Student Information Form*; Alexander W. Astin, Margo R. King, and Gerald T. Richardson; University of California, Los Angeles.*

[573]

Cooperative Mathematics Tests: Algebra I and II. Grades 8–9, 10–12; 1962–65; Educational Testing Service; Addison-Wesley Publishing Co., Inc.*

For additional information and a review by Robert A. Forsyth, see 8:298 (7 references); for a review by Kenneth J. Travers, see 7:500 (4 references); for a review by Paul Blommers, see 6:594. For excerpted reviews by John R. Hills and Jack C. Merwin of the series, see 7:465.

REFERENCES

1–4. See 7:500.
5–11. See 8:298.
12. HIRSCH, C. R. The effects of guided discovery and individualized instructional packages on initial learning, transfer, and retention in second-year algebra. *Journal for Research in Mathematics Education*, 1977, 8, 359–368.
13. COHN, S. J. Cognitive characteristics of the top-scoring third of the 1976 talent search contestants. *Gifted Child Quarterly*, 1978, 22, 416–420.
14. BECKER, B. J. Performance of a group of mathematically able youths on the mathematics usage and natural sciences reading tests of the American College Test Battery vs the Scholastic Aptitude Test. *Gifted Child Quarterly*, 1980, 24, 138–143.
15. SWAFFORD, J. O. Sex differences in first-year algebra. *Journal for Research in Mathematics Education*, 1980, 11, 335–346.
16. SWAFFORD, J. O., & KEPNER, H. S., JR. The evaluation of an application-oriented first-year algebra program. *Journal for Research in Mathematics Education*, 1980, 11, 190–201.
17. WOLLEAT, P. L., PEDRO, J. D., BECKER, A. D., & FENNEMA, E. Sex differences in high school students' causal attributions of performance in mathematics. *Journal for Research in Mathematics Education*, 1980, 11, 356–366.
18. ARMSTRONG, J. M. Achievement and participation of women in mathematics: Results of two national surveys. *Journal of Research in Mathematics Education*, 1981, 12, 356–372.
19. HOUSE, P. A. One small step for the mathematically gifted. *School Science & Mathematics*, 1981, 81, 195–199.

[574]

Cooperative Mathematics Tests: Algebra III. High school and college; 1963–65; Educational Testing Service; Addison-Wesley Publishing Co., Inc.*

See T2:673 (1 reference); for reviews by James R. Caldwell and Willard G. Warrington, see 7:501. For excerpted reviews by John R. Hills and Jack C. Merwin of the series, see 7:465.

[575]

Cooperative Mathematics Tests: Analytic Geometry. High school and college; 1963–65; Educational Testing Service; Addison-Wesley Publishing Co., Inc.*

For additional information and a review by L. Ray Carry, see 7:532. For excerpted reviews by John R. Hills and Jack C. Merwin of the series, see 7:465.

[576]

Cooperative Mathematics Tests: Arithmetic. Grades 7–9; 1962–65; Educational Testing Service; Addison-Wesley Publishing Co., Inc.*

See T2:709 (2 references); for a review by Alan R. Osborne, see 7:515 (2 references); for a review by O. F. Anderhalter, see 6:607. For excerpted reviews by John R. Hills and Jack C. Merwin of the series, see 7:465.

[577]

Cooperative Mathematics Tests: Calculus. High school and college; 1963–65; Educational Testing Service; Addison-Wesley Publishing Co., Inc.*

For additional information and reviews by William E. Kline and G. Edith Robinson, see 7:531. For excerpted reviews by John R. Hills and Jack C. Merwin of the series, see 7:465.

REFERENCES

1. MEZYNSKI, K., & STANLEY, J. C. Advanced placement oriented calculus for high school students. *Journal for Research in Mathematics Education*, 1980, 11, 347–355.
2. THOMPSON, S. B. Do individualized mastery and traditional instructional systems yield different course effects in college calculus? *American Educational Research Journal*, 1980, 17, 361–375.

[578]

Cooperative Mathematics Tests: Geometry. Grades 10–12; 1962–65; 2 scores: Part I (Euclidean geometry), total; Educational Testing Service; Addison-Wesley Publishing Co., Inc.*

For additional information and a review by Evan D. Shull, see 7:533 (2 references); see also 6:645 (1 reference). For excerpted reviews by John R. Hills and Jack C. Merwin of the series, see 7:465.

REFERENCES

1. See 6:645.
2–3. See 7:533.
4. WOLLEAT, P. L., PEDRO, J. D., BECKER, A. D., & FENNEMA, E. Sex differences in high school students' causal attributions of performance in mathematics. *Journal for Research in Mathematics Education*, 1980, 11, 356–366.

[579]

Cooperative Mathematics Tests: Structure of the Number System. Grades 7–8; 1963–65; Educational Testing Service; Addison-Wesley Publishing Co., Inc.*

See T2:613 (1 reference); for reviews by M. Vere DeVault and Leslie P. Steffe, see 7:466. For excerpted reviews by John R. Hills and Jack C. Merwin of the series, see 7:465.

REFERENCES

1. See T2:613.
2. KING, E. H. College mathematics: Open vs. lecture. *Improving College & University Teaching*, 1978, 26, 50–51.

[580]

Cooperative Mathematics Tests: Trigonometry. High school and college; 1962–65; Educational Testing Service; Addison-Wesley Publishing Co., Inc.*

For additional information and a review by Thomas A. Romberg, see 7:543. For excerpted reviews by John R. Hills and Jack C. Merwin of the series, see 7:465.

[581]

Cooperative Preschool Inventory, Revised Edition. Ages 3–6; 1965–70; CPI; achievement in areas necessary for success in school; test booklet title is *Preschool Inventory*; standardized on disadvantaged children; Bettye M. Caldwell; Addison-Wesley Publishing Co., Inc.*

See T2:490 (4 references); for a review by Joseph L. French, and an excerpted review by Dale Carlson, see 7:404 (5 references).

REFERENCES

1–5. See 7:404.
6–9. See T2:490.

10. ERNHART, C. B., SPANER S. D., & JORDAN, T. E. Validity of selected preschool screening tests. *Contemporary Educational Psychology*, 1977, 2, 78–89.
11. VOGEL, S. A. Morphological ability in normal and dyslexic children. *Journal of Learning Disabilities*, 1977, 10, 35–43.
12. BRIDGEMAN, B., & SHIPMAN, V. C. Preschool measures of self-esteem and achievement motivation as predictors of third-grade achievement. *Journal of Educational Psychology*, 1978, 70, 17–28.
13. SMITH, P. K., & SYDDALL, S. Play and non-play tutoring in preschool children: Is it play or tutoring which matters. *British Journal of Educational Psychology*, 1978, 48, 315–325.
14. REYNOLDS, C. R. An examination for bias in a preschool test battery across race and sex. *Journal of Educational Measurement*, 1980, 17, 137–146.
15. WRIGHT, M. J. Measuring the social competence of preschool children. *Canadian Journal of Behavioural Science*, 1980, 12, 17–32.

[582]

Cooperative Primary Tests. Grades 1.5–2.5, 2.5–3; 1965–67; CPT; Educational Testing Service; Addison-Wesley Publishing Co., Inc.*

a) GRADES 1.5–2.5. 4 scores: listening, word analysis, mathematics, reading.

b) GRADES 2.5–3. 7 scores: listening, word analysis, mathematics, reading, writing skills (spelling, capitalization-punctuation-usage, total).

For additional information and a review by Peter W. Airasian, see 8:13 (1 reference); for excerpted reviews by Gerald S. Hanna and Esin Kaya, see 7:10 (1 reference). For reviews of subtests, see 8:262 (2 reviews), 8:722 (2 reviews), and 8:751 (1 review).

REFERENCES

1. See 7:10.
2. See 8:13.
3. BELL, A. E., ABRAHAMSON, D. S., & MCRAE, K. N. Reading retardation: A 12-year prospective study. *Journal of Pediatrics*, 1977, 91, 363–370.
4. KAGAN, S., ZAHN, G. L., & GEALY, J. Competition and school achievement among Anglo-American and Mexican-American children. *Journal of Educational Psychology*, 1977, 69, 432–441.
5. LAMBERT, N. M., & NICOLL, R. C. Conceptual model for nonintellectual behavior and its relationship to early reading achievement. *Journal of Educational Psychology*, 1977, 69, 481–490.
6. BRIDGEMAN, B., & SHIPMAN, V. C. Preschool measures of self-esteem and achievement motivation as predictors of third-grade achievement. *Journal of Educational Psychology*, 1978, 70, 17–28.
7. BRIDGEMAN, B. Generality of a 'fast' or 'slow' test-taking style across a variety of cognitive tasks. *Journal of Educational Measurement*, 1980, 17, 211–217.
8. SIMPSON, C. Classroom organization and the gap between minority and non-minority student performance levels. *Educational Research Quarterly*, 1981, 6, 43–53.

[583]

Cooperative Primary Tests: Listening. Grades 1.5–2.5, 2.5–3; 1965–67; Educational Testing Service; Addison-Wesley Publishing Co., Inc.*

For reviews of the complete battery, see 7:10 (2 excerpts).

REFERENCES

1. RUDDELL, R. B. Early prediction of reading success: Profiles of good and poor readers. In M. L. Kamil & A. J. Moe (Eds.), *Reading research: Studies and applications; Twenty-eighth yearbook of the National Reading Conference.* Clemson, South Carolina: The National Reading Conference, 1979.
2. BARUFALD, J. P., & SWIFT, J. W. The influence of BSCS–elementary school sciences program instruction on first-grade students' listening skills. *Journal of Research in Science Teaching*, 1980, 17, 485–490.

[584]

Cooperative Primary Tests: Mathematics. Grades 1.5–2.5, 2.5–3; 1965–67; Educational Testing Service; Addison-Wesley Publishing Co., Inc.*

For additional information and reviews by Leroy G. Callahan and Thomas A. Romberg, see 8:262. For reviews of the complete battery, see 8:13 (1 review) and 7:10 (2 excerpts).

[585]

Cooperative Primary Tests: Reading. Grades 1.5–2.5, 2.5–3; 1965–67; Educational Testing Service; Addison-Wesley Publishing Co., Inc.*

For additional information and reviews by Shirley C. Feldmann and Nancy L. Roser, see 8:722 (1 reference). For reviews of the complete battery, see 8:13 (1 review) and 7:10 (2 excerpts).

REFERENCES

1. See 8:722.
2. FESHBACH, S., ADELMAN, H., & FULLER, W. Prediction of reading and related academic problems. *Journal of Educational Psychology*, 1977, 69, 299–308.
3. RUDDELL, R. B. Early prediction of reading success: Profiles of good and poor readers. In M. L. Kamil & A. J. Moe (Eds.), *Reading research: Studies and applications; Twenty-eighth yearbook of the National Reading Conference.* Clemson, South Carolina: The National Reading Conference, 1979.

[586]

Cooperative Primary Tests: Word Analysis. Grades 1.5–3; 1965–67; Educational Testing Service; Addison-Wesley Publishing Co., Inc.*

For additional information and a review by Shirley C. Feldmann, see 8:751. For reviews of the complete battery, see 8:13 (1 review) and 7:10 (2 excerpts).

REFERENCES

1. RUDDELL, R. B. Early prediction of reading success: Profiles of good and poor readers. In M. L. Kamil & A. J. Moe (Eds.), *Reading research: Studies and applications; Twenty-eighth yearbook of the National Reading Conference.* Clemson, South Carolina: The National Reading Conference, 1979.

[587]

Cooperative Primary Tests: Writing Skills. Grades 2.5–3; 1965–67; 3 scores: spelling, capitalization-punctuation-usage, total; Educational Testing Service; Addison-Wesley Publishing Co., Inc.*

For reviews of the complete battery, see 7:10 (2 excerpts).

[588]

Cooperative Reading Comprehension Test, Form Y. Secondary forms 5–6 and university; 1948–64 (Australian edition, 1960–64); Australian adaptation (spelling only) of Form Y of *Reading Comprehension: Cooperative English Test, Higher Level C2*; 4 scores: vocabulary, speed of comprehension, level of comprehension, total; Frederick B. Davis, Clarence Derrick, Jeanne M. Bradford, and Geraldine Spaulding; Australian Council for Educational Research [Australia].*

See T2:1544 (6 references).

REFERENCES

1–6. See T2:1544.
7. GADZELLA, B. M., GOLDSTON, J. T., & ZIMMERMANN, M. L. Effectiveness of exposure to study techniques on college students' perceptions. *Journal of Educational Research*, 1977, 71, 26–30.
8. GENTILE, L. M., & MCMILLAN, M. Some of our students' teachers can't read either. *Journal of Reading*, 1977, 21, 145–152.
9. AVER, M., LAHR, D., & DOCTER, R. Social and institutional factors in reading achievement in elementary schools. *Educational Research Quarterly*, 1978, 3, 3–18.
10. BLAKE, A. J. D. The predictive power of two written tests of Piagetian developmental level. *Journal of Research in Science Teaching*, 1980, 17, 435–441.

[589]
Cooperative Reading Comprehension Test, Forms L and M.
Secondary forms 2–4 (ages 14–16); 1960–67 (Australian edition, 1964–73); Australian adaptations (spelling only) of Forms 2A, 2B, and 2C of *Reading Comprehension: Cooperative English Test*, 1960 Revision; 3 scores: vocabulary, level of comprehension, speed of comprehension; Clarence Derrick, David P. Harris, and Biron Walker; Australian Council for Educational Research [Australia].*

REFERENCES
1. TREMBATH, R. J., & WHITE, R. T. Mastery achievement of intellectual skills. *Journal of Experimental Education*, 1979, 47, 247–252.
2. BLAKE, A. J. D. The predictive power of two written tests of Piagetian developmental level. *Journal of Research in Science Teaching*, 1980, 17, 435–441.

[590]
Cooperative School and College Ability Tests, Series II.
Grades 4–6, 7–9, 10–12, 13–14; 1955–73; SCAT; 3 scores: verbal, quantitative, total; combined SCAT-STEP test booklets available except for grades 13–14; Educational Testing Service; Addison-Wesley Publishing Co., Inc.*

For additional information and reviews by Lynn H. Fox and John H. Rosenbach, see 8:183 (48 references); see also T2:361 (62 references); for a review by H. J. Butcher and excerpted reviews by S. David Farr, Esin Kaya, and Douglas McKie (with Peggy Rae Koopman) of Series II, see 7:347 (186 references); for a review by Russell F. Green of the original edition (Series I), see 6:452 (64 references); for reviews by Frederick B. Davis, Hanford M. Fowler, and Julian C. Stanley, see 5:322 (7 references).

REFERENCES
1–7. See 5:322.
8–71. See 6:452.
72–257. See 7:347.
258–319. See T2:361.
320–367. See 8:183.
368. ATKIN, R., BRAY, R., DAVISON, M., HERZBERGER, S., HUMPHREYS, L., & SELZER, U. Ability factor differentiation, grades 5 through 11. *Applied Psychological Measurement*, 1977, 1, 65–76.
369. ATKIN, R., BRAY, R., DAVISON, M., HERZBERGER, S., HUMPHREYS, L., & SELZER, U. Cross-lagged panel analysis of sixteen cognitive measures at four grade levels. *Child Development*, 1977, 48, 944–952.
370. GOODYEAR, R. K., & FRANK, A. C. Introversion–extroversion: Some comparisons of the SVIB and OPI scales. *Measurement & Evaluation in Guidance*, 1977, 9, 206–211.
371. KEEFE, J. W. Model schools project report 14 Pius X High School. *National Association of Secondary School Principals Bulletin*, 1977, 61, 85–95.
372. LORD, F. M. A broad-range tailored test of verbal ability. *Applied Psychological Measurement*, 1977, 1, 95–100.
373. OTTEN, M. W. Inventory and expressive measures of locus of control and academic performance: A 5-year outcome study. *Journal of Personality Assessment*, 1977, 41, 644–649.
374. ROBITAILLE, D. F., SHERRILL, J. M., & KAUFMAN, D. M. The effect of computer utilization on the achievement and attitudes of ninth-grade mathematics students. *Journal for Research in Mathematics Education*, 1977, 8, 26–32.
375. SCHMITT, N. Interrater agreement in dimensionality and combination of assessment center judgments. *Journal of Applied Psychology*, 1977, 62, 171–176.
376. TRAUB, R. E., & FISHER, C. W. On the equivalence of constructed-response and multiple-choice tests. *Applied Psychological Measurement*, 1977, 1, 355–369.
377. WATERS, B. K. An empirical investigation of the stratified adaptive computerized testing model. *Applied Psychological Measurement*, 1977, 1, 141–152.
378. WERTS, C. E., & HILTON, T. L. Intellectual status and intellectual growth, again. *American Educational Research Journal*, 1977, 14, 137–146.
379. ALEAMONI, L. M., & OBOLER, L. ACT versus SAT in predicting first semester GPA. *Educational & Psychological Measurement*, 1978, 38, 393–399.
380. ALEXANDER, K. L., COOK, M., & McDILL, E. Curriculum tracking and educational stratification: Some further evidence. *American Sociological Review*, 1978, 43, 47–66.
381. COPELAND, M. L., CONRAD, C., & CHANSKY, N. M. Validity of two intelligence tests. *Psychological Reports*, 1978, 42, 662.
382. WOLFLE, L. M., & BRYANT, L. W. A causal model of nursing education and state board examination scores. *Nursing Research*, 1978, 27, 311–315.
383. HUMPHREYS, L. G., PARK, R. D., & PARSONS, C. K. Application of a simplex process model to six years of cognitive development in four demographic groups. *Applied Psychological Measurement*, 1979, 3, 51–64.
384. MITCHELL, J. V., JR. Causal attribution and self-assessment variables related to grade point average in high school. *Measurement & Evaluation in Guidance*, 1979, 12, 134–139.
385. AHERN, E. H., DIXON, P. W., KIMURA, T., OKUNA, J. S., & GIBSON, V. L. Phoneme use and the perception of meaning of written stimuli. *Psychologia*, 1980, 23, 206–218.
386. DIAMOND, E. E. The AMEG commission report on sex bias in achievement testing. *Measurement & Evaluation in Guidance*, 1980, 13, 135–147.
387. ALEXANDER, K. L., PALLAS, A. M., & COOK, M. A. Measure for measure: On the use of endogenous ability data in school–process research. *American Sociological Review*, 1981, 46, 619–631.
388. HOUSE, P. A. One small step for the mathematically gifted. *School Science & Mathematics*, 1981, 81, 195–199.
389. KIM, Y. C., MARX, M. H., & BROYLES, J. W. The stubborn-error effect in verbal discrimination learning. *Bulletin of the Psychonomic Society*, 1981, 18, 5–8.
390. WELDON, D. E., & MALPASS, R. S. Effects of attitudinal, cognitive, and situational variables on recall of biased communications. *Journal of Personality & Social Psychology*, 1981, 40, 39–52.

[591]
Cooperative Science Tests: Advanced General Science.
Grades 8–9; 1962–65; Educational Testing Service; Addison-Wesley Publishing Co., Inc.*

For additional information and a review by George G. Mallinson, see 8:826; for a review by Carl J. Olson, see 7:788 (1 reference). For excerpted reviews by Irvin J. Lehmann (with Clarence H. Nelson) and William Mehrens of the series, see 7:787.

[592]
Cooperative Science Tests: Biology.
Grades 10–12; 1963–65; 3 scores: general and human biology, the diversity of life, total; Educational Testing Service; Addison-Wesley Publishing Co., Inc.*

For additional information and a review by Clarence J. Goodnight, see 7:816. For excerpted reviews by Irvin J. Lehmann (with Clarence H. Nelson) and William Mehrens of the series, see 7:787.

[593]
Cooperative Science Tests: Chemistry.
Grades 9–12; 1963–65; 3 scores: general concepts and principles, laboratory, total; Educational Testing Service; Addison-Wesley Publishing Co., Inc.*

For additional information and a review by Edward F. DeVillafranca and John P. Penna, see 8:850. For excerpted reviews by Irvin J. Lehmann (with Clarence H. Nelson) and William Mehrens of the series, see 7:787.

[594]
Cooperative Science Tests: General Science.
Grades 7–9; 1962–65; Educational Testing Service; Addison-Wesley Publishing Co., Inc.*

For additional information, see 8:827; for a review by Clarence H. Nelson, see 7:789 (1 reference). For excerpted reviews by Irvin J. Lehmann (with Clarence H. Nelson) and William Mehrens of the series, see 7:787.

[595]
Cooperative Science Tests: Physics. Grades 10–12; 1963–65; 3 scores: general concepts and principles, laboratory, total; Educational Testing Service; Addison-Wesley Publishing Co., Inc.*

For additional information and a review by Wayne W. Welch, see 8:865; for a review by Alexander Even, see 7:857. For excerpted reviews by Irvin J. Lehmann (with Clarence H. Nelson) and William Mehrens of the series, see 7:787.

[596]
Cooperative Social Studies Tests: American Government. Grades 10–12; 1964–65; Educational Testing Service; Addison-Wesley Publishing Co., Inc.*

For additional information and a review by Howard D. Mehlinger, see 7:927.

[597]
Cooperative Social Studies Tests: American History. Grades 7–8, 10–12; 1964–65; Educational Testing Service; Addison-Wesley Publishing Co., Inc.*

See T2:1988 (1 reference); for a review by William J. Webster, see 7:912.

REFERENCES

1. See T2:1988.
2. McTEER, J. H., & JACKSON, J. C. The effect of team teaching upon achievement in and attitude toward United States history. *High School Journal*, 1977, 61, 1–6.

[598]
Cooperative Social Studies Tests: Civics. Grades 8–9; 1964–65; Educational Testing Service; Addison-Wesley Publishing Co., Inc.*

For additional information and a review by Anna S. Ochoa, see 8:920; for a review by Vincent N. Campbell, see 7:928.

[599]
Cooperative Social Studies Tests: Modern European History. Grades 10–12; 1964–65; Educational Testing Service; Addison-Wesley Publishing Co., Inc.*

For additional information and a review by John Manning, see 7:913.

[600]
Cooperative Social Studies Tests: Problems of Democracy. Grades 10–12; 1964–65; Educational Testing Service; Addison-Wesley Publishing Co., Inc.*

For additional information and a review by Hulda Grobman, see 7:929 (1 reference).

[601]
Cooperative Social Studies Tests: World History. Grades 10–12; 1964–65; Educational Testing Service; Addison-Wesley Publishing Co., Inc.*

For additional information, see 7:914.

[602]
Cooperative Topical Tests in American History. High school; 1963–65; CTTAH; 8 tests; Educational Testing Service; Addison-Wesley Publishing Co., Inc.*
a) TEST 1, EXPLORATION, COLONIZATION, AND INDEPENDENCE: 1450–1783.
b) TEST 2, FOUNDATIONS OF AMERICAN GOVERNMENT: 1781–1801.
c) TEST 3, GROWTH OF NATIONALISM AND DEMOCRACY: 1801–1840.
d) TEST 4, EXPANSION, CIVIL WAR, AND RECONSTRUCTION: 1840–1877.
e) TEST 5, DEVELOPMENT OF INDUSTRIAL AMERICA: 1865–1898.
f) TEST 6, IMPERIALISM, DOMESTIC REFORM, AND THE FIRST WORLD WAR: 1898–1920.
g) TEST 7, PROSPERITY, DEPRESSION, AND THE NEW DEAL: 1920–1940.
h) TEST 8, THE SECOND WORLD WAR AND AFTER.

For additional information and a review by Richard E. Gross, see 7:915.

[603]
★**Coopersmith Self-Esteem Inventories.** Ages 8–15, 16 and above; 1981; SEI; Stanley Coopersmith; Consulting Psychologists Press, Inc.*
a) SCHOOL FORM. Ages 8–15; 5–6 scores: general self subscale score, social self-peers subscale score, home-parents subscale score, school-academic subscale score, total self score, lie scale score.
b) ADULT FORM. Ages 16 and above.

[604]
The Cornell Class-Reasoning Test. Grades 4–12; 1964; deductive logic; no manual; Robert H. Ennis, William L. Gardiner, Richard Morrow, Dieter Paulus, and Lucille Ringel; Illinois Thinking Project, University of Illinois at Urbana-Champaign.*

See T2:1753 (1 reference).

[605]
The Cornell Conditional-Reasoning Test. Grades 4–12; 1964; deductive logic; no manual; Robert H. Ennis, William L. Gardiner, John Guzzetta, Richard Morrow, Dieter Paulus, and Lucille Ringel; Illinois Thinking Project, University of Illinois at Urbana-Champaign.*

See T2:1754 (1 reference).

[606]
The Cornell Critical Thinking Tests. Grades 7–12, 13–16; 1961–71; CCTT; 2 tests (Level X and Level Z) each measuring different aspects of critical thinking; Robert H. Ennis and Jason Millman; Illinois Thinking Project, University of Illinois at Urbana-Champaign.*

See T2:1755 (2 references) and 7:779 (10 references).

REFERENCES

1–10. See 7:779.
11–12. See T2:1755.
13. GARETT, K. K., & WULF, K. The relationship of a measure of critical thinking ability to personality variables and to indicators of academic achievement. *Educational & Psychological Measurement*, 1978, 38, 1181–1187.
14. MICHAEL, W. B., SMITH, R. A., & MICHAEL, J. J. Further development and validation of a self-concept measure involving school-related activities. *Educational & Psychological Measurement*, 1978, 38, 527–535.
15. NAPIER, J. D. Effects of knowledge of cognitive–moral development and request to fake on Defining Issues Test P-scores. *Journal of Psychology*, 1979, 101, 45–52.
16. PARDUE, S. F. Blocked– and integrated–content baccalaureate nursing programs: A comparative study. *Nursing Research*, 1979, 28, 305–311.
17. CURTIS, C. K. Developing critical thinking skills in nonacademic social studies classes. *Alberta Journal of Educational Research*, 1980, 26, 75–84.

18. MICHAEL, J. J., DEVANEY, R., & MICHAEL, W. B. The factorial validity of the Cornell Critical Thinking Test for a junior high school sample. *Educational & Psychological Measurement*, 1980, 40, 437–450.
19. LANDIS, R. E., & MICHAEL, W. B. The factorial validity of three measures of critical thinking within the context of Guilford's structure-of-intellect model for a sample of ninth grade students. *Educational & Psychological Measurement*, 1981, 41, 1147–1166.

[607]
Cornell Inventory for Student Appraisal of Teaching and Courses.
College teachers; 1972–73; student ratings; computer scoring and reporting services not available outside of Cornell University; James B. Maas and Thomas R. Owen (manual); James B. Maas.*

For additional information and a review by Wilbert J. McKeachie, see 8:367.

[608]
The Cornell Learning and Study Skills Inventory.
Grades 7–13, 13–16; 1970; CLASSI; 9 scores: goal orientation, activity structure, scholarly skills, lecture mastery, textbook mastery, examination mastery, self mastery, total, reading validity index; Walter Pauk and Russell Cassel; Psychologists and Educators, Inc.*
a) SECONDARY SCHOOL FORM. Grades 7–13.
b) COLLEGE FORM. Grades 13–16.

For additional information and reviews by Allen Berger and Richard D. Robinson, see 8:815 (1 reference); see also T2:1756 (2 references).

[609]
Cornell Medical Index—Health Questionnaire.
Ages 14 and over; 1949–56; CMI; a questionnaire for use by physicians in collecting medical and psychiatric information from patients; (French Canadian and Spanish editions available); Keeve Brodman, Albert J. Erdmann, Jr., and Harold G. Wolff; Cornell University Medical College.*

For additional information, see 8:530 (46 references); see also T2:1145 (42 references); for reviews by Eugene E. Levitt and David T. Lykken, see 7:61 (32 references); see also P:49 (77 references).

REFERENCES

1–77. See P:49.
78–109. See 7:61.
110–151. See T2:1145.
152–197. See 8:530.
198. BROWN, J. S., & RAWLINSON, M. E. Sex differences in sick role rejection and in work performance following cardiac surgery. *Journal of Health & Social Behavior*, 1977, 18, 276–292.
199. COLEMAN, J., WOLKIND, S., & ASHLEY, L. Symptoms of behavior disturbance and adjustment to school. *Journal of Child Psychology & Psychiatry & Allied Disciplines*, 1977, 18, 201–209.
200. COSTA, P. T., JR., & MCCRAE, R. R. Psychiatric symptom dimensions in the Cornell Medical Index among normal adult males. *Journal of Clinical Psychology*, 1977, 33, 941–946.
201. DUDLEY, D. L., AICKIN, M., & MARTIN, C. J. Cigarette smoking in a chest clinic population—Psychophysiologic variables. *Journal of Psychosomatic Research*, 1977, 21, 367–375.
202. MEIKLE, S., BRODY, H., & PYSH, F. An investigation into the psychological effects of hysterectomy. *Journal of Nervous & Mental Disease*, 1977, 164, 36–39.
203. MURRAY, T. J., KELLY, P., CAMPBELL, L., & STEFANIK, K. Haloperidol in the treatment of stuttering. *British Journal of Psychiatry*, 1977, 130, 370–373.
204. NORTON, J. C., POWELL, B. J., PENICK, E. C., & SAUERS, C. A. Screening alcoholics for medical index. *Journal of Studies on Alcohol*, 1977, 38, 2193–2196.
205. WALKER, B. A., & ZISKIND, E. Relationship of nailbiting to sociopathy. *Journal of Nervous & Mental Disease*, 1977, 164, 64–65.
206. WIENS, A. N., & MATARAZZO, J. D. WAIS and MMPI correlates of the Halstead–Reitan Neuropsychology Battery in normal male subjects. *Journal of Nervous & Mental Disease*, 1977, 164, 112–121.
207. DAUS, A. T., & TEMPLER, D. I. The prediction of college football perseverance by the use of the Cornell Medical Index: Study number II. *Journal of Sports Medicine & Physical Fitness*, 1978, 18, 283–285.
208. GUCKES, A. D., SMITH, D. E., & SWOOPE, C. C. Counseling and related factors influencing satisfaction with dentures. *Journal of Prosthetic Dentistry*, 1978, 39, 259–267.
209. HARKINS, E. B. Effects of empty nest transition on self-report of psychological and physical well-being. *Journal of Marriage & the Family*, 1978, 40, 549–556.
210. JAMES, S. Treatment of homosexuality II. Superiority of desensitization/arousal as compared with anticipatory avoidance conditioning: Results of a controlled trial. *Behavior Therapy*, 1978, 9, 28–36.
211. KOLBE, L. J., & IVERSON, D. C. An assessment of student health needs: Implications for the planning and utilization of college health services. *Journal of American College Health Association*, 1978, 26, 263–267.
212. RAHE, R. H., LOONEY, J. G., WARD, H. W., TUNG, T. M., & LIV, W. T. Psychiatric consultation in a Vietnamese refugee camp. *American Journal of Psychiatry*, 1978, 135, 185–190.
213. RICHMAN, N. Depression in mothers of young children. *Journal of the Royal Society of Medicine*, 1978, 71, 489–493.
214. WALLER, S., & LORCH, B. Social and psychological characteristics of alcoholics: A male–female comparison. *International Journal of the Addictions*, 1978, 13, 201–212.
215. WEISS, R. L., & AVED, B. M. Marital satisfaction and depression as predictors of physical health status. *Journal of Consulting & Clinical Psychology*, 1978, 46, 1379–1384.
216. CONGER, R. D., BURGESS, R. L., & BARRETT, C. Child abuse related to life change and perceptions of illness: Some preliminary findings. *Family Coordinators*, 1979, 28, 73–78.
217. LIN, K., TAZUMA, L., & MASUDA, M. Adaptational problems of Vietnamese refugees. *Archives of General Psychiatry*, 1979, 36, 955–961.
218. TAUB, J. M., & HAWKINS, D. R. Aspects of personality associated with irregular sleep habits in young adults. *Journal of Clinical Psychology*, 1979, 35, 296–304.
219. WEBB, W. B. Are short and long sleepers different? *Psychological Reports*, 1979, 44, 259–264.
220. ARMSTRONG, H. E., JR., GOLDENBERG, E., & STEWART, D. Correlations between Beck depression scores and physical complaints. *Psychological Reports*, 1980, 46, 740–742.
221. FARKAS, M. S., & HOYER, W. J. Processing consequences of perceptual grouping in selective attention. *Journal of Gerontology*, 1980, 35, 207–216.
222. KARSON, M. Is aesthetic judgment impaired by neuroticism. *Journal of Personality Assessment*, 1980, 44, 499–506.
223. LOPEZ, M. A. Social-skills training with institutionalized elderly: Effects of precounseling structuring and overlearning on skill acquisition and transfer. *Journal of Counseling Psychology*, 1980, 27, 286–293.
224. MASUDA, M., LIN, K., & TAZUMA, L. Adaptation problems of Vietnamese refugees. *Archives of General Psychiatry*, 1980, 37, 447–450.
225. NESS, R. C., & WINTROB, R. M. The emotional impact of fundamentalist religious participation: An empirical study of intragroup variation. *American Journal of Orthopsychiatry*, 1980, 50, 302–315.
226. POWELL, B. J., PENICK, E. C., & READ, M. R. Psychological adjustment and sex-role affiliation in an alcoholic population. *Journal of Clinical Psychology*, 1980, 36, 801–805.
227. SCHILL, T., TORES, C., & RAMANAIAH, N. Coping with loneliness and locus of control. *Psychological Reports*, 1980, 47, 1054.
228. SKINNER, H. A., & LEI, H. The multidimensional assessment of stressful life events. *Journal of Nervous & Mental Disease*, 1980, 168, 535–541.
229. SROLE, L., & KASSEN, A. The midtown Manhattan longitudinal study vs "the mental paradise lost" doctrine. *Archives of General Psychiatry*, 1980, 37, 209–221.
230. LUNDBERG, P. K., & PALUDI, M. A. Type A/B behavior patterns and the reporting of lifetime symptomatology: A=B. *Perceptual & Motor Skills*, 1981, 52, 473–474.

[610]
Cornell Word Form 2.
Adults; 1946–55; title on test is *C.W.F.–2*; civilian edition of *Cornell Word Form* designed for use in military psychiatric screening; psychosomatic and neuropsychiatric symptoms; Arthur Weider, Bela Mittelmann, David Wechsler, and Harold Wolff; Cornell University Medical College.*

See T2:1146 (1 reference) and P:50 (2 references); for a review by S. B. Sells, see 6:80 (1 reference); see also 5:44 (11 references).

[611]

Correct Spelling. Grades 10–13; 1967; "cognition of symbolic units" and "clerical aptitude"; Ralph Hoepfner and J. P. Guilford; Sheridan Psychological Services, Inc.*

[612]

Correctional Institutions Environment Scale. Residents and staff of juvenile and adult correctional facilities; 1974; CIES; a part of *The Social Climate Scales* (2227); 9 scores: involvement, support, expressiveness, autonomy, practical orientation, personal problem orientation, order and organization, clarity, staff control; Rudolf H. Moos; Consulting Psychologists Press, Inc.*

For additional information and a review by Kenneth A. Carlson, see 8:531 (16 references). For a review of *The Social Climate Scales*, see 8:681.

REFERENCES

1–16. See 8:531.
17. WATERS, J. E. Evaluating correctional environments: The social ecological perspective. *Corrective & Social Psychiatry & Journal of Behavioral Technology, Methods & Therapy*, 1980, 26, 45–52.

[613]

Correctional Policy Inventory: A Survey of Correctional Philosophy and Characteristic Methods of Dealing With Offenders. Correctional managers; 1970; 4 scores: reintegration, rehabilitation, reform, restraint; Vincent O'Leary; National Council on Crime and Delinquency.*

For additional information, see 8:1092 (2 references).

[614]

★**Corrective Reading Mastery Tests.** Students grades 4–12 and adults in the Corrective Reading Program; 1980–81; criterion-referenced; 6 tests; Siegfried Engleman and Linda Garcia Olen; Science Research Associates, Inc.*

a) COMPREHENSION A: THINKING BASICS. 1980; 19 scores: deductions, classification, true-false, description (1, 11), same (1, 11), analogies (1, 11), inductions (1, 11), statement inference, definitions, basic evidence, opposites, animal facts (1, 11), calendar facts, poems.

b) COMPREHENSION B: COMPREHENSION SKILLS. 1980; 2 subtests.

1) *Test* 1. To be completed after lesson 70 of Comprehension B; 17 scores: deductions (1, 11), basic evidence, analogies, contradictions (1, 11), body systems, body rules, sentence combinations (1, 11), parts of speech, subject-predicate, definitions (1, 11), statement inference, writing directions, following directions.

2) *Test* 2. To be completed at end of Comprehension B; 16 scores: basic evidence (1, 11), contradictions, similies, body rules, economic rules, statement inference (1, 11), following directions, definitions, sentence combinations, subject-predicate, sentence analysis, writing directions, editing, writing paragraphs.

c) COMPREHENSION C: CONCEPT APPLICATIONS. 1981; 2 subtests.

1) *Test* 1. To be completed after lesson 70 of Comprehension C; 17 scores: deductions (1, 11), maps/pictures/graphs, basic comprehension passages, supporting evidence, definitions, editing (1, 11), combining sentences, writing directions, filling out forms, identifying contradictory directions, information.

2) *Test* 2. To be completed at end of Comprehension C; 19 scores: main ideas, morals, specific-general, visual-spatial organization, outlining, deductions, argument rules (1, 11), ought statements, contradictions, words or deductions, maps/pictures/graphs, supporting evidence, editing, combining sentences, definitions, meaning from context (1, 11), information.

d) DECODING A: WORD-ATTACK BASICS. 1980; 14 scores: word identification (short and long vowels, sound combinations, final blends, initial blends, consonant digraphs, irregular words), sentence reading (time, errors), dictation (sound dictation, spelling from dictation), word completion (rhyming dictation, word completion), workbook skills (matching completion, circle game).

e) DECODING B: DECODING STRATEGIES. 1980; 2 subtests.

1) *Test* 1. To be completed after lesson 60 of Decoding B; 12 scores: word identification (short-vowel words, consonant digraphs, *ed* endings in short-vowel words, word endings *s* and *ing*, word endings *er* and *est*, sound combinations *ea/ar/ai*, sound combinations *ol/or/oa/-ow*, irregular words, vowel-conversion words), story reading (rate, accuracy, comprehension).

2) *Test* 2. To be completed at end of Decoding B; 13 scores: word identification (short-vowel words, *ed* endings and contractions, *s* and *es* endings, other endings, irregular words and difficult discriminations, vowel-conversion words, difficult multisyllabic words, sound combinations *ou/al/ar/igh/tch*, sound combinations *ir/ur/er/oi/wa*, sound combinations *orel/* soft *c/g/tion/ure*), story reading (rate, accuracy, comprehension).

f) DECODING C: SKILL APPLICATIONS. 1980; 2 subtests.

1) *Test* 1. To be completed after lesson 69 of Decoding C; 13 scores: word identification (sound combinations *ou/ai/ur*, sound combinations *ir/er/ar/al*, sound combinations *oi/ee/ea/au/aw*, sound combinations *ure/tion*, soft *c* and soft *g*, affixes *un/dis/ex/ly*, affixes *pre/ly/re/-ex*, difficult words, words with endings), vocabulary (vocabulary words), story reading (rate, accuracy, comprehension).

2) *Test* 2. To be completed at end of Decoding C; 11 scores: word identification (sound combinations, prefixes, suffixes *ible/able/by/less/ness*, suffixes *ial/tion/-ure*, affixes, endings, difficult words), vocabulary (vocabulary words), story reading (rate, accuracy, comprehension).

[615]

★**Cosmetology Student Admissions Examination.** Prospective cosmetology students; 1977–80; CSAE; 5 scores: interests, word analogies, comprehension and reasoning, manual dexterity, total; Anthony B. Colletti; Keystone Publications.* (In-print status uncertain; no reply from publisher.)

[616]

Cotswold Junior Ability Tests. Ages 8.5–9.5, 9.5–10.5; 1949–69; 2 levels; tests A, B, C, and E are out of print; C. M. Fleming; Robert Gibson & Sons, Glasgow, Ltd. [Scotland].*

a) JUNIOR MENTAL ABILITY D. Ages 8.5–9.5; 1967–69, c1957.

b) JUNIOR MENTAL ABILITY F. Ages 9.5–10.5; 1967–69, c1961.

For additional information concerning earlier forms, see 5:323.

[617]
Cotswold Personality Assessment P.A.1. Ages 11–16; 1960; manual subtitle is *A Study of Preferences and Values for Use in Schools and Clubs*; 6 scores: 3 preference scores (things, people, ideas) and 3 attitude scores (using one's hands, being with other people, talking about school); C. M. Fleming; Robert Gibson & Sons, Glasgow, Ltd. [Scotland].*

For additional information, see P:51; for reviews by Ralph D. Dutch and G. A. V. Morgan, see 6:81 (1 reference).

[618]
*****Counseling Services Assessment Blank**. College and adult counseling clients; 1968–79; CSAB; for evaluating services provided by counseling agencies; 3 problem-goal areas: vocational, personal, educational; James C. Hurst, Richard G. Weigel, and Martha L. Butler (manual); Rocky Mountain Behavioral Science Institute, Inc.* (In-print status uncertain; no reply from publisher.)

See T2:857 (3 references).

REFERENCES

1–3. See T2:857.
4. DAVIDSHOFER, C. O., BORMAN, A., & WEIGEL, R. G. The Counseling Services Assessment Blank: Is it reliable? *Journal of College Student Personnel*, 1977, 18, 215–218.
5. SHARF, R. S., & BISHOP, J. B. Counselors' feelings toward clients as related to intake judgments and outcome variables. *Journal of Counseling Psychology*, 1979, 26, 267–269.

[619]
★**Counselor Rating Scales (Short Form)**. Subjects in counseling experiments; 1978; for research use only; ratings by subjects in 3 areas: first impressions, helpfulness of counselor, helpfulness for specific problems; no manual; Thomas F. Cash; the Author.*

[620]
Course Evaluation Questionnaire. High school and college; 1971–72; CEQ; ratings by students; 5 scores: openness to students and ideas, contextual approach to learning, dynamism enthusiasm, organization clarity, quality meaningfulness; no manual; James K. Hoffmeister; Test Analysis and Development Corporation.*

For additional information and reviews by J. Stanley Ahmann and William C. McGaghie, see 8:368 (1 reference).

REFERENCES

1. See 8:368.
2. WEBER, L. J., & HUNT, T. C. A comparison of cognitive and attitudinal outcomes of two methods of teaching. *Improving College & University Teaching*, 1977, 25, 51–52.
3. MOORE, M. Course evaluation by students and self-evaluation by instructors. *Journal of Educational Research*, 1978, 72, 22–23.

[621]
★**Course-Faculty Instrument**. Business faculty and courses; 1976; CFI; Richard D. Freedman and Stephen A. Stumpf; New York University.*

REFERENCES

1. FREEDMAN, R. D., & STUMPF, S. A. Student evaluations of courses and faculty based on a perceived learning criterion: Scale construction, validation, and comparison of results. *Applied Psychological Measurement*, 1978, 2, 189–202.

2. FREEDMAN, R. D., STUMPF, S. A., & AGUANNO, J. C. Validity of the Course-Faculty Instrument (CFI): Intrinsic and extrinsic variables. *Educational & Psychological Measurement*, 1979, 39, 153–158.
3. STUMPF, S. A. Assessing academic program and department effectiveness using student evaluation data. *Research in Higher Education*, 1979, 11, 353–363.
4. STUMPF, S. A., & FREEDMAN, R. D. Expected grade covariation with student ratings of instruction: Individual versus class effects. *Journal of Educational Psychology*, 1979, 71, 293–302.
5. STUMPF, S. A., FREEDMAN, R. D., & AGUANNO, J. C. A path analysis of factors often found to be related to student ratings of teaching effectiveness. *Research in Higher Education*, 1979, 11, 111–123.
6. STUMPF, S. A., FREEDMAN, R. D., & KRIEGER, K. M. Validity extension of the Course-Faculty Instrument (CFI). *Research in Higher Education*, 1979, 11, 13–22.
7. STUMPF, S. A., & FREEDMAN, R. D. A broader role for student evaluation data. *Academy of Management Proceeding*, 1980, #80-52, 1–4.

[622]
***A Courtship Analysis**. Dating and engaged couples; 1961–79; unscored counseling and teaching aid; 12 areas: habits, religion, health, common interests, sex attitudes, adaptability, background, sense of humor, ambition, money, relationship, marriage; Gelolo McHugh; Family Life Publications, Inc.*

For additional information, see P:52; for a review by William R. Reevy of the original edition, see 6:675.

[623]
[Cox Mechanical and Manual Tests]. Boys ages 10 and over, 11–14, 14 and over; 1928–34; 6 tests; J. W. Cox; Charles J. Cox [England].* (In-print status uncertain; no reply from publisher.)

a) COX MECHANICAL TEST M. Ages 11–14, 14 and over.
b) MECHANICAL DIAGRAMS TEST. Ages 14 and over.
c) MECHANICAL EXPLANATION TEST 1. Ages 14 and over.
d) COX EYEBOARD TEST NO. 2. Ages 10 and over.
e) COX NAILBOARD TEST. Ages 10 and over.
f) COX NAILSTICK TEST. Ages 10 and over.

See T2:2242 (8 references); for reviews by C. A. Oakley and Alec Rodger, see 2:1652 (4 references).

[624]
CPH Patient Attitude Scale. Mental patients; 1972–74; test booklet title is *CPH Factor Scale*; for research use only; attitudes toward mental illness and hospitalization; 5 scores: authoritarian control, negative hospital orientation, external control, mental illness and treatment as physical, letdown of control for therapeutic gain; Marvin W. Kahn and Nelson F. Jones; Marvin W. Kahn.*

For additional information, see 8:511 (6 references).

[625]
Crane Oral Dominance Test: Spanish/English. Ages 4–8; 1976; CODT; both English and Spanish used in administration and in pupil responses; Barbara J. Crane; Crane Publishing Co.*

For additional information and excerpted reviews by Protase E. Woodford and Porfirio Sanchez, see 8:162 (1 reference).

[626]
Crawford Psychological Adjustment Scale. Psychiatric patients; 1968; CPAS; 7 scores based upon 25 behavior ratings: social-economic-environmental competence, derangement of thought processes and peculiar behavior, physical behavior, communications, social ac-

ceptability and moderation of behavior, management of hostility, total; Paul L. Crawford; the Author.*

See T2:1148 (1 reference).

[627]

Crawford Small Parts Dexterity Test. High school and adults; 1946–56; 2 scores: pins and collars, screws; John E. Crawford and Dorothea M. Crawford; The Psychological Corporation.*

See T2: 2223 (12 references); for a review by Neil D. Warren, see 5:871 (8 references); for a review by Raymond A. Katzell, see 4:752; for a review by Joseph E. Moore, see 3:667.

REFERENCES

1–8. See 5:871.
9–20. See T2:2223.
21. ZAIDEL, D., & SPERRY, R. W. Some long-term motor effects of cerebral commissurotomy in man. *Neuropsychologia*, 1977, 5, 193–204.
22. BERGLUND, M., & LEIJONQUIST, H. Prediction of cerebral dysfunction in alcoholics: A study of health insurance records. *Journal of Studies on Alcohol*, 1978, 39, 1968–1974.
23. SCHREINER, J. Prediction of retarded adults' work performance through components of general ability. *American Journal of Mental Deficiency*, 1978, 83, 77–79.
24. PERELL, I. B., EHRMAN, L., & MAROWITZ, J. W. Human handedness: The influence of learning. *Perceptual & Motor Skills*, 1981, 53, 967–977.

[628]

Creativity Attitude Survey. Grades 4–6; 1971; CAS; Charles E. Schaefer; Psychologists and Educators, Inc.*

For additional information and reviews by Philip V. Vernon and Kaoru Yamamoto, see 8:240 (1 reference); see also T2:553 (1 reference).

[629]

★**Creativity Checklist.** Grades kgn–graduate school; 1979; CCh; "objective, self-report, eight-item instrument developed specifically to identify overt creativity observed by at least one other person"; David L. Johnson; Stoelting Co.*

[630]

Creativity Tests for Children. Grades 4–6; 1971–76; CTC; "divergent production abilities"; 10 tests; J. P. Guilford and others listed below; Sheridan Psychological Services, Inc.*
a) ADDING DECORATIONS. Identical with first half of higher level test entitled *Decorations*; Arthur Gershon, Sheldon Gardner, and Philip R. Merrifield.
b) DIFFERENT LETTER GROUPS. Arthur Gershon.
c) HIDDEN LETTERS.
d) KINDS OF PEOPLE. Adaptation of higher level test entitled *Possible Jobs*; Arthur Gershon.
e) MAKING SOMETHING OUT OF IT.
f) MAKING OBJECTS. Adaptation of higher level test with the same title; Sheldon Gardner, Arthur Gershon, and Philip R. Merrifield.
g) NAMES FOR STORIES. Adaptation of higher level test entitled *Plot Titles*.
h) SIMILAR MEANINGS. Adaptation of higher level test entitled *Associational Fluency I*; Philip R. Merrifield.
i) WHAT TO DO WITH IT. Adaptation of higher level test entitled *Alternate Uses*; Philip R. Merrifield (Form A), Robert C. Wilson (Form B), and Paul R. Christensen (Form B).
j) WRITING SENTENCES.

For additional information and reviews by John W. French and Kaoru Yamamoto, see 8:241 (1 reference).

REFERENCES

1. See 8:241.
2. REIS, M., & GOLD, D. Relation of paternal availability to problem solving and sex–role orientation in young boys. *Psychological Reports*, 1977, 40, 823–829.

[631]

*****Cree Questionnaire.** Adults; 1957–81; CQ; creativity and inventiveness; 14 scores: overall creative potential, plus 13 technical dimension scores grouped under four broad headings (social orientation, work orientation, internal functioning, interests and skills); T. G. Thurstone, J. J. Mellinger, and Peter W. B. Goddard (manual); Human Resources Center, University of Chicago.*

See T2:1149 (1 reference) and P:53 (3 references); for reviews by Allyn Miles Munger and Theodor F. Naumann, see 6:84.

[632]

Crichton Vocabulary Scale. Ages 4–11; 1950; John C. Raven; H. K. Lewis & Co. Ltd. [England].* (In-print status uncertain; no reply from publisher.)

See T2:491 (3 references); for a review by Morton Bortner, see 6:518 (1 reference); for reviews by Charlotte Banks and W. D. Wall, see 4:337.

REFERENCES

1. See 6:518.
2–4. See T2:491.
5. GROAT, A. The use of English stress assignment rules by children taught either with traditional orthography or with the initial teaching alphabet. *Journal of Experimental Child Psychology*, 1979, 27, 395–409.
6. GILHOOLY, K. J., & GILHOOLY, M. L. M. The validity of age-of-acquisition ratings. *British Journal of Psychology*, 1980, 71, 105–110.

[633]

Crissey Dexterity Test. Job applicants; 1964; CDT; Orlo L. Crissey; Psychological Services, Inc.*

For additional information and a review by Lyle F. Schoenfeldt, see 7:1043 (1 reference).

[634]

Criterion Reading: Individualized Learning Management System. Grades kgn, 1, 2–3, 4–6, 7–adult basic education; 1970–71; criterion-referenced; 2 series: diagnostic (2 forms), instructional (called process skills); 5 levels together cover 451 overlapping specific-objective subtests; level 1—90 nonreading subtests in 3 areas: motor skills, visual matching, auditory matching; levels 2–5—361 subtests in 5 areas: phenology, structural analysis, verbal information, syntax, comprehension; Marie G. Hackett; Random House, Inc.* (In-print status uncertain; no reply from publisher.)

For additional information and an excerpted review by John Fremer, see 8:723 (2 references).

[635]

Criterion Test of Basic Skills. Grades kgn–8; 1976; criterion-referenced; 2 tests; Kerth Lundell, William Brown, and James Evans; Academic Therapy Publications.*
a) READING. 19 specific-objective subtests in 6 areas: letter recognition, letter sounding, blending and sequencing, special sounds, sight words, letter writing.

b) ARITHMETIC. 26 specific-objective subtests in 11 areas: counting, numbers and numerals, arithmetic, subtraction, multiplication, division, money measurement, telling time, symbols, fractions, decimals and percents.

For additional information, see 8:14.

REFERENCES

1. KRICHEV, A. Criterion Test of Basic Skills. *Psychology in the Schools*, 1978, 15, 145.

[636]

★Croft Readiness Assessment in Comprehension Kit. Children for whom diagnostic information in reading readiness is needed; 1978; CRAC-Kit; designed to be used with the five readiness subtests of the *Cooper-McGuire Diagnostic Word-Analysis Test*; provides the "directions and record-keeping system for measuring performance on oral and written language readiness" in addition to pattern readiness; 3 subtests; Marion L. McGuire and Marguerite J. Bumpus; Croft, Inc.*

a) ORAL LANGUAGE READINESS. Relates oral language with experience at all levels of abstraction; 3 scores: concrete, semi-abstract, abstract.
b) COMPREHENSION READINESS. Recognizes, at sight, "words that have recurred frequently in his language-experience stories and classroom activities"; scores same as for *a* above.
c) PATTERN READINESS. Ages 5 and over only; 4 parts: classification, sequence, causation, comparison; scores same as for *a* above for each part.

[637]

Cross Reference Test. Clerical job applicants; 1959; James W. Curtis; Psychometric Affiliates.*

For additional information and a review by Philip H. Kriedt, see 6:1039.

[638]

Crowley Occupational Interests Blank. Secondary school pupils of average ability or less; 1970–76; COIB; 10 scores: 5 interest areas (active-outdoor, office, social, practical, artistic) and 5 sources of job satisfaction (financial gain, stability, companionship, working conditions, interest); A. D. Crowley; Hobsons Press (Cambridge) Ltd. for Careers Research Advisory Centre [England].*

For additional information and reviews by Paul Kline and Stephen Sharp, see 8:1000.

[639]

★Crown-Crisp Experiential Index. Normal and psychoneurotic adults; 1979; CCEI; formerly published under the title *Middlesex Hospital Questionnaire*; designed to obtain the diagnostic information typically gained in a formal clinical psychiatric examination; 7 scores: free-floating anxiety, depression, hysteria, phobic anxiety, obsessionality, somatic anxiety, total; Sidney Crown and A. H. Crisp; Hodder & Stoughton Educational [England].*

For additional information and reviews by H. J. Eysenck and Lester M. Libo, see 8:615 (26 references); see also T2:1279 (8 references); for a review by D. F. Clark, see 7:103 (5 references).

REFERENCES

1–5. See 7:103.
6–13. See T2:1279.
14–39. See 8:615.

40. BEARD, R. W., BELSEY, E. M., LIEBERMAN, B. A., & WILKINSON, J. C. M. Pelvic pain in women. *American Journal of Obstetrics & Gynecology*, 1977, 128, 566–570.
41. BOOTH, J. B. Hyperlipidaemia and deafness: A preliminary survey. *Journal of the Royal Society of Medicine*, 1977, 70, 642–646.
42. CRISP, A. H., KALUCY, R. S., PILKINGTON, T. R. E., & GAZET, J. Some psychological consequences of ileojejunal bypass surgery. *American Journal of Clinical Nutrition*, 1977, 30, 109–120.
43. CROWN, S., LUCAS, C. J., STRINGER, P., & SUPRAMANIUM, S. Personality correlates of study difficulty and academic performance in university students. II. Conscience and self-esteem. *British Journal of Medical Psychology*, 1977, 50, 275–281.
44. FERNANDO, S. J. M. Hostility, personality, and depression. *British Journal of Medical Psychology*, 1977, 50, 243–249.
45. HAFNER, J. R. The husbands of agoraphobic women and their influence on treatment outcome. *British Journal of Psychiatry*, 1977, 131, 289–294.
46. HAFNER, J. R. The husbands of agoraphobia women: Assortative mating or pathogenic interaction? *British Journal of Psychiatry*, 1977, 130, 233–239.
47. STONEHILL, E., & CRISP, A. H. Psychoneurotic characteristics of patients with anorexia nervosa before and after treatment and at follow-up 4–7 years later. *Journal of Psychosomatic Research*, 1977, 21, 187–193.
48. STRINGER, P., CROWN, S., LUCAS, C. J., & SUPRAMANIUM, S. Personality correlates of study difficulty and academic performance in university students. I. The Middlesex Hospital Questionnaire and Dynamic Personality Inventory. *British Journal of Medical Psychology*, 1977, 50, 267–274.
49. CRISP, A. H., JONES, M. G., & SLATER, P. The Middlesex Hospital Questionnaire: A validity study. *British Journal of Medical Psychology*, 1978, 51, 269–280.
50. CRISP, A. H., RALPH, P. C., McGUINNESS, B., & HARRIS, G. Psychoneurotic profiles in the adult population. *British Journal of Medical Psychology*, 1978, 51, 293–301.
51. DASBERG, H., & SHALIF, I. On the validity of the Middlesex Hospital Questionnaire: A comparison of diagnostic self-ratings in psychiatric out-patients, general practice patients, and "normals" based on the Hebrew version. *British Journal of Medical Psychology*, 1978, 51, 281–291.
52. THOMAS, D., & ABBAS, K. A. Comparison of transcendental meditation and progressive relaxation in reducing anxiety. *British Medical Journal*, 1978, 2, 1749.
53. MILTON, F., & HAFNER, J. The outcome of behavior therapy for agoraphobia in relation to marital adjustment. *Archives of General Psychiatry*, 1979, 36, 807–811.
54. BAGLEY, C. The factorial reliability of the Middlesex Hospital Questionnaire in normal subjects. *British Journal of Medical Psychology*, 1980, 53, 53–58.
55. KLINE, P. The Crown–Crisp Experiential Index. *British Journal of Psychiatry*, 1980, 136, 199.
56. FENTON, G. W., FENWICK, P. B. C., DOLLIMORE, J., DUNN, T. L., & HIRSCH, S. R. EEG spectral analysis in schizophrenia. *British Journal of Psychiatry*, 1980, 136, 445–455.
57. FREEMAN, C. P. L., WEEKS, D., & KENDELL, R. E. ECT: II: Patients who complain. *British Journal of Psychiatry*, 1980, 137, 17–25.
58. HARRIS, B. Prospective trial of L-trytophan in maternity blues. *British Journal of Psychiatry*, 1980, 137, 233–235.
59. HSU, L. K. G., & CRISP, A. H. The Crown–Crisp Experiential Index (CCEI) profile in anorexia nervosa. *British Journal of Psychiatry*, 1980, 136, 567–573.
60. WEEKS, D., FREEMAN, C. P. L., & KENDELL, R. E. ECT: III: Enduring cognitive deficits? *British Journal of Psychiatry*, 1980, 137, 26–37.
61. MAVISSAKALIAN, M., & MICHELSON, L. The Middlesex Hospital Questionnaire: A validity study with American psychiatric patients. *British Journal of Psychiatry*, 1981, 139, 336–340.

[640]

★CSMS Number Operations. Ages 11–12; 1978; designed to assess conceptual understanding of the four basic number operations when applied to whole numbers; 3 scores labeled codes: part 1 code (indicates understanding of addition, subtraction, multiplication, division), part 2 code (indicates performance on story problems), combined code (total); Margaret Brown; NFER-Nelson Publishing Co. [England].*

[641]

★CSMS Science Reasoning Tasks. Ages 10–16 and older children and adults; 1977–79; criterion-referenced; assessment of ability to use concrete and formal reasoning

[642]
★CTBS Readiness Test

strategies; 7 tests: Spatial Relationships, Volume and Heaviness, The Pendulum, Equilibrium in the Balance, Inclined Plane, Chemical Combinations, Flexible Rods; M. Shayer, H. Wylam, P. Adey, and D. Küchmann; NFER-Nelson Publishing Co. [England].*

[642]
★CTBS Readiness Test. Grades kgn–0 to 1–3; 1973–77; originally developed as readiness measure (CTBS/S, Level A) of the CTBS Series; 11 scores: alphabet skills (letter forms, letter names, total), listening for information, letter sounds, visual and auditory discrimination (visual discrimination, sound matching, total), language, total, mathematics; CTB/McGraw-Hill.*

[643]
Culture Fair Intelligence Test. Ages 4–8 and mentally retarded adults, 8–14 and average adults, grades 9–16 and superior adults; 1933–73; CFIT; formerly called *Culture Free Intelligence Test*; 2 editions; Raymond B. Cattell and A. K. S. Cattell (Scales 2 and 3).

a) IPAT CULTURE FAIR INTELLIGENCE TEST. 1933–73; formerly called *IPAT Culture Free Intelligence Test*; test booklet title is *Test of g: Culture Fair*, formerly *Test of g: Culture Free*; (Spanish edition of Scales 2 and 3 available); Institute for Personality and Ability Testing, Inc.*

1) *Scale 1.* Ages 4–8 and mentally retarded adults; 1933–69.
2) *Scale 2.* Ages 8–14 and average adults; 1949–73.
3) *Scale 3.* Grades 9–16 and superior adults; 1950–73.

b) CATTELL CULTURE FAIR INTELLIGENCE TEST. 1960–61; parts 1 or 2 may be administered alone although use of both parts is recommended; 2 levels; Bobbs-Merrill Co., Inc.*

1) *Scale 2.* Ages 8–14 and average adults.
2) *Scale 3.* Grades 9–16 and superior adults.

For additional information, see 8:184 (38 references); see also T2:364 (61 references); for reviews by John E. Milholland and Abraham J. Tannenbaum, see 6:453 (15 references); for a review by I. MacFarlane Smith of *a*, see 5:343 (11 references); for reviews by Raleigh M. Drake and Gladys C. Schwesinger, see 4:300 (2 references).

REFERENCES

1–2. See 4:300.
3–13. See 5:343.
14–28. See 6:453.
29–88. See T2:364.
89–126. See 8:184.
127. AMANTE, D., VAN HOUTEN, V. W., GRIEVE, J. H., BADER, C. A., & MARGULES, P. H. Neuropsychological deficit, ethnicity, and socioeconomic status. *Journal of Consulting & Clinical Psychology*, 1977, 45, 524–535.
128. GÖKHAN, N., BINYILDIZ, P., GÜRSES, C., & ARMAN, A. Physical ability and mental development of 9–12 age group children living in Istanbul. *Journal of Sports Medicine & Physical Fitness*, 1977, 17, 207–212.
129. HUNDAL, P. S., & HORN, J. L. On the relationships between short-term learning and fluid and crystallized intelligence. *Applied Psychological Measurement*, 1977, 1, 11–21.
130. KELLAGHAN, T. Relationships between home environment and scholastic behavior in a disadvantaged population. *Journal of Educational Psychology*, 1977, 69, 754–760.
131. LOKAN, J. The differential prediction of grades in a special vocational high school. *Measurement & Evaluation in Guidance*, 1977, 10, 7–16.
132. NICHOLS, M. P., & KNOPF, I. J. Refining computerized test interpretations: An in-depth approach. *Journal of Personality Assessment*, 1977, 41, 157–159.
133. OTTO, L. B., & ALWIN, D. F. Athletics, aspirations, and attainments. *Sociology of Education*, 1977, 50, 102–113.

134. RICHARDS, M. A. One integrated curriculum: An empirical evaluation. *Nursing Research*, 1977, 26, 90–95.
135. DEFRIES, J. C., SINGER, S. M., FOCH, T. T., & LEWITTER, F. I. Familial nature of reading disability. *British Journal of Psychiatry*, 1978, 132, 361–367.
136. Deo Saran, R. A. Social class and academic guidance: A social-psychological analysis. *Canadian Journal of Behavioural Science*, 1978, 10, 239–247.
137. ENO, L. Predicting achievement and the theory of fluid and crystallized intelligence. *Psychological Reports*, 1978, 43, 847–852.
138. ENO, L., WOEHLKE, P., & DEICHMANN, J. A factor analytic study of ability, achievement, and personality characteristics of college students. *College Student Journal*, 1978, 12, 366–371.
139. FREEDMAN, B. J., ROSENTHAL, L., DONAHOE, C. P., JR., SCHLUNDT, D. G., & MCFALL, R. M. A social-behavioral analysis of skill deficits in delinquent and nondelinquent adolescent boys. *Journal of Consulting & Clinical Psychology*, 1978, 46, 1448–1462.
140. HICKS, R. A., & BEVERIDGE, R. Handedness and intelligence. *Cortex*, 1978, 14, 304–307.
141. HULFISH, S. Relationship of role identification, self-esteem, and intelligence to sex differences in field independence. *Perceptual & Motor Skills*, 1978, 47, 835–842.
142. JAMES, M. A., & KNIEF, L. Interaction of general, fluid, and crystallized ability and instruction in sixth-grade mathematics. *Journal of Educational Psychology*, 1978, 70, 319–323.
143. O'NEILL, G. P. Post-secondary aspirations of high school seniors in different school contexts: A Canadian study. *Alberta Journal of Educational Research*, 1978, 24, 137–155.
144. PRAWAT, R. S., & KERASOTES, D. Basic memory processes in reading. *Merrill–Palmer Quarterly*, 1978, 24, 181–188.
145. RUBIN, K. H., BROWN, I. D. R., & PRIDDLE, R. L. The relationships between measures of fluid, crystallized, and "Piagetian" intelligence in elementary-school-aged children. *Journal of Genetic Psychology*, 1978, 132, 29–36.
146. TORGESEN, J. K., BOWEN, C., & IVEY, C. Task structure versus modality of presentation: A study of the construct validity of the Visual-Aural Digit Span Test. *Journal of Educational Psychology*, 1978, 70, 451–456.
147. UNDHEIM, J. O. Broad ability factors in 12- to 13-year-old children, the theory of fluid and crystallized intelligence, and the differentiation hypothesis. *Journal of Educational Psychology*, 1978, 70, 433–443.
148. WILLOWS, D. M. A picture is not always worth a thousand words: Pictures as distractors in reading. *Journal of Educational Psychology*, 1978, 70, 255–262.
149. WILLOWS, D. M. Individual differences in distraction by pictures in a reading situation. *Journal of Educational Psychology*, 1978, 70, 837–847.
150. DYER, J. W., RILEY, J., & YEKOVICH, F. R. An analysis of three study skills: Notetaking, summarizing, and rereading. *Journal of Educational Research*, 1979, 73, 3–7.
151. HEILBRUN, A. B., JR. Psychopathy and violent crime. *Journal of Consulting & Clinical Psychology*, 1979, 47, 509–516.
152. IRELAND, J. F., & KAHN, M. W. How fair is the culture I.Q. test? *International Journal of Social Psychiatry*, 1979, 25, 1–3.
153. LAVRAKAS, P. J., & MAIER, R. A. Differences in human ability to judge veracity from the audio medium. *Journal of Research in Personality*, 1979, 13, 139–153.
154. RASBURY, W. C., FENNELL, R. S., III, EASTMAN, B. G., GARIN, E. H., & RICHARDS, G. Cognitive performance of children with renal disease. *Psychological Reports*, 1979, 45, 231–239.
155. SINGH, S., & SEHGAL, M. Rorschach hostility content and its relation to anxiety, neuroticism and P-E-N measures. *Journal of Clinical Psychology*, 1979, 35, 436–441.
156. STAYTON, S. E., & DIENER, R. G. Personality characteristics of juvenile delinquent heroin users. *International Journal of the Addictions*, 1979, 14, 585–587.
157. TORGESEN, J. K., & MURPHEY, H. A. Verbal vs. nonverbal and complex vs. simple responses in the paired-associate learning of poor readers. *Journal of General Psychology*, 1979, 101, 219–226.
158. BALTES, P. B., CORNELIUS, S. W., SPIRO, A., NESSELROADE, J. R., & WILLIS, S. L. Integration versus differentiation of fluid-crystallized intelligence in old age. *Developmental Psychology*, 1980, 16, 625–635.
159. BURNS, R. B. Relation of aptitudes to learning at different points in time during instruction. *Journal of Educational Psychology*, 1980, 72, 785–795.
160. BUTKOWSKY, I. S., & WILLOWS, D. M. Cognitive-motivational characteristics of children varying in reading ability: Evidence for learned helplessness in poor readers. *Journal of Educational Psychology*, 1980, 72, 408–422.
161. CHAMBERS, J. A., BARRON, F., & SPRECHER, J. W. Identifying gifted Mexican-American students. *Gifted Child Quarterly*, 1980, 24, 123–128.

162. Decker, S. N., & DeFries, J. C. Cognitive abilities in families with reading disabled children. *Journal of Learning Disabilities*, 1980, 13, 53–58.
163. Elsayed, M., Ismail, A. H., & Young, R. J. Intellectual differences of adult men related to age and physical fitness before and after an exercise program. *Journal of Gerontology*, 1980, 35, 383–387.
164. Hays, J. R., & Smith, A. L. Comparison of WISC–R and culture fair intelligence test scores for three ethnic groups of juvenile delinquents. *Psychological Reports*, 1980, 46, 931–934.
165. Hill, D. S. A comparison of the performance of normal, learning disabled, and educable mentally retarded children on Cattell's ability constructs. *Journal of Learning Disabilities*, 1980, 13, 38–41.
166. James, J. F., Gregory, D., Jones, R. K., & Rundell, O. H. Psychiatric morbidity in prisons. *Hospital & Community Psychiatry*, 1980, 31, 674–677.
167. Singh, S., & Aurora, R. Motives, work values, and child–rearing practices of females with full–time employment and full–time housekeeping. *Indian Journal of Social Work*, 1980, 41, 157–162.
168. Sternberg, R. J. Representation and process in linear syllogistic reasoning. *Journal of Experimental Psychology: General*, 1980, 109, 119–159.
169. Weiss, S. C. Culture Fair Intelligence Test and Draw–A–Person scores from a rural Peruvian sample. *Journal of Social Psychology*, 1980, 111, 147–148.
170. Zoref, L., & Williams, P. A look at content bias in IQ tests. *Journal of Educational Measurement*, 1980, 17, 313–322.
171. Aron, A., Orme–Johnson, D., & Brubaker, P. The transcendental meditation program in the college curriculum: A 4–year longitudinal study of effects on cognitive and affective functioning. *College Student Journal*, 1981, 15, 140–146.
172. Hofland, B. F., Willis, S. L., & Baltes, P. B. Fluid intelligence performance in the elderly: Intraindividual variability and conditions of assessment. *Journal of Educational Psychology*, 1981, 73, 573–586.
173. Nenty, H. J., & Dinero, T. E. A cross–cultural analysis of the fairness of the Cattell Culture Fair Intelligence Test using the Rasch model. *Applied Psychological Measurement*, 1981, 5, 355–368.
174. Puhan, B. N. Effects of marker variables on WAIS communalities. *Educational & Psychological Measurement*, 1981, 41, 55–59.
175. Thomas, E. C., & Holcomb, H. Nurturing productive thinking in able students. *Journal of General Psychology*, 1981, 104, 67–79.
176. White, A. P., & Zammarelli, J. E. Convergence principals: Information in the answer sets of some multiple–choice intelligence tests. *Applied Psychological Measurement*, 1981, 5, 21–27.
177. Willows, D. M., & Ryan, E. B. Differential utilization of syntactic and semantic information by skilled and less skilled readers in the intermediate grades. *Journal of Educational Psychology*, 1981, 73, 607–615.

[644]

★**Culture-Free Self-Esteem Inventories for Children and Adults.** Grades 3–9 and adults; 1981; 3 forms; (French and Spanish editions available); James Battle; Special Child Publications.*

a) FORM A. Grades 3–9; 60 items yielding 6 scores: general, social/peer related, academics/school related, parents/home related, lie, total.
b) FORM B. Grades 3–9; 30 items, derived from Form A.
c) FORM AD. Adults; 40 items yielding 5 scores: general, social, personal, lie, total.

REFERENCES
1. Battle, J. J. Relationship between self–esteem and depression. *Psychological Reports*, 1978, 42, 745–746.

[645]

Current and Past Psychopathology Scales. Psychiatric patients and nonpatients; 1966–68; CAPPS; the *Psychiatric Evaluation Form-Diagnostic Version* and the *Psychiatric History Schedule* have been stapled together and given a new title; rating scale and optional interview guide for use in diagnosing or describing mental illness if any; judgments based upon various sources of information (subject, informant, case records, nurse's reports, etc.); the PEF-D section, which deals with the patient's current functioning over the past month, yields 8 summary scale scores: reality testing-social disturbance, depression-anxiety, impulse control, somatic concern-functioning, disorganization, obsessive-guilt-phobic, elation-grandiosity, summary; the PHS section, which deals with the patient's past functioning from age 12 up to the past month, yields 18 summary scale scores: depression-anxiety, impulse control, social-sexual relations, reality testing, dependency, somatic concern-functioning, obsessive-compulsive, anger-excitability, manic, sexual disturbance, memory-orientation, disorganized, organicity, neurotic childhood, phobia, retardation-stubborn, hysterical symptoms, intellectual performance; no manual; Robert L. Spitzer and Jean Endicott; Research Assessment and Training Unit, New York State Psychiatric Institute.*

For additional information and reviews by William J. Eichman and Raymond D. Fowler, Jr., see 7:62 (3 references); see also P:53A (1 reference).

REFERENCES
1. See P:53A.
2–4. See 7:62.
5. Mirin, S. M., Meyer, R. E., & McNarnee, B. H. Psychopathology and mood during heroin use. *Archives of General Psychiatry*, 1976, 33, 1503–1508.
6. Johnson, J. H., Klingler, D. E., & Williams, T. A. An external criterion study of the MMPI validity indices. *Journal of Clinical Psychology*, 1977, 33, 154–156.
7. Johnson, J. H., Klingler, D. E., & Williams, T. A. Recognition in episodic long–term memory in schizophrenia. *Journal of Clinical Psychology*, 1977, 33, 643–647.
8. Klingler, D. E., Johnson, J. H., Giannetti, R. A., & Williams, T. A. Comparison of the clinical utility of the MMPI basic scales and specific MMPI state-trait scales: A test of Dahlstrom's hypothesis. *Journal of Consulting & Clinical Psychology*, 1977, 45, 1086–1092.
9. Klingler, D. E., Johnson, J. H., & Williams, T. A. A validation study of the WIST as a group administered instrument for assessment for schizophrenic thinking. *Journal of Clinical Psychology*, 1977, 33, 658–661.
10. Mendlewicz, J., & Rainer, J. D. Adoption study supporting genetic transmission in manic–depressive illness. *Nature*, 1977, 268, 327–329.
11. Wender, P. H., Rosenthal, D., Rainer, J. D., Greenhill, L., & Sarlin, B. Schizophrenics adopting parents. *Archives of General Psychiatry*, 1977, 34, 777–783.
12. Zax, M., Sameroff, A. J., & Babigian, H. M. Birth outcomes in the offspring of mentally disordered women. *American Journal of Orthopsychiatry*, 1977, 47, 218–230.
13. Carlin, A. S., Detzer, E., & Strauss, F. F. Psychopathology and nonmedical drug use: A comparison of patient and nonpatient drug users. *International Journal of the Addictions*, 1978, 13, 337–348.
14. Collins, P. J., Kietzman, M. L., Sutton, S., & Shapiro, E. Visual temporal integration in psychiatric patients. *Journal of Psychiatric Research*, 1978, 14, 203–213.
15. Giannetti, R. A., Johnson, J. H., Klingler, D. E., & Williams, T. A. Comparison of linear and configural MMPI diagnostic methods with an uncontaminated criterion. *Journal of Consulting & Clinical Psychology*, 1978, 46, 1046–1052.
16. Gift, T. E., Strauss, J. S., & Ritzler, B. A. The failure to detect low IQ in psychiatric assessment. *American Journal of Psychiatry*, 1978, 135, 345–349.
17. Lewis, D. C., Mayer, J., Hersch, R. G., & Black, R. Narcotic antagonist treatment: Clinical experience with naltrexone. *International Journal of the Addictions*, 1978, 13, 961–973.
18. Mendlewicz, J., Verbanck, P., Linkowski, P., & Wilmotte, J. Lithium accumulation in erythrocytes of manic–depressive patients: An *in vivo* twin study. *British Journal of Psychiatry*, 1978, 133, 436–444.
19. Johnson, J. H., Klingler, D. E., Giannetti, R. A., & Williams, T. A. The reliability of diagnosis by technician, computer, and algorithm. *Journal of Clinical Psychology*, 1980, 36, 447–451.
20. Johnson, J. H., Klingler, D. E., & Giannetti, R. A. A study of mental status and anamnestic factors related to the decision for inpatient or outpatient treatment. *Journal of Clinical Psychology*, 1979, 35, 844–850.
21. Dorus, W., & Senay, E. C. Depression, demographic dimensions, and drug abuse. *American Journal of Psychiatry*, 1980, 137, 699–704.
22. Green, A. H., Liang, V., Gaines, R., & Sultan, S. Psychopathological assessment of child–abusing, neglecting, and normal mothers. *Journal of Nervous & Mental Disease*, 1980, 168, 356–360.
23. Johnson, J. H., & Harris, W. G. Personality and behavioral characteristics related to divorce in a population of male applicants for psychiatric evaluation. *Journal of Abnormal Psychology*, 1980, 89, 510–513.
24. Johnson, J. H., Klingler, D. E., & Giannetti, R. A. Band width in diagnostic classification using the MMPI as a predictor. *Journal of Consulting & Clinical Psychology*, 1980, 48, 340–349.

25. MENDLEWICZ, J., LINKOWSKI, P., & REES, J. A. A double-blind comparison of dothiepin and amitriptyline in patients with primary affective disorder: Serum levels and clinical response. *British Journal of Psychiatry*, 1980, 136, 154–160.
26. HARVEY, P., WINTERS, K., WEINTRAUB, S., & NEALE, J. M. Distractibility in children vulnerable to psychopathology. *Journal of Abnormal Psychology*, 1981, 90, 298–304.
27. MENDLEWICZ, J., & BARON, M. Morbidity risks in subtypes of unipolar depressive illness: Differences between early and late onset forms. *British Journal of Psychiatry*, 1981, 139, 463–466.

[646]
Current News Test. Grades 9–12; 1951–82; 2 new tests issued annually; spring term review (covering mid December-mid April) issued each May, fall term review (covering September-mid December) issued each January; available only as part of the Newsweek Educational Program; no manual; Newsweek Educational Division.*
For additional information, see 6:985.

[647]
Curtis Completion Form. Grades 11–16 and adults; 1950–68; CCF; emotional maturity and adjustment; James W. Curtis; Western Psychological Services.*
See T2:1454 (1 reference) and P:421 (3 references); for reviews by Irwin G. Sarason and Laurance F. Shaffer, see 6:208 (2 references); for a review by Alfred B. Heilbrun, Jr., see 5:128.

[648]
Curtis Interest Scale. Grades 9–16 and adults; 1959; 10 scores (business, mechanics, applied arts, direct sales, production, science, entertainment, interpersonal, computation, farming) and 1 rating (desire for responsibility); James W. Curtis; Psychometric Affiliates.*
See T2:2177 (1 reference); for reviews by Warren T. Norman and Leona E. Tyler, see 6:1052.

[649]
[Curtis Object Completion and Space Form Tests]. Applicants for mechanical and technical jobs; 1960–61; 2 tests; James W. Curtis; Psychometric Affiliates.*
a) OBJECT-COMPLETION TEST.
b) SPACE FORM TEST.
For additional information and reviews by Richard S. Melton and I. Macfarlane Smith, see 6:1085.

[650]
Curtis Verbal-Clerical Skills Tests. Applicants for clerical positions; 1963–65; 4 tests: computation, checking, comprehension, logical reasoning ability; James W. Curtis; Psychometric Affiliates.*
For additional information, see 7:990.

[651]
Cutrona Child Study Profile of Psycho-Educational Abilities. Grades kgn–3 and special education classes; 1970–75; ratings in 10 areas: general behavior, gross-motor development, fine-motor development, body image and awareness, tactile-kinesthetic development, visual-motor perception, auditory perception, time orientation, non-verbal conceptualization, numerical conceptualization; Michael P. Cutrona; Cutronics Educational Institute.*
For additional information and a review by J. Lee Wiederholt, see 8:426.

[652]
Cutrona Reading Inventory. Grades kgn–6, 7–12 and adult; 1975; word pronunciation; criterion-referenced; 3 grade scores: independent reading, instructional reading, frustration reading; 94–100% indicates "independent reading grade level," 75–93% indicates "instructional reading grade level," 74% and lower represents "frustration reading grade level"; no manual; M. P. Cutrona; Cutronics Educational Institute.*
a) A BASIC SCREENING. Grades kgn–6.
b) ADVANCED LEVEL. Grades 7–12 and adult.
For additional information, see 8:784.

[653]
The D-K Scale of Lateral Dominance. Grades 2–6; 1969; DKSLD; 6 dominance scores: hand, foot, visual, auditory, intermodal, intramodal; Russell A. Dusewicz and Keith M. Kershner; Foundation for Research in Mental Development.* (In-print status uncertain; no reply from publisher.)
For additional information and a review by Donald A. Leton, see 7:865 (2 references).

REFERENCES

1–2. See 7:865.
3. KERSHNER, J. R. Rotation of mental images and asymmetries in word recognition. *Canadian Journal of Psychology*, 1979, 33, 39–50.

[654]
The Dailey Vocational Tests. Grades 8–12 and adults; 1964–65; DVT; 3 tests; John T. Dailey and Kenneth B. Hoyt (manual); Riverside Publishing Co.*
a) TECHNICAL AND SCHOLASTIC TEST.
b) SPATIAL VISUALIZATION TEST.
c) BUSINESS ENGLISH TEST.
See T2:2105 (1 reference); for reviews by Thomas S. Baldwin and Benjamin Shimberg, and excerpted reviews by Betty W. Ellis and Jack C. Merwin, see 7:976 (5 references).

[655]
[Daily Behavior System]. Children and adults with problem behaviors; 1971–74; form for recording by observer of daily frequency over a 1-week period of 4 "target behaviors" determined locally; 2 formats; Jerome S. Stumphauzer; Behaviormetrics Publishing Co.*
a) DAILY BEHAVIOR GRAPH. 1971–72.
b) DAILY BEHAVIOR CARD. 1974.
For additional information, see 8:534.

[656]
★**The D.A.L.E. System: Developmental Assessment of Life Experiences.** Profound to severely mentally retarded, less impaired mental abilities; 1975–79; DALE; "an inventory to assess competencies in community living"; criterion-referenced; 2 levels; Gertrude A. Barber, John P. Mannino, and Robert J. Will; Barber Center Press, Inc.*
a) LEVEL 1. Profound to severely mentally retarded; 1979; ratings in 5 areas: sensory motor, language, self-help, cognition, socialization.
b) LEVEL 2. Moderate to mild mentally retarded; 1979; ratings in 5 areas: personal hygiene, personal management, communications, residence/home management, community access.

[657]
★**Damron Reading/Language Kit.** Psycholinguistic ages 2–10; 1978; "provides specific remedial instruction for any student, particularly the learning-disabled student, through an individual educational program"; behavioral objectives in 12 categories: reception (auditory, visual), association (auditory, visual), expression (verbal, manual), closure (grammatic, visual, auditory), sequential memory (auditory, visual), sound blending; O. Rex Damron; CTB/McGraw-Hill.*

[658]
DAT Career Planning Program. Grades 8–12; 1972–75; CPP; a counseling program based on the *Differential Aptitude Tests* (DAT) and the *DAT Career Planning Questionnaire* (CPQ); yields a computer printout for student, the *DAT Career Planning Report*, consisting of a profile of DAT scores and a page of narrative statements discussing compatibility of student's occupational preferences, school interests, educational aspirations, and tested abilities; 2 parts; counselor's manual by Donald E. Super; The Psychological Corporation.*
a) DIFFERENTIAL APTITUDE TESTS.
b) DAT CAREER PLANNING QUESTIONNAIRE.

For additional information and reviews by Richard W. Johnson and Stanley R. Strong, see 8:1001. For excerpted reviews of this and the DAT, see 8:485 (2 excerpts).

[659]
*****A Dating Problems Checklist.** High school and college; 1961–79; DPCL; 7 areas: dating conditions, home-parents-family, personality and emotional self, sex attitudes, social poise, physical self, dating and definite commitments; Gelolo McHugh; Family Life Publications, Inc.*

For additional information, see P:55; for reviews by Clifford R. Adams and Robert A. Harper of the original edition, see 6:676.

[660]
A Dating Scale. Adolescents and adults; 1962; liberalism of attitudes toward dating; Panos D. Bardis; the Author.*

For additional information and a review by Charles F. Warnath, see 8:335 (3 references).

[661]
★**Decoding Inventory.** Grades 1 and over; 1979; DI; "screening measure designed to assess student performance in auditory and visual discrimination, phonics, structural analysis and use of context clues"; initial screening measure used to decide appropriate level to be administered to the individual student; Lyndon W. Searfoss and H. Donald Jacobs; Kendall/Hunt Publishing Co.*
a) LEVEL R-READINESS. Students whose performance was less than 50% on specified parts of Level 1; 2 parts: auditorily discriminating words, visually discriminating words.
b) LEVEL 1-BASIC. Reading level grades 1–3; 8 parts: naming letters, hearing initial consonants, hearing final consonants, hearing initial consonant clusters, pronouncing vowel and consonant clusters, hearing syllables, dividing shorter words into syllables, using context clues.

c) LEVEL 2-ADVANCED. Reading level grades 4 and over; 7 parts: hearing syllables, pronouncing vowels and consonant clusters, hearing initial consonant clusters, hearing final consonants, hearing initial single consonants, dividing longer words into syllables, using context clues.

[662]
Decorations. Grades 9–16 and adults; 1963; "divergent production of figural implications" or "ability to add meaningful details"; Arthur Gershon, Sheldon Gardner, Philip R. Merrifield, and J. P. Guilford; Sheridan Psychological Services, Inc.*

See T2:555 (5 references) and 6:548 (1 reference).

[663]
★**Deductive Reasoning Test.** Candidates for graduate scientists and higher level professional occupations; 1972–73; DRT; J. M. Verster; National Institute for Personnel Research [South Africa].*

[664]
A Deep Test of Articulation. Reading levels grade 2 and under, grade 3 and over; 1964; DTA; Eugene T. McDonald; Stanwix House, Inc.*

See T2:2069 (2 references); for reviews by Edgar R. Garrett and Harold A. Peterson, see 7:951 (6 references).

REFERENCES

1–6. See 7:951.
7–8. See T2:2069.
9. HOFFMAN, P. R., SCHUCKERS, G. H., & RATUSNIK, D. L. Contextual–coarticulatory inconsistency of /r/ misarticulation. *Journal of Speech & Hearing Research*, 1977, 20, 631–643.
10. MANNING, W. H., WITTSTRUCK, M. L., LOYD, R. R., & CAMPBELL, T. F. Automatization of correct production at two levels of articulatory acquisition. *Journal of Speech & Hearing Disorders*, 1977, 42, 358–363.
11. ELBERT, M., & McREYNOLDS, L. V. An experimental analysis of misarticulating children's generalization. *Journal of Speech & Hearing Research*, 1978, 21, 136–150.
12. MANNING, W. H., LOUKO, L. J., & DiSALVO, V. S. A right–ear effect for auditory feedback control of children's newly acquired phonemes. *Journal of Speech & Hearing Research*, 1978, 21, 580–588.
13. MANNING, W. H., & SCHEER, B. R. Using competing speech to estimate articulatory automatization in children: The possible effect of masking level and subject grade. *Journal of Communication Disorders*, 1978, 11, 391–397.
14. DIGGS, C. C. Linguistic significance of omissions. *ASHA*, 1979, 21, 754.
15. MARQUARDT, T. P., REINHART, J. B., & PETERSON, H. A. Markedness analysis of phonemic substitution errors in apraxia of speech. *Journal of Communication Disorders*, 1979, 12, 481–494.

[665]
Defense Mechanism Inventory. Ages 16 and over; 1968–69; DMI; for research use only; 5 scores: turning against object, projection, principalization, turning against self, reversal; David Ihilevich and Goldine C. Gleser; Goldine C. Gleser.*

For additional information, see 8:535 (30 references); see also T2:1152 (5 references); for a review by James A. Walsh, see 7:63 (4 references).

REFERENCES

1–4. See 7:63.
5–9. See T2:1152.
10–39. See 8:535.
40. BLACHA, M. D., & FANCHER, R. E. A content validity study of the Defense Mechanism Inventory. *Journal of Personality Assessment*, 1977, 41, 402–404.
41. O'LEARY, M. R., ROHSENOW, D. J., SCHAU, E. J., & DONOVAN, D. M. Defensive style and treatment outcome among men alcoholics. *Journal of Studies on Alcohol*, 1977, 38, 1036–1040.

42. CRAMER, P., & CARTER, T. The relationship between sexual identification and the use of defense mechanisms. *Journal of Personality Assessment,* 1978, 42, 63–73.
43. DUDLEY, G. E. Effects of sex, social desirability, and birth order on the Defense Mechanisms Inventory. *Journal of Consulting & Clinical Psychology,* 1978, 46, 1419–1422.
44. RADER, G. E., BEKKER, L. D., BROWN, L., & RICHARDT, C. Psychological correlates of unwanted pregnancy. *Journal of Abnormal Psychology,* 1978, 87, 373–376.
45. RICHERT, A. J., & KETTERING, R. Psychological defense as a moderator variable. *Psychological Reports,* 1978, 42, 291–294.
46. ROHSENOW, D. J., ERICKSON, R. C., & O'LEARY, M. R. The Defense Mechanism Inventory and alcoholics. *International Journal of the Addictions,* 1978, 13, 403–414.
47. EVANS, R. G. The relationship of the Marlowe–Crowne scale and its components to defensive preferences. *Journal of Personality Assessment,* 1979, 43, 406–410.
48. GORDON, N. G., & BRACKNEY, B. E. Defense mechanism preference and dimensions of psychopathology. *Psychological Reports,* 1979, 44, 188–190.
49. KIPPER, D. A., & GINOT, E. Accuracy of evaluating videotape feedback and defense mechanisms. *Journal of Consulting & Clinical Psychology,* 1979, 47, 493–499.
50. SEIF, M. N., & ATKINS, A. L. Some defensive and cognitive aspects of phobias. *Journal of Abnormal Psychology,* 1979, 88, 42–51.
51. JUNI, S., & MASLING, J. Reaction to aggression and the Defense Mechanism Inventory. *Journal of Personality Assessment,* 1980, 44, 484–486.
52. SEGALL, S. R. A test of two theories of dream forgetting. *Journal of Clinical Psychology,* 1980, 36, 739–742.
53. MILLER, I. W., III, & NORMAN, W. H. Effects of attributions for success on the alleviation of learned helplessness and depression. *Journal of Abnormal Psychology,* 1981, 90, 113–124.

[666]

★The Defining Issues Test. Grades 9–12 and college and adults; 1979; DIT; experimental forms for research use only; James R. Rest; Minnesota Moral Research Projects.*

REFERENCES

1. BLOOM, R. B. Discipline: Another face of moral reasoning. *College Student Journal,* 1978, 12, 356–359.
2. GRIFFORE, R. J., & LEWIS, J. Characteristics of teachers' moral judgment. *Educational Research Quarterly,* 1978, 3, 20–30.
3. TJOSVOLD, D., & JOHNSON, D. W. Controversy within a cooperative or competitive context and cognitive perspective–taking. *Contemporary Educational Psychology,* 1978, 3, 376–386.
4. WILLIAMS, D. M. A study of moral education in Surrey, B.C. secondary schools. *Alberta Journal of Educational Research,* 1979, 25, 89–102.
5. OLEJNIK, A. B. Adults' moral reasoning with children. *Child Development,* 1980, 51, 1285–1288.
6. PRESSLEY, M., SCHMIERER, D., & HOPE, D. J. Adults' judgment about adolescents' moral judgments. *Child Development,* 1980, 51, 1289–1291.
7. TAN–WILLIAM, C. Fostering creativity and its effect on moral reasoning of prospective teachers. *Journal of Creative Behavior,* 1980, 14, 258–263.
8. TAN–WILLMAN, C., & GUTTERIDGE, D. Creative thinking and moral reasoning of academically gifted secondary school adolescents. *Gifted Child Quarterly,* 1981, 25, 149–153.

[667]

★Degrees of Reading Power. Students grades 3–5, 5–7, 7–9, 9–12, 12–14; 1979–81; DRP; measure of reading comprehension; 5 levels labeled forms plus screening test; The College Board.*

[668]

Del Rio Language Screening Test. Ages 3 to 6–11; DRLST; identification of children (English- or Spanish-speaking) "with deviant language performance who need further evaluation"; 5 scores: receptive vocabulary, sentence repetition-length, sentence repetition-complexity, oral commands, story comprehension; 2 editions: Spanish, English; Allen S. Toronto, D. Leverman, Cornelia Hanna, Peggy Rosenzweig, and Antoneta Maldonado; National Educational Laboratory Publishers, Inc.* (In-print status uncertain; no reply from publisher.)

For additional information and an excerpted review by Leonard Baca, see 8:427 (1 reference).

[669]

Delaware County Silent Reading Test, Second Edition. Grades 1^2, 2^1, 2^2, 3^1, 3^2, 4, 5, 6, 7, 8; 1965; 5 scores: interpretation, organization, vocabulary, structural analysis, total; no manual; Judson E. Newburg and Nicholas A. Spennato; Delaware County Intermediate Unit.*

For additional information and a review by Allen Berger, see 7:686.

[670]

The Demos D Scale: An Attitude Scale for the Identification of Dropouts. Grades 7–12; 1965–70; DDS; also called *Demos Dropout Scale*; 5 attitude scores: teachers, education, peers and parents, school behavior, total; George D. Demos; Western Psychological Services.*

See T2:1153 (1 reference); for reviews by John R. Braun and Leonard V. Gordon, see 7:64.

[671]

The Dennis Test of Child Development. Grades kgn–1; 1966–74; DCD; 7 scores: gross motor, fine motor, visual perception, attention (auditory), language, mental age level, developmental quotient; William H. Dennis; the Author.*

For additional information, see 8:212.

[672]

Dennis Test of Scholastic Aptitude. Grades 4–8, 5–8; DTSA; 1961–63; William H. Dennis; the Author.*

For additional information, see 7:348.

[673]

*Dental Admission Testing Program. Dental school applicants; 1946–77; DATP; formerly called *Dental Aptitude Testing Program*; tests administered 2 times annually (April, October) at centers established by the publisher; 6 scores: quantitative reasoning (mathematics, problems in math usage), reading comprehension, natural sciences, perceptual ability, PAT; Council on Dental Education, American Dental Association.

For additional information and reviews by Robert L. Linn and Christine H. McGuire of an earlier edition, see 8:1085 (7 references); see also T2:2337 (8 references), 7:1091 (28 references), 5:916 (6 references), and 4:788 (2 references).

REFERENCES

1–2. See 4:788.
3–8. See 5:916.
9–36. See 7:1091.
37–44. See T2:2337.
45–51. See 8:1085.
52. KRESS, G. C., JR., & DOGON, I. L. A correlational study of preadmission predictor variables and dental school performance. *Journal of Dental Education,* 1981, 45, 207–210.
53. WILSON, S., SUDDICK, R. P., SHAY, J. S., & HUSTMYER, F. E., JR. Correlations of scores on embedded figures and mirror tracing with preclinical technique grades and PMAT scores of dental students. *Perceptual & Motor Skills,* 1981, 53, 31–35.

[674]
Dental Hygiene Aptitude Testing Program. Dental hygiene school applicants; 1947–72; DHATP; tests administered 3 times annually (February, May, November) at centers established by the American Dental Hygienists' Association; 4 scores: numerical ability, study-reading, science, general information; prepared for the American Dental Hygienists' Association by The Psychological Corporation.*

For additional information, see 7:1092.

[675]
The Denver Articulation Screening Exam. Economically disadvantaged ages 2.5 to 6.0; 1971–73; DASE; picture cards for use with "hard-to-test" children; Amelia F. Drumwright; LADOCA Publishing Foundation.*

For additional information and a review by Harold A. Peterson, see 8:958 (4 references).

REFERENCES

1–4. See 8:958.
5. CONWAY, D., LYTTON, H., & PYSH, F. Twin–singleton language differences. *Canadian Journal of Behavioural Science*, 1980, 12, 262–271.

[676]
★**Denver Audiometric Screening Test.** Ages 3–6; 1973; DAST; criterion-referenced; to identify children who have a serious hearing loss; 3 ratings for each ear: pass, fail, uncertain; William K. Frankenburg, Marion Downs, and Elyner Kazuk; LADOCA Publishing Foundation.*

[677]
★**Denver Community Mental Health Questionnaire-Revised.** Mental health clients; 1978; DCMHQ-R; 13 scales covering 4 areas: personal distress, alcohol and drug abuse, social and community functioning, client satisfaction; James A. Ciarlo; the Author.*

REFERENCES

1. QUALLS, P. E., JUSTICE, B., & ALLEN, R. H. Isolation and psychosocial functioning. *Psychological Reports*, 1980, 46, 279–285.
2. CIARLO, J. A., EDWARDS, D. W., KIRESUK, T. J., NEWMAN, F. L., & BROWN, T. R. The assessment of client/patient outcome techniques for use in mental health programs. Final Report, National Institute of Mental Health Contract No. 278–80–0005 (DB), Rockville, Maryland, October 1981.

[678]
Denver Developmental Screening Test. Ages 2 weeks to 6 years; 1968–70; DDST; 4 scores: gross motor, fine motor-adaptive, language, personal-social; William K. Frankenburg, Josiah B. Dodds, and Alma W. Fandal (manual); LADOCA Publishing Foundation.*

See T2:492 (6 references); for reviews by Alice E. Moriarity and Emmy E. Werner, see 7:405 (6 references).

REFERENCES

1–6. See 7:405.
7–12. See T2:492.
13. BELL, E. F., & WARBURTON, D. Two reciprocal translocations associated with microcephaly and retardation. *Journal of Medical Genetics*, 1977, 14, 141–142.
14. KOPP, C. B., KHOKA, E. W., & SIGMAN, M. A comparison of sensorimotor development among infants in India and the United States. *Journal of Cross–Cultural Psychology*, 1977, 8, 435–451.
15. MORRIS, J. J., & CLARIZIO, S. Improvement in IQ of high-risk, disadvantaged preschool children enrolled in a developmental program. *Psychological Reports*, 1977, 41, 1111–1114.
16. RITTER, D. R. Preschool attainment record as a measure of developmental skills. *Journal of Consulting & Clinical Psychology*, 1977, 45, 1184.
17. SEITZ, S., & GESKE, D. Mothers and graduate trainees' judgments of children: Some effects of labeling. *American Journal of Mental Deficiency*, 1977, 81, 362–370.
18. STERLING, H. M., & STERLING, P. J. Experiences with the QNST. *Academic Therapy*, 1977, 12, 339–342.
19. APPELBAUM, A. S. Validity of the revised Denver Developmental Screening Test for referred and nonreferred samples. *Psychological Reports*, 1978, 43, 227–233.
20. DAVIDSON, P. W., WILLOUGHBY, R. H., O'TUAMA, L. A., SWISHER, C. N., & BENJAMINS, D. Neurological and intellectual sequelae of Reye's Syndrome. *American Journal of Mental Deficiency*, 1978, 82, 535–541.
21. FIELD, T., HALLOCK, N., TING, G., DEMPSEY, J., DABIRI, C., & SHUMAN, H. H. A first–year follow–up of high–risk infants formulating a cumulative risk index. *Child Development*, 1978, 49, 119–131.
22. GARRITY, L. I., & SERVOS, A. B. Comparison of measures of adaptive behaviors in preschool children. *Journal of Consulting & Clinical Psychology*, 1978, 46, 288–293.
23. PAINTER, M. J., DEPP, R., & O'DONOGHUE, P. D. Fetal heart rate patterns and development in the first year of life. *American Journal of Obstetrics & Gynecology*, 1978, 132, 271–277.
24. SCHEIDT, P. C., STANLEY, F., & BRYLA, D. A. One year follow-up of infants exposed to ultrasound in utero. *American Journal of Obstetrics & Gynecology*, 1978, 131, 743–748.
25. SINGH, N., DONOVAN, C. M., & HANSHAW, J. B. Neonatal lead intoxication in a prenatally exposed infant. *Journal of Pediatrics*, 1978, 93, 1019–1021.
26. GARDNER, L. I., NEU, R. L., SHAH, R. S., PINTO, W., JR., CO, M., LEHR, E. R., & BARG, G. A. Family with three apparently balanced t(3;15)(p27;q22) translocation carriers. *American Journal of Diseases of Children*, 1979, 133, 1002–1005.
27. GARDNER, R. A. Throwing balls in a basket as a test of motor coordination: Normative data on 1350 school children. *Journal of Clinical Child Psychology*, 1979, 8, 152–155.
28. KROHN, E. J., & TRAXLER, A. J. Relationship of the McCarthy Scales of Children's Abilities to other measures of preschool cognitive, motor, and perceptual development. *Perceptual & Motor Skills*, 1979, 49, 783–790.
29. LEUNG, A. K. C., MCARTHUR, R. G., ROSS, S. A., MCMILLAN, D. D., & SAUVE, R. S. Thyroxine–binding globulin deficiency in Beckwith Syndrome. *Journal of Pediatrics*, 1979, 95, 752–754.
30. VENHAM, L. L., MURRAY, P., & GAULIN-KREMER, E. Personality factors affecting the preschool child's response to dental stress. *Journal of Dental Research*, 1979, 58, 2046–2051.
31. FIELD, T. M., WIDMAYER, S. M., STRINGER, S., & IGNATOFF, E. Teenage, lower–class, black mothers and their preterm infants: An intervention and developmental follow–up. *Child Development*, 1980, 51, 426–436.
32. KATOFF, L., & REUTER, J. Review of developmental screening tests for infants. *Journal of Clinical Child Psychology*, 1980, 9, 30–34.
33. TESKA, J. A., & STONEBURNER, R. L. The concept and practice of second–level screening. *Psychology in the Schools*, 1980, 17, 192–195.
34. FLEMING, J. An evaluation of the use of the Denver Developmental Screening Test. *Nursing Research*, 1981, 30, 290–293.
35. LICHTENSTEIN, R. Comparative validity of two preschool screening tests: Correlational and classification approaches. *Journal of Learning Disabilities*, 1981, 14, 68–72.
36. MAJERES, R. L., & TIMMER, T. Imitation preference as a function of motor competence. *Perceptual & Motor Skills*, 1981, 52, 175–180.
37. ROTHBERG, A. D., MAISELS, J., BAGNATO, S., MURPHY, J., GIFFORD, K., MCKINLEY, K., PALMER, E. A., & VANNUCCI, R. C. Outcome for survivors of mechanical ventilation weighing less than 1,250 gm at birth. *Journal of Pediatrics*, 1981, 98, 106–111.

[679]
★**Denver Eye Screening Test.** Ages 6 months and over; 1973; DEST; criterion-referenced; detects problems in visual acuity and non-straight eyes; 3 ratings for each eye: normal, abnormal, untestable; 2 parts; William K. Frankenburg, Arnold D. Goldstein, and John Barker; LADOCA Publishing Foundation.*

a) PART 1: VISION TEST. Ages 6 months–2.5 years, 2.5–3, 3 years and over.
b) PART 2: TESTS FOR NON-STRAIGHT EYES. Ages 6 months and over.

[680]

★Denver Prescreening Developmental Questionnaire. Ages 3 months–6 years; 1975–76; PDQ; ratings by parents; criterion-referenced; "designed to detect developmental lags"; William K. Frankenburg; LADOCA Publishing Foundation.*

[681]

Depression Adjective Check Lists. Grades 9–16 and adults; 1967; DACL; Bernard Lubin; EdITS/Educational and Industrial Testing Service.*

For additional information, see 8:536 (20 references); see also T2:1154 (2 references); for reviews by Leonard D. Goodstein and Douglas M. McNair, see 7:65 (3 references); see also P:57 (4 references).

REFERENCES

1–4. See P:57.
5–7. See 7:65.
8–9. See T2:1154.
10–29. See 8:536.
30. BARNES, M. R. Effects of antidepressive program on verbal behavior. *Journal of Clinical Psychology*, 1977, 33, 545–549.
31. GIAMBRA, L. M. Independent dimensions of depression: A factor analysis of three self-report depression measures. *Journal of Clinical Psychology*, 1977, 33, 928–935.
32. HORNSTRA, R. K., & KLASSEN, D. The course of depression. *Comprehensive Psychiatry*, 1977, 18, 119–125.
33. ABRAMS, D., & KING, G. D. An empirical investigation of the modeling of depression. *Psychological Reports*, 1978, 42, 823–832.
34. CHRISTENFELD, R., LUBIN, B., & SATIN, M. Concurrent validity of the Depression Adjective Check List in a normal population. *American Journal of Psychiatry*, 1978, 135, 582–584.
35. GIAMBRA, L. M., & TRAYNOR, T. D. Depression and daydreaming: An analysis based on self-ratings. *Journal of Clinical Psychology*, 1978, 34, 14–25.
36. HAMMEN, C. L., & PETERS, S. D. Interpersonal consequences of depression: Responses to men and women enacting a depressed role. *Journal of Abnormal Psychology*, 1978, 87, 322–332.
37. KUIPER, N. A. Depression and causal attributions for success and failure. *Journal of Personality & Social Psychology*, 1978, 36, 236–246.
38. LEWINSOHN, P. M., & AMENSON, C. S. Some relations between pleasant and unpleasant mood-related events and depression. *Journal of Abnormal Psychology*, 1978, 87, 644–654.
39. LIVINGSTON, J. E., MACLEOD, P. M., & APPLEGARTH, D. A. Vitamin B$_6$ status in women with postpartum depression. *American Journal of Clinical Nutrition*, 1978, 31, 886–891.
40. LUBIN, B., MARONE, J. G., & NATHAN, R. G. Comparison of self-administered and examiner-administered Depression Adjective Check Lists. *Journal of Consulting & Clinical Psychology*, 1978, 46, 384–385.
41. LUBIN, B., ROTH, A. V., DEAN, L. M., & HORNSTRA, R. K. Correlates of depressive mood among normals. *Journal of Clinical Psychology*, 1978, 34, 650–653.
42. MORGAN, W. P., & HORSTMAN, D. H. Psychometric correlates of pain perception. *Perceptual & Motor Skills*, 1978, 47, 27–39.
43. BAUCOM, D. H., & DANKER-BROWN, P. Influence of sex roles on the development of learned helplessness. *Journal of Consulting & Clinical Psychology*, 1979, 47, 928–936.
44. CUTLER, N. R., & COHEN, H. B. The effect of one night's sleep loss on mood and memory in normal subjects. *Comprehensive Psychiatry*, 1979, 20, 61–66.
45. JOHNSON, J. E., PETZEL, T. P., & ROHDE, M. J. Depressives' cognitive appraisal of their mood states. *Journal of Clinical Psychology*, 1979, 35, 766–768.
46. LEWINSOHN, P. M., & TALKINGTON, J. Studies on the measurement of unpleasant events and relations with depression. *Applied Psychological Measurement*, 1979, 3, 83–101.
47. LUBIN, B., & LEVITT, E. E. Norms for the Depression Adjective Check Lists: Age group and sex. *Journal of Clinical Psychology*, 1979, 47, 192.
48. MCLEAN, P. D., & HAKSTIAN, A. R. Clinical depression: Comparative efficacy of outpatient treatments. *Journal of Consulting & Clinical Psychology*, 1979, 47, 818–836.
49. O'HARA, M. W., & REHM, L. P. Self-monitoring, activity levels, and mood in the development and maintenance of depression. *Journal of Abnormal Psychology*, 1979, 88, 450–453.
50. TURNER, R. W., WARD, M. F., & TURNER, D. J. Behavioral treatment for depression: An evaluation of therapeutic components. *Journal of Clinical Psychology*, 1979, 35, 166–175.
51. ZEMORE, R., & EAMES, N. Psychic and somatic symptoms of depression among young adults, institutionalized aged and noninstitutionalized aged. *Journal of Gerontology*, 1979, 34, 716–722.
52. ZEMORE, R., & ELGAARD, F. Irrational beliefs and reactions to failure. *Canadian Journal of Behavioural Science*, 1979, 11, 245–251.
53. BLUMBERG, N. L. Effects of neonatal risk, maternal attitude, and cognitive style on early postpartum adjustment. *Journal of Abnormal Psychology*, 1980, 89, 139–150.
54. BREWER, D., DOUGHTIE, E. B., & LUBIN, B. Induction of mood and mood shift. *Journal of Clinical Psychology*, 1980, 36, 215–226.
55. CARSON, T. P., & ADAMS, H. E. Activity valence as a function of mood change. *Journal of Abnormal Psychology*, 1980, 89, 368–377.
56. HARMON, T. M., NELSON, R. O., & HAYES, S. C. Self-monitoring of mood versus activity by depressed clients. *Journal of Consulting & Clinical Psychology*, 1980, 48, 30–38.
57. LUBIN, B., CAPLAN, M. E., & COLLINS, J. F. Additional evidence for comparability of set two (lists E, F, and G) of the Depression Adjective Check Lists. *Psychological Reports*, 1980, 46, 849–850.
58. POST, R. D., & LOBITZ, W. C. The utility of Mezzich's MMPI regression formula as a diagnostic criterion in depression research. *Journal of Consulting & Clinical Psychology*, 1980, 48, 673–674.
59. POST, R. D., LOBITZ, W. C., & GASPARIKOVA-KRASNEC, M. The utilization of positive and negative feedback in the self-evaluation responses of depressed and nondepressed psychiatric patients. *Journal of Nervous & Mental Disease*, 1980, 168, 481–486.
60. RAPS, C. S., REINHARD, K. E., & SELIGMAN, M. E. P. Reversal of cognitive and affective deficits associated with depression and learned helplessness. *Journal of Abnormal Psychology*, 1980, 89, 342–349.
61. ROTH, A., KLASSEN, D., & LUBIN, B. Effects of follow-up procedures on survey results. *Psychological Reports*, 1980, 47, 275–278.
62. SANCHEZ, V., & LEWINSOHN, P. M. Assertive behavior and depression. *Journal of Consulting & Clinical Psychology*, 1980, 48, 119–120.
63. ZEMORE, R., & JOHANSEN, L. J. Depression, helplessness, and failure attributions. *Canadian Journal of Behavioural Science*, 1980, 12, 167–174.
64. BAUCOM, D. H., & AIKEN, P. A. Effect of depressed mood on eating among obese and nonobese dieting and nondieting persons. *Journal of Personality & Social Psychology*, 1981, 41, 577–585.
65. CONSTANTINO, R. E. Bereavement crisis intervention for widows in grief and mourning. *Nursing Research*, 1981, 30, 351–353.
66. CRESSWELL, D. L., & LANYON, R. I. Validation of a screening battery for psychogeriatric assessment. *Journal of Gerontology*, 1981, 36, 435–440.
67. GOLUB, S., & HARRINGTON, D. M. Premenstrual and menstrual mood changes in adolescent women. *Journal of Personality & Social Psychology*, 1981, 41, 961–965.
68. HODGSON, J. W. Cognitive versus behavioral–interpersonal approaches to the group treatment of depressed college students. *Journal of Counseling Psychology*, 1981, 28, 243–249.
69. JOESTING, J. Running and depression. *Perceptual & Motor Skills*, 1981, 52, 422.
70. LEIGHT, K. A., & ELLIS, H. C. Emotional mood states, strategies, and state–dependency in memory. *Journal of Verbal Learning & Verbal Behavior*, 1981, 20, 251–266.
71. MILLER, I. W., III, & NORMAN, W. H. Effects of attributions for success on the alleviation of learned helplessness and depression. *Journal of Abnormal Psychology*, 1981, 90, 113–124.
72. PETZEL, T. P., JOHNSON, J. E., JOHNSON, H. H., & KOWALSKI, J. Behavior of depressed subjects in problem solving groups. *Journal of Research in Personality*, 1981, 15, 389–398.
73. POLIVY, J. On the induction of emotion in the laboratory: Discrete moods or multiple affect states? *Journal of Personality & Social Psychology*, 1981, 41, 803–817.
74. ROTH, A. V., & LUBIN, B. Factors underlying the Depression Adjective Check Lists. *Educational & Psychological Measurement*, 1981, 41, 383–387.
75. WECKOWICZ, T. E., TAM, C. I., BAY, K. S., COLLIER, G., & BEELEN, L. Perception of reinforcement and psychomotor retardation in depressed patients. *Canadian Journal of Behavioural Science*, 1981, 13, 129–143.

[682]

★Depressive Experience Questionnaire. Adolescents and adults (patients and normals); 1979; DEQ; 3 scores: dependency, self criticism, efficacy; Sidney J. Blatt, Joseph P. D'Afflitti, and Donald M. Quinlan; Sidney J. Blatt.*

REFERENCES

1. BLATT, S. J., WEIN, S. J., CHEVRON, E., & QUINLAN, D. M. Parental representations and depression in normal young adults. *Journal of Abnormal Psychology*, 1979, 88, 388–397.

[683]
★**Derogatis Sexual Functioning Inventory.** Adults; 1975–79; DSFI; 12 scores: information, experience, drive, attitudes, psychological symptoms, affects, gender role definition, fantasy, body image, sexual satisfaction, total, patient's evaluation of current functioning; Leonard R. Derogatis; the Author.*

REFERENCES

1. DEROGATIS, L. R., MEYER, J. K., & VAZQUEZ, N. A psychological profile of the transsexual: I. The male. *Journal of Nervous & Mental Disease*, 1978, 166, 234–254.
2. DEROGATIS, L. R., & MELISARATOS, N. The DSFI: A multidimensional measure of sexual functioning. *Journal of Sex & Marital Therapy*, 1979, 5, 244–280.
3. DEROGATIS, L. R., & MEYER, J. K. The invested partner in sexual disorders: A profile. *American Journal of Psychiatry*, 1979, 136, 1545–1549.
4. DEROGATIS, L. R., & MEYER, J. K. A psychological profile of the sexual dysfunctions. *Archives of Sexual Behavior*, 1979, 8, 201–223.
5. DEROGATIS, L. R. Psychological assessment of psychosexual functioning. *Psychiatric Clinics of North America*, 1980, 3, 113–131.
6. DEROGATIS, L. R., MEYER, J. K., & BOLAND, P. A psychological profile of the transsexual: II. The female. *Journal of Nervous & Mental Disease*, 1981, 169, 157–168.

[684]
★**Description of Body Scale.** Adolescents and adults; 1980; DOBS; may be rated by an observer; 5 scores: masculinity-femininity of body, consistency of present body description, ideal body description, self-ideal body description difference score, incongruence between present and ideal body description; Carney, Weedman and Associates.*

[685]
★**Descriptive Tests of Language Skills.** Beginning students in two- and four-year institutions; 1977; DTLS; tests may be used independently or in combination with other tests in the series; 5 tests; published by The College Board and Educational Testing Service.
a) DTLS READING COMPREHENSION TEST.
b) DTLS VOCABULARY TEST.
c) DTLS USAGE TEST.
d) DTLS LOGICAL RELATIONSHIPS TEST.
e) DTLS SENTENCE STRUCTURE TEST.

REFERENCES

1. SNOWMAN, J., LEITNER, D. W., SNYDER, V., & LOCKHART, L. A comparison of the predictive validities of selected academic tests of the American College Test (ACT) Assessment Program and the Descriptive Tests of Language Skills for college freshmen in a basic skills program. *Educational & Psychological Measurement*, 1980, 40, 1159–1166.

[686]
★**Descriptive Tests of Mathematics Skills.** Beginning students in two- and four-year institutions; 1978; DTMS; tests may be used independently or in combination with other tests in the series; 4 tests; published by The College Board and Educational Testing Service.
a) DTMS ARITHMETIC SKILLS TEST.
b) DTMS ELEMENTARY ALGEBRA TEST.
c) DTMS INTERMEDIATE ALGEBRA TEST.
d) DTMS FUNCTIONS AND GRAPHS TEST.

[687]
★**Design for Math.** Grades kgn–1, 1–2, 2–3, 3–4, 4–5, 5–6, 6 and over; 1975–79; "criterion-referenced"; a mathematics instruction system including placement tests, pre- and post-diagnostic progress tests, and instructional aides; each diagnostic test level contains 14–30 subtests covering specific objectives; 7 levels; Donald A. Kamp, John W. Armenia, Dale H. McDonald, and Lee N. VonKuster; NCS Interpretive Scoring Systems.*
a) LEVEL A. Grades kgn–1; 14 subtest scores.
b) LEVEL B. Grades 1–2; 25 subtest scores.
c) LEVEL C. Grades 2–3; 26 subtest scores.
d) LEVEL D. Grades 3–4; 27 subtest scores.
e) LEVEL E. Grades 4–5; 25 subtest scores.
f) LEVEL F. Grades 5–6; 29 subtest scores.
g) LEVEL G. Grades 6 and over; 30 subtest scores.

[688]
Detroit Clerical Aptitudes Examination. Grades 9–12; 1937–44; 12 scores: motor (circles, classification, total), visual imagery (likenesses and differences, disarranged pictures, total), trade information, educational (handwriting, arithmetic, alphabetizing, total), total; includes *Ayres Measuring Scale for Handwriting*; Harry J. Baker and Paul H. Voelker; Bobbs-Merrill Co., Inc.*

See T2:782 (3 references); for a review by E. F. Wonderlic, see 3:626 (1 reference); for reviews by Irving Lorge and M. W. Richardson of an earlier edition, see 2:1655.

[689]
Detroit General Aptitudes Examination. Grades 6–12; 1938–54; assembled from *Detroit Mechanical Aptitudes Examination, Detroit Clerical Aptitudes Examination, Detroit General Intelligence Examination,* and *Detroit Advanced Intelligence Test*; 20 scores: intelligence, mechanical, clerical, total, and 16 subtest scores; Harry J. Baker, Alex C. Crockett, and Paul H. Voelker; Bobbs-Merrill Co., Inc.*

See T2:1068 (3 references) and 5:603; for reviews by G. Frederic Kuder, Irving Lorge, and John Gray Peatman, see 2:1654.

[690]
Detroit Mechanical Aptitudes Examination, Revised. Grades 7–16; 1928–39; 12 scores: motor (circles, classification, total), visual imagery (disarranged pictures, sizes, pulleys, total), mechanical information (tool recognition, tool information, total), arithmetic, total; Harry J. Baker, Paul H. Voelker, and Alex C. Crockett; Bobbs-Merrill Co., Inc.*

See T2:2244 (11 references); for reviews by Lloyd G. Humphreys and Dewey B. Stuit, see 3:668 (4 references); for a review by Irving Lorge and an excerpted review by J. Wayne Wrightstone, see 2:1656.

[691]
*****Detroit Tests of Learning Aptitude.** Ages 3 and over; 1935–77; DTLA; 20 scores: pictorial absurdities, verbal absurdities, pictorial opposites, verbal opposites, motor speed and precision, auditory attention span (for unrelated words, for related syllables), oral commissions, social adjustment A, visual attention span (for objects, for letters), orientation, free association, memory for designs, number ability, social adjustment B, disarranged (broken) pictures, oral directions, likenesses and differences, total; Anthony D. Chiappone (Utilizing the Detroit Tests of Learning Aptitude in Assessing the Learning Process), Harry J. Baker and Bernice Leland; Bobbs-Merrill Co., Inc.*

For additional information and a review by Arthur B. Silverstein, see 8:213 (14 references); see also T2:493 (3 references) and 7:406 (10 references); for a review by F. L. Wells, see 3:275 (1 reference); for reviews by Anne Anastasi and Henry Feinburg and an excerpted review by D. A. Worcester (with S. M. Corey) of an earlier edition, see 1:1058.

REFERENCES

1. See 3:275.
2–11. See 7:406.
12–14. See T2:493.
15–28. See 8:213.
29. BLOWERS, E. A. Prediction of Metropolitan Readiness Test scores. *Alberta Journal of Educational Research*, 1977, 23, 164–168.
30. MCSPADDEN, J. V., & STRAIN, P. S. Memory thresholds and overload effects between learning disabled and achieving pupils. *Exceptional Children*, 1977, 44, 35–36.
31. WIIG, E. H., LAPOINTE, C., & SEMEL, E. M. Relationships among language processing and production abilities of learning disabled adolescents. *Journal of Learning Disabilities*, 1977, 10, 292–299.
32. BANAS, N., & WILLS, I. H. Prescriptive teaching from the DTLA. *Academic Therapy*, 1978, 14, 107–112.
33. COLLETTE–HARRIS, M., & MINKE, K. A. A behavioral experimental analysis of dyslexia. *Behaviour Research & Therapy*, 1978, 16, 291–295.
34. STREFF, M., BAREFOOT, S., WALTER, G., & CRANDALL, K. A comparative study of hearing-impaired and normal-hearing young adults—Verbal and nonverbal abilities. *Journal of Communication Disorders*, 1978, 11, 489–498.
35. STRICHART, S. S. Evaluation model for the outcomes of individual remediation programs. *Academic Therapy*, 1978, 14, 193–202.
36. WIEBE, M. J., & HARRISON, K. A. Relationships of the McCarthy Scales of Children's Abilities and the Detroit Tests of Learning Aptitude. *Perceptual & Motor Skills*, 1978, 46, 355–359.
37. BANAS, N., & WILLS, I. H. The vulnerable child: Prescriptive teaching from the DTLA, part 4. *Academic Therapy*, 1979, 14, 617–620.
38. BANAS, N., & WILLS, I. H. The vulnerable child: Prescriptive teaching from the DTLA. *Academic Therapy*, 1979, 15, 237–240.
39. BOHNING, G. A profile graph for interpreting the Detroit Tests of Learning Aptitude. *Psychology in the Schools*, 1979, 16, 338–341.
40. BRUININKS, V. L., & MAYER, J. H. Longitudinal study of cognitive abilities and academic achievement. *Perceptual & Motor Skills*, 1979, 48, 1011–1021.
41. COLLEHI, L. F. Relationship between pregnancy and birth complications and the later development of learning disabilities. *Journal of Learning Disabilities*, 1979, 12, 659–663.
42. DEWEAVER, M. J. Listening comprehension by nonblind handicapped students at three rates of speed. *Exceptional Children*, 1979, 46, 202–208.
43. KIRCHMEIMER, J. Auditory and visual factors related to spelling success. *Psychology in the Schools*, 1979, 16, 491–494.
44. TOBEY, E. A., CULLEN, J. K., JR., RAMPP, D. L., & FLEISCHER-GALLAGHER, A. M. Effects of stimulus-onset asynchrony on the dichotic performance of children with auditory-processing disorders. *Journal of Speech & Hearing Research*, 1979, 22, 197–211.
45. LARRABEE, P. E., JR., & JONES, F. R. Behavioral effects of low plus lenses. *Perceptual & Motor Skills*, 1980, 51, 913–914.
46. CHERMAK, G. D., & O'CONNELL, V. I. Comparison of performance of eight–year-old children on three auditory sequential memory tests. *Perceptual & Motor Skills*, 1981, 52, 879–882.
47. LYON, R., REITTA, S., WATSON, B., PORCH, B., & RHODES, J. Selected linguistic and perceptual abilities of empirically derived subgroups of learning disabled readers. *Journal of School Psychology*, 1981, 19, 152–166.
48. SEMEL, E. M., & WIIG, E. H. Semel Auditory Processing Program: Training effects among children with language–learning disabilities. *Journal of Learning Disabilities*, 1981, 14, 192–196.

[692]
★Developing Cognitive Abilities Test. Grades 2, 3, 4, 5–6, 7–8, 9–12; 1980–81; DCAT; 6 levels; Donald L. Beggs, John T. Mouw, John F. Cawley, John W. Wick, Jeffrey K. Smith, Miriam Cherkes, Anne M. Fitzmaurice, and Louise J. Cawley; American Testronics.*

a) LEVEL 2. Grade 2; 4 scores: verbal ability, quantitative ability, spatial ability, total.

b) LEVEL 3. Grade 3; 4 scores (verbal, quantitative, spatial, total) in 5 categories (knowledge, comprehension, application, analysis, synthesis).
c) LEVEL 4. Grade 4; scores same as for Level 3.
d) LEVELS 5–6. Grades 5–6; scores same as for Level 3.
e) LEVELS 7–8. Grades 7–8; scores same as for Level 3.
f) LEVELS 9–12. Grades 9–12; scores same as for Level 3.

[693]
Developmental Activities Screening Inventory. Ages 6–60 months; 1976–77; DASI; Rebecca F. DuBose and Mary Beth Langley; Teaching Resources Corporation.*

For additional information, see 8:214.

[694]
★Developmental Assessment for the Severely Handicapped. Individuals functioning within the 0–6 year developmental range; 1980; DASH; criterion-referenced; 5 developmental areas: language, sensory-motor, social-emotional, activities of daily living, preacademic; Mary Kay Dykes; Exceptional Resources, Inc.*

[695]
Developmental Checklist. Visually impaired multihandicapped children ages 1–8; 1974 (no date on test materials); form for recording behavior incidents in 18 areas: self help (eating, undressing, dressing, bathroom), receptive language (listening-attending, discrimination, comprehension), expressive language (prelinguistic, linguistic), social skills (interaction with adults, interaction with peers, adjustment to school), gross motor, fine motor, pre-orientation and mobility (body awareness, concepts, environmental awareness, travel skills); no manual; Ruth Zimmerman and Susan Bornstein; Boston Center for Blind Children.*

For additional information, see 8:321.

REFERENCES

1. FELDMAN, G. The only child as a separate entity: Differences between only females and other firstborn females. *Psychological Reports*, 1978, 42, 107–110.

[696]
Developmental Indicators for the Assessment of Learning. Ages 2.5–5.5; 1975, c1972–75; DIAL; a screening test to identify children with potential learning problems who require follow-up diagnosis; 4 scores: gross motor, fine motor, concepts, communications; Carol D. Mardell and Dorothea S. Goldenberg; Dial Inc.*

For additional information and reviews by J. Jeffrey Grill and James J. McCarthy, see 8:428 (3 references).

REFERENCES

1–3. See 8:428.
4. LICHTENSTEIN, R. Comparative validity of two preschool screening tests: Correlational and classification approaches. *Journal of Learning Disabilities*, 1981, 14, 68–72.
5. OBRZUT, J. E., BOLOCOFSKY, D. N., HEATH, C. P., & JONES, J. J. An investigation of the DIAL as a pre–kindergarten screening instrument. *Educational & Psychological Measurement*, 1981, 41, 1231–1241.

[697]
Developmental Potential of Preschool Children. Handicapped children ages 2–6; 1958–62; DPPC; title on record form is *Educational Evaluation of Preschool Children*; subtitle on report form is *Inventory of Developmental Levels*; level and pattern of intellectual, sensory, and emotional functioning and "readiness to profit from

an educational program"; Else Haeussermann; Grune & Stratton, Inc.*

For additional information, see P:59.

[698]
Developmental Profile II. Birth to age 9; 1972–80; identical with original 1972 edition except for deletion of items for ages 10–12; ratings in 5 areas: physical, self-help, social, academic, communication; Gerald D. Alpern, Thomas J. Boll, and Marsha S. Shearer; Psychological Development Publications.

For additional information and a review by Jane V. Hunt of the original edition, see 8:215 (1 reference).

REFERENCES

1. See 8:215.
2. HENDRICKSON, N. J., & HANSEN, S. L. Toddlers: Competence and behavioral patterns. *Child Study Journal*, 1977, 7, 79–97.
3. HOLYROYD, J., & GOLDENBERG, I. The use of goal attainment scaling to evaluate a ward treatment program for disturbed children. *Journal of Clinical Psychology*, 1978, 34, 732–739.
4. WACHS, T. D., & DeREMER, P. Adaptive behavior and Uzgiris-Hunt Scale performance of young developmentally disabled children. *American Journal of Mental Deficiency*, 1978, 83, 171–176.
5. GREENBERG, M. T., & MARVIN, R. S. Attachment patterns in profoundly deaf preschool children. *Merrill–Palmer Quarterly*, 1979, 25, 265–279.
6. LIVINGOOD, A. B., & BORENGASSER, M. A. Cerebral gigantism in infancy: Implications for psychological and social development. *Child Psychiatry & Human Development*, 1981, 12, 46–53.

[699]
Developmental Task Analysis. Grades kgn–6; 1969; ratings by parent or other observer in 5 areas: social and personal, motor, perceptual, language, thinking; no manual; Robert E. Valett; Fearon Education.*

For additional information, see 8:429.

[700]
★Developmental Tasks for Kindergarten Readiness. Children prior to kindergarten entrance; 1978; DTKR; 12 subtest scores: social interaction, name printing, body concepts, auditory sequencing, auditory association, visual discrimination, visual memory, visual motor, color naming, relational concepts, number knowledge, alphabet knowledge; Walter J. Lesiak, Jr.; Clinical Psychology Publishing Co., Inc.*

[701]
Developmental Test of Visual-Motor Integration. Ages 2–8, 2–15; 1967; VMI; Keith E. Beery and Norman A. Buktenica (test); Follett Publishing Co.*

For additional information and reviews by Donald A. Leton and James A. Rice, see 8:870 (24 references); see also T2:1875 (6 references); for a review by Brad S. Chissom, see 7:867 (5 references).

REFERENCES

1–5. See 7:867.
6–11. See T2:1875.
12–35. See 8:870.
36. BROWN, M. J. Comparison of the Developmental Test of Visual-Motor Integration and the Bender-Gestalt test. *Perceptual & Motor Skills*, 1977, 45, 981–982.
37. BUKTENICA, N. A. Perceptual/social aspects of learning to read: A transactional process. *Peabody Journal of Education*, 1977, 54, 154–161.
38. MARTIN, R., SEWELL, T., & MANNI, J. Effects of race and social class on preschool performance on the Developmental Test of Visual-Motor Integration. *Psychology in the Schools*, 1977, 14, 466–470.
39. MATHIS, H. J., & HARSHMAN, H. W. Therapeutic program for the learning disabled child. *Physical Therapy*, 1977, 57, 823–825.
40. PRYZWANSKY, W. B. The use of the Developmental Test of Visual-Motor Integration as a group screening instrument. *Psychology in the Schools*, 1977, 14, 419–422.
41. RASKIN, L. M., & PITCHER-BAKER, G. Kinetic family drawings by children with perceptual-motor delays. *Journal of Learning Disabilities*, 1977, 10, 370–374.
42. YSSELDYKE, J. E. Aptitude–treatment interaction research with first grade children. *Contemporary Educational Psychology*, 1977, 2, 1–9.
43. CULATTA, B. The relationship between perceptual dysfunction and language disorders: A case report. *Journal of Communication Disorders*, 1978, 11, 51–63.
44. CUNNINGHAM, M. M. Perceptual ability and associational learning in normal and learning disabled children. *Perceptual & Motor Skills*, 1978, 47, 1200.
45. DAVIDSON, P. W., WILLOUGHBY, R. H., O'TUAMA, L. A., SWISHER, C. N., & BENJAMINS, D. Neurological and intellectual sequelae of Reye's Syndrome. *American Journal of Mental Deficiencies*, 1978, 82, 535–541.
46. FLYNN, T. M., & FLYNN, L. A. Evaluation of the predictive ability of five screening measures administered during kindergarten. *Journal of Experimental Education*, 1978, 46, 65–70.
47. KLEIN, A. E. The validity of the Beery Test of Visual-Motor Integration in predicting achievement in kindergarten, first, and second grades. *Educational & Psychological Measurement*, 1978, 38, 457–461.
48. LARSON, B. A. Use of the motorvator in improving gross–motor coordination, visual perception and IQ scores: A pilot study. *Journal of Music Therapy*, 1978, 15, 145–149.
49. LINDGREN, S. D. Finger localization and the prediction of reading disability. *Cortex*, 1978, 14, 87–101.
50. McINTYRE, C. W., MURRAY, M. E., CRONIN, C. M., & BLACKWELL, S. L. Span of apprehension in learning disabled boys. *Journal of Learning Disabilities*, 1978, 11, 468–475.
51. MURRAY, M. E. The relationship between personality adjustment and success in remedial programs in dyslexic children. *Contemporary Educational Psychology*, 1978, 3, 330–339.
52. PARK, R. Performance on geometric figure copying tests as predictors of types of errors in decoding. *Reading Research Quarterly*, 1978–79, 14, 100–118.
53. RAMEY, C. T., STEDMAN, D. J., BORDERS-PATTERSON, A., & MENGEL, W. Predicting school failure from information available at birth. *American Journal of Mental Deficiency*, 1978, 82, 525–534.
54. RASKIN, L. M., BLOOM, A. S., KLEE, S. H., & REESE, A. The assessment of developmentally disabled children with the WISC-R, Binet, and other tests. *Journal of Clinical Psychology*. 1978, 34, 111–114.
55. SATZ, P., & FRIEL, J. Predictive validity of an abbreviated screening battery. *Journal of Learning Disabilities*, 1978, 11, 347–351.
56. ZENTALL, S. S., ZENTALL, T. R., & BARACK, R. C. Distraction as a function of within-task stimulation for hyperactive and normal children. *Journal of Learning Disabilities*, 1978, 11, 540–548.
57. BEADLE, K. R. Clinical interactions of verbal language, learning and behavior. *Journal of Clinical Child Psychology*, 1979, 8, 201–205.
58. BRUININKS, V. L., & MAYER, J. H. Longitudinal study of cognitive abilities and academic achievement. *Perceptual & Motor Skills*, 1979, 48, 1011–1021.
59. COLARUSSO, R. P., MATHIS, G., & SHESSEL, D. Teacher effectiveness in identifying high-risk kindergarten children. *Journal of Learning Disabilities*, 1979, 12, 684–686.
60. CURTIS, C. J., MICHAEL, J. J., & MICHAEL, W. B. The predictive validity of the Developmental Test of Visual-Motor Integration under group and individual modes of administration relative to academic performance measures of second-grade pupils without identifiable major learning disabilities. *Educational & Psychological Measurement*, 1979, 39, 401–410.
61. FINEBERG, B. L., SOWARDS, S. K., & COCHRAN, G. M. Comparison of two tests of visual-motor skills. *Perceptual & Motor Skills*, 1979, 48, 156.
62. FUCHS, D. Reading and perceptual–motor performance: Can we strengthen them simultaneously? *Journal of Special Education*, 1979, 13, 265–273.
63. KIERSCHT, M. S., & MEVWISSEN, J. Follow-up of preschool age survivors of neonatal intensive care. *Journal of Psychology*, 1979, 101, 129–134.
64. KROHN, E. J., & TRAXLERE, A. J. Relationship of the McCarthy Scales of Children's Abilities to other measures of preschool cognitive, motor, and perceptual development. *Perceptual & Motor Skills*, 1979, 49, 783–790.
65. NEEDLEMAN, H. L., GUNNOE, C., LEVITON, A., REED, R., PERESIE, H., MAHER, C., & BARRETT, P. Deficits in psychologic and classroom performance of children with elevated dentine lead levels. *New England Journal of Medicine*, 1979, 300, 689–695.
66. SABATINO, D. A. The definition and assessment of visual and auditory perception. *Journal of Clinical Child Psychology*, 1979, 8, 188–194.

67. SCHOOLER, D. L., & ANDERSON, R. L. Race differences on the Developmental Test of Visual–Motor Integration, the Slosson Intelligence Test, and the ABC Inventory. *Psychology in the Schools*, 1979, 16, 453–456.
68. SHABAD, P., WORLAND, J., LANDER, H., & DIETRICH, D. A retrospective analysis of the TATs of children at risk who subsequently broke down. *Child Psychiatry & Human Development*, 1979, 10, 49–59.
69. SNYDERMAN, S. E., SANSARICQ, C., NORTON, P. M., & MANKA, M. The nutritional therapy of histidinemia. *Journal of Pediatrics*, 1979, 95, 712–715.
70. WHITE, M. A first-grade intervention program for children at risk for reading failure. *Journal of Learning Disabilities*, 1979, 12, 231–237.
71. WHITE, M., BATINI, P., SATZ, P., & FRIEL, J. Predictive validity of a screening battery for children "at risk" for reading failure. *British Journal of Educational Psychology*, 1979, 49, 132–137.
72. ZEITSCHEL, K. A., KALISH, R. A., & COLARUSSO, R. Visual perception tests used with physically handicapped children. *Academic Therapy*, 1979, 14, 565–576.
73. BRUMBACK, R. A., STATON, R. D., & WILSON, H. Neuropsychological study of children during and after remission of endogenous depressive episodes. *Perceptual & Motor Skills*, 1980, 50, 1163–1167.
74. COLARUSSO, R., GILL, S., PLANKENHORN, A., & BROOKS, R. Predicting first-grade achievement through formal testing of 5–year-old high–risk children. *Journal of Special Education*, 1980, 14, 355–363.
75. CROFOOT, M. J., & BENNETT, T. S. A comparison of three screening tests and the WISC–R in special education evaluations. *Psychology in the Schools*, 1980, 17, 474–478.
76. DEFILIPPIS, N. A., & DERBY, R. Application of predictive measures of reading disability in a culturally disadvantaged sample. *Journal of Learning Disabilities*, 1980, 13, 456–458.
77. FINKELSTEIN, N. W., & RAMEY, C. T. Information from birth certificates as a risk index for educational handicap. *American Journal of Mental Deficiency*, 1980, 84, 546–552.
78. FRIEDMAN, R., FUERTH, J. H., & FORSYTHE, A. B. A brief screening battery for predicting school achievement at ages seven and nine years. *Psychology in the Schools*, 1980, 17, 340–346.
79. FULKERSON, S. C., & FREEMAN, W. M. Perceptual–motor deficiency in autistic children. *Perceptual & Motor Skills*, 1980, 50, 331–336.
80. GERARD, J. A., & JUNKALA, J. Task analysis, handwriting, and process–based instruction. *Journal of Learning Disabilities*, 1980, 13, 54–58.
81. REYNOLDS, C. R., WRIGHT, D., & WILKINSON, W. A. Incremental validity of the Test for Auditory Comprehension of Language and the Developmental Test of Visual–Motor Integration. *Educational & Psychological Measurement*, 1980, 40, 503–507.
82. SANDOVAL, J. Reliability and concurrent validity of Light's Retention Scale. *Psychology in the Schools*, 1980, 17, 442–445.
83. SPIRITO, A. Scores on Bender–Gestalt and Developmental Test of Visual–Motor Integration of learning–disabled children. *Perceptual & Motor Skills*, 1980, 50, 1214.
84. TESKA, J. A., & STONEBURNER, R. L. The concept and practice of second–level screening. *Psychology in the Schools*, 1980, 17, 192–195.
85. WINSBERG, B. G., BIALER, I., KUPIETZ, S., BOTTI, E., & BALKA, E. B. Home vs hospital care of children with behavior disorders. *Archives of General Psychiatry*, 1980, 37, 413–418.
86. DEMERS, S. T., WRIGHT, D., & DAPPEN, L. Comparison of scores on two visual–motor tests for children referred for learning or adjustment difficulties. *Perceptual & Motor Skills*, 1981, 53, 863–867.
87. FINER, N. N., ROBERTSON, C. M., RICHARDS, R. T., PINNEL, L. E., & PETERS, K. L. Hypoxic-ischemic encephalopathy in term neonates: Perinatal factors and outcome. *Journal of Pediatrics*, 1981, 98, 112–117.
88. FISK, R. A., & JANZEN, H. L. Identifying learning disabled students with a selected psychoeducational test battery. *Alberta Journal of Educational Research*, 1981, 27, 252–263.
89. LYON, R., REITTA, S., WATSON, B., PORCH, B., & RHODES, J. Selected linguistic and perceptual abilities of empirically derived subgroups of learning disabled readers. *Journal of School Psychology*, 1981, 19, 152–166.
90. PORTER, G. L., & BINDER, D. M. A pilot study of visual–motor developmental inter–test reliability: The Beery Developmental Test of Visual Motor Integration and the Bender Visual Motor Gestalt test. *Journal of Learning Disabilities*, 1981, 14, 124–127.
91. SAXE, G. B., & SHAHEEN, S. Piagetian theory and the atypical case: An analysis of the developmental Gerstmann Syndrome. *Journal of Learning Disabilities*, 1981, 14, 131–135.
92. SNYDER, P. P., SNYDER, R. T., & MASSONG, S. F. The visual motor integration test: High interjudge reliability, high potential for diagnostic error. *Psychology in the Schools*, 1981, 18, 55–59.

[702]
Devereux Adolescent Behavior Rating Scale. Normal and emotionally disturbed children ages 13–18; 1967; DAB; problem behaviors; 12 factor scores (unethical behavior, defiant-resistive, domineering-sadistic, heterosexual interest, hyperactive expansive, poor emotional control, need approval and dependency, emotional distance, physical inferiority-timidity, schizoid withdrawal, bizarre speech and cognition, bizarre action), 3 cluster scores (inability to delay, paranoid thought, anxious self-blame), 11 item scores (persecution, plotting, bodily concern, external influences, compulsive acts, avoids competition, withdrawn, socialization, peer dominance, physical coordination, distraction); George Spivack, Jules Spotts, and Peter E. Haimes; Devereux Foundation Press.*

For additional information and a review by Carl F. Jesness, see 7:66; see also P:60 (1 reference).

REFERENCES

1. See P:60.
2. SAKLOFSKE, D. H., & EYSENCK, S. B. G. Personality and antisocial behavior in delinquent and non–delinquent boys. *Psychological Reports*, 1980, 47, 1255–1261.

[703]
Devereux Child Behavior Rating Scale. Emotionally disturbed and mentally retarded children ages 8–12; 1966; DCB; ratings by clinicians, child care workers, parents, house parents, or others who have had "intimate living arrangement with the child over a period of time"; 17 scores: distractibility, poor self care, pathological use of senses, emotional detachment, social isolation, poor coordination and body tonus, incontinence, messiness-sloppiness, inadequate need for independence, unresponsiveness to stimulation, proneness to emotional upset, need for adult contact, anxious-fearful ideation, "impulse" ideation, inability to delay, social aggression, unethical behavior; George Spivack and Jules Spotts; Devereux Foundation Press.*

See T2:1158 (1 reference); for a review by Allan G. Barclay, see 7:67; see also P:61 (3 references).

REFERENCES

1–3. See P:61.
4. See T2:1158.
5. GREGORY, M. K. Emotional indicators on the Bender–Gestalt and the Devereux Child Behavior Rating Scale. *Psychology in the Schools*, 1977, 14, 433–437.
6. FORBES, G. B. Comparison of hyperactive and emotionally–behaviorally disturbed children on the Devereux Child Behavior Rating Scale: A potential aid in diagnosis. *Journal of Clinical Psychology*, 1978, 34, 68–71.
7. AMANAT, E., & TRYNIECHI, T. Therapeutic adaptive behavior in residential treatment. *Child Psychiatry & Human Development*, 1979, 9, 238–249.
8. PAULSEN, K., & O'DONNELL, J. P. Construct validation of children's behavior problem dimensions: Relationship to activity level, impulsivity, and soft neurological signs. *Journal of Psychology*, 1979, 101, 273–278.
9. WASSERMAN, T. H., & VOGRIN, D. J. Relationship of endorsement of rational beliefs, age, months in treatment, and intelligence to overt behavior of emotionally disturbed children. *Psychological Reports*, 1979, 44, 911–917.
10. WINSBERG, B. G., BIALER, I., KUPIETZ, S., BOTTI, E., & BALKA, E. B. Home vs. hospital care of children with behavior disorders. *Archives of General Psychiatry*, 1980, 37, 413–418.

[704]
Devereux Elementary School Behavior Rating Scale. Grades kgn–6; 1966–67; DESB; problem behaviors; 11 factor scores (classroom disturbance, impatience, disrespect-defiance, external blame, achievement anxiety, external reliance, comprehension, inattentive-withdrawn, irrelevant-responsiveness, creative initiative, need for closeness to the teacher), 3 item scores (unable to change, quits easily, slow work); George Spivack and Marshall Swift; Devereux Foundation Press.*

See T2:1159 (3 references); for a review by William M. Littell, see 7:68 (1 reference); see also P:62 (2 references).

REFERENCES

1–2. See P:62.
3. See 7:68.
4–6. See T2:1159.
7. JORGENSON, G. W. Relationship of classroom behavior to the accuracy of the match between material difficulty and student ability. *Journal of Educational Psychology*, 1977, 69, 24–32.
8. POWERS, S. M. The Vane Kindergarten Test: Temporal stability and ability to predict behavioral criteria. *Psychology in the Schools*, 1977, 14, 34–36.
9. SAKLOFSKE, D. H. Personality and behavior problems of schoolboys. *Psychological Reports*, 1977, 41, 445–446.
10. WALLBROWN, J. D., WALLBROWN, F. H., & ENGIN, A. W. The prediction of first grade achievement with behavioral ratings taken during kindergarten. *Journal of Experimental Education*, 1977, 45, 16–20.
11. WELLS, M. G., & PETERSON, G. V. Kindergarten behavior ratings as a predictor of first-grade achievement. *Journal of Learning Disabilities*, 1978, 11, 344–347.
12. ELARDO, P. T., & CALDWELL, B. M. The effects of an experimental social development program on children in the middle childhood period. *Psychology in the Schools*, 1979, 16, 93–100.
13. HORNE, M. D., & LARRIVEE, B. Behavior rating scales: Need for refining normative data. *Perceptual & Motor Skills*, 1979, 49, 383–388.
14. MORROW, B. H. Elementary school performance of offspring of young adolescent mothers. *American Educational Research Journal*, 1979, 16, 423–429.
15. MOSBY, R. J. A bypass program of supportive instruction for secondary students with learning disabilities. *Journal of Learning Disabilities*, 1979, 12, 187–190.
16. FORMAN, S. G. A comparison of cognitive training and response cost procedures in modifying aggressive behavior of elementary school children. *Behavior Therapy*, 1980, 11, 594–600.
17. LARRIVEE, B., & BOURQUE, M. L. A comparative study of two behavior rating formats. *Measurement & Evaluation in Guidance*, 1980, 12, 223–228.
18. LEE, C. C. The homework helper program: Volunteer service for academic and social enrichment in the elementary school. *School Counselor*, 1980, 28, 11–21.
19. VON ISSER, A., QUAY, H. C., & LOVE, C. T. Interrelationships among three measures of deviant behavior. *Exceptional Children*, 1980, 46, 272–276.
20. WINSBERG, B. G., BIALER, I., KUPIETZ, S., BOTTI, E., & BALKA, E. B. Home vs. hospital care of children with behavior disorders. *Archives of General Psychiatry*, 1980, 37, 413–418.
21. BRADLEY, R. H. Preschool home environment and classroom behavior. *Journal of Experimental Education*, 1981, 49, 196–199.
22. THOMSON-ROUNTREE, P., CALDWELL, B. M., & WEBB, R. An examination of the relationship between role-taking and social competence. *Child Study Journal*, 1981, 11, 253–264.
23. THOMSON-ROUNTREE, P., & MUSUN-BASKETT, L. A further examination of project AWARE: The relationship between teacher behaviors and changes in student behavior. *Journal of School Psychology*, 1981, 19, 260–266.

[705]

Devereux Test of Extremity Coordination. Emotionally handicapped and neurologically impaired ages 4–10; 1971–73; DTEC; available only as part of the Individual Motor Achievement Guided Education (IMAGE) program; title on profile booklet is *Devereux IMAGE Profile*; 5 scores: sequential motor ability, fine motor ability, static balance, perceptual motor activity, total; George E. DeHaven, James D. Bruce, Franklin W. Dale (profile), and Jon E. Olexy (profile); Devereux Foundation Press.*

See T2:1894 (1 reference).

[706]

DF Opinion Survey. Grades 12–16 and adults; 1954–56; DFOS; 10 scores: need for attention, liking for thinking, adventure vs. security, self-reliance vs. dependence, aesthetic appreciation, cultural conformity, need for freedom, realistic thinking, need for precision, need for diversion; J. P. Guilford, Paul R. Christensen, and Nicholas A. Bond, Jr.; Sheridan Psychological Services, Inc.*

See T2:1151 (7 references) and P:54 (12 references); for reviews by Andrew R. Baggaley, John W. French, and Arthur W. Meadows, see 5:45.

[707]

The D48 Test. Grades 5 and over; 1963, c1961; intelligence; translation of the French edition published in 1948; for research use only; translation and American manual by John D. Black; Consulting Psychologists Press, Inc.*

See T2:365 (13 references); for reviews by Paul C. Davis and S. S. Dunn, see 6:454 (3 references).

REFERENCES

1–3. See 6:454.
4–16. See T2:365.
17. GOUGH, H. G., LAZZARI, R., FIORAVANTI, M., & STRACCA, M. An adjective check list scale to predict military leadership. *Journal of Cross-Cultural Psychology*, 1978, 9, 381–400.
18. KILPATRICK-TABAK, B., & ROTH, S. An attempt to reverse performance deficits associated with depression and experimentally induced helplessness. *Journal of Abnormal Psychology*, 1978, 87, 141–154.
19. CARRUTHERS, R. L., JR., STACK, W. B., & CHISSOM, B. S. Parallel forms of the Dominoes Test. *Psychological Reports*, 1979, 44, 1189–1190.
20. CHISSOM, B. S., & THOMAS, P. J. Equivalence of two forms of the Dominoes Test (D–48 and D–70) with graduate students in education. *Psychological Reports*, 1979, 44, 972–974.
21. FEUERSTEIN, R., RAND, Y., HOFFMAN, M., HOFFMAN, M., & MILLER, R. Cognitive modifiability in retarded adolescents: Effects of instrumental enrichment. *American Journal of Mental Deficiency*, 1979, 83, 539–550.
22. LEICHTMAN, S. R., & ERICKSON, M. T. Cognitive, demographic, and interactional determinants of role-taking skills in fourth grade children. *Perceptual & Motor Skills*, 1979, 49, 247–253.
23. LEICHTMAN, S. R. The relatedness of role-taking skills in fourth graders: A shift of perspective. *Journal of Genetic Psychology*, 1980, 136, 301–302.

[708]

★**Diagnosing Abilities in Math.** Slow learning children in math; 1980; DAM; Francis T. Sganga; Mafex Associates, Inc.*

[709]

*****Diagnosis: An Instructional Aid: Mathematics, Levels A and B.** Grades kgn–3, 3–8; 1979–80; DIAM; 2 levels; Andria P. Troutman, consultant; Science Research Associates, Inc.*

a) LEVEL A. Grades kgn–3; 2 parts.

1) *Survey Tests.* Provides quick survey of broad areas of mathematical understandings and skills in 11 tests: numbers and numerals (numbers through 10, ordinal numbers, place value), addition, subtraction, story problems, geometry and measurement (comparisons, geometry, length, time, money).

2) *Probes.* Diagnostic tests designed to pinpoint student weaknesses in 28 tests: comparing sets, sets and numbers (parts 1, 2), 1-digit numbers (counting, comparing), ordinal numbers, 2-digit numbers (place value and comparing, place value and counting, comparing), 3-digit numbers (place value, counting and comparing), 4-digit numbers, addition (1, 2, 3, 4), subtraction (1, 2, 3), story problems (1, 2, 3), comparisons, geometry, measurement, time, money (1, 2).

b) LEVEL B. Grades 3–8; 2 parts labeled Lab B1, Lab B2, plus survey tests; 4 tests of basic facts (addition, subtraction, multiplication, division).

[710] Diagnosis: An Instructional Aid: Reading

1) *Survey Tests, Lab B*1. 11 tests: whole numbers (concepts, addition, subtraction, multiplication, division, one-step word problems, other word problems), money, time, geometry, measurement.

2) *Probes, Lab B*1. Assesses basic skills in 20 tests: whole numbers/concepts (numbers through 999, numbers through 9999, numbers greater than 10,000), whole numbers (addition, subtraction, multiplication-1, multiplication-2, division-1, division-2), whole numbers/word problems (one-step word problems-1, one-step word problems-2, multiple-step word problems, extraneous and insufficient information problems, money (1, 2), time, geometric figures, geometric relationships, measurement (1, 2).

3) *Survey Tests, Lab B*2. 13 tests: factors and multiples, concepts (fractions, decimals), decimals/fractions/mixed numbers, computation (fractions/mixed numerals, decimals), word problems (fractions, decimals), rates/ratios, percents, geometric measurement, graphs, statistics/probability.

4) *Probes, Lab B*2. Assesses more advanced skills in 21 tests: factors and multiples, fractions and mixed numerals (1, 2), decimals (1, 2), decimals/fractions/mixed numerals, fractions and mixed numerals (addition and subtraction, multiplication and division), decimals (addition and subtraction, multiplication and division), fraction word problems, decimal word problems (1, 2), rates and ratios, percents (1, 2), special applications of percents, geometric measurement (1, 2), bar and line graphs, circle graphs/statistics/probability.

For additional information and reviews by Carl J. Huberty and Larry Sowder, see 8:263.

REFERENCES

1. HAMBLETON, R. K., & EIGNOR, D. R. Guidelines for evaluating criterion-referenced tests and test manuals. *Journal of Educational Measurement*, 1978, 15, 321–327.
2. SEDLACK, R. A. Diagnosis: An Instructional Aid. Mathematics Level A. *Journal of Learning Disabilities*, 1978, 11, 596–597.

[710]

Diagnosis: An Instructional Aid: Reading. Grades 1–4, 3–6; 1973–74; criterion-referenced tests consisting of a series of diagnostic tests (called probes) and an optional "survey test"; 2 levels; Science Research Associates, Inc.*

a) DIAGNOSTIC TESTS (PROBES). The two levels together cover 518 specific-objective subtests in 5 areas: comprehension, phonetic analysis, structural analysis, study skills, vocabulary; no scores obtained for the tests or subtests.

1) *Reading Level A*. Grades 1–4; 1973; 34 tests (294 specific objectives).

2) *Reading Level B*. Grades 3–6; 1974; 30 tests (224 specific objectives); the first four tests are used to determine whether the corresponding Level A tests should be administererd.

b) SURVEY TEST. Grades 1–4, 3–6; 1973–74; an optional test to determine which diagnostic tests should be administered; test consists of 2-item subtests (except for 4 3-item subtests in Level B) paralleling the diagnostic tests.

For additional information and a review by Richard C. Cox, see 8:752.

REFERENCES

1. HAMBLETON, R. K., & EIGNOR, D. R. Guidelines for evaluating criterion-referenced tests and test manuals. *Journal of Educational Measurement*, 1978, 15, 321–327.

[711]

★**Diagnostic Analysis of Reading Errors.** Adolescents and adults; 1971–79; DARE; "uses the forty-six-item word list of the *Wide Range Achievement Test* (Spelling, Level II)"; 4 scores: correct, error (sound substitutions, omissions, reversals); Jacquelyn Gillespie and Jacqueline Shohet; Jastak Associates, Inc.*

[712]

★**Diagnostic Analysis of Reading Tasks.** Grades 2.5 and below, 2.5 and above; 1976; criterion-referenced test comprised of nonsense words for diagnosing problems in encoding, transcribing sounds, and decoding of written symbols; 2 levels; Ethel Steinbert; Slosson Educational Publications, Inc.*

a) DART I. Grades 2.5 and below; item scores in 3 areas: encoding, decoding, auditory screening.

b) DART II. Grades 2.5 and above; item scores in 6 areas: encoding (sections A, B), decoding (sections A, B, medial diphthongs and diagraphs, irregular letter clusters).

[713]

Diagnostic Chart for Fundamental Processes in Arithmetic. Grades 2–8; 1925; G. T. Buswell and Lenore John; Bobbs-Merrill Co., Inc.*

See T2:713 (2 references); for a review by Leo J. Brueckner, see 4:413; for reviews by H. E. Benz and Foster E. Grossnickle, see 2:1456 (1 reference).

[714]

Diagnostic Decimal Tests. Ages 9–12, 10–12, 10–13; 1966; 3 tests; E. W. Seville; Australian Council for Educational Research [Australia].*

a) DIAGNOSTIC DECIMAL TESTS 1. Ages 9–12; addition and subtraction.

b) DIAGNOSTIC DECIMAL TESTS 2. Ages 10–12; simple multiplication and simple division.

c) DIAGNOSTIC DECIMAL TESTS 3. Ages 10–13; long multiplication and long division.

[715]

Diagnostic Fractions Test 3. Ages 7–11; 1957–66; E. W. Seville; Australian Council for Educational Research [Australia].*

For additional information, see 7:516.

[716]

Diagnostic Mathematics Inventory. Grades 1.5–2.5, 2.5–3.5, 3.5–4.5, 4.5–5.5, 5.5–6.5, 6.5–7.5, 7.5–8.5; 1971–75; DMI; revision of the *Prescriptive Mathematics Inventory* (PMI); 2 criterion-referenced tests covering objectives in "both traditional and modern mathematics"; John Gessel; CTB/McGraw-Hill.*

a) DIAGNOSTIC MATHEMATICS INVENTORY. Grades 1.5–2.5, 2.5–3.5, 3.5–4.5, 4.5–5.5, 5.5–6.5, 6.5–7.5, 7.5–8.5; 1971–75; no scores other than 37–109 item scores, each item measuring a specific objective; 7 overlapping levels covering 325 objectives.

1) *Level A/Red*. Grades 1.5–2.5; 1975; 37 item scores in 11 areas.

2) *Level B/Green*. Grades 2.5–3.5; 1975; 54 item scores in 14 areas.

3) *Level C/Blue*. Grades 3.5–4.5; 1975; 92 item scores in 22 areas.

4) *Level D/Orange*. Grades 4.5–5.5; 1971–75; items essentially the same as Orange Level of PMI except for 2 new items and change to multiple choice format; 87 item scores for 24 areas.

5) *Level E/Aqua*. Grades 5.5–6.5; 1971–75; items essentially the same as Aqua Level of PMI except for 1 new item and change to multiple choice format; 109 item scores in 16 areas.

6) *Level F/Purple*. Grades 6.5–7.5; 1971–75; items essentially the same as Purple Level of PMI except for 4 new items and change to multiple choice format; 163 item scores in 19 areas.

7) *Level G/Brown*. Grades 7.5–8.5; 1971–75; revision of Level C of PMI; 179 item scores.

b) DMI INTERIM EVALUATION TESTS. Grades 1.5–2.5, 2.5–3.5, 3.5–4.5, 4.5–5.5, 5.5–6.5, 6.5–7.5; 1973–75; IET; revision of *PMI Interim Evaluation Tests*; for continuing assessment of progress toward DMI category objectives after units of instruction; 11–39 tests yielding 37–151 scores; 6 overlapping levels covering 257 objectives (same objectives as for *a* except for exclusion of the Level G objectives).

1) *Level A/Red*. Grades 1.5–2.5; 1975; 11 tests; 37 scores.

2) *Level B/Green*. Grades 2.5–3.5; 1975; 14 tests; 52 scores.

3) *Level C/Blue*. Grades 3.5–4.5; 1975; 22 tests; 88 scores.

4) *Level D/Orange*. Grades 4.5–5.5; 1973–75; items essentially the same as Orange Level of PMI-IET except for 1 new objective; 24 tests; 82 scores.

5) *Level E/Aqua*. Grades 5.5–6.5; 1973–75; items essentially the same as Aqua Level of PMI-IET; 32 tests; 101 scores.

6) *Level F/Purple*. Grades 6.5–7.5; 1973–75; items essentially the same as Purple Level of PMI-IET except for 5 new objectives; 39 tests; 151 scores.

For additional information and reviews by Walter N. Durost and Thomas C. O'Brien, see 8:264.

REFERENCES

1. HAMBLETON, R. K., & EIGNOR, D. R. Guidelines for evaluating criterion–referenced tests and test manuals. *Journal of Educational Measurement*, 1978, 15, 321–327.

[717]

Diagnostic Number Tests 1–2. Ages 8–11, 9–12; 1951–66; formerly called *Diagnostic Arithmetic Tests 1–2*; 2 tests; E. W. Seville; Australian Council for Educational Research [Australia].*

a) TEST 1. Ages 8–11.

b) TEST 2. Ages 9–12.

For additional information, see 7:517.

[718]

★**Diagnostic Reading Inventory.** Students grades 3–12 with reading problems; 1977–79; DRI; for reading levels grades 1–8; H. Donald Jacobs and Lyndon W. Searfoss; Kendall/Hunt Publishing Co.*

[719]

*****Diagnostic Reading Scales.** Grades 1–7 and poor readers in grades 8–12; 1963–81; DRS-81; previous edition ('72) still available; 3 derived scores: instructional level, independent level, potential level, plus 12 raw scores: initial consonants, final consonants, consonant digraphs, consonant blends, initial consonant substitution, initial consonant sounds recognized auditorily, auditory discrimination, short and long vowel sounds, vowels with r, vowel diphthongs and digraphs, common syllables or phonograms, blending; George D. Spache; CTB/McGraw-Hill.*

For additional information, reviews by Nancy L. Roser and Robert L. Schreiner, and an excerpted review by Jerry Stafford of an earlier edition, see 8:753 (15 references); see also T2:1624 (4 references); for a review by Rebecca C. Barr, see 7:717 (7 references); for a review by N. Dale Bryant, see 6:821.

REFERENCES

1–7. See 7:717.
8–11. See T2:1624.
12–26. See 8:753.
27. ALLINGTON, R. L., CHODOS, L., DOMARACKI, J., & TRUEX, S. Passage dependency: Four diagnostic oral reading tests. *Reading Teacher*, 1977, 30, 369–375.
28. LAHEY, B. B., MCNEES, M. P., & SCHNELLE, J. F. The functional independence of three reading behaviors: A behavior systems analysis. *Corrective & Social Psychiatry & Journal of Behavior Technology, Methods & Therapy*, 1977, 23, 44–47.
29. CLARK, C. R., BRUININKS, R. H., & GLAMAN, G. V. Kindergarten predictors of three aspects of reading achievement. *Perceptual & Motor Skills*, 1978, 46, 411–419.
30. DORVAL, B., WALLACH, L., & WALLACH, M. A. Field evaluation of a tutorial reading program emphasizing phoneme identification skills. *Reading Teacher*, 1978, 31, 784–790.
31. DEWEAVER, M. J. Listening comprehension by nonblind handicapped students at three rates of speed. *Exceptional Children*, 1979, 46, 202–208.
32. MUIA, J. A., & CONNORS, E. T. Clinical Reading practices: Some legal considerations. *National Reading Conference Yearbook*, 1979, 145–149.
33. SHIELDS, P. H. The language of poor black children and reading performance. *Journal of Negro Education*, 1979, 48, 196–208.
34. WEAVER, P. A., & ROSNER, J. Relationships between visual and auditory perceptual skills and comprehension in students with learning disabilities. *Journal of Learning Disabilities*, 1979, 12, 617–621.
35. CURTIS, M. E. Development of components of reading skills. *Journal of Educational Psychology*, 1980, 72, 656–669.
36. DISTEFANO, P., & VALENCIA, S. The effects of syntactic maturity on comprehension of graded reading passages. *Journal of Educational Research*, 1980, 73, 247–251.
37. DWYER, E. J. Analysis of reading achievement, listening comprehension, and paradigmatic language of selected second grade students by race and sex. *Southern Journal of Education Research*, 1980, 14, 205–218.
38. D'ANGELO, K. Correction behavior of good and poor readers. *Reading World*, 1981, 21, 123–129.
39. FAY, G., TRUPIN, E., & TOWNES, B. D. The young disabled reader: Acquisition strategies and associated deficits. *Journal of Learning Disabilities*, 1981, 14, 32–35.

[720]

Diagnostic Reading Tests. Various grades kgn–13; 1947–74; DRT; 3 levels; Committee on Diagnostic Reading Tests, Inc.*

a) DIAGNOSTIC READING TESTS: KINDERGARTEN THROUGH FOURTH GRADES. Various grades kgn–4 (except for section 4, part 1); 1957–68; 2 sections, 5 booklets.

1) *Survey Section*. Grades kgn–1, 1, 2, 3–4; 1957–68; 4 levels.

(*a*) Reading Readiness Booklet. Grades kgn–1; 5 scores: relationships, eye-hand coordination, visual discrimination, auditory discrimination, vocabulary.

(*b*) Booklet 1. Grade 1; 12 scores: visual discrimination, auditory discrimination (3 subscores plus total), vocabulary (3 subscores plus total), story reading (2 subscores plus total).

[721] ★Diagnostic Screening Test: Achievement

(c) Booklet 2. Grade 2; 3 scores: word recognition, comprehension, total.
(d) Booklet 3. Grades 3–4; details same as for (c) above.
2) *Section 4: Word Attack, Part 1: Oral.* Grades 1–8; 1958–68.
b) DIAGNOSTIC READING TESTS: LOWER LEVEL. Grades 4–8; 1947–72; 2 sections, 4 booklets.
1) *Survey Section.* Grades 4–8; 1952–72; 3 parts in 2 booklets.
(a) Booklet 1: Part 1, Word Recognition and Comprehension. 2 scores: word recognition, comprehension.
(b) Booklet 2: Parts 2 and 3, Vocabulary-Story Reading. 3 scores: vocabulary, rate of reading, story comprehension.
2) *Section 4: Word Attack.* Various grades 1–13; 1947–69; 2 parts.
(a) Part 1, Oral. Grades 1–8; see a 2 above.
(b) Part 2, Silent. Grades 4–13; 1947–69; 3 scores: identification of sounds, syllabication, total.
c) DIAGNOSTIC READING TESTS: UPPER LEVEL. Grades 7–13; 1947–73; 5 sections, 6 booklets.
1) *Survey Section.* 1947–73; 5 scores: rate of reading, comprehension check, vocabulary, total comprehension, total.
2) *Section 1: Vocabulary (Revised).* 1947–68; 5 scores: English, mathematics, science, social studies, total.
3) *Section 2: Comprehension: Silent and Auditory.* 1947–68.
4) *Section 3: Rates of Reading: Part 1, General.* 1947–68; 4 scores: normal rate of reading, comprehension at normal rate, maximum rate of reading, comprehension at maximum rate.
5) *Section 4: Word Attack.* 1947–68; 2 parts.
(a) Part 1, Oral. 1948–68.
(b) Part 2, Silent. Grades 4–13; see b 2 (b) above.

For additional information, see 8:754 (4 references); see also T2:1626 (21 references); for reviews by Albert J. Kingston and B. H. Van Roekel, see 6:823 (21 references); for reviews by Frederick B. Davis, William W. Turnbull, and Henry Weitz, see 4:531 (19 references).

REFERENCES

1–19. See 4:531.
20–40. See 6:823.
41–61. See T2:1626.
62–65. See 8:754.
66. TILLMAN, C. E. Readability and other factors in college reading tests: A critique of the Diagnostic Reading Test, the Nelson–Denny Reading Test, and the McGraw-Hill Basic Reading Test. *National Reading Conference Yearbook,* 1977, 253–259.
67. TAUB, H. A., & KLINE, G. E. Recall of prose as a function of age and input modality. *Journal of Gerontology,* 1978, 33, 725–730.
68. ZAIS, R. S. The decline of academic performance in the classroom and the reading scores of prospective teachers: Some observations. *High School Journal,* 1978, 62, 52–57.
69. JANICKE, E. M. Massive oral decoding. *Academic Therapy,* 1981, 17, 157–161.
70. LEINHARDT, G., ZIGMOND, N., & COOLEY, W. W. Reading instruction and its effects. *American Educational Research Journal,* 1981, 18, 343–361.

[721]

★**Diagnostic Screening Test: Achievement.** Grades kgn–13; 1977; 5 scores: science, social studies, literature and the arts, practical knowledge, total achievement; Thomas D. Gnagey and Patricia A. Gnagey; Facilitation House.*

[722]

★**Diagnostic Screening Test: Language, Second Edition.** Grades 1–12; 1977–80; 8 scores: punctuation, spelling rules, sentence structure, grammar, capitalization, formal knowledge of language, applied knowledge of language, total language; Thomas D. Gnagey and Patricia A. Gnagey; Facilitation House.*

[723]

*****Diagnostic Screening Test: Math, Third Edition.** Grades 1–12; 1980; 31 scores: 5 basic processes scores (addition, subtraction, multiplication, division, total), 6 specialized processes scores (money, time, percent, U.S. measurement, metric measurement, total), 11 consolidation index scores, and 9 concept scores; Thomas D. Gnagey; Facilitation House.*

For additional information, see 8:265.

[724]

*****Diagnostic Screening Test: Reading, Third Edition.** Grades 1–12; 1981; identical with *Diagnostic Screening Test: Reading* ('76) except for the addition of one graded reading passage, a listening comprehension subtest, and an alternate form; 16 scores: comfort reading level, instructional reading level, frustration reading level, comprehension reading level, listening level, phonics-/sight ratio, word attack skill analysis (c-v/c, v-r, v-l, v-v, c-v-c, silent e, mix, site, total), consolidation index; Thomas D. Gnagey, Facilitation House.*

For a review by P. David Pearson of an earlier edition, see 8:755.

[725]

*****Diagnostic Screening Test: Spelling, Third Edition.** Grades 1–12; 1979; 12 scores: 3 scores (verbal, written, total) in each of 3 categories (phonics, sight, total) plus 3 consolidation index scores; Thomas D. Gnagey; Facilitation House.*

For additional information, see 8:72.

[726]

★**Diagnostic Skills Battery.** Grades 1–2, 3–4, 5–6, 7–8; 1976–80; DSB; "criterion- and norm-referenced"; 4 levels; O. F. Anderhalter; Scholastic Testing Service, Inc.*

a) LEVEL 12. Grades 1–2; 2 scores: reading, mathematics.
b) LEVEL 34. Grades 3–4; 3 scores: reading, language arts, mathematics.
c) LEVEL 56. Grades 5–6; 3 scores: reading, language arts, mathematics.
d) LEVEL 78. Grades 7–8; 3 scores: reading, language arts, mathematics.

[727]

Diagnostic Teacher-Rating Scale. Grades 4–12; 1938–52; ratings by pupils; originally published in 1938 for use in grades 4–8; 8 ratings: liking for teacher, ability to explain, kindness-friendliness-understanding, fairness in grading, discipline, work required, liking for lessons, total; Mary Amatora; Educators'-Employers' Tests & Services Associates.*

For additional information, see 6:696; for a review by Dorothy M. Clendenen, see 5:534 (5 references); see also 4:795 (2 references).

[728]
Diagnostic Test for Students of English as a Second Language. Applicants from non-English language countries for admission to American colleges; 1953; A. L. Davis; McGraw-Hill Book Co., Inc.*

See T2:227 (1 reference); for reviews by Nelson Brooks and Herschel T. Manuel, see 5:255.

[729]
Diagnostic Test of Speechreading. Deaf children ages 4–9; 1970; DTS; 5 scores: words, phrases, sentences, subtotal for phrases and sentences, total; Helmer R. Myklebust and Arthur I. Neyhus; Grune & Stratton, Inc.*

[730]
★**Diagnostic Word Patterns Tests.** Grades 3 and over; 1969–78; criterion-referenced test of sound-symbol relationships in spelling and word recognition; 3 tests; Evelyn Buckley; Educators Publishing Service, Inc.*
a) TEST 1. 1978; no scores, 10 areas: vowel-consonant pattern, vowel-consonant-consonant pattern, consonant-consonant-vowel-consonant pattern, consonant-consonant-vowel-consonant-consonant pattern, generalization for k and ck, common consonant digraphs, adding -ed, generalization for ch and tch, common letter combination patterns, nonphonetic words.
b) TEST 2. 1978; no scores, 10 areas: vowel-consonant-silent e pattern, ai and ay, oa and ow, ea and ee, ie and igh, ou and ow, au and aw, vowel controlled by r pattern, oo, nonphonetic words.
c) TEST 3. 1978; no scores, 10 areas: ea and e, oi and oy, suffixes, l-l-l generalization, vowel controlled by r pattern, suffixes, silent-e words with suffixes, two-syllable words with short vowels, two-syllable words with short and long vowels, nonphonetic words.

[731]
The Diebold Personnel Tests. Programmers and systems analysts for automatic data processing and computing installations; 1959; 5 tests; John Diebold & Associates.* (In-print status uncertain; no reply from publisher.)
a) SYMBOLS BLOCK DIAGRAM TEST.
b) CODE INDEX TEST.
c) RELATIONS IN NUMBERS TEST.
d) CODE MATCHING TEST.
e) WORD SEQUENCE TEST.
For additional information, see 6:1142.

[732]
*****Differential Aptitude Tests (Forms V and W).** Grades 8–12 and adults; 1947–82; DAT; also used as a part of the *DAT Career Planning Program*; 9 scores: verbal reasoning, numerical ability, total, abstract reasoning, clerical speed and accuracy, mechanical reasoning, space relations, spelling, language usage; George K. Bennett, Harold G. Seashore, and Alexander G. Wesman; The Psychological Corporation.*

For additional information and reviews by Thomas J. Bouchard, Jr. and Robert L. Linn and an excerpted review by Gerald S. Hanna, see 8:485 (56 references); see also T2:1069 (64 references); for a review by M. Y. Quereshi and an excerpted review by Jack C. Merwin of earlier forms, see 7:673 (139 references); for reviews by J. A. Keats and Richard E. Schutz, see 6:767 (52 references); for reviews by John B. Carroll and Norman Frederiksen, see 5:605 (49 references); for reviews by Harold Bechtoldt, Ralph F. Berdie, and Lloyd G. Humphreys, see 4:711 (27 references); for an excerpted review, see 3:620.

REFERENCES

1–28. See 4:711.
29–77. See 5:605.
78–129. See 6:767.
130–268. See 7:673.
269–332. See T2:1069.
333–388. See 8:485.
389. *Counseling From Profiles: A Casebook for the Differential Aptitude Tests*, Second Edition. New York: The Psychological Corporation, 1977.
390. GOLD, A. M. The use of separate–sex norms on aptitude tests: Friend or foe? *Measurement & Evaluation in Guidance*, 1977, 10, 162–171.
391. HAKSTIAN, A. R., & BENNET, R. W. Validity studies using the Comprehensive Ability Battery (CAB): I. Academic achievement criteria. *Educational & Psychological Measurement*, 1977, 37, 425–437.
392. HODGSON, M. L., & CRAMER, S. H. The relationship between selected self–estimated and measured abilities in adolescents. *Measurement & Evaluation in Guidance*, 1977, 10, 98–105.
393. KNAPP, R. R., KNAPP, L., & MICHAEL, W. B. Stability and concurrent validity of the career Ability Placement Survey (APS) against the DAT and the GATB. *Educational & Psychological Measurement*, 1977, 37, 1081–1085.
394. SHERMAN, J., & FENNEMA, E. The study of mathematics by high school girls and boys: Related variables. *American Educational Research Journal*, 1977, 14, 159–168.
395. WECKOWICZ, T. E., COLLIER, G., & SPRENG, L. Field dependence, cognitive functions, personality traits, and social values in heavy cannabis users and nonuser controls. *Psychological Reports*, 1977, 41, 291–302.
396. WHITELY, S. E. Information–processing on intelligence test items: Some response components. *Applied Psychological Measurement*, 1977, 1, 465–476.
397. ADAMOWICZ, J. K., & HUDSON, B. R. Visual short–term memory, response delay, and age. *Perceptual & Motor Skills*, 1978, 46, 267–270.
398. CHATTERJI, S., & MUKERJEE, M. Concurrent validity of the non-language test of verbal intelligence. *Educational & Psychological Measurement*, 1978, 38, 433–436.
399. HAKSTIAN, A. R., & BENNET, R. W. Validity studies using the Comprehensive Ability Battery (CAB): II. Relationships with the DAT and GATB. *Educational & Psychological Measurement*, 1978, 38, 1003–1015.
400. HAKSTIAN, A. R., & CATTELL, R. B. Higher–stratum ability structures on a basis of twenty primary abilities. *Journal of Educational Psychology*, 1978, 70, 657–669.
401. McKELVIE, S. J., & ROHRBERG, M. M. Individual differences in reported visual imagery and cognitive performance. *Perceptual & Motor Skills*, 1978, 46, 451–458.
402. SCHMITT, N., MELLON, P. M., & BYLENGA, C. Sex differences in validity for academic and employment criteria, and different types of predictors. *Journal of Applied Psychology*, 1978, 63, 145–150.
403. WALSH, D. M., & WALSH, M. D. Relationship between extraversion and neuroticism, and intelligence for students in grade nine English and mathematics. *Psychological Reports*, 1978, 43, 15–19.
404. GREENE, R. L., HARRIS, M. E., & MACON, R. S. Another look at personal validation. *Journal of Personality Assessment*, 1979, 43, 419–423.
405. PUHAN, B. N., & MISHRA, A. B. The factorial structure of the Differential Aptitude Test across two developmental groups. *Psychological Studies*, 1979, 24, 5–11.
406. CHIAPPETTA, E. L., & McBRIDE, J. W. Exploring the effects of general remediation on ninth–graders' achievement of the mole concept. *Science Education*, 1980, 64, 609–614.
407. DIAMOND, E. E. The AMEG commission report on sex bias in achievement testing. *Measurement & Evaluation in Guidance*, 1980, 13, 135–147.
408. OMIZO, M. M. The Differential Aptitude Tests as predictors of success in a high school for engineering program. *Educational & Psychological Measurement*, 1980, 40, 197–203.
409. PRITCHARD, R. D., HOLLENBECK, J., & DELEO, P. J. The effects of continuous and partial schedules of reinforcement on effort, performance, and satisfaction. *Organizational Behavior & Human Performance*, 1980, 25, 336–353.
410. REVELLE, W., HUMPHREYS, M. S., SIMON, L., & GILLILAND, K. The interactive effect of personality, time of day, and caffeine: A test of the arousal model. *Journal of Experimental Psychology: General*, 1980, 109, 1–31.

411. SHERMAN, J. A. Predicting mathematics grades of high school girls and boys: A further study. *Contemporary Educational Psychology*, 1980, 5, 249–255.
412. STERNBERG, R. J. Representation and process in linear syllogistic reasoning. *Journal of Experimental Psychology: General*, 1980, 109, 119–159.
413. PUHAN, B. N. Effects of marker variables on WAIS communalities. *Educational & Psychological Measurement*, 1981, 41, 55–59.
414. SEWELL, T. E., PALMO, A. J., & MANNI, J. L. High school dropout, psychological, academic, and vocational factors. *Urban Education*, 1981, 16, 65–76.

[733]
Differential Test Battery. Ages 11 to "top university level" (range for Test 1 extends downward to age 7); 1955–59; 12 tests in 7 booklets; J. R. Morrisby; distributed by Educational & Industrial Test Services Ltd. [England].*

a) TEST 1, COMPOUND SERIES TEST. Ages 7 and over; "mental work power"; 1955.
b) GENERAL ABILITY TESTS. Ages 11 and over; 1955; 3 tests.
  1) *Test 2, General Ability Tests: Verbal.*
  2) *Test 3, General Ability Tests: Numerical.*
  3) *Test 4, General Ability Tests: Perceptual.*
c) TEST 5, SHAPES TEST. Ages 11 and over; 1955; spatial ability.
d) TEST 6, MECHANICAL ABILITY TEST. Ages 11 and over; 1955.
e) SPEED TESTS. Ages 11 and over; 1955–59; 6 tests in a single booklet.
  1) *Test 7 (Speed Test 1), Routine Number and Name Checking.*
  2) *Test 8 (Speed Test 2), Perseveration.*
  3) *Test 9 (Speed Test 3), Word Fluency.*
  4) *Test 10 (Speed Test 4), Ideational Fluency.*
  5) *Test 11 (Speed Test 5), Motor Speed.*
  6) *Test 12 (Speed Test 6), Motor Skill.*

See T2:1070 (6 references) and 6:768; for reviews by E. A. Peel, Donald E. Super, and Philip E. Vernon, see 5:606.

REFERENCES

1–6. See T2:1070.
7. McCALLUM, D. I., SMITH, I. M., & ELIOT, J. Further investigation of components of mathematical ability. *Psychological Reports*, 1979, 44, 1127–1133.
8. GIESBRECHT, E. High school students' achievement of selected mathematical competencies. *School Science & Mathematics*, 1980, 80, 277–286.

[734]
★**Dimensions of Self-Concept.** Grades 4–6, 7–12; 1977–78; DOSC; self-report instrument; 5 factor scales: level of aspiration, anxiety, academic interest and satisfaction, leadership and initiative, identification vs. alienation; 2 levels; William B. Michael and Robert A. Smith; Los Angeles Unified School District.*

REFERENCES

1. LEHN, T., VLADOVIC, R., & MICHAEL, W. B. The short–term predictive validity of a standardized reading test and of scales reflecting six dimensions of academic self–concept relative to selected high school achievement criteria for four ethnic groups. *Educational & Psychological Measurement*, 1980, 40, 1017–1031.
2. MICHAEL, W. B., LEHN, T., VLADOVIC, R., & COOPER, T. Cognitive and affective factor dimensions in each of four high school samples of different ethnicity. *Educational & Psychological Measurement*, 1980, 40, 1043–1050.
3. OMIZO, M. M. The effects of relaxation and biofeedback training on Dimensions of Self–Concept (DOSC) among hyperactive male children. *Educational Research Quarterly*, 1980, 5, 22–30.
4. OMIZO, M. M., HAMMETT, V. L., LOFFREDO, D. A., & MICHAEL, W. B. The Dimensions of Self–Concept (DOSC) as predictors of academic achievement among Mexican–American junior high students. *Educational & Psychological Measurement*, 1981, 41, 835–842.
5. TAYLOR, L. K., & MICHAEL, W. B. A correlational study of academic self–concept, intellectual achievement, responsibility, social cognition, and reading. *Educational Research Quarterly*, 1981, 6, 13–23.

[735]
Dimock L Inventory. High school and adults; 1969–74; for research use only; "flexible, participative, and non-authoritarian leadership"; 4 scores: friendliness (the friendliness scale of *The Guilford-Zimmerman Temperament Survey*), participative leadership style, authoritarianism (items from various forms of the California F Scale), total; Hedley G. Dimock; Sheridan Psychological Services, Inc.*

For additional information, see 8:537.

[736]
Diplomacy Test of Empathy. Business and industry; 1957–60; DTE; revision of *Primary Empathic Abilities*; test booklet title is *Diplomacy Test of Empathic Ability*; Willard A. Kerr; Psychometric Affiliates.*

See T2:1160 (1 reference) and P:64 (2 references); for reviews by Arthur H. Brayfield and Richard S. Hatch, see 6:85 (1 reference); for a review by Robert L. Thorndike of the earlier test, see 5:99.

[737]
★**Distar Mastery Tests.** Preschool–grade 3; 1978; DMT; criterion-referenced; determines mastery for the Distar reading, language, and arithmetic programs; 6 tests; Science Research Associates, Inc.*

a) READING I. 3 scores: sound recognition, vocabulary, comprehension.
b) READING II. 5 scores: letter recognition, sound recognition, vocabulary, deductive thinking rules, comprehension.
c) LANGUAGE I. 7 to 8 scores: description of objects and actions, actions, instructional words, classification, information, applications, shapes, statement production (optional).
d) LANGUAGE II. 7 to 8 scores: word skills, sentence skills, reasoning skills, directional skills, information, applications, take-homes, statement production (optional).
e) ARITHMETIC I. 9 scores: symbol identification, groups, horizontal addition and algebra addition, horizontal and vertical subtraction, vertical addition, oral story problems, ordinal counting, more-less, written story problems.
f) ARITHMETIC II. 7 scores: column addition, column subtraction, telling time, multiplying and reducing fractions, measurement, coins, written story problems.

[738]
★**Distar Mastery Tests: Arithmetic I.** Preschool–grade 3; 1978; criterion-referenced; 9 scores: symbol identification, groups, horizontal addition and algebra addition, horizontal and vertical subtraction, vertical addition, oral story problems, ordinal counting, more-less, written story problems; Science Research Associates, Inc.*
For the complete battery entry, see 737.

[739]
★**Distar Mastery Tests: Arithmetic II.** Preschool–grade 3; 1978; criterion-referenced; 7 scores: column addition, column subtraction, telling time, multiplying and reducing fractions, measurement, coins, written story

problems; Science Research Associates, Inc.* For the complete battery entry, see 737.

[740]

★**Distar Mastery Tests: Language I.** Preschool–grade 3; 1978; criterion-referenced; 7 to 8 scores: description of objects and actions, actions, instructional words, classification, information, applications, shapes, statement production (optional); Science Research Associates, Inc.* For the complete battery entry, see 737.

[741]

★**Distar Mastery Tests: Language II.** Preschool–grade 3; 1978; criterion-referenced; 7 to 8 scores: word skills, sentence skills, reasoning skills, directional skills, information, applications, take-homes, statement production (optional); Science Research Associates, Inc.* For the complete battery entry, see 737.

[742]

★**Distar Mastery Tests: Reading I.** Preschool–grade 3; 1978; criterion–referenced; 3 scores: sound recognition, vocabulary, comprehension; Science Research Associates, Inc.* For the complete battery entry, see 737.

[743]

★**Distar Mastery Tests: Reading II.** Preschool–grade 3; 1978; criterion-referenced; 5 scores: letter recognition, sound recognition, vocabulary, deductive thinking rules, comprehension; Science Research Associates, Inc.* For the complete battery entry, see 737.

[744]

★**Do I Know How to Apply For a Job?** Job applicants; no date on test materials; Lawrence W. Hess; Bobbs-Merrill Co., Inc.*

[745]

__Dole Vocational Sentence Completion Blank.__ Grades 7–12; 1952–82; DVSCB; 27 scores in 3 major areas: concerns (problem, achievement, independence, satisfaction, material, vocation, effectiveness, recognition), general emphasis (relaxation, intellectual, active, other people, recreational), specific preference areas (outdoor, mechanical, computational, scientific, persuasive, artistic, literary, musical, social service, clerical, domestic, academic, armed forces, household arts), plus 2 miscellaneous scores (other, omit), and 9 optional categories (peace of mind, security, value, obligation, health, religion, social studies, negative academic, unclassifiable); Arthur A. Dole; Stoelting Co.

[746]

Domain Phonic Tests. Ages 5–9; 1972; no scores (except for auditory discrimination subtest), 6 areas: initial single consonants, final single consonants, consonant blends, single vowels, vowel blends, auditory discrimination; J. McLeod and J. Atkinson; Oliver & Boyd [Scotland].*

For additional information, see 8:756.

[747]

Doppelt Mathematical Reasoning Test. Grades 16–17 and employees; 1954–68; DMRT; distribution restricted and test administered at specified licensed university centers; Jerome E. Doppelt; The Psychological Corporation.*

For additional information, see 7:349 (2 references); for a review by W. V. Clemans, see 6:456 (2 references).

REFERENCES

1–2. See 6:456.
3–4. See 7:349.
5. URSANO, R. J. The Vietnam era prisoner of war: Precaptivity personality and the development of psychiatric illness. *American Journal of Psychiatry*, 1981, 138, 315–318.

[748]

Doren Diagnostic Reading Test of Word Recognition Skills, 1973 Edition. Grades 1–4; 1956–73; DDRT; 13 scores: letter recognition, beginning sounds, whole word recognition, words within words, speech consonants, ending sounds, blending, rhyming, vowels, discriminate guessing, spelling, sight words, total; Margaret Doren; American Guidance Service.*

For additional information, a review by Robert L. Schreiner, and excerpted reviews by Alex Bannatyne, Wayne Otto, and Shirley Feldmann, see 8:757 (3 references); see also T2:1627 (2 references); for reviews by B. H. Van Roekel and Verna L. Vickery of an earlier edition, see 5:659.

[749]

Dos Amigos Verbal Language Scales. Ages 5–0 to 13–5; 1973–74; language development in English and Spanish of "presumably bilingual" children; 3 scores: English, Spanish, dominant language; Donald E. Critchlow; Academic Therapy Publications.*

For additional information and an excerpted review by Richard V. Teschner, see 8:163 (2 references).

[750]

Draw-A-Man Test for Indian Children. Ages 6–10; 1956–66; adaptation of *Goodenough Intelligence Test*; Pramila Phatak; distributed by Anand Agencies [India].* (In-print status uncertain; no reply from publisher.)

See T2:372 (1 reference); for an excerpted review by M. A. Faroqi, see 7:350 (4 references).

[751]

The Draw-A-Person. Ages 5 and over; 1963; DAP; William H. Urban; Western Psychological Services.*

For additional information and reviews by Dale B. Harris and Philip M. Kitay, see 7:165.

REFERENCES

1. BARKER, T. E., & BLACK, F. W. Klinefelter Syndrome in a military population. *Archives of General Psychiatry*, 1976, 33, 607–610.
2. BELL, A. E., ABRAHAMSON, D. S., & McRAE, K. N. Reading retardation: A 12-year prospective study. *Journal of Pediatrics*, 1977, 91, 363–370.
3. BOWD, A. D. Field–dependence and performance on Piagetian invariance tasks: A cross–cultural comparison. *Journal of Genetic Psychology*, 1977, 130, 157–158.
4. HARTLAGE, L. C., & HARTLAGE, P. L. Relationships between neurological, behavioral, and academic variables. *Journal of Clinical Child Psychology*, 1977, 6, 52–53.
5. KIMBALL, J. G. The Southern California Sensory Integration Tests and the Bender Gestalt: A correlational study. *American Journal of Occupational Therapy*, 1977, 31, 295–299.
6. LATORRE, R. A., & GREGOIRE, P. A. Gender role in university mental health clients. *Journal of Individual Psychology*, 1977, 33, 246–249.
7. REKERS, G. A., WILLIS, T. J., YATES, C. E., ROSEN, A. C., & LOW, B. P. Assessment of childhood gender behavior change. *Journal of Child Psychology & Psychiatry & Allied Disciplines*, 1977, 18, 53–65.
8. TEDFORD, W. H., JR., & PENK, M. L. Intelligence and imagery in personality. *Journal of Personality Assessment*, 1977, 41, 405–413.

9. WOOD, N. E. Directed art, visual perception, and learning disabilities. *Academic Therapy*, 1977, 12, 455–462.
10. WYSOCKI, A. C., & WYSOCKI, B. A. Human figure drawing of sex offenders. *Journal of Clinical Psychology*, 1977, 33, 278–284.
11. COLLETTE–HARRIS, M., & MINKE, K. A. A behavioral experimental analysis of dyslexia. *Behaviour Research & Therapy*, 1978, 16, 292–295.
12. KOFF, E., RIERDAN, J., & SILVERSTONE, E. Changes in representation of body image as a function of menarcheal status. *Developmental Psychology*, 1978, 14, 635–642.
13. KOHN, M. L., & SCHOOLER, C. The reciprocal effects of the substantive complexity of work and intellectual flexibility: A longitudinal assessment. *American Journal of Sociology*, 1978, 84, 24–52.
14. LEWIS, C. E., SCHER, M., & DIETZ, D. Reviewing results of psychological tests in a patient group. *Hospital & Community Psychiatry*, 1978, 29, 306–308.
15. MILLER, J., SCHOOLER, C., KOHN, M. L., & MILLER, K. Women and work: The psychological effects of occupational conditions. *American Journal of Sociology*, 1978, 85, 66–94.
16. PALUDI, M. A. Machover revisited: Impact of sex–role orientation on sex sequence on the Draw–A–Person Test. *Perceptual & Motor Skills*, 1978, 47, 713–714.
17. RIDER, B. Sensorimotor treatment of chronic schizophrenics. *American Journal of Occupational Therapy*, 1978, 32, 451–455.
18. SCHOFIELD, J. W. An exploratory study of the Draw–A–Person as a measure of racial identity. *Perceptual & Motor Skills*, 1978, 46, 311–321.
19. STANLEY, G., & PERSHIN, P. Rating preschool development of name–writing and Draw–A–Person. *Perceptual & Motor Skills*, 1978, 47, 187–190.
20. VAN DYNE, W. T., & CARSKADON, T. G. Relationships among three components of self-concept and same–sex and opposite–sex human figure drawings. *Journal of Clinical Psychology*, 1978, 34, 537–538.
21. WALLER, R. W., & KEELEY, S. M. Effects of explanation and information feedback on the illusory correlation phenomenon. *Journal of Consulting & Clinical Psychology*, 1978, 46, 342–343.
22. BELFER, M. L., HARRISON, A. M., & MURRAY, J. E. Body image and the process of reconstructive surgery. *American Journal of Diseases of Children*, 1979, 133, 532–535.
23. BRUNNER, R. L., O'GRADY, D. J., PARTIN, J. C., PARTIN, J. S., & SCHUBERT, W. K. Neuropsychologic consequences of Reye Syndrome. *Journal of Pediatrics*, 1979, 95, 706–711.
24. BUHRICH, N., & McCONAGHY, N. Tests of gender feelings and behavior in homosexuality, transvestism, and transsexualism. *Journal of Clinical Psychology*, 1979, 35, 187–191.
25. CARR, A. C., GOLDSTEIN, E. G., HUNT, H. F., & KERNBERG, O. F. Psychological tests and borderline patients. *Journal of Personality Assessment*, 1979, 43, 582–590.
26. HARKULICH, J. F., MARCHNER, T. J., & BROWN, E. B. Neurological, neuropsychological, and behavioral correlates of Klinefelter's Syndrome. *Journal of Nervous & Mental Disease*, 1979, 167, 359–363.
27. KUHLMAN, T. L. A validation study of the Draw–A–Person as a measure of racial identity acceptance. *Journal of Personality Assessment*, 1979, 43, 457–460.
28. PALUDI, M. A., & BAUER, W. D. Impact of sex of experimenter on the Draw–A–Person Test. *Perceptual & Motor Skills*, 1979, 49, 456–458.
29. RIEDER, D. O., & NICHOLS, P. L. Offspring of schizophrenics III. *Archives of General Psychiatry*, 1979, 36, 665–674.
30. SCIDA, J., & VANNICELLI, M. Sex-role conflict and women's drinking. *Journal of Studies on Alcohol*, 1979, 40, 28–44.
31. SERAFINE, M. L. A measure of meter conservation in music, based on Piaget's theory. *Genetic Psychology Monographs*, 1979, 99, 185–229.
32. UNGERLEIDER, J. T., & WELLISCH, D. K. Coercive persuasion (brainwashing), religious cults, and deprogramming. *American Journal of Psychiatry*, 1979, 136, 279–282.
33. WORLAND, J., LANDER, H., & HESSELBROCK, V. Psychological evaluation of clinical disturbance in children at risk for psychopathology. *Journal of Abnormal Psychology*, 1979, 88, 13–26.
34. GOLDMAN, R. K., & VELASCO, M. M., JR. Toward the development of a rational scale in the use of Human–Figure Drawing as a kindergarten screening measure. *Perceptual & Motor Skills*, 1980, 50, 571–577.
35. HILL, E. F. A comparison of three psychological testings of a transsexual. *Journal of Personality Assessment*, 1980, 44, 52–101.
36. KAY, S. R. Progressive figure drawings in the developmental assessment of mentally retarded psychotics. *Perceptual & Motor Skills*, 1980, 50, 583–590.
37. NIELSEN, H. H. A longitudinal study of the psychological aspects of myelomeningocele. *Scandinavian Journal of Psychology*, 1980, 21, 45–54.
38. SUTER, B., SEEGMILLER, B. R., & DUNIVANT, N. Effects of age, sex, and income level on sex-role differentiation in preschoolers. *Journal of Psychology*, 1980, 104, 217–220.
39. TEGLASI, H. Acceptance of the traditional female role and sex of the first person drawn on the Draw–A–Person Test. *Perceptual & Motor Skills*, 1980, 51, 267–271.
40. VRANA, F., & PIHL, R. O. Selective attention deficit in learning disabled children: A cognitive interpretation. *Journal of Learning Disabilities*, 1980, 13, 42–45.
41. KERNBERG, O. F., GOLDSTEIN, E. G., CARR, A. C., HUNT, H. F., BAUER, S. F., & BLUMENTHAL, R. Diagnosing borderline personality: A pilot study using multiple diagnostic methods. *Journal of Nervous & Mental Disease*, 1981, 169, 225–231.
42. PONTIUS, A. Geometric figure–rotation task and face representation in dyslexia: Role of spatial relations and orientation. *Perceptual & Motor Skills*, 1981, 53, 607–614.
43. TOLOR, A., & BARBIERI, R. J. Different facets of sex anxiety. *Perceptual & Motor Skills*, 1981, 52, 546.
44. URSANO, R. J. The Viet Nam era prisoner of war: Precaptivity personality and the development of psychiatric illness. *American Journal of Psychiatry*, 1981, 138, 315–318.

[752]

Draw-A-Person Quality Scale. Ages 16–25; 1955–65; DPQS; level of intellectual functioning; Mazie Earle Wagner and Herman J. P. Schubert; Herman J. P. Schubert.*

For additional information, see P:423 (3 references); for a review by Philip L. Harriman, see 5:129 (3 references).

[753]

Driver Attitude Survey. Drivers; 1962–70; DAS; 6 scores: violations, accidents, alcohol, faking, deviance, misses; Donald H. Schuster and J. P. Guilford; Sheridan Psychological Services, Inc.*

See T2:844 (4 references) and 7:574 (3 references).

[754]

[Driver Selection Forms and Tests]. Truck drivers; 1943–73; all revised forms essentially the same as or identical with earlier forms; no manual; Dartnell Corporation.*

a) EMPLOYMENT APPLICATION. 1946–64.
b) TELEPHONE CHECK. 1946–73; Robert N. McMurry.
c) DRIVER INTERVIEW. 1946–64.
d) PHYSICAL EXAMINATION RECORD. 1946–54.
e) SELECTION AND EVALUATION SUMMARY. 1950–72; Robert N. McMurry.
f) STANDARDIZED TEST: TRAFFIC AND DRIVING KNOWLEDGE FOR DRIVERS OF MOTOR TRUCKS. 1946–64; Amos E. Neyhart and Helen L. Neyhart.
g) ROAD TEST IN TRAFFIC FOR TESTING, SELECTING, RATING, AND TRAINING TRUCK DRIVERS. 1943–64; 3 scores: specific driving skills, general driving habits and attitudes, total; Amos E. Neyhart.

For additional information and a review by Joseph E. Moore, see 6:1197; for a review by S. Rains Wallace, Jr., see 4:789.

[755]

Drug Abuse Knowledge Test. Grades 10–12; 1972–73, c1969; DAKT; test booklet title is *Drug Abuse Test*; Madge Attwood; the Author.* (In-print status uncertain; no reply from publisher.)

For additional information and a review by James E. Bryan, see 8:411.

[756]

★**Drumcondra Attainment Tests.** Grades 2, 3–4, 5–6, 7, 8, 9; 1976–78; 6 levels; Educational Research Centre [Ireland].*

a) LEVEL I. Grade 2; 1978.
 1) *Mathematics.* 4 scores: computation, concepts, problem solving, total.

2) *English.* 4 scores: vocabulary, word analysis, comprehension, total.
b) LEVEL II. Grades 3–4; 1978.
 1) *Mathematics.* 4 scores: computation, concepts, problem solving, total.
 2) *Irish.* 5 scores: vocabulary, comprehension, reading total, usage, spelling.
 3) *English.* 7 scores: vocabulary, comprehension, reading total, capitalization/punctuation, usage/grammar, language total, spelling.
c) LEVEL III. Grades 5–6; 1977.
 1) *Mathematics.* 4 scores: same as Level II.
 2) *Irish.* 5 scores: same as Level II.
 3) *English.* 7 scores: same as Level II.
d) LEVEL IV. Grade 7; 1977.
 1) *Mathematics.* 4 scores: same as Level II.
 2) *Irish.* 5 scores: same as Level II.
 3) *English.* 7 scores: same as Level II.
e) LEVEL V. Grade 8; 1976.
 1) *Mathematics.* 4 scores: same as Level II.
 2) *Irish.* 5 scores: same as Level II.
 3) *English.* 7 scores: same as Level II.
f) LEVEL VI. Grade 9; 1978.
 1) *Mathematics.* 4 scores: same as Level II.
 2) *Irish.* 5 scores: same as Level II.
 3) *English.* 7 scores: same as Level II.

[757]
★**DTLS Logical Relationships Test.** Beginning students in two- and four-year institutions; 1977; measures logical relationship skills in the following areas: categorizing ideas, using appropriate connectives, making analogies, recognizing principles of organization; published by The College Board and Educational Testing Service.

[758]
★**DTLS Reading Comprehension Test.** Beginning students in two- and four-year institutions; 1977; measures reading comprehension skills in the following areas: understanding main ideas, understanding direct statements, drawing inferences; published by The College Board and Educational Testing Service.

[759]
★**DTLS Sentence Structure Test.** Beginning students in two- and four-year institutions; 1977; measures sentence structure skills in the following areas: using complete sentences, using coordination and subordination appropriately, placing modifiers appropriately; published by The College Board and Educational Testing Service.

[760]
★**DTLS Usage Test.** Beginning students in two- and four-year institutions; 1977; measures usage skills in the following areas: pronouns, modifiers, diction and idioms, verbs; published by The College Board and Educational Testing Service.

[761]
★**DTLS Vocabulary Test.** Beginning students in two- and four-year institutions; 1977; measures vocabulary skills; published by The College Board and Educational Testing Service.

[762]
★**DTMS Arithmetic Skills Test.** Beginning students in two- and four-year institutions; 1978; measures arithmetic skills in the following areas: operations with whole numbers, operations with fractions, operations with decimals and percents, applications involving computations; published by The College Board and Educational Testing Service.

[763]
★**DTMS Elementary Algebra Test.** Beginning students in two- and four-year institutions; 1978; measures algebra skills in the following areas: operations with real numbers, operations with algebraic expressions, solutions of equations and inequalities and word problems; published by The College Board and Educational Testing Service.

[764]
★**DTMS Functions and Graphs Test.** Beginning students in two- and four-year institutions; 1978; measures functions and graphs skills in the following areas: algebraic functions, exponential and logarithmic functions, trigonometric functions; published by The College Board and Educational Testing Service.

[765]
★**DTMS Intermediate Algebra Test.** Beginning students in two- and four-year institutions; 1978; measures algebra skills in the following areas: algebraic operations, solution of equations and inequalities, coordinate plane and graphs; published by The College Board and Educational Testing Service.

[766]
Durrell Analysis of Reading Difficulty, Third Edition. Grades 1–6; 1937–80; earlier edition still available; 16 to 21 scores: oral reading, silent reading, listening comprehension, word recognition, word analysis, listening vocabulary, sounds in isolation (letters, blends and diagraphs, phonograms, initial affixes, final affixes), spelling, phonic spelling of words, visual memory of words (primary, secondary), identifying sounds in words, prereading phonics abilities inventories (optional, including syntax matching, letter names in spoken words, phonemes in spoken words, naming lower case letters, writing letters from dictation); Donald D. Durrell and Jane H. Catterson; The Psychological Corporation.

See T2:1628 (18 references); for reviews by James Maxwell and George D. Spache of an earlier edition, see 5:660; for a review by Helen M. Robinson of the original edition, see 4:561 (2 references); for reviews by Guy L. Bond and Miles A. Tinker, see 2:1533; for a review by Marion Monroe, see 1:1098.

REFERENCES
1–2. See 4:561.
3–20. See T2:1628.
21. ALLINGTON, R. L., CHODOS, L., DOMARACKI, J., & TRUEX, S. Passage dependency: Four diagnostic oral reading tests. *Reading Teacher,* 1977, 30, 369–375.
22. CASSIDY, A. M., & VUKELICH, C. The effects of group size on kindergarten children's listening comprehension performance. *Psychology in the Schools,* 1977, 14, 449–455.
23. WONG, B., WONG, R., & FOTH, D. Recall and clustering of verbal materials among normal and poor readers. *Bulletin of the Psychonomic Society,* 1977, 10, 375–378.

24. MURRAY, M. E. The relationship between personality adjustment and success in remedial programs in dyslexic children. *Contemporary Educational Psychology*, 1978, 34, 330–339.
25. WONG, B. The effects of directive cues on the organization of memory and recall in good and poor readers. *Journal of Educational Research*, 1978, 72, 32–38.
26. KIRCHMEIMER, J. Auditory and visual factors related to spelling success. *Psychology in the Schools*, 1979, 16, 491–494.
27. LOVETT, M. W. The selective encoding of sentential information in normal reading development. *Child Development*, 1979, 50, 897–900.
28. MUIA, J. A., & CONNORS, E. T. Clinical reading practices: Some legal considerations. *National Reading Conference Yearbook*, 1979, 145–149.
29. TOBEY, E. A., CULLEN, J. K., JR., RAMPP, D. L., & FLEISCHER-GALLAGHER, A. M. Effects of stimulus–onset asynchrony on the dichotic performance of children with auditory–processing disorders. *Journal of Speech & Hearing Research*, 1979, 22, 197–211.
30. CLARKE, W. M., & HOOPS, H. R. Predictive measures of speech proficiency in cerebral palsied speakers. *Journal of Communication Disorders*, 1980, 13, 385–394.
31. FULLER, G. B., & LOVINGER, S. L. Personality characteristics of three subgroups of children with reading disabilities. *Perceptual & Motor Skills*, 1980, 50, 303–308.
32. HARBER, J. R. Are auditory perceptual skills requisite for reading success? *Reading World*, 1980, 19, 272–279.
33. MATHEWS, R. C., COON, R. C., & ROSENTHAL, G. T. Broken text as a predictor of reading ability in the early grades. *Reading World*, 1980, 20, 57–64.
34. CUNNINGHAM, M. D., & MURPHY, P. J. The effects of bilateral EEG biofeedback on verbal, visual–spatial, and creative skills in learning disabled male adolescents. *Journal of Learning Disabilities*, 1981, 14, 204–208.

[767]

Dvorine Pseudo-Isochromatic Plates. Ages 3 and over; 1944–58; also called *Dvorine Color Vision Test*; Israel Dvorine; The Psychological Corporation.*

See T2:1911 (13 references) and 6:955 (12 references); for excerpted reviews by Elsie Murray, Laurance F. Shaffer, and Miles A. Tinker, see 5:773 (13 references); for excerpted reviews by Knight Dunlap, Carel C. Koch, Elsie Murray (reply by Israel Dvorine), and Miles A. Tinker, see 3:462 (4 references).

REFERENCES

1–4. See 3:462.
5–17. See 5:773.
18–29. See 6:955.
30–42. See T2:1911.
43. HOYENGA, K. B., & WALLACE, B. Sex differences in the perception of autokinetic movement of an afterimage. *Journal of General Psychology*, 1979, 100, 93–101.

[768]

★**Dyadic Parent-Child Interaction Coding System: A Manual.** Children ages 2–10 and their parents; 1981; DPICS; behavioral rating by clinician in 3 standard situations; Sheila M. Eyberg and Elizabeth A. Robinson; Sheila M. Eyberg.*

REFERENCES

1. ROBINSON, E. A., & EYBERG, S. M. The Dyadic Parent-Child Interaction Coding System: Standardization and validation. *Journal of Consulting & Clinical Psychology*, 1981, 49, 245–250.

[769]

Dynamic Personality Inventory. Ages 15 or 17 and over with IQs of 80 and over; 1956–76; DPI; 33 scores: hypocrisy, passivity, seclusion-introspection, orality, oral aggression, emotional dependence, emotional independence, verbal aggression, impulsiveness, unconventionality, hoarding, attention to details, conservatism, submissiveness, insistence on law and order, insularity, phallic symbol interest, narcissism, exhibitionism, drive for achievement, agoraphilia, sensuality, exploration and adventure, sexuality, tactile impression enjoyment, creative interest, masculine interests, feminine interests, social role seeking, social activity interest, need to give affection, ego defense persistence, initiative; also available, in abbreviated form and without scores for orality, phallic symbol interest and sexuality, under the title *Likes and Interest Test* for use with apprentices and employee applicants ages 15 and over; Tadeusz G. Grygier and Patricia Grygier (1976 manual). (Canadian distributor: Institute of Psychological Research, Inc. [Canada].)*

For additional information and a review by Stephen Sharp, see 8:539 (12 references); see also T2:1162 (4 references), 7:70 (9 references) and P:65 (6 references); for a review by S. B. Sells, see 6:86 (7 references).

REFERENCES

1–7. See 6:86.
8–13. See P:65.
14–22. See 7:70.
23–26. See T2:1162.
27–38. See 8:539.
39. CROWN, S., LUCAS, C. J., STRINGER, P., & SUPRAMANIUM, S. Personality correlates of study difficulty and academic performance in university students. II. Conscience and self-esteem. *British Journal of Medical Psychology*, 1977, 50, 275–281.
40. HAMPSON, S. E., & KLINE, P. Personality dimensions differentiating certain groups of abnormal offenders from non–offenders. *British Journal of Criminology*, 1977, 17, 310–331.
41. KLINE, P., & STOREY, R. A factor analytic study of the oral character. *British Journal of Social & Clinical Psychology*, 1977, 16, 317–328.
42. STRINGER, P., CROWN, S., LUCAS, C. J., & SUPRAMANIUM, S. Personality correlates of study difficulty and academic performance in university students. I. The Middlesex Hospital Questionnaire and Dynamic Personality Inventory. *British Journal of Medical Psychology*, 1977, 50, 267–274.
43. HARRIS, W. J., DRUMMOND, R. J., SCHULTZ, E. W., & KING, D. R. The factor structure of three teacher rating scales and a self-report inventory of children's source traits. *Journal of Learning Disabilities*, 1978, 11, 583–585.
44. KLINE, P., & MOHAN, J. Oral personality traits among female students in North India: A cross–cultural study. *Psychological Studies*, 1978, 23, 1–4.
45. KLINE, P., & STOREY, R. The Dynamic Personality Inventory: What does it measure? *British Journal of Psychology*, 1978, 69, 375–383.
46. GRYGIER, T. Deficiencies of the Dynamic Personality Inventory– and the limitations of factor analysis. *British Journal of Medical Psychology*, 1979, 52, 259–262.

[770]

Dyslexia Schedule. Children having reading difficulties and first grade entrants; 1968–69; an 89-item questionnaire to be completed by parents; score based on 23 discriminating items, 21 of which are published separately under the title *School Entrance Check List* (SECL) for screening use; John McLeod; Educators Publishing Service, Inc.*

For additional information and a review by Martin Kling, see 7:729 (3 references).

REFERENCES

1–3. See 7:729.
4. BELL, A. E., ABRAHAMSON, D. S., & McRAE, K. N. Reading retardation: A 12-year prospective study. *Journal of Pediatrics*, 1977, 91, 363–370.

[771]

★**Early Childhood Environment Rating Scale.** Early childhood settings; 1980; provides rating scales for the assessment of various environmental characteristics of early childhood facilities; 7 areas: personal care routines of children, furnishings and display for children, language-reasoning experiences, fine and gross motor activities, creative activities, social development, adult needs; Thelma Harms and Richard M. Clifford; Teachers College Press.*

[772]

Early School Personality Questionnaire. Ages 6–8; 1966–76, c1963–76; ESPQ; 13 first-order factor scores (reserved vs. warmhearted, dull vs. bright, affected by feelings vs. emotionally stable, undemonstrative vs. excitable, obedient vs. dominant, sober vs. enthusiastic, disregards rules vs. conscientious, shy vs. venturesome, tough-minded vs. tender-minded, vigorous vs. circumspect individualism, forthright vs. shrewd, self-assured vs. guilt-prone, relaxed vs. tense), 4 second-order factor scores (extraversion, anxiety, tough poise, independence); Richard W. Coan and Raymond B. Cattell; Institute for Personality and Ability Testing, Inc.*

For additional information and reviews by Jacob O. Sines and Robert L. Thorndike, see 8:540 (8 references); see also T2:1163 (3 references); for a review by Lovick C. Miller, see 7:71 (8 references); see also P:66 (7 references).

REFERENCES

1–7. See P:66.
8–15. See 7:71.
16–18. See T2:1163.
19–26. See 8:540.
27. HARRIS, W. J., KING, D. R., & DRUMMOND, R. J. Personality variables of children nominated as emotionally handicapped by classroom teachers. *Psychology in the Schools*, 1978, 15, 361–363.
28. SHADE, B. J. Regional differences in personality of Afro-American children. *Journal of Social Psychology*, 1979, 107, 71–76.
29. BOLTON, B. Comments on "Comments on the reliability of a personality questionnaire used in physical education and sport research". *Psychological Reports*, 1980, 46, 1133–1134.
30. MINDINGALL, A., LIBB, J. W., & WELCH, M. Locus of control and personality functioning of learning disabled children. *Journal of Clinical Psychology*, 1980, 36, 137–141.

[773]

***Eckstein Audiometers.** Grades kgn and over; 1959–72; 5 models (solid state); Eckstein Bros., Inc.*

a) PORTABLE AUDIOMETERS. 1961–72.
  1) *EB Tetra-Tone Audiometer.* 1968–69; for screening in schools and medical offices; Model 46.
  2) *EB Miniature Audiometer.* 1961; for air conduction screening and threshold testing in schools and medical offices; Model 60.
  3) *EB Audiometer Model 350-I.* 1965–72; air conduction threshold testing in industry.
  4) *EB Full Range Portable Audiometers.* 1970–72; 2 models (may be AC operated).
    (*a*) Model 390. For pure tone air conduction testing.
    (*b*) Model 390MB. Diagnostic model for pure tone air and bone conduction testing.

For reference to earlier models, see T2:2034; see also 6:945.

[774]

[Economics/Objective Tests]. 1 semester high school; 1970; 5 tests; no manual; Perfection Form Co.* (In-print status uncertain; no reply from publisher.)

a) CONCEPTS IN ECONOMICS.
b) PRICE, INCOME AND PERSONAL GROWTH.
c) MONEY, BANKING AND INSURANCE.
d) INTERNATIONAL TRADE.
e) FINAL TEST.

[775]

***Edinburgh Reading Tests.** Ages 7–0 to 9–0, 8–6 to 10–6, 10–0 to 12–6, 12–0 to 16–0; 1972–81; upward and downward extensions plus second editions for stages 2 and 3 of *Edinburgh Reading Tests*; Hodder & Stoughton Educational [England].*

a) STAGE 1. Ages 7–0 to 9–0; 1977; 5 scores: vocabulary, syntax, sequences, comprehension, total; test by The Godfrey Thomson Unit, University of Edinburgh, in association with The Scottish Education Department and The Educational Institute of Scotland; manual by D. J. Carroll.

b) STAGE 2. Ages 8–6 to 10–6; 1972–80; 7 scores: vocabulary, comprehension of sequences, retention of significant details, use of content, reading rate, comprehension of essential ideas, total; test by The Godfrey Thomson Unit, University of Edinburgh, in association with The Scottish Education Department and The Educational Institute of Scotland; manual by M. J. Hutchings and E. M. J. Hutchings.

c) STAGE 3. Ages 10–0 to 12–6; 1973–81; 6 scores: reading for facts, comprehension of sequences, retention of main ideas, comprehension of points of view, vocabulary, total; test by Moray House College of Education, in association with The Scottish Education Department and The Educational Institute of Scotland; manual by J. F. McBride and P. C. McNaught.

d) STAGE 4. Ages 12–0 to 16–0; 1977; 6 scores: skimming, vocabulary, reading for facts, points of view, comprehension, total; test by The Godfrey Thomson Unit, University of Edinburgh, in association with The Scottish Education Department and The Educational Institute of Scotland; manual by D. J. Carroll.

For reviews by Douglas A. Pidgeon and Earl F. Rankin of the first editions of Stages 2 and 3, see 8:724.

REFERENCES

1. YOUNGMAN, M. B. Six reactions to school transfer. *British Journal of Educational Psychology*, 1978, 48, 280–289.
2. TURNBULL, H., & DAVIDSON, G. A regional survey of attainment in reading and mathematics. *British Journal of Educational Psychology*, 1980, 50, 91.

[776]

Education Apperception Test. Preschool and elementary school; 1973; EAT; 18 photographs attempting to evoke phantasy in 4 areas: reaction toward authority, reaction toward learning, peer relationship, home attitude toward school; no scores; Jack M. Thompson and Robert A. Sones; Western Psychological Services.*

For additional information, a review by Lovick C. Miller, and an excerpted review by Alan Krichev, see 8:541 (1 reference); see also T2:1458 (1 reference).

[777]

Educational Goal Attainment Tests. Grades 7–12; 1975; EGAT; for measurement of groups, not individuals; 88 scores (including 46 subscores): 44 knowledge, 26 attitude, 18 behavior; 10 tests (each student takes only one test); (Spanish edition available except *d*); test by Bruce W. Tuckman and Alberto P. S. Montare; Phi Delta Kappa, Inc.*

a) ARTS AND LEISURE. 10 scores: 4 knowledge, 4 attitude, 2 behavior.
b) CAREERS. 10 scores: 6 knowledge, 2 attitude, 2 behavior.
c) CIVICS. 12 scores: 6 knowledge, 3 attitude, 3 behavior.
d) ENGLISH LANGUAGE. 4 scores.
e) GENERAL KNOWLEDGE. 6 scores.
f) HUMAN RELATIONS. 11 scores: 4 knowledge, 5 attitude, 2 behavior.

g) LATIN AMERICA. 6 scores: 3 knowledge, 3 Spanish language.
h) LIFE SKILLS. 12 scores: 5 knowledge, 2 attitude, 5 behavior.
i) REASONING. 3 scores.
j) SELF TEST. 14 scores: 10 attitude, 4 behavior.
For additional information, see 8:16.

REFERENCES

1. TUCKMAN, B. W., & MONTARE, A. P. S. The many uses of PDK's goal attainment tests. *Phi Delta Kappan*, 1977, 58, 610–613.

[778]

Educational Interest Inventory, Revised Edition. High school and college; 1962–77; EII; 22 scores: literature, music, art, communications, education, business administration, engineering, industrial arts, agriculture, nursing, library arts, home economics, botany, zoology, physics, chemistry, earth science, history and political science, sociology, psychology, economics, mathematics; James E. Oliver; Educational Guidance, Inc.

For additional information and reviews by Fred H. Borgen and Thomas T. Frantz, see 8:1002 (1 reference); see also T2:2178 (1 reference) and 7:1017 (6 references).

[779]

Educational Values Assessment Questionnaire. Adults; 1973; EVAQ; for research use only; rating scale "on the beliefs people have about what is important educationally for the child of elementary or junior high school age"; 8 scores: community involvement, strictness/standards, professional specialists, innovation, health-recreation-practical training, economic considerations, parent education, special handling of difficult children; Harry Gottesfeld; Human Sciences Press.* (In-print status uncertain; no reply from publisher.)

For additional information and a review by Warren G. Findley, see 8:369.

[780]

Edwards Personal Preference Schedule. College and adults; 1953–59; EPPS; 15 scores: achievement, deference, order, exhibition, autonomy, affiliation, intraception, succorance, dominance, abasement, nurturance, change, endurance, heterosexuality, aggression; Allen L. Edwards; The Psychological Corporation.*

For additional information, see 8:542 (334 references); see also T2:1164 (226 references); for reviews by Alfred B. Heilbrun, Jr. and Michael G. McKee, see 7:72 (391 references); see also P:67 (363 references); for reviews by John A. Radcliffe and Lawrence J. Stricker and an excerpted review by Edward S. Bordin, see 6:87 (284 references); for reviews by Frank Barron, Åke Bjerstedt, and Donald W. Fiske and excerpted reviews by John W. Gustad and Laurance F. Shaffer, see 5:47 (50 references).

REFERENCES

1–50. See 5:47.
51–326. See 6:87.
327–689. See P:67.
690–1080. See 7:72.
1081–1306. See T2:1164.
1307–1640. See 8:542.
1641. DUCKRO, R. DUCKRO, P., & BEAL, D. Relationship of self-disclosure and mental health in black females. *Journal of Consulting & Clinical Psychology*, 1976, 44, 940–944.
1642. ABRAMSON, P. R., MOSHER, D. L., ABRAMSON, L. M., & WOYCHOWSKI, B. Personality correlates of the Mosher Guilt Scales. *Journal of Personality Assessment*, 1977, 41, 375–382.
1643. ADAMS, A. J., & STONE, T. H. Satisfaction of need for achievement in work and leisure time activities. *Journal of Vocational Behavior*, 1977, 11, 174–181.
1644. ANCOLI, S., & GREEN, K. F. Authoritarianism, introspection, and alpha wave biofeedback training. *Psychophysiology*, 1977, 14, 40–43.
1645. BELL, E. C., & BLAKENEY, R. N. Personality correlates of conflict resolution modes. *Human Relations*, 1977, 30, 849–857.
1646. HAMMER, M., & ROSS, M. B. Psychological needs of imprisoned adult females with high and low conscience development. *Corrective & Social Psychiatry & Journal of Behavior Technology, Methods & Therapy*, 1977, 23, 73–78.
1647. HOFFMAN, H., & BONYNGE, E. R. Personalities of female alcoholics who became counselors. *Psychological Reports*, 1977, 41, 37–38.
1648. JOHNSGARD, K. Personality and performance: A psychological study of amateur sports car race drivers. *Journal of Sports Medicine & Physical Fitness*, 1977, 17, 97–104.
1649. KISH, G. B., WOODY, M. M., & FRANKEL, A. The development of a scale to measure task completion motivation. *Journal of Clinical Psychology*, 1977, 33, 128–133.
1650. LORR, M., O'CONNOR, J. P., & SEIFERT, R. F. A comparison of four personality inventories. *Journal of Personality Assessment*, 1977, 41, 520–526.
1651. MELIKIAN, L. H., & DE KARAPETIAN, A. Personality change over time: Assimilation of an ethnic minority in Lebanon. *Journal of Social Psychology*, 1977, 103, 185–191.
1652. NAVRAN, L. The common import component scoring of the Edwards Personal Preference Schedule. *Journal of Personality Assessment*, 1977, 41, 285–290.
1653. PANDEY, J., & GRIFFITT, W. Benefactors' sex and nurturance need, recipient's dependency, and the effect of number of potential helpers on helping behavior. *Journal of Personality*, 1977, 45, 79–99.
1654. PARDINE, P., & NAPOLI, A. Personality correlates of successful biofeedback training. *Perceptual & Motor Skills*, 1977, 45, 1099–1103.
1655. PATRICK, A. W., & ZUCKERMAN, M. An application of the state-trait concept to the need for achievement. *Journal of Research in Personality*, 1977, 11, 459–465.
1656. PHILLIPS, E. L., GERSHENSON, J., & LYONS, G. On time-limited writing therapy. *Psychological Reports*, 1977, 41, 707–712.
1657. PILLAY, M., & CRISP, A. H. Some psychological characteristics of patients with anorexia nervosa whose weight has been newly restored. *British Journal of Medical Psychology*, 1977, 50, 375–380.
1658. PLAX, T. G., & ROSENFELD, L. B. Antecedents of change in attitudes of males and females. *Psychological Reports*, 1977, 41, 811–821.
1659. RAMANAIAH, N. V. Stylistic components of human judgment: The generality of individual differences. *Applied Psychological Measurement*, 1977, 1, 23–29.
1660. ROSENFELD, L. B., & PLAX, T. G. Clothing as communication. *Journal of Communication*, 1977, 27, 24–31.
1661. THORSON, J. A. Variations in death anxiety related to college students' sex, major field of study, and certain personality traits. *Psychological Reports*, 1977, 40, 857–858.
1662. VAITENAS, R., & WIENER, Y. Developmental, emotional, and interest factors in voluntary mid-career change. *Journal of Vocational Behavior*, 1977, 11, 291–304.
1663. WIENER, Y., & VAITENAS, R. Personality correlates of voluntary mid career change in enterprising occupations. *Journal of Applied Psychology*, 1977, 62, 706–712.
1664. YAMAUCHI, H., & DOI, K. Factorial study of achievement-related motives. *Psychological Reports*, 1977, 41, 796–801.
1665. BACA, H. R. Personality differences among business students. *College Student Journal*, 1978, 12, 274–281.
1666. BARKER, E. T., MCLAUGHLIN, A. J., & BARNETT, W. H. Do-it-yourself human relations training: An evaluative study with one year follow-up. *School Guidance Worker*, 1978, 33, 24–28.
1667. BURNS, B. J., LAPINE, L., & ANDREWS, P. M. Personality profile of pediatric nurse practitioners associated with role change. *Nursing Research*, 1978, 27, 286–290.
1668. GOLDBERG, L. R. The reliability of reliability: The generality and correlates of intra-individual consistency in responses to structured personality inventories. *Applied Psychological Measurement*, 1978, 2, 269–291.
1669. HAZZARD, M. E., & O'FARRELL, E. Personality testing for better staffing in mental health facilities. *Journal of Psychiatric Nursing*, 1978, 16, 41–51.
1670. LEARD, H. M., & HUM, A. The personality characteristics of counsellors-in-training which correlate with ratings of effectiveness and grades. *Canadian Counsellor*, 1978, 13, 28–32.
1671. MCCLAIN, E. Feminists and nonfeminists: Contrasting profiles in independence and affiliation. *Psychological Reports*, 1978, 43, 435–441.
1672. MCCLAIN, E. W. Personality difference between intrinsically religious and nonreligious students: A factor analytic study. *Journal of Personality Assessment*, 1978, 42, 159–166.
1673. PATRICK, O. L. Ethnic students' perceptions of effective teachers. *Educational Research Quarterly*, 1978, 3, 67–73.

1674. RABEN, C. S., SNYDER, R. A., HOFFMAN, R. G., & FARR, J. L. An examination of the construct validity and reliability of the Ghiselli Self-Description Inventory as a measure of self-esteem. *Applied Psychological Measurement*, 1978, 2, 73-81.

1675. ROESSLER, R., LESTER, J. W., BUTLER, W. T., RANKIN, B., & COLLINS, F. Cognitive and noncognitive variables in the prediction of preclinical performance. *Journal of Medical Education*, 1978, 53, 678-680.

1676. ROODIN, P., BROUGHTON, A., & VAUGHT, G. M. Birth order of volunteers for group and individual psychological experiments: A negative note. *Psychological Reports*, 1978, 42, 575-580.

1677. SPOLTER, B. M., TOKAR, J. T., & GOCKA, E. F. Dependency and alcohol recidivism. *Psychological Reports*, 1978, 43, 538.

1678. STUART, I. R., MURGATROYD, D., & DENMARK, F. L. Perceptual style, locus of control and personality variables among East Indians and Blacks in Trinidad. *International Journal of Social Psychiatry*, 1978, 24, 26-32.

1679. SULLIVAN, J. A. Comparison of manifest needs of nurses and physicians in primary care practice. *Nursing Research*, 1978, 27, 255-259.

1680. ULLAGADDI, S., KELLER, J., & DHARANENDRAIAH, A. S. An adaptation of Edwards Personal Preference Schedule. *Psychological Studies*, 1978, 23, 75-82.

1681. WOODMANSEE, J. J. Validation of the nurturance scale of the Edwards Personal Preference Schedule. *Psychological Reports*, 1978, 42, 495-498.

1682. BARNES, G. E. The alcoholic personality: A reanalysis of the literature. *Journal of Studies on Alcohol*, 1979, 40, 571-634.

1683. BELCASTRO, F. P. Personality and interest characteristics of completers and noncompleters of a secondary teacher program. *College Student Journal*, 1979, 13, 73-76.

1684. BOCK, D. G., & MUNRO, M. E. The effects of organization, need for order, sex of the source, and sex of the rater on the organization trait error. *Southern Speech Communication Journal*, 1979, 44, 364-372.

1685. FALBO, T., & KIRKLAND, C. L. Relationships between father's age, birth order, family size, and need achievement. *Bulletin of the Psychonomic Society*, 1979, 13, 179-182.

1686. FINCHUM, K. G., & FREITAG, C. B. Achievement, aggression, and perceived adult age stages. *Journal of Psychology*, 1979, 102, 179-184.

1687. KNOPKE, H. J. Predicting student attrition in a baccalaureate curriculum. *Nursing Research*, 1979, 28, 224-227.

1688. LEMIRE, D. One investigation of the stereotypes associated with fraternities and sororities. *Journal of College Student Personnel*, 1979, 20, 54-57.

1689. NORMAN, R. D. Test profile similarity of identical twins: An unusual case and some controls. *Journal of Psychology*, 1979, 103, 7-13.

1690. PASEWARK, R. A., & SAWYER, R. N. Edwards Personal Preference Schedule scores of rural high school students. *Educational & Psychological Measurement*, 1979, 39, 81-84.

1691. PLAX, T. G., & ROSENFELD, L. B. Receiver differences and the comprehension of spoken messages. *Journal of Experimental Education*, 1979, 48, 23-28.

1692. PUTNAM, L. L. Preference for procedural order in task-oriented small groups. *Communication Monographs*, 1979, 46, 193-218.

1693. SCISSONS, E. H. Profiles of ability: Characteristics of Canadian engineers. *Engineering Education*, 1979, 69, 822-836.

1694. STIMPSON, D. V., & STIMPSON, M. F. Relation of personality characteristics and color preferences. *Perceptual & Motor Skills*, 1979, 49, 60-62.

1695. DOYLE, S. X., & SHAPIRO, B. P. What counts most in motivating your sales force? *Harvard Business Review*, 1980, 58, 133-140.

1696. EIDELSON, R. J. Interpersonal satisfaction and level of involvement: A curvilinear relationship. *Journal of Personality & Social Psychology*, 1980, 39, 460-470.

1697. ERDWINS, C. J., TYER, Z. E., & MELLINGER, J. C. Personality traits of mature women in student versus homemaker roles. *Journal of Psychology*, 1980, 105, 189-195.

1698. HARMON, M. H. The Barron Ego Strength Scale: A study of personality correlates among normals. *Journal of Clinical Psychology*, 1980, 36, 433-436.

1699. HORNBOSTEL, L. K., & McCALL, J. N. Sibling differences in need-achievement associated with birth order, child-spacing, sex, and sibling's sex. *Journal of Individual Psychology*, 1980, 36, 36-43.

1700. KAHN, A. M. Modifications in nursing student attitudes as measured by the EPPS: A significant reversal from the past. *Nursing Research*, 1980, 29, 61-63.

1701. KIDD, A. H., & KIDD, R. M. Personality characteristics and preferences in pet ownership. *Psychological Reports*, 1980, 46, 939-949.

1702. KOEHLER, G. Personality needs of German wives and satisfaction with life in the Philippines. *Psychologia*, 1980, 23, 78-86.

1703. LESTER, D., BABCOCK, S. D., CASSISI, J. P., GENZ, J. L., & BUTLER, A. J. P. The personalities of English and American police. *Journal of Social Psychology*, 1980, 111, 153-154.

1704. PINO, C. J. Interpersonal needs, counselor style, and personality change among seminarians during the 1970's. *Review of Religious Research*, 1980, 21, 351-367.

1705. PLAX, T. G., & ROSENFELD, L. B. Individual differences in the credibility and attitude change relationship. *Journal of Social Psychology*, 1980, 111, 79-89.

1706. RIDLEY, S. E., & BAYTON, J. E. Personality needs, social status, and preferences for an "ideal woman" in black and white college males. *Journal of Negro Education*, 1980, 49, 165-172.

1707. ASSOR, A., ARONOFF, J., & MESSÉ, L. Attribute relevance as a moderator of the effects of motivation on impression formation. *Journal of Personality & Social Psychology*, 1981, 41, 789-796.

1708. IRWIN, H. J. The psychological function of out-of-body experiences: So who needs the out-of-body experience? *Journal of Nervous & Mental Disease*, 1981, 169, 244-248.

1709. KAHN, M. W., & STEPHEN, L. S. Counselor training as a treatment method for alcohol and drug abuse. *International Journal of the Addictions*, 1981, 16, 1415-1424.

1710. URSANO, R. J. The Viet Nam era prisoner of war: Preceptivity personality and the development of psychiatric illness. *American Journal of Psychiatry*, 1981, 138, 315-318.

[781]

Effective Study Test. Grades 8-12, 11-13; 1964-72; EST; 6 scores: reality orientation, study organization, writing behavior, reading behavior, examination behavior, total; (Spanish edition available); William F. Brown; Effective Study Materials.*

For additional information and a review by A. Garr Cranney, see 8:816 (2 references).

REFERENCES

1-2. See 8:816.

3. KIRKLAND, K., & HOLLANDSWORTH, J. G., JR. Test anxiety, study skills, and academic performance. *Journal of College Student Personnel*, 1979, 20, 431-436.

4. KIRKLAND, K., & HOLLANDSWORTH, J. G., JR. Effective test taking: Skills-acquisition versus anxiety-reduction techniques. *Journal of Consulting & Clinical Psychology*, 1980, 48, 431-439.

[782]

Effectiveness Motivation Scale. Ages 3-5; 1976; manual title is *Stott-Sharp Effectiveness Motivation Scale*; ratings by teachers; 3 scores: E (strength of effectiveness motivation), W (withdrawal), Q (inconsequence); John D. Sharp, D. H. Stott, J. B. Albin (manual), and H. L. Williams (manual); NFER-Nelson Publishing Co. [England].*

For additional information, see 8:665.

[783]

The Ego-Ideal and Conscience Development Test. Ages 12-18; 1969; EICDT; 9 scores: home and family, inner development, community relations, rules and law, school and education, romance and psychosexual, economic sufficiency, self-actualization, total; R. N. Cassel; Monitor.*

For additional information and a review by George M. Guthrie, see 8:544; see also 7:74 (5 references).

[784]

Ego State Inventory. Adolescents and adults; 1974; ESI; 5 scores: punitive parent, nurturing parent, adult, rebellious child, adaptive child; David Gordon McCarley; Stoelting Co.*

For additional information and reviews by George M. Guthrie and Alfred B. Heilbrun, Jr., see 8:545 (1 reference).

[785]

The Ego Strength Q-Sort Test. Grades 9-16 and adults; 1956-58; ESQST; 6 scores: ego-status, social status, goal setting and striving, good mental health, physical status, total; Russell N. Cassel; Psychometric Affiliates.*

See T2:1167 (1 reference) and P:69; for reviews by Allen L. Edwards and Harrison G. Gough, see 6:88 (3 references).

[786]
Eidetic Parents Test. Clinical patients and marriage and family counselees; 1972; EPT; verbal reporting by patients of subjective visual images (eidetics) of parents in 30 increasingly surrealistic situations; no scores; Akhter Ahsen; Brandon House, Inc.*

For additional information, a review by Charles F. Warnath, and excerpted reviews by Gregory Sarmousakis, Barry Bricklin, and Manas Raychaudhuri, see 8:546 (8 references).

[787]
Eight State Questionnaire. Ages 16 and over; 1976, c1971–76; test booklet title is 8SQ; 8 scores: anxiety, stress, depression, regression, fatigue, guilt, extraversion, arousal; James P. Curran and Raymond B. Cattell; Institute for Personality and Ability Testing, Inc.*

For additional information and a review by Benjamin Kleinmuntz, see 8:547 (5 references).

REFERENCES

1–5. See 8:547.
6. GILLILAND, K. The interactive effect of introversion–extraversion with caffeine induced arousal on verbal performance. *Journal of Research in Personality*, 1980, 14, 482–492.

[788]
★**Ekwall Reading Inventory.** Grades kgn, 1, 2, 3, 4, 5, 6, 7, 8, 9; 1979; the *Quick Survey Word List* and the *El Paso Phonics Survey* are included to "determine if a student has the necessary skills to read material written at an adult level successfully"; Eldon E. Ekwall; Allyn and Bacon, Inc.* (In-print status uncertain; no reply from publisher.)

[789]
★**El Circo.** Ages 4–6; 1980; for use by teachers to assess Spanish-speaking children's comprehension of simple mathematical concepts and basic linguistic structures in both Spanish and English; Educational Testing Service; Addison-Wesley Publishing Co., Inc.*

a) LANGUAGE CHECK. To assess if a child's Spanish skills are sufficient to take the other measures in Spanish; item scores and mode of response scores (Spanish, English, mixture Spanish-English, nonverbal).
b) PRACTICE MATERIALS. Item scores.
c) WHAT WORDS ARE FOR. Item scores in 4 areas: verb tenses, prepositions, possessives, miscellaneous (negations, embedded sentences, active and passive voices, reflexives, indirect objectives).
d) CUANTO Y CUANTOS. Item scores in 3 areas: counting, relational terms, numerical concepts.
e) PARA QUE SIRVEN LAS PALABRAS. Item scores in 4 areas: verb tenses, prepositions, indirect objects, miscellaneous (plurals, adjectival agreement, reflexives, object pronouns, possessives).

[790]
Electrical Sophistication Test. Job applicants; 1963–65; Stanley G. Ciesla; Psychometric Affiliates.*

For additional information and a review by Charles F. Ward, see 7:1125.

[791]
Elementary Algebra: Minnesota High School Achievement Examinations. High school; 1951–70; a new, revised, or previously inactive form issued each May; Achievement Examinations for Secondary Schools, High School Achievement Examinations, and Midwest High School Achievement Examinations have also been used as series titles; edited by V. L. Lohmann; American Guidance Service.*

For additional information concerning out of print and inactive forms, see 7:504, 6:597, and 5:446; for a review by Lynnette B. Plumlee of Form A (1955), see 5:448.

[792]
★**Eliot-Price Perspective Test.** Grades 2 and over; 1974; for research use only; spatial visualization ability; John Eliot and Lewis Price; University of Maryland.* (In-print status uncertain; no reply from publisher.)

REFERENCES

1. ELIOT, J. Classification of figural spatial tests. *Perceptual & Motor Skills*, 1980, 51, 847–851.

[793]
Elizur Test of Psycho-Organicity: Children and Adults. Ages 6 and over, 10 and over; 1959–69; ETPO; brain injury; 3 scores: drawings, digits, blocks; Abraham Elizur; Western Psychological Services.*

For additional information, reviews by Joseph M. Wepman and Aubrey J. Yates, and an excerpted review by Muriel D. Lezak, see 7:75 (5 references).

REFERENCES

1–5. See 7:75.
6. JACKSON, R. E., & CULBERTSON, W. C. The Elizur Test of Psycho-Organicity and the Hooper Visual Organization Test as measures of childhood neurological impairment. *Journal of Clinical Psychology*, 1977, 33, 213–214.

[794]
Embedded Figures Test. Ages 10 and over; 1950–71; EFT; field dependence; colored versions of the original black-and-white figures by K. Gottschaldt; Herman A. Witkin and manual coauthors Philip K. Oltman, Evelyn Raskin, and Stephen A. Karp; Consulting Psychologists Press, Inc.*

For additional information, see 8:548 (134 references); see also T2:1169 (149 references) and P:71 (47 references); for reviews by Harrison G. Gough and Leona E. Tyler, see 6:89 (24 references); see also 5:49 (9 references).

REFERENCES

1–9. See 5:49.
10–33. See 6:89.
34–80. See P:71.
81–229. See T2:1169.
230–363. See 8:548.
364. BARRETT, G. V., MICHAL, W. L., PANEK, P. E., STERNS, H. L., & ALEXANDER, R. A. Information processing skills predictive of accident involvement for younger and older commercial drivers. *Industrial Gerontology*, 1977, 4, 173–182.
365. CHAPMAN, M. Father absence, stepfathers, and the cognitive performance of college students. *Child Development*, 1977, 48, 1155–1158.
366. COHLER, B. J., GRUNEBAUM, H. V., WEISS, J. L., GAMER, E., & GALLANT, D. H. Disturbance of attention among schizophrenic, depressed and well mothers and their young children. *Journal of Child Psychology & Psychiatry & Allied Disciplines*, 1977, 18, 115–135.
367. DAWSON, J. L. M. Alaskan eskimo's hand, eye, auditory dominance and cognitive style. *Psychologia*, 1977, 20, 121–135.
368. DERSHOWITZ, Z. Jewish culture and psychological differentiation—Partial replication. *Journal of Genetic Psychology*, 1977, 130, 137–144.

369. DUNCAN, J., & LAIRD, J. D. Cross-modality consistencies in individual differences in self-attribution. *Journal of Personality*, 1977, 45, 191-206.

370. EXNER, J. E., & MURRILLO, L. G. A long term follow-up of schizophrenics treated with regressive ECT. *Diseases of the Nervous System*, 1977, 38, 162-168.

371. FRANCO, E. A., & MAGARO, P. A. The relationship of A-B, field dependency, and emotional openness in paranoid and nonparanoid schizophrenics. *Journal of Clinical Psychology*, 1977, 33, 39-42.

372. GAMER, E., GALLANT, D., GRUNEBAUM, H. V., & COHLER, B. J. Children of psychotic mothers. *Archives of General Psychiatry*, 1977, 34, 592-597.

373. HOFFMAN, C., & KAGAN, S. Lateral eye movements and field dependence-independence. *Perceptual & Motor Skills*, 1977, 45, 767-778.

374. KAPUR, N., & BUTTERS, N. Visuoperceptive deficits in long-term alcoholics with Korsakoff's psychosis. *Journal of Studies on Alcohol*, 1977, 38, 2025-2035.

375. LUDWIG, A. M., & CAIN, R. B. The relationship of alcohol withdrawal experiences to impaired cognitive functioning. *Journal of Studies on Alcohol*, 1977, 38, 1795-1798.

376. MORRISON, F. J., YARBOROUGH, C., KLEIN, R. E., & LASKY, R. Cognitive style in rural preschool Guatemalan children: A serendipitous finding. *Journal of Genetic Psychology*, 1977, 130, 221-228.

377. OLTMAN, P. K., EHRLICHMAN, H., & COX, P. W. Field independence and laterality in the perception of faces. *Perceptual & Motor Skills*, 1977, 45, 255-260.

378. SIEGEL, H. B. Body boundary and field-dependence. *Perceptual & Motor Skills*, 1977, 45, 1097-1098.

379. SPELLACY, F. Neuropsychological differences between violent and nonviolent adolescents. *Journal of Clinical Psychology*, 1977, 33, 966-969.

380. SZETO, J. W., & SALOME, R. A. The effects of scanning practice and perceptual training upon several visual functions: Implications for drawing. *Studies in Art Education*, 1977, 19, 45-51.

381. TEMPLE, I. G., & WILLIAMS, H. G. Rate and level of learning as functions of information-processing characteristics of the learner and the task. *Journal of Motor Behavior*, 1977, 9, 179-192.

382. WECKOWICZ, T. E., COLLIER, G., & SPRENG, L. Field dependence, cognitive functions, personality traits, and social values in heavy cannabis users and nonuser controls. *Psychological Reports*, 1977, 41, 291-302.

383. WEINRAUB, M., & LEWIS, M. The determinants of children's responses to separation. *Monographs of the Society for Research in Child Development*, 1977, 42, 1-78.

384. WILD, C. M., & SHAPIRO, L. N. Mechanisms of change from individual to family performance in male schizophrenics and their parents. *Journal of Nervous & Mental Disease*, 1977, 165, 41-56.

385. ALLEN, M. J., & CHOLET, M. E. Strength of association between sex and field dependence. *Perceptual & Motor Skills*, 1978, 47, 419-421.

386. DOR-SHAV, N. K. On the long-range effects of concentration camp internment on Nazi victims: 25 years later. *Journal of Consulting & Clinical Psychology*, 1978, 46, 1-11.

387. GHUMAN, P. A. S. A comparative study of cognitive styles of three ethnic groups. *British Journal of Educational Psychology*, 1978, 48, 358.

388. GHUMAN, P. A. S. Nature of intellectual development of Punjabi children. *International Journal of Psychology*, 1978, 13, 281-294.

389. GRUNEBAUM, H., COHLER, B. J., KAUFFMAN, C., & GALLANT, D. Children of depressed and schizophrenic mothers. *Child Psychiatry & Human Development*, 1978, 8, 219-228.

390. HUGHES, R. N. Sex differences in field dependence: Effects of unlimited time on Group Embedded Figures Test performance. *Perceptual & Motor Skills*, 1978, 47, 1246.

391. HUGHES, R. N., HALL, C. J., & CHAMBERS, R. L. Field dependence and the Eysenck Personality Inventory: A replication. *Perceptual & Motor Skills*, 1978, 47, 1132.

392. JONES, E. E. Black-White personality differences: Another look. *Journal of Personality Assessment*, 1978, 42, 244-252.

393. KAGAN, J., LAPIDUS, D. R., & MOORE, M. Infant antecedents of cognitive functioning: A longitudinal study. *Child Development*, 1978, 49, 1005-1023.

394. KIRTON, M. Field dependence and adaption-innovation theories. *Perceptual & Motor Skills*, 1978, 47, 1239-1245.

395. KOHN, M. L., & SCHOOLER, C. The reciprocal effects of the substantive complexity of work and intellectual flexibility: A longitudinal assessment. *American Journal of Sociology*, 1978, 84, 24-52.

396. KOULAK, D., DE KONINCK, J., & OCZKOWSKI, G. Field dependence and the effect of REM deprivation on thirst. *Perceptual & Motor Skills*, 1978, 46, 559-562.

397. LATORRE, R. A. The unitary construct variously named overinclusion and cognitive style. *Journal of Psychology*, 1978, 99, 113-117.

398. LIBEN, L. S. Performance on Piagetian spatial tasks as a function of sex, field dependence, and training. *Merrill-Palmer Quarterly*, 1978, 24, 97-110.

399. LOO, R. Personality dimensions and reversible perspective in Embedded Figures Test. *Perceptual & Motor Skills*, 1978, 46, 1016-1018.

400. LUDWIG, A. M., BENDFELDT, F., WIKLER, A., & CAIN, R. B. "Loss of control" in alcoholics. *Archives of General Psychiatry*, 1978, 35, 370-373.

401. MACVANE, J. R., LANGE, J. D., BROWN, W. A., & ZAYAT, M. Psychological functioning of bipolar manic-depressives in remission. *Archives of General Psychiatry*, 1978, 35, 1351-1354.

402. MILLER, J., SCHOOLAR, C., KOHN, M. L., & MILLER, K. Women and work: The psychological effects of occupational conditions. *American Journal of Sociology*, 1978, 85, 66-94.

403. REHERMANN, O., & BRUN, B. Embedded Figures Test compared with clinical tests of abstraction and memory in intellectual impairment. *Scandinavian Journal of Psychology*, 1978, 19, 175-180.

404. ROBINSON, J. A., & BENNIK, C. D. Field articulation and working memory. *Journal of Research in Personality*, 1978, 12, 439-449.

405. SCHMIDT, J. P. The interactive effects of instructional set, field dependence, and extraversion on the Holtzman Inkblot Technique. *Journal of Clinical Psychology*, 1978, 34, 533-536.

406. SPELLACY, F. Neuropsychological discrimination between violent and non-violent men. *Journal of Clinical Psychology*, 1978, 34, 49-52.

407. SPELLACY, F., & PETER, B. Dyscalculia and elements of the developmental Gerstmann Syndrome in school children. *Cortex*, 1978, 14, 197-206.

408. WALSH, M. D. Effect of color on perception in the Embedded Figures Test. *Perceptual & Motor Skills*, 1978, 47, 1288.

409. WALSH, M. D. Factor analytic study of the Embedded Figures and Rod and Frame Tests. *Perceptual & Motor Skills*, 1978, 47, 531-537.

410. ZOCCOLOTTI, P., & OLTMAN, P. K. Field dependence and lateralization of verbal and configurational processing. *Cortex*, 1978, 14, 155-168.

411. BABAD, E. Y. Personality correlates of susceptibility to biasing information. *Journal of Personality & Social Psychology*, 1979, 37, 195-202.

412. BARNES, G. E. The alcoholic personality: A reanalysis of the literature. *Journal of Studies on Alcohol*, 1979, 40, 571-634.

413. BERGER, E., & GOLDBERGER, L. Field dependence and short-term memory. *Perceptual & Motor Skills*, 1979, 49, 87-96.

414. BERNSTEIN, B. L., & LECOMTE, C. Supervisory-type feedback effects: Feedback discrepancy level, trainee psychological differentiation, and immediate responses. *Journal of Counseling Psychology*, 1979, 26, 295-303.

415. DOEBLER, L. K., & EICKE, F. J. Effects of teacher awareness of the educational implications of field-dependent/field-independent cognitive style on selected classroom variables. *Journal of Educational Psychology*, 1979, 71, 226-232.

416. DORETHY, R., & REEVES, D. Mental functioning, perceptual differentiation, personality, and achievement among art and non-art majors. *Studies in Art Education*, 1979, 20, 52-63.

417. FEVERSTEIN, R., RAND, Y., HOFFMAN, M., HOFFMAN, M., & MILLER, R. Cognitive modifiability in retarded adolescents: Effects of instrumental enrichment. *American Journal of Mental Deficiency*, 1979, 83, 539-550.

418. GOLDMAN, B. L., DOMITOR, P. J., & MURRAY, E. J. Effects of Zen meditation on anxiety reduction and perceptual functioning. *Journal of Consulting & Clinical Psychology*, 1979, 47, 551-556.

419. GUNDLACH, R. H., & GESELL, G. P. Extent of psychological differentiation and creativity. *Perceptual & Motor Skills*, 1979, 48, 319-333.

420. HOPKINS, J., PERLMAN, T., HECHTMAN, L., & WEISS, G. Cognitive style in adults originally diagnosed as hyperactives. *Journal of Child Psychology & Psychiatry & Allied Disciplines*, 1979, 20, 209-216.

421. INABINETTE, N. The influence of cognitive style on reading. *Claremont Reading Conference Yearbook*, 1979, 183-192.

422. JOHNSON, S., FLINN, J. M., & TYER, Z. E. Effect of practice and training in spatial skills on embedded figures scores of males and females. *Perceptual & Motor Skills*, 1979, 48, 975-984.

423. LATORRE, R. A., & PIPER, W. E. Gender identity and gender role in schizophrenia. *Journal of Abnormal Psychology*, 1979, 88, 68-72.

424. McCANNE, T. R., & HATHAWAY, K. M. Autonomic and somatic responses associated with performance of the Embedded Figures Test. *Psychophysiology*, 1979, 16, 8-14.

425. NAHINSKY, I. D., MORGAN, M. S., & OESCHGER, D. E. Cognitive strategies, field dependence, and the abstraction process. *Journal of Research in Personality*, 1979, 13, 490-504.

426. NEDD, A. N. B., & MARSH, N. R. Social traditionalism and personality: An empirical investigation of the interrelationships between social values and personality attributes. *International Journal of Psychology*, 1979, 14, 73-82.

427. PATSIOKAS, A. T., CLUM, G. A., & LUSCOMB, R. L. Cognitive characteristics of suicide attempters. *Journal of Consulting & Clinical Psychology*, 1979, 47, 478-484.

428. SABATELLI, R. M., DREYER, A. S., & BUCK, R. Cognitive style and sending and receiving of facial cues. *Perceptual & Motor Skills*, 1979, 49, 203-212.

429. SHEVRIN, H., SMOKLER, I. A., & WOLF, E. Field independence, lateralization and defensive style. *Perceptual & Motor Skills*, 1979, 49, 195–202.

430. ZOCCOLOTTI, P., PASSAFIUME, D., & PIZZAMIGLIO, L. Hemispheric superiorities on a unilateral tactile test: Relationship to cognitive dimensions. *Perceptual & Motor Skills*, 1979, 49, 735–742.

431. BEITEL, P. A. Multivariate relationships among visual–perceptual attributes and gross–motor tasks with different environmental demands. *Journal of Motor Behavior*, 1980, 12, 29–40.

432. BLUMBERG, N. L. Effects of neonatal risk, maternal attitude, and cognitive style on early postpartum adjustment. *Journal of Abnormal Psychology*, 1980, 89, 139–150.

433. GUYOT, G. W., FAIRCHILD, L., & HILL, M. Physical fitness and Embedded Figures Test performance of elementary school children. *Perceptual & Motor Skills*, 1980, 50, 411–414.

434. LAOSA, L. M. Maternal teaching strategies and cognitive styles in Chicano families. *Journal of Educational Psychology*, 1980, 72, 45–54.

435. LAWRENCE, D. M., & MORTON, V. Associating Embedded Figures Test performance with extreme hysteria and psychasthenia MMPI scores in a psychiatric population. *Perceptual & Motor Skills*, 1980, 50, 432–434.

436. LEBOEUF, A. An experiment to test generalization of feedback from frontalis EMG. *Perceptual & Motor Skills*, 1980, 50, 27–31.

437. NEDD, A. N. B., & MARSH, N. R. A cross–cultural test of the personality integration hypothesis. *Journal of Personality*, 1980, 48, 293–305.

438. RUBINSTEIN, R. A. Field–dependence and Piagetian operational thought in northern Belize. *Child Study Journal*, 1980, 10, 67–76.

439. RUGGIERI, V., BERGERONE, C., CEI, A., & CERIDONO, D. Relationships between ocular dominance and field–dependence/independence. *Perceptual & Motor Skills*, 1980, 51, 1247–1251.

440. RUGGIERI, V., & MAZZA, P. Effects of muscle tone and changes in autonomic balance on cognitive style. *Psychological Reports*, 1980, 46, 916–918.

441. SARACHO, O. The relationship between the teachers' cognitive style and their perceptions of their students' academic achievements. *Educational Research Quarterly*, 1980, 5, 40–49.

442. WIENS, A. N., HARPER, R. G., & MATARAZZO, J. D. Personality correlates of nonverbal interview behavior. *Journal of Clinical Psychology*, 1980, 36, 205–215.

443. BEARDSWORTH, T., & BUCKNER, T. The ability to recognize oneself from a video recording of one's movements without seeing one's body. *Bulletin of the Psychonomic Society*, 1981, 18, 19–22.

444. BROVERMAN, D. M., VOGEL, W., KLAIBER, E. L., MAJCHER, D., SHEA, D., & PAUL, V. Changes in cognitive task performance across menstrual cycle. *Journal of Comparative & Physiological Psychology*, 1981, 95, 646–656.

445. CHATTERJEA, R. G., & PAUL, B. Field dependency, recognition capacity and extraversion. *Psychologia*, 1981, 24, 217–222.

446. DANAHY, S., & KAHN, M. W. Consistency of field dependence in treated alcoholics. *International Journal of the Addictions*, 1981, 16, 1271–1275.

447. RUGGIERI, V., CEI, A., BERGERONE, C., & GUERRERA, A. Cognitive style and perspective reversal. *Perceptual & Motor Skills*, 1981, 53, 745–746.

448. SAMPSEL, B. D., WIDAMAN, K. F., & WINER, G. A. Relation in children of psychological differentiation and reasoning by class inclusion. *Perceptual & Motor Skills*, 1981, 53, 439–446.

449. TOBACYK, J. Personality differentiation, effectiveness of personality integration, and mood in female college students. *Journal of Personality & Social Psychology*, 1981, 41, 348–356.

450. WENDER, P. H., REIMHERR, F. W., & WOOD, D. R. Attentional deficit disorder ("minimal brain dysfunction") in adults. *Archives of General Psychiatry*, 1981, 38, 449–456.

451. WILSON, S., SUDDICK, R. P., SHAY, J. S., & HUSTMYER, F. E., JR. Correlations of scores on embedded figures and mirror tracing with preclinical technique grades and PMAT scores of dental students. *Perceptual & Motor Skills*, 1981, 53, 31–35.

[795]

Emo Questionnaire. Adults; 1958–78; "designed to assess an individual's personal-emotional adjustment"; 10 diagnostic dimensions: rationalization, inferiority feelings, hostility, depression, fear and anxiety, organic reaction, projection, unreality, sex, withdrawal, plus buffer score; 4 second-order adjustment factors: internal, external, somatic, general; George O. Baehr and Melany E. Baehr (test); Human Resources Center, University of Chicago.

See T2:1170 (1 reference) and P:72; for reviews by Bertram D. Cohen and W. Grant Dahlstrom, see 6:90 (1 reference).

[796]

Emotions Profile Index. College and adults; 1974; EPI; 9 scores: timid, aggressive, trustful, distrustful, controlled, dyscontrolled, gregarious, depressed, bias; Robert Plutchik and Henry Kellerman; Western Psychological Services.*

For additional information and review by Douglas N. Jackson, see 8:549 (33 references).

REFERENCES

1–33. See 8:549.
34. KELLERMAN, H. Shostrom's mate selection model, the Pair Attraction Inventory, and the Emotions Profile Index. *Journal of Psychology*, 1977, 95, 37–43.
35. PLUTCHIK, R., & PLATMAN, S. R. Personality connotations of psychiatric diagnosis. Implications for a similarity model. *Journal of Nervous & Mental Disease*, 1977, 165, 418–422.

[797]

Empathy Inventory. Nursing instructors; 1966–70; EI; empathy for nursing school students; John R. Thurston, Helen L. Brunclik, and John F. Feldhusen (manual); Nursing Research Associates.* (In-print status uncertain; no reply from publisher.)

For additional information, see 7:1114 (2 references).

[798]

The Empathy Test. Ages 13 and over; 1947–61; ET; Willard A. Kerr and Boris J. Speroff; Psychometric Affiliates.*

See T2:1171 (10 references) and P:73 (1 reference); for a review by Wallace B. Hall, see 6:91 (9 references); for a review by Robert L. Thorndike, see 5:50 (20 references).

[799]

Employee Aptitude Survey. Ages 16 and over; 1952–63; EAS; 10 tests; G. Grimsley (*a–h*), F. L. Ruch (*a–g, i, j*), N. D. Warren (*a–g*), and J. S. Ford (*a, c, e–g, j*); Psychological Services, Inc.*

a) TEST 1, VERBAL COMPREHENSION. 1952–63.
b) TEST 2, NUMERICAL ABILITY. 1952–63.
c) TEST 3, VISUAL PURSUIT. 1956–63.
d) TEST 4, VISUAL SPEED AND ACCURACY. 1952–63.
e) TEST 5, SPACE VISUALIZATION. 1952–63.
f) TEST 6, NUMERICAL REASONING. 1952–63.
g) TEST 7, VERBAL REASONING. 1952–63.
h) TEST 8, WORD FLUENCY. 1953–63.
i) TEST 9, MANUAL SPEED AND ACCURACY. 1953–63.
j) TEST 10, SYMBOLIC REASONING. 1956–63.

See T2:1071 (14 references); for reviews by Paul F. Ross and Erwin K. Taylor, and an excerpted review by John O. Crites, see 6:769 (4 references); for reviews by Dorothy C. Adkins and S. Rains Wallace, see 5:607.

REFERENCES

1–4. See 6:769.
5–18. See T2:1071.
19. DENISI, A. S., & SHAW, J. B. Investigation of the uses of self-reports of abilities. *Journal of Applied Psychology*, 1977, 62, 641–644.
20. LUNNEBORG, C. E. Choice reaction time: What role in ability measurement? *Applied Psychological Measurement*, 1977, 1, 309–330.
21. ROSE, R. G. An examination of the responses to a multivalue logic test. *Journal of General Psychology*, 1980, 102, 275–281.

22. SCHUH, A. J. Verbal listening skill in the interview and personal characteristics of listeners. *Bulletin of the Psychonomic Society*, 1980, 15, 125–127.

[800]
Employee Performance Appraisal. Business and industry; 1962; 7 merit ratings by supervisors: quantity of work, quality of work, job knowledge, initiative, interpersonal relationships, dependability, potential; no manual; Martin M. Bruce; Martin M. Bruce, Ph.D., Publishers.*

For additional information and a review by Jean Maier Palormo, see 6:1116.

[801]
Employee Progress Appraisal Form. Rating of office employees; 1944; Albert N. Gillett; National Foremen's Institute, Inc.* (In-print status uncertain; no reply from publisher.)

[802]
[Employee Rating and Development Forms]. Executive, industrial, office, and sales personnel; 1950–65; Robert N. McMurry; Dartnell Corporation.*
a) [PATTERNED MERIT REVIEW FORMS.] 1950–64; 5 forms; no manual.
 1) *Patterned Merit Review—Executive.* 1955–59.
 2) *Patterned Merit Review Form—Plant and Office.* 1950–64.
 3) *Patterned Merit Review—Sales.* 1955–59.
 4) *Patterned Merit Review—Technical, Office, Special Skills.* 1956–64.
 5) *Statement of Supervisory Expectancies.* 1958–64.
b) PATTERNED EXIT INTERVIEW. 1953–65.
c) PERSONAL HISTORY REVIEW FORM. 1957; no manual.

For additional information and a review by Richard S. Barrett, see 6:1117; for reviews by Harry W. Karn and Floyd L. Ruch, see 4:781.

[803]
Emporia American History Test. 1, 2 semesters high school; 1962–64; first published 1962–63 in the Every Pupil Scholarship Test series; Shirley Meares and M. W. Sanders; Bureau of Educational Measurements.*

For additional information and a review by Howard R. Anderson, see 7:918.

[804]
Emporia Arithmetic Tests. Grades 1, 2–3, 4–6, 7–8; 1962–64; first published 1962–63 in the Every Pupil Scholarship Test series; 4 tests; M. W. Sanders, Ieleen Engelson (manual, *d*), Ruth Otterstrom (manual, *c*), and Patricia M. Pease (manual, *a*, *b*); Bureau of Educational Measurements.*
a) EMPORIA PRIMARY ARITHMETIC TEST. 1, 2 semesters in grade 1.
b) EMPORIA ELEMENTARY ARITHMETIC TEST. 1, 2 semesters in grades 2–3.
c) EMPORIA INTERMEDIATE ARITHMETIC TEST. 1, 2 semesters in grades 4–6.
d) EMPORIA JUNIOR HIGH SCHOOL ARITHMETIC TEST. 1, 2 semesters in grades 7–8.

For additional information and reviews by Marilyn N. Suydam and Blaine R. Worthen, see 7:519.

[805]
Emporia Biology Test. 1, 2 semesters high school; 1962–64; first published 1962–63 in the Every Pupil Scholarship Test series; Ted F. Andrews and M. W. Sanders; Bureau of Educational Measurements.*

For additional information, see 7:817.

[806]
Emporia Chemistry Test. 1, 2 semesters high school; 1962–64; first published 1962–63 in the Every Pupil Scholarship Test series; A. T. Ericson and M. W. Sanders; Bureau of Educational Measurements.*

For additional information and a review by Peter A. Dahl, see 8:851.

[807]
Emporia Clothing Test. High school; 1962–64; first published 1962–63 in the Every Pupil Scholarship Test series; Margaret C. Parkman, Patricia Duncan, and M. W. Sanders; Bureau of Educational Measurements.*

For additional information, see 7:620.

[808]
Emporia Elementary Health Test. 1, 2 semesters in grades 6–8; 1962–64; first published 1962–63 in the Every Pupil Scholarship Test series; Gary Adamson and M. W. Sanders; Bureau of Educational Measurements.*

For additional information and a review by James E. Bryan, see 7:602.

[809]
Emporia First Year Latin Test. 1 year high school; 1962–64; first published 1962–63 in the Every Pupil Scholarship Test series; Bernadine Sitts, Minnie M. Miller, Lillian A. Wall, and M. W. Sanders; Bureau of Educational Measurements.*

For additional information, see 7:306.

[810]
Emporia Foods Test. High school; 1962–64; first published 1962–63 in the Every Pupil Scholarship Test series; Margaret C. Parkman, Patricia Duncan, and M. W. Sanders; Bureau of Educational Measurements.*

For additional information, see 7:621.

[811]
Emporia General Science Test. 1, 2 semesters high school; 1962–64; first published 1962–63 in the Every Pupil Scholarship Test series; Donald Cross and M. W. Sanders; Bureau of Educational Measurements.*

For additional information and a review by Barbara F. Esser, see 7:791.

[812]
Emporia High School Health Test. High school and college; 1962–64; first published 1962–63 in the Every Pupil Scholarship Test series; Ron Blaylock and M. W. Sanders; Bureau of Educational Measurements.*

For additional information, see 7:603.

[813]
Emporia Industrial Arts Test. High school; 1962–64; first published 1962–63 in the Every Pupil Scholarship Test series; David E. Hill, Elton Amburn, and M.

[814] Emporia Physics Test

W. Sanders; Bureau of Educational Measurements.*
For additional information, see 7:629.

[814]

Emporia Physics Test. 1, 2 semesters high school; 1962–64; first published 1962–63 in the Every Pupil Scholarship Test series; Gerald L. Witten and M. W. Sanders; Bureau of Educational Measurements.*

For additional information and a review by Theodore G. Phillips, see 7:859.

[815]

Emporia Reading Tests. Grades 1, 2–3, 4–6, 7–8; 1962–64; first published in the Every Pupil Scholarship Test series; 4 tests; M. W. Sanders, Marjorie Barnett (*a–b*), Donald E. Carline (*c–d*), Ed. L. Eaton (*d*), Angie Seybold (*c*), and Stafford E. Studer (*d*); Bureau of Educational Measurements.*

a) EMPORIA PRIMARY READING TEST. 1, 2 semesters grade 1.
b) EMPORIA ELEMENTARY READING TEST. 1, 2 semesters grades 2–3.
c) EMPORIA INTERMEDIATE READING TEST. 1, 2 semesters grades 4–6.
d) EMPORIA JUNIOR HIGH SCHOOL READING TEST. 1, 2 semesters grades 7–8.

For additional information and a review by Ronald W. Mitchell, see 7:687.

[816]

Emporia Second Year Latin Test. 2 years high school; 1962–64; first published 1962–63 in the Every Pupil Scholarship Test series; Bernadine Sitts, Minnie M. Miller, Lillian A. Wall, and M. W. Sanders; Bureau of Educational Measurements.*

For additional information, see 7:307.

[817]

Emporia State Algebra II Test. High school; 1974; ESAT; total score for individuals plus group item scores for 7 goals with 17 "criterion objectives": important terms, axioms and theorems, exponents-radicals-fractions, linear and quadratic equations, graphing equations, written problems, additional topics; no manual; J. Stanley Laughlin and Howard P. Schwartz; Bureau of Educational Measurements.*

For additional information, see 8:299.

[818]

Endeavor Instructional Rating System. College; 1973–79; EIRS; student ratings of courses and instructors; 9 scores: 7 item scores (hard work, advanced planning, class discussion, personal help, presentation clarity, grade accuracy, increased knowledge), 2 composite scores (student's perception of achievement, student-instructor rapport); Peter W. Frey; Endeavor Information Systems, Inc.*

For additional information and a review by Kenneth O. Doyle, Jr., see 8:370 (5 references).

REFERENCES

1–5. See 8:370.
6. AMES, R., & LAU, S. An attributional approach to the validity of student ratings of instruction. *Contemporary Educational Psychology*, 1979, 4, 26–39.

7. MARSH, H. W. Students' evaluations of tertiary instruction: Testing the applicability of American surveys in an Australian setting. *Australian Journal of Education*, 1981, 25, 177–193.

[819]

Engineer Performance Description Form. Nonsupervisory college graduate engineers; 1975 (no date on test materials); EPDF; ratings by immediate supervisors; 7 scores yielding ratings for overall performance level plus 6 areas of development: communication, relating to others, administrative ability, motivation, technical knowledge and ability, self-sufficiency; John C. South; the Author.*

For additional information, see 8:1087 (1 reference).

REFERENCES

1. See 8:1087.
2. SOUTH, J. C. Fakability and the Engineer Performance Description Form. *Personnel Psychology*, 1980, 33, 371–376.

[820]

English Knowledge and Comprehension Test. High school; 1965; S. Chatterji and M. Mukerjee; S. Chatterji [India].* (In-print status uncertain; no reply from publisher.)

For additional information, see 7:261.

[821]

★**English Language Skills Assessment in a Reading Context.** Beginning, intermediate, and advanced students of English as a second language from upper elementary to college and adult students; 1980–81; ELSA; criterion-referenced; Cecelia Doherty and Donna Ilyin (technical manual); Newbury House Publishers, Inc.*

[822]

English Literature Anthology Tests. High school; 1959–70; slight revisions of the *Objective Tests in English Anthology* by Carl H. Larson and the *Alternate Objective Tests in English Anthology* by Dorothy A. Mason; 9 tests; no manual; Perfection Form Co.* (In-print status uncertain; no reply from publisher.)

a) BEGINNINGS OF ENGLISH LITERATURE. 1959–70.
b) THE EIGHTEENTH CENTURY. 1959–70.
c) THE ELIZABETHAN PERIOD. 1959–70.
d) THE ENGLISH NOVEL. 1964–70.
e) THE PURITAN PERIOD. 1959–70.
f) THE ROMANTIC PERIOD. 1959–70.
g) THE TWENTIETH CENTURY. 1959–70.
h) THE VICTORIAN PERIOD. 1959–79.
i) FINAL EXAMINATION. 1959–70.

For additional information concerning the earlier tests, see 7:224.

[823]

English Picture Vocabulary Test. Ages 5–8, 7–11, 11 and over; 1962–68; EPVT; derived from *Peabody Picture Vocabulary Test*; 3 levels; M. A Brimer and Lloyd M. Dunn; Educational Evaluation Enterprises [England].* (In-print status uncertain; no reply from publisher.)

a) TEST 1. Ages 5–8; 1962–66.
b) TEST 2. Ages 7–11; 1962–66.
c) TEST 3. Ages 11 and over; 1968.

See T2:495 (3 references); for a review by Kenneth Lovell of Tests 1–2, see 7:408 (5 references); for reviews by L. B. Birch and Philip M. Levy, see 6:520.

REFERENCES

1–5. See 7:408.
6–9. See T2:495.
10. BEVERIDGE, M., & MITTLER, P. Feedback, language and listener performance in severely retarded children. *British Journal of Disorders of Communication*, 1977, 12, 149–157.
11. COX, M. V. Perspective ability: The conditions of change. *Child Development*, 1977, 48, 1724–1727.
12. EVANS, D. The development of language abilities in mongols: A correlational study. *Journal of Mental Deficiency Research*, 1977, 21, 103–117.
13. JEHU, D., MORGAN, R. T. T., TURNER, R. K., & JONES, A. A controlled trial of the treatment of nocturnal enuresis in residential homes for children. *Behaviour Research & Therapy*, 1977, 15, 1–16.
14. LAWTON, J. T. Effects of advance organizer lessons on children's use and understanding of the causal and logical "because." *Journal of Experimental Education*, 1977, 46, 41–46.
15. COX, M. V. Perspective ability: A training program. *Journal of Educational Research*, 1978, 71, 127–133.
16. DOUGLAS, J. E., & SUTTON, A. The development of speech and mental processes in a pair of twins: A case study. *Journal of Child Psychology & Psychiatry & Allied Disciplines*, 1978, 19, 49–56.
17. LAWTON, J. T. Effects of an elementary strategy on operations of exclusion. *Journal of Experimental Education*, 1978, 46, 34–41.
18. SWANN, W. S. On shared knowledge: Teachers and severely subnormal children. *British Journal of Educational Psychology*, 1978, 48, 340–350.
19. VERSEY, J. Scalogram analysis and cognitive development: Evidence from a longitudinal study. *British Journal of Educational Psychology*, 1978, 48, 71–78.
20. WHELDALL, K. The influence of intonational style on the young child's ability to understand sentences: A research note on passives. *British Journal of Disorders of Communication*, 1978, 13, 147–152.
21. LEWIS, A. The early identification of children with learning difficulties. *Journal of Learning Disabilities*, 1980, 13, 51–57.
22. NELSON, H. E., & WARRINGTON, E. K. An investigation of memory functions in dyslexic children. *British Journal of Psychology*, 1980, 71, 487–503.
23. NOLAN, M., MCCARTNEY, E., MCARTHUR, K., & ROWSON, V. J. A study of the hearing and receptive vocabulary of the trainees of an adult training centre. *Journal of Mental Deficiency Research*, 1980, 24, 271–286.
24. WHELDALL, K., & POBORCA, B. Conservation without conversation? An alternative, non-verbal paradigm for assessing conservation of liquid quantity. *British Journal of Psychology*, 1980, 71, 117–134.
25. WILLIAMS, A. J., WILLIAMS, M. A., WALKER, C. A., & BUSH, P. G. The Robin Anomalad (Pierre Robin Syndrome)–A follow up study. *Archives of Diseases in Childhood*, 1981, 56, 663–668.

[824]

English Placement Test. Entrants to courses in English as a second language; 1972–78; EPT; tests by M. Spaan, L. Strowe, A. Corrigan, B. Dobson, E. Kellman, and S. Tyma; English Language Institute, University of Michigan.*

For additional information and a review by John L. D. Clark, see 8:102.

[825]

English Progress Tests. Various ages 7–3 to 15–6; 1952–72; 13 tests; tests B, C, D, and F are out of print; NFER-Nelson Publishing Co. [England].*
a) ENGLISH PROGRESS TEST A. Ages 8–0 to 9–0; 1952–60; A. F. Watts.
b) ENGLISH PROGRESS TEST E. Ages 12–0 to 13–0; 1956; M. A. Brimer and A. F. Watts.
c) ENGLISH PROGRESS TEST G. Ages 13–0 to 15–6; 1962; test by S. M. Unwin.
d) ENGLISH PROGRESS TEST A2. Ages 7–3 to 8–11; 1962–66; test by Betsy Barnard.
e) ENGLISH PROGRESS TEST B2. Ages 8–6 to 10–0; 1959–60; manual by Valerie C. Land.
f) ENGLISH PROGRESS TEST C2. Ages 9–6 to 11–0; 1961; Valerie Land.
g) ENGLISH PROGRESS TEST D2. Ages 10–6 to 12–0; 1963–64; Jennifer Henchman.
h) ENGLISH PROGRESS TEST E2. Ages 11–0 to 13–0; 1962–72; test by S. M. Unwin.
i) ENGLISH PROGRESS TEST F2. Ages 12–0 to 13–6; 1963–72; test by Jennifer Henchman and Elsa Hendry.
j) ENGLISH PROGRESS TEST B3. Ages 8–0 to 9–6; 1970–72.
k) ENGLISH PROGRESS TEST C3. Ages 9–0 to 10–9; 1970–72.
l) ENGLISH PROGRESS TEST D3. Ages 10–0 to 11–8; 1970–72.
m) ENGLISH PROGRESS TEST F3. Ages 12–0 to 13–6; 1969.

For additional information, see 7:192; for reviews by Neil Gourlay and Stanley Nisbet of Tests A–F, see 5:187.

[826]

English Test F3. Ages 12–13; 1952; formerly called *English Test FG*; G. A. V. Morgan; NFER-Nelson Publishing Co. [England].*

For additional information and reviews by Reginald Edwards, S. C. Richardson, and Cleveland A. Thomas, see 5:192.

[827]

English Test: Municipal Tests: National Achievement Tests. Grades 3–6, 6–8; 1938–56; subtest of *Municipal Battery*; 5 scores: language usage-words, language usage-sentences, punctuation and capitalization, expressing ideas, total; Robert K. Speer and Samuel Smith; Psychometric Affiliates.*

See T2:77 (1 reference) and 5:190. For reviews of the complete battery, see 5:18 (1 review), 4:20 (1 review), and 2:1191 (2 reviews).

[828]

English Test: National Achievement Tests. Grades 3–8, 7–12; 1936–57; 2 levels; Robert K. Speer and Samuel Smith; Psychometric Affiliates.*
a) GRADES 3–8. 1936–38; 7 scores: capitalization, punctuation, language usage (sentences), language usage (words), expressing ideas, letter writing, total.
b) GRADES 7–12. 1936–57; 7 scores: word usage, punctuation, vocabulary, language usage (sentences), expressing ideas, expressing feeling, total.

See T2:78 (1 reference) and 5:191; for a review by Winifred L. Post, see 4:162; for a review by Harry A. Greene, see 3:126.

[829]

English Tests for Outside Reading. Grades 9–10, 11–12; 1939; 100 tests on specific literary works; Henrietta Silliman; the Author.* (In-print status uncertain; no reply from publisher.)

For additional information, see 2:1301.

[830]

English Usage Test for Non-Native Speakers of English. Non-native speakers of English; 1955–72; distribution restricted to the Agency for International Development and the Bureau of Educational and Cultural Affairs of the U. S. Department of State; David P. Harris and Leslie A. Palmer assisted by B. Jean Longmire (Forms L and U-B); American Language Institute.*

For additional information, see 7:262.

[831]
Entrance Examination for Schools of Nursing. Applicants to schools of registered nursing; 1938–77; EESN; tests administered at centers established by the publisher; tests also available to schools for local administration; 7 scores: verbal ability, numerical ability, life sciences, physical sciences, reading skill, total (scholastic aptitude), arithmetic (first half of numerical ability subtest); The Psychological Corporation.*

For additional information and reviews by Carolyn Dawson and Christine H. McGuire, see 8:1121; see also T2:2379 (1 reference), 7:1115 (3 references), and 6:1156 (2 references).

[832]
Entrance Examination for Schools of Practical/Vocational Nursing. Applicants to schools of practical nursing; 1942–75; EESPN; tests administred at regional centers established by the publisher; tests also available to schools for local administration; 7 scores: verbal ability, numerical ability, science, reading comprehension, total (academic ability), arithmetic (first half of numerical ability subtest), reading speed; The Psychological Corporation.*

For additional information, see 8:1122 and 7:1116 (2 references).

[833]
Entrance Level Firefighter. Prospective firefighters; 1974–77; various titles used by publisher; 9 scores: 8 scores listed below plus total; distribution restricted to civil service commissions and municipal officials; McCann Associates.*

a) BOOK 1. 5 scores: interest in firefighting, compatibility, map reading, spatial relations, visual pursuit.
b) BOOK 2. 3 scores: understanding and interpreting table and test material about firefighting, basic building construction knowledges, mechanical aptitude.

For additional information, see 8:1106.

[834]
★**Environmental Language Inventory.** Children with severe delay in expressive language; 1974–78; ELI; revision of earlier ('74) edition of ELI; measures what and how to teach a child whose communication is limited to one- and two-word utterances; items scores are derived on 3 dimensions (8 semantic-grammatical rules, utterance length, intelligibility) across 4 communication situations (conversation 1, imitation, conversation 2, free play); James D. MacDonald; Charles E. Merrill Publishing Co.*

[835]
Environmental Participation Index. Culturally disadvantaged ages 12 and over; 1966–67; EPI; cultural deprivation; 3 scores: possessions, activities, total; Harold Mathis; the Author.* (In-print status uncertain; no reply from publisher.)

For additional information and a review by Carl F. Jesness, see 7:660 (2 references).

[836]
★**Environmental Prelanguage Battery.** Children with language-delays functioning at or below the single-word level; 1978; EPB; revision of first edition (1975); criterion-referenced; item scores in 14 or 15 areas: foundations in communication (functional play, motor imitation), early receptive language (identifying objects, understanding action verbs, identifying pictures), following directions (optional), non-verbal total, sound imitation, single words (noun imitation, noun production, action verb production, other categories), beginning social conversation (two-word phrase imitation, more word phrase production), verbal total; DeAnna S. Horstmeier and James D. MacDonald; Charles E. Merrill Publishing Co.*

[837]
Environmental Response Inventory. College and adults; 1971–74; ERI; for research use only; "ways people think about and relate to the everyday physical environment"; 9 scores: pastoralism, urbanism, environmental adaptation, stimulus seeking, environmental trust, antiquarianism, need for privacy, mechanical orientation, communality; George E. McKechnie; Consulting Psychologists Press, Inc.*

For additional information and reviews by James M. Richards, Jr. and Lawrence J. Stricker, see 8:550 (1 reference).

REFERENCES

1. See 8:550.
2. KEGEL–FLOM, P. Predictors of rural practice location. *Journal of Medical Education*, 1977, 52, 204–209.
3. JORGENSON, D. O. Measurement of desire for control of the physical environment. *Psychological Reports*, 1978, 42, 603–608.
4. GIFFORD, R. Enviromental dispositions and the evaluation of architectural interiors. *Journal of Research in Personality*, 1980, 14, 386–399.

[838]
*****ERB Comprehensive Testing Program II.** Grades 1–2, 2–3, 3.5–6, 6.5–9, 9.5–12; 1974–82; CTP II; aptitude test (grades 4–12) available as separate; 5 levels; Educational Records Bureau.*

a) ACHIEVEMENT TESTS, LEVEL 1. Grades 1–2; 1974–82; 4 scores: listening, word analysis, mathematics, reading.
b) ACHIEVEMENT TESTS, LEVEL 2. Grades 2–3; 1974–82; 7 scores: listening, word analysis, mathematics, reading, writing skills (spelling, capitalization-punctuation-usage, total).
c) APTITUDE/ACHIEVEMENT TEST, LEVEL 3. Grades 3.5–6; 1974–82; 11 scores: aptitude (verbal, quantitative, total), mathematics (basic concepts, computation), reading (vocabulary, total), mechanics of writing (spelling, capitalization and punctuation, total), English expression.
d) APTITUDE/ACHIEVEMENT TEST, LEVEL 4. Grades 6.5–9; 1974–82; scores same as for Level 3.
e) APTITUDE/ACHIEVEMENT TEST, LEVEL 5. Grades 9.5–12; 1974–82; scores same as for Level 3.

For additional information concerning an earlier edition, see 8:15.

[839]
ERB Modern Second Year Algebra Test. High school; 1968–69; no manual; Frederic P. Bonan, Philip Avirett, Karl S. Kalman (Form X), Stephen S. Ober, Foye Perry, Randolph Stone, Reinhoud H. van der Linde

(Form X), Frederick Watson, and Arthur Weeks (Form Y); Educational Records Bureau.*

For additional information, see 7:503.

[840]

Erotometer: A Technique for the Measurement of Heterosexual Love. Older adolescents and adults; 1971; Panos D. Bardis; the Author.*

For additional information, see 8:337 (1 reference).

[841]

★**E.S. Survey.** Job applicants and employees; 1970; "emotional stability and control"; Robert W. Cormack and Alan L. Strand; Personnel Security Corporation.*

[842]

The Essential Intelligence Test. Ages 8–12; 1940–52; manual title is *Essential Junior Intelligence Test*; Fred J. Schonell and R. H. Adams; Oliver & Boyd [Scotland].*

See T2:373 (7 references); for a review by R. Winterbourn, see 5:333; for a review by F. W. Warburton, see 4:290.

[843]

Essential Mathematics. Ages 7–14; 1976; EM; no scores, ratings by teachers on 22 items; L. M. Bental; NFER-Nelson Publishing Co. [England].*

For additional information, see 8:269.

[844]

Essentials of English Tests, Revised Edition. Grades 7–13; 1939–61; 6 scores: spelling, grammatical usage, word usage, sentence structure, punctuation and capitalization, total; original edition by Dora V. Smith and Constance M. McCullough, revision by Carolyne Green; American Guidance Service.*

See T2:81 (1 reference); for a review by J. Raymond Gerberich, see 6:266; for reviews by Charlotte W. Croon and Gerald V. Lannholm and an excerpted review by William J. Jones, see 3:128.

[845]

*****Estes Attitude Scales: Measures of Attitudes Toward School Subjects.** Grades 2–6, 6–12; 1975–81; EAS; 2 levels; Thomas H. Estes, Julie Johnstone Estes, Herbert C. Richards, and Doris Roettger; PRO-ED.*
a) ELEMENTARY FORM. Grades 2–6; 1981; 3 scores: mathematics, reading, science.
b) SECONDARY FORM. Grades 6–12; 1981; 5 scores: English, mathematics, reading, science, social studies.

For addtional information, see 8:371 (5 references).

REFERENCES

1–5. See 8:371.
6. CHESTER, R. D., & DULIN, K. L. Three approaches to the measurement of secondary school student's attitudes towards books and reading. *Research in the Teaching of English*, 1977, 11, 193–200.
7. PAYNE, D. A. Estes Attitude Scales. *Journal of Educational Measurement*, 1977, 14, 291–293.
8. ROETTGER, D., SZYMCZUK, M., & MILLARD, J. Validation of a reading attitude scale for elementary students and an investigation of the relationship between attitude and achievement. *Journal of Educational Research*, 1979, 72, 138–142.
9. RUDDELL, R. B. Early prediction of reading success: Profiles of good and poor readers. In M. L. Kamil & A. J. Moe (Eds.), *Reading research: Studies and applications; Twenty-eighth yearbook of the National Reading Conference.* Clemson, South Carolina: The National Reading Conference, 1979.
10. SUMMERS, E. G. The validity of the Estes Reading Attitude Scale for intermediate grades. *Alberta Journal of Educational Research*, 1980, 26, 36–43.
11. VACCA, R. T. A study of holistic and subskill instructional approaches to reading comprehension. *Journal of Reading*, 1980, 23, 512–518.

[846]

ETSA Tests. Job applicants; 1960–73, c1957–66; formerly called *Apitest*; 8 tests; publisher recommends use of Tests 1A, 8A, and one other; manual and technical handbook by S. Trevor Hadley and George A. W. Stouffer, Jr.; tests by Psychological Services Bureau; Educators'-Employers' Tests & Services Associates.*
a) ETSA TEST 1A, GENERAL MENTAL ABILITY TEST.
b) ETSA TEST 2A, OFFICE ARITHMETIC TEST.
c) ETSA TEST 3A, GENERAL CLERICAL ABILITY TEST.
d) ETSA TEST 4A, STENOGRAPHIC SKILLS TEST.
e) ETSA TEST 5A, MECHANICAL FAMILIARITY TEST.
f) ETSA TEST 6A, MECHANICAL KNOWLEDGE TEST.
g) ETSA TEST 7A, SALES APTITUDE TEST.
h) ETSA TEST 8A, PERSONAL ADJUSTMENT INDEX.

For additional information and reviews by Marvin D. Dunnette and Raymond A. Katzell, see 6:1025.

[847]

Evaluation Aptitude Test. Candidates for college and graduate school entrance; 1951–52; 5 scores: neutral syllogisms, emotionally toned syllogisms, total, emotional bias, indecision; DeWitt E. Sell; Psychometric Affiliates.*

For additional information and reviews by J. Thomas Hastings and Walker H. Hill, see 5:691.

[848]

Evaluation Disposition Toward the Environment. High school and college; 1976; EDEN; environmental values; 7 scores: aesthetic, experiential, knowledge seeking, prudent, active, responsible, practical; scoring must be done by publisher; Norman J. Milchus; Person-O-Metrics, Inc.*

For additional information, see 8:551.

[849]

Evaluation Modality Test. Adults; 1956; EMT; 4 scores: realism, moralism, individualism, total; Hugo O. Engelmann; Psychometric Affiliates.*

For additional information, see P:74; for a review by Wilson H. Guertin, see 5:51.

[850]

Evanston Early Identification Scale, Field Research Edition. Ages 5–0 to 6–3; 1967; EEIS; for identifying children who can be expected to have difficulty in school; Myril Landsman and Harry Dillard; the Authors.*

For additional information and reviews by James J. McCarthy and Jerome Rosner, see 7:747 (1 reference).

[851]

Everyday Skills Tests. Grades 6–12; 1975, c1969–75; EST; 2 tests, each consisting of subtests A (criterion-referenced) and B (norm-referenced); subtests B identical with subtests of *Comprehensive Tests of Basic Skills* ('69) for grades 6–8; CTB/McGraw-Hill.*
a) READING. 18 scores (15 specific objectives, 3 study skills scores).

b) MATHEMATICS. 10 scores (9 specific objectives, mathematics computation).

For additional information and reviews by Ronald K. Hambleton and Gerald S. Hanna, see 8:18.

[852]

Examining for Aphasia, Revised Edition. Adolescents and adults; 1946–54; Jon Eisenson; The Psychological Corporation.*

See T2:2071 (3 references) and P:76 (2 references); for a review by T. R. Miles and excerpted reviews by Louis M. DiCarlo and Laurance F. Shaffer, see 5:52 (3 references); for a review by D. Russell Davis and excerpted reviews by Nolan D. C. Lewis and one other, see 4:42; for a review by C. R. Strother and an excerpted review, see 3:39.

[853]

[Executive, Industrial, and Sales Personnel Forms]. Applicants for executive, industrial, office, or sales positions; 1949–68; Robert N. McMurry; Dartnell Corporation.*

a) [EXECUTIVE PERSONNEL FORMS.] 1949–68; 7 forms.
 1) *Application for Executive Position.* 1949–64.
 2) *Patterned Interview Form-Executive Position.* Applicants for management positions; 1949–65.
 3) *Patterned Interview Form.* Applicants for positions of supervisor, foreman, engineer; 1955–68.
 4) *Telephone Check on Executive Applicant.* 1950–64.
 5) *Selection and Evaluation Summary.* 1950–64.
 6) *Position Analysis.* 1956–58.
 7) *Physical Record.* 1958.

b) [INDUSTRIAL PERSONNEL FORMS.] 1949–64; 10 forms.
 1) *Application for Position.* 1950–64.
 2) *Application for Employment.* 1950–59.
 3) *Application for Office Position.* 1953–64.
 4) *Patterned Interview (Short Form).* 1949–64.
 5) *Patterned Interview Form.* Same as *a* (3) above.
 6) *Telephone Check [With Previous Employers].* 1949–59.
 7) *Telephone Check With Schools.* 1949–57.
 8) *Selection and Evaluation Summary.* Same as *a* (5) above.
 9) *Position Analysis.* Same as *a* (6) above.
 10) *Physical Record.* Same as *a* (7) above.

c) [SALES PERSONNEL FORMS.] 1949–68; 10 forms.
 1) *Application for Sales Position.* 1950–67.
 2) *Patterned Interview Form-Sales Position.* 1950–64.
 3) *Telephone Check on Sales Applicant.* 1949–64.
 4) *Sales Application Verification.* 1953–59.
 5) *Home Interview Report Form.* 1954–59.
 6) *Selection and Evaluation Summary.* Same as *a* (5) above.
 7) *Sales Position Analysis.* 1962–65.
 8) *Physical Record.* Same as *a* (7) above.
 9) *Salesman Performance Inventory.* 1965; 20 scores: general appraisal, physical and personal factors, external influences, job knowledge, motivational factors, identification with the company, company policies, planning and organization, administrative duties, personal relationships, prospecting, sales approaches, analyzing prospect needs, product presentation, handling objections, closing skills, follow-ups and call-backs, customer relations, special situations, related duties.

 10) *Man Specification Sheet—Sales.* 1968.

For additional information and a review by John P. Foley, Jr., see 6:1119 (1 reference); for a review by Floyd L. Ruch, see 4:773.

[854]

★**Executive Profile Survey.** Business executives; 1967–78; EPS; self-administered; computer processing mandatory; 11 profile dimensions: ambitious, self-assertive, enthusiastic, creative, innovative, self-directed, receptive, adaptable, composed, perceptive, systematic; Virgil R. Lang and Samuel E. Krug (manual); Institute for Personality and Ability Testing, Inc.*

[855]

Experiential World Inventory. Disturbed adolescents and adults; 1970; EWI; 8 scores: 5 perception scores (sensory, time, body, self, others), ideation, dysphoria, impulse regulation; A. Moneim El-Meligi and Humphry Osmond; Mens Sana Publishing Inc.*

For additional information and reviews by Goldine C. Gleser and Maurice Lorr, see 8:552 (2 references); see also T2:1173 (1 reference).

[856]

Expressional Growth Through Handwriting Evaluation Scale. Grades 1, 2, 3, 4, 5, 6, 7, 8–9, high school; 1958–68; formerly called *Evaluation Scales for Guiding Growth in Handwriting*; no manual; original edition by Frank N. Freeman; Zaner-Bloser Co.*

For additional information and a review by Theodore L. Harris, see 6:713 (2 references).

[857]

★**Expressive One-Word Picture Vocabulary Test.** Ages 2–12; 1979; EOWPVT; verbal intelligence; (Spanish edition available); Morrison F. Gardner; Academic Therapy Publications.*

[858]

★**Eyberg Child Behavior Inventory.** Children ages 2–16; 1978–80; ECBI; ratings by parents or others well acquainted with child on 2 scales: the problem scale, the intensity scale; no manual; Sheila Eyberg; the Author.*

REFERENCES

1. EYBERG, S. M., & ROSS, A. W. Assessment of child behavior problems: The validation of a new inventory. *Journal of Clinical Child Psychology*, 1978, 7, 113–116.
2. ROBINSON, E. A., EYBERG, S. M., & ROSS, A. W. Inventory of child problem behaviors: The standardization of an inventory of child conduct problem behaviors. *Journal of Clinical Child Psychology*, 1980, 9, 22–29.

[859]

Eysenck Personality Inventory. Grades 9–16 and adults; 1963–69; EPI; revision of *Maudsley Personality Inventory*; for revised edition of EPI, see *Eysenck Personality Questionnaire*; 3 scores: extraversion, neuroticism, lie; H. J. Eysenck and Sybil B. G. Eysenck.

a) UNITED STATES EDITION. Grades 9–16 and adults; 1963–69; a printing with title *Eysenck Personal Inventory* is available for industrial use; (Spanish edition available); EdITS/Educational and Industrial Testing Service.*

b) BRITISH EDITION. Adults; 1963–64; Hodder & Stoughton Educational [England].*

For additional information and a review by Auke Tellegen, see 8:553 (405 references); see also T2:1174

(140 references); for reviews by Victor B. Cline and Richard I. Lanyon and excerpted reviews by A. W. Heim and James Linden, see 7:76 (121 references); see also P:77 (52 references); for a review by James C. Lingoes, see 6:93 (1 reference).

REFERENCES

1. See 6:93.
2–53. See P:77.
54–174. See 7:76.
175–314. See T2:1174.
315–719. Se 8:553.
720. DELAHUNT, J., & CURRAN, J. P. Effectiveness of negative practice and self-control techniques in the reduction of smoking behavior. *Journal of Consulting & Clinical Psychology*, 1976, 44, 1002–1007.
721. AVERETT, M., & McMANIS, D. L. Relationship between extraversion and assertiveness and related personality characteristics. *Psychological Reports*, 1977, 41, 1187–1193.
722. BEARD, R. W., BELSEY, E. M., LIEBERMAN, B. A., & WILKINSON, J. C. M. Pelvic pain in women. *American Journal of Obstetrics & Gynecology*, 1977, 128, 566–570.
723. BEST, C. L., & KILPATRICK, D. G. Psychological profiles of rape crisis counselors. *Psychological Reports*, 1977, 40, 1127–1134.
724. BIANCHI, G. N., & FERGUSSON, D. M. The effect of mental state on EPI scores. *British Journal of Psychiatry*, 1977, 131, 306–309.
725. BROWNE, J. A., & HOWARTH, E. A comprehensive factor analysis of personality questionnaire items: A test of twenty putative factor hypotheses. *Multivariate Behavioral Research*, 1977, 12, 399–427.
726. BUCK, P. S., & LINDEN, J. D. Sex differences in perceived accuracy of falsified personality inventory feedback. *Journal of Consulting & Clinical Psychology*, 1977, 45, 1194.
727. CUNNINGHAM, M. R. Personality and the structure of the nonverbal communication of emotion. *Journal of Personality*, 1977, 45, 564–584.
728. DE JULIO, S., & DUFFY, K. Neuroticism and proxeinic behavior. *Perceptual & Motor Skills*, 1977, 45, 51–55.
729. DIAS, S., & CARIFO, J. A note on sex differences in achievement motivation. *Educational & Psychological Measurement*, 1977, 37, 513–517.
730. EDMUNDS, G. Extraversion, neuroticism and different aspects of self-reported aggression. *Journal of Personality Assessment*, 1977, 41, 66–70.
731. FRIGAN, J. Y. Autokinetic word technique and personality. *Perceptual & Motor Skills*, 1977, 45, 911–915.
732. GATH, A. The impact of an abnormal child upon the parents. *British Journal of Psychiatry*, 1977, 130, 405–410.
733. GIBSON, H. B., CORCORAN, M. E., & CURRAN, J. D. Hypnotic susceptibility and personality: The consequences of diazepam and the sex of the subjects. *British Journal of Psychology*, 1977, 68, 51–59.
734. GOH, D. S., & FARLEY, F. H. Personality effects on cognitive test performance. *Journal of Psychology*, 1977, 96, 111–122.
735. HAFNER, J. R. The husbands of agoraphobic women and their influence on treatment outcome. *British Journal of Psychiatry*, 1977, 131, 289–294.
736. HAMPSON, S. E., & KLINE, P. Personality dimensions differentiating certain groups of abnormal offenders from non-offenders. *British Journal of Criminology*, 1977, 17, 310–331.
737. HANSFORD, B. C., & NEIDHART, H. An Australian evaluation of the Junior Eysenck Personality Inventory. *British Journal of Educational Psychology*, 1977, 47, 330–334.
738. HESKIN, K. J., BOLTON, N., BANISTER, P. A., & SMITH, F. V. Prisoners' personality: A factor analytically derived structure. *British Journal of Social & Clinical Psychology*, 1977, 16, 203–206.
739. HUGHES, R. N., & BUSHNELL, J. A. Further relationships between IPAT Anxiety Scale performance and infantile feeding experiences. *Journal of Clinical Psychology*, 1977, 33, 698–700.
740. HUMMEL, H., & LESTER, D. Extraversion and simple reaction time. *Perceptual & Motor Skills*, 1977, 45, 1236.
741. HUNDLEBY, J. D., & ROSS, B. E. Comparison of measures of psychopathy. *Journal of Consulting & Clinical Psychology*, 1977, 45, 702–703.
742. ISMAIL, A. H., & YOUNG, R. J. Effect of chronic exercise on the multivariate relationships between selected biochemical and personality variables. *Multivariate Behavioral Research*, 1977, 12, 49–67.
743. JACOBS, K. W. Intercorrelations of the sensation-seeking scale, Eysenck Personality Inventory, and Rotter's Internal–External Control Scale. *Southern Journal of Educational Research*, 1977, 11, 9–15.
744. JOHNSON, R. C., & DANKO, G. P. Reinforcing the speaker: Effects of the speech, speaker, and listener. *Psychological Record*, 1977, 27, 489–492.
745. JOUBERT, C. E. Some correlations between Famous Sayings test and Eysenck Personality Inventory variables. *Psychological Reports*, 1977, 40, 697–698.
746. KHAVARI, K. A., MABRY, E., & HUMES, M. Personality correlates of hallucinogen use. *Journal of Abnormal Psychology*, 1977, 86, 172–178.
747. KIPPER, D. A., ZIGLER-SHANI, Z., SEN, D. M., & INSLER, V. Psychogenic infertility, neuroticism and the feminine role: A methodological inquiry. *Journal of Psychosomatic Research*, 1977, 21, 353–358.
748. KIRTON, M. Characteristics of high lie scorers. *Psychological Reports*, 1977, 40, 279–280.
749. KLINE, P., & STOREY R. A factor analytic study of the oral character. *British Journal of Social & Clinical Psychology*, 1977, 16, 317–328.
750. KLOPFER, F., JACKSON, T. T., WOLFE, W. G., & JEFFREY, G. S. The Felt Figure Replacement Technique as a personality assessment device: Validity reconsidered. *Journal of Personality Assessment*, 1977, 41, 392–395.
751. KUNDU, R., & CHAKROBARTI, P. K. Standardization of Kundu's introversion–extraversion inventory. *Manas*, 1977, 24, 65–73.
752. LANG, R. J., & VERNON, P. E. Dimensionality of the perceived self: The Tennessee Self Concept Scale. *British Journal of Social & Clinical Psychology*, 1977, 16, 363–371.
753. LEBOEUF, A. The effects of EMG feedback training on state anxiety in introverts and extraverts. *Journal of Clinical Psychology*, 1977, 33, 251–253.
754. LEIGH, J. M., WALKER, J., & JANAGANATHAN, P. Effect of preoperative anaesthetic visit on anxiety. *British Medical Journal*, 1977, 2, 987–989.
755. LESTER, D. Deviation in Sheldonian physique–temperament match and neuroticism. *Psychological Reports*, 1977, 41, 942.
756. LOO, R., & TOWNSEND, P. J. Components underlying the relation between field dependence and extraversion. *Perceptual & Motor Skills*, 1977, 45, 528–530.
757. MEHRABIAN, A. Individual differences in stimulus screening and arousability. *Journal of Personality*, 1977, 45, 237–250.
758. NIAS, D. K. B. Husband–wife similarities. *Social Science*, 1977, 52, 206–211.
759. OPOLOT, J. A. Reliability and validity of Smith's Quick Measure of Achievement. *British Journal of Social & Clinical Psychology*, 1977, 16, 395–396.
760. PALLIS, D. J., & JENKINS, J. S. Extraversion, neuroticism, and intent in attempted suicides. *Psychological Reports*, 1977, 41, 19–22.
761. PENK, W. E., & KIDD, R. V. Differences in word association commonality of schizophrenics: The self-editing–deficit model vs. the partial-collapse-of-response-hierarchy hypothesis. *Journal of Clinical Psychology*, 1977, 33, 32–39.
762. PILKONIS, P. A. Shyness, public and private, and its relationship to other measures of social behavior. *Journal of Personality*, 1977, 45, 585–595.
763. POWER, R. P., & MACRAE, K. D. Characteristics of items in the Eysenck Personality Inventory which affect responses when students simulate. *British Journal of Psychology*, 1977, 68, 491–498.
764. PRYKE, M. M., & HARPER, J. F. The Eysenck Personality Inventory Lie Scale-Some further Australian data. *Journal of Personality Assessment*, 1977, 41, 632–634.
765. REKER, G. T. The Purpose-in-Life Test in an inmate population: An empirical investigation. *Journal of Clinical Psychology*, 1977, 33, 688–693.
766. RIM, Y. Significance of work and personality. *Journal of Occupational Psychology*, 1977, 50, 135–138.
767. SEDDON, G. M. The effects of chronological age on the relationship of academic achievement with extraversion and neuroticism: A follow-up study. *British Journal of Educational Psychology*, 1977, 47, 187–192.
768. SHIRBERG, L. D., BLESS, D. M., CARLSON, K. A., FILLEY, F. S., KWIATKOWSKI, J., & SMITH, M. E. Personality characteristics, academic performance, and clinical competence in communicative disorders majors. *ASHA*, 1977, 19, 311–321.
769. SIPPRELLE, R. C., ASCOUGH, J. C., DETRIO, D. M., & HORST, P. A. Neuroticism, extroversion, and response to stress. *Behavior Research & Therapy*, 1977, 15, 411–418.
770. SKEVINGTON, S. M. Stress and anxiety neurosis: A study of recovery. *Journal of Psychosomatic Research*, 1977, 21, 439–450.
771. SMITH, D. E., & SMITH, D. D. Eysenck's psychoticism scale and reconviction. *British Journal of Criminology*, 1977, 17, 387–388.
772. STELMACK, R. M., ACHORN, E., & MICHAUD, A. Extraversion and individual differences in auditory evoked response. *Psychophysiology*, 1977, 14, 368–373.
773. STONEHILL, E., & CRISP, A. H. Psychoneurotic characteristics of patients with anorexia nervosa before and after treatment and at follow-up 4–7 years later. *Journal of Psychosomatic Research*, 1977, 21, 187–193.
774. STONES, M. J. A further study of response set and the Eysenck Personality Inventory (EPI). *Journal of Clinical Psychology*, 1977, 33, 147–150.
775. STONES, M. J. Self-ratings and the Eysenck Personality Inventory (EPI). *Journal of Clinical Psychology*, 1977, 33, 713–717.

776. SUTTON, J. M., JR., & McINTIRE, W. G. Relationship of ordinal position and sex to neuroticism in adults. *Psychological Reports*, 1977, 41, 843-846.
777. THAUBERGER, P. C., & SYDIAHA-SYMOR, D. The relationship between an avoidance of existential confrontation and neuroticism: A psychometric test. *Journal of Humanistic Psychology*, 1977, 17, 89-91.
778. TSOI, W. F., KOK, L. P., & LONG, F. Y. Male transsexualism in Singapore: A description of 56 cases. *British Journal of Psychiatry*, 1977, 131, 405-409.
779. VEERARAGHAVAN, V., & SEN, A. An experimental investigation of inaccessibility of memory trace. *Manas*, 1977, 24, 77-176.
780. VENO, A., & PAMMENT, P. Astrological factors and personality: A southern hemisphere replication. *Journal of Psychology*, 1977, 101, 73-77.
781. WIDOM, C. S. A methodology for studying noninstitutionalized psychopaths. *Journal of Consulting & Clinical Psychology*, 1977, 45, 674-683.
782. BARON, A., & GALIZIO, M. Semantic representations of drug terms by industrial workers. *Journal of Clinical Psychology*, 1978, 34, 543-554.
783. BATTEN, D. E. Information processing rate as a function of introversion-exroversion. *Perceptual & Motor Skills*, 1978, 47, 15-18.
784. BECKMAN, L. J. Self-esteem of women alcoholics. *Journal of Studies on Alcohol*, 1978, 39, 491-498.
785. BERG, I., & FIELDING, D. An evaluation of in-patient treatment in adolsecent school phobia. *British Journal of Psychiatry*, 1978, 132, 500-505.
786. BLUNT, P. Personality characteristics of a group of white South African managers: Some implications for placement procedures. *International Journal of Psychology*, 1978, 13, 139-146.
787. CAMPBELL, A., & RUSHTON, J. P. Bodily communication and personality. *British Journal of Social & Clinical Psychology*, 1978, 17, 31-36.
788. CLIFFORD, B. R., & SCOTT, J. Individual and situational factors in eyewitness testimony. *Journal of Applied Psychology*, 1978, 63, 352-359.
789. DOUGLASS, F. M., & KHAVARI, K. A. The drug use index: A measure of the extent of polydrug usage. *International Journal of the Addictions*, 1978, 13, 981-993.
790. FLEMING, O., & SEAGER, C. P. Incidence of depressive symptoms in users of the oral contraceptive. *British Journal of Psychiatry*, 1978, 132, 431-440.
791. FULLER, A. R. Personality and paired-associate learning. *International Journal of Psychology*, 1978, 13, 123-128.
792. GUCKES, A. D., SMITH, D. E., & SWOOPE, C. C. Counseling and related factors influencing satisfaction with dentures. *Journal of Prosthetic Dentistry*, 1978, 39, 259-267.
793. HARGIE, O. D. W., TITTMAR, H. G., & DICKSON, D. A. Personality correlates of student attitudes to microteaching. *Contemporary Education*, 1978, 50, 39-44.
794. HARRINGTON, N. The craving factor in the treatment of smoking. *British Journal of Social & Clinical Psychology*, 1978, 17, 363-371.
795. HUGHES, R. N., HALL, C. J., & CHAMBERS, R. L. Field dependence and the Eysenck Personality Inventory: A replication. *Perceptual & Motor Skills*, 1978, 47, 1132.
796. JAMES, S. Treatment of homosexuality II. Superiority of desensitization/arousal as compared with anticipatory avoidance conditioning: Results of a controlled trial. *Behavior Therapy*, 1978, 9, 28-36.
797. JOUBERT, C. E. Multidimensionality of locus of control and the Eysenck Personality Inventory. *Psychological Reports*, 1978, 43, 338.
798. KANTOR, H. I., MILTON, L. J., & ERNST, M. L. Comparative psychologic effects of estrogen administration on institutional and noninstitutional elderly women. *Journal of the American Geriatrics Society*, 1978, 26, 9-16.
799. KANTOROWITZ, D. A. Personality and conditioning of tumescence and detumescence. *Behaviour Research & Therapy*, 1978, 16, 117-123.
800. KARLE, W., HART, J., CORRIERE, R., GOLD, S., & MAPLE, C. Preliminary study of psychological changes in feeling study. *Psychological Reports*, 1978, 43, 1327-1334.
801. KIPPER, D. A., & GILADI, D. Effectiveness of structured psychodrama and systematic desensitization in reducing test anxiety. *Journal of Counseling Psychology*, 1978, 25, 499-505.
802. KIRTON, M. Field dependence and adaption-innovation theories. *Perceptual & Motor Skills*, 1978, 47, 1239-1245.
803. KLINE, P., & MOHAN, J. Oral personality traits among female students in North India: A cross-cultural study. *Psychological Studies*, 1978, 23, 1-4.
804. KLINE, P., & STOREY, R. The Dynamic Personality Inventory: What does it measure? *British Journal of Psychology*, 1978, 69, 375-383.
805. KONDO, C. Y., BLAN, J. A., TRAVIS, T. A., & KNOTT, J. R. Resting levels of alpha and the Eysenck Personality Inventory. *British Journal of Psychiatry*, 1978, 132, 378-380.
806. LANG, R. J. Multivariate classification of day-care patients: Personality as a continuum. *Journal of Consulting & Clinical Psychology*, 1978, 46, 1212-1226.
807. LAPIERRE, Y. D., OYEWUMI, L. K., GHADIRIAN, A., & BUTTER, H. J. A placebo-controlled study of bromazepam and diazepam in anxiety neurosis. *Current Therapeutic Research*, 1978, 23, 475-484.

808. LAYNE, C. Harmful effects of clinical training upon students' personalities. *Perceptual & Motor Skills*, 1978, 47, 777-778.
809. LAYNE, C. Relationship between the "Barnum effect" and personality inventory responses. *Journal of Clinical Psychology*, 1978, 34, 94-97.
810. LIDBERG, L., LEVANDER, S. E., SCHALLING, D., & LIDBERG, Y. Necker cube reversals, arousal and psychopathy. *British Journal of Social & Clinical Psychology*, 1978, 17, 355-361.
811. LIDDELL, A., & MORGAN, G. Superstitious compulsions. *British Journal of Medical Psychology*, 1978, 51, 369-374.
812. LOO, R. Field dependence and Eysenck's neuroticism scale. *Perceptual & Motor Skills*, 1978, 47, 522.
813. LOO, R. Personality dimensions and reversible perspective in Embedded Figures Test. *Perceptual & Motor Skills*, 1978, 46, 1016-1018.
814. LUNGHI, M. E., MILLER, P. M., & McQUILLAN, W. Psychosocial factors in osteoarthritis of the hip. *Journal of Psychosomatic Research*, 1978, 22, 57-63.
815. MANGAN, G. L. The relationship of mobility of inhibition to rate of inhibitory growth and measures of flexibility, extraversion, and neuroticism. *Journal of General Psychology*, 1978, 99, 271-279.
816. McCABE, J. J. C. Attitudes, personality and induction—A research note. *British Journal of Teacher Education*, 1978, 4, 143-145.
817. McCLURE, R. F. Towards quick identification of students with problems. *Psychological Reports*, 1978, 43, 937-938.
818. McCRAE, R. R., COSTA, P. T., JR., & BOSSE, R. Anxiety, extraversion and smoking. *British Journal of Social & Clinical Psychology*, 1978, 17, 269-273.
819. MELLSTROM, M., JR., ZUCKERMAN, M., & CICALA, G. A. General versus specific traits in the assessment of anxiety. *Journal of Consulting & Clinical Psychology*, 1978, 46, 423-431.
820. MORGAN, W. P., & HORSTMAN, D. H. Psychometric correlates of pain perception. *Perceptual & Motor Skills*, 1978, 47, 27-39.
821. MUNJACK, D. J., KANNO, P. H., & OZIEL, J. L. Ejaculatory disorders: Some psychometric data. *Psychological Reports*, 1978, 43, 783-787.
822. PENICK, E. C., REOD, M. R., CROWLEY, P. A., & POWELL, B. J. Differentiation of alcoholics by family history. *Journal of Studies on Alcohol*, 1978, 39, 1944-1948.
823. REVILL, S. I., & DODGE, J. A. Psychological determinants of infantile pyloric stenosis. *Archives of Diseases in Childhood*, 1978, 53, 66-68.
824. ROESSLER, R., LESTER, J. W., BUTLER, W. T., RANKIN, B., & COLLINS, F. Cognitive and noncognitive variables in the prediction of preclinical performance. *Journal of Medical Education*, 1978, 53, 678-680.
825. ROMINE, P. G., & CROWELL, O. Construct validity: Person-orientation and value-orientation scales of the California Psychological Inventory. *Psychological Reports*, 1978, 42, 317-318.
826. ROSENTHAL, D. A., & LINES, R. Handwriting as a correlate of extraversion. *Journal of Personality Assessment*, 1978, 42, 45-48.
827. SCHMIDT, J. P. The interactive effects of instructional set, field dependence, and extraversion on the Holtzman Inkblot Technique. *Journal of Clinical Psychology*, 1978, 34, 533-536.
828. SCHROEDER, J. E., & KOENIG, K. P. Extroversion and reminiscence following a frustrating paired-associate task. *Journal of General Psychology*, 1978, 98, 5-14.
829. SHADBOLT, D. R. Interactive relationships between measured personality and teaching strategy variables. *British Journal of Educational Psychology*, 1978, 48, 227-231.
830. SHEARD, M. J., & MARINI, J. L. Treatment of human aggressive behavior: Four case studies of the effect of lithium. *Comprehensive Psychiatry*, 1978, 19, 37-45.
831. SMART, R. G., GRAY, G., & BENNETT, C. Predictors of drinking and signs of heavy drinking among high school students. *International Journal of the Addictions*, 1978, 13, 1079-1094.
832. SMITH, B. D., & WIGGLESWORTH, M. J. Extraversion and neuroticism in orienting reflex dishabituation. *Journal of Research in Personality*, 1978, 12, 284-296.
833. SMITHERS, A. G., & LOBLEY, D. M. Dogmatism, social attitudes and personality. *British Journal of Social & Clinical Psychology*, 1978, 17, 135-142.
834. VELICER, W. F., & STEVENSON, J. F. The relation between item format and the structure of the Eysenck Personality Inventory. *Applied Psychological Measurement*, 1978, 2, 293-304.
835. WALSH, D. M., & WALSH, M. D. Relationship between extraversion and neuroticism, and intelligence for students in grade nine English and mathematics. *Psychological Reports*, 1978, 43, 15-19.
836. WASHINGTON, E. R., & ALCORN, J. D. The effects of school integration on social insight among black students classified as introverts or extraverts. *Southern Journal of Educational Research*, 1978, 12, 47-58.
837. WATKINS, D. The development and evaluation of self-esteem measuring instruments. *Journal of Personality Assessment*, 1978, 42, 171-182.
838. WEINSTEIN, N. D. Individual differences in reactions to noise: A longitudinal study in a college dormitory. *Journal of Applied Psychology*, 1978, 63, 458-466.

839. WELLISCH, D. K., JAMISON, K. R., & PASNAV, R. O. Psychosocial aspects of mastectomy: II. The man's perspective. *American Journal of Psychiatry*, 1978, 135, 543-546.
840. ANDERSON, C. C. Clarifying what values? *Canadian Counsellor*, 1979, 14, 36-40.
841. ANDREASEN, N. C., & WINOKUR, G. Newer experimental methods for classifying depression. *Archives of General Psychiatry*, 1979, 36, 447-452.
842. BARLOW, D. H., ABEL, G. G., & BLANCHARD, E. B. Gender identity change in transsexuals. *Archives of General Psychiatry*, 1979, 36, 1001-1007.
843. BRUCHON-SCHWEITZER, M. Dimensionality of body perception and personality. *Perceptual & Motor Skills*, 1979, 48, 840-842.
844. BURDICK, J. A., CHEBIB, F. S., & LEICHTY, J. Extraversion and neuroticism in a midwest community mental health center. *Psychological Reports*, 1979, 45, 241-242.
845. BYRNE, D. G. Anxiety as state and trait following survived myocardial infarction. *British Journal of Social & Clinical Psychology*, 1979, 18, 417-423.
846. CANTWELL, D. P., BAKER, L., & RUTTER, M. Families of autistic and dysphasic children. *Archives of General Psychiatry*, 1979, 36, 682-687.
847. CRAIG, M. J., HUMPHREYS, M. S., ROCKLIN, T., & REVELLE, W. Impulsivity, neuroticism, and caffeine: Do they have addictive effects on arousal? *Journal of Research in Personality*, 1979, 13, 404-419.
848. CRISP, A. H., HSU, L. K. G., & STONEHILL, E. Personality, body weight and ultimate outcome in anorexia nervosa. *Journal of Clinical Psychiatry*, 1979, 40, 332-335.
849. EPSTEIN, S. The stability of behavior: I. On predicting most of the people much of the time. *Journal of Personality & Social Psychology*, 1979, 37, 1097-1126.
850. GANGE, J. J., GEEN, R. G., & HARKINS, S. G. Autonomic differences between extraverts and introverts during vigilance. *Psychophysiology*, 1979, 16, 392-397.
851. GAUQUELIN, M., GAUQUELIN, F., & EYSENCK, S. B. G. Personality and position of the planets at birth: An empirical study. *British Journal of Social & Clinical Psychology*, 1979, 18, 71-75.
852. GUPTA, B. S., & PODDAR, M. Personality traits among Hindi-knowing Indian students. *Journal of Social Psychology*, 1979, 107, 279-280.
853. GUR, R. C., & SACKEIM, H. A. Self-deception: A concept in search of a phenomenon. *Journal of Personality & Social Psychology*, 1979, 37, 147-169.
854. HAGBERG, J. M., MULLIN, J. P., BAHRKE, M., & LIMBURG, J. Physiological profiles and selected psychological characteristics of national class American cyclists. *Journal of Sports Medicine & Physical Fitness*, 1979, 19, 341-346.
855. HARGIE, O. D. W., DICKSON, D. A., & TITTMAR, H. G. The determinants of students' attitudes to microteaching: An empirical analysis. *Programmed Learning & Educational Technology*, 1979, 16, 159-163.
856. HELPS, R., & DALTON, P. The effectiveness of an intensive group speech therapy programme for adult stammerers. *British Journal of Disorders of Communication*, 1979, 14, 17-30.
857. HEMMING, J. H. Personality and extinction of a conditioned electrodermal response. *British Journal of Social & Clinical Psychology*, 1979, 18, 105-110.
858. Hoffman, J. A., & Teyber, E. C. Some relationships between sibling age spacing and personality. *Merrill-Palmer Quarterly*, 1979, 25, 77-80.
859. HOJAT, M., & FOROUGHI, D. Iranian subjects' responses as ideal person on the Eysenck Personality Inventory. *Psychological Reports*, 1979, 45, 499-502.
860. HUXLEY, P. J., GOLDBERG, D. P., MAGUIRE, G. P., & KINCEY, V. A. The prediction of the course of minor psychiatric disorders. *British Journal of Psychiatry*, 1979, 135, 535-543.
861. IBRAHIM, A. S. Extraversion and neuroticism across cultures. *Psychological Reports*, 1979, 44, 799-803.
862. JACKSON, M. P. Extraversion, neuroticism, and date of birth: A southern hemisphere study. *Journal of Psychology*, 1979, 101, 197-198.
863. KAPOOR, T. N., MOHAN, J., & CHANDER, A. An experimental study of motivational determinants of fatigue. *Psychological Studies*, 1979, 24, 11-23.
864. KNOTT, V. J. Personality, arousal and individual differences in cigarette smoking. *Psychological Reports*, 1979, 45, 423-428.
865. KNOTT, V. J., & VENABLES, P. H. EEG alpha correlates of alcohol consumption in smokers and nonsmokers. *Journal of Studies on Alcohol*, 1979, 40, 247-257.
866. LEE, H. B., & COMREY, A. L. Distortions in a commonly used factor analytic procedure. *Multivariate Behavioral Research*, 1979, 14, 301-321.
867. LESTER, D., & WILSON, C. Handwriting and security-insecurity. *Perceptual & Motor Skills*, 1979, 48, 1002.
868. LYNCH, B. E., & HENRY, D. R. A validity study of the psychological stress evaluator. *Canadian Journal of Behavioural Science*, 1979, 11, 89-94.

869. MOLDOFSKY, H., BRODER, I., DAVIES, G., & LEZNOFF, A. Videotape educational program for people with asthma. *Canadian Medical Association Journal*, 1979, 120, 669-672.
870. MORELLI, G., KROTINGER, H., & MOORE, S. Neuroticism and Levenson's Locus of Control Scale. *Psychological Reports*, 1979, 44, 153-154.
871. MULLANEY, J. A., & TRIPPETT, C. J. Alcohol dependence and phobias: Clinical description and relevance. *British Journal of Psychiatry*, 1979, 135, 565-573.
872. NAGPAL, M., & GUPTA, B. S. Personality, reinforcement and verbal operant conditioning. *British Journal of Psychology*, 1979, 70, 471-476.
873. NAISMITH, L. D., ROBINSON, J. F., SHAW, G. B., & MACINTYRE, M. M. J. Psychological rehabilitation after myocardial infarction. *British Medical Journal*, 1979, 1, 439-446.
874. PARKER, G. Parental characteristics in relation to depressive disorders. *British Journal of Psychiatry*, 1979, 134, 138-147.
875. PENK, W. E., CHARLES, H. L., & VAN HOOSE, T. A. Psychological test comparison of day hospital and inpatient treatment. *Journal of Clinical Psychology*, 1979, 35, 837-839.
876. PERONE, M., DEWAARD, R. J., & BARON, A. Satisfaction with real and simulated jobs in relation to personality variables and drug use. *Journal of Applied Psychology*, 1979, 64, 660-668.
877. PLOUFFE, L., & STELMACK, R. M. Neuroticism and the effect of stress on the pupillary light reflex. *Perceptual & Motor Skills*, 1979, 49, 635-642.
878. RABAVILAS, A. D., BAULOUGOURIS, J. C., PERISSAKI, C., & STEFANIS, C. Pre-morbid personality traits and responsiveness to flooding in obsessive-compulsive patients. *Behavioural Research & Therapy*, 1979, 17, 575-580.
879. RIM, Y. Personality and means of influence in marriage. *Human Relations*, 1979, 32, 871-875.
880. ROBBINS, A. S., KRAUSS, D. R., HEINRICH, R., ABRASS, I., DREYER, J., & CLYMAN, B. Interpersonal skills training: Evaluation in an internal medicine residency. *Journal of Medical Education*, 1979, 54, 885-894.
881. SACKEIM, H. A., & GUR, R. C. Self-deception, other-deception, and self-reported psychopathology. *Journal of Consulting & Clinical Psychology*, 1979, 47, 213-215.
882. SATTERLY, D. J. Covariance of cognitive styles, intelligence and achievement. *British Journal of Educational Psychology*, 1979, 49, 179-181.
883. SCHNIDMAN, R. E., & LAYNE, C. Comprehensive assessment of assertion training in controlled single-case studies. *Psychological Reports*, 1979, 44, 243-246.
884. SHANMUGARN, T. E. Personality factors underlying drug abuse among college students. *Psychological Studies*, 1979, 24, 23-34.
885. SHIGEHISA, T. Intersensory facilitation of visual and auditory perception in relation to cultural factors. *Japanese Psychological Research*, 1979, 21, 78-87.
886. SKOLNICK, N. J., & ZUCKERMAN, M. Personality change in drug abusers: A comparison of therapeutic community and prison groups. *Journal of Consulting & Clinical Psychology*, 1979, 47, 768-770.
887. SMART, R. G., & GRAY, G. Parental and peer influences as correlates of problem drinking among high school students. *International Journal of the Addictions*, 1979, 14, 905-917.
888. SPANOS, N. P., & HEWITT, E. C. Glossolalia: A test of the "trance" and psychopathology hypotheses. *Journal of Abnormal Psychology*, 1979, 88, 427-434.
889. STEER, R. A., FINE, E. W., & SCOLES, P. E. Classification of men arrested for driving while intoxicated, and treatment implications. *Journal of Studies on Alcohol*, 1979, 40, 222-229.
890. STELMACK, R. M., BOURGEOIS, R. P., CHIAN, J. Y. C., & PICKARD, C. W. Extraversion and the orienting reaction habituation rate to visual stimuli. *Journal of Research in Personality*, 1979, 13, 49-58.
891. TEASDALE, J. D., & FOGARTY, S. J. Differential effects of induced mood on retrieval of pleasant and unpleasant events from episodic memory. *Journal of Abnormal Psychology*, 1979, 88, 248-257.
892. THAUBERGER, P. C., & SYDIAHA, D. Acceptance of self and others and existential persuasion. *Psychological Reports*, 1979, 44, 483-488.
893. BECKMAN, L. J., DAY, T., BARDSLEY, P., & SEEMAN, A. Z. The personality characteristics and family backgrounds of women alcoholics. *International Journal of the Addictions*, 1980, 15, 147-154.
894. BERNADT, M. W., SILVERSTONE, T., & SINGLETON, W. Behavioural and subjective effects of beta-adrenergic blockade in phobic subjects. *British Journal of Psychiatry*, 1980, 137, 452-457.
895. BRANDENBURG-HRUSKA, N. A., WEINMAN, M., & MATHEW, R. J. Frequency and severity of psychophysiological symptoms in a normal population. *Psychological Reports*, 1980, 46, 1059-1064.
896. BRIGGS, S. R., CHEEK, J. M., & BUSS, A. H. An analysis of the self-monitoring scale. *Journal of Personality & Social Psychology*, 1980, 38, 679-686.
897. COSTA, P. T., JR., & MCCRAE, R. R. Influence of extraversion and neuroticism on subjective well-being: Happy and unhappy people. *Journal of Personality & Social Psychology*, 1980, 38, 668-678.

898. CRANDALL, J. E. Adler's concept of social interest: Theory, measurement, and implications for adjustment. *Journal of Personality & Social Psychology*, 1980, 39, 481–495.

899. CROOKES, T. G. Sociability and behaviour disturbance. *British Journal of Criminology*, 1980, 19, 60–66.

900. CRUISE, R. J., BLITCHINGTON, W. P., & FLUTCHER, W. G. A. Temperament Inventory: An instrument to empirically verify the four-factor hypothesis. *Educational & Psychological Measurement*, 1980, 40, 943–954.

901. DELMONTE, M. M. Personality characteristics and regularity of meditation. *Psychological Reports*, 1980, 46, 703–712.

902. FENTON, G. W., FENWICK, P. B. C., DOLLIMORE, J., DUNN, T. L., & HIRSCH, S. R. EEG spectral analysis in schizophrenia. *British Journal of Psychiatry*, 1980, 136, 445–455.

903. FISCH, H., HAMMOND, K. R., JOYCE, C. R. B., & O'REILLY, M. Effects of psychotherapeutic drugs on multiple cue probability learning and retention. *Current Therapeutic Research*, 1980, 28, 34–46.

904. FORGAS, J. P. Images of crime: A multidimensional analysis of individual differences in crime perception. *International Journal of Psychology*, 1980, 15, 287–299.

905. FRIEDMAN, H. S., PRINCE, L. M., RIGGIO, R. E., & DIMATTEO, M. R. Understanding and assessing nonverbal expressiveness: The affective communication test. *Journal of Personality & Social Psychology*, 1980, 39, 333–351.

906. GABRYS, J. B. Effect of verbal alert and individual differences in extraversion on memory for syntax: A study with replication. *Perceptual & Motor Skills*, 1980, 51, 615–625.

907. GILLESPIE, C. R., & EYSENCK, M. W. Effects of introversion-extraversion on continuous recognition memory. *Bulletin of the Psychonomic Society*, 1980, 15, 233–235.

908. GOMEZ, J., & DALLY, P. Psychometric rating in the assessment of progress in anorexia nervosa. *British Journal of Psychiatry*, 1980, 136, 290–296.

909. GREEN, D. E., & WALKEY, F. H. A nonmetric analysis of Eysenck's Personality Inventory. *Multivariate Behavioral Research*, 1980, 15, 157–163.

910. HARRISON, B., & WHISSELL, C. M. Neuroticism, practice, and sex differences in a digit-symbol task. *Perceptual & Motor Skills*, 1980, 50, 487–490.

911. HIMADI, W. G., ARKOWITZ, H., HINTON, R., & PERL, J. Minimal dating and its relationship to other social problems and general adjustment. *Behavior Therapy*, 1980, 11, 345–352.

912. HORVATH, T., FRIEDMAN, J., & MEARES, R. Attention in hysteria: A study of Janet's hypothesis by means of habituation and arousal measures. *American Journal of Psychiatry*, 1980, 137, 217–220.

913. JACKSON, M., & FIEBERT, M. S. Introversion–extraversion and astrology. *Journal of Psychology*, 1980, 105, 155–156.

914. JONES, B. M., JONES, M. K., & HATCHER, E. M. Cognitive deficits in women alcoholics as a function of gynecological status. *Journal of Studies on Alcohol*, 1980, 41, 140–146.

915. KARLE, W., CORRIERE, R., HART, J., & WOLDENBERG, L. The functional analysis of dreams: A new theory of dreaming. *Journal of Clinical Psychology*, 1980, 36, 43–47.

916. KASSINOVE, H., MILLER, N., & KALIN, M. Effects of pretreatment with rational emotive bibliotherapy and rational emotive audiotherapy on clients waiting at community mental health center. *Psychological Reports*, 1980, 46, 851–857.

917. LANG, A. R., SEARLES, J., LAUERMAN, R., & ADESSO, V. Expectancy, alcohol, and sex guilt as determinants of interest in and reaction to sexual stimuli. *Journal of Abnormal Psychology*, 1980, 89, 644–653.

918. LAYNE, C., & ALLY, G. How and why people accept personality feedback. *Journal of Personality Assessment*, 1980, 44, 541–546.

919. LIPSKY, M. J., KASSINOVE, H., & MILLER, N. J. Effects of rational–emotive therapy, rational role reversal, and rational–emotive imagery on the emotional adjustment of community mental health center patients. *Journal of Consulting & Clinical Psychology*, 1980, 48, 366–374.

920. MCCRAE, R. R., & COSTA, P. T., JR. Openness to experience and ego level in Loevinger's Sentence Completion Test: Dispositional contributions to developmental models of personality. *Journal of Personality & Social Psychology*, 1980, 39, 1179–1190.

921. MCCREARY, C. P., TURNER, J., & DAWSON, E. Emotional disturbance and chronic low back pain. *Journal of Clinical Psychology*, 1980, 36, 709–715.

922. MEHRABIAN, A., & O'REILLY, E. Analysis of personality measures in terms of basic dimensions of temperament. *Journal of Personality & Social Psychology*, 1980, 38, 492–503.

923. MEITES, K., LOVALLO, W., & PISHKIN, V. A comparison of four scales for anxiety, depression, and neuroticism. *Journal of Clinical Psychology*, 1980, 36, 427–432.

924. METZNER, R. Correlations between Eysenck's, Jung's and Sheldon's typologies. *Psychological Reports*, 1980, 47, 343–348.

925. MORELLI, G., & ANDREWS, L. Rationality and its relation to extraversion and neuroticism. *Psychological Reports*, 1980, 47, 1111–1114.

926. NELSON–JONES, R., & COXHEAD, P. Neuroticism, social desirability and anticipations and attributions affecting self–disclosure. *British Journal of Medical Psychology*, 1980, 53, 169–180.

927. O'HAIRE, T. D., & MARCIA, J. E. Some personality characteristics associated with Ananda Marga meditators: A pilot study. *Perceptual & Motor Skills*, 1980, 51, 447–452.

928. OLSON, A. T., & GILLINGHAM, D. E. Systematic desensitization of mathematics anxiety among preservice elementary teachers. *Alberta Journal of Educational Research*, 1980, 26, 120–127.

929. OSWALD, W. T., & VELICER, W. F. Item format and the structure of the Eysenck Personality Inventory: A replication. *Journal of Personality Assessment*, 1980, 44, 283–288.

930. POWELL, B. J., PENICK, E. C., & READ, M. R. Psychological adjustment and sex–role affiliation in an alcoholic population. *Journal of Clinical Psychology*, 1980, 36, 801–805.

931. PRICE, K. P., & BLACKWELL, S. Trait levels of anxiety and psychological responses to stress in migraineurs and normal controls. *Journal of Clinical Psychology*, 1980, 36, 658–660.

932. REVELLE, W., HUMPHREYS, M. S., SIMON, L., & GILLILAND, K. The interactive effect of personality, time of day, and caffeine: A test of the arousal model. *Journal of Experimental Psychology: General*, 1980, 109, 1–31.

933. SITTON, L. R., ADAMS, I. G., & ANDERSON, H. N. Personality correlates of students' patterns of changing answers on multiple–choice tests. *Psychological Reports*, 1980, 47, 655–660.

934. SLADE, P., & JENNER, F. A. Attitudes to female roles, aspects of menstruation and complaining of menstrual symptoms. *British Journal of Social & Clinical Psychology*, 1980, 19, 109–113.

935. SPANOS, N. P., STAM, H. J., RADTKE, H. L., & NIGHTINGALE, M. E. Absorption in imaginings, sex–role orientation, and the recall of dreams by males and females. *Journal of Personality Assessment*, 1980, 44, 277–282.

936. STANDING, L., & STACE, G. The effects of environmental noise on anxiety level. *Journal of General Psychology*, 1980, 103, 263–272.

937. THAUBERGER, P. C., DAVIS, J., & CLELAND, J. F. Some indices of existential confrontation from a sample of maximum security inmates. *Perceptual & Motor Skills*, 1980, 51, 131–137.

938. THOMPSON, J. C., GRIEBSTEIN, M. G., & KUHLENSCHMIDT, S. L. Effects of EMG biofeedback and relaxation training in the prevention of academic underachievement. *Journal of Counseling Psychology*, 1980, 27, 97–106.

939. WIENS, A. N., HARPER, R. G., & MATARAZZO, J. D. Personality correlates of nonverbal interview behavior. *Journal of Clinical Psychology*, 1980, 36, 205–215.

940. AITKEN, R. C. B., LISTER, J. A., & MAIN, C. J. Identification of features associated with flying phobia in aircrew. *British Journal of Psychiatry*, 1981, 139, 38–42.

941. BERRIER, G. D., GALASSI, J. P., & MULLINIX, S. D. A comparison of matched clinical and analogue subjects on variables pertinent to the treatment of assertion deficits. *Journal of Consulting & Clinical Psychology*, 1981, 49, 980–981.

942. CHATTERJEA, R. G., & PAUL, B. Field dependency, recognition capacity and extraversion. *Psychologia*, 1981, 24, 217–222.

943. DUNNETT, S., KOUN, S., & BARBER, P. J. Social desirability in the Eysenck Personality Inventory. *British Journal of Psychology*, 1981, 72, 19–26.

944. FRANCIS, L., PEARSON, P. R., CARTER, M., & KAY, W. K. Are introverts more religious? *British Journal of Social Psychology*, 1981, 20, 101–104.

945. GARFINKEL, P. E., & WARING, E. M. Personality, interests, and emotional disturbance in psychiatric residents. *American Journal of Psychiatry*, 1981, 138, 51–55.

946. HARBERG, E., ROEPER, P., OZGOREN, F., & FELDSTEIN, A. M. Handedness and temperament. *Perceptual & Motor Skills*, 1981, 52, 283–290.

947. HERSEN, M., BELLACK, A. S., & HIMMELHOCH, J. M. A comparison of solicited and nonsolicited female unipolar depressives for treatment outcome research. *Journal of Consulting & Clinical Psychology*, 1981, 49, 611–613.

948. HIGGINS, R. L., & FRAZELL, K. Arousal in alcoholics and social drinkers progressing through a drinking sequence. *International Journal of the Addictions*, 1981, 16, 1223–1231.

949. KELLETT, J., MARZILLIER, J. S., & LAMBERT, C. Social skills and somatotype. *British Journal of Medical Psychology*, 1981, 54, 149–155.

950. KOVACS, M., RUSH, A. J., BECK, A. T., & HOLLON, S. D. Depressed outpatients treated with cognitive therapy or pharmacotherapy. *Archives of General Psychiatry*, 1981, 38, 33–39.

951. MATHEW, R. J., WEINMAN, M. L., & MIRABI, M. Physical symptoms of depression. *British Journal of Psychiatry*, 1981, 139, 293–296.

952. ORGAN, D. W. Direct, indirect and trace effects of personality variables on role adjustment. *Human Relations*, 1981, 34, 573–587.

953. OSBORNE, J. W., & STEEVES, L. Relation between self–actualization, neuroticism and extraversion. *Perceptual & Motor Skills*, 1981, 53, 996–998.

954. RINIERIS, P., STEFANIS, C., & RABARILAS, A. Relationships between obsessional personality traits, neuroticism, and extraversion in normal subjects. *Comprehensive Psychiatry*, 1981, 22, 488–489.

955. ROCKLIN, T., & REVELLE, W. The measurement of extraversion: A comparison of the Eysenck Personality Inventory and the Eysenck Personality Questionnaire. *British Journal of Social Psychology*, 1981, 20, 279–284.

956. SCARR, S., WEBBER, P. L., WENBERG, R. A., & WITTIG, M. A. Personality resemblance among adolescents and their parents in biologically related and adoptive families. *Journal of Personality & Social Psychology*, 1981, 40, 885–898.

957. SMITH, B. D., RYPMA, C. B., & WILSON, R. J. Dishabituation and spontaneous recovery of the electrodermal orienting response: Effects of extraversion, impulsivity, sociability, and caffeine. *Journal of Research in Personality*, 1981, 15, 233–240.

958. SMITH, B. D., WILSON, R. J., & RYPMA, C. B. Overhabituation and dishabituation: Effects of extraversion and amount of training. *Journal of Research in Personality*, 1981, 15, 475–487.

959. STEER, R. A., HERLICK, L., & DIAMOND, H. Retention in ambulatory detoxification. *International Journal of the Addictions*, 1981, 16, 1505–1508.

960. THALBOURNE, M. A. Extraversion and the sheep–goat variable: A conceptual replication. *Journal of the American Society for Psychical Research*, 1981, 75, 105–119.

961. WALKEY, F. H., & GREEN, D. E. The structure of the Eysenck Personality Inventory: A comparison between simple and more complex analyses of a multiple scale questionnaire. *Multivariate Behavioral Research*, 1981, 16, 361–372.

962. WALSH, R. N., BUDTZ-OLSEN, I., LEADER, C., & CUMMINS, R. A. The menstrual cycle, personality, and academic performance. *Archives of General Psychiatry*, 1981, 38, 219–221.

963. WOLFSON, S. L. Effects of Machiavellianism and communication on helping behaviour during an emergency. *British Journal of Social Psychology*, 1981, 20, 189–195.

964. WORSLEY, A. In the eye of the beholder: Social and personal characteristics of teenagers and their impressions of themselves and fat and slim people. *British Journal of Medical Psychology*, 1981, 54, 231–242.

[860]
Eysenck Personality Questionnaire. Ages 7–15, 16 and over; 1975–76; EPQ; revision of *Eysenck Personality Inventory* (1963–69) and *Junior Eysenck Personality Inventory* (1963–70); 4 scores: psychoticism (P), extraversion (E), neuroticism (N), lie (L); 2 editions; 2 levels; H. J. Eysenck and Sybil B. G. Eysenck.

a) UNITED STATES EDITION. 1975–76; EdITS/Educational and Industrial Testing Service.*

 1) *Junior.* Ages 7–15.
 2) *Adult.* Ages 16 and over.

b) BRITISH EDITION. 1975; Hodder & Stoughton Educational [England].*

 1) *Junior.* Ages 7–15.
 2) *Adult.* Ages 16 and over.

For additional information and reviews by Jack Block, Paul Kline, Lawrence J. Stricker, and Auke Tellegen, see 8:554 (84 references).

REFERENCES

1–84. See 8:554.

85. BISHOP, D. V. M. The P scale and psychosis. *Journal of Abnormal Psychology*, 1977, 86, 127–134.

86. BLOCK, J. P scale and psychosis: Continued concerns. *Journal of Abnormal Psychology*, 1977, 86, 431–434.

87. EYSENCK, S. B. G., ADELAJA, O., & EYSENCK, H. J. A comparative study of personality in Nigerian and English subjects. *Journal of Social Psychology*, 1977, 102, 171–178.

88. EYSENCK, S. B. G., & EYSENCK, H. J. Personality differences between prisoners and controls. *Psychological Reports*, 1977, 40, 1023–1028.

89. EYSENCK, S. B. G., & EYSENCK, H. J. The place of impulsiveness in a dimensional system of personality. *British Journal of Social & Clinical Psychology*, 1977, 16, 57–68.

90. EYSENCK, S. B. G., RUST, J., & EYSENCK, H. J. Personality and the classification of adult offenders. *British Journal of Criminology*, 1977, 17, 169–179.

91. GENTHNER, R. W., & MOUGHAN, J. Introverts' and extraverts' responses to nonverbal attending behavior. *Journal of Counseling Psychology*, 1977, 24, 144–146.

92. GOSSOP, M. R., & KRISTJANSSON, I. Crime and personality. A comparison of convicted and non–convicted drug–dependent males. *British Journal of Criminology*, 1977, 17, 264–273.

93. HAMILTON, M. Eysenck Personality Questionnaire (Junior and Adult). *British Journal of Medical Psychology*, 1977, 50, 205.

94. HUMPHREY, M. Eysenck Personality Questionnaire (Junior and Adult). *British Journal of Medical Psychology*, 1977, 50, 203–204.

95. IBRAHIM, A. Containment and exclusiveness: Their measurement and correlates. *International Journal of Psychology*, 1977, 12, 219–229.

96. NORRISH, M., TOOLEY, M., & GODFREY, S. Clinical, physiological and psychological study of asthmatic children attending a hospital clinic. *Archives of Diseases in Childhood*, 1977, 52, 912–917.

97. ROY, A. Nonconvulsive psychogenia attacks investigated for temporal lobe epilepsy. *Comprehensive Psychiatry*, 1977, 18, 591–593.

98. SANDERSON, H. Dependency on mother in boys who steal. *British Journal of Criminology*, 1977, 17, 180–184.

99. SILVERMAN, G. Aspects of intensity of affective constructs in depressed patients. *British Journal of Psychiatry*, 1977, 130, 174–176.

100. WILLIAMS, M., BERG-CROSS, G., & BERG-CROSS, L. Handwriting characteristics and their relationship to Eysenck's extraversion–introversion and Kagan's impulsivity–reflectivity dimensions. *Journal of Personality Assessment*, 1977, 41, 291–298.

101. WOODY, E., & CLARIDGE, G. Psychoticism and thinking. *British Journal of Social & Clinical Psychology*, 1977, 16, 241–248.

102. ZIRKEL, K., STEWART, R. A. C., & PRESTON, C. Personality and attitudinal correlates of ability to increase alpha production in EEG biofeedback training. *Psychologia*, 1977, 20, 107–110.

103. BARACK, L. I., & WIDOM, C. S. Eysenck's theory of criminality applied to women awaiting trail. *British Journal of Psychiatry*, 1978, 133, 452–456.

104. EYSENCK, S. B. G., & EYSENCK, H. J. Impulsiveness and venturesomeness: Their position in a dimensional system of personality description. *Psychological Reports*, 1978, 43, 1247–1255.

105. EYSENCK, S., & ZUCKERMAN, M. The relationship between sensation–seeking and Eysenck's dimensions of personality. *British Journal of Psychology*, 1978, 69, 483–487.

106. GOH, D. S., & MOORE, C. Personality and academic achievement in three educational levels. *Psychological Reports*, 1978, 43, 71–79.

107. GOSSOP, M. R. A comparative study of oral and intravenous drug-dependent patients on three dimensions of personality. *International Journal of the Addictions*, 1978, 13, 135–142.

108. GRIFFITHS, R. D. P., & GIDLINGHAM, P. The influence of videotape feedback on the self-assessment of psychiatric patients. *British Journal of Psychiatry*, 1978, 133, 156–161.

109. HINTON, J., WEBSTER, S., & O'NEILL, M. Simple behaviour rating scales for maximum security patients: Development and validation. *British Journal of Social & Clinical Psychology*, 1978, 17, 255–259.

110. KIRTON, M. Field dependence and adaption–innovation theories. *Perceptual & Motor Skills*, 1978, 47, 1239–1245.

111. RAHMAN, M. A., & EYSENCK, S. B. G. Psychoticism and response to treatment in neurotic patients. *Behaviour Research & Therapy*, 1978, 16, 183–189.

112. ROY, A. Self mutilation. *British Journal of Medical Psychology*, 1978, 51, 201–203.

113. SAKLOFSKE, D. H., MCKERRACHER, D. W., & EYSENCK, S. B. G. Eysenck's theory of criminality: A scale of criminal propensity as a measure of antisocial behavior. *Psychological Reports*, 1978, 43, 683–686.

114. VANDENBERG, S. G., & PRICE, R. A. Replication of the factor structure of the Comrey Personality Scales. *Psychological Reports*, 1978, 42, 343–352.

115. Zuckerman, M., Eysenck, S., & Eysenck, H. J. Sensation seeking in England and America: Cross–cultural, age and sex comparisons. *Journal of Consulting & Clinical Psychology*, 1978, 46, 139–149.

116. CARTER, H., & LOO, R. Relationships between field dependence and Eysenck's personality dimensions. *Journal of Psychology*, 1979, 103, 45–49.

117. CHARMAN, D. K. Do different personalities have different asymmetries? A brief communique of an initial experiment. *Cortex*, 1979, 15, 655–657.

118. COHEN, D., & SCHMIDT, J. P. Ambiversion: Characteristics of midrange responders on the introversion-extraversion continuum. *Journal of Personality Assessment*, 1979, 43, 514–516.

119. EYSENCK, H. J. Personality factors in a random sample of the population. *Psychological Reports*, 1979, 44, 1023–1027.

120. EYSENCK, M. W., & EYSENCK, M. C. Memory scanning, introversion-extroversion, and levels of processing. *Journal of Research in Personality*, 1979, 13, 305–315.

121. GAUQUELIN, M., GAUQUELIN, F., & EYSENCK, S. B. G. Personality and position of the planets at birth: An empirical study. *British Journal of Social & Clinical Psychology*, 1979, 18, 71–75.

122. GÖTZ, K. O., & GÖTZ, K. Personality characteristics of professional artists. *Perceptual & Motor Skills*, 1979, 49, 327–334.

123. HERSEN, M., KAZDIN, A. E., BELLACK, A. S., & TURNER, S. M. Effects of live modeling, covert modeling and rehearsal on assertiveness in psychiatric patients. *Behaviour Research & Therapy*, 1979, 17, 369–377.
124. LOJK, L., EYSENCK, S. B. G., & EYSENCK, H. J. National differences in personality: Yugoslavia and England. *British Journal of Psychology*, 1979, 70, 381–387.
125. LOO, R. Neo–Pavlovian properties of higher nervous activity and Eysenck's personality dimensions. *International Journal of Psychology*, 1979, 14, 265–274.
126. LOO, R. Note on the relationship between trait anxiety and the Eysenck Personality Questionnaire. *Journal of Clinical Psychology*, 1979, 35, 110.
127. LOO, R. A psychometric investigation of the Eysenck Personality Questionnaire. *Journal of Personality Assessment*, 1979, 43, 54–58.
128. MCLEAN, P. D., & HAKSTIAN, A. R. Clinical depression: Comparative efficacy of outpatient treatments. *Journal of Consulting & Clinical Psychology*, 1979, 47, 818–836.
129. MILLER, S. M. Coping with impending stress: Psychophysiological and cognitive correlates of choice. *Psychophysiology*, 1979, 16, 572–581.
130. POWELL, G. E., STEWART, R. A., & GRYLLS, D. G. The personality of young smokers. *British Journal of Addiction*, 1979, 74, 311–315.
131. ROBINSON, T. N., JR., & ZAHN, T. P. Covariation of two–flash threshold and autonomic arousal for high and low scores on a measure of psychoticism. *British Journal of Social & Clinical Psychology*, 1979, 18, 431–441.
132. ROY, A. Are there different types of neurotic depression? *British Journal of Medical Psychology*, 1979, 52, 147–150.
133. SCHWARTZ, S. Differential effects of personality on access to various long-term memory codes. *Journal of Research in Personality*, 1979, 13, 396–403.
134. SINGH, S., & SEHGAL, M. Rorschach hostility content and its relation to anxiety, neuroticism and P–E–N measures. *Journal of Clinical Psychology*, 1979, 35, 436–441.
135. WUDEL, P. Time estimation and personality dimensions. *Perceptual & Motor Skills*, 1979, 48, 1320.
136. WUDEL, P., & LOO, R. Birth order and person variables. *Psychological Reports*, 1979, 45, 280.
137. EYSENCK, H. J. Personality, marital satisfaction, and divorce. *Psychological Reports*, 1980, 47, 1235–1238.
138. EYSENCK, S. B. G., & MCGURK, B. J. Impulsiveness and venturesomeness in a detention center population. *Psychological Reports*, 1980, 47, 1299–1306.
139. GOSSOP, M. R., & EYSENCK, S. B. G. A further investigation into the personality of drug addicts in treatment. *British Journal of Addiction*, 1980, 75, 305–311.
140. GRIFFITH, J. H., FRITH, C. D., & EYSENCK, S. B. G. Psychoticism and thought disorder in psychiatric patients. *British Journal of Social & Clinical Psychology*, 1980, 19, 65–71.
141. HELMES, E. A psychometric investigation of the Eysenck Personality Questionnaire. *Applied Psychological Measurement*, 1980, 4, 43–55.
142. IWAWAKI, S., EYSENCK, S. B. G., & EYSENCK, H. J. Japanese and English personality structure: A cross–cultural study. *Psychologia*, 1980, 23, 195–205.
143. JANNOUN, L., MUNBY, M., CATALAN, J., & GELDER, M. A home–based treatment program for agoraphobia: Replication and controlled evaluation. *Behavior Therapy*, 1980, 11, 294–305.
144. LUNDBERG, U. Type A behavior and its relation to personality variables in Swedish male and female university students. *Scandinavian Journal of Psychology*, 1980, 21, 133–138.
145. O'CONNER, K. Electrocortical positivity and personality. *Perceptual & Motor Skills*, 1980, 51, 924–926.
146. ROBINSON, K. M., & KUMAR, R. Delayed onset of maternal affection after childbirth. *British Journal of Psychiatry*, 1980, 136, 347–353.
147. RUSSELL, D., PEPLAU, L. A., & CUTRONA, C. E. The revised UCLA Loneliness Scale: Concurrent and discriminant validity evidence. *Journal of Personality & Social Psychology*, 1980, 39, 472–480.
148. WILLIAMS, D. G. Effects of cigarette smoking on immediate memory and performance in different kinds of smoker. *British Journal of Psychology*, 1980, 71, 83–90.
149. FURNHAM, A. Personality and activity preference. *British Journal of Social & Clinical Psychology*, 1981, 20, 57–68.
150. GOLDBERG, L. R. Unconfounding situational atttributions from uncertain, neutral, and ambiguous ones: A psychometric analysis of descriptions of oneself and various types of others. *Journal of Personality & Social Psychology*, 1981, 41, 517–552.
151. HURLBURT, G. Psychoticism, teacher appraisal, and life styles of a Canadian high school sample. *Alberta Journal of Educational Research*, 1981, 27, 211–216.
152. RAMSHAW, J. E., & STANLEY, G. Individual differences in life-style response to coronary artery bypass surgery. *British Journal of Medical Psychology*, 1981, 54, 83–89.
153. ROBINSON, T. N., JR. Eye–color, sex and personality: A case of negative findings for Worthy's sociability hypothesis. *Perceptual & Motor Skills*, 1981, 52, 855–863.
154. ROCKLIN, T., & REVELLE, W. The measurement of extraversion: A comparison of the Eysenck Personality Inventory and the Eysenck Personality Questionnaire. *British Journal of Social Psychology*, 1981, 20, 279–284.
155. WARD, E. S., & HEMSLEY, D. R. Social and psychological factors associated with length of stay on an inpatient drug dependency treatment unit. *International Journal of the Addictions*, 1981, 16, 1281–1288.
156. WECKOWICZ, T. E., TAM, C. I., BAY, K. S., COLLIER, G., & BEELEN, L. Perception of reinforcement and psychomotor retardation in depressed patients. *Canadian Journal of Behavioural Science*, 1981, 13, 129–143.

[861]

The Eysenck-Withers Personality Inventory (For I. Q. 50–80 Range). Institutionalized subnormal adults; 1965–66; EWPI; more than two thirds of the items are from the *Junior Eysenck Personality Inventory*; 3 scores: extraversion, neuroticism, lie; Sybil B. G. Eysenck; Hodder & Stoughton Educational [England].*

For additional information and reviews by Paul Kline and Robert D. Wirt, see 7:77 (2 references); see also P:78 (1 reference).

REFERENCES

1. See P:78.
2–3. See 7:77.
4. HAMPSON, S. E., & KLINE, P. Personality dimensions differentiating certain groups of abnormal offenders from non–offenders. *British Journal of Criminology*, 1977, 17, 310–311.
5. WAKEFIELD, J. A., WOOD, K. A., WALLACE, F. R., & FRIEDMAN, A. F. A curvilinear relationship between extraversion and performance for adult retardates. *Psychological Reports*, 1978, 43, 387–392.

[862]

★**The Facial Interpersonal Perception Inventory.** Ages 5 and over; 1980; FIPI; 15 scores: total positive self-perception, pleasant-unpleasant (PU), accepting-rejecting (AR), sleep-tension (ST), inconsistency, between factor inconsistency, within factor inconsistency, inconsistency F ratio, total self-ideal self-perception incongruence, PU incongruence, AR incongruence, ST incongruence, between factor incongruence, within factor incongruence, incongruence F ratio; Joseph J. Luciani and Richard E. Carney; Carney, Weedman and Associates.*

[863]

The Factorial Interest Blank. Ages 11–16; 1967; FIB; 8 scores: rural-practical, sociable, humanitarian, entertainment, physical, literate, aesthetic, scientific-mechanical; P. H. Sandall; distributed by NFER-Nelson Publishing Co. [England].*

See T2:2179 (1 reference); for reviews by David P. Campbell and Hugh F. Priest, see 7:1018 (1 reference).

[864]

Faculty Morale Scale for Institutional Improvement. College faculty; 1954–63; A Local Chapter Committee, American Association of University Professors; Psychometric Affiliates.*

For additional information, see 6:697.

[865]

Fairview Development Scale: For the Infirm Mentally Retarded. Severely and profoundly mentally retarded; 1971–74; FDS; ratings by professional and nonprofessional personnel; 11 scores: perceptual and motor skills (ambulation, total), self-help skills (toilet training, dressing, feeding, grooming, total), language, social interaction, self-direction, total; Alan Boroskin, Robert T. Ross (test), and James S. Giampiccolo, Jr. (manual); Research Department, Fairview State Hospital.* (In-print status uncertain; no reply from publisher.)

For additional information, see 8:556.

[866]
Fairview Language Evaluation Scale. Mentally retarded; 1971; FLES; rating scale of language age 0–72 months; Alan Boroskin; Research Department, Fairview State Hospital.* (In-print status uncertain; no reply from publisher.)

For additional information and reviews by Ronald K. Sommers and Lawrence J. Turton, see 8:960 (2 references).

[867]
Fairview Problem Behavior Record. Mentally retarded; 1971; FPBR; checklist of 29 problem behaviors in 5 areas (aggressive, hyperactive, sexual, covert, inappropriate) plus an adjective checklist; Robert T. Ross; Research Department, Fairview State Hospital.* (In-print status uncertain; no reply from publisher.)

[868]
Fairview Self-Help Scale. Mentally retarded; 1969–70; FSHS; behavior rating scale yielding 11 scores: motor dexterity (ambulation, total), self-help skills (toilet training, dressing, eating, grooming, total), communication skills, social interaction, self-direction, total; Robert T. Ross; Research Department, Fairview State Hospital.* (In-print status uncertain; no reply from publisher.)

See T2:1179 (3 references).

REFERENCES

1–3. See T2:1179.
4. WEBB, R. C., & KOLLER, J. R. Effects of sensorimotor training on intellectual and adaptive skills of profoundly retarded adults. *American Journal of Mental Deficiency,* 1979, 83, 490–496.
5. COTTEN, P. D., SISON, G. F. P., & STARR, S. Comparing elderly mentally retarded and non–mentally retarded individuals: Who are they? What are their needs? *Gerontologist,* 1981, 21, 359–365.

[869]
Fairview Social Skills Scale: For Mildly and Moderately Retarded. Mentally retarded; 1971–74; FSSS; behavior rating scale yielding 11 scores: self-help skills (locomotion, toilet training, dressing, eating, grooming, total), communication, social interaction, occupation, self-direction, total; Robert T. Ross and James S. Giampiccolo, Jr.; Research Department, Fairview State Hospital.* (In-print status uncertain; no reply from publisher.)

[870]
A Familism Scale. Adolescents and adults; 1959; "ideal-typical familism" (in-group feelings, emphasis on family goals, common property, mutual support, desire to perpetuate); 3 scores: nuclear, extended, total; Panos D. Bardis; the Author.*

For additional information and an excerpted review by Mansell J. Blair, see 8:338 (8 references).

[871]
Family Adjustment Test. Ages 12 and over; 1952–54; FAT; test booklet title is *Elias Family Opinion Survey;* 11 scores: attitudes toward mother, attitudes toward father, father-mother attitude quotient, oedipal, struggle for independence, parent-child friction-harmony, interparental friction-harmony, family inferiority-superiority, rejection of child, parental qualities, total; Gabriel Elias; Psychometric Affiliates.*

See T2:1181 (12 references) and P:80 (1 reference); for a review by John Elderkin Bell, see 6:95; for a review by Albert Ellis, see 5:53 (6 references).

[872]
***Family Environment Scale.** Family members; 1974–81; FES; a part of *The Social Climate Scales* (2227); 10 scores: cohesion, expressiveness, conflict, independence, achievement orientation, intellectual-cultural orientation, active recreational orientation, moral-religious emphasis, organization, control, plus a derived nonprofiled family incongruence score; Rudolf H. Moos, Bernice S. Moos (manual); Consulting Psychologists Press, Inc.*

For additional information and a review by Philip H. Dreyer, see 8:557 (4 references). For a review of *The Social Climate Scales,* see 8:681.

REFERENCES

1–4. See 8:557.
5. KAROLY, P., & ROSENTHAL, M. Training parents in behavior modification: Effects on perceptions of family interaction and deviant child behavior. *Behavior Therapy,* 1977, 8, 406–410.
6. EICHEL, E. Assessment with a family focus. *Journal of Psychiatric Nursing,* 1978, 16, 11–14.
7. KAGEL, S. A., WHITE, R. M., & COYNE, J. C. Father–absent and father–present families of disturbed and nondisturbed adolescents. *American Journal of Orthopsychiatry,* 1978, 48, 342–352.
8. OLLENDICK, D. G., LA BERTEAUX, P. J., & HORNE, A. M. Relationships among maternal attitudes, perceived family environments, and preschoolers' behavior. *Perceptual & Motor Skills,* 1978, 46, 1092–1094.
9. DRUCKMAN, J. M. A family–oriented policy and treatment program for female juvenile status offenders. *Journal of Marriage & the Family,* 1979, 41, 627–636.
10. MARTINEZ, M. E., HAYS, J. R., & SOLWAY, K. S. Comparative study of delinquent and non–delinquent Mexican–American youths. *Psychological Reports,* 1979, 44, 215–221.
11. MOOS, R. H., BROMET, E., TSU, V., & MOOS, B. Family characteristics and the outcome of treatment for alcoholism. *Journal of Studies on Alcohol,* 1979, 40, 78–88.
12. BOSS, P. G. The relationship of psychological father presence, wife's personal qualities and wife/family dysfunction in families of missing fathers. *Journal of Marriage & the Family,* 1980, 42, 541–549.
13. CRONKITE, R. C., & MOOS, R. H. Determinants of the post treatment functioning of alcoholic patients: A conceptual framework. *Journal of Consulting & Clinical Psychology,* 1980, 48, 305–316.
14. FINNEY, J. W., MOOS, R. H., & MEWBORN, C. R. Post treatment experiences and treatment outcome of alcoholic patients six months and two years after hospitalization. *Journal of Consulting & Clinical Psychology,* 1980, 48, 17–29.
15. FOWLER, P. C. Family environment and early behavioral development: A structural analysis of dependencies. *Psychological Reports,* 1980, 47, 611–617.
16. MAYNARD, P., MAYNARD, N., McCUBBIN, H. I., & SHAO, D. Family life and the police profession: Coping patterns wives employ in managing job stress and the family environment. *Family Relations,* 1980, 29, 495–501.
17. KINTER, M., BOSS, P. G., & JOHNSON, J. The relationship between dysfunctional family environments and family member food intake. *Journal of Marriage & the Family,* 1981, 43, 633–641.
18. PRASINOS, S., & TITTLER, B. I. The family relationships of humor–oriented adolescents. *Journal of Personality,* 1981, 49, 295–305.

[873]
Family Pre-Counseling Inventory. Adolescents and their parents; 1975; no scores, 5 areas (specific positive actions of other, specific positive changes desired of other, assets of respondent, respondent's goals, shared activities) plus rating scale (decision making-communication-behavior exchanges); Richard B. Stuart and Freida Stuart; Research Press.*

For additional information and reviews by James A. Armentrout and Philip H. Dreyer, see 8:339.

[874]

Family Relations Test. Ages 3–7, 7–15, adults; 1957–78; 1978 revision consists of minor changes in the wording of 5 items, changes in the administration of the test, and the inclusion of normative data; Eva Bene and James Anthony (a); NFER-Nelson Publishing Co. [England].

a) CHILDREN'S VERSION. Ages 3–7, 7–15; 1957–78; 2 levels.
  1) *Younger children.* Ages 3–7.
  2) *Older children.* Ages 7–15.
b) ADULT VERSION. Adults; 1965.
c) MARRIED COUPLES VERSION. Adults; 1976.

For additional information, see 8:558 (18 references); see also T2:1182 (4 references); for an excerpted review by B. Semeonoff of *a* and *b*, see 7:79 (7 references); see also P:81 (12 references); for reviews by John E. Bell, Dale B. Harris, and Arthur R. Jensen of *a*, see 5:132 (1 reference).

REFERENCES

1. See 5:132.
2–13. See P:81.
14–20. See 7:79.
21–24. See T2:1182.
25–42. See 8:558.
43. GEDDIS, D. C., TURNER, I. F., & EARDLEY, J. Diagnostic value of a psychological test in cases of suspected child abuse. *Archives of Diseases in Childhood,* 1977, 52, 708–712.
44. JAFFE, E. D. Perceptions of family relationships by institutionalized and noninstitutionalized dependent children. *Child Psychiatry & Human Development,* 1977, 8, 81–93.
45. REKERS, G. A., & VARNI, J. W. Self monitoring and self-reinforcement processes in a pre-transsexual boy. *Behaviour Research & Therapy,* 1977, 15, 177–180.
46. REKERS, G. A., WILLIS, T. J., YATES, C. E., ROSEN, A. C., & LOW, B. P. Assessment of childhood gender behavior change. *Journal of Child Psychology & Psychiatry & Allied Disciplines,* 1977, 18, 53–65.
47. ABELSOHN, D. S., & VAN DER SPUY, H. I. J. The age variable in alcoholism. *Journal of Studies on Alcohol,* 1978, 39, 800–808.
48. PHILIPP, R. L., & ORR, R. R. Family relations as perceived by emotionally disturbed and normal boys. *Journal of Personality Assessment,* 1978, 42, 121–127.
49. SPINETTA, J. J., & MALONEY, L. J. The child with cancer: Patterns of communication and denial. *Journal of Consulting & Clinical Psychology,* 1978, 46, 1540–1541.
50. CAIRNS, N. U., CLARK, G. M., SMITH, S. D., & LANSKY, S. B. Adaptation of siblings to childhood malignancy. *Journal of Pediatrics,* 1979, 95, 484–487.
51. MEIJER, A. Emotional disorders of asthmatic children. *Child Psychiatry & Human Development,* 1979, 9, 161–169.
52. RICH, Y., & ROTHCHILD, G. Personality differences between well and poorly behaved adolescents in school. *Psychological Reports,* 1979, 44, 1143–1148.
53. MEIJER, A. Maternal feelings toward asthmatic children. *Child Psychiatry & Human Development,* 1980, 11, 33–40.
54. PFOUTS, J. H. Birth order, age-spacing, IQ differences, and family relations. *Journal of Marriage & the Family,* 1980, 42, 517–531.
55. REGEV, E., BEIT-HALLAHMI, B., & SHARABANY, R. Affective expression in Kibbutz-communal, Kibbutz-familial, and city-raised children in Israel. *Child Development,* 1980, 51, 232–237.
56. MEIJER, A., & HOVNE, R. Child psychiatric problems in "autonomous dysfunction." *Child Psychiatry & Human Development,* 1981, 12, 96–105.

[875]

Family Violence Scale. Adolescents and adults; 1973; ratings of family violence during childhood; Panos D. Bardis; the Author.*

For additional information, see 8:340 (1 reference).

[876]

Famous Sayings. Grades 9–16 and business and industry; 1958, c1957–58; FS; 4 scores: conventional mores, hostility, fear of failure, social acquiescence; Bernard M. Bass; Psychological Test Specialists.*

See T2:1183 (8 references) and P:82 (4 references); for reviews by Wesley C. Becker and Robert L. Thorndike, see 6:96 (17 references).

REFERENCES

1–17. See 6:96.
18–21. See P:82.
22–29. See T2:1183.
30. JOUBERT, C. E. Some correlations between Famous Sayings Test and Eysenck Personality Inventory variables. *Psychological Reports,* 1977, 40, 697–698.

[877]

Farnsworth Dichotomous Test for Color Blindness: Panel D-15. Ages 12 and over; 1947; Dean Farnsworth; The Psychological Corporation.*

See T2:1912 (16 references); for a review by Elsie Murray, see 4:656 (2 references); for an excerpted review, see 3:464.

REFERENCES

1–2. See 4:656.
3–18. See T2:1912.
19. HORNE, E. P., & TURNBULL, C. E. Variables of color, duration, frequency, presentation order, and sex in the estimation of dot frequency. *Journal of General Psychology,* 1977, 50, 135–142.
20. SINGERMAN, L. J., BERKOW, J. W., & PATZ, A. Dominant slowly progressive macular dystrophy. *American Journal of Ophthalmology,* 1977, 83, 680–693.

[878]

The Farnsworth-Munsell 100-Hue Test for the Examination of Color Discrimination. Mental ages 12 and over; 1942–57; Dean Farnsworth; Munsell Color Co.*

See T2:1913 (23 references) and 5:775 (1 reference); for a review by Elsie Murray, see 4:657 (2 references).

REFERENCES

1–2. See 4:657.
3. See 5:775.
4–26. See T2:1913.
27. DONALDSON, G. B. Instrumentation for the Farnsworth-Munsell 100-Hue Test. *Journal of the Optical Society of America,* 1977, 2, 248–249.
28. JOHNSON, G. F. S., & LEEMAN, M. M. Analysis of familial factors in bipolar affective illness. *Archives of General Psychiatry,* 1977, 34, 1074–1083.
29. WHITELEY, A. M., & WARRINGTON, E. K. Prosopagnosia: A clinical, psychological, and anatomical study of three patients. *Journal of Neurology, Neurosurgery & Psychiatry,* 1977, 40, 395–403.
30. SWARINGER, S., LAYMAN, S., & WILSON, A. Sex differences in color naming. *Perceptual & Motor Skills,* 1978, 47, 440–442.
31. FINE, B. J., & KOBRICK, J. L. Field dependence, practice, and low illumination as related to the Farnsworth-Munsell 100-Hue Test. *Perceptual & Motor Skills,* 1980, 51, 1167–1177.

[879]

Farnum Music Test. Grades 4–9; 1969–70; instrument readiness; the music notation subtest was formerly published under title of *The Farnum Music Notation Test* ('53); 5 scores: notation, cadence, patterns, symbol, total; Stephen E. Farnum; Bond Publishing Co.*

For additional information and reviews by Roger P. Phelps and Walter L. Wehner, see 8:93.

[880]

The Farnum String Scale: A Performance Scale for All String Instruments. Grades 7–12; 1969; 4

tests: violin, viola, cello, string bass; Stephen E. Farnum; Hal Leonard Publishing Corporation.* (In-print status uncertain; no reply from publisher.)

For additional information and a review by Walter L. Wehner, see 8:94.

[881]

Fast-Tyson Health Knowledge Test. High school and college; 1970–81; 11 scores: personal health, exercise-relaxation-sleep, nutrition and diet, consumer health, contemporary health problems, tobacco-alcohol-drugs-narcotics, safety and first aid, communicable and noncommunicable diseases, mental health, sex and family, total; Charles G. Fast and Harry L. Tyson, Jr.; Charles G. Fast.

For additional information and a review by James E. Bryan of the 1975 edition, see 8:412.

[882]

F.A.T.S.A. Test (Flowers Auditory Test of Selective Attention). Grades 1–6; 1972; FATSA; Arthur Flowers; Perceptual Learning Systems.*

For additional information and reviews by Stephen B. Hood and Eugene C. Sheeley, see 8:935.

[883]

Fear Survey Schedule. College and adults; 1964–77; FSS; self-ratings on 108 fears; Joseph Wolpe and Peter J. Lang; EdITS/Educational and Industrial Testing Service.*

For additional information and a review by Charles D. Spielberger, see 8:559 (32 references); see also T2:1185 (14 references); for a review by R. G. Demaree, see 7:80 (17 references).

REFERENCES

1–17. See 7:80.
18–31. See T2:1185.
32–63. See 8:559.
64. BAMBER, J. H. The factorial structure of adolescent responses to a Fear Survey Schedule. *Journal of Genetic Psychology*, 1977, 130, 229–238.
65. BARRERA, M., JR., & ROSEN, G. M. Detrimental effects of a self-reward contracting program on subjects' involvement in self-administered desensitization. *Journal of Consulting & Clinical Psychology*, 1977, 45, 1180–1181.
66. BORKOVEC, T. D., & O'BRIEN, G. T. Relation of autonomic perception and its manipulation to the maintenance and reduction of fear. *Journal of Abnormal Psychology*, 1977, 86, 163–171.
67. GATCHEL, R. J., HATCH, J. P., WATSON, P. J., SMITH, D., & GAAS, E. Comparative effectiveness of voluntary heart rate control and muscular relaxation as active coping skills for reducing speech anxiety. *Journal of Consulting & Clinical Psychology*, 1977, 45, 1093–1100.
68. HAFNER, J. R. The husbands of agoraphobic women: Assortative mating or pathogenic interaction? *British Journal of Psychiatry*, 1977, 130, 233–239.
69. HAFNER, J. R. The husbands of agoraphobic women and their influence on treatment outcome. *British Journal of Psychiatry*, 1977, 131, 289–294.
70. HEKMAT, H. Semantic behavior therapy: Unidimensional or multidimensional. *Behavior Therapy*, 1977, 8, 805–809.
71. ISRAEL, A. C., BECKER, R. E., & NEILANS, T. H. Contribution of pretesting to several measures of semantic desensitization effectiveness. *Journal of Consulting & Clinical Psychology*, 1977, 45, 1197–1198.
72. LEVIN, S. M., BARRY, S. M., GAMBARO, S., WOLFINSOHN, L., & SMITH, A. Variations of covert sensitization in the treatment of pedophilic behavior: A case study. *Journal of Consulting & Clinical Psychology*, 1977, 45, 896–907.
73. MAY, J. R. A psychophysiological study of self and externally regulated phobic thoughts. *Behavior Therapy*, 1977, 8, 849–861.
74. MAY, J. R. Psychophysiology of self-regulated phobic thoughts. *Behavior Therapy*, 1977, 8, 150–159.
75. MOSS, M. K., & AREND, R. A. Self-directed contact desensitization. *Journal of Consulting & Clinical Psychology*, 1977, 45, 730–738.
76. OLLENDICK, T. H., & NETTLE, M. D. An evaluation of the relaxation component of induced anxiety. *Behavior Therapy*, 1977, 8, 561–566.
77. RIMM, D. C., JANDA, L. H., LANCASTER, D., WAYNE, N. M., & DITTMAR, K. An exploratory investigation of the origin and maintenance of phobias. *Behaviour Research & Therapy*, 1977, 15, 231–238.
78. ROSEN, G. M., GLASGOW, R. E., & BARRERA, M., JR. A two-year follow-up on systematic desensitization with data pertaining to the external validity of laboratory fear assessment. *Journal of Consulting & Clinical Psychology*, 1977, 45, 1188–1189.
79. RUDESTAM, K. E., & BEDROSIAN, R. An investigation of the effectiveness of desensitization and flooding with two types of phobias. *Behaviour Research & Therapy*, 1977, 15, 23–30.
80. ZUCKERMAN, M. Development of a situation-specific trait-state test for the prediction and measurement of affective responses. *Journal of Consulting & Clinical Psychology*, 1977, 45, 513–523.
81. CARRERA, R. N., & LOTT, D. R. The effect of group implosive therapy on snake phobias. *Journal of Clinical Psychology*, 1978, 34, 177–181.
82. DUA, J. K., & BURNHARN, D. K. A laboratory comparison of systematic desensitization, flooding, and punishment procedures in the extinction of the human avoidance response. *Australian Journal of Psychology*, 1978, 30, 79–87.
83. DYCKMAN, J. M., & COWAN, P. A. Imagining vividness and the outcome of in vivo and imagined scene desensitization. *Journal of Consulting & Clinical Psychology*, 1978, 46, 1155–1156.
84. EMMELKAMP, P. M. G., KUIPERS, A. C. M., & EGGERAAT, J. B. Cognitive modification versus prolonged exposure in vivo: A comparison with agoraphobics as subjects. *Behaviour Research & Therapy*, 1978, 16, 33–41.
85. KENNY, F. T., MOWBRAY, R. M., & LALANI, S. Faradic disruption of obsessive ideation in the treatment of obsessive neurosis: A controlled study. *Behavior Therapy*, 1978, 9, 209–221.
86. MELLSTROM, M., JR., ZUCKERMAN, M., & CICALA, G. A. General versus specific traits in the assessment of anxiety. *Journal of Consulting & Clinical Psychology*, 1978, 46, 423–431.
87. ODOM, J. V., NELSON, R. O., & WEIN, K. S. The differential effectiveness of five treatment procedures on three response systems in a snake phobia analog study. *Behavior Therapy*, 1978, 9, 936–942.
88. OST, L. Fading vs systematic desensitization in the treatment of snake and spider phobia. *Behaviour Research & Therapy*, 1978, 16, 379–389.
89. SLUTSKY, J. M., & ALLEN, G. J. Influence of contextual cues on the efficacy of desensitization and a credible placebo in alleviating public speaking anxiety. *Journal of Consulting & Clinical Psychology*, 1978, 46, 119–125.
90. WEERTS, T. C., & LANG, P. J. Psychophysiology of fear imagery: Differences between focal phobia and social performance anxiety. *Journal of Consulting & Clinical Psychology*, 1978, 46, 1157–1159.
91. ABRAMS, D. B., & WILSON, G. T. Effects of alcohol on social anxiety in women: Cognitive versus physiological processes. *Journal of Abnormal Psychology*, 1979, 88, 161–173.
92. CARSRUD, A. L., & CARSRUD, K. B. The relationship of sex role and levels of defensiveness to self-reports of fear and anxiety. *Journal of Clinical Psychology*, 1979, 35, 573–575.
93. GATCHEL, R. J., HATCH, J. P., MAYNARD, A., TURNS, R., & TAUNTON-BLACKWOOD, A. Comparison of heart rate biofeedback, false biofeedback and systematic desensitization in reducing speech anxiety: Short- and long-term effectiveness. *Journal of Consulting & Clinical Psychology*, 1979, 47, 620–622.
94. HOLLANDSWORTH, J. G., JR. Self-report assessment of social fear, discomfort, and assertive behavior. *Psychological Reports*, 1979, 44, 1230.
95. HORNSVELD, R. H. J., KRAAIMAAT, F. W., & VAN DAMBAGGEN, R. M. J. Anxiety/discomfort and handwashing in obsessive-compulsive and psychiatric control patients. *Behaviour Research & Therapy*, 1979, 17, 223–228.
96. HUDESMAN, J., & WIESNER, E. The effect of counselor anxiety on the systematic desensitization of test-anxious college students. *Journal of College Student Personnel*, 1979, 20, 415–418.
97. MILTON, F., & HAFNER, J. The outcome of behavior therapy for agoraphobia in relation to marital adjustment. *Archives of General Psychiatry*, 1979, 36, 807–811.
98. MORRIS, R. J., & MAGRATH, K. H. Contribution of therapist warmth to the contact desensitization treatment of acrophobia. *Journal of Consulting & Clinical Psychology*, 1979, 47, 786–788.
99. MULLANEY, J. A., & TRIPPETT, C. J. Alcohol dependence and phobias: Clinical description and relevance. *British Journal of Psychiatry*, 1979, 135, 565–573.
100. SEIF, M. N., & ATKINS, A. L. Some defensive and cognitive aspects of phobias. *Journal of Abnormal Psychology*, 1979, 88, 42–51.
101. SLEDGE, W. H., & BOYDSTUN, J. A. Vasovagal syncope in aircrew. Psychosocial aspects. *Journal of Nervous & Mental Disease*, 1979, 167, 114–124.

102. TRUDEL, G. The effects of instructions, level of fear, duration of exposure and repeated measures on the behavioral avoidance test. *Behaviour Research & Therapy*, 1979, 17, 113–118.
103. WESSBERG, H. W., MARIOTTO, M. J., CONGER, A. J., FARRELL, A. D., & CONGER, J. C. Ecological validity of role plays for assessing heterosocial anxiety and skill of male college students. *Journal of Consulting & Clinical Psychology*, 1979, 47, 525–535.
104. WIESELBERG, N., DYCKMAN, J. M., & ABRAMOWITZ, S. I. The desensitization derby: In vivo down the backstretch, imaginal at the wire? *Journal of Clinical Psychology*, 1979, 35, 647–650.
105. ARRINDELL, W. A. Dimensional structure and psychopathology correlates of the Fear Survey Schedule (FSS–III) in a phobic population: A factorial definition of agoraphobia. *Behaviour Research & Therapy*, 1980, 18, 229–242.
106. BERNADT, M. W., SILVERSTONE, T., & SINGLETON, W. Behavioural and subjective effects of beta–adrenergic blockade in phobic subjects. *British Journal of Psychiatry*, 1980, 137, 452–457.
107. BROWN, S. D. Coping skills training: An evaluation of a psychoeducational program in a community mental health setting. *Journal of Counseling Psychology*, 1980, 27, 340–345.
108. HOKANSON, J. E., SACCO, W. P., BLUMBERG, S. R., & LANDRUM, G. C. Interpersonal behavior of depressive individuals in a mixed–motive game. *Journal of Abnormal Psychology*, 1980, 89, 320–332.
109. MUNBY, M., & JOHNSTON, D. W. Agoraphobia: The long–term follow–up of behavioural treatment. *British Journal of Psychiatry*, 1980, 137, 418–427.
110. SHEEHAN, D. V., BALLENGER, J., & JACOBSEN, G. Treatment of endogenous anxiety with phobic, hysterical, and hypochondriacal symptoms. *Archives of General Psychiatry*, 1980, 37, 51–59.
111. SHERRY, G. S., & LEVINE, B. A. An examination of procedural variables in flooding therapy. *Behavior Therapy*, 1980, 11, 148–155.
112. WILSON, G. T., ABRAMS, D. B., & LIPSCOMB, T. R. Effects of intoxication levels and drinking pattern on social anxiety in men. *Journal of Studies on Alcohol*, 1980, 41, 250–264.
113. BENSON, B. A. Personality correlates of self–punitive behavior. *Journal of Abnormal Psychology*, 1981, 90, 183–185.
114. CROZIER, W. R. Shyness and self–esteem. *British Journal of Social Psychology*, 1981, 20, 220–222.
115. KALOUPEK, D. G., PETERSON, D. A., BOYD, T. L., & LEVIS, D. J. The effects of exposure to a spatial ordered fear stimulus: A study of generalization of extinction effects. *Behavior Therapy*, 1981, 12, 130–137.
116. LINDER, L. H. Group behavioral treatment of agoraphobia: A preliminary report. *Comprehensive Psychiatry*, 1981, 22, 226–233.

[884]
Fels Parent Behavior Rating Scales. 1937–49; FPBRS; "for the use of the trained home visitor in appraising certain aspects of parent-child relationships"; 30 scores: adjustment of home, activeness of home, discord in home, sociability of family, coordination of household, child-centeredness of home, duration of contact with mother, intensity of contact with mother, restrictiveness of regulation, readiness of enforcement, severity of actual penalties, justification of policy, democracy of policy, clarity of policy, effectiveness of policy, disciplinary friction, quantity of suggestion, coerciveness of suggestion, accelerational attempt, general babying, general protectiveness, readiness of criticism, direction of criticism, readiness of explanation, solicitousness for welfare, acceptance of child, understanding, emotionality toward child, affectionateness toward child, rapport with child; Alfred L. Baldwin, Joan Kalhorn, Fay Huffman Breese, and Horace Champney; Fels Researh Institute.*

See T2:1186 (6 references) and P:84 (8 references); for a review by Dale B. Harris, see 4:43 (15 references).

[885]
Field Work Performance Report. Occupational therapy students; 1973–74; FWPR; ratings by supervisors; 6 scores: data gathering, treatment planning, treatment implementation, communication skills, professional characteristics, total; Jane Estner Slaymaker, Linda M. Crocker, and John E. Muthard; American Occupational Therapy Association, Inc.*

For additional information, see 8:1107.

REFERENCES
1. See 8:1107.
2. DEITZ, J. C., & SLAYMAKER, J. Pilot study of a revised Field Work Performance Report rating procedure. *American Journal of Occupational Therapy*, 1977, 33, 249–254.
3. FORD, A. L. A prediction of internship performance. *American Journal of Occupational Therapy*, 1977, 33, 230–234.

[886]
★**Figure Classification Test.** Applicants for industrial work with 7 to 9 years of schooling; 1976; T. R. Taylor; National Institute for Personnel Research [South Africa].*

[887]
Fire Promotion Tests. Prospective firemen promotees; 1960–69; 5 tests; McCann Associates.*
a) LIEUTENANT. 1962–69; 4 scores: pre-fire practices, extinguishment practices, fire supervision, total.
b) CAPTAIN. 1962–69; 5 scores: pre-fire practices, extinguishment practices, overhaul-salvage-rescue, fire supervision, total.
c) ASSISTANT FIRE CHIEF. 1961–69; 5 scores: fire administration, firefighting knowledge, fire prevention, fire supervision, total.
d) DEPUTY FIRE CHIEF. 1967–69; test also used for battalion chief; 5 scores: same as for *c*.
e) FIRE CHIEF. 1969; 5 scores: same as for *c*.
For additional information, see 7:1106.

[888]
Firefighter Test: B-2(m). Prospective firemen; 1954–72; distribution restricted to member public personnel agencies and nonmember agencies approved by the publisher; International Personnel Management Association.*
For additional information, see 6:1143.

[889]
Fireman Examination. Prospective firemen; 1961–62; 8 or 9 scores: learning ability (verbal, quantitative, total), fireman aptitude (interest, common sense, mechanical, total), easy verbal learning (form 70 only), total; distribution restricted to civil service commissions and municipal officials; McCann Associates.*
For additional information, see 6:1145.

[890]
*****The FIRO Awareness Scales.** Grades 4–8, 9–16 and adults; William C. Schutz and Marilyn Wood (*b*); Consulting Psychologists Press, Inc.*
a) FIRO-B [FUNDAMENTAL INTERPERSONAL RELATIONS ORIENTATION-BEHAVIOR]. Grades 9–15 and adults; 1957–82; 6 scores of behavior toward others: inclusion (expressed, wanted), control (expressed, wanted), affection (expressed, wanted).
b) FIRO-BC. Grades 4–8; 1972, c1966; 6 scores: same as for FIRO-B.
c) FIRO-F [FUNDAMENTAL INTERPERSONAL RELATIONS ORIENTATION-FEELINGS]. Grades 9–16 and adults; 1957–67; 6 scores of feelings toward others: inclusion (expressed, wanted), control (expressed, wanted), affection (expressed, wanted).
d) LIPHE [LIFE INTERPERSONAL HISTORY ENQUIRY]. Grades 9–16 and adults; 1962; retrospective childhood relationships with parents; 12 scores (6 scores for each parent): inclusion (behavior, feelings), control (behavior,

feelings), affection behavior-feeling, perceived parental approval.

e) COPE [COPING OPERATIONS PREFERENCE ENQUIRY]. Grades 9–16 and adults; 1962–76; 5 scores: denial, isolation, projection, regression-dependency, turning-against-self.

f) MATE [MARITAL ATTITUDES EVALUATION]. Grades 9–16 and adults; 1967–76; 5 scores: inclusion (behavior, feelings), control (behavior, feelings), affection.

g) VAL-ED [EDUCATIONAL VALUES]. Grades 9–16 and adults; 1967–77; 12 scores: importance, mind, teacher-student (control, affection), teacher-community (inclusion, control, affection), administrator-teacher (inclusion, control, affection), administrator-community (control, affection).

For additional information, see 8:555 (147 references); see also T2:1176 (58 references); for a review by Bruce Bloxom, see 7:78 (70 references); see also P:79 (30 references) and 6:94 (15 references).

REFERENCES

1–15. See 6:94.
16–45. See P:79.
46–115. See 7:78.
116–174. See T2:1176.
175–321. See 8:555.
322. BUGEN, L. A. Composition and orientation effects on group cohesion. *Psychological Reports*, 1977, 40, 175–181.
323. BUHMEYER, K. J., & JOHNSON, A. H. Personality profiles of physician extenders. *Psychological Reports*, 1977, 40, 655–662.
324. CAMPBELL, B. K., & BARNLUND, D. C. Communication patterns and problems of pregnancy. *American Journal of Orthopsychiatry*, 1977, 47, 134–139.
325. CARRON, A. V., & BENNETT, B. B. Compatibility in the coach athlete dyad. *Research Quarterly*, 1977, 48, 671–679.
326. HARRIS, M. E., & ROY, W. J. Dream content and its relation to self-reported interpersonal behavior. *Psychiatry*, 1977, 40, 363–368.
327. HIRSCHFELD, R. M. A., MATTHEWS, S. M., MOSHER, L. R., & MENN, A. Z. Being with madness: Personality characteristics of three treatment staffs. *Hospital & Community Psychiatry*, 1977, 28, 267–273.
328. NELSON, V. L., NIELSON, E. C., & CHECKETTS, K. T. Interpersonal attitudes of suicidal individuals. *Psychological Reports*, 1977, 40, 983–989.
329. SMITH, D. G. College classroom interactions and critical thinking. *Journal of Educational Psychology*, 1977, 69, 180–190.
330. BABLADELIS, G. Sex-role concepts and flexibility on measures of thinking, feeling, and behaving. *Psychological Reports*, 1978, 42, 99–105.
331. BRUININKS, V. L. Patterns and personality correlates of teachers' interactions with students. *Psychological Reports*, 1978, 42, 239–242.
332. BRUININKS, V. L. Peer status and personality characteristics of learning disabled and nondisabled students. *Journal of Learning Disabilities*, 1978, 11, 484–489.
333. BUHMEYER, K. J., & JOHNSON, A. H. Predicting success in a physician–extender training program. *Psychological Reports*, 1978, 42, 507–513.
334. CARRON, A. V., & GARVIE, G. T. Compatibility and successful performance. *Perceptual & Motor Skills*, 1978, 46, 1121–1122.
335. DEL GAUDIO, A. C., CARPENTER, P. J., & MORROW, G. R. Male and female treatment differences: Can they be generalized? *Journal of Consulting & Clinical Psychology*, 1978, 46, 1577–1578.
336. FROST, T., STIMPSON, D. V., & MAUGHAN, M. R. C. Some correlates of trust. *Journal of Psychology*, 1978, 99, 103–108.
337. GREENBERG, E. A., OBITZ, F. W., & KAYE, B. W. Relationships among control orientation, the FIRO–B, and the Ward Atmosphere Scale in hospitalized men alcoholics. *Journal of Studies on Alcohol*, 1978, 39, 68–76.
338. HATLEY, R. V., & TULL, M. J. Effects of organization development on teacher effectiveness and teacher–student relationships. *Southern Journal of Educational Research*, 1978, 12, 125–149.
339. HEIMOVICS, R. D., & ZEMELMAN, D. The influence of interpersonal relationships on group decision making. *Educational Administration Quarterly*, 1978, 14, 61–73.
340. SAXON, S., & BLAINE, J. D. Compulsive heroin use and interpersonal orientation. *International Journal of the Addictions*, 1978, 13, 349–358.
341. WOLKON, G. H., DAVIS, L. C., & STAPLES, F. R. Personality changes and compatibility in the psychiatric resident supervisor relationship. *Journal of Medical Education*, 1978, 53, 59–63.
342. BEUTLER, L. E., ORÓ–BEUTLER, M. E., & MITCHELL, R. Systematic comparison of two parent training programs in child management. *Journal of Counseling Psychology*, 1979, 26, 531–533.
343. DRENNEN, W., & PUGH, M. The use of a contract to facilitate sensitivity training. *Journal of Humanistic Psychology*, 1979, 19, 77–84.
344. GLUCK, G. A. The Kramer–Froehle controversy: A contribution to construct validity of the FIRO–B questionnaire. *Journal of Personality Assessment*, 1979, 43, 541–543.
345. HAWLEY, K. E., & HEINEN, J. S. Compatibility and task group performance. *Human Relations*, 1979, 32, 579–590.
346. KLEIN, J. Submission and independence in learning security. *Psychological Reports*, 1979, 44, 943–948.
347. LUBIN, B., & SMITH, P. B. Affect levels in one-day experimental groups. *Psychological Reports*, 1979, 45, 117–118.
348. MCWILLIAMS, S. A. Effects of reciprocal peer counseling on college student personality development. *Journal of the American College Health Association*, 1979, 27, 210–213.
349. O'LEARY, M., DONOVAN, D. M., CHANEY, E. F., & O'LEARY, D. E. Interpersonal attractiveness and clinical decisions in alcoholism treatment. *American Journal of Psychiatry*, 1979, 136, 618–622.
350. O'LEARY, M. R., DONOVAN, D. M., CHANEY, E. F., & SPELTZ, M. L. Correlates of clinicians' perceptions in alcoholism treatment. *Journal of Clinical Psychiatry*, 1979, 40, 344–347.
351. PUTNAM, L. L. Preference for procedural order in task-oriented small groups. *Communication Monographs*, 1979, 46, 193–218.
352. SHEPARD, L. A. Self-acceptance: The evaluative component of the self-concept construct. *American Educational Research Journal*, 1979, 16, 139–160.
353. TESCH, F. E. Interpersonal proximity and impression formation: A partial examination of Hall's proxemic model. *Journal of Social Psychology*, 1979, 107, 43–55.
354. WOUDENBERG, R. A., & POLAND, W. D. Four years of encounter groups: Changes in female and male composition. *Journal of College Student Personnel*, 1979, 20, 513–520.
355. CHILES, J. A., STAUSS, F. S., & BENJAMIN, L. S. Marital conflict and sexual dysfunction in alcoholic and non-alcoholic couples. *British Journal of Psychiatry*, 1980, 137, 266–273.
356. EASTERDAY, K. E., & PAUL, O. D. A study of the relationship of student–teacher compatibility on student achievement in algebra. *Southern Journal of Educational Research*, 1980, 14, 127–143.
357. MALLOY, T. E. A computer program for the computation of interpersonal compatibility. *Educational & Psychological Measurement*, 1980, 40, 161–162.
358. MALLOY, T. E. Use of the interpersonal compatibility construct in research on psychotherapy. *Psychological Reports*, 1980, 46, 120–122.
359. MALLOY, T. E., & FYFE, B. Interpersonal correlates of pessimism. *Psychological Reports*, 1980, 46, 871–874.
360. PAPA, L. L. Responses to life events as predictors of suicidal behavior. *Nursing Research*, 1980, 29, 362–369.
361. PINO, C. J. Interpersonal needs, counselor style, and personality change among seminarians during the 1970's. *Review of Religious Research*, 1980, 21, 351–367.
362. TORPY, D. M. The interpersonal orientation of the English midwife. *Journal of Psychology*, 1980, 104, 259–260.
363. BURTON, M. D. Identifying potential participants for college extracurricular activities. *College Student Journal*, 1981, 15, 251–253.
364. JONES, W. H., FREEMON, J. E., & GOSWICK, R. A. The persistence of loneliness: Self and other determinants. *Journal of Personality*, 1981, 49, 27–48.
365. KLARREICH, S. H. Group training in problem solving skills and group counselling: A study comparing two treatment approaches with adolescent probationers. *Corrective & Social Psychiatry & Journal of Behavior Technology, Methods & Therapy*, 1981, 27, 1–13.
366. POOLE, M. S. Decision development in small groups I: A comparison of two models. *Communication Monographs*, 1981, 48, 1–24.

[891]
First Grade Screening Test.
First grade entrants; 1966–69; FGST; intellectual deficiency, central nervous system dysfunction, and emotional disturbance; John E. Pate and Warren W. Webb; American Guidance Service.*

See T2:979 (3 references); for an excerpted review by Grayce A. Ransom, see 7:748.

REFERENCES

1–3. See T2:979.
4. HASE, H. D. Predicting performance in the first grade with the First-Grade Screening Test. *Psychology in the Schools*, 1977, 14, 407–412.
5. Gacka, R. C. The Basic School Skills Inventory as a preschool screening instrument. *Journal of Learning Disabilities*, 1978, 11, 593–595.

6. GACKA, R. C. A diagnostic preschool screening program. *Academic Therapy*, 1979, 14, 417–424.
7. LEINHARDT, G. Transition rooms: Promoting maturation or reducing education? *Journal of Educational Psychology*, 1980, 72, 55–61.

[892]
First Year Algebra Test: National Achievement Tests. 1 year high school; 1958–62; Ray Webb and Julius H. Hlavaty; Psychometric Affiliates.*

For additional information and a review by Donald L. Meyer, see 6:600.

[893]
First Year Arabic Final Examination, 1972 Edition. 1 year college; 1964–72; 1964 edition called *First-Year Arabic Qualifying Examination*; no manual; Sami A. Hanna; Middle East Center, University of Utah.* (Inprint status uncertain; no reply from publisher.)

For additional information concerning the 1964 edition, see 7:258.

[894]
First Year French Test. High school and college; 1956–68; Jean Leblon and Minnie M. Miller; Bureau of Educational Measurements.*

For additional information, see 7:273; for reviews by Nelson Brooks and Mary E. Turnbull of an earlier edition, see 5:266.

[895]
First Year Spanish Test. High school and college; 1947–68; FYST; revision of Kansas First Year Spanish Test; Oscar F. Hernández and Minnie M. Miller; Bureau of Educational Measurements.*

For additional information and a review by Charles W. Stansfield, see 8:164.

[896]
The Fisher-Logemann Test of Articulation Competence. Preschool to adult, grade 3 to adult; 1971; FLTAC; Hilda B. Fisher and Jerilyn A. Logemann; Riverside Publishing Co.*

a) PICTURE TEST. Preschool to adult; no scores, 3 areas: singleton consonants, consonant blends, vowel phonemes and diphthongs; a shortened screening form consisting of 11 of the singleton consonants may be administered.

b) SENTENCE ARTICULATION TEST. Grade 3 to adult; no scores, 5 areas: consonant pairs, singleton consonants, nasals, vowel phonemes, diphthongs.

For additional information and reviews by Marie C. Fontana and Lawrence J. Turton, see 8:961.

REFERENCES
1. MCCORMICK, D. P. Pediatric evaluation of children with school problems. *American Journal of Diseases of Children*, 1977, 131, 318–322.
2. STEPHENS, M. I., & DANILOFF, R. A methodological study of factors affecting the judgment of misarticulated /s/. *Journal of Communications Disorders*, 1977, 10, 207–220.
3. LOGEMANN, J. A., FISHER, H. B., BOSHES, B., & BLONSKY, E. R. Frequency and cooccurrence of vocal tract dysfunctions in the speech of a large sample of Parkinson patients. *Journal of Speech & Hearing Disorders*, 1978, 43, 47–57.
4. KUPPERMAN, P., BLIGH, S., & GOODBAN, M. Activating articulation skills through theraplay. *Journal of Speech & Hearing Disorders*, 1980, 45, 540–548.
5. METZ, D. E., CARD, S. C., & SPECTOR, P. B. A distinctive–features approach to the remediation of voicing errors produced by hearing-impaired adults. *Journal of Communication Disorders*, 1980, 13, 231–237.
6. BLACHE, S. E., PARSONS, S. L., & HUMPHREYS, J. M. A minimal-word–pair model for teaching the linguistic significance of distinctive feature properties. *Journal of Speech & Hearing Disorders*, 1981, 46, 291–296.
7. LOGEMANN, J. A., & FISHER, H. B. Vocal tract control in Parkinson's Disease: Phonetic feature analysis of misarticulations. *Journal of Speech & Hearing Disorders*, 1981, 46, 348–352.
8. NORRIS, M., & HARDEN, J. Natural processes in the phonologies of four error-rate groups. *Journal of Communication Disorders*, 1981, 14, 195–213.
9. TOOMBS, M. S., SINGH, S., & HAYDEN, M. E. Markedness of features in the articulatory substitutions of children. *Journal of Speech & Hearing Disorders*, 1981, 46, 184–191.

[897]
The Five Task Test: A Performance and Projective Test of Emotionality, Motor Skill and Organic Brain Damage. Ages 8 and over; 1955; FTT; Charlotte Buhler and Kathryn Mandeville; Western Psychological Services.*

For additional information, see P:428; for reviews by Dorothy H. Eichorn and Bert R. Sappenfield and an excerpted review by Laurance F. Shaffer, see 5:133.

[898]
Flags: A Test of Space Thinking. Industrial employees; 1959, c1956–59; L. L. Thurstone (test), T. E. Jeffrey (test), and Measurement Research Division, Human Resources Center, University of Chicago (manual); the Center.*

See T2:2245 (1 reference); for a review by I. Macfarlane Smith, see 6:1086.

REFERENCES
1. See T2:2245.
2. ADAMOWICZ, J. K. Visual short-term memory, age, and imaging ability. *Perceptual & Motor Skills*, 1978, 46, 571–576.

[899]
Flanagan Aptitude Classification Tests. Grades 9–12, 10–12 and adults; 1951–60; FACT; 2 editions; John C. Flanagan; Science Research Associates, Inc.*

a) SEPARATE BOOKLET 16-TEST EDITION. Grades 10–12 and adults; 1951–60; 16 tests.
  1) *FACT 1A, Inspection.* 1953–56.
  2) *FACT 2A and 2B, Coding.* 1953–56.
  3) *FACT 3A and 3B, Memory.* 1953–56.
  4) *FACT 4A, Precision.* 1953–56.
  5) *FACT 5A, Assembly.* 1953–56.
  6) *FACT 6A, Scales.* 1953–56.
  7) *FACT 7A, Coordination.* 1953–56.
  8) *FACT 8A, Judgment and Comprehension.* 1953–56.
  9) *FACT 9A, Arithmetic.* 1953–56.
  10) *FACT 10A, Patterns.* 1953–56.
  11) *FACT 11A, Components.* 1953–56.
  12) *FACT 12A, Tables.* 1953–56.
  13) *FACT 13A and 13B, Mechanics.* 1953–56.
  14) *FACT 14A, Expression.* 1953–56.
  15) *FACT 15A, Reasoning.* 1957–60.
  16) *FACT 16A, Ingenuity.* 1957–60.

b) 19-TEST EDITION. Grades 9–12; 1957–60; 19 tests (same as for *a* plus vocabulary, planning, alertness) in 2 booklets.

See T2:1072 (1 reference); for an excerpted review by Harold D. Murphy (with John P. McQuary), see 7:675 (10 references); for reviews by Norman Frederiksen and William B. Michael, see 6:770 (7 references); for reviews by Harold P. Bechtoldt, Ralph F. Berdie, and John B. Carroll, see 5:608.

REFERENCES
1–7. See 6:770.

8–17. See 7:675.
18. See T2:1072.
19. DIAMOND, E. E. The AMEG commission report on sex bias in achievement testing. *Measurement & Evaluation in Guidance*, 1980, 13, 135–147.
20. MARTIN, J. D., BLAIR, G. E., & HERRMANN, W. J. Correlations between scores on Torrance Tests of Creative Thinking and ingenuity subtest of the Flanagan Aptitude Classification Tests. *Psychological Reports*, 1981, 48, 195–198.

[900]
Flanagan Industrial Tests. Business and industry; 1960–75; FIT; short speeded forms of the *Flanagan Aptitude Classification Tests* designed for use with adults; 18 tests: Arithmetic, Assembly, Components, Coordination, Electronics, Expression, Ingenuity, Inspection, Judgment and Comprehension, Mathematics and Reasoning, Mechanics, Memory, Patterns, Planning, Precision, Scales, Tables, Vocabulary; John C. Flanagan; Science Research Associates, Inc.*

For additional information and reviews by David O. Herman and Arthur C. MacKinney, see 8:981 (3 references); for reviews by C. J. Adcock and Robert C. Droege and an excerpted review by John L. Horn, see 7:977 (1 reference).

[901]
★**Flexibility Language Dominance Test, Spanish/English.** Spanish/English bilingual students ages 10 and over; 1978; 3 scores: Spanish total, English total, difference score interpreted according to a 7 level dominance rating system; Gary D. Keller; Publishers Test Service.*

[902]
The Flint Infant Security Scale. Ages 3–24 months; 1974; FISS; mental health; Betty M. Flint; Guidance Centre, University of Toronto [Canada].*

For additional information and a review by Jane V. Hunt, see 8:560 (1 reference).

[903]
Florida Cumulative Guidance Record, Revised. Grades 1–12; 1950–77; Edward Drew Co.*

[904]
★**Florida International Diagnostic-Prescriptive Vocational Competency Profile.** Adolescents and adults (educable and trainable mentally retarded, specific learning disabled, seriously emotionally disturbed, economically disadvantaged); 1979–80; "designed to evaluate individuals' general functional level and six specific domains of vocational competency"; 7 scores: vocational self-help skills, social-emotional adjustment, work attitudes-responsibility, cognitive-learning ability, perceptual-motor skills, general work habits, total; Howard Rosenberg and Dennis G. Tesolowski; Stoelting Co.*

[905]
Flowers-Costello Tests of Central Auditory Abilities. Grades kgn–6; 1970; 3 scores: low pass filtered speech, competing messages, total; Arthur Flowers, Mary Rose Costello, and Victor Small; Perceptual Learning Systems.*

See T2:2035 (2 references).

REFERENCES
1–2. See T2:2035.

3. AYRES, A. J. Cluster analyses of measures of sensory integration. *American Journal of Occupational Therapy*, 1977, 31, 362–366.
4. AYRES, A. J. Dichotic listening performance in learning-disabled children. *American Journal of Occupational Therapy*, 1977, 31, 441–446.
5. AYRES, A. J. Learning disabilities and the vestibular system. *Journal of Learning Disabilities*, 1978, 11, 18–29.

[906]
★**Fluharty Preschool Speech and Language Screening Test.** Ages 2–6; 1978; 4 scores: identification total, articulation total, comprehension total, repetition total; Nancy Buono Fluharty; Teaching Resources Corporation.*

[907]
Ford-Hicks French Grammar Completion Tests. High school; 1944; test booklet title is *Dents' Modern Language Tests: French Grammar*; H. E. Ford and R. K. Hicks; J. M. Dent & Sons (Canada) Ltd. [Canada].* (In-print status uncertain; no reply from publisher.)

For additional information, see 6:372.

[908]
The Forer Structured Sentence Completion Test. Ages 10–18, adults; 1957–67; FSSCT; Bertram R. Forer; Western Psychological Services.*

See T2:1461 (3 references) and P:429 (4 references); for reviews by Charles N. Cofer and Percival M. Symonds, see 5:134 (5 references).

[909]
The Forer Vocational Survey. Adolescents and adults; 1957; FVS; vocational adjustment; Bertram R. Forer; Western Psychological Services.*

For additional information, see P:430; for reviews by Benjamin Balinsky and Charles N. Cofer and an excerpted review by Laurence Siegel, see 5:135.

[910]
Form Relations Group Test. Ages 14 and over; 1926–46; National Institute of Industrial Psychology; NFER-Nelson Publishing Co. [England].*

See T2:2247 (9 references); for a review by A. T. Welford, see 4:757 (10 references).

[911]
Forms From Diagnostic Methods in Speech Pathology. Children and adults with speech problems; 1952–63; 20 forms consisting of coordination forms, rating scales, attitude surveys, and biographical questionnaires; Wendell Johnson, Frederic L. Darley, and D. C. Spriestersbach; Interstate Printers & Publishers, Inc.*
a) FORM 1, CHART OF SIGNIFICANT VARIATIONS IN SEVERITY OF THE STUTTERING PROBLEM SINCE ONSET.
b) FORM 2, GENERAL SPEECH BEHAVIOR RATING.
c) FORM 3, ARTICULATION TEST. Special printing of combined record and analysis sheets of *Templin-Darley Screening and Diagnostic Tests of Articulation*.
d) FORM 4, SPEECH MECHANISM EXAMINATION.
e) FORM 5, GENERAL VOICE QUALITY EXAMINATION.
f) FORM 6, SUPPLEMENTARY EXAMINATION FOR BREATHINESS.
g) FORM 7, SUPPLEMENTARY EXAMINATION FOR HARSHNESS.
h) FORM 8, SUPPLEMENTARY EXAMINATION FOR NASALITY.

[912] The Forty-Eight Item Counseling Evaluation Test

i) FORM 9, MEASURES OF SPEECH AND LANGUAGE DEVELOPMENT.
j) FORM 10, MEASURES OF RATE OF SPEAKING AND ORAL READING.
k) FORM 11, MEASURES OF DISFLUENCY OF SPEAKING AND ORAL READING.
l) FORM 12, SPEAKING-TIME LOG.
m) FORM 13, CHECK LIST OF STUTTERING REACTIONS.
n) FORM 14, SCALE FOR RATING SEVERITY OF STUTTERING.
o) FORM 15, IOWA SCALE OF ATTITUDE TOWARD STUTTERING.
p) FORM 16, STUTTERER'S SELF-RATINGS OF REACTIONS TO SPEECH SITUATIONS.
q) FORM 17, MEASURES OF ADAPTATION OF STUTTERING AND ORAL READING RATE.
r) FORM 18, MEASURES OF STUTTERING CONSISTENCY.
s) FORM 19, IOWA UNIMANUAL HAND USAGE QUESTIONNAIRE.
t) FORM 20, IOWA PERFORMANCE TEST OF SELECTED MANUAL ACTIVITIES.

For additional information, see 6:308 (1 reference).

REFERENCES

1. See 6:308.
2. MURRAY, T. J., KELLY, P., CAMPBELL, L., & STEFANIK, K. Haloperidol in the treatment of stuttering. *British Journal of Psychiatry*, 1977, 130, 370-373.
3. SOMMERS, R. K., & STARKEY, K. L. Dichotic verbal processing in Down's Syndrome children having qualitatively different speech and language skills. *American Journal of Mental Deficiency*, 1977, 82, 44-53.
4. METZ, D. E., CONTURE, E. G., & CARUSO, A. Voice onset time, frication, and aspiration during stutterers' fluent speech. *Journal of Speech & Hearing Research*, 1979, 22, 649-656.
5. ANDREWS, G., & HARVEY, R. Regression to the mean in pretreatment measures of stuttering. *Journal of Speech & Hearing Disorders*, 1981, 46, 204-207.

[912]
The Forty-Eight Item Counseling Evaluation Test. Adolescents and adults; ICET; 1963-71; 7 scores: 6 problem areas (anxiety-tension-stress, compulsive-obsessive-rigid behavior, depressive-defeatist thoughts and feelings, friendship-socialization, religious-philosophical goals, inadequacy feelings and behavior), total; Frank B. McMahon; Western Psychological Services.*

For additional information and a review by W. Leslie Barnette, Jr., see 8:561 (2 references); see also T2:1187 (1 reference); for a review by John O. Crites, see 7:81 (1 reference).

[913]
Fountain Valley Teacher Support System in Mathematics. Grades kgn, 1, 2, 3, 4, 5, 6, 7, 8; 1972-74; FVTSS-M; criterion-referenced; the 9 levels together cover 786 specific-objective subtests in 9 areas: applications, functions and graphs, geometry, logical thinking, measurement, numbers and operations, problem solving, sets, statistics and probability; Richard L. Zweig Associates, Inc.* (In-print status uncertain; no reply from publisher.)

For additional information and a review by Randy Demaline, see 8:270.

REFERENCES

1. HAMBLETON, R. K., & EIGNOR, D. R. Guidelines for evaluating criterion-referenced tests and test manuals. *Journal of Educational Measurement*, 1978, 15, 321-327.

[914]
Fountain Valley Teacher Support System in Reading. Grades 1, 2, 3, 4, 5, 6; 1971-75; FVTSS-R; criterion-referenced; 6 levels together cover 367 specific-objective subtests in 5 areas: comprehension, phonetic analysis, structural analysis, study skills, vocabulary development; Richard L. Zweig Associates, Inc.* (In-print status uncertain; no reply from publisher.)

For additional information and reviews by Anthony J. Nitko and Gus P. Plessas, see 8:725 (1 reference).

[915]
Fountain Valley Teacher Support System in Secondary Reading. Grades 7-12; 1976; FVTSSSR; upward extension of the *Fountain Valley Teacher Support System in Reading*; criterion-referenced; 61 specific-objective subtests in 3 areas: comprehension, study skills, vocabulary development; Richard L. Zweig Associates, Inc.* (In-print status uncertain; no reply from publisher.)

For additional information and reviews by Gilbert Sax and Carleton B. Shay, see 8:758.

[916]
Four Tone Screening for Older Children and Adults. Ages 8 and over; 1973; for the detection of hearing impairments; Zenith Hearing Instrument Corporation.* (In-print status uncertain; no reply from publisher.)

[917]
Franck Drawing Completion Test. Ages 6 and over; 1951-76; FDCT; masculinity-femininity; Kate Franck; Australian Council for Educational Research [Australia].*

For additional information, see 8:562 (23 references); see also T2:1463 (38 references) and P:432 (5 references); for a review by Arthur W. Meadows, see 5:136 (5 references).

REFERENCES

1-5. See 5:136.
6-10. See P:432.
11-48. See T2:1463.
49-71. See 8:562.
72. DOMINO, G. Transcendental meditation and creativity: An empirical investigation. *Journal of Applied Psychology*, 1977, 62, 358-362.
73. SMALL, A. C., BILLER, H. B., GROSS, R. B., & PROCHASKA, J. O. Congruency of sex-role identification in normal and disturbed adolescent males. *Psychological Reports*, 1977, 41, 39-46.
74. BECKMAN, L. J. Sex-role conflict in alcoholic women: Myth or reality. *Journal of Abnormal Psychology*, 1978, 87, 408-417.
75. BUHRICH, N., & MCCONAGHY, N. Tests of gender feelings and behavior in homosexuality, transvestism, and transsexualism. *Journal of Clinical Psychology*, 1979, 35, 187-191.
76. DOMINO, G. Creativity and the home environment. *Gifted Child Quarterly*, 1979, 23, 818-828.
77. ZUCKER, R. A., BATTISTICH, V. A., & LANGER, G. B. Sexual behavior, sex-role adaptation and drinking in young women. *Journal of Studies on Alcohol*, 1981, 42, 457-465.

[918]
French Comprehension Tests. Grades kgn-2, 1-5; 1975-76; FCT; Henri C. Barik; Ontario Institute for Studies in Education [Canada].* (In-print status uncertain; no reply from publisher.)

For additional information and an excerpted review by Alison D'Anglejan, see 8:120 (1 reference).

REFERENCES

1. See 8:120.

2. SWAIN, M., & BARIK, H. C. The role of curricular approach, rural–urban background, and socioeconomic status in second language learning: The Cornwall area study. *Alberta Journal of Educational Research*, 1978, 24, 1–16.

[919]
Frost–Safran School Situations Test. Ages 9–12; 1964–71; SST; 8 response categories: hostility, anxiety, depression, guilt and self-criticism, inadequacy and rejection, happiness, neutral, indeterminate; Barry P. Frost, Carl Safran, and Georgina Adamson (manual); Psychoeducational Clinic, University of Calgary [Canada].*

REFERENCES

1. FROST, B. P., & ADAMSON, G. A study of the concurrent validity of the Frost–Safran School Situations Test. *Personality*, 1971, 2, 227–237.

[920]
Frost Self Description Questionnaire. Ages 8–14; 1972–73; FSDQ; 14 scores: anxiety (test, social, worry and tension, concentration, separation from family, spatial separation, body damage, free floating), aggression (externalized, internalized, projective), denial, affiliation, submissiveness; (Spanish edition available; Japanese and Afrikaans editions available from author); Barry P. Frost; Psychoeducational Clinic, University of Calgary [Canada].*

For additional information and a review by Harrison G. Gough, see 8:563 (1 reference); see also T2:1189 (3 references).

[921]
★**Frost Self Description Questionnaire: Extended Scales.** Ages 9–14; 1972–79; extension of *Frost Self Description Questionnaire*; Barry P. Frost; Psychoeducational Clinic, University of Calgary [Canada].*

a) FORM 1. 3 scores: externalized aggression, internalized aggression, projective aggression.

b) FORM 2. 4 scores: free floating anxiety, body damage anxiety, separation anxiety, worry and tension.

c) FORM 3. 5 scores: test anxiety, concentration anxiety, social anxiety, denial, affiliation.

[922]
Frostig Movement Skills Test Battery, Experimental Edition. Ages 6–12; 1972; FMSTB; 6 summary scores: hand-eye coordination, strength, balance, visually guided movement, flexibility, total; R. E. Orpet; Consulting Psychologists Press, Inc.*

For additional information and reviews by Thomas Oakland and Carl L. Rosen, see 8:871 (4 references).

REFERENCES

1–4. See 8:871.
5. WHYTE, L. Prescriptive teaching: Changes in stage of logico-mathematical thinking and spatial development in a group of opportunity class children. *Alberta Journal of Educational Research*, 1976, 22, 34–43.
6. JEFFREY, H., SCOTT, J., CHANDLER, D., & DUGDALE, A. E. Deafness after bacterial meningitis. *Archives of Diseases in Childhood*, 1977, 52, 555–559.
7. MONTGOMERY, P., & RICHTER, E. Effect of sensory integrative therapy on the neuromotor development of retarded children. *Physical Therapy*, 1977, 57, 799–806.
8. VAN ETTEN, C., & WATSON, B. Improving motor abilities. *Journal of Learning Disabilities*, 1977, 10, 511–513.
9. BASSIN, S. L., & BREIHAN, S. K. Relationship of performance on motor activities and reading achievement. *Perceptual & Motor Skills*, 1978, 46, 811–814.
10. FEIN, D., TINDER, P., & WATERHOUSE, L. Stimulus generalization in autistic and normal children. *Journal of Child Psychology & Psychiatry & Allied Disciplines*, 1979, 20, 325–335.

[923]
Full-Range Picture Vocabulary Test. Ages 2 and over; 1948; Robert B. Ammons and Helen S. Ammons; Psychological Test Specialists.*

For additional information and a review by Jerome M. Sattler, see 8:216 (6 references); see also T2:496 (33 references) and 6:521 (30 references); for reviews by William D. Altus and William M. Cruickshank, see 4:340 (10 references).

REFERENCES

1–10. See 4:340.
11–40. See 6:521.
41–73. See T2:496.
74–79. See 8:216.
80. FRIESWYK, S. H., JR. Schizophrenic discrimination learning as a function of aversive social and physical reinforcement. *Journal of Abnormal Psychology*, 1977, 86, 47–53.
81. GOLOMB, C. Representational development of the human figure: A look at the neglected variables of SES, IQ, sex, and verbalization. *Journal of Genetic Psychology*, 1977, 131, 207–222.
82. WALLBROWN, F. H. Shedd's formulations concerning the hyperkinetic syndrome–An empirical test of selected features. *Perceptual & Motor Skills*, 1978, 46, 809–810.
83. KATZ-GARRIS, L., HADLEY, T. J., GARRIS, R. P., & BARNHILL, B. A factor analytic study of the Adaptive Behavior Scale. *Psychological Reports*, 1980, 47, 807–814.

[924]
★**The Fullerton Language Test for Adolescents, Experimental Edition.** Ages 11–18; 1980; 8 scores: auditory synthesis, morphology competency, oral commands, convergent production, divergent production, syllabication, grammatic competency, idioms; Arden R. Thorum; Consulting Psychologists Press, Inc.*

[925]
Functional Communication Profile. Aphasic adults; 1956–69; FCP; ratings by experienced clinician following nonstructured interview; 6 scores: movement, speaking, understanding, reading, other, total; Martha Taylor Sarno; Institute of Rehabilitation Medicine.* (In-print status uncertain; no reply from publisher.)

For additional information and reviews by Raphael M. Haller and Harvey Halpern, see 8:962 (11 references).

REFERENCES

1–11. See 8:962.
12. LEVITA, E. Effects of speech therapy on aphasics' responses to functional communication profile. *Perceptual & Motor Skills*, 1978, 47, 151–154.
13. DAVID, R. M., ENDERBY, P., & BAINTON, D. Progress report on an evaluation of speech therapy for aphasia. *British Journal of Disorders of Communication*, 1979, 14, 85–88.
14. WALKER, S. A., & WILLIAMS, B. O. The response of a disabled elderly population to speech therapy. *British Journal of Disorders of Communication*, 1980, 15, 19–23.

[926]
Functional Grammar Test. High school and college; 1970; FGT; Joyce E. Lackey; Psychometric Affiliates.*

[927]
Furness Test of Aural Comprehension in Spanish. 1–3 years high school or 1–2 years college; 1945–51; 2 editions; Edna Lue Furness; National Textbook Co.* (In-print status uncertain; no reply from publisher.)

a) ORIGINAL EDITION. 1945–46; 4 scores: vocabulary, completion, identification, total.

b) RECORDED EDITION. 1951; 5 scores: vocabulary, completion, identification, question-answer, total.

See T2:310 (1 reference) and 4:262; for reviews by Frederick B. Agard and Walter V. Kaulfers of *a*, see 3:213.

REFERENCES

1. See T2:310.
2. RODRIGUEZ–BROWN, F. V. Furness Test of Aural Comprehension in Spanish. *Modern Language Journal*, 1978, 62, 432.

[928]

GAP Reading Comprehension Test. Grades 2–7; 1965–70; GAP; cloze technique with approximately every tenth word omitted; 2 editions; J. McLeod.*

a) AUSTRALIAN EDITION. 1965–67; Heinemann Educational Australia Pty Ltd. [Australia].

b) BRITISH EDITION. 1965–70; manual edited by Derick Unwin; Heinemann Educational Books Ltd. [England]. *Out of print.*

See T2:1550 (3 references); for reviews by Donald B. Black and Earl F. Rankin, see 7:688.

REFERENCES

1–3. See T2:1550.
4. NEVILLE, M. H., & PUGH, A. K. Context in reading and listening: Variations in approach to cloze tasks. *Reading Research Quarterly*, 1976–1977, 12, 13–31.
5. JACKSON, M., & ACKENSTEIN, G. The visuothematic approach in the classroom. *Academic Therapy*, 1977, 12, 327–337.
6. YOUNGMAN, M. B. Six reactions to school transfer. *British Journal of Educational Psychology*, 1978, 48, 280–289.
7. JORM, A. F. Children with reading and spelling retardation: Functioning of whole-word and correspondence rule mechanisms. *Journal of Child Psychology & Psychiatry & Allied Disciplines*, 1981, 22, 171–178.

[929]

GAPADOL. Ages 10–16; 1972; upward extension for "adolescent children" of *GAP Reading Comprehension Test*; cloze technique; J. McLeod and J. Anderson; Heinemann Educational Australia Pty Ltd. [Australia].*

For additional information and a review by Ira E. Aaron, see 8:726.

REFERENCES

1. HOWELL, E. R., SMITH, G. A., & STANLEY, G. Reading disability and visual spatial frequency specific effects. *Australian Journal of Psychology*, 1981, 33, 97–102.

[930]

Garnett College Test in Engineering Science. 1–2 years technical college; 1966–71; GCTES; 3 scores: mechanics, heat-electricity-magnetism, total; I. Macfarlane Smith; NFER-Nelson Publishing Co. [England].*

For additional information concerning the earlier edition, see 7:1093.

[931]

Gates Associative Learning Tests. Grades 1.5–7.0; (no date available); 4 scores: visual-visual (2 scores), auditory-visual (2 scores); The Reading Clinic, Temple University.*

[932]

*Gates-MacGinitie Reading Tests. Grades 1.0–1.9, 1.5–1.9, 2, 3, 4–6, 7–9, 10–12; 1926–78; GMRT; first edition of *Gates-MacGinitie Reading Tests* still available; 7 levels; Walter H. MacGinitie (test and manual), Joyce Kamons, Ruth L. Kowalski, Ruth K. MacGinitie, Timothy Mackay (manual); Riverside Publishing Co.*

a) BASIC R. Grades 1.0–1.9; 1978.

b) LEVEL A. Grades 1.5–1.9; 1978; 3 scores: vocabulary, comprehension, total.

c) LEVEL B. Grade 2; 1978; scores same as Level A.

d) LEVEL C. Grade 3; 1978; scores same as Level A.

e) LEVEL D. Grades 4–6; 1978; scores same as Level A.

f) LEVEL E. Grades 7–9; 1978; scores same as Level A.

g) LEVEL F. Grades 10–12; 1978; remaining details same as Level E.

For additional information, see 8:726A (34 references); for reviews by Carolyn L. Burke and Byron H. Van Roekel and an excerpted review by William R. Powell of an earlier edition, see 7:689.

REFERENCES

1–18. See T2:1552.
19–52. See 8:726A.
53. BACHMAN, J. G., & O'MALLEY, P. M. Self–esteem in young men: A longitudinal analysis of the impact of educational and occupational attainment. *Journal of Personality & Social Psychology*, 1977, 35, 365–380.
54. BELL, A. E., ABRAHAMSON, D. S., & MCRAE, K. N. Reading retardation: A 12-year prospective study. *Journal of Pediatrics*, 1977, 91, 363–370.
55. BOLSTAD, O. D., & JOHNSON, S. M. The relationship between teachers' assessment of students and students' actual behavior in the classroom. *Child Development*, 1977, 48, 570–578.
56. CASSIDY, A. M., & VUKELICH, C. The effects of group size on kindergarten children's listening comprehension performance. *Psychology in the Schools*, 1977, 14, 449–455.
57. DEVITO, P. J. Reading achievement of Rhode Island compensatory education students: A school effects study. *Contemporary Educational Psychology*, 1977, 2, 332–344.
58. FOCH, T. T., DEFRIES, J. C., MCCLEARN, G. E., & SINGER, S. M. Familial patterns of impairment in reading disability. *Journal of Educational Psychology*, 1977, 69, 316–329.
59. FRIEDMAN, J. B., & GILLOOLEY, W. B. Perceptual development in the profoundly deaf as related to early reading. *Journal of Special Education*, 1977, 11, 347–354.
60. GLAZZARD, M. The effectiveness of three kindergarten predictors for first-grade achievement. *Journal of Learning Disabilities*, 1977, 10, 95–99.
61. GRAVES, D. H. Research update, research for the classroom: Promising research studies. *Language Arts*, 1977, 54, 453–458.
62. GUTHRIE, J. T., & SEIFERT, M. Letter–sound complexity in learning to identify words. *Journal of Educational Psychology*, 1977, 69, 686–696.
63. KIRBY, J. R., & DAS, J. P. Reading achievement, IQ, and simultaneous-successive processing. *Journal of Educational Psychology*, 1977, 69, 564–570.
64. LONG, J. V., SCHAFFRAN, J. A., & KELLOGG, T. M. Effects of out-of-level survey testing on reading achievement scores of Title I, ESEA students. *Journal of Educational Measurement*, 1977, 14, 203–213.
65. PETERS, C. W. Predicting reading performance at the secondary level through the utilization of a student self-assessment inventory. *National Reading Conference Yearbook*, 1977, 131–135.
66. POTTS, M., & LEYMAN, L. Intervention in the motor domain: A training study with first- and second-grade slow readers. *Psychology in the Schools*, 1977, 14, 200–206.
67. ULLMAN, D. G. Children's lateral preference patterns: Frequency and relationships with achievement and intelligence. *Journal of School Psychology*, 1977, 15, 36–43.
68. VOGEL, S. A. Morphological ability in normal and dyslexic children. *Journal of Learning Disabilities*, 1977, 10, 35–43.
69. WILLIAMS, J. D., BREKKE, B. W., & PETERSON, W. Effect of visual motor program on school achievement: A longitudinal study. *Perceptual & Motor Skills*, 1977, 45, 786.
70. ARLIN, M., & ROTH, G. Pupils' use of time while reading comics and books. *American Educational Research Journal*, 1978, 15, 201–216.
71. BALDAUF, R. B., & PROPST, I. K. Preliminary evidence regarding the validity of a modified cloze procedure for lower elementary ESL students. *Educational & Psychological Measurement*, 1978, 38, 451–455.
72. BALOW, B., FUCHS, D., & KASBOHM, M. Teaching nonreaders to read: An evaluation of the basic skill centers in Minneapolis. *Journal of Learning Disabilities*, 1978, 11, 351–354.
73. BURROWS, E. H., & NEYLAND, D. Reading skills, auditory comprehension of language, and academic achievement. *Journal of Speech & Hearing Disorders*, 1978, 43, 467–472.
74. DAVID, J. L., & PELAVIN, S. H. Evaluating compensatory education: Over what period of time should achievement be measured? *Journal of Educational Measurement*, 1978, 15, 91–99.
75. ELGART, D. B. Oral reading, silent reading, and listening comprehension: A comparative study. *Journal of Reading Behavior*, 1978, 10, 203–207.

76. HOLLINGSWORTH, P. M. An experimental approach to the impress method of teaching reading. *Reading Teacher*, 1978, 31, 624-626.

77. HOWE, T., & SZYMCZUK, M. Cohort analysis of reading scores in several IGE elementary schools. *Educational Research Quarterly*, 1978, 3, 52-61.

78. JOHNSON, C. D., & CRANO, W. D. Effects of spatial skills training on reading performance. *Journal of Experimental Education*, 1978, 46, 25-28.

79. LESIAK, J. The reflection–impulsivity dimension and reading ability. *Reading World*, 1978, 17, 333-339.

80. MARGOLIS, H., & BRANNIGAN, G. G. Conceptual tempo as a parameter for predicting reading achievement. *Journal of Educational Research*, 1978, 71, 342-345.

81. MERRICKS, A. R., & CROCKER, R. K. The influence of science process activities and selected science reading materials on reading achievement of first and third grade pupils. *School Science & Mathematics*, 1978, 78, 684-690.

82. MICHAEL, W. B., SMITH, R. A., & MICHAEL, J. J. Further development and validation of a self–concept measure involving school-related activities. *Educational & Psychological Measurement*, 1978, 38, 527-535.

83. PATTON, J. E., & OFFENBACH, S. I. Effects of visual and auditory distractors on learning disabled and normal children's recognition memory performance. *Journal of Educational Psychology*, 1978, 70, 788-795.

84. READANCE, J. E., & BALDWIN, R. S. Effects of impulsivity-reflectivity and type of phonics instruction on reading achievement. *National Reading Conference Yearbook*, 1978, 36-40.

85. READANCE, J. E., & BALDWIN, R. S. The relationship of cognitive style and phonics instruction. *Journal of Educational Research*, 1978, 72, 44-52.

86. SADICK, T. L., & GINSBURG, B. E. The development of the lateral functions and reading ability. *Cortex*, 1978, 14, 3-11.

87. SMART, W. D., & OLLILA, L. The effect of sentence-combining practice on written compositions and reading comprehension. *Alberta Journal of Educational Research*, 1978, 24, 113-120.

88. WASSERMAN, S. Key vocabulary: Impact on beginning reading. *Young Children*, 1978, 33, 33-38.

89. WILLOWS, D. M. Individual differences in distraction by pictures in a reading situation. *Journal of Educational Psychology*, 1978, 70, 837-847.

90. WILLOWS, D. M. A picture is not always worth a thousand words: Pictures as distractors in reading. *Journal of Educational Psychology*, 1978, 70, 255-262.

91. ATCHISON, M. J., & CANTER, G. J. Variables influencing phonemic discrimination performance in normal and learning–disabled children. *Journal of Speech & Hearing Disorders*, 1979, 44, 543-556.

92. BALDAUF, R. B., JR., & PROPST, I. K., JR. Matching and multiple-choice cloze tests. *Journal of Educational Research*, 1979, 72, 321-326.

93. FUCHS, D. Reading and perceptual–motor performance: Can we strengthen them simultaneously? *Journal of Special Education*, 1979, 13, 265-273.

94. GILLET, J. W., & RICHARDS, H. C. Reading comprehension test performance and hierarchical classification. *Journal of Reading Behavior*, 1979, 11, 380-385.

95. GLAZZARD, P. Kindergarten predictors of school achievement. *Journal of Learning Disabilities*, 1979, 12, 689-694.

96. GREENE, C. E., & SZABO, M. Effects of reduced reading level on achievement in ISCS. *Science Education*, 1979, 63, 37-44.

97. HOLMES, D. R., & MCKEEVER, W. F. Material specific serial memory deficit in adolescent dyslexics. *Cortex*, 1979, 15, 51-62.

98. MASSARO, D. W., VENEZKY, R. L., & TAYLOR, G. A. Orthographic regularity, positional frequency, and visual processing of letter strings. *Journal of Experimental Psychology: General*, 1979, 108, 107-124.

99. OLLENDICK, D. G. Parental locus of control and the assessment of children's personality characteristics. *Journal of Personality Assessment*, 1979, 43, 401-405.

100. PROPST, I. K., & BALDAUF, R. B., JR. Use matching cloze tests for elementary ESL students. *Reading Teacher*, 1979, 32, 683-690.

101. REED, H. B. C., JR. Biological defects and special education–An issue in personnel preparation. *Journal of Special Education*, 1979, 13, 9-33.

102. TAYLOR, B. M. Good and poor reader's recall of familiar and unfamiliar text. *Journal of Reading Behavior*, 1979, 11, 375-380.

103. YAP, K. O. Vocabulary–building blocks of comprehension. *Journal of Reading Behavior*, 1979, 11, 49-59.

104. BIERSNER, R. J., & LAROCCO, J. M. Determinants of reading performance and achievement. *Perceptual & Motor Skills*, 1980, 50, 715-721.

105. BUTKOWSKY, I. S., & WILLOWS, D. M. Cognitive–motivational characteristics of children varying in reading ability: Evidence for learned helplessness in poor readers. *Journal of Educational Psychology*, 1980, 72, 408-422.

106. DUFFELMEYER, F. A. A comparison of reading test results in grades nine and twelve. *Journal of Reading*, 1980, 23, 606-608.

107. GRIMMETT, S. A., & MCCOY, M. Effects of parental communication on reading performance of third grade children. *Reading Teacher*, 1980, 34, 303-308.

108. JENKINS, B. L., LONGMAID, W. H., O'BRIEN, S. F., & SHELDON, C. N. Children's use of hypothesis testing when decoding words. *Reading Teacher*, 1980, 33, 664-667.

109. JONGSMA, E. Gates–MacGinitie Reading Tests. *Journal of Reading*, 1980, 23, 340-345.

110. LESLIE, L. Mediation or production deficiency in disabled readers? *Perceptual & Motor Skills*, 1980, 50, 519-530.

111. MARTIN, R. D., & BASTIAN, J. Relationship between behavioral indices of aggression and hostile content on the TAT for incarcerated young women. *Perceptual & Motor Skills*, 1980, 51, 327-332.

112. MASSARO, D. W., & TAYLOR, G. A. Reading ability and utilization of orthographic structure in reading. *Journal of Educational Psychology*, 1980, 72, 730-742.

113. MINTON, M. J. The effect of sustained silent reading upon comprehension and attitudes among ninth graders. *Journal of Reading*, 1980, 23, 498-502.

114. MOLDLENHAUER, D. L., & MILLER, W. H. Television and reading achievement. *Journal of Reading*, 1980, 23, 615-619.

115. POLK, C. L. H., & GOLDENSTEIN, D. Early reading and concrete operations. *Journal of Psychology*, 1980, 106, 111-116.

116. WHALEY, W. J., & KIBBY, M. W. Word synthesis and beginning reading achievement. *Journal of Educational Research*, 1980, 73, 132-138.

117. ABIDIN, R. R., & SELTZER, J. Special education outcomes: Implications for implementation of Public Law 94-142. *Journal of Learning Disabilities*, 1981, 14, 28-31.

118. MARR, M. B., & KAMIL, M. L. Single word decoding and comprehension: A constructive replication. *Journal of Reading Behavior*, 1981, 13, 81-86.

119. MCMAHON, R. J., FOREHAND, R., & GRIEST, D. L. Effects of knowledge of social learning principles on enhancing treatment outcome and generalization in a parent training program. *Journal of Consulting & Clinical Psychology*, 1981, 49, 526-532.

120. MILLER, J. W., & MCKENNA, M. C. Disabled readers: Their intellectual and perceptual capacities at differing ages. *Perceptual & Motor Skills*, 1981, 52, 467-472.

121. NEUMAN, S. B. Effect of teaching auditory perceptual skills on reading achievement in first grade. *Reading Teacher*, 1981, 34, 422-426.

122. PATBERG, J. P., DEWITZ, P., & SAMUELS, S. J. The effect of context on the size of the perceptual unit used in word recognition. *Journal of Reading Behavior*, 1981, 13, 33-48.

123. ROBERGE, J. J., & CRAVEN, P. A. Effects of reading comprehension on conditional reasoning from connected prose passages. *Journal of General Psychology*, 1981, 105, 253-260.

124. RYCKMAN, D. B. Reading achievement, IQ, and simultaneous–successive processing among normal and learning–disabled children. *Alberta Journal of Educational Research*, 1981, 27, 74-83.

125. SCHWANTES, F. M. Effects of story context on children's ongoing word recognition. *Journal of Reading Behavior*, 1981, 13, 305-311.

126. SEWELL, T. E., PALMO, A. J., & MANNI, J. L. High school dropout, psychological, academic, and vocational factors. *Urban Education*, 1981, 16, 65-76.

127. STARK, R. E., & TALLAL, P. Selection of children with specific language deficits. *Journal of Speech & Hearing Disorders*, 1981, 46, 114-122.

128. TALLAL, P., STARK, R., KALLMAN, C., & MELLITS, D. A reexamination of some nonverbal perceptual abilities of language–impaired and normal children as a function of age and sensory modality. *Journal of Speech & Hearing Research*, 1981, 24, 351-357.

129. WILLOWS, D. M., & RYAN, E. B. Differential utilization of syntactic and semantic information by skilled and less skilled readers in the intermediate grades. *Journal of Educational Psychology*, 1981, 73, 607-615.

[933]

★**Gates-MacGinitie Reading Tests, Canadian Edition.** Grades 1.0–1.9, 1.5–1.9, 2, 3, 4–6, 7–9, 10–12; 1978–81; GMRTCE; based on the second edition (1978) of the *Gates-MacGinitie Reading Tests*; 7 levels; Walter H. MacGinitie (test and manual), Joyce Kamons, Ruth Kowalski, Ruth K. MacGinitie, and Timothy Mackay (manual); Nelson Canada [Canada].*

a) BASIC R. Grades 1.0–1.9; 1979–80.

b) LEVEL A. Grades 1.5–1.9; 1979–80; 3 scores: vocabulary, comprehension, total.

c) LEVEL B. Grade 2; 1979–80; scores and forms same as for Level A.

d) LEVEL C. Grade 3; 1979–80; scores and forms same as for Level A.
e) LEVEL D. Grades 4–6; 1979–80; scores and forms same as for Level A.
f) LEVEL E. Grades 7–9; 1979–80; scores and forms same as for Level A.
g) LEVEL F. Grades 10–12; 1979–80; scores and forms same as for Level A.

[934]
Gates-MacGinitie Reading Tests: Survey F. Grades 10–12; 1969–72; lower levels of the Gates-MacGinitie Reading Tests listed separately in this volume; 4 scores: speed and accuracy (number attempted, number correct), vocabulary, comprehension; Arthur I. Gates and Walter H. MacGinitie; Riverside Publishing Co.*

For additional information and a review by Albert J. Kingston, see 8:727 (2 references); for a review by Jason Millman, see 7:690.

REFERENCES

1–2. See 8:727.
3. KERSHNER, J. R. Cerebral dominance in disabled readers, good readers, and gifted children: Search for a valid model. *Child Development*, 1977, 48, 61–67.
4. KINCAID, J. P., & GAMBLE, L. G. Ease of comprehension of standard and readable automobile insurance policies as a function of reading ability. *Journal of Reading Behavior*, 1977, 9, 85–87.
5. RAVEN, R. J., & COLE, R. Relationships between Piaget's operative comprehension and physiology modeling processes of community college students. *Science Education*, 1978, 62, 481–489.
6. RATEKIN, N. Reading achievement of disabled learners. *Exceptional Children*, 1979, 45, 454–458.
7. RYDER, R. J., & GRAVES, M. F. Secondary students' internalization of letter–sound correspondences. *Journal of Educational Research*, 1980, 73, 172–178.
8. PAIGE, W. D. The effects of the level of readability and use of a glossary on the comprehension of technical material. *Journal of Industrial Teacher Education*, 1981, 18, 43–52.

[935]
***Gates-McKillop-Horowitz Reading Diagnostic Tests, Second Edition.** Grades 1–6; 1962–81; revision of *Gates-McKillop Reading Diagnostic Tests*; 23 scores: omissions, additions, repetitions, mispronunciations (directional errors, wrong beginning, wrong middle, wrong ending, wrong in several parts, accent errors, total), reading sentences, words-flash, words-untimed, word attack (syllabication, recognizing and blending common word parts, reading words, giving letter sounds, naming capital letters, naming lowercase letters), vowels, auditory (blending, discrimination), spelling; Arthur I. Gates, Anne S. McKillop, and Elizabeth Cliff Horowitz; Teachers College Press.*

For additional information and a review by Harry Singer of an earlier edition, see 8:759 (8 references); see also T2:1629 (11 references); for reviews by N. Dale Bryant and Gabriel M. Della-Piana, see 6:824 (2 references); for a review by George D. Spache of the earlier edition, see 5:662; for a review by Worth J. Osburn, see 4:563 (2 references); for a review by T. L. Torgerson, see 3:510 (3 references).

REFERENCES

1–3. See 3:510.
4–5. See 4:563.
6–7. See 6:824.
8–18. See T2:1629.
19–26. See 8:759.

27. FRAUENHEIM, J. G. Academic achievement characteristics of adult males who were diagnosed as dyslexic in childhood. *Journal of Learning Disabilities*, 1978, 11, 476–483.
28. MERCURE, R., & WARREN, S. A. Inadequate and adequate readers' performance on a dichotic listening task. *Perceptual & Motor Skills*, 1978, 46, 709–710.
29. GUTERMAN, S. S. IQ tests in research on social stratification. The cross–class validity of the tests as measures of scholastic aptitude. *Sociology of Education*, 1979, 52, 163–173.
30. MUIA, J. A., & CONNORS, E. T. Clinical reading practices: Some legal considerations. *National Reading Conference Yearbook*, 1979, 145–149.
31. RATEKIN, N. Reading achievement of disabled learners. *Exceptional Children*, 1979, 45, 454–458.
32. WILSON, K. L. The effects of integration and class on black educational attainment. *Sociology of Education*, 1979, 52, 84–98.
33. ANDERSSON, K. E., RICHARDS, H. C., & HALLAHAN, D. P. Piagetian task performance of learning disabled children. *Journal of Learning Disabilities*, 1980, 13, 37–41.

[936]
G.C. Anecdotal Record Form. Teachers' recordings of student actions; 1943; formerly called *V.G.C. Anecdotal Record Form*; Guidance Centre, University of Toronto [Canada].*

[937]
The Geist Picture Interest Inventory. Grades 8–16 and adults; 1959–71; GPII; 18 (males) or 19 (females) scores: 11 or 12 interest scores (persuasive, clerical, mechanical, musical, scientific, outdoor, literary, computational, artistic, social service, dramatic, personal service-females only) and 7 motivation scores (family, prestige, financial, intrinsic and personality, environmental, past experience, could not say); Harold Geist; Western Psychological Services.*

See T2:2180 (18 references); for reviews by Milton E. Hahn and Benjamin Shimberg, and an excerpted review by David V. Tiedeman, see 6:1054 (12 references).

[938]
General Chemistry Test: National Achievement Tests. Grades 10–16; 1958–59; 4 scores: uses-processes-results, formulae and valence, miscellaneous facts, total; no manual; Lester D. Crow and Roy S. Cook; Psychometric Affiliates.*

For additional information and a review by J. A. Campbell, see 6:918.

[939]
General Clerical Ability Test: ETSA Test 3A. Job applicants; 1960–72, c1957–59; manual and technical handbook by S. Trevor Hadley and George A. W. Stouffer, Jr.; test by Psychological Services Bureau; Educators'-Employers' Tests & Services Associates.*

For reviews of the complete battery, see 6:1025 (2 reviews).

[940]
General Clerical Test. Grades 9–16 and clerical job applicants; 1944–72; formerly called *Psychological Corporation General Clerical Test*; 4 scores: clerical speed and accuracy, numerical ability, verbal facility, total; The Psychological Corporation. (British edition: 1971–79; technical manual by Peter Saville, Janice Hare, Laura Finlayson, and Stephen Blinkhorn; norm supplement by David Pintilie and Gill Nyfield; NFER-Nelson Publishing Co. [England].)*

For additional information and a review by Charles J. Cranny, see 8:1033 (1 reference); see also T2:2129 (11 references); for reviews by Edward E. Cureton and G. A. Satter, see 4:730 (4 references); for reviews by Edward N. Hay, Thelma Hunt, Raymond A. Katzell, and E. F. Wonderlic, see 3:630.

[941]

General Health Questionnaire. Adolescents and adults; 1969–78; GHQ; "self-administered screening test aimed at detecting psychiatric disorders among respondents in community settings"; 5 scores for scaled form only: somatic symptoms, anxiety and insomnia, social dysfunction, severe depression, total; David Goldberg; NFER-Nelson Publishing Co. [England].

For additional information, see 8:565 (15 references).

REFERENCES

1–15. See 8:565.
16. BALLINGER, C. B. Psychiatric morbidity and the menopause: Survey of a gynecological out-patient clinic. *British Journal of Psychiatry*, 1977, 131, 83–89.
17. COOPER, S. F., LEACH, C., STORER, D., & TONGE, W. L. The children of psychiatric patients: Clinical findings. *British Journal of Psychiatry*, 1977, 131, 514–522.
18. KNIGHTS, E. B., & FOLSTEIN, M. F. Unsuspected emotional and cognitive disturbance in medical patients. *Annals of Internal Medicine*, 1977, 87, 723–724.
19. PARKER, G. Cyclone Tracy and Darwin evacuees: On the restoration of the species. *British Journal of Psychiatry*, 1977, 130, 548–555.
20. ROY, A. Nonconvulsive psychogenia attacks investigated for temporal lobe epilepsy. *Comprehensive Psychiatry*, 1977, 18, 591–593.
21. ANDREWS, G., TENNANT, C., HEWSON, D. M., & VAILLANT, G. E. Life event stress, social support, coping style, and risk of psychological impairment. *Journal of Nervous & Mental Disease*, 1978, 166, 307–316.
22. CORSER, C. M., & PHILIP, A. Emotional disturbance in newly registered general practice patients. *British Journal of Psychiatry*, 1978, 132, 172–176.
23. HENDERSON, S., BYRNE, D. G., DUNCAN-JONES, P., ADCOCK, S., SCOTT, R., & STEELE, G. P. Social bonds in the epidemiology of neurosis: A preliminary communication. *British Journal of Psychiatry*, 1978, 132, 463–466.
24. HENDERSON, S., DUNCAN-JONES, P., McAULEY, H., & RITCHIE, K. The patient's primary group. *British Journal of Psychiatry*, 1978, 132, 74–86.
25. ROY, A. Vulnerability factors and depression in women. *British Journal of Psychiatry*, 1978, 133, 106–110.
26. TENNANT, C., & ANDREWS, G. The cause of life events in neurosis. *Journal of Psychosomatic Research*, 1978, 22, 41–45.
27. TENNANT, C., & ANDREWS, G. The pathogenic quality of life event stress in neurotic impairment. *Archives of General Psychiatry*, 1978, 35, 859–863.
28. FINLAY-JONES, R. A., & MURPHY, E. Severity of psychiatric disorder and the 30-item General Health Questionnaire. *British Journal of Psychiatry*, 1979, 134, 609–616.
29. NEWSON-SMITH, J. G. B., & HIRSCH, S. R. A comparison of social workers and psychiatrists in evaluating parasuicide. *British Journal of Psychiatry*, 1979, 134, 335–342.
30. SMITH, A. H. W. Psychiatric aspects of sterilization: A prospective survey. *British Journal of Psychiatry*, 1979, 135, 304–309.
31. TARNOPOLSKY, A., HAND, D. J., McKLEAN, E. K., ROBERTS, H., & WIGGINS, R. D. Validity and uses of a screening questionnaire (GHQ) in the community. *British Journal of Psychiatry*, 1979, 134, 508–515.
32. BANKS, M. H., GLEGG, C. W., JACKSON, P. R., KEMP, N. J., STAFFORD, E. M., & WALL, T. D. The use of the General Health Questionnaire as an indicator of mental states in occupational studies. *Journal of Occupational Psychology*, 1980, 53, 187–194.
33. BRODY, D. S. Physician recognition of behavioral, psychological, and social aspects of medical care. *Archives of Internal Medicine*, 1980, 140, 1286–1289.
34. HENDERSON, S., BYRNE, D. G., DUNCAN-JONES, P., SCOTT, R., & ADCOCK, S. Social relationships, adversity and neurosis: A study of associations in a general population sample. *British Journal of Psychiatry*, 1980, 137, 574–583.
35. HEPWORTH, S. J. Moderating factors of the psychological impact of unemployment. *Journal of Occupational Psychology*, 1980, 53, 139–145.
36. LUCAS, M. J., & FOLSTEIN, M. F. Nursing assessment of mental disorders on a general medical unit. *Journal of Psychiatric Nursing*, 1980, 18, 31–33.
37. MACDONALD, A. J., & BOUCHIER, I. A. D. Non-organic gastrointestinal illness: A medical and psychiatric study. *British Journal of Psychiatry*, 1980, 136, 276–283.
38. RYLE, A. Some measures of goal attainment in focused integrated active psychotherapy: A study of fifteen cases. *British Journal of Psychiatry*, 1980, 137, 475–486.
39. SINGERMAN, B., RIEDNER, E., & FOLSTEIN, M. Emotional disturbance in hearing clinic patients. *British Journal of Psychiatry*, 1980, 137, 58–62.
40. STAFFORD, E. M., JACKSON, P. R., & BANKS, M. H. Employment, work involvement and mental health in less qualified young people. *Journal of Occupational Psychology*, 1980, 53, 291–304.
41. ANDREWS, G., & HARVEY, R. Regression to the mean in pretreatment measures of stuttering. *Journal of Speech & Hearing Disorders*, 1981, 46, 204–207.
42. CATALAN, J., BRADLEY, M., GALLWEY, J., & HAWTON, K. Sexual dysfunction and psychiatric morbidity in patients attending a clinic for sexually transmitted diseases. *British Journal of Psychiatry*, 1981, 138, 292–296.
43. CORDESS, C., FOLSTEIN, M., & DRACHMAN, D. Psychiatric effects of alternate day steroid therapy. *British Journal of Psychiatry*, 1981, 138, 504–506.
44. GARFINKEL, P. E., & WARING, E. M. Personality, interests, and emotional disturbance in psychiatric residents. *American Journal of Psychiatry*, 1981, 138, 51–55.
45. HENDERSON, S. Social relationships, adversity and neurosis: An analysis of prospective observations. *British Journal of Psychiatry*, 1981, 138, 391–398.
46. MACBRIDE, A., LANCEE, W., & FREEMAN, S. J. J. The psychosocial impact of a labour dispute. *Journal of Occupational Psychology*, 1981, 54, 125–133.
47. ROY, A. Vulnerability factors and depression in men. *British Journal of Psychiatry*, 1981, 138, 75–77.
48. SHELDON, A. R., COCHRANE, J., VACHON, M. L. S., LYALL, W. A. L., ROGERS, J., & FREEMAN, S. J. J. A psychosocial analysis of risk of psychological impairment following bereavement. *Journal of Nervous & Mental Disease*, 1981, 169, 253–255.
49. SINGH, B., & RAPHAEL, B. Postdisaster morbidity of the bereaved: A possible role for preventive psychiatry? *Journal of Nervous & Mental Disease*, 1981, 169, 203–212.

[942]

General Mental Ability Test: ETSA Test 1A. Job applicants; 1960–72, c1957–66; manual and technical handbook by S. Trevor Hadley and George A. W. Stouffer, Jr.; test by Psychological Services Bureau; Educators'-Employers' Tests & Services Associates.*

For reviews of the complete battery, see 6:1025 (2 reviews).

REFERENCES

1. HUNDAL, P. S., & HORN, J. L. On the relationships between short-term learning and fluid and crystallized intelligence. *Applied Psychological Measurement*, 1977, 1, 11–21.

[943]

General Municipal Employees Performance (Efficiency) Rating System. Municipal employees; 1967–69; ratings by immediate supervisors; 8 summary ratings: quality of work, quantity of work, work habits, personal traits, relationships with people, supervisory ability, administrative ability, total; McCann Associates.*

For additional information, see 7:1107.

[944]

General Office Clerical Test: National Business Entrance Tests. Grades 11–16 and adults; 1948–72; National Business Education Association.* (In-print status uncertain; no reply from publisher.)

For additional information and a review by Mary Ellen Oliverio, see 8:325; see also 6:32 (1 reference). For reviews of the complete battery, see 6:33 (1 review), 5:515 (3 reviews), and 3:396 (1 review).

[945]

General Physics Test: National Achievement Tests. Grades 10–16; 1958–62; 3 scores: uses and application of principles, miscellaneous facts and scientists, total; no manual; Lester D. Crow and Roy S. Cook; Psychometric Affiliates.*

For additional information and a review by Theodore G. Phillips, see 6:930.

[946]
General Science Test. Matriculants and higher; 1955(?)–70; GST; revision of *Test A/12: Technical and Scientific Knowledge Test* and *Test A/13: Technical Reading Comprehension*; 2 scores: technical and scientific knowledge, technical reading comprehension; National Institute for Personnel Research [South Africa].*

See T2:1784 (1 reference).

[947]
General Science Test: National Achievement Tests. Grades 7–9; 1936–50; 7 scores: general concepts, identifications, men of science, definitions, use of objects, miscellaneous facts, total; Robert K. Speer, Lester D. Crow, and Samuel Smith; Psychometric Affiliates.*

For additional information and a review by Robert M. W. Travers, see 5:712; for reviews by Francis D. Curtis and G. W. Hunter, see 2:1602.

[948]
Geometry (Including Plane and Solid Geometry): Minnesota High School Achievement Examinations. High school; 1969–71; a new, revised, or previously inactive form issued each May; edited by V. L. Lohmann; American Guidance Service.*

For additional information, see 7:534.

[949]
George Washington University Series Nursing Tests. Prospective nurses; 1931–50; 5 tests; Thelma Hunt; Center for Psychological Service.* (In-print status uncertain; no reply from publisher.)
a) APTITUDE TEST FOR NURSING. 1931–50; F. A. Moss (Form 1).
b) ARITHMETIC TEST FOR PROSPECTIVE NURSES. 1940–50.
c) READING COMPREHENSION TEST FOR PROSPECTIVE NURSES. 1940–50.
d) GENERAL SCIENCE TEST FOR PROSPECTIVE NURSES. 1944–50.
e) INTEREST-PREFERENCE TEST FOR PROSPECTIVE NURSES. 1944–50.

See T2:2381 (3 references), 4:818 (2 references), and 3:699 (6 references).

REFERENCES
1–6. See 3:699.
7–8. See 4:818.
9–11. See T2:2381.
12. ALICHNE, M. C., & BELLUCCI, J. T. Prediction of freshman students' success in a baccalaureate nursing program. *Nursing Research*, 1981, 30, 49–53.

[950-1]
The Gerontological Apperception Test. Ages 66 and over; 1971; GAT; no scores; Robert L. Wolk and Rochelle B. Wolk; Human Sciences Press.* (In-print status uncertain; no reply from publisher.)

For additional information, a review by Joyce Parr Schaie, and an excerpted review by Margaret Mercer, see 8:566 (5 references); see also T2:1464 (2 references).

REFERENCES
1–2. See T2:1464.
3–7. See 8:566.
8. CICIRELLI, V. G. Relationship of siblings to the elderly person's feelings and concerns. *Journal of Gerontology*, 1977, 32, 317–322.

[952]
★**Gesell Preschool Test.** Ages 2.5–6; 1980; abbreviated adaptation of the *Gesell Developmental Schedules* and the *Gesell Developmental Tests*; maturity ratings in four basic fields of behavior: motor, adaptive, language, personal-social; Jacqueline Haines, Louise Bates Ames, and Clyde Gillespie; Programs for Education, Inc.*

[953]
*The Gesell School Readiness Test. Ages 5–9; 1964–80; formerly called *Gesell Developmental Tests*; Frances L. Ilg, Louise Bates Ames, Jacqueline Haines, and Clyde Gillespie; Programs for Education, Inc.*

See T2:1703 (4 references); for excerpted reviews by L. J. Borstelmann and Edith Meyer Taylor, see 7:750 (5 references).

REFERENCES
1–5. See 7:750.
6–9. See T2:1703.
10. LOPATA, D. J., & PASNAK, R. Accelerated conservation acquisition and IQ gains by blind children. *Genetic Psychology Monographs*, 1976, 93, 3–25.
11. FISH, B. Neurobiologic antecedents of schizophrenia in children. *Archives of General Psychiatry*, 1977, 34, 1297–1313.
12. ILG, F. L., AMES, L. B., HAINES, J., & GILLESPIE, C. *School Readiness: Behavior tests used at the Gesell Institute*. New York: Harper & Row, Publishers, Inc., 1978.
13. LYNN, A. M., STUNTZ, J. T., & WARD, B. H. Pneumocephalus: An unusual presentation of a persistent neurenteric fistula. *Journal of Pediatrics*, 1978, 93, 818–820.
14. CANNON, R. A., BYRNE, W. J., AMENT, M. E., GATES, B., O'CONNOR, M., & FONKALSRUD, E. W. Home parenteral nutrition in infants. *Journal of Pediatrics*, 1980, 96, 1098–1104.
15. VAN CAMP, S. S. An analysis of auditory attending skills. *Journal of Learning Disabilities*, 1980, 13, 56–60.

[954]
Getting Along. Grades 7–9; 1964–65; GA; 4 scores: self acceptance, acceptance by others, facing reality, total; Trudys Lawrence; the Author.*

For additional information, see 8:567; see also P:89 (2 references).

[955]
The Gibson Spiral Maze. Ages 8.5 and over; 1961–65; GSM; psychomotor performance associated with maladjustment, delinquency, mental illness, and accident proneness; 2 scores: time, error; H. B. Gibson; Hodder & Stoughton Educational [England].*

See T2:1191 (3 references); for a review by D. F. Clark, and excerpted reviews by C. H. Ammons and J. C.

Raven, see 7:82 (4 references); see also P:90 (2 references).

REFERENCES

1–2. See P:90.
3–6. See 7:82.
7–9. See T2:1191.
10. GILLEARD, C. J. Psychomotor performance of elderly psychiatric patients on the Gibson Spiral Maze test. *Perceptual & Motor Skills*, 1979, 48, 678.

[956]
★Gifted and Talented Screening Form. Grades kgn–9; 1979–80; GTSF; self-report checklist; 10 talent area scores: academic, creativity, arts (visual, performing, total), intelligence, leadership, psychomotor (athletics, mechanics, total); David L. Johnson; Stoelting Co.*

[957]
Gillingham-Childs Phonics Proficiency Scales. Grades 2–8; 1966–73; GCPPS; criterion-referenced; 2 levels; Educators Publishing Service, Inc.*

a) SERIES 1: BASIC READING AND SPELLING. 1966–70; 17 subtest scores in each of 2 areas: reading, spelling; Sally B. Childs, Anna Gillingham (test), and Bessie W. Stillman (test).

b) SERIES 2: ADVANCED READING. 1970–73; 20 subtest scores; Sally B. Childs and Ralph de S. Childs.

For additional information and reviews by Shirley C. Feldmann and Lawrence M. Kasdon, see 8:760.

[958]
Gilmore Oral Reading Test. Grades 1–8; 1951–68; GORT; 3 scores: accuracy, comprehension, rate; John V. Gilmore and Eunice C. Gilmore; The Psychological Corporation.*

For additional information and an excerpted review by Jerry Stafford, see 8:785 (17 references); see also T2:1679 (5 references); for reviews by Albert J. Harris and Kenneth J. Smith, see 7:737 (17 references); for reviews by Lydia A. Duggins and Maynard C. Reynolds of the original edition, see 5:671.

REFERENCES

1–17. See 7:737.
18–22. See T2:1679.
23–39. See 8:785.
40. ALLINGTON, R. L., CHODOS, L., DOMARACKI, J., & TRUEX, S. Passage dependency: Four diagnostic oral reading tests. *Reading Teacher*, 1977, 30, 369–375.
41. SCULLEN, T., & CURD, D. The reading moms: A program that works. *Phi Delta Kappan*, 1977, 58, 498–499.
42. SILBERBERG, N. E., & SILBERBERG, M. C. A note on reading tests and their role in defining reading difficulties. *Journal of Learning Disabilities*, 1977, 10, 100–103.
43. BIEGER, E. Effectiveness of visual training of letters and words on reading skills of non-readers. *Journal of Educational Research*, 1978, 71, 157–161.
44. MCINTYRE, C. W., MURRAY, M. E., CRONIN, C. M., & BLACKWELL, S. L. Span of apprehension in learning disabled boys. *Journal of Learning Disabilities*, 1978, 11, 468–475.
45. MURRAY, M. E. The relationship between personality adjustment and success in remedial programs in dyslexic children. *Contemporary Educational Psychology*, 1978, 3, 330–339.
46. RUBENSTEIN, J. S., ARMENTROUT, J. A., LEVIN, S., & HERALD, D. The parent–therapist program: Alternate care for emotionally disturbed children. *American Journal of Orthopsychiatry*, 1978, 48, 654–662.
47. WILLIAMS, F., & OAKLAND, T. A three-year auditory perception program for low–SES minority children. *Journal of Special Education*, 1978, 12, 331–344.
48. CHEEK, M. C. A correlation of oral reading, spelling, and graphemic option knowledge. *Reading World*, 1979, 18, 384–388.
49. KLEIN, P. S., & SCHWARTZ, A. A. Effects of training auditory sequential memory and attention on reading. *Journal of Special Education*, 1979, 13, 365–374.
50. RICHARDSON, E., DIBENEDETTO, B., CHRIST, A., & PRESS, M. Relationship of auditory and visual skills to reading retardation. *Journal of Learning Disabilities*, 1980, 13, 77–82.
51. TAMOR, L. Subjective text difficulty: An alternative approach to defining the difficulty level of written text. *Journal of Reading Behavior*, 1981, 13, 165–172.
52. VELLUTINO, F. R., SCANLON, D. M., DE SETTO, L., & PRUZEK, R. M. Developmental trends in the salience of meaning versus structural attributes of written words. *Psychological Research*, 1981, 43, 131–153.

[959]
★Gochnour Idiom Screening Test: An English Idiom Comprehension Test for the Deaf. Junior high through college level deaf students; 1977; GIST; Elizabeth A. Gochnour; Interstate Printers & Publishers, Inc.*

REFERENCES

1. SCHEIN, J. D. Gochnour Screening Test. *ASHA*, 1978, 20, 674–675.

[960]
Goldman-Fristoe Test of Articulation. Ages 2 and over; 1969–72; GFTA; 3 subtests: sounds in words, sounds in sentences, stimulability; subtest and total scores not recommended; Ronald Goldman and Macalyne Fristoe; American Guidance Service.*

For additional information, reviews by Margaret C. Byrne and Ralph L. Shelton, and an excerpted review by Dorothy Sherman, see 7:952 (4 references).

REFERENCES

1–4. See 7:952.
5. HOFFMAN, P. R., SCHUCKERS, G. H., & RATUSNIK, D. L. Contextual–coarticulatory inconsistency of /r/ misarticulation. *Journal of Speech & Hearing Research*, 1977, 20, 631–643.
6. MULLEN, P. A., & WHITEHEAD, R. L. Stimulus picture identification in articulation testing. *Journal of Speech & Hearing Disorders*, 1977, 42, 113–118.
7. PAYNTER, E. T., & BUMPAS, T. C. Imitative and spontaneous articulatory assessment of three–year-old children. *Journal of Speech & Hearing Disorders*, 1977, 42, 119–125.
8. STEPHENS, M. I., & DANILOFF, R. A methodological study of factors affecting the judgment of misarticulated /s/. *Journal of Communication Disorders*, 1977, 10, 207–220.
9. ELBERT, M., & MCREYNOLDS, L. V. An experimental analysis of misarticulating children's generalization. *Journal of Speech & Hearing Research*, 1978, 21, 136–150.
10. SOMMERS, R. K., ERIDGE, S., & PETERSON, M. K. How valid are children's language tests? *Journal of Special Education*, 1978, 12, 393–407.
11. GARDNER, L. I., NEU, R. L., SHAH, R. S., PINTO, W., JR., CO, M., LEHR, E. R., & BARG, G. A. Family with three apparently balanced t(3;15) (p27;q22) translocation carriers. *American Journal of Diseases of Children*, 1979, 133, 1002–1005.
12. HOWARD–PEEBLES, P. N., & MARKITON, R. I. A tetra-x female, cytogenetic testing, dermatoglyphic studies, and speech impairment. *American Journal of Mental Deficiency*, 1979, 84, 252–255.
13. PANAGOS, J. M., QUINE, M. E., & KUCH, R. J. Syntactic and phonological influences on children's articulation. *Journal of Speech & Hearing Research*, 1979, 22, 841–848.
14. TOBEY, E. A., CULLEN, J. K., JR., RAMPP, D. L., & FLEISCHER–GALLAGHER, A. M. Effects of stimulus–onset asynchrony on the dichotic performance of children with auditory–processing disorders. *Journal of Speech & Hearing Research*, 1979, 22, 197–211.
15. CANTWELL, D. P., BAKER, L., & MATTISON, R. E. Psychiatric disorders in children with speech and language retardation. *Archives of General Psychiatry*, 1980, 37, 423–426.
16. GEFFNER, D. Feature characteristics of spontaneous speech production in young deaf children. *Journal of Communication Disorders*, 1980, 13, 443–454.
17. MELNICK, C. R., MICHALS, K. K., & MATALON, R. Linguistic development of children with phenylketonuria and normal intelligence. *Journal of Pediatrics*, 1981, 98, 269–272.
18. SINGH, S., HAYDEN, M. E., & TOOMBS, M. S. The role of distinction features in articulation errors. *Journal of Speech & Hearing Disorders*, 1981, 46, 174–183.
19. TOOMBS, M. S., SINGH, S., & HAYDEN, M. E. Markedness of features in the articulatory substitutions of children. *Journal of Speech & Hearing Disorders*, 1981, 46, 184–191.

20. WEISMER, G., DINNSEN, D., & ELBERT, M. A study of the voicing distinction associated with omitted word–final stops. *Journal of Speech & Hearing Disorders*, 1981, 46, 320–328.

[961]
Goldman-Fristoe-Woodcock Auditory Skills Test Battery. Ages 3 and over; 1974–76; also called *G-F-W Battery*; 12 tests in 5 easel-kits; Ronald Goldman, Macalyne Fristoe, and Richard W. Woodcock; American Guidance Service.*

a) GFW AUDITORY SELECTIVE ATTENTION TEST. 5 scores: quiet, fan-like noise, cafeteria noise, voice, total.
b) GFW DIAGNOSTIC AUDITORY DISCRIMINATION TEST. 3 parts in 2 easel-kits.
  1) Part 1.
  2) Parts 2 and 3. Administered to those below 25th percentile on part 1; 2 scores: total of parts 1 and 2, total of parts 1, 2, and 3.
c) GFW AUDITORY MEMORY TESTS. 3 tests: recognition memory, memory for content, memory for sequence.
d) GFW SOUND-SYMBOL TESTS. 7 tests: sound mimicry, sound recognition, sound analysis, sound blending, sound-symbol association, reading of symbols, spelling of sounds.

For additional information and reviews by Katharine G. Butler and Thomas Oakland, see 8:937.

REFERENCES
1. PARNELL, M. M., & AMERMAN, J. D. Maturational influences on perception of coarticulatory effects. *Journal of Speech & Hearing Research*, 1978, 21, 682–701.
2. CARROLL, J. L. Goldman–Fristoe–Woodcock Auditory Skills Test Battery. *Journal of School Psychology*, 1979, 17, 294–296.
3. PRICHARD, C. L., TEKIELI, M. E., & KOZUP, J. M. Developmental apraxia: Diagnostic considerations. *Journal of Communication Disorders*, 1979, 12, 337–348.
4. SABATINO, D. A. The definition and assessment of visual and auditory perception. *Journal of Clinical Child Psychology*, 1979, 8, 188–194.
5. HO, H., FOCH, T. T., & PLOMIN, R. Developmental stability of the relative influence of genes and environment on specific cognitive abilities during childhood. *Developmental Psychology*, 1980, 16, 340–346.
6. PLOMIN, R., & FOCH, T. T. A twin study of objectively assessed personality in childhood. *Journal of Personality & Social Psychology*, 1980, 39, 680–688.
7. BRANDES, P. J., & EHINGER, D. M. The effects of early middle ear pathology on auditory perception and academic achievement. *Journal of Speech & Hearing Disorders*, 1981, 46, 301–307.

[962]
Goldman-Fristoe-Woodcock Test of Auditory Discrimination. Ages 4 and over; 1970; GFW; speech-sound discrimination scores under 2 conditions: quiet, background noise; 3 parts; Ronald Goldman, Macalyne Fristoe, and Richard W. Woodcock; American Guidance Service.*

For additional information and an excerpted review by Alex Bannatyne, see 8:938 (18 references); see also T2:2037 (4 references); for reviews by Eugene C. Sheeley and Ralph L. Shelton and an excerpted review by Barton B. Proger, see 7:938.

REFERENCES
1–4. See T2:2037.
5–22. See 8:938.
23. BLOWERS, E. A. Prediction of Metropolitan Readiness Test scores. *Alberta Journal of Educational Research*, 1977, 23, 164–168.
24. FOCH, T. T., DEFRIES, J. C., MCCLEARN, G. E., & SINGER, S. M. Familial patterns of impairment in reading disability. *Journal of Educational Psychology*, 1977, 69, 316–329.
25. BURROWS, E. H., & NEYLAND, D. Reading skills, auditory comprehension of language, and academic achievement. *Journal of Speech & Hearing Disorders*, 1978, 43, 467–472.
26. SCUDDER, R. R. Auditory temporal processing by children with articulation disorders. *ASHA*, 1978, 20, 811. (Abstract)
27. BEADLE, K. R. Clinical interactions of verbal language, learning and behavior. *Journal of Clinical Child Psychology*, 1979, 8, 201–205.
28. BRUININKS, V. L., & MAYER, J. H. Longitudinal study of cognitive abilities and academic achievement. *Perceptual & Motor Skills*, 1979, 48, 1011–1021.
29. HRESKO, W. P. Elicited imitation ability of children from learning disabled and regular classes. *Journal of Learning Disabilities*, 1979, 12, 456–461.
30. SEXTON, L. C., & TRELOAR, J. H. Auditory and visual perception, sex, and academic aptitude as predictors of achievement for first-grade children. *Measurement & Evaluation in Guidance*, 1979, 12, 140–146.
31. CONNERS, C. K., & TAYLOR, E. Pemoline, methylphenidate, and placebo in children with minimal brain dysfunction. *Archives of General Psychiatry*, 1980, 37, 922–930.
32. COOK, J. E., NOLAN, G. A., & ZANOTTI, R. J. Treating auditory perception problems: The NIM helps. *Academic Therapy*, 1980, 15, 473–481.
33. HASBROUCK, J. M. Performance of students with auditory figure-ground disorders under conditions of unilateral and bilateral ear occlusion. *Journal of Learning Disabilities*, 1980, 13, 548–551.
34. HORNBY, P. A. Achieving second language fluency through immersion education. *Foreign Language Annals*, 1980, 13, 107–113.
35. HUMPHREY, T. The effect of music ear training upon the auditory discrimination abilities of trainable mentally retarded adolescents. *Journal of Music Therapy*, 1980, 17, 70–74.
36. JORDON, L. S. Receptive and expressive language problems occurring in combination with a seizure disorder: A case report. *Journal of Communication Disorders*, 1980, 13, 295–303.
37. BOUNTRESS, N. G., & LADERBERG, C. M. A comparison of two tests of speech–sound discrimination. *Journal of Communication Disorders*, 1981, 14, 149–156.

[963]
Goldstein-Scheerer Tests of Abstract and Concrete Thinking. Brain damaged adults; 1941–51; 5 tests; Kurt Goldstein, Martin Scheerer, and Louis Rosenberg (*c*, record booklet); The Psychological Corporation.*

a) GOLDSTEIN-SCHEERER CUBE TEST. 1941–45.
b) GELB-GOLDSTEIN COLOR SORTING TEST. 1941–51.
c) GOLDSTEIN-SCHEERER OBJECT SORTING TEST. 1941–51.
d) WEIGL-GOLDSTEIN-SCHEERER COLOR FORM SORTING TEST. 1941–45.
e) GOLDSTEIN-SCHEERER STICK TEST. 1941–45.

See T2:1192 (36 references) and P:91 (19 references); for a review by R. W. Payne, see 6:101 (23 references); see also 5:57 (21 references); for reviews by Kate Levine Kogan, C. R. Strother (with Ludwig Immergluck), and O. L. Zangwill, see 3:41 (28 references).

REFERENCES
1–28. See 3:41.
29–49. See 5:57.
50–72. See 6:101.
73–91. See P:91.
92–127. See T2:1192.
128. EXNER, J. E., & MURRILLO, L. G. A long term follow-up of schizophrenics treated with regressive ECT. *Diseases of the Nervous System*, 1977, 38, 162–168.
129. KNIGHT, R. A., SIMS-KNIGHT, J. E., & PETCHERS-CASSELL, M. Overinclusion, broad scanning, and picture recognition in schizophrenics. *Journal of Clinical Psychology*, 1977, 33, 635–642.
130. OLESKER, W. Physiognomic perception and flexibility of concept formation. *Perceptual & Motor Skills*, 1977, 45, 99–102.

[964]
Goodenough-Harris Drawing Test. Ages 3–15; 1926–63; revision and extension of the *Goodenough Intelligence Test*; Florence L. Goodenough and Dale B. Harris; The Psychological Corporation.*

For additional information, see 8:187 (87 references); see also T2:381 (93 references); for reviews by Anne Anastasi and James A. Dunn, and excerpted reviews by M. L. Kellmer Pringle, Marjorie P. Honzik, Carol Hunter, Adolph G. Woltmann, Marvin S. Kaplan, and

Mary J. Rouse, see 7:352 (158 references); see also 6:460 (43 references); and 5:335 (34 references); for a review by Naomi Stewart of the original edition, see 4:292 (60 references).

REFERENCES

1–60. See 4:292.
61–94. See 5:335.
95–137. See 6:460.
138–295. See 7:352.
296–388. See T2:381.
389–475. See 8:187.

476. BURNS, C. J., & VELICHER, W. F. Art instruction and the Goodenough–Harris Drawing Test in fifth-graders. *Psychology in the Schools*, 1977, 14, 109–112.
477. COYLE, R. T., CLANCE, P. R., & JOESTING, J. Kinesthetic enrichment and Goodenough–Harris Draw-A-Man scores of black children from lower socioeconomic background. *Perceptual & Motor Skills*, 1977, 45, 201–202.
478. DUGDALE, A. E., & CHEN, S. T. Factors influencing school achievement of children from low socioeconomic groups in Malaysia. *International Journal of Psychology*, 1977, 12, 39–50.
479. KAY, S. R. Developmental assessment of cognitive style in mentally retarded psychotics. *Journal of Clinical Psychology*, 1977, 33, 953–958.
480. LEVINSON, B. M., & BLOCK, Z. Goodenough–Harris drawings of Jewish children of Orthodox background. *Psychological Reports*, 1977, 41, 155–158.
481. LEWIS, H. P., & LIVSON, N. Personality correlates of IQ discrepancy: Stanford–Binet and Goodenough–Harris. *Journal of Genetic Psychology*, 1977, 131, 237–242.
482. MCCORMICK, D. P. Pediatric evaluation of children with school problems. *American Journal of Diseases of Children*, 1977, 131, 318–322.
483. BURKE, J., LEWY, R., WILLIAMS, J. D., BREKKE, B., HARLOW, S. D., & PETERSON, W. The effects of three experimental programs on reading readiness. *Journal of Learning Disabilities*, 1978, 11, 515–518.
484. CALHOUN, G., WHITLEY, J. D., & ANSOLABEHERE, E. M. An investigation of the Goodenough–Harris Drawing Test and the (Coopersmith) Self Esteem Inventory. *Educational & Psychological Measurement*, 1978, 38, 1229–1232.
485. FELLOWS, B. J., & CREAMER, M. An investigation of the role of "hypnosis", hypnotic susceptibility and hypnotic induction in the production of age regression. *British Journal of Social & Clinical Psychology*, 1978, 17, 165–171.
486. FIRESTONE, P., POITRAS-WRIGHT, H., & DOUGLAS, V. The effects of caffeine on hyperactive children. *Journal of Learning Disabilities*, 1978, 11, 133–141.
487. FLYNN, T. M., & FLYNN, L. A. Evaluation of the predictive ability of five screening measures administered during kindergarten. *Journal of Experimental Education*, 1978, 46, 65–70.
488. MAY, D. C. Effects of color reversal of figure and ground drawing materials on drawing performance. *Exceptional Children*, 1978, 44, 254–260.
489. MAY, D. C., & DENSON, T. A. The reliability of children's drawings as indicators of brain damage. *Educational Research Quarterly*, 1978, 3, 43–48.
490. SMITH, P. K., & SYDDALL, S. Play and non-play tutoring in preschool children: Is it play or tutoring which matters? *British Journal of Educational Psychology*, 1978, 48, 315–325.
491. WALLBROWN, F. H. Shedd's formulations concerning the hyperkinetic syndrome–An empirical test of selected features. *Perceptual & Motor Skills*, 1978, 46, 809–810.
492. BABAD, E. Y. Personality correlates of susceptibility to biasing information. *Journal of Personality & Social Psychology*, 1979, 37, 195–202.
493. BEADLE, K. R. Clinical interactions of verbal language, learning and behavior. *Journal of Clinical Child Psychology*, 1979, 8, 201–205.
494. BLAHA, J., FAWAZ, N., & WALLBROWN, F. H. Information processing components of Koppitz Errors on the Bender Visual–motor Gestalt Test. *Journal of Clinical Psychology*, 1979, 35, 784–790.
495. BROWN, E. V. Sexual self-identification as reflected in children's drawings when asked to draw-a-person. *Perceptual & Motor Skills*, 1979, 49, 35–38.
496. DUGDALE, A. E., & CHEN, S. T. Ethnic differences in the Goodenough–Harris Draw-A-Man and Draw-A-Woman Tests. *Archives of Diseases in Childhood*, 1979, 54, 880–885.
497. KAGITCIBASI, C. The effects of socioeconomic development on draw-a-man scores in Turkey. *Journal of Social Psychology*, 1979, 108, 3–8.
498. KROHN, E. J., & TRAXLERE, A. J. Relationship of the McCarthy Scales of Children's Abilities to other measures of preschool cognitive, motor, and perceptual development. *Perceptual & Motor Skills*, 1979, 49, 783–790.

499. TOBACK, C., & RAJKUMAR, S. The emotional disturbance underlying alopecia areata, alopecia totalis, and trichotillomania. *Child Psychiatry & Human Development*, 1979, 10, 114–117.
500. WHITE, T. H. Correlations among the WISC-R, PIAT, and DAM. *Psychology in the Schools*, 1979, 16, 497–501.
501. CHAVEZ, E. L., & GONZALES-SINGH, E. Hispanic assessment: A case study. *Professional Psychology*, 1980, 11, 163–168.
502. COLBERT, C. Visual and figural elaboration in preadolescents. *Studies in Art Education*, 1980, 22, 25–35.
503. CONNERS, C. K., & TAYLOR, E. Pemoline, methylphenidate, and placebo in children with minimal brain dysfunction. *Archives of General Psychiatry*, 1980, 37, 922–930.
504. CULP, R. E., PACKARD, V. N., & HUMPHRY, R. Sensorimotor versus cognitive–perceptual training effects on the body concept of preschoolers. *American Journal of Occupational Therapy*, 1980, 34, 259–262.
505. CZEIZEL, A., LÁNYI-ENGLEMAYER, A., KLUJBER, L., MÉTNEKI, J., & TUSNÁDY, G. Etiological study of mental retardation in Budapest, Hungary. *American Journal of Mental Deficiency*, 1980, 85, 120–128.
506. FRIEDMAN, R., FUERTH, J. H., & FORSYTHE, A. B. A brief screening battery for predicting school achievement at ages seven and nine years. *Psychology in the Schools*, 1980, 17, 340–346.
507. GORDON, N., LEFKOWITZ, M. M., & TESINY, E. P. Childhood depression and the Draw-A-Person Test. *Psychological Reports*, 1980, 47, 251–257.
508. GRIFFING, P. The relationship between socioeconomic status and sociodramatic play among black kindergarten children. *Genetic Psychology Monographs*, 1980, 101, 3–34.
509. KINSBOURNE, M., & LEMPERT, H. Human figure representation by blind children. *Journal of General Psychology*, 1980, 102, 33–37.
510. LEWIS, H. P., & LIVSON, N. Cognitive development, personality and drawing: Their interrelationships in a replicated longitudinal study. *Studies in Art Education*, 1980, 22, 8–11.
511. MARBACH, E. S., & YAWKEY, T. D. The effect of imaginative play actions on language development in five-year old children. *Psychology in the Schools*, 1980, 17, 257–263.
512. SMART, R., WILTON, K., & KEELING, B. Teacher factors and special class placement. *Journal of Special Education*, 1980, 14, 217–229.
513. TESINY, E. P., LEFKOWITZ, M. M., & GORDON, N. H. Childhood depression, locus of control, and school achievement. *Journal of Educational Psychology*, 1980, 72, 506–510.
514. WEISS, S. C. Culture Fair Intelligence Test and Draw-A-Person scores from a rural Peruvian sample. *Journal of Social Psychology*, 1980, 111, 147–148.
515. WHITEHOUSE, D., SHAH, U., & PALMER, F. B. Comparison of sustained–release and standard methylphenidate in the treatment of minimal brain dysfunction. *Journal of Clinical Psychiatry*, 1980, 41, 282–285.
516. NAGLIERI, J. A., & MAXWELL, S. Inter-rater reliability and concurrent validity of the Goodenough–Harris and McCarthy draw-a-child scoring systems. *Perceptual & Motor Skills*, 1981, 53, 343–348.
517. SCOTT, L. H. Measuring intelligence with the Goodenough–Harris Drawing Test. *Psychological Bulletin*, 1981, 89, 483–505.

[965]

Gordon Occupational Check List. High school students not planning to enter college; 1961–67; 5 or 11 scores: business, outdoor, arts, technology, service, and 6 optional response summarization scores (preceding 5 areas and total); Leonard V. Gordon; The Psychological Corporation.*

For additional information and reviews by John N. McCall and Bert W. Westbrook, see 7:1019; for reviews by John O. Crites and Kenneth B. Hoyt, see 6:1056.

[966]

***Gordon Personal Profile-Inventory.** Grades 9–16 and adults; 1951–78; GPP-I; a combination of the *Gordon Personal Inventory* and the *Gordon Personal Profile*; separate booklet editions are still available; 9 scores: ascendancy, responsibility, emotional stability, sociability, self-esteem, cautiousness, original thinking, personal relations, vigor; Leonard V. Gordon; The Psychological Corporation.*

For additional information concerning the *Gordon Personal Inventory*, see 8:568 (34 references); for reviews by Charles F. Dicken and Alfred B. Heilbrun, Jr., see 6:102 (13 references); for reviews by Benno G. Fricke and John A. Radcliffe and excerpted reviews by Laurance F. Shaffer and Laurence Siegel, see 5:58.

For additional information concerning the *Gordon Personal Profile*, see 8:569 (52 references); see also T2:1194 (56 references) and P:93 (23 references); for reviews by Charles F. Dicken and Alfred B. Heilbrun, Jr., see 6:103 (25 references); for reviews by Benno G. Fricke and John A. Radcliffe and an excerpted review by Laurance F. Shaffer, see 5:59 (16 references).

References in this volume are for GPI and GPP, with the numbering sequence continuing from the GPP.

REFERENCES

1–16. See 5:59.
17–41. See 6:103.
42–64. See P:93.
65–120. See T2:1194.
121–172. See 8:569.
173. RICHARDS, M. A. One integrated curriculum: An empirical evaluation. *Nursing Research*, 1977, 26, 90–95.
174. WIENER, Y., & VAITENAS, R. Personality correlates of voluntary midcareer change in enterprising occupations. *Journal of Applied Psychology*, 1977, 62, 706–712.
175. GILLIS, J. S., & LEE, D. C. Relationships between the 16PF, GPP, and GPI. *Educational and Psychological Measurement*, 1979, 39, 7–12.
176. HORTON, R. L. Some relationships between personality and consumer decision making. *Journal of Marketing Research*, 1979, 16, 233–246.
177. SCHANINGER, C. M., LESSIG, V. P., & PANTON, D. B. The complementary use of multivariate procedures to investigate nonlinear and interactive relationships between personality and product usage. *Journal of Marketing Research*, 1980, 17, 119–124.
178. URSANO, R. J. The Viet Nam era prisoner of war: Precaptivity personality and the development of psychiatric illness. *American Journal of Psychiatry*, 1981, 138, 315–318.

[967]

The Gottesfeld Community Mental Health Critical Issues Test. Mental health professionals; 1974; for research use only; 6 scores: community context, radicalism, traditional psychotherapy, prevention, extending the definition of mental health, role diffusion; Harry Gottesfeld; Human Sciences Press.* (In-print status uncertain; no reply from publisher.)

For additional information and a review by Lester M. Libo, see 8:570 (2 references).

[968]

Gottschaldt Figures [NIPR]. Job applicants with at least 10 years of education; 1943–56; adaptation of U.S. Army Air Forces Test AC121; test in English and Afrikaans; no manual; National Institute for Personnel Research [South Africa].*

REFERENCES

1. RICHARDSON, A. The meaning and measurement of memory imagery. *British Journal of Psychology*, 1977, 68, 29–43.
2. BRANCONNIER, R. J., & COLE, J. O. The impairment index as a symptom–independent parameter of drug efficacy in geriatric psychopharmacology. *Journal of Gerontology*, 1978, 33, 217–223.

[969]

Gottschalk-Gleser Content Analysis Scales. Ages 14 and over; 1969; GGCAS; content analysis by 2 or more scorers of 5-minute verbal samples tape recorded and then typed; 13 scores: anxiety (death, mutilation, separation, guilt, shame, diffuse, total), hostility directed outward (overt, covert, total), hostility directed inward, ambivalent hostility, social alienation-personal disorganization (schizophrenic); Louis A. Gottschalk, Goldine C. Gleser, and Carolyn N. Winget (manual); University of California Press.* (In-print status uncertain; no reply from publisher.)

See T2:1195 (26 references); for a review by S. B. Sells, and an excerpted review by Kurt Salzinger, see 7:83 (10 references).

REFERENCES

1–10. See 7:83.
11–36. See T2:1195.
37. VINEY, L. L. An evaluation of an Australian youth work programme. *Australian Psychologist*, 1981, 16, 37–47.

[970]

[Government/Objective Test]. 1 semester in grades 11–12; 1970; 6 tests; no manual; Perfection Form Co.* (In-print status uncertain; no reply from publisher.)
a) FUNDAMENTALS OF GOVERNMENT.
b) THE EXECUTIVE BRANCH (POLITICAL PARTIES AND ELECTION).
c) THE LEGISLATIVE BRANCH.
d) THE AMERICAN JUDICIARY SYSTEM AND CIVIL LIBERTIES.
e) AMERICAN GOVERNMENT-STATE AND LOCAL GOVERNMENT.
f) FINAL TEST.

[971]

*****Goyer Organization of Ideas Test.** College and adults; 1966–79; GOIT; Robert S. Goyer; the Author.*

For additional information, see 8:817 (1 reference).

[972]

Graded Arithmetic-Mathematics Test. Ages 6–21; 1949–76; 2 editions; P. E. Vernon and K. M. Miller (*b*); Hodder & Stoughton Educational [England]. (British norms supplement available from NFER-Nelson Publishing Co. [England].)*
a) DECIMAL CURRENCY EDITION. Ages 7–21; 1949–71.
b) METRIC EDITION. Ages 6–13, 12–16; 1949–76; may be orally administered.

For additional information, see 8:271; see also T2:618 (8 references); for a review by Stanley Nisbet of the original edition, see 5:476.

REFERENCES

1–8. See T2:618.
9. GLOSSOP, J. A., APPLEYARD, R., & ROBERTS, C. Achievement relative to a measure of general intelligence. *British Journal of Educational Psychology*, 1979, 49, 249–257.
10. MADAUS, G. F., KELLAGHAN, T., RAKOW, E. A., & KING, D. J. The sensitivity of measures of school effectiveness. *Harvard Educational Review*, 1979, 49, 207–230.
11. REID, I., & CROUCHER, A. The Crandall Intellectual Achievement Responsibility Questionnaire: A British validation study. *Educational & Psychological Measurement*, 1980, 40, 245–249.

[973]

Graduate Management Admission Test. Business graduate students; 1954–77; GMAT; formerly called *Admission Test for Graduate Study in Business*; test administered 4 times annually (January, March, July, November) at centers established by the publisher; 3 scores: verbal, quantitative, total; Graduate Management Admission Council, Educational Testing Service.*

For additional information, see 8:1074 (11 references); see also T2:2325 (5 references); for reviews by Jerome E. Doppelt and Gary R. Hanson of earlier forms, see 7:1080 (10 references).

REFERENCES
1–10. See 7:1080.
11–15. See T2:2325.
16–26. See 8:1074.
27. IRVINE, C. A correlation study of the relationship between the candidacy examination requirements and business education graduate students' academic success at the University of Northern Iowa, 1962–1972. *Journal of Business Education*, 1977, 52, 192.
28. PFEFFER, J. Effects of an MBA and socioeconomic origins on business school graduates' salaries. *Journal of Applied Psychology*, 1977, 62, 698–705.
29. HENDEL, D. D., & DOYLE, K. O., JR. Predicting success for graduate study in business for English-speaking and non-English-speaking students. *Educational & Psychological Measurement*, 1978, 38, 411–414.
30. POGROW, S. Program characteristics and the use of student data to predict attrition from doctoral programs. *College Student Journal*, 1978, 12, 348–353.
31. WERTHEIM, E. G., WIDOM, C. S., & WORTEL, L. H. Multivariate analysis of male and female professional career choice correlates. *Journal of Applied Psychology*, 1978, 63, 234–242.
32. BREAUGH, J. A., & MANN, R. B. The utility of discriminant analysis for predicting graduation from a master of business administration program. *Educational & Psychological Measurement*, 1981, 41, 495–501.

[974]
The Graduate Record Examinations Advanced Chemistry Test. Graduate school candidates; 1939–76; test administered 5 times annually (January, April, June, October, December) at centers established by the publisher; an inactive form is available for local administration; Educational Testing Service.*

For additional information, see 8:852 (1 reference); see also 7:848 (1 reference); for a review by Max D. Engelhart of an earlier form, see 6:919. For reviews of the GRE program, see 7:667 (1 review) and 5:601 (1 review).

[975]
The Graduate Record Examinations Advanced Computer Science Test. Graduate school candidates; 1976; test administered 3 times annually (April, October, December) at centers established by the publisher; Educational Testing Service.*

For additional information, see 8:1080.

[976]
The Graduate Record Examinations Advanced Economics Test. Graduate school candidates; 1939–76; test administered 5 times annually (January, April, June, October, December) at centers established by the publisher; an inactive form is available for local administration; Educational Testing Service.*

For additional information, and a review by Irving Morrissett, see 8:897; see also 6:987 (1 reference). For reviews of the GRE program, see 7:667 (1 review) and 5:601 (1 review).

[977]
The Graduate Record Examinations Advanced Education Test. Graduate school candidates; 1946–76; test administered 5 times annually (January, April, June, October, December) at centers established by the publisher; an inactive form is available for local administration; Educational Testing Service.*

For additional information, see 8:372 (3 references); see also 7:578 (9 references); for a review by D. Welty Lefever of an earlier form, see 6:698 (7 references); for a review by Harry N. Rivlin, see 5:537. For reviews of the GRE program, see 7:667 (1 review) and 5:601 (1 review).

REFERENCES
1–7. See 6:698.
8–16. See 7:578.
17. See T2:863.
18–20. See 8:372.
21. DOLE, A. A., & BAGGALEY, A. Prediction of performance in a doctoral education program by the Graduate Record Examinations and other measures. *Educational & Psychological Measurement*, 1979, 39, 421–427.

[978]
The Graduate Record Examinations Advanced Engineering Test. Graduate school candidates; 1939–76; test administered 5 times annually (January, April, June, October, December) at centers established by the publisher; 3 scores: engineering, mathematics usage, total; an inactive form is available for local administration; Educational Testing Service.*

For additional information, see 8:1088 (1 reference). For reviews of the GRE program, see 7:667 (1 review) and 5:601 (1 review).

[979]
The Graduate Record Examinations Advanced French Test. Graduate school candidates; 1939–76; test administered 5 times annually (January, April, June, October, December) at centers established by the publisher; 3 scores: interpretive reading skills, literature and civilization, total; an inactive form is available for local administration; Educational Testing Service.*

For additional information and reviews by Helen L. Jorstad and Stanley L. Shinall, see 8:121; for a review by Nelson Brooks of an earlier form, see 6:376; for a review by Walter V. Kaulfers of an earlier form, see 5:270. For reviews of the GRE program, see 7:667 (1 review) and 5:601 (1 review).

[980]
The Graduate Record Examinations Advanced (General) Biology Test. Graduate school candidates; 1939–76; test administered 5 times annually (January, April, June, October, December) at centers established by the publisher; 4 scores: cellular and subcellular, organismal, population, total; an inactive form is available for local administration; Educational Testing Service.*

For additional information, see 8:835; for a review by Clark W. Horton of an earlier form, see 5:727. For reviews of the GRE program, see 7:667 (1 review) and 5:601 (1 review).

[981]
The Graduate Record Examinations Advanced Geography Test. Graduate school candidates; 1966–76; test administered 5 times annually (January, April, June, October, December) at centers established by the publisher; 3 scores: human geography, physical geography, total; an inactive form is available for local administration; Educational Testing Service.*

For additional information, see 8:904. For a review of the GRE program, see 7:667 (1 review).

[982]
The Graduate Record Examinations Advanced Geology Test. Graduate school candidates; 1939–76; test administered 5 times annually (January, April, June, October, December) at centers established by the publisher; 4 scores: stratigraphy-paleontology-geomorphology,

structural geology and geophysics, mineralogy-petrology-geochemistry, total; an inactive form is available for local administration; Educational Testing Service.*

For additional information, see 8:855; see also 7:852 (1 reference). For reviews of the GRE program, see 7:667 (1 review) and 5:601 (1 review).

[983]
The Graduate Record Examinations Advanced German Test. Graduate school candidates; 1939–76; test administered 5 times annually (January, April, June, October, December) at centers established by the publisher; an inactive form is available for local administration; Educational Testing Sevice.*

For additional information and a review by Vincent J. Dell'Orto, see 8:132; see also T2:269 (1 reference). For a review of the GRE program, see 7:667 (1 review) and 5:601 (1 review).

[984]
The Graduate Record Examinations Advanced History Test. Graduate school candidates; 1939–76; test administered 5 times annually (January, April, June, October, December) at centers established by the publisher; 3 scores: European history, American history, total; an inactive form is available for local administration; Educational Testing Service.*

For additional information, see 8:913; see also 7:919 (1 reference); for a review by Robert H. Ferrell of an earlier form, see 5:818. For reviews of the GRE program, see 7:667 (1 review) and 5:601 (1 review).

[985]
The Graduate Record Examinations Advanced Literature in English Test. Graduate school candidates; 1939–76; test administered 5 times annually (January, April, June, October, December) at centers established by the publisher; an inactive form is available for local administration; Educational Testing Service.*

For additional information and a review by Edward M. White, see 8:69; see also 7:219 (1 reference); for a review by Robert C. Pooley of an earlier form, see 5:215. For reviews of the GRE program, see 7:667 (1 review) and 5:601 (1 review).

[986]
The Graduate Record Examinations Advanced Mathematics Test. Graduate school candidates; 1939–76; test administered 5 times annually (January, April, June, October, December), at centers established by the publisher; an inactive form is available for local administration; Educational Testing Service.*

For additional information, see 8:272 (1 reference); for a review by Paul C. Rosenbloom of an earlier form, see 6:578; for a review by Eric F. Gardner, see 5:427 (1 reference). For reviews of the GRE program, see 7:667 (1 review) and 5:601 (1 review).

[987]
The Graduate Record Examinations Advanced Music Test. Graduate school candidates; 1951–76; test administered 5 times annually (January, April, June, October, December) at centers established by the publisher; 3 scores: music theory, music history, total; an inactive form is available for local administration; Educational Testing Service.*

For additional information, see 8:95; for a review by William S. Larson of an earlier form, see 5:247. For reviews of the GRE program, see 7:667 (1 review).

[988]
The Graduate Examinations Advanced Philosophy Test. Graduate school candidates; 1939–76; test administered 5 times annually (January, April, June, October, December) at centers established by the publisher; an inactive form is available for local administration; Educational Testing Service.*

For additional information, see 8:455; see also 7:637 (1 reference). For reviews of the GRE program, see 7:667 (1 review) and 5:601 (1 review).

[989]
The Graduate Record Examinations Advanced Physics Test. Graduate school candidates; 1939–76; test administered 5 times annually (January, April, June, October, December) at centers established by the publisher; an inactive form is available for local administration; Educational Testing Service.*

For additional information, see 8:866 (1 reference); for a review by Theodore G. Phillips, see 6:931; for a review by Leo Nedelsky, see 5:754. For reviews of the GRE program, see 7:667 (1 review) and 5:601 (1 review).

[990]
The Graduate Record Examinations Advanced Political Science Test. Graduate school candidates; 1939–76; test administered 5 times annually (January, April, June, October, December) at centers established by the publisher; an inactive form is available for local administration; Educational Testing Service.*

For additional information, see 8:921; for a review by Christine McGuire of an earlier form, see 5:835. For reviews of the GRE program, see 7:667 (1 review) and 5:601 (1 review).

[991]
The Graduate Record Examinations Advanced Psychology Test. Graduate school candidates; 1939–76; 3 scores: experimental, social, total; test administered 5 times annually (January, April, June, October, December) at centers established by the publisher; an inactive form is available for local administration; Educational Testing Service.*

For additional information, see 8:461 (3 references); see also T2:1005 (2 references) and 7:644 (9 references); for a review by Harold Seashore of an earlier form, see 5:583. For reviews of the GRE program, see 7:667 (1 review) and 5:601 (1 review).

REFERENCES

1–9. See 7:644.
10–11. See T2:1005.
12–14. See 8:461.
15. FREDERIKSEN, N., & WARD, W. C. Measures for the study of creativity in scientific problem-solving. *Applied Psychological Measurement*, 1978, 2, 1–24.
16. WARD, W. C., FREDERICKSEN, N., & CARLSON, S. B. Construct validity of free-response and machine-scorable forms of a test. *Journal of Educational Measurement*, 1980, 17, 11–29.

[992]
The Graduate Record Examinations Advanced Sociology Test. Graduate school candidates; 1939–76; test administered 5 times annually (January, April, June, October, December) at centers established by the publisher; an inactive form is available for local administration; Educational Testing Service.*

For additional information, see 8:926; for a review by J. Richard Wilmeth, see 6:1021. For reviews of the GRE program, see 7:667 (1 review) and 5:601 (1 review).

[993]
The Graduate Record Examinations Advanced Spanish Test. Graduate school candidates; 1946–76; test administered 5 times annually (January, April, June, October, December) at centers established by the publisher; 4 scores: interpretive reading skills, peninsular topics, Spanish-American topics, total; an inactive form is available for local administration; Educational Testing Service.*

For additional information and a review by Alan Garfinkel, see 8:165; for a review by Gino Parisi of an earlier form, see 7:319. For reviews of the GRE program, see 7:667 (1 review) and 5:601 (1 review).

[994]
Graduate Record Examinations: Aptitude and Advanced. Graduate school candidates; 1939–76; GRE; tests administered on specified dates at centers established by the publisher; 21 tests: Aptitude Test, Advanced Biology, Advanced Chemistry, Advanced Computer Science, Advanced Economics, Advanced Education, Advanced Engineering, Advanced French, Advanced Geography, Advanced Geology, Advanced German, Advanced History, Advanced Literature in English, Advanced Mathematics, Advanced Music, Advanced Philosophy, Advanced Physics, Advanced Political Science, Advanced Psychology, Advanced Sociology, Advanced Spanish; inactive forms of the achievement tests (except Advanced Computer Science) are available to colleges for local administration in the *Undergraduate Assessment Program*; Educational Testing Service.*

For additional information, see 8:476 (6 references); for a review by Leona E. Tyler of an earlier program, see 7:667 (10 references); see also 6:762 (1 reference); for a review by Harold Seashore, see 5:601 (12 references); see also 4:527 (24 references). For reviews of individual tests, see 8:69 (1 review), 8:121 (2 reviews), 8:132 (1 review), 8:165 (1 review), 8:897 (1 review), 7:319 (1 review), 6:9 (2 reviews), 6:376 (1 review), 6:461 (2 reviews), 6:578 (1 review), 6:698 (1 review), 6:919 (1 review), 6:931 (1 review), 6:1021 (1 review), 5:10 (2 reviews), 5:215 (1 review), 5:247 (1 review), 5:270 (1 review), 5:336 (1 review), 5:427 (1 review), 5:537 (1 review), 5:583 (1 review), 5:727 (1 review), 5:754 (1 review), 5:818 (1 review), 5:835 (1 review), and 4:293 (2 reviews).

REFERENCES
1–24. See 4:527.
25–36. See 5:601.
37. See 6:762.
38–47. See 7:667.
48–53. See 8:476.
54. THOMAS, B. Differential utility of predictors in graduate nursing education. *Nursing Research*, 1977, 26, 100–102.
55. VECCHIO, R., & COSTIN, F. Predicting teacher effectiveness from graduate admissions predictors. *American Educational Research Journal*, 1977, 14, 169–176.
56. HEREFORD, S. M. The Keller plan within a conventional academic environment. An empirical "meta-analytic" study. *Engineering Education*, 1979, 70, 250–260.
57. KAGAN, D. M., & STOCK, W. A. Equivalencing MAT and GRE scores using simple linear transformation and regression methods. *Journal of Experimental Education*, 1980, 49, 34–37.
58. KIRNAN, J. P., & GEISINGER, K. F. The prediction of graduate school success in psychology. *Educational & Psychological Measurement*, 1981, 41, 815–820.

[995]
The Graduate Record Examinations Aptitude Test. Graduate school candidates; 1949–76; GREAT; test administered 6 times annually (January, February, April, June, October, December) at centers established by the publisher; 2 scores: verbal, quantitative; (Braille and large-type editions available); Educational Testing Service.*

For additional information, see 8:188 (45 references); see also T2:382 (15 references) and 7:353 (43 references); for reviews by Robert L. French and Warren W. Willingham of an earlier edition, see 6:461 (17 references); for a review by John T. Dailey, see 5:336 (7 references); for reviews by J. P. Guilford and Carl I. Hovland, see 4:293 (2 references). For reviews of the GRE program, see 7:667 (1 review) and 5:601 (1 review).

REFERENCES
1–2. See 4:293.
3–9. See 5:336.
10–26. See 6:461.
27–69. See 7:353.
70–84. See T2:382.
85–129. See 8:188.
130. MAXWELL, S. E., & JONES, L. V. Female and male admission to graduate school: An illustrative inquiry. *Journal of Educational Statistics*, 1976, 1, 1–37.
131. AYERS, J. B., & PETERS, R. M. Predictive validity of the Test of English as a Foreign Language for Asian graduate students in engineering, chemistry, or mathematics. *Educational & Psychological Measurement*, 1977, 37, 461–463.
132. HARNETT, R. T., & CENTRA, J. A. The effects of academic departments on student learning. *Journal of Higher Education*, 1977, 48, 491–507.
133. LIN, P., & HUMPHREYS, L. G. Predictions of academic performance in graduate and professional school. *Applied Psychological Measurement*, 1977, 1, 249–257.
134. LORD, F. M. A broad-range tailored test of verbal ability. *Applied Psychological Measurement*, 1977, 1, 95–100.
135. OTTEN, M. W. Inventory and expressive measures of locus of control and academic performance: A 5-year outcome study. *Journal of Personality Assessment*, 1977, 41, 644–649.
136. WEIKEL, W. J., & LOESCH, L. C. Cognitive correlates of counsellor trainees' needs awareness. *Canadian Counsellor*, 1977, 11, 128–130.
137. FREDERIKSEN, N., & WARD, W. C. Measures for the study of creativity in scientific problem-solving. *Applied Psychological Measurement*, 1978, 2, 1–24.
138. GREEN, S. G. Aptitude test scores, past performance, and causal attributions about the poorly performing student. *Journal of Educational Psychology*, 1978, 70, 242–247.
139. SCHMIDT, F. L., JOHNSON, R. H., & GUGEL, J. F. Utility of policy capturing as an approach to graduate admissions decision making. *Applied Psychological Measurement*, 1978, 2, 347–357.
140. WEAVER, W. T. Educators in supply and demand: Effects on quality. *School Review*, 1978, 86, 552–593.
141. CAMP, J., & CLAWSON, T. The relationship between the Graduate Record Examinations Aptitude Test and graduate grade point average in a master of arts in counseling program. *Educational & Psychological Measurement*, 1979, 39, 429–431.
142. DOLE, A. A., & BAGGALEY, A. Prediction of performance in a doctoral education program by the Graduate Record Examinations and other measures. *Educational & Psychological Measurement*, 1979, 39, 421–427.

143. FURST, E. J., & ROELFS, P. J. Validation of the Graduate Record Examination and the Miller Analogies Test in a doctoral program in education. *Educational & Psychological Measurement*, 1979, 39, 147–151.
144. GRINNELL, R. M., JR., & KYTE, N. S. Anxiety level as an indicator of academic performance during first semester of graduate work. *Journal of Psychology*, 1979, 101, 199–201.
145. HEBERT, D. J., & HOLMES, A. F. Graduate Record Examinations Aptitude Test scores as a predictor of graduate grade point average. *Educational & Psychological Measurement*, 1979, 39, 415–420.
146. HEINRICH, D. L. The causal influence of anxiety on academic achievement for students of differing intellectual ability. *Applied Psychological Measurement*, 1979, 3, 351–359.
147. OMIZO, M. M., & MICHAEL, W. B. The prediction of performance in a counselor education master's degree program. *Educational & Psychological Measurement*, 1979, 39, 433–437.
148. BOZARTH, J. D., & SETTLES, R. B. Graduate Record Examination, race, and same performance outcomes. *Rehabilitation Counseling*, 1980, 23, 291–294.
149. CENTRA, J. A. Graduate degree aspirations of ethnic student groups. *American Educational Research Journal*, 1980, 17, 459–478.
150. DIAMOND, E. E. The AMEG commission report on sex bias in achievement testing. *Measurement & Evaluation in Guidance*, 1980, 13, 135–147.
151. DONLON, T. F., HICKS, M. M., & WALLMARK, M. M. Sex differences in item responses on the Graduate Record Examination. *Applied Psychological Measurement*, 1980, 4, 9–20.
152. GILLILAND, K. The interactive effect of introversion–extraversion with caffeine induced arousal on verbal performance. *Journal of Research in Personality*, 1980, 14, 482–492.
153. WARD, W. C., FREDERIKSEN, N., & CARLSON, S. B. Construct validity of free-response and machine-scorable forms of a test. *Journal of Educational Measurement*, 1980, 17, 11–29.
154. HENK, W. A. Effects of modified deletion strategies and scoring procedures on cloze test performance. *Journal of Reading Behavior*, 1981, 13, 347–357.
155. POWERS, D. E., & SWINTON, S. S. Extending the measurement of graduate admission abilities beyond the verbal and quantitative domains. *Applied Psychological Measurement*, 1981, 5, 141–158.

[996]

The Graduate School Foreign Language Testing Program. Graduate level degree candidates required to demonstrate foreign language reading proficiency; 1963–76; GSFLT; test administered 4 times annually (February, April, June, October) at participating institutions; 4 tests listed separately; in section 2 of each test, candidate elects 1 set of passages (humanities, natural sciences, or social sciences) related to their major field; Educational Testing Service.*
a) FRENCH.
b) GERMAN.
c) RUSSIAN.
d) SPANISH.
For additional information, see 8:101; see also 7:668 (3 references). For reviews of the individual tests, see 8:122 (1 review), 8:133 (1 review), 8:151 (1 review), 7:320 (1 review), 6:377 (1 review), and 6:391 (1 review).

[997]

Graduate School Foreign Language Test: French. Graduate level degree candidates required to demonstrate reading proficiency in French; 1963–76; tests administered 4 times annually (February, April, June, October) at participating institutions; Educational Testing Service.*
For additional information and a review by Stanley L. Shinall, see 8:122; see also 7:275 (3 references); for a review by Clarence E. Turner of an earlier edition, see 6:377.

[998]

Graduate School Foreign Language Test: German. Graduate level degree candidates required to demonstrate reading proficiency in German; 1963–76; GSFLTG; tests administered 4 times annually (February, April, June, October) at participating institutions; Educational Testing Service.*
For additional information and a review by Vincent J. Dell'Orto, see 8:133; see also 7:288 (3 references); for a review by Jack M. Stein of an earlier edition, see 6:391.

[999]

Graduate School Foreign Language Test: Russian. Graduate level degree candidates required to demonstrate reading proficiency in Russian; 1963–76; GSFLTR; tests administered 4 times annually (February, April, June, October) at participating institutions; Educational Testing Service.*
For additional information and a review by William D. Buffington, see 8:151; see also 7:310 (4 references).

[1000]

Graduate School Foreign Language Test: Spanish. Graduate level degree candidates required to demonstrate reading proficiency in Spanish; 1963–76; GSFLTS; tests administered 4 times annually (February, April, June, October) at participating institutions; Educational Testing Service.*
For additional information, see 8:166; for a review by Robert Lado of an earlier form, see 7:320 (3 references).

[1001]

Grammar and Usage Test Series. Grades 7–9, 10–12; 1950–70; 2 levels; no manual; Perfection Form Co.*
(In-print status uncertain; no reply from publisher.)
a) JUNIOR HIGH SCHOOL SERIES. Grades 7–9; formerly called *Objective Tests in English*; 6 tests.
1) *Plurals and Possessives.*
2) *Punctuation.*
3) *Parts of Speech.*
4) *Pronoun Usage.*
5) *Word Usage.*
6) *Final Examination.*
b) SENIOR HIGH SCHOOL SERIES. Grades 10–12; formerly called *Objective Test in Grammar*; 7 tests.
1) *Plurals and Possessives.*
2) *Punctuation.*
3) *Parts of Speech.*
4) *Pronoun Usage.*
5) *Verbals.*
6) *Word Usage.*
7) *Final Examination.*
For additional information concerning the earlier tests, see 4:171 and 4:172.

[1002]

The Graphoscopic Scale: A Projective Psychodiagnostic Method. Ages 5–16, 15 and over; 1953–69; author uses acronym PGS, denoting *Pikunas Graphoscopic Scale*; drawing completion technique; 5 scores: self-expressive balance, intelligence, creativity index, adjustment, total (called diagnostic and prognostic rating); Justin Pikunas; University Press of America.*
See T2:1465 (1 reference) and P:433 (8 references).

[1003]

Grason-Stadler Audiometers. Ages 6 and over; 1950–73; 6 audiometers (AC operated); Grason-Stadler

Co., Inc.* (Availability uncertain; no reply from manufacturer.)

a) DIAGNOSTIC AND SPEECH AUDIOMETERS. 1950–72; for pure tone (air and bone conduction) and speech testing in clinics and research; permits Békésy audiometry (except for manual model of 1701).

1) 1701 *Audiometer*. 1969–71; 3 sweep-frequency models: manual, automatic (117V, 234V).

2) 1702 *Audiometer*. 1972; fixed-frequency automatic and manual model.

3) 1704 *Audiometer*. 1972; fixed-frequency manual model.

b) SCREENING AUDIOMETERS. 1971–73.

1) 1703 *Recording Audiometer*. 1971; for pure tone air conduction testing in employment screening and hearing conservation programs; permits Békésy audiometry; 4 models: desk top (50HZ, 60HZ), portable (50HZ, 60HZ).

2) 1707 *Audiometer*. 1973; for use in schools and industry; portable manual model.

c) 1720 OTOADMITTANCE METER. 1971; for testing of middle ear pathologies in clinics and research; automatic model.

See T2:2038 (11 references) and 6:946 (6 references).

[1004]

Grassi Basic Cognitive Evaluation. Ages 3–9; 1973; GBCE; "identification of developmental deficits"; 29 scores: discriminations (5 scores), conceptualization (5 scores), identifications (3 scores), orientation (3 scores), visualization, number concepts (3 scores), kinesthesia (2 scores), auditory perception, sequencing (2 scores), recall (2 scores), total, basic learning quotient (ratio of a GBCE score to mental age on the *Stanford-Binet Intelligence Scale*); Joseph R. Grassi; Joseph R. Grassi, Inc.*

For additional information and reviews by J. Jeffrey Grill and Lester Mann, see 8:430.

REFERENCES

1. GRASSI, J. R., & LA MORTO-CORSE, A. Identification and remediation of basic cognitive deficits in disadvantaged children. *Journal of Learning Disabilities*, 1979, 12, 483–487.

[1005]

The Grassi Block Substitution Test: For Measuring Organic Brain Pathology. Mental patients; 1947–66; GBST; formerly called *The Fairfield Block Substitution Test*; manual out of print; Joseph R. Grassi; Joseph R. Grassi, Inc.*

See T2:1196 (7 references) and P:94 (13 references); for excerpted reviews by J. G. McMurray and one other, see 5:60 (5 references).

REFERENCES

1–5. See 5:60.
6–18. See P:94.
19–25. See T2:1196.
26. BERGMAN, H., HOHN, L., & AGREN, G. Neuropsychological impairment and a test of the predisposition hypothesis with regard to field dependence in alcoholics. *Journal of Studies on Alcohol*, 1981, 42, 15–23.

[1006]

Gravidometer. Older adolescents and adults; 1974; knowledge of human pregnancy; no manual; Panos D. Bardis; the Author.*

For additional information, see 8:341.

[1007]

Gray Oral Reading Test. Grades 1–16 and adults; 1963–67; GORT; William S. Gray; edited by Helen M. Robinson; PRO-ED.*

See T2:1681 (11 references); for reviews by Emery P. Bliesmer, Albert J. Harris, and Paul R. Lohnes, see 6:842.

REFERENCES

1–11. See T2:1681.
12. ALLINGTON, R. L., CHODOS, L., DOMARACKI, J., & TRUEX, S. Passage dependency: Four diagnostic oral reading tests. *Reading Teacher*, 1977, 30, 369–375.
13. BADIAN, N. A. Auditory–visual integration, auditory memory, and reading in retarded and adequate readers. *Journal of Learning Disabilities*, 1977, 10, 49–114.
14. HOLMES, D. L., & PEPER R. J. An evaluation of the use of spelling error analysis in the diagnosis of reading disabilities. *Child Development*, 1977, 48, 1708–1711.
15. JORGENSON, G. W. Relationship of classroom behavior to the accuracy of the match between material difficulty and student ability. *Journal of Educational Psychology*, 1977, 69, 24–32.
16. MALATESTA, C. Z., CIRCO, J., & SMITH, B. A discriminating, non-discriminatory test battery for a prison population. *Corrective & Social Psychiatry & Journal of Behavior Technology, Methods & Therapy*, 1977, 23, 15–17.
17. McCORMICK, D. P. Pediatric evaluation of children with school problems. *American Journal of Diseases of Children*, 1977, 131, 318–322.
18. PRESTON, M. S., & GUTHRIE, J. T., KIRSCH, I., GERTMAN, D., & CHILDS, B. VERs in normal and disabled adult readers. *Psychophysiology*, 1977, 14, 8–14.
19. REICHURDT, K. W. Playing dead or running away–Defense reactions during reading. *Journal of Reading*, 1977, 20, 706–711.
20. SILBERBERG, N. E., & SILBERBERG M. C. A note on reading tests and their role in defining reading difficulties. *Journal of Learning Disabilities*, 1977, 10, 100–103.
21. FISCHER, F. W., LIBERMAN, I. Y., & SHANKWEILER, D. Reading reversals and development dyslexia: A further study. *Cortex*, 1978, 14, 496–510.
22. GROSS, K., ROTHENBERG, S., & SCHOTTENFELD, S. Duration thresholds for letter identification in left and right visual fields for normal and reading–disabled children. *Neuropsychologia*, 1978, 16, 709–715.
23. HOLTZMAN, R. N. N, RUDEL, R. G., & GOLDENSOHN, E. S. Paroxysmal alexia. *Cortex*, 1978, 14, 592–603.
24. PARK, R. Performance on geometric figure copying tests as predictors of types of errors in decoding. *Reading Research Quarterly*, 1978–1979, 14, 100–118.
25. RUSSELL, H. L., & CARTER, J. L. Biofeedback training with children: Consultation, questions, applications and alternatives. *Journal of Clinical Child Psychology*, 1978, 7, 23–25.
26. COLLETTE, M. A. Dyslexia and classic pathognomic signs. *Perceptual & Motor Skills*, 1979, 48, 1055–1062.
27. DYKMAN, R. A., ACKERMAN, P. T., & OGLESBY, D. M. Selective and sustained attention in hyperactive, learning–disabled, and normal boys. *Journal of Nervous & Mental Disease*, 1979, 167, 288–297.
28. GOLD, P. Suspected neurological impairment and cognitive abilities: A longitudinal study. *Psychological Reports*, 1979, 45, 215–218.
29. GOLD, P. Suspected neurological impairment (SNI) and cognitive abilities: A longitudinal study of selected skills and predictive accuracy. *Journal of Clinical Child Psychology*, 1979, 8, 35–38.
30. GOLD, P., & BERK, R. A. Prediction of the academic success of children with suspected neurological impairments. *Journal of Clinical Psychology*, 1979, 35, 505–509.
31. McCORMICK, C., & SAMUELS, S. J. Word recognition by second graders: The unit of perception and interrelationships among accuracy, latency, and comprehension. *Journal of Reading Behavior*, 1979, 11, 107–118.
32. MOYER, S. B. Rehabilitation of alexia: A case study. *Cortex*, 1979, 15, 139–144.
33. REED, H. B. C., JR. Biological defects and special education – An issue in personnel preparation. *Journal of Special Education*, 1979, 13, 9–33.
34. WHITE, D. R., & JACOBS, E. The prediction of first–grade reading achievement from WPPSI scores of preschool children. *Psychology in the Schools*, 1979, 16, 189–192.
35. CANTWELL, D. P., BAKER, L., & MATTISON, R. E. Psychiatric disorders in children with speech and language retardation. *Archives of General Psychiatry*, 1980, 37, 423–426.
36. DYKMAN, R. A., ACKERMAN, P. T., & OGLESBY, D. M. Correlates of problem solving in hyperactive, learning disabled, and control boys. *Journal of Learning Disabilities*, 1980, 13, 23–32.

37. MATHEWS, R. C., COON, R. C., & ROSENTHAL, G. T. Broken text as a predictor of reading ability in the early grades. *Reading World*, 1980, 20, 57–64.
38. WHALEY, W. J., & KIBBY, M. W. Word synthesis and beginning reading achievement. *Journal of Educational Research*, 1980, 73, 132–138.
39. WILKINSON, A. C. Children's understanding in reading and listening. *Journal of Educational Psychology*, 1980, 72, 561–574.
40. ZAGER, R., ARBIT, J., & FRIEDLAND, J. Structure of a psychodiagnostic test battery for children. *Journal of Clinical Psychology*, 1980, 36, 313–318.
41. ACKERMAN, P. T., OGLESBY, D. M., & DYKMAN, R. A. A contrast of hyperactive, learning disabled, and hyperactive–learning disabled boys. *Journal of Clinical Child Psychology*, 1981, 10, 168–173.
42. GOLD, P. Suspected neurological impairment (SNI) and cognitive abilities: A longitudinal study of selected skills and predictive accuracy. *Journal of Clinical Child Psychology*, 1981, 8, 35–38.
43. TASCHOW, H. G. Innercity Canadian native and non–native pupils' achievement in reading, writing, and speaking. *Reading Teacher*, 1981, 34, 799–803.

[1008]
The Gretsch-Tilson Musical Aptitude Test.
Grades 4–12; 1938; Lowell Mason Tilson; Fred Gretsch Co., Inc.* (In-print status uncertain; no reply from publisher.)
For additional information, see 7:244 (2 references).

[1009]
Grid Test of Schizophrenic Thought Disorder.
Adults; 1967; GTSTD; 2 scores: intensity, consistency; D. Bannister and Fay Fransella; Psychological Test Publications [England].*
For additional information and a review by Robert W. Payne, see 8:571 (30 references); see also T2:1198 (8 references); for a review by David Jones, see 7:84 (7 references); see also P:96 (8 references).

REFERENCES

1–8. See P:96.
9–15. See 7:84.
16–23. See T2:1198.
24–53. See 8:571.
54. JOENSEN, E., LUND, Y., & RICHARDT, C. A comparison between the Grid Test of Schizophrenic Thought Disorder and diagnostic psychological testing. *Scandinavian Journal of Psychology*, 1977, 18, 153–156.
55. HIGGINS, K., & SHERMAN, M. The effect of motivation on loose thinking in schizophrenics as measured by the Bannister–Fransella grid test. *Journal of Clinical Psychology*, 1978, 34, 624–628.
56. POOLE, A. D. The Grid Test of Schizophrenic Thought Disorder and psychiatric symptomatology. *British Journal of Medical Psychology*, 1979, 52, 183–186.

[1010]
Group Cohesiveness: A Study of Group Morale.
Adults; 1958, c1957–58; GC; title on test is *A Study of Group Morale*; 5 scores: satisfaction of individual motives, satisfaction of interpersonal relations, homogeneity of attitude, satisfaction with leadership, total; Bernard Goldman; Psychometric Affiliates.*
See T2:1199 (1 reference) and P:97; for reviews by Eric F. Gardner and Cecil A. Gibb, see 6:104 (1 reference).

[1011]
Group Diagnostic Reading Aptitude and Achievement Tests.
Grades 3–9; 1939; 15 scores: reading (paragraph understanding, speed), word discrimination (vowels, consonants, reversals, additions and omissions), arithmetic, spelling, visual ability (letter memory, form memory), auditory ability (letter memory, discrimination and orientation), motor ability (copying text, crossing out letters), vocabulary; Marion Monroe and Eva Edith Sherman; C. H. Nevins Printing Co.*

See T2:1631 (3 references) and 6:825.

REFERENCES

1–3. See T2:1631.
4. FRAUENHEIM, J. G. Academic achievement characteristics of adult males who were diagnosed as dyslexic in childhood. *Journal of Learning Disabilities*, 1978, 11, 476–483.

[1012]
Group Diagnostic Spelling Test.
Grades 9–13; 1958; Thomas G. Kemp; Reading Laboratory and Clinic.* (In-print status uncertain; no reply from publisher.)
For additional information, see 6:319.

[1013]
Group Embedded Figures Test.
Ages 10 and over; 1971; GEFT; adaptation of the individually administered *Embedded Figures Test*; Philip K. Oltman, Evelyn Raskin, Herman A. Witkin, and Stephen A. Karp (manual); Consulting Psychologists Press, Inc.*
For additional information and reviews by Leonard D. Goodstein and Alfred E. Hall, see 8:572 (47 references); see also T2:1201 (3 references); for references to reviews of the individual test, see 8:548.

REFERENCES

1–3. See T2:1201.
4–50. See 8:572.
51. DRUMMOND, R. J., & McINTIRE, W. G. The role of cognitive style in student evaluation of instruction. *College Student Journal*, 1977, 11, 220–223.
52. FOSTER, L. M. Group Embedded Figures Test performance in different instrumental behavior styles. *Journal of Clinical Psychology*, 1977, 33, 571–574.
53. JONES, P. A. Modernization–relevant values and achievement of native and rural populations assessed within traditional and modern environments. *Annals of the New York Academy of Science*, 1977, 285, 582–592.
54. LAWSON, A. E., & WOLLMAN, W. T. Cognitive level, cognitive style, and value judgment. *Science Education*, 1977, 61, 397–407.
55. LOCKHEED, M. E. Cognitive style effects on sex status in student work groups. *Journal of Educational Psychology*, 1977, 69, 158–165.
56. LOO, R., & TOWNSEND, P. J. Components underlying the relation between field dependence and extraversion. *Perceptual & Motor Skills*, 1977, 45, 528–530.
57. NEDD, A. N. B., & SCHWARTZ, H. A cross–cultural investigation of the relative importance of child rearing and socioeconomic antecedents of field–dependence–independence. *Journal of Psychology*, 1977, 96, 63–70.
58. Noppe, L. D., & Gallagher, J. M. A cognitive style approach to creative thought. *Journal of Personality Assessment*, 1977, 41, 85–90.
59. O'LEARY, M. R., DONOVAN, D. M., & CHANEY, E. F. The relationship of perceptual field orientation to measures of cognitive functioning and current adaptive abilities in alcoholics and nonalcoholics. *Journal of Nervous & Mental Disease*, 1977, 165, 275–282.
60. POWERS, J. E., & LIS, D. J. Field dependence–independence and performance with the passive transformation. *Perceptual & Motor Skills*, 1977, 45, 759–765.
61. WITKIN, H. A., MOORE, C. A., OLTMAN, P. K., GOODENOUGH, D. R., FRIEDMAN, F., OWEN, D. R., & RASKIN, E. Role of the field–dependent and field–independent cognitive styles in academic evolution: A longitudinal study. *Journal of Educational Psychology*, 1977, 69, 197–211.
62. BOSS, M. W., & AMIN, M. E. Psychological differentiation and performance on conditional reasoning tasks. *Perceptual & Motor Skills*, 1978, 47, 935–940.
63. DAVIDSON, W. B., & HOUSE, W. J. Influence of reflection–impulsivity and cognitive style on time estimation under different ambient conditions. *Perceptual & Motor Skills*, 1978, 46, 1083–1091.
64. DAVIDSON, W. B., & HOUSE, W. J. On the relationship between reflection–impulsivity and field–dependence–independence. *Perceptual & Motor Skills*, 1978, 47, 306.
65. FORBES, J. B., & BARRETT, G. V. Individual abilities and task demands in relation to performance and satisfaction on two repetitive monitoring tasks. *Journal of Applied Psychology*, 1978, 63, 188–196.
66. HOFFMAN, D. A. Field independence and intelligence: Their relation to leadership and self–concept in sixth–grade boys. *Journal of Educational Psychology*, 1978, 70, 827–832.

67. HUGHES, R. N. Sex differences in field dependence: Effects of unlimited time on Group Embedded Figures Test performance. *Perceptual & Motor Skills*, 1978, 47, 1246.
68. HULFISH, S. Relationship of role identification, self-esteem, and intelligence to sex differences in field independence. *Perceptual & Motor Skills*, 1978, 47, 835–842.
69. LOO, R. Field dependence and Eysenck's neuroticism scale. *Perceptual & Motor Skills*, 1978, 47, 522.
70. MECK, D. S., BOURGEOIS, A., & LEUNES, A. Relation of combined measures of locus of control and psychological differentiation to personality adjustment. *Psychological Reports*, 1978, 43, 547–552.
71. MORRIS, T. L., & BERGUM, B. O. A note on the relationship between field-independence and creativity. *Perceptual & Motor Skills*, 1978, 46, 1114.
72. PACKER, J., & BAIN, J. D. Cognitive style and teacher-student compatibility. *Journal of Educational Psychology*, 1978, 70, 864–871.
73. ROCK, M. H., & GOLDBERGER, L. Relationship between agoraphobia and field dependence. *Journal of Nervous & Mental Disease*, 1978, 166, 781–786.
74. RUSH, M. C., PHILLIPS, J. S., & PANEK, P. E. Subject recruitment bias: The paid volunteer subject. *Perceptual & Motor Skills*, 1978, 47, 443–449.
75. SIGNORELLA, M. L., & JAMISON, W. Sex differences in the correlations among field dependence, spatial ability, sex role orientation, and performance on Piaget's water-level task. *Developmental Psychology*, 1978, 14, 689–690.
76. ADAMS, V. M., & MCLEOD, D. G. The interaction of field dependence/independence and the level of guidance of mathematics instruction. *Journal for Research in Mathematics Education*, 1979, 10, 347–355.
77. ANNIS, L. F. Effect of cognitive style and learning passage organization on study technique effectiveness. *Journal of Educational Psychology*, 1979, 71, 620–626.
78. AVOLIO, B. J., ALEXANDER, R. A., BARRETT, G. V., & STERNS, H. L. Analyzing preference for pace as a component of task performance. *Perceptual & Motor Skills*, 1979, 49, 667–674.
79. Bennink, C. D., & Spoelstra, T. Individual differences in field articulation as a factor in language comprehension. *Journal of Research in Personality*, 1979, 13, 480–489.
80. CARTER, H., & LOO, R. Relationships between field dependence and Eysenck's personality dimensions. *Journal of Psychology*, 1979, 103, 45–49.
81. CHALIP, L. Learning on the Group Embedded Figures Test. *Perceptual & Motor Skills*, 1979, 48, 1070.
82. DOUGLAS, C. B. Differences in attitude and ability of biology majors, nonmajors, and preservice teachers. *Improving College & University Teaching*, 1979, 27, 110–113.
83. GOODENOUGH, D. R., OLTMAN, P. K., FRIEDMAN, F., MOORE, C. A., WITKIN, H. A., OWEN, D., & RASKIN, E. Cognitive styles in the development of medical careers. *Journal of Vocational Behavior*, 1979, 14, 341–351.
84. LIS, D. J., & POWERS, J. E. Reliability and validity of the Group Embedded Figures Test for a grade school sample. *Perceptual & Motor Skills*, 1979, 48, 660–662.
85. MCLEOD, D. B., & ADAMS, V. M. The interaction of field independence with small-group instruction in mathematics. *Journal of Experimental Education*, 1979–1980, 48, 118–124.
86. PANEK, P. E., BARRETT, G. V., ALEXANDER, R. A., & STERNS, H. L. Age and self-selected performance pace on a visual monitoring inspection task. *Aging & Work*, 1979, 2, 183–191.
87. PARASINIS, I., & LONG, G. L. Relationships among spatial skills, communication skills, and field independence in deaf students. *Perceptual & Motor Skills*, 1979, 49, 879–887.
88. PELLEGRENO, D., & STICKLE, F. Field-dependence/field-independence and labeling of facial affect. *Perceptual & Motor Skills*, 1979, 48, 489–490.
89. PETRAKIS, E. Perceptual style of varsity tennis players. *Perceptual & Motor Skills*, 1979, 48, 266.
90. PRESTON, J. C., & KING, L. L. Correlations between Witkin's Group Embedded Figures Test and Nickel's Rod and Frame Test. *Perceptual & Motor Skills*, 1979, 48, 670.
91. SAVARESE, J. M., & MILLER, R. J. Artistic preferences and cognitive-perceptual style. *Studies in Art Education*, 1979, 20, 45–51.
92. STONE, E. F. Field independence and perceptions of task characteristics: A laboratory investigation. *Journal of Applied Psychology*, 1979, 64, 305–310.
93. WALKER, R. D., O'LEARY, M. R., CHANEY, E. F., & FAURIA, T. M. Influence of cognitive style on an incidental memory task. *Perceptual & Motor Skills*, 1979, 48, 195–198.
94. WEISS, H. M., & SHAW, J. B. Social influences on judgments about tasks. *Organizational Behavior & Human Performance*, 1979, 24, 126–140.
95. WORMACK, L. Cognitive predictors of articulation in writing. *Perceptual & Motor Skills*, 1979, 48, 1151–1156.
96. WORMACK, L. Restructuring ability and patterns of physics achievement. *Perceptual & Motor Skills*, 1979, 48, 451–458.
97. WUDEL, P., & LOO, R. Birth order and person variables. *Psychological Reports*, 1979, 45, 280.
98. BARNES, G. E. Characteristics of the clinical alcoholic personality. *Journal of Studies on Alcohol*, 1980, 41, 894–910.
99. BLAKE, A. J. D. The predictive power of two written tests of Piagetian developmental level. *Journal of Research in Science Teaching*, 1980, 17, 435–441.
100. BOLOCOFSKY, D. N. Motivational effects of classroom competition as a function of field dependence. *Journal of Educational Research*, 1980, 73, 213–217.
101. BOURGEOIS, A., LEVENSON, H., & WAGNER, C. Success on a biofeedback task: Effects of congruence-incongruence between locus of control and psychological differentiation. *Journal of Personality Assessment*, 1980, 44, 487–492.
102. BUFFARDI, L., & GIBSON, J. F. Relation between raters' characteristics and halo error. *Perceptual & Motor Skills*, 1980, 51, 1003–1011.
103. CARTER, H., & LOO, R. Group Embedded Figures Test: Psychometric data. *Perceptual & Motor Skills*, 1980, 50, 32–34.
104. COOPERMAN, E. W. Field differentiation and intelligence. *Journal of Psychology*, 1980, 105, 29–33.
105. DUFFY, R. A. An analysis of aesthetic sensitivity and creativity with other variables in grades four, six, eight, and ten. *Journal of Educational Research*, 1980, 73, 26–30.
106. FLEXER, B. K., & ROBERGE, J. J. IQ, field dependence-independence, and the development of formal operational thought. *Journal of General Psychology*, 1980, 103, 191–201.
107. FRY, P. S., & CHARRON, P. A. Effects of cognitive style and counselor-client compatibility on client growth. *Journal of Counseling Psychology*, 1980, 27, 529–538.
108. MCLEOD, D. B., & ADAMS, V. M. Aptitude-treatment interaction in mathematics instruction using expository and discovery methods. *Journal for Research in Mathematics Education*, 1980, 11, 225–234.
109. O'LEARY, M. R., CALSYN, D. A., & FAURIA, T. The Group Embedded Figures Test: A measure of cognitive style or cognitive impairment. *Journal of Personality Assessment*, 1980, 44, 532–537.
110. PANEK, P. E., FUNK, L. G., & NELSON, P. K. Reliability and validity of the Group Embedded Figures Test across the life span. *Perceptual & Motor Skills*, 1980, 50, 1171–1174.
111. READANCE, J. E., BALDWIN, R. S., BEAN, T. W., & DISHNER, E. K. Field dependence-independence as a variable in cloze test performance. *Journal of Reading Behavior*, 1980, 12, 65–67.
112. SARACHO, O. The relationship between the teachers' cognitive style and their perceptions of their students' academic achievements. *Educational Research Quarterly*, 1980, 5, 40–49.
113. SARACHO, O. N., & DAYTON, C. M. Relationship of teachers' cognitive styles to pupils' academic achievement gains. *Journal of Educational Psychology*, 1980, 72, 544–549.
114. SAURENMAN, D. A., & MICHAEL, W. B. Differential placement of high-achieving and low-achieving gifted pupils in grades four, five, and six on measures of field dependence-field independence, creativity, and self-concept. *Gifted Child Quarterly*, 1980, 24, 81–86.
115. SHYMANSKY, J. A., & YORE, L. D. A study of teaching strategies, student cognitive development, and cognitive style as they relate to student achievement in science. *Journal of Research in Science Teaching*, 1980, 17, 369–382.
116. SPIRO, R. J., & TIRRE, W. C. Individual differences in schema utilization during discourse processing. *Journal of Educational Psychology*, 1980, 72, 204–208.
117. WIDIGER, T. A., KNUDSON, R. M., & RORER, L. G. Convergent and discriminant validity of measures of cognitive styles and abilities. *Journal of Personality & Social Psychology*, 1980, 39, 116–129.
118. WORMACK, L. Restructuring ability among premedical and predental minority students. *Journal of Research in Science Teaching*, 1980, 17, 577–582.
119. AVOLIO, B. J., ALEXANDER, R. A., BARETT, G. V., & STERNS, H. L. Designing a measure of visual selective attention to assess individual differences in information processing. *Applied Psychological Measurement*, 1981, 5, 29–42.
120. BENSON, B. A. Personality correlates of self-punitive behavior. *Journal of Abnormal Psychology*, 1981, 90, 183–185.
121. DILLON, R. F. Analogical reasoning under different methods of test administration. *Applied Psychological Measurement*, 1981, 5, 341–347.
122. HANSEN, J., & STANSFIELD, C. The relationship of field-dependent-independent cognitive styles to foreign language achievement. *Language Learning*, 1981, 31, 349–367.
123. HART, M. E., PAYNE, D. A., & LEWIS, L. A. Prediction of basic science learning outcomes with cognitive style and traditional admissions criteria. *Journal of Medical Education*, 1981, 56, 137–139.
124. HUBBLE, M. A., NOBLE, F. C., & ROBINSON, S. E. The effect of counselor touch in an initial counseling session. *Journal of Counseling Psychology*, 1981, 28, 533–535.

125. IPPEL, M. J. Generalizability of performance-scores on embedded figures material. *Educational & Psychological Measurement*, 1981, 41, 315-331.
126. KISSINGER, J. F., & MUNJAS, B. A. Nursing process, student attributes, and teaching methodologies. *Nursing Research*, 1981, 30, 242-246.
127. LIVINGSTON, S. A. Nonverbal communication tests as predictors of success in psychology and counseling. *Applied Psychological Measurement*, 1981, 5, 325-331.
128. LUSK, E. J., & WRIGHT, H. Differences in sex and curricula on learning the Group Embedded Figures Test. *Perceptual & Motor Skills*, 1981, 53, 8-10.
129. LUSK, E. J., & WRIGHT, H. Note on learning the Group Embedded Figures Test. *Perceptual & Motor Skills*, 1981, 53, 370.
130. MAHLIOS, M. C. Effects of teacher-student cognitive style on patterns of dyadic classroom interaction. *Journal of Experimental Education*, 1981, 41, 147-157.
131. MAHLIOS, M. C. Instructional design and cognitive styles of teachers in elementary schools. *Perceptual & Motor Skills*, 1981, 52, 335-338.
132. O'LEARY, M. R., FAURIA, T., CALSYN, D. A., & FEHRENBACH, P. A. Cognitive style, personality traits, and treatment attrition among alcoholics. *International Journal of the Addictions*, 1981, 16, 1143-1148.
133. PETRAKIS, E. Cognitive styles of physical education majors. *Perceptual & Motor Skills*, 1981, 53, 574.
134. PETRAKIS, E. Relationship between figure-ground perception and viewing time in a ball-catching task. *Perceptual & Motor Skills*, 1981, 53, 899-904.
135. PETRAKIS, E., & HANSON, C. J. Cognitive style and choice of leisure activities by older adults. *Perceptual & Motor Skills*, 1981, 52, 839-842.
136. PROVOST, G. L. Teaching strategies, modes of evaluation and field-dependence factor. *Perceptual & Motor Skills*, 1981, 52, 163-173.
137. SCOTT, N., SMITH, D. U., & ROSENBERG, I. K. Cognitive style and instructional materials for medical students. *Journal of Medical Education*, 1981, 56, 565-571.
138. SHADE, B. J. Racial variation in perceptual differentiation. *Perceptual & Motor Skills*, 1981, 52, 243-248.

[1014]

Group Encounter Survey. Group members; 1963-73; GES; feelings and behavior of individuals as members of task groups; 5 scores (individual attitudes, leadership preferences, conflict resolution, intergroup relations, total) for each of 5 group membership styles; no manual; Jay Hall and Martha S. Williams; Teleometrics Int'l.*

For additional information, see 8:1048 (2 references).

[1015]

*Group Environment Scale. Group members and leaders; 1974-81; GES; a part of *The Social Climate Scales* (2227): 10 scores: cohesion, leader support, expressiveness, independence, task orientation, self-discovery, anger and aggression, order and organization, leader control, innovation; Rudolf H. Moos and Barrie Humphrey (test); Consulting Psychologists Press, Inc.*

For additional information and reviews by David P. Campbell and Robyn M. Dawes, see 8:573. For a review of *The Social Climate Scales*, see 8:681.

REFERENCES

1. SCHROEDER, C. C. Designing ideal staff environments through milieu management. *Journal of College Student Personnel*, 1979, 20, 129-135.

[1016]

★Group Inventory for Finding Creative Talent. Grades kgn-2, 3-4, 5-6; 1976-80; GIFT; 3 dimension scores: imagination, independence, many interests; (Spanish, French, Hebrew, and German editions available); Sylvia B. Rimm; Educational Assessment Service, Inc.*

REFERENCES

1. RIMM, S., & DAVIS, G. A. Five years of international research with GIFT: An instrument for the identification of creativity. *Journal of Creative Behavior*, 1980, 14, 35-46.

[1017]

★Group Inventory For Finding Interests. Grades 6-9, 9-12; 1979-80; GIFFI; for screening the creatively gifted; 5 dimension scores: creative arts and writing, challenge-inventiveness, confidence, imagination, many interests; (Spanish and Hebrew editions available); Sylvia B. Rimm and Gary A. Davis; Educational Assessment Service, Inc.*

[1018]

★Group Literacy Assessment. End of junior school and beginning of secondary school; 1981; GLA; 3 scores: proof-reading, fill the gaps, total; Frank A. Spooncer; Hodder & Stoughton Educational [England].*

[1019]

Group Mathematics Test, Second Edition. Ages 6.5-8.5; 1970-80; GMT; 3 scores: oral, computation, total; D. Young; Hodder & Stoughton Educational [England].

For additional information and a review by John Cook of an earlier edition, see 8:273.

[1020]

The Group Personality Projective Test. Ages 11 and over; 1956-61; GPPT; formerly called *Kahn Stick Figure Personality Test*; 7 scores: tension reduction quotient, nurturance, withdrawal, neuroticism, affiliation, succorance, total; Russell N. Cassel and Theodore C. Kahn; Psychological Test Specialists.*

See T2:1466 (5 references); for reviews by Edwin I. Mergargee, Stuart Oskamp, and Marvin Reznikoff, see 7:167 (5 references); see also P:434 (2 references) and 6:214 (7 references).

REFERENCES

1-7. See 6:214.
8-9. See P:434.
10-14. See 7:167.
15-19. See T2:1466.
20. AMMONS, R. B., & AMMONS, C. H. Use and evaluation of the Group Personality Projective Test: Partial summary through December, 1977. *Perceptual & Motor Skills*, 1978, 47, 1069-1070.
21. CARROLL, J. L., & FULLER, G. B. Personality correlates of the Group Personality Projective Test vs. personality factors. *Psychological Reports*, 1978, 43, 1019-1022.
22. SPERL, B., & MIDLARSKY, E. Applicability of the Group Personality Projective Test within a prison population. *Journal of Clinical Psychology*, 1978, 34, 539-542.

[1021]

Group Phonics Analysis. Reading level grades 1-3; 1971; GPA; criterion-referenced; no scores; 11 areas: number reading, letter reading, hearing consonants, alphabetization, recognition (vowels, short sounds, long vowel sounds in words), vowel digraph rule, finale e rule, open and closed syllables, syllabification; Edward Fry; Jamestown Publishers.*

For additional information, a review by Patrick Groff, and an excerpted review by Paula Altman Fuld, see 8:761 (1 reference).

[1022]

Group Projection Sketches for the Study of Small Groups. Groups of 3-40 people (ages 16 and over); 1949; manual out of print; William E. Henry and Harold Guetzkow; William E. Henry.* (In-print status uncertain; no reply from publisher.)

See T2:1467 (1 reference) and P:435; for a review by Cecil A. Gibb, see 5:138 (1 reference); for reviews by Robert R. Holt and N. W. Morton, see 4:106.

[1023]
Group Psychotherapy Suitability Evaluation Scale. Patients in group therapy; 1965–68; SES; also called *Suitability Evaluation Scale*; title on test is *Group Psychotherapy Evaluation Scale*; ratings by therapists; 6 ratings: amount of communication, quality of relatedness and communication, quality of content in relatedness, capacity for change and involvement, amount of therapist verbal activity, direction of therapist verbal activity; Clifton E. Kew; Educational Testing Service.*

For additional information, see P:99 (1 reference).

[1024]
Group Reading Assessment. End of first year junior school; 1962–64; Frank A. Spooncer; Hodder & Stoughton Educational [England].*

For additional information and reviews by David J. Carroll and Thomas Kellaghan, see 8:728.

[1025]
***Group Reading Test, Second Edition.** Ages 6–5 to 12–10; 1968–80; identical with earlier edition ('68) except for new norms; D. Young; Hodder & Stoughton Educational [England].*

For a review by Ralph D. Dutch of the original edition, see 8:729.

[1026]
Group Test for Indian South Africans. Standards 4–6, 7–8, 9–10; 1967–71; GTISA; adaptation for Indian pupils of the *New South African Group Test*; 3 scores: verbal, nonverbal, total; 3 levels; Human Sciences Research Council [South Africa].*

a) JUNIOR. Standards 4–6; 1968–71; Indian standardization by F. W. O. Heinichen, R. J. Prinsloo, and S. Oosthuizen.
b) INTERMEDIATE. Standards 7–8; 1967–69.
c) SENIOR. Standards 9–10; 1968–69.

[1027]
Group Test 20. Ages 15 and over; 1936–72; checking of names and numbers; 2 scores: speed, accuracy; National Institute of Industrial Psychology; NFER-Nelson Publishing Co. [England].*

See T2:2130 (1 reference); for a review by E. G. Chambers, see 4:723 (2 references).

[1028]
Group Test 36. Ages 10–14; 1937–45; verbal intelligence; National Institute of Industrial Psychology; NFER-Nelson Publishing Co. [England].*

See T2:384 (4 references) and 4:296.

[1029]
Group Test 75. Ages 12–13; 1957; nonverbal intelligence; National Institute of Industrial Psychology; NFER-Nelson Publishing Co. [England].*

See T2:385 (1 reference) and 5:338.

[1030]
Group Test 80A. Ages 15 and over; 1943–51; spatial perception; National Institute of Industrial Psychology; NFER-Nelson Publishing Co. [England].*

See T2:2248 (2 references); for reviews by E. G. Chambers and John Liggett, see 5:877.

[1031]
Group Test 81. Ages 14 and over; 1949–69; spatial perception; National Institute of Industrial Psychology; NFER-Nelson Publishing Co. [England].*

For additional information, see 8:1044; see also T2:2249 (6 references); for a review by E. G. Chambers, see 4:758 (5 references).

[1032]
Group Test 82. Ages 14.5 and over; 1959–70; subtest of *N.I.I.P. Engineering Apprentice Selection Test Battery*; spatial perception; National Institute of Industrial Psychology; NFER-Nelson Publishing Co. [England].*

For additional information, see 7:1052.

[1033]
Group Test 91. Industrial applicants; 1949–68; verbal intelligence; National Institute of Industrial Psychology; NFER-Nelson Publishing Co. [England].*

See T2:386 (1 reference) and 7:354.

[1034]
Group Test 95. Ages 14 and over; [1972]; verbal intelligence; no manual; National Institute of Industrial Psychology; NFER-Nelson Publishing Co. [England].*

[1035]
Group Tests 61A, 64, and 66A. Clerical applicants; 1956–72; 3 tests; National Institute of Industrial Psychology; NFER-Nelson Publishing Co. [England].*

a) GROUP TEST 61A. 1956–71; decimalized version of *Group Test 61*; filing, classification, and checking; 2 scores: speed, accuracy.
b) GROUP TEST 64. 1957–71; spelling.
c) GROUP TEST 66A. 1957–72; decimalized version of *Group Test 66*; arithmetic; 2 scores: basic operations, problems.

For additional information, see 7:991.

[1036]
Group Tests 70 and 70B. Ages 15 and over; 1939–70; subtest of *N.I.I.P. Engineering Apprentice Selection Test Battery*; nonverbal intelligence; National Institute of Industrial Psychology; NFER-Nelson Publishing Co. [England].*

See T2:388 (9 references) and 7:355 (5 references); for a review by George Westby of form 70, see 4:297 (5 references).

[1037]
Group Tests 72 and 73. Industrial applicants; 1949–68; nonverbal intelligence; National Institute of Industrial Psychology; NFER-Nelson Publishing Co. [England].*

For additional information, see 7:356 (1 reference).

[1038]
Group Tests 90A and 90B. Ages 15 and over; 1950–70; subtest of *N.I.I.P. Engineering Apprentice Selection Test Battery*; verbal intelligence; National Institute of Industrial Psychology; NFER-Nelson Publishing Co. [England].*

See T2:390 (2 references) and 7:357 (1 reference); for a review by John Liggett of form 90A, see 5:340.

REFERENCES

1. See 7:357.
2-3. See T2:390.
4. GIBSON, H. B. The British study of values: 1. Prediction of drop-out from a psychology degree course. *British Journal of Social & Clinical Psychology*, 1979, 18, 29–34.

[1039]
[Guidance Cumulative Folder and Record Forms]. Grades kgn–12; 1941–70; folder and 5 insert sheets; Chronicle Guidance Publications, Inc.*
a) INTERVIEW RECORD SHEET. 1958.
b) OBSERVATION RECORD SHEET. 1958; reports by teachers.
c) PERSONALITY REPORT SHEET. 1958; ratings by teachers.
d) FOUR YEAR EDUCATIONAL PLAN. Grades 9–12; 1961.
e) DIVISION OF VOCATIONAL EDUCATION-COOPERATIVE TRAINING. Grades 11–12; 1970; vocational education report.

For additional information, see 6:746.

[1040]
Guidance Inventory. High school; 1960–73; GI; identification of problems related to underachievement and need for counseling; 1973 manual is a condensation of manual copyrighted 1960; Ralph Gallagher; the Author.* (In-print status uncertain; no reply from publisher.)

For additional information, see P:100; for a review by John W. M. Rothney, see 6:106.

[1041]
Guidance Test Battery for Secondary Pupils (Standard 8). 1969–71; 7 scores: English vocabulary, English sentences, series completion, arithmetic, Afrikaans vocabulary, Afrikaans sentences, verbal reasoning; all test materials (except language subtests) in both English and Afrikaans; J. D. van Staden, G. J. Ligthelm, J. P. du Toit, A. P. J. Pottas, and G. Engelbrecht (revision); Human Sciences Research Council [South Africa].*

[1042]
Guilford-Holley L Inventory. College and adults; 1953–63; GHLI; leadership behavior; 5 scores: benevolence, ambition, meticulousness, discipline, aggressiveness; J. P. Guilford and J. W. Holley; Sheridan Psychological Services, Inc.*

See T2:1204 (1 reference); for reviews by Harrison G. Gough and Warren T. Norman, see 7:85 (1 reference).

[1043]
The Guilford-Shneidman-Zimmerman Interest Survey. Grades 9–16 and adults; 1948; 18 scores: artistic (appreciative, expressive), linguistic (appreciative, expressive), scientific (investigatory, theoretical), mechanical (manipulative, designing), outdoor (natural, athletic), business-political (mercantile, leadership), social activity (persuasive, gregarious), personal assistance (personal service, social welfare), office work (clerical, numerical); J. P. Guilford, Edwin Shneidman, and Wayne S. Zimmerman; Sheridan Psychological Services, Inc.*

See T2:2184 (2 references); for reviews by George K. Bennett and Wilbur L. Layton, see 4:739 (2 references).

[1044]
The Guilford-Zimmerman Aptitude Survey. Grades 9–16 and adults; 1947–56; GZAS; 7 parts, 7 scores; J. P. Guilford and Wayne S. Zimmerman; Sheridan Psychological Services, Inc.*
a) PART 1, VERBAL COMPREHENSION.
b) PART 2, GENERAL REASONING.
c) PART 3, NUMERICAL OPERATIONS.
d) PART 4, PERCEPTUAL SPEED.
e) PART 5, SPATIAL ORIENTATION.
f) PART 6, SPATIAL VISUALIZATION.
g) PART 7, MECHANICAL KNOWLEDGE.

For additional information and a review by M. Y. Quereshi, see 8:486 (9 references); see also T2:1074 (19 references) and 6:772 (17 references); for reviews by Anne Anastasi, Harold Bechtoldt, John B. Carroll, and P. E. Vernon, see 4:715 (15 references).

REFERENCES

1–15. See 4:715.
16–32. See 6:772.
33–51. See T2:1074.
52–60. See 8:486.
61. LIBEN, L. S. Performance on Piagetian spatial tasks as a function of sex, field dependence, and training. *Merrill–Palmer Quarterly*, 1978, 24, 97–110.
62. MCKELVIE, S. J., & ROHRBERG, M. M. Individual differences in reported visual imagery and cognitive performance. *Perceptual & Motor Skills*, 1978, 46, 451–458.
63. WALSH, M. D. Factor analytic study of the Embedded Figures and Rod and Frame Tests. *Perceptual & Motor Skills*, 1978, 47, 531–537.
64. GUR, R. C., & SACKEIM, H. A. Self–deception: A concept in search of a phenomenon. *Journal of Personality & Social Psychology*, 1979, 37, 147–169.

[1045]
The Guilford-Zimmerman Interest Inventory. Grades 10–16 and adults; 1962–63; 10 scores: mechanical, natural, aesthetic, service, clerical, mercantile, leadership, literary, scientific, creative; Joan S. Guilford and Wayne S. Zimmerman; Sheridan Psychological Services, Inc.*

See T2:2185 (7 references); for a review by Kenneth B. Hoyt, see 6:1057.

[1046]
***Guilford-Zimmerman Temperament Survey.** Grades 12–16 and adults; 1949–78; GZTS; revision and condensation of 3 tests: *Guilford-Martin Inventory of Factors, Guilford-Martin Personnel Inventory*, and *Inventory of Factors STDCR*; 10 scores: general activity, restraint, ascendance, sociability, emotional stability, objectivity, friendliness, thoughtfulness, personal relations, masculinity; J. P. Guilford and Wayne S. Zimmerman; Sheridan Psychological Services, Inc.*

For additional information, see 8:574 (72 references); see also T2:1207 (188 references), P:104 (132 references), and 6:110 (120 references); for a review by David R. Saunders, see 5:65 (48 references); for reviews by William Stephenson and Neil Van Steenberg and an excerpted review by Laurance F. Shaffer, see 4:49 (5 references).

REFERENCES

1–5. See 4:49.
6–53. See 5:65.
54–173. See 6:110.
174–305. See P:104.
306–494. See T2:1207.
495–566. See 8:574.

567. GUILFORD, J. S., ZIMMERMAN, W. S., & GUILFORD, J. P. *The Guilford–Zimmerman Temperament Survey handbook: Twenty-five years of research and application.* San Diego, CA: EdITS, 1976.

568. BLANCHARD, E. B., TURNER, J., ESCHETTE, N., & COURY, V. M. Assertiveness training for dental students. *Journal of Dental Education,* 1977, 41, 206–208.

569. BROWNE, J. A., & HOWARTH, E. A comprehensive factor analysis of personality questionnaire items: A test of twenty putative factor hypotheses. *Multivariate Behavioral Research,* 1977, 12, 399–427.

570. GIAMBRA, L. M. A factor analytic study of daydreaming, imaginal process, and temperament: A replication on an adult male life–span sample. *Journal of Gerontology,* 1977, 32, 675–680.

571. HUMMEL, H., & LESTER, D. Extraversion and simple reaction time. *Perceptual & Motor Skills,* 1977, 45, 1236.

572. NICHOLS, M. P., & KNOPF, I. J. Refining computerized test interpretations: An in-depth approach. *Journal of Personality Assessment,* 1977, 41 157–159.

573. SCHNEIDER, K. S. Personality correlates of altruistic behavior under four experimental conditions. *Journal of Social Psychology,* 1977, 102, 113–116.

574. WECKOWICZ, T. E., COLLIER, G., & SPRENG, L. Field dependence, cognitive functions, personality traits, and social values in heavy cannabis users and nonuser controls. *Psychological Reports,* 1977, 41, 291–302.

575. BROUSSEAU, K. R. Personality and job experience. *Organizational Behavior & Human Performance,* 1978, 22, 235–252.

576. DOUGLAS, K., & ARENBERG, D. Age changes, cohort differences, and cultural change on the Guilford–Zimmerman Temperament Survey. *Journal of Gerontology,* 1978, 33, 737–747.

577. SCHUH, A. J. Personality correlates of achievement in a personnel evaluation course. *Educational & Psychological Measurement,* 1978, 38, 1189–1191.

578. TURNER, R. G., SCHEIER, M. F., CARVER, C. S., & ICKES, W. Correlates of self-consciousness. *Journal of Personality Assessment,* 1978, 42, 285–289.

579. VICINO, F. L., & BASS, B. M. Lifespace variables and managerial success. *Journal of Applied Psychology,* 1978, 63, 81–88.

580. BRUCHON-SCHWEITZER, M. Dimensionality of body perception and personality. *Perceptual & Motor Skills,* 1979, 48, 840–842.

581. EPSTEIN, S. The stability of behavior: I. On predicting most of the people much of the time. *Journal of Personality & Social Psychology,* 1979, 37, 1097–1126.

582. COSTA, P. T., JR., McCRAE, R. R., & ARENBERG, D. Enduring dispositions in adult males. *Journal of Personality & Social Psychology,* 1980, 38, 793–800.

583. McCRAE, R. R., COSTA, P. T., JR., & ARENBERG, D. Constancy of adult personality structure in males: Longitudinal, cross-sectional and times-of-measurement analyses. *Journal of Gerontology,* 1980, 35, 877–883.

584. McDUFFIE, T. E., JR., & BRUCE, M. H. Predicting achievement and success in an AT biology program. *Journal of Research in Science Teaching,* 1980, 17, 449–454.

585. SCHUH, A. J. Verbal listening skill in the interview and personal characteristics of the listeners. *Bulletin of the Psychonomic Society,* 1980, 15, 125–127.

586. BERNARD, L. C. The multidimensional aspects of masculinity-feminity. *Journal of Personality & Social Psychology,* 1981, 41, 797–802.

587. BROUSSEAU, K. R., & PRINCE, J. B. Job-person dynamics: An extension of longitudinal research. *Journal of Applied Psychology,* 1981, 66, 59–62.

588. COSTA, P. T., JR., McCRAE, R. R., & NORRIS, A. H. Personal adjustment to aging: Longitudinal prediction from neuroticism and extraversion. *Journal of Gerontology,* 1981, 36, 78–85.

589. HIRSCHFELD, R. M. A. Situational depression: Validity of the concept. *British Journal of Psychiatry,* 1981, 139, 297–305.

590. URSANO, R. J. The Viet Nam era prisoner of war: Precaptivity personality and the development of psychiatric illness. *American Journal of Psychiatry,* 1981, 138, 315–318.

[1047]
H-T-P: House-Tree-Person Projective Technique. Ages 3 and over; 1946–66; John N. Buck and Isaac Jolles (children's interrogation folder); Western Psychological Services.*

See T2:1469 (61 references) and P:437 (24 references); for a review by Mary R. Haworth, see 6:215 (32 references); for a review by Philip L. Harriman, see 5:139 (61 references); for reviews by Albert Ellis and Ephraim Rosen and an excerpted review, see 4:107 (14 references); for reviews by Morris Krugman and Katherine W. Wilcox, see 3:47 (5 references).

[1048]
Hackman-Gaither Vocational Interest Inventory: Standard Edition. Grades 9–12 and adults; 1962–68; HGVII; positive (like), negative (dislike), and total scores for each of 8 areas: business contact, artistic, scientific-technical, health and welfare, business-clerical, mechanical, service, outdoor; Roy B. Hackman and James W. Gaither; Psychological Service Center of Philadelphia.*

For additional information and a review by Henry Weitz, see 7:1020 (21 references); see also 6:1058 (4 references).

[1049]
★**Hahnemann Elementary School Behavior Rating Scale.** Elementary school students in both regular and open classrooms; 1975; HESB; ratings by teachers; 14 item scores: originality, independent learning, involvement, productive with peers, intellectual dependency with peers, failure anxiety, unreflectiveness, irrelevant talk, disruptive social involvement, negative feelings, holding back/withdrawn, critical-competitive, blaming, approach to teacher, plus 2 added items, inattention, academic achievement; George Spivack and Marshall Swift; Department of Mental Health Sciences, Hahnemann Medical College and Hospital.*

[1050]
Hahnemann High School Behavior Rating Scale. Grades 7–12; 1971–72; HHSB; ratings by teachers; 13 scores: reasoning ability, originality, verbal interaction, rapport with teacher, anxious producer, general anxiety, quiet-withdrawn, poor work habits, lack intellectual independence, dogmatic-inflexible, verbal negativism, disturbance-restless, expressed inability; George Spivack and Marshall Swift; Department of Mental Health Sciences, Hahnemann Medical College and Hospital.*

REFERENCES

1. BEHAR, L., & STEPHENS, D. Wilderness camping: An evaluation of a residential treatment program for emotionally disturbed children. *American Journal of Orthopsychiatry,* 1978, 48, 644–653.

2. WALTON, E. G., & RUSSELL, R. D. Affective mental health education with sight and sound experiences. *Journal of School Health,* 1978, 48, 661–666.

[1051]
Hall Occupational Orientation Inventory. Grades 3–7, 8–16 and adults, low-literate adults; 1968–76, c1965–76; HOOI; 22 scores: creativity-independence, risk, information-knowledge, belongingness, security, aspiration, esteem, self-actualization, personal satisfaction, routine-dependence, data orientation, things orientation, people orientation, location concern, aptitude concern, monetary concern, physical abilities concern, environment concern, co-worker concern, qualifications concern, time concern, defensiveness; L. G. Hall and R. B. Tarrier (manual); Scholastic Testing Service, Inc.*

For additional information and reviews by Robert H. Dolliver and Austin C. Frank, see 8:1003 (5 references); see also T2:2187 (3 references); for a review by Donald G. Zytowski of the original edition, see 7:1021 (4 references).

REFERENCES

1–4. See 7:1021.
5–7. See T2:2187.
8–12. See 8:1003.
13. AMEG COMMISSION ON SEX BIAS IN MEASUREMENT. A case history of change: A review of responses to the challenge of sex bias in career interest inventories. *Measurement & Evaluation in Guidance*, 1977, 10, 148–152.
14. COVINGTON, J. E. Hall Occupational Orientation Inventory (3rd edition). *Measurement & Evaluation in Guidance*, 1979, 11, 230–233.
15. GILLINGHAM, W. H., & LOUNSBURY, J. E. A description and evaluation of a career exploration course. *Journal of College Student Personnel*, 1979, 20, 525–529.
16. TILLAR, T. C., JR., & HUTCHINS, D. E. The effectiveness of the components of a model program of career exploration for college freshmen. *Journal of College Student Personnel*, 1979, 20, 539–545.

[1052]

★Halstead-Reitan Neuropsychological Test Battery. Ages 5–8, 9–14, 15 and over; 1979; consists of three neuropsychological test batteries, one for each age level; 1 combined score: Halstead impairment index; Ralph M. Reitan; Neuropsychology Laboratory, University of Arizona.*

a) REITAN-INDIANA NEUROPSYCHOLOGICAL TEST BATTERY FOR CHILDREN. Ages 5–8; 13 tests: category, tactual performance (6-figure board; 3 scores: time, memory, localization), finger tapping, matching pictures, individual performance (4 subtests: matching figures, star, matching V's, concentric squares), marching, progressive figures, color form, Miles' abc test of ocular dominance, target, aphasia screening, sensory perceptual, tactile form recognition (2 scores: error, time).

b) HALSTEAD NEUROPSYCHOLOGICAL TEST BATTERY FOR CHILDREN. Ages 9–14; 11 tests: category, tactual performance (same as *a* above), Seashore rhythm test, speech-sounds perception, trail making, finger tapping, aphasia screening, actual form recognition (same as *a* above), sensory-perceptual, grip strength, lateral dominance.

c) HALSTEAD NEUROPSYCHOLOGICAL TEST BATTERY FOR ADULTS. Ages 15 and over; 13 tests: same as *b* above, except tactual performance has a 10-figure board for this level.

REFERENCES

1. WOLF, B., PAULSEN, E. P., & HSIA, Y. E. Asymptomatic propionyl CoA carboxylase deficiency in a 13-year-old girl. *Journal of Pediatrics*, 1979, 95, 563–565.
2. PARKER, E. S., & NOBLE, E. P. Alcohol and the aging process in social drinkers. *Journal of Studies on Alcohol*, 1980, 41, 170–178.
3. WILKINSON, D. A., & CARLEN, P. C. Neuropsychological and neurological assessment of alcoholism. *Journal of Studies on Alcohol*, 1980, 41, 129–139.
4. WILIMAS, J., GOFF, J. R., ANDERSON, H. R., LANGSTON, J. W., & THOMPSON, E. Efficacy of transfusion therapy for one to two years in patients with sickle cell disease and cerebrovascular incidents. *Journal of Pediatrics*, 1980, 96, 205–208.

[1053]

The Hand Test. Ages 6 and over; 1959–71; HT; 10 scores: interpersonal, environmental, maladjustive, withdrawal, affection-dependence-communication, direction-aggression, total responses, average initial response time, highest minus lowest response time, pathological; Edwin E. Wagner; Western Psychological Services.*

For additional information, see 8:575 (29 references); see also T2:1470 (15 references) and P:438 (12 references); for a review by Goldine C. Gleser and an excerpted review by Irving R. Stone, see 6:216 (6 references).

REFERENCES

1–6. See 6:216.
7–18. See P:438.
19–33. See T2:1470.
34–62. See 8:575.
63. WANG, P. L., & SMYERS, P. L. Psychological status after stroke as measured by the Hand Test. *Journal of Clinical Psychology*, 1977, 33, 879–882.
64. GREENE, R. S. Study of structural analysis: Comparing differential diagnosis based on psychiatric evaluation, the MMPI, and structural analysis of the Hand Test and Rorschach. *Perceptual & Motor Skills*, 1978, 46, 503–511.
65. HOOVER, T. O. The Hand Test: Fifteen years later. *Journal of Personality Assessment*, 1978, 42, 128–138.
66. MARTIN, J. D., BLAIR, G. E., & BRENT, D. The relationship of scores on Elizur's hostility system on the Rorschach to the acting–out score on the Hand Test. *Educational & Psychological Measurement*, 1978, 38, 587–591.
67. PANEK, P. E., WAGNER, E. E., & AVOLIO, B. J. Differences in Hand Test responses of healthy females across the life span. *Journal of Personality Assessment*, 1978, 42, 139–142.
68. PANEK, P. E., WAGNER, E. E., BARRETT, G. V., & ALEXANDER, R. A. Selected Hand Test personality variables related to accidents in female drivers. *Journal of Personality Assessment*, 1978, 42, 355–357.
69. RUSH, M. C., PHILLIPS, J. S., & PANEK, P. E. Subject recruitment bias: The paid volunteer subject. *Perceptual & Motor Skills*, 1978, 47, 443–449.
70. STONER, S. Sex differences in responses of children to the Hand Test. *Perceptual & Motor Skills*, 1978, 46, 759–762.
71. WAGNER, E. E. A theoretical explanation of the dissociative reaction and a confirmatory case presentation. *Journal of Personality Assessment*, 1978, 42, 312–316.
72. WAGNER, E. E., KLEIN, I., & WALTER, T. Differentiation of brain damage among low IQ subjects with three projective techniques. *Journal of Personality Assessment*, 1978, 42, 49–55.
73. MALONEY, P., & WAGNER, E. E. Interscorer reliability of the Hand Test with normal subjects. *Perceptual & Motor Skills*, 1979, 49, 181–182.
74. PANEK, P. E., & STONER, S. Test–retest reliability of the Hand Test with normal subjects. *Journal of Personality Assessment*, 1979, 43, 135–137.
75. PANEK, P. E., & WAGNER, E. E. Relationship between Hand Test variables and mental retardation: A confirmation and extension. *Journal of Personality Assessment*, 1979, 43, 600–603.
76. PANEK, P. E., WAGNER, E. E., & SUEN, H. Hand Test indices of violent and destructive behavior for institutionalized mental retardates. *Journal of Personality Assessment*, 1979, 43, 376–378.
77. DAUBNEY, J. H., & WAGNER, E. E. Prediction of success in an accelerated BS/MD medical school program using two projective techniques. *Perceptual & Motor Skills*, 1980, 51, 1179–1183.
78. HARAMIS, S. L., & WAGNER, E. E. Differentiation between acting–out and non–acting–out alcoholics with the Rorschach and the Hand Test. *Journal of Clinical Psychology*, 1980, 36, 791.
79. PANEK, P. E., & HAYSLIP, B. Construct validation of the Hand Test withdrawal score on institutionalized older adults. *Perceptual & Motor Skills*, 1980, 51, 595–598.
80. PANEK, P. E., & WAGNER, E. E. Mental retardation as a facade self phenomenon: Construct validation. *Perceptual & Motor Skills*, 1980, 51, 823–828.
81. STETSON, D., & WAGNER, E. E. A note on the use of the Hand Test in cross–cultural research: Comparison of Iranian, Chinese and American students. *Journal of Personality Assessment*, 1980, 44, 603.
82. STONER, S., & LUNDQUIST, T. Test–retest reliability of the Hand Test with older adults. *Perceptual & Motor Skills*, 1980, 50, 217–218.
83. WAGNER, E. E., & WAGNER, C. F. The facade compulsive: A type of latent schizophrenia. *Perceptual & Motor Skills*, 1980, 50, 831–837.

[1054]

Hand-Tool Dexterity Test. Adolescents and adults; 1946–65; HTDT; George K. Bennett; The Psychological Corporation.*

For additional information, see 7:1044 (4 references); for reviews by C. H. Lawshe, Jr. and Neil D. Warren, see 3:659 (2 references).

REFERENCES

1–2. See 3:659.
3–6. See 7:1044.

7. MOELLER, G., CHATTIN, C., ROGERS, W., LAXAR, K., & RYACK, B. Performance effects with repeated exposure to the diving environment. *Journal of Applied Psychology*, 1981, 66, 502–510.

[1055]

The Handicap Problems Inventory. Ages 16 and over with physical disabilities; 1960; HPI; 4 scores: personal, family, social, vocational; George N. Wright and H. H. Remmers; University Book Store.*

See T2:1210 (7 references) and P:105 (2 references); for a review by Dorothy M. Clendenen, see 6:111.

[1056]

Hannaford Industrial Safety Attitude Scales. Industry; 1959; attitude toward safety; 2 editions; Earle S. Hannaford; Center for Safety.* (In-print status uncertain; no reply from publisher.)
a) INDUSTRIAL SAFETY ATTITUDE SCALE FOR MALE EMPLOYEES.
b) INDUSTRIAL SAFETY ATTITUDE SCALE FOR MALE SUPERVISORS.

For additional information and a review by David O. Herman, see 6:690.

[1057]

*****Harding Skyscraper.** Ages 17 and over with intelligence level in top 1% of population; 1973–75; no manual; Chris. Harding; the Author.*

For additional information, see 8:189 (2 references).

[1058]

★**Harding Stress-Fair Compatibility Test.** Adults; 1980; HSFCT; measures compatibility between people; 11 scores: intellective, extraversion, sensitivity, idealism, motivation, awareness, independence, reasonability, objectivity, dominance, compatibility; Chris. Harding; the Author.*

[1059]

*****The Harrington-O'Shea Career Decision-Making System.** Grades 7–12 and college and adults; 1974–82; CDM; "self-administered and self-interpreted" inventory; 6 scores (arts, business, clerical, crafts, scientific, social) used to identify 3 or more occupational areas, for intensive career exploration, from among 18 career clusters (art work, clerical work, customer services, data analysis, education work, entertainment, legal work, literary work, management, manual work, math-science, medical-dental, musical work, personal service, sales work, skilled crafts, social services, technical) and questions in 5 areas (abilities, future plans, job values, occupational preferences, school subject preferences); Thomas F. Harrington and Arthur J. O'Shea; American Guidance Service.*
a) SELF-SCORED EDITION. (Available in English and Spanish).
b) MACHINE-SCORED EDITION. (Profile or Narrative Report, both computerized).

For additional information and a review by Carl G. Willis of an earlier edition, see 8:1004.

REFERENCES

1. HARRINGTON, T. F., & O'SHEA, A. J. Applicability of the Holland (1973) model of vocational development with Spanish-speaking clients. *Journal of Counseling Psychology*, 1980, 27, 246–251.
2. O'SHEA, A. J., & HARRINGTON, T. F. The scorer reliability of self-scored interest inventories. *Measurement & Evaluation in Guidance*, 1980, 12, 229–232.

3. WESTBROOK, B. W., ROGERS, B., & COVINGTON, J. E. Harrington/O'Shea System for Career Decision-Making. *Measurement & Evaluation in Guidance*, 1980, 13, 185–188.

[1060]

Harris Tests of Lateral Dominance. Ages 7 and over; 1947–58; 13–15 scores: knowledge of right and left, hand dominance (7 scores, 1 optional), eye dominance (4 scores, 1 optional), foot dominance (3 scores); Albert J. Harris, distributed by The Psychological Corporation.*

See T2:1877 (20 references) and 5:761 (1 reference); for reviews by William G. Peacher and Miles A. Tinker of an earlier edition, see 4:644; for an excerpted review, see 3:466.

REFERENCES

1. See 5:761.
2–21. See T2:1877.
22. WHYTE, L. Prescriptive teaching: Changes in stage of logico-mathematical thinking and spatial development in a group of opportunity class children. *Alberta Journal of Educational Research*, 1976, 22, 34–43.
23. BOUMA, H., & LEGEIN, C. P. Foveal and parafoveal recognition of letters and words by dyslexics and by average readers. *Neuropsychologia*, 1977, 15, 69–80.
24. HAGGERTY, R., & STAMM, J. S. Dichotic auditory fusion levels in children with learning disabilities. *Neuropsychologia*, 1978, 16, 349–360.
25. COLLETTE, M. A. Dyslexia and classic pathognomic signs. *Perceptual & Motor Skills*, 1979, 48, 1055–1062.
26. RICHARDSON, J. T. E., & FIRLEJ, M. D. E. Laterality and reading attainment. *Cortex*, 1979, 15, 581–595.
27. SEARLEMAN, A. Subject variables and cerebral organization for language. *Cortex*, 1980, 16, 239–254.
28. ETAUGH, C., & LEVY, R. B. Hemispheric specialization for tactile-spatial processing in pre-school children. *Perceptual & Motor Skills*, 1981, 53, 621–622.

[1061]

The Harrison-Stroud Reading Readiness Profiles. Grades kgn–1; 1949–56; 7 scores: using symbols, making visual discriminations (2 scores), using the context, making auditory discriminations, using context and auditory clues, giving the names of letters; M. Lucile Harrison and James B. Stroud; Riverside Publishing Co.*

See T2:1705 (17 references); for a review by S. S. Dunn, see 5:677 (2 references); for a review by William S. Gray, see 4:568.

[1062]

The Hartman Value Profile. Ages 12 and over; 1965–72; HVP; formerly called *The Hartman Value Inventory*; also called the *Axiometric Test*; 57 scores: 15 capacity to value one's self scores, 7 scores resulting from both capacities, 2 retest scores, and 18 deviation scores; Robert S. Hartman and Mario Cardenas Trigos; Research Concepts.* (In-print status uncertain; no reply from publisher.)

See T2:1211 (2 references) and P:106 (2 references).

[1063]

Harvard Group Scale of Hypnotic Susceptibility. College and adults; 1959–62; HGSHS; adaptation for group administration of Form A of the *Stanford Hypnotic Susceptibility Scale*; Ronald E. Shor and Emily Carota Orne; Consulting Psychologists Press, Inc.*

For additional information, see 8:576 (46 references); see also T2:1212 (19 references) and P:107 (12 references); for a review by Seymore Fisher, see 6:112 (4 references).

REFERENCES

1–3. See 6:112.

4-15. See P:107.
16-34. See T2:1212.
35-80. See 8:576.

81. DEVOGE, J. T., JOHNSON, C. A., DOMELSMITH, D. E., & WHATLEY, J. L. Effects of sex and degree of personal contact on hypnotic susceptibility. *Psychological Reports*, 1977, 41, 467-473.

82. EDMONSTON, W. E., JR. Body morphology and the capacity for hypnosis. *Annals of the New York Academy of Science*, 1977, 296, 105-118. 1977, 296, 105-118.

83. EVANS, F. J. Hypnosis and sleep: The control of altered states of awareness. *Annals of the New York Academy of Science*, 1977, 296, 162-174.

84. GRAHAM, C., & EVANS, F. J. Hypnotizability and the deployment of waking attention. *Journal of Abnormal Psychology*, 1977, 86, 631-638.

85. KIHLSTROM, J. F., & EVANS, F. J. Residual effect of suggestions for posthypnotic amnesia: A reexamination. *Journal of Abnormal Psychology*, 1977, 86, 327-333.

86. KNOX, V. J., & SHUM, K. Reduction of cold-pressor pain with acupuncture analgesia in high- and low-hypnotic subjects. *Journal of Abnormal Psychology*, 1977, 86, 639-643.

87. OBSTOJ, I., & SHEEHAN, P. W. Aptitude for trance, task generalizabilities, and incongruity response in hypnosis. *Journal of Abnormal Psychology*, 1977, 86, 543-552.

88. PERRY, C. Uncancelled hypnotic suggestions: The effects of hypnotic depth and hypnotic skill on their posthypnotic persistence. *Journal of Abnormal Psychology*, 1977, 86, 570-574.

89. PERRY, C. Variables influencing the posthypnotic persistence of an unacceptable hypnotic suggestion. *Annals of the New York Academy of Science*, 1977, 296, 264-273.

90. SCHWARTZ, S., & BURDSAL, C. A factor-analytic examination of the relationship of personality variables to hypnotizability. *Journal of Clinical Psychology*, 1977, 33, 356-360.

91. SHEEHAN, P. W. Incongruity in trance behavior: A defining property of hypnosis? *Annals of the New York Academy of Science*, 1977, 296, 194-207.

92. STERN, J. A., BROWN, M., VLETT, G. A., & SLETTEN, I. A comparison of hypnosis, acupuncture, morphine, valium, aspirin, and placebo in the management of experimentally induced pain. *Annals of the New York Academy of Science*, 1977, 296, 175-193.

93. DUMAS, R. A., & SPITZER, S. E. Influences of subject self-selection on the EEG alpha-hypnotizability correlation. *Psychophysiology*, 1978, 15, 606-608.

94. FELLOWS, B. J., & CREAMER, M. An investigation of the role of "hypnosis", hypnotic susceptibility and hypnotic induction in the production of age regression. *British Journal of Social & Clinical Psychology*, 1978, 17, 165-171.

95. KIHLSTROM, J. F., & EVANS, F. J. Generic recall during posthypnotic amnesia. *Bulletin of the Psychonomic Society*, 1978, 12, 57-60.

96. PERRY, C., & WALSH, B. Inconsistencies and anomalies of response as a defining characteristic of hypnosis. *Journal of Abnormal Psychology*, 1978, 87, 574-577.

97. SHEEHAN, P. W., MCCONKEY, K. M., & CROSS, D. Experimental analysis of hypnosis: Some observations on hypnotic phenomena. *Journal of Abnormal Psychology*, 1978, 87, 570-573.

98. SPANOS, N. P., RIVERS, S. M., & GOTTLIEB, J. Hypnotic responsivity, meditation, and laterality of eye movements. *Journal of Abnormal Psychology*, 1978, 87, 566-569.

99. WALLACE, B. Restoration of eidetic imagery via hypnotic age regression: More evidence. *Journal of Abnormal Psychology*, 1978, 87, 673-675.

100. BOWERS, P. Hypnosis and creativity: The search for the missing link. *Journal of Abnormal Psychology*, 1979, 88, 564-572.

101. D'EON, J. L., MAH, C. D., PAWLAK, A. E., & SPANOS, N. P. Effect of hypnotists' and subjects' sex on hypnotic susceptibility. *Perceptual & Motor Skills*, 1979, 48, 1232-1234.

102. DEYOUB, P. L. Hypnotizability and obesity. *Psychological Reports*, 1979, 45, 975-984.

103. EVANS, F. J. Contextual forgetting: Posthypnotic source amnesia. *Journal of Abnormal Psychology*, 1979, 88, 556-563.

104. KARLIN, R. A. Hypnotizability and attention. *Journal of Abnormal Psychology*, 1979, 88, 92-95.

105. MASLACH, C. Negative emotional biasing of unexplained arousal. *Journal of Personality & Social Psychology*, 1979, 37, 953-969.

106. NASH, M. R., JOHNSON, L. S., & TIPTON, R. D. Hypnotic age regression and the occurrence of transitional object relationships. *Journal of Abnormal Psychology*, 1979, 88, 547-555.

107. PERRY, C., GELFAND, R., & MARCOVITCH, P. The relevance of hypnotic susceptibility in the clinical context. *Journal of Abnormal Psychology*, 1979, 88, 592-603.

108. ROLL, W. G., SOLFVIN, G. F., & KRIEGER, J. Meditation and ESP: An overview of four studies. *Journal of Parapsychology*, 1979, 43, 44-45.

109. SPANOS, N. P., & HEWITT, E. C. Glossolalia: A test of the "trance" and psychopathology hypotheses. *Journal of Abnormal Psychology*, 1979, 88, 427-434.

110. SPANOS, N. P., RADTKE-BODORIK, H. L., FERGUSON, J. D., & JONES, B. The effects of hypnotic susceptibility, suggestions for analgesis, and the utilization of cognitive strategies on the reduction of pain. *Journal of Abnormal Psychology*, 1979, 88, 282-292.

111. SPANOS, N. P., & STAM, H. J. The elicitation of visual hallucinations via brief instructions in a normal sample. *Journal of Nervous & Mental Disease*, 1979, 167, 488-494.

112. SPANOS, N. P., STEGGLES, S., RADTKE-BODORIK, H. L., & RIVERS, S. M. Nonanalytic attending, hypnotic susceptibility, and psychological well-being in trained meditators and nonmeditators. *Journal of Abnormal Psychology*, 1979, 88, 85-87.

113. STAM, H. J., & SPANOS, N. P. Lateral eye-movements and indices of nonanalytic attending in right-handed females. *Perceptual & Motor Skills*, 1979, 48, 123-127.

114. WALLACE, B. Hypnotic susceptibility and the perception of afterimages and dot stimuli. *American Journal of Psychology*, 1979, 92, 681-691.

115. CRANNEY, J., & MCCONKEY, K. M. Seating preference, hypnotizability and imagery ability. *Perceptual & Motor Skills*, 1980, 5, 1175-1178.

116. HOWARD, M. L., & COE, W. C. The effects of context and subjects' perceived control in breaching post-hypnotic amnesia. *Journal of Personality*, 1980, 48, 342-359.

117. HURLEY, J. D. Differential effects of hypnosis, biofeedback training, and trophotropic responses on anxiety, ego strength, and locus of control. *Journal of Clinical Psychology*, 1980, 36, 503-507.

118. KARLIN, R., MORGAN, D., & GOLDSTEIN, L. Hypnotic analgesia: A preliminary investigation of quantitated hemispheric electroencephalographic and attentional correlates. *Journal of Abnormal Psychology*, 1980, 89, 591-594.

119. MCCONKEY, K. M., SHEEHAN, P. W., & CROSS, D. G. Posthypnotic amnesia: Seeing is not remembering. *British Journal of Social & Clinical Psychology*, 1980, 19, 99-107.

120. MCKNIGHT, R. T. Prediction of hypnotizability from personality variables of the California Psychological Inventory: A multiple regression analysis. *Psychological Reports*, 1980, 47, 1319-1322.

121. OTTESON, J. P. Stylistic and personality correlates of lateral eye movements: A factor analytic study. *Perceptual & Motor Skills*, 1980, 50, 995-1010.

122. RADTKE-BODORIK, H. L., PLANAS, M., & SPANOS, N. P. Suggested amnesia, verbal inhibition, and disorganized recall for a long word list. *Canadian Journal of Behavioural Science*, 1980, 12, 87-97.

123. SABOURIN, M., BRISSON, M., & DESCHAMBAULT, A. Evaluation of hypnotically-suggested selective deafness by heart-rate conditioning and reaction time. *Psychological Reports*, 1980, 47, 995-1002.

124. SHEEHAN, P. W. Factors influencing rapport in hypnosis. *Journal of Abnormal Psychology*, 1980, 89, 263-281.

125. SPANOS, N. P., GOTTLIEB, J., & RIVERS, S. M. The effects of short-term meditation practice on hypnotic responsivity. *Psychological Record*, 1980, 30, 343-348.

126. SPANOS, N. P., PAWLAK, A. E., MAH, C. D., & D'EON, J. L. Lateral eye-movements, hypnotic susceptibility and imaginal ability in right-handers. *Perceptual & Motor Skills*, 1980, 50, 287-294.

127. SPANOS, N. P., RADTKE-BODORIK, H. L., & STAM, H. J. Disorganized recall during suggested amnesia: Fact not artifact. *Journal of Abnormal Psychology*, 1980, 89, 1-19.

128. SPANOS, N. P., STAM, H. J., D'EON, J. L., PAWLAK, A. E., & RADTKE-BODORIK, H. L. Effects of social-psychological variables on hypnotic amnesia. *Journal of Personality & Social Psychology*, 1980, 39, 737-750.

129. SPANOS, N. P., STAM, H. J., RADTKE, H. L., & NIGHTINGALE, M. E. Absorption in imaginings, sex-role orientation, and the recall of dreams by males and females. *Journal of Personality Assessment*, 1980, 44, 277-282.

130. ST. JEAN, R. Hypnotic time distortion and learning: Another look. *Journal of Abnormal Psychology*, 1980, 89, 20-24.

131. STAM, H. J., RADTKE-BODORIK, H. L., & SPANOS, N. P. Repression and hypnotic amnesia: A failure to replicate and an alternative formulation. *Journal of Abnormal Psychology*, 1980, 89, 551-559.

132. BURGER, J. M. Locus of control, motivation, and expectancy: Predicting hypnotic susceptibility from personality variables. *Journal of Research in Personality*, 1981, 15, 523-527.

133. CRAWFORD, H. J. Hypnotic susceptibility as related to gestalt closure tasks. *Journal of Personality & Social Psychology*, 1981, 40, 376-383.

134. SCHUYLER, B. A., & COE, W. C. A physiological investigation of volitional and nonvolitional experience during posthypnotic amnesia. *Journal of Personality & Social Psychology*, 1981, 40, 1160-1169.

135. ST. JEAN, R., & COE, W. C. Recall and recognition memory during post hypnotic amnesia: A failure to confirm the disrupted-search hypothesis and the memory disorganization hypothesis. *Journal of Abnormal Psychology*, 1981, 90, 231-241.

136. STAM, H. J., SPANOS, N. P., RADTKE, H. L., & JONES, B. Further investigation of the relationship between hypnotic susceptibility and classroom seating. *Perceptual & Motor Skills*, 1981, 52, 831-836.

137. VAN DYNE, W. T., & STAVA, L. J. Analysis of relationships among hypnotic susceptibility, personality type, and vividness of mental imagery. *Psychological Reports*, 1981, 48, 23–26.

[1064]

Hay Aptitude Test Battery. Clerical and plant workers; 1947–82; tape cassette available for administration; 4 tests; Edward N. Hay; E. F. Wonderlic & Associates, Inc.
a) THE WARM UP TEST I.
b) NUMBER PERCEPTION TEST.
c) NAME FINDING TEST.
d) NUMBER SERIES COMPLETION TEST.

See T2:2132 (2 references) and 5:849 (2 references); for reviews by Reign H. Bittner and Edward E. Cureton, see 4:725 (8 references).

[1065]

Health and Safety Education Test: National Achievement Tests. Grades 3–6; 1947–60; 5 scores: good habits, cause and effect, facts, application of rules, total; no manual; Lester D. Crow and Loretta C. Ryan; Psychometric Affiliates.*

For additional information, see 6:724; for a review by Clarence H. Nelson, see 5:555.

[1066]

Health Education Test: Knowledge and Application: Acorn National Achievement Tests, Revised Edition. Grades 7–13; 1946–56; 3 scores: knowledge, application, total; John H. Shaw and Maurice E. Troyer; Psychometric Affiliates.*

See T2:928 (1 reference) and 5:557 (1 reference); for reviews by H. H. Remmers and Mabel E. Rugen, see 3:421.

[1067]

Health Knowledge Test for College Freshmen: National Achievement Tests. Grade 13; 1956; A. Frank Bridges; Psychometric Affiliates.*

For additional information and a review by James E. Bryan, see 5:558 (3 references).

[1068]

Health Test: National Achievement Tests. Grades 3–8; 1937–57; 5 scores: recognizing best habits, health comparisons, causes and effects, health facts, total; Robert K. Speer and Samuel Smith; Psychometric Affiliates.*

For additional information and a review by Benno G. Fricke, see 5:560; for a review by Jacob S. Orleans, see 4:485.

[1069]

Healy Pictorial Completion Tests. Ages 5 and over; [1914–21]; 2 tests, William Healy; Stoelting Co.*
a) TEST I. 1914; modification appears in *Arthur Point Scale of Performance Tests*.
b) TEST II. [1917–21]; subtest of *Arthur Point Scale of Performance Tests*.

See T2:558 (37 references).

[1070]

★The Hearing Measurement Scale. Adults; 1979; HMS: self-administered questionnaire for the assessment of hearing handicap; 8 scores: speech hearing, hearing for nonspeech sounds, spatial localization, emotional response to hearing impairment, speech distortion, tinnitus, personal opinion of hearing, total; William G. Noble; University of New England [Australia].* (In-print status uncertain; no reply from publisher.)

[1071]

[Hearing of Speech Tests]. Ages 3–12; 1966; "administered live voice over speech audiometry test equipment in standard audiological test rooms"; 2 tests; Bruce M. Siegenthaler and George S. Haspiel; Speech Pathology & Audiology, Pennsylvania State University.*
a) THRESHOLD BY IDENTIFICATION OF PICTURES. TIP.
b) DISCRIMINATION BY IDENTIFICATION OF PICTURES. DIP.

See T2:2039 (1 reference); for a review by Eugene C. Sheeley, see 7:939 (7 references).

REFERENCES

1–7. See 7:939.
8. See T2:2039.
9. SIEGENTHALER, B. M., & KNELLINGER, L. D. Dichotic listening by brain–injured adults: Observation of divergent test responses. *Journal of Communication Disorders*, 1981, 14, 399–409.

[1072]

The Hellenic Affiliation Scale: An Inventory of Student Behavior and Beliefs for Use by School Personnel, Experimental Form. College; 1967; HAS; title on test is *H.A.S.*; fraternity or sorority affiliation proneness; LeRoy A. Stone, Marlo A. Skurdal, and David R. Skeen; LeRoy A. Stone.* (In-print status uncertain; no reply from publisher.)

See T2:1213 (1 reference) and P:108.

[1073]

The Henmon-Nelson Tests of Mental Ability. Grades kgn–2, 3–6, 6–9, 9–12; 1931–74; Tom A. Lamke, Martin J. Nelson, and Joseph L. French; Riverside Publishing Co.*
a) PRIMARY BATTERY. Grades kgn–2; 1973–74.
b) 1973 REVISION. Grades 3–6, 6–9, 9–12; 1931–73.

For additional information and a review by Eric F. Gardner, see 8:190 (14 references); see also T2:391 (52 references); for a review by Norman E. Wallen and an excerpted review by John O. Crites of an earlier edition, see 6:462 (11 references); for reviews by D. Welty Lefever and Leona E. Tyler and an excerpted review by Laurance F. Shaffer, see 5:342 (14 references); for a review by H. M. Fowler, see 4:299 (25 references); for reviews by Anne Anastasi, August Dvorak, Howard Easley, and J. P. Guilford and an excerpted review by Francis N. Maxfield, see 2:1398.

REFERENCES

1–25. See 4:299.
26–39. See 5:342.
40–50. See 6:462.
51–102. See T2:391.
103–116. See 8:190.
117. HAUSER, R. M., & DAYMONT, T. N. Schooling, ability, and earnings: Cross–sectional findings 8 to 14 years after high school graduation. *Sociology of Education*, 1977, 50, 182–206.
118. YOST, M., AVILA, L., & VEXLER, E. B. Effect on learning of postinstructional responses to questions of differing degrees of complexity. *Journal of Educational Psychology*, 1977, 69, 399–408.

119. AHLGREN, A., & WALBERG, H. J. Basic dimensions in characteristics of classroom groups. *Alberta Journal of Educational Research*, 1978, 24, 244-256.
120. FREEDMAN, B. J., ROSENTHAL, L., DONAHOE, C. P., JR., SCHLUNDT, D. G., & MCFALL, R. M. A social-behavioral analysis of skill deficits in delinquent and nondelinquent adolescent boys. *Journal of Consulting & Clinical Psychology*, 1978, 46, 1448-1462.
121. KLING, J. O., DAVIS, W. E., & KNOST, E. K. Henmon–Nelson IQ scores as predictors of WAIS full scale IQ in alcoholics. *Journal of Clinical Psychology*, 1978, 34, 1001–1002.
122. RICH, N. S. Occupational knowledge: To what extent is rural youth handicapped? *Vocational Guidance Quarterly*, 1978, 27, 320-325.
123. WALSH, M. D. Factor analytic study of the Embedded Figures and Rod and Frame Tests. *Perceptual & Motor Skills*, 1978, 47, 531-537.
124. WILSON, K. L. Toward an improved explanation of income attainment: Recalibrating education and occupation. *American Journal of Sociology*, 1978, 84, 684-697.
125. HOTCHKISS, L., CURRY, E., HALLER, A. O., & WIDAMAN, K. The Occupational Aspiration Scale: An evaluation and alternate form for females. *Rural Sociology*, 1979, 44, 95-118.
126. WATSON, C. G., PLEMEL, D., & BURKE, M. Proverb test deficit in schizophrenic and brain-damaged patients. *Journal of Nervous & Mental Disease*, 1979, 167, 561-565.
127. WANG, C. S. Y., & SEWELL, W. H. Residence, migration, and earnings. *Rural Sociology*, 1980, 45, 185-206.
128. ROSSO, B. R., & EMANS, R. Children's use of phonic generalizations. *Reading Teacher*, 1981, 34, 653-657.
129. STERNBERG, R. J., CONWAY, B. E., KETRON, J. L., & BERNSTEIN, M. People's conceptions of intelligence. *Journal of Personality & Social Psychology*, 1981, 41, 37-55.

[1074]

★Henshaw Secondary Mathematics Test. Grades 9-10; 1980; HSMT; "redesigned from *A Diagnostic Test in Basic Algebra* and *A Diagnostic Test in Basic Geometry* "; 10 scores: four processes, set language and solution of truth sets, construction of equations and inequations and formulae, co-ordinates and graphs of relations, simultaneous and quadratic equations and factors, plane and solid figures, transformations and similar figures and symmetry, angles, congruence-chords of circle-tangents, total; John Henshaw; Australian Council for Educational Research [Australia].*

[1075]

Hess School Readiness Scale. Ages 3.5-7.0; 1975; HSRS; prediction of school success based upon mental ability; Richard J. Hess; Mafex Associates, Inc.*

For additional information and a review by Richard C. Cox, see 8:798 (3 references).

[1076]

★Heterosocial Adequacy Test. Male college students; 1978-79; HAT; a behavioral role-playing test for the assessment of heterosocial skills; Michael G. Perri, C. Steven Richards, and Jerry D. Goodrich; the Authors.*

[1077]

Hidden Figures Test. Grades 6-16; 1962-63; HFT; also included in the *Kit of Factor Referenced Cognitive Tests*; for research use only; flexibility of closure; 2 tests; Educational Testing Service.*
a) FORM CF-1. 1962-63; manual by John W. French, Ruth B. Ekstrom, and Leighton B. Price.
b) FORM 5. 1962.
See T2:559 (18 references) and 7:440 (31 references).

REFERENCES

1-31. See 7:440.
32-49. See T2:559.
50. MILLER, I. W., III, & MAGARO, P. A. Toward a multivariate theory of personality styles: Measurement and reliability. *Journal of Clinical Psychology*, 1977, 33, 460-466.
51. NELSON, B. A., & CHAVIS, G. L. Cognitive style and complex concept acquisition. *Contemporary Educational Psychology*, 1977, 2, 91-98.
52. RIDGEWAY, C. L. Note on parental similarity, acceptance of authority, and field independence. *Perceptual & Motor Skills*, 1977, 45, 811-814.
53. WILLIAMS, J. R. Follow-up study of relationships between perceptual style measures and telephone company vehicle accidents. *Journal of Applied Psychology*, 1977, 62, 751-754.
54. BIALYSTOK, E., & FRÖHLICH, M. Variables of classroom achievement in second language learning. *Modern Language Journal*, 1978, 62, 327-336.
55. KAPUR, M. A short screening battery of tests to detect organic brain dysfunctions. *Journal of Clinical Psychology*, 1978, 34, 104-111.
56. MCLEOD, D. B., CARPENTER, T. P., MCCORNACK, R. L., & SKVARCIUS, R. S. Cognitive style and mathematics learning: The interaction of field independence and instructional treatment in numeration systems. *Journal for Research in Mathematics Education*, 1978, 9, 163-174.
57. PETERSON, P. L., MARX, R. W., & CLARK, C. M. Teacher planning, teacher behavior, and student achievement. *American Educational Research Journal*, 1978, 15, 417-432.
58. STANKOV, L. Fluid and crystallized intelligence and broad perceptual factors among 11 to 12 year olds. *Journal of Educational Psychology*, 1978, 70, 324-334.
59. WALSH, M. D. Factor analytic study of the Embedded Figures and Rod and Frame Tests. *Perceptual & Motor Skills*, 1978, 47, 531-537.
60. WEISSENBERG, P. Field independence and attitudes toward population control. *Perceptual & Motor Skills*, 1978, 47, 185-186.
61. CARKIN, S. Hidden-Figures-Test performance: Lasting effects on unilateral penetrating head injury and transient effects of bilateral cingulotomy. *Neuropsychologia*, 1979, 17, 585-605.
62. FILSINGER, E. E. Psychological differentiation and socioeconomic and demographic backgrounds of a diverse group of college students. *Psychological Reports*, 1979, 45, 187-195.
63. GOLDBERG, L. R. A general scheme for the analytic decomposition of objective test scores: Illustrative demonstrations using the Rod-and-Frame Test and the Muller-Lyer illusion. *Journal of Research in Personality*, 1979, 13, 245-265.
64. MCLEOD, D. B., & ADAMS, V. M. Individual differences in cognitive style and discovery approaches to learning mathematics. *Journal of Educational Research*, 1979, 72, 317-320.
65. MCLEOD, D. B., & ADAMS, V. M. The interaction of field independence with discovery learning in mathematics. *Journal of Experimental Education*, 1979, 48, 32-35.
66. MCLEOD, D. B., & ADAMS, V. M. The interaction of field independence with small-group instruction in mathematics. *Journal of Experimental Education*, 1979-1980, 48, 118-124.
67. ROACH, D. A. Effects of some social variables on field dependence. *Perceptual & Motor Skills*, 1979, 48, 559-562.
68. Ross, L. Heroin addiction and cognitive style: Disembedding performance in the male heroin addict. *British Journal of Addiction*, 1979, 74, 51-56.
69. SEIF, M. N., & ATKINS, A. L. Some defensive and cognitive aspects of phobias. *Journal of Abnormal Psychology*, 1979, 88, 42-51.
70. WATKINS, D., & ASTILLA, E. Field dependence and self-esteem in Filipino girls. *Psychological Reports*, 1979, 44, 574.
71. WATKINS, D., & ASTILLA, E. Stability of self-esteem of Filipino girls. *Psychological Reports*, 1979, 45, 993-994.
72. FILSINGER, E. E. Difference between own and friend's socioeconomic status as a predictor of psychological differentiation. *Psychological Reports*, 1980, 46, 613-614.
73. FROST, A. G., & LINDAUER, M. S. Preferences for figural complexity as a function of cognitive style. *Bulletin of the Psychonomic Society*, 1980, 16, 221-224.
74. HUNT, D. Intentional-incidental learning and simultaneous-successive processing. *Canadian Journal of Behavioral Science*, 1980, 12, 373-383.
75. MCLEOD, D. B., & ADAMS, V. M. Aptitude-treatment interaction in mathematics instruction using expository and discovery methods. *Journal for Research in Mathematics Education*, 1980, 11, 225-234.
76. MCLEOD, D. B., & BRIGGS, J. T. Interactions of field independence and general reasoning with inductive instruction in mathematics. *Journal for Research in Mathematics Education*, 1980, 11, 94-103.
77. FILSINGER, E. E. Parental attitudes toward child rearing and the psychological differentiation of adolescents. *Journal of Genetic Psychology*, 1981, 139, 277-284.
78. IPPEL, M. J. Generalizability of performance-scores on embedded figures material. *Educational & Psychological Measurement*, 1981, 41, 315-331.
79. LANG, C., LEHRL, S., & HUK, W. A case of bilateral temporal lobe agenesis. *Journal of Neurology, Neurosurgery & Psychiatry*, 1981, 44, 626-630.
80. LAU, S., FIGUERRES, C., & DAVIS, J. K. Re-examination of the relationship between locus of control and field independence/dependence. *Perceptual & Motor Skills*, 1981, 53, 555-561.

81. PARKES, K. R. Field dependence and the differentiation of affective states. *British Journal of Psychiatry*, 1981, 139, 52–58.
82. ROACH, D. A. Predictors of mathematics achievement in Jamaican elementary school children. *Perceptual & Motor Skills*, 1981, 52, 785–786.
83. WATKINS, D., & ASTILLA, E. Field independence as a predictor of Filipino university engineering grades. *Educational & Psychological Measurement*, 1981, 41, 893–895.

[1078]
Hiett Simplified Shorthand Test (Gregg). 1, 2 semesters high school; 1951–63; an identical edition, entitled *Hiett Diamond Jubilee Shorthand Test* ('63), is available without a manual; Victor C. Hiett and H. E. Schrammel (manual); Bureau of Educational Measurements.*

For additional information, see 7:555; for a review by Gale W. Clark, see 5:512.

[1079]
High Level Battery: Test A/75. Adults with at least 12 years of education; 1960–72; formerly listed as *National Institute for Personnel Research High Level Battery*; 6 tests in a single booklet: mental alertness, arithmetical problems, reading comprehension (English, Afrikaans), vocabulary (English, Afrikaans); manual by D. P. M. Beukes; National Institute for Personnel Research [South Africa].*

For additional information, see 6:778 (1 reference).

[1080]
*****High School Characteristics Index.** Grades 9–13; 1960–70; HSCI; previously listed under *Stern Environment Indexes*; 40 scores: 30 press scores (abasement-assurance, achievement, adaptability-defensiveness, affiliation, aggression-blame avoidance, change-sameness, conjunctivity-disjunctivity, counteraction, deference-restiveness, dominance-tolerance, ego achievement, emotionality-placidity, energy-passivity, exhibitionism-inferiority avoidance, fantasied achievement, harm avoidance-risk taking, humanities and social science, impulsiveness-deliberation, narcissism, nurturance, objectivity-projectivity, order-disorder, play-work, practicalness-impracticalness, reflectiveness, science, sensuality-puritanism, sexuality-prudishness, supplication-autonomy, understanding), 7 factor scores (intellectual climate, expressiveness, group social life, personal dignity, achievement standards, orderliness/-control, peer group dominance) based on combinations of the press scores, and 3 second-order factor scores (development press, orderliness/control, peer group dominance); a short form entitled *Elementary and Secondary School Index* (ESI) is available for administration to students grades 4–13; George G. Stern; Evaluation Research Associates.*

See T2:1395 (38 references); for reviews by Wilbur L. Layton and Rodney W. Skager, see 7:143 (59 references); see also P:256 (65 references) and 6:92 (19 references).

REFERENCES

1–19. See 6:92.
20–84. See P:256.
85–143. See 7:143.
144–181. See T2:1395.
182. PAYNE, R., & MANSFIELD, R. Correlates of individual perceptions of organizational climate. *Journal of Occupational Psychology*, 1978, 51, 209–218.

[1081]
High School Interest Questionnaire. "Coloured pupils" in standards 7–10; 1973–74; 8 scores: language, performing arts, fine arts, social, science, technical, business, office work; J. B. Wolfaardt; Human Sciences Research Council [South Africa].*

For additional information, see 8:1005.

[1082]
High School Reading Test: National Achievement Tests. Grades 7–12; 1939–52; 6 scores: vocabulary, word discrimination, sentence meaning, noting details, interpreting paragraphs, total; Robert K. Speer and Samuel Smith; Psychometric Affiliates.*

For additional information and a review by Victor H. Noll, see 5:634; for a review by Holland Roberts, see 4:536; for a review by Robert L. McCaul, see 3:488.

[1083]
★**High School Subject Tests.** Grades 9–12; 1980; part of Comprehensive Assessment Program; 15 tests: Algebra, Geometry, General Mathematics, Biology, Chemistry, Physical Science, American Government, American History, World Geography, World History, Writing and Mechanics, Literature and Vocabulary, Language, Consumer Education, Health; Louis A. Gatta, Robert B. Adams, Marjorie C. Frey, Melton E. Golmon, Karen J. Kuehner, Vincent F. Malek, and John W. McConnell; American Testronics.*

[1084]
★**High School Subject Tests: Algebra.** Grades 9–12; 1980; American Testronics.* For the complete program entry, see 1083.

[1085]
★**High School Subject Tests: American Government.** Grades 9–12; 1980; American Testronics.* For the complete program entry, see 1083.

[1086]
★**High School Subject Tests: American History.** Grades 9–12; 1980; American Testronics.* For the complete program entry, see 1083.

[1087]
★**High School Subject Tests: Biology.** Grades 9–12; 1980; American Testronics.* For the complete program entry, see 1083.

[1088]
★**High School Subject Tests: Chemistry.** Grades 9–12; 1980; American Testronics.* For the complete program entry, see 1083.

[1089]
★**High School Subject Tests: Consumer Education.** Grades 9–12; 1980; American Testronics.* For the complete program entry, see 1083.

[1090]
★**High School Subject Tests: General Mathematics.** Grades 9–12; 1980; American Testronics.* For the complete program entry, see 1083.

[1091]

★High School Subject Tests:Geometry. Grades 9–12; 1980; American Testronics.* For the complete program entry, see 1083.

[1092]

★High School Subject Tests: Health. Grades 9–12; 1980; American Testronics.* For the complete program entry, see 1083.

[1093]

★High School Subject Tests: Language. Grades 9–12; 1980; Louis A. Gatta, Robert B. Adams, Marjorie C. Frey, Melton E. Golmon, Karen J. Kuehner, Vincent F. Malek, and John W. McConnell; American Testronics.* For the complete program entry, see 1083.

[1094]

★High School Subject Tests: Literature and Vocabulary. Grades 9–12; 1980; American Testronics.* For the complete program entry, see 1083.

[1095]

★High School Subject Tests: Physical Science. Grades 9–12; 1980; American Testronics.* For the complete program entry, see 1083.

[1096]

★High School Subject Tests: World Geography. Grades 9–12; 1980; American Testronics.* For the complete program entry, see 1083.

[1097]

★High School Subject Tests: World History. Grades 9–12; 1980; American Testronics.* For the complete program entry, see 1083.

[1098]

★High School Subject Tests: Writing and Mechanics. Grades 9–12; 1980; American Testronics.* For the complete program entry, see 1083.

[1099]

Hill Interaction Matrix. Prospective members and members, leaders of psychotherapy groups; 1954–68; HIM; matrix of 4 columns (topics, groups, personal, relationship) and 4 rows (conventional, assertive, speculative, confrontive) produces 16 scores, 8 marginal total scores, grand total, and other derivative scores; 3 editions; Wm. Fawcett Hill; the Author.*

a) HIM A AND B. Prospective members and members of psychotherapy groups; 1954–68; 2 editions: HIM-A, HIM-B.

b) HIM-G. Observers and leaders of psychotherapy groups; 1967–68; no manual.

For additional information, see 8:577 (35 references); see also T2:1214 (29 references).

REFERENCES

1–29. See T2:1214.
30–64. See 8:577.
65. LEE, F., & BEDNAR, R. L. Effects of group structure and risk-taking disposition on group behavior, attitudes, and atmosphere. *Journal of Counseling Psychology*, 1977, 24, 191–199.
66. ZARLE, T. H., & BOYD, R. C. An evaluation of modeling and experiential procedures for self-disclosure training. *Journal of Counseling Psychology*, 1977, 24, 118–124.
67. EVENSEN, E. P., & BEDNAR, R. L. Effects of specific cognitive and behavioral structure on early group behavior and atmosphere. *Journal of Counseling Psychology*, 1978, 25, 66–75.
68. ROE, J. E., & EDWARDS, K. J. Relationship of two process measurement systems for group therapy. *Journal of Consulting & Clinical Psychology*, 1978, 46, 1545–1556.
69. PIPER, W. E., DOAN, B. D., EDWARDS, E. M., & JONES, B. D. Cotherapy behavior, group therapy process, and treatment outcome. *Journal of Consulting & Clinical Psychology*, 1979, 47, 1081–1089.
70. ROSE, G. S., & BEDNAR, R. L. Effects of positive and negative self-disclosure and feedback on early group development. *Journal of Counseling Psychology*, 1980, 27, 63–70.
71. SILBERGELD, S., THUNE, E. S., & MANDERSCHEID, R. W. Marital role dynamics during brief group psychotherapy: Assessment of verbal interactions. *Journal of Clinical Psychology*, 1980, 36, 480–492.
72. THUNE, E. S., MANDERSCHEID, R. W., & SILBERGELD, S. Personal vs relationship orientation as a dimension of sex-role differentiation. *Psychological Reports*, 1980, 46, 455–465.
73. THUNE, E. S., MANDERSCHEID, R. W., & SILBERGELD, S. Status or sex roles as determinants of interaction patterns in small, mixed-sex groups. *Journal of Social Psychology*, 1980, 112, 51–65.

[1100]

★Hill Performance Test of Selected Positional Concepts. Visually impaired children ages 6–10; 1981; revision of *Concepts Involved in Body Position and Space*; 5 scores: ability to identify positional relationships of body parts, ability to move various body parts in relationship to each other, ability to move body in relationship to objects, ability to form object to object relationships, total; Everett W. Hill; Stoelting Co.*

[1101]

Hiskey-Nebraska Test of Learning Aptitude. Ages 3–17 (deaf and hearing); 1941–66; HNTLA; revision of *Nebraska Test of Learning Aptitude*; Marshall S. Hiskey; the Author.*

For additional information and a review by Brian F. Bolton, see 8:217 (11 references); see also T2:499 (1 reference); for a review by T. Ernest Newland, see 7:410 (14 references); for a review by William Sloan of an earlier edition, see 5:409 (8 references); for a review by Mildred C. Templin, see 4:353 (1 reference); see also 3:289 (3 references).

REFERENCES

1–3. See 3:289.
4. See 4:353.
5–12. See 5:409.
13–26. See 7:410.
27. See T2:499.
28–38. See 8:217.
39. BOLTON, B. Differential ability structure in deaf and hearing children. *Applied Psychological Measurement*, 1978, 2, 147–149.
40. CRANDALL, K. E. Inflectional morphemes in the manual English of young hearing-impaired children and their mothers. *Journal of Speech & Hearing Research*, 1978, 21, 372–386.
41. HURLEY, O. L., HIRSHOREN, A., KAVALE, K., & HUNT, J. T. Intercorrelations among tests of general mental ability and achievement for black and white deaf children. *Perceptual & Motor Skills*, 1978, 46, 1107–1113.
42. RICHMAN, L. C. Language mediation hypothesis: Implications of verbal/performance discrepancy and reading ability. *Perceptual & Motor Skills*, 1978, 47, 391–398.
43. HIRSHOREN, A., HURLEY, O. L., & KAVALE, K. Psychometric characteristics of the WISC-R performance scale with deaf children. *Journal of Speech & Hearing Disorders*, 1979, 44, 73–79.
44. HURLEY, O. L. Predictive validity of two mental ability tests with black deaf children. *Journal of Negro Education*, 1979, 48, 14–19.
45. KLEIN, P. S., & SCHWARTZ, A. A. Effects of training auditory sequential memory and attention on reading. *Journal of Special Education*, 1979, 13, 365–374.
46. RICHMAN, L. C. Language variables related to reading ability of children with verbal deficits. *Psychology in the Schools*, 1979, 16, 299–305.

47. JORDON, L. S. Receptive and expressive language problems occurring in combination with a seizure disorder: A case report. *Journal of Communication Disorders*, 1980, 13, 295-303.
48. KARAGAN, N. J., RICHMAN, L. C., & SORENSEN, J. P. Analysis of verbal disability in Duchene Muscular Dystrophy. *Journal of Nervous & Mental Disease*, 1980, 168, 419-423.
49. KLEBANOFF, M. A., & NEFF, J. M. Familial dysautonomia associated with recurrent osteomyelitis in a non-Jewish girl. *Journal of Pediatrics*, 1980, 96, 75-77.
50. RICHMAN, L. C. Cognitive patterns and learning disabilities in cleft palate children with verbal deficits. *Journal of Speech & Hearing Research*, 1980, 23, 447-456.
51. RICHMAN, L. C., & LINDGREN, S. D. Verbal mediation deficits: Relation to behavior and achievement in children. *Journal of Abnormal Psychology*, 1981, 90, 99-104.
52. STARK, R. E., & TALLAL, P. Selection of children with specific language deficits. *Journal of Speech & Hearing Disorders*, 1981, 46, 114-122.

[1102]

Holborn Reading Scale. Ages 5.5-11.0; 1948; 2 scores: word recognition, comprehension; A. F. Watts; Harrap Ltd. [England].*

See T2:1682 (2 references); for a review by Stanley Nisbet, see 5:635 (1 reference); for a review by C. M. Fleming, see 4:537.

[1103]

Hollingsworth-Sanders Geography Test. 1, 2 semesters in grades 5-7; 1962-64; first published 1962-63 in the Every Pupil Scholarship Test series; Leon Hollingsworth and M. W. Sanders; Bureau of Educational Measurements.*

For additional information and a review by Dana G. Kurfman, see 7:906.

[1104]

Hollingsworth-Sanders Intermediate History Test. 1, 2 semesters in grades 5-6; 1962-64; first published 1962-63 in the Every Pupil Scholarship Test series; Leon Hollingsworth and M. W. Sanders; Bureau of Educational Measurements.*

For additional information and a review by Dana G. Kurfman, see 8:914.

[1105]

Hollingsworth-Sanders Junior High School Literature Test. 1, 2 semesters in grades 7-8; 1962-64; first published 1962-63 in the Every Pupil Scholarship Test series; Leon Hollingsworth and M. W. Sanders; Bureau of Educational Measurements.*

For additional information and a review by Paul B. Diederich, see 7:220.

[1106]

*****Holtzman Inkblot Technique.** Ages 5 and over; 1958-73; HIT; 20-22 scores: reaction time, rejection, location, space, form definiteness, form appropriateness, color, shading, movement, pathognomic verbalization, integration, content (human, animal, anatomy, sex, abstract), anxiety, hostility, barrier, penetration, balance, popular; 2 formats: individual, group; Wayne H. Holtzman, Joseph S. Thorpe (book), Jon D. Swartz (book), and E. Wayne Herron (book); The Psychological Corporation.*

For additional information and a review by Rolf A. Peterson, see 8:578 (96 references); see also T2:1471 (42 references); for excerpted reviews by Raymond J. McCall and David G. Martin, see 7:169 (106 references); see also P:439 (90 references); for reviews by Richard W. Coan, H. J. Eysenck, Bertram R. Forer, and William N. Thetford, see 6:217 (22 references).

REFERENCES

1-22. See 6:217.
23-112. See P:439.
113-218. See 7:169.
219-260. See T2:1471.
261-356. See 8:578.

357. AVERBACH, S. M., & EDINGER, J. D. The effects of surgery-induced stress on anxiety as measured by the Holtzman Inkblot Technique. *Journal of Personality Assessment*, 1977, 41, 19-24.
358. DIAZ-GUERRERO, R. A Mexican psychology. *American Psychologist*, 1977, 32, 934-944.
359. GREENBERG, E., ARONOW, E., & RAUCHWAY, A. Inkblot content and interpersonal distance. *Journal of Clinical Psychology*, 1977, 33, 882-887.
360. JANOWSKY, D. S., HUEY, L., STORMS, L., & JUDD, L. L. Methylphenidate hydrochloride effects on psychological tests in acute schizophrenic and nonpsychotic patients. *Archives of General Psychiatry*, 1977, 34, 189-194.
361. JUDD, L. L., HUBBARD, B., JANOWSKY, D. S., HUEY, L. Y., & ATTEWELL, P. A. The effect of lithium carbonate on affect, mood, & personality of normal subjects. *Archives of General Psychiatry*, 1977, 34, 346-351.
362. SANDERS, J. L. Personality correlates of the abstract response on the Holtzman Inkblot Technique. *Journal of Personality Assessment*, 1977, 41, 349-350.
363. SANDERS, S. J., TEDFORD, W. H., JR., & HARDY, B. W. Effects of musical stimuli on creativity. *Psychological Record*, 1977, 27, 463-471.
364. FISHER, S. Body experience before and after surgery. *Perceptual & Motor Skills*, 1978, 46, 699-702.
365. GLAUBMAN, H., & HARTMANN, E. Daytime state and night-time sleep: A sleep study after a marathon group experience. *Perceptual & Motor Skills*, 1978, 46, 711-715.
366. MULLEN, J. M., DUDLEY, H. K., & CRAIG, E. M. Dangerousness and the mentally ill offender: Results of a pilot study. *Hospital & Community Psychiatry*, 1978, 29, 424-425.
367. SCHMIDT, J. P. The interactive effects of instructional set, field dependence, and extraversion on the Holtzman Inkblot Technique. *Journal of Clinical Psychology*, 1978, 34, 533-536.
368. VILKKI, J. Effects of thalamic lesions on complex perception and memory. *Neuropsychologia*, 1978, 16, 427-437.
369. FISHER, S., WRIGHT, D. M., & MOELIS, I. Effects of maternal themes upon death imagery. *Journal of Personality Assessment*, 1979, 43, 595-599.
370. GINSBERG, A., & GIOIELLI, M. M. P. A comparative study of acculturation and adaptation of descendants of Japanese born in Brazil (Nissei) compared with Japanese and Brazilians. *Human Development*, 1979, 22, 340-357.
371. GOLDMAN, B. L., DOMITOR, P. J., & MURRAY, E. J. Effects of Zen meditation on anxiety reduction and perceptual functioning. *Journal of Consulting & Clinical Psychology*, 1979, 47, 551-556.
372. SEIF, M. N., & ATKINS, A. L. Some defensive and cognitive aspects of phobias. *Journal of Abnormal Psychology*, 1979, 88, 42-51.
373. SHAPIRO, A. K., STRUENING, E. L., & SHAPIRO, E. The reliability and validity of a placebo test. *Journal of Psychiatric Research*, 1979, 15, 253-290.
374. THEBERGE, L., & KERNALEGUEN, A. Importance of cosmetics related to aspects of the self. *Perceptual & Motor Skills*, 1979, 48, 827-830.
375. GREENBERG, R. P., & FISHER, S. Freud's penis-baby equation: Exploratory tests of a controversial theory. *British Journal of Medical Psychology*, 1980, 53, 333-342.
376. HARTUNG, J., & SKORKA, D. The HIT profile of psychedelic drug users. *Journal of Personality Assessment*, 1980, 44, 237-245.
377. HILL, E. F. A comparison of three psychological testings of a transsexual. *Journal of Personality Assessment*, 1980, 44, 52-101.
378. LOCKWOOD, J. L., & ROLL, S. Effects of fantasy behavior, level of fantasy predisposition, age, and sex on direction of aggression in young children. *Journal of Genetic Psychology*, 1980, 136, 255-264.
379. ROSEGRANT, J. Adaptive regression of two types. *Journal of Personality Assessment*, 1980, 44, 592-599.
380. VINCENT, K. R. Semi-automated full battery. *Journal of Clinical Psychology*, 1980, 36, 437-446.
381. KIRKPATRICK, M., SMITH, C., & ROY, R. Lesbian mothers and their children: A comparative study. *American Journal of Orthopsychiatry*, 1981, 51, 545-551.

[1107]

Home Index. Grades 4-12; 1949-82; for research use only; 5 scores: social status, ownership, socio-civic involvement, aesthetic involvement, total; Harrison G. Gough; the Author.*

For additional information, see 8:468 (3 references); see also T2:1040A (8 references).

REFERENCES

1–8. See T2:1040A.
9–11. See 8:468.
12. SEROW, R. C. Social adaptation in the high school. The effects of enrollment density and personal background. *Urban Education*, 1980, 15, 169–182.

[1108]
★**Home Observation for Measurement of the Environment.** Birth to age 3, preschool; 1978–79; HOME; 7 or 9 scores listed below; 2 levels; Bettye M. Caldwell and Robert H. Bradley; the Authors.*

a) LEVEL 1. Birth to 3 years; 7 scores: emotional and verbal responsivity of mother, acceptance of child's behavior, organization of the physical and temporal environment, provision of appropriate play materials, maternal involvement with the child, opportunities for variety, total.

b) LEVEL 2. Preschool; 9 scores: stimulation through toys and games and reading materials, language stimulation, physical environment, pride and affection and warmth, stimulation of academic behavior, modeling and encouragement of social maturity, variety of stimulation, physical punishment, total.

REFERENCES

1. HONIG, A. S., TANNENBAUM, J., & CALDWELL, B. M. Maternal behavior in verbal report and in laboratory observation: A methodological study. *Child Psychiatry & Human Development*, 1973, 3, 216–230.
2. CALDWELL, B. M., BRADLEY, R. H., & ELARDO, R. Early stimulation. *Mental Retardation & Developmental Disabilities Abstracts*, 1975, 7, 152–194.
3. BRADLEY, R. H., & CALDWELL, B. M. Home Observation for Measurement of the Environment: A validation study of screening efficiency. *American Journal of Mental Deficiency*, 1977, 81, 417–420.
4. BRADLEY, R. H., CALDWELL, B. M., & ELARDO, R. Home environment, social status, and mental test performance. *Journal of Educational Psychology*, 1977, 69, 697–701.
5. BRADLEY, R. H., STUCK, G. B., COOP, R. H., & WHITE, K. P. A new scale to assess locus of control in three achievement domains. *Psychological Reports*, 1977, 41, 656.
6. ELARDO, R., BRADLEY, R., & CALDWELL, B. M. A longitudinal study of the relation of infants' home environments to language development at age three. *Child Development*, 1977, 48, 595–603.
7. BRADLEY, R. H., & CALDWELL, B. M. Home environment and locus of control. *Journal of Clinical Child Psychology*, 1979, 8, 107–111.
8. BRADLEY, R. H., & CALDWELL, B. M. Home Observation for Measurement of the Environment: A revision of the preschool scale. *American Journal of Mental Deficiency*, 1979, 84, 235–244.
9. BRADLEY, R. H., CALDWELL, B. M., & ELARDO, R. Home environment and cognitive development in the first 2 years: A cross-lagged panel analysis. *Developmental Psychology*, 1979, 15, 246–250.
10. LAVECK, B., HAMMOND, M. A., & LAVECK, G. D. Minor congenital anomalies and behavior in different home environments. *Journal of Pediatrics*, 1980, 96, 940–943.
11. MILAR, C. R., SCHROEDER, S. R., MUSHAK, P., DOLCOURT, J. L., & GRANT, L. Contributions of the caregiving environment to increased lead burden of children. *American Journal of Mental Deficiency*, 1980, 84, 339–344.
12. BRADLEY, R. H., & CALDWELL, B. M. Home environment and infant social behavior. *Infant Mental Health Journal*, 1981, 2, 18–22.
13. BRADLEY, R. H., & CALDWELL, B. M. The HOME Inventory: A validation of the preschool scale for black children. *Child Development*, 1981, 52, 708–710.
14. NIHIRA, K., MINK, I. T., & MEYERS, C. E. Relationship between home environment and school adjustment of TMR children. *American Journal of Mental Deficiency*, 1981, 86, 8–15.

[1109]
The Hooper Visual Organization Test. Ages 14 and over; 1957–66; HVOT; organic brain pathology; H. Elston Hooper; Western Psychological Services.*

See T2:1216 (5 references) and P:111 (7 references); for reviews by Ralph M. Reitan and Otfried Spreen, see 6:116 (4 references).

REFERENCES

1–4. See 6:116.
5–11. See P:111.
12–16. See T2:1216.
17. BELL, A. E., ABRAHAMSON, D. S., & MCRAE, K. N. Reading retardation: A 12-year prospective study. *Journal of Pediatrics*, 1977, 91, 363–370.
18. JACKSON, R. E., & CULBERTSON, W. C. The Elizur Test of Psycho–Organicity and the Hooper Visual Organization Test as measures of childhood neurological impairment. *Journal of Clinical Psychology*, 1977, 33, 213–214.
19. ORNSTEIN, P. Cognitive deficits in chronic alcoholics. *Psychological Reports*, 1977, 40, 719–724.
20. BOTWINICK, J., WEST, R., & STORANDT, M. Predicting death from behavioral test performance. *Journal of Gerontology*, 1978, 33, 755–762.
21. CUMMINGS, J., HEBBEN, N. A., OBLER, L., & LEONARD, P. Nonphasic misnaming and other behavioral features of an unusual toxic encephalopathy: Case study. *Cortex*, 1980, 16, 315–323.
22. GERNER, R., ESTABROOK, W., STEVER, J., & JARVIK, L. Treatment of geriatric depression with trazodone, imipramine, and placebo: A double–blind study. *Journal of Clinical Psychiatry*, 1980, 41, 216–220.

[1110]
Horn Art Aptitude Inventory. Grades 12–16 and adults; 1939–53; 2 scores: scribbling and doodling, imagery; Charles C. Horn; Stoelting Co.*

For additional information and review by Orville Palmer, see 5:242; for a review by Edwin Ziegfeld, see 3:171 (1 reference).

[1111]
Hoskins-Sanders Literature Test. 1, 2 semesters grades 9–13; 1962–64; first published 1962–63 in the Every Pupil Scholarship Test series; Thomas Hoskins and M. W. Sanders; Bureau of Educational Measurements.*

For additional information and a review by Alan C. Purves, see 7:221.

[1112]
★**How A Child Learns.** Grades 1–8; 1970–71; manual title is *Classroom Analysis of Learning Skills and Disabilities: An Observational Approach*; observation of activities of children which is guided through analysis of children's learning channels and leads to a written prescriptive teaching plan; 4 areas: auditory, visual, verbal, manual; Thomas Gnagey and Patricia Gnagey (manual); Facilitation House.*

[1113]
How Supervise? Supervisors; 1943–71; Quentin W. File and H. H. Remmers (manual); The Psychological Corporation.*

See T2:2448 (11 references); for a review by Joel T. Campbell, see 6:1189 (9 references); see also 5:926 (18 references); for a review by Milton M. Mandell, see 4:774 (8 references); for reviews by D. Welty Lefever, Charles I. Mosier, and C. H. Ruedisili, see 3:687 (5 references).

[1114]
★**Howarth Mood Adjective Check List.** College and adults; 1979–80; HMACL; 10 scores: aggression,

scepticism, egotism, outgoingness, control, anxiety, cooperative, fatigue, concentration, sadness; Edgar Howarth; the Author.*

[1115]
★**Howarth Personality Questionnaire.** College and adults; 1971–80; HPQ; 10 scores: sociability, anxiety, dominance, conscience, hypochondriac-medical, impulsive, cooperative-considerateness, inferiority, persistence, suspicion vs. trust; Edgar Howarth, the Author.*

[1116]
Hoyum-Sanders English Tests. 1, 2 semesters in grades 2–4, 5–6, 7–8; 1962–64; first published 1962–63 in the Every Pupil Scholarship Test series; 3 tests; Vera Davis Hoyum and M. W. Sanders; Bureau of Educational Measurements.*

a) HOYUM-SANDERS ELEMENTARY ENGLISH TEST. 1, 2 semesters in grades 2–4.
b) HOYUM-SANDERS INTERMEDIATE ENGLISH TEST. 1, 2 semesters in grades 5–6.
c) HOYUM-SANDERS JUNIOR HIGH SCHOOL ENGLISH TEST. 1, 2 semesters in grades 7–8.

For additional information and a review by Paul B. Diederich, see 7:196.

REFERENCES

1. SLAVIN, R. E. Student teams and comparison among equals: Effects on academic performance and student attitudes. *Journal of Educational Psychology*, 1978, 70, 532–538.
2. SLAVIN, R. E. Effects of individual learning expectations on student achievement. *Journal of Educational Psychology*, 1980, 72, 520–524.
3. SLAVIN, R. E. Effects of student teams and peer tutoring on academic achievement and time-on-task. *Journal of Experimental Education*, 1980, 48, 252–257.

[1117]
Human Figure Drawing Techniques. This is a dummy entry to serve as a catchall for references on the use of human figure drawings in general. References dealing with specific tests are listed under the relevant tests: *Goodenough-Harris Drawing Test, Machover Draw-A-Person Test, Draw-A-Person Quality Scale,* and *H-T-P: House-Tree-Person Projective Technique.*

For additional information, see 8:581 (108 references); see also T2:1475 (150 references) and P:442A (181 references).

REFERENCES

1–181. See P:442A.
182–331. See T2:1474.
332–439. See 8:581.
440. DOR-SHAV, N. K. On the long-range effects of concentration camp internment on Nazi victims: 25 years later. *Journal of Consulting & Clinical Psychology*, 1978, 46, 1–11.
441. BRANNIGAN, G. G., MARGOLIS, H., & MORAN, P. W. Cognitive tempo and children's human figure drawings. *Perceptual & Motor Skills*, 1979, 49, 414.
442. CLANCE, P. R., MITCHELL, M., & ENGELMAN, S. R. Body cathexis in children as a function of awareness training and yoga. *Journal of Clinical Child Psychology*, 1980, 9, 82–85.
443. LAOSA, L. M. Maternal teaching strategies and cognitive styles in Chicano families. *Journal of Educational Psychology*, 1980, 72, 45–54.
444. KIRKPATRICK, M., SMITH, C., & ROY, R. Lesbian mothers and their children: A comparative study. *American Journal of Orthopsychiatry*, 1981, 51, 545–551.

[1118]
Human Relations Inventory. Grades 9–16 and adults; 1954–59; HRI; social conformity; Raymond E. Bernberg; Psychometric Affiliates.*

See T2:1221 (4 references), P:114 (1 reference), and 6:119 (6 references); for reviews by Raymond C. Norris and John A. Radcliffe, see 5:68.

[1119]
★**Hunter-Grundin Literacy Profiles.** Ages 6.5–8, 7.10–9.3, 9–10; 1979–80; ratings by teacher in part; 4 to 5 tests: Attitude to Reading (Levels 1 and 2 only), Reading for Meaning, Spelling, Free Writing, Spoken Language; 3 levels; Elizabeth Hunter-Grundin and Hans U. Grundin; Test Agency [England].*

[1120]
IBM 3881 Optical Mark Reader. 1972; for reading IBM 3881 answer sheets (maximum of 2,480 response positions) marked with ordinary lead pencils; 3 models: Model 1 reads up to 4,000 sheets per hour and transmits data directly to a computer (System/3, System/370 Model 115, 125, 13X, 14X, 15X, 4331, 4341, 3031, 3032, 3033, and 3081); Model 2 reads up to 3,700 sheets per hour and uses IBM 3410 magnetic tape subsystem to record data on magnetic tape for use with various computers; Model 3 records test results on an IBM diskette (the diskette drive and controls are built into the Model 3); International Business Machines Corporation.*

[1121]
★**ICES: Instructor and Course Evaluation System.** College students; 1976–78; instructors choose items from a pool of over 450 covering student perceptions of teaching styles, student outcomes, and course characteristics; no manual; Office of Instructional Resources, University of Illinois at Urbana-Champaign.*

[1122]
Ideal Leader Behavior Description Questionnaire. Supervisors; 1957; ILBDQ; employee ratings of a supervisor; test booklet title is *Ideal Leader Behavior (What You Expect of Your Leader)*; same as *Leader Behavior Description Questionnaire* except that the reponses indicate what a supervisor ought to be rather than what he is; original edition by John K. Hemphill and Alvin E. Coons; current edition by Personnel Research Board, Ohio State University; Publications Sales Division, Ohio State University Press.*

See T2:2449 (6 references) and 7:1145 (10 references).

[1123]
The IES Test. Ages 10 and over and latency period girls; 1956–58; 14 scores: 3 scores each for *a–c* (impulses, ego, superego) plus 5 scores listed in *d* below; 4 tests; Lawrence A. Dombrose and Morton S. Slobin; Psychological Test Specialists.*

a) ARROW-DOT TEST. 1957–58; reaction to goal barriers.
b) PICTURE STORY COMPLETION TEST. 1956–58; conception of outside world.
c) PHOTO-ANALYSIS TEST. 1956–58; desired self-gratifications.
d) PICTURE TITLE TEST. 1956–58; recognition and acceptance of ego pressures; 5 scores: impulse, ego, superego, defense, superego plus defense.

See T2:1475 (16 references) and P:443 (26 references); for reviews by Douglas P. Crowne and Walter

Katkovsky and an excerpted review by John O. Crites, see 6:220 (15 references).

REFERENCES

1-15. See 6:220.
16-41. See P:443.
42-57. See T2:1475.
58. BAEHR, M. E., & FROEMEL, E. C. The Arrow-Dot Test as a prediction of police officer performance. *Perceptual & Motor Skills*, 1977, 45, 683-693.
59. AMMONS, R. B., & AMMONS, C. H. Use and evaluation of the IES test: Partial summary through December, 1977: II. Theses, reports, and reviews. *Perceptual & Motor Skills*, 1978, 47, 1110.
60. SHEARD, M. H., & MARINI, J. L. Treatment of human aggressive behavior: Four case studies of the effect of lithium. *Comprehensive Psychiatry*, 1978, 19, 37-45.

[1124]

★**Illinois Children's Language Assessment Test.** Ages 3-6; 1977; 21 scores: matching colors, recognizing colors, naming colors, matching forms, auditory retention, repetition, auditory comprehension, recognizing objects, naming objects, matching objects to test pictures, stimulability, articulation test, oral musculature, free association (matching, placing), matching objects to test pictures, determining function, explaining pictures, Draw-A-Man, copying geometric forms, total; Phyllis B. Arlt; Interstate Printers & Publishers, Inc.*

REFERENCES

1. FORCUCCI, R. Illinois Children's Language Assessment Test. *ASHA*, 1978, 20, 434-435.

[1125]

Illinois Course Evaluation Questionnaire. College; 1965-74; CEQ; ratings by students; 30 scores: general course attitude (4 item scores, total), method of instruction (4 item scores, total), course content (4 item scores, total), interest and attention (4 item scores, total), instructor-general (2 item scores, total), instructor-specific (5 item scores, total), total; Richard E. Spencer (Forms 66 and 32), Lawrence M. Aleamoni, and Dale C. Brandenburg (manual); Office of Instructional Resources, University of Illinois at Urbana-Champaign.*

For additional information and a review by Robert J. Menges, see 8:373 (10 references); see also T2:864 (1 reference) and 7:579 (2 references).

REFERENCES

1-2. See 7:579.
3. See T2:864.
4-13. See 8:373.
14. BRENDEN, D. R. Face-to-face and telelecture interaction sessions when presenting a course by telelecture. *Journal of Industrial Teacher Education*, 1977, 14, 53-59.
15. MOORE, M. The evaluation of instruction at the Israel Institute of Technology. *Educational & Psychological Measurement*, 1977, 37, 1039-1041.
16. WEBER, C. R. A comparison of values clarification and lecture-discussion methods in teaching college health science. *College Student Journal*, 1977, 11, 98-104.
17. BLOUNT, H. P., GUPTA, V. G., & STALLINGS, W. M. The effects of different instructions on student ratings of university courses and teachers. *Journal of Educational Research*, 1978, 71, 149-152.
18. POTTER, E. L. The relationship of teacher training and teaching experience to assessment of teaching performance of community/junior college faculty. *Journal of Educational Research*, 1978, 72, 81-85.
19. RYBACK, D., & SANDERS, J. J. Humanistic versus traditional teaching styles and student satisfaction. *Journal of Humanistic Psychology*, 1980, 20, 87-90.

[1126]

Illinois Test of Psycholinguistic Abilities, Revised Edition. Ages 2-10; 1961-68; ITPA; 11-13 scores: auditory reception, visual reception, visual sequential memory, auditory association, auditory sequential memory, visual association, visual closure, verbal expression, grammatic closure, manual expression, auditory closure (optional), sound blending (optional), total; Samuel A. Kirk, James J. McCarthy, and Winifred D. Kirk; University of Illinois Press.*

For additional information, reviews by James Lumsden and J. Lee Wiederholt, and an excerpted review by R. P. Waugh, see 8:431 (269 references); see also T2:981 (113 references); for reviews by John B. Carroll and Clinton I. Chase, see 7:442 (239 references); see also 6:549 (22 references).

REFERENCES

1-22. See 6:549.
23-261. See 7:442.
262-374. See T2:981.
375-643. See 8:431.
644. LEONG, C. K. Spatial-temporal information-processing in children with specific reading disability. *Reading Research Quarterly*, 1976-1977, 12, 204-215.
645. WHYTE, L. Prescriptive teaching: Changes in stage of logico-mathematical thinking and spatial development in a group of opportunity class children. *Alberta Journal of Educational Research*, 1976, 22, 34-43.
646. ARNDT, W. B., SHELTON, R. L., JOHNSON, A. F., & FURR, M. L. Identification and description of homogeneous subgroups within a sample of misarticulating children. *Journal of Speech & Hearing Research*, 1977, 20, 263-292.
647. AYRES, A. J. Cluster analyses of measures of sensory integration. *American Journal of Occupational Therapy*, 1977, 31, 363-366.
648. BELL, A. E., ABRAHAMSON, D. S., & MCRAE, K. N. Reading retardation: A 12-year prospective study. *Journal of Pediatrics*, 1977, 91, 363-370.
649. BLOWERS, E. A. Prediction of Metropolitan Readiness Test scores. *Alberta Journal of Educational Research*, 1977, 23, 164-168.
650. BURNS, E. The effects of skewness on the interpretation of ITPA scaled scores. *Journal of School Psychology*, 1977, 15, 219-224.
651. CAMP, B. W. Verbal mediation in young aggressive boys. *Journal of Abnormal Psychology*, 1977, 86, 145-153.
652. CAMP, B. W., VAN DOORNINCK, W. J., ZIMET, S. G., & DAHLEM, N. W. Verbal abilities in young aggressive boys. *Journal of Educational Psychology*, 1977, 69, 129-135.
653. CHERRY, F. F., & EATON, E. L. Physical and cognitive development in children of low-income mothers working in the child's early years. *Child Development*, 1977, 48, 158-166.
654. DELACEY, P. R., & NURCOMBE, B. Effects of enrichment preschooling at Bourke: A further follow-up study. *Australian Journal of Education*, 1977, 21, 80-90.
655. ELARDO, R., BRADLEY, R., & CALDWELL, B. M. A longitudinal study of the relation of infants' home environments to language development at age three. *Child Development*, 1977, 48, 595-603.
656. EVANS, D. The development of language abilities in Mongols: A correlational study. *Journal of Mental Deficiency Research*, 1977, 21, 103-117.
657. EVESHAM, M. Teaching language skills to children with language disorders. *British Journal of Disorders of Communication*, 1977, 12, 23-29.
658. FOCH, T. T., DEFRIES, J. C., MCCLEARN, G. E., & SINGER, S. M. Familial patterns of impairment in reading disability. *Journal of Educational Psychology*, 1977, 69, 316-329.
659. GRILL, J. J., & BARTEL, N. R. Language bias in tests: ITPA grammatic closure. *Journal of Learning Disabilities*, 1977, 10, 229-235.
660. HARE, B. A. Perceptual deficits are not a cue to reading problems in second grade. *Reading Teacher*, 1977, 30, 624-628.
661. HARTH, R., & JUSTEN, J. E., III. The validity of the ITPA Visual Closure Subtest. *Academic Therapy*, 1977, 12, 261-265.
662. JOHNSON, A. F., SHELTON, R. L., ARNDT, W. B., & FURR, M. L. Factor analysis of measures of articulation, language, auditory processing, reading-spelling, and maxillofacial structure. *Journal of Speech & Hearing Research*, 1977, 20, 319-324.
663. KIRK, S. A., VON ISSER, A., & ELKINS, J. Ethnic differences in head start children. *Journal of Clinical Child Psychology*, 1977, 6, 91-92.
664. LEDOUX, J. E., RISSE, G. L., SPRINGER, S. P., WILSON, D. H., & GAZZANIGA, M. S. Cognition and commissurotomy. *Brain*, 1977, 100, 87-104.
665. LESIAK, J. The Gates-MacGinitie Readiness Skills Test and Illinois Test of Psycholinguistic Abilities as predictors of first grade reading. *Psychology in the Schools*, 1977, 14, 4-10.
666. MADIGAN, R. J., & PETERSON, W. J. Television on the Bering Strait. *Journal of Communication*, 1977, 27, 183-187.

667. MARGOLIS, H. Auditory perceptual test performance and the reflection–impulsivity dimension. *Journal of Learning Disabilities*, 1977, 10, 164–172.

668. MCCORMICK, D. P. Pediatric evaluation of children with school problems. *American Journal of Diseases of Children*, 1977, 131, 318–322.

669. MCDERMOTT, P. A. Measures of diagnostic data usage as discriminants among training and experience levels in school psychology. *Psychology in the Schools*, 1977, 14, 323–331.

670. MIYASHITA, T. Factor analytic study of the ITPA and the Frostig test. *Japanese Psychological Research*, 1977, 19, 187–192.

671. PRIOR, M. R. Psycholinguistic disabilities of autistic and retarded children. *Journal of Mental Deficiency Research*, 1977, 21, 37–45.

672. RICHEK, M. A. Readiness skills that predict initial word learning using 2 different methods of instruction. *Reading Research Quarterly*, 1977–1978, 13, 200–222.

673. ROBBINS, R. L., & HARWAY, N. I. Goal setting and reactions to success and failure in children with learning disabilities. *Journal of Learning Disabilities*, 1977, 10, 35–62.

674. ROE, K. V. Correlations between Gesell scores in infancy and performance on verbal and nonverbal tests in early childhood. *Perceptual & Motor Skills*, 1977, 45, 1131–1134.

675. SHELTON, R. L., JOHNSON, A. F., & ARNDT, W. B. Delayed judgment speech–sound discrimination and /r/ or /s/ articulation status and improvement. *Journal of Speech & Hearing Research*, 1977, 20, 704–717.

676. STEWART, D. W. The factorial structure of the ITPA and WISC subtests in three diagnostic groups. *Journal of Clinical Psychology*, 1977, 33, 199–205.

677. THOMSON, A. J., SEARLE, M., & RUSSELL, G. Quality of survival after severe birth asphyxia. *Archives of Diseases in Childhood*, 1977, 52, 620–626.

678. VOGEL, S. A. Morphological ability in normal and dyslexic children. *Journal of Learning Disabilities*, 1977, 10, 35–43.

679. VON ISSER, A. Psycholinguistic abilities in children with epilepsy. *Exceptional Children*, 1977, 43, 270–275.

680. VON ISSER, A., & KIRK, S. A. The effects of head start on psycholinguistic functions. *Journal of Clinical Child Psychology*, 1977, 6, 93.

681. WIIG, E. H., LAPOINT, C., & SEMEL, E. M. Relationships among language processing and production abilities of learning disabled adolescents. *Journal of Learning Disabilities*, 1977, 10, 292–299.

682. WILLIAMS, A. M., MARKS, C. J., & BIALER, I. Validity of the Peabody Picture Vocabulary Test as a measure of hearing vocabulary in mentally retarded and normal children. *Journal of Speech & Hearing Research*, 1977, 20, 197–204.

683. WING, L., GOULD, J., YEATES, S. R., & BRIERLEY, L. M. Symbolic play in severely mentally retarded and in autistic children. *Journal of Child Psychology & Psychiatry & Allied Disciplines*, 1977, 18, 167–178.

684. AYRES, A. J. Learning disabilities and the vestibular system. *Journal of Learning Disabilities*, 1978, 11, 18–29.

685. BOWEN, C., GELABERT, T., & TORGESEN, J. Memorization processes involved in performance on the visual–sequential memory subtest of the Illinois Test of Psycholinguistic Abilities. *Journal of Educational Psychology*, 1978, 70, 887–893.

686. BURR, D. B., & ROHR, A. Patterns of psycholinguistic development in the severely mentally retarded: A hypothesis. *Social Biology*, 1978, 25, 15–22.

687. COLARUSSO, R. P., & DANGEL, H. An informal assessment of psycholinguistic abilities. *Academic Therapy*, 1978, 14, 203–208.

688. CULATTA, B. The relationship between perceptual dysfunction and language disorders: A case report. *Journal of Communication Disorders*, 1978, 11, 51–63.

689. DAS, J. P., LEONG, C. K., & WILLIAMS, N. H. The relationship between learning disability and simultaneous–successive processing. *Journal of Learning Disabilities*, 1978, 11, 618–625.

690. DE GAFFENREID, H., BLOOM, A., & WAGNER, M. A comparison of an ITPA estimated psycholinguistic quotient and WISC-R IQs for developmentally disabled children. *Journal of Clinical Psychology*, 1978, 34, 943–945.

691. DEFRIES, J. C., SINGER, S. M., FOCH, T. T., & LEWITTER, F. I. Familial nature of reading disability. *British Journal of Psychiatry*, 1978, 132, 361–367.

692. DESMOND, M. M., FISHER, E. S., VORDERMAN, A. L., SCHAFFER, H. G., ANDREW, L. P., ZION, T. E., & CATLIN, F. I. The longitudinal course of congenital rubella encephalitis in nonretarded children. *Journal of Pediatrics*, 1978, 93, 584–591.

693. ELKINS, J. Empirical evidence for a model of reading disability research. *Australian Journal of Education*, 1978, 22, 303–309.

694. HAGGERTY, R., & STAMM, J. S. Dichotic auditory fusion levels in children with learning disabilities. *Neuropsychologia*, 1978, 16, 349–360.

695. JURKOVIC, G. J. Relation of psycholinguistic development to imaginative play of disadvantaged preschool children. *Psychology in the Schools*, 1978, 15, 560–564.

696. KAUFMAN, A. S. The importance of basic concepts in the individual assessment of preschool children. *Journal of School Psychology*, 1978, 16, 207–211.

697. KAZELSKIS, R. A correction for loading bias in a principal components analysis. *Educational & Psychological Measurement*, 1978, 38, 253–257.

698. KIRK, S. A., & KIRK, W. D. Uses and abuses of the ITPA. *Journal of Speech & Hearing Disorders*, 1978, 43, 58–75.

699. LAVINE, S. B. The paired comparisons method of identifying developmental discrepancies with the ITPA. *Journal of Learning Disabilities*, 1978, 11, 506–510.

700. MABEE, W. S. An investigation of the learning disability construct by the JAN technique. *Journal of Experimental Education*, 1978, 46, 19–24.

701. MAGGIORE, R. P. Reliability of proposed short form of Illinois Test of Psycholinguistic Abilities. *Exceptional Children*, 1978, 45, 198–204.

702. MARGOLIS, H., & BRANNIGAN, G. G. Conceptual tempo as a parameter for predicting reading achievement. *Journal of Educational Research*, 1978, 71, 342–345.

703. MCLEAD, T. M., & CRUMP, W. D. The relationship of visuospatial skills and verbal ability to learning disabilities in mathematics. *Journal of Learning Disabilities*, 1978, 11, 237–241.

704. MORRISON, D., & POTHIER, P. Effects of sensory–motor training on the language development of retarded preschoolers. *American Journal of Orthopsychiatry*, 1978, 48, 310–319.

705. PATTON, J. E., & OFFENBACH, S. I. Effects of visual and auditory distractors on learning disabled and normal children's recognition memory performance. *Journal of Educational Psychology*, 1978, 70, 788–795.

706. RAMANAIAH, N. V., O'DONNELL, J. P., & ADAMS, M. A test of the theoretical model of the revised Illinois Test of Psycholinguistic Abilities. *Applied Psychological Measurement*, 1978, 2, 519–525.

707. ROE, K. V. Infant's mother–stranger discrimination at 3 months as a predictor of cognitive development at 3 and 5 years. *Developmental Psychology*, 1978, 14, 191–192.

708. ROHR, A., & BURR, D. B. Etiological differences in patterns of psycholinguistic development of children of IQ 30–60. *American Journal of Mental Deficiency*, 1978, 82, 549–553.

709. RUBIN, R. A., & BALOW, B. Prevalence of teacher identified behavior problems: A longitudinal study. *Exceptional Children*, 1978, 45, 102–111.

710. SILVERSTEIN, A. B. Note on the construct validity of the ITPA. *Psychology in the Schools*, 1978, 15, 371–372.

711. STREFF, M., BAREFOOT, S., WALTER, G., & CRANDALL, K. A comparative study of hearing–impaired and normal–hearing young adults–Verbal and nonverbal abilities. *Journal of Communication Disorders*, 1978, 11, 489–498.

712. STRICHART, S. S. Evaluation model for the outcomes of individual remediation programs. *Academic Therapy*, 1978, 14, 193–202.

713. SUITER, M. L., & POTTER, R. E. The effects of paradigmatic organization on verbal recall. *Journal of Learning Disabilities*, 1978, 11, 247–250.

714. TEASDALE, G. R., TIERNEY, R. J., AMES, W. S., & WRAY, R. H. A cross–cultural comparison of item analysis data on the revised ITPA. *Australian Psychologist*, 1978, 13, 391–399.

715. TIERNEY, R. J., & AMES, W. S. An examination of the diagnostic claims of the revised Illinois Test of Psycholinguistic Abilities. *Journal of Learning Disabilities*, 1978, 11, 586–590.

716. WEITHORN, C. J., & KAGEN, E. Interaction of language development and activity level on performance of first–graders. *American Journal of Orthopsychiatry*, 1978, 48, 148–159.

717. BEADLE, K. R. Clinical interactions of verbal language, learning and behavior. *Journal of Clinical Child Psychology*, 1979, 8, 201–205.

718. BELKA, D. E., & WILLIAMS, H. G. Prediction of later cognitive behavior from early school perceptual–motor, perceptual, and cognitive performances. *Perceptual & Motor Skills*, 1979, 49, 131–141.

719. BRUININKS, V. L., & MAYER, J. H. Longitudinal study of cognitive abilities and academic achievement. *Perceptual & Motor Skills*, 1979, 48, 1011–1021.

720. COLARUSSO, R. P., MATHIS, G., & SHESSEL, D. Teacher effectiveness in identifying high–risk kindergarten children. *Journal of Learning Disabilities*, 1979, 12, 684–686.

721. COLLEHI, L. F. Relationship between pregnancy and birth complications and the later development of learning disabilities. *Journal of Learning Disabilities*, 1979, 12, 659–663.

722. CRAWFORD, J. H., & FRY, M. A. Trait–task interaction in intra– and intermodal matching of auditory and visual trigrams. *Contemporary Educational Psychology*, 1979, 4, 1–10.

723. DEWART, H. M. Language comprehension processes of mentally retarded children. *American Journal of Mental Deficiency*, 1979, 84, 177–183.

724. FISHBEIN, H. D. Braille–phonics: A new technique for aiding the reading disabled. *Journal of Learning Disabilities*, 1979, 12, 60–64.

725. GILBERT, K. A., & HEMMING, H. Environmental change and psycholinguistic ability of mentally retarded adults. *American Journal of Mental Deficiency*, 1979, 83, 453–459.

726. HARBER, J. R. Measures of visual closure. *Perceptual & Motor Skills*, 1979, 48, 206.
727. HARKULICH, J. F., MARCHNER, T. J., & BROWN, E. B. Neurological, neuropsychological, and behavioral correlates of Klinefelter's Syndrome. *Journal of Nervous & Mental Disease*, 1979, 167, 359-363.
728. INAGAKI, K. Relationship of curiosity to perceptual and verbal fluency in young children. *Perceptual & Motor Skills*, 1979, 48, 789-790.
729. KLEIN, P. S., & SCHWARTZ, A. A. Effects of training auditory sequential memory and attention on reading. *Journal of Special Education*, 1979, 13, 365-374.
730. KONSTANTAREAS, M. M., WEBSTER, C. D., & OXMAN, J. Manual language acquisition and its influence on other areas of functioning in four autistic and autistic-like children. *Journal of Child Psychology & Psychiatry & Allied Disciplines*, 1979, 20, 337-350.
731. LUDLOW, C. L., RICHARDS-MUNN, B., & CULLISON, B. L. The effect of drugs on communicative abilities of hyperactive and normal children. *ASHA*, 1979, 21, 759. (Abstract)
732. MCNUTT, J. C., & LERI, S. M. Language differences between institutionalized and noninstitutionalized retarded children. *American Journal of Mental Deficiency*, 1979, 83, 339-345.
733. MORGAN, S. R. Psycho-educational profile of emotionally disturbed abused children. *Journal of Clinical Child Psychology*, 1979, 8, 3-6.
734. MURAMOTO, O., SUGISHITA, M., SUGITA, H., & TOYOKURA, Y. Effect of physostigmine on constructional and memory tasks in Alzheimer's Disease. *Archives of Neurology*, 1979, 36, 501-503.
735. PETTIT, J. M., & HELMS, S. B. Hemispheric language dominance of language-disordered, articulation-disordered, and normal children. *Journal of Learning Disabilities*, 1979, 12, 71-76.
736. RIEDER, D. O., & NICHOLS, P. L. Offspring of schizophrenics III. *Archives of General Psychiatry*, 1979, 36, 665-674.
737. RUBIN, R. A., & BALOW, B. Measures of infant development and socioeconomic status as predictors of later intelligence and school achievement. *Developmental Psychology*, 1979, 15, 225-227.
738. RUBIN, R. A., BALOW, B., & FISCH, R. O. Neonatal serum, bilirubin levels related to cognitive development at ages 4 through 7 years. *Journal of Pediatrics*, 1979, 94, 601-604.
739. STECKOL, K. F., & LEONARD, L. B. The use of grammatical morphemes by normal and language-impaired children. *Journal of Communication Disorders*, 1979, 12, 291-301.
740. TAYLOR, L. J. Family environments, language, and intelligence. *Canadian Journal of Behavioural Science*, 1979, 11, 1-10.
741. TEMPLE, I. G., WILLIAMS, H. G., & BATEMAN, N. J. A test battery to assess intrasensory and intersensory development of young children. *Perceptual & Motor Skills*, 1979, 48, 643-659.
742. TOBEY, E. A., CULLEN, J. K., JR., RAMPP, D. L., & FLEISCHER-GALLAGHER, A. M. Effects of stimulus-onset asynchrony on the dichotic performance of children with auditory-processing disorders. *Journal of Speech & Hearing Research*, 1979, 22, 197-211.
743. TREPANIER, M. L., & LIBEN, L. S. The operative basis of performance on Piagetian memory tasks: Evidence from normal and learning disabled children. *Developmental Psychology*, 1979, 15, 668-669.
744. WEITHORN, C. J., & KAGEN, E. Training first graders of high-activity level to improve performance through verbal self-direction. *Journal of Learning Disabilities*, 1979, 12, 82-88.
745. WENTLAND, T. J. ITPA interchannel differences. *Perceptual & Motor Skills*, 1979, 48, 699-702.
746. WOLFF, S., & BARLOW, A. Schizoid personality in childhood: A comparative study of schizoid, autistic and normal children. *Journal of Child Psychology & Psychiatry & Allied Disciplines*, 1979, 20, 29-46.
747. ZAIDEL, E. Performance on the ITPA following cerebral commissurotomy and hemispherectomy. *Neuropsychologia*, 1979, 17, 259-280.
748. BELKA, D. E., & WILLIAMS, H. G. Canonical relationships among perceptual-motor, perceptual, and cognitive behaviors in children. *Research Quarterly for Exercise & Sport*, 1980, 51, 463-477.
749. BERLER, E. S., & ROMANCZYK, R. G. Assessment of the learning disabled and hyperactive child: An analysis and critique. *Journal of Learning Disabilities*, 1980, 13, 10-12.
750. BRAGGIO, J. T., BRAGGIO, S. M., HALL, A. D., ALLMAN, T. W., PEYTON, L. J., & KARAN, D. Validating optimal response modes of learning disabled children. *Perceptual & Motor Skills*, 1980, 51, 1335-1345.
751. BRUMBACK, R. A., STATON, R. D., & WILSON, H. Neuropsychological study of children during and after remission of endogenous depressive episodes. *Perceptual & Motor Skills*, 1980, 50, 1163-1167.
752. CANTWELL, D. P., BAKER, L., & MATTISON, R. E. Psychiatric disorders in children with speech and language retardation. *Archives of General Psychiatry*, 1980, 37, 423-426.
753. COLARUSSO, R., GILL, S., PLANKENHORN, A., & BROOKS, R. Predicting first-grade achievement through formal testing of 5-year-old high-risk children. *Journal of Special Education*, 1980, 14, 355-363.

754. DANSKY, J. L. Cognitive consequences of sociodramatic play and exploration training for economically disadvantaged preschoolers. *Journal of Child Psychology & Psychiatry & Allied Disciplines*, 1980, 21, 47-58.
755. DOYLE, A. B., RAPPARD, P., & CONNOLLY, J. Two solitudes in the preschool classroom. *Canadian Journal of Behavioural Science*, 1980, 12, 221-232.
756. FINKELSTEIN, N. W., GALLAGHER, J. J., & FARRAN, D. C. Attentiveness and responsiveness to auditory stimuli of children at risk for mental retardation. *American Journal of Mental Deficiency*, 1980, 85, 135-144.
757. GREEN, H. G. Latency to respond and performance on visual association of the Illinois Test of Psycholinguistic Abilities. *Perceptual & Motor Skills*, 1980, 51, 453-454.
758. GREEN, H. G. Preschool children's conceptual tempo and performance on visual discrimination tasks. *Journal of Psychology*, 1980, 106, 21-25.
759. HAMMILL, D. D., & NEWCOMER, P. L. Response to Maggiore's criticisms of the short form ITPA. *Exceptional Children*, 1980, 46, 434-438.
760. HARBER, J. R. Are auditory perceptual skills requisite for reading success? *Reading World*, 1980, 19, 272-279.
761. HICKS, C. The ITPA visual sequential memory task: An alternative interpretation and the implication for good and poor readers. *British Journal of Educational Psychology*, 1980, 50, 16-25.
762. JOHNSON, J. I., LEDER, S. B., & EGELSTON, R. L. Influence of intonation on auditory sequential memory skills. *Perceptual & Motor Skills*, 1980, 50, 703-708.
763. JORDON, L. S. Receptive and expressive language problems occurring in combination with a seizure disorder: A case report. *Journal of Communication Disorders*, 1980, 13, 295-303.
764. KLEECK, A. V., & CARPENTER, R. L. The effects of children's language comprehension level on adults' child-directed talk. *Journal of Speech & Hearing Research*, 1980, 23, 546-569.
765. LEONG, C. K. Cognitive patterns of "retarded" and below-average readers. *Contemporary Educational Psychology*, 1980, 5, 101-117.
766. MARGOLIS, H., LEONARD, H. S., BRANNIGAN, G. G., & HEVERLY, M. A. The validity of form F of the Matching Familiar Figures Test with kindergarten children. *Journal of Experimental Child Psychology*, 1980, 29, 12-22.
767. MCCLURE, J., KALK, M., & KEENAN, V. Use of grammatical morphemes by beginning readers. *Journal of Learning Disabilities*, 1980, 13, 34-39.
768. MCLESKY, J., KANDASWAMY, S., & COLARUSSO, R. A canonical correlation analysis of the WISC and ITPA for a group of learning-disabled children. *Journal of Special Education*, 1980, 14, 253-259.
769. MUSSELWHITE, C. R., ST. LOUIS, K. O., & PENICK, P. B. A communicative interaction analysis system for language-disordered children. *Journal of Communication Disorders*, 1980, 13, 315-324.
770. PEREZ, F. M. Performance of bilingual children on the Spanish version of the ITPA. *Exceptional Children*, 1980, 46, 536-541.
771. RICHARDSON, E., DIBENEDETTO, B., CHRIST, A., & PRESS, M. Relationship of auditory and visual skills to reading retardation. *Journal of Learning Disabilities*, 1980, 13, 77-82.
772. RILEY, G. D., & RILEY, J. Motoric and linguistic variables among children who stutter: A factor analysis. *Journal of Speech & Hearing Disorders*, 1980, 45, 504-514.
773. TORGESEN, J. K., & HOUCK, D. G. Processing deficiencies of learning-disabled children who perform poorly on the Digit Span Test. *Journal of Educational Psychology*, 1980, 72, 141-160.
774. TSUSHIMA, W. T., & TOWNE, W. S. ITPA performances of young children with and without questionable brain disorders. *Journal of Learning Disabilities*, 1980, 13, 13-15.
775. WINSBERG, B. G., BIALER, I., KUPIETZ, S., BOTTI, E., & BALKA, E. B. Home vs hospital care of children with behavior disorders. *Archives of General Psychiatry*, 1980, 37, 413-418.
776. BLOSKOVICS, M., ENGEL, R., PODOSIN, R. L., AZEN, C. G., & FRIEDMAN, E. G. EEG pattern in phenylketonuria under early initiated dietary treatment. *American Journal of Diseases of Children*, 1981, 135, 802-808.
777. CHERMAK, G. G., & O'CONNELL, V. I. Comparison of performance of eight-year-old children on three auditory sequential memory tests. *Perceptual & Motor Skills*, 1981, 52, 879-882.
778. DEAN, R. S., & KUNDERT, D. K. The effects of abstractiveness in mediation with learning-problem children. *Journal of Clinical Child Psychology*, 1981, 10, 173-175.
779. DEAN, R. S., & KUNDERT, D. K. Intelligence and teachers' ratings as predictors of abstract and concrete learning. *Journal of School Psychology*, 1981, 19, 78-85.
780. ELFENBEIN, J. L., WAZIRI, M., & MORRIS, H. L. Verbal communication skills of six children with craniofacial anomalies. *Cleft Palate Journal*, 1981, 18, 59-64.
781. ELKINS, J., & SULTMANN, W. F. TPA and Learning Disability: A Discriminant Analysis. *Journal of Learning Disabilities*, 1981, 14, 88-92.

782. GARMAN, D. Language development and first grade reading achievement. *Reading World*, 1981, 21, 40–49.
783. GREESON, L. E. Modeling, intelligence, and language development. *Journal of Genetic Psychology*, 1981, 139, 195–203.
784. LYON, R., REITTA, S., WATSON, B., PORCH, B., & RHODES, J. Selected linguistic and perceptual abilities of empirically derived subgroups of learning disabled readers. *Journal of School Psychology*, 1981, 19, 152–166.
785. NEUMAN, S. B. Effect of teaching auditory perceptual skills on reading achievement in first grade. *Reading Teacher*, 1981, 34, 422–426.
786. SEMEL, E. M., & WIIG, E. H. Semel auditory processing program: Training effects among children with language–learning disabilities. *Journal of Learning Disabilities*, 1981, 14, 192–196.
787. STARK, R. E., & TALLAL, P. Selection of children with specific language deficits. *Journal of Speech & Hearing Disorders*, 1981, 46, 114–122.
788. STATON, R. D., WILSON, H., & BRUMBACK, R. A. Cognitive improvement associated with tricyclic antidepressant treatment of childhood major depressive illness. *Perceptual & Motor Skills*, 1981, 53, 219–234.

[1127]
Illinois Tests in the Teaching of English. High school English teachers; 1969–72; ITTE; criterion-referenced; 4 tests; William H. Evans and Paul H. Jacobs; Southern Illinois University Press.*
a) KNOWLEDGE OF LANGUAGE.
b) ATTITUDE AND KNOWLEDGE IN WRITTEN COMPOSITION, COMPETENCY TEST B. 3 scores: attitudes (2 scores), knowledge.
c) KNOWLEDGE OF LITERATURE.
d) KNOWLEDGE OF THE TEACHING OF ENGLISH.
For additional information, see 8:52 (1 reference).

[1128]
★**Ilyin Oral Interview.** Junior high and secondary and adult students; 1972–76; IOI; designed to assess the ability of non-native English speakers to communicate verbally with content and structural accuracy; Donna Ilyin; Newbury House Publishers, Inc.*
REFERENCES
1. AGOR, B. J., GENZEL, R., GRANITE, D., & BRILL, J. V. Comments on Kenneth J. Mattran's "Native speaker reactions to speakers of ESL: implications for adult basic education oral English proficiency testing". *TESOL Quarterly*, 1978, 12, 485–488.

[1129]
The Immediate Test: A Quick Verbal Intelligence Test. Adults; 1951; Raymond J. Corsini; Sheridan Psychological Services, Inc.*
See T2:500 (2 references); for reviews by Jerome E. Doppelt and Ivan Norman Mensh, see 4:342 (1 reference).

[1130]
★**Impact Message Inventory: Form II.** College students and adults; 1976–79; self-report inventory; assesses "momentary emotional and other engagements of one person by another during ongoing transactions in counseling/psychotherapy and other dyads"; 15 subscales: dominant, competitive, hostile, mistrusting, detached, inhibited, submissive, succorant, abasive, deferent, agreeable, nurturant, affiliative, sociable, exhibitionistic; Donald J. Kiesler, J. C. Anchin, M. J. Perkins, B. M. Chirico, E. M. Kyle, and E. J. Federman; Donald J. Kiesler.*
REFERENCES
1. PERKINS, M. J., KIESLER, D. J., ANCHIN, J. C., CHIRICO, B. M., KYLE, E. M., & FEDERMAN, E. J. The Impact Message Inventory: A new measure of relationship in counseling/psychotherapy and other dyads. *Journal of Counseling Psychology*, 1979, 26, 363–367.

[1131]
An Incomplete Sentence Test. Employees, college; 1949–53; 2 editions; George Spache; Reading Laboratory and Clinic.* (In-print status uncertain; no reply from publisher.)
a) AN INCOMPLETE SENTENCE TEST FOR INDUSTRIAL USE. Employees; 1949.
b) AN INCOMPLETE SENTENCE TEST [COLLEGE EDITION]. College; 1953; no manual.
For additional information, see P:444; for a review by Benjamin Balinsky, see 5:142.
REFERENCES
1. IMODA, F., & RULLA, L. M. Sociometric differentiation and self in male religious vocationers. *Group Psychotherapy, Psychodrama & Sociometry*, 1978, 31, 20–32.

[1132]
★**Incomplete Sentences Task.** Grades 7–12, college-age adolescents; 1979–80; IST; self-administered projective and psychometric test; "designed to detect potential emotional problems that might, for example, interfere with classroom learning"; 3 scores: hostility, anxiety, dependency; Barbara Lanyon; Stoelting Co.*

[1133]
Independent Activities Questionnaire. High school and college; 1965–67; IAQ; for research use only; non-academic achievement; 25 scores: 20 scale scores (agriculture, art and design, business, collecting, drama, electronics, exploring, games, handicraft, home responsibility, leadership, mathematics, mechanics, music, politics, public speaking, scholarship, science, sports, writing) and 5 derived scores (arts and crafts, speech, sciences, arts and sciences, social activities); Stephen P. Klein (manual); Educational Testing Service.*
See T2:1230 (1 reference) and P:122 (2 references).

[1134]
★**Independent Living Behavior Checklist.** Behaviorally impaired adults; 1979; ILBC; criterion-referenced; 6 areas: mobility skills, self-care skills, home maintenance and safety skills, food skills, social and communication skills, functional academic skills; Richard T. Walls, Thomas Zane, and John E. Thvedt; West Virginia Rehabilitation Research and Training Center.*

[1135]
Indiana-Oregon Music Discrimination Test. Grades 5 through graduate school; 1934–75 (no date on test materials); revision of *Oregon Music Discrimination Test* ('34) by Kate Hevner; music appreciation; first 30 items (Test E) primarily for grades 5–9, first 37 items (Test J) primarily for grades 7–9, all 43 items (Test S) primarily for grades 9 and over; original test by Kate Hevner, revision by Newell H. Long; Midwest Music Tests.*
For additional information and reviews by Richard Colwell and Paul R. Lehman, see 8:96 (16 references).
REFERENCES
1–16. See 8:96.
17. MARTIN, P. J. Distinguishing school orchestra members. *Council for Research in Music Education. Bulletin*, 1979, 59, 62–67.

[1136]
Indiana Physical Fitness Test. Grades 4–12; 1964; modification of *Indiana University Motor Fitness Index*; 4

scores: straddle chins, squat thrusts, push ups, vertical jump; Karl W. Bookwalter and Harold J. Walter (norms); Indiana Public Health Foundation, Inc.*

For additional information, see 7:606.

[1137]

Individual Career Exploration. Grades 8–12; 1976; ICE; self-administered and self-scored inventory of interests, experience, occupational choices, and abilities in 8 occupational groups: service, business contact, organization, technology, outdoor, science, general culture, arts and entertainment; 5 scores: first-choice occupational group, second-choice group, decision level (motivation), job values (most important, second most important); Anna Miller-Tiedeman in consultation with Anne Roe (classification of occupations booklet); Scholastic Testing Service, Inc.*

For additional information and a review by Richard S. Melton, see 8:1006.

[1138]

Individual Phonics Criterion Test. Grades 1–8; 1971; IPCT; formerly called *Phonics Criterion Test*; criterion-referenced; no scores, 14 areas: easy consonants, short vowels, long and silent vowels, difficult consonants, consonant digraphs, consonant second sounds, schwa sounds, long vowel digraphs, vowel plus r, broad o, diphthongs, difficult vowels, consonant blends, consonant exceptions; no manual; Edward Fry; Jamestown Publishers.*

For additional information and a review by Joyce E. Hood, see 8:762.

[1139]

Individual Pupil Monitoring System—Mathematics, Forms S and T. Grades 1, 2, 3, 4, 5, 6, 7, 8; 1973; IPMS—Mathematics; criterion-referenced; 24 tests (each test booklet is called an "Assessment Module"): 3 tests (fall, winter, spring) at each of 8 grade levels; each test contains 11 to 22 5-item (levels 1–3) or 10-item (levels 4–8) subtests covering specific objectives; 3 types of scores: individual scores for each objective (a 5- or 10-item subtest), individual mean scores for each test, class mean scores for each objective; Riverside Publishing Co.*

For additional information and reviews by Aaron D. Buchanan and Thomas A. Romberg, see 8:274.

REFERENCES

1. HAMBLETON, R. K., & EIGNOR, D. R. Guidelines for evaluating criterion–referenced tests and test manuals. *Journal of Educational Measurement*, 1978, 15, 321–327.

[1140]

Individual Pupil Monitoring System—Reading. Grades 1, 2, 3, 4, 5, 6; 1974; IPMS—Reading; criterion-referenced; the general skills structure is the same for all grades although some specific skills are not tested in all grades; each test booklet contains from 11 to 29 5-item tests; "each test measuring mastery of one behavioral objective"; 2 types of scores: individual scores for each objective (a 5-item subtest), class mean score for each objective; 3 tests; Riverside Publishing Co.*

a) WORD-ATTACK. Overlapping behavioral objectives in 3 areas: phonics, structure, context.

b) VOCABULARY AND COMPREHENSION. Overlapping behavioral objectives in 2 areas: vocabulary, comprehension.

c) DISCRIMINATION/STUDY SKILLS. Overlapping behavioral objectives in 2 areas: discrimination, study skills.

For additional information and reviews by Dale D. Johnson and Byron H. Van Roekel, see 8:763.

REFERENCES

1. HAMBLETON, R. K., & EIGNOR, D. R. Guidelines for evaluating criterion–referenced tests and test manuals. *Journal of Educational Measurement*, 1978, 15, 321–327.

[1141]

Individual Scale for Indian South Africans. Ages 8–17; 1971; ISISA; adaptation for Indian pupils of the *New South African Individual Scale*; 13 scores: verbal (vocabulary, comprehension, similarities, problems, memory, total), nonverbal (pattern completion, blocks, absurdities, form board, mazes, total), total; R. J. Prinsloo and F. W. O. Heinichen in collaboration with D. J. Swart; Human Sciences Research Council [South Africa].*

[1142]

Individualized Criterion Referenced Testing: Math. Grades 1, 2, 3, 4, 5, 6, 7, 8; 1973–77; ICRTM; 8 levels consisting of 39 tests covering 312 overlapping specific-objective subtests (2 items each) not classified other than by grade; separate 2-item tests, called *Benchmarks: Math*, are available for each of the 312 objectives; Educational Development Corporation.* (In-print status uncertain; no reply from publisher.)

For additional information and a review by Jane Dass, see 8:275.

[1143]

Individualized Criterion Referenced Testing: Reading. Grades kgn, 1, 2, 3, 4, 5, 6, 7, 8; 1973–76; ICRTR; 9 levels consisting of 46 tests covering 345 overlapping specific-objective subtests not classified other than by grade; separate 2-item tests, called *Benchmarks: Reading*, are available for each of the 288 objectives for grades 1–8; Educational Development Corporation.* (In-print status uncertain; no reply from publisher.)

For additional information and reviews by Ruth N. Hartley and Martin Kling, see 8:764.

[1144]

Industrial Arts Aptitude Battery: Woodworking Test. Grades 7–14; 1974; Robert Dale Hogan, Elton Amburn, and Dale Kevin Hogan; Bureau of Educational Measurements.*

For additional information, see 8:419 (1 reference).

[1145]

★**Industrial Reading Test.** Grade 9 and over vocational students and applicants or trainees in technical or vocational training programs; 1976–78; IRT; ability to comprehend written technical materials; Psychological Measurement Division; The Psychological Corporation.*

[1146]

The Industrial Sentence Completion Form. Employee applicants; 1963; ISCF; experimental form; no manual; Martin M. Bruce; Martin M. Bruce, Ph.D., Publishers.*

For additional information, see P:445.

[1147]

★**Infant Rating Scale.** Ages 5, 7; 1981; IRS; ratings by teachers for screening and early intervention; 2 levels; Geoff A. Lindsay; Hodder & Stoughton Educational [England].*
a) LEVEL 1. Age 5; 6 scores: language, early learning, behaviour, social integration, general development, total.
b) LEVEL 2. Age 7; 6 scores: language/education, fine motor skills, behaviour, social integration, general development, total.

[1148]

Inferred Self-Concept Scale. Grades 1–6; 1969–73; ISCS; ratings by teachers and counselors; E. L. McDaniel; Western Psychological Services.*

For additional information and a review by Norman D. Sundberg, see 8:584; see also T2:1231 (1 reference).

[1149]

★**Informal Evaluation of Oral Reading Grade Level.** Ages 5–11 and adolescents and adults with reading difficulties; 1973; 2 scores: oral comprehension level, reading level (independent, instructional, or frustration); Deborah Edel; Book-Lab, Inc.*

[1150]

Information Test on Drugs and Drug Abuse. Grades 9–16 and adults; 1957–68; for research use only; no manual; H. Frederick Kilander; Glenn C. Leach, Publisher.*

[1151]

Information Test on Human Reproduction. Grades 9–16 and adults; 1950–67; for research use only; no manual; H. Frederick Kilander; Glenn C. Leach, Publisher.*

See T2:934 (1 reference).

[1152]

Informeter: An International Technique for the Measurement of Political Information. Older adolescents and adults; 1972; no manual; Panos D. Bardis; the Author.*

For additional information, see 8:922.

[1153]

The Ingram Edinburgh Articulation Test. Ages 3–0 to 6–0; 1971; EAT; formerly called *The Edinburgh Articulation Test*; T. T. S. Ingram, A. Anthony, D. Bogle, and M. W. McIsaac; Churchill Livingstone [Scotland].*
(United States distributor: Longman, Inc.)

For additional information, reviews by Harold A. Peterson and Joel Stark, and excerpted reviews by P. Margot Harrison, Hazel Francis, and Robert Fawcus, see 8:959 (5 references); see also T2:2070 (1 reference).

REFERENCES

1. See T2:2070.
2–6. See 8:959.
7. JOHNSON, S., & SOMERS, H. Spontaneous and imitated responses in articulation testing. *British Journal of Disorders of Communication*, 1978, 13, 107–116.
8. D'SOUZA, S. W., MCCARTNEY, E., NOLAN, M., & TAYLOR, I. G. Hearing, speech, and language in survivors of severe perinatal asphyxia. *Archives of Diseases in Childhood*, 1981, 56, 245–252.
9. HOWELL, J., SKINNER, C., GRAY, M., & BROOMFIELD, S. A study of the comparative effectiveness of different language tests with two groups of children. *British Journal of Disorders of Communication*, 1981, 16, 31–42.
10. WILLIAMS, A. J., WILLIAMS, M. A., WALKER, C. A., & BUSH, P. G. The Robin Anomalad (Pierre Robin Syndrome)—A follow up study. *Archives of Diseases in Childhood*, 1981, 56, 663–668.

[1154-5]

★**Initial Placement Inventory.** Grades 1, 2, 3, 4, 5, 6, 7, 8; 1980; IPI; designed to help place students in SERIES "r", Macmillan Reading Program; 8 scores in 3 areas: silent reading (number of correct answers, reading level, placement level), word recognition (number of words correct), oral reading (number of decoding errors, reading level, number of correct comprehension questions, reading level); Madeline A. Weinstein; Macmillan Publishing Co., Inc.*

[1156]

*****The Instant Word Recognition Test.** Primary grades and remedial reading situations; 1971–77; criterion-referenced test; item scores only; Edward Fry; Jamestown Publishers.*

For additional information, a review by Priscilla Drum, and an excerpted review by Paula Altmann Fuld of the 1971 edition, see 8:780 (1 reference).

[1157]

★**The Instant Words Criterion Test.** Elementary students; 1980; criterion-referenced test of students' sight reading abilities with 300 common words with and without suffixes; item scores only; Edward Fry; Jamestown Publishers.*

[1158]

Institutional Functioning Inventory. College faculty and administrators; 1968–70; IFI; a measure of perceived institutional vitality; the first half of the inventory may be used with students; for research use only; 11 scores: intellectual-aesthetic extracurriculum, freedom, human diversity, concern for improvement of society, concern for undergraduate learning, democratic governance, meeting local needs, self-study and planning, concern for advancing knowledge, concern for innovation, institutional esprit; Richard E. Peterson, John A. Centra, Rodney T. Hartnett and Robert L. Linn; Educational Testing Service.*

For additional information, see 8:586 (24 references); see also T2:1234 (2 references); for reviews by Paul L. Dressel and Clifford E. Lunneborg, see 7:89 (3 references).

REFERENCES

1–3. See 7:89.
4–5. See T2:1234.

6–29. See 8:586.
30. PETERSON, A. V. Men share their perceptions of university student life environment. *College Student Journal*, 1977, 11, 128–131.
31. STAPPENBECK, H. A practical approach to institutional self–study in higher education. *North Central Association Quarterly*, 1978, 52, 464–471.
32. BORLING, J. E. The effects of sedative music on alpha rhythms and focused attention in high–creative and low–creative subjects. *Journal of Music Therapy*, 1981, 18, 101–108.

[1159]

Institutional Goals Inventory. College faculty and students and other subgroups; 1972–77; IGI; for measurement of groups, not individuals; "to help college communities delineate goals and establish priorities among them"; 3 scores (goal is, goal should be, discrepancy) for total group and each subgroup for each of 90 goal statements and each of 20 goal summary areas (based on 80 of the goal statements): academic development, intellectual orientation, individual personal development, humanism/altruism, cultural/aesthetic awareness, traditional religiousness, vocational preparation, advanced training, research, meeting local needs, public service, social egalitarianism, social criticism/activism, freedom, democratic governance, community, intellectual/aesthetic environment, innovation, off-campus learning, accountability/ efficiency; 20 local goal statements may be added; (French Canadian and English Canadian editions available); comparative data by Richard E. Peterson and Norman P. Uhl; Institutional Research Program for Higher Education; Educational Testing Service.*

For additional information and reviews by Clifford E. Lunneborg and M. Y. Quereshi, see 8:375 (31 references); see also T2:1235 (2 references).

[1160]

★**Instructional Styles Inventory.** Instructors; 1976; may be used either in conjunction with or independent of *Learning Styles Inventory* (1310); self-report inventory; 17 scores in 4 areas: conditions (peer, organization, goal setting, competition, instructor, detail, independence, authority), content (numeric, qualitative, inanimate, people), mode (talking, readings, iconics, direct experience), influence; Albert A. Canfield and Judith S. Canfield; Humanics Media.*

[1161]

★**Instrument for Disability Screening, [Developmental Edition].** Primary grade children; 1980; IDS; ratings by teachers; 9 scores: hyperactive/aggressive, visual, speech/auditory, reading, drawing/writing, inactivity, concepts, psychomotor development, total; James R. Beatty; the Author.*

REFERENCES
1. BEATTY, J. R. The analysis of an instrument for screening learning disabilities. *Journal of Learning Disabilities*, 1975, 8, 58–64.
2. BEATTY, J. R. Identifying decision–making policies in the diagnosis of learning disabilities. *Journal of Learning Disabilities*, 1977, 10, 13–21.
3. BEATTY, J. R. Construct validation of an instrument for screening learning disabilities. *Journal of Learning Disabilities*, 1979, 12, 58–65.

[1162]

The Integration Level Test Series. Adults; 1965–66; ILTS; for research use only; 8 tests; no manual (except for *Sex Inventory* and *Ideological Survey*); Frederick C. Thorne; Clinical Psychology Publishing Co., Inc.*

a) PERSONAL HEALTH SURVEY. PHS; physical and mental symptoms related to mental health; 12 scores: general health, general development, gastro-intestinal system, cardio-vascular system, miscellaneous systems, central nervous system, neuro-muscular systems, anxiety-fear states, anger-frustration states, schizophrenia, affective psychoses, character disorders.

b) THE SEX INVENTORY. SI; 2 editions.

1) *Male Form.* 9 scores: sex drive and interest, sexual maladjustment and frustration, neurotic conflict associated with sex, sexual cathexes and fixations, repression of sexuality, loss of sex controls, homosexuality, sex role confidence, promiscuity and sociopathic tendency.

2) *Female Form.* 11 scores: sex drive and interest, sex maladjustment and frustration, neurotic conflict over sex, sexual cathexes and fixations, sexual repression, sex control, homosexuality, sex role confidence, sexual psychopathy, nymphomania, sexual frigidity.

c) THE IDEOLOGICAL SURVEY. IS; factors contributing to a person's conception of the place of man in the world; 13 scores: 5 scores reflecting individualism and capitalism (morality and reason, rational self-interest, self-sufficiency, self-responsibility, earning and creativity), 8 scores reflecting collectivism and socialism (altruism and morality, socialism, collectivism, insecurity and defensiveness, dependency, inadequacy, rationalizing failure, work attitudes).

d) SOCIAL STATUS STUDY. SSS; 10 role scores: citizen, social person, social class, parent and family, financial manager, sex partner, worker, marriage partner, leader-follower, political.

e) THE PERSONAL DEVELOPMENT STUDY. PDS; utilization of classical Freudian mechanisms in personality structure; 10 scores: repression, regression, projection, identification, rationalization, reaction formations, extrapunitiveness, intropunitiveness, impunitiveness, miscellaneous mechanisms.

f) THE EXISTENTIAL STUDY. EA; also called *Existential Analysis*; state of being in the world; 7 scores: self-status, self-actualization, existential morale, existential vacuum, humanistic identification, existence and destiny, suicide.

g) THE LIFE STYLE ANALYSIS. LSA; Adlerian life style patterns in relation to the Murray need systems; 30 scores: 10 characteristic life styles (normal coping, individual, exploitive, pampered-spoiled, defiant-resistive, domineering-authoritarian, conforming, escapist, oneupmanship, evasive-ignoring), 20 Murray needs (abasement, achievement, affiliation, aggression, autonomy, blame avoidance, counteraction, defendance, deference, dominance, exhibition, harm avoidance, inferiority avoidance, nurturance, order, play, rejection, sentience, succorance, understanding).

h) THE FEMININITY STUDY. FS; special situational problems of women in modern culture; 11 scores: feminine social role, female parent role, feminine career role, female homemaker role, female role confidence, female sex identification, development and maturation, sex drive and interests, promiscuity, homosexuality, health and neurotic conflict.

See T2:1237 (5 references) and P:125A (12 references).

REFERENCES
1–12. See P:125A.
13–17. See T2:1237.
18. PISHKIN, V., & THORNE, F. C. A factorial study of personal development of unmarried mothers, college, alcoholic, and schizophrenic populations. *Journal of Clinical Psychology*, 1977, 33, 609–617.
19. THORNE, F. C. The personal development study. *Journal of Clinical Psychology*, 1977, 33, 604–608.

20. THORNE, F. C., & PISHKIN, V. The factorial structure of personal development mechanisms in unmarried mothers, college, alcoholic, and schizophrenic populations. *Journal of Clinical Psychology*, 1977, 33, 618–624.

21. HOWELLS, K., & WRIGHT, E. The sexual attitudes of aggressive sexual offenders. *British Journal of Criminology*, 1978, 18, 170–174.

[1163]

*Interest Check List, 1979 Edition. Grades 9–12 and adults; 1946–79; ICL; interviewing aid; 1979 edition a completely new revision oriented to the occupational coding structure of the *USES Guide for Occupational Exploration*; developed and published by the United States Employment Service; distributed by the United States Government Printing Office.*

See T2:2190 (2 references) and 5:860; for reviews by Milton L. Blum and Howard R. Taylor of the original edition, see 4:741.

[1164]

★Interest Determination, Exploration and Assessment System. Grades 6–12; 1977–80; IDEAS; self-scorable; 14 scores: mechanical/fixing, electronics, nature/outdoors, science, numbers, writing, arts/crafts, social service, child care, medical service, business, sales, office practices, food service; Charles B. Johansson; NCS Interpretive Scoring Systems.*

[1165]

Interest Inventory for Elementary Grades: George Washington University Series. Grades 4–6; 1941; IIEG; 11 scores: reading, movies, radio, games and toys, hobbies, things to own, school subjects, people, occupations, activities, total; Mitchell Dreese and Elizabeth Mooney; Center for Psychological Service.* (In-print status uncertain; no reply from publisher.)

See T2:1238 (1 reference) and P:126 (4 references); for reviews by Harold D. Carter and Lee J. Cronbach, see 3:52 (1 reference).

[1166]

Interest Questionnaire for Indian South Africans. Standards 6–10; 1969–71; IQISA; 7 scores: language, arts, social service, science, mechanics, business, office work; S. Oosthuizen; Human Sciences Research Council [South Africa].*

[1167]

Intermediate Personality Questionnaire for Indian Pupils (Standards 6 to 8). Standards 6–8; 1974; IPQI; 10 scores: social extraversion, verbal intelligence, emotional stability, adventuresomeness, creativity, dominance, perseverance, relaxedness, spirit of enterprise, environmental relatedness; S. Oosthuizen; Human Sciences Research Council [South Africa].*

For additional information, see 8:587.

[1168]

Inter-Person Perception Test. Ages 6 and over; 1969; IPPT; F. K. Heussenstamm and R. Hoepfner; Monitor.*

For additional information and reviews by Jane Loevinger and Norman D. Sundberg, see 8:588.

REFERENCES

1. LIVINGSTON, S. A. Nonverbal communication tests as predictors of success in psychology and counseling. *Applied Psychological Measurement*, 1981, 5, 325–331.

[1169]

★Interpersonal Behavior Survey. Grades 9–16 and adults; 1980; IBS; distinguishes assertive behaviors from aggressive behaviors; 21 scores: denial, infrequency, impression management, general aggressiveness-rational, hostile stance, expression of anger, disregard for rights, verbal aggressiveness, physical aggressiveness, passive aggressiveness, general assertiveness-rational, self-confidence, initiating assertiveness, defending assertiveness, frankness, praise, requesting help, refusing demands, conflict avoidance, dependency, shyness, plus 2 additional scores (general aggressiveness-empirical, general assertiveness-empirical) and 10 short-form scores; Paul A. Mauger, David R. Adkinson, Suzanne K. Zoss (test), Gregory Firestone (test), and J. David Hook (test); Western Psychological Services.*

[1170]

Interpersonal Check List. Adults; 1955–73; ICL; for research use only; 4 summary scores (dominance, love, average intensity, acquiescence) or 20 detail scores (managerial, self-confident, competitive, critical, hostile, resentful, distrustful, self-critical, submissive, dependent, trusting, agreeable, friendly, sympathetic, nurturant, impressive, 4 level of intensity scores) at 1–2 levels of personality: descriptions by others, descriptions by self (including ego ideal); Rolfe LaForge, Timothy Leary (test), Robert Suczek (test), and Mervin Freedman (test); Rolfe LaForge.*

See T2:1240 (115 references) and P:127 (70 references); for a review by P. M. Bentler, see 6:127 (39 references).

REFERENCES

1–39. See 6:127.
40–109. See P:127.
110–224. See T2:1240.

225. HUME, N., & GOLDSTEIN, G. Is there an association between astrological data and personality? *Journal of Clinical Psychology*, 1977, 33, 711–713.

226. HURWITZ, J. I., & DAYA, D. K. Non-help–seeking wives of employed alcoholics: A multilevel interpersonal profile. *Journal of Studies on Alcohol*, 1977, 38, 1730–1739.

227. LUBER, R. F., & WELLS, R. A. Structured, short–term multiple family therapy: An educational approach. *International Journal of Group Psychotherapy*, 1977, 27, 43–58.

228. REIN, I. Medical and nursing students: Concepts of self and ideal self, typical and ideal work partner. *Journal of Personality Assessment*, 1977, 41, 368–374.

229. RO-TROCK, G. K., WELLISCH, D. K., & SCHOOLAR, J. C. A family therapy outcome study in an inpatient setting. *American Journal of Orthopsychiatry*, 1977, 47, 514–522.

230. BURKE, E. L., ZILBERG, N. J., AMINI, F., SALASNEK, S., & FORKIN, D. Some empirical evidence for Erickson's concept of negative identity in delinquent adolescent drug abusers. *Comprehensive Psychiatry*, 1978, 19, 141–152.

231. FERGUSON, L. R., & ALLEN, D. R. Congruence of parental perception, marital satisfaction, and child adjustment. *Journal of Consulting & Clinical Psychology*, 1978, 46, 345–346.

232. FITZGERALD, J. M. Actual and perceived sex and generational differences in interpersonal style: Structural and quantitative issues. *Journal of Gerontology*, 1978, 33, 394–401.

233. DRENNEN, W., & PUGH, M. The use of a contract to facilitate sensitivity training. *Journal of Humanistic Psychology*, 1979, 19, 77–84.

234. LEWIS, R. A., FRENEAU, P. J., & ROBERTS, C. L. Fathers and the postparental transition. *Family Coordinator*, 1979, 28, 514–520.

235. TRUCKENMILLER, J. L., & SCHAIE, K. W. Multilevel structural validation of Leary's interpersonal diagnosis system. *Journal of Consulting & Clinical Psychology*, 1979, 47, 1030–1045.

236. UNGERLEIDER, J. T., & WELLISCH, D. K. Coercive persuasion (brainwashing), religious cults, and deprogramming. *American Journal of Psychiatry*, 1979, 136, 279–282.

237. HARTLAGE, L. C., & SPEER, E. V. Patient preferences with regard to ideal therapist characteristics. *Journal of Clinical Psychology*, 1980, 36, 288–291.

238. LYONS, J., HIRSCHBERG, N., & WILKINSON, L. The radex structure of the Leary interpersonal behavior circle. *Multivariate Behavioral Research*, 1980, 15, 249–257.
239. LEES–HALEY, P. R. College norms for the Leary Interpersonal Checklist. *Journal of Consulting & Clinical Psychology*, 1981, 49, 302–303.
240. MCCORMICK, C. C., & KAVANAGH, J. A. Scaling interpersonal checklist items to a circular model. *Applied Psychological Measurement*, 1981, 5, 421–447.

[1171]
Interpersonal Communication Inventory. Grades 9–16 and adults; 1969–76; ICI; Millard J. Bienvenu, Sr.; the Author.*

For additional information, see 8:589 (3 references); see also T2:1241 (1 reference).

REFERENCES

1. See T2:1241.
2–4. See 8:589.
5. CAMPBELL, B. K., & BARNBIND, D. C. Communication patterns and problems of pregnancy. *American Journal of Orthopsychiatry*, 1977, 47, 134–139.
6. ALLRED, G. H., & GRAFF, T. T. Improving students' interpersonal communication. *Journal of College Student Personnel*, 1980, 21, 155–162.

[1172]
★**Interpersonal Conflict Scales.** Adults; 1981; experimental edition; "designed for the reporting of perceived feelings to statements about spouse behavior"; 8 scores: agreement in thinking, communication, disagreement in behavior, perception of the other's feelings, companionship and sharing, emotional satisfaction, security, recognition; Carol Hoskins and Philip Merrifield; Family Life Publications, Inc.*

[1173]
★**Interpersonal Style Inventory.** High school and college and adults; 1977–82; ISI; 15 scores: directive-nondirective, sociable-detached, help seeking-self sufficient, nurturant-withholding, conscientious-expedient, trusting-cynical, tolerant-hostile, sensitive-lacks awareness, independent-conforming, rule free-rule bound, deliberate-impulsive, orderly-casual, persistent-lacks perseverance, stable/relaxed-anxious, approval seeking-admits frailties; Maurice Lorr and Richard P. Youniss; Maurice Lorr.*

REFERENCES

1. LORR, M., O'CONNOR, J. P., & SEIFERT, R. F. A comparison of four personality inventories. *Journal of Personality Assessment*, 1977, 41, 520–526.

[1174]
Intra- and Interpersonal Relations Scale. Bantu pupils in Forms IV and V; 1973–75; IIPS; 4 scores: self-image, mother-child relationship, father-child relationship, ideal self; G. G. Minnaar; Human Science Research Council [South Africa].*

For additional information, see 8:590.

[1175]
Introducing Career Concepts Inventory. Grades 5–7, 7–9; 1975; to be used as part of an instructional program; 2 levels; A. Joanne Holloway and Joan T. Naper; Science Research Associates, Inc.*

a) SERIES 1. Grades 5–7; 7 scores: interests, focus, school subjects, abilities, work features, work settings, total.
b) SERIES 2. Grades 7–9; 7 scores: work styles, work roles, skill development, training needs, income patterns, employment opportunities, total.

For additional information, see 8:1007.

[1176]
Intuitive Mechanics (Weights & Pulleys). Engineering students and industrial workers; 1956–59; ability to visualize internal movement or displacement of parts; L. L. Thurstone and T. E. Jeffrey; Human Resources Center, University of Chicago.*

[1177]
Inventory No. 2. Ages 16 and over; 1956; "a mental ability test"; Stevens, Thurow and Associates, Inc.*

For additional information, see 6:463.

[1178]
Inventory of Anger Communication. High school and adults; 1974–76; IAC; Millard J. Bienvenu, Sr.; the Author.*

For additional information, see 8:591 (1 reference).

[1179]
An Inventory of Certain Feelings. Applicants for employment; 1952; preoccupation with anxieties; Maurice H. Krout; distributed by Johanna Krout Tabin.*

[1180]
★**Inventory of Individually Perceived Group Cohesiveness.** Group members grades 5 and over; 1979–80; IIPGC; "self-report, 20-item measure of an individual's perceptions of cooperation, control, and task influence processes operating in a group"; 4 scores: cooperation, control, task influence, total; David L. Johnson; Stoelting Co.*

[1181]
★**Inventory of Interests.** Adolescents and adults; 1971; designed for use by counselors; ratings in 2 areas: occupations, subjects for study; (Spanish edition available); Guidance Testing Associates.* (In-print status uncertain; no reply from publisher.)

[1182]
An Inventory of Primary Skills. Grades kgn–1; 1970; IPS; administered by parent; 20 scores: self information, body identification, body spatial relations, copying designs, alphabet printing, writing numbers, symbol matching, sentence copying, counting, basic arithmetic, copying house, draw-a-man, sight vocabulary, paragraph reading, alphabet knowledge, number knowledge, class concepts, position in space concepts, descriptive concepts, total; no manual; Robert E. Valett; Fearon Education.*

[1183]
An Inventory of Religious Activities and Interests. High school and college students considering church-related occupations and theological school students; 1967–70; IRAI; for research use only; 11 scales: counselor, administrator, teacher, scholar, evangelist, spiritual guide, preacher, reformer, priest, musician, check scale; Sam C. Webb; Ministry Inventories.*

See T2:1025A (2 references); for a review by Donald G. Zytowski, see 7:1023.

REFERENCES

1–2. See T2:1025A.
3. WEBB, S. C., HULTGEN, D. D., & CRADDICK, R. A. Predicting occupational choice by clinical and statistical methods. *Journal of Counseling Psychology*, 1977, 24, 98–110.

[1184]
★**Inventory of Self-Hypnosis.** College and adults; 1978; adaptation of *Harvard Group Scale of Hypnotic Susceptibility, Form A*; self-administered instructions designed to teach self-hypnosis; 13 ratings: head falling, eye closure, lowering left hand, immobilization of right arm, finger lock, rigidity of left arm, hands moving together, inability to shake head, vivid imagining of a fly, eyelids glued shut, touching left ankle, blanketing fog, total; Ronald E. Shor; Consulting Psychologists Press, Inc.*

[1185]
Inventory of Teacher Knowledge of Reading, Revised Edition. Elementary school teachers and college students in methods courses; 1971–75; no manual; A. Sterl Artley and Veralee B. Hardin; Lucas Brothers Publishers.*

For additional information and an excerpted review by Daniel T. Fishco, see 8:781 (6 references).

REFERENCES

1–6. See 8:781.
7. RORIE, I. L. Analysis and validation of the revised Inventory of Teacher Knowledge of Reading. *Journal of Reading*, 1978, 21, 606–607.
8. ELLSWORTH, R., & MILLER, J. W. A validation study of the Inventory of Teacher Knowledge of Reading. *Educational & Psychological Measurement*, 1980, 40, 537–542.
9. JONES, L. L., & HAYES, A. E. How valid are surveys of teacher needs? *Educational & Psychological Measurement*, 1980, 37, 390–392.

[1186]
Inventory of Vocational Interests: Acorn National Aptitude Tests. Grades 7–16 and adults; 1943–60; 5 scores: mechanical, academic, artistic, business and economic, farm-agricultural; Andrew Kobal, J. Wayne Wrightstone, and Karl R. Kunze; Psychometric Affiliates.*

For additional information and a review by John W. French, see 6:1060; for reviews by Marion A. Bills, Edward S. Bordin, Harold D. Carter, and Patrick Slater, see 3:638.

[1187]
Inventory-Survey Tests. Grades 4–6, 7–8; 1968–69; IST; 6 scores: word meaning, sentence meaning, paragraph meaning, word analysis, dictionary skills, total; 2 levels, only 1 level currently in print; Marion Monroe; Scott, Foresman & Co.*
a) INVENTORY-SURVEY TEST FOR INTERMEDIATE GRADES. Grades 4–6.
b) INVENTORY-SURVEY TEST FOR UPPER GRADES. Grades 7–8. *Out of print.*

[1188]
Iowa Algebra Aptitude Test, Third Edition. Grade 8; 1931–69; IAAT; H. A. Greene and Darrell Sabers; Bureau of Educational Research and Service.*

See T2:681 (7 references); for reviews by W. L. Bashaw and Cyril J. Hoyt, and an excerpted review by Russell A. Chadbourn, see 7:505 (8 references); for reviews by Harold Gulliksen and Emma Spaney of an earlier edition, see 4:393; for a review by David Segel, see 3:327 (2 references); for reviews by Richard M. Drake and M. W. Richardson, see 2:1441 (1 reference).

[1189]
Iowa Geometry Aptitude Test, Third Edition. High school; 1935–69; IGAT; revision of *Iowa Plane Geometry Aptitude Test*; James Maxey and Darrell Sabers; Bureau of Educational Research and Service.*

See T2:751 (2 references); for a review by Lynnette B. Plumlee, see 7:537 (2 references); for a review by Philip H. DuBois of an earlier edition, see 3:360; for reviews by Edward E. Cureton and Charles C. Weidemann, see 2:1469.

[1190]
★**Iowa Parent Behavior Inventory.** Parents; 1976–79; IPBI; ratings by parents of their behavior in relation to their child; Sedahlia Jasper Crase, Samuel G. Clark, and Damaris Pease; Iowa State University Research Foundation, Inc.*
a) MOTHER FORM. 1977; 6 scores: parental involvement, limit setting, responsiveness, reasoning guidance, free expression, intimacy.
b) FATHER FORM. 1977; 5 scores: parental involvement, limit setting, responsiveness, reasoning guidance, intimacy.

[1191]
Iowa Silent Reading Tests. Grades 6–9, 9–14, 11–16; 1927–73; ISRT; 3 levels; coordinating editor: Roger Farr; The Psychological Corporation.*
a) LEVEL 1. Grades 6–9; 5 scores: vocabulary, reading comprehension, total, directed reading, reading efficiency.
b) LEVEL 2. Grades 9–14; 5 scores: same as for *a*.
c) LEVEL 3. Grades 11–16; 4 scores: vocabulary, reading comprehension, total, reading efficiency.

For additional information, reviews by Nikola N. Filby and A. Ralph Hakstian, and excerpted reviews by Frederick B. Davis, and Russell Hunter and Ralph Hoepfner, see 8:730 (9 references); see also T2:1560 (42 references); for a review by Worth R. Jones of an earlier edition, see 6:794 (40 references); for reviews by Frederick B. Davis and William W. Turnbull and excerpted reviews by Earl R. Gabler and Margaret Pankaskie, see 3:489 (21 references); for reviews by Ivan A. Booker and Holland D. Roberts, see 2:1547 (6 references).

REFERENCES

1–6. See 2:1547.
7–27. See 3:489.
28–67. See 6:794.
68–109. See T2:1560.
110–118. See 8:730.
119. ALEXANDER, C. F. Adding to usefulness of standardized reading tests in college programs. *Journal of Reading*, 1977, 20, 288–291.
120. HAYWARD, K. G., ORLANDO, V. P., & BLIESMER, E. P. Effectiveness of a study management course for "non-traditional" students. *National Reading Conference Yearbook*, 1977, 17–20.
121. COIL, A. College reading needs: Beyond 'filling the bin.' *42nd Claremont Reading Conference Yearbook*, 1978, 219–225.
122. COULSON, J. E. National evaluation of the Emergency School Aid Act (ESAA): A review of methodological issues. *Journal of Educational Statistics*, 1978, 3, 1–60.
123. FOWLER, B., & KROLL, B. M. Verbal skills as factors in the passageless validation of reading comprehension tests. *Perceptual & Motor Skills*, 1978, 47, 335–338.
124. MCPHAIL, I. P. A psycholinguistic approach to training urban high school students in test-taking strategies. *Journal of Negro Education*, 1978, 47, 168–176.
125. SMITH-BURKE, M., GINGRICH, P. S., & EAGLEEYE, D. Differential effects of prior context, style and deletion pattern on cloze comprehension. *National Reading Conference Yearbook*, 1978, 133–137.

126. WAID, L. R., KANOY, R. C., III, BLICK, K. A., & WALKER W. E. Relationship of state–trait anxiety and type of practice to reading comprehension. *Journal of Psychology*, 1978, 98, 27–36.
127. DIVESTA, F. J., HAYWARD, K. G., & ORLANDO, V. P. Development trends in monitoring text for comprehension. *Child Development*, 1979, 50, 97–105.
128. GRABE, M., & PRENTICE, W. The impact of reading competence on the ability to take a perspective. *Journal of Reading Behavior*, 1979, 11, 21–25.
129. WEINER, M., & ZIBRIN, M. Dissimilarities in grade–equivalent scores on different standardized tests of achievement: A threat to criterion-related validity. *Educational & Psychological Measurement*, 1979, 39, 923–928.

[1192]
*Iowa Tests of Basic Skills, Forms 7 and 8.
Grades kgn.1–1.5, kgn.8–1.9, 1.7–2.6, 2.7–3.5, 3, 4, 5, 6, 7, 8–9; 1955–79; ITBS; previous edition still available; A. N. Hieronymus, E. F. Lindquist, H. D. Hoover, and others; Riverside Publishing Co.*

a) PRIMARY BATTERY: LEVELS 5–8. Grades kgn.1–1.5, kgn.8–1.9, 1.7–2.6, 2.7–3.5; 1978–79.

1) *level* 5. Grades kgn.1–1.5; 5 scores: listening, vocabulary, word analysis, language, mathematics.

2) *level* 6. Grades kgn.8–1.9; 6 scores: listening, vocabulary, word analysis, reading, language, mathematics.

3) *level* 7. Grades 1.7–2.6; 2 batteries.
  (*a*) Basic Battery. 9 scores: vocabulary, word analysis, reading comprehension (pictures, sentences, stories), language skills (spelling), mathematics skills (concepts, problems, computation).
  (*b*) Complete Battery. 15 scores: 9 scores from Basic Battery plus listening, language skills (capitalization, punctuation, usage), work study skills (visual materials, reference materials).

4) *level* 8. Grades 2.7–3.5; details same as for Level 7.

b) MULTILEVEL EDITION: LEVELS 9–14. Grades 3, 4, 5, 6, 7, 8–9; 1978–79.

For additional information and reviews by Larry A. Harris and Fred Pyrczak of Forms 5–6, see 8:19 (58 references); see also T2:19 (87 references) and 6:13 (17 references); for reviews by Virgil E. Herrick, G. A. V. Morgan, and H. H. Remmers, and an excerpted review by Laurence Siegel of Forms 1–2, see 5:16. For reviews of the modern mathematics supplement, see 7:481 (2 reviews).

REFERENCES
1–17. See 6:13.
18–104. See T2:19.
105–162. See 8:19.

163. EARLY, G. H., GRISSOM, W. M., LABRENTZ, E. L., DEFELICE, G., & MCCLAIN, N. J. Intermodal abilities as predictors of academic achievement. *Academic Therapy*, 1976–1977, 12, 163–169.
164. AMES, C., AMES, R., & FELKER, D. W. Effects of competitive reward structure and valence of outcome on children's achievement attributions. *Journal of Educational Psychology*, 1977, 69, 1–8.
165. CECCONI, C. P., HOOD, S. B., & TUCKER, R. K. Influence of reading level difficulty on the disfluencies of normal children. *Journal of Speech & Hearing Research*, 1977, 20, 475–484.
166. COHEN, R. B., & BRADLEY, R. H. Teaching superordinate concepts with simulation games. *Alberta Journal of Educational Research*, 1977, 23, 298–304.
167. COKER, H., & LORENTZ, J. L. Growth in reading as a correlate of pupil classroom behavior. In P. D. Pearson & J. Hansen (Eds.), *Reading: Theory, research, and practice; Twenty-sixth yearbook of the National Reading Conference*. Clemson, South Carolina: The National Reading Conference Inc., 1977.
168. GOOD, T. L., & GROUWS, D. A. Teaching effects: A process–product study in fourth-grade mathematics classrooms. *Journal of Teacher Education*, 1977, 28, 49–54.
169. GORDON, D. A. Children's beliefs in internal–external control and self-esteem as related to academic achievement. *Journal of Personality Assessment*, 1977, 41, 383–386.
170. KAISER, H. E., & SILLIN, P. C. Guidance effectiveness in the elementary schools. *Elementary School Guidance & Counseling*, 1977, 12, 61–64.
171. LEHRER, B. E., & HIERONYMUS, A. N. Predicting achievement using intellectual, academic–motivational and selected non-intellectual factors. *Journal of Experimental Education*, 1977, 45, 44–51.
172. MCCAIG, R. A. What your director of instruction needs to know about standardized English tests. *Language Arts*, 1977, 54, 491–495.
173. MCKINNEY, J. D., & FORMAN, S. G. Factor structure of the Wallach–Kogan tests of creativity and measures of intelligence and achievement. *Psychology in the Schools*, 1977, 14, 41–44.
174. MCPARTLAND, J. M., & EPSTEIN, J. L. Open schools and achievement: Extended tests of a finding of no relationship. *Sociology of Education*, 1977, 50, 133–144.
175. MICHAELS, L. A., & FORSYTH, R. A. Construction and validation of an instrument measuring certain attitudes toward mathematics. *Educational & Psychological Measurement*, 1977, 37, 1043–1049.
176. NICHOLS, N. J., & MCKINNEY, A. W. Black or white socio-economically disadvantaged pupils– They aren't necessarily inferior. *Journal of Negro Education*, 1977, 46, 443–449.
177. PAYNE, D. A., PERKINS, M. L., ELLETT, C. D., & SHELLENBERGER, S. The validity of student assessments of principals' competencies. *Journal of Educational Research*, 1977, 70, 156–159.
178. PENMAN, K. A., CHRISTOPHER, J. R., & WOOD, G. S. Using gross motor activity to improve language arts concepts by third grade students. *Research Quarterly*, 1977, 48, 134–137.
179. RENTZ, R. R., & BASHAW, W. L. The National Reference Scale for Reading: An application of the Rasch model. *Journal of Educational Measurement*, 1977, 14, 161–179.
180. RIE, E. D., & RIE, H. E. Recall, retention, and Ritalin. *Journal of Consulting & Clinical Psychology*, 1977, 45, 967–972.
181. SALVIA, J., ALGOZZINE, R., & SHEARE, J. B. Attractiveness and school achievement. *Journal of School Psychology*, 1977, 15, 60–67.
182. SHEEHAN, D. S., & MARCUS, M. The effects of teacher race and student race on vocabulary and mathematics achievement. *Journal of Educational Research*, 1977, 70, 123–126.
183. THOMPSON, A. J., & SILVERMAN, E. M. Children's comprehension of time-compressed speech: Effects of speaker's familiarities. *Perceptual & Motor Skills*, 1977, 45, 1253–1254.
184. WILLIAMS, J. D., BREKKE, B. W., & PETERSON, W. Effect of visual motor program on school achievement: A longitudinal study. *Perceptual & Motor Skills*, 1977, 45, 786.
185. AMES, C. Children's achievement attributions and self-reinforcement: Effects of self-concept and competitive reward structure. *Journal of Educational Psychology*, 1978, 70, 345–355.
186. BERGER, N. S. Why can't John read? Perhaps he's not a good listener? *Journal of Learning Disabilities*, 1978, 11, 633–638.
187. BRUNING, R. H., BURTON, J. K., & BALLERING, M. Visual and auditory memory: Relationships to reading achievement. *Contemporary Educational Psychology*, 1978, 3, 340–351.
188. BUSSE, T. V., & SERAYDARIAN, L. The relationships between first name desirability and school readiness, IQ, and school achievement. *Psychology in the Schools*, 1978, 15, 297–302.
189. CARTER, D. E., SPERO, A. J., & WALSH, J. A. A comparison of the Visual Aural Digit Span and the Bender Gestalt as discriminators of low achievement in the primary grades. *Psychology in the Schools*, 1978, 15, 194–198.
190. COHEN, R. B., & BRADLEY, R. H. Simulation games, learning, and retention. *Elementary School Journal*, 1978, 78, 247–253.
191. COSTA, A. L. Competency based education: Let's examine the assumptions. *Thrust*, 1978, 7, 26–28.
192. CUNNINGHAM, J. W., & CUNNINGHAM, P. M. Validating a limited–cloze procedure. *Journal of Reading Behavior*, 1978, 10, 211–213.
193. FLOOD, J. E. The influence of first sentences on reader expectations within prose passages. *Reading World*, 1978, 17, 306–315.
194. FORMAN, S. G., & MCKINNEY, J. D. Creativity and achievement of second graders in open and traditional classrooms. *Journal of Educational Psychology*, 1978, 70, 101–107.
195. GOOD, T. L., & BECKERMAN, T. M. An examination of teachers' effects on high, middle, and low aptitude students' performance on a standardized achievement test. *American Educational Research Journal*, 1978, 15, 477–482.
196. GOOD, T. L., GROUWS, D. A., & BECKERMAN, T. M. Curriculum pacing: Some empirical data in mathematics. *Journal of Curriculum Studies*, 1978, 10, 75–81.
197. HALL, P. K., & TOMBLIN, J. B. A follow–up study of children with articulation and language disorders. *Journal of Speech & Hearing Disorders*, 1978, 43, 227–241.
198. HUNTER, J. A., & LOWE, J. D. The use of the WISC–R, Otis, Iowa, and SRBCSS in identifying gifted elementary students. *Southern Journal of Educational Research*, 1978, 12, 59–65.

199. JERSE, F. W., & FAKOURI, M. E. Juvenile delinquency and academic deficiency. *Contemporary Education*, 1978, 49, 106-109.

200. KOSMOSKI, G. J., & VOCKELL, E. L. The learning center: Stimulus to cognitive and affective growth. *Elementary School Journal*, 1978, 79, 47-54.

201. LORENTZ, J. L., & COKER, H. Observed patterns of teacher-pupil classroom behavior as predictors of student growth in reading. *National Reading Conference Yearbook*, 1978, 16-19.

202. MEYER, R. A. Mathematical problem-solving performance and intellectual abilities of fourth-grade children. *Journal for Research in Mathematics Education*, 1978, 9, 334-348.

203. MILLS, C. Is sex role related to intellectual abilities? *Gifted Child Quarterly*, 1978, 22, 536-538.

204. PORTER, A. C., SCHMIDT, W. H., FLODEN, R. E., & FREEMAN, D. J. Practical significance in program evaluation. *American Educational Research Journal*, 1978, 15, 529-539.

205. PRIGGE, G. R. The differential effects of the use of manipulative aids on the learning of geometric concepts by elementary school children. *Journal of Research in Mathematics Education*, 1978, 9, 361-367.

206. RUHLAND, D., GOLD, M., & FELD, S. Role problems and the relationship of achievement motivation to scholastic performance. *Journal of Educational Psychology*, 1978, 70, 950-959.

207. SHEEHAN, D. S., & MARCUS, M. Teacher performance on the National Teacher Examinations and student mathematics and vocabulary achievement. *Journal of Educational Research*, 1978, 71, 134-136.

208. SIMMONS, R. G., BROWN, L., BUSH, D. M., & BLYTH, D. A. Self-esteem and achievement of black and white adolescents. *Social Problems*, 1978, 26, 86-96.

209. THOMPSON, B., ALSTON, H. L., CUNNINGHAM, C. H., & WAKEFIELD, J. A., JR. The relationship of a measure of structure of intellect abilities and academic achievement. *Educational & Psychological Measurement*, 1978, 38, 1207-1210.

210. THOMPSON, B., ALSTON, H. L., & SAY, M. W. Correspondence across three ethnic groups of constructs measured by the Iowa Tests of Basic Skills. *Psychology in the Schools*, 1978, 15, 347-349.

211. WELLS, M. G., & PETERSON, G. V. Kindergarten behavior rating as a predictor of first-grade achievement. *Journal of Learning Disabilities*, 1978, 11, 344-347.

212. BRUININKS, V. L., & MAYER, J. H. Longitudinal study of cognitive abilities and academic achievement. *Perceptual & Motor Skills*, 1979, 48, 1011-1021.

213. DONLON, T. F., EKSTROM, R. B., & LOCKHEED, M. E. The consequences of sex bias in the content of major achievement test batteries. *Measurement & Evaluation in Guidance*, 1979, 11, 202-216.

214. FELD, S., RUHLAND, D., & GOLD, M. Developmental changes in achievement motivation. *Merrill-Palmer Quarterly*, 1979, 25, 43-60.

215. FREDRICK, W. C., WALBERG, H. J., & RASHER, S. P. Time, teacher comments, and achievement in urban high schools. *Journal of Educational Research*, 1979, 73, 63-65.

216. GEORGE, W. C. The talent-search concept: An identification strategy for the intellectually gifted. *Journal of Special Education*, 1979, 13, 221-237.

217. GRAY-LITTLE, B., & APPELBAUM, M. I. Instrumentality effects in the assessment of racial differences in self-esteem. *Journal of Personality & Social Psychology*, 1979, 37, 1221-1229.

218. GUTTENTAG, R. E. Picture-naming interference with good and poor readers. *Perceptual & Motor Skills*, 1979, 49, 67-70.

219. JONES, M. B., & PIKULSKI, J. J. Cloze for the content area teacher. *Reading World*, 1979, 18, 253-258.

220. KENDALL, J. R., & HOOD, J. Investigating the relationship between comprehension and word recognition: Oral reading analysis of children with comprehension or word recognition disabilities. *Journal of Reading Behavior*, 1979, 11, 41-48.

221. LAMB, P. Cloze procedure as a comprehension measure in grade two. *National Reading Conference Yearbook*, 1979, 100-103.

222. MORRIS, J. D., MORGAN, F. B., & MAYNOR, W. On selecting the best set of regression predictors. *Journal of Experimental Education*, 1979-1980, 48, 100-103.

223. PLAKE, B. S. The interpretation of norm-based scores from individualized testing using the Iowa Tests of Basic Skills. *Psychology in the Schools*, 1979, 16, 8-13.

224. ROETTGER, D., SZYMCZUK, M., & MILLARD, J. Validation of a reading attitude scale for elementary students and an investigation of the relationship between attitude and achievement. *Journal of Educational Research*, 1979, 72, 138-142.

225. SCHELL, L. M., & COURTNEY, D. The effect of male teachers on the academic achievement of father-absent sixth grade boys. *Journal of Educational Research*, 1979, 72, 194-196.

226. SHEEHAN, D. S. Black achievement in a desegregated school district. *Journal of Social Psychology*, 1979, 107, 185-192.

227. SILVERMAN, B. Test bias and ability level testing. *Journal of School Psychology*, 1979, 17, 255-259.

228. BLISS, L. B. A test of Lord's assumption regarding examinee guessing behavior on multiple-choice tests using elementary school students. *Journal of Educational Measurement*, 1980, 17, 147-153.

229. BOOK, R. M. Identification of educationally at-risk children during the kindergarten year: A four-year follow-up study of group test performance. *Psychology in the Schools*, 1980, 17, 153-158.

230. CHARLES, R. I. Exemplification and characterization moves in the classroom teaching of geometry concepts. *Journal for Research in Mathematics Education*, 1980, 11, 10-21.

231. COLARUSSO, R., GILL, S., PLANKENHORN, A., & BROOKS, R. Predicting first-grade achievement through formal testing of 5-year-old high-risk children. *Journal of Special Education*, 1980, 14, 355-363.

232. CROSS, L. H., & CROSS, G. M. Teachers' evaluative comments and pupil perception of control. *Journal of Experimental Education*, 1980, 49, 68-71.

233. CUMMINGS, J. A., & NELSON, R. B. Basic concepts in the oral directions of group achievement tests. *Journal of Educational Research*, 1980, 73, 259-261.

234. DIAMOND, E. E. The AMEG commission report on sex bias in achievement testing. *Measurement & Evaluation in Guidance*, 1980, 13, 135-147.

235. FORSYTH, R. A., & SPRATT, K. F. Measuring problem solving ability in mathematics with multiple-choice items: The effect of item format on selected item and test characteristics. *Journal of Educational Measurement*, 1980, 17, 31-43.

236. FOX, G. L., & INAZU, J. K. Patterns and outcomes of mother-daughter communication about sexuality. *Journal of Social Issues*, 1980, 36, 7-29.

237. GETTINGER, M., & WHITE, M. A. Evaluating curriculum fit with class ability. *Journal of Educational Psychology*, 1980, 72, 338-344.

238. GUSKEY, T. R., NORDSTROM, C., & WICK, J. W. Evaluation of a voluntary busing program through cohort comparisons. *Urban Education*, 1980, 15, 3-32.

239. HALLER, E. J., & DAVIS, S. A. Does socioeconomic status bias the assignment of elementary school students to reading groups? *American Educational Research Journal*, 1980, 17, 409-418.

240. IWANICKI, E. F. A new generation of standardized achievement test batteries: A profile of their major features. *Journal of Educational Measurement*, 1980, 17, 155-162.

241. KNIFONG, J. D. Computational requirements of standardized word problem tests. *Journal for Research in Mathematics Education*, 1980, 11, 3-9.

242. KOLATA, G. B. Math and sex: Are girls born with less ability? *Science*, 1980, 210, 1234-1235.

243. LOYD, B. H., FORSYTH, R., & HOOVER, H. D. Relationship of elementary and secondary school achievement test scores to later academic success. *Educational & Psychological Measurement*, 1980, 40, 1117-1124.

244. LOYD, B. H., & HOOVER, H. D. Vertical equating using the Rasch model. *Journal of Educational Measurement*, 1980, 17, 179-193.

245. PAYNE, M. C., JR., DAVENPORT, R. K., DOMANGUE, J. C., & SCROKA, R. D. Reading comprehension and perception of sequentially organized patterns: Intramodal and cross-modal comparisons. *Journal of Learning Disabilities*, 1980, 13, 39-44.

246. PLAKE, B. S. A comparison of a statistical and subjective procedure to ascertain item validity: One step in the test validation process. *Educational & Psychological Measurement*, 1980, 40, 397-404.

247. PLAKE, B. S., HOOVER, H. D., & LOYD, B. H. An investigation of the Iowa Tests of Basic Skills for sex bias: A developmental look. *Psychology in the Schools*, 1980, 17, 47-52.

248. ROGERS, B. G., WILSON, B. J., & HEWETT, G. Canonical variates in longitudinal achievement data. *Psychology in the Schools*, 1980, 17, 496-499.

249. WALBERG, H. J., BOLE, R. E., & WAXMAN, H. C. School-based family socialization and reading achievement in the inner city. *Psychology in the Schools*, 1980, 17, 509-514.

250. GUSKEY, T. R. Comparison of a Rasch model scale and the grade-equivalent scale for vertical equating of test scores. *Applied Psychological Measurement*, 1981, 5, 187-201.

251. HALLER, E. J., & DAVIS, S. A. Teacher perceptions, parental social status and grouping for reading instruction. *Sociology of Education*, 1981, 54, 162-174.

252. HESS, T. M., & RADTKE, R. C. Processing and memory factors in children's reading comprehension skill. *Child Development*, 1981, 52, 479-488.

253. HOSTICKA, A., & TRAUGH, C. A descriptive study of pre-service teachers' attitudes toward and aptitude in mathematics. *College Student Journal*, 1981, 15, 32-37.

254. KLEIN, A. Redundancy in the Iowa Tests of Basic Skills. *Educational & Psychological Measurement*, 1981, 41, 537-544.

255. MAESTAS, L. C. Ethnicity and high school student achievement across rural and urban districts. *Educational Research Quarterly*, 1981, 6, 33-42.

256. OMIZO, M. M., HAMMETT, V. L., LOFFREDO, D. A., & MICHAEL, W. B. The dimensions of self-concept (DOSC) as predictors of

academic achievement among Mexican–American junior high school students. *Educational & Psychological Measurement*, 1981, 41, 835–842.

257. PANAGOS, J. L., HOLMES, R. L., THURMAN, R. L., YARD, G. J., & SPANER, S. D. Operation SAIL. One effective model for the assimilation of new students into a school district. *Urban Education*, 1981, 15, 451–468.

258. SCHWANTES, F. M. Effects of story context on children's ongoing word recognition. *Journal of Reading Behavior*, 1981, 13, 305–311.

259. SMEAD, V., & CHASE, C. I. Student expectations as they relate to achievement in eighth grade mathematics. *Journal of Educational Research*, 1981, 75, 115–120.

[1193]

Iowa Tests of Educational Development, [Seventh Edition]. Grades 9–12; 1942–81; ITED; previous edition still available; 9 scores: correctness and appropriateness of expression (Test E), ability to do quantitative thinking (Test Q), social studies (Test SS), natural sciences (Test NS), literacy materials (Test L), vocabulary (Test V), sources of information (Test SI), total, reading total; prepared under the direction of Leonard S. Feldt, Robert A. Forsyth and E. F. Lindquist with the assistance of Stephanie D. Alnot and Paul S. Belgrade; Science Research Associates, Inc.

For additional information and reviews by C. Mauritz Lindvall and John E. Milholland of an earlier form, see 8:20 (15 references); see also T2:20 (85 references); for reviews by Ellis Batton Page and Alexander G. Wesman of earlier forms, see 6:14 (23 references); for reviews by J. Murray Lee and Stephen Wiseman, see 5:17 (9 references); for a review by Eric F. Gardner, see 4:17 (3 references); for reviews by Henry Chauncey, Gustav J. Froehlich, and Lavone A. Hanna, see 3:12.

REFERENCES

1–3. See 4:17.
4–12. See 5:17.
13–35. See 6:14.
36–120. See T2:20.
121–135. See 8:20.

136. HIRSCH, C. R. The effects of guided discovery and individualized instructional packages on initial learning, transfer, and retention in second-year algebra. *Journal for Research in Mathematics Education*, 1977, 8, 359–368.

137. NEWMAN, A. P. Twelve year study of pupils who were underachieving in reading first grade. In P. D. Pearson & J. Hansen (Eds.), *Reading: Theory, research, and practice; Twenty-sixth yearbook of the National Reading Conference*. Clemson, South Carolina: The National Reading Conference, Inc., 1977.

138. RAVEN, R. J., & CALVEY, H. Achievement on a test of Piaget's operative comprehension as a function of a process–oriented elementary school science program. *Science Education*, 1977, 61, 159–166.

139. FITZPATRICK, J. L. Academic underachievement, other–direction, and attitudes toward women's roles in bright adolescent females. *Journal of Educational Psychology*, 1978, 70, 645–650.

140. HALL, P. K., & TOMBLIN, J. B. A follow-up study of children with articulation and language disorders. *Journal of Speech & Hearing Disorders*, 1978, 43, 227–241.

141. VANDERPLOEG, A. J., & MUELLER, S. G. An examination of the Armed Services Vocational Aptitude Battery. *Measurement & Evaluation in Guidance*, 1978, 11, 70–77.

142. BRISCO, C. M., & JACOBS, K. W. Alphabetical order of surname and intelligence in elementary school. *Southern Journal of Educational Research*, 1979, 13, 153–158.

143. DIAMOND, E. E. The AMEG commission report on sex bias in achievement testing. *Measurement & Evaluation in Guidance*, 1980, 13, 135–147.

144. LOYD, B. H., FORSYTH, R., & HOOVER, H. D. Relationship of elementary and secondary school achievement test scores to later academic success. *Educational & Psychological Measurement*, 1980, 40, 1117–1124.

145. MELICAN, G. J., & FELDT, L. S. An empirical study of the Zajonc–Markus hypothesis for achievement test score declines. *American Educational Research Journal*, 1980, 17, 5–19.

146. FORSYTH, R., & GILMER, J. Some empirical results related to the robustness of the Rasch model. *Applied Psychological Measurement*, 1981, 5, 175–186.

147. JEPSEN, D. A., & PREDIGER, D. J. Dimensions of adolescent career development. A multi–instrument analysis. *Journal of Vocational Behavior*, 1981, 19, 350–368.

148. KOLEN, M. Comparison of traditional and item response theory methods for equating tests. *Journal of Educational Measurement*, 1981, 18, 1–11.

149. STANDIFER, C. E., & MAPLES, E. G. Achievement and attitude of third–grade students using two types of calculators. *School Science & Mathematics*, 1981, 81, 17–24.

[1194]

Iowa Tests of Music Literacy. Grades 4–12, 7–12; 1970–71, c1970; ITML; 9 scores: tonal concepts (aural perception, reading recognition, notational understanding, total), rhythmic concepts (aural perception, reading recognition, notational understanding, total), total; Edwin Gordon; Bureau of Educational Research and Service.*

For additional information and a review by Paul R. Lehman, see 8:97 (16 references); see also T2:199 (5 references) and 7:245 (2 references).

[1195]

★IOX Basic Skill System. End of grades 5 or 6, grades 9–12; 1978–79; "minimal competency assessment"; criterion-referenced; 3 tests: reading, writing, mathematics; 2 levels; Instructional Objectives Exchange.*

[1196]

★The IOX Basic Skill Word List. Grades 1–12; 1980; "a resource for reading instruction and readability determination"; Instructional Objectives Exchange.*

[1197]

The IPAT Anxiety Scale Questionnaire. Ages 14 and over; 1957–76; ASQ; also called *IPAT Anxiety Scale*; title on test is *Self Analysis Form, 1976 Edition*; total score plus 7 optional scores (recommended only for experimental use): covert anxiety, overt anxiety, 5 component scores (apprehension, tension, low self-control, emotional instability, suspicion); Raymond B. Cattell, Samuel E. Krug (manual), and Ivan H. Scheier (manual); Institute for Personality and Ability Testing, Inc. (South African adaptation entitled *The IPAT Anxiety Scale*: Ages 15 and over; 1968; adaptation by Elizabeth M. Madge; Human Sciences Research Council [South Africa].)*

For additional information and reviews by Richard I. Lanyon and Paul McReynolds, see 8:582 (85 references); see also T2:1225 (120 references) and P:116 (45 references); for a review by Jacob Cohen of the earlier edition, see 6:121 (23 references); for reviews by J. P. Guilford and E. Lowell Kelly and an excerpted review by Laurance F. Shaffer, see 5:70.

REFERENCES

1–23. See 6:121.
24–68. See P:116.
69–188. See T2:1225.
189–273. See 8:582.

274. ESLER, M., JULIUS, S., ZWEIFLER, A., RANDALL, O., HARBURG, E., GARDINER, H., & DEQUATTRO, V. Mild high–renin essential hypertension: Neurogenic human hypertension. *New England Journal of Medicine*, 1977, 296, 405–411.

275. HASKELL, S. D., & HANDLER, L. Personality and background predictors of a young wife's desired family size. *Journal of Clinical Psychology*, 1977, 33, 755–759.

276. HUGHES, R. N., & BUSHNELL, J. A. Further relationships between IPAT Anxiety Scale performance and infantile feeding experiences. *Journal of Clinical Psychology*, 1977, 33, 698–700.

277. KAZARIAN, S. S., & EVANS, D. R. Modification of obsessional ruminations. A comparative study. *Canadian Journal of Behavioural Science*, 1977, 9, 91–100.

278. MOORE, A. M., & MATSON, J. L. A comparison of modeling, desensitization, flooding, study skills, and control groups for reducing test anxiety. *Behavior Therapy*, 1977, 8, 1–8.

279. OLESKI, M. S. The effect of indefinite pretrial incarceration on the anxiety level of an urban jail population. *Journal of Clinical Psychology*, 1977, 33, 1006–1008.
280. PENK, W. E., & KIDD, R. V. Differences in word association commonality of schizophrenics: The self–editing–deficit model vs. the partial–collapse–of–response–hierarchy hypothesis. *Journal of Clinical Psychology*, 1977, 33, 32–39.
281. PERSKY, H., O'BRIEN, C. P., FINE, E., HOWARD, W. J., KHAN, M. A., & BECK, R. W. The effect of alcohol and smoking on testosterone function and aggression in chronic alcoholics. *American Journal of Psychiatry*, 1977, 134, 621–625.
282. RUDESTAM, K. E., & BEDROSIAN, R. An investigation of the effectiveness of desensitization and flooding with two types of phobias. *Behaviour Research & Therapy*, 1977, 15, 23–30.
283. SHAND, J., & GRAU, B. Perceived self and ideal self ratings in relation to high and low levels of anxiety in college women. *Journal of Psychology*, 1977, 95, 55–57.
284. SNYDER, A. L., & DEFFENBACHER, J. L. Comparison of relaxation as a self–control and systematic desensitization in the treatment of test anxiety. *Journal of Consulting & Clinical Psychology*, 1977, 45, 1022–1023.
285. WILKINS, W. E., HJELLE, L. A., & THOMPSON, M. Anxiety and actualization: A reconceptualization. *Journal of Clinical Psychology*, 1977, 33, 1001–1005.
286. ZAX, M., SAMEROFF, A. J., & BABIGIAN, H. M. Birth outcomes in the offspring of mentally disordered women. *American Journal of Orthopsychiatry*, 1977, 47, 218–230.
287. DONNELLY, E. F., MURPHY, D. L., & GOODWIN, F. K. Primary affective disorder: Anxiety in unipolar and bipolar depressed groups. *Journal of Clinical Psychology*, 1978, 34, 621–623.
288. FOA, E. B., & GOLDSTEIN, A. Continuous exposure and complete response prevention in the treatment of obsessive–compulsive neurosis. *Behavior Therapy*, 1978, 9, 821–829.
289. KENNY, F. T., MOWBRAY, R. M., & LALANI, S. Faradic disruption of obsessive ideation in the treatment of obsessive neurosis: A controlled study. *Behavior Therapy*, 1978, 9, 209–221.
290. MYHILL, J., & LORR, M. The Coopersmith Self–Esteem Inventory: Analysis and partial validation of a modified adult form. *Journal of Clinical Psychology*, 1978, 34, 72–76.
291. REVIERE, R., & POSEY, T. B. Correlates of two measures of fear of success in women. *Psychological Reports*, 1978, 42, 609–610.
292. WILKINS, W. E., & KRAUSS, H. H. Anxiety and actualization: Further research. *Journal of Clinical Psychology*, 1978, 34, 958–960.
293. ANANTH, J., SOLYOM, L., BRYNTWICK, S., & KRISHNAPPA, U. Chlorimipramine therapy for obsessive–compulsive neurosis. *American Journal of Psychiatry*, 1979, 136, 700–701.
294. DAVIS, S., CHANDLER, E., CUYLER, R., MARULLO, S., ROSENKRANTZ, A., JENSEN, S., & KREFFT, K. The concurrent validation of a screening device for distinguishing emotional problems in college students. *Journal of the American College Health Association*, 1979, 27, 316–320.
295. DEFFENBACHER, J. L., & PARKS, D. H. A comparison of traditional and self–control desensitization. *Journal of Counseling Psychology*, 1979, 26, 93–97.
296. FEHR, L. A., & STAMPS, L. E. The Mosher Guilt Scales: A construct validity extension. *Journal of Personality Assessment*, 1979, 43, 257–260.
297. GOTTLIEB, H., FISCHOFF, S., & LAMONT, J. Interaction of anxiety and note-taking on verbal conditioning in clinical interviews. *Psychological Reports*, 1979, 44, 503–510.
298. KARMOS, A. H. The development and validation of a nonverbal measure of self–esteem: The sliding person test. *Educational & Psychological Measurement*, 1979, 39, 479–484.
299. KARMOS, A. H., & KARMOS, J. S. Construct validity analyses of a "nonverbal" measure of self–esteem: The Sliding Person Test. *Psychological Reports*, 1979, 44, 895–910.
300. MCLACHLAN, J. F. C., WALDERMAN, R. L., BIRCHMORE, D. F., & MARSDEN, L. R. Self–evaluation, role satisfaction, and anxiety in the woman alcoholic. *International Journal of the Addictions*, 1979, 14, 809–832.
301. PENK, W. E., CHARLES, H. L., & VAN HOOSE, T. A. Psychological test comparison of day hospital and inpatient treatment. *Journal of Clinical Psychology*, 1979, 35, 837–839.
302. REDFERING, D. L. Relationship between attitudes toward feminism and levels of dogmatism, achievement, and anxiety. *Journal of Psychology*, 1979, 101, 297–304.
303. AHMED, S. M. S. Reactions to crowding in different settings. *Psychological Reports*, 1980, 46, 1279–1284.
304. BROWN, S. D. Coping skills training: An evaluation of a psychoeducational program in a community mental health setting. *Journal of Counseling Psychology*, 1980, 27, 340–345.
305. DICKEY, P. A. A comparison of the incremental difference between the beginning and ending heart rate when shorthand writers are informed and not informed of speeds of dictation. *Delta Pi Epsilon Journal*, 1980, 22, 20–31.
306. EGELAND, B., BREITENBUCHER, M., & ROSENBERG, D. Prospective study of the significance of life stress in the etiology of child abuse. *Journal of Consulting & Clinical Psychology*, 1980, 48, 195–205.
307. FIELDING, R. A note on behavioural treatment in the rehabilitation of myocardial infarction patients. *British Journal of Social & Clinical Psychology*, 1980, 19, 157–161.
308. HIGHLAND, A. C. Confounding of the repression–sensitization scale, controlled for social desirability, with the IPAT anxiety scale. *Psychological Reports*, 1980, 47, 1003–1006.
309. HURLEY, J. D. Differential effects of hypnosis, biofeedback training, and trophotropic responses on anxiety, ego strength, and locus of control. *Journal of Clinical Psychology*, 1980, 36, 503–507.
310. LEHRER, P. M., SCHOICKET, S., CARRINGTON, P., & WOOLFOLK, R. L. Psychophysiological and cognitive responses to stressful stimuli in subjects practicing progressive relaxation and clinically standardized meditation. *Behaviour Research & Therapy*, 1980, 18, 293–303.
311. ROMIROWSKY, S. Psychological adaptation patterns in response to cardiac surgery. *Journal of Rehabilitation*, 1980, 46, 50–52.
312. ROTHPEARL, A. Personality traits in martial artists: A descriptive approach. *Perceptual & Motor Skills*, 1980, 50, 395–401.
313. STANDING, L., & STACE, G. The effects of environmental noise on anxiety level. *Journal of General Psychology*, 1980, 103, 263–272.
314. THAUBERGER, P. C., DAVIS, J., & CLELAND, J. F. Some indices of existential confrontation from a sample of maximum security inmates. *Perceptual & Motor Skills*, 1980, 51, 131–137.
315. TOTH, J. C. Effect of structured preparation for transfer on patient anxiety on leaving coronary care unit. *Nursing Research*, 1980, 29, 28–34.
316. VAUGHN, B., DEINARD, A., & EGELAND, B. Measuring temperament in pediatric practice. *Journal of Pediatrics*, 1980, 96, 510–514.
317. GERZI, S., & BERMAN, E. Emotional reactions of expectant fathers to their wives' first pregnancy. *British Journal of Medical Psychology*, 1981, 54, 259–265.
318. HAURI, P. Treating psychophysiologic insomnia with biofeedback. *Archives of General Psychiatry*, 1981, 38, 752–758.
319. HIEBERT, B., & FOX, E. E. Reactive effects of self–monitoring anxiety. *Journal of Counseling Psychology*, 1981, 28, 187–193.
320. KREITLER, S., & KREITLER, H. Test item content: Does it matter? *Educational & Psychological Measurement*, 1981, 41, 635–642.
321. NAYLOR, F. D. A state–trait curiosity inventory. *Australian Psychologist*, 1981, 16, 172–183.

[1198]

IPAT Depression Scale. Adults; 1976; all items from *Clinical Analysis Questionnaire*; test booklet title is *Personal Assessment Inventory*; Samuel Krug and James E. Laughlin; Institute for Personality and Ability Testing, Inc.*

For additional information and reviews by Allan L. LaVoie and David T. Lykken, see 8:583.

REFERENCES

1. DAVIS, S., CHANDLER, E., CUYLER, R., MARULLO, S., ROSENKRANTZ, A., JENSEN, S., & KREFFT, K. The concurrent validation of a screening device for distinguishing emotional problems in college students. *Journal of the American College Health Association*, 1979, 27, 316–320.

[1199]

***IPMA Fire Service Tests.** Prospective fire service personnel; 1973–80; distribution restricted to persons who have completed a Test Security Agreement with the publisher; International Personnel Management Association.*

a) FIREFIGHTER. 1973–80; 84 items in 4 areas: decision-making and reasoning ability, understanding instructions, mechanical aptitude, reading ability.

b) FIRE INSPECTOR. [1974]

1) *Fire Inspector.* 125 items in 8 areas: reading comprehension, records and reports, public speaking, interviewing, combustible materials, fire inspection hazards, fire prevention, public relations.

2) *Senior Fire Inspector.* 60 items same as in 1 above plus 35 additional items in 4 areas: fire safety, supervision, evidence, building inspection.

c) FIRE DRIVER. 1974; 110 items in 13 areas: fire combat, automotive terms, ventilation, automotive maintenance, ladders, public relations, fire hazards, gauges, hydraulics, automotive operations, forcible entry, salvage, hoses.

d) RADIO OPERATOR. 1974.

1) *Radio Operator.* 100 items in 9 areas: reading comprehension, vocabulary, arithmetic, filing, English usage, pronunciation, radio operation, electricity, radio I (terminology, principles, equipment, trouble shooting).

2) *Senior Radio Operator.* 30 items same as in 1 above plus 30 additional items in 2 areas: supervision, radio II (terminology, principles, equipment, trouble shooting).

e) FIRE ENGINEER. [1968]; 110 items in 3 areas: automotive terminology/operations, fire equipment/combat and first aid, pumps/gauges/hydraulics.

f) FIRE SERVICE SUPERVISOR (SERGEANT/LIEUTENANT). [1974]; 150 items in 13 areas: fire combat, equipment, first aid, inspection, hazards, building construction, sprinklers, alarms, salvage, supervision, reports, training, hydraulics.

g) FIRE SERVICE ADMINISTRATOR (CAPTAIN). 1974; 150 items in 3 areas: combat equipment/fire combat/combat command/fire chemistry, inspection/building construction/salvage/sprinklers/alarms/hazards, supervisors/administration/training/report writing.

h) FIRE SERVICE ADMINISTRATOR (BATTALION CHIEF). 1974; 175 items in 3 areas: combat equipment/techniques/command, inspection/building construction/alarm systems/extinguishers/hazards, supervision/administration/training/public relations/report writing.

i) FIRE SERVICE ADMINISTRATOR (DEPUTY CHIEF). 1974; 175 items in 15 areas: reading comprehension, vocabulary, fire combat, combat equipment, physical, hydraulics, first aid, automotive, prevention and protection, sprinklers and alarms, arson, public relations, training, performance evaluation, supervision.

j) FIRE SERVICE ADMINISTRATOR (CHIEF). 1974; 150 items in 22 areas: reading comprehension, special problems, combat techniques, fire command, pumpers, extinguishers, training, fire inspection, records and reports, combat equipment, hydraulics, fire chemistry, supervision, planning, NBFU Standards, fire hazards, public relations, education, fire training, budget, personnel, administration.

[1200]

IPMA Police Service Tests. Prospective police service personnel; 1973–79; distribution restricted to persons who have completed a Test Security Agreement with the publisher; International Personnel Management Association.

a) MULTIJURISDICTIONAL POLICE OFFICER EXAMINATION. 1976–79; MPOE; 150 items in 10 areas: verbal comprehension, spatial scanning, visualization, semantic ordering, memory for ideas, spatial orientation, problem sensitivity, induction, memory for relationship, paired associates memory.

b) POLICE OFFICER. 1973; 71 items in 4 areas: human relations, decision-making and reasoning ability, data and rule interpretation, reading comprehension.

c) POLICE DETECTIVE. 1974; 165 items in 15 areas: reading comprehension, crime classification, patrol, search and seizure, arrest, interrogation, identification, criminology, crime prevention, vice, courts and trials, fingerprints, supervision, public relations, juvenile delinquency.

d) IDENTIFICATION OFFICER. [1972]; 100 items in 4 areas: fingerprinting (equipment, classification, filming, techniques), tabular interpretation, filing, photography (equipment, papers, film, errors, exposure, records and reports, processing).

e) POLICE RADIO DISPATCHER. 1974; 120 items in 14 areas: reading comprehension, abstract reasoning, arithmetic calculations, filing skill, tabular interpretation, pronunciation, terminology, radio equipment, radio dispatching, radio operations, radio logs, radio communications, radio repairs, radio symbols.

f) POLICE SUPERVISOR (CORPORAL, SERGEANT). 1974; 145 items in 10 areas: patrol (techniques, traffic, accident), investigation, first aid, civil disturbance, juvenile delinquency, drugs, courts and trials (evidence, search and seizure, arrest, warrants, testimony), community relations, report writing, supervision (training, leadership).

g) POLICE ADMINISTRATOR (LIEUTENANT). 1974; 145 items in 16 areas: patrol, crime prevention, criminology, identification, interrogation, investigation, vice, juvenile delinquency, riot control, courts and trials, evidence, supervision, public relations, records and reports, uniform crime reports, reading comprehension.

h) POLICE ADMINISTRATOR (CAPTAIN). 1974; 170 items in 17 areas: accident investigation, traffic, investigation, identification, interrogation, patrol, vice, crime prevention, courts and trials, administration-coordination, administration-planning, administration-budgeting, administration-general, uniform crime reporting, public relations, training, supervision.

i) POLICE ADMINISTRATOR (ASSISTANT CHIEF). 1974; 200 items in 25 areas: reading, vocabulary, criminology, patrol, search and seizure, arrest, evidence, courts and trials, interrogation, office organization, identification, vice, probation and parole, crime prevention, reports, work assignments, supervision, personnel, employee relations, public relations, training, juvenile delinquency, special problems, patrol organization, administration.

j) POLICE ADMINISTRATOR (CHIEF). 1974; 180 items in 29 areas: reading comprehension, tabular interpretation, crime classification, patrol, search and seizure, arrest, stolen property recovery, evidence, courts and trials, interrogation, investigation, accident investigation, traffic, criminology, identification, fingerprints, crime prevention, juvenile delinquency, vice, reports, special problems, supervision I, training, personnel I, public relations, administration, crime statistics, supervision II, personnel II.

[1201]

It Scale for Children. Ages 5–6; 1956; ITSC; for research use only; sex role preference; Daniel G. Brown; Psychological Test Specialists.*

For additional information, see 8:592 (23 references); see also T2:1247 (25 references) and P:131 (7 references); for reviews by Philip L. Harriman and Boyd R. McCandless, see 6:129 (18 references).

REFERENCES

1–18. See 6:129.
19–25. See P:131.
26–50. See T2:1247.
51–73. See 8:592.
74. DIXIT, R. C., & GUPTA, S. Sex–role preferences among young children of rural and urban social groups. *Psychologia*, 1977, 20, 111–119.
75. GOLD, D., & ANDRES, D. Maternal employment and child development at three age levels. *Journal of Research & Development in Education*, 1977, 10, 20–29.

76. REKERS, G. A., & VARNI, J. W. Self monitoring and self-reinforcement processes in a pre–transsexual boy. *Behaviour Research & Therapy*, 1977, 15, 177–180.
77. GOLD, D., & ANDRES, D. Relations between maternal employment and development of nursery school children. *Canadian Journal of Behavioural Science*, 1978, 10, 116–129.
78. GOLD, D., & ANDRES, D. The development of Francophone nursery–school children with employed and nonemployed mothers. *Canadian Journal of Behavioural Science*, 1979, 11, 169–173.

[1202]

★Item Analysis of Slosson Intelligence Test. Children and adults; 1978; to aid in screening for strengths and weaknesses in the major areas of learning; Slosson Educational Publications, Inc.*

[1203]

Jackson Personality Inventory. Grades 10–16 and adults; 1976; JPI; 16 scores: anxiety, breadth of interest, complexity, conformity, energy level, innovation, interpersonal affect, organization, responsibility, risk taking, self esteem, social adroitness, social participation, tolerance, value orthodoxy, infrequency; Douglas N. Jackson; Research Psychologists Press, Inc.*

For additional information and reviews by Lewis R. Goldberg and David T. Lykken, see 8:593 (6 references).

REFERENCES

1–6. See 8:593.
7. AHAMMER, I. M., & BENNETT, K. Viewing "older people": A comparative method–comparative sample approach. *Australian Journal of Psychology*, 1977, 29, 97–110.
8. JACKSON, D. N. Reliability of the Jackson Personality Inventory. *Psychological Reports*, 1977, 40, 613–614.
9. HOOD, R. W., JR., HALL, J. R., WATSON, P. J., & BIDERMAN, M. Personality correlates of the reports of mystical experience. *Psychological Reports*, 1979, 44, 804–806.
10. VAN TUINEN, M., & RAMARAIAH, N. V. A multimethod analysis of selected self–esteem measures. *Journal of Research in Personality*, 1979, 13, 16–24.
11. HIGHLEN, P. S., & RUSSELL, B. Effects of counselor gender and counselor and client sex role on females' counselor preference. *Journal of Counseling Psychology*, 1980, 27, 157–165.
12. SKINNER, H. A., & LEI, H. The multidimensional assessment of stressful life events. *Journal of Nervous & Mental Disease*, 1980, 168, 535–541.

[1204]

★Jackson Vocational Interest Survey. High school and over; 1976–77; JVIS; "developed to assist high school and college students and adults with educational and career planning"; 34 basic interest scale scores: creative arts, performing arts, mathematics, physical science, engineering, life science, social science, adventure, nature-agriculture, skilled trades, personal service, family activity, medical service, dominant leadership, job security, stamina, accountability, teaching, social service, elementary education, finance, business, office work, sales, supervision, human relations management, law, professional advising, author-journalism, academic achievement, technical writing, independence, planfulness, interpersonal confidence; Douglas N. Jackson; Research Psychologists Press, Inc.*

REFERENCES

1. COVINGTON, J. E. Jackson Vocational Interest Survey. *Measurement & Evaluation in Guidance*, 1979, 12, 49–52.

[1205]

Jansky Screening Index. Kgn; 1972; JSI; Jeannette Jansky and Katrina de Hirsch (manual); Matt-Jansky.* (In-print status uncertain; no reply from publisher.)

For additional information, see 8:800 (14 references).

REFERENCES

1–14. See 8:800.
15. ROTHENBERG, J. J., LEHMAN, L. B., & HACKMAN, J. D. An individualized learning disabilities program in the regular classroom. *Journal of Learning Disabilities*, 1979, 12, 496–499.

[1206]

★Jenkins Activity Survey. Employed adults ages 25–65; 1965–79; JAS; a measure of type A behavior, the coronary prone behavior pattern; 4 scores: type A, speed and impatience, job involvement, hard-driving and competitive; C. David Jenkins, Stephen J. Zyzanski, and Ray H. Rosenman; The Psychological Corporation.*

REFERENCES

1. NIELSON, W. R., & DOBSON, K. S. The coronary-prone behavior pattern and trait anxiety: Evidence for discriminant validity. *Journal of Consulting & Clinical Psychology*, 1980, 48, 546–547.

[1207]

Jensen Alternation Board. Ages 5 and over; 1959–60; JAB; learning age; Milton B. Jensen; Lafayette Instrument Co.*

See T2:560A (3 references) and 6:550 (2 references).

[1208]

Jesness Behavior Checklist. Ages 10 and over; 1970–71; JBC; ratings by observers and self-ratings in 14 areas: unobtrusiveness, friendliness, responsibility, considerateness, independence, rapport, enthusiasm, sociability, conformity, calmness, effective communication, insight, social control, anger control; Carl F. Jesness; Consulting Psychologists Press, Inc.*

For additional information and reviews by Dorcas Susan Butt and Edwin I. Megargee, see 8:594 (3 references).

REFERENCES

1–3. See 8:594.
4. LUKIN, P. R. Recidivism and changes made by delinquents during residential treatment. *Journal of Research in Crime & Delinquency*, 1981, 18, 101–112.

[1209]

The Jesness Inventory. Disturbed children and adolescents ages 8–18, adults; 1962–72; JI; 11 scores: social maladjustment, value orientation, immaturity, autism, alienation, manifest aggression, withdrawal, social anxiety, repression, denial, asocial index; Carl F. Jesness; Consulting Psychologists Press, Inc.*

a) YOUTH EDITION. Disturbed children and adolescents ages 8–18; 1962–72.

b) ADULT EDITION. Adults; 1972, c1962; experimental form.

For additional information and a review by Dorcas Susan Butt, see 8:595 (14 references); see also T2:1249 (5 references); for a review by Sheldon A. Weintraub of *a*, see 7:94 (10 references); see also P:133 (3 references).

REFERENCES

1–3. See P:133.
4–13. See 7:94.
14–18. See T2:1249.
19–32. See 8:595.
33. SHARK, M. L., & HANDAL, P. J. Reliability and validity of the Jesness Inventory: A caution. *Journal of Consulting & Clinical Psychology*, 1977, 45, 692–695.
34. WOODBURY, R., & PATE, D. H. Vocational and personality dimensions of adjudicated delinquents. *Measurement & Evaluation in Guidance*, 1977, 10, 106–112.

35. HARBISON, J., JARDINE, E., & CURRAN, J. D. The use of the Jesness Inventory with Northern Ireland populations. *British Journal of Criminology*, 1978, 18, 387–390.
36. STOTT, M. W. R., & OLCZAK, P. V. Relating personality characteristics to juvenile offense categories: Differences between status offenders and juvenile delinquents. *Journal of Clinical Psychology*, 1978, 34, 80–84.
37. WODARSKI, J. S. The prediction of anti-social behavior: An application of regression analysis. *Corrective & Social Psychiatry & Journal of Behavioral Technology, Methods & Therapy*, 1978, 24, 102–110.
38. BRANDT, D. E. Development of intake criteria in a day treatment program for delinquent boys. *Psychological Reports*, 1979, 44, 1028–1030.
39. SIMONDS, J. F., & KASHANI, J. Drug abuse and criminal behavior in delinquent boys committed to a training school. *American Journal of Psychiatry*, 1979, 136, 1444–1448.
40. STAYTON, S. E., & DIENER, R. G. Personality characteristics of juvenile delinquent heroin users. *International Journal of the Addictions*, 1979, 14, 585–587.
41. PUTNINS, A. L. Reliability of the Jesness Inventory. *Applied Psychological Measurement*, 1980, 4, 127–129.

[1210]

JEVS Work Sample Evaluation System. High school and adults; 1969–76; also called *Philadelphia J.E.V.S. Work Sample Battery*; simulated work activities for evaluation of performance, interest, and work behavior of rehabilitation, minority group, and school populations; 28 tests: Nut-Bolt-Washer Assembly, Rubber Stamping, Washer Threading, Budgette Assembly, Sign Making, Tile Sorting, Nut Packing, Collating Leather Samples, Grommet Assembly, Union Assembly, Belt Assembly, Ladder Assembly, Metal Square Fabrication, Hardware Assembly, Telephone Assembly, Lock Assembly, Filing by Numbers, Proofreading, Filing by Letters, Nail and Screw Sorting, Adding Machine, Payroll Computation, Computing Postage, Resistor Reading, Pipe Assembly, Blouse Making, Vest Making, Condensing Principle; 2 scores: time and quality ratings of 1 (lowest 40%), 2 (middle 20%), 3 (highest 40%) for each test, plus 27 ratings by evaluator: behavior in interpersonal situations (5 ratings), worker characteristics (9 ratings), learning and comprehension (6 ratings), discriminations, manipulative skills (5 ratings), significant worker characteristics (2 ratings); Jewish Employment and Vocational Service, Inc.*

For additional information, see 8:982 (3 references).

[1211]

★**JIIG-CAL Occupational Interests Guide.** High school and college students; 1980; also called *Job Ideas and Information Generator-Computer Assisted Learning*; revision of the still-in-print *APU Occupational Interest Guide*; one component of a program including a jobfile and computer programs; self-ratings on 2 of six sections chosen by the student (unskilled, semi-skilled, skilled craft, skilled technician, semi-professional, graduate professional) yielding six preference scores: interest in practical work/using your hands/science and engineering, working with living things, clerical/secretarial/saleswork including business and some aspects of law, work involving neatness and an eye for colour and shape, interest in working with people in need, interest in working where you meet people including acting and writing; S. J. Closs (classroom guide, manual, and test materials), P. R. MacLean, M. V. Walker (classroom guide); Hodder & Stoughton Educational [England].*

[1212]

★**Job Activity Preference Questionnaire.** Business and industry; 1972–81; JAPQ; restructured and simplified version of the *Position Analysis Questionnaire* used for measuring vocational preferences and experiences; weighted combinations of 150 items into 16 dimensions of work: making decisions/communicating and having responsibility, operating vehicles, using machines-tools-instruments, performing physical activities, operating keyboard and office equipment, monitoring and/or controlling equipment and/or processes, working under uncomfortable conditions, working with art-decor entertainment, performing supervisory duties, performing estimating activities, processing written information, working with buyers-customers-salespersons, working under hazardous conditions, performing paced and/or repetitive activities, working with aerial and aquatic equipment, catering/serving/smelling/tasting; Robert C. Mecham, Alma F. Harris (test), Ernest J. McCormick (test), and P. R. Jeanneret (test); PAQ Services, Inc.*

[1213]

★**Job Analysis and Interest Measurement.** Adults; 1957–77; JAIM; for counseling, job analysis, and research use; coping skills and work-relevant attitudes influencing job success or failure and job satisfaction; 2 editions; Regis Walther; JAIM Research, Inc.*

a) [MACHINE SCORED EDITION.] 1957–77; 32 scores: orientations (optimism, self confidence, interpersonal trust, unconventional), self management (plan ahead, orderliness, perseverance, emotional control, schedule activities), interpersonal style (self assertive, supportive of others, take leadership, move toward aggressor, move away from aggressor, move against aggressor), cognitive style (concrete-practical, systematic-methodical), relationship to authority (act independently, work as an assistant), supervisory style (directive leadership, motivate by rewards, motivate by results), work preferences (social interaction, mechanical activities, group participation, activity-frequent change, job challenge), values (status attainment, social service, approval from others, intellectual achievement, role conformity).

b) [SELF–SCORED EDITION.] 1971; manual title is *Exercises in Self Understanding: A Workbook for Trainers*; 9 tests.

1) *Basic Beliefs Inventory.* 3 scores: optimism, self-confidence, basic trust.

2) *Activity Preference Inventory.* 4 scores: job challenge, social interaction, mechanical activities, activity-frequent change.

3) *Personal Values Inventory.* 5 scores: status attainment, social service, approval from others, intellectual achievement, dependability.

4) *Self Management Inventory.* 5 scores: plan ahead, orderliness, perseverance, emotional control, schedule activities.

5) *Relationship to Authority Inventory.* 5 scores: work as supervisor, work as an assistant, work with group, work alone, act independently.

6) *Reaction to Aggression Inventory.* 3 scores: move toward aggressor, move away from aggressor, move against aggressor.

7) *Leadership Style Inventory.* 4 scores: directive leadership, external controls, motivates by rewards, motivates by results.

8) *Information Processing Inventory.* 3 scores: systematic-methodical, concrete-practical, open system.

9) *Interpersonal Style Inventory.* 3 scores: self assertiveness, supportive of others, take leadership.
See T2:1250 (10 references) and 7:95 (14 references).

REFERENCES

1–14. See 7:95.
15–24. See T2:1250.
25. WALTHER, R. H. ASTD members–Their perceptions and training goals. *Training & Development Journal,* 1971, 32–37.
26. TROJANOWICZ, R. C. *Juvenile delinquency: Concepts and control.* Englewood Cliffs, N. J.: Prentice-Hall, 1973.
27. PUTHAM, L. L. Preference for procedural order in task–oriented small groups. *Communication Monographs,* 1979, 46, 193–218.

[1214]

[Job Application Forms]. Job applicants and employees; 1957–71; 8 application forms; no manual for *b–h*; Hilton Shepherd Co., Inc.*

a) JOB APPLICATION FORM. Job applicants; [1960].
b) PERSONNEL INVENTORY FORM. Employees being considered for transfer or promotion; [1960].
c) EMPLOYMENT APPLICATION FORM. Job applicants; 1960–66.
d) PERSONNEL RECORD FOLDER. 1960–68.
e) CONTENT CONTROL SHEET. 1960–68.
f) MEDICAL EMPLOYMENT FORM. Administrators, nurses, and technologists; 1960–67.
g) EMPLOYMENT APPLICATION. Nonmedical personnel; 1960–67.
h) BANK EMPLOYMENT FORM. Applicants for positions in banks and financial institutions; 1971.

For additional information, see 7:1069.

[1215]

Job Attitude Analysis. Production and clerical workers; 1961–70; an inventory for employment interviewing and vocational counseling; P. L. Mellenbruch; Psychometric Affiliates.*

For additional information, see 7:980 (1 reference).

[1216]

Job Attitude Scale. Adults; 1971; JAS; intrinsic and extrinsic factors in job satisfaction and motivation; 17 scores: praise and recognition, growth in skill, creative work, responsibility, advancement, achievement, salary security, personnel policies, competent supervision, relations-peers, relations-subordinates, relations-supervisor, working conditions, status, family needs, general intrinsic; an abbreviated edition for obtaining only the general intrinsic score is available; Shoukry D. Saleh; the Author [Canada].*

For additional information, see 8:1049 (9 references).

[1217]

★Job Awareness Inventory. Average and special needs students in grades 10–12; 1980–81; JAI; "criterion-referenced"; 5 scores: occupations, do you know how to, general information, interview actions, total; Teen Makowski; Mafex Associates, Inc.*

[1218]

Job Performance Scale. Employees; 1971; ratings by supervisors which may be used for local validation of *Wonderlic Personnel Test;* ratings in 3 areas: ability to perform, attitude, total; 3 parts which may be used separately or in combination; no manual; only accessories are for conducting validation research; E. F. Wonderlic & Associates, Inc.*

a) PRIMARY RATING NO. 1.
b) PRIMARY RATING NO. 2.
c) RATER'S PERFORMANCE SUMMARY. For ranking of all employees rated.

For additional information, see 8:1059.

[1219]

Job-Tests Program. Adults; 1947–81; battery of aptitude tests, personality tests, and performance appraisal forms used in various combinations in different jobs in business and industry; 4 series; Industrial Psychology, Inc.

a) APTITUDE-INTELLIGENCE TEST SERIES. 1947–81; 15 tests; Joseph E. King (1–8, 10–15) and H. B. Osborn, Jr. (9).

1) *Office Terms.* 1947–81; tests ability to understand the special terms used in business.
2) *Numbers.* 1947–81; tests ability to work rapidly and accurately with numbers.
3) *Perception.* 1947–81; tests ability to perceive details in and recognize differences in words and numbers quickly.
4) *Judgment.* 1947–81; tests ability to figure out solutions to problems.
5) *Fluency.* 1947–81; tests ability to think of words rapidly.
6) *Parts.* 1949–81; tests ability to see the whole in relation to its parts.
7) *Memory.* 1948–81; tests ability to remember visual, verbal, and numerical materials.
8) *Sales Terms.* 1948–56; tests ability to understand words and information in the sales and contact fields.
9) *Factory Terms.* 1948–57; tests ability to understand words and information in the factory and mechanical fields.
10) *Tools.* 1948–76; tests ability to recognize pictures of common tools, equipment, and machines.
11) *Precision.* 1948–57; tests ability to see details in pictures, to recognize differences and likenesses rapidly.
12) *Blocks.* 1948–56; adapted from Army General Classification Test; tests ability to visualize objects on the basis of three dimensional cues.
13) *Dimension.* 1948–56; tests ability to visualize objects when seen from different angles.
14) *Dexterity.* 1949–56; tests ability to perform routine motor tasks rapidly; three paper and pencil subtests: maze, checks, dots.
15) *Motor.* 1948–56; tests ability to coordinate eye and hand movements in a specific motoric task; motor apparatus required.

b) EMPLOYEE ATTITUDE SERIES. 1954–60; 3 tests; R. B. Cattell, J. E. King (1–3), and A. K. Schuettler (1–2).

1) *CPF (Contact Personality Factor).* 1954; test of extroversion versus introversion, or contact versus non-contact personality; also published by Institute for Personality and Ability Testing as Form A of IPAT Contact Personality Factor Test.
2) *NPF (Neurotic Personality Factor).* 1954; tests general stability, emotional balance, lack of neurotic tendencies; also published by Institute for Personality and Ability Testing as IPAT Neurotic Personality Factor Test.

3) *16 PF (Sixteen Personality Factor).* 1956; measures 16 basic factors of personality; Industrial Edition A.

c) JOB TEST FIELD SERIES. 1960–81; 28 recommended test batteries (Junior Clerk, Numbers Clerk, Office Machine Operator, Contact Clerk, Senior Clerk, Secretary, Unskilled Worker, Semi-Skilled Worker, Factory Machine Operator, Vehicle Operator, Inspector, Skilled Worker, Sales Clerk, Salesperson, Sales Engineer, Scientist, Engineer, Office Technical, Writer, Designer, Instructor, Office Supervisor, Sales Supervisor, Factory Supervisor, General Clerk, Dental Office Assistant, Dental Technician, Optometric Assistant).

d) MERIT RATING SERIES. 1957; developed to aid management in obtaining a reliable and accurate rating of an employee's job performance or efficiency, from the immediate supervisor; provides strengths and weaknesses on such performance traits as quantity, quality, job knowledge, personal work-habits, potential, etc.; 5 forms tailored to each of the major job families.

1) *Clerical.*
2) *Mechanical.*
3) *Sales.*
4) *Technical.*
5) *Supervisor.*

See T2:1078 (12 references); for reviews by William H. Helme and Stanley I. Rubin, see 6:774; for a review by Harold P. Bechtoldt of the Factored Aptitude Series, see 5:602; for a review by D. Welty Lefever and an excerpted review by Laurance F. Shaffer of an earlier edition of this series, see 4:712 (1 reference).

[1220]

Johnson Basic Sight Vocabulary. Grades 1–2; 1976; JBSVT; 2 overlapping levels (grades 1, 2) in a single booklet; Dale D. Johnson; Chapman, Brook & Kent.*

For additional information and a review by Doris E. Nason, see 8:79.

REFERENCES

1. MAVROGENES, N. A. Johnson Basic Sight Vocabulary Test. *Reading Teacher,* 1979, 33, 366–367.

[1221]

Johnson-Kenney Screening Test. Ages 5.5–6.5; 1970–73; JKST; 12 scores: number concepts (counting and recognition, writing numbers), visual motor coordination, discrimination of form, symbol recognition, spatial relations, position in space, perceiving relationships, auditory discrimination, color recognition, total, draw a person; Rosalie C. Johnson and Rose K. Kenney (test); J-K Screening Service.* (In-print status uncertain; no reply from publisher.)

For additional information and a review by Frank R. Vellutino, see 8:433 (2 references).

[1222]

★**The Jones-Mohr Listening Test.** Persons in educational and training programs; 1976; "a tape-assisted learning program" John E. Jones and Lawrence Mohr; University Associates, Inc.*

[1223]

Jones Personality Rating Scale. Grades 9–12 and adults; 1939; 8 ratings: dependability, cultural refinement, leadership, industriousness, mental alertness, thoroughness, personal appearance, ability to get along with others; Harold J. Jones; Jones Teaching Aids.* (In-print status uncertain; no reply from publisher.)

For additional information, see P:134.

[1224]

*****Jordan Left-Right Reversal Test, Second Revised Edition.** Ages 6–12, 9–12; 1973–80; visual reversals of letter and number; Brian T. Jordan; Academic Therapy Publications.*

For additional information and reviews by Barbara K. Keogh and Richard J. Reisboard, and excerpted reviews by Alex Bannatyne and Alan Krichev, see 8:434 (5 references)

REFERENCES

1–5. See 8:434.
6. STRICHART, S. S. Use of the Jordan Left–Right Reversal Test with learning disabled children. *Perceptual & Motor Skills,* 1978, 47, 1291–1297.
7. MCKIERNAN, J., & AVAKIAN, M. Directional awareness training. Remediation of receptive letter reversals. *Academic Therapy,* 1980, 16, 193–197.

[1225]

★**Joseph Pre-School and Primary Self-Concept Screening Test.** Ages 3–6 to 9–11; 1979; identifies children, at an early age, who may later develop learning problems; may be used with non-verbal children; 1 score: Global Self Concept; Jack Joseph; Stoelting Co.*

[1226]

Journalism Test. High school; 1957; 16 scores: news values, arrangement of facts, paragraphing, sentence variety, news source, sports, feature values, speech-interview, editorials, news style, columns, advertising, make up, headlines, terminology, copyreading; no manual; Frances Miller and Kenneth Stratton; Stratton-Christian Press.*

For additional information, see 7:1108.

[1227]

★**Judgement of Occupational Behavior-Orientation.** Grades 6–adult; 1981; commonly called JOB-O; 9 scales: education, interest, inclusion, control, affection, physical activity, hands/tools/machinery,problem-solving, creating/ideas; (Spanish and Vietnamese editions available); Arthur Cutler, Francis Ferry, Robert Kauk, and Robert Robinett; CFKR Career Materials, Inc.*

[1228]

Junior Aptitude Tests for Indian South Africans. Standards 6–8; 1971; JATISA; 10 scores: verbal reasoning, series completion, social insight, language usage, numerical reasoning, spatial perception (2 dimensional, 3 dimensional), visual arts, clerical speed and accuracy, mechanical insight; S. Oosthuizen; Human Sciences Research Council [South Africa].*

[1229]

Junior Eysenck Personality Inventory. Ages 7–15; 1963–70; JEPI; 3 scores: extraversion, neuroticism, lie; (Spanish edition available); Sybil B. G. Eysenck; EdITS/Educational and Industrial Testing Service.*

For additional information, see 8:596 (37 references); see also T2:1252 (14 references); for reviews by Maurice Chazan and Robert D. Wirt and excerpted reviews by

Gertrude H. Keir and B. Semeonoff, see 7:96 (19 references); see also P:135 (7 references).

REFERENCES

1–7. See P:135.
8–26. See 7:96.
27–40. See T2:1252.
41–77. See 8:596.
78. BELL, A. E., ABRAHAMSON, D. S., & MCRAE, K. N. Reading retardation: A 12-year prospective study. *Journal of Pediatrics*, 1977, 91, 363–370.
79. HORNSTEIN, D., SOLOMON, S. J., & HOUSTON, B. K. Preliminary report on a juvenile court testing program. *Corrective & Social Psychiatry & Journal of Behavior Technology, Methods & Therapy*, 1977, 23, 11–14.
80. SAKLOFSKE, D. H. Antisocial behavior and psychoticism in adolescent schoolboys. *Psychological Reports*, 1977, 41, 425–426.
81. SAKLOFSKE, D. H. Personality and behavior problems of schoolboys. *Psychological Reports*, 1977, 41, 445–446.
82. STEWART, R. A. C. Factor analysis and rotation of responses to the Junior Eysenck Personality Inventory. *Psychological Reports*, 1977, 40, 599–601.
83. ZEGANS, L. S., & ZEGANS, S. Relevance of the extraversion and neuroticism scales of the Junior EPI to adolescent boys in a residential treatment setting. *British Journal of Medical Psychology*, 1977, 50, 329–340.
84. BERG, I., & FIELDING, D. An evaluation of hospital inpatient treatment in adolescent school phobia. *British Journal of Psychiatry*, 1978, 132, 500–505.
85. POOLE, M. E. Identifying early school leaving. *Australian Journal of Education*, 1978, 22, 13–24.
86. POWELL, G. E., & STEWART, R. A. The relationship of age, sex and personality to social attitudes in children aged 8–15 years. *British Journal of Social & Clinical Psychology*, 1978, 17, 307–317.
87. SAKLOFSKE, D. H., & EYSENCK, S. B. G. Cross-cultural comparison of personality: New Zealand children and English children. *Psychological Reports*, 1978, 42, 1111–1116.
88. TAPASAK, R. C., ROODIN, P. A., & VAUGHT, G. M. Effects of extraversion, anxiety, and sex on children's verbal fluency and coding task performance. *Journal of Psychology*, 1978, 100, 49–55.
89. FOUTS, G. T., & CLICK, M. Effect of live and TV models on observational learning in introverted and extraverted children. *Perceptual & Motor Skills*, 1979, 48, 863–867.
90. GABRYS, J. B. The Babcock story recall of behaviorally disordered children scoring high or low on extraversion. *Perceptual & Motor Skills*, 1979, 48, 157–158.
91. JAMISON, R. N. Cigarette smoking and personality in male and female adolescents. *Psychological Reports*, 1979, 44, 842.
92. MARTIN, P. J. Distinguishing school orchestra members. *Council for Research in Music Education Bulletin*, 1979, 59, 62–67.
93. NIAS, D. K. B. The classification and correlates of children's academic and recreational interests. *Journal of Child Psychology & Psychiatry & Allied Disciplines*, 1979, 20, 73–79.
94. RIDING, R. J. The effect of extraversion and detail content on the recall of prose by eleven-year-old children. *British Journal of Educational Psychology*, 1979, 49, 297–303.
95. VOGRIN, D., & KASSINOVE, H. Effects of behavior rehearsal, audiotaped observation, and intelligence on assertiveness and adjustment in third-grade children. *Psychology in the Schools*, 1979, 16, 422–429.
96. DOWLING, J. R. Adjustment from primary to secondary school: A one year follow-up. *British Journal of Educational Psychology*, 1980, 50, 26–32.
97. DUFFY, R. A. An analysis of aesthetic sensitivity and creativity with other variables in grades four, six, eight, and ten. *Journal of Educational Research*, 1980, 73, 26–30.
98. DYKMAN, R. A., ACKERMAN, P. T., & OGLESBY, D. M. Correlates of problem solving in hyperactive, learning disabled, and control boys. *Journal of Learning Disabilities*, 1980, 13, 23–32.
99. GABRYS, J. B. Effect of verbal alert and individual differences in extraversion on memory for syntax: A study with replication. *Perceptual & Motor Skills*, 1980, 51, 615–625.
100. GABRYS, J. B. Stability of scores on the Junior Eysenck Personality Inventory in an outpatient population. *Perceptual & Motor Skills*, 1980, 51, 743–746.
101. IWAWAKI, S., EYSENCK, S. B. G., & EYSENCK, H. J. The universality of typology: A comparison between English and Japanese school children. *Journal of Social Psychology*, 1980, 112, 3–9.
102. MAQSUD, M. Extraversion, neuroticism, intelligence and academic achievement in northern Nigeria. *British Journal of Educational Psychology*, 1980, 50, 71–73.
103. MAQSUD, M. Personality and academic attainment of primary school children. *Psychological Reports*, 1980, 46, 1271–1275.
104. SAKLOFSKE, D. H., & EYSENCK, S. B. G. Personality and antisocial behavior in delinquent and non-delinquent boys. *Psychological Reports*, 1980, 47, 1255–1261.
105. ACKERMAN, P. T., OGLESBY, D. M., & DYKMAN, R. A. A contrast of hyperactive, learning disabled, and hyperactive–learning disabled boys. *Journal of Clinical Child Psychology*, 1981, 10, 168–173.

[1230]
Junior High School Mathematics Test: Acorn Achievement Tests. Grades 7–9; 1942–52; 4 scores: concepts, problem analysis, problems, total; Harry Eisner; Psychometric Affiliates.*

For additional information and a review by Myron F. Rosskopf, see 5:429; for a review by William Betz, see 3:310.

[1231]
Junior High School Record. Grades 7–10; 1955; also available in combination with the *Personality Record (Revised)*; National Association of Secondary-School Principals.* (In-print status uncertain; no reply from publisher.)

[1232]
Junior High School Test of Economics. Grades 7–9; 1973–74; Leon M. Schur, Robert Donegan, Marlin L. Tanck, David Zitlow, and Gerald A. Weston; Joint Council on Economic Education.*

For additional information and a review by Lee H. Ehman, see 8:898.

[1233]
Jr.-Sr. High School Personality Questionnaire. Ages 12–18; 1953–75; HSPQ; 14 primary factor scores: reserved vs. warmhearted (A), dull vs. bright (B), affected by feelings vs. emotionally stable (C), undemonstrative vs. excitable (D), obedient vs. assertive (E), sober vs. enthusiastic (F), disregards rules vs. conscientious (G), shy vs. adventurous (H), tough-minded vs. tender-minded (I), zestful vs. circumspect individualism (J), self-assured vs. apprehensive (O), sociably group-dependent vs. self-sufficient (Q_2), uncontrolled vs. controlled (Q_3), relaxed vs. tense (Q_4), plus 4 second-order factor scores: introversion vs. extraversion (I), low anxiety vs. high anxiety (II), tender minded emotionality vs. tough poise (III), dependence vs. independence (IV); 2 editions.

a) IPAT EDITION. 1953–75; Raymond B. Cattell and Mary D. L. Cattell; Institute for Personality and Ability Testing, Inc. (British adaptation: Ages 12–18; 1973; supplement by Peter Saville and Laura Finlayson; NFER-Nelson Publishing Co. [England]. South African adaptation entitled *High School Personality Questionnaire* of 1963 IPAT edition: Ages 13–18; 1967; adaptation by E. M. Madge; Human Sciences Research Council [South Africa].)*

b) BOBBS-MERRILL EDITION. 1958–60; Raymond B. Cattell, Richard W. Coan, and Halla Beloff; Bobbs-Merrill Co., Inc.*

For additional information, see 8:597 (68 references); see also T2:1253 (37 references); for reviews by Robert Hogan and Douglas N. Jackson, see 7:97 (53 references); see also P:136 (29 references); for reviews by C. J. Adcock and Philip E. Vernon of an earlier edition (the current Bobbs-Merrill edition), see 6:131 (17 references); see also 5:72 (4 references).

REFERENCES

1–4. See 5:72.
5–21. See 6:131.

22-51. See P:136.
52-104. See 7:97.
105-141. See T2:1253.
142-209. See 8:597.
210. BARTON, K., DIELMAN, T. E., & CATTELL, R. B. Child-rearing practices related to child personality. *Journal of Social Psychology*, 1977, 101, 75-85.
211. BELL, A. E., ABRAHAMSON, D. S., & McRAE, K. N. Reading retardation: A 12-year prospective study. *Journal of Pediatrics*, 1977, 91, 363-370.
212. DYSON, R. S. The relationship between musical abilities and certain personality characteristics in secondary schoolchildren: A pilot study. *Council for Research in Music Education. Bulletin*, 1977, 50, 11-13.
213. HORNSTEIN, D., SOLOMON, S. J., & HOUSTON, B. K. Preliminary report on a juvenile court testing program. *Corrective & Social Psychiatry & Journal of Behavior Technology, Methods & Therapy*, 1977, 23, 11-14.
214. HUMMEL-ROSSI, B., & MERRIFIELD, P. Student personality factors related to teacher reports of their interactions with students. *Journal of Educational Psychology*, 1977, 69, 375-380.
215. MERRIFIELD, P. R., & HUMMEL-ROSSI, B. Relationships of indices of eighth grade academic achievement to sex and to measures of differentiated aptitudes and personality traits. *Educational & Psychological Measurement*, 1977, 37, 487-492.
216. POWER, C. N. Effects of student characteristics and level of teacher-student interaction on achievement and attitudes. *Contemporary Educational Psychology*, 1977, 2, 265-274.
217. WILLIAMS, R. E. Programmed instruction for creativity. *Programmed Learning & Educational Technology*, 1977, 14, 50-64.
218. BROWN, B. J., DRUCE, N. R., & SAWYER, C. E. Individual differences and absconding behavior. *British Journal of Criminology*, 1978, 18, 62-70.
219. VERMA, G. Conservatism and personality factors in a sample of adolescents. *Contemporary Educational Psychology*, 1978, 3, 51-56.
220. WHITTAKER, E. M. The personality structure of boys in a regional assessment centre. *British Journal of Educational Psychology*, 1978, 48, 92-97.
221. ANDERSON, B. J., LEMKE, E. A., & LEWIS, M. L. Identification of self-concept using the High School Personality Questionnaire. *Perceptual & Motor Skills*, 1979, 48, 731-734.
222. GUSTAFSSON, J. E. Attitudes towards the school, the teacher, and classmates at the class and individual level. *British Journal of Educational Psychology*, 1979, 49, 124-131.
223. HAIGHT, J. M. Spontaneous Psi cases: A survey and preliminary study of ESP, attitude, and personality relationships. *Journal of Parapsychology*, 1979, 43, 179-203.
224. MARTIN, P. J. Distinguishing school orchestra members. *Council for Research in Music Education. Bulletin*, 1979, 59, 62-67.
225. NUTTALL, E. V., & NUTTALL, R. L. Child-spacing effects on intelligence, personality, and social competence. *Journal of Psychology*, 1979, 102, 3-12.
226. SHERMAN, J. L., KRUG, S. E., & BIRENBAUM, M. Checking the reliability and validity of HSPQ profiles. *Journal of Personality Assessment*, 1979, 43, 644-647.
227. SOLHKHAH, N., HELLER, R. M., & ADERMAN, M. Facial imagery and personality development. *Perceptual & Motor Skills*, 1979, 48, 243-250.
228. ZAK, I. Modal personality of young Jews and Arabs in Israel. *Journal of Social Psychology*, 1979, 109, 3-10.
229. BOLTON, B. Comments on "Comments on the reliability of a personality questionnaire used in physical education and sport research". *Psychological Reports*, 1980, 46, 1133-1134.
230. LATUS, G., & BAUMAN, E. Personality and environmental correlates of academic achievement in Ojibwa Indian youth. *International Journal of Psychology*, 1980, 15, 71-82.
231. SCHUERGER, J. M., FEO, A. F., & NOWAK, M. J. Personality matches across media in a large high-school sample. *Multivariate Behavioral Research*, 1981, 16, 373-378.

[1234]

Juvenile Justice Policy Inventory. Juvenile justice professionals; 1973; JJPI; 4 scores: reintegration, rehabilitation, reform, restraint; Vincent O'Leary; National Council on Crime and Delinquency.*

For additional information, see 8:316.

[1235]

Ka-Ro Inkblot Test. Ages 3 and over; 1970; designed as "a Rorschach parallel series"; Yasufumi Kataguchi and the Ka-Ro Research Group (manual and record booklet); Kaneko Shobo Publisher [Japan].* (In-print status uncertain; no reply from publisher.)

For additional information and excerpted reviews by Jon D. Swartz and Daniel Brower, see 8:598 (4 references); see also 7:171 (1 reference).

[1236]

Kahn Intelligence Tests. Ages 1 month and over (particularly the verbally or culturally handicapped); 1960; KIT; uses same test objects as *Kahn Test of Symbol Arrangement*; main scale plus 6 optional scales: brief scale, concept formation, recall, motor coordination, scale for use with the deaf, scale for use with the blind; Theodore C. Kahn; Psychological Test Specialists.*

See T2:502 (1 reference); for a review by Marjorie P. Honzik, see 7:411 (6 references); see also 6:524 (2 references).

REFERENCES

1-2. See 6:524.
3-8. See 7:411.
9. See T2:502.
10. MATHEWSON, P. D. The Kahn Intelligence Test (experimental form) recall scale as a measure of retention. *Journal of Consulting & Clinical Psychology*, 1977, 45, 148.
11. REAM, J. H., III. Evaluation of intelligence in youthful offenders: The Kahn Intelligence Tests. *Perceptual & Motor Skills*, 1978, 46, 835-838.

[1237]

Kahn Test of Symbol Arrangement. Ages 6 and over; 1949-60; KTSA; Theodore C. Kahn; Psychological Test Specialists.*

See T2:1478 (27 references), P:447 (36 references), and 6:224 (10 references); for reviews by Cherry Ann Clark and Richard Jessor and an excerpted review by Laurance F. Shaffer, see 5:145 (16 references); for a review by Edward Joseph Shoben, Jr., see 4:110 (2 references).

REFERENCES

1-2. See 4:110.
3-18. See 5:145.
19-28. See 6:224.
29-64. See P:447.
65-91. See T2:1478.
92. KIPPER, D. A. The Kahn Test of Symbol Arrangement and criminality. *Journal of Clinical Psychology*, 1977, 33, 777-781.
93. DAVIS, L. L. Mental health of cancer patients as a function of group psychotherapy. *Unpublished Ph.D. dissertation, California Graduate Institute*, 1979.
94. REEVES, W. H. Auditory learning disabilities and emotional disturbance: Diagnostic differences. *Journal of Learning Disabilities*, 1980, 13, 30-33.
95. ROSE, A. Characteristics of extreme KTSA scorers. *Perceptual & Motor Skills*, 1980, 50, 553-554.

[1238]

Kansas Spelling Tests. 1, 2 semesters in grades 3, 4-6, 7-8; 1962-64; first published 1962-63 in the Every Pupil Scholarship Test series; 3 tests; Connie Moritz, Alice Robinson, Mary T. Williams, and M. W. Sanders; Bureau of Educational Measurements.*

a) KANSAS ELEMENTARY SPELLING TEST. 1, 2 semesters in grade 3.
b) KANSAS INTERMEDIATE SPELLING TEST. 1, 2 semesters in grades 4-6.
c) KANSAS JUNIOR HIGH SCHOOL SPELLING TEST. 1, 2 semesters in grades 7-8.

For additional information and a review by Thomas D. Horn, see 8:74.

[1239]
Kasanin-Hanfmann Concept Formation Test.
Normal and schizophrenic adults; 1940; CFT; also called *Vigotsky Test*; Jacob Kasanin and Eugenia Hanfmann; Stoelting Co.*

See T2:1140 (9 references), P:47 (7 references), and 6:78 (11 references); for a review by Kate Levine Kogan (with William S. Kogan), see 4:35 (8 references); for a review by O. L. Zangwill, see 3:27 (21 references).

REFERENCES

1–19. See 3:27.
20–27. See 4:35.
28–38. See 6:78.
39–45. See P:47.
46–54. See T2:1140.
55. REEVES, W. H. Auditory learning disabilities and emotional disturbance: Diagnostic differences. *Journal of Learning Disabilities*, 1980, 13, 30–33.

[1240]
Katz Adjustment Scales. Normal and mentally disordered adults; 1961–76; KAS; adjustment and social behavior in the community; for research use only; test booklet title is *KAS Behavior Inventories*; Martin M. Katz, Samuel B. Lyerly (manual), and Henri A. Lowery (supplement); Martin M. Katz.*

a) SCALES DESIGNED FOR RELATIVE'S RATINGS (R SCALES). 5 scales; 18 scores: 13 factor scores for Form R1, 1 score for each of Forms R2–R5 and 1 score (level of dissatisfaction with performance) based on differences between corresponding items on Forms R2 and R3.

1) *Form R1, Relative's Ratings of Patient's Symptoms and Social Behavior.* Primarily for use prior to hospitalization or following discharge; 13 factor scores: belligerence, verbal expansiveness, negativism, helplessness, suspiciousness, anxiety, withdrawal and retardation, general psychopathology, nervousness, confusion, bizarreness, hyperactivity, emotional stability.

2) *Form R2, Level of Performance of Socially Expected Activities.*

3) *Form R3, Level of Expectations for Performance of Social Activities.*

4) *Form RS4, Level of Free Time Activities.* Adaptation of *Your Activities and Attitudes.*

5) *Form R5, Level of Satisfaction With Free Time Activities.* Items are identical to those in Form RS4.

b) SCALES DESIGNED FOR PATIENTS' SELF-RATINGS (S SCALES). 5 scales; 6 scores: 1 score for each of Forms S1, S2, S3, RS4, S5, and 1 score (level of dissatisfaction with performance) based on differences between corresponding items on Forms S2 and S3.

1) *Form S1, Symptom Discomfort.* Adaptation of Johns Hopkins Symptom Distress Scale.

2) *Forms S2, S3, RS4, and S5.* Identical to the corresponding R scales except that they are adapted for self-rating.

For additional information, see 8:599 (23 references); see also T2:1255 (12 references) and P:138 (10 references).

REFERENCES

1–10. See P:138.
11–22. See T2:1255.
23–48. See 8:599.
49. BECKER, R. E., & SHASKAN, E. G. Platelet monoamine oxidase activity in schizophrenic patients. *American Journal of Psychiatry*, 1977, 134, 512–517.

50. EXNER, J. E., & MURRILLO, L. G. A long term follow–up of schizophrenics treated with regressive ECT. *Diseases of the Nervous System*, 1977, 38, 162–168.
51. LINN, M. W., & CAFFEY, E. M., JR. Foster placement for the older psychiatric patient. *Journal of Gerontology*, 1977, 32, 340–345.
52. MATTES, J. A., ROSEN, B., KLEIN, D. F., & MILLAN, D. Comparison of the clinical effectiveness of 'short' versus 'long' stay psychiatric hospitalization: III. Further results of a 3-year posthospital follow-up. *Journal of Nervous & Mental Disease*, 1977, 165, 395–402.
53. SHAFFER, J. W., SCHMIDT, C. W., ZLOTOWITZ, H. I., & FISHER, R. S. Social adjustment profiles of female drivers involved in fatal and nonfatal accidents. *American Journal of Psychiatry*, 1977, 134, 801–804.
54. ENGLEHARDT, D. M., RUDORFER, L., & ROSEN, B. Haloperidol and thiothixene in the long–term treatment of chronic schizophrenic outpatients in an urban community: Social and vocational adjustment. *Journal of Clinical Psychiatry*, 1978, 39, 834–840.
55. LAPIERRE, Y. D. A controlled study of penfluridol in the treatment of chronic schizophrenia. *American Journal of Psychiatry*, 1978, 135, 956–959.
56. ODDY, M., HUMPHREY, M., & UTTLEY, D. Stresses upon the relatives of head–injured patients. *British Journal of Pyschiatry*, 1978, 133, 507–513.
57. STRAUSS, J. S., KOKES, R. F., RITZLER, B. A., HARDER, D. W., & VAN ORD, A. Patterns of disorder in first admission psychiatric patients. *Journal of Nervous & Mental Disease*, 1978, 166, 611–623.
58. ANDREASEN, N. C., & WINOKUR, G. Newer experimental methods for classifying depression. *Archives of General Psychiatry*, 1979, 36, 447–452.
59. GOLDSTEIN, S. E., & BIRNBOM, F. Nylidrin HCl in the treatment of symptoms of the aged: A double–blind placebo controlled study. *Journal of Clinical Psychiatry*, 1979, 4, 520–524.
60. STRAUSS, J. S., HARDER, D. W., & CHANDLER, M. Egocentrism in children of parents with a history of psychotic disorders. *Archives of General Psychiatry*, 1979, 36, 191–196.
61. SUMMERS, F. Characteristics of new patient admissions to aftercare. *Hospital & Community Psychiatry*, 1979, 30, 199–202.
62. VANNICELLI, M., SHAAK, M., & NAHOR, A. Nontransitional residential treatment: A two year follow–up of a successful community. *American Journal of Orthopsychiatry*, 1979, 49, 522–526.
63. CROOK, T., HOGARTY, G. E., & ULRICH, R. F. Inter–rater reliability of informants' rating: Katz Adjustment Scales, R form. *Psychological Reports*, 1980, 47, 427–432.
64. GRAY, J. A follow–up study of psychiatric patients in a sheltered workshop program. *Hospital & Community Psychiatry*, 1980, 31, 563–566.
65. KOKES, R. F., HARDER, D. W., FISHER, L., & STRAUSS, J. S. Child competence and psychiatric risk. V. Sex of patient parent and dimension of psychotherapy. *Journal of Nervous & Mental Disease*, 1980, 168, 348–352.
66. STERN, M. J., & CLEARY, P. National exercise and heart disease project: Psychosocial changes observed during a low–level exercise program. *Archives of Internal Medicine*, 1981, 141, 1463–1467.

[1241]
Katz-Zalk Opinion Questionnaire. Grades 1–6; 1973–75; prepublication form called Projective Prejudice Test; racial attitudes; 3 scores: negative, positive, total; no manual; Phyllis A. Katz and Sue R. Zalk; Sue R. Zalk.*

For additional information, see 8:600 (3 references).

[1242]
Kaufman Development Scale. Birth to age 9 and mentally retarded all ages; 1972–74; KDS; 7 scores: gross motor, fine motor, receptive, expressive, personal behavior, inter-personal behavior, total; H. Kaufman; Stoelting Co.*

For additional information and a review by Dorothy H. Eichorn, see 8:218.

[1243]
★Keele Pre-School Assessment Guide. Children in nursery school; 1980; KPAG; experimental form; criterion-referenced; ratings by teachers or counselors in 5 areas: social behavior, cognition, physical skills, socialization, language; Stephen Tyler; NFER-Nelson Publishing Co. [England].*

[1244]
Kelvin Measurement of Ability in Infant Classes. Ages 5–8; 1935; C. M. Fleming; Robert Gibson & Sons, Glasgow, Ltd. [Scotland].*

See T2:395 (1 reference) and 5:346.

[1245]
★**The Kendrick Battery for the Detection of Dementia in the Elderly.** Ages 55 and over; 1979; battery should be repeated six weeks after initial testing; 2 tests; Andrew J. Gibson and Don C. Kendrick; NFER-Nelson Publishing Co. [England].*
a) OBJECT LEARNING TEST. A test of memory recall.
b) DIGIT COPYING TEST. A test of speed performance.

[1246]
★**Kent Infant Development Scale.** Ages 2–13 months; 1978–81; KID; ratings by parent or caregiver; 6 scores: cognitive, motor, social, language, self-help, full scale; Jeanette Reuter, Lewis Katoff, and Virginia Dunn (manual); Kent Developmental Metrics.*

REFERENCES

1. REUTER, J., KATOFF, L., & DUNN, V. The Kent Infant Development Scale. *Proceedings University of Pittsburgh–Prevention of Psychosocial Disorders of Infancy*, 1981, 88–89.

[1247]
Kent-Rosanoff Free Association Test. Ages 4 and over; 1910; K-R; G. H. Kent and A. J. Rosanoff; Stoelting Co.*

See T2:1480 (44 references) and P:448 (34 references); for a review by Jerry S. Wiggins, see 6:226 (82 references).

REFERENCES

1–82. See 6:226.
83–116. See P:448.
117–160. See T2:1480.
161. INNES, J. M. Extremity and "don't know" set in questionnaire response. *British Journal of Social & Clinical Psychology*, 1977, 16, 9–12.
162. JANOWSKY, D. S., HUEY, L., STORMS, L., & JUDD, L. L. Methylphenidate hydrochloride effects on psychological tests in acute schizophrenic and nonpsychotic patients. *Archives of General Psychiatry*, 1977, 34, 189–194.
163. STORMS, L. H. Changes in schizophrenics' word association commonalities during hospitalization. *Journal of Nervous & Mental Disease*, 1977, 164, 284–286.
164. COURSEY, R. D., BUCHSBAUM, M. S., & MURPHY, D. L. Psychological characteristics of subjects identified by platelet MAO activity and evoked potentials as biologically at risk for psychopathology. *Journal of Abnormal Psychology*, 1980, 89, 151–164.
165. STAM, H. J., RADTKE-BODORIK, H. L., & SPANOS, N. P. Repression and hypnotic amnesia: A failure to replicate and an alternative formulation. *Journal of Abnormal Psychology*, 1980, 89, 551–559.

[1248]
Kepner Mid-Year Algebra Achievement Tests. 1 semester high school; 1969; KMAAT; Henry S. Kepner, Jr. and Darrell Sabers; Bureau of Educational Research and Service.*

For additional information, a review by Gerald L. Ericksen, and an excerpted review by Arthur Mittman, see 7:506.

[1249]
★**Kerby Learning Modality Test, Revised 1980.** Ages 5, 6–8, 8–11; 1980, c1978–80; KLMT; diagnostic test for screening of perceptual modality functioning; 13 scores: visual (discrimination, memory, closure, motor coordination, total), auditory (discrimination, memory, closure, motor coordination, total), motor (visual, auditory, total); Maude L. Kerby; Western Psychological Services.*

[1250]
Key Math Diagnostic Arithmetic Test. Preschool–grade 6; 1971–76; "originally developed for testing educable mentally retarded children" (items "require almost no reading or writing ability"); 15 or 16 scores: content (numeration, fractions, geometry and symbols), operations (addition, subtraction, multiplication, division, mental computation, numerical reasoning), applications (word problems, missing elements, money, measurement, time), total, metric supplement (optional); Austin J. Connolly, William Nachtman, and E. Milo Pritchett; American Guidance Service.*

For additional information and an excerpted review by Alex Bannatyne, see 8:305 (10 references).

REFERENCES

1–10. See 8:305.
11. FINCHAM, F., & MELTZER, L. Learning disabilities and arithmetic achievement. *Journal of Learning Disabilities*, 1977, 10, 508–510.
12. GREENSTEIN, J., & STRAIN, P. S. The utility of the key math diagnostic arithmetic test for adolescent learning disabled students. *Psychology in the Schools*, 1977, 14, 275–282.
13. BRUININKS, V. L. Actual and perceived peer status of learning-disabled students in mainstream programs. *Journal of Special Education*, 1978, 12, 51–58.
14. BRUININKS, V. L. Peer status and personality characteristics of learning disabled and nondisabled students. *Journal of Learning Disabilities*, 1978, 11, 484–489.
15. MCLEAD, T. M., & CRUMP, W. D. The relationship of visuospatial skills and verbal ability to learning disabilities in mathematics. *Journal of Learning Disabilities*, 1978, 11, 237–241.
16. VAN ETTEN, C., & WATSON, B. Arithmetic skills: Assessment and instruction. *Journal of Learning Disabilities*, 1978, 11, 42–43.
17. HAMRICK, K. B. Oral language and readiness for the written symbolization of addition and subtraction. *Journal for Research in Mathematics Education*, 1979, 10, 188–194.
18. REED, H. B. C., JR. Biological defects and special education—An issue in personnel preparation. *Journal of Special Education*, 1979, 13, 9–33.
19. SANDOVAL, J. Reliability and concurrent validity of Light's Retention Scale. *Psychology in the Schools*, 1980, 17, 442–445.
20. SCHUSTER, D. H., & VINCENT, L. Teaching math and reading with suggestion and music. *Academic Therapy*, 1980, 16, 69–72.
21. BRODER, P. K., DUNIVANT, N., SMITH, E. C., & SUTTON, L. P. Further observations on the link between learning disabilities and juvenile delinquency. *Journal of Educational Psychology*, 1981, 73, 838–850.
22. KARMOS, J. S., SCHEER, J., MILLER, A., & BARDO, H. The relationship of math achievement to impulsivity in mathematically deficient elementary school students. *School Science & Mathematics*, 1981, 81, 685–688.

[1251]
Keystone Tests of Binocular Skill. Grades 1, 2–3, 4–5, 8 and over; 1938–49; adaptation of *Standardized Oral Reading Check Tests* for use with the Keystone Telebinocular to identify children who can read better with one eye than with both eyes together; 2 scores (time, errors) for both eyes, left eye, right eye; Keystone View.*

For additional information, see 6:957 (1 reference).

REFERENCES

1. See 6:957.
2. HAYWOOD, K. M. Eye movements during coincidence–anticipation performance. *Journal of Motor Behavior*, 1977, 9, 313–318.

[1252]
[**Keystone Visual Screening Tests**]. Preschool and over; 1933–71; visual screening tests which can be administered by lay personnel as a basis for referrals to eye specialists; basic instrument used is the Keystone Telebinocular; an attachment, the Keystone Periometer, can be

added to any of the three models for measuring the extent of the lateral field of vision; Keystone View.*

a) KEYSTONE VISUAL SURVEY TESTS. Grades 1 (2 or 4 for some tests) and over; 1933–61; screening tests for use in referring students to eye specialists on the basis of failures made on both of two successive testings a week or so apart, preferably administered by different persons; revision of the *Betts Ready to Read Tests*; "the regular tests for acuity both far and near should not be used until the end of the second grade"; the color tests should not be used below grade 4; low scores for children under 7 may represent visual immaturity rather than visual deficiency; Keystone Telebinocular No. 1103 required for administration; 15 tests: simultaneous vision, vertical posture, lateral posture (2 scores), fusion (2 scores), usable vision (6 scores), depth perception, color perception (2 scores); 10 additional tests for use with the Keystone Telebinocular No. 1103 are listed below.

1) *Keystone Massachusetts School Vision Test.* Grades 1 and over; 1959; 5 scores: visual acuity at a distance, hyperopia (far, near), phoria (far, near); no manual; not to be confused with out of print *Massachusetts Vision Test.*
2) *Keystone Michigan School Vision Test.* Grades 1 and over; 1959; 5 scores: visual acuity at a distance, hyperopia (far, near), phoria (far, near); no manual.
3) *Keystone New York School Vision Test.* Grades kgn–8; 1958; 5 scores: visual acuity at a distance (each eye), farsightedness, lateral phoria (far, near).
4) *Keystone Plus-Lens Test.* Ages 5 and over; 1957–71; farsightedness; referral to an eye specialist on the basis of this test alone is not warranted.
5) *Keystone Preschool Test.* Ages 4–6; 1956; "gross visual acuity" at far point; no manual.
6) *Keystone Ready-to-Read Tests.*
7) *Keystone Tests of Binocular Skill.*
8) *Keystone Rapid Screening Test.* Grades 1 and over; 1967; students failing to pass all tests should be administered the longer *Keystone Visual Survey Tests*; 9 pass-fail scores: fusion (2 scores), hyperphoria, depth perception, color perception, usable vision (4 scores).
9) *Near-Point Visual Acuity Test.* Nonreaders; 1967; usable vision of each eye and both eyes together at reading distance; no manual.
10) *Spache Binocular Reading Test.*

b) KEYSTONE OCCUPATIONAL VISUAL SERVICE TESTS. Employees; 1935–61; screening tests for "determining an employee's visual status so that an appropriate job placement may be made" and for referring employees to eye specialists; Keystone Telebinocular No. 1102 is required for administration; 15 scores: vertical balance (2 scores), lateral balance (2 scores), fusion (2 scores), usable vision (6 scores), depth perception, color vision (2 scores); an additional test for use with the Keystone Telebinocular No. 1102 follows:

1) *Keystone Industrial Short Tests.* Employees; 1948; 12 pass-fail scores: hyperphoria (2 scores), fusion (2 scores), depth perception, color perception, usable vision (6 scores); "failure of any test indicates the need for examination on the complete battery of tests."

c) KEYSTONE DRIVER VISION TESTS. Driver applicants; 1950–70; 11 scores: vertical balance, lateral balance, fusion, usable vision (3 scores), depth perception, color perception (2 scores), tunnel vision (2 scores); Keystone Telebinocular No. 1101; periometer attachment necessary for funnel vision test.

See T2:1918 (27 references) and 5:780 (18 references); for a review by F. Nowell Jones and an excerpted review of an earlier model of the occupational telebinocular, see 3:467 (43 references).

REFERENCES

1–43. See 3:467.
44–61. See 5:780.
62–88. See T2:1918.
89. MARTINETTI, R. F. Effect of stimulus perspective on perception of oscillation. *Perceptual & Motor Skills*, 1981, 52, 911–917.

[1253]

★**Khatena-Torrance Creative Perception Inventory.** Ages 12 and over; 1976; 13 scores: creative perception index (2 scores), environmental sensitivity, initiative, self-strength, intellectuality, individuality, artistry, acceptance of authority, self-confidence, inquisitiveness, awareness of others, disciplined imagination; Joe Khatena and E. Paul Torrance; Stoelting Co.*

REFERENCES

1. KHATENA, J. The Khatena–Torrance Creative Perception Inventory for identification diagnosis facilitation and research. *Gifted Child Quarterly*, 1977, 21, 517–525.
2. KHATENA, J., & BELLAROSA, A. Further validity evidence of something about myself. *Perceptual & Motor Skills*, 1978, 47, 906.

[1254]

Kilander-Leach Health Knowledge Test. Grades 12–16; 1936–72; KLHKT; formerly called *Kilander Health Knowledge Test*; original test by H. Frederick Kilander, revision by Glenn C. Leach; Glenn C. Leach, Publisher.*

See T2:935 (5 references); for a review by James E. Bryan, see 7:609 (2 references); see also 5:562 (3 references); for excerpted reviews by Lois M. Shoemaker and one other of an earlier form, see 2:1503.

[1255]

Kindergarten Auditory Screening Test. Grades kgn–1; 1971; KAST; 3 scores: speech in environmental noise, phonemic synthesis, same/different; Jack Katz; Follett Publishing Co.*

For additional information and a review by Nicholas W. Bankson, see 8:940 (3 references).

REFERENCES

1–3. See 8:940.
4. MARGOLIS, H. Auditory perceptual test performance and the reflection–impulsivity dimension. *Journal of Learning Disabilities*, 1977, 10, 164–172.
5. MARGOLIS, H., & BRANNIGAN, G. G. Conceptual tempo as a parameter for predicting reading achievement. *Journal of Educational Research*, 1978, 71, 342–345.
6. SABATINO, D. A. The definition and assessment of visual and auditory perception. *Journal of Clinical Child Psychology*, 1979, 8, 188–194.

[1256]

Kindergarten Behavioural Index: A Screening Technique for Reading Readiness. Grades kgn–1; 1972; KBI; behavior checklist; 38 scores: self identity, handedness, directionality (3 scores), visual-motor coordination (7 scores), rhythm, speech, language structure (2 scores), language sequencing (5 scores), sequential memory (4 scores), language association, behaviour (8 scores), attention (3 scores), total; Enid M. Banks; Australian Council for Educational Research [Australia].*

[1257]
Kit of Factor Referenced Cognitive Tests. Various grades 6–16; 1954–63; formerly called *Kit of Reference Tests for Cognitive Factors*, 1963 *Revision*; for research use only; groups of 1–5 tests measuring 24 (16 in the 1954 Kit) "of the better established factors in the cognitive area"; 4 of the 16 factors presented in the 1954 Kit have been dropped and 12 new factors added; "whereas the tests in the first Kit [1954] were usually exact copies of those used in earlier factor studies, most of the tests in the present edition have been newly adapted"; although most tests have been "adapted" or revised, the same titles are used in both the 1954 and 1963 Kits; unless otherwise indicated, all tests were prepared by the Educational Testing Service; tests compiled and manual written by John W. French, Ruth B. Ekstrom, and Leighton A. Price; Educational Testing Service.*

a) FACTOR CF: FLEXIBILITY OF CLOSURE. Grades 6–16; 1962; 3 tests.
  1) *Hidden Figures Test, Cf-1.*
  2) *Hidden Patterns Test, Cf-2.*
  3) *Copying Test, Cf-3. Out of print.*

b) FACTOR CS: SPEED OF CLOSURE. Grades 6–16; 1962; 2 tests.
  1) *Gestalt Completion Test, Cs-1.*
  2) *Concealed Words Test, Cs-2.*

c) FACTOR FA: ASSOCIATIONAL FLUENCY. Grades 6–16; 1957–62; 3 tests.
  1) *Controlled Associations Test, Fa-1.* 1962. *Out of print.*
  2) *Associational Fluency 1, Form A, [Fa-2].* 1957; Paul R. Christensen and J. P. Guilford; Sheridan Psychological Services, Inc.
  3) *Associations 4, Fa-3.* 1962; J. P. Guilford. *Out of print.*

d) FACTOR FE: EXPRESSIONAL FLUENCY. Grades 8–16; 1958–62; 3 tests.
  1) *Expressional Fluency, [Fe-1].* 1958; Paul R. Christensen and J. P. Guilford; Sheridan Psychological Services, Inc.
  2) *Simile Interpretations, Fe-2.* 1962; J. P. Guilford. *Out of print.*
  3) *Word Arrangement, Fe-3.* 1962; J. P. Guilford. *Out of print.*

e) FACTOR FI: IDEATIONAL FLUENCY. Grades 8–16; 1962; 3 tests. *Out of print.*
  1) *Topics Test, Fi-1.*
  2) *Theme Test, Fi-2.*
  3) *Thing Categories Test, Fi-3.*

f) FACTOR FW: WORD FLUENCY. Grades 6–16; 1962; 3 tests. *Out of print.*
  1) *Word Endings Test, Fw-1.*
  2) *Word Beginnings Test, Fw-2.*
  3) *Word Beginnings and Endings Test, Fw-3.*

g) FACTOR I: INDUCTION. Grades 8–16; 1962; 3 tests.
  1) *Letter Sets Test, I-1.*
  2) *Locations Test, I-2.*
  3) *Figure Classification, I-3.*

h) FACTOR LE: LENGTH ESTIMATION. Grades 6–16; 1962; 3 tests.
  1) *Estimation of Length Test, Le-1.*
  2) *Shortest Road Test, Le-2. Out of print.*
  3) *Nearer Point Test, Le-3.*

i) FACTOR MA: ASSOCIATIVE (ROTE) MEMORY. Grades 6–16; 1962; 3 tests. *Out of print.*
  1) *Picture-Number Test, Ma-1.*
  2) *Object-Number Test, Ma-2.*
  3) *First and Last Names Test, Ma-3.*

j) FACTOR MK: MECHANICAL KNOWLEDGE. 1962; 3 tests. *Out of print.*
  1) *Tool Knowledge Test, Mk-1.* Grades 6–16.
  2) *Mechanical Information Test, Mk-2.* Grades 8–16.
  3) *Electrical Information Test, Mk-3.* Grades 8–16.

k) FACTOR MS: MEMORY SPAN. Grades 6–16; 1962; 3 tests.
  1) *Auditory Number Span Test, Ms-1. Out of print.*
  2) *Visual Number Span Test, Ms-2. Out of print.*
  3) *Auditory Letter Span Test, Ms-3.*

l) FACTOR N: NUMBER FACILITY. Grades 6–16; 1953–62; 3 tests; 1962 tests essentially the same as tests copyrighted 1953 except for an increase in items.
  1) *Addition Test, N-1.*
  2) *Division Test, N-2.*
  3) *Subtraction and Multiplication Test, N-3.*

m) FACTOR O: ORIGINALITY. Grades 10–16; 1958–62; 3 tests. *Out of print.*
  1) *Plot Titles, O-1.* 1962.
  2) *Symbol Production, O-2.* 1962.
  3) *Consequences, O-3 [10–Item Edition].* 1958; P. R. Christensen, P. R. Merrifield, and J. P. Guilford.

n) FACTOR P: PERCEPTUAL SPEED. Grades 6–16; 1962; 3 tests.
  1) *Finding A's Test, P-1.*
  2) *Number Comparison Test, P-2. Out of print.*
  3) *Identical Pictures Test, P-3.*

o) FACTOR R: GENERAL REASONING. 1955–62; 4 tests.
  1) *Mathematics Aptitude Test, R-1.* Grades 6–12; 1962. *Out of print.*
  2) *Mathematics Aptitude Test, R-2.* Grades 11–16; 1962.
  3) *Ship Destination Test, [R-3].* 1955; Paul R. Christensen and J. P. Guilford; Sheridan Psychological Services, Inc.
  4) *Necessary Arithmetic Operations Test, R-4.* Grades 6–16; 1962.

p) FACTOR RE: SEMANTIC REDEFINITION. Grades 10–16; 1962; 3 tests. *Out of print.*
  1) *Gestalt Transformation, Re-1.*
  2) *Object Synthesis, Re-2.* J. P. Guilford.
  3) *Picture Gestalt, Re-3.* J. P. Guilford. For a revision, see *New Uses.*

q) FACTOR RS: SYLLOGISTIC REASONING. Grades 11–16; 1955–62; 3 tests.
  1) *Nonsense Syllogisms Test, Rs-1.* 1962.
  2) *Logical Reasoning, [Rs-2].* 1955; Alfred F. Hertzka and J. P. Guilford; Sheridan Psychological Services, Inc.
  3) *Inference Test, Rs-3.* 1962.

r) FACTOR S: SPATIAL ORIENTATION. 1947–62; 3 tests.
  1) *Card Rotations Test, S-1.* Grades 8–16; 1962.
  2) *Cube Comparisons Test, S-2.* Grades 8–16; 1962.
  3) *Guilford-Zimmerman Aptitude Survey: Part 5, Spatial Orientation, [S-3].* 1947; J. P. Guilford and Wayne S. Zimmerman; Sheridan Psychological Services, Inc.

s) FACTOR SEP: SENSITIVITY TO PROBLEMS. Grades 8–16; 1962; 3 tests. *Out of print.*
  1) *Apparatus Test, Sep-1.* J. P. Guilford.
  2) *Seeing Problems, Sep-2.*
  3) *Seeing Deficiencies, Sep-3.* J. P. Guilford.

t) FACTOR SS: SPATIAL SCANNING. Grades 6–16; 1962; 3 tests.
  1) *Maze Tracing Speed Test, Ss-1.*

2) *Choosing a Path, Ss-2.*
3) *Man Planning Test, Ss-3.*

u) FACTOR V: VERBAL COMPREHENSION. 1962; 5 tests.
1) *Vocabulary Test, V-1.* Grades 7–12. *Out of print.*
2) *Vocabulary Test, V-2.* Grades 7–12.
3) *Wide Range Vocabulary Test, V-3.* Grades 7–16.
4) *Advanced Vocabulary Test, V-4.* Grades 11–16.
5) *Vocabulary Test, V-5.* Grades 11–16. *Out of print.*

v) FACTOR VZ: VISUALIZATION. Grades 9–16; 1962; 3 tests.
1) *Form Board Test, Vz-1.*
2) *Paper Folding Test, Vz-2.*
3) *Surface Development Test, Vz-3.*

w) FACTOR XA: FIGURAL ADAPTIVE FLEXIBILITY. Grades 11–16; 1962; 3 tests. *Out of print.*
1) *Match Problems 2, Xa-1.*
2) *Match Problems 5, Xa-2.*
3) *Planning Air Maneuvers, Xa-3.*

x) FACTOR XS: SEMANTIC SPONTANEOUS FLEXIBILITY. Grades 6–16; 1960–62; 3 tests.
1) *Utility Test, Xs-1.* 1962. *Out of print.*
2) *Alternate Uses, [Xs-2].* 1960; Paul R. Christensen, J. P. Guilford, Philip R. Merrifield, and Robert C. Wilson; Sheridan Psychological Services, Inc.
3) *Object Naming, Xs-3.* 1962; J. P. Guilford. *Out of print.*

See T2:561 (103 references) and 6:551.

REFERENCES

1–103. See T2:561.
104. ALPAUGH, P. K., & BIRREN, J. E. Variables affecting creative contributions across the adult life span. *Human Development*, 1977, 20, 240–248.
105. CORY, C. H., RIMLAND, B., & BRYSON, R. A. Using computerized tests to measure new dimensions of abilities: An exploratory study. *Applied Psychological Measurement*, 1977, 1, 101–110.
106. CUMMINS, J. Cognitive factors associated with the attainment of intermediate levels of bilingual skills. *Modern Language Journal*, 1977, 61, 3–12.
107. LUNNEBORG, C. E. Choice reaction time: What role in ability measurement? *Applied Psychological Measurement*, 1977, 1, 309–330.
108. MAYER, R. E. Problem–solving performance with task overload: Effects of self–pacing and trait anxiety. *Bulletin of the Psychonomic Society*, 1977, 9, 283–286.
109. PLATNICK, D. M., & RICHARDS, L. G. Individual differences related to performance on two word–recognition tasks. *American Journal of Psychology*, 1977, 90, 133–144.
110. RICHARDSON, A. The meaning and measurement of memory imagery. *British Journal of Psychology*, 1977, 68, 29–43.
111. ROYER, P. N. Effects of specificity and position of written instructional objects on learning from lecture. *Journal of Educational Psychology*, 1977, 69, 40–45.
112. SCHMECK, R. R., RIBICH, F., & RAMANAIAH, N. Development of a self–report inventory for assessing individual differences in learning processes. *Applied Psychological Measurements*, 1977, 1, 413–431.
113. SZETO, J. A., & SALOME R. A. The effects of scanning practice and perceptual training upon several visual functions: Implications for drawing. *Studies in Art Education*, 1977, 19, 45–51.
114. TRAUB, R. E., & FISHER, C. W. On the equivalence of constructed–response and multiple–choice tests. *Applied Psychological Measurement*, 1977, 1, 355–369.
115. ALLEN, M. J. An empirical demonstration of the factor differentiation hypothesis. *Multivariate Behavioral Research*, 1978, 13, 63–75.
116. ANDERSON, R. C., SPIRO, R. J., & ANDERSON, M. C. Schemata as scaffolding for the representation of information in connected discourse. *American Educational Research Journal*, 1978, 15, 433–440.
117. ANDRE, M. E. D. A., & ANDERSON, T. H. The development and evaluation of a self–questioning study technique. *Reading Research Quarterly*, 1978–1979, 14, 605–623.
118. ANNIS, L., & DAVIS, J. K. Study techniques and cognitive style: Their effect on recall and recognition. *Journal of Educational Research*, 1978, 71, 175–178.
119. ARNDT, S., & BERGER, D. E. Cognitive mode and asymmetry in cerebral functioning. *Cortex*, 1978, 14, 78–86.
120. BECKER, J. P., & YOUNG, C. D., JR. Designing instructional methods in mathematics to accommodate different patterns of aptitude. *Journal for Research in Mathematics Education*, 1978, 9, 4–18.
121. CABAN, J. P., HAMBLETON, R. K., COFFING, D. G., CONWAY, M. T., & SWAMINATHAN, H. Mental imagery as an approach to spelling instruction. *Journal of Experimental Education*, 1978, 46, 15–21.
122. CUNNINGHAM, W. R., SEPKOSKI, C. M., & OPEL, M. R. Fatigue effects on intelligence test performance in the elderly. *Journal of Gerontology*, 1978, 33, 541–545.
123. DEFRIES, J. C., SINGER, S. M., FOCH, T. T., & LEWITTER, F. I. Familial nature of reading disability. *British Journal of Psychiatry*, 1978, 132, 361–367.
124. FORBES, J. B., & BARRETT, G. V. Individual abilities and task demands in relation to performance and satisfaction on two repetitive monitoring tasks. *Journal of Applied Psychology*, 1978, 63, 188–196.
125. GINTHER, J. R. Pretraining Chicano students before administration of a mathematics predictor test. *Journal for Research in Mathematics Education*, 1978, 9, 118–125.
126. KIRBY, J. R., & DAS, J. P. Skills underlying Coloured Progressive Matrices. *Alberta Journal of Educational Research*, 1978, 24, 94–99.
127. MEYER, R. A. Mathematical problem–solving performance and intellectual abilities of fourth–grade children. *Journal for Research in Mathematics Education*, 1978, 9, 334–348.
128. PETERSON, P. L., & CLARK, C. M. Teachers' reports of their cognitive processes during teaching. *American Educational Research Journal*, 1978, 15, 555–565.
129. PETERSON, P. L., MARX, R. W., & CLARK, C. M. Teacher planning, teacher behavior, and student achievement. *American Educational Research Journal*, 1978, 15, 417–432.
130. PETRUSIC, W. M., VARRO, L., & JAMIESON, D. G. Mental rotation validation of two spatial ability tests. *Psychological Research*, 1978, 40, 139–148.
131. PLEMONS, J. K., WILLIS, S. L., & BALTES, P. B. Modifiability of fluid intelligence in aging: A short–term longitudinal training approach. *Journal of Gerontology*, 1978, 33, 224–231.
132. RAMSEY, P. H. Factor analysis of the WAIS and twenty French–kit reference tests. *Applied Psychological Measurement*, 1978, 2, 505–517.
133. RESICK, P. A., & PAYNE, R. B. Sex and practice distribution effects in children. *Bulletin of the Psychonomic Society*, 1978, 11, 380–382.
134. RUSSELL, M., & SINES, J. O. Further evidence that M–F is bipolar and multidimensional. *Journal of Clinical Psychology*, 1978, 34, 643–649.
135. SIGNORELLA, M. L., & JAMISON, W. Sex differences in the correlations among field dependence, spatial ability, sex role orientation, and performance on Piaget's water–level task. *Developmental Psychology*, 1978, 14, 689–690.
136. STANKOV, L., & SPILSBURY, G. The measurement of auditory abilities of blind, partially sighted, and sighted children. *Applied Psychological Measurement*, 1978, 2, 491–503.
137. WEISZ, J. R., QUINLAN, D. M., O'NEILL, P., & O'NEILL, P. C. The Rorschach and structured tests of perception as indices of intellectual development in mentally retarded and nonretarded children. *Journal of Experimental Child Psychology*, 1978, 25, 326–336.
138. CARTER, R. C. Mental abilities during a simulated dive to 427 meters underwater. *Journal of Applied Psychology*, 1979, 64, 449–454.
139. COSDEN, M. A., ELLIS, H. C., & FEENEY, D. M. Cognitive flexibility–rigidity, repetition effects, and memory. *Journal of Research in Personality*, 1979, 13, 386–395.
140. HILL, D. M., & OBENAUF, P. A. Spatial visualization, problem solving, and cognitive development in freshman teacher education students. *Science Education*, 1979, 63, 665–670.
141. KATZ, A. N., & POAG, J. R. Sex differences in instructions to "be creative" on divergent and non–divergent test scores. *Journal of Personality*, 1979, 47, 518–530.
142. MCLEOD, D. B., & ADAMS, V. M. Individual differences in cognitive style and discovery approaches to learning mathematics. *Journal of Educational Research*, 1979, 72, 317–320.
143. MCLEOD, D. B., & ADAMS, V. M. The interaction of field independence with small–group instruction in mathematics. *Journal of Experimental Education*, 1979–1980, 48, 118–124.
144. MILLER, W. G., SNOWMAN, J., & O'HARA, T. Application of alternative statistical techniques to examine the hierarchical ordering in Bloom's taxonomy. *American Educational Research Journal*, 1979, 16, 241–248.
145. MYROW, D. L. Learner choice and task engagement. *Journal of Experimental Education*, 1979, 47, 200–207.
146. RANDHAWA, B. S., & HUNT, D. Some further evidence on successive and simultaneous integration and individual differences. *Canadian Journal of Behavioural Science*, 1979, 11, 340–355.
147. SAVARESE, J. M., & MILLER, R. J. Artistic preferences and cognitive–perceptual style. *Studies in Art Education*, 1979, 20, 45–51.
148. THREADGILL, J. The interaction of learner aptitude with types of questions accompanying a written lesson on logical implications. *Journal for Research in Mathematics Education*, 1979, 10, 337–346.

149. WEBB, N. L. Processes, conceptual knowledge, and mathematical problem solving ability. *Journal for Research in Mathematics Education*, 1979, 10, 83–93.
150. WHITELY, S. E. Estimating measurement error on highly speeded tests. *Applied Psychological Measurement*, 1979, 3, 141–154.
151. WORMACK, L. Cognitive predictors of articulation in writing. *Perceptual & Motor Skills*, 1979, 48, 1151–1156.
152. WORMACK, L. Restructuring ability and patterns of physics achievement. *Perceptual & Motor Skills*, 1979, 48, 451–458.
153. YOUNG, C. D., JR., & BECKER, J. P. The interaction of cognitive aptitudes with sequences of figural and symbolic treatments of mathematical inequalities. *Journal for Research in Mathematics Education*, 1979, 10, 24–36.
154. ZOCCOLOTTI, P., PASSAFIUME, D., & PIZZAMIGLIO, L. Hemispheric superiorities on a unilateral tactile test: Relationship to cognitive dimensions. *Perceptual & Motor Skills*, 1979, 49, 735–742.
155. ANDRE, T., MUELLER, C., WOMACK, S., SMID, K., & TUTTLE, M. Adjunct application questions facilitate later application, or do they? *Journal of Educational Psychology*, 1980, 72, 533–543.
156. BALTES, P. B., CORNELIUS, S. W., SPIRO, A., NESSELROADE, J. R., & WILLIS, S. L. Integration versus differentiation of fluid/crystallized intelligence in old age. *Developmental Psychology*, 1980, 16, 625–635.
157. BURNS, R. B. Relation of aptitudes to learning at different points in time during instruction. *Journal of Educational Psychology*, 1980, 72, 785–795.
158. DICKSTEIN, L. S. Inference errors in deductive reasoning. *Bulletin of the Psychonomic Society*, 1980, 16, 414–416.
159. ELMORE, P. B., & VASU, E. S. Relationship between selected variables and statistics achievement: Building a theoretical model. *Journal of Educational Psychology*, 1980, 72, 457–467.
160. HERTEL, P. T., COSSLEN, M., & JOHNSON, P. J. Passage recall: Schema change and cognitive flexibility. *Journal of Educational Psychology*, 1980, 72, 133–140.
161. HO, H. Z., FOCH, T. T., & PLOMIN, R. Developmental stability of the relative influence of genes and environment on specific cognitive abilities during childhood. *Developmental Psychology*, 1980, 16, 340–346.
162. HUNT, D. Intentional–incidental learning and simultaneous–successive processing. *Canadian Journal of Behavioral Science*, 1980, 12, 373–383.
163. KINNEY, J. A. S., & LURIA, S. M. Factor analysis of perceptual and cognitive abilities tested by different methods. *Perceptual & Motor Skills*, 1980, 50, 59–69.
164. KORAN, J. J., JR., KORAN, M. L., & BAKER, S. D. Differential response to cueing and feedback in the acquisition of an inductively presented biological concept. *Journal for Research in Science Teaching*, 1980, 17, 167–172.
165. KORAN, M. L., & KORAN, J. J., JR. Interaction of learner characteristics with pictorial adjuncts in learning from science text. *Journal for Research in Science Teaching*, 1980, 17, 477–483.
166. MARSELLA, A. J., & GOLDEN, C. J. The structure of cognitive abilities in Americans of Japanese and of European ancestry in Hawaii. *Journal of Social Psychology*, 1980, 112, 19–30.
167. MULLIGAN, G., & MARTIN, W. Adaptors, innovators and the Kirton Adaption Innovation Inventory. *Psychological Reports*, 1980, 46, 883–892.
168. STANKOV, L. Ear differences and implied cerebral lateralization on some intellective auditory factors. *Applied Psychological Measurement*, 1980, 4, 21–38.
169. STERNBERG, R. J. Representation and process in linear syllogistic reasoning. *Journal of Experimental Psychology: General*, 1980, 109, 119–159.
170. STERNBERG, R. J., & WEIL, E. M. An aptitude x strategy interaction in linear syllogistic reasoning. *Journal of Educational Psychology*, 1980, 72, 226–239.
171. TENNYSON, C. L., TENNYSON, R. D., & ROTHEN, W. Content structure and instructional control strategies as design variables in concept acquisition. *Journal of Educational Psychology*, 1980, 72, 499–505.
172. TENNYSON, R. D. Instructional control strategies and content structure as design variables in concept acquisition using computer–based instruction. *Journal of Educational Psychology*, 1980, 72, 525–532.
173. WARD, W. C., FREDERICKSEN, N., & CARLSON, S. B. Construct validity of free response and machine–scorable forms of a test. *Journal of Educational Measurement*, 1980, 17, 11–29.
174. WEDIGER, T. A., KNUDSON, R. M., & RORER, L. G. Convergent and discriminant validity of measures of cognitive styles and abilities. *Journal of Personality & Social Psychology*, 1980, 39, 116–129.
175. BORLING, J. E. The effects of sedative music on alpha rhythms and focused attention in high–creative and low–creative subjects. *Journal of Music Therapy*, 1981, 18, 101–108.
176. COPPAGE, S. J., & PAYNE, R. B. An experimental test of current theories of psychomotor reminiscence. *Perceptual & Motor Skills*, 1981, 52, 343–352.
177. CUNNINGHAM, W. R. Ability factor structure differences in adulthood and old age. *Multivariate Behavioral Research*, 1981, 16, 3–22.
178. DREHER, M. J., & SINGER, H. The validity of the instantiation hypothesis. *Journal of Reading Behavior*, 1981, 13, 223–235.
179. DURAPAU, V. J., JR., & CARRY, L. R. Interaction of general reasoning ability and processing strategies in geometry instruction. *Journal for Research in Mathematics Education*, 1981, 12, 15–26.
180. KISSINGER, J. F., & MUNJAS, B. A. Nursing process, student attributes, and teaching methodologies. *Nursing Research*, 1981, 30, 242–246.
181. ROBINSON, J. A. Context effects in retrospective judgments of personal experiences. *Bulletin of the Psychonomic Society*, 1981, 17, 147–150.

[1258]

★**Knowledge and Attitudes of Drug Usage.** Grades 4–6, 7–12; 1973; "an IOX measurable objectives collection"; utilizes knowledge, direct report, indirect, archival, observation, and planning information measures; 2 levels; Instructional Objectives Exchange.*
a) INTERMEDIATE LEVEL. Grades 4–6; 4 objectives: drug experience, school description check list, life decisions, facts about drugs (2 forms), plus basis of belief measure.
b) SECONDARY LEVEL. Grades 7–12; 8 objectives: drug use inventory (personal opinions), drug experience, school description check list, problems-problems, life decisions, facts about drugs (2 forms), teacher observation form, community drug report, plus basis of belief measure.

[1259]

Knowledge of Occupations Test. High school; 1974; KOT; 9 scores: earnings, licensing and certification, job descriptions, employment trends, training, terminology, graphs, tools, total; Leroy G. Baruth; Psychologists and Educators, Inc.*

For additional information and reviews by David O. Herman and Dean H. Nafziger, see 8:1008 (1 reference).

[1260]

★**Knox's Cube Test.** Ages 3–8, 9 and over; 1980; KCT; non-verbal mental test; attention span and short-term memory; Mark H. Stone and Benjamin D. Wright; Stoelting Co.*

[1261]

Knuth Achievement Tests in Music: Recognition of Rhythm and Melody. Grades 3–4, 5–6, 7–12; 1936–68; KATM; manual title is *Achievement Tests in Music*; reissue of the 1936 edition using filmstrips and prerecorded tapes; William E. Knuth; Creative Arts Research Associates, Inc.* (In-print status uncertain; no reply from publisher.)

See T2:201 (5 references) and 7:246 (1 reference); for a review by Carl E. Seashore, see 2:1332 (1 reference); for reviews by Jay W. Fay and James L. Mursell, see 1:1085.

[1262]

★**Kohlberg's Moral Judgment Interview.** Ages 10 and over; 1983; moral development; Anne Colby, Lawrence Kohlberg, et al.; Cambridge University Press.*

REFERENCES

1. BENSON, A. L. Morality of schizophrenic adolescents. *Journal of Abnormal Psychology*, 1980, 89, 674–677.
2. COLBY, A., KOHLBERG, L., GIBBS, J., & LIEBERMAN, M. A longitudinal study of moral judgment. *Society for Research & Child Development*, Monograph Series, 1981 (in press).

[1263]

★**Kohn Problem Checklist.** Children ages 3–6 in preschool programs; 1979; ratings by teachers or other observers; 2 factor scores: apathy-withdrawal, anger-defiance; Martin Kohn, Barbara Parnes, and Bernice L. Rosman; Martin Kohn.*

[1264]

★Kohn Social Competence Scale. Children ages 3–6 in half-day, full-day preschool programs; 1979; ratings by teachers or other observers; 2 factor scores: interest-participation versus apathy-withdrawal, cooperation-compliance versus anger-defiance; 2 scales; Martin Kohn, Barbara Parnes, and Bernice L. Rosman; Martin Kohn.*
a) 73-ITEM SOCIAL COMPETENCE SCALE. Children ages 3–6 in full-day preschool programs.
b) 64-ITEM SOCIAL COMPETENCE SCALE. Children ages 3–6 in half-day preschool programs.

[1265]

The Kohs Block-Design Test. Mental ages 5–20; [1919]; formerly called *The Block-Design Test*; modifications appear in *Arthur Point Scale of Performance Tests, New Guinea Performance Scales, Ohwaki-Kohs Tactile Block Design Intelligence Test for the Blind*, and *Pacific Design Construction Test*; S. C. Kohs; Stoelting Co.*

See T2:545 (74 references).

REFERENCES

1–74. See T2:545.
75. BERGLUND, M., LEIJONQUIST, H., & HÖRLÉN. M. Prognostic significance and reversibility of cerebral dysfunction in alcoholics. *Journal of Studies on Alcohol*, 1977, 38, 1761–1770.
76. BERGLUND, M., & LEIJONQUIST, H. Prediction of cerebral dysfunction in alcoholics: A study of health insurance records. *Journal of Studies on Alcohol*, 1978, 39, 1968–1974.
77. BRATT, H. M. Hemisphere asymmetry in school age children. *School Science & Mathematics*, 1979, 79, 158–160.
78. POWELL, G. E. Categories of aphasia: A cluster-analysis of Schuell Test profiles. *British Journal of Disorders of Communication*, 1979, 14, 111–122.

[1266]

★Kraner Preschool Math Inventory. Ages 3–0 to 6–6; 1976–77; KPMI; criterion-referenced test measures quantitative concepts acquisition and a norm-referenced subtest (Math/Screen) derived from KPMI measures mathematics language development; Robert E. Kraner; Teaching Resources Corporation.*
a) KPMI. Ages 3–0 to 6–6; 1976; criterion-referenced; no scores, 7 areas: counting, cardinal numbers, quantities, sequence, positional, directional, geometry/measurement.
b) MATH/SCREEN TEST. Ages 5–6 to 6–6; 1977; norm-referenced; 8 scores: numeral recognition, numeral comprehension, comparisons, sequence, position, direction, geometry/measurement, total.

REFERENCES

1. MELINE, T. Kraner Preschool Math Inventory. *ASHA*, 1978, 20, 675.

[1267]

★Krantz Health Opinion Survey. College; 1980; HOS; measures preferences for different health-care treatment approaches; 3 scores: information, behavioral involvement, total; David S. Krantz, Andrew Baum, and Margaret V. Wideman; David S. Krantz.*

REFERENCES

1. KRANTZ, D. S., BAUM, A., & WIDEMAN, J. V. Assessment of preferences for self-treatment and information in health care. *Journal of Personality & Social Psychology*, 1980, 39, 977–990.

[1268]

K.S.U. Speech Discrimination Test. Persons with hearing loss grades 3 and over; 1967–69; no manual; Kenneth W. Berger; Audiotone.* (In-print status uncertain; no reply from publisher.)

For additional information and a review by Harris Winitz, see 8:939 (3 references).

[1269]

Kuder General Interest Survey. Grades 6–12; 1934–76; KGIS; 11 scores: outdoor, mechanical, computational, scientific, persuasive, artistic, literary, musical, social service, clerical, verification; G. Frederic Kuder; Science Research Associates, Inc.*

For additional information, see 8:1009 (16 references); for reviews by Barbara A. Kirk, Paul R. Lohnes, and John N. McCall, and excerpted reviews by T. R. Husek and Robert F. Stahmann, see 7:1024 (8 references).

REFERENCES

1–8. See 7:1024.
9–24. See 8:1009.
25. AMEG COMMISSION ON SEX BIAS IN MEASUREMENT. A case history of change: A review of responses to the challenge of sex bias in career interest inventories. *Measurement & Evaluation in Guidance*, 1977, 10, 148–152.
26. BECKER, S. Personality correlates of the discrepancy between expressed and inventoried interest scores. *Measurement & Evaluation in Guidance*, 1977, 10, 24–30.
27. BRAUN, N. J., & KNOCHE, M. Prediction of job performance using psychological appraisal testing: A validity study. *Australian Psychologist*, 1978, 13, 379–389.
28. EPPERSON, D. L., & HAMMOND, D. C. Use of interest inventories with native Americans: A case for local norms. *Journal of Counseling Psychology*, 1981, 28, 213–220.

[1270]

Kuder Occupational Interest Survey. Grades 11–16 and adults; 1956–76; KOIS; items same as those in *Kuder Preference Record—Occupational* but scored differently; 114 occupational scores and 48 college-major scores; G. Frederic Kuder; Science Research Associates, Inc.*

For additional information, see 8:1010 (41 references); see also T2:2194 (13 references); for reviews by Robert H. Dolliver and W. Bruce Walsh, and excerpted reviews by Frederick G. Brown and Robert F. Stahmann, see 7:1025 (19 references).

REFERENCES

1–19. See 7:1025.
20–32. See T2:2194.
33–73. See 8:1010.
74. AMEG COMMISSION ON SEX BIAS IN MEASUREMENT. A case history of change: A review of responses to the challenge of sex bias in career interest inventories. *Measurement & Evaluation in Guidance*, 1977, 10, 148–152.
75. TITTLE, C. K., & DENKER, E. R. Kuder Occupational Interest Survey profiles of reentry women. *Journal of Counseling Psychology*, 1977, 24, 293–300.
76. ZYTOWSKI, D. G. The effects of being interest-inventoried. *Journal of Vocational Behavior*, 1977, 11, 153–157.
77. TITTLE, C. K., DENKER, E. R., & KAGEN, E. Differentiating the interests of mature women: A factor analysis of the KOIS. *Measurement & Evaluation in Guidance*, 1978, 11, 34–43.
78. ZYTOWSKI, D. G., & LAING, J. Validity of other-gender-normed scales on the Kuder Occupational Interest Survey. *Journal of Counseling Psychology*, 1978, 25, 205–209.
79. HANSEN, C. J., & ZYTOWSKI, D. G. The Kuder Occupational Interest Inventory as a moderator of its predictive validity. *Educational & Psychological Measurement*, 1979, 39, 107–118.
80. DIAMOND, E. E. A response to Weinrach's "Discrepancy identification: A model for the interpretation of the Kuder DD and other interest inventories". *Vocational Guidance Quarterly*, 1980, 29, 53–55.
81. HARMON, L. W., & ZYTOWSKI, D. G. Reliability of Holland codes across interest measures for adult females. *Journal of Counseling Psychology*, 1980, 27, 478–483.

82. LESTER, D. Relationships between subscale scores of police officers on the Kuder Occupational Interest Survey. *Psychological Reports*, 1980, 46, 1276.
83. LESTER, D., & PURGARIE, C. Predicting graduation from a police academy with the Kuder Occupational Interest Survey. *Psychological Reports*, 1980, 47, 78.
84. WEINRACH, S. G. Discrepancy identification: A model for the interpretation of the Kuder DD and other interest inventories. *Vocational Guidance Quarterly*, 1980, 29, 42–52.
85. DIAMOND, E. E. Sex–typical and sex–atypical interests of Kuder Occupational Interest Survey criterion groups: Implications for counseling. *Journal of Counseling Psychology*, 1981, 28, 229–242.

[1271]

Kuder Preference Record—Vocational. Grades 9–16 and adults; 1934–76; KPR-V; also called *Kuder C*; for revision and downward extension, see *Kuder General Interest Survey* (Kuder E); 11 scores: outdoor, mechanical, computational, scientific, persuasive, artistic, literary, musical, social service, clerical, verification; Frederic Kuder; Science Research Associates, Inc.*

For additional information and a review by Lenore W. Harmon, see 8:1011 (36 references); see also T2:2195 (302 references); for a review by Martin Katz, see 6:1063 (148 references); for reviews by Clifford P. Froehlich and John Pierce-Jones, see 5:863 (211 references); for reviews by Edward S. Bordin, Harold D. Carter, and H. M. Fowler, see 4:742 (144 references); for reviews by Ralph F. Berdie, E. G. Chambers, and Donald E. Super and an excerpted review by Arthur H. Brayfield of an earlier edition, see 3:640 (60 references); for reviews by A. B. Crawford and Arthur E. Traxler, see 2:1671 (2 references).

REFERENCES

1–2. See 2:1671.
3–62. See 3:640.
63–208. See 4:742.
209–419. See 5:863.
420–567. See 6:1063.
568–869. See T2:2195.
870–905. See 8:1011.

906. MALATESTA, C. Z., CIRCO, J., & SMITH, B. A discriminating, non–discriminatory test battery for a prison population. *Corrective & Social Psychiatry & Journal of Behavior Technology, Methods, & Therapy*, 1977, 23, 15–17.
907. WIGGINS, J. D., & WESLANDER, D. Expressed vocational choices and later employment compared with Vocational Preference Inventory and Kuder Preference Record–Vocational scores. *Journal of Vocational Behavior*, 1977, 11, 158–165.
908. BERNARD, M. L., & GILLILAND, B. E. Sex bias in counseling: An examination of certain counselor characteristics and their effect on counseling behavior. *School Counselor*, 1981, 29, 34–40.
909. PRYOR, R. G. L. Interests and values as preferences: A validation of the work aspect preference scale. *Australian Psychologist*, 1981, 16, 258–272.

[1272]

Kuhlmann-Anderson Test, Seventh Edition. Grades kgn, 1, 2, 3–4, 4–5, 5–7, 7–9, 9–12; 1927–67; KAT, also MAP; publisher uses title *Kuhlmann-Anderson Measure of Academic Potential* in promotional literature; 8 levels; F. Kuhlmann (fourth and earlier editions) and Rose G. Anderson; Scholastic Testing Service, Inc.*

a) BOOKLETS K, A, B, AND CD. Grades kgn, 1, 2, 3–4; 1927–65.
b) SEPARATE ANSWER SHEET EDITION. Grades 4–5, 5–7, 7–9, 9–12; 1927–67.
  1) *Booklets D and EF.* Grades 4–5, 5–7; 1927–67.
  2) *Booklets G and H.* Grades 7–9, 9–12; 1927–65; 3 scores: verbal, quantitative, total.

See T2:398 (53 references); for reviews by William B. Michael and Douglas A. Pidgeon, and an excerpted review by Frederick B. Davis, see 6:466 (11 references); see also 5:348 (15 references); for reviews by Henry E. Garrett and David Segel of an earlier edition, see 4:302 (10 references); for reviews by W. G. Emmett and Stanley S. Marzolf, see 3:236 (25 references); for a review by Henry E. Garrett, see 2:1404 (15 references); for reviews by Psyche Cattell, S. A. Courtis, and Austin H. Turney, see 1:1049.

REFERENCES

1–15. See 2:1404.
16–40. See 3:236.
41–50. See 4:302.
51–65. See 5:348.
66–76. See 6:466.
77–129. See T2:398.

130. GARGIULO, R. M. The effects of labels and instruction on concept attainment in the educable mentally retarded. *Contemporary Educational Psychology*, 1977, 2, 284–291.
131. KAUFFMAN, J. M., EPSTEIN, M. H., & CHLEBNIKOW, B. Emotionally disturbed boy's work for self and others. *Child Study Journal*, 1977, 7, 179–188.
132. PERNEY, L. R., HYDE, E. M., & MACHOCK, B. J. Black intelligence–A re–evaluation. *Journal of Negro Education*, 1977, 46, 450–455.
133. JOHNSON, R. A., YARBOROUGH, B. H. The effects of marks on the development of academically talented elementary pupils. *Gifted Child Quarterly*, 1978, 22, 498–505.
134. PICHE, G. L., RUBIN, D. L., & MICHLIN, M. L. Age and social class in children's use of persuasive communicative appeals. *Child Development*, 1978, 49, 773–780.
135. YARBOROUGH, B. M., & JOHNSON, R. A. The relationship between intelligence levels and benefits from innovative, nongraded elementary schooling and traditional, graded schooling. *Educational Research Quarterly*, 1978, 3, 28–38.
136. PELHAM, W. E. Selective attention deficits in poor readers? Dichotic listening, speeded classification, and auditory and visual central and incidental learning tasks. *Child Development*, 1979, 50, 1050–1061.
137. AVIEZER, Y., & SIMPSON, S. Variability and instability in perceptual and reading functions of brain–injured children. *Journal of Learning Disabilities*, 1980, 13, 41–47.
138. GUSKEY, T. R., NORDSTROM, C., & WICK, J. W. Evaluation of a voluntary busing program through cohort comparisons. *Urban Education*, 1980, 15, 3–32.
139. LOPER, A. B., & HALLAHAN, D. P. A comparison of different statistical procedures for determining the relationship between cognitive tempo and reading achievement. *Journal of General Psychology*, 1980, 102, 89–97.
140. MANDELL, A. Problem–solving strategies of sixth-grade students who are superior problem solvers. *Science Education*, 1980, 64, 203–211.
141. YARBOROUGH, B. H., & JOHNSON R. A. How meaningful are marks in promoting growth in reading? *Reading Teacher*, 1980, 33, 644–651.
142. YARBOROUGH, B. H., & JOHNSON, R. A. A six-year study of sex differences in intellectual functioning, reading/language arts achievement, and affective development. *Journal of Psychology*, 1980, 106, 55–61.

[1273]

Kundu's Neurotic Personality Inventory. Adults; 1965; test booklet title is *K.N.P.I.*; KNPI; Ramanath Kundu; the Author [India].*

See T2:1257 (2 references) and P:140 (5 references).

[1274]

Kwalwasser Music Talent Test. Grades 4–6, 7–16 and adults; 1953; Jacob Kwalwasser; Belwin-Mills Publishing Corporation.*

See T2:203 (4 references); for reviews by Paul R. Farnsworth and Kate Hevner Mueller, see 5:248.

[1275]

Kwalwasser-Ruch Test of Musical Accomplishment. Grades 4–12; 1924–27; Jacob Kwalwasser and G. M. Ruch; Bureau of Educational Research and Service.*

See T2:204 (6 references); for reviews by William S. Larson and James L. Mursdell, see 2:1333 (1 reference).

[1276]

★**The Lake St. Clair Incident.** Adults; 1977–78; LSC; to examine group and individual decision-making processes, help individuals and groups perceive and evaluate their interactions and styles of communicating, and utilize the instrument to simply have fun or create an environment; 3 scores: autocratic, consultive, consensual; Albert A. Canfield; Humanics Media.*

[1277]

Language Arts: IOX Objectives-Based Tests. Grades kgn–6; 1973–74; criterion-referenced; 108 tests (spirit masters for local duplicating) in 3 areas; series description by W. James Popham; tests developed under the direction of Nola Paxton, Linda Paulson, Nancy Fess, and Rae Jeane Popham; Instructional Objectives Exchange.*
a) MECHANICS AND USAGE. 34 tests.
b) WORD FORMS AND SYNTAX. 42 tests.
c) COMPOSITION, LIBRARY, AND LITERARY SKILLS. 32 tests.

For additional information and reviews by Stephen M. Koziol, Jr. and William J. Wright, see 8:53.

[1278]

Language Arts: Minnesota High School Achievement Examinations. Grades 7, 8, 9, 10, 11, 12; 1951–70; a new, revised, or previously inactive form issued each May; Achievement Examinations for Secondary Schools, High School Achievement Examinations, and Midwest High School Achievement Examinations have also been used as series titles; 6 levels; edited by V. L. Lohmann; American Guidance Service.*
a) LANGUAGE ARTS GRADE 7.
b) LANGUAGE ARTS GRADE 8.
c) LANGUAGE ARTS GRADE 9.
d) LANGUAGE ARTS GRADE 10.
e) LANGUAGE ARTS GRADE 11.
f) LANGUAGE ARTS GRADE 12.

For additional information, see 7:197; for a review by Marvin D. Glock of Forms E (1962) and F (1963), see 6:268; see also 5:185; for a review by Roger A. Richards of Form A (1955) and Form B (1957), see 5:186.

[1279]

Language Arts Test: Content Evaluation Series. Grades 7–9; 1969; 3 tests in 1 booklet; Elsa Graser (*a*), Leonard Freyman (*b*), and Ruth Reeves (*c*); Riverside Publishing Co.*
a) LANGUAGE ABILITY TEST: CONTENT EVALUATION SERIES.
b) COMPOSITION TEST: CONTENT EVALUATION SERIES.
c) LITERATURE TEST: CONTENT EVALUATION SERIES.

For additional information and reviews by Joan J. Michael and Blaine R. Worthen, see 7:198.

[1280]

★**Language Assessment Battery.** Grades kgn–2, 3–6, 7–12; 1976; LAB; 3 levels; 2 editions: English, Spanish; prepared by Board of Education of the City of New York; Riverside Publishing Co.*
a) LEVEL I. Grades kgn–2; 3 tests: listening and speaking, reading, writing.
b) LEVEL II. Grades 3–6; 4 tests: listening, reading, writing, speaking.
c) LEVEL III. Grades 7–12; 4 tests: listening, reading, writing, speaking.

[1281]

★**Language Assessment Scales.** Grades kgn–5, 6–12 and over; 1981–82; LAS; 6 or 7 scores: minimal pairs, lexical, phonemes, sentence comprehension, oral production, total, observation of pragmatic language (optional); (Spanish edition ('81) available for Form A only); Edward A. De Avila and Sharon E. Duncan; Linguametrics Group.*

REFERENCES

1. BRAINARD, C. Language Assessment Scales. *Modern Language Journal*, 1978, 62, 350–351.
2. DALTON, S. Validation of the Language Assessment Scales. *Educational & Psychological Measurement*, 1979, 39, 1001–1003.
3. DEAVILA, E., & DUNCAN, S. Language Assessment Scales I. *Language Arts*, 1979, 56, 89–90.
4. DEAVILA, E. A., & DUNCAN, S. E. *A convergent approach to oral language assessment: Theoretical and technical specifications on the Language Assessment Scales.* San Rafael, California: Linguametrics Group, 1981.

[1282]

*****Language Facility Test.** Ages 3 and over; 1965–80; LFT; identical with *Language Facility Test* ('68) except for slight changes in manual; measures language and grammar in English or Spanish; 2 scoring systems (9-point qualitative scale for evaluating communication in primary language, error analysis for standard English) for verbal responses to 12 pictures; John T. Dailey; Allington Corporation.*

See T2:2078; for a review by Nicholas Anastasiow of an earlier form, see 7:955 (1 reference).

REFERENCES

1. See 7:955.
2. HERNANDEZ-CHAVEZ, E., & BURT, M. K. Language facility test. *Modern Language Journal*, 1978, 62, 282–283.

[1283]

★**Language Imitation Test.** Severely educational subnormal children ages 5 and over; no date on test materials; LIT; experimental form; 6 subtests: sound imitation, word imitation, syntactic control (2 subtests), word organization control, sentence completion; Paul Berry and Peter Mittler; NFER-Nelson Publishing Co. [England].*

[1284]

★**Language Proficiency Test.** Grades 9 and over; 1981; LPT; 6–9 scores: aural/oral (commands, short answers [optional], comprehension [optional]), reading (vocabulary, comprehension), writing (grammar, sentence response, paragraph response, translation [optional]); Joan Gerard and Gloria Weinstock; Academic Therapy Publications.*

[1285]

Language Proficiency Tests. Black pupils in Forms IV, V; 1974–75; LPTE; tests for Form IV and Form V are identical with English subtests of Form A and Form B, respectively, of *General Tests of Language and Arithmetic for Students* ('72); 4 scores: language usage, vocabulary, reading comprehension, total; (Afrikaans edition available); J. C. Chamberlain; Human Sciences Research Council [South Africa].*

For additional information, see 8:104.

[1286]

Language Sampling, Analysis, and Training, Revised Edition. Children with language delay; 1974–77; Dorothy Tyack and Robert Gottsleben; Consulting Psychologists Press, Inc.
a) TRANSCRIPTION SHEETS.
b) WORD/MORPHEME TALLY AND SUMMARY. 6 scores: 3 totals (sentences, words, morphemes) and 3 means (word/sentence, morphemes/sentence, word-morpheme index).
c) SEQUENCE OF LANGUAGE ACQUISITION. Assessment of 6 areas: noun phrase constituents, verb phrase constituents, constructions, complex sentences, negation, questions.
d) BASELINE AND GOAL DATA.
e) TRAINING WORKSHEET.
f) SCORE SHEET.
For additional information, see 8:964.

[1287]

Language-Structured Auditory Retention Span Test. Mental ages 3.7 to adult; 1973–75; LARS; immediate recall of words and sentences presented orally; 2 scores: mental age, "quotient" (MA/CA); Luis Carlson; Academic Therapy Publications.*

For additional information, a review by James B. Lingwall, and an excerpted review by Alan Krichev, see 8:941 (1 reference).

[1288]

Language Usage: Differential Aptitude Tests. Grades 8–12 and adults; 1947–77; George K. Bennett, Harold G. Seashore, and Alexander G. Wesman; The Psychological Corporation. For the complete battery entry, see 732.

For additional information regarding an earlier edition, see 8:50; see also T2:93 (2 references). For reviews of the complete battery, see 8:485 (2 reviews, 1 excerpt), 7:673 (1 review, 1 excerpt), 6:767 (2 reviews), 5:605 (2 reviews), 4:711 (3 reviews), and 3:620 (1 excerpt).

[1289]

★Laterality Preference Schedule. Children and adults; 1978; LPS; 6 scores: general laterality, visually guided activity, visual, auditory, strength, foot use; Raymond S. Dean; the Author.*

REFERENCES

1. DEAN, R. S. Cerebral laterality and reading comprehension. *Neuropsychologia*, 1978, 16, 633–636.
2. DEAN, R. S. Reliability and predictive validity of the Dean Laterality Preference Schedule with preadolescents. *Perceptual & Motor Skills*, 1978, 47, 1345–1346.
3. SCHWARTZ, N. H., & DEAN, R. S. Laterality preference patterns of learning disabled children. *Perceptual & Motor Skills*, 1978, 47, 869–870.
4. DEAN, R. S. Cerebral laterality and verbal–performance discrepancies in intelligence. *Journal of School Psychology*, 1979, 17, 145–150.
5. DEAN, R. S. Cerebral lateralization and reading dysfunction. *Journal of School Psychology*, 1980, 18, 324–332.
6. DEAN, R. S., SCHWARTZ, N. H., & SMITH, L. S. Lateral preference patterns as a discriminator of learning difficulties. *Journal of Consulting & Clinical Psychology*, 1981, 49, 227–235.

[1290]

★The Laurita-Trembley Diagnostic Word Processing Test. Grades 1.9–4.9, 5.0–college; 1979; criterion-referenced; 4 scores: (raw, word count, vertical word processing, horizontal word processing), derived from 6 areas: vowel discrimination, direct phonic processing, indirect structural processing (long and short vowel), prefixes and suffixes (long and short vowel); Raymond E. Laurita and Phillip W. Trembley; L & T Educational Materials, Inc.*

[1291]

Law Enforcement Perception Questionnaire. Law enforcement personnel; 1970; LEPQ; attitudes toward law enforcement and law enforcement personnel; Frank Lee; Psychometric Affiliates.*

[1292]

Law School Admission Test. Law school entrants; 1948–82; LSAT; test administered 4 times annually (February, June, October, December) at centers established by the publisher; LSAT total score plus an unscored writing sample; administered by Law School Admission Services; Law School Admission Council.

For additional information, see 8:1093 (7 references); see also T2:2349 (7 references); for a review by Leo A. Munday of earlier forms, see 7:1098 (23 references); see also 5:928 (7 references); for a review by Alexander G. Wesman, see 4:815 (6 references).

REFERENCES

1–6. See 4:815.
7–13. See 5:928.
14–36. See 7:1098.
37–43. See T2:2349.
44–50. See 8:1093.
51. MARCO, G. L. Use of the logistic model as an alternative to linear interpolation for computing percentile ranks. *Journal of Educational Measurement*, 1977, 14, 271–275.
52. BART, W. M. An empirical inquiry into the relationship between test factor structure and test hierarchical structure. *Applied Psychological Measurement*, 1978, 2, 331–335.
53. WERTHEIM, E. G., WIDOM, C. S., & WORTEL, L. H. Multivariate analysis of male and female professional career choice correlates. *Journal of Applied Psychology*, 1978, 63, 234–242.
54. KAYE, D. An "A" is an "A" is an "A": An exploratory analysis of a new method for adjusting undergraduate grades for law school admissions purposes. *Journal of Legal Education*, 1981, 31, 233–241.
55. LINN, R. L., HARNISCH, D. L., & DUNBAR, S. B. Corrections for range restriction: An empirical investigation of conditions resulting in conservative corrections. *Journal of Applied Psychology*, 1981, 66, 655–663.
56. LINN, R. L., HARNISCH, D. L., & DUNBAR, S. B. Validity generalization and situational specificity: An analysis of the prediction of first-year grades in law school. *Applied Psychological Measurement*, 1981, 5, 281–289.

[1293]

Lawshe-Kephart Personnel Comparison System. For rating any aspect of employee performance by the paired comparison technique; 1946–48; C. H. Lawshe, Jr. and N. C. Kephart; Village Book Cellar.* (In-print status uncertain; no reply from publisher.)

For additional information and a review by Reign H. Bittner, see 4:778 (1 reference).

[1294]

★An LD Program that Works. Learning disabled children; 1979; approaches for implementing a learning disabilities program based on the Midland School in New Jersey; Edward G. Scagliotta; Mafex Associates, Inc.*

[1295]

Leader Behavior Description Questionnaire. Supervisors; 1957; LBDQ; "2 scores (consideration, initiating structure) based upon responses by 4–10 raters"; 2 tests; original edition by John K. Hemphill and Alvin E. Coons; current edition by Personnel Research Board, Ohio

State University; Publication Sales Division, Ohio State University Press.*

a) LEADER BEHAVIOR DESCRIPTION QUESTIONNAIRE. Employee ratings of a specific supervisor; manual by Andrew W. Halpin.

b) IDEAL LEADER BEHAVIOR DESCRIPTION QUESTIONNAIRE. Employee ratings of what a supervisor ought to be; test booklet title is *Ideal Leader Behavior (What You Expect of Your Leader)*; no manual.

For additional information and a review by Robert L. Dipboye, see 8:1174 (138 references); see also T2:2451 (35 references) and 7:1146 (108 references).

REFERENCES

1–108. See 7:1146.
109–143. See T2:2451.
144–281. See 8:1174.
282. INDIRESAN, J. Multivariate analysis of factors affecting the job satisfaction of engineering teachers. *Indian Journal of Psychometry & Education*, 1975, 6, 16–27.
283. ADAMS, E. F., LAKER, D. R., & HULIN, C. L. An investigation of the influence of job level and functional specialty on job attitudes and perceptions. *Journal of Applied Psychology*, 1977, 62, 335–343.
284. BIRD, A. M. Development of a model for predicting team performance. *Research Quarterly*, 1977, 48, 24–32.
285. BLEDSOE, J. C., & BROWN, S. E. On the independence of consideration and initiating structure: A factor analysis of the Leader Behavior Description Questionnaire. *Psychological Reports*, 1977, 41, 431–434.
286. LEE, D. M., & ALVARES, K. M. Effects of sex on descriptions and evaluations of supervisory behavior in a simulated industrial setting. *Journal of Applied Psychology*, 1977, 62, 405–410.
287. MITCHELL, T. R., LARSON, J. R., JR., & GREEN, S. G. Leader behavior, situational moderators, and group performance: An attributional analysis. *Organizational Behavior & Human Performance*, 1977, 18, 254–268.
288. RUSH, M. C., THOMAS, J. C., & LORD, R. G. Implicit leadership theory: A potential threat to the internal validity of leader behavior questionnaires. *Organizational Behavior & Human Performance*, 1977, 20, 93–110.
289. BROWN, S. E., & BLEDSOE, J. C. Job satisfaction of school superintendents as related to perceptions of leader's behavior. *Psychological Reports*, 1978, 42, 171–174.
290. CHRISTENSEN, C. E., MILNER, K., & CHRISTENSEN, J. E. An analysis of faculty perceptions of leadership qualities of male and female physical education departments. *Research Quarterly for Exercise & Sport*, 1978, 49, 269–277.
291. HYNES, K., FELDHUSEN, J. F., & RICHARDSON, W. B. Application of a three–stage model of instruction to youth leadership training. *Journal of Applied Psychology*, 1978, 63, 623–628.
292. KENIS, I. Leadership behavior, subordinate personality, and satisfaction with supervision. *Journal of Psychology*, 1978, 98, 99–107.
293. GILMORE, D. C., BEEHR, T. A., & RICHTER, D. J. Effects of leader behaviors on subordinate performance and satisfaction: A laboratory experiment with student employees. *Journal of Applied Psychology*, 1979, 64, 166–172.
294. MOBLEY, W. H., HAND, H. H., BAKER, R. L., & MEGLINO, B. M. Conceptual and empirical analysis of military recruit training attrition. *Journal of Applied Psychology*, 1979, 64, 10–18.
295. VOSSTRACHE, C. Players' perceptions of leadership qualities for coaches. *Research Quarterly for Exercise & Sport*, 1979, 50, 679–686.
296. BLEDSOE, J. C., BROWN, S. E., & DALTON, S. L. Perception of leadership behavior of the school business manager. *Perceptual & Motor Skills*, 1980, 50, 1147–1150.
297. BLEDSOE, J. C., BROWN, S. E., & DALTON, S. L. Real and ideal leadership of school business managers as perceived by several publics. *Southern Journal of Educational Research*, 1980, 14, 171–176.
298. CASHMAN, J. F., & SNYDER, R. A. Perceptions of leaders' behavior: Situational and personal determinants. *Psychological Reports*, 1980, 46, 615–624.
299. EREZ, M. Correlates of leadership style: Field–dependence and social intelligence versus social orientation. *Perceptual & Motor Skills*, 1980, 50, 231–238.
300. INDIRESAN, J. Perception of leadership style and satisfaction of different need areas. *Indian Journal of Social Work*, 1980, 41, 21–28.
301. LEWIS, R. G., & GINGERICH, W. Leadership characteristics: Views of Indian and non–Indian students. *Social Casework*, 1980, 8, 494–497.
302. MOORE, L. M., & RICKEL, A. V. Characteristics of women in traditional and non–traditional managerial roles. *Personnel Psychology*, 1980, 33, 317–333.

303. POWELL, G. N., & BUTTERFIELD, D. A. The female leader: Attributional effects of group performance. *Psychological Reports*, 1980, 47, 891–897.
304. SCHRIESHEIM, C. A., & DENISI, A. S. Item presentation as an influence on questionnaire validity: A field experiment. *Educational & Psychological Measurement*, 1980, 40, 175–182.
305. RUSH, M. C., & BEAUVAIS, L. L. A critical analysis of format-induced versus subject–imposed bias in leadership ratings. *Journal of Applied Psychology*, 1981, 66, 722–727.
306. RUSH, M. C., PHILLIPS, J. S., & LORD, R. G. Effects of a temporal delay in rating on leader behavior descriptions: A laboratory investigation. *Journal of Applied Psychology*, 1981, 66, 442–450.
307. SCHRIESHEIM, C. A. The effect of grouping or randomizing items on leniency response bias. *Educational & Psychological Measurement*, 1981, 41, 401–411.

[1296]
Leader Behavior Description Questionnaire, Form 12.

Supervisors; 1957–63; LBDQ–12; revision of *Leader Behavior Description Questionnaire* with 10 additional scores; for research use only; employee ratings of a supervisor; 12 scores: representation, demand reconciliation, tolerance of uncertainty, persuasiveness, initiation of structure, tolerance of freedom, role assumption, consideration, production emphasis, predictive accuracy, integration, superior orientation; scores based upon responses of 4 to 10 raters; original edition by John K. Hemphill and Alvin E. Coons; manual by Ralph M. Stogdill; current edition by Bureau of Business Research, Ohio State University; Publications Sales Division, Ohio State University Press.*

For additional information and a review by Robert L. Dipboye, see 8:1175 (101 references); see also T2:2452 (19 references) and 7:1147 (48 references).

REFERENCES

1–48. See 7:1147.
49–67. See T2:2452.
68–168. See 8:1175.
169. BLEDA, P. R., GITTER, G. A., & D'AGOSTINO, R. B. Enlisted men's perceptions of leader attributes and satisfaction with military life. *Journal of Applied Psychology*, 1977, 62, 43–49.
170. OSBORN, R. N., HUNT, J. G., & SKARET, D. J. Managerial influence in a complex configuration with two unit heads. *Human Relations*, 1977, 30, 1025–1038.
171. ADAMS, E. F. A multivariate study of subordinate perceptions of and attitudes toward minority and majority managers. *Journal of Applied Psychology*, 1978, 63, 277–288.
172. JOHNS, G. Attitudinal and nonattitudinal predictors of two forms of absence from work. *Organizational Behavior & Human Performance*, 1978, 22, 431–444.
173. SHERIDAN, J. E., & VREDENBURGH, D. J. Usefulness of leadership behavior and social power variables in predicting job tension, performance, and turnover of nursing employees. *Journal of Applied Psychology*, 1978, 63, 89–95.
174. SCHRIESHEIM, C. A, KINICKI, A. J., & SCHRIESHEIM, J. F. The effect of leniency of leader behavior descriptions. *Organizational Behavior & Human Performance*, 1979, 23, 1–29.
175. VOSSTRACHE, C. Players' perceptions of leadership qualities for coaches. *Research Quarterly for Exercise & Sport*, 1979, 50, 679–686.
176. CASHMAN, J. F., & SNYDER, R. A. Perceptions of leaders' behavior: Situational and personal determinants. *Psychological Reports*, 1980, 46, 615–624.
177. GREENE, C. N., & SCHRIESHEIM, C. A. Leader–group interactions: A longitudinal field investigation. *Journal of Applied Psychology*, 1980, 65, 50–59.
178. SCHRIESHEIM, J. F. The social context of leader–subordinate relations: An investigation of the effects of group cohesiveness. *Journal of Applied Psychology*, 1980, 65, 183–194.
179. BUTTERFIELD, D. A. Effect of group performance, leader sex, and rater sex on ratings of leader behavior. *Organizational Behavior & Human Performance*, 1981, 28, 129–141.
180. KOERNER, B. L. Selected correlates of job performance of community health nurses. *Nursing Research*, 1981, 30, 43–48.
181. SCHRIESHEIM, C. A. Leniency effects on convergent and discriminant validity for grouped questionnaire items: A further investigation. *Educational & Psychological Measurement*, 1981, 41, 1093–1099.

182. SCHRIESHEIM, C. A., & DENISI, A. S. Task dimensions as moderators of the effects of instrumental leadership: A two-sample replicated test of path-goal leadership theory. *Journal of Applied Psychology*, 1981, 66, 589-597.
183. SCHRIESHEIM, C. A., & HILL, K. D. Controlling acquiescence response bias by item reversals: The effect on questionnaire validity. *Educational & Psychological Measurement*, 1981, 41, 1101-1114.
184. VECCHIO, R. P. Situational and behavioral moderators of subordinate satisfaction with supervision. *Human Relations*, 1981, 34, 947-963.

[1297]

The Leadership Ability Evaluation. Grades 9-16 and adults; 1961; LAE; social climate created in influencing others; 5 scores: laissez faire, democratic-cooperative, autocratic-submissive, autocratic-aggressive, decision pattern; Russell N. Cassel and Edward J. Stancik; Western Psychological Services.*

See T2:1259 (3 references) and P:142; for reviews by John D. Black and Cecil A. Gibb, see 6:133 (4 references).

[1298]

★**Leadership and Self-Development Scale.** College; 1976-79; 9 scores: assertiveness, risk taking, self-concept, setting goals, decision making, obtaining a followership, conflict resolution, group roles, evaluation; Virginia Hoffman and Patricia B. Elmore; Patricia B. Elmore.*

REFERENCES

1. BRITTON, V., & ELMORE, P. B. Leadership and self-development workshop for women. *Journal of College Student Personnel*, 1977, 18, 318.
2. BRITTON, V., & ELMORE, P. B. Developing leadership skills in women students. *NASPA Journal*, 1979, 17, 10-14.

[1299]

Leadership Evaluation and Development Scale. Prospective supervisors; 1964-65; LEADS; Harley W. Mowry (question booklets and casebook from materials prepared by the Armstrong Cork Company); Psychological Services, Inc.*

For additional information and reviews by Walter C. Borman and Frank J. Landy, see 8:1176; for a review by Cecil A. Gibb, see 7:1148 (1 reference).

[1300]

Leadership Opinion Questionnaire. Supervisors and prospective supervisors; 1960-69; LOQ; attitudes of supervisors toward ideal supervisory behavior; 2 scores: consideration, structure; Edwin A. Fleishman; Science Research Associates, Inc.*

For additional information, see 8:1177 (52 references); see also T2:2454 (15 references); for a review by Cecil A. Gibb, see 7:1149 (41 references); for reviews by Jerome E. Doppelt and Wayne K. Kirchner, see 6:1190 (6 references).

REFERENCES

1-6. See 6:1190.
7-47. See 7:1149.
48-62. See T2:2454.
63-114. See 8:1177.
115. ZEDECK, S., & KAFRY, D. Capturing rater policies for processing evaluation data. *Organizational Behavior & Human Performance*, 1977, 18, 269-294.
116. LANDY, F. J., & LAMIELL-LANDY, A. Dimensions of teacher behavior. *Journal of Applied Psychology*, 1978, 63, 522-526.
117. PASMORE, W. A., & KING, D. C. Understanding organizational change: A comparative study of multifaceted interventions. *Journal of Applied Behavioral Science*, 1978, 14, 455-468.
118. TAYLOR, I. A. Characteristics of "creative leaders". *Journal of Creative Behavior*, 1978, 12, 221-222. (Abstract)

119. BATLIS, N. C., & GREEN, P. C. Leadership style emphasis and related personality attributes. *Psychological Reports*, 1979, 44, 587-592.
120. DAGENAIS, F. Birth order and leadership style. *Journal of Social Psychology*, 1979, 109, 151-152.
121. DAGENAIS, F. Response bias and the Leadership Opinion Questionnaire scales. *Journal of General Psychology*, 1979, 100, 161-162.
122. JOHNSON, C. A., & ADERMAN, M. Leadership style and personal history information. *Journal of Psychology*, 1979, 102, 243-251.
123. PUTNAM, L. L. Preference for procedural order in task-oriented small groups. *Communication Monographs*, 1979, 46, 193-218.
124. DRORY, A., & BEN-PORAT, A. Leadership style and leniency bias in evaluation of employees' performance. *Psychological Reports*, 1980, 46, 735-739.

[1301]

Leadership Practices Inventory. Supervisors; 1955-67; LPI; for use with the author's management development program in leadership and communication; 2 scores (desirable practices marked as ideal, desirable practices marked as in actual practice) for each of: 4 leadership styles (using style answer form), 5 management areas (using area answer form), and 2 derived totals; Charles W. Nelson; Management Research Associates.* (In-print status uncertain; no reply from publisher.)

[1302]

The Leadership Q-Sort Test (A Test of Leadership Values). Adults; 1958; LQST; 7 scores: personal integrity, consideration of others, mental health, technical information, decision making, teaching and communication, total; Russell N. Cassel; Psychometric Affiliates.*

For additional information, see P:143; for reviews by Joel T. Campbell, Cecil A. Gibb, and William Stephenson, see 6:134 (6 references).

[1303]

Learning Ability Profile. Grades 5-16 and adults; 1975-78; LAP; 5 scores: total and 4 derived scores (certainty, problem solving, flexibility, frustration); Margherita M. Henning; Harvard Personnel Testing [Canada]. (U.S. distributor: Wolfe Computer Aptitude Testing.)

For additional information, see 8:191.

[1304]

★**Learning Disability Rating Procedure.** Grades kgn-12; 1981; LDRP; 11 scores: IQ, reading decoding, listening comprehension, comprehension variance, socially inappropriate behavior, expressive verbal language development, learning motivation, expressive writing development, independent work level/distractibility, severe discrepancy level, total; Gerald J. Spadafore and Sharon J. Spadafore; Academic Therapy Publications.*

[1305]

★**Learning Efficiency Test.** Ages 6 and over; 1981; LET; 6 scores (ordered immediate recall, unordered immediate recall, ordered short term recall, unordered short term recall, ordered long term recall, unordered long term recall) for both visual memory and auditory memory; Raymond E. Webster; Academic Therapy Publications.*

[1306]

Learning Methods Test. Grades kgn, 1, 2, 3; 1954-55; LMT; comparative effectiveness of four methods of teaching new words: visual, phonic, kinesthetic, combination; Robert E. Mills; The Mills Center.*

See T2:1666 (3 references); for reviews by Thomas E. Culliton, Jr. and William Eller, see 6:836 (1 reference).

[1307]

★Learning Staircase. Developmental ages 1½–7; 1976; criterion-referenced; "designed to answer the needs of early childhood special education classes"; 20 content areas (modules): adjectives, auditory memory, auditory perception, body image, classification, colors, fine motor, gross motor, number concepts, preverbal, reading readiness, same and different, sequence, spatial relationships, time, toilet training, verbal comprehension, verbal expression, visual memory, vocabulary; Lila Coughran and Marilyn Goff; Teaching Resources Corporation.*

[1308]

★Learning Style Identification Scale. Grades 1–8; 1981; LSIS; ratings by teachers; 4 scores obtained by rating 4 areas: intrapersonal information, extrapersonal information, cognitive development, self-concept; Paul J. Malcom, William C. Lutz, Mary A. Gerken, and Gary M. Hoeltke; Publishers Test Service.*

[1309]

★Learning Styles Inventory [Creative Learning Press, Inc.]. Grades 4–12 and teachers; 1978; LSI; "a measure of student preference for instructional techniques"; 9 factor scores: projects, drill and recitation, peer teaching, discussion, teaching games, independent study, programmed instruction, lecture, simulation; Joseph S. Renzulli and Linda H. Smith; Creative Learning Press, Inc.*

[1310]

★Learning Styles Inventory [Humanics Media]. Grades 6 through post-graduate level; 1976–80; may be used either in conjunction with or independent of *Instructional Styles Inventory* (1160); self-report inventory; 17 scores in 4 areas: conditions (peer, organization, goal setting, competition, instructor, detail, independence, authority), content (numeric, qualitative, inanimate, people), mode (listening, reading, iconic, direct experience), expectation; Albert A. Canfield; Humanics Media.*

[1311]

★Learning through Listening. Ages 10–11, 13–14, 17–18; 1976–80; 6 scores: content, contextual constraints, phonology, register, relationship, total; Andrew Wilkinson, Leslie Stratta, and Peter Dudley; Macmillan Education [England].*

[1312]

Leavell Hand-Eye Coordinator Tests. Ages 8–14; 1958–61; for determining need for training on the Delacato Stereo-Reader; 7 scores: hand-foot preference, eye-ear preference, hand dexterity preference, visual imagery (3 scores), total; Ullin W. Leavell; Keystone View.*

For additional information, see 6:937.

[1313]

Lee Test of Algebraic Ability, Revised. Grades 7–8; 1930–64; TAA; identical with the 1930 edition except for adaptation to machine scoring; J. Murray Lee; Bobbs-Merrill Co., Inc.*

See T2:684 (3 references); for reviews by W. L. Bashaw and Cyril J. Hoyt, and an excerpted review by William Mehrens, see 7:508 (2 references); for a review by S. S. Wilks, see 2:1443 (1 reference).

[1314]

★Leeds Scales for the Self-Assessment of Anxiety and Depression. Psychiatric patients; 1976; self-rating scale; 4 scores: depression (general, specific), anxiety (general, specific); R. P. Snaith, G. W. K. Bridge, and Max Hamilton; Psychological Test Publications [England].*

[1315]

The Leicester Number Test: Basic Number Concepts. Ages 7–1 to 9–0; 1970–73; Charles Gillham and K. A. Hesse; Hodder & Stoughton Educational [England].*

For additional information and a review by John Cook, see 8:277.

[1316]

Leisure Activities Blank. Ages 15 and over; 1974–75; LAB; for research use only; 16 scores: past participation (mechanics, crafts, intellectual, slow living, sports, glamour sports), future participation (adventure, mechanics, crafts, easy living, intellectual, ego-recognition, slow living, clean living), validity scores (frequent past, frequent future); George E. McKechnie; Consulting Psychologists Press, Inc.*

For additional information and reviews by David P. Campbell and Leonard S. Feldt, see 8:602 (3 references).

REFERENCES

1–3. See 8:602.
4. CHAMPOUX, J. E. An exploratory study of the role of job scope, need for achievement, and social status in the relationship between work and nonwork. *Sociology & Social Research*, 1981, 65, 153–176.
5. PETRAKIS, E., & HANSON, C. J. Cognitive style and choice of leisure activities by older adults. *Perceptual & Motor Skills*, 1981, 52, 839–842.

[1317]

Leisure Interest Inventory. High school and college and adults; 1969; LII; 5 scores: games, art, sociability, mobility, immobility; Edwina E. Hubert; the Author.*

For additional information, see 8:603.

[1318]

The Leiter Adult Intelligence Scale. Adults; 1949–72; LAIS; revision of *Leiter-Partington Adult Performance Scale*; includes the *The FR-CR Test*, *Partington's Pathways Test*, *The Leiter Adaptation of Arthur's Stencil Design Test*, and *The Leiter Adaptation of the Painted Cube Test*; 3 scores: verbal, performance, total; Russell Graydon Leiter; Stoelting Co.*

See T2:504 (12 references); for reviews by Paul C. Davis and Frank B. Jex, and an excerpted review by Laurance F. Shaffer, see 6:525 (15 references); for reviews by Harold A. Delp and Herschel Manuel and an excerpted review by Laurance F. Shaffer of the original edition, see 4:350 (4 references). For a review of *The FR-CR Test*, see 4:339; for an excerpted review of *The Leiter Adaptation of Arthur's Stencil Design Test*, see 4:347; for an excerpted review of *The Leiter Adaptation of the Painted Cube Test*, see 4:348; for reviews of *Partington's Pathways Test*, see 4:355 (1 review, 1 excerpt).

[1319]

Leiter International Performance Scale. Ages 2–18, 3–8, 1936–55; 2 editions; Russell Graydon Leiter and Grace Arthur (*b*); Stoelting Co.*

a) 1948 REVISION. Ages 2–18; 1936–52.

b) ARTHUR ADAPTATION. Ages 3–8; 1952–55; author recommends use with *Arthur Point Scale of Performance Tests.*

See T2:505 (18 references); for a review by Emmy E. Werner, see 6:526 (10 references); see also 5:408 (17 references); for a review by Gwen F. Arnold and an excerpted review by Laurance F. Shaffer of *a*, see 4:349 (25 references).

REFERENCES

1–25. See 4:349.
26–42. See 5:408.
43–52. See 6:526.
53–70. See T2:505.
71. BARRY, N. J., JR., & OVERMANN, P. B. Comparison of the effectiveness of adult and peer models with EMR children. *American Journal of Mental Deficiency,* 1977, 82, 33–36.
72. COHEN, D. J., CAPARULO, B. K., SHAYWITZ, B. A., & BOWERS, M. B. Dopamine and serotonin metabolism in neuropsychiatrically disturbed children. *Archives of General Psychiatry,* 1977, 34, 545–550.
73. MANSDORF, I. J. Learning concepts through modeling: Using different instructional procedures with institutionalized mentally retarded adults. *American Journal of Mental Deficiency,* 1977, 82, 287–291.
74. MORRIS, J. J., & CLARIZIO, S. Improvement in IQ of high-risk, disadvantaged preschool children enrolled in a developmental program. *Psychological Reports,* 1977, 41, 1111–1114.
75. DUVALL, S. W., & MALONEY, M. P. Comparison of the WAIS and Leiter International Performance Scale in a large urban community mental health setting. *Psychological Reports,* 1978, 43, 235–238.
76. GERKEN, K. C. Performance of Mexican American children on intelligence tests. *Exceptional Children,* 1978, 44, 438–443.
77. HOLYROYD, J., & GOLDENBERG, I. The use of goal attainment scaling to evaluate a ward treatment program for disturbed children. *Journal of Clinical Psychology,* 1978, 34, 732–739.
78. TOOMEY, K. E., MOHANDAS, T., SPARKES, R. S., KABACK, M. M., & RIMOIN, D. L. Segregation of an insertional chromosome rearrangement in 3 generations. *Journal of Medical Genetics,* 1978, 15, 382–387.
79. WHITE, F., LYNCH, J. I., & HAYDEN, M. E. Use of the Leiter International Performance Scale with adult aphasics. *Journal of Clinical Psychology,* 1978, 34, 667–671.
80. BARTOLUCCI, G., & PIERCE, S. J. A preliminary comparison of phonological development in autistic, normal, and mentally retarded subjects. *British Journal of Disorders of Communication,* 1979, 12, 137–147.
81. KORSAGER, S., & ANDERSEN, M. Thyroid replacement therapy in Down's Syndrome with hypothyroidism. *Journal of Mental Deficiency Research,* 1979, 23, 105–110.
82. DILLON, R., SNOWMAN, J., & TZENG, O. Recognition memory in hearing–impaired children: A levels-of-processing approach. *Journal of Experimental Child Psychology,* 1980, 29, 502–506.
83. KOEGEL, R. L., EGEL, A. L., & WILLIAMS, J. A. Behavioral contrast and generalization across settings in the treatment of autistic children. *Journal of Experimental Child Psychology,* 1980, 30, 422–437.
84. RATCLIFFE, M. W., & RATCLIFFE, K. J. A comparison of the Wechsler Intelligence Scale for Children–Revised and Leiter International Performance Scale for a group of educationally handicapped adolescents. *Journal of Clinical Psychology,* 1980, 36, 310–312.
85. KAMHI, A. G. Developmental vs. difference theories of mental retardation: A new look. *American Journal of Mental Deficiency,* 1981, 86, 1–7.
86. KAMHI, A. G. Nonlinguistic symbolic and conceptual abilities of language–impaired and normally developing children. *Journal of Speech & Hearing Research,* 1981, 24, 446–453.

[1320]

The Level of Aspiration Board. Mental ages 12.5 and over; 1940–50; LAB; 2 scores: mean difference between performance and estimate, shifts; J. B. Rotter; distributed by Edward Butler.* (In-print status uncertain; no reply from publisher.)

See T2:1261 (28 references) and P:144 (9 references).

[1321]

★**Lewis Counseling Inventory.** Adolescents in school; 1978; identifies those students in need of guidance and counseling; 8 scores: relationship with teachers, relationship with family, irritability, social confidence, relationship with peers, health, total, lie scale; D. G. Lewis and P. D. Pumfrey; NFER-Nelson Publishing Co. [England].*

[1322]

★**Lexington Developmental Scales.** Ages birth–6 years; 1973–77; may be used by parents and volunteers; "particularly helpful in pre and post testing"; contains behavioral and experimental items rated by examiner in 4 areas: motor, language, cognitive, personal and social; United Cerebral Palsy of the Bluegrass, John V. Irwin, Margaret Norris Ward, Ann B. Greis, Carol C. Deen, Valerie C. Cooley, Alice A. Awvenshine, Rhea A. Taylor, C. A. Coleman; United Cerebral Palsy of the Bluegrass.*

REFERENCES

1. FOLGER, M. K., & LEONARD, L. B. Language and sensorimotor development during the early period of referential speech. *Journal of Speech & Hearing Research,* 1978, 21, 519–527.

[1323]

★**Library Skills Test.** Grades 7–12 and college freshmen; 1980; LST; Illinois Association of College and Research Libraries; Scholastic Testing Service, Inc.*

[1324]

Library Tests. College; 1967–72; 3 tests; no manual; Perfection Form Co.* (In-print status uncertain; no reply from publisher.)

a) TEST 1: LIBRARY SURVEY TEST. General knowledge of library.

b) TEST 2: LIBRARY SOURCES AND SKILLS TEST. More detailed knowledge of library.

c) TEST 3: LIBRARY SOURCES AND USES OF INFORMATION. Thorough knowledge of library and research techniques.

[1325]

The Life Adjustment Inventory. High school; 1951; LAI; 14 scores: adjustment to curriculum, reading and study skills, communication and listening skills, social skills and etiquette, boy-girl relationships, religion-moral-ethics, functional citizenship, vocational orientation and preparation, physical and mental health, family living, orientation to science, consumer education, art appreciation and creativity, use of leisure time; J. Wayne Wrightstone and Ronald C. Doll; Psychometric Affiliates.*

For additional information, see P:145 (1 reference); for reviews by John W. M. Rothney and Helen Schacter, see 4:67.

[1326]

★**Life Skills, Forms 1 and 2.** Grades 9–12 and adults; 1979–80; 3 scores: reading, mathematics, total; Kenneth Majer and Dena Wadell; Riverside Publishing Co.*

[1327]

★**Life Style Questionnaire.** Ages 14 and over; 1980; LSQ; provides information regarding the interests, attitudes, and behaviors of people at work; 13 scores: 6

interest scores (expressive/imaginative, logical/analytical, managerial/enterprising, precise/administrative, active/concrete, supportive/social) and 7 attitude scores (low risk vs. high risk, carefree vs. perseverance, uncompetitive vs. competitive, unemotional vs. sensitive, isolate vs. group member, reject career vs. want career, opinions changing vs. opinions stable); James S. Barrett; Test Agency [England].*

[1328]
★Light's Retention Scale, Revised Edition 1981. Grades kgn–12; 1981; LRS; ratings by teachers and parents; a nonpsychometric instrument used as a counseling tool with a specific retention candidate; H. Wayne Light; Academic Therapy Publications.*

REFERENCES

1. SANDOVAL, J. Reliability and concurrent validity of Light's Retention Scale. *Psychology in the Schools*, 1980, 17, 442–445.

[1329]
Ligondé Equivalence Test. Adults who left elementary or secondary school 15 to 20 years ago; 1967; LET; also called *School Equivalence Test*; (French edition available); Paultre Ligondé; Institute of Psychological Research, Inc. [Canada].*

For additional information and a review by J. Douglas Ayers, see 8:21.

[1330]
Lincoln Diagnostic Spelling Tests. Grades 2–4 or 2–5, 4–8, 8–12 or 9–12; 1941–62; 2 editions; A. L. Lincoln.
a) EDUCATIONAL RECORDS BUREAU EDITION. Grades 2–4 or 2–5, 4–8, 8–12; 1941–62; 3 levels; Educational Records Bureau.*
 1) *Lincoln Primary Spelling Test*. Grades 2–4 in independent schools or 2–5 in public schools; 1960–62.
 2) *Lincoln Intermediate Spelling Test*. Grades 4–8; 1941–62.
 3) *Lincoln Diagnostic Spelling Test*. Grades 8–12; 1941–62.
b) BOBBS-MERRILL COMPANY EDITION. Grades 9–12; 1949–56; 1956 tests same as Forms 1, 2 of *Lincoln Diagnostic Spelling Test* published 1941 and 1942, Bobbs-Merrill Co., Inc.* *Out of Print*.

See T2:152 (3 references); for a review by Gus P. Plessas, see 6:320 (6 references); for reviews by Walter Scribner Guiler and George Spache of the tests for grades 4–12, see 4:202.

[1331]
The Lincoln-Oseretsky Motor Development Scale. Ages 6–14; 1948–56; revision of *Oseretsky Tests of Motor Proficiency*; William Sloan; Stoelting Co.*

See T2:1895 (27 references); for a review by Anna Espenschade, see 5:767 (10 references).

REFERENCES

1–10. See 5:767.
11–37. See T2:1895.
38. GARDNER, R. A. Throwing balls in a basket as a test of motor coordination: Normative data on 1350 school children. *Journal of Clinical Psychology*, 1979, 8, 152–155.
39. MALOY, C. F., & SATTLER, J. M. Motor and cognitive proficiency of learning disabled and normal children. *Journal of School Psychology*, 1979, 17, 213–218.
40. CHARLOP, M., & ATWELL, C. W. The Charlop–Atwell Scale of Motor Coordination: A quick and easy assessment of young children. *Perceptual & Motor Skills*, 1980, 50, 1291–1308.
41. WINSBERG, B. G., BIALER, I., KUPIETZ, S., BOTTI, E., & BALKA, E. B. Home vs. hospital care of children with behavior disorders. *Archives of General Psychiatry*, 1980, 37, 413–418.
42. WENDER, P. H., REIMHERR, F. S., & WOOD, D. R. Attentional deficit disorder ('minimal brain dysfunction') in adults. *Archives of General Psychiatry*, 1981, 38, 449–456.

[1332]
Lindamood Auditory Conceptualization Test, Revised Edition. Preschool children and over; 1971–79; LACT; 3 scores: isolated sounds in sequence, sounds within a syllable pattern, total; Charles H. Lindamood and Patricia C. Lindamood; Teaching Resources Corporation.

For additional information and reviews by Katharine G. Butler and James A. Till of an earlier edition, see 8:942 (5 references).

REFERENCES

1–5. See 8:942.
6. CUNNINGHAM, M. M. Perceptual ability and associational learning in normal and learning disabled children. *Perceptual & Motor Skills*, 1978, 47, 1200.
7. FREEMAN, B. A., & BEASLEY, D. S. Discrimination of time altered sentential approximations and monosyllables by children with reading problems. *Journal of Speech & Hearing Research*, 1978, 21, 497–506.

[1333]
Lippincott Reading Readiness Test (Including Readiness Check List). Grades kgn–1; 1965–73; Pierce H. McLeod; J. B. Lippincott Co.* (In-print status uncertain; no reply from publisher.)

For additional information and a review by Edward R. Sipay, see 7:753 (1 reference).

REFERENCES

1. See 7:753.
2. COLLIGAN, R. C. Concurrent validity of the Myklebust Pupil Rating Scale in a kindergarten population. *Journal of Learning Disabilities*, 1977, 10, 317–320.
3. COLLIGAN, R. C. Predictive utility of the Myklebust Pupil Rating Scale: A two-year follow-up. *Journal of Learning Disabilities*, 1979, 12, 264–267.

[1334]
★Listening Comprehension. Grades 1–3; 1976; 7 scores: following directions, sequencing, using context in listening, finding main ideas, forming sensory images from oral description, sensing emotion and moods through word usage and manner of delivery, making inferences and drawing conclusions; Susan Hohl and B. Cheney Edwards; Educators Publishing Service, Inc.*

[1335]
★Listening Comprehension Group Tests. Adult education students of English as a second language; 1981; LCGT; 2 tests; Donna Ilyin and Susan Rubin (technical guide); Newbury House Publishers, Inc.*
a) LISTENING COMPREHENSION PICTURE TEST. Beginning and intermediate adult education students of English as a second language; LCPT; does not require reading or writing skills.
b) LISTENING COMPREHENSION WRITTEN TEST. Intermediate and advanced students of English as a second language; LCWT.

[1336]

Literature Tests/Objective. High school; 1929–71; 2 series; no manual; Perfection Form Co.* (In-print status uncertain; no reply from publisher.)
a) 50-QUESTION SERIES. 1950–71; 284 tests on specific literary works; formerly called *Book Review Tests.*
b) 100-QUESTION SERIES. 1929–70; 174 tests on specific literary works; formerly called *Objective Tests in English.*

For additional information concerning earlier editions, see 6:295 and 6:304.

[1337]

Logical Reasoning. Grades 9–16 and adults; 1955; Alfred F. Hertzka and J. P. Guilford; Sheridan Psychological Services, Inc.*

See T2:1761 (10 references); for reviews by Duncan Howie and Charles R. Langmuir, see 5:694 (1 reference).

[1338]

★**The Lollipop Test: A Diagnostic Screening Test of School Readiness.** First grade entrants; 1981; criterion-referenced; 4 scores: identification of colors and shapes and copying shapes, picture description and position and spatial recognition, identification of numbers and counting, identification of letters and writing; Alex L. Chew; Humanics Ltd.*

[1339]

★**London House Personnel Selection Inventory.** Job applicants; 1975–80; PSI; 9 scores: 3 scores (percentile score, risk category, low risk confidence) for each of 3 areas (dishonesty, violence, drug abuse); London House Management Consultants, Inc.*

REFERENCES

1. JONES, J. W. Acquisitional processes underlying illicit alcohol abuse in underage children: An observational learning model. *Psychological Reports*, 1979, 45, 735–740.
2. JONES, J. W. Attitudinal correlates of employees' deviance: Theft, alcohol use, and nonprescribed drug use. *Psychological Reports*, 1980, 47, 71–77.

[1340]

★**London Reading Test.** Ages 10–7 to 12–4; 1978–80; LRT; Margaret Biscoe, Ced Bradshaw, Sheila Clarke, Miles Halliwell, David Morgan, Theresa Nunn, Helen Quigley, Irene Zelickman, and Gloria Callaway (practice test); NFER-Nelson Publishing Co. [England].*

[1341]

Lorge-Thorndike Intelligence Tests. Grades kgn–13; 1954–66; LTIT; 2 editions; Irving Lorge, Robert L. Thorndike, and Elizabeth Hagen (*b*); Riverside Publishing Co.*
a) SEPARATE LEVEL EDITION. Grades kgn–1, 2–3, 4–6, 7–9, 10–12; 1954–62; 5 levels; 2 tests (verbal, nonverbal) for levels 3–5.
  1) *Level 1, Nonverbal Battery.* Grades kgn–1.
  2) *Level 2, Nonverbal Battery.* Grades 2–3.
  3) *Level 3.* Grades 4–6.
  4) *Level 4.* Grades 7–9.
  5) *Level 5.* Grades 10–12.
b) MULTI-LEVEL EDITION. Grades 3–13; 1954–66; revision of levels 3–5 of the separate level edition; 3 scores: verbal, nonverbal, composite; 8 levels (grades 3, 4, 5, 6, 7, 8–9, 10–11, 12–13) in a single booklet.

See T2:400 (38 references); for a review by Carol K. Tittle of the multi-level edition, see 7:360 (95 references); see also 6:467 (11 references); for reviews by Frank S. Freeman, John E. Milholland, and D. A. Pidgeon of the separate level edition, see 5:350 (6 references).

REFERENCES

1–6. See 5:350.
7–17. See 6:467.
18–112. See 7:360.
113–150. See T2:400.
151. BADIAN, N. A. Auditory–visual integration, auditory memory, and reading in retarded and adequate readers. *Journal of Learning Disabilities*, 1977, 10, 49–114.
152. BEARISON, D. J., & LEVEY, L. M. Children's comprehension of referential communication: Decoding ambiguous messages. *Child Development*, 1977, 48, 716–720.
153. BRODZINSKY, D. M., FEVER, V., & OWENS, J. Detection of linguistic ambiguity by reflective, impulsive, fast/accurate, and slow inaccurate children. *Journal of Educational Psychology*, 1977, 69, 237–243.
154. GOLDBERG, R. A., SCHWARTZ, S., & STEWART, M. Individual differences in cognitive processes. *Journal of Educational Psychology*, 1977, 69, 9–14.
155. KENNEDY, S. P., & SUZUKI, N. S. Spontaneous elaboration in Mexican–American and Anglo–American high school seniors. *American Educational Research Journal*, 1977, 14, 383–388.
156. KERCKHOFF, A. C., & CAMPBELL, R. T. Black–white differences in the educational attainment process. *Sociology of Education*, 1977, 50, 15–27.
157. KIRBY, J. R., & DAS, J. P. Reading achievement, IQ, and simultaneous–successive processing. *Journal of Educational Psychology*, 1977, 69, 564–570.
158. LEHRER, B. E., & HIERONYMOUS, A. N. Predicting achievement using intellectual, academic–motivational and selected non–intellectual factors. *Journal of Experimental Education*, 1977, 45, 44–51.
159. MALGADY, R. G. Children's interpretation and appreciation of similes. *Child Development*, 1977, 48, 1734–1738.
160. MIRON, M. A validation study of a transferred group intelligence test. *International Journal of Psychology*, 1977, 12, 193–205.
161. NICHOLS, N. J., & MCKINNEY, A. W. Black or white socioeconomically disadvantaged pupils – they aren't necessarily inferior. *Journal of Negro Education*, 1977, 46, 443–449.
162. PALMER, L. L. Characteristics of near–point and far–point binocular and monocular sighting in classroom and opthalmological populations. *Perceptual & Motor Skills*, 1977, 45, 707–711.
163. WEGNER, D. M. Attribute generality: The development and articulation of attributes in person perception. *Journal of Research in Personality*, 1977, 11, 329–339.
164. WHITELY, S. E. Information–processing on intelligence test items: Some response components. *Applied Psychological Measurement*, 1977, 1, 465–476.
165. ANDERSON, C. C., & MAGUIRE, T. O. The effect of TV viewing on the educational performance of elementary school children. *Alberta Journal of Educational Research*, 1978, 24, 156–163.
166. ANDERSON, L. W., & SCOTT, C. C. The relationship among teaching methods, student characteristics, and student involvement in learning. *Journal of Teacher Education*, 1978, 29, 52–57.
167. AUGUST, G. J., & RYCHLAK, J. F. Role of intelligence and task difficulty in the affective learning styles of children with high and low self-concepts. *Journal of Educational Psychology*, 1978, 70, 406–413.
168. BAKER, A. M., & KAUFFMAN, J. M. Screening LD children with the Lorge-Thorndike. *Academic Therapy*, 1978, 13, 549–552.
169. BRETT, A. The influence of affective education on the cognitive performance of kindergarden children. *Child Study Journal*, 1978, 8, 165–174.
170. BREUNING, S. E., & ZELLA, W. F. Effects of individualized incentives on norm-referenced IQ test performance of high school students in special education classes. *Journal of School Psychology*, 1978, 16, 220–226.
171. BUSSE, T. V., & SERAYDARIAN, L. The relationships between first name desirability and school readiness, IQ, and school achievement. *Psychology in the Schools*, 1978, 15, 297–302.
172. CLARK, A., BREKKE, B., & WILLIAMS, J. Conservation of weight with adolescents and young people. *Journal of Teaching & Learning: The University of North Dakota*, 1978, 4, 3–14.
173. ENO, L. Predicting achievement and the theory of fluid and crystallized intelligence. *Psychological Reports*, 1978, 43, 847–852.
174. ENO, L., WOEHLKE, P., & DEICHMANN, J. A factor analytic study of ability, achievement, and personality characteristics of college students. *College Student Journal*, 1978, 12, 366–371.

175. KIRBY, J. R., & DAS, J. P. Information processing and human abilities. *Journal of Educational Psychology*, 1978, 70, 58–66.
176. MCCLURE, L. F., CHINSKY, J. M., & LARCEN, S. W. Enhancing social problem-solving performance in an elementary school setting. *Journal of Educational Psychology*, 1978, 70, 504–513.
177. MORGAN, W. R., ALWIN, D. F., & GRIFFIN, L. J. Social origins, parental values, and the transmission of inequality. *American Journal of Sociology*, 1978, 85, 156–166.
178. PICHE, G. L., RUBIN, D. L., & MICHLIN, M. L. Age and social class in children's use of persuasive communicative appeals. *Child Development*, 1978, 49, 773–780.
179. POIZNER, S. B., NICEWANDER, A. W., & GETTYS, C. F. Alternative response and scoring methods for multiple-choice items: An empirical study of probabilistic and ordinal response modes. *Applied Psychological Measurement*, 1978, 2, 83–96.
180. SPIEGEL, M. R., & BRYANT, N. D. Is speed of processing information related to intelligence and achievement? *Journal of Educational Psychology*, 1978, 70, 904–910.
181. BAILEY, R. C., & HATCH, V. Interpersonal perceptions of intelligence in late childhood and early adolescent friendships. *Journal of Genetic Psychology*, 1979, 135, 109–114.
182. BRODZINSKY, D. M., MESSER, S. B., & TEU, J. D. Sex differences in children's expression and control of fantasy and overt aggression. *Child Development*, 1979, 50, 372–379.
183. GETTINGER, M., & WHITE, M. A. Which is the stronger correlate of school learning? Time to learn or measured intelligence? *Journal of Educational Psychology*, 1979, 71, 405–412.
184. JOHNSON, R. A. Verbal originality in the absence of sight: Blind versus sighted adolescents. *Child Study Journal*, 1979, 9, 261–271.
185. KENDALL, J. R., & HOOD, J. Investigating the relationship between comprehension and word recognition: Oral reading analysis of children with comprehension or word recognition disabilities. *Journal of Reading Behavior*, 1979, 11, 41–48.
186. KIRCHMEIMER, J. Auditory and visual factors related to spelling success. *Psychology in the Schools*, 1979, 16, 491–494.
187. LUNDSTEEN, S. W., & WILSON, J. A. R. Permanency of gains for children's problem solving processes and subabilities. *Educational Research Quarterly*, 1979, 4, 41–49.
188. MAYFIELD, B. Teacher perception of creativity, intelligence and achievement. *Gifted Child Quarterly*, 1979, 23, 812–817.
189. MESSER, S. B., & BRODZINSKY, D. M. The relation of conceptual tempo to aggression and its control. *Child Development*, 1979, 50, 758–766.
190. SCHWARTZ, S. Differential effects of personality on access to various long-term memory codes. *Journal of Research in Personality*, 1979, 13, 396–403.
191. SILLIMAN, E. R. Relationship between pictorial interpretation and comprehension of three spatial relations in school-age children. *Journal of Speech & Hearing Research*, 1979, 22, 366–388.
192. GREENE, J. C. Individual and teacher/class effects in aptitude treatment studies. *American Educational Research Journal*, 1980, 17, 291–302.
193. HICKS, C. The development of creative thinking and its relationship to IQ and reading achievement. *Reading World*, 1980, 20, 44–52.
194. JENSEN, A. R. Uses of sibling data in educational and psychological research. *American Educational Research Journal*, 1980, 17, 153–170.
195. JOHNSON, R. A. Sensory images in the absence of sight: Blind versus sighted adolescents. *Perceptual & Motor Skills*, 1980, 51, 177–178.
196. LESLIE, L. Mediation or production deficiency in disabled readers? *Perceptual & Motor Skills*, 1980, 50, 519–530.
197. RIBORDY, S. C., HOMES, D. S., & BUCHSBAUM, H. K. Effects of affective and cognitive distractions on anxiety reduction. *Journal of Social Psychology*, 1980, 112, 121–127.
198. STANDING, L., BOND, B., SMITH, P., & ISLEY, C. Is the immediate memory span determined by subvocalization rate? *British Journal of Psychology*, 1980, 71, 525–539.
199. BARRATT, E. S., PATTON, J., OLSSON, N. G., & ZUCKER, G. Impulsivity and paced tapping. *Journal of Motor Behavior*, 1981, 13, 286–300.
200. FISK, R. A., & JANZEN, H. L. Identifying learning disabled students with a selected psychoeducational test battery. *Alberta Journal of Educational Research*, 1981, 27, 252–263.
201. SAIGH, P. A. The validity of the Lorge Thorndike Nonverbal Battery as a predictor of the academic achievement of international students. *Educational & Psychological Measurement*, 1981, 41, 1315–1318.
202. SHEPARD, L., CAMILLI, G., & AVERILL, M. Comparison of procedures for detecting test item bias with both internal and external ability criteria. *Journal of Educational Statistics*, 1981, 6, 317–375.
203. SWANSON, L. Vigilance deficit in learning disabled children: A signal detection analysis. *Journal of Child Psychology & Psychiatry & Allied Disciplines*, 1981, 22, 393–399.
204. THOMSON–ROUNTREE, P., CALDWELL, B. M., & WEBB, R. An examination of the relationship between role–taking and social competence. *Child Study Journal*, 1981, 11, 253–264.

[1342]

Lorimer Braille Recognition Test: A Test of Ability in Reading Braille Contractions. Students (ages 7–13) in grade 2 Braille; 1962; John Lorimer; Association for the Education and Welfare of the Visually Handicapped [England].*
For additional information, see 6:854 (1 reference).

[1343]

★**Louisville Behavior Checklist.** Ages 4–6, 7–12, 13–17; 1977–81; LBC; "social and emotional behaviors indicative of psychopathological disorders"; 3 levels; 13 to 20 scales; Lovick C. Miller; Western Psychological Services.*
a) FORM E1. Ages 4–6; 1977–81; 20 scales: infantile aggression, hyperactivity, antisocial behavior, aggression, social withdrawal, sensitivity, fear, inhibition, intellectual deficit, immaturity, cognitive disability, normal irritability, prosocial deficit, rare deviance, neurotic behavior, psychotic behavior, somatic behavior, sexual behavior, school disturbance predictor, severity level.
a) FORM E2. Ages 7–12; 1977–81; 19 scales: same as for Form E1 except academic disability replaces intellectual deficit, learning disability replaces cognitive disability, and school disturbance predictor is omitted.
c) FORM E3. Ages 13–17; 1981; 13 scales: egocentric-exploitive, destructive-assaultive, social delinquency, adolescent turmoil, apathetic isolation, neuroticism, dependent-inhibited, academic disability, neurological or psychotic abnormality, general pathology, longitudinal, severity level, total pathology.

REFERENCES

1. SACKS, S., & DELEAN, G. Training the disturbed enuretic. *Behaviour Research & Therapy*, 1978, 16, 296–299.

[1344]

*****A Love Attitudes Inventory.** Grade 12 and college; 1971; LAI; David Knox; Family Life Publications, Inc.*
See T2:821 (1 reference).

[1345]

LRA Standard Mastery Tasks in Language. Grades 1, 2; 1970; 2 levels; Donald E. P. Smith, Judith M. Smith, and Raymond Cabot (*a*); Learning Research Associates, Inc.* (In-print status uncertain; no reply from publisher.)
a) PRIMARY 1. Grade 1; 2 scores: letter matching, sound matching.
b) PRIMARY 2. Grade 2; 5 scores: letter naming, letter writing, word naming, word writing, word attack.

[1346]

★**The Luria-Nebraska Neuropsychological Battery.** Ages 15 and over; 1980; uses cards adapted from *Luria's Neuropsychological Investigation* by Anne-Lise Christensen; 14 scores: motor, rhythm, tactile, visual, receptive speech, expressive speech, writing, reading, arithmetic, memory, intellectual processes, pathognomic, left hemisphere, right hemisphere; Charles J. Golden, Thomas A. Hammeke, and Arnold D. Purisch; Western Psychological Services.*

[1347] The Lüscher Color Test

REFERENCES

1. LEWIS, G. P., GOLDEN, C. J., MOSES, J. A., JR., OSMON, D. C., PURISCH, A. D., & HAMMEKE, T. A. Localization of cerebral dysfunction with a standardized version of Luria's Neuropsychological Battery. *Journal of Consulting & Clinical Psychology*, 1979, 47, 1003–1019.
2. BERG, R. A., & GOLDEN, C. J. Identification of neuropsychological deficits in epilepsy using the Luria–Nebraska Neuropsychological Battery. *Journal of Consulting & Clinical Psychology*, 1981, 49, 745–747.
3. GOLDEN, C. J., FROSS, K. H., & GRABER, B. Split–half reliability and item–scale consistency of the Luria–Nebraska Neuropsychological Battery. *Journal of Consulting & Clinical Psychology*, 1981, 49, 304–305.
4. GOLDEN, C. J., MOSES, J. A., JR., FISHBURNE, F. J., ENGUM, E., LEWIS, G. P., WISNIEWSKI, A. M., CONLEY, F. K., & BERG, R. A. Cross-validation of the Luria–Nebraska Neuropsychological Battery for the presence, lateralization, and localization of brain damage. *Journal of Consulting & Clinical Psychology*, 1981, 49, 491–507.
5. GOLDEN, C. J., MOSES, J. A., JR., GRABER, B., & BERG, R. Objective clinical rules for interpreting the Luria–Nebraska Neuropsychological Battery: Derivation, effectiveness, and validation. *Journal of Consulting & Clinical Psychology*, 1981, 49, 616–618.
6. MALLOY, P. F., & WEBSTER, J. S. Detecting mild brain impairment using the Luria–Nebraska Neuropsychological Battery. *Journal of Consulting & Clinical Psychology*, 1981, 49, 768–770.
7. McKAY, S. E., GOLDEN, C. J., MOSES, J. A., JR., FISHBURNE, F., & WISNIEWSKI, A. Correlation of the Luria–Nebraska Neuropsychological Battery with the WAIS. *Journal of Consulting & Clinical Psychology*, 1981, 49, 940–946.
8. PRIFITERA, A., & RYAN, J. J. Validity of the Luria–Nebraska intellectual processes scale as a measure of adult intelligence. *Journal of Consulting & Clinical Psychology*, 1981, 49, 755–756.

[1347]
The Lüscher Color Test. Adults; 1947–69; LCT; an 8-color patch version (also called *Short Lüscher Test*) of the 73-color patch *Full Lüscher Test* available in German edition only; a personality test sold through bookstores for self-administration or administration to others; translated and edited by Ian A. Scott; Max Lüscher; Random House, Inc.* (In-print status uncertain; no reply from publisher.)

See T2:1263 (2 references); for a review by S. G. Lee, and excerpted reviews by C. H. Ammons (with R. B. Ammons), Bernard I. Murstein, and David Sanford, see 7:98.

REFERENCES

1–2. See T2:1263.
3. COHEN, E., & HUNTER, I. Severity of depression differentiated by a color selection test. *American Journal of Psychiatry*, 1978, 135, 611–612.
4. HENRY, D. L., & JACOBS, K. W. Color eroticism and color preference. *Perceptual & Motor Skills*, 1978, 47, 106.
5. BRAUN, C. M. J., & BONTA, J. L. Cross-cultural validity, reliability, and stimulus characteristics of the Lüscher Color Test. *Journal of Personality Assessment*, 1979, 43, 459–460.
6. SEEFELDT, F. M. The Lüscher Color Test: Sex differences in color preference. *Perceptual & Motor Skills*, 1979, 48, 896–898.
7. STIMPSON, D. V., & STIMPSON, M. F. Relation of personality characteristics and color preferences. *Perceptual & Motor Skills*, 1979, 49, 60–62.
8. COROTTO, L. V., & HAFNER, J. L. The Lüscher Color Test: Relationship between color preferences and behavior. *Perceptual & Motor Skills*, 1980, 50, 1066.
9. HAFNER, J. L., & COROTTA, L. V. Age, sex, race, and the Lüscher Color Test. *Perceptual & Motor Skills*, 1980, 50, 1144–1146.
10. LEDFORD, R. S., & HOKE, W. E. Self-report as a validity check for the Lüscher Color Test. *Perceptual & Motor Skills*, 1981, 53, 545–546.

[1348]
Luther Hospital Sentence Completions. Prospective nursing students; 1959–70; LHSC; nonquantitative interpretations of responses in 7 attitudinal areas: nursing, self, home-family, responsibility, others, classwork and studies, love and marriage; an abbreviated edition, consisting of 40 of the 90 items, is also available under the title *Nursing Sentence Completions* (NSC); these 40 items may be scored quantitatively in either edition to obtain a score for predicting success in training; the authors refer to the scoring key as the *Nursing Education Scale* (NES); John R. Thurston, Helen L. Brunclik, P. A. Finn (test), and John Feldhusen (manual); Nursing Research Associates.* (In-print status uncertain; no reply from publisher.)

See T2:2382 (2 references) and 7:1117 (5 references).

[1349]
M-B History Record: Self-Administered Form. Psychiatric patients and penal groups; 1957–72; MBHR; 8 scores: family disunity, conflict with parents, health awareness, introversion, school and job failure, social misfit, breakdowns and addiction, inconsistency; an optional marriage section may also be administered when appropriate; Peter F. Briggs; Clinical Psychology Publishing Co., Inc.*

For additional information and reviews by W. Grant Dahlstrom and Douglas N. Jackson, see 8:604 (3 references); see also T2:1265 (7 references), P:148 (3 references), and 6:136 (2 references).

[1350]
M-Scale: An Inventory of Attitudes Toward Black/White Relations in the United States. College and adults; 1968–69; MS; "reliability coefficient appears to be too low (r=.27) to use the Scale as a predictive instrument"; James H. Morrison; the Author.*

For additional information and a review by Marvin E. Shaw, see 8:605 (1 reference); see also T2:1266 (1 reference).

[1351]
The MACC Behavioral Adjustment Scale, Revised 1971. Psychiatric patients; 1957–71; MACC; 5 scores: mood, cooperation, communication, social contact, total adjustment; same as the 1962 edition except for format and a few changes in wording; Robert B. Ellsworth; Western Psychological Services.*

See T2:1264 (11 references) and P:147 (10 references); for a review by Wilson H. Guertin, see 6:135 (2 references); for a review by Maurice Lorr, see 5:82.

REFERENCES

1–2. See 6:135.
3–12. See P:147.
13–23. See T2:1264.
24. MAY, P. R. A., TUMA, A. H., & DIXON, W. J. For better or for worse? Outcome variance with psychotherapy and other treatments for schizophrenia. *Journal of Nervous & Mental Disease*, 1977, 165, 231–239.
25. ALDEN, L. Treatment environment and patient improvement. *Journal of Nervous & Mental Disease*, 1978, 166, 327–334.
26. COSTELLO, R. M. Premorbid social competence construct generalizability across ethnic groups: Path analyses with two premorbid social competence components. *Journal of Consulting & Clinical Psychology*, 1978, 46, 1164–1165.
27. TUMA, A. H., MAY, P. R. A., YALE, C., & FORSYTHE, A. B. Therapist experience, general clinical ability, and treatment outcome in schizophrenia. *Journal of Consulting & Clinical Psychology*, 1978, 46, 1120–1126.
28. VAN PUTTEN, T., & MAY, P. R. A. "Akinetic depression" in schizophrenia. *Archives of General Psychiatry*, 1978, 35, 1101–1107.
29. LONOWSKI, D. J., STERLING, F. E., & KING, H. A. Electromyographic assessment of dimethylaminoethanol (DEANOL) in treatment of jardive dyskinesia. *Psychological Reports*, 1979, 45, 415–419.
30. TUMA, A. H., & MAY, P. R. A. And if that doesn't work, what next...? A study of treatment failures in schizophrenia. *Journal of Nervous & Mental Disease*, 1979, 167, 566–571.
31. COROTTO, L. V., & HAFNER, J. L. The Lüscher Color Test: Relationship between color preferences and behavior. *Perceptual & Motor Skills*, 1980, 50, 1066.
32. COSTELLO, R. M. Alcoholism aftercare and outcome: Cross-lagged panel and path analyses. *British Journal of Addiction*, 1980, 75, 49–53.

33. KATZ–GARRIS, L., HADLEY, T. J., GARRIS, R. P., & BARNHILL, B. A factor analytic study of the Adaptive Behavior Scale. *Psychological Reports*, 1980, 47, 807–814.
34. MAY, P. R. A., VAN PUTTEN, T., & YALE, C. Predicting outcome of antipsychotic drug treatment from early response. *American Journal of Psychiatry*, 1980, 137, 1088–1089.
35. HADDAD, L. B. Intra–institutional relocation: Measured impact upon geriatric patients. *Journal of the American Geriatrics Society*, 1981, 29, 86–88.
36. MAY, P. R. A., VAN PUTTEN, T., JENDEN, D. J., YALE, C., & DIXON, W. J. Chlorpromazine levels and the outcome of treatment in schizophrenic patients. *Archives of General Psychiatry*, 1981, 38, 202–207.

[1352]
Machine Calculation Test: National Business Entrance Tests. Grades 11–16 and adults; 1941–72; earlier tests called *Key-Driven Calculating Machine Ability Test*; National Business Association.* (In-print status uncertain; no reply from publisher.)

For additional information, see 6:39; for a review by Dorothy C. Adkins of earlier forms, see 5:514; for a review by Elizabeth Fehrer, see 3:384. For reviews of the complete battery, see 6:33 (1 review), 5:515 (3 reviews), and 3:396 (1 review).

[1353]
Machover Draw-A-Person Test. Ages 2 and over; 1949; MDAP; also called *Machover Figure Drawing Test*; Karen Machover; Charles C Thomas, Publisher.*

For additional information, see 8:606 (26 references); see also T2:1481 (83 references) and P:451 (85 references); for a review by Philip M. Kitay, see 6:229 (84 references); see also 5:148 (39 references); for reviews by Philip L. Harriman and Naomi Stewart, see 4:111 (13 references).

[1354]
★**The Macmillan Diagnostic Reading Pack.** Reading ages 5–6, 6–7, 7–8, 8–9 years; 1980; 4 levels; Ted Ames; Macmillan Education [England].*

a) STAGE 1. Reading ages 5–6 years; item scores in 3 areas: visual skills (32 key words, letter-matching, upper and lower case matching, visual memory-recognition, visual memory reproduction), auditory skills (transcribing sounds, sound value of letters, auditory discrimination, short-term auditory memory), phonic blending (blending 2 and 3 letter words, auditory blending).

b) STAGE 2. Reading ages 6–7 years; item scores in 5 areas: key words (68 key words, 32 key words), phonic recognition (initial and final consonant blends and digraphs, consonant and vowel sounds), phonic blending (consonant blends and digraphs, blending 2 and 3 letter words), phonic spelling (spelling 2 and 3 letter words, transcribing sounds), oral reading (accuracy, comprehension).

c) STAGE 3. Reading ages 7–8 years; item scores in 5 areas: key words (68 key words, 32 key words), phonic recognition (long vowels and vowel digraphs, final and initial consonant blends and consonant digraphs), phonic blending (vowel digraphs, consonant blends and digraphs), phonic spelling (spelling of short vowel words containing consonant blends and digraphs, spelling 2 and 3 letter words), oral reading (accuracy, comprehension).

d) STAGE 4. Reading ages 8–9 years; item scores in 4 areas: phonic recognition (long vowels and vowel digraphs, final consonant blends), phonic blending (vowel digraphs, consonant blends and digraphs), phonic spelling (spelling of regular single syllable words, spelling of short vowel words containing consonant blends and digraphs), oral reading (accuracy, comprehension).

[1355]
★**The Macmillan Reader Placement Test.** Grades 1 and over; 1967–72; part of Macmillan Reading Program; can be used as supplement to *Macmillan Mastery Tests*; 2 tests: word pronunciation, oral reading: Edward R. Sipay, senior authors: Albert J. Harris and Mae Knight Clark; Macmillan Publishing Co., Inc.*

[1356]
MacQuarrie Test for Mechanical Ability. Grades 7 and over; 1925–43; 8 scores: tracing, tapping, dotting, copying, location, blocks, pursuit, total; T. W. MacQuarrie; CTB/McGraw-Hill.*

See T2:2251 (38 references) and 4:759 (15 references); for reviews by John R. Kinzer, C. H. Lawshe, Jr., and Alec Rodger, see 3:661 (43 references).

REFERENCES

1–43. See 3:661.
44–58. See 4:759.
59–96. See T2:2251.
97. ZAIDEL, D., & SPERRY, R. W. Some long–term motor effects of cerebral commissurotomy in man. *Neuropsychologia*, 1977, 15, 193–204.
98. KIELHOFNER, G., BURKE, J. P., & IGI, C. H. A model of human occupation, part 4. Assessment and intervention. *American Journal of Occupational Therapy*, 1980, 34, 777–788.

[1357]
*****Maferr Inventory of Feminine Values.** Junior and senior high school, college and adults; 1955–79; MIFV; for research use only; perception of sex roles; 2 levels; Anne G. Steinmann and David J. Fox, with Mary Toro; Maferr Foundation, Inc.*

a) MAFERR DEVELOPMENTAL INVENTORY OF FEMININE VALUES. Junior and senior high school; 1966; 5 tests: female self perception, female perception of ideal women, female perception of man's ideal woman, female perception of mother's ideal, female perception of father's ideal.

b) ADULT INVENTORY. College and adults; 1955–79; 5 tests (3 for women, 2 for men): woman's self-perception, woman's ideal woman, woman's perception of man's ideal woman, man's ideal woman, man's perception of woman's ideal woman; (Finnish, French, German, Greek, Japanese, Portuguese, and Spanish editions available).

For additional information and reviews by Goldine C. Gleser and Lenore W. Harmon, see 8:607 (28 references); see also T2:1267 (11 references).

[1358]
*****Maferr Inventory of Masculine Values.** Junior and senior high school, college and adults; 1966–79; MIMV; for research use only; perception of sex role; 2 levels; Anne G. Steinmann and David J. Fox, with Mary Toro; Maferr Foundation, Inc.*

a) MAFERR DEVELOPMENTAL INVENTORY OF MASCULINE VALUES. Junior and senior high school; 1966; 5 tests: male self perception, male perception of ideal man, male perception of woman's ideal man, male perception of mother's ideal, male perception of father's ideal.

b) ADULT INVENTORY. College and adults; 1966–79; 5 tests (3 for men, 2 for women): man's self perception, man's ideal man, man's perception of woman's ideal man, woman's ideal man, woman's perception of man's ideal man; (Finnish, French, German, Greek, Japanese, Portuguese, and Spanish editions available).

For additional information and a review by Leonard D. Goodstein, see 8:608 (4 references); see also T2:1268 (1 reference).

[1359]

*Maico Audiometers. Grades kgn and over; 1936–81; 8 models; Maico Hearing Instruments, Inc.
a) ADVANCED DIAGNOSTIC AUDIOMETER. For pure tone (air and bone conduction) and speech testing by health care professionals; Model MA32.
b) PORTABLE AUDIOMETERS. For testing in schools and industry; 4 models.
  1) *Model MA*39. For air conduction testing.
  2) *Model MA*40. For air and bone conduction testing.
  3) *Model MA*41. For air conduction with bone and speech testing.
  4) *Model MA*27. Ultra portable audiometer for air conduction testing.
c) DUAL CHANNEL RESEARCH AND DIAGNOSTIC AUDIOMETER. For pure tone (air and bone conduction) and speech testing in clinical and research work; Model MA24B.
d) COMPUTERIZED AUDIOMETERS. For use by employers; 2 models.
  1) *Model MA*26.
  2) *Model MA*28.

For reference to earlier models, see T2:2043 (1 reference); see also 6:947 (2 references) and 5:763 (4 references). For comments by Louis M. DiCarlo on screening audiometers in general and specific comments on an earlier Maico portable model and three other portable audiometers, see 6:942.

[1360]

★The Major-Minor-Finder. Ages 16–adult; 1978–81; M-M-F; Arthur Cutler, Francis Ferry, Robert Kauk, and Robert Robinett; CFKR Career Materials, Inc.*

[1361]

Make A Picture Story. Ages 6 and over; 1947–52; MAPS; Edwin S. Shneidman; The Psychological Corporation.*

See T2:1482 (10 references) and P:452 (4 references); for a review by Arthur R. Jensen, see 6:230 (10 references); see also 5:149 (18 references); for reviews by Albert I. Rabin and Charles R. Strother, see 4:113 (19 references).

REFERENCES

1–19. See 4:113.
20–38. See 5:149.
39–48. See 6:230.
49–52. See P:452.
53–62. See T2:1482.
63. REKERS, G. A., & VARNI, J. W. Self monitoring and self–reinforcement processes in a pre–transsexual boy. *Behaviour Research & Therapy*, 1977, 15, 177–180.
64. REKERS, G. A., WILLIS, T. J., YATES, C. E., ROSEN, A. C., & LOW, B. P. Assessment of childhood gender behavior change. *Journal of Child Psychology & Psychiatry & Allied Disciplines*, 1977, 18, 53–65.
65. SUMMERS, F., & WALSH, F. The nature of the symbiotic bond between mother and schizophrenic. *American Journal of Orthopsychiatry*, 1977, 47, 484–494.
66. SUMMERS, F., & WALSH, F. Symbiosis and confirmation between father and schizophrenic. *American Journal of Orthopsychiatry*, 1979, 49, 136–148.

[1362]

Making Objects. Grades 9–16 and adults; 1963; "divergent production of figural systems" or "figural expressional fluency"; Sheldon Gardner, Arthur Gershon, Philip R. Merrifield, and J. P. Guilford; Sheridan Psychological Services, Inc.*

See T2:562 (8 references) and 6:552 (1 reference).

REFERENCES

1. See 6:552.
2–9. See T2:562.
10. COHEN, D., SCHAIE, K. W., & GRIBBIN, K. The organization of spatial abilities in older men and women. *Journal of Gerontology*, 1977, 32, 578–585.
11. DURIO, H. F. A factor analysis of response task constraint in measures of creative aptitude. *Gifted Child Quarterly*, 1979, 23, 829–836.

[1363]

Management Relations Survey. Managers; 1970; ratings by employees; 4 scores: exposure and feedback scores in each of 2 areas (your manager's practices, your practices with management); Jay Hall; Teleometrics Int'l.*

For additional information and a review by Walter C. Borman, see 8:1178 (1 reference).

[1364]

Management Style Diagnosis Test, Second Edition. Managers; 1965–75; MSDT; manager's perception of own managerial style; 8 managerial style scores (deserter, missionary, autocrat, compromiser, bureaucrat, developer, benevolent autocrat, executive) based upon combinations of dichotomized task orientation, relationships orientation, and effectiveness scores plus a style synthesis score (average of last 3 scores); W. J. Reddin; Organizational Tests Ltd. [Canada].*

For additional information and a review by Abraham K. Korman, see 8:1179 (5 references).

[1365]

Management Transactions Audit. Managers; 1973; MTA; manager's views as to how he would handle 18 specific complaints, challenges, and uncertainties on the part of subordinates, colleagues, and superiors; 3 transaction scores (parent subsystem, adult subsystem, child subsystem) and 2 tension indexes (disruptive, constructive) for each of 3 relationships (subordinates, colleagues, superiors); no manual; Jay Hall and C. Leo Griffith; Teleometrics Int'l.*

For additional information and reviews by Stephan J. Motowidlo and Ronald N. Taylor, see 8:1180.

[1366]

Managerial Philosophies Scale. Managers; 1975; MPS; "manager's assumptions and working theories about the nature of those whose activities he or she coordinates"; 2 scores: theory X (reductive management beliefs), theory Y (developmental management beliefs); no manual; Jacob Jacoby and James R. Terborg; Teleometrics Int'l.*

For additional information, see 8:1181.

REFERENCES

1. BROWN, S. E., & LADAWAN, T. Perceived satisfaction with leadership as related to subordinate and superordinate managerial philosophies. *Perceptual & Motor Skills*, 1979, 48, 355–359.

[1367]

The Manchester Scales of Social Adaptation. Ages 6–15; 1966; MSSA; adaptation of *Vineland Social*

Maturity Scale; 13 scores: social perspective (general, sport, current affairs, aesthetic, scientific, total), self-direction (socialisation of play, freedom of movement, self-help, handling of money, responsibility in home, total), total; E. A. Lunzer; NFER-Nelson Publishing Co. [England].*

For additional information, reviews by G. A. V. Morgan and M. L. Kellmer Pringle, and an excerpted review by Maurice Chazan, see 7:99 (1 reference).

REFERENCES

1. See 7:99.
2. LONG, C. G., & MOORE, J. R. Parental expectations for their epileptic children. *Journal of Child Psychology & Psychiatry & Allied Disciplines*, 1979, 20, 299–312.

[1368]

Mandel Social Adjustment Scale. Psychiatric patients and others; 1959; MSAS; 8 scores: occupational, family life, economic, health, religion, residence, community and social, total; Nathan G. Mandel; the Author.* (In-print status uncertain; no reply from publisher.)

For additional information, see P:151 (2 references).

[1369]

The Manson Evaluation. Adults; 1948; ME; identification of alcoholics, potential alcoholics, and severely maladjusted adults; 8 scores: anxiety, depressive fluctuations, emotional sensitivity, resentfulness, incompleteness, aloneness, interpersonal relations, total; Morse P. Manson; Western Psychological Services.*

See T2:1271 (2 references) and P:152 (1 reference); for a review by Dugal Campbell, see 6:137 (5 references); for reviews by Charles H. Honzik and Albert L. Hunsicker, see 4:68 (4 references).

[1370]

Manual Accuracy and Speed Test. Ages 4 and over; 1971; MAST; also called *Minnesota MAST*; 10 scores: 2 scores (best hand, worst hand) for 5 subtests (alternate tapping, large peg placement, small peg placement, nails transfer, steadiness); Peter F. Briggs and Auke Tellegen; Lafayette Instrument Co.*

See T2:1896 (1 reference).

REFERENCES

1. See T2:1896.
2. DENISI, A. S., & SHAW, J. B. Investigation of the uses of self-reports of abilities. *Journal of Applied Psychology*, 1977, 62, 641–644.

[1371]

Marianne Frostig Developmental Test of Visual Perception, Third Edition. Ages 3–8; 1961–66; DTVP; 7 scores: eye-motor coordination, figure-ground discrimination, form constancy, position in space, spatial relations, total, perceptual quotient; Marianne Frostig in collaboration with D. Welty Lefever, John R. B. Whittlesey, and Phyllis Maslow (monograph); Consulting Psychologists Press, Inc.*

For additional information, see 8:882 (72 references); see also T2:1921 (43 references); for reviews by Brad S. Chissom, Newell C. Kephart, and Lester Mann see 7:871 (117 references); for reviews by James M. Anderson and Mary C. Austin, see 6:553 (7 references).

REFERENCES

1–7. See 6:553.
8–124. See 7:871.
125–167. See T2:1921.

168–239. See 8:882.
240. BASSETT, J. E., GAYTON, W. F., BLANCHARD, E. B., & OZMON, K. L. Birth order and perceptual motor performance. *Perceptual & Motor Skills*, 1977, 45, 1076–1078.
241. HARE, B. A. Perceptual deficits are not a cue to reading problems in second grade. *Reading Teacher*, 1977, 30, 624–628.
242. HARTH, R., & JUSTEN, J. E., III. The validity of the ITPA Visual Closure Subtest. *Academic Therapy*, 1977, 12, 261–265.
243. KAUFMAN, H. S., & BIREN, P. L. Persistent reversers: Poor readers, writers, spellers? *Academic Therapy*, 1977, 12, 209–217.
244. MATHIS, H. J., & HARSHMAN, H. W. Therapeutic program for the learning disabled child. *Physical Therapy*, 1977, 57, 823–825.
245. MIYASHITA, T. Factor analytic study of the ITPA and the Frostig test. *Japanese Psychological Research*, 1977, 19, 187–192.
246. WOOD, N. E. Directed art, visual perception, and learning disabilities. *Academic Therapy*, 1977, 12, 455–462.
247. BREKKE, B., WILLIAMS, J. D., & FOLLMAN, D. E. Comparative assessment of visual perceptual abilities in the trainable mentally retarded. *Perceptual & Motor Skills*, 1978, 47, 735–738.
248. BROCK, P. B., HISAMA, T., & CASEY, J. P. Correlates among Frostig Visual Perception scores and IQs of mildly mentally impaired and intellectually superior primary children. *Perceptual & Motor Skills*, 1978, 46, 262.
249. DONOVAN, G., & MITCHELL, M. M. Analysis of the Developmental Test of Visual Perception and the Motorfree Visual Perception Test. *Perceptual & Motor Skills*, 1978, 46, 1284–1286.
250. O'DONNELL, J. P., PAULSEN, K. A., & McGAUN, J. D. Matching familiar figures test: A unidimensional measure of reflection–impulsivity? *Perceptual & Motor Skills*, 1978, 47, 1247–1253.
251. ZENTALL, S. S., ZENTALL, T. R., & BARACK, R. C. Distraction as a function of within–task stimulation for hyperactive and normal children. *Journal of Learning Disabilities*, 1978, 11, 540–548.
252. BELKA, D. E., & WILLIAMS, H. G. Prediction of later cognitive behavior from early school perceptual-motor, perceptual, and cognitive performances. *Perceptual & Motor Skills*, 1979, 49, 131–141.
253. HILLMAN, L. S., HILLMAN, R. E., & DODSON, W. E. Diagnosis, treatment, and follow-up of neonatal mepivacaine intoxication secondary to paracervical and pudendal blocks during labor. *Journal of Pediatrics*, 1979, 95, 472–477.
254. NEEDLEMAN, H. L. GUNNOE, C., LEVITON, A., REED, R., PERESIE, H., MAHER, C., & BARRETT, P. Deficits in psychologic and classroom performance of children with elevated dentine lead levels. *New England Journal of Medicine*, 1979, 300, 689–695.
255. SABATINO, D. A. The definition and assessment of visual and auditory perception. *Journal of Clinical Child Psychology*, 1979, 8, 188–194.
256. BACHARA, G. H., & PHELAN, W. J. Visual perception and language levels of deaf children. *Perceptual & Motor Skills*, 1980, 51, 272.
257. BELKA, D. E., & WILLIAMS, H. G. Canonical relationships among perceptual–motor, perceptual, and cognitive behaviors in children. *Research Quarterly for Exercise & Sport*, 1980, 51, 463–477.
258. GERARD, J. A., & JUNKALA, J. Task analysis, handwriting, and process–based instruction. *Journal of Learning Disabilities*, 1980, 13, 54–58.
259. GLUCKMAN, S., & BARLING, J. Effects of a remedial program on visual–motor perception in spina bifida children. *Journal of Genetic Psychology*, 1980, 136, 195–202.
260. JOHNSON, V. M. Analysis of factors influencing special educational placement decisions. *Journal of School Psychology*, 1980, 18, 191–202.
261. BLOSKOVICS, M., ENGEL, R., PODOSIN, R. L., AZEN, C. G., & FRIEDMAN, E. G. EEG pattern in phenylketonuria under early initiated dietary treatment. *American Journal of Diseases of Children*, 1981, 135, 802–808.
262. COOPER, C., & ARNOLD, P. Hearing impairment and visual perceptual processes in reading. *British Journal of Disorders of Communication*, 1981, 16, 43–49.
263. SNYDER, P. P., SNYDER, R. T., & MASSONG, S. F. The visual motor integration test: High interjudge reliability, high potential for diagnostic error. *Psychology in the Schools*, 1981, 18, 55–59.
264. STEIN, G. M., GIBBONS, R. D., & MELDMAN, M. J. Lateral eye movement and handedness as measures of functional brain asymmetry in learning disability. *Cortex*, 1981, 16, 223–229.

[1372]

***A Marital Communication Inventory.** Adults; 1968–79; MCI; Millard J. Bienvenu, Sr.; Family Life Publications, Inc.*

For additional information and a review by Bernard I. Murstein of an earlier edition, see 8:342 (6 references); see also T2:823 (1 reference) and 7:565 (1 reference).

REFERENCES

1. See 7:565.
2. See T2:823.

3–8. See 8:342.
9. Ro-Trock, G. K., Wellisch, D. K., & Schoolar, J. C. A family therapy outcome study in an inpatient setting. *American Journal of Orthopsychiatry*, 1977, 47, 514–522.
10. Schumm, W. R., & Jackson, R. W. Marital communication or marital adjustment? A brief report on the Marital Communication Inventory. *Psychological Reports*, 1980, 46, 441–442.
11. Schumm, W. R., Race, G. S., Morris, J. E., Anderson, S. A., Griffin, C. L., McCutchen, M. B., & Benigas, J. E. Dimensionality of the Marital Communication Inventory and marital conventionalization: A third report. *Psychological Reports*, 1981, 48, 163–171.

[1373]

Marital Pre-Counseling Inventory. Married couples beginning counseling; 1972–73; 13 areas: family locater for a typical week, positive aspects of spouse's behavior, specific behaviors wanted from spouse, specific behaviors wanted by spouse, self-assessment, goals, interests, power in decision-making, areas of satisfaction and dissatisfaction, communication effectiveness, sexual satisfaction, child management, perception of value of the marriage; latter 6 areas include rating scales with scoring optional; Richard B. Stuart; Research Press.*

For additional information, see 8:343.

REFERENCES
1. Miaoulis, C. N., & Gutsch, K. U. A study of the innovative use of time and planned short term treatment in conjoint counseling. *Southern Journal of Educational Research*, 1979, 13, 135–143.

[1374]

★**Marital Satisfaction Inventory.** Married couples beginning counseling; 1979–81; MSI; self-report measure of marital interaction and extent of marital distress; 11 scales: conventionalization, global distress, affective communication, problem-solving communication, time together, disagreement about finances, sexual dissatisfaction, role orientation, family history of distress, dissatisfaction with children, conflict over childrearing; Douglas K. Snyder; Western Psychological Services.*

[1375]

A Marriage Adjustment Form. Adults; 1939–61; MAF; problems checklist; Ernest W. Burgess; distributed by Family Life Publications, Inc.*

See T2:826 (3 references) and P:154 (1 reference); for a review by Lester W. Dearborn, see 6:681.

[1376]

The Marriage Adjustment Inventory. Marital counselees; 1962; MAI; problems checklist; 52 scores: 4 scores (self-evaluation, spouse-evaluation, husband-wife evaluation, total) in each of 12 areas (family relationships, dominance, immaturity, neurotic traits, sociopathic traits, money-management, children, interests, physical, abilities, sexual, incompatibility) and total scores for self-evaluation, spouse-evaluation, husband-wife evaluation, total; Morse P. Manson and Arthur Lerner; Western Psychological Services.*

For additional information, see P:155; for reviews by Clifford R. Adams and Albert Ellis, see 6:682.

REFERENCES
1. Hendrick, S. S. Self-disclosure and marital satisfaction. *Journal of Personality & Social Psychology*, 1981, 40, 1150–1159.

[1377]

A Marriage Analysis, Experimental Edition. Married couples in counseling; 1966; 8 scores: role concepts, self image, feelings toward spouse, emotional openness, knowledge of spouse, sexual adjustment and security, common traits, meaning of marriage; Daniel C. Blazier and Edgar T. Goosman; Family Life Publications, Inc.*

For additional information and reviews by Robert C. Challman and Robert A. Harper, see 7:566.

[1378]

Marriage Counseling Kit. Premarital couples; 1972; card sort for comparing and discussing opinions relevant to marriage; 3 ratings (agree, disagree, not sure) in each of 3 categories (with statement, with each other, with counselor's opinion) for each of 85 items, total category scores; no manual; James R. Hine; Interstate Printers & Publishers, Inc.*

For additional information, see 8:344.

[1379]

★**A Marriage Evaluation.** Marital counselees; 1977; 6 scores: readiness before marriage, decision making, communication, values, personal growth in marriage, commitment and expectations; Henry C. Blount, Jr.; Family Life Publications, Inc.*

[1380]

*****The Marriage Expectation Inventories.** Engaged and married couples; 1972–79; MEI; Patrick J. McDonald, Ellen B. Pirro (inventories), Charles Cleveland (inventories), and Claudette McDonald (manual); Family Life Publications, Inc.*

a) FORM 1. Engaged couples; no scores, 9 areas: love, communication, freedom, sex, money, selfishness, religious expectations, relatives, expectations related to children.

b) FORM 2. Married couples; no scores, 8 areas: love, communication, freedom, sex, money, selfishness, religious expectations, relatives.

For additional information and a review by James Leslie McCary of an earlier edition, see 8:345.

[1381]

Marriage Inventory. Married couples in counseling; 1971; no manual; David Knox; Family Life Publications, Inc.*

For additional information and a review by Donald L. Mosher, see 8:346.

[1382]

A Marriage Prediction Schedule. Adults; 1939–61; MPS; Ernest W. Burgess; Family Life Publications, Inc.*

For additional information, see P:158; for a review by Lester W. Dearborn, see 6:684; see also 5:84 (8 references).

[1383]

*****A Marriage Role Expectation Inventory.** Adolescents and adults; 1960–79; MREI; 9 scores: authority, homemaking, children, personality, social participation, sexual relations, education, employment and support, total; Marie S. Dunn in collaboration with J. N. DeBonis; Family Life Publications, Inc. *

See T2:833 and P:159 (6 references); for a review by Robert C. Challman of an earlier edition, see 6:685 (6 references).

REFERENCES
1-6. See 6:685 or P:159.
7. MELEIS, A. I., & SWENDSEN, L. A. Role supplementation: An empirical test of nursing intervention. *Nursing Research*, 1978, 27, 11-18.

[1384]
Marriage Scale (For Measuring Compatibility of Interests). Premarital and marital counselees; 1970-73; attitudes toward 21 "major factors in a happy marriage"; item scores only; J. Gustav White; Psychologists and Educators, Inc.*

For additional information, see 8:347.

[1385]
Martin S-D Inventory. Clients and patients; 1970; MSDI; a self-report by patients; depression and suicide-proneness; William T. Martin; Psychologists and Educators, Inc.*

For additional information and a review by Charles Neuringer, see 8:609 (1 reference).

[1386]
★**Martinek-Zaichkowsky Self-Concept Scale for Children.** Grades 1-8; 1977; MZSCS; a non-verbal, culture-free instrument measuring global self-concept; Thomas J. Martinek and Leonard D. Zaichkowsky; Psychologists and Educators, Inc.*

REFERENCES
1. MARTINEK, T. J., ZAICHKOWSKY, L. D., & CHEFFERS, J. T. F. Decision-making in elementary age children: Effects on motor skills and self-concept. *Research Quarterly*, 1977, 48, 349-357.
2. MCGEE, R. Measuring affective behavior in physical education. *Journal of Physical Education & Recreation*, 1977, 48, 29-30.
3. MARTINEK, T. J. Students' expectations as related to a teacher's expectations and self-concepts of elementary age children. *Perceptual & Motor Skills*, 1980, 50, 555-561.

[1387]
Maryland Parent Attitude Survey. Parents; [1957-66]; MPAS; parental attitudes toward child rearing; for research use only; 4 scores: disciplinarian, indulgent, protective, rejecting; Donald K. Pumroy; the Author.*

See T2:1273 (4 references) and P:160 (6 references).

REFERENCES
1-6. See P:160.
7-10. See T2:1273.
11. SCHNABL-DICKEY, E. A. Relationships between parents' child-rearing attitudes and the jumping and throwing performance of their preschool children. *Research Quarterly*, 1977, 48, 382-390.
12. DIEBOLD, M. H., CURTIS, W. S., & DUBOSE, R. F. Developmental scales versus observational measures for deaf-blind children. *Exceptional Children*, 1978, 44, 275-278.
13. GELSO, C. J., BIRK, J. M., & POWERS, R. Intergenerational relationships in the development of child rearing attitudes. *Journal of Genetic Psychology*, 1978, 133, 31-41.
14. SLOUGH, N. M., KOGAN, K. L., & TYLER, N. B. Derivation of parent norms for the Maryland Parent Attitude Survey: Application to parents of developmentally delayed children. *Psychological Reports*, 1978, 42, 183-189.
15. KRAUTHAMER, C. Maternal attitudes of alcoholic and nonalcoholic class women. *International Journal of the Addictions*, 1979, 14, 639-644.

[1388]
★**Maslach Burnout Inventory.** Staff members in human service and educational institutions; 1981; MBI; research edition; test title is *Human Services Survey*; 2 scores (frequency, intensity) for each of 3 subscales: emotional exhaustion, depersonalization, personal accomplishment; Christina Maslach and Susan E. Jackson; Consulting Psychologists Press, Inc.*

[1389]
Mastery: An Evaluation Tool: Mathematics. Grades kgn, 1, 2, 3, 4, 5, 6, 7, 8-9; 1974-76; criterion-referenced; 15-40 subtest scores in 10 areas: fractional numbers, geometry, integers, measurement, numbers and numerals, sets and functions and graphing, sets and logical thinking and geometry, statistics and probability, whole number computations, whole numbers; each test consists of 15-40 3-item single-objective subtests; Science Research Associates, Inc.*

For additional information and a review by Mary Montgomery Lindquist, see 8:278.

REFERENCES
1. HAMBLETON, R. K., & EIGNOR, D. R. Guidelines for evaluating criterion-referenced tests and test manuals. *Journal of Educational Measurement*, 1978, 15, 321-327.

[1390]
Mastery: An Evaluation Tool: Reading. Grades kgn, 1, 2, 3, 4, 5, 6, 7, 8, 9; 1974-76; SOBAR (System for Objective-Based Assessment-Reading); criterion-referenced; 23-35 subtest scores in 6 areas: comprehension (grades kgn-9), letter recognition (kgn), phonic analysis (kgn-4), structural analysis (1-9), study skills (1-9), vocabulary (kgn-9); each test consists of 23-35 3-item single-objective subtests; customized tests covering locally chosen objectives are available in both English and Spanish; Center for the Study of Evaluation, University of California at Los Angeles; Science Research Associates, Inc.*

For additional information, a review by Thorsten R. Carlson, and an excerpted review by Frank Greene, see 8:766 (1 reference).

REFERENCES
1. See 8:766.
2. HAMBLETON, R. K., & EIGNOR, D. R. Guidelines for evaluating criterion-referenced tests and test manuals. *Journal of Educational Measurement*, 1978, 15, 321-327.

[1391]
★**Mastery: An Evaluation Tool: Selected Short SOBAR Reading Tests.** Grades 3-9; 1975-76; "provide an alternative to the full-length catalog *mastery* test in SOBAR Reading"; criterion-referenced; 9 tests; Center for the Study of Evaluation, University of California at Los Angeles; Science Research Associates, Inc.*

a) PHONIC ANALYSIS. Grades 3-5; 1975.
b) STRUCTURAL ANALYSIS. Grades 3-9; 1975.
c) STUDY SKILLS. Grades 4-9; 1975.
d) VOCABULARY I. Grades 4-5; 1975.
e) VOCABULARY II. Grades 6-7; 1975.
f) VOCABULARY III. Grades 8-9; 1975.
g) COMPREHENSION I. Grades 4-5; 1975.
h) COMPREHENSION II. Grades 6-7; 1975.
i) COMPREHENSION III. Grades 8-9; 1975.

[1392]
★**Mastery: An Evaluation Tool: Selected Short SOBAR Reading Tests: Comprehension I.** Grades 4-5; 1975; criterion-referenced; Center for the Study of Evaluation, University of California at Los Angeles; Science Research Associates, Inc.*

For the complete program entry, see 1391.

[1393]
★**Mastery: An Evaluation Tool: Selected Short SOBAR Reading Tests: Comprehension II.**
Grades 6–7; 1975; criterion-referenced; Center for the Study of Evaluation, University of California at Los Angeles; Science Research Associates, Inc.*

For the complete program entry, see 1391.

[1394]
★**Mastery: An Evaluation Tool: Selected Short SOBAR Reading Tests: Comprehension III.**
Grades 8–9; 1975; criterion-referenced; Center for the Study of Evaluation, University of California at Los Angeles; Science Research Associates, Inc.*

For the complete program entry, see 1391.

[1395]
★**Mastery: An Evaluation Tool: Selected Short SOBAR Reading Tests: Phonic Analysis.** Grades 3–5; 1975; criterion-referenced; Center for the Study of Evaluation, University of California at Los Angeles; Science Research Associates, Inc.*

For the complete program entry, see 1391.

[1396]
★**Mastery: An Evaluation Tool: Selected Short SOBAR Reading Tests: Structural Analysis.**
Grades 3–9; 1975; criterion-referenced; Center for the Study of Evaluation, University of California at Los Angeles; Science Research Associates, Inc.*

For the complete program entry, see 1391.

[1397]
★**Mastery: An Evaluation Tool: Selected Short SOBAR Reading Tests: Study Skills.** Grades 4–9; 1975; criterion-referenced; Center for the Study of Evaluation, University of California at Los Angeles; Science Research Associates, Inc.*

For the complete program entry, see 1391.

[1398]
★**Mastery: An Evaluation Tool: Selected Short SOBAR Reading Tests: Vocabulary I.** Grades 4–5; 1975; criterion-referenced; Center for the Study of Evaluation, University of California at Los Angeles; Science Research Associates, Inc.*

For the complete program entry, see 1391.

[1399]
★**Mastery: An Evaluation Tool: Selected Short SOBAR Reading Tests: Vocabulary II.** Grades 4–5; 1975; criterion-referenced; Center for the Study of Evaluation, University of California at Los Angeles; Science Research Associates, Inc.*

For the complete program entry, see 1391.

[1400]
★**Mastery: An Evaluation Tool: Selected Short SOBAR Reading Tests: Vocabulary III.** Grades 8–9; 1975; criterion-referenced; Center for the Study of Evaluation, University of California at Los Angeles; Science Research Associates, Inc.*

For the complete program entry, see 1391.

[1401]
★**Mastery: Survival Skills Tests.** Grades 7–12; 1976; objectives-based tests in reading and mathematics relating to skills essential for everyday living; Science Research Associates, Inc.*

[1402]
★**Mastery Tests.** Reading level grades 1–3, 4–6; 1968–70; part of The Macmillan Reading Program; may be used independent of or in conjunction with the *Macmillan Reader Placement Test*; 2 levels; Edward R. Sipay; Macmillan Publishing Co., Inc.*

a) MASTERY TESTS FOR THE PRIMARY GRADES. Reading level grades 1–3; 7 tests, 4 scores for each: word recognition, word analysis, comprehension, total.
1) *Mastery Test To Accompany Opening Books, RE/A Magic Box, RE/Things You See, RE.* Grade 1.
2) *Mastery Test To Accompany Worlds of Wonder, RE.* Grade 1.
3) *Mastery Test To Accompany Lands of Pleasure, RE.* Grade 1.
4) *Mastery Test To Accompany Enchanted Gates, RE.* Grade 2.
5) *Mastery Test To Accompany Shining Bridges, RE.* Grade 2.
6) *Mastery Test To Accompany Better Than Gold, RE.* Grade 3.
7) *Mastery Test To Accompany More Than Words, RE.* Grade 3.

b) MASTERY TESTS FOR THE INTERMEDIATE GRADES. Reading level grades 4–6; 3 tests, 3 scores for each: word recognition, comprehension, total.
1) *Mastery Test To Accompany The Magic Word.* Grade 4.
2) *Mastery Test To Accompany Bold Journeys.* Grade 5.
3) *Mastery Test To Accompany Into New Worlds.* Grade 6.

[1403]
Match Problems. Grades 9–16 and adults; 1963; formerly called *Match Problems 2*; "divergent production of figural transformation" or "originality in dealing with concrete visual material"; Raymond M. Berger and J. P. Guilford; Sheridan Psychological Services, Inc.*

See T2:564 (15 references) and 6:554 (7 references).

REFERENCES

1–7. See 6:554.
8–22. See T2:564.
23. ALPAUGH, P. K., & BIRREN, J. E. Variables affecting creative contributions across the adult life span. *Human Development*, 1977, 20, 240–248.

[1404]
Match Problems V. Grades 9–16; 1962–69; "divergent production of figural transformations"; 1969 test identical with test copyrighted 1962 except for one new and one revised item; no manual; Philip R. Merrifield and J. P. Guilford; Sheridan Psychological Services, Inc.*

For additional information, see 6:551w2.

REFERENCES

1. ALPAUGH, P. K., & BIRREN, J. E. Variables affecting creative contributions across the adult life span. *Human Development*, 1977, 20, 240–248.
2. COHEN, D., SCHAIE, K. W., & GRIBBIN, K. The organization of spatial abilities in older men and women. *Journal of Gerontology*, 1977, 32, 578–585.

[1405]

Mathematics Anxiety Rating Scale. Grades 7–12, college and adults; 1972–79; 2 levels; Richard M. Suinn; Rocky Mountain Behavioral Science Institute, Inc. (In-print status uncertain; no reply from publisher.)
a) MATHEMATICS ANXIETY RATING SCALE-A. Grades 7–12; 1979; MARS-A.
b) MATHEMATICS ANXIETY RATING SCALE. College and adults; 1972; MARS.

For additional information and reviews by William E. Kline and James A. Walsh of *b*, see 8:610 (3 references).

REFERENCES

1–3. See 8:610.
4. HENDEL, D. D., & DAVIS, S. O. Effectiveness of an intervention strategy for reducing mathematics anxiety. *Journal of Counseling Psychology,* 1978, 25, 429–434.
5. MICHAELS, L. A., & FORSYTH, R. A. Measuring attitudes toward mathematics? Some questions to consider. *Arithmetic Teacher,* 1978, 26, 22–25.
6. MORRIS, L. W., KELLAWAY, D. S., & SMITH, D. H. Mathematics Anxiety Rating Scale: Predicting anxiety experiences and academic performance in two groups of students. *Journal of Educational Psychology,* 1978, 70, 589–594.
7. OLSON, A. T., & GILLINGHAM, D. E. Systematic desensitization of mathematics anxiety among preservice elementary teachers. *Alberta Journal of Educational Research,* 1980, 26, 120–127.
8. ROUNDS, J. B., JR., & HENDEL, D. D. Mathematics anxiety and attitudes toward mathematics. *Measurement & Evaluation in Guidance,* 1980, 13, 83–89.
9. ROUNDS, J. B., JR., & HENDEL, D. D. Measurement and dimensionality of mathematics anxiety. *Journal of Counseling Psychology,* 1980, 27, 138–149.
10. SHERWOOD, R. D., & GABEL, D. Basic science skills for prospective elementary teachers: Measuring and predicting success. *Science Education,* 1980, 64, 195–201.
11. PLAKE, B. S., SMITH, E. P., & DAMSTEEGT, D. C. A validity investigation of the Achievement Anxiety Test. *Educational & Psychological Measurement,* 1981, 41, 1215–1222.
12. SOVCHIK, R., MERCONI, L. J., & STEINER, E. Mathematics anxiety of preservice elementary mathematics methods students. *School Science & Mathematics,* 1981, 81, 643–648.

[1406]

Mathematics Attainment Test EF. Ages 11–0 to 13–0; 1972; NFER-Nelson Publishing Co. [England].*

[1407]

Mathematics Attainment Tests C1 and C3. Ages 9–3 to 10–8; 1965–69; 2 tests; NFER-Nelson Publishing Co. [England].*
a) MATHEMATICS ATTAINMENT TEST C1. 1965–69; formerly called *Junior Mathematics Test C1.*
b) MATHEMATICS ATTAINMENT TEST C3. 1966–69; formerly called *Junior Mathematics Test C3.*

For additional information and a review by John Cook, see 7:470.

[1408]

Mathematics Attainment Tests DE1 and DE2. Ages 10–0 to 12–0; 1966–70; 2 tests; NFER-Nelson Publishing Co. [England].*
a) MATHEMATICS ATTAINMENT TEST DE1. 1966–70; modification of *Mathematics Test 17*; 1970 test essentially the same as test published 1966 except for 12 items revised for metrication and decimalization.
b) MATHEMATICS ATTAINMENT TEST DE2. 1967–70; formerly called *Intermediate Mathematics Test 1.*

For additional information, see 7:471.

[1409]

Mathematics Attainment Tests (Oral). Ages 7–0 to 8–6, 8–6 to 9–8; 1965–72; 2 levels; NFER-Nelson Publishing Co. [England].*
a) MATHEMATICS ATTAINMENT TEST A (ORAL). Ages 7–0 to 8–6; 1969–72; formerly called *Junior Mathematics Test A1.*
b) MATHEMATICS ATTAINMENT TEST B (ORAL). Ages 8–6 to 9–8; 1965–69; formerly called *Junior Mathematics Test B1.*

For additional information and a review by John Cook, see 7:472.

[1410]

★Mathematics Attitude Inventory. Grades 7–12; 1979; MAI; 6 scores: perception of the mathematics teacher, anxiety toward mathematics, value of mathematics in society, self-concept in mathematics, enjoyment of mathematics, motivation in mathematics; Richard S. Sandman; Minnesota Research and Evaluation Center, University of Minnesota.*

REFERENCES

1. SANDMAN, R. S. Mathematics Attitude Inventory and MAI user's manual. *Journal for Research in Mathematics Education,* 1980, 11, 148–149.

[1411]

★Mathematics Evaluation Procedures K–2. Grades kgn–4; 1980; criterion-referenced; 104 objectives in 3 areas: number (problem solving and graphs), shape, measurement (length, mass, volume, area, time, money, temperature); North Sydney Region Infants' Mistresses' Council; Australian Council for Educational Research [Australia].*

[1412]

Mathematics: IOX Objectives-Based Tests. Grades kgn–6, 7–9; 1973–76; criterion-referenced; 280 tests (spirit masters for local duplicating) in 7 areas; series description by W. James Popham; tests developed under the direction of Ira Moskow, Denis Purcell, and Don May (3); Instructional Objectives Exchange.*
a) GRADES KGN–6.
 1) *Sets and Numbers.* 35 tests.
 2) *Operations and Properties.* 40 tests.
 3) *Numeration and Relations.* 38 tests.
 4) *Measurement.* 38 tests.
 5) *Geometry.* 36 tests.
b) GRADES 7–9.
 1) *Elements, Symbolism, and Measurement.* 42 tests.
 2) *Geometry, Operations, and Relations.* 51 tests.

For additional information and reviews by Anthony J. Nitko and Marilyn N. Suydam, see 8:279.

[1413]

Mathematics: Minnesota High School Achievement Examinations. Grades 7, 8, 9; 1951–70; a new, revised, or previously inactive form issued each May; Achievement Examinations for Secondary Schools, High School Achievement Examinations, and Midwest High School Achievement Examinations have also been used as series titles; 3 levels; edited by V. L. Lohmann; American Guidance Service.*
a) MATHEMATICS GRADE 7. 1962–70; Form E ('62).
b) MATHEMATICS GRADE 8. 1962–70; Form E ('62).
c) MATHEMATICS GRADE 9. 1951–70; Form 4 ('54).

For additional information concerning out of print and inactive forms, see 7:473, 6:582, and 5:424; for a review by Gerald L. Ericksen of Form F ('63) of the test for grade 9, see 6:577.

[1414]
Mathematics Test: Content Evaluation Series. Grades 7–9; 1969; Gilbert Ulmer; Riverside Publishing Co.*

For additional information and a review by Robert A. Forsyth, see 7:475.

[1415]
A Mathematics Test for Grades Four, Five and Six. Grades 4–6; 1969; 13 scores: numeration systems, set terminology, mathematical structure, addition and subtraction, multiplication, division, common fractions, decimal fractions and per cent, measurements, geometry, problems, graphs and scales, total; Stanley J. LeJeune; Psychometric Affiliates.*

For additional information and a review by William H. Nibbelink, see 8:280; for a review by Arthur Mittman, see 7:476.

[1416]
Mathematics Test for Seniors. Standards 9, 10; 1973; J. F. Vorster (test) and S. J. P. Kruger (manual); Human Sciences Research Council [South Africa].*

For additional information, see 8:281.

[1417]
Mathematics Test: McGraw-Hill Basic Skills System. Grades 11–14; 1970; also called *MHBSS Mathematics Test*; although designed for use with the MHBSS instructional program, the test may be used independently; 4 scores: arithmetic, elementary algebra, intermediate algebra, total; McGraw-Hill Book Co., Inc.*

For additional information and reviews by James Braswell and Carl J. Huberty, see 7:477.

[1418]
***Mathematics Topic Tests: Elementary Level.** Grades 4–9; 1974–80; criterion-referenced; 7 tests; Frances Crook Morrison; published in cooperation with the Research Centre of The Ottawa Board of Education by Guidance Centre, University of Toronto [Canada].*

a) TEST 1, NUMBER AND NUMERATION. Grades 5–9; 40 item scores plus total.

b) TEST 2, ADDITION AND SUBTRACTION WITH WHOLE NUMBERS. Grades 4–6; 32 item scores plus total.

c) TEST 3, MULTIPLICATION AND DIVISION WITH WHOLE NUMBERS. Grades 5–8; 24 item scores plus total.

d) TEST 4, OPERATIONS WITH FRACTIONS. Grades 5–7; 32 item scores plus total.

e) TEST 5, MULTIPLICATION AND DIVISION WITH FRACTIONS. Grades 6–9; 31 item scores plus total.

f) TEST 6, MEASUREMENT, GRAPHS, AND GEOMETRY. Grades 5–8; 33 item scores plus total.

g) TEST 7, OPERATIONS WITH DECIMALS. Grades 5–8; 39 item scores plus total.

For a review by Thomas E. Kieren of an earlier edition, see 8:282.

[1419]
Maudsley Personality Inventory. College and adults; 1959–62; MPI; for revised edition, see *Eysenck Personality Inventory*; 2 scores: neuroticism, extraversion; H. J. Eysenck.

a) BRITISH EDITIONS. 1959; Hodder & Stoughton Educational [England].*

b) UNITED STATES EDITION. 1962; Robert R. Knapp (manual); EdITS/Educational and Industrial Testing Service.*

For additional information, see 8:611 (129 references); see also T2:1275 (273 references) and P:161 (149 references); for reviews by Arthur R. Jensen, James C. Lingoes, William Stephenson, and Philip E. Vernon and excerpted reviews by Edward S. Bordin, A. Bursill, and G. A. Foulds, see 6:138 (120 references).

REFERENCES

1–117. See 6:138.
118–266. See P:161.
267–539. See T2:1275.
540–668. See 8:611.
669. BROWNE, J. A., & HOWARTH, E. A comprehensive factor analysis of personality questionnaire items: A test of twenty putative factor hypotheses. *Multivariate Behavioral Research*, 1977, 12, 399–427.
670. HIRSCHFIELD, R. M. A., KLERMAN, G. L., GOUGH, H. G., BARRETT, J., KORCHIN, S. J., & CHODOFF, P. A measure of interpersonal dependence. *Journal of Personality Assessment*, 1977, 41, 610–618.
671. KAVANAGH, T., & SHEPARD, R. J. Sexual activity after myocardial infarction. *Canadian Medical Association Journal*, 1977, 116, 1250–1253.
672. LONG, G. T., CALHOUN, L. G., & SELBY, J. W. Personality characteristics related to cross-situational consistency of interpersonal distance. *Journal of Personality Assessment*, 1977, 41, 274–278.
673. PAYKEL, E. S. Depression and appetite. *Journal of Psychosomatic Research*, 1977, 21, 401–407.
674. SCHAEFFER, D. S. Scores on neuroticism pathology, mood, and Rorschach and diagnosis of affective disorder. *Psychological Reports*, 1977, 40, 1135–1141.
675. WEISSMAN, M. M., & KLERMAN, G. L. The chronic depressive in the community: Unrecognized and poorly treated. *Comprehensive Psychiatry*, 1977, 18, 523–532.
676. BAEKGAARD, W., NYBORG, H., & NIELSEN, J. Neuroticism and extraversion in Turner's Syndrome. *Journal of Abnormal Psychology*, 1978, 87, 583–586.
677. COHEN, D. B., MCGRATH, M. J., BELL, L. W., HANLON, M. J., & SIMON, N. REM motivation induced by brief REM deprivation: The influence of cognitive, gender, and personality. *Journal of Personality & Social Psychology*, 1978, 36, 741–751.
678. LESTER, D., & WRIGHT, T. Murderers and overcontrolled hostility. *Psychological Reports*, 1978, 43, 1202.
679. MENDHIRATTA, S. S., WIG, N. N., & VERMA, S. K. Some psychological correlates of long-term heavy cannabis users. *British Journal of Psychiatry*, 1978, 132, 482–486.
680. SHEPHARD, R. J., & KAVANAGH, T. Patient reactions to a regular conditioning programme following myocardial infarction. *Journal of Sports Medicine & Physical Fitness*, 1978, 18, 371–378.
681. SHIOMI, K. Differences in decision time between extraverts and introverts under the "task-oriented situation" and the "ego-oriented situation". *Psychological Reports*, 1978, 42, 563–566.
682. SHIOMI, K. Relations of pain threshold and pain tolerance in cold water with scores on Maudsley Personality Inventory and Manifest Anxiety Scale. *Perceptual & Motor Skills*, 1978, 47, 1155–1158.
683. WAGMAN, M. The comparative effects of didactic-correction and self-contradiction on fallacious scientific and personal reasoning. *Journal of General Psychology*, 1978, 99, 67–80.
684. WEISSMAN, M. M., PRUSOFF, B. A., & KLERMAN, G. L. Personality and the prediction of long-term outcome of depression. *American Journal of Psychiatry*, 1978, 135, 797–800.
685. ZALESKI, Z., & GALKOWSKA, M. Neuroticism and marital satisfaction. *Behaviour Research & Therapy*, 1978, 16, 285–286.
686. ANANTH, J., SOLYOM, L., BRYNTWICK, S., & KRISHNAPPA, U. Chlorimipramine therapy for obsessive-compulsive neurosis. *American Journal of Psychiatry*, 1979, 136, 700–701.
687. BEDFORD, A., EDINGTON, A., & KELLNER, R. Changes in self-rating of symptoms: A comparison of questionnaire graphic scales with test cards. *British Journal of Psychiatry*, 1979, 134, 108–110.
688. HIRSCHFELD, R., & KLERMAN, G. L. Personality attributes and affective disorders. *American Journal of Psychiatry*, 1979, 136, 67–70.
689. LAVRAKAS, P. J., & MAIER, R. A. Differences in human ability to judge veracity from the audio medium. *Journal of Research in Personality*, 1979, 13, 139–153.
690. PETHÖ, B., TOLNA, J., & TUSNÁDY, G. Multi-trait-multi-method assessment of predictive variables of outcome in schizophrenia

spectrum disorders. A nosological evaluation. *Journal of Psychiatric Research,* 1979, 15, 163-174.
691. RAY, J. J. The authoritarian as measured by a personality scale: Solid citizen or misfit? *Journal of Clinical Psychology,* 1979, 35, 744-747.
692. ROUNSAVILLE, B. J., WEISSMAN, M. M., PRUSOFF, B. A., & HERCEG-BARON, R. L. Marital disputes and treatment outcome in depressed women. *Comprehensive Psychiatry,* 1979, 20, 483-490.
693. SANFORD, J. Personality and paranormal experience: The relationship between social adjustment, extroversion, neuroticism, and the report of psychic phenomena. *Journal of Parapsychology,* 1979, 43, 54-55.
694. SHIOMI, K. Differences in reaction times of extraverts and introverts to Rapaport's Word Association Test. *Psychological Reports,* 1979, 45, 75-80.
695. WAGMAN, M. Systematic dilemma counseling: Theory, method, research. *Psychological Reports,* 1979, 44, 55-72.
696. DOLKE, A. M., & SUTARIA, R. Personality characteristics and job attitudes. *Indian Journal of Social Work,* 1980, 41, 275-283.
697. RAY, J. J. Are authoritarians extraverted? *British Journal of Social & Clinical Psychology,* 1980, 19, 147-148.
698. RAY, J. J., & SINGH, S. Effects of individual differences on productivity among farmers in India. *Journal of Social Psychology,* 1980, 112, 11-17.
699. SHIOMI, K. Performance differences between extraverts and introverts on exercises using an ergometer. *Perceptual & Motor Skills,* 1980, 50, 356-358.
700. WAGMAN, M. PLATO DCS: An interactive computer system for personal counseling. *Journal of Counseling Psychology,* 1980, 27, 16-30.
701. WANDER, B. D., & COTTON, C. C. Relation of marginality to extraversion–introversion dimension. *Psychological Reports,* 1980, 47, 1015-1021.
702. ZUCKERMAN, D. M., PRUSOFF, B. A., WEISSMAN, M. M., & PADIAN, N. S. Personality as a predictor of psychotherapy and pharmacotherapy outcome for depressed outpatients. *Journal of Consulting & Clinical Psychology,* 1980, 48, 730-735.
703. HIRSCHFELD, R. M. A. Situational depression: Validity of the concept. *British Journal of Psychiatry,* 1981, 139, 297-305.
704. LAPORTE, D. J., MCLELLAN, A. T., O'BRIEN, C. P., & MARSHALL, J. R. Treatment response in psychiatrically impaired drug abusers. *Comprehensive Psychiatry,* 1981, 22, 411-419.
705. MATUSSEK, P., SÖLDNER, M., & NAGEL, D. Identification of the endogenous depressive syndrome based on the symptoms and the characteristics of the course. *British Journal of Psychiatry,* 1981, 138, 361-372.
706. SINGH, V. K., & GUPTA, B. S. Personality and drugs in visual figural after-effects. *International Journal of Psychology,* 1981, 16, 35-44.
707. SMITH, D. I., & KIRKHAM, R. W. Relationship between some personality characteristics and driving record. *British Journal of Social Psychiatry,* 1981, 20, 229-231.

[1420]
Maxfield-Buchholz Scale of Social Maturity for Use With Preschool Blind Children. Infancy-6 years; 1958; revision of *Maxfield-Fjeld Adaptation of the Vineland Social Maturity Scale*; manual title is *A Social Maturity Scale for Blind Preschool Children*; Kathryn E. Maxfield and Sandra Buchholz; American Foundation for the Blind, Inc.*

For additional information, see P:162 and 6:139 (2 references).

REFERENCES

1-2. See 6:139.
3. ROTHBERG, A. D., MAISELS, J., BAGNATO, S., MURPHY, J., GIFFORD, K., MCKINLEY, K., PALMER, E. A., & VANNUCCI, R. C. Outcome for survivors of mechanical ventilation weighing less than 1,250 gm at birth. *Journal of Pediatrics,* 1981, 98, 106-111.

[1421]
★**McCall-Crabbs Standard Test Lessons in Reading.** Reading level grades 3, 4, 5, 6, 7, 8; 1926-79; fourth revised edition of *McCall-Crabbs Standard Test Lessons in Reading*; item and grade equivalent scores; original test by William A. McCall and Lelah Crabbs Schroeder; revised by Robert P. Starr; Teachers College Press.*

[1422]
[McCann Typing Tests]. Applicants for typing positions; 1961-64; 3 scores: speed, accuracy, total; McCann Associates.*

For additional information, see 6:50.

[1423]
★**McCarthy Individualized Diagnostic Reading Inventory, Revised Edition.** Grades kgn-12; 1971-76; 3 levels of qualitative ratings of reading (independent, instructional, frustration) and item scores classified above or below 90% mastery criterion; William G. McCarthy; Educators Publishing Service, Inc.*

[1424]
McCarthy Scales of Children's Abilities. Ages 2.5-8.5; 1972, c1970-72; MSCA; 6 scores: verbal, perceptual-performance, quantitative, composite (general cognitive), memory, motor; Dorothea McCarthy; The Psychological Corporation.*

For additional information, reviews by Jane V. Hunt, Jerome M. Sattler, and Arthur B. Silverstein, and excerpted reviews by Everett E. Davis, Linda Hufano and Ralph Hoepfner, R. B. Ammons and C. H. Ammons, and Alan Krichev, see 8:219 (29 references).

REFERENCES

1-29. See 8:219.
30. EISER, C., & LANSDOWN, R. Retrospective study of intellectual development in children treated for acute lymphoblastic leukaemia. *Archives of Diseases in Childhood,* 1977, 52, 525-529.
31. KAUFMAN, A. S. A McCarthy short form for rapid screening of preschool, kindergarten, and first-grade children. *Contemporary Educational Psychology,* 1977, 2, 149-157.
32. MOORE, C. L., & BURNS, W. J. Brief screening for developmentally delayed preschoolers. *Perceptual & Motor Skills,* 1977, 45, 1169-1170.
33. ASHEM, B., & JANES, M. D. Deleterious effects of chronic undernutrition on cognitive abilities. *Journal of Child Psychology & Psychiatry & Allied Disciplines,* 1978, 19, 23-31.
34. BRYANT, C. K., & ROFFE, M. W. A reliability study of the McCarthy Scales of Children's Abilities. *Journal of Clinical Psychology,* 1978, 34, 401-406.
35. EISER, C. An evaluation of the McCarthy Scales of Children's Abilities. *British Journal of Educational Psychology,* 1978, 48, 351-353.
36. GERKEN, K. C., HANCOCK, K. A., & WADE, T. H. A comparison of the Stanford-Binet Intelligence Scale and the McCarthy Scales of Children's Abilities with preschool children. *Psychology in the Schools,* 1978, 15, 468-472.
37. HOLYROYD, J., & GOLDENBERG, I. The use of goal attainment scaling to evaluate a ward treatment program for disturbed children. *Journal of Clinical Psychology,* 1978, 34, 732-739.
38. KAUFMAN, A. S. The importance of basic concepts in the individual assessment of preschool children. *Journal of School Psychology,* 1978, 16, 207-211.
39. KAUFMAN, A. S., ZALMA, R., & KAUFMAN, N. L. The relationship of hand dominance to the motor coordination, mental ability, and right-left awareness of young normal children. *Child Development,* 1978, 49, 885-888.
40. O'DONNELL, J. P., PAULSEN, K. A., & MCGAUN, J. D. Matching Familiar Figures Test: A unidimensional measure of reflection-impulsivity? *Perceptual & Motor Skills,* 1978, 47, 1247-1253.
41. PHILLIPS, B. L., PASEWARK, R. A., & TINDALL, R. C. Relationship among McCarthy Scales of Children's Abilities, WPPSI, and Columbia Mental Maturity Scale. *Psychology in the Schools,* 1978, 15, 352-356.
42. RAMEY, C. T., & CAMPBELL, F. A. Compensatory education for disadvantaged children. *School Review,* 1978, 87, 171-189.
43. REYNOLDS, C. R. The McCarthy drawing tests as a group instrument. *Contemporary Educational Psychology,* 1978, 3, 169-174.
44. TIVAN, T., & PILLEMER, D. B. The importance of small but consistent group differences on standardized tests: The case of sex differences on the McCarthy Scales of Children's Abilities. *Journal of Clinical Psychology,* 1978, 34, 443-445.
45. WIEBE, M. J., & HARRISON, K. A. Relationships of the McCarthy Scales of Children's Abilities and the Detroit Tests of Learning Aptitude. *Perceptual & Motor Skills,* 1978, 46, 355-359.

46. GOH, D. S, & YANGQUIST, J. A comparison of the McCarthy Scales of Children's Abilities and WISC–R. *Journal of Learning Disabilities*, 1979, 12, 344–348.
47. GOLD, D., REIS, M., & BERGER, C. Male teachers and development of nursery–school children. *Psychological Reports*, 1979, 44, 457–458.
48. KROHN, E. J., & TRAXLERE, A. J. Relationship of the McCarthy Scales of Children's Abilities to other measures of preschool cognitive, motor, and perceptual development. *Perceptual & Motor Skills*, 1979, 49, 783–790.
49. LEVENSON, R. L., JR., & ZINO, T. C., II. Assessment of cognitive deficiency with the McCarthy scales and Stanford–Binet: A correlational analysis. *Perceptual & Motor Skills*, 1979, 48, 291–295.
50. LEVENSON, R. L., JR., & ZINO, T. C., II. Using McCarthy scales extrapolated general cognitive indexes below 50: Some words of caution. *Psychological Reports*, 1979, 45, 350.
51. MOORE, C. L., & BURNS, W. J. The performance of neurologically impaired and normal Ss on four screening techniques. *Journal of Clinical Psychology*, 1979, 35, 420–424.
52. NAGLIERI, J. A., & HARRISON, P. L. Comparison of McCarthy general cognitive indexes and Stanford–Binet IQs for educable mentally retarded children. *Perceptual & Motor Skills*, 1979, 48, 1251–1254.
53. Oberklaid, F., Dworkin, P. H., & Levine, M. D. Developmental behavioral dysfunction in preschool children. *American Journal of Diseases of Children*, 1979, 133, 1126–1131.
54. RAMEY, C. T., & CAMPBELL, F. A. Early childhood education for psychosocially disadvantaged children: Effects on psychological processes. *American Journal of Mental Deficiency*, 1979, 83, 645–648.
55. REYNOLDS, C. R. Objectivity of scores for the McCarthy drawing tests. *Psychology in the Schools*, 1979, 16, 367–368.
56. ROFFE, M. W., & BRYANT, C. K. How reliable are MSCA profile interpretations? *Psychology in the Schools*, 1979, 16, 14–18.
57. RUMMO, J. H., ROUTH, D. K., RUMMO, N. J., & BROWN, J. F. Behavioral and neurological effects of symptomatic and asymptomatic lead exposure in children. *Archives of Environmental Health*, 1979, 34, 120–124.
58. SHELLENBERGER, S., & LACHTERMAN, T. Cognitive and motor functioning on the McCarthy scales by Spanish-speaking children. *Perceptual & Motor Skills*, 1979, 49, 863–866.
59. TAYLOR, R. L. Comparison of the McCarthy Scales of Children's Abilities and the Peabody Picture Vocabulary Test. *Psychological Reports*, 1979, 45, 196–198.
60. TAYLOR, R. L., SLOCUMB, P. R., & O'NEILL, J. A short form of the McCarthy Scales of Children's Abilities: Methodological and clinical applications. *Psychology in the Schools*, 1979, 16, 347–350.
61. ERNHART, C. B., CALLAHAN, R., & LANDA, B. The McCarthy scales: Predictive validity and stability of scores for urban black children. *Educational & Psychological Measurement*, 1980, 40, 1183–1188.
62. ERNHART, C. B., & LANDA, B. Cumulative deficit, a longitudinal analysis of scores on McCarthy scales. *Psychological Reports*, 1980, 47, 283–286.
63. FERRARI, M. Comparisons of the Peabody Picture Vocabulary Test and the McCarthy Scales of Children's Abilities with a sample of autistic children. *Psychology in the Schools*, 1980, 17, 466–469.
64. GOH, D. S., & SIMONS, M. R. Comparison of learning disabled and general education children on the McCarthy Scales of Children's Abilities. *Psychology in the Schools*, 1980, 17, 429–436.
65. HARRISON, P. L., KAUFMAN, A. S., & NAGLIERI, J. A. Subtest patterns and recategorized groupings of the McCarthy scales for EMR Children. *American Journal of Mental Deficiency*, 1980, 85, 129–134.
66. HO, H., FOCH, T. T., & PLOMIN, R. Developmental stability of the relative influence of genes and environment on specific cognitive abilities during childhood. *Developmental Psychology*, 1980, 16, 340–346.
67. HYND, G. W., QUACKENBUSH, R., KRAMER, R., CONNOR, R., & WEED, W. Concurrent validity of the McCarthy Scales of Children's Abilities with native American primary-grade children. *Measurement & Evaluation in Guidance*, 1980, 13, 29–34.
68. KAUFMAN, N. L., & KAUFMAN, A. S. Creativity in children with minimal brain dysfunction. *Journal of Creative Behavior*, 1980, 14, 73. (Abstract)
69. KEITH, T. Z., & BOLEN L. M. Factor structure of the McCarthy scales for children experiencing problems in school. *Psychology in the Schools*, 1980, 17, 320–326.
70. KRAMER, M. S., ROOKS, Y., WASHINGTON, L. A., & PEARSON, H. A. Pre- and postnatal growth and development in sickle cell anemia. *Journal of Pediatrics*, 1980, 96, 857–860.
71. NAGLIERI, J. A. Comparison of McCarthy General Cognitive Index and WISC–R IQ for educable mentally retarded, learning disabled, and normal children. *Psychological Reports*, 1980, 47, 591–596.
72. NAGLIERI, J. A. McCarthy and WISC–R correlations with WRAT achievement scores. *Perceptual & Motor Skills*, 1980, 51, 392–394.
73. PAULSEN, K. A., & O'DONNELL, J. P. Relationship between minor physical anomalies and "soft signs" of brain damage. *Perceptual & Motor Skills*, 1980, 51, 402.
74. REYNOLDS, C. R. An examination for bias in a preschool test battery across race and sex. *Journal of Educational Measurement*, 1980, 17, 137–146.
75. REYNOLDS, C. R., & KAUFMAN, A. S. Lateral eye movement behavior in children. *Perceptual & Motor Skills*, 1980, 50, 1023–1037.
76. TAYLOR, R. L., & IVIMEY, J. K. Diagnostic use of the WISC–R and McCarthy scales: A regression analysis approach to learning disabilities. *Psychology in the Schools*, 1980, 17, 327–330.
77. TAYLOR, R. L., & IVIMEY, J. K. Predicting academic achievement: Preliminary analysis of the McCarthy scales. *Psychological Reports*, 1980, 46, 1232.
78. VANE, J. R., & MOTTA, R. W. Test response inconsistency in young children. *Journal of School Psychology*, 1980, 18, 25–33.
79. WATKINS, E. O., & WIEBE, M. J. Construct validity of the McCarthy Scales of Children's Abilities: Regression analysis with preschool children. *Educational & Psychological Measurement*, 1980, 40, 1173–1182.
80. BRACKEN, B. A. McCarthy scales as a learning disability diagnostic aid: A closer look. *Journal of Learning Disabilities*, 1981, 14, 128–130.
81. DENNEHY, S. E. Two short forms of the McCarthy Scales of Children's Abilities applied to a sample of Victorian children. *Australian Psychologist*, 1981, 16, 93–100.
82. HUCHCROFT, S. A., WEARING, M. P, & BUCK, C. W. Late results of Cesarean and vaginal delivery in cases of breech presentation. *Canadian Medical Association Journal*, 1981, 125, 726–730.
83. MISHRA, S. P. Factor analysis of the McCarthy scales for groups of White and Mexican–American children. *Journal of School Psychology*, 1981, 19, 178–182.
84. NAGLIERI, J. A., KAUFMAN, A. S., & HARRISON, P. L. Factor structure of the McCarthy scales for school–age children with low GCI's. *Journal of School Psychology*, 1981, 19, 226–232.
85. NAGLIERI, J. A., & MAXWELL, S. Inter-rater reliability and concurrent validity of the Goodenough–Harris and McCarthy draw-a-child scoring systems. *Perceptual & Motor Skills*, 1981, 53, 343–348.
86. PALFREY, J. S., LEVINE, M. D., OBERKLAID, F., LERNER, M., & AUFSEESER, C. L. An analysis of observed attention and activity patterns in preschool children. *Journal of Pediatrics*, 1981, 98, 1006–1011.
87. REYNOLDS, C. R., McBRIDE, R. D., & GIBSON, L. J. Black–white IQ discrepancies may be related to differences in hemisphericity. *Contemporary Educational Psychology*, 1981, 6, 180–184.
88. VALENCIA, R. R., HENDESON, R. W., & RANKIN, R. J. Relationship of family constellation and schooling to intellectual performance of Mexican American children. *Journal of Educational Psychology*, 1981, 73, 524–532.
89. WEIL, W. B., SPENCER, M., BENJAMIN, D., & SEAGULL, E. The effect of polybrominated biphenyl on infants and young children. *Journal of Pediatrics*, 1981, 98, 47–51.

[1425]

★McCarthy Screening Test. Ages 4–6.5; 1970–78; MST; "adaptation of the *McCarthy Scales of Children's Abilities*"; criterion-referenced; percentile cut-off scores provided for classification as "at-risk" for learning problems; 6 tests: right-left orientation, verbal memory, draw-a-design, numerical memory, conceptual grouping, leg coordination; The Psychological Corporation.*

REFERENCES

1. TAYLOR, R. L., & IVIMEY, J. K. Predicting academic achievement: Preliminary analysis of the McCarthy scales. *Psychological Reports*, 1980, 46, 1232.
2. UMANSKY, W., & COHEN, L. R. Race and sex differences on the McCarthy Screening Test. *Psychology in the Schools*, 1980, 17, 400–404.

[1426]

The McCormick Job Performance Measurement "Rate-$-Scales." Employees; 1971; 5 ratings by supervisors: responsibility, attitude, time in grade, efficiency, total; Ronald R. McCormick; Trademark Design Products, Inc.*

For additional information and a review by Alan R. Bass, see 8:1060 (1 reference).

[1427]

McCullough Word-Analysis Tests. Grades 4–6; 1962–63, c1960–63; MWAT; 10 scores: phonetic (initial blends and digraphs, phonetic discrimination, matching letters to vowel sounds, sounding whole words, interpreting phonetic symbols, total), structural (dividing words

into syllables, root words in affixed forms, total), total; Constance M. McCullough; Chapman, Brook & Kent.*
See T2:1634 (1 reference); for a review by Larry A. Harris, see 7:719 (2 references); for reviews by Emery P. Bliesmer and Albert J. Harris, see 6:826.

[1428]
The McGlade Road Test for Use in Driver Licensing, Education and Employment. Prospective drivers; 1961–62; manual title is *A New Road Test for Use in Driver Licensing, Education & Employment* (out of print); Francis S. McGlade; Center for Safety.* (In-print status of test uncertain; no reply from publisher.)
For additional information, see 6:691 (1 reference).

[1429]
McGrath Diagnostic Reading Test. Grades 1–13; 1974–76; the *McGrath Test of Reading Skills* must also be administered, since its 3 subtests are subtests of this test; 19 scores: letter recognition (2 scores), oral spelling, MTRS subtests (oral word recognition, oral paragraph reading, word meanings), comprehension (2 scores), consonant sounds, blends, short vowels, auditory fusion, auditory memory (2 scores), laterality (3 scores), visual perception and memory, visual discrimination; Joseph E. McGrath; McGrath Publishing Co.* (In-print status uncertain; no reply from publisher.)
For additional information, see 8:765.

[1430]
McGrath Test of Reading Skills, Second Edition. Grades 1–13; 1965–67; 4 scores: oral word recognition, oral paragraph reading, silent reading vocabulary, oral reading rate; Joseph E. McGrath; McGrath Publishing Co.* (In-print status uncertain; no reply from publisher.)
For additional information and a review by Byron H. Van Roekel, see 7:692.

[1431]
McGrath's Preliminary Screening Test in Reading. Grades 1–13; 1973–76; earlier forms entitled *Oral Word-Recognition Test*; items are from the word recognition subtest of the *McGrath Test of Reading Skills*; word pronunciation; no manual; Joseph E. McGrath; McGrath Publishing Co.* (In-print status uncertain; no reply from publisher.)
For additional information, see 8:786.

[1432]
★**McGrath's Silent Reading Paragraphs Test, Comprehension.** Grades 1, 2, 3, 4, 5, 6, 7, 8, 9, 10, 11, 12, 13; 1976; MSRPTC; Joseph E. McGrath; McGrath Publishing Co.* (In-print status uncertain; no reply from publisher.)

[1433]
*****The McGuire-Bumpus Diagnostic Comprehension Test.** Reading levels grades 1.5–2.5, 2.5–3.5, 4–6; 1971–79; MBDCT; although designed as part of the Croft Inservice Program: Reading Comprehension Skills, the test may be used independently; criterion-referenced; 4 tests, 12 scores listed below; "mastery" (defined as 2 or fewer errors on each test) required on previous test before administering Tests B, C, and D; Marion L. McGuire and Marguerite J. Bumpus; Croft, Inc.*

a) LITERAL READING. 4 scores: selecting details, translating details, identifying signal words, selecting the main idea.
b) INTERPRETIVE READING. 3 scores: determining implied details, identifying organizational patterns, inferring the main idea.
c) ANALYTIC READING. 3 scores: identifying the problem, developing hypotheses, determining relevant details.
d) CRITICAL READING. 2 scores: selecting criteria for judgement, making a judgement.

[1434]
McHugh-McParland Reading Readiness Test. Grades kgn–1; 1966–68; 5 scores: rhyming words, beginning sounds, visual discrimination, identifying letters, total; Walter J. McHugh and Myrtle McParland; Cal-State Bookstore.* (In-print status uncertain; no reply from publisher.)
For additional information and reviews by Rebecca C. Barr and Edward R. Sipay, see 7:754.

REFERENCES
1. SHEPARD, L. Construct and predictive validity of the California Entry Level Test. *Educational & Psychological Measurement*, 1979, 39, 867–877.

[1435]
*****McLeod Phonic Worksheets.** Reading level grade 3.5 and under; 1972–77; formerly called *Domain Phonic Tests*; criterion-referenced; 6 areas: initial single consonants, final single consonants, single vowels, consonant blends and digraphs, vowel blends, auditory discrimination; John McLeod and Joan Atkinson; Educators Publishing Service, Inc.*
For additional information, see 8:756.

[1436]
Means-Ends Problem-Solving Procedure. Adults; 1975; MEPS; "individual's ability to orient himself to, and conceptualize means of moving towards a goal"; 2 major scores (relevant means, relevancy scores) and other minor scores; Jerome J. Platt and George Spivack; Department of Mental Health Sciences, Hahnemann Medical College and Hospital.*
For additional information, see 8:612 (11 references).

REFERENCES
1–11. See 8:612.
12. COCHE, E., & DOUGLAS, A. A. Therapeutic effects of problem-solving training and play-reading groups. *Journal of Clinical Psychology*, 1977, 33, 821–827.
13. GOTLIB, I. H., & ASARNOW, R. F. Interpersonal and impersonal problem-solving skills in mildly and clinically depressed university students. *Journal of Consulting & Clinical Psychology*, 1979, 47, 86–95.
14. STEINLAUF, B. Problem-solving skills, locus of control, and the contraceptive effectiveness of young women. *Child Development*, 1979, 50, 268–271.
15. GILBRIDE, T. V., & HEBERT, J. Pathological characteristics of good and poor interpersonal problem-solvers among psychiatric outpatients. *Journal of Clinical Psychology*, 1980, 36, 121–127.
16. HIGGINS, J. P., & THIES, A. P. Problem solving and social position among emotionally disturbed boys. *American Journal of Orthopsychiatry*, 1981, 51, 356–358.
17. MARSH, D. T., SERAFICA, F. C., & BARENBOIM, C. Interrelationships among perspective taking, interpersonal problem solving, and interpersonal functioning. *Journal of Genetic Psychology*, 1981, 138, 37–48.

[1437]
Meares-Sanders Junior High School History Test. 1, 2 semesters in grades 7–8; 1962–64; first

[1438] ★Measure of Arousal Seeking Tendency

published 1962–63 in the Every Pupil Scholarship Test series; Shirley Meares and M. W. Sanders; Bureau of Educational Measurements.*

For additional information and a review by Ina V. S. Mullis, see 8:915.

[1438]
★**Measure of Arousal Seeking Tendency.** College; 1978; no manual; Albert Mehrabian; the Author.*

REFERENCES

1. MEHRABIAN, A. Characteristic individual reactions to preferred and unpreferred environments. *Journal of Personality*, 1978, 46, 717–731.

[1439]
★**Measure of Child Stimulus Screening and Arousability.** Ages 3 months to 7 years; 1978; ratings by parents; no manual; Albert Mehrabian and Carol A. Falender; Albert Mehrabian.*

REFERENCES

1. MEHRABIAN, A., & FALENDER, C. A. A questionnaire measure of individual differences in child stimulus screening. *Educational & Psychological Measurement*, 1978, 38, 1119–1127.
2. MEHRABIAN, A., & O'REILLY, E. Analysis of personality measures in terms of basic dimensions of temperament. *Journal of Personality & Social Psychology*, 1980, 38, 492–503.

[1440]
★**Measure of Individual Differences in Dominance-Submissiveness.** College; 1978; no manual; Albert Mehrabian; the Author.*

[1441]
The Measurement of Self Concept in Kindergarten Children. Kgn; 1967; MSCKC; experimental form; projective drawing technique; 3 scores: self concept, non-self concept, discrepancy; Lucienne Y. Levine and J. Clayton Lafferty; Research Concepts.* (In-print status uncertain; no reply from publisher.)

For additional information, see P:454.

[1442]
★**Measures of Achieving Tendency.** College; 1975; Albert Mehrabian and Lewis Bank; Albert Mehrabian.*

REFERENCES

1. SINGER, R. N., & MCCAUGHAN, L. R. Motivational effects of attributions, expectancy, and achievement motivation during the learning of a novel motor task. *Journal of Motor Behavior*, 1978, 10, 245–253.

[1443]
★**Measures of Affiliative Tendency and Sensitivity to Rejection.** College students and adults; 1976; 2 scores: affiliative tendency, sensitivity to rejection; no manual; Albert Mehrabian; the Author.*

REFERENCES

1. MEHRABIAN, A. Questionnaire measures of affiliative tendency and sensitivity to rejection. *Psychological Reports*, 1976, 38, 199–209.

[1444]
★**Measures of Individual Differences in Temperament.** College students and adults; 1978; 3 scores: trait pleasure, trait arousal, trait dominance; no manual; Albert Mehrabian; the Author.*

REFERENCES

1. MEHRABIAN, A. Measures of individual differences in temperament. *Educational & Psychological Measurement*, 1978, 38, 1105–1117.

[1445]
★**Measures of Language Skills for Two- to-Seven-Year-Old Children.** Ages 2–7; 1978; MLS 2–7; 6 linguistically oriented tests: vocabulary comprehension, grammar comprehension, inflection production, grammar formedness judgment, grammar imitation, grammar equivalence judgment; Christy Moynihan and Albert Mehrabian; Albert Mehrabian.

[1446]
Measures of Musical Abilities. Ages 7–14; 1966; MMA; Arnold Bentley; Harrap Ltd. [England].*

See T2:206 (3 references); for reviews by Richard Colwell and John McLeish, and excerpted reviews by Richard R. Bentley and Paul R. Farnsworth, see 7:247 (13 references).

REFERENCES

1–13. See 7:247.
14–16. See T2:206.
17. VAUGHAN, M. M. Musical creativity: Its cultivation and measurement. *Council for Research in Music Education. Bulletin*, 1977, 50, 72–77.

[1447]
★**Measures of Occupational Stress, Strain, and Coping.** Employed adults; 1981; experimental form; 3 questionnaires; Samuel H. Osipow and Arnold R. Spokane; Marathon Consulting & Press.*

a) OCCUPATIONAL ENVIRONMENT SCALES. OES; 7 scales: role overload, role insufficiency, role ambiguity, role boundary, responsibility, physical environment, full scale total.

b) PERSONAL STRAIN QUESTIONNAIRE. PSQ; 5 scales: vocational strain, psychological strain, interpersonal strain, physical strain, full scale total.

c) PERSONAL RESOURCES QUESTIONNAIRE. PRQ; 5 scales: recreation, self-care, social support, rational/cognitive coping, full scale total.

[1448]
★**Measures of Pleasure-, Arousal-, and Dominance-Inducing Qualities of Parental Attitudes.** Ages 3 months–8 years; 1979; ratings by parents to measure pleasure, arousal and dominance levels experienced by the child; 3 scores: pleasure-inducing, arousal-inducing, dominance-inducing; C. A. Falender and A. Mehrabian; A. Mehrabian.*

REFERENCES

1. FALENDER, C. A., & MEHRABIAN, A. The emotional climate for children as inferred from parental attitudes: A preliminary validation of three scales. *Educational & Psychological Measurement*, 1980, 40, 1033–1042.

[1449]
★**Measures of Self-Concept K–12.** Grades kgn–3, 4–6, 7–12; 1972; "an IOX measureable objectives collection"; criterion-referenced; utilizes direct self-report, inferential self-report, and observation; 3 levels; Instructional Objectives Exchange.*

a) PRIMARY. Grades kgn–3; 10 objectives: self-appraisal (5 objectives: comprehensive, peer, school, family, general), television actors, the class play, parental approval, work posting, perceived approval situation.

b) INTERMEDIATE. Grades 4–6; 11 objectives: self-appraisal (same as *a* above), what would you do, parental approval, the class play, how about you, work posting, perceived approval situation.

c) SECONDARY. Grades 7–12; 9 objectives: self-appraisal (same as *a* above), what would you do, word choice, for all I know, perceived approval situation.

REFERENCES

1. McGee, R. Measuring affective behavior in physical education. *Journal of Physical Education & Recreation*, 1977, 48, 29–30.

[1450]
Mechanical Aptitude Test: Acorn National Aptitude Tests. Grades 7–16 and adults; 1943–52; 5 scores: comprehension of mechanical tasks, use of tools and materials (verbal), matching tools and operations, use of tools and materials (nonverbal), total; 1952 test identical with test copyrighted 1943; Andrew Kobal, J. Wayne Wrightstone, and Karl R. Kunze; Psychometric Affiliates.*

For additional information, see 5:878; for reviews by Reign H. Bittner, James M. Porter, Jr., and Alec Rodger, see 3:669.

[1451]
Mechanical Comprehension Test, Second Edition. Male technical apprentices and trainee engineer applicants; 1966–68; manual by P. D. Griffiths; National Institute for Personnel Research [South Africa].*

For additional information, see 7:1053.

REFERENCES

1. Booth, R. F., & Newman, K. Social status and minority recruit performance in the navy: Some implications for affirmative action programs. *Sociological Quarterly*, 1977, 18, 564–573.
2. Greener, J. M., & Osburn, H. G. An empirical study of the accuracy of corrections for restriction in range due to explicit selection. *Applied Psychological Measurement*, 1979, 3, 31–41.
3. Wilder, D. A., & Thompson, J. E. Intergroup contact with independent manipulations of in-group and out-group interaction. *Journal of Personality & Social Psychology*, 1980, 38, 589–603.

[1452]
Mechanical Familiarity Test: ETSA Test 5A. Job applicants; 1960–72; c1957–59; manual and technical handbook by S. Trevor Hadley and George A. W. Stouffer, Jr.; test by Psychological Services Bureau; Educators'-Employers' Tests & Services Associates.*

For reviews of the complete battery, see 6:1025 (2 reviews).

[1453]
Mechanical Information Test. Ages 15 and over; 1948–70; MIT; subtest of *N.I.I.P. Engineering Apprentice Selection Test Battery*; National Institute of Industrial Psychology; NFER-Nelson Publishing Co. [England].*

For additional information, see 7:1054 (1 reference).

[1454]
Mechanical Knowledge Test: ETSA Test 6A. Job applicants; 1960–72; c1957–59; manual and technical handbook by S. Trevor Hadley and George A. W. Stouffer, Jr.; test by Psychological Services Bureau; Educators'-Employers' Tests & Services Associates.*

For reviews of the complete battery, see 6:1025 (2 reviews).

[1455]
Mechanical Movements: A Test of Mechanical Comprehension. Industrial employees; 1959–63, c1956–63; abbreviated version of a Thurstone test developed about 1918; L. L. Thurstone (test), T. E. Jeffrey (test), and Measurement Research Division, Human Resources Center, University of Chicago (manual); the Center.*

For additional information and a review by William A. Owens, see 6:1089.

[1456]
***Mechanical Reasoning: Differential Aptitude Tests.** Grades 8–12 and adults; 1947–77; George K. Bennett, Harold G. Seashore, and Alexander G. Wesman; The Psychological Corporation.* For the complete battery entry, see 732.

For additional information regarding an earlier edition, see 8:1042 (2 references); see also T2:2256 (11 references). For reviews of the complete battery, see 8:485 (2 reviews, 1 excerpt), 7:673 (1 review, 1 excerpt), 6:767 (2 reviews), 5:605 (2 reviews), 4:711 (3 reviews), and 3:620 (1 excerpt).

REFERENCES

1–11. See T2:2256.
12–13. See 8:1042.
14. Lokan, J. The differential prediction of grades in a special vocational high school. *Measurement & Evaluation in Guidance*, 1977, 10, 7–16.
15. Cohn, S. J. Cognitive characteristics of the top-scoring third of the 1976 talent search contestants. *Gifted Child Quarterly*, 1978, 22, 416–420.
16. Arnold, P., & Walter, G. Communication and reasoning skills of deaf and hearing signers. *Perceptual & Motor Skills*, 1979, 49, 192–194.
17. Becker, B. J. Performance of a group of mathematically able youths on the mathematics usage and natural sciences reading tests of the American College Test Battery vs the Scholastic Aptitude Test. *Gifted Child Quarterly*, 1980, 24, 138–143.

[1457]
Medical School Instructor Attitude Inventory. Medical school faculty members; 1961; 6 scores: democratic-autocratic attitude toward teaching, critical-complimentary attitude toward medical schools, liberal-traditional attitude toward medical education, appreciative-depreciative attitude toward medical students, favorable-unfavorable attitude toward full-time teachers, favorable-unfavorable attitude toward part-time teachers; Edwin F. Rosinski; the Author.*

For additional information, see 6:1138 (1 reference).

[1458]
Medical Sciences Knowledge Profile. Citizens or permanent resident aliens in the United States and Canada; publication date not available; MSKP; program of the Association of American Medical Colleges; test is administered once a year at centers throughout the United States and foreign countries; 8 scores: anatomy, behavioral sciences, biochemistry, introductory clinical diagnosis, microbiology, pathology, pharmacology, physiology; National Board of Medical Examiners.

[1459]
The Meeting Street School Screening Test. Grades kgn–1; 1969; MSSST; 4 scores: motor patterning, visual-perceptual-motor, language, total; Peter K. Hainsworth and Marian L. Sigueland; Crippled Children and Adults of Rhode Island, Inc.*

For additional information, a review by Roy A. Kress, and an excerpted review by Alex Bannatyne, see 8:435 (8 references); see also T2:984 (1 reference); for an excerpted review by William Yule, see 7:756 (4 references).

REFERENCES

1-4. See 7:756.
5. See T2:984.
6-13. See 8:435.
14. McCormick, D. P. Pediatric evaluation of children with school problems. *American Journal of Diseases of Children*, 1977, 131, 318-322.
15. Pope, J., Lehrer, B., & Stevens, J. A multiphasic reading screening procedure. *Journal of Learning Disabilities*, 1980, 13, 47-51.
16. Swanson, B. B., Payne, D. A., & Jackson, B. A predictive validity study of the Metropolitan Readiness Test and Meeting Street School Screening Test against first grade Metropolitan Achievement Test scores. *Educational & Psychological Measurement*, 1981, 41, 575-578.

[1460]

The Meier Art Tests. Grades 7-16 and adults, 9-16 and adults; 1929-63; 2 tests; Norman Charles Meier; Bureau of Educational Research and Service.*
a) THE MEIER ART TESTS: 1, ART JUDGMENT. Grades 7-16 and adults; 1929-42; revision of *Meier-Seashore Art Judgment Test*.
b) THE MEIER ART TESTS: 2, AESTHETIC PERCEPTION. Grades 9-16 and adults; 1963.

See T2:189 (15 references); for an excerpted review by Laurence Siegel of test 2, see 7:240 (7 references); for a review by Harold A. Schultz, see 6:346 (8 references); for a review by Harold A. Schultz of test 1, see 4:224 (9 references); for a review by Edwin Ziegfeld, see 3:172 (4 references); for reviews by Paul R. Farnsworth and Aulus Ward Saunders of the original edition of test 1, see 2:1326 (15 references).

REFERENCES

1-15. See 2:1326.
16-19. See 3:172.
20-28. See 4:224.
29-36. See 6:346.
37-43. See 7:240.
44-48. See T2:189.
49. Berger, G. H., & Gaunitz, S. C. B. Self-rated imagery and vividness of task pictures in relation to visual memory. *British Journal of Psychology*, 1977, 68, 283-288.
50. Hall, G. E., & Reschly, D. J. Effects of differing external feedback conditions on rates of self-reinforcement. *Journal of General Psychology*, 1977, 97, 109-115.
51. Judd, L. L., Hubbard, B., Janowsky, D. S., Huey, L. Y., & Takahashi, K. I. The effect of lithium carbonate on the cognitive functions of normal subjects. *Archives of General Psychiatry*, 1977, 34, 355-357.
52. DiGuisto, E. L., & Bond, N. W. One-trial conditioned suppression: Effects of instructions on extinction. *American Journal of Psychology*, 1978, 91, 313-319.
53. Berger, G. H., & Gaunitz, S. C. B. Self-rated imagery and encoding strategies in visual memory. *British Journal of Psychology*, 1979, 70, 21-24.
54. Gor, R. E. Cognitive concomitants of hemispheric dysfunction in schizophrenia. *Archives of General Psychiatry*, 1979, 36, 269-274.
55. Hill, K. A., & Junus, F. Individual differences in concept learning of painting styles. *Perceptual & Motor Skills*, 1979, 49, 255-261.
56. Karson, M. Is aesthetic judgment impaired by neuroticism. *Journal of Personality Assessment*, 1980, 44, 499-506.

[1461]

Melvin-Smith Receptive-Expressive Observation. Grades 1-12; 1973-76; REO; "identifying learning problems and directing remediation"; 4 scores: visual vocal, auditory vocal, visual motor, auditory motor; Joan M. Smith; Educational Research Consultants, Inc.*

For additional information, see 8:436 (1 reference).

[1462]

Memory-For-Designs. Ages 8.5 and over; 1946-60; MFD; brain damage; Frances K. Graham and Barbara S. Kendall; Psychological Test Specialists.*

For additional information, see 8:613 (34 references); see also T2:1277 (16 references); for a review by R. W. Payne, see 7:101 (26 references); see also P:163 (15 references); for a review by Otfried Spreen, see 6:140 (18 references); see also 4:69 (5 references).

REFERENCES

1-5. See 4:69.
6-23. See 6:140.
24-38. See P:163.
39-64. See 7:101.
65-80. See T2:1277.
81-114. See 8:613.
115. Krywaniuk, L. W., & Das, J. P. Cognitive strategies in native children: Analysis and intervention. *Alberta Journal of Educational Research*, 1976, 22, 271-280.
116. Leong, C. K. Spatial-temporal information-processing in children with specific reading disability. *Reading Research Quarterly*, 1976-1977, 12, 204-215.
117. Blusewicz, M. J., Dustman, R. E., Schenkenberg, T., & Beck, E. C. Neuropsychological correlates of chronic alcoholism and aging. *Journal of Nervous & Mental Disease*, 1977, 165, 348-355.
118. Chaney, E. F., Erickson, R. C., & O'Leary, M. R. Brain damage and five MMPI items with alcoholic patients. *Journal of Clinical Psychology*, 1977, 33, 307-308.
119. Dolan, M. P., & Norton, J. C. A programmed training technique that uses reinforcement to facilitate acquisition and retention in brain-damaged patients. *Journal of Clinical Psychology*, 1977, 33, 496-501.
120. Kirby, J. R., & Das, J. P. Reading achievement, IQ, and simultaneous-successive processing. *Journal of Educational Psychology*, 1977, 69, 564-570.
121. Kumar, S. Short term memory for a nonverbal tactual task after cerebral commissurotomy. *Cortex*, 1977, 13, 55-61.
122. Ledoux, J. E., Risse, G. L., Springer, S. P., Wilson, D. H., & Gazzaniga, M. S. Cognition and commissurotomy. *Brain*, 1977, 100, 87-104.
123. Mednick, B. Intellectual and behavioral functioning of ten- to twelve-year-old children who showed certain transient symptoms in the neonatal period. *Child Development*, 1977, 48, 844-853.
124. Richardson, A. The meaning and measurement of memory imagery. *British Journal of Psychology*, 1977, 68, 29-43.
125. Richmond, B. O., & Aliotti, N. C. Developmental skills of advantaged and disadvantaged children on perceptual tasks. *Psychology in the Schools*, 1977, 14, 461-466.
126. Tsushima, W. T., & Towne, W. S. Effects of paint sniffing on neuropsychological test performance. *Journal of Abnormal Psychology*, 1977, 86, 402-407.
127. Arbit, J., & Zager, R. Psychometrics of a neuropsychological test battery. *Journal of Clinical Psychology*, 1978, 34, 460-465.
128. Berglund, M., & Leijonquist, H. Prediction of cerebral dysfunction in alcoholics: A study of health insurance records. *Journal of Studies on Alcohol*, 1978, 39, 1968-1974.
129. Das, J. P., Leong, C. K., & Williams, N. H. The relationship between learning disability and simultaneous-successive processing. *Journal of Learning Disabilities*, 1978, 11, 618-625.
130. Gustafson, L., & Hagberg, B. Recovery in hydrocephalic dementia after shunt operation. *Journal of Neurology, Neurosurgery & Psychiatry*, 1978, 41, 940-947.
131. Jarman, R. Patterns of cognitive ability in retarded children: A reexamination. *American Journal of Mental Deficiency*, 1978, 82, 344-348.
132. Jarman, R. F. Cross-modal and intramodal matching: Relationships to simultaneous and successive synthesis and levels of performance among three intelligence groups. *Alberta Journal of Educational Research*, 1978, 24, 100-112.
133. Joslyn, D., Grundvig, J. L., & Chamberlain, C. J. Predicting confabulation from the Graham-Kendall Memory-For-Designs Test. *Journal of Consulting & Clinical Psychology*, 1978, 46, 181-182.
134. Kirby, J. R., & Das, J. P. Information processing and human abilities. *Journal of Educational Psychology*, 1978, 70, 58-66.
135. Lewis, C. E., Scher, M., & Dietze, D. Reviewing results of psychological tests in a patient group. *Hospital & Community Psychiatry*, 1978, 29, 306-308.
136. McManis, D. L., Figley, C., Richert, M., & Fabre, T. Memory-For-Designs, Bender-Gestalt, Trail Making Test, and WISC-R performance of retarded and adequate readers. *Perceptual & Motor Skills*, 1978, 46, 443-450.
137. Persinger, B. D., & Holmes, C. B. Closure difficulty, figure-size expansion, and figure-size constriction on 240 Graham-Kendall Memory-For-Designs records. *Perceptual & Motor Skills*, 1978, 47, 343-347.
138. Streff, M., Barefoot, S., Walter, G., & Crandall, K. A comparative study of hearing-impaired and normal-hearing young adults—

verbal and nonverbal abilities. *Journal of Communication Disorders*, 1978, 11, 489–498.

139. CARROLL, J. A., FULLER, G. B., & CARROLL, J. L. Comparison of culturally deprived school achievers and underachievers on memory function and perception. *Perceptual & Motor Skills*, 1979, 48, 59–62.

140. FINE, E. W., & STEER, R. A. Short-term spatial memory deficits in men arrested for driving while intoxicated. *American Journal of Psychiatry*, 1979, 136, 594–597.

141. JARMAN, R. F. Cognitive processes and syntactical structure: Analysis of paradigmatic and syntagmatic associations. *Psychological Research*, 1979, 41, 153–167.

142. JARMAN, R. F. Simultaneous and successive cognitive processes in the Mueller–Lyer Illusion. *Journal of Genetic Psychology*, 1979, 134, 23–32.

143. KAUFMAN, D., & KAUFMAN, P. Strategy training and remedial techniques. *Journal of Learning Disabilities*, 1979, 12, 416–419.

144. MOLLOY, G. N., & DAS, J. P. Intellectual abilities and processes: An exploratory study with implications for person–teaching method interactions. *Australian Journal of Education*, 1979, 23, 83–92.

145. NAVARRO, D. J. Women A.A. members and nonalcoholics: Scores on the Holmes and MacAndrew scales of the MMPI. *Journal of Studies on Alcohol*, 1979, 40, 496–498.

146. ORRASCHEL, H., MEDNICK, S., SCHULSINGER, F., & ROCK, D. The children of psychiatrically disturbed parents. *Archives of General Psychiatry*, 1979, 36, 691–695.

147. PERSINGER, B. D., JR., & HOLMES, C. B. The effects of personality traits on Memory-For-Designs performance. *Journal of Clinical Psychology*, 1979, 35, 798–801.

148. STONES, M. J. Rekitting the Wechsler Paired–Associate Task: The Waterford Index. *Journal of Clinical Psychology*, 1979, 35, 626–630.

149. ASHMAN, A. F., & DAS, J. P. Relation between planning and simultaneous–successive processing. *Perceptual & Motor Skills*, 1980, 51, 371–382.

150. BERGMAN, H., BORG, S., & HOLM, L. Neuropsychological impairment and exclusive abuse of sedatives or hypnotics. *American Journal of Psychiatry*, 1980, 137, 215–217.

151. DUSTMAN, R. E., & BECK, E. C. Memory-For-Designs Test: Comparison of performance of young and old adults. *Journal of Clinical Psychology*, 1980, 36, 770–774.

152. KISH, G. B., HAGEN, J. M., WOODY, M. M., & HARVEY, H. L. Alcoholics recovery from cerebral impairment as a function of duration of abstinence. *Journal of Clinical Psychology*, 1980, 36, 584–589.

153. LEONG, C. K. Cognitive patterns of "retarded" and below-average readers. *Contemporary Educational Psychology*, 1980, 5, 101–117.

154. VAUGHAN, M. The validity of the Modified Word Learning Test. *Journal of Clinical Psychology*, 1980, 36, 467–471.

155. BERGMAN, H., HOHN, L., & AGREN, G. Neuropsychological impairment and a test of the predisposition hypothesis with regard to field dependence in alcoholics. *Journal of Studies on Alcohol*, 1981, 42, 15–23.

156. DAVIES, A. D. M., SPELMAN, M. S., & DAVIES, M. G. Combining psychometric data on brain damage and the influence of aging. *Perceptual & Motor Skills*, 1981, 52, 583–592.

157. FABIAN, M. S., PARSONS, O. A., & SILBERSTEIN, J. A. Impaired perceptual–cognitive functioning in women alcoholics: Cross-validated findings. *Journal of Studies on Alcohol*, 1981, 42, 217–229.

158. LYON, R., REITTA, S., WATSON, B., PORCH, B., & RHODES, J. Selected linguistic and perceptual abilities of empirically derived subgroups of learning disabled readers. *Journal of School Psychology*, 1981, 19, 152–166.

159. PERSINGER, B. D., JR., & HOLMES, C. B. Extreme constriction of figure size as a personality trait indicator on Memory-For-Designs. *Perceptual & Motor Skills*, 1981, 53, 216–218.

160. RIEGE, W. H., & INMAN, V. Age difference in nonverbal memory tasks. *Journal of Gerontology*, 1981, 36, 51–58.

161. RIEGE, W. H., KELLY, K., & KLANE, L. T. Age and error differences on Memory–For–Designs. *Perceptual & Motor Skills*, 1981, 52, 507–513.

162. SILBERSTEIN, J. A., & PARSONS, O. A. Neuropsychological impairment in female alcoholics: Replication and extension. *Journal of Abnormal Psychology*, 1981, 90, 179–182.

[1463]

Memory for Events. Grades 9–13; 1969; "memory for semantic systems"; J. P. Guilford; Sheridan Psychological Services, Inc.*

[1464]

Memory for Meanings. Grades 7–16; 1969; "memory for semantic units"; Ralph Hoepfner and J. P. Guilford; Sheridan Psychological Services, Inc.*

[1465]

Menometer. Adolescents and adults; 1974; knowledge of physical aspects of human menstruation; no manual; Panos D. Bardis; the Author.*

For additional information, see 8:413.

[1466]

★**Menstrual Distress Questionnaire.** Adult women; 1968–77; MDQ; this instrument has also been administered to men with modifications in instructions and purpose; 8 scores: pain, concentration, behavior change, autonomic reactions, water retention, negative affect, arousal, control; Rudolf H. Moos; the Author.*

REFERENCES

1. MOOS, R. H., & LEIDERMAN, D. B. Toward a menstrual cycle symptom typology. *Journal of Psychosomatic Research*, 1978, 22, 31–40.
2. DOTY, R. L., SNYDER, P. J., HUGGINS, G. R., & LOWRY, L. D. Endocrine, cardiovascular, and psychological correlates of olfactory sensitivity changes during the human menstrual cycle. *Journal of Comparative & Physiological Psychology*, 1981, 95, 45–60.
3. GOLUB, S., & HARRINGTON, D. M. Premenstrual and menstrual mood changes in adolescent women. *Journal of Personality & Social Psychology*, 1981, 41, 961–965.
4. Klein, J. R., Litt, I. F., Rosenberg, A., & Udall, L. The effect of aspirin on dysmenorrhea in adolescents. *Journal of Pediatrics*, 1981, 98, 987–990.

[1467]

Mental Alertness: Tests B/1 and B/2. Job applicants with 9–11, 12 or more years of education; 1945–68; 2 levels; no manual; National Institute for Personnel Research [South Africa].*

a) TEST B/2. Job applicants with 9–11 years of education; 1945–68; revision of Test A (G) of the South African Air Force.

b) TEST B/1. Job applicants with 12 or more years of education; 1945–62; revision of Test A (F) of the South African Air Force.

For additional information, see 7:362.

[1468]

Merit Rating Series. Industry; 1948–59; formerly called *Employee Evaluation Services*; 5 scales; Joseph E. King; Industrial Psychology, Inc.*

a) PERFORMANCE: CLERICAL. 1956; 5 scores: quantity, accuracy, job knowledge, personal-work habits, overall.

b) PERFORMANCE: MECHANICAL. 1953–57; 5 scores: production, quality, job knowledge, personal-work habits, overall.

c) PERFORMANCE: SALES. 1953–57; 5 scores: volume, accuracy, job knowledge, personal-work habits, overall.

d) PERFORMANCE: TECHNICAL. 1953–57; 5 scores: same as for *b*.

e) PERFORMANCE: SUPERVISOR. 1953–57; 4 scores: department operation, employee relations, job knowledge, personal-work habits.

For additional information and a review by Seymour Levy, see 6:1123; for a review by Brent Baxter of the original series, see 4:770 (1 reference).

[1469]

Merrill-Demos DD Scale: An Attitude Scale for the Identification of Potential or Actual Primary and Secondary Drug Abuse and Delinquent Behavior. Grades 3–9; 1971; MDDD; formerly called *The TPSC Scale*; 5 attitude scores: teachers, police, school, community, total; Merrill J. Weijola and George D. Demos; Sheridan Psychological Services, Inc.*

For additional information, see 8:614.

[1470]

★**Merrill Language Screening Test.** Ages 64–85 months; 1980; MLST; 3 or 4 scores: expressive language, receptive language, elicited language, articulation (optional); Myrna Mumm, Wayne Secord, Katherine Dykstra; Charles E. Merrill Publishing Co.*

[1471]

Merrill-Palmer Scale of Mental Tests. Ages 24–63 months; 1926–31, c1926–1948; Rachel Stutsman; Stoelting Co.*

See T2:507 (17 references); for a review by Marjorie P. Honzik, see 6:527 (16 references); for reviews by Nancy Bayley, B. M. Castner, Florence L. Goodenough, and Florence M. Teagarden, see 2:1406 (13 references).

REFERENCES

1–13. See 2:1406.
14–29. See 6:527.
30–46. See T2:507.
47. DuBose, R. F. Predictive value of infant intelligence scales with multiple handicapped children. *American Journal of Mental Deficiency*, 1977, 81, 388–390.
48. Goldman, J. G. Reflections of personality functioning in psychological testing of disadvantaged three to five year olds. *Journal of Personality Assessment*, 1977, 41, 39–42.
49. Gould, J. The use of the Vineland Social Maturity Scale, the Merrill-Palmer Scale of Mental Tests (non-verbal items) and the Reynell Developmental Language Scales with children in contact with the services for severe mental retardation. *Journal of Mental Deficiency Research*, 1977, 21, 213–226.
50. Roe, K. V. Correlations between Gesell scores in infancy and performance on verbal and nonverbal tests in early childhood. *Perceptual & Motor Skills*, 1977, 45, 1131–1134.
51. Wing, L., Gould, J., Yeates, S. R., & Brierley, L. M. Symbolic play in severely mentally retarded and in autistic children. *Journal of Child Psychology & Psychiatry & Allied Disciplines*, 1977, 18, 167–178.
52. Hall, P. K., & Tomblin, J. B. A follow-up study of children with articulation and language disorders. *Journal of Speech & Hearing Disorders*, 1978, 43, 227–241.
53. Freeman, B. J., Guthrie, D., Ritvo, E., Schroth, P., Glass, R., & Frankel, F. Behavior observation scale: Preliminary analysis of the similarities and differences between autistic and mentally retarded children. *Psychological Reports*, 1979, 44, 519–524.
54. Cohen, R. S., Stevenson, D. K., Malachowski, N., Ariagno, R. L., Johnson, J. D., & Sunshine, P. Late morbidity among survivors of respiratory failure treated with tolazoline. *Journal of Pediatrics*, 1980, 97, 644–647.

[1472]

★**Meta-Motivation Inventory.** Managers and persons in leadership positions; 1979; MMI; self-administered measure of personal and managerial style; 22 scores: deterministic (approval, conventional, dependency, avoidance, helplessness), motivation (perfection, assertiveness, independence, achievement, meta-achievement), need for control (persuasiveness, manipulation, reactive, authoritarian, exploitive), concern for people (cooperation, affiliation, humanistic, synergy, meta-humanistic), self-actualization, stress; John A. Walker; Meta-Visions.* (Also distributed by Humanics Media.)

[1473]

Metropolitan Achievement Tests, 5th Edition (1978). Grades kgn.0–kgn.5, kgn.5–1.4, 1.5–2.4, 2.5–3.4, 3.5–4.9, 5.0–6.9, 7.0–9.9, 10.0–12.9; 1931–80; MAT; 2 batteries; Irving H. Balow, Roger Farr, Thomas P. Hogan, and George A. Prescott; The Psychological Corporation.

a) SURVEY BATTERY. Grades kgn.0–kgn.5, kgn.5–1.4, 1.5–2.4, 2.5–3.4, 3.5–4.9, 5.0–6.9, 7.0–9.9, 10.0–12.9; 1977–79; subtests in reading and mathematics, (grades kgn.5–12.9) available as separates; partial batteries without science and social studies available (grades kgn.0–12.9); complete batteries available (grades 1.5–9.9); practice tests available (grades kgn.0–6.9); 8 levels.

1) *Preprimer.* Grades kgn.0–kgn.5; 4 scores: reading, mathematics, language, total.

2) *Primer.* Grades kgn.5–1.4; 4 scores: same as 1 above.

3) *Primary* 1. Grades 1.5–2.4; 7 scores: reading, mathematics, language, basics total, science, social studies, complete total.

4) *Primary* 2. Grades 2.5–3.4; 7 scores: same as for 3 above.

5) *Elementary.* Grades 3.5–4.9; 7 scores: same as for 3 above.

6) *Intermediate.* Grades 5.0–6.9; 7 scores: same as for 3 above.

7) *Advanced* 1. Grades 7.0–9.9; 7 scores: same as for 3 above.

8) *Advanced* 2. Grades 10.0–12.9; 4 scores: reading, mathematics, language, total.

b) INSTRUCTIONAL TESTS. Grades kgn.5–1.4, 1.5–2.4, 2.5–3.4, 3.5–4.9, 5.0–6.9, 7.0–9.9; 1977–80; practice tests listed with survey battery above can be used with corresponding levels of instructional tests; 6 levels.

1) *Primer.* Grades kgn.5–1.4; 3 tests.

(*a*) Reading Instructional Test. 6 scores: reading comprehension, visual discrimination, letter recognition, auditory discrimination, sight vocabulary, phoneme/grapheme-consonants.

(*b*) Language Instructional Test. 4 scores: listening comprehension, spelling, study skills, total.

(*c*) Mathematics Instructional Test. 4 scores: numeration, geometry and measurement, operations and problem solving, total.

2) *Primary* 1. Grades 1.5–2.4; 3 tests.

(*a*) Reading Instructional Test. 6 scores: reading comprehension, auditory discrimination, sight vocabulary, phoneme/grapheme-consonants, vocabulary in context, word part clues.

(*b*) Language Instructional Test. 7 scores: listening comprehension, punctuation and capitalization, usage, grammar and syntax, spelling, study skills, total.

(*c*) Mathematics instructional test. 5 scores: numeration, geometry and measurement, problem solving, operations-whole numbers, total.

3) *Primary* 2. Grades 2.5–3.4; 3 tests.

(*a*) Reading Instructional Test. 6 scores: reading comprehension, sight vocabulary, phoneme/-grapheme-consonants, phoneme/grapheme-vowels, vocabulary in content, word part clues.

(*b*) Language Instructional Test. 7 scores: listening comprehension, punctuation and capitalization, usage, grammar and syntax, spelling, study skills, total.

(*c*) Mathematics Instructional Test. 5 scores: numeration, geometry and measurement, problem solving, operations-whole numbers, total.

4) *Elementary.* Grades 3.5–4.9; 3 tests.

(*a*) Reading Instructional Test. 7 scores: reading comprehension, sight vocabulary, phoneme/-grapheme-consonants, phoneme/grapheme-vowels, vocabulary in context, word part clues, rate of comprehension.

(b) Language Instructional Test. 7 scores: listening comprehension, punctuation and capitalization, usage, grammar and syntax, spelling, study skills, total.

(c) Mathematics Instructional Test. 6 scores: numeration, geometry and measurement, problem solving, operations-whole numbers, operations-laws and properties, total.

5) *Intermediate.* Grades 5.0–6.9; 3 tests.

(a) Reading Instructional Test. 7 scores: reading comprehension, phoneme/grapheme-consonants, phoneme/grapheme-vowels, vocabulary in context, word part clues, rate of comprehension, skimming and scanning.

(b) Language Instructional Test. 6 scores: punctuation and capitalization, usage, grammar and syntax, spelling, study skills, total.

(c) Mathematics Instructional Test. 8 scores: numeration, geometry and measurement, problem solving, operations-whole numbers, operations-laws and properties, operations-fractions and decimals, graphs and statistics, total.

6) *Advanced* 1. Grades 7.0–9.9; 3 tests.

(a) Reading Instructional Test. 4 scores: reading comprehension, vocabulary in context, skimming and scanning, rate of comprehension.

(b) Language Instructional Test. 6 scores: same as for Intermediate level 5 above.

(c) Mathematics Instructional Test. 8 scores: same as for Intermediate level 5 above.

For reviews by Norman E. Gronlund and Richard M. Wolf and an excerpted review by Joseph A. Wingard and Peter M. Bentler of an earlier edition, see 8:22 (41 references); see also T2:22 (20 references) and 7:14 (25 references); for reviews by Henry S. Dyer and Warren G. Findley of an earlier edition, see 6:15 (16 references); for a review by Warren G. Findley, see 4:18 (10 references); see also 3:13 (7 references); for reviews by E. V. Pullias and Hugh B. Wood, see 2:1189 (3 references); for reviews by Jack W. Dunlap, Charles W. Odell, and Richard Ledgerwood, see 1:874. For reviews of subtests, see 8:283 (1 review), 8:732 (2 reviews), 6:627 (2 reviews), 6:797 (1 review), 6:877 (2 reviews), 6:970 (2 reviews), 4:416 (1 review), 4:543 (2 reviews), 2:1458.1 (2 reviews), 2:1551 (1 review), 1:892 (2 reviews), and 1:1105 (2 reviews).

REFERENCES

1–3. See 2:1189.
4–10. See 3:13.
11–20. See 4:18.
21–36. See 6:15.
37–61. See 7:14.
62–81. See T2:22.
82–122. See 8:22.

123. EARLY, G. H., GRISSOM, W. M., LABRENTZ, E. L., DeFELICE, G., & McCLAIN, N. J. Intermodal abilities as predictors of academic achievement. *Academic Therapy*, 1976–1977, 12, 163–169.

124. BIEMILLER, A. Relationships between oral reading rates for letters, words, and simple text in the development of reading achievement. *Reading Research Quarterly*, 1977–1978, 13, 223–253.

125. BUKTENICA, N. A. Perceptual/social aspects of learning to read: A transactional process. *Peabody Journal of Education*, 1977, 54, 154–161.

126. CANTRELL, R. P., STENNER, A. J., & KATZENMEYER, W. G. Teacher knowledge, attitudes, and classroom teaching correlates of student achievement. *Journal of Educational Psychology*, 1977, 69, 172–179.

127. COOPER, H. M. Controlling personal rewards: Professional teachers' differential use of feedback and the effects of feedback on the student's motivation to perform. *Journal of Educational Psychology*, 1977, 69, 419–427.

128. CRAWFORD, J., BROPHY, J. E., EVERTSON, C. M., & COULTER, C. L. Classroom dyadic interaction: Factor structure of process variables and achievement correlates. *Journal of Educational Psychology*, 1977, 69, 761–772.

129. FITZPATRICK, J. L., PARR, G. D., & BUTLER, C. G. Fast-accurate and slow-inaccurate conceptual tempos: Are they distinct groups? *Perceptual & Motor Skills*, 1977, 45, 643–647.

130. FOCH, T. T., DeFRIES, J. C., McCLEARN, G. E., & SINGER, S. M. Familial patterns of impairment in reading disability. *Journal of Educational Psychology*, 1977, 69, 316–329.

131. GABEL, H., GRAYBILL, D., & CONNORS, G. Parent-teacher communication in relation to child academic achievement and self-concept. *Peabody Journal of Education*, 1977, 54, 142–145.

132. HALL, W. C., JR., & MYERS, C. B. The effect of a training program in the Taba teaching strategies on teaching methods and teacher perceptions of their teaching. *Peabody Journal of Education*, 1977, 54, 162–167.

133. LEINHARDT, G. Program evaluation: An empirical study of individualized instruction. *American Educational Research Journal*, 1977, 14, 277–293.

134. PIHL, R. O., & PARKES, M. Hair element content in learning disabled children. *Science*, 1977, 198, 204–206.

135. PLANTE, A. J. The Connecticut "pairing" model proves effective in bilingual/bicultural education. *Phi Delta Kappan*, 1977, 58, 427.

136. RENTZ, R. R., & BASHAW, W. L. The National Reference Scale for Reading: An application of the Rasch model. *Journal of Educational Measurement*, 1977, 14, 161–179.

137. SEATON, H. W. The effects of a visual perception training program on reading achievement. *Journal of Reading Behavior*, 1977, 9, 188–192.

138. SILBERBERG, N. E., & SILBERBERG, M. C. A note on reading tests and their role in defining reading difficulties. *Journal of Learning Disabilities*, 1977, 10, 100–103.

139. SIMONS, E. S. The effects of kinetic structure on knowledge about and performance of a psychomotor skill: Teaching students to use the compound microscope. *Educational Horizons*, 1977, 55, 156–162.

140. SLINDE, J. A., & LINN, R. L. Vertically equated tests: Fact or phantom? *Journal of Educational Measurement*, 1977, 14, 23–32.

141. SMITH, M. D., DOKECKI, P. R., & DAVIS, E. E. School related factors influencing the self-concepts of children with learning problems. *Peabody Journal of Education*, 1977, 54, 185–195.

142. SMITH, M. K., & McMANIS, D. L. Concurrent validity of the Peabody Individual Achievement Test and the Wide Range Achievement Test. *Psychological Reports*, 1977, 41, 1279–1284.

143. TROTMAN, F. K. Race, IQ, and the middle class. *Journal of Educational Psychology*, 1977, 69, 266–273.

144. ASBURY, C. A. Cognitive factors related to discrepant arithmetic achievement of white and black first graders. *Journal of Negro Education*, 1978, 47, 337–342.

145. BELMONT, I., & BELMONT, L. Stability or change in reading achievement over time: Developmental and educational implications. *Journal of Learning Disabilities*, 1978, 11, 80–88.

146. BRUNING, R. H., BURTON, J. K., & BALLERING, M. Visual and auditory memory: Relationships to reading achievement. *Contemporary Educational Psychology*, 1978, 3, 340–351.

147. BURIEL, R. Relationship of three field-dependence measures to the reading and math achievement of Anglo American and Mexican American children. *Journal of Educational Psychology*, 1978, 70, 167–174.

148. COSTA, A. L. Competency based education: Let's examine the assumptions. *Thrust*, 1978, 7, 26–28.

149. HARDMAN, M. L. A functional administrative teaching model for academic programming with the trainable mentally retarded. *Education & Training of the Mentally Retarded*, 1978, 13, 23–28.

150. HAUTALA, L. W., & MASON, G. E. In search of success. *Southern Journal of Educational Research*, 1978, 12, 235–248.

151. HOGABOAM, T. W., & PERFETTI, C. A. Reading skill and the role of verbal experience in decoding. *Journal of Educational Psychology*, 1978, 70, 717–729.

152. HOUSE, E. R., GLASS, G. V., McLEAN, L. D., & WALKER, D. F. No simple answer: Critique of the Follow Through evaluation. *Harvard Educational Review*, 1978, 48, 128–160.

153. JENKINS, J. R., & PANY, D. Standardized achievement tests: How useful for special education? *Exceptional Children*, 1978, 44, 448–453.

154. KAIL, R. V., & MARSHALL, C. V. Reading skill and memory scanning. *Journal of Educational Psychology*, 1978, 70, 508–514.

155. LEWIS, J., & TODD, R. The relationship of cognitive abilities scores with social studies achievement. *Educational & Psychological Measurement*, 1978, 38, 463–464.

156. MORINE-DERSHIMER, G. The anatomy of teacher prediction. *Educational Research Quarterly*, 1978, 4, 59–65.

157. OAKLAND, T. Predictive validity of readiness tests for middle and lower socioeconomic status Anglo, Black, and Mexican American children. *Journal of Educational Psychology*, 1978, 70, 574–582.

158. PERFETTI, C. A., FINGER, E., & HOGABOAM, T. Sources of vocalization latency differences between skilled and less skilled young readers. *Journal of Educational Psychology*, 1978, 70, 730–739.
159. PINE, M. A. Self-concept, informal education, reading achievement in grade one. *Reading Teacher*, 1978, 31, 412–417.
160. PORTER, A. C., SCHMIDT, W. H., FLODEN, R. E., & FREEMAN, D. J. Practical significance in program evaluation. *American Educational Research Journal*, 1978, 15, 529–539.
161. RASBURY, W. C., FALGOUT, J. C., & PERRY, N. W., JR. A Yudin-type short form of the WISC–R: Two aspects of validation. *Journal of Clinical Psychology*, 1978, 34, 120–126.
162. RAYDER, N. F., LARSON, J. C., & ABRAMS, A. I. Effect of socio-contextual variables on child achievement. *Journal of Teacher Education*, 1978, 29, 58–63.
163. ROGERS, C. M., SMITH, M. D., & COLEMAN, J. M. Social comparison in the classroom: The relationship between academic achievement and self-concept. *Journal of Educational Psychology*, 1978, 70, 50–57.
164. RUHLAND, D., GOLD, M., & FELD, S. Role problems and the relationship of achievement motivation to scholastic performance. *Journal of Educational Psychology*, 1978, 70, 950–959.
165. RUST, J. O., MILLER, L. S., & WILSON, W. H. Using a control group to evaluate a resource room program. *Psychology in the Schools*, 1978, 15, 503–506.
166. SMITH, M. D., ZINGALE, S. A., & COLEMAN, J. M. The influence of adult expectancy/child performance discrepancies upon children's self-concepts. *American Educational Research Journal*, 1978, 15, 259–265.
167. STRANG, L., SMITH, M. D., & ROGERS, C. M. Social comparison, multiple reference groups, and the self-concepts of academically handicapped children before and after mainstreaming. *Journal of Educational Psychology*, 1978, 70, 487–497.
168. TURNER, R. R. Locus of control, academic achievement, and Follow Through in Appalachia. *Contemporary Educational Psychology*, 1978, 3, 367–375.
169. WILLIAMS, F., & OAKLAND, T. A three-year auditory perception program for low-SES minority children. *Journal of Special Education*, 1978, 12, 331–344.
170. ANDERSON, L. M., EVERTSON, C. M., & BROPHY, J. E. An experimental study of effective teaching in first-grade reading groups. *Elementary School Journal*, 1979, 79, 193–223.
171. BRYAN, T., & PEARL, R. Self-concepts and locus of control of learning disabled children. *Journal of Clinical Child Psychology*, 1979, 8, 223–226.
172. DONLON, T. F., EKSTROM, R. B., & LOCKHEED, M. E. The consequences of sex bias in the content of major achievement test batteries. *Measurement & Evaluation in Guidance*, 1979, 11, 202–216.
173. DOYLE, R. E., GOTTLIEB, B., & SCHNEIDER, D. Underachievers achieve–A case for intensive counseling. *School Counselor*, 1979, 26, 134–143.
174. EVANS, M., TAYLOR, N., & BLUM, I. Children's written language awareness and its relation to reading acquisition. *Journal of Reading Behavior*, 1979, 11, 7–19.
175. FELD, S., RUHLAND, D., & GOLD, M. Developmental changes in achievement motivation. *Merrill–Palmer Quarterly*, 1979, 25, 43–60.
176. FULLER, G. B., & FRIEDRICH, D. Visual-motor test performance: Race and achievement variables. *Journal of Clinical Psychology*, 1979, 35, 621–623.
177. JENSEN, M., & BECK, M. D. Gender balance analysis of the Metropolitan Achievement Tests, 1978 Edition. *Measurement & Evaluation in Guidance*, 1979, 12, 25–34.
178. KAUFMAN, D., & KAUFMAN, P. Strategy training and remedial techniques. *Journal of Learning Disabilities*, 1979, 12, 416–419.
179. LEINHARDT, G., SEEWALD, A. M., & ENGEL, M. Learning what's taught: Sex differences in instruction. *Journal of Educational Psychology*, 1979, 71, 432–439.
180. O'CONNER, P. D., STUCK, G. B., & WYNE, M. D. Effects of a short-term intervention resource-room program on task orientation and achievement. *Journal of Special Education*, 1979, 13, 375–385.
181. PANUNTO, B., & WHITE, D. Achievement and the prediction of achievement in English first and second language children. *Alberta Journal of Educational Research*, 1979, 25, 61–67.
182. RAYDER, N. F., ABRAMS, A. I., & LARSON, J. C. The effect of socio-contextual variables on child achievement. *Journal of Teaching & Learning*, 1979, 4, 9–23.
183. RESCHLY, D. J., & SABERS, D. C. Analysis of test bias in four groups with the regression definition. *Journal of Educational Measurement*, 1979, 16, 1–9.
184. REYNOLD, W. M. Development and validation of a scale to measure learning-related classroom behaviors. *Educational & Psychological Measurement*, 1979, 39, 1011–1018.
185. SHEPARD, L. Construct and predictive validity of the California entry level test. *Educational & Psychological Measurement*, 1979, 39, 867–877.
186. SMITH, M. D. Prediction of self-concept among learning disabled children. *Journal of Learning Disabilities*, 1979, 12, 664–669.
187. SMITH, S. M. Standardized tests used in correctional institutions. *Journal of Employment Counseling*, 1979, 16, 178–188.
188. STEPHAN, W. G., & ROSENFIELD, D. Black self-rejection: Another look. *Journal of Educational Psychology*, 1979, 71, 708–716.
189. TOMLINSON–KEASEY, C., & KELLY, R. R. Is hemispheric specialization important to scholastic achievement? *Cortex*, 1979, 15, 97–107.
190. WYNE, M. D., & STUCK, G. B. Time-on-task and reading performance in underachieving children. *Journal of Reading Behavior*, 1979, 11, 119–128.
191. ALLEN, M., & WELLMAN, M. M. Hand position during writing, cerebral laterality and reading: Age and sex differences. *Neuropsychologia*, 1980, 18, 33–40.
192. BERLER, E. S., & ROMANCZYK, R. G. Assessment of the learning disabled and hyperactive child: An analysis and critique. *Journal of Learning Disabilities*, 1980, 13, 10–12.
193. CARTER, D. E., & WALSH, J. A. Father absence and the black child: A multivariate analysis. *Journal of Negro Education*, 1980, 49, 134–143.
194. CORNO, L. Individual and class level effects of a parent-assisted instruction in classroom memory support strategies. *Journal of Educational Psychology*, 1980, 72, 278–292.
195. CUMMINGS, J. A., & NELSON, R. B. Basic concepts in the oral directions of group achievement tests. *Journal of Educational Research*, 1980, 73, 259–261.
196. DIAMOND, E. E. The AMEG commission report on sex bias in achievement testing. *Measurement & Evaluation in Guidance*, 1980, 13, 135–147.
197. FORSETH, S. D. Art activities, attitudes, and achievement in elementary mathematics. *Studies in Art Education*, 1980, 21, 22–27.
198. HOGAN, T. P., & MISHLER, C. Relationships between essay tests and objective tests of language skills for elementary school students. *Journal of Educational Measurement*, 1980, 17, 219–227.
199. IWANICKI, E. F. A new generation of standardized achievement test batteries: A profile of their major features. *Journal of Educational Measurement*, 1980, 17, 155–162.
200. KAUFMAN, N. L. Differential validity of reversal errors as predictors of first-grade reading achievement for blacks and whites. *Psychology in the Schools*, 1980, 17, 460–465.
201. KNIFONG, J. D. Computational requirements of standardized work problem tests. *Journal for Research in Mathematics Education*, 1980, 11, 3–9.
202. MORINE–DERSHIMER, G. The anatomy of teacher prediction. *Educational Research Quarterly*, 1980, 3, 59–65.
203. PATCHEN, M., HOFMANN, G., & BROWN, W. R. Academic performance of black high school students under different conditions of contact with peers. *Sociology of Education*, 1980, 53, 33–51.
204. REYNOLDS, C. R. An examination for bias in a preschool test battery across race and sex. *Journal of Educational Measurement*, 1980, 17, 137–146.
205. ROBERGE, J. J., & FLEXER, B. K. Control of variables and propositional reasoning in early adolescence. *Journal of General Psychology*, 1980, 103, 3–12.
206. RYDER, R. J., & GRAVES, M. F. Secondary students' internalization of letter-sound correspondences. *Journal of Educational Research*, 1980, 73, 172–178.
207. SMITH, W. E., & BECK, M. D. Determining instructional reading level with the 1978 Metropolitan Achievement Tests. *Reading Teacher*, 1980, 34, 313–319.
208. SNYDER, R. T., MASSONG, S. R., & ASHMORE, R. J. Relationship of Bender memory to achievement in arithmetic by first graders. *Perceptual & Motor Skills*, 1980, 51, 795–798.
209. VRANA, F., & PIHL, R. O. Selective attention deficit in learning disabled children: A cognitive interpretation. *Journal of Learning Disabilities*, 1980, 13, 42–45.
210. WESTBROOK, B. W., CUTTS, C. C., MADISON, S. S., & ARCIA, M. A. The validity of the Crite's model of career maturity. *Journal of Vocational Behavior*, 1980, 16, 249–281.
211. WINSBERG, B. G., BIALER, I., KUPIETZ, S., BOTTI, E., & BALKA, E. B. Home vs hospital care of children with behavior disorders. *Archives of General Psychiatry*, 1980, 37, 413–418.
212. ARMSTRONG, J. M. Achievement and participation of women in mathematics: Results of two national surveys. *Journal of Research in Mathematics Education*, 1981, 12, 356–372.
213. BANDURA, A., & SCHUNK, D. H. Cultivating competence, self-efficacy, and intrinsic interest through proximal self-motivation. *Journal of Personality & Social Psychology*, 1981, 41, 586–598.
214. BAUMANN, J. F. Effect of ideational prominence on children's reading comprehension of expository prose. *Journal of Reading Behavior*, 1981, 13, 49–56.
215. CHAMPION, D. W., LOWE, R. C., & CAVIOR, N. Egocentrism in elementary school children: Validity and application of assessment techniques. *Psychological Reports*, 1981, 48, 27–34.

216. ELDREDGE, A. R. An investigation to determine the relationships among self-concept, locus of control, and reading achievement. *Reading World*, 1981, 21, 59–64.
217. GREEN, K. D., VOSK, B., FOREHAND, R., & BECK, S. An examination of differences among sociometrically identified accepted, rejected, and neglected children. *Child Study Journal*, 1981, 11, 117–124.
218. HYND, G. W., OBRZUT, J. E., & OBRZUT, A. Are lateral and perceptual assymmetries related to WISC-R and achievement test performance in normal and learning–disabled children? *Journal of Consulting & Clinical Psychology*, 1981, 49, 977–979.
219. KAZIMOUR, K. K., & RESCHLY, D. J. Investigation of the norms and concurrent validity for the Adaptive Behavior Inventory for Children (ABIC). *American Journal of Mental Deficiency*, 1981, 85, 504–511.
220. LINN, R. L., LEVINE, M. V., HASTINGS, C. N., & WARDROP, J. L. Item bias in a test of reading comprehension. *Applied Psychological Measurement*, 1981, 5, 159–173.
221. SWANSON, B. B., PAYNE, D. A., & JACKSON, B. A predictive validity study of the Metropolitan Readiness Test and Meeting Street School Screening Test against first grade Metropolitan Achievement Test Scores. *Educational & Psychological Measurement*, 1981, 41, 575–578.

[1474]
★**Metropolitan Achievement Tests: Language Instructional Test.** Grades kgn.5–1.4, 1.5–2.4, 2.5–3.4, 3.5–4.9, 5.0–6.9, 7.0–9.9; 1977–80; 6 levels; Irving H. Balow, Roger Farr, Thomas P. Hogan, and George A. Prescott; The Psychological Corporation.*

For the complete battery entry, see 1473.

a) PRIMER. Grades kgn.5–1.4; 4 scores: listening comprehension, spelling, study skills, total.

b) PRIMARY 1. Grades 1.5–2.4; 7 scores: listening comprehension, punctuation and capitalization, usage, grammar and syntax, spelling, study skills, total.

c) PRIMARY 2. Grades 2.5–3.4; 7 scores: same as for *b* above.

d) ELEMENTARY. Grades 3.5–4.9; 7 scores: same as for *b* above.

e) INTERMEDIATE. Grades 5.0–6.9; 6 scores: same as for *b* above with the exception of listening comprehension.

f) ADVANCED 1. Grades 7.0–9.9; 6 scores: same as for *b* above with the exception of listening comprehension.

For additional information and reviews of an earlier edition of the complete battery, see 8:22 (2 reviews, 1 excerpt), 6:15 (2 reviews), 4:18 (1 review), 2:1189 (2 reviews), and 1:874 (3 reviews).

[1475]
★**Metropolitan Achievement Tests: Mathematics Instructional Test.** Grades kgn.5–1.4, 1.5–2.4, 2.5–3.4, 3.5–4.9, 5.0–6.9, 7.0–9.9; 1977–80; 6 levels; Irving H. Balow, Roger Farr, Thomas P. Hogan, and George A. Prescott; The Psychological Corporation.*

For the complete battery entry, see 1473.

a) PRIMER. Grades kgn.5–1.4; 4 scores: numeration, geometry and measurement, operations and problem solving, total.

b) PRIMARY 1. Grades 1.5–2.4; 5 scores: numeration, geometry and measurement, problem solving, operations-whole numbers, total.

c) PRIMARY 2. Grades 2.5–3.4; 5 scores: same as for *b* above.

d) ELEMENTARY. Grades 3.5–4.9; 6 scores: same as for *b* above plus operations-laws and properties.

e) INTERMEDIATE. Grades 5.0–6.9; 8 scores: same as for *b* above plus operations-laws and properties, operations-fractions and decimals, graphs and statistics.

f) ADVANCED 1. Grades 7.0–9.9; 8 scores: same as for *e* above.

[1476]
★**Metropolitan Achievement Tests: Reading Instructional Test.** Grades kgn.5–1.4, 1.5–2.4, 2.5–3.4, 3.5–4.9, 5.0–6.9, 7.0–9.9; 1977–80; 6 levels; Irving H. Balow, Roger Farr, Thomas P. Hogan, and George A. Prescott; The Psychological Corporation.* For the complete battery entry, see 1473.

a) PRIMER. Grades kgn.5–1.4; 6 scores: reading comprehension, visual discrimination, letter recognition, auditory discrimination, sight vocabulary, phoneme/grapheme-consonants.

b) PRIMARY 1. Grades 1.5–2.4; 6 scores: reading comprehension, auditory discrimination, sight vocabulary, phoneme/grapheme-consonants, vocabulary in context, word part clues.

c) PRIMARY 2. Grades 2.5–3.4; 6 scores: reading comprehension, sight vocabulary, phoneme/grapheme-consonants, phoneme/grapheme-vowels, vocabulary in context, word part clues.

d) ELEMENTARY. Grades 3.5–4.9; 7 scores: same as for *c* above plus rate of comprehension.

e) INTERMEDIATE. Grades 5.0–6.9; 7 scores: reading comprehension, phoneme/grapheme-consonants, phoneme/grapheme-vowels, vocabulary in context, word part clues, rate of comprehension, skimming and scanning.

f) ADVANCED 1. Grades 7.0–9.9; 4 scores: reading comprehension, vocabulary in context, skimming and scanning, rate of comprehension.

For additional information and reviews of an earlier edition of the complete battery, see 8:22 (2 reviews, 1 excerpt), 6:15 (2 reviews), 4:18 (1 review), 2:1189 (2 reviews), and 1:874 (3 reviews).

[1477]
★**Metropolitan Achievement Tests: Survey Battery: Mathematics, 1978 Edition.** Grades kgn.5–1.4, 1.5–2.4, 2.5–3.4, 3.5–4.9, 5.0–6.9, 7.0–9.9, 10.0–12.9; 1977–79; 7 levels; Irving H. Balow, Roger Farr, Thomas P. Hogan, and George A. Prescott; The Psychological Corporation.* For the complete battery entry, see 1473.

a) PRIMER. Grades kgn.5–1.4.
b) PRIMARY 1. Grades 1.5–2.4.
c) PRIMARY 2. Grades 2.5–3.4.
d) ELEMENTARY. Grades 3.5–4.9.
e) INTERMEDIATE. Grades 5.0–6.9.
f) ADVANCED 1. Grades 7.0–9.9.
g) ADVANCED 2. Grades 10.0–12.9.

For additional information and a review by C. Alan Riedesel of the 1970 edition, see 8:283 (5 references); see also T2:637 (4 references) and 7:480 (4 references); for reviews by O. F. Anderhalter and E. W. Hamilton of the 1958 edition, see 6:627 (1 reference); for a review by Robert L. Burch of an earlier edition, see 4:416; for reviews by Peter L. Spencer and Harry Grove Wheat, see 2:1458.1; for reviews by Foster E. Grossnickle and Guy M. Wilson, see 1:892. For reviews of an earlier edition of the complete battery, see 8:22 (2 reviews, 1 excerpt), 6:15 (2 reviews), 4:18 (1 review), 2:1189 (2 reviews), and 1:874 (3 reviews).

[1478] *Metropolitan Achievement Tests: Survey Battery: Reading

REFERENCES

1. See 6:627.
2–5. See 7:480.
6–9. See T2:637.
10–14. See 8:283.
15. ALMEIDA, E. Effects of parental involvement in teacher training. *International Journal of Psychology*, 1978, 13, 221–236.
16. BARNETT, M. A., & KAISER, D. L. The relationship between intellectual–achievement responsibility attributions and performance. *Child Study Journal*, 1978, 8, 209–215.
17. RONSHAUSEN, N. L. The effect on mathematics achievement of programmed tutoring as a method of individualized, one-to-one instruction. *Journal of Experimental Education*, 1979, 47, 268–276.
18. CROCKER, L., & BENSON, J. Does answer–changing affect test quality? *Measurement & Evaluation in Guidance*, 1980. 12, 233–239.

[1478]
Metropolitan Achievement Tests: Survey Battery: Reading, 1978 Edition. Grades kgn.5–1.4, 1.5–2.4, 2.5–3.4, 3.5–4.9, 5.0–6.9, 7.0–9.9, 10.0–12.9; 1977–79; 7 levels; Irving H. Balow, Roger Farr, Thomas P. Hogan, and George A. Prescott; The Psychological Corporation. For the complete battery entry, see 1473.

a) PRIMER. Grades kgn.5–1.4.
b) PRIMARY 1. Grades 1.5–2.4.
c) PRIMARY 2. Grades 2.5–3.4.
d) ELEMENTARY. Grades 3.5–4.9.
e) INTERMEDIATE. Grades 5.0–6.9.
f) ADVANCED 1. Grades 7.0–9.9.
g) ADVANCED 2. Grades 10.0–12.9.

For additional information and reviews by Fred Pyrczak and Darrell L. Sabers of the 1970 edition, see 8:732 (32 references); see also T2:1567 (12 references) and 7:696 (16 references); for a review by H. Alan Robinson of the 1958 edition, see 6:797 (4 references); for reviews by James R. Hobson and Margaret G. McKim of an earlier edition, see 4:543; for a review by D. A. Worcester, see 2:1551; for reviews by Ivan A. Booker and Joseph C. Dewey, see 1:1105. For reviews of an earlier edition of the complete battery, see 8:22 (2 reviews, 1 excerpt), 6:15 (2 reviews), 4:18 (1 review), 2:1189 (2 reviews), and 1:874 (3 reviews).

REFERENCES

1–4. See 6:797.
5–20. See 7:696.
21–32. See T2:1567.
33–64. See 8:732.
65. CARTELLI, L. M. The effects of paradigmatic language training on the reading process: An experimental study. *National Reading Conference Yearbook*, 1977, 267–271.
66. DILLARD, J. M., WARRIOR–BENJAMIN, J., & PERRIN, D. W. Efficacy of test–wiseness on test anxiety and reading achievement among black youth. *Psychological Reports*, 1977, 41, 1135–1140.
67. SEATON, H. W., & SMITH, S. D. The use of receptive and expressive language development activities for improving students' reading achievement. *National Reading Conference Yearbook*, 1977, 82–87.
68. BECK, M. D. The effect of item response changes on scores on an elementary reading achievement test. *Journal of Educational Research*, 1978, 71, 153–156.
69. CARTELLI, L. M. Paradigmatic language training for learning disabled children. *Journal of Learning Disabilities*, 1978, 11, 313–318.
70. TURNER, R. R. Locus of control, academic achievement, and Follow Through in Appalachia. *Contemporary Educational Psychology*, 1978, 3, 367–375.
71. CORNO, L. A hierarchical analysis of selected naturally occurring aptitude–treatment interactions in the third grade. *American Educational Research Journal*, 1979, 16, 391–409.
72. CARTELLI, L. M. Reading comprehension: A matter of referents. *Academic Therapy*, 1980, 15, 421–430.
73. DWYER, E. J. Analysis of reading achievement, listening comprehension, and paradigmatic language of selected second grade students by race and sex. *Southern Journal of Educational Research*, 1980, 14, 205–218.
74. LEWIS, J. The relationship between attitude toward reading and reading success. *Educational & Psychological Measurement*, 1980, 40, 261–262.
75. MARTIN, J., VELDMAN, D. J., & ANDERSON, L. M. Within–class relationships between student achievement and teacher behaviors. *American Educational Research Journal*, 1980, 17, 479–490.
76. SUMMERS, E. G. The validity of the Estes Reading Attitude Scale for intermediate grades. *Alberta Journal of Educational Research*, 1980, 26, 36–43.
77. WESTBROOK, B. W., CUTTS, C. C., MADISON, S. S., & ARCIA, M. A. The validity of the Crite's model of career maturity. *Journal of Vocational Behavior*, 1980, 16, 249–281.
78. DIVGI, D. R. Model–free evaluation of equating and scaling. *Applied Psychological Measurement*, 1981, 5, 203–208.
79. NEUMAN, S. B. Effect of teaching auditory perceptual skills on reading achievement in first grade. *Reading Teacher*, 1981, 34, 422–426.

[1479]
Metropolitan Readiness Tests, 1976 Edition. First half kgn, second half kgn and first grade entrants; 1933–76; MRT; Joanne R. Nurss and Mary E. McGauvran; The Psychological Corporation.*

a) LEVEL 1. First half kgn; 1974–76; 9 or 10 scores: auditory memory, rhyming, visual skills (letter recognition, visual matching, total), language skills (school language listening, quantitative language, total), total, copying (optional).

b) LEVEL 2. Second half kgn and first grade entrants; 1933–76; 4–6 scores: auditory skills, visual skills, language skills, total, quantitative skills (optional), copying (optional).

For additional information, see 8:802 (111 references); see also T2:1716 (55 references); for reviews by Robert Dykstra and Harry Singer of an earlier edition, see 7:757 (124 references); for a review by Eric F. Gardner and an excerpted review by Fay Griffith, see 4:570 (3 references); for a review by Irving H. Anderson, see 3:518 (5 references); for a review by W. J. Osburn, see 2:1552 (10 references).

REFERENCES

1–10. See 2:1552.
11–15. See 3:518.
16–18. See 4:570.
19–142. See 7:757.
143–197. See T2:1716.
198–308. See 8:802.
309. BACKER, J. C., WOODEN, S., & MULLER, D. Individualized, success oriented instructions in achievement and self–concept of first graders. *Perceptual & Motor Skills*, 1977, 45, 721–722.
310. BECHER, R. M., & WOLFGANG, C. H. An exploration of the relationship between symbolic representation in dramatic play and art and the cognitive and reading readiness levels of kindergarten children. *Psychology in the Schools*, 1977, 14, 377–381.
311. BROWN, T. J. Predictive and explanatory relationship among preschool temperament and home environment variables and subsequent reading readiness and achievement. *Florida Journal of Educational Research*, 1977, 19, 25–29.
312. BUKTENICA, N. A. Perceptual/social aspects of learning to read: A transactional process. *Peabody Journal of Education*, 1977, 54, 154–161.
313. CASSIDY, A. M., & VUKELICH, C. The effects of group size on kindergarten children's listening comprehension performance. *Psychology in the Schools*, 1977, 14, 449–455.
314. COLLIGAN, R. C. Concurrent validity of the Myklebust Pupil Rating Scale in a kindergarten population. *Journal of Learning Disabilities*, 1977, 10, 317–320.
315. ESLER, W. K., MIDGETT, J., & BIRD, R. C. Elementary science materials and the exceptional child. *Science Education*, 1977, 61, 181–184.
316. HUSHAK, L. J. The role of schools in reducing the variance of cognitive skills. *Journal of Educational Research*, 1977, 70, 115–122.
317. JOHNSON, D. L., BREKKE, B., & HARLOW, S. D. Appropriateness of the Motor–Free Visual Perception Test when used with the mentally retarded. *Education & Training of the Mentally Retarded*, 1977, 12, 312–315.
318. O'LEARY, S. G., & SCHNEIDER, M. R. Special class placement for conduct problem children. *Exceptional Children*, 1977, 44, 24–30.
319. RANDEL, M. A., FRY, M. A., & RALLS, E. M. Two readiness measures as predictors of first– and third–grade reading achievement. *Psychology in the Schools*, 1977, 14, 37–40.

320. RICHMOND, M. G., & MCNINCH, G. Word learning: Concrete vs abstract acquisition. *Perceptual & Motor Skills*, 1977, 45, 292–294.
321. SEATON, H. W., & SMITH, S. D. The use of receptive and expressive language development activities for improving students' reading achievement. *National Reading Conference Yearbook*, 1977, 82–87.
322. SHEEHAN, D. S., & MARCUS, M. The effects of teacher race and student race on vocabulary and mathematics achievement. *Journal of Educational Research*, 1977, 70, 123–126.
323. TOKAR, E. B., & HOLTHOUSE, N. D. The validity of the subtests of 1976 edition of the Metropolitan Readiness Tests. *Educational & Psychological Measurement*, 1977, 37, 1099–1101.
324. ASBURY, C. A. Cognitive factors related to discrepant arithmetic achievement of white and black first graders. *Journal of Negro Education*, 1978, 47, 337–342.
325. BREKKE, B., WILLIAMS, J. D., & FOLLMAN, D. E. Comparative assessment of visual perceptual abilities in the trainable mentally retarded. *Perceptual & Motor Skills*, 1978, 47, 735–738.
326. BUSSE, T. V., & SERAYDARIAN, L. The relationships between first name desirability and school readiness, IQ, and school achievement. *Psychology in the Schools*, 1978, 15, 297–302.
327. FLYNN, T. M., & FLYNN, L. A. Evaluation of the predictive ability of five screening measures administered during kindergarten. *Journal of Experimental Education*, 1978, 46, 65–70.
328. FOWLER, P. C., & RICHARDS, H. C. Father absence, educational preparedness, and academic achievement: A test of the confluence model. *Journal of Educational Psychology*, 1978, 70, 595–601.
329. MARGOLIS, H., & BRANNIGAN, G. G. Conceptual tempo as a parameter for predicting reading achievement. *Journal of Educational Research*, 1978, 71, 342–345.
330. OAKLAND, T. Predictive validity of readiness tests for middle and lower socioeconomic status Anglo, Black, and Mexican American children. *Journal of Educational Psychology*, 1978, 70, 574–582.
331. QUORN, K. C., & YORE, L. D. Comparison studies of reading readiness program skills acquisition by different methods: Formal reading readiness program, informal reading readiness program, and a kindergarten science program. *Science Education*, 1978, 62, 459–465.
332. RUBIN, R. A., & BALOW, B. Prevalence of teacher identified behavior problems: A longitudinal study. *Exceptional Children*, 1978, 45, 102–111.
333. RUBIN, R. A., BALOW, B., DORLE, J., & ROSEN, M. Preschool prediction of low achievement in basic school skills. *Journal of Learning Disabilities*, 1978, 11, 664–667.
334. SADICK, T. L., & GINSBURG, B. E. The development of the lateral functions and reading ability. *Cortex*, 1978, 14, 3–11.
335. SHEEHAN, D. S., & MARCUS, M. Teacher performance on the National Teacher Examinations and student mathematics and vocabulary achievement. *Journal of Educational Research*, 1978, 71, 134–136.
336. SWAIN, M., & BARIK, H. C. The role of curricular approach, rural-urban background, and socioeconomic status in second language learning: The Cornwall area study. *Alberta Journal of Educational Research*, 1978, 24, 1–16.
337. TALMAGE, H., & WALBERG, H. J. Naturalistic, decision-oriented evaluation of a district reading program. *Journal of Reading Behavior*, 1978, 10, 185–195.
338. VUKELICH, C., & MCADAM, J. A. Mothers' ability to predict their children's reading readiness skills. *Reading Teacher*, 1978, 32, 345–348.
339. WEITHORN, C. J., & KAGEN, E. Interaction of language development and activity level on performance of first graders. *American Journal of Orthopsychiatry*, 1978, 48, 148–159.
340. WILLIAMS, F., & OAKLAND, T. A three-year auditory perception program for low-SES minority children. *Journal of Special Education*, 1978, 12, 331–344.
341. ANDERSON, L. M., EVERTSON, C. M., & BROPHY, J. E. An experimental study of effective teaching in first-grade reading groups. *Elementary School Journal*, 1979, 79, 193–223.
342. BELKA, D. E., & WILLIAMS, H. G. Prediction of later cognitive behavior from early school perceptual–motor, perceptual, and cognitive performances. *Perceptual & Motor Skills*, 1979, 49, 131–141.
343. BLUM, I. H., TAYLOR, N. E., & BLUM, R. A. Methodological considerations and developmental trends in children's awareness of word boundaries. *National Reading Conference Yearbook*, 1979, 33–38.
344. CLEMINSHAW, H. K., & GUIDUBALDI, J. The effect of time and structure on kindergarten student social and academic performance. *Journal of Educational Research*, 1979, 73, 92–101.
345. COLLIGAN, R. C. Predictive utility of the Myklebust Pupil Rating Scale: A two-year follow-up. *Journal of Learning Disabilities*, 1979, 12, 264–267.
346. DICKSON, W. P., HESS, R. D., MIYAKE, N., & AZUMA, H. Referential communication accuracy between mother and child as a predictor of cognitive development in the United States and Japan. *Child Development*, 1979, 50, 53–59.
347. EVANS, M., TAYLOR, N., & BLUM, I. Children's written language awareness and its relation to reading acquisition. *Journal of Reading Behavior*, 1979, 11, 7–19.

348. GREENLAW, M. J., & MOORE, D. An analysis of current research on the Metropolitan Readiness Test and first grade reading achievement. *National Reading Conference Yearbook*, 1979, 23–28.
349. LITCHER, J. H., ROBERGE, L. P., MEYER, M., & KARNES, L. R. Alternative learning experiences for high-risk, first-grade students. *Journal of Learning Disabilities*, 1979, 12, 686–688.
350. MCCARRON, L., & HORN, P. W. Haptic visual discrimination and intelligence. *Journal of Clinical Psychology*, 1979, 35, 117–120.
351. NAGLE, R. J. The predictive validity of the Metropolitan Readiness Tests, 1976 Edition. *Educational & Psychological Measurement*, 1979, 39, 1043–1045.
352. REYNOLDS, C. R. A factor analytic study of the Metropolitan Readiness Test. *Contemporary Educational Psychology*, 1979, 4, 315–317.
353. REYNOLDS, C. R. The invariance of the factorial validity of the Metropolitan Readiness Tests for blacks, whites, males, and females. *Educational & Psychological Measurement*, 1979, 39, 1047–1052.
354. RONSHAUSEN, N. L. The effect on mathematics achievement of programmed tutoring as a method of individualized, one-to-one instruction. *Journal of Experimental Education*, 1979, 47, 268–276.
355. ROTHENBERG, J. J., LEHMAN, L. B., & HACKMAN, J. D. An individualized learning disabilities program in the regular classroom. *Journal of Learning Disabilities*, 1979, 12, 496–499.
356. RUBIN, R. A., & BALOW, B. Measures of infant development and socioeconomic status as predictors of later intelligence and school achievement. *Developmental Psychology*, 1979, 15, 225–227.
357. RUBIN, R. A., BALOW, B., & FISCH, R. O. Neonatal serum, bilirubin levels related to cognitive development at ages 4 through 7 years. *Journal of Pediatrics*, 1979, 94, 601–604.
358. RUDDELL, R. B. Early prediction of reading success: Profiles of good and poor readers. In M. L. Kamil & A. J. Moe (Eds.), *Reading research: Studies and applications; Twenty-eighth yearbook of the National Reading Conference*. Clemson, South Carolina: The National Reading Conference, 1979.
359. WEITHORN, C. J., & KAGEN E. Training first graders of high-activity level to improve performance through verbal self-direction. *Journal of Learning Disabilities*, 1979, 12, 82–88.
360. ABRAMS, A. I., BODY, B., & RAYDER, N. F. Problems and solutions in evaluating child outcomes of large-scale educational programs. *Journal of Experimental Education*, 1980, 48, 153–165.
361. ALLEN, M., & WELLMAN, M. M. Hand position during writing, cerebral laterality and reading: Age and sex differences. *Neuropsychologia*, 1980, 18, 33–40.
362. BELKA, D. E., & WILLIAMS, H. G. Canonical relationships among perceptual–motor, perceptual, and cognitive behaviors in children. *Research Quarterly for Exercise & Sport*, 1980, 51, 463–477.
363. CASSIDY, J., & VUKELICH, C. Do the gifted read early? *Reading Teacher*, 1980, 33, 578–582.
364. GUSKEY, T. R., NORDSTROM, C., & WICK, J. W. Evaluation of a voluntary busing program through cohort comparisons. *Urban Education*, 1980, 15, 3–32.
365. HESS, R. D., KASHIWAGI, K., AZUMA, H., PRICE, G. C., & DICKSON, W. P. Maternal expectations for mastery of developmental tasks in Japan and the United States. *International Journal of Psychology*, 1980, 15, 259–271.
366. KAUFMAN, N. L. Differential validity of reversal errors as predictors of first-grade reading achievement for blacks and whites. *Psychology in the Schools*, 1980, 17, 460–465.
367. MARTIN, J., VELDMAN, D. J., & ANDERSON, L. M. Within-class relationships between student achievement and teacher behaviors. *American Educational Research Journal*, 1980, 17, 479–490.
368. PELLEGRINI, A. D. The relationship between kindergartner's play and achievement in prereading, language, and writing. *Psychology in the Schools*, 1980, 17, 530–535.
369. REISMAN, F. K., & TORRANCE, E. P. Alternative procedures for assessing intellectual strengths of young children. *Psychological Reports*, 1980, 46, 227–230.
370. REYNOLDS, C. R. An examination for bias in a preschool test battery across race and sex. *Journal of Educational Measurement*, 1980, 17, 137–146.
371. ROGERS, B. G., WILSON, B. J., & HEWETT, G. Canonical variates in longitudinal achievement data. *Psychology in the Schools*, 1980, 17, 496–499.
372. SAWYER, W. E., & SAWYER, J. C. Preschool experience and reading readiness skills: Predicting the most efficient reading instruction. *Educational Research*, 1980, 9, 10.
373. SZASZ, C. W., BAADE, L. E., & PASKEWICZ, C. W. Emotional and developmental aspects of human figure drawings in predicting school readiness. *Journal of School Psychology*, 1980, 18, 67–73.
374. YARBOROUGH, B. H., & JOHNSON, R. A. How meaningful are marks in promoting growth in reading? *Reading Teacher*, 1980, 33, 644–651.
375. YARBOROUGH, B. H., & JOHNSON, R. A. A six-year study of sex differences in intellectual functioning, reading/language arts achievement, and affective development. *Journal of Psychology*, 1980, 106, 55–61.

376. BELKA, D. E. Prediction of kindergartners' behavior on Metropolitan Readiness Tests from preschool perceptual and perceptual–motor performances: A validation study. *Perceptual & Motor Skills*, 1981, 52, 899–902.

377. DUNLEAVY, R. A., HANSEN, J. L., SZASZ, C. W., & BAADE, L. E. Early kindergarten identification of academically not–ready children by use of Human Figure Drawing Developmental Score. *Psychology in the Schools*, 1981, 18, 35–38.

378. OBRZUT, J. E., BOLOCOFSKY, D. N., HEATH, C. P., & JONES, J. J. An investigation of the DIAL as a pre–kindergarten screening instrument. *Educational & Psychological Measurement*, 1981, 41, 1231–1241.

379. SEEFELDT, C. Social and emotional adjustment of first grade children with and without Montessori preschool experience. *Child Study Journal*, 1981, 11, 231–246.

380. SOUSLEY, S. A., & GARGIULO, R. M. Effect of conceptual tempo on kindergarten reading readiness. *Perceptual & Motor Skills*, 1981, 53, 127–134.

381. SWANSON, B. B., PAYNE, D. A., & JACKSON, B. A predictive validity study of the Metropolitan Readiness Test and Meeting Street School Screening Test against first grade Metropolitan Achievement Test scores. *Educational & Psychological Measurement*, 1981, 41, 575–578.

[1480]
The Michigan Picture Test—Revised. Ages 8–14; 1953–80; MPT-R; 4 scores: tension, verb tense, direction of forces, combined maladjustment index, plus 5 tentative test variables: psychosexual level, interpersonal relationships, personal pronouns, popular objects, level of interpretation; Max L. Hutt; Grune & Stratton, Inc.

See P:455 (11 references); for reviews by William E. Henry and Morris Krugman, and excerpted reviews by Laurance F. Shaffer and Edwin S. Shneidman of an earlier edition, see 5:150 (7 references).

[1481]
★Michigan Prescriptive Program in English. Persons striving to obtain 10th grade equivalency or pass the G.E.D. Test; 1973–75; a pretest is administered and scored and a prescribed course of study is implemented to help the student correct problem areas; William E. Lockhart; Ann Arbor Publishers.*

[1482]
★Michigan Prescriptive Program in Mathematics. Persons striving to obtain 10th grade equivalency or pass the G.E.D. test in math; 1978–79; a pretest is administered and scored and from the results a prescribed course of study is implemented to help the student correct problem areas; William E. Lockhart; Ann Arbor Publishers.*

[1483]
Michigan Test of Aural Comprehension. College applicants from non-English language countries; 1969–72; MTAC; John Upshur, Mary Spaan, and Rudolph Thrasher; English Language Institute, University of Michigan.*

For additional information and a review by John B. Carroll, see 8:105.

REFERENCES

1. MADSEN, H. S. An indirect measure of listening comprehension. *Modern Language Journal*, 1979, 63, 429–435.

[1484]
Michigan Test of English Language Proficiency. College applicants from non-English language countries; 1961–77; MTELP; tests by J. Upshur, A. S. Palmer, M. Spaan, R. Thrasher, J. Peterson, and B. Hockman; manual by Division of Testing and Certification; English Language Institute, University of Michigan.*

For additional information and a review by Edward J. Cervenka, see 8:106 (5 references); see also T2:233 (1 reference) and 7:264 (2 references); for a review by John B. Carroll, see 6:360.

REFERENCES

1–2. See 7:264.
3. See T2:233.
4–8. See 8:106.
9. BALDAUF, R. B., JR., & AYABE, H. I. Acculturation and educational achievement in American Samoan adolescents. *Journal of Cross–Cultural Psychology*, 1977, 8, 241–255.
10. BALDAUF, R. B. The validity of the Michigan Test of English Language Proficiency as a general measure of high school English achievement in American Samoa. *Educational & Psychological Measurement*, 1978, 38, 429–432.
11. BRIÉRE, E. J. Limited English speakers and the Miranda rights. *Teachers of English to Speakers of Other Languages Quarterly*, 1978, 12, 235–245.
12. THOMAS, R. E., & RICHARDSON, J. W. Study of English proficiency standards for foreign graduate students. *Journal of the American Association of Collegiate Registrars*, 1978, 53, 201–208.
13. MADSEN, H. S. An indirect measure of listening comprehension. *Modern Language Journal*, 1979, 63, 429–435.
14. ABADZI, H. The use of multivariate statistical procedures in international student admissions. *Journal of College Student Personnel*, 1980, 21, 195–201.
15. BALDAUF, R. B., JR., & DAWSON, R. L. T. The predictive validity of the Michigan Test of English Language Proficiency for teacher trainees in Papua New Guinea. *Educational & Psychological Measurement*, 1980, 40, 1201–1205.

[1485]
Mill Hill Vocabulary Scale. Ages 4 and over, 11–14, 14 and over; 1943–58; intelligence; 2 editions, only 1 edition currently available; John C. Raven; H. K. Lewis & Co. Ltd. [England].* (In-print status uncertain; no reply from publisher.)

a) ORAL DEFINITIONS FORM. Ages 4 and over; consists of all words from both forms of the junior and senior levels below.

b) WRITTEN TEST. Ages 11–14, 14 and over. (Australian edition of senior level: Australian Council for Educational Research [Australia].) *Out of print*.

See T2:403 (32 references); for a review by Morton Bortner, see 6:471 (16 references); see also 4:303 (7 references); for a review by David Wechsler, see 3:239 (3 references).

REFERENCES

1–3. See 3:239.
4–10. See 4:303.
11–26. See 6:471.
27–58. See T2:403.
59. HALL, J. N., BAKER, R. D., & HUTCHINSON, K. A controlled evaluation of token economy procedures with chronic schizophrenic patients. *Behaviour Research & Therapy*, 1977, 15, 261–283.
60. KUSUMO, K. S., & VAUGHN, M. Effects of lithium salts on memory. *British Journal of Psychiatry*, 1977, 131, 453–457.
61. LARNER, S. Encoding in senile dementia and elderly depressives: A preliminary study. *British Journal of Social & Clinical Psychology*, 1977, 16, 379–390.
62. MCGLONE, J. Sex differences in the cerebral organization of verbal functions in patients with unilateral brain lesions. *Brain*, 1977, 100, 775–793.
63. RICHARDSON, A. The meaning and measurement of memory imagery. *British Journal of Psychology*, 1977, 68 29–43.
64. SHARP, J. R., ROSENBAUM, G., GOLDMAN, M. S., & WHITMAN, R. D. Recoverability of psychological functioning following alcohol abuse: Acquisition of meaningful synonyms. *Journal of Consulting & Clinical Psychology*, 1977, 45, 1023–1028.
65. TOONE, B. K., & RON, M. A study of predictive factors in depressive disorders of poor outcome. *British Journal of Psychiatry*, 1977, 131, 587–591.

66. WIJESINGHE, O. B. A. The effect of varying the rate of presentation on the information transmission of schizophrenic and control groups. *British Journal of Psychiatry*, 1977, 130, 509–513.
67. COURT, J. H. A researcher's bibliography for Raven's Progressive Matrices and Mill Hill Vocabulary Scales. *Australian Psychologist*, 1978, 13, 248.
68. CUTTING, J. Specific psychological deficits in alcoholism. *British Journal of Psychiatry*, 1978, 133, 119–122.
69. EMLER, N. P., HEATHER, N., & WINTON, M. Delinquency and the development of moral reasoning. *British Journal of Social & Clinical Psychology*, 1978, 17, 325–331.
70. RICHARD, G. P., & BURLEY, P. M. Alcoholics beliefs about and attitudes to controlled drinking. *British Journal of Social & Clinical Psychology*, 1978, 17, 159–163.
71. CHICK, J., WATERHOUSE, L., & WOLFF, S. Psychological construing in schizoid children grown up. *British Journal of Psychiatry*, 1979, 135, 425–430.
72. CUTTING, J. Differential impairment of memory in Korsakoff's Syndrome. *Cortex*, 1979, 15, 501–506.
73. CUTTING, J. Memory in functioning psychosis. *Journal of Neurology, Neurosurgery & Psychiatry*, 1979, 42, 1031–1037.
74. KENDRICK, D. C., GIBSON, A. J., & MOYES, I. C. A. The Revised Kendrick Battery: Clinical studies. *British Journal of Social & Clinical Psychology*, 1979, 18, 329–340.
75. KENDRICK, D. C., & MOYES, I. C. A. Activity, depression, medication and performance on the revised Kendrick battery. *British Journal of Social & Clinical Psychology*, 1979, 18, 341–350.
76. BESSON, J. A. O. A diagnostic pointer to adult metachromatic leucodystrophy. *British Journal of Psychiatry*, 1980, 137, 186–187.
77. BROOKS, D. N., AUGHTON, M. E., BOND, M. R., JONES, P., & RIZVI, S. Cognitive sequelae in relationship to early indices of severity of brain damage after severe blunt head injury. *Journal of Neurology, Neurosurgery & Psychiatry*, 1980, 43, 529–534.
78. ELLENBERG, L., ROSENBAUM, G., GOLDMAN, M. S., & WHITMAN, R. D. Recoverability of psychological functioning following alcohol abuse: Lateralization effects. *Journal of Consulting & Clinical Psychology*, 1980, 48, 503–510.
79. GIBSON, A. J., MOYES, I. C. A., & KENDRICK, D. Cognitive assessment of the elderly long-stay patient. *British Journal of Psychiatry*, 1980, 137, 551–557.
80. GILHOOLY, K. J., & GILHOOLY, M. L. M. The validity of age-of-acquisition ratings. *British Journal of Psychology*, 1980, 71, 105–110.
81. HEMSLEY, D. R., & RICHARDSON, P. H. Shadowing by context in schizophrenia. *Journal of Nervous & Mental Disease*, 1980, 168, 141–145.
82. JOHNSON, O., & HARLEY, C. Handedness and sex differences in cognitive tests of brain laterality. *Cortex*, 1980, 16, 73–82.
83. MARSH, R. W. The significance for intelligence of differences in birthweight and health within monozygotic twin pairs. *British Journal of Psychology*, 1980, 71, 63–67.
84. REID, I., & CROUCHER, A. The Crandall intellectual achievement responsibility questionnaire: A British validation study. *Educational & Psychological Measurement*, 1980, 40, 245–249.
85. WAUGH, N. C. Age-related differences in acquisition of a verbal habit. *Perceptual & Motor Skills*, 1980, 50, 435–438.
86. WEEKS, D., FREEMAN, C. P. L., & KENDELL, R. E. ECT:III: Enduring cognitive deficits? *British Journal of Psychiatry*, 1980, 137, 26–37.
87. DAVIES, A. D. M., SPELMAN, M. S., & DAVIES, M. G. Combining psychometric data on brain damage and the influence of aging. *Perceptual & Motor Skills*, 1981, 52, 583–592.

[1486]
Miller Analogies Test. Candidates for graduate school; 1926–75; MAT; Forms J and R also published under the title *Advanced Personnel Test* for use in business; distribution restricted and test administered at specified licensed university centers; Braille and large-type editions available; W. S. Miller (test); The Psychological Corporation.*

For additional information, see 8:192 (31 references); see also T2:404 (15 references) and 7:363 (57 references); for reviews by Lloyd G. Humphreys, William B. Schrader, and Warren W. Willingham, see 6:472 (26 references); for a review by John T. Dailey, see 5:352 (28 references); for reviews by J. P. Guilford and Carl I. Hovland, see 4:304 (16 references).

REFERENCES

1–16. See 4:304.
17–44. See 5:352.
45–70. See 6:472.
71–127. See 7:363.
128–142. See T2:404.
143–173. See 8:192.
174. DEFFENBACHER, J. L. Relationship of worry and emotionality to performance on the Miller Analogies Test. *Journal of Educational Psychology*, 1977, 69, 191–195.
175. IRVINE, C. A correlation study of the relationship between the candidacy examination requirements and business education graduate students' academic success at the University of Northern Iowa, 1962–1972. *Journal of Business Education*, 1977, 52, 192.
176. MEINERS, M. L., & DABBS, J. M., JR. Ear temperature and brain blood flow: Laterality effects. *Bulletin of the Psychonomic Society*, 1977, 10, 194–196.
177. WECKOWICZ, T. E., COLLIER, G., & SPRENG, L. Field dependence, cognitive functions, personality traits, and social values in heavy cannabis users and nonuser controls. *Psychological Reports*, 1977, 41, 291–302.
178. GASTORF, J. W., & SULS, J. Performance evaluation via social comparison: Performance similarity versus related-attribute similarity. *Social Psychology*, 1978, 41, 297–305.
179. VICINO, F. L., & BASS, B. M. Lifespace variables and managerial success. *Journal of Applied Psychology*, 1978, 63, 81–88.
180. WERTHEIM, E. G., WIDOM, C. S., & WORTEL, L. H. Multivariate analysis of male and female professional career choice correlates. *Journal of Applied Psychology*, 1978, 63, 234–242.
181. FURST, E. J., & ROELFS, P. J. Validation of the Graduate Record Examination and the Miller Analogies Test in a doctoral program in education. *Educational & Psychological Measurement*, 1979, 39, 147–151.
182. GREENER, J. M., & OSBURN, H. G. An empirical study of the accuracy of corrections for restriction in range due to explicit selection. *Applied Psychological Measurement*, 1979, 3, 31–41.
183. MURRAY, R. E. Variability in MAT results within the field of education. *Psychological Reports*, 1979, 45, 665–666.
184. SULS, J., GAES, G., & GASTORF, J. Evaluating a sex-related ability: Comparisons with same-, opposite-, and combined-sex norms. *Journal of Research in Personality*, 1979, 13, 294–304.
185. GORDON, M. Predictive strategies in diagnostic tasks. *Nursing Research*, 1980, 29, 39–45.
186. KAGAN, D. M., & STOCK, W. A. Equivalencing MAT and GRE scores using simple linear transformation and regression methods. *Journal of Experimental Education*, 1980, 49, 34–37.
187. PIHL, R. O., SEGAL, Z., & YANKOFSKY, L. The effect of alcohol and placebo on affective reactions of social drinkers to a procedure designed to induce depressive affect anxiety and hostility. *Journal of Clinical Psychology*, 1980, 36, 337–342.
188. KIRNAN, J. P., & GEISINGER, K. F. The prediction of graduate school success in psychology. *Educational & Psychological Measurement*, 1981, 41, 815–820.
189. URSANO, R. J. The Viet Nam era prisoner of war: Precaptivity personality and the development of psychiatric illness. *American Journal of Psychiatry*, 1981, 138, 315–318.

[1487]
★Millon Behavioral Health Inventory. Physical and behavioral medicine patients ages 17 and over; 1981–82; MBHI; 8th grade reading level required; machine scorable only; 17 to 20 scores in 3 to 4 areas: basic coping style (introversive, inhibited, cooperative, sociable, confident, forceful, respectful, sensitive), psychogenic attitudes (chronic tension, recent stress, premorbid pessimism, future dispair, social alienation, somatic anxiety), prognostic indices (pain treatment responsivity, life threat reactivity, emotional vulnerability), plus scores for patients exhibiting specific disease syndromes: psychosomatic correlates (allergic inclination, gastrointestinal susceptibility, cardiovascular tendency); Theodore Millon, Catherine J. Green, and Robert B. Meagher; NCS Interpretive Scoring Systems.*

[1488]
★Millon Clinical Multiaxial Inventory. Adults receiving psychotherapy or participating in psychological assessment; 1976–81; MCMI; report discusses relationships between the more transient DSM-III clinical disorders (Axis I) and the more enduring personality

[1488] ★Millon Clinical Multiaxial Inventory

disorders (Axis II); 22 scores: 8 basic personality styles (schizoid, avoidant, dependent, histrionic, narcissistic, antisocial, compulsive, passive-aggressive), 3 pathological personality syndromes (schizotypal, borderline, paranoid), 6 symptom disorder scales of moderate severity (anxiety, somatoform, hypomanic, dysthymia, alcohol abuse, drug abuse), 3 symptom disorder scales of extreme severity (psychotic thinking, psychotic depression, psychotic delusions), plus 2 additional correction scales which provide a means to identify and adjust possible test-taking distortions; Theodore Millon; NCS Interpretive Scoring Systems.*

REFERENCES

1. GILBRIDE, T. V., & HEBERT, J. Pathological characteristics of good and poor interpersonal problem-solvers among psychiatric outpatients. *Journal of Clinical Psychology*, 1980, 36, 121–127.
2. SNIBBE, J. R., PETERSON, P. J., & SOSNER, B. Study of psychological characteristics of a workers' compensation sample using the MMPI and Millon Clinical Multiaxial Inventory. *Psychological Reports*, 1980, 47, 959–966.
3. BOSWELL, P. C., & MURRAY, E. J. Depression, schizophrenia, and social attraction. *Journal of Consulting & Clinical Psychology*, 1981, 49, 641–647.

[1489]
Milwaukee Academic Interest Inventory. Grades 12–14; 1973–74; MAII; 8 scores: 6 field variables (physical science, healing occupations, behavioral science, economics, humanities-social studies, elementary education) plus 2 discriminant variables (commercial vs. nurturant interests, natural science vs. social studies interests); Andrew R. Baggaley; Western Psychological Services.*

For additional information and a review by Austin C. Frank, see 8:1012 (1 reference); see also T2:2196 (4 references).

REFERENCES

1–4. See T2:2196.
5. See 8:1012.
6. BAGGALEY, A. R., & DOLE, A. A. Life goals and academic interests as predictors of extracurricular activities of secondary school sophomores. *Contemporary Educational Psychology*, 1977, 2, 172–180.

[1490]
Minimum Essentials for Modern Mathematics. Grades 6–8; 1963–71; Ernest Hayes; Hayes Educational Tests.*

For additional information and a review by Gerald L. Ericksen, see 6:587.

[1491]
★Minimum Essentials Test. Grades 8–12 and adults; 1980–81; MET; 4–5 scores: basic skills (reading, language, mathematics, plus optional writing), life skills; William K. Rice, Jr., Thomas R. Guskey, Carole Lachman Perlman, and Marion F. Rice; American Testronics.*

[1492]
Minnesota Child Development Inventory. Ages 1–6; 1968–74; MCDI; observations by mother; 8 scores: general development, gross motor, fine motor, expressive language, comprehension-conceptual, situation comprehension, self help, personal-social; Harold R. Ireton and Edward J. Thwing; Behavior Science Systems, Inc.

For additional information and a review by William L. Goodwin, see 8:220 (3 references).

REFERENCES

1–3. See 8:220.
4. COLLIGAN, R. C. The Minnesota Child Development Inventory as an aid in the assessment of developmental disability. *Journal of Clinical Psychology*, 1977, 33, 162–163.
5. CLARKE-STEWART, K. A. And daddy makes three: The father's impact on mother and young child. *Child Development*, 1978, 49, 466–478.
6. GARRITY, L. I., & SERVOS, A. B. Comparison of measures of adaptive behaviors in preschool children. *Journal of Consulting & Clinical Psychology*, 1978, 46, 288–293.
7. CLARKE-STEWART, K. A., VANDER STOEP, L. P., & KILLIAN, G. A. Analysis and replication of mother–child relations at two years of age. *Child Development*, 1979, 50, 777–793.
8. ULLMAN, D. G., & KAUSCH, D. F. Early identification of developmental strengths and weaknesses in preschool children. *Exceptional Children*, 1979, 46, 8–13.
9. CHAMBERLIN, R. W., & SZUMOWSKI, E. K. A follow-up study of parent education in pediatric office practices: Impact at age two and a half. *American Journal of Public Health*, 1980, 70, 1180–1188.

[1493]
Minnesota Clerical Test. Grades 8–12 and adults; 1933–79; MCT; 2 scores: number comparison, name comparison; Dorothy M. Andrew, Donald G. Paterson, and Howard P. Longstaff; The Psychological Corporation.

See T2:2135 (23 references) and 6:1040 (10 references); for a review by Donald D. Super, see 5:850 (46 references); for reviews by Thelma Hunt, R. B. Selover, Erwin K. Taylor, and E. F. Wonderlic, see 3:627 (22 references); for a review by W. D. Commins, see 2:1664 (18 references).

REFERENCES

1–18. See 2:1664.
19–40. See 3:627.
41–86. See 5:850.
87–96. See 6:1040.
97–119. See T2:2135.
120. HALL, W. B., & GOUGH, H. G. Selecting statistical clerks with the Minnesota Clerical Test. *Journal of Psychology*, 1977, 96, 297–301.
121. LUNNEBORG, C. E. Choice reaction time: What role in ability measurement? *Applied Psychological Measurement*, 1977, 1, 309–330.
122. DIAZ, A. P. D. L. Construction defect in the Minnesota Clerical Test. *Professional Psychology*, 1978, 9, 7–8.
123. CHISSOM, B. S., & THOMAS, P. J. Equivalence of two forms of the Dominoes Test (D–48 and D–70) with graduate students in education. *Psychological Reports*, 1979, 44, 972–974.
124. OLIVAS, L. A comparison of programmed and conventional teller-training instruction. *Business Education Forum*, 1979, 34, 54–55.

[1494]
Minnesota Engineering Analogies Test. Candidates for graduate school and industry; 1954–70; MEAT; distribution restricted and test administered at specified licensed university centers; Marvin D. Dunnette; The Psychological Corporation.*

For additional information, see 7:1095 (2 references); see also 6:1133 (2 references); for reviews by A. Pemberton Johnson and William B. Schrader, see 5:933 (6 references).

REFERENCES

1–6. See 5:933.
7–8. See 6:1133.
9–10. See 7:1095.
11. URSANO, R. J. The Vietnam era prisoner of war: Precaptivity personality and the development of psychiatric illness. *American Journal of Psychiatry*, 1981, 138, 315–318.

[1495]
Minnesota Importance Questionnaire, 1975 Revision. Vocational counselees; 1967–75; MIQ; intrapersonal vocational needs of an individual for specified job-

related reinforcers; 21 or 22 scores (20 of which parallel scores of *Minnesota Job Description Questionnaire* and *Minnesota Satisfaction Questionnaire*): ability utilization, achievement, activity, advancement, authority, company policies and practices, compensation, co-workers, creativity, independence, moral values, recognition, responsibility, security, social service, social status, supervision—human relations, supervision—technical, variety, working conditions, autonomy (ranked form only), validity; (Spanish edition available); David J. Weiss, René V. Dawis, Lloyd H. Lofquist, Evan G. Gay, and Darwin D. Hendel (manual); Vocational Psychology Research.*

For additional information and reviews by Lewis E. Albright and Sheldon Zedeck, see 8:1050 (40 references); see also T2:2283 (8 references) and 7:1063 (29 references).

REFERENCES

1–29. See 7:1063.
30–37. See T2:2283.
38–77. See 8:1050.
78. AMEG COMMISSION ON SEX BIAS IN MEASUREMENT. A case history of change: A review of responses to the challenge of sex bias in career interest inventories. *Measurement & Evaluation in Guidance*, 1977, 10, 148–152.
79. ELIZUR, D., & TZINER, A. Vocational needs, job rewards, and satisfaction: A canonical analysis. *Journal of Vocational Behavior*, 1977, 10, 205–211.
80. HENDEL, D. D. Behavioral validation of a vocational needs scale. *Applied Psychological Measurement*, 1977, 1, 307–308.
81. HENDEL, D. D. Intransitivity on paired–comparisons instruments: The relationship of the total circular triad score to stimulus circular triads. *Applied Psychological Measurement*, 1977, 1, 403–411.
82. TINSLEY, H. E. A., & TINSLEY, D. J. Different needs, interests, and abilities of effective and ineffective counselor trainees: Implications for counselor selection. *Journal of Counseling Psychology*, 1977, 24, 83–86.
83. ROUNDS, J. B., JR., MILLER, T. W., & DAWIS, R. V. Comparability of multiple rank order and paired comparison methods. *Applied Psychological Measurement*, 1978, 2, 415–420.
84. BALSLEY, I. W. A psychological battery approach to the assessment and evaluation of shorthand skills. *Balance Sheet LVI*, 1979, 1, 13–20.
85. HENDEL, D. D. Paired comparisons intransitivity: Is it relatively stable over time? *Educational & Psychological Measurement*, 1979, 39, 779–784.
86 HUBER, C. H. Career planning with mildly retarded students: A model for school counselors. *Vocational Guidance Quarterly*, 1979, 27, 223–229.
87. LEVY, M. F., REICHMAN, W., & HERRINGTON, S. Congruence between personality and job characteristics in alcoholics and nonalcoholics. *Journal of Social Psychology*, 1979, 107, 213–217.
88. ROUNDS, J. B., JR., DAWIS, R. V., & LOFQUIST, L. H. Life history correlates of vocational needs for a female adult sample. *Journal of Counseling Psychology*, 1979, 26, 487–496.
89. YUEN, R. K. W., TINSLEY, D. J., & TINSLEY, H. E. A. The vocational needs and background characteristics of homemaker–oriented women and career-oriented women. *Vocational Guidance Quarterly*, 1980, 28, 250–256.
90. LEVY, M. F., REICHMAN, W., & HERRINGTON, S. Abstinent alcoholics' adjustment to work. *Journal of Studies on Alcohol*, 1981, 42, 529–532.
91. MURRAY, S. G. Personality characteristics of adult women with low or high profiles on the SCII or SVIB occupational scales. *Journal of Applied Psychology*, 1981, 66, 422–430.

[1496]

★**Minnesota Infant Development Inventory.** Birth to 15 months; 1977–80; observations by mother; no scores, 5 developmental areas: gross motor, fine motor, language, comprehension, personal-social; Harold Ireton and Edward Thwing; Behavior Science Systems, Inc.*

[1497]

Minnesota Job Description Questionnaire. Employees and supervisors; 1967–68; MJDQ; for research use only; primarily for group measurement of occupational reinforcer patterns (ORP's) to match with intrapersonal vocational needs as measured by *Minnesota Importance Questionnaire*; 22 scores (20 of which parallel scores of *Minnesota Importance Questionnaire* and *Minnesota Satisfaction Questionnaire*): ability utilization, achievement, activity, advancement, authority, company policies and practices, compensation, coworkers, creativity, independence, moral values, recognition, responsibility, security, social service, social status, supervision—human relations, supervision—technical, variety, working conditions, autonomy, neutral point; scoring must be done by publisher; Fred H. Borgen, David J. Weiss, Howard E. A. Tinsley, René V. Dawis, and Lloyd H. Lofquist; Vocational Psychology Research.*

For additional information and a review by Sheldon Zedeck, see 8:1051 (15 references); see also T2:2284 (8 references).

REFERENCES

1–8. See T2:2284.
9–23. See 8:1051.
24. ELIZUR, D., & TZINER, A. Vocational needs, job rewards, and satisfaction: A canonical analysis. *Journal of Vocational Behavior*, 1977, 10, 205–211.
25. ROUNDS, J. B., JR., SHUBSACHS, A. P. W., DAWIS, R. V., & LOFQUIST, L. H. A test of Holland's environment formulations. *Journal of Applied Psychology*, 1978, 63, 609–616.
26. SHUBSACHS, A. P. W., ROUNDS, J. B., JR., DAWIS, R. V., & LOFQUIST, L. H. Perception of work reinforcer systems: Factor structure. *Journal of Vocational Behavior*, 1978, 13, 54–62.
27. FISCHER, D. G., & SOBKOW, J. A. Worker's estimation of ability requirements of their jobs. *Perceptual & Motor Skills*, 1979, 48, 519–531.

[1498]

Minnesota Multiphasic Personality Inventory. Ages 16 and over; 1943–67; MMPI; 14 scores: 4 validity scales [question (?), lie (L), validity (F, '43), test taking attitude (K, '46)] and 10 clinical scales [hypochondriasis (Hs, '43), depression (D, '43), hysteria (Hy, '43), psychopathic deviate (Pd, '43), masculinity and femininity (Mf, '43), paranoia (Pa, '43), psychasthenia (Pt, '43), schizophrenia (Sc, '43), hypomania (Ma, '43), social introversion (Si, '51)]; 3 editions differing in format; (Spanish edition available); Starke R. Hathaway and J. Charnley McKinley; published by University of Minnesota Press; distributed by NCS Interpretive Scoring Systems.*

a) INDIVIDUAL FORM ("THE CARD SET").

b) OLD GROUP FORM ("THE BOOKLET FORM"). Items same as in individual form.

c) NEW GROUP FORM (FORM R). New sequence of items with the 399 items used to obtain the 14 scores appearing first and the 167 research items last; shortened versions consist of the first 399 items or if K and Si scales are not wanted, 366 items.

For additional information and reviews by Henry A. Alker and Glen D. King, see 8:616 (1188 references); see also T2:1281 (549 references); for reviews by Malcolm D. Gynther and David A. Rodgers, see 7:104 (831 references); see also P:166 (1066 references); for reviews by C. J. Adcock and James C. Lingoes, see 6:143 (626 references); for reviews by Albert Ellis and Warren T. Norman, see 5:86 (496 references); for a review by Arthur L. Benton, see 4:71 (211 references); for reviews by Arthur L. Benton, H. J. Eysenck, L. S. Penrose, and Julian B. Rotter, and an excerpted review, see 3:60 (76 references).

REFERENCES

1–72. See 3:60.

73–283. See 4:71.
284–779. See 5:86.
780–1394. See 6:143.
1395–2460. See P:166.
2461–3291. See 7:104.
3292–3840. See T2:1281.
3841–5028. See 8:616.

5029. BARKER, T. E., & BLACK, F. W. Klinefelter Syndrome in a military population. *Archives of General Psychiatry*, 1976, 33, 607–610.

5030. COX, G., COSTANZO, P. R., & COIE, J. D. A survey instrument for the assessment of popular conceptions of mental illness. *Journal of Consulting & Clinical Psychology*, 1976, 44, 901–909.

5031. GYNTHER, M., & ULLOM, J. Objections to MMPI items as a function of interpersonal trust, race, and sex. *Journal of Consulting & Clinical Psychology*, 1976, 44, 1020.

5032. KOSS, M. P., BUTCHER, J. N., & HOFFMAN, N. G. The MMPI critical items: How well do they work? *Journal of Consulting & Clinical Psychology*, 1976, 44, 921–928.

5033. MEGARGEE, E. I., & DORHOUT, B. Revision and refinement of an MMPI-based typology of youthful offenders. *FCI Research Reports*, 1976, 6, 1–17.

5034. WOOD, D. R., REIMHERR, F. W, WENDER, P. H., & JOHNSON, G. E. Diagnosis and treatment of minimal brain dysfunction in adults. *Archives of General Psychiatry*, 1976, 33, 1453–1460.

5035. AKERS, T. K., TUCKER, D. M., ROTH, R. S., & VIDILOFF, J. S. Personality correlates of EEG change during meditation. *Psychological Reports*, 1977, 40, 439–442.

5036. ARNOLD, L. S., QUINSEY, V. L., & VELNER, I. Overcontrolled hostility among men found not guilty by reason of insanity. *Canadian Journal of Behavioural Science*, 1977, 9, 333–340.

5037. ATSAIDES, J. P., NEURINGER, C., & DAVIS, K. L. Development of an institutionalized chronic alcoholic scale. *Journal of Consulting & Clinical Psychology*, 1977, 45, 609–611.

5038. BAER, D. M., & FEDIO, P. Quantitative analysis of interictal behavior in temporal lobe epilepsy. *Archives of Neurology*, 1977, 34, 454–467.

5039. BASSETT, J. E., SCHELLMAN, G. C., GAYTON, W. F., & TAVORMINA, J. Efficacy of the Mini-Mult validity scales with prisoners. *Journal of Clinical Psychology*, 1977, 33, 729–731.

5040. BASSOS, C., SEEMAN, W., & SCHUMSKY, D. Context effect in the MMPI. *Journal of Clinical Psychology*, 1977, 33, 178–180.

5041. BECK, E. A., & MCINTYRE, S. C. MMPI patterns of shoplifters within a college population. *Psychological Reports*, 1977, 41, 1035–1040.

5042. BEST, C. L., & KILPATRICK, D. G. Psychological profiles of rape crisis counselors. *Psychological Reports*, 1977, 40, 1127–1134.

5043. BLOOM, W. Relevant MMPI norms for young adult air force trainees. *Journal of Personality Assessment*, 1977, 41, 505–510.

5044. BOLLER, F., VRTUNSKI, B., MACK, J. L., & KIM, Y. Neuropsychological correlates of hypertension. *Archives of Neurology*, 1977, 34, 701–705.

5045. BONYNGE, E. R., & HOFFMAN, H. Personality measurements in selection of applicants for an alcohol counselor training program. *Psychological Reports*, 1977, 41, 493–494.

5046. BOWEN, R. C., & SHEPEL, L. Physical and psychological complications after intestinal bypass for obesity. *Canadian Medical Association Journal*, 1977, 116, 871–875.

5047. BRAHEN, L. S., CAPONE, T., WIECHERT, V., & DESIDERIO, D. Naltrexone and cyclazocine. *Archives of General Psychiatry*, 1977, 34, 1181–1184.

5048. BRODERICK, E. F., JR. Legal preparation of a case of traumatic impotence. *Journal of Forensic Sciences*, 1977, 22, 795–798.

5049. BROWN, J. S., & RAWLINSON, M. E. Sex differences in sick role rejection and in work performance following cardiac surgery. *Journal of Health & Social Behavior*, 1977, 18, 276–292.

5050. BROWNE, J. A., & HOWARTH, E. A comprehensive factor analysis of personality questionnaire items: A test of twenty putative factor hypotheses. *Multivariate Behavioral Research*, 1977, 12, 399–427.

5051. BURKE, H., & MARCUS, R. MacAndrew MMPI alcoholism scale: Alcoholism and drug addictiveness. *Journal of Psychology*, 1977, 96, 141–148.

5052. BUSH, M. The relationship between impaired selective attention and severity of psychopathology in acute psychiatric patients. *British Journal of Medical Psychology*, 1977, 50, 251–265.

5053. CADOW, B. The MMPI and CPI as measures of a prison treatment population. *FCI Research Reports*, 1977, 9, 1–12.

5054. CALSYN, D. A., SPENGLER, D. M., & FREEMAN, C. W. Application of the somatization factor of the MMPI-168 with low back pain patients. *Journal of Clinical Psychology*, 1977, 33, 1017–1020.

5055. CAMPBELL, H. G., CLARKSON, Q. D., & SINSABAUGH, L. L. MMPI identification of nonrehabilitants among disabled veterans. *Journal of Personality Assessment*, 1977, 41, 266–269.

5056. CARLIN, A. S., & STAUSS, F. F. Descriptive and functional classifications of drug abusers. *Journal of Consulting & Clinical Psychology*, 1977, 45, 222–227.

5057. CEGALIS, J. A., LEEN, D., & SOLOMON, E. J. Attention in schizophrenia: An analysis of selectivity in the functional visual field. *Journal of Abnormal Psychology*, 1977, 86, 470–482.

5058. CHANEY, E. F., ERICKSON, R. C., & O'LEARY, M. R. Brain damage and five MMPI items with alcoholic patients. *Journal of Clinical Psychology*, 1977, 33, 307–308.

5059. CLAVELLE, P. R., & BUTCHER, J. N. An adaptive typological approach to psychiatric screening. *Journal of Consulting & Clinical Psychology*, 1977, 45, 851–859.

5060. CLOPTON, J. R., & NEURINGER, C. Fortran computer programs for the development of new MMPI scales. *Educational & Psychological Measurement*, 1977, 37, 783–786.

5061. CLOPTON, J. R., & NEURINGER, C. MMPI cannot say scores: Normative data and degree of profile distortion. *Journal of Personality Assessment*, 1977, 41, 511–513.

5062. COLLIGAN, R. C., & OSBORNE, D. MMPI profiles from adolescent medical patients. *Journal of Clinical Psychology*, 1977, 33, 188–189.

5063. COLLINS, H. A., BURGER, G. K., & TAYLOR, G. A. Personality patterns of drug abusers as shown by MMPI profiles. *Journal of Clinical Psychology*, 1977, 33, 897–900.

5064. COSTELLO, R. M. Construction and cross-validation of an MMPI black-white scale. *Journal of Personality Assessment*, 1977, 41, 514–519.

5065. COWGELL, V. G. Interpersonal effects of a suicidal communication. *Journal of Consulting & Clinical Psychology*, 1977, 45, 592–599.

5066. CRARY, W. G., & WEXLER, M. Meniere's Disease: A psychosomatic disorder? *Psychological Reports*, 1977, 41, 603–645.

5067. CROAKE, J. W., & OLSON, T. D. Family constellation and personality. *Journal of Individual Psychology*, 1977, 33, 9–17.

5068. CROSS, L. H., & FRARY, R. B. An empirical test of Lord's theoretical results regarding formula scoring of multiple-choice tests. *Journal of Educational Measurement*, 1977, 14, 313–321.

5069. CROWLEY, T. J., HOEHN, M. M., RUTLEDGE, C. O., STALLINGS, M. A., HEATON, R. K., SUNDELL, S., & STILSON, D. Dopamine excretion and vulnerability to drug-induced Parkinsonism. *Archives of General Psychiatry*, 1977, 35, 97–104.

5070. DAVIS, D. A., & WIDSETH, J. C. Prediction of help-seeking with the MMPI: The problem of base rates. *Journal of Clinical Psychology*, 1977, 33, 995–1000.

5071. DIKMEN, S., & REITAN, R. M. MMPI correlates of adaptive ability deficits in patients with brain lesions. *Journal of Nervous & Mental Disease*, 1977, 165, 247–254.

5072. DINNING, W. D., & EVANS, R. G. Discriminant and convergent validity of the SCL-90 in psychiatric inpatients. *Journal of Personality Assessment*, 1977, 41, 304–310.

5073. DUDLEY, D. L., AICKIN, M., & MARTIN, C. J. Cigarette smoking in a chest clinic population-Psychophysiologic variables. *Journal of Psychosomatic Research*, 1977, 21, 367–375.

5074. DWORKIN, R. H., & WIDOM, C. S. Undergraduate MMPI profiles and longitudinal prediction of adult social outcome. *Journal of Consulting & Clinical Psychology*, 1977, 45, 620–625.

5075. EDELSON, R. I., & PAUL, G. L. Staff "attitude" and "atmosphere" scores as a function of ward size and patient chronicity. *Journal of Consulting & Clinical Psychology*, 1977, 45, 874–884.

5076. ERICKSON, R. C., & O'LEARY, M. Using the MMPI 168 with alcoholics. *Journal of Clinical Psychology*, 1977, 33, 133–135.

5077. EVANS, D. R. Use of the MMPI to predict effective hotline workers. *Journal of Clinical Psychology*, 1977, 33, 1113–1114.

5078. EVANS, R., & DINNING, W. D. Future outlook and psychopathology among psychiatric patients. *Psychological Reports*, 1977, 41, 1309–1310.

5079. EXNER, J. E., & MURRILLO, L. G. A long term follow-up of schizophrenics treated with regressive ECT. *Diseases of the Nervous System*, 1977, 38, 162–168.

5080. EXNER, J. E., JR, WYLIE, J., LEUVA, A., & PARRILL, T. Some psychological characteristics of prostitutes. *Journal of Personality Assessment*, 1977, 41, 474–485.

5081. FASCHINGBAUER, T. R., & EGLEVSKY, D. A. Relation of dogmatism to creativity: Origence and intellectence. *Psychological Reports*, 1977, 40, 391–394.

5082. FEINMAN, J. M., & FINE, H. J. The relationship between sphere dominance and non-pathological behavior with a further examination of the somato-affective sphere. *Journal of Clinical Psychology*, 1977, 33, 959–965.

5083. FISHKIN, S. M., LOVALLO, W. R., & PISHKIN, V. Relationship between schizophrenic thinking and MMPI for process and reactive patients. *Journal of Clinical Psychology*, 1977, 33, 116–119.

5084. FOWLES, D. C., ROBERTS, R., & NAGEL, K. E. The influence of introversion/extroversion on the skin conductance response to stress and stimulus intensity. *Journal of Research in Personality*, 1977, 11, 129–146.

5085. FREEMAN, C., CALSYN, D., & O'LEARY, M. Application of Faschingbauer's abbreviated MMPI with medical patients. *Journal of Consulting & Clinical Psychology*, 1977, 45, 706–707.

5086. Freeman, C. W., O'Leary, M. R., & Calsyn, D. Application of the Faschingbauer abbreviated MMPI with alcoholic patients. *Journal of Clinical Psychology*, 1977, 33, 303-306.
5087. Furlong, M. J., & Leton, D. A. The validity of MMPI scales to identify potential child abusers. *Journal of Clinical Child Psychology*, 1977, 6, 55-57.
5088. Gendreau, P., Andrews, D. A., & Wormith, J. S. Personality characteristics of incarcerated speed abusers. *Canadian Journal of Behavioural Science*, 1977, 9, 341-347.
5089. Glenn, R. N., & Janda, L. H. Self-ideal discrepancy and acceptance of false personality interpretations. *Journal of Personality Assessment*, 1977, 41, 311-316.
5090. Globus, G., Friedmann, J., Huntley, A., Naitoh, P., Mullaney, D., & Johnson, L. Performance and mood during and after gradual sleep reduction. *Psychophysiology*, 1977, 14, 245-250.
5091. Goldsmith, H. H., & Gottesman, I. I. An extension of construct validity for personality scales using twin-based criteria. *Journal of Research in Personality*, 1977, 11, 381-397.
5092. Gottlieb, H., Strite, L. C., Koller, R., Madorsky, A., Hockersmith, V., Kleeman, M., & Wagner, J. Comprehensive rehabilitation of patients having chronic low back pain. *Archives of Physical Medicine & Rehabilitation*, 1977, 58, 101-108.
5093. Graf, K., Baer, P. E., & Comstock, B. S. MMPI changes in briefly hospitalized non-narcotic drug users. *Journal of Nervous & Mental Disease*, 1977, 165, 126-133.
5094. Greyson, B. Telepathy in mental illness: Deluge or delusion. *Journal of Nervous & Mental Disease*, 1977, 165, 184-200.
5095. Griffiths, R. D. P. The prediction of psychiatric patients' work adjustment in the community. *British Journal of Social & Clinical Psychology*, 1977, 16, 165-173.
5096. Groesch, S. J., & Davis, W. E. Psychiatric patients' religion and MMPI responses. *Journal of Clinical Psychology*, 1977, 33, 168-171.
5097. Guilleminault, C., Eldridge, F. L., Tilkian, A., Simmons, F. B., & Dement, W. C. Sleep apnea syndrome due to upper airway obstruction. *Archives of Internal Medicine*, 1977, 137, 296-300.
5098. Halperin, K. M., Neuringer, C., Davies, P. S., & Goldstein, G. Validation of the schizophrenia-organicity scale with brain-damaged and non-brain-damaged schizophrenics. *Journal of Consulting & Clinical Psychology*, 1977, 45, 949-950.
5099. Hanlon, T. E., McCabe, O. L., Savage, C., & Kurland, A. A. Narcotic antagonist treatment of addict parolees-The failure of an effective approach. *Comprehensive Psychiatry*, 1977, 18, 211-219.
5100. Heath, D. H. Academic predictors of adult maturity and competence. *Journal of Higher Education*, 1977, 48, 613-632.
5101. Heath, D. H. Maternal competence, expectation, and involvement. *Journal of Genetic Psychology*, 1977, 131, 169-182.
5102. Heath, D. H. Some possible effects of occupation on the maturing of professional men. *Journal of Vocational Behavior*, 1977, 11, 263-281.
5103. Hedlund, J. L. MMPI clinical scale correlates. *Journal of Consulting & Clinical Psychology*, 1977, 45, 739-750.
5104. Hedlund, J. L., Cho, D. W., & Wood, J. B. Comparative validity of MMPI-168 factors and clinical scales. *Multivariate Behavioral Research*, 1977, 12, 327-329.
5105. Hedlund, J. L., Cho, D. W., & Wood, J. B. MMPI-168 factor structure: A replication with public mental health patients. *Journal of Consulting & Clinical Psychology*, 1977, 45, 711-712.
5106. Heilbrun, A. B., & Heilbrun, K. S. The black minority criminal and violent crime: The role of self control. *British Journal of Criminology*, 1977, 17, 332-347.
5107. Helmes, E., Reed, P. L., & Jackson, D. N. Desirability and frequency scale values and endorsement proportions for items of Personality Research Form-E. *Psychological Reports*, 1977, 41, 435-444.
5108. Hirschfield, R. M. A., Klerman, G. L., Gough, H. G., Barrett, J., Korchin, S. J., & Chodoff, P. A measure of interpersonal dependence. *Journal of Personality Assessment*, 1977, 41, 610-618.
5109. Holland, T. R. Multivariate analysis of personality correlates of alcohol and drug abuse in a prison population. *Journal of Abnormal Psychology*, 1977, 86, 644-650.
5110. Hume, N., & Goldstein, G. Is there an association between astrological data and personality? *Journal of Clinical Psychology*, 1977, 33, 711-713.
5111. Hundleby, J. D., & Ross, B. E. Comparison of measures of psychopathy. *Journal of Consulting & Clinical Psychology*, 1977, 45, 702-703.
5112. Hurwitz, J. I., & Daya, D. K. Non-help-seeking wives of employed alcoholics: A multilevel interpersonal profile. *Journal of Studies on Alcohol*, 1977, 38, 1730-1739.
5113. Ibrahim, A. Containment and exclusiveness: Their measurement and correlates. *International Journal of Psychology*, 1977, 12, 219-229.
5114. Janowsky, D. S., Huey, L., Storms, L., & Judd, L. L. Methylphenidate hydrochloride effects on psychological tests in acute schizophrenic and nonpsychotic patients. *Archives of General Psychiatry*, 1977, 34, 189-194.

5115. Jarnecke, R. W., & Chambers, E. D. MMPI content scales: Dimensional structure, construct validity, and interpretive norms in a psychiatric population. *Journal of Consulting & Clinical Psychology*, 1977, 45, 1126-1131.
5116. Jenkins, C. D., Zyzanski, S. J., Ryan, T. J., Flessas, A., & Tannenbaum, S. I. Social insecurity and coronary-prone type A responses as identifiers of severe atherosclerosis. *Journal of Consulting & Clinical Psychology*, 1977, 45, 1060-1067.
5117. Johnsgard, K. Personality and performance: A psychological study of amateur sports car race drivers. *Journal of Sports Medicine & Physical Fitness*, 1977, 17, 97-104.
5118. Johnson, D. W., & Norem-Hebeisen, A. Attitudes toward interdependence among persons and psychological health. *Psychological Reports*, 1977, 40, 843-850.
5119. Johnson, J. H., Klingler, D. E., & Williams, T. A. An external criterion study of the MMPI validity indices. *Journal of Clinical Psychology*, 1977, 33, 154-156.
5120. Justice, B., McBee, G. W., & Allen, R. H. Life events, psychological distress and social functioning. *Psychological Reports*, 1977, 40, 467-473.
5121. Karoly, P., & Rosenthal, M. Training parents in behavior modification: Effects on perceptions of family interaction and deviant child behavior. *Behavior Therapy*, 1977, 8, 406-410.
5122. Kavanagh, T., & Shephard, R. J. Sexual activity after myocardial infarction. *Canadian Medical Association Journal*, 1977, 116, 1250-1253.
5123. Kimball, H. C., & Cundick, B. F. Emotional impact of videotape and reenacted feedback on subjects with high and low defenses. *Journal of Counseling Psychology*, 1977, 24, 377-382.
5124. King, G. D., Gideon, D. A., Haynes, C. D., Dempsey, R. L., & Jenkins, C. W. Intellectual and personality changes associated with carotid endarterectomy. *Journal of Clinical Psychology*, 1977, 33, 215-220.
5125. King, G. D., & Kelley, C. K. Behavioral correlates for spike-4, spike-9, and 4-9/9-4 MMPI profiles in students at a university mental health center. *Journal of Clinical Psychology*, 1977, 33, 718-724.
5126. King, G. D., & Kelley, C. K. MMPI behavioral correlates of spike-5 two-point code types with scale 5 as one elevation. *Journal of Clinical Psychology*, 1977, 33, 180-185.
5127. King, H. F., Carroll, J. L., & Fuller, G. B. Comparison of nonpsychiatric blacks and whites on the MMPI. *Journal of Clinical Psychology*, 1977, 33, 725-728.
5128. Kish, G. B., Woody, M. M., & Frankel, A. The development of a scale to measure task completion motivation. *Journal of Clinical Psychology*, 1977, 33, 128-133.
5129. Klinger, D. E., Johnson, J. H., Giannetti, R. A., & Williams, T. A. Comparison of the clinical utility of the MMPI basic scales of Dahlstrom's hypothesis. *Journal of Consulting & Clinical Psychology*, 1977, 45, 1086-1092.
5130. Klingler, D. E., Johnson, J. H., & Williams, T. A. A retest of MMPI prediction of admission to a psychiatric hospital. *Journal of Clinical Psychology*, 1977, 33, 1029-1031.
5131. Klingler, D. E., Johnson, J. H., & Williams, T. A. A validation study of the WIST as a group administered instrument for assessment of schizophrenic thinking. *Journal of Clinical Psychology*, 1977, 33, 658-661.
5132. Koh, S. D., Szoc, R., & Peterson, R. A. Short-term memory scanning in schizophrenic young adults. *Journal of Abnormal Psychology*, 1977, 86, 451-460.
5133. Krasnoff, A. Failure of MMPI scales to predict treatment completion. *Journal of Studies on Alcohol*, 1977, 38, 1440-1442.
5134. Kuldau, J. M., & Dirks, S. J. Controlled evaluation of a hospital-originated community transitional system. *Archives of General Psychiatry*, 1977, 34, 1331-1340.
5135. Lang, R. J., & Vernon, P. E. Dimensionality of the perceived self: The Tennessee Self Concept Scale. *British Journal of Social & Clinical Psychology*, 1977, 16, 363-371.
5136. Lanyon, R. I. Effect of biofeedback-based relaxation on stuttering during reading and spontaneous speech. *Journal of Consulting & Clinical Psychology*, 1977, 45, 860-866.
5137. Leonard, C. V. The MMPI as a suicide predictor. *Journal of Consulting & Clinical Psychology*, 1977, 45, 367-377.
5138. Leventhal, G. Female criminality: Is "women's lib" to blame? *Psychological Reports*, 1977, 41, 1179-1182.
5139. Levin, S. M., Barry, S. M., Gambaro, S., Wolfinsohn, L., & Smith, A. Variations of covert sensitization in the treatment of pedophilic behavior: A case study. *Journal of Consulting & Clinical Psychology*, 1977, 45, 896-907.
5140. Lewinsohn, P. M., Zeiss, A. M., Zeiss, R. A., & Haller, R. Endogeneity and reactivity as orthogonal dimensions in depression. *Journal of Nervous & Mental Disease*, 1977, 164, 327-332.
5141. Lick, J. R., & Heffler, D. Relaxation training and attention placebo in the treatment of severe insomnia. *Journal of Consulting & Clinical Psychology*, 1977, 45, 153-161.

5142. LINDSEY, C. J., MARTIN, P. J., & STERNE, A. L. Patient characteristics and expectancy measures as factors that influence the expectancy–improvement relationship. *Journal of Clinical Psychology*, 1977, 33, 1125–1127.

5143. LINTON, P. H., & ESTOCK, R. E. The anxiety phobic depersonalization syndrome: Role of the cognitive perceptual style. *Diseases of the Nervous System*, 1977, 38, 138–141.

5144. LISKOW, B. I., CLAYTON, P., WOODRUFF, R., GUZE, S., & CLONINGER, R. Briquet's Syndrome, hysterical personality, and the MMPI. *American Journal of Psychiatry*, 1977, 134, 1137–1139.

5145. LYLE, O. E., & GOTTESMAN, I. I. Premorbid psychometric indicators of the gene for Huntington's Disease. *Journal of Consulting & Clinical Psychology*, 1977, 45, 1011–1022.

5146. MARKS, P. A., & HALLER, D. Now I lay me down for keeps: A study of adolescent suicide attempts. *Journal of Clinical Psychology*, 1977, 33, 390–400.

5147. MARTIN, P. J., FRIEDMEYER, M. H., MOORE, J. E., & CLAVEAUX, R. A. Patients' experiences and improvement in treatment: The shape of the link. *Journal of Clinical Psychology*, 1977, 33, 827–833.

5148. MARTIN, P. J., GUHR, K. E., HUNTER, M. L., & ACREE, N. J. Therapists' expectancies and patients' improvement in treatment: The shape of the link. *Psychological Reports*, 1977, 40, 443–453.

5149. MARTIN, P. J., MOORE, J. E., STERNE, A. L., & MCNAIRY, R. M. Therapists prophesy. *Journal of Clinical Psychology*, 1977, 33, 502–510.

5150. MARTIN, P. J., STERNE, A. L., MOORE, J. E., & LINDSEY, C. J. Patients' expectancies and hospital outcome. *Journal of Clinical Psychology*, 1977, 33, 254–258.

5151. MATARAZZO, J. D., & WIENS, A. N. Black Intelligence Test of Cultural Homogeneity and Wechsler Adult Intelligence Scale scores of black and white police applicants. *Journal of Applied Psychology*, 1977, 62, 57–63.

5152. MATTHEWS, C. G., DIKMEN, S., & HARLEY, J. P. Age of onset and psychometric correlates of MMPI profiles in major motor epilepsy. *Diseases of the Nervous System*, 1977, 38, 173–176.

5153. MAY, P. R. A., TUMA, A. H., & DIXON, W. J. For better or for worse? Outcome variance with psychotherapy and other treatments for schizophrenia. *Journal of Nervous & Mental Disease*, 1977, 165, 231–239.

5154. MCCREARY, C. P., & MENSH, I. N. Personality differences associated with age in law offenders. *Journal of Gerontology*, 1977, 32, 164–167.

5155. MCCREARY, C., & PADILLA, E. MMPI differences among black, Mexican–American, and white male offenders. *Journal of Clinical Psychology*, 1977, 33, 171–177.

5156. MCLACHLAN, J. F. C. A scale for the evaluation of psychological distress. *Journal of Clinical Psychology*, 1977, 33, 159–161.

5157. MCWILLIAMS, J., & BROWN, C. C. Treatment termination variables, MMPI scores and frequencies of relapse in alcoholics. *Journal of Studies on Alcohol*, 1977, 38, 477–486.

5158. MERBAUM, M. Some personality characteristics of soldiers exposed to extreme war stress: A follow–up study of post–hospital adjustment. *Journal of Clinical Psychology*, 1977, 33, 558–562.

5159. MIDDENTS, G. J. A pilot project for assessing nonacademic characteristics of premedical students. *Journal of Medical Education*, 1977, 52, 343–344.

5160. MLOTT, S. R., LIRA, F. T., & MILLER, W. C. Psychological assessment of the burn patient. *Journal of Clinical Psychology*, 1977, 33, 425–430.

5161. MONROE, L. J., & MARKS, P. A. MMPI differences between adolescent poor and good sleepers. *Journal of Consulting & Clinical Psychology*, 1977, 45, 151–152.

5162. MONTANDON, H. E. Psychophysiological aspects of the Kirlian phenomenon: A confirmatory study. *Journal of the American Society for Psychical Research*, 1977, 71, 45–49.

5163. MORF, M., SYROTUIK, J., & KRZNARIC, S. Real data simulation of a two–stage statistical diagnostic system. *Journal of Consulting & Clinical Psychology*, 1977, 45, 822–828.

5164. MOSS, C. S., HOSFORD, R. E., ANDERSON, W. R., & PETRACCA, M. Personality variables of blacks participating in a prison riot. *Journal of Consulting & Clinical Psychology*, 1977, 45, 505–512.

5165. MURSTEIN, B. I., CERRETO, M., & MACDONALD, M. G. A theory and investigation of the effect of exchange-orientation on marriage and friendship. *Journal of Marriage & the Family*, 1977, 39, 543–548.

5166. NADITCH, M. P. LSD flashbacks and ego functioning. *Journal of Abnormal Psychology*, 1977, 86, 352–359.

5167. NEWMARK, C. S., KONANC, J., APONTE, C., & GARD, B. Changes in psychiatric admission MMPI profiles over a period of 15 to 20 years. *Journal of Clinical Psychology*, 1977, 33, 741–743.

5168. NEWMARK, C. S., WOODY, G., & ZIFF, D. Understanding and similarity in relation to marital satisfaction. *Journal of Clinical Psychology*, 1977, 33, 83–86.

5169. NICHOLS, M. P., & KNOPF, I. J. Refining computerized test interpretations: An in-depth approach. *Journal of Personality Assessment*, 1977, 41, 157–159.

5170. NORTON, J. C., & ROMANO, P. Validation of the Watson–Thomas rules for MMPI diagnosis. *Diseases of the Nervous System*, 1977, 38, 773–775.

5171. O'LEARY, M., CALSYN, D. A., CHANEY, E. F., & FREEMAN, C. W. Predicting alcohol treatment program drop–outs. *Diseases of the Nervous System*, 1977, 38, 993–995.

5172. O'LEARY, M. R., DONOVAN, D. M., CYSEWSKI, B., & CHANEY, E. F. Perceived locus of control, experienced control, and depression: A trait description of the learned helplessness model of depression. *Journal of Clinical Psychology*, 1977, 33, 164–168.

5173. OSBORNE, D. Comparison of MMPI scores of pregnant women and female medical patients. *Journal of Clinical Psychology*, 1977, 33, 448–450.

5174. OSBORNE, D. MMPI characteristics of multigravidas and primigravidas in the third trimester of pregnancy. *Psychological Reports*, 1977, 40, 81–82.

5175. OTTOMANELLI, G. A. Patient improvement, measured by the MMPI and *Pyp*, related to paraprofessional and professional counselor assignment. *International Journal of the Addictions*, 1977, 13, 503–507.

5176. OVERALL, J. E., & HIGGINS, C. W. An application of actuarial methods in psychiatric diagnosis. *Journal of Clinical Psychology*, 1977, 33, 973–980.

5177. PALLIS, D. J., & BIRTCHNELL, J. Seriousness of suicide attempt in relation to personality. *British Journal of Psychiatry*, 1977, 130, 253–259.

5178. PASSINI, F. T., WATSON, C. G., DEHNEL, L., & HERDER, J. Alpha wave biofeedback training therapy in alcoholics. *Journal of Clinical Psychology*, 1977, 33, 292–299.

5179. PATTON, J. F., & FREITAG, C. B. Correlational study of death anxiety, general anxiety and locus of control. *Psychological Reports*, 1977, 40, 51–54.

5180. PENK, W. E., & KIDD, R. V. Differences in word association commonality of schizophrenics: The self–editing–deficit model vs. the partial–collapse–of–response–hierarchy hypothesis. *Journal of Clinical Psychology*, 1977, 33, 32–39.

5181. PERR, I. N. Psychiatric evaluation of traumatic impotence: Evolution of a case. *Journal of Forensic Sciences*, 1977, 22, 781–790.

5182. PERSKY, H., O'BRIEN, C. P., FINE, E., HOWARD, W. J., KHAN, M. A., & BECK, R. W. The effect of alcohol and smoking on testosterone function and aggression in chronic alcoholics. *American Journal of Psychiatry*, 1977, 134, 621–625.

5183. PHILLIPS, E. L., GERSHENSON, J., & LYONS, G. On time-limited writing therapy. *Psychological Reports*, 1977, 41, 707–712.

5184. PIPER, W. E., DEBBANE, E. G., & GARANT, J. Group psychotherapy outcome research: Problems and prospects of a first–year project. *International Journal of Group Psychotherapy*, 1977, 27, 321–341.

5185. PLEMONS, G. A comparison of MMPI scores of Anglo– and Mexican–American psychiatric patients. *Journal of Consulting & Clinical Psychology*, 1977, 45, 149–150.

5186. POMERANTZ, A. S., GREENBERG, I., & BLACKBURN, G. L. MMPI profiles of obese men and women. *Psychological Reports*, 1977, 41, 731–734.

5187. PROKOP, C. K. The role of psychologic evaluation in determining the personal meanings of aging and illness. *Geriatrics*, 1977, 32, 125–139.

5188. RADER, C. M. MMPI profile types of exposers, rapists, & assaulters in a court services population. *Journal of Consulting & Clinical Psychology*, 1977, 45, 61–69.

5189. RAMANAIAH, N. V. Stylistic components of human judgment: The generality of individual differences. *Applied Psychological Measurement*, 1977, 1, 23–29.

5190. RAMANAIAH, N. V., SCHILL, T., & LEUNG, L. S. A test of the hypothesis about the two-dimensional nature of the Marlowe-Crowne Social Desirability Scale. *Journal of Research in Personality*, 1977, 11, 251–259.

5191. REILLEY, R. R., & LITTLE, D. K. Hierarchical grouping of MMPI group profiles. *Psychological Reports*, 1977, 41, 1323–1330.

5192. RHODES, R. J., & RICE, A. S. MMPI correlates of the Popoff index of depression. *Psychological Reports*, 1977, 40, 35–41.

5193. ROSENBAUM, M., & RAZ, D. Denial, locus of control and depression among physically disabled and nondisabled men. *Journal of Clinical Psychology*, 1977, 33, 672–676.

5194. RUFF, C. F., AYERS, J. L., & TEMPLER, D. I. The Watson and the Hovey MMPI scales: Do they measure organicity or "functional" psychopathology? *Journal of Clinical Psychology*, 1977, 33, 732–734.

5195. RUSSELL, E. W. MMPI profiles of brain–damaged and schizophrenic subjects. *Journal of Clinical Psychology*, 1977, 33, 190–193.

5196. RUTSCHMANN, J., CORNBLATT, B., & ERLENMEYER-KIMLING, L. Sustained attention in children at risk for schizophrenia. *Archives of General Psychiatry*, 1977, 34, 571–575.

5197. RYAN, J. J., & SOUHEAVER, G. T. Further evidence that concerns the validity of an MMPI key for separation of brain–damaged and schizophrenic patients. *Journal of Clinical Psychology*, 1977, 33, 753–754.

5198. RYCHLAK, J. F., & INGWELL, R. H. Causal orientation and personal adjustment of hospitalized veterans. *Journal of Personality Assessment*, 1977, 41, 299–303.

5199. SAPPINGTON, A. A. Direct manipulation of physiological arousal in induced anxiety therapy–biofeedback approach. *Journal of Clinical Psychology*, 1977, 33, 1070–1075.

5200. SAPPINGTON, J. Reactive schizophrenia and perceptual sensitization. *Perceptual & Motor Skills*, 1977, 45, 807–810.

5201. SHARMA, S. Sex differences in self-reported anxiousness for different situations and modes of response among university students in India. *Psychologia*, 1977, 21, 155–160.

5202. SHWEDER, R. A. Illusory correlation and the MMPI controversy. *Journal of Consulting & Clinical Psychology*, 1977, 45, 917–924.

5203. SINES, J. O. M–F: Bipolar and probably multidimensional. *Journal of Clinical Psychology*, 1977, 33, 1038–1041.

5204. SPELLACY, F. Neuropsychological differences between violent and nonviolent adolescents. *Journal of Clinical Psychology*, 1977, 33, 966–969.

5205. STRASSBERG, D. S., & KANGAS, J. MMPI correlates of self-disclosure. *Journal of Clinical Psychology*, 1977, 33, 739–740.

5206. STREINER, D. L., GOODMAN, J. T., & MCLEAN, A. Correspondence between the MMPI and the Midi–Mult. *Psychological Reports*, 1977, 40, 551–554.

5207. SUMMERS, F., & WALSH, F. The nature of the symbiotic bond between mother and schizophrenic. *American Journal of Orthopsychiatry*, 1977, 47, 484–494.

5208. TARTER, R. E., & BUONPHANE, N. Differentiation of alcoholics. *Archives of General Psychiatry*, 1977, 34, 761–768.

5209. TAYLOR, J. B. Item homogeneity, scale reliability, and the self concept hypothesis. *Educational & Psychological Measurement*, 1977, 37, 349–361.

5210. THORNTON, C. C., GOTTHEIL, E., GELLENS, H. K., & ALTERMAN, A. I. Voluntary versus involuntary abstinence in the treatment of alcoholics. *Journal of Studies on Alcohol*, 1977, 38, 1740–1748.

5211. THORSTEINSSON, G., STONNINGTON, H. H., STILWELL, G. K., & ELVEBACK, L. R. Transcutaneous electrical stimulation: A double blind trial of its efficacy for pain. *Archives of Physical Medicine & Rehabilitation*, 1977, 58, 8–13.

5212. TSOI, W. F., KOK, L. P., & LONG, F. Y. Male transsexualism in Singapore: A description of 56 cases. *British Journal of Psychiatry*, 1977, 131, 405–409.

5213. VERINIS, J. S., & ESPINDOLA, E. Therapeutic effects of psychological testing. *Psychological Reports*, 1977, 41, 527–530.

5214. WALLS, R., MCGLYNN, F. D., & TINGSTROM, D. H., III. An evaluation of three short forms extracted from the group form MMPI responses of incarcerated offenders. *Journal of Clinical Psychology*, 1977, 33, 431–435.

5215. WALLS, R. T., TSENG, M. S., & ELLIS, W. D. Time and money for vocational rehabilitation of clients with psychotic and psychoneurotic disabilities. *Journal of Occupational Psychology*, 1977, 50, 37–44.

5216. WATSON, C. G., & JACOBS, L. Evidence for a dual-factor concept of psychopathological emotional deficit: Anhedonia and sensation-seeking. *Journal of Clinical Psychology*, 1977, 33, 385–389.

5217. WATSON, C. G., & SCHULD, D. Psychosomatic factors in the etiology of neoplasms. *Journal of Consulting & Clinical Psychology*, 1977, 45, 455–461.

5218. WEINBERGER, D. R., & KELLY, M. J. Catatonia and malignant syndrome: A possible complication of neuroleptic administration: Report of a case involving haloperidol. *Journal of Nervous & Mental Disease*, 1977, 165, 263–268.

5219. WIENS, A. N., & MATARAZZO, J. D. WAIS and MMPI correlates of the Halstead–Reitan Neuropsychology Battery in normal male subjects. *Journal of Nervous & Mental Disease*, 1977, 164, 112–121.

5220. WEISS, R. W., & RUSSAKOFF, S. Relationship of MMPI scores of drug-abusers to personal variables and type of treatment program. *Journal of Psychology*, 1977, 96, 25–29.

5221. WIDOM, C. S. A methodology for studying noninstitutionalized psychopaths. *Journal of Consulting & Clinical Psychology*, 1977, 45, 674–683.

5222. WILCOX, P., & DAWSON, J. G. Role-played and hypnotically induced simulation of psychopathology on the MMPI. *Journal of Clinical Psychology*, 1977, 33, 743–745.

5223. WILSON, A. S., MABRY, E. A., & KHAVARI, K. A. Use of MMPI profiles for occupational classification of alcoholics. *Journal of Studies on Alcohol*, 1977, 38, 471–476.

5224. WILSON, A. S., MABRY, E. A., KHAVARI, K. A., & DALPES, D. Discriminant analysis of MMPI profiles for demographic classifications of male alcoholics. *Journal of Studies on Alcohol*, 1977, 38, 47–57.

5225. WINSTEAD, D. K., PARKER, M., & WILLI, F. J. P. Propoxyphene on demand. *Archives of General Psychiatry*, 1977, 34, 1463–1468.

5226. ZHEUTLIN, S., & GOLDSTEIN, S. G. The prediction of psychosocial adjustment subsequent to cardiac insult. *Journal of Clinical Psychology*, 1977, 33, 706–710.

5227. ZIARNIK, J. P., FREEMAN, C. W., SHERRARD, D. J., & CALSYN, D. A. Psychological correlates of survival on renal dialysis. *Journal of Nervous & Mental Disease*, 1977, 164, 210–213.

5228. ALTERMAN, A. I., DRULEY, K. A., CONNOLLY, R., & BUSH, D. A comparison of moral reasoning in drug addicts and nonaddicts. *Journal of Clinical Psychology*, 1978, 34, 790–794.

5229. APFELDORF, M. Alcoholism scales of the MMPI. Contributions and future directions. *International Journal of the Addictions*, 1978, 13, 17–53.

5230. ARCHER, R. P., SUTKER, P. B., WHITE, J. L., & ORVIN, G. H. Personality relationships among parents and adolescent offspring in inpatient treatment. *Psychological Reports*, 1978, 42, 207–214.

5231. ARMENTROUT, J. A., & HAVER, A. L. MMPI's of rapists of adults, rapists of children, and non–rapist sex offenders. *Journal of Clinical Psychology*, 1978, 34, 330–332.

5232. BARKER, B. M., & BARKER, H. R. Norms for MMPI factor scales. *Journal of Clinical Psychology*, 1978, 34, 429–430.

5233. BLOOM, L. J., SHELTON, J. L., & MICHAELS, A. C. Dysmenorrhea and personality. *Journal of Personality Assessment*, 1978, 42, 272–276.

5234. BROWN, J. B., & DUNBAR, P. W. MMPI differences between fee-paying and non-fee-paying psychotherapy clients. *Journal of Clinical Psychology*, 1978, 34, 953–954.

5235. BUCK, J. A., & GRAHAM, J. R. The 4–3 MMPI profile type: A failure to replicate. *Journal of Consulting & Clinical Psychology*, 1978, 46, 344.

5236. BURKHART, B. R., CHRISTIAN, W. L., & GYNTHER, M. D. Item subtlety and faking on the MMPI: A paradoxical relationship. *Journal of Personality Assessment*, 1978, 42, 76–80.

5237. BURKHART, B. R., GYNTHER, M. D., & CHRISTIAN, W. L. Psychological mindedness, intelligence, and item subtlety endorsement patterns on the MMPI. *Journal of Clinical Psychology*, 1978, 34, 76–79.

5238. BUTCHER, J. N., & TELLEGEN, A. Common methodological problems in MMPI research. *Journal of Consulting & Clinical Psychology*, 1978, 46, 620–628.

5239. CARLIN, A. S., DETZER, E., & STAUSS, F. F. Psychopathology and nonmedical drug use: A comparison of patient and nonpatient drug users. *International Journal of the Addictions*, 1978, 13, 337–348.

5240. CARLSON, R. W. MMPI content and repression–sensitization scales. *Psychological Reports*, 1978, 43, 1115–1119.

5241. CHRISTIAN, W. L., BURKHART, B. R., & GYNTHER, M. D. Subtle–obvious ratings of MMPI items: New interest in an old concept. *Journal of Consulting & Clinical Psychology*, 1978, 46, 1178–1186.

5242. CLOPTON, J. R. Alcoholism and the MMPI: A review. *Journal of Studies on Alcohol*, 1978, 39, 1540–1558.

5243. CLOPTON, J. R. MMPI scale development methodology. *Journal of Personality Assessment*, 1978, 42, 148–151.

5244. CLOPTON, J. R., & KLEIN, G. L. An initial look at the redundancy of specialized MMPI scales. *Journal of Consulting & Clinical Psychology*, 1978, 46, 1436–1438.

5245. COX, W. M. Spelling accuracy as a function of repression-sensitization. *British Journal of Educational Psychology*, 1978, 48, 84–85.

5246. DAVIS, D. A., & WIDSETH, J. C. A Minnesota Multiphasic Personality Inventory indicator of psychological distress in male students. *Journal of Counseling Psychology*, 1978, 25, 469–472.

5247. DIRKS, J. F., KINSMAN, R. A., JONES, N. F., & FROSS, K. H. New developments in panic-fear research in asthma: Validity and stability of the MMPI panic-fear scale. *British Journal of Medical Psychology*, 1978, 51, 119–126.

5248. DODRILL, C. B. A neuropsychological battery for epilepsy. *Epilepsia*, 1978, 19, 611–623.

5249. DONNELLY, E. F., GOODWIN, F. K., WALDMAN, I. N., & MURPHY, D. L. Prediction of anti–depressant responses to lithium. *American Journal of Psychiatry*, 1978, 135, 552–556.

5250. DONOVAN, D. M., CHANEY, E. F., & O'LEARY, M. R. Relationship to drinking styles, benefits, and consequences. *Journal of Nervous & Mental Disease*, 1978, 166, 553–561.

5251. EDINGER, J. D., & AUERBACH, S. M. Development and validation of a multidimensional multivariate model for accounting for infractions in a correctional setting. *Journal of Personality & Social Psychology*, 1978, 36, 1472–1489.

5252. ERRICKSON, E., DARNELL, M. H., & LABECK, L. Brief treatment of hallucinatory behavior with behavioral techniques. *Behavior Therapy*, 1978, 9, 663–665.

5253. ESHBAUGH, D. M., TOSI, D. J., & HOYT, C. Some personality patterns and dimensions of male alcoholics: A multivariate description. *Journal of Personality Assessment*, 1978, 42, 409–417.

5254. EXNER, J. E., JR., ARMBRUSTER, G., & MITTMAN, B. The Rorschach response process. *Journal of Personality Assessment*, 1978, 42, 27–38.

5255. FASCHINGBAUER, T. R., JOHNSON, D. T., & NEWMARK, C. S. The interpretative validity of the FAM: Long term psychotherapists' ratings of psychiatric inpatients. *Journal of Personality Assessment*, 1978, 42, 74–75.

5256. FENTON, G. W., FENWICK, P. B. C., FERGUSON, W., & LAM, C. T. The contingent negative variation in antisocial behavior: A pilot study of Broadmoor patients. *British Journal of Psychiatry*, 1978, 132, 368–377.

5257. FIX, J. A., DAUGHTON, D., KASS, I., PATIL, K. D., KASS, M., & POLENZ, D. Personality traits affecting vocational rehabilitation success in patients with chronic obstructive pulmonary disease. *Psychological Reports,* 1978, 43, 939–944.

5258. FRIEDRICH, W. N., & LOFTSGARD, S. O. A comparison of the MacAndrew Alcoholism Scale and the Michigan Alcoholism Screening Test in a sample of problem drinkers. *Journal of Studies on Alcohol,* 1978, 39, 1940–1944.

5259. GAINES, T., & MORRIS, R. Relationships between MMPI measures of psychopathology and WAIS subtest scores and intelligence quotients. *Perceptual & Motor Skills,* 1978, 47, 399–402.

5260. GARETT, K., & WULF, K. The relationship of a measure of critical thinking ability to personality variables and to indicators of academic achievement. *Educational & Psychological Measurement,* 1978, 38, 1181–1187.

5261. GASPARRINI, W. G., SATZ, P., HEILMAN, K. M., & COOLIDGE, F. L. Hemispheric asymmetries of affective processing as determined by the Minnesota Multiphasic Personality Inventory. *Journal of Neurology, Neurosurgery & Psychiatry,* 1978, 41, 470–473.

5262. GAYTON, W. F., BASSETT, J. E., TAVORMINA, J., & OZMON, K. L. Repression–sensitization and health behavior. *Journal of Consulting & Clinical Psychology,* 1978, 46, 1542–1544.

5263. GERBER, G. L. Coping effectiveness and dreams as a function of personality and dream recall. *Journal of Clinical Psychology,* 1978, 34, 526–532.

5264. GIANNETTI, R. A., JOHNSON, J. H., KLINGLER, D. E., & WILLIAMS, T. A. Comparison of linear and configural MMPI diagnostic methods with an uncontaminated criterion. *Journal of Consulting & Clinical Psychology,* 1978, 46, 1046–1052.

5265. GISPERT, M., & FALK, R. Adolescent sexual activity: Contraception and abortion. *American Journal of Obstetrics & Gynecology,* 1978, 132, 620–628.

5266. GOLDBERG, L. R. The reliability of reliability: The generality and correlates of intra–individual consistency in responses to structured personality inventories. *Applied Psychological Measurement,* 1978, 2, 269–291.

5267. GOMES–SCHWARTZ, B. Effective ingredients in psychotherapy: Prediction of outcome from process variables. *Journal of Consulting & Clinical Psychology,* 1978, 46, 1023–1035.

5268. GRANT, I., ADAMS, K. M., CARLIN, A. S., RENNICK, P. M., JUDD, L. L., SCHOOFF, K., & REED, R. Organic impairment in polydrug users: Risk factors. *American Journal of Psychiatry,* 1978, 135, 178–184.

5269. GREEN, L. Temporal and stimulus factors in self-monitoring by obese persons. *Behavior Therapy,* 1978, 9, 328–341.

5270. GREENE, R. L. An empirically derived MMPI carelessness scale. *Journal of Clinical Psychology,* 1978, 34, 407–410.

5271. GREENOUGH, T. J., KEEGAN, D. L., & ASH, D. G. Psychological and social adjustment of blind subjects and the 16PF. *Journal of Clinical Psychology,* 1978, 34, 84–87.

5272. GRIFFITHS, R. D. P., & GILLINGHAM, P. The influence of videotape feedback on the self-assessment of psychiatric patients. *British Journal of Psychiatry,* 1978, 133, 156–161.

5273. GYNTHER, M. D., LACHAR, D., & DAHLSTROM, W. G. Are special norms for minorities needed? Development of an MMPI F scale for blacks. *Journal of Consulting & Clinical Psychology,* 1978, 46, 1403–1408.

5274. HAERTZEN, C. A., MARTIN, W. R., HEWETT, B. B., & SANDQUIST, V. Measurement of psychopathy as a state. *Journal of Psychology,* 1978, 100, 201–204.

5275. HAIER, R. J., ROSENTHAL, D., & WENDER, P. H. MMPI assessment of psychopathology in the adopted–away offspring of schizophrenics. *Archives of General Psychiatry,* 1978, 35, 171–175.

5276. HALMI, K. A., DEKIRMENJIAN, H., DAVIS, J. M., CASPAR, R., & GOLDBERG, S. Catecholamine metabolism in anorexia nervosa. *Archives of General Psychiatry,* 1978, 35, 458–460.

5277. HANBACK, J. W., & REVELLE, W. Arousal and perceptual sensitivity in hypochondriacs. *Journal of Abnormal Psychology,* 1978, 87, 523–530.

5278. HARPER, D. C. Personality characteristics of physically impaired adolescents. *Journal of Clinical Psychology,* 1978, 34, 97–103.

5279. HARPER, D. C., & RICHMAN, L. C. Personality profiles of physically impaired adolescents. *Journal of Clinical Psychology,* 1978, 34, 636–642.

5280. HASLAM, M. T. Separation experiences and other emotional traumata in childhood, and their relationship to subsequent adolescent breakdown. *International Journal of Social Psychiatry,* 1978, 24, 295–303.

5281. HASTINGS, A. C. The Oakland poltergeist. *Journal of the American Society of Psychical Research,* 1978, 72, 233–256.

5282. HEAPS, R. A. Relating physical and psychological fitness: A psychological point of view. *Journal of Sports Medicine & Physical Fitness,* 1978, 18, 399–408.

5283. HEATH, D. H. What meaning and effect does fatherhood have for the maturing of professional men? *Merrill–Palmer Quarterly,* 1978, 24, 265–278.

5284. HEATON, R. K., CHELUNE, G. J., & LEHMAN, R. A. W. Using neuropsychological and personality tests to assess the likelihood of patient employment. *Journal of Nervous & Mental Disease,* 1978, 166, 408–416.

5285. HEATON, R. K., SMITH, H. H., JR., LEHMAN, R. A. W., & VOGT, A. T. Prospects for faking believable deficits on neuropsychological testing. *Journal of Consulting & Clinical Psychology,* 1978, 46, 892–900.

5286. HOFFMAN, H., & WEHLER, R. Pre– and posttraining MMPI scores of women alcoholism counselors. *Journal of Studies on Alcohol,* 1978, 39, 1952–1955.

5287. HOLLAND, T. R. Dimensions, patterns, and personality correlates of drug abuse in an offender population. *Journal of Consulting & Clinical Psychology,* 1978, 46, 577–578.

5288. HOLLAND, T. R., & WATSON, C. G. Utilization of the Goldberg MMPI profile classification rules for the assessment of psychopathology in different clinical populations. *Journal of Clinical Psychology,* 1978, 34, 893–901.

5289. HOWELLS, K., & WRIGHT, E. The sexual attitudes of aggressive sexual offenders. *British Journal of Criminology,* 1978, 18, 170–174.

5290. HUESMANN, L. R., LEFKOWITZ, M. M., & ERON, L. D. Sum of MMPI scales F, 4, and 9 as a measure of aggression. *Journal of Consulting & Clinical Psychology,* 1978, 46, 1071–1078.

5291. IVNIK, R. J. Neuropsychological stability in multiple sclerosis. *Journal of Consulting & Clinical Psychology,* 1978, 46, 913–923.

5292. JOHNSON, J. H., WILLIAMS, T. A., & KLINGLER, D. E. An exploratory study of the interaction between personality and psychopathology. *Journal of Clinical Psychology,* 1978, 34, 371–379.

5293. JUSTICE, B., MCBEE, G. W., & ALLEN, R. H. Sex differences in psychological distress and social functioning. *Psychological Reports,* 1978, 43, 659–662.

5294. KELLEY, C., & KING, G. D. Behavioral correlates for within–normal–limit MMPI profiles with and without elevated K in students at a university mental health center. *Journal of Clinical Psychology,* 1978, 34, 695–699.

5295. KENDALL, P. C., EDINGER, J., & EBERLY, C. Taylor's MMPI correction factor for spinal cord injury: Empirical endorsement. *Journal of Consulting & Clinical Psychology,* 1978, 46, 370–371.

5296. KOH, S. D., & PETERSON, R. A. Encoding orientation and the remembering of schizophrenic young adults. *Journal of Abnormal Psychology,* 1978, 87, 303–313.

5297. KOKOSH, J. Two–point MMPI code types and academic achievement: Replication and reanalysis. *Psychological Reports,* 1978, 42, 623–626.

5298. KOULACK, D., DE KONINCK, J., & OCZKOWSKI, G. Field dependence and the effect of REM deprivation on thirst. *Perceptual & Motor Skills,* 1978, 46, 559–562.

5299. LACHAR, D., & ALEXANDER, R. S. Veridicality of self–report: Replicated correlates of the Wiggins MMPI content scales. *Journal of Consulting & Clinical Psychology,* 1978, 46, 1349–1356.

5300. LAPIERRE, Y. D., OYEWUMI, L. K., GHADIRIAN, A., & BUTTER, H. J. A placebo–controlled study of bromazepam and diazepam in anxiety neurosis. *Current Therapeutic Research,* 1978, 23, 475–484.

5301. LAYNE, C. Relationship between the "Barnum effect" and personality inventory responses. *Journal of Clinical Psychology,* 1978, 34, 94–97.

5302. LEFKOWITZ, M. M., HUESMANN, L. R., & ERON, L. D. Parental punishment. *Archives of General Psychiatry,* 1978, 35, 186–191.

5303. LEVITT, E. E. A note on MMPI scale development methodology. *Journal of Personality Assessment,* 1978, 42, 503–504.

5304. LEWINSOHN, P. M., & AMENSON, C. S. Some relations between pleasant and unpleasant mood–related events and depression. *Journal of Abnormal Psychology,* 1978, 87, 644–654.

5305. LEWIS, C. E., SCHER, M., & DIETZE, D. Reviewing results of psychological tests in a patient group. *Hospital & Community Psychiatry,* 1978, 29, 306–308.

5306. LOTHSTEIN, L. M., & JONES, P. Discriminating violent individuals by means of various psychological tests. *Journal of Personality Assessment,* 1978, 42, 237–243.

5307. LOUKS, J. L., FREEMAN, C. W., & CALSYN, D. A. Personality organization as an aspect of back pain in a medical setting. *Journal of Personality Assessment,* 1978, 42, 152–158.

5308. MACANDREW, C. Women alcoholics' responses to scale 4 of the MMPI. *Journal of Studies on Alcohol,* 1978, 39, 1841–1854.

5309. MARTIN, J. D., STOKES, E. H., & AYERS, J. L. A correlation of Barron's Ego Strength Scale and Rokeach's Dogmatism Scale. *Educational & Psychological Measurement,* 1978, 38, 583–586.

5310. MARTINDALE, C., ROSS, M., HINES, D., & ABRAMS, L. Independence of interaction and interpersonal attraction in a psychiatric hospital population. *Journal of Abnormal Psychology,* 1978, 87, 247–255.

5311. MCGURK, B. J. Personality types among "normal" homicides. *British Journal of Criminology,* 1978, 18, 146–161.

5312. MILLER, W. H., & KEIRN, W. C. Personality measurement in parents of retarded and emotionally disturbed children: A replication. *Journal of Clinical Psychology,* 1978, 34, 686–690.

5313. MILLER, W. R. Behavioral treatment of problem drinkers: A comparative outcome study of three controlled drinking therapies. *Journal of Consulting & Clinical Psychology*, 1978, 46, 74–86.

5314. MILLIGAN, W. L. Computer controlled oral test administration: A method and example. *Educational & Psychological Measurement*, 1978, 38, 823–828.

5315. MORAN, M., WATSON, C. G., BROWN, J., WHITE, C., & JACOBS, L. Systems releasing action therapy with alcoholics: An experimental evaluation. *Journal of Clinical Psychology*, 1978, 34, 769–774.

5316. MUNJACK, D. J., KANNO, P. H., & OZIEL, J. L. Ejaculatory disorders: Some psychometric data. *Psychological Reports*, 1978, 43, 783–787.

5317. MYERS, L. B., & LEVY, G. W. Description and prediction of the intractable inmate. *Journal of Research in Crime & Delinquency*, 1978, 15, 214–228.

5318. NASH, M. M. A Micro-Mult for screening psychiatric disturbance. *Psychological Reports*, 1978, 42, 985–986.

5319. NEWMAN, O. S., HEATON, R. K., & LEHMAN, A. W. Neuropsychological and MMPI correlates of patients' future employment characteristics. *Perceptual & Motor Skills*, 1978, 46, 635–642.

5320. NEWMARK, C. S., & FASCHINGBAUER, T. R. Bibliography of short forms of the MMPI. *Journal of Personality Assessment*, 1978, 42, 496–502.

5321. NEWMARK, C. S., GENTRY, L., SIMPSON, M., & JONES, T. MMPI criteria for diagnosing schizophrenia. *Journal of Personality Assessment*, 1978, 42, 366–373.

5322. NEWMARK, C. S., ZIFF, D. R., FINCH, A. J., JR., & KENDALL, P. C. Comparing the empirical validity of the standard form with two abbreviated MMPIs. *Journal of Consulting & Clinical Psychology*, 1978, 46, 53–61.

5323. NICHOLS, M. P., & BIERENBAUM, H. Success of cathartic therapy as a function of patient variables. *Journal of Clinical Psychology*, 1978, 34, 726–728.

5324. NORTON, J. C. The Trail Making Test and Bender Background Interference Procedure as screening devices. *Journal of Clinical Psychology*, 1978, 34, 916–922.

5325. O'LEARY, M. R., CHANEY, E. F., BROWN, L. S., & SCHUCKIT, M. A. The use of the Goldberg indices with alcoholics: A cautionary note. *Journal of Clinical Psychology*, 1978, 34, 988–990.

5326. OLSEN, E. J., BANK, L., & JARVIK, L. F. Gerovital-H_3: A clinical trial as an antidepressant. *Journal of Gerontology*, 1978, 33, 514–520.

5327. OLTMANNS, T. F. Selective attention in schizophrenic and manic psychoses: The effect of distraction on information processing. *Journal of Abnormal Psychology*, 1978, 87, 212–225.

5328. OMRAN, A. R., SHORE, R. E., MARKOFF, R. A., FRIEDHOFF, A., ALBERT, R. E., BARR, H., DAHLSTROM, G., & PASTERNACK, B. S. Follow-up study of patients treated by X-ray epilation for tinea capitis: Psychiatric evaluation. *American Journal of Public Health*, 1978, 68, 561–567.

5329. OSBORNE, D. MMPI changes between the first and third trimester of pregnancy. *Journal of Clinical Psychology*, 1978, 34, 92–93.

5330. OSBORNE, D., & SWENSON, W. M. Muscle tension and personality. *Journal of Clinical Psychology*, 1978, 34, 391–392.

5331. OTTOMANELLI, G., WILSON, P., & WHYTE, R. MMPI evaluation of 5-year methadone treatment status. *Journal of Consulting & Clinical Psychology*, 1978, 46, 579–581.

5332. PAGE, R. D., & SCHAUB, L. H. EMG biofeedback applicability for differing personality types. *Journal of Clinical Psychology*, 1978, 34, 1014–1020.

5333. PANTO, L. T., & SCHWARTZ, M. L. Differentiation of neurologic and pseudo-neurologic patients with combined MMPI Mini-Mult and pseudo-neurologic scale. *Journal of Clinical Psychology*, 1978, 34, 56–60.

5334. PATALANO, F. Personality dimensions of drug abusers who enter a drug-free therapeutic community. *Psychological Reports*, 1978, 42, 1063–1069.

5335. PENK, W. E., ROBINOWITZ, R., & FUDGE, J. W. Differences in interpersonal orientation of heroin, amphetamine, and barbiturate users. *British Journal of Addiction*, 1978, 73, 82–88.

5336. PENK, W. E., ROBINOWITZ, R., WOODWARD, W. A., & HESS, J. L. Differences in MMPI scores of black and white compulsive heroin users. *Journal of Abnormal Psychology*, 1978, 87, 505–513.

5337. PETERS, P. K., SWENSON, W. M., & MULDER, D. W. Is there a characteristic personality profile in amyotrophic lateral sclerosis? A Minnesota Multiphasic Personality Inventory study. *Archives of Neurology*, 1978, 35, 321–322.

5338. PETERSON, R., SUSHINSKY, L., & DEMASK, R. S. Are locus of control and depression related? *Psychological Reports*, 1978, 43, 727–731.

5339. PETZEL, T. P. Social desirability ratings of MMPI items as related to position of first person pronouns. *Psychological Reports*, 1978, 42, 1075–1078.

5340. POYTHRESS, N. G., & BLANEY, P. H. The validity of MMPI interpretations based on the Minimult and the FAM. *Journal of Personality Assessment*, 1978, 42, 143–147.

5341. QUEEN, L., & FREITAG, C. B. A comparison of externality, anxiety, and life satisfaction in two aged populations. *Journal of Psychology*, 1978, 98, 71–74.

5342. RAPPAPORT, E. The relation between trait anxiety and the Harris MMPI Pd subscales among psychiatric inpatients. *Journal of Clinical Psychology*, 1978, 34, 388–390.

5343. RASKIN, D. C., & HARE, R. D. Psychotherapy and detection of deception in a prison population. *Psychophysiology*, 1978, 15, 126–136.

5344. RATHUS, S. A. A factor structure of the MMPI-168 with and without regression weights. *Psychological Reports*, 1978, 42, 643–651.

5345. REDFERING, D. L., & JONES, J. G. Effects of defensiveness on the State–Trait Anxiety Inventory. *Psychological Reports*, 1978, 43, 83–89.

5346. RHODES, R. J. A further look at the Popoff index of depression. *Psychological Reports*, 1978, 42, 309–310.

5347. RHODES, R. J., & CHANG, A. F. A further look at the institutionalized chronic alcoholic scale. *Journal of Clinical Psychology*, 1978, 34, 779–780.

5348. RICHARDS, W. A. Mystical and archetypal experiences of terminal patients in DPT-assisted psychotherapy. *Journal of Religion & Health*, 1978, 17, 117–126.

5349. ROESSLER, R., LESTER, J. W., BUTLER, W. T., RANKIN, B., & COLLINS, F. Cognitive and noncognitive variables in the prediction of preclinical performance. *Journal of Medical Education*, 1978, 53, 678–680.

5350. ROSENBLATT, A. I., & PRITCHARD, D. A. Moderators of racial differences on the MMPI. *Journal of Consulting & Clinical Psychology*, 1978, 46, 1572–1573.

5351. RUSSELL, M., & SINES, J. O. Further evidence that M-F is bipolar and multidimensional. *Journal of Clinical Psychology*, 1978, 34, 643–649.

5352. RYHÄNEN, P., HELKALA, E., IHALAINEN, O., HOLLMÉN, A., RANTAKYLÄ, S., MERILÄ, M., TUOHINO, V., PIETARILA, M., & HORTTONEN, L. Effects of anesthesia on the psychological function of patients. *Annals of Clinical Research*, 1978, 10, 318–322.

5353. SACCO, W. P., & HOKANSON, J. E. Expectations of success and anagram performance of depressives in a public and private setting. *Journal of Abnormal Psychology*, 1978, 87, 122–130.

5354. SACCO, W. P., & HOKANSON, J. E. Performance satisfaction of depressives under high and low success conditions. *Journal of Clinical Psychology*, 1978, 34, 907–909.

5355. SAPSFORD, R. J. Life-sentence prisoners: Psychological changes during sentence. *British Journal of Criminology*, 1978, 18, 128–145.

5356. SCHNEIDER, S., & RICE, D. R. Neurologic manifestations of childhood hysteria. *Journal of Pediatrics*, 1978, 94, 153–156.

5357. SCHUCK, J., LEVENTHAL, D., & CARBONELL, J. A test of the schizophrenic's ability to process information in one or two sensory modes. *British Journal of Social & Clinical Psychology*, 1978, 17, 243–249.

5358. SHARP, L. F., & CHASON, L. R. The use of moderator variables in predicting college student attrition. *Journal of College Student Personnel*, 1978, 19, 388–393.

5359. SHEALY, A. E. Comparison of two non-intellectual scales of intelligence and their relationship to intellectual changes following surgery. *Psychological Reports*, 1978, 42, 51–56.

5360. SHEALY, A. E., & WALKER, D. R. Minnesota Multiphasic Personality Inventory prediction of intellectual changes following cardiac surgery. *Journal of Nervous & Mental Disease*, 1978, 166, 263–267.

5361. SHEARD, M. H., & MARINI, J. L. Treatment of human aggressive behavior: Four case studies of the effect of lithium. *Comprehensive Psychiatry*, 1978, 19, 37–45.

5362. SHEPHARD, R. J., & KAVANAGH, T. Patient reactions to a regular conditioning programme following myocardial infarction. *Journal of Sports Medicine & Physical Fitness*, 1978, 18, 371–378.

5363. SIBERSCHATZ, G. Selective attention and changes in clinical state. *Journal of Research in Personality*, 1978, 12, 197–204.

5364. SIMONO, R. B. Careers in the clergy: The myth of feminity. *Educational & Psychological Measurement*, 1978, 38, 507–511.

5365. SKINNER, H. A. Differentiating the contribution of elevation, scatter, and shape in profile similarity. *Educational & Psychological Measurement*, 1978, 38, 297–308.

5366. SKINNER, H. A., & JACKSON, D. N. A model of psychopathology based on an integration of MMPI actuarial systems. *Journal of Consulting & Clinical Psychology*, 1978, 46, 231–238.

5367. SMITH, R. J., & GRIFFITH, J. E. Psychopathy, the Machiavellian, and anomie. *Psychological Reports*, 1978, 42, 258.

5368. SPAULING, W. The relationship of some information-processing factors to severely disturbed behavior. *Journal of Nervous & Mental Disease*, 1978, 166, 417–428.

5369. SPELLACY, F. Neuropsychological discrimination between violent and non-violent men. *Journal of Clinical Psychology*, 1978, 34, 49–52.

5370. STAUDENMAYER, H., KINSMAN, R. A., & JONES, N. F. Attitudes toward respiratory illness and hospitalization in asthma. Relationships with personality, symptomatology, and treatment response. *Journal of Nervous & Mental Disease*, 1978, 166, 624–634.

5371. STEIN, M. K., DOWNING, R. W., & RICKELS, K. Self–estimates in anxious and depressed outpatients treated with pharmacotherapy. *Psychological Reports*, 1978, 43, 487–492.

5372. STERONKO, R. J., & WOODS, D. J. Impairment in early stages of visual information processing in non–psychotic schizotypic individuals. *Journal of Abnormal Psychology*, 1978, 87, 481–490.

5373. SUAREZ, Y., CROWE, M. J., & ADAMS, H. E. Depression: Avoidance learning and physiological correlates in clinical and analog populations. *Behaviour Research & Therapy*, 1978, 16, 21–31.

5374. SUTKER, P. B., ALLAIN, A. N., & GEYER, S. Female criminal violence and differential MMPI characteristics. *Journal of Consulting & Clinical Psychology*, 1978, 46, 1141–1143.

5375. SUTKER, P. B., ARCHER, R. P., & ALLAIN, A. N. Drug abuse patterns, personality characteristics, and relationships with sex, race and sensation seeking. *Journal of Consulting & Clinical Psychology*, 1978, 46, 1374–1378.

5376. TALBOTT, J. A., & GILLEN, C. Differences between nonprofessional recovering alcoholic counselors treating bowery alcoholics: A study of therapist variables. *Psychiatric Quarterly*, 1978, 50, 333–342.

5377. TAMEZ, E. G., MOORE, M. J., & BROWN, P. L. Relaxation training as a nursing intervention versus pro re nata medication. *Nursing Research*, 1978, 27, 160–165.

5378. TARR, L. H. Developmental sex–role theory and sex–role attitudes in late adolescents. *Psychological Reports*, 1978, 42, 807–814.

5379. TEMPLER, D. I., RUFF, C. F., BARTHLOW, V. L., HALCOMB, P. H., & AYERS, J. L. Psychometric assessment of alcoholism in convicted felons. *Journal of Studies on Alcohol*, 1978, 39, 1948–1951.

5380. TODD, P. B., & MARGAREY, C. J. Ego defenses and affects in women with breast symptoms: A preliminary measurement paradigm. *British Journal of Medical Psychology*, 1978, 51, 177–189.

5381. TOWNE, W. S., & TSUSHIMA, W. T. The use of the low back and the dorsal scales in the identification of functional low back patients. *Journal of Clinical Psychology*, 1978, 34, 88–91.

5382. TREVITHICK, L., & HOSCH, H. M. MMPI correlates of drug addiction based on drug of choice. *Journal of Consulting & Clinical Psychology*, 1978, 46, 180.

5383. TSUJIMOTO, R. N., & NARDI, P. M. A comparison of Kohlberg's and Hogan's theories of moral development. *Social Psychology Quarterly*, 1978, 41, 235–245.

5384. TUMA, A. H., MAY, P. R. A., YALE, C., & FORSYTHE, A. B. Therapist characteristics and the outcome of treatment in schizophrenia. *Archives of General Psychiatry*, 1978, 35, 81–85.

5385. TUMA, A. H., MAY, P. R. A., YALE, C., & FORSYTHE, A. B. Therapist experience, general clinical ability, and treatment outcome in schizophrenia. *Journal of Consulting & Clinical Psychology*, 1978, 46, 1120–1126.

5386. TURNER, J., & MCCREARY, C. Short forms of the MMPI with back pain patients. *Journal of Consulting & Clinical Psychology*, 1978, 46, 354–355.

5387. VAN KAMMEN, D. P., & MURPHY, D. L. Prediction of imipramine antidepressant response by a one–day d–amphetamine trial. *American Journal of Psychiatry*, 1978, 135, 1179–1184.

5388. VESTRE, N. D., GREENE, R. L., & MARKS, M. W. Psychological adjustment of persons seeking sensitivity group experiences. *Psychological Reports*, 1978, 42, 1295–1298.

5389. VINCENT, K. R. Validity of the MMPI 168 on private clinic subpopulations. *Journal of Clinical Psychology*, 1978, 34, 61–62.

5390. WADE, T. C., BAKER, T. B., MORTON, T. L., & BAKER, L. J. The status of psychological testing in clinical psychology: Relationships between test use and professional activities and orientations. *Journal of Personality Assessment*, 1978, 42, 3–10.

5391. WAID, L. R., KANOY, R. C., III, BLICK, K. A., & WALKER, W. E. Relationship of state–trait anxiety and type of practice to reading comprehension. *Journal of Psychology*, 1978, 98, 27–36.

5392. WATSON, C. G., DAVIS, W. E., & GASSER, B. The separation of organics from depressives with ability– and personality–based tests. *Journal of Clinical Psychology*, 1978, 34, 393–397.

5393. WATSON, C. G., HERDER, J., & PASSINI, F. T. Alpha biofeedback therapy in alcoholics: An 18–month follow up. *Journal of Clinical Psychology*, 1978, 34, 765–769.

5394. WATSON, C. G., & PLEMEL, D. An MMPI scale to separate brain–damaged from functional psychiatric patients in neuropsychiatric settings. *Journal of Consulting & Clinical Psychology*, 1978, 46, 1127–1132.

5395. WATSON, C. G., PLEMEL, D., & JACOBS, L. An MMPI sign to separate organic from functional psychiatric patients. *Journal of Clinical Psychology*, 1978, 34, 398–401.

5396. WEIMER, S. R. Using fairy tales in psychotherapy. *Bulletin of the Menninger Clinic*, 1978, 42, 25–34.

5397. WEISS, R. W., & RUSSAKOFF, S. The sex role identity of male drug abusers. *Journal of Clinical Psychology*, 1978, 34, 1010–1013.

5398. WILSON, S., & KENNARD, D. The extraverting effect of treatment in a therapeutic community for drug abusers. *British Journal of Psychiatry*, 1978, 132, 296–299.

5399. ZIEGLER, R., KOHUTEK, K., & OWEN, P. A multimodal treatment approach for incarcerated alcoholics. *Journal of Clinical Psychology*, 1978, 34, 1005–1009.

5400. ZIESAT, H. A., JR. Are family patterns related to the development of chronic low back pain? *Perceptual & Motor Skills*, 1978, 46, 1062.

5401. ZIESAT, H. A., JR. Correlates of the tourniquet ischemia pain ratio. *Perceptual & Motor Skills*, 1978, 47, 147–150.

5402. ZIESAT, H. A., JR., & GENTRY, W. D. The Pain Apperception Test: An investigation of concurrent validity. *Journal of Clinical Psychology*, 1978, 34, 786–789.

5403. ZISOOK, S., ROGERS, P. J., FASCHINGBAUER, T. R., & DEVAUL, R. A. Absence of hostility in outpatients after administration of halazepam—A new benzodiazepine. *Journal of Clinical Psychiatry*, 1978, 39, 683–686.

5404. ADEBIMPE, V. R., GIGANDET, J., & HARRIS, E. MMPI diagnosis of black psychiatric patients. *American Journal of Psychiatry*, 1979, 136, 85–87.

5405. ALLEN, R. H., WEINMAN, M. L., LORIMER, R., CLAGHORN, J. L., MCBEE, G., & JUSTICE, B. The effects of response bias on sex differences in a psychiatric population. *Journal of Nervous & Mental Disease*, 1979, 167, 437–441.

5406. ANDERSON, W. P., & KUNCE, J. T. Sex offenders: Three personality types. *Journal of Clinical Psychology*, 1979, 35, 671–676.

5407. ANISKIEWICZ, A. S. Autonomic components of vicarious conditioning and psychopathy. *Journal of Clinical Psychology*, 1979, 35, 60–67.

5408. ARCHER, R. P., WHITE, J. L., & ORVIN, G. H. MMPI characteristics and correlates among adolescent psychiatric inpatients. *Journal of Clinical Psychology*, 1979, 35, 498–504.

5409. ARTWOHL, A. Correlation between Rotter's I-E scale and Barron's Ego Strength Scale. *Psychological Reports*, 1979, 45, 498.

5410. BAIRD, P. Relationships between certain MMPI factors and psychotherapeutic preferences. *Psychological Reports*, 1979, 44, 1317–1318.

5411. BALLOUN, K. D., & HOLMES, D. S. Effects of repeated examinations on the ability to detect guilt with a polygraphic examination: A laboratory experiment with a real crime. *Journal of Applied Psychology*, 1979, 64, 316–322.

5412. BARNES, G. E. The alcoholic personality: A reanalysis of the literature. *Journal of Studies on Alcohol*, 1979, 40, 571–634.

5413. BARRERA, M., JR. An evaluation of a brief group therapy for depression. *Journal of Clinical Psychology*, 1979, 47, 413–415.

5414. BAUCOM, D. H., & GREENE, R. L. The universality of generalized personality statements. *Journal of Personality Assessment*, 1979, 43, 497–500.

5415. BILLINGS, A. Conflict resolution in distressed and nondistressed married couples. *Journal of Consulting & Clinical Psychology*, 1979, 47, 368–376.

5416. BIRTCHNELL, J. Early parent death and the clinical scales of the MMPI. *British Journal of Psychiatry*, 1979, 132, 574–579.

5417. BISHOP, E. R., & TORCH, E. M. Dividing "hysteria": A preliminary investigation of conversion disorder and psychalgia. *Journal of Nervous & Mental Disease*, 1979, 167, 348–356.

5418. BLACKBURN, R. Psychopathy and personality: The dimensionality of self–report and behavior rating data in abnormal offenders. *British Journal of Social & Clinical Psychology*, 1979, 18, 111–119.

5419. BLAZER, D. G., II, & HOUPT, J. L. Perception of poor health in the healthy older adult. *Journal of the American Geriatrics Society*, 1979, 27, 330–334.

5420. BLOCKBURN, R. Cortical and autonomic arousal in primary and secondary psychopaths. *Psychophysiology*, 1979, 16, 143–150.

5421. BLUE, L. A., & BLUE, F. R. Effects of biofeedback on muscular tension in selected personality states. *Journal of Psychology*, 1979, 101, 11–14.

5422. BOHN, M. J., JR. Classification of offenders in an institution for young adults. *FCI Research Reports*, 1979, 10, 1–27.

5423. BOLTON, B. The relationship between two personality questionnaires: The Mini–Mult and the 16PF–E. *Journal of Personality Assessment*, 1979, 43, 289–292.

5424. BURKE, H. R. Renal patients and their MMPI profiles. *Journal of Psychology*, 1979, 101, 229–236.

5425. CARSON, C. C., III, OSBORNE, D., & SEGURA, J. W. Psychological characteristics of patients with female urethral syndrome. *Journal of Clinical Psychology*, 1979, 35, 312–313.

5426. CLAYTON, M. R., & GRAHAM, J. R. Predictive validity of Barron's Es scale: The role of symptom acknowledgment. *Journal of Consulting & Clinical Psychology*, 1979, 47, 424–425.

5427. CLOPTON, J. R., & BAUCOM, D. H. MMPI ratings of suicide risk. *Journal of Personality Assessment*, 1979, 43, 293–296.

5428. CLOPTON, J. R., PALLIS, D. J., & BIRTCHNELL, J. Minnesota Multiphasic Personality Inventory profile patterns of suicide attempters. *Journal of Consulting & Clinical Psychology*, 1979, 47, 135–139.

5429. COLLINS, H. A. Profiles of addicts. *Psychological Reports*, 1979, 44, 603–608.

5430. DAVIS, W. E., PURSELL, S. A., & BURNHAM, R. A. Alcoholism, sex–role orientation and psychological distress. *Journal of Clinical Psychology*, 1979, 35, 209–212.

5431. DAWLEY, H. H., JR., & WINSTEAD, D. K. An attitude survey of the effects of marijuana on sexual enjoyment. *Journal of Clinical Psychology*, 1979, 35, 212–217.

5432. DIETVORST, T. F., SWENSON, W. M., NIVEN, R. G., & MORSE, R. M. Analysis of the MMPI profiles of physicians in treatment for drug dependency. *Journal of Studies on Alcohol*, 1979, 40, 1023–1029.

5433. DIRKS, J. F., KINSMAN, R. A., STAUDENMAYER, H., & KLEIGER, J. H. Panic–fear in asthma. Symptomatology as an index of signal anxiety and personality as an index of ego resources. *Journal of Nervous & Mental Disease*, 1979, 167, 615–619.

5434. DIRKS, J. F., PALEY, A., & FRUSS, K. H. Panic-fear research in asthma and the nuclear conflict theory of asthma: Similarities, differences and clinical implications. *British Journal of Medical Psychology*, 1979, 52, 71–76.

5435. DOUGLASS, F. M., IV, KHAVARI, K. A., & FARBER, P. D. A comparison of classical and latent trait item analysis procedures. *Educational & Psychological Measurement*, 1979, 39, 337–352.

5436. EDINGER, J. D. Cross–validation of the Megargee MMPI typology for prisoners. *Journal of Consulting & Clinical Psychology*, 1979, 47, 234–242.

5437. EDINGER, J. D., NELSON, W. M., III, BAILEY, K. G., WALLACE, J., & LYMAN, R. The utility of Wechsler Adult Intelligence Scale profile analysis with prisoners. *Journal of Clinical Psychology*, 1979, 35, 807–814.

5438. ELENEWSKI, J. J., & CARRERA, R. N. Levels of adjustment, depression and attitudes toward death among good and poor sleepers. *Journal of Clinical Psychology*, 1979, 35, 493–497.

5439. FRANKS, D. D., & THACKER, B. T. Assessing familial factors in alcoholism from MMPI profiles. *American Journal of Psychiatry*, 1979, 136, 1084–1085.

5440. GENDREAU, P., GRANT, B. A., LEIPCIGER, M., & COLLINS, S. Norms and recidivism rates for the MMPI and selected experimental scales on a Canadian delinquent sample. *Canadian Journal of Behavioural Science*, 1979, 11, 21–31.

5441. GOLDEN, C. J., SWEET, J. J., & OSMON, D. C. The diagnosis of brain–damage by the MMPI: A comprehensive evaluation. *Journal of Personality Assessment*, 1979, 43, 138–142.

5442. GOLDEN, R. R., & MEEHL, P. E. Detection of the schizoid taxon with MMPI indicators. *Journal of Abnormal Psychology*, 1979, 88, 217–233.

5443. GOLDSMITH, L. A. Adaptive regression, humor, and suicide. *Journal of Consulting & Clinical Psychology*, 1979, 47, 628–630.

5444. GORDON, N. G., & BRACKNEY, B. E. Defense mechanism preference and dimensions of psychopathology. *Psychological Reports*, 1979, 44, 188–190.

5445. GOTTHEIL, E., EXLINE, R. V., & WINKELMAYER, R. Judging emotions of normal and schizophrenic subjects. *American Journal of Psychiatry*, 1979, 136, 1049–1054.

5446. GRANT, I., ADAMS, K., & REED, R. Normal neuropsychological abilities of alcoholic men in their late thirties. *American Journal of Psychiatry*, 1979, 136, 1263–1269.

5447. GREENE, R. L. Response consistency on the MMPI: The TR index. *Journal of Personality Assessment*, 1979, 43, 69–71.

5448. GYNTHER, M. D., BURKHART, B. R., & HOVANITZ, C. Do face-valid items have more predictive validity than subtle items? The case of the MMPI Pd scale. *Journal of Consulting & Clinical Psychology*, 1979, 47, 295–300.

5449. HAIER, R. J., RIEDER, R. O., KHOURI, P. J., & BUCHSBAUM, M. S. Extreme MMPI scores and the research diagnostic criteria. *Archives of General Psychiatry*, 1979, 36, 528–534.

5450. HARTLAGE, L. C., & TOLLISON, C. D. MMPI correlates of looking left or right during mental tasks. *Journal of Clinical Psychology*, 1979, 35, 92–94.

5451. HARTMANN, E., & SPINWEBER, C. L. Sleep induced by L-tryptophan. Effects of dosages within the normal dietary intake. *Journal of Nervous & Mental Disease*, 1979, 167, 497–499.

5452. HEATON, R. K., VOGT, A. T., HOEHN, M. M., LEWIS, J. A., CROWLEY, T. J., & STALLINGS, M. A. Neuropsychological impairment with schizophrenia vs. acute and chronic cerebral lesions. *Journal of Clinical Psychology*, 1979, 35, 46–53.

5453. HEILBRUN, A. B., JR. Psychopathy and violent crime. *Journal of Consulting & Clinical Psychology*, 1979, 47, 509–516.

5454. HIBBS, B. J., KOBOS, J. C., & GONZALEZ, J. Effects of ethnicity, sex, and age on MMPI profiles. *Psychological Reports*, 1979, 45, 591–597.

5455. HOLLAND, T. R. Ethnic group differences in MMPI profile pattern and factorial structure among adult offenders. *Journal of Personality Assessment*, 1979, 43, 72–77.

5456. IMPERIO, A. M., CULLINAN, T. F., & RIKLAN, M. MMPI characteristics associated with cerebral palsy and dystonia musculorum deformans. *Perceptual & Motor Skills*, 1979, 48, 1003–1007.

5457. JONES, I. H., & FREI, D. Exhibitionism–A biological hypothesis. *British Journal of Medical Psychology*, 1979, 52, 63–70.

5458. KEEGAN, J. F., & LACHAR, D. The MMPI as a predictor of early termination from polydrug abuse treatment. *Journal of Personality Assessment*, 1979, 43, 379–384.

5459. KEELER, M. H., TAYLOR, C. I., & MILLER, W. C. Are all recently detoxified alcoholics depressed? *American Journal of Psychiatry*, 1979, 136, 586–588.

5460. KELLEY, C. K., & KING, G. D. Behavioral correlates of infrequent two–point MMPI code types at a university mental health center. *Journal of Clinical Psychology*, 1979, 35, 576–585.

5461. KELLEY, C. K., & KING, G. D. Behavioral correlates of the 2–7–8 MMPI profile type in students at a university mental health center. *Journal of Consulting & Clinical Psychology*, 1979, 47, 679–685.

5462. KELLEY, C. K., & KING, G. D. Cross validation of the 2–8/8–2 MMPI code type for young adult psychiatric outpatients. *Journal of Personality Assessment*, 1979, 43, 143–149.

5463. KENNARD, D., & WILSON, S. The modification of personality disturbance in a therapeutic community for drug abusers. *British Journal of Medical Psychology*, 1979, 52, 215–221.

5464. KLEIN, J. Submission and independence in learning security. *Psychological Reports*, 1979, 44, 943–948.

5465. KRAUTHAMER, C. The personality of alcoholic middle–class women: A comparative study with the MMPI. *Journal of Clinical Psychology*, 1979, 35, 442–448.

5466. KUPERMAN, S. K., GOLDEN, C. J., & BLUME, H. G. Predicting pain treatment results by personality variables in organic and functional patients. *Journal of Clinical Psychology*, 1979, 35, 832–837.

5467. KUPERMAN, S. K., GOLDEN, C. J., OSMON, D., & BLUME, H. G. Prediction of neurosurgical results by psychological evaluation. *Perceptual & Motor Skills*, 1979, 48, 311–315.

5468. LACHAR, D., BERMAN, W., GRISELL, J. L., & SCHOOFF, K. A heroin addiction scale for the MMPI: Effectiveness in differential diagnosis in a psychiatric setting. *International Journal of the Addictions*, 1979, 14, 135–142.

5469. LACHAR, D., GDOWSKI, C. L., & KEEGAN, J. F. MMPI profiles of men alcoholics, drug addicts and psychiatric patients. *Journal of Studies on Alcohol*, 1979, 40, 45–56.

5470. LACHAR, D., LEWIS, R., & KUPKE, T. MMPI in differentiation of temporal lobe and nontemporal lobe epilepsy: Investigation of three levels of test performance. *Journal of Consulting & Clinical Psychology*, 1979, 47, 186–188.

5471. LACHAR, D., & WROBEL, T. A. Validating clinicians' hunches: Construction of a new MMPI critical item set. *Journal of Consulting & Clinical Psychology*, 1979, 47, 277–284.

5472. LANE, J. B., & LACHAR, D. Correlates of broad MMPI categories. *Journal of Clinical Psychology*, 1979, 35, 560–566.

5473. LANE, P. J., & KLING, J. S. Construct validation of the overcontrolled hostility scale of the MMPI. *Journal of Consulting & Clinical Psychology*, 1979, 47, 781–782.

5474. LA TORRE, R. A., & PIPER, W. E. Gender identity and gender role in schizophrenia. *Journal of Abnormal Psychology*, 1979, 88, 68–72.

5475. LEGGETT, J., & ARCHER, R. P. Locus of control and depression among psychiatric inpatients. *Psychological Reports*, 1979, 45, 835–838.

5476. LEON, G. R., GILLUM, B., GILLUM, R., & GOUZE, M. Personality stability and change over a 30-year period—Middle age to old age. *Journal of Consulting & Clinical Psychology*, 1979, 47, 517–524.

5477. LESTER, D., & CLOPTON, J. R. Suicide and overcontrol. *Psychological Reports*, 1979, 44, 758.

5478. LEWINSOHN, P. M., & TALKINGTON, J. Studies on the measurement of unpleasant events and relations with depression. *Applied Psychological Measurement*, 1979, 3, 83–101.

5479. LOBITZ, W. C., & POST, R. D. Parameters of self–reinforcement and depression. *Journal of Abnormal Psychology*, 1979, 88, 33–41.

5480. MACANDREW, C. MAC scale scores of three samples of men under conditions of conventional versus independent scale administration. *Journal of Studies on Alcohol*, 1979, 40, 138–141.

5481. MANDELZYS, N. Correlates of offense severity and recidivism probability in a Canadian sample. *Journal of Clinical Psychology*, 1979, 35, 897–907.

5482. MARTIN, J. D., BLAIR, G. E., & BOTTOMS, S. A. H. A correlation of Barron's Ego Strength Scale and Smith's Non-Conformity Scale. *Educational & Psychological Measurement*, 1979, 39, 959–963.

5483. MARTIN, J. D., BLAIR, G. E., GRAH, C. R., & SHOAFF, J. E. Correlation of the scores on Barron's Ego Strength Scale with the scores on the Bender Gestalt Test. *Educational & Psychological Measurement*, 1979, 39, 187–191.

5484. MARUTA, T., SWANSON, D. W., & FINLAYSON, R. E. Drug abuse and dependency in patients with chronic pain. *Mayo Clinic Proceedings*, 1979, 54, 241–244.

5485. MCCREARY, C., TURNER, J., & DAWSON, E. The MMPI as a predictor of response to conservative treatment for low back pain. *Journal of Clinical Psychology*, 1979, 35, 278–284.

5486. MCLEAN, P. D., & HAKSTIAN, A. R. Clinical depression: Comparative efficacy of outpatient treatments. *Journal of Consulting & Clinical Psychology*, 1979, 47, 818–836.

5487. MERZBACHER, C. F. A diet and exercise regimen: Its effect upon mental acuity and personality, a pilot study. *Perceptual & Motor Skills*, 1979, 48, 367–371.

5488. MEZZICH, A. C., & MEZZICH, J. E. A data-based typology of depressed adolescents. *Journal of Personality Assessment*, 1979, 43, 238-246.

5489. MEZZICH, A. C., & MEZZICH, J. E. Symptomatology of depression in adolescence. *Journal of Personality Assessment*, 1979, 43, 267-275.

5490. MINTZ, J., LUBORSKY, L., & CHRISTOPH, P. Measuring the outcomes of psychotherapy: Findings of the Penn psychotherapy project. *Journal of Consulting & Clinical Psychology*, 1979, 47, 319-334.

5491. MIRABILE, C. S., JR., & GLUECK, B. C. Motion sickness—Key to neurobiologic variation. *Journal of Clinical Psychology*, 1979, 40, 171-174.

5492. MONCRIEFF, M., & PEARSON, D. Comparison of MMPI profiles of assaultive and non-assaultive exhibitionists and voyeurs. *Corrective & Social Psychiatry Journal of Behavior Technology, Methods & Therapy*, 1979, 25, 91-93.

5493. MOSS, C. S., HOSFORD, R. E., & ANDERSON, W. R. Sexual assault in a prison. *Psychological Reports*, 1979, 44, 823-828.

5494. MURRELL, M. E., & LESTER, D. Masculinity in police officers. *Psychological Reports*, 1979, 44, 14.

5495. MYLET, M., STYFCO, S. J., & ZIGLER, E. The interrelationship between self-image disparity and social competence, defensive style, and adjustment status. *Journal of Nervous & Mental Disease*, 1979, 167, 553-560.

5496. NAVARRO, D. J. Women A.A. members and nonalcoholics: Scores on the Holmes and MacAndrew scales of the MMPI. *Journal of Studies on Alcohol*, 1979, 40, 496-498.

5497. O'LEARY, M. R., DONOVAN, D. M., CHANEY, E. F., & O'LEARY, D. E. Interpersonal attractiveness and clinical decisions in alcoholism treatment. *American Journal of Psychiatry*, 1979, 136, 618-622.

5498. O'LEARY, M. R., DONOVAN, D. M., CHANEY, E. F., & SPELTZ, M. L. Correlates of clinician's perceptions of patients in alcoholism treatment. *Journal of Clinical Psychiatry*, 1979, 40, 344-347.

5499. O'LEARY, M. R., ROHSENOW, D. J., & CHANEY, E. F. The use of multivariate personality strategies in predicting attrition from alcoholism treatment. *Journal of Clinical Psychiatry*, 1979, 40, 190-193.

5500. PAGE, R. D., & SCHAUB, L. H. Efficacy of a three- versus a five-week alcohol treatment program. *International Journal of the Addictions*, 1979, 14, 697-714.

5501. PANTON, J. H. Long post-validation of the MMPI Escape (EC) and Prison Adjustment (AP) Scales. *Journal of Clinical Psychology*, 1979, 35, 101-107.

5502. PANTON, J. H. An MMPI item content scale to measure religious identification within a state prison population. *Journal of Clinical Psychology*, 1979, 35, 588-591.

5503. PANTON, J. H. MMPI profile configurations associated with incestuous and non-incestuous child molesting. *Psychological Reports*, 1979, 45, 335-338.

5504. PEAKE, T. H. Therapist-patient agreement and outcome in group therapy. *Journal of Clinical Psychology*, 1979, 35, 637-646.

5505. PENA-RAMOS, A., & HORNBERGER, R. MMPI and drug treatment in alcohol withdrawal. *Journal of Clinical Psychiatry*, 1979, 40, 361-364.

5506. PENK, W. E., CARPENTER, J. C., & RYLEE, K. E. MMPI correlates of social and physical anhedonia. *Journal of Consulting & Clinical Psychology*, 1979, 47, 1046-1052.

5507. PENK, W. E., FUDGE, J. W., ROBINOWITZ, R., & NEMAN, R. S. Personality characteristics of compulsive heroin, amphetamine, and barbiturate users. *Journal of Consulting & Clinical Psychology*, 1979, 47, 583-585.

5508. PENNINGTON, B. H., PETERSON, L. P., & BARKER, H. R., JR. The diagnostic use of the MMPI in organic brain dysfunction. *Journal of Clinical Psychology*, 1979, 35, 484-492.

5509. PICKENS, R., ERRICKSON, E., THOMPSON, T., HESTON, L., & ECKERT, E. D. MMPI correlates of performance on a behavior therapy ward. *Behaviour Research & Therapy*, 1979, 17, 17-24.

5510. POST, R. D., & GASPARIKOVA-KRASNEC, M. MMPI validity scales and behavioral disturbance in psychiatric inpatients. *Journal of Personality Assessment*, 1979, 43, 155-159.

5511. RAND, S. W. Correspondence between psychological reports based on the Mini-Mult and the MMPI. *Journal of Personality Assessment*, 1979, 43, 160-163.

5512. REHM, L. P., FUCHS, C. Z., ROTH, D. M., KORNBLITH, S. J., & ROMANO, J. M. A comparison of self-control and assertion skills treatments of depression. *Behavior Therapy*, 1979, 10, 429-442.

5513. RENAER, M., VERTOMMEN, H., NIJS, P., WAGEMANS, L., & VAN HEMELRIJCK, T. Psychological aspects of chronic pelvic pain in women. *American Journal of Obstetrics & Gynecology*, 1979, 134, 75-80.

5514. ROBBINS, J. M. Objective versus subjective responses to abortion. *Journal of Consulting & Clinical Psychology*, 1979, 47, 994-995.

5515. SACKS, J. G., & LEVY, N. M. Objective personality changes in residents of a therapeutic community. *American Journal of Psychiatry*, 1979, 136, 796-799.

5516. SCHER, S. S. Overt versus covert modeling with overcontrolled youthful offenders. *FCI Research Reports*, 1979, 10, 1-20.

5517. SCHIFF, I., REGESTEIN, Q., TULCHINSKY, D., & RYAN, K. J. Effects of estrogens on sleep and psychological state of hypogonadal women. *JAMA*, 1979, 242, 2405-2407.

5518. SCHNEIDER, S. J. Disability payments for psychiatric patients: Is patient assessment affected? *Journal of Clinical Psychology*, 1979, 35, 259-264.

5519. SCHROEDER, D. J., & PIERCY, D. C. A comparison of MMPI two-point codes in four alcoholism treatment facilities. *Journal of Clinical Psychology*, 1979, 35, 656-663.

5520. SCHWARTZ, M. F., & GRAHAM, J. R. Construct validity of the MacAndrew Alcoholism Scale. *Journal of Consulting & Clinical Psychology*, 1979, 47, 1090-1095.

5521. SCOTT, N. A., & CONN, M. G. Correspondence of the MMPI and the MMPI-168 among incarcerated female felons. *Journal of Personality Assessment*, 1979, 43, 473-478.

5522. SENDBUEHLER, J. M., KINCEL, R. L., NEMETH, G., & OERTEL, J. Dimension of seriousness in attempted suicide: Significance of the MF scale in suicidal MMPI profiles. *Psychological Reports*, 1979, 44, 343-361.

5523. SHAPIRO, A. K., STRUENING, E. L., & SHAPIRO, E. The reliability and validity of a placebo test. *Journal of Psychiatric Research*, 1979, 15, 253-290.

5524. SIMPSON, G. B., BOURNE, L. E., JR., JUSTESEN, D. R., & RHODES, R. J. Schizophrenic and paranoid thinking in conceptual performance. *Bulletin of the Psychonomic Society*, 1979, 13, 97-100.

5525. SINES, L. K., BAUCOM, D. H., & GRUBA, G. H. A validity scale sign calling for caution in the interpretation of MMPIs among psychiatric inpatients. *Journal of Personality Assessment*, 1979, 43, 604-607.

5526. SKOLNICK, N. J., & ZUCKERMAN, M. Personality change in drug abusers: A comparison of therapeutic community and prison groups. *Journal of Consulting & Clinical Psychology*, 1979, 47, 768-770.

5527. SMITH, R. B., BURGESS, A. E., GUINEE, V. J., & REIFSNIDER, L. C. A curvilinear relationship between alcoholic withdrawal tremor and personality. *Journal of Clinical Psychology*, 1979, 35, 199-203.

5528. SMITH, S. M. Standardized tests used in correctional institutions. *Journal of Employment Counseling*, 1979, 16, 178-188.

5529. SOBEL, H. J., & WORDEN, J. W. The MMPI as a predictor of psychosocial adaptation to cancer. *Journal of Consulting & Clinical Psychology*, 1979, 47, 716-724.

5530. STEIN, M. K., DOWNING, R. W., & RICKELS, K. The Minnesota Multiphasic Personality Inventory in predicting response to pharmacotherapy of neurotic outpatients. *Journal of Nervous & Mental Disease*, 1979, 167, 542-547.

5531. STEINBERG, F. A. The delineation of an MMPI symptom pattern unique to lithium responders. *American Journal of Psychiatry*, 1979, 136, 567-569.

5532. STENN, P. G., MOTHERSILL, K. J., & BROOKE, R. I. Biofeedback and a cognitive behavioral approach to treatment of myofascial pain dysfunction syndrome. *Behavior Therapy*, 1979, 10, 29-36.

5533. STREINER, D. L., & MILLER, H. R. A table for prorating incomplete Form R MMPIs. *Journal of Consulting & Clinical Psychology*, 1979, 47, 474-477.

5534. STRUPP, H. H., & HADLEY, S. W. Specific vs nonspecific factors in psychotherapy. *Archives of General Psychiatry*, 1979, 36, 1125-1136.

5535. SUMMERS, F., & WALSH, F. Symbiosis and confirmation between father and schizophrenic. *American Journal of Orthopsychiatry*, 1979, 49, 136-148.

5536. SUTKER, P. B., ARCHER, R. P., & ALLAIN, A. N. Voluntarism and self-reported psychopathology among opiate addicts. *Journal of Abnormal Psychology*, 1979, 88, 59-67.

5537. SUTKER, P. B., ARCHER, R. P., BRANTLEY, P. J., & KILPATRICK, D. G. Alcoholics and opiate addicts: Comparison of personality characteristics. *Journal of Studies on Alcohol*, 1979, 40, 635-644.

5538. TAMKIN, A. S. Rorschach card rejection and its relationships to defensiveness, intelligence, and sex. *Psychological Reports*, 1979, 44, 1003-1006.

5539. TEMPLER, D. I., BARTHLOW, V. L., HALCOMB, P. H., RUFF, C. F., & AYERS, J. L. The death anxiety of convicted felons. *Corrective & Social Psychiatry & Journal of Behavior Technology, Methods & Therapy*, 1979, 25, 18-20.

5540. TEMPLER, D. I., & DAUS, A. T. An athlete adjustment prediction scale. *Journal of Sports Medicine & Physical Fitness*, 1979, 19, 413-416.

5541. THOMPSON, R. J. Utility of the Faschingbauer abbreviated MMPI as a function of patient group and sex. *Journal of Clinical Psychology*, 1979, 35, 546-553.

5542. TSAI, M., FELDMAN-SUMMERS, S., & EDGAR, M. Childhood molestation: Variables related to differential impacts on psychosexual functioning in adult women. *Journal of Abnormal Psychology*, 1979, 88, 407-417.

5543. TSUSHIMA, W. T., & TOWNE, W. S. Clinical limitations of the low back scale. *Journal of Clinical Psychology*, 1979, 35, 306-308.

5544. TSUSHIMA, W. T., & WEDDING, D. MMPI results of male candidates for transsexual surgery. *Journal of Personality Assessment*, 1979, 43, 385-387.

5545. UNGERLEIDER, J. T., & WELLISCH, D. K. Coercive persuasion (brainwashing), religious cults, and deprogramming. *American Journal of Psychiatry*, 1979, 136, 279–282.

5546. VINCENT, L. R., & VINCENT, K. R. Ego development and psychopathology. *Psychological Reports*, 1979, 44, 408–410.

5547. WARD, L. C., WRIGHT, H. W., & TAULBEE, E. S. An improvement in the statistical validity of the MMPI-168 through modified scoring. *Journal of Consulting & Clinical Psychology*, 1979, 47, 618–619.

5548. WATSON, C. G., & BURANEN, C. The frequency and identification of false positive conversion reactions. *Journal of Nervous & Mental Disease*, 1979, 167, 243–247.

5549. WATSON, C. G., DALY, W. K., ZIMMERMAN, A., & ANDERSON, D. Effects of patient attitude and staff indulgence on improvement in schizophrenics: A test of impression management theory. *Journal of Abnormal Psychology*, 1979, 88, 338–340.

5550. WATSON, C. G., JACOBS, L., & HERDER, J. Correlates of alpha, beta, and theta wave production. *Journal of Clinical Psychology*, 1979, 35, 364–369.

5551. WEBB, L. J., & ALLEN, R. Sex differences in mental health. *Journal of Psychology*, 1979, 101, 89–96.

5552. WEBB, W. B. Are short and long sleepers different? *Psychological Reports*, 1979, 44, 259–264.

5553. WEINBERG, J. C., MANDEL, H. P., & MILLER, G. H. The relationship between various dietary factors and MMPI subscales: Implications for clinical practice. *Journal of Clinical Psychology*, 1979, 35, 880–886.

5554. WEYBREW, B. B., & NODDIN, E. M. Hand preference and the MMPI profiles of nuclear submariners. *Psychological Reports*, 1979, 45, 107–110.

5555. WHITE, R. B., JR. Relationship of scores on the escapism scale of the MMPI to escape from minimum security federal custody. *Journal of Clinical Psychology*, 1979, 35, 467–470.

5556. WILLIS, K. A., WEHLER, R., & RUSH, W. A. MacAndrew scale scores of smoking and nonsmoking alcoholics. *Journal of Studies on Alcohol*, 1979, 40, 906–907.

5557. WOOD, D., DEL NUOVO, A., BUCKY, S. F., SCHEIN, S., & MICHALIK, M. Psychodrama with an alcohol abuser population. *Group Psychotherapy, Psychodrama & Sociometry*, 1979, 32, 75–88.

5558. WOLLERT, R. W., & BUCHWALD, A. M. Subclinical depression and performance expectations, evaluations of performance, and actual performance. *Journal of Nervous & Mental Disease*, 1979, 167, 237–242.

5559. WORMITH, J. S., & HASENPUSCH, B. Multidimensional measurement of delayed gratification preference with incarcerated offenders. *Journal of Clinical Psychology*, 1979, 35, 218–225.

5560. ZARANTONELLO, M. M., JOHNSON, J. E., & PETZEL, T. P. The effects of ego-involvement and task difficulty on actual and perceived performance of depressed college students. *Journal of Clinical Psychology*, 1979, 35, 285–288.

5561. ZEISS, A. M., LEWINSOHN, P. M., & MUÑOZ, R. F. Nonspecific improvement effects in depression using interpersonal skills training, pleasant activity schedules, or cognitive training. *Journal of Consulting & Clinical Psychology*, 1979, 47, 427–439.

5562. ZEMORE, R., & EAMES, N. Psychic and somatic symptoms of depression among young adults, institutionalized aged and noninstitutionalized aged. *Journal of Gerontology*, 1979, 34, 716–722.

5563. ZIELINSKI, J. J. Psychological test data of depressed, nondepressed and relapsed alcoholics receiving pharmacological aversion. *British Journal of Addiction*, 1979, 74, 175–182.

5564. ADAMS, P. L., & HOROVITZ, J. H. Coping patterns of mothers of poor boys. *Child Psychiatry & Human Development*, 1980, 10, 144–155.

5565. ADAMS, P. L., & HOROVITZ, J. H. Psychopathology and fatherlessness in poor boys. *Child Psychiatry & Human Development*, 1980, 10, 135–143.

5566. ALKALAY, I., KAPLAN, A. S., SHARMA, R., & KIMBEL, P. Chronic obstructive pulmonary disease: Rehabilitation program with continuation on an outpatient basis. *Journal of the American Geriatrics Society*, 1980, 28, 88–92.

5567. ALLEN, R. H., WEINMAN, M., LORIMOR, R., & CLAGHORN, J. L. A multi-tiered screening system for the least restrictive setting. *American Journal of Psychiatry*, 1980, 137, 968–971.

5568. ARCHER, R. P. Generalized expectancies of control, trait anxiety, and psychopathology among psychiatric inpatients. *Journal of Consulting & Clinical Psychology*, 1980, 48, 736–742.

5569. BAER, P. E., DUNBAR, P. W., HAMILTON, J. E., II, & BEUTLER, L. E. Therapists' perceptions of the psychotherapeutic process: Development of a psychotherapy process inventory. *Psychological Reports*, 1980, 46, 563–570.

5570. BARNES, G. E. Characteristics of the clinical alcoholic personalities. *Journal of Studies on Alcohol*, 1980, 41, 894–910.

5571. BARON, M., PERLMAN, R., & LEVITT, M. Paranoid schizophrenia and platelet MAO activity. *American Journal of Psychiatry*, 1980, 137, 1465–1466.

5572. BATTLE, J. Relationship between self-esteem and depression among high school students. *Perceptual & Motor Skills*, 1980, 51, 157–158.

5573. BATZEL, L. W., DODRILL, C. B., & FRASER, R. T. Further validation of the WPSI Vocational Scale: Comparisons with other correlates of employment in epilepsy. *Epilepsia*, 1980, 21, 235–242.

5574. BENNETT, F. W., & CIMBOLIC, P. Use of local norms to improve high-point code-type concordance of two short forms of the MMPI. *Journal of Personality Assessment*, 1980, 44, 639–643.

5575. BERNSTEIN, I. H. Security guards' MMPI profiles: Some normative data. *Journal of Personality Assessment*, 1980, 44, 377–380.

5576. BETZ, N. E., & BANDER, R. S. Relationship of MMPI Mf and CPI Fe scales to fourfold sex role classifications. *Journal of Personality & Social Psychology*, 1980, 39, 1245–1248.

5577. BLASHFIELD, R. K., & MOREY, L. C. A comparison of four clustering methods using MMPI Monte Carlo data. *Applied Psychological Measurement*, 1980, 4, 57–64.

5578. BLAZER, D. The diagnosis of depression in the elderly. *Journal of the American Geriatrics Society*, 1980, 28, 52–58.

5579. BLAZER, D., & WILLIAMS, C. D. Epidemiology of dysphoria and depression in an elderly population. *American Journal of Psychiatry*, 1980, 137, 439–444.

5580. BOHN, M. J., JR. Inmate classification and the reduction of institution violence. *Corrections Today*, 1980, 42, 48–55.

5581. BUCHSBAUM, M. S., & SOSTEK, A. J. An adaptive-rate continuous performance test: Vigilance characteristics and reliability for 400 male students. *Perceptual & Motor Skills*, 1980, 51, 707–713.

5582. BURDICK, B. M., & HOLMES, C. B. Use of the lithium response scale with an outpatient psychiatric sample. *Psychological Reports*, 1980, 47, 69–70.

5583. BURKHART, B. R., GYNTHER, M. D., & FROMUTH, M. E. The relative predictive validity of subtle vs. obvious items on the MMPI depression scale. *Journal of Clinical Psychology*, 1980, 36, 748–751.

5584. BUSBY, K., & DE KONINCK, J. Short-term effects of strategies for self-regulation on personality dimensions and dream content. *Perceptual & Motor Skills*, 1980, 50, 751–765.

5585. BUTCHER, J. N., KENDALL, P. C., & HOFFMAN, N. MMPI short forms: Caution. *Journal of Consulting & Clinical Psychology*, 1980, 48, 275–278.

5586. CASPER, R. C., ECKERT, E. D., HALMI, K. A., GOLDBERG, S. C., & DAVIS, J. M. Bulimia: Its incidence and clinical importance in patients with anorexia nervosa. *Archives of General Psychiatry*, 1980, 37, 1030–1035.

5587. CEGALIS, J. A., & TEGTMEYER, P. F. Visual selectivity in schizophrenia. *Journal of Nervous & Mental Disease*, 1980, 168, 229–235.

5588. CHELUNE, G. J., SULTAN, F. E., & WILLIAMS, C. L. Loneliness, self-disclosure, and interpersonal effectiveness. *Journal of Counseling Psychology*, 1980, 27, 462–468.

5589. CHILES, J. A., STAUSS, F. S., & BENJAMIN, L. S. Marital conflict and sexual dysfunction in alcoholic and non-alcoholic couples. *British Journal of Psychiatry*, 1980, 137, 266–273.

5590. COLLIGAN, R. C., OSBORNE, D., & OFFORD, K. P. Linear transformation and the interpretation of MMPI T scores. *Journal of Clinical Psychology*, 1980, 36, 162–165.

5591. CONLEY, J. J., & KAMMEIER, M. L. MMPI item responses of alcoholics in treatment: Comparisons with normals and psychiatric patients. *Journal of Consulting & Clinical Psychology*, 1980, 48, 668–669.

5592. COURSEY, R. D., BUCHSBAUM, M. S., & MURPHY, D. L. Psychological characteristics of subjects identified by platelet MAO activity and evoked potentials as biologically at risk for psychopathology. *Journal of Abnormal Psychology*, 1980, 89, 151–164.

5593. COWAN, J. D., KAY, D. C., NEIDERT, G. L., ROSS, F. E., & BELMORE, S. M. Defeated and joyless: Potential measures of change in drug abuser characteristics. *Journal of Nervous & Mental Disease*, 1980, 168, 391–399.

5594. CRAIG, R. J. Characteristics of inner city heroin addicts applying for treatment in a veteran administration hospital drug program (Chicago). *International Journal of the Addictions*, 1980, 15, 409–418.

5595. DATTORE, P. J., SHONTZ, F. C., & COYNE, L. Premorbid personality differentiation of cancer and noncancer groups: A test of the hypothesis of cancer proneness. *Journal of Consulting & Clinical Psychology*, 1980, 48, 388–393.

5596. DE LA FUENTE, J. R., & ROSENBAUM, A. H. Neuroendocrine dysfunction and blood levels of tricyclic antidepressants. *American Journal of Psychiatry*, 1980, 137, 1260–1261.

5597. DIRKS, J. F., SCHRAA, J. C., BROWN, E. L., & KINSMAN, R. A. Psychomaintenance in asthma: Hospitalization rates and financial impact. *British Journal of Medical Psychology*, 1980, 53, 349–354.

5598. DIXIT, R. C., & VISHNOI, P. L. Employment of the mothers as a determinant of mother–daughter relationship and the development of masculinity–femininity among young girls. *Psychologia*, 1980, 23, 167–172.

5599. DONNELLY, E. F., MURPHY, D. L., & WALDMAN, I. N. Denial and somatization as characteristics of bipolar depressed groups. *Journal of Clinical Psychology*, 1980, 36, 159–162.

5600. EISENMANN, R. Effective manipulation by psychopaths. *Corrective & Social Psychiatry & Journal of Behavior Technology, Methods & Therapy*, 1980, 26, 116–118.

5601. ELMORE, P. B., & VASU, E. S. Relationship between selected variables and statistics achievement: Building a theoretical model. *Journal of Educational Psychology*, 1980, 72, 457–467.

5602. ERON, L. D., & HUESMANN, L. R. Adolescent aggression and television. *Annals of the New York Academy of Science*, 1980, 347, 319–331.

5603. ESHBAUGH, D. M., TOSI, D. J., & HOYT, C. N. Women alcoholics: A typological description using the MMPI. *Journal of Studies on Alcohol*, 1980, 41, 310–317.

5604. EVANS, R. G., & DINNING, W. D. A validation study of Forms A and B of the Whitaker Index of Schizophrenic Thinking. *Journal of Personality Assessment*, 1980, 44, 416–419.

5605. FAGAN, T. J., & LIRA, F. T. The primary and secondary sociopathic personality: Differences in frequency and severity of antisocial behaviors. *Journal of Abnormal Psychology*, 1980, 89, 493–496.

5606. FIX, A. J., DAUGHTON, D., KASS, I., BELL, C. W., & GOLDEN, C. J. Emotional, intellectual and physiological predictors of vocational outcome of pulmonary rehabilitation patients. *Psychological Reports*, 1980, 46, 379–382.

5607. FRANCES, R. J., TIMM, S., & BUCKY, S. Studies of familial and nonfamilial alcoholism. *Archives of General Psychiatry*, 1980, 37, 564–566.

5608. FREEMAN, C. W., CALSYN, D. A., SHERRAD, D. J., & PAIGE, A. B. Psychological assessment of renal dialysis patients using standard psychometric techniques. *Journal of Consulting & Clinical Psychology*, 1980, 48, 537–539.

5609. GEIST, C. R., & BOYD, S. T. Personality characteristics of army helicopter pilots. *Perceptual & Motor Skills*, 1980, 51, 253–254.

5610. GIDEON, W. L., LITTEL, A. S., & MARTIN, D. W. Evaluation of a training program for certified alcoholism counselors. *Journal of Studies on Alcohol*, 1980, 41, 8–19.

5611. GILLUM, R., LEON, G. R., KAMP, J., & BECERRA–ALDAMA, J. Prediction of cardio–vascular and other disease onset and mortality from 30-year longitudinal MMPI data. *Journal of Consulting & Clinical Psychology*, 1980, 48, 405–406.

5612. GOLD, S. N. Relations between level of ego development and adjustment patterns in adolescents. *Journal of Personality Assessment*, 1980, 44, 630–638.

5613. GOLDEN, R. R., & MEEHL, P. E. Detection of biological sex: An empirical test of cluster methods. *Multivariate Behavioral Research*, 1980, 15, 475–496.

5614. GREENE, R. L., BAUCOM, D. H., & MACON, R. S. Students' acceptance of high and low generalized personality interpretations. *Journal of Clinical Psychology*, 1980, 36, 166–170.

5615. GROSSCUP, S. J., & LEWINSOHN, P. M. Unpleasant and pleasant events, and mood. *Journal of Clinical Psychology*, 1980, 36, 252–259.

5616. GYNTHER, M. D., & GREEN, S. B. Accuracy may make a difference, but does a difference make for accuracy?: A response to Pritchard and Rosenblatt. *Journal of Consulting & Clinical Psychology*, 1980, 48, 268–272.

5617. HACKNEY, G. R., & RIBORDY, S. C. An empirical investigation of emotional reactions to divorce. *Journal of Clinical Psychology*, 1980, 36, 105–110.

5618. HAIER, R. J., BUCHSBAUM, M. S., MURPHY, D. L., GOTTESMAN, I. I., & COURSEY, R. D. Psychiatry vulnerability, monamine oxidase, and the average evoked potential. *Archives of General Psychiatry*, 1980, 37, 341–345.

5619. HARMON, T. M., NELSON, R. O., & HAYES, S. C. Self-monitoring of mood versus activity by depressed clients. *Journal of Consulting & Clinical Psychology*, 1980, 48, 30–38.

5620. HEIMBERG, R. G., & HARRISON, D. F. Use of the Rathus Assertiveness Schedule with offenders: A question of questions. *Behavior Therapy*, 1980, 11, 278–281.

5621. HERMANN, B. P., SCHWARTZ, M. S., KARNES, W. E., & VAHDAT, P. Psychopathology in epilepsy: Relationship of seizure type to age at onset. *Epilepsia*, 1980, 21, 15–23.

5622. HEWETT, B. B., & MARTIN, W. R. Psychometric comparisons of sociopathic and psychopathological behaviors of alcoholics and drug abusers versus a low drug use control population. *International Journal of the Addictions*, 1980, 15, 77–105.

5623. HOKANSON, J. E., SACCO, W. P., BLUMBERG, S. R., & LANDRUM, G. C. Interpersonal behavior of depressive individuals in a mixed-motive game. *Journal of Abnormal Psychology*, 1980, 89, 320–332.

5624. HOLDEN, C. Identical twins reared apart. *Science*, 1980, 207, 1323–1328.

5625. HOLLAND, T. R., & LEVI, M. Canonical versus factor analytic perspectives on the structure of associations between the MMPI and the Buss–Durkee Hostility Inventory. *Journal of Personality Assessment*, 1980, 44, 479–483.

5626. HOLLAND, T. R., LEVI, M., & WATSON, C. G. Personality patterns among hospitalized vs. incarcerated psychopaths. *Journal of Clinical Psychology*, 1980, 36, 826–832.

5627. HOLLAND, T. R., & WATSON, C. G. Multivariate analysis of WAIS–MMPI relationships among brain–damaged, schizophrenic, neurotic, and alcoholic patients. *Journal of Clinical Psychology*, 1980, 36, 352–359.

5628. HORTON, A. M., JR., & JOHNSON, C. H. Rational–emotive therapy and depression: A clinical case study. *Perceptual & Motor Skills*, 1980, 51, 853–854.

5629. HOVANITZ, C. A., & GYNTHER, M. D. The prediction of impulsive behavior: Comparative valididies of obvious vs. subtle MMPI hypomania (MA) items. *Journal of Clinical Psychology*, 1980, 36, 422–427.

5630. HUNT, D. D., & HAMPSON, J. L. Follow-up of 17 biologic male transsexuals after sex–reassignment surgery. *American Journal of Psychiatry*, 1980, 137, 432–438.

5631. JOHNSON, D. D., DORR, K. E., SWENSON, W. M., & SERVICE, J. Reactive hypoglycemia. *JAMA*, 1980, 243, 1151–1155.

5632. JOHNSON, J. H., & HARRIS, W. G. Personality and behavioral characteristics related to divorce in a population of male applicants for psychiatric evaluation. *Journal of Abnormal Psychology*, 1980, 89, 510–513.

5633. JOHNSON, J. H., KLINGLER, D. E., & GIANNETTI, R. A. Band width in diagnostic classification using the MMPI as a predictor. *Journal of Consulting & Clinical Psychology*, 1980, 48, 340–349.

5634. JONES, B. M., JONES, M. K., & HATCHER, E. M. Cognitive deficits in women alcoholics as a function of gynecological status. *Journal of Studies on Alcohol*, 1980, 41, 140–146.

5635. KALES, J. D., KALES, A., SOLDATOS, C. R., CALDWELL, A. B., CHARNEY, D. S., & MARTIN, E. D. Night terrors. Clinical characteristics and personality patterns. *Archives of General Psychiatry*, 1980, 37, 1413–1417.

5636. KALES, A., SOLDATOS, C. R., CALDWELL, A. B., CHARNEY, D. S., KALES, J. D., MARKEL, D., & CADIEUX, R. Nightmares: Clinical characteristics and personality patterns. *American Journal of Psychiatry*, 1980, 137, 1197–1201.

5637. KALES, A., SOLDATOS, C. R., CALDWELL, A. B., KALES, J. D., HUMPHREY, F. J., II, CHARNEY, D. S., & SCHWEITZER, P. K. Somnambulism. Clinical characteristics and personality patterns. *Archives of General Psychiatry*, 1980, 37, 1406–1410.

5638. KEANE, S. P., & GIBBS, M. Construct validation of the Sc scale of the MMPI. *Journal of Clinical Psychology*, 1980, 36, 152–158.

5639. KELLEY, C. K., & KING, G. D. Two- and three-point classification of MMPI profiles in which scales 2, 7, and 8 are the highest elevations. *Journal of Personality Assessment*, 1980, 44, 25–33.

5640. KINSMAN, R. A., DIRKS, J. D., & JONES, N. F. Levels of psychological experience in asthma: General and illness–specific concomitants of panic–fear personality. *Journal of Clinical Psychology*, 1980, 36, 552–561.

5641. KINSMAN, R. A., DIRKS, J. D., DAHLEM, N. W., & HELLER, A. S. Anxiety in asthma: Panic–fear symptomatology and personality in relation to manifest anxiety. *Psychological Reports*, 1980, 46, 196–198.

5642. KLEIGER, J. H., & JONES, N. F. Characteristics of alexithymic patients in a chronic respiratory illness population. *Journal of Nervous & Mental Disease*, 1980, 168, 465–470.

5643. KOH, S. D., MARUSARZ, T. Z., & ROSEN, A. J. Remembering of sentences by schizophrenic young adults. *Journal of Abnormal Psychology*, 1980, 89, 291–294.

5644. KRANTZ, D. S., BAUM, A., & WIDEMAN, M. V. Assessment of preferences for self–treatment and information in health care. *Journal of Personality & Social Psychology*, 1980, 39, 977–990.

5645. KURLYCHEK, R. T., & JORDON, L. MMPI profiles and code types of responsible and non–responsible criminal defendants. *Journal of Clinical Psychology*, 1980, 36, 590–593.

5646. LAWRENCE, D. M., & MORTON, V. Associating Embedded Figures Test performance with extreme hysteria and psychasthenia MMPI scores in a psychiatric population. *Perceptual & Motor Skills*, 1980, 50, 432–434.

5647. LEAVITT, F., BERGER, J. C., HOEPPNER, J., & NORTHROP, G. Presurgical adjustment in male transsexuals with and without hormonal treatment. *Journal of Nervous & Mental Disease*, 1980, 168, 693–697.

5648. LEAVITT, F., & GARRON, D. C. Validity of a back pain classification scale for detecting psychological disturbances as measured by the MMPI. *Journal of Clinical Psychology*, 1980, 36, 186–189.

5649. LEWINSOHN, P. M., MISCHEL, W., CHAPLIN, W., & BARTON, R. Social competence and depression: The role of illusory self-perceptions. *Journal of Abnormal Psychology*, 1980, 89, 203–212.

5650. LEYNES, C. Keep or adopt: A study of factors influencing pregnant adolescents' plans for their babies. *Child Psychiatry & Human Development*, 1980, 11, 105–112.

5651. LINNOILA, M., ERWIN, C. W., & CLEVELAND, W. P. Effects of age and alcohol on psychomotor performance of men. *Journal of Studies on Alcohol*, 1980, 41, 488–495.

5652. LOBERG, T. Alcohol misuse and neuropsychological deficits in men. *Journal of Studies on Alcohol*, 1980, 41, 119–128.

5653. LOWMAN, J. Measurement of family affective structure. *Journal of Personality Assessment*, 1980, 44, 130–141.

5654. MacCrimmon, D. J., Cleghorn, J. M., Asarnow, R. F., & Steffy, R. A. Children at risk for schizophrenia. *Archives of General Psychiatry*, 1980, 37, 671–674.

5655. Major, L. F., Lerner, P., Goodwin, F. K., Ballenger, J. C., Brown, G. L., & Lovenberg, W. Dopamine B–hydroxylase in CSF. *Archives of General Psychiatry*, 1980, 37, 308–310.

5656. Maloney, M. P., Duvall, S. W., & Friesen, J. Evaluation of response consistency on the MMPI. *Psychological Reports*, 1980, 46, 295–298.

5657. McAllister, H. A. Self–disclosure and liking: Effects for senders and receivers. *Journal of Personality*, 1980, 48, 409–418.

5658. McCreary, C. P., Turner, J., & Dawson, E. Emotional disturbance and chronic low back pain. *Journal of Clinical Psychology*, 1980, 36, 709–715.

5659. McGill, J. C. MMPI score differences among Anglo, Black and Mexican–American welfare recipients. *Journal of Clinical Psychology*, 1980, 36, 147–151.

5660. McGuire, J. P., & Leak, G. K. Prediction of self–disclosure from objective personality assessment techniques. *Journal of Clinical Psychology*, 1980, 36, 201–204.

5661. McGurk, B. J., & McGurk, R. E. Personality types among prisoners and prison officers. *British Journal of Criminology*, 1980, 19, 31–49.

5662. Merian, E. M., Stefan, D., Schoenfeld, L. S., & Kobos, J. C. Screening of police applicants: A 5–item MMPI research index. *Psychological Reports*, 1980, 47, 155–158.

5663. Michels, P. J., & Layne, C. Inventory responding models people's acceptance of feedback "derived"from tests and from interviews. *Journal of Personality Assessment*, 1980, 44, 302–306.

5664. Mill, T. W., & Paciello, R. A. Discriminative dimensions of the MMPI as a function of age and psychopathology. *Journal of Clinical Psychology*, 1980, 36, 758–759.

5665. Mozdzierz, G. J., & Semyck, R. W. The Social Interest Index: A study of construct validity. *Journal of Clinical Psychology*, 1980, 36, 417–422.

5666. Munjack, D. J., Kanno, P. H., Staples, F. R., & Leonard, M. D. Some psychometric data on ejaculatory disorders: A further note. *Psychological Reports*, 1980, 46, 1047–1050.

5667. Nacev, V. Dependency and ego–strength as indicators of patients' attendance in psychotherapy. *Journal of Clinical Psychology*, 1980, 36, 691–695.

5668. Nagelberg, D. B., & Shemberg, K. B. Mental health on the college campus: An epidemiological study. *Journal of the American College Health Association*, 1980, 28, 228–230.

5669. Nation, J. R., & Cooney, J. B. The change and maintenance effectiveness of persistence training regarding the treatment of laboratory induced and naturally occurring depression. *Bulletin of the Psychonomic Society*, 1980, 16, 121–124.

5670. Nerviano, V. J., McCarty, D., & McCarty, S. M. MMPI profile patterns of men alcoholics in two contrasting settings. *Journal of Studies on Alcohol*, 1980, 41, 1143–1152.

5671. Newmark, C. S., & Hutchins, T. C. Age and MMPI indices of schizophrenia. *Journal of Clinical Psychology*, 1980, 36, 768–769.

5672. Newmark, C. S., Woody, G. G., Ziff, D. R., & Finch, A. J., Jr. MMPI short forms: A different perspective. *Journal of Consulting & Clinical Psychology*, 1980, 48, 279–283.

5673. O'Leary, M. R., Donovan, D. M., Chaney, E. F., & O'Leary, D. E. Relationship of alcoholic personality subtypes to treatment follow–up measures. *Journal of Nervous & Mental Disease*, 1980, 168, 475–480.

5674. Patalano, F. Comparison of MMPI scores of drug abusers and Mayo Clinic normative groups. *Journal of Clinical Psychology*, 1980, 36, 576–579.

5675. Patalano, F. MMPI two–point code–type frequencies of drug abusers in a therapeutic community. *Psychological Reports*, 1980, 46, 1019–1022.

5676. Penk, W. E., & Robinowitz, R. A test of the voluntarism hypothesis among nonvolunteering opiate addicts who voluntarily return to treatment. *Journal of Abnormal Psychology*, 1980, 89, 234–239.

5677. Penk, W. E., Robinowitz, R., Woodward, W. A., & Hess, J. L. MMPI factor scale differences among heroin addicts differing in race and admission status. *International Journal of the Addictions*, 1980, 15, 329–337.

5678. Penk, W. E., Robinowitz, R., Woodward, W. A., & Parr, W. C. An MMPI comparison of polydrug and heroin abusers. *Journal of Abnormal Psychology*, 1980, 89, 299–302.

5679. Penk, W. E., Vebersax, J. S., Andrews, R. H., & Charles, H. L. Client correlates of community informant adjustment ratings. *Journal of Personality Assessment*, 1980, 44, 157–166.

5680. Penny, G. D., & Rust, J. O. Effect of a walking–jogging program on personality characteristics of middle–aged females. *Journal of Sports Medicine & Physical Fitness*, 1980, 20, 221–226.

5681. Peyser, J. M., Edwards, K. R., & Poser, C. M. Psychological profiles in patients with multiple sclerosis. *Archives of Neurology*, 1980, 37, 437–440.

5682. Pino, C. J. Interpersonal needs, counselor style, and personality change among seminarians during the 1970's. *Review of Religious Research*, 1980, 21, 351–367.

5683. Pollack, D., & Shore, J. H. Validity of the MMPI with native Americans. *American Journal of Psychiatry*, 1980, 137, 946–950.

5684. Post, R. D., & Lobitz, W. C. The utility of Mezzich's MMPI regression formula as a diagnostic criterion in depression research. *Journal of Consulting & Clinical Psychology*, 1980, 48, 673–674.

5685. Post, R. D., Lobitz, W. C., & Gasparikova–Krasnec, M. The utilization of positive and negative feedback in the self–evaluation responses of depressed and nondepressed psychiatric patients. *Journal of Nervous & Mental Disease*, 1980, 168, 481–486.

5686. Pritchard, D. A., & Rosenblatt, A. Racial bias in the MMPI: A methodological review. *Journal of Consulting & Clinical Psychology*, 1980, 48, 263–267.

5687. Pritchard, D. A., & Rosenblatt, A. Reply to Gynther and Green. *Journal of Consulting & Clinical Psychology*, 1980, 48, 273–274.

5688. Prokop, C. K., Bradley, L. A., Margolis, R., & Gentry, W. D. Multivariate analysis of the MMPI profiles of patients with multiple pain complaints. *Journal of Personality Assessment*, 1980, 44, 246–252.

5689. Quinsey, V. L., Arnold, L. S., & Pruesse, M. G. MMPI profiles of men referred for a pretrial psychiatric assessment as a function of offense type. *Journal of Clinical Psychology*, 1980, 36, 410–417.

5690. Ramanaiah, N. V., & Martin, H. J. On the two–dimensional nature of the Marlowe–Crowne Social Desirability Scale. *Journal of Personality Assessment*, 1980, 44, 507–514.

5691. Ramani, S. V., Quesney, L. F., Olson, D., & Gumnit, R. J. Diagnosis of hysterical seizures in epileptic patients. *American Journal of Psychiatry*, 1980, 137, 705–709.

5692. Rathus, S. A., Fox, J. A., & Ortins, J. B. The MacAndrew Scale as a measure of substance abuse and delinquency among adolescents. *Journal of Clinical Psychology*, 1980, 36, 579–583.

5693. Richman, L. C., & Harper, D. C. Personality profiles of physically impaired young adults. *Journal of Clinical Psychology*, 1980, 36, 668–671.

5694. Robinowitz, R., Woodward, W. A., & Penk, W. E. MMPI comparison of black heroin users volunteering or not volunteering for treatment. *Journal of Consulting & Clinical Psychology*, 1980, 48, 540–542.

5695. Sanchez, V. C., Lewinsohn, P. M., & Larson, D. W. Assertion training: Effectiveness in the treatment of depression. *Journal of Clinical Psychology*, 1980, 36, 526–529.

5696. Schoenfeld, L. S., Kobos, J. C., & Phinney, I. R. Screening police applicants: A study of reliability with the MMPI. *Psychological Reports*, 1980, 47, 419–425.

5697. Schultz, K. J., & Koulack, D. Dream affect and the menstrual cycle. *Journal of Nervous & Mental Disease*, 1980, 168, 436–438.

5698. Scott, N. A. The applicability of the Beall–Panton MMPI Escape Index to female felons. *Journal of Clinical Psychology*, 1980, 36, 360–363.

5699. Shealy, R. C., Lowe, J. D., & Ritzler, B. A. Sleep onset insomnia: Personality characteristics and treatment outcome. *Journal of Consulting & Clinical Psychology*, 1980, 48, 659–661.

5700. Siddall, J. W., & Keogh, N. J. Psychotherapeutic drug recommendations based on the Mini–Mult. *Psychological Reports*, 1980, 47, 1283–1288.

5701. Silva, J. A., & Yesavage, J. A. Covariance of affective and schizophrenic symptoms in schizoaffective psychosis. *Journal of Nervous & Mental Disease*, 1980, 168, 559–561.

5702. Snibbe, J. R., Peterson, P. J., & Sosner, B. Study of psychological characteristics of a workers' compensation sample using the MMPI and Millon Clinical Multiaxial Inventory. *Psychological Reports*, 1980, 47, 959–966.

5703. Solway, K. S., Hays, J. R., Schreiner, D., & Cansler, D. Clinical study of youths petitioned for certification as adults. *Psychological Reports*, 1980, 46, 1067–1073.

5704. Srole, L., & Kassen, A. The midtown Manhattan longitudinal study vs "the mental paradise lost" doctrine. *Archives of General Psychiatry*, 1980, 37, 209–221.

5705. Staples, R. B., Ficher, I. V., Shapiro, M., Martin, K., & Gonick, P. A re–evaluation of MMPI discriminators of biogenic and psychogenic impotence. *Journal of Consulting & Clinical Psychology*, 1980, 48, 543–545.

5706. Stevens, M. R., & Reilley, R. R. MMPI Short Forms: A literature review. *Journal of Personality Assessment*, 1980, 44, 368–376.

5707. Stricklin, A. B., & Penk, M. L. Levels of imagery and personality dimensions in a female prison population. *Journal of Personality Assessment*, 1980, 44, 390–395.

5708. Strupp, H. H. Success and failure in time–limited psychotherapy. A systematic comparison of two cases: Comparison 1. *Archives of General Psychiatry*, 1980, 37, 595–603.

5709. STRUPP, H. H. Success and failure in time–limited psychotherapy. A systematic comparison of two cases: Comparison 2. *Archives of General Psychiatry*, 1980, 37, 708–716.

5710. STRUPP, H. H. Success and failure in time–limited psychotherapy. Further evidence (Comparison 4). *Archives of General Psychiatry*, 1980, 37, 947–954.

5711. STRUPP, H. H. Success and failure in time–limited psychotherapy with special reference to the performance of a lay counselor. *Archives of General Psychiatry*, 1980, 37, 831–841.

5712. SUTKER, P. B., ARCHER, R. P., & ALLAIN, A. N. Psychopathology of drug abusers: Sex and ethnic considerations. *International Journal of the Addictions*, 1980, 15, 605–613.

5713. SUTKER, P. B., BRANTLEY, P. J., & ALLAIN, A. N. MMPI response patterns and alcohol consumption in DUI offenders. *Journal of Consulting & Clinical Psychology*, 1980, 48, 350–355.

5714. SWANSON, D. W., & MARUTA, T. Patients complaining of extreme pain. *Mayo Clinic Proceedings*, 1980, 55, 563–566.

5715. TAMKIN, A. S. Rorschach experience balance, introversion, and sex. *Psychological Reports*, 1980, 46, 843–848.

5716. THARP, V. K., MALTZMAN, I., SYNDULKO, K., & ZISKIND, E. Autonomic activity during anticipation of an aversive tone in noninstitutionalized sociopaths. *Psychophysiology*, 1980, 17, 123–128.

5717. THAUBERGER, P. C., DAVIS, J., & CLELAND, J. F. Some indices of existential confrontation from a sample of maximum security inmates. *Perceptual & Motor Skills*, 1980, 51, 131–137.

5718. TORKI, M. A. Validation of the MMPI MF scale in Kuwait. *Psychological Reports*, 1980, 47, 1152–1154.

5719. VECKER, A. E., BOUTILIER, L. R., & RICHARDSON, E. H. "Indianism" and MMPI scores of men alcoholics. *Journal of Studies on Alcohol*, 1980, 41, 357–362.

5720. VINCENT, K. R. Semi–automated full battery. *Journal of Clinical Psychology*, 1980, 36, 437–446.

5721. WADDON, T. A., & LUCAS, R. A. MMPI as a predictor of weight loss. *Psychological Reports*, 1980, 46, 984–986.

5722. WALLACE, J. E., MACCRIMMON, D. J., & GOLDBERG, W. M. Acute hyperthyroidism: Cognitive and emotional correlates. *Journal of Abnormal Psychology*, 1980, 89, 519–527.

5723. WAMPLER, R. S., LAUER, J. B., LANTZ, J. B., WAMPLER, K. S., EVENS, M. G., & MADURA, J. A. Psychological effects of intestinal bypass surgery. *Journal of Counseling Psychology*, 1980, 27, 492–499.

5724. WARD, L. C. Conversion equations for modified scoring of the MMPI-168. *Journal of Personality Assessment*, 1980, 44, 644–646.

5725. WARD, L. C., & SELBY, R. B. An abbreviation of the MMPI with increased comprehension and readability. *Journal of Clinical Psychology*, 1980, 36, 180–186.

5726. WARD, L. C., & WARD, J. W. MMPI readability reconsidered. *Journal of Personality Assessment*, 1980, 44, 387–389.

5727. WATSON, C. G., DALY, W. K., & ZIMMERMAN, A. Staff attitudes and treatment effectiveness. *Journal of Clinical Psychology*, 1980, 36, 601–605.

5728. WATSON, C. G., & HERDER, J. Effectiveness of alpha biofeedback therapy: Negative results. *Journal of Clinical Psychology*, 1980, 36, 508–513.

5729. WATSON, C. G., & JACOBS, L. Interrelationships and correlates of four measures of pleasure deficit. *Journal of Clinical Psychology*, 1980, 36, 142–147.

5730. WEINBERGER, L. J., & BRADLEY, L. A. Effects of "favorability" and type of assessment device upon acceptance of general personality interpretations. *Journal of Personality Assessment*, 1980, 44, 44–47.

5731. WEITKAMP, L. R., PARDUE, L. H., & HUNTZINGER, R. S. Genetic marker studies in a family with unipolar depression. *Archives of General Psychiatry*, 1980, 37, 1187–1192.

5732. WETZEL, R. D., MARGULIES, T., DAVIS, R., & KARAM, E. Hopelessness, depression, and suicide intent. *Journal of Clinical Psychiatry*, 1980, 41, 159–160.

5733. YOUNG, R. C., GOULD, E., GLICK, I. D., & HARGREAVES, W. Personality inventory correlates of outcome in a follow–up study of psychiatric hospitalization. *Psychological Reports*, 1980, 46, 903–906.

5734. YOUNGREN, M. A., & LEWINSOHN, P. M. The functional relation between depression and problematic interpersonal behavior. *Journal of Abnormal Psychology*, 1980, 89, 333–341.

5735. AMENSON, C. S., & LEWINSOHN, P. M. An investigation into the observed sex difference in prevalence of unipolar depression. *Journal of Abnormal Psychology*, 1981, 90, 1–13.

5736. APFELDORF, M., & HUNLEY, P. J. The MacAndrew Scale: A measure of the diagnosis of alcoholism. *Journal of Studies on Alcohol*, 1981, 42, 80–86.

5737. BERNARD, L. C. The multidimensional aspects of masculinity–femininity. *Journal of Personality & Social Psychology*, 1981, 41, 797–802.

5738. BEUTLER, L. E., & MITCHELL, R. Differential psychotherapy outcome among depressed and impulsive patients as a function of analytic and experimental treatment procedures. *Psychiatry*, 1981, 44, 297–306.

5739. BLANCHARD, J. S. Readability of the MMPI. *Perceptual & Motor Skills*, 1981, 52, 985–986.

5740. CARP, F. M., & CARP, A. Mental health characteristics and acceptance–rejection of old age. *American Journal of Orthopsychiatry*, 1981, 51, 230–241.

5741. CHASSIN, L., EASON, B. J., & YOUNG, R. D. Identifying with a deviant label: The validation of a methodology. *Social Psychology Quarterly*, 1981, 1, 31–36.

5742. COLEMAN, R. M., MILES, L. E., GUILLEMINAULT, C. C., ZARCONE, V. P., VAN DEN HOED, J., & DEMENT, W. C. Sleep–wake disorders in the elderly: A polysomnographic analysis. *Journal of the American Geriatrics Society*, 1981, 29, 289–296.

5743. CUNNINGHAM, J. A., & STRASSBERG, D. S. Neuroticism and disclosure reciprocity. *Journal of Counseling Psychology*, 1981, 28, 455–458.

5744. DOANE, J. A., GOLDSTEIN, M. J., & RODNICK, E. H. Parental patterning of affective style and the development of schizophrenia spectrum disorders. *Family Process*, 1981, 20, 337–349.

5745. DOANE, J. A., WEST, K. L., GOLDSTEIN, M. J., RODNICK, E. H., & JONES, J. E. Parental communication deviance and affective style. *Archives of General Psychiatry*, 1981, 38, 679–685.

5746. DODRILL, C. B. An economical method for the evaluation of general intelligence in adults. *Journal of Consulting & Clinical Psychology*, 1981, 49, 668–673.

5747. ENGEL, K. L., & PAUL, G. L. Staff performance: Do attitudinal "effectiveness profiles" really assess it? *Journal of Nervous & Mental Disease*, 1981, 169, 529–540.

5748. FOUREMAN, W. C., PARKS, R., GARDIN, T. H. The MMPI as a predictor of retention in a therapeutic community for heroin addicts. *International Journal of the Addictions*, 1981, 16, 893–903.

5749. GARFINKEL, P. E., & WARING, E. M. Personality, interests, and emotional disturbance in psychiatric residents. *American Journal of Psychiatry*, 1981, 138, 51–55.

5750. GOLDBERG, L. R. Unconfounding situational attributions from uncertain, neutral, and ambiguous ones: A psychometric analysis of descriptions of oneself and various types of others. *Journal of Personality & Social Psychology*, 1981, 41, 517–552.

5751. HAURI, P. Treating psychophysiologic insomnia with biofeedback. *Archives of General Psychiatry*, 1981, 38, 752–758.

5752. HIRSCHFELD, R. M. A. Situational depression: Validity of the concept. *British Journal of Psychiatry*, 1981, 139, 297–305.

5753. KAHN, M. W., & STEPHEN, L. S. Counselor training as a treatment method for alcohol and drug abuse. *International Journal of the Addictions*, 1981, 16, 1415–1424.

5754. KELTIKANGAS–JÄRVINEN, L., JÄRVINEN, H., & LEHTONEN, T. Psychic disturbances in patients with chronic prostatitis. *Annals of Clinical Research*, 1981, 13, 45–49.

5755. LEON, G. R., BUTCHER, J. N., KLEINMAN, M., GOLDBERG, A., & ALMAGOR, M. Survivors of the holocaust and their children: Current status and adjustment. *Journal of Personality & Social Psychology*, 1981, 41, 503–516.

5756. LEON, G. R., KAMP, J., GILLUM, R., & GILLUM, B. Life stress and dimensions of functioning in old age. *Journal of Gerontology*, 1981, 36, 66–69.

5757. LINDER, L. H. Group behavioral treatment of agoraphobia: A preliminary report. *Comprehensive Psychiatry*, 1981, 22, 226–233.

5758. LEMAIRE, T. E., & CLOPTON, J. R. Expressions of hostility in mild depression. *Psychological Reports*, 1981, 48, 259–262.

5759. MAY, P. R. A., TUMA, A. H., DIXON, W. J., YALE, C., THIELE, D. A., & KRAUDE, W. H. Schizophrenia. A follow–up study of the results of five forms of treatment. *Archives of General Psychiatry*, 1981, 38, 776–784.

5760. MCDANIEL, S. H., STILES, W. B., & MCGAUGHEY, K. J. Correlations of male college students' verbal response mode use in psychotherapy with measures of psychological disturbance and psychotherapy outcome. *Journal of Consulting & Clinical Psychology*, 1981, 49, 571–582.

5761. O'LEARY, M. R., FAURIA, T., CALSYN, D. A., & FEHRENBACH, P. A. Cognitive style, personality traits, and treatment attrition among alcoholics. *International Journal of the Addictions*, 1981, 16, 1143–1148.

5762. PENK, W. E., BROWN, A. S., ROBERTS, W. R., DOLAN, M. P., ATKINS, H. G., & ROBINOWITZ, R. Visual memory of black and white male heroin and nonheroin drug users. *Journal of Abnormal Psychology*, 1981, 90, 486–489.

5763. PETZEL, T. P., JOHNSON, J. E., JOHNSON, H. H., & KOWALSKI, J. Behavior of depressed subjects in problem solving groups. *Journal of Research in Personality*, 1981, 15, 389–398.

5764. PLOTKIN, W. B., & RICE, K. M. Biofeedback as a placebo: Anxiety reduction facilitated by training in either suppression or enhancement of alpha brainwaves. *Journal of Consulting & Clinical Psychology*, 1981, 49, 590–596.

5765. REICH, P., DESILVA, R. A., LOWN, B., & MURAWSKI, B. J. Acute psychological disturbances preceding life–threatening ventricular arrhythmias. *JAMA*, 1981, 246, 233–235.

5766. SAUNDERS, G. R., & SHUCKIT, M. A. MMPI scores in young men with alcoholic relatives and controls. *Journal of Nervous & Mental Disease*, 1981, 169, 456–458.

5767. ROFFE, M. W. Predictive correlates of treatment program completion in a sample of male alcoholics. *International Journal of the Addictions*, 1981, 16, 849–857.

5768. SCHEIBER, S. C., COHEN, I., YAMAMURA, H., NOVAL, R., & BEUTLER, L. Dialysis for schizophrenia: An uncontrolled study of 11 patients. *American Journal of Psychiatry*, 1981, 138, 662–665.

5769. STERN, M. J., & CLEARY, P. National exercise and heart disease project: Psychosocial changes observed during a low-level exercise program. *Archives of Internal Medicine*, 1981, 141, 1463–1467.

5770. STRASSBERG, D. S., REIMHERR, F., WARD, M., RUSSELL, S., & COLE, A. The MMPI and chronic pain. *Journal of Consulting & Clinical Psychology*, 1981, 49, 220–226.

5771. TUCKER, D. M., STENSLIE, C. E., ROTH, R. S., & SHEARER, S. L. Right frontal lobe activation and right hemisphere performance. *Archives of General Psychiatry*, 1981, 38, 169–174.

5772. URSANO, R. J., BOYDSTUN, J. A., & WHEATLEY, R. D. Psychiatric illness in U.S. Air Force Viet Nam prisoners of war: A five-year follow-up. *American Journal of Psychiatry*, 1981, 138, 310–314.

5773. WARD, L. C., WRIGHT, H. W., & TAULBEE, E. S. A comparison of two short forms of the MMPI in a sample of men alcoholics. *Journal of Studies on Alcohol*, 1981, 42, 514–516.

5774. WATSON, C. G., & PLEMBEL, D. A test of the interference and normal associate bias theories of schizophrenic cognitive deficit. *Journal of Nervous & Mental Disease*, 1981, 169, 185–190.

5775. WEITZMAN, E. D., CZEISLER, C. A., COLEMAN, R. M., SPIELMAN, A. J., ZIMMERMAN, J. C., DEMENT, W., RICHARDSON, G., & POLLAK, C. P. Delayed sleep phase syndrome: A chronological disorder with sleep-onset insomnia. *Archives of General Psychiatry*, 1981, 38, 737–746.

5776. WENDER, P. H., REIMHERR, F. W., & WOOD, D. R. Attentional deficit disorder ("minimal brain dysfunction") in adults. *Archives of General Psychiatry*, 1981, 38, 449–456.

5777. ZAGER, L. D., & MEGARGEE, E. I. Seven MMPI alcohol and drug abuse scales: An empirical investigation of their interrelationships, convergent and discriminant validity, and degree of racial bias. *Journal of Personality & Social Psychology*, 1981, 40, 532–544.

[1499]
[Re Minnesota Multiphasic Personality Inventory.] Behaviordyne Psychodiagnostic Laboratory Service. A computerized scoring and interpreting service for qualified users of the MMPI or the *California Psychological Inventory*; 1969–76; formerly called *OPTIMUM Psychodiagnostic Consultation Service*; various types of interpretive reports are available: types 1 (for industrial psychologists and personnel counselors), 2 (for counselors and caseworkers), 3 (for correctional counselors), 5 (for physicians), 6 (standard report for psychiatrists and psychologists), 7 (detailed report for use before psychoanalysis or intensive psychotherapy), 7B (brief type 7 report); brief form of the other types of reports also available; additional options available with each type of report: self-report (separate printout of narrative second-person statements for presentation to client), penal option (inclusion of forensic statements, with reports 2, 6, 7, and 7B only), research option (inclusion of data on factor loadings and 166 clinical scales); although the reports may be based on either the CPI or the MMPI, publisher recommends that the CPI be used for types 1–3 reports and the MMPI for types 5–7 reports; the interpretive report is a computer printout presenting a graph of 12 MMPI standard scales (excludes Si and ? scales), a 2–7 page narrative report, an "echo sheet" of item responses, and a "data page" (reports 5, 6, and 7 only) listing: standard scores on 14 MMPI scales, ratings on 9 psychosis indices, rankings of the 8 MMPI clinical scales, mismark and/or blank count, and ranking on addiction and alcohol tendencies; no manual; original system by Joseph C. Finney, Charles Dwight Auvenshine, David Fulton Smith, and Donald E. Skeeters; Behaviordyne, Inc.*

For additional information and reviews by Fred L. Adair and James N. Butcher, see 8:619 (5 references); see also T2:1282 (2 references); for reviews by William J. Eichman, see 7:105 and 7:107 (9 references).

[1500]
[Re Minnesota Multiphasic Personality Inventory.] Caldwell Report: An MMPI Interpretation. A computerized scoring and interpreting service for qualified users of the MMPI; 1969; the 5 page interpretive report presents narrative sentences in 4 areas (test taking attitude, symptoms and personality characteristics, diagnostic impression, treatment considerations), a list of MMPI critical items with significant responses circled, profiled scores on 3 validity scales (excludes ? scale), 10 clinical scales, and scores on 12 other scales: (family discord, authority problems, persecutory ideas, poignancy, naivete, amorality, psychomotor acceleration, imperturbability, ego inflation, alcoholism, overcontrolled hostility, functional low back pain); no manual; Alex B. Caldwell; Caldwell Report.*

For additional information and reviews by Fred L. Adair and James N. Butcher, see 8:620 (4 references).

[1501]
[Re Minnesota Multiphasic Personality Inventory.] Psychological Assessment Services. A computerized scoring and interpreting service for qualified professional personnel in correctional and court-related facilities; 1973–75; a modification for use in criminal justice settings of the Fowler-Roche program for clinical use; the interpretive report is a 7–9 page computer printout presenting a narrative report, scores on 4 validity scales, 10 clinical scales, and 32 other scales: 14 special scales (first factor, second factor, ego strength, low back pain, caudality, dependency, dominance, responsibility, prejudice, social status, control, manifest anxiety, social desirability, maladjustment), 13 content scales (social maladjustment, depression, feminine interests, poor morale, religious fundamentalism, authority conflict, psychoticism, organic symptoms, family problems, manifest hostility, phobias, hypomania, poor health), and 4 prison scales (adjustment to prison, habitual criminalism, parole violator, overcontrolled hostility), reproduction of critical items with responses, a profile of the validity and clinical scores, additional narrative statements based on 10 of the content scales, and a summary data sheet of scores and item responses; 3 of the 14 special scales are utilized in the computerized narrative statements; no manual; program by Raymond D. Fowler, Jr.; Psychological Assessment Services.*

For additional information and reviews by Fred L. Adair and James N. Butcher, see 8:622.

[1502]
[Re Minnesota Multiphasic Personality Inventory.] Roche MMPI Computerized Interpretation Service. A computerized scoring and interpreting service for clinical psychologists and physicians in clinical practice and research; 1966–76; 2 reports available: complete report (interpretive), scores and profile only (technical); the interpretive report is a 5–8 page computer printout presenting a narrative report, scores on 4 validity scales, 10 clinical scales, and 22 other scales: 12 special scales (ego strength, maladjustment, first factor, second factor, dependency, dominance, responsibility, prejudice, social status, control, manifest anxiety, social desirability) and 10

content scales (depression, poor morale, psychoticism, phobias, organic symptoms, authority conflict, manifest hostility, family problems, hypomania, social maladjustment), reproduction of critical items with responses, the MacAndrews scales elevation, and a profile of the validity and clinical scales; only the validity and clinical scales are utilized in the computerized narrative statements; the technical report is a 2 page computer printout presenting a profile of the validity and clinical scales, scores on these scales plus the 12 special scales, the MacAndrews scale elevation, and a list of item responses; (Spanish testbook available); manual by Raymond D. Fowler, Jr.; Roche Psychiatric Service Institute.*

For additional information and a review by James N. Butcher, see 8:624 (7 references); see also T2:1285 (2 references); for reviews by William J. Eichman and Benjamin Kleinmuntz, see 7:105 and 7:109 (6 references); see also P:169 (9 references).

[1503]
Minnesota Percepto-Diagnostic Test (Revised). Ages 5-16; 1962-69; MPDT; brain damage and emotional disturbances; G. B. Fuller and J. T. Laird (test); Clinical Psychology Publishing Co., Inc.*

For additional information, see 8:872 (22 references); see also T2:1485 (17 references) and P:457 (19 references); for reviews by Richard W. Coan and Eugene E. Levitt of the original edition, see 6:231 (2 references).

REFERENCES

1-2. See 6:231.
3-21. See P:457.
22-38. See T2:1485.
39-60. See 8:872.
61. REICHURDT, K. W. Playing dead or running away—Defense reactions during reading. *Journal of Reading*, 1977, 20, 706-711.
62. ROCHFORD, J., GRANT, I., & LAVIGNE, G. Medical students and drugs: Further neuropsychological and use pattern considerations. *International Journal of the Addictions*, 1977, 12, 1057-1065.
63. WALLBROWN, J. D., WALLBROWN, F. H., & ENGIN, A. W. The validity of two clinical tests of visual–motor perception. *Journal of Clinical Psychology*, 1977, 33, 491-495.
64. CROOKES, T. G. Factors in the rotation of reproduced figures. *Journal of Clinical Psychology*, 1978, 34, 446-449.
65. CARROLL, J. A., FULLER, G. B., & CARROLL, J. L. Comparison of culturally deprived school achievers and underachievers on memory function and perception. *Perceptual & Motor Skills*, 1979, 48, 59-62.
66. FULLER, G. B., & FRIEDRICH, D. Visual–motor test performance: Race and achievement variables. *Journal of Clinical Psychology*, 1979, 35, 621-623.
67. STONES, M. J. Rekitting the Wechsler Paired–Associate Task: The Waterford Index. *Journal of Clinical Psychology*, 1979, 35, 626-630.
68. CONNERS, C. K., & TAYLOR, E. Pemoline, methylphenidate, and placebo in children with minimal brain dysfunction. *Archives of General Psychiatry*, 1980, 37, 922-930.
69. FULLER, G. B., & LOVINGER, S. L. Personality characteristics of three sub-groups of children with reading disabilities. *Perceptual & Motor Skills*, 1980, 50, 303-308.
70. PUTNAM, L. R. Minnesota Percepto–Diagnostic Test and reading achievement. *Perceptual & Motor Skills*, 1981, 53, 235-238.

[1504]
★Minnesota Preschool Inventory. Ages 3-4, 4-6; 1975-80; MPI; observations by mothers; "to identify children whose development and/or adjustment pose a high risk for failure in kindergarten"; 2 forms; Harold Ireton and Edward Thwing; Behavior Science Systems, Inc.*

a) [ORIGINAL FORM]. Ages 4-6; 1975-79; 7 developmental scales: self-help, fine motor, expressive language, comprehension, memory, letter recognition, number comprehension; 4 adjustment scales: immaturity, hyperactivity, behavior problems, emotional problems; 4 symptom categories: motor, language, somatic, sensory.
b) FORM 34. Ages 3-4; 1980; 4 developmental scales: self-help, fine motor, expressive language, comprehension; 4 adjustment scales: immaturity, hyperactivity, behavior problems, emotional problems; 5 symptom scales: motor, language, somatic, vision, hearing.

[1505]
Minnesota Preschool Scale. Ages 1.5-6.0; 1932-40; MPS; 3 scores: verbal, nonverbal, total; Florence L. Goodenough, Katherine M. Maurer, and M. J. Van Wagenen; American Guidance Service.*

See T2:509 (2 references); for a review by Marjorie P. Honzik, see 6:528 (3 references); see also 4:351 (2 references); for a review by Beth L. Wellman, see 3:286 (2 references); for reviews by Rachel Stutsman Ball, Nancy Bayley, and Florence M. Teagarden of the original edition, see 2:1407 (3 references).

REFERENCES

1-3. See 2:1407.
4-5. See 3:286.
6-7. See 4:351.
8-10. See 6:528.
11-12. See T2:509.
13. JOHNSON, E. G. A battery of tasks to examine Luria's theory of the development of verbal control of motor behavior in Australian preschoolers. *Genetic Psychology Monographs*, 1980, 102, 269-298.
14. NIELSEN, H. H. A longitudinal study of the psychological aspects of myelomeningocele. *Scandinavian Journal of Psychology*, 1980, 21, 45-54.

[1506]
Minnesota Rate of Manipulation Test, 1969 Edition. Grade 7 to adults; 1931-69; MRMT; revision of *Minnesota Manual Dexterity Test*; 5 scores: placing, turning, displacing, 1-hand turning and placing, 2-hand turning and placing; test by Minnesota Employment Stabilization Research Institute; American Guidance Service.*

See T2:2227 (10 references); for a review by Lyle F. Schoenfeldt, see 7:1046 (10 references); see also 6:1077 (24 references); for reviews by Edwin E. Ghiselli and John R. Kinzer and an excerpted review, see 3:663 (23 references); for reviews by Lorene Teegarden and Morris S. Viteles, see 2:1662 (4 references).

REFERENCES

1-4. See 2:1662.
5-26. See 3:663.
27-50. See 6:1077.
51-60. See 7:1046.
61-70. See T2:2227.
71. ELFANT, I. L. Correlation between kinesthetic discrimination and manual dexterity. *American Journal of Occupational Therapy*, 1977, 31, 23-28.
72. ZAIDEL, D., & SPERRY, R. W. Some long-term motor effects of cerebral commissurotomy in man. *Neuropsychologia*, 1977, 6, 193-204.
73. DASTOOR, D. P., KLINGNER, A., MULLER, H. F., & KACHANOFF, R. A psychogeriatric assessment program. V. Three-year follow-up. *Journal of the American Geriatrics Society*, 1979, 27, 162-169.
74. HUSAK, W. S., & MAGILL, R. A. Correlations among perceptual-motor ability, self-concept and reading achievement in early elementary grades. *Perceptual & Motor Skills*, 1979, 48, 447-450.
75. MULLER, H. F., DASTOOR, D. P., KLINGNER, A., COLE, M., & BOILLAT, J. Amantadine in senile dementia: Electroencephalographic and clinical effects. *Journal of the American Geriatrics Society*, 1979, 27, 9-16.

[1507]
Minnesota Reading Examination for College Students. Grades 9-16; 1930-35; 2 scores: vocabulary, paragraph reading; Melvin E. Haggerty and Alvin C. Eurich; University of Minnesota Press.*

See T2:1568 (7 references); for a review by James M. McCallister, see 3:491 (3 references); for a review by W. C. McCall, see 2:1554 (3 references); for a review by Ruth Strang, see 1:1106.

[1508]
Minnesota Satisfaction Questionnaire. Business and industry; 1963–67; MSQ; job satisfaction; David J. Weiss, René V. Dawis, George W. England, and Lloyd H. Lofquist; Vocational Psychology Research.*

a) LONG FORM. 21 scores: ability utilization, achievement, activity, advancement, authority, company policies and practices, compensation, coworkers, creativity, independence, moral values, recognition, responsibility, security, social service, social status, supervision—human relations, supervision—technical, variety, working conditions, general satisfaction.

b) SHORT FORM. 3 scores: intrinsic, extrinsic, general.

For additional information and a review by Robert M. Guion, see 8:1052 (82 references); see also T2:2285 (11 references); for reviews by Lewis E. Albright and John P. Foley, Jr., see 7:1064 (18 references).

REFERENCES

1–18. See 7:1064.
19–29. See T2:2285.
30–111. See 8:1052.
112. ARVEY, R. D., & GROSS, R. H. Satisfaction levels and correlates of satisfaction in the homemaker job. *Journal of Vocational Behavior*, 1977, 10, 13–24.
113. BLEDSOE, J. C., & BROWN, S. E. Factor structure of the Minnesota Satisfaction Questionnaire. *Perceptual & Motor Skills*, 1977, 45, 301–302.
114. ELIZUR, D., & TZINER, A. Vocational needs, job rewards, and satisfaction: A canonical analysis. *Journal of Vocational Behavior*, 1977, 10, 205–211.
115. FOLKINS, C., O'REILLY, C., III, ROBERTS, K., & MILLER, S. Physical environment and job satisfaction in a community mental health center. *Community Mental Health Journal*, 1977, 13, 24–30.
116. ILGEN, D. R., & HOLLENBACK, J. H. The role of job satisfaction in absence behavior. *Organizational Behavior & Human Performance*, 1977, 19, 148–161.
117. KATZ, R., & VAN MAANEN, J. The loci of work satisfaction: Job, interaction, and policy. *Human Relations*, 1977, 30, 469–486.
118. KUTIE, R. C. An analysis of the job dimensions of word processing secretaries, administrative support secretaries, and traditional secretaries and the correlation of these job dimensions with job satisfaction factors. *Business Education Forum*, 1977, 32, 38–40.
119. MCLEAN, G. N. Effectiveness of model office, cooperative office education, and office procedures courses based on employee satisfaction and satisfactoriness eighteen months after graduation. *Delta Pi Epsilon Journal*, 1977, 19(4), 21–28.
120. SCHWAB, D. P., & HENEMAN, H. G., III. Age and satisfaction with dimension of work. *Journal of Vocational Behavior*, 1977, 10, 212–220.
121. BROWN, S. E., & BLEDSOE, J. C. Job satisfaction of school superintendents as related to perceptions of leader's behavior. *Psychological Reports*, 1978, 42, 171–174.
122. DIPBOYE, R. L., ZULTOWSKI, W. H., DEWHIRST, H. D., & ARVEY, R. D. Self-esteem as a moderator of the relationship between scientific interests and the job satisfaction of physicists and engineers. *Journal of Applied Psychology*, 1978, 63, 289–294.
123. FEILD, H. S., HOLLEY, W. H., & ARMENAKIS, A. A. Computerized answer sheets: What effects on response to a mail survey. *Educational & Psychological Measurement*, 1978, 38, 755–759.
124. FRONTZ, H. O. Sources of job satisfaction and dissatisfaction among psychiatric aides. *Hospital & Community Psychiatry*, 1978, 29, 229–230.
125. KENIS, I. Leadership behavior, subordinate personality, and satisfaction with supervision. *Journal of Psychology*, 1978, 98, 99–107.
126. MOTOWIDLO, S. J., & BORMAN, W. C. Relationships between military morale, motivation, satisfaction, and unit effectiveness. *Journal of Applied Psychology*, 1978, 63, 47–52.
127. PHILLIPS, E., & HAYS, J. R. Job satisfaction and perceived congruence of attitude between workers and supervisors in a mental health setting. *Perceptual & Motor Skills*, 1978, 47, 55–59.
128. SCHRIESHEIM, C. A. Job satisfaction, attitudes toward unions, and voting in a union representation election. *Journal of Applied Psychology*, 1978, 63, 548–552.
129. ARVEY, R. D., & DEWHIRST, H. D. Relationships between diversity of interests, age, job satisfaction and job performance. *Journal of Occupational Psychology*, 1979, 52, 17–23.
130. BLEDSOE, J. C., & BABER, W. C. Factor invariance in the measurement of job satisfaction. *Perceptual & Motor Skills*, 1979, 48, 985–986.
131. DIPBOYE, R. L., ZULTOWSKI, W. H., DEWHIRST, H. D., & ARVEY, R. D. Self-esteem as a moderator of performance–satisfaction relationships. *Journal of Vocational Behavior*, 1979, 15, 193–206.
132. DITTRICH, J. E., & CARRELL, M. R. Organizational equity perceptions, employee job satisfaction, and departmental absence and turnover rates. *Organizational Behavior & Human Performance*, 1979, 24, 29–40.
133. CHELOHA, R. S., & FARR, J. L. Absenteeism, job involvement, and job satisfaction in an organizational setting. *Journal of Applied Psychology*, 1980, 65, 467–473.
134. FRY, L. W., & GREENFELD, S. An examination of attitudinal differences between policewomen and policemen. *Journal of Applied Psychology*, 1980, 65, 123–126.
135. IVANCEVICH, J. M. A longitudinal study of behavioral expectation scales: Attitudes and performance. *Journal of Applied Psychology*, 1980, 65, 139–146.
136. SCHMITT, N., & MELLON, P. M. Life and job satisfaction: Is the job central? *Journal of Vocational Behavior*, 1980, 16, 51–58.
137. BERGMANN, T. J. Managers and their organizations: An interactive approach to multidimensional job satisfaction. *Journal of Occupational Psychology*, 1981, 54, 275–288.
138. JOHNSTON, G. S., YEAKEY, C. C., & WINTER, R. A. A study of the relationship between the job satisfaction of principals and the perceived level of teacher militancy. *Alberta Journal of Educational Research*, 1981, 27, 352–365.

[1509]
Minnesota Satisfactoriness Scales. Employees; 1965–70; MSS; ratings by supervisors; 5 scores: performance, conformance, dependability, personal adjustment, general satisfactoriness; Dennis L. Gibson, David J. Weiss, René V. Dawis, and Lloyd H. Lofquist; Vocational Psychology Research.*

For additional information and a review by Jerome E. Doppelt, see 8:1061 (9 references).

REFERENCES

1–9. See 8:1061.
10. MCLEAN, G. N. Effectiveness of model office, cooperative office education, and office procedures courses based on employee satisfaction and satisfactoriness eighteen months after graduation. *Delta Pi Epsilon Journal*, 1977, 19(4), 21–28.
11. PETERS, J. W. R. The relationship of the satisfactoriness of North Dakota vocationally trained employees to selected factors of the employee, the supervisor, and the organization. *Business Education Forum*, 1978, 33, 42–43.

[1510]
Minnesota Scholastic Aptitude Test. High school and college; 1969–72, c1940–72; MSAT; a short form of the *Ohio State University Psychological Test*, Form 23; originally prepared for use in Minnesota secondary schools; Wilbur L. Layton; original test by Herbert A. Toops; Wilbur L. Layton.*

For additional information and a review by William B. Michael, see 8:193 (10 references); see also T2:405 (31 references).

REFERENCES

1–31. See T2:405.
32–41. See 8:193.
42. DUFF, T. B. Measurement of personal economic understandings developed in basic business. *Business Education Forum*, 1977, 32, 35–37.
43. KIM, P. Y. Personal economic understanding and college business and economics courses. *Delta Pi Epsilon Journal*, 1977, 14, 22–35.
44. FOWLER, B., & KROLL, B. M. Verbal skills as factors in the passageless validation of reading comprehension tests. *Perceptual & Motor Skills*, 1978, 47, 335–338.

45. LATTA, R. M., DOLPHIN, W. D., & GRABE, M. Individual differences model applied to instruction and evaluation of large college classes. *Journal of Educational Psychology*, 1978, 70, 960–970.
46. MCLEAN, G. N. The relationship between typewriting performance and shorthand transcription skills. *Delta Pi Epsilon Journal*, 1978, 20(1), 20–25.
47. WHITELY, S. E., & DOYLE, K. O., JR. Validity and generalizability of student ratings from between–classes and within–class data. *Journal of Educational Psychology*, 1979, 71, 117–124.
48. STINARD, T. A., & DOLPHIN, W. D. Which students benefit from self–paced mastery instruction and why. *Journal of Educational Psychology*, 1981, 73, 754–763.

[1511]

*Minnesota Spatial Relations Test, Revised Edition. Ages 16 and over; 1930–79; MSRT; revision of H. C. Link's *Spatial Relations Test*; 2 scores: time, error; American Guidance Service.*

See T2:2258 (23 references); for a review by Milton L. Blum, see 3:664 (18 references); for a review by Lorene Teegarden, see 2:1663 (10 references).

[1512]

Minnesota Speed of Reading Test for College Students. Grades 12–16; 1936; Alvin C. Eurich; University of Minnesota Press.*

See T2:1749 (13 references); for a review by J. R. Gerberich, see 2:1555 (2 references); for reviews by Frederick B. Davis and Ruth Strang, see 1:1107.

[1513]

Minnesota Test for Differential Diagnosis of Aphasia. Adults; 1965–73, c1948–73; MTDDA; used to classify subjects into 5 major and 2 minor categories of aphasia; 47 tests (9 auditory, 9 visual and reading, 15 speech and language, 10 visuomotor and writing, and 4 numerical relations and arithmetic processes); Hildred Schuell and Joyce W. Sefer (technical manual); University of Minnesota Press.*

See T2:2080 (4 references); for reviews by David Jones and Seymour Rigrodsky, see 7:958 (7 references); see also P:172 (8 references).

REFERENCES

1–8. See P:172.
9–15. See 7:958.
16–19. See T2:2080.
20. APRIL, R. S., & TSE, P. C. Crossed aphasia in a Chinese bilingual dextral. *Archives of Neurology*, 1977, 34, 766–770.
21. KIMURA, D. Acquisition of a motor skill after left–hemisphere damage. *Brain*, 1977, 100, 527–542.
22. MCGLONE, J. Sex differences in the cerebral organization of verbal functions in patients with unilateral brain lesions. *Brain*, 1977, 100, 775–793.
23. WIIG, E. H., LAPOINT, C., & SEMEL, E. M. Relationships among language processing and production abilities of learning disabled adolescents. *Journal of Learning Disabilities*, 1977, 10, 292–299.
24. COUGHLAN, A. K., & WARRINGTON, E. K. Word comprehension and word–retrieval in patients with localized cerebral lesions. *Brain*, 1978, 101, 163–185.
25. LOZANO, R. A., & DREYER, D. E. Some effects of delayed auditory feedback on dyspraxia of speech. *Journal of Communication Disorders*, 1978, 11, 407–415.
26. WALLER, M. R., & DARLEY, F. L. The influence of context on the auditory comprehension of paragraphs by aphasic subjects. *Journal of Speech & Hearing Research*, 1978, 21, 732–745.
27. DAVID, R. M., ENDERBY, P., & BAINTON, D. Progress report on an evaluation of speech therapy for aphasia. *British Journal of Disorders of Communication*, 1979, 14, 85–88.
28. MARQUARDT, T. P., REINHART, J. B., & PETERSON, H. A. Markedness analysis of phonemic substitution errors in apraxia of speech. *Journal of Communication Disorders*, 1979, 12, 481–494.
29. POWELL, G. E. Categories of aphasia: A cluster–analysis of Schuell Test profiles. *British Journal of Disorders of Communication*, 1979, 14, 111–122.
30. ROSS, A. J. A study of the application of blissymbolics as a means of communication for a young brain damaged adult. *British Journal of Disorders of Communication*, 1979, 14, 103–109.
31. BARRON, J., WHITELEY, S. J., HORN, A. C., RALSTON, A. R., & ACKRILL, P. A new approach to the early detection of dialysis encephalopathy. *British Journal of Disorders of Communication*, 1980, 15, 75–85.
32. POWELL, G. E., BAILEY, S., & CLARK, E. A very short version of the Minnesota Aphasia Test. *British Journal of Social & Clinical Psychology*, 1980, 19, 189–194.
33. BAILEY, S., POWELL, G. E., & CLARK, E. A note on intelligence and recovery from aphasia: The relationships between Raven's matrices and scores and change on the Schuell Aphasia Test. *British Journal of Disorders of Communication*, 1981, 16, 193–203.

[1514]

★Miskimins Self-Goal-Other Discrepancy Scale. Children and adults; 1967–79; MSGO; 8 scores: 7 factor scores (self-goal culturally typical goals, self-goal culturally atypical goals, self-others overvaluing others, self-others critical others, self-others globally critical others, self-others critical others-personal, negativistic or random responding), total; R. W. Miskimins; Rocky Mountain Behavioral Science Institute, Inc.* (In-print status uncertain; no reply from publisher.)

REFERENCES

1. JACKSON, B. The self–concepts of business education students at the secondary level. *Delta Pi Epsilon Journal*, 1978, 20, 1–11.

[1515]

The Missouri Children's Picture Series. Ages 5–16; 1971, c1963–64; MCPS; 8 scores: conformity, masculinity-femininity, maturity, aggression, inhibition, activity level, sleep disturbance, somatization; Jacob O. Sines, Jerome D. Pauker, and Lloyd K. Sines; Psychological Assessment and Services, Inc.*

For additional information, reviews by Dale B. Harris and Lovick C. Miller, and an excerpted review by George Gilmore, see 8:625 (11 references); see also T2:1287 (4 references).

REFERENCES

1–4. See T2:1287.
5–15. See 8:625.
16. BAKER, E., ULLMAN, D. G., & STEIN, M. D. Increased reliability of an objective personality measure for children. *Psychology in the Schools*, 1978, 15, 191–193.
17. DEFILIPPIS, N. A. Concurrent validity of the Missouri Children's Picture Series. *Journal of Clinical Psychology*, 1979, 35, 433–435.
18. DROTAR, D., OWENS, R., GOTTHOLD, J. Personality adjustment of children and adolescents with hypopituitarism. *Child Psychiatry & Human Development*, 1980, 11, 59–66.

[1516]

MKM Binocular Preschool Test. Preschool; 1963–65; "near point performance"; Leland D. Michael and James W. King; MKM, Inc.*

For additional information, see 7:868.

[1517]

MKM Monocular and Binocular Reading Test. Grades 1–2, 3 and over; 1963–64; "to detect children who are likely to have reading problems associated with poor binocular coordination and macular suppression"; Leland D. Michael and James W. King; MKM, Inc.*

See T2:1920 (1 reference) and 7:869.

[1518]

MKM Picture Arrangement Test. Grades kgn–6; 1963–65; "directionality"; Leland D. Michael and James W. King; MKM, Inc.*

For additional information, see 7:870.

[1519]
MLA-Cooperative Foreign Language Tests: French. 1–2 years high school or 2 semesters college, 3–4 years high school or 4 semesters college; 1963–65; 4 tests in a single booklet: listening, speaking, reading, writing; writing test available as separate; prepared by Educational Testing Service in cooperation with the Modern Language Association of America; Addison-Wesley Publishing Co., Inc.*

For additional information and a review by Daniel R. Dupecher, see 8:123 (1 reference); see also T2:256 (1 reference); for a review by Michio Peter Hagiwara, see 7:277 (5 references). For an excerpted review by John L. D. Clark of the series, see 7:254.

[1520]
MLA-Cooperative Foreign Language Tests: German. 1–2 years high school or 2 semesters college, 3–4 years high school or 4 semesters college; 1963–65; 4 tests in a single booklet: listening, speaking, reading, writing; writing test available as separate; prepared by Educational Testing Service in cooperation with the Modern Language Association of America; Addison-Wesley Publishing Co., Inc.*

For additional information and a review by Herbert Lederer, see 8:134 (1 reference); see also T2:272 (1 reference); for a review by T. F. Naumann, see 7:290 (2 references). For an excerpted review by John L. D. Clark of the series, see 7:254.

[1521]
MLA-Cooperative Foreign Language Tests: Italian. 1–2 years high school or 2 semesters college, 3–4 years high school or 4 semesters college; 1963–65; 4 tests in a single booklet: listening, speaking, reading, writing; writing test available as separate; prepared by Educational Testing Service in cooperation with the Modern Language Association of America; Addison-Wesley Publishing Co., Inc.*

For additional information and a review by Josephine Bruno Pane, see 7:302. For an excerpted review by John L. D. Clark of the series, see 7:254.

[1522]
MLA-Cooperative Foreign Language Tests: Russian. 1–2 years high school or 2 semesters college, 3–4 years high school or 4 semesters college; 1963–65; 4 tests in a single booklet: listening, speaking, reading, writing; writing test available as separate; prepared by Educational Testing Service in cooperation with the Modern Language Association of America; Addison-Wesley Publishing Co., Inc.*

For additional information and a review by Richard Schupbach, see 8:152; see also T2:301 (1 reference); for an excerpted review by Raymond L. Bair, see 7:312 (2 references). For an excerpted review by John L. D. Clark of the series, see 7:254.

[1523]
MLA-Cooperative Foreign Language Tests: Spanish. 1–2 years high school or 2 semesters college, 3–4 years high school or 4 semesters college; 1963–65; 4 tests in a single booklet: listening, speaking, reading, writing; writing test available as separate; prepared by Educational Testing Service in cooperation with the Modern Language Association of America; Addison-Wesley Publishing Co., Inc.*

For additional information and a review by Robert Lado, see 7:322 (2 references). For an excerpted review by John L. D. Clark of the series, see 7:254.

[1524]
Modern Algebra Test: Content Evaluation Series. 1 year high school; 1972; Gerald S. Hanna; Riverside Publishing Co.*

For additional information and reviews by Jeremy Kilpatrick and J. R. Jefferson Wadkins, see 8:300.

[1525]
Modern Economics Test: Content Evaluation Series. Grades 10–12; 1971; Morris G. Sica, Sylvia Lane, and John D. Lafky; Riverside Publishing Co.*

For additional information and reviews by Lee H. Ehman and Irving Morrissett, see 8:899.

[1526]
Modern Geometry Test: Content Evaluation Series. Grades 10–12; 1971; Gerald S. Hanna; Riverside Publishing Co.*

For additional information and reviews by Len Pikaart and J. R. Jefferson Wadkins, see 8:311.

[1527]
Modern Language Aptitude Test. Grades 9 and over; 1959, c1955–58; MLAT; earlier experimental form called *Psi-Lambda Foreign Language Aptitude Battery*; 6 scores: number learning, phonetic script, spelling clues, words in sentences, paired associates, total; John B. Carroll and Stanley M. Sapon; The Psychological Corporation.*

See T2:221 (34 references); for reviews by Wayne D. Fisher (with Bertram B. Masia) and Marion F. Shaycoft, and excerpted reviews by Edward S. Bordin, Harold B. Dunkel, Herschel T. Manuel, and Laurence Siegel, see 6:357 (10 references).

REFERENCES

1–10. See 6:357.
11–44. See T2:221.
45. JAMES, C. J., & JORSTAD, H. L. Evaluating foreign language proficiency of prospective French and German teachers using standardized and native-rater instruments. *Foreign Language Annals*, 1977, 10, 549–560.
46. JOINER, E. G. Communicative versus non-communicative language practice in the teaching of beginning college French. *Modern Language Journal*, 1977, 61, 236–242.
47. NIEMAN, L. L., & SMITH, W. F. Individualized instruction: Its effects upon achievement and interest in beginning Spanish. *Modern Language Journal*, 1978, 62, 157–167.

[1528]
Modern Photography Comprehension Test. Photography students; 1953–69; MPCT; revision of *What Do You Know About Photography?*; Martin M. Bruce; Martin M. Bruce, Ph.D., Publishers.*

For additional information and a review by David P. Campbell, see 7:547.

[1529]
Monroe Diagnostic Reading Examination for Diagnosis of Special Difficulty in Reading. Grades 1–4; [1928–29]; a combination of assessment procedures consisting of the *Revised Stanford–Binet Scales*, Gray's *Standardized Oral Reading Paragraphs*, Monroe's *Standardized Silent Reading Tests*, an adaptation of *Ayres Spelling Scale*, the arithmetic computation subtest of

Stanford Achievement Test: Arithmetic, and 9 additional tests: alphabet repeating and reading, *Iota Word Test*, letter naming, recognition of orientation, mirror reading, mirror writing, number reversals, word discrimination, sounding; Marion Monroe; Stoelting Co.*

See T2:1623 (4 references).

[1530]
Monroe's Standardized Silent Reading Test. Grades 3–5, 6–8, 9–12; 1919–59; 2 scores: rate, comprehension; Walter S. Monroe; Bobbs-Merrill Co., Inc.*

See T2:1569 (27 references); for reviews by Charles R. Langmuir and Agatha Townsend, see 6:798 (5 references).

[1531]
Mooney Problem Check List, 1950 Revision. Grades 7–9, 9–12, 13–16, adults; 1941–50; MPCL; 4 levels; Ross L. Mooney and Leonard V. Gordon (manuals, *c*, and *d*); The Psychological Corporation.*

a) JUNIOR HIGH SCHOOL FORM. Grades 7–9; 1942–50; 7 scores: health and physical development, school, home and family, money-work-the future, boy and girl relations, relations to people in general, self-centered concerns.

b) HIGH SCHOOL FORM. Grades 9–12; 1941–50; 11 scores: health and physical development, finances-living conditions-employment, social and recreational activities, social-psychological relations, personal-psychological relations, courtship-sex-marriage, home and family, morals and religion, adjustment to school work, the future-vocational and educational, curriculum and teaching procedure.

c) COLLEGE FORM. Grades 13–16; 1941–50; 11 scores: same as for High School Form.

d) ADULT FORM. Adults; 1950; 9 scores: health, economic security, self-improvement, personality, home and family, courtship, sex, religion, occupation.

For additional information, see 8:626 (48 references); see also T2:1289 (92 references) and P:173 (55 references); for a review by Thomas C. Burgess, see 6:145 (25 references); see also 5:89 (26 references); for reviews by Harold E. Jones and Morris Krugman, see 4:73 (13 references); for reviews by Ralph C. Bedell and Theodore F. Lentz, of an earlier form of *a–c*, see 3:67 (17 references).

REFERENCES

1–17. See 3:67.
18–30. See 4:73.
31–56. See 5:89.
57–81. See 6:145.
82–136. See P:173.
137–228. See T2:1289.
229–276. See 8:626.
277. BERRY, G. L. Counseling needs of disadvantaged veterans. *Journal of College Student Personnel*, 1977, 18, 406–412.
278. PLUTCHIK, R., HYMAN, I., CONTE, H., & KARASU, T. B. Medical symptoms and life stresses in psychiatric emergency-room patients. *Journal of Abnormal Psychology*, 1977, 86, 447–449.
279. ANASTASIOW, N. J., EVERETT, M., O'SHAUGHNESSY, T. E., EGGLESTON, P. J., & EKLUND, S. J. Improving teenage attitudes toward children, child handicaps, and hospital settings: A child development curriculum for potential parents. *American Journal of Orthopsychiatry*, 1978, 48, 663–672.
280. DOMINO, G., & DEGROOTE, M. V. A comparison of counseling seekers and nonseekers on the Mooney Problem Checklist. *Journal of College Student Personnel*, 1978, 19, 33–36.
281. GUPTA, M., & GUPTA, P. Family problems of adolescent girls and their effect on verbal learning. *Psychological Studies*, 1978, 23, 25–29.
282. PALLADINO, J. J., & DOMINO, G. Differences between counseling center clients and nonclients on three measures. *Journal of College Student Personnel*, 1978, 19, 497–501.
283. PALLADINO, J. J., & TRYON, G. S. Have the problems of entering freshmen changed? *Journal of College Student Personnel*, 1978, 19, 313–316.
284. ROBYAK, J. E. Study skills versus non–study skills students: A discriminant analysis. *Journal of Educational Research*, 1978, 71, 161–166.
285. ROBYAK, J. E., & DOWNEY, R. G. Effectiveness of a study skills course for students of different academic achievement levels and personality types. *Journal of Counseling Psychology*, 1978, 25, 544–550.
286. SWEARINGEN, D. J. What does the patient think? An evaluation of a general psychiatric ward. *Hospital & Community Psychiatry*, 1978, 29, 182–184.
287. TRYON, G. S. Differences between counseling seekers and nonseekers on the Mooney Problem Checklist. *Journal of College Student Personnel*, 1978, 19, 501–505.
288. WOUDENBERG, R. A., & PAYNE, P. A. An examination of the training therapy principle. *Journal of College Student Personnel*, 1978, 19, 141–145.
289. CALISTE, E. R. "Students" adjustment from open to structured schools. *Contemporary Education*, 1979, 50, 138–145.
290. GARWOOD, S. G., & ALLEN, L. Self-concept and identified problem differences between pre– and postmenarcheal adolescents. *Journal of Clinical Psychology*, 1979, 35, 528–537.
291. PARADISE, L. V., & WILDER, D. H. The relationship between client reluctance and counseling effectiveness. *Counselor Education & Supervision*, 1979, 19, 35–41.
292. SEAY, T. A., & ALTEKRUSE, M. K. Verbal and nonverbal behavior in judgments of facilitative conditions. *Journal of Counseling Psychology*, 1979, 26, 108–119.
293. SWAN, M., & WILSON, L. J. Sexual and marital problems in a psychiatric out–patient population. *British Journal of Psychiatry*, 1979, 135, 310–314.
294. COURSEY, R. D., BUCHSBAUM, M. S., & MURPHY, D. L. Psychological characteristics of subjects identified by platelet MAO activity and evoked potentials as biologically at risk for psychopathology. *Journal of Abnormal Psychology*, 1980, 89, 151–164.
295. NIDIFFER, F. D. Combining cognitive and behavioral approaches to suicidal depression: A 42–month follow–up. *Psychological Reports*, 1980, 47, 539–542.

[1532]
Moore Eye-Hand Coordination and Color-Matching Test. Ages 2–6, 7 and over; 1949–68; 2 levels; Joseph E. Moore; Joseph E. Moore and Associates.*

a) THE MOORE EYE-HAND COORDINATION TEST: PRESCHOOL FORM. Ages 2–6.

b) MOORE EYE-HAND COORDINATION AND COLOR-MATCHING TEST. Ages 7 and over; 2 scores: eye-hand coordination, color matching.

See T2:1880 (2 references) and 5:872 (1 reference); for reviews by Norman Frederiksen and Jay L. Otis, see 4:750 (6 references).

[1533]
Moray House English Tests. Ages 8.5–10.5, 10–12, 12–14; 1935–70; 3 levels; Godfrey Thomson Unit, University of Edinburgh; Hodder & Stoughton Educational [England].*

a) MORAY HOUSE JUNIOR ENGLISH TEST. Ages 8.5–10.5; 1952–70.

b) MORAY HOUSE ENGLISH TEST. Ages 10–12; 1935–69.

c) MORAY HOUSE ENGLISH TEST (ADV.). Ages 12–14; 1947–58.

See T2:95 (6 references) and 7:202 (1 reference); for a review by M. Alan Brimer, see 6:271 (7 references).

REFERENCES

1–7. See 6:271.
8. See 7:202.
9–14. See T2:95.
15. BEHRENS, L. T., & VERNON, P. E. Personality correlates of over-achievement and under-achievement. *British Journal of Educational Psychology*, 1978, 48, 290–297.

[1534]
Moray House Mathematics Tests. Ages 8.5–10.5, 10–12; 1964–70; 2 levels; distribution restricted to education authorities; Godfrey Thomson Unit, University of Edinburgh; Hodder & Stoughton Educational [England].*
a) MORAY HOUSE JUNIOR MATHEMATICS TEST. Ages 8.5–10.5; 1964–70.
b) MORAY HOUSE MATHEMATICS TEST. Ages 10–12; 1964–69.
For additional information, see 7:482.

[1535]
Moray House Verbal Reasoning Tests. Ages 8.5–10.5, 10–12, 12–14.5, 13.5 and over; 1930–72; formerly listed as *Moray House Intelligence Tests*; 5 levels, 4 levels currently available; Godfrey Thomson Unit, University of Edinburgh; Hodder & Stoughton Educational [England].*
a) MORAY HOUSE JUNIOR REASONING TEST FOR NINE YEAR OLDS. Ages 8.5–10.5; 1947–70; formerly called *Moray House Junior Intelligence Test*.
b) MORAY HOUSE VERBAL REASONING TEST. Ages 10–12; 1930–72; formerly called *Moray House Intelligence Tests*; 1–3 new forms issued annually; distribution of forms 75–89 restricted to education authorities.
c) MORAY HOUSE VERBAL REASONING TEST: VERNIER TEST 2. Ages 10–12 of above average ability; 1954–57. Out of print.
d) MORAY HOUSE VERBAL REASONING TEST (ADV.). Ages 12–14.5; 1940–68.
e) MORAY HOUSE VERBAL REASONING TEST (ADULT) 1. Ages 13.5 and over; 1952–70; formerly called *Moray House Adult Intelligence Test* 1.

See T2:409 (18 references), 7:364 (3 references), 6:474 (13 references), and 5:353 (2 references); for a review by Patrick Slater of earlier forms, see 3:241 (2 references); for a review by C. Ebblewhite Smith, see 2:1409.

REFERENCES
1–2. See 3:241.
3–4. See 5:353.
5–17. See 6:474.
18–20. See 7:364.
21–38. See T2:409.
39. DOWLING, J. R. Adjustment from primary to secondary school: A one year follow-up. *British Journal of Educational Psychology*, 1980, 50, 26–32.
40. SEYMOUR, P. H. K., & MOIR, W. L. N. Intelligence and semantic judgement time. *British Journal of Psychology*, 1980, 71, 53–61.

[1536]
The Moreton Mathematics Tests. Grades 3–5, 5–7; 1970–74; MMT; metric revision; 2 levels; R. J. Andrews, J. Elkins, and R. G. Cochrane; Teaching and Testing Resources [Australia].*
a) LEVEL 2. Grades 3–5; 1970–74; 2 tests called Forms N (numerical operations), P (mathematical applications).
b) LEVEL 3. Grades 5–7; 1972–74; numerical operations.
For additional information, see 8:285; see also T2:641 (1 reference).

[1537]
The Mother-Child Relationship Evaluation. Mothers; 1961; MCRE; experimental form; 5 scores: 4 direct scores (acceptance, overprotection, overindulgence, rejection) and 1 derived score (confusion-dominance); Robert M. Roth; Western Psychological Services.*

For additional information, see P:174; for reviews by John Elderkin Bell and Dale B. Harris, see 6:146.

REFERENCES
1. KRAUTHAMER, C. Maternal attitudes of alcoholic and nonalcoholic upper middle class women. *International Journal of the Addictions*, 1979, 14, 639–644.
2. EPSTEIN, J., BERG-CROSS, G., & BERG-CROSS, L. Maternal expectations and birth order in families with learning disabled and normal children. *Journal of Learning Disabilities*, 1980, 13, 45–52.
3. MEIJER, A., & HOVNE, R. Child psychiatric problems in "autonomous dysfunction." *Child Psychiatry & Human Development*, 1981, 12, 96–105.

[1538]
Motivation Analysis Test. Ages 17 and over; 1959–75; MAT; 40–45 scores: 4 motivation scores (integrated, unintegrated, total, conflict) for each of 5 drives (mating, assertiveness, fear, narcism-comfort, pugnacity-sadism) and each of 5 sentiment structures (superego, self-sentiment, career, home-parental, sweetheart-spouse), plus 5 optional scores (total integration, total personal interest, total conflict, autism-optimism, information-intelligence); Raymond B. Cattell, John L. Horn, and Arthur B. Sweney, with the assistance of John A. Radcliffe; Institute for Personality and Ability Testing, Inc.*

For additional information, see 8:627 (31 references); see also T2:1291 (13 references); for reviews by Henry A. Alker and Andrew L. Comrey, and an excerpted review by Gilbert E. Mazer of the 1964 test, see 7:110 (18 references); see also P:175 (6 references).

REFERENCES
1–6. See P:175.
7–24. See 7:110.
25–37. See T2:1291.
38–68. See 8:627.
69. STEWART, D. W. The self–sentiment: Comment on internal consistency of Cattell's theory. *Psychological Reports*, 1977, 40, 267–270.
70. KAWASH, G., & BUSCH, N. Personal dynamic conflict as a predictor of expressed marital happiness. *Journal of Clinical Psychology*, 1978, 34, 171–176.
71. JAMES, J. F., GREGORY, D., JONES, R. K., & RUNDELL, O. H. Psychiatric morbidity in prisons. *Hospital & Community Psychiatry*, 1980, 31, 674–677.

[1539]
***Motivation and Potential for Adoptive Parenthood Scale.** Adults seeking to adopt children; 1977; MPAPS; ratings by caseworkers; 3 scores: motivation, potential, total; Byron W. Lindholm and John Touliatos; Monitor.*
For additional information, see 8:317.

[1540]
Motor-Free Visual Perception Test. Ages 4–8; 1972; MVPT; Ronald P. Colarusso and Donald D. Hammill; Academic Therapy Publications.*
For additional information, a review by Carl L. Rosen, and an excerpted review by Alan Krichev, see 8:883 (9 references).

REFERENCES
1–9. See 8:883.
10. HUDGINS, A. L. Assessment of visual–motor disabilities in young children: Toward differential diagnosis. *Psychology in the Schools*, 1977, 14, 252–260.
11. JOHNSON, D. L., BREKKE, B., & HARLOW, S. D. Appropriateness of the Motor-Free Visual Perception Test when used with the mentally retarded. *Education & Training of the Mentally Retarded*, 1977, 12, 312–315.
12. DONOVAN, G., & MITCHELL, M. M. Analysis of the Developmental Test of Visual Perception and the Motor–Free Visual Perception Test. *Perceptual & Motor Skills*, 1978, 46, 1284–1286.

13. COLARUSSO, R. P., MATHIS, G., & SHESSEL, D. Teacher effectiveness in identifying high-risk kindergarten children. *Journal of Learning Disabilities*, 1979, 12, 684-686.
14. HARBER, J. R. Measures of visual closure. *Perceptual & Motor Skills*, 1979, 48, 206.
15. SABATINO, D. A. The definition and assessment of visual and auditory perception. *Journal of Clinical Child Psychology*, 1979, 8, 188-194.
16. SEXTON, L. C., & TRELOAR, J. H. Auditory and visual perception, sex, and academic aptitude as predictors of achievement for first-grade children. *Measurement & Evaluation in Guidance*, 1979, 12, 140-146.
17. ZEITSCHEL, K. A., KALISH, R. A., & COLARUSSO, R. Visual perception tests used with physically handicapped children. *Academic Therapy*, 1979, 14, 565-576.
18. COLARUSSO, R., GILL, S., PLANKENHORN, A., & BROOKS, R. Predicting first-grade achievement through formal testing of 5-year-old high-risk children. *Journal of Special Education*, 1980, 14, 355-363.
19. GERARD, J. A., & JUNKALA, J. Task analysis, handwriting, and process-based instruction. *Journal of Learning Disabilities*, 1980, 13, 54-58.
20. HILL, D. S. A comparison of the performance of normal, learning disabled, and educable mentally retarded children on Cattell's ability constructs. *Journal of Learning Disabilities*, 1980, 13, 38-41.
21. BRANDES, P. J., & EHINGER, D. M. The effects of early middle ear pathology on auditory perception and academic achievement. *Journal of Speech & Hearing Disorders*, 1981, 46, 301-307.

[1541]

The Multi-Aptitude Test. College courses in testing; 1955; miniature battery of 10 tests for instructional use; Edward E. Cureton, Louise Witmer Cureton, and students; The Psychological Corporation.*

For additional information and a review by H. H. Remmers, see 5:612 (1 reference).

[1542]

Multidimensional Assessment of Philosophy of Education. Teachers and prospective teachers; 1973-76; MAPE; 6 scores: classroom climate (unstructured vs. controlling), individual differences (acknowledges vs. disregards), teaching style (personal vs. impersonal), learning emphasis (social vs. textbook), procedures and planning (utilizes vs. distrusts), theoretical base (idealistic vs. pragmatic); Wilson H. Guertin, John H. Litcher, William D. Hedges, and John T. Wilson; Parauniversity Resources.*

For additional information, see 8:379 (1 reference).

[1543]

The Multidimensional Maturity Scale. Grades kgn-12; 1968; MMS; ratings (based upon records, interviews, observations, and tests) in 6 areas: physiological, emotional, psychosexual, mental, educational, social; Barnard J. Hartman; Priority Innovations, Inc.*

For additional information, see 7:111.

[1544]

Multi-Ethnic Awareness Survey. Grades 7-12 and teachers; 1977; no manual; Gregory C. Coffin, Nancy Stackpole Coffin, Robert E. Rhodes, and Bessie Lasley Rhodes; Coffin Associates.* (In-print status uncertain; no reply from publisher.)

For additional information, see 8:318.

[1545]

Multijurisdictional Police Officer Examination. Prospective police officers; 1976; MPOE; distribution restricted to public personnel agencies; developed by Educational Testing Service for the International Association of Chiefs of Police and the publisher; technical report by Michael Rosenfeld and Richard F. Thornton; International Personnel Management Association.*

For additional information, see 8:1094.

[1546]

★**Multiphasic Environmental Assessment Procedure.** 1979; MEAP; measures and describes sheltered care settings; 5 tests; Rudolf H. Moos, Sonne Lemke, Barbara Mehren (handbook and scoring booklet), and Mary Gauvain (handbook and scoring booklet); Social Ecology Laboratory, Dept. of Psychiatry at Stanford University Medical Center.*

a) PHYSICAL AND ARCHITECTURAL FEATURES CHECKLIST. Sheltered care facility; PAF; 9 scores: physical amenities, social-recreational aids, prosthetic aids, orientational aids, safety features, architectural choice, space availability, staff facilities, community accessibility.

b) POLICY AND PROGRAM INFORMATION FORM. Policy and program-related characteristics; POLIF; 10 scores: selectivity, expectations for functioning, tolerance for deviance, policy charity, policy choice, resident control, provision for privacy, availability of health services, availability of daily living assistance, availability of social-recreational activities.

c) RESIDENT AND STAFF INFORMATION FORM. Residents and staff; RESIF; ratings by evaluator; 9 scores: staff richness, resident social resources, resident heterogeneity, resident functional abilities, resident activity level, resident integration in the community, utilization of health services, utilization of daily living assistance, utilization of social-recreational activities.

d) RATING SCALE. Sheltered care facility; RS; ratings in 4 areas: physical attractiveness, environmental diversity, resident functioning, staff functioning.

e) SHELTERED CARE ENVIRONMENT SCALE. Social environment; SCES; 7 scores: cohesion, conflict, independence, self-exploration, organization, resident influence, physical comfort.

REFERENCES

1. Moos, R. H., & LEMKE, S. Assessing the social environments of sheltered care settings. *Gerontologist*, 1979, 19, 74-82.
2. LEMKE, S., & MOOS, R. H. Assessing the institutional policies of sheltered care settings. *Journal of Gerontology*, 1980, 35, 96-107.
3. Moos, R. H., & LEMKE, S. Assessing the physical and architectural features of sheltered care settings. *Journal of Gerontology*, 1980, 35, 571-583.
4. LEMKE, S., & MOOS, R. H. The suprapersonal environments of sheltered care settings. *Journal of Gerontology*, 1981, 36, 233-243.

[1547]

Multiple Affect Adjective Check List. Grades 8-16 and adults; 1960-67; MAACL; extension of *Affect Adjective Check List*; 3 scores: anxiety, depression, hostility; Marvin Zuckerman and Bernard Lubin; EdITS/Educational and Industrial Testing Service.*

For additional information, see 8:628 (102 references); see also T2:1293 (56 references); for reviews by E. Lowell Kelly and Edwin I. Megargee, see 7:112 (60 references); see also P:176 (28 references).

REFERENCES

1-28. See P:176.
29-88. See 7:112.
89-144. See T2:1293.
145-246. See 8:628.
247. BEAR. Efficacy of alpha biofeedback training in elevating mood. *Journal of Consulting & Clinical Psychology*, 1977, 45, 334.
248. BLEDA, P. R., & SANDMAN, P. H. In smoke's way: Socioemotional reactions to another's smoking. *Journal of Applied Psychology*, 1977, 62, 452-458.
249. BLOOM, L. J., HOUSTON, B. K., HOLMES, D. S., & BURISH, T. G. The effectiveness of attentional diversion and situation redefinition for reducing stress due to a nonambiguous threat. *Journal of Research in Personality*, 1977, 11, 83-94.

250. BOND, J. B., JR. Change in anxiety level as a factor in test performance. *Alberta Journal of Educational Research*, 1977, 23, 97–102.

251. COLE, C. S., & COYNE, J. C. Situational specificity of laboratory-induced learned helplessness. *Journal of Abnormal Psychology*, 1977, 86, 615–623.

252. GATCHEL, R. J., MCKINNEY, M. E., & KOEBERNICK, L. F. Learned helplessness, depression, and physiological responding. *Psychophysiology*, 1977, 14, 25–31.

253. HANDLEY, S. L., DUNN, T. L., BAKER, J. M., COCKSHOTT, C., & GOULD, S. Mood changes in puerperium, and plasma tryptophon and cortisol concentrations. *British Medical Journal*, 1977, 2, 18–20.

254. HODGSON, R. W. Evidence of two kinds of fear aroused by threat appeals. *Psychological Reports*, 1977, 41, 788–790.

255. ISMAIL, A. H., & YOUNG, R. J. Effect of chronic exercise on the multivariate relationships between selected biochemical and personality variables. *Multivariate Behavioral Research*, 1977, 12, 49–67.

256. ISRAEL, E., & BEIMAN, I. Live versus recorded relaxation training: A controlled investigation. *Behavior Therapy*, 1977, 8, 251–254.

257. JOHNSON, R. C., & DANKO, G. P. Reinforcing the speaker: Effects of the speech, speaker, and listener. *Psychological Record*, 1977, 27, 489–492.

258. JOHNSTON, M., & HACKMANN, A. Cross-validation and response sets in repeated use of mood questionnaires. *British Journal of Social & Clinical Psychology*, 1977, 16, 235–239.

259. KAZARIAN, S. S., & EVANS, D. R. Modification of obsessional ruminations: A comparative study. *Canadian Journal of Behavioural Science*, 1977, 9, 91–100.

260. KILMANN, P. R., WAGNER, M. K., & SOTILE, W. M. The differential impact of self-monitoring on smoking behavior: An exploratory study. *Journal of Clinical Psychology*, 1977, 33, 912–914.

261. KIRSCHENBAUM, D. S., & KAROLY, P. When self-regulation fails: Tests of some preliminary hypotheses. *Journal of Consulting & Clinical Psychology*, 1977, 45, 1116–1125.

262. KUJOTH, R. K., & TOPETZES, N. J. A rational–emotive approach to mental health for college students. Study 1. *College Student Journal*, 1977, 11, 1–6.

263. KUJOTH, R. K., & TOPETZES, N. J. A rational–emotive approach to mental health for college students. Study 2. *College Student Journal*, 1977, 11, 7–11.

264. MCFARLAIN, R. A., COHEN, G. H., YODER, J., & GUIDRY, L. Psychological test and demographic variables associated with retention of narcotic addicts in treatment. *International Journal of the Addictions*, 1977, 12, 399–410.

265. MONTGOMERY, G. K. Effects of performance evaluation and anxiety on cardiac response in anticipation of difficult problem solving. *Psychophysiology*, 1977, 14, 251–257.

266. PASSINI, F. T., WATSON, C. G., DEHNEL, L., & HERDER, J. Alpha wave bio-feedback training therapy in alcoholics. *Journal of Clinical Psychology*, 1977, 33, 292–299.

267. PERSKY, H., O'BRIEN, C. P., FINE, E., HOWARD, W. J., KHAN, M. A., & BECK, R. W. The effect of alcohol and smoking on testosterone function and aggression in chronic alcoholics. *American Journal of Psychiatry*, 1977, 134, 621–625.

268. PRESSNER, J. A., & SAVITSKY, J. C. Effect of contingent and noncontingent feedback and subject expectancies on electroencephalogram biofeedback training. *Journal of Consulting & Clinical Psychology*, 1977, 45, 713–714.

269. PRYER, M. W., & DISTEFANO, M. K., JR. Correlates of locus of control among male alcoholics. *Journal of Clinical Psychology*, 1977, 33, 300–303.

270. REARDON, J. P., & TOSI, D. J. The effects of rational stage directed imagery on self-concept and reduction of psychological stress in adolescent delinquent females. *Journal of Clinical Psychology*, 1977, 33, 1084–1092.

271. SAPPINGTON, A. A. Direct manipulation of physiological arousal in induced anxiety therapy–biofeedback approach. *Journal of Clinical Psychology*, 1977, 33, 1070–1075.

272. SAPPINGTON, A. A. Two short versions of the Multiple Affect Adjective Check List. *Journal of Clinical Psychology*, 1977, 33, 700–705.

273. SHERIDAN, E. P., & MELHUS, G. E. A programmed personal growth laboratory. *Psychological Reports*, 1977, 41, 143–150.

274. WEISSBERG, M. A comparison of direct and vicarious treatments of speech anxiety: Desensitization, desensitization with coping imagery, & cognitive modification. *Behavior Therapy*, 1977, 8, 606–620.

275. WEISSBERG, M., & LAMB, D. Comparative effects of cognitive modification, systematic desensitization, and speech preparation in the reduction of speech and general anxiety. *Communication Monographs*, 1977, 44, 27–36.

276. WOODS, D. J. The repression–sensitization variable and self-reported arousal: Effects of stress and instructional set. *Journal of Consulting & Clinical Psychology*, 1977, 45, 173–183.

277. WYRICK, R. A., & WYRICK, L. C. Time experience during depression. *Archives of General Psychiatry*, 1977, 34, 1441–1443.

278. BECKMAN, L. J. Self-esteem of women alcoholics. *Journal of Studies on Alcohol*, 1978, 39, 491–498.

279. BEIMAN, I., ISRAEL, E., & JOHNSON, S. A. During training and posttraining effects of live and taped extended progressive relaxation, self-relaxation, and electromyogram biofeedback. *Journal of Consulting & Clinical Psychology*, 1978, 46, 314–321.

280. BERNDT, D. J. Construct validation of the personal and sociopolitical dimensions of Rotter's Internal–External Locus of Control Scale. *Psychological Reports*, 1978, 42, 1259–1263.

281. BLOOM, L. J., & TRAUTT, G. M. Therapeugenic factors in psychotherapy: The use of psychological tests. *Journal of Clinical Psychology*, 1978, 34, 513–518.

282. CHALUS, G. A. The mechanisms underlying attributive projection. *Journal of Personality*, 1978, 46, 362–382.

283. FORD, J. D. Therapeutic relationship in behavior therapy: An empirical analysis. *Journal of Consulting & Clinical Psychology*, 1978, 46, 1302–1314.

284. HOUSTON, B. K., BLOOM, L. J., BURISH, T. G., & CUMMINGS, E. M. Positive evaluation of stressful experiences. *Journal of Personality*, 1978, 46, 205–214.

285. KIMLICKA, T. M., & CROSS, H. J. A comparison of chronic versus casual marijuana users on personal values and behavioral orientations. *International Journal of the Addictions*, 1978, 13, 1145–1156.

286. PACHMAN, J. S., FOY, D. W., & VAN ERD, M. Goal choice of alcoholics: A comparison of those who choose total abstinence vs. those who choose responsible, controlled drinking. *Journal of Clinical Psychology*, 1978, 34, 781–783.

287. PAOLINO, T. J., JR., MCCRADY, B. S., & KOGAN, K. B. Alcoholic marriages: A longitudinal empirical assessment of alternative theories. *British Journal of Addiction*, 1978, 73, 129–138.

288. PISHKIN, V., FISHKIN, S. M., SHURLEY, J. T., LAWRENCE, B. E., & LOVALLO, W. R. Cognitive and psychophysiologic response to doxepin and chlordiazepoxide. *Comprehensive Psychiatry*, 1978, 19, 171–178.

289. RANK, D., & SUEDFELD, P. Positive reactions of alcoholic men to sensory deprivation. *International Journal of the Addictions*, 1978, 13, 807–815.

290. REVILL, S. I., & DODGE, J. A. Psychological determinants of infantile pyloric stenosis. *Archives of Diseases in Childhood*, 1978, 53, 66–68.

291. RUPERT, P. A., & HOLMES, D. S. Effects of multiple sessions of true and placebo heartrate biofeedback training on the heart rates and anxiety levels of anxious patients during and following treatment. *Psychophysiology*, 1978, 15, 582–590.

292. RUSSELL, D., PEPLAU, L. A., & FERGUSON, M. L. Developing a measure of loneliness. *Journal of Personality Assessment*, 1978, 42, 290–294.

293. SHEARD, M. H., & MARINI, J. L. Treatment of human aggressive behavior: Four case studies of the effect of lithium. *Comprehensive Psychiatry*, 1978, 19, 37–45.

294. SIBERSCHATZ, G. Selective attention and changes in clinical state. *Journal of Research in Personality*, 1978, 12, 197–204.

295. SIEGEL, J. M., & LOFTUS, E. F. Impact of anxiety and life stress upon eyewitness testimony. *Bulletin of the Psychonomic Society*, 1978, 12, 479–480.

296. WATSON, C. G., HERDER, J., & PASSINI, F. T. Alpha biofeedback therapy in alcoholics: An 18-month follow up. *Journal of Clinical Psychology*, 1978, 34, 765–769.

297. ALLOY, L. B., & ABRAMSON, L. Y. Judgment of contingency in depressed and nondepressed students: Sadder but wiser? *Journal of Experimental Psychology: General*, 1979, 108, 441–485.

298. BAKER, B. S., & LYNN, M. R. Psychiatric nursing consultation: The use of an inservice model to assist nurses in the grief process. *Journal of Psychiatric Nursing*, 1979, 17, 15–19.

299. BAUER, R. M., & CRAIGHEAD, W. E. Psychophysiological responses to the imagination of fearful and neutral situations: The effects of imagery instructions. *Behavior Therapy*, 1979, 10, 389–403.

300. BRADY, C. A., PACK, J., & BABICH, J. M. Effects of three intake procedures on mothers of disturbed children. *Psychological Reports*, 1979, 44, 459–466.

301. BURISH, T. G., & HOUSTON, B. K. Causal projection, similarity projection, and coping with threat to self-esteem. *Journal of Personality*, 1979, 47, 57–70.

302. CARSRUD, A. L., & CARSRUD, K. B. The relationship of sex role and levels of defensiveness to self-reports of fear and anxiety. *Journal of Clinical Psychology*, 1979, 35, 573–575.

303. CRAIGHEAD, W. E., KIMBALL, W. H., & REHAK, P. J. Mood changes, physiological responses, and self-statements during social rejection imagery. *Journal of Consulting & Clinical Psychology*, 1979, 47, 385–396.

304. CUTLER, N. R., & COHEN, H. B. The effect of one night's sleep loss on mood and memory in normal subjects. *Comprehensive Psychiatry*, 1979, 20, 61–66.

305. FROST, R. O., GRAF, M., & BECKER, J. Self-devaluation and depressed mood. *Journal of Consulting & Clinical Psychology*, 1979, 47, 958–962.

306. GUR, R. C., & SACKEIM, H. A. Self-deception: A concept in search of a phenomenon. *Journal of Personality & Social Psychology,* 1979, 37, 147–169.
307. HOWES, M. J., & HOKANSON, J. E. Conversational and social responses to depressive interpersonal behavior. *Journal of Abnormal Psychology,* 1979, 88, 625–634.
308. JAREMKO, M. E., & LINDSEY, R. Stress-coping abilities of individuals high and low in jealousy. *Psychological Reports,* 1979, 44, 547–553.
309. JOHNSON, J. H., SARASON, I. G., & SIEGEL, J. M. Arousal seeking as a moderator of life stress. *Perceptual & Motor Skills,* 1979, 49, 665–666.
310. LUBIN, B., & SMITH, P. B. Affect levels in one-day experimental groups. *Psychological Reports,* 1979, 45, 117–118.
311. PITTMAN, N. L., & PITTMAN, T. S. Effects of amount of helplessness training and internal–external locus of control on mood and performance. *Journal of Personality & Social Psychology,* 1979, 37, 39–47.
312. SAPPINGTON, A. A., CORSSEN, G., BECKER, A. T., & TAVAKOLI, M. Ketamine-facilitated induced anxiety therapy and its effect upon clients' reactions to stressful situations. *Journal of Clinical Psychology,* 1979, 35, 425–429.
313. SELIGMAN, M. E. P., ABRAMSON, L. Y., SEMMEL, A., & VONBAEYER, C. Depressive attributional style. *Journal of Abnormal Psychology,* 1979, 88, 242–247.
314. WATSON, C. G., JACOBS, L., & HERDER, J. Correlates of alpha, beta, and theta wave production. *Journal of Clinical Psychology,* 1979, 35, 364–369.
315. WOUDENBERG, R. A., & POLAND, W. D. Four years of encounter groups: Changes in female and male composition. *Journal of College Student Personnel,* 1979, 20, 513–520.
316. ZEMORE, R., & ELGAARD, F. Irrational beliefs and reactions to failure. *Canadian Journal of Behavioural Science,* 1979, 11, 245–251.
317. BANDLER, W., & KOHOUT, L. J. Semantics of implication operators and fuzzy relational products. *International Journal of Man-Machine Studies,* 1980, 12, 89–116.
318. BARRIOS, B. A., GINTER, E. J., SCALISE, J. J., & MILLER, F. G. Treatment of test anxiety by applied relaxation and cue-controlled relaxation. *Psychological Reports,* 1980, 46, 1287–1296.
319. BECKMAN, L. J., DAY, T., BARDSLEY, P., & SEEMAN, A. Z. The personality characteristics and family backgrounds of women alcoholics. *International Journal of the Addictions,* 1980, 15, 147–154.
320. BURGER, J. M., & ARKIN, R. M. Prediction, control, and learned helplessness. *Journal of Personality & Social Psychology,* 1980, 38, 482–491.
321. CRANDALL, J. E. Adler's concept of social interest: Theory, measurement, and implications for adjustment. *Journal of Personality & Social Psychology,* 1980, 39, 481–495.
322. GOLIN, S., JARRETT, S., STEWART, M., & DRAYTON, W. Cognitive theory and the generality of pessimism among depressed persons. *Journal of Abnormal Psychology,* 1980, 89, 101–104.
323. GORDON, W. A., FREIDENBERGS, I., DILLER, L., HIBBARD, M., WOLF, C., LEVINE, L., LIPKINS, R., EZRACHI, O., & LUCIDO, D. Efficacy of psychosocial intervention with cancer patients. *Journal of Consulting & Clinical Psychology,* 1980, 48, 743–759.
324. HACKNEY, G. R., & RIBORDY, S. C. An empirical investigation of emotional reactions to divorce. *Journal of Clinical Psychology,* 1980, 36, 105–110.
325. HANDLEY, S. L., DUNN, T. L., WALDRON, G., & BAKER, J. M. Trytophan, cortisol and puerperal mood. *British Journal of Psychiatry,* 1980, 136, 498–508.
326. HUTCHINGS, D. F., DENNEY, D. R., BASGALL, J., & HOUSTON, B. K. Anxiety management and applied relaxation in reducing general anxiety. *Behaviour Research & Therapy,* 1980, 18, 181–190.
327. JAREMKO, M. E., HADFIELD, R., & WALKER, W. E. Contribution of an educational phase to stress inoculation of speech anxiety. *Perceptual & Motor Skills,* 1980, 50, 495–501.
328. JAREMKO, M. E. The use of stress inoculation training in the reduction of public speaking anxiety. *Journal of Clinical Psychology,* 1980, 36, 735–738.
329. KEANE, T. M., & LISMAN, S. A. Alcohol and social anxiety in males: Behavioral, cognitive, and physiological effects. *Journal of Abnormal Psychology,* 1980, 89, 213–223.
330. LIPSKY, M. J., KASSINOVE, H., & MILLER, N. J. Effects of rational–emotive therapy, rational role reversal, and rational–emotive imagery on the emotional adjustment of community mental health center patients. *Journal of Consulting & Clinical Psychology,* 1980, 48, 366–374.
331. MCCOLLAM, J. B., BURISH, T. G., MAISTO, S. A., & SOBELL, M. B. Alcohol's effects on physiological arousal and self-reported affect and sensations. *Journal of Abnormal Psychology,* 1980, 89, 224–233.
332. MCGRATH, M. J., & COHEN, D. REM drive and function: A study of the interactive effects of personality and presleep condition. *Journal of Abnormal Psychology,* 1980, 89, 737–743.
333. MEYER, J. P., & MULHERIN, A. From attribution to helping: An analysis of the mediating effects of affect and expectancy. *Journal of Personality & Social Psychology,* 1980, 39, 201–210.
334. MOLINARI, V., & KHANNA, P. Locus of control and the denial of anxiety. *Psychological Reports,* 1980, 47, 131–140.
335. NIELSON, W. R., & DOBSON, K. S. The coronary-prone behavior pattern and trait anxiety: Evidence for discriminant validity. *Journal of Consulting & Clinical Psychology,* 1980, 48, 546–547.
336. PIHL, R. O., SEGAL, Z., & YANKOFSKY, L. The effect of alcohol and placebo on affective reactions of social drinkers to a procedure designed to induce depressive affect anxiety and hostility. *Journal of Clinical Psychology,* 1980, 36, 337–342.
337. PITTMAN, T. S., & PITTMAN, N. L. Deprivation of control and the attribution process. *Journal of Personality & Social Psychology,* 1980, 39, 377–389.
338. PITTNER, M. S., & HOUSTON, B. K. Response to stress, cognitive coping strategies, and the type A behavior pattern. *Journal of Personality & Social Psychology,* 1980, 39, 147–157.
339. POLIVY, J., & DOYLE, C. Laboratory induction of mood states through the reading of self-referent mood statements: Affective changes or demand characteristics? *Journal of Abnormal Psychology,* 1980, 89, 286–290.
340. SIDEROFF, S. I., & JARVIK, M. E. Conditioned responses to a videotape showing heroin-related stimuli. *International Journal of the Addictions,* 1980, 15, 529–536.
341. SILBERFARB, P. M., PHILBERT, D., & LEVINE, P. M. Psychosocial aspects of neoplastic disease: II. Affective and cognitive effects of chemotherapy in cancer patients. *American Journal of Psychiatry,* 1980, 137, 597–601.
342. SOLOMON, S., HOLMES, D. S., & MCCAUL, K. D. Behavioral control over aversive events: Does control that requires effort reduce anxiety and physiological arousal? *Journal of Personality & Social Psychology,* 1980, 39, 729–736.
343. WATSON, C. G., & HERDER, J. Effectiveness of alpha biofeedback therapy: Negative results. *Journal of Clinical Psychology,* 1980, 36, 508–513.
344. YOUNG, J. A., & PIHL, R. O. Self-control of the effects of alcohol intoxication. *Journal of Studies on Alcohol,* 1980, 41, 567–571.
345. ALLOY, L. B., ABRAMSON, L. Y., & VISCUSI, D. Induced mood and the illusion of control. *Journal of Personality & Social Psychology,* 1981, 41, 1129–1140.
346. AUSTIN, M. F., & GRANT, T. N. Interview training for college students disadvantaged in the labor market: Comparison of five instructional techniques. *Journal of Counseling Psychology,* 1981, 28, 72–75.
347. FRANCIS, K. T. Perceptions of anxiety, hostility and depression in subjects exhibiting the coronary-prone behavior pattern. *Journal of Psychiatric Research,* 1981, 16, 183–190.
348. HIGGINS, R. L., & FRAZELL, K. Arousal in alcoholics and social drinkers progressing through a drinking sequence. *International Journal of the Addictions,* 1981, 16, 1223–1231.
349. JOESTING, J. Affect changes before, during and after a 50 mile run. *Perceptual & Motor Skills,* 1981, 52, 162.
350. KALOUPEK, D. G., PETERSON, D. A., BOYD, T. L., & LEVIS, D. J. The effects of exposure to a spatial ordered fear stimulus: A study of generalization of extinction effects. *Behavior Therapy,* 1981, 12, 130–137.
351. NIELSEN, S. L., & SARASON, I. G. Emotion, personality, and selective attention. *Journal of Personality & Social Psychology,* 1981, 41, 945–960.
352. PERSKY, H., STAUSS, D., LIEF, H. I., MILLER, W. R., & O'BRIEN, C. P. Effect of the research process on human sexual behavior. *Journal of Psychiatric Research,* 1981, 16, 41–52.
353. POLIVY, J. On the induction of emotion in the laboratory: Discrete moods or multiple affect states? *Journal of Personality & Social Psychology,* 1981, 41, 803–817.
354. REICH, P., DESILVA, R. A., LOWN, B., & MURAWSKI, B. J. Acute psychological disturbances preceding life-threatening ventricular arrhythmias. *JAMA,* 1981, 246, 233–235.

[1548]

★**Multiple Assessment Programs and Services.** Entering and continuing college students; 1982; MAPS; "designed to help colleges determine the placement levels and remediation requirements of incoming as well as continuing students"; provides data in the following assessment areas: remediation, placement, exemption, selection, instruction, guidance and counseling; 3 biographical questionnaires and 60 tests derived from the following programs: *Comparative Guidance and Placement Program, Descriptive Tests of Language Skills, Descriptive Tests of Mathematics Skills, Institutional Admissions Testing Program, Institutional Test of Standard Written English,* and *Testing Academic Achievement*; program administered by The College Board and Educational Testing Service.

[1549]
The Multiple Purpose Self Trainer. High school and adults; 1951–67; a teaching-testing pull-tab device for use with any set of objective questions keyed to the given answer pattern; Charles W. Nelson; Management Research Associates.* (In-print status uncertain; no reply from publisher.)
a) SCALE OF VALUES FORM.
b) TRUE-FALSE FORM.

[1550]
★Multivariate Vocational Evaluation System. High school and adults; no date; MOVE; formerly called *The Hester Evaluation System*; 26 separate tests measuring 27 aptitudes: arm-hand steadiness, two-arm coordination, manual dexterity, finger dexterity, wrist-finger speed, two-hand coordination, machine feeding, hand/tool dexterity, perceptual accuracy, multi-limb coordination, perceptual speed, oral directions, visual-motor reversal, aiming, decision speed, lifting ability, reaction time, response orientation, hand strength, abstract reasoning, arithmetic grade level, spatial perception, depth perception, fine perceptual motor coordination, verbal reasoning, numerical reasoning, reading grade level; Evaluation Systems, Inc.*

[1551]
Murphy-Durrell Reading Readiness Analysis. First grade entrants; 1949–65, c1947–65; MDRRA; revision of *Murphy-Durrell Diagnostic Reading Readiness Test*; 6 scores: sound recognition, letter names (capitals, lower case, total), learning rate, total; Helen A. Murphy and Donald D. Durrell; The Psychological Corporation.*

For additional information and an excerpted review by Jerry Stafford, see 8:803 (13 references); see also T2:1717 (7 references); for reviews by Rebecca C. Barr and Harry Singer, see 7:758 (10 references); for reviews by Joan Bollenbacher and S. S. Dunn of the earlier edition, see 5:679 (2 references); see also 4:571 (2 references).

REFERENCES
1–2. See 4:571.
3–4. See 5:679.
5–14. See 7:758.
15–21. See T2:1717.
22–34. See 8:803.
35. PINE, M. A. Self-concept, informal education, reading achievement in grade one. *Reading Teacher*, 1978, 31, 412–417.

[1552]
Musical Aptitude Profile. Grades 4–12; 1965; MAP; 11 scores: tonal imagery (melody, harmony, total), rhythm imagery (tempo, meter, total), musical sensitivity (phrasing, balance, style, total), total; Edwin Gordon; Riverside Publishing Co.*

For additional information, see 8:98 (25 references); see also T2:209 (11 references); for reviews by Robert W. Lundin and John McLeish, see 7:249 (33 references).

REFERENCES
1–33. See 7:249.
34–44. See T2:209.
45–69. See 8:98.
70. ERLINGS, B. A pilot investigation of relationships between elementary keyboard sightreading achievement by music majors in college and selected musical profile tests. *Council for Research in Music Education. Bulletin*, 1977, 50, 14–17.
71. GREENBERG, M. A. Robert Harvey McDowell: The development and implementation of a rhythmic ability test designed for four-year-old preschool children. *Bulletin of the Council for Research in Music Education*, 1977, 51, 45–57.
72. SCHLEUTER, S. L., & DEYARMAN, R. Musical aptitude stability among primary school children. *Bulletin of the Council for Research in Music Education*, 1977, 51, 14–22.
73. COX, M. O. A descriptive analysis of the response to beat, meter, and rhythm pattern by children, grades one to six. *Council for Research in Music Education*, 1981, 65, 47–52.

[1553]
★Mutually Responsible Facilitation Inventory. Adults; 1973; MRFI; provides a framework for planning the remediation of interpersonal adjustment problems; no scores, 5 areas: individuals must believe that they are important to others, individuals must recognize that others believe they can and will behave according to the rules, people desire positive mutually facilitating relationships, each individual must be meaningfully involved with other people, individuals should be able to give and accept love; Thomas D. Gnagey; Facilitation House.*

[1554]
★My Vocational Situation. High school and college and adults; 1980; MVS; problems checklist for the selection of vocational assistance; 3 scores: vocational identity, occupational information, personal or environmental barriers; John L. Holland, Denise Daiger, and Paul G. Power; Consulting Psychologists Press, Inc.*

[1555]
Myers-Briggs Type Indicator. Grades 9–16 and adults; 1943–76; MBTI; 4 scores: extraversion vs. introversion, sensation vs. intuition, thinking vs. feeling, judgment vs. perception; Katharine C. Briggs and Isabel Briggs Myers; Consulting Psychologists Press, Inc.*

For additional information and a review by Richard W. Coan, see 8:630 (115 references); see also T2:1294 (120 references) and P:177 (56 references); for reviews by Gerald A. Mendelsohn and Norman D. Sundberg and an excerpted review by Laurence Siegel, see 6:147 (10 references).

REFERENCES
1–10. See 6:147.
11–66. See P:177.
67–186. See T2:1294.
187–301. See 8:630.
302. BUHMEYER, K. J., & JOHNSON, A. H. Personality profiles of physician extenders. *Psychological Reports*, 1977, 40, 655–662.
303. CARLYN, M. An assessment of the Myers–Briggs Type Indicator. *Journal of Personality Assessment*, 1977, 41, 461–473.
304. CARPENTER, J. C. Personal approach: An empirical construct and some findings. *Journal of Personality*, 1977, 45, 169–189.
305. CARSKADON, T. G. Test–retest reliabilities of continuous scores on the Myers–Briggs Type Indicator. *Psychological Reports*, 1977, 41, 1011–1012.
306. ELIOT, J., & HARDY, R. C. Internality and extroversion–introversion. *Perceptual & Motor Skills*, 1977, 45, 430.
307. EVERED, R. D. Organizational activism and its relation to "reality" and mental imagery. *Human Relations*, 1977, 30, 311–334.
308. HANEWICZ, W. B. Police personality: A Jungian perspective. *Crime & Delinquency*, 1977, 24, 152–172.
309. HIRSCHFELD, R. M. A., MATTHEWS, S. M., MOSHER, L. R., & MENN, A. Z. Being with madness: Personality characteristics of three treatment staffs. *Hospital & Community Psychiatry*, 1977, 28, 267–273.
310. PARHAM, J. A. W. Academic success of persistent and nonpersistent students voluntarily enrolled in a university reading program. *Journal of Reading*, 1977, 20, 693–696.
311. REZLER, A. G., & BUCKLEY, J. M. A comparison of personality types among female student health professionals. *Journal of Medical Education*, 1977, 52, 475–477.
312. ROBYAK, J. E., & PATTON, M. J. Effectiveness of a study skills course for students of different personality types. *Journal of Counseling Psychology*, 1977, 24, 200–207.

313. BLOSSER, P. An alternative to the M.A.T. program. *Science Education*, 1978, 62, 309–317.
314. BRUHN, J. G., BUNCE, H., III, & GREASER, R. C. Correlations of Myers–Briggs Type Indicator with other personality and achievement variables. *Psychological Reports*, 1978, 43, 771–776.
315. BRUHN, J. G., FLOYD, C. S., & BUNCE, H. Training effects on attitudes and personality characteristics of nurse practitioners. *Psychological Reports*, 1978, 42, 703–713.
316. BUHMEYER, K. J. Selection and attrition profiles of physician–extender students. *Psychological Reports*, 1978, 43, 1009–1010.
317. BUHMEYER, K. J., & JOHNSON, A. H. Predicting success in a physician–extender training program. *Psychological Reports*, 1978, 42, 507–513.
318. CARSKADON, T. G., & KNUDSON, M. L. Relationship between conceptual systems and psychological types. *Psychological Reports*, 1978, 42, 483–486.
319. HAMMERS, C. P. Predicting success in individualized and traditional beginning shorthand courses. *Business Education Forum*, 1978, 33, 37–38.
320. LEARD, H. M., & HUM, A. The personality characteristics of counsellors–in–training which correlate with ratings of effectiveness and grades. *Canadian Counsellor*, 1978, 13, 28–32.
321. O'HARA–DEVEREAUX, M., BROWN, T. C., MENTINK, J., & MORGAN, W. A. Biographical data, personality, and vocational interests of family nurse practitioners. *Psychological Reports*, 1978, 43, 1259–1268.
322. ROBYAK, J. E., & DOWNEY, R. G. Effectiveness of a study skills course for students of different academic achievement levels and personality types. *Journal of Counseling Psychology*, 1978, 25, 544–550.
323. RUTSOHN, P. Understanding personality types: Does it matter? *Improving College & University Teaching*, 1978, 26, 249–254.
324. ARNOLD, L., CALKINS, V., & BRUMWELL, M. Influence of decision–makers' characteristics on outcome of a selection process in medical school. *Psychological Reports*, 1979, 44, 535–544.
325. BROOKS, F. R., & JOHNSON, R. W. Self–descriptive adjectives associated with a Jungian personality inventory. *Psychological Reports*, 1979, 44, 747–750.
326. CARR, G. D., & BARR, S. Z. Consider a new method for teaching college macroeconomics. *Journal of Business Education*, 1979, 54, 310–312.
327. CIONINI, L., MAGARO, P., SMITH, P., & VELECOGNA, F. Relationship between sex, age, education and field–dependence: A cross–cultural comparison. *Perceptual & Motor Skills*, 1979, 49, 581–582.
328. JONES, R. D., & WEINHOUSE, S. Running as self therapy. *Journal of Sports Medicine & Physical Fitness*, 1979, 19, 397–404.
329. ROBYAK, J. E., & DOWNEY, R. G. A discriminant analysis of the study skills and personality types of underachieving and nonunderachieving study skills students. *Journal of College Student Personnel*, 1979, 20, 306–309.
330. SCHROEDER, C. C. Designing ideal staff environments through milieu management. *Journal of College Student Personnel*, 1979, 20, 129–135.
331. WESTMAN, A. S., & CANTER, F. M. Relationship between certain Circadian behavior patterns and Jungian personality types. *Psychological Reports*, 1979, 44, 1199–1204.
332. BRUHN, J. G., BUNCE, H., III, & FLOYD, C. S. Correlates of job satisfaction among pediatric nurse practitioners. *Psychological Reports*, 1980, 46, 807–814.
333. CARLSON, R. A. Studies of Jungian typology: II. Representations of the personal world. *Journal of Personality & Social Psychology*, 1980, 38, 801–810.
334. KELLER, H. T., & TETLOW, E. W. Participation in community theater and type of personality. *Psychological Reports*, 1980, 47, 711–714.
335. O'HAIRE, T. D., & MARCIA, J. E. Some personality characteristics associated with Ananda Marga meditators: A pilot study. *Perceptual & Motor Skills*, 1980, 51, 447–452.
336. RADONSKY, V. E. Personality characteristics of the published and nonpublished occupational therapist. *American Journal of Occupational Therapy*, 1980, 34, 209–212.
337. SCHROEDER, C. C., WARNER, R., & MALONE, D. R. Effects of assignment to living units by personality types on environmental perceptions and student development. *Journal of College Student Personnel*, 1980, 21, 443–449.
338. CARL, H. A study for the improvement of listening comprehension and for the assessment of personality factors as they relate to listening. *Journal of Business Education*, 1981, 56, 328–329.
339. COHEN, D., COHEN, M., & CROSS, H. A construct validity study of the Myers–Briggs Type Indicator. *Educational & Psychological Measurement*, 1981, 41, 883–891.
340. DETTMER, P. Improving teacher attitudes toward characteristics of the creatively gifted. *Gifted Child Quarterly*, 1981, 25, 11–16.
341. MILLER, A., & COOLEY, E. Moderator variables for the relationship between life change and disorders. *Journal of General Psychology*, 1981, 104, 223–233.
342. SCHMIDT, J. J. Counseling and consulting: Separate processes or the same? *Personnel & Guidance Journal*, 1981, 60, 168–171.
343. VAN DYNE, W. T., & STAVA, L. J. Analysis of relationships among hypnotic susceptibility, personality type, and vividness of mental imagery. *Psychological Reports*, 1981, 48, 23–26.

[1556]

National Business Entrance Tests. Grades 11–16 and adults; 1938–72; formerly called *National Clerical Ability Tests* and *United-NOMA Business Entrance Tests*; subtests available as separates; 3 series; National Business Education Association.* (In-print status uncertain; no reply from publisher.)

a) [GENERAL TESTING SERIES (SERIES 2500).] 1938–72; 6 tests.

1) *Business Fundamentals and General Information Test.* 1938–72.
2) *Bookkeeping Test.* 1938–72
3) *General Office Clerical Test.* 1948–72.
4) *Machine Calculation Test.* 1941–72.
5) *Stenographic Test.* 1938–72.
6) *Typewriting Test.* 1941–72.

b) [SHORT FORM SERIES.] 1938–55; 2 tests. *Out of print.*

1) *Stenographic Test.* 1938–55.
2) *Typewriting Test.* 1941–55.

c) [OFFICIAL TESTING SERIES (SERIES 2000 AND 2100).] 1938–65; administered only at NBET Centers which may be established in any community; 6 tests.

1) *Business Fundamentals and General Information Test.* 1938–65.
2) *Bookkeeping Test.* 1938–65.
3) *General Office Clerical Test.* 1948–65.
4) *Machine Calculation Test.* 1941–65.
5) *Stenographic Test.* 1938–65.
6) *Typewriting Test.* 1941–65.

For additional information and a review by Melvin R. Marks, see 6:33 (5 references); for reviews by Edward N. Hay, Jacob S. Orleans, and Wimburn L. Wallace of earlier forms, see 5:515; see also 4:453 (1 reference); for a review by Paul S. Lomax, see 3:396; see also 2:1476 (9 references). For a review of the typewriting test, see 6:55; earlier editions of the machine calculation test, see 5:514 (1 review) and 3:384 (1 review); the stenographic test, see 5:522 (1 review) and 3:391 (2 reviews); the typewriting test, see 5:526 (1 review) and 3:394 (2 reviews); the bookkeeping test, see 3:368 (2 reviews); the business fundamentals test, see 3:369 (2 reviews); and the clerical test, see 3:379 (2 reviews).

[1557]

National Educational Development Tests. Grades 7–8, 9–10; 1959–74; tests administered each fall and spring by individual schools; materials listed are for 1976–77 testing; 7 scores: English usage, mathematics usage, social studies reading, natural sciences reading, word usage, total, learning ability; Test of Learning Ability by Thelma Gwinn Thurstone; Science Research Associates, Inc.*

a) GRADES 7–8. 1963–74.

b) GRADES 9–10. 1959–74; test booklet includes the optional *Educational Planning Questionnaire* called the Counselor's Program; *Educational Planning Questionnaire* by Samuel A. Stouffer.

For additional information and a review by Gerald S. Hanna, see 8:23 (2 references); see also T2:24 (1 reference) and 7:16 (2 references); for reviews by Willis W. Clark, Arthur E. Traxler, and Alexander G. Wesman of an earlier form of *b*, see 6:17.

REFERENCES

1–2. See 7:16.
3. See T2:24.
4–5. See 8:23.
6. COLE, J. N. The effects of non-prose textual characteristics on retention of major concepts and supporting details with and without specific instruction in their use. In P. D. Pearson & J. Hansen (Eds.), *Reading: Theory, research, and practice; Twenty-sixth yearbook of the National Reading Conference.* Clemson, South Carolina: The National Reading Conference, Inc., 1977.
7. MARTIN, J. D., & KIDWELL, J. C. Intercorrelations of the Wechsler Intelligence Scale for Children–Revised, the Slosson Intelligence Test, and the National Educational Development Test. *Educational & Psychological Measurement,* 1977, 37, 1117–1120.
8. HECHT, L. W. Measuring student behavior during group instruction. *Journal of Educational Research,* 1978, 71, 283–290.
9. DOEBLER, L. K., & FOREMAN, S. T. National Educational Development Tests as a predictor of College Entrance Examination Board Scholastic Aptitude Test scores. *Educational & Psychological Measurement,* 1979, 39, 909–911.
10. MURPHY, M. J., NELSON, D. A., & CHEAP, T. L. Rated and actual performance of high school students as a function of sex and attractiveness. *Psychological Reports,* 1981, 48, 103–106.

[1558]

National Engineering Aptitude Search Test: The Junior Engineering Technical Society. Grades 9–12; 1963–71, c1947–68; tests admininistered each spring at chapter centers of the Junior Engineering Technical Society; 5 scores: verbal, numerical, science, total, mechanical comprehension; The Psychological Corporation.*

For additional information concerning an earlier form, see 6:1134.

[1559]

National German Examination for High School Students. 2, 3, or 4 years high school; 1960–76; also called *AATG National Standardized Testing Program;* formerly called *AATG German Test* and *National German Contest for High School Students;* tests administered annually in February/March under auspices of high school guidance departments or centers established by the publisher; American Association of Teachers of German with the technical assistance of Educational Testing Service; program administered by American Association of Teachers of German, Inc.*

For additional information, see 8:135; for reviews by Gilbert C. Kettelkamp and Theodor F. Naumann of an earlier edition, see 6:382.

[1560]

National Institute for Personnel Research Intermediate Battery. Standards 7–10 and job applicants with 9–12 years of education; 1964–69; 7 tests in a single booklet: mental alertness, arithmetical problems, computation, spot-the-error (speed, accuracy), reading comprehension, vocabulary, spelling; manual by Anne-Marie Wilcocks; National Institute for Personnel Research [South Africa].*

See T2:1084 (2 references) and 7:678.

[1561]

National Institute for Personnel Research Normal Battery. Standards 6–10 and job applicants with 8–11 years of education; 1960–73; 5 tests in a single booklet: mental alertness, reading comprehension, vocabulary, spelling, computation; manual by S. M. A. Waterhouse; National Institute for Personnel Research [South Africa].*

See T2:1085 (2 references) and 6:779.

[1562]

National Occupational Competency Testing Program. Teachers and prospective teachers in skilled trades; 1973–82; NOCTI; tests administered each spring and fall at centers approved by the publisher; 41 tests: Air Conditioning and Refrigeration, Airframe and Power Plant Mechanic, Architectural Drafting, Audio Visual Communications, Auto Body Repair, Auto Mechanic, Baking, Brick Masonry, Building Construction Occupations, Building Trades Maintenance, Cabinet Making and Millwork, Carpentry, Civil Technology, Commercial Art, Computer Technology, Cosmetology, Diesel Engine Repair, Drafting Occupations, Electrical Installation, Electronics Communications, Electronics Technology, Heating, Industrial Electrician, Industrial Electronics, Machine Drafting, Machine Trades, Major Appliance Repair, Masonry, Materials Handling, Mechanical Technology, Painting and Decorating, Plumbing, Power Sewing, Printing, Quantity Food Preparation, Radio/TV Repair, Sheet Metal, Small Engine Repair, Textile Production/Fabrication, Tool and Die Making, Welding; 2 parts: written, performance; norms by Leon S. Tunkel and Raymond S. Klein; National Occupational Competency Testing Institute.*

For additional information and a review by Thomas S. Baldwin, see 8:1153 (6 references). For reviews of separate tests, see 8:1129 (1 review), 8:1131 (1 review), 8:1133 (2 reviews), 8:1134 (1 review), 8:1135 (1 review), 8:1138 (1 review), 8:1139 (1 review), 8:1140 (1 review), 8:1141 (1 review), 8:1142 (1 review), 8:1143 (1 review), 8:1147 (1 review), 8:1150 (1 review), 8:1151 (1 review), and 8:1152 (1 review).

REFERENCES

1–6. See 8:1153.
7. GUTCHER, D., & THOMPSON, D. Structured and non-structured work experience programs. *Journal of Industrial Teacher Education,* 1977, 15, 75–85.
8. SCHENCK, J. P. Occupational competence of trade and industrial teacher education students using three work experience combinations. *Journal of Industrial Teacher Education,* 1979, 16, 5–10.

[1563]

[National Science Foundation Graduate Fellowship Testing Program.] Applicants for N.S.F. fellowships for graduate study in the sciences; 1951–72; applicant takes 2 tests from the *Graduate Record Examinations*: the Aptitude Test and 1 Advanced Test (Biology, Chemistry, Economics, Engineering, Geography, Geology, Mathematics, Physics, Political Science, Psychology, or Sociology); program administered for the National Science Foundation by Educational Testing Service.*

[1564]

Naylor-Harwood Adult Intelligence Scale. Ages 18 and over; 1955–72; NHAIS; Australian adaptation of *Wechsler Adult Intelligence Scale;* 14 scores: verbal (information, comprehension, arithmetic, similarities, memory for digits, vocabulary, total), performance (letter symbol, picture completion, block design, picture arrangement, object assembly, total), total; manual by G. F. K. Naylor and Elsie Harwood; Australian Council for Educational Research [Australia].*

For additional information, see 8:221.

[1565]
N.B. Spelling Tests. Standards 1–3, 3–5, 6–8, 8–10 for English pupils and 3–5, 6–8, 9–10 for Afrikaans pupils; [1962–64]; Human Sciences Research Council [South Africa].*

For additional information, see 7:228.

[1566]
[NCRI Achievement Tests in Hebrew.] Grades 5–7, 7–9; 1965–67; Simon Bugatch and Judah Pilch (test); National Curriculum Research Institute, Jewish Education Service of North America, Inc.*

See T2:281 (1 reference) and 7:298.

[1567]
Neale Analysis of Reading Ability, Second Edition. Ages 6–13; 1957–66; NARA; 3 scores (accuracy, comprehension, rate of reading) plus 3 optional supplementary tests (names and sounds of letters, auditory discrimination through simple spelling, blending and recognition of syllables); (Braille edition ('77, by J. Lorimer) available from NFER-Nelson Publishing Co. [England]); Marie D. Neale; Macmillan Education [England].*

See T2:1683 (7 references); for reviews by M. Alan Brimer and Magdalen D. Vernon, and an excerpted review, see 6:843.

REFERENCES

1–7. See T2:1683.
8. JEHU, D., MORGAN, R. T. T., TURNER, R. K., & JONES, A. A controlled trial of the treatment of nocturnal enuresis in residential homes for children. *Behaviour Research & Therapy*, 1977, 15, 1–16.
9. JORM, A. F. Effect of word imagery on reading performance as a function of reader ability. *Journal of Educational Psychology*, 1977, 69, 46–54.
10. RIDING, R. J., & PUGH, J. C. Iconic memory and reading performance in nine-year-old children. *British Journal of Educational Psychology*, 1977, 47, 132–137.
11. RYLE, A., & MACDONALD, J. Responses to reading as perceived by boys with and without specific reading retardation and behavioural disorders: A repertory grid study. *Journal of Child Psychology & Psychiatry & Allied Disciplines*, 1977, 18, 323–334.
12. DAS, J. P., LEONG, C. K., & WILLIAMS, N. H. The relationship between learning disability and simultaneous-successive processing. *Journal of Learning Disabilities*, 1978, 11, 618–625.
13. LOVEGROVE, W., & BROWN, C. Development of information processing in normal and disabled readers. *Perceptual & Motor Skills*, 1978, 46, 1047–1059.
14. TIZARD, B., & HODGES, J. The effect of early institutional rearing on the development of eight-year-old children. *Journal of Child Psychology & Psychiatry & Allied Disciplines*, 1978, 19, 99–118.
15. BISHOP, D. V. M., JANCEY, C., & STEEL, A. M. Orthoptic status and reading disability. *Cortex*, 1979, 15, 659–666.
16. LONG, C. G., & MOORE, J. R. Parental expectations for their epileptic children. *Journal of Child Psychology & Psychiatry & Allied Disciplines*, 1979, 20, 299–312.
17. BEDWELL, C. H., GRANT, R., & MCKEOWN, J. R. Visual and ocular control anomalies in relation to reading difficulty. *British Journal of Educational Psychology*, 1980, 50, 61–70.
18. GREEN, P., & KOTENKO, V. Superior speech comprehension in schizophrenics under monaural versus binaural listening conditions. *Journal of Abnormal Psychology*, 1980, 89, 399–408.
19. CHADWICK, O., RUTTER, M., THOMPSON, J., & SHAFFER, D. Intellectual performance and reading skills after localized head injury in childhood. *Journal of Child Psychology & Psychiatry & Allied Disciplines*, 1981, 22, 117–139.
20. SNOWLING, M., & FRITH, M. The role of sound, shape and orthographic cues in early reading. *British Journal of Psychology*, 1981, 72, 83–87.

[1568]
***Nelson-Denny Reading Test, Forms E and F.** Grades 9–12 and adults; 1929–81; NDRT; previous editions (Forms A and B, '60) and (Forms C and D, '73) still available; 4 scores: vocabulary, comprehension, total, rate; James I. Brown, J. Michael Bennett, and Gerald Hanna; Riverside Publishing Co.*

For additional information and reviews by Robert A. Forsyth and Alton L. Raynor of Forms C and D, see 8:735 (31 references); see also T2:1572 (46 references); for reviews by David B. Orr and Agatha Townsend and an excerpted review by John O. Crites of Forms A and B, see 6:800 (13 references); for a review by Ivan A. Booker, see 4:544 (17 references); for a review by Hans C. Gordon, see 2:1557 (6 references).

REFERENCES

1–6. See 2:1557.
7–23. See 4:544.
24–36. See 6:800.
37–82. See T2:1572.
83–113. See 8:735.
114. GRIGGS, B. M. A systems approach to the development and evaluation of a minicourse for nurses. *Nursing Research*, 1977, 26, 34–41.
115. JONES, J. D., & OSBORNE, T. An educational support program: The results of merging academics and student personnel services. *Journal of College Student Personnel*, 1977, 18, 251–254.
116. MANGIERI, J. N., & OLSEN, H. D. Self-concept-of-achievement ability and reading proficiency of black and white males in an adult education course. *Journal of Negro Education*, 1977, 46, 456–461.
117. MIDDENTS, G. J. A pilot project for assessing nonacademic characteristics of premedical students. *Journal of Medical Education*, 1977, 52, 343–344.
118. PYRCZAK, F. Does it pay to guess when there is a "penalty" for guessing? *Journal of Reading*, 1977, 21, 222–230.
119. ROSSMAN, J. F. How one high school set up a reading program for 500 students. *Journal of Reading*, 1977, 20, 393–397.
120. SMITH, B. D. Do we need differential diagnosis at the college level? No. *Journal of Reading*, 1977, 21, 62–66.
121. TILLMAN, C. E. Readability and other factors in college reading tests: A critique of the Diagnostic Reading Test, the Nelson-Denny Reading Test, and the McGraw-Hill Basic Reading Test. *National Reading Conference Yearbook*, 1977, 253–259.
122. BRABENDER, V., & DICKHAUS, R. C. Effect of hypnosis on comprehension of complex verbal material. *Perceptual & Motor Skills*, 1978, 47, 1322.
123. BRUHN, J. G., BUNCE, H., III, & GREASER, R. C. Correlations of Myers–Briggs Type Indicator with other personality and achievement variables. *Psychological Reports*, 1978, 43, 771–776.
124. BUTTER, E. J., & VALLANO, T. W. Auditory and visual cognitive styles and adult performance. *Perceptual & Motor Skills*, 1978, 47, 995–998.
125. COIL, A. College reading needs: Beyond 'filling the bin.' *42nd Claremont Reading Conference Yearbook*, 1978, 219–225.
126. EANET, M. G. An investigation of the REAP reading/study procedure: Its rationale and efficacy. *National Reading Conference Yearbook*, 1978, 229–232.
127. JONGSMA, E. A., POUND, R. E., & TIPS, M. L. The effects of instruction in testwiseness in a college reading improvement course. In P. D. Pearson & J. Hansen (Eds.), *Reading: Disciplined inquiry in process and practice; Twenty-seventh yearbook of the National Reading Conference*, 1978, 27, 237–241.
128. MAXWELL, M. Learning style and other correlates of performance on a scanning experiment. *Journal of Reading Behavior*, 1978, 10, 49–55.
129. PRATT, D. F., & GOSS, A. E. Study and test formats in learning factual information. *Bulletin of the Psychonomic Society*, 1978, 11, 301–304.
130. STIGGINS, R. J., SCHMEISER, C. B., & FERGUSON, R. L. Validity of the ACT assessment as an indicator of reading ability. *Applied Psychological Measurement*, 1978, 2, 337–344.
131. BECK, F. W., & GUEDRY, P. Reading phase of academic skills enhancement programs. *Journal of College Student Personnel*, 1979, 20, 276.
132. DUFFELMEYER, F. A. The effect of rewriting prose material on reading comprehension. *Reading World*, 1979, 19, 1–11.
133. ENTIN, E. B., & KLARE, G. R. Differential relationships of two versions of Cloze Tests to vocabulary and reading comprehension. *National Reading Conference Yearbook*, 1979, 68–71.
134. GEIS, L., & CARNEY, M. L. Reading ability, college grades, and attrition: A two-year study. *National Reading Conference Yearbook*, 1979, 163–167.
135. GLOVER, J. A. Levels of questions asked in interview and reading sessions by creative and relatively noncreative college students. *Journal of Genetic Psychology*, 1979, 135, 103–108.
136. GLOVER, J. A., ZIMMER, J. W., & BRUNING, R. H. Utility of the Nelson–Denny as a predictor of structure and thematicity in memory from prose. *Psychological Reports*, 1979, 45, 44–46.

137. STALEY, N. K., & SMYTH, T. J. C. An evaluation of the effectiveness of a college reading program using four criteria. *National Reading Conference Yearbook*, 1979, 182-185.
138. WILLOUGHBY, T. L., KELLY, B., & CASALE, U. Validity of the Study Practices Inventory for pharmacy students. *Educational & Psychological Measurement*, 1979, 39, 491-494.
139. ZIMMER, J. W., GLOVER, J. A., RONNING, R. R., & PETERSEN, C. On the utility of the Nelson-Denny Reading Test as a covariate in research on prose-processing. *Perceptual & Motor Skills*, 1979, 48, 641-642.
140. ABARTIS, C., & COLLINS, C. The effect of writing instruction and reading methodology upon college students' reading skills. *Journal of Reading*, 1980, 23, 408-413.
141. ANGELO, J. K. B. Effects of sensory integration treatment on the low-achieving college student. *American Journal of Occupational Therapy*, 1980, 34, 671-675.
142. ERWIN, T. D., & MILLIKAN, J. L. The relationship of the Nelson-Denny Reading Test to the Scholastic Aptitude Verbal Tests. *Measurement & Evaluation in Guidance*, 1980, 13, 169-171.
143. GEROW, J. R., & MURPHY, D. P. The validity of the Nelson-Denny Reading Test as a predictor of performance in introductory psychology. *Educational & Psychological Measurement*, 1980, 40, 553-555.
144. GLOVER, J. A., ZIMMER, J. W., & BRUNING, R. H. Information processing approaches among creative students. *Journal of Psychology*, 1980, 105, 93-97.
145. MASSARO, D. W., & TAYLOR, G. A. Reading ability and utilization of orthographic structure in reading. *Journal of Educational Psychology*, 1980, 72, 730-742.
146. MATHEWS, N. N., HUNT, E. B., & MACLEOD, C. M. Strategy choice and strategy training in sentence-picture verification. *Journal of Verbal Learning & Verbal Behavior*, 1980, 19, 531-548.
147. PETERSEN, C., GLOVER, J. A., & RONNING, R. R. An examination of three prose learning strategies on reading comprehension. *Journal of General Psychology*, 1980, 102, 39-52.
148. SCHMECK, R. R. Relationships between measures of learning style and reading comprehension. *Perceptual & Motor Skills*, 1980, 50, 461-462.
149. SHANNON, A. J. Effects of methods of standardized reading achievement test administration on attitude toward reading. *Journal of Reading*, 1980, 23, 684-686.
150. BLACK, J. T., & HARDING, I. W. Developing reading skills in the high shcool physics class. *Physics Teacher*, 1981, 19, 106-112.
151. CUMMINS, R. P. The Nelson-Denny Reading Test (Forms E & F). *Journal of Reading*, 1981, 25, 54-59.

[1569]

*The Nelson Reading Skills Test, Forms 3 and 4. Grades 3.0-4.5, 4.6-6.9, 7.0-9.9; 1931-77; RST; revision of *The Nelson Reading Test*; 3 levels; Gerald Hanna, Leo M. Schell, and Robert Schreiner; Riverside Publishing Co.*

a) LEVEL A. Grades 3.0-4.5; 2 to 5 scores: word meaning, reading comprehension, sound-symbol correspondence (optional), root words (optional), syllabication (optional).

b) LEVEL B. Grades 4.6-6.9; 2 to 3 scores: word meaning, reading comprehension, reading rate (optional).

c) LEVEL C. Grades 7.0-9.9; 2 to 3 scores: word meaning, reading comprehension, reading rate (optional).

See T2:1573 (5 references); for a review by H. Alan Robinson of an earlier edition, see 6:802; for a review by William D. Sheldon of the original edition, see 4:545 (1 reference); for a review by Constance M. McCullough, see 3:492; for an excerpted review by Albert Grant, see 2:1558.

REFERENCES

1. See 4:545.
2-6. See T2:1573.
7. SCHERICH, H. H., & HANNA, G. S. Passage-dependency data in the selection of reading comprehension test items. *Educational & Psychological Measurement*, 1977, 37, 991-997.
8. DRAHOZAL, E. C., & HANNA, G. S. Reading comprehension subscores: Pretty bottles for ordinary wine. *Journal of Reading*, 1978, 21, 416-420.

[1570]

The Nelson Reading Test, Revised Edition. Grades 3-9; 1931-62; revision of *The Nelson Silent Reading Test: Vocabulary and Paragraph*; 3 scores: vocabulary, paragraph comprehension, total; M. J. Nelson; Riverside Publishing Co.*

See T2:1573 (5 references); for a review by H. Alan Robinson, see 6:802; for a review by William D. Sheldon of the original edition, see 4:545 (1 reference); for a review by Constance M. McCullough, see 3:492; for an excerpted review by Albert Grant, see 2:1558.

REFERENCES

1. See 4:545.
2-6. See T2:1573.
7. LOKAN, J. The differential prediction of grades in a special vocational high school. *Measurement & Evaluation in Guidance*, 1977, 10, 7-16.
8. MODJESKI, R. B., & MICHAEL, W. B. The relationship of the General Educational Performance Index measure to other indicators of educational development in each of three samples from an United States Army population. *Educational & Psychological Measurement*, 1978, 38, 377-391.
9. READANCE, J. E., BALDWIN, R. S., BEAN, T. W., & DISHNER, E. K. Field dependence-independence as a variable in cloze test performance. *Journal of Reading Behavior*, 1980, 12, 65-67.
10. VACCA, R. T. A study of holistic and subskill instructional approaches to reading comprehension. *Journal of Reading*, 1980, 23, 512-518.
11. HANNA, G. S., & SCHERICH, H. H. An empirical evaluation of three definitions of context dependence. *Journal of Reading Behavior*, 1981, 13, 75-80.
12. ROACH, D. A. Predictors of mathematics achievement in Jamaican elementary school children. *Perceptual & Motor Skills*, 1981, 52, 785-786.

[1571]

★Neurological Dysfunctions of Children. Ages 3-10; 1979; NDOC; consists of 16 tasks a child is to perform, measurement of child's head circumference, information on child's developmental history and further information gathered from examiner observations and health records; items are evaluated on a yes/no basis and interpreted in clusters, not as separate item ratings; James W. Kuhns; Publishers Test Service.*

[1572]

★Neuropsychological Questionnaire. Children, adults; 1978; Fernando Melendez; Psychological Assessment Resources, Inc.*

[1573]

The Neuroticism Scale Questionnaire. Ages 13 and over; 1961; NSQ; test booklet title is *NSQ*; 5 scores: depressiveness, submissiveness, overprotection, anxiety, total; Ivan H. Scheier and Raymond B. Cattell; Institute for Personality and Ability Testing, Inc.*

See T2:1295 (27 references) and P:178 (10 references); for reviews by E. Lowell Kelly and Jerome D. Pauker and an excerpted review by John O. Crites (reply by Ivan H. Scheier), see 6:148 (1 reference).

REFERENCES

1. See 6:148.
2-11. See P:178.
12-38. See T2:1295.
39. SMITH, J. C. Personality correlates of continuation and outcome in mediation and erect sitting control treatments. *Journal of Consulting & Clinical Psychology*, 1978, 46, 272-279.
40. MATHEW, R. J., CLAGHORN, J. L., & LARGEN, J. Craving for alcohol in sober alcoholics. *American Journal of Psychiatry*, 1979, 136, 594-597.
41. SINGH, S., & SEHGAL, M. Rorschach hostility content and its relation to anxiety, neuroticism and P-E-N measures. *Journal of Clinical Psychology*, 1979, 35, 436-441.
42. WEINSTEIN, L., & DEMANN, A. F. Autonomy-control variation in child rearing and neurotic tendency in young adults: An exploratory study. *Bulletin of the Psychonomic Society*, 1981, 17, 193-194.

[1574]

New Guinea Performance Scales. Pre-literates ages 17 and over; 1961–71; NGPS; based (except *f*) on the unpublished *PIR Test* used for screening for the Pacific Island Regiment; test (except *e*) is essentially the same as the *Queensland Test* except for minor differences in some of the testing materials and differences in administration, scoring, and norms population; 6 tests; 7 scores: 6 scores listed below plus total; I. G. Ord; Society for New Guinea Psychological Research and Publications [Papua New Guinea].* (In-print status uncertain; no reply from publisher.)

a) CUBE IMITATION TEST. An adaptation of *Knox Cube Test: Pintner Modification.*
b) BEAD THREADING TEST.
c) PASSALONG TEST. Modification of a subtest of *Alexander Performance Scale*; test booklet title is *Passalong Test (New Guinea Version).*
d) FORM ASSEMBLY TEST.
e) OBSERVATION TEST.
f) DESIGN CONSTRUCTION TEST. Published separately as *Pacific Design Construction Test.*

For additional information, see 7:412 (4 references).

[1575]

The New Iowa Spelling Scale. Grades 2–8; 1954; master word list with difficulty values by grades from which teacher may compile tests; Harry A. Greene; Bureau of Educational Research and Service.*

For additional information, see 6:322 (1 reference).

REFERENCES

1. See 6:322.
2. CHEEK, M. C. A correlation of oral reading, spelling, and graphemic option knowledge. *Reading World*, 1979, 18, 384–388.
3. BRYANT, N. D., DRABIN, I. R., & GETTINGER, M. Effects of varying unit size on spelling achievement in learning disabled children. *Journal of Learning Disabilities*, 1981, 14, 200–203.

[1576]

New Medical College Admission Test. Applicants for admission to member colleges of the Association of American Medical Colleges and to other participating institutions; 1946–77; New MCAT; revision, first administered in spring 1977, of *Medical College Admission Test*; administered 2 times annually (spring, fall) at centers established by the publisher; 6 scores: biology, chemistry, physics, science problems, skills analysis (reading, quantitative); 4 parts: science knowledge, science problems, reading skills analysis, quantitative skills analysis; constructed under the direction of AAMC by the American Institutes for Research; program administered at the direction of Association of American Medical Colleges.*

For additional information, see 8:1101 (40 references); see also T2:2355 (30 references); for reviews by Nancy S. Cole and James M. Richards, Jr. of earlier forms, see 7:1100 (57 references); for reviews by Robert L. Ebel and Philip H. DuBois, see 6:1137 (43 references); for a review by Alexander G. Wesman, see 5:932 (4 references); for a review by Morey J. Wantman, see 4:817 (11 references).

REFERENCES

1–11. See 4:817.
12–15. See 5:932.
16–58. See 6:1137.
59–115. See 7:1100.
116–145. See T2:2355.
146–185. See 8:1101.
186. BARBEE, R. A., & DINHAM, S. M. Student decision-making and performance in a flexible-time curriculum. *Journal of Medical Education*, 1977, 52, 882–887.
187. COOPER, J. A. D. The New Medical College Admissions Test. *Journal of Medical Education*, 1977, 52, 77.
188. GORDON, T. L., & JOHNSON, D. G. Study of U. S. medical school applicants, 1975–76. *Journal of Medical Education*, 1977, 52, 707–730.
189. GOUGH, H. G., & DUCKER, D. G. Social class in relation to medical school performance and choice of specialty. *Journal of Psychology*, 1977, 96, 31–43.
190. GOUGH, H. G., & HALL, W. B. A comparison of medical students from medical and non-medical families. *Journal of Medical Education*, 1977, 52, 541–547.
191. GOUGH, H. G., & HALL, W. B. A comparison of physicians who did or did not respond to a postal questionnaire. *Journal of Applied Psychology*, 1977, 62, 777–780.
192. GOUGH, H. G., & HALL, W. B. Number of children wanted and expected by American physicians. *Journal of Psychology*, 1977, 96, 45–53.
193. HALEY, H. B., HUYNH, H., PAIVA, R. E. A., & JUAN, I. R. Students' attitudes toward cancer: Change in medical school. *Journal of Medical Education*, 1977, 52, 500–507.
194. LANE, M. S., & FEITZ, R. H. MCAT performance by selected characteristics of medical school aspirants. *Journal of Medical Education*, 1977, 52, 219–221.
195. REID, J. C., & BLAIN, B. B. Identifying students who will be in academic difficulty in medical school. *Journal of Medical Education*, 1977, 52, 66–67.
196. ROOS, N. P., GAUMONT, M., & COLWILL, N. L. Female and physicians: A sex role incongruity. *Journal of Medical Education*, 1977, 52, 345–346.
197. STACHNIK, T. J., & SIMONS, R. C. A comparison of D.O. and M.D. student performance. *Journal of Medical Education*, 1977, 52, 920–925.
198. STILLMAN, P. L., BROWN, D. R., REDFIELD, D. L., & SABERS, D. L. Construct validation of the Arizona Clinical Interview Rating Scale. *Educational & Psychological Measurement*, 1977, 37, 1031–1038.
199. WALDMAN, B. Economic and racial disadvantage as reflected in traditional medical school selection factors. *Journal of Medical Education*, 1977, 52, 961–970.
200. BENENSON, T. F., STIMMEL, B., & SMITH, H., JR. Concurrent criterion validity of a modified pass/fail grading system and associated error rates. *Educational & Psychological Measurement*, 1978, 38, 405–410.
201. CLAUDY, J. G. Biserial weights: A new approach to test item option weighting. *Applied Psychological Measurement*, 1978, 2, 25–30.
202. GIVNER, N., & KLINTBERG, I. Admissions and performance differences between students admitted to medical school after three and four years of college. *College & University*, 1978, 53, 297–300.
203. KUPFER, D. J., DREW, F. L., CURTIS, E. K., & RUBINSTEIN, D. N. Personality style and empathy in medical students. *Journal of Medical Education*, 1978, 53, 507–509.
204. MARSHALL, R. J., JR., FULTON, J. P., & WESSEN, A. F. Physician career outcomes and the process of medical education. *Journal of Health & Social Behavior*, 1978, 19, 124–138.
205. MURDEN, R., GALLOWAY, G. M., REID, J. C., & COLWILL, J. M. Academic and personal predictors of clinical success in medical school. *Journal of Medical Education*, 1978, 53, 711–719.
206. ROESSLER, R., LESTER, J. W., BUTLER, W. T., RANKIN, B., & COLLINS, F. Cognitive and noncognitive variables in the prediction of preclinical performance. *Journal of Medical Education*, 1978, 53, 678–680.
207. BRANDT, E. N., HOLMSTROM, F., & PADGETT, W. B. Admissions to UT medical schools, an analysis: Characteristics of accepted applicants. *Texas Medicine*, 1979, 75, 87–92.
208. VELOSKI, J., HERMAN, M. W., GONELLA, J. S., ZELEZNIK, C., & KELLOW, W. F. Relationships between performance in medical school and first postgraduate year. *Journal of Medical Education*, 1979, 54, 909–916.
209. CULLEN, T. J., DOHNER, C. W., PECKHAM, P. H., SAMSON, W. E., & SCHWARZ, M. R. Predicting first-quarter test scores from the New Medical College Admission Test. *Journal of Medical Education*, 1980, 55, 393–398.
210. ERDMAN, J. B. Validating the MCAT. *Journal of Medical Education*, 1980, 55, 463–464.
211. FRIEDMAN, C. P., & BAKEWELL, W. E., JR. Incremental validity of the new MCAT. *Journal of Medical Education*, 1980, 55, 399–404.
212. GIVNER, N., KLINTBERG, I., & HYNES, K. Effect of retaking the Medical College Admissions Test on applicants' scores. *Psychological Reports*, 1980, 47, 411–415.
213. HYNES, K., & GIVNER, N. An empirical investigation of change in MCAT scores upon retest. *Journal of Medical Education*, 1980, 55, 201–202.
214. MCGUIRE, F. L. The new MCAT and medical student performance. *Journal of Medical Education*, 1980, 55, 405–408.

215. THOMAE-FORGUES, M., & ERDMANN, J. B. MCAT scores and academic records of natural science and humanities majors applying to medical school, 1978–79. *Journal of Medical Education*, 1980, 55, 971–972.
216. BROOKS, C. M., JACKSON, J. R., HOFFMAN, H. H., & HAND, G. S., JR. Validity of the new MCAT for predicting GPA and NBME Part I examination performance. *Journal of Medical Education*, 1981, 56, 767–769.
217. DAWSON-SAUNDERS, B., & DOOLEN, D. R. An alternative method to predict performance: Canonical redundancy analysis. *Journal of Medical Education*, 1981, 56, 295–300.
218. DISEKER, R. A., & MICHIELUTTE, R. An analysis of empathy in medical students before and following clinical experience. *Journal of Medical Education*, 1981, 56, 1004–1010.
219. FOSTER, P. J. Clinical discussion groups: Verbal participation and outcomes. *Journal of Medical Education*, 1981, 56, 831–838.
220. GOLMON, M. E., & BERRY, C. A. Comparative predictive validity of the new MCAT using different admissions criteria. *Journal of Medical Education*, 1981, 56, 981–986.
221. HART, M. E., PAYNE, D. A., & LEWIS, L. A. Prediction of basic science learning outcomes with cognitive style and traditional admissions criteria. *Journal of Medical Education*, 1981, 56, 137–139.
222. HYNES, K., & GIVNER, N. Restriction of range effects on the new MCAT'S predictive validity. *Journal of Medical Education*, 1981, 56, 352–353.
223. JONES, R. F., & THOMAE-FORGUES, M. A factor comparison of old and new MCAT scales. *Journal of Medical Education*, 1981, 56, 161–166.
224. MILSTEIN, R. M., WILKINSON, L., BURROW, G. N., & KESSEN, W. Admission decisions and performance during medical school. *Journal of Medical Education*, 1981, 56, 77–82.
225. SLOTNICK, H. B. Identifying and remediating specific deficiencies of entering medical students. *Journal of Medical Education*, 1981, 56, 91–102.

[1577]
New Mexico Career Education Test Series. Grades 9–12; 1973; "designed to assess specific learner objectives in the area of career education"; criterion-referenced; 6 tests; Charles C. Healy and Stephen P. Klein; Monitor.*
a) NM ATTITUDE TOWARD WORK TEST. NMATWT.
b) NM CAREER PLANNING TEST. NMCPT.
c) NM CAREER ORIENTED ACTIVITIES CHECKLIST. NMCOAC.
d) NM KNOWLEDGE OF OCCUPATIONS TEST. NMKOT.
e) NM JOB APPLICATION PROCEDURES TEST. NMJAPT.
f) NM CAREER DEVELOPMENT TEST. NMCDT.

For additional information, a review by Jack L. Bodden, and excerpted reviews by Dale Prediger and Bert W. Westbrook, see 8:1013 (2 references).

REFERENCES
1–2. See 8:1013.
3. YEN, F. B., & HEALY, C. C. The effects of work experience on two scales of career development. *Measurement & Evaluation in Guidance*, 1977, 10, 175–177.

[1578]
New South African Group Test. Ages 8–11, 10–14, 13–17; 1931–65; NSAGT; 3 scores: verbal, nonverbal, total; 3 levels; Human Sciences Research Council [South Africa].*
a) JUNIOR. Ages 8–11; 1931–65.
b) INTERMEDIATE. Ages 10–14; 1931–63.
c) SENIOR. Ages 13–17; 1931–65.

See T2:411 (1 reference) and 7:365 (3 references).

REFERENCES
1–3. See 7:365.
4. See T2:411.
5. FINCHAM, F. A comparison of moral judgment in learning disabled and normal achieving boys. *Journal of Psychology*, 1977, 96, 153–160.
6. FINCHAM, F. Conservation and cognitive role-taking ability in learning disabled boys. *Journal of Learning Disabilities*, 1979, 12, 25–31.

[1579]
*****The New Sucher-Allred Reading Placement Inventory.** Reading level grades 1–9; 1968–81; SAR-PI; 3 major scores: independent, instructional, and frustrational grade reading levels; Floyd Sucher and Ruel A. Allred; Economy Co.

For additional information, reviews by Marjorie S. Johnson and James L. Wardrop, and excerpted reviews by Jerry Johns and Jerry Stafford, see 8:746 (3 references); see also T2:1604 (1 reference).

REFERENCES
1. See T2:1604.
2–4. See 8:746.
5. ANDERSON, W. W. Focus on measurement and evaluation. Commercial informal reading inventories: A comparative review. *Journal of Reading*, 1977, 17, 99–104.

[1580]
New Uses. Grades 10–16; 1962–69; "convergent production of semantic transformations"; revision of *Picture Gestalt*; Ralph Hoepfner and J. P. Guilford; Sheridan Psychological Services, Inc.*

REFERENCES
1. ALPAUGH, P. K., & BIRREN, J. E. Variables affecting creative contributions across the adult life span. *Human Development*, 1977, 20, 240–248.
2. RUSCH, R., & STEINER, J. Problems in scoring, agreement among raters, and internal consistency of selected marker tests. *Journal of Experimental Education*, 1979, 47, 276–282.

[1581]
Newsweek NewsQuiz. Grades 9–12; 1951–82; 6 tests (spirit masters for local duplicating) issued annually during school year (October, November, December, February, March, and April); available only as part of the Newsweek Educational Program; no manual; Newsweek Educational Division.*

For additional information, see 6:986.

[1582]
N.I.I.P. Engineering Apprentice Selection Test Battery. Engineering apprentices; 1936–72; 6 tests, 7 scores: 6 scores listed below and combined score for *a–e*; subtests available only as separates; National Institute of Industrial Psychology; NFER-Nelson Publishing Co. [England].*
a) GROUP TEST 82. Spatial perception.
b) GROUP TESTS 90A AND 90B. Verbal intelligence.
c) GROUP TESTS 70 AND 70B. Nonverbal intelligence.
d) ARITHMETIC TESTS EA2A AND EA4. Arithmetic attainment.
e) VINCENT MECHANICAL DIAGRAMS TEST. Mechanical ability.
f) MECHANICAL INFORMATION TEST.

For additional information, see 7:1096 (1 reference).

[1583]
NIIP Group Test 36. Ages 10–13; 1937–74; formerly called *Group Test 36*; verbal intelligence; National Institute of Industrial Psychology; NFER-Nelson Publishing Co. [England].*

For additional information, see 8:195; see also T2:384 (4 references).

[1584]
19 Field Interest Inventory. Standards 8–10 and college and adults; 1970–71; FII; 21 scores: fine arts, performing arts, language, historical, service, social work, sociability, public speaking, law, creative thought, science,

[1585]
NLN Achievement Tests for Schools Preparing Registered Nurses. Students in state-approved schools preparing registered nurses; 1943–73; tests loaned to schools for their own use; 3 levels; National League for Nursing, Inc.*

a) [BASIC ACHIEVEMENT TESTS.] Course-end tests; 1943–73; 9 tests.
  1) *Anatomy and Physiology.* 1943–64.
  2) *Chemistry.* 1943–63; 4 scores: inorganic, organic, biochemistry, total.
  3) *Microbiology.* 1943–71.
  4) *Normal Nutrition.* 1946–72; formerly called *Nutrition and Diet Therapy.*
  5) *Basic Pharmacology.* 1944–67; formerly called *Pharmacology and Therapeutics.*
  6) *Medical-Surgical Nursing.* 1956–62; 4 scores: medical nursing, surgical nursing, medical-surgical nursing, total.
  7) *Obstetric Nursing.* 1945–68; 4 scores: antepartal care, partal and postpartal care of mothers, care of newborn, total.
  8) *Nursing of Children.* 1945–68; 3 scores: growth and development, care of the sick child, total.
  9) *Psychiatric Nursing.* 1945–68; 3 scores: psychiatric nursing practices, facts and principles, total.

b) COMPREHENSIVE ACHIEVEMENT TESTS. Students about to graduate; 1957–68; 8 tests.
  1) *Diet Therapy and Applied Nutrition.* 1962.
  2) *Pharmacology in Clinical Nursing (Application of Facts and Principles).* 1960–67.
  3) *Natural Sciences in Nursing.* 1957–68; 3 scores: facts and principles (knowledge, application, total).
  4) *Maternity and Child Nursing.* 1958–67; 3 scores: care of the normal pregnant woman and normal child, care of sick children, total.
  5) *Disaster Nursing.* 1961; 3 scores: general nursing applied to disasters, facts and principles of disasters and disaster nursing, total.
  6) *Medical-Surgical Nursing, Part 1.* 1961; 4 scores: orthopedic nursing, neurological-neurosurgical nursing, eye-ear-nose-and-throat nursing, total.
  7) *Medical-Surgical Nursing, Part 2.* 1962; 3 scores: medical nursing, surgical nursing, total.
  8) *Communicable Disease Nursing.* 1946–63; 3 scores: prevention and transmission, disease manifestations and other aspects, total.

c) [BACCALAUREATE LEVEL TESTS.] For baccalaureate programs only; 1956–73; 5 tests.
  1) *Maternal Child Nursing.* 1964; 4 scores: growth and development (including pregnancy), conditions and care of the sick child, other relevant aspects, total.
  2) *Medical-Surgical Nursing.* 1967; 4 scores: part A, part B, knowledge, application.
  3) *Applied Natural Sciences.* 1967; 4 scores: part A, part B, knowledge, application.
  4) *Community Health Nursing.* 1956–73; earlier forms called *Public Health Nursing*; 4 scores: family health, community health, science and general information, total.
  5) *Psychiatric Nursing.* 1972; 3 scores: facts and principles, psychiatric nursing practice, total.

See T2:2383 (4 references), 7:1118 (10 references), and 6:1157 (1 reference).

REFERENCES
1. See 6:1157.
2–11. See 7:1118.
12–15. See T2:2383.
16. WOLFLE, L. M., & BRYANT, L. W. A causal model of nursing education and state board examination scores. *Nursing Research*, 1978, 27, 311–315.

[1586]
NLN Practical Nursing Achievement Tests. Students in state-approved schools of practical nursing; 1950–64; tests loaned to schools for their own use; 3 tests; National League for Nursing, Inc.*

a) THREE UNITS OF CONTENT. 1957–64; TUC; 4 scores: body structure and function, basic nursing procedures, nutrition and diet therapy, total.

b) NURSING INCLUDING ASPECTS OF PHARMACOLOGY. 1950–64; NIP; 4 scores: medical-surgical, maternal-child, pharmacology, total.

c) ELEMENTARY PSYCHIATRIC NURSING. 1958; for aide-training programs.

See T2:2385 (2 references) and 7:1120 (1 reference).

[1587]
NLN Pre-Nursing and Guidance Examination. Applicants for admission to state-approved schools preparing registered nurses; 1941–72; PNG; tests administered throughout the year at centers established by the publisher; 4 tests, 7 scores: 6 scores listed below, composite; National League for Nursing, Inc.*

a) NLN TEST OF ACADEMIC APTITUDE. Special printing of level 1 (for grades 12–14) of *Cooperative School and College Ability Tests: Series 2*; 3 scores: quantitative, verbal, total.

b) NLN READING TEST. Special printing of level 1 (for grades 12–14) of *Sequential Tests of Educational Progress, Series 2: Reading.*

c) NLN SCIENCE TEST. Special printing of level 1 (for grades 12–14) of *Sequential Tests of Educational Progress, Series 2: Science.*

d) NLN SOCIAL STUDIES TEST. Special printing of level 1 (for grades 12–14) of *Sequential Tests of Educational Progress, Series 2: Social Studies.*

See T2:2387 (18 references) and 6:1162 (8 references).

[1588]
NM Concepts of Ecology Test. Grades 6–8, 9–12; 1973; NMCET; criterion-referenced; Educational Evaluation Associates for and in cooperation with the New Mexico State Department of Education; Monitor.*

For additional information and a review by Jacqueline V. Mallinson, see 8:859.

[1589]
NM Consumer Mathematics Test. Grades 9–12; 1973; NMCMT; criterion-referenced; Educational Evaluation Associates for and in cooperation with the New Mexico State Department of Education; Monitor.*

For additional information and reviews by James Braswell and Carl J. Huberty, see 8:312.

[1590]
NM Consumer Rights and Responsibilities Test. Grades 9–12; 1973; NMCRRT; criterion-referenced; Educational Evaluation Associates for and in cooperation with the New Mexico State Department of Education; Monitor.*

For additional information and reviews by William E. Coffman and Norman Eagle, see 8:416.

[1591]
NOCTI Examination: Air Conditioning and Refrigeration. Teachers and prospective teachers; 1973–77; test administered each spring and fall at centers approved by the publisher; 5 scores for written part (total and 4 subscores), 3 scores for performance part (process, product, total); National Occupational Competency Testing Institute.*

For additional information and a review by Richard A. Swanson, see 8:1129. For a review of the NOCTI program, see 8:1153.

REFERENCES
1. GUTCHER, D., & THOMPSON, D. Structured and non–structured work experience programs. *Journal of Industrial Teacher Education*, 1977, 15, 75–85.

[1592]
NOCTI Examination: Airframe and Power Plant Mechanic. Teachers and prospective teachers; 1973–77; test administered each spring and fall at centers approved by the publisher; 4 scores for written part (total and 3 subscores), 3 scores for performance part (process, product, total); National Occupational Competency Testing Institute.*

For additional information, see 8:1130. For a review of the NOCTI program, see 8:1153.

[1593]
NOCTI Examination: Architectural Drafting. Teachers and prospective teachers; 1973–77; test administered each spring and fall at centers approved by the publisher; 5 scores for written part (total and 4 subscores), 3 scores for performance part (process, product, total); National Occupational Competency Testing Institute.*

For additional information and a review by Gary E. Lintereur, see 8:1131. For a review of the NOCTI program, see 8:1153.

REFERENCES
1. GUTCHER, D., & THOMPSON, D. Structured and non–structured work experience programs. *Journal of Industrial Teacher Education*, 1977, 15, 75–85.

[1594]
NOCTI Examination: Auto Body Repair. Teachers and prospective teachers; 1973–77; test administered each spring and fall at centers approved by the publisher; 5 scores for written part (total and 4 subscores), 3 scores for performance part (process, product, total); National Occupational Competency Testing Institute.*

For additional information, see 8:1132. For review of the NOCTI program, see 8:1153.

[1595]
NOCTI Examination: Auto Mechanic. Teachers and prospective teachers; 1973–77; test administered each spring and fall at centers approved by the publisher; 5 scores for written part (total and 4 subscores), 3 scores for performance part (process, product, total); National Occupational Competency Testing Institute.*

For additional information and reviews by Charles W. Pendleton and Kenneth E. Poucher, see 8:1133 (1 reference). For a review of the NOCTI program, see 8:1153.

REFERENCES
1. See 8:1133.
2. GUTCHER, D., & THOMPSON, D. Structured and non–structured work experience programs. *Journal of Industrial Teacher Education*, 1977, 15, 75–85.

[1596]
NOCTI Examination: Cabinet Making and Millwork. Teachers and prospective teachers; 1973–77; test administered each spring and fall at centers approved by the publisher; 5 scores for written part (total and 4 subscores), 3 scores for performance part (process, product, total); National Occupational Competency Testing Institute.*

For additional information and a review by Gary E. Lintereur, see 8:1134. For a review of the NOCTI program, see 8:1153.

[1597]
NOCTI Examination: Carpentry. Teachers and prospective teachers; 1973–77; test administered each spring and fall at centers approved by the publisher; 5 scores for written part (total and 4 subscores), 3 scores for performance part (process, product, total); National Occupational Competency Testing Institute.*

For additional information and a review by Daniel L. Householder, see 8:1135 (1 reference). For a review of the NOCTI program, see 8:1153.

[1598]
NOCTI Examination: Civil Technology. Teachers and prospective teachers; 1973–77; test administered each spring and fall at centers approved by the publisher; 5 scores for written part (total and 4 subscores), 3 scores for performance part (process, product, total); National Occupational Competency Testing Institute.*

For additional information, see 8:1136. For a review of the NOCTI program see 8:1153.

[1599]
NOCTI Examination: Cosmetology. Teachers and prospective teachers; 1973–77; test administered each spring and fall at centers approved by the publisher; 5 scores for written part (total and 4 subscores), 3 scores for performance part (process, product, total); National Occupational Competency Testing Institute.*

For additional information, see 8:1137. For a review of the NOCTI program, see 8:1153.

[1600]
NOCTI Examination: Diesel Engine Repair. Teachers and prospective teachers; 1973–77; test administered each spring and fall at centers approved by the publisher; 5 scores for written part (total and 4 subscores),

[1601]
NOCTI Examination: Electrical Installation.
Teachers and prospective teachers; 1973–77; test administered each spring and fall at centers approved by the publisher; 5 scores for written part (total and 4 subscores), 3 scores for performance part (process, product, total); National Occupational Competency Testing Institute.*

For additional information and a review by Alan R. Suess, see 8:1139 (1 reference). For a review of the NOCTI program, see 8:1153.

REFERENCES

1. See 8:1139.
2. GUTCHER, D., & THOMPSON, D. Structured and non-structured work experience programs. *Journal of Industrial Teacher Education*, 1977, 15, 75–85.

[1602]
NOCTI Examination: Electronics Communications. Teachers and prospective teachers; 1973–77; test administered each spring and fall at centers approved by the publisher; 5 scores for written part (total and 4 subscores), 3 scores for performance part (process, product, total); National Occupational Competency Testing Institute.*

For additional information and a review by Emil H. Hoch, see 8:1140. For a review of the NOCTI program, see 8:1153.

[1603]
NOCTI Examination: Industrial Electrician. Teachers and prospective teachers; 1973–77; test administered each spring and fall at centers approved by the publisher; 5 scores for written part (total and 4 subscores), 3 scores for performance part (process, product, total); National Occupational Competency Testing Institute.*

For additional information and a review by Alan R. Suess, see 8:1141. For a review of the NOCTI program, see 8:1153.

[1604]
NOCTI Examination: Industrial Electronics. Teachers and prospective teachers; 1973–77; test administered each spring and fall at centers approved by the publisher; 5 scores for written part (total and 4 subscores), 3 scores for performance part (process, product, total); National Occupational Competency Testing Institute.*

For additional information and a review by Emil H. Hoch, see 8:1142. For a review of the NOCTI program, see 8:1153.

[1605]
NOCTI Examination: Machine Drafting. Teachers and prospective teachers; 1973–77; test administered each spring and fall at centers approved by the publisher; 5 scores for written part (total and 4 subscores), 3 scores for performance part (process, product, total); National Occupational Competency Testing Institute.*

For additional information and a review by Tim L. Wentling, see 8:1143. For a review of the NOCTI program, see 8:1153.

[1606]
NOCTI Examination: Machine Trades. Teachers and prospective teachers; 1973–77; test administered each spring and fall at centers approved by the publisher; 5 scores for written part (total and 4 subscores), 3 scores for performance part (process, product, total); National Occupational Competency Testing Institute.*

For additional information, see 8:1144 (1 reference). For a review of the NOCTI program, see 8:1153.

[1607]
NOCTI Examination: Masonry. Teachers and prospective teachers; 1973–77; test administered each spring and fall at centers approved by the publisher; 5 scores for written part (total and 4 subscores), 3 scores for performance part (process, product, total); National Occupational Competency Testing Institute.*

For additional information, see 8:1145. For a review of the NOCTI program, see 8:1153.

[1608]
NOCTI Examination: Mechanical Technology. Teachers and prospective teachers; 1973–77; test administered each spring and fall at centers approved by the publisher; 5 scores for written part (total and 4 subscores), 3 scores for performance part (process, product, total); National Occupational Competency Testing Institute.*

For additional information, see 8:1146. For a review of the NOCTI program, see 8:1153.

[1609]
NOCTI Examination: Plumbing. Teachers and prospective teachers; 1973–77; test administered each spring and fall at centers approved by the publisher; 5 scores for written part (total and 4 subscores), 3 scores for performance part (process, product, total); National Occupational Competency Testing Institute.*

For additional information and a review by Richard C. Erickson, see 8:1147. For a review of the NOCTI program, see 8:1153.

[1610]
NOCTI Examination: Printing. Teachers and prospective teachers; 1973–77; test administered each spring and fall at centers approved by the publisher; 5 scores for written part (total and 4 subscores), 3 scores for performance part (process, product, total); 2 tests: letterpress, offset; National Occupational Competency Testing Institute.*

For additional information, see 8:1148. For a review of the NOCTI program, see 8:1153.

REFERENCES

1. GUTCHER, D., & THOMPSON, D. Structured and non-structured work experience programs. *Journal of Industrial Teacher Education*, 1977, 15, 75–85.

[1611]
NOCTI Examination: Quantity Food Preparation. Teachers and prospective teachers; 1973–77; test administered each spring and fall at centers approved by the publisher; 5 scores for written part (total and 4 subscores), 3 scores for performance part (process, product, total); National Occupational Competency Testing Institute.*

For additional information, see 8:1149. For a review of the NOCTI program, see 8:1153.

[1612]
NOCTI Examination: Sheet Metal. Teachers and prospective teachers; 1973–77; test administered each spring and fall at centers approved by the publisher; 5 scores for written part (total and 4 subscores), 3 scores for performance part (process, product, total); National Occupational Competency Testing Institute.*

For additional information and a review by Daniel L. Householder, see 8:1150. For a review of the NOCTI program, see 8:1153.

REFERENCES
1. CAUTER, E. V., & NENDLEWICZ, J. 24–hour dopamine–beta–hydroxlase pattern: A possible biological index of manic depression. *Life Sciences*, 1978, 22, 147–156.

[1613]
NOCTI Examination: Small Engine Repair. Teachers and prospective teachers; 1973–77; test administered each spring and fall at centers approved by the publisher; 5 scores for written part (total and 4 subscores), 3 scores for performance part (process, product, total); National Occupational Competency Testing Institute.*

For additional information and a review by Kenneth E. Poucher, see 8:1151. For a review of the NOCTI program, see 8:1153.

[1614]
NOCTI Examination: Welding. Teachers and prospective teachers; 1973–77; test administered each spring and fall at centers approved by the publisher; 5 scores for written part (total and 4 subscores), 3 scores for performance part (process, product, total); National Occupational Competency Testing Institute.*

For additional information and a review by Richard C. Erickson, see 8:1152. For a review of the NOCTI program, see 8:1153.

[1615]
Non-Language Test of Verbal Intelligence—Form 768. Class 8 (ages 11–13); 1968; 4 scores: analogy, classification, opposites, picture arrangement; S. Chatterji and Manjula Mukerjee; Statistical Publishing Society [India].*

See T2:412 (2 references).

REFERENCES
1–2. See T2:412.
3. CHATTERJI, S,. & MUKERJEE, M. Concurrent validity of the Non-Language Test of Verbal Intelligence. *Educational & Psychological Measurement*, 1978, 38, 433–436.

[1616]
★**Non-Readers Intelligence Test, Third Edition.** Ages 6–5 to 8–11 and with less able children up to the age of 13–11; 1964–78; NRIT; D. Young; Hodder & Stoughton Educational [England].*

For additional information concerning an earlier edition, see 7:366.

[1617]
*****Non-Verbal Intelligence Tests for Deaf and Hearing Subjects.** Ages 3–16; 1939–70; NITDHS; administered orally or in pantomine; 9 scores: mosaic, picture memory, arrangement, analogies, completion, Knox cubes, drawing, sorting, IQ; (Dutch, German, and French editions available); J. Th. Snijders and N. Snijders-Oomen; distributed by Swets Test Services [The Netherlands].* (U.S. distributor: Swets North America, Inc.)

See T2:512 (5 references); for a review by J. S. Lawes see 6:529 (2 references).

[1618]
Non-Verbal Reasoning Test. Job applicants and industrial employees; 1961; Raymond J. Corsini (test) and Measurement Research Division, Human Resources Center, University of Chicago (manual); the Center.*

See T2:414 (2 references); for reviews by James E. Kennedy and David G. Ryans, see 6:478.

[1619]
★**Nonverbal Test of Cognitive Skills.** Ages 6–13; 1981; NTCS; 2 derived scores: cognitive skills age, cognitive skills index; G. Orville Johnson and Herbert F. Boyd; Charles E. Merrill Publishing Co.*

[1620]
Non-Verbal Tests. Ages 8 to 11–0, 10 to 12, 10 to 15; 1947–65; 3 levels; NFER-Nelson Publishing Co. [England].*

a) NON-VERBAL TESTS 1–2. Ages 10–12; 1947–59; 2 forms.
  1) *Non-Verbal Test 1.* 1947–59; test booklet title is *A Scale of Non-Verbal Mental Ability*; J. W. Jenkins. (An Australian adaptation, *Jenkins Non-Verbal Test*, is available from Australian Council for Educational Research [Australia].)
  2) *Non-Verbal Test 2.* 1948–51; D. M. Lee and J. W. Jenkins.
b) NON-VERBAL TEST DH. Ages 10 to 15; 1953–58; formerly called *Non-Verbal Test 3*; B. Calvert (test) and I. Macfarlane Smith (original manual).
c) NON-VERBAL TEST BD. Ages 8 to 11–0; 1953–65; formerly called *Non-Verbal Test 5*; D. A. Pidgeon.

See T2:415 (12 references) and 7:367 (1 reference); for reviews by T. R. Miles and John Nisbet, see 6:479 (1 reference); for a review by Cyril A. Rogers, see 5:356 (1 reference); for a review by E. A. Peel of the original edition, see 4:307 (3 references).

REFERENCES
1–3. See 4:307.
4. See 5:356.
5. See 6:479.
6. See 7:367.
7–18. See T2:415.
19. RAE, G. Relation of auditory-visual integration to reading and intelligence. *Journal of General Psychology*, 1977, 97, 3–8.
20. YOUNGMAN, M. B. Six reactions to school transfer. *British Journal of Educational Psychology*, 1978, 48, 280–289.
21. MCCALLUM, D. I., SMITH, I. M., & ELIOT, J. Further investigation of components of mathematical ability. *Psychological Reports*, 1979, 44, 1127–1133.
22. EVANS, G., GEORGEFF, M., & POOLE, M. E. Training in information selection for communication. *Australian Journal of Education*, 1980, 24, 137–154.
23. HOWELL, E. R., SMITH, G. A., & STANLEY, G. Reading disability and visual spatial frequency specific effects. *Australian Journal of Psychology*, 1981, 33, 97–102.

[1621]
Northampton Activity Rating Scale. Mental patients; 1951; NARS; "behavior exhibited by mental

patients in rehabilitation and activity therapies of the hospital environment"; Isidor W. Scherer; the Author.*
For additional information, see P:180.

[1622]
Northwestern Syntax Screening Test. Ages 3–7; 1969–71; NSST; 2 scores: receptive, expressive; Laura Lee; Northwestern University Press.*

For additional information, reviews by Marie C. Fontana and R. Duane Logue, and an excerpted review by Maryl Bannatyne, see 8:967 (26 references); see also T2:2084 (3 references).

REFERENCES

1–3. See T2:2084.
4–29. See 8:967.
30. ARNDT, W. B. A psychometric evaluation of the Northwestern Syntax Screening Test. *Journal of Speech & Hearing Disorders,* 1977, 42, 316–319.
31. ARNDT, W. B., SHELTON, R. L., JOHNSON, A. F., & FURR, M. L. Identification and description of homogeneous subgroups within a sample of misarticulating children. *Journal of Speech & Hearing Research,* 1977, 20, 263–292.
32. BYRNE, M. C. A clinician looks at the Northwestern Syntax Screening Test. *Journal of Speech & Hearing Disorders,* 1977, 42, 320–322.
33. GRILL, J. J., & BARTEL, N. R. Language bias in tests: ITPA grammatic closure. *Journal of Learning Disabilities,* 1977, 10, 229–235.
34. LEE, L. L. Reply to Arndt and Byrne. *Journal of Speech & Hearing Disorders,* 1977, 42, 323–327.
35. WIIG, E. H., LAPOINT, C., & SEMEL, E. M. Relationships among language processing and production abilities of learning disabled adolescents. *Journal of Learning Disabilities,* 1977, 10, 292–299.
36. BEDROSIAN, J. L., & PRUTTING, C. A. Communicative performance of mentally retarded adults in four conversational settings. *Journal of Speech & Hearing Research,* 1978, 21, 79–95.
37. CHAPMAN, D. L., & FRIEDMAN, D. Comparison of three expressive syntax measures with four year olds. *ASHA,* 1978, 20, 832.
38. DOEHRING, D. G., BONNYCASTLE, D. E., & LING, A. H. Rapid reading skills of integrated hearing–impaired children. *Volta Review,* 1978, 80, 399–409.
39. LAMBERTS, F., & YSSELDYKE, J. E. Group oral language training with TMH children based on learning to think material. *Education & Training of the Mentally Retarded,* 1978, 13, 309–315.
40. NELSON, N. W., & MCROSKEY, R. L. Comprehension of standard English at varied speaking rates by children whose major dialect is black English. *Journal of Communication Disorders,* 1978, 11, 37–50.
41. PALEN, C., & MIDDLESWORTH, K. L. Comparing pictorial testing and grammatical preference in children's language comprehension. *ASHA,* 1978, 20, 832. (Abstract)
42. RINGLER, N., TRAUSE, M. A., KLAUS, M., & KENNELL, J. The effects of extra postpartum contact and maternal speech patterns on children's IQs, speech, and language comprehension at five. *Child Development,* 1978, 49, 862–865.
43. SCHMAUCH, V. A., PANAGOS, J. M., & KLICH, R. J. Syntax influences the accuracy of consonant production in language–disordered children. *Journal of Communication Disorders,* 1978, 11, 315–323.
44. SOMMERS, R. K., ERIDGE, S., & PETERSON, M. K. How valid are children's language tests? *Journal of Special Education,* 1978, 12, 393–407.
45. WILCOX, M. J., & LEONARD, L. B. Experimental acquisition of wh–questions in language–disordered children. *Journal of Speech & Hearing Research,* 1978, 21, 220–239.
46. BROWNS, F. Beginning reading instruction with hearing–impaired children. *Volta Review,* 1979, 81, 100–108.
47. STECKOL, K. F., & LEONARD, L. B. The use of grammatical morphemes by normal and language–impaired children. *Journal of Communication Disorders,* 1979, 12, 291–301.
48. WHITE, M. A first–grade intervention program for children at risk for reading failure. *Journal of Learning Disabilities,* 1979, 12, 231–237.
49. JORDON, L. S. Receptive and expressive language problems occurring in combination with a seizure disorder: A case report. *Journal of Communication Disorders,* 1980, 13, 295–303.
50. KLEECK, A. V., & CARPENTER, R. L. The effects of children's language comprehension level on adults' child–directed talk. *Journal of Speech & Hearing Research,* 1980, 23, 546–569.
51. KLEIN, A. Test–retest reliability and predictive validity of the Northwestern Syntax Screening Test. *Educational & Psychological Measurement,* 1980, 40, 1167–1172.
52. RATUSNIK, D. L., KLEE, T. M., & RATUSNIK, C. M. Northwestern Syntax Screening Test: A short form. *Journal of Speech & Hearing Disorders,* 1980, 45, 200–208.
53. BLISS, L. S., & ALLEN, D. V. Black English responses on selected language tests. *Journal of Communication Disorders,* 1981, 14, 225–233.
54. CHAPMAN, D. L., & NATION, J. E. Patterns of language performance in educable mentally retarded children. *Journal of Communication Disorders,* 1981, 14, 245–254.
55. MELNICK, C. R., MICHALS, K. K. & MATALON, R. Linguistic development of children with phenylketonuria and normal intelligence. *Journal of Pediatrics,* 1981, 98, 269–272.
56. STARK, R. E., & TALLAL, P. Selection of children with specific language deficits. *Journal of Speech & Hearing Disorders,* 1981, 46, 114–122.

[1623]
The Nottingham Number Test. Ages 9–1 to 11–0; 1973; NNT; upward extension of *Leicester Number Test*; 3 scores: number concepts, number skills, total; W. E. C. Gillham and K. A. Hesse; Hodder & Stoughton Educational [England].*

For additional information, see 8:306.

[1624]
NTE Core Battery. College seniors and teachers; 1940–82; test administered 3 times annually (February, July, November) at centers established by the publisher; 3 scores: communication skills, general knowledge, professional knowledge; Educational Testing Service.*

For additional information, see 8:382 (2 references). For reviews of the testing program, see 8:381 (2 reviews), 7:582 (2 reviews), 6:700 (1 review), 5:538 (3 reviews), and 4:802 (1 review).

REFERENCES

1–2. See 8:382.
3. DAVIS, H. A comparison of academic achievement of black PE majors at predominately black and predominately white institutions. *Journal of Physical Education and Recreation,* 1977, 48, 24–25.

[1625]
NTE Programs. College seniors and teachers; 1940–82; NTE; tests administered 3 times annually (February, July, November) at centers established by the publisher (French, German, Guidance Counselor, Music Education, and Spanish not offered in July); a composite NTE score is available for examinees taking both *a* and *b*; Educational Testing Service.*

a) NTE CORE BATTERY. 1982; 3 scores: communication skills, general knowledge, professional knowledge.
b) TEACHING AREA EXAMINATIONS. 1940–77; 26 tests, also listed separately: Art Education, Audiology, Biology and General Science, Business Education, Chemistry-Physics-General Science, Early Childhood Education, Education in the Elementary School, Education of Mentally Retarded, Educational Administration and Supervision, English Language and Literature, French, German, Guidance Counselor, Home Economics Education, Industrial Arts Education, Introduction to the Teaching of Reading, Mathematics, Media Specialist—Library and Audio-Visual Services, Music Education, Physical Education, Reading Specialist, Social Studies, Spanish, Speech-Communication and Theatre, Speech Pathology, Texas Government.

For additional information and reviews by Jack C. Merwin and James V. Mitchell, Jr., see 8:381 (15 references); see also T2:869 (8 references); for reviews by Wayne H. Holtzman and Edwin Wandt of an earlier program, see 7:582 (25 references); for a review by Harold Seashore, see 6:700 (5 references); for reviews by William A. Brownell, Walter W. Cook, and Lawrence G. Derthick, see 5:538 (6 references); for a review by Harry

N. Rivlin, see 4:802 (43 references). For reviews of individual tests, see 8:54 (1 review), 8:86 (1 review), 8:124 (1 review), 8:136 (1 review), 8:169 (1 review), 8:326 (1 review), 8:734 (1 review), 8:828 (1 review), 8:891 (1 review), 8:966 (1 review), 7:250 (2 reviews), 7:556 (1 review), 6:259 (1 review), 6:345 (1 review), 6:350 (1 review), 6:583 (1 review), and 6:974 (1 review).

REFERENCES

1–43. See 4:802.
44–49. See 5:538.
50–54. See 6:700.
55–79. See 7:582.
80–87. See T2:869.
88–102. See 8:381.
103. DAVIS, H. A comparison of academic achievement of black PE majors at predominately black and predominately white institutions. *Journal of Physical Education & Recreation*, 1977, 48, 24–25.
104. AYERS, J. B., & QUALLS, G. S. Concurrent and predictive validity of the National Teachers Examinations. *Journal of Educational Research*, 1979, 73, 86–92.
105. PANACKAL, A. A. Rigid and flexible course requirements and achievement in a college of education. *College Student Journal*, 1980, 14, 135–141.
106. WILLSON, V. L., & STOLLER, J. E. Predicting teacher NTE scores in mathematics and science. *Educational & Psychological Measurement*, 1981, 41, 479–485.

[1626]
NTE Specialty Area Tests: Art Education Specialty Area Test. College seniors and teachers; 1961–76; test administered 3 times annually (February, July, November) at centers established by the publisher; Educational Testing Service.*

For additional information and a review by Laura H. Chapman, see 8:86; for a review by Harold A. Schultz of earlier forms, see 6:345. For reviews of the testing program, see 8:381 (2 reviews), 7:582 (2 reviews), and 6:700 (1 review).

[1627]
NTE Specialty Area Tests: Audiology Specialty Area Test. College seniors and teachers; 1970–77; test administered 3 times annually (February, July, November) at centers established by the publisher; Educational Testing Service.*

For additional information, see 8:943. For reviews of the testing program, see 8:381 (2 reviews) and 7:582 (2 reviews).

[1628]
NTE Specialty Area Tests: Biology and General Science Specialty Area Test. College seniors and teachers; 1940–77; test administered 3 times annually (February, July, November) at centers established by the publisher; Educational Testing Service.*

For additional information, see 8:828. For reviews of the testing program, see 8:381 (2 reviews), 7:582 (2 reviews), 6:700 (1 review), and 5:538 (3 reviews).

[1629]
NTE Specialty Area Tests: Business Education Specialty Area Test. College seniors and teachers; 1956–77; test administered 3 times annually (February, July, November) at centers established by the publisher; Educational Testing Service.*

For additional information and a review by Leonard J. West, see 8:326; for a review by Ray G. Price of an earlier form, see 7:556. For reviews of the testing program, see 8:381 (2 reviews), 7:582 (2 reviews), 6:700 (1 review), and 5:538 (3 reviews).

[1630]
NTE Specialty Area Tests: Chemistry, Physics, and General Science Specialty Area Test. College seniors and teachers; 1940–77; tests administered 3 times annually (February, July, November) at centers established by the publisher; Educational Testing Service.*

For additional information and a review by Jacqueline V. Mallinson, see 8:829. For reviews of the testing program, see 8:381 (2 reviews), 7:582 (2 reviews), 6:700 (1 review), and 5:538 (3 reviews).

[1631]
NTE Specialty Area Tests: Early Childhood Education Specialty Area Test. College seniors and teachers; 1953–77; test administered 3 times annually (February, July, November) at centers established by the publisher; Educational Testing Service.*

For additional information, see 8:383. For reviews of the testing program, see 8:381 (2 reviews), 7:582 (2 reviews), 6:700 (1 review), and 5:538 (3 reviews).

[1632]
NTE Specialty Area Tests: Education in the Elementary School Specialty Area Test. College seniors and teachers; 1940–76; test administered 3 times annually (February, July, November) at centers established by the publisher; Educational Testing Service.*

For additional information, see 8:385. For reviews of the testing program, see 8:381 (2 reviews), 7:582 (2 reviews), 6:700 (1 review), 5:538 (3 reviews), and 4:802 (1 review).

[1633]
NTE Specialty Area Tests: Education of the Mentally Retarded Specialty Area Test. College seniors and teachers; 1970–77; test administered 3 times annually (February, July, November) at centers established by the publisher; Educational Testing Service.*

For additional information, see 8:386. For reviews of the testing program, see 8:381 (2 reviews) and 7:582 (2 reviews).

[1634]
NTE Specialty Area Tests: Educational Administration and Supervision Specialty Area Test. Prospective school administrators; 1971–77; test administered 3 times annually (February, July, November) at centers established by the publisher; Educational Testing Service.*

For additional information, see 8:384. For reviews of the testing program, see 8:381 (2 reviews).

[1635]
NTE Specialty Area Tests: English Language and Literature Specialty Area Test. College seniors and teachers; 1940–76; test administered 3 times annually (February, July, November) at centers established by the publisher; Educational Testing Service.*

For additional information and a review by Roger A. Richards, see 8:54; see also 7:203 (1 reference); for a review by Holland Roberts of an earlier form, see 6:259. For reviews of the testing program, see 8:381 (2 reviews),

7:582 (2 reviews), 6:700 (1 review), 5:538 (3 reviews), and 4:802 (1 review).

[1636]
NTE Specialty Area Tests: French Specialty Area Test. College seniors and teachers; 1970–76; test administered 2 times annually (February, November) at centers established by the publisher; derived from *MLA Foreign Language Proficiency Tests for Teachers and Advanced Students: French*; Educational Testing Service.*

For additional information and a review by Joseph A. Murphy, see 8:124. For reviews of the testing program, see 8:381 (2 reviews), 7:582 (2 reviews), and 4:802 (1 review).

[1637]
NTE Specialty Area Tests: German Specialty Area Test. College seniors and teachers; 1970–76; test administered 2 times annually (February, November) at centers established by the publisher; derived from *MLA Foreign Language Proficiency Tests for Teachers and Advanced Students: German* ; Educational Testing Service.*

For additional information and a review by Randall L. Jones, see 8:136. For reviews of the testing program, see 8:381 (2 reviews) and 7:582 (2 reviews).

[1638]
NTE Specialty Area Tests: Guidance Counselor Specialty Area Test. Prospective guidance counselors; 1972–76; test administered 2 times annually (February, November) at centers established by the publisher; Educational Testing Service.*

For additional information, see 8:387. For reviews of the testing program, see 8:381 (2 reviews).

[1639]
NTE Specialty Area Tests: Home Economics Education Specialty Area Test. College seniors and teachers; 1960–77; test administered 3 times annually (February, July, November) at centers established by the publisher; Educational Testing Service.*

For additional information, see 8:417. For reviews of the testing program, see 8:381 (2 reviews), 7:582 (2 reviews), and 6:700 (1 review).

[1640]
NTE Specialty Area Tests: Industrial Arts Education Specialty Area Test. College seniors and teachers; 1947–76; test administered 3 times annually (February, July, November) at centers established by the publisher; Educational Testing Service.*

For additional information, see 8:420. For reviews of the testing program, see 8:381 (2 reviews), 7:582 (2 reviews), 6:700 (1 review), 5:538 (3 reviews), and 4:802 (1 review).

[1641]
NTE Specialty Area Tests: Introduction to the Teaching of Reading Specialty Area Test. College seniors and teachers; 1972–76; test administered 3 times annually (February, July, November) at centers established by the publisher; Educational Testing Service.*

For additional information, see 8:733. For reviews of the testing program, see 8:381 (2 reviews).

[1642]
NTE Specialty Area Tests: Mathematics Specialty Area Tests. College seniors and teachers; 1940–76; test administered 3 times annually (February, July, November) at centers established by the publisher; Educational Testing Service.*

For additional information, see 8:286; for a review by Paul Blommers of an earlier form, see 6:583. For reviews of the testing program, see 8:381 (2 reviews), 7:582 (2 reviews), 6:700 (1 review), 5:538 (3 reviews), and 4:802 (1 review).

[1643]
NTE Specialty Area Tests: Media Specialist-Library and Audio-Visual Services Specialty Area Test. College seniors and teachers; 1970–76; test administered 3 times annually (February, July, November) at centers established by the publisher; Educational Testing Service.*

For additional information, see 8:388. For reviews of the testing program, see 8:381 (2 reviews) and 7:582 (2 reviews).

[1644]
NTE Specialty Area Tests: Music Education Specialty Area Test. College seniors and teachers; 1957–76; test administered 2 times annually (February, November) at centers established by the publisher; Educational Testing Service.*

For additional information, see 8:99; for reviews by Paul R. Lehman and Roger P. Phelps of earlier forms, see 7:250; for a review by William S. Larson, see 6:350. For reviews of the testing program, see 8:381 (2 reviews), 7:582 (2 reviews), 6:700 (1 review), and 5:538 (3 reviews).

[1645]
NTE Specialty Area Tests: Physical Education Specialty Area Test. College seniors and teachers; 1954–77; test administered 3 times annually (February, July, November) at centers established by the publisher; a combined version replacing the former *Men's Physical Education* and *Women's Physical Education* tests; Educational Testing Service.*

For additional information, see 8:414. For reviews of the testing program, see 8:381 (2 reviews), 7:582 (2 reviews), 6:700 (1 review), and 5:538 (3 reviews).

[1646]
NTE Specialty Area Tests: Reading Specialist Specialty Area Test. College seniors and teachers; 1969–76; test administered 3 times annually (February, July, November) at centers established by the publisher; formerly entitled *National Teacher Examinations: Reading Specialist—Elementary School*; Educational Testing Service.*

For additional information and a review by H. Alan Robinson, see 8:734. For reviews of the testing program, see 8:381 (2 reviews) and 7:582 (2 reviews).

[1647]
NTE Specialty Area Tests: Social Studies Specialty Area Test. College seniors and teachers; 1940–76; tests administered 3 times annually (February, July,

November) at centers established by the publisher; Educational Testing Service.*

For additional information and a review by Jack L. Nelson, see 8:891. For a review by Harry D. Berg of an earlier form, see 6:974. For reviews of the testing program, see 8:381 (2 reviews), 7:582 (2 reviews), 6:700 (1 review), 5:538 (3 reviews), and 4:802 (1 review).

[1648]
NTE Specialty Area Tests: Spanish Specialty Area Test. College seniors and teachers; 1970–76; test administered 2 times annually (February, November) at centers established by the publisher; derived from *MLA Foreign Language Proficiency Tests for Teachers and Advanced Students: Spanish*; Educational Testing Service.*

For additional information and a review by Charles W. Stansfield, see 8:169. For reviews of the testing program see 8:381 (2 reviews), 7:582 (2 reviews), and 4:802 (1 review).

[1649]
NTE Specialty Area Tests: Speech-Communication and Theatre Specialty Area Test. College seniors and teachers; 1970–77; tests administered 3 times annually (February, July, November) at centers established by the publisher; Educational Testing Service.*

For additional information, see 8:965. For reviews of the testing program, see 8:381 (2 reviews) and 7:582 (2 reviews).

[1650]
NTE Specialty Area Tests: Speech Pathology Specialty Area Test. College seniors and teachers; 1970–77; test administered 3 times annually (February, July, November) at centers established by the publisher; Educational Testing Service.*

For additional information and a review by Margaret C. Byrne, see 8:966. For reviews of the testing program, see 8:381 (2 reviews) and 7:582 (2 reviews).

[1651]
NTE Specialty Area Tests: Texas Government Specialty Area Test. College seniors and teachers; 1972–76; test administered 3 times annually (February, July, November) at centers established by the publisher; Educational Testing Service.*

For additional information, see 8:923. For reviews of the testing program, see 8:381 (2 reviews).

[1652]
Number Test DE. Ages 10.5–12.5; 1965; formerly called *Number Test I*; E. L. Barnard; NFER-Nelson Publishing Co. [England].*

For additional information, see 7:522.

REFERENCES

1. McCallum D. I., Smith, I. M., & Eliot, J. Further investigation of components of mathematical ability. *Psychological Reports*, 1979, 44, 1127–1133.

[1653]
*****Numerical Ability: Differential Aptitude Tests.** Grades 8–12 and adults; 1947–77; George K. Bennett, Harold G. Seashore, and Alexander G. Wesman; The Psychological Corporation.* For the complete battery entry, see 732.

For additional information regarding an earlier edition, see 8:267 (2 references); see also T2:644 (11 references). For reviews of the complete battery, see 8:485 (2 reviews, 1 excerpt), 7:673 (1 review, 1 excerpt), 6:767 (2 reviews), 5:605 (2 reviews), 4:711 (3 reviews), and 3:620 (1 excerpt).

REFERENCES

1–11. See T2:644.
12–13. See 8:267.
14. Silver, E. A. Student perceptions of relatedness among mathematical verbal problems. *Journal of Research in Mathematics Education*, 1979, 10, 195–210.

[1654]
Nurse Attitudes Inventory. Prospective nursing students; 1965–70; NAI; a multiple choice test based upon *Luther Hospital Sentence Completions*; 9 scores: attitudes (nursing, self, home-family, responsibility, others-love-marriage, academic), verification (V-1, V-2), total; the authors refer to the scoring key used to obtain the total score as the *Nursing Education Scale*, abbreviated NES-NAI to distinguish it from the *Nursing Education Scale* based upon either the *Luther Hospital Sentence Completions* or the *Nursing Sentence Completions*; John R. Thurston, Helen L. Brunclik, and John F. Feldhusen (manual); Nursing Research Associates.* (In-print status uncertain; no reply from publisher.)

For additional information, see 7:1122 (5 references).

[1655]
Nurses' Observation Scale for Inpatient Evaluation. Mental patients; 1965–66; NOSIE; manual title is *NOSIE–30: A Treatment-Sensitive Ward Behavior Scale*; 7 scores: social competence, social interest, personal neatness, irritability manifest psychosis, retardation, total; Gilbert Honigfeld, Roderic D. Gillis, and C. James Klett (manual); Behavior Arts Center.*

For additional information and a review by William J. Eichman, see 8:631 (37 references); see also T2:1298 (11 references) and 7:114 (24 references).

REFERENCES

1–24. See 7:114.
25–35. See T2:1298.
36–72. See 8:631.
73. Clark, M. L., Paredes, A., Costiloe, J. P., Fulkerson, F. G., & Wood, F. Evaluation of two dose levels of loxapine succinate in chronic schizophrenia. *Diseases of the Nervous System*, 1977, 38, 7–10.
74. Dolan, M. P., & Norton, J. C. A programmed training technique that uses reinforcement to facilitate acquisition and retention in brain–damaged patients. *Journal of Clinical Psychology*, 1977, 33, 496–501.
75. Ehrensing, R. H., Kastin, A. J., Larsons, P. F., & Bishop, G. A. Melanocyte–stimulating–hormone release–inhibiting factor–I and tardive dyskinesia. *Diseases of the Nervous System*, 1977, 38, 303–307.
76. Heath, R. G. Modulation of emotion with a brain pacemaker. *Journal of Nervous & Mental Disease*, 1977, 165, 300–317.
77. Hedlund, J. L. MMPI clinical scale correlates. *Journal of Consulting & Clinical Psychology*, 1977, 45, 739–750.
78. Kay, S. R. Developmental assessment of cognitive style in mentally retarded psychotics. *Journal of Clinical Psychology*, 1977, 33, 953–958.
79. Lin, T. Addicts' demographic characteristics and ward behaviors in a community–like hospital setting. *International Journal of the Addictions*, 1977, 12, 65–71.
80. McCreadie, R. G., & MacDonald, I. M. High dosage haloperidol in chronic schizophrenia. *British Journal of Psychiatry*, 1977, 131, 310–316.
81. Mielke, D. H., Gallant, D. M., & Kessler, C. An evaluation of a unique new antipsychotic agent, sulpiride: Effects on serum prolactin and growth hormone levels. *American Journal of Psychiatry*, 1977, 134, 1371–1375.
82. Philip, A. E. Cross–cultural study of the factorial dimensions of the NOSIE. *Journal of Clinical Psychology*, 1977, 33, 467–468.

83. PHILLIPSON, O. T., MCKEOWN, J. M., BAKER, J., & HEALEY, A. F. Correlation between plasma chlorpromazine and its metabolites and clinical ratings in patients with acute relapse of schizophrenic and paranoid psychosis. *British Journal of Psychiatry,* 1977, 131, 172–184.
84. RAASOCH, J., WILLMUTH, R., THOMSON, L., & HYDE, R. Intra-hospital transfer: Effects on chronically ill psychogeriatric patients. *Journal of the American Geriatrics Society,* 1977, 25, 281–284.
85. SILVESTRI, R. Implosive therapy treatment of emotionally disturbed retardates. *Journal of Consulting & Clinical Psychology,* 1977, 45, 14–22.
86. SIMPSON, G. B., BRANCHEY, M. H., & LEE, J. H. A trial of naltrexone in chronic schizophrenia. *Current Therapeutic Research,* 1977, 22, 909–913.
87. VIUKARI, M., & LINNOILA, M. Serum medazepam, diazepam, and N-desmethyldiazepam levels after single and multiple oral doses of medazepam. *Annals of Clinical Research,* 1977, 9, 284–286.
88. BEARD, M. T., ENELOW, C. T., & OWENS, J. G. Activity therapy as a reconstructive plan on the social competence of chronic hospitalized patients. *Journal of Psychiatric Nursing,* 1978, 16, 33–41.
89. BRANCHEY, M. H., LEE, J. H., SIMPSON, J. M., ELGART, B., & VICENCIO, A. Loxapine succinate as a neuroleptic agent: Evaluation in two populations of elderly psychiatric patients. *Journal of the American Geriatrics Society,* 1978, 26, 263–267.
90. CAPOTE, B., & PAPIKH, N. Cyclandelate in the treatment of senility: A controlled study. *Journal of the American Geriatrics Society,* 1978, 26, 360–362.
91. ERRICKSON, E., DARNELL, M. H., & LABECK, L. Brief treatment of hallucinatory behavior with behavioral techniques. *Behavior Therapy,* 1978, 9, 663–665.
92. GARDOS, G., TECCE, J. J., HARTMANN, E., BOWERS, P., & COLE, J. O. Treatment with mesoridazine and thioridazine in chronic schizophrenia: I. Assessment of clinical and electrophysiologic responses in refractory hallucinating schizophrenics. *Comprehensive Psychiatry,* 1978, 19, 517–525.
93. GARDOS, G., TECCE, J. J., HARTMANN, E., BOWERS, P., & COLE, J. O. Treatment with mesoridazine and thioridazine in chronic schizophrenia: II. Potential predictors of drug response. *Comprehensive Psychiatry,* 1978, 19, 527–532.
94. LANG, R. J. Multivariate classification of day-care patients: Personality as a continuum. *Journal of Consulting & Clinical Psychology,* 1978, 46, 1212–1226.
95. MACDONALD, M. L. Reality orientation versus sheltered workshops as treatment for the institutionalized aging. *Journal of Gerontology,* 1978, 33, 416–421.
96. MCCREADIE, R. G., MAIN, C. J., & DUNLAP, R. A. Token economy, pimozide and chronic schizophrenia. *British Journal of Psychiatry,* 1978, 133, 179–181.
97. OLTMANNS, T. F. Selective attention in schizophrenic and manic psychoses: The effect of distraction on information processing. *Journal of Abnormal Psychology,* 1978, 87, 212–225.
98. RIDER, B. Sensorimotor treatment of chronic schizophrenics. *American Journal of Occupational Therapy,* 1978, 32, 451–455.
99. ROTROSEN, J., ANGRIST, B. M., GERSHON, S., ARONSON, M., GRUEN, P., SACHAR, E. J., DENNING, R. K., MATTHYSSE, S., STANLEY, M., & WILK, S. Thiethylperazine. *Archives of General Psychiatry,* 1978, 35, 1113–1118.
100. SIMON, P., FERMANIAN, J., GINESTET, D., GOUJET, M. A., & PERON-MAGNAN, P. Standard and long-acting depot neuroleptics in chronic schizophrenics. *Archives of General Psychiatry,* 1978, 35, 893–897.
101. SINGH, A. N., SAXENA, B., & NELSON, H. L. A controlled clinical study of trazodone in chronic schizophrenic patients with pronounced depressive symptomatology. *Current Therapeutic Research,* 1978, 23, 485–501.
102. SUGERMAN, A. A. A controlled trial of a new antidepressant, WIN 27147–2. *Current Therapeutic Research,* 1978, 24, 227–231.
103. VAN PUTTEN, T., & MAY, P. R. A. "Akinetic depression" in schizophrenia. *Archives of General Psychiatry,* 1978, 35, 1101–1107.
104. COWLEY, L. M., & GLEN, R. S. Double-blind study of thioridazine and haloperidol in geriatric patients with a psychosis associated with organic brain syndrome. *Journal of Clinical Psychiatry,* 1979, 4, 411–419.
105. ELLIOTT, P. A., BARLOW, F., HOOPER, A., & KINGERLEE, P. E. Maintaining patients' improvements in a token economy. *Behaviour Research & Therapy,* 1979, 17, 355–367.
106. GELENBERG, A. J., & DOLLER, J. C. Clozapine versus chlorpromazine for the treatment of schizophrenia: Preliminary results from a double-blind study. *Journal of Clinical Psychiatry,* 1979, 40, 238–240.
107. LINGJAERDE, O., ENGSTRAND, E., ELLINGSEN, P., STYLO, D. A., & ROBAK, O. H. Antipsychotic effect of diazepam when given in addition to neuroleptics in chronic psychotic patients: A double-blind clinical trial. *Current Therapeutic Research,* 1979, 26, 505–514.
108. MCMORDIE, W. R., & SWINT, E. B. Predictive utility, sex of rater difference, and interrater reliabilities of the NOSIE–30. *Journal of Clinical Psychology,* 1979, 35, 773–775.
109. PHILIP, A. E. Prediction of successful rehabilitation by nurse rating scale. *British Journal of Psychiatry,* 1979, 134, 422–426.

110. SHEPPARD, G. P. High–dose propranolol in schizophrenia. *British Journal of Psychiatry,* 1979, 134, 470–476.
111. DENIKER, P., LOO, H., & COTTEREAU, M. J. Parental loxapine in severely disturbed schizophrenic patients. *Journal of Clinical Psychiatry,* 1980, 41, 23–26.
112. DITTMAR, N. D., & FRANKLIN, J. L. State hospital patients discharged to nursing homes: How are they doing? *Hospital & Community Psychiatry,* 1980, 31, 255–258.
113. HALL, R. C. W., GARDNER, E. R., STICKNEY, S. K., LECANN, A. F., & POPKIN, M. K. Physical illness manifesting as psychiatric disease. II. Analysis of a state hospital inpatient population. *Archives of General Psychiatry,* 1980, 37, 989–995.
114. KAY, S. R. Progressive figure drawings in the developmental assessment of mentally retarded psychotics. *Perceptual & Motor Skills,* 1980, 50, 583–590.
115. MALIK, S. C., & KUMAR, K. Loxapine in adolescent schizophrenia: A comparative study with trifluoperazine. *Current Therapeutic Research,* 1980, 28, 432–446.
116. RIFKIN, A., SARAF, K., KANE, J., ROSS, D., & KLEIN D. F. A comparison of trimipramine and imipramine: A controlled study. *Journal of Clinical Psychiatry,* 1980, 41, 124–129.
117. VYAS, B. K., & KALLA, V. A six–month double–blind comparison of loxapine succinate and chlorpromazine in chronic schizophrenic patients. *Current Therapeutic Research,* 1980, 28, 16–30.
118. AHLFORS, U. G. A comparison of amoxapine and imipramine in the treatment of depression in hospitalized patients. *Current Therapeutic Research,* 1981, 30, 856–866.
119. BECKER, R. E. Properiziazine: Effectiveness against hostility and aggression as compared to chlorpromazine. *Current Therapeutic Research,* 1981, 29, 925–928.
120. BRANCHEY, M. H., BRANCHEY, L. B., & RICHARDSON, M. Effects of neuroleptic adjustment on clinical condition and tardive dyskinesia in schizophrenic patients. *American Journal of Psychiatry,* 1981, 138, 608–612.
121. LAPIERRE, Y. D., CHAUDHRY, R., & SEPOS, V. A long–term efficacy and toxicity study of fluspirilene in chronic schizophrenia. *Current Therapeutic Research,* 1981, 30, 793–802.
122. PARK, S., HARDESTY, A. S., & GARCIA, E. Effects of triiodothyronine and chlorpromazine combination treatment in schizophrenia. *Current Therapeutic Research,* 1981, 29, 929–935.
123. PEET, M., BETHELL, M. S., COATES, A., KHAMNEE, A. K., HALL, P., COOPER, S. J., KING, D. J., & YATES, R. A. Propranolol in schizophrenia: I. Comparison of propranolol, chlorpromazine and placebo. *British Journal of Psychiatry,* 1981, 139, 105–111.
124. VAN PUTTEN, T., MAY, P. R. A., MARDER, S. R., & WITTMAN, L. A. Subjective response to antipsychotic drugs. *Archives of General Psychiatry,* 1981, 38, 187–190.

[1656]

★Nutrition Achievement Tests. Grades kgn–2, 3–4, 5–6; 1979; Judy K. Brun, Alyce M. Fanslow, Cheryl O. Hausafus, et al.; National Dairy Council and Iowa State University.*

[1657]

Nutrition Information Test. Grades 9–16 and adults; 1942–68; for research use only; no manual; H. Frederick Kilander; Glenn C. Leach, Publisher.*

See T2:953 (2 references) and 3:425 (1 reference).

[1658]

★Nutrition Knowledge and Interest Questionnaire. Grades 9 and above; 1981; for measurement of groups, not individuals; 6 objectives: analyzes physical/mental-emotional/social and economic factors that affect an individual's diet, interprets relationships between nutritional status and disease, assesses the interrelationships of diet/activity and other factors in regulating weight, distinguishes between food fads and fallacies and diets based on scientific principles of nutrition, examines emerging trends in society that are affecting dietary patterns, develops a plan of nutritional behaviors that promotes health for an individual and his or her family; G. Darrell Passwater; Teachers College Press.*

[1659]
★OARS Multidimensional Functional Assessment Questionnaire. Ages 60 and over; 1975–78; MFAQ; can be administered in clinical or survey settings to the subject or to someone who knows the subject well; ratings ranging from excellent to totally impaired for each of 5 scales: social resources, economic resources, mental health, physical health, activities of daily living; Center for the Study of Aging and Human Development; Duke University Medical Center.*

REFERENCES

1. BLAZER, D. The diagnosis of depression in the elderly. *Journal of the American Geriatrics Society*, 1980, 28, 52–58.

[1660]
The Object Relations Technique. Ages 11 and over; 1955–73; ORT; Herbert Phillipson; distributed by NFER-Nelson Publishing Co. [England].*

See T2:1486 (5 references) and P:458 (5 references); for a review by H. R. Beech and an excerpted review by Leopold Bellak, see 6:233 (7 references); for a review by George Westby, see 5:151 (6 references).

[1661]
Object Sorting Scales. Ages 16 and over; 1966; OSS; modification of *Goldstein-Scheerer Object Sorting Test*; 2 scores: schizotypy, brain damage; S. H. Lovibond; Australian Council for Educational Research [Australia].*

For additional information and a review by Robert W. Payne, see 8:632 (5 references); see also T2:1299 (11 references).

[1662]
★Objective-Analytic (O-A) Test Battery. Ages 14 and over; 1955–78; O-A; measures one to ten personality factors; Raymond B. Cattell and James M. Schuerger; Institute for Personality and Ability Testing, Inc.*

[1663]
Objective Tests in Constructive English. Grades 7, 8, 9, 10–12; 1955–64; no manual; Gunnar Horn; Perfection Form Co.* (In-print status uncertain; no reply from publisher.)

[1664]
Objective Tests in Punctuation. Grades 7, 8, 9, 10–12; 1955–64; no manual; Gunnar Horn; Perfection Form Co.* (In-print status uncertain; no reply from publisher.)

[1665]
Objectives-Referenced Bank of Items and Tests: Mathematics. Grades kgn–12 and adults; 1975; ORBIT:M; customized, criterion-referenced tests (consisting of 4-item, single-objective subtests) covering up to 50 objectives locally chosen from a list of 507 objectives (443 specific objectives and 64 category objectives) in 18 areas: addition, subtraction, multiplication, division, number and numeration, number theory, number sentences, number properties, set theory, common scales, geometry, measurement, graphs, coordinate geometry, word problems, probability and statistics, algebra, ratio and proportion and per cent; subtests are categorized according to "grade range in which each objective is typically introduced and mastered"; CTB/McGraw-Hill.*

a) MULTI-OBJECTIVE TESTS.
b) SINGLE-OBJECTIVE SUBTESTS.

For additional information and reviews by Arthur Mittman and Alan Osborne, see 8:287.

[1666]
Objectives-Referenced Bank of Items and Tests: Reading and Communication Skills. Grades kgn–12 and adults; 1975; ORBITS; customized, criterion-referenced tests (consisting of 4-item, single-objective subtests) covering up to 50 objectives locally chosen from a list of 335 objectives (233 specific objectives and 102 category objectives) in 10 areas: visual discrimination, phonic analysis, structural analysis, word meaning, literal comprehension, interpretive comprehension, critical comprehension, reference skills, language mechanics, language expression; subtests are categorized according to grade level of the most difficult word in the subtest; 2 formats; CTB/McGraw-Hill.*

a) MULTI-OBJECTIVE TESTS.
b) SINGLE-OBJECTIVE SUBTESTS. 335 subtests.

For additional information, see 8:767.

[1667]
Observation Test for Policeman. Prospective policemen; 1962; for use with *Policeman Examination*; distribution restricted to civil service commissions and municipal officials; McCann Associates.*

For additonal information, see 6:1146.

[1668]
★ Occ-U-Sort. Grades 7 and over and adults; 1981; an occupational card-sort system based on the *Dictionary of Occupational Titles* and Holland's 6 types: realistic, investigative, artistic, social, enterprising, conventional; Lawrence K. Jones; Publishers Test Service.*

REFERENCES

1. JONES, L.K. Occu–Sort: Development and evaluation of an occupational card sort system. *Vocational Guidance Journal*, 1979, 28, 56–62.
2. JONES, L.K., & DEVAULT, R.M. Evaluation of a self-guided career exploration system: The Occu-Sort. *School Counselor*, 1979, 26, 334–341.
3. JONES, L.K. Holland's typology and the new Guide for Occupations: Bridging the gap. *Vocational Guidance Quarterly*, 1980, 29, 70–76.
4. JONES, L.K. Issues in developing an occupational card sort. *Measurement & Evaluation in Guidance*, 1980, 12, 206–215.
5. HARRIS, M. B., & JONES, L. Occu–Sort: A new career planning tool. *Journal of College Placement*, 1981, 42, 47–50.

[1669]
Occupational Check List. Ages 15 and over ("above average ability"); 1972–76; OCL; 6 scores: practical, enterprising, scientific, clerical, artistic, social; A. D. Crowley; Hobsons Press (Cambridge) Ltd. for Careers Research and Advisory Centre [England].*

For additional information and a review by David G. Hawkridge, see 8:1014.

[1670]
O'Connor Finger Dexterity Test. Ages 14 and over; 1920–26 (?); Johnson O'Connor; Stoelting Co. (Also published by Lafayette Instrument Co.)*

See T2:2228 (14 references) and 6:1078 (32 references); for a review by Morris S. Viteles, see 2:1659 (15 references).

REFERENCES

1–15. See 2:1659.

16-47. See 6:1078.
48-61. See T2:2228.
62. GLOSS, D. S., & WARDLE, M. G. Use of a test of psychomotor ability in an expanded role. *Perceptual & Motor Skills*, 1981, 53, 659-662.

[1671]
O'Connor Tweezer Dexterity Test. Ages 14 and over; 1920-28(?); Johnson O'Connor; Stoelting Co. (Also published by Lafayette Instrument Co.)*

See T2:2229 (9 references) and 6:1079 (23 references); for a review by Morris S. Viteles, see 2:1678 (13 references).

REFERENCES

1-13. See 2:1678.
14-36. See 6:1079.
37-45. See T2:2229.
46. WEINSTEIN, P., KIYAK, H. A., NILGROM, P., RATENER, P., & MORRISON, K. Manual dexterity as a predictor of quality of care among dental practitioners. *Journal of Dental Education*, 1979, 43, 165-169.

[1672]
O'Connor Wiggly Block. Ages 16 and over; 1928-51; Johnson O'Connor; Stoelting Co. (Also published by Lafayette Instrument Co.)*

See T2:2259 (3 references) and 6:1091 (27 references).

[1673]
★**The Offer Self-Image Questionnaire for Adolescents.** Ages 14-18; 1971-77; OSIQ; 12 scores: impulse control, emotional tone, body and self-image, social relationships, morals, sexual attitudes, family relationships, mastery of the external world, vocational and educational goals, psychopathology, superior adjustment, total; Daniel Offer, E. Ostrov (manual), and K. I. Howard (manual); Daniel Offer.*

For additional information, see 8:633 (10 references).

REFERENCES

1-10. See 8:633.
11. CASPER, R. C., OFFER, D., & OSTROV, E. The self-image of adolescents with acute anorexia nervosa. *Journal of Pediatrics*, 1981, 98, 656-661.

[1674]
Office Arithmetic Test: ETSA Test 2A. Job applicants; 1960-72, c1957-59; manual and technical handbook by S. Trevor Hadley and George A. W. Stouffer, Jr.; test by Psychological Services Bureau; Educators'-Employers' Tests & Services Associates.*

For reviews of the complete battery, see 6:1025 (2 reviews).

[1675]
Office Information and Skills Test: Content Evaluation Series. Grade 12; 1971-72; 4 or 7 scores: office information, error location and correction, timed typewriting (errors, speed), transcription (optional, 3 scores); G. Elizabeth Ripka; Riverside Publishing Co.*

For additional information and a review by Mary Ellen Oliverio, see 8:327.

[1676]
Office Skills Achievement Test. Employees; 1962-63; 7 scores: business letter, grammar, checking, filing, arithmetic, written directions, total; Paul L. Mellenbruch; Psychometric Affiliates.*

For additional information and reviews by Douglas G. Schultz and Paul W. Thayer, see 6:1043.

[1677]
★**Office Skills Tests.** Applicants for clerical postions; 1977; 12 tests: checking, coding, filing, forms completion, grammar, numerical skills, oral directions, punctuation, reading comprehension, spelling, typing, vocabulary; Science Research Associates, Inc.*

[1678]
★**Ohio Accounting/Computing Clerk Achievement Test.** Grades 11-12; 1980; OACCAT; available only as a part of the *Ohio Vocational Education Achievement Test Program*; 11 scores: sales & receivables, payroll records, maintaining inventory records and files, completing the accounting cycle, worksheet information, processing purchases and payables, specialized accounting and office functions, cash receipts and payments, mechanical and electronic data accounting, employment procedures, total; Vocational Instructional Materials Laboratory, Ohio State University.

[1679]
★**Ohio Agricultural Business Achievement Test.** Grades 11-12; 1980; OAGBAT; available only as a part of the *Ohio Vocational Education Achievement Test Program*; 10 scores: agricultural careers, human relations, office procedures, agricultural services—animals, advertising & promotions, agricultural services—plants, sales, marketing & storage, money management, total; Vocational Instructional Materials Laboratory, Ohio State University.

[1680]
★**Ohio Agricultural Mechanic Achievement Test.** Grades 11-12; 1981; OAGMAT; available only as a part of the *Ohio Vocational Education Achievement Test Program*; 15 scores: service and repair engines, carburetion systems, diesel engines, cooling systems, hydraulic systems, brakes and steering, equipment assembly, charging systems and accessories, cranking systems, ignition systems, power trains and transmissions, metal fabrication and refinishing, heating/ventilation and air conditioning, personal development, total; Vocational Instuctional Materials Laboratory, Ohio State University.

[1681]
★**Ohio Apparel and Accessories Achievement Test.** Grades 11-12; 1982; OAAAT; available only as a part of the *Ohio Vocational Education Achievement Test Program*; 11 scores: cashiering, merchandise display, sales, stockkeeping and inventory control, first line management, product knowledge, receiving and marking merchandise, support functions, customer services, obtain employment, total; Vocational Instructional Materials Laboratory, Ohio State University.

[1682]
*****Ohio Auto Body Mechanic Achievement Test.** Grades 11-12; 1969-79; OABAT; available only as a part of the *Ohio Vocational Education Achievement Test Program*; 15 scores: welding, repair and straighten, patch and fill, fiberglass repair, panel replacement, refinishing, trim and hardware, glass replacement, frame and unit body repair, suspension systems, engine cooling systems, air conditioning, electrical systems, shop management and operations, total; Vocational Instructional Materials Laboratory, Ohio State University.

For additional information concerning an earlier edition, see 8:1154.

[1683]
*Ohio Automotive Mechanics Achievement Test. Grades 11–12; 1959–78; OAMAT; available only as a part of the *Ohio Vocational Education Achievement Test Program*; 17 scores: service management, lubrication and preventive maintenance, engine service and repair, cooling systems, fuel and exhaust systems, ignition systems, cranking systems, charging system, accessory systems, transmissions, drive line, emission systems, brake systems, steering systems, suspension systems, heating/ventilation and air conditioning systems, total; Vocational Instructional Materials Laboratory, Ohio State University.

For additional information concerning an earlier edition, see 8:1155 (1 reference).

[1684]
*Ohio Carpentry Achievement Test. Grades 11–12; 1970–81; OCAT; available only as a part of the *Ohio Vocational Education Achievement Test Program*; 12 scores: blueprint reading, surveying, foundations, floor framing, wall and ceiling framing, insulation, mathematics and estimating, roof framing, roofing, exterior finish, interior finish, total; Vocational Instructional Materials Laboratory, Ohio State University.

For additional information concerning an earlier edition, see 8:1156.

[1685]
★Ohio Clerk-Stenographer Achievement Test. Grades 11–12; 1981; OCSAT; available only as a part of the *Ohio Vocational Education Achievement Test Program*; 8 scores: dictation, correspondence, financial records, communications, copy reproduction, record management, personal development/employment, total; Vocational Instructional Materials Laboratory, Ohio State University.

[1686]
★Ohio Clerk Typist Achievement Test. Grades 11–12; 1982; OCTAT; available only as a part of the *Ohio Vocational Education Achievement Test Program*; 11 scores: letters and envelopes and memos, filing, proofreading and editing, mail procedures, employment procedures/human relations, reports and manuscripts and forms, accounting/calculating, telephone and receptionist duties, machine transcription/word processing, reprographics, total; Vocational Instructional Materials Laboratory, Ohio State University.

[1687]
★Ohio Commercial Art Achievement Test. Grades 11–12; 1980; OCAAT; available only as a part of the *Ohio Vocational Education Achievement Test Program*; 11 scores: drawing, design, illustration, technique, color, drafting, mechanical, photography, layout, typography, total; Vocational Instructional Materials Laboratory, Ohio State University.

[1688]
★Ohio Communication Products Electronics Achievement Test. Grades 11–12; 1973–83; OCPEAT; available only as a part of the *Ohio Vocational Education Achievement Test Program*; 14 scores: personal development, D/C electronics, A/C electronics, active electronic devices, electronic circuitry, electronic test equipment, audio systems, radio receiver systems, T.V. receiver systems, transmitter systems, antenna and transmission systems, special systems, digital logic systems, total; Vocational Instructional Materials Laboratory, Ohio State University.

For additional information concerning an earlier edition, see 8:1157.

[1689]
★Ohio Community and Home Services Achievement Test. Grades 11–12; 1982; OCHSAT; available only as a part of the *Ohio Vocational Education Achievement Test Program*; 16 scores: personal care to patient, vital signs, lift/move and transport patients, perform special care, infant and child care, provide food service, care and cleaning equipment, care of furnishings, care of resilient and masonry floors, care of draperies/upholstery and carpets, provide room care, care of restrooms, care of public areas, provide laundry service, careers and employment, total; Vocational Instructional Materials Laboratory, Ohio State University.

[1690]
Ohio Construction Electricity Achievement Test. Grades 11–12; 1973–77; OCEAT; available only as part of the *Ohio Vocational Education Achievement Test Program*; 19 scores: orientation, DC electricity, magnetism, DC power sources, DC motors and controllers, instrumentation, AC electricity, AC circuits, three-phase AC electricity, transformers, AC motors and starters, electronics, planning and layout, branch circuits, wiring methods, lighting, heating and air conditioning, low-voltage systems, total; Vocational Instructional Materials Laboratory, Ohio State University.*

For additional information concerning an earlier edition, see 8:1158.

[1691]
*Ohio Cosmetology Achievement Test. Grades 11–12; 1967–80; OCOAT; available only as part of the *Ohio Vocational Education Achievement Test Program*; 11 scores: sanitation, scalp care, manicuring, hair shaping, hair styling, facials, permanent waving, hair coloring, applied science, shop management and mathematics, total; Vocational Instructional Materials Laboratory, Ohio State University.

For additional information concerning an earlier edition, see 8:1159.

[1692]
★Ohio Data Processing Achievement Test. Grades 11–12; 1981; ODPAT; available only as a part of the *Ohio Vocational Education Achievement Test Program*; 10 scores: computer systems, clerical procedures, programming languages, automated electronic D. P. equipment, flow charting, data entry, operations, business math/accounting, employment procedures, total; Vocational Instructional Materials Laboratory, Ohio State University.

[1693]
★Ohio D. E. Food Service Personnel Achievement Test. Grades 11–12; 1981; ODEFSPAT; available only as a part of the *Ohio Vocational Education

Achievement Test Program; 13 scores: restaurant management, inventory and purchasing procedures, business principles, waiter/waitressing, cashiering, employment procedures, human relations, communications, selling principles, advertising, product/service information, safety and housekeeping, total; Vocational Instructional Materials Laboratory, Ohio State University.

[1694]
*Ohio Dental Assisting Achievement Test. Grades 11–12; 1970–82; ODAAT; available only as a part of the *Ohio Vocational Education Achievement Test Program*; 15 scores: anatomy, microbiology and sterilization, dental emergencies and pharmacology, dental laboratory, restorative and impression materials, preventive dentistry, ethics and personal development, radiology, dental office management, chairside assisting—basic, chairside assisting—prosthetics, chairside assisting—oral surgery and pathology, chairside assisting—other specialties, expanded duties, total; Vocational Instructional Materials Laboratory, Ohio State University.

For additional information concerning an earlier edition, see 8:1086.

[1695]
★Ohio Diesel Mechanic Achievement Test. Grades 11–12; 1981; ODMAT; available only as a part of the *Ohio Vocational Education Achievement Test Program*; 15 scores: service and repair engines, fuel systems, intake systems, charging and cranking systems, electrical and ignition systems, hydraulic systems, cooling systems, drive line, steering systems, suspension systems, brake systems, heating and air conditioning systems, lubrication & preventive maintenance, service management, total; Vocational Instructional Materials Laboratory, Ohio State University.

[1696]
*Ohio Diversified Health Occupations Achievement Test. Grades 11–12; 1975–77; ODHOAT; available only as a part of the *Ohio Vocational Education Achievement Test Program*; 16 scores: orientation, emergency first aid, dental assisting skills, medical assisting skills, communications and office skills, laboratory skills, preparing for the world of work, asepsis, vital signs, positioning and draping, physical examinations, transfer and ambulation, patient units, patient personal care, pre-operative and post-operative care, total; Vocational Instructional Materials Laboratory, Ohio State University.

For additional information concerning an earlier edition, see 8:1102.

[1697]
Ohio Drafting Achievement Test. Grades 11–12; 1962–78; ODAT; available only as a part of the *Ohio Vocational Education Achievement Test Program*; 18 scores: geometric drawing, orthographic projection, pictorial drawings, sectional views, auxiliary views, drafting materials/equipment/reproduction, dimensioning, production/working drawings, fastening methods, industrial materials and processes, intersections and developments, mechanisms, architectural drawings, structural drawings, electrical drawings, civil engineering drawings, mathematics, total; Vocational Instructional Materials Laboratory, Ohio State University.

For additional information and a review by Richard A. Swanson of an earlier edition, see 8:1160; see also T2:2428 (1 reference).

[1698]
★Ohio Fabric Services Achievement Test. Grades 11–12; 1981; OFSAT; available only as a part of the *Ohio Vocational Education Achievement Test Program*; 16 scores: alteration specialist, custom dressmaker, custom tailor, fabric coordinator, fashion coordinator, power machine operator, dry cleaner, interior design specialist, drapery consultant, drapery maker, drapery installer, slipcover maker, upholsterer, refinisher, careers and employment, total; Vocational Instructional Materials Laboratory, Ohio State University.

[1699]
★Ohio Farm Management Achievement Test. Grades 11–12; 1982; OFMAT; available only as a part of the *Ohio Vocational Education Achievement Test Program*; 12 scores: plan and supervise work, maintain and analyze farm records, buildings and structures, finance farm operations, maintain inventory of supplies, plan crop enterprise, market farm products, plan livestock enterprise, equipment and machinery, general management duties, employment procedures, total; Vocational Instructional Materials Laboratory, Ohio State University.

[1700]
★Ohio Food Marketing Key Employee Achievement Test. Grades 11–12; 1980; OFMKEAT; available only as a part of the *Ohio Vocational Education Achievement Test Program*; 12 scores: employment procedures, human relations, business principles, communications, financial operations, public relations, service technology, product information, pricing, operations, advertising and display, total; Vocational Instructional Materials Laboratory, Ohio State University.

[1701]
★Ohio General Merchandising Achievement Test. Grades 11–12; 1980; OGMAT; available only as a part of the *Ohio Vocational Education Achievement Test Program*; 13 scores: employment procedures, human relations, business principles, communications, financial transactions, selling, marketing, cashiering, inventory procedures, housekeeping & security, advertising & display, product & service technology, total; Vocational Instructional Materials Laboratory, Ohio State University.

[1702]
★Ohio General Office Clerk Achievement Test. Grades 11–12; 1980; OGOCAT; available only as a part of the *Ohio Vocational Education Achievement Test Program*; 12 scores: typing forms and reports, reprographics, employment seeking, composition and editing, records management, receptionist duties, letters and correspondence, financial records, telephone communications, word processing, accounting functions, total; Vocational Materials Laboratory, Ohio State University.

[1703]
*Ohio Heating, Air Conditioning, and Refrigeration Achievement Test. Grades 11–12; 1976–77; OHARAT; available only as a part of the *Ohio Vocational Education Achievement Test Program*; 11 scores: refrigera-

tion and air conditioning (installing, troubleshooting electrical, troubleshooting mechanical, service and repair electrical, service and repair mechanical), warm air heating systems (installing, troubleshooting electrical, troubleshooting mechanical, service and repair electrical, service and repair mechanical), total; Vocational Instructional Materials Laboratory, Ohio State University.

For additional information concerning an earlier edition, see 8:1161.

[1704]
★**Ohio H. Ec. Food Services Achievement Test.** Grades 11–12; 1981; OHEFSAT; available only as a part of the *Ohio Vocational Education Achievement Test Program*; 11 scores: baker, cook/chef, pantry worker, caterer, dietary aide, dining room service, cafeteria line, sanitation and safety, storeroom operations, careers and employment, total; Vocational Instructional Materials Laboratory, Ohio State University.

[1705]
★**Ohio Horticulture Achievement Test.** Grades 11–12; 1979; OHAT; available only as a part of the *Ohio Vocational Education Achievement Test Program*; 11 scores: soil and plant science, production floriculture, retail floriculture, garden center, personal development, fruit and vegetable production, turf services, nursery, landscaping, equipment and mechanics, total; Vocational Instructional Materials Laboratory, Ohio State University.

[1706]
*****Ohio Industrial Electronics Achievement Test.** Grades 11–12; 1973–83; OIEAT; available only as part of the *Ohio Vocational Education Achievement Test Program*; 14 scores: personal development, sell and install and test equipment, fabricate circuits and enclosures, D.C. electronics, A.C. electronics, semi-conductors, test equipment, analog electronic circuits, digital logic, digital electronic circuits, troubleshooting and analysis, special electronic devices, electro-mechanical devices, total; Vocational Instructional Materials Laboratory, Ohio State University.

For additional information, see 8:1162.

[1707]
Ohio Lithographic Printing Achievement Test. Grades 11–12; 1976–77; OLPAT; available only as a part of the *Ohio Vocational Education Achievement Test Program*; 10 scores: layout and design, composing, paste-up, proofing, camera and film processing, stripping, platemaking and proofs, off-set presses, finishing operations, total; Vocational Instructional Materials Laboratory, Ohio State University.

For additional information, see 8:1163.

[1708]
*****Ohio Machine Trades Achievement Test.** Grades 11–12; 1958–77; OMTAT; available only as a part of the *Ohio Vocational Education Achievement Test Program*; 14 scores: orientation and safety, bench work, power sawing, drilling machines, engine lathes, turret lathes, blueprint reading, milling machine, shaper-planer, abrasive machining, heat treating and applied metallurgy, applied math, applied science, total; Vocational Instructional Materials Laboratory, Ohio State University.

For additional information concerning an earlier edition see 8:1164; see also T2:2427 (2 references).

[1709]
★**Ohio Masonry Achievement Test.** Grades 11–12; 1982; OMSAT; available only as a part of the *Ohio Vocational Education Achievement Test Program*; 11 scores: prepare materials and job site, lay brick and block to a line, lay brick and block with a plumb rule, fireplaces and chimneys, arches, miscellaneous masonry construction, concrete masonry, surveying, mathematics and blueprint reading, personal development, total; Vocational Instructional Materials Laboratory, Ohio State University.

[1710]
Ohio Medical Assisting Achievement Test. Grades 11–12; 1974–77; OMAAT; available only as a part of the *Ohio Vocational Education Achievement Test Program*; 10 scores: orientation, body systems, clinical assistant skills, medications, sterilization, medical office skills, laboratory skills, electrocardiography, x-ray, total; Vocational Instructional Materials Laboratory, Ohio State University.*

For additional information concerning an earlier edition, see 8:1103.

[1711]
★**Ohio Nursery School Teacher Aide/Child Care Achievement Test.** Grades 11–12; 1979; ONTAAT; available only as a part of the *Ohio Vocational Education Achievement Test Program*; 13 scores: child care careers, center administration, maintenance, program planning, evaluation, special need children, health and safety, activity selection, structured activity preparation, unstructured activity supervision, routine activity supervision, nutrition and snacks, total; Vocational Instructional Materials Laboratory, Ohio State University.

[1712]
The Ohio Penal Classification Test. Penal institutions; 1952–54; also available for industrial use under the title *Ohio Classification Test* ('57); 5 scores: block counting, digit-symbol, number series, memory span, total; DeWitt E. Sell; manual for industrial edition by the author and Robert W. Scollay and Leroy N. Vernon; Psychometric Affiliates.*

See T2:418 (2 references); for a review by Norman Eagle, see 5:358.

[1713]
★**Ohio Production Agriculture Achievement Test.** Grades 11–12; 1982; OPAAT; available only as a part of the *Ohio Vocational Education Achievement Test Program*; 13 scores: beef production, small grain production, sheep production, soybean production, crop chemical application, agricultural construction, operator maintenance, dairy production, corn production, swine production, forage production, employment procedures, total; Vocational Instructional Materials Laboratory, Ohio State University.

[1714]
★**Ohio School Library/Media Test.** Grades 4–12; 1978; OSLMT; 6 scores: organization, selection, utilization, comprehension, production, total; Anne M. Hyland; WARD Artcraft Printing Co.*

[1715]
Ohio Sheet Metal Achievement Test. Grades 11–12; 1964–77; OSMAT; available only as a part of the *Ohio Vocational Education Achievement Test Program*; 15 scores: blueprint reading, applied science, applied math, hand tool operations, machine operations, soldering, special operations, mechanical drawing, freehand sketching, metals, non-metallic, layout operations, fabricating operations, welding, total; Vocational Instructional Materials Laboratory, Ohio State University.*

For additional information, see 8:1165; see also T2:2430 (1 reference).

[1716]
Ohio State University Psychological Test. Grades 9–16 and adults; 1919–68; OSUPT; 4 scores: same-opposites, analogies, reading comprehension, total; Herbert A. Toops; originally published by the Ohio College Association; now distributed by Wilbur L. Layton.*

See T2:419 (89 references); for a review by Cyril J. Hoyt (with W. Wesley Tennyson), see 5:359 (29 references); for a review by George A. Ferguson, see 4:308 (23 references); for a review by J. P. Guilford, see 3:244 (28 references); for reviews by Louis D. Hartson, Theos A. Langlie, and Rudolf Pintner, see 1:1051.

[1717]
The Ohio State University Test for Identifying Misarticulations. Speech clinicians and senior speech majors; 1965; various titles used by publisher; "reliability of speech clinicians and researchers in the recognition of misarticulations"; 4 scores: isolated words, phrases, 3-word groups, total; Ruth Beckey Irwin; Department of Photography and Cinema, Ohio State University.* (In-print status uncertain; no reply from publisher.)

For additional information, see 8:968 (1 reference).

[1718]
The Ohio Tests of Articulation and Perception of Sounds. Ages 5–8; 1973; OTAPS; 8 scores: articulation (sounds in words, sounds in phrases, nonsense words in context, stimulability of nonsense words), listening (identification of sounds by self, by examiner, comparator perception of sounds by self, by examiner); Ruth Beckey Irwin and Marcia Stevenson Abbate (test); Stanwix House, Inc.*

For additional information and a review by Harris Winitz, see 8:928 (4 references); see also T2:2023 (4 references).

REFERENCES
1–4. See T2:2023.
5–8. See 8:928.
9. MATTHEWS, B. A. J., & SEYMOUR, C. M. The performance of learning disabled children on tests of auditory discrimination. *Journal of Learning Disabilities*, 1981, 14, 9–12.

[1719]
***Ohio Vocational Education Achievement Test Program.** Grades 11–12; 1964–83; formerly called *Ohio Trade and Industrial Education Achievement Test Program*; tests administered annually in March at participating schools; each student must take 2 tests: the intelligence test and an occupational test; Vocational Instructional Materials Laboratory, Ohio State University.

a) INTELLIGENCE TEST. Short Form Test of Academic Aptitude, Level 5 (grades 9–12).
b) OCCUPATIONAL TESTS. 1964–83; 38 tests based on occupational analyses or course outlines prepared for use in Ohio.
1) *Ohio Accounting/Computing Clerk Achievement Test.*
2) *Ohio Agricultural Business Achievement Test.*
3) *Ohio Agricultural Mechanic Achievement Test.*
4) *Ohio Apparel and Accessories Sales Achievement Test.*
5) *Ohio Auto Body Mechanic Achievement Test.*
6) *Ohio Automotive Mechanics Achievement Test.*
7) *Ohio Carpentry Achievement Test.*
8) *Ohio Clerk-Stenographer Achievement Test.*
9) *Ohio Clerk Typist Achievement Test.*
10) *Ohio Commercial Art Achievement Test.*
11) *Ohio Communication Products Electronics Achievement Test.*
12) *Ohio Community and Home Services Achievement Test.*
13) *Ohio Construction Electricity Achievement Test.*
14) *Ohio Cosmetology Achievement Test.*
15) *Ohio D. E. Food Service Personnel Achievement Test.*
16) *Ohio Data Processing Achievement Test.*
17) *Ohio Dental Assisting Achievement Test.*
18) *Ohio Diesel Mechanic Achievement Test.*
19) *Ohio Diversified Health Occupations Achievement Test.*
20) *Ohio Drafting Achievement Test.*
21) *Ohio Fabric Services Achievement Test.*
22) *Ohio Farm Management Achievement Test.*
23) *Ohio Food Marketing Key Employee Achievement Test.*
24) *Ohio General Merchandising Achievement Test.*
25) *Ohio General Office Clerk Achievement Test.*
26) *Ohio H. Ec. Food Services Achievement Test.*
27) *Ohio Heating, Air Conditioning, and Refrigeration Achievement Test.*
28) *Ohio Horticulture Achievement Test.*
29) *Ohio Industrial Electronics Achievement Test.*
30) *Ohio Lithographic Printing Achievement Test.*
31) *Ohio Machine Trades Achievement Test.*
32) *Ohio Masonry Achievement Test.*
33) *Ohio Medical Assisting Achievement Test.*
34) *Ohio Nursery School Teacher Aide/Child Care Achievement Test.*
35) *Ohio Production Agriculture Achievement Test.*
36) *Ohio Sheet Metal Achievement Test.*
37) *Ohio Welding Achievement Test.*
38) *Ohio Word Processing Achievement Test.*

For additional information concerning an earlier edition, see 8:1166; see also T2:2431 (1 reference).

REFERENCES
1. See T2:2431.
2. KAPES, J. T., & MARTIN, R. B. Exploring the use of Holland's Vocational Preference Inventory with male vocational–technical students. *Journal of Industrial Teacher Education*, 1978, 15, 27–35.
3. HINES, C. V., ALTSCHULD, J. W., & RINDERER, R. E. A study of the construct validity of six vocational achievement tests in the Ohio Vocational Education Achievement Test Program. *Journal of Industrial Teacher Education*, 1981, 19, 3–13.

[1720]
***Ohio Vocational Interest Survey, Second Edition.** Grades 7–college and adults; 1969–81; OVIS II; 23 scores: manual work, basic services, machine operation, quality control, clerical, health services, crafts and precise

operations, skilled personal services, sports and recreation, customer services, regulations enforcement, communications, numerical, visual arts, agriculture and life sciences, engineering and physical sciences, music, performing arts, marketing, legal services, management, education and social work, medical services; handbook by David W. Winefordner; The Psychological Corporation.*

For additional information, see 8:1016 (24 references); see also T2:2201 (3 references); for reviews by Thomas T. Frantz and John W. M. Rothney of an earlier edition, see 7:1029 (4 references).

REFERENCES

1-4. See 7:1029.
5-7. See T2:2201.
8-31. See 8:1016.
32. AMEG COMMISSION ON SEX BIAS IN MEASUREMENT. A case history of change: A review of responses to the challenge of sex bias in career interest inventories. *Measurement & Evaluation in Guidance*, 1977, 10, 148-152.
33. WOODBURY, R., & PATE, D. H. Vocational and personality dimensions of adjudicated delinquents. *Measurement & Evaluation in Guidance*, 1977, 10, 106-112.

[1721]

*Ohio Welding Achievement Test. Grades 11-12; 1969-79; OWAT; available only as a part of the *Ohio Vocational Education Achievement Test Program*; 8 scores: labor and management, oxyacetylene welding, shielded metal arc welding, tungsten arc welding, gas metal arc welding, resistance welding, blueprints and math, total; Vocational Instructional Materials Laboratory, Ohio State University.

For additional information concerning an earlier edition, see 8:1167.

[1722]

★Ohio Word Processing Achievement Test. Grades 11-12; 1982; OWPAT; available only as a part of the *Ohio Vocational Education Achievement Test Program*; 11 scores: typing and transcription, reprographics, word processing concepts and procedures, business transactions, proofreading and editing, automated word processing equipment, receptionist duties, composition and dictation, records management, employment procedures, total; Vocational Instructional Materials Laboratory, The Ohio State University.

[1723]

Oliphant Auditory Discrimination Memory Test. Grades 1-8; 1971; OADMT; Genevieve G. Oliphant; Educators Publishing Service, Inc.*

For additional information and a review by Lear Ashmore, see 8:944; see also T2:2049 (1 reference).

[1724]

Oliphant Auditory Synthesizing Test. Grades 1-8; 1971; OAST; Genevieve Oliphant; Educators Publishing Service, Inc.*

For additional information and a review by Lon L. Emerick, see 8:945; see also T2:2050 (1 reference).

[1725]

★Oliver: Parent-Administered Communication Inventory. All ages "who have yet to develop age appropriate communication"; 1978; component of *The Environmental Language Intervention Program*; ratings by parents or caregivers; James D. MacDonald; Charles E. Merrill Publishing Co.*

[1726]

Omnibus Personality Inventory. College; 1968, c1959-68; OPI; 15 scores: thinking introversion (TI), theoretical orientation (TO), estheticism (Es), complexity (Co), autonomy (Au), religious orientation (RO), social extroversion (SE), impulse expression (IE), personal integration (PI), anxiety level (AL), altruism (Am), practical outlook (PO), masculinity-femininity (MF), response bias (RB), intellectual disposition category (IDC) based on the first 6 scores; Paul Heist, George Yonge, T. R. McConnell (test), and Harold Webster (test); The Psychological Corporation.*

For additional information and a review by Edgar Howarth, see 8:634 (134 references); see also T2:1302 (62 references); for reviews by Richard W. Coan and Paul McReynolds, see 7:116 (82 references); see also P:184 (60 references); for reviews by Paul M. Kjeldergaard and Norman E. Wallen and an excerpted review by Laurence Siegel of earlier forms, see 6:150 (11 references).

REFERENCES

1-11. See 6:150.
12-70. See P:184.
71-152. See 7:116.
153-214. See T2:1302.
215-348. See 8:634.
349. BROWNE, J. A., & HOWARTH, E. A comprehensive factor analysis of personality questionnaire items: A test of twenty putative factor hypotheses. *Multivariate Behavioral Research*, 1977, 12, 399-427.
350. GOODYEAR, R. K., & FRANK, A. C. Introversion-extroversion: Some comparisons of the SVIB and OPI scales. *Measurement & Evaluation in Guidance*, 1977, 9, 206-211.
351. KAZANAS, H. C., & MORRISON, R. E. Relationships of personality traits and the meaning and value of work for junior college students. *Journal of College Student Personnel*, 1977, 18, 486-490.
352. KUH, G. D. Factors associated with post-college changes in personality characteristics. *Journal of College Student Personnel*, 1977, 18, 362-370.
353. PETERS, W. H., & BLUES, A. G. Teacher intellectual disposition as it relates to student openness in written response to literature. *Research in the Teaching of English*, 1977, 12, 127-136.
354. SHAPIRO, H. M. Perceived family structure as an explanation of Jewish intellectuality. *Sociological Quarterly*, 1977, 18, 448-463.
355. TINSLEY, H. E. A., & TINSLEY, D. J. Relationship between scores on the Omnibus Personality Inventory and counselor trainee effectiveness. *Journal of Counseling Psychology*, 1977, 24, 522-526.
356. WEBER, C. R. A comparison of values clarification and lecture-discussion methods in teaching college health science. *College Student Journal*, 1977, 11, 98-104.
357. YONGE, G. D. Instructional artifacts on personality inventories. *Psychological Reports*, 1977, 40, 899-903.
358. EISERT, D. C., & TOMLINSON-KEASEY, C. Cognitive and interpersonal growth during the college freshman year: A structural analysis. *Perceptual & Motor Skills*, 1978, 46, 995-1005.
359. ENO, L. Predicting achievement and the theory of fluid and cystallized intelligence. *Psychological Reports*, 1978, 43, 847-852.
360. ENO, L., WOEHLKE, P., & DEICHMANN, J. A factor analytic study of ability, achievement, and personality characteristics of college students. *College Student Journal*, 1978, 12, 366-371.
361. LACY, W. B. Interpersonal relationships as mediators of structural effects: College student socialization in a traditional and experimental university environment. *Sociology of Education*, 1978, 51, 201-211.
362. O'HARA-DEVEREAUX, M., BROWN, T. C., MENTINK, J., & MORGAN, W. A. Biographical data, personality, and vocational interests of family nurse practitioners. *Psychological Reports*, 1978, 43, 1259-1268.
363. SLOAN, T. S., & BROWN, D. R. The Clark-Trow typology and applicants to a six-year A.B.-M.D. program. *Journal of College Student Personnel*, 1978, 19, 6-10.
364. YONGE, G. D., & REGAN, M. C. Female sex-role expectations and authoritarianism. *Psychological Reports*, 1978, 43, 415-418.
365. BLIMLING, G. S., & PAULSEN, F. M. The educational developmental group enrichment (EDGE) program: A comprehensive model for student development in residence halls. *National Association for Women Deans, Administrators & Counselors. Journal*, 1979, 42, 24-33.

366. DAGENAIS, G. Response bias and the Leadership Opinion Questionnaire scales. *Journal of General Psychology*, 1979, 100, 161–162.
367. KUH, G. D., & ARDAIOLO, F. P. A comparison of the personality characteristics of adult learners and traditional age freshmen. *Journal of College Student Personnel*, 1979, 20, 329–335.
368. ERWIN, T. D., & DELWORTH, U. An instrument to measure Chickering's Vector of Identity. *NASPA Journal*, 1980, 17, 19–24.
369. HARMON, M. H. The Barron Ego Strength Scale: A study of personality correlates among normals. *Journal of Clinical Psychology*, 1980, 36, 433–436.
370. HOLMES, C. M., SHOLLEY, B. K., & WALKER, W. E. Leader, follower, and isolate personality patterns in black and white emergent leadership groups. *Journal of Psychology*, 1980, 105, 41–46.
371. MELEIS, A. I., & DAGENAIS, F. Response bias and self-report of honesty. *Journal of General Psychology*, 1980, 103, 303–304.
372. SHUGER, D., & DEBOUT, J. Contrasts in Gestalt and analytic therapy. *Journal of Humanistic Psychology*, 1980, 20, 21–39.
373. BLUME, F. The role of personal growth groups at Johnston College. *Journal of Humanistic Psychology*, 1981, 21, 47–61.
374. MELEIS, A. I., & DAGENAIS, F. Sex-role identity and perception of professional self in graduates of three nursing programs. *Nursing Research*, 1981, 30, 162–167.

[1727]

One Hole Test. Job applicants; 1972; OHT; 2 machines; Gavriel Salvendy and W. Douglas Seymour; Lafayette Instrument Co.*

a) LEVEL ONE. 3 scores: number of pins inserted in first and last of 7 or 15 one-minute trials, total.

b) LEVEL TWO. 9 scores: same as above plus first and last trial time for each of 3 categories (grasp, position, reach and move).

See T2:2230 (1 reference).

[1728]

Ontario School Record System, 1972 Edition. Grades kgn–13; 1950–72; OSRS; 3 parts: *Ontario Student Record Folder, Ontario School Office Index Card, Student Achievement Form*; Ministry of Education, Ontario; Guidance Centre, University of Toronto [Canada].*

For additional information concerning an earlier edition, see 6:747.

[1729]

Opinion, Attitude, and Interest Survey. High school seniors and college students; 1962–68, c1955–65; OAIS; factors related to academic success and educational interest; 14 scores: 3 response bias scores (set for true, infrequent response, social undesirability), 3 academic promise scores (achiever personality, intellectual quality, creative personality), 3 adjustment scores (social, emotional, masculine orientation), and 5 interest scores (business, humanities, social science, physical science, biological science); Benno G. Fricke; OAIS Testing Program.* (In-print status uncertain; no reply from publisher.)

See T2:1303 (55 references) and P:185 (19 references); for reviews by John O. Crites and Harold Webster, see 6:151 (4 references).

REFERENCES

1–4. See 6:151.
5–23. See P:185.
24–78. See T2:1303.
79. SHARF, R. S. Evaluation of a computer-based narrative interpretation of a test battery. *Measurement & Evaluation in Guidance*, 1978, 11, 50–53.
80. WILDER, D. H., PARADISE, L. V., & HOFFER, G. L. Academic performance and its personality correlates in a college sample of blacks and whites. *Psychological Reports*, 1978, 42, 765.

[1730]

Opinions Toward Adolescents. College and adults; 1971–72; OTA; 8 scores: liberal-conservative, punitive-permissive, restrictive-accepting, authoritarian-democratic, mistrust-trust, prejudice-acceptance, understanding-misunderstanding, skepticism-sincerity (test taking attitude); William T. Martin; Psychologists and Educators, Inc.*

For additional information and a review by W. Grant Dahlstrom, see 8:635.

[1731]

*****Optometry College Admission Test.** Optometry college applicants; 1971–79; OCAT; tests administered 2 times annually (March, October) at centers established by the publisher; 6 scores: biology, chemistry, physics, verbal ability, quantitative ability, study-reading; sponsored by the Association of Schools and Colleges of Optometry; prepared and administered by The Psychological Corporation.*

For additional information and a review by Penelope Kegel-Flom of earlier forms, see 8:1104 (3 references).

[1732]

★**Oral English/Spanish Proficiency Placement Test.** Ages 4–20; 1974–76; OE/SPPT; performance rated by examiner; 2 tests: English, Spanish; Steve Moreno; Moreno Educational Co.*

[1733]

★**Oral Language Dominance Measure.** Bilingual (Spanish, English) students grades kgn–3; 1978–80; OLDM; 2 scores: English, Spanish; (Spanish edition available); El Paso Public Schools.*

[1734]

★**Oral Language Evaluation.** Elementary students; 1977; language development in English and Spanish of bilingual children on a 6 level continuum (labeling, basic sentences, language expansion, connecting-relating-modifying, storytelling-concrete, storytelling-abstract); Nicholas J. Silvaroli, Jann T. Skinner and J. O. "Rocky" Maynes, Jr.; EMC Publishing.*

REFERENCES

1. HARRIS, M. M., & READANCE, J. E. Oral Language Evaluation. *Language Arts*, 1979, 56, 88–89.

[1735]

★**Oral Language Proficiency Measure.** Grades 4–6; 1977–79; OLPM; assesses language dominance (English, Spanish); (Spanish edition available); El Paso Public Schools.*

[1736]

★**Oral Language Sentence Imitation Diagnostic Inventory-F.** Ages 5–7; 1977–78; OLSIDI-F; may be used in conjunction with or independent of the *Oral Language Sentence Imitation Screening Test*; 27 subtests: present progressive, prepositions, plural, past irregular, possessive, uncontractible copula, articles, past regular, third person regular, third person irregular, uncontractible auxiliary, contractible copula, contractible auxiliary, personal pronouns/subjective, personal pronouns/objective, reflexive pronouns, possessive pronouns/determiner, possessive pronouns/nominal, negatives, wh questions, interrogative reversals, modals, do insertions, embedded sentences, infinitives, coordinations or conjunctions, future tense; Linda Zachman, Rosemary Huisingh, Carol Jorgensen, and Mark Barrett; LinguiSystems, Inc.*

REFERENCES

1. COMKOWYCZ, S., & GRADY, L. Authors' response to OLSIST and OLSIDI reviews. *ASHA*, 1979, 21, 1036–1037.

[1737]

★Oral Language Sentence Imitation Screening Test. Ages 3–4, 4–5, 5–7; 1976–78; OLSIST; may be used in conjunction with or independent of the *Oral Language Sentence Imitation Diagnostic Inventory-F*; Linda Zachman, Rosemary Huisingh, Carol Jorgensen, and Mark Barrett; LinguiSystems, Inc.*

REFERENCES

1. COMKOWYCZ, S., & GRADY, L. Authors' response to OLSIST and OLSIDI reviews. *ASHA*, 1979, 21, 1036–1037.

[1738]

Oral Rating Form for Rating Language Proficiency in Speaking and Understanding English. Non-native speakers of English; 1959–67; also called *AULC Interview Rating Form*; distribution restricted to government agencies; 6 ratings by interviewers: comprehension, pronunciation, grammar and word-order, vocabulary, general speed of speech and sentence length, total; [David P. Harris]; American Language Institute.*

For additional information, see 7:265.

[1739]

Oral Reading Criterion Test. Reading level grades 1–7; 1971; ORCT; criterion-referenced; 3 reading level scores: independent, instructional, frustration; no manual; Edward Fry; Jamestown Publishers.*

For additional information and an excerpted review by Paula Altman Fuld, see 8:787 (1 reference).

[1740]

Oral Verbal Intelligence Test. Ages 7.5–14; 1973; OVIT; D. Young; Hodder & Stoughton Educational [England].*

For additional information and a review by A. E. G. Pilliner, see 8:197.

[1741]

Oral Word-Recognition Test. Grades 1–13; 1973; catalog uses the title *A Preliminary Screening Test in Reading*; items are from the word recognition subtest of the *McGrath Test of Reading Skills*; no directions for administration and scoring; Joseph E. McGrath; McGrath Publishing Co.* (In-print status uncertain; no reply from publisher.)

For additional information, see 8:788.

[1742]

The Oregon Academic Ranking Test. Gifted children grades 3–7; 1965; OART; for rapid identification of the top 3 percent; 9 scores: making sentences, making comparisons, numbers, secret words, working problems, reasoning, completing sentences, sayings, total; Charles H. Derthick; Western Psychological Services.*

For additional information and a review by Robert H. Bauernfeind, see 7:369.

[1743]

Organic Integrity Test. Ages 5 and over; 1960–67; OIT; form perception as an indication of brain deficit unrelated to intelligence; H. C. Tien; Psychodiagnostic Test Co.*

See T2:1305 (10 references); for reviews by Ralph M. Reitan and Joseph M. Wepman, see 7:117 (8 references); see also P:186 (12 references).

[1744]

★Organization Health Survey. Managers and administrators and supervisors in government and industry; 1978–80; OHS; 8 scales: productivity, leadership, organization structure, communication, conflict management, human resource management, participation, creativity; P. T. Kehoe and W. J. Reddin; Organizational Tests Ltd. [Canada].*

[1745]

*Organizational Climate Index. Employees; 1958–70; OCI; previously listed under *Stern Environment Indexes*; a short form is available; 3 factor structures and norm groups; *School Work Environment*: 38 scores: 30 press scores (abasement-assurance, achievement, adaptability-defensiveness, affiliation, aggression-blame avoidance, change-sameness, conjunctivity-disjunctivity, counteraction, deference-restiveness, dominance-tolerance, ego achievement, emotionality-placidity, energy-passivity, exhibitionism-inferiority avoidance, fantasied achievement, harm avoidance-risk taking, humanities and social science, impulsiveness-deliberation, narcissism, nurturance, objectivity-projectivity, order-disorder, play-work, practicalness-impracticalness, reflectiveness, science, sensuality-puritanism, sexuality-prudishness, supplication-autonomy, understanding), 6 factor scores (intellectual climate, achievement standards, personal dignity, organizational effectiveness, orderliness, impulse control) based on combinations of the press scores, 2 second-order factor scores (development, task effectiveness); *College Work Environment*: 38 scores: 30 press scores listed above, 6 factor scores (achievement standards, intellectual climate, practicalness, supportiveness, orderliness, impulse control) based on combinations of the press scores, 2 second-order factor scores (development press, control press); *Industrial Sites*: 38 scores: 30 press scores listed above, 6 factor scores (intellectual climate, organizational effectiveness, personal dignity, orderliness, work, impulse control) based on combinations of the press scores, 2 second-order factor scores (development press, control press); George G. Stern and Carl R. Steinhoff; Evaluation Research Associates.*

See T2:1395 (38 references); for reviews by Wilbur L. Layton and Rodney W. Skager, see 7:143 (59 references); see also P:256 (65 references) and 6:92 (19 references).

REFERENCES

1–19. See 6:92.
20–84. See P:256.
85–143. See 7:143.
144–181. See T2:1395.
182. PAYNE, R., & MANSFIELD, R. Correlates of individual perceptions of organizational climate. *Journal of Occupational Psychology*, 1978, 51, 209–218.

[1746]
Organizational Value Dimensions Questionnaire: Business Form. Adults; 1965–66; OVDQ; for research use only; attitudes toward business and industrial firms in general; manual title *Value Scale—The Business Firm*; 9 scores: organizational magnitude and structure, internal consideration, competition and strategy, social responsibility, quality, change, member identification and control, external political participation, member equality and participation; Carroll L. Shartle and Ralph M. Stogdill; Publications Sales Division, Ohio State University Press.*

For additional information and a review by William G. Mollenkopf, see 8:1075.

[1747]
★**Orientation and Motivation Inventory.** Grades 11 and 12 and college freshmen and sophomores; 1981; OMI; 12 scales: theoretical vs. practical, altruistic vs. help withholding, approval seeking vs. admitting frailties, novelty seeking vs. liking sameness, achievement motivated vs. nonambitious, psychological minded vs. nonpsychological minded, power seeking vs. power avoiding, planful-organized vs. casual-unregulated, materially oriented vs. nonacquisitive, adventure seeking vs. cautious, person-oriented vs. impersonal, recognition seeking vs. recognition avoiding; Maurice Lorr, Richard P. Youniss, and Edward C. Stefic; Maurice Lorr.*

[1748]
The Orientation Inventory. College and industry; 1962–77; OI; kinds of satisfactions and rewards sought in jobs; 3 scores: self-orientation, interaction-orientation, task-orientation; Bernard M. Bass; Consulting Psychologists Press, Inc.*

For additional information and a review by Thomas J. Bouchard, Jr., see 8:636 (15 references); see also T2:1306 (26 references) and P:187 (13 references); for reviews by Richard S. Barrett and H. Bradley Sagen, see 6:153 (2 references).

REFERENCES
1–2. See 6:153.
3–15. See P:187.
16–41. See T2:1306.
42–56. See 8:636.
57. WOUDENBERG, R. A., & POLAND, W. D. Four years of encounter groups: Changes in female and male composition. *Journal of College Student Personnel*, 1979, 20, 513–520.

[1749]
★**Orleans-Hanna Algebra Prognosis Test.** Grades 7–11; 1928–82; Gerald S. Hanna and Joseph B. Orleans; The Psychological Corporation.*

See T2:688 (11 references); for reviews by W. L. Bashaw and Cyril J. Hoyt of an earlier edition, see 7:510 (3 references); for reviews by Harold Gulliksen and Emma Spaney, see 4:396 (1 reference); for a review by S. S. Wilks, see 2:1444 (4 references).

[1750]
O'Rourke Clerical Aptitude Test, Junior Grade. Applicants for clerical positions; 1926–58; 2 parts; no manual; L. J. O'Rourke; O'Rourke Publications.*
a) CLERICAL PROBLEMS. 1926–35.
b) REASONING TEST. 1926–58.

See T2:2138 (1 reference) and 5:851 (1 reference); for a review by Raymond A. Katzell, see 3:629 (3 references).

[1751]
O'Rourke Mechanical Aptitude Test. Grades 7–12 and adults; 1926–57; some forms entitled *O'Rourke Mechanical Aptitude Test-Junior Grade*; L. J. O'Rourke; O'Rourke Publications.*

See T2:2260 (1 reference) and 5:882; for reviews by Jay L. Otis and George A. Satter, see 3:672 (8 references); for a review by Herbert A. Landry, see 2:1668.

[1752]
Ortho-Rater. Adults; 1942–58; 12 scores for each model: binocular action of the eyes (4 tests), fineness of visual discrimination (6 tests), perception of depth, color discrimination; 2 models; Bausch & Lomb, Inc.* (In-print status uncertain; no reply from publisher.)
a) MASTER ORTHO-RATER. 1942–58.
b) MODIFIED ORTHO-RATER. 1952–58.

See T2:1923 (31 references) and 5:783 (59 references); for reviews by Henry A. Imus and F. Nowell Jones, see 3:471 (41 references).

[1753]
The "Orton" Intelligence Test, No. 4. Ages 10–14; 1931; Robert Gibson & Sons, Glasgow, Ltd. [Scotland].*

For additional information, see 1:1052.

[1754]
★**Otis-Lennon School Ability Test.** Grades 1, 2–3, 4–5, 6–8, 9–12; 1977–79; OLSAT; revision of still-in-print *Otis-Lennon Mental Ability Test*; Arthur S. Otis and Roger T. Lennon; The Psychological Corporation.*

For additional information concerning an earlier edition, see 8:198 (35 references); see also T2:424 (10 references); for a review by John E. Milholland and excerpted reviews by Arden Grotelueschen and Arthur E. Smith, see 7:370 (6 references).

REFERENCES
1–6. See 7:370.
7–16. See T2:424.
17–51. See 8:198.
52. BRODZINSKY, D. M., FEUER, V., & OWENS, J. Detection of linguistic ambiguity by reflective, impulsive, fast/accurate, and slow inaccurate children. *Journal of Educational Psychology*, 1977, 69, 237–243.
53. BUKTENICA, N. A. Perceptual/social aspects of learning to read: A transactional process. *Peabody Journal of Education*, 1977, 54, 154–161.
54. CANTRELL, R. P., STENNER, A. J., & KATZENMEYER, W. G. Teacher knowledge, attitudes, and classroom teaching correlates of student achievement. *Journal of Educational Psychology*, 1977, 69, 172–179.
55. CASKEY, W. E., & LARSON, G. L. Two modes of administration of the Bender Visual–Motor Gestalt Test of kindergarten children. *Perceptual & Motor Skills*, 1977, 45, 1003–1006.
56. HUGHES, R. J. An experimental study in teaching mathematical concepts utilizing computer–assisted instruction in business machines. *Business Education Forum*, 1977, 32, 44–45.
57. LORD, F. M. A broad–range tailored test of verbal ability. *Applied Psychological Measurement*, 1977, 1, 95–100.
58. MARTIN, J. D., & MARTIN, E. M. The relationship of the Purpose in Life (PIL) Test to the Personal Orientation Inventory (POI), the Otis-Lennon Mental Ability Test scores, and grade point averages of high school students. *Educational & Psychological Measurement*, 1977, 37, 1103–1105.
59. MARTORANO, S. C. A developmental analysis of performance on Piaget's formal operations tasks. *Developmental Psychology*, 1977, 13, 666–672.
60. MCINTIRE, W. G., & DRUMMOND, R. J. Multiple predictors of self–concept in children. *Psychology in the Schools*, 1977, 14, 295–298.

61. MURPHY, R. Societal values and the reaction of teachers to student's backgrounds. *Canadian Review of Sociology & Anthropology*, 1977, 14, 48–56.

62. PETTY, N. E., & HARRELL, E. H. Effect of programmed instruction related to motivation, anxiety, and test wiseness on group IQ test performance. *Journal of Educational Psychology*, 1977, 69, 630–635.

63. RUPLEY, W. H. Stability of teacher effect on pupils' reading achievement over a two year period and its relation to instructional emphasis. In P. D. Pearson & J. Hansen (Eds.), *Reading: Theory, research, and practice; Twenty-sixth yearbook of the National Reading Conference*. Clemson, South Carolina: The National Reading Conference, Inc., 1977.

64. RUPLEY, W. H. Teacher instructional emphases and student achievement in reading. *Peabody Journal of Education*, 1977, 54, 286–291.

65. TROTMAN, F. K. Race, IQ, and the middle class. *Journal of Educational Psychology*, 1977, 69, 266–273.

66. ULLMAN, D. G. Children's lateral preference patterns: Frequency and relationships with achievement and intelligence. *Journal of School Psychology*, 1977, 15, 36–43.

67. BARNETT, M. A., & KAISER, D. L. The relationship between intellectual-achievement responsibility attributions and performance. *Child Study Journal*, 1978, 8, 209–215.

68. BERGER, N. S. Why can't John read? Perhaps he's not a good listener? *Journal of Learning Disabilities*, 1978, 11, 633–638.

69. BREUNING, S. E., & ZELLA, W. F. Effects of individualized incentives on norm-referenced IQ test performance of high school students in special education classes. *Journal of School Psychology*, 1978, 16, 220–226.

70. BRUHN, J. G., BUNCE, H., III, & GREASER, R. C. Correlations of Myer-Briggs Type Indicator with other personality and achievement variables. *Psychological Reports*, 1978, 43, 771–776.

71. BRUNING, R. H., BURON, J. K., & BALLERING, M. Visual and auditory memory: Relationships to reading achievement. *Contemporary Educational Pyschology*, 1978, 3, 340–351.

72. COPELAND, M. L., CONRAD, C., & CHANSKY, N. M. Validity of two intelligence tests. *Psychological Reports*, 1978, 42, 662.

73. COUNTS, D. K., HOLLANDSWORTH, J. G., JR., & ALCORN, J. D. Use of electromyographic biofeedback and cue-controlled relaxation in the treatment of test anxiety. *Journal of Consulting & Clinical Psychology*, 1978, 46, 990–996.

74. COVIN, T. M. Comparison of the Pintner and Otis-Lennon scores of Caucasian boys in first grade. *Psychological Reports*, 1978, 42, 984.

75. GROSS, K., ROTHENBERG, S., & SCHOTTENFELD, S. Duration thresholds for letter identification in left and right visual fields for normal and reading-disabled children. *Neuropsychologia*, 1978, 16, 709–715.

76. HOGABOAM, T. W., & PERFETTI, C. A. Reading skill and the role of verbal experience in decoding. *Journal of Educational Psychology*, 1978, 70, 717–729.

77. KAIL, R. V., & MARSHALL, C. V. Reading skill and memory scanning. *Journal of Educational Psychology*, 1978, 70, 508–514.

78. MATEFY, R. E. Evaluation of a remediation program using senior citizens as psychoeducational agents. *Community Mental Health Journal*, 1978, 14, 327–336.

79. PERFETTI, C. A., FINGER, E., & HOGABOAM, T. Sources of vocalization latency differences between skilled and less skilled young readers. *Journal of Educational Psychology*, 1978, 70, 730–739.

80. RASBURY, W. C., FALGOUT, J. C., & PERRY, N. W., JR. A Yudin-type short form of the WISC-R: Two aspects of validation. *Journal of Clinical Psychology*, 1978, 34, 120–126.

81. RAVEN, R. J., & MURRAY, R. B. Effect of high school chemistry experiences on Piaget's operative comprehension. *Science Education*, 1978, 62, 467–470.

82. SWAIN, M., & BARIK, H. C. The role of curricular approach, rural-urban background, and socioeconomic status in second language learning: The Cornwall area study. *Alberta Journal of Educational Research*, 1978, 24, 1–16.

83. SWANSON, L. Verbal encoding effects on the visual short-term memory of learning disabled and normal readers. *Journal of Educational Psychology*, 1978, 70, 539–544.

84. BHUSHAN, V. Evidence regarding the validity of an adaptation of the Learning Environment Inventory from English to French. *Educational & Psychological Measurement*, 1979, 39, 453–461.

85. CHAPMAN, J. W., & BOERSMA, F. J. Learning disabilities, locus of control, and mother attitudes. *Journal of Educational Psychology*, 1979, 71, 250–258.

86. DAVIDSON, C. W., & HOFFEY, P. Relationship between achievement in high school biology and type of science course completed, sex, and intelligence quotients of students. *Southern Journal of Educational Research*, 1979, 13, 133–138.

87. DORETHY, R., & REEVES, D. Mental functioning, perceptual differentiation, personality, and achievement among art and non–art majors. *Studies in Art Education*, 1979, 20, 52–63.

88. HAASE, R. F., LEE, D. Y., & BANKS, D. L. Cognitive correlates of polychronicity. *Perceptual & Motor Skills*, 1979, 49, 271–282.

89. HOWELL, F. M., & FRESE, W. Race, sex, and aspirations: Evidence for the "race convergence" hypothesis. *Sociology of Education*, 1979, 52, 34–46.

90. JOHNSON, R. A. Verbal originality in the absence of sight: Blind versus sighted adolescents. *Child Study Journal*, 1979, 9, 261–271.

91. LEE, S. S. Memory span, IQ, and memory aids effects on learning of logico-conceptual rules. *Contemporary Educational Psychology*, 1979, 4, 334–347.

92. LOVETT, M. W. The selective encoding of sentential information in normal reading development. *Child Development*, 1979, 50, 897–900.

93. PELHAM, W. E. Selective attention deficits in poor readers? Dichotic listening, speeded classification, and auditory and visual central and incidental learning task. *Child Development*, 1979, 50, 1050–1061.

94. PULLIS, J. M. A measurement of alternate-form reliability for published shorthand takes. *Business Education Forum*, 1979, 34 (1), 57.

95. RUPLEY, W. H., ASHE, M., & BUCKLAND, P. The relation between the discrimination of letter–like forms and word recognition. *Reading World*, 1979, 19, 113–123.

96. SILLIMAN, E. R. Relationship between pictorial interpretation and comprehension of three spatial relations in school–age children. *Journal of Speech & Hearing Research*, 1979, 22, 366–388.

97. SPITZ, H. H., & BYRNES, M. M. Development progression of performance on the tower of Hanoi problem. *Bulletin of the Psychonomic Society*, 1979, 14, 379–381.

98. TALOUMIS, T. Scores on Piagetian area tasks as predictors of achievement in mathematics over a four-year period. *Journal for Research in Mathematics Education*, 1979, 10, 120–134.

99. BENNINGA, J. S. Integration of self–concept and moral judgment: Two studies. *Journal of Genetic Psychology*, 1980, 136, 25–36.

100. CASKEY, W. E., JR., & LARSON, G. L. Scores on group and individually administered Bender–Gestalt Test and Otis–Lennon IQs of kindergarten children. *Perceptual & Motor Skills*, 1980, 50, 387–390.

101. DUNN, R. S., & PRICE, G. E. The learning style characteristics of gifted students. *Gifted Child Quarterly*, 1980, 24, 33–36.

102. GETTINGER, M., & WHITE, M. A. Evaluating curriculum fit with class ability. *Journal of Educational Psychology*, 1980, 72, 338–344.

103. JOHNSON, R. A. Sensory images in the absence of sight: Blind versus sighted adolescents. *Perceptual & Motor Skills*, 1980, 51, 177–178.

104. KIRKLAND, K., & HOLLANDSWORTH, J. G., JR. Effective test taking: Skills-acquisition versus anxiety-reduction techniques. *Journal of Consulting & Clinical Psychology*, 1980, 48, 431–439.

105. LOUCKS, S., BURSTEIN, A. G., & GONZALEZ, J. Concurrent validity of the Kent EGY Scale in a Mexican–American population. *Journal of School Psychology*, 1980, 18, 79–80.

106. PRITCHARD, R. D., HOLLENBACK, J., & DELEO, P. J. The effects of continuous and partial schedules of reinforcement on effort, performance, and satisfaction. *Organizational Behavior & Human Performance*, 1980, 25, 336–353.

107. RASKIND, L. T., & NAGLE, R. J. Modeling effects on the intelligence test performance of test-anxious children. *Psychology in the Schools*, 1980, 17, 351–355.

108. ROGERS, B. G., WILSON, B. J., & HEWETT, G. Canonical variates in longitudinal achievement data. *Psychology in the Schools*, 1980, 17, 496–499.

109. RUSCELLO, D. M., MOREAU, V. K., & SHOLTIS, D. Awareness of certain articulatory gestures in normal–speaking and articulatory–defective children. *Journal of Communication Disorders*, 1980, 13, 59–64.

110. SWANSON, L. Conceptual rule learning in normal and learning disabled children. *Journal of General Psychology*, 1980, 102, 255–263.

111. WATKINS, D., & ASTILLA, E. Intellective and non–intellective predictors of academic achievement at a Filipino university. *Educational & Psychological Measurement*, 1980, 40, 245–249.

112. WATKINS, D., & ASTILLA, E. Relationship between field independence, intelligence, and school achievement for Filipino girls. *Perceptual & Motor Skills*, 1980, 51, 593–594.

113. WATKINS, D., & ASTILLA, E. Self-esteem and school achievement of Filipino girls. *Journal of Psychology*, 1980, 105, 3–5.

114. WESTBROOK, B. W., CUTTS, C. C., MADISON, S. S., & ARCIA, M. A. The validity of the Crite's model of career maturity. *Journal of Vocational Behavior*, 1980, 16, 249–281.

115. ALICHNE, M. C., & BELLUCCI, J. T. Prediction of freshman students' success in a baccalaureate nursing program. *Nursing Research*, 1981, 30, 49–53.

116. CHAPMAN, J. W., CULLEN, J. L., BOERSMA, F. J., & MAGUIRE, T. O. Affective variables and school achievement: A study of possible causal influences. *Canadian Journal of Behavioural Science*, 1981, 13, 181–192.

117. HOWELL, F. M., & FRESE, W. Educational plans as motivation or attitude? Some additional evidence. *Social Psychology Quarterly*, 1981, 44, 218–236.

118. LEHMAN, J. D., KAHLE, J. B., & NORDLAND, F. Cognitive development and creativity: A study in two high schools. *Science Education*, 1981, 65, 197–206.

[1755]
Otis Self-Administering Tests of Mental Ability.
Ages 9–14, 12.5 and over; 1936–77; manuals by D. Spearritt; Australian Council for Educational Research [Australia].*

See T2:426 (139 references) and 5:363 (52 references); for a review by Frederic Kuder, see 3:250 (71 references). For additional information concerning the original Australian edition, see 2:1412.

[1756]
Otto Pre-Marital Counseling Schedules. Adult couples; 1961, c1951–61; checklist for use as a discussion stimulator; 3 parts; Herbert A. Otto; Consulting Psychologists Press, Inc.*
a) PRE-MARITAL SURVEY SECTION.
b) FAMILY FINANCE SECTION.
c) SEXUAL ADJUSTMENT SECTION.

For additional information, see P:189 (2 references); for reviews by Robert C. Challman and William R. Reevy, see 6:686.

[1757]
Pain Apperception Test. Adults; 1956–75; PAT; 10 scores: 3 scores (intensity, duration, total) in each of 3 areas (felt pain sensations, anticipation of pain vs. felt-sensation, self-inflicted vs. other-inflicted pain), total; Donald V. Petrovich; Western Psychological Services.*

For additional information and a review by Charles D. Spielberger, see 8:639 (3 references); see also T2:1488 (10 references).

REFERENCES

1–10. See T2:1488.
11–13. See 8:639.
14. ZIESAT, H. A., JR. Correlates of the tourniquet ischemia pain ratio. *Perceptual & Motor Skills*, 1978, 47, 147–150.
15. ZIESAT, H. A., JR., & GENTRY, W. D. The Pain Apperception Test: An investigation of concurrent validity. *Journal of Clinical Psychology*, 1978, 34, 786–789.
16. ELTON, D., BURROWS, G. D., & STANLEY, G. V. The relationship between psychophysical and perceptual variables and chronic pain. *British Journal of Social & Clinical Psychology*, 1979, 18, 425–430.

[1758]
Pair Attraction Inventory. College and adults; 1970–71; PAI; for research use only; 7 scores: mother-son, daddy-doll, bitch-nice guy, master-servant, hawks, doves, person-person; Everett L. Shostrom; EdITS/Educational and Industrial Testing Service.*

For additional information and a review by James R. Clopton, see 8:349 (10 references).

REFERENCES

1–10. See 8:349.
11. KELLERMAN, H. Shostrom's Mate Selection Model, the Pair Attraction Inventory, and the Emotions Profile Index. *Journal of Psychology*, 1977, 95, 37–43.
12. SHOSTROM, F. L., & KNAPP, R. R. Relationship between clinical ratings and inventory measures of intrapersonal styles: Validity of the Pair Attraction Inventory. *Educational & Psychological Measurement*, 1977, 37, 541–543.
13. MIAOULIS, C. N., & GUTSCH, K. U. A study of the innovative use of time and planned short term treatment in conjoint counseling. *Southern Journal of Educational Research*, 1979, 13, 135–143.

[1759]
★**PAL-C Scale.** Counseling, mental health, or medical services clients; 1978–81; also called *Profile of Adaptation to Life-Clinical Scale*; self-report questionnaire pre- and posttreatment; 7 scores: negative emotions, psychological well being, income management, physical symptoms, alcohol/drugs, close interpersonal relationships, child relationship; Robert B. Ellsworth and Shanae L. Ellsworth (scale and manual); Consulting Psychologists Press, Inc.*

[1760]
★**PAL-H Scale.** Counseling, mental health, or medical services clients; 1978–81; also called *Profile of Adaptation to Life-Holistic Scale*; self-report questionnaire pre- and posttreatment; 7 scores: negative emotions, psychological well being, income management, physical symptoms, alcohol/drugs, close interpersonal relationships, child relationship, plus 5 life style areas correlated with good adjustment: social activity, self activity, nutrition and exercise, personal growth, spiritual awareness; Robert B. Ellsworth and Shanae L. Ellsworth (scale and manual); Consulting Psychologists Press, Inc.*

[1761]
*****A Parent-Adolescent Communication Inventory.** Ages 13 and over; 1968–79; PACI; Millard J. Bienvenu, Sr.; Family Life Publications, Inc.*

See T2:1310 (1 reference); for a review by David B. Orr of an earlier edition, see 7:119 (3 references).

REFERENCES

1–3. See 7:119.
4. See T2:1310.
5. RO-TROCK, G. K., WELLISCH, D. K., & SCHOOLAR, J. C. A family therapy outcome study in an inpatient setting. *American Journal of Orthopsychiatry*, 1977, 47, 514–522.
6. FLORA, R. R. The effect of self concept upon adolescents' communication with parents. *Journal of School Health*, 1978, 48, 100–102.

[1762]
★**Parent As A Teacher Inventory.** Mothers and fathers with children ages 3–9; 1978–82; PAAT; 6 scores: creativity, frustration, control, play, teaching-learning process, total; (Spanish edition of the inventory and profile available); Robert D. Strom; Scholastic Testing Service, Inc.*

REFERENCES

1. STROM, R., & JOHNSON, A. Assessment for parent education. *Journal of Experimental Education*, 1978, 47, 9–16.
2. STROM, R., & HILL, J. Childrearing expectations of Hopi and Navajo parents of preschoolers. *Journal of Instructional Psychology*, 1979, 6, 15–27.
3. STROM, R., HATHAWAY, C., & SLAUGHTER, H. The correlation of maternal attitudes and preschool children's performance on the McCarthy Scales of Children's Abilities. *Journal of Instructional Psychology*, 1981, 8, 139–145.
4. STROM, R., REES, R., SLAUGHTER, H., & WURSTER, S. Childrearing expectations of families with atypical children. *American Journal of Orthopsychiatry*, 1981, 51, 285–296.

[1763]
Parent Opinion Inventory. Parents of school children; 1976; POI; attitudes toward elementary and secondary school programs; for measurement of groups, not individuals; National Study of School Evaluation.*

For additional information, see 8:390.

[1764]
Parent Readiness Evaluation of Preschoolers. Ages 3–9 to 5–8; 1968–69; PREP; administered by parent; 17 scores: verbal (general information, comprehension, opposites, identification, verbal association, verbal description, listening, language, total), performance (concepts, motor co-ordination, visual-motor association, visual interpretation, auditory memory, visual memory, total),

total; A. Edward Ahr and Benita Simons (handbook); Priority Innovations, Inc.*

For additional information and reviews by S. Alan Cohen, Robert E. Valett, and David P. Weikart, see 7:759.

[1765]

*PARS Scale. Mental patients and clinical clients; 1974–81; also called *Personal Adjustment and Role Skills Scale*; pre- and posttreatment ratings by significant other; 8 scores: interpersonal relations, alienation, anxiety, confusion, alcohol-drug use, house activity, child relations, work; Robert B. Ellsworth and Shanae L. Ellsworth (scale and manual); Consulting Psychologists Press, Inc.*

For additional information and a review by William J. Eichman of an earlier edition, see 8:638 (6 references).

REFERENCES

1–6. See 8:638.
7. MORGUELAN, F. N., MICHAEL, W. B., & ALLEN, R. E. The design and development of a measure consisting of demographic–biographical and symptom–related items for prediction of community adjustment of schizophrenic patients. *Educational & Psychological Measurement*, 1978, 38, 491–499.
8. PENK, W. E. Effects of ambiguous and unambiguous stimulus word differences on popular responses of schizophrenics. *Journal of Clinical Psychology*, 1978, 34, 838–843.
9. PENK, W. E., & ROBINOWITZ, R. Measuring aspects of treatment outcome among psychosocial compulsive drug users. *Journal of Clinical Psychology*, 1978, 34, 222–229.
10. ELLSWORTH, R. B., CASEY, N. A., HICKEY, R. H., TWEMLOW, S. W., COLLINS, J. F., SCHOONOVER, R. A., HYER, L., & NESSELROADE, J. R. Some characteristics of effective psychiatric treatment programs. *Journal of Consulting & Clinical Psychology*, 1979, 47, 799–817.
11. FONTANA, A. F., MARCUS, J. L., HUGHES, L. A., & DOWDS, B. N. Subjective evaluation of life events. *Journal of Consulting & Clinical Psychology*, 1979, 47, 906–911.
12. PAGE, R. D., & SCHAUB, L. H. Efficacy of a three-versus a five-week alcohol treatment program. *International Journal of the Addictions*, 1979, 14, 697–714.
13. PENK, W. E., VEBERSAX, J. S., ANDREWS, R. H., & CHARLES, H. L. Client correlates of community informant adjustment ratings. *Journal of Personality Assessment*, 1980, 44, 157–166.
14. WRIGHT, B. M., & STOFFELMAYR, B. E. Distress in clients and significant others: The question of causality. *Family Process*, 1980, 19, 401–410.

[1766]

A Partial Index of Modernization: Measurement of Attitudes Toward Morality. Children and adults; 1972; Panos D. Bardis; the Author.*

For additional information, see 8:464 (1 reference).

[1767]

Pattern Relations Test. College graduates; 1968–69; PRT; abstract reasoning; test in English and Afrikaans; D. Daneel (test) and Delene Barker (manual); National Institute for Personnel Research [South Africa].*

[1768]

★The Patterned Elicitation Syntax Screening Test. Ages 3–7.5; 1981; PESST; "designed to determine, with a small expenditure of time, whether a child's expressive grammatical skills are age appropriate"; Edna Carter Young and Joseph J. Perachio; Communication Skill Builders, Inc.*

[1769]

Peabody Individual Achievement Test. Grades kgn–12; 1970; PIAT; 6 scores: mathematics, reading recognition, reading comprehension, spelling, general information, total; Lloyd M. Dunn and Frederick C. Markwardt, Jr.; American Guidance Service.*

For additional information and excerpted reviews by Alex Bannatyne and Barton B. Proger, see 8:24 (36 references); see also T2:26 (2 references); for a review by Howard B. Lyman, see 7:17.

REFERENCES

1–2. See T2:26.
3–38. See 8:24.
39. DEAN, R. S. Analysis of the PIAT with Anglo and Mexican-American children. *Journal of School Psychology*, 1977, 15, 329–333.
40. DEAN, R. S. Internal consistency of the PIAT with Mexican-American children. *Psychology in the Schools*, 1977, 14, 167–168.
41. DEBELL, S. M., & VANCE, H. B. Concurrent validity of three measures of arithmetic achievement. *Perceptual & Motor Skills*, 1977, 45, 848.
42. DOWNING, C. J. Teaching children behavior change techniques. *Elementary School Guidance & Counseling*, 1977, 11, 277–283.
43. FOCH, T. T., DEFRIES, J. C., MCCLEARN, G. E., & SINGER, S. M. Familial patterns of impairment in reading disability. *Journal of Educational Psychology*, 1977, 69, 316–329.
44. FOSTER, G., & KEECH, V. Teacher reactions to the label of educable mentally retarded. *Education & Training of the Mentally Retarded*, 1977, 12, 307–311.
45. JORGENSON, G. W., KLEIN, N., & KUMAR, V. K. Achievement and behavior correlates of matched levels of student ability and material difficulty. *Journal of Educational Research*, 1977, 71, 100–103.
46. MADIGAN, R. J., & PETERSON, W. J. Television on the Bering Strait. *Journal of Communication*, 1977, 27, 183–187.
47. MILLER, S. R., & SABATINO, D. A. Evaluating the instructional effectiveness of supplemental special educational materials. *Exceptional Children*, 1977, 43, 457–461.
48. SMITH, M. K., & MCMANIS, D. L. Concurrent validity of the Peabody Individual Achievement Test and the Wide Range Achievement Test. *Psychological Reports*, 1977, 41, 1279–1284.
49. YSSELDYKE, J. E. Aptitude–treatment interaction research with first grade children. *Contemporary Educational Psychology*, 1977, 2, 1–9.
50. BOLL, T. J., RICHARDS, H., & BERENT, S. Tactile–perceptual functioning and academic performance in brain–impaired and unimpaired children. *Perceptual & Motor Skills*, 1978, 47, 491–495.
51. BRUININKS, V. L. Peer status and personality characteristics of learning disabled and nondisabled students. *Journal of Learning Disabilities*, 1978, 11, 484–489.
52. DEFRIES, J. C., SINGER, S. M., FOCH, T. T., & LEWITTER, F. I. Familial nature of reading disability. *British Journal of Psychiatry*, 1978, 132, 361–367.
53. HARMER, W. R., & WILLIAMS, F. The Wide Range Achievement Test and the Peabody Individual Achievement Test: A comparative study. *Journal of Learning Disabilities*, 1978, 11, 667–670.
54. HARPER, G. F., GUIDUBALDI, J., & KEHLE, T. J. Is academic achievement related to classroom behavior? *Elementary School Journal*, 1978, 78, 203–207.
55. HEATON, R. K., CHELUNE, G. J., & LEHMAN, R. A. W. Using neuropsychological and personality tests to assess the likelihood of patient employment. *Journal of Nervous & Mental Disease*, 1978, 166, 408–416.
56. JENKINS, M. B., KRIEL, R. L., BOYD, L., & BARNWELL, A. Trisomy 21 with 47, +18 lymphocyte cell line: Double mitotic nondisjunction. *Journal of Medical Genetics*, 1978, 15, 396–397.
57. JENKINS, J. R., & PANY, D. Standardized achievement test: How useful for special education? *Exceptional Children*, 1978, 44, 448–453.
58. KIEFFER, D. M., & GOLDEN, C. J. The Peabody Individual Achievement Test with normal and special school populations. *Psychological Reports*, 1978, 42, 395–401.
59. KUPIETZ, S. S., & RICHARDSON, E. Children's vigilance performance and inattentiveness in the classroom. *Journal of Child Psychology & Psychiatry & Allied Disciplines*, 1978, 19, 145–154.
60. MILLER, T. L., & SABATINO, D. A. An evaluation of the teacher consultant model as an approach to mainstreaming. *Exceptional Children*, 1978, 45, 86–91.
61. NILES, J. A., & TAYLOR, B. M. The development of orthographic sensitivity during the school year by primary grade children. *National Reading Conference Yearbook*, 1978, 41–44.
62. PETERSEN, C. R., & HART, D. H. Use of multiple discriminant function analysis in evaluation of a state–wide system for identification of educationally handicapped children. *Psychological Reports*, 1978, 43, 743–755.
63. RICHMOND, B. O., & WAITS, C. Special education–Who needs it? *Exceptional Children*, 1978, 44, 279–280.
64. SANNER, R., & MCMANIS, D. L. Concurrent validity of the Peabody Individual Achievement Test and the Wide Range Achievement

Test for middle-class elementary school children. *Psychological Reports*, 1978, 42, 19–24.

65. SWANSON, L. Verbal encoding effects on the visual short-term memory of learning disabled and normal readers. *Journal of Educational Psychology*, 1978, 70, 539–544.

66. WIKOFF, R. L. Correlational and factor analysis of the Peabody Individual Achievement Test and the WISC–R. *Journal of Consulting & Clinical Psychology*, 1978, 46, 322–325.

67. BECK, F. W., LINDSEY, J. D., & FACZIENDE, R. A comparison of the General Information Subtest of the Peabody Individual Achievement Test with the information subtest of the Wechsler Intelligence Scale for Children–Revised. *Educational & Psychological Measurement*, 1979, 39, 1073–1077.

68. BROWNING, R., SALVIA, J., & YSSELDYKE, J. E. Technical characteristics of the Peabody Individual Achievement Test as a function of item arrangement and basal and ceiling rules. *Psychology in the Schools*, 1979, 16, 4–7.

69. DEAN, R. S. The use of the PIAT with emotionally disturbed children. *Journal of Learning Disabilities*, 1979, 12, 629–631.

70. DWORKIN, N. E. Changing teachers' negative expectations. *Academic Therapy*, 1979, 14, 517–531.

71. ESLER, W. K. Fun and gains with science. *School Science & Mathematics*, 1979, 79, 637–640.

72. LORENZ, L., & VOCKELL, E. Using neurological impress method with learning disabled readers. *Journal of Learning Disabilities*, 1979, 12, 420–422.

73. MILLER, W. H. A comparison of the Wide Range Achievement Test and the Peabody Individual Achievement Test for educationally handicapped children. *Journal of Learning Disabilities*, 1979, 12, 65–68.

74. PALMER, D. J. Regular-classroom teachers' attributions and instructional prescriptions for handicapped and nonhandicapped pupils. *Journal of Special Education*, 1979, 13, 325–337.

75. RESCHLY, D. J., & LAMPRECHT, M. J. Expectancy effects of labels: Fact or artifact? *Exceptional Children*, 1979, 46, 55–58.

76. REYNOLDS, C. R. Factor structure of the Peabody Individual Achievement Test at five grade levels between grades one and 12. *Journal of School Psychology*, 1979, 17, 270–274.

77. ROSKAM, K. Music therapy as an aid for increasing auditory awareness and improving reading skill. *Journal of Music Therapy*, 1979, 16, 31–42.

78. SATTERFIELD, J. H., CANTWELL, D. P., & SATTERFIELD, B. T. Multimodality treatment. *Archives of General Psychiatry*, 1979, 36, 965–974.

79. STONEBURNER, R. L., & BROWN, B. A. A comparison of PIAT and WRAT performances of learning disabled adolescents. *Journal of Learning Disabilities*, 1979, 12, 631–634.

80. WALDEN, J. A comparison of the PIAT and WRAT: A closer look. *Psychology in the Schools*, 1979, 16, 342–346.

81. WHITE, T. H. Correlations among the WISC–R, PIAT, and DAM. *Psychology in the Schools*, 1979, 16, 497–501.

82. WIKOFF, R. L. Determining basals for the Peabody Individual Achievement Test. *Psychology in the Schools*, 1979, 16, 172–174.

83. WIKOFF, R. L. The WISC–R as a predictor of achievement. *Psychology in the Schools*, 1979, 16, 364–366.

84. BERG, A., & HAMMITT, K. B. Assessing the psychiatric patient's ability to meet the literacy demands of hospitalization. *Hospital & Community Psychiatry*, 1980, 31, 266–268.

85. COOPER, S. An approach to the educational assessment of the learning disabled child. *Journal of Clinical Child Psychology*, 1980, 9, 59–62.

86. DECKER, S. N., & DEFRIES, J. C. Cognitive abilities in families with reading disabled children. *Journal of Learning Disabilities*, 1980, 13, 53–58.

87. GARREN, R. B. Hemispheric laterality differences among four levels of reading achievement. *Perceptual & Motor Skills*, 1980, 50, 119–123.

88. HO, H., FOCH, T. T., & PLOMIN, R. Developmental stability of the relative influence of genes and environment on specific cognitive abilities during childhood. *Developmental Psychology*, 1980, 16, 340–346.

89. JOHNSON, V. M. Analysis of factors influencing special educational placement decisions. *Journal of School Psychology*, 1980, 18, 191–202.

90. REYNOLDS, C. R., & GUTKIN, T. B. Statistics related to profile interpretation of the Peabody Individual Achievement Test. *Psychology in the Schools*, 1980, 17, 316–319.

91. RICHARDSON, E., DIBENEDETTO, B., CHRIST, A., & PRESS, M. Relationship of auditory and visual skills to reading retardation. *Journal of Learning Disabilities*, 1980, 13, 77–82.

92. ROBINSON, E. H., III, & BROSH, M. C. Communication skills training for resource teachers. *Journal of Learning Disabilities*, 1980, 13, 55–58.

93. SATTERFIELD, J. H., SATTERFIELD, B. T., & CANTWELL, D. P. Multimodality treatment: A two-year evaluation of 61 hyperactive boys. *Archives of General Psychiatry*, 1980, 37, 915–919.

94. SCULL, J. W., & BRAND, L. H. The WRAT and the PIAT with learning disabled children. *Journal of Learning Disabilities*, 1980, 13, 64–66.

95. STEIN, C. L. E., & GOLDMAN, J. Beginning reading instruction for children with minimal brain dysfunction. *Journal of Learning Disabilities*, 1980, 13, 219–222.

96. TREMBLEY, P. W., CAPONIGRO, J. D., & GAFFNEY, V. T. Effects of programming from the WRAT and the PIAT for students determined to have learning disabilities in arithmetic. *Journal of Learning Disabilities*, 1980, 13, 63–65.

97. WHEELER, L., & REILLY, T. F. Self-concept and its relationship to academic achievement for EMR adolescents. *Journal of Special Education*, 1980, 17, 78–83.

98. ALLINGTON, R. L. Sensitivity to orthographic structure in educable mentally retarded children. *Contemporary Educational Psychology*, 1981, 6, 135–139.

99. BADIAN, N. A. Recategorized WISC–R scores of disabled and adequate readers. *Journal of Educational Research*, 1981, 75, 109–114.

100. BRANDES, P. J., & EHINGER, D. M. The effects of early middle ear pathology on auditory perception and academic achievement. *Journal of Speech & Hearing Disorders*, 1981, 46, 301–307.

101. CORDONI, B. K., & SNYDER, M. K. A comparison of learning disabled college students' achievement from WRAT and PIAT grade, standard, and subtest scores. *Psychology in the Schools*, 1981, 18, 28–34.

102. ELLIOT, M. Quantitative evaluation procedures for learning disabilities. *Journal of Learning Disabilities*, 1981, 14, 84–87.

103. LYON, R., REITTA, S., WATSON, B., PORCH, B., & RHODES, J. Selected linguistic and perceptual abilities of empirically derived subgroups of learning disabled readers. *Journal of School Psychology*, 1981, 19, 152–166.

104. SATTERFIELD, J. H., SATTERFIELD, B. T., & CANTWELL, D. P. Three-year modality treatment study of 100 hyperactive boys. *Journal of Pediatrics*, 1981, 98, 650–655.

105. SILVERSTEIN, A. B. Pattern analysis on the PIAT. *Psychology in the Schools*, 1981, 18, 13–14.

[1770]

★Peabody Mathematics Readiness Test. Grades kgn–1; 1979; PMRT; 6 scores: number, containment, size, shape, configuration, drawing test; Otto C. Bassler, Morris I. Beers, Lloyd I. Richardson, and Richard L. Thurman; Scholastic Testing Service, Inc.*

[1771]

Peabody Picture Vocabulary Test-Revised. Ages 2.5–40; 1959–81; PPVT-R; "designed primarily to measure a subject's receptive (hearing) vocabulary for Standard American English"; Lloyd M. Dunn and Leota M. Dunn; American Guidance Service.

For additional information and references of an earlier edition, see 8:222 (213 references); see also T2:516 (77 references) and 7:417 (201 references); for reviews by Howard B. Lyman and Ellen V. Piers, see 6:530 (21 references).

REFERENCES

1–21. See 6:530.
22–223. See 7:417.
224–301. See T2:516.
302–514. See 8:222.

515. APPELBAUM, A. S., & TUMA, J. M. Social class and test performance: Comparative validity of the Peabody with the WISC and WISC–R for two socioeconomic groups. *Psychological Reports*, 1977, 40, 139–145.

516. APRIL, R. S., & TSE, P. C. Crossed aphasia in a Chinese bilingual dextral. *Archives of Neurology*, 1977, 34, 766–770.

517. BATES, E., & SILVERN, L. Social adjustment and politeness in preschoolers. *Journal of Communication*, 1977, 27, 104–111.

518. BENDER, N. N. Verbal mediation as an instructional technique with young trainable mentally retarded children. *Journal of Special Education*, 1977, 11, 449–455.

519. BEN-ZEEV, S. The influence of bilingualism on cognitive strategy and cognitive development. *Child Development*, 1977, 48, 1009–1018.

520. BLOWERS, E. A. Prediction of Metropolitan Readiness Test scores. *Alberta Journal of Educational Research*, 1977, 23, 164–168.

521. BOGNER, C. N., & BROWN, A. W. Mothers learn to teach their own children. *Phi Delta Kappan*, 1977, 58, 500–501.

522. BOUCHER, J. Alternation and sequencing behavior, and response to novelty in autistic children. *Journal of Child Psychology & Psychiatry & Allied Disciplines*, 1977, 18, 67–72.

523. BUGENTAL, D. B., WHALEN, C. K., & HENKER, B. Causal attributions of hyperactive children and motivational assumptions of two

behavior-change approaches: Evidence for an interactionist position. *Child Development*, 1977, 48, 874–884.

524. CLINGMAN, J. M., AUERBACK, S. M., BOWMAN, P. C., & PARRISH, J. M. Differential effects of candy, social, and token rewards on the IQ scores of children of above average intelligence. *Psychology in the Schools*, 1977, 14, 95–98.

525. COLARUSSO, R., MCLESKEY, J., & GILL, S. H. Use of the Peabody Picture Vocabulary Test and the Slosson Intelligence Test with urban black kindergarten children. *Journal of Special Education*, 1977, 11, 427–432.

526. COVIN, T. M. Relationship of Peabody and WISC–R IQs of candidates for special education. *Psychological Reports*, 1977, 40, 189–190.

527. COVIN, T. M. Relationship of the SIT and PPVT to the WISC–R. *Journal of School Psychology*, 1977, 15, 259–260.

528. DELACEY, P. R., & NURCOMBE, B. Effects of enrichment preschooling at Bourke: A further follow-up study. *Australian Journal of Education*, 1977, 21, 80–90.

529. DRUCKER, S. A., DREWES, A. A., & RUBIN, L. ESP in relation to cognitive development and IQ in young children. *Journal of the American Society for Pyschical Research*, 1977, 71, 289–298.

530. ERNHART, C. B., SPANER, S. D., & JORDON, T. E. Validity of selected preschool screening tests. *Contemporary Educational Psychology*, 1977, 2, 78–89.

531. EVESHAM, M. Teaching language skills to children with language disorders. *British Journal of Disorders of Communication*, 1977, 12, 23–29.

532. FIELD, D. The importance of the verbal content in the training of Piagetian conservation skills. *Child Development*, 1977, 48, 1583–1592.

533. FOWLER, R. L., & CLINGMAN, J. The influence of intrinsic and extrinsic reward on the intratest performance of high- and low-scoring children. *Psychological Record*, 1977, 27, 603–610.

534. GAINES, R. Developmental assessment of pattern detection of matrices. *Child Development*, 1977, 48, 445–451.

535. GALLAGHER, T. M. Revision behaviors in the speech of normal children developing language. *Journal of Speech & Hearing Research*, 1977, 20, 303–318.

536. GAMER, E., GALLANT, D., GRUNEBAUM, H. V., & COHLER, B. J. Children of psychotic mothers. *Archives of General Psychiatry*, 1977, 34, 592–597.

537. GOODMAN, J. F. Aging and intelligence in young retarded adults: A cross-sectional study of fluid abilities in three samples. *Psychological Reports*, 1977, 41, 255–263.

538. GOTTLIEB, D. E., TAYLOR, S. E., & RUDERMAN, A. Cognitive bases of children's moral judgments. *Developmental Psychology*, 1977, 13, 547–556.

539. GUTHRIE, J. T., & SEIFERT, M. Letter-sound complexity in learning to identify words. *Journal of Educational Psychology*, 1977, 69, 686–696.

540. HALL, J. N., BAKER, R. D., & HUTCHINSON, K. A controlled evaluation of token economy procedures with chronic schizophrenic patients. *Behaviour Research & Therapy*, 1977, 15, 261–283.

541. HALL, V. C., HUPPERTZ, J. W., & LEVI, A. Attention and achievement exhibited by middle- and lower-class black and white elementary school boys. *Journal of Educational Psychology*, 1977, 69, 115–120.

542. HALL, V. C., & KAYE, D. B. Patterns of early cognitive development among boys in four subcultural groups. *Journal of Educational Psychology*, 1977, 69, 66–87.

543. HASLAM, R. H. A., ALLEN, J. R., DORSEN, M. M., KANOFSKY, D. L., MELLITS, E. D., & NORRIS, D. A. The sequelae of group B B-hemolytic streptococcal meningitis in early infancy. *American Journal of Diseases of Children*, 1977, 131, 845–849.

544. HATCH, G. L., & COVIN, T. M. Comparability of WISC and Peabody IQs of young children from three heterogeneous groups. *Psychological Reports*, 1977, 40, 1345–1346.

545. IRWIN, R. J., & NEWLAND, J. K. Children's knowledge of left and right: Research note. *Journal of Child Psychology & Psychiatry & Allied Disciplines*, 1977, 18, 271–277.

546. JOHNSON, E. G. The development of color knowledge in preschool children. *Child Development*, 1977, 48, 308–311.

547. JOHNSTON, R. P., & SINGLETON, C. H. Social class and communication style: The ability of middle and working class five year olds to encode and decode abstract stimuli. *British Journal of Psychology*, 1977, 68, 237–244.

548. KENDALL, P. C., & LITTLE, V. L. Correspondence of brief intelligence measures to the Wechsler scales with delinquents. *Journal of Consulting & Clinical Psychology*, 1977, 45, 660–666.

549. KIBBY, M. W. Note on relationship of word difficulty and word frequency. *Psychological Reports*, 1977, 41, 12–14.

550. KIER, R. J., STYFCO, S. J., & ZIGLER, E. Success expectancies and the probability learning of children of low and middle socioeconomic status. *Developmental Psychology*, 1977, 13, 444–449.

551. KIMBALL, J. G. The Southern California Sensory Integration Tests and the Bender Gestalt: A correlational study. *American Journal of Occupational Therapy*, 1977, 31, 295–299.

552. LEE, D. Y. Evaluation of a group counseling program designed to enhance social adjustment of mentally retarded adults. *Journal of Counseling Psychology*, 1977, 24, 318–323.

553. LYTTON, H., CONWAY, D., & SAUVÉ, R. The impact of twinship on parent-child interaction. *Journal of Personality & Social Psychology*, 1977, 35, 97–107.

554. LYTTON, H., MARTIN, N. G., & EAVES, L. Environmental and genetic causes of variation in ethological aspects of behavior in two-year old boys. *Social Biology*, 1977, 24, 200–211.

555. MADIGAN, R. J., & PETERSON, W. J. Television on the Bering Strait. *Journal of Communication*, 1977, 27, 183–187.

556. MANOSEVITZ, M., FLING, S., & PRENTICE, N. M. Imaginary companions in young children: Relationships with intelligence, creativity and waiting ability. *Journal of Child Psychology & Psychiatry & Allied Disciplines*, 1977, 18, 73–78.

557. MARGOLIS, H. Auditory perceptual test performance and the reflection–impulsivity dimension. *Journal of Learning Disabilities*, 1977, 10, 164–172.

558. MARSH, G., & MINEO, R. J. Training preschool children to recognize phonemes in words. *Journal of Educational Psychology*, 1977, 69, 748–753.

559. MCCORMICK, D. P. Pediatric evaluation of children with school problems. *American Journal of Diseases of Children*, 1977, 131, 318–322.

560. MCGLONE, J. Sex differences in the cerebral organization of verbal functions in patients with unilateral brain lesions. *Brain*, 1977, 100, 775–793.

561. MOORE, C. L., & BURNS, W. J. Brief screening for developmentally delayed preschoolers. *Perceptual & Motor Skills*, 1977, 45, 1169–1170.

562. PIHL, R. O., & PARKES, M. Hair element content in learning disabled children. *Science*, 1977, 198, 204–206.

563. PRICE-WILLIAMS, D. R., & RAMIREZ, M., III. Divergent thinking, cultural differences, and bilingualism. *Journal of Social Psychology*, 1977, 103, 3–11.

564. PRIOR, M. R. Psycholinguistic disabilities of autistic and retarded children. *Journal of Mental Deficiency Research*, 1977, 21, 37–45.

565. QUAY, L. C., MATHEWS, M., & SCHWARZMUELLER, B. Communication encoding and decoding in children from different socioeconomic and racial groups. *Developmental Psychology*, 1977, 14, 415–416.

566. RICHMOND, B. O., & LONG, M. WISC R and PPVT scores for black and white mentally retarded children. *Journal of School Psychology*, 1977, 15, 261–263.

567. RINGEL, S. P., CARROLL, J. E., & SCHOLD, S. C. The spectrum of mild X-linked recessive muscular dystrophy. *Archives of Neurology*, 1977, 34, 408–416.

568. ROE, K. V. Correlations between Gesell scores in infancy and performance on verbal and nonverbal tests in early childhood. *Perceptual & Motor Skills*, 1977, 45, 1131–1134.

569. SALTZ, E., DIXON, D., & JOHNSON, J. Training disadvantaged preschoolers on various fantasy activities: Effects on cognitive functioning and impulse control. *Child Development*, 1977, 48, 367–380.

570. SMITH, J. D. Perceptual decentering in EMR and nonretarded children. *American Journal of Mental Deficiency*, 1977, 81, 499–501.

571. SOBOTKA, K. R., BLACK, F. W., HILL, S. D., & PORTER, R. J. Some psychological correlates of developmental dyslexia. *Journal of Learning Disabilities*, 1977, 10, 363–369.

572. SOBOTKA, K. R., & MAY, J. G. Visual evoked potentials and reaction time in normal and dyslexic children. *Psychophysiology*, 1977, 14, 18–23.

573. SOMERVILL, J. W., & BROPHY, P. D. Teacher's perceptions of distractibility: Two-year follow-up. *Perceptual & Motor Skills*, 1977, 45, 640.

574. TAYLOR, A. M., THURLOW, M. L., & TURNURE, J. E. Vocabulary development of educable retarded children. *Exceptional Children*, 1977, 43, 444–449.

575. THOMAS, P. J. Administration of a dialectical Spanish version and standard English version of the Peabody Picture Vocabulary Test. *Psychological Reports*, 1977, 40, 747–750.

576. TONER, I. J., HOLSTEIN, R. B., & HETHERINGTON, E. M. Reflection–impulsivity and self-control in preschool children. *Child Development*, 1977, 48, 239–245.

577. TRIVEDI, A. A comparison of three intelligence tests for the assessment of mental retardation. *Journal of Mental Deficiency Research*, 1977, 21, 289–297.

578. TSUSHIMA, W. T., & TOWNE, W. S. Effects of paint sniffing on neuropsychological test performance. *Journal of Abnormal Psychology*, 1977, 86, 402–407.

579. VOGEL, J. M. The development of recognition memory for the left–right orientation of pictures. *Child Development*, 1977, 48, 1532–1543.

580. VOGEL, S. A. Morphological ability in normal and dyslexic children. *Journal of Learning Disabilities*, 1977, 10, 35–43.

581. WEINBERG, W. A. Reply, a letter in reference to "depression in childhood." *Journal of Pediatrics*, 1977, 85, 292–293.

582. WEINRAUB, M., & LEWIS, M. The determinants of children's responses to separation. *Monographs of the Society for Research in Child Development*, 1977, 42, 1–78.

583. WILLIAMS, A. M., MARKS, C. J., & BIALER, I. Validity of the Peabody Picture Vocabulary Test as a measure of hearing vocabulary in mentally retarded and normal children. *Journal of Speech & Hearing Research*, 1977, 20, 197–204.

584. WOOD, N. E. Directed art, visual perception, and learning disabilities. *Academic Therapy*, 1977, 12, 455–462.

585. ADAMS, J. Visual and tactual integration and cerebral dysfunction in children with learning disabilities. *Journal of Learning Disabilities*, 1978, 11, 197–204.

586. ASBURY, C. A. Cognitive factors related to discrepant arithmetic achievement of white and black first graders. *Journal of Negro Education*, 1978, 47, 337–342.

587. BARRETT, C. A., & NICHOLLS, J. G. Motivational factors in the Peabody Picture Vocabulary Test. *Journal of Cross-Cultural Psychology*, 1978, 9, 349–357.

588. BEDROSIAN, J. L., & PRUTTING, C. A. Communicative performance of mentally retarded adults in four conversational settings. *Journal of Speech & Hearing Research*, 1978, 21, 79–95.

589. BLACHER-DIXON, J., & SIMEONSSON, R. J. Effect of shared experience on role-taking performance of retarded children. *American Journal of Mental Deficiency*, 1978, 83, 21–28.

590. BLITCHINGTON, W. P. Birth order and vocabulary development. *Michigan Academician*, 1978, 10, 433–442.

591. BURNS, W. J., & BURNS, K. A. Checklist of perceptual-motor and language skills for developmentally handicapped preschoolers. *Perceptual & Motor Skills*, 1978, 46, 1211–1214.

592. BURROWS, E. H., & NEYLAND, D. Reading skills, auditory comprehension of language, and academic achievement. *Journal of Speech & Hearing Disorders*, 1978, 43, 467–472.

593. CAREY, J. C., & HALL, B. D. Confirmation of the Cohen Syndrome. *Journal of Pediatrics*, 1978, 93, 239–244.

594. COCHRAN, J. W., FOX, J. H., & KELLY, M. P. Reversible mental symptoms in temporal arthritis. *Journal of Nervous & Mental Disease*, 1978, 166, 446–447.

595. COHN-JONES, L., & SEIM, R. Perceptual and intellectual factors affecting number concept development in retarded and nonretarded children. *American Journal of Mental Deficiency*, 1978, 83, 9–15.

596. COUGHLAN, A. K., & WARRINGTON, E. K. Word comprehension and word-retrieval in patients with localized cerebral lesions. *Brain*, 1978, 101, 163–185.

597. DAVIDSON, P. W., WILLOUGHBY, R. H., O'TUAMA, L. A., SWISHER, C. N., & BENJAMINS, D. Neurological and intellectual sequelae of Reye's Syndrome. *American Journal of Mental Deficiency*, 1978, 82, 535–541.

598. DEHORN, A., & KLINGE, V. Correlations and factor analysis of the WISC-R and the Peabody Picture Vocabulary Test for an adolescent psychiatric sample. *Journal of Consulting & Clinical Psychology*, 1978, 46, 1160–1161.

599. DOEHRING, D. G., BONNYCASTLE, D. E., & LING, A. H. Rapid reading skills of integrated hearing-impaired children. *Volta Review*, 1978, 80, 399–409.

600. EDELBROCK, C., & SUGAWARA, A. I. Acquisition of sex-typed preferences in preschool-aged children. *Developmental Psychology*, 1978, 14, 614–623.

601. ELBERT, M., & MCREYNOLDS, L. V. An experimental analysis of misarticulating children's generalization. *Journal of Speech & Hearing Research*, 1978, 21, 136–150.

602. FINCHAM, F., & BORLING, J. Locus of control and generosity in learning disabled, normal achieving, and gifted children. *Child Development*, 1978, 49, 530–533.

603. FINITZO-HIEBER, T., & TILLMAN, T. W. Room acoustic effects on monosyllabic word discrimination ability for normal and hearing-impaired children. *Journal of Speech & Hearing Research*, 1978, 21, 440–458.

604. FLYNN, T. M., & FLYNN, L. A. Evaluation of the predictive ability of five screening measures administered during kindergarten. *Journal of Experimental Education*, 1978, 46, 65–70.

605. GARRITY, L. I., & SERVOS, A. B. Comparison of measures of adaptive behaviors in preschool children. *Journal of Consulting & Clinical Psychology*, 1978, 46, 288–293.

606. GENESEE, F., TUCKER, G. R., & LAMBERT, W. E. The development of ethnic identity and ethnic role taking skills in children from different school settings. *International Journal of Psychology*, 1978, 13, 39–57.

607. HOLLINGSWORTH, P. M. An experimental approach to the impress method of teaching reading. *Reading Teacher*, 1978, 31, 624–626.

608. HORAN, M. D., & HICK, T. L. Peabody Picture Vocabulary Test scoring by Fortran. *Educational & Psychological Measurement*, 1978, 38, 197.

609. HUTCHERSON, R. Correlating the Boehm and PPVT. *Academic Therapy*, 1978, 13, 285–288.

610. JORDAN, L. S., HARDY, J. C., & MORRIS, H. L. Performance of children with good and poor articulation on tasks of tongue placement. *Journal of Speech & Hearing Research*, 1978, 21, 429–439.

611. LAMBERTS, F., & YSSELDYKE, J. E. Group oral language training with TMH children based on learning to think material. *Education & Training of the Mentally Retarded*, 1978, 13, 309–315.

612. LAWTON, J. T., & FOWELL, N. Effects of advance organizers on preschool children's learning of math concepts. *Journal of Experimental Education*, 1978, 47, 76–81.

613. LILES, B. Z., COOKER, H. S., KASS, M., & CAREY, B. J. The effects of pause time on auditory comprehension of language-disordered children. *Journal of Communication Disorders*, 1978, 11, 365–374.

614. LINDGREN, S. D. Finger localization and the predicting of reading disability. *Cortex*, 1978, 14, 87–101.

615. LONGSTRETH, L. E., & ZOLTAN, V. Developmental changes in retention: Independent of age? *Journal of Experimental Child Psychology*, 1978, 26, 115–121.

616. MALONEY, M. P., NELSON, D., DUVALL, S., & KIRKENDALL, A. Performance of psychiatric inpatients on three standard tests of intelligence. *Psychological Reports*, 1978, 43, 1289–1290.

617. MARGOLIS, H., & BRANNIGAN, G. G. Conceptual tempo as a parameter for predicting reading achievement. *Journal of Educational Research*, 1978, 71, 342–345.

618. MORRISON, D., & POTHIER, P. Effects of sensory-motor training on the language development of retarded preschoolers. *American Journal of Orthopsychiatry*, 1978, 48, 310–319.

619. PENNER, K. A., & VINSON, B. P. Facilitation of verb recognition by MR subjects through syntactic cuing. *ASHA*, 1978, 20, 771. (Abstract)

620. RAMEY, C. T., STEDMAN, D. J., BORDERS-PATTERSON, A., & MENGEL, W. Predicting school failure from information available at birth. *American Journal of Mental Deficiency*, 1978, 82, 525–534.

621. ROSEN, R. C., & LIGHTNER, E. S. Phenotypic malformations in association with maternal trimethadione therapy. *Journal of Pediatrics*, 1978, 92, 240–244.

622. RUBIN, K. H. Role taking in childhood: Some methodological considerations. *Child Development*, 1978, 49, 428–433.

623. RUBIN, K. H., BROWN, I. D. R., & PRIDDLE, R. L. The relationships between measures of fluid, crystallized, and "Piagetian" intelligence in elementary-school-aged children. *Journal of Genetic Psychology*, 1978, 132, 29–36.

624. SATZ, P., & FRIEL, J. Predictive validity of an abbreviated screening battery. *Journal of Learning Disabilities*, 1978, 11, 347–351.

625. SCHMAUCH, V. A., PANAGOS, J. M., & KLICH, R. J. Syntax influences the accuracy of consonant production in language-disordered children. *Journal of Communication Disorders*, 1978, 11, 315–323.

626. SHALLICE, T., & EVANS, M. E. The involvement of the frontal lobes in cognitive estimation. *Cortex*, 1978, 14, 294–303.

627. SHEARD, M. H., & MARINI, J. L. Treatment of human aggressive behavior: Four case studies of the effect of lithium. *Comprehensive Psychiatry*, 1978, 19, 37–45.

628. SNOW, C. E., & HOEFNAGEL-HOHLE, M. The critical period for language acquisition: Evidence from second language learning. *Child Development*, 1978, 49, 1114–1128.

629. SOMMERS, R. K., ERIDGE, S., & PETERSON, M. K. How valid are children's language tests? *Journal of Special Education*, 1978, 12, 393–407.

630. SPELLACY, F., & PETER, B. Dyscalculia and elements of the developmental Gerstmann Syndrome in school children. *Cortex*, 1978, 14, 197–206.

631. ULLMAN, D. G., BARKLEY, R. A., & BROWN, W. The behavioral symptoms of hyperkinetic children who successfully responded to stimulant drug treatment. *American Journal of Orthopsychiatry*, 1978, 48, 425–437.

632. VANCE, H., PRICHARD, K. K., & WALLBROWN, F. H. Comparison of the WISC-R and PPVT for a group of mentally retarded students. *Psychology in the Schools*, 1978, 15, 349–351.

633. WASHINGTON, D. S., & NAREMORE, R. C. Children's use of spatial prepositions in two- and three-dimensional tasks. *Journal of Speech & Hearing Research*, 1978, 21, 151–165.

634. WEISZ, J. R., QUINLAN, D. M., O'NEILL, P., & O'NEILL, P. C. The Rorschach and structured tests of perception as indices of intellectual development in mentally retarded and nonretarded children. *Journal of Experimental Child Psychology*, 1978, 25, 326–336.

635. WHITE, D., & PANUNTO, B. Verbal and nonverbal abilities in English first and second language children. *Psychological Reports*, 1978, 42, 191–197.

636. WILLIAMS, F., & OAKLAND, T. A three-year auditory perception program for low-SES minority children. *Journal of Special Education*, 1978, 12, 331–344.

637. BARKLEY, R. A., & CUNNINGHAM, C. E. Stimulant drugs and activity level in hyperactive children. *American Journal of Orthopsychiatry*, 1979, 49, 491–499.

638. BARLING, J. Verbal proficiency: A confounding variable in the reliability of children's attitude scales? *Child Development*, 1979, 50, 1254–1256.

639. Barling, J., & Fincham, F. Effects of self- and externally imposed reinforcement (material and social) on intelligence test performance of above-average IQ children. *Journal of Genetic Psychology*, 1979, 135, 63–70.

640. Beadle, K. R. Clinical interactions of verbal language, learning and behavior. *Journal of Clinical Child Psychology*, 1979, 8, 201–205.

641. Bountress, N., & Richards, J. Speech, language and hearing disorders in an adult penal institution. *Journal of Speech & Hearing Disorders*, 1979, 44, 293–300.

642. Carroll, J. A., Fuller, G. B., & Carroll, J. L. Comparison of culturally deprived school achievers and underachievers on memory function and perception. *Perceptual & Motor Skills*, 1979, 48, 59–62.

643. Clarke-Stewart, K. A., Vander Stoep, L. P., & Killian, G. A. Analysis and replication of mother-child relations at two years of age. *Child Development*, 1979, 50, 777–793.

644. Colarusso, R. P., Mathis, G., & Shessel, D. Teacher effectiveness in identifying high-risk kindergarten children. *Journal of Learning Disabilities*, 1979, 12, 684–686.

645. Coppage, K. W., & Veal, M. C. Establishing functional language in an autistic child: A cooperative approach. *Journal of Communication Disorders*, 1979, 12, 447–460.

646. Cunningham, C. E., & Barkley, R. A. The interactions of normal and hyperactive children with their mothers in free play and structured tasks. *Child Development*, 1979, 50, 217–224.

647. Desberg, P., Marsh, G., Schneider, L. A., & Duncan-Rose, C. The effects of social dialect on auditory sound blending and word recognition. *Contemporary Educational Psychology*, 1979, 4, 140–144.

648. Dewart, H. M. Language comprehension processes of mentally retarded children. *American Journal of Mental Deficiency*, 1979, 84, 177–183.

649. Dickson, W. P., Hess, R. D., Miyake, N., & Azuma, H. Referential communication accuracy between mother and child as a predictor of cognitive development in the United States and Japan. *Child Development*, 1979, 50, 53–59.

650. Dworkin, N. E. Changing teachers' negative expectations. *Academic Therapy*, 1979, 14, 517–531.

651. Emmerich, W., Cocking, R. R., & Sigel, I. E. Relationships between cognitive and social functioning in preschool children. *Developmental Psychology*, 1979, 15, 495–504.

652. Fein, D., Tinder, P., & Waterhouse, L. Stimulus generalization in autistic and normal children. *Journal of Child Psychology & Psychiatry & Allied Disciplines*, 1979, 20, 325–335.

653. Feldman, A., & Acredolo, L. The effect of active versus passive exploration on memory for spatial location in children. *Child Development*, 1979, 50, 698–704.

654. Fuller, G. B., & Friedrich, D. Visual–motor test performance: Race and achievement variables. *Journal of Clinical Psychology*, 1979, 35, 621–623.

655. Gardner, L. I., Neu, R. L., Shah, R. S., Pinto, W., Jr., Co, M., Lehr, E. R., & Barg, G. A. Family with three apparently balanced t(3;15)(p27;q22) translocation carriers. *American Journal of Diseases of Children*, 1979, 133, 1002–1005.

656. Glenwick, D. S., & Barocas, R. Training impulsive children in verbal self-control by use of natural change agents. *Journal of Special Education*, 1979, 13, 387–398.

657. Gold, D., Reis, M., & Berger, C. Male teachers and development of nursery–school children. *Psychological Reports*, 1979, 44, 457–458.

658. Greenberg, J. The child's capacity to perceive metaphor in art objects: A paradigmatic case of aesthetic development. *Journal of Creative Behavior*, 1979, 13, 232–246.

659. Hedge, M. N., & Gierut, J. The operant training and generalization of pronouns and a verb form in a language delayed child. *Journal of Communication Disorders*, 1979, 12, 23–24.

660. Herjanic, B. M., Barredo, V. H., Herjanic, M., & Tomelleri, C. J. Children of heroin addicts. *International Journal of the Addictions*, 1979, 14, 919–931.

661. Hillman, L. S., Hillman, R. E., & Dodson, W. E. Diagnosis, treatment, and follow–up of neonatal mepivacaine intoxication secondary to paracervical and pudenal blocks during labor. *Journal of Pediatrics*, 1979, 95, 472–477.

662. Holmes, D. R., & McKeever, W. F. Material specific serial memory deficit in adolescent dyslexics. *Cortex*, 1979, 15, 51–62.

663. Hresko, W. P. Elicited imitation ability of children from learning disabled and regular classes. *Journal of Learning Disabilities*, 1979, 12, 456–461.

664. Kendall, J. R., & Hood, J. Investigating the relationship between comprehension and word recognition: Oral reading analysis of children with comprehension or word recognition disabilities. *Journal of Reading Behavior*, 1979, 11, 41–48.

665. Kendall, P. C., & Wilcox, L. E. Self–control in children: Development of a rating scale. *Journal of Consulting & Clinical Psychology*, 1979, 47, 1020–1029.

666. Kierscht, M. S., & Mevwissen, J. Follow–up of preschool age survivors of neonatal intensive care. *Journal of Psychology*, 1979, 101, 129–134.

667. Klein, P. S., & Schwartz, A. A. Effects of training auditory sequential memory and attention on reading. *Journal of Special Education*, 1979, 13, 365–374.

668. Kuczaj, S. A., II. Evidence for a language learning strategy: On the relative ease of acquisition of prefixes and suffixes. *Child Development*, 1979, 50, 1–13.

669. Layton, T. L., & Stick, S. L. Use of mean morphological units to assess language development. *Journal of Communication Disorders*, 1979, 12, 35–44.

670. Ludlow, C. L., Richards-Munn, B., & Cullison, B. L. The effect of drugs on communicative abilities of hyperactive and normal children. *ASHA*, 1979, 21, 759. (Abstract)

671. Marlowe, W., Egner, K., & Foreman, D. Story comprehension as a function of modality and reading ability. *Journal of Learning Disabilities*, 1979, 12, 194–197.

672. Martin, R. L., Cloninger, C. R., & Guze, S. B. The evaluation of diagnostic concordance in follow–up studies: II. A blind, prospective follow–up of female criminals. *Journal of Psychiatric Research*, 1979, 15, 107–125.

673. Mize, J. M., Callaway, B., & Smith, J. W. Comparison of reading disabled children's scores on the WISC-R, Peabody Picture Vocabulary Test, and Slosson Intelligence Test. *Psychology in the Schools*, 1979, 16, 356–358.

674. Monson, L. B., Greenspan, S., & Simeonsson, R. J. Correlates of social competence in retarded children. *American Journal of Mental Deficiency*, 1979, 83, 627–630.

675. Moore, C. L., & Burns, W. J. The performance of neurologically impaired and normal Ss on four screening techniques. *Journal of Clinical Psychology*, 1979, 35, 420–424.

676. Murray, J. D. Spontaneous private speech and performance on a delayed match–to–sample task. *Journal of Experimental Child Psychology*, 1979, 27, 286–302.

677. Myers, B., & Goldstein, D. Cognitive development in bilingual and monolingual lower–class children. *Psychology in the Schools*, 1979, 16, 137–142.

678. Needleman, H. L., Gunnoe, C., Leviton, A., Reed, R., Peresie, H., Maher, C., & Barrett, P. Deficits in psychologic and classroom performance of children with elevated dentine lead levels. *New England Journal of Medicine*, 1979, 300, 689–695.

679. Panunto, B., & White, D. Achievement and the prediction of achievement in English first and second language children. *Alberta Journal of Educational Research*, 1979, 25, 61–67.

680. Powazek, M., & Billmeier, G. J., Jr. Assessment of intellectual development after surgery for craniofacial dysostosis. *American Journal of Diseases of Children*, 1979, 133, 151–153.

681. Prior, M. R., & Bradshaw, J. L. Hemisphere functioning in autistic children. *Cortex*, 1979, 15, 73–81.

682. Prior, M. R., & Hall, L. C. Comprehension of transitive and intransitive phrases by autistic, retarded, and normal children. *Journal of Communication Disorders*, 1979, 12, 103–111.

683. Richman, L. C. Language variables related to reading ability of children with verbal deficits. *Psychology in the Schools*, 1979, 16, 299–305.

684. Ritterman, S. I., Ford, M. A., & Zenner, A. A. Influence of social reinforcement and syntactic cues on the PPVT. *ASHA*, 1979, 21, 686. (Abstract)

685. Shankweiler, D., Liberman, I. Y., Mark, L. S., Fowler, C. A., & Fischer, F. W. The speech code and learning to read. *Journal of Experimental Psychology: Human Learning and Memory*, 1979, 5, 531–545.

686. Silvern, L. E., Waterman, J. M., Sobesky, W., & Ryan, V. L. Effects of a developmental model of perspective taking training. *Child Development*, 1979, 50, 243–246.

687. Smith, M., III, Johnston, D. R., & Coop, R. H. The acquisition of dimensional and expressive terms in young children. *Child Study Journal*, 1979, 9, 239–249.

688. Stone, N. W., & Levin, H. S. Neuropsychological testing of developmentally delayed young children: Problems and progress. *Journal of Learning Disabilities*, 1979, 12, 271–274.

689. Stratford, B. Attraction to "good form" in Down's Syndrome. *Journal of Mental Deficiency Research*, 1979, 23, 243–251.

690. Stratford, B. Discrimination of size, form, and order in Mongol and other mentally handicapped children. *Journal of Mental Deficiency Research*, 1979, 23, 45–53.

691. Taylor, R. L. Comparison of the McCarthy Scales of Children's Abilities and the Peabody Picture Vocabulary Test. *Psychological Reports*, 1979, 45, 196–198.

692. Tobey, E. A., Cullen, J. K., Jr., Rampp, D. L., & Fleischer-Gallagher, A. M. Effects of stimulus–onset asynchrony on the dichotic performance of children with auditory–processing disorders. *Journal of Speech & Hearing Research*, 1979, 22, 197–211.

[1771] *Peabody Picture Vocabulary Test-Revised

693. TOMLINSON-KEASEY, C., & KELLY, R. R. Is hemispheric specialization important to scholastic achievement? *Cortex*, 1979, 15, 97–107.

694. TOMLINSON-KEASEY, C., & KELLY, R. R. A task analysis of hemispheric functioning. *Neuropsychologia*, 1979, 17, 345–351.

695. TOWER, R. B., SINGER, D. G., SINGER, J. L., & BIGGS, A. Differential effects of television programming on preschooler's cognition, imagination, and social play. *American Journal of Orthopsychiatry*, 1979, 49, 265–281.

696. TREPANIER, M. L., & LIBEN, L. S. The operative basis of performance on Piagetian memory tasks: Evidence from normal and learning disabled children. *Developmental Psychology*, 1979, 15, 668–669.

697. VANCE, H. B., LEWIS, R., & DEBELL, S. Correlations of the Wechsler Intelligence Scale for Children–Revised, Peabody Picture Vocabulary Test, and Slosson Intelligence Test for a group of learning disabled students. *Psychology in the Schools*, 1979, 44, 735–738.

698. VANCE, H. B., & SINGER, M. G. Correlations between the Quick Test Forms 1 and 3 and Peabody Picture Vocabulary Test for children and youth with learning problems. *Psychological Reports*, 1979, 44, 315–318.

699. VENHAM, L. L., MURRAY, P., & GAULIN-KREMER, E. Personality factors affecting the preschool child's response to dental stress. *Journal of Dental Research*, 1979, 58, 2046–2051.

700. WALDEN, J. A comparison of the PIAT and WRAT: A closer look. *Psychology in the Schools*, 1979, 16, 342–346.

701. WALKER, B. B., & SANDMAN, C. A. Influences of an analog of the neuropeptide ACTH 4–9 on mentally retarded adults. *American Journal of Mental Deficiency*, 1979, 83, 346–352.

702. WALTERS, J. Strategies for requesting in Spanish and English. *Language Learning*, 1979, 29, 277–293.

703. WARRINGTON, E., & SHALLICE, T. Semantic access dyslexia. *Brain*, 1979, 102, 43–63.

704. WATSON, J. S., HAYES, L. A., & VIETZI, P. Bidimensional sorting in preschoolers with an instrumental learning task. *Child Development*, 1979, 50, 1178–1183.

705. WEBSTER, R. E. Visual and aural short–term memory capacity deficits in mathematics disabled students. *Journal of Educational Research*, 1979, 72, 276–283.

706. WESTBY, C. E. Language performance of stuttering and nonstuttering children. *Journal of Communication Disorders*, 1979, 12, 133–145.

707. WHALEN, C. K., HENKER, B., COLLINS, B. E., McAULIFFE, S., & VAUX, A. Peer interaction in a structured communication task: Comparisons of normal and hyperactive boys and of methyphenidate (Ritalin) and placebo effects. *Child Development*, 1979, 50, 388–401.

708. WHITE, M. A first–grade intervention program for children at risk for reading failure. *Journal of Learning Disabilities*, 1979, 12, 231–237.

709. WHITE, M., BATINI, P., SATZ, P., & FRIEL, J. Predictive validity of a screening battery for children "at risk" for reading failure. *British Journal of Educational Psychology*, 1979, 49, 132–137.

710. ZABEL, R. H. Recognition of emotions in facial expressions by emotionally disturbed and nondisturbed children. *Psychology in the Schools*, 1979, 16, 119–126.

711. AYRES, A. J., & TICKLE, L. S. Hyper–responsivity to touch and vestibular stimuli as a predictor of positive response to sensory integration procedures by autistic children. *American Journal of Occupational Therapy*, 1980, 34, 375–381.

712. BERLER, E. S., & ROMANCZYK, R. G. Assessment of the learning disabled and hyperactive child: An analysis and critique. *Journal of Learning Disabilities*, 1980, 13, 10–12.

713. BLANCHARD, J. S. Preliminary investigation of transfer between single–word decoding ability and contextual reading comprehension by poor readers in grade six. *Perceptual & Motor Skills*, 1980, 51, 1271–1281.

714. BROWN, R. T. Locus of control and its relationship to intelligence and achievement. *Psychological Reports*, 1980, 46, 1249–1250.

715. BRUMBACK, R. A., JACKOWAY, M. L., & WEINBERG, W. A. Relation of intelligence to childhood depression in children referred to an educational diagnostic center. *Perceptual & Motor Skills*, 1980, 50, 11–17.

716. CANNING, P. M., ORR, R., & ROURKE, B. P. Sex differences in perceptual, visual–motor, linguistic and concept–formation abilities of retarded readers? *Journal of Learning Disabilities*, 1980, 13, 37–41.

717. CANTWELL, D. P., BAKER, L., & MATTISON, R. E. Psychiatric disorders in children with speech and language retardation. *Archives of General Psychiatry*, 1980, 37, 423–426.

718. CHAVEZ, E. L., & GONZALES-SINGH, E. Hispanic assessment: A case study. *Professional Psychology*, 1980, 11, 163–168.

719. COLARUSSO, R., GILL, S., PLANKENHORN, A., & BROOKS, R. Predicting first–grade achievement through formal testing of 5–year–old high–risk children. *Journal of Special Education*, 1980, 14, 355–363.

720. COLEMAN, M., BROWN, G., & GANONG, L. A comparison of PPVT and SIT scores of young children. *Psychology in the Schools*, 1980, 17, 178–180.

721. CONWAY, D., LYTTON, H., & PYSH, F. Twin–singleton language differences. *Canadian Journal of Behavioural Science*, 1980, 12, 264–271.

722. CROFOOT, M. J., & BENNETT, T. S. A comparison of three screening tests and the WISC–R in special education evaluations. *Psychology in the Schools*, 1980, 17, 474–478.

723. CULL, J. G., & HARDY, R. E. Comparison of expressive and receptive measures of intelligence. *Journal of Psychology*, 1980, 105, 211–213.

724. DE FILIPPIS, N. A., & DERBY, R. Application of predictive measures of reading disability in a culturally disadvantaged sample. *Journal of Learning Disabilities*, 1980, 13, 51–53.

725. DOYLE, A. B., RAPPARD, P., & CONNOLLY, J. Two solitudes in the preschool classroom. *Canadian Journal of Behavioural Science*, 1980, 12, 221–232.

726. ENRIGHT, R. D., FRANKLIN, C. C., & MANHEIM, L. A. Children's distributive justice reasoning: A standardized and objective scale. *Developmental Psychology*, 1980, 16, 193–202.

727. FARLEY, F. H., & REYNOLDS, V. J. Arousal and cognition: Picture vocabulary performance and individual differences in physiological arousal. *Perceptual & Motor Skills*, 1980, 50, 579–582.

728. FERRARI, M. Comparisons of the Peabody Picture Vocabulary Test and the McCarthy Scales of Children's Abilities with a sample of autistic children. *Psychology in the Schools*, 1980, 17, 466–469.

729. FIELDS, T. A., & ASHMORE, L. L. Effect of elicitation variables on analysis of language samples for normal and language–disordered children. *Perceptual & Motor Skills*, 1980, 50, 911–919.

730. FINKELSTEIN, N. W., & RAMEY, C. T. Information from birth certificates as a risk index for educational handicap. *American Journal of Mental Deficiency*, 1980, 84, 546–552.

731. FOX, R., & ROTATORI, A. F. Incidental learning in mildly retarded children. *Journal of General Psychology*, 1980, 102, 121–125.

732. FULLER, G. B., & LOVINGER, S. L. Personality characteristics of three sub–groups of children with reading disabilities. *Perceptual & Motor Skills*, 1980, 50, 303–308.

733. GRIFFITH, P. L., & ROBINSON, J. H. Influence of iconicity and phonological similarity on sign learning by mentally retarded children. *American Journal of Mental Deficiency*, 1980, 85, 291–298.

734. HATANO, G., MIYAKE, K., & TAJIMA, N. Mother behavior in an unstructured situation and child's acquisition of number conservation. *Child Development*, 1980, 51, 379–385.

735. HEDGE, M. N. An experimental–clinical analysis of grammatical and behavioral distinctions between verbal auxiliary and copula. *Journal of Speech & Hearing Research*, 1980, 23, 864–877.

736. HODAPP, A. F., & HODAPP, J. Correlation of PPVT and WISC–R: A function of diagnostic category. *Psychology in the Schools*, 1980, 17, 33–36.

737. HULIT, L. M., HOWARD, M. R., & FOSTER, S. K. Effects of delay interval and pictorial cues on a sentence imitation task. *Perceptual & Motor Skills*, 1980, 51, 91–100.

738. HUNT, J. M., & PARASKEVOPOULOS, J. Children's psychological development as a function of the inaccuracy of their mothers' knowledge of their abilities. *Journal of Genetic Psychology*, 1980, 136, 285–298.

739. JOHNSON, F. L. Communicative purpose in children's referential language. *Communication Monographs*, 1980, 47, 46–55.

740. JORDON, L. S. Receptive and expressive language problems occurring in combination with a seizure disorder: A case report. *Journal of Communication Disorders*, 1980, 13, 295–303.

741. KLEECK, A. V., & CARPENTER, R. L. The effects of children's language comprehension level on adults' child–directed talk. *Journal of Speech & Hearing Research*, 1980, 23, 546–569.

742. KRAMER, M. S., ROOKS, Y., WASHINGTON, L. A., & PEARSON, H. A. Pre– and postnatal growth and development in sickle cell anemia. *Journal of Pediatrics*, 1980, 96, 857–860.

743. LEEPER, H. A., Jr., PANNBACKER, M., & ROGINSKI, J. Oral language characteristics of adult cleft–palate speakers compared on the basis of cleft type and sex. *Journal of Communication Disorders*, 1980, 13, 133–146.

744. MARBACH, E. S., & YAWKEY, T. D. The effect of imaginative play actions on language development in five–year old children. *Psychology in the Schools*, 1980, 17, 257–263.

745. MARGOLIS, H., LEONARD, H. S. BRANNIGAN, G. G., & HEVERLY, M. A. The validity of form F of the Matching Familiar Figures Test with kindergarten children. *Journal of Experimental Child Psychology*, 1980, 29, 12–22.

746. MEDWAY, F. J., & EGELSON, R. Teacher ratings of internal and external students in open and traditional class environments. *Psychology in the Schools*, 1980, 17, 390–395.

747. MUSSELWHITE, C. R., ST. LOUIS, K. O., & PENICK, P. B. A communicative interaction analysis system for language–disordered children. *Journal of Communication Disorders*, 1980, 13, 315–324.

748. PHILLIPS, D. A., & ZIGLER, E. Children's self–image disparity: Effects of age, socioeconomic status, ethnicity, and gender. *Journal of Personality & Social Psychology*, 1980, 39, 689–700.

749. POLK, C. L. H., & GOLDENSTEIN, D. Early reading and concrete operations. *Journal of Psychology*, 1980, 106, 111–116.

750. POWELL, B. J., PENICK, E. C., & READ, M. R. Psychological adjustment and sex–role affiliation in an alcoholic population. *Journal of Clinical Psychology*, 1980, 36, 801–805.

751. PRIOR, M., & McGILLIVRAY, J. The performance of autistic children on three learning set tasks. *Journal of Child Psychology & Psychiatry & Allied Disciplines*, 1980, 21, 313–323.

752. RAPOPORT, J. L., BUCHSBAUM, M. S., WEINGARTNER, H., ZAHN, T. P., LUDLOW, C., & MIKKELSEN, E. J. Dextroamphetamine: Its cognitive and behavioral effects in normal and hyperactive boys and normal men. *Archives of General Psychiatry*, 1980, 37, 933–943.

753. SAFFRAN, E. M. Reading in deep dyslexia in not ideographic. *Neuropsychologia*, 1980, 18, 219–223.

754. SATTLER, J. M., AVILA, V., HOUSTON, W. B., & TONEY, D. H. Performance of bilingual Mexican–American children on Spanish and English versions of the Peabody Picture Vocabulary Test. *Journal of Consulting & Clinical Psychology*, 1980, 48, 782–784.

755. SATTLER, J. M., BOHANAN, A. L., & MOORE, M. K. Relationship between PPVT and WISC–R in children with reading disabilities. *Psychology in the Schools*, 1980, 17, 331–334.

756. SCARLETT, W. G. Social isolation from agemates among nursery school children. *Journal of Child Psychology & Psychiatry & Allied Disciplines*, 1980, 21, 231–240.

757. SCHULTZ, C. L., & NYSTUL, M. S. Mother–child interaction behavior as an outcome of theoretical models of parent group education. *Journal of Individual Psychology*, 1980, 36, 3–15.

758. SINGER, D. G., & SINGER, J. L. Television viewing and aggressive behavior in preschool children: A field study. *Annals of the New York Academy of Science*, 1980, 347, 289–303.

759. SMITH, A. N., & SPENCE, C. M. National day care study: Optimizing the day care environment. *American Journal of Orthopsychiatry*, 1980, 50, 718–721.

760. SMITH, T. P., & RIBORDY, S. C. Correlates of reflection–impulsivity in kindergarten males: Intelligence, socioeconomic status, race, father's absence, and teachers' ratings. *Psychological Reports*, 1980, 47, 1187–1191.

761. SPACE, L. G., & CROMWELL, R. L. Personal constructs among depressed patients. *Journal of Nervous & Mental Disease*, 1980, 168, 150–158.

762. SPARKS, S., & HUTCHINSON, B. Cri Du Chat: Report of a case. *Journal of Communication Disorders*, 1980, 13, 9–13.

763. STIPEK, D. A causal analysis of the relationship between locus of control and academic achievement in first grade. *Contemporary Educational Psychology*, 1980, 5, 90–99.

764. TESKA, J. A., & STONEBURNER, R. L. The concept and practice of second–level screening. *Psychology in the Schools*, 1980, 17, 192–195.

765. TOWER, R. B. Parents' self-concepts and preschool children's behaviors. *Journal of Personality & Social Psychology*, 1980, 39, 710–718.

766. VRANA, F., & PIHL, R. O. Selective attention deficit in learning disabled children: A cognitive interpretation. *Journal of Learning Disabilities*, 1980, 13, 42–45.

767. WHALEY, W. J., & KIBBY, M. W. Word synthesis and beginning reading achievement. *Journal of Educational Research*, 1980, 73, 132–138.

768. WILIMAS, J., GOFF, J. R., ANDERSON, H. R., JR., LANGSTON, J. W., & THOMPSON, E. Efficacy of transfusion therapy for one to two years in patients with sickle cell disease and cerebrovascular accidents. *Journal of Pediatrics*, 1980, 96, 205–208.

769. WILSON, R. S., KASZNIAK, A. W., KLAWANS, H. L., & GARRON, D. C. High speed memory scanning in Parkinsonism. *Cortex*, 1980, 16, 67–72.

770. ZOREF, L., & WILLIAMS, P. A look at content bias in IQ tests. *Journal of Educational Measurement*, 1980, 17, 313–322.

771. ALLINGTON, R. L. Sensitivity to orthographic structure in educable mentally retarded children. *Contemporary Educational Psychology*, 1981, 6, 135–139.

772. BRACKEN, B. A., & PRASSE, D. P. Comparison of the PPVT, PPVT–R, and intelligence tests used for the placement of black, white and hispanic EMR students. *Journal of School Psychology*, 1981, 19, 304–311.

773. CAMPBELL, A. L., JR., BOGEN, J. E., & SMITH, A. Disorganization and reorganization to cognitive and sensorimotor functions in cerebral commissurotomy: Compensatory roles of the forebrain commissures and cerebral hemispheres in man. *Brain*, 1981, 104, 493–511.

774. CHAMPION, D. W., LOWE, R. C., & CAVIOR, N. Egocentrism in elementary school children: Validity and application of assessment techniques. *Psychological Reports*, 1981, 48, 27–34.

775. CHAPMAN, D. L., & NATION, J. E. Patterns of language performance in educable mentally retarded children. *Journal of Communication Disorders*, 1981, 14, 245–254.

776. CLARK, C. R. Learning words using traditional orthography and the symbols of rebus, bliss, and carrier. *Journal of Speech & Hearing Disorders*, 1981, 46, 191–196.

777. COHEN, R., WOLL, G., & EHRENSTEIN, W. H. Recognition deficits resulting from focused attention in aphasia. *Psychological Research*, 1981, 43, 391–405.

778. ELFENBEIN, J. L., WAZIRI, M., & MORRIS, H. L. Verbal communication skills of six children with craniofacial anomalies. *Cleft Palate Journal*, 1981, 18, 59–64.

779. ELLIOTT, D. Visual and kinesthetic memory and integration of mentally retarded and nonretarded adults. *American Journal of Mental Deficiency*, 1981, 86, 194–200.

780. FASH, D. S., & MADISON, C. L. Parents' language interaction with young children: A comparative study of mothers' and fathers'. *Child Study Journal*, 1981, 11, 137–153.

781. FAY, W. H., & ANDERSON, D. E. Children's echo–reactions as a function of increasing lexical difficulty: A developmental study. *Journal of Genetic Psychology*, 1981, 138, 259–267.

782. FURLONG, M. J. Torque: An at-risk indicator of reading or behavior problems? *Journal of Clinical Child Psychology*, 1981, 10, 165–167.

783. GOODMAN, N., & ANDREWS, J. Cognitive development of children in family and group day care. *American Journal of Orthopsychiatry*, 1981, 51, 271–284.

784. GURALNICK, M. J. The social behavior of preschool children at different developmental levels: Effects of group composition. *Journal of Experimental Child Psychology*, 1981, 31, 115–130.

785. JOHNSTON, C. W., & PIROZZOLO, F. J. Eye movements and cognitive strategies. *Perceptual & Motor Skills*, 1981, 53, 623–632.

786. KEISER, H., MONTAGUE, J., WOLD, D., MAUNE, S., & PATTISON, D. Hearing loss of Down Syndrome adults. *American Journal of Mental Deficiency*, 1981, 85, 467–472.

787. KOOTZ, J. P., MARINELLI, B., & COHEN, D. J. Sensory receptor sensitivity in autistic children. *Archives of General Psychiatry*, 1981, 38, 271–273.

788. KORNSE, D. D., MANNI, J. L., RUBENSTEIN, H., & GRAZIANI, L. J. Developmental apraxia of speech and manual dexterity. *Journal of Communication Disorders*, 1981, 14, 321–330.

789. KRAMER, J. J., & ENGLE, R. W. Teaching awareness of strategic behavior in combination with strategy training: Effects on children's memory performance. *Journal of Experimental Child Psychology*, 1981, 32, 513–530.

790. LAYTON, T. L., & HARDY, C. A. Semantic–syntactic relations in the oral speech of an autistic adolescent. *Journal of General Psychology*, 1981, 105, 323–324.

791. LICHTENSTEIN, R. Comparative validity of two preschool screening tests: Correlational and classification approaches. *Journal of Learning Disabilities*, 1981, 14, 68–72.

792. McREYNOLDS, L. V., & ELBERT, M. Criteria for phonological process analysis. *Journal of Speech & Hearing Disorders*, 1981, 46, 197–204.

793. MEADE, E. R. Impulse control and cognitive functioning in lower– and middle–SES children: A developmental study. *Merrill–Palmer Quarterly*, 1981, 27, 271–285.

794. MELNICK, C. R., MICHALS, K. K., & MATALON, R. Linguistic development of children with phenylketonuria and normal intelligence. *Journal of Pediatrics*, 1981, 98, 269–272.

795. MERITS–PATTERSON, R., & REED, C. G. Disfluencies in the speech of language–delayed children. *Journal of Speech & Hearing Research*, 1981, 24, 55–58.

796. MILLER, J. W., & McKENNA, M. C. Disabled readers: Their intellectual and perceptual capacities at differing ages. *Perceptual & Motor Skills*, 1981, 52, 467–472.

797. NORRIS, M., & HARDEN, J. Natural processes in the phonologies of four error–rate groups. *Journal of Communication Disorders*, 1981, 14, 195–213.

798. OWENS, A., & BEATTY–DESANA, J. Communication functioning in trisomy 9p. *Journal of Communication Disorders*, 1981, 14, 113–122.

799. PEARL, R., DONAHUE, M., & BRYAN, T. Children's responses to nonexplicit requests for clarification. *Perceptual & Motor Skills*, 1981, 53, 919–925.

800. PETERS, R. D., & DAVIES, K. Effects of self–instruction training on cognitive impulsivity of mentally retarded adolescents. *American Journal of Mental Deficiency*, 1981, 85, 377–382.

801. POLLITT, E., LEIBEL, R. L., & GREENFIELD, D. Brief fasting, stress, and cognition in children. *American Journal of Clinical Nutrition*, 1981, 34, 1526–1533.

802. POWELL, G., MOORE, D., & CALLAWAY, B. A concurrent validity study of the Woodcock Word Comprehension Test. *Psychology in the Schools*, 1981, 18, 24–27.

803. RUBENSTEIN, J. L., HOWES, C., & BOYLE, P. A two-year follow-up of infants in community–based day care. *Journal of Child Psychology & Psychiatry & Allied Disciplines*, 1981, 22, 209–218.

804. RYCKMAN, D. B. Reading achievement, IQ, and simultaneous–successive processing among normal and learning–disabled children. *Alberta Journal of Educational Research*, 1981, 27, 74–83.

805. SEMEL, E. M., & WIIG, E. H. Semel Auditory Processing Program: Training effects among children with language–learning disabilities. *Journal of Learning Disabilities*, 1981, 14, 192–196.

806. SHALLICE, T. Phonological agraphia and the lexical route in writing. *Brain*, 1981, 104, 413–429.

807. SNOWLING, M. J. Phonemic deficits in developmental dyslexia. *Psychological Research*, 1981, 43, 219–234.
808. SNOWLING, M., & FRITH, U. The role of sound, shape and orthographic cues in early reading. *British Journal of Psychology*, 1981, 72, 83–87.
809. STATON, R. D., & BRUMBACK, R. A. Non-specificity of motor hyperactivity as a diagnostic criterion. *Perceptual & Motor Skills*, 1981, 52, 323–332.
810. STIPEK, D. J., LAMB, M. E., & ZIGLER, E. F. OPTI: A measure of children's optimism. *Educational & Psychological Measurement*, 1981, 41, 131–143.
811. STRANGE, W., & BROEN, P. A. The relationship between perception and production of /w/, /r/, and /l/ by three-year-old children. *Journal of Experimental Psychology*, 1981, 31, 81–102.
812. TUNMER, W. E., & FLETCHER, C. M. The relationship between conceptual tempo, phonological awareness, and word recognition in beginning readers. *Journal of Reading Behavior*, 1981, 13, 173–185.
813. WARRINGTON, E. K. Concrete word dyslexia. *British Journal of Psychology*, 1981, 72, 175–196.
814. WATTERS, R. G., WHEELER, L. J., & WATTERS, W. E. The relative efficiency of two orders for training autistic children in the expressive and receptive use of manual signs. *Journal of Communication Disorders*, 1981, 14, 273–285.
815. WETHERBY, A. M., KOEGEL, R. L., & MENDEL, M. Central auditory nervous system dysfunction in echolalic autistic individuals. *Journal of Speech & Hearing Research*, 1981, 24, 420–429.

[1772]

★Peek-a-Boo Test. Ages 3–6 and children not yet able to read; 1975; visual ability; 9 non-language tests in 6 areas: acuity, vertical eye coordination, lateral eye coordination, fusion, depth perception, color discrimination; Patricia J. Hill; Keystone View.

[1773]

★Peer Attitudes Toward the Handicapped Scale. Grades 4–8; 1981; PATHS; self-report assessment technique; 3 subscales: physical, learning, behavioral, plus total score; Michael T. Bagley and John F. Greene; PRO-ED.*

[1774]

Pennsylvania Bi-Manual Worksample. Ages 16 and over; 1943–45; 2 scores: assembly, disassembly; John R. Roberts; American Guidance Service.*

See T2:2231 (8 references); for reviews by Edwin E. Ghiselli, Thomas W. Harrell, Albert Gibson Packard, and Neil D. Warren, see 3:665 (3 references).

REFERENCES

1–3. See 3:665.
4–11. See T2:2231.
12. ZAIDEL, D., & SPERRY, R. W. Some long-term motor effects of cerebral commissurotomy in man. *Neuropsychologia*, 1977, 6, 193–204.

[1775]

Per-Flu-Dex Tests. College and industry; 1955; 7 tests; Frank J. Holmes; Psychometric Affiliates.*
a) PER-SYMB TEST. Symbol number substitution.
b) PER-VERB TEST. Letter perception and counting.
c) PER-NUMB TEST. Number counting and perception.
d) FLU-VERB TEST. Word completion and verbal fluency.
e) FLU-NUMB TEST. Arithmetic computation.
f) THE DEX-MAN SCALE. Manual speed of movement.
g) DEX-AIM TEST. Aiming accuracy and speed.
See T2:2286 (2 references); for reviews by Andrew L. Comrey and John W. French, see 5:901.

[1776]

Perception of Values Inventory. Grades kgn–3, 4–12 and adults; 1973–74; 8 scores (affection, respect, skill, enlightenment, power/influence, wealth, well-being, rectitude/responsibility) in each of 3 areas (attitude toward others, toward self, from others); 2 levels; Bert K. Simpson, Lida C. Colwell (*a*), and Louise B. Taylor (*a*); Carney, Weedman and Associates.*
a) ME AND YOU INVENTORY. Grades kgn–3; 1974; MYI.
b) PERCEPTION OF VALUES INVENTORY. Grades 4–12 and adults; 1973; PVI.

For additional information and a review by John R. Braun, see 8:640 (1 reference).

[1777]

Perceptual Battery. Job applicants with at least 10 years of education; 1961–63; spatial relations; National Institute for Personnel Research [South Africa].*

For additional information, see 7:1055.

[1778]

★The Perceptual Maze Test. Ages 6–16, adults; 1955–78; PMT; brain damage; Alick Elithorn, Janice Smith (manual), and David Jones (manual); Medical Research Council [England].*
a) NEUROPSYCHIATRIC SETS A + B. Ages 8 through adults; 1978.
b) GROUP VERSION A + B. Ages 8 through adults; 1960.
c) CHILDREN'S VERSION. Ages 6–16; 1969.
d) STANDARD SETS. Ages 8 through adult; 1968.

See T2:1311 (1 reference); for reviews by Manfred J. Meier and Aubrey J. Yates of an earlier edition, see 7:120 (3 references); see also P:190A (23 references).

[1779]

Perceptual Motor Test. Grades 1–3; 1972–73; "developed initially to predict potential learning problems of children entering the first grade and to diagnose deficiencies in children manifesting learning difficulties in the primary grades"; 2 scores (reading potential, writing potential) based on 9 subtest scores: posture, flexibility, balance, awareness, bilaterality, unilaterality, crosslaterality, hand-eye-foot preference, eye control; Paul Smith; Educational Activities, Inc.* (In-print status uncertain; no reply from publisher.)

For additional information and reviews by Richard E. Darnell and James A. Rice, see 8:880.

REFERENCES

1. BOYD, M. A., WOOD, W. W., & CONRY, R. F. Prediction of preclinical operative dentistry performance in two instructional methods. *Journal of Dental Education*, 1980, 44, 328–331.
2. KRESS, G. C., JR., & DOGON, I. L. A correlational study of preadmission predictor variables and dental school performance. *Journal of Dental Education*, 1981, 45, 207–210.

[1780]

Perceptual Speed (Identical Forms). Grades 9–16 and industrial employees; 1956–66; L. L. Thurstone (test), T. E. Jeffrey (test), and Norman J. Kantor (manual); Human Resources Center, University of Chicago.*

See T2:570 (2 references) and 7:444 (2 references); for a review by Leroy Wolins, see 6:556.

[1781]

★Performance Assessment in Reading. Junior high school students; 1978–79; PAIR; Reading Support Services Center of the Los Angeles Unified School District; CTB/McGraw-Hill.*

[1782]
[Performance Review Forms]. Employees, managers; 1960–61; 2 forms; Seymour Levy; Martin M. Bruce, Ph.D., Publishers.*
a) EMPLOYEE PERFORMANCE APPRAISAL. Employees, managers; 1960; for summarizing a performance review interview; 2 editions: forms for employees, managers.
b) MANAGERIAL PERFORMANCE REVIEW. Managers; 1961; ratings by supervisors preparatory to performance review interview.

For additional information, see 6:1125.

[1783]
Personal Adjustment Index: ETSA Test 8A. Job applicants; 1960–73, c1957–59; revision of *Personal Adjustability Test*; 8 scores: community spirit, attitude toward cooperation, attitude toward health, attitude toward authority, nervous tendencies, leadership, job stability, total; manual and technical handbook by S. Trevor Hadley and George A. W. Stouffer, Jr.; test by Psychological Services Bureau; Educators'-Employers' Tests & Services Associates.*

For reviews of the complete battery, see 6:1025 (2 reviews).

[1784]
Personal Audit. Grades 9–16 and adults; 1941–45; PA; emotional adjustment; 2 editions; Clifford R. Adams and William M. Lepley; Science Research Associates, Inc.*
a) FORM SS (SHORT FORM). 6 scores: seriousness, firmness, frankness, tranquility, stability, tolerance.
b) FORM LL (LONG FORM). 9 scores: 6 scores same as for short form plus steadiness, persistence, contentment.

See T2:1314 (4 references) and P:192 (6 references); for a review by William Seeman, see 4:75 (3 references); for a review by Percival M. Symonds, see 3:64 (10 references).

[1785]
★Personal Background Inventory. Job applicants; 1973–78; PBI; 10 scores: group participation and school achievement, drive, mobility, financial responsibility, family responsibility, job and personal stability, educational-vocational consistency, parental family adjustment, parental success in education and employment, health; Melany E. Baehr and Frances M. Burns (inventory), Robert E. Penny III (manual); Human Resources Center, University of Chicago.*

[1786]
★Personal Career Development Profile. Ages 16 and over; 1949–79; PCDP; computer-interpreted report of the *Sixteen Personality Factor Questionnaire*; profile divided into 8 sections: overview, problem solving patterns, patterns for coping with stressful conditions, patterns of interpersonal interaction, patterns for career-occupational-avocational interests, personal-career development considerations, 50 occupational comparisons, test data for professional use only; Verne Walter; Institute for Personality and Ability Testing, Inc.*

[1787]
★Personal Distress Inventory and Scales. Psychiatric patients and normal adults; 1978; PDIS; 4 tests; Alan Bedford and Graham Foulds; NFER-Nelson Publishing Co. [England].*
a) DELUSIONS-SYMPTOMS-STATES INVENTORY. DSSI; 84 items divided into 4 classes containing 12 sets: dysthymic states (anxiety, depression, elation), neurotic symptoms (conversion, dissociative, phobic, compulsive, ruminative), integrated delusions (persecution, grandeur, contrition), delusions of disintegration (disintegration).
b) DELUSIONS-SYMPTOMS-STATES INVENTORY/STATE OF ANXIETY AND DEPRESSION. DSSI/sAD; consists of the 7 state of anxiety and 7 state of depression items from the DSSI.
c) DELUSIONS-SYMPTOMS-STATES INVENTORY/NEUROTIC SYMPTOMS. DSSI/NS; authors recommend use with DSSI/sAD for populations where delusional items are inappropriate; consists of the 5 sets of neurotic symptoms (35 items) from the full DSSI.
d) PERSONALITY DEVIANCE SCALE. PDS; derived from the *Hostility-Direction of Hostility Questionnaire*; 3 scales consisting of 2 subscales each: extrapunitive (hostile thoughts, denigratory attitudes), intropunitive (lack of self-confidence, over-dependency on others), dominance (domineering social attitude, uninhibited hostile acts).

[1788]
Personal History Index. Job applicants; 1963–67; PHI; for research use only; 8 scores: school achievement, higher educational achievement, drive, leadership and group participation, financial responsibility, early family responsibility, parental family adjustment, stability; Melany E. Baehr, Robert K. Burns, and Robert N. McMurry; Human Resources Center, University of Chicago.*

For additional information and a review by John K. Hemphill, see 7:981 (5 references).

[1789]
Personal Orientation Inventory. Grades 9–16 and adults; 1962–68; POI; 12 scores: time competence, inner directed, self-actualizing value, existentiality, feeling reactivity, spontaneity, self regard, self acceptance, nature of man, synergy, acceptance of aggression, capacity for intimate contact; Everett L. Shostrom; EdITS/Educational and Industrial Testing Service.*

For additional information and an excerpted review by Donald J. Tosi and Cathy A. Lindamood, see 8:641 (433 references); see also T2:1315 (80 references); for reviews by Bruce Bloxom and Richard W. Coan, see 7:121 (97 references); see also P:193 (26 references).

REFERENCES

1–26. See P:193.
27–123. See 7:121.
124–203. See T2:1315.
204–636. See 8:641.
637. BUHMEYER, K. J., & JOHNSON, A. H. Personality profiles of physician extenders. *Psychological Reports*, 1977, 40, 655–662.
638. CARLOCK, C. J., & MARTIN, P. Y. Sex composition and the intensive group experience. *Social Work*, 1977, 22, 27–32.
639. FARRELL, M., HALEY, M., & MAGNASCO, J. Teaching interpersonal skills. *Nursing Outlook*, 1977, 25, 322–325.
640. FISCHER, J., & KNAPP, R. R. The validity of the Personal Orientation Inventory for measuring the effects of training for therapeutic practice. *Educational & Psychological Measurement*, 1977, 37, 1069–1074.
641. FOULDS, M. L., & HANNIGAN, P. S. Gestalt workshops and measured changes in self–actualization: Replication and refinement study. *Journal of College Student Personnel*, 1977, 18, 200–205.
642. KELLEY, V. R., KELLEY, P. L., GAURON, E. F., & RAWLINGS, E. I. Training helpers in rural mental health delivery. *Social Work*, 1977, 22, 229–231.

643. KENNEDY, E. C., HECKLER, V. J., KOBLER, F. J., & WALKER, R. E. Clinical assessment of a profession: Roman Catholic clergymen. *Journal of Clinical Psychology*, 1977, 33, 120–128.
644. KNICKERBOCKER, B., & DAVIDSHOFER, C. Attitudinal outcomes of the life planning workshop. *Journal of Counseling Psychology*, 1977, 25, 103–109.
645. LESTER, D., & COLVIN, L. M. Fear of death, alienation, and self-actualization. *Psychological Reports*, 1977, 41, 526.
646. MARTIN, J. D., & MARTIN, E. M. The relationship of the Purpose in Life (PIL) Test to the Personal Orientation Inventory (POI), the Otis-Lennon Mental Ability Test scores, and grade point averages of high school students. *Educational & Psychological Measurement*, 1977, 37, 1103–1105.
647. NEVILL, D. D. Sex roles and personality correlates. *Human Relations*, 1977, 30, 751–759.
648. NIESZ, N. L. Periodicity and self-actualization in women. *Journal of Clinical Psychology*, 1977, 33, 1014–1017.
649. NOLL, R. L., WILLOWER, D. J., & BARNETTE, J. J. Teacher self-actualization and pupil control ideology-behavior consistency. *Alberta Journal of Educational Research*, 1977, 23, 65–70.
650. OTTEN, M. W. Sex differences on the Personal Orientation Inventory. *Journal of Personality Assessment*, 1977, 41, 63–65.
651. SCHAFER, W. D., & JONES, J. R. A modified split–half approach to internal consistency estimates for the Personal Orientation Inventory. *Psychological Reports*, 1977, 41, 1020–1022.
652. SHERIDAN, E. P., & MELHUS, G. E. A programmed personal growth laboratory. *Psychological Reports*, 1977, 41, 143–150.
653. TWEMLOW, S. W., & BOWEN, W. T. Sociocultural predictors of self-actualization in EEG–biofeedback–treated alcoholics. *Psychological Reports*, 1977, 40, 591–598.
654. WEBER, C. R. A comparison of values clarification and lecture-discussion methods in teaching college health science. *College Student Journal*, 1977, 11, 98–104.
655. WEISS, K. L. Two media programs for mature women students. *Journal of College Student Personnel*, 1977, 18, 527–528.
656. WILKINS, W. E., HJELLE, L. A., & THOMPSON, M. Anxiety and actualization: A reconceptualization. *Journal of Clinical Psychology*, 1977, 33, 1001–1005.
657. WISE, G. W. The Personal Orientation Inventory: A study of internal consistency. *Psychological Reports*, 1977, 40, 1000–1002.
658. YONGE, G. D. Instructional artifacts on personality inventories. *Psychological Reports*, 1977, 40, 899–903.
659. BUHMEYER, K. J. Selection and attrition profiles of physician-extender students. *Psychological Reports*, 1978, 43, 1009–1010.
660. BUHMEYER, K. J., & JOHNSON, A. H. Predicting success in a physician–extender training program. *Psychological Reports*, 1978, 42, 507–513.
661. DIETCH, J. Love, sex roles, and psychological health. *Journal of Personality Assessment*, 1978, 42, 626–634.
662. DODS, L. Y., & TREPPA, J. A. Contrasting personality profiles of male and female medical students. *Journal of Psychology*, 1978, 98, 3–10.
663. DRENNEN, W., & CHERMOL, B. Relaxation and placebo-suggestion as uncontrolled variables in TM research. *Journal of Humanistic Psychology*, 1978, 18, 89–93.
664. ESPOSITO, R. P., McADOO, H., & SCHER, L. The Johari window test: A research note. *Journal of Humanistic Psychology*, 1978, 18, 79–81.
665. HIX, J. A., & HENSLEY, J. H. Sensitivity of the POI to instructional set in military and college populations. *Measurement & Evaluation in Guidance*, 1978, 11, 117–122.
666. HOGAN, H. W., & McWILLIAMS, J. M. Factors related to self-actualization. *Journal of Psychology*, 1978, 100, 117–122.
667. HUSA, H. F. Self-actualization in an educational psychology course for college freshman honors students. *Psychological Reports*, 1978, 42, 1333–1334.
668. KARLE, W., HART, J., CORRIERE, R., GOLD, S., & MAPLE, C. Preliminary study of psychological changes in feeling study. *Psychological Reports*, 1978, 43, 1327–1334.
669. KAY, E., LYONS, A., NEWMAN, W., & MANKIN, D. A test–retest study of the Personal Orientation Inventory. *Journal of Humanistic Psychology*, 1978, 18, 87–89.
670. KIDD, N. V., & HUDSON, G. R. Single–sex counseling groups and mini courses for women students. *Journal of College Student Personnel*, 1978, 19, 483–488.
671. KIMLICKA, T. M., & CROSS, H. J. A comparison of chronic versus casual marijuana users on personal values and behavioral orientations. *International Journal of the Addictions*, 1978, 13, 1145–1156.
672. KNAPP, R. R., CARDENAS, C., & MICHAEL, W. B. Cross–cultural validation of the effects of dissimulation on a measure of actualizing. *Educational & Psychological Measurement*, 1978, 38, 1157–1163.
673. KNAPP, R. R., & KNAPP, L. Conceptual and statistical refinement and extension of the measurement of the Personal Orientation Dimensions. *Educational & Psychological Measurement*, 1978, 38, 523–526.
674. LAMBERT, M. J., SEGGER, J. F., STALEY, J. S., SPENCER, B., & NELSON, D. Reported self-concept and self-actualizing value changes as a function of academic classes with wilderness experience. *Perceptual & Motor Skills*, 1978, 46, 1035–1040.
675. LUCAS, L. F., & TSUJIMOTO, R. N. Self–actualization and moral judgment. *Psychological Reports*, 1978, 43, 838.
676. MACVANE, J. R., LANGE, J. D., BROWN, W. A., & ZAYAT, M. Psychological functioning of bipolar manic–depressives in remission. *Archives of General Psychiatry*, 1978, 35, 1351–1354.
677. MATHES, E. W. Self–actualization, metavalues, and creativity. *Psychological Reports*, 1978, 43, 215–222.
678. MATHES, E. W., & EDWARDS, L. L. An empirical test of Maslow's theory of motivation. *Journal of Humanistic Psychology*, 1978, 18, 75–77.
679. OAKLAND, J. A., FREED, F., LOVEKIN, A., DAVIS, J. P., JR., & CAMILLERI, R. A critique of Shostrom's Personal Orientation Inventory. *Journal of Humanistic Psychology*, 1978, 18, 75–85.
680. POLLAK, J. M. Relationships between psychoanalytic personality pattern, death anxiety, and self–actualization. *Perceptual & Motor Skills*, 1978, 46, 846.
681. RICHARDS, W. A. Mystical and archetypal experiences of terminal patients in DPT–assisted psychotherapy. *Journal of Religion & Health*, 1978, 17, 117–126.
682. SCROGGINS, W. F., & IVEY, A. E. Teaching and maintaining microcounseling skills with a residence hall staff. *Journal of College Student Personnel*, 1978, 19, 158–162.
683. SOBOL, E. G. Self–actualization and the baccalaureate nursing student's response to stress. *Nursing Research*, 1978, 27, 238–244.
684. TAYLOR, I. A. Characteristics of "creative leaders". *Journal of Creative Behavior*, 1978, 12, 221–222. (Abstract)
685. TOSI, D. J., & ESHBAUGH, D. M. A cognitive–experiential approach to the interpersonal and intrapersonal development of counselors and therapists. *Journal of Clinical Psychology*, 1978, 34, 494–500.
686. TRAVIS, C. B., & ANTHONY, S. E. Some psychological consequences of integration. *Journal of Negro Education*, 1978, 47, 151–158.
687. TREPPA, J. A., & DODS, L. Y. Some personality correlates of the A–B Therapist Scale for male and female students. *Journal of Clinical Psychology*, 1978, 34, 519–522.
688. WEHLER, R., & HOFFMANN, H. Personal Orientation Inventory scores of female alcoholism counselors before and after training. *Psychological Reports*, 1978, 43, 500–502.
689. WILKINS, W. E., & KRAUSS, H. H. Anxiety and actualization: Further research. *Journal of Clinical Psychology*, 1978, 34, 958–960.
690. DRENNEN, W., & PUGH, M. The use of a contract to facilitate sensitivity training. *Journal of Humanistic Psychology*, 1979, 19, 77–84.
691. GREENBERG, L. S., & CLARKE, K. M. Differential effects of the two-chair experiment and empathic reflections at a conflict marker. *Journal of Counseling Psychology*, 1979, 26, 1–8.
692. HAMPTON, J. D., & KERASOTES, D.L. Faculty level of self-actualization in relation to student rating of instructors. *Educational & Psychological Measurement*, 1979, 39, 971–975.
693. HATTIE, J. Stability of results across many studies: Sex differences on the Personal Orientation Inventory. *Journal of Personality Assessment*, 1979, 43, 627–628.
694. HYMAN, R. B. Construct validity of Shostrom's Personal Orientation Inventory: A systematic summary. *Measurement & Evaluation in Guidance*, 1979, 12, 174–184.
695. JOHNSON, S., & JOHNSON, N. Effects of various group approaches on self-actualization of graduate counseling students. *Journal of Counseling Psychology*, 1979, 26, 444–447.
696. KING, M. Parental self-actualization and children's self-concept. *Psychological Reports*, 1979, 44, 80–82.
697. KIPP, D. J. The Personal Orientation Inventory: A predictive device for resident advisors. *Journal of College Student Personnel*, 1979, 20, 382–384.
698. McWILLIAMS, S. A. Effects of reciprocal peer counseling on college student personality development. *Journal of the American College Health Association*, 1979, 27, 210–213.
699. MORRIS, G. B. Teachers' attitudes in relation to rational–emotive and self-actualization theories. *Psychological Reports*, 1979, 44, 229–230.
700. PARITAKY, R., & MAGOON, T. Human potential seminar outcomes as measured by the Personal Orientation Inventory and goal attainment inventories. *Journal of Counseling Psychology*, 1979, 26, 30–36.
701. PETEROY, E. T. Effects of member and leader expectations on group outcome. *Journal of Counseling Psychology*, 1979, 26, 534–537.
702. ROBBINS, A. S., KRAUSS, D. R., HEINRICH, R., ABRASS, I., DREYER, J., & CLYMAN, B. Interpersonal skills training: Evaluation in an internal medicine residency. *Journal of Medical Education*, 1979, 54, 885–894.
703. ROLL, W. G., SOLFVIN, G. F., & KRIEGER, J. Meditation and ESP: An overview of four studies. *Journal of Parapsychology*, 1979, 43, 44–45.
704. SCHROEDER, J. J., & KOBLER, F. J. Power holders in the church: A psychological profile of Catholic bishops in the United States. *Journal of Clinical Psychology*, 1979, 35, 713–719.

705. SHEPARD, L. A. Self-acceptance: The evaluative component of the self-concept construct. *American Educational Research Journal*, 1979, 16, 139-160.
706. SKOLNICK, N. J., & ZUCKERMAN, M. Personality change in drug abusers: A comparison of therapeutic community and prison groups. *Journal of Consulting & Clinical Psychology*, 1979, 47, 768-770.
707. CRANDALL, J. E. Adler's concept of social interest: Theory, measurement, and implications for adjustment. *Journal of Personality & Social Psychology*, 1980, 39, 481-495.
708. CROSS, D. G., SHEEHAN, P. W., & KHAN, J. A. Alternative advice and counsel in psychotherapy. *Journal of Consulting & Clinical Psychology*, 1980, 48, 615-625.
709. DEMING, A. L. Self-actualization level as a predictor of practicum supervision effectiveness. *Journal of Counseling Psychology*, 1980, 27, 213-216.
710. FOREST, J., & SICZ, G. Data discrepancies in the Personal Orientation Inventory manual. *Journal of Personality Assessment*, 1980, 44, 538-540.
711. FOREST, J., & SICZ, G. Subjects' perceived difficulties in the Personal Orientation Inventory. *Perceptual & Motor Skills*, 1980, 51, 986.
712. GOLDSTEIN, J. O. Comparison of graduating AD and baccalaureate nursing students' characteristics. *Nursing Research*, 1980, 29, 46-49.
713. KARLE, W., CORRIERE, R., HART, J., & WOLDENBERG, L. The functional analysis of dreams: A new theory of dreaming. *Journal of Clinical Psychology*, 1980, 36, 43-47.
714. KUIKEN, D., & POWELL, R. Spatio-temporal displacement and expression of feeling in dreams of emotionally expressive persons. *Perceptual & Motor Skills*, 1980, 51, 455-461.
715. LEWANDOWSKI, L. A., & KRAMER, M. Role transformation of special care unit nurses: A comparative study. *Nursing Research*, 1980, 29, 170-179.
716. MONTI, P. M., CURRAN, J. P., CORRIVEAU, D. P., DELANCEY, A. L., & HAGERMAN, S. M. Effects of social skills training groups and sensitivity training groups with psychiatric patients. *Journal of Consulting & Clinical Psychology*, 1980, 48, 241-248.
717. MURPHY, T. J. The relationship between self-actualization and adjustment among American Catholic priests. *Educational & Psychological Measurement*, 1980, 40, 457-461.
718. OCLATIS, K. A., & STINER, A. Relationship between patients' in-process evaluations of therapy and psychotherapy outcome. *Journal of Clinical Psychology*, 1980, 36, 259-264.
719. PANZARELLA, R. The phenomenology of aesthetic peak experiences. *Journal of Humanistic Psychology*, 1980, 20, 69-85.
720. SHADISH, W. R., JR. Nonverbal interventions in clinical groups. *Journal of Consulting & Clinical Psychology*, 1980, 48, 164-168.
721. SHUGER, D., & DEBOUT, J. Contrasts in Gestalt and analytic therapy. *Journal of Humanistic Psychology*, 1980, 20, 21-39.
722. SICZ, G., & FOREST, J. Norms for the Personal Orientation Inventory profile sheet. *Psychological Reports*, 1980, 46, 376-378.
723. STONES, C. R. A Jesus community in South Africa: Self-actualization or need for security. *Psychological Reports*, 1980, 46, 287-290.
724. CROSS, D. G., SHEEHAN, P. W., & KHAN, J. A. In defense of alternative advice and counsel and the ways in which it can be researched. *Journal of Consulting & Clinical Psychology*, 1981, 49, 734-737.
725. GODDARD, R. C. Increase in assertiveness and actualization as a function of didactic training. *Journal of Counseling Psychology*, 1981, 28, 279-287.
726. GOLDMAN, J. A., & OLCZAK, P. V. Effect of test sensitization and knowledge about self-actualization on taking the Personal Orientation Survey. *Educational & Psychological Measurement*, 1981, 41, 49-53.
727. HATTIE, J. A four-stage factor analytic approach to studying behavioral domains. *Applied Psychological Measurement*, 1981, 5, 77-88.
728. HENINGTON, M. Effect of intensive multicultural, non-sexist instruction on secondary student teachers. *Educational Research Quarterly*, 1981, 6, 65-75.
729. JOHNSON, G. B. A prediction of student teacher evaluation. *College Student Journal*, 1981, 15, 299-303.
730. MARTIN, J. D., BLAIR, G. E., & CASH, M. Correlation of the self-actualizing value subscale of the Personal Orientation Inventory with the self-acceptance, socialization, and self-control scales of the California Psychological Inventory. *Educational & Psychological Measurement*, 1981, 41, 589-593.
731. MARTIN, J. D., BLAIR, G. E., RUDOLPH, L. B., & MELMAN, B. S. Intercorrelations among scale scores of the Personal Orientation Inventory for nursing students. *Psychological Reports*, 1981, 48, 199-202.
732. NYSTUL, M. The effects of birth order and family size on self-actualization. *Journal of Individual Psychology*, 1981, 37, 107-112.
733. OSBORNE, J. W., & STEEVES, L. Relation between self-actualization, neuroticism and extraversion. *Perceptual & Motor Skills*, 1981, 53, 996-998.
734. REKER, G. T., & PEACOCK, E. J. The Life Attitude Profile (LAP): A multidimensional instrument for assessing attitudes toward life. *Canadian Journal of Behavioural Science*, 1981, 13, 264-273.

[1790]

The Personal Preference Scale. Ages 15 and over; 1947-54; PPS; 10 scores: active-inactive, sociable-individualistic, permissive-critical, consistent-inconsistent, efficient-inefficient, self effacing-egocentric, masculine-effeminoid, feminine-masculinoid, emotionally mature-emotionally immature, socially mature-socially immature; Maurice H. Krout and Johanna Krout; [Johanna Krout Tabin].*

See T2:1316 (2 references), P:194 (5 references), and 5:93 (2 references).

REFERENCES

1-2. See 5:93.
3-7. See P:194.
8-9. See T2:1316.
10. SWANSON, G. E. Travels through inner space: Family structure and openness to absorbing experiences. *American Journal of Sociology*, 1978, 83, 890-919.

[1791]

★**Personal Questionnaire Rapid Scaling Technique.** Adolescents and adults; 1977-80; PQRST; designed to monitor fluctuations in feelings, beliefs, and symptoms; David J. Mulhall; NFER-Nelson Publishing Co. [England].*

[1792]

★**Personal Relations Inventory.** High school and over; 1980; PRI; measures 4 types of assertiveness and includes a scale consisting of Crowne-Marlowe Social Desirability items (1960); 5 scale scores: defense of rights, social assertiveness, directiveness, independence, approval seeking; Maurice Lorr and William W. More; Maurice Lorr.*

[1793]

★**The Personal Sphere Model.** Adolescents and adults; 1978; PSM; projective measure of "libidinal attachments"; 18 scores: 7 impressionistic evaluations and 11 measurable variables; Raoul A. Schmiedeck; Grune & Stratton, Inc.*

[1794]

Personal Values Inventory. Grades 12-13; 1941-69; PVI; for predicting academic achievement; 12 scores: high school self report, need for achievement, direction of aspirations, socioeconomic status, peer influence, home influence, planning, persistence, self control, total of persistence and self control, faking, self insight; separate editions for men and women; George E. Schlesser, John A. Finger, and Thomas Lynch (manual); Colgate University Testing Service.*

See T2:1318 (3 references); for reviews by Henry A. Alker and Robert R. Knapp, see 7:122 (2 references); see also P:195 (15 references).

REFERENCES

1-15. See P:195.
16-17. See 7:122.
18-20. See T2:1318.
21. DEBOER, G. E. The direct and indirect contributions of a series of intellective and non-intellective student attributes to the prediction of high school and college achievement: A path analytic model. *Educational & Psychological Measurement*, 1981, 41, 487-494.

[1795]

The Personality Inventory. Grades 9-16 and adults; 1931-38; PI, also BPI; commonly called *Bernreuter*

[1796] ★Personality Inventory for Children

Personality Inventory; 6 scores: neurotic tendency, self-sufficiency, introversion-extroversion, dominance-submission, confidence, sociability; Robert G. Bernreuter; Consulting Psychologists Press, Inc.*

See T2:1320 (124 references) and P:198 (20 references); for reviews by Wesley C. Becker and Donald J. Veldman, see 6:157 (22 references); see also 5:95 (39 references); for a review by Leona E. Tyler, see 4:77 (188 references); for reviews by Charles I. Mosier and Theodore Newcomb, see 2:1239 (71 references).

[1796]

★**Personality Inventory for Children.** Ages 3–16; 1977; PIC; 33 scores: 1 screening scale (adjustment), 3 validity scales [lie, F (identifies deviant response sets), defensiveness], 12 clinical scales: achievement, intellectual screening, development, somatic concern, depression, family relations, delinquency, withdrawal, anxiety, psychosis, hyperactivity, social skills, plus 17 experimental scales: adolescent maladjustment, aggression, asocial, cerebral dysfunction, delinquency prediction, ego strength, excitement, externalization, internalization, infrequency, introversion-extroversion, K (identifies denial of symptoms), learning disabilities prediction, reality distortion, sex role, social desirability, somatization; Robert D. Wirt, Philip D. Seat, David Lachar (manual), James K. Klinedinst (manual), and William E. Broen (test); Western Psychological Services.*

REFERENCES

1. LACHAR, D., BUTKUS, M., & HRYHORCZUK, L. Objective personality assessment of children: An exploratory study of the Personality Inventory for Children (PIC) in a child psychiatric setting. *Journal of Personality Assessment*, 1978, 42, 529–537.
2. DEHORN, A. B., LACHAR, D., & GDOWSKI, C. L. Profile classification strategies for the Personality Inventory for Children. *Journal of Consulting & Clinical Psychology*, 1979, 47, 874–881.
3. LACHAR, D., & GDOWSKI, C. L. Problem–behavior factor correlates of Personality Inventory for Children profile scales. *Journal of Consulting & Clinical Psychology*, 1979, 47, 39–48.
4. KURDEK, L. A. Developmental relations among childrens' perspective taking, moral judgment, and parent–rated behaviors. *Merrill-Palmer Quarterly*, 1980, 26, 103–121.
5. BENNETT, T. S., & WELSH, M. C. Validity of a configural interpretation of the intellectual screening and achievement scales of the Personality Inventory for Children. *Educational & Psychological Measurement*, 1981, 41, 863–868.

[1797]

Personality Rating Scale. Grades 4–12; 1944–62; PRS; identical with *Child Personality Scale* ('51) except for format; originally called *22-Trait Personality Rating Scale*; modification for use with children of E. Lowell Kelly's *36-Trait Personality Rating Scale*; ratings by classmates and teachers or self-ratings; 22 ratings: pep, intelligence, sociability, nervousness-calmness, popularity, religiousness, punctuality, courtesy, cooperation, generosity, persistence, honesty, neatness, patience, interests, disposition, good sport, boisterous-quiet, entertaining, thoughtfulness, sense of humor, dependability; S. Mary Amatora; Educators'-Employers' Tests & Services Associates.*

See T2:1321 (2 references) and P:199; for a review by Laurance F. Shaffer, see 6:158 (4 references); for reviews by Robert H. Bauernfeind and Dale B. Harris, see 5:41 (18 references).

[1798]

Personality Research Form. Grades 7–16 and adults, college; 1965–74; PRF; 3 editions; Douglas N. Jackson; Research Psychologists Press, Inc.*

a) STANDARD EDITION. College; 1965–68; 15 scores: achievement, affiliation, aggression, autonomy, dominance, endurance, exhibition, harm avoidance, impulsivity, nurturance, order, play, social recognition, understanding, infrequency.

b) LONG EDITION. College; 1965–67; 22 scores: same as for Standard Edition plus abasement, change, cognitive structure, defendence, sentience, succorance, desirability; contains the 300 items of the Standard Edition plus 140 additional items intermixed.

c) WIDE RANGE FORM. Grades 7–16 and adults; 1974; test booklet title is *PRF-Form E*; 22 scores: same as for Long Edition.

For additional information and a review by Robert Hogan, see 8:643 (132 references); see also T2:1322 (23 references); for reviews by Anne Anastasi, E. Lowell Kelly, and Jerry S. Wiggins, and excerpted reviews by John O. Crites, Lonnie D. Valentine, Jr., and Ruth Wessler with Jane Loevinger of *a* and *b*, see 7:123 (27 references); see also P:201 (13 references).

REFERENCES

1–13. See P:201.
14–40. See 7:123.
41–63. See T2:1322.
64–195. See 8:643.
196. BARNSTEIN, P. H., CARMODY, T. P., RELINGER, H., ZOHN, C. J., DEVINE, D. A., & BUGGE, I. D. Reduction of smoking behavior: A multivariable treatment package and the programming of response maintenance. *Psychological Record*, 1977, 27, 733–741.
197. BEJAR, I. I. An application of the continuous response level model to personality measurement. *Applied Psychological Measurement*, 1977, 1, 509–521.
198. BONYNGE, E. R., & HOFFMAN, H. Personality measurements in selection of applicants for an alcohol counselor training program. *Psychological Reports*, 1977, 41, 493–494.
199. BRADLEY, G., & BRADLEY, L. A. Experimenter prestige and feedback related to acceptance of genuine personality interpretations and self-attitude. *Journal of Personality Assessment*, 1977, 41, 178–185.
200. DIAS, S., & CARIFO, J. A note on sex differences in achievement motivation. *Educational & Psychological Measurement*, 1977, 37, 513–517.
201. DIAZ-GUERRERO, R. A Mexican psychology. *American Psychologist*, 1977, 32, 934–944.
202. GAYTON, W. F., HAVU, G. F., OZMON, K. L., & TAVORMINA, J. A comparison of the Bem Sex Role Inventory and the PRF ANDRO Scale. *Journal of Personality Assessment*, 1977, 41, 619–621.
203. GOLDBERG, L. R. What if we administered the "wrong" inventory? The prediction of scores on the Personality Research Form scales from those on the California Psychological Inventory and vice versa. *Applied Psychological Measurement*, 1977, 1, 339–354.
204. HARPER, F. B. W. Practice teaching performance and resultant achievement motivation. *Alberta Journal of Educational Research*, 1977, 23, 104–108.
205. HELMES, E., & JACKSON, D. N. The item factor structure of the Personality Research Form. *Applied Psychological Measurement*, 1977, 1, 185–194.
206. HELMES, E., REED, P. L., & JACKSON, D. N. Desirability and frequency scale values and endorsement proportions for items of Personality Research Form–E. *Psychological Reports*, 1977, 41, 435–444.
207. HESS, A. K., & NEVILLE, D. Testwiseness: Some evidence for the effect of personality testing on subsequent test results. *Journal of Personality Assessment*, 1977, 41, 170–177.
208. HUBA, G. J., SEGAL, B., & SINGER, J. L. Organization of needs in male and female drug and alcohol users. *Journal of Consulting & Clinical Psychology*, 1977, 45, 34–44.
209. KUNCEL, R. B. Ordering items by endorsement value and its effect upon test validity. *Educational & Psychological Measurement*, 1977, 37, 897–905.
210. KUNCEL, R. B. The subject–item interaction in itemmetric research. *Educational & Psychological Measurement*, 1977, 37, 665–678.
211. LAMONT, L. M., & LUNDSTROM, W. J. Identifying successful industrial salesmen by personality and personal characteristics. *Journal of Marketing Research*, 1977 14, 517–529.
212. LONG, G. T., CALHOUN, L. G., & SELBY, J. W. Personality characteristics related to cross–situational consistency of interpersonal distance. *Journal of Personality Assessment*, 1977, 41, 274–278.

213. LORR, M., O'CONNOR, J. P., & SEIFERT, R. F. A comparison of four personality inventories. *Journal of Personality Assessment*, 1977, 41, 520–526.

214. LORR, M., & SEIFERT, R. F. First-order factor structure of the Personality Research Form. *Journal of Personality Assessment*, 1977, 41, 270–273.

215. MEHRABIAN, A. Individual differences in stimulus screening and arousability. *Journal of Personality*, 1977, 45, 237–250.

216. MEYER, J. P., & PEPPER, S. Need compatibility and marital adjustment in young married couples. *Journal of Personality & Social Psychology*, 1977, 35, 331–342.

217. PIHL, R. O., & SPIERS, P. Some personality differences among the multidisciplinary team. *Journal of Clinical Psychology*, 1977, 33, 269–272.

218. RANDOLPH, D. L., CASTON, E. E., & WRIGHT, J. Prediction of job satisfaction of psychologists via personality tests. *Southern Journal of Educational Research*, 1977, 11, 229–239.

219. ROGERS, T. B., KUIPER, N. A., & KIRKER, W. S. Self-reference and the encoding of personal information. *Journal of Personality & Social Psychology*, 1977, 35, 677–688.

220. SANDERS, J. L. Personality correlates of the abstract response on the Holtzman Inkblot Technique. *Journal of Personality Assessment*, 1977, 41, 349–350.

221. SCHNEIDER, F. W., & GREEN, J. E. Need for affiliation and sex as moderators of the relationship between need for achievement and academic performance. *Journal of School Psychology*, 1977, 15, 269–277.

222. SKINNER, H. A., & JACKSON, D. N. The missing person in personnel classification: A tale of two models. *Canadian Journal of Behavioural Science*, 1977, 9, 147–160.

223. SNYDER, C. R., & FROMKIN, H. L. Abnormality as a positive characteristic: The development and validation of a scale measuring need for uniqueness. *Journal of Abnormal Psychology*, 1977, 86, 518–527.

224. STEERS, R. M. Individual differences in participative decision-making. *Human Relations*, 1977, 30, 837–847.

225. STONE, E. F., MOWDAY, R. T., & PORTER, L. W. High order need strengths as moderators of the job scope–job satisfaction relationship. *Journal of Applied Psychology*, 1977, 62, 466–471.

226. WEIKEL, W. J., & LOESCH, L. C. Cognitive correlates of counsellor trainees' needs awareness. *Canadian Counsellor*, 1977, 11, 128–130.

227. WORELL, J., & WORELL, L. Support and opposition to the women's liberation movement: Some personality and parental correlates. *Journal of Research in Personality*, 1977, 11, 10–20.

228. BARNES, D. F., & BERZINS, J. I. A and B undergraduate interviewers of schizophrenic and neurotic inpatients: A test of the interaction hypothesis. *Journal of Consulting & Clinical Psychology*, 1978, 46, 1368–1373.

229. BERZINS, J. I., WELLING, M. A., & WETTER, R. E. A new measure of psychological androgyny based on the Personality Research Form. *Journal of Consulting & Clinical Psychology*, 1978, 46, 126–138.

230. BLOOM, L. J., SHELTON, J. L., & MICHAELS, A. C. Dysmenorrhea and personality. *Journal of Personality Assessment*, 1978, 42, 272–276.

231. CAHILL, M. C., & BELFER, P. L. Word association times, felt effects, and personality characteristics of science students given a placebo energizer. *Psychological Reports*, 1978, 42, 231–238.

232. CHAPMAN, L. J., CHAPMAN, J. P., & RAULIN, M. L. Body image aberration in schizophrenia. *Journal of Abnormal Psychology*, 1978, 87, 399–407.

233. CRAWFORD, J. Interactions of learner characteristics with the difficulty level of the instruction. *Journal of Educational Psychology*, 1978, 70, 523–531.

234. DAVIDSON, W. B., & HOUSE, W. J. Influence of reflection-impulsivity and cognitive style on time estimation under different ambient conditions. *Perceptual & Motor Skills*, 1978, 46, 1083–1091.

235. DAVIDSON, W. B., & HOUSE, W. J. On the relationship between reflection–impulsivity and field–dependence–independence. *Perceptual & Motor Skills*, 1978, 47, 306.

236. DIENER, E., & DEFOUR, D. Does television violence enhance program popularity? *Journal of Personality & Social Psychology*, 1978, 36, 333–341.

237. DWORKIN, R. H., & KIHLSTROM, J. F. An S–R Inventory of Dominance for research on the nature of person–situation interactions. *Journal of Personality*, 1978, 46, 43–56.

238. HERBERT, G. R. A comparative analysis of personality characteristics of industrial arts teachers in the United States. *Journal of Industrial Teacher Education*, 1978, 16, 33–44.

239. KELLY, J. A., FURMAN, W., & YOUNG, V. Problems associated with the typological measurement of sex roles and androgyny. *Journal of Consulting & Clinical Psychology*, 1978, 46, 1574–1576.

240. KELLY, J. A., & WORELL, L. Personality characteristics, parent behaviors, and sex of subject in relation to cheating. *Journal of Research in Personality*, 1978, 12, 179–188.

241. KONDO, C. Y., POWELL, B. J., & PENICK, E. C. Clinical correlates of the PRF androgyny scale in an alcoholic population. *Journal of Personality Assessment*, 1978, 42, 611–612.

242. LEENAARS, A. A., BRINGMANN, W. G., & BALANCE, W. D. G. The effects of positive vs negative wording on subjects' validity ratings of "true" and "false" feedback statements. *Journal of Clinical Psychology*, 1978, 34, 369–370.

243. MEHRABIAN, A. Measures of individual differences in temperament. *Educational & Psychological Measurement*, 1978, 38, 1105–1117.

244. MEHRABIAN, A., & BANK, L. A questionnaire measure of individual differences in achieving tendency. *Educational & Psychological Measurement*, 1978, 38, 475–478.

245. MORF, M. E., & KRANE, W. R. A topology of test–takers based on true responding and item endorsement. *Psychological Reports*, 1978, 43, 531–537.

246. WEINSTEIN, N. D. Individual differences in reactions to noise: A longitudinal study in a college dormitory. *Journal of Applied Psychology*, 1978, 63, 458–466.

247. ANOLIK, S. A. Personality, family, educational, and criminological characteristics of bright delinquents. *Psychological Reports*, 1979, 44, 727–734.

248. ANTILL, J. K., & CUNNINGHAM, J. D. Self-esteem as a function of masculinity in both sexes. *Journal of Consulting & Clinical Psychology*, 1979, 47, 783–785.

249. BARNES, G. E. The alcoholic personality: A reanalysis of the literature. *Journal of Studies on Alcohol*, 1979, 40, 571–634.

250. BARNETT, L. R., & NIETZEL, M. T. Relationship of instrumental and affectional behaviors and self–esteem to marital satisfaction in distressed and nondistressed couples. *Journal of Consulting & Clinical Psychology*, 1979, 47, 946–957.

251. BATES, J. E., FREELAND, C. A. B., & LOUNSBURY, M. L. Measurement of infant difficultness. *Child Development*, 1979, 50, 794–803.

252. BURSTEIN, A. G., LOUCKS, S., KOBOS, J. C., & STANTON, B. Psychological characteristics of medical students and residents. *Journal of Medical Education*, 1979, 54, 56–58.

253. CLINGMAN, J. M., MCALLISTER, S., & LUSHENE, R. L. Some psychological correlates of hemophilia. *Journal of Personality Assessment*, 1979, 43, 629–632.

254. CREALOCK, C. The influence of "fear of success" and "need for achievement" on the vocational aspirations of male and female high school students. *Canadian Counsellor*, 1979, 14, 32–35.

255. GREEN, S. B., BURKHART, B. R., & HARRISON, W. H. Personality correlates of self-report, role–playing, and in vivo measures of assertiveness. *Journal of Consulting & Clinical Psychology*, 1979, 47, 16–24.

256. HOLDEN, R. R., & JACKSON, D. N. Item subtlety and face validity in personality assessment. *Journal of Consulting & Clinical Psychology*, 1979, 47, 459–468.

257. JACKSON, D. N., CHAN, D. W., & STRICKER, L. J. Implicit personality theory: Is it illusory? *Journal of Personality*, 1979, 47, 1–10.

258. KOBASA, S. C. Stressful life events, personality, and health: An inquiry into hardiness. *Journal of Personality & Social Psychology*, 1979, 37, 1–11.

259. KUIPER, N. A., & ROGERS, T. B. Encoding of personal information: Self–other differences. *Journal of Personality & Social Psychology*, 1979, 37, 499–514.

260. LOUCKS, S., KOBOS, J. C., STANTON, B., BURSTEIN, A. G., & LAWLIS, G. F. Sex-related psychological characteristics of medical students. *Journal of Psychology*, 1979, 102, 119–123.

261. MOWDAY, R. T., STONE, E. F., & PORTER, L. W. The interaction of personality and job scope in predicting turnover. *Journal of Vocational Behavior*, 1979, 15, 78–89.

262. MUCOWSKI, R. J. A typology of occupational patterns of Roman Catholic religious priests in mid–life. *Counseling & Values*, 1979, 24, 16–24.

263. MUNGAS, D. M., TRONTEL, E. H., WINEGARDNER, J., BROWN, D. S., SWEENEY, T. M., & WALTERS, H. A. The Personality Research Form as a therapy outcome measure of social behavior. *Journal of Clinical Psychology*, 1979, 35, 822–832.

264. MUNGAS, D. M., & WALTERS, H. A. Pretesting effects in the evaluation of social skills training. *Journal of Consulting & Clinical Psychology*, 1979, 47, 216–218.

265. PAUNONEN, S. V., & JACKSON, D. N. Nonverbal trait interference. *Journal of Personality & Social Psychology*, 1979, 37, 1645–1659.

266. PUTNAM, L. L. Preference for procedural order in task–oriented small groups. *Communication Monographs*, 1979, 46, 193–218.

267. ROGERS, T. B., KUIPER, N. A., & ROGERS, P. J. Symbolic distance and congruity effects for paired–comparisons judgments of degree of self-reference. *Journal of Research in Personality*, 1979, 13, 433–449.

268. STENN, P. G., MOTHERSILL, K. J., & BROOKE, R. I. Biofeedback and a cognitive behavioral approach to treatment of myofascial pain dysfunction syndrome. *Behavior Therapy*, 1979, 10, 29–36.

269. STONE, E. F., GANSTER, D. C., WOODMAN, R. W., & FUSILIER, M. R. Relationships between growth need strength and selected individual differences measures employed in job design research. *Journal of Vocational Behavior*, 1979, 14, 329–340.

270. VALE, D. W., & RIKER, H. C. Sex–role differences in student leadership training. *Journal of College Student Personnel,* 1979, 20, 58–62.
271. VAN TUINEN, M., & RAMARAIAH, N. V. A multimethod analysis of selected self-esteem measures. *Journal of Research in Personality,* 1979, 13, 16–24.
272. ANTILL, J. K., & CUNNINGHAM, J. D. The relationship of masculinity, femininity, and androgyny to self–esteem. *Australian Journal of Psychology,* 1980, 32, 195–207.
273. BRENNER, O. C., & TOMKIEWICZ, J. Relationship between aggression and managerial effectiveness. *Psychological Reports,* 1980, 47, 271–274.
274. BURSTEIN, A. G., LOUCKS, S., KOBOS, J., JOHNSON, G., TALBERT, R. L., & STANTON, B. A longitudinal study of personality characteristics on medical students. *Journal of Medical Education,* 1980, 55, 786–787.
275. BUSS, D. M., & CRAIK, K. H. The frequency concept of disposition: Dominance and prototypically dominant acts. *Journal of Personality,* 1980, 48, 379–392.
276. CLABBY, J. F., JR. The Wit: A personality analysis. *Journal of Personality Assessment,* 1980, 44, 307–310.
277. EGELAND, B., BREITENBUCHER, M., & ROSENBERG, D. Prospective study of the significance of life stress in the etiology of child abuse. *Journal of Consulting & Clinical Psychology,* 1980, 48, 195–205.
278. EPSTEIN, J., BERG–CROSS, G., & BERG–CROSS, L. Maternal expectations and birth order in families with learning disabled and normal children. *Journal of Learning Disabilities,* 1980, 13, 45–52.
279. FRIEDMAN, H. S., DiMATTEO, M. R., & TARANTA, A. A study of the relationship between individual differences in nonverbal expressiveness and factors of personality and social interaction. *Journal of Research in Personality,* 1980, 14, 351–364.
280. FRIEDMAN, H. S., PRINCE, L. M., RIGGIO, R. E., & DiMATTEO, M. R. Understanding and assessing nonverbal expressiveness: The affective communication test. *Journal of Personality & Social Psychology,* 1980, 39, 333–351.
281. HARRIS, J. G., JR. Nomovalidation and idiovalidation. A quest for the true personality profile. *American Psychologist,* 1980, 35, 729–744.
282. HIGHLEN, P. S., & RUSSELL, B. Effects of counselor gender and counselor and client sex role on females' counselor preference. *Journal of Counseling Psychology,* 1980, 27, 157–165.
283. HIRSCHBERG, N., & JENNINGS, S. J. Beliefs, personality, and person perception: A theory of individual differences. *Journal of Research in Personality,* 1980, 14, 235–249.
284. JACKSON, D. N., PEACOCK, A. C., & SMITH, J. P. Impressions of personality in the employment interview. *Journal of Personality & Social Psychology,* 1980, 39, 294–307.
285. KANTNER, J. E., & ELLERBUSCH, R. C. Androgyny and occupational choice. *Psychological Reports,* 1980, 47, 1289–1290.
286. KLOCKARS, A. J., & WALKUP, H. R. The PRF and peer ratings. *Educational & Psychological Measurement,* 1980, 40, 1099–1103.
287. MEHRABIAN, A., & O'REILLY, E. Analysis of personality measures in terms of basic dimensions of temperament. *Journal of Personality & Social Psychology,* 1980, 38, 492–503.
288. MILLER, W. R., TAYLOR, C. A., & WEST, J. C. Focused versus broad–spectrum behavior therapy for problem drinkers. *Journal of Consulting & Clinical Psychology,* 1980, 48, 590–601.
289. PENICK, E. C., POWELL, B. J., READ, M. R., & MAHONEY, D. Sex–role typing: A methodological note. *Psychological Reports,* 1980, 47, 143–146.
290. PIHL, R. O., & CARON, M. The relationship between geographic mobility, adjustment, and personality. *Journal of Clinical Psychology,* 1980, 36, 190–194.
291. POWELL, B. J., PENICK, E. C., & READ, M. R. Psychological adjustment and sex–role affiliation in an alcoholic population. *Journal of Clinical Psychology,* 1980, 36, 801–805.
292. RODRIGUEZ, R., NIETZEL, M. T., & BERZINS, J. I. Sex role orientation and assertiveness among female college students. *Behavior Therapy,* 1980, 11, 353–366.
293. ROTHSTEIN, M., & JACKSON, D. N. Decision making in the employment interview: An experimental approach. *Journal of Applied Psychology,* 1980, 65, 271–283.
294. SANDILANDS, M. L., & McMULLIN, J. A. Territorial marking and dominance: A field study in the halls of academia. *Psychological Reports,* 1980, 46, 1018.
295. SEGAL, B., HUBA, G. J., & SINGER, J. L. Reasons for drug and alcohol use by college students. *International Journal of the Addictions,* 1980, 15, 489–498.
296. SKINNER, H. A., & LEI, H. The multidimensional assessment of stressful life events. *Journal of Nervous & Mental Disease,* 1980, 168, 535–541.
297. STARK-ADAMEC, C., & PIHL, R. O. Personality and non–medical use of drugs. *Psychological Reports,* 1980, 46, 103–110.
298. VAUGHN, B., DEINARD, A., & EGELAND, B. Measuring temperament in pediatric practice. *Journal of Pediatrics,* 1980, 96, 510–514.

299. WEINBERGER, L. J., & BRADLEY, L. A. Effects of "favorability" and type of assessment device upon acceptance of general personality interpretations. *Journal of Personality Assessment,* 1980, 44, 44–47.
300. AUSTIN, M. F., & GRANT, T. N. Interview training for college students disadvantaged in the labor market: Comparison of five instructional techniques. *Journal of Counseling Psychology,* 1981, 28, 72–75.
301. BRUNNGUELL, D., CRICHTON, L., & EGELAND, B. Maternal personality and attitude in disturbances of child rearing. *American Journal of Orthopsychiatry,* 1981, 51, 680–691.
302. BUSS, D. M., & CRAIK, K. H. The act frequency analysis of interpersonal dispositions: Aloofness, gregariousness, dominance and submissiveness. *Journal of Personality,* 1981, 49, 175–192.
303. CARROLL, J. F. X., MALLOY, T. E., ROSCIOLI, D. L., & GODARD, D. R. Personality similarities and differences in four diagnostic groups of women alcoholics and drug addicts. *Journal of Studies on Alcohol,* 1981, 42, 432–440.
304. GELINEAU, E. P. A psychometric approach to the measurement of color preference. *Perceptual & Motor Skills,* 1981, 53, 163–174.
305. GIFFORD, R. Sociability: Traits, settings, and interactions. *Journal of Personality & Social Psychology,* 1981, 41, 340–347.
306. HOHN, R. L., DES LAURIERS, M., & DEATON, W. Learners' characteristics and performance effects in self–paced instruction. *Psychological Reports,* 1981, 40, 1011–1012.
307. MUNGAS, D. M., TRONTEL, E. H., & WINEGARDNER, J. Multivariable–multimethod analysis of the dimensions of interpersonal behavior. *Journal of Research in Personality,* 1981, 15, 107–121.
308. ORY, J. C., & POGGIO, J. P. Response–mode variation effects on affective measures. *Educational & Psychological Measurement,* 1981, 41, 625–634.
309. SKINNER, H. A. Comparison of clients assigned to in-patient and out-patient treatment for alcoholism and drug addiction. *British Journal of Psychiatry,* 1981, 138, 312–330.
310. SKINNER, H. A. Primary syndromes of alcohol abuse: Their measurement and correlates. *British Journal of Addiction,* 1981, 76, 63–76.
311. SOLOMON, M. J. Dimensions of interpersonal behavior: A convergent validation within a cognitive interactionist framework. *Journal of Personality,* 1981, 49, 15–26.

[1799]

[Personnel Interviewing Forms]. Business and industry; 1956; 4 forms; no manual; Judd-Safian Associates; Martin M. Bruce, Ph.D., Publishers.*

a) INITIAL INTERVIEW TABULATION. For recording ratings in 10 areas: appearance, voice and speech, poise, health, education, manner, responsiveness, experience, job stability, motivation.

b) PERSONAL HISTORY AUDIT. Job applicants.

c) DEPTH INTERVIEW PATTERN. For interviewing in 5 areas: work evaluation, educational and social evaluation, economic evaluation, personality evaluation, ambitions evaluation.

d) EMPLOYMENT REFERENCE INQUIRY. For securing employee evaluation from previous employers.

For additional information, see 6:1127.

[1800]

★**Personnel Performance Problems Inventory.** Management and administrative personnel; 1977–80; PPPI; delegation problems; 5 scores: responsibility, authority, accountability, results, conditions; Albert A. Canfield; Humanics Media.*

[1801]

Personnel Rating Scale. Employees; 1965–66; 11 ratings by supervisors: cooperativeness, quality of work, adaptability, dependability, emotional stability, quantity of work, sociability, persistence, initiative, work knowledge, overall; Psychological Publications Press.* (In-print status uncertain; no reply from publisher.)

For additional information, see 7:1071.

[1802]

The Personnel Reaction Blank, Revised Edition. Adults; 1954–72; PRB; worker dependability and conscientiousness; Harrison G. Gough; Consulting Psychologists Press, Inc.*

See T2:1323 (1 reference) and P:202.

[1803]

Personnel Relations Survey. Managers; 1967; 6 scores: exposure and feedback scores for each of 3 relationships (with colleagues, employees, and supervisors); Jay Hall and Martha S. Williams; Teleometrics Int'l.*

For additional information and a review by Robert M. Guion, see 8:1183 (3 references).

[1804]

Personnel Research Institute Classification Test. Adults; 1943–54; formerly called *Classification Test for Industrial and Office Personnel*; Jay L. Otis, Evelyn Katz (Form A), Robert W. Henderson (A), Mary Aiken (A), David J. Chesler (Form B), and Gardner E. Lindzey (B); Psychological Research Services.*

See T2:431 (1 reference); for reviews by James R. Glennon and Melvin R. Marks, see 6:484 (2 references). For reviews by Louise Witmer Cureton and Albert K. Kurtz of this and other tests in the *Personnel Research Institute Clerical Battery*, see 4:729.

[1805]

[Personnel Research Institute Clerical Battery]. Applicants for clerical positions; 1945–48; 7 tests; Psychological Research Services.*

a) NUMBER COMPARISON TEST FOR CLERICAL AND INDUSTRIAL INSPECTION OPERATIONS. 1945–46; Jay L. Otis and Louise W. Garman.
b) NAME COMPARISON TEST FOR CLERICAL AND INDUSTRIAL INSPECTION OPERATIONS. 1945–46; Jay L. Otis and Louise W. Garman.
c) TABULATION TEST. 1947; Jay L. Otis and David J. Chesler.
d) FILING TEST. 1947; Jay L. Otis and David J. Chesler.
e) ALPHABETIZING TEST. 1947; David J. Chesler.
f) ARITHMETIC REASONING TEST.
g) SPELLING TEST FOR CLERICAL WORKERS.

See T2:2140 (6 references); for reviews by Louise Witmer Cureton and Albert K. Kurtz, see 4:729. For reference to a review of the spelling test, see T2:159.

[1806]

Personnel Research Institute Factory Series Test. Applicants for routine industrial positions; 1950–56; Jay L. Otis and Alfred H. Exton; Psychological Research Services.*

For additional information and a review by N. M. Downie, see 6:485.

[1807]

Personnel Research Institute Test of Shorthand Skills. Stenographers; 1951–54; title on test is *Otis and Laurent Test of Shorthand Skills*; 2 scores: transliteration, transcription; Jay L. Otis and Harry Laurent; Psychological Research Services.*

For additional information and a review by Irol Whitmore Balsley, see 6:43.

[1808]

Personnel Tests for Industry. Trade school and adults; 1945–69; PTI; 3 tests; The Psychological Corporation. (British norms supplement: 1978; Gill Nyfield; NFER-Nelson Publishing Co. [England].)*

a) PTI-VERBAL TEST. 1952–69; PTI-V; Alexander G. Wesman.
b) PTI-NUMERICAL TEST. 1952–69; PTI-N; Jerome E. Doppelt.
c) PTI-ORAL DIRECTIONS TEST. 1945–54; ODT; Charles R. Langmuir.

See T2:433 (5 references) and 7:373 (3 references); for a review by Erwin K. Taylor, see 5:366; see also 4:309 (1 reference); for reviews by Charles D. Flory, Irving Lorge, and William W. Turnbull of the *Oral Directions Test*, see 3:245.

REFERENCES

1. See 4:309.
2–4. See 7:373.
5–9. See T2:433.
10. DENISI, A. S., & SHAW, J. B. Investigation of the uses of self-reports of abilities. *Journal of Applied Psychology*, 1977, 62, 641–644.
11. DISTEFANO, M. K., JR., & PRYER, M. W. General ability and opinions about mental illness among psychiatric aides. *Psychological Reports*, 1978, 42, 190.
12. WOOD, D. A. The predictive validity of verbal and numerical subtests of the Personnel Tests for Industry (PTI) in a sample of highly skilled employees. *Educational & Psychological Measurement*, 1980, 40, 431–435.

[1809]

Pertinent Questions. Grades 9–16 and adults; 1960; experimental form; conceptual foresight; Raymond M. Berger, J. P. Guilford, and P. R. Merrifield (manual); Sheridan Psychological Services, Inc.*

See T2:571 (1 reference) and 6:557 (3 references).

[1810]

★Phoneme Baseline Recording Forms. Grades kgn–6 and mentally retarded and learning disabled children; 1979; speech articulation problems; 6 scores (isolation, syllables, words, sentences, reading or story-retelling, spontaneous speech) for each of 13 phonemes; Mary Pizzuti; Communication Skill Builders, Inc.*

[1811]

★The Phonetic Reading Chain Oral Reading Diagnostic Decoding Test. Students having difficulties in phonics; no date; PRCORDDT; designed to be used with the Phonetic Reading Chain program; Ruth Worden Frank; Mafex Associates, Inc.*

[1812]

Phonics Criterion Test. Reading level grades 1–3; 1971; PCT; no scores, 99 phoneme grapheme correspondences in 14 areas: easy consonants, short vowels, long and silent vowels, difficult consonants, consonant digraphs, consonant second sounds, schwa sounds, long vowel digraphs, vowel plus r, broad o, diphthongs, difficult vowels, consonant blends, consonant exceptions; Edward Fry; Jamestown Publishers.*

[1813]

***Phonovisual Diagnostic Tests, [1975 Revision].** Grades 3–12; 1975; phonetics skills as taught by the Phonovisual Method; Edna B. Smith and Mazie C. Lloyd; Phonovisual Products, Inc.*

See T2:1638; for reviews by Charles M. Brown and George D. Spache of an earlier edition, see 6:829.

[1814]
Photo Articulation Test. Ages 3–12; 1969; PAT; 4 scores: tongue sounds, lip sounds, vowel sounds, total; Kathleen Pendergast, Stanley E. Dickey, John W. Selmar, and Anton L. Soder; Interstate Printers & Publishers, Inc.*

For additional information and a review by Lawrence D. Shriberg, see 8:969 (1 reference); see also 7:962 (2 references).

REFERENCES

1–2. See 7:962.
3. See 8:969.
4. CHAPEY, R. Diagnosis and intervention of adult articulation errors based on distinctive feature theory and the Mysak feedback model of therapy. *Journal of Communication Disorders*, 1977, 10, 245–252.
5. OLLER, D. K., JENSEN, H. T., & LAFAYETTE, R. H. The relatedness of phonological processes of a hearing–impaired child. *Journal of Communication Disorders*, 1978, 11, 97–105.
6. SCHMAUCH, V. A., PANAGOS, J. M., & KLICH, R. J. Syntax influences the accuracy of consonant production in language–disordered children. *Journal of Communication Disorders*, 1978, 11, 315–323.
7. BLACHE, S. E., PARSONS, S. L., & HUMPHREYS, J. M. A minimal–word–pair model for teaching the linguistic significance of distinctive feature properties. *Journal of Speech & Hearing Disorders*, 1981, 46, 291–296.
8. SINGH, S., HAYDEN, M. E., & TOOMBS, M. S. The role of distinction features in articulation errors. *Journal of Speech & Hearing Disorders*, 1981, 46, 174–183.

[1815]
PHSF Relations Questionnaire. Standards 6–10 and college and adults; 1969–71; PHSF; 12 scores: personal (self-confidence, self-esteem, self-control, nervousness, health), home (family influences, personal freedom), social (sociability—group, sociability—specific person, moral sense), formal relations, validity scale; F. A. Fouché and P. E. Grobbelaar; Human Sciences Research Council [South Africa].*

For additional information, see 7:118.

[1816]
Physics: Minnesota High School Achievement Examinations. High school; 1951–70; a new, revised, or old inactive form issued each May; edited by V. L. Lohmann; American Guidance Service.*

For additional information concerning out of print and inactive forms, see 7:861, 5:756, and 5:759; for a review by Irvin J. Lehmann of Form E (1962) and Form F (1963), see 6:934.

[1817]
Physiognomic Cue Test. College and adults; 1974–75; PCT; "attribution of human or human-like behavior to inanimate forms"; 3 scores: feeling-physiognomic, thing-physiognomic, total; Morris I. Stein; Human Sciences Press.* (In-print status uncertain; no reply from publisher.)

For additional information, see 8:645.

REFERENCES

1. OLESKER, W. Physiognomic perception and empathy. *Perceptual & Motor Skills*, 1977, 45, 83–86.
2. ORMONT, R. J. Physiognomic perception and educational–vocational preference. *Perceptual & Motor Skills*, 1978, 46, 603–610.
3. SEIF, M. N., & ATKINS, A. L. Some defensive and cognitive aspects of phobias. *Journal of Abnormal Psychology*, 1979, 88, 42–51.
4. BILOTTA, J., & LINDAUER, M. S. Artistic and nonartistic backgrounds as determinants of the cognitive response to the arts. *Bulletin of the Psychonomic Society*, 1980, 15, 354–356.

[1818]
Pictographic Self Rating Scale. High school and college; 1955–57; attitude toward classroom and study activities; Einar R. Ryden; Psychometric Affiliates.*

For additional information and reviews by Stanley E. Davis and John D. Krumboltz, see 6:701 (2 references).

[1819]
Pictorial Interest Inventory. Adult males, particularly poor readers and nonreaders; 1959; for research use only; 11 scores: clerical and sales, personal service, protective and custodial, farming, mechanical, building and maintenance, skilled-sedentary, vehicle operators, electrical workers, natural processors, assembly line workers; Barron B. Scarborough; the Author.* (In-print status uncertain; no reply from publisher.)

[1820]
Pictorial Inventory of Careers. Grades 3–14 and disadvantaged adults; 1972; PIC; developmental edition called *Pictorial Inventory of Occupational Training Interest*; 21 scores: agriculture, business and office (data processing, secretarial), communications (fine arts, media), criminal justice, electrical/electronics, engineering technology (applied, civil/drafting), environmental and natural resources, health services, home economics and food service, mid-management and supervision, science and laboratory, service (air transportation, fire science, personal, public), trade and industry construction, mechanics, metal trades; slide projector necessary for administration; Tom Kosuth and Earl Clancy; Educators Assistance Institute.* (In-print status uncertain; no reply from publisher.)

REFERENCES

1. WESTBROOK, B. W. Pictorial Inventory of Careers test review. *Measurement & Evaluation in Guidance*, 1978, 10, 243–244.

[1821]
Pictorial Study of Values: Pictorial Allport-Vernon. Ages 14 and over; 1957; PSV; test booklet title is *The Pictorial Study*; 7 scores: aesthetic, economic, political, religious, social, theoretical, strength of liking things in general; Charles Shooster; Psychometric Affiliates.*

See T2:1325 (1 reference) and P:204 (1 reference); for reviews by Andrew R. Baggaley and Harrison G. Gough, see 5:96.

[1822]
★**Pictorial Test of Bilingualism and Language Dominance.** Grades kgn–2; 1975–76; "provides procedures for the objective measurement of language facility in English and Spanish"; 4 scores: English oral vocabulary, Spanish oral vocabulary, bilingual oral vocabulary, total oral vocabulary; Darwin Nelson, Michael J. Fellner, and C. L. Norrell; Stoelting Co.*

[1823]
Pictorial Test of Intelligence. Ages 3–8; 1964; PTI; prepublication titles were *North Central Individual Test of Mental Ability* and *Pictorial Intelligence Test*; 7 scores: picture vocabulary, form discrimination, information and comprehension, similarities, size and number, immediate recall, total; Joseph L. French; Riverside Publishing Co.*

For additional information and an excerpted review by Thomas A. Smith, see 8:223 (11 references); see also

T2:517 (1 reference); for reviews by Philip Himelstein and T. Ernest Newland, see 7:418 (17 references); see also 6:531 (2 references).

REFERENCES

1-2. See 6:531.
3-19. See 7:418.
20. See T2:517.
21-31. See 8:223.
32. SALTZ, E., DIXON, D., & JOHNSON, J. Training disadvantaged preschoolers on various fantasy activities: Effects on cognitive functioning and impulse control. *Child Development*, 1977, 48, 367-380.
33. HYND, G. W., KRAMER, R., QUACKENBUSH, R., & CONNER, R. Clinical utility of the WISC-R and the French Pictorial Test of Intelligence with native American primary grade children. *Perceptual & Motor Skills*, 1979, 49, 480-482.
34. SAWYER, R. N., STANLEY, G. E., & WATSON, T. E. A factor analytic study of the construct validity of the Pictorial Test of Intelligence. *Educational & Psychological Measurement*, 1979, 39, 613-623.

[1824]

Picture Articulation & Language Screening Test. Grade 1; 1976; PALST; 3 parts: language abilities, initial and final sounds (administered only if part 1 score is below cutoff point), sounds in isolation (optional); no manual; William C. Rodgers; Word Making Productions.* (In-print status uncertain; no reply from publisher.)

For additional information, see 8:970.

[1825]

Picture Identification Test. High school and college; 1959-71; PIT; 3 scores (judgment, attitude, association) and an effectiveness rating for each of 22 needs (abasement, achievement, affiliation, aggression, autonomy, blame avoidance, counteraction, defendance, deference, dominance, exhibition, gratitude, harm avoidance, inferiority avoidance, nurturance, order, play, rejection, sentience, sex, succorance, understanding), average; no manual for examiners; Jay L. Chambers; the Author.*

See T2:1490 (2 references) and P:463 (17 references).

REFERENCES

1-17. See P:463.
18-19. See T2:1490.
20. CHAMBERS, J. L., & SURMA, M. B. Need associations and psychopathology. *Journal of Personality Assessment*, 1977, 41, 358-367.
21. GRANGER, R. C., MATHEWS, M., QUAY, L. C., & VERNER, R. Teacher judgements of the communication effectiveness of children using different speech patterns. *Journal of Educational Psychology*, 1977, 69, 793-796.
22. CHAMBERS, J. L., & SURMA, M. E. Dimensions of Picture Identification Test need associations. *Journal of Personality Assessment*, 1979, 43, 128-134.

[1826]

Picture Interest Exploration Survey. Grades 7-12; 1974; PIES; career interest inventory based upon 156 slides, each showing "a worker's hand performing a task" representative of an occupation; 13 scores: industrial production, office, service, education, sales, construction, transportation activities, scientific and technical, mechanics and repairmen, health, social scientists and social service, art-design and communications, agriculture; Elizabeth F. Mahoney; Education Achievement Corporation.* (In-print status uncertain; no reply from publisher.)

For additional information, see 8:1018.

[1827]

Picture Situation Test. Adult males; 1971; PST; "reaction to aggression provoking stimuli in a social situation"; 4 scores: type of aggression (direct, denial), effect of response (constructive, destructive); A. J. Templer (manual); National Institute for Personnel Research [South Africa].*

[1828]

The Picture Story Test Blank. Clinical clients; 1965-66; PSTB; manual title is *Picture Story Test Booklet*; for recording protocols of picture story tests; Psychological Research and Development Institute; Psychological Publications Press.* (In-print status uncertain; no reply from publisher.)

For additional information, see P:465.

[1829]

Picture Test A. Ages 7-0 to 8-1; 1955-70; formerly called *Picture Test* 1 and, earlier, *Picture Intelligence Test* 1; Joan E. Stuart; NFER-Nelson Publishing Co. [England].*

For additional information, see 7:374; for reviews by Charlotte E. K. Banks and M. L. Kellmer Pringle, see 5:367.

[1830]

The Picture World Test. Ages 6 and over; 1955-65; PWT; Charlotte Buhler and Morse P. Manson; Western Psychological Services.*

For additional information, see P:466 (1 reference); for a review by Walter Kass and an excerpted review by Laurance F. Shaffer, see 5:153.

[1831]

The Piers-Harris Children's Self Concept Scale (The Way I Feel About Myself). Grades 3-12; 1969; CSCS; Ellen V. Piers and Dale B. Harris (test); Counselor Recordings and Tests.* (In-print status uncertain; no reply from publisher.)

For additional information, see 8:646 (95 references); see also T2:1326 (10 references); for a review by Peter M. Bentler, see 7:124 (8 references).

REFERENCES

1-8. See 7:124.
9-18. See T2:1326.
19-113. See 8:646.
114. ANILOFF, L. The relationship between high school program and self-concept, occupational aspiration, and occupational expectation among ninth grade students. *Journal of Business Education*, 1977, 53, 136.
115. AUGUST, G. J., & FELKER, D. W. Role of affective meaningfulness and self-concept in the verbal learning styles of white and black children. *Journal of Educational Psychology*, 1977, 69, 253-260.
116. BRUYA, L. D. Effect of selected movement skills on positive self-concept. *Perceptual & Motor Skills*, 1977, 45, 252-254.
117. CALHOUN, G., & ELLIOT, R. N. Self concept and academic achievement of educable retarded and emotionally disturbed pupils. *Exceptional Children*, 1977, 43, 379-380.
118. DAY, B., & BRICE, R. Academic achievement, self-concept development, and behavior patterns of six-year-old children in open classrooms. *Elementary School Journal*, 1977, 78, 133-139.
119. DILLARD, J. M., WARRIOR-BENJAMIN, J., & PERRIN, D. W. Efficacy of test-wiseness on test anxiety and reading achievement among black youth. *Psychological Reports*, 1977, 41, 1135-1140.
120. ELDRIDGE, M. S., WITMER, J. M., BARCIKOWSKI, R., & BAUER, L. The effects of a group guidance program on the self-concepts of EMR children. *Measurement & Evaluation in Guidance*, 1977, 9, 184-191.
121. GABEL, H., GRAYBILL, D., & CONNORS, G. Parent-teacher communication in relation to child academic achievement and self-concept. *Peabody Journal of Education*, 1977, 54, 142-145.
122. GALLUZZI, E. G., & ZUCKER, K. B. Level of adjustment and the self- and others-concepts. *Psychology in the Schools*, 1977, 14, 104-108.
123. GORDON, D. A. Children's beliefs in internal-external control and self-esteem as related to academic achievement. *Journal of Personality Assessment*, 1977, 41, 383-386.

124. KAISER, H. E., & SILLIN, P. C. Guidance effectiveness in the elementary schools. *Elementary School Guidance & Counseling*, 1977, 12, 61–64.

125. KETCHAM, B., & SNYDER, R. T. Self–attitudes of the intellectually and socially advantaged student: Normative study of the Piers–Harris Children's Self–Concept Scale. *Psychological Reports*, 1977, 40, 111–116.

126. MCINTIRE, W. G., & DRUMMOND, R. J. Multiple predictors of self–concept in children. *Psychology in the Schools*, 1977, 14, 295–298.

127. MOYAL, B. R. Locus of control, self–esteem, stimulus appraisal, and depressive symptoms in children. *Journal of Consulting & Clinical Psychology*, 1977, 45, 951–952.

128. OANH, N. T., & MICHAEL, W. B. The predictive validity of each of ten measures of self–concept relative to teachers' ratings of achievement in mathematics and reading of Vietnamese children and of those from five other ethnic groups. *Educational & Psychological Measurement*, 1977, 37, 1005–1016.

129. PIERS, E. V. Children's self–esteem, level of esteem certainty, and responsibility for success and failure. *Journal of Genetic Psychology*, 1977, 130, 295–304.

130. SMITH, M. D., DOKECKI, P. R., & DAVIS, E. E. School related factors influencing the self–concepts of children with learning problems. *Peabody Journal of Education*, 1977, 54, 185–195.

131. SMITH, M. D., & ROGERS, C. M. Item instability on the Piers–Harris Children's Self–Concept Scale for academic underachievers with high, middle, and low self concepts: Implications for construct validity. *Educational & Psychological Measurement*, 1977, 37, 553–558.

132. WINNE, P. H., MARX, R. W., & TAYLOR, T. D. A multitrait-multimethod study of three self–concept inventories. *Child Development*, 1977, 48, 893–901.

133. AMES, C. Children's achievement attributions and self–reinforcement: Effects of self–concept and competitive reward structure. *Journal of Educational Psychology*, 1978, 70, 345–355.

134. AUGUST, G. J., & RYCHLAK, J. F. Role of intelligence and task difficulty in the affective learning styles of children with high and low self–concepts. *Journal of Educational Psychology*, 1978, 70, 406–413.

135. BOERSMA, F. J., & CHAPMAN, J. W. Comparison of students' perception of ability scale with the Piers–Harris Children's Self–Concept Scale. *Perceptual & Motor Skills*, 1978, 47, 827–832.

136. BRADY, P. J., FIGUERRES, C. I., FELKER, D. W., & GARRISON, W. M. Predicting student self–concept, anxiety, and responsibility from self–evaluation and self–praise. *Psychology in the Schools*, 1978, 15, 434–438.

137. CHEONG, G. S. C., & WADDEN, E. P. The relationship between teachers' experimental and dogmatic attitudes, and their pupils' self–concept. *Alberta Journal of Educational Research*, 1978, 24, 121–125.

138. GRAYBILL, D. Relationship of maternal child–rearing behaviors to children's self–esteem. *Journal of Psychology*, 1978, 100, 45–47.

139. HOFFMAN, D. A. Field independence and intelligence: Their relation to leadership and self–concept in sixth–grade boys. *Journal of Educational Psychology*, 1978, 70, 827–832.

140. KOENIG, C. R., JOHNSON, D. J., & GRAVES, M. Comparison of two methods of developing manipulative skills of children in upper elementary grades. *Perceptual & Motor Skills*, 1978, 47, 605–606.

141. KOSMOSKI, G. J., & VOCKELL, E. L. The learning center: Stimulus to cognitive and affective growth. *Elementary School Journal*, 1978, 79, 47–54.

142. MANNARINO, A. P. Friendship patterns and self–concept development in preadolescent males. *Journal of Genetic Psychology*, 1978, 133, 105–110.

143. MARTINEK, T. J., CHEFFERS, J. T. F., & ZAICHKOWSKY, L. D. Physical activity, motor development and self concept: Race and age differences. *Perceptual & Motor Skills*, 1978, 46, 147–154.

144. MARX, R. W., & WINNE, P. H. Construct interpretations of three self–concept inventories. *American Educational Research Journal*, 1978, 15, 99–109.

145. MATEFY, R. E. Evaluation of a remediation program using senior citizens as psychoeducational agents. *Community Mental Health Journal*, 1978, 14, 327–336.

146. MORAN, M., MICHAEL, W. B., & DEMBO, M. H. The factorial validity of three frequently employed self–report measures of self–concept. *Educational & Psychological Measurement*, 1978, 38, 547–563.

147. MURRAY, M. E. The relationship between personality adjustment and success in remedial programs in dyslexic children. *Contemporary Educational Psychology*, 1978, 3, 330–339.

148. PARISH, T. S., & TAYLOR, J. C. A further report on the validity and reliability of the Personal Attribute Inventory for children as a self–concept scale. *Educational & Psychological Measurement*, 1978, 38, 1225–1228.

149. PARISH, T. S., & TAYLOR, J. C. The Personal Attribute Inventory for Children: A report on its validity and reliability as a self–concept scale. *Educational & Psychological Measurement*, 1978, 38, 565–569.

150. PRYTULA, R. E., PHELPS, M. R., MORRISSEY, E. F., & DAVIS, S. F. Figure drawing size as a reflection of self–concept or self–esteem. *Journal of Clinical Psychology*, 1978, 34, 207–214.

151. ROGERS, C. M., SMITH, M. D., & COLEMAN, J. M. Social comparison in the classroom: The relationship between academic achievement and self–concept. *Journal of Educational Psychology*, 1978, 70, 50–57.

152. SAVAGE, J. E., JR., ADAIR, A., & FRIEDMAN, P. Community–social variables related to black parent–absent families. *Journal of Marriage & the Family*, 1978, 40, 779–785.

153. SHEARE, J. B. The impact of resource programs upon the self–concept and peer acceptance of learning disabled children. *Psychology in the Schools*, 1978, 15, 406–412.

154. SHEARN, D. F., & RANDOLPH, D. L. Effects of reality therapy methods applied in the classroom. *Psychology in the Schools*, 1978, 15, 79–83.

155. SMITH, M. D., ZINGALE, S. A., & COLEMAN, J. M. The influence of adult expectancy/child performance discrepancies upon children's self–concepts. *American Educational Research Journal*, 1978, 15, 259–265.

156. STRANG, L., SMITH, M. D., & ROGERS, C. M. Social comparison, multiple reference groups, and the self–concepts of academically handicapped children before and after mainstreaming. *Journal of Educational Psychology*, 1978, 70, 487–497.

157. AMES, C., & FELKER, D. W. Effects of self–concept on children's causal attributions and self–reinforcement. *Journal of Educational Psychology*, 1979, 71, 613–619.

158. BELFER, M. L., HARRISON, A. M., & MURRAY, J. E. Body image and the process of reconstructive surgery. *American Journal of Diseases of Children*, 1979, 133, 532–535.

159. BLOOM, R. B., SHEA, R. J., & EUN, B. S. The Piers–Harris Self–Concept Scale: Norms for behaviorally disordered children. *Psychology in the Schools*, 1979, 16, 483–487.

160. BOERSMA, F. J., CHAPMAN, J. W., & MAGUIRE, T. O. The student's perception of ability scale: An instrument for measuring academic self–concept in elementary school children. *Educational & Psychological Measurement*, 1979, 39, 1035–1041.

161. BRYAN, T., & PEARL, R. Self–concepts and locus of control of learning disabled children. *Journal of Clinical Child Psychology*, 1979, 8, 223–226.

162. CAIRNS, N. U., CLARK, G. M., SMITH, S. D., & LANSKY, S. B. Adaptation of siblings to childhood malignancy. *Journal of Pediatrics*, 1979, 95, 484–487.

163. COKER, G. A comparison of self–concepts and academic achievement of visually handicapped children enrolled in a regular school and in a residential school. *Education of the Visually Handicapped*, 1979, 11, 67–74.

164. EDMONDSON, R. J. Utilization of HDP and TA programs to enhance self esteem. *Elementary School Guidance & Counseling*, 1979, 13, 299–301.

165. ELKIND, D., & BOWEN, R. Imaginary audience behavior in children and adolescents. *Developmental Psychology*, 1979, 15, 38–44.

166. GORDON, D. A., JONES, R. H., & NOWICKI, S., JR. A measure of intensity of parental punishment. *Journal of Personality Assessment*, 1979, 43, 485–496.

167. HAMMOND, J. M. Children of divorce: Implications for counselors. *School Counselor*, 1979, 27, 7–14.

168. HAMMOND, J. M. Children of divorce: A study of self–concept, academic achievement, and attitudes. *Elementary School Journal*, 1979, 80, 55–62.

169. HAMMOND, J. M. A comparison of elementary children from divorced and intact families. *Phi Delta Kappan*, 1979, 61, 219.

170. HERJANIC, B. M., BARREDO, V. H., HERJANIC, M., & TOMELLERI, C. J. Children of heroin addicts. *International Journal of the Addictions*, 1979, 14, 919–931.

171. HUDGINS, E. W. Examining the effectiveness of affective education. *Psychology in the Schools*, 1979, 16, 581–585.

172. KAPP, K. Self concept of the cleft lip or palate child. *Cleft Palate Journal*, 1979, 16, 171–176.

173. KARMOS, A. H. The development and validation of a nonverbal measure of self–esteem: The sliding person test. *Educational & Psychological Measurement*, 1979, 39, 479–484.

174. MARTINEZ, M. E., HAYS, J. R., & SOLWAY, K. S. Comparative study of delinquent and non–delinquent Mexican–American youths. *Psychological Reports*, 1979, 44, 215–221.

175. PLATTEN, M. R., & WILLIAMS, L. R. A comparative analysis of the factorial structures of two administrations of the Piers–Harris Children's Self Concept Scale to one group of elementary school children. *Educational & Psychological Measurement*, 1979, 39, 471–478.

176. RASCHKE, H. J., & RASCHKE, V. J. Family conflict and children's self–concepts: A comparison of intact and single–parent families. *Journal of Marriage & the Family*, 1979, 41, 367–374.

177. RICH, C. E., BARCIKOWSKI, R. S., & WITMER, J. M. The factorial validity of the Piers–Harris Children's Self Concept Scale for a sample of intermediate–level EMR students enrolled in elementary school. *Educational & Psychological Measurement*, 1979, 39, 479–484.

178. SMITH, M. D. Prediction of self–concept among learning disabled children. *Journal of Learning Disabilities*, 1979, 12, 664–669.

179. STEPHENS, N., & DAY, H. D. Sex–role identity, parental identification, and self–concept of adolescent daughters from mother–

absent, father–absent, and intact families. *Journal of Psychology*, 1979, 103, 193–202.

180. STEWART, D. J., CRUMP, W. D., & McLEAN, J. E. Response instability on the Piers–Harris Children's Self–Concept Scale. *Journal of Learning Disabilities*, 1979, 12, 351–355.

181. VAN PUTTE, A. W. Relationship of school setting to self concept in physically disabled children. *Journal of School Health*, 1979, 49, 576–578.

182. WAKSMAN, S. A. An evaluation of social learning procedures designed to aid students with conduct problems. *Psychology in the Schools*, 1979, 16, 416–421.

183. WOLF, T. M., HUNTER, S. M., & WEBBER, L. S. Psychosocial measures and cardiovascular risk factors in children and adolescents. *Journal of Psychology*, 1979, 101, 139–146.

184. BAGLEY, C. R., & VERMA, G. K. The structures and validity of self–concept measures in multi–ethnic populations. *British Journal of Educational Psychology*, 1980, 50, 77.

185. BOWLSBY, R. A., II, & ISO-AHOLA, S. E. Self–concepts of children in summer baseball programs. *Perceptual & Motor Skills*, 1980, 51, 1202.

186. BRUMBACK, R. A., STATON, R. D., & WILSON, H. Neuropsychological study of children during and after remission of endogenous depressive episodes. *Perceptual & Motor Skills*, 1980, 50, 1163–1167.

187. BUTLER, L., MIEZITIS, S., FRIEDMAN, R., & COLE, E. The effect of two school–based intervention programs on depressive symptoms in preadolescents. *American Educational Research Journal*, 1980, 17, 111–119.

188. CANGELOSI, A., GRESSARD, C. F., & MINES, R. A. The effects of a rational thinking group on self–concepts in adolescents. *School Counselor*, 1980, 27, 357–361.

189. GALLUZZI, E. G., KIRBY, E. A., & ZUCKER, K. B. Students' and teachers' perception of classroom environment and self– and others– concepts. *Psychological Reports*, 1980, 46, 747–753.

190. GREEN, K. E., & KOLFF, C. Two promising measures of health education program outcomes and asthmatic children. *Journal of School Health*, 1980, 50, 332–336.

191. HALL, J. A., & HALBERSTADT, A. G. Masculinity and femininity in children: Development of the Children's Personal Attributes Questionnaire. *Developmental Psychology*, 1980, 16, 270–280.

192. KANOY, R. C., III, JOHNSON, B. W., & KANOY, K. W. Locus of control and self–concept in achieving and underachieving bright elementary students. *Psychology in the Schools*, 1980, 17, 395–399.

193. KINARD, E. M. Emotional development in physically abused children. *American Journal of Orthopsychiatry*, 1980, 50, 686–696.

194. LEE, C. C. The Homework Helper Program: Volunteer service for academic and social enrichment in the elementary school. *School Counselor*, 1980, 28, 11–21.

195. LUCKER, G. W., & GRABER, L. W. Physiognomic features and facial appearance judgments in children. *Journal of Psychology*, 1980, 104, 261–268.

196. MARTINEK, T. J. Students' expectations as related to a teacher's expectations and self–concepts of elementary age children. *Perceptual & Motor Skills*, 1980, 50, 555–561.

197. MARX, R. W., & WINNE, P. H. Self–concept validation research: Some current complexities. *Measurement & Evaluation in Guidance*, 1980, 13, 72–82.

198. PECK, R., BLATTSTEIN, D., BLATTSTEIN, A., & FOX, R. Comparison of self, peer, and teacher ratings of student coping as predictors of achievement, self–esteem, and attitudes. *Journal of Teacher Education*, 1980, 31, 45–52.

199. TIDWELL, R. A psycho–educational profile of 1,593 gifted high school students. *Gifted Child Quarterly*, 1980, 24, 63–86.

200. WERRY, J. S., AMAN, M. G., & DIAMOND, E. Imipramine and methylphenidate in hyperactive children. *Journal of Child Psychology & Psychiatry & Allied Disciplines*, 1980, 21, 27–35.

201. ABIDIN, R. R., & SELTZER, J. Special education outcomes: Implications for implementation of Public Law 94–142. *Journal of Learning Disabilities*, 1981, 14, 28–31.

202. BRIDGWATER, C. A. Construct validity of the Personality Research Form: Further evidence. *Educational & Psychological Measurement*, 1981, 41, 533–535.

203. CAMPBELL, R. L. Intellectual development, achievement, and self–concept of elementary minority school children. *School Science & Mathematics*, 1981, 81, 200–204.

204. CHAPMAN, J. W., CULLEN, J. L., BOERSMA, F. J., & MAGUIRE, T. O. Affective variables and school achievement: A study of possible causal influences. *Canadian Journal of Behavioural Science*, 1981, 13, 181–192.

205. DELUTY, R. H. Adaptiveness of aggressive, assertive, and submissive behavior for children. *Journal of Clinical Child Psychology*, 1981, 10, 155–158.

206. ELDREDGE, A. R. An investigation to determine the relationships among self–concept, locus of control, and reading achievement. *Reading World*, 1981, 21, 59–64.

207. FELDHUSEN, J. F., & KOLLOFF, M. B. ME: A self–concept scale for gifted students. *Perceptual & Motor Skills*, 1981, 53, 319–323.

208. FRANKLIN, M. R., JR., DULEY, S. M., ROUSSEAU, E. W., & SABERS, D. L. Construct validation of the Piers–Harris Children's Self Concept Scale. *Educational & Psychological Measurement*, 1981, 41, 439–443.

209. JALALI, B., JALALI, M., CROCETTI, G., & TURNER, F. Adolescents and drug use: Toward a more comprehensive approach. *American Journal of Orthopsychiatry*, 1981, 51, 120–130.

210. JOHNSON, D. S. Naturally acquired learned helplessness: The relationship of school failure to achievement behavior, attributions, and self–concept. *Journal of Educational Psychology*, 1981, 73, 174–180.

211. JONES, J. D. An investigation into the effects of teachers' verbal interactions, and students' self–concept. *College Student Journal*, 1981, 15, 38–46.

212. KLEIN, J. R., LITT, I. F., ROSENBERG, A., & UDALL, L. The effect of aspirin on dysmenorrhea in adolescents. *Journal of Pediatrics*, 1981, 98, 987–990.

213. MASSAD, C. M. Sex role identity and adjustment during adolescence. *Child Development*, 1981, 52, 1290–1298.

214. MOLLA, P. M. Self–concept in children with and without physical disabilities. *Journal of Psychiatric Nursing*, 1981, 19, 22–27.

215. PANDINA, R. J., & WHITE, H. R. Patterns of alcohol and drug use of adolescent students and adolescents in treatment. *Journal of Studies on Alcohol*, 1981, 42, 441–456.

216. PLATTEN, M. R., & WILLIAMS, L. R. Replication of a test–retest factorial validity study with the Piers–Harris Children's Self Concept Scale. *Educational & Psychological Measurement*, 1981, 41, 453–462.

217. PUCKETT, J. R., & FORD, H. T., JR. Self–concept scores and participation in recreation–league team sports. *Perceptual & Motor Skills*, 1981, 52, 249–250.

218. STATON, R. D., WILSON, H., & BRUMBACK, R. A. Cognitive improvement associated with tricyclic antidepressant treatment of childhood major depressive illness. *Perceptual & Motor Skills*, 1981, 53, 219–234.

219. WAY, J. W. Achievement and self–concept in multiage classrooms. *Educational Research Quarterly*, 1981, 6, 69–75.

220. WOLF, T. M., HUNTER, S. M., WEBBER, L. S., & BERENSON, G. S. Self–concept, locus of control, goal blockage, and coronary–prone behavior pattern in children and adolescents: Bogalusa heart study. *Journal of General Psychology*, 1981, 105, 13–26.

[1832]

A Pill Scale. Older adolescents and adults; 1969; attitudes toward oral contraception; Panos D. Bardis; the Author.*

For additional information, see 8:350 (3 references).

[1833]

Pimsleur Language Aptitude Battery. Grades 6–12; 1966–67; 5 scores: grade-point average, interest, verbal, auditory, total; Paul Pimsleur; The Psychological Corporation.*

See T2:223 (5 references); for a review by A. Ralph Hakstian, and an excerpted review by Donald C. Ryberg, see 7:256 (5 references).

[1834]

Pintner-Manikin Test. Ages 2 and over; [1917]; subtest of *Merrill-Palmer Scale of Mental Tests* and *Arthur Point Scale of Performance Tests, Form 1*; R. Pintner; Stoelting Co.

See T2:563 (1 reference).

[1835]

Pintner-Paterson Feature Profile Test. Ages 4 and over; [1917–23]; modification of *Knox-Kempf Feature Profile Test* ['14]; subtest of *Arthur Point Scale of Performance Tests* and *Performance Tests of Intelligence*; R. Pintner and D. G. Paterson; Stoelting Co.

See T2:556 (1 reference).

[1836]

★**PIP Developmental Charts.** Mentally handicapped children birth to age 5; 1976; behavioral checklist to establish the level of development; profile of 5 areas of

[1837]
Plane Geometry: National Achievement Tests.
High school; 1958–70; Ray Webb and Julius H. Hlavaty; Psychometric Affiliates.*

For additional information and a review by Dorothy L. Jones, see 7:540.

[1838]
Plane Trigonometry: National Achievement Tests. Grades 10–16; 1958–60; 1959; Ray Webb and Julius H. Hlavaty; Psychometric Affiliates.*

For additional information, see 6:656.

[1839]
Planning Career Goals. Grades 8–12; 1975–76; PCG; revision of tests in the 1960–61 *Project Talent Test Battery*; values, abilities, information, and interests considered relevant to each of 12 occupational groups (engineering, physical science, mathematics, and architecture; medical and biological sciences; business administration; general teaching and social service; humanities, law and social and behavioral science; fine arts and performing arts; technical jobs; proprietors and sales workers; mechanics and industrial trades; construction trades; secretarial-clerical and office workers; general labor and public and community service); American Institutes for Research; CTB/McGraw-Hill.*

a) LIFE AND CAREER PLANS.
b) PCG ABILITY MEASURES. 10 scores: vocabulary, English, reading, comprehension, creativity, mechanical reasoning, visualization, abstract reasoning, quantitative reasoning, mathematics, computation, plus a weighted average of stanine scores on the 3–5 tests which best predict membership in each of the 12 occupational groups.
c) PCG INFORMATION MEASURES. 12 occupational group scores as listed above.
d) PCG INTEREST INVENTORY. 12 occupational group scores as listed above.

For additional information and reviews by Dean H. Nafziger and Donald E. Super, see 8:1019.

REFERENCES
1. BEARD, J. G. Planning Career Goals. *Measurement & Evaluation in Guidance*, 1978, 11, 57–59.

[1840]
Plot Titles. Grades 9–16; 1962–69; PT; 2 scores: ideational fluency, originality; Raymond M. Berger and J. P. Guilford; Sheridan Psychological Services, Inc.*

See T2:572 (23 references) and 6:551M1.

REFERENCES
1–23. See T2:572.
24. ALPAUGH, P. K., & BIRREN, J. E. Variables affecting creative contributions across the adult life span. *Human Development*, 1977, 20, 240–248.

[1841]
PMA Readiness Level. Grades kgn–1; 1946–74; revision of 1962 edition of *SRA Primary Mental Abilities* for grades kgn–1; 5 tests; Thelma Gwinn Thurstone; Science Research Associates, Inc.*

a) AUDITORY DISCRIMINATION. 1974.
b) VERBAL MEANING. 1946–74.
c) PERCEPTUAL SPEED. 1946–74.
d) NUMBER FACILITY. 1946–74.
e) SPATIAL RELATIONS. 1946–74.

For additional information and a review by Robert Dykstra, see 8:804.

[1842]
Poetry Test/Objective. Grades 7–9, 10–12; no manual; Perfection Form Co.* (In-print status uncertain; no reply from publisher.)

[1843]
Police Officer A-1(M). Prospective police officers; 1973; abbreviated revision of *Test for Police Officer A-1*; distribution restricted to public personnel agencies; International Personnel Management Association.*

For additional information, see 8:1095 (1 reference).

[1844]
Police Performance Rating System. Policemen; 1964–69; PPRS; ratings by immediate supervisors; 7 summary ratings: quality of work, interpersonal relationship traits, quantity of work, character traits, quality of supervision given, quality of administrative work, total; McCann Associates.*

For additional information, see 7:1109.

[1845]
Police Promotion Tests. Prospective policemen promotees; 1960–69; 6 tests; McCann Associates.*

a) SERGEANT. 1962–69; 6 or 7 scores: patrol, other police knowledges, crime investigation, law, supervision, reading comprehension (Form B only), total.
b) LIEUTENANT. 1962–69; 6 or 8 scores: same as for *a* plus administration (Form B only).
c) DETECTIVE. 1962–69; 4 scores: crime investigation, investigative judgment, law, total.
d) CAPTAIN. 1962–68; 6 scores: police supervision, police administration, crime investigation, other police knowledges, law (Form A only), reading comprehension (Form B only), total.
e) ASSISTANT CHIEF. 1968–69; 6 scores: same as for *d*.
f) CHIEF OF POLICE. 1960–69; 6 scores: same as for *d*.

For additional information, see 7:1110.

[1846]
Police Sergeant. Prospective sergeants; 1975–77; various titles used by publisher; 6 scores: police supervisory principles and practices, legal knowledges, technical police knowledges, police judgment, understanding and interpreting police table and text materials, total; distribution restricted to civil service commissions and municipal officials; McCann Associates.*

For additional information, see 8:1096.

[1847]
Policeman Examination. Prospective policemen; 1960–62; 8 or 9 scores: learning ability (verbal, quantitative, total), police aptitude (interest, common sense, public relations, total), easy verbal learning (forms 70 only), total; distribution restricted to civil service commissions and municipal officials; McCann Associates.*

For additional information, see 6:1150.

[1848]
Politte Sentence Completion Test. Grades 1–8, 7–12; 1970–71; PSCT; no scores; 2 levels; Alan J. Politte; Psychologists and Educators, Inc.*
a) ELEMENTARY SCHOOL FORM. Grades 1–8; 1970–71.
b) INTERMEDIATE AND SECONDARY FORM. Grades 7–12; 1971.

[1849]
Polyfactorial Study of Personality. Adults; 1959; PSP; 11 scores: hypochondriasis, sexual identification, anxiety, social distance, sociopathy, depression, compulsivity, repression, paranoia, schizophrenia, hyperaffectivity; Ronald H. Stark; Martin M. Bruce, Ph.D., Publishers.*

For additional information, see P:206; for reviews by Bertram D. Cohen and Donald R. Peterson and an excerpted review by Edward S. Bordin, see 6:160.

[1850]
★Pope Inventory of Basic Reading Skills. Reading level grades 4 and less; 1974; "evaluates the word attack skills of readers who have difficulty in sounding out words that are unfamiliar to them"; ratings by teachers in 12 areas: knowledge of left and right, sight vocabulary, hears and writes initial consonants, hears and writes final consonants, blends sounds to make words, visually recognizes consonants and sounds them correctly, reads short vowels in words, reads long vowels in words, reads correctly words that lend themselves to reversal, hears and writes consonant combinations, visually recognizes consonant combinations and sounds them correctly, reads vowel combinations; no manual; Lillie Pope; Book-Lab, Inc.*

[1851]
***Porch Index of Communicative Ability.** Aphasic adults; 1967–81; PICA; for a downward extension, see 1852; revision consists of revised manual ('81) which incorporates material from earlier editions "as well as new information that will make both scoring and interpretation more clinically and psychometrically powerful"; 22 scores: gestural (8 unnamed subtest scores and total), verbal (4 unnamed subtest scores and total), graphic (6 unnamed subtest scores and total), total; Bruce E. Porch; Consulting Psychologists Press, Inc.*

For additional information and a review by Margaret C. Byrne, see 8:971 (14 references); see also T2:2087 (2 references); for a review by Daniel R. Boone, see 7:963 (1 reference).

REFERENCES

1. See 7:963.
2–3. See T2:2087.
4–17. See 8:971.
18. GROHER, M. Language and memory disorders following closed head trauma. *Journal of Speech & Hearing Research*, 1977, 20, 212–223.
19. JOHNSON, J. P., SOMMERS, R. K., & WEIDNER, W. F. Dichotic ear preference in aphasia. *Journal of Speech & Hearing Research*, 1977, 20, 116–129.
20. LOVE, R. J., & WEBB, W. G. The efficacy of cueing techniques in Broca's aphasia. *Journal of Speech & Hearing Disorders*, 1977, 42, 170–178.
21. MARTIN, A. D. Aphasia testing: A second look at the Porch Index of Communicative Ability. *Journal of Speech & Hearing Disorders*, 1977, 42, 547–562.
22. PODRAZA, B. L., & DARLEY, F. L. Effect of auditory prestimulation on naming in aphasia. *Journal of Speech & Hearing Research*, 1977, 20, 669–683.
23. WARREN, R. L., HUBBARD, D. J., & KNOX, A. W. Short-term memory scan in normal individuals with aphasia. *Journal of Speech & Hearing Research*, 1977, 20, 497–509.
24. DERIE, F., & PABLO, R. Y. The social behavior of elderly aphasic versus nonaphasic long–term patients. *Journal of the American Geriatrics Society*, 1978, 26, 82–88.
25. DISIMONI, F. G., & HOLT, D. L. Ability of short PICA versions to predict standard form overall score. *ASHA*, 1978, 20, 825. (Abstract)
26. DUMOND, D. L., HARDY, J. C., & VAN DEMARK, A. A. Presentation by order of difficulty of test tasks to persons with aphasia. *Journal of Speech & Hearing Research*, 1978, 21, 350–360.
27. HANSON, W. R., & CICCIARELLI, A. W. The time, amount, and pattern of language improvement in adult aphasics. *British Journal of Disorders of Communication*, 1978, 13, 59–63.
28. MARSHALL, R. C., TOMPKINS, C. A., & PHILLIPS, D. S. Treatment scheduling: Effects on communication of aphasic subjects. *ASHA*, 1978, 20, 825. (Abstract)
29. NOLL, J. D., & RANDOLPH, S. R. Auditory semantic, syntactic, and retention errors made by aphasic subjects on The Token Test. *Journal of Communication Disorders*, 1978, 11, 543–553.
30. WALLER, M. R., & DARLEY, F. L. The influence of context on the auditory comprehension of paragraphs by aphasic subjects. *Journal of Speech & Hearing Research*, 1978, 21, 732–745.
31. CHAPEY, R., & LUBINSKI, R. Semantic judgment ability in adult aphasia. *Cortex*, 1979, 15, 247–255.
32. COOPER, L. D., & RIGRODSKY, S. Verbal training to improve explanations of conservation with aphasic adults. *Journal of Speech & Hearing Research*, 1979, 22, 818–828.
33. CULTON, G. L., & FERGUSON, P. A. Comprehension training with aphasic subjects: The development and application of five automated language programs. *Journal of Communication Disorders*, 1979, 12, 69–82.
34. MILLS, R. H., KNOX, A. W., JUOLA, J. F., & SALMON, S. J. Cognitive loci of impairments in picture naming by aphasic subjects. *Journal of Speech & Hearing Research*, 1979, 22, 73–87.
35. SHIRLEY, J. G., GAETH, J. H., & ALLEN, D. V. Sensitivity of two aphasia tests to site of lesion. *ASHA*, 1979, 21, 717.
36. SOMMERS, R. K., HARBAUGH, D., McCREIGHT, K., & STEVENSON, M. J. Prediction: PICA scores and scores from an auditory/visual sequencing task. *ASHA*, 1979, 21, 717. (Abstract)
37. WALLER, M. R., & DARLEY, F. L. Effect of prestimulation on sentence comprehension by aphasic subjects. *Journal of Communication Disorders*, 1979, 12, 461–479.
38. BROOKSHIRE, R. H., & NICHOLAS, L. E. Verification of active and passive sentences by aphasic and nonaphasic subjects. *Journal of Speech & Hearing Research*, 1980, 23, 878–893.
39. DISIMONI, F. G., KEITH, R. L., & DARLEY, F. L. Prediction of PICA overall score by short versions of the test. *Journal of Speech & Hearing Research*, 1980, 23, 511–516.
40. LINCOLN, N. B., & ELLS, P. A shortened version of the PICA. *British Journal of Disorders of Communication*, 1980, 15, 183–187.
41. MARSHALL, R. C., TOMPKINS, C. A., & PHILLIPS, D. S. Effects of scheduling on the communicative assessment of aphasic patients. *Journal of Communication Disorders*, 1980, 13, 105–114.
42. PORCH, B. E., COLLINS, M., WETZ, R. T., & FRIDEN, T. P. Statistical prediction of change in aphasia. *Journal of Speech & Hearing Research*, 1980, 23, 312–321.
43. SAMPLES, J. M., & LANE, V. W. Language gains in global aphasia over a three–year period: A case study. *Journal of Communication Disorders*, 1980, 13, 49–57.
44. YORKSTON, K. M., & BEUKELMAN, D. R. An analysis of connected speech samples of aphasic and normal speakers. *Journal of Speech & Hearing Disorders*, 1980, 45, 27–36.
45. CROSSON, B., & WARREN, R. L. Dichotic ear preference for C-V-C words in Wernicke's and Broca's aphasia. *Cortex*, 1981, 17, 249–258.
46. DUFFY, R. J., & DUFFY, J. R. Three studies of deficits in pantomimic expression and pantomimic recognition in aphasia. *Journal of Speech & Hearing Research*, 1981, 24, 70–84.
47. ELMORE-NICHOLAS, L., & BROOKSHIRE, R. H. Effects of pictures and picturability on sentence verification by aphasic and nonaphasic subjects. *Journal of Speech & Hearing Research*, 1981, 24, 292–298.
48. LINCOLN, N. B., PICKERSGILL, M. J., & VALENTINE, J. D. Is the Porch Index of Communicative Ability an equal interval scale? *British Journal of Disorders of Communication*, 1981, 16, 185–191.
49. NANCE, A. L., & OCHSNER, G. J. Language modality performance patterns in aphasia. *Journal of Communication Disorders*, 1981, 14, 421–428.

[1852]
***Porch Index of Communicative Ability in Children.** Ages 3–6, 6–12; 1973–79; PICAC; for an upward extension, see 1851; 2 levels; Bruce E. Porch; Consulting Psychologists Press, Inc.*
a) BASIC BATTERY. Ages 3–6; 15 subtest scores: verbal (function, naming, completion, imitation), gestural function, auditory (function, commands, names), reading

names, visual (pictures, matching), graphic (dictated, spelled, copying, geometric forms) plus 7 derived scores: overall, gestural, verbal, graphic, general comprehension, visual, auditory.

b) ADVANCED BATTERY. Ages 6–12; 20 subtest scores (same as for a except for deletion of visual matching and graphic geometric forms and the addition of reading [function, backwards], verbal description, graphic [function, names, drawing], drawing copying) plus 7 derived scores (same as for a).

For additional information and a review by Lon L. Emerick, see 8:972.

[1853]

The Porteus Maze Test. Ages 3 and over; 1914–65; PMT; 2 scores: quantitative, qualitative; 2 editions and 2 supplements; Stanley D. Porteus.
a) VINELAND REVISION. Ages 3 and over; 1914–24; 13 mazes: years 3–12, 14, adult 1, 2; Stoelting Co.*
b) VINELAND REVISION: NEW SERIES. Ages 3 and over; 1914–65; 12 mazes: years 3–12, 14, adult 1; The Psychological Corporation.*
c) PORTEUS MAZE EXTENSION. Ages 7 and over; 1953–65; for use only as a practice-free retest of b; 8 mazes: years 7–12, 14, adult; The Psychological Corporation.*
d) PORTEUS MAZE SUPPLEMENT. Ages 7 and over; 1959–65; for use only as a third retest after b and c; 8 mazes: years 7–12, 14, adult; The Psychological Corporation.*

For additional information, see 8:224 (25 references); see also T2:518 (52 references); for reviews by Richard F. Docter and John L. Horn, and excerpted reviews by William D. Altus, H. B. Gibson, D. C. Kendrick, and Laurance F. Shaffer, see 7:419 (67 references); see also 6:532 (38 references) and 5:412 (28 references); for reviews by C. M. Louttit and Gladys C. Schwesinger, see 4:356 (56 references).

REFERENCES

1–56. See 4:356.
57–84. See 5:412.
85–122. See 6:532.
123–189. See 7:419.
190–241. See T2:518.
242–266. See 8:224.
267. BUGENTAL, D. B., WHALEN, C. K., & HENKER, B. Causal attributions of hyperactive children and motivational assumptions of two behavior–change approaches: Evidence for an interactionist position. *Child Development*, 1977, 48, 874–884.
268. GOODMAN, J. F. Aging and intelligence in young retarded adults: A cross-sectional study of fluid abilities in three samples. *Psychological Reports*, 1977, 41, 255–263.
269. HAMPSON, S. E., & KLINE, P. Personality dimensions differentiating certain groups of abnormal offenders from non-offenders. *British Journal of Criminology*, 1977, 17, 310–331.
270. JUDD, L. L., HUBBARD, R. B., HUEY, L. Y., ATTWELL, P. A., JANOWSKY, D. S., & TAKAHASHI, K. I. Lithium carbonate and ethanol induced "highs" in normal subjects. *Archives of General Psychiatry*, 1977, 34, 463–467.
271. MALATESTA, C. Z., CIRCO, J., & SMITH, B. A discriminating, non-discriminatory test battery for a prison population. *Corrective & Social Psychiatry & Journal of Behavior Technology, Methods & Therapy*, 1977, 23, 15–17.
272. SPELLACY, F. Neuropsychological differences between violent and nonviolent adolescents. *Journal of Clinical Psychology*, 1977, 33, 966–969.
273. WIDOM, C. S. A methodology for studying noninstitutionalized psychopaths. *Journal of Consulting & Clinical Psychology*, 1977, 45, 674–683.
274. ALTSHULER, K. Z. Toward a psychology of deafness? *Journal of Communication Disorders*, 1978, 11, 159–169.
275. BUGENTAL, D. B., COLLINS, S., COLLINS, L., & CHANEY, L. A. Attributional and behavioral changes following two behavior management interventions with hyperactive boys: A follow-up study. *Child Development*, 1978, 49, 247–250.
276. EZEILO, B. Validating Panga Munthu Test and Porteus Maze Test (Wooden Form) in Zambia. *International Journal of Psychology*, 1978, 13, 333–342.
277. FIRESTONE, P., POITRAS-WRIGHT, H., & DOUGLAS, V. The effects of caffeine on hyperactive children. *Journal of Learning Disabilities*, 1978, 11, 133–141.
278. RIDDLE, M., & ROBERTS, A. H. Psychosurgery and the Porteus Maze Tests. *Archives of General Psychiatry*, 1978, 35, 493–497.
279. SPELLACY, F. Neuropsychological discrimination between violent and non-violent men. *Journal of Clinical Psychology*, 1978, 34, 49–52.
280. SPITZ, H. H., & DeRISI, D. T. Porteus Maze Test performance of retarded young adults and nonretarded children. *American Journal of Mental Deficiency*, 1978, 83, 40–43.
281. FEUERSTEIN, R., RAND, Y., HOFFMAN, M., HOFFMAN, M., & MILLER, R. Cognitive modifiability in retarded adolescents: Effects of instrumental enrichment. *American Journal of Mental Deficiency*, 1979, 83, 539–550.
282. GLENWICK, D. S., & BAROCAS, R. Training impulsive children in verbal self-control by use of natural change agents. *Journal of Special Education*, 1979, 13, 387–398.
283. HERJANIC, B. M., BARREDO, V. H., HERJANIC, M., & TOMELLERI, C. J. Children of heroin addicts. *International Journal of the Addictions*, 1979, 14, 919–931.
284. JACKSON, A. M., FARLEY, G. K., ZIMET, S. G., & GOTTMAN, J. M. Optimizing the WISC-R test performance of low- and high-impulsive emotionally disturbed children. *Journal of Learning Disabilities*, 1979, 12, 622–625.
285. KENDALL, P. C., & WILCOX, L. E. Self-control in children: Development of a rating scale. *Journal of Consulting & Clinical Psychology*, 1979, 47, 1020–1029.
286. SATTERFIELD, J. H., CANTWELL, D. P., & SATTERFIELD, B. T. Multimodality treatment. *Archives of General Psychiatry*, 1979, 36, 965–974.
287. WEISS, S. C. Some observations on Porteus Maze performance among the Campa Indians of Eastern Peru. *Journal of Social Psychology*, 1979, 108, 123–124.
288. WORMITH, J. S., & HASENPUSCH, B. Multidimensional measurement of delayed gratification preference with incarcerated offenders. *Journal of Clinical Psychology*, 1979, 35, 218–225.
289. ASHMAN, A. F., & DAS, J. P. Relation between planning and simultaneous-successive processing. *Perceptual & Motor Skills*, 1980, 51, 371–382.
290. BESSON, J. A. O. A diagnostic pointer to adult metachromatic leucodystrophy. *British Journal of Psychiatry*, 1980, 137, 186–187.
291. CONNERS, C. K., & TAYLOR, E. Pemoline, methylphenidate, and placebo in children with minimal brain dysfunction. *Archives of General Psychiatry*, 1980, 37, 922–930.
292. CUMMINGS, J., HEBBEN, N. A., OBLER, L., & LEONARD, P. Nonaphasic misnaming and other neurobehavorial features of an unusual toxic encephalopathy: Case study. *Cortex*, 1980, 16, 315–323.
293. GOW, L., & WARD, J. Effects of modification of conceptual tempo on acquisition of work skills. *Perceptual & Motor Skills*, 1980, 50, 107–116.
294. HOVANITZ, C. A., & GYNTHER, M. D. The prediction of impulsive behavior: Comparative validities of obvious vs. subtle MMPI hypomania (MA) items. *Journal of Clinical Psychology*, 1980, 36, 422–427.
295. KENDALL, P. C., & WILCOX, L. E. Cognitive-behavioral treatment for impulsivity: Concrete versus conceptual training in non-self-controlled problem children. *Journal of Consulting & Clinical Psychology*, 1980, 48, 80–91.
296. O'KEEFE, E. J. Impulsivity and risk taking in nondelinquent boys. *Perceptual & Motor Skills*, 1980, 50, 722.
297. HOLMES, C. S. Reflective training and causal attributions in impulsive mildly retarded children. *Journal of Clinical Child Psychology*, 1981, 10, 194–199.
298. KENDALL, P. C. One-year follow-up of concrete versus conceptual cognitive-behavorial self-control training. *Journal of Consulting & Clinical Psychology*, 1981, 49, 748–749.
299. STATON, R. D., WILSON, H., & BRUMBACK, R. A. Cognitive improvement associated with tricyclic antidepressant treatment of childhood major depressive illness. *Perceptual & Motor Skills*, 1981, 53, 219–234.
300. WENDER, P. H., REIMHERR, F. W., & WOOD, D. R. Attentional deficit disorder ("minimal brain dysfunction") in adults. *Archives of General Psychiatry*, 1981, 38, 449–456.

[1854]

Portland Prognostic Test for Mathematics. Grades 6.9–8.0, 8.5–9.0; 1960–71; Ernest Hayes; Hayes Educational Tests.*

See T2:646 (1 reference); for a review by Cyril J. Hoyt, see 6:588 (1 reference).

[1855]
Position Analysis Questionnaire. Business and industry; 1969–73; PAQ; "analysis of jobs in terms of 187 job elements that reflect... the basic human behaviors in jobs, regardless of the specific 'technological' area or level of the job"; each position should be rated by 3 or more analysts; 32 job dimension scores (watching devices/materials for information, interpreting what is heard or seen, using data originating with people, watching things from a distance, evaluating information from things, being aware of environmental conditions, being aware of body movement and balance, making decisions, processing information, controlling machines/processes, using hands and arms to control/modify, using feet/hands to operate equipment/vehicles, performing activities requiring general body movement, using hands and arms to move/position things, using fingers vs. general body movement, performing skilled/technical activities, communicating judgements-decisions-information, exchanging job-related information, performing staff/related activities, contacting supervisor or subordinates, dealing with the public, being in a hazardous/unpleasant environment, engaging in personally demanding situations, engaging in businesslike work situations, being alert to detail/changing conditions, performing unstructured vs. structured work, working on a variable vs. regular schedule, having decision making-communication-social responsibility, performing skilled activities, being physically active/related environmental conditions, operating equipment/vehicles, processing information) plus estimated means, standard deviations, and validity coefficients of 9 GATB scores (intelligence, verbal, numerical, spatial, form perception, clerical perception, motor coordination, finger dexterity, manual dexterity) for job incumbents; Ernest J. McCormick, P. R. Jeanneret, and Robert C. Mecham; published by PAQ Services, Inc.; distributed by University Book Store.*

For additional information and a review by Alan R. Bass, see 8:983 (17 references).

REFERENCES

1–17. See 8:983.
18. ARVEY, R. D., PASSINO, E. M., & LOUNSBURY, J. W. Job analysis results as influenced by sex of incumbent and sex of analyst. *Journal of Applied Psychology*, 1977, 62, 411–416.
19. DUNHAM, R. B. Relationships of perceived job design characteristics to job ability requirement and job value. *Journal of Applied Psychology*, 1977, 62, 760–763.
20. KUTIE, R. C. An analysis of the job dimensions of word processing, secretaries, administrative support secretaries, and traditional secretaries and the correlation of these job dimensions with job satisfaction factors. *Business Education Forum*, 1977, 32, 38–40.
21. ROUNDS, J. B., JR., SHUBSACHS, A. P. W., DAWIS, R. V., & LOFQUIST, L. H. A test of Holland's environment formulations. *Journal of Applied Psychology*, 1978, 63, 609–616.
22. TAYLOR, L. R. Empirically derived job families as a foundation for the study of validity generalization: Study I. *Personnel Psychology*, 1978, 31, 325–340.
23. TAYLOR, L. R., & COLBERT, G. A. Empirically derived job families as a foundation for the study of validity generalization: Study II. *Personnel Psychology*, 1978, 31, 341–353.
24. CORNELIUS, E. T., III, CARRON, T. S., & COLLINS, M. N. Job analysis models and job classification. *Personnel Psychology*, 1979, 32, 693–708.
25. MCCORMICK, E. J., DENISI, A. S., & SHAW, J. B. Use of the Position Analysis Questionniare for establishing the job component validity of tests. *Journal of Applied Psychology*, 1979, 64, 51–56.
26. MURRANKA, P. A. Task inventories and position analysis for correspondence secretaries, administrative secretaries and supervisors in word processing. *Business Education Forum*, 1979, 34, 54.
27. SMITH, J. E., & HAKEL, M. D. Convergence among data sources, response bias, and reliability and validity of a structured job analysis questionnaire. *Personnel Psychology*, 1979, 32, 677–692.
28. LEVINE, E. L., ASH, R. A., & BENNETT, N. Exploratory comparative study of four job analysis methods. *Journal of Applied Psychology*, 1980, 65, 524–535.
29. ARVEY, R. D., MAXWELL, S. E., GUTENBERG, R. L., & CAMP, C. Detecting job differences: A Monte Carlo study. *Personnel Psychology*, 1981, 34, 709–730.

[1856]
Possible Jobs. Grades 6–16 and adults; 1963; "divergent production of semantic implications" or "ability to suggest alternative deductions"; Arthur Gershon and J. P. Guilford; Sheridan Psychological Services, Inc.*

See T2:573 (9 references) and 6:558 (1 reference).

REFERENCES

1. See 6:558.
2–10. See T2:573.
11. DOMINO, G. Creativity and the home environment. *Gifted Child Quarterly*, 1979, 23, 818–828.

[1857]
★Potential for Foster Parenthood Scale. Applicants for foster parenthood; 1977 (no date on test materials); PFPS; ratings by caseworker; 10 scores: health, employment and income, time, opportunities for cultural and intellectual development, opportunities for religious and spiritual development, marriage, ability and motivation for foster parenthood, flexibility, working with the agency and child's own parents, total; John Touliatos and Byron W. Lindholm; John Touliatos.*

[1858]
The Potter-Nash Aptitude Test for Lumber Inspectors and Other General Personnel Who Handle Lumber. Employees in woodworking industries; 1958; test booklet title is *The P-N Test*; arithmetic; F. T. Potter and N. Nash; N. Nash.* (In-print status uncertain; no reply from publisher.)

For additional information, see 6:1152.

[1859]
Power Reading Survey Test. Grades 1–3, 4–6, 7–12; 1973–75; criterion-referenced tests covering 195 overlapping objectives in 3 areas: word recognition, comprehension, study skills; William E. Blanton, James L. Laffey, Edward L. Robbins, and Carl B. Smith; BFA Educational Media.* (In-print status uncertain; no reply from publisher.)

For additional information, reviews by Ira E. Aaron and William R. Merz, and an excerpted review by Jessie J. DuBois, see 8:768 (1 reference).

[1860]
★Practical Articulation Kit. Grades 2–12; 1972; can be used as a screening device or game for language building; Martha M. McDonough; Interstate Printers & Publishers, Inc.*

[1861]
PRADI Autobiographical Form. Clinical clients; 1966; PAF; Psychological Research and Development Institute and Sheldon J. Lachman (manual); Psychological Publications Press.* (In-print status uncertain; no reply from publisher.)

For additional information, see P:190.

[1862]

PRADI Draw-A-Person Test. Clinical clients; 1966; DAPT; Psychological Research and Development Institute; Psychological Publications Press.* (In-print status uncertain; no reply from publisher.)

For additional information, see P:459.

[1863]

★**Pre-Academic Learning Inventory.** Ages 4.5–6; 1975; 9 areas: language development, speech development, concept development, body concept, auditory channel development, visual channel development, visual-motor integration, eye-hand coordination, gross motor coordination, plus a behavorial checklist; Mildred H. Wood and Fay M. Layne; Academic Therapy Publications.*

[1864]

Predictive Ability Test, Adult Edition. Ages 17 and over; 1974; PAT; ability to predict; Myles I. Friedman; the Author.*

For additional information, see 8:242 (1 reference).

[1865]

Predictive Screening Test of Articulation. Grade 1; 1968–75; PSTA; identification of children unlikely to master normal articulation by end of grade 2 without speech therapy; Charles Van Riper and Robert L. Erickson; Office of Self-Instructional Programs, Division of Continuing Education, Western Michigan University.*

For additional information and a review by Ralph L. Shelton, see 8:973 (7 references); see also T2:2088 (2 references) and 7:964 (1 reference).

[1866]

Preliminary Scholastic Aptitude Test/National Merit Scholarship Qualifying Test. Grades 10–12; 1959–76; PSAT/NMSQT; formerly called *Preliminary Scholastic Aptitude Test*; "a shortened version of the *College Board Scholastic Aptitude Test*"; for guidance in grades 10–12 and scholarship testing in grade 11; administered in October at participating secondary schools; special administration arrangements available for the physically handicapped; 3 scores: verbal, mathematical, selection index (for scholarship consideration by NMSC); Braille and large-type editions available; program administered by The College Board, the National Merit Scholarship Corporation, and Educational Testing Service.*

For additional information and reviews by Jerome E. Doppelt and J. Thomas Hastings, see 8:199 (15 references); see also T2:436 (4 references) and 7:375 (10 references); for a review by Wayne S. Zimmerman of earlier forms, see 6:487 (2 references).

REFERENCES

1–2. See 6:487.
3–12. See 7:375.
13–16. See T2:436.
17–31. See 8:199.
32. PALMER, L. L. Characteristics of near–point and far–point binocular and monocular sighting in classroom and opthalmological populations. *Perceptual & Motor Skills*, 1977, 45, 707–711.
33. THIBEAULT, R. J., ZETLER, A. G., & WILSON, A. P. The achievement of bus transported pupils. *Journal of Teaching & Learning*, 1977, 2, 17–22.
34. ALEXANDER, K. L., COOK, M., & McDILL, E. Curriculum tracking and educational stratification: Some further evidence. *American Sociological Review*, 1978, 43, 47–66.
35. BRASWELL, J. S. The College Board Scholastic Aptitude Test: An overview of the mathematical portion. *Mathematics Teacher*, 1978, 71, 168–180.
36. DOYLE, K. O., JR., & CRICHTON, L. I. Student, peer and self evaluations of college instructors. *Journal of Educational Psychology*, 1978, 70, 815–826.
37. ALDERMAN, D. L., & POWERS, D. E. The effects of special preparation on SAT–verbal scores. *American Educational Research Journal*, 1980, 17, 239–251.
38. DIAMOND, E. E. The AMEG commission report on sex bias in achievement testing. *Measurement & Evaluation in Guidance*, 1980, 13, 135–147.

[1867]

Premarital Communication Inventory. Premarital counselees; 1968–74; PCI; Millard J. Bienvenu, Sr.; the Author.*

For additional information and a review by James R. Clopton, see 8:351.

[1868]

★**Pre-Marital Counseling Inventory.** Premarital counselees; 1975; PMCI; interview form for obtaining and analyzing data in 6 areas: family background, past marital history, history of present relationship, roles for husband and wife, expectations, looking ahead; Richard B. Stuart and Freida Stuart; Research Press.*

[1869]

★**The Premarital Counseling Kit.** Pre-marital counselees; 1978; Millard J. Bienvenu, Sr.; Family Life Publications, Inc.*

a) FORM 1: BASIC INFORMATION.
b) FORM 2: COMMUNICATION INVENTORY.
c) FORM 3: INCOMPLETE SENTENCES.
d) FORM 4: STRENGTHS AND POSSIBLE PROBLEM AREAS.
e) FORM 5: EVALUATION SUMMARY.
f) FORM 6: MARRIAGE PREPARATION PROGRAMMING.

[1870]

PreReading Expectancy Screening Scales. First grade entrants; 1973; PRESS; predicting reading problems in beginning readers; 4 scores: visual sequencing, visual/auditory spatial, auditory sequencing, letter identification; Lawrence C. Hartlage and David G. Lucas; Psychologists and Educators, Inc.*

For additional information and reviews by Robert Dykstra and Joyce E. Hood, see 8:805 (1 reference).

[1871]

Pre-Reading Screening Procedures. First grade entrants of average or superior intelligence; 1968–69; PSP; identification of children "who make errors in perception and recall of language symbols which often indicate a Specific Language Disability, or dyslexia"; 7 or 8 scores: visual (discrimination of letter forms, discrimination of word forms, visual perception memory), visual-motor (copying, visual perception memory), auditory discrimination, letter knowledge, individual auditory tests (optional); Beth H. Slingerland; Educators Publishing Service, Inc.*

See T2:1721 (1 reference); for reviews by Colleen B. Jamison and Roy A. Kress, see 7:732 (1 reference).

REFERENCES

1. See 7:732.
2. See T2:1721.

3. LITCHER, J. H., ROBERGE, L. P., MEYER, M., & KARNES, L. R. Alternative learning experiences for high–risk, first–grade students. *Journal of Learning Disabilities*, 1979, 12, 686–688.

[1872]

Preschool and Early Primary Skills Survey, Preliminary Edition. Ages 3–3 to 7–2; 1971; PEPSS; 4 or 5 scores: picture recognition, picture relationship, picture sequence, total, form completion (optional); John A. Long, Jr., Morton Morris, and George A. W. Stouffer, Jr.; distribution by Mafex Associates, Inc.*

[1873]

Preschool and Kindergarten Performance Profile. Preschool and kgn; 1970; PKPP; ratings by teachers; 11 scores: social (interpersonal relations, emotional behavior, safety), intellectual (communication, basic concepts, perceptual development, imagination and creative expression), physical (self-help, gross motor skills, fine visual motor skills), total; Alfred J. DiNola, Bernard P. Kaminsky, and Allan E. Sternfeld; Educational Performance Associates, Inc.

[1874]

Preschool Attainment Record, Research Edition. Ages 6 months to 7 years; 1966–67; PAR; 9 scores: ambulation, manipulation, rapport, communication, responsibility, information, ideation, creativity, total; Edgar A. Doll; American Guidance Service.*

See T2:519 (2 references); for a review by Roberta R. Collard, and an excerpted review by C. H. Ammons, see 7:420 (5 references).

REFERENCES

1–5. See 7:420.
6–7. See T2:519.
8. ERNHART, C. B., SPANER, S. D., & JORDAN, T. E. Validity of selected preschool screening tests. *Contemporary Educational Psychology*, 1977, 2, 78–89.
9. RITTER, D. R. Preschool attainment record as a measure of developmental skills. *Journal of Consulting & Clinical Psychology*, 1977, 45, 1184.
10. HUG, N., BARCLAY, A., COLLINS, H., & LAMP, R. Validity and factor structure of the preschool attainment record in head start children. *Journal of Psychology*, 1978, 99, 71–74.
11. KATOFF, L., & REUTER, J. Review of developmental screening tests for infants. *Journal of Clinical Child Psychology*, 1980, 9, 30–34.

[1874A]

The Preschool Behavior Questionnaire. Ages 3–6; 1974; PBQ; 4 scores: hostile-aggressive, anxious-fearful, hyperactive-distractable, total; Lenore Behar and Samuel Stringfield; Lenore Behar.*

[1875]

Preschool Embedded Figures Test. Ages 3–5; 1972; PEFT; downward extension of *Children's Embedded Figures Test*; Susan W. Coates; Consulting Psychologists Press, Inc.*

See T2:1331 (1 reference).

REFERENCES

1. See T2:1331.
2. CONNER, J. M., & SERBIN, L. A. Behaviorally based masculine– and feminine–activity–preference scales for preschoolers: Correlates with other classroom behaviors and cognitive tests. *Child Development*, 1977, 48, 1411–1416.
3. EMMERICH, W. Structure and development of personal–social behaviors in economically disadvantaged preschool children. *Genetic Psychology Monographs*, 1977, 95, 191–245.
4. O'BRIEN, R. A. Relationship of parent–child communication to child's exploratory behavior and self–differentiation. *Nursing Research*, 1980, 29, 150–156.

5. FOORMAN, B. R. A neoPiagetian analysis of four–year–olds' performance on Piaget's water–level task. *Perceptual & Motor Skills*, 1981, 52, 631–639.
6. MOSKOWITZ, D. S., DREYER, A. S., & KRONSBERG, S. Preschool children's field independence: Prediction from antecedent and concurrent maternal and child behavior. *Perceptual & Motor Skills*, 1981, 52, 607–616.

[1876]

★**Preschool Language Assessment Instrument, Experimental Edition.** Ages 3–6; 1978; PLAI; "designed to assess young children's skills in coping with the language demands of the teaching situation"; 4 area scores: matching perception, selective analysis of perception, reordering perception, reasoning about perception; Marion Blank, Susan A. Rose, and Laura J. Berlin; Grune & Stratton, Inc.*

[1877]

*****Preschool Language Scale, Revised Edition.** Ages 2–6; 1969–79; PLS; 3 scores: auditory comprehension, verbal ability, total, plus an articulation section; (Spanish edition available); Irla Lee Zimmerman, Violette G. Steiner, and Roberta Evatt Pond; Charles E. Merrill Publishing Co.*

For additional information and an excerpted review by Barton B. Proger, see 8:929 (3 references); see also T2:2024 (1 reference); for a review by Joel Stark and an excerpted review by C. H. Ammons, see 7:965.

REFERENCES

1. See T2:2024.
2–4. See 8:929.
5. DIEBOLD, M. H., CURTIS, W. S., & DUBOSE, R. F. Developmental scales versus observational measures for deaf-blind children. *Exceptional Children*, 1977, 44, 275–278.
6. SEATON, H. W., & SMITH, S. D. The use of receptive and expressive language development activities for improving student's reading achievement. *National Reading Conference Yearbook*, 1977, 82–87.
7. DAVIDSON, P. W., WILLOUGHBY, R. H., O'TUAMA, L. A., SWISHER, C. N., & BENJAMINS, D. Neurological and intellectual sequelae of Reye's Syndrome. *American Journal of Mental Deficiency*, 1978, 82, 535–541.
8. LEWKOWICZ, N. K., & LOW, L. Y. Effects of visual aids and word structure on phonemic segmentation. *Contemporary Educational Psychology*, 1979, 4, 238–252.
9. STEWART, J. M., MARTIN, M. E., & BRADY, G. M. Communicative disorders at a health–care center. *Journal of Communication Disorders*, 1979, 12, 349–359.
10. BURG, C., RAPOPORT, J. L., BARTLEY, L. S., QUINN, P. O., & TIMMINS, P. Newborn minor physical anomalies and problem behavior at age three. *American Journal of Psychiatry*, 1980, 137, 791–796.
11. RUBENSTEIN, J. L., HOWES, C., & BOYLE, P. A two-year follow-up of infants in community-based day care. *Journal of Child Psychology & Allied Disciplines*, 1981, 22, 209–218.

[1878]

★**Preschool Screening Instrument.** Ages 4–5; 1979; PSSI; 6 scores: human figure drawing, visual motor perception/fine motor, gross motor, language development, speech, behavior; Stephen Paul Cohen; Stoelting Co.*

[1879]

Preschool Self-Concept Picture Test. Ages 4–5; 1966–68; PSCPT; comparison of self-concept and ideal self-concept; Rosestelle B. Woolner; the Author.*

For additional information, see P:212 (1 reference).

[1880]

Prescriptive Reading Inventory. Grades kgn.0–1.0, kgn.5–2.0, 1.5–2.5, 2.0–3.5, 3.0–4.5, 4.0–6.5; 1972–77; PRI; 2 criterion-referenced tests; 30 to 42 scores (mastery, needs review, nonmastery) covering 90 reading objectives for Levels A–D and 30 objectives (10 specific, 20 category) for Levels 1 and 2; CTB/McGraw-Hill.*

a) PRESCRIPTIVE READING INVENTORY. 1972–76.

1) *Level 1.* Grades kgn.0–1.0; 1976; 30 scores: 2 scores (each based on 3 items) plus total in each of 10 categories (sound discrimination, sound matching, form matching, visual reasoning, sound-symbol correspondence, letter names, oral language, literal comprehension, interpretive comprehension, attention skills).

2) *Level 2.* Grades kgn.5–2.0; 1976; 30 scores: 2 scores (each based on 3 items) plus total in each of 10 categories (sound discrimination, sound matching, sound-symbol correspondence, visual reasoning, oral language, sight vocabulary, initial reading, attention skills, literal comprehension, interpretive comprehension).

3) *Level A.* Grades 1.5–2.5; 1972–76; 34 scores (each based on 3–5 items): recognition of sounds and symbols (2 scores), phonic analysis (4 scores), structural analysis (9 scores), translation (7 scores), literal comprehension (3 scores), interpretive comprehension (7 scores), critical comprehension (2 scores).

4) *Level B.* Grades 2.0–3.5; 1972–76; 41 scores (each based on 3–6 items): recognition of sounds and symbols (2 scores), phonic analysis (8 scores), structural analysis (8 scores), translation (7 scores), literal comprehension (3 scores), interpretive comprehension (12 scores), critical comprehension (1 score).

5) *Level C.* Grades 3.0–4.5; 1972–76; 42 scores (each based on 3–8 items): phonic analysis (4 scores), structural analysis (8 scores), translation (8 scores), literal comprehension (5 scores), interpretive comprehension (13 scores), critical comprehension (4 scores).

6) *Level D.* Grades 4.0–6.5; 1972–76; 38 scores (each based on 3–6 items): phonic analysis (3 scores), structural analysis (5 scores), translation (6 scores), literal comprehension (3 scores), interpretive comprehension (12 scores), critical comprehension (9 scores).

b) PRI INTERIM TESTS. 1972–77; "short, teacher-scored tests for each of PRI's objectives"; 20–42 tests (14–25 single-sheet skills tests and 9–24 comprehension tests in 3–7 booklets) each based on 3 (Levels 1 and 2) or 5 (Levels A–D) items; 6 levels (1, 2, A, B, C, D).

For additional information and reviews by Roger Farr and Carolyn E. Massad, see 8:769 (5 references).

REFERENCES

1–5. See 8:769.
6. HAMBLETON, R. K., & EIGNOR, D. R. Guidelines for evaluating criterion–referenced tests and test manuals. *Journal of Educational Measurement,* 1978, 15, 321–327.

[1881]

Prescriptive Reading Inventory Interim Tests. Grades 1.5–2.5, 2.0–3.5, 3.0–4.5, 4.0–6.5; 1973; experimental edition; primarily for use after study of a behavior prescribed by the *Prescriptive Reading Inventory;* 163 scores (mastery, needs review, non-mastery) covering 90 reading objectives; mastery interpreted as 80 percent correct; also identifies "students who failed to show mastery of at least 60% of the objectives" in any of the following categories: recognition of sounds and symbols (grades 1.5–3.5 only), phonic analysis, structural analysis, translation, literal comprehension, interpretive comprehension, critical comprehension; 4 levels; CTB/McGraw-Hill.*

a) A (RED) LEVEL. Grades 1.5–2.5; 25 skills tests, 10 comprehension tests in 3 booklets; no manual.

b) B (GREEN) LEVEL. Grades 2.0–3.5; 25 skills tests, 19 comprehension tests in 6 booklets.

c) C (BLUE) LEVEL. Grades 3.0–4.5; 20 skills tests, 27 comprehension tests in 8 booklets.

d) D (ORANGE) LEVEL. Grades 4.0–6.5; 14 skills tests, 28 comprehension tests in 8 booklets.

[1882]

★**Prescriptive Reading Performance Test.** Grades 1–12 and adult; 1978; PRPT; measures reading level, paragraph reading comprehension, word attack skills, spelling performance; 7 scores: identified words (phonetic, sight, total), error words (phonetic, sight, phonetic equivalent, total); Janet B. Fudala; Western Psychological Services.*

[1883]

Present State Examination. Adult psychiatric patients; 1967–74; PSE; clinical interview questionnaire for rating by psychiatrist of psychiatric symptoms reported by patient as occurring during preceding month; 38 syndrome scores and various derived scores; no scoring instructions except description of computer program; J. K. Wing, J. E. Cooper, and N. Sartorius; Cambridge University Press.*

For additional information, a review by Raymond D. Fowler, Jr., and excerpted reviews by Jack Zusman, Isabel C. A. Moyes, Clive A. Sims, and David Goldberg, see 8:649 (26 references).

REFERENCES

1–26. See 8:649.
27. MCCABE, M. S. Reactive psychosis and schizophrenia with good prognosis. *Archives of General Psychiatry,* 1976, 33, 571–576.
28. PHILLIPSON, O. T., MCKEOWN, J. M., BAKER, J., & HEALEY, A. F. Correlation between plasma chlorpromazine and its metabolites and clinical ratings in patients with acute relapse of schizophrenic and paranoid psychosis. *British Journal of Psychiatry,* 1977, 131, 172–184.
29. SYLPH, J. A., & KEDWARD, H. B. Alternatives to the mental hospital. *Archives of General Psychiatry,* 1977, 34, 909–912.
30. BROCKINGTON, I. F., KENDELL, R. E., KELLETT, J. M., CURRY, S. H., & WAINWRIGHT, S. Trials of lithium, chlorpromazine and amitriptyline in schizoaffective patients. *British Journal of Psychiatry,* 1978, 133, 162–168.
31. CHAMBERS, C. A., & NAYLOR, G. J. A controlled trial of L–tryptophan in mania. *British Journal of Psychiatry,* 1978, 132, 555–559.
32. CHEADLE, A. J., FREEMAN, H. L., & KORER, J. Chronic schizophrenic patients in the community. *British Journal of Psychiatry,* 1978, 132, 221–227.
33. HENDERSON, S., BYRNE, D. G., DUNCAN–JONES, P., ADCOCK, S., SCOTT, R., & STEELE, G. P. Social bonds in the epidemiology of neurosis: A preliminary communication. *British Journal of Psychiatry,* 1978, 132, 463–466.
34. HENDERSON, S., DUNCAN–JONES, P., MCAULEY, H., & RITCHIE, K. The patient's primary group. *British Journal of Psychiatry,* 1978, 132, 74–86.
35. LEFF, J. P. Psychiatrists' versus patients' concepts of unpleasant emotions. *British Journal of Psychiatry,* 1978, 133, 306–313.
36. SHULMAN, R., GRIFFITHS, J., & DIEWOLD, P. Catechol–o–methyl transferase activity in patients with depressive illness and anxiety states. *British Journal of Psychiatry,* 1978, 132, 133–138.
37. SILVERSTEIN, M. L., & HARROW, M. First–rank symptoms in the postacute schizophrenic: A follow–up study. *American Journal of Psychiatry,* 1978, 135, 1481–1486.
38. STRAUSS, J. S., KIKES, R. F., RITZLER, B. A., HARDER, D. W., & VAN ORD, A. Patterns of disorder in first admission psychiatric patients. *Journal of Nervous & Mental Disease,* 1978, 166, 611–623.
39. BHROLCHÁIN, M. N., BROWN, G. W., & HARRIS, T. O. Psychotic and neurotic depression: 2. Clinical characteristics. *British Journal of Psychiatry,* 1979, 134, 94–107.
40. BOND, P. A., CUNDALL, R. L., & FALLOON, I. R. H. Monoamine oxidase (MAO) of platelets, plasma, lymphocytes and granulocytes in schizophrenia. *British Journal of Psychiatry,* 1979, 134, 360–365.

41. BROCKINGTON, I. F., KENDELL, R. E., WAINWRIGHT, S., HILLIER, V. F., & WALKER, J. The distinction between the affective psychoses and schizophrenia. *British Journal of Psychiatry*, 1979, 135, 243–248.

42. CUTTING, J. Memory in functional psychosis. *Journal of Neurology, Neurosurgery & Psychiatry*, 1979, 42, 1031–1037.

43. FINLAY-JONES, R. A., & MURPHY, E. Severity of psychiatric disorder and the 30-item general health questionnaire. *British Journal of Psychiatry*, 1979, 134, 609–616.

44. FREEMAN, H., CHEADLE, A. J., & KORES, J. R. Use of hospital services by chronic schizophrenics in the community. *British Journal of Psychiatry*, 1979, 134, 417–421.

45. FREEMAN, S. J. J., FORMO, A., ALAMPUR, A. G., & SOMMERS, A. F. Psychiatric disorder in a skid-row mission population. *Comprehensive Psychiatry*, 1979, 20, 454–462.

46. GRUZELIER, J. H., & HAMMOND, N. V. Gains, losses, and lateral differences in the hearing of schizophrenic patients. *British Journal of Psychiatry*, 1979, 70, 319–330.

47. HIRSCH, S. R., PIATT, S., KNIGHTS, A., & WEYMAN, A. Shortening hospital stay for psychiatric care: Effect on patients and their families. *British Medical Journal*, 1979, 1, 442–446.

48. HORVATH, T., & MEARES, R. The sensory filter in schizophrenia: A study of habituation, arousal, and the dopamine hypothesis. *British Journal of Psychiatry*, 1979, 134, 39–45.

49. JOHNSTONE, E. C., FRITH, C. D., GOLD, A., & STEVENS, M. The outcome of severe acute schizophrenic illnesses after one year. *British Journal of Psychiatry*, 1979, 134, 28–33.

50. KNIGHTS, A., OKASHA, M. S., SALIH, M. A., & HIRSCH, S. R. Depressive and extrapyramidal symptoms and clinical effects: A trial of fluphenazine versus flupenthixol in maintenance of schizophrenic out-patients. *British Journal of Psychiatry*, 1979, 135, 515–523.

51. LURIA, R. E., & BERRY, R. Reliability and descriptive validity of PSE syndromes. *Archives of General Psychiatry*, 1979, 36, 1187–1195.

52. MURRAY, R. M., OON, M. C. H., RODNIGHT, R., BIRLEY, J. L. T., & SMITH, A. Increased excretion of dimethyltryptamine and certain features of psychosis. *Archives of General Psychiatry*, 1979, 36, 644–649.

53. NEWSON-SMITH, J. G. B., & HIRSCH, S. R. A comparison of social workers and psychiatrists in evaluating parasuicide. *British Journal of Psychiatry*, 1979, 134, 335–342.

54. ORLEY, J., & WING, J. K. Psychiatric disorders in two African villages. *Archives of General Psychiatry*, 1979, 36, 513–520.

55. SCHULTZ, C. L., & HERRON, W. G. Comparison of process–reactive measures in schizophrenia. *Journal of Clinical Psychology*, 1979, 35, 270–277.

56. SERBAN, G. Mental status, functioning, and stress in chronic schizophrenic patients in community care. *American Journal of Psychiatry*, 1979, 136, 948–952.

57. SERBAN, G., & GIDYNSKI, C. B. Relationship between cognitive defect, affect response and community adjustment in chronic schizophrenia. *British Journal of Psychiatry*, 1979, 134, 602–608.

58. STRAUSS, J. S., GABRIEL, K. R., KOKES, R. F., RITZLER, B. A., VAN ORD, A., & TARANA, E. Do psychiatric patients fit their diagnoses? Patterns of symptomatology as described with the biplot. *Journal of Nervous & Mental Disease*, 1979, 167, 105–113.

59. YOZAWITZ, A., BRUDER, G., SUTTON, S., SHARPE, L., GURLAND, B., FLEISS, J., & COSTA, L. Dichotic perception: Evidence for right hemisphere dysfunction in affective psychosis. *British Journal of Psychiatry*, 1979, 135, 224–237.

60. CARPENTER, L., & BROCKINGTON, I. F. A study of mental illness in Asians, West Indians and Africans living in Manchester. *British Journal of Psychiatry*, 1980, 137, 201–205.

61. CHECKLEY, S. A., MURRAY, R. M., OON, M. C. H., RODNIGHT, R., & BIRLEY, J. L. T. A longitudinal study of urinary excretion of N, N-dimethyltryptamine in psychotic patients. *British Journal of Psychiatry*, 1980, 137, 236–239.

62. CHOWDHURY, M. E. H., & CHACON, C. Depot fluphenazine and flupenthixol in the treatment of stabilized schizophrenics. A double-blind comparative trial. *Comprehensive Psychiatry*, 1980, 21, 135–139.

63. OWENS, D. G. C., & JOHNSTONE, E. C. The disabilities of chronic schizophrenia–their nature and the factors contributing to their development. *British Journal of Psychiatry*, 1980, 136, 384–395.

64. CUTTING, J. Physical illness and psychosis. *British Journal of Psychiatry*, 1980, 136, 109–119.

65. FENTON, G. W., FENWICK, P. B. C., DOLLIMORE, J., DUNN, T. L., & HIRSCH, S. R. EEG spectral analysis in schizophrenia. *British Journal of Psychiatry*, 1980, 136, 445–455.

66. GRIFFITH, J. H., FRITH, C. D., & EYSENCK, S. B. G. Psychoticism and thought disorder in psychiatric patients. *British Journal of Social & Clinical Psychology*, 1980, 19, 65–71.

67. GRUZELIER, J., THORNTON, S., STANIFORTH, D., ZAKI, S., & YORKSTON, N. Active and passive avoidance learning in controls and schizophrenic patients on racemic propranolol and neuroleptics. *British Journal of Psychiatry*, 1980, 137, 131–137.

68. HARDER, D. W., STRAUSS, J. S., KOKES, R. F., RITZLER, B. A., & GIFT, T. E. Life events and psychopathology severity among first psychiatric admissions. *Journal of Abnormal Psychology*, 1980, 89, 165–180.

69. HENDERSON, S., BYRNE, D. G., DUNCAN-JONES, P., SCOTT, R., & ADCOCK, S. Social relationships, adversity and neurosis: A study of associations in a general population sample. *British Journal of Psychiatry*, 1980, 137, 574–583.

70. KELLY, W. F., CHECKLEY, S. A., & BENDER, D. A. Cushing's Syndrome, tryptophan and depression. *British Journal of Psychiatry*, 1980, 136, 125–132.

71. KNIGHTS, A., HIRSCH, S. R., & PLATT, S. D. Clinical change as a function of brief admission to hospital in a controlled study using the Present State Examination. *British Journal of Psychiatry*, 1980, 137, 170–180.

72. LEFF, J., & VAUGHN, C. The interaction of life events and relatives' expressed emotion in schizophrenia and depressive neurosis. *British Journal of Psychiatry*, 1980, 136, 146–153.

73. LURIA, R. E., & BERRY, R. Teaching the Present State Examination in America. *American Journal of Psychiatry*, 1980, 137, 26–31.

74. MURPHY, E., & BROWNE, G. W. Life events, psychiatric disturbance and physical illness. *British Journal of Psychiatry*, 1980, 136, 326–338.

75. PEREZ, M. M., & TRIMBLE, M. R. Epileptic psychosis–diagnostic comparison with process schizophrenia. *British Journal of Psychiatry*, 1980, 137, 245–249.

76. RITZLER, B., ZAMBIANCO, D., HARDER, D., KASKEY, M. Psychotic patterns of the concept of the object on the Rorschach Test. *Journal of Abnormal Psychology*, 1980, 89, 46–55.

77. ROBIN, A., COPAS, J. B., & FREEMAN-BROWNE, D. L. Problem areas and mental and behavioral status in schizophrenia, neurosis, and depression. *Journal of Nervous & Mental Disease*, 1980, 168, 412–418.

78. TUNE, L. E., CREESE, I., DEPAULO, J. R., SLAVNEY, P. R., COYLE, J. T., & SNYDER, S. H. Clinical state and serum neuroleptic levels measured by radioreceptor assay in schizophrenia. *American Journal of Psychiatry*, 1980, 137, 187–190.

79. WEEKS, D., FREEMAN, C. P. L., & KENDELL, R. E. ECT: III: Enduring cognitive deficits? *British Journal of Psychiatry*, 1980, 137, 26–37.

80. BLACKBURN, I. M., BISHOP, S., GLEN, A. I. M., WHALLEY, L. J., & CHRISTIE, J. E. The efficacy of cognitive therapy in depression: A treatment trial using cognitive therapy and pharmacotherapy, each alone and in combination. *British Journal of Psychiatry*, 1981, 139, 181–189.

81. CORDESS, C., FOLSTEIN, M., & DRACHMAN, D. Psychiatric effects of alternate day steroid therapy. *British Journal of Psychiatry*, 1981, 138, 504–506.

82. DASILVA, L., & JOHNSTONE, E. C. A follow-up study of severe puerperal psychiatric illness. *British Journal of Psychiatry*, 1981, 139, 346–354.

83. DEAN, C., & KENDALL, R. E. The symptomatology of puerperal illness. *British Journal of Psychiatry*, 1981, 139, 128–133.

84. JOHNSTONE, E. C., OWENS, D. G. C., GOLD, A., CROW, T. J., & MACMILLAN, J. F. Institutionalization and the defects of schizophrenia. *British Journal of Psychiatry*, 1981, 139, 195–203.

85. KNIGHTS, A., & HIRSCH, S. R. "Revealed" depression and drug treatment for schizophrenia. *Archives of General Psychiatry*, 1981, 38, 806–811.

86. LEFF, J., & VAUGHN, C. The role of maintenance therapy and relatives' expressed emotion in the relapse of schizophrenia: A two-year follow-up. *British Journal of Psychiatry*, 1981, 139, 102–104.

87. MANSCHRECK, T. C., MAHER, B. A., RUCKLOS, M. E., VEREEN, D. R., JR., & ADER, D. N. Deficient motor synchrony in schizophrenia. *Journal of Abnormal Psychology*, 1981, 90, 321–328.

88. OKASHA, A., & ASHOUR, A. Psycho-demographic study of anxiety in Egypt: The PSE in its Arabic version. *British Journal of Psychiatry*, 1981, 139, 70–73.

89. ROUNSAVILLE, B. J., CACCIOLA, J., WEISSMAN, M. M., & KLEBER, H. D. Diagnostic concordance in a follow-up study of opiate addicts. *Journal of Psychiatric Research*, 1981, 16, 191–201.

90. SILVERSTEIN, M. L., & HARROW, M. Scheiderian first-rank symptoms in schizophrenia. *Archives of General Psychiatry*, 1981, 38, 288–293.

91. STURGEON, D., KUIPERS, L., BERKOWITZ, R., TURPIN, G., & LEFF, J. Psychophysiological responses of schizophrenic patients to high and low expressed emotion relatives. *British Journal of Psychiatry*, 1981, 138, 40–45.

92. TENNANT, C., BEBBINGTON, P., & HURRAY, J. The short-term outcome of neurotic disorders in the community: The relation of remission to clinical factors and to "neutralizing" life events. *British Journal of Psychiatry*, 1981, 139, 213–220.

93. TENNANT, C., SMITH, A., BEBBINGTON, P., & HURRY, J. Parental loss in childhood. Relationship to adult psychiatric impairment and contact with psychiatric services. *Archives of General Psychiatry*, 1981, 38, 309–314.

94. TUNE, L. E., CREESE, I., DEPAULO, J. R., SLAVNEY, P. R., SNYDER, S. H. Neuroleptic serum levels measured by radioreceptor assay

and clinical response in schizophrenic patients. *Journal of Nervous & Mental Disease*, 1981, 169, 60–63.
95. VADHER, A., & NDETEI, D. M. Life events and depression in a Kenyan setting. *British Journal of Psychiatry*, 1981, 139, 134–137.
96. WALKER, E., HOPPES, E., EMORY, E., MEDNICK, S., & SCHULSINGER, F. Environmental factors related to schizophrenia in psychophysiologically labile high-risk males. *Journal of Abnormal Psychology*, 1981, 90, 313–320.

[1884]
The Press Test. Industrial employees; 1961–80; PT; ability to work under stress; 5 scores: reading speed, color-naming speed, color-naming speed with distraction, difference between color-naming speed with and without distraction, difference between reading speed and color-naming speed; Melany E. Baehr, Raymond J. Corsini, and Ronald Graef (manual); Human Resources Center, University of Chicago.

See T2:1333 (1 reference) and P:213 (1 reference); for reviews by William H. Helm and Allyn Miles Munger, see 6:163.

REFERENCES
1. See P:213.
2. See T2:1333.
3. OSTROGA–PARKER, J., & WILSONCROFT, W. E. Color perception and deafness: College–level comparisons. *Journal of Communication Disorders*, 1979, 12, 361–367.
4. ROE, W. T., WILSONCROFT, W. E., & GRIFFITHS, R. S. Effects of motor and verbal practice on the Stroop task. *Perceptual & Motor Skills*, 1980, 50, 647–650.

[1885]
[Pressey Classification and Verifying Tests]. Grades 1–2, 3–6, 7–12 and adults; 1922–58; 3 levels; S. L. Pressey (except *a*) and L. C. Pressey; Bobbs-Merrill Co., Inc.*

a) PRIMARY CLASSIFICATION TEST. Grades 1–2; 1922.
b) PRESSEY INTERMEDIATE CLASSIFICATION-VERIFYING TESTS. Grades 3–6; 1922–58; 2 tests.
 1) *Pressey Intermediate Classification Test.*
 2) *Pressey Intermediate Verifying Test.*
c) PRESSEY SENIOR CLASSIFICATION-VERIFYING TESTS. Grades 7–12 and adults; 1922–58; 2 tests.
 1) *Pressey Senior Classification Test.*
 2) *Pressey Senior Verifying Test.*

See T2:438 (15 references); for a review by Walter N. Durost, see 6:488 (11 references).

[1886]
Pressey Diagnostic Reading Tests. Grades 3–9; 1929; 4 scores: speed, vocabulary, paragraph meaning, total; S. L. Pressey and L. C. Pressey; Bobbs-Merrill Co., Inc.*

See T2:1576 (3 references).

[1887]
Pressey Diagnostic Tests in English Composition. Grades 7–12; 1923–24; 4 tests; Bobbs-Merrill Co., Inc.*

a) CAPITALIZATION. S. L. Pressey, E. V. Bowers, and Blythe Pearce.
b) PUNCTUATION. S. L. Pressey, Helen Ruhlen, and Blythe Pearce.
c) GRAMMAR. F. R. Conkling, S. L. Pressey, and L. C. Pressey.
d) SENTENCE STRUCTURE. F. R. Conkling, S. L. Pressey, and L. C. Pressey.

See T2:104 (7 references); for reviews by Harry A. Greene and Jean Hoard, see 2:1274.

[1888]
★PRI Reading Systems. Grades kgn–1, 1–2, 2–3, 4–6, 7–9; 1980; PRI/RS; criterion-referenced; part of a system which provides materials for placement, diagnosis, instruction, monitoring, prescription, enrichment, and reinforcement; 2 systems which assess 4 basic skill areas (oral language, word attack and usage, comprehension, applications); 5 levels; CTB/McGraw-Hill.*

a) SYSTEM 1. A graded approach; 2 tests per level (instructional and category).
 1) *Level A.* Grades kgn–1; 3 areas: oral language, oral comprehension, word analysis.
 2) *Level B.* Grades 1–2; 7 areas: oral language, oral comprehension, word analysis, vocabulary, word usage, literal comprehension, interpretive and critical comprehension.
 3) *Level C.* Grades 2–3; 7 areas: word analysis, vocabulary, word usage, literal comprehension, interpretive and critical comprehension, content area reading, study skills.
 4) *Level D.* Grades 4–6; 7 areas same as for 3 above.
 5) *Level E.* Grades 7–9; 7 areas same as for 3 above.
b) SYSTEM 2. A multi-graded approach; 2 tests.
 1) *Placement Test.* Used to determine skill area instructional levels; 4 areas.
  (*a*) Oral Language. Grades kgn–2 (Levels A, B); 2 parts: oral language, oral comprehension.
  (*b*) Word Attack and Usage. Grades kgn–3, 2–9 (Levels A–C, C–E); 3 parts: word analysis, vocabulary, word usage.
  (*c*) Comprehension. Grades 1–3, 2–9 (Levels B–C, C–E); 2 parts: literal comprehension, interpretive and critical comprehension.
  (*d*) Applications. Grades 2–9 (Levels C–E); 2 parts: study skills, content area reading.
 2) *Skill Area Diagnostic Test.* 8 areas.
  (*a*) Oral Language. Grades kgn–2 (Levels A, B); 2 parts: oral language, oral comprehension.
  (*b*) Word Analysis. Grades kgn–5 (Levels A–D).
  (*c*) Vocabulary. Grades 1–9 (Levels B–E).
  (*d*) Word Usage. Grades 1–9 (Levels B–E).
  (*e*) Literal Comprehension. Grades 1–9 (Levels B–E).
  (*f*) Interpretive and Critical Comprehension. Grades 1–9 (Levels B–E).
  (*g*) Study Skills. Grades 1–9 (Levels B–E).
  (*h*) Content Area Reading. Grades 2–9 (Levels C–E).

[1889]
Primary Academic Sentiment Scale. Ages 4–4 to 7–3; 1968; PASS; motivation for learning and level of maturity and parental independence; 2 scores: sentiment, dependency; Glen Robbins Thompson; Priority Innovations, Inc.*

For additional information and a review by Jerome Rosner, see 7:760.

[1890]
[Primary Mathematics Survey Tests]. Grades 2, 3; 1973; subtest of *Primary Survey Tests*; 2 levels, only 1 currently available; E. Glenadine Gibb and Marion

Monroe; handbooks by Kenneth S. Goodman, John C. Manning, Andrew Schiller, and Joseph M. Wepman; Scott, Foresman & Co.*

a) EARLY PRIMARY MATHEMATICS SURVEY TEST. Grade 2.
b) LATE PRIMARY MATHEMATICS SURVEY TEST. Grade 3. *Out of print.*

[1891]

★Primary Measures of Music Audiation. Kgn–3; 1979; 3 scores: tonal, rhythm, composite; Edwin E. Gordon; G.I.A. Publications, Inc.*

REFERENCES

1. GORDON, E. E. The assessment of music aptitudes of very young children. *Gifted Child Quarterly*, 1980, 24, 107–111.

[1892]

Primary Mechanical Ability Tests. Applicants for positions requiring mechanical ability; 1940–50; 4 tests; 5 scores: 4 scores listed below, total; J. H. Hazelhurst; Stevens, Thurow & Associates, Inc.*

a) TEST 1, CROSSES.
b) TEST 2, BOLTS.
c) TEST 3, TOOLS.
d) TEST 4, MISSING LINES.

For additional information, see 6:1087.

[1893]

Primary Reading Assessment Units. Grades 1–3; 1973; PRAU; 10 tests; 1–3 levels; Ellen Campbell, Patricia Tracy, and Eileen McErlaine (except technical report); Ontario Institute for Studies in Education [Canada].* (In-print status uncertain; no reply from publisher.)

a) RECOGNIZING FEELINGS. Grade 1.
b) FINDING REASONS, PREDICTING RESULTS. Grades 1, 2.
c) CHOOSING IDEAS AND DETAILS. Grades 1, 2, 3.
d) DISCOVERING IDEAS AND DETAILS. Grades 1, 2, 3.
e) FINDING THE RIGHT ORDER. Grade 2.
f) FOLLOWING DIRECTIONS. Grade 2.
g) READING GRAPHS. Grade 2.
h) FINDING OUT WHAT THE WRITER MEANS. Grades 2, 3.
i) READING CHARTS. Grade 3.
j) READING MAPS. Grade 3.

For additional information, see 8:737.

[1894]

Primary Reading Profiles. Grades 1–2, 2–3; 1953–68; PRP; 6 scores: reading aptitude, auditory association, word recognition, word attack, reading comprehension, total; James B. Stroud, Albert N. Hieronymus, and Paul McKee; Riverside Publishing Co.*

See T2:1641 (2 references); for reviews by James R. Hobson and Verna L. Vickery, see 5:665.

REFERENCES

1–2. See T2:1641.
3. ARNDT, W. B., SHELTON, R. L., JOHNSON, A. F., & FURR, M. L. Identification and description of homogeneous subgroups within a sample of misarticulating children. *Journal of Speech & Hearing Research*, 1977, 20, 263–292.
4. BELKA, D. E., & WILLIAMS, H. G. Prediction of later cognitive behavior from early school perceptual–motor, perceptual, and cognitive performances. *Perceptual & Motor Skills*, 1979, 49, 131–141.
5. BERNDT, L., & HOGE, R. D. Relations among reading ability, reading mode, and recognition memory. *Canadian Journal of Behavioral Science*, 1979, 11, 252–255.
6. BELKA, D. E., & WILLIAMS, H. G. Canonical relationships among perceptual–motor, perceptual, and cognitive behaviors in children. *Research Quarterly for Exercise & Sport*, 1980, 51, 463–477.
7. RUSS, S. W. Primary process integration on the Rorschach and achievement in children. *Journal of Personality Assessment*, 1980, 44, 338–344.

[1895]

[Primary Reading Survey Tests]. Grades 2, 3; 1973; subtest of *Primary Survey Tests*; 2 levels; Kenneth S. Goodman, John C. Manning, Marion Monroe, Andrew Schiller, Joseph M. Wepman, and E. Glenadine Gibb (handbooks); Scott, Foresman & Co.*

a) EARLY PRIMARY READING SURVEY TEST. Grade 2.
b) LATE PRIMARY READING SURVEY TEST. Grade 3.

REFERENCES

1. MARJORIBANKS, K. Ethnicity, family environment, school attitudes and academic achievement. *Australian Journal of Education*, 1978, 22, 249–261.

[1896]

Primary Self-Concept Inventory. Grades kgn–6; 1973–74; PSCI; self-concept relevant to school success; 10 scores: personal self (physical size, emotional state, total), social self (peer acceptance, helpfulness, total), intellectual self (success, student self, total), total; Douglas G. Muller and Robert Leonetti; Teaching Resources Corporation.*

For additional information and a review by Rick Crandall, see 8:650 (6 references).

REFERENCES

1–6. See 8:650.
7. BACKER, J. C., WOODEN, S., & MULLER, D. Individualized, success oriented instructions in achievement and self-concept of first graders. *Perceptual & Motor Skills*, 1977, 45, 721–722.
8. MULLER, D., CHAMBLISS, J., & WOOD, M. Relationships between area-specific measures of self-concept, self-esteem and academic achievement for junior high school students. *Perceptual & Motor Skills*, 1977, 45, 1117–1118.
9. TORSHEN, K. P., KROEKER, L. P., & PETERSON, R. A. Self-concept assessment for young children: Development of a self-report, peer comparison measure. *Contemporary Educational Psychology*, 1977, 2, 325–331.
10. MOORE, F. B., & PARR, G. D. Models of bilingual education: Comparisons of effectiveness. *Elementary School Journal*, 1978, 79, 93–97.
11. SUMMERLIN, M. L., & WARD, G. R. The effect of parental participation in a parent group on a child's self-concept. *Journal of Psychology*, 1978, 100, 227–232.
12. HUSAK, W. S., & MAGILL, R. A. Correlations among perceptual–motor ability, self-concept and reading achievement in early elementary grades. *Perceptual & Motor Skills*, 1979, 48, 447–450.
13. LARNED, D. T., & MULLER, D. Development of self-concept in grades one through nine. *Journal of Psychology*, 1979, 102, 143–155.
14. NIHIRA, K., MINK, I. T., & MEYERS, C. E. Relationship between home environment and school adjustment of TMR children. *American Journal of Mental Deficiency*, 1981, 86, 8–15.

[1897]

[Primary Survey Tests]. Grades 2, 3; 1973; 4 scores: reading, spelling, language, mathematics; subtests in reading and mathematics available as separates; 2 levels; E. Glenadine Gibb, Kenneth S. Goodman, John C. Manning, Marion Monroe, Andrew Schiller, and Joseph M. Wepman; Scott, Foresman & Co.*

a) EARLY PRIMARY SURVEY TEST. Grade 2.
b) LATE PRIMARY SURVEY TEST. Grade 3.

[1898]

Primary Test of Economic Understanding. Grades 2–3; 1971; PTEU; Donald G. Davison and John H. Kilgore; Bureau of Business and Economic Research,

[1899]

University of Iowa; distributed by Joint Council on Economic Education.*

For additional information and reviews by James O. Hodges and Anna S. Ochoa, see 8:900 (1 reference); see also T2:1967 (1 reference).

[1899]

The Primary Visual Motor Test. Ages 4–8; 1964–70; PVMT; Mary R. Haworth; Grune & Stratton, Inc.*

For additional information and excerpted reviews by Mary D. Sheridan and Sarah A. Aleman, see 8:873 (5 references); for a review by Dale B. Harris and an excerpted review by A. Barclay, see 7:873 (1 reference).

REFERENCES

1. See 7:873.
2–6. See 8:873.
7. HAWORTH, M. R. Visual motor performance of psychotic children. *Journal of Consulting & Clinical Psychology*, 1981, 49, 947–958.

[1900]

The Pritchard-Fox Phoneme Auditory Discrimination Tests: Test Four. Grades kgn and over; 1970; PADT; 13 scores: 4 scores (initial, terminal, medial, total) in each of 3 categories (consonants, vowels, total), total; Alan S. Pritchard and Barbara S. Fox; Alpha Educational Associates.* (In-print status uncertain; no reply from publisher.)

For additional information, see 7:943.

[1901]

Process Diagnostic. Group members; 1974–75; PD; ratings of self and fellow group members on individual contributions to group performance; 9 scores in 3 group climates: problem solving (integrative, content-bound, process-bound), fight (frustration, status-striving, perceptual difference), flight (fear, indifference, impotence) for each group member and total group; no manual; Jay Hall; Teleometrics Int'l.*

For additional information and a review by Paul W. Thayer, see 8:1053.

[1902]

*****A Process for the Assessment of Effective Student Functioning.** Grades kgn–3, 3–7; 1979; formerly called *A Process for In-School Screening of Children With Emotional Handicaps*; catalog uses the title *Pupil Behavior Rating Scale* (PBRS); ratings by teachers, peers, and self; 6 scores: classroom adaptation, interpersonal behavior, intrapersonal behavior, total, peer rating, self rating; Nadine M. Lambert, Carolyn S. Hartsough, and Eli M. Bower; Publishers Test Service.*

See T2:1336 (6 references) and P:215 (1 reference); for reviews by Alan O. Ross and J. Robert Williams, see 6:164 (3 references).

[1903]

★**Profile of a School.** Students and parents and school personnel; 1973–78; POS; for measurement of groups, not individuals; "questionnaires are designed to record the actual human behavior that occurs within the organization as seen not only by its leaders, but also by other members of the school system"; 18 major index scores, each based on 2 or more related items; Jane Gibson Likert and Rensis Likert; Rensis Likert Associates, Inc.*

For an additional listing of Rensis Likert profiles, see 1905.

[1904]

Profile of Mood States. College and psychiatric outpatients; 1971; POMS; earlier experimental forms called *Lorr Outpatient Mood Scale* and *Psychiatric Outpatient Mood Scale*; 6 scores: tension-anxiety, depression-dejection, anger-hostility, vigor-activity, fatigue-inertia, confusion-bewilderment; Douglas M. McNair, Maurice Lorr, and Leo F. Droppleman; EdITS/Educational and Industrial Testing Service.*

For additional information and reviews by William J. Eichman and Thaddeus E. Weckowicz, see 8:651 (33 references); see also T2:1337 (16 references).

REFERENCES

1–16. See T2:1337.
17–49. See 8:651.
50. BEST, C. L., & KILPATRICK, D. G. Psychological profiles of rape crisis counselors. *Psychological Reports*, 1977, 40, 1127–1134.
51. BROWN, W. A., CORRIVEAU, D. P., & MONTI, P. M. Anger arousal by a motion picture: A methodological note. *American Journal of Psychiatry*, 1977, 134, 930–931.
52. COWGELL, V. G. Interpersonal effects of a suicidal communication. *Journal of Consulting & Clinical Psychology*, 1977, 45, 592–599.
53. FREED, E. X., RILEY, E. P., & ORNSTEIN, P. Assessment of alcoholics' moods at the beginning and end of a hospital treatment program. *Journal of Clinical Psychology*, 1977, 33, 887–894.
54. GLOBUS, G., FRIEDMANN, J., HUNTLEY, A., NAITOH, P., MULLANEY, D., & JOHNSON, L. Performance and mood during and after gradual sleep reduction. *Psychophysiology*, 1977, 14, 245–250.
55. GOLDBERG, H. L., & FINNERTY, R. J. A double-blind study of prazepam versus placebo in single daily doses in the treatment of anxiety. *Comprehensive Psychiatry*, 1977, 18, 147–155.
56. Goot eeevning – arrgh. *Science News*, 1977, 112, 105.
57. HUGHES, J. M. Adolescent children of alcoholic parents and the relationship of Alateen to these children. *Journal of Consulting & Clinical Psychology*, 1977, 45, 946–947.
58. JUDD, L. L., HUBBARD, R. B., HUEY, L. Y., ATTEWELL, P. A., JANOWSKY, D. S., & TAKAHASHI, K. I. Lithium carbonate and ethanol induced "highs" in normal subjects. *Archives of General Psychiatry*, 1977, 34, 463–467.
59. JUDD, L. L., HUBBARD, R. B., JANOWSKY, D. S., HUEY, L. Y., & ATTEWELL, P. A. The effect of lithium carbonate on affect, mood, and personality of normal subjects. *Archives of General Psychiatry*, 1977, 34, 346–351.
60. LIRA, F. T., WHITE, M. J., & FINCH, A. J., JR. Anxiety and mood states in delinquent adolescents. *Journal of Personality Assessment*, 1977, 41, 532–536.
61. MEIKLE, S., BRODY, H., & PYSH, F. An investigation into the psychological effects of hysterectomy. *Journal of Nervous & Mental Disease*, 1977, 164, 36–39.
62. SCHUBERT, D. S. P. Alertness and clear thinking as characteristics of high naturally occurring autonomic nervous system arousal. *Journal of General Psychology*, 1977, 97, 179–184.
63. STITT, F. W., FRANE, M., & FRANE, J. W. Mood change in rheumatoid arthritis: Factor analysis as a tool in clinical research. *Journal of Chronic Diseases*, 1977, 30, 135–145.
64. TUTONE, R. M. Correlates of illness susceptibility. *British Journal of Medical Psychology*, 1977, 50, 79–86.
65. BRANCONNIER, R. J., & COLE, J. P. The Impairment Index as a symptom-independent parameter of drug efficacy in geriatric psychopharmacology. *Journal of Gerontology*, 1978, 33, 217–223.
66. DEL GAUDIO, A. C., CARPENTER, P. J., & MORROW, G. R. Male and female treatment differences: Can they be generalized? *Journal of Consulting & Clinical Psychology*, 1978, 46, 1577–1578.
67. FAGAN, T. J., & LIRA, F. T. Profile of Mood States: Racial differences in a delinquent population. *Psychological Reports*, 1978, 43, 348–350.
68. GILBERT, G. S., PARKER, J. C., & CLAIBORN, C. D. Differential mood changes in alcoholics as a function of anxiety management strategies. *Journal of Clinical Psychology*, 1978, 34, 229–232.
69. GLAUBMAN, H., & HARTMANN, E. Daytime state and night-time sleep: A sleep study after a marathon group experience. *Perceptual & Motor Skills*, 1978, 46, 711–715.
70. HASKELL, D. S., GAMBILL, J. D., GARDOS, G., McNAIR, D. M., & FISHER, S. Doxepin or diazepam for anxious and anxious-depressed outpatients? *Journal of Clinical Psychiatry*, 1978, 39, 135–139.
71. JACOBSON, A. F., WEISS, B. L., STEINBOOK, R. M., BRAUZER, B., & GOLDSTEIN, B. J. The measurement of psychological states by use of factors derived from a combination of items from mood and symptom checklists. *Journal of Clinical Psychology*, 1978, 34, 677–685.

72. KANTOR, H. I., MILTON, L. J., & ERNST, M. L. Comparative psychologic effects of estrogen administration on institutional and noninstitutional elderly women. *Journal of the American Geriatrics Society*, 1978, 26, 9–16.

73. LAUGHREN, T. P., BROWN, W. A., & PETRUCCI, J. A. Effects of thioridazine on serum testosterone. *American Journal of Psychiatry*, 1978, 135, 982–984.

74. LEWIS, D. C., MAYER, J., HERSCH, R. G., & BLACK, R. Narcotic antagonist treatment: Clinical experience with naltrexone. *International Journal of the Addictions*, 1978, 13, 961–973.

75. LIRA, F. T., & FAGAN, T. J. The Profile of Mood States: Normative data on a delinquent population. *Psychological Reports*, 1978, 42, 640–642.

76. MILEY, D. P., ABRAMS, A. A., ATKINSON, H., & JANOWSKY, D. S. Successful treatment of thalamic pain with apomorphine. *American Journal of Psychiatry*, 1978, 135, 1230–1233.

77. MILLER, W. R. Behavioral treatment of problem drinkers: A comparative outcome study of three controlled drinking therapies. *Journal of Consulting & Clinical Psychology*, 1978, 46, 74–86.

78. MIRABI, M., MATHEW, R. J., & CLAGHORN, J. L. When is a neuroleptic appropriate in psychoneurosis? *Current Therapeutic Research*, 1978, 23, 101–104.

79. MORGAN, W. P., & HORSTMAN, D. H. Psychometric correlates of pain perception. *Perceptual & Motor Skills*, 1978, 47, 27–39.

80. PAGE, R. D., & SCHAUB, L. H. EMG biofeedback applicability for differing personality types. *Journal of Clinical Psychology*, 1978, 34, 1014–1020.

81. PENICK, E. C., READ, M. R., CROWLEY, P. A., & POWELL, B. J. Differentiation of alcoholics by family history. *Journal of Studies on Alcohol*, 1978, 39, 1944–1948.

82. STEER, R. A. Moods and biorhythms of heroin addicts. *Psychological Reports*, 1978, 43, 829–830.

83. STEER, R. A., & FINE, E. W. Mood differences of men arrested once and men arrested twice for driving while intoxicated *Journal of Studies on Alcohol*, 1978, 39, 922–925.

84. TAYLOR, C. B., FERGUSON, J. M., & READING, J. C. Gradual weight loss and depression. *Behavior Therapy*, 1978, 9, 622–625.

85. WORSLEY, A., & CHANG, A. Oral contraceptives and emotional state. *Journal of Psychosomatic Research*, 1978, 22, 13–16.

86. BARRANCO, S. F., THRASH, M. L., HACKETT, E., FREY, J., WARD, J., & NORRIS, E. Early onset of response to doxepin treatment. *Journal of Clinical Psychiatry*, 1979, 40, 265–269.

87. CAREY, R. G., & POSAVEC, E. J. Holistic care in a cancer care center. *Nursing Research*, 1979, 28, 213–216.

88. CUTLER, N. R., & COHEN, H. B. The effect of one night's sleep loss on mood and memory in normal subjects. *Comprehensive Psychiatry*, 1979, 20, 61–66.

89. GYNTHER, M. D., BURKHART, B. R., & HOVANITZ, C. Do face-valid items have more predictive validity than subtle items? The case of the MMPI Pd scale. *Journal of Consulting & Clinical Psychology*, 1979, 47, 295–300.

90. HAGBERG, J. M., MULLIN, J. P., BAHRKE, M., & LIMBURG, J. Physiological profiles and selected psychological characteristics of national class American cyclists. *Journal of Sports Medicine & Physical Fitness*, 1979, 19, 341–346.

91. JUDD, L. L. Effect of lithium on mood, cognition, and personality function in normal subjects. *Archives of General Psychiatry*, 1979, 36, 860–865.

92. KALTREIDER, N. B., GOLDSMITH, S., & MARGOLIS, A. J. The impact of midtrimester abortion techniques on patients and staff. *American Journal of Obstetrics & Gynecology*, 1979, 35, 235–238.

93. KILPATRICK, D. G., VERONEN, L. J., & RESICK, P. A. The aftermath of rape: Recent empirical findings. *American Journal of Orthopsychiatry*, 1979, 49, 658–669.

94. MATHEW, R. J., CLAGHORN, J. L., & LARGEN, J. Craving for alcohol in sober alcoholics. *American Journal of Psychiatry*, 1979, 136, 594–597.

95. PEAKE, T. H. Therapist–patient agreement and outcome in group therapy. *Journal of Clinical Psychology*, 1979, 35, 637–646.

96. PERONE, M., DEWAARD, R. J., & BARON, A. Satisfaction with real and simulated jobs in relation to personality variables and drug use. *Journal of Applied Psychology*, 1979, 64, 660–668.

97. POLLOCK, V., CHO, D. W., REKER, D., & VOLAVKA, J. Profile of Mood States: The factors and their physiological correlates. *Journal of Nervous & Mental Disease*, 1979, 167, 612–614.

98. SCHUBERT, D. S. P. A biphasic change in mood with a tricyclic antidepressant. *Journal of Nervous & Mental Disease*, 1979, 167, 248–249.

99. SHAPIRO, A. K., STRUENING, E. L., & SHAPIRO, E. The reliability and validity of a placebo test. *Journal of Psychiatric Research*, 1979, 15, 253–290.

100. SOBEL, H. J., & WORDEN, J. W. The MMPI as a predictor of psychosocial adaptation to cancer. *Journal of Consulting & Clinical Psychology*, 1979, 47, 716–724.

101. SOLOFF, P. H., & BARTEL, A. G. Effects of denial on mood and performance in cardiovascular rehabilitation. *Journal of Chronic Diseases*, 1979, 32, 307–313.

102. STEER, R. A., & SCHUT, J. Mood components of heroin addicted men: Psychosocial correlates. *International Journal of the Addictions*, 1979, 14, 1171–1176.

103. VAN DYKE, C., JATLOW, P., UNGERER, J., BARASH, P., & BYCK, R. Cocaine and lidocaine have similar psychological effects after intranasal application. *Life Sciences*, 1979, 24, 271–274.

104. VANNICELLI, M. Treatment contracts in an inpatient alcoholism treatment setting. *Journal of Studies on Alcohol*, 1979, 40, 457–471.

105. VANNICELLI, M., SHAAK, M., & NAHOR, A. Nontransitional residential care: A two year follow–up of a successful community. *American Journal of Orthopsychiatry*, 1979, 49, 522–526.

106. WELDON, E., CLARKIN, J. E., HENNESSY, J. J., & FRANCES, A. Day hospital versus outpatient treatment: A controlled study. *Psychiatric Quarterly*, 1979, 51, 144–150.

107. WEXLER, B. E., & HENINGER, G. R. Alterations in cerebral laterality during acute psychotic illness. *Archives of General Psychiatry*, 1979, 36, 278–284.

108. BROWN, W. A., & SHUEY, I. Response to dexamethasone and subtype of depression. *Archives of General Psychiatry*, 1980, 37, 747–751.

109. BURKHART, B. R., GYNTHER, M. D., & FROMUTH, M. E. The relative predictive validity of subtle vs. obvious items on the MMPI depression scale. *Journal of Clinical Psychology*, 1980, 36, 748–751.

110. COWAN, J. D., KAY, D. C., NEIDERT, G. L., ROSS, F. E., & BELMORE, S. M. Defeated and joyless: Potential measures of change in drug abuser characteristics. *Journal of Nervous & Mental Disease*, 1980, 168, 391–399.

111. GORDON, L. B. Preferential drug abuse: Defenses and behavioral correlates. *Journal of Personality Assessment*, 1980, 44, 345–350.

112. HYNAN, M., HARPER, S., WOOD, C., & KALLAS, C. Parametric effects of blocking and winning in a competition paradigm of human aggression. *Bulletin of the Psychonomic Society*, 1980, 16, 295–298.

113. JUDD, L. L., JANOWSKY, D. S., SEGAL, D. S., & HUEY, L. Y. Naloxone–induced behavioral and physiological effects in normal and manic subjects. *Archives of General Psychiatry*, 1980, 37, 583–586.

114. LOUCKS, S. Loneliness, affect, and self–concept: Construct validity of the Bradley Loneliness Scale. *Journal of Personality Assessment*, 1980, 44, 142–147.

115. MILLER, W. R., TAYLOR, C. A., & WEST, J. C. Focused versus broad-spectrum behavior therapy for problem drinkers. *Journal of Consulting & Clinical Psychology*, 1980, 48, 590–601.

116. ROBBINS, B. J., & BROTHERTON, P. L. Mood change with alcohol intoxication. *British Journal of Social & Clinical Psychology*, 1980, 19, 149–155.

117. STEER, R. A., EMERY, G. D., & BECK, A. T. Correlates of self-reported and clinically assessed depression in male heroin addicts. *Journal of Clinical Psychology*, 1980, 36, 798–800.

118. VILA, J., & BEECH, H. R. Premenstrual symptomatology: An interaction hypothesis. *British Journal of Social & Clinical Psychology*, 1980, 19, 73–80.

119. WEEKS, D. G., MICHELA, J. L., PEPLAU, L. A., & BRAGG, M. E. Relation between loneliness and depression: A structural equation analysis. *Journal of Personality & Social Psychology*, 1980, 39, 1238–1244.

120. WILSON, V. E., MORLEY, N. C., & BIRD, E. I. Mood profiles of marathon runners, joggers and non-exercisers. *Perceptual & Motor Skills*, 1980, 50, 117–118.

121. WOLCHIK, S. A., BIGGS, V. W., WINCZE, J. P., SAKHEIM, D. K., BARLOW, D. H., & MAVISSAKALIAN, M. The effect of emotional arousal on subsequent sexual arousal in men. *Journal of Abnormal Psychology*, 1980, 89, 595–598.

122. WRIGHT, B. M., & STOFFELMAYR, B. E. Distress in clients and significant others: The question of causality. *Family Process*, 1980, 19, 401–410.

123. BOBRUFF, A., GARDOS, G., TARSY, D., RAPKIN, R. M., COLE, J. O., & MOORE, P. Clonazepam and phenobarbital in tardive dyskinesia. *American Journal of Psychiatry*, 1981, 138, 189–193.

124. DORNBUSH, R. L., SHAPIRO, B., & FREEDMAN, A. M. Effects of an ACTH short chain neuropeptide in man. *American Journal of Psychiatry*, 1981, 138, 962–964.

125. ELLIS, E. M., ATKESON, B. M., & CALHOUN, K. S. An assessment of long–term reaction to rape. *Journal of Abnormal Psychology*, 1981, 90, 263–266.

126. JOESTING, J. Comparison of personalities of athletes who sail with those who run. *Perceptual & Motor Skills*, 1981, 52, 514.

127. KILPATRICK, D. G., RESICK, P. A., & VERONEN, L. J. Effects of a rape experience: A longitudinal study. *Journal of Social Issues*, 1981, 37, 105–122.

128. LEFCOURT, H. M., MILLER, R. S., WARE, E. E., & SHERK, D. Locus of control as a modifier of the relationship between stressors and moods. *Journal of Personality & Social Psychology*, 1981, 41, 357–369.

129. NORBECK, J. S., LINDSEY, A. M., & CARRIERI, V. L. The development of an instrument to measure social support. *Nursing Research*, 1981, 30, 264–269.
130. SILVA, J. M., III, SCHULTZ, B. B., HASLAM, R. W., & MURRAY, D. A psychophysiological assessment of elite wrestlers. *Research Quarterly for Exercise & Sport*, 1981, 52, 348–358.
131. SPIEGEL, D., BLOOM, J. R., & YALOM, I. Group support for patients with metastatic cancer. A randomized prospective outcome study. *Archives of General Psychiatry*, 1981, 38, 527–533.
132. SWETT, C., JR. Effects of oxazepam and EMG biofeedback on induced stress. *Current Therapeutic Research*, 1981, 29, 165–169.
133. TAYLOR, C. B., DEBUSK, R. F., DAVIDSON, D. M., HOUSTON, N., & BURNETT, K. Optimal methods for identifying depression following hospitalization for myocardial infarction. *Journal of Chronic Diseases*, 1981, 34, 127–133.

[1905]

★[Profiles from Rensis Likert Associates, Inc.]. 1974–78; for measurement of groups, not individuals; 6 questionnaires; Rensis Likert and Jane Gibson Likert; Rensis Likert Associates, Inc.*

a) PROFILE OF CONFLICT CHARACTERISTICS. 1974; "designed to describe the nature and extent of conflict within and between organizations or groups."
b) PROFILE OF GROUP MEMBER BEHAVIOR. 1977; "designed to describe the overall behavior of the members of any group engaged in group problem solving."
c) PROFILE OF GROUP PROBLEM SOLVING. 1977; "designed to enable each member of a group to describe the group's problem solving behavior."
d) PROFILE OF LEADERSHIP BEHAVIOR. 1977; "designed to describe the behavior of the leader in any group engaged in problem solving."
e) PROFILE OF ORGANIZATIONAL CHARACTERISTICS. 1977–78; "developed to enable persons to describe the management system of style used in their organization."
f) PROFILE OF OWN BEHAVIOR. 1977; "designed to enable a member of a group engaged in problem solving to describe his/her own behavior."

For an additional listing of a Rensis Likert profile, see 1903.

[1906]

★Program for Assessing Youth Employment Skills. Adolescents and young adults with low verbal skills; 1967–79; PAYES; 7 subtests: job-holding skills, attitude toward supervision, self-confidence, job knowledge, job-seeking skills, practical reasoning, vocational interest inventory; Educational Testing Service; Cambridge, The Adult Education Co.*

[1907]

Programmer Aptitude/Competence Test System. Computer programmers and applicants for programmer training; 1970; PACTS; 2 tests; Haverly Systems, Inc.*

a) PACTS APTITUDE TEST. Applicants for programmer training; "ability to learn programming"; 3 scores (correctness, quality, overall grade) for each of 15 problems plus a single overall aptitude rating.
b) PACTS COMPETENCE TEST. Experienced programmers; tests tailored to meet individual needs, local objectives, and time available by selecting 5 to 9 problems in programming (a maximum of 20 may be selected) out of 30 available; a work performance test which requires the use of computer facilities; 5 scores (percent correct, percent of objective, straight score, numeric grade, letter grade) for each problem and 3 final scores (straight score, numeric grade, letter grade).

See T2:2336 (1 reference).

[1908]

*Progress Assessment Chart of Social Development. Mentally handicapped ages birth–1, 1–7, 6–15, adults; 1963–80; PAC; behavior checklist for assessing progress; for *a*, *b*, *f*, 4 areas: self-help, communication, socialization, occupation; for *c*, *d*, *e*, *g*, 5 areas: same as those above plus personal assessment; 8 checklists; (Dutch, French, German, Norwegian, Portuguese, Spanish, and Swedish editions available); H. C. Gunzburg; SEFA (Publications) Ltd. [England].*

a) ELEMENTARY PROGRESS ASSESSMENT CHART. Birth–1 year; 1979; S/E PAC.
b) PRIMARY PROGRESS ASSESSMENT CHART, EIGHTH EDITION. Ages 1–7; 1966–77; P-PAC.
c) PROGRESS ASSESSMENT CHART 1, THIRTEENTH EDITION. Ages 6–16; 1963–77; PAC-1.
d) PROGRESS ASSESSMENT CHART 1A, THIRD EDITION. 1972–80; PAC-1A; extension of PAC-1 relevant to social education.
e) PROGRESS ASSESSMENT CHART 2, TWELFTH EDITION. Adolescents and adults; 1963–77; PAC-2.
f) PROGRESS ASSESSMENT CHART FOR DOWN'S SYNDROME, THIRD EDITION. Ages 6–15 and over; 1973–77; M/PAC-1; adaptation of *c* above.
g) PROGRESS ASSESSMENT CHART I FOR THE SEVERELY HANDICAPPED. Ages 1–5; 1982; S/PAC-1; measures level of skill when verbally requested by another.
h) PROGRESS ASSESSMENT CHART 2 FOR THE SEVERELY HANDICAPPED ADULT. Adults; 1976–77; S/PAC-2.

See T2:1338 (3 references), 7:125 (1 reference), and P:216 (5 references).

REFERENCES

1–5. See P:216.
6. See 7:125.
7–9. See T2:1338.
10. WEINSTOCK, A., WULKAN, P., COLON, C. J., COLEMAN, J., & GONCALVES, S. Stress inoculation and interinstitutional transfer of mentally retarded individuals. *American Journal of Mental Deficiency*, 1979, 83, 385–390.

[1909]

★The Progress Evaluation Scales. Ages 6–12, 13–17, adult mental health clients, developmentally disabled; 1972–81; PES; ratings of present status and goals by patient, therapist, and significant-other; 7 scales: family interaction, occupation, getting along with others, feelings and mood, use of free time, problems, attitude toward self; 4 levels; manual by David Ihilevich and Goldine C. Gleser; Shiawassee County Community Mental Health Services Board.*

a) CHILDREN'S FORM. Mental health clients ages 6–12.
b) ADOLESCENT'S FORM. Mental health clients ages 13–17.
c) ADULT FORM. Adult mental health clients.
d) DEVELOPMENTALLY DISABLED FORM. Developmentally disabled clients.

REFERENCES

1. IHILEVICH, D., GLESER, G. C., GRITTER, G. W., KROMAN, L. J., & WATSON, A. S. Measuring program outcome: The Progress Evaluation Scales. *Evaluation Review*, 1981, 5, 451–477.

[1910]

Progressive Achievement Tests of Listening Comprehension. Standards 1–4 and Forms I–IV (ages 7–14); 1971–72; PATLC; manual by Warwick B. Elley and Neil A. Reid; New Zealand Council for Educational Research [New Zealand].*

For additional information and a review by Roger A. Richards, see 8:453 (2 references).

REFERENCES

1-2. See 8:453.
3. EVANS, G., GEORGEFF, M., & POOLE, M. E. Training in information selection for communication. *Australian Journal of Education*, 1980, 24, 137-154.

[1911]
Progressive Achievement Tests of Mathematics. Standards 2-4 and Forms I-IV (ages 8-14); 1974-75; PATM; 7 overlapping levels called Parts 2 (Standard 2), 3 (3), 4 (4), 5 (Form I), 6 (II), 7 (III), 8 (IV) in 2 booklets; manual by Neil A. Reid and David C. Hughes; New Zealand Council for Educational Research [New Zealand].*

For additional information and a review by Harold C. Trimble, see 8:288.

REFERENCES

1. SEPIE, A. C., & KEELING B. The relationship between types of anxiety and under-achievement in mathematics. *Journal of Educational Research*, 1978, 72, 15-19.

[1912]
Progressive Achievement Tests of Reading. Standards 2-4 and Forms I-IV; 1969-70; PATR; raw scores are converted into "levels of achievement" regardless of age or class and into percentile ranks within half-year age groups; 2 tests; 7 overlapping levels called Parts 2 (Standard 2), 3 (3), 4 (4), 5 (Form I), 6 (II), 7 (III), 8 (IV) in a single booklet; Warwick B. Elley and Neil A. Reid; New Zealand Council for Educational Research [New Zealand]. (Australian edition: Grades 3-9; 1970-73; manual by M. L. Clark; Australian Council for Educational Research [Australia].)*
a) READING COMPREHENSION.
b) READING VOCABULARY.

For additional information and a review by Douglas A. Pidgeon, see 8:738 (1 reference); see also T2:1579 (1 reference); for excerpted reviews by Milton L. Clark and J. Elkins, see 7:699.

REFERENCES

1. See T2:1579.
2. See 8:738.
3. BALDAUF, R. N., JR., DAWSON, R. L. T., PRIOR, J., & PROPST, I. K., JR. Can matching cloze be used with secondary ESL pupils. *Journal of Reading*, 1980, 23, 435-440.
4. NICHOLSON, T., & IMLACH, R. Where do their answers come from? A study of the inferences children make when answering questions about narrative stories. *Journal of Reading Behavior*, 1981, 13, 111-129.

[1913]
*★Progressive Achievement Tests of Study Skills.** Standards 3-4 and Forms I-V (ages 9-15); 1978-79; standardized and developed for use in New Zealand; Neil A. Reid, A. Cedric Croft, and Peter F. Jackson; New Zealand Council for Educational Research [New Zealand].*
a) SERIES 1: KNOWLEDGE AND USE OF REFERENCE MATERIALS. Standards 3-4 and Forms I-V.
b) SERIES 2: READING MAPS, GRAPHS, TABLES AND DIAGRAMS. Standards 3-4 and Forms I-V.
c) SERIES 3: READING STUDY SKILLS. Forms I-V.

REFERENCES

1. JACKSON, P. F. Answer changing on objective tests. *Journal of Educational Research*, 1978, 71, 313-315.

[1914]
Progressive Matrices. Ages 5 and over; 1938-65; PM; 3 levels; J. C. Raven. (U.S. distributor: The Psychological Corporation.)*
a) STANDARD PROGRESSIVE MATRICES. Ages 6 and over; 1938-60.
b) COLOURED PROGRESSIVE MATRICES. Ages 5-11 and mental patients and senescents; 1947-63.
c) ADVANCED PROGRESSIVE MATRICES. Ages 11 and over of above-average intellectual ability; 1943-65; 2 editions.
1) *Set 1.* For use either as a practice test for Set 2 or as a rough screening test.
2) *Set 2, 1962 Revision.* For use either as "a test of intellectual capacity" when used without a time limit or as "a test of intellectual efficiency" when used with a time limit ("usually of 40 minutes").

For additional information, see 8:200 (190 references); see also T2:439 (122 references) and 7:376 (194 references); for a review by Morton Bortner, see 6:490 (78 references); see also 5:370 (62 references); for reviews by Charlotte Banks, W. D. Wall, and George Westby, see 4:314 (32 references); for reviews by Walter C. Shipley and David Wechsler of the 1938 edition, see 3:258 (13 references); for a review by T. J. Keating, see 2:1417 (8 references).

REFERENCES

1-8. See 2:1417.
9-21. See 3:258.
22-53. See 4:314.
54-115. See 5:370.
116-193. See 6:490.
194-387. See 7:376.
388-509. See T2:439.
510-699. See 8:200.
700. KRYWANIUK, L. W., & DAS, J. P. Cognitive strategies in native children: Analysis and intervention. *Alberta Journal of Educational Research*, 1976, 22, 271-280.
701. LEONG, C. K. Spatial-temporal information-processing in children with specific reading disability. *Reading Research Quarterly*, 1976-1977, 12, 204-215.
702. APRIL, R. S., & TSE, P. C. Crossed aphasia in a Chinese bilingual dextral. *Archives of Neurology*, 1977, 34, 766-770.
703. BASHI, J. Effects of inbreeding on cognitive performance. *Nature*, 1977, 266, 440-442.
704. BELMONT, L. Birth order, intellectual competence, and psychiatric status. *Journal of Individual Psychology*, 1977, 33, 97-104.
705. BELMONT, L., WITTES, J., & STEIN, Z. Relation of birth order, family size and social class to psychological functions. *Perceptual & Motor Skills*, 1977, 45, 1107-1116.
706. BEN-ZEEV, S. The influence of bilingualism on cognitive strategy and cognitive development. *Child Development*, 1977, 48, 1009-1018.
707. BOUCHER, J. Alternation and sequencing behavior, and response to novelty in autistic children. *Journal of Child Psychology & Psychiatry & Allied Disciplines*, 1977, 18, 67-72.
708. CONRAD, R. Lip-reading by deaf and hearing children. *British Journal of Educational Psychology*, 1977, 47, 60-65.
709. COX, M. V. Perspective ability: The conditions of change. *Child Development*, 1977, 48, 1724-1727.
710. CRAWFORD, D. A. The HDHQ results of long-term prisoners: Relationships with criminal and institutional behaviour. *British Journal of Social & Clinical Psychology*, 1977, 16, 391-394.
711. GAINOTTI, G., CALTAGIRONE, C., & MICELI, G. Poor performance of right brain-damaged patients on Raven's coloured matrices: Derangement of general intelligence or of specific abilities? *Neuropsychologia*, 1977, 15, 675-680.
712. GOODMAN, J. F. Aging and intelligence in young retarded adults: A cross-sectional study of fluid abilities in three samples. *Psychological Reports*, 1977, 41, 255-263.
713. HALL, V. C., HUPPERTZ, J. W., & LEVI, A. Attention and achievement exhibited by middle- and lower-class black and white

elementary school boys. *Journal of Educational Psychology*, 1977, 69, 115–120.

714. HALL, V. C., & KAYE, D. B. Patterns of early cognitive development among boys in four subcultural groups. *Journal of Educational Psychology*, 1977, 69, 66–87.

715. JOHNSON, E. G., HILTON, S., MACDONALD, I., SCHEAFFE, P., STARK, J., STONE, L., & WATERER, B. The predictive validity of the Raven's Progressive Matrices Test with migrant children. *Australian Journal of Education*, 1977, 21, 187–188.

716. JORM, A. F. Effect of word imagery on reading performance as a function of reader ability. *Journal of Educational Psychology*, 1977, 69, 46–54.

717. KANEKAR, S. Academic performance in relation to anxiety and intelligence. *Journal of Social Psychology*, 1977, 101, 153–154.

718. KIPPER, D. A. The Kahn Test of Symbol Arrangement and Criminality. *Journal of Clinical Psychology*, 1977, 33, 777–781.

719. KIRBY, J. R., & DAS, J. P. Reading achievement, IQ, and simultaneous–successive processing. *Journal of Educational Psychology*, 1977, 69, 564–570.

720. KURDESK, L. A. Structural components and intellectual correlates of cognitive perspective taking in first–through fouth–grade children. *Child Development*, 1977, 48, 1503–1511.

721. LEINHARDT, G. Program evaluation: An empirical study of individualized instruction. *American Educational Research Journal*, 1977, 14, 277–293.

722. LINCOLN, N. B., & STAPLES, D. J. Psychological aspects of some chronic progressive neuromuscular disorders. *Journal of Chronic Diseases*, 1977, 30, 207–215.

723. MALATESTA, C. Z., CIRCO, J., & SMITH, B. A discriminating, non–discriminatory test battery for a prison population. *Corrective & Social Psychiatry & Journal of Behavior Technology, Methods & Therapy*, 1977, 23, 15–17.

724. MAQSUD, M. The influence of social heterogeneity and sentimental credibility on moral judgments of Nigerian Muslim adolescents. *Journal of Cross–Cultural Psychology*, 1977, 8, 113–122.

725. MCGINTY, R. L. The effects of instructions in sentential logic on selected abilities of second– and third–grade children. *Journal of Research in Mathematics Education*, 1977, 8, 88–96.

726. MILGRAM, R. M., & MILGRAM, N. A. The effect of test content and context on the anxiety–intelligence relationship. *Journal of Genetic Psychology*, 1977, 130, 121–127.

727. OPOLOT, J. A. Reliability and validity of Smith's Quick Measure of Achievement. *British Journal of Social & Clinical Psychology*, 1977, 16, 395–396.

728. PAGE, R. D., & SCHAUB, L. H. Intellectual functioning in alcoholics during six months' abstinence. *Journal of Studies on Alcohol*, 1977, 38, 1240–1246.

729. SIMON, A., & WARD, L. O. Age, gender, intelligence, and religious worries in secondary school pupils. *Irish Journal of Education*, 1977, 11, 96–101.

730. SIMON, A., & WARD, L. O. Influence of age, abilities, and angle on pupils' judgements of size of angles. *Perceptual & Motor Skills*, 1977, 45, 949–950.

731. SRIVASTAVA, A. K. Social–class interaction in the language effectiveness of bright secondary school students. *Psychologia*, 1977, 20, 226–233.

732. STEVENS, D. P., STAGG, R., & MACKAY, I. R. What happens when hospitalized patients see their own records. *Annals of Internal Medicine*, 1977, 86, 474–477.

733. TAYLOR, L. J., & SKANES, G. R. A cross–cultural examination of some of Jensen's hypothesis. *Canadian Journal of Behavioural Science*, 1977, 9, 315–322.

734. TOWNSEND, M. A. R., & KEELING, B. The relationship of level I and level II cognitive processes to a test of associative responding. *Journal of Educational Research*, 1977, 70, 127–130.

735. VOSS, H. G., & KELLER, H. Critical evaluation of the Obscure Figures Test as an instrument for measuring "cognitive innovation". *Perceptual & Motor Skills*, 1977, 45, 495–502.

736. WARD, L. O. Variables influencing auditory–visual integration in normal and retarded readers. *Journal of Reading Behavior*, 1977, 9, 290–295.

737. WHEELER, T. J., WATKINS, E. J., & MCLAUGHLIN, S. P. Reading retardation and cross–laterality in relation to short–term information processing tasks. *British Journal of Educational Psychology*, 1977, 47, 126–131.

738. ZEDECK, S., & KAFRY, D. Capturing rater policies for processing evaluation data. *Organizational Behavior & Human Performance*, 1977, 18, 269–294.

739. BECKER, L. D. Learning characteristics of educationally handicapped and retarded children. *Exceptional Children*, 1978, 44, 502–511.

740. BERGLUND, M., & LEIJONQUIST, H. Prediction of cerebral dysfunction in alcoholics: A study of health insurance records. *Journal of Studies on Alcohol*, 1978, 39, 1968–1974.

741. BRIDGEMAN, B., & SHIPMAN, V. C. Preschool measures of self–esteem and achievement motivation as predictors of third–grade achievement. *Journal of Educational Psychology*, 1978, 70, 17–28.

742. CARLSON, J. S. Measuring intellectual capabilities of hearing–impaired children: Effects of testing–the–limits procedures. *Volta Review*, 1978, 80, 216–224.

743. CARLSON, J. S., & WIEDL, K. H. Use of testing–the–limits procedures in the assessment of intellectual capabilities in children with learning difficulties. *American Journal of Mental Deficiency*, 1978, 82, 559–564.

744. COUGHLAN, A. K., & WARRINGTON, E. K. Word comprehension and word–retrieval in patients with localized cerebral lesions. *Brain*, 1978, 101, 163–185.

745. COURT, J. H. A researcher's bibliography for Raven's Progressive Matrices and Mill Hill Vocabulary Scales. *Australian Psychologist*, 1978, 13, 248.

746. COX, M. V. Perspective ability: A training program. *Journal of Educational Research*, 1978, 71, 127–133.

747. CUMMINS, J., & DAS, J. P. Simultaneous and successive syntheses and linguistic processes. *International Journal of Psychology*, 1978, 13, 129–138.

748. CUMMINS, J., & MULCAHY, R. Orientation to language in Ukranian–English bilingual children. *Child Development*, 1978, 49, 1239–1242.

749. DAS, J. P., & CUMMINS, J. Academic performance and cognitive processes in EMR children. *American Journal of Mental Deficiency*, 1978, 83, 197–199.

750. DAS, J. P., LEONG, C. K., & WILLIAMS, N. H. The relationship between learning disability and simultaneous–successive processing. *Journal of Learning Disabilities*, 1978, 11, 618–625.

751. DAS, J. P., & SOYSA, P. Late effects of malnutrition on cognitive competence. *International Journal of Psychology*, 1978, 13, 295–303.

752. DENES, F., SEMENZA, C., STOPPA, E., & GRADENIGO, G. Selective improvement by unilateral brain–damaged patients on Raven Coloured Progressive Matrices. *Neuropsychologia*, 1978, 16, 749–752.

753. ELGEROT, A. Psychological and physiological changes during tobacco–abstinence in habitual smokers. *Journal of Clinical Psychology*, 1978, 34, 759–764.

754. FRANK, H., & WILCOX, C. Development and preliminary cross–validation of two-step procedure for firefighter selection. *Psychological Reports*, 1978, 43, 27–36.

755. FREEMAN, J. The gifted child syndrome. *British Journal of Educational Psychology*, 1978, 48, 358.

756. GAINOTTI, G., CALTAGIRONE, C., & MICELI, G. Immediate visual–spatial memory in hemisphere damaged patients: Impairment of verbal coding and of perceptual processing. *Neuropsychologia*, 1978, 16, 501–507.

757. GARRITY, L. I., & SERVOS, A. B. Comparison of measures of adaptive behaviors in preschool children. *Journal of Consulting & Clinical Psychology*, 1978, 46, 288–293.

758. GENESEE, F., TUCKER, G. R., & LAMBERT, W. E. The development of ethnic identity and ethnic role taking skills in children from different school settings. *International Journal of Psychology*, 1978, 13, 39–57.

759. GHUMAN, P. A. S. Nature of intellectual development of Punjabi children. *International Journal of Psychology*, 1978, 13, 281–294.

760. GOH, D. S., & MOORE, C. Personality and academic achievement in three educational levels. *Psychological Reports*, 1978, 43, 71–79.

761. GOUGH, H. G., LAZZARI, R., FIORAVANTI, M., & STRACCA, M. An Adjective Check List scale to predict military leadership. *Journal of Cross–Cultural Psychology*, 1978, 9, 381–400.

762. HARBER, J. R. The influence of abstract reasoning ability and degree of bidialectism on third and fifth graders' reading performance. *Educational Research Quarterly*, 1978, 3, 34–39.

763. HOLTZMAN, R. N. N., RUDEL, R. G., & GOLDENSOHN, E. S. Paroxysmal alexia. *Cortex*, 1978, 14, 592–603.

764. HOUSE, E. R., GLASS, G. V., MCLEAN, L. D., & WALKER, D. F. No simple answer: Critique of the follow through evaluation. *Harvard Educational Review*, 1978, 48, 128–160.

765. JARMAN, R. F. Cross–modal and intramodal matching: Relationships to simultaneous and successive synthesis and levels of performance among three intelligence groups. *Alberta Journal of Educational Research*, 1978, 24, 100–112.

766. JARMAN, R. F. Patterns of cognitive ability in retarded children: A reexamination. *American Journal of Mental Deficiency*, 1978, 82, 344–348.

767. JOHNSON, E. S. Validation of concept–learning strategies. *Journal of Experimental Psychology: General*, 1978, 107, 237–266.

768. KEATING, D. P. A search for social intelligence. *Journal of Educational Psychology*, 1978, 70, 218–223.

769. KEATING, D. P., & BOBBITT, B. L. Individual and developmental differences in cognitive–processing components of mental ability. *Child Development*, 1978, 49, 155–167.

770. KIRBY, J. R., & DAS, J. P. Information processing and human abilities. *Journal of Educational Psychology*, 1978, 70, 58–66.

771. KIRBY, J. R., & DAS, J. P. Skills underlying Coloured Progressive Matrices. *Alberta Journal of Educational Research*, 1978, 24, 94–99.

772. KROEGER, E. The role of training in the assessment of learning ability in migrant children: Overcoming lack in performance or competence. *British Journal of Educational Psychology*, 1978, 48, 361–362.

773. KUMAR, P., & GAIROLA, L. Some psychological factors related to family planning among women. *Indian Journal of Social Work*, 1978, 39, 129–132.

774. KURDEK, L. A. Relationship between cognitive perspective taking and teachers' ratings of children's classroom behavior in grades one through four. *Journal of Genetic Psychology*, 1978, 132, 21–27.

775. LUNNEBORG, C. E. Some information–processing correlates of measures of intelligence. *Multivariate Behavioral Research*, 1978, 13, 153–161.

776. MARJORIBANKS, K. Ethnicity, family environment and cognitive performance. *Psychological Reports*, 1978, 42, 1277–1278.

777. MARJORIBANKS, K. Ethnicity, school attitudes, intelligence and academic achievement. *International Journal of Psychology*, 1978, 13, 167–178.

778. McGURK, B. J., BOLTON, N., & SMITH, M. Some psychological, educational and criminological variables related to recidivism in deliquent boys. *British Journal of Social & Clinical Psychology*, 1978, 17, 251–254.

779. McKENNA, P., & WARRINGTON, E. K. Category-specific naming preservation: A single case study. *Journal of Neurology, Neurosurgery & Psychiatry*, 1978, 41, 571–574.

780. OGUNLADE, J. O. The predictive validity of the Raven Progressive Matrices with some Nigerian children. *Educational & Psychological Measurement*, 1978, 38, 465–467.

781. RABINOWITZ, S., & VAN DER SPUY, H. I. J. Selection criteria for dialysis and renal transplant. *American Journal of Psychiatry*, 1978, 135, 861–862.

782. RAYDER, N. F., LARSON, J. C., & ABRAMS, A. I. Effect of socio-contextual variables on child achievement. *Journal of Teacher Education*, 1978, 29, 58–63.

783. ROSENTHAL, D., & MORRISON, S. On being a minority in the classroom: A study of the influence of ethnic mix on cognitive functioning and attitudes in working class children. *Australian Journal of Education*, 1978, 22, 144–160.

784. RUBIN, K. H., BROWN, I. D. R., & PRIDDLE, R. L. The relationships between measures of fluid, crystallized, and "Piagetian" intelligence in elementary–school–aged children. *Journal of Genetic Psychology*, 1978, 132, 29–36.

785. SABINI, J. P., & SILVER, M. Objectifiability and calling rights into play: An empirical study. *Human Relations*, 1978, 31, 791–807.

786. SHALLICE, T., & EVANS, M. E. The involvement of the frontal lobes in cognitive estimation. *Cortex*, 1978, 14, 294–303.

787. STREFF, M., BAREFOOT, S., WALTER, G., & CRANDALL, K. A comparative study of hearing–impaired and normal–hearing young adults–verbal and nonverbal abilities. *Journal of Communication Disorders*, 1978, 11, 489–498.

788. SUTKER, P. B., ALLAIN, A. N., & GEYER, S. Female criminal violence and differential MMPI characteristics. *Journal of Consulting & Clinical Psychology*, 1978, 46, 1141–1143.

789. SUTKER, P. B., ALLAIN, A. N., SMITH, C. J., & COHEN, G. H. Addict descriptions of therapeutic community, multimodality, and methadone maintenance treatment clients and staff. *Journal of Consulting & Clinical Psychology*, 1978, 46, 508–517.

790. VANDENBERG, S. G., & PRICE, R. A. Replication of the factor structure of the Comrey Personality Scales. *Psychological Reports*, 1978, 42, 343–352.

791. VERNON, P. E., RYBA, K. A., & LANG, R. J. Simultaneous and successive processing: An attempt at replication. *Canadian Journal of Behavioural Science*, 1978, 10, 1–15.

792. VERSEY, J. Scalogram analysis and cognitive development: Evidence from a longitudinal study. *British Journal of Educational Psychology*, 1978, 48, 71–78.

793. WHITE, D., & PANUNTO, B. Verbal and nonverbal abilities in English first and second language children. *Psychological Reports*, 1978, 42, 191–197.

794. CAPPA, S. F., & VIGNOLO, L. A. "Transcortical" features of aphasia following left thalamic hemorrhage. *Cortex*, 1979, 15, 121–130.

795. CLARK, P., & RUTTER, M. Task difficulty and task performance in autistic children. *Journal of Child Psychology & Psychiatry & Allied Disciplines*, 1979, 20, 271–285.

796. CORNO, L. A hierarchical analysis of selected naturally occurring aptitude–treatment interactions in the third grade. *American Educational Research Journal*, 1979, 16, 391–409.

797. CUMMINS, J., & MULCAHY, R. Simultaneous and successive processing and narrative speech. *Canadian Journal of Behavioural Science*, 1979, 11, 64–71.

798. DILLON, R. F. Improving validity by testing for competence: Refinement of a paradigm and its application to the hearing–impaired. *Educational & Psychological Measurement*, 1979, 39, 363–371.

799. DOBSON, K. S., & NEUFELD, R. W. J. Stress–related appraisals: A regression analysis. *Canadian Journal of Behavioural Science*, 1979, 11, 274–285.

800. EVANS, M. A. A comparative study of young children's classroom activities and learning outcomes. *British Journal of Educational Psychology*, 1979, 49, 15–26.

801. GROAT, A. The use of English stress assignment rules by children taught either with traditional orthography or with the initial teaching alphabet. *Journal of Experimental Child Psychology*, 1979, 27, 395–409.

802. HENDRICKSON, E., LEVY, R., & POST, F. Averaged evoked responses in relation to cognitive and affective state of elderly psychiatric patients. *British Journal of Psychiatry*, 1979, 134, 494–501.

803. JARMAN, R. F. Cognitive processes and syntactical structure: Analysis of paradigmatic and syntagmatic associations. *Psychological Research*, 1979, 41, 153–167.

804. JARMAN, R. F. Simultaneous and successive cognitive processes in the Mueller–Lyer Illusion. *Journal of Genetic Psychology*, 1979, 134, 23–32.

805. KAUFMAN, D., & KAUFMAN, P. Strategy training and remedial techniques. *Journal of Learning Disabilities*, 1979, 12, 416–419.

806. KAYE, D. B., HALL, V. C., & BARON, M. B. Factors influencing rule discovery in children. *Journal of Educational Psychology*, 1979, 71, 654–668.

807. KERTESZ, A. Visual agnosia: The dual deficit of perception and recognition. *Cortex*, 1979, 15, 403–419.

808. KURDEK, L. A. Children's coordination of differing cognitive perspectives. *Journal of Genetic Psychology*, 1979, 135, 279–285.

809. LAPSLEY, D. K., & ENRIGHT, R. D. The effects of social desirability, intelligence, and milieu on an American validation of the Conservatism Scale. *Journal of Social Psychology*, 1979, 107, 9–14.

810. LEGARETTA, D. The effects of program models on language acquisition by Spanish speaking children. *Teachers of English to Speakers of Other Languages Quarterly*, 1979, 13, 521–534.

811. MAIR, W. G. P., WARRINGTON, E. K., & WEISKRANTZ, L. Memory disorder in Korsakoff's psychosis. A neuropathological and neuropsychological investigation of two cases. *Brain*, 1979, 102, 749–783.

812. MARJORIBANKS, K. Ethclass, the achievement syndrome, and children's cognitive performance. *Journal of Educational Research*, 1979, 72, 327–333.

813. MOLLOY, G. N., & DAS, J. P. Intellectual abilities and processes: An exploratory study with implications for person–teaching method interactions. *Australian Journal of Education*, 1979, 23, 83–92.

814. MYERS, B., & GOLDSTEIN, D. Cognitive development in bilingual and monolingual lower–class children. *Psychology in the Schools*, 1979, 16, 137–142.

815. NIAS, D. K. B. The classification and correlates of children's academic and recreational interests. *Journal of Child Psychology & Psychiatry & Allied Disciplines*, 1979, 20, 73–79.

816. PANUNTO, B., & WHITE, D. Achievement and the prediction of achievement in English first and second language children. *Alberta Journal of Educational Research*, 1979, 25, 61–67.

817. PETERSON, P. L., & JANICKI, T. C. Individual characteristics and children's learning in large–group and small–group approaches. *Journal of Educational Psychology*, 1979, 71, 677–687.

818. POWELL, G. E. Categories of aphasia: A cluster–analysis of Schuell Test profiles. *British Journal of Disorders of Communication*, 1979, 14, 111–122.

819. RAYDER, N. F., ABRAMS, A. I., & LARSON, J. C. The effect of socio–contextual variables on child achievement. *Journal of Teaching & Learning*, 1979, 4, 9–23.

820. RICH, Y., & ROTHCHILD, G. Personality differences between well and poorly behaved adolescents in school. *Psychological Reports*, 1979, 44, 1143–1148.

821. SIMON, A., & WARD, L. O. Some variables influencing judgments of the size of angles. *Contemporary Educational Psychology*, 1979, 4, 11–14.

822. VALENCIA, R. R. Comparison of intellectual performance of Chicano and Anglo third–grade boys on the Raven's Coloured Progressive Matrices. *Psychology in the Schools*, 1979, 16, 448–453.

823. WEAVER, P. A., & ROSNER, J. Relationships between visual and auditory perceptual skills and comprehension in students with learning disabilities. *Journal of Learning Disabilities*, 1979, 12, 617–621.

824. WYKE, M. A., & ASSO, D. Perception and memory for spatial relations in children with developmental dysphasia. *Neuropsychologia*, 1979, 17, 231–239.

825. BALTES, P. B., CORNELIUS, S. W., SPIRO, A., NESSELROADE, J. R., & WILLIS, S. L. Integration versus differentiation of fluid–crystallized intelligence in old age. *Developmental Psychology*, 1980, 16, 625–635.

826. BARCLAY, J. R., & WU, W. Classroom climates in Taiwanese and American elementary schools: A cross–cultural study. *Contemporary Educational Psychology*, 1980, 5, 65–82.

827. BART, W. M., BAXTER, J., & FREY, S. The relationships of spatial ability and sex to formal reasoning capabilities. *Journal of Psychology*, 1980, 104, 191–198.

828. BATTLE, J., BLOWERS, T., & YEUDALL, L. An exploratory study of self-esteem and brain dysfunction in elementary school children. *Psychological Reports*, 1980, 46, 149–150.

829. BESSON, J. A. O. A diagnostic pointer to adult metachromatic leucodystrophy. *British Journal of Psychiatry*, 1980, 137, 186–187.

830. BIERSNER, R. J., & LAROCCO, J. M. Determinants of reading performance and achievement. *Perceptual & Motor Skills*, 1980, 50, 715–721.

831. BIZMAN, A., YINON, Y., RONCO, B., & SCHACHAR, T. Regaining self-esteem through helping behavior. *Journal of Psychology*, 1980, 105, 203–209.

832. BRIDGEMAN, B. Generality of a "fast" or "slow" test-taking style across a variety of cognitive tasks. *Journal of Educational Measurement*, 1980, 17, 211–217.

833. BROOKS, D. N., AUGHTON, M. E., BOND, M. R., JONES, P., & RIZVI, S. Cognitive sequela in relationship to early indices of severity of brain damage after severe blunt head injury. *Journal of Neurology, Neurosurgery & Psychiatry*, 1980, 43, 529–534.

834. CARLSON, J. S., & JENSEN, C. M. The factorial structure of the Raven Coloured Progressive Matrices Test: A reanalysis. *Educational & Psychological Measurement*, 1980, 40, 1111–1116.

835. CHRISTIE, D. J., & GLICKMAN, C. D. The effects of classroom noise on children: Evidence for sex differences. *Psychology in the Schools*, 1980, 17, 405–408.

836. CORNO, L. Individual and class level effects of a parent-assisted instruction in classroom memory support strategies. *Journal of Educational Psychology*, 1980, 72, 278–292.

837. DALGLEISH, B. Communicative experience and visually derived concepts: The acquisition of the concept of symmetry by oral and signing deaf and hearing children. *British Journal of Disorders of Communication*, 1980, 15, 9–17.

838. DILLON, R. F. Cognitive style and elaboration of logical abilities in hearing-impaired children. *Journal of Experimental Child Psychology*, 1980, 30, 389–400.

839. DILLON, R. F. Matching students to their preferred testing conditions: Improving the validity of cognitive assessment. *Educational & Psychological Measurement*, 1980, 40, 999–1004.

840. DILLON, R., SNOWMAN, J., & TZENG, O. Recognition memory in hearing-impaired children: A levels-of-processing approach. *Journal of Experimental Child Psychology*, 1980, 29, 502–506.

841. GUTHRIE, A., & ELLIOT, W. A. The mature and reversibility of cerebral impairment in alcoholism: Treatment implications. *Journal of Studies on Alcohol*, 1980, 41, 147–155.

842. HOOSAIN, R. Mental speed, response time, and intelligence. *Perceptual & Motor Skills*, 1980, 51, 799–803.

843. IDOL-MAESTAS, L. Oral language responses of children with reading difficulties. *Journal of Special Education*, 1980, 14, 385–404.

844. JARMAN, R. F., & NELSON, J. G. Torque and cognitive ability: Some contradictions to Blau's proposals. *Journal of Clinical Psychology*, 1980, 36, 458–464.

845. JONES, B. M., JONES, M. K., & HATCHER, E. M. Cognitive deficits in women alcoholics as a function of gynecological status. *Journal of Studies on Alcohol*, 1980, 41, 140–146.

846. KEATING, D. P., & CLARK, L. V. Development of physical and social reasoning in adolescence. *Developmental Psychology*, 1980, 16, 23–30.

847. KURDEK, L. A. Developmental relations among children's perspective taking, moral judgment, and parent-rated behaviors. *Merrill-Palmer Quarterly*, 1980, 26, 103–121.

848. LARSEN, W. W. Cognitive tempo and intellectual performance in college students. *Psychological Reports*, 1980, 47, 989–990.

849. LEONG, C. K. Cognitive patterns of "retarded" and below-average readers. *Contemporary Educational Psychology*, 1980, 101–117.

850. LUNDBERG, I., OLOFSSON, A., & WALL, S. Reading and spelling skills in the first school years predicted from phonemic awareness skills in kindergarten. *Scandinavian Journal of Psychology*, 1980, 21, 159–173.

851. MAQSUD, M. Extraversion, neuroticism, intelligence and academic achievement in northern Nigeria. *British Journal of Educational Psychology*, 1980, 50, 71–73.

852. MAQSUD, M. Personality and academic attainment of primary school children. *Psychological Reports*, 1980, 46, 1271–1275.

853. MARSH, R. W. The significance for intelligence of differences in birth-weight and health within monozygotic twin pairs. *British Journal of Psychology*, 1980, 71, 63–67.

854. MISHRA, S. P. The influence of examiners' ethnic attributes on intelligence test scores. *Psychology in the Schools*, 1980, 17, 117–122.

855. OSCAR-BERMAN, M., & ZOLA-MORGAN, S. M. Comparative neuropsychology of Karsakoff's Syndrome. I-Spatial and visual reversal learning. *Neuropsychologia*, 1980, 18, 499–512.

856. OSCAR-BERMAN, M., & ZOLA-MORGAN, S. M. Comparative neuropsychology and Karsakoff's Syndrome. II-Two-choice visual discrimination learning. *Neuropsychologia*, 1980, 18, 513–525.

857. PANELS, P. E., & STONER, S. B. Age differences on Raven's Coloured Progressive Matrices. *Perceptual & Motor Skills*, 1980, 50, 997–998.

858. PARSONS, O. A. Cognitive dysfunction in alcoholics and social drinkers. *Journal of Studies on Alcohol*, 1980, 41, 105–118.

859. PENK, W. E., ROBINOWITZ, R., WOODWARD, W. A., & HESS, J. L. MMPI factor scale differences among heroin addicts differing in race and admission status. *International Journal of the Addictions*, 1980, 15, 329–337.

860. PIHL, R. O., SEGAL, Z., & YANKOFSKY, L. The effect of alcohol and placebo on affective reactions of social drinkers to a procedure designed to induce depressive affect anxiety and hostility. *Journal of Clinical Psychology*, 1980, 36, 337–342.

861. PLATT, L. J., ANDREWS, G., YOUNG, M., & QUINN, P. T. Dysarthia of adult cerebral palsy: I. Intelligibility and articulatory impairment. *Journal of Speech & Hearing Research*, 1980, 23, 28–40.

862. QUINSEY, V. L., ARNOLD, L. S., & PRUESSE, M. G. MMPI profiles of men referred for a pretrial psychiatric assessment as a function of offense type. *Journal of Clinical Psychology*, 1980, 36, 410–417.

863. ROSE, R. G. An examination of the response to a multivalue logic test. *Journal of General Psychology*, 1980, 102, 275–281.

864. ROSENTHAL, D. A., SOMERVILLE, S. C., & SHEAHAN, R. K. The development of formal operational reasoning: Effects of two training procedures with ten-year olds. *Genetic Psychology Monographs*, 1980, 102, 219–268.

865. RUSSELL, J., & MAXWELL, M. Children's water-level drawing: A problem of ignoring internal frameworks. *Perceptual & Motor Skills*, 1980, 51, 1001–1002.

866. SCHMIDTKE, A., & SCHALLER, S. Comparative study of factor structure of Raven's Coloured Progressive Matrices. *Perceptual & Motor Skills*, 1980, 51, 1244–1246.

867. SCHULTZ, N. R., JR., HOYER, W. J., & KAYE, D. B. Trait anxiety, spontaneous flexibility, and intelligence in young and elderly adults. *Journal of Consulting & Clinical Psychology*, 1980, 48, 289–291.

868. SHEWAN, C. M., & KERTESZ, A. Reliability and validity characteristics of the Western Aphasia Battery (WAB). *Journal of Speech & Hearing Disorders*, 1980, 45, 308–324.

869. WAUGH, N. C. Age-related differences in acquisition of a verbal habit. *Perceptual & Motor Skills*, 1980, 50, 435–438.

870. WEEKS, D., FREEMAN, C. P. L., & KENDELL, R. E. ECT: III: Enduring cognitive deficits? *British Journal of Psychiatry*, 1980, 137, 26–37.

871. WIDIGER, T. A., KNUDSON, R. M., & RORER, L. G. Convergent and discriminant validity of measures of cognitive styles and abilities. *Journal of Personality & Social Psychology*, 1980, 39, 116–129.

872. WOLL, S. B., FRAPS, C. L., WEEKS, D. G., PENDERGRASS, J., & VANDERPLAS, M. A. Role of sentence context in the encoding of trait descriptors. *Journal of Personality & Social Psychology*, 1980, 39, 59–68.

873. ZAGAR, R., ARBIT, J., & FRIEDLAND, J. Structure of a psychodiagnostic test battery for children. *Journal of Clinical Psychology*, 1980, 36, 313–318.

874. BAILEY, S., POWELL, G. E., & CLARK, E. A note on intelligence and recovery from aphasia: The relationship between Raven's matrices scores and change on the Schuell Aphasia Test. *British Journal of Disorders of Communication*, 1981, 16, 193–203.

875. BASSO, A., CAPITANI, E., LUZZATTI, C., & SPINNLER, H. Intelligence and left hemisphere disease: The role of aphasia, apraxia and size of lesion. *Brain*, 1981, 104, 721–734.

876. BLOCK, J., BUSS, D. M., BLOCK, J. H., & GJERDE, P. F. The cognitive style of breadth of categorization: Longitudinal consistency of personality correlates. *Journal of Personality & Social Psychology*, 1981, 40, 770–779.

877. BRANDES, P. J., & EHINGER, D. M. The effects of early middle ear pathology on auditory perception and academic achievement. *Journal of Speech & Hearing Disorders*, 1981, 46, 301–307.

878. CAMPBELL, A. L., JR., BOGEN, J. E., & SMITH, A. Disorganization and reorganization to cognitive and sensorimotor functions in cerebral commissurotomy: Compensatory roles of the forebrain commissures and cerebral hemispheres in man. *Brain*, 1981, 104, 493–511.

879. CLARK, E. A note on intelligence and recovery from aphasia: The relationship between Raven's matrices scores and change on the Schuell Aphasia Test. *British Journal of Disorders of Communication*, 1981, 16, 193–203.

880. DAVIES, A. D. M., SPELMAN, M. S., & DAVIES, M. G. Combining psychometric data on brain damage and the influence of aging. *Perceptual & Motor Skills*, 1981, 52, 583–592.

881. DELOCHE, G., ANDREEWSKY, E., & DESI, M. Lexical meaning: A case report, some striking phenomena, theoretical implications. *Cortex*, 1981, 17, 147–152.

882. DILLON, R. F. Analogical reasoning under different methods of test administration. *Applied Psychological Measurement*, 1981, 5, 341–347.

883. DILLON, R. F., POHLMANN, J. T., & LOHMAN, D. F. A factor analysis of Raven's Advanced Progressive Matrices freed of difficulty factors. *Educational & Psychological Measurement*, 1981, 41, 1295–1302.

884. DILLON, R. F., & WISHER, R. A. The predictive validity of eye movement indices for technical school qualifying test performance. *Applied Psychological Measurement*, 1981, 5, 43–49.

885. FABIAN, M. S., PARSONS, O. A., & SILBERSTEIN, J. A. Impaired perceptual–cognitive functioning in women alcoholics: Cross-validated findings. *Journal of Studies on Alcohol*, 1981, 42, 217–229.
886. LANG, C., LEHRL, S., & HUK, W. A case of bilateral temporal lobe agenesis. *Journal of Neurology, Neurosurgery & Psychiatry*, 1981, 44, 626–630.
887. LEAL, L. L., BAXTER, E. G., MARTIN, J., & MARX, R. W. Cognitive modification and systematic desensitization with test anxious high school students. *Journal of Counseling Psychology*, 1981, 28, 525–528.
888. LYON, R., REITTA, S., WATSON, B., PORCH, B., & RHODES, J. Selected linguistic and perceptual abilities of empirically derived subgroups of learning disabled readers. *Journal of School Psychology*, 1981, 19, 152–166.
889. NAGLIERI, J. A., KAUFMAN, A. S., KAUFMAN, N. L., & KAMPHAUS, R. W. Cross validation of Das' simultaneous and successive processes with novel tasks. *Alberta Journal of Educational Research*, 1981, 27, 264–271.
890. NYBERG, V. R., & BLACKMORE, D. E. A longitudinal study of grade III achievement in Edmonton public schools. *Alberta Journal of Educational Research*, 1981, 27, 154–159.
891. PENK, W. E., BROWN, A. S., ROBERTS, W. R., DOLAN, M. P., ATKINS, H. G., & ROBINOWITZ, R. Visual memory of black and white male heroin and nonheroin drug users. *Journal of Abnormal Psychology*, 1981, 90, 486–489.
892. PETERSON, P. L., JANICKI, T. C., & SWING, S. R. Ability x treatment interaction effects on children's learning in large-group and small-group approaches. *American Educational Research Journal*, 1981, 18, 453–473.
893. PUHAN, B. N. Effects of marker variables on WAIS communalities. *Educational & Psychological Measurement*, 1981, 41, 55–59.
894. RYCKMAN, D. B. Reading achievement, IQ, and simultaneous-successive processing among normal and learning disabled children. *Alberta Journal of Educational Research*, 1981, 27, 74–83.
895. SEWELL, T. E., PALMO, A. J., & MANNI, J. L. High school dropout, psychological, academic, and vocational factors. *Urban Education*, 1981, 16, 65–76.
896. SHEPARD, L., CAMILLI, G., & AVERILL, M. Comparison of procedures for detecting testing test item bias with both internal and external ability criteria. *Journal of Education Statistics*, 1981, 6, 317–375.
897. SKINNER, H. A. Primary syndromes of alcohol abuse: Their measurement and correlates. *British Journal of Addiction*, 1981, 76, 63–76.
898. STONE, B., & DAY, M. C. A developmental study of the processes underlying solution of figural matrices. *Child Development*, 1981, 52, 359–362.
899. ZAIDEL, E., ZAIDEL, D. W., & SPERRY, R. W. Left and right intelligence: Case studies of Raven's Progressive Matrices following brain bisection and hemidecortication. *Cortex*, 1981, 17, 167–186.

[1915]
Project MEMPHIS Instruments for Individual Program Planning and Evaluation. Preschool handicapped children; 1974; MEMPHIS (Memphis Educational Model Providing Handicapped Infant Services); for use in early childhood education programs for exceptional children; 3 parts which "may be used in totality or in part"; Alton D. Quick, Thomas L. Little, and A. Ann Campbell; Fearon Education.*

a) COMPREHENSIVE DEVELOPMENTAL SCALE. Ratings by teacher; 5 scores: personal-social, gross motor, fine motor, language, percepto-cognitive.

b) DEVELOPMENTAL SKILL ASSIGNMENT RECORD. Non-evaluative form for listing up to 4 skills in each of 5 areas in *a* above which "child needs to learn next to promote later school success."

c) CONTINUOUS RECORD FOR EDUCATIONAL-DEVELOPMENTAL GAIN. For evaluation during and after locally determined training period, of performance level of skills listed in *b* above; pass-fail score for each skill on each date evaluated (up to 24 dates), plus percent of skills mastered (of those assigned) in each of the 5 areas and total.

For additional information and an excerpted review by Karin Taylor Oddsen, see 8:438 (2 references).

[1916]
★**Projective Assessment of Aging Method.** Elderly; 1979; PAAM; thoughts and feelings about significant themes and problems of aging; Bernard D. Starr, Marcella Bakur Weiner, and Marilyn Rabetz; Springer Publishing Co., Inc.*

a) STANDARD FORM. 14 pictures with male/female alternatives for 3 pictures.

b) ALTERNATIVES. 14 pictures; more specialized themes.

[1917]
A Projective Index of Body Awareness. Mental patients; 1969; Wilfred A. Cassell; the Author.*

For additional information, see 8:652.

[1918]
★**Proof-Reading Tests of Spelling.** Standards 2–4 and Forms 1–2 (ages 8–13); 1981; PRETOS; measures a child's ability to discriminate between words spelled correctly and incorrectly in the context of meaningful paragraphs; 2 scores: production, recognition; Cedric Croft, Alison Gilmore, Neil Reid, and Peter Jackson; New Zealand Council for Educational Research [New Zealand].*

[1919]
Proverbs Test. Grades 5–16 and adults; 1954–56; 2 scores: abstract, concrete; Donald R. Gorham; Psychological Test Specialists.*

See T2:440 (33 references); for reviews by Eugene L. Gaier and Alfred B. Heilbrun, Jr., see 5:371 (4 references).

REFERENCES

1–4. See 5:371.
5–37. See T2:440.
38. BROGA, M. I., & NEUFELD, R. W. J. Dimensions of thinking among process and reactive schizophrenics. *Psychological Record*, 1977, 27, 265–277.
39. HARROW, M., & QUINLAN, D. Is disordered thinking unique to schizophrenia? *Archives of General Psychiatry*, 1977, 34, 15–21.
40. POWELL, J. C. The developmental sequence of cognition as revealed by wrong answers. *Alberta Journal of Educational Research*, 1977, 23, 43–51.
41. AMMONS, R. B., & AMMONS, C. H. Use and evaluation of Proverbs Test: Partial summary through March, 1976. *Perceptual & Motor Skills*, 1978, 47, 1044–1046.
42. HARROW, M., & PROSEN, M. Intermingling and disordered logic as influences on schizophrenic 'thought disorders.' *Archives of General Psychiatry*, 1978, 35, 1213–1218.
43. HARROW, M., & PROSEN, M. Schizophrenic thought disorders: Bizarre associations and intermingling. *American Journal of Psychiatry*, 1979, 136, 293–296.
44. WATSON, C. G., PLEMEL, D., & BURKE, M. Proverb Test deficit in schizophrenic and brain-damaged patients. *Journal of Nervous & Mental Disease*, 1979, 167, 561–565.
45. KNIGHT, R. A., EPSTEIN, B., & ZIELONY, R. D. The validity of the Whitaker index of schizophrenic thinking. *Journal of Clinical Psychology*, 1980, 36, 632–639.
46. PHILLIPS, W. M., PHILLIPS, A. M., & SHEARN, C. R. Objective assessment of schizophrenic thinking. *Journal of Clinical Psychology*, 1980, 36, 79–89.
47. REEVES, W. H. Auditory learning disabilities and emotional disturbance: Diagnostic differences. *Journal of Learning Disabilities*, 1980, 13, 30–33.
48. REICH, J. H. Proverbs and the modern mental status exam. *Comprehensive Psychiatry*, 1981, 22, 528–531.

[1920]
PSB-Aptitude for Practical Nursing Examination. Applicants for admission to practical nursing schools; 1961–72; revision of *PSB-Entrance Examination for Schools of Practical Nursing*; 5 scores: general mental ability, spelling, natural sciences, judgement in practical

nursing situations, personal adjustment index; Anna S. Evans, Joan R. Yanuzzi, and George A. W. Stouffer, Jr., with the technical assistance of the Psychological Services Bureau; the Bureau.*

For additional information concerning the earlier edition, see 6:1163.

[1921]
Pseudo-Isochromatic Plates for Testing Color Perception. Ages 7 and over; 1940–65; red-green deficiency; originally published in 1940 as 46-plate test including 14 plates from Ishihara's *Test for Colour-Blindness* and 31 plates from Stilling's original pseudo-isochromatic diagrams; an 18-plate selection of the 46-plate edition was prepared in 1947 as suggested by LeGrand H. Hardy, Gertrude Rand, and M. Catherine Rittler; the current 1965 edition is a 14-plate selection—11 plates from the 18-plate edition and 3 plates from the 46-plate edition; not to be confused with the 21-plate *AO H–R–R Pseudoisochromatic Plates* ('57) now out of print; American Optical Corporation.*

See T2:1924 (21 references) and 4:661 (8 references); for an excerpted review of the 46-plate test, see 3:473 (9 references).

REFERENCES

1–9. See 3:473.
10–17. See 4:661.
18–38. See T2:1924.
39. DUNCKLEY, R. A. Conflict performance as a function of instructional set and absolute strength. *Journal of Research in Personality*, 1977, 11, 243–250.

[1922]
Psychiatric Evaluation Form. Psychiatric patients and nonpatients; 1967–68; PEF; interview guide and rating scale for recording scaled judgments (based upon various sources of information: subject, informant, case records, nurses' notes, etc.) of a person's functioning over a one week period in 19 psychopathological dimensions and role impairment in 3 occupational roles and 2 social roles; Robert L. Spitzer, Jean Endicott, Alvin Mesnikoff, and George Cohen; Research Assessment and Training Unit, New York State Psychiatric Institute.* [The Diagnostic Version, PEF-D (same as regular edition except for the addition of 12 scales and the coverage of a person's functioning over the past month) is available only as a part of *Current and Past Psychopathology Scales*.]

See T2:1339 (4 references); for reviews by Goldine C. Gleser and Jerome D. Pauker, see 7:126 (1 reference).

REFERENCES

1. See 7:126.
2–5. See T2:1339.
6. GLICK, I. D., HARGREAVES, W. A., DRUES, J., & SHOWSTACK, J. A. Short vs. long hospitalization. *Archives of General Psychiatry*, 1976, 33, 78–83.
7. GLICK, I. D., HARGREAVES, W. A., DRUES, J., SHOWSTACK, J. A., & KATZOW, J. J. Short vs. long hospitalization: A prospective controlled study. *Archives of General Psychiatry*, 1977, 34, 314–317.
8. GOULD, E., & GLICK, I. D. The effects of family presence and brief family intervention on global outcome for hospitalized schizophrenic patients. *Family Process*, 1977, 16, 503–510.
9. HARGREAVES, W. A., GLICK, I. D., DRUES, J., SHOWSTACK, J. A., & FEIGENBAUM, E. Short vs. long hospitalization: A prospective controlled study. *Archives of General Psychiatry*, 1977, 34, 305–311.
10. HEDLUND, J. L. MMPI clinical scale correlates. *Journal of Consulting & Clinical Psychology*, 1977, 45, 739–750.
11. SCHWARTZ, C. C., & MYERS, J. K. Life events and schizophrenia. *Archives of General Psychiatry*, 1977, 34, 1242–1245.
12. GLESER, G. C., GREEN, B. L., & WINGET, C. N. Quantifying interview data on psychic impairment of disaster survivors. *Journal of Nervous & Mental Disease*, 1978, 166, 209–216.
13. VANNICELLI, M., WASHBURN, S., SCHEFF, B. J., & LONGABAUGH, R. Comparison of usual and experimental patients in a psychiatric day center. *Journal of Consulting & Clinical Psychology*, 1978, 46, 87–93.
14. FENTON, F. R., TESSIER, L., & STRUENING, E. L. A comparative trial of home and hospital psychiatric care. *Archives of General Psychiatry*, 1979, 36, 1073–1079.
15. YOUNG, R. C., GLICK, I. D., HARGREAVES, W. A., BRAFF, D., & DROES, J. Therapist A–B score and treatment outcome with psychiatric inpatients: A table of random numbers. *British Journal of Medical Psychology*, 1979, 52, 119–121.
16. BOWDEN, C. L., SCHOENFELD, L. S., & ADAMS, R. L. A correlation between dropout status and improvement in a psychiatric clinic. *Hospital & Community Psychiatry*, 1980, 31, 192–195.
17. KANAS, N., ROGERS, M., KRETH, E., PATTERSON, L., & CAMPBELL, R. The effectiveness of group psychotherapy during the first three weeks of hospitalization. A controlled study. *Journal of Nervous & Mental Disease*, 1980, 168, 487–492.
18. VANNICELLI, M., WASHBURN, S. L., & SCHEFF, B. J. Family attitudes toward mental illness: Immutable with respect to time, treatment setting, and outcome. *American Journal of Orthopsychiatry*, 1980, 50, 151–155.
19. YOUNG, R. C., GOULD, E., GLICK, I. D., & HARGREAVES, W. Personality inventory correlates of outcome in a follow-up study of psychiatric hospitalization. *Psychological Reports*, 1980, 46, 903–906.
20. LINDY, J. D., GRACE, M. C., & GREEN, B. L. Survivors: Outreach to a reluctant population. *American Journal of Orthopsychiatry*, 1981, 51, 468–478.

[1923]
The Psychiatric Status Schedules: Subject Form, Second Edition. Psychiatric patients and nonpatients; 1966–68; PSS; a standardized interview schedule for gathering from a subject information needed to fill out a matching inventory designed to evaluate social and role functioning as well as mental status; most of the sections dealing with signs and symptoms of psychiatric disorder are from the *Mental Status Schedule*; 18 symptom scores (inappropriate affect-appearance-behavior, interview belligerence-negativism, agitation-excitement, retardation-lack of emotion, speech disorganization, grandiosity, suspicion-persecution-hallucinations, reported overt anger, depression-anxiety, suicide-self-mutilation, somatic concerns, social isolation, daily routine-leisure time impairment, antisocial impulses or acts, alcoholic abuse, drug abuse, disorientation memory, denial of illness), 5 role functioning scores (wage earner, housekeeper, student or trainee, mate, parent), 5 summary symptom and role scales (subjective distress, behavioral disturbance, impulse control disturbance, reality testing disturbance, summary role), and 20 supplemental scores (anxiety, auditory hallucinations, catatonic behavior, conversion reaction, delusions-hallucinations, depression-suicide, disassociation, elated mood, guilt, lack of emotion, obsessions-compulsions, persecutory delusions, phobia, psychomotor retardation, sex deviation, silliness, somatic delusions or hallucinations, visual hallucinations, miscellaneous, validity check); Robert L. Spitzer, Jean Endicott, and George Cohen; Research Assessment and Training Unit, New York State Psychiatric Institute.*

See T2:1340 (6 references); for a review by Hans H. Strupp, see 7:127 (5 references).

REFERENCES

1–5. See 7:127.
6–11. See T2:1340.
12. DOHRENWEND, B. P., YAGER, T. J., EGRI, G., & MENDELSOHN, F. S. The psychiatric status schedule as a measure of dimensions of psychopathology in the general population. *Archives of General Psychiatry*, 1978, 35, 731–777.

13. VANNICELLI, M., WASHBURN, S., SCHEFF, B. J., & LONGABAUGH, R. Comparison of usual and experimental patients in a psychiatric day center. *Journal of Consulting & Clinical Psychology*, 1978, 46, 87–93.
14. ENDICOTT, J., COHEN, J., NEE, J., FLEISS, J. L., & HERZ, M. I. Brief vs. standard hospitalization. *Archives of General Psychiatry*, 1979, 36, 706–712.
15. HEATON, R. K., VOGT, A. T., HOEHN, M. M., LEWIS, J. A., CROWLEY, T. J., & STALLINGS, M. A. Neuropsychological impairment with schizophrenia vs. acute and chronic cerebral lesions. *Journal of Clinical Psychology*, 1979, 35, 46–53.
16. PIPER, W. E., DOAN, B. D., EDWARDS, E. M., & JONES, B. D. Cotherapy behavior, group therapy process, and treatment outcome. *Journal of Consulting & Clinical Psychology*, 1979, 47, 1081–1089.
17. WAXLER, N. E. Is outcome for schizophrenia better in nonindustrialized societies? The case of Sri Lanka. *Journal of Nervous & Mental Disease*, 1979, 167, 144–158.
18. KENNEDY, P., & HIRD, F. Description and evaluation of a short-stay admission ward. *British Journal of Psychiatry*, 1980, 136, 205–215.
19. MACCRIMMON, D. J., CLEGHORN, J. M., ASARNOW, R. F., & STEFFY, R. A. Children at risk for schizophrenia. *Archives of General Psychiatry*, 1980, 37, 671–674.
20. MCKENNA, G. J., & KHANTZIAN, E. J. Ego functions and psychopathology in narcotics and polydrug users. *International Journal of the Addictions*, 1980, 15, 259–268.
21. SILBERFARB, P. M., MAVER, H., CROUTHAMEL, C. S. Psychosocial aspects of neoplastic disease: I. Functional status of breast cancer patients during different treatment regimens. *American Journal of Psychiatry*, 1980, 137, 450–455.
22. SPITZER, R. L., ENDICOTT, J., COHEN, J., & NEE, J. The psychiatric status schedule for epidemiological research. *Archives of General Psychiatry*, 1980, 37, 1193–1197.
23. STRUPP, H. H. Success and failure in time–limited psychotherapy. A systematic comparison of two cases: Comparison 1. *Archives of General Psychiatry*, 1980, 37, 595–603.
24. VANNICELLI, M., WASHBURN, S. L., & SCHEFF, B. J. Family attitudes toward mental illness: Immutable with respect to time, treatment setting, and outcome. *American Journal of Orthopsychiatry*, 1980, 50, 151–155.
25. WINSBERG, B. G., BIALER, I., KUPIETZ, S., BOTTI, E., & BALKA, E. B. Home vs. hospital care of children with behavior disorders. *Archives of General Psychiatry*, 1980, 37, 413–418.
26. CROWLEY T. J., & HYDINGER-MACDONALD, M. Motility, Parkinsonism, and prolactin with thiothixene and thioridazine. *Archives of General Psychiatry*, 1981, 38, 668–675.
27. MCDANIEL, S. H., STILES, W. B., & MCGAUGHEY, K. J. Correlations of male college students verbal response mode use in psychotherapy with measures of psychological disturbance and psychotherapy outcome. *Journal of Consulting & Clinical Psychology*, 1981, 49, 571–582.
28. SCHEIBER, S. C., COHEN, I., YAMAMURA, H., NOVAL, R., & BEUTLER, L. Dialysis for schizophrenia: An uncontrolled study of 11 patients. *American Journal of Psychiatry*, 1981, 138, 662–665.
29. SZAPOCZNIK, J., SANTISTEBAN, D., HERVIS, O., SPENCER, F., & KURTINES, W. M. Treatment of depression among Cuban American elders: Some validation evidence for a life enhancement counseling approach. *Journal of Consulting & Clinical Psychology*, 1981, 49, 752–754.

[1924]
Psychodiagnostic Test Report Blank. Psychologists; 1965–74; for imparting information derived from client's test data to referring professionals; Leopold Bellak; C.P.S., Inc.*

For additional information, see 8:463 (1 reference).

[1925]
★**Psycho-Educational Battery.** Grades kgn–6, 7–16 and adults; 1976; PEB; 2 levels; Lillie Pope; Book-Lab, Inc.*

a) LEVEL Y. Grades kgn–6; evaluations in 22 areas: motor performance, awareness of time and place, intensity, knowledge of left and right, tactile and kinesthetic perception, knowledge of letters and digits, no tendency to reverse, sight vocabulary, paragraph reading, phonics evaluation, spelling, counting, recognition of coins and size relationships, knowledge of colors, competence with language of space relationships, auditory word discrimination, concept development, auditory memory, visual memory, speech, arithmetic, behavior and learning style.

b) LEVEL O. Grades 7–16 and adults; evaluations in 13 areas: motor performance, awareness of time and place, interests, sight words, reading paragraphs, inventory of basic reading skills, spelling, concept development, auditory memory, auditory word discrimination, speech, arithmetic basic functions, behavior and learning style.

[1926]
★**Psychoeducational Evaluation of the Pre-school Child: A Manual Utilizing the Haeussermann Approach.** Pre-school children; 1972; "an educational evaluation"; no scores; Eleonora Jedrysek, Zelda S. Klapper, Lillie Pope, and Joseph Wortis; Grune & Stratton, Inc.*

[1927]
A Psychoeducational Inventory of Basic Learning Abilities. Ages 5–12 with suspected learning disabilities; 1968; rating scale of 53 basic learning abilities in 6 areas: gross motor development, sensory-motor integration, perceptual-motor skills, language development, conceptual skills, social skills; no manual; Robert E. Valett; Fearon Education.*

[1928]
Psychoeducational Profile of Basic Learning Abilities. Ages 2–14 with learning disabilities; 1966; booklet for recording clinical and standardized test data in 5 areas: motor integration and physical development, perceptual abilities, language, social-personal adaptivity, general intellectual functioning; Robert E. Valett; Consulting Psychologists Press, Inc.*

For additional information, see 7:548.

[1929]
*****Psycho-Epistemological Profile.** College and adults; 1968–80; PEP; experimental form; 3 scores: metaphoric, rational, empirical; J. R. Royce and L. P. Mos; Center for Advanced Study in Theoretical Psychology, University of Alberta [Canada].* (United States distributor: Psychometric Affiliates.)

For additional information, see 8:653 (2 references).

[1930]
★**Psycholinguistic Rating Scale.** Grades kgn–1.4, 1.5–2.9, 3.0–5.9, 6.0–8.9; 1982; PRS; designed to measure relevant classroom psycholinguistic behaviors; ratings by teachers in 8–10 areas: auditory reception, auditory association, auditory memory, auditory closure, verbal expression, visual reception, visual association, visual memory, plus visual closure and manual expression for all but the advanced level; Kenneth L. Hobby; Western Psychological Services.*

[1931]
Psychological Screening Inventory. Ages 16 and over; 1968–73; PSI; "a brief mental health screening device used in situations where time and professional manpower may be at a premium"; 5 scores: alienation, social nonconformity, discomfort, expression, defensiveness; Richard I. Lanyon; Research Psychologists Press, Inc.*

For additional information and a review by Stephen L. Golding, see 8:654 (32 references); see also T2:1342 (7 references).

REFERENCES

1–7. See T2:1342.
8–39. See 8:654.
40. BRUCH, M. A. Psychological Screening Inventory as a predictor of college student adjustment. *Journal of Consulting & Clinical Psychology*, 1977, 45, 237–244.
41. MEHRYAR, A. H., HEKMAT, H., & KHAJAVI, A. F. Some personality correlates of contemplated suicide. *Psychological Reports*, 1977, 40, 1291–1294.
42. FRANKLE, A. H. Sequential response shift rate: A correlate of human adaptivity measurable with existing personality inventories. *Journal of Psychology*, 1978, 98, 129–143.
43. JOHNSON, R. W., & JOHNSON, J. H. A cross–validation of the Sn scale on the Psychological Screening Inventory with female hitchhikers. *Journal of Clinical Psychology*, 1978, 34, 366–367.
44. LANYON, R. I. Factor structure of Psychological Screening Inventory scales. *Psychological Reports*, 1978, 42, 383–386.
45. MCGURK, B. J., BOLTON, N., & SMITH, M. Some psychological, educational and criminological variables related to recidivism in delinquent boys. *British Journal of Social & Clinical Psychology*, 1978, 17, 251–254.
46. MECK, D. S., BOURGEOIS, A., & LEUNES, A. Relation of combined measures of locus of control and psychological differentiation to personality adjustment. *Psychological Reports*, 1978, 43, 547–552.
47. PAOLINO, T. J., JR., MCCRADY, B. S., & KOGAN, K. B. Alcoholic marriages: A longitudinal empirical assessment of alternative theories. *British Journal of Addiction*, 1978, 73, 129–138.
48. SARASON, I. G., JOHNSON, J. H., & SIEGEL, J. M. Assessing the impact of life changes: Development of the life experiences survey. *Journal of Consulting & Clinical Psychology*, 1978, 46, 932–946.
49. SMITH, R. E., JOHNSON, J. H., & SARASON, I. G. Life change, the sensation seeking motive, and psychological distress. *Journal of Consulting & Clinical Psychology*, 1978, 46, 348–349.
50. HARTMAN, L. M. The preventive reduction of psychological risk in asymptomatic adolescents. *American Journal of Orthopsychiatry*, 1979, 49, 121–135.
51. JANSEN, M. A., & LITWACK, L. The effects of assertive training on counselor trainees. *Counselor Education & Supervision*, 1979, 19, 27–34.
52. SCHWARZ, J. C., & ZUROFF, D. C. Family structure and depression in female college students: Effect of parental conflict, decision–making power, and inconsistency of love. *Journal of Abnormal Psychology*, 1979, 88, 398–406.
53. SURWIT, R. S., BRADNER, M. N., FENTON, C. H., & PILON, R. N. Individual differences in response to the behavioral treatment of Raynaud's Disease. *Journal of Consulting & Clinical Psychology*, 1979, 47, 363–367.
54. MECK, D. S., & BAITHER, R. The relation of age to personality adjustment among DWI offenders. *Journal of Clinical Psychology*, 1980, 36, 342–345.
55. SCHWARZ, J. C., & GETTER, H. Parental conflict and dominance in late adolescent maladjustment: A triple interaction model. *Journal of Abnormal Psychology*, 1980, 89, 573–580.
56. CRESSWELL, D. L., & LANYON, R. I. Validation of a screening battery for psychogeriatric assessment. *Journal of Gerontology*, 1981, 36, 435–440.
57. MCGURK, B. J., MCEWAN, A. W., & GRAHAM, F. Personality types and recidivism among young delinquents. *British Journal of Criminology*, 1981, 21, 159–165.

[1932]

Psychometric Behavior Checklist. Adults; 1960; PBC; also called *Maryland Test Behavior Checklist*; for recording unusual test taking behavior; Bernard G. Berenson, Kathryn C. Biersdorf, Thomas M. Magoon, Martha J. Maxwell, Donald K. Pumroy, and Marjorie H. Richey; University Counseling Center.*

For additional information, see P:219; see also 6:166 (1 reference).

[1933]

Psychotic Inpatient Profile. Mental patients; 1961–68; PIP; ratings by nurses and psychiatric aides; revision of *Psychotic Reaction Profile*; 12 scores: excitement, hostile belligerence, paranoid projection, anxious depression, retardation, seclusiveness, care needed, psychotic disorganization, grandiosity, perceptual disorganization, depressive mood, disorientation; 10 of the scores are "essentially equivalent" to the 10 scores obtained on the *Inpatient Multidimensional Psychiatric Scale*, the 2 new scores are seclusiveness and care needed; Maurice Lorr and Norris D. Vestre; Western Psychological Services.*

For additional information and a review by Thaddeus E. Weckowicz, see 8:655 (10 references); see also T2:1345 (1 reference); for a review by Goldine C. Gleser, see 7:128 (4 references); for a review of the original edition, see 6:167.

REFERENCES

1–4. See 7:128.
5. See T2:1345.
6–15. See 8:655.
16. KAVANAUGH, P. B., & AULD, F. Evidence for validity of the Differential Personality Inventory. *Journal of Clinical Psychology*, 1977, 33, 456–459.
17. KNIGHT, R. A., & BLANEY, P. H. The interrater reliability of the Psychotic Inpatient Profile. *Journal of Clinical Psychology*, 1977, 33, 647–653.
18. ALDEN, L. Treatment environment and patient improvement. *Journal of Nervous & Mental Disease*, 1978, 166, 327–334.
19. MISHARA, B. L. Geriatric patients who improve in token economy and general milieu treatment programs: A multivariate analysis. *Journal of Consulting & Clinical Psychology*, 1978, 46, 1340–1348.
20. YOUNG, R. C., & PANDI, G. R. Common factors in two methods for assessing psychiatric inpatients. *Journal of Clinical Psychology*, 1978, 34, 693–694.
21. WALKER, L. G. The effect of some incentives on the work performance of psychiatric patients at a rehabilitation workshop. *British Journal of Psychiatry*, 1979, 134, 427–435.
22. HADDAD, L. B. Intra–institutional relocation: Measured impact upon geriatric patients. *Journal of the American Geriatrics Society*, 1981, 29, 86–88.
23. HADDAD, L. B. Utilizing rating instruments for evaluating behavioral characteristics differentiating elderly patients selected for skilled nursing, intermediate, and psychiatric care. *Journal of Gerontology*, 1981, 36, 583–585.

[1934]

*****The Pupil Rating Scale Revised: Screening for Learning Disabilities.** Ages 5–14; 1971–81; ratings by teachers, counselors, or school psychologists; 8 scores: verbal (auditory comprehension, spoken language, total), nonverbal (orientation, motor coordination, personal-social behavior, total), total; Helmer R. Myklebust; Grune & Stratton, Inc.*

For additional information, a review by Nicholas J. Anastasiow of an earlier edition and an excerpted review by Barton B. Proger, see 8:439 (5 references).

REFERENCES

1–5. See 8:439.
6. COLLIGAN, R. C. Concurrent validity of the Myklebust Pupil Rating Scale in a kindergarten population. *Journal of Learning Disabilities*, 1977, 10, 317–320.
7. QUINN, J. A., & WILSON, B. J. Programming effects on learning disabled children: Performance and affect. *Psychology in the Schools*, 1977, 14, 196–199.
8. HARRIS, W. J., DRUMMOND, R. J., SCHULTZ, E. W., & KING, D. R. The factor structure of three teacher rating scales and a self–report inventory of children's source traits. *Journal of Learning Disabilities*, 1978, 11, 583–585.
9. RAMEY, C. T., STEDMAN, D. J., BORDERS–PATTERSON, A., & MENGEL, W. Predicting school failure from information available at birth. *American Journal of Mental Deficiency*, 1978, 82, 525–534.
10. COLLIGAN, R. C. Predictive utility of the Myklebust Pupil Rating Scale: A two–year follow–up. *Journal of Learning Disabilities*, 1979, 12, 264–267.
11. FINKELSTEIN, N. W., & RAMEY, C. T. Information from birth certificates as a risk index for educational handicap. *American Journal of Mental Deficiency*, 1980, 84, 546–552.
12. PIHL, R. O., & NAGY, K. A. The applicability of the Myklebust Pupil Rating Scale. *Journal of Learning Disabilities*, 1980, 13, 58–62.
13. VRANA, F., & PIHL, R. O. Selective attention deficit in learning disabled children: A cognitive interpretation. *Journal of Learning Disabilities*, 1980, 13, 42–45.

[1935]
Pupil Record of Educational Behavior. Preschool through "upper primary levels"; 1971; PREB; unscored record of performance in 27 areas: visual-motor perception (copying geometric forms, color, form, puzzles, coloring and cutting, pegboard designs, incomplete pictures, block designs, self concept, writing, following directions, motor coordination), auditory perception (listening, beginning consonant sounds, rhymes), language development (matching letters, oral language, sequence, comprehension, recall, word recognition, definitions), mathematical concepts (matching numbers, counting, number concepts, problem solving, computation); (Spanish edition available); Ruth Cheves; Teaching Resources Corporation.*

For additional information and a review by Phyllis L. Newcomer, see 8:440.

[1936]
Purdue Clerical Adaptability Test, Revised Edition. Applicants for clerical positions; 1949–56; 6 scores: spelling, computation, checking, word meaning, copying, reasoning; C. H. Lawshe, Joseph Tiffin, and Herbert Moore; distributed by University Book Store.*

See T2:2142 (2 references); for reviews by Mary Ellen Oliverio and Donald Spearritt, see 5:853 (2 references); for reviews by Edward N. Hay, Joseph E. Moore, and Alec Rodger of an earlier edition, see 4:732.

[1937]
Purdue Creativity Test. Applicants for engineering positions; 1960, c1957–60; test booklet title is *Creativity Test*; 3 scores: fluency, flexibility, total; C. H. Lawshe and D. H. Harris; distributed by University Book Store.*

See T2:2347 (1 reference); for reviews by Samuel T. Mayo and Philip R. Merrifield, see 6:1136 (2 references).

REFERENCES

1–2. See 6:1136.
3. See T2:2347.
4. MAGNUSSON, D., & BACKTEMAN, G. Longitudinal stability of person characteristics: Intelligence and creativity. *Applied Psychological Measurement*, 1978, 2, 489–490.

[1938]
Purdue Hand Precision Test. Ages 17 and over; 1941; 3 scores: attempts, correct responses, error time; Joseph Tiffin; Lafayette Instrument Co.*

For additional information, see 6:1080 (2 references).

[1939]
The Purdue High School English Test. Grades 9–12; 1931–62; abbreviated modification of *New Purdue Placement Test in English*; 6 scores: grammar, punctuation, effective expression, vocabulary, spelling, total; H. H. Remmers, R. D. Franklin, G. S. Wykoff, and J. H. McKee; Riverside Publishing Co.*

See T2:105 (12 references); for reviews by Charlotte Croon Davis and Benjamin Rosner, see 6:276.

[1940]
Purdue Industrial Mathematics Test. Adults; 1946; C. H. Lawshe, Jr. and Dennis H. Price; University Book Store.*

See T2:650 (6 references); for reviews by Clyde H. Coombs and C. C. Upshall, see 3:314.

[1941]
Purdue Industrial Supervisors Word-Meaning Test. Supervisors; 1952; Joseph Tiffin and Donald A. Long; University Book Store.*

See T2:170 (3 references); for reviews by Jerome E. Doppelt and Bernadine Meyer, see 5:237 (2 references).

[1942]
Purdue Industrial Training Classification Test. Grades 9–12 and adults; 1942; shop mathematics; C. H. Lawshe and A. C. Moutoux; University Book Store.*

See T2:2433 (2 references); for reviews by D. Welty Lefever and Charles I. Mosier, see 3:675 (2 references).

[1943]
The Purdue Instructor Performance Indicator. College teachers; 1960; ratings by students; John H. Snedeker and H. H. Remmers; University Book Store.*

See T2:880 (1 reference); for a review by C. Robert Pace, see 6:704 (3 references).

[1944]
Purdue Interview Aids. Applicants for industrial employment; 1943; 3 tests; C. H. Lawshe; distributed by University Book Store.*
a) CAN YOU READ A WORKING DRAWING?
b) CAN YOU READ A MICROMETER?
c) CAN YOU READ A SCALE?

For additional information and a review by William W. Waite, see 4:775.

[1945]
The Purdue Master Attitude Scales. Grades 7–16; 1934–60; PMAS; formerly listed as *Generalized Attitude Scales*; *a–h* have space for insertion of any 5 attitude variables; 15 original scales, only 9 currently available; H. H. Remmers (editor and manual author); University Book Store.*
a) A SCALE FOR MEASURING ATTITUDE TOWARD ANY SCHOOL SUBJECT. 1934–60; original forms by Ella B. Silance.
b) A SCALE FOR MEASURING ATTITUDES TOWARD ANY VOCATION. 1934–60; original forms by Harold E. Miller.
c) A SCALE FOR MEASURING ATTITUDE TOWARD ANY INSTITUTION. 1934–60; original forms by Ida B. Kelley.
d) A SCALE FOR MEASURING ATTITUDE TOWARD ANY DEFINED GROUP. 1934–60; revision of *A Scale for Measuring Attitude Toward Races and Nationalities*; original forms by H. H. Grice.
e) A SCALE FOR MEASURING ATTITUDES TOWARD ANY PROPOSED SOCIAL ACTION. 1935–60; original forms by Dorothy M. Thomas.
f) A SCALE FOR MEASURING ATTITUDES TOWARD ANY PRACTICE. 1934–60; original forms by H. W. Bues.
g) A SCALE FOR MEASURING ATTITUDE TOWARD ANY HOME-MAKING ACTIVITY. 1934–60; original forms by Beatrix Kellar.
h) A SCALE FOR MEASURING INDIVIDUAL AND GROUP "MORALE." 1936–60; original forms by Laurence Whisler.
i) HIGH SCHOOL ATTITUDE SCALE. 1935–60; original forms by F. H. Gillespie.
j) A SCALE FOR MEASURING ATTITUDE TOWARD ANY DISCIPLINARY PROCEDURE. 1936; V. R. Clouse. *Out of print.*

k) A SCALE FOR MEASURING ATTITUDE TOWARD ANY TEACHER. 1935; L. D. Hoshaw. *Out of print.*
l) A SCALE FOR MEASURING ATTITUDES TOWARD ANY PLAY. 1935; Mildred Dimmitt. *Out of print.*
m) A SCALE FOR MEASURING ATTITUDES TOWARD ANY SELECTION OF POETRY. 1935; J. E. Hadley. *Out of print.*
n) A SCALE FOR MEASURING ATTITUDES TOWARD ANY SOCIAL SITUATION. 1938; Elna Huffman. *Out of print.*
o) A SCALE TO MEASURE ATTITUDE TOWARD ANY ADVERTISEMENT. 1938; Ruth E. Henion. *Out of print.*

See T2:1348 (17 references) and P:223 (1 reference); for a review by Donald T. Campbell, see 6:168; for reviews by Donald T. Campbell and Kenneth E. Clark of the original forms, see 4:46 (37 references); for reviews by W. D. Commins and Theodore Newcomb, see 2:1202 (9 references); for a review by Stephen M. Corey, see 1:897; for a review by Lee J. Cronback of earlier forms of the High School Attitude Scale, see 3:46.

REFERENCES

1-9. See 2:1202.
10-46. See 4:46.
47. See P:223.
48-64. See T2:1348.
65. BACON, M. L. Factors affecting retention and loss of associate-degree students in University of Kentucky community colleges. *Journal of Business Education*, 1977, 53, 45–50.
66. HUGHES, R. J. An experimental study in teaching mathematical concepts utilizing computer-assisted instruction in business machines. *Business Education Forum*, 1977, 32, 44–45.

[1946]

Purdue Mechanical Adaptability Test. Males ages 15 and over; 1945–50; C. H. Lawshe, Jr. and Joseph Tiffin; University Book Store.*

See T2:2263 (5 references) and 4:762 (6 references); for reviews by Jay L. Otis and Dewey B. Stuit, see 3:676.

[1947]

Purdue Non-Language Personnel Test. Business and industry; 1957–69; abbreviated revision of *Purdue Non-Language Test*; Joseph Tiffin; University Book Store.*

See T2:442 (1 reference) and 7:377; for reviews by John D. Hundleby and Benjamin Rosner of the earlier test, see 6:491.

[1948]

Purdue Pegboard. Grades 9–16 and adults; 1941–68; PP; 5 scores: right hand, left hand, both hands, right plus left plus both hands, assembly; Purdue Research Foundation under the direction of Joseph Tiffin; Science Research Associates, Inc.*

See T2:2234 (51 references) and 6:1081 (15 references); for a review by Neil D. Warren, see 5:873 (11 references); see also 4:751 (12 references); for reviews by Edwin F. Ghiselli, Thomas W. Harrell, and Albert Gibson Packard, see 3:666 (3 references).

REFERENCES

1-3. See 3:666.
4-15. See 4:751.
16-26. See 5:873.
27-41. See 6:1081.
42-92. See T2:2234.
93. APRIL, R. S., & TSE, P. C. Crossed aphasia in a Chinese bilingual dextral. *Archives of Neurology*, 1977, 34, 766–770.
94. BLEDA, P. R., & SANDMAN, P. H. In smoke's way: Socioemotional reactions to another's smoking. *Journal of Applied Psychology*, 1977, 62, 452–458.
95. BOLLER, F., VRTUNSKI, B., MACK, J. L., & KIM, Y. Neuropsychological correlates of hypertension. *Archives of Neurology*, 1977, 34, 701–705.
96. ZAIDEL, D., & SPERRY, R. W. Some long-term motor effects of cerebral commissurotomy in man. *Neuropsychologia*, 1977, 6, 193–204.
97. SCHREINER, J. Prediction of retarded adults' work performance through components of general ability. *American Journal of Mental Deficiency*, 1978, 83, 77–79.
98. GARDNER, R. A., & BROMAN, M. The Purdue Pegboard: Normative data on 1334 school children. *Journal of Clinical Child Psychology*, 1979, 8, 156–162.
99. BATTLE, J., BLOWERS, T., & YEUDALL, L. An exploratory study of self-esteem and brain dysfunction in elementary school children. *Psychological Reports*, 1980, 46, 149–150.
100. HAMM, N. H., & CURTIS, D. Normative data for the Purdue Pegboard on a sample of adult candidates for vocational rehabilitation. *Perceptual & Motor Skills*, 1980, 50, 309–310.
101. LUNDBERG, P. K. Assessment of drugs' side effects: Visual analogue scale versus check-list format. *Perceptual & Motor Skills*, 1980, 50, 1067–1073.
102. MOSSHOLDER, K. W. Effects of externally mediated goal setting on intrinsic motivation: A laboratory experiment. *Journal of Applied Psychology*, 1980, 65, 202–210.
103. PEYSER, J. M., EDWARDS, K. R., & POSER, C. M. Psychological profiles in patients with multiple sclerosis. *Archives of Neurology*, 1980, 37, 437–440.
104. SAPPINGTON, J. T. Measures of lateral dominance: Interrelationships and temporal stability. *Perceptual & Motor Skills*, 1980, 50, 783–790.
105. SIEGEL, D., & DAVIS, C. Transfer effects of learning at specific speeds on performance over a range of speeds. *Perceptual & Motor Skills*, 1980, 50, 83–89.

[1949]

The Purdue Perceptual-Motor Survey. Ages 6–10; 1966; PPMS; to identify those children lacking perceptual-motor abilities necessary for acquiring academic success; 22 scores: balance and posture (walking board [3 scores], jumping), body image and differentiation (identification of body parts, imitation of movements, obstacle course, Krauss-Weber, angels in the snow), perceptual-motor match (chalkboard [4 scores], rhythmic writing [3 scores]), ocular control (4 scores), form perception (2 scores); Eugene G. Roach and Newell C. Kephart; Charles E. Merrill Publishing Co.*

For additional information, see 8:874 (21 references); see also T2:1883 (9 references); for reviews by Colleen B. Jamison and Daniel Landis, see 7:874 (25 references).

REFERENCES

1-25. See 7:874.
26-34. See T2:1883.
35-55. See 8:874.
56. WHYTE, L. Prescriptive teaching: Changes in stage of logico-mathematical thinking and spatial development in a group of opportunity class children. *Alberta Journal of Educational Research*, 1976, 22, 34–43.
57. POTTS, M., & LEYMAN, L. Intervention in the motor domain: A training study with first- and second-grade slow readers. *Psychology in the Schools*, 1977, 14, 200–206.
58. LARSON, B. A. Use of the motorvator in improving gross-motor coordination, visual perception and IQ scores: A pilot study. *Journal of Music Therapy*, 1978, 15, 145–149.
59. BAKER-NOBLES, L., & BINK, M. P. Sensory integration in the rehabilitation of blind adults. *American Journal of Occupational Therapy*, 1979, 33, 559–564.
60. WYCKOFF, W. L. Relationship of students' ranks and developmental readiness scores. *Perceptual & Motor Skills*, 1980, 50, 8–10.
61. STEIN, G. M., GIBBONS, R. D., & MELDMAN, M. J. Lateral eye movement and handedness as measures of functional brain asymmetry in learning disability. *Cortex*, 1981, 16, 223–229.

[1950]

The Purdue Rating Scale for Administrators and Executives. Administrators and executives; 1950–51; 36 ratings plus factor scores; 3 profile folders; H. H. Remmers and R. L. Hobson; University Book Store.*

a) REPORT FORM A. College administrators; 3 factor scores: fairness to subordinates, administrative achievement, democratic orientation.

b) REPORT FORM B. Business executives; 2 factor scores: social responsibility for subordinates and society, executive achievement.

c) REPORT FORM C. School administrators.

See T2:1349 (1 reference) and P:224; for reviews by John P. Foley, Jr. and Herbert A. Tonne, see 5:101 (1 reference); for a review by Kenneth L. Heaton, see 4:83 (7 references).

[1951]

The Purdue Rating Scale for Instruction. College teachers; 1927–65; PRSI; revision of *The Purdue Rating Scale for Instructors*; student ratings on 26 characteristics of the instructor and teaching situation; H. H. Remmers, D. N. Elliott (scale), and J. A. Weisbrodt (manual and response card); University Book Store.*

See T2:881 (9 references) and 7:588 (9 references); for a review by C. Robert Pace, see 6:705 (5 references); for a review by Kenneth L. Heaton, see 4:803 (26 references).

[1952]

Purdue Reading Test for Industrial Supervisors. Supervisors; 1955; Joseph Tiffin and Roy Dunlap; University Book Store.*

See T2:1739 (3 references); for reviews by Jerome E. Doppelt and Louis C. Nanassy, see 5:644 (1 reference).

[1953]

The Purdue Student-Teacher Opinionaire. Student teachers; 1969–76; PSTO; for measurement of groups, not individuals; 2 editions; Ralph R. Bentley and Jo-Ann Price; University Book Store.*

a) FORM A. 1969–70; 100 median item scores grouped by 12 factors (rapport with supervising teacher, rapport with principal, teaching as a profession, rapport with university supervisor, community support of education, student teacher load, rapport with students, rapport with other teachers, satisfaction with housing, professional preparation, school facilities, curriculum issues), 12 median factor scores, and total.

b) [FORM B]. 1976; an abbreviated revision of Form A; 60 median item scores grouped by 9 factors (rapport with supervising teacher, rapport with principal, rapport with university supervisor, teaching as a profession, school facilities and services, professional preparation, rapport with students, rapport with other teachers, student teacher load), 9 median factor scores, and total.

For additional information and reviews by Kenneth O. Doyle, Jr. and Elazar J. Pedhazur, see 8:391 (8 references); see also T2:882 (2 references) and 7:589 (1 reference).

REFERENCES

1. See 7:589.
2–3. See T2:882.
4–11. See 8:391.
12. MAHAN, J. M., & SMITH, M. F. Student teacher satisfaction with alternative field experiences: Expectations versus realities. *High School Journal*, 1977, 61, 16–26.
13. MAHAN, J. M., & LACEFIELD, W. Educational attitude changes during year-long student teaching. *Journal of Experimental Education*, 1978, 46, 4–15.

[1954]

The Purdue Teacher Evaluation Scale. Teachers grades 7–12; 1969–75; PTES; ratings by students; 60 item scores and 6 scale scores: ability to motivate students, ability to control students, subject matter orientation, student-teacher communication, teaching methods and procedures, fairness; Ralph R. Bentley and Allan R. Starry; University Book Store.*

For additional information and reviews by Craig S. Scott and Richard W. Watkins, see 8:392 (5 references); see also 7:590 (1 reference).

[1955]

The Purdue Teacher Opinionaire. Teachers; 1961–75; PTO; revision of *The Purdue Teacher Morale Inventory*; for measurement of groups, not individuals; 100 or 120 median item scores grouped by 10 or 12 factors (teacher rapport with principal, satisfaction with teaching, rapport among teachers, teacher salary, teacher load, curriculum issues, teachers status, community support of education, school facilities and services, community pressures, teacher rapport with school board [optional], teacher rapport with superintendent [optional]), 10 or 12 median factor scores, and total; Ralph R. Bentley and Averno M. Rempel; University Book Store.*

For additional information, see 8:393 (63 references); see also T2:884 (16 references); for reviews by Bert A. Goldman and Benjamin Rosner, see 7:591 (26 references).

REFERENCES

1–26. See 7:591.
27–42. See T2:884.
43–105. See 8:393.
106. ASKOV, E. N., DUPUIS, M. M., & LEE, J. W. An effective inservice model for content area reading in the secondary schools. *National Reading Conference Yearbook*, 1978, 6–12.
107. COOPER, J. F. The job satisfaction and productivity of junior college teachers. *College Student Journal*, 1978, 12, 382–386.
108. DUPUIS, M. M., & ASKOV, E. N. Content area differences in attitudes toward teaching reading. *High School Journal*, 1978, 62, 83–88.
109. HEWITSON, M. Participative decision making for teachers–Placebo or panacea? *Australian Journal of Education*, 1978, 22, 189–205.
110. ASKOV, E. N., & DUPUIS, M. M. Guidelines for inservice programs to teach reading in content courses. *Journal of Teacher Education*, 1979, 30, 16–18.
111. DUPUIS, M. M., & ASKOV, E. N. Combining university and school–based inservice education in content area reading. *National Reading Conference Yearbook*, 1979, 28, 223–227.
112. DUPUIS, M. M., ASKOV, E. N., & LEE, J. W. Changing attitudes toward content area reading: The content area reading project. *Journal of Educational Research*, 1979, 73, 66–74.
113. PARDUE, S. F. Blocked– and integrated–content baccalaureate nursing programs: A comparative study. *Nursing Research*, 1979, 28, 305–311.

[1956]

Purdue Trade Information Test for Sheetmetal Workers. Sheetmetal workers; 1958; Joseph Tiffin, B. R. Modisette, and Warren B. Griffin; University Book Store.*

For additional information, see 5:942.

[1957]

Purdue Trade Information Test in Carpentry. Vocational school and adults; 1952; Joseph Tiffin and Robert F. Mengelkoch; University Book Store.*

For additional information and a review by P. L. Mellenbruch, see 5:943 (1 reference).

[1958]
Purdue Trade Information Test in Engine Lathe Operation. Vocational school and adults; 1955; Robert Cochran and Joseph Tiffin; University Book Store.*

For additional information and a review by William J. Micheels, see 5:944.

[1959]
Purdue Trade Information Test in Welding, Revised Edition. Vocational school and adults; 1952; Joseph Tiffin and Warren B. Griffin; distributed by University Book Store.*

For additional information and a review by Richard A. Swanson, see 8:1168; see also T2:2438 (1 reference).

[1960]
The Purpose in Life Test. Adults; 1962–69; PIL; James C. Crumbaugh and Leonard T. Maholick; Psychometric Affiliates.*

For additional information, see 8:656 (54 references); see also T2:1350 (4 references); for reviews by John R. Braun and George Domino, see 7:130 (7 references).

REFERENCES

1–7. See 7:130.
8–11. See T2:1350.
12–65. See 8:656.
66. CRUMBAUGH, J. C. The Seeking of Noetic Goals test (SONG): A complimentary scale to the Purpose in Life Test (PIL). *Journal of Clinical Psychology*, 1977, 33, 900–907.
67. JACOBSON, G. R., RITTER, D. P., & MUELLER, L. Purpose in life and personal values among adult alcoholics. *Journal of Clinical Psychology*, 1977, 33, 314–316.
68. MARTIN, J. D., & MARTIN, E. M. The relationship of the Purpose in Life (PIL) Test to the Personal Orientation Inventory (POI), the Otis-Lennon Mental Ability Test scores, and grade point averages of high school students. *Educational & Psychological Measurement*, 1977, 37, 1103–1105.
69. MORRISON, R. F. Career adaptivity: The effective adaptation of managers of changing role demands. *Journal of Applied Psychology*, 1977, 62, 549–558.
70. REKER, G. T. The Purpose-in-Life Test in an inmate population: An empirical investigation. *Journal of Clinical Psychology*, 1977, 33, 688–693.
71. SODERSTROM, D., & WRIGHT, E. W. Religious orientation and meaning in life. *Journal of Clinical Psychology*, 1977, 33, 65–68.
72. BOLT, M. Purpose in life and death concern. *Journal of Genetic Psychology*, 1978, 132, 159–160.
73. BYNUM, J. E., COOPER, B. L., & ACUFF, F. G. Retirement reorientation: Senior adult education. *Journal of Gerontology*, 1978, 33, 253–261.
74. ROBERTSON, S. A. Some personality correlates of time competence, temporal extension and temporal evaluation. *Perceptual & Motor Skills*, 1978, 46, 743–750.
75. CRUMBAUGH, J. C., & CARR, G. L. Treatment of alcoholics with logotherapy. *International Journal of the Addictions*, 1979, 14, 847–853.
76. FORGAS, J., & MENYHART, J. The perception of political leaders: A multidimensional analysis. *Australian Journal of Psychology*, 1979, 31, 213–223.
77. JENKS, J., KAHANE, J., BOBINSKI, V., & PIERMARINI, T. The relationship between perceived college student satisfaction and goal-directedness. *Measurement & Evaluation in Guidance*, 1979, 11, 225–229.
78. REKER, G. T., & COUSINS, J. B. Factor structure, construct validity and reliability of the Seeking of Noetic Goals (SONG) and Purpose in Life (PIL) tests. *Journal of Clinical Psychology*, 1979, 35, 85–91.
79. THOMPSON, W. E., & BYNUM, J. E. Purpose in life and college selection. *College & University*, 1979, 54, 223–230.
80. CRANDALL, J. E. Adler's concept of social interest: Theory, measurement, and implications for adjustment. *Journal of Personality & Social Psychology*, 1980, 39, 481–495.
81. PHILLIPS, W. M. Purpose in life, depression, and locus of control. *Journal of Clinical Psychology*, 1980, 36, 661–667.
82. STONES, C. R., & PHILBRICK, J. L. Purpose in life in South Africa: A comparison of American and South African beliefs. *Psychological Reports*, 1980, 47, 739–742.
83. BROOKINGS, J. B., DANA, R. H., & BOLTON, B. A multitrait-multimethod analysis of alienation. *Journal of Psychology*, 1981, 109, 59–64.
84. HICKS, T. M. A study of the background, level of job satisfaction, maturity, and morale of "delayed vocation" Catholic priests. *Review of Religious Research*, 1981, 22, 328–345.
85. PALOUTZIAN, R. F. Purpose in life and value changes following conversion. *Journal of Personality & Social Psychology*, 1981, 41, 1153–1160.
86. REKER, G. T., & PEACOCK, E. J. The Life Attitude Profile (LAP): A multidimensional instrument for assessing attitudes toward life. *Canadian Journal of Behavioural Science*, 1981, 13, 264–273.

[1961]
The Q-Tags Test of Personality. Ages 6 and over, 12 and over; 1967–69; QTTP; 2 forms; Arthur G. Storey and Louis I. Masson (manual); Institute of Psychological Research, Inc. [Canada].*

a) [BIOGRAPHICAL FORM.] Ages 6 and over; 13 scores: 6 factor scores (affective, assertive, effective, hostility, reverie, social) in each of 2 areas (he or she is, he or she should be), correlation of self and idealself.
b) [AUTOBIOGRAPHICAL FORM.] Ages 12 and over; 13 scores: 6 factor scores (same as *a* above) in each of 2 areas (I am, I wish I were), correlation of self and idealself.

See T2:1351 (2 references); for a review by Joan Preston, see 7:131 (2 references); see also P:225 (5 references).

[1962]
★The Quality of School Life Scale. Grades 4–12; 1977–78; QSL; self-report questionnarie; 3 subscales, 4 scores: satisfaction with school, commitment to classwork, reactions to teachers, total; Joyce L. Epstein under the direction of James M. McPartland, Johns Hopkins University; Riverside Publishing Co.*

[1963]
★Queensland University Aphasia and Language Test. Ages 2–10; 1978; QUALT; ratings by examiner; designed to test the 4 main channels of verbal communication (auditory, oral expression, reading, writing); 4 scores corresponding to the 4 channels above; John H. Tyrer and Mervyn J. Eadie; Australian Council for Educational Research [Australia].*

[1964]
★Questionnaire Measure of Stimulus Screening and Arousability. College and adults; 1976; Albert Mehrabian; the Author.*

[1965]
QUESTS: A Life-Choice Inventory. Grades 9–12; 1974–76; 6 scores: needs recognition, values clarification, adaptive autonomy, perception of reality, self-worth, total; scoring must be done by publisher; Norman J. Milchus, Omar D. Numey, and David N. Rodwell; Person-O-Metrics, Inc.*

For additional information, see 8:657.

[1966]
★Quick Language Assessment Inventory. Grades kgn–6; 1974; designed for children suspected of needing English as a second language; parents or guardians provide information about child's English and Spanish background; Steve Moreno; Moreno Educational Co.*

[1967]

★Quick Neurological Screening Test, Revised Edition. Ages 5 and over; 1974–79; QNST; screening for early identification of learning disabilities; Margaret Mutti, Harold M. Sterling, and Norma V. Spalding; Academic Therapy Publications.*

[1968]

Quick Screening Scale of Mental Development. Ages 6 months to 10 years; 1963; 6 mental age ratings: body coordination, manual performance, speech and language, listening attention and number, play interests, general mental level (mean of preceding 5 ratings); Katharine M. Banham; Psychometric Affiliates.*

For additional information and a review by Boyd R. McCandless, see 6:533.

[1969]

The Quick Test. Ages 2 and over; 1958–62; QT; picture vocabulary; R. B. Ammons and C. H. Ammons; Psychological Test Specialists.*

For additional information, see 8:225 (33 references); see also T2:522 (15 references); for excerpted reviews by Peter F. Merenda and B. Semeonoff, see 7:422 (30 references); for reviews by Boyd R. McCandless and Ellen V. Piers, see 6:534 (3 references).

REFERENCES

1–3. See 6:534.
4–33. See 7:422.
34–48. See T2:522.
49–81. See 8:225.
82. BACHMAN, J. G., & O'MALLEY, P. M. Self-esteem in young men: A longitudinal analysis of the impact of educational and occupational attainment. *Journal of Personality & Social Psychology*, 1977, 35, 365–380.
83. ERNHART, C. B., SPANER, S. D., & JORDON, T. E. Validity of selected preschool screening tests. *Contemporary Educational Psychology*, 1977, 2, 78–89.
84. KAY, S. R. Developmental assessment of cognitive style in mentally retarded psychotics. *Journal of Clinical Psychology*, 1977, 33, 953–958.
85. KENDALL, P. C., & LITTLE, V. L. Correspondence of brief intelligence measures to the Wechsler scales with delinquents. *Journal of Consulting & Clinical Psychology*, 1977, 45, 660–666.
86. NEWMAN, E. H. Resolution of inconsistent attitude communications in normal and schizophrenic subjects. *Journal of Abnormal Psychology*, 1977, 86, 41–46.
87. NICHOLSON, C. L. Correlations between the Quick Test and the Wechsler Intelligence Scale for Children–Revised. *Psychological Reports*, 1977, 40, 523–526.
88. PENTECOSTE, J. C., & LOWE, W. F. The Quick Test as a predictive instrument for college success. *Psychological Reports*, 1977, 41, 759–762.
89. THORNTON, C. C., GOTTHEIL, E., GELLENS, H. K., & ALTERMAN, A. I. Voluntary versus involuntary abstinence in the treatment of alcoholics. *Journal of Studies on Alcohol*, 1977, 38, 1740–1748.
90. CIULA, B. A., & CODY, J. J. Comparative study of validity of the WAIS and Quick Test as predictors of functioning intelligence in a psychiatric facility. *Psychological Reports*, 1978, 42, 971–974.
91. DEWOLFE, A. S., & FEDIRKA, P. J. Interference in word associations in schizophrenia. *Journal of Clinical Psychology*, 1978, 34, 302–305.
92. LARUSSO, L. Sensitivity of paranoid patients to nonverbal cues. *Journal of Abnormal Psychology*, 1978, 87, 463–471.
93. MALONEY, M. P., NELSON, D., DUVALL, S., & KIRKENDALL, A. Performance of psychiatric inpatients on three standard tests of intelligence. *Psychological Reports*, 1978, 43, 1289–1290.
94. ROTATORI, A. F. Test-retest reliability of the Quick Test for mentally retarded children. *Perceptual & Motor Skills*, 1978, 46, 162.
95. SMOLEN, R. C. Expectancies, mood, and performance of depressed and nondepressed psychiatric inpatients on chance and skill tasks. *Journal of Consulting & Clinical Psychology*, 1978, 87, 91–101.
96. SPAULING, W. The relationships of some information–processing factors to severely disturbed behavior. *Journal of Nervous & Mental Disease*, 1978, 166, 417–428.
97. WECKOWICZ, T. E., TAM, C. I., MASON, J., & BAY, K. S. Speed in test performance in depressed patients. *Journal of Abnormal Psychology*, 1978, 87, 578–582.
98. ZIMMERMAN, R. R., SCHROLL, E. F., ACKLES, P., BARRETT, R., & AUSTER, M. Performance of institutional retardates on standard and new forms of the Quick Test. *Perceptual & Motor Skills*, 1978, 46, 263–266.
99. GUTERMAN, S. S. IQ tests in research on social stratification. The cross–class validity of the tests as measures of scholastic aptitude. *Sociology of Education*, 1979, 52, 163–173.
100. HILL, K. A., & JUNUS, F. Individual differences in concept learning of painting styles. *Perceptual & Motor Skills*, 1979, 49, 255–261.
101. PERSINGER, B. D., JR. Clinical use of the Quick Test with sheltered workshop clients. *Perceptual & Motor Skills*, 1979, 49, 565–566.
102. QUERY, W. T. Changes in scores on California Psychological Inventory among seminarians: What happened to the class of '68. *Psychological Reports*, 1979, 45, 129–130.
103. TENG, E. L. Dichotic ear effects with digits and tones: A within–subject comparison. *Perceptual & Motor Skills*, 1979, 49, 391–399.
104. VANCE, H. B., & SINGER, M. G. Correlations between the Quick Test forms 1 and 3 and Peabody Picture Vocabulary Test for children and youth with learning problems. *Psychological Reports*, 1979, 44, 315–318.
105. WILSON, K. L. The effects of integration and class on black educational attainment. *Sociology of Education*, 1979, 52, 84–98.
106. DEFILIPPIS, N. A., & FULMER, K. Effects of age and IQ level on the validity of one short intelligence test used for screening purposes. *Educational & Psychological Measurement*, 1980, 40, 543–545.
107. EICH, W. F. Use of brief intelligence tests administered in pediatric practice. *Psychological Reports*, 1980, 46, 551–554.
108. ERNHART, C. B., CALLAHAN, R., & LANDA, B. The McCarthy scales: Predictive validity and stability of scores for urban black children. *Educational & Psychological Measurement*, 1980, 40, 1183–1188.
109. HIRSCH, F. J., & HIRSCH, S. J. The Quick Test as a screening device for gifted students. *Psychology in the Schools*, 1980, 17, 37–39.
110. HOWARD, D. V., LASAGA, M. I., & MCANDREWS, M. P. Semantic activation during memory encoding across the adult life span. *Journal of Gerontology*, 1980, 35, 884–890.
111. KAY, S. R. Progressive figure drawings in the developmental assessment of mentally retarded psychotics. *Perceptual & Motor Skills*, 1980, 50, 583–590.
112. LOWELL, W. E. The development of hierarchical classification skills in science. *Journal of Research in Science Teaching*, 1980, 17, 425–433.
113. MALONEY, M. P., DUVALL, S. W., & FRIESEN, J. Evaluation of response consistency on the MMPI. *Psychological Reports*, 1980, 46, 295–298.
114. MILAR, C. R., SCHROEDER, S. R., MUSHAK, P., DOLCOURT, J. L., & GRANT, L. Contributions of the caregiving environment to increased lead burden of children. *American Journal of Mental Deficiency*, 1980, 84, 339–344.
115. PETEROY, E. T. Prediction of WAIS scores from Quick Test scores for white and black patients at a mental health center. *Psychological Reports*, 1980, 47, 259–262.
116. RANDOLPH, G. C., RANDOLPH, J. J., CIULA, B. A., PADGET, J., & CUNEO, D. Retrospective comparison of Quick Test IQs of new admissions and a random sample of patients in a maximum security mental hospital.
117. SAKLOFSKE, D. H., & KELLY, I. W. The Quick Test: Its relationship with the Canadian Test of Basic Skills and the Canadian Lorge–Thorndike Intelligence Tests. *Psychological Reports*, 1980, 46, 802.
118. VANCE, H., BLIXT, S., & ELLIS, C. R. Equivalence of forms one and three of the Quick Test. *Psychological Reports*, 1980, 46, 1184–1186.
119. VANCE, H., PRICHARD, K. K., & JEHLE, W. O. Quick Test alternate–form reliability for rural mountain children and youth with learning problems. *Psychological Reports*, 1980, 47, 1109–1110.
120. FABES, R. A., MORAN, J. D., III, & MCCULLERS, J. C. The hidden costs of reward and WAIS subscale performance. *American Journal of Psychology*, 1981, 94, 387–398.
121. FORBACH, G. B., & EVANS, R. G. The Remote Associates Test as a predictor of productivity in brainstorming groups. *Applied Psychological Measurement*, 1981, 5, 333–340.
122. GRONWALL, D., & WRIGHTSON, P. Memory and information processing capacity after closed head injury. *Journal of Neurology, Neurosurgery & Psychiatry*, 1981, 44, 889–895.
123. KENNEDY, K. J. Age effects on trail making test performance. *Perceptual & Motor Skills*, 1981, 52, 671–675.
124. LAW, J. G., JR., PRICE, D. R., & HERBERT, D. A. Study of Quick Test, WAIS, and premorbid estimates of intelligence for neuropsychiatric patients. *Perceptual & Motor Skills*, 1981, 52, 919–922.
125. RIZZO, J. M., & STEPHENS, M. I. Performance of children with normal and impaired oral language production on a set of auditory comprehension tests. *Journal of Speech & Hearing*, 1981, 46, 150–159.

[1970]

Quick Word Test. Grades 4–6, 7–12 and superior students grades 11–12 and average adults, college and professional adults; 1957–78; QWT; 3 levels; Edgar F.

Borgatta and Raymond J. Corsini; F. E. Peacock Publishers Test Division.*

a) ELEMENTARY LEVEL. Grades 4–6; 1967.

b) LEVEL 1. Grades 7–12 and superior students grades 11–12 and average adults; 1957–78.

c) LEVEL 2. College and professional adults; 1957–78.

For additional information, a review by Jum C. Nunnally, and excerpted reviews by Jack C. Merwin and Gilbert Sax and Ethel A. Oda, see 7:378 (8 references).

REFERENCES

1–8. See 7:378.
9. FENNEMA, E., & SHERMAN, J. Sex–related differences in mathematics achievement, spatial visualization and affective factors. *American Educational Research Journal*, 1977, 14, 51–71.
10. OLIVER, L. W. Evaluating career counseling outcome for three modes of test interpretation. *Measurement & Evaluation in Guidance*, 1977, 10, 153–161.
11. SHERMAN, J., & FENNEMA, E. The study of mathematics by high school girls and boys: Related variables. *American Educational Research Journal*, 1977, 14, 159–168.
12. ADAMOWICZ, J. K. Visual short–term memory, age, and imaging ability. *Perceptual & Motor Skills*, 1978, 46, 571–576.
13. ADAMOWICZ, J. K., & HUDSON, B. R. Visual short–term memory, response delay, and age. *Perceptual & Motor Skills*, 1978, 46, 267–270.
14. HISCOCK, M. Imagery assessment through self–report: What do imagery questionnaires measure? *Journal of Consulting & Clinical Psychology*, 1978, 46, 223–230.
15. WATKINS, M. Correlation between Quick Word Test and Sixteen Personality Factor Questionnarie B Factor scores. *Psychological Reports*, 1978, 42, 653–654.
16. MARTIN, J. D., BLAIR, G. E., & VICKERS, D. M. Correlation of the Quick Word Test and Wide Range Vocabulary Test with the Shipley Institute of Living Scale. *Educational & Psychological Measurement*, 1979, 39, 935–937.
17. SHERMAN, J. Predicting mathematics performance in high school girls and boys. *Journal of Educational Psychology*, 1979, 71, 242–249.

[1971]

★**Quickscreen.** Grades kgn, 1, 2; 1979–80; QS; designed to screen for speech, language, and learning problems; 5 or 6 areas scored depending on level: name, auditory comprehension, visual-motor figures, auditory-vocal, words (b), cognitive (c), yielding a total score indicating degree of risk; Janet B. Fudala; Western Psychological Services.*

[1972]

The RAD Scales. Supervisors; 1957; RAD; experimental; self-ratings of perceived degrees of responsibility, authority, and delegation of authority; 3 scores: responsibility, authority, delegation; Ralph M. Stogdill; Publications Sales Division, Ohio State University Press.*

For additional information and a review by Michael J. Kavanagh, see 8:1184 (6 references); see also T2:2457 (5 references) and 7:1150 (20 references).

[1973]

★**Rapid Exam for Early Referral.** Ages 3–6; 1980; REFER; 4 scores: write loops, touch body parts, count 1 to 10, touch circles; Carl H. Koenig and Harold P. Kunzelmann; Charles E. Merrill Publishing Co.*

[1974]

★**Rating of Behavior Scale.** Children and adolescents and adults; 1980; ROBS; measures sex-role adoption and attitudes for both present and ideal roles; may be rated by an observer; 13 scores: total level of activity, level of activity in masculine sex-role behaviors (M), level of activity in feminine sex-role behaviors (F), total variation in present activity levels (K), variation between average levels of activity in the M and F scores (K_1), inconsistency within the two sex-role categories (K_2), F ratio between K_1 and K_2 (K_3), total incongruence between present and ideal sex-role behavior (C), incongruence between actual and ideal masculine sex-role behavior (M_1), incongruence between actual and ideal feminine sex-role behaviors (F_1), variation between averages for M_1 and F_1 differences in actual and ideal behaviors (C_1), variation due to inconsistency within M_1 and F_1 categories (C_2), F ratio between C_1 and C_2 (C_3); Carney, Weedman and Associates.*

[1975]

RBH Arithmetic Fundamentals Test. Business and industry; 1951–63; Richardson, Bellows, Henry & Co., Inc.*

For additional information and a review by John W. Lombard, see 7:523.

[1976]

The RBH Arithmetic Reasoning Test. Business and industry; 1948–63; Richardson, Bellows, Henry & Co., Inc.*

For additional information and a review by John W. Lombard, see 7:524.

REFERENCES

1. SCHMIDT, F. L., HUNTER, J. E., & CAPLAN, J. R. Validity generalization results for two job groups in the petroleum industry. *Journal of Applied Psychology*, 1981, 66, 261–273.

[1977]

RBH Classifying Test. Business and industry; 1950–63; 3 scores: speed, accuracy, rights minus wrongs; Richardson, Bellows, Henry & Co., Inc.*

For additional information and a review by Douglas G. Schultz, see 7:995.

[1978]

RBH Number Checking Test. Business and industry; 1957–63; 2 scores: checking forward, checking backward; Richardson, Bellows, Henry & Co., Inc.*

For additional information and a review by Douglas G. Schultz, see 7:997.

[1979]

RBH Scientific Reading Test. Employees in technical companies; 1950–69; Richardson, Bellows, Henry & Co., Inc.*

For additional information and a review by Samuel T. Mayo, see 7:772.

[1980]

RBH Shop Arithmetic Test. Industry; 1948–63; Richardson, Bellows, Henry & Co., Inc.*

See T2:729 (1 reference); for a review by John W. Lombard, see 7:525; see also 6:636 (2 references).

[1981]

RBH Test of Chemical Comprehension. Employee applicants and applicants for nurses training; 1951–68; "chemical facts" of an "everyday nature"; Richardson, Bellows, Henry & Co., Inc.*

For additional information, see 7:849.

REFERENCES

1. CALLENDER, J. C., & OSBURN, H. G. An empirical comparison of coefficient alpha, Guttman's lambda–2, and msplit maximized split–half reliability estimates. *Journal of Educational Measurement*, 1979, 16, 89–99.

2. GREENER, J. M., & OSBURN, H. G. An empirical study of the accuracy of corrections for restriction in range due to explicit selection. *Applied Psychological Measurement*, 1979, 3, 31-41.
3. SCHMIDT, F. L., HUNTER, J. E., & CAPLAN, J. R. Validity generalization results for two job groups in the petroleum industry. *Journal of Applied Psychology*, 1981, 66, 261-273.

[1982]

RBH Test of Dictation Speed. Stenographers; 1958-63; no manual; Richardson, Bellows, Henry & Co., Inc.*

For additional information, see 6:48.

[1983]

RBH Test of Language Skills. Business and industry; 1949-63; Richardson, Bellows, Henry & Co., Inc.*
For additional information, see 6:285.

[1984]

RBH Test of Learning Ability. Business and industry; 1947-63; TLA; 3 editions; Richardson, Bellows, Henry & Co., Inc.*
a) FORMS S AND T.
b) FORMS DS-12 AND DT-12. Identical with Forms S and T except for removal of directions from testing time; formerly titled *Test for Office Personnel*.
c) FORM ST. Consists of Forms S and T combined.

See T2:444 (1 reference); for a review by Erwin K. Taylor, see 7:379 (2 references); see also 6:504 (2 references).

REFERENCES
1-2. See 6:504.
3-4. See 7:379.
5. See T2:444.
6. GREENER, J. M., & OSBURN, H. G. An empirical study of the accuracy of corrections for restriction in range due to explicit selection. *Applied Psychological Measurement*, 1979, 3, 31-41.

[1985]

RBH Test of Non-Verbal Reasoning. Business and industry; 1948-63; catalog uses title *The RBH Non-Verbal Reasoning Test*; Richardson, Bellows, Henry & Co., Inc.*

For additional information and a review by Erwin K. Taylor, see 7:380 (1 reference); see also 6:505 (3 references).

[1986]

RBH Test of Reading Comprehension. Business and industry; 1951-63; Richardson, Bellows, Henry & Co., Inc.*
For additional information and reviews by Thorsten R. Carlson and Willard A. Kerr, see 7:701.

REFERENCES
1. BROWN, L. L., & SHERBENOU, R. J. A comparison of teacher perceptions of student reading ability, reading performance, and classroom behavior. *Reading Teacher*, 1981, 34, 557-560.

[1987]

RBH Test of Typing Speed. Applicants for clerical positions; 1958-63; 2 scores: net speed, accuracy; Richardson, Bellows, Henry & Co., Inc.*
For additional information, see 6:53.

[1988]

Reactions to Everyday Situations. Ages 16 and over; 1970-72; RES; anxiety; Sheena M. A. Waterhouse (test) and Valerie J. Fairbairn (manual); National Institute for Personnel Research [South Africa].*

[1989]

A Reading and Vocabulary Test for Students of English as a Second Language. Non-native speakers of English; 1960-72; distribution restricted to the Agency for International Development and the Bureau of Educational and Cultural Affairs of the U.S. Department of State; David P. Harris and Leslie A. Palmer; American Language Institute.*
For additional information, see 7:267.

[1990]

Reading Classification Test. Ages 7.5-11.5; 1972-76; adaptation of oral word reading subtest of *Individual Reading Test*; word pronunciation; H. J. Williamson and I. L. Ball; Educational Resources [Australia].*
For additional information, see 8:789 (1 reference).

[1991]

Reading Comprehension: Cooperative English Tests. Grades 9-12, 13-14; 1940-60; separate booklet edition of reading subtest of *Cooperative English Tests*; 4 scores: vocabulary, level of comprehension, speed of comprehension, total; revision by Clarence Derrick, David P. Harris, and Biron Walker; Addison-Wesley Publishing Co., Inc.*

See T2:1583 (51 references); for reviews by W. V. Clemans and W. G. Fleming, see 6:806 (12 references); see also 5:645 (21 references) and 4:547 (20 references); for reviews by Robert Murray Bear and J. B. Stroud of an earlier edition, see 3:497 (15 references); see also 2:1564 (2 references). For reviews of the complete battery, see 6:256 (2 reviews, 1 excerpt) and 3:120 (3 reviews).

REFERENCES
1-2. See 2:1564.
3-17. See 3:497.
18-37. See 4:547.
38-58. See 5:645.
59-70. See 6:806.
71-121. See T2:1583.
122. GABLE, R. K., ROBERTS, A. D., & OWEN, S. V. Affective and cognitive correlates of classroom achievement. *Educational & Psychological Measurement*, 1977, 37, 977-986.
123. ZIMMERMANN, M. L., GOLDSTON, J. T., & GADZELLA, B. M. Prediction of academic performance for college students by sex and race. *Psychological Reports*, 1977, 41, 1183-1186.
124. SENI, C. L., GADZELLA, B. M., GOLDSTON, J. T., & ZIMMERMANN, M. L. Differences and changes of internally oriented students on study habits. *College Student Journal*, 1978, 12, 294-298.

[1992]

Reading Comprehension Test DE. Ages 10-12.5; 1963-71; formerly called *Reading Comprehension Test 1*; E. L. Barnard; NFER-Nelson Publishing Co. [England].*
For additional information, see 7:702.

[1993]

Reading Efficiency Tests. Grades 7-16 and adults; 1966-74; MRET; formerly called *Maintaining Reading Efficiency Tests*; 3 scores: rate, comprehension accuracy, reading efficiency; 5 forms; no manual; Lyle L. Miller; Developmental Reading Distributors.*
a) TEST 1, HISTORY OF BRAZIL, 1970 REVISION. 1966-70.
b) TEST 2, HISTORY OF JAPAN, 1970 REVISION. 1966-70.
c) TEST 3, HISTORY OF INDIA. 1970.
d) TEST 4, HISTORY OF NEW ZEALAND. 1970.
e) TEST 5, HISTORY OF SWITZERLAND. 1970.

For additional information and a reveiw by Alton L. Raygor, see 8:731.

[1993A]
Reading/Everyday Activities in Life. Ages 10 and over; 1972; R/EAL; functional literacy; criterion-referenced; (Spanish edition available); Marilyn Lichtman; Westwood Press.*

For additional information and reviews by Albert J. Kingston and Richard D. Robinson, see 8:812 (1 reference).

REFERENCES

1. See 8:812.
2. ESON, M. E., YEN, J. K., & BOURKE, R. S. Assessment of recovery from serious head injury. *Journal of Neurology, Neurosurgery & Psychiatry*, 1978, 41, 1036–1042.

[1994]
Reading Eye II. Grades 1, 2, 3, 4, 5, 6, 7–8, 9–16 and adults; 1959–69; a portable electronic eye-movement recorder with test materials; 5 reading component scores (fixations, regressions, average span of recognition, average duration of fixation, rate with comprehension), 3 ratings (grade level of reading, relative efficiency, directional attack), and 2 diagnostic categories (visual adjustment, general adjustment to reading); Stanford E. Taylor, Helen Frackenpohl, and James L. Pettee; Educational Developmental Laboratories, Inc.*

See T2:1672 (5 references); for a review by John J. Geyer, see 7:734 (9 references); for reviews by Arthur S. McDonald and George D. Spache of an earlier model, see 6:838 (3 references).

[1995]
Reading for Understanding Placement Test. Grades 3–8, 8–12, 5–16; 1959–69; designed for use with the self-teaching reading exercises prepared by the same author; 3 levels; Thelma Gwinn Thurstone; Science Research Associates, Inc.*

a) JUNIOR EDITION. Grades 3–8; 1963.
b) SENIOR EDITION. Grades 8–12; 1963–65.
c) GENERAL EDITION. Grades 5–16; 1959–69.

See T2:1588 (2 references).

REFERENCES

1–2. See T2:1588.
3. WEST, E. M. The use of an unobstructive screening device to approximate reading levels of adults. *National Reading Conference Yearbook*, 1978, 190–192.

[1996]
Reading-Free Vocational Interest Inventory. Educable mentally retarded at the high school level; 1975; RFVII; formerly called *AAMD-Becker Reading-Free Vocational Interest Inventory*; 2 forms; Ralph L. Becker; Elbern Publications.*

a) MALE FORM. 11 scores: automotive, building trades, clerical, animal care, food service, patient care, horticulture, janitorial, personal service, laundry service, materials handling.
b) FEMALE FORM. 8 scores: laundry service, light industrial, clerical, personal service, food service, patient care, horticulture, housekeeping.

For additional information and reviews by Esther E. Diamond and George Domino, see 8:988 (6 references).

REFERENCES

1–6. See 8:988.

7. HUBER, C. H. Career planning with mildly retarded students: A model for school counselors. *Vocational Guidance Quarterly*, 1979, 27, 223–229.
8. BECKER, R. L., SCHULL, C., & CAMBELL, K. Vocational interest evaluation of TMR adults. *American Journal of Mental Deficiency*, 1981, 85, 350–356.

[1997]
Reading: IOX Objectives-Based Tests. Grades kgn–6; 1973–76; criterion-referenced; 78 tests in 2 areas; series description by W. James Popham; tests developed under the direction of John McNeil, Nola Paxton, and Linda Paulson; Instructional Objectives Exchange.*

a) WORD ATTACK SKILLS. 38 tests.
b) COMPREHENSION SKILLS. 40 tests.

For additional information and reviews by Rebecca C. Barr and Barton B. Proger, see 8:771.

[1998]
★**Reading Readiness Inventory.** Ages 4–7; 1976; behavior checklist for use by teachers in judging reading readiness; no scores, 4 areas: physiological, environmental, emotional-motivational-personality, intellectual; John Downing and Derek Thackray; Hodder & Stoughton Educational [England].*

[1999]
Reading Skills Diagnostic Test. Grades 2–8; 1967–71; 6 scores: letter identification, simple phonics, consistent words, inconsistent words, letters in context, words in context; Richard H. Bloomer; Brador Publications, Inc.*

For additional information and reviews by Ira E. Aaron and Edward R. Sipay, see 8:772; see also T2:1644 (1 reference).

[2000]
Reading Test AD. Ages 7–6 to 11–1; 1956–70; formerly called *Sentence Reading Test* 1; A. F. Watts; NFER-Nelson Publishing Co. [England].*

See T2:1591 (3 references) and 7:703; for reviews by Reginald R. Dale and Stephen Wiseman, see 5:652.

[2001]
Reading Test (Comprehension and Speed): Municipal Tests: National Achievement Tests. Grades 3–6, 6–8; 1938–57; subtest of *Municipal Battery*; 5 scores: following directions, sentence meaning, paragraph meaning, reading speed, total; Robert K. Speer and Samuel Smith; Psychometric Affiliates.*

For additional information and a review by Larry A. Harris, see 8:741. For reviews of the complete battery, see 5:18 (1 review), 4:20 (1 review), and 2:1191 (2 reviews).

[2002]
Reading Test: McGraw-Hill Basic Skills System. Grades 11–14; 1970; also called *MHBSS Reading Test*; although designed for use with the MHBSS instructional program, the test may be used independently; 7 scores: 2 reading rates (recreational, study), flexibility, retention, skimming and scanning, paragraph comprehension, total; Alton L. Raygor; McGraw-Hill Book Co., Inc.*

For additional information and a review by Donald B. Black, see 7:704.

REFERENCES

1. GROBE, S. F., & GROBE, C. H. Reading skills as a correlate of writing ability in college freshmen. *Reading World*, 1977, 17, 50–54.

2. PARHAM, J. A. W. Academic success of persistent and nonpersistent students voluntarily enrolled in a university reading program. *Journal of Reading*, 1977, 20, 693–696.
3. TILLMAN, C. E. Readability and other factors in college reading tests: A critique of the Diagnostic Reading Test, the Nelson–Denny Reading Test, and the McGraw-Hill Basic Reading Test. *National Reading Conference Yearbook*, 1977, 253–259.
4. MICHAEL, W. B., & SHAFFER, P. The comparative validity of the California State University and Colleges English Placement Test (CSUC-EPT) in the prediction of fall semester grade point average and English course grades of first-semester entering freshmen. *Educational & Psychological Measurement*, 1978, 38, 985–1001.
5. SANTA, C. M., & TRUSCOTT, R. B. A college reading program: The integration of reading, writing, speaking and thinking within the content areas. *College Student Journal*, 1979, 13, 391–397.
6. FAIGLEY, L., DALY, J. A., & WITTE, S. P. The role of writing apprehension in writing performance and competence. *Journal of Educational Research*, 1981, 75, 16–21.

[2003]

Reading Tests A and BD. 1, 2–4 years primary school; 1967–73; 2 levels; NFER-Nelson Publishing Co. [England].*
a) READING TEST A. 1 year primary school; 1968–73; formerly called *Primary Reading Test 1*.
b) READING TEST BD. 2–4 years primary school; 1967–69; formerly called *Primary Reading Test 2*.
For additional information, see 7:705.

REFERENCES

1. RAE, G. Relation of auditory–visual integration to reading and intelligence. *Journal of General Psychology*, 1977, 97, 3–8.

[2004]

Reading Tests EH 1–3. First 4 years of secondary school; 1961–66; formerly called *Secondary Reading Tests 1–3*; 3 tests; S. M. Bate; NFER-Nelson Publishing Co. [England].*
a) TEST 1, VOCABULARY.
b) TEST 2, COMPREHENSION.
c) TEST 3, CONTINUOUS PROSE. Reading speed.

REFERENCES

1. McCALLUM, D. I., SMITH, I. M., & ELIOT, J. Further investigation of components of mathematical ability. *Psychological Reports*, 1979, 44, 1127–1133.

[2005]

Rehabilitation Client Rating Scale. Vocational rehabilitation counselees; 1974; RCRS; formerly called *Queens Counsellor Rating Scale*; 5 scores: work attributes, impulsivity, emotional maladjustment, social adjustment, devious behavior; John S. Hicks; the Author.*
For additional information, see 8:1062 (1 reference).

[2006]

Reicherter-Sanders Typewriting I and II. 1, 2 semesters high school; 1962–64; first published 1962–63 in the Every Pupil Scholarship Test series; Richard F. Reicherter and M. W. Sanders; Bureau of Educational Measurements.*
For additional information and a review by Lawrence W. Erickson, see 7:557.

[2007]

***Reid Report/Reid Survey.** Job applicants; 1969–80; for predicting the likelihood of employee theft; Reid Psychological Systems.*
For additional information and a review by Stanley L. Brodsky of the *Reid Report*, see 8:658 (3 references); see also T2:1353 (1 reference) and 7:132 (1 reference).

[2008]

A Religion Scale. Adolescents and adults; 1961; attitudes toward religion; Panos D. Bardis; the Author.*
For additional information, see 8:465 (2 references).

[2009]

A Religious Attitudes Inventory. Religious counselees; 1964; W. E. Crane and J. Henry Coffer, Jr.; Family Life Publications, Inc.*
For additional information, see 7:650.

[2010]

Research Personnel Review Form. Research and engineering and scientific firms; 1959–60; for supervisor's evaluation of research personnel in preparation for a performance review interview; Morris I. Stein; the Author.*
For additional information, see 6:1164.

[2011]

Reversal Test. Grade 1 entrants; 1954; Åke W. Edfeldt; Psykologiförlaget AB [Sweden].*

[2012]

***Revised Behavior Problem Checklist.** Children ages 5–12 and adolescents; 1979–82; RBPC; ratings by anyone well acquainted with the child; 6 scores: conduct-disorder, socialized aggression, attention-problems-immaturity, anxiety-withdrawal, psychotic behavior, motor excess; Herbert C. Quay and Donald R. Peterson; Herbert C. Quay.

REFERENCES

1. RICHMAN, L. C. Parents and teachers: Differing views of behavior of cleft palate children. *Cleft Palate Journal*, 1978, 15, 360–364.
2. LUEGER, R. J. Person and situation factors influencing transgression in behavior–problem adolescents. *Journal of Abnormal Psychology*, 1980, 89, 453–458.
3. HALE, R. L., & ZUCKERMAN, C. Application of confirmatory factor analysis to verify the construct validity of the Behavior Problem Checklist and the Bristol Social Adjustment Guides. *Educational & Psychological Measurement*, 1981, 41, 843–850.
4. LINDHOLM, B. W., & TOULIATOS, J. Development of children's behavior problems. *Journal of Genetic Psychology*, 1981, 139, 47–53.
5. LINDHOLM, B. W., & TOULIATOS, J. Mothers' and fathers' perception of their childrens' psychological adjustment. *Journal of Genetic Psychology*, 1981, 139, 245–255.
6. RICHMAN, L. C., & LINDGREN, S. D. Manual for the Behavior Problem Checklist. *Journal of Abnormal Psychology*, 1981, 90, 99–104.

[2013]

***Revised Beta Examination, Second Edition.** Ages 16–64; 1931–78; BETA-II; non-verbal intellectual ability; 7 scores: mazes, coding, paper form boards, picture completion, clerical checking, picture absurdities, total; 1946 revision by Robert M. Lindner and Milton Gurvitz; basic revision by C. E. Kellogg and N. W. Morton; The Psychological Corporation.*
See T2:447 (29 references); for a review by Bert A. Goldman of an earlier edition, see 6:494 (13 references); see also 5:375 (14 references); for reviews by Raleigh M. Drake and Walter C. Shipley, see 3:259 (5 references); for reviews by S. D. Porteus and David Wechsler, see 2:1419 (4 references).

[2014]

***The Revised Developmental Screening Inventory—1980.** Ages 1–36 months; 1966–80; DSI; test consists of selected items from *Gesell Developmental*

Schedules; ratings in 5 areas: adaptive, gross motor, fine motor, language, personal-social; Hilda Knobloch, Frances Stevens, and Anthony Malone; Hilda Knobloch.

See T2:494 (2 references) and 7:407 (1 reference).

REFERENCES

1. See 7:407.
2–3. See T2:494.
4. GRAVES, P. L. Nutrition and infant behavior: A replication study in the Katmandu Valley, Nepal. *American Journal of Clinical Nutrition*, 1978, 31, 541–55.
5. KATOFF, L., & REUTER, J. Review of developmental screening tests for infants. *Journal of Clinical Child Psychology*, 1980, 9, 30–34.

[2015]
Revised Minnesota Paper Form Board Test.
Grades 9–16 and adults; 1930–70; orginial test by Donald G. Paterson, Richard M. Elliott, L. Dewey Anderson, Herbert A. Toops, and Edna Heidbreder; revision by Rensis Likert and William H. Quasha; The Psychological Corporation. (British norms supplement available from NFER-Nelson Publishing Co. [England].)*

See T2:2266 (37 references), 7:1056 (19 references), and 6:1092 (16 references); for a review by D. W. McElwain, see 5:884 (29 references); for reviews by Clifford E. Jurgensen and Raymond A. Katzell, see 4:763 (38 references); for a review by Dewey B. Stuit, see 3:677 (48 references); for a review by Alec Rodger, see 2:1673 (9 references).

REFERENCES

1–9. See 2:1673.
10–57. See 3:677.
58–95. See 4:763.
96–124. See 5:884.
125–140. See 6:1092.
141–159. See 7:1056.
160–196. See T2:2266.
197. DENISI, A. S., & SHAW, J. B. Investigation of the uses of self-reports of abilities. *Journal of Applied Psychology*, 1977, 62, 641–644.
198. WALLACE, I. G. The role of overt letter rearrangement in anagram solving in subjects of high and low spatial ability and anagrams of two levels of difficulty. *Journal of General Psychology*, 1977, 96, 117–124.
199. PAIVIO, A. Comparisons of mental clocks. *Journal of Experimental Psychology: Human Perception & Performance*, 1978, 4, 61–71.
200. PETRUSIC, W. M., VARRO, L., & JAMIESON, D. G. Mental rotation validation of two spatial ability tests. *Psychological Research*, 1978, 40, 139–148.
201. RICHARDSON, A. The meaning and measurement of memory imagery. *British Journal of Psychology*, 1977, 68, 29–43.
202. KIRTON, M. Field dependence and adaption–innovation theories. *Perceptual & Motor Skills*, 1978, 47, 1239–1245.
203. MYERS, L. B., & LEVY, G. W. Description and prediction of the intractable inmate. *Journal of Research in Crime & Delinquency*, 1978, 15, 214–228.
204. KERTESZ, A. Visual agnosia: The dual deficit of perception and recognition. *Cortex*, 1979, 15, 403–419.
205. SERGENT, J., & LAMBERT, W. E. 'Learned helplessness' or 'learned incompetence'? *Canadian Journal of Behavioural Science*, 1979, 11, 257–274.
206. WILLIAMS, J. D., & BREKKE, B. W. Relationships among different stages of Piagetian tasks and spatial relations in adolescents. *Journal of Genetic Psychology*, 1979, 134, 179–184.
207. BART, W. M., BAXTER, J., & FREY, S. The relationships of spatial ability and sex to former reasoning capabilities. *Journal of Psychology*, 1980, 104, 191–198.
208. DABBS, J. M., JR., & CHOO, G. Left–right carotid blood flow predicts specialized mental ability. *Neuropsychologia*, 1980, 18, 711–713.
209. DORAN, R. L., & DIETRICH, M. C. Psychomotor abilities of science and nonscience high school students. *Journal of Research in Science Teaching*, 1980, 17, 495–502.
210. ORNSTEIN, R., JOHNSTONE, J., HERRON, J., & SWENCIONIS, C. Differential right hemisphere engagement in visuospatial tasks. *Neuropsychologia*, 1980, 18, 49–64.
211. STERNBERG, R. J. Representation and process in linear syllogistic reasoning. *Journal of Experimental Psychology: General*, 1980, 109, 119–159.
212. ARMSTRONG, J. M. Achievement and participation of women in mathematics: Results of two national surveys. *Journal of Research in Mathematics Education*, 1981, 12, 356–372.
213. BLAGER, F. B., & ALPINER, J. G. Correlation between visual–spatial ability and speech reading. *Journal of Communication Disorders*, 1981, 14, 331–339.
214. CUNNINGHAM, M. D., & MURPHY, P. J. The effects of bilateral EEG biofeedback on verbal, visual–spatial, and creative skills in learning disabled male adolescents. *Journal of Learning Disabilities*, 1981, 14, 204–208.
215. RUOFF, P., DOERR, H., FULLER, P., MARTIN, D., & RUOFF, L. O. Motor and cognitive interactions during lateralized cerebral functions in children: An EEG study. *Cortex*, 1981, 17, 5–18.

[2016]
***Revised Pre-Reading Screening Procedures.**
First grade entrants; 1968–80; "to identify first grade academic needs"; 12 scores in 5 areas: visual, visual-kinesthetic-motor, auditory, auditory-visual, auditory-visual-kinesthetic-motor; Beth H. Slingerland; Educators Publishing Service, Inc.*

See T2:1721 (1 reference); for reviews by Colleen B. Jamison and Roy A. Kress of the earlier edition, see 7:732 (1 reference).

[2017]
★**Revised Token Test.** Preliminary normative data based on the following standardization samples: non-brain-damaged, left hemisphere brain-damaged, right hemisphere brain-damaged; 1978; a reconstruction of the *Token Test*; auditory processing inefficiencies; 22 scores: 10 subtest mean scores, overall mean score, 11 linguistic element mean scores; Malcolm Ray McNeil and Thomas E. Prescott; University Park Press.*

REFERENCES

1. HAGEMAN, C. F. Prediction and pattern of auditory processing using Revised Token Test. *ASHA*, 1979, 21, 717–718.
2. MCNEIL, M. R., CINQUANTA, C. M. D., LANGLOIS, A., & PRESCOTT, T. E. Ordinality and intervality of the Revised Token Test's scoring system. *ASHA*, 1979, 21, 717.
3. NOLL, J. D. Revised Token Test. *ASHA*, 1979, 21, 620–622.
4. BLANCHARD, S. L., & PRESCOTT, T. E. The effects of temporal expansion upon auditory comprehension in aphasic adults. *British Journal of Disorders of Communication*, 1980, 15, 115–127.
5. BROOKSHIRE, R. H., & NICHOLAS, L. E. Verification of active and passive sentences by aphasic and nonaphasic subjects. *Journal of Speech & Hearing Research*, 1980, 23, 878–893.

[2018]
***Reynell Developmental Language Scales (Revised).** Ages 1–7; 1969–77; RDLS; 3 scales; Joan K. Reynell with the statistical assistance of Michael Curwen; NFER-Nelson Publishing Co. [England].*

a) VERBAL COMPREHENSION SCALE A. Requires no speech, but some hand function.

b) VERBAL COMPREHENSION SCALE B. Adaptation of Scale A for use with children with neither speech nor hand function.

c) EXPRESSIVE LANGUAGE SCALE. 4 scores: structure, vocabulary, content, total.

For additional information and reviews by Katharine G. Butler and Joel Stark, see 8:974 (3 references); see also T2:2025 (3 references).

REFERENCES

1–3. See T2:2025.
4–6. See 8:974.
7. COHEN, D. J., CAPARULO, B. K., SHAYWITZ, B. A., & BOWERS, M. B. Dopamine and serotonin metabolism in neuropsychiatrically disturbed children. *Archives of General Psychiatry*, 1977, 34, 545–550.
8. EVESHAM, M. Teaching language skills to children with language disorders. *British Journal of Disorders of Communication*, 1977, 12, 23–29.

9. GOULD, J. The use of the Vineland Social Maturity Scale, the Merrill-Palmer Scale of Mental Tests (non-verbal items) and the Reynell Developmental Language Scales with children in contact with the services for severe mental retardation. *Journal of Mental Deficiency Research*, 1977, 21, 213–226.
10. WING, L., GOULD, J., YEATES, S. R., & BRIERLEY, L. M. Symbolic play in severely mentally retarded and in autistic children. *Journal of Child Psychology & Psychiatry & Allied Disciplines*, 1977, 18, 167–178.
11. DOUGLAS, J. E., & SUTTON, A. The development of speech and mental processes in a pair of twins: A case study. *Journal of Child Psychology & Psychiatry & Allied Disciplines*, 1978, 19, 49–56.
12. SMITH, P. K., & SYDDALL, S. Play and non-play tutoring in pre-school children: Is it play or tutoring which matters. *British Journal of Educational Psychology*, 1978, 48, 315–325.
13. BEVERIDGE, M., SPENCER, J., & MIHLER, P. Self-blame and communication failure in retarded adolescents. *Journal of Child Psychology & Psychiatry & Allied Disciplines*, 1979, 20, 129–138.
14. KONSTANTAREAS, M. M., WEBSTER, C. D., & OXMAN, J. Manual language acquisition and its influence on other areas of functioning in four autistic and autistic-like children. *Journal of Child Psychology & Psychiatry & Allied Disciplines*, 1979, 20, 337–350.
15. SIEGEL, L. S. Infant perceptual, cognitive, and motor behaviors as predictors of subsequent cognitive and language development. *Canadian Journal of Psychology*, 1979, 33, 382–395.
16. TEW, B. The "cocktail party syndrome" in children with hydrocephalus and spina bifida. *British Journal of Disorders of Communication*, 1979, 14, 89–101.
17. SILVA, P. A., & FERGUSSON, D. Some factors contributing to language development in three year old children: A report from the Dunedin multidisciplinary child development study. *British Journal of Disorders of Communication*, 1980, 15, 205–214.
18. BATH, D. Developing the speech therapy service in day nurseries: A progress report. *British Journal of Disorders of Communication*, 1981, 16, 159–173.
19. D'SOUZA, S. W., MCCARTNEY, E., NOLAN, M., & TAYLOR, I. G. Hearing, speech, and language in survivors of severe perinatal asphyxia. *Archives of Diseases in Childhood*, 1981, 56, 245–252.
20. HOWELL, J., SKINNER, C., GRAY, M., & BROOMFIELD, S. A study of the comparative effectiveness of different language tests with two groups of children. *British Journal of Disorders of Communication*, 1981, 16, 31–42.
21. SIEGEL, L. S. Infant tests as predictors of cognitive and language development at two years. *Child Development*, 1981, 52, 545–557.
22. WILLIAMS, A. J., WILLIAMS, M. A., WALKER, C. A., & BUSH, P. G. The Robin Anomalad (Pierre Robin Syndrome)—A follow up study. *Archives of Diseases in Childhood*, 1981, 56, 663–668.

[2019]
★**Reynell-Zinkin Scales: Developmental Scales for Young Visually Handicapped Children Part 1—Mental Development.** Ages 0–5; 1979; 6 scales: social adaptation, sensorimotor understanding, exploration of environment, response to sound and verbal comprehension, expressive language, communication; Joan Reynell and Pamela Zinkin (test); NFER-Nelson Publishing Co. [England].*

[2020]
Rhode Island Profile of Early Learning Behavior. Grades kgn–2; 1972; formerly called *Rhode Island Pupil Identification Scale*; behavior checklist for identification of learning problems; 3 behavior ratings: classroom, written work, total; Harry S. Novack, Elisa Bonaventura, and Peter F. Merenda; Jamestown Publishers.*

For additional information and a review by Dennis J. Deloria of the earlier edition, see 8:441 (5 references).

REFERENCES

1–5. See 8:441.
6. FLOOK, W. M., & VELICER, W. F. School readiness and teachers' ratings: A validation study. *Psychology in the Schools*, 1977, 14, 140–146.
7. MERENDA, P. F., BONAVENTURA, E., & NOVACK, H. S. An intensive study of the reliability of Rhode Island Pupil Identification Scale. *Psychology in the Schools*, 1977, 14, 282–289.

[2021]
Richmond Tests of Basic Skills. Junior school (ages 8–1 to 11–0) and secondary school (11–1 to 14–0); 1975, c1955–75; RTBS; British adaptation of *Iowa Tests of Basic Skills*, Multilevel Edition; 11 scores: vocabulary, reading comprehension, language (spelling, use of capital letters, punctuation, usage), work-study skills (map reading, reading graphs and tables, knowledge and use of reference materials), mathematics skills (mathematics concepts, mathematics problem solving); 6 overlapping levels (ages 8–1 to 9–0, 9–1 to 10–0, 10–1 to 11–0, 11–1 to 12–0, 12–1 to 13–0, 13–1 to 14–0) in a single booklet; original test by A. N. Hieronymus and E. F. Lindquist; adaptation by Norman France and Ian Fraser (teacher's guide and norms supplement); NFER-Nelson Publishing Co. [England].*

For additional information and reviews by Michael Berger and Thomas Kellaghan, see 8:25.

[2022]
The Riley Articulation and Language Test, Revised. Grades kgn–2; 1966–71; RALT; for screening of children most in need of speech therapy; 4 scores: language proficiency, intelligibility, articulation function, language function; Glyndon D. Riley; Western Psychological Services.*

For additional information and reviews by Ralph L. Shelton and Lawrence D. Shriberg, see 8:975 (1 reference); for a review by Raphael M. Haller of the original edition, see 7:967 (1 reference).

[2023]
*****Riley Motor Problems Inventory, Revised 1976.** Ages 4–9; 1972–76; RMPI; formerly called *Motor Problems Inventory*; 14 scores: oral motor tasks ("puh", "puh-tuh-kuh", tongue laterality, subtest total), fine motor tasks (eye-hand laterality, finger coordination, two-finger tap, subtest total), gross motor tasks (thigh-slap, hop, balance, walk-run-skip, subtest total), total; Glyndon D. Riley; Western Psychological Services.*

For additional information and a review by Brad S. Chissom of an earlier edition, see 8:879.

REFERENCES

1. RILEY, G. D., & RILEY, J. Motoric and linguistic variables among children who stutter: A factor analysis. *Journal of Speech & Hearing Disorders*, 1980, 45, 504–514.

[2024]
Riley Preschool Developmental Screening Inventory. Ages 3–5; 1969; RPDSI; school readiness; 2 scores: design, make-a-boy (girl); Clara M. D. Riley; Western Psychological Services.*

For additional information and a review by Doris E. Nason, see 8:806.

REFERENCES

1. MOORE, C. L., & BURNS, W. J. Brief screening for developmentally delayed preschoolers. *Perceptual & Motor Skills*, 1977, 45, 1169–1170.
2. MOORE, C. L., & BURNS, W. J. The performance of neurologically impaired and normal Ss on four screening techniques. *Journal of Clinical Psychology*, 1979, 35, 420–424.

[2025]
Ring and Peg Tests of Behavior Development. Birth to age 6; 1958–75; experimental; 6 scores: ambulative, manipulative, communicative, social adaptive, emo-

tive, total; Katharine M. Banham; Psychometric Affiliates.*

For additional information, see 8:226; for reviews by Jane V. Hunt and Emmy E. Werner, see 7:423.

[2026]
Risk-Taking-Attitude-Values Inventory. Ages 3 and over; 1972–79; RTAVI; importance and nearness ratings for each of 8 value goals (affection, respect, skill, enlightenment, power, wealth, well-being, rectitude) and ratings in 4 areas (usefulness, expectancy, ways of changing, frequency) for several specific behaviors; 5 levels; Richard E. Carney; Carney, Weedman and Associates.*

a) PRESCHOOL-PRIMARY FORM. Ages 3–8.
b) ELEMENTARY LEVEL. Grades 4–7.
c) SECONDARY LEVEL. Grades 7–12 and adults.
d) POST HIGH SCHOOL LEVEL. College.
e) MATURE ADULT LEVEL. Adult.

For additional information and a review by Stuart Oskamp, see 8:659 (1 reference); see also T2:1354A (1 reference).

[2027]
Rock-A-Bye, Baby: A Group Projective Test for Children. Ages 5–10; 1959, c1951–56; sibling rivalry; 5 scores: self concept, jealousy index, aggression to parents, guilt index, anxiety index, index of obsessive trends; Mary R. Haworth and Adolf G. Woltmann; Audio-Visual Services, Pennsylvania State University.* (In-print status uncertain; no reply from publisher.)

See T2:1497 (1 reference), P:468, and 6:236 (4 references).

[2028]
★**Rockford Infant Developmental Evaluation Scales.** Birth to 4 years; 1979; RIDES; developmental checklist offering an informal assessment of developmental function; 3 ways of administering items: ask parents for information, observe spontaneous actions and informal play, present specific tasks or set up situation that will elicit a particular kind of response; developmental behaviors arranged by age range into five skill areas: personal-social/self-help, fine motor/adaptive, receptive language, expressive language, gross motor; developed by Project RHISE, Children's Development Center, Rockford, IL.; Scholastic Testing Service, Inc.*

[2029]
Rokeach Value Survey. Ages 11 and over; 1967–73; RVS; test booklet title is *Value Survey*; manual title is *The Nature of Human Values*; rankings of 18 terminal values ("end-states of existence") and 18 instrumental values ("modes of behavior"); Milton Rokeach; Free Press (manual), Halgren Tests (test).*

For additional information and reviews by Jacob Cohen and Tom Kitwood, see 8:660 (155 references); see also T2:1355 (39 references).

REFERENCES

1–39. See T2:1355.
40–194. See 8:660.
195. BALKIN, J., KATZ, C., LEVIN, J., & BRANDT, D. Police in college: The value gap revisited. *Psychological Reports*, 1977, 41, 1023–1029.
196. BRAHEN, L. S., CAPONE, T., WIECHERT, V., & DESIDERIO, D. Naltrexone and cyclazocine. *Archives of General Psychiatry*, 1977, 34, 1181–1184.
197. LOYE, D., GORNEY, R., & STEELE, G. An experimental field study. *Journal of Communication*, 1977, 27, 206–216.
198. SIMMONS, D. D. Early adolescent personal values in American sponsored extraterritorial and stateside schools. *Journal of Psychology*, 1977, 95, 161–167.
199. SKEEL, D. J. What values are most important? *Today's Education*, 1977, 66, 63–64.
200. WECKOWICZ, T. E., COLLIER, G., & SERENG, L. Field dependence, cognitive functions, personality traits, and social values in heavy cannabis users and nonuser controls. *Psychological Reports*, 1977, 41, 291–302.
201. BOLT, M. The Rokeach Value Survey: Preferred or preferable? *Perceptual & Motor Skills*, 1978, 47, 322.
202. HEATH, R. L., & FOGEL, D. S. Terminal and instrumental? An inquiry into Rokeach's Value Survey. *Psychological Reports*, 1978, 42, 1147–1154.
203. KATZ, B., & BEECH, R. P. Values of counselors and clients participating in a storefront counseling center in a ghetto community. *Counseling & Values*, 1978, 23, 10–16.
204. KIMLICKA, T. M., & CROSS, H. J. A comparison of chronic versus casual marijuana users on personal values and behavioral orientations. *International Journal of the Addictions*, 1978, 13, 1145–1156.
205. MARTINI, J. L. Patient–therapist value congruence and ratings of client improvement. *Counseling & Values*, 1978, 23, 25–32.
206. MARTINI, J. L., & BROOK, R. C. Value comparisons between alcoholics, nonalcoholics, and therapists. *International Journal of the Addictions*, 1978, 13, 1169–1176.
207. SMITHERS, A. G., & LOBLEY, D. M. Dogmatism, social attitudes and personality. *British Journal of Social & Clinical Psychology*, 1978, 17, 135–142.
208. TALBOTT, J. A., & GILLEN C. Differences between nonprofessional recovering alcoholic counselors treating bowery alcoholics: A study of therapist variables. *Psychiatric Quarterly*, 1978, 50, 333–342.
209. TOWNSEND, P. C. Value orientations and initial commitment to behavioral and client–centered psychotherapies. *Counseling Values*, 1978, 23, 49–52.
210. ZENZEN, M. J., & HAMMER, L. Z. Value measurement and existential wholeness: A critique of the Rokeachean approach to value research. *Journal of Value Inquiry*, 1978, 12, 142–156.
211. ABBOTT, K., & PENN, R. Value preferences in dissimilar campus living groups. *Journal of College Student Personnel*, 1979, 20, 122–129.
212. COCHRANE, R., BILLIG, M., & HOGG, M. Politics and values in Britain: A test of Rokeach's two-value model. *British Journal of Social & Clinical Psychology*, 1979, 18, 159–167.
213. FEATHER, N. T. Accuracy of judgment of value systems: A field study of own and attributed value priorities in Papua New Guinea. *International Journal of Psychology*, 1979, 14, 151–162.
214. FEATHER, N. T. Value correlates of conservatism. *Journal of Personality & Social Psychology*, 1979, 37, 1617–1630.
215. GILGEN, A. R., & CHO, J. H. Performance of Eastern and Western-oriented college students on the Value Survey and the Ways of Life Scale. *Psychological Reports*, 1979, 45, 263–268.
216. KINDELAN, K. M., & MCCARREY, M. W. Spouse's value systems: Similarity, type and attributed marital adjustment. *Psychological Reports*, 1979, 44, 1295–1302.
217. LINDER, F., & BAUER, D. Interpersonal perception of the values freedom and equality. *Perceptual & Motor Skills*, 1979, 48, 167–170.
218. SMITH, M. D. Hockey violence: A test of the violent subculture hypothesis. *Social Problems*, 1979, 27, 235–247.
219. TOBACYK, J. Sex differences in predictability of self–disclosure for instrumental and terminal values. *Psychological Reports*, 1979, 44, 985–986.
220. YOUNG, R. A. The effects of value confrontation and reinforcement counseling on the career planning attitudes and behavior of adolescent males. *Journal of Vocational Behavior*, 1979, 15, 1–11.
221. BLOMQUIST, B. L., CRUISE, P. D., & CRUISE, R. J. Values of baccalaureate nursing students in secular and religious schools. *Nursing Research*, 1980, 29, 379–383.
222. BROWN, N. W., & LAWSON, R. Values in parochial and public schools: Alike or different. *Psychological Reports*, 1980, 47, 279–282.
223. CRANDALL, J. E. Adler's concept of social interest: Theory, measurement, and implications for adjustment. *Journal of Personality & Social Psychology*, 1980, 39, 481–495.
224. FEATHER, N. T. Conservatism, acquiescence, and the effects of sample heterogeneity. *Australian Journal of Psychology*, 1980, 32, 11–16.
225. FEATHER, N. T. Similarity of values systems within the same nation: Evidence from Australia and Papua New Guinea. *Australian Journal of Psychology*, 1980, 32, 17–30.
226. GOVERNALI, J. F., & SECHRIST, W. C. Clarifying values in a health education setting: An experimental analysis. *Journal of School Health*, 1980, 50, 151–154.
227. HLASNY, R. G., & MCCARREY, M. W. Similarity of values and warmth effects on clients' trust and perceived therapist's effectiveness. *Psychological Reports*, 1980, 46, 1111–1118.

228. HOGAN, H. W. German and American authoritarianism, self-estimated intelligence and value priorities. *Journal of Social Psychology*, 1980, 111, 145–146.
229. KATZ, B., & BEECH, R. P. Values and counselors 1968–1978: Stability or change? *Personnel & Guidance Journal*, 1980, 58, 609–612.
230. MAHONEY, J., & PECHURA, C. M. Values and volunteers: Axiology of altruism in a crisis center. *Psychological Reports*, 1980, 47, 1007–1012.
231. MCFARLANE, A. H., NORMAN, G. R., STREINER, D. L., ROY, R., & SCOTT, D. J. A longitudinal study of the influence of the psychosocial environment on health status: A preliminary report. *Journal of Health & Social Behavior*, 1980, 21, 124–133.
232. MCKERNAN, J., & RUSSELL, J. L. Differences of religion and sex in the values systems of Northern Ireland adolescents. *British Journal of Social & Clinical Psychology*, 1980, 19, 115–118.
233. MUNSON, J. M., & POSNER, B. Z. Concurrent validation of two value inventories in predicting job classification and success for organizational personnel. *Journal of Applied Psychology*, 1980, 65, 536–542.
234. MUNSON, J. M., & POSNER, B. Z. The factorial validity of a modified Rokeach Value Survey for four diverse samples. *Educational & Psychological Measurement*, 1980, 40, 1073–1079.
235. ROSEN, A., & NORDQUIST, T. A. Ego development level and values in a yogic community. *Journal of Personality & Social Psychology*, 1980, 39, 1152–1160.
236. VECCHIOTTI, D. I., & KORN, J. H. Comparison of student and recruiter values. *Journal of Vocational Behavior*, 1980, 16, 43–50.
237. WEISBORD, A., SHERMAN, M. F., & SHERMAN, N. C. Values as a function of religious commitment in Judaism. *Journal of Social Psychology*, 1980, 110, 101–107.
238. COLANGELO, N., & PARKER, M. Value differences among gifted adolescents. *Counseling & Values*, 1981, 26, 35–41.
239. FEATHER, N. T. Values and attitudes of medical students at an Australian university. *Journal of Medical Education*, 1981, 56, 818–830.
240. GAYLE, G. M. H. Another look at personality motivation and second language learning in a bilingual context. *Alberta Journal of Educational Research*, 1981, 27, 145–153.
241. MEDLUNG, J. M., & MCCARREY, M. Marital adjustment over segments of the family life cycle: The issue of spouses' value similarity. *Journal of Marriage & the Family*, 1981, 43, 195–203.
242. SAYEED, O. B., & SINHA, P. Personal value systems and job content/context factors. *Indian Journal of Social Work*, 1981, 42, 155–163.
243. STEFFERUD, B., & BOLTON, B. Nonverbal counseling behavior and therapists' stated value orientations. *Counseling & Values*, 1981, 26, 19–25.

[2030]

Rorschach. Ages 3 and over; 1921–51; variously referred to by such titles as Rorschach Method, Rorschach Test, Rorschach Ink Blot Test, Rorschach Psychodiagnostics; many variations and modifications are in use with no one method of scoring and interpreting generally accepted; this entry refers only to the Psychodiagnostic Plates first published in 1921; the references which follow also include references to various accessories and parallel plates not developed by Hermann Rorschach; Hermann Rorschach; Hans Huber [Switzerland]. (United States distributor: Grune & Stratton, Inc.)*

For additional information and reviews by Richard H. Dana and Rolf A. Peterson, see 8:661 (360 references); see also T2:1499 (376 references); for reviews by Alvin G. Burstein, John F. Knutson, Charles C. McArthur, Albert I. Rabin, and Marvin Resnikoff, see 7:175 (455 references); see also P:470 (719 references); for reviews by Richard H. Dana, Leonard D. Eron, and Arthur R. Jensen, see 6:237 (734 references); for reviews by Samuel J. Beck, H. J. Eysenck, Raymond J. McCall, and Laurance F. Shaffer, see 5:154 (1078 references); for a review by Helen Sargent, see 4:117 (621 references); for reviews by Morris Krugman and J. R. Wittenborn, see 3:73 (452 references); see also 2:1246 (147 references).

REFERENCES

1–147. See 2:1246.
148–598. See 3:73.
599–1219. See 4:117.
1220–2297. See 5:154.
2298–3030. See 6:237.

3031–3749. See P:470.
3750–4204. See 7:175.
4205–4580. See T2:1499.
4581–4940. See 8:661.
4941. BARKER, T. E., & BLACK, F. W. Klinefelter Syndrome in a military population. *Archives of General Psychiatry*, 1976, 33, 607–610.
4942. BELL, A. E., ABRAHAMSON, D. S., & MCRAE, K. N. Reading retardation: A 12–year prospective study. *Journal of Pediatrics*, 1977, 91, 363–370.
4943. BERK, S. N., MOORE, M. E., & RESNICK, J. H. Psychosocial factors as mediators of acupuncture therapy. *Journal of Consulting & Clinical Psychology*, 1977, 45, 612–619.
4944. BLATT, S. J., & FEIRSTEIN, A. Cardiac response and personality organization. *Journal of Consulting & Clinical Psychology*, 1977, 45, 115–123.
4945. BRAHEN, L. S., CAPONE, T., WIECHERT, V., & DESIDERIO, D. Naltrexone and cyclazocine: A controlled treatment study. *Archives of General Psychiatry*, 1977, 34, 1181–1184.
4946. COHEN, L., & WEINER, F. J. Adolescent Rorschach responses as a function of age at first institutionalization. *Journal of Personality Assessment*, 1977, 41, 227–229.
4947. DANA, R. H., HINMAN, S., & BOLTON, B. Dimensions of examinees' response to the Rorschach: An empirical synthesis. *Psychological Reports*, 1977, 40, 1147–1153.
4948. EBERT, J. N., EWING, J. H., ROGERS, M. H., & REYNOLDS, D. J. Changes in primary process expression in hospitalized schizophrenics treated with phenothiazines: Two projective tasks compared. *Journal of Genetic Psychology*, 1977, 130, 83–94.
4949. EXNER, J. E., & MURRILLO, L. G. A long term follow–up of schizophrenics treated with regressive ECT. *Diseases of the Nervous System*, 1977, 38, 162–168.
4950. EXNER, J. E., JR., & WYLIE, J. Some Rorschach data concerning suicide. *Journal of Personality Assessment*, 1977, 41, 339–348.
4951. EXNER, J. E., JR., WYLIE, J., LEUVA, A., & PARRILL, T. Some psychological characteristics of prostitutes. *Journal of Personality Assessment*, 1977, 41, 474–485.
4952. FEINMAN, J. M., & FINE, H. J. The relationship between sphere dominance and non–pathological behavior with a further examination of the somato–affective sphere. *Journal of Clinical Psychology*, 1977, 33, 959–965.
4953. FISH, B. Neurobiologic antecedents of schizophrenia in children. *Archives of General Psychiatry*, 1977, 34, 1297–1313.
4954. FRIESWYK, S. The assessment of a relationship disposition, "fantasy withdrawal", from Rorschach face sheet data. *Journal of Clinical Psychology*, 1977, 33, 1132–1140.
4955. HARROW, M., & QUINLAN, D. Is disordered thinking unique to schizophrenia? *Archives of General Psychiatry*, 1977, 34, 15–21.
4956. HEATH, D. H. Academic predictors of adult maturity and competence. *Journal of Higher Education*, 1977, 48, 613–632.
4957. HEATH, D. H. Maternal competence, expectation, and involvement. *Journal of Genetic Psychology*, 1977, 131, 169–182.
4958. HEATH, D. H. Some possible effects of occupation on the maturing of professional men. *Journal of Vocational Behavior*, 1977, 11, 263–281.
4959. KWAWER, J. S. Male homosexual psychodynamics and the Rorschach Test. *Journal of Personality Assessment*, 1977, 41, 10–18.
4960. MATARAZZO, J. D., & WIENS, A. N. Black Intelligence Test of Cultural Homogeneity and Wechsler Adult Intelligence Scale scores of black and white police applicants. *Journal of Applied Psychology*, 1977, 62, 57–63.
4961. MCCRAW, R. K., & TUMA, J. M. Rorschach content categories of juvenile diabetics. *Psychological Reports*, 1977, 40, 818.
4962. MCDERMOTT, P. A. Measures of diagnostic data usage as discriminants among training and experience levels in school psychology. *Psychology in the Schools*, 1977, 14, 323–331.
4963. MERCURIO, R., & VACC, N. A. Relationship of two measures of conformity. *Perceptual & Motor Skills*, 1977, 45, 538.
4964. NICHOLS, M. P., & KNOPF, I. J. Refining computerized test interpretations: An in–depth approach. *Journal of Personality Assessment*, 1977, 41, 157–159.
4965. PROKOP, C. K. The role of psychologic evaluation in determining the personal meanings of aging and illness. *Geriatrics*, 1977, 32, 125–139.
4966. RIVARD, E., & DUDEK, S. Z. Primary process thinking in the same children at two developmental levels. *Journal of Personality Assessment*, 1977, 41, 120–130.
4967. SCHAEFFER, D. S. Scores on neuroticism pathology, mood, and Rorschach and diagnosis of affective disorder. *Psychological Reports*, 1977, 40, 1135–1141.
4968. SCHORI, T. R., & THOMAS, C. B. Precursors of premature disease and death: Rorschach and figure–drawing factors. *Psychological Reports*, 1977, 40, 1115–1122.
4969. SHAKOW, D. The nature of deterioration in schizophrenic conditions. *Psychological Issues*, 1977, 10, 4–86.

4970. SIEGEL, H. B. Body boundary and field–dependence. *Perceptual & Motor Skills*, 1977, 45, 1097–1098.

4971. SYNDER, C. R., & CLAIR, M. S. Does insecurity breed acceptance? Effects of trait and situational insecurity on acceptance of positive and negative diagnostic feedback. *Journal of Consulting & Clinical Psychology*, 1977, 45, 843–850.

4972. URIST, J. The Rorschach Test and the assessment of object relations. *Journal of Personality Assessment*, 1977, 41, 3–9.

4973. VEERARAGHAVAN, V., & SEN, A. An experimental investigation of inaccessibility of memory trace. *Manas*, 1977, 24, 77–176.

4974. VESTEWIG, R. E., & PARADISE, C. A. Multidimensional scaling of the TAT and the measurement of achievement motivation. *Journal of Personality Assessment*, 1977, 41, 595–603.

4975. VORHAUS, P. G. Watchman, what of the future? *Journal of Personality Assessment*, 1977, 41, 427–433.

4976. WEINBERGER, D. R., & KELLY, M. J. Catatonia and malignant syndrome: A possible complication of neuroleptic administration: Report of a case involving haloperidol. *Journal of Nervous & Mental Disease*, 1977, 165, 263–268.

4977. WEISS, W. V., & KATZ, M. Rorschach form level and the process–reactive dimension in schizophrenia. *Journal of Clinical Psychology*, 1977, 33, 875–878.

4978. WENDER, P. H., ROSENTHAL, D., RAINER, J. D., GREENHILL, L., & SARLIN, B. Schizophrenics adopting parents. *Archives of General Psychiatry*, 1977, 34, 777–783.

4979. WILD, C. M., & SHAPIRO, L. N. Mechanisms of change from individual to family performance in male schizophrenics and their parents. *Journal of Nervous & Mental Disease*, 1977, 165, 41–56.

4980. WULACH, J. S. Piagetian cognitive development and primary process thinking in children. *Journal of Personality Assessment*, 1977, 41, 230–237.

4981. ALTSHULER, K. Z. Toward a psychology of deafness? *Journal of Communication Disorders*, 1978, 11, 159–169.

4982. BAKER, M. The Torrance Tests of Creative Thinking and the Rorschach Inkblot Test: Relationships between two measures of creativity. *Perceptual & Motor Skills*, 1978, 46, 539–547.

4983. BERGMAN, H., NORLIN, B., BORG, S., KÖPPEN, S., STARCK, A., & ZOTTERMAN, A. Structuring and articulation of Rorschach inkblots in relation to alcohol consumption: A co–twin control study. *Perceptual & Motor Skills*, 1978, 46, 947–952.

4984. BLUMETTI, A. E., & GREENBERG, R. P. Reality testing and Rorschach perceptual regression in female patients. *Journal of Personality Assessment*, 1978, 42, 39–44.

4985. CHALUS, G. A. The mechanisms underlying attributive projection. *Journal of Personality*, 1978, 46, 362–382.

4986. DOR-SHAV, N. K. On the long-range effects of concentration camp internment on Nazi victims: 25 years later. *Journal of Consulting & Clinical Psychology*, 1978, 46, 1–11.

4987. EXNER, J. E., JR., ARMBRUSTER, G., & MITTMAN, B. The Rorschach response process. *Journal of Personality Assessment*, 1978, 42, 27–38.

4988. EXNER, J. E., JR., ARMBRUSTER, G. L., & VIGLIONE, D. The temporal stability of some Rorschach features. *Journal of Personality Assessment*, 1978, 42, 474–482.

4989. FRANK, G. On the validity of hypotheses derived from the Rorschach: III. The relationship between shading and anxiety. *Perceptual & Motor Skills*, 1978, 46, 531–538.

4990. FRANK, G. On validity of hypotheses derived from the Rorschach: IV. The unique affective pull of the cards. *Perceptual & Motor Skills*, 1978, 47, 179–184.

4991. GARWOOD, J. Six-month prognostic norms derived from studies of the Rorschach prognostic scale. *Journal of Personality Assessment*, 1978, 42, 22–26.

4992. GELLER, A. M., & ATKINS, A. Cognitive and personality factors in suicidal behavior. *Journal of Consulting & Clinical Psychology*, 1978, 46, 860–868.

4993. GREENBERG, R. P., & CARDWELL, G. F. Rorschach developmental level and intelligence factors. *Journal of Consulting & Clinical Psychology*, 1978, 46, 844–848.

4994. HAGGARD, E. A. On quantitative Rorschach scales. *Educational & Psychological Measurement*, 1978, 38, 703–724.

4995. HÄNNINEN, H., NURMINEN, M., TOLONEN, M., & MARTELIN, T. Psychological tests as indicators of excessive exposure to carbon disulfide. *Scandinavian Journal of Psychology*, 1978, 19, 163–174.

4996. HEATH, D. H. What meaning and effects does fatherhood have for the maturing of professional men? *Merrill–Palmer Quarterly*, 1978, 24, 265–278.

4997. HOUCK, R. L., & DAWSON, J. G. Comparative study of persisters and leavers in seminary training. *Psychological Reports*, 1978, 42, 1131–1137.

4998. KESTENBAUM, J. M., & LYNCH, D. Rorschach suicide predictors: A crossvalidational study. *Journal of Clinical Psychology*, 1978, 34, 754–758.

4999. KURTZ, R. M., & GARFIELD, S. L. Illusory correlation: A further exploration of Chapman's Paradigm. *Journal of Consulting & Clinical Psychology*, 1978, 46, 1009–1015.

5000. LEVY, D. L., HOLZMAN, P. S., & PROCTOR, L. R. Vestibular responses in schizophrenia. *Archives of General Psychiatry*, 1978, 35, 972–981.

5001. LION, L. S. Psychological effects of jogging: A preliminary study. *Perceptual & Motor Skills*, 1978, 47, 1215–1218.

5002. MARTIN, J. D., BLAIR, G. E., & BRENT, D. The relationship of scores on Elizur's hostility system on the Rorschach to the acting–out score on the Hand Test. *Educational & Psychological Measurement*, 1978, 38, 587–591.

5003. MCCULLY, R. S. The laugh of Satan: A study of a familial murderer. *Journal of Personality Assessment*, 1978, 42, 81–91.

5004. MORELAND, K. L. Measurement of delay of gratification. *Journal of Personality Assessment*, 1978, 42, 354.

5005. PRANDONI, J. R., & SWARTZ, C. P. Rorschach protocols for three diagnostic categories of adult offenders: Normative data. *Journal of Personality Assessment*, 1978, 42, 115–120.

5006. RABINOWITZ, S., & VAN DER SPUY, H. I. J. Selection criteria for dialysis and renal transplant. *American Journal of Psychiatry*, 1978, 135, 861–862.

5007. RIERDAN, J., LANG, E., & EDDY, S. Suicide and transparency responses on the Rorschach: A replication. *Journal of Consulting & Clinical Psychology*, 1978, 46, 1162–1163.

5008. RITZLER, B. A. The Nuremberg mind revisited: A quantitative approach to Nazi Rorschachs. *Journal of Personality Assessment*, 1978, 42, 344–353.

5009. RYHÄNEN, P., HELKALA, E., IHALAINEN, O., HOLLMÉN, A., RANTAKYLÄ, S., MERILÄ, M., TUOHINO, V., PIETARILA, M., & HORTTONEN, L. Effects of anasthesia on the psychological function of patients. *Annals of Clinical Research*, 1978, 10, 318–322.

5010. SILVERMAN, L. H., ROSS, D. L., ADLER, J. M., & LUSTIG, D. A. Simple research paradigm for demonstrating subliminal psychodynamic activation: Effects of Oedipal stimuli on dart–throwing accuracy in college males. *Journal of Abnormal Psychology*, 1978, 87, 341–357.

5011. TOLONEN, M., & HANNINEN, H. Psychological tests specific to individual carbon disulfide exposure. *Scandinavian Journal of Psychology*, 1978, 19, 241–245.

5012. WADE, T. C., BAKER, T. B., MORTON, T. L., & BAKER, L. J. The status of psychological testing in clinical psychology: Relationships between test use and professional activities and orientations. *Journal of Personality Assessment*, 1978, 42, 3–10.

5013. WAGNER, E. E. A theoretical explanation of the dissociative reaction and a confirmatory case presentation. *Journal of Personality Assessment*, 1978, 42, 312–316.

5014. WAGNER, E. E. Personality correlates of Rorschach scoring determinants: Hypotheses derived from structural analysis. *Journal of Personality Assessment*, 1978, 42, 466–473.

5015. WAGNER, E. E., KLEIN, I., & WALTER, T. Differentiation of brain damage among low IQ subjects with three projective techniques. *Journal of Personality Assessment*, 1978, 42, 49–55.

5016. WAGNER, E. E., & WAGNER, C. F. Similar Rorschach patterning in three cases of anorexia nervosa. *Journal of Personality Assessment*, 1978, 42, 426–432.

5017. WALLER, R. W., & KEELEY, S. M. Effects of explanation and information feedback on the illusory correlation phenomenon. *Journal of Consulting & Clinical Psychology*, 1978, 46, 342–343.

5018. WEINER, I. B., & EXNER, J. E., JR. Rorschach indices of disordered thinking in patient and nonpatient adolescents and adults. *Journal of Personality Assessment*, 1978, 42, 339–343.

5019. WEISZ, J. R., QUINLAN, D. M., O'NEILL, P., & O'NEILL, P. C. The Rorschach and structured tests of perception as indices of intellectual development in mentally retarded and nonretarded children. *Journal of Experimental Child Psychology*, 1978, 25, 326–336.

5020. YANOVSKI, A., & FOGEL, M. L. Effects of instructions for visual imagery on Rorschach responses. *Perceptual & Motor Skills*, 1978, 47, 1323–1335.

5021. ARONOW, E., REZNIKOFF, M., & RAUCHWAY, A. Some old and new directions in Rorschach testing. *Journal of Personality Assessment*, 1979, 43, 227–234.

5022. BARNES, G. E. The alcoholic personality: A reanalysis of the literature. *Journal of Studies on Alcohol*, 1979, 40, 571–634.

5023. BARTSCH, J. R., & DAWSON, J. G. Rorschach content analysis of the use of sexual imagery by Catholic seminarians. *Psychological Reports*, 1979, 45, 647–655.

5024. BROOKS, C. R. Rorschach variables and their relationship to WISC-R IQ among children referred. *Psychology in the Schools*, 1979, 16, 369–373.

5025. CARR, A. C., GOLDSTEIN, E. G., HUNT, H. F., & KERNBERG, O. F. Psychological tests and borderline patients. *Journal of Personality Assessment*, 1979, 43, 582–590.

5026. DANESINO, A., DANIELS, J., & MCLAUGHLIN, T. J. Jo-Jo, Josephine and Joanne: A study of multiple personality by means of the Rorschach Test. *Journal of Personality Assessment*, 1979, 43, 300-313.

5027. EDELL, W. S., & CHAPMAN, L. J. Anhedonia, perceptual abberation, and the Rorschach. *Journal of Consulting & Clinical Psychology*, 1979, 47, 377-384.

5028. HAIMO, S. F., & HOLZMAN, P. S. Thought disorder in schizophrenics and normal controls: Social class and race differences. *Journal of Consulting & Clinical Psychology*, 1979, 47, 963-967.

5029. HARDER, D. W. The assessment of ambitious-narcissistic character style with three projective tests: The Early Memories, TAT, and Rorschach. *Journal of Personality Assessment*, 1979, 43, 23-32.

5030. HARDER, D. W., & RITZLER, B. A. A comparison of Rorschach developmental level and form-level systems as indicators of psychosis. *Journal of Personality Assessment*, 1979, 43, 347-354.

5031. IKEGAMI, T. Cognitive style in children: The relation between reflection-impulsivity and Rorschach scores. *Psychologia*, 1979, 22, 207-221.

5032. JUNI, S., MASLING, J., & BRANNON, R. Interpersonal touching and orality. *Journal of Personality Assessment*, 1979, 43, 235-237.

5033. KENDRA, J. M. Predicting suicide using the Rorschach Inkblot Test. *Journal of Personality Assessment*, 1979, 43, 452-456.

5034. KWAWER, J. S. Borderline phenomena, interpersonal relations, and the Rorschach Test. *Bulletin of the Menninger Clinic*, 1979, 43, 515-524.

5035. LITWACK, T. R., WEIDEMANN, C. F., & YAGER, J. The fear of object loss, responsiveness to subliminal stimuli, and schizophrenic psychopathology. *Journal of Nervous & Mental Disease*, 1979, 167, 79-90.

5036. MORRISON, H. L. Psychiatric observations and interpretations of bite mark evidence in multiple murders. *Journal of Forensic Sciences*, 1979, 24, 492-502.

5037. NEWMARK, C. S., KONANC, J. T., SIMPSON, M., BOREN, R. B., & PRILLAMAN, K. Predictive validity of the Rorschach prognostic rating scale with schizophrenic patients. *Journal of Nervous & Mental Disease*, 1979, 167, 135-143.

5038. PETHÖ, B., TOLNA, J., & TUSNÁDY, G. Multi-trait-multi-method assessment of predictive variables of outcome in schizophrenia spectrum disorders. A nosological evaluation. *Journal of Psychiatric Research*, 1979, 15, 163-174.

5039. SCHWARTZ, F., & LAZAR, Z. The scientific status of the Rorschach. *Journal of Personality Assessment*, 1979, 43, 3-11.

5040. SERGENT, J., & BINIK, Y. M. On the use of symmetry in the Rorschach Test. *Journal of Personality Assessment*, 1979, 43, 355-359.

5041. SHABAD, P., WORLAND, J., LANDER, H., & DIETRICH, D. A retrospective analysis of the TATs of children at risk who subsequently broke down. *Child Psychiatry & Human Development*, 1979, 10, 49-59.

5042. SHEVRIN, H., SMOKLER, I. A., & WOLF, E. Field independence, lateralization and defensive style. *Perceptual & Motor Skills*, 1979, 49, 195-202.

5043. SINGER, B. A. Defensiveness in exhibitionists. *Journal of Personality Assessment*, 1979, 43, 526-531.

5044. SMOKLER, I. A., & SHERVIN, H. Cerebral lateralization and personality style. *Archives of General Psychiatry*, 1979, 36, 949-954.

5045. TAMKIN, A. S. Rorschach card rejection and its relationships to defensiveness, intelligence, and sex. *Psychological Reports*, 1979, 44, 1003-1006.

5046. WORLAND, J. Rorschach developmental level in the offspring of patients with schizophrenia and manic-depressive illness. *Journal of Personality Assessment*, 1979, 43, 591-594.

5047. WORLAND, J., LANDER, H., & HESSELBROCK, V. Psychological evaluation of clinical disturbance in children at risk for psychopathology. *Journal of Abnormal Psychology*, 1979, 88, 13-26.

5048. YANOVSKI, A., & FOGEL, M. L. Visual imagery reactivity: Relationships to Rorschach responses, diagnostic classification and therapeutic potential. *Psychological Reports*, 1979, 45, 1003-1010.

5049. ALBERT, S., FOX, H. M., & KAH, M. W. Faking psychosis on the Rorschach: Can expert judges detect malingering. *Journal of Personality Assessment*, 1980, 44, 115-119.

5050. ALHEIDT, P. The effect of reading ability on Rorschach performance. *Journal of Personality Assessment*, 1980, 44, 3-10.

5051. AMOS, S. P. A test-operate-test-exit model for Rorschach scoring. *Journal of Personality Assessment*, 1980, 44, 234-236.

5052. BASH, I. Y., & ALPERT, M. The determination of malingering. *Annals of the New York Academy of Science*, 1980, 347, 86-99.

5053. BONHEUR, H., & ROSNER, R. Sex offenders: A descriptive analaysis of cases studied at a forensic psychiatry clinic. *Journal of Forensic Sciences*, 1980, 25, 3-14.

5054. CARLSON, R. W. Temporal factors associated with Rorschach space responses. *Perceptual & Motor Skills*, 1980, 51, 1261-1262.

5055. COURSEY, R. D., BUCHSBAUM, M. S., & MURPHY, D. L. Psychological characteristics of subjects identified by platelet MAO activity and evoked potentials as biologically at risk for psychopathology. *Journal of Abnormal Psychology*, 1980, 89, 151-164.

5056. DAUBNEY, J. H., & WAGNER, E. E. Prediction of success in an accelerated BS/MD medical school program using two projective techniques. *Perceptual & Motor Skills*, 1980, 51, 1179-1183.

5057. DE LA FUENTE, J. R., & ROSENBAUM, A. H. Neuroendocrine dysfunction and blood levels of tricyclic antidepressants. *American Journal of Psychiatry*, 1980, 137, 1260-1261.

5058. EXNER, J. E., JR. But it's only an inkblot. *Journal of Personality Assessment*, 1980, 44, 563-577.

5059. FISHER, L., & JONES, J. E. Child competence and psychiatric risk. II. Areas of relationship between child and family functioning. *Journal of Nervous & Mental Disease*, 1980, 168, 332-337.

5060. FULLER, G. B., & LOVINGER, S. L. Personality characteristics of three sub-groups of children with reading disabilities. *Perceptual & Motor Skills*, 1980, 50, 303-308.

5061. GORDON, L. B. Preferential drug abuse: Defenses and behavioral correlates. *Journal of Personality Assessment*, 1980, 44, 345-350.

5062. GRALA, C. The concept of splitting and its manifestations of the Rorschach Test. *Bulletin of the Menninger Clinic*, 1980, 44, 253-271.

5063. HARAMIS, S. L., & WAGNER, E. E. Differentiation between acting-out and non-acting-out alcoholics with the Rorschach and the Hand Test. *Journal of Clinical Psychology*, 1980, 36, 791.

5064. LAGRECA, A. M. Can children remember to be creative? An interview study of children's thinking processes. *Child Development*, 1980, 51, 572-575.

5065. LOUCKS, S., BURSTEIN, A. G., BOROS, T., & KREGOR, E. The affective ratio in Rorschach's test as a function of age. *Journal of Personality Assessment*, 1980, 44, 590-591.

5066. LOVITT, R., & WEINER, M. Conservation withdrawal vs. depression in medically ill patients: Rorschach case study. *Journal of Personality Assessment*, 1980, 44, 460-464.

5067. MASLING, J., SHIFFNER, J., & SHENFELD, M. Client perception of the counselor and orality. *Journal of Counseling Psychology*, 1980, 27, 294-298.

5068. MCCULLY, R. S. A commentary on Adolf Eichmann's Rorschach. *Journal of Personality Assessment*, 1980, 44, 311-318.

5069. MICHELS, P. J., & LAYNE, C. Inventory responding models people's acceptance of feedback "derived" from tests and from interviews. *Journal of Personality Assessment*, 1980, 44, 302-306.

5070. OSTROV, E., MAROHN, R. C., OFFER, D., CURTISS, G., & FECZKO, M. The adolescent antisocial behavior check list. *Journal of Clinical Psychology*, 1980, 36, 594-601.

5071. PANEK, P. E., & WAGNER, E. E. Mental retardation as a facade self phenomenon: Construct validation. *Perceptual & Motor Skills*, 1980, 51, 823-828.

5072. RITZLER, B., ZAMBIANCO, D., HARDER, D., & KASKEY, M. Psychotic patterns of the concept of the object on the Rorschach Test. *Journal of Abnormal Psychology*, 1980, 89, 46-55.

5073. ROSE, D., & BITTER, E. J. The Palo Alto Destructive Content Scale as a predictor of physical assaultiveness in men. *Journal of Personality Assessment*, 1980, 44, 228-233.

5074. RUSS, S. W. Primary process integration on the Rorschach and achievement in children. *Journal of Personality Assessment*, 1980, 44, 338-344.

5075. SALLEY, R. D., KHANNA, P., BYRUM, W., & HUTT, L. D. REM sleep and EEG abnormalities in criminal psychopaths. *Perceptual & Motor Skills*, 1980, 51, 715-722.

5076. SCHLESINGER, L. B., & FOX, C. F. Achromatic Rorschach perceptions: Some implications for the diagnosis of depression. *Perceptual & Motor Skills*, 1980, 50, 199-202.

5077. TAMKIN, A. S. Rorschach experience balance, introversion, and sex. *Psychological Reports*, 1980, 46, 843-848.

5078. WAGNER, E. E., & WAGNER, C. F. The facade compulsive: A type of latent schizophrenia. *Perceptual & Motor Skills*, 1980, 50, 831-837.

5079. WEINBERGER, L. J., & BRADLEY, L. A. Effects of "favorability" and type of assessment device upon acceptance of general personality interpretations. *Journal of Personality Assessment*, 1980, 44, 44-47.

5080. WIDIGER, T. A., & SCHILLING, K. M. Toward a construct validation of the Rorschach. *Journal of Personality Assessment*, 1980, 44, 450-459.

5081. YANOVSKI, A., & FOGEL, M. L. Clinical comparisons and Rorschach response differences between visual imagery reactors and nonreactors. *Journal of Personality Assessment*, 1980, 44, 578-589.

5082. DANA, R. H., BONGE, D., & STAUFFACHER, R. Personality dimensions in Rorschach reports: An empirical synthesis. *Perceptual & Motor Skills*, 1981, 52, 711-715.

5083. GORDON, M., & OSHMAN, H. Rorschach indices of children classified as hyperactive. *Perceptual & Motor Skills*, 1981, 52, 703-707.

5084. JUNI, S. Career choice and orality. *Journal of Vocational Behavior*, 1981, 19, 78-83.

5085. JUNI, S. Maintaining anonymity vs. requesting feedback as a function of oral dependency. *Perceptual & Motor Skills*, 1981, 52, 239-242.

5086. JUNI, S., & FRENZ, A., JR. Psychosexual fixation and perceptual defense. *Perceptual & Motor Skills*, 1981, 52, 83-89.

5087. KELTIKANGAS-JÄVINEN, L., JÄVINEN, H., & LEHTONEN, T. Psychic disturbances in patients with chronic prostatitis. *Annals of Clinical Research*, 1981, 13, 45–49.

5088. KERNBERG, O. F., GOLDSTEIN, E. G., CARR, A. C., HUNT, H. F., BAUER, S. F., & BLUMENTHAL, R. Diagnosing borderline personality: A pilot study using multiple diagnostic methods. *Journal of Nervous & Mental Disease*, 1981, 169, 225–231.

5089. LAMBERT, N. M. The clinical validity of the process for assessment of effective student functioning. *Journal of School Psychology*, 1981, 19, 323–334.

5090. LERNER, H. D., SUGARMAN, A., & GAUGHRAN, J. Borderline and schizophrenic patients: A comparative study of defensive structure. *Journal of Nervous & Mental Disease*, 1981, 169, 705–711.

5091. OGAWA, T. Personality characteristics of Parkinson's disease. *Perceptual & Motor Skills*, 1981, 52, 375–378.

5092. SINGER, M. T., & LARSON, D. G. Borderline personality and the Rorschach Test. *Archives of General Psychiatry*, 1981, 38, 693–698.

5093. SPEAR, W. E., & LAPIDUS, L. B. Qualitative differences in manifest object representations: Implications for a multidimensional model of psychological functioning. *Journal of Abnormal Psychology*, 1981, 90, 157–167.

5094. STRAUSS, H., HADAR, M., SHAVIT, H., & ITSKOWITZ, R. Relationship between creativity, repression, and anxiety in first graders. *Perceptual & Motor Skills*, 1981, 53, 275–282.

5095. URSANO, R. J. The Viet Nam era prisoner of war: Precaptivity personality and the development of psychiatric illness. *American Journal of Psychiatry*, 1981, 138, 315–318.

[2031]

*The Rosenzweig Picture-Frustration Study. Ages 4–13, 12–18, 14 and over; 1944–81; test booklet title is *Rosenzweig P-F Study*; 15 scores: directions of aggression (extraggression, intraggression, imaggression), types of aggression (obstacle-dominance, ego (etho)-defense, need-persistence), 9 combinations of the preceding categories; Saul Rosenzweig; the Author.*

a) FORM FOR CHILDREN. Ages 4–13; 1948–81.

b) REVISED FORM FOR ADOLESCENTS. Ages 12–18; 1964.

c) REVISED FORM FOR ADULTS. Ages 14 and over; 1944–78.

For additional information, see 8:662 (39 references); see also T2:1500 (106 references) and P:471 (63 references); for a review of *a* and *c* by Åka Bjerstedt, see 6:238 (61 references); for reviews by Richard H. Dana and Bert R. Sappenfield, see 5:155 (109 references); for reviews by Robert C. Challman and Percival M. Symonds, see 4:129 (77 references).

REFERENCES

1–77. See 4:129.
78–186. See 5:155.
187–247. See 6:238.
248–310. See P:471.
311–416. See T2:1500.
417–455. See 8:662.
456. ROSENZWEIG, S. An investigation of the reliability of the Rosenzweig Picture-Frustration (P-F) Study, Children's Form. *Journal of Personality Assessment*, 1978, 42, 483–488.
457. SHEARD, M. H., & MARINI, J. L. Treatment of human aggressive behavior: Four case studies of the effect of lithium. *Comprehensive Psychiatry*, 1978, 19, 37–45.
458. COCHÉ, E., & MEEHAN, J. Factor and cluster analyses with the Rosenzweig Picture Frustration Study. *Journal of Personality Assessment*, 1979, 43, 39–44.
459. DROTAR, D., OWENS, R., & GOTTHOLD, J. Personality adjustment of children and adolescents with hypopituitarism. *Child Psychiatry & Human Development*, 1980, 11, 59–66.
460. KINARD, E. M. Emotional development in physically abused children. *American Journal of Orthopsychiatry*, 1980, 50, 686–696.
461. LOCKWOOD, J. L., & ROLL, S. Effects of fantasy behavior, level of fantasy predisposition, age, and sex on direction of aggression in young children. *Journal of Genetic Psychology*, 1980, 136, 255–264.
462. ROMIROWSKY, S. Psychological adaptation patterns in response to cardiac surgery. *Journal of Rehabilitation*, 1980, 46, 50–52.

[2032]

Ross Test of Higher Cognitive Processes. Grades 4–6; 1976–79; 9 scores: analogies, deductive reasoning, missing premises, abstract relations, sequential synthesis, questioning strategies, analysis of relevant and irrelevant information, analysis of attributes, total; John D. Ross and Catherine M. Ross; Academic Therapy Publications.

For additional information, see 8:201.

REFERENCES

1. KRICHEV, A. Ross Test of Higher Cognitive Processes. *Psychology in the Schools*, 1978, 15, 145–146.

[2033]

Roswell-Chall Auditory Blending Test. Grades 1–4; 1963; Florence G. Roswell and Jeanne S. Chall; Essay Press, Inc.* (In-print status uncertain; no reply from publisher.)

See T2:1674 (7 references); for reviews by Ira E. Aaron and B. H. Van Roekel, see 6:830 (2 references).

[2034]

Roswell-Chall Diagnostic Reading Test of Word Analysis Skills, Revised and Extended. Reading level grades 1–4; 1956–1978; 15 scores: words (high frequency words), decoding (consonant sounds, consonant diagraphs, consonant blends, short vowel sounds, short and long vowel sounds, rule of silent e, vowel diagraphs, diphthongs and vowels controlled by r, syllabication, total), letter names (naming capital letters, naming lower case letters), encoding (encoding single consonants, encoding regular words); Florence G. Roswell and Jeanne S. Chall; Essay Press, Inc. (In-print status uncertain; no reply from publisher.)

See T2:1643 (2 references); for reviews by Ira E. Aaron and Emmett Albert Betts of an earlier form, see 6:831 (1 reference); for a review by Byron H. Van Roekel of the original form, see 5:667.

REFERENCES

1. See 6:831.
2–3. See T2:1643.
4. KUPIETZ, S. S., & RICHARDSON, E. Children's vigilance performance and inattentiveness in the classroom. *Journal of Child Psychology & Allied Disciplines*, 1978, 19, 145–154.
5. REED, H. B. C., JR. Biological defects and special education—An issue in personnel preparation. *Journal of Special Education*, 1979, 13, 9–33.
6. RICHARDSON, E., DIBENEDETTO, B., CHRIST, A., & PRESS, M. Relationship of auditory and visual skills to reading retardation. *Journal of Learning Disabilities*, 1980, 13, 77–82.

[2035]

Rothwell-Miller Interest Blank. Ages 13 and over; 1958; RMIB; formerly called *Rothwell Interest Blank, Miller Revision*; 12 scores: outdoor, mechanical, computational, scientific, personal contact, aesthetic, literary, musical, social service, clerical, practical, medical; Kenneth M. Miller and J. W. Rothwell; Australian Council for Educational Research [Australia].*

For additional information, see 5:867.

[2036]

Rothwell-Miller Interest Blank, [British Edition]. Ages 11 and over; 1958–68; British adaptation of original Australian edition; 12 scores: outdoor, mechanical, computational, scientific, persuasive, aesthetic, literary, musical, social service, clerical, practical, medical; original test by J. W. Rothwell; 1958 and 1968 revisions by Kenneth M. Miller; NFER-Nelson Publishing Co. [England].*

For additional information and reviews by A. W. Heim and Clive Jones, see 7:1034 (2 references).

[2037]
The Rotter Incomplete Sentences Blank. Grades 9–12, 13–16, adults; 1950; RISB; test sheet title is *Incomplete Sentences Blank*; Julian B. Rotter and Janet E. Rafferty (manual); The Psychological Corporation.*

For additional information, see 8:663 (21 references); see also T2:1501 (48 references), P:472 (35 references), 6:239 (17 references), and 5:156 (18 references); for reviews by Charles N. Cofer and William Schofield and an excerpted review by Adolf G. Woltmann, see 4:130 (6 references).

REFERENCES

1–6. See 4:130.
7–24. See 5:156.
25–41. See 6:239.
42–76. See P:472.
77–124. See T2:1501.
125–145. See 8:663.
146. BARKER, T. E., & BLACK, F. W. Klinefelter Syndrome in a military population. *Archives of General Psychiatry*, 1976, 33, 607–610.
147. ABRAMOWITZ, S. I., ABRAMOWITZ, C. V., & NASSI, A. J. Comparative family conflict among student left political activists. *Journal of Clinical Psychology*, 1977, 33, 87–92.
148. MITROFF, I. I., & FITZGERALD, I. On the psychology of the Apollo moon scientists: A chapter in the psychology of science. *Human Relations*, 1977, 30, 657–674.
149. RABINOWITZ, A., & SHOUVAL, R. Fantasy as a medium for the reduction of trait versus state aggression. *Journal of Research in Personality*, 1977, 11, 180–190.
150. VAITENAS, R., & WIENER, Y. Developmental, emotional, and interest factors in voluntary mid–career change. *Journal of Vocational Behavior*, 1977, 11, 291–304.
151. PRANDONI, J. R., & SWARTZ, C. P. Rorschach protocols for three diagnostic categories of adult offenders: Normative data. *Journal of Personality Assessment*, 1978, 42, 115–120.
152. ZUROFF, D. C., & SCWHARZ, J. C. Effects of transcendental meditation and muscle relaxation on trait anxiety, maladjustment, locus of control, and drug use. *Journal of Consulting & Clinical Psychology*, 1978, 46, 264–271.
153. SMITH, S. M. Standardized tests used in correctional institutions. *Journal of Employment Counseling*, 1979, 16, 178–188.
154. KROUSE, H. J., & KROUSE, J. H. Psychological factors in post mastectomy adjustment. *Psychological Reports*, 1981, 48, 275–278.
155. LAH, M. I., & ROTTER, J. B. Changing college student norms on the Rotter Incomplete Sentences Blank. *Journal of Consulting & Clinical Psychology*, 1981, 49, 985.
156. URSANO, R. J. The Viet Nam era prisoner of war: Precaptivity personality and the development of psychiatric illness. *American Journal of Psychiatry*, 1981, 138, 315–318.

[2038]
Roughness Discrimination Test. Blind children in grades kgn–1; 1965; RDT; test of tactual ability of predicting Braille reading readiness; Carson Y. Noland and June E. Morris; American Printing House for the Blind, Inc.*

For additional information, see 7:551 (4 references).

[2039]
Rucker-Gable Educational Programming Scale. Teachers and administrators; 1973–74; RGEPS; attitude toward and knowledge of appropriate program placement for mentally retarded, emotionally disturbed, or learning disabled children; 30 item scores plus 7 scores (mental retardation, emotional disturbance, learning disabilities, severity of handicap [mild, moderate, severe], total), in each of 2 areas: attitude, knowledge; Chauncy N. Rucker and Robert K. Gable; Rucker-Gable Assoc.*

For additional information and a review by James J. McCarthy, see 8:442 (9 references).

REFERENCES
1–9. See 8:442.
10. GILLUNG, T. B., & RUCKER, C. N. Labels and teacher expectations. *Exceptional Children*, 1977, 43, 464–465.
11. JOHNSON, A. B., & CARTWRIGHT, C. A. The roles of information and experience in improving teachers' knowledge and attitudes about mainstreaming. *Journal of Special Education*, 1979, 13, 453–462.
12. PFEIFFER, S. I. The influence of diagnostic labeling on special education placement decisions. *Psychology in the Schools*, 1980, 17, 346–350.

[2040]
[Rush Hughes (PB 50): Phonetically Balanced Lists 5–12]. Grades 2 and over; 1951; auditory discrimination; 8 lists on two records; no manual; [Central Institute for the Deaf]; [Technisonic Studios, Inc.].* (In-print status uncertain; no reply from the publisher.)

See T2:2053 (6 references) and 6:951 (6 references).

[2041]
Russell-Sanders Bookkeeping Test. 1, 2 semesters high school; 1962–64; first published 1962–63 in the Every Pupil Scholarship Test series; Raymond B. Russell and M. W. Sanders; Bureau of Educational Measurements.*

For additional information and a review by Bernard H. Newman, see 7:558.

[2042]
Rutgers Social Attribute Inventory. Adults; 1959; RSAI; perception of others (either real persons or generalized classes); 24 trait ratings: good natured-stubborn, intelligent-unintelligent, tense-relaxed, strong-weak, childish-mature, old fashioned-modern, dominating-submissive, thin-fat, adventurous-cautious, lazy-ambitious, optimistic-pessimistic, masculine-feminine, young-old, responsible-irresponsible, crude-refined, tall-short, suspicious-trusting, talkative-quiet, thrifty-wasteful, dependent-self reliant, unsympathetic-sympathetic, good looking-plain, conventional-unconventional, rich-poor; William D. Wells; Psychometric Affiliates.*

For additional information, see P:231; for reviews by David B. Orr and John Pierce-Jones, see 6:169.

[2043]
The Ruth Fry Symbolic Profile. Ages 14 and over; 1959–61; RFSP; no manual; Ruth Thacker Fry; C. G. Jung Educational Center.* (In-print status uncertain; no reply from publisher.)

[2044]
S-D Proneness Checklist. Clients and patients; 1970; SDPC; ratings by interviewer or informant; 3 scores: depression, suicide, total; no manual; William T. Martin; Psychologists and Educators, Inc.*

For additional information and a review by Charles Neuringer, see 8:664.

[2045]
Safran Culture Reduced Intelligence Test. Grades 1–6, 4 and over; 1960–69; SCRIT; C. Safran; the Author [Canada].* (In-print status uncertain; no reply from publisher.)

[2046]
Safran Student's Interest Inventory, Revised Edition. Grades 8–12; 1960–76; SSII; revision of *Safran Vocational Interest Test*; 11 scores: 7 interest scores (economic, technical, outdoor, service, humane, artistic, scientific) and 4 ability self-ratings (academic, mechanical, social, clerical); Carl Safran, Douglas W. Feltham, and Edgar N. Wright; Nelson Canada [Canada].*

For additional information, see 8:1021; for a review by Thomas T. Frantz of an earlier edition, see 7:1035; see also 6:1069 (1 reference).

See T2:453 (1 reference); for a review by Lee J. Cronbach, see 7:384 (6 references); see also 6:497 (1 reference).

REFERENCES
1. See 6:1069.
2. BORGEN, W. A., LACROIX, H., & GOETZ, E. Career exploration through group counseling. *School Guidance Worker*, 1978, 34, 46–47.

[2047]
St. Lucia Graded Word Reading Test. Grades 2–7; 1969; R. J. Andrews; Teaching and Testing Resources [Australia].*

REFERENCES
1. ELKINS, J. Empirical evidence for a model of reading disability research. *Australian Journal of Education*, 1978, 22, 303–309.

[2048]
St. Lucia Reading Comprehension Test. Grades 2–4; 1974; J. Elkins and R. J. Andrews; Teaching and Testing Resources [Australia].*

For additional information, see 8:743.

REFERENCES
1. BALDAUF, R. B., JR., DAWSON, R. L. T., PRIOR, J., & PROPST, I. K., JR. Can matching cloze be used with secondary ESL pupils. *Journal of Reading*, 1980, 23, 435–440.

[2049]
Sales Aptitude Test: ETSA Test 7A. Job applicants; 1960–72, c1957–59; 8 scores: sales judgment, interest in selling, personality factors, occupational identification, level of aspiration, insight into human nature, awareness of sales approach, total; manual and technical handbook by S. Trevor Hadley and George A. W. Stouffer, Jr.; test by Psychological Services Bureau; Educators'-Employers' Tests & Services Associates.*

For reviews of the complete battery, see 6:1025 (2 reviews).

[2050]
★**Sales Attitudes Check List.** Applicants for sales positions; 1960–67; SACL; forced choice rating scale; Erwin K. Taylor; Science Research Associates, Inc.*

[2051]
Sales Comprehension Test. Applicants for sales positions; 1947–71; Martin M. Bruce; Martin M. Bruce, Ph.D., Publishers.*

See T2:2406 (3 references) and 6:1178 (7 references); for a review by Raymond A. Katzell, see 5:947 (10 references).

[2052]
[Sales Motivation]. Sales managers, salespeople; 1972; 2 tests, 5 scores for each: basic-creature comfort, safety and order, belonging and affiliation, ego-status, actualization and self-expression; no manual; Jay Hall and Norman J. Seim; Teleometrics Int'l.*

a) INCENTIVES MANAGEMENT INDEX. Sales manager; IMI; practices and attitudes regarding motivational needs of subordinates.

b) SALES MOTIVATION SURVEY. Salespeople; SMS; motivational needs and values.

For additional information, see 8:1124.

[2053]
★**Sales Motivation Inventory, Revised.** Applicants for sales positions; 1953–77; SMI; minor wording changes in items and revised scoring key; (French edition available); Martin M. Bruce; Martin M. Bruce, Ph.D., Publishers.*

See T2:2408 (5 references); for a review by S. Rains Wallace, see 5:948 (2 references).

[2054]
[Sales Relations]. Salespeople, customers; 1972; views regarding behavior in 20 sales situations; 2 tests (same items except for first and third person expression), 2 scores (exposure, feedback) in each of 3 areas (salesperson's views of his own behavior, customer's views of salesperson's behavior, customer's preferences for salesperson's behavior) plus categorization into 1 of 4 sales types (no sell, soft sell, hard sell, awareness sell); no manual; Jay Hall and C. Leo Griffith (*b*); Teleometrics Int'l.*

a) SALES RELATIONS SURVEY. Salespeople; SRS; salesperson's views as to how he would behave.

b) CUSTOMER REACTION SURVEY. Customers; CRS; customer's views of how a salesperson would behave and how customer would prefer that he behave.

For additional information and a review by Raymond A. Katzell, see 8:1125.

[2055]
The Sales Sentence Completion Blank. Applicants for sales positions; 1961; Norman Gekoski; Martin M. Bruce, Ph.D., Publishers.*

For additional information, a review by William E. Kendall, and an excerpted review by John O. Crites, see 6:1181.

[2056]
Sales Style Diagnosis Test. Salespeople; 1975; SSDT; salesperson's perception of own sales style; 6 scores: orientation (task, relationships), effectiveness, style (dominant, supporting, synthesis); no manual; W. J. Reddin and David Forman; Organizational Tests Ltd. [Canada].*

For additional information, see 8:1126.

[2057]
Sales Transaction Audit. Salespeople; 1972; STA; salesperson's views as to how he would handle 18 specific complaints, challenges, and uncertainties on the part of customers; 3 transaction scores (parent subsystem, adult subsystem, child subsystem) and 2 tension indexes (disruptive, constructive); no manual; Jay Hall and C. Leo Griffith; Teleometrics Int'l.*

For additional information and a review by Stephen L. Cohen, see 8:1127.

[2058]

Salford Sentence Reading Test. Ages 6–10 to 10–6; 1976; SSRT; G. E. Bookbinder; Hodder & Stoughton Educational [England].*

For additional information and a review by J. Douglas Ayers, see 8:791.

[2059]

San Francisco Vocational Competency Scale. Mentally retarded adults; 1968; SFVCS; for rating workers in "sheltered workshops"; Samuel Levine and Freeman F. Elzey; The Psychological Corporation.*

See T2:2315 (1 reference); for an excerpted review by N. M. Downie, see 7:1073.

[2060]

Sand: Concepts About Print Test. Ages 5–0 to 7–0; 1972; early detection of reading difficulties; Marie M. Clay; Heinemann Educational Books Ltd. [New Zealand].* (United States distributor: Heinemann Educational Books, Inc.)

For additional information, see 8:774.

REFERENCES

1. GOODMAN, Y. M. Sand: Concepts About Print Test. *Reading Teacher*, 1981, 34, 445–448.

[2061]

Sanders-Buller World History Test. 1, 2 semesters high school; 1962–64; first published 1962–63 in the Every Pupil Scholarship Test series; M. W. Sanders and Robert Buller; Bureau of Educational Measurements.*

For additional information and a review by John Manning, see 7:922.

[2062]

Sanders-Fletcher Spelling Test. 1, 2 semesters in grades 9–13; 1962–64; first published 1962–63 in the Every Pupil Scholarship Test series; Gwen Fletcher and M. W. Sanders; Bureau of Educational Measurements.*

For additional information and a review by Thomas D. Horn, see 7:229.

[2063]

Sanders-Fletcher Vocabulary Test. 1, 2 semesters in grades 9–13; 1938–64; first published 1938 in the Every Pupil Scholarship Test series; Gwen Fletcher and M. W. Sanders; Bureau of Educational Measurements.*

For additional information and reviews by C. Mauritz Lindvall and William A. Mehrens, see 8:80.

[2064]

★Santostefano Tests of Cognitive Control. Children and adults; 1971–78; manual reprinted in part from *A Biodevelopmental Approach to Clinical Child Psychology: Cognitive Controls and Cognitive Therapy*; 5 tests; Sebastiano Santostefano; the Author.*

a) BODY SCHEMA AND TEMPO REGULATION TEST. Children; assessment of "the unique and habitual ways a child constructs cognitive schema of body positions, mobility and tempos"; 7 subtests: positions of the total body, positions of large parts of the body, positions of small parts of the body, touching small ambiguous shapes, moving the body at various tempos through the space of a room, moving a representation of the body at various tempos, moving a pencil at various tempos across the space of a sheet of paper.

b) SCATTERED SCANNING TEST. Younger children, older children; assesses the "manner in which the individual directs attention at and scans a visual field."

c) THE FRUIT DISTRACTION TEST. Ages 3–15 years; assesses the "selective deployment of attention" to relevant information; FDT; 3 scores: reading time distractability, reading error distractability, number of recalls of peripheral figures, plus optional reading variability score.

d) THE LEVELING-SHARPENING HOUSE TEST. Ages 3 years–adults; 1971; LSHT; assesses the "manner in which an individual manages information that remains stable and changes over time."

e) THE OBJECT SORT TEST II. Ages 4–adolescence and adults; assesses the manner in which "an individual relates, categorizes, and conceptualizes information"; O-SII; total score plus optional additional score; other test materials available from The Psychological Corporation.

[2065]

SAQS Chicago Q Sort. College and adults; 1956–57; SAQS; Raymond Corsini; Psychometric Affiliates.*

See T2:1358 (5 references) and P:232 (2 references); for reviews by William Stephenson and Clifford H. Swensen, Jr., see 5:103 (2 references).

[2066]

Sare-Sanders Constitution Test. High school and college; 1962–64; first published 1962–63 in the Every Pupil Scholarship Test series; Harold V. Sare and M. W. Sanders; Bureau of Educational Measurements.*

For additional information, see 7:932.

[2067]

Sare-Sanders Sociology Test. High school and college; 1958; Harold Sare and Merritt U. Sanders; Bureau of Educational Measurements.*

For additional information and a review by J. Richard Wilmeth, see 6:1022.

[2068]

A Scale to Measure Attitudes Toward Disabled Persons. Disabled and nondisabled adults; 1957–66; ATDP; title on test is *ATDP Scale*; Harold E. Yuker, J. R. Block, and Janet H. Younng; Human Resources Center.* (In-print status uncertain; no reply from publisher.)

For additional information, see 8:666 (31 references); see also T2:1363 (40 references) and P:235 (14 references).

REFERENCES

1–14. See P:235.
15–54. See T2:1363.
55–85. See 8:666.
86. TICHENOR, C. C., & RUNDALL, T. G. Attitudes of physical therapists toward cancer: A pilot study. *Physical Therapy*, 1977, 57, 160–165.
87. KINNE, R. D., & STIEFEL, D. J. Assessment of student attitude and confidence in a program of dental education in care of the disabled. *Journal of Dental Education*, 1979, 43, 271–275.
88. SPEAKMAN, H. G. B., & HOFFMANN, C. M. The "fakeability" of the Attitudes Toward Disabled Persons Scale: Form B. *Physical Therapy*, 1979, 59, 866–868.

[2069]

★Scales for Rating the Behavioral Characteristics of Superior Students. Population unspecified, developed from research with students grades 4–6; 1976;

SRBCSS; scales for rating by teachers; 10 scores: learning, motivational, creativity, leadership, artistic, musical, dramatics, communication (precision, expressiveness), planning; Joseph S. Renzulli, Linda H. Smith, Alan J. White, Carolyn M. Callahan, and Robert K. Hartman; Creative Learning Press, Inc.*

[2070]

★SCC Clerical Skills Series. Job applicants; 1975–76; "developed from an extensive job analysis of public service positions"; 6 tests; distribution restricted to public personnel agencies who have completed a Test Security Agreement; Selection Consultation Center; International Personnel Management Association.*

a) 361.1 CLERICAL SKILLS SERIES. 6 scores: punctuating, vocabulary, filing, reading, grammar, spelling.
b) 362.1 CLERICAL SKILLS SERIES. 6 scores: name and number checking, vocabulary, reading, numerical skills, coding I, coding II.
c) 363.1 CLERICAL SKILLS SERIES. 5 scores: name and number checking, vocabulary, filing, coding I, coding II.
d) 364.1 ORAL INSTRUCTION.
e) 365.1 TYPING TEST.
f) 367.1 DICTATION/TRANSCRIPTION.

[2071]

Scholastic Achievement Test for English Lower Standards 2 and 3. Standards 2, 3; 1973–74; English as a second language; 4 scores: language usage, vocabulary, reading comprehension, total; L. J. R. Kritzinger and S. R. Clark (test); Human Sciences Research Council [South Africa].*

For additional information, see 8:107.

[2072]

Scholastic Achievement Test for English Lower Standards 9 and 10. Standards 9–10; English as a second language; 4 scores: language usage, vocabulary, reading comprehension, total; L. J. R. Kritzinger; Human Sciences Research Council [South Africa].*

For additional information, see 8:108.

[2073]

Scholastic Achievement Test in Arithmetic. Grades 1/substandard A, 2/substandard B, standards 1, 2, 3, 4; 1973–74; 4 scores: mechanical, comprehension, application, total; (Afrikaans edition available); J. A. Holtzhausen and S. J. P. Kruger (manual); Human Sciences Research Council [South Africa].*

For additional information, see 8:308.

[2074]

Scholastic Achievement Test of English Second Language Standard 1. Standard 1; 1974–75; 5 scores: spelling, language usage, vocabulary, reading comprehension, total; L. J. R. Kritzinger; Human Sciences Research Council [South Africa].*

For additional information, see 8:109.

[2075]

Scholastic Achievement Tests for English First Language. Grade 2/sub B, standards 1, 2, 3, 4, 6, 9–10; 1973–75; various titles used for various levels as listed below; L. J. R. Kritzinger and S. R. Clark (tests in *a* below); Human Sciences Research Council [South Africa].*

a) ENGLISH HIGHER ACHIEVEMENT TEST. Grade 2/sub B, standards 1, 2, 3; 1973; manual title is *Scholastic Achievement Tests English Higher*; 3 or 4 scores: vocabulary, language usage (standards 1–3), reading comprehension, spelling.
b) STANDARD 4. 1974–75; manual title is *Scholastic Achievement Test for English Home Language*; 5 scores: spelling, language usage, vocabulary, reading comprehension, total.
c) STANDARD 6. 1974–75; 4 scores: language usage, vocabulary, reading comprehension, total.
d) STANDARDS 9 AND 10. 1973; title on test materials is *Scholastic Achievement Test for English Higher*; 4 scores: same as for standard 6.

For additional information, see 8:55.

[2076]

Scholastic Proficiency Battery. Standards 8–10; 1969–71; SPB; 5 scores: social sciences, commercial sciences, natural sciences, arithmetic, languages (either English or Afrikaans); F. A. Fouché, N. F. Alberts, and V. H. Paul (test); Human Sciences Research Council [South Africa].*

For additional information, see 7:23.

[2077]

The Schonell Reading Tests. Ages 5–15, 6–9, 7–11, 9–13; 1942–55; 7 tests, only 4 currently available; Fred J. Schonell; Oliver & Boyd [Scotland].*

a) TEST R1, GRADED WORD READING TEST. Ages 5–15; also called *Graded Reading Vocabulary Test*.
b) TEST R2, SIMPLE PROSE READING TEST. Ages 6–9; also called *My Dog Test*.
c) TEST R3, SILENT READING TEST A. Ages 7–11.
d) TEST R4, SILENT READING TEST B. Ages 9–13.
e) TEST R5, TEST OF ANALYSIS AND SYNTHESIS OF WORDS CONTAINING COMMON PHONIC UNITS. *Out of print.*
f) TEST R6, TEST OF DIRECTIONAL ATTACK ON WORDS. *Out of Print.*
g) TEST R7, VISUAL WORD DISCRIMINATION TEST. *Out of print.*

See T2:1646 (18 references); for a review by R. W. McCulloch, see 5:651 (4 references); for a review by M. L. Kellmer Pringle, see 4:552 (3 references); for a review by Edith I. M. Thomson, see 3:499.

REFERENCES

1–3. See 4:552.
4–7. See 5:651.
8–25. See T2:1646.
26. SIMON, A., & WARD, L. O. Influence of age, abilities, and angle on pupils' judgements of size of angles. *Perceptual & Motor Skills*, 1977, 45, 949–950.
27. WHEELER, T. J., WATKINS, E. J., & MCLAUGHLIN, S. P. Reading retardation and cross-laterality in relation to short-term information processing tasks. *British Journal of Educational Psychology*, 1977, 47, 126–131.
28. LOVEGROVE, W., & BROWN, C. Development of information processing in normal and disabled readers. *Perceptual & Motor Skills*, 1978, 46, 1047–1059.
29. MCGURK, B. J., BOLTON, N., & SMITH, M. Some psychological, educational and criminological variables related to recidivism in delinquent boys. *British Journal of Social & Clinical Psychology*, 1978, 17, 251–254.
30. PERMAN, B. E. Reading attainment in hearing–impaired children: A comparison of higher and lower achievers. *Journal of Communication Disorders*, 1978, 11, 227–235.
31. BOERSMA, F. J., CHAPMAN, J. W., & BATTLE, J. Academic self-concept change in special education students: Some suggestions for interpreting self-concept scores. *Journal of Special Education*, 1979, 13, 433–442.

32. CUMMINS, J. P., & DAS, J. P. Cognitive processing, academic achievement, and WISC–R performance in EMR children. *Journal of Consulting & Clinical Psychology*, 1980, 48, 777–779.
33. NELSON, H. E., & WARRINGTON, E. K. An investigation of memory functions in dyslexic children. *British Journal of Psychology*, 1980, 71, 487–503.
34. SHALLICE, T. Phonological agraphia and the lexical route in writing. *Brain*, 1981, 104, 413–429.

[2078]

School Administration and Supervision. Prospective elementary school administrators and supervisors; 1968–71; available to school systems for local use as part of the *School Personnel Research and Evaluation Services*; originally available as part of the discontinued *School Administrative and Supervisory Examination Services*; Educational Testing Service.*

[2079]

School Apperception Method. Grades kgn–9; 1968; SAM; Irving L. Solomon and Bernard D. Starr; Springer Publishing Co., Inc.*

For additional information and reviews by Willard E. Reitz and Norman D. Sundberg, see 7:176 (1 reference); see also P:473 (2 references).

[2080]

School Atmosphere Questionnaire. Grades 7–12; 1971; SAQ; ratings by students; 3 scores: enthusiasm for school, school acceptance understanding, school dynamism enthusiasm; no manual; James K. Hoffmeister; Test Analysis and Development Corporation.*

For additional information and a review by Hulda Grobman, see 8:394.

[2081]

★**School Attitude Measure.** Grades 4–6, 7–8, 9–12; 1980; SAM; 5 scores: motivation for schooling, academic self-concept (performance based), academic self-concept (reference based), sense of control over performance, instructional mastery; Lawrence J. Dolen and Marci Morrow Enos; American Testronics.*

[2082]

The School Attitude Survey: Feelings I Have About School. Grades 3–6; 1970; SAS; 4 areas: about the things we learn, about the teacher and me, about the other children and me, about me and my classroom; Harold F. Burks; Arden Press.* (In-print status uncertain; no reply from publisher.)

For additional information and a review by Patricia W. Lunneborg, see 8:667; see also T2:1364 (1 reference).

[2083]

★**School Behavior Checklist.** Ages 4–6, 7–13; 1977–81; SBC; 7 or 9 scales: low need achievement, aggression, anxiety, cognitive deficit (Form A1 only), hostile isolation, extraversion, normal irritability (Form A1 only), school disturbance (Form A1 only), total disability, academic disability (Form A2 only); Lovick C. Miller; Western Psychological Services.*

[2084]

★**School/Home Observation and Referral System.** Preschool–grade 3; 1978; SHORS; provides a systematic approach for "the identification and referral of children who have problems that may interfere with learning"; ratings by parents and teachers on 7 checklists: health, motor abilities, hearing, vision, speech and language, learning, behavior; Joyce Evans; CTB/McGraw-Hill.*

[2085]

School Interest Inventory. Grades 7–12; 1966, c1959–66; SII; revision of *Life Adjustment Scale, Number 1* (58); for identifying potential dropouts who "should receive counseling"; William C. Cottle; Riverside Publishing Co.*

See T2:1365 (1 reference); for reviews by Gene V Glass and Leonard V. Gordon, and an excerpted review by William L. Goodwin, see 7:134 (7 references); see also P:236 (9 references).

[2086]

The School Inventory. High school; 1936; SI; attitudes toward teachers and school; Hugh M. Bell; Consulting Pyschologists Press, Inc.*

See T2:1366 (2 references) and P:237 (2 references); for a review by Ross W. Matteson, see 4:84 (3 references); for reviews by Robert G. Bernreuter and J. B. Maller, see 2:1252 (4 references).

REFERENCES

1–4. See 2:1252.
5–7. See 4:84.
8–9. See P:237.
10–11. See T2:1366.
12. BELL, A. E., ABRAHAMSON, D. S., & MCRAE, K. N. Reading retardation: A 12-year prospective study. *Journal of Pediatrics*, 1977, 91, 363–370.

[2087]

The School Motivation Analysis Test. Ages 12–17; 1961–76; SMAT; downward extension of *Motivation Analysis Test*; 45 scores: 4 motivation scores (unintegrated, integrated, total, difference [conflict]) for each of 6 drives (assertiveness, mating, fear, narcism, pugnacity-sadism, protectiveness) and each of 4 sentiments (self-sentiment, superego, school, home) plus 5 derived scores (total autism-optimism, general information-intelligence, total integration, total personal interest, total conflict); Arthur B. Sweney, Raymond B. Cattell, and Samuel E. Krug; Institute for Personality and Ability Testing, Inc.*

For additional information and reviews by Jacob Cohen and Paul McReynolds, see 8:668 (11 references); see also T2:1367 (2 references) and 7:135 (10 references).

REFERENCES

1–10. See 7:135.
11–12. See T2:1367.
13–23. See 8:668.
24. CAPPADONA, D. L., & KERZNER-LIPSKY, D. Prediction of school mathematical achievement from motivation, self-concept, teachers' ratings and ability measures. *School Science & Mathematics*, 1979, 79, 140–144.
25. HAKSTIAN, A. R., & GALE, C. A. Validity studies using the Comprehensive Ability Battery (CAB): III. Performance in conjunction with personality and motivational traits. *Educational & Psychological Measurement*, 1979, 39, 389–400.

[2088]

School Personnel Research and Evaluation Services. Teachers and prospective administrators and supervisors; 1971, c1967–71; SPRES; derived from discontinued *School Administrative and Supervisory Examination Services*; tests available to school systems for local use; 20 tests; Educational Testing Service.*

a) COMMON EXAMINATIONS. 1971, c1970–71; reprinting of inactive 1970 form of *National Teacher Examinations: Common Examinations*; 5 scores: professional education, written English expression, social studies-literature—the fine arts, science and mathematics, total.
b) SPECIALTY EXAMINATIONS. 1971, c1967–71; all tests are reprints of inactive forms (1967–69) of *National Teacher Examinations* except School Administration and

Supervision, Secondary School Administration, and Secondary School Supervision, which were originally published as part of the *School Administrative and Supervisory Examination Services*; 19 tests: Art Education, Biology and General Science, Business Education, Chemistry-Physics-General Science, Early Childhood Education, Education in the Elementary School, English Language and Literature, French, Home Economics Education, Industrial Arts Education, Mathematics, Music Education, Physical Education, Reading Specialist-Elementary School, School Administration and Supervision, Secondary School Administration, Secondary School Supervision, Social Studies, Spanish.

For reference to reviews of the *National Teacher Examinations*, See T2:869.

[2089]
School Problem Screening Inventory, Fifth Edition. Grades kgn–12; 1974–78; SPSI; ratings by teachers; 10 scores: learning disabilities (visual-motor, auditory-verbal, total), mental retardation, general learning skill deficit, behavior disorder (under-controlled, over-controlled, total), educational handicap, general maladjustment; Thomas D. Gnagey; Facilitation House.*

For additional information, see 8:444.

[2090]
The School Readiness Checklist. Ages 5–6; 1963–68; booklet title is *Ready or Not*; checklist to be used by parents; John J. Austin, J. Clayton Lafferty, Frederick Leaske (manual), and Fred Cousino (manual); Research Concepts.* (In-print status uncertain; no reply from publisher.)

For additional information and a review by Dennis J. Deloria, see 7:762.

[2091]
School Readiness Survey, Second Edition. Ages 4–6; 1967–75; to be administered and scored by parents with school supervision; 8 scores: number concepts, discrimination of form, color naming, symbol matching, speaking vocabulary, listening vocabulary, general information, total, plus unscored general readiness checklist; F. L. Jordan and James Massey; Consulting Psychologists Press, Inc.*

For additional information and a review by John Downing, see 8:807 (3 references); for excerpted reviews by Dale E. Bennett and Byron Egeland, see 7:763.

[2092]
The School Survey of Interpersonal Relationships. Teachers; 1971; SSIR; a measure of a "school's interpersonal learning climate"; 3 main scores: affective (teachers feelings toward students and other staff members), cognitive (teachers' knowledge regarding students and other staff members), total, and 7 subscores (teachers' feelings toward or perception of principal, fellow teachers, counselors, non-teaching staff, self, students in general, different types of students); Joe Wittmer; Remediation Associates, Inc.* (In-print status uncertain; no reply from publisher.)

See T2:890 (2 references).

[2093]
School Vision Tester. Grades kgn and over; 1957–74; 6 tests: tumbling E acuity (each eye), farsightedness (each eye), muscle balance (far, near); the instrument is the same as the *Ortho-Rater* except for the test slides; the standard *Ortho-Rater* may be used to extend testing; Bausch & Lomb, Inc.* (Availability uncertain; no reply from manufacturer.)

For additional information and a review by Carl L. Rosen, see 7:875 (1 reference); for a review by Helen M. Robinson, see 6:958 (2 references).

[2094]
School Weekly News Quiz. High school; 1947–74; revision of *New York Times Current Affairs Test*; although title implies weekly publication, 8 tests (spirit masters for local duplication) issued annually during school year (October–May); available only as part of the New York Times Daily School Service Program; no manual; New York Times.* (Availability uncertain; no reply from publisher.)

For additional information concerning the earlier edition, see 6:983.

[2095]
Schubert General Ability Battery. Grades 12–16 and adults; 1946–65; 5 scores: vocabulary, analogies, arithmetic problems, syllogisms, total; Herman J. P. Schubert and Daniel S. P. Schubert (test); Herman J. P. Schubert.*

For additional information, see 7:386 (1 reference); for a review by William B. Schrader, see 5:382.

[2096]
Science Attitude Questionnaire. Secondary school; 1970–71; SAQ; also called *Attitudes to Science Questionnaire*; for research use only; 5 scores: science interest, social implications of science, learning activities, science teachers, schools; test by Larry S. Skurnik and Patricia M. Jeffs with a contribution by Taysir Kawa; manual by Desmond Nuttall; NFER-Nelson Publishing Co. [England].*

[2097]
Science: Minnesota High School Achievement Examinations. Grades 7, 8, 9; 1951–70; a new, revised, or previously inactive form issued each May; Achievement Examinations for Secondary Schools, High School Achievement Examinations, and Midwest High School Achievement Examinations have also been used as series titles; 3 levels; edited by V. L. Lohmann; American Guidance Service.*

a) SCIENCE GRADE 7 (LIFE SCIENCE). 1962–70.
b) SCIENCE GRADE 8 (EARTH SCIENCE). 1962–70.
c) SCIENCE GRADE 9 (PHYSICAL SCIENCE). 1951–70; 1963 and earlier forms called *General Science*; Form 4 ('54), entitled *General Science III: Achievement Examinations for Secondary Schools*, is available from another publisher.

For additional information concerning out of print and inactive forms, see 7:798, 6:875, and 5:710; for reviews by Elizabeth Hagen and Jacqueline V. Mallinson of Form E (1962) and Form F (1963) for grades 7 and 8, see 6:881.

[2098]
Science Tests: Content Evaluation Series. Grades 8–9; 1969; 2 tests in 1 booklet; Ernestine O'Connell; Riverside Publishing Co.*
a) PHYSICAL SCIENCE TEST: CONTENT EVALUATION SERIES.
b) EARTH SCIENCE TEST: CONTENT EVALUATION SERIES.

For additional information and a review by Jacqueline V. Mallinson, see 7:799.

[2099]
Scientific Knowledge and Aptitude Test. High school; 1964; SKAT; S. Chatterji and M. Mukerjee; S. Chatterji [India].* (In-print status uncertain; no reply from publisher.)

See T2:1793 (1 reference) and 7:800 (1 reference).

[2100]
★**SCL-90-R.** Psychiatric and medical patients; 1975–79; designed primarily to reflect psychological symptom patterns; analogue for ratings by professionals is available; scored in terms of 9 primary symptom dimensions: somatization, obsessive-compulsive, interpersonal sensitivity, depression, anxiety, hostility, phobic anxiety, paranoid ideation, psychoticism, plus 3 indices of distress: global severity index, positive symptom distress index, positive symptom total; Leonard R. Derogatis; the Author.*

REFERENCES
1. DEROGATIS, L. R., RICKELS, K., & ROCK, A. F. The SCL-90 and the MMPI: A step in the validation of a new self-report scale. *British Journal of Psychology,* 1976, 128, 280–289.
2. DEROGATIS, L. R., & CLEARY, P. A. Confirmation of the dimensional structure of the SCL-90: A study in construct validation. *Journal of Clinical Psychology,* 1977, 33, 981–989.
3. DEROGATIS, L. R., & CLEARY, P. A. Factorial invariance across gender for the primary symptom dimensions of the SCL-90. *British Journal of Social & Clinical Psychology,* 1977, 16, 347–356.
4. DEROGATIS, L. R., ABELOFF, M. D., & MELISARATOS, N. Psychological coping mechanisms and survival time in metastic breast cancer. *JAMA,* 1979, 242, 1504–1508.
5. KILPATRICK, D. G., VERONEN, L. J., & RESICK, P. A. The aftermath of rape: Recent empirical findings. *American Journal of Orthopsychiatry,* 1979, 49, 658–669.
6. STEER, R. A., & HENRY, M. Relationship of level of functioning to self-reported and rated psychopathology. *Journal of Clinical Psychology,* 1979, 35, 769–772.
7. ARRINDELL, W. A. Dimensional structure and psychopathology correlates of the Fear Survey Schedule (FSS-III) in a phobic population: A factorial definition of agoraphobia. *Behaviour Research & Therapy,* 1980, 18, 229–242.
8. HALLE, E., SCHMIDT, C. W., & MEYER, J. K. The role of grandmothers in transsexualism. *American Journal of Psychiatry,* 1980, 137, 497–498.
9. RAVARIS, C. L., ROBINSON, D. S., IVES, J. O., NIES, A., & BARTLETT, D. Phenelzinc and amitriptyline in the treatment of depression. A comparison of present and past studies. *Archives of General Psychiatry,* 1980, 37, 1075–1080.
10. WRIGHT, B. M., & STOFFELMAYR, B. E. SCL-90-R: Administration, scoring, and procedures manual – I. *Family Process,* 1980, 19, 401–410.
11. KILPATRICK, D. G., RESICK, P. A., & VERONEN, L. J. Effects of a rape experience: A longitudinal study. *Journal of Social Issues,* 1981, 37, 105–122.
12. PRUSOFF, B. A., WEISSMAN, M. M., CHARNEY, J., DOCHERTY, J., KLEBER, H., RORENSAVILLE, B. J., SHOLOMKAS, A. J., & SHOLOMKAS, D. Speed of symptom reduction in depressed outpatients treated with amoxapine and amitriptyline. *Current Therapeutic Research,* 1981, 30, 843–855.
13. STEINGLASS, P. The impact of alcoholism on the family: Relationship between degree of alcoholism and psychiatric symptomatology. *Journal of Studies on Alcohol,* 1981, 42, 288–303.

[2101]
Scott Mental Alertness Test. Applicants for office positions; 1923; Scott Co.; Stoelting Co.*
See T2:456 (1 reference).

[2102]
SCREEN. Grades kgn–3; 1975; "for school use on a research basis"; 10 scores: 6 test scores (self-concept and school adjustment, visual skills, auditory skills, figure copying, basic knowledge, general readiness) and teacher ratings in 4 areas (cognitive-perceptual skills, behavioral adjustment, social adjustment, immaturity); scoring must be done by publisher; Gerald M. Senf and Andrew L. Comrey; SCREEN, Inc.* (In-print status uncertain; no reply from publisher.)

For additional information and a review by Barton B. Proger, see 8:443 (2 references).

[2103]
A Screening Deep Test of Articulation. Grades kgn and over; 1968; SDTA; Eugene T. McDonald; Stanwix House, Inc.*

See T2:2090 (1 reference); for reviews by Edgar R. Garrett and Harold A. Peterson, see 7:968 (2 references).

REFERENCES
1–2. See 7:968.
3. See T2:2090.
4. McNUTT, J. C. Oral sensory and motor behaviors of children with /s/ or /r/ misarticulations. *Journal of Speech & Hearing Research,* 1977, 20, 694–703.
5. PALOW, N. G. Clinical and educational materials. *ASHA,* 1977, 19, 49.
6. SHELTON, R. L., JOHNSON, A. F., & ARNDT, W. B. Delayed judgement speech–sound discrimination and /r/ or /s/ articulation status and improvement. *Journal of Speech & Hearing Research,* 1977, 20, 704–717.
7. SCHISSEL, R. J., & FLOURNOY, J. E. An investigation of the variability of judgments of experienced and inexperienced listeners in their use of a screening test of articulation. *Journal of Communication Disorders,* 1978, 11, 459–468.
8. SHELTON, R. L., JOHNSON, A. F., RUSCELLO, D. M., & ARNDT, W. B. Assessment of parent-administered listening training for preschool children with articulation deficits. *Journal of Speech & Hearing Disorders,* 1978, 43, 242–254.
9. DWORKIN, J. P. Characteristics of frontal lespers clustered according to severity. *Journal of Speech & Hearing Disorders,* 1979, 45, 37–44.
10. SCHISSEL, R. J., & JAMES, L. B. A comparison of childrens' performance on two tests of articulation. *Journal of Speech & Hearing Disorders,* 1979, 44, 363–372.
11. SCHISSEL, R. J. The role of selected auditory skills in the misarticulation of /s/, /r/, and /o/ by third grade children. *British Journal of Disorders of Communication,* 1980, 15, 129–138.
12. SCHISSEL, R. J., & McDONALD, E. T. Effects of time between stimuli on the relationship of speech–sound discrimination skills to consistency of correct production of [s] and [r]. *Journal of Communication Disorders,* 1980, 13, 83–91.

[2104]
Screening Speech Articulation Test. Ages 3.5–8.5; 1955–70; Merlin J. Mecham, J. Lorin Jex, and J. Dean Jones; Communication Research Associates, Inc.*

For additional information of an earlier edition, see 6:314.

[2105]
*****Screening Test for Auditory Perception.** Grades 1–6; 1969–81; STAP; designed for the detection of weaknesses rather than strengths in the auditory perception of students; 6 scores: ability to recognize the two basic vowel sounds, ability to differentiate between initial single consonant sounds and blends, ability to discriminate between rhyming and nonrhyming words, ability to retain

and identify rhythmic sound patterns, ability to detect subtle differences in paired words, total; Geraldine M. Kimmell and Jack Wahl; Academic Therapy Publications.*

For additional information and reviews by Ann Brickner and Rosslyn Gaines of an earlier edition, see 7:944 (1 reference).

REFERENCES

1. See 7:944.
2. KOENKE K. A comparison of three auditory discrimination–perception tests. *Academic Therapy*, 1978, 14, 463–468.

[2106]
Screening Test for the Assignment of Remedial Treatments. Ages 4–6 to 6–5; 1968; START; 5 scores: visual memory, auditory memory, visual copying, visual discrimination, total; A. Edward Ahr; Priority Innovations, Inc.*

For additional information and an excerpted review by Barton B. Proger, see 8:445 (2 references); see also T2:988 (1 reference); for a review by Evelyn Deno, see 7:764.

[2107]
Screening Test of Academic Readiness. Ages 4–0 to 6–5; 1966; STAR; 9 scores: picture vocabulary, letters, picture completion, copying, picture description, human figure drawing, relationships, numbers, total (IQ); A. Edward Ahr; Priority Innovations, Inc.*

For additional information, a review by Mildred H. Huebner, and an excerpted review by Jon Magoon (with Richard C. Cox), see 7:765 (5 references).

REFERENCES

1–5. See 7:765.
6. KLEIN, A. E. The validity of the Screening Test of Academic Readiness in predicting achievement in first and second grades. *Educational & Psychological Measurement*, 1977, 37, 493–497.
7. KLEIN, A. E. The reliability and predictive validity of the Slosson Intelligence Test for pre–kindergarten pupils. *Educational & Psychological Measurement*, 1978, 38, 1211–1217.
8. KLEIN, A. E. The validity of the Beery Test of Visual–Motor Integration in predicting achievement in kindergarten, first and second grades. *Educational & Psychological Measurement*, 1978, 38, 457–461.
9. GARDNER, L. I., NEU, R. L., SHAH, R. S., PINTO, W., JR., CO, M., LEHR, E. R., & BARG, G. A. Family with three apparently balanced t(3;15) (p27; q22) translocation carriers. *American Journal of Diseases of Children*, 1979, 133, 1002–1005.
10. KLEIN, A. E. Some evidence concerning the factorial validity of the screening test of academic readiness. *Educational & Psychological Measurement*, 1980, 40, 239–244.

[2108]
★**Screening Test of Adolescent Language.** Junior and senior high school; 1980; STAL; pinpoint children at risk who have not been identified as having a language problem; 4 subtests: vocabulary, auditory memory span, language processing, proverb explanation; Elizabeth M. Prather, Sheila Van Ausdal Breecher, Marimyn Lee Stafford, and Elizabeth Matthews Wallace; University of Washington Press.*

[2109]
Screening Test of Spanish Grammar. Spanish-speaking children ages 3–6; 1973; STSG; syntax screening; 2 scores: receptive, expressive; Allen S. Toronto; Northwestern University Press.*

For additional information and a review by Diana S. Natalicio, and excerpted reviews by Alex Bannatyne and Huberto Molina, see 8:171 (3 references).

REFERENCES

1–3. See 8:171.
4. RUEDA, R., & PEROZZI, J. A. A comparison of two Spanish tests of receptive language. *Journal of Speech & Hearing Disorders*, 1977, 42, 210–215.

[2110]
Screening Test for Identifying Children With Specific Language Disability. Grades 1–2.5, 2.5–3.5, 3.5–4, 5–6; 1962–74; 8 or 9 tests listed below plus 2 optional individual auditory tests (echolalia, story telling); Beth H. Slingerland; Educators Publishing Service, Inc.*
a) FORMS A, B, C, REVISED EDITION. Grades 1–2.5, 2.5–3.5, 3.5–4; 1962–70; 13 scores: visual copying far point, visual copying near point, total, visual perception-memory, visual discrimination, visual perception-memory with kinesthetic memory, auditory recall (letters, numbers, spelling), auditory discrimination of sounds, auditory-visual association, total errors (excluding visual copying), total errors plus self-corrections and poor formations; revisions by Beth H. Slingerland and Alice S. Ansara.
b) FORM D. Grades 5–6; 1974; 9 tests, 14 scores: visual copying far point, visual copying near point, total, visual perception-memory, visual discrimination, visual perception-memory with kinesthetic memory, auditory recall (letters, numbers, spelling), auditory discrimination of sounds, auditory-visual association, auditory perception and individual orientation, total errors (excluding visual copying), total errors and confusions.

For additional information and an excerpted review by Barton B. Proger, see 8:446 (3 references); see also T2:989 (4 references); for reviews by Evelyn Deno and Joseph M. Wepman of *a*, see 7:969 (3 references).

[2111]
★**SEARCH—A Scanning Instrument for the Identification of Potential Learning Disability, Second Edition, Expanded.** Children ages 63 to 80 months; 1975–81; total score and stanine-based profile of 10 components: visual matching, visual recall, designs, auditory sequencing, auditory discrimination, articulation, sound-symbol association, directionality, finger schema, pencil grip; (Spanish and Portuguese editions available); Archie A. Silver and Rosa A. Hagin; Walker Educational Book Corporation.*

REFERENCES

1. ARNOLD, L. E., BARNEBEY, N., MCMANUS, J., SMELTZER, D. J., CONRAD, A., WINER, G., & DESGRANGES, L. Prevention by specific perceptual remediation for vulnerable first graders. *Archives of General Psychiatry*, 1977, 34, 1279–1294.
2. SILVER, A. A., HAGIN, R. A., & BEECHER, R. Scanning, diagnosis, and intervention in the prevention of reading disabilities. *Journal of Learning Disabilities*, 1978, 11, 437–449.

[2112]
The Seashore-Bennett Stenographic Proficiency Test: A Standard Recorded Stenographic Worksample. Adults; 1946–56; Harold Seashore and George K. Bennett; The Psychological Corporation.*

For additional information, see 5:519 (2 references); for a review by Harold F. Rothe, see 4:455 (1 reference); for a review by Ann Brewington, see 3:386.

[2113]
Seashore Measures of Musical Talents. Grades 4–16 and adults; 1919–60; 6 scores: pitch, loudness, rhythm, time, timbre, tonal memory; Carl E. Seashore,

Don Lewis, and Joseph R. Saetveit; The Psychological Corporation.*

See T2:211 (97 references); for reviews by Kenneth L. Bean and Robert W. Lundin, see 6:353 (13 references); see also 5:251 (9 references); for reviews by John McLeish and Herbert D. Wing of the 1939 revision, see 4:229 (16 references); for reviews by Paul R. Farnsworth, William S. Larson, and James L. Mursell, see 3:177 (46 references); see also 2:1338 (60 references).

REFERENCES

1–55. See 2:1338.
56–101. See 3:177.
102–117. See 4:229.
118–126. See 5:251.
127–139. See 6:353.
140–236. See T2:211.

237. BOLLER, F., VRTUNSKI, B., MACK, J. L., & KIM, Y. Neuropsychological correlates of hypertension. *Archives of Neurology*, 1977, 34, 701–705.
238. FRIEDMAN, M. J., CULVER, C. M., & FERRELL, R. B. On the safety of long–term treatment with lithium. *American Journal of Psychiatry*, 1977, 134, 1123–1126.
239. SPELLACY, F. Neuropsychological differences between violent and nonviolent adolescents. *Journal of Clinical Psychology*, 1977, 33, 966–969.
240. TSUSHIMA, W. T., & TOWNE, W. S. Effects of paint sniffing on neuropsychological test performance. *Journal of Abnormal Psychology*, 1977, 86, 402–407.
241. DECUIR, A. A., & BRASWELL, C. E. A musical profile for a sample of learning–disabled children and adolescents: A pilot study. *Perceptual & Motor Skills*, 1978, 46, 1080–1082.
242. DODRILL, C. B. A neuropsychological battery for epilepsy. *Epilepsia*, 1978, 19, 611–623.
243. DODRILL, C. B., & DIKMEN, S. S. The Seashore Tonal Memory Test as a neuropsychological measure. *Journal of Consulting & Clinical Psychology*, 1978, 46, 192–193.
244. HEATON, R. K., SMITH, H. H., JR., LEHMAN, R. A. W., & VOGT, A. T. Prospects for faking believable deficits on neuropsychological testing. *Journal of Consulting & Clinical Psychology*, 1978, 46, 892–900.
245. IVNIK, R. J. Neuropsychological stability in multiple sclerosis. *Journal of Consulting & Clinical Psychology*, 1978, 46, 913–923.
246. IVNIK, R. J. Neuropsychological test performance as a function of the duration of MS–related symptomatology. *Journal of Clinical Psychiatry*, 1978, 39, 304–312.
247. SPELLACY, F. Neuropsychological discrimination between violent and nonviolent men. *Journal of Clinical Psychology*, 1978, 34, 49–52.
248. STANKOV, L. Fluid and crystallized intelligence and broad perceptual factors among 11 and 12 year olds. *Journal of Educational Psychology*, 1978, 70, 324–334.
249. STANKOV, L., & SPILSBURY, G. The measurement of auditory abilities of blind, partially sighted, and sighted children. *Applied Psychological Measurement*, 1978, 2, 491–503.
250. BYRNE, B., & SINCLAIR, J. Memory for tonal sequence and timbre: A correlation with familial handedness. *Neuropsychologia*, 1979, 17, 539–542.
251. DECUIR, A. A., & MARANTO, C. D. Analysis of visual and auditory rhythmic perception abilities of piano majors. *Perceptual & Motor Skills*, 1979, 49, 659–664.
252. NEEDLEMAN, H. L., GUNNOE, C., LEVITON, A., REED, R., PERESIE, H., MAHER, C., & BARRETT, P. Deficits in psychologic and classroom performance of children with elevated dentine lead levels. *New England Journal of Medicine*, 1979, 300, 689–695.
253. REED, H. B. C., JR. Biological defects and special education – An issue in personnel preparation. *Journal of Special Education*, 1979, 13, 9–33.
254. DIKMEN, S., & MORGAN, S. F. Neuropsychological factors related to employability and occupational status in persons with epilepsy. *Journal of Nervous & Mental Disease*, 1980, 168, 236–240.
255. RIEGLER, J. Most comfortable loudness level of geriatric patients as a function of seashore loudness discrimination scores, detection threshold, age, sex, setting, and musical background. *Journal of Music Therapy*, 1980, 17, 214–222.
256. STANKOV, L. Ear differences and implied cerebral lateralization on some intellective auditory factors. *Applied Psychological Measurement*, 1980, 4, 21–38.
257. STANKOV, L., & HORN, J. L. Human abilities revealed through auditory tests. *Journal of Educational Psychology*, 1980, 72, 21–44.
258. MOORE, J. L., & HANNAY, H. J. Verbal–performance IQ-discrepancy and rhythm test performance. *Perceptual & Motor Skills*, 1981, 52, 819–826.
259. RYCKMAN, D. B. Reading achievement, IQ, and simultaneous-successive processing among normal and learning–disabled children. *Alberta Journal of Educational Research*, 1981, 27, 74–83.
260. SUNG, Y. H., & DAWIS, R. V. Level and factor structure differences in selected abilities across race and sex groups. *Journal of Applied Psychology*, 1981, 66, 613–624.

[2114]

Second Year French Test. High school and college; 1956–68; Jean Leblon and Minnie M. Miller; Bureau of Educational Measurements.*

For additional information and a review by John L. D. Clark, see 7:280; for reviews by Geraldine Spaulding and Clarence E. Turner of an earlier edition, see 5:271.

[2115]

Second Year Spanish Test. High school and college; 1953–68; revision of *Kansas Second Year Spanish Test*; Oscar F. Hernández and Minnie M. Miller; Bureau of Educational Measurements.*

For additional information, see 7:326.

[2116]

★**Secondary Level English Proficiency Test.** Students in grades 7–11 whose native language is not English; no dates; SLEP; 4 areas: listening comprehension, grammar, vocabulary, reading comprehension; Educational Testing Service.

[2117]

Secondary School Administration. Prospective secondary school administrators; 1968–71; available to school systems for local use as part of the *School Personnel Research and Evaluation Services*; originally available as part of the discontinued *School Administrative and Supervisory Examination Services*; Educational Testing Service.*

[2118]

Secondary School Admission Test: General School Ability and Reading. Grades 5–7, 8–10; 1957–77; SSAT; tests administered 5 times annually (January, March, April, June, December) at centers established by the publisher; 4 scores: ability (verbal, quantitative, total), reading comprehension; program administered for the Secondary School Admission Test Board, Inc. by Educational Testing Service.*

For additional information, see 8:478; see also 7:24 (1 reference); for reviews by Charles O. Neidt and David V. Tiedeman of earlier forms, see 6:24 (1 reference).

[2119]

Secondary-School Record. Grades 9–12; 1941–64; SSR; National Association of Secondary-School Principals.* (In-print status uncertain; no reply from publisher.)
a) TRANSCRIPT.
b) STUDENT DESCRIPTION SUMMARY. For summarizing ratings by several teachers of 8 characteristics on *Student Description Form*.

For additional information concerning an earlier edition, see 4:516 (1 reference).

[2120]

Secondary School Supervision. Prospective secondary school supervisors; 1968–71; available to school systems for local use as part of the *School Personnel Research and Evaluation Services*; originally available as part of the discontinued *School Administrative and Supervisory Examination Services*; Educational Testing Service.*

[2121]

Security-Insecurity Inventory. Grades 9–16 and adults; 1945–52; SII; test booklet title is the *The S-I Inventory*; A. H. Maslow, E. Birsh, I. Honigmann, F. McGrath, A. Plason, and M. Stein; Consulting Psychologists Press, Inc.*

See T2:1370 (39 references) and P:239 (16 references); for reviews by Nelson G. Hanawalt and Harold Webster, see 5:107 (10 references).

REFERENCES

1–10. See 5:107.
11–26. See P:239.
27–65. See T2:1370.
66. SHRIVASTAVA, G. P. A short form of the Maslow Security-Insecurity Inventory. *Manas*, 1976, 23, 115–119.
67. PESTONJIE, D. M., & AHMAD, N. Alienation and insecurity as related to occupational levels. *Indian Journal of Social Work*, 1977, 23, 263–268.
68. SINGH, M. P., & MANDAL, G. Social factors related to frustration among agricultural scientists. *Indian Journal of Social Work*, 1977, 23, 235–239.
69. SNYDER, C. R., & CLAIR, M. S. Does insecurity breed acceptance?: Effects of trait and situational insecurity on acceptance of positive and negative diagnostic feedback. *Journal of Consulting & Clinical Psychology*, 1977, 45, 843–850.
70. MATHES, E. W., & EDWARDS, L. L. An empirical test of Maslow's theory of motivation. *Journal of Humanistic Psychology*, 1978, 18, 75–77.

[2122]

★**SEED Developmental Profiles.** Birth to 48 months; 1976; functional assessment designed to be used to establish a developmental profile of a child's performance; 8 developmental profile areas: social-emotional, gross motor, fine motor, adaptive-reasoning, receptive language, expressive language, feeding, dressing and simple hygiene, plus a master developmental profile; Joan Herst, Shelia Wolfe, Gloria Jorgensen, and Sandra Pallan; Sewall Rehabilitation Center.* (In-print status uncertain; no reply from publisher.)

[2123]

Seeing Problems. Grades 9–16; 1962–69; Philip R. Merrifield and J. P. Guilford; Sheridan Psychological Services, Inc.*

See T2:577 (15 references) and 6:551s2.

[2124]

★**The Seeking of Noetic Goals Test.** Adolescents and adults; 1977; SONG; complementary scale to the *Purpose of Life Test* to measure the strength of motivation to find life meaning; James C. Crumbaugh; Psychometric Affiliates.*

REFERENCES

1. REKER, G. T., & COUSINS, J. B. Factor structure, construct validity and reliability of the Seeking of Noetic Goals (SONG) and Purpose in Life (PIL) tests. *Journal of Clinical Psychology*, 1979, 35, 85–91.

[2125]

Seguin-Goddard Formboard. Ages 5–14; [1911]; modifications appear in *Arthur Point Scale of Performance Tests* and *Merrill-Palmer Scale of Mental Test*; E. Sequin, H. H. Goddard, and N. Norsworthy; Stoelting Co.

See T2:578 (25 references).

REFERENCES

1–25. See T2:578.

26. REED, H. B. C., JR. Biological defects and special education – An issue in personnel preparation. *Journal of Special Education*, 1979, 13, 9–33.

[2126]

[Selection Interview Forms]. Business and industry; 1962; 2 forms; Benjamin Balinsky; Martin M. Bruce, Ph.D., Publishers.*
a) SELECTION INTERVIEW FORM.
b) INTERVIEW RATING FORM.
For additional information, see 6:1128.

[2127]

★**Self-Actualization Inventory.** Managers and students of administration; 1978; SAI; "degree to which six needs are unfulfilled"; 6 scales: physical, security, relationships, respect, independence, self-actualization; W. J. Reddin and Ken Rowell; Organizational Tests Ltd. [Canada].*

[2128]

Self-Administered Dependency Questionnaire. Ages 8–15; 1973–74; SADQ; revision of *Highland Dependency Questionnnaire*; test booklet title is *The Self-Administered HDQ*; ratings by mothers of frequency of dependent behavior of their children; 4 scores: affection, assistance, communication, travel; no manual; Ian Berg; the Author [England].* (In-print status uncertain; no reply from publisher.)

For additional information, see 8:669 (6 references).

REFERENCES

1–6. See 8:669.
7. SANDERSON, H. Dependency on mother in boys who steal. *British Journal of Criminology*, 1977, 17, 180–184.
8. BERG, I., & FIELDING, D. An evaluation of hospital in-patient treatment in adolescent school phobia. *British Journal of Psychiatry*, 1978, 132, 500–505.

[2129]

A Self Appraisal Scale for Teachers. Teachers; 1957; Howard Wilson; A. R. A.*

For additional information, see 5:541.

[2130]

Self-Concept Adjective Checklist. Grades kgn–8; 1971; SCAC; Alan J. Politte; Psychologists and Educators, Inc.*

[2131]

The Self-Concept and Motivation Inventory: What Face Would You Wear? Age 4–kgn, grades 1–3, 3–6, 7–12; 1967–77; SCAMIN; George A. Farrah, Norman J. Milchus, and William Reitz; Person-O-Metrics, Inc.*
a) PRE-SCHOOL/KINDERGARTEN FORM. Age 4–kgn; 3 or 4 scores: motivation (goal and achievement needs, achievement investment), self-concept, total (optional).
b) EARLY ELEMENTARY FORM. Grades 1–3; 4 or 5 scores: motivation (goal and achievement needs, achievement investment), self-concept (role expectations, self-adequacy), total (optional).
c) LATER ELEMENTARY FORM. Grades 3–6; 4–11 scores: same part scores as for Early Elementary Form plus 6 optional scores of support climate scores (parents, teachers, peers and siblings, academic self, academic activity climate, school climate, total (optional).
d) SECONDARY FORM. Grades 7–12; 4–20 scores: same part scores as for Early Elementary Form plus 16 optional

scores: sources of support climate (parents, teachers, peers, academic self, physical and social self, adults and counselors, academic activity climate, school climate), immediate-intrinsic orientation (evaluated competition, tasks and projects, discovery and creativity, skills), fulfillment orientation (aspiration, cooperation and conformity, responsibility, acceptance and praise).

For additional information and a review by Lorrie Shepard, see 8:670 (4 references).

REFERENCES

1-4. See 8:670.
5. DRUMMOND, R. J., & MCINTIRE, W. G. Evaluating the factor structure of "self-concept" in children. A cautionary note. *Measurement & Evaluation in Guidance*, 1977, 9, 172–176.
6. VENHAM, L. L., MURRAY, P., & GAULIN-KREMER, E. Personality factors affecting the preschool child's response to dental stress. *Journal of Dental Research*, 1979, 58, 2046–2051.
7. SOULE, J. C., DRUMMOND, J., & MCINTIRE, W. G. Dimensions of self-concept for children in kindergarten and grades 1 and 2. *Psychological Reports*, 1981, 48, 83–88.

[2132]
Self-Concept as a Learner Scale. Grades 4–12; 1967–72; SCAL; 5 scores: motivation, task orientation, problem solving, class membership, total; no manual; Walter B. Waetjen; the Author.*

For additional information, see 8:671 (1 reference).

REFERENCES

1. See 8:671.
2. KEEFE, J. W. Model schools project report 14 Pius X High School. *National Association of Secondary School Principals Bulletin*, 1977, 61, 85–95.
3. TIDWELL, R. A psycho-educational profile of 1,593 gifted high school students. *Gifted Child Quarterly*, 1980, 24, 63–68.

[2133]
★**Self-Description Inventory.** Grades 9 and over; 1975–77; SDI; measures normal personality and vocationally-oriented dimensions; 22 scores: 11 personal description scales (cautious—adventurous, nonscientific—analytical, tense—relaxed, insecure—confident, conventional—imaginative, impatient—patient, unconcerned—altruistic, reserved—outgoing, soft-spoken—forceful, lackadaisical—industrious, unorganized—orderly), 6 vocationally-oriented scales (realistic, investigative, artistic, social, enterprising, conventional), 5 administrative indices [total responses, response percentages (yes, sometimes, no), response check]; Charles B. Johansson; NCS Interpretive Scoring Systems.*

[2134]
*****The Self Directed Search: A Guide to Educational and Vocational Planning.** High school and college and adults; 1970–79; SDS; "a self-administered, self-scored, and self-interpreted vocational counseling tool"; 6 scores (realistic, investigative, artistic, social, enterprising, conventional) for each of 3 scales (activities, competencies, occupations) and for self-ratings of abilities, summary; 2 forms; (Spanish ('79) and Vietnamese ('77) editions available); John L. Holland; Consulting Psychologists Press, Inc.*

a) STANDARD FORM. 1970–78. (New Zealand adaptation: 1982; Brian Keeling and Bryan F. Tuck; New Zealand Council for Educational Research [New Zealand].)*

b) FORM E. 1972–79; "simplified for a 4th grade reading level."

For additional information, a review by John O. Crites, and excerpted reviews by Fred Brown, Richard Seligman, Catherine C. Cutts, and Robert H. Dolliver and Robert N. Hansen of an earlier edition, see 8:1022 (88 references); see also T2:2211 (1 reference.)

REFERENCES

1. See T2:2211.
2–89. See 8:1022.
90. CUTTS, C. C. Self Directed Search. *Measurement & Evaluation in Guidance*, 1977, 10, 117–120.
91. DOLLIVER, R. H., & HANSEN, R. N. Self Directed Search. *Measurement & Evaluation in Guidance*, 1977, 10, 120–123.
92. ESPOSITO, R. P. The relationship between the motive to avoid success and vocational choice. *Journal of Vocational Behavior*, 1977, 10, 347–357.
93. HODGSON, M. L., & CRAMER, S. H. The relationship between selected self-estimated and measured abilities in adolescents. *Measurement & Evaluation in Guidance*, 1977, 10, 98–105.
94. HOLLAND, J. L. Self Directed Search. *Measurement & Evaluation in Guidance*, 1977, 10, 123–128.
95. HOLLAND, J. L., & HOLLAND, J. E. Vocational indecision: More evidence and speculation. *Journal of Counseling Psychology*, 1977, 24, 404–414.
96. KELSO, G. I., HOLLAND, J. L., & GOTTREDSON, G. D. The relation of self-reported competencies to aptitude test scores. *Journal of Vocational Behavior*, 1977, 10, 99–103.
97. LUCAS, R. W. A study of patients' attitudes to computer interrogation. *International Journal of Man–Machine Studies*, 1977, 9, 69–86.
98. McGOWAN, A. S. Vocational maturity and anxiety among vocationally undecided and indecisive students. The effectiveness of Holland's Self-Directed Search. *Journal of Vocational Behavior*, 1977, 10, 196–204.
99. O'NEIL, J. M., & MAGOON, T. M. The predictive power of Holland's investigative personality type and consistency levels using the Self Directed Search. *Journal of Vocational Behavior*, 1977, 10, 39–46.
100. SIEBEL, C. E., & WALSH, W. B. A modification of the instructions to Holland's Self-Directed Search. *Journal of Vocational Behavior*, 1977, 11, 282–290.
101. TOUCHTON, J. G., & MAGOON, T. M. Occupational daydreams as predictors of vocational plans of college women. *Journal of Vocational Behavior*, 1977, 10, 156–166.
102. WALSH, W. B., HORTON, J. A., & GUFFEY, R. L. Holland's theory and college degreed working men and women. *Journal of Vocational Behavior*, 1977, 10, 180–186.
103. ATTARIAN, P. J. Early recollections: Predictors of vocational choice. *Journal of Individual Psychology*, 1978, 34, 56–61.
104. BINGHAM, R. P., & WALSH, W. B. Concurrent validity of Holland's theory for college-degreed black women. *Journal of Vocational Behavior*, 1978, 13, 242–250.
105. GANSTER, D. C., & LOVELL, J. E. An evaluation of a career development seminar using Crite's Career Maturity Inventory. *Journal of Vocational Behavior*, 1978, 13, 172–180.
106. KEELING, B., & TUCK, B. F. Raw scores versus same-sex normed scores: An experimental study of the validity of Holland's SDS with adolescents of both sexes. *Journal of Vocational Behavior*, 1978, 13, 263–271.
107. MALETT, S. D., SPOKANE, A. R., & VANCE, F. L. Effects of vocationally relevant information on the expressed and measured interests of freshman males. *Journal of Counseling Psychology*, 1978, 25, 292–298.
108. MOUNT, M. K., & MUCHINSKY, P. M. Concurrent validation of Holland's hexagonal model with occupational workers. *Journal of Vocational Behavior*, 1978, 13, 348–354.
109. MOUNT, M. K., & MUCHINSKY, P. M. Person–environment congruence and employee job satisfaction: A test of Holland's theory. *Journal of Vocational Behavior*, 1978, 13, 84–100.
110. O'NEIL, J. M., MAGOON, T. M., & TRACEY, T. J. Status of Holland's investigative personality types and their consistency levels seven years later. *Journal of Counseling Psychology*, 1978, 25, 530–535.
111. PRICE, G. E., MICHAL, R. D., & O'NEIL, J. M. Using the computer to minimize SDS user error rate and facilitate SDS interpretation and research. *Measurement & Evaluation in Guidance*, 1978, 11, 150–154.
112. UTZ, P., & HARTMAN, B. An analysis of the discriminatory power of Holland's types for business majors in three concentration areas. *Measurement & Evaluation in Guidance*, 1978, 11, 175–182.
113. BLIMLING, G. S., & PAULSEN, F. M. The Educational Developmental Group Enrichment (EDGE) program: A comprehensive model for student development in residence halls. *Journal of the National Association for Women Deans, Administrators & Counselors*, 1979, 42, 24–33.
114. BYRNE, T. P., REARDON, R. C., & KELLY, F. D. Differential client satisfaction with Holland's Self-Directed Search. *Journal of College Student Personnel*, 1979, 20, 502–506.

115. DOTY, M. S., & BETZ, N. E. Comparison of the concurrent validity of Holland's theory for men and women in an enterprising occupation. *Journal of Vocational Behavior*, 1979, 15, 207–216.
116. FITZSIMMONS, G., & MELNYCHUK, D. The concurrent validity of the Canadian Occupational Interest Inventory and Self Directed Search. *Canadian Counsellor*, 1979, 13, 219–224.
117. HEPPNER, P. P., & KRAUSE, J. B. A career seminar course. *Journal of College Student Personnel*, 1979, 20, 300–305.
118. LUNNEBORG, P. W. Service vs. technical interest–Biggest sex difference of all? *Vocational Guidance Quarterly*, 1979, 28, 146–153.
119. O'NEIL, J. M., PRICE, G. E., & TRACEY, T. J. The stimulus value, treatment effects, and sex differences when completing the Self-Directed Search and Strong–Campbell Interest Inventory. *Journal of Counseling Psychology*, 1979, 26, 45–50.
120. TAKAI, R., & HOLLAND, J. L. Comparison of the Vocational card sort, the SDS, and the Vocational Exploration and Insight Kit. *Vocational Guidance Quarterly*, 1979, 27, 312–318.
121. TALBOT, D. B., & BIRK, J. M. Does the Vocational Exploration and Insight Kit equal the sum of its parts?: A comparison study. *Journal of Counseling Psychology*, 1979, 26, 359–362.
122. TAYLOR, K. F., KELSO, G. I., COX, G. N., ALLOWAY, W. J., & MATTHEWS, J. P. Applying Holland's vocational categories to leisure activities. *Journal of Occupational Psychology*, 1979, 52, 199–207.
123. WALSH, W. B., BINGHAM, R., & HORTON, J. A. Holland's theory and college–degreed working black and white women. *Journal of Vocational Behavior*, 1979, 15, 217–223.
124. ATANASOFF, G. E., & SLANEY, R. B. Three approaches to counselor–free career exploration among college women. *Journal of Counseling Psychology*, 1980, 27, 332–339.
125. BARKER, S., WHITE, P., REARDON, R., & JOHNSON, P. An evaluation of the effectiveness of an adaptation of the Self–Directed Search for use by the blind. *Rehabilitation Counseling Bulletin*, 1980, 23, 177–182.
126. BATESKY, J. A., MALACOS, J. A., & PURCELL, K. M. Comparison of personality characteristics of physical education and recreation majors, and factors which affect career choice. *Perceptual & Motor Skills*, 1980, 51, 1291–1298.
127. BENNINGER, W. B., & WALSH, W. B. Holland's theory and non–college–degreed working men and women. *Journal of Vocational Behavior*, 1980, 17, 81–88.
128. BYRNE, T. P. Self-esteem and satisfaction with Holland's SDS. *Canadian Counsellor*, 1980, 14, 160–162.
129. HARMON, L. W., & ZYTOWSKI, D. G. Reliability of Holland codes across interest measures for adult females. *Journal of Counseling Psychology*, 1980, 27, 478–483.
130. LYNCH, R. M., & LYNCH, J. Birth order and vocational preference. *Journal of Experimental Education*, 1980, 49, 15–18.
131. O'NEIL, J. M. Reply to Prediger. *Journal of Counseling Psychology*, 1980, 27, 304.
132. PREDIGER, D. J. The determination of Holland types characterizing occupational groups. *Journal of Vocational Behavior*, 1980, 16, 33–42.
133. PREDIGER, D. J. On the virtues of raw–scored interest inventories: Reaction to O'Neil, Price, and Tracey (1979). *Journal of Counseling Psychology*, 1980, 27, 302–303.
134. REARDON, R., & KAHNWEILER, W. Comparison of pencil–and–paper and tactile–board forms of the Self–Directed Search. *Journal of Counseling Psychology*, 1980, 27, 328–331.
135. SALTOUN, J. Fear of failure in career development. *Vocational Guidance Quarterly*, 1980, 29, 35–41.
136. TRACEY, T. J., & SEDLACEK, W. E. Comparison of error rates on the original Self–Directed Search and the 1977 revision. *Journal of Counseling Psychology*, 1980, 27, 299–301.
137. TUCK, B. F., & KEELING, B. Sex and cultural differences in the factorial structure of the Self–Directed Search. *Journal of Vocational Behavior*, 1980, 16, 105–114.
138. ARANYA, N., BARAK, A., & AMERNIC, J. A test of Holland's theory in a population of accountants. *Journal of Vocational Behavior*, 1981, 19, 15–24.
139. JOHNSON, J. A., & HOGAN, R. Vocational interests, personality and effective police performance. *Personnel Psychology*, 1981, 34, 49–53.
140. JOHNSON, J. A., SMITHER, R., & HOLLAND, J. L. Evaluating vocational interventions: A tale of two career development seminars. *Journal of Counseling Psychology*, 1981, 28, 180–183.
141. PREDIGER, D. J. A note on Self–Directed Search validity for females. *Vocational Guidance Quarterly*, 1981, 30, 117–129.
142. RACHMAN, D., AMERNIC, J., & ARANYA, N. A factor–analytic study of the construct validity of Holland's Self Directed Search test. *Educational & Psychological Measurement*, 1981, 41, 425–437.
143. WIGGINS, J. D., & MOODY, A. A field–based comparison of four career–exploration approaches. *Vocational Guidance Quarterly*, 1981, 30, 15–20.
144. YANICO, B. J. Sex-role self–concept and attitudes related to occupational daydreams and future fantasies of college women. *Journal of Vocational Behavior*, 1981, 19, 290–301.

[2135]

Self-Esteem Questionnaire. Ages 9 and over; 1971–76; SEQ; 2 scores: self esteem, self other satisfaction; James K. Hoffmeister; Test Analysis and Development Corporation.*

For additional information and a review by Rick Crandall, see 8:672.

REFERENCES

1. WATSON, J. Conceptual systems of undergraduate nursing students as compared with university students at large, and practicing nurses. *Nursing Research*, 1978, 27, 151–155.
2. HARTMAN, L. M. The preventive reduction of psychological risk in asymptomatic adolescents. *American Journal of Orthopsychiatry*, 1979, 49, 121–135.
3. GIBSON, D. E. Reminiscence, self–esteem and self–other satisfaction in adult male alcoholics. *Journal of Psychiatric Nursing*, 1980, 18, 7–11.

[2136]

The Self Explorations Inventory. College and adults; 1966; SEI; for research use only; no scores, 12 questions allowing for "projective-type" responses; Sheldon J. Lachman; Psychological Publications Press.* (In-print status uncertain; no reply from publisher.)

For additional information, see 7:177.

[2137]

★**Self-Motivated Career Planning.** High school and college and adults; 1949–78; SMCP; self-administered vocational counseling tool; Verne Walter and Melvin Wallace; Institute for Personality and Ability Testing, Inc.*

[2138]

Self Perception Inventory [Psychologists and Educators, Inc.]. Ages 12 and over; 1967–69; SPI; 12 scores: general adjustment (consistency, self-actualization, supervision, total), general maladjustment (uncommon response, rigidity-dogmatism, authoritarianism, anxiety, depression, paranoia, total), time; William T. Martin; Psychologists and Educators, Inc.*

For additional information and a review by John R. Braun, see 8:674 (1 reference); see also 7:136 (3 references).

[2139]

Self-Perception Inventory [SOARES Associates]. Grades 1–12, high school age and adults, teachers and student teachers; 1965–80; SPI; subject's perceptions of self, subject's perceptions of how others perceive him/her, and perceptions others have of him/her; 3 levels; (Spanish, French, and Italian editions available); Anthony T. Soares and Louise M. Soares; SOARES Associates.

a) STUDENT FORMS. Grades 1–12; 1967–80; 8 scores: self-concept, reflected self—classmates, reflected self—teachers, reflected self—parents, ideal concept, perceptions of others (male and female scales), student self, perceptions of other—student self (male and female scales).

b) ADULT FORMS. High school age and adults; 1967–80; 6 scores: self-concept, reflected self—friends, reflected self—teachers, reflected self—parents, ideal concept, perceptions of others (male and female scales), plus various discrepancy scores (optional).

c) TEACHER FORMS. Teachers, students teachers, their students; 1965–80; 7 scores: self-concept—teacher, reflected self—cooperating teacher, reflected self—supervisor, ideal self—teacher, teacher perception, reflected teacher perception, student perceptions, plus various discrepancy scores (optional).

For additional information and a review by Lorrie Shepard of the original edition, see 8:673 (2 references).

REFERENCES

1–2. See 8:673.
3. FROEHLICH, L. H., & JEPSON, D. A. Stability and change in self-perception scores over the secondary school years. *Measurement & Evaluation in Guidance*, 1980, 12, 240–246.

[2140]

★**Self Profile Q-Sort.** Grades 2–8; 1972–74; SPQS; no scores, examiners may develop their own criteria for evaluation of items; Alan J. Politte; Psychologists and Educators, Inc.*

[2141]

A Self-Rating Scale for Leadership Qualifications. Adults; 1942–48; E. J. Benge; National Foremen's Institute, Inc.* (In-print status uncertain; no reply from publisher.)

For additional information, see 5:906.

[2142]

Self-Report Inventory. College; 1959–67; SRI; for research use only; Form R-3; 10 scores: self, others, children, authority, work, reality, parents, hope, total, intensity; Oliver H. Bown and Donald J. Veldman (preliminary manual); distributed by Research and Development Center for Teacher Education, University of Texas.*

See T2:1378 (23 references).

[2143]

Self-Scoring Mathematics Placement Tests. Students entering postsecondary institutions with open-door policies; 1976, c1962–76; subtests of *CGP Self-Scoring Placement Tests in English and Mathematics*; self-scoring edition of the mathematics tests in the *Comparative Guidance and Placement Program*; 4 tests; tests may be administered separately but usually administered in following pairs: computation and applied arithmetic for students with less than 1 year high school algebra, computation and elementary algebra for students with 1 year, elementary and advanced algebra for students with more than 1 year; published by The College Board and Educational Testing Service.*
a) COMPUTATION PLACEMENT TEST.
b) APPLIED ARITHMETIC PLACEMENT TEST.
c) ELEMENTARY ALGEBRA PLACEMENT TEST.
d) INTERMEDIATE ALGEBRA PLACEMENT TEST.

For additional information and a review by Arthur Mittman, see 8:289. For reviews of the complete battery, see 8:7 (2 reviews). For reference to reviews of the CGP Program, see 8:475.

[2144]

Self-Scoring Reading Placement Test. Students entering post-secondary institutions with open-door policies; 1976, c1962–76; subtest of *CGP Self-Scoring Placement Tests in English and Mathematics*; self-scoring edition of the reading test (Form UPG) in the *Comparative Guidance and Placement Program*; published by The College Board and Educational Testing Service.*

For additional information, see 8:739. For reviews of the battery, see 8:7 (2 reviews). For reference to reviews of the CGP Program, see 8:475.

[2145]

Self-Scoring Written English Expression Placement Test. Students entering postsecondary institutions with open-door policies; 1976, c1962–76; subtest of *CGP Self-Scoring Placement Tests in English and Mathematics*; self-scoring edition of the sentences test in the *Comparative Guidance and Placement Program*; published by The College Board and Educational Testing Service.*

For additional information and reviews by Joseph J. Foley and David P. Harris, see 8:61. For reviews of the complete battery, see 8:7 (2 reviews). For reference to reviews of the CGP Program, see 8:475.

[2146]

★**SELF (Self-concept Evaluation of Location Form).** Adolescents and adults; 1978–80; SELF; 15 scores: total positive self-concept, evaluation factor, potency factor, activity factor, self-concept inconsistency, between factor inconsistency, within factor inconsistency, inconsistency F ratio, total self-ideal self incongruence, evaluation incongruence, potency incongruence, activity incongruence, between factors incongruence, within factor incongruence, incongruence F ratio; Richard E. Carney, Gil Spielberg, and Clifford W. Weedman; Carney, Weedman and Associates.*

[2147]

Self Valuation Test. Ages 7–15, adults; 1957; test booklet title is *S.V.T.*; verbal and nonverbal projective test employing several stimuli simultaneously; 2 levels; John Liggett; J. & P. Bealls Ltd. [England].* (In-print status uncertain; no reply from publisher.)
a) [FORM FOR CHILDREN.] Ages 7–15.
b) [FORMS FOR ADULTS.] Adults; forms also available under the title *Faces Test*.

See T2:1505 (1 reference), P:473A (3 references), and 5:157 (2 references).

[2148]

The Senior Apperception Technique. Ages 65 and over; 1973; SAT; Leopold Bellak and Sonya Sorel Bellak; C.P.S., Inc.*

For additional information and a review by K. Warner Schaie, see 8:676 (1 reference).

REFERENCES

1. See 8:676.
2. SCHROTH, M. L. Sex and generational differences in Senior Apperception Technique projections. *Perceptual & Motor Skills*, 1978, 47, 1299–1304.
3. FOOTE, J., & KAHN, M. W. Discriminative effectiveness of the Senior Apperception test with impaired and nonimpaired elderly persons. *Journal of Personality Assessment*, 1979, 43, 360–364.

[2149]

Senior Aptitude Tests. Standards 8–10 and college and adults; 1969–71; SAT; 12 scores: verbal comprehension, numerical fluency, word fluency, visual perception speed, reasoning (deductive, inductive), spatial visualization (2 dimensional, 3 dimensional), memory (paragraphs, symbols), psychomotor coordination, writing speed; F. A. Fouché and N. F. Alberts; Human Sciences Research Council [South Africa].*

For additional information, see 7:681.

[2150]
Senior English Test. Technical college entrants; 1963–71; distribution restricted to colleges of further education; NFER-Nelson Publishing Co. [England].*

For additional information and reviews by M. A. Brimer and David A. Walker, see 7:207.

[2151]
★**Senior High Assessment of Reading Performance.** Grades 9–12; 1976–80; SHARP; "competencies in reading skills necessary for everyday life"; Los Angeles Unified School District; CTB/McGraw-Hill.*

[2152]
Senior Mathematics Test. Technical college entrants; 1963–71; distribution restricted to colleges of further education; NFER-Nelson Publishing Co. [England].*

For additional information, see 7:487.

[2153]
Senior South African Individual Scale. Ages 6–17; 1964; NSAIS; 12 scores: verbal (vocabulary, comprehension, reasoning, problems, memory, total), non-verbal (pattern completion, blocks, absurdities, form board, total), total; both power and power-time scores are obtained for 4 subtests (problems, pattern completion, blocks, absurdities), verbal total, nonverbal total, and overall total; Human Sciences Research Council [South Africa].*

For additional information, see 7:413 (1 reference).

REFERENCES
1. See 7:413.
2. EVANS, D., BOWIE, M. D., HANSEN, J. D. L., MOODIE, A. D., & VAN DER SPUY, H. I. J. Intellectual development and nutrition. *Journal of Pediatrics*, 1980, 97, 358–363.

[2154]
Sentence Completion Blank. College and adults; 1955–66; SCB; Sheldon J. Lachman; Psychological Publications Press.* (In-print status uncertain; no reply from publisher.)

For additional information, see 7:178.

[2155]
Sentence Completion Test. High school and college; 1972; SCT; 35 item scores in 6 areas: self concept, parental attitude, peer attitude, need for achievement, learning attitude, body image; Floyd S. Irvin; Psychologists and Educators, Inc.*

See T2:1507 (5 references).

REFERENCES
1–5. See T2:1507.
6. HARRIS, M. M. Oral and written syntax of second graders. *Research in the Teaching of English*, 1977, 11, 117–132.
7. LORR, M., & MANNING, T. T. Measurement of ego development by sentence completion and personality test. *Journal of Clinical Psychology*, 1978, 34, 354–360.
8. LORR, M., & MANNING, T. T. Personality correlates of the sex role types. *Journal of Clinical Psychology*, 1978, 34, 884–888.
9. LICHTENBERG, J. W., & HECK, E. J. Interactional structure of interviews conducted by counselors of differing levels of cognitive complexity. *Journal of Counseling Psychology*, 1979, 26, 15–22.
10. ALBERT, R. S. Exceptionally gifted boys and their parents. *Gifted Child Quarterly*, 1980, 24, 174–179.
11. ROSEN, A., & NORDQUIST, T. A. Ego development level and values in a yogic community. *Journal of Personality & Social Psychology*, 1980, 39, 1152–1160.
12. ROZSNAFSZKY, J. The relationship of level of ego development to Q-sort personality ratings. *Journal of Personality & Social Psychology*, 1981, 41, 99–120.
13. SWENSEN, C. H., ESKEW, R. W., & KOHLHEPP, K. A. Stage of family life cycle, ego development, and the marriage relationship. *Journal of Marriage & the Family*, 1981, 43, 841–853.
14. URSANO, R. J. The Viet Nam era prisoner of war: Precaptivity personality and the development of psychiatric illness. *American Journal of Psychiatry*, 1981, 138, 315–318.

[2156]
★**Sentence Comprehension Test, Experimental Edition.** Ages 3–5; 1979; SCT; measures child's level of skill in receptive language; 15 subtests: simple intransitive, simple transitive, intransitive with adjective, transitive with adjective, plural, past tense, future tense, passive, simple negative, transitive negative, comparative, superlative, simple prepositions, harder prepositions, embedded phrase; Kevin Wheldall, Peter Mittler, and Angela Hobsbaum; NFER-Nelson Publishing Co. [England].*

[2157]
★**Sentence Imitation Screening Tests.** Ages 3–6; 1979; responses recorded on tape; Merlin J. Mecham and J. Dean Jones; Communication Research Associates, Inc.*

[2158]
★**Separation Anxiety Test.** Ages 11–18; 1972–80; provides a measure of emotional and personality patterns which adolescents show in reaction to separation experiences; 28 scores: 18 association responses (rejection, impaired concentration, phobic feeling, anxiety, loneliness, withdrawal, somatic, adaptive reaction, anger, projection, empathy, evasion, fantasy, well-being, sublimation, intrapunitive, identity stress, total), plus 10 derived response patterns (attachment, individuation, hostility, painful tension, reality avoidance, concentration impairment and sublimation, self-love loss, identity stress, absurd responses, attachment-individuation balance); Henry G. Hansburg; Robert E. Krieger Publishing Co., Inc.*

[2159]
★**Sequenced Inventory of Communication Development.** Ages 4 months–4 years; 1975–79; SICD; 2 scales; Dona Lea Hedrick, Elizabeth M. Prather, and Annette R. Tobin; University of Washington Press.*

a) RECEPTIVE SCALE. 3 scores: awareness, discrimination, understanding.

b) EXPRESSIVE SCALE. 4 scores: imitation, initiating, responsive, verbal output.

REFERENCES
1. LAMBERTS, F. Review of a test for communicative behaviors. *Journal of Learning Disabilities*, 1978, 11, 355–356.
2. WINKLER, S. Sequenced Inventory of Communication Development. *ASHA*, 1979, 21, 622–623.
3. LAVECK, B., HAMMOND, M. A., & LAVECK, G. D. Minor congenital anomalies and behavior in different home environments. *Journal of Pediatrics*, 1980, 96, 940–943.
4. OWENS, A., & BEATTY-DESANA, J. Communication functioning in trisomy. *Journal of Communication Disorders*, 1981, 14, 113–122.

[2160]
Sequential Tests of Educational Progress, Series II. Grades 4–6, 7–9, 10–12, 13–14 (except *b*, *c*2); 1956–72; STEP; combined SCAT-STEP test booklets available except for grades 13–14; 7 tests listed separately; Educational Testing Service; Addison-Wesley Publishing Co., Inc.*

a) ENGLISH EXPRESSION. Grades 4–6, 7–9, 10–12, 13–14; 1969–72.
b) MECHANICS OF WRITING. Grades 4–6, 7–9, 10–12; 1956–72; 3 scores: spelling, capitalization and punctuation, total.
c) MATHEMATICS. Grades 4–6, 7–9, 10–12, 13–14; 1956–72; 2 tests.
  1) *Mathematics Basic Concepts.* Grades 4–6, 7–9, 10–12, 13–14; 1956–72.
  2) *Mathematics Computation.* Grades 4–6, 7–9, 10–12; 1969–72.
d) READING. Grades 4–6, 7–9, 10–12, 13–14; 1956–72.
e) SCIENCE. Grades 4–6, 7–9, 10–12, 13–14; 1956–72.
f) SOCIAL STUDIES. Grades 4–6, 7–9, 10–12, 13–14; 1956–72.

For additional information and reviews by John H. Rosenbach and Richard E. Schutz, see 8:28 (5 references); see also T2:35 (37 references); for reviews by Harold Seashore and John E. Stecklein of the original edition (Series I), see 6:25 (6 references); for reviews by Robert W. B. Jackson and Wilbur L. Layton and an excerpted review by Laurence Siegel, see 5:24. For reviews of subtests, see 8:56 (2 reviews), 8:57 (1 review), 8:290 (1 review), 8:744 (2 reviews), 8:830 (2 reviews), 8:892 (2 reviews), 6:292 (2 reviews, 1 excerpt), 6:590 (2 reviews), 6:810 (2 reviews), 6:882 (2 reviews), 6:971 (2 reviews), 5:206 (3 reviews), 5:207 (3 reviews), 5:438 (3 reviews), 5:578 (2 reviews), 5:653 (3 reviews), 5:716 (3 reviews), and 5:792 (3 reviews).

REFERENCES

1–6. See 6:25.
7–43. See T2:35.
44–48. See 8:28.
49. ATKIN, R., BRAY, R., DAVISON, M., HERZBERGER, S., HUMPHREYS, L., & SELZER, U. Ability factor differentiation, grades 5 through 11. *Applied Psychological Measurement*, 1977, 1, 65–76.
50. ATKIN, R., BRAY, R., DAVISON, M., HERZBERGER, S., HUMPHREYS, L., & SELZER, U. Cross-lagged panel analysis of sixteen cognitive measures at four grade levels. *Child Development*, 1977, 48, 944–952.
51. DRABA, R. E., & STEINKELLNER, L. L. Screening applicants for teacher training. *Educational Forum*, 1977, 42, 101–109.
52. KEEFE, J. W. Model schools project report 14 Pius X High School. *National Association of Secondary School Principals Bulletin*, 1977, 61, 85–95.
53. LORD, F. M. A broad-range tailored test of verbal ability. *Applied Psychological Measurement*, 1977, 1, 95–100.
54. MORGAN, A. M., RACHELSON, S., & LLOYD, B. Science activities as contributors to the development of reading skills in first grade students. *Science Education*, 1977, 61, 135–144.
55. RENTZ, R. R., & BASHAW, W. L. The National Reference Scale for Reading: An application of the Rasch model. *Journal of Educational Measurement*, 1977, 14, 161–179.
56. WERTS, C. E., & HILTON, T. L. Intellectual status and intellectual growth, again. *American Educational Research Journal*, 1977, 14, 137–146.
57. ALEXANDER, K. L., COOK, M., & McDILL, E. Curriculum tracking and educational stratification: Some further evidence. *American Sociological Review*, 1978, 43, 47–66.
58. COPELAND, M. L., CONRAD, C., & CHANSKY, N. M. Validity of two intelligence tests. *Psychological Reports*, 1978, 42, 662.
59. FISCHER, D. G., HUNT, D., & RANDHAWA, B. S. Empirical validity of Ertl's brain-wave analyzer (BWAO2). *Educational & Psychological Measurement*, 1978, 38, 1017–1030.
60. MYERS, J. A. Compressed speech increases learning efficiency. *Education of the Visually Handicapped*, 1978, 10, 56–64.
61. SEIDNER, C. J., LEWIS, S. C., SHERWIN, N. V., & TROLL, E. W. Cognitive and affective outcomes for pupils in an open-space elementary school: A comparative study. *Elementary School Journal*, 1978, 78, 208–219.
62. STIGGINS, R. J., SCHMEISER, C. B., & FERGUSON, R. L. Validity of the ACT assessment as an indicator of reading ability. *Applied Psychological Measurement*, 1978, 2, 337–344.
63. WOLFLE, L. M., & BRYANT, L. W. A causal model of nursing education and state board examination scores. *Nursing Research*, 1978, 27, 311–315.
64. DONLON, T. F., EKSTROM, R. B., & LOCKHEED, M. E. The consequences of sex bias in the content of major achievement test batteries. *Measurement & Evaluation in Guidance*, 1979, 11, 202–216.
65. HUMPHREYS, L. G., PARK, R. D., & PARSONS, C. K. Applications of a simplex process model to six years of cognitive development in four demographic groups. *Applied Psychological Measurement*, 1979, 3, 51–64.
66. PETERSON, P. L., & JANICKI, T. C. Individual characteristics and children's learning in large-group and small-group approaches. *Journal of Educational Psychology*, 1979, 71, 677–687.
67. SLINDE, J. A., & LINN, R. L. The Rasch model, objective measurement, equating, and robustness. *Applied Psychological Measurement*, 1979, 3, 437–452.
68. SMITH, N. M. Allocation of time and achievement in elementary social studies. *Journal of Educational Research*, 1979, 72, 231–236.
69. TOEWS, W. Study of the cognitive structures of unified and subject-centered science students and those of their teachers. *Science Education*, 1979, 63, 173–182.
70. WEINER, M., & ZIBRIN, M. Dissimilarities in grade-equivalent scores on different standardized tests of achievement: A threat to criterion-related validity. *Educational & Psychological Measurement*, 1979, 39, 923–928.
71. AHERN, E. H., DIXON, P. W., KIMURA, T., OKUNA, J. S., & GIBSON, V. L. Phoneme use and the perception of meaning of written stimuli. *Psychologia*, 1980, 23, 206–218.
72. DIAMOND, E. E. The AMEG commission report on sex bias in achievement testing. *Measurement & Evaluation in Guidance*, 1980, 13, 135–147.
73. DRURY, D. W. Black self-esteem and desegregated schools. *Sociology of Education*, 1980, 53, 88–103.
74. IWANICKI, E. F. A new generation of standardized achievement test batteries: A profile of their major features. *Journal of Educational Measurement*, 1980, 17, 155–162.
75. MARX, R. W., & WINNE, P. H. Self-concept validation research: Some current complexities. *Measurement & Evaluation in Guidance*, 1980, 13, 72–82.
76. MASSARO, D. W., & TAYLOR, G. A. Reading ability and utilization of orthographic structure in reading. *Journal of Educational Psychology*, 1980, 72, 730–742.
77. WORMACK, L. Restructuring ability among premedical and predental minority students. *Journal of Research in Science Teaching*, 1980, 17, 577–582.
78. ALEXANDER, K. L., PALLAS, A. M., & COOK, M. A. Measure for measure: On the use of endogenous ability data in school-process research. *American Sociological Review*, 1981, 46, 619–631.
79. SWANSON, L. Vigilance deficit in learning disabled children: A signal detection analysis. *Journal of Child Psychology & Psychiatry & Allied Disciplines*, 1981, 22, 393–399.

[2161]

Sequential Tests of Educational Progress: English Expression, Series II. Grades 4–6, 7–9, 10–12, 13–14; 1969–72; Educational Testing Service; Addison-Wesley Publishing Co., Inc.*

For additional information and reviews by John C. Sherwood and William J. Wright, see 8:56. For reviews of the complete battery, see 8:28 (2 reviews).

[2162]

Sequential Tests of Educational Progress: Mathematics, Series II. Grades 4–6, 7–9, 10–12, 13–14 (except *b*); 1956–72; Educational Testing Service; Addison-Wesley Publishing Co., Inc.*

a) MATHEMATICS BASIC CONCEPTS. Grades 4–6, 7–9, 10–12, 13–14; 1956–72.
b) MATHEMATICS COMPUTATION. Grades 4–6, 7–9, 10–12; 1969–72.

For additional information and a review by Len Pikaart, see 8:290 (1 reference); see also T2:652 (15 references); for reviews by Arthur Mittman and Douglas A. Pidgeon of the original edition (Series I) of *a*, see 6:590 (5 references); for reviews by Paul F. Dresel, Gordon Fifer, and Tom A. Lamke, see 5:438. For reviews of the complete battery, see 8:28 (2 reviews), 6:25 (2 reviews), and 5:24 (2 reviews, 1 excerpt).

REFERENCES

1-5. See 6:590.
6-20. See T2:652.
21. See 8:290.
22. SHERMAN, J. Mathematics, spatial visualization, and related factors: Changes in girls and boys, grades 8-11. *Journal of Educational Psychology*, 1980, 72, 476-482.

[2163]
Sequential Tests of Educational Progress: Mechanics of Writing, Series II. Grades 4-6, 7-9, 10-12; 1956-72; 3 scores: spelling, capitalization and punctuation, total; Educational Testing Service; Addison-Wesley Publishing Co., Inc.*

For additional information and a review by Joseph J. Foley, see 8:57 (3 references); see also T2:113 (13 references); for reviews by Hillel Black and Albert N. Hieronymus and an excerpted review by Dean A. Allen of the original edition (Series I), see 6:292 (3 references); for reviews by Charlotte Croon Davis, John M. Stalnaker, and Louis C. Zahner, see 5:207. For reviews of the complete battery, see 8:28 (2 reviews), 6:25 (2 reviews), and 5:24 (2 reviews, 1 excerpt).

[2164]
Sequential Tests of Educational Progress: Reading, Series II. Grades 4-6, 7-9, 10-12, 13-14; 1956-72; Educational Testing Service; Addison-Wesley Publishing Co., Inc.*

For additional information and reviews by Richard T. Johnson and James L. Wardrop, see 8:744 (7 references); see also T2:1599 (25 references); for reviews by Emmett Albert Betts and Paul R. Lohnes of the original edition (Series I), see 6:810 (6 references); for reviews by Eric F. Gardner, James R. Hobson, and Stephen Wiseman, see 5:653. For reviews of the complete battery, see 8:28 (2 reviews), 6:25 (2 reviews), and 5:24 (2 reviews, 1 excerpt).

REFERENCES

1-6. See 6:810.
7-31. See T2:1599.
32-38. See 8:744.
39. BRASEL, K. E., & QUIGLEY, S. P. Influence of certain language and communication environments in early childhood on the development of language in deaf individuals. *Journal of Speech & Hearing Research*, 1977, 20, 95-107.
40. DAVIS, D. F. Language and social class: Conflict with established theory. *Research in the Teaching of English*, 1977, 11, 207-217.
41. BEAN, T. W. Decoding strategies of Hawaiian Islands dialect speakers in grades four, five, and six. *Reading World*, 1978, 17, 295-305.
42. HANNA, G. S., & OASTER, T. R. How important is passage dependence in reading comprehension? *Journal of Educational Research*, 1978, 71, 345-348.
43. HANNA, G. S. An improved design for examining the importance of context dependence. *Journal of Reading Behavior*, 1979, 11, 329-337.
44. LUNDSTEEN, S. W., & WILSON, J. A. R. Permanency of gains for children's problem solving processes and subabilities. *Educational Research Quarterly*, 1979, 4, 41-49.

[2165]
Sequential Tests of Educational Progress: Science, Series II. Grades 4-6, 7-9, 10-12, 13-14; 1956-72; Educational Testing Service; Addison-Wesley Publishing Co., Inc.*

For additional information and reviews by Wayne W. Welch and Victor L. Willson, see 8:830 (4 references); see also T2:1794 (18 references); for reviews by John C. Flanagan and George G. Mallinson of the original edition (Series I), see 6:882 (2 references); for reviews by Palmer O. Johnson, Julian C. Stanley (with M. Jacinta Mann), and Robert M. W. Travers, see 5:716. For reviews of the complete battery, see 8:28 (2 reviews), 6:25 (2 reviews), and 5:24 (2 reviews, 1 excerpt).

REFERENCES

1-2. See 6:882.
3-20. See T2:1794.
21-24. See 8:830.
25. RUST, J. O., STRANG, H. R., & BRIDGEMAN, B. How knowledge of results and goal setting function during academic tests. *Journal of Experimental Education*, 1977, 45, 52-55.
26. RAVEN, R. J., & ADRIAN, M. Relationships among science achievement, self-concept, and Piaget's operative comprehension. *Science Education*, 1978, 62, 471-479.

[2166]
Sequential Tests of Educational Progress: Social Studies, Series II. Grades 4-6, 7-9, 10-12, 13-14; 1956-72; original series (Series I) still available; Educational Testing Service; Addison-Wesley Publishing Co., Inc.*

For additional information and reviews by Howard D. Mehlinger and Ina V. S. Mullis, see 8:892 (1 reference); see also T2:1948 (13 references); for reviews by Jonathon C. McLendon and Donald W. Oliver of the original edition (Series I), see 6:971 (1 reference); for reviews by Richard E. Gross, S. A. Rayner, and Ralph W. Tyler, see 5:792. For reviews of the complete battery, see 8:28 (2 reviews), 6:25 (2 reviews), and 5:24 (2 reviews, 1 excerpt).

[2167]
★**The Sex Attitudes Survey and Profile, Trial Edition.** Marital and premarital counselees and adult sex education students; 1976; SAS; 107 items concerning sex attitudes; Gelolo McHugh and Thomas G. McHugh; Family Life Publications, Inc.*

[2168]
Sex Knowledge and Attitude Test, Second Edition. College and adults; 1971-73; SKAT; designed to serve both as a test and as a teaching aid; 5 scores: attitude (heterosexual relations, sexual myths, autoeroticism, abortion), knowledge; Harold I. Lief and David M. Reed; Center for the Study of Sex Education in Medicine.* (In-print status uncertain; no reply from publisher.)

For additional information and a review by Eugene E. Levitt, see 8:352 (7 references).

REFERENCES

1-7. See 8:352.
8. DELEMOS, H. Changes in helping professional's knowledge and attitudes following a human sexuality workshop led by a nurse. *Journal of Psychiatric Nursing*, 1977, 15, 11-21.
9. ELSTEIN, M., GORDON, A. D. G., & BUCKINGHAM, M. S. Sexual knowledge and attitudes of general practitioners in Wessex. *British Medical Journal*, 1977, 1, 369-371.
10. LAMBERTI, J. W., & CHAPEL, J. L. Development and evaluation of a sex education program for medical students. *Journal of Medical Education*, 1977, 52, 582-586.
11. FYFE, B. Effects of a sexual enhancement workshop on young adults. *Journal of Clinical Psychology*, 1979, 35, 873-875.

[2169]
*****Sex Knowledge Inventory.** Students in sex education classes in high school and college and adults; 1950-79; SKI; Gelolo McHugh; Family Life Publications, Inc.*

a) SEX KNOWLEDGE INVENTORY: VOCABULARY AND ANATOMY, 1977 REVISION. High school and college students and adults; 1950-77.

b) SEX KNOWLEDGE INVENTORY: 1979 REVISION. College students and adults; 1950–79.

See T2:838 (2 references) and 7:570 (6 references); for a review by Clifford R. Adams, see 6:687 (3 references); for a review by Albert Ellis and an excerpted review by Donald F. Schroeder, see 4:488.

[2170]

Sexometer. Adolescents and adults; 1974; sex information; Panos D. Bardis; the Author.*

For additional information, see 8:353 (1 reference).

[2171]

Sexual Adjustment Inventory. 1975; SAI; Freida Stuart, Richard B. Stuart, William L. Maurice, and George Szasz; Research Press.*

For additional information, see 8:354.

[2172]

★**The Sexual Communication Inventory.** Premarital and marital counselees; 1980; experimental edition; Millard J. Bienvenu, Sr.; Family Life Publications, Inc.*

[2173]

The Sexual Compatibility Test. Couples; 1974–76; SCT; 33 scores: 7 major scores (activity level, desired activity level, pleasure, estimate of mate's pleasure, desired pleasure, desire for mate's pleasure, problem solving) in each of 12 areas, 3 special scores (problem solving, sexual satisfaction, deception), 6 dysfunction scores, 4 derived scores, treatment predictor index; Arthur L. Foster; the Author.*

For additional information, see 8:355.

[2174]

★**The Sexual Concerns Checklist, Experimental Edition.** Junior high and high school, adults; 1980; survey instrument to be used prior to teaching or counseling about sex; Lester A. Kirkendall; Family Life Publications, Inc.*

[2175]

Shapes Analysis Test. Ages 14 and over; 1972; SAT; spatial perception; 3 scores: 2-dimensional, 3-dimensional, total; A. W. Heim, K. P. Watts, and V. Simmonds; Test Agency [England].*

For additional information and a review by Charles T. Myers, see 8:1046 (2 references).

[2176]

★**Sheltered Employment Work Experience Program.** Mentally retarded teenagers and adults; 1975–82; SEWEP; ratings by professional in 10 major vocational competency areas: factory work training, carpentry, print shop, laundry, building maintenance, general and outdoor maintenance, transportation aide, library aide, food service, housekeeping, plus personal/social development and general vocational development; Barber Center Press, Inc.*

[2177]

Sheridan Gardiner Test of Visual Acuity. Ages 5 and over; 1970; Mary D. Sheridan and Peter A. Gardiner; Keeler Instruments Ltd. [England].* (United States distributor: Keeler Instruments Inc.)

See T2:1926 (1 reference).

[2178]

Ship Destination Test. Grades 9 and over; 1955–56; general reasoning; Paul R. Christensen and J. P. Guilford; Sheridan Psychological Services, Inc.*

See T2:457 (13 references); for a review by William B. Schrader, see 6:500 (8 references); for a review by C. J. Adcock, see 5:383.

[2179]

Shipley-Institute of Living Scale for Measuring Intellectual Impairment. Adults; 1939–46; SILS; formerly called *Shipley-Hartford Retreat Scale for Measuring Intellectual Impairment*; 4 scores: vocabulary, abstractions, total, conceptual quotient; Walter C. Shipley; distributed by Barbara S. Boyle.*

For additional information, see 8:677 (39 references); see also T2:1380 (34 references); for a review by Aubrey J. Yates, see 7:138 (21 references); see also P:244 (38 references), 6:173 (13 references), and 5:111 (23 references); for reviews by E. J. G. Bradford, William A. Hunt, and Margaret Ives, see 3:95 (25 references).

REFERENCES

1–25. See 3:95.
26–48. See 5:111.
49–61. See 6:173.
62–99. See P:244.
100–120. See 7:138.
121–154. See T2:1380.
155–193. See 8:677.

194. BARKER, T. E., & BLACK, F. W. Klinefelter Syndrome in a military population. *Archives of General Psychiatry*, 1976, 33, 607–610.
195. CHANEY, E. F., ERICKSON, R. C., & O'LEARY, M. R. Brain damage and five MMPI items with alcoholic patients. *Journal of Clinical Psychology*, 1977, 33, 307–308.
196. COHLER, B. J., GRUNEBAUM, H. V., WEISS, J. L., GAMER, E., & GALLANT, D. H. Disturbance of attention among schizophrenic, depressed and well mothers and their young children. *Journal of Child Psychology & Psychiatry & Allied Disciplines*, 1977, 18, 115–135.
197. JOHNSON, J. H., KLINGLER, D. E., & WILLIAMS, T. A. An external criterion study of the MMPI validity indices. *Journal of Clinical Psychology*, 1977, 33, 154–156.
198. KLINGLER, D. E., JOHNSON, J. H., & WILLIAMS, T. A. A validation study of the WIST as a group administered instrument for assessment of schizophrenic thinking. *Journal of Clinical Psychology*, 1977, 33, 658–661.
199. LYLE, O. E., & GOTTESMAN, I. I. Premorbid psychometric indicators of the gene for Huntington's Disease. *Journal of Consulting & Clinical Psychology*, 1977, 45, 1011–1022.
200. MAISTO, S. A., & ADESSO, V. J. Effect of instructions and feedback on blood alcohol level discrimination training in nonalcoholic drinkers. *Journal of Consulting & Clinical Psychology*, 1977, 45, 625–636.
201. MARTIN, J. D., BLAIR, G. E., STOKES, E. H., & LESTER, E. H. A validity and reliability study of the Slosson Intelligence Test and the Shipley Institute of Living Scale. *Educational & Psychological Measurement*, 1977, 37, 1107–1110.
202. MARTIN, P. J., FRIEDMEYER, M. H., & STERNE, A. L. IQ deficit in schizophrenia: A test of competing theories. *Journal of Clinical Psychology*, 1977, 33, 667–672.
203. MAY, P. R. A., TUMA, A. H., & DIXON, W. J. For better or for worse? Outcome variance with psychotherapy and other treatments for schizophrenia. *Journal of Nervous & Mental Disease*, 1977, 165, 231–239.
204. ORNSTEIN, P. Cognitive deficits in chronic alcoholics. *Psychological Reports*, 1977, 40, 719–724.
205. PAGE, R. D., & SCHAUB, L. H. Intellectual functioning in alcoholics during six months' abstinence. *Journal of Studies on Alcohol*, 1977, 38, 1240–1246.
206. PISHKIN, V., LOVALLO, W. R., LENK, R. G., & BOURNE, L. E., JR. Schizophrenic cognitive dysfunction: A deficit in rule transfer. *Journal of Clinical Psychology*, 1977, 33, 335–342.
207. RYCHLAK, J. F., & INGWELL, R. H. Causal orientation and personal adjustment of hospitalized veterans. *Journal of Personality Assessment*, 1977, 41, 299–303.
208. TEDFORD, W. H., JR., & PENK, M. L. Intelligence and imagery in personality. *Journal of Personality Assessment*, 1977, 41, 405–413.
209. WALKER, B. A., & ZISKIND, E. Relationship of nailbiting to sociopathy. *Journal of Nervous & Mental Disease*, 1977, 164, 64–65.

210. ABRAMSON, L. Y., GARBER, J., EDWARDS, N. B., & SELIGMAN, M. E. P. Expectancy changes in depression and schizophrenia. *Journal of Abnormal Psychology*, 1978, 87, 102–109.
211. ALTERMAN, A. I., DRULEY, K. A., CONNOLLY, R., & BUSH, D. A comparison of moral reasoning in drug addicts and nonaddicts. *Journal of Clinical Psychology*, 1978, 34, 790–794.
212. CHANEY, E. F., O'LEARY, M. R., & MARLATT, G. A. Skill training with alcoholics. *Journal of Consulting & Clinical Psychology*, 1978, 46, 1092–1104.
213. DIETVORST, T. F., SWENSON, W. M., & MORSE, R. M. Intellectual assessment in a midwestern alcoholism treatment population. *Journal of Clinical Psychology*, 1978, 34, 244–249.
214. ENDLER, P. B., & EIMON, M. C. Postural and reflex integration in schizophrenic patients. *American Journal of Occupational Therapy*, 1978, 32, 456–459.
215. FUNDERBURK, S. J., & FERJO, N. Clinical observations in Klinefelter (47, XXY) Syndrome. *Journal of Mental Deficiency Research*, 1978, 22, 207–212.
216. GRUNEBAUM, H., COHLER, B. J., KAUFFMAN, C., & GALLANT, D. Children of depressed and schizophrenic mothers. *Child Psychiatry & Human Development*, 1978, 8, 219–228.
217. LEWIS, C. E., SCHER, M., & DIETZE, D. Reviewing results of psychological tests in a patient group. *Hospital & Community Psychiatry*, 1978, 29, 306–308.
218. PAGE, R. D., & SCHAUB, L. H. EMG biofeedback applicability for differing personality types. *Journal of Clinical Psychology*, 1978, 34, 1014–1020.
219. SUTKER, P. B., ALLAIN, A. N., & GEYER, S. Female criminal violence and differential MMPI characteristics. *Journal of Consulting & Clinical Psychology*, 1978, 46, 1141–1143.
220. SUTKER, P. B., ARCHER, R. P., & ALLAIN, A. N. Drug abuse patterns, personality characteristics, and relationships with sex, race, and sensation seeking. *Journal of Consulting & Clinical Psychology*, 1978, 46, 1374–1378.
221. WATSON, C. G., KUCALA, T., & JACOBS, L. The prediction of outcome from anhedonia and process–reactive scales. *Journal of Clinical Psychology*, 1978, 34, 889–892.
222. FERGUSON, B. Hospitalized adults' role–taking ability, psychiatric status and reported symptomatology. *Psychological Reports*, 1979, 44, 319–324.
223. MARTIN, J. D., BLAIR, G. E., & VICKERS, D. M. Correlation of the Quick Word Test and Wide Range Vocabulary Test with the Shipley Institute of Living Scale. *Educational & Psychological Measurement*, 1979, 39, 935–937.
224. MARTIN, J. D., BLAIR, G. E., & VICKERS, D. M. Correlation of the Slosson Intelligence Test with the California Short–Form Test of Mental Maturity and the Shipley Institute of Living Scale. *Educational & Psychological Measurement*, 1979, 39, 193–196.
225. MARUTA, T., SWANSON, D. W., & FINLAYSON, R. E. Drug abuse and dependency in patients with chronic pain. *Mayo Clinic Proceedings*, 1979, 54, 241–244.
226. MYLET, M., STYFCO, S. J., & ZIGLER, E. The interrelationship between self–image disparity and social competence, defensive style, and adjustment status. *Journal of Nervous & Mental Disease*, 1979, 167, 553–560.
227. O'LEARY, M., DONOVAN, D. M., CHANEY, E. F., & O'LEARY, D. E. Interpersonal attractiveness and clinical decisions in alcoholism treatment. *American Journal of Psychiatry*, 1979, 136, 618–622.
228. O'LEARY, M. R., DONOVAN, D. M., CHANEY, E. F., & SPELTZ, M. L. Correlates of clinicians' perceptions of patients in alcoholism treatment. *Journal of Clinical Psychiatry*, 1979, 40, 344–347.
229. WATSON, C. G., DALY, W. K., ZIMMERMAN, A., & ANDERSON, D. Effects of patient attitude and staff indulgence on improvement in schizophrenics: A test of impression management theory. *Journal of Abnormal Psychology*, 1979, 88, 338–340.
230. YOUNG, A., & REARDEN, J. Black Intelligence Test of Cultural Homogeneity and Shipley–Institute of Living Scale scores for black Chicago youths. *Psychological Reports*, 1979, 45, 457–458.
231. YU, H. K., & JOHNSON, J. H. Imagery in the associative learning of schizophrenics. *Journal of Clinical Psychology*, 1979, 35, 265–269.
232. ADI, H., & PULOS, S. Individual differences and formal operational performance of college students. *Journal for Research in Mathematics Education*, 1980, 11, 150–156.
233. ARCHER, R. P., BEDELL, J. R., & AMUSO, K. F. Personality, demographic, and intellectual variables associated with readiness for discharge from psychiatric treatment. *Journal of Psychology*, 1980, 104, 67–74.
234. COHLER, B. J., GALLANT, D. H., GRUNEBAUM, H. U., WEISS, J. L., & GAMER, E. Child–care attitudes and development of young children of mentally ill and well mothers. *Psychological Reports*, 1980, 46, 31–46.
235. ECKARDT, M. J., RYBACK, R. S., & PAUTLER, C. P. Neuropsychological deficits in alcoholic men in their mid thirties. *American Journal of Psychiatry*, 1980, 137, 932–936.

236. FEIFEL, H., & NAGY, V. T. Death orientation and life–threatening behavior. *Journal of Abnormal Psychology*, 1980, 89, 38–45.
237. HEWETT, B. B., & MARTIN, W. R. Psychometric comparisons of sociopathic and psychopathological behaviors of alcoholics and drug abusers versus a low drug use control population. *International Journal of the Addictions*, 1980, 15, 77–105.
238. JOHNSON, J. H., & HARRIS, W. G. Personality and behavioral characteristics related to divorce in a population of male applicants for psychiatric evaluation. *Journal of Abnormal Psychology*, 1980, 89, 510–513.
239. JONES, B. M., JONES, M. K., & HATCHER, E. M. Cognitive deficits in women alcoholics as a function of gynecological status. *Journal of Studies on Alcohol*, 1980, 41, 140–146.
240. JONES, M. K., & JONES, B. M. The relationship of age and drinking habits to the effects of alcohol on memory in women. *Journal of Studies on Alcohol*, 1980, 41, 179–186.
241. KNIGHT, R. A., EPSTEIN, B., & ZIELONY, R. D. The validity of the Whitaker Index of Schizophrenic Thinking. *Journal of Clinical Psychology*, 1980, 36, 632–639.
242. MOZDZIERZ, G. J., & SEMYCK, R. W. The social interest index: A study of construct validity. *Journal of Clinical Psychology*, 1980, 36, 417–422.
243. O'LEARY, M. R., CALSYN, D. A., & FAURIA, T. The Group Embedded Figures Test: A measure of cognitive style or cognitive impairment. *Journal of Personality Assessment*, 1980, 44, 532–537.
244. PARKER, E. S., & NOBLE, E. P. Alcohol and the aging process in social drinkers. *Journal of Studies on Alcohol*, 1980, 41, 170–178.
245. PARSONS, O. A. Cognitive dysfunction in alcoholics and social drinkers. *Journal of Studies on Alcohol*, 1980, 41, 105–118.
246. PHILLIPS, W. M., PHILLIPS, A. M., & SHEARN, C. R. Objective assessment of schizophrenic thinking. *Journal of Clinical Psychology*, 1980, 36, 79–89.
247. RAHAIM, S., WAID, L. R., KENNELLY, K. J., & STRICKLIN, A. Differences in self–monitoring of expressive behavior in depressed and nondepressed individuals. *Psychological Reports*, 1980, 46, 1051–1056.
248. SUTKER, P. B., ARCHER, R. P., & ALLAIN, A. N. Psychopathology of drug abusers: Sex and ethnic considerations. *International Journal of the Addictions*, 1980, 15, 605–613.
249. SWANSON, D. W., & MARUTA, T. Patients complaining of extreme pain. *Mayo Clinic Proceedings*, 1980, 55, 563–566.
250. VAUGHN, B., DEINARD, A., & EGELAND, B. Measuring temperament in pediatric practice. *Journal of Pediatrics*, 1980, 96, 510–514.
251. BELMORE, S. M. Age–related changes in processing explicit and implicit language. *Journal of Gerontology*, 1981, 36, 316–322.
252. BRUNNGUELL, D., CRICHTON, L., & EGELAND, B. Maternal personality and attitude in disturbances of child rearing. *American Journal of Orthopsychiatry*, 1981, 51, 680–691.
253. FABIAN, M. S., PARSONS, O. A., & SILBERSTEIN, J. A. Impaired perceptual–cognitive functioning in women alcoholics: Cross–validated findings. *Journal of Studies on Alcohol*, 1981, 42, 217–229.
254. HERSEN, M., BELLACK, A. S., & HIMMELHOCH, J. M. A comparison of solicited and nonsolicited female unipolar depressives for treatment outcome research. *Journal of Consulting & Clinical Psychology*, 1981, 49, 611–613.
255. LAPORTE, D. J., MCLELLAN, A. T., O'BRIEN, C. P., & MARSHALL, J. R. Treatment response in psychiatrically impaired drug abusers. *Comprehensive Psychiatry*, 1981, 22, 411–419.
256. MARTIN, J. D., BLAIR, G. E., SADOWSKI, C., & WHEELER, K. J. Intercorrelations among the Slosson Intelligence Test, the Shipley–Institute of Living Scale, and the Intellectual Efficiency Scale of the California Psychological Inventory. *Educational & Psychological Measurement*, 1981, 41, 595–598.
257. OLSON, R. P., GANLEY, R., DEVINE, V. T., & DORSEY, G. C., JR. Long–term effects of behavioral versus insight–oriented therapy with inpatient alcoholics. *Journal of Consulting & Clinical Psychology*, 1981, 49, 866–877.

[2180]

The Short Employment Tests. Applicants for clerical positions; 1951–78; SET; 4 scores: verbal, numerical, clerical, total; 3 tests; George K. Bennett and Marjorie Gelink; The Psychological Corporation.

a) V [VERBAL].
b) N [NUMERICAL].
c) CA [CLERICAL].

For additional information and reviews by Ronald N. Taylor and Paul W. Thayer, see 8:1037 (4 references); see also T2:2151 (6 references); for a review by Leonard W. Ferguson, see 6:1045 (9 references); for a review by P. L. Mellenbruch, see 5:854 (16 references).

REFERENCES

1-16. See 5:854.
17-25. See 6:1045.
26-31. See T2:2151.
32-35. See 8:1037.
36. MOTOWIDLO, S. J., LOEHR, V., & DUNNETTE, M. D. A laboratory study of the effects of goal specificity on the relationship between probability of success and performance. *Journal of Applied Psychology*, 1978, 63, 172–179.

[2181]
Short Form Test of Academic Aptitude. Grades 1.5–3.4, 3.5–4, 5–6, 7–9, 9–12; 1936–74; SFTAA; revision of *California Short-Form Test of Mental Maturity*; 3 scores: language, nonlanguage, total; Elizabeth T. Sullivan, Willis W. Clark, and Ernest W. Tiegs; CTB/McGraw-Hill.*

For additional information, a review by Lynn H. Fox, and an excerpted review by David M. Shoemaker, see 8:202 (9 references).

REFERENCES

1-9. See 8:202.
10. O'REILLY, R. P., & STREETER, R. E. Report on the development and validation of a system for measuring literal comprehension in a multiple-choice cloze format: Preliminary factor analytic results. *Journal of Reading Behavior*, 1977, 9, 45–69.
11. PALMER, L. L. Characteristics of near-point and far-point binocular and monocular sighting in classroom and ophthalmological populations. *Perceptual & Motor Skills*, 1977, 45, 707–711.
12. RUDY, K. R. The Short Form Test of Academic Aptitude (SFTAA) as a determinant of minimal brain dysfunction in children. *Journal of General Psychology*, 1977, 96, 169–176.
13. HOFFMAN, D. A. Field independence and intelligence: Their relation to leadership and self-concept in sixth-grade boys. *Journal of Educational Psychology*, 1978, 70, 827–832.
14. YEN, W. M. Measuring individual differences with an information-processing model. *Journal of Educational Psychology*, 1978, 70, 72–86.
15. CAPPADONA, D. L., & KERZNER-LIPSKY, D. Prediction of school mathematical achievement from motivation, self-concept, teachers' ratings and ability measures. *School Science & Mathematics*, 1979, 79, 140–144.
16. SCHELL, L. M., & COURTNEY, D. The effect of male teachers on the academic achievement of father-absent sixth grade boys. *Journal of Educational Research*, 1979, 72, 194–196.
17. SMITH, J. K., & KRAJKOVICH, J. G. Validation of the Image of Science and Scientists Scale. *Educational & Psychological Measurement*, 1979, 39, 495–498.
18. SPITZ, H. H., & BYRNES, M. M. Developmental progression of performance on the tower of Hanoi problem. *Bulletin of the Psychonomic Society*, 1979, 14, 379–381.
19. HILL, D. S. A comparison of the performance of normal, learning disabled, and educable mentally retarded children on Cattell's ability constructs. *Journal of Learning Disabilities*, 1980, 13, 38–41.
20. SCHNEIDER, L. S., & RENNER, J. W. Concrete and formal teaching. *Journal of Research in Science Teaching*, 1980, 17, 503–517.
21. HINES, C. V., ALTSCHULD, J. W., & RINDERER, R. E. A study of the construct validity of six vocational achievement tests in the Ohio Vocational Education Achievement Program. *Journal of Industrial Teacher Education*, 1981, 19, 3–13.

[2182]
Short Occupational Knowledge Test for Auto Mechanics. Job applicants; 1969–70; score is pass, fail, or unclassifiable; Bruce A. Campbell and Suellen O. Johnson; Science Research Associates, Inc.*

For additional information and a review by Emory E. Wiseman, see 7:1137.

[2183]
Short Occupational Knowledge Test for Bookkeepers. Job applicants; 1970; score is pass, fail, or unclassifiable; Bruce A. Campbell and Suellen O. Johnson; Science Research Associates, Inc.*

For additional information, see 7:1000.

[2184]
Short Occupational Knowledge Test for Carpenters. Job applicants; 1969–70; score is pass, fail, or unclassifiable; Bruce A. Campbell and Suellen O. Johnson; Science Research Associates, Inc.*

For additional information and a review by Robert S. Swanson, see 8:1169.

[2185]
Short Occupational Knowledge Test for Draftsmen. Job applicants; 1969–70; score is pass, fail, or unclassifiable; Bruce A. Campbell and Suellen O. Johnson; Science Research Associates, Inc.*

For additional information and a review by Tim L. Wentling, see 8:1170.

[2186]
Short Occupational Knowledge Test for Electricians. Job applicants; 1969–70; score is pass, fail, or unclassifiable; Bruce A. Campbell and Suellen O. Johnson; Science Research Associates, Inc.*

For additional information and a review by Charles F. Ward, see 7:1140.

[2187]
Short Occupational Knowledge Test for Machinists. Job applicants; 1969–70; score is pass, fail, or unclassifiable; Bruce A. Campbell and Suellen O. Johnson; Science Research Associates, Inc.*

For additional information, see 7:1141.

[2188]
Short Occupational Knowledge Test for Office Machine Operators. Job applicants; 1970; score is pass, fail, or unclassifiable; Bruce A. Campbell and Suellen O. Johnson; Science Research Associates, Inc.*

For additional information, see 7:1001.

[2189]
Short Occupational Knowledge Test for Plumbers. Job applicants; 1970; score is pass, fail, or unclassifiable; Bruce A. Campbell and Suellen O. Johnson; Science Research Associates, Inc.*

For additional information, see 7:1142.

[2190]
Short Occupational Knowledge Test for Secretaries. Job applicants; 1969–70; score is pass, fail, or unclassifiable; Bruce A. Campbell and Suellen O. Johnson; Science Research Associates, Inc.*

For additional information and a review by Albert K. Kurtz, see 8:1038.

[2191]
Short Occupational Knowledge Test for Tool and Die Makers. Job applicants; 1970; score is pass, fail, or unclassifiable; Bruce A. Campbell and Suellen O. Johnson; Science Research Associates, Inc.*

For additional information, see 7:1143.

[2192]
Short Occupational Knowledge Test for Truck Drivers. Job applicants; 1970; score is pass, fail, or unclassifiable; Bruce A. Campbell and Suellen O. Johnson; Science Research Associates, Inc.*

For additional information, see 7:1155.

[2193]
Short Occupational Knowledge Test for Welders. Job applicants; 1969–70; score is pass, fail, or unclassifiable; Bruce A. Campbell and Suellen O. Johnson; Science Research Associates, Inc.*

For additional information and a review by Richard A. Swanson, see 8:1171.

[2194]
Short Tests of Clerical Ability. Applicants for office positions; 1959–73; STCA; 7 tests; Jean M. Palormo; Science Research Associates, Inc.*

a) ARITHMETIC. 3 scores: computation, business arithmetic, total.
b) BUSINESS VOCABULARY.
c) CHECKING.
d) CODING.
e) DIRECTIONS–ORAL AND WRITTEN.
f) FILING.
g) LANGUAGE.

For additional information and reviews by Lorraine D. Eyde and Dean R. Malsbary, see 8:1039 (1 reference); for reviews by Philip H. Kriedt and Paul W. Thayer, see 6:1046.

[2195]
Shorthand Aptitude Test. High school; 1953–54; V. Brownless, S. Dunn, and the Queensland Department of Public Instruction; Australian Council for Educational Research [Australia].*

For additional information and a review by James Lumsden, see 5:520.

[2196]
★**Shutt Primary Language Indicator Test.** Grades kgn–6; 1976; SPLIT; revised from a 1974 individually administered SPLIT appropriate for Mexican-Americans only; present edition appropriate for Cuban, Puerto Rican, and Mexican-American children; 6 scores: listening comprehension (Spanish, English), verbal fluency (Spanish, English), reading comprehension and grammar (Spanish, English, for grades 3–6 only); D. L. Shutt; Webster Division, McGraw-Hill Book Co.*

[2197]
Siebrecht Attitude Scale. Grades 9–16 and adults; 1941–58; attitude toward safe driving practices; Elmer B. Siebrecht; Center for Safety.* (In-print status uncertain; no reply from publisher.)

See T2:850 (2 references) and 6:693 (3 references).

[2198]
Simile Interpretations. Grades 10–16; 1962–69; "divergent production of semantic systems"; Paul R. Christensen, J. P. Guilford, and Ralph Hoepfner; Sheridan Psychological Services, Inc.*

See T2:579 (1 reference).

[2199]
Similes. Grades 4–16; 1971; literary creativity; Charles E. Schaefer; Research Psychologists Press, Inc.*

For additional information and reviews by Philip M. Clark and Norman Frederiksen, see 8:245 (3 references); see also T2:580 (1 reference).

REFERENCES
1. See T2:580.
2–4. See 8:245.
5. DOMINO, G. Transcendental meditation and creativity: An empirical investigation. *Journal of Applied Psychology*, 1977, 62, 358–362.
6. KHATENA, J., & BELLAROSA, A. Sex differences, sense modality, and production of original verbal images. *Perceptual & Motor Skills*, 1978, 47, 1336.
7. TORRANCE, E. P., & MOURAD, S. Some creativity and style of learning and thinking correlates of Guglielmino's self-directed learning readiness scale. *Psychological Reports*, 1978, 43, 1167–1171.
8. DOMINO, G. Creativity and the home environment. *Gifted Child Quarterly*, 1979, 23, 818–828.
9. DURIO, H. F. A factor analysis of response task constraint in measures of creative aptitude. *Gifted Child Quarterly*, 1979, 23, 829–836.

[2200]
★**Simons Measurements of Music Listening Skills.** Grades kgn–3; 1974–76; SMMLS; "a criterion-referenced test"; 10 scores: melodic direction, steps/jumps, harmony—one tone or more, harmony—chord, meter, tonal patterns, rhythm patterns, dynamics, tempo, total; Gene M. Simons; Stoelting Co.*

[2201]
★**The Single and Double Simultaneous (Face-Hand) Stimulation Test.** Ages 18–75; 1979; SDSS; measures specific somatosensory functions of individuals with suspected disease or injury of the central nervous system; Carmen C. Centofanti and Aaron Smith; Western Psychological Services.*

REFERENCES
1. CAMPBELL, A. L., BOGEN, J. E., & SMITH, A. Disorganization and reorganization of cognitive and sensorimotor functions in cerebral commissurotomy: Compensatory roles of the forebrain commissures and cerebral hemispheres in man. *Brain*, 1981, 104, 493–511.

[2202]
Sipay Word Analysis Tests. Grades 1–adult; 1974; SWAT; criterion-referenced; item, part, trial, and total test scores are reported as fractions (number correct over number presented); 17 tests; Edward R. Sipay; Educators Publishing Service, Inc.*

a) SURVEY TEST. For determining which specific tests and parts of other tests should be administered; each referral is based upon the first failed item in 3 trials.
b) TEST 1, LETTER NAMES. 2 parts: lower case, upper case; 30 scores.
c) TEST 2, SYMBOL-SOUND ASSOCIATION: SINGLE LETTERS. 2 parts (sounds, words) for consonants, vowels; 28 scores.
d) TEST 3, SUBSTITUTION: SINGLE LETTERS. 3 parts: initial consonants, final consonants, medial vowels; 7 scores.
e) TEST 4, CONSONANT-VOWEL-CONSONANT TRIGRAMS. 3 parts: initial consonants, final consonants, vowels; 4 scores.
f) TEST 5, INITIAL CONSONANT BLENDS AND DIGRAPHS. 3 parts: blends, digraphs, triple cluster; 12 scores.
g) TEST 6, FINAL CONSONANT BLENDS AND DIGRAPHS. 2 parts: blends, digraphs; 8 scores.
h) TEST 7, VOWEL COMBINATIONS. 4 parts: vowel digraphs, diphthongs, vowel combinations (more common, less common); 16 scores.
i) TEST 8, OPEN-SYLLABLE GENERALIZATION. 6 scores.
j) TEST 9, FINAL SILENT E GENERALIZATION. 6 scores.
k) TEST 10, VOWEL VERSATILITY. 6 scores.
l) TEST 11, VOWELS + R. 3 parts: single vowel + r, 2 vowels + r, single vowel + r + silent e; 12 scores.

m) TEST 12, SILENT CONSONANTS. 4 scores.
n) TEST 13, VOWEL SOUNDS OF Y. 4 scores.
o) TEST 14, VISUAL ANALYSIS. 3 parts: monosyllabic words, root words and affixes, syllabication; 53 scores.
p) TEST 15, VISUAL BLENDING. 2 parts: component elements into syllables, syllables into words; 9 scores.
q) TEST 16, CONTRACTIONS. 17 scores.

For additional information, reviews by Roy A. Kress and William J. Valmont, and excerpted reviews by Virginia L. Brown and Shirley C. Feldmann, see 8:775 (4 references).

[2203]
Situational Attitude Scale. College and adults; 1972, c1969–72; SAS; "attitudes of whites toward blacks"; 11 scores: 10 situations scores, total; William E. Sedlacek and Glenwood C. Brooks, Jr.; University Counseling Center.*

For additional information and reviews by Ralph Mason Dreger and Marvin E. Shaw, see 8:678 (1 reference); see also T2:1381 (3 references).

[2204]
★**Situational Leadership.** Managers, leaders, administrators, supervisors, and staff; 1973–80; SL; the related programs, *Situational Leadership Simulator* and *The Essentials of Situational Leadership*, are also available; 6 tests; Paul Hersey and Joseph W. Keilty; Learning Resources Corporation.*

a) INTERACTION INFLUENCE ANALYSIS. 1980; IIA; ratings by observers; 9 scores for both leaders and followers: directing, questioning, supporting, attentive listening, accepting, rational responding, nonattentive listening, rejecting, irrational responding.
b) LEADER EFFECTIVENESS AND ADAPTABILITY DESCRIPTION. 1973; LEAD; ratings by self and others.
c) MATURITY STYLE MATCH. 1979; MSM; ratings in 4 areas: major objectives, maturity, integration of style and maturity, maturity style match matrix.
d) MATURITY SCALE. 1977; MS; 2 scores (job maturity, psychological maturity) for each of 5 major objectives or responsibilities.
e) POWER PERCEPTION PROFILE. 1979; PPP; 7 scores: coercive, connection, expert, information, legitimate, referent, reward.
f) LEADERSHIP SCALE. 1980; LS; 2 scores (total task-behavior, total relationship-behavior) for each of 5 major objectives or responsibilities.

[2205]
★**Situational Parenting.** Parents and their children; 1980; combination of *Maturity Style Match* and *Parent-Self and Parent-Other*, which are available separately; ratings by parents and children; helps family members learn how to vary their behavior to fit the situation; 2 tests; no manual; Paul Hersey (*a*, *b*), Kenneth H. Blanchard (*a*, *b*), Joseph W. Keilty (*a*), John Donoghue (*b*), and Anna Donoghue (*b*); Learning Resources Corporation.*

a) MATURITY STYLE MATCH. Determines how the parenting style used matches the child's maturity level; 4 areas: parent style, maturity, integration of style and maturity, maturity style match matrix.
b) PARENT-SELF AND PARENT-OTHER. Parents and children ages up to 8, 9–15, 16 and over; provides feedback on parenting styles; 3 scores: parenting style, flexibility, adaptability.

[2206]
Situational Preference Inventory. Grades 9–16 and adults; 1968–73; SPI; "individual styles of social interaction"; 3 scores: cooperational, instrumental, analytic; Carl N. Edwards; the Author.*

See T2:1382 (2 references).

[2207]
★**Six Inventories to Assess Affective Impact of Basic Skills Instructional Programs.** Older primary level and secondary level students; 1979; "for use in connection with minimum competency testing programs"; Romeria Tidwell and W. James Popham; Instructional Objectives Exchange.*

[2208]
Sixteen Personality Factor Questionnaire. Ages 16 and over; 1949–80; 16PF; 24 scores; 16 primary factor scores: reserved vs. outgoing (A), less intelligent vs. more intelligent (B), affected by feelings vs. emotionally stable (C), humble vs. assertive (E), sober vs. happy-go-lucky (F), expedient vs. conscientious (G), shy vs. venturesome (H), tough-minded vs. tender-minded (I), trusting vs. suspicious (L), practical vs. imaginative (M), forthright vs. astute (N), self-assured vs. apprehensive (O), conservative vs. experimenting (Q_1), group-dependent vs. self-sufficient (Q_2), undisciplined self-conflict vs. controlled (Q_3), relaxed vs. tense (Q_4), plus 8 second order factors (worksheet available): introversion vs. extraversion (Q_I), low anxiety vs. high anxiety (Q_{II}), sensitivity/emotionalism vs. tough poise (Q_{III}), dependence vs. independence (Q_{IV}), discreetness (Q_V), prodigal subjectivity (Q_{VI}), "may be identifiable as fluid intelligence" (Q_{VII}), "probably best regarded as the real superego factor" (Q_{VIII}); Raymond B. Cattell, Herbert W. Eber, and Maurice M. Tatsuoka (handbook); Institute for Personality and Ability Testing, Inc.*

a) FORMS A AND B, 1967–68 EDITION. 1949–79; authors recommend that both forms (374 items) be used; (German and Spanish editions available).
b) FORMS C AND D, 1969 EDITION. Reading levels grade 6 and over; 1954–79; author recommends administration of both forms; (Spanish editions available for Form C); industrial edition of 1956 Form C published under title *Employee Attitude Series: 16PF*, published by Industrial Psychology, Inc.
c) FORM E. Reading levels grades 3–4; 1965–76; tape cassette is available for oral administration to persons reading below the grade 3 level; (Spanish edition available).

For additional information and reviews by Bruce M. Bloxom, Brian F. Bolton, and James A. Walsh, see 8:679 (619 references); see also T2:1383 (244 references); for reviews by Thomas J. Bouchard, Jr. and Leonard G. Rorer, see 7:139 (295 references); see also P:245 (249 references); for a review by Maurice Lorr of an earlier edition, see 6:174 (81 references); for a review by C. J. Adcock, see 5:112 (21 references); for reviews by Charles M. Harsh, Ardie Lubin, and J. Richard Wittenborn, see 4:87 (8 references).

REFERENCES

1–8. See 4:87.

9–29. See 5:112.
30–108. See 6:174.
109–357. See P:245.
358–652. See 7:139.
653–896. See T2:1383.
897–1515. See 8:679.

1516. BREWER, B. R., & APOSTOL, R. A. Relationships among personality, empathy, and counselor effectiveness. *Journal of Teaching & Learning: The University of North Dakota*, 1976, 2, 7–15.

1517. ALKER, H. A., & OWEN, D. W. Biological, trait, and behavioral–sampling predictions of performance in a stressful life setting. *Journal of Personality & Social Psychology*, 1977, 35, 717–723.

1518. BERNARDIN, H. J. The relationship of personality variables to organizational withdrawal. *Personnel Psychology*, 1977, 30, 17–27.

1519. BROWN, J. J., & HART, D. H. Correlates of females' sexual fantasies. *Perceptual & Motor Skills*, 1977, 45, 819–825.

1520. BROWNE, J. A., & HOWARTH, E. A comprehensive factor analysis of personality questionnaire items: A test of twenty putative factor hypotheses. *Multivariate Behavioral Research*, 1977, 12, 399–427.

1521. CAMPBELL, J. B., & CHUN, K. Interinventory predictability and content overlap of the 16PF and the CPI. *Applied Psychological Measurement*, 1977, 1, 51–63.

1522. CARRUTH, B. R., MANGEL, M., & ANDERSON, H. L. Assessing change–proneness and nutrition–related behaviors. *Journal of the American Dietetic Association*, 1977, 70, 47–53.

1523. CHEN, K., & MONSALUD, A. Personality correlates of semantic habits in the deaf. *Journal of Psychology*, 1977, 95, 305–307.

1524. CLARK, D. F. Personality characteristics of applicants and members of children's panels. *British Journal of Criminology*, 1977, 17, 228–236.

1525. COLLINS, H. A., BURGER, G. K., & TAYLOR, G. A. Personality patterns of drug abusers as shown by MMPI profiles. *Journal of Clinical Psychology*, 1977, 33, 897–900.

1526. COOPER, C. L. Adverse and growthful effects of experiential learning groups: The role of the trainer, participant, and group characteristics. *Human Relations*, 1977, 30, 1103–1129.

1527. COSTA, P. T., JR., FOZARD, J. L., & McCRAE, R. R. Personological interpretation of factors from the Strong Vocational Interest Blank scales. *Journal of Vocational Behavior*, 1977, 10, 231–243.

1528. DIAS, S., & CARIFO, J. A note on sex differences in achievement motivation. *Educational & Psychological Measurement*, 1977, 37, 513–517.

1529. ESLER, M., JULIUS, S., ZWEIFLER, A., RANDALL, O., HARBURG, E., GARDINER, H., & DEQUATTRO, V. Mild high–renin essential hypertension: Neurogenic human hypertension. *New England Journal of Medicine*, 1977, 296, 405–411.

1530. FERGUSON, N. Simultaneous speech, interruptions and dominance. *British Journal of Social & Clinical Psychology*, 1977, 16, 295–302.

1531. GARSON, A., JR., WILLIAMS, R. B. J., & RECKLESS, J. Long–term follow–up of patients with tetralogy of fallot: Physical health and psychopathology. *Journal of Pediatrics*, 1977, 85, 429–433.

1532. GOEBEL, B., & HARRIS, E. Impact of sex–role values on cognitive performance. *Psychological Reports*, 1977, 41, 1251–1256.

1533. GROSSMAN, F. M. Instructional specialty, sex, and imaginativeness of prospective teachers. *Psychological Reports*, 1977, 40, 1174.

1534. HAMPSON, S. E., & KLINE, P. Personality dimensions differentiating certain groups of abnormal offenders from non–offenders. *British Journal of Criminology*, 1977, 17, 310–331.

1535. HARTUNG, G. H., & FARGE, E. J. Personality and physiological traits in middle–aged runners and joggers. *Journal of Gerontology*, 1977, 32, 541–548.

1536. HERRMAN, D. J., POST, A. L., WITTMAIER, B. C., & ELSASSER, T. C. Relationship between personality factors and adaptation to stress in a military institution. *Psychological Reports*, 1977, 40, 831–834.

1537. HESKIN, K. J., BOLTON, N., BANISTER, P. A., & SMITH, F. V. Prisoners' personality: A factor analytically derived structure. *British Journal of Social & Clinical Psychology*, 1977, 16, 203–206.

1538. HUNDLEBY, J. D., & ROSS, B. E. Comparison of measures of psychopathy. *Journal of Consulting & Clinical Psychology*, 1977, 45, 702–703.

1539. HYMAN, C. A. A report on the psychological test results of battering parents. *British Journal of Social & Clinical Psychology*, 1977, 16, 221–224.

1540. ISMAIL, A. H., & YOUNG, R. J. Effect of chronic exercise on the multivariate relationships between selected biochemical and personality variables. *Multivariate Behavioral Research*, 1977, 12, 49–67.

1541. JOHNSGARD, K. Personality and performance: A psychological study of amateur sports car race drivers. *Journal of Sports Medicine & Physical Fitness*, 1977, 17, 97–104.

1542. KAESTNER, E., & GOLDSTEIN, M. Reliability of a personality test for narcotic addicts in treatment. *Journal of Consulting & Clinical Psychology*, 1977, 45, 1192–1193.

1543. KISH, G. B., WOODY, M. M., & FRANKEL, A. The development of a scale to measure task completion motivation. *Journal of Clinical Psychology*, 1977, 33, 128–133.

1544. KLINE, P., & STOREY, R. A factor analytic study of the oral character. *British Journal of Social & Clinical Psychology*, 1977, 16, 317–328.

1545. LAMONT, L. M., & LUNDSTROM, W. J. Identifying successful industrial salesmen by personality and personal characteristics. *Journal of Marketing Research*, 1977, 14, 517–529.

1546. McCUTCHEON, L. E. Dumber by the dozen? Not necessarily! *Psychological Reports*, 1977, 40, 109–110.

1547. MERCURIO, R., & VACC, N. A. Relationship of two measures of conformity. *Perceptual & Motor Skills*, 1977, 45, 538.

1548. NERVIANO, V. J., & WEITZEL, W. D. The 16PF and CPI: A comparison. *Journal of Clinical Psychology*, 1977, 33, 400–406.

1549. NICHOLS, M. P., & KNOPF, I. J. Refining computerized test interpretations: An in–depth approach. *Journal of Personality Assessment*, 1977, 41, 157–159.

1550. PATEL, K. Personality factors predicting creative profiles. *Psychologia*, 1977, 20, 74–82.

1551. PIPER, W. E., DEBBANE, E. G., & GARANT, J. Group psychotherapy outcome research: Problems and prospects of a first-year project. *International Journal of Group Psychotherapy*, 1977, 27, 321–341.

1552. SORENSEN, G., & McCOOSKEY, J. C. The prediction of interaction behavior in small groups: Zero history vs. intact groups. *Communication Monographs*, 1977, 44, 73–80.

1553. STANKOV, L. Some experiences with the F scale in Yugoslavia. *British Journal of Social & Clinical Psychology*, 1977, 16, 111–121.

1554. STEWART, D. W. The self–sentiment: Comment on internal consistency of Cattell's theory. *Psychological Reports*, 1977, 40, 267–270.

1555. STROUP, A. L., & MANDERSCHEID, R. W. CPI and 16PF second–order factor congruence. *Journal of Clinical Psychology*, 1977, 33, 1023–1026.

1556. TURNER, R. G., & HIBBS, C. Vocational interest and personality correlates of differential abilities. *Psychological Reports*, 1977, 40, 727–730.

1557. TURNER, R. G., & HORN, J. M. Personality, husband–wife similarity, and Holland's occupational types. *Journal of Vocational Behavior*, 1977, 10, 111–120.

1558. WHITE, W. C., & ANDREWS, J. V. An experiential–behavioral approach to the treatment of social incompetence. *Journal of American College Health Association*, 1977, 25, 186–188.

1559. YOUNG, R. J., & ISMAIL, A. H. Comparison of selected physiological and personality variables in regular and nonregular adult male exercisers. *Research Quarterly*, 1977, 48, 617–622.

1560. ABELSOHN, D. S., & VAN DER SPUY, H. I. J. The age variable in alcoholism. *Journal of Studies on Alcohol*, 1978, 39, 800–808.

1561. BARKER, E. T., McLAUGHLIN, A. J., & BARNETT, W. H. Do-it-yourself human relations training: An evaluative study with one year follow-up. *School Guidance Worker*, 1978, 33, 24–28.

1562. BEDFORD, A., & McIVER, D. Foulds' "general instability" and "psychopathy" 16PF scales and their relationship to psychiatric mood state. *Journal of Clinical Psychology*, 1978, 34, 417–418.

1563. BERNARD, L. C., & EPSTEIN, D. J. Sex role conformity in homosexual and heterosexual males. *Journal of Personality Assessment*, 1978, 42, 505–511.

1564. BOSKIND-LODAHL, M., & WHITE, W. C. The definition and treatment of bulimarexia in college women–A pilot study. *Journal of the American College Health Association*, 1978, 27, 84–86.

1565. BRADLEY, R., & REDFERING, D. L. Drug abuses in the military: Correlates of successful rehabilitation. *Journal of Clinical Psychology*, 1978, 34, 233–237.

1566. CAMPBELL, A., & RUSHTON, J. P. Bodily communication and personality. *British Journal of Social & Clinical Psychology*, 1978, 17, 31–36.

1567. CARROLL, J. L., & FULLER, G. B. Personality correlates of the group personality projective test vs personality factors. *Psychological Reports*, 1978, 43, 1019–1022.

1568. COOPER, C. L., MALLINGER, M., & KAHN, R. Identifying sources of occupational stress among dentists. *Journal of Occupational Psychology*, 1978, 51, 227–239.

1569. DIXON, P. N. Effects of a behavior modification skills training on several personality factors among teacher trainees. *College Student Journal*, 1978, 12, 320–323.

1570. DIXON, P. N., & ELIAS, S. F. Differences in attitudes toward role playing by various personality factors. *College Student Journal*, 1978, 12, 439–443.

1571. DOR-SHAV, N. K. On the long-range effects of concentration camp internment on Nazi victims: 25 years later. *Journal of Consulting & Clinical Psychology*, 1978, 46, 1–11.

1572. GEORGE, L. K. The impact of personality and social status factors upon levels of activity and psychological well-being. *Journal of Gerontology*, 1978, 33, 840–847.

1573. GIACOBBE, G. A., & GRAHAM, R. M. The responses of aggressive emotionally disturbed and normal boys to selected musical stimuli. *Journal of Music Therapy*, 1978, 15, 118–135.

1574. GOLDEN, C. J. Cross–cultural second order factor structure of the 16PF. *Journal of Personality Assessment*, 1978, 42, 167–170.

1575. GREENOUGH, T. J., KEEGAN, D. L., & ASH, D. G. Psychological and social adjustment of blind subjects and the 16PF. *Journal of Clinical Psychology*, 1978, 34, 84–87.

1576. HAMPSON, S. E., GILMOUR, R., & HARRIS, P. L. Accuracy in self-perception: The "fallacy of personal validation". *British Journal of Social & Clinical Psychology*, 1978, 17, 231–235.

1577. HANDLEY, H. M., & HICKSON, J. F. Background and career orientations of women with mathematical aptitude. *Journal of Vocational Behavior*, 1978, 13, 255–262.

1578. HARRIS, J. E., & BODDEN, J. L. An activity group experience for disengaged elderly persons. *Journal of Counseling Psychology*, 1978, 25, 325–330.

1579. HUNDAL, P. S., & SINGH, S. Some correlates of progressive farm behavior. *Journal of Occupational Psychology*, 1978, 51, 327–332.

1580. JAMES, S. Treatment of homosexuality II. Superiority of desensitization/arousal as compared with anticipatory avoidance conditioning: Results of a controlled trial. *Behavior Therapy*, 1978, 9, 28–36.

1581. KLINE, P., & STOREY, R. The Dynamic Personality Inventory: What does it measure? *British Journal of Psychology*, 1978, 69, 375–383.

1582. KRUG, S. E. Further evidence on 16PF distortion scales. *Journal of Personality Assessment*, 1978, 42, 513–518.

1583. LANGEVIN, R., PAITICH, P., FREEMAN, R., MANN, K., & HANDY, L. Personality characteristics and sexual anomalies in males. *Canadian Journal of Behavioural Science*, 1978, 10, 222–238.

1584. LEARD, H. M., & HUM, A. The personality characteristics of counsellors–in–traning which correlate with ratings of effectiveness and grades. *Canadian Counsellor*, 1978, 13, 28–32.

1585. McCLAIN, E. Feminists and nonfeminists: Contrasting profiles in independence and affiliation. *Psychological Reports*, 1978, 43, 435–441.

1586. McCLAIN, E. W. Personality difference between intrinsically religious and nonreligious students: A factor analytic study. *Journal of Personality Assessment*, 1978, 42, 159–166.

1587. McCRAE, R. R., COSTA, P. T., JR., & BOSSE, R. Anxiety, extraversion and smoking. *British Journal of Social & Clinical Psychology*, 1978, 17, 269–273.

1588. McGURK, B. J., BOLTON, N., & SMITH, M. Some psychological, educational and criminological variables related to recidivism in delinquent boys. *British Journal of Social & Clinical Psychology*, 1978, 17, 251–254.

1589. O'HARA-DEVEREAUX, M., BROWN, T. C., MENTINK, J., & MORGAN, W. A. Biographical data, personality, and vocational interests of family nurse practitioners. *Psychological Reports*, 1978, 43, 1259–1268.

1590. ROBERTSON, S. A. Some personality correlates of time competence, temporal extension and temporal evaluation. *Perceptual & Motor Skills*, 1978, 46, 743–750.

1591. SARGENT, C. L. Hypnosis as a psi–conducive state: A controlled replication study. *Journal of Parapsychology*, 1978, 42, 257–275.

1592. SMITH, J. C. Personality correlates of continuation and outcome in meditation and erect sitting control treatments. *Journal of Consulting & Clinical Psychology*, 1978, 46, 272–299.

1593. STROUP, A. L., & MANDERSCHEID, R. W. Analytical, sample, and gender variations in 16PF second-order personality factors. *Journal of Experimental Education*, 1978–1979, 47, 118–125.

1594. WARD, G. R., CUNNINGHAM, C. H., & SUMMERLIN, M. L. Personality profiles and dogmatism in undergraduate teacher education students. *Psychology in the Schools*, 1978, 15, 33–36.

1595. WATKINS, M. Correlation between Quick Word Test and Sixteen Personality Factor Questionnaire B Factor scores. *Psychological Reports*, 1978, 42, 653–654.

1596. WIKOFF, R. L., & KAFKA, G. F. Interrelationships between the choice of college major, the ACT and the Sixteen Personality Factor Questionnaire. *Journal of Educational Research*, 1978, 71, 320–324.

1597. WILSON, S., & KENNARD, D. The extraverting effect of treatment in a therapeutic community for drug abusers. *British Journal of Psychiatry*, 1978, 132, 296–299.

1598. WILSON, S., & MANDELBROTE, B. Drug rehabilitation and criminality. *British Journal of Criminology*, 1978, 18, 381–386.

1599. BARNES, G. E. The alcoholic personality: A reanalysis of the literature. *Journal of Studies on Alcohol*, 1979, 40, 571–634.

1600. BATLIS, N. C., & GREEN, P. C. Leadership style emphasis and related personality attributes. *Psychological Reports*, 1979, 44, 587–592.

1601. BLEDSOE, J. C. Personality characteristics differentiating internal and external college women. *Journal of Psychology*, 1979, 103, 81–86.

1602. BOLTON, B. The relationship between two personality questionnaires: The Mini-Mult and the 16PF-E. *Journal of Personality Assessment*, 1979, 43, 289–292.

1603. BOLTON, B. The Tennessee Self-Concept Scale and the Normal Personality Sphere (16PF). *Journal of Personality Assessment*, 1979, 43, 608–613.

1604. BOLTON, B., & RENFROW, N. E. Personality characteristics associated with aerobic exercise in adult females. *Journal of Personality Assessment*, 1979, 43, 504–508.

1605. BONAPORTE, B. H. Ego defensiveness, open–closed mindedness, and nurses' attitude toward culturally different patients. *Nursing Research*, 1979, 28, 166–172.

1606. BRADY, C. A., PACK, J., & BABICH, J. M. Effects of three intake procedures on mothers of disturbed children. *Psychological Reports*, 1979, 44, 459–466.

1607. BRUCHON-SCHWEITZER, M. Dimensionality of body perception and personality. *Perceptual & Motor Skills*, 1979, 48, 840–842.

1608. BUBENZER, D. L., ZARSKI, J. J., & WALTER, D. A. Measuring social interest: A validation study. *Journal of Individual Psychology*, 1979, 35, 202–213.

1609. BURDSAL, C., & BOLTON, B. An item factoring of 16PF-E: Further evidence concerning Cattell's Normal Personality Sphere. *Journal of General Psychology*, 1979, 100, 103–109.

1610. ELMORE, R. F., & ELLETT, C. D. A canonical analysis of personality characteristics, personal and teaching practices beliefs, and dogmatism of beginning teacher education students. *Journal of Experimental Education*, 1979, 47, 112–117.

1611. FARGE, E. J., HARTUNG, G. H., & BORLAND, C. M. Runners and meditators: A comparison of personality profiles. *Journal of Personality Assessment*, 1979, 43, 501–503.

1612. FILSINGER, E. E., & STILWELL, S. R. Empirically derived personality types among male and female college students. *Journal of Psychology*, 1979, 102, 275–287.

1613. GILL, R. W. T. The in-tray (in–basket) exercise as a measure of management potential. *Journal of Occupational Psychology*, 1979, 52, 185–197.

1614. GILLIS, J. S., & LEE, D. C. Relationships between the 16PF, GPP, and GPI. *Educational & Psychological Measurement*, 1979, 39, 7–12.

1615. HART, L. S. A 16PF study of men and women alcoholics. *Journal of Studies of Alcohol*, 1979, 40, 1082–1084.

1616. HILL, K. A., & JUNUS, F. Individual differences in concept learning of painting styles. *Perceptual & Motor Skills*, 1979, 49, 255–261.

1617. HOOVER, T. Performance prediction of students in teacher education. *Journal of Experimental Education*, 1979, 47, 192–195.

1618. HUDGINS, E. W. Examining the effectiveness of affective education. *Psychology in the Schools*, 1979, 16, 581–585.

1619. JONES, R. D., & WEINHOUSE, S. Running as self therapy. *Journal of Sports Medicine & Physical Fitness*, 1979, 19, 397–404.

1620. KAPPES, B. M., & PARISH, T. S. The Personal Attribute Inventory: A measure of self-concepts and personality profiles. *Educational & Psychological Measurement*, 1979, 39, 955–958.

1621. KAPUR, R. L., & PANDURANGI, A. K. A comparative study of reactive psychosis and acute psychosis without precipitating stress. *British Journal of Psychiatry*, 1979, 135, 544–550.

1622. KENNARD, D., & WILSON, S. The modification of personality disturbance in a therapeutic commmunity for drug abusers. *British Journal of Medical Psychology*, 1979, 52, 215–221.

1623. LEVY, M. F., REICHMAN, W., & HERRINGTON, S. Congruence between personality and job characteristics in alcoholics and nonalcoholics. *Journal of Social Psychology*, 1979, 107, 213–217.

1624. NEUFELDT, D. E., & HOLMES, C. B. Relationship between personality traits and fear of death. *Psychological Reports*, 1979, 45, 907–910.

1625. NOERAGER, J. P. An assessment of CAD-A personality instrument developed specifically for marketing research. *Journal of Marketing Research*, 1979, 16, 53–59.

1626. OMIZO, M. M., MORROW, J. R., WARD, G. R., DISCH, J. G., & MICHAEL, W. B. The validity of a composite of nineteen personality variables in differentiating between American world class Olympic contenders and undergraduate education majors. *Educational & Psychological Measurement*, 1979, 39, 977–983.

1627. PERSINGER, B. D., JR., & HOLMES, C. B. The effects of personality traits on Memory–For–Designs performance. *Journal of Clinical Psychology*, 1979, 35, 798–801.

1628. PIPER, W. E., DOAN, B. D., EDWARDS, E. M., & JONES, B. D. Cotherapy behavior, group therapy process, and treatment outcome. *Journal of Consulting & Clinical Psychology*, 1979, 47, 1081–1089.

1629. RENFROW, N. E., & BOLTON, B. Personality characteristics associated with aerobic exercise in adult males. *Journal of Personality Assessment*, 1979, 43, 261–266.

1630. SCHERER, C. Effects of early field experience on student teachers' self–concepts and performance. *Journal of Experimental Education*, 1979, 47, 208–214.

1631. SHELTON, J., & HARRIS, T. L. Personality characteristics of art students. *Psychological Reports*, 1979, 44, 949–950.

1632. SIMONO, R. B., DAWSON, G., & MURPHY, H. Factor M as a correlate of physical fitness: Imagination or just more energy. *Journal of Clinical Psychology*, 1979, 35, 309–311.

1633. SLEDGE, W. H., & BOYDSTUN, J. A. Vasovagal syncope in aircrew. Psychosocial aspects. *Journal of Nervous & Mental Disease*, 1979, 167, 114–124.

1634. STAMP, P. Girls and mathematics: Parental variables. *British Journal of Educational Psychology*, 1979, 49, 39–50.

1635. STAR, B., CLARK, C. G., GOETZ, K. M., & O'MALIA, L. Psychosocial aspects of wife battering. *Social Casework*, 1979, 8, 479–487.

1636. TOBACYK, J., BAILEY, L., & MYERS, H. Preference for paintings and personality traits. *Psychological Reports*, 1979, 45, 787–793.

1637. WARD, G. R., MORROW, J. R., & OMIZO, M. The prediction of performance of Olympic athletes in discus, hammer, javelin, and shotput from measures of personality characteristics. *Educational & Psychological Measurement*, 1979, 39, 197–201.

1638. WATSON, C. G., BURKE, M., & PLEMEL, D. The relationship of personality style to abstract thinking deficits in schizophrenia. *Journal of Clinical Psychology*, 1979, 35, 247–249.

1639. WEAVER, H. M., HOUNSHELL, P. B., & COBLE, C. B. Effects of science methods courses with and without field experience on attitudes of preservice elementary teachers. *Science Education*, 1979, 63, 655–664.

1640. WORMITH, J. S., & HASENPUSCH, B. Multidimensional measurement of delayed gratification preference with incarcerated offenders. *Journal of Clinical Psychology*, 1979, 35, 218–225.

1641. YARBER, W. L., & KAPLAN, R. Personality comparisons of college students reporting previous sexually transmissible disease infection and students never infected. *Journal of the American College Health Association*, 1979, 27, 307–310.

1642. ZAK, I., MEIR, E. I., & KRAEMER, R. The common space of personality traits and vocational interests. *Journal of Personality Assessment*, 1979, 43, 424–428.

1643. BERNARD, L. C. Multivariate analysis of new sex role formulations and personality. *Journal of Personality & Social Psychology*, 1980, 38, 323–336.

1644. BOLTON, B. Comments on "Comments on the reliability of a personality questionnaire used in physical education and sport research". *Psychological Reports*, 1980, 46, 1133–1134.

1645. BOLTON, B. Personality (16PF) correlates of WAIS scales: A replication. *Applied Psychological Measurement*, 1980, 4, 399–401.

1646. BROWN, R. A. Personality measure in gamma and delta alcoholics: A brief note. *Journal of Clinical Psychology*, 1980, 36, 345–346.

1647. BURDSAL, C., & BUEL, C. L. A short term community based early stage intervention program for behavior problem youth. *Journal of Clinical Psychology*, 1980, 36, 226–241.

1648. BURKE, R. J., & WEIR, T. Personality, value and behavioral correlates of the type A individual. *Psychological Reports*, 1980, 46, 171–181.

1649. BUSBY, K., & DE KONINCK, J. Short–term effects of strategies for self–regulation on personality dimensions and dream content. *Perceptual & Motor Skills*, 1980, 50, 751–765.

1650. COSTA, P. T., JR., & MCCRAE, R. R. Influence of extraversion and neuroticism on subjective well–being: Happy and unhappy people. *Journal of Personality & Social Psychology*, 1980 38, 668–678.

1651. ELLINGTON, J. E., MARSH, L. A., & CRITELLI, J. W. Personality characteristics of women with masculine names. *Journal of Social Psychology*, 1980, 111, 211–218.

1652. ELMORE, R. F., & ELLETT, C. D. Personality characteristics, beliefs systems, and cognitive performance of exiting teacher education students. *Journal of Experimental Education*, 1980, 48, 104–109.

1653. ELSAYED, M., ISMAIL, A. H., & YOUNG, R. J. Intellectual differences of adult men related to age and physical fitness before and after an exercise program. *Journal of Gerontology*, 1980, 35, 383–387.

1654. FLOCKEN, J. M. Personality characteristics of communicative disorders graduate students. *ASHA*, 1980, 22, 7–16.

1655. GOLDBERG, L. R., NORMAN, W. T., & SCHWARTZ, E. The comparative validity of questionnaire data (16PF scales) and objective test data (O-A Battery) in predicting five peer–rating criteria. *Applied Psychological Measurement*, 1980, 4, 183–194.

1656. GRAHAM, F. M., & GUTSCH, K. U. Alcoholism: Establishing a baseline criterion against which to measure therapeutic effectiveness. *Southern Journal of Educational Research*, 1980, 14, 33–45.

1657. HART, L. S., & STUELAND, D. Classifying women alcoholics by Cattell's 16PF: A preliminary investigation of an alcoholic typology. *Journal of Studies on Alcohol*, 1980, 41, 911–921.

1658. IMADA, A. S., FLETCHER, C., & DALESSIO, A. Individual correlates of an occupational stereotype: A reexamination of the stereotype of accountants. *Journal of Applied Psychology*, 1980, 65, 436–439.

1659. KARSON, M. Is aesthetic judgment impaired by neuroticism. *Journal of Personality Assessment*, 1980, 44, 499–506.

1660. MARSHALL, D. D. A caution on the use of semantic dimension personality self–ratings as sufficient self–reports. *Measurement & Evaluation in Guidance*, 1980, 13, 90–94.

1661. MCCRAE, R. R., & COSTA, P. T., JR. Openness to experience and ego level in Loevinger's Sentence Completion Test: Dispositional contributions to developmental models of personality. *Journal of Personality & Social Psychology*, 1980, 39, 1179–1190.

1662. MITCHELL, R. B. An investigation of job satisfaction among correspondence secretaries and the impact of supervision. *Delta Pi Epsilon Journal*, 1980, 22, 32–40.

1663. MULLINS, D., & HAYS, J. R. Personality characteristics and employability of mentally retarded adults. *Psychological Reports*, 1980, 47, 1063–1067.

1664. PRINS, D., MANDELKORN, T., & CERF, F. A. Principal and differential effects of haloperidol and placebo treatments upon speech disfluencies in stutterers. *Journal of Speech & Hearing Research*, 1980, 23, 614–629.

1665. SHANNON, L. R., & HOUSTON, S. Personality factors of college students from two different enrollment periods. *Journal of Experimental Education*, 1980, 48, 302–306.

1666. SIERACKI, S., & MELLINGER, J. Religious correlates of Hogan's survey of ethical attitudes. *Psychological Reports*, 1980, 46, 267–276.

1667. SLADE, P., & JENNER, F. A. Attitudes to female roles, aspects of menstruation and complaining of menstrual symptoms. *British Journal of Social & Clinical Psychology*, 1980, 19, 109–113.

1668. SMART, R., WILTON, K., & KEELING, B. Teacher factors and special class placement. *Journal of Special Education*, 1980, 14, 217–229.

1669. TWA, R. J., & GREENE, M. Prediction of success in student teaching as a criterion for selection in teacher education programs. *Alberta Journal of Educational Research*, 1980, 26, 1–13.

1670. WARD, G. R., PORTER, S., & OMIZO, M. M. Personality characteristics and motivational needs of preservice and inservice teachers: Implications for practice. *Journal of Teaching & Learning*, 1980, 5, 38–47.

1671. WENDT, J. C., WARD, G. R., & JACKSON, A. S. Personality determinants of Herzberg's conceptualization of the maintenance–motivator. *Journal of Teaching & Learning*, 1980, 5, 26–38.

1672. WETZEL, R. D., CLONINGER, C. R., HONG, B., & REICH, T. Personality as a subclinical expression of the affective disorders. *Comprehensive Psychiatry*, 1980, 21, 197–205.

1673. WHITAKER, D. B. Personality traits as manifested in game behavior. *Perceptual & Motor Skills*, 1980, 51, 870.

1674. WIEBE, K. F., & FLECK, J. R. Personality correlates of intrinsic, extrinsic, and nonreligious orientations. *Journal of Psychology*, 1980, 105, 181–187.

1675. YOUNG, M., & REEVE, T. G. Discriminant analysis of personality and body–image factors of females differing in percent body fat. *Perceptual & Motor Skills*, 1980, 50, 547–552.

1676. AITKEN, R. C. B., LISTER, J. A., & MAIN, C. J. Identification of features associated with flying phobia in aircrew. *British Journal of Psychiatry*, 1981, 139, 38–42.

1677. CAMPAGNA, W. D., & O'TOOLE, J. J. A comparison of the personality profiles of Roman Catholic and male Protestant seminarians. *Counseling & Values*, 1981, 26, 62–67.

1678. DEAN, R. S., & GARABEDIAN, A. A. The personality characteristics of the rigid learner. *Journal of School Psychology*, 1981, 19, 143–151.

1679. DEAN, R. S., & GARABEDIAN, A. A. Personality dimensions concomitant with adolescents' perceived body weight. *Journal of Clinical Child Psychology*, 1981, 10, 86–89.

1680. DEFIORE, R. M., KRAMER, T. J., & MUNZ, D. C. Predictors of motivation for job changing: Maintenance versus motivation seekers. *Perceptual & Motor Skills*, 1981, 52, 967–973.

1681. DIXON, P. N., PARR, G. D., & ELIAS, S. F. Personality related to attitudes toward a behavior modification training activity. *College Student Journal*, 1981, 15, 69–73.

1682. DOWD, R., & INNES, J. M. Sport and personality: Effects of type of sport and level of competition. *Perceptual & Motor Skills*, 1981, 53, 79–89.

1683. ELLIOTT, A. G. P. Some implications of lie scale scores in real–life selection. *Journal of Occupational Psychology*, 1981, 54, 9–16.

1684. FOX, S., HABOUCHA, S., & DINUR, Y. The predictive validity of the Sixteen Personality Factor Questionnaire relative to three independent criterion measures of military performance. *Educational & Psychological Measurement*, 1981, 41, 515–521.

1685. LAWLOR, M., & COCHRAN, L. Does invalidation produce loose construing? *British Journal of Medical Psychology*, 1981, 54, 41–50.

1686. LEVY, M. F., REICHMAN, W., & HERRINGTON, S. Abstinent alcoholics' adjustment to work. *Journal of Studies on Alcohol*, 1981, 42, 529–532.

1687. MACBRIDE, A., LANCEE, W., & FREEMAN, S. J. J. The psychosocial impact of a labour dispute. *Journal of Occupational Psychology*, 1981, 54, 125–133.

1688. MCGURK, B. J., MCEWAN, A. W., & GRAHAM, F. Personality types and recidivism among young delinquents. *British Journal of Criminology*, 1981, 21, 159–165.

1689. MILGRAM, R. M., & ARAD, R. Ideational fluency as a predictor of original problem solving. *Journal of Educational Psychology*, 1981, 73, 568–572.

1690. MILONE, M. N., JR., COLLINS, J. L., & ASHCROFT, S. C. Personality characteristics of counselor trainees preparing for work with deaf persons. *Rehabilitation Counseling Bulletin*, 1981, 24, 354–361.

1691. PERSINGER, B. D., JR., & HOLMES, C. B. Extreme constriction of figure size as a personality trait indicator on Memory–For–Designs. *Perceptual & Motor Skills*, 1981, 53, 216–218.

1692. RAUSTE–VON WRIGHT, M., VON WRIGHT, J., & FRANKENHAEUSER, M. Relationships between sex–related psychological characteristics during adolescence and cate cholamine excretion during achievement stress. *Psychophysiology*, 1981, 18, 362–370.

1693. RENFROW, N. E., & BOLTON, B. Physiological and psychological characteristics associated with women's participation in intercollegiate athletics. *Perceptual & Motor Skills*, 1981, 53, 90.
1694. SHELDON, A. R., COCHRANE, J., VACHON, M. L. S., LYALL, W. A. L., ROGERS, J., & FREEMAN, S. J. J. A psychosocial analysis of risk of psychological impairment following bereavement. *Journal of Nervous & Mental Disease*, 1981, 169, 253–255.
1695. SQUIER, R. W., & MEW, J. R. C. The relationship betwen facial structure and personality characteristics. *British Journal of Social Psychology*, 1981, 20, 151–160.
1696. TOBACYK, J., MYERS, H., & BAILEY, L. Preference for photographs and personality traits. *Perceptual & Motor Skills*, 1981, 52, 763–766.
1697. VALLIANT, P. M., SIMPSON–HOUSLEY, P., & McKELVIE, S. J. Personality in athletic and non–athletic college groups. *Perceptual & Motor Skills*, 1981, 52, 963–966.

[2209]

Sketches. Grades 9 and over; 1967; "divergent production of figural units" or "visual-figural fluency"; S. Gardner, A. Gershon, P. R. Merrifield, and J. P. Guilford; Sheridan Psychological Services, Inc.*

See T2:581 (1 reference).

[2210]

★**Skills and Attributes Inventory.** Job incumbents and superiors; 1976–79; SAI; 13 scores: general functioning intelligence, visual acuity, visual and coordination skills, physical coordination, mechanical skills, graphic clerical skills, general clerical skills, leadership ability, tolerance in interpersonal relations, organization identification, conscientiousness and reliability, efficiency under stress, solitary work; Melany E. Baehr and Robert E. Penny III (manual); Human Resources Center, University of Chicago.*

[2211]

★**Skills for Independent Living.** Educable mentally retarded secondary school students and low achieving nonretarded secondary school students; 1981; SIL; resource kit based on objectives tested in the *Social and Prevocational Information Battery* and the *Tests for Everyday Living*; life skills in 9 areas: purchasing habits, budgeting, banking, job search skills, job-related behavior, home management, health care, hygiene and grooming, functional signs; Larry K. Irvin, Andrew S. Halpern, and Jacqueline D. Becklund; CTB/McGraw-Hill.*

[2212]

★**Skills Inventory For Parents.** Parents of handicapped or developmentally delayed children; 1978; SIP; "changes in parental skills as a result of both group and individualized programming in a home-based prescriptive infant program"; 7 skill areas: parental involvement with the program as a whole, home visits and prescriptions, teaching skills, encouragement of language development, physical care, environment, broker-advocacy skills; Jean B. Waltrip; Child Development Resources.*

[2213]

Sklar Aphasia Scale, Revised 1973. Brain damaged adults; 1966–73; SAS; 5 scores: auditory decoding, visual decoding, oral encoding, graphic encoding, total; Maurice Sklar; Western Psychological Services.*

For additional information and a review by Manfred J. Meier, see 8:976 (1 reference); for reviews by Arthur L. Benton and Daniel R. Boone of the original edition, see 7:970; see also P:247 (2 references).

REFERENCES

1–2. See P:247.
3. See 8:976.
4. COHEN, R., ENGEL, D., KELTER, S., LIST, G., & STROHNER, H. Validity of the Sklar Aphasia Scale. *Journal of Speech & Hearing Research*, 1977, 20, 146–154.

[2214]

★**Slingerland Screening Tests for Identifying Children with Specific Language Disability.** Grades 1–beginning of 2, 2–beginning of 3, 3–4, 5–6; 1962–80; Beth H. Slingerland; Educators Publishing Service, Inc.*

REFERENCES

1. BURNS, W. J., & BURNS, K. A. The Slingerland Screening Tests: Local norms. *Journal of Learning Disabilities*, 1977, 10, 450–454.
2. DINERO, T. E., DONAH, C. H., & LARSON, G. L. The Slingerland Screening Tests for Identifying Children with Specific Language Disability: Screening for learning disabilities in first grade. *Perceptual & Motor Skills*, 1979, 49, 971–978.

[2215]

Sloan Achromatopsia Test. Individuals suspected of total color blindness; 1955–61; Louise L. Sloan; Munsell Color Co.*

[2216]

Slosson Drawing Coordination Test for Children and Adults. Ages 1.5 and over; 1962–67; SDCT; brain dysfunction and perceptual disorders; Richard L. Slosson; Slosson Educational Publications, Inc.*

For additional information and reviews by Arthur L. Benton and James C. Reed, see 7:140.

REFERENCES

1. RUSSELL, H. L., & CARTER, J. L. Biofeedback training with children: Consultation, questions, applications and alternatives. *Journal of Clinical Child Psychology*, 1978, 7, 23–25.

[2217]

*****Slosson Intelligence Test.** Ages 2 weeks and over; 1961–81; SIT; based in part upon *Stanford-Binet Intelligence Scale, Third Revision* and *Gesell Developmental Schedules*; 1981 edition includes 1981 norms tables, sections on updated validity, independent sampling, other research findings, and an extended bibliography, no change in test items; Richard L. Slosson; Slosson Educational Publications, Inc.*

For additional information, see 8:227 (62 references); see also T2:524 (12 references); for reviews by Philip Himelstein and Jane V. Hunt, see 7:424 (31 references).

REFERENCES

1–31. See 7:424.
32–43. See T2:524.
44–105. See 8:227.
106. LOPATA, D. J., & PASNAK, R. Accelerated conservation acquisition and IQ gains by blind children. *Genetic Psychology Monographs*, 1976, 93, 3–25.
107. BALDWIN, A. Y. Tests can underpredict: A case study. *Phi Delta Kappan*, 1977, 58, 620–621.
108. CAGNEY, M. A. Children's ability to understand standard English and black dialect. *Reading Teacher*, 1977, 30, 607–610.
109. COLARUSSO, R., McLESKEY, J., & GILL, S. H. Use of the Peabody Picture Vocabulary Test and the Slosson Intelligence Test with urban black kindergarten children. *Journal of Special Education*, 1977, 11, 427–432.
110. COVIN, T. M. Comparison of SIT and WISC-R IQs among special education candidates. *Psychology in the Schools*, 1977, 14, 19–23.
111. COVIN, T. M. Relationship of the SIT and PPVT to the WISC–R. *Journal of School Psychology*, 1977, 15, 259–260.
112. ESLER, W. K., MIDGETT, J., & BIRD, R. C. Elementary science materials and the exceptional child. *Science Education*, 1977, 61, 181–184.

113. LEBRON-RODRIGUEZ, D. E., & PASNAK, R. Induction of the intellectual gains in blind children. *Journal of Experimental Child Psychology*, 1977, 24, 505–515.

114. MARTIN, J. D., BLAIR, G. E., STOKES, E. H., & LESTER, E. H. A validity and reliability study of the Slosson Intelligence Test and the Shipley Institute of Living Scale. *Educational & Psychological Measurement*, 1977, 37, 1107–1110.

115. MARTIN, J. D., & KIDWELL, J. C. Intercorrelations of the Wechsler Intelligence Scale for Children–Revised, the Slosson Intelligence Test, and the National Educational Development Test. *Educational & Psychological Measurement*, 1977, 37, 1117–1120.

116. PRESTON, M. S., GUTHRIE, J. T., KIRSCH, I., GERTMAN, D., & CHILDS, B. VERs in normal and disabled adult readers. *Psychophysiology*, 1977, 14, 8–14.

117. ROGERS, S. Characteristics of the cognitive development of profoundly retarded children. *Child Development*, 1977, 48, 837–843.

118. STERNBERG, L., EPSTEIN, M. H., & ADAMS, D. Performance characteristics of retarded and normal students on pattern recognition tasks. *Contemporary Educational Psychology*, 1977, 2, 209–218.

119. TRIVEDI, A. A comparison of three intelligence tests for the assessment of mental retardation. *Journal of Mental Deficiency Research*, 1977, 21, 289–297.

120. ULLMAN, D. G. Children's lateral preference patterns: Frequency and relationships with achievement and intelligence. *Journal of School Psychology*, 1977, 15, 36–43.

121. WONG, B., WONG, R., & FOTH, D. Recall and clustering of verbal materials among normal and poor readers. *Bulletin of the Psychonomic Society*, 1977, 10, 375–378.

122. BURKE, J., LEWY, R., WILLIAMS, J. D., BREKKE, B., HARLOW, S. D., & PETERSON, W. The effects of three experimental programs on reading readiness. *Journal of Learning Disabilities*, 1978, 11, 515–518.

123. CLARK, A., BREKKE, B., & WILLIAMS, J. Conservation of weight with adolescents and young people. *Journal of Teaching & Learning: The University of North Dakota*, 1978, 4, 3–14.

124. FLYNN, T. M., & FLYNN, L. A. Evaluation of the predictive ability of five screening measures administered during kindergarten. *Journal of Experimental Education*, 1978, 46, 65–70.

125. HALE, R. L., DOUGLAS, B., CUMMINS, A., RITTGARN, G., BREED, B., & DABBERT, D. The Slosson as a predictor of Wide Range Achievement Test performance. *Psychology in the Schools*, 1978, 15, 507–509.

126. HARPER, G. F., GUIDUBALDI, J., & KEHLE, T. J. Is academic achievement related to classroom behavior? *Elementary School Journal*, 1978, 78, 203–207.

127. HUG, N., BARCLAY, A., COLLINS, H., & LAMP, R. Validity and factor structure of the preschool attainment record in Head Start children. *Journal of Psychology*, 1978, 99, 71–74.

128. JENKINS, J. R., & PANY, D. Standardized achievement tests: How useful for special education? *Exceptional Children*, 1978, 44, 448–453.

129. KLEIN, A. E. The reliability and predictive validity of the Slosson Intelligence Test for pre-kindergarten pupils. *Educational & Psychological Measurement*, 1978, 38, 1211–1217.

130. LARSON, B. A. Use of the motorvator in improving gross–motor coordination, visual perception and IQ scores: A pilot study. *Journal of Music Therapy*, 1978, 15, 145–149.

131. MYERS, J. A. Compressed speech increases learning efficiency. *Education of the Visually Handicapped*, 1978, 10, 56–64.

132. OAKLAND, T. Predictive validity of readiness tests for middle and lower socioeconomic status Anglo, Black, and Mexican American children. *Journal of Educational Psychology*, 1978, 70, 574–582.

133. RICHMOND, B. O., & WAITS, C. Special education–Who needs it? *Exceptional Children*, 1978, 44, 279–280.

134. ROTATORI, A. F., & EPSTEIN, M. The Slosson Intelligence Test as a quick screening test of mental ability with profoundly and severely retarded children. *Psychological Reports*, 1978, 42, 1117–1118.

135. RUSSELL, H. L., & CARTER, J. L. Biofeedback training with children: Consultation, questions, applications and alternatives. *Journal of Clinical Child Psychology*, 1978, 7, 23–25.

136. SHIMONI, N. A case study approach to delivering and evaluating services by a school psychologist. *Journal of School Psychology*, 1978, 16, 257–264.

137. WONG, B. The effects of directive cues on the organization of memory and recall in good and poor readers. *Journal of Educational Research*, 1978, 72, 32–38.

138. BAUM, D. D. An investigation of the predictive validity of the Slosson Intelligence Test with learning disabled kindergarten children. *Educational & Psychological Measurement*, 1979, 39, 1067–1072.

139. BAUM, D. D., & KELLY, T. J. The validity of the Slosson Intelligence Test with learning disabled kindergartners. *Journal of Learning Disabilities*, 1979, 12, 268–270.

140. BLAHA, J., FAWAZ, N., & WALLBROWN, F. H. Information processing components of Koppitz Errors on the Bender Visual–Motor Gestalt Test. *Journal of Clinical Psychology*, 1979, 35, 784–790.

141. COLARUSSO, R. P., MATHIS, G., & SHESSEL, D. Teacher effectiveness in identifying high–risk kindergarten children. *Journal of Learning Disabilities*, 1979, 12, 684–686.

142. FUDALA, J. B. Differential evaluation of students with the S.I.T. *Academic Therapy*, 1979, 15, 61–64.

143. GARDNER, L. I., NEU, R. L., SHAH, R. S., PINTO, W., JR., CO, M., LEHR, E. R., & BARG, G. A. Family with three apparently balanced t(3;15)(p27;q22) translocation carriers. *American Journal of Diseases of Children*, 1979, 133, 1002–1005.

144. HORODEZKY, B. Comparative difficulty of beginning reading vocabulary: Set II. *Alberta Journal of Educational Research*, 1979, 25, 259–263.

145. KARNES, F. A., & BROWN, K. E. Comparison of the SIT with the WISC-R for gifted students. *Psychology in the Schools*, 1979, 16, 478–482.

146. LITCHER, J. H., ROBERGE, L. P., MEYER, M., & KARNES, L. R. Alternative learning experiences for high–risk, first–grade students. *Journal of Learning Disabilities*, 1979, 12, 686–688.

147. LOWRANCE, D., & ANDERSON, H. N. A comparison of the Slosson Intelligence Test and the WISC-R with elementary school children. *Psychology in the Schools*, 1979, 16, 361–364.

148. MARTIN, J. D., BLAIR, G. E., & VICKERS, D. M. Correlation of the Slosson Intelligence Test with the California Short–Form Test of Mental Maturity and the Shipley Institute of Living Scale. *Educational & Psychological Measurement*, 1979, 39, 193–196.

149. MIZE, J. M., CALLAWAY, B., & SMITH, J. W. Comparison of reading disabled children's scores on the WISC-R, Peabody Picture Vocabulary Test, and Slosson Intelligence Test. *Psychology in the Schools*, 1979, 16, 356–358.

150. REYNOLDS, W. M. A caution against the use of the Slosson Intelligence Test in the diagnosis of mental retardation. *Psychology in the Schools*, 1979, 16, 77–79.

151. ROTATORI, A. F., SEDLACK, B., & FREAGON, S. Usefulness of the Slosson Intelligence Test with severely and profoundly retarded children. *Perceptual & Motor Skills*, 1979, 48, 334.

152. SCHOOLER, D. L., & ANDERSON, R. L. Race differences on the Developmental Test of Visual–Motor Integration, the Slosson Intelligence Test, and the ABC Inventory. *Psychology in the Schools*, 1979, 16, 453–456.

153. SPITZ, H. H., & BYRNES, M. M. Developmental progression of performance on the tower of Hanoi problem. *Bulletin of the Psychonomic Society*, 1979, 14, 379–381.

154. SWANSON, L. Auditory recall of conceptually, phonetically, and linguistically similar words by normal and learning–disabled children. *Journal of Special Education*, 1979, 13, 63–67.

155. THOMPSON, H. J., ROBERTS, R. N., & WHIDDON, M. F. Inadequacy of brief IQ measures in the classification of mentally retarded prisoners. *American Journal of Mental Deficiency*, 1979, 83, 416–417.

156. VANCE, H. B., LEWIS, R., & DEBELL, S. Correlations of the Wechsler Intelligence Scale for Children-Revised, Peabody Picture Vocabulary Test, and Slosson Intelligence Test for a group of learning disabled students. *Psychology in the Schools*, 1979, 44, 735–738.

157. ABROMS, K. I., & GOLLIN, J. B. Developmental study of gifted preschool children and measures of psychosocial giftedness. *Exceptional Children*, 1980, 46, 334–341.

158. BOHNING, G. Item analysis of Slosson Intelligence Test: A review. *Psychology in the Schools*, 1980, 17, 339.

159. BOOK, R. M. Identification of educationally at–risk children during the kindergarten year: A four-year follow-up study of group test performance. *Psychology in the Schools*, 1980, 17, 153–158.

160. CASSIDY, J., & VUKELICH, C. Do the gifted read early? *Reading Teacher*, 1980, 33, 578–582.

161. CIANFLONE, R., & ZULLO, T. G. The relationship of an early measure of intelligence to the ability to learn sight vocabulary words and to later reading achievement. *Educational & Psychological Measurement*, 1980, 40, 1197–1200.

162. COLARUSSO, R., GILL, S., PLANKENHORN, A., & BROOKS, R. Predicting first-grade achievement through formal testing of 5-year-old high-risk children. *Journal of Special Education*, 1980, 14, 355–363.

163. COLEMAN, M., BROWN, G., & GANONG, L. A comparison of PPVT and SIT scores of young children. *Psychology in the Schools*, 1980, 17, 178–180.

164. COOK, J. E., NOLAN, G. A., & ZANOTTI, R. J. Treating auditory perception problems: The NIM helps. *Academic Therapy*, 1980, 15, 473–481.

165. CROFOOT, M. J., & BENNETT, T. S. A comparison of three screening tests and the WISC–R in special education evaluations. *Psychology in the Schools*, 1980, 17, 474–478.

166. DIRKS, J., WESSELS, K., QUARFOTH, J., & QUENON, B. Can short–form WISC-R IQ tests identify children with high full scale IQ? *Psychology in the Schools*, 1980, 17, 40–46.

167. EICH, W. F. Use of brief intelligence tests administered in pediatric practice. *Psychological Reports*, 1980, 46, 551–554.

168. FOX, R., & ROTATORI, A. F. Incidental learning in mildly retarded children. *Journal of General Psychology*, 1980, 102, 121–125.

169. GRAY, S. W., & RUTTLE, K. The family-oriented home visiting program: A longitudinal study. *Genetic Psychology Monographs*, 1980, 102, 299-316.
170. LITROWNIK, A. J., & FREITAS, J. L. Self-monitoring in moderately retarded adolescents: Reactivity and accuracy as a function of valence. *Behavior Therapy*, 1980, 11, 245-255.
171. MCCLURE, J., KALK, M., & KEENAN, V. Use of grammatical morphemes by beginning readers. *Journal of Learning Disabilities*, 1980, 13, 34-39.
172. PFOUTS, J. H. Birth order, age-spacing, IQ differences, and family relations. *Journal of Marriage & the Family*, 1980, 42, 517-531.
173. POPE, J., LEHRER, B., & STEVENS, J. A multiphasic reading screening procedure. *Journal of Learning Disabilities*, 1980, 13, 47-51.
174. RUST, J. O., & LOSE, B. D. Screening for giftedness with the Slosson and the Scale for Rating Behavioral Characteristics of Superior Students. *Psychology in the Schools*, 1980, 17, 446-451.
175. SMART, R., WILTON, K., & KEELING, B. Teacher factors and special class placement. *Journal of Special Education*, 1980, 14, 217-229.
176. SMITH, S., BRUNSON, B., & NYMAN, B. WAIS and Slosson IQs of mentally retarded adults. *Psychological Reports*, 1980, 46, 870.
177. TESKA, J. A., & STONEBURNER, R. L. The concept and practice of second-level screening. *Psychology in the Schools*, 1980, 17, 192-195.
178. ZOREF, L., & WILLIAMS, P. A look at content bias in IQ tests. *Journal of Educational Measurement*, 1980, 17, 313-322.
179. BARAHOL, R. M., WATERMAN, J., & MARTIN, H. P. The social cognitive development of abused children. *Journal of Consulting & Clinical Psychology*, 1981, 49, 508-516.
180. KATZ, R. B., SHANKWEILER, D., & LIBERMAN, I. Y. Memory for item order and phonetic recoding in the beginning reader. *Journal of Experimental Child Psychology*, 1981, 32, 474-484.
181. MARTIN, J. D., BLAIR, G. E., SADOWSKI, C., & WHEELER, K. J. Intercorrelations among the Slosson Intelligence Test, the Shipley-Institute of Living Scale, and the intellectual efficiency scale of the California Psychological Inventory. *Educational & Psychological Measurement*, 1981, 41, 595-598.
182. MILLER, J. W., & MCKENNA, M. C. Disabled readers: Their intellectual and perceptual capacities at differing ages. *Perceptual & Motor Skills*, 1981, 52, 467-472.
183. OBRZUT, J. E., BOLOCOFSKY, D. N., HEATH, C. P., & JONES, J. J. An investigation of the DIAL as a pre-kindergarten screening instrument. *Educational & Psychological Measurement*, 1981, 41, 1231-1241.
184. POWELL, G., MOORE, D., & CALLAWAY, B. A concurrent validity study of the Woodcock Word Comprehension Test. *Psychology in the Schools*, 1981, 18, 24-27.
185. VELLUTINO, F. R., SCANLON, D. M., DE SETTO, L., & PRUZEK, R. M. Developmental trends in the salience of meaning versus structural attributes of written words. *Psychological Research*, 1981, 43, 131-153.
186. ZEKULIN-HARTLEY, X. Y. Hemispheric asymmetry in Down's syndrome children. *Canadian Journal of Behavioural Science*, 1981, 13, 210-217.
187. ZIFCAK, M. Phonological awareness and reading acquisition. *Contemporary Educational Psychology*, 1981, 6, 117-126.

[2218]

Slosson Oral Reading Test. Grades 1-8 and high school; 1963; SORT; no manual; Richard L. Slosson; Slosson Educational Publications, Inc.*

See T2:1688 (5 references) and 6:844.

REFERENCES

1-5. See T2:1688.
6. AYRES, A. J. Dichotic listening performance in learning-disabled children. *American Journal of Occupational Therapy*, 1977, 31, 441-446.
7. DOEHRING, D. G., & HOSHKO, I. M. Classification of reading problems by the Q-technique of factor analysis. *Cortex*, 1977, 13, 281-294.
8. RYAN, E. B., MCNAMARA, S. R., & KENNEY, M. Linguistic awareness and reading performance among beginning readers. *Journal of Reading Behavior*, 1977, 9, 399-400.
9. AYRES, A. J. Learning disabilities and the vestibular system. *Journal of Learning Disabilities*, 1978, 11, 18-29.
10. DOEHRING, D. G., BONNYCASTLE, D. E., & LING, A. H. Rapid reading skills of integrated hearing-impaired children. *Volta Review*, 1978, 80, 399-409.
11. OAKLAND, T. Predictive validity of readiness tests for middle and lower socioeconomic status Anglo, Black, and Mexican American children. *Journal of Educational Psychology*, 1978, 70, 574-582.
12. BROWNS, F. Beginning reading instruction with hearing-impaired children. *Volta Review*, 1979, 81, 100-108.
13. CASSIDY, J., & VUKELICH, C. Do the gifted read early? *Reading Teacher*, 1980, 33, 578-582.
14. CERMAK, S. A., COSTER, W., & DRAKE, C. Representational and nonrepresentational gestures in boys with learning disabilities. *American Journal of Occupational Therapy*, 1980, 34, 19-26.
15. COOPER, S. An approach to the educational assessment of the learning disabled child. *Journal of Clinical Child Psychology*, 1980, 9, 59-62.
16. DWYER, E. J. Analysis of reading achievement, listening comprehension and paradigmatic language of selected second grade students by race and sex. *Southern Journal of Educational Research*, 1980, 14, 205-218.
17. PRAWAT, R. S., & JARVIS, R. Gender difference as a factor in teachers' perceptions of students. *Journal of Educational Psychology*, 1980, 72, 743-749.
18. WEST, J., SONSTEGARD, M., & HAGERMAN, H. A study of counseling and consulting in Appalachia. *Elementary School Guidance & Counseling*, 1980, 15, 5-13.
19. WHALEY, W. J., & KIBBY, M. W. Word synthesis and beginning reading achievement. *Journal of Educational Research*, 1980, 73, 132-138.
20. POWELL, G., MOORE, D., & CALLAWAY, B. A concurrent validity study of the Woodcock Word Comprehension Test. *Psychology in the Schools*, 1981, 18, 24-27.

[2219]

Smedley Hand Dynamometer. Ages 6-18; [1920(?)-53]; strength of grip; F. Smedley; Stoelting Co.*

See T2:1901 (10 references).

[2220]

★**Smith-Johnson Nonverbal Performance Scale.** Ages 2-4; 1977; "effective in evaluating the language- and/or hearing-impaired child"; 14 scores: formboard, block building, pencil drawing, bead stringing, knot tying, color items, scissors, paper folding, cube tapping, form discrimination, completion items, manikin, block patterns, sorting; Alathena J. Smith and Ruth E. Johnson; Western Psychological Services.*

[2221]

★**Snijders-Oomen Non-Verbal Intelligence Scale for Young Children.** Ages 2.5-7; 1939-76; SON 2½-7; also called *Non-Verbal Intelligence Scale S.O.N. 2½-7*; this is the lower level (upper level for ages 7-17 in preparation) of a revision of still-in-print 1958 edition of *Non-Verbal Intelligence Tests for Deaf and Hearing Subjects* (S.O.N. 1958) for ages 3-16; 6 scores: sorting, mosaic, combination, memory, copying, total; (Dutch and German editions available); J. Th. Snijders and N. Snijders-Oomen; Swets Test Services [The Netherlands].*

For additional information, see 8:228; see also T2:512 (5 references); for a review by J. S. Lawes of the 1958 edition, see 6:529 (2 references).

REFERENCES

1-2. See 6:529.
3-7. See T2:512.
8. YULE, W. Snijders-Oomen Non-Verbal Intelligence Scale- S.O.N. 2½-7. *Journal of Child Psychology & Psychiatry & Allied Disciplines*, 1978, 19, 78-79.

[2222]

Snyder Knuth Music Achievement Test. Elementary education and music majors; 1968; Alice Snyder Knuth; Creative Arts Research Associates, Inc.* (In-print status uncertain; no reply from publisher.)

For additional information and reviews by Richard Colwell and Edwin Gordon, see 7:251 (3 references).

[2223]

SOBER Español. Grades kgn-3; 1975; customized criterion-referenced test covering 10-30 objectives (3 items per objective) locally chosen from a list of 203 objectives in 4 areas: encoding, decoding, vocabulary, comprehension; Ricardo J. Cornejo; Science Research Associates, Inc.*

For additional information and excerpted reviews by Y. Arturo Cabrera and George Hughes, see 8:170 (2 references).

[2224]
Social and Prevocational Information Battery. Educable mentally retarded grades 7–12, trainable mentally retarded grades 7–12; 1975–79; 10 scores: purchasing habits, budgeting, banking, job related behavior, job search skills, home management, health care, hygiene and grooming, functional signs, total; 2 levels; Larry K. Irvin, Andrew S. Halpern and authors listed below; CTB/McGraw-Hill.

a) SOCIAL AND PREVOCATIONAL INFORMATION BATTERY. Educable mentally retarded grades 7–12; 1975; SPIB; Paul Raffeld and Robert Link.

b) SOCIAL AND PREVOCATIONAL INFORMATION BATTERY, FORM T. Trainable mentally retarded grades 7–12; 1979; SPIB-T; revision of *Social and Prevocational Information Battery* to broaden use to moderately retarded examinees, also screens students through administration of pretest to ensure examinee can handle the testing situation; William M. Reynolds.

For a review by C. Edward Meyers of the original edition only, see 8:984 (2 references).

REFERENCES

1–2. See 8:984.
3. IRVIN, L. K., & HALPERN, A. S. Reliability and validity of the Social and Prevocational Information Battery for mildly retarded individuals. *American Journal of Mental Deficiency*, 1977, 81, 603–605.
4. IRVIN, L. K., HALPERN, A. S., & REYNOLDS, W. M. Assessing social and prevocational awareness in mildly and moderately retarded individuals. *American Journal of Mental Deficiency*, 1977, 82, 266–272.
5. DANKER-BROWN, P., SIGELMAN, C. K., & FLEXER, R. W. Sex bias in vocational programming for handicapped students. *Journal of Special Education*, 1978, 12, 451–458.
6. FLEXER, R., SIGELMAN, C. K., DESANCTIS, M., & DANKER-BROWN, P. Relationships of IQ to experiences and adjustment in work-study programs for handicapped youth. *Rehabilitation Counseling Bulletin*, 1979, 23, 15–23.
7. HALPERN, A. S., & IRVIN, L. K. Alternative approaches to the measurement of adaptive behavior. *American Journal of Mental Deficiency*, 1979, 84, 304–310.
8. HUBER, C. H. Career planning with mildly retarded students: A model for school counselors. *Vocational Guidance Quarterly*, 1979, 27, 223–229.
9. IRVIN, L. K., HALPERN, A. S., & LANDMAN, J. T. Assessment of retarded student achievement with standardized true/false and multiple-choice tests. *Journal of Educational Measurement*, 1980, 17, 51–58.

[2225]
Social Attitude Scale. High school graduates and above; 1971–72; liberalism-conservatism; for measurement of groups; no manual; William W. Rambo; Department of Psychology, Oklahoma State University.* (In-print status uncertain; no reply from publisher.)

For additional information, see 8:680 (2 references).

[2226]
★Social Behavior Assessment. Grades kgn–6; 1978–80; SBA; ratings by teachers; 4 areas: environmental behaviors, interpersonal behaviors, self-related behaviors, task related behaviors; Thomas M. Stephens; Cedars Press, Inc.*

REFERENCES

1. STEPHENS, T. M. *Social skills in the classroom*. Columbus OH: Cedars Press, 1978.

[2227]
The Social Climate Scales. Members of various groups; 1974; SCS; 8 tests; for reviews and additional references and information, see the separate test entries; Rudolf H. Moos and associates; Consulting Psychologists Press, Inc.*

a) CLASSROOM ENVIRONMENT SCALE. Junior high and high school students and teachers.

b) COMMUNITY ORIENTED PROGRAMS ENVIRONMENT SCALE. Members and staff of community oriented psychiatric facilities.

c) CORRECTIONAL INSTITUTIONS ENVIRONMENT SCALE. Residents and staff of juvenile and adult correctional facilities.

d) GROUP ENVIRONMENT SCALE. Group members and leaders.

e) FAMILY ENVIRONMENT SCALE. Family members.

f) UNIVERSITY RESIDENCE ENVIRONMENT SCALE. Students in university living groups.

g) WARD ATMOSPHERE SCALE. Patients and staff of hospital-based psychiatric treatment programs.

h) WORK ENVIRONMENT SCALE. Employees and supervisors in work units.

For additional information and a review by James M. Richards, Jr., see 8:681(84 references).

[2228]
Social Intelligence Test: George Washington University Series. Grades 9–16 and adults; 1930–55; SIT; 3 editions; F. A. Moss, Thelma Hunt, K. T. Omwake, and L. G. Woodward (*a* and manual); Center for Psychological Service.* (In-print status uncertain; no reply from publisher.)

a) SECOND EDITION. 1930–55; 6 scores: judgment in social situations, recognition of the mental state of the speaker, memory for names and faces, observation of human behavior, sense of humor, total.

b) SHORT EDITION. 1944–55; 5 scores: same as for Second Edition except for omission of memory for names and faces.

c) SP (SPECIAL) EDITION. 1947–55; 3 scores: judgment in social situations, observation of human behavior, total.

See T2:1386 (15 references), P:250 (3 references), 6:176 (14 references), and 4:89 (7 references); for reviews by Glen U. Cleeton and Howard R. Taylor, see 3:96 (9 references); for a review by Robert L. Thorndike, see 2:1253 (20 references).

REFERENCES

1–20. See 2:1253.
21–29. See 3:96.
30–36. See 4:89.
37–50. See 6:176.
51–53. See P:250.
54–68. See T2:1386.
69. BURLEY, P. M., & MCGUINNESS, J. Effects of social intelligence on the Milgram paradigm. *Psychological Reports*, 1977, 40, 767–770.
70. POMERANTZ, S., & HOUSE, W. C. Liberated versus traditional women's performance satisfaction and perceptions of ability. *Journal of Psychology*, 1977, 95, 205–211.
71. KEATING, D. P. A search for social intelligence. *Journal of Educational Psychology*, 1978, 70, 218–223.

[2229]
★Social Interaction and Creativity in Communication System. Grades 1 and over; 1979; SICCS; 8 categories: appraisal, prescriptive, informational, question-

ing, self-reference, self-initiated, productivity, quantity; David L. Johnson; Stoelting Co.*

[2230]

Social Relations Test. Adult males; 1960–66; test booklet title is *S.R.T.*; no manual; [J. C. de Ridder and Lynette Shaw]; Industrial Psychological Services [South Africa].* (In-print status uncertain; no reply from publisher.)

See T2:1509 (2 references) and P:473B (1 reference).

[2231]

★**Social Skills for Severely Retarded Adults— An Inventory and Training Program.** Severely or profoundly handicapped adolescents and adults; 1980; 10 areas of social behavior: appropriate physical interaction, touching/manipulating objects, reacts to name, social smiling, eye contact, social interaction with trainer, traveling with trainer, group interaction, development of leisure skills, waiting; Sandra E. McClennen, Ronald R. Hoekstra, and James E. Bryan; Research Press.*

[2232]

Social Studies Grade 10 (American History): Minnesota High School Achievement Examinations. Grade 10; 1951–70; a new, revised, or previously inactive form issued each May; Achievement Examinations for Secondary Schools, High School Achievement Examinations, and Midwest High School Achievement Examinations have also been used as series titles; edited by V. L. Lohmann; American Guidance Service.*

For additional information, concerning out of print and inactive forms, see 7:923, 6:1008, and 5:807; for a review by Howard R. Anderson of Form A (1955) and Form B (1957), see 5:810.

[2233]

Social Studies Grade 11 (World History): Minnesota High School Achievement Examinations. Grade 11; 1951–70; a new, revised, or previously inactive form issued each May; Achievement Examinations for Secondary Schools, High School Achievement Examinations, and Midwest High School Achievement Examinations have also been used as series titles; edited by V. L. Lohmann; American Guidance Service.*

For additional information concerning out of print and inactive forms, see 7:924, 6:1009, and 5:821.

[2234]

Social Studies Grade 12 (American Problems): Minnesota High School Achievement Examinations. Grade 12; 1951–70; a new, revised, or previously inactive form issued each May; Achievement Examinations for Secondary Schools, High School Achievement Examinations, and Midwest High School Achievement Examinations have also been used as series titles; edited by V. L. Lohmann; American Guidance Service.*

For additional information concerning out of print and inactive forms, see 7:893, 6:976, 5:789, and 5:795.

[2235]

Social Studies: Minnesota High School Achievement Examinations. Grades 7, 8, 9; 1961–70; a new, revised, or previously inactive form issued each May; Midwest High School Achievement Examinations used as series title through 1962; 3 levels; edited by V. L. Lohmann; American Guidance Service.*

a) SOCIAL STUDIES GRADE 7. 1961–70.
b) SOCIAL STUDIES GRADE 8. 1962–70.
c) SOCIAL STUDIES GRADE 9. 1962–70.

For additional information concerning out of print and inactive forms, see 7:892 and 6:973.

[2236]

Socio-Economic Status Scales. Urban students, adults, rural families; 1962–64; 2 editions; Manasayan [India].*

a) SOCIO-ECONOMIC STATUS SCALE (URBAN). Urban students, adults; 1962; 3 ratings (education, occupation, income) yielding a total status score; B. Kuppuswamy.
b) SOCIO-ECONOMIC STATUS SCALE (RURAL). Rural families; 1964; 9 ratings (caste, occupation, education, social participation, land, house, farm powers, material possessions, family type and size) yielding a total status score; Udai Pareek and G. Trivedi.

See T2:1041 (1 reference); for excerpted reviews by Anwar Ansari, E. G. Parameswaran, and one other, see 7:661 (1 reference); for an excerpted review by D. Gopal Rao, see 6:757.

REFERENCES

1. See 7:661.
2. See T2:1041.
3. HUNDAL, P. S., & SINGH, S. Some correlates of progressive farm behavior. *Journal of Occupational Psychology*, 1978, 51, 327–332.
4. GOPAL, A. K., SHARMA, V. K., & SINGH, A. K. Motivational differences among high and low creative university students. *Psychologia*, 1980, 23, 240–246.

[2237]

★**Socio-Sexual Knowledge & Attitudes Test.** Developmentally disabled ages 18–42 and non-retarded persons of all ages; 1976–80; SSKAT; criterion-referenced; 240 sex knowledge and sex attitude items covering 14 topic areas: anatomy terminology, menstruation, dating, marriage, intimacy, intercourse, pregnancy and childbirth, birth control, masturbation, homosexuality, venereal disease, alcohol and drugs, community risks and hazards, terminology check; Joel R. Wish, Katherine Fiechtl McCombs, and Barbara Edmonson; Stoelting Co.*

REFERENCES

1. EDMONSON, B., MCCOMBS, K., & WISH, J. What retarded adults believe about sex. *American Journal of Mental Deficiency*, 1979, 84, 11–18.

[2238]

Solid Geometry: National Achievement Tests. High school; 1958–60; Ray Webb and Julius H. Hlavaty (manual); Psychometric Affiliates.*

For additional information and a review by Sheldon S. Myers, see 6:653.

[2239]

*****Somatic Inkblot Series.** Ages 3 and over; 1969–80; SIS; manual title is *Body Symbolism and the Somatic Inkblot Series*; diagnostic aid for body awareness assessment; Wilfred A. Cassell; the Author.*

For additional information, see 8:518 (2 references).

REFERENCES

1–2. See 8:518.
3. CASSELL, W. A. *Body Symbolism and the Somatic Inkblot Series.* Anchorage: Aurora Publishing Co., 1980.

[2240]

The Sound-Apperception Test. Ages 16 and over; 1965; "unstructured sounds much like auditory equivalents of ink blots" and 16 "semi-structured sound effects that reveal fantasy and dynamics of interpersonal situations"; 10 scores: reality orientation, like-indifferent-dislike, loss of life, physical aggression, nonphysical aggression, internalized emotional stress, positive reassurance, total, failure, success; Kenneth L. Bean; Sound Apperception Test Distributor.*

For additional information, see P:474 (3 references).

[2241]

*****South African Personality Questionnaire.** Grades 12 and over; 1974; SAPQ; 5 scores: social unresponsiveness vs. social responsiveness, tranquillity vs. anxiety, amity vs. hostility, flexibility vs. rigidity, submissiveness vs. dominance; (Afrikaans edition available); D. W. Steyn (manual); National Institute for Personnel Research [South Africa].*

[2242]

The South African Picture Analysis Test. Ages 5–13; 1960, c1959; SAPAT; 8 interpretive categories: condition of hero, environmental pressure, needs, reactions, characteristics of stories (4 categories); B. F. Nel and A. J. K. Pelser; Swets Test Services [The Netherlands].* (United States distributor: Swets North America, Inc.)

For additional information, see P:475; for reviews by S. G. Lee and Johann M. Schepers and an excerpted review by Wilson H. Guertin, see 6:240.

[2243]

Southern California Motor Accuracy Test. Ages 4–7 with nervous system dysfunction; 1964; SCMAT; also available as a subtest of *Southern California Sensory Integration Tests*; test consists of tracing a line design; 2 scores: accuracy, adjusted (accuracy and speed); A. Jean Ayres; Western Psychological Services.*

See T2:1902 (2 references); for a review by Newell C. Kephart, and an excerpted review by C. H. Ammons, see 7:878 (9 references).

REFERENCES

1–9. See 7:878.
10–11. See T2:1902.
12. HUDGIN, A. L. Assessment of visual–motor disabilities in young children: Toward differential diagnosis. *Psychology in the Schools*, 1977, 14, 252–260.
13. RAPP, D. J. Does diet affect hyperactivity? *Journal of Learning Disabilities*, 1978, 11, 383–389.
14. FULKERSON, S. C., & FREEMAN, W. M. Perceptual–motor deficiency in autistic children. *Perceptual & Motor Skills*, 1980, 50, 331–336.

[2244]

Southern California Sensory Integration Tests. Ages 4–10 with learning problems; 1962–72; SCSIT; a battery of tests consisting of *The Ayres Space Test* (SV), *Southern California Figure-Ground Visual Perception Test* (FG), *Southern California Kinesthesia and Tactile Perception Tests* (KIN, MFP, FI, GRA, LTS, DTS), *Southern California Perceptual-Motor Tests* (MAC, IP, CML, BMC, RLD, SBO, SBC), and two new tests: design copying (DC), position in space (PS); 17 scores: space visualization (SV), figure-ground perception (FG), kinesthesia (KIN), manual form perception (MFP), finger identification (FI), graphesthesia (GRA), localization of tactile stimuli (LTS), double tactile stimuli perception (DTS), motor accuracy (MAC), imitation of postures (IP), crossing midline of body (CML), bilateral motor coordination (BMC), right-left discrimination (RLD), standing balance with eyes open (SBO), standing balance with eyes closed (SBC), design copying (DC), position in space (PS); A. Jean Ayres; Western Psychological Services.*

For additional information and reviews by Homer B. C. Reed, Jr. and Alida S. Westman, see 8:875 (5 references); see also T2:1887 (18 references). For reviews of *The Ayres Space Test*, see 6:63 (2 reviews); *Southern California Figure-Ground Visual Perception Tests*, see 7:876 (1 review); *Southern California Kinesthesia and Tactile Perception Tests*, see 7:877 (1 review); *Southern California Motor Accuracy Test*, see 7:878 (1 review, 1 excerpt); *Southern California Perceptual-Motor Tests*, see 7:879 (1 review, 1 excerpt).

REFERENCES

1–18. See T2:1887.
19–23. See 8:875.
24. AYRES, A. J. Cluster analyses of measures of sensory integration. *American Journal of Occupational Therapy*, 1977, 31, 363–366.
25. AYRES, A. J. Dichotic listening performance in learning–disabled children. *American Journal of Occupational Therapy*, 1977, 31, 441–446.
26. AYRES, A. J. Effect of sensory integrative therapy on the coordination of children with choreoathetoid movements. *American Journal of Occupational Therapy*, 1977, 31, 291–293.
27. ELFANT, I. L. Correlation between kinesthetic discrimination and manual dexterity. *American Journal of Occupational Therapy*, 1977, 31, 23–28.
28. KIMBALL, J. G. The Southern California Sensory Integration Tests (Ayres) and the Bender Gestalt: A correlational study. *American Journal of Occupational Therapy*, 1977, 31, 295–299.
29. AYRES, A. J. Learning disabilities and the vestibular system. *Journal of Learning Disabilities*, 1978, 11, 18–29.
30. CULATTA, B. The relationship between perceptual dysfunction and language disorders: A case report. *Journal of Communication Disorders*, 1978, 11, 51–63.
31. DE PAUW, K. P. Enhancing the sensory integration of aphasic students. *Journal of Learning Disabilities*, 1978, 11, 142–146.
32. ENDLER, P. B., & EIMON, M. C. Postural and reflex integration in schizophrenic patients. *American Journal of Occupational Therapy*, 1978, 32, 456–459.
33. OTTENBACHER, K. Identifying vestibular processing dysfunction in learning–disabled children. *American Journal of Occupational Therapy*, 1978, 32, 217–221.
34. BAKER-NOBLES, L., & BINK, M. P. Sensory integration in the rehabilitation of blind adults. *American Journal of Occupational Therapy*, 1979, 33, 559–564.
35. OTTENBACHER, K., WATSON, P. J., SHORT, M. A., & BIDERMAN, M. D. Nystagmus and ocular fixation difficulties in learning disabled children. *American Journal of Occupational Therapy*, 1979, 33, 717–721.
36. TEMPLE, I. G., WILLIAMS, H. G., & BATEMAN, N. J. A test battery to assess intrasensory and intersensory development of young children. *Perceptual & Motor Skills*, 1979, 48, 643–659.
37. WHITE, M. A first-grade intervention program for children at risk for reading failure. *Journal of Learning Disabilities*, 1979, 12, 231–237.
38. ANGELO, J. K. B. Effects of sensory integration treatment on the low-achieving college student. *American Journal of Occupational Therapy*, 1980, 34, 671–675.
39. BRUNT, D. Characteristics of upper limb movements in a sample of meningomyelocele children. *Perceptual & Motor Skills*, 1980, 51, 431–437.
40. CERMAK, S. A., QUINTERO, E. J., & COHEN, P. M. Developmental age trends in crossing the body midline in normal children. *American Journal of Occupational Therapy*, 1980, 34, 313–319.
41. DRAKE, B. L. Gross motor skills and hand grip in the elderly. *American Journal of Occupational Therapy*, 1980, 34, 274–276.
42. OTTENBACHER, K. Excessive postrotary nystagmus duration in learning disabled children. *American Journal of Occupational Therapy*, 1980, 34, 40–44.
43. CHAPPARO, C. J., NELSON, J. G., YERXA, E. J., & WILSON, L. Incidence of sensory integrative dysfunction among children with orofacial cleft. *American Journal of Occupational Therapy*, 1981, 35, 96–100.
44. COUPER, J. L. Dance therapy: Effects on motor performance of children with learning disabilities. *Physical Therapy*, 1981, 61, 23–26.

[2245]
Southgate Group Reading Tests. Ages 6–7.5, 7–8; 1960–62, c1959–62; 2 tests; Vera Southgate; Hodder & Stoughton Educational [England].*
a) TEST 1—WORD SELECTION. Ages 6–7.5; 1960–61, c1959.
b) TEST 2—SENTENCE COMPLETION TEST. Ages 7–8; 1962.

For additional information, reviews by M. L. Kellmer Pringle and Magdalen D. Vernon, and an excerpted review by P. E. Vernon of Test 1, see 6:812.

REFERENCES
1. ELKINS, J. Empirical evidence for a model of reading disability research. *Australian Journal of Education*, 1978, 22, 303–309.
2. MCMICHAEL, P. The hen or the egg? Which comes first—antisocial emotional disorders or reading disability. *British Journal of Educational Psychology*, 1979, 49, 226–238.
3. MCMICHAEL, P. Reading difficulties, behavior, and social status. *Journal of Educational Psychology*, 1980, 72, 76–86.

[2246]
***Space Relations: Differential Aptitude Tests.** Grades 8–12 and adults; 1947–77; George K. Bennett, Harold G. Seashore, and Alexander G. Wesman; The Psychological Corporation.* For the complete battery entry, see 732.

For additional information regarding an earlier edition, see 8:1043 (2 references); see also T2:2268 (18 references). For reviews of the complete battery, see 8:485 (2 reviews, 1 excerpt), 7:673 (1 review, 1 excerpt), 6:767 (2 reviews), 5:605 (2 reviews), 4:711 (3 reviews), and 3:620 (1 excerpt).

REFERENCES
1–18. See T2:2268.
19–20. See 8:1043.
21. FENNEMA, E., & SHERMAN, J. Sex-related differences in mathematics achievement, spatial visualization and affective factors. *American Educational Research Journal*, 1977, 14, 51–71.
22. MEINERS, M. L., & DABBS, J. M., JR. Ear temperature and brain blood flow: Laterality effects. *Bulletin of the Psychonomic Society*, 1977, 10, 194–196.
23. SHERMAN, J., & FENNEMA, E. The study of mathematics by high school girls and boys: Related variables. *American Educational Research Journal*, 1977, 14, 159–168.
24. TAPLEY, S. M., & BRYDEN, M. P. An investigation of sex differences in spatial ability: Mental rotation of three-dimensional objects. *Canadian Journal of Psychology*, 1977, 31, 122–130.
25. BECK, M. M., TAFT, T. B., JR., & ZIMMER, S. E. Predicting clinical performance: A two-step approach. *Journal of Dental Education*, 1978, 9, 524–527.
26. FENNEMA, E. H., & SHERMAN, J. A. Sex-related differences in mathematics achievement and related factors: A further study. *Journal for Research in Mathematics Education*, 1978, 9, 189–203.
27. DYER, J. W., RILEY, J., & YEKOVICH, F. R. An analysis of three study skills: Notetaking, summarizing, and rereading. *Journal of Educational Research*, 1979, 73, 3–7.
28. PARASINIS, I., & LONG, G. L. Relationships among spatial skills, communication skills, and field independence in deaf students. *Perceptual & Motor Skills*, 1979, 49, 879–887.
29. SHERMAN, J. Predicting mathematics performance in high school girls and boys. *Journal of Educational Psychology*, 1979, 71, 242–249.
30. BECKER, B. J. Performance of a group of mathematically able youths on the mathematics usage and natural sciences reading tests of the American College Test Battery vs the Scholastic Aptitude Test. *Gifted Child Quarterly*, 1980, 24, 138–143.
31. BEITEL, P. A. Multivariate relationships among visual–perceptual attributes and gross–motor tasks with different environmental demands. *Journal of Motor Behavior*, 1980, 12, 29–40.
32. GRAYDON, J. Spatial ability in highly skilled women squash players. *Perceptual & Motor Skills*, 1980, 50, 968–970.
33. SHERMAN, J. Mathematics, spatial visualization, and related factors: Changes in girls and boys, grades 8–11. *Journal of Educational Psychology*, 1980, 72, 476–482.
34. STERNBERG, R. J., & WEIL, E. M. An aptitude X strategy interaction in linear syllogistic reasoning. *Journal of Educational Psychology*, 1980, 72, 226–239.

[2247]
Spache Binocular Reading Test. Nonreaders and grade 1, grades 1.5–2, 3 and over; 1943–55; eye preference in reading; 3 levels; George D. Spache; Keystone View.*
a) TEST 1. Nonreaders and grade 1.
b) TEST 2, MY BIG RED CAR. Grades 1.5–2.
c) TEST 3, THE QUEEN. Grades 3 and over.

See T2:1929 (2 references); for a review by Helen M. Robinson, see 6:959; see also 5:784 (4 references); for a review by Albert J. Harris of Test 3, see 3:461 (4 references).

[2248]
★Spanish/English Reading Comprehension Test. Grades 1–6, 7–12 and adults; 1978; based on Mexican curriculum materials; Steve Moreno; Moreno Educational Co.*

[2249]
SPAR Reading Test. Ages 7–0 to 15–11; 1976; based upon *Group Reading Test* and uses the same scoring stencils; may be administered with *SPAR Spelling Test* or independently; D. Young; Hodder & Stoughton Educational [England].*

For additional information and a review by J. Douglas Ayers, see 8:742.

[2250]
SPAR Spelling Test. Ages 7–0 to 15–11; 1976; may be administered with *SPAR Reading Test* or independently; no specific form, the 30 test items are chosen locally from a list of 300 words divided into 2 "banks": Spelling Banks A, B; D. Young; Hodder & Stoughton Educational [England].*

For additional information and a review by J. Douglas Ayers, see 8:76.

[2251]
Spatial Orientation Memory Test. Ages 5–9; 1971–75; SOMT; Joseph M. Wepman and Dainis Turaids; Language Research Associates, Inc.*

For additional information and a review by John J. Geyer, see 8:876.

REFERENCES
1. OTTESON, J. P. Stylistic and personality correlates of lateral eye movements: A factor analytic study. *Perceptual & Motor Skills*, 1980, 50, 995–1010.
2. MILLER, J. W., & MCKENNA, M. C. Disabled readers: Their intellectual and perceptual capacities at differing ages. *Perceptual & Motor Skills*, 1981, 52, 467–472.

[2252]
Specific Language Disability Test. "Average to high IQ" children in grades 6–8; 1967–68; SLDT; upward extension of *Screening Tests for Identifying Children With Specific Language Disability*; 10 tests (visual copying far point, visual copying near point, visual discrimination, visual perception memory for words, visual perception memory in association with kinesthetic memory, auditory discrimination, auditory perception and recall, auditory-visual discrimination, comprehension, spelling) with 4 scores (omissions, errors, self-corrections, reversals) for

each; Neva Malcomesius; Educators Publishing Service, Inc.*

For additional information and reviews by S. Alan Cohen and Robert E. Valett, see 7:971.

[2253]
Speed Scale for Determining Independent Reading Level. Grades 1–12; 1975; 3 grade level scores: word recognition [pronunciation], comprehension [vocabulary], independent reading [average of pronunciation and vocabulary levels]; Ward Cramer and Roger Trent; Academic Therapy Publications.*

For additional information and a review by J. Jaap Tuinman, see 8:782.

[2254]
*****Spelling: Differential Aptitude Tests.** Grades 8–12 and adults; 1947–77; revision of the spelling subtest of Form B of the DAT *Language Usage* (1947), later called Form M of the DAT *Language Usage—Spelling* (1962); George K. Bennett, Harold G. Seashore, and Alexander G. Wesman; The Psychological Corporation.* For the complete battery entry, see 732.

For additional information regarding an earlier edition, see 8:73; see also T2:157 (2 references). For reviews of the complete battery, see 8:485 (2 reviews, 1 excerpt), 7:673 (1 review, 1 excerpt), 6:767 (2 reviews), 5:605 (2 reviews), 4:711 (3 reviews), and 3:620 (1 excerpt).

[2255]
Spelling Errors Test. Grades 2–4, 5–6, 7–8; 1948–55; George Spache; Reading Laboratory and Clinic.* (In-print status uncertain; no reply from publisher.)

For additional information, see 5:228 (1 reference).

[2256]
Spelling Test for Clerical Workers: [Personnel Research Institute Clerical Battery]. Stenographic applicants and high school; 1947; Jay L. Otis, David J. Chesler, and Irene Salmi; Psychological Research Services.*

See T2:159 (1 reference); for a review by Harold H. Bixler, see 4:211. For reviews of the complete battery, see 4:729 (2 reviews).

[2257]
Spelling Test: McGraw-Hill Basic Skills System. Grades 11–14; 1970; also called *MHBSS Spelling Test*; although designed for use with the MHBSS instructional program, the test may be used independently; Alton L. Raygor; McGraw-Hill Book Co., Inc.*

For additional information and reviews by Thomas D. Horn and Albert H. Yee, see 7:230.

[2258]
Spelling Test: National Achievement Tests. Grades 3–4, 5–8, 7–9, 10–12; 1936–57; Robert K. Speer and Samuel Smith; Psychometric Affiliates.*

For additional information and a review by James A. Fitzgerald, see 5:230; for a review by W. J. Osburn, see 1:1161.

[2259]
★**Spellmaster.** Grades 1–adult; 1974–75; "criterion-referenced test"; Claire R. Cohen in collaboration with Rhoda M. Abrams; Learnco Inc.*

[2260]
*****SRA Achievement Series.** Grades kgn–1, 1–2, 2–3, 3–4, 4–6, 6–8, 8–9, 9–12; 1978–81; earlier form entitled *Achievement Series: SRA Assessment Survey*; 8 levels; Robert A. Naslund, Louis P. Thorpe, and D. Welty Lefever; Science Research Associates, Inc.*

a) LEVEL A. Grades kgn–1; 11 scores: 8 achievement scores: reading (visual discrimination, auditory discrimination, letters and sounds, listening comprehension, total), mathematics (concepts, total), composite, plus 3 educational ability series (EAS) scores: verbal, nonverbal, total.

b) LEVEL B. Grades 1–2; 13 scores: 10 achievement: reading (auditory discrimination, letters and sounds, listening comprehension, vocabulary, comprehension, total), mathematics (concepts, computation, total), composite, plus same 3 EAS scores as *a*.

c) LEVEL C. Grades 2–3; 16 scores: 13 achievement: reading (letters and sounds, listening comprehension, vocabulary, comprehension, total), mathematics (concepts, computation, total), language arts (mechanics, usage, spelling, total), composite, plus same 3 EAS scores as *a*.

d) LEVEL D. Grades 3–4; 14 scores: 11 achievement: reading (vocabulary, comprehension, total), mathematics (concepts, computation, total), language arts (mechanics, usage, spelling, total), composite, plus same 3 EAS scores as *a*.

e) LEVEL E. Grades 4–6; 18 scores: 15 achievement: reading (vocabulary, comprehension, total), mathematics (concepts, computation, problem solving, total), language arts (mechanics, usage, spelling, total), reference materials, social studies, science, composite, plus same 3 EAS scores as *a*.

f) LEVEL F. Grades 6–8; 18 scores: same as *e*.

g) LEVEL G. Grades 8–9; 18 scores: same as *e*.

h) LEVEL H. Grades 9–12; 17 scores: 14 achievement: reading (vocabulary, comprehension, total), mathematics (concepts/computation, problem solving, total), language arts (mechanics/usage, spelling, total), reference materials, social studies, science, survey of applied skills, composite, plus same 3 EAS scores as *a*.

For reviews by Robert H. Bauernfeind and Frederick G. Brown of earlier forms, see 8:1 (11 references); see also T2:29 (3 references); for reviews by Miriam M. Bryan and Fred M. Smith, see 7:18 (9 references); for a review by Jacob S. Orleans, see 6:21 (3 references); for reviews by Warren G. Findley and Worth R. Jones, see 5:21.

REFERENCES

1–3. See 6:21.
4–12. See 7:18.
13–15. See T2:29.
16–26. See 8:1.
27. BALDAUF, R. B., JR., & AYABE, H. I. Acculturation and educational achievement in American Samoan adolescents. *Journal of Cross–Cultural Psychology*, 1977, 8, 241–255.
28. LEONARD, P. Model schools project report: 5. Edgewood Junior High School. *National Association of Secondary School Principals Bulletin*, 1977, 61, 25–35.
29. MCINTIRE, W. G., & DRUMMOND, R. J. Multiple predictors of self-concept in children. *Psychology in the Schools*, 1977, 14, 295–298.
30. RENTZ, R. R., & BASHAW, W. L. The National Reference Scale for Reading: An application of the Rasch model. *Journal of Educational Measurement*, 1977, 14, 161–179.
31. RUPLEY, W. H. Stability of teacher effect on pupils' reading achievement over a two year period and its relation to instructional emphasis. In P. D. Pearson & J. Hansen (Eds.), *Reading: Theory, research, and practice; Twenty-sixth yearbook of the National Reading Conference.* Clemson, South Carolina: The National Reading Conference, Inc., 1977.

32. SLINDE, J. A., & LINN, R. L. Vertically equated tests: Fact or phantom? *Journal of Educational Measurement*, 1977, 14, 23–32.
33. BARNETT, M. A., & KAISER, D. L. The relationship between intellectual–achievement responsibility attributions and performance. *Child Study Journal*, 1978, 8, 209–215.
34. BOEGLI, R. G., & WASIK, B. H. Use of the token economy system to intervene on a schoolwide level. *Psychology in the Schools*, 1978, 15, 72–78.
35. FOWLER, P. C., & RICHARDS, H. C. Father absence, educational preparedness, and academic achievement: A test of the confluence model. *Journal of Educational Psychology*, 1978, 70, 595–601.
36. JOHNSON, R. A., & YARBOROUGH, B. H. The effects of marks on the development of academically talented elementary pupils. *Gifted Child Quarterly*, 1978, 22, 498–505.
37. YARBOROUGH, B. H., & JOHNSON, R. A. The relationship between intelligence levels and benefits from innovative, nongraded elementary schooling and traditional, graded schooling. *Educational Research Quarterly*, 1978, 3, 28–38.
38. EBMEIER, H., & GOOD, T. L. The effects of instructing teachers about good teaching on the mathematics achievement of fourth grade students. *American Educational Research Journal*, 1979, 16, 1–16.
39. GAVER, D., & RICHARDS, H. C. Dimensions of naturalistic observation for the prediction of academic success. *Journal of Educational Research*, 1979, 72, 123–127.
40. GETTINGER, M., & WHITE, M. A. Which is the stronger correlate of school learning? Time to learn or measured intelligence? *Journal of Educational Psychology*, 1979, 71, 405–412.
41. HILTZHEIMER, N. B., & GUMAER, J. Behavior management and classroom guidance in an inner–city school. *Elementary School Guidance & Counseling*, 1979, 13, 272–278.
42. HUSAK, W. S., & MAGILL, R. A. Correlations among perceptual–motor ability, self–concept and reading achievement in early elementary grades. *Perceptual & Motor Skills*, 1979, 48, 447–450.
43. SEXTON, L. C., & TRELOAR, J. H. Auditory and visual perception, sex, and academic aptitude as predictors of achievement for first-grade children. *Measurement & Evaluation in Guidance*, 1979, 12, 140–146.
44. SLINDE, J. A., & LINN, R. L. The Rasch model, objective measurement, equating, and robustness. *Applied Psychological Measurement*, 1979, 3, 437–452.
45. DIAMOND, E. E. The AMEG commission report on sex bias in achievement testing. *Measurement & Evaluation in Guidance*, 1980, 13, 135–147.
46. IWANICKI, E. F. A new generation of standardized achievement test batteries: A profile of their major features. *Journal of Educational Measurement*, 1980, 17, 155–162.
47. KANE, B. J., & ALLEY, G. R. A peer–tutored instructional management program in computational mathematics for incarcerated, learning disabled juvenile delinquents. *Journal of Learning Disabilities*, 1980, 13, 148–151.
48. MANDELL, A. Problem–solving strategies of sixth–grade students who are superior problem solvers. *Science Education*, 1980, 64, 203–211.
49. WRIGHT, D., REYNOLDS, C. R., & DAPPEN, L. Criterion-related validity of three common preschool assessment instruments for boys and girls. *Psychological Reports*, 1980, 47, 1291–1296.
50. YARBOROUGH, B. H., & JOHNSON, R. A. How meaningful are marks in promoting growth in reading? *Reading Teacher*, 1980, 33, 644–651.
51. STANDIFER, C. E., & MAPLES, E. G. Achievement and attitude of third–grade students using two types of calculators. *School Science & Mathematics*, 1981, 81, 17–24.

[2261]

SRA Arithmetic Index. Job applicants ages 14 and over with poor educational backgrounds; 1968–74; total score and a proficiency level (addition and subtraction of whole numbers, multiplication and division of whole numbers, fractions, or decimals and percentages); combined manual for this and *SRA Reading Index*; manual by Bruce A. Campbell with the assistance of LaVonne Macaitis; Science Research Associates, Inc.*

For additional information, see 8:307 (3 references). For a review by Dorothy C. Adkins of this test and the *SRA Reading Index*, see 7:20.

[2262]

SRA Attitude Survey. Employees; 1951–74; formerly called *SRA Employee Inventory*; employee attitudes toward work environment; for group measurement only; Science Research Associates, Inc.*

a) THE CORE SURVEY. 1951–74; 78 item scores (percentages of both favorable response and no response for total group, subgroup) in 15 areas: job demands, working conditions, pay, employee benefits, friendliness and cooperation of fellow employees, supervisor-employee interpersonal relations, confidence in management, technical competence of supervision, effectiveness of administration, communication, job security, status and recognition, identification with company, growth and advancement opportunity, reactions to the inventory; (French, Spanish, and Portuguese editions available); a special edition for hospital employees is available; original survey by Robert K. Burns, L. L. Thurstone, David G. Moore, and Melany E. Baehr.

b) ANONYMOUS COMMENTS. Optional supplement to *a*.

c) CUSTOM-BUILT SURVEY. Optional supplement to *a* of up to 21 custom items.

d) FUNCTION-SPECIFIC SURVEYS. Supervisors and sales representatives; 1972–74; optional supplement to *a*; attitudes regarding their particular job areas and problems; 31 item scores (percentages of favorable response and no response for total group, subgroup) in 5 areas listed below; 2 surveys.

1) *Survey for Supervisors.* 5 areas: job fulfillment conditions, authority and responsibility, relations with peers and subordinates, relations with superiors, management reponsiveness.

2) *Survey for Sales Representatives.* 5 areas: training, sales support, demands and rewards, sales supervision, management responsiveness.

For additional information, see 8:1054 (9 references). For reviews by Erwin K. Taylor and Albert S. Thompson of original edition of *a*, see 5:905 (10 references).

[2263]

SRA Clerical Aptitudes. Grades 9–12 and adults; 1947–73; 4 scores: office vocabulary, office arithmetic, office checking, total; Richardson, Bellows, Henry & Co., Inc.; Science Research Associates, Inc.*

For additional information, see 8:328; see also T2:791 (2 references); for reviews by Edward N. Hay and G. A. Satter, see 4:732.

[2264]

★**SRA Coping Skills: A Survey plus Activities.** Grade 7–adult; 1978; 9 scores: working, community resources, consumer economics, household management, health and safety, personal law, government, stress, total; Science Research Associates, Inc.*

[2265]

SRA Mechanical Aptitudes. Grades 9–12 and adults; 1947–50; 4 scores: mechanical knowledge, space relations, shop arithmetic, total; Richardson, Bellows, Henry & Co., Inc.; Science Research Associates, Inc.*

See T2:2267 (8 references); for reviews by Alec Rodger and Douglas G. Schultz, see 4:764.

[2266]

SRA Nonverbal Form. Ages 12 and over; 1946–73; formerly called *SRA Non-Verbal Classification Form*; Robert N. McMurry and Joseph E. King; Science Research Associates, Inc.*

[2267]

SRA Pictorial Reasoning Test. Ages 14 and over; 1966–73; PRT; "to measure the learning potential of individuals from diverse backgrounds with reading difficulties"; test by Robert N. McMurry and Phyllis D. Arnold; manual by Bruce A. Campbell with the editorial assistance of Marita Schofield; Science Research Associates, Inc.*

See T2:449 (12 references); for a review by W. D. Commins, see 4:318; for an excerpted review, see 3:261 (incorrectly listed under 3:260 in the first printing of The Third Mental Measurements Yearbook).

For additional information, reviews by Raymond A. Katzell and John E. Milholland, and a excerpted review by John L. Horn, see 7:381.

[2268]

SRA Placement and Counseling Program. Grades 4.5–6.5, 6–8.5, 8–10.5; 1978–81; PAC; formerly published as part of the SRA Achievement Series; modular program including achievement, ability, and interest measures to assist in screening, placement, and counseling of students; 4 tests; Leonard W. Biedermann; Science Research Associates, Inc.

a) 3R. Grades 4.5–6.5, 6–8.5, 8–10.5; composed of items from the same subtests of the 1978 Achievement Series; can be used in the screening, placement, and counseling programs; 12 scores: reading (vocabulary, comprehension, total), mathematics (computation, concepts, problem solving, total), language arts (mechanics, usage, spelling, total), composite.

b) BACKGROUND TESTS (OPTIONAL). Grades 4.5–6.5, 6–8.5, 8–10.5; same full tests as those in the 1978 Achievement Series; can be used in the screening, placement, and counseling programs; 3 scores: reference materials, social studies, science.

c) EDUCATION ABILITY SERIES (OPTIONAL). Grades 4.5–6.5, 6–8.5, 8–10.5; EAS; optional test which can be used in the placement and counseling programs; available only as an add-on to PAC; 3 scores: verbal, nonverbal, total.

d) KUDER E GENERAL INTEREST SURVEY (OPTIONAL). Grades 6–10; KGIS; to be used in the counseling program; 11 scores: outdoor, mechanical, computational, scientific, persuasive, artistic, literary, musical, social service, clerical, verification.

[2269]

SRA Primary Mental Abilities, 1962 Edition. Grades kgn–1, 2–4, 4–6, 6–9, 9–12; 1946–65; PMA; earlier editions titled Tests of Primary Mental Abilities and Chicago Tests of Primary Mental Abilities; 5 levels; L. L. Thurstone (earlier editions) and Thelma Gwinn Thurstone; Science Research Associates, Inc.*

a) GRADES K–1. 5 scores: verbal meaning, perceptual speed, number facility, spatial relations, total.

b) GRADES 2–4. 5 scores: same as for grades kgn–1.

c) GRADES 4–6. 6 scores: same as for grades kgn–1 plus reasoning.

d) GRADES 6–9. 5 scores: verbal meaning, number facility, reasoning, spatial relations, total.

e) GRADES 9–12. 5 scores: same as for grades 6–9.

For additional information, see 8:488 (67 references); see also T2:1087 (57 references); for reviews by M. Y. Quereshi and Richard E. Schutz, see 7:680 (98 references); for a review by John E. Milholland, see 6:780 (50 references); for reviews by Norman Frederiksen and Albert K. Kurtz of an earlier edition, see 5:614 (58 references); for reviews by Anne Anastasi, Ralph F. Berdie, John B. Carroll, Stuart A. Courtis, and P. E. Vernon, see 4:716 (42 references); for reviews by Cyril Burt, James R. Hobson, and F. L. Wells, see 3:225 (52 references); for a review by Florence L. Goodenough of a, see 3:264; for reviews by Henry E. Garrett, Truman L. Kelley, C. Spearman, Godfrey H. Thomson, and Robert C. Tryon and excerpted reviews by A. B. Crawford and John M. Stalnaker, see 2:1427 (11 references).

REFERENCES

1–10. See 2:1427.
11–60. See 3:225.
61–102. See 4:716.
103–161. See 5:614.
162–211. See 6:780.
212–309. See 7:680.
310–366. See T2:1087.
367–433. See 8:488.
434. ARZI, Y., & AMIR, Y. Intellectual and academic achievements and adjustment of under–priviledged children in homogeneous and heterogeneous classrooms. Child Development, 1977, 48, 726–729.
435. CAMP, B. W. Verbal mediation in young aggressive boys. Journal of Abnormal Psychology, 1977, 86, 145–153.
436. COHEN, D., SCHAIE, K. W., & GRIBBIN, K. The organization of spatial abilities in older men and women. Journal of Gerontology, 1977, 32, 578–585.
437. FOCH, T. T., DEFRIES, J. C., MCCLEARN, G. E., & SINGER, S. M. Familial patterns of impairment in reading disability. Journal of Educational Psychology, 1977, 69, 316–329.
438. HIGGINS, E. T. Communication development as related to channel, incentive, and social class. Genetic Psychology Monographs, 1977, 96, 75–141.
439. LABOUVIE-VIEF, G., LEVIN, J. R., HURLBUT, N. L., & URBERG, K. In pursuit of the elusive relationship between selected cognitive abilities and learning. Contemporary Educational Psychology, 1977, 2, 239–250.
440. MCCALL, R. B. Childhood IQ's as predictors of adult educational and occupational status. Science, 1977, 197, 482–483.
441. MCKINNEY, J. D., & FORMAN, S. G. Factor structure of the Wallach–Kogan tests of creativity and measures of intelligence and achievement. Psychology in the Schools, 1977, 14, 41–44.
442. RANDEL, M. A., FRY, M. A., & RALLS, E. M. Two readiness measures as predictors of first– and third–grade reading achievement. Psychology in the Schools, 1977, 14, 37–40.
443. SCHAIE, K. W., & PARHAM, I. A. Cohort–sequential analyses of adult intellectual development. Developmental Psychology, 1977, 13, 649–653.
444. SNYDER, S. S., & FELDMAN, D. H. Internal and external influences on cognitive developmental change. Child Development, 1977, 48, 937–943.
445. STERNBERG, L., EPSTEIN, M. H., & ADAMS, D. Performance characteristics of retarded and normal students on pattern recognition tasks. Contemporary Educational Psychology, 1977, 2, 209–218.
446. YSSELDYKE, J. E. Aptitude–treatment interaction research with first grade children. Contemporary Educational Psychology, 1977, 2, 1–9.
447. ASBURY, C. A. Cognitive factors related to discrepant arithmetic achievement of white and black first graders. Journal of Negro Education, 1978, 47, 337–342.
448. FISCHER, D. G., HUNT, D., & RANDHAWA, B. S. Empirical validity of Ertl's brain–wave analyzer (BWAO2). Educational & Psychological Measurement, 1978, 38, 1017–1030.
449. FORMAN, S. G., & MCKINNEY, J. D. Creativity and achievement of second graders in open and traditional classrooms. Journal of Educational Psychology, 1978, 70, 101–107.
450. FURNEAUX, W. D., & REES, R. The structure of mathematical ability. British Journal of Psychology, 1978, 69, 507–512.
451. GILDEMEISTER, J. E., & FRIEDMAN, P. Cognitive style and visual analysis in first graders of high and low verbal ability. Perceptual & Motor Skills, 1978, 47, 759–766.
452. HAKSTIAN, A. R., & CATTELL, R. B. Higher–stratum ability structures on a basis of twenty primary abilities. Journal of Educational Psychology, 1978, 70, 657–669.
453. HÄRNQUIST, K. Primary mental abilities at collective and individual levels. Journal of Educational Psychology, 1978, 70, 706–716.
454. HERTZOG, C., SCHAIE, K. W., & GRIBBIN, K. Cardiovascular disease and changes in intellectual functioning from middle to old age. Journal of Gerontology, 1978, 33, 872–883.

455. JAMES, M. A., & KNIEF, L. Interaction of general, fluid, and crystallized ability and instruction in sixth-grade mathematics. *Journal of Educational Psychology*, 1978, 70, 319-323.
456. KIRBY, J. R., & DAS, J. P. Information processing and human abilities. *Journal of Educational Psychology*, 1978, 70, 58-66.
457. KIRBY, J. R., & DAS, J. P. Skills underlying Coloured Progressive Matrices. *Alberta Journal of Educational Research*, 1978, 24, 94-99.
458. KIRTON, M. Have adaptors and innovators equal levels of creativity. *Psychological Reports*, 1978, 42, 695-698.
459. MCLEAD, T. M., & CRUMP, W. D. The relationship of visuospatial skills and verbal ability to learning disabilities in mathematics. *Journal of Learning Disabilities*, 1978, 11, 237-241.
460. MEYER, R. A. Mathematical problem-solving performance and intellectual abilities of fourth-grade children. *Journal of Research in Mathematics Education*, 1978, 9, 334-348.
461. BRISCO, C. M., & JACOBS, K. W. Alphabetical order of surname and intelligence in elementary school. *Southern Journal of Educational Research*, 1979, 13, 153-158.
462. BRUININKS, V. L., & MAYER, J. H. Longitudinal study of cognitive abilities and academic achievement. *Perceptual & Motor Skills*, 1979, 48, 1011-1021.
463. CAMMOCK, T., & CAIRNS, E. Concurrent validity of a children's version of the Stroop Color-Word Test: The Fruit Distraction Test. *Perceptual & Motor Skills*, 1979, 49, 611-616.
464. GOLDBERG, L. R. A general scheme for the analytic decomposition of objective test scores: Illustrative demonstrations using the Rod-and-Frame Test and the Müller-Lyer Illusion. *Journal of Research in Personality*, 1979, 13, 245-265.
465. KAIL, R., CARTER, P., & PELLEGRINO, J. The locus of sex differences in spatial ability. *Perception & Psychophysics*, 1979, 26, 182-186.
466. MADAUS, G. F., KELLAGHAN, T., RAKOW, E. A., & KING, D. J. The sensitivity of measures of school effectiveness. *Harvard Educational Review*, 1979, 49, 207-230.
467. RAND, Y., TANNENBAUM, A. J., & FEUERSTEIN, R. Effects of instrumental enrichment on the psychoeducational development of low-functioning adolescents. *Journal of Educational Psychology*, 1979, 71, 751-763.
468. SCOTT, R., & STUMME, J. Intrachild variabilities: Will curtailment of testing harm minority children? *Psychology in the Schools*, 1979, 16, 68-71.
469. SEXTON, L. C., & TRELOAR, J. H. Auditory and visual perception, sex, and academic aptitude as predictors of achievement for first-grade children. *Measurement & Evaluation in Guidance*, 1979, 12, 140-146.
470. SHARP, D., COLE, M., & LAVE, C. Education and cognitive development: The evidence from experimental research. *Monographs of the Society for Research in Child Development*, 1979, 44, 51-58.
471. TALOUMIS, T. Scores on Piagetian area tasks as predictors of achievement in mathematics over a four-year period. *Journal for Research in Mathematics Education*, 1979, 10, 120-134.
472. ZOCCOLOTTI, P., PASSAFIUME, D., & PIZZAMIGLIO, L. Hemispheric superiorities on a unilateral tactile test: Relationship to cognitive dimensions. *Perceptual & Motor Skills*, 1979, 49, 735-742.
473. BERLIN, D. F., & LANGUIS, M. L. Age and sex differences in measures of brain lateralization. *Perceptual & Motor Skills*, 1980, 50, 959-967.
474. DECKER, S. N., & DEFRIES, J. C. Cognitive abilities in families with reading disabled children. *Journal of Learning Disabilities*, 1980, 13, 53-58.
475. FRIEZE, I. H., & SNYDER, H. N. Children's beliefs about the causes of success and failure in school settings. *Journal of Educational Psychology*, 1980, 72, 186-196.
476. GRIBBIN, K., SCHAIE, K. W., & PARHAM, I. Complexity of life style and maintenance of intellectual abilities. *Journal of Social Issues*, 1980, 36, 47-61.
477. KAIL, R., PELLEGRINO, J., & CARTER, P. Developmental changes in mental rotation. *Journal of Experimental Child Psychology*, 1980, 29, 102-116.
478. KRAUSS, I. K., QUAYHAGEN, M., & SCHAIE, K. W. Spatial rotation in the elderly: Performance factors. *Journal of Gerontology*, 1980, 35, 199-206.
479. PETERSON, P. L., JANICKI, T. C., & SWING, S. R. Aptitude-treatment interaction effects of three social studies teaching approaches. *American Educational Research Journal*, 1980, 17, 339-360.
480. ROGERS, B. G., WILSON, B. J., & HEWETT, G. Canonical variates in longitudinal achievement data. *Psychology in the Schools*, 1980, 17, 496-499.
481. MCGLONE, J. Sexual variation in behaviour during spatial and verbal tasks. *Canadian Journal of Psychology*, 1981, 35, 277-282.
482. PIZZAMIGLIO, L., & ZOCCOLOTTI, P. Sex and cognitive influence on visual hemifield superiority for face and letter recognition. *Cortex*, 1981, 17, 215-226.
483. POSLUSZNY, R., & BARTON, K. Dichaptic task performance as a function of ability pattern, sex, and hand preference. *Perceptual & Motor Skills*, 1981, 53, 435-438.

[2270]

SRA Reading Index. Job applicants ages 14 and over with poor educational backgrounds; 1968-74; total score and a proficiency level (picture-word association, word decoding, phrase comprehension, sentence comprehension, or paragraph comprehension); combined manual for this and *SRA Arithmetic Index*; manual by Bruce A. Campbell with the assistance of LaVonne Macaitis; Science Research Associates, Inc.*

For additional information, see 8:813 (3 references). For a review by Dorothy C. Adkins of this test and the *SRA Arithmetic Index*, see 7:20.

[2271]

SRA Reading Record. Grades 6-12; 1947-59; 5 scores: reading rate, comprehension, everyday reading skills, vocabulary, total; Guy T. Buswell; Science Research Associates, Inc.*

See T2:1597 (1 reference); for a review by William W. Turnbull, see 4:550 (2 references); for a review by Frances Oralind Triggs and an excerpted review, see 3:502.

[2272]

SRA Sales Attitudes Check List. Applicants for sales positions; 1960; modification of *Sales Personnel Description Form*; Erwin K. Taylor and the Personnel Research & Development Corporation; Science Research Associates, Inc.*

For additional information and a review by John P. Foley, Jr., see 6:1177.

[2273]

SRA Test of Mechanical Concepts. High school and adults; 1976; 4 scores: mechanical interrelationships, mechanical tools and devices, spatial relations, total; Steven J. Stanard and Kathleen Wahl Bode; Science Research Associates, Inc.*

For additional information and reviews by Lorraine D. Eyde and Lyle F. Schoenfeldt, see 8:1045.

[2274]

SRA Typing 5. Prospective employees; 1975; 3 tests, 2 scores for each: speed, accuracy; Steven J. Stanard and LaVonne A. Macaitis (manual); Science Research Associates, Inc.*

a) FORM A—TYPING SPEED.
b) FORM B—BUSINESS LETTER.
c) FORM C—NUMERICAL.

For additional information and reviews by Charles J. Cranny and Lawrence W. Erickson, see 8:1035.

[2275]

SRA Typing Skills. Applicants for clerical positions; 1947-73; 2 scores: speed, accuracy; Marion W. Richardson and Ruth A. Pedersen; Science Research Associates, Inc.*

For additional information, see 8:1036; see also T2:792 (1 reference); for reviews by Lawrence W. Erickson and Jacob S. Orleans, see 6:51 (2 references).

[2276]

SRA Verbal Form. Grades 7-16 and adults; 1946-73; formerly called *SRA Verbal Classification Form*; abbreviated adaptation of *Thurstone Test of Mental Alertness* which is an abbreviated adaptation of *American Council on Education Psychological Examination for High School Students*, 1940 Edition; 3 scores: quantitative, linguistic, total; test by Thelma Gwinn Thurstone and L. L. Thurstone; manual by Bruce A. Campbell with the editorial assistance of LaVonne Macaitis and Marita Schofield; Science Research Associates, Inc.*

See T2:452 (1 reference) and 7:383 (2 references); for reviews by W. D. Commins and Willis C. Schaefer, see 4:319.

REFERENCES

1–2. See 7:383.
3. See T2:452.
4. MORRISON, R. F. Career adaptivity: The effective adaptation of managers of changing role demands. *Journal of Applied Psychology*, 1977, 62, 549–558.
5. SEROW, R. C. Social adaptation in the high school: The effects of enrollment density and personal background. *Urban Education*, 1980, 15, 169–182.
6. SILVA, P. A., & BRADSHAW, J. Some factors contributing to intelligence at age of school entry. *British Journal of Educational Psychology*, 1980, 50, 10–15.

[2277]

★**Staff Burnout Scale for Health Professionals.** Health professionals; 1980; SBS-HP; 2 scores: lie, total; John W. Jones; London House Management Consultants, Inc.*

REFERENCES

1. JONES, J. W. Attitudinal correlates of employee theft of drugs and hospital supplies among nursing personnel. *Nursing Research*, 1981, 30, 349–351.
2. JONES, J. W. *The burnout syndrome. Current research, theory, interventions.* Park Ridge, IL.: London House Press, 1981.
3. JONES, J. W. Dishonesty, burnout, and unauthorized work break extensions. *Personality & Social Psychology Bulletin*, 1981, 7, 406–409.
4. QUATTROCHI–TUBIN, S., JONES, J. W., & BREEDLOVE, V. The burnout syndrome in geriatric counselors and service workers. *Activities, Adaptation & Aging*, in press.
5. SOTO, C., & JONES, J. W. Staff burnout and negligent counseling practices among crisis phone counselors. *Crisis Intervention*, in press.

[2278]

*****The Staffordshire Test of Computation, 1974 Revision.** Ages 7–15; 1938–74; revision of *The Staffordshire Arithmetic Test*; M. E. Hebron and W. Pattinson; Harrap Ltd. [England].*

See T2:737 and 5:486; for a review by Stephen Wiseman of the original edition, see 3:352 (1 reference).

[2279]

*****Stamp Behaviour Study Technique.** Ages 3–5; 1968–78; BST; checklist for recording teacher's observation of behavior in 4 areas: attitudes to self and others, expression of negative feelings, use of powers, integration of home and kindergarten life; Isla M. Stamp; Australian Council for Educational Research [Australia].*

[2280]

Standard Reading Inventory. Grades 1–7; 1966, c1963–66; SRI; 4 scores (independent reading level, minimum instructional level, maximum instructional level, frustration level), 6–9 subtest scores (vocabulary in isolation, vocabulary in context, oral word recognition errors, total oral errors, recall after oral reading, recall after silent reading, total comprehension, oral speed, silent speed) at each of 11 reading levels (preprimer, 1^1, 1^2, 2^1, 2^2, 3^1, 3^2, 4, 5, 6, 7), and various ratings and checklists; Robert A. McCracken; Klamath Printing Co.*

See T2:1649 (2 references); for a review by H. Alan Robinson, see 7:723 (8 references).

REFERENCES

1–8. See 7:723.
9–10. See T2:1649.
11. GRACENIN, C. T., & COOK, J. E. Alpha biofeedback and LD children. *Academic Therapy*, 1977, 12, 275–279.
12. KENDALL, J. R., & HOOD, J. Investigating the relationship between comprehension and word recognition: Oral reading analysis of children with comprehension or word recognition disabilities. *Journal of Reading Behavior*, 1979, 11, 41–48.
13. COOK, J. E., NOLAN, G. A., & ZANOTTI, R. J. Treating auditory perception problems: The NIM helps. *Academic Therapy*, 1980, 15, 473–481.
14. LESLIE, L. Mediation or production deficiency in disabled readers? *Perceptual & Motor Skills*, 1980, 50, 519–530.

[2281]

The Standard Reading Tests. Reading ages up to 9–0; 1958; SRT; 12 tests; J. C. Daniels and Hunter Diack; Hart-Davis Educational Ltd. [England].*
a) TEST 1, THE STANDARD TEST OF READING SKILL.
b) TEST 2, COPYING ABSTRACT FIGURES.
c) TEST 3, COPYING A SENTENCE.
d) TEST 4, VISUAL DISCRIMINATION AND ORIENTATION TEST.
e) TEST 5, LETTER-RECOGNITION TEST.
f) TEST 6, AURAL DISCRIMINATION TEST.
g) TEST 7, DIAGNOSTIC WORD-RECOGNITION TESTS.
h) TEST 8, ORAL WORD-RECOGNITION TEST.
i) TEST 9, PICTURE WORD-RECOGNITION TEST.
j) TEST 10, SILENT PROSE-READING AND COMPREHENSION TEST.
k) TEST 11, GRADED SPELLING TEST.
l) TEST 12, GRADED TEST OF READING EXPERIENCE.

See T2:1650 (1 reference); for a review by M. L. Kellmer Pringle, see 7:724; for a review by L. B. Birch, see 6:833 (1 reference).

REFERENCES

1. See 6:833.
2. See T2:1650.
3. JACKSON, M., & ACKENSTEIN, G. The visuothematic approach in the classroom. *Academic Therapy*, 1977, 12, 327–337.
4. WILLIAMS, A. J., WILLIAMS, M. A., WALKER C. A., & BUSH, P. G. The Robin Anomalad (Pierre Robin Syndrome)–A follow up study. *Archives of Diseases in Childhood*, 1981, 56, 663–668.

[2282]

*****Standardized Bible Content Tests.** Bible college; 1956–81; SBCT; Commission on Testing and Measurement of the American Association of Bible Colleges; the Association.*

For additional information, see 8:466; see also 7:651 (1 reference).

[2283]

*****Standardized Oral Reading Check Tests.** Grades 1, 2–3, 4–5, 6–8; 1923 (no date on test materials); 2 scores: rate, accuracy; 4 levels; William S. Gray; Bobbs-Merrill Co., Inc.*
a) SET 1. Grade 1.
b) SET 2. Grades 2–3.
c) SET 3. Grades 4–5.
d) SET 4. Grades 6–8.

For additional information and a review by Kenneth J. Smith, see 8:792; see also T2:1689 (7 references); for reviews by David H. Russell and Clarence R. Stone, see 2:1570 (1 reference).

[2284]
Standardized Oral Reading Paragraphs Test.
Grades 1.4–8.0; 1915–55; 3 scores: paragraph score, total raw score, B-scores (grade equivalents); William S. Gray; Bobbs-Merrill Co., Inc.*

For additional information and a review by Kenneth J. Smith, see 8:793; see also T2:1690 (19 references); for reviews by David Kopel and Clarence R. Stone, see 2:1571 (7 references).

[2285]
A Standardized Road-Map Test of Direction Sense. Ages 7–18; 1965; right-left directional orientation; John Money; Academic Therapy Publications.*

For additional information and an excerpted review by Alan Krickev, see 8:877 (2 references); for a review by James C. Reed and excerpted reviews by C. H. Ammons and Joseph L. French, see 7:880 (6 references).

REFERENCES

1–6. See 7:880.
7–8. See 8:877.
9. KRICHEV, A. A Standardized Road–Map Test of Direction Sense. *Psychology in the Schools*, 1977, 14, 247–248.
10. TAPLEY, S. M., & BRYDEN, M. P. An investigation of sex differences in spatial ability: Mental rotation of three–dimensional objects. *Canadian Journal of Psychology*, 1977, 31, 122–130.
11. ESON, M. E., YEN, J. K., & BOURKE, R. S. Assessment of recovery from serious head injury. *Journal of Neurology, Neurosurgery & Psychiatry*, 1978, 41, 1036–1042.

[2286]
Stanford Achievement Test, 1973 Edition. Grades 1.5–2.4, 2.5–3.4, 3.5–4.4, 4.5–5.4, 5.5–6.9, 7.0–9.5; 1923–75; SAT; subtest in mathematics and reading available as separates; partial batteries are available without science, social science, and listening comprehension (grades 2.5–6.9), without science and social science (grades 7.0–9.5); 1–2 forms; Richard Madden, Eric F. Gardner, Herbert C. Rudman, Bjorn Karlsen, and Jack C. Merwin; The Psychological Corporation.*
a) PRIMARY LEVEL 1. Grades 1.5–2.4; 12 or 13 scores: reading (word, comprehension, word plus comprehension), word study skills, total, mathematics (concepts, computation and applications, total), auditory (vocabulary, listening comprehension, total), total, spelling (optional); 3 editions.
b) PRIMARY LEVEL 2. Grades 2.5–3.4; 16 scores: reading (word, comprehension, word plus comprehension), word study skills, total, mathematics (concepts, computation, applications, total), spelling, social science, science, auditory (vocabulary, listening comprehension, total), total; 3 editions.
c) PRIMARY LEVEL 3. Grades 3.5–4.4; 15 scores: reading comprehension, word study skills, total, mathematics (concepts, computation, applications, total), spelling, language, social science, science, auditory (vocabulary, listening comprehension, total), total; 3 editions.
d) INTERMEDIATE LEVEL 1. Grades 4.5–5.4; 15 scores: same as for primary level 3.
e) INTERMEDIATE LEVEL 2. Grades 5.5–6.9; 15 scores: same as for primary level 3.
f) ADVANCED. Grades 7.0–9.5; 12 scores: vocabulary, reading comprehension, total, mathematics (concepts, computation, applications, total), spelling, language, social science, science, total.

For additional information, reviews by Robert L. Ebel and A. Harry Passow, and excerpted reviews by Irvin J. Lehmann and Lawrence M. Kasdon, see 8:29 (51 references); see also T2:36 (87 references); for an excerpted review by Peter F. Merenda of the 1964 edition, see 7:25 (44 references); for a review by Miriam M. Bryan and an excerpted review by Robert E. Stake (with J. Thomas Hastings), see 6:26 (13 references); for a review by N. L. Gage of an earlier edition, see 5:25 (19 references); for reviews by Paul R. Hanna (with Claude E. Norcross) and Virgil E. Herrick, see 4:25 (20 references); for reviews by Walter W. Cook and Ralph C. Preston, see 3:18 (33 references). For reviews of subtests, see 8:291 (2 reviews), 8:745 (2 reviews), 7:209 (2 reviews), 7:527 (1 review), 7:708 (1 review), 7:802 (1 review), 7:895 (1 review), 6:637 (1 review), 5:656 (2 reviews), 5:698 (2 reviews), 5:799 (1 review), 4:419 (1 review), 4:555 (1 review), 4:593 (2 reviews), 3:503 (1 review), and 3:595 (1 review).

REFERENCES

1–34. See 3:18.
35–54. See 4:25.
55–73. See 5:25.
74–86. See 6:26.
87–130. See 7:25.
131–217. See T2:36.
218–268. See 8:29.
269. BROWN, J. A., & KAMEEN, M. C. Pupil personal competence perceptions and academic performance. *Contemporary Education*, 1976, 47, 195–201.
270. AMES, S. G., BECKER, L. D., & DALTON, S. The predictive validity of the Stanford Early School Achievement Test. *Educational & Psychological Measurement*, 1977, 37, 505–507.
271. BALDWIN, A. Y. Tests can underpredict: A case study. *Phi Delta Kappan*, 1977, 58, 620–621.
272. BELL, A. E., ABRAHAMSON, D. S., & MCRAE, K. N. Reading retardation: A 12-year prospective study. *Journal of Pediatrics*, 1977, 91, 363–370.
273. BRASEL, K. E., & QUIGLEY, S. P. Influence of certain language and communication environments in early childhood on the development of language in deaf individuals. *Journal of Speech & Hearing Research*, 1977, 20, 95–107.
274. CALHOUN, G., & ELLIOTT, R. N. Self concept and academic achievement of educable retarded and emotionally disturbed pupils. *Exceptional Children*, 1977, 43, 379–380.
275. CANAVAN–GUMPERT, D. Generating reward and cost orientations through praise and criticism. *Journal of Personality & Social Psychology*, 1977, 35, 501–513.
276. DAY, B., & BRICE, R. Academic achievement, self–concept development, and behavior patterns of six-year-old children in open classrooms. *Elementary School Journal*, 1977, 78, 133–139.
277. FITZPATRICK, J. L., PARR, G. D., & BUTLER, C. G. Fast-accurate and slow–inaccurate conceptual tempos: Are they distinct groups? *Perceptual & Motor Skills*, 1977, 45, 643–647.
278. FOCH, T. T., DEFRIES, J. C., MCCLEARN, G. E., & SINGER, S. M. Familial patterns of impairment in reading disability. *Journal of Educational Psychology*, 1977, 69, 316–329.
279. GIBBS, V., & PROCTOR, S. Reading together: An experiment with the neurological–impress method. *Contemporary Education*, 1977, 48, 156–157.
280. HOPPER, G. Parental understanding of their child's test results as interpreted by elementary school teachers. *Measurement & Evaluation in Guidance*, 1977, 10, 84–89.
281. MERRIFIELD, P. R., & HUMMEL–ROSSI, B. Relationships of indices of eighth grade academic achievement to sex and to measures of differentiated aptitudes and personality traits. *Educational & Psychological Measurement*, 1977, 37, 487–492.
282. RANDEL, M. A., FRY, M. A., & RALLS, E. M. Two readiness measures as predictors of first– and third–grade reading achievement. *Psychology in the Schools*, 1977, 14, 37–40.
283. ROSSMAN, J. F. How one high school set up a reading program for 500 students. *Journal of Reading*, 1977, 20, 393–397.
284. ROTH, R. A. How effective are CBTE programs? *Phi Delta Kappan*, 1977, 58, 757–760.
285. RUBIN, R. A., DORLE, J., & SANDIDGE, S. Self–esteem and school performance. *Psychology in the Schools*, 1977, 14, 503–507.
286. SMITH, M. K., & MCMANIS, D. L. Concurrent validity of the Peabody Individual Achievement Test and the Wide Range Achievement Test. *Psychological Reports*, 1977, 41, 1279–1284.

287. BAKER, A. M., & KAUFFMAN, J. M. Screening LD children with the Lorge–Thorndike. *Academic Therapy*, 1978, 13, 549–552.

288. BRUNING, R. H., BURTON, J. K., & BALLERING, M. Visual and auditory memory: Relationships to reading achievement. *Contemporary Educational Psychology*, 1978, 3, 340–351.

289. BUSSE, T. V., & SERAYDARIAN, L. The relationships between first name desirability and school readiness, IQ, and school achievement. *Psychology in the Schools*, 1978, 15, 297–302.

290. COSTA, A. L. Competency based education: Let's examine the assumptions. *Thrust*, 1978, 7, 26–28.

291. FITZPATRICK, J. L. Academic underachievement, other–direction, and attitudes toward women's roles in bright adolescent females. *Journal of Educational Psychology*, 1978, 70, 645–650.

292. HURLEY, O. L., HIRSHOREN, A., KAVALE, K., & HUNT, J. T. Intercorrelations among tests of general mental ability and achievement for black and white deaf children. *Perceptual & Motor Skills*, 1978, 46, 1107–1113.

293. KLEIN, A. E. The reliability and predictive validity of the Slosson Intelligence Test for pre–kindergarten pupils. *Educational & Psychological Measurement*, 1978, 38, 1211–1217.

294. KLEIN, A. E. The validity of the Beery Test of Visual–Motor integration in predicting achievement in kindergarten, first, and second grades. *Educational & Psychological Measurement*, 1978, 38, 457–461.

295. KNOX, B. J., & GLOVER, J. A. A note on preschool experience effects on achievement, readiness, and creativity. *Journal of Genetic Psychology*, 1978, 132, 151–152.

296. MATEFY, R. E. Evaluation of a remediation program using senior citizens as psychoeducational agents. *Community Mental Health Journal*, 1978, 14, 327–336.

297. MORAN, R. T. Keying results on the CELT–Structure Test to U.S. grade level instructional materials. *Teachers of English to Speakers of Other Languages Quarterly*, 1978, 12, 139–143.

298. NELSON, W. M., III, EDINGER, J. D., & WALLACE, J. The utility of two Wechsler Adult Intelligence Scale short forms with prisoners. *Journal of Personality Assessment*, 1978, 42, 302–311.

299. PORTER, A. C., SCHMIDT, W. H., FLODEN, R. E., & FREEMAN, D. J. Practical significance in program evaluation. *American Educational Research Journal*, 1978, 15, 529–539.

300. RICH, N. S. Occupational knowledge: To what extent is rural youth handicapped? *Vocational Guidance Quarterly*, 1978, 27, 320–325.

301. RUBIN, R. A., & BALOW, B. Prevalence of teacher identified behavior problems: A longitudinal study. *Exceptional Children*, 1978, 45, 102–111.

302. SANNER, R., & MCMANIS, D. L. Concurrent validity of the Peabody Individual Achievement Test and the Wide Range Achievement Test for middle–class elementary school children. *Psychological Reports*, 1978, 42, 19–24.

303. STEINBAUER, E., & HELLER, M. S. The Boehm Test of Basic Concepts as a predictor of academic achievement in grades 2 and 3. *Psychology in the Schools*, 1978, 15, 357–360.

304. THOMAS, J. L. The influence of pictures with written text and achievement on reading comprehension of elementary students. *Southern Journal of Educational Research*, 1978, 13, 37–46.

305. COKER, G. A comparison of self–concepts and academic achievement of visually handicapped children enrolled in a regular school and in a residential school. *Education of the Visually Handicapped*, 1979, 11, 67–74.

306. COLLIGAN, R. C. Predictive utility of the Myklebust Pupil Rating Scale: A two–year follow–up. *Journal of Learning Disabilities*, 1979, 12, 264–267.

307. DOYLE, R. E., GOTTLIEB, B., & SCHNEIDER, D. Underachievers achieve–A case for intensive counseling. *School Counselor*, 1979, 26, 134–143.

308. EVANS, M. A. A comparative study of young children's classroom activities and learning outcomes. *British Journal of Educational Psychology*, 1979, 49, 15–26.

309. GAGNE, E. D., MOORE, J. W., HAUCK, W. E., & HOY, R. V. The effect on children's performance of a discrepancy between adult expectancy and feedback statements. *Journal of Experimental Education*, 1979, 47, 320–324.

310. GEORGE, W. C. The talent–search concept: An identification strategy for the intellectually gifted. *Journal of Special Education*, 1979, 13, 221–237.

311. GETTINGER, M., & WHITE, M. A. Which is the stronger correlate of school learning? Time to learn or measured intelligence? *Journal of Educational Psychology*, 1979, 71, 405–412.

312. HURLEY, O. L. Predictive validity of two mental ability tests with black deaf children. *Journal of Negro Education*, 1979, 48, 14–19.

313. KLEIN, A. E. Additional evidence of the predictive validity of the Stanford Early School Achievement Test. *Educational & Psychological Measurement*, 1979, 39, 1053–1059.

314. KLEIN, A. E. Further evidence on the redundancy of the Stanford Achievement Test. *Educational & Psychological Measurement*, 1979, 39, 1061–1065.

315. LUNDSTEEN, S. W., & WILSON, J. A. R. Permanency of gains for children's problem solving processes and subabilities. *Educational Research Quarterly*, 1979, 4, 41–49.

316. MORROW, B. H. Elementary school performance of offspring of young adolescent mothers. *American Educational Research Journal*, 1979, 16, 423–429.

317. MOSBY, R. J. A bypass program of supportive instruction for secondary students with learning disabilities. *Journal of Learning Disabilities*, 1979, 12, 187–190.

318. NAGLE, R. J. The predictive validity of the Metropolitan Readiness Tests, 1976 Edition. *Educational & Psychological Measurement*, 1979, 39, 1043–1045.

319. PELHAM, W. E. Selective attention deficits in poor readers? Dichotic listening, speeded classification, and auditory and visual central and incidental learning tasks. *Child Development*, 1979, 50, 1050–1061.

320. RINGLER, L. H., SMITH–BURKE, M. T., & MEYERS, R. S. Interactive model of teacher education. In M. L. Kamil & A. J. Moe (Eds.), *Reading research: Studies and applications; Twenty–eighth yearbook of the National Reading Conference*. Clemson, South Carolina: The National Reading Conference, Inc., 1979.

321. RUBIN, R. A., & BALOW, B. Measures of infant development and socioeconomic status as predictors of later intelligence and school achievement. *Developmental Psychology*, 1979, 15, 225–227.

322. SEIDMAN, E., RAPPAPORT, J., KRAMER, J., LINNEY, J. A., HERZBERGER, S., & ALDEN, L. Assessment of classroom behavior: A multiattribute, multisource approach to instrument development and validation. *Journal of Educational Psychology*, 1979, 71, 451–464.

323. TALOUMIS, T. Scores on Piagetian area tasks as predictors of achievement in mathematics over a four–year period. *Journal for Research in Mathematics Education*, 1979, 10, 120–134.

324. TOMLINSON–KEASEY, C., & KELLY, R. R. Is hemispheric specialization important to scholastic achievement? *Cortex*, 1979, 15, 97–107.

325. WILLIAMSON, W. E. The concurrent validity of the 1965 Wide Range Achievement Test with neurologically impaired and emotionally handicapped pupils. *Journal of Learning Disabilities*, 1979, 12, 201–203.

326. BESTGEN, B. J., REYS, R. E., RYBOLT, J. F., & WYATT, J. W. Effectiveness of systematic instruction on attitudes and computational estimation skills of preservice elementary teachers. *Journal for Research in Mathematics Education*, 1980, 11, 124–136.

327. BOOK, R. M. Identification of educationally at–risk children during the kindergarten year: A four–year follow–up study of group test performance. *Psychology in the Schools*, 1980, 17, 153–158.

328. BROOKS, C. R., & RIGGS, S. T. WISC–R, WISC, and reading achievement relationships among hearing–impaired children attending public schools. *Volta Review*, 1980, 82, 96–102.

329. DIAMOND, E. E. The AMEG commission report on sex bias in achievement testing. *Measurement & Evaluation in Guidance*, 1980, 13, 135–147.

330. FORSETH, S. D. Art activities, attitudes, and achievement in elementary mathematics. *Studies in Art Education*, 1980, 21, 22–27.

331. JENSEN, A. R. Uses of sibling data in educational and psychological research. *American Educational Research Journal*, 1980, 17, 153–170.

332. KLEINKE, D. J. Item order, response location, and examinee sex and handedness and performance on a multiple–choice test. *Journal of Educational Research*, 1980, 73, 225–229.

333. KNIFONG, J. D. Computational requirements of standardized word problem tests. *Journal for Research in Mathematics Education*, 1980, 11, 3–9.

334. LEE, C. C. The Homework Helper Program: Volunteer service for academic and social enrichment in the elementary school. *School Counselor*, 1980, 28, 11–21.

335. LEINHARDT, G. Transition rooms: Promoting maturation or reducing education? *Journal of Educational Psychology*, 1980, 72, 55–61.

336. MESSERLY, C. L., & ARAM, D. M. Academic achievement of hearing–impaired students of hearing parents and of hearing impaired parents: Another look. *Volta Review*, 1980, 82, 25–32.

337. PRITCHARD, R. D., HOLLENBACK, J., & DELEO, P. J. The effects of continuous and partial schedules of reinforcement on effort, performance, and satisfaction. *Organizational Behavior & Human Performance*, 1980, 25, 336–353.

338. SHERMAN, L. W., & HOFFMANN, R. J. Achievement as a momentary event, as a continuing state, locus of control: A clarification. *Perceptual & Motor Skills*, 1980, 51, 1159–1166.

339. SWAFFORD, J. O., & KEPNER, H. S., JR. The evaluation of an application–oriented first–year algebra program. *Journal for Research in Mathematics Education*, 1980, 11, 190–201.

340. TREMBLEY, P. W., CAPONIGRO, J. D., & GAFFNEY, V. T. Effects of programming from the WRAT and the PIAT for students determined to have learning disabilities in arithmetic. *Journal of Learning Disabilities*, 1980, 13, 63–65.

341. VICTOR, J. B., & HALVERSON, C. F., JR. Children's friendship choices: Effects of school behavior. *Psychology in the Schools*, 1980, 17, 409–414.

342. ABIDIN, R. R., & SELTZER, J. Special education outcomes; implications for implementation of Public Law 94-142. *Journal of Learning Disabilities*, 1981, 14, 28-31.
343. ARMSTRONG, J. M. Achievement and participation of women in mathematics: Results of two national surveys. *Journal of Research in Mathematics Education*, 1981, 12, 356-372.
344. BRIDGE, C. A., & TIERNEY, R. J. The inferential operations of children across text with narrative and expository tendencies. *Journal of Reading Behavior*, 1981, 13, 201-214.
345. CAMPBELL, R. L. Intellectual development, achievement, and self-concept of elementary minority school children. *School Science & Mathematics*, 1981, 81, 200-204.
346. SHUMWAY, R. J., WHEATLEY, G. H., COBURN, T. G., WHITE, A. L., REYS, R. E., & SCHOEN, H. L. Initial effects of calculators in elementary school mathematics. *Journal for Research in Mathematics Education*, 1981, 12, 119-141.
347. STANOVICH, K. E., CUNNINGHAM, A. E., & WEST, R. F. A longitudinal study of the development of automatic recognition skills in first graders. *Journal of Reading Behavior*, 1981, 13, 57-74.
348. WILLIAMS, P. R., & FORTUNA, S., JR. Reading management systems: Not sufficient, not necessary. *Alberta Journal of Educational Research*, 1981, 27, 93-94.

[2287]
Stanford Achievement Test: Mathematics Tests, 1973 Edition. Grades 1.5-2.4, 2.5-3.4, 3.5-4.4, 4.5-5.4, 5.5-6.9, 7.0-9.5; 1923-75; 2 editions for primary levels 1-3; Richard Madden, Eric F. Gardner, Herbert C. Rudman, Bjorn Karlsen, and Jack C. Merwin; The Psychological Corporation.*

a) PRIMARY LEVEL 1. Grades 1.5-2.4; 3 scores: concepts, computation and applications, total.
b) PRIMARY LEVEL 2. Grades 2.5-3.4; 4 scores: concepts, computation, applications, total.
c) PRIMARY LEVEL 3. Grades 3.5-4.4; 4 scores: same as for primary level 2.
d) INTERMEDIATE LEVEL 1. Grades 4.5-5.4; 4 scores: same as for primary level 2.
e) INTERMEDIATE LEVEL 2. Grades 5.5-6.9; 4 scores: same as for primary level 2.
f) ADVANCED. Grades 7.0-9.5; 4 scores: same as for primary level 2.

For additional information and reviews by E. G. Begle and Marilyn N. Suydam, see 8:291 (5 references); see also T2:655 (17 references); for a review by Harold C. Trimble of the 1964 edition, see 7:527 (6 references); for a review by C. Alan Riedesel of an earlier edition, see 6:637 (7 references); for a review by Robert L. Burch, see 4:419. For reviews of the complete battery, see 8:29 (2 reviews, 2 excerpts), 7:25 (1 excerpt), 6:26 (1 review, 1 excerpt), 5:25 (1 review), 4:25 (2 reviews), and 3:18 (2 reviews).

REFERENCES

1-7. See 6:637.
8-13. See 7:527.
14-30. See T2:655.
31-35. See 8:291.
36. RUBIN, R. A. Stability of self-esteem ratings and their relation to academic achievement: A longitudinal study. *Psychology in the Schools*, 1978, 15, 430-433.
37. RUBIN, R. A., BALOW, B., DORLE, J., & ROSEN, M. Preschool prediction of low achievement in basic school skills. *Journal of Learning Disabilities*, 1978, 11, 664-667.
38. LAMBERT, N. M., & URBANSKI, C. Behavioral profiles of children with different levels of achievement. *Journal of School Psychology*, 1980, 18, 58-66.
39. SWAFFORD, J. O. Sex differences in first-year algebra. *Journal for Research in Mathematics Education*, 1980, 11, 335-346.
40. VAIDYA, S., & CHANSKY, N. Cognitive development and cognitive style as factors in mathematics achievement. *Journal of Educational Psychology*, 1980, 72, 326-330.
41. SMITH, L. T., & HALEY, J. M. Inservice education: Teacher response and student achievement. *School Science & Mathematics*, 1981, 81, 189-194.

[2288]
Stanford Achievement Test: Reading Tests, 1973 Edition. Grades 1.5-2.4, 2.5-3.4, 3.5-4.4, 4.5-5.4, 5.5-6.9, 7.0-9.5; 1923-75; 2 editions for primary levels 1-3; Richard Madden, Eric F. Gardner, Herbert C. Rudman, Bjorn Karlsen, and Jack C. Merwin; The Psychological Corporation.*

a) PRIMARY LEVEL 1. Grades 1.5-2.4; 6 scores: reading (word, comprehension, word plus comprehension), word study skills total, vocabulary.
b) PRIMARY LEVEL 2. Grades 2.5-3.4; 6 scores: same as for primary level 1.
c) PRIMARY LEVEL 3. Grades 3.5-4.4; 4 scores: comprehension, word study skills, total, vocabulary.
d) INTERMEDIATE LEVEL 1. Grades 4.5-5.4; 4 scores: same as for primary level 3.
e) INTERMEDIATE LEVEL 2. Grades 5.5-6.9; 4 scores: same as for primary level 3.
f) ADVANCED. Grades 7.0-9.5; 3 scores: vocabulary, comprehension, total.

For additional information and reviews by Gene V Glass and Earl F. Rankin, see 8:745 (22 references); see also T2:1603 (32 references); for a review by Arthur E. Traxler of the 1964 edition, see 7:708 (16 references); see also 6:813 (1 reference); for reviews by Helen M. Robinson and Agatha Townsend of an earlier edition, see 5:656; for a review by James R. Hobson, see 4:555 (4 references); for a review by Margaret G. McKim, see 3:503. For reviews of the complete battery, see 8:29 (2 reviews, 2 excerpts), 7:25 (1 excerpt), 6:26 (1 review, 1 excerpt), 5:25 (1 review), 4:25 (2 reviews), and 3:18 (2 reviews).

REFERENCES

1-4. See 4:555.
5. See 6:813.
6-21. See 7:708.
22-53. See T2:1603.
54-75. See 8:745.
76. DEWITZ, P. Criterion-referenced tests and the Reading Miscue Inventory: Re-evaluating diagnostic procedures. *41st Claremont Reading Conference Yearbook*, 1977, 148-158.
77. GIBBS, V., & PROCTOR, S. Reading together: An experiment with the neurological-impress method. *Contemporary Education*, 1977, 48, 156-157.
78. HARE, B. A. Perceptual deficits are not a cue to reading problems in second grade. *Reading Teacher*, 1977, 30, 624-628.
79. KELLY, D. H. How the school and teachers create deviants. *Contemporary Education*, 1977, 48, 202-205.
80. KENDER, J. P., & RUBENSTEIN, H. Recall versus reinspection in IRI Comprehension Tests. *Reading Teacher*, 1977, 30, 776-779.
81. ANDERSON, C. C., & MAGUIRE, T. O. The effect of TV viewing on the educational performance of elementary school children. *Alberta Journal of Educational Research*, 1978, 24, 156-163.
82. AVER, M., LAHR, D., & DOCTER, R. Social and institutional factors in reading achievement in elementary schools. *Educational Research Quarterly*, 1978, 3, 3-18.
83. BEAN, T. W. Decoding strategies of Hawaiian Islands dialect speakers in grades four, five, and six. *Reading World*, 1978, 17, 295-305.
84. RUBIN, R. A. Stability of self-esteem ratings and their relation to academic achievement: A longitudinal study. *Psychology in the Schools*, 1978, 15, 430-433.
85. VORIH, L., & ROSIER, P. Rock Point Community School: An example of a Navajo-English bilingual elementary school program. *Teachers of English to Speakers of Other Languages Quarterly*, 1978, 12, 263-269.
86. BENSON, G. P., HAYCRAFT, J. L., STEYAERT, J. P., & WEIGEL, D. J. Mobility in sixth graders as related to achievement, adjustment, and socioeconomic status. *Psychology in the Schools*, 1979, 16, 444-447.
87. RITZEN, J. M., WINKLER, D. R., & HARGREAVES-HEAP, S. Teacher preferences and the level and distribution of scholastic achievement. *Journal of Experimental Education*, 1979, 47, 311-319.
88. LAMBERT, N. M., & URBANSKI, C. Behavioral profiles of children with different levels of achievement. *Journal of School Psychology*, 1980, 18, 58-66.

89. MATHEWS, R. C., COON, R. C., & ROSENTHAL, G. T. Broken text as a predictor of reading ability in the early grades. *Reading World*, 1980, 20, 57–64.
90. MCCAUGHEY, M. W., JUOLA, J. F., SCHADLER, M., & WARD, N. J. Whole–word units are used before orthographic knowledge in perceptual development. *Journal of Experimental Child Psychology*, 1980, 30, 411–421.

[2289]
Stanford-Binet Intelligence Scale, Third Revision.

Ages 2 and over; 1916–73; S-B; revised IQ tables by Samuel R. Pinneau; norms supplement by Robert L. Thorndike; Lewis M. Terman and Maud A. Merrill; Riverside Publishing Co. (British edition: Harrap Ltd. [England].)*

For additional information, see 8:229 (176 references); see also T2:525 (428 references); for a review by David Freides, see 7:425 (258 references); for a review by Elizabeth D. Fraser and excerpted reviews by Benjamin Balinski, L. B. Birch, James Maxwell, Marie D. Neale, and Julian C. Stanley, see 6:536 (110 references); for reviews by Mary R. Haworth and Norman D. Sundberg of the second revision, see 5:413 (121 references); for a review by Boyd R. McCandless, see 4:358 (142 references); see also 3:292 (217 references); for excerpted reviews by Cyril Burt, Grace H. Kent, and M. Krugman, see 2:1420 (132 references); for reviews by Francis N. Maxfield, J. W. M. Rothney, and F. L. Wells, see 1:1062.

REFERENCES

1–134. See 2:1420.
135–351. See 3:292.
352–493. See 4:358.
494–620. See 5:413.
621–728. See 6:536.
729–986. See 7:425.
987–1414. See T2:525.
1415–1590. See 8:229.

1591. LOPATA, D. J., & PASNAK, R. Accelerated conservation acquisition and IQ gains by blind children. *Genetic Psychology Monographs*, 1976, 93, 3–25.
1592. WHYTE, L. Prescriptive teaching: Changes in stage of logico-mathematical thinking and spatial development in a group of opportunity class children. *Alberta Journal of Educational Research*, 1976, 22, 34–43.
1593. BARRY, K., APOLLONI, T., & COOKE, T. A. Improving the personal hygiene of mildly retarded men in a community based residential training program. *Corrective & Social Psychiatry & Journal of Behavior Technology, Methods & Therapy*, 1977, 23, 65–68.
1594. BELL, A. E., ABRAHAMSON, D. S., & MCRAE, K. N. Reading retardation: A 12-year prospective study. *Journal of Pediatrics*, 1977, 91, 363–370.
1595. BEVERIDGE, M., & MITTLER, P. Feedback, language and listener performance in severely retarded children. *British Journal of Disorders of Communication*, 1977, 12, 149–157.
1596. BLOOM, A. S., KLEE, S. H., & RASKIN, L. M. A comparison of the Stanford–Binet abbreviated and complete forms for developmentally disabled children. *Journal of Clinical Psychology*, 1977, 33, 477–480.
1597. BRADLEY, R. H., & CALDWELL, B. M. Home observation for measurement of the environment: A validation study of screening efficiency. *American Journal of Mental Deficiency*, 1977, 81, 417–420.
1598. BROOKS, C. R. WISC, WISC–R, S–BL&M, WRAT: Relationships and trends among children ages six to ten referred for psychological evaluation. *Psychology in the Schools*, 1977, 14, 30–33.
1599. BROWNE, T., STOTSKY, B. A., & EICHORN, J. A selective comparison of psychological, developmental, social, and academic factors among emotionally disturbed children in three treatment settings. *Child Psychiatry & Human Development*, 1977, 7, 231–253.
1600. CALEF, R. S., CALEF, R. A., PIPER, E., & WILSON, S. A. Imagined verbal transformations as a function of age and verbal intelligence. *Bulletin of the Psychonomic Society*, 1977, 10, 109–110.
1601. CARTELLI, L. M. The effects of paradigmatic language training on the reading process: An experimental study. *National Reading Conference Yearbook*, 1977, 267–271.
1602. CHASEY, W. C. Motor skill overlearning effects on retention and relearning by retarded boys. *Research Quarterly*, 1977, 48, 41–46.
1603. CHERRY, F. F., & EATON, E. L. Physical and cognitive development in children of low-income mothers working in the child's early years. *Child Development*, 1977, 48, 158–166.

1604. DOBBINS, D. A., & RARICK, G. L. The performance of intellectually normal and educable mentally retarded boys on tests of throwing accuracy. *Journal of Motor Behavior*, 1977, 9, 23–28.
1605. ESCOBAR, V., EASTMAN, J., WEAVER, D., & MELNICK, M. Maxillofacial dysostosis. *Journal of Medical Genetics*, 1977, 14, 355–358.
1606. EVANS, D. The development of language abilities in mongols: A correlational study. *Journal of Mental Deficiency & Research*, 1977, 21, 103–117.
1607. EVANS, T., PIERCE, L., YORK, R., & BROWN, L. Increasing the speech intensity of a retarded–emotionally disturbed student in a public school classroom. *Child Study Journal*, 1977, 7, 131–144.
1608. FINLEY, K. H., BUSE, S. T., POPPER, R. W., HONZIK, M. P., COLLART, D. S., & RIGGS, N. Intellectual functioning of children with tetralogy of fallot: Influence of open-heart surgery and earlier palliative operations. *Journal of Pediatrics*, 1977, 85, 318–323.
1609. GAMER, E., GRUNEBAUM, H., COHLER, B. J., & GALLANT, D. H. Children at risk: Performance of three-year-olds and their mentally ill and well mothers on an interaction task. *Child Psychiatry & Human Development*, 1977, 8, 102–114.
1610. GOLDEN, M., MONTARE, A., & BRIDGER, W. Verbal control of delay behavior in two-year-old boys as a function of social class. *Child Development*, 1977, 48, 1107–1111.
1611. GOLOMB, C. Representational development of the human figure: A look at the neglected variables of SES, IQ, Sex, and verbalization. *Journal of Genetic Psychology*, 1977, 131, 207–222.
1612. GOODMAN, J. F. Medical Diagnosis and intelligence levels in young mentally retarded children. A follow-up study. *Journal of Mental Deficiency Research*, 1977, 21, 205–212.
1613. HAGEN, R. L., DURHAM, T., & SHANNON, D. Administration of digit span on the Wechsler and Binet: Differences that matter. *Journal of Clinical Psychology*, 1977, 33, 480–482.
1614. HALL, V. C., & KAYE, D. B. Patterns of early cognitive development among boys in four subcultural groups. *Journal of Educational Psychology*, 1977, 69, 66–87.
1615. HASLAM, R. H. A., ALLEN, J. R., DORSEN, M. M., KANOFSKY, D. L., MELLITS, E. D., & NORRIS, D. A. The sequelae of group B β-hemolytic streptococcal meningitis in early infancy. *American Journal of Diseases of Children*, 1977, 131, 845–849.
1616. HUNTER, A. G. W., MCALPINE, P. J., RUDD, N. L., & FRASER, F. C. A "new" syndrome of mental retardation with characteristic facies and brachyphalangy. *Journal of Medical Genetics*, 1977, 14, 430–437.
1617. KAUFMAN, A. S., & VAN HAGEN, J. Investigation of the WISC–R for use with retarded children: Correlation with the 1972 Stanford–Binet and comparison of WISC and WISC–R profiles. *Psychology in the Schools*, 1977, 14, 10–14.
1618. KELLAGHAN, T. Relationships between home environment and scholastic behavior in a disadvantaged population. *Journal of Educational Psychology*, 1977, 69, 754–760.
1619. KIBBY, M. W. Note on relationship of word difficulty and word frequency. *Psychological Reports*, 1977, 41, 12–14.
1620. KLONOFF, H., LOW, M. D., & CLARK, C. Head injuries in children: A prospective five year follow-up. *Journal of Neurology, Neurosurgery & Psychiatry*, 1977, 40, 1211–1219.
1621. LERER, R. J., & LERER, M. P. Responses of adolescents with minimal brain dysfunction to methylphenidate. *Journal of Learning Disabilities*, 1977, 10, 223–228.
1622. LERER, R. J., LERER, M. P., & ARTNER, J. The effects of methylphenidate on the handwriting of children with minimal brain dysfunction. *Journal of Pediatrics*, 1977, 91, 127–132.
1623. LEVINSON, B. M., & BLOCK, Z. Goodenough–Harris drawings of Jewish children of Orthodox background. *Psychological Reports*, 1977, 41, 155–158.
1624. LEWIS, H. P., & LIVSON, N. Personality correlates of IQ discrepancy: Stanford–Binet and Goodenough–Harris. *Journal of Genetic Psychology*, 1977, 131, 237–242.
1625. LLOYD, B. B., & EASTON, B. The intellectual development of Yoruba children. *Journal of Cross-Cultural Psychology*, 1977, 8, 3–16.
1626. MACWHINNEY, B., & OSSER, H. Verbal planning functions in children's speech. *Child Development*, 1977, 48, 978–985.
1627. MCCALL, R. B. Childhood IQ's as predictors of adult educational and occupational status. *Science*, 1977, 197, 482–483.
1628. MCCALL, R. B., EICHORN, D. H., & HOGARTY, P. S. Transitions in early mental development. *Monographs of the Society for Research in Child Development*, 1977, 42, 1–108.
1629. MIRANDA, S. B., HACK, M., FANTZ, R. L., FANAROFF, A. A., & KLAUS, M. H. Neonatal pattern vision: A predictor of future mental performance? *Journal of Pediatrics*, 1977, 91, 642–647.
1630. MOEN, J. L., WILCOX, R. D., & BURNS, J. K. PKU as a factor in the development of self-esteem. *Journal of Pediatrics*, 1977, 90, 1027–1029.
1631. MORRIS, J. J., & CLARIZIO, S. Improvement in IQ of high-risk, disadvantaged preschool children enrolled in a developmental program. *Psychological Reports*, 1977, 41, 1111–1114.

1632. MULLER, D. P. R., LLOYD, J. K., & BIRD, A. C. Long-term management of abetalipoproteinaemia: Possible role for vitamin E. *Archives of Diseases in Childhood*, 1977, 52, 209–214.

1633. PODRUCH, P. E., & WEISSKOPF, B. Trisomy for the short arms of chromosome 9 in two generations, with balanced translocations t(15p+;9q-) in three generations. *Journal of Pediatrics*, 1977, 85, 92–95.

1634. RESCH, R. C., LILLESKOV, R. K., SCHUR, H. M., & MIHALOV, T. Infant day care as a treatment intervention: A follow-up comparison study. *Child Psychiatry & Human Development*, 1977, 7, 147–155.

1635. RIE, E. D., & RIE, H. E. Recall, retention, and Ritalin. *Journal of Consulting & Clinical Psychology*, 1977, 45, 967–972.

1636. ROE, K. V. Correlations between Gesell scores in infancy and performance on verbal and nonverbal tests in early childhood. *Perceptual & Motor Skills*, 1977, 45, 1131–1134.

1637. RUST, J. O., & OSTER, G. D. Accuracy of feelings of correctness on the WAIS and Binet. *Psychological Reports*, 1977, 41, 1275–1278.

1638. SEWELL, T., & MANNI, J. Comparison of scores of normal children on the WISC-R and Stanford-Binet, Form LM, 1972. *Perceptual & Motor Skills*, 1977, 45, 1057–1058.

1639. SEWELL, T. E. A comparison of the WPPSI and Stanford-Binet Intelligence Scale (1972) among lower SES black children. *Psychology in the Schools*, 1977, 14, 158–161.

1640. SHAKOW, D. The nature of deterioration in schizophrenic conditions. *Psychological Issues*, 1977, 10, 4–86.

1641. SHAPIRO, S., HEINONEN, O. P., SISKIND, V., KAUFMAN, D. W., MONSON, R. R., & SLONE, D. Antenatal exposure to doxylamine succinate and dicyclomine hydrochloride (Bendectin) in relation to congenital malformations, perinatal mortality rate, birth weight, and intelligence quotient score. *American Journal of Obstetrics & Gynecology*, 1977, 128, 480–485.

1642. SHORR, D. N., MCCLELLAND, S. E., & ROBINSON, H. B. Corrected mental age scores for the Stanford-Binet Intelligence Scale. *Measurement & Evaluation in Guidance*, 1977, 10, 144–147.

1643. SLONE, D., SISKIND, V., HEINONEN, O. P., MONSON, R. R., KAUFMAN, D. W., & SHAPIRO, S. Antenatal exposure to phenothiazines in relation to cogenital malformations, perinatal mortality rate, birth weight, and intelligence quotient score. *American Journal of Obstetrics & Gynecology*, 1977, 128, 486–488.

1644. STEHBENS, J. A., BAKER, G. L., & KITCHELL, M. Outcome at ages 1, 3, and 5 years of children born to diabetic women. *American Journal of Obstetrics & Gynecology*, 1977, 127, 408–413.

1645. STERNBERG, L., EPSTEIN, M. H., & ADAMS, D. Performance characteristics of retarded and normal students on pattern recognition tasks. *Contemporary Educational Psychology*, 1977, 2, 209–218.

1646. THOMPSON, R. J., JR. Consequences of using the 1972 Stanford-Binet Intelligence Scale norms. *Psychology in the Schools*, 1977, 14, 444–448.

1647. THORNDIKE, R. L. Causation of Binet IQ decrements. *Journal of Educational Measurement*, 1977, 14, 197–202.

1648. WEISZ, J. R. A follow-up developmental study of hypothesis behavior among mentally retarded and nonretarded children. *Journal of Experimental Child Psychology*, 1977, 24, 108–122.

1649. WILLERMAN, L., & FIEDLER, M. F. Intellectually precocious preschool children: Early development and later intellectual accomplishments. *Journal of Genetic Psychology*, 1977, 131, 13–20.

1650. ANDERT, J. N., HUSTAK, T. L., & DINNING, W. D. Bender-Gestalt reproduction times for retarded adults. *Journal of Clinical Psychology*, 1978, 34, 927–929.

1651. AYRES, A. J. Learning disabilities and the vestibular system. *Journal of Learning Disabilities*, 1978, 11, 18–29.

1652. BEDROSIAN, J. L., & PRUTTING, C. A. Communicative performance of mentally retarded adults in four conversational settings. *Journal of Speech & Hearing Research*, 1978, 21, 79–95.

1653. CAMPBELL, M., GELLER, B., SMALL, A. M., PETTI, T. A., & FERRIS, S. H. Minor physical anomalies in young psychotic children. *American Journal of Psychiatry*, 1978, 135, 573–575.

1654. CAREY, J. C., & HALL, B. D. Confirmation of the Cohen Syndrome. *Journal of Pediatrics*, 1978, 93, 239–244.

1655. COCHRAN, J. W., FOX, J. H., & KELLY, M. P. Reversible mental symptoms in temporal arthritis. *Journal of Nervous & Mental Disease*, 1978, 166, 446–447.

1656. DAVIDSON, P. W., WILLOUGHBY, R. H., O'TUAMA, L. A., SWISHER, C. N., & BENJAMINS, D. Neurological and intellectual sequelae of Reye's Syndrome. *American Journal of Mental Deficiency*, 1978, 82, 535–541.

1657. DESOUSA, A. L., KLEIMAN, M. B., & MEALEY, J., JR. Quadriplegia and cortical blindness in hemophilus influenzae meningitis. *Journal of Pediatrics*, 1978, 93, 253–254.

1658. DIEBOLD, M. H., CURTIS, W. S., & DUBOSE, R. F. Developmental scales versus observational measures for deaf-blind children. *Exceptional Children*, 1978, 44, 275–278.

1659. DOUGLAS, J. E., & SUTTON, A. The development of speech and mental processes in a pair of twins: A case study. *Journal of Child Psychology & Psychiatry & Allied Disciplines*, 1978, 19, 49–56.

1660. DOYLE, A. B., & SOMERS, K. The effects of group and family day care on infant attachment behaviours. *Canadian Journal of Behavioural Science*, 1978, 10, 38–45.

1661. DUBE, G. G., & RUDOLF, J. A. Performance of black head start children on the Vane Kindergarten Test and the Stanford-Binet as related to age and sex variables. *Journal of Clinical Psychology*, 1978, 34, 431–437.

1662. ESON, M. E., YEN, J. K., & BOURKE, R. S. Assessment of recovery from serious head injury. *Journal of Neurosurgery & Psychiatry*, 1978, 41, 1036–1042.

1663. FRANZINI, L. R., & LITROWNIK, A. J. Influence of the modeling of grouped stimuli during rehearsal on digit recall in children. *Psychological Record*, 1978, 28, 115–122.

1664. FUNDERBURK, S. J., & FERJO, N. Clinical observations in Klinefelter (47, XXY) syndrome. *Journal of Mental Deficiency Research*, 1978, 22, 207–212.

1665. GERKEN, K. C., HANCOCK, K. A., & WADE, T. H. A comparison of the Stanford-Binet Intelligence Scale and the McCarthy Scales of Children's Abilities with preschool children. *Psychology in the Schools*, 1978, 15, 468–472.

1666. GOLDSTEIN, D., MEYER, W. J., & EGELAND, B. Cognitive performance and competence characteristics of lower- and middle-class preschool children. *Journal of Genetic Psychology*, 1978, 132, 177–183.

1667. GOODMAN, J. F., & CAMERON, J. The meaning of IQ constancy in young retarded children. *Journal of Genetic Psychology*, 1978, 132, 109–119.

1668. HALL, P. K., & TOMBLIN, J. B. A follow-up study of children with articulation and language disorders. *Journal of Speech & Hearing Disorders*, 1978, 43, 227–241.

1669. HASKINS, R., RAMEY, C. T., STEDMAN, D. J., BLACHER-DIXON, J., & PIERCE, J. E. Effects of repeated assessment on standardized test performance by infants. *American Journal of Mental Deficiency*, 1978, 83, 233–239.

1670. HINDLEY, C. B., & OWEN, C. F. The extent of individual changes in I.Q. for ages between 6 months and 17 years, in a British longitudinal sample. *Journal of Child Psychology & Psychiatry & Allied Disciplines*, 1978, 19, 329–350.

1671. HOLYROYD, J., & GOLDENBERG, I. The use of goal attainment scaling to evaluate a ward treatment program for disturbed children. *Journal of Clinical Psychology*, 1978, 34, 732–739.

1672. KAUFMAN, A. S. The importance of basic concepts in the individual assessment of preschool children. *Journal of School Psychology*, 1978, 16, 207–211.

1673. KAUFMAN, A. S., & WATERSTREET, M. A. Determining a child's strong and weak areas of functioning on the Stanford-Binet: A simplification of Sattler's SD method. *Journal of School Psychology*, 1978, 16, 72–78.

1674. KILLAN, J. B., & HUGHES, L. C. A comparison of short forms of the Wechsler Intelligence Scale for Children-Revised in the screening of gifted referrals. *Gifted Child Quarterly*, 1978, 22, 111–115.

1675. LANDIG, H., & NAUMANN, T. F. Aspects of intelligence in gifted preschoolers. *Gifted Child Quarterly*, 1978, 22, 85–89.

1676. LANGEVIN, R., PAITICH, D., FREEMAN, R., MANN, K., & HANDY, L. Personality characteristics and sexual anomalies in males. *Canadian Journal of Behavioural Science*, 1978, 10, 222–238.

1677. LITROWNIK, A. J., FREITAS, J. L., & FRANZINI, L. R. Self-regulation in mentally retarded children: Assessment and training of self-monitoring skills. *American Journal of Mental Deficiency*, 1978, 82, 499–506.

1678. MANS, L., CICCHETTI, D., & SROUFE, L. A. Mirror reactions of Down's Syndrome infants and toddlers: Cognitive underpinnings of self-recognition. *Child Development*, 1978, 49, 1247–1250.

1679. MARHOLIN, D., II, POHL, R. E., III, STEWART, R. M., TOUCHETTE, P. E., TOWNSEND, N. M., & KOLODNY, E. H. Effects of diet and behavior therapy on social and motor behavior of retarded phenylketonuric adults: An experimental analysis. *Pediatric Research*, 1978, 12, 179–187.

1680. MORRISON, D., & POTHIER, P. Effects of sensory-motor training on the language development of retarded preschoolers. *American Journal of Orthopsychiatry*, 1978, 48, 310–319.

1681. O'DONNELL, J. P., PAULSEN, K. A., & MCGAUN, J. D. Matching familiar figures test: A unidimensional measure of reflection-impulsivity? *Perceptual & Motor Skills*, 1978, 47, 1247–1253.

1682. RAMEY, C. T., & CAMPBELL, F. A. Compensatory education for disadvantaged children. *School Review*, 1978, 87, 171–189.

1683. RASKIN, L. M., BLOOM, A. S., KLEE, S. H., & REESE, A. The assessment of developmentally disabled children with the WISC-R, Binet, and other tests. *Journal of Clinical Psychology*, 1978, 34, 111–114.

1684. ROE, K. V. Infant's mother-stranger discrimination at 3 months as a predictor of cognitive development at 3 and 5 years. *Developmental Psychology*, 1978, 14, 191–192.

1685. ROSEN, R. C., & LIGHTNER, E. S. Phenotypic malformations in association with maternal trimethadione therapy. *Journal of Pediatrics*, 1978, 92, 240–244.

1686. RUBIN, R. A., & BALOW, B. Prevalence of teacher identified behavior problems: Longitudinal study. *Exceptional Children*, 1978, 45, 102–111.

1687. SACHS, H. K., KRALL, V., McCAUGHRAN, D. A., ROZENFELD, I. H., YOUNGSMITH, N., GROWE, G., LAZAR, B. S., NOVAR, L., O'CONNELL, L., & RAYSON, B. I.Q. following treatment of lead poisoning: A patient–sibling comparison. *Journal of Pediatrics*, 1978, 93, 428–431.

1688. SCHUEPFER, T., & GHOLSON, B. Effects of IQ and mental age on hypothesis testing in normal and retarded children: A methodological analysis. *Developmental Psychology*, 1978, 14, 423–424.

1689. SINGER, J. H. Evaluating program placement in an institution for the mentally retarded: A multivariate approach. *Journal of Special Education*, 1978, 12, 133–142.

1690. STREISSGUTH, A. P., HERMAN, C. S., & SMITH, D. W. Intelligence, behavior, and dysmorphogenesis in the fetal alcohol syndrome: A report of 20 patients. *Journal of Pediatrics*, 1978, 92, 363–367.

1691. TROUTMAN, J. G. Cognitive predictors of final grades in finite mathematics. *Educational & Psychological Measurement*, 1978, 38, 401–404.

1692. WADE, T. C., BAKER, T. B., MORTON, T. L., & BAKER, L. J. The status of psychological testing in clinical psychology: Relationships between test use and professional activities and orientations. *Journal of Personality Assessment*, 1978, 42, 3–10.

1693. WHITE, C. A., GOPLERUD, C. P., KISKER, C. T., STEHBENS, J. A., KITCHELL, M., & TAYLOR, J. C. Intrauterine fetal transfusion, 1965–1976, with an assessment of the surviving children. *American Journal of Obstetrics & Gynecology*, 1978, 130, 933–940.

1694. WILTON, K., & BARBOUR, A. Mother–child interaction in high-risk and contrast preschoolers of low socioeconomic status. *Child Development*, 1978, 49, 1136–1145.

1695. ZESKIND, P. S., & RAMEY, C. T. Fetal malnutrition: An experimental study of its consequences on infant development in two care giving environments. *Child Development*, 1978, 49, 1155–1162.

1696. ABRAHAMSON, D. S., & BELL, A. E. Assessment of the school readiness section of the early detection inventory: Preschool prediction across situational factors. *Journal of School Psychology*, 1979, 17, 162–171.

1697. BEADLE, K. R. Clinical interactions of verbal language, learning and behavior. *Journal of Clinical Child Psychology*, 1979, 8, 201–205.

1698. BENNETT, F. C., SELLS, C. J., & BRAND, C. Influences on measured intelligence in Down's Syndrome. *American Journal of Diseases of Children*, 1979, 133, 700–703.

1699. BOSSARD, M. D., & GALUSHA, R. The utility of the Stanford–Binet in predicting WRAT performance. *Psychology in the Schools*, 1979, 16, 488–490.

1700. BRUNNER, R. L., O'GRADY, D. J., PARTIN, J. C., PARTIN, J. S., & SCHUBERT, W. K. Neuropsychologic consequences of Reye Syndrome. *Journal of Pediatrics*, 1979, 95, 706–711.

1701. CAMFIELD, C. S., CHAPLIN, S., DOYLE, A., SHAPIRO, S. H., CUMMINGS, C., & CAMFIELD, P. R. Side effects of phenobarbital in toddlers: Behavioral and cognitive aspects. *Journal of Pediatrics*, 1979, 95, 361–365.

1702. CLARKE–STEWART, K. A., VANDER STOEP, L. P., & KILLIAN, G. A. Analysis and replication of mother–child relations at two years of age. *Child Development*, 1979, 50, 777–793.

1703. CLARREN, S. K., SMITH, D. W., HARVEY, M. A. S., WARD, R. H., & MYRIANTHOPOULOS, N. C. Hyperthermia—A prospective evaluation of a possible teratogenic agent in man. *Journal of Pediatrics*, 1979, 95, 81–83.

1704. CRAWFORD, J. H., & FRY, M. A. Trait–task interaction in intra- and intermodal matching of auditory and visual trigrams. *Contemporary Educational Psychology*, 1979, 4, 1–10.

1705. DAUPHINAIS, S. M., & BRADLEY, R. W. IQ change and occupational level: A longitudinal study with third Harvard growth study participants. *Journal of Vocational Behavior*, 1979, 15, 367–375.

1706. FORNESS, S. R., SILVERSTEIN, A. B., & GUTHRIE, D. Relationship between classroom behavior and achievement of mildly mentally retarded children. *American Journal of Mental Deficiency*, 1979, 84, 260–265.

1707. GOLD, P. Suspected neurological impairment and cognitive abilities: A longitudinal study. *Psychological Reports*, 1979, 45, 215–218.

1708. GOLD, P. Suspected neurological impairment (SNI) and cognitive abilities: A longitudinal study of selected skills and predictive accuracy. *Journal of Clinical Child Psychology*, 1979, 8, 35–38.

1709. GOLD, P., & BERK, R. A. Prediction of the academic success of children with suspected neurological impairments. *Journal of Clinical Psychology*, 1979, 35, 505–509.

1710. GRASSI, J. R., LA MORTO-CORSE, A. Identification and remediation of basic cognitive deficits in disadvantaged children. *Journal of Learning Disabilities*, 1979, 12, 483–487.

1711. HARKULICH, J. F., MARCHNER, T. J., & BROWN, E. B. Neurological, neuropsychological, and behavioral correlates of Klinefelter's Syndrome. *Journal of Nervous & Mental Disease*, 1979, 167, 359–363.

1712. HILLMAN, L. S., HILLMAN, R. E., & DODSON, W. E. Diagnosis, treatment, and follow-up of neonatal mepivacaine intoxication secondary to paracervical and pudendal blocks during labor. *Journal of Pediatrics*, 1979, 95, 472–477.

1713. HINDLEY, C. B., & OWEN, C. F. An analysis of individual patterns of DQ and IQ curves from 6 months to 17 years. *British Journal of Psychology*, 1979, 70, 273–293.

1714. JOHNSON, R. A. Verbal originality in the absence of sight: Blind versus sighted adolescents. *Child Study Journal*, 1979, 9, 261–271.

1715. KIERSCHT, M. S., & MEVWISSEN, J. Follow-up of preschool age survivors of neonatal intensive care. *Journal of Psychology*, 1979, 101, 129–134.

1716. KNOBBE, T., MEIER, P., WENAR, C., & CORDERO, L. Psychological development of children who received intrauterine transfusions. *American Journal of Obstetrics & Gynecology*, 1979, 133, 877–879.

1717. KOFF, E., KAMMERER, B., BOYLE, P., & PUESCHEL, S. M. Intelligence and phenylketonuria: Effects of diet termination. *Journal of Pediatrics*, 1979, 94, 534–537.

1718. KONSTANTAREAS, M. M., WEBSTER, C. D., & OXMAN, J. Manual language acquisition and its influence on other areas of functioning in four autistic and autistic–like children. *Journal of Child Psychology & Psychiatry & Allied Disciplines*, 1979, 20, 337–350.

1719. KROHN, E. J., & TRAXLERE, A. J. Relationship of the McCarthy Scales of Children's Abilities to other measures of preschool cognitive, motor, and perceptual development. *Perceptual & Motor Skills*, 1979, 49, 783–790.

1720. LEVENSON, R. L., JR., & ZINO, T. C., II. Assessment of cognitive deficiency with the McCarthy scales and Stanford–Binet: A correlational analysis. *Perceptual & Motor Skills*, 1979, 48, 291–295.

1721. LUDLOW, J. R., & ALLEN, L. M. The effect of early intervention and pre-school stimulus on the development of the Down's Syndrome child. *Journal of Mental Deficiency Research*, 1979, 23, 29–44.

1722. LYTLE, W. G., & CAMPBELL, N. J. Do special programs affect the social status of the gifted? *Elementary School Journal*, 1979, 80, 93–97.

1723. MARTIN, F. Is it necessary to retest children in special education classes? *Journal of Learning Disabilities*, 1979, 12, 388–392.

1724. MERRITT, T. A., WHITE, C. L., JACOB, J., KURLINSKI, J., MARTIN, J., DISESSA, T. G., EDWARDS, D., FRIEDMAN, W. F., & GLUCK, L. Patient ductus arteriosus treated with ligation or indomethacin: A follow-up study. *Journal of Pediatrics*, 1979, 95, 588–594.

1725. NAGLIERI, J. A., & HARRISON, P. L. Comparison of McCarthy general cognitive indexes and Stanford–Binet IQs for educable mentally retarded children. *Perceptual & Motor Skills*, 1979, 48, 1251–1254.

1726. PANEK, P. E., & HAACK, R. Abbreviated forms of the Stanford–Binet, L–M: Reliability and effects on classification of institutionalized mentally retarded adults. *Psychological Reports*, 1979, 45, 676–678.

1727. PANEK, P. E., & WAGNER, E. E. Relationship between Hand Test variables and mental retardation: A confirmation and extension. *Journal of Personality Assessment*, 1979, 43, 600–603.

1728. PERRY, J. D., GUIDUBALDI, J., & KEHLE, T. J. Kindergarten competencies as predictors of third-grade classroom behavior and achievement. *Journal of Educational Psychology*, 1979, 71, 443–450.

1729. POWAZEK, M., & BILLMEIER, G. J., JR. Assessment of intellectual development after surgery for craniofacial dysostosis. *American Journal of Diseases of Children*, 1979, 133, 151–153.

1730. RAMEY, C. T., FARRAN, D. C., & CAMPBELL, F. A. Predicting IQ from mother–infant interactions. *Child Development*, 1979, 50, 804–814.

1731. ROTATORI, A. F., SEDLACK, B., & FREAGON, S. Usefulness of the Slosson Intelligence Test with severely and profoundly retarded children. *Perceptual & Motor Skills*, 1979, 48, 334.

1732. RUBIN, R. A., & BALOW, B. Measures of infant development and socioeconomic status as predictors of later intelligence and school achievement. *Developmental Psychology*, 1979, 15, 225–227.

1733. RUBIN, R. A., BALOW, B., & FISCH, R. O. Neonatal serum, bilirubin levels related to cognitive development at ages 4 through 7 years. *Journal of Pediatrics*, 1979, 94, 601–604.

1734. SEGAL, S., RUTMAN, J. Y., & FRIMPTER, G. W. Galactokinase deficiency and mental retardation. *Journal of Pediatrics*, 1979, 95, 750–752.

1735. SIEGEL, L. S. Infant perceptual, cognitive, and motor behaviors as predictors of subsequent cognitive and language development. *Canadian Journal of Psychology*, 1979, 33, 382–395.

1736. TOBEY, E. A., CULLEN, J. K., JR., RAMPP, D. L., & FLEISCHER–GALLAGHER, A. M. Effects of stimulus-onset asynchrony on the dichotic performance of children with auditory–processing disorders. *Journal of Speech & Hearing Research*, 1979, 22, 197–211.

1737. VANDIVER, P. L., & VANDIVER, S. S. A "nonbiased assessment" of intelligence testing. *Educational Forum*, 1979, 44, 97–108.

1738. WATERS, E., WIPPMAN, J., & SROUFE, L. A. Attachment, positive affect, and competence in the peer group: Two studies in construct validation. *Child Development*, 1979, 50, 821–829.

1739. WEISZ, J. R. Perceived control and learned helplessness among mentally retarded and nonretarded children: A developmental analysis. *Developmental Psychology*, 1979, 15, 311–319.

1740. BAKEMAN, R., & BROWN, J. V. Early interaction: Consequences for social and mental development at three years. *Child Development*, 1980, 51, 437–447.

1741. BERBAUM, M. L., & MORELAND, R. L. Intellectual development within the family: A new application of the confluence model. *Developmental Psychology*, 1980, 16, 506–515.

1742. BOOK, R. M. Identification of educationally at-risk children during the kindergarten year: A four-year follow-up study of group test performance. *Psychology in the Schools*, 1980, 17, 153–158.

1743. BOSSARD, M. D., REYNOLDS, C. R., & GUTKIN, T. B. A regression analysis of test bias on the Stanford–Binet Intelligence Scale for black and white children referred for psychological services. *Journal of Clinical Child Psychology*, 1980, 9, 52–54.

1744. BRADLEY, R. H., & CALDWELL, B. M. The relation of home environment, cognitive competence, and IQ among males and females. *Child Development*, 1980, 51, 1140–1148.

1745. BURG, C., RAPOPORT, J. L., BARTLEY, L. S., QUINN, P. O., & TIMMINS, P. Newborn minor physical anomalies and problem behavior at age three. *American Journal of Psychiatry*, 1980, 137, 791–796.

1746. BURGER, A. L., BLACKMAN, L. S., & TAN, N. Maintenance and generalization of a sorting and retrieval strategy by EMR and nonretarded individuals. *American Journal of Mental Deficiency*, 1980, 84, 373–380.

1747. CLARKE–STEWART, K. A., UMEH, B. J., SNOW, M. E., & PEDERSON, J. A. Development and prediction of children's sociability form 1 to 2 1/2 years. *Developmental Psychology*, 1980, 16, 290–302.

1748. COHEN, R. S., STEVENSON, D. K., NALACHOWSKI, N., ARIAGNO, R. L., JOHNSON, J. D., & SUNSHINE, P. Late morbidity among survivors of respiratory failure treated with tolazoline. *Journal of Pediatrics*, 1980, 97, 644–647.

1749. COHLER, B. J., GALLANT, D. H., GRUNEBAUM, H. U., WEISS, J. L., & GAMER, E. Child–care attitudes and development of young children of mentally ill and well mothers. *Psychological Reports*, 1980, 46, 31–46.

1750. CONNOLLY, B., MORGAN, S., RUSSELL, F. F., & RICHARDSON, B. Early intervention with Down's syndrome children. *Physical Therapy*, 1980, 60, 1405–1408.

1751. CARTELLI, L. M. Reading comprehension: A matter of referents. *Academic Therapy*, 1980, 15, 421–430.

1752. CUDEK, R., MCCORMICK, D. J., & CLIFF, N. Implied orders tailored testing: Simulation with the Stanford–Binet. *Applied Psychological Measurement*, 1980, 4, 157–163.

1753. CZEIZEL, A., LÁNYI–ENGLEMAYER, A., KLUJBER, L., MÉTNEKI, J., & TUSNÁDY, G. Etiological study of mental retardation in Budapest, Hungary. *American Journal of Mental Deficiency*, 1980, 85, 120–128.

1754. DWYER, J. T., MILLER, L. G., ARDUINO, N. L., ANDREW, E. M., DIETZ, W. H., JR., REED, J. C., & REED, H. B. C., JR. Mental age and IQ of predominantly vegetarian children. *Journal of the American Dietetic Association*, 1980, 76, 142–147.

1755. ENRIGHT, R. D. An integration of social cognitive development and cognitive processing: Educational applications. *American Educational Research Journal*, 1980, 17, 21–41.

1756. GRAY, S. W., & RUTTLE, K. The family–oriented home visiting program: A longitudinal study. *Genetic Psychology Monographs*, 1980, 102, 299–316.

1757. HERMAN, C. S., KIRCHNER, G. L., STREISSGUTH, A. P., & LITTLE, R. E. Vigilance paradigm for preschool children used to relate vigilance behavior to IQ and prenatal exposure to alcohol. *Perceptual & Motor Skills*, 1980, 50, 863–867.

1758. HUNT, J. M., & PARASKEVOPOULOS, J. Children's psychological development as a function of the inaccuracy of their mothers' knowledge of their abilities. *Journal of Genetic Psychology*, 1980, 136, 285–298.

1759. ILMER, S., & DREWS, J. Differential analysis of selected prompts and neurological variables in motor assessment of moderately mentally retarded children. *American Journal of Mental Deficiency*, 1980, 84, 508–517.

1760. JOHNSON, R. A. Sensory images in the absence of sight: Blind versus sighted adolescents. *Perceptual & Motor Skills*, 1980, 51, 177–178.

1761. JOHNSON, V. M. Analysis of factors influencing special educational placement decisions. *Journal of School Psychology*, 1980, 18, 191–202.

1762. LEWIS, H. P., & LIVSON, N. Cognitive development, personality and drawing: Their interrelationships in a replicated longitudinal study. *Study in Art Education*, 1980, 22, 8–11.

1763. MARSH, R. W. The significance for intelligence of differences in birth-weight and health within monozygotic twin pairs. *British Journal of Psychology*, 1980, 71, 63–67.

1764. MULLIGAN, J. C., PAINTER, M. J., O'DONOGHUE, P. A., MACDONALD, H. M., ALLEN, A. C., & TAYLOR, P. M. Neonatal asphyxia. II. Neonatal mortality and long-term sequelae. *Journal of Pediatrics*, 1980, 96, 903–907.

1765. PALISIN, H. The Neonatal Perception Inventory: Failure to replicate. *Child Development*, 1980, 51, 737–742.

1766. REYNOLDS, C. R., & KAUFMAN, A. S. Lateral eye movement behavior in children. *Perceptual & Motor Skills*, 1980, 50, 1023–1037.

1767. RUDRUD, E., FERRARA, J., & ZIARNIK, J. Living placement and absenteeism in community–based training programs. *American Journal of Mental Deficiency*, 1980, 84, 401–404.

1768. SHAYWITZ, S. E., COHEN, D. J., & SHAYWITZ, B. A. Behavior and learning difficulties in children of normal intelligence born to alcoholic mothers. *Journal of Pediatrics*, 1980, 96, 978–982.

1769. SILVA, P. A., & BRADSHAW, J. Some factors contributing to intelligence at age of school entry. *British Journal of Educational Psychology*, 1980, 50, 10–15.

1770. SILVERSTEIN, A. B. Extrapolated Stanford–Binet IQs for mentally retarded and mentally gifted individuals. *Psychological Reports*, 1980, 46, 900–902.

1771. SPARKS, S., & HUTCHINSON, B. Cri Du Chat: Report of a case. *Journal of Communication Disorders*, 1980, 13, 9–13.

1772. TERESTMAN, N. Mood quality and intensity in nursery school children as predictors of behavioral disorders. *American Journal of Orthopsychiatry*, 1980, 50, 125–138.

1773. THIEL, G. W., & REYNOLDS, C. R. Predictive validity of the revised Stanford–Binet Intelligence Scale with trainable mentally retarded students. *Educational & Psychological Measurement*, 1980, 40, 509–512.

1774. TORGESEN, J. K., & HOUCK, D. G. Processing deficiencies of learning-disabled children who perform poorly on the Digit Span Test. *Journal of Educational Psychology*, 1980, 72, 141–160.

1775. VANE, J. R., & MOTTA, R. W. Test response inconsistency in young children. *Journal of School Psychology*, 1980, 18, 25–33.

1776. WADDELL, D. D. The Stanford–Binet: An evaluation of the technical data available since the 1972 restandardization. *Journal of School Psychology*, 1980, 18, 203–209.

1777. WRIGHT, M. J. Measuring the social competence of preschool children. *Canadian Journal of Behavioural Science*, 1980, 12, 17–32.

1778. ZOREF, L., & WILLIAMS, P. A look at content bias in IQ tests. *Journal of Educational Measurement*, 1980, 17, 313–322.

1779. BLOSKOVICS, M., ENGEL, R., PODOSIN, R. L., AZEN, C. G., & FRIEDMAN, E. G. EEG pattern in phenylketonuria under early initiated dietary treatment. *American Journal of Diseases of Children*, 1981, 135, 802–808.

1780. BRINICH, P. M. Relationship between intellectual functioning and communicative competence in deaf children. *Journal of Communication Disorders*, 1981, 14, 429–434.

1781. ELLIOT, M. Quantitative evaluation procedures for learning disabilities. *Journal of Learning Disabilities*, 1981, 14, 84–87.

1782. FINER, N. N., ROBERTSON, C. M., RICHARDS, R. T., PINNEL, L. E., & PETERS, K. L. Hypoxic–ischemic encephalopathy in term neonates: Perinatal factors and outcome. *Journal of Pediatrics*, 1981, 98, 112–117.

1783. GOLD, P. Suspected neurological impairment (SNI) and cognitive abilities: A longitudinal study of selected skills and predictive accuracy. *Journal of Clinical Child Psychology*, 1981, 8, 35–38.

1784. GREESON, L. E. Modeling, intelligence, and language development. *Journal of Genetic Psychology*, 1981, 139, 195–203.

1785. HASWELL, K., HOCK, E., & WENAR, C. Oppositional behavior of preschool children: Theory and intervention. *Family Relations*, 1981, 30, 440–446.

1786. LICHTENSTEIN, R. Comparative validity of two preschool screening tests: Correlational and classification approaches. *Journal of Learning Disabilities*, 1981, 14, 68–72.

1787. LORBER, J., & SALFIELD, S. A. W. Results of selective treatment of spina bifida cystica. *Archives of Diseases in Childhood*, 1981, 56, 822–830.

1788. MELNICK, C. R., MICHALS, K. K. & MATALON, R. Linguistic development of children with phenylketonuria and normal intelligence. *Journal of Pediatrics*, 1981, 98, 269–272.

1789. MOESCHLER, J. B., BENNETT, F. C. & CROMWELL, L. D. Use of the CT scan in the medical evaluation of the mentally retarded child. *Journal of Pediatrics*, 1981, 98, 63–65.

1790. RICHARDSON, S. A., KOLLER, H., KATZ, M., & MCLAREN, J. A functional classification of seizures and its distribution in a mentally retarded population. *American Journal of Mental Deficiency*, 1981, 85, 457–466.

1791. SIMON, A., & WARD, L. O. Effects of age and intelligence on children's classification ability. *Journal of General Psychology*, 1981, 104, 111–117.

1792. TORRANCE, E. P. Predicting the creativity of elementary school children (1958–80)–And the teacher who "made a difference." *Gifted Child Quarterly*, 1981, 25, 55–62.

1793. WATTERS, R. G., WHEELER, L. J., & WATTERS, W. E. The relative efficiency of two orders for training autistic children in the expressive and receptive use of manual signs. *Journal of Communication Disorders*, 1981, 14, 273–285.

[2290]
[Re Stanford-Binet Intelligence Scale] A Clinical Profile for the Stanford Binet Intelligence Scale

[2291] *Stanford Diagnostic Mathematics Test

(L-M). Ages 5 and over; 1965; title on profile is *A Profile for the Stanford Binet (L-M)*; an item classification system for use by school psychologists in analyzing and reporting performance in 6 categories: general comprehension, visual-motor ability, arithmetic reasoning, memory and concentration, vocabulary and verbal fluency, judgment and reasoning; Robert E. Valett; Consulting Psychologists Press, Inc.*

For additional information, see 7:426.

[2291]

Stanford Diagnostic Mathematics Test. Grades 1.5–4.5, 3.5–6.5, 5.5–8.5, 7.5–13; 1976–78; SDMT; 4 scores: number system and numeration, computation, applications, total; 4 levels; Leslie S. Beatty, Richard Madden, Eric F. Gardner, and Bjorn Karlsen; The Psychological Corporation.

a) RED LEVEL. Grades 1.5–4.5.
b) GREEN LEVEL. Grades 3.5–6.5.
c) BROWN LEVEL. Grades 5.5–8.5.
d) BLUE LEVEL. Grades 7.5–13.

For additional information and reviews by Glenda Lappan and Larry Sowder, see 8:292.

REFERENCES

1. HAMBLETON, R. K., & EIGNOR, D. R. Guidelines for evaluating criterion–referenced tests and test manuals. *Journal of Educational Measurement*, 1978, 15, 321–327.

[2292]

Stanford Diagnostic Reading Test, 1976 Edition. Grades 1–6 to 3–5, 2–6 to 5–5, 4–6 to 9–5, 9–0 to 13–0; 1966–78; SDRT; revision and extension of earlier edition; 4 levels; Bjorn Karlsen, Richard Madden, and Eric F. Gardner; The Psychological Corporation.

a) RED LEVEL. Grades 1–6 to 3–5: 6 scores: auditory vocabulary, auditory discrimination, phonetic analysis, comprehension (word reading, reading comprehension, total).

b) GREEN LEVEL. Grades 2–6 to 5–5; 7 scores: auditory vocabulary, auditory discrimination, phonetic analysis, structural analysis, comprehension (literal, inferential, total).

c) BROWN LEVEL. Grades 4–6 to 9–5; 7 scores: auditory vocabulary, comprehension (literal, inferential, total), phonetic analysis, structural analysis, reading rate.

d) BLUE LEVEL. Grades 9–0 to 13–0; 12 scores: comprehension (literal, inferential, total), vocabulary (word meaning, word parts, total), decoding (phonetic analysis, structural analysis, total), rate (fast reading, scanning and skimming, total).

For a review by Byron H. Van Roekel, see 8:777 (13 references); see also T2:1651 (2 references); for a review by Lawrence M. Kasdon of Levels 1–2 of the earlier edition, see 7:725 (3 references).

REFERENCES

1–3. See 7:725.
4–5. See T2:1651.
6–18. See 8:777.
19. CANNEY, G., & SCHREINER, R. A study of the effectiveness of selected syllabication rules and phonogram patterns forward attack. *Reading Research Quarterly*, 1976–77, 12, 102–124.
20. BADIAN, N. A. Auditory–visual integration, auditory memory, and reading in retarded and adequate readers. *Journal of Learning Disabilities*, 1977, 10, 49–114.
21. BOWLING, E. N., & LAFFEY, J. L. Children's retrospective oral responses to silent reading test items. *National Reading Conference Yearbook*, 1977, 236–243.
22. MIKULECKY, L, & WOLF, A. Effect of uninterrupted sustained silent reading and of reading games on changes in secondary student's reading attitudes. *National Reading Conference Yearbook*, 1977, 126–130.
23. RICKARDS, J. P., & HATCHER, C. W. Interspersed meaningful learning questions as semantic cues for poor comprehenders. *Reading Research Quarterly*, 1977–78, 13, 538–553.
24. THURMOND, V. B. The effect of black English on the reading performance of high school students. *Journal of Educational Research*, 1977, 70, 156–163.
25. HAMBLETON, R. K., & EIGNOR, D. R. Guidelines for evaluating criterion–referenced tests and test manuals. *Journal of Educational Measurement*, 1978, 15, 321–327.
26. ZINCK, R. A. The relation of comprehension to semantic and syntactic language cues utilized during oral and silent reading. *National Reading Conference Yearbook*, 1978, 154–160.
27. KURTH, R. J. A comparison of small group and individualized instruction in junior college remedial reading programs. *National Reading Conference Yearbook*, 1979, 174–176.
28. OLSHAVSKY, J. E., & KLETZING, K. Prediction: One strategy for reading success in high school. *Journal of Reading*, 1979, 22, 512–516.
29. CUMMINGS, J. A., & NELSON, R. B. Basic concepts in the oral directions of group achievement tests. *Journal of Educational Research*, 1980, 73, 259–261.
30. HICKS, C. The development of creative thinking and its relationship to IQ and reading achievement. *Reading World*, 1980, 20, 44–52.
31. ALVERMAN, D. E. The compensatory effect of graphic organizers on descriptive text. *Journal of Educational Research*, 1981, 75, 44–48.
32. BROWN, L. L., & SHERBENOU, R. J. A comparison of teacher perceptions of student reading ability, reading performance, and classroom behavior. *Reading Teacher*, 1981, 34, 557–560.
33. ROSSO, B. R., & EMANS, R. Children's use of phonic generalizations. *Reading Teacher*, 1981, 34, 653–657.

[2293]

Stanford Early School Achievement Test. Grades kgn.1–1.1, 1.1–1.8; 1969–71; SESAT; 2 levels; Richard Madden and Eric F. Gardner; The Psychological Corporation.*

a) LEVEL 1. Grades kgn.1–1.1; 1969; 5 scores: environment, mathematics, letters and sounds, aural comprehension, total.

b) LEVEL 2. Grades 1.1–1.8; 1970–71; 7 scores: environment, mathematics, letters and sounds, aural comprehension, word reading, sentence reading, total.

For additional information and a review by Courtney B. Cazden, see 8:30 (6 references); see also T2:38 (1 reference); for reviews by Elizabeth Hagen and William A. Mehrens of Level 1, see 7:28.

REFERENCES

1. See T2:38.
2–7. See 8:30.
8. AMES. S. G., BECKER, L. D., & DALTON, S. The predictive validity of the Stanford Early School Achievement Test. *Educational & Psychological Measurement*, 1977, 37, 505–507.
9. KLEIN, A. E. The validity of the Screening Test of Academic Readiness in predicting achievement in first and second grades. *Educational & Psychological Measurement*, 1977, 37, 493–499.
10. BURROWS, E. H., & NEYLAND, D. Reading skills, auditory comprehension of language, and academic achievement. *Journal of Speech & Hearing Disorders*, 1978, 43, 467–472.
11. KLEIN, A. E., The reliability and predictive validity of the Slosson Intelligence Test for pre–kindergarten pupils. *Educational & Psychological Measurement*, 1978, 38, 1211–1217.
12. KLEIN, A. E. The validity of the Beery Test of Visual–Motor Integration in predicting achievement in kindergarten, first, and second grades. *Educational & Psychological Measurement*, 1978, 38, 457–461.
13. KLEIN, A. E. Additional evidence of the predictive validity of the Stanford Early School Achievement Test. *Educational & Psychological Measurement*, 1979, 39, 1053–1059.
14. KLEIN, A. Test-retest reliability and predictive validity of the Northwestern Syntax Screening Test. *Educational & Psychological Measurement*, 1980, 40, 1167–1172.
15. STAUFFER, A. J., & HINZMAN, J. An investigation into the validity of race and socio–economic status as factors for equalizing student knowledge along with an identification of deficiencies in knowledge. *Educational & Psychological Measurement*, 1980, 40, 525–529.

16. Winsberg, B. G., Bialer, I., Kupietz, S., Botti, E., & Balka, E. B. Home vs. hospital care of children with behavior disorders. *Archives of General Psychiatry*, 1980, 37, 413–418.

[2294]
Stanford Hypnotic Susceptibility Scale.
College and adults; 1959–62; SHSS; for a downward extension, see *The Children's Hypnotic Susceptibility Scale*; André M. Weitzenhoffer and Ernest R. Hilgard; Consulting Psychologists Press, Inc.*

For additional information, see 8:682 (40 references); see also T2:1389 (31 references) and P:253 (18 references); for reviews by Milton V. Kline and C. Scott Moss, see 6:178 (17 references).

REFERENCES

1–17. See 6:178.
18–35. See P:253.
36–66. See T2:1389.
67–106. See 8:682.
107. Dolby, R. M., & Sheehan, P. W. Cognitive processing and expectancy behavior in hypnosis. *Journal of Abnormal Psychology*, 1977, 86, 334–345.
108. Gibson, H. B. Animal hypnosis and human hypnosis: New experimental evidence relating to an old controversy. *Psychologia*, 1977, 20, 136–144.
109. Gibson, H. B., Corcoran, M. E., & Curran, J. D. Hypnotic susceptibility and personality: The consequences of diazepam and the sex of the subjects. *British Journal of Psychology*, 1977, 68, 51–59.
110. Graham, C., & Evans, F. J. Hypnotizability and the deployment of waking attention. *Journal of Abnormal Psychology*, 1977, 86, 631–638.
111. Obstoj, I., Sheehan, P. W. Aptitude for trance, task generalizabilities, and incongruity response in hypnosis. *Journal of Abnormal Psychology*, 1977, 86, 543–552.
112. Perry, C. Uncancelled hypnotic suggestions: The effects of hypnotic depth and hypnotic skill on their posthypnotic persistence. *Journal of Abnormal Psychology*, 1977, 86, 570–574.
113. Perry, C. Variables influencing the posthypnotic persistence of an uncanceled hypnotic suggestion. *Annals of the New York Academy of Science*, 1977, 296, 264–273.
114. Sheehan, P. W. Incongruity in trance behavior: A defining property of hypnosis? *Annals of the New York Academy of Science*, 1977, 296, 194–207.
115. Wagstaff, G. F. An experimental study of compliance and post-hypnotic amnesia. *British Journal of Social & Clinical Psychology*, 1977, 16, 225–228.
116. Wickramasekera, I. E. On attempts to modify hypnotic susceptibility: Some psychophysiological procedures and promising directions. *Annals of the New York Academy of Science*, 1977, 296, 143–151.
117. Zamansky, H. S. Suggestion and counter-suggestion in hypnotic behavior. *Journal of Abnormal Psychology*, 1977, 86, 346–351.
118. Hilgard, E. R., Macdonald, H., Morgan, A. H., & Johnson, L. S. The reality of hypnotic analgesia: A comparison of highly hypnotizables with simulators. *Journal of Abnormal Psychology*, 1978, 87, 239–246.
119. Perry, C., & Walsh, B. Inconsistencies and anomalies of response as a defining characteristic of hypnosis. *Journal of Abnormal Psychology*, 1978, 87, 574–577.
120. Shapiro, D., Jr. Behavioral and attitudinal changes resulting from a "Zen experience" workshop and Zen meditation. *Journal of Humanistic Psychology*, 1978, 18, 21–29.
121. Swanson, G. E. Travels through inner space: Family structure and openness to absorbing experiences. *American Journal of Sociology*, 1978, 83, 890–916.
122. Yanovski, A., & Fogel, M. L. Effects of instructions for visual imagery on Rorschach responses. *Perceptual & Motor Skills*, 1978, 47, 1323–1335.
123. Blum, G. S., & Barbour, J. S. Selective inattention to anxiety-linked stimuli. *Journal of Experimental Psychology: General*, 1979, 108, 182–224.
124. Bowers, K. S. Time distortion and hypnotic ability: Underestimating the duration of hypnosis. *Journal of Abnormal Psychology*, 1979, 88, 435–439.
125. Bowers, P. Hypnosis and creativity: The search for the missing link. *Journal of Abnormal Psychology*, 1979, 88, 564–572.
126. Coe, W. C., & Ryken, K. Hypnosis and risks to human subjects. *American Psychologist*, 1979, 34, 673–681.
127. Evans, F. J. Contextual forgetting: Posthypnotic source amnesia. *Journal of Abnormal Psychology*, 1979, 88, 556–563.
128. Hunt, S. M. Hypnosis as obedience behaviour. *British Journal of Social & Clinical Psychology*, 1979, 18, 21–27.
129. Katz, N. W. Comparative efficacy of behavioral training, training plus relaxation, and a sleep/trance hypnotic induction in increasing hypnotic susceptibility. *Journal of Consulting & Clinical Psychology*, 1979, 47, 119–127.
130. Perry, C., Gelfand, R., & Marcovitch, P. The relevance of hypnotic susceptibility in the clinical context. *Journal of Abnormal Psychology*, 1979, 88, 592–603.
131. Pettigrew, C. G., & Dawson, J. G. Death Anxiety: "state" or "trait"? *Journal of Clinical Psychology*, 1979, 35, 154–158.
132. Sackeim, H. A., Paulhus, D., & Weiman, A. L. Classroom seating and hypnotic susceptibility. *Journal of Abnormal Psychology*, 1979, 88, 81–84.
133. Sheehan, P. W., & Dolby, R. M. Motivated involvement in hypnosis: The illustration of clinical rapport through hypnotic dreams. *Journal of Abnormal Psychology*, 1979, 88, 573–583.
134. Fourie, D. P. Relationship aspects of hypnotic susceptibility. *Perceptual & Motor Skills*, 1980, 51, 1032–1034.
135. Howard, M. L., & Coe, W. C. The effects of context and subjects' perceived control in breaching post-hypnotic amnesia. *Journal of Personality*, 1980, 48, 342–359.
136. Karlin, R., Morgan, D., & Goldstein, L. Hypnotic analgesia: A preliminary investigation of quantitated hemispheric electroencephalographic and attentional correlates. *Journal of Abnormal Psychology*, 1980, 89, 591–594.
137. Sheehan, P. W. Factors influencing rapport in hypnosis. *Journal of Abnormal Psychology*, 1980, 89, 263–281.
138. St. Jean, R. Hypnotic time distortion and learning: Another look. *Journal of Abnormal Psychology*, 1980, 89, 20–24.
139. Crawford, H. J. Hypnotic susceptibility as related to gestalt closure tasks. *Journal of Personality & Social Psychology*, 1981, 40, 376–383.
140. Piedmont, R. L. Effects of hypnosis and biofeedback upon the regulation of peripheral skin temperature. *Perceptual & Motor Skills*, 1981, 53, 855–862.

[2295]
★Stanford Mental Arithmetic Test.
Grades 1, 2, 3, 4, 5, 6; 1975; SMAT; Jane Sachar; the Author.*

REFERENCES

1. Sachar, J. An instrument for evaluating mental arithmetic skills. *Journal for Research in Mathematics Education*, 1978, 9, 233–237.
2. Sherman, J. Mathematics, spatial visualization, and related factors: Changes in girls and boys, grades 8–11. *Journal of Educational Psychology*, 1980, 72, 476–482.

[2296]
Stanford-Ohwaki-Kohs Block Design Intelligence Test for the Blind: American Revision of the Ohwaki-Kohs Test.
Blind and partially sighted ages 16 and over; 1965–66; uses same testing materials as *The Ohwaki-Kohs Tactile Block Design Intelligence Test for the Blind*; Richard M. Suinn and William L. Dauterman; Western Psychological Services.*

For additional information, see 7:427.

[2297]
Stanford Profile Scales of Hypnotic Susceptibility, Revised Edition.
College and adults; 1963–67; SPSHS; 25 scores: agnosia and cognitive distortion (4 item scores plus total), positive hallucinations (4 item scores plus total), negative hallucinations (4 item scores plus total), dreams and regressions (4 item scores plus total), amnesia and post-hypnotic compulsions (3 item scores plus total), total susceptibility; one of the item scores for amnesia and post-hypnotic compulsions is derived from Form A of the *Stanford Hypnotic Susceptibility Scale* and provision is also made for profiling 3 additional scores (loss of motor coordination and 2 subscores) from this scale; Ernest R. Hilgard and André M. Weitzenhoffer (test), (revised standardization data by Ernest R. Hilgard, Leslie M. Cooper, Lillian W. Lauer, and Arlene H. Morgan); Consulting Psychologists Press, Inc.*

See T2:1390 (3 references) and P:254 (4 references); for reviews by Seymour Fisher and Eugene E. Levitt of the original edition, see 6:179.

REFERENCES

1–4. See P:254.
5–7. See T2:1390.
8. PASCARELLA, E. T. Student motivation as a differential predictor of course outcomes in personalized system of instruction and conventional instructional methods. *Journal of Educational Research*, 1977, 71, 21–26.
9. PERRY, C. Uncancelled hypnotic suggestions: The effects of hypnotic depth and hypnotic skill on their posthypnotic persistence. *Journal of Abnormal Psychology*, 1977, 86, 570–574.
10. HILGARD, E. R., HILGARD, J. R., MACDONALD, H., MORGAN, A. H., & JOHNSON, L. S. Covert pain in hypnotic analgesia: Its reality as tested by the real-simulator design. *Journal of Abnormal Psychology*, 1978, 87, 655–663.
11. CRAWFORD, H. J., MACDONALD, H., & HILGARD, E. R. Hypnotic deafness: A psychophysical study of responses to tone intensity as modified by hypnosis. *American Journal of Psychology*, 1979, 92, 193–214.
12. NASH, M. R., JOHNSON, L. S., & TIPTON, R. D. Hypnotic age regression and the occurrence of transitional object relationships. *Journal of Abnormal Psychology*, 1979, 88, 547–555.

[2298]

Stanford Test of Academic Skills. Grades 8–10, 11–12 and grade 13 in junior/community college; 1972–75; TASK; also called *Stanford TASK*; 3 scores: reading, English, mathematics; Eric F. Gardner, Robert Callis, Jack C. Merwin, and Richard Madden; The Psychological Corporation.*

For additional information and reviews by Clinton I. Chase and Robert L. Thorndike, see 8:31.

REFERENCES

1. RAVEN, R. J., & ADRIAN, M. Relationships among science achievement, self-concept, and Piaget's operative comprehension. *Science Education*, 1978, 62, 471–479.
2. WEINER, M., & ZIBRIN, M. Dissimilarities in grade–equivalent scores on different standardization tests of achievement: A threat to criterion–related validity. *Educational & Psychological Measurement*, 1979, 39, 923–928.
3. SMITH, C. F., JR., & WESTERN, R. D. Passage independence: A neglected issue in the measurement of reading proficiency. *Reading World*, 1980, 19, 352–356.

[2299]

STARS Test (Short Term Auditory Retrieval and Storage). Grades 1–6; 1972; STARS; recognition of pairs and triads of words presented simultaneously; Arthur Flowers; Perceptual Learning Systems.*

For additional information, see 8:946.

[2300]

State-Trait Anxiety Inventory. Grades 9–16 and adults; 1968–70; STAI; for a downward extension, see 2301; title on test is *Self-Evaluation Questionnaire*; 2 scores: state anxiety, trait anxiety; C. D. Spielberger, R. L. Gorsuch, and R. Lushene; Consulting Psychologists Press, Inc.*

For additional information and reviews by Ralph Mason Dreger and Edward S. Katkin, see 8:683 (268 references); see also T2:1391 (45 references) and 7:141 (20 references).

REFERENCES

1–20. See 7:141.
21–65. See T2:1391.
66–333. See 8:683.
334. AKAMATSU, T. J., & THELEN, M. H. Observer states and traits and the imitative process: A test of a new formulation. *Journal of Research in Personality*, 1977, 11, 165–179.
335. AVERBACH, S. M., & EDINGER, J. D. The effects of surgery-induced stress on anxiety as measured by the Holtzman Inkblot Technique. *Journal of Personality Assessment*, 1977, 41, 19–24.
336. BARKER, B. M., BARKER, H. R., JR., & WADSWORTH, A. P. Factor analysis of the items of the State–Trait Anxiety Inventory. *Journal of Clinical Psychology*, 1977, 33, 450–455.
337. BEDELL, J. A. Effects of instructions on the measurement of state anxiety in children. *Journal of Consulting & Clinical Psychology*, 1977, 45, 941–942.
338. BEST, C. L., & KILPATRICK, D. G. Psychological profiles of rape crisis counselors. *Psychological Reports*, 1977, 40, 1127–1134.
339. BEUTLER, L. E., JOHNSON, D. T., MORRIS, K., & NEVILLE, C. W., JR. Effect of time–specific sets and patients' personality style on state and trait anxiety. *Psychological Reports*, 1977, 40, 1003–1010.
340. BIERSNER, R. J., HARRIS, J. A., & RYMAN, D. H. Emotional predisposition to psychotropic drug effects. *Journal of Consulting & Clinical Psychology*, 1977, 45, 943–945.
341. COOK, D. W., & KUNCE, J. T. Reducing counselor anxiety by using modeling strategies. *Journal of Employment Counseling*, 1977, 14, 110–115.
342. CRARY, W. G., & WEXLER, M. Meniere's Disease: A psychosomatic disorder? *Psychological Reports*, 1977, 41, 603–645.
343. DEARDORFF, P. A., KENDALL, P. C., FINCH, A. J., JR., & SITARZ, A. M. Empathy, locus of control and anxiety in college students. *Psychological Reports*, 1977, 40, 1236–1238.
344. DILLBECK, M. C. The effect of the transcendental meditation technique on anxiety level. *Journal of Clinical Psychology*, 1977, 33, 1076–1078.
345. DINNING, W. D., & EVANS, R. G. Discriminant and convergent validity of the SCL-90 in psychiatric inpatients. *Journal of Personality Assessment*, 1977, 41, 304–310.
346. EVANS, R., & DINNING, W. D. Future outlook and psychopathology among psychiatric patients. *Psychological Reports*, 1977, 41, 1309–1310.
347. GILL, D. L. Influence of group success–failure and relative ability on intrapersonal variables. *Research Quarterly*, 1977, 48, 685–694.
337. BEDELL, J. A. Effects of instructions on the measurement of state anxiety in children. *Journal of Consulting & Clinical Psychology*, 1977, 45, 941–942.
349. GRANVOLD, D. K., & OLLERENSHAW, S. J. Interpersonal skill training through a dating feedback group. *Group Psychotherapy, Psychodrama & Sociometry*, 1977, 30, 49–59.
350. HARKINS, S. W., & CHAPMAN, C. R. The perception of induced dental pain in young and elderly women. *Journal of Gerontology*, 1977, 32, 428–435.
351. HOLLEMBEAK, N., JOHNSON, E. P., & TRACY, D. B. Validity of a non-projective anxiety scale for preschool children. *Psychological Reports*, 1977, 41, 212–214.
352. ISRAEL, E., & BEIMAN, I. Live versus recorded relaxation training: A controlled investigation. *Behavior Therapy*, 1977, 8, 251–254.
353. JOESTING, J. Test–retest correlates for the State–Trait Anxiety Inventory. *Psychological Reports*, 1977, 40, 671–672.
354. JOESTING, J., & WHITEHEAD, G. I., II. Relationship of state and trait anxiety to grades in educational psychology. *Psychological Reports*, 1977, 40, 705–706.
355. JOHNSTON, M., & HACKMANN, A. Cross-validation and response sets in repeated use of mood questionnaires. *British Journal of Social & Clinical Psychology*, 1977, 16, 235–239.
356. KAESTNER, E., ROSEN, L., & APPEL, P. Patterns of drug abuse: Relationships with ethnicity, sensation seeking, and anxiety. *Journal of Consulting & Clinical Psychology*, 1977, 45, 462–468.
357. LEBOEUF, A. The effects of EMG feedback training on state anxiety in introverts and extraverts. *Journal of Clinical Psychology*, 1977, 33, 251–253.
358. MAYER, R. E. Problem–solving performance with task overload: Effects of self-pacing and trait anxiety. *Bulletin of the Psychonomic Society*, 1977, 9, 283–286.
359. MEHRABIAN, A. Individual differences in stimulus screening and arousability. *Journal of Personality*, 1977, 45, 237–250.
360. MELNICK, J., & WICHER, D. Social risk taking propensity and anxiety as predictors of group performance. *Journal of Counseling Psychology*, 1977, 24, 415–419.
361. MUELLER, J. H. Test anxiety, input modality, and levels of organization in free recall. *Bulletin of the Psychonomic Society*, 1977, 9, 67–69.
362. MUELLER, J. H., CARLOMUSTO, M., & MORLER, M. Recall as a function of method of presentation and individual differences in test anxiety. *Bulletin of the Psychonomic Society*, 1977, 10, 447–450.
363. NIXON, G. F., & STEFFECK, J. C. Reliability of the State–Trait Anxiety Inventory. *Psychological Reports*, 1977, 40, 357–358.
364. OHLSON, E. L., & MEIN, L. The difference in level of anxiety in undergraduate mathematics and nonmathematics majors. *Journal for Research in Mathematics Education*, 1977, 8, 48–56.
365. OLLENDICK, T. H., & NETTLE, M. D. An evaluation of the relaxation component of induced anxiety. *Behavior Therapy*, 1977, 8, 561–566.

366. PASSINI, F. T., WATSON, C. G., DEHNEL, L., & HERDER, J. Alpha wave bio-feedback training therapy in alcoholics. *Journal of Clinical Psychology*, 1977, 33, 292-299.
367. REEVES, R. A., & MAY, W. W. Effects of state-trait anxiety and task difficulty on paired-associate learning. *Psychological Reports*, 1977, 41, 179-185.
368. ROUSE, L. O., & SOLOMON, G. F. Base line procedures for application of EEG alpha biofeedback to the rehabilitation of criminal offenders. *Corrective & Social Psychiatry & Journal of Behavioral Technology, Methods & Therapy*, 1977, 23, 56-61.
369. RYAN, J., & SOUHEAVER, G. T. The role of sleep in electrosleep therapy for anxiety. *Diseases of the Nervous System*, 1977, 38, 515-517.
370. SHARMA, S. Sex differences in self-reported anxiousness for different situations and modes of response among university students in India. *Psychologia*, 1977, 21, 155-160.
371. SHARMA, S., & DANG, R. A study of trait anxiety in relation to types of stressful situations among males and females. *Psychological Studies*, 1977, 22, 49-53.
372. VALLE, R. S., & DEGOOD, D. E. Effects of state-trait anxiety on the ability to enhance and suppress EEG alpha. *Psychophysiology*, 1977, 14, 1-8.
373. WANKEL, L. M. Audience size and trait anxiety effects upon state anxiety and motor performance. *Research Quarterly*, 1977, 48, 181-186.
374. WAXER, P. H. Nonverbal cues for anxiety: An examination of emotional leakage. *Journal of Abnormal Psychology*, 1977, 86, 306-314.
375. WHITEHEAD, W. E., BLACKWELL, B., DESILVA, H., & ROBINSON, A. Anxiety and anger in hypertension. *Journal of Psychosomatic Research*, 1977, 21, 383-389.
376. WINSTEAD, D. K., PARKER, M., & WILLI, F. J. P. Propoxyphene on demand. *Archives of General Psychiatry*, 1977, 34, 1463-1468.
377. ZUCKERMAN, M. Development of a situation-specific trait-state test for the prediction and measurement of affective responses. *Journal of Consulting & Clinical Psychology*, 1977, 45, 513-523.
378. ABDEL-HALIM, A. A. Employee affective responses to organizational stress: Moderating effects of job characteristics. *Personnel Psychology*, 1978, 31, 561-579.
379. ARCHER, R. B., & STEIN, D. K. Personal control expectancies and state anxiety. *Psychological Reports*, 1978, 42, 551-558.
380. ARNOLD, B. R., & PAROTT, R. Job interviewing: Stress-management and interpersonal-skills training for welfare-rehabilitation clients. *Rehabilitation Counseling Bulletin*, 1978, 22, 44-51.
381. AUERBACH, S., & KENDALL, P. C. Sex differences in anxiety response and adjustment to dental surgery: Effects of general vs. specific preoperative information. *Journal of Clinical Psychology*, 1978, 34, 309-313.
382. BANDER, R. S., RUSSELL, R. K., & WEISKOTT, G. N. Effects of varying amounts of assertive training on level of assertiveness and anxiety reduction in women. *Psychological Reports*, 1978, 43, 144-146.
383. BEATTY, M. J., & BEHNKE, R. R. Effects of compressed speech on learner anxiety. *Southern Speech Communication Journal*, 1978, 43, 296-301.
384. BEIMAN, I., ISRAEL, E., & JOHNSON, S. A. During training and posttraining effects of live and taped extended progressive relaxation, self-relaxation, and electromyogram biofeedback. *Journal of Consulting & Clinical Psychology*, 1978, 46, 314-321.
385. BEIMAN, I., O'NEIL, P., WACHTEL, D., FRUGÈ, E., JOHNSON, S., & FEUERSTEIN, M. Validation of a self-report/behavioral subject selection procedure for analog fear research. *Behavior Therapy*, 1978, 9, 169-177.
386. BETZ, N. E. Prevalence, distribution, and correlates of math anxiety in college students. *Journal of Counseling Psychology*, 1978, 25, 441-448.
387. BURTON, C. A., & NICHOLS, M. P. The behavioral target complaints form: A nonreaction measure of psychotherapeutic outcome. *Psychological Reports*, 1978, 42, 219-226.
388. COUNTS, D. K., HOLLANDSWORTH, J. G., JR., & ALCORN, J. D. Use of electromyographic biofeedback and cue-controlled relaxation in the treatment of test anxiety. *Journal of Consulting & Clinical Psychology*, 1978, 46, 990-996.
389. DEFFENBACHER, J. L., & SHELTON, J. L. Comparison of anxiety management training and desensitization in reducing test and other anxieties. *Journal of Counseling Psychology*, 1978, 25, 277-282.
390. DODS, L. Y., & TREPPA, J. A. Contrasting personality profiles of male and female medical students. *Journal of Psychology*, 1978, 98, 3-10.
391. EBERST, R. M. The reduction in the intensity of meaning attached to sex words. *Journal of School Health*, 1978, 48, 355-361.
392. FEINBERG, L. B., & HALPERIN, S. Affective and cognitive correlates of course performance in introductory statistics. *Journal of Experimental Education*, 1978, 46, 11-18.
393. FIEDLER, D., & BEACH, L. R. On the decision to be assertive. *Journal of Consulting & Clinical Psychology*, 1978, 46, 537-546.
394. FISHER, S. Anxiety and sex role in body landmark functions. *Journal of Research in Personality*, 1978, 12, 87-99.
395. FRANCO, J. N. Reduction of dental anxiety: An exploratory study. *Perceptual & Motor Skills*, 1978, 46, 302.
396. GOLDFRIED, M. R., LINEHAN, M. M., & SMITH, J. L. Reduction of test anxiety through cognitive restructuring. *Journal of Consulting & Clinical Psychology*, 1978, 46, 32-39.
397. GREDEN, J. F., FONTAINE, P., LUBETSKY, M., & CHAMBERLIN, K. Anxiety and depression associated with caffeinism among psychiatric inpatients. *American Journal of Psychiatry*, 1978, 135, 963-966.
398. GRIFFITHS, T. J., STEEL, D. H., & VACCARO, P. Anxiety levels of beginning scuba students. *Perceptual & Motor Skills*, 1978, 47, 312-314.
399. HOELTER, J. W., & HOELTER, J. A. The relationship between fear of death and anxiety. *Journal of Psychology*, 1978, 99, 225-226.
400. HOLROYD, K. A. Effects of social anxiety and social evaluation on beer consumption and social interaction. *Journal of Studies on Alcohol*, 1978, 39, 737-744.
401. HUBBLE, M. A., & GELSO, C. J. Effect of counselor attire in an initial interview. *Journal of Counseling Psychology*, 1978, 25, 581-584.
402. HYMEN, S. P., & WARREN, R. An evaluation of rational-emotive imagery as a component of rational-emotive therapy in the treatment of test anxiety. *Perceptual & Motor Skills*, 1978, 46, 847-853.
403. KENDALL, P. C. Anxiety: States, traits-situations? *Journal of Consulting & Clinical Psychology*, 1978, 46, 280-287.
404. KENDALL, P. C., FINCH, A. J., JR., & MONTGOMERY, L. E. Vicarious anxiety: A systematic evaluation of a vicarious threat to self-esteem. *Journal of Consulting & Clinical Psychology*, 1978, 46, 997-1008.
405. KING, G. D., HANNAY, H. J., MASEK, B. J., & BURNS, J. W. Effects of anxiety and sex on neuropsychological tests. *Journal of Consulting & Clinical Psychology*, 1978, 46, 375-376.
406. LAMB, D., Use of behavioral measures in anxiety research. *Psychological Reports*, 1978, 43, 1079-1085.
407. LEDERMAN, R. P., LEDERMAN, E., WORK, B. A., & MCCANN, D. The relationship of maternal anxiety, plasma catecholamines, and plasma cortisol to progress in labor. *American Journal of Obstetrics & Gynecology*, 1978, 132, 495-500.
408. LEHREN, P. M. Psychophysiological effects of progressive relaxation in anxiety neurotic patients and of progressive relaxation and alpha feedback in nonpatients. *Journal of Consulting & Clinical Psychology*, 1978, 46, 389-404.
409. LENT, R. W., & RUSSELL, R. K. Treatment of test anxiety by cue-controlled desensitization and study-skills training. *Journal of Counseling Psychology*, 1978, 25, 217-224.
410. LEWIS, C. E., BIGLAN, A., & STEINBOCK, E. Self-administered relaxation training and money deposits in the treatment of recurrent anxiety. *Journal of Consulting & Clinical Psychology*, 1978, 46, 1274-1283.
411. LION, L. S. Psychological effects of jogging: A preliminary study. *Perceptual & Motor Skills*, 1978, 47, 1215-1218.
412. LOGUE, P. E., GENTRY, W. D., LINNOILA, M. K., & ERWIN, C. W. Effect of alcohol consumption on state anxiety changes in male and female nonalcoholics. *American Journal of Psychiatry*, 1978, 135, 1079-1081.
413. LOO, R. Cautionary note on the use of short state-anxiety measures. *Perceptual & Motor Skills*, 1978, 46, 633-634.
414. LOO, R. Personality dimensions and reversible perspective in Embedded Figures Test. *Perceptual & Motor Skills*, 1978, 46, 1016-1018.
415. MECK, D. S., BOURGEOIS, A., & LEUNES, A. Relation of combined measures of locus of control and psychological differentiation to personality adjustment. *Psychological Reports*, 1978, 43, 547-552.
416. MELLSTROM, M., JR., ZUCKERMAN, M., & CICALA, G. A. General versus specific traits in the assessment of anxiety. *Journal of Consulting & Clinical Psychology*, 1978, 46, 423-431.
417. MENASCO, M. B., & HAWKINS, D. I. A field test of the relationship between cognitive dissonance and state anxiety. *Journal of Marketing Research*, 1978, 15, 650-655.
418. MILLER, D. J., MUELLER, J. H., GOLDSTEIN, A. G., & POTTER, L. L. Depth of processing and test anxiety in landscape recognition. *Bulletin of the Psychonomic Society*, 1978, 11, 341-343.
419. MILLER, M. P., MURPHY, P. J., & MILLER, T. P. Comparison of electromyographic feedback and progressive relaxation training in treating circumscribed anxiety stress reactions. *Journal of Consulting & Clinical Psychology*, 1978, 46, 1291-1298.
420. MORAN, M., WATSON, C. G., BROWN, J., WHITE, C., & JACOBS, L. Systems releasing action therapy with alcholics: An experimental evaluation. *Journal of Clinical Psychology*, 1978, 34, 769-774.
421. MORGAN, W. P., & HORSTMAN, D. H. Psychometric correlates of pain perception. *Perceptual & Motor Skills*, 1978, 47, 27-39.
422. MUELLER, J. H. The effects of individual differences in test anxiety and type of orienting task on levels of organization in free recall. *Journal of Research in Personality*, 1978, 12, 100-116.
423. MUELLER, J. H., CARLOMUSTO, M., & MARLER, M. Recall and organization in memory as a function of rate of presentation and individual differences in test anxiety. *Bulletin of the Psychonomic Society*, 1978, 12, 133-136.
424. NAYLOR, F. D. Success and failure experiences and the factor structure of the State-Trait Anxiety Inventory. *Australian Journal of Psychology*, 1978, 30, 217-222.

425. Neufeld, R. W. J. Veridicality of cognitive mapping of stressor effects: Sex differences. *Journal of Personality*, 1978, 46, 623–644.
426. O'Grady, K. E., & Janda, L. H. Psychometric correlates of the Mosher Forced Choice Guilt Inventory. *Journal of Consulting & Clinical Psychology*, 1978, 46, 1581–1582.
427. Parker, J. C., Gilbert, G. S., & Thoreson, R. W. Reduction of autonomic arousal in alcoholics: A comparison of relaxation and meditation techniques. *Journal of Consulting & Clinical Psychology*, 1978, 46, 879–886.
428. Peters, R. A. Effects of anxiety, curiosity, and perceived instructor threat on student verbal behavior in the college classroom. *Journal of Educational Psychology*, 1978, 70, 388–395.
429. Powazek, M., Goff, J. R., Scyving, J., & Paulson, M. A. Emotional reactions of children to isolation in a cancer hospital. *Journal of Pediatrics*, 1978, 92, 834–837.
430. Purvis, J. W., & Morgan, W. P. Influence on repeated maximal testing on anxiety and work capacity in college women. *Research Quarterly for Exercise & Sport*, 1978, 49, 512–519.
431. Rappaport, E. The relation between anxiety and the Harris MMPI P_D subscales among psychiatric inpatients. *Journal of Clinical Psychology*, 1978, 34, 388–390.
432. Redfering, D. L., & Jones, J. G. Effects of defensiveness on the State–Trait Anxiety Inventory. *Psychological Reports*, 1978, 43, 83–89.
433. Reeves, R. A., Edmonds, E. M., & Transou, D. L. Effects of color and trait anxiety on state anxiety. *Perceptual & Motor Skills*, 1978, 46, 855–858.
434. Ross, G. R. Reducing irrational personality traits, trait anxiety, and intra–interpersonal needs in high school students. *Measurement & Evaluation in Guidance*, 1978, 11, 44–49.
435. Rupert, P. A., & Holmes, D. S. Effects of multiple sessions of true and placebo heart rate biofeedback training on the heart rates and anxiety levels of anxious patients during and following treatment. *Psychophysiology*, 1978, 15, 582–590.
436. Schmidt, J. P. The interactive effects of instructional set, field dependence, and extraversion on the Holtzman Inkblot Technique. *Journal of Clinical Psychology*, 1978, 34, 533–536.
437. Schnitzer, B. R. Anxiety, depression, and dyspnea in patients with chronic obstructive pulmonary disease. *American Review of Respiratory Disease*, 1978, 117, 211. (Abstract)
438. Sharp, G. L., & Muller, D. The effects of lowering self–concept on associative learning. *Journal of Psychology*, 1978, 100, 233–241.
439. Shipley, R. H., Butt, J. H., Horwitz, B., & Farbry, J. E. Preparation for a stressful medical procedure: Effect of amount of stimulus preexposure and coping style. *Journal of Consulting & Clinical Psychology*, 1978, 46, 499–507.
440. Smith, J. C. Personality correlates of continuation and outcome in meditation and erect sitting control treatments. *Journal of Consulting & Clinical Psychology*, 1978, 46, 272–279.
441. Sobol, E. G. Self–actualization and the baccalaureate nursing student's response to stress. *Nursing Research*, 1978, 27, 238–244.
442. Sturges, P. T. Delay of informative feedback in computer–assisted testing. *Journal of Educational Psychology*, 1978, 70, 378–387.
443. Sweeney, D. R., Maas, J. W., & Heninger, G. R. State anxiety, physical activity, and urinary 3-methoxy-4-hydroxyphenethylene glycol excretion. *Archives of General Psychiatry*, 1978, 35, 1418–1423.
444. Tenenbaum, G., & Milgram, R. M. Trait and state anxiety in Israeli student athletes. *Journal of Clinical Psychology*, 1978, 34, 691–693.
445. Treppa, J. A., & Dods, L. Y. Some personality correlates of the A–B therapist scale for male and female medical students. *Journal of Clinical Psychology*, 1978, 34, 519–522.
446. Trussell, R. P. Use of graduated behavior rehearsal, feedback, and systematic desensitization for speech anxiety. *Journal of Counseling Psychology*, 1978, 25, 14–20.
447. Tyrer, P., Lewis, P., & Lee, I. Effects of subliminal and supraliminal stress on symptoms of anxiety. *Journal of Nervous & Mental Disease*, 1978, 166, 88–95.
448. Waid, L. R., Kanoy, R. C., III, Blick, K. A., & Walker, W. E. Relationship of state–trait anxiety and type of practice to reading comprehension. *Journal of Psychology*, 1978, 98, 27–36.
449. Watson, C. G., Herder, J., & Passini, F. T. Alpha biofeedback therapy in alcoholics: An 18-month follow up. *Journal of Clinical Psychology*, 1978, 34, 765–769.
450. Weinberg, R. S. The effects of success and failure on the patterning of neuromuscular energy. *Journal of Motor Behavior*, 1978, 10, 53–61.
451. Weinberg, R. S., & Ragan, J. Motor performance under three levels of trait anxiety and stress. *Journal of Motor Behavior*, 1978, 10, 169–176.
452. Zisook, S., Rogers, P., McClelland, M., Faschingbauer, T., & Lloyd, C. State–trait anxiety and anxiolytic treatment. *Current Therapeutic Research*, 1978, 23, 403–406.
453. Abrams, D. B., & Wilson, G. T. Effects of alcohol on social anxiety in women: Cognitive versus physiological processes. *Journal of Abnormal Psychology*, 1979, 88, 161–173.
454. Aquino, N. S., Trent, P. J., & Deutsch, J. E. Factors related to foreign nurse graduates' test–taking performance. *Nursing Research*, 1979, 28, 111–114.
455. Archer, R. P. Relationships between locus of control, trait anxiety, and state anxiety: An interactionist perspective. *Journal of Personality*, 1979, 47, 305–316.
456. Bauer, G. P., & Schlottmann, R. S. Effects of state anxiety and demand conditions on modeling behavior. *Psychological Reports*, 1979, 45, 511–516.
457. Bedell, J. R., Archer, R. P., & Rosmann, M. Relaxation therapy, desensitization, and the treatment of anxiety–based disorders. *Journal of Clinical Psychology*, 1979, 35, 840–843.
458. Boswell, P. C., & Murray, E. J. Effects of meditation on psychological and physiological measures of anxiety. *Journal of Consulting & Clinical Psychology*, 1979, 47, 606–607.
459. Burish, T. G., & Houston, B. K. Causal projection, similarity projection, and coping with threat to self–esteem. *Journal of Personality*, 1979, 47, 57–70.
460. Carr-Kaffashan, L., & Woolfolk, R. L. Active and placebo effects in treatment of moderate and severe insomnia. *Journal of Consulting & Clinical Psychology*, 1979, 47, 1072–1080.
461. Chandler, T. A., Cosner, T., & Spies, C. A. Anxiety and attribution as predictors of non–completion of a course. *Psychological Reports*, 1979, 45, 413–414.
462. Courtois, M. R., & Mueller, J. H. Processing multiple physical features in facial recognition. *Bulletin of the Psychonomic Society*, 1979, 14, 74–76.
463. Fehr, L. A., & Stamps, L. E. Guilt and shyness: A profile of social discomfort. *Journal of Personality Assessment*, 1979, 43, 481–484.
464. Fisher, S., Wright, D. M. & Moelis, I. Effects of maternal themes upon death imagery. *Journal of Personality Assessment*, 1979, 43, 595–599.
465. Franco, J. N., & Craft, D. B. Personality and environmental variables associated with dental anxiety. *Perceptual & Motor Skills*, 1979, 49, 529–530.
466. Gentil, M. L. F., & Lader, M. Effects of anxiety on attitudes–A semantic differential study. *British Journal of Medical Psychology*, 1979, 52, 133–139.
467. Goldman, B. L., Domitor, P. J., & Murray, E. J. Effects of Zen meditation on anxiety reduction and perceptual functioning. *Journal of Consulting & Clinical Psychology*, 1979, 47, 551–556.
468. Gotlib, I. H., & Asarnow, R. F. Interpersonal and impersonal problem–solving skills in mildly and clinically depressed university students. *Journal of Consulting & Clinical Psychology*, 1979, 47, 86–95.
469. Griffiths, T. J., Steel, D. H., & Vaccaro, P. Relationship between anxiety and performance in scuba diving. *Perceptual & Motor Skills*, 1979, 48, 1009–1010.
470. Grinnell, R. M., Jr., & Kyte, N. S. Anxiety level as an indicator of academic performance during first semester of graduate work. *Journal of Psychology*, 1979, 101, 199–201.
471. Hatch, J. P., & Gatchel, R. J. Development of physiological response patterns concomitant with the learning of voluntary heart rate control. *Journal of Comparative & Physiological Psychology*, 1979, 93, 306–313.
472. Heinrich, D. L. The causal influence of anxiety on academic achievement for students of differing intellectual ability. *Applied Psychological Measurement*, 1979, 3, 351–359.
473. Jaremko, M. E., & Lindsey, R. Stress–coping abilities of individuals high and low in jealousy. *Psychological Reports*, 1979, 44, 547–553.
474. Kanter, N. J., & Goldfried, M. R. Relative effectiveness of rational restructuring and self–control desensitization in the reduction of interpersonal anxiety. *Behavior Therapy*, 1979, 10, 472–490.
475. Kendall, P. C., Williams, L., Pechacek, T. F., Graham, L. E., Shisslak, C., & Herzoff, N. Cognitive–behavioral and patient education interventions in cardiac catheterization procedures: The Palo Alto Medical Psychology Project. *Journal of Consulting & Clinical Psychology*, 1979, 47, 49–58.
476. Kilpatrick, D. G., Veronen, L. J., & Resick, P. A. The aftermath of rape: Recent empirical findings. *American Journal of Orthopsychiatry*, 1979, 49, 658–669.
477. Lewis, M. S., Gottesman, D., & Gutstein, S. The course and duration of crisis. *Journal of Consulting & Clinical Psychology*, 1979, 47, 128–134.
478. Logan, P., & Loo, R. Application of the μ index to the State–Trait Anxiety Inventory. *Psychological Reports*, 1979, 44, 860–862.
479. Logan, P., & Loo, R. Source of covariation between the state and trait scales of the State–Trait Anxiety Inventory. *Journal of Psychology*, 1979, 103, 3–5.
480. Loo, R. The State–Trait Anxiety Inventory A–trait scale: Dimensions and their generalization. *Journal of Personality Assessment*, 1979, 43, 50–53.

481. MATHEW, R. J., HO BENG, T., KRALIK, P., & CLAGHORN, J. L. Anxiety and serum prolactin. *American Journal of Psychiatry*, 1979, 136, 716–717.
482. MATHEW, R. J., WEINMAN, M., & CLAGHORN, J. L. Xerostomia and sialorrhea in depression. *American Journal of Psychiatry*, 1979, 136, 1476–1477.
483. MILLER, S. M. Coping with impending stress: Psychophysiological and cognitive correlates of choice. *Psychophysiology*, 1979, 16, 572–581.
484. MUELLER, J. H., BAILIS, K. L., & GOLDSTEIN, A. G. Depth of processing and anxiety in facial recognition. *British Journal of Psychology*, 1979, 70, 511–515.
485. MUELLER, J. H., MILLER, D. J., & HUTCHINGS, J. L. Anxiety and orienting tasks in picture recognition. *Bulletin of the Psychonomic Society*, 1979, 13, 145–148.
486. NOWICKI, S., JR., WINOGRAD, E., & MILLARD, B. A. Memory for faces: A social learning analysis. *Journal of Research in Personality*, 1979, 13, 460–468.
487. OLLENDICK, D. G. Parental locus of control and the assessment of children's personality characteristics. *Journal of Personality Assessment*, 1979, 43, 401–405.
488. PETERSON, P. L. Aptitude x treatment interaction effects of teacher structuring and student participation in college instruction. *Journal of Educational Psychology*, 1979, 71, 521–533.
489. RAPHAEL, D., MOSS, S. W., & ROSSER, M. E. Evidence concerning the construct validity of conceptual level as a personality variable. *Canadian Journal of Behavioural Science*, 1979, 11, 327–339.
490. RAPPAPORT, E. Effects of dogmatism on state anxiety during the analysis and synthesis of new beliefs. *Journal of Personality Assessment*, 1979, 43, 284–288.
491. RAPPAPORT, E. General versus situation-specific trait anxiety in prediction of state anxiety during group therapy. *Psychological Reports*, 1979, 44, 715–718.
492. RAY, C. Examination stress and performance on a color-word interference test. *Perceptual & Motor Skills*, 1979, 49, 400–402.
493. SCOTT, J. C., & NELSON, D. L. Anxiety and encoding strategy. *Bulletin of the Psychonomic Society*, 1979, 13, 297–299.
494. SHIPLEY, R. H., BUTT, J. H., & HORWITZ, E. A. Preparation to reexperience a stressful medical examination: Effect of repetitious videotape exposure and coping style. *Journal of Consulting & Clinical Psychology*, 1979, 47, 485–492.
495. SMITHER, R., & RODRIGUEZ-GIEGLING, M. Marginality, modernity, and anxiety in Indochinese refugees. *Journal of Cross-Cultural Psychology*, 1979, 10, 469–478.
496. STAMPS, L. E., & FEHR, L. A. Heart rate changes and anxiety: A methodological clarification. *Journal of General Psychology*, 1979, 100, 319–320.
497. STEINLAUF. B. Problem-solving skills, locus of control, and the contraceptive effectiveness of young women. *Child Development*, 1979, 50, 268–271.
498. TULLMAN, G. M., TULLMAN, M. J., ROGERS, B. J., & ROSEN, J. B. Anxiety in dental patients: A study of three phases of state anxiety in three treatment groups. *Psychological Reports*, 1979, 45, 407–412.
499. VAN DER PLOEG, H. M. Relationship of state–trait anxiety to academic performance in Dutch medical students. *Psychological Reports*, 1979, 45, 223–227.
500. WATSON, C. G., JACOBS, L., & HERDER, J. Correlates of alpha, beta, and theta wave production. *Journal of Clinical Psychology*, 1979, 35, 364–369.
501. WEINBERG, R. S., & HUNT, V. V. Effects of structural integration on state-trait anxiety. *Journal of Clinical Psychology*, 1979, 35, 319–322.
502. WOOD, D., DEL NUOVO, A., BUCKY, S. F., SCHEIN, S., & MICHALIK, M. Psychodrama with an alcohol abuser population. *Group Psychotherapy, Psychodrama & Sociometry*, 1979, 32, 75–88.
503. WUDEL, P. Time estimation and personality dimensions. *Perceptual & Motor Skills*, 1979, 48, 1320.
504. WUDEL, P., & LOO, R. Birth order and person variables. *Psychological Reports*, 1979, 45, 280.
505. ARCHER, R. P. Generalized expectancies of control, trait anxiety, and psychopathology among psychiatric inpatients. *Journal of Consulting & Clinical Psychology*, 1980, 48, 736–742.
506. ARCHER, R. P., BEDELL, J. R., & AMUSO, K. F. Personality, demographic, and intellectual variables associated with readiness for discharge from psychiatric treatment. *Journal of Psychology*, 1980, 104, 67–74.
507. BARRIOS, B. A., GINTER, E. J., SCALISE, J. J., & MILLER, F. G. Treatment of test anxiety by applied relaxation and cue-controlled relaxation. *Psychological Reports*, 1980, 46, 1287–1296.
508. BARSTOW, J. Stress variance in hospice nursing. *Nursing Outlook*, 1980, 28, 751–754.
509. BEATTY, M. J., BEHNKE, R. R., & FROELICH, D. L. Effects of achievement incentive and presentation rate on listening comprehension. *Quarterly Journal of Speech*, 1980, 66, 193–200.
510. BENNETT, B., HALL, C., & GUAY, M. An approach combining relaxation training, imagery and practice examinations for the control of test anxiety. *Perceptual & Motor Skills*, 1980, 51, 977–978.
511. BISTLINE, J. L., JAREMKO, M. E., & SOBLEMAN, S. The relative contributions of covert reinforcement and cognitive restructuring to test anxiety reduction. *Journal of Clinical Psychology*, 1980, 36, 723–728.
512. BLUMBERG, N. L. Effects of neonatal risk, maternal attitude, and cognitive style on early postpartum adjustment. *Journal of Abnormal Psychology*, 1980, 89, 139–150.
513. BRADENBURG-HRUSKA, N. A., WEINMAN, M., & MATHEW, R. J. Frequency and severity of psychophysiological symptoms in a normal population. *Psychological Reports*, 1980, 46, 1059–1064.
514. BREWER, D., DOUGHTIE, E. B., & LUBIN, B. Induction of mood and mood shift. *Journal of Clinical Psychology*, 1980, 36, 215–226.
515. BROOKS, G. R., & RICHARDSON, F. C. Emotional skills training: A treatment program for duodenal ulcer. *Behavior Therapy*, 1980, 11, 198–207.
516. BUSBY, K., & DE KONINCK, J. Short-term effects of strategies for self-regulation on personality dimensions and dream content. *Perceptual & Motor Skills*, 1980, 50, 751–765.
517. CHATTERJEA, R. G., CHATTOPADHYAY, P. K., ROY, A. R., BISWAS, P. K., BHATTACHARYYA, A. K., & BASU, A. K. Role of trait anxiety and induced arousal in two-flash threshold of neurotic patients. *Psychological Reports*, 1980, 46, 231–234.
518. CRABBS, M. A., & HOPPER, G. The relationship between cognitive and somatic measures in the assessment of anxiety. *Bulletin of the Psychonomic Society*, 1980, 15, 218–220.
519. DEFFENBACHER, J. L., & MICHAELS, A. C. Two self-control procedures in the reduction of targeted and nontargeted anxieties–A year later. *Journal of Counseling Psychology*, 1980, 27, 9–15.
520. DEFFENBACHER, J. L, MICHAELS, A. C., DALEY, P. C., & MICHAELS, T. A comparison of homogeneous and heterogeneous anxiety management training. *Journal of Counseling Psychology*, 1980, 27, 630–634.
521. DEFFENBACHER, J. L., MICHAELS, A. C., MICHAELS, T., & DALEY, P. C. Comparison of anxiety management training and self-control desensitization. *Journal of Counseling Psychology*, 1980, 27, 232–239.
522. EVANS, R. G., & DINNING, W. D. A validation study of Forms A and B of the Whitaker Index of Schizophrenic Thinking. *Journal of Personality Assessment*, 1980, 44, 416–419.
523. FAGAN, T. J., & LIRA, F. T. The primary and secondary sociopathic personality: Differences in frequency and severity of antisocial behaviors. *Journal of Abnormal Psychology*, 1980, 89, 493–496.
524. FIELD, T. M., WIDMAYER, S. M., STRINGER, S., & IGNATOFF, E. Teenage, lower-class, black mothers and their preterm infants: An intervention and developmental follow-up. *Child Development*, 1980, 51, 426–436.
525. GILL, D. L. Comparison of three measures of pre-competition arousal. *Perceptual & Motor Skills*, 1980, 51, 765–766.
526. GRIEST, D. L., FOREHAND, R., WELLS, K. C., & McMAHON, R. J. An examination of differences between nonclinic and behavior-problem clinic-referred children and their mothers. *Journal of Abnormal Psychology*, 1980, 89, 497–500.
527. GROSS, T. F., & MASTENBROOK, M. Examination of the effects of state anxiety on problem-solving efficiency under high and low memory conditions. *Journal of Educational Psychology*, 1980, 72, 605–609.
528. HALL, E. G. Comparison of postperformance state anxiety of internals and externals following failure or success on a simple motor task. *Research Quarterly for Exercise & Sport*, 1980, 51, 306–314.
529. HALL, E. G., CHURCH, G. E., & STONE, M. Relationship of birth order to selected personality characteristics of nationally ranked Olympic weight lifters. *Perceptual & Motor Skills*, 1980, 51, 971–976.
530. HAWKINS, R. C., II, DOELL, S. R., LINDSETH, P., JEFFERS, V., & SKAGGS, S. Anxiety reduction in hospitalized schizophrenics through thermal biofeedback and relaxation training. *Perceptual & Motor Skills*, 1980, 51, 475–782.
531. HESTER, S. B., & FOWLER, S. C. Limb tremor as an indicator of emotional arousal. *Journal of Nervous & Mental Disease*, 1980, 168, 679–684.
532. HUTCHINGS, D. F., DENNEY, D. R., BASGALL, J. & HOUSTON, B. K. Anxiety management and applied relaxation in reducing general anxiety. *Behaviour Research Therapy*, 1980, 18, 181–190.
533. ILLFELDER, J. K. Fear of success, sex role attitudes, and career salience and anxiety levels of college women. *Journal of Vocational Behavior*, 1980, 16, 7–17.
534. JANNOUN, L., MUNBY, M., CATALAN, J., & GELDER, M. A home-based treatment program for agoraphobia: Replication and controlled evaluation. *Behavior Therapy*, 1980, 11, 294–305.
535. JONES, L. K., & CHENERY, M. F. Multiple subtypes among vocationally undecided college students.: A model and assessment instrument. *Journal of Counseling Psychology*, 1980, 27, 469–477.
536. KAPPES, B. M. Concurrent validity of the Personal Attribute Inventory as a self-concept scale. *Perceptual & Motor Skills*, 1980, 51, 752–754.

537. Kassinove, H., Miller, N., & Kalin, M. Effects of pretreatment with rational emotive bibliotherapy and rational emotive audiotherapy on clients waiting at community mental health center. *Psychological Reports*, 1980, 46, 851–857.

538. Kellerman, J., Zeltzer, L., Ellenberg, L., Dash, J., & Rigler, D. Psychological effects of illness in adolescence. I. Anxiety, self-esteem, and perception of control. *Journal of Pediatrics*, 1980, 97, 126–131.

539. Knox, W. J. An exploratory study of state–trait anxiety as a function of automated relaxation training, desired changes and drinking behavior. *Journal of Clinical Psychology*, 1980, 36, 332–337.

540. Lamb, D. H., & Strand, K. H. The effect of a brief relaxation treatment for dental anxiety on measures of state and trait anxiety. *Journal of Clinical Psychology*, 1980, 36, 270–274.

541. Lang, A. R., Searles, J., Lauerman, R., & Adesso, V. Expectancy, alcohol, and sex guilt as determinants of interest in and reaction to sexual stimuli. *Journal of Abnormal Psychology*, 1980, 89, 644–653.

542. Lehrer, P. M., Schoicket, S., Carrington, P., & Woolfolk, R. L. Psychophysiological and cognitive responses to stressful stimuli in subjects practicing progressive relaxation and clinically standardized meditation. *Behaviour Research and Therapy*, 1980, 18, 293–303.

543. Lipscomb, T. R., Nathan, P. E., Wilson, G. T., & Abrams, D. B. Effects of tolerance on the anxiety–reducing function of alcohol. *Archives of General Psychiatry*, 1980, 37, 577–582.

544. Lipsky, M. J., Kassinove, H., & Miller, N. J. Effects of rational–emotive therapy, rational role reversal, and rational–emotive imagery on the emotional adjustment of community mental health center patients. *Journal of Consulting & Clinical Psychology*, 1980, 48, 366–374.

545. Lopez, M. A. Social-skills training with institutionalized elderly: Effects of precounseling structuring and overlearning on skill acquisition and transfer. *Journal of Counseling Psychology*, 1980, 27, 286–293.

546. Margalit, C., Teichman, Y., & Levitt, R. Emotional reaction to physical threat: Reexamination with female subjects. *Journal of Consulting & Clinical Psychology*, 1980, 48, 403–404.

547. Mehrabian, A., & O'Reilly, E. Analysis of personality measures in terms of basic dimensions of temperament. *Journal of Personality & Social Psychology*, 1980, 38, 492–503.

548. Mueller, J. H., & Fisher, D. Field independence and input grouping in free recall. *Bulletin of the Psychonomic Society*, 1980, 16, 397–400.

549. Mueller, J. H., & Wherry, K. L. Orienting strategies at study and test in facial recognition. *American Journal of Psychology*, 1980, 93, 107–117.

550. Naylor, F. D., Elsworth, G. R., & Astbury, J. A. Interactions of factorial components and testing occasions in the determination of scores on the A–state scale of the State–Trait Anxiety Inventory. *Australian Journal of Psychology*, 1980, 32, 217–223.

551. Nielson, W. R., & Dobson, K. S. The coronary–prone behavior pattern and trait anxiety: Evidence for discriminant validity. *Journal of Consulting & Clinical Psychology*, 1980, 48, 546–547.

552. Oclatis, K. A., & Stiner, A. Relationship between patients' in-process evaluations of therapy and psychotherapy outcome. *Journal of Clinical Psychology*, 1980, 36, 259–264.

553. Olson, A. T., Gillingham, D. E. Systematic desensitization of mathematics anxiety among preservice elementary teachers. *Alberta Journal of Educational Research*, 1980, 26, 120–127.

554. Olson, D. R, & Schlottmann, R. S. Role of model's affect in test anxiety. *Psychological Reports*, 1980, 47, 956–958.

555. Peterson, P. L., Janicki, T. C., & Swing, S. R. Aptitude-treatment interaction effects of three social studies teaching approaches. *American Educational Research Journal*, 1980, 17, 339–360.

556. Pihl, R. O., & Caron, M. The relationship between geographic mobility, adjustment, and personality. *Journal of Clinical Psychology*, 1980, 36, 190–194.

557. Pilkonis, P. A., Feldman, H., Himmelhoch, J., & Cornes, C. Social anxiety and psychiatric diagnosis. *Journal of Nervous & Mental Disease*, 1980, 168, 13–18.

558. Price, K. P., & Blackwell, S. Trait levels of anxiety and psychological responses to stress in migraineurs and normal controls. *Journal of Clinical Psychology*, 1980, 36, 658–660.

559. Reed, M., & Saslow, C. The effects of relaxation instructions and EMG biofeedback on test anxiety, general anxiety, and locus of control. *Journal of Clinical Psychology*, 1980, 36, 683–690.

560. Reynolds, C. R. Concurrent validity of What I Think and Feel: The Revised Children's Manifest Anxiety Scale. *Journal of Consulting & Clinical Psychology*, 1980, 48, 774–775.

561. Ribordy, S. C., Holmes, D. S., & Buchsbaum, H. K. Effects of affective and cognitive distractions on anxiety reduction. *Journal of Social Psychology*, 1980, 111, 121–127.

562. Russell, D., Peplau, L. A., & Cutrona, C. E. The Revised UCLA Loneliness Scale: Concurrent and discriminant validity evidence. *Journal of Personality & Social Psychology*, 1980, 39, 472–480.

563. Saxena, A. K., & Rastogi, G. D. A study of trait–state anxiety in high and low hostile subjects. *Psychologia*, 1980, 23, 138–145.

564. Seta, J. J., & Hassan, R. K. Awareness of prior success or failure: A critical factor in task performance. *Journal of Personality & Social Psychology*, 1980, 39, 70–76.

565. Standing, L., & Stace, G. The effects of environmental noise on anxiety level. *Journal of General Psychology*, 1980, 103, 263–272.

566. Suess, W. M., Alexander, A. B., Smith, D. D., Sweeney, H. W., & Marion, R. J. The effects of psychological stress on respiration: A preliminary study of anxiety and hyperventilation. *Psychophysiology*, 1980, 17, 535–540.

567. Thompson, J. C., Griebstein, M. G., & Kuhlenschmidt, S. L. Effects of EMG biofeedback and relaxation training in the prevention of academic underachievement. *Journal of Counseling Psychology*, 1980, 27, 97–106.

568. Trent, J. T., & Maxwell, W. A. State and trait components of test anxiety and their implications for treatment. *Psychological Reports*, 1980, 47, 475–480.

569. VanDercar, D. H., Greaner, J., Hibler, N. S., Spielberger, C. D., & Block, S. A description and analysis of the operation and validity of the psychological stress evaluator. *Journal of Forensic Sciences*, 1980, 25, 175–188.

570. Vontver, L., Irby, D., Rakestraw, P., Haddock, M., Prince, E., & Stenchever, M. The effects of two methods of pelvic examination instruction on student performance and anxiety. *Journal of Medical Education*, 1980, 55, 778–785.

571. Walker, L. J. S., & Walker, J. L. Trait anxiety in mothers: Differences associated with employment status, family size and age of children. *Psychological Reports*, 1980, 47, 295–299.

572. Wallach, H. F., Riege, W. H., & Cohen, M. J. Recognition memory for emotional words: A comparative study of young, middle-aged and older persons. *Journal of Gerontology*, 1980, 35, 371–375.

573. Watson, C. G., & Herder, J. Effectiveness of alpha biofeedback therapy: Negative results. *Journal of Clinical Psychology*, 1980, 36, 508–513.

574. White, B. C., Lincoln, C. A., Pearce, N. W., Reeb, R., & Vaida, C. Anxiety and muscle tension as consequences of caffeine withdrawal. *Science*, 1980, 209, 1547–1548.

575. Wiens, A. N., Harper, R. G., & Matarazzo, J. D. Personality correlates of nonverbal interview behavior. *Journal of Clinical Psychology*, 1980, 36, 205–215.

576. Woods, D. J., & Oppenheimer, K. C. Torque, hemispheric dominance, and psychosocial adjustment. *Journal of Abnormal Psychology*, 1980, 89, 567–572.

577. Zeltzer, L., Kellerman, J., Ellenberg, L., Dash, J., & Rigler, D. Psychologic effects of illness in adolescence. II. Impact of illness in adolescents–Crucial issues and coping styles. *Journal of Pediatrics*, 1980, 97, 132–138.

578. Altmaier, E. M., & Woodward, M. Group vicarious desensitization of test anxiety. *Journal of Counseling Psychology*, 1981, 28, 467–469.

579. Bander, R. S., Betz, N. E. The relationship of sex and sex role to trait and situationally specific anxiety types. *Journal of Research in Personality*, 1981, 15, 312–322.

580. Barratt, E. S., Patton, J., Olsson, N. G., & Zucker, G. Impulsivity and paced tapping. *Journal of Motor Behavior*, 1981, 13, 286–300.

581. Behnke, R. R., Beatty, M. J. A cognitive–physiological model of speech anxiety. *Communication Monographs*, 1981, 48, 158–163.

582. Brown, G. S., & Strange, C. The relationship of academic major and career choice status to anxiety among college freshmen. *Journal of Vocational Behavior*, 1981, 19, 328–334.

583. Dye, C. J., & Erber, J. T. Two group procedures for the treatment of nursing home patients. *Gerontologist*, 1981, 21, 539–544.

584. Ferrell, W. L., & Galassi, J. P. Assertion training and human relations training in the treatment of chronic alcoholics. *International Journal of the Addictions*, 1981, 16, 959–968.

585. Forman, S. G. Stress–management training: Evaluation of effects on school psychological services. *Journal of School Psychology*, 1981, 19, 233–241.

586. Francis, K. T. Perceptions of anxiety, hostility and depression in subjects exhibiting the coronary–prone behavior pattern. *Journal of Psychiatric Research*, 1981, 16, 183–190.

587. Frank, E., Turner, S. M., Stewart, B. D., Jacob, M., & West, D. Past psychiatric symptoms and the response to sexual assault. *Comprehensive Psychiatry*, 1981, 22, 479–487.

588. Golub, S., & Harrington, D. M. Premenstrual and menstrual mood changes in adolescent women. *Journal of Personality & Social Psychology*, 1981, 41, 961–965.

589. Hartfield, M. J., & Cason, C. L. Effect of information on emotional responses during barium enema. *Nursing Research*, 1981, 30, 151–155.

590. Heidt, P. Effect of therapeutic touch on anxiety level of hospitalized patients. *Nursing Research*, 1981, 30, 32–37.

591. HOFLAND, B. F., WILLIS, S. L., & BALTES, P. B. Fluid intelligence performance in the elderly: Intraindividual variability and conditions of assessment. *Journal of Educational Psychology*, 1981, 73, 573–586.
592. HUBBLE, M. A., NOBLE, F. C., & ROBINSON, S. E. The effect of counselor touch in an initial counseling session. *Journal of Counseling Psychology*, 1981, 28, 533–535.
593. KILPATRICK, D. G., RESICK, P. A., & VERONEN, L. J. Effects of a rape experience: A longitudinal study. *Journal of Social Issues*, 1981, 37, 105–122.
594. LEAL, L. L., BAXTER, E. G., MARTIN, J., & MARX, R. W. Cognitive modification and systematic desensitization with test anxious high school students. *Journal of Counseling Psychology*, 1981, 28, 525–528.
595. LOGUE, P. E., LINNOILA, M., WALLMAN, L., & ERWIN, C. W. Effects of ethanol and psychomotor tests on state anxiety: Interaction with menstrual cycle in women. *Perceptual & Motor Skills*, 1981, 52, 643–648.
596. LOHR, J. W. & BONGE, D. On the distinction between illogical and irrational beliefs and their relationship to anxiety. *Psychological Reports*, 1981, 48, 191–194.
597. MATHEW, R. J., WEINMAN, M. L., & MIRABI, M. Physical symptoms of depression. *British Journal of Psychiatry*, 1981, 139, 293–296.
598. NEUGER, G. J., O'LEARY, D. S., FISHBURNE, F. J., BARTH, J. T., BERENT, S., GIORDANI, B., & BOLL, T. J. Order effects on the Halstead–Reitan Neuropsychological Test Battery and allied procedures. *Journal of Consulting & Clinical Psychology*, 1981, 49, 722–730.
599. PARKER, K. P. Anxiety and complications in patients on hemodialysis. *Nursing Research*, 1981, 30, 334–336.
600. PILKONAS, P. A., FELDMAN, H., & HIMMELHOCH, J. Social anxiety and substance abuse in affective disorders. *Comprehensive Psychiatry*, 1981, 22, 451–457.
601. PLAKE, B. S., SMITH, E. P., & DAMSTEEGT, D. C. A validity investigation of the Achievement Anxiety Test. *Educational & Psychological Measurement*, 1981, 41, 1215–1222.
602. PLAKE, B. S., THOMPSON, P. A., & LOWRY, S. Effect of item arrangement, knowledge of arrangement, and test anxiety on two scoring methods. *Journal of Experimental Education*, 1981, 49, 214–219.
603. PLOTKIN, W. D., & RICE, K. M. Biofeedback as a placebo: Anxiety reduction facilitated by training in either suppression or enhancement of alpha brainwaves. *Journal of Consulting & Clinical Psychology*, 1981, 49, 590–596.
604. POLIVY, J. On the induction of emotion in the laboratory: Discrete moods or multiple affect states? *Journal of Personality & Social Psychology*, 1981, 41, 803–817.
605. RAPHAEL, D., & XELOWSKI, H. Adolescents' anxiety and intolerance of ambiguity scores as predictors of dropping-out of a study. *Psychological Reports*, 1981, 48, 229–230.
606. RUBIN, S. A two-track model of bereavement: Theory and application in research. *American Journal of Orthopsychiatry*, 1981, 51, 101–109.
607. SCHANDRY, R. Heart beat perception and emotional experience. *Psychophysiology*, 1981, 18, 483–488.
608. SILVA, J. M., III, SCHULTZ, B. B., HASLAM, R. W., & MURRAY, D. A psychophysiological assessment of elite wrestlers. *Research Quarterly for Exercise & Sport*, 1981, 52, 348–358.
609. TEICHMAN, M. State–trait anxiety in methadone maintenance patients. *International Journal of the Addictions*, 1981, 16, 1125–1128.
610. THYER, B. A., & PAPSDORF, J. C. Concurrent validity of the Rational Behavior Inventory. *Psychological Reports*, 1981, 48, 255–258.

[2301]

State-Trait Anxiety Inventory for Children. Ages 4–6; 1970–73; STAIC; downward extension of *State-Trait Anxiety Inventory*; title on test is *How-I-Feel Questionnaire*; 2 scores: state anxiety, trait anxiety; Charles D. Spielberger in collaboration with C. Drew Edwards, Robert E. Lushene, Joseph Montuori, and Denna Platzek; Consulting Psychologists Press, Inc.*

For additional information and a review by Norman S. Endler, see 8:684 (19 references); see also T2:1392 (2 references).

REFERENCES

1–2. See T2:1392.
3–21. See 8:684.
22. KIEFFER, L. F. Relationship of trait anxiety, peer presence, task difficulty, and skill acquisition of sixth-grade boys. *Research Quarterly*, 1977, 48, 550–562.
23. LIRA, F. T., WHITE, M. J., & FINCH, A. J., JR. Anxiety and mood states in delinquent adolescents. *Journal of Personality Assessment*, 1977, 41, 532–536.
24. NELSON, W. M., III, FINCH, A. J., JR, KENDALL, P. C., & GORDON, R. H. Anxiety and locus of conflict in normal children. *Psychological Reports*, 1977, 41, 375–378.
25. RITCHIE, J., VILLIGER, J., & DUIGNAN, P. Sex role differentiation in children: A preliminary investigation. *Australian & New Zealand Journal of Sociology*, 1977, 13, 142–145.
26. FINCH, A. J., JR., KENDALL, P. C., DANNENBURG, M. A., & MORGAN, J. R. Effects of task difficulty on state–trait anxiety in emotionally disturbed children. *Journal of Genetic Psychology*, 1978, 133, 253–259.
27. KASE, J. B., SIKES, S. M., & SPIELBERGER, C. D. Emotional reactions to frightening and neutral scenes in story theatre. *Communication Monographs*, 1978, 45, 181–186.
28. POWAZEK, M., GOFF, J. R., SCYVING, J., & PAULSON, M. A. Emotional reactions of children to isolation in a cancer hospital. *Journal of Pediatrics*, 1978, 92, 834–837.
29. POWERS, P. S., & GIRGENTI, J. R. Analysis of a system. *Journal of Psychiatric Nursing*, 1978, 16, 17–22.
30. SMITH, I. D. Sex differences in self-concept revisited. *Australian Psychologist*, 1978, 13, 161–166.
31. BOYLE, G. Delimitation of state–trait curiosity in relation to state anxiety and learning task performance. *Australian Journal of Education*, 1979, 23, 70–82.
32. KLORMAN, R., MICHAEL, R., HILPERT, P. L., & SVEEN, O. B. A further assessment of predictors of the child's behavior in dental treatment. *Journal of Dental Research*, 1979, 58, 2338–2343.
33. OLLENDICK, D. G. Locus of control and anxiety as mediating variables of locus of conflict in disadvantaged youth. *Journal of Psychology*, 1979, 101, 23–25.
34. OLLENDICK, T. H., & HERSEN, M. Social skills training for juvenile delinquents. *Behaviour Research & Therapy*, 1979, 17, 547–554.
35. VOGRIN, D., & KASSINOVE, H. Effects of behavior rehearsal, audiotaped observation, and intelligence on assertiveness and adjustment in third–grade children. *Psychology in the Schools*, 1979, 16, 422–429.
36. NELSON, W. M., III. A cognitive–behavioral treatment for disproportionate dental anxiety and pain: A case study. *Journal of Clinical Child Psychology*, 1981, 10, 79–82.

[2302]

Statistically Validated Written Tests for Police Officer. Prospective police officers; 1976–81; 2 forms; McCann Associates.

a) FORM 125. 5 scores: observational ability, police aptitude, police public relations, police judgment, total.

b) FORM 100. 8 scores: observational ability, ability to exercise judgment and common sense, interest in police work, ability to exercise judgment-map reading, ability to exercise judgment-dealing with people, ability to read and comprehend police text material, reasoning ability, total.

[2303]

★**The Steenburgen Diagnostic-Prescriptive Math Program.** Grades 1–3, 4–6; 1978; "a criterion-referenced test"; no manual; Fran Steenburgen; Academic Therapy Publications.*

[2304]

Stenographic Dictation Test. Applicants for stenographic positions; 1962–64; McCann Associates.*

For additional information, see 6:46.

[2305]

Stenographic Skill-Dictation Test. Applicants for stenographic positions; 1950–73; formerly called *Test for Stenographic Skill*; Edward N. Hay; E. F. Wonderlic & Associates, Inc.*

For additional information and reviews by Reign H. Bittner and Clifford E. Jurgensen, see 4:459.

[2306]

Stenographic Skills Test: ETSA Test 4A. Job applicants; 1960–72, c1957–59; manual and technical handbook by S. Trevor Hadley and George A. W.

Stouffer, Jr.; test by Psychological Services Bureau; Educators'-Employers' Tests & Services Associates.*

For reviews of the complete battery, see 6:1025 (2 reviews).

[2307]

Stenographic Test: National Business Entrance Tests. Grades 11–16 and adults; 1938–72; earlier tests called *Stenographic Ability Test*; National Business Education Association.* (In-print status uncertain; no reply from publisher.)

See T2:795 (3 references); see also 6:47 (1 reference); for a review by Edward B. Greene of earlier forms, see 5:522; for reviews by Ann Brewington and Elizabeth Fehrer, see 3:391. For reviews of the complete battery, see 6:33 (1 review), 5:515 (3 reviews), and 3:396 (1 review).

[2308]

Stern Activities Index. Grades 7–16 and adults; 1950–72; SAI; personal needs; 2 editions; George G. Stern; Evaluation Research Associates.*

a) [FORM 1158.] 1950–70; 48 scores: 30 need scores (abasement-assurance, achievement, adaptability-defensiveness, affiliation, aggression-blame avoidance, changesameness, conjunctivity-disjunctivity, counteraction, deference-restiveness, dominance-tolerance, ego achievement, emotionality-placidity, energy-passivity, exhibitionism-inferiority avoidance, fantasied achievement, harm avoidance-risk taking, humanities and social science, impulsiveness-deliberation, narcissism, nurturance, objectivity-projectivity, order-disorder, play-work, practicalness-impracticalness, reflectiveness, science, sensuality-puritanism, sexuality-prudishness, supplication-autonomy, understanding), 12 factor scores (self-assertion, audacity-timidity, intellectual interests, motivation, applied interests, orderliness, submissiveness, closeness, sensuousness, friendliness, expressiveness-constraint, egoism-diffidence), 4 second-order factor scores (achievement orientation, dependency needs, emotional expression, educability), 1 validity score, 1 academic aptitude score; also 5 composite culture factor scores (expressive, intellectual, protective, vocational, collegiate) based on combinations of needs scores with environmental press scores.

b) FORM 1158-SHORT FORM. 1972; 18 scores: same as for *a* except for omission of 30 need scores.

See T2:1394 (23 references); for reviews by Wilbur L. Layton and Rodney W. Skager of *a*, see 7:142 (61 references); see also P:255 (41 references) and 6:180 (27 references).

[2309]

[Stevens-Thurow Personnel Forms]. Business and industry; 1951–72; 12 record and rating forms; Stevens, Thurow & Associates, Inc.*

a) PERSONAL HISTORY RECORD. Applicants, employees; 1951–72.
b) APPLICATION FOR POSITION. Applicants for clerical positions; 1951.
c) APPLICATION FOR EMPLOYMENT. Applicants for shop or plant positions; 1951.
d) PRELIMINARY INTERVIEW. Prospective employees; 1954.
e) INTERVIEWER'S GUIDE AND RATING FORM FOR PROSPECTIVE EMPLOYEES. Prospective employees; 1956–67.
f) EMPLOYMENT INTERVIEW SCHEDULE. Prospective employees; 1956.
g) WORK REFERENCE INVESTIGATION. 1951–63.
h) JOB DESCRIPTION [SHORT FORM]. 1956.
i) JOB DESCRIPTION QUESTIONNAIRE [LONG FORM]. 1952.
j) APPRAISAL REPORT FOR MANAGEMENT PERSONNEL. Manager's rating of employees; 1959.
k) APPRAISAL REPORT FOR MANAGEMENT PERSONNEL (SUPPLEMENTARY FORM FOR SALES MANAGERS). 1959.
l) WORK BEHAVIOR INVENTORY. Supervisor's rating of employees; 1951–63.

For additional information, see 6:1129.

[2310]

Steward Basic Factors Inventory (1960 Edition). Applicants for sales and office positions; 1957–63; revision of *Steward Sales Aptitude Inventory*; originally called *Steward Vocational Fitness Inventory*; 14 scores: business knowledge (vocabulary, arithmetic, total), dominance, personal adjustment, occupational interests (clerical, artistic, supervisory, accounting, writing, selling, mechanical, total), total; Verne Steward; Steward-Mortensen & Associates.* (In-print status uncertain; no reply from publisher.)

For additional information and reviews by Leonard V. Gordon and Lyman W. Porter, see 6:1182.

[2311]

Steward Life Insurance Knowledge Test. Applicants for life insurance agent or supervisory positions; 1952–56; 5 scores: arithmetic, vocabulary, principles, functions, total; Verne Steward; Steward-Mortensen & Associates.* (In-print status uncertain; no reply from publisher.)

For additional information, see 5:950.

[2312]

Steward Occupational Objectives Inventory, 1957 Edition. Applicants for supervisory positions in life insurance companies or agencies; 1956–57; formerly called *Steward Supervisory Personnel Inventory*; ratings in 8 areas: caliber level, life insurance knowledge, selling skills, leadership ability, supervisory skills, personal adjustment, survival on job, supplementary items; Verne Steward; Steward-Mortensen & Associates.* (In-print status uncertain, no reply from publisher.)

For additional information, see 5:951.

[2313]

Steward Personal Background Inventory (1960 Revised Edition). Applicants for sales positions; 1949–60; revision of *Personal Inventory of Background Factors*; ratings of 5 factors (caliber, aptitude, adjustment, survival, supplementary) in 7 areas (health, education, experience, financial status, activities, family status, miscellaneous); Verne Steward; Steward-Mortensen & Associates.* (In-print status uncertain; no reply from publisher.)

For additional information and reviews by Leonard V. Gordon and Lyman W. Porter, see 6:1183.

[2314]

Steward Personnel Tests (Short Form), 1958 Edition. Applicants for sales and office positions; 1957–58; abbreviated version of *Steward Sales Aptitude Inventory* and *Steward Vocational Fitness Inventory*; 10 scores: business knowledge, arithmetic, occupational interests (clerical, artistic, supervisory, accounting, writing, selling, mechanical, selling activities); Verne Steward; Steward-Mortensen & Associates.* (In-print status uncertain; no reply from publisher.)

For additional information and reviews by Leonard V. Gordon and Lyman W. Porter, see 6:1029.

[2315]
Stogdill Behavior Cards: A Test-Interview for Delinquent Children. Delinquents having a reading grade score 4.5 or higher; 1941–50; Ralph M. Stogdill; distributed by Stoelting Co.*

For additional information, see P:16; see also 6:65 (1 reference); for reviews by W. C. Kvaraceus and Simon H. Tulchin, see 3:25 (3 references).

[2316]
Strait Biblical Knowledge Test. Grades 9–16 and adults; 1975; 2 tests labeled Forms I, II; Jim Strait; Bureau of Educational Measurements.*
a) FORM I: OLD TESTAMENT.
b) FORM II: NEW TESTAMENT.
For additional information, see 8:467.

[2317]
Stromberg Dexterity Test. Trade school and adults; 1945–51; SDT; Eleroy L. Stromberg; The Psychological Corporation.*

See T2:2235 (8 references); for a review by Julian C. Stanley, see 4:755 (1 reference).

REFERENCES

1. See 4:755.
2–9. See T2:2235.
10. ZAIDEL, D., & SPERRY, R. W. Some long-term motor effects of cerebral commissurotomy in man. *Neuropsychologia*, 1977, 5, 193–204.
11. DORAN, R. L., & DIETRICH, M. C. Psychomotor abilities of science and nonscience high school students. *Journal of Research in Science Teaching*, 1980, 17, 495–502.

[2318]
*****Strong-Campbell Interest Inventory.** Ages 16 and over; 1927–81; SCII; 193 scoring scales (6 general occupational themes, 23 basic interests scales, 162 occupational scales, 2 special scales) and 26 administrative indexes; GENERAL OCCUPATIONAL THEMES: realistic, investigative, artistic, social, enterprising, conventional; BASIC INTEREST SCALES: adventure, agriculture, art, athletics, business management, domestic arts, law/politics, mathematics, mechanical activities, medical science, medical service, merchandising, military activities, music/dramatics, nature, office practices, public speaking, religious activities, sales, science, social service, teaching, writing; OCCUPATIONAL SCALES: accountant (2 scales: female, male), advertising executive (f, m), agribusiness manager (m), air force officer (f, m), architect (f, m), army officer (f, m), art teacher (f, m), banker (f, m), beautician (f, m), biologist (f, m), business education teacher (f, m), buyer (f, m), chamber of commerce executive (f, m), chemist (f, m), chiropractor (f, m), college professor (f, m), commercial artist (f, m), computer programmer (f, m), credit manager (f, m), dental assistant (f), dental hygienist (f), dentist (f, m), department store manager (f, m), dietitian (f, m), elected public official (f, m), elementary education teacher (f, m), engineer (f, m), English teacher (f, m), executive housekeeper (f, m), farmer (f, m), fine artist (f, m), flight attendant (f, m), foreign language teacher (f, m), forester (f, m), geographer (f, m), geologist (f, m), guidance counselor (f, m), home economics teacher (f), interior decorator (f, m), investment fund manager (m), IRS agent (f, m), lawyer (f, m), librarian (f, m), licensed practical nurse (f, m), life insurance agent (f, m), marketing executive (f, m), mathematician (f, m), mathscience teacher (f, m), medical technologist (f, m), minister (f, m), musician (f, m), navy officer (f, m), nursing home administrator (f, m), occupational therapist (f, m), optometrist (f, m), personnel director (f, m), pharmacist (f, m), photographer (f, m), physical education teacher (f, m), physical therapist (f, m), physician (f, m), physicist (f, m), police officer (f, m), psychologist (f, m), public administrator (f, m), public relations director (f, m), purchasing agent (f, m), radiologic technologist (f, m), realtor (f, m), recreation leader (f, m), registered nurse (f, m), reporter (f, m), restaurant manager (f, m), school administrator (f, m), secretary (f), skilled crafts (m), social science teacher (f, m), social worker (f, m), sociologist (f, m), special education teacher (f, m), speech pathologist (f, m), systems analyst (f, m), veterinarian (f, m), vocational agriculture teacher (m), YWCA director (f), YMCA director (M); SPECIAL SCALES: academic comfort, introversion-extroversion; ADMINISTRATIVE INDEXES: total response, infrequent response, response percentages (like, indifferent, dislike) for each of the 7 inventory sections plus total for all parts; original inventory by Edward K. Strong, Jr., revision by David P. Campbell (test and manual) and Jo-Ida C. Hansen (manual); Stanford University Press.*

For reviews by John O. Crites, Robert H. Dolliver, Patricia W. Lunneborg, and excerpted reviews by Richard W. Johnson, David P. Campbell, and Jean C. Steinhauer, see 8:1023 (289 references); these references are for SVIB–M, SVIB–W, and SCII).

For references on the *Strong Vocational Interest Blank For Men*, see T2:2212 (133 references); for reviews by Martin R. Katz and Charles J. Krauskopf and excerpted reviews by David P. Campbell and John W. M. Rothney, see 7:1036 (485 references); for reviews by Alexander W. Astin and Edward J. Furst, see 6:1070 (189 references); see also 5:868 (153 references); for reviews by Edward S. Bordin and Elmer D. Hinckley, see 4:747 (98 references); see also 3:647 (102 references); for reviews by Harold D. Carter, John G. Darley, and N. W. Morton, see 2:1680 (71 references); for a review by John G. Darley, see 1:1178. For references on the *Strong Vocational Interest Blank For Women*, see T2:2213 (30 references); for reviews by Dorothy M. Clendenen and Barbara A. Kirk, see 7:1037 (92 references); see also 6:1071 (12 references) and 5:869 (19 references); for a review by Gwendolen Schneidler Dickson, see 3:649 (38 references); for a review by Ruth Strang, see 2:1681 (10 references); for a review by John G. Darley, see 1:1179.

REFERENCES

1–71. See 2:1680.
72–175. See 3:647.
176–273. See 4:747.
274–426. See 5:868.
427–614. See 6:1070.
615–1099. See 7:1036.
1100–1232. see T2:2212.
1233–1521. See 8:1023.

1522. AMEG COMMISSION ON SEX BIAS IN MEASUREMENT. A case history of change: A review of responses to the challenge of sex bias in career interest inventories. *Measurement & Evaluation in Guidance*, 1977, 10, 148–152.

1523. CATRON, D. W., & ZULTOWSKI, W. H. Strong–Campbell general occupational themes: Profiles of four academic divisions. *Measurement & Evaluation in Guidance*, 1977, 10, 38–43.

1524. COSTA, P. T., JR., FOZARD, J. L., & MCCRAE, R. R. Personological interpretation of factors from the Strong Vocational Interest Blank scales. *Journal of Vocational Behavior*, 1977, 10, 231–243.

1525. DOLLIVER, R. H., & WILL, J. A. Ten-year follow-up of the Tyler Vocational Card Sort and the Strong Vocational Interest Blank. *Journal of Counseling Psychology*, 1977, 24, 48–54.

1526. FABRY, J., & POGGIO, J. P. The factor compatibility and communality of coded-expressed and inventoried interests. *Measurement & Evaluation in Guidance*, 1977, 10, 90–97.

1527. GOODYEAR, R. K., & FRANK, A. C. Introversion–extroversion: Some comparisons of the SVIB and OPI scales. *Measurement & Evaluation in Guidance*, 1977, 9, 206–211.

1528. GOTTLIEB, H., STRITE, L. C., KOLLER, R., MADORSKY, A., HOCKERSMITH, V., KLEEMAN, M., & WAGNER, J. Comprehensive rehabilitation of patients having chronic low back pain. *Archives of Physical Medicine & Rehabilitation*, 1977, 58, 101–108.

1529. GOUGH, H. G., & HALL, W. B. A comparison of physicians who did or did not respond to a postal questionnaire. *Journal of Applied Psychology*, 1977, 62, 777–780.

1530. GROTEVANT, H. D., SCARR, S., & WEINBERG, R. A. Patterns of interest similarity in adoptive and biological families. *Journal of Personality & Social Psychology*, 1977, 35, 667–676.

1531. HANSEN, J. C. Coding SCII items according to Holland's vocational theory. *Measurement & Evaluation in Guidance*, 1977, 10, 75–83.

1532. HANSEN, J. C. Evaluation of accuracy and consistency of machine scoring the SCII. *Measurement & Evaluation in Guidance*, 1977, 10, 141–143.

1533. JOHNSON, R. W. Relationships between male and female interest scales for the same occupations. *Journal of Vocational Behavior*, 1977, 11, 239–252.

1534. KEGEL-FLOM, P. Predictors of rural practice location. *Journal of Medical Education*, 1977, 52, 204–209.

1535. KLEIN, K. L., & WEINER, Y. Interest congruency as a moderator of the relationships between job tenure and job satisfaction and mental health. *Journal of Vocational Behavior*, 1977, 10, 92–98.

1536. LUNNEBORG, P. W. Construct validity of the Strong–Campbell Interest Inventory and Vocational Interest Inventory among college counseling clients. *Journal of Vocational Behavior*, 1977, 10, 187–195.

1537. LUNNEBORG, P. W., & GERRY, M. H. Sex differences in changing sex-stereotyped vocational interests. *Journal of Counseling Psychology*, 1977, 24, 247–250.

1538. MATARAZZO, J. D., & WIENS, A. N. Black Intelligence Test of Cultural Homogeneity and Wechsler Adult Intelligence Scale scores of black and white police applicants. *Journal of Applied Psychology*, 1977, 62, 57–63.

1539. MEUSER, D. M., & EDWARDS, H. P. Comparing the vocational interests of arts and science freshmen using the Strong–Campbell Interest Inventory. *Canadian Counsellor*, 1977, 11, 123–127.

1540. MEUSER, P. E., & MCINNIS, C. E. Differentiation of university freshmen in arts and science on the general occupational themes of the Strong–Campbell Interest Inventory. *Canadian Counsellor*, 1977, 11, 166–172.

1541. MIDDENTS, G. J. A pilot project for assessing nonacademic characteristics of premedical students. *Journal of Medical Education*, 1977, 52, 343–344.

1542. NICHOLS, M. P., & KNOPF, I. J. Refining computerized test interpretations: An in-depth approach. *Journal of Personality Assessment*, 1977, 41, 157–159.

1543. OLIVER, L. W. Evaluating career counseling outcome for three modes of test interpretation. *Measurement & Evaluation in Guidance*, 1977, 10, 153–161.

1544. RAMANAIAH, N. V. Stylistic components of human judgment: The generality of individual differences. *Applied Psychological Measurement*, 1977, 1, 23–29.

1545. RICE, J. K., & GOERING, M. L. Women in transition: A life-planning workshop model. *Journal of National Association for Women Deans, Administrators, & Counselors*, 1977, 40, 57–61.

1546. STEDMAN, M. E., & BREEN, M. J. Teacher interest and pupil attitudes. *Educational & Psychological Measurement*, 1977, 37, 1091–1094.

1547. TAYLOR, G. A., BIDUS, D. R., & COLLINS, H. A. The vocational interests of drug-dependent patients. *Psychological Reports*, 1977, 41, 959–963.

1548. TINSLEY, H. E. A., & TINSLEY, D. J. Different needs, interests, and abilities of effective and ineffective counselor trainees: Implications for counselor selection. *Journal of Counseling Psychology*, 1977, 24, 83–86.

1549. VAITENAS, R., & WIENER, Y. Developmental, emotional, and interest factors in voluntary mid-career change. *Journal of Vocational Behavior*, 1977, 11, 291–304.

1550. WORTHINGTON, E. L., JR., & DOLLIVER, R. H. Validity studies of the Strong Vocational Interest Inventories. *Journal of Counseling Psychology*, 1977, 24, 208–216.

1551. BORGEN, F. H., & SELING, M. J. Expressed and inventoried interests revisited: Perspicacity in the person. *Journal of Counseling Psychology*, 1978, 25, 536–543.

1552. CRAMER, P., & CARTER, T. The relationship between sexual identification and the use of defense mechanisms. *Journal of Personality Assessment*, 1978, 42, 63–73.

1553. DIPBOYE, R. L., ZULTOWSKI, W. H., DEWHIRST, H. D., & ARVEY, R. D. Self-esteem as a moderator of the relationship between scientific interests and the job satisfaction of physicists and engineers. *Journal of Applied Psychology*, 1978, 63, 289–294.

1554. FRANK, H., & WILCOX, D. Development and preliminary cross-validation of two-step procedure for firefighter selection. *Psychological Reports*, 1978, 43, 27–36.

1555. JOHNSON, R. W., KIRK, K. W., OHVALL, R. A., & BARBRE, A. R. The use of the Strong–Campbell Interest Inventory with female and male pharmacy students. *Measurement & Evaluation in Guidance*, 1978, 11, 99–105.

1556. JOHNSON, R. W. A "unisex" occupational scale for the Strong–Campbell Interest Inventory. *Applied Psychological Measurement*, 1978, 2, 527–532.

1557. GROTEVANT, H. D. Sibling constellations and sex typing of interests in adolescence. *Child Development*, 1978, 49, 540–542.

1558. HANSEN, J. C. Age differences and empirical scale construction. *Measurement & Evaluation in Guidance*, 1978, 11, 78–87.

1559. MALETT, S. D., SPOKANE, A. R., & VANCE, F. L. Effects of vocationally relevant information on the expressed and measured interests of freshman males. *Journal of Counseling Psychology*, 1978, 25, 292–298.

1560. O'HARA-DEVEREAUX, M., BROWN, T. C., MENTINK, J., & MORGAN, W. A. Biographical data, personality, and vocational interests of family nurse practitioners. *Psychological Reports*, 1978, 43, 1259–1268.

1561. PATTERSON, V., & HEILBRON, D. Therapist personality and treatment outcome: A test of the interaction hypothesis using the Campbell A-B scale. *Psychiatric Quarterly*, 1978, 50, 320–332.

1562. ROBBINS, P. I., THOMAS, L. E., HARVEY, D. W., & KANDEFER, C. Career change and congruence of personality type: An examination of DOT-derived work environment designations. *Journal of Vocational Behavior*, 1978, 13, 15–25.

1563. RUBINSTEIN, M. R. Integrative interpretation of vocational interest inventory results. *Journal of Counseling Psychology*, 1978, 25, 306–309.

1564. SCHMITT, N. Achievement level and sex differences in levels of interests and the interest-educational choice relationship. *College Student Journal*, 1978, 12, 167–173.

1565. SHAFFER, J. W., STEPHENS, J. H., & ZLOTOWITZ, H. I. Absence of significant A-B scale differences among medical specialties. *Educational & Psychological Measurement*, 1978, 38, 291–295.

1566. SHARF, R. S. Evaluation of a computer-based narrative interpretation of a test battery. *Measurement & Evaluation in Guidance*, 1978, 11, 50–53.

1567. SIMONO, R. B. Careers in the clergy: The myth of femininity. *Educational & Psychological Measurement*, 1978, 38, 507–511.

1568. SLANEY, R. B. Expressed and inventoried vocational interests: A comparison of instruments. *Journal of Counseling Psychology*, 1978, 25, 520–529.

1569. SPOKANE, A. R., MALETT, S. D., & VANCE, F. L. Consistent curricular choice and congruence of subsequent changes. *Journal of Vocational Behavior*, 1978, 13, 45–53.

1570. TINSLEY, D. J., & FAUNCE, P. S. Vocational interests of career and homemaker oriented women. *Journal of Vocational Behavior*, 1978, 13, 327–337.

1571. TRYON, G. S. Differences between counseling seekers and nonseekers on the Mooney Problem Checklist. *Journal of College Student Personnel*, 1978, 19, 501–505.

1572. WIENER, Y., & KLEIN, K. L. The relationship between vocational interests and job satisfaction: Reconciliation of divergent results. *Journal of Vocational Behavior*, 1978, 13, 298–304.

1573. WOLFE, J. H. Comparative cluster analysis of patterns of vocational interest. *Multivariate Behavioral Research*, 1978, 13, 33–44.

1574. ARVEY, R. D., & DEWHIRST, H. D. Relationships between diversity of interests, age, job satisfaction and job performance. *Journal of Occupational Psychology*, 1979, 52, 17–23.

1575. BARNOWE, J. T., FROST, P. J., & JAMAL, M. When personality meets situation: Exploring influences on choice of business major. *Journal of Occupational Psychology*, 1979, 52, 167–176.

1576. BELCASTRO, F. P. Personality and interest characteristics of completers and noncompleters of a secondary teacher preparation program. *College Student Journal*, 1979, 13, 73–76.

1577. BLAKE, R., & FABRY, J. Reliability of the Strong–Campbell Interest Inventory with high school seniors. *Measurement & Evaluation in Guidance*, 1979, 12, 19–24.

1578. BLIMLING, G. S., & PAULSEN, F. M. The Educational Developmental Group Enrichment (EDGE) program: A comprehensive model for student development in residence halls. *Journal of the National Association for Women Deans, Administrators & Counselors*, 1979, 42, 24–33.

1579. BRUSH, D. H., & SCHOENFELDT, L. F. Interrelationships among interests, life–history, and educational criteria. *Applied Psychological Measurement*, 1979, 3, 165–175.

1580. CAIRO, P. C. The validity of the Holland and basic interest scales of the Strong Vocational Interest Blank: Leisure activities versus occupational membership as criteria. *Journal of Vocational Behavior*, 1979, 15, 68–77.

1581. CREASER, J. W., & CARSELLO, C. J. Isolating factors related to paraprofessional effectiveness. *Journal of Counseling Psychology*, 1979, 26, 259–262.

1582. DOTY, M. S., & BETZ, N. E. Comparison of the concurrent validity of Holland's theory for men and women in an enterprising occupation. *Journal of Vocational Behavior*, 1979, 15, 207–216.

1583. GILLINGHAM, W. H., & LOUNSBURY, J. E. A description and evaluation of a career exploration course. *Journal of College Student Personnel*, 1979, 20, 525–529.

1584. GOTTHEIL, E., EXLINE, R. V., & WINKELMAYER, R. Judging emotions of normal and schizophrenic subjects. *American Journal of Psychiatry*, 1979, 136, 1049–1054.

1585. GROTEVANT, H. D. Environmental influences on vocational interest development in adolescents from adoptive and biological families. *Child Development*, 1979, 50, 854–860.

1586. LEVY, M. F., REICHMAN, W., & HERRINGTON, S. Congruence between personality and job characteristics in alcoholics and nonalcoholics. *Journal of Social Psychology*, 1979, 107, 213–217.

1587. LUNNEBORG, P. W. Service vs. technical interest–Biggest sex difference of all? *Vocational Guidance Quarterly*, 1979, 28, 146–153.

1588. MILLER, M. J., & COCHRAN, J. R. Evaluating the use of technology in reporting SCII results to students. *Measurement & Evaluation in Guidance*, 1979, 12, 166–173.

1589. NAVRAN, L., & WALKER, R. W. Longitudinal changes in vocational interests of Canadian military college cadets. *Canadian Counsellor*, 1979, 13, 136–139.

1590. OHLDE, C. D. Relationship between self–esteem and response style. *Journal of Counseling Psychology*, 1979, 26, 455–458.

1591. O'NEIL, J. M., PRICE, G. E., & TRACEY, T. J. The stimulus value, treatment effects, and sex differences when completing the Self–Directed Search and Strong–Campbell Interest Inventory. *Journal of Counseling Psychology*, 1979, 26, 45–50.

1592. REILLY, R., & ECHTERNACHT, G. Some problems with the criterion–keying approach to occupational interest scale development. *Educational & Psychological Measurement*, 1979, 39, 85–94.

1593. REUTERFORS, D. L., SCHNEIDER, L. J., & OVERTON, T. D. Academic achievement: An examination of Holland's congruency, consistency, and differentiation predictions. *Journal of Vocational Behavior*, 1979, 14, 181–189

1594. ROUNDS, J. B., JR., DAVISON, M. L., & DAWIS, R. V. The fit between Strong–Campbell Interest Inventory general occupational themes and Holland's hexagonal model. *Journal of Vocational Behavior*, 1979, 15, 303–315.

1595. ROUNDS, J. B., JR., & DAWIS, R. V. Factor analysis of Strong Vocational Interest Blank items. *Journal of Applied Psychology*, 1979, 64, 132–143.

1596. SPOKANE, A. R. Occupational preference and the validity of the Strong–Campbell Interest Inventory for college women and men. *Journal of Counseling Psychology*, 1979, 26, 312–318.

1597. SPOKANE, A. R. Validity of the Holland categories for college women and men. *Journal of College Student Personnel*, 1979, 20, 335–340.

1598. THOMAS, L. E. Personality and work environment congruence of mid–life career changes. *Journal of Occupational Psychology*, 1979, 52, 177–183.

1599. ZALINSKI, J. S., & ABRAHAMS, N. M. The effects of item context in faking personnel selection inventories. *Personnel Psychology*, 1979, 32, 161–166.

1600. ATANASOFF, G. E., & SLANEY, R. B. Three approaches to counselor–free career exploration among college women. *Journal of Counseling Psychology*, 1980, 27, 332–339.

1601. EMLING, R. C., GREEN, P. A., & STEVENS, F. W., JR. A comparison of interests of first year dental students and fellows of the Academy of General Dentistry on the Strong–Campbell Interest Inventory. *Journal of Dental Research*, 1980, 59, 786–794.

1602. HANSEN, J. C., & STOCCO, J. L. Stability of vocational interests of adolescents and young adults. *Measurement & Evaluation in Guidance*, 1980, 13, 173–178.

1603. HARMON, L. W., ZYTOWSKI, D. G. Reliability of Holland codes across interest measures for adult females. *Journal of Counseling Psychology*, 1980, 27, 478–483.

1604. O'NEIL, J. M. Reply to Prediger. *Journal of Counseling Psychology*, 1980, 27, 304.

1605. PREDIGER, D. J. On the virtues of raw–scored interest inventories: Reaction to O'Neil, Price, and Tracey (1979). *Journal of Counseling Psychology*, 1980, 27, 302–303.

1606. BARTLUNG, H. C., & HOOD, A. An 11–year follow-up of measured interest and vocational choice. *Journal of Counseling Psychology*, 1981, 28, 27–35.

1607. BERNARD, L. C. The multidimensional aspects of masculinity–feminity. *Journal of Personality & Social Psychology*, 1981, 41, 797–802.

1608. BETZ, N. E., & WOLFE, L. K. Comparison of the utility of two approaches to sex–balanced interest scales for college women. *Journal of Vocational Behavior*, 1981, 19, 61–77.

1609. DOLLIVER, R. H. A review of female–male score differences on the Strong–Campbell Twin Occupational Scales. *Journal of Counseling Psychology*, 1981, 28, 334–341.

1610. DOLLIVER, R. H., & WORTHINGTON, E. L., JR. Concurrent validity of other–sex and same–sex twin Strong–Campbell Interest Inventory occupation scales. *Journal of Counseling Psychology*, 1981, 28, 126–134.

1611. GARFINKEL, P. E., & WARING, E. M. Personality, interests, and emotional disturbance in psychiatric residents. *American Journal of Psychiatry*, 1981, 138, 51–55.

1612. HOFFMAN, M. A., SPOKANE, A. R., & MAGOON, T. M. Effects of feedback mode on counseling outcomes using the Strong–Campbell Interest Inventory: Does the counselor really matter? *Journal of Counseling Psychology*, 1981, 28, 119–125.

1613. JOHNSON, J. A., SMITHER, R., & HOLLAND, J. L. Evaluating vocational interventions: A tale of two career development seminars. *Journal of Counseling Psychology*, 1981, 28, 180–183.

1614. LETOURNEAU, J. E., & BEAULNE, C. Characteristics of female optometry students on the SCII. *American Journal of Optometry & Physiological Optics*, 1981, 58, 179–182.

1615. LEVY, M. F., REICHMAN, W., & HERRINGTON, S. Abstinent alcoholics' adjustment to work. *Journal of Studies on Alcohol*, 1981, 42, 529–532.

1616. LINDSEY, J. D., TELLER, H. E., & FRITH, G. H. The relationship of auditory processing impairments and adolescents' vocational interest and social behavior. *Volta Review*, 1981, 83, 82–94.

1617. MOSSHOLDER, K. W., DEWHIRST, H. D., & ARVEY, R. D. Vocational interest and personality differences between development and research personnel: A field study. *Journal of Vocational Behavior*, 1981, 19, 233–243.

1618. MURRAY, S. G. Personality characteristics of adult women with low or high profiles on the SCII or SVIB occupational scales. *Journal of Applied Psychology*, 1981, 66, 422–430.

1619. NAYLOR, F. D. A state-trait curiosity inventory. *Australian Psychologist*, 1981, 16, 172–183.

1620. SLANEY, R. B., & SLANEY, F. M. A comparison of measures of expressed and inventoried vocational interests among counseling center clients. *Journal of Counseling Psychology*, 1981, 28, 515–518.

[2319]

★Stroop Color and Word Test. Ages 7 and over; 1978; diagnosis of brain dysfunction; 3 scores: word, color, color-word; Charles J. Golden; Stoelting Co.*

REFERENCES

1. JARMAN, R. F., & KRYWANIUK, L. W. Simultaneous and successive syntheses: A factor analysis of speed of information processing. *Perceptual & Motor Skills*, 1978, 46, 1167–1172.

[2320]

★Structure of Intellect Learning Abilities Test. Grades kgn–1, preschool–grade 3, 7–12, adults; 1975–81; 8 forms; Mary Meeker and Robert Meeker; SOI Institute.*

a) BASIC FORM. Grades 2–12; 1975; 26 scores in 5 test areas: comprehension (cognition of figural units, cognition of figural classes, cognition of figural systems, cognition of figural transformations, cognition of symbolic relations, cognition of symbolic systems, cognition of semantic units, cognition of semantic relations, cognition of semantic systems), memory [memory of figural units, memory of symbolic units (visual, auditory), memory of symbolic systems (visual, auditory), visual memory of symbolic implications], evaluation (evaluation of figural units, evaluation of figural classes, evaluation of symbolic classes, evaluation of symbolic systems), convergent production (convergent production of figural units, convergent production of symbolic systems, convergent production of symbolic transformations, convergent production of symbolic implications), divergent production (divergent production of figural units, divergent production of semantic units, divergent production of symbolic relations); (Spanish and French translations available).

b) PROCESS AND DIAGNOSTIC SCREENING TEST. Preschool–grade 3; 1975; 11 scores based on the Basic Form but specifically developed for this age group; (Spanish edition available).

c) SPECIAL EDITION FORM. Grades kgn–1 and adult form for special education and deaf populations; 1975; 14 scores testing reading and arithmetic abilities taken from Basic Form and reformatted with larger figures and characters.

d) READING FORM. Grades 7–12; 1975; 11 scores relating to reading, language arts, and social science selected from the Basic Form.

e) ARITHMETIC FORM. Grades 7–12; 1975; 12 scores relating to arithmetic, mathematics, and science selected from the Basic Form.

f) DEVELOPMENTAL VISION FORM. Grades 2–12; 1975; 9 scores selected from the Basic Form which have been found to be the best indicators of vision performance difficulties.

g) GIFTED SCREENING FORM. Grades 2–6; 1975; not advised for minority disadvantaged; 12 scores selected from the Basic Form for the purpose of screening for gifted.

h) CAREER AND VOCATION FORM. Adults; 1975; 24 scores same as in Basic Form with deletion of visual memory of symbolic units, visual memory of symbolic systems, and visual memory of symbolic implications, and the addition of memory of semantic implications.

REFERENCES

1. CUNNINGHAM, C. H., THOMPSON, B., ALSTON, H. L., & WAKEFIELD, J. A., JR. Use of S.O.I. abilities for prediction. *Gifted Child Quarterly*, 1978, 22, 506–512.
2. THOMPSON, B., ALSTON, H. L., CUNNINGHAM, C. H., & WAKEFIELD, J. A., JR. The relationship of a measure of structure of intellect abilities and academic achievement. *Educational & Psychological Measurement*, 1978, 38, 1207–1210.

[2321]

Structure Tests—English Language. High school and over; 1976; STEL; 3 levels: beginning, intermediate, advanced; no manual; Jeanette Best and Donna Ilyin; Newbury House Publishers, Inc.*

For additional information, see 8:58.

REFERENCES

1. POCK, A. C. Structure Tests–English Language. *Modern Language Journal*, 1977, 61, 427.

[2322]

Structured and Scaled Interview to Assess Maladjustment. Mental patients; 1974; SSIAM; social adjustment; 11 ratings (5 deviant behavior, friction with others, 3 distress, 2 inferential) in each of 5 areas (work, social-leisure, family, marriage, sex) plus 11 overall ratings; Barry J. Gurland, Neil J. Yorkston, Anthony R. Stone, and Jerome D. Frank; Springer Publishing Co., Inc.*

For additional information, a review by Bertram D. Cohen, and an excerpted review by J. K. Wing, see 8:685 (7 references).

REFERENCES

1–7. See 8:685.
8. BOTHWELL, S., & WEISSMAN, M. M. Social impairment four years after an acute depressive episode. *American Journal of Orthopsychiatry*, 1977, 47, 231–237.
9. STERN, M. J., PASCALE, L., & ACKERMAN, A. Life adjustment postmyocardial infarction: Determining predictive variables. *Archives of Internal Medicine*, 1977, 137, 1680–1685.
10. PAYKEL, E. S., WEISSMAN, M. M., & PRUSOFF, B. A. Social maladjustment and severity of depression. *Comprehensive Psychiatry*, 1978, 19, 121–128.
11. WEISSMAN, M. M., PRUSOFF, B. A., THOMPSON, W. D., HARDING, P. S., & MYERS, J. K. Social adjustment by self–report in a community sample and in psychiatric outpatients. *Journal of Nervous & Mental Disease*, 1978, 166, 317–326.
12. HERJANIC, B. M., BARREDO, V. H., HERJANIC, M., & TOMELLERI, C. J. Children of heroin addicts. *International Journal of the Addictions*, 1979, 14, 919–931.
13. PETHÖ, B., TOLNA, J., & TUSNÁDY, G. Multi–trait–multi–method assessment of predictive variables of outcome in schizophrenia spectrum disorders. A nosological evaluation. *Journal of Psychiatric Research*, 1979, 15, 163–174.
14. PIPER, W. E., DOAN, B. D., EDWARDS, E. M., & JONES, B. D. Cotherapy behavior, group therapy process, and treatment outcome. *Journal of Consulting & Clinical Psychology*, 1979, 47, 1081–1089.
15. SERBAN, G. Mental status, functioning, and stress in chronic schizophrenic patients in community care. *American Journal of Psychiatry*, 1979, 136, 948–952.
16. SERBAN, G., & GIDYNSKI, C. B. Relationship between cognitive defect, affect response and community adjustment in chronic schizophrenia. *British Journal of Psychiatry*, 1979, 134, 602–608.
17. RASKIN, M., BALI, L. R., & PEEKE, H. V. Muscle biofeedback and transcendental meditation. *Archives of General Psychiatry*, 1980, 37, 93–97.

[2323]

Structured-Objective Rorschach Test: Preliminary Edition. Adults; 1958; SORT; also called *S-O Rorschach Test*; 15 scores (for deriving 26 traits): whole-blot (W), major details (D), minor details (Dd), white space (S), form resemblance (F), poor form resemblance (F-), human movement (M), animal movement (FM), color and form resemblance (FC), color and poor form resemblance (CF), shading (Fch), animal figure (A), human figure (H), modal responses (P), rare responses (O); Joics B. Stone; [S-O Publishers].* (In-print status uncertain; no reply from publisher.)

See T2:1513 (10 references) and P:477 (33 references); for reviews by Jesse G. Harris, Jr. and Boris Semeonoff and excerpted reviews by Edward S. Bordin and Laurence Siegel, see 6:242 (16 references).

[2324]

STS Closed High School Placement Test. Grade 9 entrants; 1955–77; HSPT; new series issued annually; 7 scores: ability (verbal, quantitative, total), skills (reading, modern mathematics or arithmetic, language), composite; Scholastic Testing Service, Inc.*

For additional information and reviews by Leonard S. Cahen and Irvin J. Lehmann, see 8:26 (1 reference); see also 7:21 (2 references); for reviews by Marion F. Shaycoft and James R. Hayden of an earlier series, see 6:6; for reviews by William C. Cottle and Robert A. Jones of the 1955 "open" test, see 5:15.

REFERENCES

1–2. See 7:21.
3. See 8:26.
4. DIAMOND, E. E. The AMEG commission report on sex bias in achievement testing. *Measurement & Evaluation in Guidance*, 1980, 13, 135–147.

[2325]
STS Educational Development Series: Scholastic Tests. Grades 2-3, 3-4, 4-6, 6-9, 9-12; 1963-80; EDS; a battery of ability and achievement tests and questions on interests and plans; the latest forms, Forms R, S, T, and U contain "up-to-date objectives and modern views of social studies and career planning"; 14 reports and scores for grades 4-12: 3 interest areas (career plans, school plans, school interests), 3 ability scores (verbal, nonverbal, total), 7 achievement scores (reading, English, mathematics, basic skills total, science, USA in the world [Forms B, C], social studies [Forms R, S, T, U], solving everyday problems [Forms B, C], career planning [Forms R, S, T, U]), composite of ability and achievement scores; 9 reports and scores for grades 2-4: same as above except for omission of career plans, school plans, science, USA in the world, and solving everyday problems; a basic skills battery (reading, English, and mathematics), a core achievement battery (reading, English, mathematics, science, and social studies), and an ability/skills battery (verbal, nonverbal, reading, English, and mathematics) are also available as separates (except for primary levels for which only the basic skills battery is available separately); 5 levels; O. F. Anderhalter, R. H. Bauernfeind, V. M. Cashen, Mary E. Greig, Walter M. Lifton, George Mallinson, Jacqueline Mallinson, Joseph F. Papenfuss, and Neil Vail; Scholastic Testing Service, Inc.

a) LOWER PRIMARY LEVEL. Grades 2-3; 1968-78.
b) UPPER PRIMARY LEVEL. Grades 3-4; 1972-80.
c) ELEMENTARY LEVEL. Grades 4-6; 1970-79.
d) ADVANCED LEVEL. Grades 6-9; 1963-78.
e) SENIOR LEVEL. Grades 9-12; 1965-78.

For additional information and reviews by Samuel T. Mayo and William A. Mehrens of forms copyrighted 1976 and earlier, see 8:27; see also T2:33 (1 reference); for a review by Robert D. North of forms copyrighted 1968 and earlier, see 7:22.

REFERENCES

1. See T2:33.
2. ASHER, S. R. Influence of topic interest on black children's and white children's comprehension. *Child Development*, 1979, 50, 686-690.

[2326]
STS Junior Inventory. Grades 4-8; 1957-72; problems checklist; revision of *SRA Junior Inventory* with deletion of items construed by some as invading the personal privacy of the student and his family; H. H. Remmers and Robert H. Bauernfeind; Scholastic Testing Service, Inc.*

See T2:1360 (6 references) and P:232A; for a review by Warren R. Baller and excerpted reviews by Laurance F. Shaffer and Laurence Siegel of the original edition, see 5:104 (5 references); for a review by Dwight L. Arnold, see 4:90.

[2327]
STS Youth Inventory. Grades 7-12; 1956-71; problems checklist; revision of *SRA Youth Inventory* with deletion of items construed by some as invading the personal privacy of the student and his family; 5 scores: my school, after high school, about myself, getting along with others, things in general; Hermann H. Remmers and Benjamin Shimberg; Scholastic Testing Service, Inc.*

See T2:1361 (12 references); for a review by Forrest L. Vance and an excerpted review by Laurence Siegel of the original edition, see 6:170 (12 references); see also 5:105 (12 references); for reviews by Kenneth E. Clark and Frank S. Freeman, see 4:91 (7 references).

[2328]
Student Attitude Inventory. College; 1967; formerly called *Study of Professional Education Attitude Inventory*; for research purposes only; 7 scales: academic, intellectual, political-economic liberalism, social liberalism, pragmatism, dogmatism, cynicism; D. S. Anderson and J. S. Western; Australian Council for Educational Research [Australia].*

For additional information, see 7:145 (2 references).

REFERENCES

1-2. See 7:145.
3. LEHRER, B. E., & HIERONYMOUS, A. N. Predicting achievement using intellectual, academic-motivational and selected non-intellectual factors. *Journal of Experimental Education*, 1977, 45, 44-51.
4. VANNICELLI, M., SHAAK, M., & NAHOR, A. Nontransitional residential care: A two year follow-up of a successful community. *American Journal of Orthopsychiatry*, 1979, 49, 522-526.

[2329]
Student Description Form. Grades 9-12; 1964; SDF; rating by teachers to be used on *Secondary-School Record—Student Description Summary*; 8 ratings: participation in discussion, involvement in classroom activities, pursuit of independent study, evenness of performance, critical and questioning attitude, depth of understanding, personal responsibility, consideration for others; National Association of Secondary-School Principals.* (In-print status uncertain; no reply from publisher.)

For additional information, see P:258.

[2330]
★Student Developmental Task Inventory (Revised, Second Edition). Ages 17-23; 1979; SDTI-2; manual is entitled *Assessing Student Development* and is a preliminary manual for both the *Student Developmental Task Inventory (Revised, Second Edition)* and the *Student Developmental Profile and Planning Record*; designed to assess the personal growth and development of individual undergraduate college students; 3 task scores (each comprised of 3 subtask scores): developing autonomy (emotional autonomy, instrumental autonomy, interdependence), developing purpose (appropriate educational plans, mature career plans, mature life style plans), developing mature interpersonal relationships (intimate relationships with opposite sex, mature relationships with peers, tolerance); Roger B. Winston, Jr., Theodore K. Miller, and Judith S. Prince; Student Development Associates.*

[2331]
Student Disability Survey. Grades 1-9; SDS; 1975; test booklet title is *School Disability Survey*; ratings by teachers; 5 scores: poor academic, poor intellectuality, poor attention, poor classroom involvement, excessive aggressiveness; Harold F. Burks; Arden Press.* (In-print status uncertain; no reply from publisher.)

For additional information and a review by James E. Ysseldyke, see 8:447.

[2332]
Student Evaluation Scale. Grades 1-12; 1970; SES; ratings by teachers; 3 scores: educational response, social-

emotional response, total; William T. Martin and Sue Martin; Psychologists and Educators, Inc.*

[2333]
Student Information Form. Entering college freshmen; 1966–76; SIF; for measurement of groups, not individuals; survey questionnaire of "an ongoing longitudinal study of the American higher education system" called the Cooperative Institutional Research Program (CIRP); also for immediate utilization by participating institutions; data collected from each student include demographic characteristics, secondary school background, finances, orientation to college, aspirations, attitudes and values, and 10 optional locally designed items; report to participating institutions yields 163 (plus 10 optional) item percentage scores (male, female, total) and national norms for comparable institutions; separate reports for up to 8 independent "special breakout groups" available; no manual; 1976 norms booklet by Alexander W. Astin, Margo R. King, and Gerald T. Richardson; questionnaire by Higher Education Research Institute; program sponsored by the American Council on Education and administered by the Higher Education Research Institute of the University of California, Los Angeles.*

For additional information and a review by Albert B. Hood, see 8:397 (15 references).

[2334]
Student Instructional Report. College teachers; 1971–77; SIR; ratings and background data by students concerning the instructor, course, and student; 39 item scores plus up to 10 optional locally prepared items; (Canadian English edition, Canadian French edition, and Spanish edition available); Institutional Research Program for Higher Education; Educational Testing Service.*

For additional information and reviews by Frank Costin and William C. McGaghie, see 8:398 (16 references); see also T2:894 (1 reference).

REFERENCES
1. See T2:894.
2–17. See 8:398.
18. CENTRA, J. A. Student ratings of instruction and their relationship to student learning. *American Educational Research Journal*, 1977, 14, 17–24.
19. MORSTAIN, B. R. Relationship of student and instructor educational orientations with course ratings. *Journal of Educational Psychology*, 1977, 49, 388–398.
20. DAS, H., FROST, P. J., & BARNOWE, J. T. Behaviorally anchored scales for assessing behavioral science teaching. *Canadian Journal of Behavioural Science*, 1979, 11, 79–88.

[2335]
Student Opinion Inventory. High School; 1974; SOI; attitude toward school; for measurement of groups, not individuals; National Study of School Evaluation.*
a) PART A. 34 single item scores or 7 subscale scores (teacher, counselor, administration, student, curriculum and instruction, participation, school image).
b) PART B. Recommendations for school improvement; 12 items, no scores.

For additional information, see 8:399.

REFERENCES
1. BEJAR, I. I., & DOYLE, K. O. Factorial invariance in student ratings of instruction. *Applied Psychological Measurement*, 1981, 5, 307–312.

[2336]
Student Orientations Survey. College students; 1971–76; SOS; for research use only; educational attitudes; 80 group item scores (frequencies and percentages) and 10 scores: purpose (achievement, inquiry), process (assignment learning, independent study), power (assessment, interaction), peer relations (affiliation, informal association), public position (affirmation, involvement); scoring must be done by publisher; Barry R. Morstain and R. M. Gray (Form D); Barry R. Morstain.*

For additional information and reviews by Albert B. Hood and C. Robert Pace, see 8:400 (4 references).

REFERENCES
1–4. See 8:400.
5. MORSTAIN, B. R. An analysis of students' satisfaction with their academic program. *Journal of Higher Education*, 1977, 48, 1–16.
6. MORSTAIN, B. R. Relationship of student and instructor educational orientations with course ratings. *Journal of Educational Psychology*, 1977, 49, 388–398.
7. WATKINS, D., & MORSTAIN, B. The educational orientations of lectures and their students: A case study of an Australian university. *Australian Journal of Education*, 1980, 24, 155–163.

[2337]
Student Reactions to College. 1 or more semesters of a two-year college, 1 or more semesters of a four-year college; 1971–74; SRC; for measurement of groups, not individuals; percentage response distributions for 150 items in 10 areas (instruction and classroom experience, counseling and advising, administrative regulations, class scheduling/registration, student activities, studying, faculty contact, student goals and planning, daily living, library/bookstore) plus 20 optional locally constructed items, for total group and for each of 5 locally identified subgroups; scoring must be done by publisher; Jonathan R. Warren and Pamela J. Roelfs (technical report); Educational Testing Service.*

For additional information and reviews by Lawrence M. Aleamoni and Eric F. Gardner, see 8:401 (1 reference).

[2338]
A Student's Rating Scale of an Instructor. High school and college; 1952–69; no manual; Russell M. Eidsmoe; the Author.* (In-print status uncertain; no reply from publisher.)

See T2:896 (1 reference); for a review by James R. Hayden of an earlier form, see 6:702.

[2339]
★**Students Typewriting Tests.** Students completing typewriting instruction of first semester, second semester, third semester, fourth semester; no date available; STT; 4 tests; National Business Education Association.* (In-print status uncertain; no reply from publisher.)
a) TYPEWRITING I: FIRST SEMESTER. 5 scores: timed writing, theme writing, centering, letter writing, total.
b) TYPEWRITING II: SECOND SEMESTER. 5 scores: timed writing, business letter with corrections, tabulation, manuscript, total.
c) TYPEWRITING III: THIRD SEMESTER. 5 scores: timed writing, business letter with tabulation, interoffice memorandum, business form, total.
d) TYPEWRITING IV: FOURTH SEMESTER. 5 scores: timed writing, form letters, rough-draft tabulation, business forms, total.

[2340]
Study Attitudes and Methods Survey. High school and college; 1972–76; SAMS; 6 scores: academic interest, academic drive, study methods, study anxiety, manipulation, alienation toward authority; William B. Michael, Joan J. Michael, and Wayne S. Zimmerman; EdITS/Educational and Industrial Testing Service.*

For additional information and reviews by Allen Berger and John W. Lombard, see 8:818 (6 references); see also T2:1766 (4 references).

REFERENCES

1–4. See T2:1766.
5–10. See 8:818.
11. ZIMMERMAN, W. S., PARKS, H., & GRAY, K. The validity of traditional cognitive measures and of scales of the study attitudes and methods survey in the prediction of the academic success of educational opportunity program students. *Educational & Psychological Measurement*, 1977, 37, 465–470.
12. UHLEMANN, M. R., THOMPSON, A. P., & REBERG, B. J. Validity of study skill tests with first year university students. *Canadian Counsellor*, 1979, 14, 17–20.

[2341]
★Study Habits Evaluation and Instruction Kit. Forms 4–6 (ages 14–17); 1979; SHEIK; test booklet titled *Inventory of Study Habits*; self-administered; 7 scale scores: the place of study, study times, organization for study, textbook reading skills, taking notes, studying for examinations, examination technique; Peter F. Jackson, Neil A. Reid, and A. Cedric Croft; New Zealand Council for Educational Research [New Zealand].*

[2342]
Study Habits Inventory, Revised Edition. Grades 12–16; 1934–41; C. Gilbert Wrenn; Consulting Psychologists Press, Inc.*

See T2:1768 (14 references); for a review by Douglas E. Scates, see 3:540 (8 references); for reviews by Edward S. Jones and William A. McCall, see 2:1574.

REFERENCES

1–8. See 3:540.
9–22. See T2:1768.
23. SRIVASTAVA, A. K. Social-class interaction in the language effectiveness of bright secondary school students. *Psychologia*, 1977, 20, 226–233.
24. ROBYAK, J. E. Study skills versus non-study skills students: A discriminant analysis. *Journal of Educational Research*, 1978, 71, 161–166.

[2343]
Study of Values: A Scale for Measuring the Dominant Interests in Personality, Third Edition. Grades 10–16 and adults; 1931–70; SV, also AVL, for British adaptation, see *Study of Values: British Edition*; 6 scores: theoretical, economic, aesthetic, social, political, religious; Gordon W. Allport, Philip E. Vernon, and Gardner Lindzey; Riverside Publishing Co.*

For additional information, see 8:686 (191 references); see also T2:1403 (149 references); for a review by Robert Hogan, see 7:146 (212 references); see also P:259 (195 references); for reviews by John D. Hundleby and John A. Radcliffe, see 6:182 (137 references); for a review by N. L. Gage of the second edition, see 5:114 (57 references); for reviews by Harrison G. Gough and William Stephenson and an excerpted review by Laurance F. Shaffer, see 4:92 (25 references); for a review by Paul E. Meehl of the original edition, see 3:99 (61 references).

REFERENCES

1–61. See 3:99.
62–86. See 4:92.
87–143. See 5:114.
144–280. See 6:182.
281–475. See P:259.
476–687. See 7:146.
688–836. See T2:1403.
837–1027. See 8:686.
1028. BUHMEYER, K. J., & JOHNSON, A. H. Personality profiles of physician extenders. *Psychological Reports*, 1977, 40, 655–662.
1029. FEHR, L. A., & HEINTZELMAN, M. E. Personality and attitude correlates of religiosity: A source of controversy. *Journal of Psychology*, 1977, 95, 63–66.
1030. HALEY, H. B., HUYNH, H., PAIVA, R. E. A., & JUAN, I. R. Students' attitudes toward cancer: Change in medical school. *Journal of Medical Education*, 1977, 52, 500–507.
1031. JACOBSON, G. R., RITTER, D. P., & MUELLER, L. Purpose in life and personal values among adult alcoholics. *Journal of Clinical Psychology*, 1977, 33, 314–316.
1032. PAIVA, R. E. A., JUAN, I. R., HUYNH, H., & HALEY, H. B. Medical students' religious affiliation as related to values and attitudes toward patient care. *Psychological Reports*, 1977, 41, 747–758.
1033. PLAX, T. G., & ROSENFELD, L. B. Antecedents of change in attitudes of males and females. *Psychological Reports*, 1977, 41, 811–821.
1034. ROSENFELD, L. B., & PLAX, T. G. Clothing as communication. *Journal of Communication*, 1977, 27, 24–31.
1035. WECKOWICZ, T. E., COLLIER, G., & SPRENG, L. Field dependence, cognitive functions, personality traits, and social values in heavy cannabis users and nonuser controls. *Psychological Reports*, 1977, 41, 291–302.
1036. ZIRKEL, K., STEWART, R. A. C., & PRESTON, C. Personality and attitudinal correlates of ability to increase alpha production in EEG biofeedback training. *Psychologia*, 1977, 20, 107–110.
1037. BUHMEYER, K. J., & JOHNSON, A. H. Predicting success in a physician–extender training program. *Psychological Reports*, 1978, 42, 507–513.
1038. GOETHALS, G. R., & FROST, M. Value change and the recall of earlier values. *Bulletin of the Psychonomic Society*, 1978, 11, 73–74.
1039. HEGARTY, W. H., & SIMS, H. P., JR. Some determinants of unethical decision behavior: An experiment. *Journal of Applied Psychology*, 1978, 63, 451–457.
1040. HISCOCK, M. Imagery assessment through self–report: What do imagery questionnaires measure? *Journal of Consulting & Clinical Psychology*, 1978, 46, 223–230.
1041. MILLS, C. Is sex role related to intellectual abilities? *Gifted Child Quarterly*, 1978, 22, 536–538.
1042. AMERIKANER, M. Personality integration, values, and the goals of counseling: An open systems approach. *Counseling & Values*, 1979, 24, 56–64.
1043. BRUCHON-SCHWEITZER, M. Dimensionality of body perception and personality. *Perceptual & Motor Skills*, 1979, 48, 840–842.
1044. FEHR, L. A., & STAMPS, L. E. The Mosher Guilt Scales: A construct validity extension. *Journal of Personality Assessment*, 1979, 43, 257–260.
1045. HUBBARD, H. R., & BLEDSOE, J. C. Some effects of an experimental curriculum designed to meet the religious needs of gifted adolescents. *Psychological Reports*, 1979, 44, 1047–1050.
1046. ORCUTT, M. A., & WALSH, W. B. Traditionality and congruence of career aspirations for college women. *Journal of Vocational Behavior*, 1979, 14, 1–11.
1047. PLAX, T. G., & ROSENFELD, L. B. Receiver differences and the comprehension of spoken messages. *Journal of Experimental Education*, 1979, 48, 23–28.
1048. SHANKER, P., CLARK, L., & ASTHANA, H. Value profiles and value contradictions in Canadian, East Indian, and West Indian students. *Psychologia*, 1979, 22, 189–194.
1049. ALBERT, R. S. Exceptionally gifted boys and their parents. *Gifted Child Quarterly*, 1980, 24, 174–179.
1050. SHEPARD, K. F., & HALLINAN, M. Impact of similarity of interviewer–interviewee and interviewer–interviewer on ratings in a selection interview. *Psychological Reports*, 1980, 47, 1087–1092.
1051. DUNBAR, R. E., SMITH, P. C., BEARSE, L. N., JOHNSON, S. M., SALICK, M. R., ERENKRANTZ, B. D., & IRONSON, G. H. Multidimensional scaling and standardized testing of value systems. *Perceptual & Motor Skills*, 1981, 52, 559–573.
1052. FISHER, E. P., & FISHER, R. L. Parents of disturbed enuretic and nonenuretic children. *Perceptual & Motor Skills*, 1981, 52, 181–182.

[2344]
Study of Values: British Edition, 1965. College and adults; 1965; adaptation of *Study of Values: A Scale for Measuring the Dominant Interests in Personality, Third Edition*; 6 scores: theoretical, economic, aesthetic, social,

political, religious; original test by Gordon W. Allport, Philip E. Vernon, and Gardner Lindzey; adaptation by Sylvia Richardson; NFER-Nelson Publishing Co. [England].*

See T2:1404 (4 references) and P:259A.

REFERENCES

1-4. See T2:1404.
5. GIBSON, H. B. The British study of values: I. Prediction of drop–out from a psychology degree course. *British Journal of Social & Clinical Psychology*, 1979, 18, 29–34.
6. GIBSON, H. B. The British study of values: II. The effects of "test-faking" and of maturation on a psychology degree course. *British Journal of Social & Clinical Psychology*, 1979, 18, 35–39.

[2345]
The Study Skills Counseling Evaluation. High school and college; 1962; George Demos; Western Psychological Services.*

For additional information and reviews by Stanley E. Davis and W. G. Fleming, see 6:865.

[2346]
Study Skills Surveys. Grades 9–16; 1965–70; SSS; 4 scores: study organization, study techniques, study motivation, total; (Spanish edition available); William F. Brown; Effective Study Materials.*

For additional information, see 8:819.

REFERENCES

1. FREMAUW, W. J., & FEINDLER, E. L. Peer versus professional models for study skills training. *Journal of Counseling Psychology*, 1978, 25, 576–580.

[2347]
Study Skills Test: McGraw-Hill Basic Skills System. Grades 11–14; 1970; also called *MHBSS Study Skills Test*; although designed for use with the MHBSS instructional program, the test may be used independently; 6 scores: problem solving, underlining, library information, study skills information, total, inventory of study habits and attitudes; Alton L. Raygor; McGraw-Hill Book Co., Inc.*

For additional information and a review by Walter Pauk, see 7:781.

REFERENCES

1. HANEY, R., MICHAEL, W. B., & MARTOIS, J. The prediction of success of three ethnic samples on a state board certification examination for nurses from performance on academic course variables and on standardized achievement and study skills measures. *Educational & Psychological Measurement*, 1977, 37, 949–964.
2. ROBYAK, J. E. The relationship between study problems and most and least preferred instructional style. *College Student Journal*, 1978, 12, 72–76.
3. ROBYAK, J. E. Study skills versus non–study skills students: A discriminant analysis. *Journal of Educational Research*, 1978, 71, 161–166.
4. ROBYAK, J. E., & DOWNEY, R. G. Effectiveness of a study skills course for students of different academic achievement levels and personality types. *Journal of Counseling Psychology*, 1978, 25, 544–550.
5. THOMPSON, A. P., REBERG, B. J., & UHLEMANN, M. R. Canadian normative data for the McGraw–Hill Study Skills Test from a Canadian university. *Canadian Journal of Behavioural Science*, 1978, 10, 267–269.
6. ROBYAK, J. E., & DOWNEY, R. G. A discriminant analysis of the study skills and personality types of underachieving and nonunderachieving study skills students. *Journal of College Student Personnel*, 1979, 20, 306–309.
7. UHLEMANN, M. R., THOMPSON, A. P., & REBERG, B. J. Validity of study skill tests with first year university students. *Canadian Counsellor*, 1979, 14, 17–20.

[2348]
Stycar Hearing Tests. Ages 6 months to 7 years (normal and mentally retarded); 1958–76; SHT; Mary D. Sheridan; NFER-Nelson Publishing Co. [England].*

For additional information and a review by Ronald Goldman, see 8:947.

REFERENCES

1. THOMSON, A. J., SEARLE, M., & RUSSELL, G. Quality of survival after severe birth asphyxia. *Archives of Diseases in Childhood*, 1977, 52, 620–626.

[2349]
Stycar Language Test. Mental ages 11–20 months, 21 months–5.5 years, 3–6 years, with marked speech and language difficulties; 1976; SLT; no scores; M. D. Sheridan; NFER-Nelson Publishing Co. [England].*

a) COMMON OBJECTS TEST. Mental ages 11–20 months.
b) MINIATURE TOYS TESTS. Mental ages 21 months–5.5 years.
c) PICTURE BOOK TEST. Mental ages 3–6.

For additional information and a review by Ronald Goldman, see 8:977 (1 reference).

[2350]
Stycar Vision Tests. Normal and handicapped children 6 months and over; 1958–76; SVT; 5 levels; Mary D. Sheridan; distributed by NFER-Nelson Publishing Co. [England].*

a) MINIATURE TOYS TEST. Nonspeaking handicapped children mental ages 21 months and over who are unable to recognize letters; 1958–76.
b) GRADED BALLS TEST. Ages 6–30 months (also handicapped children with mental ages within this range); 1968–76.
c) AGES 3, 4–5. 1958–76; 2 levels: 5-letter booklet for 3 year olds, 7-letter booklet for 4–5 year olds.
d) AGES 5–7. 1958–76; 9-letter charts.
e) PANDA TEST. Severely visually handicapped children ages 6–30 months (also handicapped children with mental ages within this range); 1973–76.

For additional information, see 8:884 (8 references); see also T2:1931 (5 references).

REFERENCES

1-5. See T2:1931.
6-13. See 8:884.
14. THOMSON, A. J., SEARLE, M., & RUSSELL, G. Quality of survival after severe birth asphyxia. *Archives of Diseases in Childhood*, 1977, 52, 620–626.

[2351]
[Styles of Leadership and Management]. Views regarding leadership (*a*) or managerial (*b*) practices in 12 situations; 2 tests (same items except for first and third person expression); each test yields 5 scores (philosophy, planning and goal setting, implementation, evaluation, total) for each of 5 leadership (*a*) or managerial (*b*) styles (based on varying degrees of concern for people vs. concern for production); no manual; Jay Hall, Martha S. Williams (*a* 1, *b*) and Jerry B. Harvey (*b*); Teleometrics Int'l.*

a) LEADERSHIP. Leaders, others; 1968–71.

1) *Styles of Leadership Survey.* Leaders; 1968; SLS; leader's views of his own leadership practices and philosophy.

2) *Leadership Appraisal Survey.* Others; 1971; LAS; views of the practices and philosophy of one's leader.

b) MANAGEMENT. Managers, employees; 1964–73.

1) *Styles of Management Inventory.* Managers; 1964–73; SMI; manager's view of his own managerial practices and attitudes.

2) *Management Appraisal Survey.* Employees; 1967–73; MAS; employee's views on the managerial practices and attitudes of his superior.

For additional information and a review by Abraham K. Korman, see 8:1185 (8 references).

REFERENCES

1–8. See 8:1185.
9. HALL, J., & DONNELL, S. M. Managerial achievement: The personal side of behavior. *Human Relations*, 1979, 32, 77–101.

[2352]

Subsumed Abilities Test. Ages 9 and over; 1957–63; 5 scores: recognition, abstraction, conceptualization, total (demonstrated abilities) potential abilities; Joseph R. Sanders; Martin M. Bruce, Ph.D., Publishers.*

See T2:582 (2 references); for a review by Naomi Stewart, see 6:560.

[2353]

Suinn Test Anxiety Behavior Scale. College and adults; 1971; STABS; no manual; Richard M. Suinn; Rocky Mountain Behavioral Science Institute, Inc.* (In-print status uncertain; no reply from publisher.)

For additional information and a review by Norman S. Endler, see 8:687 (20 references); see also T2:1406 (3 references).

REFERENCES

1–3. See T2:1406.
4–23. See 8:687.
24. HOLROYD, K. A. Cognition and desensitization in the group treatment of test anxiety. *Journal of Consulting & Clinical Psychology*, 1976, 44, 991–1001.
25. DENNEY, D. R., & RUPERT, P. A. Desensitization and self-control in the treatment of test anxiety. *Journal of Counseling Psychology*, 1977, 24, 272–280.
26. REISTER, B. W., STOCKTON, R. A., & MAULTSBY, M. C. Counseling the test anxious: An alternative. *Journal of College Student Personnel*, 1977, 18, 506–510.
27. DEFFENBACHER, J. L., & SHELTON, J. L. Comparison of anxiety management training and desensitization in reducing test and other anxieties. *Journal of Counseling Psychology*, 1978, 25, 277–282.
28. GOLDFRIED, M. R., LINEHAN, M. M., & SMITH, J. L. Reduction of test anxiety through cognitive restructuring. *Journal of Consulting & Clinical Psychology*, 1978, 46, 32–39.
29. KIPPER, D. A., & GILADI, D. Effectiveness of structured psychodrama and systematic desensitization in reducing test anxiety. *Journal of Counseling Psychology*, 1978, 25, 499–505.
30. MCGLYNN, F. D., KINJO, K., & DOHERTY, G. Effects of cue-controlled relaxation, a placebo treatment, and no treatment on changes in self-reported test anxiety among college students. *Journal of Clinical Psychology*, 1978, 34, 707–714.
31. ROMANO, J. L., & CABIANCA, W. A. EMG biofeedback training versus systematic desensitization for test anxiety reduction. *Journal of Counseling Psychology*, 1978, 25, 8–13.
32. SHELTON, J. L., & MADRAZO-PETERSON, R. Treatment outcome and maintenance in systematic desensitization: Professional versus paraprofessional effectiveness. *Journal of Counseling Psychology*, 1978, 25, 331–335.
33. BARRIOS, B. A., GINTER, E. J., SCALISE, J. J., & MILLER, F. G. Treatment of test anxiety by applied relaxation and cue-controlled relaxation. *Psychological Reports*, 1980, 46, 1287–1296.
34. BISTLINE, J. L., JAREMKO, M. E., & SOBLEMAN, S. The relative contributions of covert reinforcement and cognitive restructuring to test anxiety reduction. *Journal of Clinical Psychology*, 1980, 36, 723–728.
35. HARRIS, G., & JOHNSON, S. B. Comparison of individualized covert modeling, self-control desensitization, and study skills training for alleviation of test anxiety. *Journal of Consulting & Clinical Psychology*, 1980, 48, 186–194.
36. ROUNDS, J. B., JR., & HENDEL, D. D. Measurement and dimensionality of mathematics anxiety. *Journal of Counseling Psychology*, 1980, 27, 138–149.

37. TRENT, J. T., & MAXWELL, W. A. State and trait components of test anxiety and their implications for treatment. *Psychological Reports*, 1980, 47, 475–480.
38. WALTERS, G. D. Attrition of clients as a function of treatment modality and initial anxiety level. *Psychological Reports*, 1980, 47, 47–50.

[2354]

Supervisory Behavior Description. Supervisors; 1970–72; SBD; ratings by subordinates; 2 scores: consideration, structure; Edwin A. Fleishman; Management Research Institute.* (In-print status uncertain; no reply from publisher.)

For additional information and a review by Michael J. Kavanagh, see 8:1186 (31 references).

REFERENCES

1–31. See 8:1186.
32. MATSUI, T. Impacts of management styles on the relations between supervisor needs and leadership patterns. *Journal of Applied Psychology*, 1978, 63, 658–661.
33. MATSUI, T., & OHTSUKA, Y. Within–person expectancy theory predictions of supervisory consideration and structure behavior. *Journal of Applied Psychology*, 1978, 63, 128–131.
34. MATSUI, T., OHTSUKA, Y., & KIKUCHI, A. Consideration and structure behavior as reflections of supervisory interpersonal values. *Journal of Applied Psychology*, 1978, 63, 259–262.
35. WEISS, H. M. Social learning of work values in organizations. *Journal of Applied Psychology*, 1978, 63, 711–718.

[2355]

Supervisory Index. Supervisors; 1960–69; SI; 5 attitude scores: management, supervision, employees, human relations practices, total; Norman Gekoski and Solomon L. Schwartz; Science Research Associates, Inc.*

See T2:2459 (1 reference) and 7:1151 (1 reference); for reviews by Arthur H. Brayfield and Albert K. Kurtz, see 6:1192 (1 reference).

REFERENCES

1. See 6:1192.
2. See 7:1151.
3. See T2:2459.
4. MEYER, D. E., & ROSENTRETTER, G. A job analysis approach to test validity. *College Student Journal*, 1978, 12, 100–102.

[2356]

Supervisory Inventory on Communication. Supervisors and prospective supervisors; 1965–72; SIC; Donald L. Kirkpatrick; the Author.*

For additional information, see 7:1152 (1 reference).

[2357]

Supervisory Inventory on Discipline. Supervisors; 1973; manual subtitle is (*For Union and Non-Union Firms*); SID; Earl J. Wyman; the Author.*

[2358]

Supervisory Inventory on Grievances. Supervisors; 1970; SIG; Earl J. Wyman and Donald L. Kirkpatrick; Earl J. Wyman.*

[2359]

Supervisory Inventory on Human Relations. Supervisors and prospective supervisors; 1960–72; SIHR; Donald L. Kirkpatrick and Earl Planty (test); Donald L. Kirkpatrick.*

See T2:2463 (1 reference); for a review by Seymour Levy of the original edition, see 6:1193 (1 reference).

[2360]
Supervisory Inventory on Labor Relations. Supervisors in unionized firms; 1972; SILR; Earl J. Wyman; the Author.*

[2361]
Supervisory Inventory on Safety. Supervisors and prospective supervisors; 1967–69; SIS; Donald L. Kirkpatrick; the Author.*

For additional information, see 7:1153.

[2362]
★**Supervisory Practices Inventory, Form A.** Managers or administrators; 1981; SPT; self-scoring; 10 areas: setting objectives, planning, organizing, delegating, problem identification, decision making, subordinate development, performance evaluation, conflict resolution, team building; Judith S. Canfield and Albert A. Canfield; Humanics Media.*

[2363]
Supervisory Practices Test, Revised. Supervisors; 1957–76; SPT; (French and German editions available); Martin M. Bruce; Martin M. Bruce, Ph.D., Publisher.*

For additional information, see 8:1187; see also T2:2466 (2 references) and 6:1194 (4 references); for reviews by Clifford E. Jurgensen and Mary Ellen Oliverio, see 5:955.

REFERENCES

1–4. See 6:1194.
5–6. See T2:2466.
7. MEYER, D. E., & ROSENTRETTER, G. A job analysis approach to test validity. *College Student Journal*, 1978, 12, 100–102.

[2364]
★**Survey of Basic Competencies.** Ages 3–15; 1979; "designed for preliminary assessment, rapid screening for potential school learning problems, and for entry into the full *Assessment of Basic Competencies* (208) diagnostic battery"; 4 subtest scores (information processing, language, reading, mathematics) plus a composite score; Jwalla P. Somwaru; Scholastic Testing Service, Inc.*

[2365]
Survey of Educational Leadership Practices. Teachers and school administrators; 1955–67; SELP; an adaptation of *Leadership Practices Inventory*; 2 scores (desirable practices marked as ideal, desirable practices marked as in actual practice) for total, each of 4 leadership styles (using style answer form), and each of 5 management areas (using area answer form); J. J. Valenti and Charles W. Nelson; Management Research Associates.* (In-print status uncertain; no reply from publisher.)

See T2:897 (1 reference).

[2366]
Survey of Interpersonal Values. Grades 9–16 and adults; 1960–76; SIV; 6 scores: support, conformity, recognition, independence, benevolence, leadership; Leonard V. Gordon; Science Research Associates, Inc.*

For additional information and reviews by John D. Black and Allan L. LaVoie, see 8:688 (51 references); see also T2:1407 (78 references) and P:261 (48 references); for reviews by Lee J. Cronbach, Leonard D. Goodstein, and John K. Hemphill and an excerpted review by Laurence Siegel, see 6:184 (12 references).

REFERENCES

1–12. See 6:184.
13–60. See P:261.
61–138. See T2:1407.
139–189. See 8:688.
190. BASSETT, J. E., SCHELLMAN, G. C., KOHAUT, S. M., & GAYTON, W. F. Norms for prisoners and reliability on two value surveys. *Psychological Reports*, 1977, 41, 383–386.
191. HALEY, H. B., HUYNH, H., PAIVA, R. E. A., & JUAN, I. R. Students' attitudes toward cancer: Change in medical school. *Journal of Medical Education*, 1977, 52, 500–507.
192. PAIVA, R. E. A., JUAN, I. R., HUYNH, H., & HALEY, H. B. Medical students' religious affiliation as related to values and attitudes toward patient care. *Psychological Reports*, 1977, 41, 747–758.
193. BROCK, A. M. Impact of a management–oriented course on knowledge and leadership skills exhibited by baccalaureate nursing students. *Nursing Research*, 1978, 27, 217–221.
194. MATSUI, T., OHTSUKA, Y., & KIKUCHI, A. Consideration and structure behavior as reflections of supervisory interpersonal values. *Journal of Applied Psychology*, 1978, 63, 259–262.
195. PLUTCHIK, R., CONTE, H., & KANDLER, H. Variables related to the selection of psychiatric residents. II. A replication study. *Comprehensive Psychiatry*, 1978, 19, 65–71.
196. WILLIAMS, M. A., BLOCH, D. W., & BLAIR, E. M. Values and value changes of graduate nursing students: Their relationship to faculty values and to selected educational factors. *Nursing Research*, 1978, 27, 181–189.
197. LINN, L. S. Interns' attitudes and values as antecedents of clinical performance. *Journal of Medical Education*, 1979, 54, 238–240.
198. ROSEN, B. Interpersonal values among child–abusive women. *Psychological Reports*, 1979, 45, 819–822.
199. GORDON, L. V., & KELLY, E. Perceptibility of student–clients' interpersonal values by high school counselors. *Psychological Reports*, 1980, 46, 1107–1110.
200. GORDON, L. V., & MCAVIN, M. W. Attributions of interpersonal values and counseling effectiveness. *Psychological Reports*, 1980, 47, 847–852.
201. ROSEN, B., & STEIN, M. T. Women who abuse their children. *American Journal of Diseases of Children*, 1980, 134, 947–950.
202. ALICHNE, M. C., & BELLUCCI, J. T. Prediction of freshman students' success in a baccalaureate nursing program. *Nursing Research*, 1981, 30, 49–53.
203. HARVILL, L. M. Anticipatory socialization of medical students. *Journal of Medical Education*, 1981, 56, 431–433.

[2367]
Survey of Management Perception. Supervisors; 1956–58; SMP; a projective test requiring the subject to write stories (setting, characters, plot, outcome) about 9 pictures and a story "that could happen in your own company"; no manual; Charles W. Nelson; Management Research Associates.* (In-print status uncertain; no reply from publisher.)

[2368]
*****Survey of Object Visualization.** Grades 9–16 and adults; 1945–70; Daniel R. Miller; Psychological Services, Inc.

For additional information and a review by William J. Micheels, see 5:887 (5 references); for reviews by Charles M. Harsh, Clifford E. Jurgensen, Shailer Peterson, and Patrick Slater of the original edition, see 3:681.

[2369]
*****Survey of Organizations.** Employees; 1967–80; SOO; derived from the 1974 edition of the *Survey of Organizations* and the 1976 edition of the *Organization Survey Profile*; for measurement of groups, not individuals; 28 scores for each of 3 to 5 hierarchical groups: organizational climate, guidance system (communication flow, decision-making practices, concern for people, influence and control), job design (job challenge, job reward, job clarity), shape (organization of work, absence of bureaucracy, coordination), coordination moderators (work interdependence, emphasis on cooperation), super-

visory leadership (support, team building, goal emphasis, work facilitation, encouragement of participation), perceived causes of supervisory leadership (interpersonal competence, involvement, administrative scope), peer relationships (support, team building, goal emphasis, work facilitation), end results (group functioning, satisfaction, goal integration); developed by Rensis Likert Associates, Inc., and the Institute for Social Research, University of Michigan; University Associates, Inc.*

For additional information, reviews by Robert Fitzpatrick and Stephan J. Motowidlo, and an excerpted review by John Toplis of an earlier edition, see 8:985 (12 references).

REFERENCES

1–12. See 8:985.
13. MOTOWIDLO, S. J., & BORMAN, W. C. Relationships between military morale, motivation, satisfaction, and unit effectiveness. *Journal of Applied Psychology*, 1978, 63, 47–52.
14. KOCH, J. L. Effects of goal specificity and performance feedback to work groups on peer leadership, performance, and attitudes. *Human Relations*, 1979, 32, 819–840.

[2370]

Survey of Personal Values. Grades 11–16 and adults; 1964–67; SPV; 6 scores: practical mindedness, achievement, variety, decisiveness, orderliness, goal orientation; Leonard V. Gordon; Science Research Associates, Inc.*

See T2:1409 (5 references); for a review by Gene V Glass, see 7:148 (6 references); see also P:263 (3 references).

REFERENCES

1–3. See P:263.
4–9. See 7:148.
10–14. See T2:1409.
15. BASSETT, J. E., SCHELLMAN, G. C., KOHAUT, S. M., & GAYTON, W. F. Norms for prisoners and reliability on two value surveys. *Psychological Reports*, 1977, 41, 383–386.
16. MORRISON, R. F. Career adaptivity: The effective adaptation of managers of changing role demands. *Journal of Applied Psychology*, 1977, 62, 549–558.
17. WILLIAMS, M. A., BLOCH, D. W., & BLAIR, E. M. Values and value changes of graduate nursing students: Their relationship to faculty values and to selected educational factors. *Nursing Research*, 1978, 27, 181–189.
18. ALICHNE, M. C., & BELLUCCI, J. T. Prediction of freshman students' success in a baccalaureate nursing program. *Nursing Research*, 1981, 30, 49–53.
19. DEFIORE, R. M., KRAMER, T. J., & MUNZ, D. C. Predictors of motivation for job changing: Maintenance versus motivation seekers. *Perceptual & Motor Skills*, 1981, 52, 967–973.

[2371]

Survey of Primary Reading Development. Grades 1–2, 2–4; 1957–64; SPRD; J. Richard Harsh and Dorothy Soeberg; Educational Testing Service (Berkeley Office).*

For additional information and a review by Allen Berger, see 7:709; for reviews by Thomas C. Barrett and Russell G. Stauffer of the test for grades 1–2, see 6:814.

[2372]

Survey of School Attitudes. Grades 1–4, 4–8; 1975–77, c1973–75; SSA; "criterion-referenced and norm-referenced"; 4 scores: reading/language, mathematics, science, social studies; Thomas P. Hogan; The Psychological Corporation.*

For additional information and reviews by Carleton B. Shay and Victor L. Willson, see 8:402.

REFERENCES

1. BECK, M. D. What *are* pupils' attitudes toward the school curriculum? *Elementary School Journal*, 1977, 78, 73–78.
2. HOGAN, T. P. Students' interest in particular mathematics topics. *Journal for Research in Mathematics Education*, 1977, 8, 115–122.
3. MILLER, J. V. Survey of School Attitudes. *Measurement & Evaluation in Guidance*, 1978, 11, 54–57.
4. SULLIVAN, R. J. Students' interests in specific science topics. *Science Education*, 1979, 63, 591–598.
5. WOLF, F. M., & BLIXT, S. L. A cross–sectional cross lagged panel analysis of mathematics achievement and attitudes: Implications for the interpretation of the direction of predictive validity. *Educational & Psychological Measurement*, 1981, 41, 829–834.

[2373]

*Survey of Space Relations Ability. Grades 9–16 and adults; 1944–70; Harry W. Case and Floyd Ruch; Psychological Services, Inc.

For additional information and a review by D. W. McElwain, see 5:888 (4 references); for reviews by E. G. Chambers, Clifford E. Jurgensen, and James M. Porter, Jr., see 3:682.

[2374]

Survey of Study Habits and Attitudes. Grades 7–12, 12–14; 1953–67; SSHA; original edition called *Brown-Holtzman Survey of Study Habits and Attitudes*; 7 scores: study habits (delay avoidance, work methods, total), study attitudes (teacher approval, education acceptance, total), total; (Spanish edition available); William F. Brown and Wayne H. Holtzman; The Psychological Corporation.*

For additional information, see 8:820 (45 references); see also T2:1772 (33 references); for a review by Carleton B. Shay and excerpts by Martin J. Higgins and Albert E. Roark (with Scott A. Harrington), see 7:782 (69 references); see also 6:856 (12 references); for reviews by James Deese and C. Gilbert Wrenn (with Roy D. Lewis) of the original edition, see 5:688 (14 references).

REFERENCES

1–14. See 5:688.
15–26. See 6:856.
27–95. See 7:782.
96–128. See T2:1772.
129–173. See 8:820.
174. GADZELLA, B. M., GOLDSTON, J. T., & ZIMMERMANN, M. L. Effectiveness of exposure to study techniques on college students' perceptions. *Journal of Educational Research*, 1977, 71, 26–30.
175. GOLDSTON, J., ZIMMERMANN, M., SENI, C., & GADZELLA, B. M. Study habits and attitudes characteristic of sex and locus–of–control groups. *Psychological Reports*, 1977, 40, 271–274.
176. HABURTON, E. Impact of an experimental reading–study skills course on high–risk student success in a community college. *National Reading Conference Yearbook*, 1977, 110–114.
177. TRYON, G. S., & SY, M. J. The effectiveness of study skills instruction with students in an adult degree program. *Journal of College Student Personnel*, 1977, 18, 478–481.
178. ZIMMERMANN, M. L., GOLDSTON, J. T., & GADZELLA, B. M. Prediction of academic performance for college students by sex and race. *Psychological Reports*, 1977, 41, 1183–1186.
179. BLUSTEIN, D. L., & STREITMAN, J. Peer modeling influences on the study attitudes of underachievers. *Journal of College Student Personnel*, 1978, 19, 567–568.
180. GOLDMAN, G. Contract teaching of academic skills. *Journal of Counseling Psychology*, 1978, 25, 320–324.
181. GROVER, P. L., JR., & TESSIER, K. E. Diagnosis and treatment of academic frustration syndrome. *Journal of Medical Education*, 1978, 53, 734–740.
182. KELLER, J. M., GOLDMAN, J. A., & SUTTERER, J. R. Locus of control in relation to academic attitudes and performance in a personalized system of instruction course. *Journal of Educational Psychology*, 1978, 70, 414–421.
183. LENT, R. W., & RUSSELL, R. K. Treatment of test anxiety by cue–controlled desensitization and study–skills training. *Journal of Counseling Psychology*, 1978, 25, 217–224.

184. MAXWELL, M. Learning style and other correlates of performance on a scanning experiment. *Journal of Reading Behavior*, 1978, 10, 49–55.
185. MCPHAIL, I. P. A summer reading/study skills program for black and minority health professions students. *Reading World*, 1978, 18, 48–66.
186. PALLADINO, J. J., & DOMINO, G. Differences between counseling center clients and nonclients on three measures. *Journal of College Student Personnel*, 1978, 19, 497–501.
187. ROBYAK, J. E. The relationship between study problems and most and least preferred instructional style. *College Student Journal*, 1978, 12, 72–76.
188. ROBYAK, J. E., & DOWNEY, R. G. Effectiveness of a study skills course for students of different academic achievement levels and personality types. *Journal of Counseling Psychology*, 1978, 25, 544–550.
189. SENI, C. L., GADZELLA, B. M., GOLDSTON, J. T., & ZIMMERMANN, M. L. Differences and changes of internally oriented students on study habits. *College Student Journal*, 1978, 12, 294–298.
190. TRYON, G. S. Differences between counseling seekers and nonseekers on the Mooney Problem Checklist. *Journal of College Student Personnel*, 1978, 19, 501–505.
191. DANESEREAU, D. F., COLLINS, K. W., MCDONALD, B. A., HOLLEY, C. D., GARLAND, J., DIEKHOFF, G., & EVANS, S. H. Development and evaluation of a learning strategy training program. *Journal of Educational Psychology*, 1979, 71, 64–73.
192. GADZELLA, B. M. The effects of student-to-student counseling on students' perceptions of study habits and attitudes. *Journal of College Student Personnel*, 1979, 20, 424–430.
193. O'PRAY, R. J. The relationship of achievement in collegiate business program and faculty–remedial student discrepancy over student study habits and attitudes. *Business Education Forum*, 1979, 34, 55.
194. ROBYAK, J. E., & DOWNEY, R. G. A discriminant analysis of the study skills and personality types of underachieving and nonunderachieving study skills students. *Journal of College Student Personnel*, 1979, 20, 306–309.
195. TARPEY, E. A., & HARRIS, J. B., JR. Study skills courses make a difference! *Journal of College Student Personnel*, 1979, 20, 62–67.
196. BRAY, J. H., MAXWELL, S. E., & SCHMECK, R. R. A psychometric investigation of the Survey of Study Habits and Attitudes. *Applied Psychological Measurement*, 1980, 4, 195–201.
197. SCHMECK, R. R. Relationships between measures of learning style and reading comprehension. *Perceptual & Motor Skills*, 1980, 50, 461–462.
198. ALTMAIER, E. M., & WOODWARD, M. Group vicarious desensitization of test anxiety. *Journal of Counseling Psychology*, 1981, 28, 467–469.
199. KIRSCHENBAUM, D. S., HUMPHREY, L. L., & MALETT, S. D. Specificity of planning in adult self-control: An applied investigation. *Journal of Personality & Social Psychology*, 1981, 40, 941–950.

[2375]

Survey Test of Vocabulary. Grades 3–12; 1931–65; no manual; L. J. O'Rourke; O'Rourke Publications.*

See T2:173 (2 references), 7:234, and 5:239 (3 references); for reviews by Verner M. Sims and Clifford Woody, see 3:167 (1 reference).

[2376]

Surveys of Research Administration and Environment. Research and engineering and scientific firms; 1959–60; 2 forms for gathering information and opinions on the company and its research activities; Morris I. Stein; the Author.*
a) STEIN SURVEY FOR ADMINISTRATORS. Supervisors and administrators; also part of *Technical Personnel Recruiting Inventory*.
b) STEIN RESEARCH ENVIRONMENT SURVEY. Research and technical personnel.

For additional information, see 6:1166.

[2377]

★**SWCEL-P Oral Placement Test for Adults.** Non-English and limited English speaking students; 1976; OPTA; designed to measure English oral production and aural comprehension proficiencies; no author indicated, developed under a program directed by Allen Ferrel; Southwestern Cooperative Educational Laboratory.

[2378]

★**SWCEL-P Test of Oral Language Proficiency.** Non-English and limited English speaking students; 1976; 4 scores: vocabulary, pronunciation, syntax, total; Southwestern Cooperative Educational Laboratory.

[2379]

Sweet Technical Information Test. Ages 14–17; 1973–75; STIT; suitability of students "for technical and practical occupations at trade and subprofessional level"; R. Sweet; Australian Council for Educational Research [Australia].*

For additional information, see 8:1172.

[2380]

Symbol Digit Modalities Test. Ages 8 and over; 1973; SDMT; "early screening of apparently normal children and adults for possible covert manual motor, visual, learning and/or other cerebral defects"; Aaron Smith; Western Psychological Services.*

For additional information and reviews by Brad S. Chissom and James C. Reed, see 8:878; see also T2:1889 (4 references).

REFERENCES

1–4. See T2:1889.
5. WATSON, C. G., DAVIS, W. E., & GASSER, B. The separation of organics from depressives with ability- and personality-based tests. *Journal of Clinical Psychology*, 1978, 34, 393–397.
6. CAMPBELL, A. L., JR., BOGEN, J. E., & SMITH, A. Disorganization and reorganization to cognitive and sensorimotor functions in cerebral commissurotomy: Compensatory roles of the forebrain commissures and cerebral hemispheres in man. *Brain*, 1981, 104, 493–511.

[2381]

Symbol Elaboration Test. Ages 6 and over; 1950–53; SET; Johanna Krout; [Johanna Krout Tabin].*

For additional information, see P:478; for a review by Richard H. Dana, see 5:160 (1 reference).

[2382]

Symbol Identities. Grades 10 and over; 1967; "evaluation of symbolic units"; Ralph Hoepfner and J. P. Guilford; Sheridan Psychological Services, Inc.*

[2383]

Symbolic Play Test, Experimental Edition. Ages 1–3; 1976; SPT; language potential; Marianne Lowe and Anthony J. Costello; NFER-Nelson Publishing Co. [England].*

For additional information, see 8:930.

REFERENCES

1. WHITTAKER, C. A. A note on developmental trends in the symbolic play of hospitalized profoundly retarded children. *Journal of Child Psychology & Psychiatry & Allied Disciplines*, 1980, 21, 253–261.

[2384]

Symonds Picture-Story Test. Grades 7–12; 1948; SPST; Percival M. Symonds; Teachers College Press.*

See T2:1515 (9 references) and P:479 (5 references); for reviews by Walter Kass and Kenneth R. Newton, see 5:161 (2 references); for a review by E. J. G. Bradford and an excerpted review by Robert R. Holt, see 4:132 (2 references).

[2385]

★**Syntax One.** Developmental ages 5 and over; 1976–82; criterion-referenced; for children whose syntax skills lag behind other language-related skills; no scores other than an items correct score; 11 syntactical construct areas: the + noun + is + an adjective, the + noun + is + a + noun, the + noun + is + verb-ing, the + noun + is + verb-ing + the or a + noun, pronoun + is + verb-ing + possessive or the + noun, is + the + noun + verb-ing + the + noun, the + noun + is + preposition + the + nouns, the + noun + is + not + (anything else), did + the + noun + verb + (anything) and the + noun + did + not + (anything else), the + noun + verb-ed + (anything else), will + the + noun + verb + (anything) and the + noun + will + verb + (anything else); Carolyn Ausberger; Communication Skill Builders, Inc.*

[2386]

★**Syntax Two**. Developmental ages 5 and over; 1980; criterion-referenced; to develop awareness of the function and form of questions in order to obtain information in problem-solving situations; 12 goal areas: what + will + (the + noun) (pronoun) + verb, what + will + (the + noun) (pronoun) + do, what + did + the + noun + do, what + did + the + noun + verb, noun phrase + does + not + (anything else) and does + noun phrase + (anything else), do + (noun phrase [plural]) (pronoun [plural]) + (anything else) and noun phrase (plural) + do + not + (anything else), what + do + noun phrase (plural) + (anything else) and do + noun phrase (plural) + (anything else) contrasted with constructions of the form what + does + noun phrase (singular) + (anything else) and does + noun phrase (singular) + (anything else), what + auxiliary + the + noun + verb-ing, where + auxiliary + noun phrase (+ go), where + noun phrase + verb phrase, what + verb phrase and who + verb phrase, what auxiliary + noun phrase + verb and who + auxiliary + noun phrase + verb; Carolyn Ausberger; Communication Skill Builders, Inc.*

[2387]

★**System of Multicultural Pluralistic Assessment**. Ages 5–11; 1977–79; SOMPA; comprehensive method of measuring the cognitive abilities, perceptual-motor abilities, and adaptive behavior of children through 3 distinct assessment models: medical model (defines as abnormal any organic condition interfering with physiological functioning), social system model (derived from the social deviance perspective in sociology), pluralistic model (compares test scores of child to test scores of other children of similar sociocultural background to evaluate as normal, subnormal, or supranormal); (Spanish edition available); Jane R. Mercer and June F. Lewis; The Psychological Corporation.*

a) STUDENT ASSESSMENT. Ages 5–11; 1978; 6 instruments: Physical Dexterity Tasks, Bender Visual Motor Gestalt Test, Weight by Height, Visual Acuity (Snellen Test), Auditory Acuity (audiometer), WISC-R (WPPSI for children under 6 years); the following instruments are not available in the SOMPA kit and must be obtained by the tester: Bender Gestalt, Snellen Test, audiometer, WISC-R or WPPSI.

b) PARENT INTERVIEW. Parents; 1977; 3 instruments: Sociocultural Scales (11 questions), Adaptive Behavior Inventory for Children (ABIC) (242 questions), Health History Inventory (45 questions); all 3 instruments contained within SOMPA materials.

REFERENCES

1. BACA, L., & CERVANTES, H. The assessment of minority students: Are adaptive behavior scales the answer? *Psychology in the Schools*, 1978, 15, 366–370.
2. HOLDEN, C. California court is forum for latest round in IQ debate. *Science*, 1978, 201, 1106–1109.
3. OAKLAND, T., & FEIGENBAUM, D. Multiple sources of test bias on the WISC–R and Bender–Gestalt Test. *Journal of Consulting & Clinical Psychology*, 1979, 47, 968–974.
4. GOTTS, E. E. System of Multicultural Pluralistic Assessment (SOMPA). Basic kit. *Journal of School Psychology*, 1980, 18, 295–297.
5. OAKLAND, T. An evaluation of the ABIC, pluralistic norms, and estimated learning potential. *Journal of School Psychology*, 1980, 18, 3–11.
6. VACC, N. A., & ATWELL, B. Relationship of the Adaptive Behavior Inventory for Children and intelligence. *Psychological Reports*, 1980, 47, 402.
7. KAZIMOUR, K. K., & RESCHLY, D. J. Investigation of the norms and concurrent validity for the Adaptive Behavior Inventory for Children (ABIC). *American Journal of Mental Deficiency*, 1981, 85, 504–511.
8. RESCHLY, D. J. Evaluation of the effects of SOMPA measures on classification of students as mildly mentally retarded. *American Journal of Mental Deficiency*, 1981, 86, 16–20.
9. WALL, S. M., & PARADISE, L. V. A comparison of parent and teacher reports of selected adaptive behaviors of children. *Journal of School Psychology*, 1981, 19, 73–77.

[2388]

Szondi Test. Ages 5 and over; 1937–65; ST; 8 factors, 4 vectors (each vector is a total of 2 factors): homosexual, sadistic, sexual vector, epileptic, hysteric, paroxysmal vector, catatonic, paranoic, schizophrenic vector, depressive, manic, contact vector; Lipot Szondi; Hans Huber [Switzerland].* (United States distributor: Grune & Stratton, Inc.)

See T2:1516 (24 references), P:480 (24 references), 6:243 (21 references), and 5:162 (74 references); for reviews by Ardie Lubin and Albert I. Rabin, see 4:134 (67 references); for a review by Susan K. Deri, see 3:100.

[2389]

★**The TA Survey**. Employee screening; 1970–81; to evaluate trust attitudes of candidate as a predictor of theft proneness; previously part of the *Personnel Security Preview*; Alan L. Strand and Robert W. Cormack; Personnel Security Corporation.*

[2390]

The Tapping Test: A Predictor of Typing and Other Tapping Operations. High school; 1959–70; John C. Flanagan, Grace Fivars (manual), Shirley A. Tuska (manual), and Carol F. Hershey (manual); Psychometric Techniques Associates.*

See T2:796 (3 references); for reviews by Ray G. Price and Henry Weitz, see 6:52 (2 references).

REFERENCES

1–2. See 6:52.
3–5. See T2:796.
6. ANDREW, J. M. Laterality on the Tapping Test among legal offenders. *Journal of Clinical Child Psychology*, 1978, 7, 149–150.
7. DODRILL, C. B. The hand dynamometer as a neuropsychological measure. *Journal of Consulting & Clinical Psychology*, 1978, 46, 1432–1435.

[2391]

TARC Assessment Inventory for Severely Handicapped Children. Severely handicapped ages 3–16; 1975; TARC; behavior checklist; 17 scores: self-help (4 scores plus total), motor (3 scores plus total), communication (3 scores plus total), social (2 scores plus total), total; Wayne Sailor and Bonnie Jean Mix; H & H Enterprises, Inc.*

For additional information, see 8:689.

[2392] ★Task Assessment For Prescriptive Teaching

REFERENCES

1. WESTLING, D. L., KOORLAND, M. A., & TAIT, P. E. Interrater reliability of the TARC Assessment System. *Education & Training of the Mentally Retarded*, 1981, 16, 31–36.

[2392]
★**Task Assessment For Prescriptive Teaching.** Ages 6 and over; 1979; TAPT; criterion-referenced; item scores in 23 areas: reading (pre-skills, letters, consonant/symbol sound, vowel/symbol sound, blending skills, academic/instructional words, community/functional words, word structure analysis, question orientation and context, thought expression, informational resources), mathematics (pre-skills, addition, subtraction, monetary concepts, time concepts, multiplication, division, fractions, decimals, percentages, weights and measures, practical skills with calculator); Daniel Hofeditz and Duane Wilke; Scholastic Testing Service, Inc.*

[2393]
Tasks of Emotional Development Test. Ages 6–11, 12–18; 1960–71; TED; 2 levels; Haskel Cohen and Geraldine Rickard Weil; T.E.D. Associates.*

a) LATENCY. Ages 6–11; 5 scores (perception, outcome, affect, motivation, spontaneity) in each of 12 areas (peer socialization, trust, aggression toward peers, attitudes for learning, respect for property of others, separation from mother figure, identification with same-sex parent, acceptance of siblings, acceptance of need-frustration, acceptance of parents' affection to one another, orderliness and responsibility, self-image).

b) ADOLESCENCE. Ages 12–18; 5 scores in each of 13 areas: same as for latency level plus heterosexual socialization.

For additional information and excerpted reviews by Edward Earl Gotts, C. H. Ammons and R. B. Ammons, see 8:691 (7 references); see also T2:1517 (2 references) and P:481 (1 reference).

REFERENCES

1. See P:481.
2–3. See T2:1517.
4–10. See 8:691.
11. FRANK, R. A., & COHEN, D. J. Psychosocial concomitants of biological maturation in pre-adolescence. *American Journal of Psychiatry*, 1979, 136, 1518–1524.
12. KINARD, E. M. Emotional development in physically abused children. *American Journal of Orthopsychiatry*, 1980, 50, 686–696.

[2394]
TAV Selection System. Adults; 1963–68; TAV; vocational selection and counseling; 7 tests; R. R. Morman; TAV Selection System.*

a) TAV ADJECTIVE CHECK LIST. 1963–68; 3 scores: toward people (T), away from people (A), versus people (V).
b) TAV JUDGMENTS. 1964–68; 3 scores: same as in *a*.
c) TAV PERSONAL DATA. 1964–68; 3 scores: same as in *a*.
d) TAV PREFERENCES. 1963–68; 3 scores: same as in *a*.
e) TAV PROVERBS AND SAYINGS. 1966–68; 3 scores: same as in *a*.
f) TAV SALESMAN REACTIONS. 1967–68; 3 scores: same as in *a*.
g) TAV MENTAL AGILITY. 1965–68; 3 scores: follow directions and carefulness, weights and balance, verbal comprehension.

For additional information and a review by Robert G. Demaree, see 8:986 (1 reference); see also T2:2113 (3 references); for an excerpted review by John O. Crites, see 7:983 (1 reference); see also P:263A (11 references).

[2395]
The Taylor-Helmstadter Pair Comparison Scale of Aesthetic Judgment. Ages 4 and over; 1973; Anne P. Taylor; the Author.*

For additional information, see 8:87.

REFERENCES

1. FITZNER, D. H. The effects of combined art teaching approaches on the development of aesthetic sensitivity among selected elderly adults. *Studies in Art Education*, 1980, 21, 28–37.

[2396]
Taylor-Johnson Temperament Analysis. Grades 7–12, 9–16 and adults; 1941–77; TJTA; revision of *Johnson Temperament Analysis*; individual, premarital, and marital counseling; 9 trait scores (nervous-composed, depressive-lighthearted, active/social-quiet, expressive/-responsive-inhibited, sympathetic-indifferent, subjective-objective, dominant-submissive, hostile-tolerant, self disciplined-impulsive) plus test-taking attitude scale; 2 editions; (French, German, Portuguese, and Spanish editions and edition for the blind available); original edition by Roswell H. Johnson; revision by Robert M. Taylor; Psychological Publications, Inc.*

a) SECONDARY EDITION. 1972–77; grades 7–12 (reading level grades 5 and over); simplified version of *b* for self-evaluation only; W. Lee Morrison (test).

b) REGULAR EDITION. 1941–77; grades 9–16 and adults (reading level grades 8 and over); 2 forms; Lucile P. Morrison (manual).

1) *[Criss-Cross Form.]* May be used to evaluate self or significant other.
2) *Non-Criss-Cross Form.*

For additional information and a review by Robert F. Stahmann, see 8:692 (18 references); see also T2:840 (3 references); for a review by Donald L. Mosher of *b*, see 7:572 (1 reference); see also P:264 (3 references) and 6:130 (10 references); for a review by Albert Ellis of the original edition, see 4:62 (6 references); for a review by H. Meltzer, see 3:57.

REFERENCES

1–6. See 4:62.
7–16. See 6:130.
17–19. See P:264.
20. See 7:572.
21–23. See T2:840.
24–41. See 8:692.
42. MOSS, D. M., III. Three levels of mate selection and marital interaction. *Journal of Religion & Health*, 1977, 16, 288–304.

[2397]
Teacher Attitude Inventory. Teachers and prospective teachers; 1974; TAI; for research use only; 7 attitude scores: teaching profession, class-room teaching, pupil-centered practice, educational process, pupils, teachers, total; S. P. Ahluwalia; the Author [India].* (In-print status uncertain; no reply from publisher.)

For additional information, see 8:403.

[2398]
Teacher-Image Questionnaire. Grades 7–12; 1968 (no date on test materials); TIQ; ratings by students "to provide teachers with confidential feedback designed to help them work more effectively with students"; 17 ratings: knowledge of subject, clarity of presentation,

fairness, control, attitude toward students, success in stimulating interest, enthusiasm, attitude toward student ideas, encouragement of student participation, sense of humor, assignments, appearance, openness, self-control, consideration of others, effectiveness, average; scoring must be done by publisher; Educator Feedback Center, Western Michigan University; the Center.* (In-print status uncertain; no reply from publisher.)

For additional information and a review by Edward F. Iwanicki, see 8:405 (2 references).

[2399]
Teacher Opinionaire on Democracy. Teachers; 1949; democratic aspects of teacher philosophy; Enola Ledbetter and Theodore F. Lentz; Character Research Association.*

See T2:901 (2 references); for reviews by George W. Hartmann and C. Robert Pace, see 4:805.

[2400]
Teacher Self-Rating Inventory. Teachers; 1971; TSRI; no manual; Harold F. Burks; Arden Press.* (In-print status uncertain; no reply from publisher.)

[2401]
★**Teacher's Handbook of Diagnostic Inventories, Second Edition.** Grades kgn–8; 1974–79; "to assess the learning needs of individual students"; 4 areas: spelling, reading, handwriting, arithmetic; Philip H. Mann, Patricia A. Suiter, and Rose Marie McClung; Allyn and Bacon, Inc.* (In-print status uncertain; no reply from publisher.)

[2402]
★**Teacher's Handbook of Diagnostic Screening, Second Edition.** Ages 4, 6 and over; 1974–79; "to check for the minimum level of readiness abilities necessary for success in basic language tasks"; 18 areas: visual motor, visual figure-ground, visual discrimination, visual closure, visual memory, auditory discrimination, auditory closure, auditory memory (sentences), alphabet-speech (auditory-visual association), visual language classification, visual language association, auditory language classification, auditory language association, manual language expression, speech, verbal language expression, written language expression, nonverbal language; Philip H. Mann, Patricia A. Suiter, and Rose Marie McClung; Allyn and Bacon, Inc.* (In-print status uncertain; no reply from publisher.)

[2403]
Teaching Aptitude Test: George Washington University Series. Grades 12–16; 1927; F. A. Moss, T. Hunt, and F. C. Wallace; Center for Psychological Service.* (In-print status uncertain; no reply from publisher.)

See T2:904 (2 references); for a review by May V. Seagoe, see 4:806; for a review by A. S. Barr, see 3:405 (8 references).

[2404]
The Teaching Research Motor-Development Scale. Moderately and severely retarded (preschool–grade 12); 1972; 74 scores: standing and crouching on tiptoes (3 scores), standing heel to toe and on one foot (6 scores), jumping (4 scores), walking (5 scores), imitations of movements, touching nose and fingertips (3 scores), close and open hands, tapping with feet and fingers, stepping over, ducking under, passing between, placing matchsticks and coins in a box (4 scores), winding thread (4 scores), tapping and drawing lines (4 scores), mazes (4 scores), cutting (6 scores), catching and bouncing and throwing a ball (13 scores), pull-up (3 scores), sit-up (2 scores), push-up (3 scores), running (3 scores), total; H. D. Fredericks, Victor L. Baldwin, Philip Doughty, and L. James Walter; Charles C Thomas, Publisher.*

[2405]
Team Effectiveness Survey. Team members; 1968–69; TES; ratings of self and fellow team members on individual contributions to team action; 4 scores for each team member: exposure (open and candid expression of one's feelings), feedback (active solicitation of information from others), defensive, supportive, plus total team effectiveness score; no manual; Jay Hall; Teleometrics Int'l.*

For additional information and a review by William G. Mollenkopf, see 8:1055.

[2406]
Technical and Scholastic Test: The Dailey Vocational Tests. Grades 8–12 and adults; 1964–65; TST; 3 scores for males in grades 8–10 and females: technical, scholastic, total; 11 scores for others: technical (electricity, electronics, mechanics, science, total), scholastic (arithmetic, algebra, vocabulary, total), total, mechanical (mechanics and arithmetic); John T. Dailey and Kenneth B. Hoyt (manual); Riverside Publishing Co.*

For reviews of the complete battery, see 7:976 (2 reviews, 2 excerpts).

[2407]
Technical Personnel Recruiting Inventory. Research and engineering and scientific firms; 1959–60; 3 parts; Morris I. Stein; the Author.*

a) INDIVIDUAL QUALIFICATION FORM. Supervisors; description of an available research position.
b) PERSONAL DATA FORM FOR SCIENTIFIC, ENGINEERING, AND TECHNICAL PERSONNEL. Job applicants.
c) STEIN SURVEY FOR ADMINISTRATORS. Administrators; description of company's research environment; also part of *Surveys of Research Administration and Environment.*

For additional information, see 6:1167.

[2408]
Technical Tests. Standards 6–8 (ages 13–15); 1962; 5 scores: arithmetic, mechanical insight, spatial relations (2 scores), tool test; Human Sciences Research Council [South Africa].*

For additional information, see 6:1187.

[2409]
★**Temperament and Values Inventory.** Grades 9 and over; 1976–77; TVI; measures work-related dimensions of temperament and reward values; 14 scores: 7 temperament scales (routine-flexible, quiet-active, attentive-distractible, serious-cheerful, consistent-changeable, reserved-sociable, reticent-persuasive), 7 reward values scales (social recognition, managerial/sales benefits, leadership, social service, task specificity, philosophical curiosi-

[2410] *Temperament Comparator

ty, work independence); Charles B. Johansson and Patricia L. Webber (test); NCS Interpretive Scoring Systems.*

[2410]

Temperament Comparator. Managers, supervisors, salesmen, and professionals; 1958–81; 24 scores: 18 trait scores (calm, cautious, decisive, demonstrative, emotionally stable, energetic, enthusiastic, even-tempered, lively, persevering, prompt starter, quick worker, seeks company, self-confident, serious, socially at ease, steady worker, talkative), 5 factor scores (extroversive/impulsive vs. reserved/cautious, emotionally responsive vs. emotionally controlled, self-reliant/individually oriented vs. dependent/group oriented, excitable/high energy vs. placid/low energy, socially oriented vs. not socially oriented), and consistency; Melany E. Baehr, R. W. Pranis, and Marie Schmieder (manual); Human Resources Center, University of Chicago.

See T2:1413 (1 reference) and P:265; for reviews by Lawrence J. Stricker and Robert L. Thorndike, see 6:187 (1 reference).

[2411]

★Temperament Inventory. College and adults; 1977–80; TI; 4 scores: phlegmatic, sanguine, choleric, melancholy; (Spanish, French, and German editions available); Robert J. Cruise, W. Peter Blitchington, and W. G. A. Futcher (manual); Andrews University Press.*

REFERENCES

1. CRUISE, R. J., BLITCHINGTON, W. P., & FUTCHER, W. G. A. Temperament Inventory: An instrument to empirically verify the four-factor hypothesis. *Educational & Psychological Measurement*, 1980, 40, 943–954.

[2412]

Templin-Darley Tests of Articulation. Ages 3 and over; 1960–69; TDTA; 2 editions; Mildred C. Templin and Frederic L. Darley; Bureau of Educational Research and Service.*

a) TEMPLIN-DARLEY SCREENING AND DIAGNOSTIC TESTS OF ARTICULATION. Ages 3–8; 1960; 2 tests: screening test, total diagnostic test.

b) TEMPLIN-DARLEY TESTS OF ARTICULATION, [SECOND EDITION]. Ages 3 and over; 1960–69; 10 scores: screening test, consonant singles—initial and final, vowels, diphthongs and combination, clusters (4 scores), Iowa Pressure Articulation Test, total diagnostic test.

See T2:2095 (8 references); for a review by Raphael M. Haller of b, see 7:972 (16 references); for excerpted reviews by Harry Hollien and Al Knox of a, see 6:315 (9 references).

REFERENCES

1–9. See 6:315.
10–25. See 7:972.
26–33. See T2:2095.
34. ARNDT, W. B., SHELTON, R. L., JOHNSON, A. F., & FURR, M. L. Identification and description of homogeneous subgroups within a sample of misarticulating children. *Journal of Speech & Hearing Research*, 1977, 20, 263–292.
35. KELLY, D. H. Oral vibrotactile sensation: An evaluation of children with normal and defective articulation. *Journal of Communication Disorders*, 1977, 10, 359–368.
36. SHELTON, R. L., JOHNSON, A. F., & ARNDT, W. B. Delayed judgment speech–sound discrimination and /r/ or /s/ articulation status and improvement. *Journal of Speech & Hearing Research*, 1977, 20, 704–717.

37. STEPHENS, M. I., & DANILOFF, R. A methodological study of factors affecting the judgment of misarticulated /s/. *Journal of Communication Disorders*, 1977, 10, 207–220.
38. JORDAN, L. S., HARDY, J. C., & MORRIS, H. L. Performance of children with good and poor articulation on tasks of tongue placement. *Journal of Speech & Hearing Research*, 1978, 21, 429–439.
39. MCWILLIAMS, B. J., & MATTHEWS, H. P. A comparison of intelligence and social maturity in children with unilateral complete clefts and those with isolated cleft palates. *Cleft Palate Journal*, 1979, 16, 363–372.
40. PETTIT, J. M., & HELMS, S. B. Hemispheric language dominance of language–disordered, articulation–disordered, and normal children. *Journal of Learning Disabilities*, 1979, 12, 71–76.
41. CLARKE, W. M., & HOOPS, H. R. Predictive measures of speech proficiency in cerebral palsied speakers. *Journal of Communication Disorders*, 1980, 13, 385–394.
42. DANILOFF, R. G., WILCOX, K., & STEPHENS, M. I. An acoustic–articulatory description of children's defective /s/ productions. *Journal of Communication Disorders*, 1980, 13, 347–363.
43. RUSCELLO, D. M., MOREAU, V. K., & SHOLTIS, D. Awareness of certain articulatory gestures in normal–speaking and articulatory–defective children. *Journal of Communication Disorders*, 1980, 13, 59–64.
44. SINGH, S., HAYDEN, M. E., & TOOMBS, M. S. The role of distinction features in articulation errors. *Journal of Speech & Hearing Disorders*, 1981, 46, 174–183.
45. STARK, R. E., & TALLAL, P. Selection of children with specific language deficits. *Journal of Speech & Hearing Disorders*, 1981, 46, 114–122.
46. STRANGE, W., & BROEN, P. A. The relationship between perception and production of /w/, /r/, and /l/ by three–year–old children. *Journal of Experimental Psychology*, 1981, 31, 81–102.
47. TOOMBS, M. S., SINGH, S., & HAYDEN, M. E. Markedness of features in the articulatory substitutions of children. *Journal of Speech & Hearing Disorders*, 1981, 46, 184–191.

[2413]

Tennessee Self Concept Scale. Ages 12 and over; 1964–65; TSCS; 2 scoring systems referred to as Counseling Form and Clinical Research Form; William H. Fitts; Counselor Recordings and Tests.* (In-print status uncertain; no reply from publisher.)

a) COUNSELING FORM. 14 profiled scores: self criticism, 9 self esteem scores (identity, self satisfaction, behavior, physical self, moral-ethical self, personal self, family self, social self, total), 3 variability of response scores (variation across the first 3 self esteem scores, variation across the last 5 self esteem scores, total), distribution score.

b) CLINICAL AND RESEARCH FORM. 29 profiled scores: the 14 scores in a above and the following 15: response bias, net conflict, total conflict, 6 empirical scales (defensive positive, general maladjustment, psychosis, personality disorder, neurosis, personality integration), deviant signs, 5 scores consisting of counts of each type of response made.

For additional information, see 8:693 (384 references); see also T2:1415 (80 references); for reviews by Peter M. Bentler and Richard M. Suinn and an excerpted review by John O. Crites, see 7:151 (88 references); see also P:266 (30 references).

REFERENCES

1–30. See P:266.
31–118. See 7:151.
119–198. See T2:1415.
199–582. See 8:693.
583. ARZI, Y., & AMIR, Y. Intellectual and academic achievements and adjustment of under–privileged children in homogeneous and heterogeneous classrooms. *Child Development*, 1977, 48, 726–729.
584. BARRETT, T. C., & TINSLEY, H. E. A. Measuring vocational self–concept crystallization. *Journal of Vocational Behavior*, 1977, 11, 305–313.
585. BARRETT, T. C., & TINSLEY, H. E. A. Vocational self–concept crystallization and vocational indecision. *Journal of Counseling Psychology*, 1977, 24, 301–307.
586. BERTINETTI, J. F., & FABRY, J. An investigation of the construct validity of the Tennessee Self–Concept Scale. *Journal of Clinical Psychology*, 1977, 33, 416–418.

587. CURTIS, J., & ALTMANN, H. The relationship between teachers' self-concept and the self-concept of students. *Child Study Journal*, 1977, 7, 17-27.

588. DARDEN, B. J., & BAYTON, J. A. Self-concept and black's assessment of black leading roles in motion pictures and television. *Journal of Applied Psychology*, 1977, 62, 620-623.

589. FRYREAR, J. L., NUELL, L. R., & WHITE, P. Enhancement of male juvenile delinquents self-concepts through photographed social interactions. *Journal of Clinical Psychology*, 1977, 33, 833-838.

590. HABURTON, E. Impact of an experimental reading-study skills course on high-risk student success in a community college. *National Reading Conference Yearbook*, 1977, 110-114.

591. HALL, W. M., & VALINE, W. J. The relationship between self-concept and marital adjustment for commuter college students. *Journal of College Student Personnel*, 1977, 18, 298-300.

592. HASKELL, S. D., & HANDLER, L. Personality and background predictors of a young wife's desired family size. *Journal of Clinical Psychology*, 1977, 33, 755-759.

593. HUTT, M. L., DATES, B. G., & REID, D. M. The predictive ability of HABGT Scales for a male delinquent population. *Journal of Personality Assessment*, 1977, 41, 492-496.

594. JONES, W. H., NICHOL, S. S., & PROKOP, C. Self-concept as a function of political ideology and activism. *Psychological Reports*, 1977, 40, 1295-1296.

595. KILMANN, P. R., WAGNER, M. K., & SOTILE, W. M. The differential impact of self-monitoring on smoking behavior: An exploratory study. *Journal of Clinical Psychology*, 1977, 33, 912-914.

596. LANG, R. J., & VERNON, P. E. Dimensionality of the perceived self: The Tennessee Self Concept Scale. *British Journal of Social & Clinical Psychology*, 1977, 16, 363-371.

597. LINDBLAD, R. A. Self concept of white, middle socioeconomic status addicts: A controlled study. *International Journal of the Addictions*, 1977, 12, 137-151.

598. MALDONADO, B. M., & CROSS, W. C. Today's Chicano refutes the stereotype. *College Student Journal*, 1977, 11, 146-152.

599. MILLEN, L., & ROLL, S. Relationships between sons' feelings of being understood by their fathers and measures of the sons' psychological functioning. *Journal of Genetic Psychology*, 1977, 130, 19-25.

600. MILLIKIN, N. L. Self concept: A comparison of four groups of university students. *Business Education Forum*, 1977, 32, 48.

601. NEVILL, D. D. Sex roles and personality correlates. *Human Relations*, 1977, 30, 751-759.

602. NYSTUL, M. S., & GARDE, M. Comparison of self-concepts of transcendental meditators and nonmeditators. *Psychological Reports*, 1977, 41, 303-306.

603. PLAX, T. G., & ROSENFELD, L. B. Antecedents of change in attitudes of males and females. *Psychological Reports*, 1977, 41, 811-821.

604. POUND, R. E., HANSEN, J. C., & PUTNAM, B. A. An empirical analysis of the Tennessee Self Concept Scale. *Educational & Psychological Measurement*, 1977, 37, 545-551.

605. REARDON, P., & TOSI, D. J. The effects of rational stage directed imagery on self-concept and reduction of psychological stress in adolescent delinquent females. *Journal of Clinical Psychology*, 1977, 33, 1084-1092.

606. ROSENFELD, L. B., & PLAX, T. G. Clothing as communication. *Journal of Communication*, 1977, 27, 24-31.

607. SHAPIRO, A., & SWENSON, C. H. Self-disclosure as a function of self-concept and sex. *Journal of Personality Assessment*, 1977, 41, 144-149.

608. SHUEMAN, S. A., & SEDLACEK, W. E. An evaluation of a women's studies program. *Journal of the National Association for Women Deans, Administrators, & Counselors*, 1977, 41, 7-12.

609. WEST, J. H., & RAY, P. B. The helper therapy principal in relationship to self-concept change in commuter peer counselors. *Journal of College Student Personnel*, 1977, 18, 301-305.

610. WHITESIDE, M. Self concept differences among education and liberal arts undergraduates, teachers and other professionals. *College Student Journal*, 1977, 11, 69-73.

611. WHITESIDE, M. Self-concept differences among high and low creative college students. *Journal of College Student Personnel*, 1977, 18, 224-227.

612. BLOOM, L. J., SHELTON, J. L., & MICHAELS, A. C. Dysmenorrhea and personality. *Journal of Personality Assessment*, 1978, 42, 272-276.

613. BRADLEY, R., & REDFERING, D. L. Drug abuses in the military: Correlates of successful rehabilitation. *Journal of Clinical Psychology*, 1978, 34, 233-237.

614. CARROLL, J. F. X., KLEIN, M. I., & SANTO, Y. Comparison of the similarities and differences in the self-concepts of male alcoholics and addicts. *Journal of Consulting & Clinical Psychology*, 1978, 46, 575-576.

615. CERNIGLIA, R. P., HORENSTEIN, D., & CHRISTENSEN, E. W. Group decision-making and self-management in the treatment of psychiatric patients. *Journal of Clinical Psychology*, 1978, 34, 489-493.

616. DOHERTY, P. A., & SCHMIDT, M. R. Sex-typing and self-concept in college women. *Journal of College Student Personnel*, 1978, 19, 493-497.

617. FLORA, R. R. The effect of self concept upon adolescents' communication with parents. *Journal of School Health*, 1978, 48, 100-102.

618. GARRISON, W. M. SELFCON: Tennessee Self Concept Scale scoring program. *Applied Psychological Measurement*, 1978, 2, 332.

619. GREENWALD, D. P. Self-report assessment in high- and low-dating college women. *Behavior Therapy*, 1978, 9, 297-299.

620. HULFISH, S. Relationship of role identification, self-esteem, and intelligence to sex differences in field independence. *Perceptual & Motor Skills*, 1978, 47, 835-842.

621. KNOUSE, S. B., TAUBER, R. T., & SKONIECZKA, K. The effects of one-session training upon résumé writing skills. *Vocational Guidance Quarterly*, 1978, 27, 326-333.

622. LAMBERT, M. J., SEGGER, J. F., STALEY, J. S., SPENCER, B., & NELSON, D. Reported self-concept and self-actualizing value changes as a function of academic classes with wilderness experience. *Perceptual & Motor Skills*, 1978, 46, 1035-1040.

623. LANG, R. J. Multivariate classification of day-care patients: Personality as a continuum. *Journal of Consulting & Clinical Psychology*, 1978, 46, 1212-1226.

624. LEVIN, J., KARNI, E., & FRANKEL, Y. Analysis of the Tennessee Self-Concept Scale as a faceted instrument. *Psychological Reports*, 1978, 43, 619-623.

625. MANGANIELLO, J. A. Opiate addiction: A study identifying three systematically related psychological correlates. *International Journal of the Addictions*, 1978, 13, 839-847.

626. MORAN, M., MICHAEL, W. B., & DEMBO, M. H. The factorial validity of three frequently employed self-report measures of self-concept. *Educational & Psychological Measurement*, 1978, 38, 547-563.

627. O'LEARY, M. R., CHANEY, E. F., & HUDGINS, W. Self-concept: Effects of alcoholism, hospitalization and treatment. *Psychological Reports*, 1978, 42, 655-661.

628. POUND, R. E. Using self-concept subscales in predicting career maturity for race and sex subgroups. *Vocational Guidance Quarterly*, 1978, 27, 61-70.

629. PUTNAM, B. A., HOSIE, T. W., & HANSEN, J. C. Sex differences in self-concept variables and vocational attitude maturity of adolescents. *Journal of Experimental Education*, 1978, 47, 23-27.

630. RABEN, C. S., SNYDER, R. A., HOFFMAN, R. G., & FARR, J. L. An examination of the construct validity and reliability of the Ghiselli Self-Description Inventory as a measure of self-esteem. *Applied Psychological Measurement*, 1978, 2, 73-81.

631. REDDY, W. B., LANGMEYER, D., & ASCH, P. A. S. Self-concept, school self-image, satisfaction, and involvement in an alternative high school. *Psychology in the Schools*, 1978, 15, 66-71.

632. REVIERE, R., & POSEY, T. B. Correlates of two measures of fear of success in women. *Psychological Reports*, 1978, 42, 609-610.

633. SMITH, J. C. Personality correlates of continuation and outcome in meditation and erect sitting control treatments. *Journal of Consulting & Clinical Psychology*, 1978, 46, 272-279.

634. STONER, S., & KAISER, L. Sex differences in self-concepts of adolescents. *Psychological Reports*, 1978, 43, 305-306.

635. WHITESIDE, M. Correlates of achievement motivation. *Journal of College Student Personnel*, 1978, 19, 548-551.

636. YARWORTH, J. S., & GAUTHIER, W. J. Relationship of student self-concept and selected personal variables to participation in school activities. *Journal of Educational Psychology*, 1978, 70, 335-344.

637. ANDERSON, B. J., LEMKE, E. A., & LEWIS, M. L. Identification of self-concept using the High School Personality Questionnaire. *Perceptual & Motor Skills*, 1979, 48, 731-734.

638. ARMENTROUT, D. P. The impact of chronic pain on the self-concept. *Journal of Clinical Psychology*, 1979, 35, 517-521.

639. BOLTON, B. The Tennessee Self-Concept Scale and the Normal Personality Sphere (16PF). *Journal of Personality Assessment*, 1979, 43, 608-613.

640. BRINKMANN, J. R., & HOSKINS, T. A. Physical conditioning and altered self-concept in rehabilitated hemiplegic patients. *Physical Therapy*, 1979, 59, 859-865.

641. CAMPBELL, R. L., WILLIAMS, W. E., & SUTTON, E. Black student teacher's self-concept and attitudes toward their training program. *Journal of Negro Education*, 1979, 48, 149-155.

642. COOLEY, R. S., & SEEMAN, J. Personality integration and social schemata. *Journal of Personality*, 1979, 47, 288-304.

643. DICKSTEIN, E. B., & HARDY, B. W. Self-esteem, autonomy, and moral behavior in college men and women. *Journal of Genetic Psychology*, 1979, 134, 51-55.

644. FISHER, L., ROWLEY, P. T., & LIPKIN, M., JR. Predicting immediate outcome of genetic counseling following genetic screening. *Social Biology*, 1979, 26, 289-301.

645. GARWOOD, S. G., & ALLEN, L. Self-concept and identified problem differences between pre- and postmenarcheal adolescents. *Journal of Clinical Psychology*, 1979, 35, 528-537.

646. GLAUBMAN, H., ORBACH, I., GROSS, Y., AVIRAM, O., FRIEDER, I., FRIEMAN, M., & PELLED, O. REM need in adolescents as indicated by

resistance to REM deprivation. *Perceptual & Motor Skills*, 1979, 48, 251–254.

647. GRAY-LITTLE, B., & APPELBAUM, M. I. Instrumentality effects in the assessment of racial differences in self-esteem. *Journal of Personality & Social Psychology*, 1979, 37, 1221–1229.

648. HEAD, D. N. A comparison of self-concept scores for visually impaired adolescents in several class settings. *Education of the Visually Handicapped*, 1979, 11, 51–55.

649. HILYER, J. C., JR., & MITCHELL, W. Effect of systematic physical fitness training combined with counseling on the self-concept of college students. *Journal of Counseling Psychology*, 1979, 26, 427–436.

650. ISRALSKY, M., GOLDBERG, R. T., & SCHWACHMAN, H. Vocational rehabilitation of the person with cystic fibrosis. *Rehabilitation Counseling Bulletin*, 1979, 23, 114–119.

651. JACKSON, R. L. Material good need fulfillment as a correlate of self–esteem. *Journal of Social Psychology*, 1979, 108, 139–140.

652. KING, E., & PRICE, F. T. Black self–concept: A new perspective. *Journal of Negro Education*, 1979, 48, 216–221.

653. KING, M. Parental self–actualization and children's self–concept. *Psychological Reports*, 1979, 44, 80–82.

654. McGOUGH, R. L., & KAZANAS, H. C. Relationship of self–concept meaning and value of disadvantaged and non–disadvantaged students. *Journal of Industrial Teacher Education*, 1979, 16, 45–55.

655. NYSTUL, M. S., & GARDE, M. The self–concepts of regular transcendental meditators, dropout meditators, and nonmeditators. *Journal of Psychology*, 1979, 103, 15–18.

656. OHLDE, C. D. Relationship between self–esteem and response style. *Journal of Counseling Psychology*, 1979, 26, 455–458.

657. PAGE, R. D., & SCHAUB, L. H. Efficacy of a three– versus a five–week alcohol treatment program. *International Journal of the Addictions*, 1979, 14, 697–714.

658. PETRUCCI, R. J., & WHEELAN, S. A. The planned change model of personal growth on medical students' attitude toward self. *Journal of Medical Education*, 1979, 54, 342–343.

659. PLAX, T. G., & ROSENFELD, L. B. Receiver differences and the comprehension of spoken messages. *Journal of Experimental Education*, 1979, 48, 23–28.

660. SCHERER, C. Effects of early field experience on student teachers' self–concepts and performance. *Journal of Experimental Education*, 1979, 47, 208–214.

661. SCHWARZWALD, J., USHPIZ, V., & SHOHAM, M. Self–esteem and prospective mate assessment in Israeli students. *Journal of Psychology*, 1979, 103, 271–279.

662. SMITH, S. D., & SMITH, W. D. Teaching the poor: Its effect on student teacher self–concept. *Journal of Teacher Education*, 1979, 30, 45–49.

663. STANTON, H. E. Increasing lecturer self–confidence. *Australian Psychologist*, 1979, 14, 329–335.

664. STAYTON, S. E., & DIENER, R. G. Personality characteristics of juvenile delinquent heroin users. *International Journal of the Addictions*, 1979, 14, 585–587.

665. VAN TUINEN, M., & RAMARAIAH, N. V. A multimethod analysis of selected self–esteem measures. *Journal of Research in Personality*, 1979, 13, 16–24.

666. ZEITNER, R. M., & WEIGHT, D. G. The pupillometric response as a parameter of self–esteem. *Journal of Clinical Psychology*, 1979, 35, 176–183.

667. BLEDSOE, J. C., & DIXON, C. Effects of economic disadvantage on self–concepts of urban black high school students. *Journal of Psychology*, 1980, 106, 121–127.

668. BROWN, S. D. Coping skills training: An evaluation of a psychoeducational program in a community mental health setting. *Journal of Counseling Psychology*, 1980, 27, 340–345.

669. BYRNE, T. P. Self–esteem and satisfaction with Holland's SDS. *Canadian Counsellor*, 1980, 14, 160–162.

670. COURSEY, R. D., BUCHSBAUM, M. S., & MURPHY, D. L. Psychological characteristics of subjects identified by platelet MAO activity and evoked potentials as biologically at risk for psychopathology. *Journal of Abnormal Psychology*, 1980, 89, 151–164.

671. ELLIS, L. S. An investigation of nursing student self–concept levels: A pilot survey. *Nursing Research*, 1980, 29, 389–391.

672. ERDWINS, C., SMALL, A., & GROSS, R. The relationship of sex role to self–concept. *Journal of Clinical Psychology*, 1980, 36, 111–115.

673. ERDWINS, C. J., TYER, Z. E., & MELLINGER, J. C. Personality traits of mature women in student versus homemaker roles. *Journal of Psychology*, 1980, 105, 189–195.

674. FRIEDENBERG, W. P., & GILLIS, J. S. Modification of self–esteem with techniques of attitude change: A replication. *Psychological Reports*, 1980, 46, 1087–1095.

675. HEAD, D. N. The stability of self–concept scores in visually impaired adolescents. *Education of the Visually Handicapped*, 1980, 12, 66–74.

676. KERNALEGUEN, A., & CONRAD, S. G. Analysis of fine measures of self–concept. *Perceptual & Motor Skills*, 1980, 51, 855–861.

677. LARSEN, J. A., & MITCHELL, C. T. Task–centered, strength–oriented group work with delinquents. *Social Casework*, 1980, 3, 154–163.

678. LEWANDOWSKI, L. A., & KRAMER, M. Role transformation of special care unit nurses: A comparative study. *Nursing Research*, 1980, 29, 170–179.

679. LEWIS, J., BENTLEY, C., & SAWYER, A. The relationship between selected personality traits and self–esteem among female nursing students. *Educational & Psychological Measurement*, 1980, 40, 259–260.

680. LOUCKS, S. Loneliness, affect, and self–concept: Construct validity of the Bradley Loneliness Scale. *Journal of Personality Assessment*, 1980, 44, 142–147.

681. MORRAN, D. K., & STOCKTON, R. A. Effect of self–concept on group member reception of positive and negative feedback. *Journal of Counseling Psychology*, 1980, 27, 260–267.

682. PEROVICH, G. M., & MIERZWA, J. A. Group facilitation of vocational maturity and self–esteem in college students. *Journal of College Student Personnel*, 1980, 21, 206–211.

683. PLAX, T. G., & ROSENFELD, L. B. Individual differences in the credibility and attitude change relationship. *Journal of Social Psychology*, 1980, 111, 79–89.

684. REITER, S., & LEVI, A. M. Factors affecting social integration of noninstitutionalized mentally retarded adults. *American Journal of Mental Deficiency*, 1980, 85, 25–30.

685. SCHUMM, W. R., FIGLEY, C. R., & FUHS, N. N. Similarity in self–esteem as a function of duration of marriage among student couples. *Psychological Reports*, 1980, 47, 365–366.

686. STANTON, H. E. The modification of student self–concept. *Studies in Higher Education*, 1980, 5, 71–76.

687. TERRELL, F., & TAYLOR, J. Self concept of juveniles who commit black on black crimes. *Corrective & Social Psychiatry & Journal of Behavior Technology, Methods & Therapy*, 1980, 26, 107–109.

688. VOIGHT, N. L., LAWLER, A., & FULKERSON, K. F. Community–based guidance: A "Tupperware party" approach to mid–life decision making. *Personnel & Guidance Journal*, 1980, 59, 106–107.

689. WAMPLER, R. S., LAUER, J. B., LANTZ, J. B., WAMPLER, K. S., EVENS, M. G., & MADURA, J. A. Psychological effects of intestinal bypass surgery. *Journal of Counseling Psychology*, 1980, 27, 492–499.

690. WOLFF, J., & DESIDERATO, O. Transfer of assertion–training effects to roommates of program participants. *Journal of Counseling Psychology*, 1980, 27, 484–491.

691. AMMONS, P., & AMMONS, F. Parental preference among females in relation to vocational aspiration, self–concept, and leadership. *Journal of Genetic Psychology*, 1981, 138, 309–310.

692. ANDREOLI, K. G. Self–concept and health beliefs in compliant and noncompliant hypertensive patients. *Nursing Research*, 1981, 30, 323–328.

693. BOYLE, E. S., & LARSON, P. C. Factor structure of the Tennessee Self–Concept Scale for an institutionalized, disabled population. *Perceptual & Motor Skills*, 1981, 52, 575–582.

694. BOYLE, E. S., & SIELSKI, K. A. Correlates of health locus of control in an older, disabled group. *Journal of Psychology*, 1981, 109, 87–91.

695. DANAHY, S., & KAHN, M. W. Consistency of field dependence in treated alcoholics. *International Journal of the Addictions*, 1981, 16, 1271–1275.

696. EYO, I. E. British delinquents and nondelinquents on seven domains of the self–concept. *Journal of Psychology*, 1981, 109, 137–145.

697. KAHN, M. W., & STEPHEN, L. S. Counselor training as a treatment method for alcohol and drug abuse. *International Journal of the Addictions*, 1981, 16, 1415–1424.

698. KLARREICH, S. H. Group training in problem solving skills and group counselling: A study comparing two treatment approaches with adolescent probationers. *Corrective & Social Psychiatry & Journal of Behavior Technology, Methods & Therapy*, 1981, 27, 1–13.

699. LUND, N. L., CARMAN, S. M., & KRANZ, P. L. Reliability in the use of the Tennessee Self–Concept Scale for educable mentally retarded adolescents. *Journal of Psychology*, 1981, 109, 205–211.

700. McGUIRE, B., & TINSLEY, H. E. A. A contribution to the construct validity of the Tennessee Self–Concept Scale: A confirmatory factor analysis. *Applied Psychological Measurement*, 1981, 5, 449–457.

701. ROFFE, M. W. Predictive correlates of treatment program completion in a sample of male alcoholics. *International Journal of the Addictions*, 1981, 16, 849–857.

702. SEWELL, T. E., PALMO, A. J., & MANNI, J. L. High school dropout, psychological, academic, and vocational factors. *Urban Education*, 1981, 16, 65–76.

[2414]

Test A/8: Arithmetic. Technical college students and applicants for clerical and trade positions with 8–12 years of education; 1943–57; National Institute for Personnel Research [South Africa].*

See T2:740 (2 references) and 6:639.

[2415]

Test A/65. Matriculants and higher; [1956?]; also called *English Language Achievement Test*; 3 scores: spelling, comprehension, vocabulary; no manual; National Institute for Personnel Research [South Africa].*

[2416]

★Test Anxiety Profile. Grades 9–12 and college; 1980; TAP; 12 scores: 2 anxiety scores (feeling of anxiety, thought interference) for 6 different situations (multiple choice exam, math exam, essay exam, pop quiz, talking in front of class, test with a time limit); E. R. Oetting and J. L. Deffenbacher; Rocky Mountain Behavioral Science Institute, Inc.* (In-print status uncertain; no reply from publisher.)

[2417]

★Test Attitude Inventory. High school and college students; 1977–80; self-report inventory of test anxiety; 3 scores: worry, emotionality, total; Charles D. Spielberger; Consulting Psychologists Press, Inc.*

REFERENCES

1. SCOTT, J. C., & NELSON, D. L. Anxiety and encoding strategy. *Bulletin of the Psychonomic Society*, 1979, 13, 297–299.
2. MUELLER, J. H., & COURTOIS, M. R. Test anxiety and breadth of encoding experiences in free recall. *Journal of Research in Personality*, 1980, 14, 458–466.

[2418]

Test for Ability to Sell: George Washington University Series. Grades 7–16 and adults; 1929–50; F. A. Moss, Herbert Wyle, William Loman, William Middleton, Thelma Hunt, Robert George, and William Schnell; Center for Psychological Service.* (In-print status uncertain; no reply from publisher.)

For additional information, see 4:829; for a review by Floyd L. Ruch, see 3:705.

[2419]

Test for Colour-Blindness. Ages 4 and over; 1917–70; congenital color vision deficiency; Shinobu Ishihara; Kanehara Shuppan Co., Ltd. [Japan]. (United States distributor: Graham-Field.)

See T2:1932 (29 references), 7:882 (13 references), and 6:962 (58 references).

REFERENCES

1–58. See 6:962.
59–71. See 7:882.
72–100. See T2:1932.
101. HENKIN, R. I., & GILLIS, W. T. Divergent taste responsiveness to fruit of the tree. *Nature*, 1977, 265, 536–537.

[2420]

Test for Firefighter B-1(m). Firemen and prospective firemen; 1973; test booklet title is *Firefighter*; no manual; test rented to member public personnel agencies and nonmember agencies approved by the publisher; International Personnel Management Association.*

[2421]

A Test of Active Vocabulary. Grades 9–12; 1961; Paul W. Lehmann; Educational Publications.* (In-print status uncertain; no reply from publisher.)

For additional information, see 6:338.

[2422]

★Test of Adolescent Language. Grades 6–12; 1980; TOAL; 19 scores: 8 subtest scores (listening/vocabulary, listening/grammar, speaking/vocabulary, speaking/grammar, reading/vocabulary, reading/grammar, writing/vocabulary, writing/grammar), 11 composite scores (adolescent language quotient, listening, speaking, reading, writing, spoken language, written language, vocabulary, grammar, receptive language, expressive language); Donald D. Hammill, Virginia L. Brown, Stephen C. Larsen, and J. Lee Wiederholt; PRO-ED.*

[2423]

Test of Adult College Aptitude. Evening college entrants; 1966; TACA; King W. Wientge and Philip H. DuBois; TACA Development Fund.* (In-print status uncertain; no reply from publisher.)

For additional information and a review by Kenneth D. Hopkins, see 7:389.

[2424]

★Test of Auditory Comprehension. Hearing impaired ages 4–17; 1976–81; TAC; designed to be used in conjunction with the Auditory Skills Curriculum for the selection of auditory training objectives and measurement of progress; 10 scores: linguistic vs. nonlinguistic, linguistic/human-nonlinguistic/environmental, stereotypic messages, single element core noun vocabulary, recalls two critical elements, recalls four critical elements, sequences three events, recalls five details, sequences three events with competing message, recalls five details with competing message; Audiologic Services and Southwest School for the Hearing Impaired, Office of the Los Angeles County Superintendent of Schools; Foreworks.*

[2425]

Test of Auditory Discrimination. Grades kgn–6; 1975; TAD; manual title is *The Testing-Teaching Module of Auditory Discrimination*; 6 scores: initial consonants, initial consonant blends and digraphs, final consonants, final consonant blends and digraphs, vowels, auditory blending; Victoria Risko; Academic Therapy Publications.*

For additional information and reviews by Lear Ashmore and Eugene C. Sheeley, see 8:948.

REFERENCES

1. SHELTON, R. L., JOHNSON, A. F., & ARNDT, W. B. Delayed judgment speech–sound discrimination and /r/ or /s/ articulation status and improvement. *Journal of Speech & Hearing Research*, 1977, 20, 704–717.
2. KOENKE, K. A comparison of three auditory discrimination–perception tests. *Academic Therapy*, 1978, 14, 463–468.

[2426]

Test of Aural Perception in English for Japanese Students. Japanese students in American colleges; 1950; for research use only; Robert Lado and R. D. Andrade; English Language Institute, University of Michigan.*

See T2:236 (1 reference) and 6:362.

[2427]

Test of Aural Perception in English for Latin-American Students. Latin-American students of English; 1947–57; Robert Lado; English Language Institute, University of Michigan.*

See T2:237 (2 references) and 5:262.

[2428]
Test of Basic Assumptions. Adults; 1959–68, c1957–59; TBA; for experimental and research use only; 12 scores: 3 attitude scores (realist, idealist, pragmatist) for each of 4 "life areas" (organization of effort and problem solving, human abilities and the individual, general philosophy of life, economics and business); James H. Morrison and Martin Levit (test); James H. Morrison.*

For additional information, see P:268.

[2429]
Test of Behavioral Rigidity, Research Edition. Ages 21 and over; 1960, c1956–60; TBR; 4 scores: motor-cognitive rigidity, personality-perceptual rigidity, psychomotor speed, total; K. Warner Schaie; Consulting Psychologists Press, Inc.*

See T2:1418 (9 references) and P:269 (4 references); for reviews by Douglas P. Crowne and Benjamin Kleinmuntz, see 6:189 (9 references).

REFERENCES

1–9. See 6:189.
10–13. See P:269.
14–22. See T2:1418.
23. HERTZOG, C., SCHAIE, K. W., & GRIBBIN, K. Cardiovascular disease and change in intellectual functioning from middle to old age. *Journal of Gerontology*, 1978, 33, 872–883.
24. DORETHY, R., & REEVES, D. Mental functioning, perceptual differentiation, personality, and achievement among art and non-art majors. *Studies in Art Education*, 1979, 20, 52–63.
25. GRIBBIN, K., SCHAIE, K. W., & PARHAM, I. Complexity of life style and maintenance of intellectual abilities. *Journal of Social Issues*, 1980, 36, 47–61.

[2430]
★Test of Children's Learning Ability-Individual Version. Ages 7–8; 1979; TCLA; experimental form; 7 scores: concept formation (prompts, spontaneous classifications sets 1–5, spontaneous classifications set 6), verbal learning of objects, number series, verbal learning of syllables, analogies; developed from test by Judith M. Haynes; X. Perryer, S. Hegarty, M. Andrews, C. Gipps, D. Lucas, and S. Hegarty (manual); NFER-Nelson Publishing Co. [England].*

[2431]
*Test of Cognitive Skills. Grades 2–3, 3–5, 5–7, 7–9, 9–12; 1981; TCS; revision of *Short Form Test of Academic Aptitude*; 5 scores: sequences, analogies, memory, verbal reasoning, total (cognitive skills index); CTB/McGraw-Hill.*

For additional information, a review by Lynn H. Fox, and an excerpted review by David M. Shoemaker of the *Short Form Test of Academic Aptitude*, see 8:202 (9 references).

[2432]
★Test of Competence in Mathematics Level 4–5, 6–7, 8–9. Grades 4–5, 6–7, 8–9; 1979–81; Frances C. Morrison; Guidance Centre, University of Toronto [Canada].*

[2433]
Test of Concept Utilization. Ages 4.5–18.5; 1972; TCU; 24 scores: 6 equivalence scores (color, shape, homogeneous function, abstract, stimulus bound, object bound), 2 relational scores (relational function, minor relational), 3 structure scores (total equivalence, total relational, total unilateral), 6 reality match scores (color, shape, homogeneous function, abstract, relational function, total), 2 concept articulation scores (acceptable mains, inferior mains), 4 qualitative scores (action, object qualities, infusions, creations), negations; Richard L. Crager and Ann J. Spriggs (manual); Western Psychological Services.*

For additional information and a review by William C. Ward, see 8:246; see also T2:585 (1 reference).

[2434]
Test of Consumer Competencies. Grades 8–12; 1975–76; TCC; Thomas O. Stanley, E. Thomas Garman, and Richard D. Brown; Scholastic Testing Service, Inc.*

For additional information and a review by William E. Coffman, see 8:418 (1 reference).

REFERENCES
1. See 8:418.
2. STANLEY, T. O. The development of the Test of Consumer Competency. *Delta Pi Epsilon Journal*, 1977, 14, 1–15.

[2435]
Test of Creative Potential. Grades 2–12 and adults; 1973; TCP; Ralph Hoepfner and Judith Hemenway; Monitor.*

For additional information and reviews by John W. French and William A. Owens, see 8:247.

[2436]
★The Test of Early Language Development. Ages 3–0 to 7–11; 1981; TELD; standardized on the same sample of children and developed as a companion test to the *Test of Early Reading Ability*; total score with the capability for individual item analysis in the areas of receptive language, expressive language, semantics, and syntactic forms; Wayne P. Hresko, D. Kim Reid, and Donald D. Hammill; PRO-ED.*

[2437]
★Test of Early Learning Skills. Ages 3.5–5.5; 1979; TELS; abbreviated adaptation of *Assessment of Basic Competencies*; part of *Assessment of Basic Competencies Series*; 4 scores: thinking, language, number, total; Jwalla P. Somwaru; Scholastic Testing Service, Inc.*

[2438]
★The Test of Early Reading Ability. Ages 3–0 to 7–11; 1981; TERA; standardized on the same sample of children and developed as a companion test to the *Test of Early Language Development*; total score with the capability for individual item analysis in the areas of alphabet knowledge, word meaning, and reading conventions; D. Kim Reid, Wayne P. Hresko, and Donald D. Hammill; PRO-ED.*

[2439]
★Test of Economic Achievement. High school; 1978; TEA; J. D. Thexton; Guidance Centre, University of Toronto [Canada].*

[2440]
*Test of Economic Literacy. Grades 11–12; 1978–79; TEL; substantive revision of *Test of Economic Understanding*; (Spanish version available); test by TEL Working Committee, Joint Council on Economic Education; manual by John C. Soper; Joint Council on Economic Education.*

See T2:1968 (19 references); for reviews by Edward J. Furst and Christine H. McGuire, and an excerpted review by Robert L. Ebel of an earlier edition, see 7:901 (10 references).

[2441]
Test of English as a Foreign Language. College and other institutional applicants from non-English language countries; 1964–81; TOEFL; test administered monthly in approximately 135 countries; 4 scores: listening comprehension, structure and written expression, reading comprehension and vocabulary, total; program administered by The College Board, the Graduate Record Examination Board, and Educational Testing Service.

For additional information, see 8:110 (15 references); see also T2:238 (4 references); for reviews by Clinton I. Chase and George Domino of earlier forms, see 7:266 (10 references).

REFERENCES

1–10. See 7:266.
11–14. See T2:238.
15–29. See 8:110.
30. AYERS, J. B., & PETERS, R. M. Predictive validity of the Test of English as a Foreign Language for Asian graduate students in engineering, chemistry, or mathematics. *Educational & Psychological Measurement*, 1977, 37, 461–463.
31. JOHNSON, D. C. The TOEFL and domestic students: Conclusively inappropriate. *Teachers of English to Speakers of Other Languages Quarterly*, 1977, 11, 79–86.
32. HOSLEY, D. Performance differences of foreign students on the TOEFL. *Teachers of English to Speakers of Other Languages Quarterly*, 1978, 12, 99–100.
33. PALMER, L. A., & WOODFORD, P. E. English tests: Their credibility in foreign student admissions. *College & University*, 1978, 53, 500–510.
34. THOMAS, R. E., & RICHARDSON, J. W. Study of English proficiency standards for foreign graduate students. *Journal of the American Association of Collegiate Registrars*, 1978, 53, 201–208.
35. AQUINO, N. S., TRENT, P. J., & DEUTSCH, J. E. Factors related to foreign nurse graduates' test–taking performance. *Nursing Research*, 1979, 28, 111–114.
36. HOSLEY, D., & MEREDITH, K. Inter- and intra-test correlates of the TOEFL. *Teachers of English to Speakers of Other Languages Quarterly*, 1979, 13, 209–217.
37. RICKARD, R. B. Exploring perceptual strategies and reading in a second language: Performance differences between speakers of different native languages. *Teachers of English to Speakers of Other Languages Quarterly*, 1979, 13, 599–602.
38. ABADZI, H. The use of multivariate statistical procedures in international student admissions. *Journal of College Student Personnel*, 1980, 21, 195–201.

[2442]
A Test of English Usage. English-speaking high school and college students and adults; 1963–64; A. Edwin Harper, Jr., and Rhea S. Das; Manasayan [India].*

For additional information, see 6:284.

[2443]
★Test of Enquiry Skills. Junior high school; 1979; TOES; designed to measure enquiry skills among students studying science, social science, or general studies; 9 skill scores: using reference materials (library usage, index and table of contents), interpreting and processing information (scales, averages-percentages-proportions, charts and tables, graphs), critical thinking in science (comprehension of science reading, design of experimental procedures, conclusions and generalizations); Barry J. Fraser; Australian Council for Educational Research [Australia].*

[2444]
★Test of Grammatically Correct Spanish/English, Written and Oral. Grades kgn–4; 1976–78; 4 scores: vocabulary, sentence patterns, grammar, usage; Las Cruces Public Schools.*

a) WRITTEN TESTS. Grades 2–4; 2 parts: Spanish, English.
b) ORAL TESTS. Grades kgn–4; 2 parts: Spanish, English.

[2445]
Test of Language Development. Ages 4–0 to 8–11, 8–6 to 12–11; TOLD; 2 levels; Phyllis L. Newcomer and Donald D. Hammill; PRO-ED.

a) TEST OF LANGUAGE DEVELOPMENT—PRIMARY. Ages 4–0 to 8–11; 1977–82; TOLD—P; 12 scores: 5 principle subtest scores (picture vocabulary, oral vocabulary, grammatic understanding, sentence imitation, grammatic completion), 2 supplemental subtest scores (word discrimination, word articulation), and 5 composite scores (semantics, syntax, listening, speaking, total spoken language).
b) TEST OF LANGUAGE DEVELOPMENT—INTERMEDIATE. Ages 8–6 to 12–11; 1982; TOLD—I; 10 scores: 5 subtest scores (sentence combining, characteristics, word ordering, generals, grammatic comprehension), and 5 composite scores (syntax, semantics, listening, speaking, total spoken language).

For additional information, see 8:978.

REFERENCES

1. NEWCOMER, P. L., & MAGEE, P. The performance of learning (reading) disabled children on a test of spoken language. *Reading Teacher*, 1977, 30, 896–900.
2. BLACKWELL, P. Test of Language Development (TOLD). *ASHA*, 1978, 20, 580–581.
3. EVASCO, K. M., STICK, S., & SHAW, C. K. Language samples and test scores: Comparisons and suggestions for assessment. *ASHA*, 1978, 20, 771. (Abstract)
4. WIENER, F. D., LEWNAU, L. E., & ERWAY, E. Standardization of the TOLD on black American English—speaking children. *ASHA*, 1978, 20, 832. (Abstract)
5. BACHARA, G. H., & PHELAN, W. J. Visual perception and language levels of deaf children. *Perceptual & Motor Skills*, 1980, 51, 272.

[2446]
★Test of Lateral Awareness and Directionality. Grades 1–12; 1980; LAD; criterion-referenced; 3 scores: lateral awareness, directionality, total; Joseph Lockavitch and August Mauser; Academic Therapy Publications.*

[2447]
Test of Library/Study Skills. Grades 2–5, 4–9, 8–12; 1975; no manual; Irene Gullette and Frances Hatfield; Larlin Corporation.*

For additional information, see 8:821.

[2448]
Test of Listening Accuracy in Children. Grades kgn–2, 2–6; 1962–74; TLAC; formerly called *Picture Speech Discrimination Test*; Merlin J. Mecham, J. Lorin Jex, and J. Dean Jones; Communication Research Associates, Inc.*

a) INDIVIDUAL TEST VERSION. Grades kgn–2.
b) GROUP TEST VERSION. Grades 2–6.

For additional information, see 8:949; see also T2:2056 (2 references); for reviews by Ann Brickner and Richard E. Shine, see 7:946.

[2449]
★Test of Minimal Articulation Competence. Ages 3 and over; 1981; T-MAC; 3 scores: vowel/diphthong, consonant, total (developmental articulation index); Wayne Secord; Charles E. Merrill Publishing Co.*
a) COMPLETE TEST.
b) SCREENING TEST.
c) RAPID SCREENING TEST.

[2450]
Test of Motor Impairment. Ages 5-14; 1972; TMI; motor deficiency resulting from neural dysfunction; D. H. Stott, F. A. Moyes, and S. E. Henderson; Brook Educational Publishing Ltd. [Canada].*
For additional information and a review by Jerome D. Pauker, see 8:881 (2 references); see also T2:1904 (4 references).

[2451]
Test of Musicality, Fourth Edition. Grades 4-12; 1942-58; E. Thayer Gaston; Test of Musicality.*
See T2:214 (11 references); for reviews by Paul R. Farnsworth and Kate Hevner Mueller, see 5:252 (1 reference).

[2452]
Test of Nonverbal Auditory Discrimination. Grades kgn-3; 1968-75; TENVAD; 6 scores: pitch, loudness, rhythm, duration, timbre, total; Norman A. Buktenica; Follett Publishing Co.*
For additional information and a review by Nicholas W. Bankson, see 8:950 (2 references); see also T2:2057 (9 references).

REFERENCES
1-9. See T2:2057.
10-11. See 8:950.
12. BUKTENICA, N. A. Perceptual/social aspects of learning to read: A transactional process. *Peabody Journal of Education*, 1977, 54, 154-161.

[2453]
Test of Perceptual Organization. "Normals and psychiatric patients ages 12 and over"; 1967-70; TPO; formerly called *Test of Abstract Reasoning*; William T. Martin; Psychologists and Educators, Inc.*
For additional information, reviews by A. Ralph Hakstian and Robert C. Nichols, and an excerpted review by Barton B. Proger, see 8:203; see also 7:390 (1 reference).

[2454]
★Test of Performance in Computational Skills. Grades 9-12; 1977-80; TOPICS; designed to be used as a part of a diagnostic-prescriptive program; authors recommend that students be tested no later than grade 10; pass/fail score determined by performance in 7 major areas: operations (multiple operations, division, multiplication, subtraction, addition), measurement, other skills; Research and Evaluation Branch of the Los Angeles Unified School District; CTB/McGraw-Hill.*

[2455]
Test of Reading and Number: Inter-American Series. Grade 4 entrants; 1969; TRN; experimental form; 3 scores: reading, number, total; parallel editions in English and Spanish; Herschel T. Manuel; Guidance Testing Associates.* (In-print status uncertain; no reply from publisher.)
For additional information, see 7:30.

REFERENCES
1. MESTRE, J. P. Predicting academic achievement among bilingual Hispanic college technical students. *Educational & Psychological Measurement*, 1981, 41, 1255-1264.

[2456]
★The Test of Reading Comprehension: A Method for Assessing the Understanding of Written Language. Ages 6-6 to 14-6; 1978; TORC; 8 to 9 scores: general vocabulary, syntactic similarities, paragraph reading, total reading comprehension, sentence sequencing (substitute), mathematics vocabulary, social studies vocabulary, science vocabulary, reading directions; Virginia L. Brown, Donald D. Hammill, and J. Lee Wiederholt; PRO-ED.*

REFERENCES
1. JONGSMA, E. A. Test of Reading Comprehension. *Reading Teacher*, 1980, 33, 703-708.

[2457]
Test of Retail Sales Insight. Retail clerks and students; 1960-71; TRSI; earlier form called *Test of Sales Insight*; 6 scores: sales knowledge, customer motivation, merchandise procurement, sales promotion, sales closure, total; Russell Cassel; Psychologists and Educators, Inc.*

[2458]
★Test of Scholastic Abilities. Ages 9-0 to 12-5, 10-6 to 14-5, 12-6 to 14-11; 1981; "measures those verbal and numerical reasoning abilities deemed to be requisites for success in academic aspects of the New Zealand school curriculum"; 2 scores: age percentile ranks, stanines; Neil Reid, Peter Jackson, Alison Gilmore, and Cedric Croft; New Zealand Council for Educational Research [New Zealand].*

[2459]
★Test of Science-Related Attitudes. Grades 7-10; 1981; TOSRA; 7 scales: social implications of science, normality of scientists, attitude to scientific inquiry, adoption of scientific attitudes, enjoyment of science lessons, leisure interest in science, career interest in science; Barry J. Fraser; Australian Council for Educational Research [Australia].*

REFERENCES
1. FRASER, B. J. Predictive validity of an individualized classroom environment questionnaire. *Alberta Journal of Educational Research*, 1981, 27, 240-251.

[2460]
The Test of Social Inferences. Normals (ages 7-13), mildly retarded (ages 9 and over), moderately retarded (ages 12 and over); 1974; TSI; "a test of social comprehension usable with readers or non-readers"; Barbara Edmonson, John de Jung, Henry Leland, and Ethel M. Leach; Educational Activities, Inc.* (In-print status uncertain; no reply from publisher.)
For additional information, see 8:694 (10 references).

REFERENCES

1-10. See 8:694.
11. KARPF, R. J. Effects of emotions on altruism and social inference in retarded adolescents. *Psychological Reports*, 1977, 41, 135-138.

[2461]

Test of Social Insight. Grades 6-12, 13-16 and adults; 1959-63; TSI; 6 scores: withdrawal, passivity, cooperation, competition, aggression, total; Russell N. Cassel; Martin M. Bruce, Ph.D., Publishers.*

See T2:1419 (3 references) and P:270; for reviews by John D. Black and John Pierce-Jones, and an excerpted review by Edward S. Bordin, see 6:190 (4 references).

REFERENCES

1-4. See 6:190.
5-7. See T2:1419.
8. WASHINGTON, E. R., & ALCORN, J. D. The effects of school integration on social insight among black students classified as introverts or extraverts. *Southern Journal of Educational Research*, 1978, 12, 47-58.

[2462]

★Test of the Hierarchy of Inductive Knowledge. Educable mentally retarded children ages 9-14; 1979-81; THINK; developed to assess level of social problem-solving among EMR learners; 9 scores: label, detail, visual inference, statement of problem, solutions-qualifications, best, predictions-verifications, learning statement, generalization; I. Leon Smith and Sandra Greenberg; Professional Examination Service.*

[2463]

Test of Understanding in Personal Economics. High school; 1971; TUPE; Joint Council on Economic Education.*

For additional information and a review by Hulda Grobman, see 8:902 (5 references).

REFERENCES

1-5. See 8:902.
6. DUFF, T. B. Measurement of personal economic understandings developed in basic business. *Business Education Forum*, 1977, 32, 35-37.
7. KIM, P. Y. Personal economic understanding and college business and economics courses. *Delta Pi Epsilon Journal*, 1977, 14, 22-35.
8. WELLING, J. S. Personal economic understanding in general business classes: A comparison of a conventional method with an experiential method. *Journal of Business Education*, 1977, 52, 336.

[2464]

Test of Work Competency and Stability. Ages 21 and over; 1960-61, c1959-60; TWCS; for predicting work capacity and identifying persons psychologically incapable of work; 1 form consisting of an interview questionnaire (1 or 2 scores: ego strength and optionally, occupational stability) and 4-6 tests: 2 perceptual tests of intelligence (digits backward, picture arrangement), 2 psychomotor tests (tapping, steadiness), and (optionally) stress test (mirror drawing), digit symbol; (French edition available); A. Gaston Leblanc; Institute of Psychological Research, Inc. [Canada].*

For additional information and a review by Jerome D. Pauker, see 8:695; see also T2:1420 (1 reference) and 6:191 (2 references).

[2465]

★Test of Written English. Grades 1-6; 1979; TWE; 4 scores: capitalization, punctuation, written expression, total; Velma R. Andersen and Sheryl K. Thompson; Academic Therapy Publications.*

[2466]

★Test of Written Language. Grades 3-12; 1978-83; TOWL; 8 scaled scores: 5 scores for principal subtests (vocabulary, thematic maturity, spelling, word usage, style), a written language quotient (based on 5 principal subtests), 2 scores for supplemental subtests (thought units, handwriting); Donald D. Hammill and Stephen C. Larsen; PRO-ED.*

[2467]

Test on the Fundamentals of Hebrew. Grades 2-5, 3-6, 4-7; 1955-59; 4 or 5 scores: sentences (grades 3-7 only), vocabulary, stories, grammar, total; Committee on Tests of the Jewish Education Service of North America, Inc.; the Service.*

For additional information, see 6:397.

[2467A]

Test on Understanding Science. Grades 5-6, junior high school students, high school and college students and adults; 1961; TOUS; for research use only; 4 understanding scores: the scientific enterprise, scientists, methods and aims of science, total; W. W. Cooley and L. E. Klopfer; L. E. Klopfer.*

See T2:1856 (11 references); for reviews by Hulda Grobman and Victor H. Noll, see 7:804 (30 references); see also 6:925 (3 references).

[2468]

A Test on Use of the Dictionary. High school and college; 1955-63; 6 scores: pronunciation, meaning, spelling, derivation, usage, total; George D. Spache; Reading Laboratory and Clinic.* (In-print status uncertain; no reply from publisher.)

For additional information, see 6:866.

[2469]

Test Orientation Procedure. Job applicants and trainees; 1967; TOP; job applicants needing practice taking tests; no scores; George K. Bennett and Jerome E. Doppelt with the assistance of A. B. Madans and R. G. Buchanan; The Psychological Corporation.

For additional information and a review by Lewis E. Albright, see 7:1066.

[2470]

Testing Academic Achievement. High school graduates and college students; 1973-76, c1967-76; TAA; a program of tests for use by colleges in granting credit and in the placement of students; all tests are either inactive forms or discontinued tests used earlier in other testing programs of The College Board; tests are rented to colleges for local administration and scoring; program administered by The College Board and Educational Testing Service.*

a) ADVANCED PLACEMENT EXAMINATIONS. See 124.
b) CLEP GENERAL EXAMINATIONS. See 411.
c) COLLEGE PLACEMENT TESTS. See 507.

For additional information, see 8:479.

[2471]

[Tests A/9 and A/10]. Applicants for technical and apprentice jobs; 1955-57; interest in scientific fields; 2 parts; tests in English and Afrikaans; no manual; National Institute for Personnel Research [South Africa].*

a) TEST A/9: [TECHNICAL AND SCIENTIFIC KNOWLEDGE].
b) TEST A/10: [TECHNICAL READING COMPREHENSION].
For additional information, see 6:1109.

[2472]
Tests for Auditory Comprehension of Language. Ages 3–6; 1973; 2 tests which may be administered in English or Spanish; Elizabeth Carrow; Teaching Resources Corporation.*
a) SCREENING TEST FOR AUDITORY COMPREHENSION OF LANGUAGE. STACL; short form for identifying children who need further testing with long form.
b) TEST FOR AUDITORY COMPREHENSION OF LANGUAGE, FIFTH EDITION. TACL; long form.
For additional information and reviews by John T. Hatten and Huberto Molina, see 8:454 (6 references); see also T2:997A (2 references).

REFERENCES

1–2. See T2:997A.
3–8. See 8:454.
9. CARROW, E. Test for Auditory Comprehension of Language. *Modern Language Journal*, 1977, 61, 427–428.
10. DAVIS, J. M. Reliability of hearing-impaired children's responses to oral and total presentations of the Test for Auditory Comprehension of Language. *Journal of Speech & Hearing Disorders*, 1977, 42, 520–527.
11. RUEDA, R., & PEROZZI, J. A. A comparison of two Spanish tests of receptive language. *Journal of Speech & Hearing Disorders*, 1977, 42, 210–215.
12. SOMMERS, R. K., & STARKEY, K. L. Dichotic verbal processing in Down's Syndrome children having qualitatively different speech and language skills. *American Journal of Mental Deficiency*, 1977, 82, 44–53.
13. UNARES-ORAMA, N., & SANDERS, L. J. Evaluation of syntax in three-year-old Spanish-speaking Puerto Rican children. *Journal of Speech & Hearing Research*, 1977, 20, 350–357.
14. BURROWS, E. H., & NEYLAND, D. Reading skills, auditory comprehension of language, and academic achievement. *Journal of Speech & Hearing Disorders*, 1978, 43, 467–472.
15. SOMMERS, R. K., ERIDGE, S., & PETERSON, M. K. How valid are children's language tests? *Journal of Special Education*, 1978, 12, 393–407.
16. COPPAGE, K. W., & VEAL, M. C. Establishing functional language in an autistic child: A cooperative approach. *Journal of Communication Disorders*, 1979, 12, 447–460.
17. LEONARD, L. B., & REID, L. Children's judgment of utterance appropriateness. *Journal of Speech & Hearing Research*, 1979, 22, 500–515.
18. ORCHIK, D. J., KRYGIER, K. M., RAGSDALE, R., & BROWN, J. B. Language performance in mild and moderate sensorineural hearing loss. *ASHA*, 21, 1979, 698. (Abstract)
19. SABATINO, D. A. The definition and assessment of visual and auditory perception. *Journal of Clinical Child Psychology*, 1979, 8, 188–194.
20. ANDERSON, J. D., HESS, R., & RICHARDSON, K. Test-retest reliability of the Test for Auditory Comprehension of Language when it is used with mentally retarded children. *Journal of Speech & Hearing Disorders*, 1980, 45, 195–199.
21. DAVIS, S. M., & McCROSKEY, R. L. Auditory fusion in children. *Child Development*, 1980, 51, 75–80.
22. DOYLE, A. B., RAPPARD, P., & CONNOLLY, J. Two solitudes in the preschool classroom. *Canadian Journal of Behavioural Science*, 1980, 12, 221–232.
23. JOHNSON, J. I., LEDER, S. B., & EGELSTON, R. L. Influence of intonation on auditory sequential memory skills. *Perceptual & Motor Skills*, 1980, 50, 703–708.
24. JORDON, L. S. Receptive and expressive language problems occurring in combination with a seizure disorder: A case report. *Journal of Communication Disorders*, 1980, 13, 295–303.
25. KLEECK, A. V., & CARPENTER, R. L. The effects of children's language comprehension level of adults' child-directed talk. *Journal of Speech & Hearing Research*, 1980, 23, 546–569.
26. REYNOLDS, C. R., WRIGHT, D., & WILKINSON, W. A. Incremental validity of the Test for Auditory Comprehension of Language and the Developmental Test of Visual–Motor Integration. *Educational & Psychological Measurement*, 1980, 40, 503–507.
27. WRIGHT, D., REYNOLDS, C. R., & DAPPEN, L. Criterion–related validity of three common preschool assessment instruments for boys and girls. *Psychological Reports*, 1980, 47, 1291–1296.
28. ALLEN, D. V., BLISS, L. S., & TIMMONS, J. Language evaluation: Science or art? *Journal of Speech & Hearing Disorders*, 1981, 46, 66–68.
29. BATH, D. Developing the speech therapy service in day nurseries: A progress report. *British Journal of Disorders of Communication*, 1981, 16, 159–173.
30. HOWELL, J., SKINNER, C., GRAY, M., & BROOMFIELD, S. A study of the comparative effectiveness of different language tests with two groups of children. *British Journal of Disorders of Communication*, 1981, 16, 31–42.
31. OWENS, A., & BEATTY–DESANA, J. Communication functioning in trisomy 9p. *Journal of Communication Disorders*, 1981, 14, 113–122.
32. STARK, R. E., & TALLAL, P. Selection of children with specific language deficits. *Journal of Speech & Hearing Disorders*, 1981, 46, 114–122.
33. WETHERBY, A. M., KOEGEL, R. L., & MENDEL, M. Central auditory nervous system dysfunction in echolalic autistic individuals. *Journal of Speech & Hearing Research*, 1981, 24, 420–429.

[2473]
★**Tests for Everyday Living.** Junior and senior high school; 1979; TEL; 8 scores: purchasing habits, banking, budgeting, health care, home management, job search skills, job related behavior, total; Andrew S. Halpern, Larry K. Irvin, and Janet T. Landman; Publishers Test Service.*

REFERENCES

1. LANDMAN, J. T., IRVIN, L. K., & HALPERN, A. S. Measuring life skills of adolescents: Tests for Everyday Living (TEL). *Measurement & Evaluation in Guidance*, 1980, 13, 95–106.

[2474]
Tests of Academic Progress. Grades 9–12; 1964–72; TAP; 7 scores: social studies, composition, science, reading, mathematics, literature, total; 4 overlapping levels (grades 9, 10, 11, 12) in a single booklet; Dale P. Scannell, Oscar M. Haugh (composition and literature), William B. Reiner (science), Alvin H. Schild (social studies), Henry P. Smith (reading), and Gilbert Ulmer (mathematics); Riverside Publishing Co.*

For additional information and reviews by J. Stanley Ahmann and Clinton I. Chase, see 8:32 (1 reference); for a review by C. M. Lindvall of earlier Forms 1 and 2, see 7:31. For reviews of subtests, see 7:210 (2 reviews), 7:225 (3 reviews), 7:491 (2 reviews), 7:710 (1 review), 7:805 (1 review), and 7:896 (1 review).

REFERENCES

1. See 8:32.
2. JOHNSTON, J. D. Improving high school/college articulation for compensatory students through early basic skills evaluation. *National Reading Conference Yearbook*, 1977, 105–109.
3. SHERMAN, J., & FENNEMA, E. The study of mathematics by high school girls and boys: Related variables. *American Educational Research Journal*, 1977, 14, 159–168.

[2475]
★**Tests of Achievement and Proficiency, Form T.** Grades 9–12; 1978–79; TAP; revision of *Tests of Academic Progress*; Dale P. Scannell in cooperation with Oscar M. Haugh, Alvin H. Schild, and Gilbert Ulmer; Riverside Publishing Co.*
a) BASIC BATTERY. Grades 9–12; 5 scores: reading comprehension, mathematics, written expression, using sources of information, total, plus an applied proficiency skill score.
b) COMPLETE BATTERY. Grades 9–12; 7 scores: reading comprehension, mathematics, written expression, using sources of information, social studies, science, total, plus an applied proficiency skill score.

[2476]
Tests of Achievement in Basic Skills: Mathematics. Preschool–kgn, grades 1, 2, 3–4, 4–6, 7–9, 10–12; 1970–76; TABS-M; may be used separately or as part of instructional Individualized Mathematics Program (IMP); criterion-referenced; 18–69 item scores, each item measuring a specific objective, and part and total scores listed below; 7 levels; James C. Young and Robert R. Knapp (Level C manuals); EdITS/Educational and Industrial Testing Service.*

a) LEVEL K. Preschool–kgn; 1974; 18 item scores in 3 areas: arithmetic skills, geometry-measurement, modern concepts.

b) LEVEL 1. Grade 1; 1974; 36 item scores in 3 areas: arithmetic skills, geometry-measurement, modern concepts.

c) LEVEL 2. Grade 2; 1974; 41 item scores in 3 areas: arithmetic skills, geometry-measurement-application, modern concepts.

d) LEVEL A. Grades 3–4; 1973; 49 item scores in 3 areas: arithmetic skills, geometry-measurement-application, modern concepts.

e) LEVEL B. Grades 4–6; 1972–73; 73 item and total scores in 3 areas: arithmetic skills, geometry-measurement-application, modern concepts, plus total.

f) LEVEL C. Grades 7–9; 1970–71; 68 item and total scores in 3 areas: arithmetic skills, geometry-measurement-application, modern concepts, plus total.

g) LEVEL D. Grades 10–12; 1972–76; 47 item and total scores in 2 areas: arithmetic skills, arithmetic application, plus total.

For additional information, reviews by James Braswell and C. Alan Riedesel, and an excerpted review by Barton B. Proger, see 8:293 (2 references); see also 7:492 (1 reference).

[2477]
Tests of Adult Basic Education, 1976 Edition. Adults at reading levels grades 2–4, 4–6, 6–9; 1967–76, c1957–76; TABE; essentially the same as the 1970 *California Achievement Tests* for grades 2–4, 4–6, 6–9; CTB/McGraw-Hill.*

a) LEVEL E. Adults at reading levels grades 2–4; 6 scores: reading (vocabulary, comprehension, total), mathematics (computation, concepts and problems, total).

b) LEVEL M. Adults at reading levels grades 4–6; 10 scores: same as for Level E plus language (mechanics and expression, spelling, total), total.

c) LEVEL D. Adults at reading levels grades 6–9; 10 scores: same as for Level M.

d) PRACTICE EXERCISES AND LOCATOR TEST. 1967–76; for determining level of test to be administered.

For additional information and reviews by Thomas F. Donlon and Norman E. Gronlund, see 8:33 (1 reference); for a review by A. N. Hieronymus and an excerpted review by S. Alan Cohen of an earlier edition, see 7:32. For reference to reviews of the *California Achievement Tests*, see 8:10.

REFERENCES
1. See 8:33.
2. MANNING, D. T. Everyday materials improve adults' reading. *Journal of Reading*, 1978, 21, 721–724.
3. COLES, G. S., CIPOREN, F., KONIGSBERG, R., & COHEN, B. Educational therapy in a community mental health center. *Community Mental Health Journal*, 1980, 16, 79–89.

[2478]
***Tests of Basic Experiences 2.** Prekgn–beginning of grade 1, end of kgn–end of grade 1; 1970–79; TOBE 2; revision of still-in-print *Tests of Basic Experiences*; "designed to measure the differences in children's awareness of the world around them"; 2 levels each consisting of 4 tests: language, mathematics, science, social studies; Margaret H. Moss; CTB/McGraw-Hill.*

For additional information, a review by Esther E. Diamond, and excerpted reviews by Steven Thurber and Barton B. Proger of an earlier edition, see 8:34 (8 references); for a review by Courtney B. Cazden, see 7:33. For a review by Stephen M. Koziol, Jr. of the language test, see 8:59; for a review by Leroy G. Callahan of the mathematics test, see 8:294; for a review by Arlen R. Gullickson of the science test, see 8:860.

REFERENCES
1–8. See 8:34.
9. MOORE, F. B., & PARR, G. D. Models of bilingual education: Comparisons of effectiveness. *Elementary School Journal*, 1978, 79, 93–97.
10. OAKLAND, T. Predictive validity of readiness tests for middle and lower socioeconomic status Anglo, Black, and Mexican American children. *Journal of Educational Psychology*, 1978, 70, 574–582.
11. RAMEY, C., STEDMAN, D. J., BORDERS–PATTERSON, A., & MENGEL, W. Predicting school failure from information available at birth. *American Journal of Mental Deficiency*, 1978, 82, 525–534.
12. MAGLIOCCA, L. A., RINALDI, R. T., & STEPHENS, T. M. A field test of a frequency sampling screening instrument for early identification of at risk children: A report on the second year pilot study. *Child Study Journal*, 1979, 9, 213–229.
13. FAREL, A. M. Effects of preferred maternal roles, maternal employment, and sociodemographic status on school adjustment and competence. *Child Development*, 1980, 51, 1179–1186.
14. FINKELSTEIN, N. W., & RAMEY, C. T. Information from birth certificates as a risk index for educational handicap. *American Journal of Mental Deficiency*, 1980, 84, 546–552.
15. REYNOLDS, C. R. An examination for bias in a preschool test battery across race and sex. *Journal of Educational Measurement*, 1980, 17, 137–146.

[2479]
***Tests of Basic Experiences 2: Language.** Prekgn–beginning of grade 1, end of kgn–end of grade 1; 1970–79; TOBE 2; Margaret H. Moss; CTB/McGraw-Hill. For the complete battery entry, see 2478.

For additional information and a review by Stephen M. Koziol, Jr. of an earlier edition, see 8:59; see also T2:120 (1 reference) and 7:211 (1 reference). For reviews of the complete battery, see 8:34 (1 review, 2 excerpts) and 7:33 (1 review).

REFERENCES
1. See 7:211.
2. See T2:120.
3. REIS, M., & GOLD, D. Relation of paternal availability to problem solving and sex–role orientation in young boys. *Psychological Reports*, 1977, 40, 823–829.

[2480]
***Tests of Basic Experiences 2: Mathematics.** Prekgn–beginning of grade 1, end of kgn–end of grade 1; 1970–79; TOBE 2; Margaret H. Moss; CTB/McGraw-Hill. For the complete battery entry, see 2478.

For additional information and a review by Leroy G. Callahan of an earlier edition, see 8:294. For reviews of the complete battery, see 8:34 (1 review, 2 excerpts) and 7:33 (1 review).

REFERENCES
1. REIS, M., & GOLD, D. Relation of paternal availability to problem solving and sex–role orientation in young boys. *Psychological Reports*, 1977, 40, 823–829.

[2481]

*Tests of Basic Experiences 2: Science. Prekgn–beginning of grade 1, end of kgn–end of grade 1; 1970–79; TOBE 2; Margaret H. Moss; CTB/McGraw-Hill. For the complete battery entry, see 2478.

For additional information and a review by Arlen R. Gullickson of an earlier edition, see 8:860. For reviews of the complete battery, see 8:34 (1 review, 2 excerpts) and 7:33 (1 review).

[2482]

*Tests of Basic Experiences 2: Social Studies. Prekgn–beginning of grade 1, end of kgn–end of grade 1; 1970–79; TOBE 2; Margaret H. Moss; CTB/McGraw-Hill. For the complete battery entry, see 2478.

For additional information, and reviews of an earlier edition of the complete battery, see 8:34 (1 review, 2 excerpts) and 7:33 (1 review).

[2483]

*Tests of English as a Second Language. Only for use in rating English proficiency of proposed participants for AID training programs (for reasons of test security, no other use of these measures is permitted); 1967–80; ALI/GU tests; 3 tests: English Usage, Listening Comprehension, Reading and Vocabulary; David P. Harris and Leslie A. Palmer; American Language Institute.

[2484]

Tests of General Ability: Inter-American Series. Preschool, grades kgn–1.5, 2–3, 4–6, 7–9, 10–13.5; 1961–73; TGA; revision of *Tests of General Ability: Cooperative Inter-American Tests*; 6 levels; parallel editions in English and Spanish; Herschel T. Manuel; Guidance Testing Associates.* (In-print status uncertain; no reply from publisher.)
a) PRESCHOOL LEVEL. Ages 4–5; 1966–73; 3 scores: verbal-numerical, nonverbal, total.
b) LEVEL 1–PRIMARY. Grades kgn–1.5; 1962–73; 3 scores: same as in *a*.
c) LEVEL 2–PRIMARY. Grades 2–3; 1964–73; 3 scores: same as in *a*.
d) LEVEL 3–ELEMENTARY. Grades 4–6; 1961–73; 4 scores: verbal, nonverbal, numerical, total.
e) LEVEL 4–INTERMEDIATE. Grades 7–9; 1962–73; 4 scores: same as in *d*.
f) LEVEL 5–ADVANCED. Grades 10–13.5; 1962–67; 4 scores: same as in *d*.

See T2:468 (1 reference); for reviews by Russel F. Green and Richard E. Schutz, see 7:391 (2 references); for reviews by Raleigh M. Drake and Walter N. Durost of the earlier edition, see 4:325 (8 references).

REFERENCES

1–8. See 4:325.
9–10. See 7:391.
11. See T2:468.
12. PLANTE, A. J. The Connecticut pairing model proves effective in bilingual/bicultural education. *Phi Delta Kappan*, 1977, 58, 427.

[2485]

Tests of General Educational Development. Candidates for high school equivalency certificates; 1944–76; GED; tests administered throughout the year at official GED centers to civilians and military personnel; separate forms for military personnel discontinued in 1974; practice test forms, entitled *Official GED Practice Test*, are available in English and Spanish for local administration and scoring; 6 scores: correctness and effectiveness of expression, interpretation of reading materials in the social studies, interpretation of reading materials in the natural sciences, interpretation of literary materials, general mathematical ability, average; special editions available for the blind and partially sighted; General Educational Development Testing Service of the American Council on Education.

For additional information, see 8:35 (20 references); see also 7:34 (21 references); for a review by Robert J. Solomon of earlier forms, see 5:27 (39 references); for a review by Gustav J. Froehlich, see 4:26 (27 references); for reviews by Herbert S. Conrad and Warren G. Findley, see 3:20 (11 references). For reviews by Charlotte W. Croon of an earlier form of the expression subtest, see 3:122; for reviews by W. E. Hall and C. Robert Pace of an earlier form of the social studies reading subtest, see 3:528.

REFERENCES

1–11. See 3:20.
12–38. See 4:26.
39–77. See 5:27.
78–98. See 7:34.
99–109. See T2:48.
110–129. See 8:35.
130. LUCAS, W. A., & SPARTANBURG, S. C. Testing the effectiveness of video, voice, and data feedback. *Journal of Communication*, 1978, 28, 168–179.
131. MODJESKI, R. B., & MICHAEL, W. B. The relationship of the general educational performance index measure to other indicators of educational development in each of three samples from an United States Army population. *Educational & Psychological Measurement*, 1978, 38, 377–391.

[2486]

Tests of Perception of Scientists and Self. Grades 9–12; 1976; TOPOSS; 2 tests; L. D. Mackay and R. T. White; Australian Council for Educational Research [Australia].*
a) TOPOSS SELF. Congruence between student's self-perception and scientists' perception of scientists.
b) TOPOSS SCIENTISTS. Congruence between student's perception of scientists and scientists' perception of scientists.

For additional information, see 8:696.

REFERENCES

1. FRASER, B. J. Selection and validation of attitude scales for curriculum evaluation. *Science Education*, 1977, 61, 317–329.

[2487]

Tests of Proficiency in English. Non-native speakers of English ages 7–11; 1973; "content-referenced"; 1 to 19 scores depending on number of tests and levels taken; 4 tests: listening, speaking, reading, writing; 3 levels of which "child takes all he can reasonably be expected to attempt"; NFER-Nelson Publishing Co. [England].*

For additional information and a review by A. E. G. Pilliner, see 8:111.

[2488]

Tests of Reading: Inter-American Series. Grades 1, 2–3, 4–6, 7–9, 10–13; 1950–73; revision of *Tests of Reading: Cooperative Inter-American Tests*; parallel editions in English and Spanish; 5 levels; Herschel T. Manuel; Guidance Testing Associates.* (In-print status uncertain; no reply from publisher.)

a) LEVEL I, PRIMARY. Grade 1; 1966–73; 3 scores: vocabulary, comprehension, total.
b) LEVEL 2, PRIMARY. Grades 2–3; 1962–73; 5 scores: vocabulary, comprehension (level, speed, total), total.
c) LEVEL 3, ELEMENTARY. Grades 4–6; 1962–73; 5 scores: same as for Level 2.
d) LEVEL 4, INTERMEDIATE. Grades 7–9; 1962–73; 5 scores: same as for Level 2.
e) LEVEL 5, ADVANCED. Grades 10–13; 1962–67; 5 scores: same as for Level 2.

For additional information and a review by Georgia S. Adams, see 7:711 (4 references); see also 6:818 (4 references); for reviews by Jacob S. Orleans and Frederick L. Westover of the earlier edition, see 4:557 (4 references).

REFERENCES

1–4. See 4:557.
5–8. See 6:818.
9–12. See 7:711.
13. PLANTE, A. J. The Connecticut pairing model proves effective in bilingual/bicultural education. *Phi Delta Kappan*, 1977, 58, 427.

[2489]

Tests of Social Intelligence. High school and adults; 1965–66; TSI; 6 tests; 5 scores: implications (test *a*), classes (test *b*), systems (tests *c*, *d*), transformations (tests *e*, *f*), composite (tests *a*, *b*, *c*, *f*); J. P. Guilford, Maureen O'Sullivan, and R. deMille (*c*, *d*, *e*); Sheridan Psychological Services, Inc.*
a) CARTOON PREDICTIONS.
b) EXPRESSION GROUPING.
c) MISSING CARTOONS.
d) MISSING PICTURES.
e) PICTURE EXCHANGE.
f) SOCIAL TRANSLATIONS.

See T2:1421 (4 references); for a review by Douglas N. Jackson, see 7:152 (2 references); see also P:272 (1 reference).

REFERENCES

1. See P:272.
2–3. See 7:152.
4–7. See T2:1421.
8. LAVRAKAS, P. J., & MAIER, R. A. Differences in human ability to judge veracity from the audio medium. *Journal of Research in Personality*, 1979, 13, 139–153.

[2490]

Thackray Reading Readiness Profiles. Ages 4–8 to 5–8; 1974; TRRP; 3 scores: vocabulary, auditory discrimination, visual discrimination, plus unscored general ability (draw-a-man); Derek Thackray and Lucy Thackray; Hodder & Stoughton Educational [England].*

For additional information and excerpted reviews by J. M. Francis-Williams, Richard Lansdown, and Brian Preen, see 8:810 (4 references).

REFERENCES

1–4. See 8:810.
5. MCMICHAEL, P. The hen or the egg? Which comes first—Antisocial emotional disorders or reading disability. *British Journal of Educational Psychology*, 1979, 49, 226–238.
6. MCMICHAEL, P. Reading difficulties, behavior, and social status. *Journal of Educational Psychology*, 1980, 72, 76–86.

[2491]

Thematic Apperception Test. Ages 4 and over; 1935–43; TAT; Henry A. Murray; Harvard University Press.*

For additional information and a review by Jon D. Swartz, see 8:697 (241 references); see also T2:1519 (231 references); for reviews by Richard H. Dana and Leonard D. Eron, see 7:181 (297 references); see also P:484 (339 references); for a review by C. J. Adcock, see 6:245 (287 references); for reviews by Leonard D. Eron and Arthur R. Jensen, see 5:164 (311 references); for a review by Arthur L. Benton, see 4:136 (198 references); for reviews by Arthur L. Benton, Julian B. Rotter, and J. R. Wittenborn and an excerpted review, see 3:103 (102 references).

REFERENCES

1–101. See 3:103.
102–299. See 4:136.
300–610. See 5:164.
611–897. See 6:245.
898–1236. See P:484.
1237–1533. See 7:181.
1534–1764. See T2:1519.
1765–2005. See 8:697.
2006. DUCKRO, R., DUCKRO, P., & BEAL, D. Relationship of self-disclosure and mental health in black females. *Journal of Consulting & Clinical Psychology*, 1976, 44, 940–944.
2007. FISHER, J. M. Sex differences in smoking dynamics. *Journal of Health & Social Behavior*, 1976, 17, 155–162.
2008. BAILEY, B. E., & GREEN, J., III. Black Thematic Apperception Test stimulus material. *Journal of Personality Assessment*, 1977, 41, 25–30.
2009. FISH, B. Neurobiologic antecedents of schizophrenia in children. *Archives of General Psychiatry*, 1977, 34, 1297–1313.
2010. HAMM, R. J. Stability of self-concept and fear of failure. *Psychological Reports*, 1977, 40, 522.
2011. HAMPSON, S. E., & KLINE, P. Personality dimensions differentiating certain groups of abnormal offenders from non–offenders. *British Journal of Criminology*, 1977, 17, 310–331.
2012. HEILBRUN, A. B., JR. The influence of defensive styles upon the predictive validity of the Thematic Apperception Test. *Journal of Personality Assessment*, 1977, 41, 486–491.
2013. HURWITZ, J. I., & DAYA, D. K. Non–help-seeking wives of employed alcoholics: A multilevel interpersonal profile. *Journal of Studies on Alcohol*, 1977, 38, 1730–1739.
2014. INMAN, D. J. Differentiation of intrapunitive from extrapunitive female inmates. *Journal of Clinical Psychology*, 1977, 33, 95–98.
2015. JONES, J. E. Patterns of transactional style deviance in the TAT's of parents of schizophrenics. *Family Process*, 1977, 16, 327–337.
2016. KAWAMURA–REYNOLDS, M. Motivational effects of an audience in the content of imaginative thought. *Journal of Personality & Social Psychology*, 1977, 35, 912–919.
2017. KOCHANSKY, G. E., SALZMAN, C., SHADER, R. I., HARMATZ, J. S., & OGLETREE, A. M. Effects of chlordiazepoxide and oxazepam administration on verbal hostility. *Archives of General Psychiatry*, 1977, 34, 1457–1459.
2018. LEAVERTON, D. R., RUPP, J. W., & POFF, M. G. Brief therapy for monocular hysterical blindness in childhood. *Child Psychiatry & Human Development*, 1977, 7, 254–263.
2019. LIEBER, D. J. Parental focus of attention in a videotape feedback task as a function of hypothesized risk for offspring schizophrenia. *Family Process*, 1977, 16, 467–475.
2020. MCDERMOTT, P. A. Measures of diagnostic data usage as discriminants among training and experience levels in school psychology. *Psychology in the Schools*, 1977, 14, 323–331.
2021. NEEL, A. F. Social and biological factors in child development. *Psychological Reports*, 1977, 40, 1143–1146.
2022. NICHOLS, M. P., & KNOPF, I. J. Refining computerized test interpretations: An in-depth approach. *Journal of Personality Assessment*, 1977, 41, 157–159.
2023. O'GORMAN, J. G., & STAIR, L. H. Perception of hostility in the TAT as a function of defensive style. *Journal of Personality Assessment*, 1977, 41, 591–594.
2024. OPOLOT, J. A. Reliability and validity of Smith's Quick Measure of Achievement. *British Journal of Social & Clinical Psychology*, 1977, 16, 395–396.
2025. PATRICK, A. W., & ZUCKERMAN, M. An application of the state-trait concept to the need for achievement. *Journal of Research in Personality*, 1977, 11, 459–465.
2026. RABINOWITZ, A., & SHOUVAL, R. Fantasy as a medium for the reduction of trait versus state aggression. *Journal of Research in Personality*, 1977, 11, 180–190.
2027. REIDY, T. The aggressive characteristics of abused and neglected children. *Journal of Clinical Psychology*, 1977, 33, 1140–1145.

2028. STEELE, R. S. Power motivation, activation, and inspirational speeches. *Journal of Personality*, 1977, 45, 53–64.
2029. SUMMERS, F., & WALSH, F. The nature of the symbiotic bond between mother and schizophrenic. *American Journal of Orthopsychiatry*, 1977, 47, 484–494.
2030. VAITENAS, R., & WIENER, Y. Developmental, emotional, and interest factors in voluntary mid-career change. *Journal of Vocational Behavior*, 1977, 11, 291–304.
2031. VESTEWIG, R. E., & PARADISE, C. A. Multidimensional scaling of the TAT and the measurement of achievement motivation. *Journal of Personality Assessment*, 1977, 41, 595–603.
2032. WINGATE, M. E. Criteria for stuttering. *Journal of Speech & Hearing Research*, 1977, 20, 596–607.
2033. WINTER, D. G., & STEWART, A. J. Power motive reliability as a function of retest instructions. *Journal of Consulting & Clinical Psychology*, 1977, 45, 436–440.
2034. WINTER, D. G., STEWART, A. J., & MCCLELLAND, D. C. Husband's motives and wife's career level. *Journal of Personality & Social Psychology*, 1977, 35, 159–166.
2035. YAMAUCHI, H., & DOI, K. Factorial study of achievement-related motives. *Psychological Reports*, 1977, 41, 795–801.
2036. BINDELGLAS, P. M., & DEE, G. Enuresis treatment with imipramine hydrochloride: A 10-year follow-up study. *American Journal of Psychiatry*, 1978, 135, 1549–1552.
2037. CHALUS, G. A. The mechanisms underlying attributive projection. *Journal of Personality*, 1978, 46, 362–382.
2038. COCHE, E., & SPECTOR, J. TAT-derived affiliation scores and social behavior in therapy groups. *Psychological Reports*, 1978, 42, 739–744.
2039. CONLEY, J. J. Sex differences and androgyny in fantasy content. *Journal of Personality Assessment*, 1978, 42, 604–610.
2040. HASTINGS, A. C. The Oakland poltergeist. *Journal of the American Society of Psychical Research*, 1978, 72, 233–256.
2041. HUNDAL, P. S., & SINGH, S. Some correlates of progressive farm behavior. *Journal of Occupational Psychology*, 1978, 51, 327–332.
2042. IMODA, F., & RULLA, L. M. Sociometric differentiation and self in male religious vocationers. *Group Psychotherapy. Psychodrama & Sociometry*, 1978, 31, 20–32.
2043. PASQUALI, L., & CALLEGARI, A. I. Working mothers and daughters' sex-role identification in Brazil. *Child Development*, 1978, 49, 902–905.
2044. PRASAD, M. B., & SINHA, B. P. Self as a dimension of need for achievement. *Psychological Studies*, 1978, 23, 49–55.
2045. REMER, R., WATSON, J. J., & BRINLY, B. L. Valence of arousal and emotive imagery. *Psychological Reports*, 1978, 43, 167–171.
2046. ROSS, C. W. Nurse's personal death concerns and responses to dying–patient statements. *Nursing Research*, 1978, 27, 64–68.
2047. SCHNEIDER, S., & RICE, D. R. Neurologic manifestations of childhood hysteria. *Journal of Pediatrics*, 1978, 94, 153–156.
2048. SILVERMAN, L. H., ROSS, D. L., ADLER, J. M., & LUSTIG, D. A. Simple research paradigm for demonstrating subliminal psychodynamic activation: Effects of Oedipal stimuli on dart-throwing accuracy in college males. *Journal of Abnormal Psychology*, 1978, 87, 341–357.
2049. SINHA, B. P., & PRASAD, M. B. Relationship between projective and questionnaire measures of achievement motivation. *Psychological Studies*, 1978, 23, 95–97.
2050. TRIPATHI, R. R., & AGRAWAL, A. The achievement motive in leaders and nonleaders: A role analysis. *Psychologia*, 1978, 21, 97–103.
2051. WADE, T. C., BAKER, T. B., MORTON, T. L., & BAKER, L. J. The status of psychological testing in clinical psychology: Relationships between test use and professional activities and orientation. *Journal of Personality Assessment*, 1978, 42, 3–10.
2052. WINTER, D. G., & MCCLELLAND, D. C. Thematic analysis: An empirically derived measure of the effects of liberal arts education. *Journal of Educational Psychology*, 1978, 70, 8–16.
2053. BARNES, G. E. The alcoholic personality: A reanalysis of the literature. *Journal of Studies on Alcohol*, 1979, 40, 571–634.
2054. CAIRNS, N. U., CLARK, G. M., SMITH, S. D., & LANSKY, S. B. Adaptation of siblings to childhood malignancy. *Journal of Pediatrics*, 1979, 95, 484–487.
2055. CHRISTENSEN, M. G., LEE, C. A. B., & BUGG, P. W. Professional development of nurse practitioners as a function of need motivation, learning style, and locus of control. *Nursing Research*, 1979, 28, 51–56.
2056. DIENER, E., & KERBER, K. W. Personality characteristics of American gun-owners. *Journal of Social Psychology*, 1979, 107, 227–238.
2057. FALBO, T., & RICHMAN, C. L. Relationships between father's age, birth order, family size, and need achievement. *Bulletin of the Psychonomic Society*, 1979, 13, 179–182.
2058. GLAUBMAN, H., ORBACH, I., GROSS, Y., AVIRAM, O., FRIEDER, I., FRIEMAN, M., & PELLED, O. REM need in adolescents as indicated by resistance to REM deprivation. *Perceptual & Motor Skills*, 1979, 48, 251–254.
2059. GUTMANN, D., ROTHMAN, S., & LICHTER, S. R. Two kinds of radicals: A discriminant analysis of a projective test. *Journal of Personality Assessment*, 1979, 43, 12–22.
2060. HARDER, D. W. The assessment of ambitious–narcissistic character style with three projective tests: The Early Memories, TAT, and Rorschach. *Journal of Personality Assessment*, 1979, 43, 23–32.
2061. LEVY, M. F., REICHMAN, W., & HERRINGTON, S. Congruence between personality and job characteristics in alcoholics and nonalcoholics. *Journal of Social Psychology*, 1979, 107, 213–217.
2062. MANCHANDA, R., SETHI, B. B., & GUPTA, S. C. Hostility and guilt in obsessive–compulsive neurosis. *British Journal of Psychiatry*, 1979, 135, 52–54.
2063. OBUCHI, K. Perceptual vs. imaginative component of thematic response. *Japanese Psychological Research*, 1979, 21, 29–34.
2064. PANDEY, R. E. Manifestations of sexual and aggressive drives in prelatency, latency, and postlatency children. *International Journal of Social Psychiatry*, 1979, 25, 125–130.
2065. SHABAD, P., WORLAND, J., LANDER, H., & DIETRICH, D. A retrospective analysis of the TATs of children at risk who subsequently broke down. *Child Psychiatry & Human Development*, 1979, 10, 49–59.
2066. SHAPIRO, J. P. "Fear of success" imagery as a reaction to sex-role inappropriate behavior. *Journal of Personality Assessment*, 1979, 43, 33–38.
2067. SHEPARD, L. A. Self-acceptance: The evaluative component of the self–concept construct. *American Educational Research Journal*, 1979, 16, 139–160.
2068. SINGH, S. Relationships among projective and direct verbal measures of achievement motivation. *Journal of Personality Assessment*, 1979, 43, 45–49.
2069. SUMMERS, F., & WALSH, F. Symbiosis and confirmation between father and schizophrenic. *American Journal of Orthopsychiatry*, 1979, 49, 136–148.
2070. TEDESCHI, J. T. Frustration, fantasy aggression, and the exercise of coercive power. *Perceptual & Motor Skills*, 1979, 48, 215–219.
2071. TRUCKENMILLER, J. L., & SCHAIE, K. W. Multi-level structural validation of Leary's interpersonal diagnosis system. *Journal of Consulting & Clinical Psychology*, 1979, 47, 1030–1045.
2072. WOOD, M. M., & GREENFELD, S. Fear of success in high achieving male and female managers in private industry vs. the public sector. *Journal of Psychology*, 1979, 103, 289–297.
2073. WORLAND, J., LANDER, H., & HESSELBROCK, V. Psychological evaluation of clinical disturbance in children at risk for psychopathology. *Journal of Abnormal Psychology*, 1979, 88, 13–26.
2074. ZUCKERMAN, E., & JACOB, T. Task effects in family interaction. *Family Process*, 1979, 18, 47–53.
2075. AGARWAL, A., & TRIPATHI, L. B. Time perspective in achievement motivation. *Psychologia*, 1980, 23, 50–62.
2076. ASHMAN, A. F., & DAS, J. P. Relation between planning and simultaneous–successive processing. *Perceptual & Motor Skills*, 1980, 51, 371–382.
2077. BONHEUR, H., & ROSNER, R. Sex offenders: A descriptive analysis of cases studied at a forensic psychiatry clinic. *Journal of Forensic Sciences*, 1980, 25, 3–14.
2078. CRAMER, P. The development of sexual identity. *Journal of Personality Assessment*, 1980, 44, 604–612.
2079. DE BLIJ, K., & HINRICHSEN, J. J. Construct validity of Rotter's Locus of Control Scale in men alcoholics. *Journal of Studies on Alcohol*, 1980, 41, 463–475.
2080. GORDON, L. B. Preferential drug abuse: Defenses and behavioral correlates. *Journal of Personality Assessment*, 1980, 44, 345–350.
2081. GOULD, S. Need of achievement, career mobility, and the Mexican–American college graduate. *Journal of Vocational Behavior*, 1980, 16, 73–82.
2082. HILL, E. F. A comparison of three psychological testings of a transsexual. *Journal of Personality Assessment*, 1980, 44, 52–101.
2083. HYMOWITZ, P., & SPOHN, H. The effects of antipsychotic medication on the linguistic ability of schizophrenics. *Journal of Nervous & Mental Disease*, 1980, 168, 287–296.
2084. LEFKOWITZ, J., & FRASER, A. W. Assessment of achievement and power motivation of blacks and whites, using a black and white TAT, with black and white administrators. *Journal of Applied Psychology*, 1980, 65, 685–696.
2085. MARTIN, R. D., & BASTIAN, J. Relationship between behavioral indices of aggression and hostile content on the TAT for incarcerated young women. *Perceptual & Motor Skills*, 1980, 51, 327–332.
2086. MCADAMS, D. P. A thematic coding system for the intimacy motive. *Journal of Research in Personality*, 1980, 14, 413–432.
2087. MIKKELSEN, E. J., RAPOPORT, J. L., NEE, L., GRUENAU, C., MENDELSON, W., & GILLIN, J. C. Childhood enuresis. I. Sleep patterns and psychopathology. *Archives of General Psychiatry*, 1980, 37, 1139–1144.
2088. NEWMAN, A., & GRUSS, L. Role-taking ability of paranoids. *Psychological Reports*, 1980, 47, 729–730.
2089. RITZLER, B. A., SHARKEY, K. J., & CHUDY, J. F. A comprehensive projective alternative to the TAT. *Journal of Personality Assessment*, 1980, 44, 358–362.

2090. ROTHBERG, D. L. Professional achievement and locus of control: A tenuous inference reconsidered. *Psychological Reports*, 1980, 46, 183–188.
2091. SINGH, S., & AURORA, R. Motives, work values and child-rearing practices of females with full-time employment and full-time housekeeping. *Indian Journal of Social Work*, 1980, 41, 157–162.
2092. TWA, R. J., & GREENE, M. Prediction of success in student teaching as a criterion for selection in teacher education programs. *Alberta Journal of Educational Research*, 1980, 26, 1–13.
2093. VAILLANT, G. E. Natural history of male psychological health: VIII. Antecedents of alcoholism and "orality". *American Journal of Psychiatry*, 1980, 137, 181–186.
2094. WEINBERGER, L. J., & BRADLEY, L. A. Effects of "favorability" and type of assessment device upon acceptance of general personality interpretations. *Journal of Personality Assessment*, 1980, 44, 44–47.
2095. WISE, S., & GROSSMAN, F. K. Adolescent mothers and their infants: Psychological factors in early attachment and interaction. *American Journal of Orthopsychiatry*, 1980, 50, 454–468.
2096. BROOKINGS, J. B., DANA, R. H., & BOLTON, B. A multitrait-multimethod analysis of alienation. *Journal of Psychology*, 1981, 109, 59–64.
2097. CARP, F. M., & CARP, A. Mental health characteristics and acceptance–rejection of old age. *American Journal of Orthopsychiatry*, 1981, 51, 230–241.
2098. DOANE, J. A., WEST, K. L., GOLDSTEIN, M. J., RODNICK, E. H., & JONES, J. E. Parental communication deviance and affective style. *Archives of General Psychiatry*, 1981, 38, 679–685.
2099. FODOR, E. M., & FARROW, D. L. The power motive as an influence on use of power. *Journal of Personality & Social Psychology*, 1981, 37, 2091–2097.
2100. HOLMES, C. B., & DUNGAN, D. S. Gender of thematic apperception card 3 BM figure. *Perceptual & Motor Skills*, 1981, 53, 897–898.
2101. KAGAN, S., & KNIGHT, G. P. Social motives among Anglo American and Mexican American children: Experimental and projective measures. *Journal of Research in Personality*, 1981, 15, 93–106.
2102. KELTIKANGAS–JÄRVINEN, L., JÄVINEN, H., & LEHTONEN, T. Psychic disturbances in patients with chronic prostatitis. *Annals of Clinical Research*, 1981, 13, 45–49.
2103. KERNBERG, O. F., GOLDSTEIN, E. G, CARR, A. C., HUNT, H. F., BAUER, S. F., & BLUMENTHAL, R. Diagnosing borderline personality: A pilot study using multiple diagnostic methods. *Journal of Nervous & Mental Disease*, 1981, 169, 225–231.
2104. LEWIS, J. M., RODNICK, E. H., & GOLDSTEIN, M. J. Interfamilial interactive behavior, parental communication deviance, and risk for schizophrenia. *Journal of Abnormal Psychology*, 1981, 90, 448–457.
2105. McADAMS, D. P., BOOTH, L., & SELVIK, R. Religious identity among students at a private college: Social motives, ego stage, and development. *Merrill–Palmer Quarterly*, 1981, 27, 219–239.
2106. McADAMS, D. P., & POWERS, J. Themes of intimacy in behavior and thought. *Journal of Personality & Social Psychology*, 1981, 40, 573–587.
2107. PIHL, R. O., & MANDELCORN, B. The manipulation of maternal expectancy in a mother–child interaction. *Journal of Genetic Psychology*, 1981, 139, 85–95.
2108. SHILL, M. Castration fantasies and assertiveness in father-absent males. *Psychiatry*, 1981, 44, 263–272.
2109. SQUYRES, E. M. Guidelines for use in scoring TAT stories for time-span. *Perceptual & Motor Skills*, 1981, 52, 333–334.
2110. URSANO, R. J. The Viet Nam era prisoner of war: Precaptivity personality and the development of psychiatric illness. *American Journal of Psychiatry*, 1981, 138, 315–318.

[2492]

★Themes Concerning Blacks. Blacks ages 4 and over; 1972; TCB; free association or story completion responses to 20 picture cards; Robert L. Williams; Robert L. Williams & Associates, Inc.*

[2493]

Theological School Inventory. Incoming seminary students; 1962–72; TSI; motivation for entering the ministry; 12 scores (definiteness, natural leading, special leading, concept of the call, flexibility, acceptance by others, intellectual concern, self-fulfillment, leadership success, evangelistic witness, social reform, service to persons) plus unscored sections on biographical information and reactions to demands of the ministry; Educational Testing Service (test), James E. Dittes (manual and supplements), Frederick Kling (test and 1 supplement), Ellery Pierson (1 supplement), and Harry DeWire (1 supplement); Ministry Studies Board; Ministry Inventories.*

See T2:1028 (7 references) and P:273 (5 references).

[2494]

★Therapy Attitude Inventory. Parents; 1974; TAI; no manual; Sheila Eyberg; the Author.*

REFERENCES

1. EYBERG, S. M., & MATARAZZO, R. G. Training parents as therapists: A comparison between individual parent–child interaction training and parent group didactic training. *Journal of Clinical Psychology*, 1980, 36, 492–499.

[2495]

★Thinking Creatively in Action and Movement. Ages 3–8; 1981; TCAM; 3 scores: fluency, originality, imagination; E. Paul Torrance; Scholastic Testing Service, Inc.*

[2496]

Thinking Creatively With Sounds and Words, Research Edition. Grades 3–12, adults; 1973; TCSW; 2 tests (sounds and images, onomatopoeia and images) in a single booklet; E. Paul Torrance, Joe Khatena, and Bert F. Cunnington (except technical manual); Scholastic Testing Service, Inc.*

For additional information and reviews by Philip M. Clark and Mary Lee Smith, see 8:248 (16 references); see also T2:587 (17 references).

REFERENCES

1–17. See T2:587.
18–33. See 8:248.
34. TORRANCE, E. P., & MOURAD, S. Some creativity and style of learning and thinking correlates of Guglielmino's self-directed learning readiness scale. *Psychological Reports*, 1978, 43, 1167–1171.
35. JOHNSON, R. A. Verbal originality in the absence of sight: Blind versus sighted adolescents. *Child Study Journal*, 1979, 9, 261–271.
36. TORRANCE, E. P., & MOURAD, S. Role of hemisphericity in performance on selected measures of creativity. *Gifted Child Quarterly*, 1979, 23, 44–55.
37. BULL, K. S., & DAVIS, G. A. Evaluating creative potential using the statement of past creative activities. *Journal of Creative Behavior*, 1980, 14, 249–257.
38. JOHNSON, R. A. Sensory images in the absence of sight: Blind versus sighted adolescents. *Perceptual & Motor Skills*, 1980, 51, 177–178.

[2497]

This I Believe Test. Grades 10 and over; 1971–74; TIB; for research use only; for measurement of groups only; sentence completion; classification into 1 of 4 systems of concreteness-abstractness and 7 or 8 dimension scores: openness, candor, evaluativeness, externality, cynicism, optimism, complexity, criticalness (optional); no manual; O. J. Harvey; the Author.* (In-print status uncertain; no reply from publisher.)

For additional information and a review by Richard W. Coan, see 8:698 (27 references); see also T2:1521 (11 references).

REFERENCES

1–11. See T2:1521.
12–38. See 8:698.
39. RÓSEN, A. Conceptual system and personality: A multivariate study of system stage and personality correlates. *Journal of Research in Personality*, 1977, 11, 416–430.
40. WIEDERANDERS, M. R., & HARVEY, O. J. Effects of conceptual system and quality of feedback on voluntary task persistence. *Journal of Educational Psychology*, 1977, 69, 442–451.
41. CARSKADON, T. G., & KNUDSON, M. C. Relationship between conceptual systems and psychological types. *Psychological Reports*, 1978, 42, 483–486.

[2498]
Thompson Smoking and Tobacco Knowledge Test. Grades 7–16; 1964–67; no manual; Clem W. Thompson; the Author.* (In-print status uncertain; no reply from publisher.)

[2499]
Thurstone Temperament Schedule. Grades 9–16 and adults; 1949–53; TTS; 7 scores: active, vigorous, impulsive, dominant, stable, sociable, reflective; L. L. Thurstone; Science Research Associates, Inc.*

See T2:1423 (32 references), P:277 (20 references), and 6:192 (17 references); for a review by Neil J. Van Steenberg, see 5:118 (12 references); for reviews by Hans J. Eysenck, Charles M. Harsh, and David G. Ryans, and an excerpted review by Laurance F. Shaffer, see 4:93.

REFERENCES

1–12. See 5:118.
13–28. See 6:192.
29–48. See P:277.
49–80. See T2:1423.
81. GILBERT, A. R. Superiority of latency-weighted scores over unweighted scores in personality testing, exemplified by the testing of patrolmen for professional competence. *Psychologia*, 1977, 21, 90–96.
82. BUFFARDI, L., & GIBSON, J. F. Relation between raters' characteristics and halo error. *Perceptual & Motor Skills*, 1980, 51, 1003–1011.

[2500]
Thurstone Test of Mental Alertness. Grades 9–12 and adults; 1943–68; TTMA; abbreviated adaptation of *American Council on Education Psychological Examination for High School Students*, 1940 Edition; for a shorter adaptation of this rest, see *SRA Verbal Form*; 3 scores: quantitative, linguistic, total; Thelma Gwinn Thurstone and L. L. Thurstone; Science Research Associates, Inc.*

See T2:469 (5 references); for a review by Robert D. North, see 7:392 (4 references); for a review by Joshua A. Fishman, see 5:391; see also 4:326 (3 references); for reviews by Anne Anastasi and Emily T. Burr of an earlier edition, see 3:265.

[2501]
Tickmaster. Job applicants; 1954–65; environmental conditions under which applicant will be most productive; Roland Ballen; the Author.*

[2502]
The Time Appreciation Test. Ages 10 and over; 1943–46; test sheet title is *JNB Time Test*; John N. Buck; Western Psychological Services.*

See T2:588 (5 references); for reviews by E. J. G. Bradford and Charles N. Cofer, see 3:266 (2 references).

[2503]
Time Current Affairs Test. Grades 9–12 and adults; 1935–74; formerly called *Current Affairs Test*; new test issued annually in January; available only as part of the Time Education Program; no manual; Time, Inc.* (In-print status uncertain; no reply from publisher.)

[2504]
The Time Monthly News Quiz. Grades 9–12 and adults; 1969–74; 9 tests (spirit masters for local duplicating) in each of 2 areas; issued annually in August (Summer Review Quiz), September, October, November, December–January, February, March, April, and May; available only as part of the Time Education Program; no manual; Time, Inc.* (In-print status uncertain; no reply from publisher.)
a) ENGLISH REVIEW. 1973–74.
b) NEWS QUIZ. 1969–74.

[2505]
★**Time Questionnaire: Assessing Suicide Potential.** Adults; 1978–79; TQ; a semi-projective personality technique using time perspective as an index of suicide potential; for research use only; 8 scores: past, present, future, total, faking, omission, bizarre, unscorable; Robert Yufit and Bonnie Benzies; Consulting Psychologists Press, Inc.*

[2506]
Titmus Vision Tester. Ages 3 and over; 1958–69; TVT; formerly called *T/O Vision Tester*; 7 units; Titmus Optical Co., Inc.* (In-print status uncertain; no reply from publisher.)
a) SCHOOL UNIT. Grades 1–5; 1959–66; duplicates the *Massachusetts Vision Test*.
b) PEDIATRIC UNIT. Ages 3–9, grades kgn–5; 1960–66; duplicates the *Michigan Pre-School Vision Test* and the *Massachusetts Vision Test*.
c) GENERAL TESTING UNIT. Ages 3–5, grades 1–12, grades 1–16 and adults; 1959–69; includes the *Michigan Pre-School Vision Test* and the *Massachusetts Vision Test*.
d) INDUSTRIAL-OCCUPATIONAL UNIT. Industry; 1959.
e) AEROMEDICAL UNIT. Pilots; 1959–68.
f) DRIVER EDUCATION UNIT. 1959–61; no manual.
g) DRIVER LICENSING UNIT. 1959–60; no manual.

See T2:1934 (6 references); for a review by Carl L. Rosen of the school unit, see 7:883.

REFERENCES

1–6. See T2:1934.
7. IGLEHART, V. R., CONNER, D., & SINNETTE, C. H. A comprehensive school health program in Harlem: A retrospective view. *Journal of School Health*, 1977, 47, 88–93.

[2507]
T.M.R. Performance Profile for the Severely and Moderately Retarded. Ages 4 and over; 1963–67; 7 scores: social behavior, self-care, communication, basic knowledge, practical skills, body usage, total; Alfred J. DiNola, Bernard P. Kaminsky, and Allan E. Sternfeld; Educational Performance Associates, Inc.*

See T2:1412 (1 reference).

[2508]
★**T. M. R. School Competency Scales.** Trainable mentally retarded, 5 age levels in 2 booklets, ages 5–10, 11–17; 1976; ratings by teachers; 5 scores: perceptual-motor, initiative-responsibility, cognition, personal-social, language; Samuel Levine, Freeman F. Elzey, Paul Thormahlen, and Leo F. Cain; Consulting Psychologists Press, Inc.*

[2509]
★**The Token Test for Children.** Ages 3–12; 1978; assessing subtle receptive language dysfunction; Frank DiSimoni; Teaching Resources Corporation.*

REFERENCES

1. NOLL, J. D. The Token Test for Children. *ASHA*, 1979, 21, 623–624.

[2510]

Toledo Chemistry Placement Examination. College entrants; 1959–81; TCPE; 7 scores: arithmetic and algebra, general knowledge, formulas and nomenclature, equations, algebraic formulations, chemical problems, total; Albertine Krohn; Examinations Committee, American Chemical Society.*

For additional information and a review by Frank J. Fornoff, see 8:853 (3 references); see also T2:1847 (2 references); for reviews by Kenneth E. Anderson and William R. Crawford of earlier forms, see 6:920 (1 reference).

[2511]

Tooze Braille Speed Test: A Test of Basic Ability in Reading Braille. Students (ages 7–13) in grades 1 or 2 Braille; 1962; F. H. G. Tooze; Association for the Education and Welfare of the Visually Handicapped [England].*

For additional information, see 6:855.

[2512]

Torrance Tests of Creative Thinking. Kgn through graduate school; 1966–74; TTCT; revision of *Minnesota Tests of Creative Thinking*; 2 tests; E. Paul Torrance; Scholastic Testing Service, Inc.*

a) VERBAL TEST. Test booklet title is *Thinking Creatively With Words*; 3 scores: fluency, flexibility, originality.

b) FIGURAL TEST. Test booklet title is *Thinking Creatively With Pictures*; 4 scores: fluency, flexibility, originality, elaboration.

For additional information, see 8:249 (229 references); see also T2:589 (88 references); for reviews by Leonard L. Baird and Robert L. Thorndike, and excerpted reviews by Ralph Hoepfner, John L. Holland, and Michael A. Wallach, see 7:448 (243 references).

REFERENCES

1–243. See 7:448.
244–331. See T2:589.
332–560. See 8:249.

561. BURSTINER, I. Creative management training for department store middle managers: An evaluation. *Journal of Creative Behavior*, 1977, 11, 105–108.
562. CALLAHAN, C. M., & RENZULLI, J. S. The effectiveness of a creativity training program in the language arts. *Gifted Child Quarterly*, 1977, 21, 538–545.
563. COX, R. S. Rewarding instructions vs brainstorming on creativity test scores of college students. *Psychological Reports*, 1977, 41, 951–954.
564. FRANKLIN, B. S., & RICHARDS, P. N. Effects on children's divergent thinking abilities of a period of direct teaching for divergent production. *British Journal of Educational Psychology*, 1977, 47, 66–70.
565. GLOVER, J. A., & SAUTTER, F. Relation of four components of creativity to risk-taking preferences. *Psychological Reports*, 1977, 41, 227–230.
566. GOOR, A., & RAPOPORT, T. Enhancing creativity in an informal educational framework. *Journal of Educational Psychology*, 1977, 69, 636–643.
567. GOURLEY, T. J., KELLY, V., & ZUCEA, R. The application of a rational-psychedelic continuum concept of creativity to the classroom. *Gifted Child Quarterly*, 1977, 21, 103–108.
568. GREER, R. N., & BLANK, S. S. Cognitive style, conceptual tempo and problem solving: Modification through programmed instruction. *American Educational Research Journal*, 1977, 14, 295–315.
569. HALPIN, G. Day school or residential school: Which is better for development of creative thinking abilities of blind children. *Psychological Reports*, 1977, 41, 59–62.
570. HARGREAVES, D. J. Sex roles in divergent thinking. *British Journal of Educational Psychology*, 1977, 47, 25–32.
571. JOHNSON, R. A. Creative thinking in the absence of language: Deaf versus hearing adolescents. *Child Study Journal*, 1977, 7, 49–57.
572. JOINER, E. G. Communicative versus non-communi[cative] language practice in the teaching of beginning college Fren[ch]. *Language Journal*, 1977, 61, 236–242.
573. KALTSOUNIS, B., & HIGDON, G. School conformity relationship to creativity. *Psychological Reports*, 1977, 40, 715–718.
574. MALGADY, R. G. Children's interpretation and apprecia[tion of] similes. *Child Development*, 1977, 48, 1734–1738.
575. MARTIN, J. D., BLAIR, G. E., STOKES, E. H., & ARMSTRON[G] Correlation of the Object Assembly and Block Design Test of the Wechsler Adult Intelligence Scale and the Torrance Tests of Creative Thinking. *Educational & Psychological Measurement*, 1977, 37, 1095–1097.
576. PATEL, K. Personality factors predicting creative profiles. *Psychologia*, 1977, 20, 74–82.
577. POOLE, M. E., WILLIAMS, A. J., & LETT, W. R. Innercenteredness of highly creative adolescents. *Psychological Reports*, 1977, 41, 365–366.
578. ROSENTHAL, D. A., MORRISON, S. M., & PERRY, L. Teaching creativity: A comparison of two techniques. *Australian Journal of Education*, 1977, 21, 226–232.
579. UNO, T., GARGIULO, R. M., SEARS, J. D., MAUTER, M., & ROWE, J. Creativity in developmentally disabled adolescents. *Psychological Reports*, 1977, 40, 1207–1212.
580. VAUGHAN, M. M. Musical creativity: Its cultivation and measurement. *Council for Research in Music Education. Bulletin*, 1977, 50, 72–77.
581. VOSS, H. G., & KELLER, H. Critical evaluation of the Obscure Figures Test as an instrument for measuring "cognitive innovation". *Perceptual & Motor Skills*, 1977, 45, 495–502.
582. WILLIAMS, R. E. Programmed instruction for creativity. *Programmed Learning & Educational Technology*, 1977, 14, 50–64.
583. BAKER, M. The Torrance Tests of Creative Thinking and the Rorschach Inkblot Test: Relationships between two measures of creativity. *Perceptual & Motor Skills*, 1978, 46, 539–547.
584. BOLEN, L. M., & TORRANCE, E. P. The influence on creative thinking of locus of control, cooperation, and sex. *Journal of Clinical Psychology*, 1978, 34, 903–907.
585. BRUCH, C. B., & MORSE, J. A. Initial study of creative (productive) given under the Bruch–Morse model. *Gifted Child Quarterly*, 1978, 22, 526–535.
586. CARTER, J., & TORRANCE, E. P. Teacher effect in using creative thinking exercises with sixth graders. *Journal of Creative Behavior*, 1978, 12, 217. (Abstract)
587. EICHENBERGER, R. J. Creativity measurement through use of judgement criteria in physics. *Educational & Psychological Measurement*, 1978, 38, 421–427.
588. ENGELMAN, M. A. The response of older women to a creative problem-solving program. *Journal of Creative Behavior*, 1978, 12, 278. (Abstract)
589. FARLEY, F. H. Note on creativity and scholastic achievement of women as a function of birth order and family size. *Perceptual & Motor Skills*, 1978, 47, 13–14.
590. FORISHA, B. L. Creativity and imagery in men and women. *Perceptual & Motor Skills*, 1978, 47, 1255–1264.
591. FRIEDMAN, F., RAYMOND, B. A., & FELDHUSEN, J. F. The effects of environmental scanning on creativity. *Gifted Child Quarterly*, 1978, 22, 248–251.
592. HAGGARD, M. R. The effect of creative thinking–reading activities (CT–RA) on reading comprehension. *National Reading Conference Yearbook*, 1978, 233–236.
593. HOLMAN, E. R., & WHITE, W. F. Self-concept of student teachers determines their creative skills and attitudes towards teaching. *Journal of Creative Behavior*, 1978, 12, 219. (Abstract)
594. JENSEN, L. R. Diagnosis and evaluation of creativity, research and thinking skills of academically talented elementary students. *Gifted Child Quarterly*, 1978, 22, 98–110.
595. KALTSOUNIS, B. Creative performance among siblings of various ordinal birth positions. *Psychological Reports*, 1978, 42, 915–918.
596. KANDIL, S. A., & TORRANCE, E. P. Further verification of high creative potential among emotionally disturbed and behavior disordered children. *Journal of Creative Behavior*, 1978, 12, 280. (Abstract)
597. KNOX, B. J., & GLOVER, J. A. A note on preschool experience effects on achievement, readiness, and creativity. *Journal of Genetic Psychology*, 1978, 132, 151–152.
598. KVASHNY, A., & SEARS, J. T. Measurement of creativity variables in students. *Engineering Education*, 1978, 69, 269–272.
599. LANDRENEAU, E., & HALPIN, G. The influence of modeling on children's creative performance. *Journal of Educational Research*, 1978, 71, 137–139.
600. LETT, W. R., WILLIAMS, A. J., & POOLE, M. E. Challenging stereotypes of creativity in school and leisure. *Psychological Reports*, 1978, 42, 71–74.
601. MAXWELL, B. A., & REILLEY, R. R. Creativity, satisfaction, and orientation of college freshman. *Psychological Reports*, 1978, 42, 859–864.

602. MORSE, J. A., & BRUCH, C. B. A comparison of sex roles of creative–productive versus non–productive women. *Gifted Child Quarterly*, 1978, 22, 520–525.

603. MUELLER, L. K. Beneficial and detrimental modeling effects on creative response production. *Journal of Psychology*, 1978, 98, 253–260.

604. SCHROEDER, N. Failure to relate academic ability to the lateral eye–shift in elementary school children. *Perceptual & Motor Skills*, 1978, 47, 135–139.

605. TAYLOR, I. A. Characteristics of "creative leaders". *Journal of Creative Behavior*, 1978, 12, 221–222. (Abstract)

606. TORRANCE, E. P. Effects of increasing the time limits of the Just Suppose Test. *Journal of Creative Behavior*, 1978, 12, 281. (Abstract)

607. TORRANCE, E. P., & MOURAD, S. Some creativity and style of learning and thinking correlates of Guglielmino's self–directed learning readiness scale. *Psychological Reports*, 1978, 43, 1167–1171.

608. TUKKO, H., & TAYLOR, I. A. Creativity and inducing theta rhythm production through simultaneous sensory stimulation. *Journal of Creative Behavior*, 1978, 12, 282. (Abstract)

609. ARGULEWICZ, E. N., MEALOR, D. J., & RICHMOND, B. O. Creative abilities of learning disabled children. *Journal of Learning Disability*, 1979, 12, 21–24.

610. BOSSE, M. A. Do creative children behave differently? *Journal of Creative Behavior*, 1979, 13, 119–126.

611. GLOVER, J. A. Levels of questions asked in interview and reading sessions by creative and relatively noncreative college students. *Journal of Genetic Psychology*, 1979, 135, 103–108.

612. HALPIN, G., HALPIN, G., MILLER, E., & LANDRENEAU, E. Observer characteristics related to the imitation of a creative model. *Journal of Psychology*, 1979, 102, 133–142.

613. HERSHEY, M., & KEARNS, P. The effect of guided fantasy on the creative thinking and writing ability of gifted students. *Gifted Child Quarterly*, 1979, 23, 71–77.

614. HOCEVAR, D. The unidimensional nature of creative thinking in fifth grade children. *Child Study Journal*, 1979, 9, 273–277.

615. HOCEVAR, D., & MICHAEL, W. B. The effects of scoring formulas on the discriminant validity of tests of divergent thinking. *Educational & Psychological Measurement*, 1979, 39, 917–921.

616. HUBER, J., TREFFINGER, D., TRACY, D., & RAND, D. Self-instructional use of programmed creativity–training materials with gifted and regular students. *Journal of Educational Psychology*, 1979, 71, 303–309.

617. KALTSOUNIS, B. Black students' personality traits associated with originality and elaboration. *Psychological Reports*, 1979, 44, 83–87.

618. KALTSOUNIS, B. Evidence for validity of the scale, your style of learning and thinking. *Perceptual & Motor Skills*, 1979, 48, 177–178.

619. KUO, Y. Y., PASCHAL, B. J., & SCHURR, K. T. Creative thinking in Indiana and Taiwan college students. *College Student Journal*, 1979, 13, 319–327.

620. LAUGHTON, J. Nonlinguistic creative abilities and expressive syntactic abilities of hearing–impaired children. *Volta Review*, 1979, 81, 409–420.

621. LETT, W. R., WILLIAMS, A. J., & POOLE, M. E. The achievement drive and ego strength of highly creative adolescents. *Journal of Psychology*, 1979, 102, 263–266.

622. MAYFIELD, B. Teacher perception of creativity, intelligence and achievement. *Gifted Child Quarterly*, 1979, 23, 812–817.

623. SHEAN, J. M. The effect of training in creative problem solving on divergent thinking and organizational perceptions of students of school administration. *Journal of Creative Behavior*, 1979, 13, 222–223. (Abstract)

624. STASO, W. H. The effects of simulation games and creativity training on children's divergent thinking. *Gifted Child Quarterly*, 1979, 23, 415–416.

625. TAYLOR, I. A., & FISH, T. A. The creative behavior disposition scale: A Canadian validation. *Canadian Journal of Behavioural Science*, 1979, 11, 95–97.

626. THOMAS, B. Promoting creativity in nursing education. *Nursing Research*, 1979, 28, 115–119.

627. TORRANCE, E. P., & MOURAD, S. Role of hemisphericity in performance on selected measures of creativity. *Gifted Child Quarterly*, 1979, 23, 44–55.

628. TRAVIS, F. The transcendental meditation technique and creativity: A longitudinal study of Cornell University undergraduates. *Journal of Creative Behavior*, 1979, 13, 169–180.

629. TRENTHAM, L. L. Anxiety and instruction effects on sixth–grade students in a testing situation. *Psychology in the Schools*, 1979, 16, 439–443.

630. WALLINGA, C. R., & CRASE, S. J. Parental influence on creativity of fifth grade children. *Gifted Child Quarterly*, 1979, 23, 768–777.

631. WESTBY, C. E. Language performance of stuttering and nonstuttering children. *Journal of Communication Disorders*, 1979, 12, 133–145.

632. WILKS, L., & THOMPSON, P. Birth order and creativity in young children. *Psychological Reports*, 1979, 45, 443–449.

633. WILLIAMS, A. J., POOLE, M., & LETT, W. R. Actual and ideal self–perceptions of creative students. *Perceptual & Motor Skills*, 1979, 48, 995–1001.

634. BALL, O. E., & TORRANCE, E. P. Effectiveness of new materials developed for training the streamlined scoring of the TTCT, Figural A and B Forms. *Journal of Creative Behavior*, 1980, 14, 199–203.

635. BORGSTADT, C., & GLOVER, J. A. Contrasting novel and repetitive stimuli in creativity training. *Psychological Reports*, 1980, 46, 652.

636. COLBERT, C. Visual and figural elaboration in preadolescents. *Studies in Art Education*, 1980, 22, 25–35.

637. COMEAU, H. The relationship between sex, birth order, and creativity. *Journal of Creative Behavior*, 1980, 14, 71. (Abstract)

638. DEHLAVI, N. S. Relationship between creativity and personality characteristics in an Iranian sample. *Perceptual & Motor Skills*, 1980, 50, 823–828.

639. DOERR, S. L. Conjugate lateral eye movement, cerebral dominance, and the figural creativity factors of fluency, flexibility, originality, and elaboration. *Studies in Art Education*, 1980, 21, 5–11.

640. DUFFY, R. A. An analysis of aesthetic sensitivity and creativity with other variables in grades four, six, eight, and ten. *Journal of Educational Research*, 1980, 73, 26–30.

641. EBELING, K. S., & SPEAR, P. S. Preference and performance on two tasks of varying ambiguity as a function of ambiguity tolerance. *Australian Journal of Psychology*, 1980, 32, 127–133.

642. FORSETH, S. D. Art activities, attitudes, and achievement in elementary mathematics. *Studies in Art Education*, 1980, 21, 22–27.

643. GLOVER, J. A. A creativity–training workshop: Short–term, long-term, and transfer effects. *Journal of Genetic Psychology*, 1980, 136, 3–16.

644. GLOVER, J. A., ZIMMER, J. W., & BRUNING, R. H. Information processing approaches among creative students. *Journal of Psychology*, 1980, 105, 93–97.

645. GRAHAM, S., & SHEINKER, A. Creative capabilities of learning-disabled and normal students. *Perceptual & Motor Skills*, 1980, 50, 481–482.

646. HATTIE, J. Should creativity tests be administered under testlike conditions? An empirical study of three alternative conditions. *Journal of Educational Psychology*, 1980, 72, 87–98.

647. HICKS, C. The development of creative thinking and its relationship to IQ and reading achievement. *Reading World*, 1980, 20, 44–52.

648. LAGRECA, A. M. Can children remember to be creative? An interview study of children's thinking processes. *Child Development*, 1980, 51, 572–575.

649. O'HAIRE, T. D., & MARCIA, J. E. Some personality characteristics associated with Ananda Marga meditators: A pilot study. *Perceptual & Motor Skills*, 1980, 51, 447–452.

650. OKOH, N. Bilingualism and divergent thinking among Nigerian and Welsh school children. *Journal of Social Psychology*, 1980, 110, 163–170.

651. REISMAN, F. K., & TORRANCE, E. P. Alternative procedures for assessing intellectual strengths of young children. *Psychological Reports*, 1980, 46, 227–230.

652. ROSENTHAL, D. A, & CONWAY, M. Adolescents' creativity and non–conformity in school. *Psychological Reports*, 1980, 47, 668.

653. SIGG, J. M., & GARGIULO, R. M. Creativity and cognitive style in learning disabled and nondisabled school age children. *Psychological Reports*, 1980, 46, 299–305.

654. STEWART, C. A., & CLAYSON, D. A note on change in creativity by handedness over a maturational time period. *Journal of Psychology*, 1980, 104, 39–42.

655. STONE, B. G. Relationship between creativity and classroom behavior. *Psychology in the Schools*, 1980, 17, 106–108.

656. BINIK, Y. M., FAINSILBER, L., & SPEVACK, M. Obsessionality and creativity. *Canadian Journal of Behavioural Science*, 1981, 13, 25–32.

657. HARRISON, J., STRAUSS, H., & GLAUBMAN, R. The impact of open and traditional classrooms on achievement and creativity: The Israeli case. *Elementary School Journal*, 1981, 82, 27–35.

658. HARRISON, J., STRAUSS, H., & GLAUBMAN, R. Who benefits from the open classroom? The interaction of social background with class setting. *Journal of Educational Research*, 1981, 75, 87–94.

659. LEHMAN, J. D., KAHLE, J. B., & NORDLAND, F. Cognitive development and creativity: A study in two high schools. *Science Education*, 1981, 65, 197–206.

660. MARTIN, J. D., BLAIR, G. E., & HERRMANN, W. J. Correlations between scores on Torrance Tests of Creative Thinking and ingenuity subtest of the Flanagan Aptitude Classification Tests. *Psychological Reports*, 1981, 48, 195–198.

661. NEWLAND, G. A. Differences between left– and right–handers on a measure of creativity. *Perceptual & Motor Skills*, 1981, 53, 787–792.

662. RHODES, J. W. Relationships between vividness of mental imagery and creative thinking. *Journal of Creative Behavior*, 1981, 15, 90–98.

663. SHYMANSKY, J. A., & PENICK, J. E. Teacher behavior does make a difference in hands–on science classrooms. *School Science & Mathematics*, 1981, 81, 412–422.

664. STRAUSS, H., HADAR, M., SHAVIT, H., & ITSKOWITZ, R. Relationship between creativity, repression, and anxiety in first graders. *Perceptual & Motor Skills*, 1981, 53, 275–282.

665. TAN-WILLMAN, C., & GUTTERIDGE, D. Creative thinking and moral reasoning of academically gifted secondary school adolescents. *Gifted Child Quarterly*, 1981, 25, 149–153.
666. THOMAS, N. G., & BERK, L. E. Effects of school environments on the development of young children's creativity. *Child Development*, 1981, 52, 1153–1162.
667. TORRANCE, E. P. Predicting the creativity of elementary school children (1958–80)–And the teacher who "made a difference." *Gifted Child Quarterly*, 1981, 25, 55–62.

[2513]

The Toy World Test. Ages 2 and over; 1941–55; TWT; formerly called *The World Test*; Charlotte Buhler; Centre de Psychologie Appliquee [France].*

See T2:1523 (1 reference) and P:488 (1 reference); for a review by L. Joseph Stone, see 5:168 (11 references); see also 4:147 (6 references).

[2514]

*****TRACOR Audiometers.** Grades kgn and over; 1955–82; Tracor, Inc.*

a) TRACOR RA 410S: MICRO-AUTOMATED SYSTEM. For pure tone air conduction testing; can be tied into a computer or overall health information system.

b) TRACOR-RUDMOSE ARJ4C. Automatically records pure tone air conduction threshold responses; for testing in industrial hearing conservation programs.

c) TRACOR-RUDMOSE RA206: CLINICAL BEKESY AUDIOMETER. Automatic and manual; continuous or pulsed air or bone conduction.

d) TRACOR-RUDMOSE RA226: DIAGNOSTIC SPEECH AUDIOMETER. Manual; continuous or pulsed air or bone conduction; speech testing can be either live or recorded.

e) TRACOR-RUDMOSE MANUAL AUDIOMETERS. For use in clinics, hospitals, industry, and schools; 3 models:

1) *RA214: Monitoring.* For air conduction testing.

2) *RA215: Diagnostic.* For air and bone conduction testing.

3) *RA216: Speech.* For live or recorded speech air and bone conduction testing.

f) TRACOR RA115 CLINICAL AUDIOMETER. For pure tone (air and bone conduction) and live or recorded speech testing in hospitals, clinics, and medical offices; 2 models: RA115A (table model), RA115A (console).

g) TRACOR RA208: COMPLIANCE AUDIOMETER. Performs middle ear analysis; pure tone air conduction testing.

For reference to earlier models, see T2:2058.

[2515]

Trait Evaluation Index. College and adults; 1967–68; TEI; 22 scores (social orientation, compliance, benevolence, elation, ambition, motivational drive, self confidence, dynamism, independence, personal adequacy, caution, self organization, responsibility, propriety, courtesy, verbal orientation, intellectual orientation, perception, self control, fairmindedness, adaptability, sincerity), plus 4 general supplementary scores (overall adjustment, masculinity, femininity, consistency) and 3 supplementary scores for engineers (employment stability, productivity-creativity, job satisfaction); Alan R. Nelson; Martin M. Bruce, Ph.D., Publishers.*

See T2:1424 (1 reference); for reviews by Harold Borko and Jacob Cohen, see 7:155 (1 reference).

[2516]

*****Transactional Analysis Life Position Survey.** Ages 18 and over; 1976; TALPS; 2 scores: I'm OK, you're OK; Frederick D. Kramer and Bruce W. Strade; Monitor.*

For additional information, see 8:699.

[2517]

★**Transitional Assessment.** Students transfering from primary to secondary schools; 1978; also called *Transitional Assessment Modules*; 2 parts: Math (numbers, addition, subtraction, multiplication, division, properties of the four operations − × ÷ +, shapes, ratio, proportion and percentage, money, problems), English (autobiographical, descriptive, explanatory, story-writing, sentence-writing, punctuation, "cloze" technique, reading comprehension); NFER-Nelson and the Hillingdon Education Authority; NFER-Nelson Publishing Co. [England].*

[2518]

Traxler High School Reading Test, Revised. Grades 10–12; 1938–67; 5 scores: rate, story comprehension, main ideas, total comprehension, total; Arthur E. Traxler; Bobbs-Merrill Co., Inc.*

See T2:1610 (3 references); for a review by Robert A. Forsyth, see 7:712; for a review by Harold D. Carter, see 4:559 (4 references); for reviews by Alvin C. Eurich, Constance M. McCullough, and C. Gilbert Wrenn, and excerpted reviews by E. L. Abell and J. Wayne Wrightstone, see 2:1578.

[2519]

Traxler High School Spelling Test. Grades 9–12; 1937–55; Arthur E. Traxler; Bobbs-Merrill Co., Inc.*

For additional information and a review by Gus P. Plessas, see 6:326; for a review by Henry D. Rinsland, see 4:212.

[2520]

Traxler Silent Reading Test. Grades 7–10; 1934–69; 6 scores: reading rate, story comprehension, word meaning, paragraph meaning, total comprehension, total; Arthur E. Traxler; Bobbs-Merrill Co., Inc.*

See T2:1611 (1 reference); for a review by William E. Coffman, see 7:713; for a review by J. Thomas Hastings, see 4:560 (2 references); for reviews by Robert L. McCaul and Miles A. Tinker and an excerpted review by J. Wayne Wrightstone, see 2:1579 (3 references); for reviews by Frederick B. Davis and Spencer Shank, see 1:1114.

[2521]

★**Tree•Bee Test of Auditory Discrimination.** Ages 3 and over; 1978; norm-referenced and criterion-referenced; item scores in 8 areas: initial consonants, final consonants, vowels, memory, words, sentences, pairs, comprehension; Janet B. Fudala; Academic Therapy Publications.*

[2522]

The Tree Test. Ages 9 and over; 1949–52; Charles Koch; Hans Huber [Switzerland].*

For additional information, see P:489 (3 references); see also 5:170 (2 references).

[2523]
Tressler English Minimum Essentials Test, Revised Edition. Grades 8–12; 1932–56; 8 scores: grammatical correctness, vocabulary, punctuation and capitalization, the sentence and its parts, sentence sense, inflection and accent, spelling, total; J. C. Tressler; Bobbs-Merrill Co., Inc.*

For additional information and reviews by Osmond E. Palmer and Roger A. Richards, see 6:286 (1 reference).

[2524]
Triadal Equated Personality Inventory. Adult males; 1960–63; TEPI; 22 scores: dominance, self confidence, decisiveness, independence, toughness, suspiciousness, conscientiousness, introversion, restlessness, solemnity, foresight, industriousness, warmth, enthusiasm, conformity, inventiveness, persistence, sex drive, recognition drive, cooperativeness, humility-tolerance, self-control; Research Staff, United Consultants; Psychometric Affiliates.*

For additional information and a review by Jacob Cohen, see 7:156.

[2525]
Trigonometry: Minnesota High School Achievement Examinations. High school; 1961–70; a new, revised, or previously inactive form issued each May; Midwest High School Achievement Examinations used as series title in 1961; edited by V. L. Lohmann; American Guidance Service.*

For additional information concerning earlier forms, see 7:544 and 6:658.

[2526]
Twitchell-Allen Three-Dimensional Personality Test. Ages 3 and over (sighted and sightless); 1948–60; TA3DPT; formerly called *Twitchell-Allen Three-Dimensional Test*; Doris Twitchell-Allen; the Author.*

For additional information, see P:490 (2 references); see also 5:171 (3 references); for a review by Edward Joseph Shoben, Jr., see 4:143.

[2527]
Typewriting Test: National Business Entrance Tests. Grades 11–16 and adults; 1941–72; earlier tests called *Typing Ability Test*; National Business Education Association.* (In-print status uncertain; no reply from publisher.)

For additional information and a review by Leonard J. West, see 8:329; see also T2:799 (1 reference); for a review by Lawrence W. Erickson of earlier forms, see 6:55 (1 reference); for a review by Clifford E. Jurgensen, see 5:526; for reviews by E. G. Blackstone and Beatrice J. Dvorak, see 3:394. For reviews of the complete battery, see 6:33 (1 review), 5:515 (3 reviews), and 3:396 (1 review).

[2528]
Typing Skill. Typists; 1952–71; formerly called *Test for Typing Skill*; Edward N. Hay; E. F. Wonderlic & Associates, Inc.*

For additional information and a review by Bernadine Meyer, see 5:523.

[2529]
Typing Test for Business. Applicants for typing positions; 1967–68; TTB; 5 tests plus practice test (*a*); distribution restricted to personnel departments; The Psychological Corporation (test), Jerome E. Doppelt (manual), Arthur D. Hartman (manual), and Fay B. Krawchick (manual); The Psychological Corporation.*
a) PRACTICE COPY.
b) STRAIGHT COPY. 2 scores: speed, accuracy.
c) LETTERS.
d) REVISED MANUSCRIPT.
e) NUMBERS.
f) TABLES.

For additional information and reviews by Mary T. Harrison and Leonard J. West, see 7:1007.

[2530]
Understanding Communication (Verbal Comprehension). Industrial employees at the skilled level or below; 1959, c1956–59; Thelma G. Thurstone and Measurement Research Division, Human Resources Center, University of Chicago; the Center.*

See T2:1747 (1 reference); for reviews by C. E. Jurgensen and Donald E. P. Smith, see 6:840.

[2531]
Understanding in Science Test. Grades 7–9; 1975; experimental form; categorization into one of 4 Piagetian stages: early concrete (0–29 percent of possible score), late concrete (32–56 percent), early formal (56–76 percent), late formal (79–100 percent); R. P. Tisher and L. G. Dale; Australian Council for Educational Research [Australia].*

For additional information, see 8:861.

REFERENCES
1. HILL, D. M., & OBENAUF, P. A. Spatial visualization, problem solving, and cognitive development in freshman teacher education students. *Science Education*, 1979, 63, 665–670.
2. BLAKE, A. J. D. The predictive power of two written tests of Piagetian developmental level. *Journal of Research in Science Teaching*, 1980, 17, 435–441.

[2532]
★**Uniform Performance Assessment System.** All ages with developmental level birth to 6 years; 1981; UPAS; designed to monitor the progress of individuals who are learning skills normally acquired between birth and age 6; criterion-referenced; 5 subtests: pre-academic, communication, social/self-help, gross motor, inappropriate behaviors; Norris G. Haring, Owen R. White, Eugene B. Edgar, James Q. Affleck, and Alice H. Hayden; Charles E. Merrill Publishing Co.*

[2533]
United Students Typewriting Tests, Volume 14. 1, 2, 3, 4 semesters; 1932–58; Committee on Tests, UBEA Research Foundation; National Business Education Association.* (In-print status uncertain; no reply from publisher.)

For additional information, see 5:527.

[2534]
University Residence Environment Scale. Students in university living groups; 1974, URES; a part of *The Social Climate Scales* (2227); 10 scores: involvement, emotional support, independence, traditional social orien-

tation, competition, academic achievement, intellectuality, order and organization, student influence, innovation; Marvin S. Gerst and Rudolf H. Moos; Consulting Psychologists Press, Inc.*

For additional information and reviews by Fred H. Borgen and James V. Mitchell, Jr., see 8:700 (12 references). For a review of *The Social Climate Scales*, see 8:681.

REFERENCES

1–12. See 8:700.
13. RICHMAN, J. M. Homogenous housing: A transfer student adjustment program. *NASPA Journal*, 1979, 17, 43–48.
14. SCHROEDER, C. C., WARNER, R., & MALONE, D. R. Effects of assignment to living units by personality types on environmental perceptions and student development. *Journal of College Student Personnel*, 1980, 21, 443–449.
15. WINSTON, R. B., JR., HUTSON, G. S., & MCCAFFREY, S. S. Environmental influences on fraternity academic achievement. *Journal of College Student Personnel*, 1980, 21, 449–455.

[2535]

USES Basic Occupational Literacy Test. Educationally disadvantaged adults; 1971–74; BOLT; 5 tests; 3–4 levels; orders for test materials must be cleared through appropriate State Employment Security agency; developed and published by the United States Employment Service; manual, information brochure, DOT supplements, record card, and pretesting orientation booklet distributed by United States Government Printing Office; tests, answer sheets, and scoring stencils distributed by Intran Corporation.*

a) WIDE-RANGE SCALE. Screening test to determine appropriate level of BOLT to administer; 2 scores: vocabulary, arithmetic.
b) READING VOCABULARY. 4 levels: Fundamental, Basic Intermediate, High Intermediate, Advanced.
c) READING COMPREHENSION. 4 levels same as in *b*.
d) ARITHMETIC COMPUTATION. 4 levels same as in *b*.
e) ARITHMETIC REASONING. 3 levels: Fundamental, Intermediate, Advanced.

For additional information and reviews by Lee J. Cronbach and Bruce W. Tuckman, see 8:489.

[2536]

USES Clerical Skills Tests. Applicants for clerical positions; 1968; 6 tests; distribution restricted to State Employment Services affiliated with the United States Employment Service; published by United States Employment Service and distributed by United States Government Printing Office.*

a) TYPING TEST. 2 scores: speed, accuracy.
b) DICTATION TEST.
c) SPELLING TEST.
d) STATISTICAL TYPING TEST. 2 scores: speed, accuracy.
e) MEDICAL SPELLING TEST.
f) LEGAL SPELLING TEST.

For additional information, see 7:1009 (1 reference).

[2537]

***USES General Aptitude Test Battery.** Grades 9–12 and adults; 1946–82; GATB; for a nonreading adaptation, see *USES Nonreading Aptitude Test Battery*; orders for tests must be cleared through a State Employment Service office; developed and published by the United States Employment Service for use in its occupational counseling program and released by State Employment Services for use in other organizations; test booklets and manuals distributed by United States Government Printing Office and by Intran Corporation; apparatus tests (Pegboard and Finger Dexterity Board) distributed by Specialty Case Manufacturing Co. and Warwick Products Co.*

a) SCREENING AND PRETESTING EXERCISES. 1966–73.
1) *GATB-NATB Screening Device.* 1966–73; consists of the Wide-Range Scale of the *USES Basic Occupational Literacy Test*; to identify examinees who are deficient in reading skills and should be tested with the *USES Nonreading Aptitude Test Battery*.
2) *USES Pretesting Orientation Exercises.* 1968; test-taking practice for disadvantaged persons.
b) GATB, B–1002. Grades 9–12 and adults; 1952–82; 9 scores: intelligence, verbal, numerical, spatial, form perception, clerical perception, motor coordination, finger dexterity, manual dexterity; 12 tests: 8 paper and pencil tests plus 4 performance tests; (Spanish edition available).
1) *Book 1.* Forms A, B, C, D; 4 tests: name comparison, computation, three-dimensional space, vocabulary. F5
2) *Book 2.* Forms A, B, C, D; 3 tests: tool matching, arithmetic reasoning, form matching.
3) *Part 8 [Mark Making].*
4) *Pegboard.* 2 tests: place, turn.
5) *Finger Dexterity Board.* 2 tests: assemble, disassemble.

For additional information, see 8:490 (96 references); see also T2:1073 (45 references); for a review by David J. Weiss, see 7:676 (138 references); for reviews by Harold P. Bechtoldt and John B. Carroll of earlier forms, see 6:771 (55 references); for reveiws by Andrew L. Comrey, Clifford P. Froehlich, and Lloyd G. Humphreys, see 5:609 (176 references); for reviews by Milton L. Blum, Edward B. Greene, and Howard R. Taylor, see 4:714 (33 references).

REFERENCES

1–33. See 4:714.
34–209. See 5:609.
210–264. See 6:771.
265–402. See 7:676.
403–447. See T2:1073.
448–543. See 8:490.
544. ANDERSON, B. L. Schizophrenic performance during interpersonal competitive conditions. *Journal of Clinical Psychology*, 1977, 33, 970–972.
545. BACHMAN, J. G., & O'MALLEY, P. M. Self–esteem in young men: A longitudinal analysis of the impact of educational and occupational attainment. *Journal of Personality & Social Psychology*, 1977, 35, 365–380.
546. DUNHAM, R. B. Relationships of perceived job design characteristics to job ability requirement and job value. *Journal of Applied Psychology*, 1977, 62, 760–763.
547. GETSINGER, S. H. Ego-delay and vocational behavior. *Journal of Personality Assessment*, 1977, 41, 91–95.
548. KNAPP, R. R., KNAPP, L., & MICHAEL, W. B. Stability and concurrent validity of the career Ability Placement Survey (APS) against the DAT and the GATB. *Educational & Psychological Measurement*, 1977, 37, 1081–1085.
549. MALATESTA, C. Z., CIRCO, J., & SMITH, B. A discriminating, non–discriminatory test battery for a prison population. *Corrective & Social Psychiatry & Journal of Behavior Technology, Methods & Therapy*, 1977, 23, 15–17.
550. STAVIG, G. R. The semistandardized regression coefficient. *Multivariate Behavioral Research*, 1977, 12, 255–258.
551. TINSLEY, H. E. A., & TINSLEY, D. J. Different needs, interests, and abilities of effective and ineffective counselor trainees: Implications for counselor selection. *Journal of Counseling Psychology*, 1977, 24, 83–86.
552. HAKSTIAN, A. R., & BENNET, R. W. Validity studies using the Comprehensive Ability Battery (CAB): II. Relationships with the DAT and GATB. *Educational & Psychological Measurement*, 1978, 38, 1003–1015.
553. KLEIN, F. Uses of the General Aptitude Test Battery to predict success on the tests of General Educational Development. *Journal of Employment Counseling*, 1978, 15, 29–36.
554. KNAPP, L., KNAPP, R. R., STRAND, L., & MICHAEL, W. B. Comparative validity of the Career Ability Placement Survey (CAPS) and

the General Aptitude Test Battery (GATB) for predicting high school course marks. *Educational & Psychological Measurement*, 1978, 38, 1053–1056.

555. FISCHER, D. G., & SOBKOW, J. Workers' estimation of ability requirements of their jobs. *Perceptual & Motor Skills*, 1979, 48, 519–531.

556. GUERETLE, J. L., & NADEAU, G. G. Revised guidance testing program in five New Brunswick school districts: Justification for a three-year study. *School Guidance Worker*, 1979, 34, 19–24.

557. GUTERMAN, S. S. IQ tests in research on social stratification. The cross–class validity of the tests as measures of scholastic aptitude. *Sociology of Education*, 1979, 52, 163–173.

558. MCCORMICK, E. J., DENISI, A. S., & SHAW, J. B. Use of the Position Analysis Questionnaire for establishing the job component validity of tests. *Journal of Applied Psychology*, 1979, 64, 51–56.

559. SMITH, S. M. Standardized tests used in correctional institutions. *Journal of Employment Counseling*, 1979, 16, 178–188.

560. WILSON, K. L. The effects of integration and class on black educational attainment. *Sociology of Education*, 1979, 52, 84–98.

561. BOOTH, J. A. G., & LAURIN–DUMAS, M. S. The use of self-estimates aptitudes in employment counseling. *Canadian Counsellor*, 1980, 15, 25–30.

562. CHAMPAGNE, D., & QUERY, J. M. N. Urban education and training for American Indian students. *Urban Education*, 1980, 15, 93–101.

563. CORNELIUS, E. T., III, & LYNESS, K. S. A comparison of holistic and decomposed judgment strategies in job analysis by job incumbents. *Journal of Applied Psychology*, 1980, 65, 155–163.

564. DIAMOND, E. E. The AMEG commission report on sex bias in achievement testing. *Measurement & Evaluation in Guidance*, 1980, 13, 135–147.

565. WATTS, F., & EVERITT, B. S. The factorial structure of the General Aptitude Test Battery. *Journal of Clinical Psychology*, 1980, 36, 763–767.

566. BRISCOE, C. D., MUELDER, W., & MICHAEL, W. B. The concurrent validity of self–estimates of abilities relative to criteria provided by standardized test measures of the same abilities for a sample of high school students eligible for participation in the CETA program. *Educational & Psychological Measurement*, 1981, 41, 1285–1294.

[2538]

★USES Interest Inventory. Grade 12 and adults; 1981; II; 12 scores: artistic, scientific, plants and animals, protective, mechanical, industrial, business detail, selling, accommodating, humanitarian, leading-influencing, physical performing; orders for tests must be cleared through a State Employment Service office; developed and published by the United States Employment Service for use in its occupational counseling program and released by State Employment Services for use in other organizations; materials distributed by United States Government Printing Office and Intran Corporation.*

[2539]

*USES Nonreading Aptitude Test Battery, 1982 Edition. Disadvantaged grades 9–12 and adults; 1965–82; NATB; nonreading adaptation of the *USES General Aptitude Test Battery*; 9 scores: intelligence, verbal, numerical, spatial, form perception, clerical perception, motor coordination, finger dexterity, manual dexterity; 1 pretest exercise and 11 tests: 7 paper and pencil tests plus 4 performance tests; orders for test materials must be cleared through a State Employment Service office; developed and published by the United States Employment Service for use in its occupational counseling program and released by State Employment Services for use in other organizations; manuals, record and norms cards, and GATB Part 8 distributed by State Employment Services; apparatus tests (Pegboard and Finger Dexterity Board) distributed by Specialty Case Manufacturing Co. and Warwick Products Co.*

a) GATB-NATB SCREENING DEVICE. 1972–73; consists of the Wide-Range Scale of the *USES Basic Occupational Literacy Test*; to identify examinees sufficiently skilled in reading and arithmetic to be tested with the *USES General Aptitude Test Battery*.

b) USES NONREADING APTITUDE TEST BATTERY (NATB).
1) *NATB Pretest* (optional). Number Comparison.
2) *Book 1.* 3 tests: oral vocabulary, number comparison, design completion.
3) *Book 2.* 3 tests: tool matching, three-dimensional space, form matching.
4) *Part 8 [Mark Making].*
5) *Pegboard.* 2 tests: place, turn.
6) *Finger Dexterity Board.* 2 tests: assemble, disassemble.

For additional information, a review by Bruce W. Tuckman, and an excerpted review by Victor Stecker, see 8:491 (5 references); see also 7:679 (3 references).

REFERENCES

1–3. See 7:679.
4–8. See 8:491.
9. HUBER, C. H. Career planning with mildly retarded students: A model for school counselors. *Vocational Guidance Quarterly*, 1979, 27, 223–229.
10. WATKINS, M. W. Intellectual and special aptitudes of tenth grade EMH students. *Education & Training of the Mentally Retarded*, 1979, 15, 139–142.

[2540]

Uses Test. Ages 11–13; 1974; cross-cultural differences in values; for measurement of groups only; 8 scores: sustentative, benevolent, malevolent, hedonistic, esthetic, religious, hierarchical, not scorable; Wayne Dennis; Psychological Test Specialists.*

For additional information, see 8:701 (15 references).

[2541]

Utah Test of Language Development, Revised Edition. Ages 1.5 to 14.5; 1958–67; UTLD; formerly called *Utah Verbal Language Development Scale*; a "direct-test" revision of the "informant-interview" *Verbal Language Development Scale*; Merlin J. Mecham, J. Lorin Jex, and J. Dean Jones; Communication Research Associates, Inc.*

See T2:2097 (4 references); for reviews by Katharine G. Butler and William H. Perkins, see 7:973.

REFERENCES

1–4. See T2:2097.
5. HARDMAN, M. L. A functional administrative teaching model for academic programming with the trainable mentally retarded. *Education & Training of the Mentally Retarded*, 1978, 13, 23–28.
6. MASTERS, L., & MARSH, G. E., II. Middle ear pathology as a factor in learning disabilities. *Journal of Learning Disabilities*, 1978, 11, 103–106.
7. HOWARD-PEEBLES, P. N., & MARKITON, R. I. A tetra-x female, cytogenetic testing, dermatoglyphic studies, and speech impairment. *American Journal of Mental Deficiency*, 1979, 84, 252–255.
8. STECKOL, K. F., & LEONARD, L. B. The use of grammatical morphemes by normal and language–impaired children. *Journal of Communication Disorders*, 1979, 12, 291–301.
9. STEWART, J. M., MARTIN, M. E., & BRADY, G. M. Communicative disorders at a health–care center. *Journal of Communication Disorders*, 1979, 12, 349–359.

[2542]

VALCAN Vocational Interest Profile (VIP). Ages 15 and over; 1960–61; title on manual and profile is *PSYCAN Vocational Interest Profile*; formerly called *WIPCO Vocational Interest Profile*; 9 scores: numerical, mechanical, scientific, clerical, persuasive, musical, literary, artistic, service; R. N. Smith and J. R. McIntosh; distributed by University of British Columbia Bookstore [Canada].* (In-print status uncertain; no reply from publisher.)

For additional information, see 6:1072.

[2543]
Valett Developmental Survey of Basic Learning Abilities. Ages 2–7; 1966; largely a selection and adaptation of items from many scales, particularly the *Gesell Developmental Schedules*; 7 areas of development: motor integration and physical development, tactile discrimination, auditory discrimination, visual-motor coordination, visual discrimination, language development and verbal fluency, conceptual development; Robert E. Valett; Consulting Psychologists Press, Inc.*

See T2:991 (1 reference); for reviews by Lester Mann and Roger A. Ruth, see 7:767 (2 references).

[2544]
★**Valett Inventory of Critical Thinking Abilities.** Ages 4–5, 6–7, 8–9, 10–11, 12–15; 1981; VICTA; ratings by teachers or counselors; "criterion-referenced"; measures level of critical thinking at which a child is functioning; ratings in 10 areas: imagination, evaluation, humor, application, comprehension, synthesis, verbal concepts, calculation, analysis, knowledge; 5 levels; Robert E. Valett; Academic Therapy Publications.*
a) LEVEL 1. Sensory-Perceptual Exploration.
b) LEVEL 2. Intuitive Organization.
c) LEVEL 3. Concrete Relationships.
d) LEVEL 4. Representational Concepts.
e) LEVEL 5. Propositional Logic.

[2545]
★**Values Inventory.** Managers and students of management; 1978; VI; 6 scales: theoretical, power, achievement, human, industry, financial; W. J. Reddin and Ken Rowell; Organizational Tests Ltd. [Canada].*

[2546]
Values Inventory for Children. Grades 1–7; 1976; VIC; 7 scores: asocial, social conformity, me first, sociability, academic, masculinity, adult closeness; Joan S. Guilford, Willa Gupta, and Lisbeth Goldberg; Sheridan Psychological Services, Inc.*

For additional information and a review by Anne Anastasi, see 8:702 (3 references).

[2547]
The Vane Evaluation of Language Scale. Ages 2.5 to 6.5; 1975; VELS; also called VANE-L; language acquisition; 3 scores: receptive language, expressive language, memory; Julia R. Vane; Clinical Psychology Publishing Co., Inc.*

For additional information and a review by Robert L. Rosenbaum, see 8:980 (1 reference).

[2548]
Vane Kindergarten Test. Ages 4–6; 1968; VKT; 4 scores: perceptual motor, vocabulary, drawing a man, total; Julia R. Vane; Clinical Psychology Publishing Co., Inc.*

See T2:528 (7 references); for reviews by Dorothy H. Eichorn and Marcel L. Goldschmid, see 7:428 (3 references).

REFERENCES
1–3. See 7:428.
4–10. See T2:528.
11. POWERS, S. M. The Vane Kindergarten Test: Temporal stability and ability to predict behavioral criteria. *Psychology in the Schools*, 1977, 14, 34–36.
12. PRAWAT, R. S., & HANES, B. F. Sentence comprehension as a function of conservation, age, and IQ. *Child Study Journal*, 1977, 8, 43–53.
13. PRAWAT, R. S., & JONES, H. A longitudinal study of language development in children at different levels of cognitive development. *Merrill–Palmer Quarterly*, 1977, 23, 115–120.
14. DUBE, G. G., & RUDOLF, J. A. Performance of black head start children on the Vane Kindergarten Test and the Stanford–Binet as related to age and sex variables. *Journal of Clinical Psychology*, 1978, 34, 431–437.

[2549]
Vasectomy Scale: Attitudes. Older adolescents and adults; 1974; no manual; Panos D. Bardis; the Author.*

For additional information, see 8:357.

[2550]
Verbal Auditory Screening for Children. Ages 3–6; 1964–71; VASC; for the detection of preschool children requiring "more specialized diagnostic testing"; Zenetron, Inc.* (In-print status uncertain; no reply from publisher.)

For additional information and a review by Charles V. Anderson, see 8:951 (4 references); see also T2:2059 (1 reference) and 7:947 (6 references).

REFERENCES
1–6. See 7:947.
7. See T2:2059.
8–11. See 8:951.
12. MULAC, A., & TOMLINSON, C. N. Generalization of an operant remediation program for syntax with language delayed children. *Journal of Communication Disorders*, 1977, 10, 231–243.

[2551]
Verbal Language Development Scale. Birth to age 15; 1958–71; VLDS; extension of the communication section of *Vineland Social Maturity Scale*; behavior checklist for use in interviewing adult informants; Merlin J. Mecham; American Guidance Service.*

See T2:2098 (4 references); for reviews by Katharine G. Butler and William H. Perkins, see 7:974 (1 reference); see also 6:316 (7 references).

REFERENCES
1–7. See 6:316.
8. See 7:974.
9–12. See T2:2098.
13. ERNHART, C. B., SPANER, S. D., & JORDAN, T. E. Validity of selected preschool screening tests. *Contemporary Educational Psychology*, 1977, 2, 78–89.
14. DOYLE, A. B., & SOMERS, K. The effects of group and family day care on infant attachment behaviors. *Canadian Journal of Behavioural Science*, 1978, 10, 38–45.
15. KATOFF, L., & REUTER, J. Review of developmental screening tests for infants. *Journal of Clinical Child Psychology*, 1980, 9, 30–34.
16. FINER, N. N., ROBERTSON, C. M., RICHARDS, R. T., PINNELL, L. E., & PETERS, K. L. Hypoxic–ischemic encephalopathy in term neonates: Perinatal factors and outcome. *Journal of Pediatrics*, 1981, 98, 112–117.

[2552]
The Verbal Power Test of Concept Equivalence. Ages 14 and over; 1959–63; VPT; E. Francesco; Western Psychological Services.*

See T2:471 (3 references); for a review by Erwin K. Taylor, see 7:394; see also 6:508 (3 references).

[2553]
Verbal Reasoning. Job applicants and industrial employees; 1958–61; Raymond J. Corsini, Richard Renck, and Measurement Research Division, Human Resources Center, University of Chicago (manual); the Center.*

For additional information and reviews by James E. Kennedy and David G. Ryans, see 6:509.

REFERENCES

1. ZEDECK, S., & KAFRY, D. Capturing rater policies for processing evaluation data. *Organizational Behavior & Human Performance*, 1977, 18, 269-294.

[2554]
*Verbal Reasoning: Differential Aptitude Tests.

Grades 8-12 and adults; 1947-77; George K. Bennett, Harold G. Seashore, and Alexander G. Wesman; The Psychological Corporation.* For the complete battery entry, see 732.

For additional information regarding an earlier edition, see 8:186; see also T2:473 (12 references). For reviews of the complete battery, see 8:485 (2 reviews, 1 excerpt), 7:673 (1 review, 1 excerpt), 6:767 (2 reviews), 5:605 (2 reviews), 4:711 (3 reviews), and 3:620 (1 excerpt).

REFERENCES

1-12. See T2:473.
13. ARNOLD, P., & WALTER, G. Communication and reasoning skills of deaf and hearing signers. *Perceptual & Motor Skills*, 1979, 49, 192-194.
14. COOPERMAN, E. W. Field differentiation and intelligence. *Journal of Psychology*, 1980, 105, 29-33.
15. STERNBERG, R. J., & WEIL, E. M. An aptitude x strategy interaction in linear syllogistic reasoning. *Journal of Educational Psychology*, 1980, 72, 226-239.

[2555]
Veterinary Aptitude Test.

Veterinary school applicants; 1951-73; VAT; tests administered at centers established by the publisher; 5 scores: reading comprehension, quantitative ability, science information, verbal memory, total; original test by William A. Owens and Loyal C. Payne; The Psychological Corporation.*

See T2:2358 (1 reference), 7:1101, 6:1139 (3 references), and 5:957 (3 references).

[2556]
Vincent Mechanical Diagrams Test.

Ages 15 and over; 1936-70 VMD; based upon *The Vincent Mechanical Models Test A*; subtest of *N.I.I.P. Engineering Apprentice Selection Test Battery*; National Institute of Industrial Psychology; NFER-Nelson Publishing Co. [England].*

For additional information, see 7:1058.

[2557]
Vineland Social Maturity Scale.

Birth to maturity; 1935-65; VSMS; Edgar A. Doll; American Guidance Service.*

For additional information, see 8:703 (23 references); see also T2:1428 (50 references), P:281 (21 references), 6:194 (20 references), and 5:120 (15 references); for reviews by William M. Cruickshank and Florence M. Teagarden, see 4:94 (21 references); for reviews by C. M. Louttit and John W. M. Rothney and an excerpted review, see 3:107 (58 references); for reviews by Paul H. Furfey, Elaine F. Kinder, and Anna S. Starr, see 1:1143.

REFERENCES

1-58. See 3:107.
59-79. See 4:94.
80-94. See 5:120.
95-114. See 6:194.
115-135. See P:281.
136-185. See T2:1428.
186-208. See 8:703.
209. BELL, A. E., Abrahamson, D. S., & McRae, K. N. Reading retardation: A 12-year prospective study. *Journal of Pediatrics*, 1977, 91, 363-370.
210. BENNETT, V. C., & BARDON, J. I. The effects of a school program on teenage mothers and their children. *American Journal of Orthopsychiatry*, 1977, 47, 671-678.
211. BEVERIDGE, M., & MITTLER, P. Feedback, language and listener performance in severely retarded children. *British Journal of Disorders of Communication*, 1977, 12, 149-157.
212. CLOSE, D. W. Community living for severely and profoundly retarded adults: A group home study. *Education & Training of the Mentally Retarded*, 1977, 12, 256-262.
213. GOULD, J. The use of the Vineland Social Maturity Scale, the Merrill–Palmer Scale of Mental Tests (non–verbal items) and the Reynell Developmental Language Scales with children in contact with the services for severe mental retardation. *Journal of Mental Deficiency Research*, 1977, 21, 213-226.
214. HASLAM, R. H. A., ALLEN, J. R., DORSEN, M. M., KANOFSKY, D. L., MELLITS, E. D., & NORRIS, D. A. The sequelae of group B β-hemolytic streptococcal meningitis in early infancy. *American Journal of Diseases of Children*, 1977, 131, 845-849.
215. KAY, S. R. Developmental assessment of cognitive style in mentally retarded psychotics. *Journal of Clinical Psychology*, 1977, 33, 953-958.
216. MCCORMICK, D. P. Pediatric evaluation of children with school problems. *American Journal of Diseases of Children*, 1977, 131, 318-322.
217. MEDNICK, B. Intellectual and behavioral functioning of ten- to twelve-year-old children who showed certain transient symptoms in the neonatal period. *Child Development*, 1977, 48, 844-853.
218. SANCHEZ, O., MAMUNES, P., & YUNIS, J. J. Partial trisomy 20 (20q13) and partial trisomy 21 (21pter→21q21.3) *Journal of Medical Genetics*, 1977, 14, 459-462.
219. ANNIS, L. V. Social age score: Stability among profoundly retarded, institutionalized adults. *Perceptual & Motor Skills*, 1978, 46, 206.
220. DAVIDSON, P. W., WILLOUGHBY, R. H., O'TUAMA, L. A., SWISHER, C. N., & BENJAMINS, D. Neurological and intellectual sequelae of Reye's Syndrome. *American Journal of Mental Deficiency*, 1978, 82, 535-541.
221. ESON, M. E., YEN, J. K., & BOURKE, R. S. Assessment of recovery from serious head injury. *Journal of Neurology, Neurosurgery, & Psychiatry*, 1978, 41, 1036-1042.
222. HALL, P. K., & TOMBLIN, J. B. A follow-up study of children with articulation and language disorders. *Journal of Speech & Hearing Disorders*, 1978, 43, 227-241.
223. MARHOLIN, D., II, POHL, R. E., III, STEWART, R. M., TOUCHETTE, P. E., TOWNSEND, N. M., & KOLODNY, E. H. Effects of diet and behavior therapy on social and motor behavior of retarded phenylketonuric adults: An experimental analysis. *Pediatric Research*, 1978, 12, 179-187.
224. OIKAWA, K., DEONAUTH, J., & BREIDBART, S. Mental retardation and elevated serontonin levels in adults. *Life Sciences*, 1978, 23, 45-48.
225. BEVERIDGE, M., SPENCER, J., & MITTLER, P. Self-blame and communication failure in retarded adolescents. *Journal of Child Psychology & Psychiatry & Allied Disciplines*, 1979, 20, 129-138.
226. BONIFACE, D., & GRAHAM, P. The three-year-old and his attachment to a special soft object. *Journal of Child Psychology & Psychiatry & Allied Disciplines*, 1979, 20, 217-224.
227. BRUNNER, R. L., O'GRADY, D. J., PARTIN, J. C., PARTIN, J. S., & SCHUBERT, W. K. Neuropsychologic consequences of Reye Syndrome. *Journal of Pediatrics*, 1979, 95, 706-711.
228. HILLMAN, L. S., HILLMAN, R. E., & DODSON, W. E. Diagnosis, treatment, and follow-up of neonatal mepivacaine intoxication secondary to paracervical and pudenal blocks during labor. *Journal of Pediatrics*, 1979, 95, 472-477.
229. MCWILLIAMS, B. J., & MATTHEWS, H. P. A comparison of intelligence and social maturity in children with unilateral complete clefts and those with isolated cleft palates. *Cleft Palate Journal*, 1979, 16, 363-372.
230. PETHÖ, B., TOLNA, J., & TUSNÁDY, G. Multi-trait-multi-method assessment of predictive variables of outcome in schizophrenia spectrum disorders. A nosological evaluation. *Journal of Psychiatric Research*, 1979, 15, 163-174.
231. SEGAL, S., RUTMAN, J. Y., & FRIMPTER, G. W. Galactokinase deficiency and mental retardation. *Journal of Pediatrics*, 1979, 95, 750-752.
232. STODDEN, R. A., & LAZAR, A. L. The effects of treatment upon the relationship between vocational interest and vocational ability of the educable mentally retarded adolescent. *Education & Training of the Mentally Retarded*, 1979, 14, 251-256.
233. TEW, B. The "cocktail party syndrome" in children with hydrocephalus and spina bifida. *British Journal of Disorders of Communication*, 1979, 14, 89-101.
234. VENHAM, L. L., MURRAY, P., & GAULIN-KREMER, E. Personality factors affecting the preschool child's response to dental stress. *Journal of Dental Research*, 1979, 58, 2046-2051.
235. CONNOLLY, B., MORGAN, S., RUSSELL, F. F., & RICHARDSON, B. Early intervention with Down's syndrome children. *Physical Therapy*, 1980, 60, 1405-1408.

236. DANEMAN, D., & HOWARD, N. J. Neonatal thyrotoxicosis: Intellectual impairment and craniosynostosis in later years. *Journal of Pediatrics*, 1980, 97, 257-259.
237. KATOFF, L., & REUTER, J. Review of developmental screening tests for infants. *Journal of Clinical Child Psychology*, 1980, 9, 30-34.
238. KAY, S. R. Progressive figure drawings in the developmental assessment of mentally retarded psychotics. *Perceptual & Motor Skills*, 1980, 50, 583-590.
239. KLEECK, A. V., & CARPENTER, R. L. The effects of children's language comprehension level on adults' child-directed talk. *Journal of Speech & Hearing Research*, 1980, 23, 546-569.
240. KOOCHER, G. P., O'MALLEY, J. E., GOGAN, J. L., & FOSTER, D. J. Psychological adjustment among pediatric cancer survivors. *Journal of Child Psychology & Psychiatry & Allied Disciplines*, 1980, 21, 163-173.
241. ROSZKOWSKI, M. J. Concurrent validity of the Adaptive Behavior Scale as assessed by the Vineland Social Maturity Scale. *American Journal of Mental Deficiency*, 1980, 85, 86-89.
242. WILKINS, L. E., BROWN, J. A., & WOLF, B. Psychomotor development in 65 home-reared children with cri-du-chat syndrome. *Journal of Pediatrics*, 1980, 97, 401-405.
243. BUTLER, G. S., & RABINOWITZ, F. M. An investigation of factors contributing to the apparent overselective responding of mentally retarded children. *Child Development*, 1981, 52, 430-442.
244. CULLEN, S. M., CRONK, C. E., PUESCHEL, S. M., SCHNELL, R. R., & REED, R. Social development and feeding milestones of young Down's Syndrome children. *American Journal of Mental Deficiency*, 1981, 85, 410-415.
245. LAYTON, T. L., & HARDY, C. A. Semantic-syntactic relations in the oral speech of an autistic adolescent. *Journal of General Psychology*, 1981, 105, 323-324.
246. LUCCA, J. A., & SETTLES, B. H. Effects of children's disabilities on parental time use. *Physical Therapy*, 1981, 61, 196-201.

[2558]

A Violence Scale. Adolescents and adults; 1973; attitudes toward violence; Panos D. Bardis; the Author.*

For additional information, see 8:704 (1 reference).

[2559]

★**Visco Child Development Screening Test.** Ages 3-7; 1978-80; also called *ChilDSTest*; test includes parent report and observations by teacher and examiner; 13 scores: fine motor skills, gross motor skills, visual sequencing-body directions, auditory sequencing-body directions, copy figures, perceptuomotor-spatial directions, auditory sequencing, numerical counting, numerical gestalt, draw-a-picture, language, articulation, total; Susan J. Visco and Carmela R. Visco; Educational Activities, Inc.*

[2560]

★**The Visual Aural Digit Span Test.** Ages 5.5-12; 1977-78; VADS Test; 11 scores: aural-oral, visual-oral, aural-written, visual-written, aural input, visual input, oral expression, written expression, intrasensory integration, intersensory integration, total; Elizabeth M. Koppitz; Grune & Stratton, Inc.*

REFERENCES

1. KOPPITZ, E. M. The Bender Gestalt and VADS test performance of learning disabled middle school pupils. *Journal of Learning Disabilities*, 1981, 14, 96-98.
2. KOPPITZ, E. M. The Visual Aural Digit Span Test for seventh graders: A normative study. *Journal of Learning Disabilities*, 1981, 14, 93-95.

[2561]

Visual Discrimination Test. Ages 5-8; 1975; "ability to discriminate between like non-alphabetic forms"; Joseph M. Wepman, Anne Morency, and Marva Seidl; Language Research Associates, Inc.*

For additional information and reviews by Morton Bortner and Mildred H. Huebner, see 8:448 (1 reference).

REFERENCES

1. See 8:448.
2. MARGOLIS, H., BRANNIGAN, G. G., & PENNER, W. J. Modification of impulsive visual discrimination performance. *Journal of Special Education*, 1978, 12, 29-35.

[2562]

Visual Memory Scale. Ages 5-6; 1971-75; VMS; James L. Carroll; Carroll Publications.* (In-print status uncertain; no reply from publisher.)

For additional information, see 8:449 (2 references).

[2563]

Visual Memory Test. Ages 5-8; 1975; "ability to hold in immediate memory visually presented forms of a non-alphabetic nature"; Joseph M. Wepman, Anne Morency, and Marva Seidl; Language Research Associates, Inc.*

For additional information and a review by Morton Bortner, see 8:450 (2 references).

REFERENCES

1-2. See 8:450.
3. RICHEK, M. A. Readiness skills that predict initial word learning using 2 different methods of instruction. *Reading Research Quarterly*, 1977-1978, 13, 200-222.

[2564]

★**Visual Pattern Recognition Test and Diagnostic Schedule.** Ages 4-7 to 5-6; 1979; VPR; initially developed "to give student teachers some means of assessing children's readiness for reading"; Diane Montgomery; NFER-Nelson Publishing Co. [England].*

[2565]

The Visual-Verbal Test: A Measure of Conceptual Thinking. Schizophrenic patients; 1959-60; VVT; Marvin J. Feldman and James Drasgow; Western Psychological Services.*

For additional information, see P:282; for reviews by R. W. Payne and Donald R. Peterson, see 6:195 (8 references).

REFERENCES

1-8. See 6:195.
9. MANUCK, S. B., CROFT, S., & GOLD, K. S. Coronary-prone behavior pattern and cardiovascular response. *Psychophysiology*, 1978, 15, 403-411.

[2566]

Vocabulary Comprehension Scale. Ages 2-6; 1975; 66 scores: pronouns (17 item scores, total), quality (6 item scores, total), position (26 item scores, total), size (6 item scores, total), quantity (6 item scores, total); Tina E. Bangs; Teaching Resources Corporation.*

For additional information and a review by Laura A. Driscoll, see 8:81.

REFERENCES

1. GARRISON, G. Vocabulary Comprehension Scale. *ASHA*, 1977, 19, 50.

[2567]

Vocabulary Test for High School Students and College Freshmen. Grades 9-13; 1964; Arthur E. Traxler; Bobbs-Merrill Co., Inc.*

For additional information, a review by George P. Winship, Jr., and an excerpted review by Joan Bollenbacher, see 7:235 (1 reference).

[2568]
Vocabulary Test: McGraw-Hill Basic Skills System. Grades 11–14; 1970; also called *MHBSS Vocabulary Test*; although designed for use with the MHBSS instructional program, the test may be used independently; Alton L. Raygor; McGraw-Hill Book Co., Inc.*

For additional information and review by George P. Winship, Jr., see 7:236.

[2569]
Vocabulary Test: National Achievement Tests. Grades 3–8, 7–12; 1939–57; Robert K. Speer and Samuel Smith; Psychometric Affiliates.*

For additional information, see 5:241; for a review by Clifford Woody, see 3:168.

[2570]
★**Vocational Adaptation Rating Scale.** Ages 13–50 (mentally retarded individuals); 1980; VARS; ratings by parents, teachers, and other professionals; measures maladaptive behavior likely to occur in a vocational setting; frequency and severity scores in 7 areas: verbal manners, communication skills, attendance and punctuality, interpersonal behavior, respect for property and rules and regulations, grooming and personal hygiene, total; Robert G. Malgady, Peter R. Barcher, John Davis (test), and George Towner (test); Western Psychological Services.*

[2571]
The Vocational Apperception Test: Advanced Form. College; 1949; VAT; 2 forms; Robert B. Ammons, Margaret N. Butler, and Sam A. Herzig; Psychological Test Specialists.*

a) [FORM FOR MEN.] Preferences in 8 areas: teacher, executive or office worker, doctor, lawyer, engineer, personnel or social worker, salesman, laboratory technician.

b) [FORM FOR WOMEN.] Preferences in 10 areas: laboratory technician, dietician, buyer, nurse, teacher, artist, secretary, social worker, mother, housewife.

For additional information, see P:492 (3 references); for reviews by Benjamin Balinsky and William E. Henry and an excerpted review by George S. Rhodes, see 4:146 (1 reference).

[2572]
★**Vocational Behavior Checklist.** Vocational rehabilitation clients; 1978; VBC; criterion-referenced; 7 areas: pre-vocational skills, job-seeking skills, interview skills, job-related skills, work performance skills, on-the-job social skills, union-financial-security skills; Richard T. Walls, Thomas Zane, and Thomas J. Werner; West Virginia Rehabilitation Research and Training Center.*

[2573]
★**Vocational Exploration and Insight Kit.** High school and college and adults; 1970–80; VEIK; built around *Self Directed Search* but more thorough; self-administered and self-interpreted vocational counseling tool; John L. Holland and associates; Consulting Psychologists Press, Inc.*

REFERENCES
1. TALBOT, D. B., & BIRK, J. M. Does the Vocational Exploration and Insight Kit equal the sum of its parts: A comparison study. *Journal of Counseling Psychology*, 1979, 26, 359–362.

[2574]
Vocational Interest and Sophistication Assessment. Retarded adolescents and young adults; 1967–68; VISA; Joseph J. Parnicky, Harris Kahn, and Arthur D. Burdett; Joseph J. Parnicky.*

a) FORM FOR MALES. Interest and knowledge scores in each of 7 areas: garage, laundry, food service, maintenance, farm and grounds, materials handling, industry.

b) FORM FOR FEMALES. Interest and knowledge scores in each of 4 areas: business and clerical, housekeeping, food service, laundry and sewing.

For additional information and reviews by Esther E. Diamond and George Domino, see 8:1024 (3 references); see also T2:2217 (1 reference) and 7:1039 (2 references).

[2575]
*Vocational Interest, Experience, and Skill Assessment.** Grades 8–10, grade 11–adult; 1976–83; VIESA-I and II; self-scored, nationally normed vocational interest and experience inventories reporting scores related to data, ideas, people, and things work tasks, plus a structure for the self-appraisal of skills in the same work task areas; American College Testing Program.*

For additional information and a review by Charles J. Krauskopf of the earlier edition, see 8:1025.

[2576]
★**Vocational Interest Inventory.** High school; 1981; VII; must be computer-scored by publisher; 8 scores: service, business contact, organization, technical, outdoor, science, general culture, arts and entertainment; Patricia W. Lunneborg; Western Psychological Services.*

REFERENCES
1. LUNNEBORG, P. A. Construct validity of the Strong–Campbell Interest Inventory and Vocational Interest Inventory among college counseling clients. *Journal of Vocational Behavior*, 1977, 10, 187–195.
2. LUNNEBORG, P. W. Service vs. technical interest–Biggest sex difference of all? *Vocational Guidance Quarterly*, 1979, 28, 146–153.

[2577]
Vocational Interest Profile. Ages 15 and over; 1960–66; VIP; 9 scores: numerical, mechanical, scientific, clerical, persuasive, musical, artistic, literary, service; Robin N. Smith and J. R. McIntosh (test and user's guide); distributed by University of British Columbia Bookstore [Canada].* (In-print status uncertain; no reply from publisher.)

For additional information, see 7:1040 (1 reference).

REFERENCES
1. See 7:1040.
2. PREDIGER, D. J., & NOETH, R. J. Effectiveness of a brief counseling intervention in stimulating vocational exploration. *Journal of Vocational Behavior*, 1979, 14, 352–368.

[2578]
Vocational Interest Questionnaire for Pupils in Standards 6–10. 1974–75; VIQ; 10 scores: technical, outdoor, social service, natural science, office work (non-numerical, numerical), music, art, commerce, language; T. M. Coetzee; Human Sciences Research Council [South Africa].*

For additional information, see 8:1026.

[2579]

Vocational Opinion Index. Disadvantaged trainees in vocational skills programs; 1973–76; VOI; a measure of "Job Readiness Posture (JRP)"....a term used to define an individual's attitudes, perceptions and motivations that impact on his/her ability to get and/or hold a job"; 13 scores divided into 3 areas: attractions to work (overall, benefits to children, benefits to worker, better life style, independence), losses associated with work (overall, personal freedom, time for family), barriers to employment (medical, child care and family, new situations and people, ability to get and hold a job, transportation); (Spanish edition available); Associates for Research in Behavior, Inc.*

For additional information, see 8:1056.

REFERENCES

1. KNEIPP, S. A., VANDERGOOT, D., & LAWRENCE, R. E. An evaluation of two job–search skills training programs in a vocational rehabilitation agency. *Rehabilitation Counseling Bulletin*, 1980, 23, 202–208.

[2580]

★**Vocational Preference Index.** Ages 8 and over; 1972–78; VPI; 7 scores: physical work, self-expression, business, mechanical, medicine, concern for nature, management control; James D. Widmayer and M. June Allard; Slosson Educational Publications, Inc.*

[2581]

*Vocational Preference Inventory, Seventh Revision.** High school and college and adults; 1953–78; VPI; "a personality inventory composed entirely of occupational titles"; 11 scores: realistic, intellectual, social, conventional, enterprising, artistic, self-control, masculinity, status, infrequency, acquiescence; John L. Holland; Consulting Psychologists Press, Inc.*

For additional information and an excerpted review by W. Bruce Walsh of an earlier edition, see 8:1028 (175 references); see also T2:1430 (48 references); for reviews by Joseph A. Johnston and Paul R. Lohnes, see 7:157 (39 references); see also P:283 (31 references); for reviews by Robert L. French and H. Bradley Sagen of an earlier edition, see 6:115 (13 references).

REFERENCES

1–13. See 6:115.
14–44. See P:283.
45–83. See 7:157.
84–131. See T2:1430.
132–306. See 8:1028.

307. CUNNINGHAM, C. H., ALSTON, H. L., DOUGHTIE, E. B., & WAKEFIELD, J. A., JR. Use of Holland's vocational theory with potential high school dropouts. *Journal of Vocational Behavior*, 1977, 10, 35–38.
308. OLIVER, L. W. Evaluating career counseling outcome for three modes of test interpretation. *Measurement & Evaluation in Guidance*, 1977, 10, 153–161.
309. RICHARDS, J. M., JR. Personality type for physicians' assistants and associates based on Vocational Preference Inventory. *Psychological Reports*, 1977, 41, 397–398.
310. SMITH, P. J. Comparison of counselees and noncounselees with reference to Holland's theory. *Journal of Counseling Psychology*, 1977, 24, 244–246.
311. TURNER, R. G., & HIBBS, C. Vocational interest and personality correlates of differential abilities. *Psychological Reports*, 1977, 40, 727–730.
312. WALSH, W. B., HORTON, J. A., & GUFFEY, R. L. Holland's theory and college–degreed working men and women. *Journal of Vocational Behavior*, 1977, 10, 180–186.
313. BINGHAM, R. P., & WALSH, W. B. Concurrent validity of Holland's theory for college–degreed black women. *Journal of Vocational Behavior*, 1978, 13, 242–250.
314. HALES, L., & HARTMAN, T. Personality, sex, and work values. *Journal of Experimental Education*, 1978, 47, 16–21.
315. KAPES, J. T., & MARTIN, R. B. Exploring the use of Holland's Vocational Preference Inventory with male vocational–technical students. *Journal of Industrial Teacher Education*, 1978, 15, 27–35.
316. LAUDEMAN, K. A., & GRIFFETH, P. Holland's theory of vocational choice and postulated value dimensions. *Educational & Psychological Measurement*, 1978, 38, 1165–1175.
317. LOESCH, L. C., & SAMPSON, J. P., JR. Job knowledge and vocational preferences. *Vocational Guidance Quarterly*, 1978, 27, 55–60.
318. MASTIE, M. M. Vocational Preference Inventory, Sixth Revision. *Measurement & Evaluation in Guidance*, 1978, 11, 123–128.
319. SALOMONE, P. R., & SLANEY, R. B. The applicability of Holland's theory to nonprofessional workers. *Journal of Vocational Behavior*, 1978, 13, 63–74.
320. DOUGHERTY, A. M., & DAVIES, M. M. Vocational preferences of incarcerated males. *Psychological Reports*, 1979, 45, 240.
321. HELMS, J. E. Perceptions of a sex–fair counselor and client. *Journal of Counseling Psychology*, 1979, 26, 504–513.
322. JONES, L. K. Occu–Sort: Development and evaluation of an occupational card sort system. *Vocational Guidance Quarterly*, 1979, 28, 56–62.
323. JONES, L. K., & DE VAULT, R. M. Evaluation of a self–guided career exploration system: The Occu-Sort. *School Counselor*, 1979, 26, 334–341.
324. LUNNEBORG, P. W. Service vs. technical interest–Biggest sex difference of all? *Vocational Guidance Quarterly*, 1979, 28, 146–153.
325. MAYNARD, M. The occupational, learning, and social support orientations of employees. *Journal of Employment Counseling*, 1979, 16, 94–109.
326. ORCUTT, M. A., & WALSH, W. B. Traditionality and congruence of career aspirations for college women. *Journal of Vocational Behavior*, 1979, 14, 1–11.
327. ROUNDS, J. B., JR., DAVISON, M. L., & DAWIS, R. V. The fit between Strong–Campbell Interest Inventory general occupational themes and Holland's hexagonal model. *Journal of Vocational Behavior*, 1979, 15, 303–315.
328. SCHENK, G. E., JOHNSTON, J. A., & JACOBSEN, K. The influence of a career group experience on the vocational maturity of college students. *Journal of Vocational Behavior*, 1979, 14, 284–296.
329. SCISSONS, E. H. Profiles of ability: Characteristics of Canadian engineers. *Engineering Education*, 1979, 69, 822–836.
330. SPOKANE, A. R., & DERBY, D. P. Congruence, personality pattern, and satisfaction in college women. *Journal of Vocational Behavior*, 1979, 15, 36–42.
331. TAKAI, R., & HOLLAND, J. L. Comparison of the Vocational Card Sort, the SDS, and the Vocational Exploration and Insight kit. *Vocational Guidance Quarterly*, 1979, 27, 312–318.
332. TAYLOR, K. F., KELSO, G. I., COX, G. N., ALLOWAY, W. J., & MATTHEWS, J. P. Applying Holland's vocational categories to leisure activities. *Journal of Occupational Psychology*, 1979, 52, 199–207.
333. WALSH, W. B., BINGHAM, R., & HORTON, J. A. Holland's theory and college–degreed working black and white women. *Journal of Vocational Behavior*, 1979, 15, 217–223.
334. WIGGINS, J. D., & WESLANDER, D. L. Personality characteristics of counselors rated as effective or ineffective. *Journal of Vocational Behavior*, 1979, 15, 175–185.
335. ALBERT, R. S. Exceptionally gifted boys and their parents. *Gifted Child Quarterly*, 1980, 24, 174–179.
336. BENNINGER, W. B., & WALSH, W. B. Holland's theory and non–college–degreed working men and women. *Journal of Vocational Behavior*, 1980, 17, 81–88.
337. EREZ, M., & SHNEORSON, Z. Personality types and motivational characteristics of academic versus professionals in industry in the same occupational discipline. *Journal of Vocational Behavior*, 1980, 17, 95–105.
338. GENTRY, J. M., WINER, J. L., SIGELMAN, C. K., & PHILLIPS, F. L. Alderian lifestyle and vocational preference. *Journal of Individual Psychology*, 1980, 36, 80–86.
339. HARRINGTON, T. F., & O'SHEA, A. J. Applicability of the Holland (1973) model of vocational development with Spanish–speaking clients. *Journal of Counseling Psychology*, 1980, 27, 246–251.
340. LAUFER, W. S. Vocational interests of criminal offenders: A typological and demographic investigation. *Psychological Reports*, 1980, 46, 315–324.
341. SCANLAN, T. J. Toward an occupational classification for self–employed men: An investigation of entrepreneurship from the perspective of Holland's theory of career development. *Journal of Vocational Behavior*, 1980, 16, 163–172.
342. SLANEY, R. B. Expressed vocational choice and vocational indecision. *Journal of Counseling Psychology*, 1980, 27, 122–129.
343. SLANEY, R. B. An investigation of racial differences on vocational variables among college women. *Journal of Vocational Behavior*, 1980, 16, 197–207.
344. ATHANASON, J. A., O'GORMAN, J., & MEYER, E. Factorial validity of the vocational interest scales of the Holland Vocational

Preference Inventory for Australian high school students. *Educational & Psychological Measurement*, 1981, 41, 523–527.

345. DiNuzzo, T. M., & Tolbert, E. L. Promoting the personal growth and vocational maturity of the re–entry woman: A group approach. *Journal of the National Association of Women Deans, Administrators & Counselors*, 1981, 45, 26–31.

346. Kiulighan, D. M., Jr., Hageseth, J. A., Tipton, R. M., & McGovern, T. V. Effects of matching treatment approaches and personality types in group vocational counseling. *Journal of Counseling Psychology*, 1981, 28, 315–320.

347. Lowe, B. The relationship between vocational interest differentiation and career undecidedness. *Journal of Vocational Behavior*, 1981, 19, 346–349.

348. Slaney, R. B., & Russell, J. E. A. An investigation of different levels of agreement between expressed and inventoried vocational interests among college women. *Journal of Counseling Psychology*, 1981, 28, 221–228.

349. Spokane, A. R., & Herzog–Spokane, R. Effects of information on preference for an occupation. *Journal of Employment Counseling*, 1981, 18, 64–72.

350. Weiser, M. A., Klimek, R. J., & Hodinko, B. Career perspectives of male prison inmates in college courses. *Journal of Vocational Behavior*, 1981, 19, 36–41.

351. Wiggins, J. D., & Moody, A. A field–based comparison of four career–exploration approaches. *Vocational Guidance Quarterly*, 1981, 30, 15–20.

[2582]

★**Wachs Analysis of Cognitive Structures.** Ages 3–6; 1977; WACS; assesses a child's cognitive development in terms of body and sense thinking, mainly by non-verbal performance tasks; 4 scores: identification of objects, object design, graphic design, general movement; Harry Wachs and Lawrence J. Vaughan; Western Psychological Services.*

[2583]

Wahler Physical Symptoms Inventory. Psychiatric patients and counselees; 1973; WPSI; H. J. Wahler; Western Psychological Services.*

See T2:1432 (1 reference).

[2584]

Wahler Self-Description Inventory. Grades 7 and over and psychiatric patients; 1971; WSDI; "the degree to which respondents *differentially* emphasize favorable and unfavorable characteristics in their self-evaluations"; 3 scores: favorable attributes, unfavorable attributes, difference; H. J. Wahler; Western Psychological Services.*

For additional information and a review by Douglas M. McNair, see 8:705; see also T2:1433 (3 references).

[2585]

Walker Problem Behavior Identification Checklist. Grades 4–6; 1970; WPBIC; ratings by teachers; 6 scores: acting-out, withdrawal, distractability, disturbed peer relations, immaturity, total; Hill M. Walker; Western Psychological Services.*

For additional information, see 7:159 (1 reference).

REFERENCES

1. See 7:159.
2. Bolstad, O. D., & Johnson, S. M. The relationship between teachers' assessment of students and students' actual behavior in the classroom. *Child Development*, 1977, 48, 570–578.
3. Kerlin, M. A., & Latham, W. L. Intervention effects of a crisis-resource program. *Exceptional Children*, 1977, 44, 32–34.
4. Kern, R. M., & Hankins, G. Adlerian group counseling with contracted homework. *Elementary School Guidance & Counseling*, 1977, 11, 284–290.
5. Richmond, B. O., & Waits, C. Special education–who needs it? *Exceptional Children*, 1978, 44, 279–280.
6. Csapo, M. The effect of self-recording and social reinforcement components of parent training programs. *Journal of Experimental Child Psychology*, 1979, 27, 479–488.
7. Csapo, M., & Friesen, J. Training parents of hard core delinquents as behavior managers of their children. *Canadian Counsellor*, 1979, 13, 68–74.
8. Hammond, J. M. Children of divorce: Implications for counselors. *School Counselor*, 1979, 27, 7–14.
9. Hammond, J. M. Children of divorce: A study of self–concept, academic achievement, and attitudes. *Elementary School Journal*, 1979, 80, 55–62.
10. Hammond, J. M. A comparison of elementary children from divorced and intact families. *Phi Delta Kappan*, 1979, 61, 219.
11. Mash, E. J., & Mercer, B. J. A comparison of the behavior of deviant and non-deviant boys while playing alone and interacting with a sibling. *Journal of Child Psychology & Psychiatry & Allied Disciplines*, 1979, 20, 197–207.
12. O'Conner, P. D., Stuck, G. B., & Wyne, M. D. Effects of a short–term intervention resource–room program on task orientation and achievement. *Journal of Special Education*, 1979, 13, 375–385.
13. Waksman, S. A. An evaluation of social learning procedures designed to aid students with conduct problems. *Psychology in the Schools*, 1979, 16, 416–421.
14. Weinrott, M. R., Corson, J. A., & Wilchesky, M. Teacher-mediated treatment of social withdrawal. *Behavior Therapy*, 1979, 10, 281–294.
15. Wyne, M. D., & Stuck, G. B. Time-on-task and reading performance in underachieving children. *Journal of Reading Behavior*, 1979, 11, 119–128.
16. Stone, B. G. Relationship between creativity and classroom behavior. *Psychology in the Schools*, 1980, 17, 106–108.
17. Waksman, S. A., & Loveland, R. J. The Portland Problem Behavior Checklist. *Psychology in the Schools*, 1980, 17, 25–29.
18. Lochman, J. E., Nelson, W. M., III, & Sims, J. P. A cognitive behavioral program for use with aggressive children. *Journal of Clinical Child Psychology*, 1981, 10, 146–148.

[2586]

Walton-Sanders English Test. 1, 2 semesters in grades 9–13; 1962–64; first published 1962–63 in the Every Pupil Scholarship Test series; Charles E. Walton and M. W. Sanders; Bureau of Educational Measurements.*

For additional information and a review by Charlotte Croon Davis, 8:60.

[2587]

Ward Atmosphere Scale. Patients and staff of hospital-based psychiatric treatment programs; 1974; WAS; a part of *The Social Climate Scales (2227)*; 10 scores (involvement, support, spontaneity, autonomy, practical orientation, personal problem orientation, anger and aggression, order and organization, program clarity, staff control) plus 3 nonprofiled outcome scores (dropout, release rate, community tenure); Rudolf H. Moos; Consulting Psychologists Press, Inc.*

For additional information and a review by Earl S. Taulbee, see 8:706 (31 references). For a review of *The Social Climate Scales*, see 8:681.

REFERENCES

1–31. See 8:706.
32. Doherty, E. G. Length of hospitalization on a short–term therapeutic community: A multivariate study by sex across time. *Archives of General Psychiatry*, 1976, 33, 87–92.
33. Edelson, R. I., & Paul, G. L. Staff "attitude" and "atmosphere" scores as a function of ward size and patient chronicity. *Journal of Consulting & Clinical Psychology*, 1977, 45, 874–884.
34. Klass, D. B., Growe, G. A., & Strizich, M. Ward treatment milieu and post hospital functioning. *Archives of General Psychiatry*, 1977, 34, 1047–1052.
35. Pratt, T. C., Linn, M. W., Carmichael, J. S., & Webb, N. L. The alcoholic's perception of the ward as a predictor of after–care attendance. *Journal of Clinical Psychology*, 1977, 33, 915–918.
36. Alden, L. Factor analysis of the Ward Atmosphere Scale. *Journal of Consulting & Clinical Psychology*, 1978, 46, 175–176.
37. Alden, L. Treatment environment and patient improvement. *Journal of Nervous & Mental Disease*, 1978, 166, 327–334.
38. Greenberg, E. A., Obitz, F. W., & Kaye, B. W. Relationships among control orientation, the FIRO–B, and the Ward Atmosphere Scale

in hospitalized men alcoholics. *Journal of Studies on Alcohol,* 1978, 39, 68–76.

39. MANDERSCHEID, R. W., KOENIG, G. R., & SILBERGELD, S. Psychosocial factors for classroom, group, and ward. *Psychological Reports,* 1978, 43, 555–561.

40. MCGEE, M. G., & WOODS, D. J. Use of Moos' Ward Atmosphere Scale in a residential setting for mentally retarded adolescents. *Psychological Reports,* 1978, 43, 580–582.

41. VERINIS, J. S., & FLAHERTY, J. A. Using the Ward Atmosphere Scale to help change the treatment environment. *Hospital & Community Psychiatry,* 1978, 29, 238–240.

42. WOLF, M. S. The effect of education on nurses' views of a therapeutic milieu. *Journal of Psychiatric Nursing,* 1978, 16, 29–33.

43. FISCHER, J. The relationship between alcoholic patients' milieu perception and measures of their drinking during a brief follow–up period. *International Journal of the Addictions,* 1979, 14, 1151–1156.

44. O'LEARY, M. R., DONOVAN, D. M., CHANEY, E. F., & SPELTZ, M. L. Correlates of clinicians' perceptions of patients in alcoholism treatment. *Journal of Clinical Psychiatry,* 1979, 40, 344–347.

45. WOODS, D. J., & BILLIG, J. M. The A–B variable and preferred inpatient treatment environment. *Journal of Clinical Psychology,* 1979, 35, 429–432.

46. ARCHER, R. P., & AMUSO, K. F. Comparison of staff's and patients' perceptions of ward atmosphere. *Psychological Reports,* 1980, 46, 959–965.

47. RHODES, L. M. Social climate perception and depression of patients and staff in a chronic hemodialysis unit. *Journal of Nervous & Mental Disease,* 1981, 169, 169–175.

[2588]

Ward Behavior Inventory. Mental patients; 1959–68; WBI; revision of *Ward Behavior Rating Scale*; ratings by ward nurses and attendants; Eugene I. Burdock, Anne S. Hardesty, Gad Hakerem (test), Joseph Zubin (test), and Yvonne M. Beck (test); Springer Publishing Co., Inc.*

For additional information and a review by Earl S. Taulbee, see 8:707 (4 references); see also T2:1435 (12 references) and P:285 (14 references).

REFERENCES

1–14. See P:285.
15–26. See T2:1435.
27–30. See 8:707.
31. EBERT, J. N., EWING, J. H., ROGERS, M. H., & REYNOLDS, D. J. Changes in primary process expression in hospitalized schizophrenics treated with phenothiazines: Two projective tasks compared. *Journal of Genetic Psychology,* 1977, 130, 83–94.
32. MCCREADIE, R. G., DINGWALL, J. M., WILES, D. H., & HEYKANTS, J. J. P. Intermittent pimozide versus fluphenazine decanoate as maintenance therapy in chronic schizophrenia. *British Journal of Psychiatry,* 1980, 137, 510–517.
33. RAO, V. A. R., BISHOP, M., & COPPEN, A. Clinical state, plasma levels of haloperidol and prolactin: A correlation study in chronic schizophrenia. *British Journal of Psychiatry,* 1980, 137, 518–521.

[2589]

★**Washington Pre-College Test.** College bound high school students; 1975–80; WPC; 2 parts: part 1, 10 scores: verbal composite, quantitative composite, English usage, spelling, reading comprehension, vocabulary, applied mathematics, mathematics achievement, spatial ability, mechanical reasoning, part 2: vocational interest inventory; The Washington Pre-College Testing Program.*

[2590]

Washington Speech Sound Discrimination Test. Ages 3–5; 1971, c1969–71; WSSDT; Elizabeth Prather, Adah Miner, Margaret Anne Addicott, and Linda Sunderland; Interstate Printers & Publishers, Inc.*

For additional information and reviews by Raphael M. Haller and Leija V. McReynolds, see 8:952 (1 reference).

[2591]

The Watkins-Farnum Performance Scale: A Standardized Achievement Test for All Band Instruments. Music students; 1942–62; John G. Watkins and Stephen E. Farnum; Hal Leonard Music, Inc.* (In-print status uncertain; no reply from publisher.)

See T2:216 (4 references); for a review by Herbert D. Wing, see 5:253 (2 references); for related reviews, see 3:1228 (4 excerpts).

[2592]

Watson Diagnostic Mathematics Test: Computation, Fourth Edition. Grades 1–3, 4–6, 7–10; 1973; WDMT; 3 levels; G. Milton Watson; Book Society of Canada Ltd. [Canada].*

a) PRIMARY. Grades 1–3; 22 scores: grade 1 level (basic concepts, counting, addition, subtraction, fractions, time, total), grade 2 level (counting, addition, subtraction, multiplication, fractions, time, total), grade 3 level (basic concepts, counting, addition, subtraction, multiplication, fractions, total), total.

b) JUNIOR. Grades 4–6; 14 scores: addition (whole numbers, fractions), subtraction (whole numbers, fractions), total, multiplication (whole numbers, fractions), division (whole numbers, fractions), total (unsorted review, decimals-percent-fractions, total), total.

c) INTERMEDIATE. Grades 7–10; 16 scores: addition (whole numbers and decimals, fractions), subtraction (whole numbers and decimals, fractions), total, multiplication (whole numbers and decimals, fractions), division (whole numbers and decimals, fractions), total (rules of signs review, fractions and decimals, percent, stretchers, total), total.

[2593]

Watson English Usage and Appreciation Test, Fourth Edition. Grades 4–8; 1966; G. Milton Watson; Book Society of Canada Ltd. [Canada].*

For additional information and a review by Vincent R. D'Oyley, see 7:213.

[2594]

*****Watson-Glaser Critical Thinking Appraisal.** Grades 9–16 and adults; 1942–80; CTA; 6 scores: inference, recognition of assumptions, deduction, interpretation, evaluation of arguments, total; Goodwin Watson and Edward M. Glaser; The Psychological Corporation.*

For additional information, see 8:822 (49 references); see also T2:1775 (35 references); for excerpted reviews by John O. Crites and G. C. Helmstadter, see 7:783 (74 references); see also 6:867 (24 references); for reviews by Walker H. Hill and Carl I. Hovland of an earlier edition, see 5:700 (8 references); for a review by Robert H. Thouless and an excerpted review by Harold P. Fawcett, see 3:544 (3 references).

REFERENCES

1–3. See 3:544.
4–11. See 5:700.
12–35. See 6:687.
36–109. See 7:783.
110–144. See T2:1775.
145–193. See 8:822.
194. GABLE, R. K., ROBERTS, A. D., & OWEN, S. V. Affective and cognitive correlates of classroom achievement. *Educational & Psychological Measurement,* 1977, 37, 977–986.
195. HALL, W. C., JR., & MYERS, C. B. The effect of a training program in the Taba teaching strategies on teaching methods and teacher

perceptions of their teaching. *Peabody Journal of Education*, 1977, 54, 162–167.

196. RICHARDS, M. A. One integrated curriculum: An empirical evaluation. *Nursing Research*, 1977, 26, 90–95.

197. ROBERTS, A. D., GABLE, R. K., & OWEN, S. V. An evaluation of minicourse curricula in secondary social studies. *Journal of Experimental Education*, 1977, 46, 4–11.

198. SMITH, D. G. College classroom interactions and critical thinking. *Journal of Educational Psychology*, 1977, 69, 180–190.

199. SCHMECK, R. R., & RIBICH, F. D. Construct validation of the Inventory of Learning Processes. *Applied Psychological Measurement*, 1978, 2, 551–562.

200. ANNIS, L. F., & ANNIS, D. B. The impact of philosophy on students' critical thinking ability. *Contemporary Educational Psychology*, 1979, 4, 219–226.

201. RIBORDY, S. C., HOLMES, D. S., & BUCHSBAUM, H. K. Effects of affective and cognitive distractions on anxiety reduction. *Journal of Social Psychology*, 1980, 112, 121–127.

202. ROSE, R. G. An examination of the responses to a multivalue logic test. *Journal of General Psychology*, 1980, 102, 275–281.

203. VIDLER, D., & HANSEN, R. Answer changing on multiple-choice tests. *Journal of Experimental Education*, 1980, 49, 18–20.

204. FOSTER, P. J. Clinical discussion groups: Verbal participation and outcomes. *Journal of Medical Education*, 1981, 56, 831–838.

205. GOLDMAN, F. W., & GOLDMAN, M. The effects of dyadic group experience in subsequent individual performance. *Journal of Social Psychology*, 1981, 115, 83–88.

206. KETEFIAN, S. Critical thinking, educational preparation, and development of moral judgement among selected groups of practicing nurses. *Nursing Research*, 1981, 30, 98–103.

207. LANDIS, R. E., & MICHAEL, W. B. The factorial validity of three measures of critical thinking within the context of Guilford's structure-of-intellect model for a sample of ninth grade students. *Educational & Psychological Measurement*, 1981, 41, 1147–1166.

208. WILSON, D. G., & WAGNER, E. E. The Watson–Glaser Critical Thinking Appraisal as a predictor of performance in a critical thinking course. *Educational & Psychological Measurement*, 1981, 41, 1319–1322.

[2595]

Watson Number-Readiness Test, Fifth Edition. Grades kgn–1; 1963; 6 scores: subjective test (teacher's ratings of social, emotional, and psychological readiness, total), objective test, total; G. Milton Watson; Book Society of Canada Ltd. [Canada].*

For additional information, see 7:529.

[2596]

Watson Reading-Readiness Test. Grades kgn–1; 1960; 6 scores: subjective test (teacher's ratings of physical, social, emotional, and psychological readiness), objective test, total; G. Milton Watson; Book Society of Canada Ltd. [Canada].*

For additional information, see 6:851.

[2597]

Weber Advanced Spatial Perception Test. Ages 13–17; 1976, c1968–76; WASP; 5 scores: form recognition, pattern perception, shape analysis, reflected figures, total; not available for use in New South Wales; P. G. Weber; Australian Council for Educational Research [Australia].*

For additional information, see 8:1047.

[2598]

*****Wechsler Adult Intelligence Scale-Revised.** Ages 16 and over; 1939–81; WAIS-R; revision of *Wechsler Adult Intelligence Scale*; 14 scores: verbal (information, comprehension, arithmetic, similarities, digit span, vocabulary, total), performance (digit symbol, picture completion, block design, picture arrangement, object assembly, total), total; David Wechsler; The Psychological Corporation. (British manual supplement (WAIS): 1971; Peter Saville; NFER-Nelson Publishing Co. [England]. South African edition: Ages 18–59; 1969; National Institute for Personnel Research [South Africa].)*

For additional information on the original edition, see 8:230 (351 references); see also T2:529 (178 references); for reviews by Alvin G. Burstein and Howard B. Lyman, see 7:429 (538 references); see also 6:538 (180 references); for reviews by Nancy Bayley and Wilson H. Guertin, see 5:414 (42 references).

REFERENCES

1–42. See 5:414.
43–222. See 6:538.
223–762. See 7:429.
763–940. See T2:529.
941–1291. See 8:230.

1292. BARKER, T. E., & BLACK, F. W. Klinefelter Syndrome in a military population. *Archives of General Psychiatry*, 1976, 33, 607–610.

1293. WOOD, D. R., REIMHERR, F. W., WENDER, P. H., & JOHNSON, G. E. Diagnosis and treatment of minimal brain dysfunction in adults. *Archives of General Psychiatry*, 1976, 33, 1453–1460.

1294. ADAMS, R. L., KOBOS, J. C., & PRESTON, J. Effect of racial-ethnic grouping, age, and IQ range on the validity of the Satz–Mogel short form of the Wechsler Adult Intelligence Scale. *Journal of Consulting & Clinical Psychology*, 1977, 45, 498–499.

1295. ALPAUGH, P. K., & BIRREN, J. E. Variables affecting creative contributions across the adult life span. *Human Development*, 1977, 20, 240–248.

1296. ALPERT, M., & ANDERSON, L. T. Imagery mediation of vocal emphasis in flat affect. *Archives of General Psychiatry*, 1977, 34, 208–212.

1297. APRIL, R. S., & TSE, P. C. Crossed aphasia in a Chinese bilingual dextral. *Archives of Neurology*, 1977, 34, 766–770.

1298. BERG, P. A., & LEVENTHAL, D. B. The effect of distractor strength versus rate of item presentation on retention in schizophrenics. *British Journal of Social & Clinical Psychology*, 1977, 16, 147–152.

1299. BLUSEWICZ, M. J., SCHENKENBERG, T., DUSTMAN, R. E., & BECK, E. C. WAIS performance in young normal, young alcoholic, and elderly normal groups: An evaluation of organicity and mental aging indices. *Journal of Clinical Psychology*, 1977, 33, 1149–1153.

1300. BOLLER, F., VRTUNSKI, B., MACK, J. L., & KIM, Y. Neuropsychological correlates of hypertension. *Archives of Neurology*, 1977, 34, 701–705.

1301. BOWEN, R. C., & SHEPEL, L. Physical and psychological complications after intestinal bypass for obesity. *Canadian Medical Association Journal*, 1977, 116, 871–875.

1302. BUSH, M. The relationship between impaired selective attention and severity of psychopathology in acute psychiatric patients. *British Journal of Medical Psychology*, 1977, 50, 251–265.

1303. CAUTHEN, N. R. Extension of the Wechsler Memory Scale norms to older age groups. *Journal of Clinical Psychology*, 1977, 33, 208–211.

1304. CEGALIS, J. A., LEEN, D., & SOLOMON, E. J. Attention in schizophrenia: An analysis of selectivity in the functional visual field. *Journal of Abnormal Psychology*, 1977, 86, 470–482.

1305. CHRISTODOULOU, G. N. The syndrome of capgras. *British Journal of Psychiatry*, 1977, 130, 556–564.

1306. COHEN, D., SCHAIE, K. W., & GRIBBIN, K. The organization of spatial abilities in older men and women. *Journal of Gerontology*, 1977, 32, 578–585.

1307. CORNBLETH, T. Effects of a protected hospital ward area on wandering and nonwandering geriatrics patients. *Journal of Gerontology*, 1977, 32, 573–577.

1308. DESILVA, W. P., & HEMSLEY, D. R. The influence of context on language perception in schizophrenia. *British Journal of Social & Clinical Psychology*, 1977, 16, 337–345.

1309. DIKMEN, S., & MATTHEWS, C. G. Effect of major motor seizure frequency upon cognitive–intellectual functions in adults. *Epilepsia*, 1977, 18, 21–29.

1310. DIKMEN, S., MATTHEWS, C. G., & HARLEY, J. P. Effect of early versus late onset of major motor epilepsy on cognitive–intellectual performance: Further considerations. *Epilepsia*, 1977, 18, 31–36.

1311. DIKMEN, S., & REITAN, R. M. MMPI correlates of adaptive ability deficits in patients with brain lesions. *Journal of Nervous & Mental Disease*, 1977, 165, 247–254.

1312. DIMOND, S. J., SCAMMELL, R. E., BROUWERS, E. Y. M., & WEEKS, R. Functions of the centre section (trunk) of the corpus callosum in man. *Brain*, 1977, 100, 543–562.

1313. DINNING, W. D., ANDERT, J. N., & HUSTAK, T. L. Reliability and stability of WAIS IQs for institutionalized adult retardates. *Psychological Reports*, 1977, 40, 929–930.

1314. DOLAN, M. P., & NORTON, J. C. A programmed training technique that uses reinforcement to facilitate acquisition and retention in brain–damaged patients. *Journal of Clinical Psychology*, 1977, 33, 496–501.

1315. DONNELLY, E. F., & WALDMAN, I. N. IQ as a predictor of antidepressant responses to imipramine. *Psychological Reports*, 1977, 41, 55–56.

1316. EXNER, J. E., & MURRILLO, L. G. A long term follow–up of schizophrenics treated with regressive ECT. *Diseases of the Nervous System*, 1977, 38, 162–168.

1317. EXNER, J. E., JR., WYLIE, J., LEUVA, A., & PARRILL, T. Some psychological characteristics of prostitutes. *Journal of Personality Assessment*, 1977, 41, 474–485.

1318. FEDERMAN, E. J., & BAILEY, K. G. Extending the Similarities Subtest of the WAIS for increased validity. *Journal of Clinical Psychology*, 1977, 33, 1055–1059.

1319. FERRIS, S. H., SATHANANTHAN, G., GERSHON, S., & CLARK, C. Senile dementia: Treatment with deanol. *Journal of the American Geriatrics Society*, 1977, 25, 241–244.

1320. FINLAYSON, M. A. J. Test complexity and brain damage at different educational levels. *Journal of Clinical Psychology*, 1977, 33, 221–223.

1321. FINLAYSON, M. A. J., JOHNSON, K. A., & REITAN, R. M. Relationship of level of education to neuropsychological measures in brain–damaged and non–brain–damaged adults. *Journal of Consulting & Clinical Psychology*, 1977, 45, 536–542.

1322. FISH, B. Neurobiologic antecedents of schizophrenia in children. *Archives of General Psychiatry*, 1977, 34, 1297–1313.

1323. FOCH, T. T., DEFRIES, J. C., MCCLEARN, G. E., & SINGER, S. M. Familial patterns of impairment in reading disability. *Journal of Educational Psychology*, 1977, 69, 316–329.

1324. FRIEDMAN, M. J., CULVER, C. M., & FERRELL, R. B. On the safety of long–term treatment with lithium. *American Journal of Psychiatry*, 1977, 134, 1123–1126.

1325. GIAMBRA, L. M. A factor analytic study of daydreaming, imaginal process, and temperament: A replication on an adult male life-span sample. *Journal of Gerontology*, 1977, 32, 675–680.

1326. GILBERT, C. Non-verbal perceptual abilities in relation to left-handedness and cerebral lateralization. *Neuropsychologia*, 1977, 15, 779–791.

1327. GLASGOW, R. E., ZEISS, R. A., BARRERA, M., JR., & LEWINSOHN, P. M. Case studies on remediating memory deficits in brain–damaged individuals. *Journal of Clinical Psychology*, 1977, 33, 1049–1054.

1328. GOLDSTEIN, S. G., FILSKOV, S. B., WEAVER, L. A., & IVES, J. O. Neuropsychological effects of electroconvulsive therapy. *Journal of Clinical Psychology*, 1977, 33, 798–806.

1329. GOLDSTEIN, G., & HALPERIN, K. M. Neuropsychological differences among subtypes of schizophrenia. *Journal of Abnormal Psychology*, 1977, 86, 34–40.

1330. GOLDSTONE, S., LHARMAN, W. T., & NURNBERG, H. G. Temporal information processing by alcoholics. *Journal of Studies on Alcohol*, 1977, 38, 2009–2024.

1331. GOODMAN, J. F. IQ decline in mentally retarded adults: A matter of fact or methodological flaw. *Journal of Mental Deficiency Research*, 1977, 21, 199–203.

1332. GOTTLIEB, H., STRITE, L. C., KOLLER, R., MADORSKY, A., HOCKERSMITH, V., KLEEMAN, M., & WAGNER, J. Comprehensive rehabilitation of patients having chronic low back pain. *Archives of Physical Medicine & Rehabilitation*, 1977, 58, 101–108.

1333. GRAND, S., MARCOS, L. R., FREEMAN, N., & BARROSO, F. Relation of psychopathology and bilingualism to kinesic aspects of interview behavior in schizophrenia. *Journal of Abnormal Psychology*, 1977, 86, 492–500.

1334. GRIFFITHS, R. D. P. The prediction of psychiatric patients' work adjustment in the community. *British Journal of Social & Clinical Psychology*, 1977, 16, 165–173.

1335. GROTEVANT, H. D., SCARR, S., & WEINBERG, R. A. Intellectual development in family constellations with adopted and natural children: A test of the Zajonc and Markus model. *Child Development*, 1977, 48, 1699–1703.

1336. HAALAND, K. Y., CLEELAND, C. S., & CARR, D. Motor performance after unilateral hemisphere damage in patients with tumor. *Archives of Neurology*, 1977, 34, 556–559.

1337. HALGIN, R., RIKLAN, M., & MISIAK, H. Levodopa, Parkinsonism, and recent memory. *Journal of Nervous & Mental Disease*, 1977, 164, 268–272.

1338. HALL, J. N., BAKER, R. D., & HUTCHINSON, K. A controlled evaluation of token economy procedures with chronic schizophrenic patients. *Behaviour Research & Therapy*, 1977, 15, 261–283.

1339. HARROW, M., & QUINLAN, D. Is disordered thinking unique to schizophrenia? *Archives of General Psychiatry*, 1977, 34, 15–21.

1340. HAYNES, J., & GORMLY, J. Anxiety and memory. *Bulletin of the Psychonomic Society*, 1977, 9, 191–192.

1341. HOFFMAN, C., & KAGAN, S. Lateral eye movements and field dependence–independence. *Perceptual & Motor Skills*, 1977, 45, 767–778.

1342. HYMAN, C. A. A report on the psychological test results of battering parents. *British Journal of Social & Clinical Psychology*, 1977, 16, 221–224.

1343. JENKYN, L. R., WALSH, D. B., CULVER, C. M., & REEVES, A. G. Clinical signs in diffuse cerebral dysfunction. *Journal of Neurology, Neurosurgery, & Psychiatry*, 1977, 40, 956–966.

1344. JUDD, L. L., HUBBARD, B., JANOWSKY, D. S., HUEY, L. Y., & TAKAHASHI, K. I. The effect of lithium carbonate on the cognitive functions of normal subjects. *Archives of General Psychiatry*, 1977, 34, 355–357.

1345. KAPUR, N., & BUTTERS, N. Visuoperceptive deficits in long–term alcoholics with Korsakoff's psychosis. *Journal of Studies on Alcohol*, 1977, 38, 2025–2035.

1346. KENDALL, P. C., & LITTLE, V. L. Correspondence of brief intelligence measures to the Wechsler scales with delinquents. *Journal of Consulting & Clinical Psychology*, 1977, 45, 660–666.

1347. KIM, S. P., SIOMOPOULOS, G., & COHEN, R. J. Verbal abstraction and culture: An exploratory study with proverbs. *Psychological Reports*, 1977, 41, 967–972.

1348. KING, G. D., GIDEON, D. A., HAYNES, C. D., DEMPSEY, R. L., & JENKINS, C. W. Intellectual and personality changes associated with carotid endarterectomy. *Journal of Clinical Psychology*, 1977, 33, 215–220.

1349. KING, G. D., & KELLEY, C. K. Behavioral correlates for Spike-4, Spike-9, and 4-9/9-4 MMPI profiles in students at a university mental health center. *Journal of Clinical Psychology*, 1977, 33, 718–724.

1350. KLJAJIĆ, I. Benton OCS and OES as actuarial indices of brain pathology. *Journal of Clinical Psychology*, 1977, 33, 792–794.

1351. KOH, S. D., SZOC, R., & PETERSON, R. A. Short–term memory scanning in schizophrenic young adults. *Journal of Abnormal Psychology*, 1977, 86, 451–460.

1352. KORBOOT, P. J., NAYLOR, G. F. K., & SOARES, A. Patterns of cognitive dysfunction in alcoholics. *Australian Journal of Psychology*, 1977, 29, 25–30.

1353. LANG, R. J., & VERNON, P. E. Dimensionality of the perceived self: The Tennessee Self Concept Scale. *British Journal of Social & Clinical Psychology*, 1977, 16, 363–371.

1354. LANSDELL, H., & DONNELLY, E. F. Factor analysis of the Wechsler Adult Intelligence Scale subtests and the Halstead–Reitan category and tapping tests. *Journal of Consulting & Clinical Psychology*, 1977, 45, 412–416.

1355. LARNER, S. Encoding in senile dementia and elderly depressives: A preliminary study. *British Journal of Social & Clinical Psychology*, 1977, 16, 379–390.

1356. LERER, R. J., & LERER, M. P. Responses of adolescents with minimal brain dysfunction to methylphenidate. *Journal of Learning Disabilities*, 1977, 10, 223–228.

1357. LEWINSOHN, P. M., DANAHER, B. G., & KIKEL, S. Visual imaginery as a mnemonic aid for brain–injured persons. *Journal of Consulting & Clinical Psychology*, 1977, 45, 717–723.

1358. LINCOLN, N. B., & STAPLES, D. J. Psychological aspects of some chronic progressive neuromuscular disorders. *Journal of Chronic Diseases*, 1977, 30, 207–215.

1359. LYLE, O. E., & GOTTESMAN, I. I. Premorbid psychometric indicators of the gene for Huntington's Disease. *Journal of Consulting & Clinical Psychology*, 1977, 45, 1011–1022.

1360. MALATESTA, C. Z., CIRCO, J., & SMITH, B. A discriminating, non–discriminatory test battery for a prison population. *Corrective & Social Psychiatry & Journal of Behavior Technology, Methods & Therapy*, 1977, 23, 15–17.

1361. MARTIN, J. D., BLAIR, G. E., STOKES, E. H., & ARMSTRONG, G. Correlation of the Object Assembly and Block Design Tests of the Wechsler Adult Intelligence Scale and the Torrance Tests of Creative Thinking. *Educational & Psychological Measurement*, 1977, 37, 1095–1097.

1362. MATARAZZO, J. D., & WIENS, A. N. Black Intelligence Test of Cultural Homogeneity and Wechsler Adult Intelligence Scale scores of black and white police applicants. *Journal of Applied Psychology*, 1977, 62, 57–63.

1363. MATHEWSON, P. D. The Kahn Intelligence Test (Experimental Form) recall scale as a measure of retention. *Journal of Consulting & Clinical Psychology*, 1977, 45, 148.

1364. MATTHEWS, K. A. Caregiver–child interactions and the type A coronary-prone behavior pattern. *Child Development*, 1977, 48, 1752–1756.

1365. McCALL, R. B. Childhood IQ's as predictors of adult educational and occupational status. *Science*, 1977, 197, 482–483.

1366. McFARLAIN, R. A., COHEN, G. H., YODER, J., & GUIDRY, L. Psychological test and demographic variables associated with retention of narcotic addicts in treatment. *International Journal of the Addictions*, 1977, 12, 399–410.

1367. McGLONE, J. Sex differences in the cerebral organization of verbal functions in patients with unilateral brain lesions. *Brain*, 1977, 100, 775–793.

1368. MIDDENTS, G. J. A pilot project for assessing nonacademic characteristics of premedical students. *Journal of Medical Education*, 1977, 52, 343–344.
1369. MITCHELL, N. B., POLLACK, R. H., & MCGREW, J. F. The relation of form perception to hue and fundus pigmentation. *Bulletin of the Psychonomic Society*, 1977, 9, 97–99.
1370. MLOTT, S. R., LIRA, F. T., & MILLER, W. C. Psychological assessment of the burn patient. *Journal of Clinical Psychology*, 1977, 33, 425–430.
1371. MUELLER, J. H. Test anxiety, input modality, and levels of organization in free recall. *Bulletin of the Psychonomic Society*, 1977, 9, 67–69.
1372. NASRALLAH, H. A., DONNELLY, E. F., BIGELOW, L. B., RIVERA-CALIMLIM, L., ROGOL, A., POTKIN, S., RAUSCHER, F. P., WYATT, R. J., & GILLIN, J. C. Inhibition of dopamine synthesis in chronic schizophrenia. *Archives of General Psychiatry*, 1977, 34, 649–655.
1373. NICHOLS, M. P., & KNOPF, I. J. Refining computerized test interpretations: An in-depth approach. *Journal of Personality Assessment*, 1977, 41, 157–159.
1374. NORTON, S. J., SCHULTZ, M. C., REED, C. M., BRAIDA, L. D., DURLACH, N. I., RABINOWITZ, W. M., & CHOMSKY, C. Analytic study of the Tadoma method: Background and preliminary results. *Journal of Speech & Hearing Research*, 1977, 20, 574–595.
1375. O'LEARY, M. R., DONOVAN, D. M., & CHANEY, E. F. The relationship of perceptual field orientation to measures of cognitive functioning and current adaptive abilities in alcoholics and nonalcoholics. *Journal of Nervous & Mental Disease*, 1977, 165, 275–282.
1376. OPOLOT, J. A. Reliability and validity of Smith's quick measure of achievement. *British Journal of Social & Clinical Psychology*, 1977, 16, 395–396.
1377. PAGE, R. D., & SCHAUB, L. H. Intellectual functioning in alcoholics during six months' abstinence. *Journal of Studies on Alcohol*, 1977, 38, 1240–1246.
1378. PHILLIPS, W. M. Structure of WAIS scores for private psychiatric inpatients. *Psychological Reports*, 1977, 44, 119–126.
1379. PICKERING, J. W., JOHNSON, D. L., & STARY, J. E. Systematic VIQ/PIQ differences on the WAIS: An artifact of this instrument? *Journal of Clinical Psychology*, 1977, 33, 1060–1064.
1380. PRINZ, P. N. Sleep patterns in the healthy aged: Relationship with intellectual function. *Journal of Gerontology*, 1977, 32, 179–186.
1381. PROKOP, C. K. The role of psychologic evaluation in determining the personal meanings of aging and illness. *Geriatrics*, 1977, 32, 125–139.
1382. PRYER, M. W., & DISTEFANO, M. K., JR. Correlates of locus of control among male alcoholics. *Journal of Clinical Psychology*, 1977, 33, 300–303.
1383. RAUSCH, R. Cognitive strategies in patients with unilateral temporal lobe excisions. *Neuropsychologia*, 1977, 15, 385–395.
1384. RAUSCH, R., SERAFETINIDES, E. A., & CRANDALL, P. H. Olfactory memory in patients with anterior temporal lobectomy. *Cortex*, 1977, 13, 445–452.
1385. REED, G. F. Obsessional cognitive: Performance on two numerical tasks. *British Journal of Psychiatry*, 1977, 130, 184–185.
1386. REED, G. F. Obsessional personality disorder and remembering. *British Journal of Psychiatry*, 1977, 130, 177–183.
1387. RITZLER, B. A. Proprioception and schizophrenia: A replication study with nonschizophrenic patient controls. *Journal of Abnormal Psychology*, 1977, 86, 501–509.
1388. RUST, J. O., & OSTER, G. D. Accuracy of feelings of correctness on the WAIS and Binet. *Psychological Reports*, 1977, 41, 1275–1278.
1389. SACCUZZO, D. P., & MILLER, S. Critical interstimulus interval in delusional schizophrenics and normals. *Journal of Abnormal Psychology*, 1977, 86, 261–266.
1390. SCARDAMALIA, M. Information processing capacity and the problem of horizontal *decalage*: A demonstration using combinatorial reasoning tasks. *Child Development*, 1977, 48, 28–37.
1391. SCHAU, E. J., & O'LEARY, M. R. Adoptive abilities of hospitalized alcoholics and matched controls: The brain-age quotient. *Journal of Studies on Alcohol*, 1977, 38, 403–409.
1392. SCHMOLLING, P., & LAPIDUS, L. B. Effect of enriched stimulus and instructional conditions on verbal abstracting ability in acute schizophrenics. *Psychological Reports*, 1977, 41, 1203–1210.
1393. SILVERSTEIN, A. B. Comparison of two criteria for determining the number of factors. *Psychological Reports*, 1977, 41, 387–390.
1394. SINES, J. O. M-F: Bipolar and probably multidimensional. *Journal of Clinical Psychology*, 1977, 33, 1038–1041.
1395. SMITH, A. D. Adult age differences in cued recall. *Developmental Psychology*, 1977, 13, 326–331.
1396. SMITH, C. A., & MORRIS, L. W. Differential effects of stimulative and sedative music on anxiety, concentration, and performance. *Psychological Reports*, 1977, 41, 1047–1053.
1397. SMITH, H. H., JR., & SMITH, L. S. WAIS functioning of cirrhotic and non-cirrhotic alcoholics. *Journal of Clinical Psychology*, 1977, 33, 309–313.
1398. SPOHN, H. E., LACOURSIERE, R. B., THOMPSON, K., & COYNE, L. Phenothiazine effects on psychological and psychophysiological dysfunction in chronic schizophrenics. *Archives of General Psychiatry*, 1977, 34, 633–644.
1399. STEFFY, A. R. F., STEFFY, R. A., MACCRIMMON, D. J., & CLEGHORN, J. M. An attentional assessment of foster children at risk for schizophrenia. *Journal of Abnormal Psychology*, 1977, 86, 267–275.
1400. STEWART, D. W., & MORRIS, L. Intelligence and academic achievement in a clinical adolescent population. *Psychology in the Schools*, 1977, 14, 513–518.
1401. STORANDT, M. Age, ability level, & method of administering and scoring the WAIS. *Journal of Gerontology*, 1977, 32, 175–178.
1402. SWIERCINSKY, D. P. Significance of crossed eye–hand dominance for the adult neuropsychological evaluation. *Journal of Nervous & Mental Disease*, 1977, 165, 134–138.
1403. THUMIN, F., & STERN, A. Two construct validity studies of the Thumin Test of Mental Dexterity. *Psychological Reports*, 1977, 40, 884–886.
1404. TODD, J., COOLIDGE, F., & SATZ, P. The Wechsler Adult Intelligence Scale discrepancy index: A neuropsychological evaluation. *Journal of Consulting & Clinical Psychology*, 1977, 45, 450–454.
1405. TSUSHIMA, W. T., & BRATTON, J. C. Effects of geographic region upon Wechsler Adult Intelligence Scale results: A Hawaii–mainland United States comparison. *Journal of Consulting & Clinical Psychology*, 1977, 45, 501–502.
1406. TURNER, R. G., & GILLILAND, L. Comparison of self-report and performance measures of attention. *Perceptual & Motor Skills*, 1977, 45, 409–410.
1407. TURNER, R. G., & WILLERMAN, L. Sex differences in WAIS item performance. *Journal of Clinical Psychology*, 1977, 33, 795–797.
1408. VANDER KOLK, C. J. Demographic, etiological, and functional variables related to intelligence in the visually impaired. *Journal of Clinical Psychology*, 1977, 33, 782–786.
1409. VOGT, A. T., & HEATON, R. K. Comparison of Wechsler Adult Intelligence Scale indices of cerebral dysfunction. *Perceptual & Motor Skills*, 1977, 45, 607–615.
1410. WEINRAUB, M., & LEWIS, M. The determinants of children's responses to separation. *Monographs of the Society for Research in Child Development*, 1977, 42, 1–78.
1411. WEINSTEIN, N. D. Noise and intellectual performance: A confirmation and extension. *Journal of Applied Psychology*, 1977, 62, 104–107.
1412. WENDER, P. H., ROSENTHAL, D., RAINER, J. D., GREENHILL, L., & SARLIN, B. Schizophrenics adopting parents. *Archives of General Psychiatry*, 1977, 34, 777–783.
1413. WHITEHEAD, A. Changes in cognitive functioning in elderly psychiatric patients. *British Journal of Psychiatry*, 1977, 130, 605–608.
1414. WIENS, A. N., & MATARAZZO, J. D. WAIS and MMPI correlates of the Halstead–Reitan Neuropsychology Battery in normal male subjects. *Journal of Nervous & Mental Disease*, 1977, 164, 112–121.
1415. WILD, C. M., & SHAPIRO, L. N. Mechanisms of change from individual to family performance in male schizophrenics and their parents. *Journal of Nervous & Mental Disease*, 1977, 165, 41–56.
1416. WILDMAN, R. W., & WILDMAN, R. W., II. Validity of verbal IQ as a short form of the Wechsler Adult Intelligence Scale. *Journal of Consulting & Clinical Psychology*, 1977, 45, 171–172.
1417. WILKIE, F. L., & EISDORFER, C. Sex, verbal ability, and pacing differences in serial learning. *Journal of Gerontology*, 1977, 32, 63–67.
1418. ANDERSON, R. Cognitive changes after amygdalotomy. *Neuropsychologia*, 1978, 16, 439–451.
1419. ANDERT, J. N., HUSTAK, T. L., & DINNING, W. D. Bender-Gestalt reproduction times for retarded adults. *Journal of Clinical Psychology*, 1978, 34, 927–929.
1420. ANDREW, J. M. Why can't delinquents read? *Perceptual & Motor Skills*, 1978, 47, 640.
1421. ARBIT, J., & ZAGER, R. Psychometrics of a neuropsychological test battery. *Journal of Clinical Psychology*, 1978, 34, 460–465.
1422. ARENBERG, D. Differences and changes with age in the Benton Visual Retention Test. *Journal of Gerontology*, 1978, 33, 534–540.
1423. ARNDT, S., & BERGER, D. E. Cognitive mode and asymmetry in cerebral functioning. *Cortex*, 1978, 14, 78–86.
1424. ASARNOW, R. F., CROMWELL, R. L., & RENNICK, P. M. Cognitive and evoked response measures of information processing in schizophrenics with and without a family history of schizophrenia. *Journal of Nervous & Mental Disease*, 1978, 166, 719–730.
1425. ASARNOW, R. F., & MACCRIMMON, D. J. Residual performance deficit in clinically remitted schizophrenics: A marker of schizophrenia? *Journal of Abnormal Psychology*, 1978, 87, 597–608.
1426. ASARNOW, R. F., & MANN, R. Size estimation in paranoid and nonparanoid schizophrenics: A test of the stimulus redundancy formulation interpretation. *Journal of Nervous & Mental Disease*, 1978, 166, 96–103.
1427. BASSO, A., TABORELLI, A., & VIGNOLO, L. A. Dissociated disorders of speaking and writing in aphasia. *Journal of Neurology, Neurosurgery, & Psychiatry*, 1978, 41, 556–563.

1428. BELFORD, B., & RUSSELL, E. W. Cortical involvement in schizophrenics. *Psychological Reports*, 1978, 42, 1039-1047.

1429. BENSON, K., COHEN, M., & ZARCONE, V., JR. REM sleep time and digit span impairment in alcoholics. *Journal of Studies on Alcohol*, 1978, 39, 1488-1498.

1430. BLACK, F. W., & STRUB, R. L. Digit repetition performance in patients with focal brain damage. *Cortex*, 1978, 14, 12-21.

1431. BOTWINICK, J., WEST, R., & STORANDT, M. Predicting death from behavioral test performance. *Journal of Gerontology*, 1978, 33, 755-762.

1432. BUCCI, W., & FREEDMAN, N. Language and hand: The dimension of referential competence. *Journal of Personality*, 1978, 46, 594-622.

1433. BURIEL, R. Relationship of three field-dependence measures to the reading and math achievement of Anglo American and Mexican American children. *Journal of Educational Psychology*, 1978, 70, 167-174.

1434. BUTTERS, N., SAX, D., MONTGOMERY, K., & TARLOW, S. Comparison of the neuropsychological deficits associated with early and advanced Huntington's Disease. *Archives of Neurology*, 1978, 35, 585-589.

1435. CAINE, E. D., HUNT, R. D., WEINGARTNER, H., & EBERT, M. H. Huntington's Dementia. *Archives of General Psychiatry*, 1978, 35, 377-384.

1436. CALVERT, E. J., & CROZIER, W. R. An analysis of verbal-performance intelligence quotient discrepancies in the Wechsler Adult Intelligence Scale results of mentally subnormal hospital patients. *Journal of Mental Deficiency Research*, 1978, 22, 147-153.

1437. CATRON, D. W. Immediate test-retest changes in WAIS scores among college males. *Psychological Reports*, 1978, 43, 279-290.

1438. CAUTHEN, N. Normative data for the tactual performance test. *Journal of Clinical Psychology*, 1978, 34, 456-460.

1439. CAUTHEN, N. R. Verbal fluency: Normative data. *Journal of Clinical Psychology*, 1978, 34, 126-129.

1440. CIULA, B. A., & CODY, J. J. Comparative study of validity of the WAIS and Quick Test as predictors of functioning intelligence in a psychiatric facility. *Psychological Reports*, 1978, 42, 971-974.

1441. CLARK, S., & LANE, M. K. Women's behavioral manifestations of traditionalist and liberated role concepts. *Journal of Psychology*, 1978, 98, 81-89.

1442. COUGHLAN, A. K., & WARRINGTON, E. K. Word comprehension and word-retrieval in patients with localized cerebral lesions. *Brain*, 1978, 101, 163-185.

1443. CUTTING, J. The relationship between Korsakov's Syndrome and "alcoholic dementia". *British Journal of Psychiatry*, 1978, 132, 240-251.

1444. CUTTING, J. Specific psychological deficits in alcoholism. *British Journal of Psychiatry*, 1978, 133, 119-122.

1445. DIETVORST, T. F., SWENSON, W. M., & MORSE, R. M. Intellectual assessment in a midwestern alcoholism treatment population. *Journal of Clinical Psychology*, 1978, 34, 244-249.

1446. DIKMEN, S., & REITAN, R. M. Neuropsychological performance in posttraumatic epilepsy. *Epilepsia*, 1978, 19, 117-183.

1447. DODRILL, C. B. A neuropsychological battery for epilepsy. *Epilepsia*, 1978, 19, 611-623.

1448. DODRILL, C. B., & WILKUS, R. J. Neuropsychological correlates of the electroencephalogram in epileptics: III. Generalized nonepileptiform abnormalities. *Epilepsia*, 1978, 19, 453-462.

1449. DONNELLY, E. F., NASRALLAH, H. A., WYATT, R. J., GILLIAN, J. C., & BIGELOW, L. B. Effects of dopamine synthesis inhibition on WAIS comprehension. *Journal of Consulting & Clinical Psychology*, 1978, 46, 385-388.

1450. DOR-SHAV, N. K. On the long-range effects of concentration camp internment on Nazi victims: 25 years later. *Journal of Consulting & Clinical Psychology*, 1978, 46, 1-11.

1451. DUVALL, S. W., & MALONEY, M. P. Comparison of the WAIS and Leiter International Performance Scale in a large urban community mental health setting. *Psychological Reports*, 1978, 43, 235-238.

1452. DYCK, D. G., & BREEN, L. J. Learned helplessness, immunization and importance of task in humans. *Psychological Reports*, 1978, 43, 315-321.

1453. ERICKSON, R. C., CALSYN, D. A., & SCHEUPBACH, C. S. Abbreviating the Halstead-Reitan Neuropsychological Test Battery. *Journal of Clinical Psychology*, 1978, 34, 922-926.

1454. FENTON, G. W., FENWICK, P. B. C., FERGUSON, W., & LAM, C. T. The contingent negative variation in antisocial behaviour: A pilot study of Broadmoor patients. *British Journal of Psychiatry*, 1978, 132, 368-377.

1455. FLETCHER, J. M., RICE, W. J., & RAY, R. M. Linear discriminant function analysis in neuropsychological research: Some uses and abuses. *Cortex*, 1978, 14, 564-577.

1456. FREDERICKS, R. S., & FINKEL, P. Schizophrenic performance on the Halstead-Reitan battery. *Journal of Clinical Psychology*, 1978, 34, 26-30.

1457. FUNDERBURK, S. J., & FERJO, N. Clinical observations in Klinefelter (47, XXY) Syndrome. *Journal of Mental Deficiency Research*, 1978, 22, 207-212.

1458. GAINES, T., & MORRIS, R. Relationships between MMPI measures of psychopathology and WAIS subtest scores and intelligence quotients. *Perceptual & Motor Skills*, 1978, 47, 399-402.

1459. GELENBERG, A. J., KLERMAN, G. L., HARTMAN, E. L., & SALT, P. Recurrent unipolar depression with a 48-hour cycle. *British Journal of Psychiatry*, 1978, 133, 123-129.

1460. GIFT, T. E., STRAUSS, J. S., & RITZLER, B. A. The failure to detect low IQ in psychiatric assessment. *American Journal of Psychiatry*, 1978, 135, 345-349.

1461. GOLDFRIED, M. R., LINEHAN, M. M., & SMITH, J. L. Reduction of test anxiety through cognitive restructuring. *Journal of Consulting & Clinical Psychology*, 1978, 46, 32-39.

1462. GRANT, E. A., STORANDT, M., & BOTWINICK, J. Incentive and practice in the psychomotor performance of the elderly. *Journal of Gerontology*, 1978, 33, 413-415.

1463. GREENBERG, R. P., & CARDWELL, G. F. Rorschach developmental level and intelligence factors. *Journal of Consulting & Clinical Psychology*, 1978, 46, 844-848.

1464. GRIFFITHS, R. D. P., & GILLINGHAM, P. The influence of videotape feedback on the self-assessment of psychiatric patients. *British Journal of Psychiatry*, 1978, 133, 156-161.

1465. GRUZELIER, J. H., & HAMMOND, N. The effect of chlorpromazine upon psycho-physiological, endocrine and information processing measures in schizophrenia. *Journal of Psychiatric Research*, 1978, 14, 167-182.

1466. GUIDRY, L. L., MCBRIDE, W. A., & WALTERS, T. J. WAIS performance of forensic versus civilly committed mental retardates. *Psychological Reports*, 1978, 43, 723-726.

1467. HAFNER, J. L., COROTTO, L. V., & CURNUTT, R. H. The development of a WAIS short form for clinical populations. *Journal of Clinical Psychology*, 1978, 34, 935-937.

1468. HAGGARD, M. R. The effect of creative thinking-reading activities (CT-RA) on reading comprehension. *National Reading Conference Yearbook*, 1978, 233-236.

1469. HÄNNINEN, H., NURMINEN, M., TOLONEN, M., & MARTELIN, T. Psychological tests as indicators of excessive exposure to carbon disulfide. *Scandinavian Journal of Psychology*, 1978, 19, 163-174.

1470. HARROW, M., & PROSEN, M. Intermingling and disordered logic as influences on schizophrenic "thought disorders". *Archives of General Psychiatry*, 1978, 35, 1213-1218.

1471. HEATON, R. K., CHELUNE, G. J., & LEHMAN, R. A. W. Using neuropsychological and personality tests to assess the likelihood of patient employment. *Journal of Nervous & Mental Disease*, 1978, 166, 408-416.

1472. HEATON, R. K., SMITH, H. H., JR., LEHMAMN, R. A. W., & VOGT, A. T. Prospects for faking believable deficits on neuropsychological testing. *Journal of Consulting & Clinical Psychology*, 1978, 46, 892-900.

1473. HEILBRUN, A. B., JR., & MADISON, J. K. An analysis of structural factors in schizophrenic delusions. *Journal of Clinical Psychology*, 1978, 34, 326-329.

1474. HENRICHS, T. F., & AMOLSCH, T. J. A note on the actuarial interpretation of WAIS profile patterns. *Journal of Personality Assessment*, 1978, 42, 418-420.

1475. HIER, D. B., LEMAY, M., ROSENBERGER, P. B., & PERLO, V. P. Developmental dyslexia. *Archives of Neurology*, 1978, 35, 90-92.

1476. HILL, A. L. WAIS subtest score characteristics of institutionalized mentally retarded samples. *Perceptual & Motor Skills*, 1978, 47, 131-134.

1477. HOLTZMAN, R. N. N., RUDEL, R. G., & GOLDENSOHN, E. S. Paroxysmal alexia. *Cortex*, 1978, 14, 592-603.

1478. HUBBLE, L. M. Comparability and equivalence of estimates of IQs from Revised Beta Examination and Wechsler Adult Intelligence Scale among older male delinquents. *Psychological Reports*, 1978, 42, 1030.

1479. INTAGLIATA, J. C. Increasing the interpersonal problem-solving skills of an alcoholic population. *Journal of Consulting & Clinical Psychology*, 1978, 46, 489-498.

1480. IVNIK, R. J. Neuropsychological stability in multiple sclerosis. *Journal of Consulting & Clinical Psychology*, 1978, 46, 913-923.

1481. IVNIK, R. J. Neuropsychological test performance as a function of the duration of MS-related symptomatology. *Journal of Clinical Psychiatry*, 1978, 39, 304-312.

1482. JENKINS, M. B., KRIEL, R. L., BOYD, L., & BARNWELL, A. Trisomy 21 with 47, +18 lymphocyte cell line: Double mitotic nondisjunction. *Journal of Medical Genetics*, 1978, 15, 396-397.

1483. KLINE, D. W., & ORME-ROGERS, C. Examination of stimulus persistence as the basis for superior visual identification performance among older adults. *Journal of Gerontology*, 1978, 33, 76-81.

1484. KLING, J. O., DAVIS, W. E., & KNOST, E. K. Henmon-Nelson IQ scores as predictors of WAIS full scale IQ in alcoholics. *Journal of Clinical Psychology*, 1978, 34, 1001-1002.

1485. LANG, R. J. Multivariate classification of day-care patients: Personality as a continuum. *Journal of Consulting & Clinical Psychology*, 1978, 46, 1212-1226.

1486. LANGEVIN, R., PAITICH, D., FREEMAN, R., MANN, K., & HANDY, L. Personality characteristics and sexual anomalies in males. *Canadian Journal of Behavioural Science*, 1978, 10, 222-238.
1487. LATCHAM, R., WHITE, A., & SIMS, A. Ganser Syndrome: The aetiological argument. *Journal of Neurology, Neurosurgery, & Psychiatry*, 1978, 41, 851-854.
1488. LAWRIW, I., & SUTKER, L. W. A further analysis of the Block Rotation Test. *Journal of Clinical Psychology*, 1978, 34, 930-934.
1489. LEVY, D. L., HOLZMAN, P. S., & PROCTOR, L. R. Vestibular responses in schizophrenia. *Archives of General Psychiatry*, 1978, 35, 972-981.
1490. LOO, R. Personality dimensions and reversible perspective in Embedded Figures Test. *Perceptual & Motor Skills*, 1978, 46, 1016-1018.
1491. LUBIN, B., MARONE, J. G., & NATHAN, R. G. Comparison of self-administered and examiner-administered Depression Adjective Check Lists. *Journal of Consulting & Clinical Psychology*, 1978, 46, 384-385.
1492. LUNNEBORG, C. E. Some information-processing correlates of measures of intelligence. *Multivariate Behavioral Research*, 1978, 13, 153-161.
1493. MALONEY, M. P., NELSON, D., DUVALL, S., & KIRKENDALL, A. Performance of psychiatric inpatients on three standard tests of intelligence. *Psychological Reports*, 1978, 43, 1289-1290.
1494. MATARAZZO, J. D., WIENS, A. N., & SHEALY, A. E. Correlation of WAIS IQ in 10 pairs of brothers. *Journal of Consulting & Clinical Psychology*, 1978, 46, 571-572.
1495. MCGLONE, J. Sex differences in functional asymmetry. *Cortex*, 1978, 14, 122-128.
1496. MCGURK, B. J. Personality types among "normal" homicides. *British Journal of Criminology*, 1978, 18, 146-161.
1497. MENDHIRATTA, S. S., WIG, N. N., & VERMA, S. K. Some psychological correlates of long-term heavy cannabis users. *British Journal of Psychiatry*, 1978, 132, 482-486.
1498. MOHS, R. C., TINKLENBERG, J. R., ROTH, W. T., & KOPELL, B. S. Slowing of short-term memory scanning in alcoholics. *Journal of Studies on Alcohol*, 1978, 39, 1908-1915.
1499. MONEY, J., CLARKE, F. C., & BECK, J. Congenital hypothyroidism and I.Q. increase: A quarter century follow-up. *Journal of Pediatrics*, 1978, 93, 432-434.
1500. MONSEN, R. B. Toward measuring how well hearing-impaired children speak. *Journal of Speech & Hearing Research*, 1978, 21, 197-219.
1501. MUELLER, J. H., CARLOMUSTO, M., & MARLER, M. Recall and organization in memory as a function of rate of presentation and individual differences in test anxiety. *Bulletin of the Psychonomic Society*, 1978, 12, 133-136.
1502. NELSON, H. E., & O'CONNELL, A. Dementia: The estimation of premorbid intelligence levels using the New Adult Reading Test. *Cortex*, 1978, 14, 234-244.
1503. NELSON, W. M., III, EDINGER, J. D., & WALLACE, J. The utility of two Wechsler Adult Intelligence Scale short forms with prisoners. *Journal of Personality Assessment*, 1978, 42, 302-311.
1504. NEWMAN, O. S., HEATON, R. K., & LEHMAN, A. W. Neuropsychological and MMPI correlates of patients' future employment characteristics. *Perceptual & Motor Skills*, 1978, 46, 635-642.
1505. NOLAN, J. D., HAVEMEYER, E., & VIG, S. Mature and young adult women's recall of textbook material. *Journal of Educational Psychology*, 1978, 70, 695-700.
1506. NORTON, J. C. The Trail Making Test and Bender Background Interference Procedure as screening devices. *Journal of Clinical Psychology*, 1978, 34, 916-922.
1507. OIKAWA, K., DEONAUTH, J., & BREIDBART, S. Mental retardation and elevated serotonin levels in adults. *Life Sciences*, 1978, 23, 45-48.
1508. OVERALL, J. E., HOFFMANN, N. G., & LEVIN, H. Effects of aging, organicity, alcoholism, and functional psychopathology on WAIS subtest profiles. *Journal of Consulting & Clinical Psychology*, 1978, 46, 1315-1322.
1509. OVERALL, J. E., & LEVIN, H. S. Correcting for cultural factors in evaluating intellectual deficit on the WAIS. *Journal of Clinical Psychology*, 1978, 34, 910-915.
1510. PERMAN, B. E. Reading attainment in hearing-impaired children: A comparison of higher and lower achievers. *Journal of Communication Disorders*, 1978, 11, 227-235.
1511. PRANDONI, J. R., & SWARTZ, C. P. Rorschach protocols for three diagnostic categories of adult offenders: Normative data. *Journal of Personality Assessment*, 1978, 42, 115-120.
1512. RABINOWITZ, S., & VAN DER SPUY, H. I. J. Selection criteria for dialysis and renal transplant. *American Journal of Psychiatry*, 1978, 135, 861-862.
1513. RADFORD, L. M., CHANEY, E. F., O'LEARY, M. R., & O'LEARY, D. E. Screening for cognitive impairment among inpatients. *Journal of Clinical Psychiatry*, 1978, 39, 712-715.
1514. RAMSEY, P. H. Factor analysis of the WAIS and twenty French-kit reference tests. *Applied Psychological Measurement*, 1978, 2, 505-517.

1515. RASKIN, A., GERSHON, S., CROOK, T. H., SATHANANTHAN, G., & FERRIS, S. The effects of hyperbaric and normobaric oxygen on cognitive impairment in the elderly. *Archives of General Psychiatry*, 1978, 35, 50-56.
1516. RAUSCH, R., LEIB, J. P., & CRANDALL, P. H. Neuropsychologic correlates of depth spike activity in epileptic patients. *Archives of Neurology*, 1978, 35, 699-705.
1517. REARN, J. H., III. Evaluation of intelligence in youthful offenders: The Kahn Intelligence Tests. *Perceptual & Motor Skills*, 1978, 46, 835-838.
1518. REYNOLDS, W. M. A question as to the validity of the verbal scale IQ as a WAIS short form. *Journal of Consulting & Clinical Psychology*, 1978, 46, 1535-1536.
1519. RICHARDSON, J. T. E. Memory and intelligence following spontaneously arrested congenital hydrocephalus. *British Journal of Social & Clinical Psychology*, 1978, 17, 261-267.
1520. RIERDAN, J., LANG, E., & EDDY, S. Suicide and transparency responses on the Rorschach: A replication. *Journal of Consulting & Clinical Psychology*, 1978, 46, 1162-1163.
1521. RINGLER, N., TRAUSE, M. A., KLAUS, M., & KENNELL, J. The effects of extra postpartum contact and maternal speech patterns on children's IQs, speech, and language comprehension at five. *Child Development*, 1978, 49, 862-865.
1522. ROBINSON, J. A., & BENNIK, C. D. Field articulation and working memory. *Journal of Research in Personality*, 1978, 12, 439-449.
1523. ROSENBLATT, A. I., & PRITCHARD, D. A. Moderators of racial differences on the MMPI. *Journal of Consulting & Clinical Psychology*, 1978, 46, 1572-1573.
1524. RUBIN, R. A., & BALOW, B. Prevalence of teacher identified behavior problems: Longitudinal study. *Exceptional Children*, 1978, 45, 102-111.
1525. RYHÄNEN, P., HELKALA, E., IHALAINEN, O., HOLLMÉN, A., RANTAKYLÄ, S., MERILÄ, M., TUOHINO, V., PIETARILA, M., & HORTTONEN, L. Effects of anasthesia on the psychological function of patients. *Annals of Clinical Research*, 1978, 10, 318-322.
1526. SALTHOUSE, T. A. The role of memory in the age decline in digit-symbol substitution performance. *Journal of Gerontology*, 1978, 33, 232-238.
1527. SCARR, S., & WEINBERG, R. A. The influence of "family background" on intellectual attainment. *American Sociological Review*, 1978, 43, 674-692.
1528. SCHREINER, J. Prediction of retarded adults' work performance through components of general ability. *American Journal of Mental Deficiency*, 1978, 83, 77-79.
1529. SHAWVER, L., & JEW, C. Predicting violent behavior from WAIS characteristics: A replication failure. *Journal of Consulting & Clinical Psychology*, 1978, 46, 206.
1530. SHEALY, A. E. Comparison of two non-intellective scales of intelligence and their relationship to intellectual changes following surgery. *Psychological Reports*, 1978, 42, 51-56.
1531. SHEALY, A. E., & WALKER, D. R. Minnesota Multiphasic Personality Inventory prediction of intellectual changes following cardiac surgery. *Journal of Nervous & Mental Disease*, 1978, 166, 263-267.
1532. SPELLACY, F. Neuropsychological discrimination between violent and non-violent men. *Journal of Clinical Psychology*, 1978, 34, 49-52.
1533. STOKOLS, D., NOVACO, R. W., & STOKOLS, J. Traffic congestion, Type A behavior, and stress. *Journal of Applied Psychology*, 1978, 63, 467-480.
1534. STREISSGUTH, A. P., HERMAN, C. S., & SMITH, D. W. Intelligence, behavior, and dysmorphogenesis in the fetal alcohol syndrome: A report of 20 patients. *Journal of Pediatrics*, 1978, 92, 363-367.
1535. SWIERCINSKY, D. P., & PATTERSON, T. W. The revised Army Alpha Examination as a predictor of intelligence and brain impairment. *Psychological Reports*, 1978, 42, 601-602.
1536. TELEFORD, R., & WORRALL, E. P. Cognitive functions in manic-depressives: Effects of lithium and physostigmine. *British Journal of Psychiatry*, 1978, 133, 424-428.
1537. THEILGAARD, A., LAURSEN, P., KJAERBY, O., PALUDAN, B., HOFFMAN, G., ZILSTORFF, K., & THOMSEN, J. Meniere's Disease. II. A neuropsychological study. *Annals of Otology, Rhinology & Laryngology*, 1978, 40, 139-146.
1538. TUCKER, G. H., & SUIB, M. R. Conjugate lateral eye movement (CLEM) direction and its relationship to performance on verbal and visuospatial tasks. *Neuropsychologia*, 1978, 16, 251-254.
1539. URBAN, M. D., ROGERS, J. G., & MEYER, W. J. Familial syndrome of mental retardation, short stature, contractures of the hands, and genital anomalies. *Journal of Pediatrics*, 1978, 94, 52-55.
1540. VERNON, P. E., RYBA, K. A., & LANG, R. J. Simultaneous and successive processing: An attempt at replication. *Canadian Journal of Behavioural Science*, 1978, 10, 1-15.
1541. WADE, T. C., BAKER, T. B., MORTON, T. L., & BAKER, L. J. The status of psychological testing in clinical psychology: Relationships between test use and professional activities and orientations. *Journal of Personality Assessment*, 1978, 42, 3-10.

1542. WAGNER, E. E., KLEIN, I., & WALTER, T. Differentiation of brain damage among low IQ subjects with three projective techniques. *Journal of Personality Assessment*, 1978, 42, 49–55.

1543. WAPNER, W., JUDD, T., & GARDNER, H. Visual agnosia in an artist. *Cortex*, 1978, 14, 343–364.

1544. WATSON, C. G., DAVIS, W. E., & GASSER, B. The separation of organics from depressives with ability- and personality-based tests. *Journal of Clinical Psychology*, 1978, 34, 393–397.

1545. WATSON, C. G., KUCALA, T., & JACOBS, L. The prediction of outcome from anhedonia and process–reactive scales. *Journal of Clinical Psychology*, 1978, 34, 889–892.

1546. WATSON, C. G., & PLEMEL, D. An MMPI scale to separate brain-damaged from functional psychiatric patients in neuropsychiatric settings. *Journal of Consulting & Clinical Psychology*, 1978, 46, 1127–1132.

1547. WECKOWICZ, T. E., TAM, C. I., MASON, J., & BAY, K. S. Speed in test performance in depressed patients. *Journal of Abnormal Psychology*, 1978, 87, 578–582.

1548. WEHLER, R., & HOFFMAN, H. Intellectual functioning in lobotomized and non-lobotomized long term chronic schizophrenic patients. *Journal of Clinical Psychology*, 1978, 34, 449–451.

1549. WEISS, G., HECHTMAN, L., & PERLMAN, T. Hyperactives as young adults: School, employer, and self-rating scales obtained during ten-year follow–up evaluation. *American Journal of Orthopsychiatry*, 1978, 48, 438–445.

1550. WIERZBICKI, M., & YOUNG, R. D. The relation of intelligence and task difficulty to appreciation of humor. *Journal of General Psychology*, 1978, 99, 25–32.

1551. WILSON, S., & KENNARD, D. The extraverting effect of treatment in a therapeutic community for drug abusers. *British Journal of Psychiatry*, 1978, 132, 296–299.

1552. WILSON, R. S., ROSENBAUM, G., BROWN, G., ROURKE, D., WHITMAN, D., & GRISELL, J. An index of premorbid intelligence. *Journal of Consulting & Clinical Psychology*, 1978, 46, 1554–1555.

1553. WILSON, S., & MANDELBROTE, B. Drug rehabilitation and criminality. *British Journal of Criminology*, 1978, 18, 381–386.

1554. ARCHER, R. P., WHITE, J. L., & ORVIN, G. H. MMPI characteristics and correlates among adolescent psychiatric inpatients. *Journal of Clinical Psychology*, 1979, 35, 498–504.

1555. BAILEY, K. G., & FEDERMAN, E. J. Factor analysis of breadth and depth dimensions on Wechsler's similarities and vocabulary subscales. *Journal of Clinical Psychology*, 1979, 35, 341–345.

1556. BALSLEY, I. W. A psychological battery approach to the assessment and evaluation of shorthand skills. *Balance Sheet*, LVI, 1979, 1, 13–20.

1557. BASSETT, J. E., & GAYTON, W. F. Wechsler object assembly and bodily concern: A behavioral extension with prisoners. *Journal of Consulting & Clinical Psychology*, 1979, 47, 984–985.

1558. BEAUVOIS, M. F., & DEROUESNE, J. Phonological alexia: Three dissociations. *Journal of Neurology, Neurosurgery, & Psychiatry*, 1979, 42, 1115–1124.

1559. BENTIN, S., & GORDON, H. W. Assessment of cognitive asymmetries in brain–damaged and normal subjects: Validation of a test battery. *Journal of Neurology, Neurosurgery, & Psychiatry*, 1979, 42, 715–723.

1560. BERGER, E., & GOLDBERGER, L. Field dependence and short-term memory. *Perceptual & Motor Skills*, 1979, 49, 87–96.

1561. BIGELOW, L. B., DONNELLY, E. P., TORREY, E. F., & LEE, C. A. Assessment of clinical status of schizophrenic patients by the WAIS comprehension subtest. *Journal of Clinical Psychiatry*, 1979, 40, 258–261.

1562. BROWN, H. S., & MAY, A. E. A test–retest reliability study of the Wechsler Adult Intelligence Scale. *Journal of Consulting & Clinical Psychology*, 1979, 47, 601–602.

1563. BUHRICH, N., & MCCONAGHY, N. Tests of gender feelings and behavior in homosexuality, transvestism, and transsexualism. *Journal of Clinical Psychology*, 1979, 35, 187–191.

1564. BURKE, M., HINTON, J., & O'NEILL, M. Past alcohol intake, intellectual functioning and psychopathic behavior. *Psychological Reports*, 1979, 44, 394.

1565. CAPPA, S. F., & VIGNOLO, L. A. "Transcortical" features of aphasia following left thalamic hemorrhage. *Cortex*, 1979, 15, 121–130.

1566. CARR, A. C., GOLDSTEIN, E. G., HUNT, H. F., & KERNBERG, O. F. Psychological tests and borderline patients. *Journal of Personality Assessment*, 1979, 43, 582–590.

1567. CATRON, D. W., & THOMPSON, C. C. Test–retest gains in WAIS scores after four retest intervals. *Journal of Clinical Psychology*, 1979, 35, 352–357.

1568. CHELUNE, G. J., HEATON, R. K., LEHMAN, R. A. W., & ROBINSON, A. Level versus pattern of neuropsychological performance among schizophrenic and diffusely brain–damaged patients. *Journal of Consulting & Clinical Psychology*, 1979, 47, 155–163.

1569. CLARKE-STEWART, K. A., VANDER STOEP, L. P., & KILLIAN, G. A. Analysis and replication of mother–child relations at two years of age. *Child Development*, 1979, 50, 777–793.

1570. COURSEY, R. D., BUCHSBAUM, M. S., & MURPHY, D. L. Platelet MAO activity and evoked potentials in the identification of subjects biologically at risk for psychiatric disorders. *British Journal of Psychiatry*, 1979, 134, 372–381.

1571. CRAFT, N. P., & KRONENBERGER, E. J. Comparability of WISC–R and WAIS IQ scores in educable mentally handicapped adolescents. *Psychology in the Schools*, 1979, 16, 502–504.

1572. CRAIG, R. J., & VERINIS, J. S. Evidence for organicity in concrete vs. overinclusive thought–disordered schizophrenics. *Journal of Clinical Psychology*, 1979, 35, 696–703.

1573. CROVITZ, H. F., HARVEY, M. T., & HORN, R. W. Problems in the acquisition of imagery mnemonics: Three brain–damaged cases. *Cortex*, 1979, 15, 225–234.

1574. DASTOOR, D. P., KLINGNER, A., MÜLLER, H. F., & KACHANOFF, R. A psychogeriatric assessment program. V. Three-year follow–up. *Journal of the American Geriatrics Society*, 1979, 27, 162–169.

1575. DAUPHINAIS, S. M., & BRADLEY, R. W. IQ change and occupational level: A longitudinal study with third Harvard growth study participants. *Journal of Vocational Behavior*, 1979, 15, 367–375.

1576. DAVIS, T. M., & RODRIGUEZ, V. L. Comparison of scores on the WAIS and its Puerto Rican counterpart, Escala De Inteligencia Wechsler Para Adultos, in an institutionalized Latin American psychiatric population. *Journal of Consulting & Clinical Psychology*, 1979, 47, 181–182.

1577. DICKSON, W. P., HESS, R. D., MIYAKE, N., & AZUMA, H. Referential communication accuracy between mother and child as a predictor of cognitive development in the United States and Japan. *Child Development*, 1979, 50, 53–59.

1578. DIETVORST, T. F., SWENSON, W. M., NIVEN, R. G., & MORSE, R. M. Analysis of the MMPI profiles of physicians in treatment for drug dependency. *Journal of Studies on Alcohol*, 1979, 40, 1023–1029.

1579. D'ORBÁN, P. T. Women who kill their children. *British Journal of Psychiatry*, 1979, 134, 560–571.

1580. DYE, O. A. Effects of practice on Trail Making Test performance. *Perceptual & Motor Skills*, 1979, 48, 296.

1581. EDINGER, J. D., NELSON, W. M., III, BAILEY, K. G., WALLACE, J., & LYMAN, R. The utility of Wechsler Adult Intelligence Scale profile analysis with prisoners. *Journal of Clinical Psychology*, 1979, 35, 807–814.

1582. GARDNER, L. I., NEU, R. L., SHAH, R. S., PINTO, W., JR., CO, M., LEHR, E. R., & BARG, G. A. Family with three apparently balanced t(3;15)(p27;q22) translocation carriers. *American Journal of Diseases of Children*, 1979, 133, 1002–1005.

1583. GRANT, I., ADAMS, K., & REED, R. Normal neuropsychological abilities of alcoholic men in their late thirties. *American Journal of Psychiatry*, 1979, 136, 1263–1269.

1584. GROSSI, D., ORSIN, A., MONETTI, C., & DE MICHELE, G. Sex differences in children's spatial and verbal memory span. *Cortex*, 1979, 15, 667–670.

1585. HAFNER, J. L., NELSON, D. A., COROTTO, L. V., & CURNUTT, R. H. The validity of a WAIS short form with a nonclinical population. *Journal of Clinical Psychology*, 1979, 35, 820–821.

1586. HAIMO, S. F., & HOLZMAN, P. S. Thought disorder in schizophrenics and normal controls: Social class and race differences. *Journal of Consulting & Clinical Psychology*, 1979, 47, 963–967.

1587. HANNAY, H. J., & SMITH, A. C. Dichhaptic perception of forms by normal adults. *Perceptual & Motor Skills*, 1979, 49, 991–1000.

1588. HARDER, D. W., & RITZLER, B. A. A comparison of Rorschach developmental level and form–level systems as indicators of psychosis. *Journal of Personality Assessment*, 1979, 43, 347–354.

1589. HARROW, M., & PROSEN, M. Schizophrenic thought disorders: Bizarre associations and intermingling. *American Journal of Psychiatry*, 1979, 136, 293–296.

1590. HART, R. R., NORMAN, W. B., & SERGENT, M. W. The auditory form of the Ohio Literacy Test: Preliminary correlational analysis with Wechsler Adult Intelligence Scale. *Psychological Reports*, 1979, 45, 629–630.

1591. HART, R. R., NORMAN, W. B., & SERGENT, M. W. Preliminary correlational analysis of the Ohio Literacy Test and the WAIS. *Psychological Reports*, 1979, 45, 897–898.

1592. HEATON, R. K., VOGT, A. T., HOEHN, M. M., LEWIS, J. A., CROWLEY, T. J., & STALLINGS, M. A. Neuropsychological impairment with schizophrenia vs. acute and chronic cerebral lesions. *Journal of Clinical Psychology*, 1979, 35, 46–53.

1593. HENDRICKSON, E., LEVY, R., & POST, F. Averaged evoked responses in relation to cognitive and affective state of elderly psychiatric patients. *British Journal of Psychiatry*, 1979, 134, 494–501.

1594. HOLLAND, T. R., & WADSWORTH, H. M. Comparison and combination of recall and background interference procedures for the Bender-Gestalt Test with brain–damaged and schizophrenic patients. *Journal of Personality Assessment*, 1979, 43, 123–127.

1595. HOLLAND, T. R., LEVI, M., & WATSON, C. G. Multivariate structure of associations between verbal and nonverbal intelligence among brain–damaged, schizophrenic, neurotic, and alcoholic patients. *Journal of Abnormal Psychology*, 1979, 88, 354–360.

1596. HOPKINS, J., PERLMAN, T., HECHTMAN, L., & WEISS, G. Cognitive style in adults originally diagnosed as hyperactives. *Journal of Child Psychology & Psychiatry & Allied Disciplines*, 1979, 20, 209–216.

1597. HOWARD-PEEBLES, P. N., & MARKITON, R. I. A tetra-X female, cytogenetic testing, dermatoglyphic studies, and speech impairment. *American Journal of Mental Deficiency*, 1979, 84, 252–255.

1598. JEEVES, M. A., SIMPSON, D. A., & GEFFEN, G. Functional consequences of the transcallosal removal of intraventricular tumours. *Journal of Neurology, Neurosurgery, & Psychiatry*, 1979, 42, 134–142.

1599. JOHNSON, R. A. Verbal originality in the absence of sight: Blind versus sighted adolescents. *Child Study Journal*, 1979, 9, 261–271.

1600. JUDD, L. L. Effect of lithium on mood, cognition, and personality function in normal subjects. *Archives of General Psychiatry*, 1979, 36, 860–865.

1601. KAY, S. R. Maturity of schizophrenic conceptual style in relation to intelligence. *Perceptual & Motor Skills*, 1979, 48, 1286.

1602. KAY, S. R. Schizophrenic WAIS pattern by diagnostic subtypes. *Perceptual & Motor Skills*, 1979, 48, 1241–1242.

1603. KERTESZ, A. Visual agnosia: The dual deficit of perception and recognition. *Cortex*, 1979, 15, 403–419.

1604. KLINGE, V. Facilitating oral hygiene in patients with chronic schizophrenia. *Journal of the American Dental Association*, 1979, 99, 644–645.

1605. KORSAGER, S., & ANDERSEN, M. Thyroid replacement therapy in Down's Syndrome with hypothyroidism. *Journal of Mental Deficiency Research*, 1979, 23, 105–110.

1606. KUPKE, T., LEWIS, R., & RENNICK, P. Sex differences in the neuropsychological functioning of epileptics. *Journal of Consulting & Clinical Psychology*, 1979, 47, 1128–1130.

1607. LACHMAN, J. L., LACHMAN, R., & THRONESBERY, C. Metamemory through adult life span. *Developmental Psychology*, 1979, 15, 543–551.

1608. LEHMAN, R. A. W., CHELUNE, G. J., & HEATON, R. K. Level and variability of performance on neuropsychological tests. *Journal of Clinical Psychology*, 1979, 35, 358–363.

1609. LELI, D. A., & FILSKOV, S. B. Relationship of intelligence to education and occupation as signs of intellectual deterioration. *Journal of Consulting & Clinical Psychology*, 1979, 47, 702–707.

1610. LEWIS, R. F., NELSON, R. W., & EGGERTSEN, C. Neuropsychological test performances of paranoid schizophrenic and brain-damaged patients. *Journal of Clinical Psychology*, 1979, 35, 54–59.

1611. LEZAK, M. D. Recovery of memory and learning functions following traumatic brain injury. *Cortex*, 1979, 15, 63–72.

1612. LIN, Y. Note on WAIS verbal–performance differences in IQ. *Perceptual & Motor Skills*, 1979, 49, 888–890.

1613. LINN, M. W., & HUNTER, K. Perception of age in the elderly. *Journal of Gerontology*, 1979, 34, 46–52.

1614. LIRA, F. T., FAGAN, T. J., & WHITE, M. J. Violent behavior and differential WAIS characteristics among black prison inmates. *Psychological Reports*, 1979, 45, 356–358.

1615. LOBITZ, W. C., & POST, R. D. Parameters of self-reinforcement and depression. *Journal of Abnormal Psychology*, 1979, 88, 33–41.

1616. MANDELZYS, N. Correlates of offense severity and recidivism probability in a Canadian sample. *Journal of Clinical Psychology*, 1979, 35, 897–907.

1617. MARCOS, L. R. Hand movements and nondominant fluency in bilinguals. *Perceptual & Motor Skills*, 1979, 48, 207–214.

1618. MARTIN, F. Is it necessary to retest children in special education classes. *Journal of Learning Disabilities*, 1979, 12, 388–392.

1619. McWILLIAMS, B. J., & MATTHEWS, H. P. A comparison of intelligence and social maturity in children with unilateral complete clefts and those with isolated cleft palates. *Cleft Palate Journal*, 1979, 16, 363–372.

1620. MERZBACHER, C. F. A diet and exercise regimen: Its effect upon mental acuity and personality, a pilot study. *Perceptual & Motor Skills*, 1979, 48, 367–371.

1621. MIGLIOLLI, M., BUCHTEL, H. A., CAMPANINI, T., & DeRISIO, C. Cerebral hemispheric lateralization of cognitive deficits due to alcoholism. *Journal of Nervous & Mental Disease*, 1979, 167, 212–217.

1622. MISHARA, B. L. Environment and face–hand test performance in the institutionalized elderly. *Journal of Gerontology*, 1979, 34, 692–696.

1623. MOYER, S. B. Rehabilitation of alexia: A case study. *Cortex*, 1979, 15, 139–144.

1624. MÜLLER, H. F., DASTOOR, D. P., KLINGNER, A., COLE, M., & BOILLAT, J. Amantadine in senile dementia: Electroencephalographic and clinical effects. *Journal of the American Geriatrics Society*, 1979, 27, 9–16.

1625. NORMAN, R. D. Test profile similarity of identical twins: An unusual case and some controls. *Journal of Psychology*, 1979, 103, 7–13.

1626. NORTON, J. C. Wechsler variables as a function of age and neurologic status. *Journal of Clinical Psychiatry*, 1979, 40, 217–219.

1627. O'DELL, S. L., MAHONEY, N. D., HORTON, W. G., & TURNER, P. E. Media-assisted parent training: Alternative models. *Behavior Therapy*, 1979, 10, 103–110.

1628. O'LEARY, M. R., DONOVAN, D. M., CHANEY, E. F., & WALKER, R. D. Cognitive impairment and treatment outcome with alcoholics: Preliminary findings. *Journal of Clinical Psychiatry*, 1979, 40, 397–398.

1629. O'LEARY, M. R., DONOVAN, D. M., CHANEY, E. F., WALKER, R. D., & SCHAU, E. J. Application of discriminant analysis to level of performance of alcoholics and nonalcoholics on Wechsler–Bellevue and Halstead–Reitan subtests. *Journal of Clinical Psychology*, 1979, 35, 204–208.

1630. PATRICK, J. Bodily concerns as predicted by the Wechsler Object Assembly and Picture Completion subtests: Methodological considerations. *Journal of Consulting & Clinical Psychology*, 1979, 47, 1134–1135.

1631. POWELL, G. E. The relationship between intelligence and verbal and spatial memory. *Journal of Clinical Psychology*, 1979, 35, 335–340.

1632. PUHAN, B. N., & MISHRA, A. B. The factorial structure of the Differential Aptitude Test across two developmental groups. *Psychological Studies*, 1979, 24, 5–11.

1633. RAMANAIAH, N. V., & ADAMS, M. L. Confirmatory factor analysis of the WAIS and the WPPSI. *Psychological Reports*, 1979, 45, 351–355.

1634. RAMEY, C. T., FARRAN, D. C., & CAMPBELL, F. A. Predicting IQ from mother–infant interactions. *Child Development*, 1979, 50, 804–814.

1635. RANKIN, J. L., & KAUSLER, D. H. Adult age differences in false recognitions. *Journal of Gerontology*, 1979, 34, 58–65.

1636. RUSSELL, E. W. Three patterns of brain damage on the WAIS. *Journal of Clinical Psychology*, 1979, 35, 611–620.

1637. RUST, J. O., BARNARD, D., & OSTER, G. D. WAIS verbal–performance differences among elderly when controlling for fatigue. *Psychological Reports*, 1979, 44, 489–490.

1638. RYAN, J. J., & BLOM, B. E. WAIS characteristics and violent behavior: Failure to generalize versus failure to replicate. *Journal of Consulting & Clinical Psychology*, 1979, 47, 581–582.

1639. SACCUZZO, D. P., KERR, M., MARCUS, A., & BROWN, R. Input capability and speed of processing in mental retardation. *Journal of Abnormal Psychology*, 1979, 88, 341–345.

1640. SAIGH, P. A., & ISLAM, M. T. The effects of imposed latency on the performance of Arab undergraduates on two WAIS subtests. *Journal of Psychology*, 1979, 102, 169–172.

1641. SAVAGE, R. D., & ADAMS, M. Cognitive functioning and neurological deficit: Duchenne Muscular Dystrophy and cerebral palsy. *Australian Psychologist*, 1979, 14, 59–75.

1642. SCHULTZ, N. R., DINEEN, J. T., ELIAS, M. F., PENTZ, C. A., III, & WOOD, W. G. WAIS performance for different age groups of hypertensive and control subjects during the administration of a diuretic. *Journal of Gerontology*, 1979, 34, 246–253.

1643. SELZ, M., & REITAN, R. M. Neuropsychological test performance of normal, learning-disabled, and brain-damaged older children. *Journal of Nervous & Mental Disease*, 1979, 167, 298–302.

1644. SELZ, M., & REITAN, R. M. Rules for neuropsychological diagnosis: Classification of brain function in older children. *Journal of Consulting & Clinical Psychology*, 1979, 47, 258–264.

1645. SHAPIRO, A. K., STRUENING, E. L., & SHAPIRO, E. The reliability and validity of a placebo test. *Journal of Psychiatric Research*, 1979, 15, 253–290.

1646. SHARP, D., COLE, M., & LAVE, C. Education and cognitive development: The evidence from experimental research. *Monographs of the Society for Research in Child Development*, 1979, 44, 59–73.

1647. SHATIN, L. Brief form of the competency screening test for mental competence to stand trial. *Journal of Clinical Psychology*, 1979, 35, 464–467.

1648. SHEVRIN, H., SMOKLER, I. A., & WOLF, E. Field independence, lateralization and defensive style. *Perceptual & Motor Skills*, 1979, 49, 195–202.

1649. SIEGLER, I. C., & BOTWINICK, J. A long-term longitudinal study of intellectual ability of older adults: The matter of selective subject attrition. *Journal of Gerontology*, 1979, 34, 242–245.

1650. SILVERSTEIN, M. L., ROSENBAUM, G., & RENNICK, P. M. Decay and interference processes in short-term retention of normal and brain-damaged patients. *Journal of Clinical Psychiatry*, 1979, 40, 86–92.

1651. SIMONDS, J. F., & KASHANI, J. Drug abuse and criminal behavior in delinquent boys committed to a training school. *American Journal of Psychiatry*, 1979, 136, 1444–1448.

1652. SMITH, S. M. Standardized tests used in correctional institutions. *Journal of Employment Counseling*, 1979, 16, 178–188.

1653. SMOKLER, I. A., & SHEVRIN, H. Cerebral lateralization and personality style. *Archives of General Psychiatry*, 1979, 36, 949–954.

1654. SPANOS, N. P., & HEWITT, E. C. Glossolalia: A test of the "trance" and psychopathology hypotheses. *Journal of Abnormal Psychology*, 1979, 88, 427–434.

1655. STONES, M. J. Rekitting the Wechsler Paired–Associate Task: The Waterford Index. *Journal of Clinical Psychology*, 1979, 35, 626–630.

1656. SWASSING, R. A hierarchical analysis of the WAIS performance of adolescent retardates. *Journal of Experimental Education*, 1979, 47, 179–181.

1657. SWIERCINSKY, D. P. Factorial pattern description and comparison of functional abilities in neurological assessment. *Perceptual & Motor Skills*, 1979, 48, 231–241.

1658. TAMKIN, A. S. Rorschach card rejection and its relationships to defensiveness, intelligence, and sex. *Psychological Reports*, 1979, 44, 1003–1006.

1659. TEMPLER, D. I., BARTHLOW, V. L., HALCOMB, P. H., RUFF, C. F., & AYERS, J. L. The death anxiety of convicted felons. *Corrective & Social Psychiatry & Journal of Behavior Technology, Methods & Therapy*, 1979, 25, 18–20.

1660. THOMPSON, H. J., ROBERTS, R. N., & WHIDDON, M. F. Inadequacy of brief IQ measures in the classification of mentally retarded prisoners. *American Journal of Mental Deficiency*, 1979, 83, 416–417.

1661. TOWNES, B. D., PRIEST, S. R., & BOURKE, V. M. Clinical neuropsychology: An evolving field. *Australian Psychologist*, 1979, 14, 169–174.

1662. TSUSHIMA, W. T., & WEDDING, D. A comparison of the Halstead–Reitan Neuropsychological Battery and computerized tomography in the identification of brain disorder. *Journal of Nervous & Mental Disease*, 1979, 167, 704–707.

1663. UNGERLEIDER, J. T., & WELLISCH, D. K. Coercive persuasion (brainwashing), religious cults, and deprogramming. *American Journal of Psychiatry*, 1979, 136, 279–282.

1664. UZZELL, B. P., ZIMMERMAN, R. A., DOLINSKAS, C. A., & OBRIST, W. D. Lateralized psychological impairment associated with CT lesions in head injured patients. *Cortex*, 1979, 15, 391–401.

1665. VINCENT, K. R. The modified WAIS: An alternative to short forms. *Journal of Clinical Psychology*, 1979, 35, 624–625.

1666. VINCENT, L. R., & VINCENT, K. R. Ego development and psychopathology. *Psychological Reports*, 1979, 44, 408–410.

1667. WAGNER, E. E., & CALDWELL, M. A. WAIS test–retest reliability for a clinical out–patient sample. *Perceptual & Motor Skills*, 1979, 48, 131–137.

1668. WARD, L. C., & SELBY, R. Further appraisal of the verbal scale as a short form of the WAIS. *Journal of Consulting & Clinical Psychology*, 1979, 47, 989–990.

1669. WEBSTER, R. E. Utility of the WAIS in predicting vocational success of psychiatric patients. *Journal of Clinical Psychology*, 1979, 35, 111–116.

1670. WILLNER, A. E., & RABINER, C. J. Psychopathology and cognitive dysfunction five years after open–heart surgery. *Comprehensive Psychiatry*, 1979, 20, 409–418.

1671. WILLERMAN, L., LOEHLIN, J. C., & HORN, J. M. Parental problem-solving speed as a correlate of intelligence in parents and their adopted and natural children. *Journal of Educational Psychology*, 1979, 71, 627–634.

1672. WORLAND, J. Rorschach developmental level in the offspring of patients with schizophrenia and manic–depressive illness. *Journal of Personality Assessment*, 1979, 43, 591–594.

1673. ZIEGLER, M. E., & DOEHRMAN, S. The generalizability of verbal IQ as an estimate of full scale IQ on the Wechsler Adult Intelligence Scale. *Journal of Clinical Psychology*, 1979, 35, 805–807.

1674. ZINKUS, P. W., & GOTTLIEB, M. I. Patterns of perceptual deficits in academically deficient juvenile delinquents. *Psychology in the Schools*, 1979, 16, 19–27.

1675. ADAMS, K. M., GRANT, I., & REED, R. Neuropsychology in alcoholic men in their late thirties: One–year follow–up. *American Journal of Psychiatry*, 1980, 137, 928–931.

1676. ANTHONY, W. Z., HEATON, R. K., & LEHMAN, R. A. W. An attempt to cross–validate two actuarial systems for neuropsychological test interpretation. *Journal of Consulting & Clinical Psychology*, 1980, 48, 317–326.

1677. AUGUST, G. J. Input organization as a mediating factor in memory: A comparison of educable mentally retarded and nonretarded individuals. *Journal of Experimental Child Psychology*, 1980, 30, 125–143.

1678. BAK, J. S., & GREENE, R. L. Changes in neuropsychological functioning in an aging population. *Journal of Consulting & Clinical Psychology*, 1980, 48, 395–399.

1679. BARRIOS, B. A., GINTER, E. J., SCALISE, J. J., & MILLER, F. G. Treatment of test anxiety by applied relaxation and cue–controlled relaxation. *Psychological Reports*, 1980, 46, 1287–1296.

1680. BASH, I. Y., & ALPERT, M. The determination of malingering. *Annals of the New York Academy of Science*, 1980, 347, 86–99.

1681. BATSHAW, M. L., ROAN, Y., JUNG, A. L., ROSENBERG, L. A., & BRUSILOW, S. W. Cerebral dysfunction in asymptomatic carriers of ornithine transcarbamylase deficiency. *New England Journal of Medicine*, 1980, 302, 482–485.

1682. BATZEL, L. W., DODRILL, C. B., & FRASER, R. T. Further validation of the WPSI Vocational Scale: Comparisons with other correlates of employment in epilepsy. *Epilepsia*, 1980, 21, 235–242.

1683. BENNETT–LEVY, J., & POWELL, G. E. The Subjective Memory Questionnaire (SMQ). An investigation into the self–reporting of "real–life" memory skills. *British Journal of Social & Clinical Psychology*, 1980, 19, 177–188.

1684. BESSON, J. A. O. A diagnostic pointer to adult metachromatic leucodystrophy. *British Journal of Psychiatry*, 1980, 137, 186–187.

1685. BLACK, F. W. WAIS verbal–performance discrepancies as predictors of lateralization in patients with discrete brain lesions. *Perceptual & Motor Skills*, 1980, 51, 213–214.

1686. BLUMBERG, N. L. Effects of neonatal risk, maternal attitude, and cognitive style on early postpartum adjustment. *Journal of Abnormal Psychology*, 1980, 89, 139–150.

1687. BOLTON, B. Personality (16PF) correlates of WAIS scales: A replication. *Applied Psychological Measurement*, 1980, 4, 399–401.

1688. BONHEUR, H., & ROSNER, R. Sex offenders: A descriptive analysis of cases studied at a forensic psychiatry clinic. *Journal of Forensic Sciences*, 1980, 25, 3–14.

1689. BOTWINICK, J., & SIEGLER, I. C. Intellectual ability among the elderly: Simultaneous cross–sectional and longitudinal comparisons. *Developmental Psychology*, 1980, 16, 49–53.

1690. BOTWINICK, J., & STORANDT, M. Recall and recognition of old information in relation to age and sex. *Journal of Gerontology*, 1980, 35, 70–76.

1691. BROOKS, D. N., AUGHTON, M. E., BOND, M. R., JONES, P., & RIZVI, S. Cognitive sequela in relationship to early indices of severity of brain damage after severe blunt head injury. *Journal of Neurology, Neurosurgery, & Psychiatry*, 1980, 43, 529–534.

1692. BUCHSBAUM, M. S., & SOSTEK, A. J. An adaptive–rate continuous performance test: Vigilance characteristics and reliability for 400 male students. *Perceptual & Motor Skills*, 1980, 51, 707–713.

1693. CEGALIS, J. A., & TEGTMEYER, P. F. Visual selectivity in schizophrenia. *Journal of Nervous & Mental Disease*, 1980, 168, 229–235.

1694. CHAVEZ, E. L., & GONZALES–SINGH, E. Hispanic assessment: A case study. *Professional Psychology*, 1980, 11, 163–168.

1695. COHEN, D., & EISDORFER, C. Serum immunoglobulins and cognitive status in the elderly: I. A population study. *British Journal of Psychiatry*, 1980, 136, 33–39.

1696. COURSEY, R. D., BUCHSBAUM, M. S., & MURPHY, D. L. Psychological characteristics of subjects identified by platelet MAO activity and evoked potentials as biologically at risk for psychopathology. *Journal of Abnormal Psychology*, 1980, 89, 151–164.

1697. CROOK, T., GILBERT, J. G., & FERRIS, S. Operationalizing memory impairment for elderly persons: The Guild Memory Test. *Psychological Reports*, 1980, 47, 1315–1318.

1698. CUMMINGS, J., HEBBEN, N. A., OBLER, L., & LEONARD, P. Nonaphasic misnaming and other neurobehavioral features of an unusual toxic encephalopathy: Case study. *Cortex*, 1980, 16, 315–323.

1699. DAUBNEY, J. H., & WAGNER, E. E. Prediction of success in an accelerated BS/MD medical school program using two projective techniques. *Perceptual & Motor Skills*, 1980, 51, 1179–1183.

1700. DELANEY, R. C., ROSEN, A. J., MATTSON, R. H., & NOVELLY, R. A. Memory function in focal epilepsy: A comparison of non–surgical, unilateral temporal lobe and frontal lobe samples. *Cortex*, 1980, 16, 103–117.

1701. DIKMEN, S., & MORGAN, S. F. Neuropsychological factors related to employability and occupational status in persons with epilepsy. *Journal of Nervous & Mental Disease*, 1980, 168, 236–240.

1702. DODRILL, C. B. Rapid evaluation of intelligence in adults with epilepsy. *Epilepsia*, 1980, 21, 359–367.

1703. DONNELLY, E. F., WALDMAN, I. N., MURPHY, D. L., WYATT, R. J., & GOODWIN, F. K. Primary affective disorder: Thought disorder in depression. *Journal of Abnormal Psychology*, 1980, 89, 315–319.

1704. DONNELLY, E. F., WEINBERGER, D. R., WALDMAN, I. N., & WYATT, R. J. Cognitive impairment associated with morphological brain abnormalities on computed tomography in chronic schizophrenic patients. *Journal of Nervous & Mental Disease*, 1980, 168, 305–308.

1705. DRACHMAN, D. A., & SAHAKIAN, B. J. Memory and cognitive function in the elderly: A preliminary trial of physostigmine. *Archives of Neurology*, 1980, 37, 674–675.

1706. ECKARDT, M. J., RYBACK, R. S., & PAUTLER, C. P. Neuropsychological deficits in alcoholic men in their mid thirties. *American Journal of Psychiatry*, 1980, 137, 932–936.

1707. EISER, C. Effects of chronic illness on intellectual development. *Archives of Diseases in Childhood*, 1980, 55, 766–770.

1708. ERMAN, M. K., & MURRAY, G. B. A case report of anorexia nervosa and Gaucher's Disease. *American Journal of Psychiatry*, 1980, 137, 858–859.

1709. EVANS, R. G. Reactions to threat by defensive and congruent internals and externals: A self–esteem analysis. *Journal of Research in Personality*, 1980, 14, 76–90.

1710. FARRAN, D. C., & RAMEY, C. T. Social class differences in dyadic involvement during infancy. *Child Development*, 1980, 51, 254–257.

1711. FEIER, C. D., & GERSTMAN, L. J. Sentence comprehension abilities throughout the adult life span. *Journal of Gerontology*, 1980, 35, 722–728.

1712. FERRIS, S. H., CROOK, T., CLARK, E., MCCARTHY, M., & RAE, D. Facial recognition memory deficits in normal aging and senile dementia. *Journal of Gerontology*, 1980, 35, 707–714.

1713. FISH, J. M., & SINKEL, P. Correlation of scores on Wechsler Memory Scale and Wechsler Adult Intelligence Scale for chronic alcoholics and normals. *Psychological Reports*, 1980, 47, 940–942.

1714. FREEMAN, C. W., CALSYN, D. A., SHERRAD, D. J., & PAIGE, A. B. Psychological assessment of renal dialysis patients using standard psychometric techniques. *Journal of Consulting & Clinical Psychology*, 1980, 48, 537–539.

1715. FULLERTON, A. M., & SMITH, A. D. Age-related differences in the use of redundancy. *Journal of Gerontology*, 1980, 35, 729–735.

1716. GERNER, R., ESTABROOK, W., STEVER, J., & JARVIK, L. Treatment of geriatric depression with trazodone, impramine, and placebo: A double-blind study. *Journal of Clinical Psychiatry*, 1980, 41, 216–220.

1717. GESCHWIND, N., SHADER, R. I., BEAR, D., NORTH, B., LEVIN, K., & CHETHAM, D. Behavioral changes with temporal lobe epilepsy: Assessment and treatment. *Journal of Clinical Psychiatry*, 1980, 41, 89–95.

1718. GORDON, H. W. Cognitive asymmetry in dyslexic families. *Neuropsychologia*, 1980, 18, 645–656.

1719. GREEN, P., & KOTENKO, V. Superior speech comprehension in schizophrenics under monaural versus binaural listening conditions. *Journal of Abnormal Psychology*, 1980, 89, 399–408.

1720. GROSSMAN, L., & SUMMERS, F. A study of the capacity of schizophrenic patients to give informed consent. *Hospital & Community Psychiatry*, 1980, 31, 205–206.

1721. HARDER, D. W., STRAUSS, J. S., KOKES, R. F., RITZLER, B. A., & GIFT, T. E. Life events and psychopathology severity among first psychiatric admissions. *Journal of Abnormal Psychology*, 1980, 89, 165–180.

1722. HASSANYEH, F., & DAVISON, K. Bipolar affective psychosis with onset before age 16 years report of 10 cases. *British Journal of Psychiatry*, 1980, 137, 530–539.

1723. HENDLER, N., CIMINI, C., MA, T., & LONG, D. A comparison of cognitive impairment due to benzodiazepines and to narcotics. *American Journal of Psychiatry*, 1980, 137, 828–830.

1724. HESS, R. D., KASHIWAGI, K., AZUMA, H., PRICE, G. C., & DICKSON, W. P. Maternal expectations for mastery of developmental tasks in Japan and the United States. *International Journal of Psychology*, 1980, 15, 259–271.

1725. HEWETT, B. B., & MARTIN, W. R. Psychometric comparisons of sociopathic and psychopathological behaviors of alcoholics and drug abusers versus a low drug use control population. *International Journal of the Addictions*, 1980, 15, 77–105.

1726. HILL, E. F. A comparison of three psychological testings of a transsexual. *Journal of Personality Assessment*, 1980, 44, 52–101.

1727. HOLDEN, C. Identical twins reared apart. *Science*, 1980, 207, 1323–1328.

1728. HOLLAND, T. R., & WATSON, C. G. Multivariate analysis of WAIS–MMPI relationships among brain-damaged, schizophrenic, neurotic, and alcoholic patients. *Journal of Clinical Psychology*, 1980, 36, 352–359.

1729. HORAN, M., ASHTON, R., & MINTO, J. Using ECT to study hemispheric specialization for sequential processes. *British Journal of Psychiatry*, 1980, 137, 119–125.

1730. HOWARD, D. V. Category norms: A comparison of the Battig and Montague (1969) norms with the responses of adults between the ages of 20 and 80. *Journal of Gerontology*, 1980, 35, 225–231.

1731. HUNT, D. D., & HAMPSON, J. L. Follow-up of 17 biologic male transsexuals after sex-reassignment surgery. *American Journal of Psychiatry*, 1980, 137, 432–438.

1732. JACOBY, R. J., & LEVY, R. Computed tomography in the elderly. 2. Senile dementia: Diagnosis and functional impairment. *British Journal of Psychiatry*, 1980, 136, 256–269.

1733. JACOBY, R. J., & LEVY, R. Computed tomography in the elderly. 3. Affective disorder. *British Journal of Psychiatry*, 1980, 136, 270–275.

1734. JOHNSON, D., & QUINLAN, D. Fluid and rigid boundaries of paranoid and nonparanoid schizophrenics on a role-playing task. *Journal of Personality Assessment*, 1980, 44, 523–531.

1735. JOHNSON, O., & HARLEY, C. Handedness and sex differences in cognitive tests of brain laterality. *Cortex*, 1980, 16, 73–82.

1736. JOHNSON, R. A. Sensory images in the absence of sight: Blind versus sighted adolescents. *Perceptual & Motor Skills*, 1980, 51, 177–178.

1737. JUDD, L. L., JANOWSKY, D. S., SEGAL, D. S., & HUEY, L. Y. Naloxone-induced behavioral and physiological effects in normal and manic subjects. *Archives of General Psychiatry*, 1980, 37, 583–586.

1738. KANE, B. J., & ALLEY, G. R. A peer-tutored instructional management program in computational mathematics for incarcerated, learning disabled juvenile delinquents. *Journal of Learning Disabilities*, 1980, 13, 148–151.

1739. KAUSLER, D. H., & PUCKETT, J. M. Frequency judgments and correlated cognitive abilities in young and elderly adults. *Journal of Gerontology*, 1980, 35, 376–382.

1740. KEISER, T. W., & LOWY, D. Heroin addiction and the Wechsler Digit Span Test. *Journal of Clinical Psychology*, 1980, 36, 347–351.

1741. KISH, G. B., HAGEN, J. M., WOODY, M. M., & HARVEY, H. L. Alcoholics recovery from cerebral impairment as a function of duration of abstinence. *Journal of Clinical Psychology*, 1980, 36, 584–589.

1742. KOOCHER, G. P., O'MALLEY, J. E., GOGAN, J. L., & FOSTER, D. J. Psychological adjustment among pediatric cancer survivors. *Journal of Child Psychology & Psychiatry & Allied Disciplines*, 1980, 21, 163–173.

1743. LAOSA, L. M. Maternal teaching strategies and cognitive styles in Chicano families. *Journal of Educational Psychology*, 1980, 72, 45–54.

1744. LEEPER, H. A., JR., PANNBACKER, M., & ROGINSKI, J. Oral language characteristics of adult cleft–palate speakers compared on the basis of cleft type and sex. *Journal of Communication Disorders*, 1980, 13, 133–146.

1745. LEVINE, D. N., CALVANIO, R., & WOLF, E. Disorders of visual behavior following bilateral posterior cerebral lesions. *Psychological Reports*, 1980, 41, 217–234.

1746. LIPSKY, M. J., KASSINOVE, H., & MILLER, N. J. Effects of rational–emotive therapy, rational role reversal, and rational–emotive imagery on the emotional adjustment of community mental health center patients. *Journal of Consulting & Clinical Psychology*, 1980, 48, 366–374.

1747. LOBERG, T. Alcohol misuse and neuropsychological deficits in men. *Journal of Studies on Alcohol*, 1980, 41, 119–128.

1748. MALONEY, M. P., DUVALL, S. W., & FRIESEN, J. Evaluation of response consistency on the MMPI. *Psychological Reports*, 1980, 46, 295–298.

1749. MARSH, G. G. Disability and intellectual function in multiple sclerosis patients. *Journal of Nervous & Mental Disease*, 1980, 168, 758–762.

1750. MILBERG, W., GREIFFENSTEIN, M., LEWIS, R., & ROURKE, D. Differentiation of temporal lobe and generalized seizure patients with the WAIS. *Journal of Consulting & Clinical Psychology*, 1980, 48, 39–42.

1751. MILLER, W. R., & ORR, J. Nature and sequence of neuropsychological deficits in alcoholics. *Journal of Studies on Alcohol*, 1980, 41, 325–337.

1752. MOLINARI, V., & KHANNA, P. Locus of control and the denial of anxiety. *Psychological Reports*, 1980, 47, 131–140.

1753. MUELLER, J. H., & FISHER, D. Field independence and input grouping in free recall. *Bulletin of the Psychonomic Society*, 1980, 16, 397–400.

1754. NAFICY, A., & WILLERMAN, L. Excessive yielding to normal biases is not a distinctive sign of schizophrenia. *Journal of Abnormal Psychology*, 1980, 89, 697–703.

1755. OSCAR-BERMAN, M., & ZOLA-MORGAN, S. M. Comparative neuropsychology and Karsakoff's Syndrome. I–spatial and visual reversal learning. *Neuropsychologia*, 1980, 18, 499–512.

1756. OSCAR-BERMAN, M., & ZOLA-MORGAN, S. M. Comparative neuropsychology and Karsakoff's Syndrome. II–two-choice visual discrimination learning. *Neuropsychologia*, 1980, 18, 513–525.

1757. OTTESON, J. P. Stylistic and personality correlates of lateral eye movements: A factor analytic study. *Perceptual & Motor Skills*, 1980, 50, 995–1010.

1758. OXMAN, T. E., & SILBERFARB, P. M. Serial cognitive testing in cancer patients receiving chemotherapy. *American Journal of Psychiatry*, 1980, 137, 1263–1265.

1759. PARKER, N. Personality change following accidents: The report of a double murder. *British Journal of Psychiatry*, 1980, 137, 401–409.

1760. PARSONS, O. A. Cognitive dysfunction in alcoholics and social drinkers. *Journal of Studies on Alcohol*, 1980, 41, 105–118.

1761. PAUL, J., & GREGORY, R. The effects of handedness and writing posture on neuropsychological test results. *Neuropsychologia*, 1980, 18, 231–235.

1762. PETEROY, E. T. Prediction of WAIS scores from Quick Test scores for white and black patients at a mental health center. *Psychological Reports*, 1980, 47, 259–262.

1763. PHILLIPS, W. M., PHILLIPS, A. M., & SHEARN, C. R. Objective assessment of schizophrenic thinking. *Journal of Clinical Psychology*, 1980, 36, 79–89.

1764. PIAZZA, D. M. The influence of sex and handedness in the hemispheric specialization of verbal and nonverbal tasks. *Neuropsychologia*, 1980, 18, 163–176.

1765. PITTNER, M. S., & HOUSTON, B. K. Response to stress, cognitive coping strategies, and the type A behavior pattern. *Journal of Personality & Social Psychology*, 1980, 39, 147–157.

1766. POECK, K., & LEHMKUHL, G. Ideatory apraxia in a left-handed patient with right-sided brain lesion. *Cortex*, 1980, 16, 273–284.

1767. PONSFORD, J. L., & DONNAN, G. A. Transient global amnesia–a hippocampal phenomenon? *Journal of Neurology, Neurosurgery, & Psychiatry*, 1980, 43, 285–287.

1768. POWELL, D. A., MILLIGAN, W. L., & FURCHTGOTT, E. Peripheral autonomic changes accompanying learning and reaction time performance in older people. *Journal of Gerontology*, 1980, 35, 57–65.

1769. PRIGATANO, G. P. Neuropsychological functioning of recidivist alcoholics treated with disulfiram: A follow-up report. *International Journal of the Addictions*, 1980, 15, 287–294.

1770. QUINSEY, V. L., ARNOLD, L. S., & PRUESSE, M. G. MMPI profiles of men referred for a pretrial psychiatric assessment as a function of offense type. *Journal of Clinical Psychology*, 1980, 36, 410–417.

1771. RICHARDS, J. S. Visual memory in left hemiplegia: A clinical evaluation of verbally mediated theories of visual memory. *Perceptual & Motor Skills*, 1980, 51, 13–14.

1772. RITZLER, B., ZAMBIANCO, D., HARDER, D., & KASKEY, M. Psychotic patterns of the concept of the object on the Rorschach Test. *Journal of Abnormal Psychology*, 1980, 89, 46–55.

1773. ROBINSON, A. L., HEATON, R. K., LEHMAN, R. A. W., & STILSON, D. W. The utility of the Wisconsin Card Sorting Test in detecting and localizing frontal lobe lesions. *Journal of Consulting & Clinical Psychology*, 1980, 48, 605–614.

1774. RUDRUD, E., FERRARA, J., & ZIARNIK, J. Living placement and absenteeism in community–based training programs. *American Journal of Mental Deficiency*, 1980, 84, 401–404.

1775. RUSSELL, E. W. Fluid and crystallized intelligence: Effects of diffuse brain damage on the WAIS. *Perceptual & Motor Skills*, 1980, 51, 121–122.

1776. RYAN, C. Learning and memory deficits in alcoholics. *Journal of Studies on Alcohol*, 1980, 41, 437–447.

1777. RYAN, J. J., SOUHEAVER, G. T., & DEWOLFE, A. S. Intellectual deficit in chronic renal failure: A comparison with neurological and medical-psychiatric patients. *Journal of Nervous & Mental Disease*, 1980, 168, 763–767.

1778. SACCUZZO, D. P., & BRAFF, D. L. Associative cognitive dysfunction in schizophrenia and old age. *Journal of Nervous & Mental Disease*, 1980, 168, 41–45.

1779. SAPPINGTON, J. T. Measures of lateral dominance: Inter-relationships and temporal stability. *Perceptual & Motor Skills*, 1980, 50, 783–790.

1780. SAUNDERS, D. R., KAPLAN, S. J., & RODD, W. G. Implications of the personality assessment system for marital counseling: A pilot study. *Psychological Reports*, 1980, 46, 151–160.

1781. SCHULTZ, N. R., JR., HOYER, W. J., & KAYE, D. B. Trait anxiety, spontaneous flexibility, and intelligence in young and elderly adults. *Journal of Consulting & Clinical Psychology*, 1980, 48, 289–291.

1782. SHAYWITZ, S. E., COHEN, D. J., & SHAYWITZ, B. A. Behavior and learning difficulties in children of normal intelligence born to alcoholic mothers. *Journal of Pediatrics*, 1980, 96, 978–982.

1783. SIGELMAN, C. K., ELIAS, S. F., & DANKER-BROWN, P. Interview behaviors of mentally retarded adults as predictors of employability. *Journal of Applied Psychology*, 1980, 65, 67–73.

1784. SILBERFARB, P. M., PHILBERT, D., & LEVINE, P. M. Psychosocial aspects of neoplastic disease: II. Affective and cognitive effects of chemotherapy in cancer patients. *American Journal of Psychiatry*, 1980, 137, 597–601.

1785. SILVERSTEIN, A. B. Estimating the general factor in the WISC and the WAIS. *Psychological Reports*, 1980, 46, 189–190.

1786. SMITH, S., BRUNSON, B., & NYMAN, B. WAIS and Slosson IQs of mentally retarded adults. *Psychological Reports*, 1980, 46, 870.

1787. SNIBBE, J. R., PETERSON, P. J., & SOSNER, B. Study of psychological characteristics of a workers' compensation sample using the MMPI and Millon Clinical Multiaxial Inventory. *Psychological Reports*, 1980, 47, 959–966.

1788. SOLWAY, K. S., HAYS, J. R., SCHREINER, D., & CANSLER, D. Clinical study of youths petitioned for certification as adults. *Psychological Reports*, 1980, 46, 1067–1073.

1789. SOPHN, H. E., & FITZPATRICK, T. Informed consent and bias in samples of schizophrenic subjects at risk for drug withdrawal. *Journal of Abnormal Psychology*, 1980, 89, 79–92.

1790. SVENDSEN, D. Relationship of IQ and occupational disability of retarded adults in Bergen, Norway. *American Journal of Mental Deficiency*, 1980, 85, 197–199.

1791. TAMKIN, A. S. Rorschach experience balance, introversion, and sex. *Psychological Reports*, 1980, 46, 843–848.

1792. TAMKIN, A. The Weigl Color-Form Sorting Test as an index of cortical function. *Journal of Clinical Psychology*, 1980, 36, 778–781.

1793. TRAUPMANN, K. L. Encoding processes and memory for categorically related words by schizophrenic patients. *Journal of Abnormal Psychology*, 1980, 89, 704–716.

1794. TYMCHUK, A. J., SIMMONS, J. Q., & NEAFSEY, S. Intellectual characteristics of adolescent childhood psychotics with high verbal ability. *Journal of Mental Deficiency Research*, 1980, 21, 133–138.

1795. VAILLANT, G. E., & MILOFSKY, E. Natural history of male psychological health: IX. Empirical evidence for Erickson's model of the life cycle. *American Journal of Psychiatry*, 1980, 137, 1348–1359.

1796. VAUGHAN, M. The validity of the Modified Word Learning Test. *Journal of Clinical Psychology*, 1980, 36, 467–471.

1797. VEGA, A., GOLDSTEIN, G., SHELLY, C., & HEGEDUS, A. Dichotic listening in psychiatric patients with and without diffuse brain damage. *Perceptual & Motor Skills*, 1980, 51, 511–518.

1798. VEROFF, A. E. The neuropsychology of aging. Qualitative analysis of visual reproductions. *Psychological Reports*, 1980, 41, 259–268.

1799. VINCENT, K. R. Semi-automated full battery. *Journal of Clinical Psychology*, 1980, 36, 437–446.

1800. WAHL, O. F., & SIEG, D. Time estimation among schizophrenics. *Perceptual & Motor Skills*, 1980, 50, 535–541.

1801. WALLACH, H. F., RIEGE, W. H., & COHEN, M. J. Recognition memory for emotional words: A comparative study of young, middle-aged and older persons. *Journal of Gerontology*, 1980, 35, 371–375.

1802. WEBER, D. B., & EPSTEIN, H. R. Contrasting adaptive behavior ratings of male and female institutionalized residents across two settings. *American Journal of Mental Deficiency*, 1980, 84, 397–400.

1803. WIENS, A. N., HARPER, R. G., & MATARAZZO, J. D. Personality correlates of nonverbal interview behavior. *Journal of Clinical Psychology*, 1980, 36, 205–215.

1804. WILKINSON, D. A., & CARLEN, P. L. Neuropsychological and neurological assessment of alcoholism. *Journal of Studies on Alcohol*, 1980, 41, 129–139.

1805. WOLF, A. S. Homicide and blackout in Alaskan natives: A report and reproduction of five cases. *Journal of Studies on Alcohol*, 1980, 41, 456–462.

1806. WOODS, B. T. The restricted effects of right hemisphere lesions after age one: Wechsler test data. *Neuropsychologia*, 1980, 18, 65–70.

1807. WORLAND, J., & HESSELBROCK, V. The intelligence of children and their parents with schizophrenia and affective illness. *Journal of Child Psychology & Psychiatry & Allied Disciplines*, 1980, 21, 191–201.

1808. ZOREF, L., & WILLIAMS, P. A look at content bias in IQ tests. *Journal of Educational Measurement*, 1980, 17, 313–322.

1809. ABRAMS, R., REDFIELD, J., & TAYLOR, M. A. Cognitive dysfunction in schizophrenia, affective disorder and organic brain disease. *British Journal of Psychiatry*, 1981, 139, 190–194.

1810. ALESANDRINI, K. L. Pictorial-verbal and analytic-holistic learning. *Journal of Educational Psychology*, 1981, 73, 358–368.

1811. BARRATT, E. S., PATTON, J., OLSSON, N. G., & ZUCKER, G. Impulsivity and paced tapping. *Journal of Motor Behavior*, 1981, 13, 286–300.

1812. BASSO, A., CAPITANI, E., LUZZATTI, C., & SPINNLER, H. Intelligence and left hemisphere disease: The roll of aphasia, apraxia and size of lesion. *Brain*, 1981, 104, 721–734.

1813. BERES, C. A., & BARON, A. Improved digit symbol substitution by older women as a result of extended practice. *Journal of Gerontology*, 1981, 36, 591–597.

1814. BLASKOVICS, M., ENGEL, R., PODOSIN, R. L., AZEN, C. G., & FRIEDMAN, E. G. EEG pattern in phenylketonuria under early initiated dietary treatment. *American Journal of Diseases of Children*, 1981, 135, 802–808.

1815. BOLTER, J., VENEKLASEN, J., & LONG, C. J. Investigation of WAIS effectiveness in discriminating between temporal and generalized seizure patients. *Journal of Consulting & Clinical Psychology*, 1981, 49, 549–553.

1816. BRAFF, D. L., & SACCUZZO, D. P. Information processing dysfunction in paranoid schizophrenia: A two-factor deficit. *American Journal of Psychiatry*, 1981, 138, 1051–1056.

1817. BROVERMAN, D. M., VOGEL, W., KLAIBER, E. L., MAJCHER, D., SHEA, D., & PAUL, V. Changes in cognitive task performance across menstrual cycle. *Journal of Comparative & Physiological Psychology*, 1981, 95, 646–656.

1818. CAMPBELL, A. L., JR., BOGEN, J. E., & SMITH, A. Disorganization and reorganization to cognitive and sensorimotor functions in cerebral commissurotomy: Compensatory roles of the forebrain commissures and cerebral hemispheres in man. *Brain*, 1981, 104, 493–511.

1819. CARP, F. M., & CARP, A. Mental health characteristics and acceptance–rejection of old age. *American Journal of Orthopsychiatry*, 1981, 51, 230–241.

1820. CEGALIS, J. A., & DEPTULA, M. S. Attention in schizophrenia: Signal detection in the visual periphery. *Journal of Nervous & Mental Disease*, 1981, 169, 751–760.

1821. DODRILL, C. B. An economical method for the evaluation of general intelligence in adults. *Journal of Consulting & Clinical Psychology*, 1981, 49, 668–673.

1822. DYE, C. J., & ERBER, J. T. Two group procedures for the treatment of nursing home patients. *Gerontologist*, 1981, 21, 539–544.

1823. ERBER, J. T., BOTWINICK, J., & STORANDT, M. The impact of memory on age differences in digit symbol performance. *Journal of Gerontology*, 1981, 36, 586–590.

1824. FABES, R. A., MORAN, J. D., III, & McCULLERS, J. C. The hidden costs of reward and WAIS subscale performance. *American Journal of Psychology*, 1981, 94, 387–398.

1825. FABIAN, M. S., PARSONS, O. A., & SILBERSTEIN, J. A. Impaired perceptual–cognitive functioning in women alcoholics: Cross-validated findings. *Journal of Studies on Alcohol*, 1981, 42, 217–229.

1826. FRY, P. S., & PRESTON, J. Achievement performance of positive and negative affect subjects and their partners under conditions of cooperation and competition. *British Journal of Social Psychology*, 1981, 20, 23–29.

1827. GOLDING, E. The effect of unilateral brain lesion on reasoning. *Cortex*, 1981, 17, 31–40.

1828. GREIFFENSTEIN, M., MILBERG, W., LEWIS, R., & ROSENBAUM, G. Temporal lobe epilepsy and schizophrenia: Comparison of reaction time deficits. *Journal of Abnormal Psychology*, 1981, 90, 105–112.

1829. HARDER, D. W., GIFT, T. E., STRAUSS, J. S., RITZLER, B. A., & KOKES, R. F. Life events and two–year outcome in schizophrenia. *Journal of Consulting & Clinical Psychology*, 1981, 49, 619–626.

1830. HEMMING, H., LAVENDER, T., & PILL, R. Quality of life of mentally retarded adults transferred from large institutions to new small units. *American Journal of Mental Deficiency*, 1981, 86, 157–169.

1831. KAUSLER, D. H., & PUCKETT, J. M. Adult age differences in memory for sex of voice. *Journal of Gerontology*, 1981, 36, 44–50.

1832. KERNBERG, O. F., GOLDSTEIN, E. G., CARR, A. C., HUNT, H. F., BAUER, S. F., & BLUMENTHAL, R. Diagnosing borderline personality: A pilot study using multiple diagnostic methods. *Journal of Nervous & Mental Disease*, 1981, 169, 225–231.

1833. KORMAN, M., MATTHEWS, R. W., & LOVITT, R. Neuropsychological effects of abuse of inhalants. *Perceptual & Motor Skills*, 1981, 53, 547–553.

1834. LAW, J. G., JR, PRICE, D. R., & HERBERT, D. A. Study of Quick Test, WAIS, and premorbid estimates of intelligence for neuropsychiatric patients. *Perceptual & Motor Skills*, 1981, 52, 919–922.

1835. LEHMKUHL, G., & POECK, K. A disturbance in the conceptual organization of actions in patients with ideational apraxia. *Cortex*, 1981, 17, 153–158.

1836. LELI, D. A., & FILSKOV, S. B. Actuarial assessment of Wechsler verbal–performance scale differences as signs of lateralized cerebral impairment. *Perceptual & Motor Skills*, 1981, 53, 492–496.

1837. LEWIS, J. D., MANTZ, D., & MELLIS, L. P. Long–term tolvene abuse. *American Journal of Psychiatry*, 1981, 138, 368–370.

1838. MCGRAW, K. O., & MALLORY, L. H. The effect of monetary incentives on backward digit span performance. *Journal of Research in Personality*, 1981, 15, 270–276.

1839. MCKAY, S. E., GOLDEN, C. J., MOSES, J. A., JR, FISHBURNE, F., & WISNIEWSKI, A. Correlation of the Luria–Nebraska Neuropsychological Battery with the WAIS. *Journal of Consulting & Clinical Psychology*, 1981, 49, 940–946.

1840. MILLER, M. J., SMALL, I. F., MILSTEIN, V., MALLOY, F., & STOUT, J. R. Electrode placement and cognitive change with ECT: Male and female response. *American Journal of Psychiatry*, 1981, 138, 384–385.

1841. MOORE, J. L., & HANNAY, H. J. Verbal–performance IQ–discrepancy and rhythm test performance. *Perceptual & Motor Skills*, 1981, 52, 819–826.

1842. NEUGER, G. J., O'LEARY, D. S., FISHBURNE, F. J., BARTH, J. T., BERENT, S., GIORDANI, B., & BOLL, T. J. Order effects on the Halstead–Reitan Neuropsychological Test Battery and allied procedures. *Journal of Consulting & Clinical Psychology*, 1981, 49, 722–730.

1843. NORTH, A. J., & ULATOWSKA, H. K. Competence in independently living older adults: Assessment and correlates. *Journal of Gerontology*, 1981, 36, 576–582.

1844. ORSINI, A., SCHIAPPA, O., & GROSSI, D. Sex and cultural differences in children's spatial and verbal memory span. *Perceptual & Motor Skills*, 1981, 53, 39–42.

1845. PLUDE, D. J., & HOYER, W. J. Adult age differences in visual search as a function of stimulus mapping and process load. *Journal of Gerontology*, 1981, 36, 598–604.

1846. PRIFITERA, A., & RYAN, J. J. Validity of the Luria–Nebraska intellectual processes scale as a measure of adult intelligence. *Journal of Consulting & Clinical Psychology*, 1981, 49, 755–756.

1847. PUHAN, B. N. Effects of marker variables on WAIS communalities. *Educational & Psychological Measurement*, 1981, 41, 55–59.

1848. RAMEY, C. T., & BROWNLEE, J. R. Improving the identification of high-risk infants. *American Journal of Mental Deficiency*, 1981, 85, 504–511.

1849. RIEGE, W. H., & INMAN, V. Age difference in nonverbal memory tasks. *Journal of Gerontology*, 1981, 36, 51–58.

1850. RIEGE, W. H., KELLY, K., & KLANE, L. T. Age and error differences on Memory-For-Designs. *Perceptual & Motor Skills*, 1981, 52, 507–513.

1851. SACCUZZO, D. P., & BRAFF, D. L. Early information processing deficit in schizophrenia. *Archives of General Psychiatry*, 1981, 38, 175–179.

1852. SCHALOCK, R. L., HARPER, R. S., & CARVER, G. Independent living placement: Five years later. *American Journal of Mental Deficiency*, 1981, 86, 170–177.

1853. SEIDENBERG, M., O'LEARY, D. S., BERENT, S., & BOLL, T. Changes in seizure frequency and test-retest scores on the Wechsler Adult Intelligence Scale. *Epilepsia*, 1981, 22, 75–83.

1854. SEWELL, T. E., PALMO, A. J., & MANNI, J. L. High school dropout, psychological, academic, and vocational factors. *Urban Education*, 1981, 16, 65–76.

1855. SHADE, B. J. Racial variation in perceptual differentiation. *Perceptual & Motor Skills*, 1981, 52, 243–248.

1856. SHALLICE, T. Phonological agraphia and the lexical route in writing. *Brain*, 1981, 104, 413–429.

1857. SILBERSTEIN, J. A., & PARSONS, O. A. Neuropsychological impairment in female alcoholics: Replication and extension. *Journal of Abnormal Psychology*, 1981, 90, 179–182.

1858. SKINNER, H. A. Comparison of clients assigned to in–patient and out–patient treatment for alcoholism and drug addiction. *British Journal of Psychiatry*, 1981, 138, 312–320.

1859. SKINNER, H. A. Primary syndromes of alcohol abuse: Their measurement and correlates. *British Journal of Addiction*, 1981, 76, 63–76.

1860. STEWART, J. H. Wechsler performance IQ scores and social behaviors of hearing–impaired students. *Volta Review*, 1981, 83, 215–222.

1861. TERRELL, F., TERRELL, S. L., & TAYLOR, J. Effects of race of examiner and cultural mistrust on the WAIS performance of black students. *Journal of Consulting & Clinical Psychology*, 1981, 49, 750–751.

1862. THIEL, G. W. Relationship of IQ, adaptive behavior, age, and environmental demand to community-placement success of mentally retarded adults. *American Journal of Mental Deficiency*, 1981, 86, 208–211.

1863. URSANO, R. J. The Viet Nam era prisoner of war: Preactivity personality and the development of psychiatric illness. *American Journal of Psychiatry*, 1981, 138, 315–318.

1864. VAN PUTTEN, T., MAY, P. R. A., MARDER, S. R., & WITTMAN, L. A. Subjective response to antipsychotic drugs. *Archives of General Psychiatry*, 1981, 38, 187–190.

1865. WARRINGTON, E. K. Concrete word dyslexia. *British Journal of Psychology*, 1981, 72, 175–196.

1866. WECHSLER, D. The psychometric tradition: Developing the Wechsler Adult Intelligence Scale. *Contemporary Educational Psychology*, 1981, 6, 82–85.

1867. WEINGARTNER, H., KAYE, W., SMALLBERG, S. A., EBERT, M. H., GILLIN, J. C., & SITARAM, N. Memory failures in progressive idiopathic dementia. *Journal of Abnormal Psychology*, 1981, 90, 187–196.

[2599]

[Re Wechsler Adult Intelligence Scale] Rhodes WAIS Scatter Profile. Ages 16 and over; 1971; a form for profiling WAIS scores; Fen Rhodes; EdITS/Educational and Industrial Testing Service.*

For additional information, see 7:430.

[2600]

[Re Wechsler Adult Intelligence Scale] WAIS Mental Description Sheet. Ages 16 and over; 1974; a form for profiling WAIS scores; John A. Blazer; Psychologists and Educators, Inc.*

For additional information, see 8:231.

REFERENCES

1. WALSH, A. C., & MELANEY, C. Huntington's Disease: Improvement with an anticoagulant–psychotherapy regimen. *Journal of the American Geriatrics Society*, 1978, 26, 127–129.

[2601]

[Re Wechsler Adult Intelligence Scale] WAIS Test Profile. Ages 16 and over; 1968–69; Consulting Psychologists Press, Inc.*

[2602]

Wechsler Intelligence Scale for Children-Revised. Ages 6–16; 1949–74; WISC-R; original edition (WISC) still available; 13–15 scores: verbal (information, comprehension, arithmetic, similarities, vocabulary, digit span [optional], total), performance (picture completion, picture arrangement, block design, object assembly, coding, mazes [optional], total); David Wechsler; The Psychological Corporation. (British edition: 1976; NFER-Nelson Publishing Co. [England].)*

For additional information, reviews by David Freides and Randolph H. Whitworth, and excerpted reviews by Carol Kehr Tittle and Joseph Petrosko, see 8:232 (548 references); see also T2:533 (230 references); for reviews by David Freides and R. T. Osborne of the original edition, see 7:431 (518 references); for a review by Alvin G. Burstein, see 6:540 (155 references); for reviews by Elizabeth D. Fraser, Gerald R. Patterson, and Albert I. Rabin, see 5:416 (111 references); for reviews by James M. Anderson, Harold A. Delp, and Boyd R. McCandless, and an excerpted review by Laurance F. Shaffer, see 4:363 (22 references).

REFERENCES

1–22. See 4:363.
23–133. See 5:416.
134–288. See 6:540.
289–807. See 7:431.
808–1037. See T2:533.
1038–1585. See 8:232.

1586. KRYWANIUK, L. W., & DAS, J. P. Cognitive strategies in native children: Analysis and intervention. *Alberta Journal of Educational Research*, 1976, 22, 271–280.

1587. WHYTE, L. Prescriptive teaching: Changes in stage of logico-mathematical thinking and spatial development in a group of opportunity class children. *Alberta Journal of Educational Research*, 1976, 22, 34–43.

1588. ABIKOFF, H., GITTELMAN-KLEIN, R., & KLEIN, D. F. Validation of a classroom observation code for hyperactive children. *Journal of Consulting & Clinical Psychology*, 1977, 45, 772–783.

1589. ACKERMAN, P. T., DYKMAN, R. A., & PETERS, J. E. Teenage status of hyperactive and nonhyperactive learning disabled boys. *American Journal of Orthopsychiatry*, 1977, 47, 577–596.

1590. ALLEN, R. M. And they call this research . . . *Psychological Reports*, 1977, 40, 926.

1591. APPELBAUM, A. S., & TUMA, J. M. Social class and test performance: Comparative validity of the Peabody with the WISC and WISC-R for two socioeconomic groups. *Psychological Reports*, 1977, 40, 139–145.

1592. ARNOLD, L. E., BARNEBEY, N., McMANUS, J., SMELTZER, D. J., CONRAD, A., WINER, G., & DESGRANGES, L. Prevention by specific perceptual remediation for vulnerable first graders. *Archives of General Psychiatry*, 1977, 34, 1279–1294.

1593. BABAD, E. Y. Pygmalion in reverse. *Journal of Special Education*, 1977, 11, 81–90.

1594. BACK, R., & DANA, R. H. Examiner sex bias and Wechsler Intelligence Scale for Children scores. *Journal of Consulting & Clinical Psychology*, 1977, 45, 500.

1595. BADIAN, N., & WOLFF, P. H. Manual asymmetries of motor sequencing in boys with reading disability. *Cortex*, 1977, 13, 343–349.

1596. BANAS, N., & WILLS, I. H. Prescriptions from WISC-R patterns. *Academic Therapy*, 1977, 13, 241–246.

1597. BAUER, R. H. Short-term memory in learning–disabled and nondisabled children. *Bulletin of the Psychonomic Society*, 1977, 10, 128–130.

1598. BECKMAN, L. The use of the Block Design subtest as an identifying instrument for spatial children. *Gifted Child Quarterly*, 1977, 21, 113–116.

1599. BEN-ZEEV, S. The influence of bilingualism on cognitive strategy and cognitive development. *Child Development*, 1977, 48, 1009–1018.

1600. BLOWERS, E. A. Prediction of Metropolitan Readiness Test scores. *Alberta Journal of Educational Research*, 1977, 23, 164–168.

1601. BRANNIGAN, G. G., & ASH, T. Cognitive tempo and WISC-R performance. *Journal of Clinical Psychology*, 1977, 33, 212.

1602. BRANNIGAN, G. G., & ASH, T. Social judgement in conceptually impulsive and reflective children. *Psychological Reports*, 1977, 41, 466.

1603. BRANNIGAN, G. G., ROSENBERG, L. A., LOPRETE, L. J., & CALNEN, T. Scoring of WISC-R comprehension, similarities, and vocabulary responses by experienced and inexperienced judges. *Psychology in the Schools*, 1977, 14, 430.

1604. BROOKS, C. R. WISC, WISC-R, S-BL&M, WRAT: Relationships and trends among children ages six to ten referred for psychological evaluation. *Psychology in the Schools*, 1977, 14, 30–33.

1605. BROWNE, T., STOTSKY, B. A., & EICHORN, J. A selective comparison of psychological developmental, social, and academic factors among emotionally disturbed children in three treatment settings. *Child Psychiatry & Human Development*, 1977, 7, 231–253.

1606. BUTLER, C., DOSTER, J. T., & LAHEY, B. B. Parent and teacher-mediated social skills training in a very withdrawn disadvantaged girl. *Corrective & Social Psychiatry & Journal of Behavior Technology, Methods & Therapy*, 1977, 23, 85–87.

1607. CAMP, B. W. Verbal mediation in young aggressive boys. *Journal of Abnormal Psychology*, 1977, 86, 145–153.

1608. CAMP, B. W., VAN DOORNINCK, W. J., ZIMET, S. G., & DAHLEM, N. W. Verbal abilities in young aggressive boys. *Journal of Educational Psychology*, 1977, 69, 129–135.

1609. CAMPBELL, S. B., SCHLEIFER, M., WEISS, G., & PERLMAN, T. A two-year follow-up of hyperactive preschoolers. *American Journal of Orthopsychiatry*, 1977, 47, 149–162.

1610. CARROLL, J. L., & CARROLL, J. A. A comparison of the WISC information and arithmetic subtests with a multiple choice procedure using kindergarten, first–, and second–grade children. *Psychology in the Schools*, 1977, 14, 416–418.

1611. CATRON, D. W., & CATRON, S. S. WISC-R vs WISC: A comparison with educable mentally retarded children. *Journal of School Psychology*, 1977, 15, 264–266.

1612. CHERRY, F. F., & EATON, E. L. Physical and cognitive development in children of low-income mothers working in the child's early years. *Child Development*, 1977, 48, 158–166.

1613. CORBETT, J., & HARRIS, R. Progressive disintegrative psychosis of childhood. *Journal of Child Psychology & Psychiatry & Allied Disciplines*, 1977, 18, 211–219.

1614. COVIN, T. M. Comparability of WISC and WISC-R scores for 30 8- and 9-year-old institutionalized Caucasian children. *Psychological Reports*, 1977, 40, 382.

1615. COVIN, T. M. Comparison of SIT and WISC-R IQs among special education candidates. *Psychology in the Schools*, 1977, 14, 19–23.

1616. COVIN, T. M. Comparison of WISC and WISC-R full scale IQs for a sample of children in special education. *Psychological Reports*, 1977, 41, 237–238.

1617. COVIN, T. M. Relationship of Peabody and WISC-R IQs of candidates for special education. *Psychological Reports*, 1977, 40, 189–190.

1618. COVIN, T. M. Relationship of the SIT and PPVT to the WISC-R. *Journal of School Psychology*, 1977, 15, 259–260.

1619. COVIN, T. M. Stability of the WISC-R for 9-year-olds with learning difficulties. *Psychological Reports*, 1977, 40, 1297–1298.

1620. COVIN, T. M., & HATCH, G. WISC full scale IQ mean differences of black children and white children aged 6 through 15 and having problems in school. *Psychological Reports*, 1977, 40, 281–282.

1621. COVIN, T. M., & HATCH, G. L. WISC-R full scale mean IQs for both black and white children, aged 6 through 15 and having difficulty in school. *Psychological Reports*, 1977, 41, 1201–1202.

1622. DALBY, J. T., KINSBOURNE, M., SWANSON, J. M., & SOBOL, M. P. Hyperactive children's underuse of learning time: Correction by stimulant treatment. *Child Development*, 1977, 48, 1448–1453.

1623. DAVIS, E. E. Matched pair comparison of WISC and WISC-R scores. *Psychology in the Schools*, 1977, 14, 161–166.

1624. DEAN, R. S. Analysis of the PIAT with Anglo and Mexican-American children. *Journal of School Psychology*, 1977, 15, 329–333.

1625. DEAN, R. S. Patterns of emotional disturbance on the WISC-R. *Journal of Clinical Psychology*, 1977, 33, 486–490.

1626. DEAN, R. S. Reliability of the WISC-R with Mexican-American children. *Journal of School Psychology*, 1977, 15, 267–268.

1627. DEAN, R. S. The validity and reliability of abbreviated versions of the WISC-R. *Educational & Psychological Measurement*, 1977, 37, 1111–1116.

1628. DEBELL, S. M., & VANCE, H. B. Concurrent validity of three measures of arithmetic achievement. *Perceptual & Motor Skills*, 1977, 45, 848.

1629. DIAZ-GUERRERO, R. A Mexican psychology. *American Psychologist*, 1977, 32, 934–944.

1630. DOBBINS, D. A., & RARICK, G. L. The performance of intellectually normal and educable mentally retarded boys on tests of throwing accuracy. *Journal of Motor Behavior*, 1977, 9, 23–28.

1631. DOEHRING, D. G., & HOSHKO, I. M. Classification of reading problems by the Q-technique of factor analysis. *Cortex*, 1977, 13, 281–294.

1632. DOPPELT, J. E., & KAUFMAN, A. S. Estimation of the differences between WISC-R and WISC IQs. *Educational & Psychological Measurement*, 1977, 37, 417–424.

1633. EISER, C., & LANSDOWN, R. Retrospective study of intellectual development in children treated for acute lymphoblastic leukaemia. *Archives of Diseases in Childhood*, 1977, 52, 525–529.

1634. EVESHAM, M. Teaching language skills to children with language disorders. *British Journal of Disorders of Communication*, 1977, 12, 23–29.

1635. FISH, B. Neurobiologic antecedents of schizophrenia in children. *Archives of General Psychiatry*, 1977, 34, 1297–1313.

1636. FOCH, T. T., DEFRIES, J. C., McCLEARN, G. E., & SINGER, S. M. Familial patterns of impairment in reading disability. *Journal of Educational Psychology*, 1977, 69, 316–329.

1637. FREDERICKSON, L. C. Measured intelligence: Species specific? Perhaps! Race specific? Perhaps not. *Journal of Genetic Psychology*, 1977, 130, 95–104.

1638. GABEL, H., GRAYBILL, D., & CONNORS, G. Parent-teacher communication in relation to child academic achievement and self-concept. *Peabody Journal of Education*, 1977, 54, 142–145.

1639. GABRYS, J. B. Methylphenidate effect on attentional and cognitive behavior in six- through twelve-year-old males. *Perceptual & Motor Skills*, 1977, 45, 1143-1149.

1640. GIRONDA, R. J. A comparison of WISC and WISC-R results of urban educable mentally retarded students. *Psychology in the Schools*, 1977, 14, 271-275.

1641. GORDON, D. A., & MACLEAN, W. E. Developmental analysis of outerdirectedness in noninstitutionalized EMR children. *American Journal of Mental Deficiency*, 1977, 81, 508-511.

1642. GOULD, J. The use of the Vineland Social Maturity Scale, the Merrill-Palmer Scale of Mental Tests (non-verbal items) and the Reynell Developmental Language Scales with children in contact with the services for severe mental retardation. *Journal of Mental Deficiency Research*, 1977, 21, 213-226.

1643. HAGEN, R. L., DURHAM, T., & SHANNON, D. Administration of digit span on the Wechsler and Binet: Differences that matter. *Journal of Clinical Psychology*, 1977, 33, 480-482.

1644. HARTH, R., & JUSTEN, J. E., III. The validity of the ITPA Visual Closure Subtest. *Academic Therapy*, 1977, 12, 261-265.

1645. HARTLAGE, L. C., & BOONE, K. E. Achievement test correlates of Wechsler Intelligence Scale for Children and Wechsler Intelligence Scale for Children-Revised. *Perceptual & Motor Skills*, 1977, 45, 1283-1286.

1646. HASLAM, R. H. A., ALLEN, J. R., DORSEN, M. M., KANOFSKY, D. L., MELLITS, E. D., & NORRIS, D. A. The sequelae of group B β-hemolytic streptococcal meningitis in early infancy. *American Journal of Diseases of Children*, 1977, 131, 845-849.

1647. HATCH, G. L., & COVIN, T. M. Comparability of WISC and Peabody IQs of young children from three heterogeneous groups. *Psychological Reports*, 1977, 40, 1345-1346.

1648. HAYDEN, B., NASBY, W., & DAVIDS, A. Interpersonal conceptual structures, predictive accuracy, and social adjustment of emotionally disturbed boys. *Journal of Abnormal Psychology*, 1977, 86, 315-320.

1649. HAYS, J. R., & SOLWAY, K. S. Violent behavior and differential Wechsler Intelligence Scale for Children characteristics. *Journal of Consulting & Clinical Psychology*, 1977, 45, 1187.

1650. HIRSHOREN, A., KAVALE, K., HURLEY, O. L., & HUNT, J. T. The reliability of the WISC-R performance scale with deaf children. *Psychology in the Schools*, 1977, 14, 412-415.

1651. JEFFREY, H., SCOTT, J., CHANDLER, D., & DUGDALE, A. E. Deafness after bacterial meningitis. *Archives of Diseases in Childhood*, 1977, 52, 555-559.

1652. JOESTING, J. Correlations of scores on Bender Visual-Motor Gestalt Test and WISC-R. *Perceptual & Motor Skills*, 1977, 45, 980.

1653. KAUFMAN, A. S., & VAN HAGEN, J. Investigation of the WISC-R for use with retarded children: Correlation with the 1972 Stanford-Binet and comparison of WISC and WISC-R profiles. *Psychology in the Schools*, 1977, 14, 10-14.

1654. KENDALL, P. C., & LITTLE, V. L. Correspondence of brief intelligence measures to the Wechsler scales with delinquents. *Journal of Consulting & Clinical Psychology*, 1977, 45, 660-666.

1655. KIBBY, M. W. Note on relationship of word difficulty and word frequency. *Psychological Reports*, 1977, 41, 12-14.

1656. KLONOFF, H., LOW, M. D., & CLARK, C. Head injuries in children: A prospective five year follow-up. *Journal of Neurology, Neurosurgery, & Psychiatry*, 1977, 40, 1211-1219.

1657. KOFF, E., BOYLE, P., & PUESCHEL, S. M. Perceptual motor functioning in children with phenylketonuria. *American Journal of Diseases of Children*, 1977, 131, 1084-1087.

1658. LEAVERTON, D. R., RUPP, J. W., & POFF, M. G. Brief therapy for monocular hysterical blindness in childhood. *Child Psychiatry & Human Development*, 1977, 7, 254-263.

1659. LEBRON-RODRIGUEZ, D. E., & PASNAK, R. Induction of intellectual gains in blind children. *Journal of Experimental Child Psychology*, 1977, 24, 505-515.

1660. LERER, R. J., & LERER, M. P. Responses of adolescents with minimal brain dysfunction to methylphenidate. *Journal of Learning Disabilities*, 1977, 10, 223-228.

1661. LERER, R. J., LERER, M. P., & ARTNER, J. The effects of methylphenidate on the handwriting of children with minimal brain dysfunction. *Journal of Pediatrics*, 1977, 91, 127-132.

1662. LEWANDOWSKI, N. G., SACCUZZO, D. P., & LEWANDOWSKI, D. G. The WISC as a measure of personality types. *Journal of Clinical Psychology*, 1977, 33, 285-291.

1663. LINCOLN, N. B., & STAPLES, D. J. Psychological aspects of some chronic progressive neuromuscular disorders. *Journal of Chronic Diseases*, 1977, 30, 207-215.

1664. LYLE, O. E., & GOTTESMAN, I. I. Premorbid psychometric indicators of the gene for Huntington's Disease. *Journal of Consulting & Clinical Psychology*, 1977, 45, 1011-1022.

1665. MADIGAN, R. J., & PETERSON, W. J. Television on the Bering Strait. *Journal of Communication*, 1977, 27, 183-187.

1666. MARGOLIS, H. Auditory perceptual test performance and the reflection-impulsivity dimension. *Journal of Learning Disabilities*, 1977, 10, 164-172.

1667. MARTIN, J. D., & KIDWELL, J. C. Intercorrelations of the Wechsler Intelligence Scale for Children-Revised, the Slosson Intelligence Test, and the National Educational Development Test. *Educational & Psychological Measurement*, 1977, 37, 1117-1120.

1668. MATTHEWS, K. A. Caregiver-child interactions and the type A coronary-prone behavior pattern. *Child Development*, 1977, 48, 1752-1756.

1669. McCORMICK, D. P. Pediatric evaluation of children with school problems. *American Journal of Diseases of Children*, 1977, 131, 318-322.

1670. McDERMOTT, P. A. Measures of diagnostic data usage as discriminants among training and experience levels in school psychology. *Psychology in the Schools*, 1977, 14, 323-331.

1671. McGONAGLE, B. A comparison between the WISC and WISC-R among a clinical referred population. *Psychology in the Schools*, 1977, 14, 423-426.

1672. MEDNICK, B. Intellectual and behavioral functioning of ten- to twelve-year-old children who showed certain transient symptoms in the neonatal period. *Child Development*, 1977, 48, 844-853.

1673. MOEN, J. L., WILCOX, R. D., & BURNS, J. K. PKU as a factor in the development of self-esteem. *Journal of Pediatrics*, 1977, 90, 1027-1029.

1674. MORAN, M. R., & BYRNE, M. C. Mastery of verb tense markers by normal and learning-disabled children. *Journal of Speech & Hearing Research*, 1977, 20, 529-542.

1675. NEEL, A. F. Social and biological factors in child development. *Psychological Reports*, 1977, 40, 1143-1146.

1676. NICHOLSON, C. L. Correlations between the Quick Test and the Wechsler Intelligence Scale for Children-Revised. *Psychological Reports*, 1977, 40, 523-526.

1677. PIERSEL, W. C., BRODY, G. H., & KRATOCHWILL, T. R. A further examination of motivational influences on disadvantaged minority group children's intelligence test performance. *Child Development*, 1977, 48, 1142-1145.

1678. REKERS, G. A., & VARNI, J. W. Self monitoring and self-reinforcement processes in a pre-transsexual boy. *Behaviour Research & Therapy*, 1977, 15, 177-180.

1679. REKERS, G. A., WILLIS, T. J., YATES, C. E., ROSEN, A. C., & LOW, B. P. Assessment of childhood gender behavior change. *Journal of Child Psychology & Psychiatry & Allied Disciplines*, 1977, 18, 53-65.

1680. RESCHLY, D. J., & DAVIS, R. A. Comparability of WISC and WISC-R scores among borderline and mildly retarded children. *Journal of Clinical Psychology*, 1977, 33, 1045-1048.

1681. RESNICK, R. J. An abbreviated form of the WISC-R: Is it valid? *Psychology in the Schools*, 1977, 14, 426-429.

1682. RICHMOND, B. O., & LONG, M. WISC-R and PPVT scores for black and white mentally retarded children. *Journal of School Psychology*, 1977, 15, 261-263.

1683. RIEDER, R. O., BROMAN, S. H., & ROSENTHAL, D. The offspring of schizophrenics. *Archives of General Psychiatry*, 1977, 34, 789-799.

1684. ROBBINS, R. L., & HARWAY, N. I. Goal setting and reactions to success and failure in children with learning disabilities. *Journal of Learning Disabilities*, 1977, 10, 35-62.

1685. ROBERTS, S. H., HOWELL, R. T., LAURENCE, K. M., & HEATHCOTE, M. E. Stable dicentric autosome, tdic (8:22) (p23:p13), in a mentally retarded girl. *Journal of Medical Genetics*, 1977, 14, 66-68.

1686. RUBIN, R. A., DORLE, J., & SANDIDGE, S. Self-esteem and school performance. *Psychology in the Schools*, 1977, 14, 503-507.

1687. RYLE, A., & MACDONALD, J. Responses to reading as perceived by boys with and without specific reading retardation and behavioural disorders: A repertory grid study. *Journal of Child Psychology & Psychiatry & Allied Disciplines*, 1977, 18, 323-334.

1688. SAMUEL, W. Observed IQ as a function of test atmosphere, tester expectation, and race of tester: A replication for female subjects. *Journal of Educational Psychology*, 1977, 69, 593-604.

1689. SATTLER, J. M., SQUIRE, L., & ANDRES, J. Scoring discrepancies between the WISC-R manual and two scoring guides. *Journal of Clinical Psychology*, 1977, 33, 1058-1059.

1690. SCARDAMALIA, M. Information processing capacity and the problem of horizontal *decalage*: A demonstration using combinatorial reasoning tasks. *Child Development*, 1977, 48, 28-37.

1691. SCHWARTING, F. G., & SCHWARTING, K. R. The relationship of the WISC-R and WRAT: A study based upon a selected population. *Psychology in the Schools*, 1977, 14, 431-433.

1692. SEWELL, T., & MANNI, J. Comparison of scores of normal children on the WISC-R and Stanford-Binet, form LM, 1972. *Perceptual & Motor Skills*, 1977, 45, 1057-1058.

1693. SILVERSTEIN, A. B. Alternative factor analytic solutions for the Wechsler Intelligence Scale for Children-Revised. *Educational & Psychological Measurement*, 1977, 37, 121-124.

1694. SILVERSTEIN, A. B. Comparison of two criteria for determining the number of factors. *Psychological Reports*, 1977, 41, 387–390.
1695. SILVERMAN, I., RASKIN, L. M., DAVIDSON, J. L., & BLOOM, A. S. Relationships among token test, age, and WISC scores for children with learning problems. *Journal of Learning Disabilities*, 1977, 10, 104–107.
1696. SMITH, M. D., COLEMAN, J. M., DOKECKI, P. R., & DAVIS, E. E. Intellectual characteristics of school labeled learning disabled children. *Exceptional Children*, 1977, 43, 352–357.
1697. SMITH, M. D., COLEMAN, J. M., DOKECKI, P. R., & DAVIS, E. E. Recategorized WISC-R scores of learning disabled children. *Journal of Learning Disabilities*, 1977, 10, 437–443.
1698. SMITH, M. D., DOKECKI, P. R., & DAVIS, E. E. School related factors influencing the self-concepts of children with learning problems. *Peabody Journal of Education*, 1977, 54, 185–195.
1699. SOBOTKA, K. R., BLACK, F. W., HILL, S. D., & PORTER, R. J. Some psychological correlates of developmental dyslexia. *Journal of Learning Disabilities*, 1977, 10, 363–369.
1700. SOBOTKA, K. R., & MAY, J. G. Visual evoked potentials and reaction time in normal dyslexic children. *Psychophysiology*, 1977, 14, 18–23.
1701. SOLLY, D. C. Comparison of WISC and WISC-R scores of mentally retarded and gifted children. *Journal of School Psychology*, 1977, 15, 255–258.
1702. SPELLACY, F. Neuropsychological differences between violent and nonviolent adolescents. *Journal of Clinical Psychology*, 1977, 33, 966–969.
1703. STERNBERG, L., EPSTEIN, M. H., & ADAMS, D. Performance characteristics of retarded and normal students on pattern recognition tasks. *Contemporary Educational Psychology*, 1977, 2, 209–218.
1704. STEWART, D. W. The factorial structure of the ITPA and WISC subtests in three diagnostic groups. *Journal of Clinical Psychology*, 1977, 33, 199–205.
1705. STEWART, D. W., & MORRIS, L. Intelligence and academic achievement in a clinical adolescent population. *Psychology in the Schools*, 1977, 14, 513–518.
1706. STRAUCH, A. B. More on the sex x race interaction on cognitive measures. *Journal of Educational Psychology*, 1977, 69, 152–157.
1707. SWANSON, H. L. Nonverbal visual short-term memory as a function of age and dimensionality in learning-disabled children. *Child Development*, 1977, 48, 51–55.
1708. TAUB, H. B., GOLDSTEIN, K. M., & CAPUTO, D. V. Indices of neonatal prematurity as discriminators of development in middle childhood. *Child Development*, 1977, 48, 797–805.
1709. TAYLOR, L. J. Sex and psychological differentiation. *Psychological Reports*, 1977, 41, 192–194.
1710. TORGESEN, J. K. Memorization processes in reading-disabled children. *Journal of Educational Psychology*, 1977, 69, 571–578.
1711. TORGESEN, J., & GOLDMAN, T. Verbal rehearsal and short-term memory in reading-disabled children. *Child Development*, 1977, 48, 56–60.
1712. TRIVEDI, A. A comparison of three intelligence tests for the assessment of mental retardation. *Journal of Mental Deficiency Research*, 1977, 21, 289–297.
1713. TSUSHIMA, W. T., & TOWNE, W. S. Effects of paint sniffing on neuropsychological test performance. *Journal of Abnormal Psychology*, 1977, 86, 402–407.
1714. TSUSHIMA, W. T., & TOWNE, W. S. Neuropsychological abilities of young children with questionable brain disorders. *Journal of Consulting & Clinical Psychology*, 1977, 45, 757–762.
1715. VANCE, H., & WALLBROWN, F. H. Hierarchical factor structure of the WISC-R for referred children and adolescents. *Psychological Reports*, 1977, 41, 699–702.
1716. VAN DONGEN, H. R., & LOONEN, M. C. B. Factors related to prognosis of acquired aphasia in children. *Cortex*, 1977, 13, 131–136.
1717. WEINBERG, W. A. Reply, a letter in reference to "depression in childhood." *Journal of Pediatrics*, 1977, 85, 292–293.
1718. WELNER, Z., WELNER, A., STEWART, M., PALKES, H., & WISH, E. A controlled study of siblings of hyperactive children. *Journal of Nervous & Mental Disease*, 1977, 165, 110–117.
1719. WHYTE, L. Logico-mathematical and spatial development in children underachieving in arithmetic. *Alberta Journal of Educational Research*, 1977, 23, 280–297.
1720. WILLERMAN, L., & FIEDLER, M. F. Intellectually precocious preschool children: Early development and later intellectual accomplishments. *Journal of Genetic Psychology*, 1977, 131, 13–20.
1721. WILSON, R. S. Twins and siblings: Concordance for school-age mental development. *Child Development*, 1977, 48, 211–216.
1722. WING, L., GOULD, J., YEATES, S. R., & BRIERLEY, L. M. Symbolic play in severely mentally retarded and in autistic children. *Journal of Child Psychology & Psychiatry & Allied Disciplines*, 1977, 18, 167–178.
1723. WITELSON, S. F. Developmental dyslexia: Two right hemispheres and none left. *Science*, 1977, 195, 309–311.

1724. WONG, B., WONG, R., & FOTH, D. Recall and clustering of verbal materials among normal and poor readers. *Bulletin of the Psychonomic Society*, 1977, 10, 375–378.
1725. WOOD, R. E. Fetal alcohol syndrome: Its implications for dentistry. *Journal of the American Dental Association*, 1977, 95, 596–599.
1726. AARON, P. G. Dyslexia, an imbalance in cerebral information-processing strategies. *Perceptual & Motor Skills*, 1978, 47, 699–706.
1727. ANDREW, J. M. Why can't delinquents read? *Perceptual & Motor Skills*, 1978, 47, 640.
1728. AYRES, A. J. Learning disabilities and the vestibular system. *Journal of Learning Disabilities*, 1978, 11, 18–29.
1729. BAKER, H., & WILLS, U. School phobia: Classification and treatment. *British Journal of Psychiatry*, 1978, 132, 492–499.
1730. BERG, I., & FIELDING, D. An evaluation of hospital in-patient treatment in adolescent school phobia. *British Journal of Psychiatry*, 1978, 132, 500–505.
1731. BOSAEUS, E. The relationship between psychological test results and EEG patterns in healthy children. *Scandinavian Journal of Psychology*, 1978, 19, 181–191.
1732. BREUNING, S. E., & ZELLA, W. F. Effects of individualized incentives on norm-referenced IQ test performance of high school students in special education classes. *Journal of School Psychology*, 1978, 16, 220–226.
1733. CARTER, D. E., SPERO, A. J., & WALSH, J. A. A comparison of the Visual Aural Digit Span and the Bender Gestalt as discriminators of low achievement in the primary grades. *Psychology in the Schools*, 1978, 15, 194–198.
1734. COHEN, R. L., & NETLEY, C. Cognitive deficits, learning disabilities, and WISC verbal–performance consistency. *Developmental Psychology*, 1978, 14, 624–634.
1735. CRNIC, K. A. Maternal sensitivity to children in problem situations. *American Journal of Orthopsychiatry*, 1978, 48, 291–299.
1736. DAS, J. P., & CUMMINGS, J. Academic performance and cognitive processes in EMR children. *American Journal of Mental Deficiency*, 1978, 83, 197–199.
1737. DEAN, R. S. Distinguishing learning disabled and emotionally disturbed children on the WISC-R. *Journal of Consulting & Clinical Psychology*, 1978, 46, 381–382.
1738. DE GAFFENREID, H., BLOOM, A., & WAGNER, M. A comparison of an ITPA estimated psycholinguistic quotient and WISC-R IQs for developmentally disabled children. *Journal of Clinical Psychology*, 1978, 34, 943–945.
1739. DEHORN, A., & KLINGE, V. Correlations and factor analysis of the WISC-R and the Peabody Picture Vocabulary Test for an adolescent psychiatric sample. *Journal of Consulting & Clinical Psychology*, 1978, 46, 1160–1161.
1740. DESMOND, M. M., FISHER, E. S., VORDERMAN, A. L., SCHAFFER, H. G., ANDREW, L. P., ZION, T. E., & CATLIN, F. I. The longitudinal course of congenital rubella encephalitis in nonretarded children. *Journal of Pediatrics*, 1978, 93, 584–591.
1741. DYCK, D. G., & BREEN, L. J. Learned helplessness, immunization and importance of task in humans. *Psychological Reports*, 1978, 43, 315–321.
1742. EISER, C. Intellectual abilities among survivors of childhood leukaemia as a function of CNS irradiation. *Archives of Diseases in Childhood*, 1978, 53, 391–395.
1743. ELLENBERG, J. H., & NELSON, K. B. Febrile seizures and later intellectual performance. *Archives of Neurology*, 1978, 35, 17–21.
1744. EME, R., STONE, S., & IZRAL, R. Spatial deficit in familial left-handed children. *Perceptual & Motor Skills*, 1978, 47, 919–922.
1745. ERIKSON, C. L., BYRD, S. H., & MILON, T. A. Suitability of the California abbreviated WISC for WISC-R subtests with the mentally retarded and slow-learner children. *Psychology in the Schools*, 1978, 15, 498–502.
1746. FAIRWEATHER, H., & HUH, S. J. On the rate of gain of information in children. *Journal of Experimental Child Psychology*, 1978, 26, 216–229.
1747. FISH, B., & DIXON, W. J. Vestibular hyporeactivity in infants at risk for schizophrenia. *Archives of General Psychiatry*, 1978, 35, 963–971.
1748. FRANZINI, L. R., & LITROWNIK, A. J. Influence of the modeling of grouped stimuli during rehearsal on digit recall in children. *Psychological Record*, 1978, 28, 115–122.
1749. FRAUENHEIM, J. G. Academic achievement characteristics of adult males who were diagnosed as dyslexic in childhood. *Journal of Learning Disabilities*, 1978, 11, 476–483.
1750. FUNDERBURK, S. J., & FERJO, N. Clinical observations in Klinefelter (47, XXY) Syndrome. *Journal of Mental Deficiency Research*, 1978, 22, 207–212.
1751. GEAR, G. H. Effects of training on teachers' accuracy in the identification of gifted children. *Gifted Child Quarterly*, 1978, 22, 90–97.
1752. GHUMAN, P. A. S. Nature of intellectual development of Punjabi children. *International Journal of Psychology*, 1978, 13, 281–294.

1753. GROSS, K., ROTHENBERG, S., & SCHOTTENFELD, S. Duration thresholds for letter identification in left and right visual fields for normal and reading–disabled children. *Neuropsychologia*, 1978, 16, 709–715.
1754. GRUNEBAUM, H., COHLER, B. J., KAUFFMAN, C., & GALLANT, D. Children of depressed and schizophrenic mothers. *Child Psychiatry & Human Development*, 1978, 8, 219–228.
1755. GUPTA, R., CECI, S. J., & SLATER, A. M. Visual discrimination in good and poor readers. *Journal of Special Education*, 1978, 12, 409–416.
1756. GUTKIN, T. B. Some useful statistics for the interpretation of the WISC–R. *Journal of Consulting & Clinical Psychology*, 1978, 46, 1561–1563.
1757. HAGGARD, M. R. The effect of creative thinking–reading activities (CT–RA) on reading comprehension. *National Reading Conference Yearbook*, 1978, 233–236.
1758. HALE, R. L. The WISC–R as a predictor of WRAT performance. *Psychology in the Schools*, 1978, 15, 172–175.
1759. HALL, P. K., & TOMBLIN, J. B. A follow–up study of children with articulation and language disorders. *Journal of Speech & Hearing Disorders*, 1978, 43, 227–241.
1760. HAMM, H. A., & EVANS, J. G. WISC–R subtest patterns of severely emotionally disturbed students. *Psychology in the Schools*, 1978, 15, 188–190.
1761. HAUER, A. L., & ARMENTROUT, J. A. Failure of the Bender–Gestalt and Wechsler tests to differentiate children with and without seizure disorders. *Perceptual & Motor Skills*, 1978, 47, 199–202.
1762. HAYS, J. R., SOLWAY, K. S., & SCHREINER, D. Intellectual characteristics of juvenile murderers versus status offenders. *Psychological Reports*, 1978, 43, 80–82.
1763. HEGARTY, S. F. Culture fairness via tests of learning ability. *British Journal of Educational Psychology*, 1978, 48, 359.
1764. HIER, D. B., LEMAY, M., ROSENBERGER, P. B., & PERLO, V. P. Developmental dyslexia. *Archives of Neurology*, 1978, 35, 90–92.
1765. HOFFMAN, J., & WEINER, B. Effects of attributions for success and failure on the performance of retarded adults. *American Journal of Mental Deficiency*, 1978, 82, 449–452.
1766. HOLDEN, C. California court is forum for latest round in IQ debate. *Science*, 1978, 201, 1106–1109.
1767. HOLYROYD, J., & GOLDENBERG, I. The use of goal attainment scaling to evaluate a ward treatment program for disturbed children. *Journal of Clinical Psychology*, 1978, 34, 732–739.
1768. HUNTER, J. A., & LOWE, J. D. The use of the WISC–R, Otis, Iowa, and SRBCSS in identifying gifted elementary students. *Southern Journal of Educational Research*, 1978, 12, 59–65.
1769. HURLEY, O. L., HIRSHOREN, A., KAVALE, K., & HUNT, J. T. Intercorrelations among tests of general mental ability and achievement for black and white deaf children. *Perceptual & Motor Skills*, 1978, 46, 1107–1113.
1770. IRWIN, M., ENGLE, P. L., YARBROUGH, C., KLEIN, R. E., & TOWNSEND, J. The relationship of prior ability and family characteristics to school attendance and school achievement in rural Guatemala. *Child Development*, 1978, 49, 415–427.
1771. JANES, C. L., & HESSELBROCK, V. M. Problem children's adult adjustment predicted from teacher's ratings. *American Journal of Orthopsychiatry*, 1978, 48, 300–309.
1772. JARMAN, R. Patterns of cognitive ability in retarded children: A reexamination. *American Journal of Mental Deficiency*, 1978, 82, 344–348.
1773. JARMAN, R. F., & KRYWANIUK, L. W. Simultaneous and successive synthesis: A factor analysis of speed of information processing. *Perceptual & Motor Skills*, 1978, 46, 1167–1172.
1774. JENSEN, L. R. Diagnosis and evaluation of creativity, research and thinking skills of academically talented elementary students. *Gifted Child Quarterly*, 1978, 22, 98–110.
1775. KAGAN, J., LAPIDUS, D. R., & MOORE, M. Infant antecedents of cognitive functioning: A longitudinal study. *Child Development*, 1978, 49, 1005–1023.
1776. KILLAN, J. B., & HUGHES, L. C. A comparison of short forms of the Wechsler Intelligence Scale for Children–Revised in the screening of gifted referrals. *Gifted Child Quarterly*, 1978, 22, 111–115.
1777. KOJIMA, H. Assessment of field dependence in young children. *Perceptual & Motor Skills*, 1978, 46, 479–492.
1778. KRYNICKI, V. E. Cerebral dysfunction in repetitively assaultive adolescents. *Journal of Nervous & Mental Disease*, 1978, 166, 59–67.
1779. LEISMAN, G. Aetiological factors in dyslexia: III. Ocular–motor factors in visual perceptual response efficiency. *Perceptual & Motor Skills*, 1978, 47, 675–678.
1780. LOMBARD, T. J., & REIDEL, R. G. An analysis of the factor structure of the WISC–R and the effect of color on the coding subtest. *Psychology in the Schools*, 1978, 15, 176–179.
1781. MACFAUL, R., DORNER, S., BRETT, E. M., & GRANT, D. B. Neurological abnormalities in patients treated for hypothyroidism from early life. *Archives of Diseases in Childhood*, 1978, 53, 611–619.
1782. MARGOLIS, H., & BRANNIGAN, G. G. Conceptual tempo as a parameter for predicting reading achievement. *Journal of Educational Research*, 1978, 71, 342–345.

1783. MARSHALL, W., HESS, A. K., & LAIR, C. V. The WISC–R and WRAT as indicators of arithmetic achievement in juvenile delinquents. *Perceptual & Motor Skills*, 1978, 47, 408–410.
1784. McINTYRE, C. W., MURRAY, M. E., CRONIN, C. M., & BLACKWELL, S. L. Span of apprehension in learning disabled boys. *Journal of Learning Disabilities*, 1978, 11, 468–475.
1785. McKAY, H., SINISTERRA, L., McKAY, A., GOMEZ, H., & LLOREDA, P. Improving cognitive ability in chronically deprived children. *Science*, 1978, 200, 270–278.
1786. McMANIS, D. L., FIGLEY, C., RICHERT, M., & FABRE, T. Memory–For–Designs, Bender–Gestalt, Trail Making Test, and WISC–R performance of retarded and adequate readers. *Perceptual & Motor Skills*, 1978, 46, 443–450.
1787. MEHAN, H. Structuring school structure. *Harvard Educational Review*, 1978, 48, 32–64.
1788. MILLER, M., STONEBURNER, R. L., & BRECHT, R. D. WISC subtest patterns as discriminators of perceptual disability. *Journal of Learning Disabilities*, 1978, 11, 449–452.
1789. MILLICHAP, J. G. Growth of hyperactive children treated with methylphenidate. *Journal of Learning Disabilities*, 1978, 11, 567–570.
1790. MOLLICK, L. R., & MESSER, S. B. The relation of reflection–impulsivity to intelligence tests. *Journal of Genetic Psychology*, 1978, 132, 157–158.
1791. MOORE, S. F., & COLE, S. Cognitive self–mediation training with hyperkinetic children. *Bulletin of the Psychonomic Society*, 1978, 12, 18–20.
1792. MORRIS, J. D., EVANS, J. G., & PEARSON, D. R. The WISC–R subtest profile of a sample of severely emotionally disturbed children. *Psychological Reports*, 1978, 42, 319–325.
1793. MORRIS, J. D., MARTIN, R. A., JOHNSON, E., BIRCH, M. C., & THOMPSON, D. Subtest order and WISC–R scores of a sample of educable mentally retarded subjects. *Psychological Reports*, 1978, 43, 383–386.
1794. MUNFORD, P. R. A comparison of the WISC and WISC–R on black child psychiatric outpatients. *Journal of Clinical Psychology*, 1978, 34, 938–943.
1795. MURRAY, M. E. The relationship between personality adjustment and success in remedial programs in dyslexic children. *Contemporary Educational Psychology*, 1978, 3, 330–339.
1796. OETTINGER, L., JR., MAJOVSKI, L. V., & GAUCH, R. R. Coding A and coding B of the WISC are not equivalent tasks. *Perceptual & Motor Skills*, 1978, 47, 987–991.
1797. OLLER, D. K., JENSEN, H. T., & LAFAYETTE, R. H. The relatedness of phonological processes of a hearing–impaired child. *Journal of Communication Disorders*, 1978, 11, 97–105.
1798. ORBACH, I., & GLAUBMAN, H. Suicidal, aggressive, and normal children's perception of personal and impersonal death. *Journal of Clinical Psychology*, 1978, 34, 850–857.
1799. PARNELL, M. M., & AMERMAN, J. D. Maturational influences on perception of coarticulatory effects. *Journal of Speech & Hearing Research*, 1978, 21, 682–701.
1800. PATTON, J. E., & OFFENBACH, S. I. Effects of visual and auditory distractors on learning disabled and normal children's recognition memory performance. *Journal of Educational Psychology*, 1978, 70, 788–795.
1801. PERMAN, B. E. Reading attainment in hearing–impaired children: A comparison of higher and lower achievers. *Journal of Communication Disorders*, 1978, 11, 227–235.
1802. PETERSEN, C. R., & HART, D. H. Use of multiple discriminant function analysis in evaluation of a state–wide system for identification of educationally handicapped children. *Psychological Reports*, 1978, 43, 743–755.
1803. PRESTON, J. Abbreviated forms of the WISC–R. *Psychological Reports*, 1978, 42, 882–887.
1804. PRISTO, L. J. Comparing WISC and WISC–R scores. *Psychological Reports*, 1978, 42, 515–518.
1805. RAPP, D. J. Does diet affect hyperactivity? *Journal of Learning Disabilities*, 1978, 11, 383–389.
1806. RASBURY, W. C., FALGOUT, J. C., & PERRY, N. W., JR. A Yudin–type short form of the WISC–R: Two aspects of validation. *Journal of Clinical Psychology*, 1978, 34, 120–126.
1807. RASKIN, L. M., BLOOM, A. S., KLEE, S. H., & REESE, A. The assessment of developmentally disabled children with the WISC–R, Binet, and other tests. *Journal of Clinical Psychology*, 1978, 34, 111–114.
1808. RAYDER, N., BODY, B., & NIMNICHT, G. Assessing follow through: Changes in intelligence test scores over two and three years of experience in the responsive program. *Journal of Experimental Education*, 1978, 47, 60–66.
1809. RESCHLY, D. J. WISC–R factor structures among Anglos, Blacks, Chicanos, and Native–American Papagos. *Journal of Consulting & Clinical Psychology*, 1978, 46, 417–422.
1810. RICHMAN, L. C. Language mediation hypothesis: Implications of verbal/performance discrepancy and reading ability. *Perceptual & Motor Skills*, 1978, 47, 391–398.

1811. RUBENSTEIN, J. S., ARMENTROUT, J. A., LEVIN, S., & HERALD, D. The parent–therapist program: Alternate care for emotionally disturbed children. *American Journal of Orthopsychiatry*, 1978, 48, 654–662.

1812. RUGEL, R. P. The value of parental report of family histories of reading disorders and pregnancy and birth complications in reading disabled and normal children. *Psychology in the Schools*, 1978, 15, 583–587.

1813. RUMSEY, J. M., & RYCHLAK, J. F. The role of affective assessment in intelligence testing. *Journal of Personality Assessment*, 1978, 42, 421–425.

1814. SACHS, H. K., KRALL, V., McCAUGHRAN, D. A., ROZENFELD, I. H., YOUNGSMITH, N., GROWE, G., LAZAR, B. S., NOVAR, L., O'CONNELL, L., & RAYSON, B. I.Q. following treatment of lead poisoning: A patient–sibling comparison. *Journal of Pediatrics*, 1978, 93, 428–431.

1815. SAIGH, P. A., & PAYNE, D. A. Effect of reinforcement of response on internal consistency of selected WISC–R subtests. *Psychological Reports*, 1978, 43, 756–758.

1816. SATTLER, J. M., ANDRES, J. R., SQUIRE, L. S., WISELY, R., & MALOY, C. F. Examiner scoring of ambiguous WISC-R responses. *Psychology in the Schools*, 1978, 15, 486–489.

1817. SCHIFF, M., DUYME, M., DUMARET, A., STEWART, J., TOMKIEWICZ, S., & FEINGOLD, J. Intellectual status of working–class children adopted early into upper–middle–class families. *Science*, 1978, 200, 1503–1504.

1818. SCHOOLER, D. L., BEEBE, M. C., & KOEPKE, T. Factor analysis of WISC-R scores for children identified as learning disabled, educable mentally impaired, and emotionally impaired. *Psychology in the Schools*, 1978, 15, 478–485.

1819. SHASBY, G., & KINGSLEY, R. F. A study of behavior and body type in troubled youth. *Journal of School Health*, 1978, 48, 103–107.

1820. SHIEK, D. A., & MILLER, J. E. Validity generalization of the WISC-R factor structure with 10 1/2-year-old children. *Journal of Consulting & Clinical Psychology*, 1978, 46, 583.

1821. SMITH, M. D. Stability of WISC-R subtest profiles for learning disabled children. *Psychology in the Schools*, 1978, 15, 4–7.

1822. SMITH, M. D., ZINGALE, S. A., & COLEMAN, J. M. The influence of adult expectancy/child performance discrepancies upon children's self–concepts. *American Educational Research Journal*, 1978, 15, 259–265.

1823. SOBOTKA, K. R., & BLACK, F. W. A procedure for the rapid computation of WISC-R factor scores. *Journal of Clinical Psychology*, 1978, 34, 117–119.

1824. SPELLACY, F., & PETER, B. Dyscalculia and elements of the developmental Gerstmann Syndrome in school children. *Cortex*, 1978, 14, 197–206.

1825. STEDMAN, J. M., LAWLIS, G. F., CORTNER, R. H., & ACHTERBERG, G. Relationships between WISC-R factors, Wide-Range Achievement Test scores, and visual–motor maturation in children referred for psychological examination. *Journal of Consulting & Clinical Psychology*, 1978, 46, 869–872.

1826. STOKES, E. H., BRENT, D., HUDDLESTON, N. J., ROZIER, J. S., & MARRERO, B. A comparison of WISC and WISC-R scores of sixth grade students: Implications for validity. *Educational & Psychological Measurement*, 1978, 38, 469–473.

1827. STRANG, L., SMITH, M. D., & ROGERS, C. M. Social comparison, multiple reference groups, and the self–concepts of academically handicapped children before and after mainstreaming. *Journal of Educational Psychology*, 1978, 70, 487–497.

1828. STREISSGUTH, A. P., HERMAN, C. S., & SMITH, D. W. Intelligence, behavior, and dysmorphogenesis in the fetal alcohol syndrome: A report of 20 patients. *Journal of Pediatrics*, 1978, 92, 363–367.

1829. SWANSON, L. Primary performance of normal and retarded children: Stimulus familiarity or spatial memory? *Child Study Journal*, 1978, 8, 101–110.

1830. SWERDLIK, M. Comparison of WISC and WISC-R scores of referred black, white and Latino children. *Journal of School Psychology*, 1978, 16, 110–125.

1831. SWERDLIK, M. E., & SCHWEITZER, J. A comparison of factor structures of the WISC and WISC-R. *Psychology in the Schools*, 1978, 15, 166–172.

1832. TAPASAK, R. C., ROODIN, P. A., & VAUGHT, G. M. Effects of extraversion, anxiety, and sex on children's verbal fluency and coding task performance. *Journal of Psychology*, 1978, 100, 49–55.

1833. TERRELL, F., TAYLOR, J., & TERRELL, S. L. Effects of type of social reinforcement on the intelligence test performance of lower–class black children. *Journal of Consulting & Clinical Psychology*, 1978, 46, 1538–1539.

1834. TIZARD, B., & HODGES, J. The effect of early institutional rearing on the development of eight year old children. *Journal of Child Psychology & Psychiatry & Allied Disciplines*, 1978, 19, 99–118.

1835. TOWNES, B. D., REITAN, R. M., & TRUPIN, E. W. Concept formation ability in brain–damaged and normal children. *Academic Therapy*, 1978, 13, 517–526.

1836. TUMA, J. M., APPELBAUM, A. S., & BEE, D. E. Comparability of the WISC and WISC-R in normal children of divergent socioeconomic backgrounds. *Psychology in the Schools*, 1978, 15, 339–346.

1837. VANCE, H., & ENGIN, A. Analysis of cognitive abilities of black children's performance on WISC-R. *Journal of Clinical Psychology*, 1978, 34, 452–456.

1838. VANCE, H. B., & HANKINS, N. Analysis of cognitive ability for rural white culturally different children. *Journal of Psychology*, 1978, 98, 15–21.

1839. VANCE, H., GAYNOR, P., & COLEMAN, M. Item analysis of the Wechsler Intelligence Scale for Children–Revised. *Psychology in the Schools*, 1978, 14, 132–139.

1840. VANCE, H., HANKINS, N., & WALLBROWN, F. Correlations between WISC-R subtests and verbal, performance, and full scale IQ scores for minority group children. *Psychology in the Schools*, 1978, 15, 154–159.

1841. VANCE, H., HANKINS, N., WALLBROWN, F., ENGIN, A., & McGEE, H. Analysis of cognitive abilities for mentally retarded children on the WISC–R. *Psychological Reports*, 1978, 28, 391–397.

1842. VANCE, H., PRICHARD, K. K., & WALLBROWN, F. H. Comparison of the WISC-R and PPVT for a group of mentally retarded students. *Psychology in the Schools*, 1978, 15, 349–351.

1843. VANCE, H., & WALLBROWN, F. H. The structure of intelligence for black children: A hierarchical approach. *Psychological Reports*, 1978, 28, 31–39.

1844. VANCE, H., WALLBROWN, F. H., & BLAHA, J. Determining WISC-R profiles for reading disabled children. *Journal of Learning Disabilities*, 1978, 11, 657–661.

1845. VANCE, H., WALLBROWN, F. H., & FREMONT, T. S. The abilities of retarded students: Further evidence concerning the stimulus trace factor. *Journal of Psychology*, 1978, 100, 77–82.

1846. VINEY, L. L., & CLARKE, A. M. Effects of modeling and instruction on problem–solving by school children with different expectations of success. *Australian Journal of Education*, 1978, 22, 179–188.

1847. WADE, T. C., BAKER, T. B., MORTON, T. L., & BAKER, L. J. The status of psychological testing in clinical psychology: Relationships between test use and professional activities and orientations. *Journal of Personality Assessment*, 1978, 42, 3–10.

1848. WAKEFIELD, J. A., WOOD, K. A., WALLACE, F. R., & FRIEDMAN, A. F. A curvilinear relationship between extraversion and performance for adult retardates. *Psychological Reports*, 1978, 43, 387–392.

1849. WALLBROWN, F. H. Shedd's formulations concerning the hyperkinetic syndrome–An empirical test of selected features. *Perceptual & Motor Skills*, 1978, 46, 809–810.

1850. WEBSTER, R. E., & SCHENCK, S. J. Diagnostic test pattern differences among LD, ED, EMH, and multi–handicapped students. *Journal of Educational Research*, 1978, 72, 75–80.

1851. WEISS, G., HECHTMAN, L., & PERLMAN, T. Hyperactives as young adults: School, employer, and self–rating scales obtained during ten–year follow–up evaluation. *American Journal of Orthopsychiatry*, 1978, 48, 438–445.

1852. WHEATON, P. J., & VANDERGRIFF, A. F. Comparison of WISC and WISC-R scores of highly gifted students in public school. *Psychological Reports*, 1978, 43, 627–630.

1853. WHITE, C. A., GOPLERUD, C. P., KISKER, C. T., STEHBENS, J. A., KITCHELL, M., & TAYLOR, J. C. Intrauterine fetal transfusion, 1965–76, with an assessment of the surviving children. *American Journal of Obstetrics & Gynecology*, 1978, 130, 933–940.

1854. WIKOFF, R. L. Correlational and factor analysis of the Peabody Individual Achievement Test and the WISC–R. *Journal of Consulting & Clinical Psychology*, 1978, 46, 322–325.

1855. WILTON, K., & BARBOUR, A. Mother–child interaction in high-risk and contrast preschoolers of low socioeconomic status. *Child Development*, 1978, 49, 1136–1145.

1856. ZINGALE, S. A., & SMITH, M. D. WISC-R patterns for learning–disabled children at three SES levels. *Psychology in the Schools*, 1978, 15, 199–204.

1857. ZINKUS, P. W., GOTTLIEB, M. I., & SCHAPIRO, M. Developmental and psychoeducational sequelae of chronic otitis media. *American Journal of Diseases of Children*, 1978, 132, 1100–1104.

1858. ALGOZZINE, R., WHORTON, J. E., & REID, W. R. Special class exit criteria: A modest beginning. *Journal of Special Education*, 1979, 13, 132–136.

1859. ANDO, H., & YOSHIMURA, I. Comprehension skill levels and prevalence of maladaptive behaviors in autistic and mentally retarded children. *Child Psychiatry & Human Development*, 1979, 9, 131–136.

1860. ANGSTADT, A., GUTSCH, K. V., & DANIELS, J. A comparison of WISC and WISC-R results among black elementary students. *Southern Journal of Educational Research*, 1979, 13, 127–132.

1861. ARCHER, R. P., WHITE, J. L., & ORVIN, G. H. MMPI characteristics and correlates among adolescent psychiatric inpatients. *Journal of Clinical Psychology*, 1979, 35, 498–504.

1862. BAILEY, B. S., & RICHMOND, B. O. Adaptive behavior of retarded, slow-learner, and average intelligence children. *Journal of School Psychology*, 1979, 17, 260–263.

1863. BAKER, H., & WILLS, U. School phobic children at work. *British Journal of Psychiatry*, 1979, 135, 561–564.

1864. BANNATYNE, A. Spatial competence, learning disabilities, auditory-vocal deficits and a WISC–R subtest recategorization. *Journal of Clinical Child Psychology*, 1979, 8, 194–200.

1865. BEAUCHAMP, D. P., SAMUELS, D. D., & GIFFORE, R. J. WISC-R information and digit span scores of American and Canadian children. *Applied Psychological Measurement*, 1979, 3, 231–236.

1866. BECK, F. W., LINDSEY, J. D., & FACZIENDE, B. A comparison of the general information subtest of the Peabody Individual Achievement Test with the information subtest of the Wechsler Intelligence Scale for Children–Revised. *Educational & Psychological Measurement*, 1979, 39, 1073–1077.

1867. BISHOP, D., & BUTTERWORTH, G. E. A longitudinal study using the WPPSI and WISC–R with an English sample. *British Journal of Educational Psychology*, 1979, 49, 156–158.

1868. BISHOP, D. V. M., JANCEY, C., & STEEL, A. M. Orthoptic status and reading disability. *Cortex*, 1979, 15, 659–666.

1869. BOERSMA, F. J., CHAPMAN, J. W., & BATTLE, J. Academic self-concept change in special education students: Some suggestions for interpreting self–concept scores. *Journal of Special Education*, 1979, 13, 433–442.

1870. BROOKS, C. R. Rorschach variables and their relationship to WISC–R IQ among children referred. *Psychology in the Schools*, 1979, 16, 369–373.

1871. BRUNNER, R. L., O'GRADY, D. J., PARTIN, J. C., PARTIN, J. S., & SCHUBERT, W. K. Neuropsychologic consequences of Reye Syndrome. *Journal of Pediatrics*, 1979, 95, 706–711.

1872. CARROLL, J. A., FULLER, G. B., & CARROLL, J. L. Comparison of culturally deprived school achievers and underachievers on memory function and perception. *Perceptual & Motor Skills*, 1979, 48, 59–62.

1873. CLARREN, S. K., SMITH, D. W., HARVEY, M. A. S., WARD, R. H., & MYRIANTHOPOULOS, N. C. Hyperthermia–A prospective evaluation of a possible teratogenic agent in man. *Journal of Pediatrics*, 1979, 95, 81–83.

1874. COLLEHI, L. F. Relationship between pregnancy and birth complications and the later development of learning disabilities. *Journal of Learning Disabilities*, 1979, 12, 659–663.

1875. CONGER, A. J., CONGER, J. C., FARRELL, A. D., & WARD, D. What can the WISC–R measure. *Applied Psychological Measurement*, 1979, 3, 421–436.

1876. CRAFT, N. P., & KRONENBERGER, E. J. Comparability of WISC–R and WAIS IQ scores in educable mentally handicapped adolescents. *Psychology in the Schools*, 1979, 16, 502–504.

1877. CRAWFORD, J. H., & FRY, M. A. Trait-task interaction in intra- and intermodal matching of auditory and visual trigrams. *Contemporary Educational Psychology*, 1979, 4, 1–10.

1878. CUTRONA, C. E., & FESHBACH, S. Cognitive and behavioral correlates of children's differential use of social information. *Child Development*, 1979, 50, 1036–1042.

1879. DEAN, R. S. Cerebral laterality and verbal–performance discrepancies in intelligence. *Journal of School Psychology*, 1979, 17, 145–150.

1880. DEAN, R. S. Distinguishing patterns for Mexican American children on the WISC–R. *Journal of Clinical Psychology*, 1979, 35, 790–794.

1881. DEFILIPPIS, N. A. Normative and validity data for the Missouri children's behavior checklist. *Journal of Clinical Psychology*, 1979, 35, 605–610.

1882. DICKSON, W. P., HESS, R. D., MIYAKE, N., & AZUMA, H. Referential communication accuracy between mother and child as a predictor of cognitive development in the United States and Japan. *Child Development*, 1979, 50, 53–59.

1883. DINERO, T. E., DONAH, C. H., & LARSON, G. L. The Slingerland Screening Tests for Identifying Children with Specific Language Disability: Screening for learning disabilities in first grade. *Perceptual & Motor Skills*, 1979, 49, 971–978.

1884. DUNLAP, W. P., RUSSELL, S. N., & INGRAM, C. Determining learning disabilities in mathematics. *Academic Therapy*, 1979, 15, 81–85.

1885. DYKMAN, R. A., ACKERMAN, P. T., & OGLESBY, D. M. Selective and sustained attention in hyperactive, learning–disabled, and normal boys. *Journal of Nervous & Mental Disease*, 1979, 167, 288–297.

1886. FROMING, W. J., & McCOLGAN, E. B. Comparing the Defining Issues Test and the moral dilemma interview. *Developmental Psychology*, 1979, 15, 658–659.

1887. FUDALA, J. B. Differential evaluation of students with the S.I.T. *Academic Therapy*, 1979, 15, 61–64.

1888. GABRYS, J. B. The Babcock story recall of behaviorally disordered children scoring high or low on extraversion. *Perceptual & Motor Skills*, 1979, 48, 157–158.

1889. GARDNER, L. I., NEU, R. L., SHAH, R. S., PINTO, W., JR., CO, M., LEHR, E. R., & BARG, G. A. Family with three apparently balanced t(3;15)(p27;q22) translocation carriers. *American Journal of Diseases of Children*, 1979, 133, 1002–1005.

1890. GLENWICK, D. S., & BAROCAS, R. Training impulsive children in verbal self-control by use of natural change agents. *Journal of Special Education*, 1979, 13, 387–398.

1891. GOH, D. S. Empirical versus random item selection in the design of intelligence test short forms–The WISC–R example. *Applied Psychological Measurement*, 1979, 3, 75–82.

1892. GOH, D. S., & YANGQUIST, J. A comparison of the McCarthy Scales of Children's Abilities and the WISC–R. *Journal of Learning Disabilities*, 1979, 12, 344–348.

1893. GOLD, P. Suspected neurological impairment and cognitive abilities: A longitudinal study. *Psychological Reports*, 1979, 45, 215–218.

1894. GOLD, P. Suspected neurological impairment (SNI) and cognitive abilities: A longitudinal study of selected skills and predictive accuracy. *Journal of Clinical Child Psychology*, 1979, 8, 35–38.

1895. GORDON, N. G., & KANTOR, D. R. Effects of clinical dosage levels of methylphenidate on two–flash thresholds and perceptual motor performance in hyperactive children. *Perceptual & Motor Skills*, 1979, 48, 721–722.

1896. GUTKIN, T. B. Bannatyne patterns of Caucasian and Mexican-American learning disabled children. *Psychology in the Schools*, 1979, 16, 178–183.

1897. GUTKIN, T. B. The WISC–R verbal comprehension, perceptual organization, and freedom from distractability deviation quotients: Data for practitioners. *Psychology in the Schools*, 1979, 16, 359–360.

1898. HALE, R. L. The utility of WISC–R subtest scores in discriminating among adequate and underachieving children. *Multivariate Behavioral Research*, 1979, 14, 245–253.

1899. HARKULICH, J. F., MARCHNER, T. J., & BROWN, E. B. Neurological, neuropsychological, and behavioral correlates of Klinefelter's Syndrome. *Journal of Nervous & Mental Disease*, 1979, 167, 359–363.

1900. HETRICK, E. W. Bender visual–motor abilities of slow learners. *Perceptual & Motor Skills*, 1979, 49, 31–34.

1901. HIRSHOREN, A., HURLEY, O. L., & KAVALE, K. Psychometric characteristics of the WISC–R performance scale with deaf children. *Journal of Speech & Hearing Disorders*, 1979, 44, 73–79.

1902. HISAMA, T. The effects of three psychoeducational variables on the achievement motivation of children with behavior disorders and learning disabilities. *Journal of Psychological Research*, 1979, 21, 41–44.

1903. HOLT, M. M., & HOBBS, T. R. The effects of token reinforcement, feedback and response cost on standardized test performance. *Behaviour Research & Therapy*, 1979, 17, 81–83.

1904. HURLEY, O. L. Predictive validity of two mental ability tests with black deaf children. *Journal of Negro Education*, 1979, 48, 14–19.

1905. HYND, G. W., KRAMER, R., QUACKENBUSH, R., & CONNER, R. Clinical utility of the WISC–R and the French Pictorial Test of Intelligence with native American primary grade children. *Perceptual & Motor Skills*, 1979, 49, 480–482.

1906. IRELAND, J. F., & KAHN, M. W. How fair is the culture I.Q. test? *International Journal of Social Psychiatry*, 1979, 25, 1–3.

1907. JACKSON, A. M., FARLEY, G. K., ZIMET, S. G., & GOTTMAN, J. M. Optimizing the WISC–R test performance of low– and high–impulsive emotionally disturbed children. *Journal of Learning Disabilities*, 1979, 12, 622–625.

1908. JOHNSON, R. A. Verbal originality in the absence of sight: Blind versus sighted adolescents. *Child Study Journal*, 1979, 9, 261–271.

1909. JOOST, M. G., & SALVENDY, G. The development and validation of an objective method for quantifying hyperactivity in children. *Journal of Psychological Researches*, 1979, 21, 18–28.

1910. KAPP, K. Self concept of the cleft lip or palate child. *Cleft Palate Journal*, 1979, 16, 171–176.

1911. KARNES, F. A., & BROWN, K. E. Comparison of the SIT with the WISC–R for gifted students. *Psychology in the Schools*, 1979, 16, 478–482.

1912. KAUFMAN, A. S. Role of speed on WISC–R performance across the age range. *Journal of Consulting & Clinical Psychology*, 1979, 47, 595–597.

1913. KHAYYER, M., & MOJDEHI, H. Intelligence: Iranian male delinquents compared with non–delinquents on selected WISC scales. *Psychological Reports*, 1979, 44, 782.

1914. KIRK, C. Patterns of word segmentation in preschool children. *Child Study Journal*, 1979, 9, 37–49.

1915. KLEIN, P. S., & SCHWARTZ, A. A. Effects of training auditory sequential memory and attention on reading. *Journal of Special Education*, 1979, 13, 365–374.

1916. KRYNICKI, V. E., & NAHAS, A. D. Differing lateralized perceptual–motor patterns in schizophrenic and non–psychotic children. *Perceptual & Motor Skills*, 1979, 49, 603–610.

1917. KUNCE, J. T., & McMAHON, R. C. Neuropsychological significance of children's Wechsler intelligence scores. *Psychological Reports*, 1979, 44, 787–790.

1918. LANGHORNE, J. E., & LONEY, J. A four-fold model for subgrouping the hyperkinetic/MBD syndrome. *Child Psychiatry & Human Development*, 1979, 9, 153–159.

1919. LEICHTMAN, S. R., & ERICKSON, M. T. Cognitive, demographic, and interactional determinants of role-taking skills in fourth grade children. *Perceptual & Motor Skills*, 1979, 49, 247–253.
1920. LITCHER, J. H., ROBERGE, L. P., MEYER, M., & KARNES, L. R. Alternative learning experiences for high-risk, first-grade students. *Journal of Learning Disabilities*, 1979, 12, 686–688.
1921. LOWRANCE, D., & ANDERSON, H. N. A comparison of the Slosson Intelligence Test and the WISC-R with elementary school children. *Psychology in the Schools*, 1979, 16, 361–364.
1922. LYTLE, W. G., & CAMPBELL, N. J. Do special programs affect the social status of the gifted? *Elementary School Journal*, 1979, 80, 93–97.
1923. MALOY, C. F., & SATTLER, J. M. Motor and cognitive proficiency of learning disabled and normal children. *Journal of School Psychology*, 1979, 17, 213–218.
1924. MARTIN, F. Is it necessary to retest children in special education classes. *Journal of Learning Disabilities*, 1979, 12, 388–392.
1925. McCARRON, L., & HORN, P. W. Haptic visual discrimination and intelligence. *Journal of Clinical Psychology*, 1979, 35, 117–120.
1926. McWILLIAMS, B. J., & MATTHEWS, H. P. A comparison of intelligence and social maturity in children with unilateral complete clefts and those with isolated cleft palates. *Cleft Palate Journal*, 1979, 16, 363–372.
1927. MILICH, R. S., & LONEY, J. The factor composition of the WISC for hyperkinetic/MBD males. *Journal of Learning Disabilities*, 1979, 12, 491–495.
1928. MIZE, J. M., CALLAWAY, B., & SMITH, J. W. Comparison of reading disabled children's scores on the WISC-R, Peabody Picture Vocabulary Test, and Slosson Intelligence Test. *Psychology in the Schools*, 1979, 16, 356–358.
1929. NEEDLEMAN, H. L., GUNNOE, C., LEVITON, A., REED, R., PERESIE, H., MAHER, C., & BARRETT, P. Deficits in psychologic and classroom performance of children with elevated dentine head levels. *New England Journal of Medicine*, 1979, 300, 689–695.
1930. OAKLAND, T., & FEIGENBAUM, D. Multiple sources of test bias on the WISC-R and Bender-Gestalt Test. *Journal of Consulting & Clinical Psychology*, 1979, 47, 968–974.
1931. O'CONNER, P. D., STUCK, G. B., & WYNE, M. D. Effects of a short-term intervention resource-room program on task orientation and achievement. *Journal of Special Education*, 1979, 13, 375–385.
1932. OLLENDICK, T. H. Discrepancies between verbal and performance IQs and subtest scatter on the WISC-R for juvenile delinquents. *Psychological Reports*, 1979, 45, 563–568.
1933. ORBACH, I., & GLAUBMAN, H. Children's perception of death as a defensive process. *Journal of Abnormal Psychology*, 1979, 88, 671–674.
1934. PAAL, N., HESTERLY, O., & WEFFER, J. W. Comparability of the WISC and the WISC-R. *Journal of Learning Disabilities*, 1979, 12, 348–351.
1935. PALMER, D. J. Regular-classroom teachers' attributions and instructional prescriptions for handicapped and nonhandicapped pupils. *Journal of Special Education*, 1979, 13, 325–337.
1936. PETERSEN, C. R., & HART, D. H. Factor structure of the WISC-R for a clinic-referred population and specific subgroups. *Journal of Consulting & Clinical Psychology*, 1979, 47, 643–645.
1937. PIROZZOLO, F. J., & RAYNER, K. Cerebral organization and reading disability. *Neuropsychologia*, 1979, 17, 485–491.
1938. POWAZEK, M., & BILLMEIER, G. J., JR. Assessment of intellectual development after surgery for craniofacial dysostosis. *American Journal of Diseases of Children*, 1979, 133, 151–153.
1939. RAMEY, C. T., FARRAN, D. C., & CAMPBELL, F. A. Predicting IQ from mother–infant interactions. *Child Development*, 1979, 50, 804–814.
1940. REED, H. B. C., JR. Biological defects and special education–An issue in personnel preparation. *Journal of Special Education*, 1979, 13, 9–33.
1941. RESCHLY, D. J., & LAMPRECHT, M. J. Expectancy effects of labels: Fact or artifact? *Exceptional Children*, 1979, 46, 55–58.
1942. RESCHLY, D. J., & SABERS, D. C. Analysis of test bias in four groups with the regression definition. *Journal of Educational Measurement*, 1979, 16, 1–9.
1943. REYNOLDS, C. R., GUTKIN, T. B., DAPPEN, L., & WRIGHT, D. Differential validity of the WISC-R for boys and girls referred for psychological services. *Perceptual & Motor Skills*, 1979, 48, 868–870.
1944. REYNOLDS, C. R., & HARTLAGE, L. Comparison of WISC and WISC-R regression lines for academic prediction with black and with white referred children. *Journal of Consulting & Clinical Psychology*, 1979, 47, 589–591.
1945. RICHMAN, L. C. Language variables related to reading ability of children with verbal deficits. *Psychology in the Schools*, 1979, 16, 299–305.
1946. RIEDER, D. O., & NICHOLS, P. L. Offspring of schizophrenics III. *Archives of General Psychiatry*, 1979, 36, 665–674.
1947. RUBIN, R. A., & BALOW, B. Measures of infant development and socioeconomic status as predictors of later intelligence and school achievement. *Developmental Psychology*, 1979, 15, 225–227.

1948. RUBIN, R. A., BALOW, B., & FISCH, R. O. Neonatal serum, bilirubin levels related to cognitive development at ages 4 through 7 years. *Journal of Pediatrics*, 1979, 94, 601–604.
1949. SACCUZZO, D. P., KERR, M., MARCUS, A., & BROWN, R. Input capability and speed of processing in mental retardation. *Journal of Abnormal Psychology*, 1979, 88, 341–345.
1950. SAIGH, P. A., & PAYNE, D. A. The effect of type of reinforcer and reinforcement schedule on performances of EMR students on four selected subtests of the WISC-R. *Psychology in the Schools*, 1979, 16, 106–110.
1951. SAMUELS, D. D., & GRIFFERE, R. J. The Plattsburgh French language immersion program: Its influence on intelligence and self-esteem. *Language Learning*, 1979, 29, 45–52.
1952. SANDOVAL, J. The WISC-R and internal evidence of test bias with minority groups. *Journal of Consulting & Clinical Psychology*, 1979, 47, 919–927.
1953. SATTERFIELD, J. H., CANTWELL, D. P., & SATTERFIELD, B. T. Multimodality treatment. *Archives of General Psychiatry*, 1979, 36, 965–974.
1954. SAVAGE, R. D., & ADAMS, M. Cognitive functioning and neurological deficit: Duchenne Muscular Dystrophy and cerebral palsy. *Australian Psychologist*, 1979, 14, 59–73.
1955. SCHNEIDER, M. A., & SPIVACK, G. An investigative study of the Bender–Gestalt: Clinical validation of its use with a reading disabled population. *Journal of Clinical Psychology*, 1979, 35, 346–351.
1956. SELZ, M., & REITAN, R. M. Neuropsychological test performance of normal, learning-disabled, and brain-damaged older children. *Journal of Nervous & Mental Disease*, 1979, 167, 298–302.
1957. SELZ, M., & REITAN, R. M. Rules for neuropsychological diagnosis: Classification of brain function in older children. *Journal of Consulting & Clinical Psychology*, 1979, 47, 258–264.
1958. SHABAD, P., WORLAND, J., LANDER, H., & DIETRICH, D. A retrospective analysis of the TATS of children at risk who subsequently broke down. *Child Psychiatry & Human Development*, 1979, 10, 49–59.
1959. SHEKIM, W. O., DEKIRMENJIAN, H., CHAPEL, J. L., JAVAID, J., & DAVIS, J. M. Norepinephrine metabolism and clinical response to dextroamphetamine in hyperactive boys. *Journal of Pediatrics*, 1979, 95, 389–394.
1960. SHELLENBERGER, S., & LACHTERMAN, T. Cognitive and motor functioning on the McCarthy scales by Spanish-speaking children. *Perceptual & Motor Skills*, 1979, 49, 863–866.
1961. SHERRETS, S., GARD, G., & LANGNER, H. Frequency of clerical errors on WISC protocols. *Psychology in the Schools*, 1979, 16, 495–496.
1962. SIMONDS, J. F., & KASHANI, J. Drug abuse and criminal behavior in delinquent boys committed to a training school. *American Journal of Psychiatry*, 1979, 136, 1444–1448.
1963. SMITH, M. D. Prediction of self-concept among learning disabled children. *Journal of Learning Disabilities*, 1979, 12, 664–669.
1964. SNYDERMAN, S. E., SANSARICQ, C., NORTON, P. M., & MANKA, M. The nutritional therapy of histidinemia. *Journal of Pediatrics*, 1979, 95, 712–715.
1965. STRAUSS, J. S., HARDER, D. W., & CHANDLER, M. Egocentrism in children of parents with a history of psychotic disorders. *Archives of General Psychiatry*, 1979, 36, 191–196.
1966. STRICHART, S. S., & LOVE, E. WISC-R performance of children referred to a university center for learning disabilities. *Psychology in the Schools*, 1979, 16, 183–188.
1967. SWANSON, E. N., & DEBALSSIE, R. R. Interpreter and Spanish administration effects on the WISC performance of Mexican-American children. *Journal of School Psychology*, 1979, 17, 231–236.
1968. SWERDLIK, M. E., & WILSON, F. R. A comparison of WISC and WISC-R subtest scatter. *Journal of Learning Disabilities*, 1979, 12, 105–107.
1969. TABACHNICK, B. G. Test scatter on the WISC-R. *Journal of Learning Disabilities*, 1979, 12, 626–628.
1970. TAYLOR, L. J. Family environments, language, and intelligence. *Canadian Journal of Behavioural Science*, 1979, 11, 1–10.
1971. TEJANI, A., MAHADEVAN, R., DOBIAS, B., NANGIA, B. S., & VARMA, P. N. Total parenteral nutrition of the neonate–A long-term follow-up. *Journal of Pediatrics*, 1979, 94, 803–805.
1972. TERVOORT, B. T., & ANSINK, B. J. Cortical word deafness in a child: A case history. *Journal of Communication Disorders*, 1979, 12, 211–216.
1973. TEW, B. The "cocktail party syndrome" in children with hydrocephalus and spina bifida. *British Journal of Disorders of Communication*, 1979, 14, 89–101.
1974. TOBACK, C., & RAJKUMAR, S. The emotional disturbance underlying alopecia areata, alopecia totalis, and trichotillomania. *Child Psychiatry & Human Development*, 1979, 10, 114–117.
1975. TOWNES, B. D., PRIEST, S. R., & BOURKE, V. M. Clinical neuropsychology: An evolving field. *Australian Psychologist*, 1979, 14, 169–174.
1976. VANCE, H. Sex differences on the WISC-R for retarded children and youth. *Psychology in the Schools*, 1979, 16, 27–31.

1977. VANCE, H., HANKINS, N., & MCGEE, H. A preliminary study of black and white differences on the revised Wechsler Intelligence Scale for Children. *Journal of Clinical Psychology*, 1979, 35, 815–819.

1978. VANCE, H. B., LEWIS, R., & DEBELL, S. Correlations of the Wechsler Intelligence Scale for Children–Revised, Peabody Picture Vocabulary Test, and Slosson Intelligence Test for a group of learning disabled students. *Psychology in the Schools*, 1979, 44, 735–738.

1979. VANCE, H., & SINGER, M. G. Recategorization of the WISC–R subtest scaled scores for learning disabled children. *Journal of Learning Disabilities*, 1979, 12, 487–491.

1980. VANDIVER, P. L., & VANDIVER, S. S. A "nonbiased assessment" of intelligence testing. *Educational Forum*, 1979, 44, 97–108.

1981. WASSERMAN, T. H., & VOGRIN, D. J. Relationship of endorsement of rational beliefs, age, months in treatment, and intelligence to overt behavior of emotionally disturbed children. *Psychological Reports*, 1979, 44, 911–917.

1982. WATKINS, M. W. Intellectual and special aptitudes of tenth grade EMH students. *Education & Training of the Mentally Retarded*, 1979, 15, 139–142.

1983. WEINER, S. G., & KAUFMAN, A. S. WISC–R versus WISC for black children suspected of learning or behavioral disorders. *Journal of Learning Disabilities*, 1979, 12, 100–105.

1984. WHITE, T. H. Correlations among the WISC–R, PIAT, and DAM. *Psychology in the Schools*, 1979, 16, 497–501.

1985. WHITE, W. G. Evaluating scaled score differences for the Bannatyne recategorization of the Wechsler subtests. *Psychology in the Schools*, 1979, 16, 174–177.

1986. WIKOFF, R. L. The WISC–R as a predictor of achievement. *Psychology in the Schools*, 1979, 16, 364–366.

1987. WILLERMAN, L., LOEHLIN, J. C., & HORN, J. M. Parental problem–solving speed as a correlate of intelligence in parents and their adopted and natural children. *Journal of Educational Psychology*, 1979, 71, 627–634.

1988. WOLF, B., PAULSEN, E. P., & HSIA, Y. E. Asymptomatic propionyl CoA carboxylase deficiency in a 13-year-old girl. *Journal of Pediatrics*, 1979, 95, 563–565.

1989. WOLFF, S., & BARLOW, A. Schizoid personality in childhood: A comparative study of schizoid, autistic and normal children. *Journal of Child Psychology & Psychiatry & Allied Disciplines*, 1979, 20, 29–46.

1990. WORKMAN, E. A., WORKMAN, B. L., & MACLIN, J. Visual and auditory stimulus presentation factors in the behavioral treatment of illegible handwriting. *Corrective & Social Psychiatry & Journal of Behavior Technology, Methods & Therapy*, 1979, 25, 129–133.

1991. WORLAND, J. Rorschach developmental level in the offspring of patients with schizophrenia and manic–depressive illness. *Journal of Personality Assessment*, 1979, 43, 591–594.

1992. WORLAND, J., LANDER, H., & HESSELBROCK, V. Psychological evaluation of clinical disturbance in children at risk for psychopathology. *Journal of Abnormal Psychology*, 1979, 88, 13–26.

1993. ZINKUS, P. W., & GOTTLIEB, M. I. Patterns of perceptual deficits in academically deficient juvenile delinquents. *Psychology in the Schools*, 1979, 16, 19–27.

1994. ANDERSSON, K. E., RICHARDS, H. C., & HALLAHAN, D. P. Piagetian task performance of learning disabled children. *Journal of Learning Disabilities*, 1980, 13, 37–41.

1995. ASHMAN, A. F., & DAS, J. P. Relation between planning and simultaneous–successive processing. *Perceptual & Motor Skills*, 1980, 51, 371–382.

1996. ASHMORE, R. J., & SNYDER, R. T. Relationship of visual and auditory short–term memory to later reading achievement. *Perceptual & Motor Skills*, 1980, 51, 15–18.

1997. BACK, R. D., & DANA, R. H. Self–help for male WISC examiners by pretest exposure to children. *Perceptual & Motor Skills*, 1980, 51, 838.

1998. BANNATYNE, A. Spatial competence, learning disabilities, auditory–vocal deficits and a WISC–R subtest recategorization. *Journal of Clinical Child Psychology*, 1980, 8, 194–200.

1999. BERLER, E. S., & ROMANCZYK, R. G. Assessment of the learning disabled and hyperactive child: An analysis and critique. *Journal of Learning Disabilities*, 1980, 13, 10–12.

2000. BERLIN, D. F., & LANGUIS, M. L. Age and sex differences in measures of brain lateralization. *Perceptual & Motor Skills*, 1980, 50, 959–967.

2001. BISHOP, D. V. M. Predictive validity of short forms of the WPPSI. *British Journal of Social & Clinical Psychology*, 1980, 19, 173–175.

2002. BLOOM, A. S., & RASKIN, L. M. WISC–R verbal–performance IQ discrepancies: A comparison of learning disabled children to the normative sample. *Journal of Clinical Psychology*, 1980, 36, 322–323.

2003. BLOOM, A., WAGNER, M., RESKIN, L., & BERGMAN, A. A comparison of intellectually delayed and primary reading disabled children on measures of intelligence and achievement. *Journal of Clinical Psychology*, 1980, 36, 788–790.

2004. BRADLEY, F. O., HANNA, G. S., & LUCAS, B. A. The reliability of scoring the WISC–R. *Journal of Consulting & Clinical Psychology*, 1980, 48, 530–531.

2005. BRAGGIO, J. T., OWEN, J. A., & BRAGGIO, S. M. Discrimination–reversal training eliminates perceptual errors of learning–disabled children. *Contemporary Educational Psychology*, 1980, 5, 11–21.

2006. BRANNIGAN, G. G., ASH, T., & MARGOLIS, H. Impulsivity-reflectivity and children's intellectual performance. *Journal of Personality Assessment*, 1980, 44, 41–43.

2007. BRIDGEMAN, B. Generality of a "fast" or "slow" test–taking style across a variety of cognitive tasks. *Journal of Educational Measurement*, 1980, 17, 211–217.

2008. BROOKS, C. R., & RIGGS, S. T. WISC–R, WISC, and reading achievement relationships among hearing–impaired children attending public schools. *Volta Review*, 1980, 82, 96–102.

2009. BROSNAN, P. G., LEWANDOWSKI, R. C., TOGURRI, A. G., PAYER, A. F., & MEYER, W. J. A new familial syndrome of 46,XY gonadal dysgenesis with anomalies of ectodermal and mesodermal structures. *Journal of Pediatrics*, 1980, 97, 586–590.

2010. BROWN, R. T. Impulsivity and psychoeducational intervention in hyperactive children. *Journal of Learning Disabilities*, 1980, 13, 19–24.

2011. BRUMBACK, R. A., JACKOWAY, M. L., & WEINBERG, W. A. Relation of intelligence to childhood depression in children referred to an educational diagnostic center. *Perceptual & Motor Skills*, 1980, 50, 11–17.

2012. BRUMBACK, R. A., STATON, R. D., & WILSON, H. Neuropsychological study of children during and after remission of endogenous depressive episodes. *Perceptual & Motor Skills*, 1980, 50, 1163–1167.

2013. BURGER, A. L., BLACKMAN, L. S., & TAN, N. Maintenance and generalization of a sorting and retrieval strategy by EMR and nonretarded individuals. *American Journal of Mental Deficiency*, 1980, 84, 373–380.

2014. BURT, M. A., & MYRICK, R. D. Developmental play: What's it all about? *Elementary School Guidance & Counseling*, 1980, 15, 14–21.

2015. CANNING, P. M., ORR, R., & ROURKE, B. P. Sex differences in perceptual, visual–motor, linguistic and concept–formation abilities of retarded readers? *Journal of Learning Disabilities*, 1980, 13, 37–41.

2016. CANTWELL, D. P., BAKER, L., & MATTISON, R. E. Psychiatric disorders in children with speech and language retardation. *Archives of General Psychiatry*, 1980, 37, 423–426.

2017. CERMAK, S. A., COSTER, W., & DRAKE, C. Representational and nonrepresentational gestures in boys with learning disabilities. *American Journal of Occupational Therapy*, 1980, 34, 19–26.

2018. CONNERS, C. K., & TAYLOR, E. Pemoline, methylphenidate, and placebo in children with minimal brain dysfunction. *Archives of General Psychiatry*, 1980, 37, 922–930.

2019. COOPER, S. An approach to the educational assessment of the learning disabled child. *Journal of Clinical Child Psychology*, 1980, 9, 59–62.

2020. CROCKETT, D., CLARK, C., & KLONOFF, H. Correlation and consistency of WISC IQ in sibling and nonsibling pairs. *Journal of Consulting & Clinical Psychology*, 1980, 48, 427–430.

2021. CROFOOT, M. J., & BENNETT, T. S. A comparison of three screening tests and the WISC–R in special education evaluations. *Psychology in the Schools*, 1980, 17, 474–478.

2022. CUMMINS, J. P., & DAS, J. P. Cognitive processing, academic achievement, and WISC–R performance in EMR children. *Journal of Consulting & Clinical Psychology*, 1980, 48, 777–779.

2023. CUMMINS, M., & NORRISH, M. Follow-up of children of diabetic mothers. *Archives of Diseases in Childhood*, 1980, 55, 259–264.

2024. DEAN, R. S. Factor structure of the WISC–R with Anglos and Mexican–Americans. *Journal of School Psychology*, 1980, 18, 234–239.

2025. DEAN, R. S. They do when compared with emotionally disturbed children: Reply to Sattler. *Journal of Consulting & Clinical Psychology*, 1980, 48, 256–257.

2026. DE BLIJ, K., & HINRICHSEN, J. J. Construct validity of Rotter's Locus of Control scale in men alcoholics. *Journal of Studies on Alcohol*, 1980, 41, 463–475.

2027. DECKER, S. N., & DEFRIES, J. C. Cognitive abilities in families with reading disabled children. *Journal of Learning Disabilities*, 1980, 13, 53–58.

2028. DEFILIPPIS, N. A., & FULMER, K. Effects of age and IQ level on the validity of one short intelligence test used for screening purposes. *Educational & Psychological Measurement*, 1980, 40, 543–545.

2029. DE LA FUENTE, J. R., & ROSENBAUM, A. H. Neuroendocrine dysfunction and blood levels of tricyclic antidepressants. *American Journal of Psychiatry*, 1980, 137, 1260–1261.

2030. DIRKS, J., WESSELS, K., QUARFOTH, J., & QUENON, B. Can short–form WISC–R IQ tests identify children with high full scale IQ? *Psychology in the Schools*, 1980, 17, 40–46.

2031. DUNLEAVY, R. A., & BAADE, L. E. Neuropsychological correlates of severe asthma in children 9–14 years old. *Journal of Consulting & Clinical Psychology*, 1980, 48, 214–219.

2032. DYKMAN, R. A., ACKERMAN, P. T., & MCCRAY, D. S. Effects of methylphenidate on selective and sustained attention in hyperactive, reading–disabled, and presumably attention–disordered boys. *Journal of Nervous & Mental Disease*, 1980, 168, 745–752.

2033. DYKMAN, R. A., ACKERMAN, P. T., & OGLESBY, D. M. Correlates of problem solving in hyperactive, learning disabled, and control boys. *Journal of Learning Disabilities*, 1980, 13, 23–32.

2034. EISER, C. Effects of chronic illness on intellectual development. *Archives of Diseases in Childhood*, 1980, 55, 766–770.

2035. ELLIS, N. C., & HENNELLY, R. A. A bilingual word–length effect: Implications for intelligence testing and the relative ease of mental calculation in Welsh and English. *British Journal of Psychology*, 1980, 71, 43–51.

2036. ENGLE, R. W., NAGLE, R. J., & DICK, M. Maintenance and generalization of a semantic rehearsal strategy in educable mentally retarded children. *Journal of Experimental Child Psychology*, 1980, 30, 438–454.

2037. ENO, L., & WOEHLKE, P. Diagnostic differences between educationally handicapped and learning disabled students. *Psychology in the Schools*, 1980, 17, 469–473.

2038. ENRIGHT, R. D. An integration of social cognitive development and cognitive processing: Educational applications. *American Educational Research Journal*, 1980, 17, 21–41.

2039. EPSTEIN, J., BERG-CROSS, G., & BERG-CROSS, L. Maternal expectations and birth order in families with learning disabled and normal children. *Journal of Learning Disabilities*, 1980, 13, 45–52.

2040. FARRAN, D. C., & RAMEY, C. T. Social class differences in dyadic involvement during infancy. *Child Development*, 1980, 51, 254–257.

2041. GABRIELLI, W. F., JR., & MEDNICK, S. A. Sinistrality and delinquency. *Journal of Abnormal Psychology*, 1980, 89, 654–661.

2042. GAJAR, A. H. Characteristics across exceptional categories: EMR, LD, & ED. *Journal of Special Education*, 1980, 14, 165–173.

2043. GETTINGER, M., & WHITE, M. A. Evaluating curriculum fit with class ability. *Journal of Educational Psychology*, 1980, 72, 338–344.

2044. GOH, D. S. Note on selection of WISC-R short forms for different uses. *Journal of Clinical Psychology*, 1980, 36, 319–321.

2045. GRIFFITH, J. J., & MEDNICK, S. A., SCHULSINGER, F., & DIDERICHSEN, B. Verbal associative disturbances in children at high risk for schizophrenia. *Journal of Abnormal Psychology*, 1980, 89, 125–131.

2046. GUTKIN, T. B., & REYNOLDS, C. R. Factorial similarity of the WISC-R for Anglos and Chicanos referred for psychological services. *Journal of School Psychology*, 1980, 18, 34–39.

2047. HASSANYEH, F., & DAVISON, K. Bipolar affective psychosis with onset before age 16 years report of 10 cases. *British Journal of Psychiatry*, 1980, 137, 530–539.

2048. HAYS, J. R., & SMITH, A. L. Comparison of WISC-R and culture fair intelligence test scores for three ethnic groups of juvenile delinquents. *Psychological Reports*, 1980, 46, 931–934.

2049. HESS, R. D., KASHIWAGI, K., AZUMA, H., PRICE, G. C., & DICKSON, W. P. Maternal expectations for mastery of developmental tasks in Japan and the United States. *International Journal of Psychology*, 1980, 15, 259–271.

2050. HIRSCH, F. J., & HIRSCH, S. J. The Quick Test as a screening device for gifted students. *Psychology in the Schools*, 1980, 17, 37–39.

2051. HO, H., FOCH, T. T., & PLOMIN, R. Developmental stability of the relative influence of genes and environment on specific cognitive abilities during childhood. *Developmental Psychology*, 1980, 16, 340–346.

2052. HODAPP, A. F., & HODAPP, J. Correlation of PPVT and WISC-R: A function of diagnostic category. *Psychology in the Schools*, 1980, 17, 33–36.

2053. HORNBY, P. A. Achieving second language fluency through immersion education. *Foreign Language Annals*, 1980, 13, 107–113.

2054. HUBBLE, L. M., & GROFF, M. WISC-R profiles of adjudicated delinquents later incarcerated or released on probation. *Psychological Reports*, 1980, 47, 481–482.

2055. INAYATULLA, M., & CANTOR, S. Effects of thioridazine on the cognitive functioning of a hypotonic schizophrenic boy. *American Journal of Psychiatry*, 1980, 137, 1459–1460.

2056. IRELAND-GALMAN, M. M., PADILLA, G. J., & MICHAEL, W. B. The relationship between performance on the Mazes Subtest of the Wechsler Intelligence Scale for Children–Revised (WISC-R) and speed of solving anagrams with simple and difficult arrangements of letter order. *Educational & Psychological Measurement*, 1980, 40, 513–524.

2057. JOHNSON, R. A. Sensory images in the absence of sight: Blind versus sighted adolescents. *Perceptual & Motor Skills*, 1980, 51, 177–178.

2058. JORDON, L. S. Receptive and expressive language problems occurring in combination with a seizure disorder: A case report. *Journal of Communication Disorders*, 1980, 13, 295–303.

2059. JORDON, V. B. Conserving kinship concepts: A developmental study in social cognition. *Child Development*, 1980, 51, 146–155.

2060. KANE, B. J., & ALLEY, G. R. A peer–tutored instructional management program in computational mathematics for incarcerated, learning disabled juvenile delinquents. *Journal of Learning Disabilities*, 1980, 13, 148–151.

2061. KARAGAN, N. J., RICHMAN, L. C., & SORENSEN, J. P. Analysis of verbal disability in Duchene Muscular Dystrophy. *Journal of Nervous & Mental Disease*, 1980, 168, 419–423.

2062. KARNES, F. A., & BROWN, K. E. Factor analysis of the WISC-R for the gifted. *Journal of Educational Psychology*, 1980, 72, 197–199.

2063. KARNES, F. A., & BROWN, K. E. Sex differences in the WISC-R scores of gifted students. *Psychology in the Schools*, 1980, 17, 361–363.

2064. KLEBANOFF, M. A., & NEFF, J. M. Familial dysautonomia associated with recurrent osteomyelitis in a non–Jewish girl. *Journal of Pediatrics*, 1980, 96, 75–77.

2065. KOOCHER, G. P., O'MALLEY, J. E., GOGAN, J. L., & FOSTER, D. J. Psychological adjustment among pediatric cancer survivors. *Journal of Child Psychology & Psychiatry & Allied Disciplines*, 1980, 21, 163–173.

2066. KRALL, V., SACHS, H., RAYSON, B., LAZAR, B., GROWE, G., & O'CONNELL, L. Effects of lead poisoning on cognitive test performance. *Perceptual & Motor Skills*, 1980, 50, 483–486.

2067. LAOSA, L. M. Maternal teaching strategies and cognitive styles in Chicano families. *Journal of Educational Psychology*, 1980, 72, 45–54.

2068. LAWLIS, G. F., STEDMAN, J. M., & CORTNER, R. H. Factor analysis of the WISC-R for a sample of bilingual Mexican–Americans. *Journal of Clinical Child Psychology*, 1980, 9, 57–58.

2069. LEICHTMAN, S. R. The relatedness of role–taking skills in fourth graders: A shift of perspective. *Journal of Genetic Psychology*, 1980, 136, 301–302.

2070. LEWIS, H. P., & LIVSON, N. Cognitive development, personality and drawing: Their interrelationships in a replicated longitudinal study. *Studies in Art Education*, 1980, 22, 8–11.

2071. MAENPAA, J., & LIEWENDAHL, K. Peripheral insensitivity to thyroid hormones in a euthyroid girl with goitre. *Archives of Diseases in Childhood*, 1980, 55, 207–212.

2072. MAISTO, A. A., & SIPE, S. An examination of encoding and retrieval processes in reading disabled children. *Journal of Experimental Child Psychology*, 1980, 30, 223–230.

2073. MARGOLIS, H., LEONARD, H. S., BRANNIGAN, G. G., & HEVERLY, M. A. The validity of form F of the Matching Familiar Figures Test with kindergarten children. *Journal of Experimental Child Psychology*, 1980, 29, 12–22.

2074. MARSH, R. W. The significance for intelligence of differences in birth–weight and health within monozygotic twin pairs. *British Journal of Psychology*, 1980, 71, 63–67.

2075. MAUER, R. G., & STEWART, M. A. Attention of deficit without hyperactivity in a child psychiatry clinic. *Journal of Clinical Psychiatry*, 1980, 41, 232–233.

2076. MCLESKY, J., KANDASWAMY, S., & COLARUSSO, R. A canonical correlation analysis of the WISC and ITPA for a group of learning–disabled children. *Journal of Special Education*, 1980, 14, 253–259.

2077. MIKKELSEN, E. J., RAPOPORT, J. L., NEE, L., GRUENAU, C., MENDELSON, W., & GILLIN, J. C. Childhood enuresis. I. Sleep patterns and psychopathology. *Archives of General Psychiatry*, 1980, 37, 1139–1144.

2078. MILLER, L. J., BURDG, N. B., & CARPENTER, D. Application of recategorized WISC-R scores for adjudicated adolescents. *Perceptual & Motor Skills*, 1980, 51, 187–191.

2079. MILLER, M. On the attempt to find WISC-R profiles for learning and reading disabilities (a response to Vance, Wallbrown, and Blaha). *Journal of Learning Disabilities*, 1980, 13, 52–54.

2080. MISHRA, S. P. The influence of examiners' ethnic attributes on intelligence test scores. *Psychology in the Schools*, 1980, 17, 117–122.

2081. MONEY, J., CLARKE, F. C., & BECK, J. Congenital hypothyroidism and I.Q. increase: A quarter century follow–up. *Journal of Pediatrics*, 1978, 93, 432–434.

2082. MORRIS, J. D., KELSEY, E., & MARTIN, R. A. Comparison of WISC-R performance of urban and rural special education students. *Psychological Reports*, 1980, 46, 671–677.

2083. MUNFORD, P. R., MEYEROWITZ, B. E., & MUNFORD, A. M. A comparison of black and white children's WISC/WISC-R differences. *Journal of Clinical Psychology*, 1980, 36, 471–475.

2084. MUNFORD, P. R., & MUNOZ, A. A comparison of the WISC and WISC-R on Hispanic children. *Journal of Clinical Psychology*, 1980, 36, 452–458.

2085. NAGLIERI, J. A. Comparison of McCarthy General Cognitive Index and WISC-R IQ for educable mentally retarded, learning disabled, and normal children. *Psychological Reports*, 1980, 47, 591–596.

2086. NAGLIERI, J. A. McCarthy and WISC-R correlations with WRAT achievement scores. *Perceptual & Motor Skills*, 1980, 51, 392–394.

2087. NAGLIERI, J. A. WISC-R subtest patterns for learning disabled and mentally retarded children. *Perceptual & Motor Skills*, 1980, 51, 605–606.

2088. NELSON, H. E., & WARRINGTON, E. K. An investigation of memory functions in dyslexic children. *British Journal of Psychology*, 1980, 71, 487–503.

2089. NEUFELD, J. S., & COZAC, E. A study of the self–concept of intellectually superior children. *Alberta Journal of Educational Research*, 1980, 26, 149–158.

2090. NEWMAN, A., DICKSTEIN, R., & GARGAN, M. Developmental effects in social facilitation and in being a model. *Journal of Psychology*, 1980, 99, 143–150.

2091. NIELSEN, H. H. A longitudinal study of the psychological aspects of myelomeningocele. *Scandinavian Journal of Psychology*, 1980, 21, 45–54.

2092. OAKLAND, T. An evaluation of the ABIC, pluralistic norms, and estimated learning potential. *Journal of School Psychology*, 1980, 18, 3–11.

2093. PLOMIN, R., & FOCH, T. T. A twin study of objectively assessed personality in childhood. *Journal of Personality & Social Psychology*, 1980, 39, 680–688.

2094. QUATTROCCHI, M., & SHERRETS, S. WISC–R: The first five years. *Psychology in the Schools*, 1980, 17, 297–312.

2095. RASKIND, L. T., & NAGLE, R. J. Modeling effects on the intelligence test performance of test-anxious children. *Psychology in the Schools*, 1980, 17, 351–355.

2096. RATCLIFFE, M. W., & RATCLIFFE, K. J. A comparison of the Wechsler Intelligence Scale for Children–Revised and Leiter International Performance Scale for a group of educationally handicapped adolescents. *Journal of Clinical Psychology*, 1980, 36, 310–312.

2097. REEVES, W. H. Auditory learning disabilities and emotional disturbance: Diagnostic differences. *Journal of Learning Disabilities*, 1980, 13, 30–33.

2098. REYNOLDS, C. R. Concurrent validity of What I Think and Feel: The Revised Children's Manifest Anxiety Scale. *Journal of Consulting & Clinical Psychology*, 1980, 48, 774–775.

2099. REYNOLDS, C. R., & GUTKIN, T. B. Stability of the WISC–R factor structure across sex at two age levels. *Journal of Clinical Psychology*, 1980, 36, 775–777.

2100. REYNOLDS, C. R., & KAUFMAN, A. S. Lateral eye movement behavior in children. *Perceptual & Motor Skills*, 1980, 50, 1023–1037.

2101. RICHARDSON, E., DiBENEDETTO, B., CHRIST, A., & PRESS, M. Relationship of auditory and visual skills to reading retardation. *Journal of Learning Disabilities*, 1980, 13, 77–82.

2102. RICHMAN, L. C. Cognitive patterns and learning disabilities in cleft palate children with verbal deficits. *Journal of Speech & Hearing Research*, 1980, 23, 447–456.

2103. RUDRUD, E., FERRARA, J., & ZIARNIK, J. Living placement and absenteeism in community-based training programs. *American Journal of Mental Deficiency*, 1980, 84, 401–404.

2104. RUST, J. O., & LOSE, B. D. Screening for giftedness with the Slosson and the Scale for Rating Behavioral Characteristics of Superior Students. *Psychology in the Schools*, 1980, 17, 446–451.

2105. SAIGH, P. A. The effects of positive nonverbal examiner comments on the WISC–R performance of Americans in Lebanon. *Journal of Psychology*, 1980, 104, 165–169.

2106. SAMUEL, W. Mood and personality correlates of IQ by race and sex of subject. *Journal of Personality & Social Psychology*, 1980, 38, 993–1004.

2107. SANDOVAL, J. Reliability and concurrent validity of Light's Retention Scale. *Psychology in the Schools*, 1980, 17, 442–445.

2108. SANDOVAL, J., & MIILLE, M. P. W. Accuracy of judgements of WISC–R item difficulty for minority groups. *Journal of Consulting & Clinical Psychology*, 1980, 48, 249–253.

2109. SATTERFIELD, J. H., SATTERFIELD, B. T., & CANTWELL, D. P. Multimodality treatment: A two-year evaluation of 61 hyperactive boys. *Archives of General Psychiatry*, 1980, 37, 915–919.

2110. SATTLER, J. M. Learning-disabled children do not have a perceptual organization deficit: Comments on Dean's WISC–R analysis. *Journal of Consulting & Clinical Psychology*, 1980, 48, 254–255.

2111. SATTLER, J. M., BOHANAN, A. L., & MOORE, M. K. Relationship between PPVT and WISC–R in children with reading disabilities. *Psychology in the Schools*, 1980, 17, 331–334.

2112. SCHLOSSER, L., & ALGOZZINE, B. Sex, behavior, and teacher expectancies. *Journal of Experimental Education*, 1980, 48, 231–236.

2113. SEYFORT, B., SPREEN, O., & LAHMER, V. A critical look at the WISC–R with native Indian children. *Alberta Journal of Educational Research*, 1980, 26, 14–24.

2114. SHAVIT, H. Effects of feedback–induced changes in expectancy for skill–related outcome on affective vs instrumental reactions. *Perceptual & Motor Skills*, 1980, 50, 951–957.

2115. SHAYWITZ, S. E., COHEN, D. J., & SHAYWITZ, B. A. Behavior and learning difficulties in children of normal intelligence born to alcoholic mothers. *Journal of Pediatrics*, 1980, 96, 978–982.

2116. SILVERSTEIN, A. B. Cluster analysis of the Wechsler Intelligence Scale for Children–Revised. *Educational & Psychological Measurement*, 1980, 40, 51–54.

2117. SILVERSTEIN, A. B. Estimating the general factor in the WISC and the WAIS. *Psychological Reports*, 1980, 46, 189–190.

2118. SILVERSTEIN, A. B. Estimating the general factor in the WISC–R. *Psychological Reports*, 1980, 47, 1185–1186.

2119. SIMON, J. M., & EVANS, J. R. WISC–R picture arrangement subtest scores and peer acceptance/rejection. *Perceptual & Motor Skills*, 1980, 51, 558.

2120. SMITH, I. L., & GREENBERG, S. Dimensions underlying a hierarchically based assessment of social problem–solving. *American Journal of Mental Deficiency*, 1980, 84, 411–414.

2121. SNOWLING, M. J. The development of grapheme–phoneme correspondence in normal and dyslexic readers. *Journal of Experimental Child Psychology*, 1980, 29, 294–305.

2122. SOLWAY, K. S., HAYS, J. R., SCHREINER, D., & CANSLER, D. Clinical study of youths petitioned for certification as adults. *Psychological Reports*, 1980, 46, 1067–1073.

2123. STABLER, B., WHITT, J. K., MOREAULT, D. M., D'ERCOLE, A. J., & UNDERWOOD, L. E. Social judgments by children of short stature. *Psychological Reports*, 1980, 46, 743–746.

2124. STEELMAN, L. C., & MERCY, J. A. Unconfounding the confluence model: A test of sibship size and birth–order effects on intelligence. *American Sociological Review*, 1980, 45, 571–582.

2125. STEINKAMP, M. W. Relationships between environmental distractions and task performance of hyperactive and normal children. *Journal of Learning Disabilities*, 1980, 13, 209–214.

2126. STEVENSON, L. P. WISC–R analysis: Implications for diagnosis and intervention. *Journal of Learning Disabilities*, 1980, 13, 60–63.

2127. SVANUM, S., & BRINGLE, R. G. Evaluation of confluence model variables on IQ and achievement test scores in a sample of 6– to 11-year-old children. *Journal of Educational Psychology*, 1980, 72, 427–436.

2128. TAYLOR, R. L., & IVIMEY, J. K. Diagnostic use of the WISC–R and McCarthy Scales: A regression analysis approach to learning disabilities. *Psychology in the Schools*, 1980, 17, 327–330.

2129. TERRELL, F., TERRELL, S. L., & TAYLOR, J. Effects of race of examiner and type of reinforcement on the intelligence test performance of lower–class black children. *Psychology in the Schools*, 1980, 17, 270–272.

2130. THOMAS, P. J. A longitudinal comparison of the WISC and WISC–R with special education pupils. *Psychology in the Schools*, 1980, 17, 437–441.

2131. THOMPSON, R. J., JR. The diagnostic utility of WISC–R measures with children referred to a developmental evaluation center. *Journal of Consulting & Clinical Psychology*, 1980, 48, 440–447.

2132. TORGESEN, J. K., & HOUCK, D. G. Processing deficiencies of learning–disabled children who perform poorly on the Digit Span Test. *Journal of Educational Psychology*, 1980, 72, 141–160.

2133. TOWNES, B. D., TRUPIN, E. W., MARTIN, D. C., & GOLDSTEIN, D. Neuropsychological correlates of academic success among elementary school children. *Journal of Consulting & Clinical Psychology*, 1980, 48, 675–684.

2134. TRAMILL, J. L., EDWARDS, R. P., & TRAMILL, J. K. Comparison of the Goodenough–Harris Drawing Test and the WISC–R for children experiencing academic difficulties. *Perceptual & Motor Skills*, 1980, 50, 543–546.

2135. TSUSHIMA, W. T., & TOWNE, W. S. ITPA performances of young children with and without questionable brain disorders. *Journal of Learning Disabilities*, 1980, 13, 13–15.

2136. TUMA, J. M., & APPELBAUM, A. S. Reliability and practice effects of WISC–R IQ estimates in a normal population. *Educational & Psychological Measurement*, 1980, 40, 671–678.

2137. TYMCHUK, A. J., SIMMONS, J. Q., & NEAFSEY, S. Intellectual characteristics of adolescent childhood psychotics with high verbal ability. *Journal of Mental Deficiency Research*, 1980, 21, 133–138.

2138. VACC, N. A., & ATWELL, B. Relationship of the Adaptive Behavior Inventory for children and intelligence. *Psychological Reports*, 1980, 47, 402.

2139. VRANA, F., & PIHL, R. O. Selective attention deficit in learning disabled children: A cognitive interpretation. *Journal of Learning Disabilities*, 1980, 13, 42–45.

2140. WALLBROWN, F. H., BLAHA, J., & VANCE, B. A reply to Miller's concerns about WISC–R profile analysis. *Journal of Learning Disabilities*, 1980, 13, 54–59.

2141. WEBER, D. B., & EPSTEIN, H. R. Contrasting adaptive behavior ratings of male and female institutionalized residents across two settings. *American Journal of Mental Deficiency*, 1980, 84, 397–400.

2142. WEBSTER, R. E., & LAFAYETTE, A. D. Distinguishing among three subgroups of handicapped students using Bannatyne's recategorization. *Journal of Educational Research*, 1980, 73, 237–240.

2143. WHEATON, P. J., VANDERGRIFF, A. F., & NELSON, W. H. Comparability of the WISC and WISC–R with bright elementary school students. *Journal of School Psychology*, 1980, 18, 271–275.

2144. WIENER, J. A theoretical model of the acquisition of peer relationships of learning disabled children. *Journal of Learning Disabilities*, 1980, 13, 42–47.

2145. WILIMAS, J., GOFF, J. R., ANDERSON, H. R., JR., LANGSTON, J. W., & THOMPSON, E. Efficacy of transfusion therapy for one to two years in patients with sickle cell disease and cerebrovascular accidents. *Journal of Pediatrics*, 1980, 96, 205–208.

2146. WINSBERG, B. G., BIALER, I., KUPIETZ, S., BOTTI, E., & BALKA, E. B. Home vs hospital care of children with behavior disorders. *Archives of General Psychiatry*, 1980, 37, 413–418.

2147. WOODS, B. T. The restricted effects of right–hemisphere lesions after age one: Wechsler test data. *Neuropsychologia*, 1980, 18, 65–70.

2148. WORLAND, J., & HESSELBROCK, V. The intelligence of children and their parents with schizophrenia and affective illness. *Journal of Child Psychology & Psychiatry & Allied Disciplines*, 1980, 21, 191–201.

2149. ZAGAR, R., ARBIT, J., & FRIEDLAND, J. Structure of a psychodiagnostic test battery for children. *Journal of Clinical Psychology*, 1980, 36, 313–318.

2150. ZENDEL, I. H., & PIHL, R. O. Torque and learning and behavior problems in children. *Journal of Consulting & Clinical Psychology*, 1980, 48, 602–604.

2151. ZOREF, L., & WILLIAMS, P. A look at content bias in IQ tests. *Journal of Educational Measurement*, 1980, 17, 313–322.

2152. ACKERMAN, P. T., OGLESBY, D. M., & DYKMAN, R. A. A contrast of hyperactive, learning disabled, and hyperactive–learning disabled boys. *Journal of Clinical Child Psychology*, 1981, 10, 168–173.

2153. ANDERSON, B., & RALLIS, K. Relationship between Bender errors, emotional indicators and performance on Bender recall. *Perceptual & Motor Skills*, 1981, 53, 497–498.

2154. AUGUST, G. J., STEWART, M. A., & TSAI, L. The incidence of cognitive disabilities in the siblings of autistic children. *British Journal of Psychiatry*, 1981, 138, 416–422.

2155. BADIAN, N. A. Recategorized WISC–R scores of disabled and adequate readers. *Journal of Educational Research*, 1981, 75, 109–114.

2156. BELL, R. C. Common space analysis of several versions of the Wechsler Intelligence Scale for Children. *Applied Psychological Measurement*, 1981, 5, 125–132.

2157. BENNETT, T. S., & WELSH, M. C. Validity of a configural interpretation of the intellectual screening and achievement scales of the Personality Inventory for Children. *Educational & Psychological Measurement*, 1981, 41, 863–868.

2158. BERLIN, D. F., & LANGUIS, M. L. Hemispheric correlates of the rod–and–frame test. *Perceptual & Motor Skills*, 1981, 52, 35–41.

2159. BLOCK, J., BUSS, D. M., BLOCK, J. H., & GJERDE, P. F. The cognitive style of breadth of categorization: Longitudinal consistency of personality correlates. *Journal of Personality & Social Psychology*, 1981, 40, 770–779.

2160. BLOOM, A., WAGNER, M., BERGMAN, A., ALTSHULER, L., & RASKIN, L. Relationship between intellectual status and reading skills for developmentally disabled children. *Perceptual & Motor Skills*, 1981, 52, 853–854.

2161. BRADLEY, L., & BRYANT, P. Visual memory and phonological skills in reading and spelling backwardness. *Psychological Research*, 1981, 43, 193–199.

2162. BRODER, P. K., DUNIVANT, N., SMITH, E. C., & SUTTON, L. P. Further observations on the link between learning disabilities and juvenile delinquency. *Journal of Educational Psychology*, 1981, 73, 838–850.

2163. BYRNE, B., & ARNOLD, L. Dissociation of the recency effect and immediate memory span: Evidence from beginning readers. *British Journal of Psychology*, 1981, 72, 371–376.

2164. CAMPBELL, A. L., JR., BOGEN, J. E., & SMITH, A. Disorganization and reorganization related to cognitive and sensorimotor functions in cerebral commissurotomy: Compensatory roles of the forebrain commissures and cerebral hemispheres in man. *Brain*, 1981, 104, 493–511.

2165. CHADWICK, O., RUTTER, M., THOMPSON, J., & SHAFFER, D. Intellectual performance and reading skills after localized head injury in childhood. *Journal of Child Psychology & Psychiatry & Allied Disciplines*, 1981, 22, 117–139.

2166. CLARIZIO, H., & BERNARD, R. Recategorized WISC–R scores of learning disabled children and differential diagnosis. *Psychology in the Schools*, 1981, 18, 5–12.

2167. DAWSON, G. D. Sex differences in dichaptic processing. *Perceptual & Motor Skills*, 1981, 53, 935–944.

2168. DEAN, R. S., & KUNDERT, D. K. The effects of abstractiveness in mediation with learning-problem children. *Journal of Clinical Child Psychology*, 1981, 10, 173–175.

2169. DEAN, R. S., & KUNDERT, D. K. Intelligence and teachers' ratings as predictors of abstract and concrete learning. *Journal of School Psychology*, 1981, 19, 78–85.

2170. ELLIOT, M. Quantitative evaluation procedures for learning disabilities. *Journal of Learning Disabilities*, 1981, 14, 84–87.

2171. GARDNER, R. A. Digits forward and digits backward as two separate tests: Normative data on 1567 school children. *Journal of Clinical Child Psychology*, 1981, 10, 131–135.

2172. GOLD, P. Suspected neurological impairment (SNI) and cognitive abilities: A longitudinal study of selected skills and predictive accuracy. *Journal of Clinical Child Psychology*, 1981, 8, 35–38.

2173. GUTKIN, T. B., & REYNOLDS, C. R. Factorial similarity of the WISC–R for white and black children from the standardization sample. *Journal of Educational Psychology*, 1981, 73, 227–231.

2174. HALE, R. L. Cluster analysis in school psychology: An example. *Journal of School Psychology*, 1981, 19, 51–56.

2175. HALE, R. L. Concurrent validity of the WISC–R factor scores. *Journal of School Psychology*, 1981, 19, 274–278.

2176. HUBBLE, L. M., & GROFF, M. Factor analysis of WISC–R scores of male delinquents referred for evaluation. *Journal of Consulting & Clinical Psychology*, 1981, 49, 738–739.

2177. HYND, G. W., OBRZUT, J. E., & OBRZUT, A. Are lateral and perceptual asymmetries related to WISC–R and achievement test performance in normal and learning–disabled children? *Journal of Consulting & Clinical Psychology*, 1981, 49, 977–979.

2178. KAZDIN, A. E., FRENCH, N. H., & SHERICK, R. B. Acceptability of alternative treatments for children: Evaluations by inpatient children, parents, and staff. *Journal of Consulting & Clinical Psychology*, 1981, 49, 900–907.

2179. KAZIMOUR, K. K., & RESCHLY, D. J. Investigation of the norms and concurrent validity for the Adaptive Behavior Inventory for Children (ABIC). *American Journal of Mental Deficiency*, 1981, 85, 504–511.

2180. KIRKPATRICK, M., SMITH, C., & ROY, R. Lesbian mothers and their children: A comparative study. *American Journal of Orthopsychiatry*, 1981, 51, 545–551.

2181. KOOTZ, J. P., MARINELLI, B., & COHEN, D. J. Sensory receptor sensitivity in autistic children. *Archives of General Psychiatry*, 1981, 38, 271–273.

2182. LAMBERT, N. M. The clinical validity of the process for assessment of effective student functioning. *Journal of School Psychology*, 1981, 19, 323–334.

2183. LATORRE, R. A., & LATORRE, A. Effect of lateral eye fixation on cognitive processes. *Perceptual & Motor Skills*, 1981, 52, 487–490.

2184. LORBER, J., & SALFIELD, S. A. W. Results of selective treatment of spina bifida cystica. *Archives of Diseases in Childhood*, 1981, 56, 822–830.

2185. LUND, N. L., CARMAN, S. M., & KRANZ, P. L. Reliability in the use of the Tennessee Self–Concept Scale for educable mentally retarded adolescents. *Journal of Psychology*, 1981, 109, 205–211.

2186. LYON, R., REITTA, S., WATSON, B., PORCH, B., & RHODES, J. Selected linguistic and perceptual abilities of empirically derived subgroups of learning disabled readers. *Journal of School Psychology*, 1981, 19, 152–166.

2187. MARUYAMA, G., RUBIN, R. A., & KINGSBURY, G. G. Self-esteem and educational achievement: Independent constructs with a common cause? *Journal of Personality & Social Psychology*, 1981, 40, 962–975.

2188. McCANN, D. C., & PRENTICE, N. M. Promoting moral judgement of elementary school children: The influence of direct reinforcement and cognitive disequilibrium. *Journal of Genetic Psychology*, 1981, 139, 27–34.

2189. MEIJER, A., & HOVNE, R. Child psychiatric problems in "autonomous dysfunction." *Child Psychiatry & Human Development*, 1981, 12, 96–105.

2190. MOESCHLER, J. B., BENNETT, F. C., & CROMWELL, L. D. Use of the CT scan in the medical evaluation of the mentally retarded child. *Journal of Pediatrics*, 1981, 98, 63–65.

2191. MOFFITT, T. E. Vocabulary and arithmetic performance of father–absent boys. *Child Study Journal*, 1981, 10, 233–241.

2192. MOFFITT, T. E., GABRIELLI, W. F., MEDNICK, S. A., & SCHULSINGER, F. Socioeconomic status, IQ, and delinquency. *Journal of Abnormal Psychology*, 1981, 90, 152–156.

2193. MORGAN, A. M. B. Correlation of Frostig visual perception scores and verbal IQ's among epileptic children. *Perceptual & Motor Skills*, 1981, 52, 97–98.

2194. MULVANEY, D. E., HUGHES, L. H., JWAIDEH, A. R., & DINSMOOR, J. A. Differential production of positive and negative discriminative stimuli by normal and retarded children. *Journal of Experimental Child Psychology*, 1981, 32, 389–400.

2195. NAGLIERI, J. A., KAUFMAN, A. S., KAUFMAN, N. L., & KAMPHAUS, R. W. Cross validation of Das' simultaneous and successive processes with novel tasks. *Alberta Journal of Educational Research*, 1981, 27, 264–271.

2196. NAGLIERI, J. A., & MAXWELL, S. Inter–rater reliability and concurrent validity of the Goodenough-Harris and McCarthy draw–a–child scoring systems. *Perceptual & Motor Skills*, 1981, 53, 343–348.

2197. O'LEARY, D. S., SEIDENBERG, M., BERENT, S., & BOLL, T. J. Effects of age of onset of tonic-clonic seizures on neuropsychological performance in children. *Epilepsia*, 1981, 22, 197–204.

2198. PIHL, R. O., & MANDELCORN, B. The manipulation of maternal expectancy in a mother–child interaction. *Journal of Genetic Psychology*, 1981, 139, 85–95.

2199. POWELL, G., MOORE, D., & CALLAWAY, B. A concurrent validity study of the Woodcock Word Comprehension Test. *Psychology in the Schools*, 1981, 18, 24–27.

2200. PRENTICE-DUNN, S., WILSON, D. R., & LYMAN, R. D. Client factors related to outcome in a residential and day treatment program for children. *Journal of Clinical Child Psychology*, 1981, 10, 188–191.

2201. RABER, S. M., & WEISZ, J. R. Teacher feedback to mentally retarded and nonretarded children. *American Journal of Mental Deficiency*, 1981, 86, 148–156.

2202. REYNOLDS, C. R., & NIGL, A. J. A regression analysis of differential validity in intellectual assessment for black and for white inner city children. *Journal of Clinical Child Psychology*, 1981, 10, 176–179.
2203. REYNOLDS, C. R., WRIGHT, D., & DAPPEN, L. A comparison of the criterion-related validity (academic achievement) of the WPPSI and the WISC-R. *Psychology in the Schools*, 1981, 18, 20–23.
2204. RIBNER, S., & KAHN, P. Scatter on the WISC as an indicator of intellectual potential. *Psychology in the Schools*, 1981, 18, 39–42.
2205. RICHARDSON, S. A., KOLLER, H., KATZ, M., & McLAREN, J. A functional classification of seizures and its distribution in a mentally retarded population. *American Journal of Mental Deficiency*, 1981, 85, 457–466.
2206. RICHMAN, L. C., & LINDGREN, S. D. Verbal mediation deficits: Relation to behavior and achievement in children. *Journal of Abnormal Psychology*, 1981, 90, 99–104.
2207. RUOFF, P., DOERR, H., FULLER, P., MARTIN, D., & RUOFF, L. O. Motor and cognitive interactions during lateralized cerebral functions in children: An EEG study. *Cortex*, 1981, 17, 5–18.
2208. SAIGH, P. A. The effects of positive examiner verbal comments on the total WISC–R performance of institutionalized EMR students. *Journal of School Psychology*, 1981, 19, 86–91.
2209. SAXE, G. B., & SHAHEEN, S. Piagetian theory and the atypical case: An analysis of the developmental Gerstmann Syndrome. *Journal of Learning Disabilities*, 1981, 14, 131–135.
2210. SCHROTH, M. L. Type I and type II abilities in children and learning rate. *Journal of Genetic Psychology*, 1981, 138, 95–102.
2211. SCHROTH, M. L. The use of IQ and MA as measures of learning rate with fluid and crystallized intelligence. *Journal of General Psychology*, 1981, 105, 235–242.
2212. SEMEL, E. M., & WIIG, E. H. Semel Auditory Processing Program: Training effects among children with language–learning disabilities. *Journal of Learning Disabilities*, 1981, 14, 192–196.
2213. SLEIGH, G., & LINDENBAUM, R. H. Benign (non–paroxysmal) familial chorea. *Paediatric perspectives. Archives of Diseases in Childhood*, 1981, 56, 616–621.
2214. SNOWLING, M. J. Phonemic deficits in developmental dyslexia. *Psychological Research*, 1981, 43, 219–234.
2215. STARK, R. E., & TALLAL, P. Selection of children with specific language deficits. *Journal of Speech & Hearing Disorders*, 1981, 46, 114–122.
2216. STATON, R. D., & BRUMBACK, R. A. Non–specificity of motor hyperactivity as a diagnostic criterion. *Perceptual & Motor Skills*, 1981, 52, 323–332.
2217. STATON, R. D., WILSON, H., & BRUMBACK, R. A. Cognitive improvement associated with tricyclic antidepressant treatment of childhood major depressive illness. *Perceptual & Motor Skills*, 1981, 53, 219–234.
2218. STEIN, G. M., GIBBONS, R. D., & MELDMAN, M. J. Lateral eye movement and handedness as measures of functional brain asymmetry in learning disability. *Cortex*, 1981, 16, 223–229.
2219. STEWART, J. H. Wechsler performance IQ scores and social behaviors of hearing–impaired students. *Volta Review*, 1981, 83, 215–222.
2220. STRAUSS, H., HADAR, M., SHAVIT, H., & ITSKOWITZ, R. Relationship between creativity, repression, and anxiety in first graders. *Perceptual & Motor Skills*, 1981, 53, 275–282.
2221. TALLAL, P., STARK, R., KALLMAN, C., & MELLITS, D. A reexamination of some nonverbal perceptual abilities of language–impaired and normal children as a function of age and sensory modality. *Journal of Speech & Hearing Research*, 1981, 24, 351–357.
2222. THOMPSON, R. J. The diagnostic utility of Bannatyne's recategorized WISC–R scores with children referred to a developmental evaluation center. *Psychology in the Schools*, 1981, 18, 43–47.
2223. TORRANCE, E. P. Predicting the creativity of elementary school children (1958–80)–And the teacher who "made a difference." *Gifted Child Quarterly*, 1981, 25, 55–62.
2224. ULLMAN, D. G., EGAN, D., FIEDLER, N., JURENEC, G., PLISKE, R., THOMPSON, P., & DOHERTY, M. E. The many faces of hyperactivity: Similarities and differences in diagnostic policies. *Journal of Consulting & Clinical Psychology*, 1981, 49, 694–704.
2225. VELLUTINO, F. R., SCANLON, D. M., DE SETTO, L., & PRUZEK, R. M. Developmental trends in the salience of meaning versus structural attributes of written words. *Psychological Research*, 1981, 43, 131–153.
2226. WALKER, N. W. Modifying impulsive responding to four WISC–R subtests. *Journal of School Psychology*, 1981, 19, 335–339.
2227. WATTERS, R. G., WHEELER, L. J., & WATTERS, W. E. The relative efficiency of two orders for training autistic children in the expressive and receptive use of manual signs. *Journal of Communication Disorders*, 1981, 14, 273–285.
2228. WERSH, J., & BRIERE, J. WISC–R subtest variability in normal Canadian children and its relationship to sex, age, and IQ. *Canadian Journal of Behavioural Science*, 1981, 13, 76–85.
2229. WILLIAMS, A. J., WILLIAMS, M. A., WALKER, C. A., & BUSH, P. G. The Robin Anomalad (Pierre Robin Syndrome)–A follow up study. *Archives of Diseases in Childhood*, 1981, 56, 663–668.
2230. YSSELDYKE, J., SHINN, M., & EPPS, S. A comparison of the WISC–R and the Woodcock–Johnson tests of cognitive ability. *Psychology in the Schools*, 1981, 18, 15–19.

[2603]
[Re Wechsler Intelligence Scale for Children—Revised] WISC-R Profile Form. Ages 6–17; 1974; Kenneth L. Hobby; Psychologists and Educators, Inc.*

For additional information, see 8:233.

[2604]
[Re Wechsler Intelligence Scale for Children] Rhodes WISC Scatter Profile. Ages 5–15; 1969; a form for profiling WISC scores; Fen Rhodes; EdITS/Educational and Industrial Testing Service.*

For additional information, see 7:433.

[2605]
[Re Wechsler Intelligence Scale for Children] WISC Test Profile and WISC-R Profile. Ages 5–15; 1968–69; Consulting Psychologists Press, Inc.*

[2606]
★Wechsler Intelligence Scales for Children-Revised: For the Deaf. Ages 6–16; 1979; Deaf WISC-R; adaptation of the performance scale; 7 scores: picture completion, picture arrangement, block design, object assembly, coding, mazes, total; Steven Ray; Northwestern State University of Louisiana.*

[2607]
Wechsler Memory Scale. Adults; 1945–46; David Wechsler and Calvin P. Stone (Form 2); The Psychological Corporation.*

For additional information, see 8:250 (36 references); see also T2:592 (70 references) and 6:561 (9 references); for reviews by Ivan Norman Mensh and Joseph Newman, see 4:364 (6 references); for a review by Kate Levine Kogan, see 3:302 (3 references).

REFERENCES

1–3. See 3:302.
4–9. See 4:364.
10–18. See 6:561.
19–88. See T2:592.
89–124. See 8:250.
125. BARKER, T. E., & BLACK, F. W. Klinefelter Syndrome in a military population. *Archives of General Psychiatry*, 1976, 33, 607–610.
126. TARTER, R. E., & SCHNEIDER, D. U. Blackouts. *Archives of General Psychiatry*, 1976, 33, 1492–1496.
127. ANDERSON, B. L. Schizophrenic performance during interpersonal competitive conditions. *Journal of Clinical Psychology*, 1977, 33, 970–972.
128. BIERSNER, R. J., HALL, D. A., NEWMAN, T. S., & LINAWEAVER, P. G. Learning rate equivalency of two narcotic gases. *Journal of Applied Psychology*, 1977, 62, 747–750.
129. BOLLER, F., VRTUNSKI, B., MACK, J. L., & KIM, Y. Neuropsychological correlates of hypertension. *Archives of Neurology*, 1977, 34, 701–705.
130. BRANCONNIER, R. J., & COLE, J. O. A memory assessment technique for use in geriatric psychopharmacology: Drug efficacy trial with naftidrofuryl. *Journal of the American Geriatrics Society*, 1977, 25, 186–188.
131. CAUTHEN, N. R. Extension of the Wechsler Memory Scale norms to older age groups. *Journal of Clinical Psychology*, 1977, 33, 208–211.
132. CORNBLETH, T. Effects of a protected hospital ward area on wandering and nonwandering geriatrics patients. *Journal of Gerontology*, 1977, 32, 573–577.
133. EXNER, J. E., & MURRILLO, L. G. A long term follow–up of schizophrenics treated with regressive ECT. *Diseases of the Nervous System*, 1977, 38, 162–168.
134. FERRIS, S. H., SATHANANTHAN, G., GERSHON, S., & CLARK, C. Senile dementia: Treatment with deanol. *Journal of the American Geriatrics Society*, 1977, 25, 241–244.
135. GROHER, M. Language and memory disorders following closed head trauma. *Journal of Speech & Hearing Research*, 1977, 20, 212–223.

136. IVISON, D. J. The Wechsler Memory Scale: Preliminary findings toward an Australian standardization. *Australian Psychologist*, 1977, 12, 303-312.

137. JURKO, M. F., & ANDY, O. J. Verbal learning dysfunction with combined centre median and amygdala lesions. *Journal of Neurology, Neurosurgery, & Psychiatry*, 1977, 40, 695-698.

138. KEAR-COLWELL, J. J. The structure of the Wechsler Memory Scale: A replication. *Journal of Clinical Psychology*, 1977, 33, 483-485.

139. LEDOUX, J. E., RISSE, G. L., SPRINGER, S. P., WILSON, D. H., & GAZZANIGA, M. S. Cognition and commissurotomy. *Brain*, 1977, 100, 87-104.

140. LINCOLN, N. B., & STAPLES, D. J. Psychological aspects of some chronic progressive neuromuscular disorders. *Journal of Chronic Diseases*, 1977, 30, 207-215.

141. MALATESTA, C. Z., CIRCO, J., & SMITH, B. A discriminating, non-discriminatory test battery for a prison population. *Corrective & Social Psychiatry & Journal of Behavior Technology, Methods & Therapy*, 1977, 23, 15-17.

142. McGLONE, J. Sex differences in the cerebral organization of verbal functions in patients with unilateral brain lesions. *Brain*, 1977, 100, 775-793.

143. NEWMAN, E. H. Resolution of inconsistent attitude communications in normal and schizophrenic subjects. *Journal of Abnormal Psychology*, 1977, 86, 41-46.

144. PRIGATANO, G. P. Wechsler Memory Scale is a poor screening test for brain dysfunction. *Journal of Clinical Psychology*, 1977, 33, 772-777.

145. PRINZ, P. N. Sleep patterns in the healthy aged: Relationship with intellectual function. *Journal of Gerontology*, 1977, 32, 179-186.

146. RAO, A. V., & NAMMALVAR, N. The course and outcome in depressive illness. *British Journal of Psychiatry*, 1977, 130, 392-396.

147. RAUSCH, R. Cognitive strategies in patients with unilateral temporal lobe excisions. *Neuropsychologia*, 1977, 15, 385-395.

148. RAUSCH, R., SERAFETINIDES, E. A., & CRANDALL, P. H. Olfactory memory in patients with anterior temporal lobectomy. *Cortex*, 1977, 13, 445-452.

149. WECKOWICZ, T. E., COLLIER, G., & SPRENG, L. Field dependence, cognitive functions, personality traits, and social values in heavy cannabis users and nonuser controls. *Psychological Reports*, 1977, 41, 291-302.

150. ARBIT, J., & ZAGER, R. Psychometrics of a neuropsychological test battery. *Journal of Clinical Psychology*, 1978, 34, 460-465.

151. BLACK, F. W., & STRUB, R. L. Digit repetition performance in patients with focal brain damage. *Cortex*, 1978, 14, 12-21.

152. BOTWINICK, J., WEST, R., & STORANDT, M. Predicting death from behavioral test performance. *Journal of Gerontology*, 1978, 33, 755-762.

153. BRANCONNIER, R. J., & COLE, J. O. The Impairment Index as a symptom-independent parameter of drug efficacy in geriatric psychopharmacology. *Journal of Gerontology*, 1978, 33, 217-223.

154. BUTTERS, N., SAX, D., MONTGOMERY, K., & TARLOW, S. Comparison of the neuropsychological deficits associated with early and advanced Huntington's Disease. *Archives of Neurology*, 1978, 35, 585-589.

155. COCHRAN, J. W., FOX, J. H., & KELLY, M. P. Reversible mental symptoms in temporal arthritis. *Journal of Nervous & Mental Disease*, 1978, 166, 446-447.

156. CUTTING, J. Specific psychological deficits in alcoholism. *British Journal of Psychiatry*, 1978, 133, 199-222.

157. DODRILL, C. B. A neuropsychological battery for epilepsy. *Epilepsia*, 1978, 19, 611-623.

158. FLETCHER, J. M., RICE, W. J., & RAY, R. M. Linear discriminant function analysis in neuropsychological research: Some uses and abuses. *Cortex*, 1978, 14, 564-577.

159. HEATON, R. K., CHELUNE, G. J., & LEHMAN, R. A. W. Using neuropsychological and personality tests to assess the likelihood of patient employment. *Journal of Nervous & Mental Disease*, 1978, 166, 408-416.

160. HOLTZMAN, R. N. N., RUDEL, R. G., & GOLDENSOHN, E. S. Paroxysmal alexia. *Cortex*, 1978, 14, 592-603.

161. JOSLYN, D., GRUNDVIG, J. L., & CHAMBERLAIN, C. J. Predicting confabulation from the Graham-Kendall Memory-For-Designs Test. *Journal of Consulting & Clinical Psychology*, 1978, 46, 181-182.

162. KEAR-COLWELL, J. J., & HELLER, M. A normative study of the Wechsler Memory Scale. *Journal of Clinical Psychology*, 1978, 34, 437-442.

163. NEMEC, R. E. Effect of controlled background interference on test performance by right and left hemiplegics. *Journal of Consulting & Clinical Psychology*, 1978, 46, 294-297.

164. NORTON, J. C. The Trail Making Test and Bender Background Interference Procedure as screening devices. *Journal of Clinical Psychology*, 1978, 34, 916-922.

165. OSBORNE, D., & DAVIS, L. J., JR. Standard scores for Wechsler Memory Scale subtests. *Journal of Clinical Psychology*, 1978, 34, 115-116.

166. RASKIN, A., GERSHON, S., CROOK, T. H., SATHANANTHAN, G., & FERRIS, S. The effects of hyperbaric and normobaric oxygen on cognitive impairment in the elderly. *Archives of General Psychiatry*, 1978, 35, 50-56.

167. RAUSCH, R., LEIB, J. P., & CRANDALL, P. H. Neuropsychologic correlates of depth spike activity in epileptic patients. *Archives of Neurology*, 1978, 35, 699-705.

168. RAWLING, P., & LYLE, J. G. Cued recall and discrimination of memory deficit. *Journal of Consulting & Clinical Psychology*, 1978, 46, 1227-1229.

169. SHEALY, A. E. Comparison of two non-intellective scales of intelligence and their relationship to intellectual changes following surgery. *Psychological Reports*, 1978, 42, 51-56.

170. SHEALY, A. E., & WALKER, D. R. Minnesota Multiphasic Personality Inventory prediction of intellectual changes following cardiac surgery. *Journal of Nervous & Mental Disease*, 1978, 166, 263-267.

171. TELEFORD, R., & WORRALL, E. P. Cognitive functions in manic-depressives: Effects of lithium and physostigmine. *British Journal of Psychiatry*, 1978, 13, 424-428.

172. VERNON, P. E., RYBA, K. A., & LANG, R. J. Simultaneous and successive processing: An attempt at replication. *Canadian Journal of Behavioural Science*, 1978, 10, 1-15.

173. ARBIT, J., & ZAGAR, R. The effects of age and sex on the factor structure of the Wechsler Memory Scale. *Journal of Psychology*, 1979, 102, 185-190.

174. CUTTING, J. Memory in functional psychosis. *Journal of Neurology, Neurosurgery & Psychiatry*, 1979, 42, 1031-1037.

175. DASTOOR, D. P., KLINGNER, A., MULLER, H. F., & KACHANOFF, R. A psychogeriatric assessment program. V. Three-year follow-up. *Journal of the American Geriatrics Society*, 1979, 27, 162-169.

176. DODRILL, C. B. Sex differences on the Halstead-Reitan Neuropsychological Battery and on other neuropsychological measures. *Journal of Clinical Psychology*, 1979, 35, 236-241.

177. GABRYS, J. B. The Babcock Story Recall of behaviorally disordered children scoring high or low on extraversion. *Perceptual & Motor Skills*, 1979, 48, 157-158.

178. GILLEARD, C. J. Note on prediction of Wechsler Memory Scale visual reproduction scores for a handicapped geriatric population. *Perceptual & Motor Skills*, 1979, 49, 878.

179. JEEVES, M. A., SIMPSON, D. A., & GEFFEN, G. Functional consequences of the transcallosal removal of intraventricular tumours. *Journal of Neurology, Neurosurgery, & Psychiatry*, 1979, 42, 134-142.

180. KASZNIAK, A. W., GARRON, D. C., & FOX, J. Differential effects of age and cerebral atrophy upon span of immediate recall and paired-associate learning in older patients suspected of dementia. *Cortex*, 1979, 15, 285-295.

181. KERTESZ, A. Visual agnosia: The dual deficit of perception and recognition. *Cortex*, 1979, 15, 403-419.

182. LOGUE, P., & WYRICK, L. Initial validation of Russell's revised Wechsler Memory Scale: A comparison of normal aging versus dementia. *Journal of Consulting & Clinical Psychology*, 1979, 47, 176-178.

183. MIGLIOLLI, M., BUCHTEL, H. A., CAMPANINI, T., & DE RISIO, C. Cerebral hemispheric lateralization of cognitive deficits due to alcoholism. *Journal of Nervous & Mental Disease*, 1979, 167, 212-217.

184. MÜLLER, H. F., DASTOOR, D. P., KLINGNER, A., COLE, M., & BOILLAT, J. Amantadine in senile dementia: Electroencephalographic and clinical effects. *Journal of the American Geriatrics Society*, 1979, 27, 9-16.

185. POWELL, G. E. The relationship between intelligence and verbal and spatial memory. *Journal of Clinical Psychology*, 1979, 35, 335-340.

186. ROSEN, H. J. Double-blind comparison of haloperidol and thioridazine in geriatric outpatients. *Journal of Clinical Psychiatry*, 1979, 40, 17-20.

187. STONES, M. J. Rekitting the Wechsler Paired-Associate Task: The Waterford Index. *Journal of Clinical Psychology*, 1979, 35, 626-630.

188. WOODS, R. T. Reality orientation and staff attention: A controlled study. *British Journal of Psychiatry*, 1979, 134, 502-507.

189. BAK, J. S., & GREENE, R. L. Changes in neuropsychological functioning in an aging population. *Journal of Consulting & Clinical Psychology*, 1980, 48, 395-399.

190. BRESLOW, R., KOCSIS, J., & BELKIN, B. Memory deficits in depression: Evidence utilizing the Wechsler Memory Scale. *Perceptual & Motor Skills*, 1980, 51, 541-542.

191. BROOKS, D. N., AUGHTON, M. E., BOND, M. R., JONES, P., & RIZVI, S. Cognitive sequela in relationship to early indices of severity of brain damage after severe blunt head injury. *Journal of Neurology, Neurosurgery, & Psychiatry*, 1980, 43, 529-534.

192. CROOK, T., GILBERT, J. G., & FERRIS, S. Operationalizing memory impairment for elderly persons: The Guild Memory Test. *Psychological Reports*, 1980, 47, 1315-1318.

193. CUMMINGS, J., HEBBEN, N. A., OBLER, L., & LEONARD, P. Nonaphasic misnaming and other neurobehavioral features of an unusual toxic encephalopathy: Case study. *Cortex*, 1980, 16, 315-323.

194. CUTTING, J. Physical illness and psychosis. *British Journal of Psychiatry*, 1980, 136, 109-119.

195. DE LA FUENTE, J. R., & ROSENBAUM, A. H. Neuroendocrine dysfunction and blood levels of tricyclic antidepressants. *American Journal of Psychiatry*, 1980, 137, 1260-1261.

196. DELANEY, R. C., ROSEN, A. J., MATTSON, R. H., & NOVELLY, R. A. Memory function in focal epilepsy: A comparison of non-surgical, unilateral temporal lobe and frontal lobe samples. *Cortex*, 1980, 16, 103–117.

197. DIKMEN, S., & MORGAN, S. F. Neuropsychological factors related to employability and occupational status in persons with epilepsy. *Journal of Nervous & Mental Disease*, 1980, 168, 236–240.

198. FISH, J. M., & SINKEL, P. Correlation of scores on Wechsler Memory Scale and Wechsler Adult Intelligence Scale for chronic alcoholics and normals. *Psychological Reports*, 1980, 47, 940–942.

199. GESCHWIND, N., SHADER, R. I., BEAR, D., NORTH, B., LEVIN, K., & CHETHAM, D. Behavioral changes with temporal lobe epilepsy: Assessment and treatment. *Journal of Clinical Psychiatry*, 1980, 41, 89–95.

200. KEAR-COLWELL, J. J., & HELLER, M. The Wechsler Memory Scale and closed head injury. *Journal of Clinical Psychology*, 1980, 36, 782–787.

201. LEVINE, D. N., CALVANIO, R., & WOLF, E. Disorders of visual behavior following bilateral posterior cerebral lesions. *Psychological Reports*, 1980, 41, 217–234.

202. LOBERG, T. Alcohol misuse and neuropsychological deficits in men. *Journal of Studies on Alcohol*, 1980, 41, 119–128.

203. McCARTY, S. M., ZIESAT, H. A., LOGUE, P. E., POWER, D. G., & ROSENSTIEL, A. K. Alternate-form reliability and age-related scores for Russell's revised Wechsler Memory Scale. *Journal of Consulting & Clinical Psychology*, 1980, 48, 296–298.

204. OSCAR-BERMAN, M., & ZOLA-MORGAN, S. M. Comparative neuropsychology and Korsakoff's Syndrome. I–spatial and visual reversal learning. *Neuropsychologia*, 1980, 18, 499–512.

205. OSCAR-BERMAN, M., & ZOLA-MORGAN, S. M. Comparative neuropsychology and Korsakoff's Syndrome. II–two-choice visual discrimination learning. *Neuropsychologia*, 1980, 18, 513–525.

206. PARSONS, O. A. Cognitive dysfunction in alcoholics and social drinkers. *Journal of Studies on Alcohol*, 1980, 41, 105–118.

207. PONSFORD, J. L., & DONNAN, G. A. Transient global amnesia–A hippocampal phenomenon? *Journal of Neurology, Neurosurgery & Psychiatry*, 1980, 43, 285–287.

208. POWELL, B. J., PENICK, E. C., & READ, M. R. Psychological adjustment and sex-role affiliation in an alcoholic population. *Journal of Clinical Psychology*, 1980, 36, 801–805.

209. RICHARDS, J. S. Visual memory in left hemiplegia: A clinical evaluation of verbally mediated theories of visual memory. *Perceptual & Motor Skills*, 1980, 51, 13–14.

210. VEROFF, A. E. The neuropsychology of aging. Qualitative analysis of visual reproductions. *Psychological Reports*, 1980, 41, 259–268.

211. VINCENT, K. R. Semi-automated full battery. *Journal of Clinical Psychology*, 1980, 36, 437–446.

212. ZIESAT, H. A., JR., LOGUE, P. E., & McCARTY, S. M. Psychological measurement of memory deficits in dialysis patients. *Perceptual & Motor Skills*, 1980, 50, 311–318.

213. BARRATT, E. S., PATTON, J., OLSSON, N. G., & ZUCKER, G. Impulsivity and paced tapping. *Journal of Motor Behavior*, 1981, 13, 286–300.

214. BOLTER, J., VENEKLASEN, J., & LONG, C. J. Investigation of WAIS effectiveness in discriminating between temporal and generalized seizure patients. *Journal of Consulting & Clinical Psychology*, 1981, 49, 549–553.

215. CUTTING, J. Response bias in Korsakoff's Syndrome. *Cortex*, 1981, 17, 107–112.

216. DERRY, P. A., & KUIPER, N. A. Schematic processing and self-reference in clinical depression. *Journal of Abnormal Psychology*, 1981, 90, 286–297.

217. GRONWALL, D., & WRIGHTSON, P. Memory and information processing capacity after closed head injury. *Journal of Neurology, Neurosurgery & Psychiatry*, 1981, 44, 889–895.

218. NORTH, A. J., & ULATOWSKA, H. K. Competence in independently living older adults: Assessment and correlates. *Journal of Gerontology*, 1981, 36, 576–582.

219. WANG, P. L., & GOLDBERG, L. A. Multidimensional assessment of human memory functioning. *Psychologia*, 1981, 24, 75–85.

220. WEINGARTNER, H., KAYE, W., SMALLBERG, S. A., EBERT, M. H., GILLIN, J. C., & SITARAM, N. Memory failures in progressive idiopathic dementia. *Journal of Abnormal Psychology*, 1981, 90, 187–196.

[2608]
Wechsler Preschool and Primary Scale of Intelligence.
Ages 4–6.5; 1967, c1949–67; WPPSI; 8 of the 11 tests provide the same measures as the *Wechsler Intelligence Scale for Children* and approximately 1/3 of the total number of items are essentially the same; 13 or 14 scores: verbal (information, vocabulary, arithmetic, similarities, comprehension, sentences [optional], total), performance (animal house, picture completion, mazes, geometric design, block design, total), total; David Wechsler; The Psychological Corporation. (British edition: 1971; manual supplement by Peter Saville; NFER-Nelson Publishing Co. [England].)*

For additional information, see 8:234 (84 references); see also T2:538 (30 references); for reviews by Dorothy H. Eichorn and A. B. Silverstein, and excerpted reviews by C. H. Ammons and O. A. Oldridge (with E. E. Allison), see 7:434 (56 references).

REFERENCES

1–56. See 7:434.
57–86. See T2:538.
87–170. See 8:234.

171. CAMPBELL, S. B., SCHLEIFER, M., WEISS, G., & PERLMAN, T. A two-year follow-up of hyperactive preschoolers. *American Journal of Orthopsychiatry*, 1977, 47, 149–162.

172. COHLER, B. J., GRUNEBAUM, H. V., WEISS, J. L., GAMER, E., & GALLANT, D. H. Disturbance of attention among schizophrenic, depressed and well mothers and their young children. *Journal of Child Psychology & Psychiatry & Allied Disciplines*, 1977, 18, 115–135.

173. CONNER, J. M., & SERBIN, L. A. Behaviorally based masculine- and feminine-activity-preference scales for preschoolers: Correlates with other classroom behaviors and cognitive tests. *Child Development*, 1977, 48, 1411–1416.

174. DELACEY, P. R., & NURCOMBE, B. Effects of enrichment preschooling at Bourke: A further follow-up study. *Australian Journal of Education*, 1977, 21, 80–90.

175. EISER, C., & LANSDOWN, R. Retrospective study of intellectual development in children treated for acute lymphoblastic leukaemia. *Archives of Diseases in Children*, 1977, 52, 525–529.

176. FAIRWEATHER, H., & BUTTERWORTH, G. The WPPSI at four years: A sex difference in verbal-performance discrepancies. *British Journal of Educational Psychology*, 1977, 47, 85–90.

177. FESHBACH, S., ADELMAN, H., & FULLER, W. Prediction of reading and related academic problems. *Journal of Educational Psychology*, 1977, 69, 299–308.

178. FREDRICKSON, L. C. Measured intelligence: Species specific? Perhaps; Race specific? Perhaps not. *Journal of Genetic Psychology*, 1977, 130, 95–104.

179. GALLIMORE, R., LAM, D. J., SPEIDEL, G. E., & THARP, R. G. The effects of elaboration and rehearsal on long-term retention of shape names by kindergarten. *American Educational Research Journal*, 1977, 14, 471–483.

180. GOLD, D., & ANDRES, D. Maternal employment and child development at three age levels. *Journal of Research & Development in Education*, 1977, 10, 20–29.

181. GOLDMAN, J. G. Reflections of personality functioning in psychological testing in disadvantaged three to five year olds. *Journal of Personality Assessment*, 1977, 41, 39–42.

182. HASLAM, R. H. A., ALLEN, J. R., DORSEN, M. M., KANOFSKY, D. L., MELLITS, E. D., & NORRIS, D. A. The sequelae of group B β-hemolytic streptococcal meningitis in early infancy. *American Journal of Diseases of Children*, 1977, 131, 845–849.

183. KAUFMAN, A. S., DARAMOLA, S. F., & DiCUIO, R. F. Interpretation of the WPPSI tests for boys and girls at three age levels. *Contemporary Educational Psychology*, 1977, 2, 232–238.

184. SEWELL, T. E. A comparison of the WPPSI and Stanford-Binet Intelligence Scale (1972) among lower SES black children. *Psychology in the Schools*, 1977, 14, 158–161.

185. SILVERSTEIN, A. B. Comparison of two criteria for determining the number of factors. *Psychological Reports*, 1977, 41, 387–390.

186. TAYLOR, L. J. Sex and psychological differentiation. *Psychological Reports*, 1977, 41, 192–194.

187. CAMPBELL, S. B., GELLER, B., SMALL, A. M., PETTI, T. A., & FERRIS, S. H. Minor physical anomalies in young psychotic children. *American Journal of Psychiatry*, 1978, 135, 573–575.

188. CULATTA, B. The relationship between perceptual dysfunction and language disorders: A case report. *Journal of Communication Disorders*, 1978, 11, 51–63.

189. DOLAN, A. B., & MATHENY, A. P., JR. A distinctive growth curve for a group of children with academic learning problems. *Journal of Learning Disabilities*, 1978, 11, 490–494.

190. DOLLINGER, S. J., & THELEN, M. H. Overjustification and children's intrinsic motivation: Comparative effects of four rewards. *Journal of Personality & Social Psychology*, 1978, 36, 1259–1269.

191. DOUGLAS, J. E., & SUTTON, A. The development of speech and mental processes in a pair of twins: A case study. *Journal of Child Psychology & Psychiatry & Allied Disciplines*, 1978, 19, 49–56.

192. GERKEN, K. C. Performance of Mexican American children on intelligence tests. *Exceptional Children*, 1978, 44, 438–443.
193. GOLD, D., & ANDRES, D. Relations between maternal employment and development of nursery school children. *Canadian Journal of Behavioural Science*, 1978, 10, 116–129.
194. GROSS, M. B. Cultural concomitants of preschoolers' preparation for learning. *Psychological Reports*, 1978, 43, 807–813.
195. HEIL, J., BARCLAY, A., & ENDRES, J. M. B. A factor analytic study of WPPSI scores of educationally deprived and normal children. *Psychological Reports*, 1978, 42, 727–730.
196. JORDAN, T. E. Influences on vocabulary attainment. A five-year prospective study. *Child Development*, 1978, 49, 1096–1106.
197. KAUFMAN, A. S. The importance of basic concepts in the individual assessment of preschool children. *Journal of School Psychology*, 1978, 16, 207–211.
198. KOJIMA, H. Assessment of field dependence in young children. *Perceptual & Motor Skills*, 1978, 46, 479–492.
199. MACFAUL, R., DORNER, S., BRETT, E. M., & GRANT, D. B. Neurological abnormalities in patients treated for hypothyroidism from early life. *Archives of Diseases in Childhood*, 1978, 53, 611–619.
200. MARGOLIS, H., & BRANNIGAN, G. G. Conceptual tempo as a parameter for predicting reading achievement. *Journal of Educational Research*, 1978, 71, 342–345.
201. MCKAY, H., SINISTERRA, L., MCKAY, A., GOMEZ, H., & LLOREDA, P. Improving cognitive ability in chronically deprived children. *Science*, 1978, 200, 270–278.
202. MOORE, C. L. Racial preference and intelligence. *Journal of Psychology*, 1978, 100, 39–43.
203. PARNELL, M. M., & AMERMAN, J. D. Maturational influences on perception of coarticulatory effects. *Journal of Speech & Hearing Research*, 1978, 21, 682–701.
204. PHILLIPS, B. L., PASEWARK, R. A., & TINDALL, R. C. Relationship among McCarthy Scales of Children's Abilities, WPPSI, and Columbia Mental Maturity Scale. *Psychology in the Schools*, 1978, 15, 352–356.
205. RAYDER, N., BODY, B., & NIMNICHT, G. Assessing follow through: Changes in intelligence test scores over two and three years of experience in the responsive program. *Journal of Experimental Education*, 1978, 47, 60–66.
206. SACHS, H. K., KRALL, V., MCCAUGHRAN, D. A., ROZENFELD, I. H., YOUNGSMITH, N., GROWE, G., LAZAR, B. S., NOVAR, L., O'CONNELL, L., & RAYSON, B. I.Q. following treatment of lead poisoning: A patient–sibling comparison. *Journal of Pediatrics*, 1978, 93, 428–431.
207. TIZARD, B., & HODGES, J. The effect of early institutional rearing on the development of eight year old children. *Journal of Child Psychology & Psychiatry & Allied Disciplines*, 1978, 19, 99–118.
208. BAUM, D. D. An investigation of the predictive validity of the Slosson Intelligence Test with learning disabled kindergarten children. *Educational & Psychological Measurement*, 1979, 39, 1067–1072.
209. BAUM, D. D., & KELLY, T. J. The validity of the Slosson Intelligence Test with learning disabled kindergartners. *Journal of Learning Disabilities*, 1979, 12, 268–270.
210. BERGAN, J. R., & PARRA, E. B. Variations in IQ testing and instruction and the letter learning and achievement of Anglo and bilingual Mexican–American children. *Journal of Educational Psychology*, 1979, 71, 819–826.
211. BISHOP, D., & BUTTERWORTH, G. E. A longitudinal study using the WPPSI and WISC–R with an English sample. *British Journal of Educational Psychology*, 1979, 49, 156–158.
212. CROWELL, D. C., & AU, K. H. Using a scale of questions to improve listening comprehension. *Language Arts*, 1979, 56, 38–43.
213. GARDNER, L. I., NEU, R. L., SHAH, R. S., PINTO, W., JR., CO, M., LEHR, E. R., & BARG, G. A. Family with three apparently balanced t(3;15) (p27;q22) translocation carriers. *American Journal of Diseases of Children*, 1979, 133, 1002–1005.
214. GOLD, D., & ANDRES, D. The development of Francophone nursery–school children with employed and nonemployed mothers. *Canadian Journal of Behavioural Science*, 1979, 11, 169–173.
215. MARTIN, F. It is necessary to retest children in special education classes. *Journal of Learning Disabilities*, 1979, 12, 388–392.
216. MCWILLIAMS, B. J., & MATTHEWS, H. P. A comparison of intelligence and social maturity in children with unilateral complete clefts and those with isolated cleft palates. *Cleft Palate Journal*, 1979, 16, 363–372.
217. RAMANAIAH, N. V., & ADAMS, M. L. Confirmatory factor analysis of the WAIS and WPPSI. *Psychological Reports*, 1979, 45, 351–355.
218. SERBIN, L. A., & CONNOR, J. M. Sex-typing of children's play preferences and patterns of cognitive performance. *Journal of Genetic Psychology*, 1979, 134, 315–316.
219. SHELLENBERGER, S., & LACHTERMAN, T. Cognitive and motor functioning on the McCarthy scales by Spanish–speaking children. *Perceptual & Motor Skills*, 1979, 49, 863–866.
220. STRAUSS, J. S., HARDER, D. W., & CHANDLER, M. Egocentrism in children of parents with a history of psychotic disorders. *Archives of General Psychiatry*, 1979, 36, 191–196.
221. TEJANI, A., MAHADEVAN, R., DOBIAS, B., NANGIA, B. S., & VARMA, P. N. Total parenteral nutrition of the neonate–A long–term follow–up. *Journal of Pediatrics*, 1979, 94, 803–805.
222. TEW, B. The "cocktail party syndrome" in children with hydrocephalus and spina bifida. *British Journal of Disorders of Communication*, 1979, 14, 89–101.
223. WHITE, D. R., & JACOBS, E. The prediction of first–grade reading achievement from WPPSI scores of preschool children. *Psychology in the Schools*, 1979, 16, 189–192.
224. ABRAMS, A. I., BODY, B., & RAYDER, N. F. Problems and solutions in evaluating child outcomes of large–scale educational programs. *Journal of Experimental Education*, 1980, 48, 153–165.
225. BISHOP, D. V. M. Predictive validity of short forms of the WPPSI. *British Journal of Social & Clinical Psychology*, 1980, 19, 173–175.
226. BRINICH, P. M. Childhood deafness and maternal control. *Journal of Communication Disorders*, 1980, 13, 75–81.
227. BRUMBACK, R. A., JACKOWAY, M. L., & WEINBERG, W. A. Relation of intelligence to childhood depression in children referred to an educational diagnostic center. *Perceptual & Motor Skills*, 1980, 50, 11–17.
228. CANTWELL, D. P., BAKER, L., & MATTISON, R. E. Psychiatric disorders in children with speech and language retardation. *Archives of General Psychiatry*, 1980, 37, 423–426.
229. COHLER, B. J., GALLANT, D. H., GRUNEBAUM, H. U., WEISS, J. L., & GAMER, E. Child–care attitudes and development of young children of mentally ill and well mothers. *Psychological Reports*, 1980, 46, 31–46.
230. COOLEY, N. R. The Wechsler Preschool and Primary Scale of Intelligence: Difficulty order of subtest questions. *Psychology in the Schools*, 1980, 14, 24–29.
231. CUMMINS, M., & NORRISH, M. Follow–up of children of diabetic mothers. *Archives of Diseases in Childhood*, 1980, 55, 259–264.
232. DANEMAN, D., & HOWARD, N. J. Neonatal thyrotoxicosis: Intellectual impairment and craniosynostosis in later years. *Journal of Pediatrics*, 1980, 97, 257–259.
233. DANSKY, J. L. Cognitive consequences of sociodramatic play and exploration training for economically disadvantaged preschoolers. *Journal of Child Psychology & Psychiatry & Allied Disciplines*, 1980, 21, 47–58.
234. FAREL, A. M. Effects of preferred maternal roles, maternal employment, and sociodemographic status on school adjustment and competence. *Child Development*, 1980, 51, 1179–1186.
235. GOUZE, K. R., & NADELMAN, L. Constancy of gender identity for self and others in children between the ages of three and seven. *Child Development*, 1980, 51, 275–278.
236. HENRY, R. M. A theoretical empirical analysis of "reasoning" in the socialization of young children. *Human Development*, 1980, 23, 105–125.
237. PALISIN, H. The Neonatal Perception Inventory: Failure to replicate. *Child Development*, 1980, 51, 737–742.
238. REYNOLDS, C. R., & KAUFMAN, A. S. Lateral eye movement behavior in children. *Perceptual & Motor Skills*, 1980, 50, 1023–1037.
239. SHAYWITZ, S. E., COHEN, D. J., & SHAYWITZ, B. A. Behavior and learning difficulties in children of normal intelligence born to alcoholic mothers. *Journal of Pediatrics*, 1980, 96, 978–982.
240. VANE, J. R., & MOTTA, R. W. Test response inconsistency in young children. *Journal of School Psychology*, 1980, 18, 25–33.
241. WRIGHT, D., REYNOLDS, C. R., & DAPPEN, L. Criterion–related validity of three common preschool assessment instruments for boys and girls. *Psychological Reports*, 1980, 47, 1291–1296.
242. AUGUST, G. J., STEWART, M. A., & TSAI, L. The incidence of cognitive disabilities in the siblings of autistic children. *British Journal of Psychiatry*, 1981, 138, 416–422.
243. BRINICH, P. M. Relationship between intellectual functioning and communicative competence in deaf children. *Journal of Communication Disorders*, 1981, 14, 429–434.
244. CARLSON, L., & REYNOLDS, C. R. Factor structure and specific variance of the WPPSI subtests at six age levels. *Psychology in the Schools*, 1981, 18, 48–54.
245. MERITS-PATTERSON, R., & REED, C. G. Disfluencies in the speech of language–delayed children. *Journal of Speech & Hearing Research*, 1981, 24, 55–58.
246. MOORE, C. L. Race: A factor in perceptual organization of black preschoolers. *Child Study Journal*, 1981, 11, 69–74.
247. REYNOLDS, C. R., MCBRIDE, R. D., & GIBSON, L. J. Black–white IQ discrepancies may be related to differences in hemisphericity. *Contemporary Educational Psychology*, 1981, 6, 180–184.
248. REYNOLDS, C. R., WRIGHT, D., & DAPPEN, L. A comparison of the criterion–related validity (academic achievement) of the WPPSI and the WISC–R. *Psychology in the Schools*, 1981, 18, 20–23.
249. STARK, R. E., & TALLAL, P. Selection of children with specific language deficits. *Journal of Speech & Hearing Disorders*, 1981, 46, 114–122.

250. STATON, R. D., & BRUMBACK, R. A. Non-specificity of motor hyperactivity as a diagnostic criterion. *Perceptual & Motor Skills*, 1981, 52, 323-332.

[2609]
[Re Wechsler Preschool and Primary Scale of Intelligence] WPPSI Test Profile. Ages 4–6.5; 1968–69; Consulting Psychologists Press, Inc.*

[2610]
Weights and Pulleys: A Test of Intuitive Mechanics. Engineering students and industrial employees; 1959, c1956–59; L. L. Thurstone (test), T. E. Jeffrey (test), and Measurement Research Division, Human Resources Center, University of Chicago (manual); the Center.*

For additional information and a review by William A. Owens, see 6:1098.

[2611]
★**Weiss Comprehensive Articulation Test.** Preschool children and over; 1978–80; WCAT; "for making a thorough diagnosis of articulation and its associated parameters"; 5 scores: articulation, articulation age, intelligibility, auditory-visual stimulability, number of misarticulations; Curtis E. Weiss; Teaching Resources Corporation.*

[2612]
★**Weller-Strawser Scales of Adaptive Behavior.** Learning disabled students ages 6–12, 13–18; 1981; WSSAB; ratings by teachers; 5 scores: social coping, relationships, pragmatic language, production, total; Carol Weller and Sherri Strawser; Academic Therapy Publications.*

[2613]
*Welsh Figure Preference Test. Ages 6 and over; 1959–80; WFPT; 27 scores: don't like total, repeat, conformance, *Barron-Welsh Art Scale*, revised art scale, male-female, neuropsychiatric, children, movement, 5 sex symbol scores, and 13 figure-structure preference scores; George S. Welsh; Consulting Psychologists Press, Inc.*

See T2:1437 (34 references) and P:287 (24 references); for a review by Harold Borko and an excerpted review by Gordon V. Anderson, see 6:197 (20 references).

REFERENCES

1-20. See 6:197.
21-44. See P:287.
45-78. See T2:1437.
79. GOOR, A., & RAPOPORT, T. Enhancing creativity in an informal educational framework. *Journal of Educational Psychology*, 1977, 69, 636-643.
80. HIRSCHFELD, R. M. A., MATTHEWS, S. M., MOSHER, L. R., & MENN, A. Z. Being with madness: Personality characteristics of three treatment staffs. *Hospital & Community Psychiatry*, 1977, 28, 267-273.
81. RIDLEY, D. R. Preference for stimulus complexity and architectural creativity. *Perceptual & Motor Skills*, 1977, 45, 815-818.
82. TORRANCE, E. P., & MOURAD, S. Role of hemisphericity in performance on selected measures of creativity. *Gifted Child Quarterly*, 1979, 23, 44-55.

[2614]
Wesman Personnel Classification Test. Grades 8–16 and adults; 1946–65; WPCT; title on Forms A and B is *Personnel Classification Test*; 3 scores: verbal, numerical, total; Alexander G. Wesman; The Psychological Corporation.*

See T2:480 (2 references); for a review by Arthur C. MacKinney, and an excerpted review by Jack C. Merwin, see 7:400 (7 references); see also 5:399 (8 references); for reviews by John C. Flanagan and Erwin K. Taylor, see 4:331 (3 references); for an excerpted review, see 3:253.

REFERENCES

1-3. See 4:331.
4-11. See 5:399.
12-18. See 7:400.
19-20. See T2:480.
21. FORBES, J. B., & BARRETT, G. V. Individual abilities and task demands in relation to performance and satisfaction on two repetitive monitoring tasks. *Journal of Applied Psychology*, 1978, 63, 188-196.
22. CHISSOM, B. S., & THOMAS, P. J. Equivalence of two forms of the Dominoes Test (D-48 and D-70) with graduate students in education. *Psychological Reports*, 1979, 44, 972-974.
23. KESSELMAN, G. A., & LOPEZ, F. E. The impact of job analysis on employment test validation for minority and nonminority accounting personnel. *Personnel Psychology*, 1979, 32, 91-108.
24. LEVY, M. F., REICHMAN, W., & HERRINGTON, S. Congruence between personality and job characteristics in alcoholics and nonalcoholics. *Journal of Social Psychology*, 1979, 107, 213-217.

[2615]
★**Western Aphasia Battery.** Adults with language disorders; 1980; administration of *Raven's Coloured Progessive Matrices* and 4 Koh's Blocks (from the *Wechsler Adult Intelligence Scale*) are required for the optional construction and cortical quotient scores, these instruments must be supplied by the examiner; designed to measure the "main clinical aspects of language function"; 17 obtained subscores which form 7 major scores: spontaneous speech, comprehension, repetition, naming, reading and writing, praxis, construction (optional), plus 2 derived scores: aphasia quotient, cortical quotient (optional); Andrew Kertesz; Grune & Stratton, Inc.*

[2616]
The Western Personality Inventory. Adults; 1948–63; WPI; a combination in one booklet of *The Alcadd Test* and *The Manson Evaluation*; identification of alcoholics and potential alcoholics; Morse P. Manson; Western Psychological Services.*

For additional information, see P:288. For reference to reviews of *The Alcadd Test* and *The Manson Evaluation*, see T2:1098 and T2:1271.

[2617]
The Western Personnel Tests. College and adults; 1962; WPT; Robert L. Gunn and Morse P. Manson; Western Psychological Services.*

See T2:481 (1 reference); for reviews by Lewis E. Albright and Erwin K. Taylor, see 6:512.

[2618]
What I Like to Do: An Inventory of Students' Interests. Grades 4–7; 1954–75; WILD; revision of *What I Like to Do: An Inventory of Children's Interests*; 15 scores in 4 areas: play (active-social, active-solo, quiet-social, quiet-solo), academic (physical science, life science, mathematics, social science), arts (performing, visual, music), occupations (physical-manual social, physical-manual solo, symbolic-linguistic social, symbolic-linguistic solo); C. E. Meyers and manual coauthors Marcella R. Bonsall, Karen Drinkard, Mary Ellen Nogrady, Linda Metz Organ, and Elayne Goldman Zinner; Science Research Associates, Inc.*

For additional information and a review by Henry Weitz, see 8:709 (1 reference); see also T2:1439 (8 references) and P:289 (4 references); for reviews by John W. M. Rothney and Naomi Stewart and an excerpted review by Laurence F. Shaffer of the original edition, see 5:122.

REFERENCES

1–4. See P:289.
5–12. See T2:1439.
13. See 8:709.
14. JOHNSON, N., FLOWERS, A., JOHNSON, S. C., & JOHNSON, J. A career awareness program for educable mentally retarded students. *Vocational Guidance Quarterly*, 1980, 28, 328–334.

[2619]

Whisler Strategy Test. Business and industry; 1959–61, c1955–61; "intelligent action"; 6 scores: 4 direct scores (number circled-boldness, number attempted-speed, number right-accuracy, net strategy) and 2 derived scores (caution, hyperaction); Laurence D. Whisler; Psychometric Affiliates.*

See T2:2292 (1 reference); for reviews by Jean Maier Palormo and Paul F. Ross, see 6:1110 (1 reference).

[2620]

Whitaker Index of Schizophrenic Thinking. Mental patients; 1973; WIST; Leighton C. Whitaker; Western Psychological Services.*

For additional information and reviews by Bertram D. Cohen and Robert W. Payne, see 8:710 (4 references).

REFERENCES

1–4. See 8:710.
5. BOURNE, L. E., JR., JUSTESEN, D. R., ABRAHAM, T., BEEKER, C., BRAUCHI, J. T., WHITAKER, L. C., & YAROUSHI, R. A. Limits to conceptual rule–learning by schizophrenic patients. *Journal of Clinical Psychology*, 1977, 33, 324–334.
6. DINNING, W. D., & EVANS, R. G. Discriminant and convergent validity of the SCL-90 in psychiatric inpatients. *Journal of Personality Assessment*, 1977, 41, 304–310.
7. EVANS, R., & DINNING, W. D. Future outlook and psychopathology among psychiatric patients. *Psychological Reports*, 1977, 41, 1309–1310.
8. FISHKIN, S. M., LOVALLO, W. R., & PISHKIN, V. Relationship between schizophrenic thinking and MMPI for process and reactive patients. *Journal of Clinical Psychology*, 1977, 33, 116–119.
9. KAVANAUGH, P. B., & AULD, F. Evidence for validity of the differential personality inventory. *Journal of Clinical Psychology*, 1977, 33, 456–459.
10. KLINGLER, D. E., JOHNSON, J. H., & WILLIAMS, T. A. A validation study of the WIST as a group administered instrument for assessment of schizophrenic thinking. *Journal of Clinical Psychology*, 1977, 33, 658–661.
11. PISHKIN, V., LOVALLO, W. R., LENK, R. G., & BOURNE, L. E., JR. Schizophrenic cognitive dysfunction: A deficit in rule transfer. *Journal of Clinical Psychology*, 1977, 33, 335–342.
12. NEWMARK, C. S., SIMPSON, M., & JONES, T. The discriminative validity of the Whitaker Index of Schizophrenic Thinking. *Journal of Personality Assessment*, 1978, 42, 636–643.
13. FISHKIN, S. M., LOVALLO, W. R., WHITAKER, L. C., & PISHKIN, V. Randomness and the "streaking" phenomenon: Attentional anomalies in performance on the Whitaker Index of Schizophrenic Thinking (WIST). *Journal of Clinical Psychology*, 1979, 35, 289–295.
14. NEWMARK, C. S., KONANC, J. T., SIMPSON, M., BOREN, R. B., & PRILLAMAN, K. Predictive validity of the Rorschach prognostic rating scale with schizophrenic patients. *Journal of Nervous & Mental Disease*, 1979, 167, 135–143.
15. SIMPSON, G. B., BOURNE, L. E., JR., JUSTESEN, D. R., & RHODES, R. J. Schizophrenic and paranoid thinking in conceptual performance. *Bulletin of the Psychonomic Society*, 1979, 13, 97–100.
16. DOBSON, D. J. G., & NEUFELD, R. W. J. Relationship between the Whitaker Index of Schizophrenic Thinking and intelligence in paranoid and nonparanoid schizophrenics. *Journal of Consulting Clinical Psychology*, 1980, 48, 92–94.
17. EVANS, R. G., & DINNING, W. D. A validation study of Forms A and B of the Whitaker Index of Schizophrenic Thinking. *Journal of Personality Assessment*, 1980, 44, 416–419.
18. KNIGHT, R. A., EPSTEIN, B., & ZIELONY, R. D. The validity of the Whitaker Index of Schizophrenic Thinking. *Journal of Clinical Psychology*, 1980, 36, 632–639.
19. NEWMARK, C. S., JONES, M. T., MCKEE, D. C., SIMPSON, M., BOREN, R. B., & PRILLAMAN, K. Using discriminant function analysis with clinical, demographic and historical variables to diagnose schizophrenia. *British Journal of Medical Psychology*, 1980, 53, 365–373.
20. PHILLIPS, W. M., PHILLIPS, A. M., & SHEARN, C. R. Objective assessment of schizophrenic thinking. *Journal of Clinical Psychology*, 1980, 36, 79–89.

[2621]

Wide Range Achievement Test, 1978 Edition. Ages 5–11, 12 and over; 1940–78; WRAT; 3 scores: spelling, arithmetic, reading; (large-print edition available); Joseph F. Jastak and Sarah Jastak; Jastak Associates, Inc.

For additional information, see 8:37 (117 references); see also T2:50 (35 references); for reviews by Jack C. Merwin and Robert L. Thorndike, see 7:36 (49 references); see also 6:27 (15 references); for reviews by Paul Douglas Courtney, Verner M. Sims, and Louis P. Thorpe of the 1946 edition, see 3:21.

REFERENCES

1–15. See 6:27.
16–64. See 7:36.
65–99. See T2:50.
100–216. See 8:37.
217. STARKMAN, S., BUTKOVICH, C., & MURRAY, T. The relationship among measures of cognitive development, learning proficiency, academic achievement, and IQ for seventh grade, low socioeconomic status black males. *Journal of Experimental Education*, 1976, 45, 52–56.
218. WOOD, D. R., REIMHERR, F. W., WENDER, P. H., & JOHNSON, G. E. Diagnosis and treatment of minimal brain dysfunction in adults. *Archives of General Psychiatry*, 1976, 33, 1453–1460.
219. ACKERMAN, P. T., DYKMAN, R. A., & PETERS, J. E. Teenage status of hyperactive and nonhyperactive learning disabled boys. *American Journal of Orthopsychiatry*, 1977, 47, 577–596.
220. ALLEN, R. M. And they call this research . . . *Psychological Reports*, 1977, 40, 926.
221. ARNDT, W. B., SHELTON, R. L., JOHNSON, A. F., & FURR, M. L. Identification and description of homogeneous subgroups within a sample of misarticulating children. *Journal of Speech & Hearing Research*, 1977, 20, 263–292.
222. ARNOLD, L. E., BARNEBEY, N., MCMANUS, J., SMELTZER, D. J., CONRAD, A., WINER, G., & DESGRANGES, L. Prevention by specific perceptual remediation for vulnerable first graders. *Archives of General Psychiatry*, 1977, 34, 1279–1294.
223. AYRES, A. J. Cluster analyses of measures of sensory integration. *American Journal of Occupational Therapy*, 1977, 31, 363–366.
224. AYRES, A. J. Dichotic listening performance in learning–disabled children. *American Journal of Occupational Therapy*, 1977, 31, 441–446.
225. BABAD, E. Y. Pygmalion in reverse. *Journal of Special Education*, 1977, 11, 81–90.
226. BEDELL, J. A. Effects of instructions on the measurement of state anxiety in children. *Journal of Consulting & Clinical Psychology*, 1977, 45, 941–942.
227. BROOKS, C. R. WISC, WISC-R, S-BL&M, WRAT: Relationships and trends among children ages six to ten referred for psychological evaluation. *Psychology in the Schools*, 1977, 14, 30–33.
228. BROWNE, T., STOTSKY, B. A., & EICHORN, J. A selective comparison of psychological, developmental, social, and academic factors among emotionally disturbed children in three treatment settings. *Child Psychiatry & Human Development*, 1977, 7, 231–253.
229. CAMP, B. W. Verbal mediation in young aggressive boys. *Journal of Abnormal Psychology*, 1977, 86, 145–153.
230. CAMP, B. W., & DOLCOURT, J. L. Reading and spelling in good and poor readers. *Journal of Learning Disabilities*, 1977, 10, 300–307.
231. CAMP, B. W., VAN DOORNINCK, W. J., ZIMET, S. G., & DAHLEM, N. W. Verbal abilities in young aggressive boys. *Journal of Educational Psychology*, 1977, 69, 129–135.
232. COLLIGAN, R. C. Concurrent validity of the Myklebust Pupil Rating Scale in a kindergarten population. *Journal of Learning Disabilities*, 1977, 10, 317–320.
233. DALBY, J. T., KINSBOURNE, M., SWANSON, J. M., & SOBOL, M. P. Hyperactive children's underuse of learning time: Correction by stimulant treatment. *Child Development*, 1977, 48, 1448–1453.

234. Dean, R. S. Analysis of the PIAT with Anglo and Mexican-American children. *Journal of School Psychology*, 1977, 15, 329-333.
235. DeBell, S. M., & Vance, H. B. Concurrent validity of three measures of arithmetic achievement. *Perceptual & Motor Skills*, 1977, 45, 848.
236. Foch, T. T., DeFries, J. C., McClearn, G. E., & Singer, S. M. Familial patterns of impairment in reading disability. *Journal of Educational Psychology*, 1977, 69, 316-329.
237. Foster, G., & Keech, V. Teacher reactions to the label of educable mentally retarded. *Education & Training of the Mentally Retarded*, 1977, 12, 307-311.
238. Greenwood, C. R., Hops, H., & Walker, H. M. The Program for Academic Survival Skills (PASS): Effects on student behavior and achievement. *Journal of School Psychology*, 1977, 15, 25-35.
239. Gruber, J. J., & Noland, M. Perceptual-motor and scholastic achievement relationships in emotionally disturbed elementary school children. *Research Quarterly*, 1977, 48, 68-73.
240. Hare, B. A. Perceptual deficits are not a cue to reading problems in second grade. *Reading Teacher*, 1977, 30, 624-628.
241. Hartlage, L. C., & Boone, K. E. Achievement test correlates of Wechsler Intelligence Scale for Children and Wechsler Intelligence Scale for Children-Revised. *Perceptual & Motor Skills*, 1977, 45, 1283-1286.
242. Hartlage, L. C., & Hartlage, P. L. Relationships between neurological, behavioral, and academic variables. *Journal of Clinical Child Psychology*, 1977, 6, 52-53.
243. Hartlage, L. C., & Steele, C. T. WISC and WISC-R correlates of academic achievement. *Psychology in the Schools*, 1977, 14, 15-18.
244. Holmes, D. L., & Peper, R. J. An evaluation of the use of spelling error analysis in the diagnosis of reading disabilities. *Child Development*, 1977, 48, 1708-1711.
245. Hornstein, D., Solomon, S. J., & Houston, B. K. Preliminary report on a juvenile court testing program. *Corrective & Social Psychiatry & Journal of Behavior Technology, Methods & Therapy*, 1977, 23, 11-14.
246. Hutt, M. L., Dates, B. G., & Reid, D. M. The predictive ability of HABGT Scales for a male delinquent population. *Journal of Personality Assessment*, 1977, 41, 492-496.
247. Jenkyn, L. R., Walsh, D. B., Culver, C. M., & Reeves, A. G. Clinical signs in diffuse cerebral dysfunction. *Journal of Neurology, Neurosurgery, & Psychiatry*, 1977, 40, 956-966.
248. Leaverton, D. R., Rupp, J. W., & Poff, M. G. Brief therapy for monocular hysterical blindness in childhood. *Child Psychiatry & Human Development*, 1977, 7, 254-263.
249. Lerer, R. J., Lerer, M. P., & Artner, J. The effects of methylphenidate on the handwriting of children with minimal brain dysfunction. *Journal of Pediatrics*, 1977, 91, 127-132.
250. McCormick, D. P. Pediatric evaluation of children with school problems. *American Journal of Diseases of Children*, 1977, 131, 318-322.
251. McDermott, P. A. Measures of diagnostic data usage as discriminants among training and experience levels in school psychology. *Psychology in the Schools*, 1977, 14, 323-331.
252. McLaughlin, T. F., & Malaby, J. E. A cost free token reinforcement program for special education students. *Corrective & Social Psychiatry & Journal of Behavior Technology, Methods & Therapy*, 1977, 23, 111-116.
253. Miller, S. R., & Sabatino, D. A. Evaluating the instructional effectiveness of supplemental special educational materials. *Exceptional Children*, 1977, 43, 457-461.
254. Morsink, C., & Otto, W. Special considerations in teaching LD children to read. *National Reading Conference Yearbook*, 1977, 163-167.
255. Nichols, M. P., & Knopf, I. J. Refining computerized test interpretations: An in-depth approach. *Journal of Personality Assessment*, 1977, 41, 157-159.
256. O'Leary, S. G., & Schneider, M. R. Special class placement for conduct problem children. *Exceptional Children*, 1977, 44, 24-30.
257. Rie, E. D., & Rie, H. E. Recall, retention, and Ritalin. *Journal of Consulting & Clinical Psychology*, 1977, 45, 967-972.
258. Rubin, R. A., Dorle, J., & Sandidge, S. Self-esteem and school performance. *Psychology in the Schools*, 1977, 14, 503-507.
259. Rudy, K. R. The Short Form Test of Academic Aptitude (SFTAA) as a determinant of minimal brain dysfunction in children. *Journal of General Psychology*, 1977, 96, 169-176.
260. Schwarting, F. G., & Schwarting, K. R. The relationship of the WISC-R and WRAT: A study based upon a selected population. *Psychology in the Schools*, 1977, 14, 431-433.
261. Silberberg, N. E., & Silberberg, M. C. A note on reading tests and their role in defining reading difficulties. *Journal of Learning Disabilities*, 1977, 10, 100-103.
262. Smith, M. K., & McManis, D. L. Concurrent validity of the Peabody Individual Achievement Test and the Wide Range Achievement Test. *Psychological Reports*, 1977, 41, 1279-1284.
263. Sobotka, K. R., Black, F. W., Hill, S. D., & Porter, R. J. Some psychological correlates of developmental dyslexia. *Journal of Learning Disabilities*, 1977, 10, 363-369.
264. Sobotka, K. R., & May, J. G. Visual evoked potentials and reaction time in normal and dyslexic children. *Psychophysiology*, 1977, 14, 18-23.
265. Stewart, D. W., & Morris, L. Intelligence and academic achievement in a clinical adolescent population. *Psychology in the Schools*, 1977, 14, 513-518.
266. Swiercinsky, D. P. Significance of crossed eye-hand dominance for the adult neuropsychological evaluation. *Journal of Nervous & Mental Disease*, 1977, 165, 134-138.
267. Torgesen, J. K. Memorization processes in reading-disabled children. *Journal of Educational Psychology*, 1977, 69, 571-578.
268. Tsushima, W. T., & Towne, W. S. Neuropsychological abilities of young children with questionable brain disorders. *Journal of Consulting & Clinical Psychology*, 1977, 45, 757-762.
269. Ullman, D. G. Children's lateral preference patterns: Frequency and relationships with achievement and intelligence. *Journal of School Psychology*, 1977, 15, 36-43.
270. Weinberg, W. A. Reply, a letter in reference to "depression in childhood." *Journal of Pediatrics*, 1977, 85, 292-293.
271. Welner, Z., Welner, A., Stewart, M., Palkes, H., & Wish, E. A controlled study of siblings of hyperactive children. *Journal of Nervous & Mental Disease*, 1977, 165, 110-117.
272. Willerman, L., & Fiedler, M. F. Intellectually precocious preschool children: Early development and later intellectual accomplishments. *Journal of Genetic Psychology*, 1977, 131, 13-20.
273. Wood, N. E. Directed art, visual perception, and learning disabilities. *Academic Therapy*, 1977, 12, 455-462.
274. Andrew, J. M. Why can't delinquents read? *Perceptual & Motor Skills*, 1978, 47, 640.
275. Ayres, A. J. Learning disabilities and the vestibular system. *Journal of Learning Disabilities*, 1978, 11, 18-29.
276. Becker, L. D., Bender, N. N., & Morrison, G. Measuring impulsivity-reflection: A critical review. *Journal of Learning Disabilities*, 1978, 11, 626-632.
277. Cohen, R. L., & Netley, C. Cognitive deficits, learning disabilities, and WISC verbal-performance consistency. *Developmental Psychology*, 1978, 14, 624-634.
278. Cunningham, M. M. Perceptual ability and associational learning in normal and learning disabled children. *Perceptual & Motor Skills*, 1978, 47, 1200.
279. Daly, D. A., & Kimbarow, M. L. Stuttering as operant behavior: Effects of the verbal stimuli, *wrong*, *right*, and *tree* on the disfluency rates of school-age stutterers and nonstutterers. *Journal of Speech & Hearing Research*, 1978, 21, 589-597.
280. Das, J. P., & Cummings, J. Academic performance and cognitive processes in EMR children. *American Journal of Mental Deficiency*, 1978, 83, 197-199.
281. Ellenberg, J. H., & Nelson, K. B. Febrile seizures and later intellectual performance. *Archives of Neurology*, 1978, 35, 17-21.
282. Hale, R. L. The WISC-R as a predictor of WRAT performance. *Psychology in the Schools*, 1978, 15, 172-175.
283. Hale, R. L., Douglas, B., Cummins, A., Rittgarn, G., Breed, B., & Dabbert, D. The Slosson as a predictor of Wide Range Achievement Test performance. *Psychology in the Schools*, 1978, 15, 507-509.
284. Hardman, M. L. A functional administrative teaching model for academic programming with the trainable mentally retarded. *Education & Training of the Mentally Retarded*, 1978, 13, 23-28.
285. Harmer, W. R., & Williams, F. The Wide Range Achievement Test and the Peabody Individual Achievement Test: A comparative study. *Journal of Learning Disabilities*, 1978, 11, 667-670.
286. Howell, K. W. Using peers in drill-type instruction. *Journal of Experimental Education*, 1978, 46, 52-56.
287. Ivnik, R. J. Neuropsychological stability in multiple sclerosis. *Journal of Consulting & Clinical Psychology*, 1978, 46, 913-923.
288. Ivnik, R. J. Neuropsychological test performance as a function of the duration of MS-related symptomatology. *Journal of Clinical Psychiatry*, 1978, 39, 304-312.
289. Jenkins, J. R., & Pany, D. Standardized achievement tests: How useful for special education? *Exceptional Children*, 1978, 44, 448-453.
290. Juola, J. F., Schadler, M., Chabot, R. J., & McCaughey, M. W. The development of visual information processing skills related to reading. *Journal of Experimental Child Psychology*, 1978, 25, 459-476.
291. Marshall, W., Hess, A. K., & Lair, C. V. The WISC-R and WRAT as indicators of arithmetic achievement in juvenile delinquents. *Perceptual & Motor Skills*, 1978, 47, 408-410.
292. McIntyre, C. W., Murray, M. E., Cronin, C. M., & Blackwell, S. L. Span of apprehension in learning disabled boys. *Journal of Learning Disabilities*, 1978, 11, 468-475.
293. Miller, T. L., & Sabatino, D. A. An evaluation of the teacher consultant model as an approach to mainstreaming. *Exceptional Children*, 1978, 45, 86-91.

294. MURRAY, M. E. The relationship between personality adjustment and success in remedial programs in dyslexic children. *Contemporary Educational Psychology*, 1978, 3, 330–339.

295. PETERSEN, C. R., & HART, D. H. Use of multiple discriminant function analysis in evaluation of a state–wide system for identification of educationally handicapped children. *Psychological Reports*, 1978, 43, 743–755.

296. RASKIN, L. M., BLOOM, A. S., KLEE, S. H., & REESE, A. The assessment of developmentally disabled children with the WISC-R, Binet, and other tests. *Journal of Clinical Psychology*, 1978, 34, 111–114.

297. RICHMAN, L. C. Language mediation hypothesis: Implications of verbal/performance discrepancy and reading ability. *Perceptual & Motor Skills*, 1978, 47, 391–398.

298. ROSENBLATT, A. I., & PRITCHARD, D. A. Moderators of racial differences on the MMPI. *Journal of Consulting & Clinical Psychology*, 1978, 46, 1572–1573.

299. RUBENSTEIN, J. S., ARMENTROUT, J. A., LEVIN, S., & HERALD D. The parent–therapist program: Alternate care for emotionally disturbed children. *American Journal of Orthopsychiatry*, 1978, 48, 654–662.

300. RUBIN, R. A., & BALOW, B. Prevalence of teacher identified behavior problems: A longitudinal study. *Exceptional Children*, 1978, 45, 102–111.

301. RUSSELL, H. L., & CARTER, J. L. Biofeedback training with children: Consultation, questions, applications and alternatives. *Journal of Clinical Child Psychology*, 1978, 7, 23–25.

302. SANNER, R., & MCMANIS, D. L. Concurrent validity of the Peabody Individual Achievement Test and the Wide Range Achievement Test for middle–class elementary school children. *Psychological Reports*, 1978, 42, 19–24.

303. SAVAGE, J. E., JR., ADAIR, A., & FRIEDMAN, P. Community–social variables related to black parent–absent families. *Journal of Marriage & the Family*, 1978, 40, 779–785.

304. SCHREINER, J. Prediction of retarded adults' work performance through components of general ability. *American Journal of Mental Deficiency*, 1978, 83, 77–79.

305. SHASBY, G., & KINGSLEY, R. F. A study of behavior and body type in troubled youth. *Journal of School Health*, 1978, 48, 103–107.

306. SILVER, A. A., HAGIN, R. A., & BEECHER, R. Scanning, diagnosis, and intervention in the prevention of reading disabilities. *Journal of Learning Disabilities*, 1978, 11, 439–445.

307. SILVERSTEIN, A. B. Note on the norms for the WRAT. *Psychology in the Schools*, 1978, 15, 152–153.

308. SPELLACY, F., & PETER, B. Dyscalculia and elements of the developmental Gerstmann Syndrome in school children. *Cortex*, 1978, 14, 197–206.

309. STEDMAN, J. M., LAWLIS, G. F., CORTNER, R. H., & ACHTERBERG, G. Relationships between WISC–R factors, Wide-Range Achievement Test scores, and visual–motor maturation in children referred for psychological examination. *Journal of Consulting & Clinical Psychology*, 1978, 46, 869–872.

310. SWANSON, L. Verbal encoding effects on the visual short–term memory of learning disabled and normal readers. *Journal of Educational Psychology*, 1978, 70, 539–544.

311. TORGESEN, J. K., BOWEN, C., & IVEY, C. Task structure versus modality of presentation: A study of the construct validity of the Visual–Aural Digit Span Test. *Journal of Educational Psychology*, 1978, 70, 451–456.

312. WEBSTER, R. E., & SCHENCK, S. J. Diagnostic test pattern differences among LD, ED, EMH, and multi–handicapped students. *Journal of Educational Research*, 1978, 72, 75–80.

313. WEST, R. F., & STANOVICH, K. E. Automatic contextual facilitation in readers. *Child Development*, 1978, 49, 717–727.

314. WHITE, C. A., GOPLERUD, C. P., KISKER, C. T., STEHBENS, J. A., KITCHELL, M., & TAYLOR, J. C. Intrauterine fetal transfusion, 1965–1976, with an assessment of the surviving children. *American Journal of Obstetrics & Gynecology*, 1978, 130, 933–940.

315. ZINKUS, P. W., GOTTLIEB, M. I., & SCHAPIRO, M. Developmental and psychoeducational sequelae of chronic otitis media. *American Journal of Diseases of Children*, 1978, 132, 1100–1104.

316. ALFORD, D. W., MOORE, M. W., & SIMON, J. L. A preliminary assessment of the validity and usefulness of the WRAT with visually handicapped residential school students. *Education of the Visually Handicapped*, 1979, 11, 102–108.

317. ALGOZZINE, R., WHORTON, J. E., & REID, W. R. Special class exit criteria: A modest beginning. *Journal of Special Education*, 1979, 13, 132–136.

318. BOERSMA, F. J., CHAPMAN, J. W., & BATTLE, J. Academic self-concept change in special education students: Some suggestions for interpreting self-concept scores. *Journal of Special Education*, 1979, 13, 433–442.

319. BOSSARD, M. D., & GALUSHA, R. The utility of the Stanford–Binet in predicting WRAT performance. *Psychology in the Schools*, 1979, 16, 488–490.

320. BRUNNER, R. L., O'GRADY, D. J., PARTIN, J. C., PARTIN, J. S., & SCHUBERT, W. K. Neuropsychologic consequences of Reye Syndrome. *Journal of Pediatrics*, 1979, 95, 706–711.

321. BRYAN, T., & PEARL, R. Self-concepts and locus of control of learning disabled children. *Journal of Clinical Psychology*, 1979, 8, 223–226.

322. CARLSON, J. S., & DILLON, R. Effects of testing conditions on Piaget matrices and order of appearance problems: A study of competence versus performance. *Journal of Educational Measurement*, 1979, 16, 19–26.

323. CARROLL, J. A., FULLER, G. B., & CARROLL, J. L. Comparisons of culturally deprived school achievers and underachievers on memory function and perception. *Perceptual & Motor Skills*, 1979, 48, 59–62.

324. COHEN, R., RUBIN, S., & HEINEN, J. R. K. Collateral increases in performance of long division resulting from on–task gains using token reinforcement and self–recording. *Psychological Reports*, 1979, 44, 651–658.

325. COLLETTE, M. A. Dyslexia and classic pathognomic signs. *Perceptual & Motor Skills*, 1979, 48, 1055–1062.

326. COLLIGAN, R. C. Predictive utility of the Myklebust Pupil Rating Scale: A two-year follow-up. *Journal of Learning Disabilities*, 1979, 12, 264–267.

327. CUTRONA, C. E., & FESHBACH, S. Cognitive and behavioral correlates of children's differential use of social information. *Child Development*, 1979, 50, 1036–1042.

328. DUNLAP, W. P., RUSSELL, S. N., & INGRAM, C. Determining learning disabilities in mathematics. *Academic Therapy*, 1979, 15, 81–85.

329. DYKMAN, R. A., ACKERMAN, P. T., & OGLESBY, D. M. Selective and sustained attention in hyperactive, learning–disabled, and normal boys. *Journal of Nervous & Mental Disease*, 1979, 167, 288–297.

330. FISHBEIN, H. D. Braille–phonics: A new technique for aiding the reading disabled. *Journal of Learning Disabilities*, 1979, 12, 60–64.

331. FORNESS, S. R., SILVERSTEIN, A. B., & GUTHRIE, D. Relationship between classroom behavior and achievement of mildly mentally retarded children. *American Journal of Mental Deficiency*, 1979, 84, 260–265.

332. GLENWICK, D. S., & BAROCAS, R. Training impulsive children in verbal self-control by use of natural change agents. *Journal of Special Education*, 1979, 13, 387–398.

333. GOLD, P. Suspected neurological impairment and cognitive abilities: A longitudinal study. *Psychological Reports*, 1979, 45, 215–218.

334. GOLD, P. Suspected neurological impairment (SNI) and cognitive abilities: A longitudinal study of selected skills and predictive accuracy. *Journal of Clinical Child Psychology*, 1979, 8, 35–38.

335. GOLD, P., & BERK, R. A. Prediction of the academic success of children with suspected neurological impairments. *Journal of Clinical Psychology*, 1979, 35, 505–509.

336. GRASSI, J. R., & LA MORTO-CORSE, A. Identification and remediation of basic cognitive deficits in disadvantaged children. *Journal of Learning Disabilities*, 1979, 12, 483–487.

337. HARKULICH, J. F., MARCHNER, T. J., & BROWN, E. B. Neurological, neuropsychological, and behavioral correlates of Klinefelter's Syndrome. *Journal of Nervous & Mental Disease*, 1979, 167, 359–363.

338. HEILBRUN, A. B., JR. Psychopathy and violent crime. *Journal of Consulting & Clinical Psychology*, 1979, 47, 509–516.

339. HERJANIC, B. M., BARREDO, V. H., HERJANIC, M., & TOMELLERI, C. J. Children of heroin addicts. *International Journal of the Addictions*, 1979, 14, 919–931.

340. HETRICK, E. W. Training parents of learning disabled children in facilitative communicative skills. *Journal of Learning Disabilities*, 1979, 12, 275–277.

341. JASON, L. A., FERONE, L., & ANDEREGG, T. Evaluating ecological, behavioral, and process consultation interventions. *Journal of School Psychology*, 1979, 17, 103–115.

342. JOOST, M. G., & SALVENDY, G. The development and validation of an objective method for quantifying hyperactivity in children. *Journal of Psychological Researches*, 1979, 21, 18–28.

343. KERSHNER, J. R. Rotation of mental images and asymmetries in word recognition. *Canadian Journal of Psychology*, 1979, 33, 39–50.

344. KLEIN, P. S., & SCHWARTZ, A. A. Effects of training auditory sequential memory and attention on reading. *Journal of Special Education*, 1979, 13, 365–374.

345. KUPKE, T., LEWIS, R., & RENNICK, P. Sex differences in the neuropsychological functioning of epileptics. *Journal of Consulting & Clinical Psychology*, 1979, 47, 1128–1130.

346. LINCOLN, A., & CHAZAN, S. Perceived competence and intrinsic motivation in learning disability children. *Journal of Clinical Child Psychology*, 1979, 8, 213–216.

347. LORENZ, L., & VOCKELL, E. Using neurological impress method with learning disabled readers. *Journal of Learning Disabilities*, 1979, 12, 420–422.

348. MARLOWE, W., EGNER, K., & FOREMAN, D. Story comprehension as a function of modality and reading ability. *Journal of Learning Disabilities*, 1979, 12, 194–197.

349. MCLAUGHLIN, T. F., DOLLIVER, P., & MALABY, J. E. A timer game: Effects for on–task behavior and generalization for academic

behavior for an entire special education class. *Contemporary Educational Psychology*, 1979, 4, 172–174.

350. MILLER, W. H. A comparison of the Wide Range Achievement Test and the Peabody Individual Achievement Test for educationally handicapped children. *Journal of Learning Disabilities*, 1979, 12, 65–68.

351. PERRY, J. D., GUIDUBALDI, J., & KEHLE, T. J. Kindergarten competencies as predictors of third-grade classroom behavior and achievement. *Journal of Educational Psychology*, 1979, 71, 443–450.

352. PITTMAN, R. B. Situational referents of an academic setting and locus of control. *Journal of Experimental Education*, 1979, 47, 290–296.

353. POWAZEK, M., & BILLMEIER, G. J., JR. Assessment of intellectual development after surgery for craniofacial dysostosis. *American Journal of Diseases of Children*, 1979, 133, 151–153.

354. REED, H. B. C., JR. Biological defects and special education–An issue in personnel preparation. *Journal of Special Education*, 1979, 13, 9–33.

355. REYNOLDS, C. R., GUTKIN, T. B., DAPPEN, L., & WRIGHT, D. Differential validity of the WISC–R for boys and girls referred for psychological services. *Perceptual & Motor Skills*, 1979, 48, 868–870.

356. REYNOLDS, C. R., & HARTLAGE, L. Comparison of WISC and WISC–R regression lines for academic prediction with black and with white referred children. *Journal of Consulting & Clinical Psychology*, 1979, 47, 589–591.

357. RICHMAN, L. C. Language variables related to reading ability of children with verbal deficits. *Psychology in the Schools*, 1979, 16, 299–305.

358. RIEDER, D. O., & NICHOLS, P. L. Offspring of schizophrenics III. *Archives of General Psychiatry*, 1979, 36, 665–674.

359. RUBIN, R. A., & BALOW, B. Measures of infant development and socioeconomic status as predictors of later intelligence and school achievement. *Developmental Psychology*, 1979, 15, 225–227.

360. RUPLEY, W. H., ASHE, M., & BUCKLAND, P. The relation between the discrimination of letter-like forms and word recognition. *Reading World*, 1979, 19, 113–123.

361. SCHWORM, R. W. Word mediation and generalization in beginning readers. *Journal of Reading Behavior*, 1979, 11, 139–151.

362. SEIDMAN, E., RAPPAPORT, J., KRAMER, J., LINNEY, J. A., HERZBERGER, S., & ALDEN, L. Assessment of classroom behavior: A multiattribute, multisource approach to instrument development and validation. *Journal of Educational Psychology*, 1979, 71, 451–464.

363. SELZ, M., & REITAN, R. M. Neuropsychological test performance of normal, learning–disabled, and brain–damaged older children. *Journal of Nervous & Mental Disease*, 1979, 167, 298–302.

364. SELZ, M., & REITAN, R. M. Rules for neuropsychological diagnosis: Classification of brain function in older children. *Journal of Consulting & Clinical Psychology*, 1979, 47, 258–264.

365. SHANKWEILER, D., LIBERMAN, I. Y., MARK, L. S., FOWLER, C. A., & FISCHER, F. W. The speech code and learning to read. *Journal of Experimental Psychology: Human Learning & Memory*, 1979, 5, 531–545.

366. SMITH, S. M. Standardized tests used in correctional institutions. *Journal of Employment Counseling*, 1979, 16, 178–188.

367. STANOVICH, K. E. The effect of orthographic structure on the word search performance of good and poor readers. *Journal of Experimental Child Psychology*, 1979, 28, 258–267.

368. STAYTON, S. E., & DIENER, R. G. Personality characteristics of juvenile delinquent heroin users. *International Journal of the Addictions*, 1979, 14, 585–587.

369. STONEBURNER, R. L., & BROWN, B. A. A comparison of PIAT and WRAT performances of learning disabled adolescents. *Journal of Learning Disabilities*, 1979, 12, 631–634.

370. STRUB, R. L., BLACK, R. W., & LEVENTHAL, B. The clinical utility of reproduction drawing tests with low IQ patients. *Journal of Clinical Psychiatry*, 1979, 40, 386–388.

371. SWANSON, L. Auditory recall of conceptually, phonetically, and linguistically similar words by normal and learning–disabled children. *Journal of Special Education*, 1979, 13, 63–67.

372. TORGESEN, J. K., & MURPHEY, H. A. Verbal vs. nonverbal and complex vs. simple responses in the paired–associate learning of poor readers. *Journal of General Psychology*, 1979, 101, 219–220.

373. WALDEN, J. A comparison of the PIAT and WRAT: A closer look. *Psychology in the Schools*, 1979, 16, 342–346.

374. WEBSTER, R. E. Visual and aural short–term memory capacity deficits in mathematics disabled students. *Journal of Educational Research*, 1979, 72, 276–283.

375. WILLIAMSON, W. E. The concurrent validity of the 1965 Wide Range Achievement Test with neurologically impaired and emotionally handicapped pupils. *Journal of Learning Disabilities*, 1979, 12, 201–203.

376. WILSON, R., PARKER, T., STEVENSON, H. W., & WILKINSON, A. Perceptual discrimination as a predictor of achievement in reading and arithmetic. *Journal of Educational Psychology*, 1979, 71, 220–225.

377. WOLF, B., PAULSEN, E. P., & HSIA, Y. E. Asymptomatic propionyl CoA carboxylase deficiency in a 13–year old girl. *Journal of Pediatrics*, 1979, 95, 563–565.

378. ZINKUS, P. W., & GOTTLIEB, M. I. Patterns of perceptual deficits in academically deficient juvenile delinquents. *Psychology in the Schools*, 1979, 16, 19–27.

379. ANDERSSON, K. E., RICHARDS, H. C., & HALLAHAN, D. P. Piagetian task performance of learning disabled children. *Journal of Learning Disabilities*, 1980, 13, 37–41.

380. ANGELO, J. K. B. Effects of sensory integration treatment on the low–achieving college student. *American Journal of Occupational Therapy*, 1980, 34, 671–675.

381. ASHMORE, R. J., & SNYDER, R. T. Relationship of visual and auditory short–term memory to later reading achievement. *Perceptual & Motor Skills*, 1980, 51, 15–18.

382. BATSHAW, M. L., ROAN, Y., JUNG, A. L., ROSENBERG, L. A., & BRUSILOW, S. W. Cerebral dysfunction in asymptomatic carriers of ornithine transcarbamylase deficiency. *New England Journal of Medicine*, 1980, 302, 482–485.

383. BERLER, E. S., & ROMANCZYK, R. G. Assessment of the learning disabled and hyperactive child: An analysis and critique. *Journal of Learning Disabilities*, 1980, 13, 10–12.

384. BOSSARD, M. D., REYNOLDS, C. R., & GUTKIN, T. B. A regression analysis of test bias on the Stanford–Binet Intelligence Scale for black and white children referred for psychological service. *Journal of Clinical Child Psychology*, 1980, 9, 52–54.

385. BROWN, R. T. Locus of control and its relationship to intelligence and achievement. *Psychological Reports*, 1980, 46, 1249–1250.

386. BRUMBACK, R. A., JACKOWAY, M. L., & WEINBERG, W. A. Relation of intelligence to childhood depression in children referred to an educational diagnostic center. *Perceptual & Motor Skills*, 1980, 50, 11–17.

387. BRUMBACK, R. A., STATON, R. D., & WILSON, H. Neuropsychological study of children during and after remission of endogenous depressive episodes. *Perceptual & Motor Skills*, 1980, 50, 1163–1167.

388. CANNING, P. M., ORR, R., & ROURKE, B. P. Sex differences in perceptual, visual–motor, linguistic and concept–formation abilities of retarded readers? *Journal of Learning Disabilities*, 1980, 13, 37–41.

389. CANTWELL, D. P., BAKER, L., & MATTISON, R. E. Psychiatric disorders in children with speech and language retardation. *Archives of General Psychiatry*, 1980, 37, 423–426.

390. CONNERS, C. K., & TAYLOR, E. Pemoline, methylphenidate, and placebo in children with minimal brain dysfunction. *Archives of General Psychiatry*, 1980, 37, 922–930.

391. COOPER, S. An approach to the educational assessment of the learning disabled child. *Journal of Clinical Child Psychology*, 1980, 9, 59–62.

392. CUMMINS, J. P., & DAS, J. P. Cognitive processing, academic achievement, and WISC–R performance in EMR children. *Journal of Consulting & Clinical Psychology*, 1980, 48, 777–779.

393. DIAMOND, E. E. The AMEG commission report on sex bias in achievement testing. *Measurement & Evaluation in Guidance*, 1980, 13, 135–147.

394. DYKMAN, R. A., ACKERMAN, P. T., & McCRAY, D. S. Effects of methylphenidate on selective and sustained attention in hyperactive, reading–disabled, and presumably attention–disordered boys. *Journal of Nervous & Mental Disease*, 1980, 168, 745–752.

395. DYKMAN, R. A., ACKERMAN, P. T., & OGLESBY, D. M. Correlates of problem solving in hyperactive, learning disabled, and control boys. *Journal of Learning Disabilities*, 1980, 13, 23–32.

396. ENO, L., & WOEHLKE, P. Diagnostic differences between educationally handicapped and learning disabled students. *Psychology in the Schools*, 1980, 17, 469–473.

397. EPSTEIN, J., BERG–CROSS, G., & BERG–CROSS, L. Maternal expectations and birth order in families with learning disabled and normal children. *Journal of Learning Disabilities*, 1980, 13, 45–52.

398. GAJAR, A. H. Characteristics across exceptional categories: EMR, LD, & ED. *Journal of Special Education*, 1980, 14, 165–173.

399. GETZ, D. J. Learning enhancement through visual training. *Academic Therapy*, 1980, 15, 457–466.

400. HEWETT, B. B., & MARTIN, W. R. Psychometric comparisons of sociopathic and psychopathological behaviors of alcoholics and drug abusers versus a low drug use control population. *International Journal of the Addictions*, 1980, 15, 77–105.

401. HORNBY, P. A. Achieving second language fluency through immersion education. *Foreign Language Annals*, 1980, 13, 107–113.

402. ITO, H. R. Long–term effects of resource room programs on learning disabled children's reading. *Journal of Learning Disabilities*, 1980, 13, 36–40.

403. JANKE, R. W. Computational errors of mentally retarded students. *Psychology in the Schools*, 1980, 17, 30–32.

404. LINCOLN, A., & CHAZAN S. Perceived competence and intrinsic motivation in learning disability children. *Journal of Clinical Child Psychology*, 1980, 8, 213–216.

405. LOPER, A. B., & HALLAHAN, D. P. A comparison of different statistical procedures for determining the relationship between cognitive tempo and reading achievement. *Journal of General Psychology*, 1980, 102, 89–97.

406. MAISTO, A. A., & SIPE, S. An examination of encoding and retrieval processes in reading disabled children. *Journal of Experimental Child Psychology*, 1980, 30, 223–230.

407. McLaughlin, T. F., Cady, M., & Bement, G. Effects of the behavioral analysis model of follow-through on the reading and arithmetic achievement by native American elementary school children. *Psychological Reports*, 1980, 47, 403-407.

408. Mikkelsen, E. J., Rapoport, J. L., Nee, L., Gruenau, C., Mendelson, W., & Gillin, J. C. Childhood enuresis. I. Sleep patterns and psychopathology. *Archives of General Psychiatry*, 1980, 37, 1139-1144.

409. Murchie, D. K., & Weckowicz, T. E. Semantic priming in nonproductive schizophrenia. *Journal of Communication Disorders*, 1980, 13, 249-261.

410. Naglieri, J. A. McCarthy and WISC-R correlates with WRAT achievement scores. *Perceptual & Motor Skills*, 1980, 51, 392-394.

411. Naglieri, J. A., & Parks, J. C. Wide Range Achievement Test: A one-year stability study. *Psychological Reports*, 1980, 47, 1028-1030.

412. Plomin, R., & Foch, T. T. A twin study of objectively assessed personality in childhood. *Journal of Personality & Social Psychology*, 1980, 39, 680-688.

413. Pope, J., Lehrer, B., & Stevens, J. A multiphasic reading screening procedure. *Journal of Learning Disabilities*, 1980, 13, 47-51.

414. Richman, L. C. Cognitive patterns and learning disabilities in cleft palate children with verbal deficits. *Journal of Speech & Hearing Research*, 1980, 23, 447-456.

415. Scull, J. W., & Brand, L. H. The WRAT and the PIAT with learning disabled children. *Journal of Learning Disabilities*, 1980, 13, 64-66.

416. Silverstein, A. B. A comparison of the 1976 and 1978 norms for the WRAT. *Psychology in the Schools*, 1980, 17, 313-315.

417. Spiro, R. J., & Tirre, W. C. Individual differences in schema utilization during discourse processing. *Journal of Educational Psychology*, 1980, 72, 204-208.

418. Steinkamp, M. W. Relationship between environmental distractions and task performance of hyperactive and normal children. *Journal of Learning Disabilities*, 1980, 13, 209-214.

419. Stipek, D. A causal analysis of the relationship between locus of control and academic achievement in first grade. *Contemporary Educational Psychology*, 1980, 5, 90-99.

420. Svanum, S., & Bringle, R. G. Evaluation of confluence model variables on IQ and achievement test scores in a sample of 6- to 11-year-old children. *Journal of Educational Psychology*, 1980, 72, 427-436.

421. Taylor, R. L., & Ivimey, J. K. Diagnostic use of the WISC-R and McCarthy Scales: A regression analysis approach to learning disabilities. *Psychology in the Schools*, 1980, 17, 327-330.

422. Thiel, G. W., & Reynolds, C. R. Predictive validity of the revised Stanford-Binet Intelligence Scale with trainable mentally retarded students. *Educational & Psychological Measurement*, 1980, 40, 509-512.

423. Trembley, P. W., Caponigro, J. D., & Gaffney, V. T. Effects of programming from the WRAT and the PIAT for students determined to have learning disabilities in arithmetic. *Journal of Learning Disabilities*, 1980, 13, 63-65.

424. Tsushima, W. T., & Towne, W. S. ITPA performance of young children with and without questionable brain disorders. *Journal of Learning Disabilities*, 1980, 13, 13-15.

425. Walker, E., Marwit, S. J., & Emory, E. A cross-sectional study of emotional recognition in schizophrenics. *Journal of Abnormal Psychology*, 1980, 89, 428-436.

426. Webster, R. E. Short-term memory in mathematics-proficient and mathematics-disabled students as a function of input-modality/output-modality pairings. *Journal of Special Education*, 1980, 14, 67-78.

427. Wilimas, J., Goff, J. R., Anderson, H. R., Jr., Langston, J. W., & Thompson, E. Efficacy of transfusion therapy for one to two years in patients with sickle cell disease and cerebrovascular accidents. *Journal of Pediatrics*, 1980, 96, 205-208.

428. Wilkinson, A. C. Children's understanding in reading and listening. *Journal of Educational Psychology*, 1980, 72, 561-574.

429. Wright, D., Reynolds, C. R., & Dappen, L. Criterion-related validity of three common preschool assessment instruments for boys and girls. *Psychological Reports*, 1980, 47, 1291-1296.

430. Zagar, R., Arbit, J., & Friedland, J. Structure of a psychodiagnostic test battery for children. *Journal of Clinical Psychology*, 1980, 36, 313-318.

431. Ackerman, P. T., Oglesby, D. M., & Dykman, R. A. A contrast of hyperactive, learning disabled, and hyperactive-learning disabled boys. *Journal of Clinical Child Psychology*, 1981, 10, 168-173.

432. August, G. J., Stewart, M. A., & Tsai, L. The incidence of cognitive disabilities in the siblings of autistic children. *British Journal of Psychiatry*, 1981, 138, 416-422.

433. Bennett, T. S., & Welsh, M. C. Validity of configural interpretation of the intellectual screening and achievement scales of the Personality Inventory for Children. *Educational & Psychological Measurement*, 1981, 41, 863-868.

434. Brandes, P. J., & Ehinger, D. M. The effects of early middle ear pathology on auditory perception and academic achievement. *Journal of Speech & Hearing Disorders*, 1981, 46, 301-307.

435. Cordoni, B. K., & Snyder, M. K. A comparison of learning disabled college students' achievement from WRAT and PIAT grade, standard, and subtest scores. *Psychology in the Schools*, 1981, 18, 28-34.

436. Cunningham, M, D., & Murphy, P. J. The effects of bilateral EEG biofeedback on verbal, visual-spatial, and creative skills in learning disabled male adolescents. *Journal of Learning Disabilities*, 1981, 14, 204-208.

437. Elliot, M. Quantitative evaluation procedures for learning disabilities. *Journal of Learning Disabilities*, 1981, 14, 84-87.

438. Fay, G., Trupin, E., & Townes, B. D. The young disabled reader: Acquisition strategies and associated deficits. *Journal of Learning Disabilities*, 1981, 14, 32-35.

439. Fisk, R. A., & Janzen, H. L. Identifying learning disabled students with a selected psychoeducational test battery. *Alberta Journal of Educational Research*, 1981, 27, 252-263.

440. Furlong, M. J. Torque: An at-risk indicator of reading or behavior problems? *Journal of Clinical Child Psychology*, 1981, 10, 165-167.

441. Gold, P. Suspected neurological impairment (SNI) and cognitive abilities: A longitudinal study of selected skills and predictive accuracy. *Journal of Clinical Child Psychology*, 1981, 8, 35-38.

442. Hale, R. L. Cluster analysis in school psychology: An example. *Journal of School Psychology*, 1981, 19, 51-56.

443. Hale, R. L. Concurrent validity of the WISC-R factor scores. *Journal of School Psychology*, 1981, 19, 274-278.

444. Ito, H. R. After the resource room-Then what? *Academic Therapy*, 1981, 16, 283-287.

445. Koppitz, E. M. The Bender Gestalt and VADS test performance of learning disabled middle school pupils. *Journal of Learning Disabilities*, 1981, 14, 96-98.

446. Korman, M., Matthews, R. W., & Lovitt, R. Neuropsychological effects of abuse of inhalants. *Perceptual & Motor Skills*, 1981, 53, 547-553.

447. Leinhardt, G., Zigmond, N., & Cooley, W. W. Reading instruction and its effects. *American Educational Research Journal*, 1981, 18, 343-361.

448. Maruyama, G., Rubin, R. A., & Kingsbury, G. G. Self-esteem and educational achievement: Independent constructs with a common cause? *Journal of Personality & Social Psychology*, 1981, 40, 962-975.

449. Panagos, J. L., Holmes, R. L., Thurman, R. L., Yard, G. J., & Spaner, S. D. Operation SAIL. One effective model for the assimilation of new students into a school district. *Urban Education*, 1981, 15, 451-468.

450. Prentice-Dunn, S., Wilson, D. R., & Lyman, R. D. Client factors related to outcome in a residential and day treatment program for children. *Journal of Clinical Child Psychology*, 1981, 10, 188-191.

451. Reynolds, C. R., & Nigl, A. J. A regression analysis of differential validity in intellectual assessment for black and white inner city children. *Journal of Clinical Child Psychology*, 1981, 10, 176-179.

452. Reynolds, C. R., Wright, D., & Dappen, L. A comparison of the criterion-related validity (academic achievement) of the WPPSI and the WISC-R. *Psychology in the Schools*, 1981, 18, 20-23.

453. Richman, L. C., & Lindgren, S. D. Verbal mediation deficits: Relation to behavior and achievement in children. *Journal of Abnormal Psychology*, 1981, 90, 99-104.

454. Semel, E. M., & Wiig, E. H. Semel Auditory Processing Program: Training effects among children with language-learning disabilities. *Journal of Learning Disabilities*, 1981, 14, 192-196.

455. Sewell, T. E., Palmo, A. J., & Manni, J. L. High school dropout, psychological, academic, and vocational factors. *Urban Education*, 1981, 16, 65-76.

456. Skinner, H. A. Comparison of clients assigned to in-patient and out-patient treatment for alcoholism and drug addiction. *British Journal of Psychiatry*, 1981, 138, 312-330.

457. Stanovich, K. E. Relationships between word decoding speed, general name-retrieval ability, and reading progress in first-grade children. *Journal of Educational Psychology*, 1981, 73, 809-815.

458. Stanovich, K. E., Cunningham, A. E., & West, R. F. A longitudinal study of the development of automatic recognition skills in first graders. *Journal of Reading Behavior*, 1981, 13, 57-74.

459. Staton, R. D., & Brumback, R. A. Non-specificity of motor hyperactivity as a diagnostic criterion. *Perceptual & Motor Skills*, 1981, 52, 323-332.

460. Staton, R. D., Wilson, H., & Brumback, R. A. Cognitive improvement associated with tricyclic antidepressant treatment of childhood major depressive illness. *Perceptual & Motor Skills*, 1981, 53, 219-234.

461. Tamor, L. Subjective text difficulty: An alternative approach to defining the difficulty level of written text. *Journal of Reading Behavior*, 1981, 13, 165-172.

462. Tunmer, W. E., & Fletcher, C. M. The relationship between conceptual tempo, phonological awareness, and word recognition in beginning readers. *Journal of Reading Behavior*, 1981, 13, 173-185.

463. Walker, E. Emotion recognition in disturbed and normal children: A research note. *Journal of Child Psychology & Psychiatry & Allied Disciplines*, 1981, 22, 263-268.

464. WENDER, P. H., REIMHERR, F. W., & WOOD, D. R. Attentional deficit disorder ("minimal brain dysfunction") in adults. *Archives of General Psychiatry*, 1981, 38, 449–456.
465. ZIFCAK, M. Phonological awareness and reading acquisition. *Contemporary Educational Psychology*, 1981, 6, 117–126.

[2622]
Wide Range Employability Sample Test. Ages 16–54 (normal and handicapped); 1972–73; WREST; originally developed for use with "mentally and physically handicapped" persons enrolled in a rehabilitation workshop for welfare clients; 12 scores: folding, stapling, packaging, measuring, assembling, tag stringing, gluing, collating, color and shade matching, pattern matching, total performance, total errors; J. F. Jastak and Dorothy E. King; Jastak Associates, Inc.*

For additional information and reviews by Frank L. Schmidt and William C. Ward, see 8:987.

[2623]
Wide Range Intelligence and Personality Test. Ages 9.5–54; 1958–74; WRIPT; formerly called *The Jastak Test of Potential Ability and Behavior Stability*; 16 scores: 10 direct scores (vocabulary, number series, coding, picture reasoning, space series, verbal reasoning, social concept, arithmetic, space completion, spelling) and 6 derived scores (language, reality, motivation, psychomotor, intelligence, capacity); Joseph F. Jastak; Jastak Associates, Inc.*

For additional information and a review by David J. Weiss, see 8:492 (1 reference); for reviews by Anne Anastasi and Benjamin Kleinmuntz and excerpted reviews by Edward S. Bordin and Earl C. Butterfield, see 6:773 (3 references).

[2624]
*****Wide Range Interest-Opinion Test.** Grades kgn–12 and adults; 1970–79; WRIOT; 26 scores: 18 occupational interests (art, literature, music, drama, sales, management, office work, personal service, protective service, social service, social science, biological science, physical science, number, mechanics, machine operation, outdoor, athletics), 8 vocational attitudes (sedentariness, risk, ambition, chosen skill level, sex stereotype, agreement, negative bias, positive bias); Joseph F. Jastak and Sarah R. Jastak; Jastak Associates, Inc.*

For additional information and a review by Donald G. Zytowski, see 8:1029.

[2625]
Wide-span Reading Test. Ages 7–15; 1972; Alan Brimer (incorporating material by Herbert Gross); NFER-Nelson Publishing Co. [England].*

For additional information and reviews by David J. Carroll and William Yule, see 8:747.

REFERENCES
1. CONRAD, R. The reading ability of deaf school-leavers. *British Journal of Educational Psychology*, 1977, 47, 138–148.

[2626]
★**Williams Awareness Sentence Completion.** Ages 15 and over; 1972–76; WASC; Black awareness and consciousness; Robert L. Williams; Robert L. Williams & Associates, Inc.*

[2627]
Williams Intelligence Test for Children With Defective Vision. Blind and partially sighted ages 5–15; 1956; M. Williams; distributed by NFER-Nelson Publishing Co. [England].*

See T2:540 (1 reference); for a review by T. Ernest Newland, see 6:541 (2 references).

[2628]
Wilson Driver Selection Test. Prospective motor vehicle operators; 1961–72; 6 scores (visual attention, depth visualization, recognition of simple detail, recognition of complex detail, eye-hand coordination, steadiness) and safety aptitude rating (based on number of subtests passed); Clark L. Wilson; Martin M. Bruce, Ph.D., Publishers.*

For additional information and reviews by Willard A. Kerr and D. H. Schuster, see 6:1200.

[2629]
Wilson-Patterson Attitude Inventory. Ages 14 and over; 1970–75; WPAI; also called *C-Scale*; revision of *Conservatism Scale* with scoring extended to 5 additional attitude scales; "despite the changed title of this test its major purpose remains that of measuring conservatism"; 6 scores: conservatism, realism, militarism-punitiveness, anti-hedonism, ethnocentrism, religion-puritanism; most of the research data presented applied to the original C-Scale; Glenn D. Wilson and John Patterson (test); NFER-Nelson Publishing Co. [England].*

For additional information and reviews by Robyn M. Dawes and Elazar J. Pedhazur, see 8:711 (78 references); see also T2:1143 (9 references) and 7:60 (9 references).

REFERENCES
1–9. See 7:60.
10–18. See T2:1143.
19–96. See 8:711.
97. HAMPSON, S. E., & KLINE, P. Personality dimensions differentiating certain groups of abnormal offenders from non-offenders. *British Journal of Criminology*, 1977, 17, 310–331.
98. HOGAN, H. W. Cross-cultural reliability and factor structure of the Wilson-Patterson Conservatism Scale. *Psychological Reports*, 1977, 41, 453–454.
99. JOE, V. C., JONES, R. N., & RYDER, S. Conservatism, openness to experience and sample bias. *Journal of Personality Assessment*, 1977, 41, 527–531.
100. KIRTON, M. J. Ray's Balanced Dogmatism Scale re-examined. *British Journal of Social & Clinical Psychology*, 1977, 16, 97–98.
101. KIRTON, M. Relatedness of married couples' scores on "adorno" type tests. *Psychological Reports*, 1977, 40, 1013–1014.
102. MARJORIBANKS, K. Arts/science students and social attitudes. *Psychological Reports*, 1977, 40, 437–438.
103. ZIRKEL, K., STEWART, R. A. C., & PRESTON, C. Personality and attitudinal correlates of ability to increase alpha production in EEG biofeedback training. *Psychologia*, 1977, 20, 107–110.
104. FEATHER, N. T. Family resemblances in conservatism: Are daughters more similar to parents than sons are? *Journal of Personality*, 1978, 46, 260–278.
105. JOE, V. C., & SMITH, J. S. Conservatism and inadequate sex information. *Psychological Reports*, 1978, 42, 402.
106. JOSEFOWITZ, N., & MARJORIBANKS, K. Religious affiliation, church attendance and social attitudes. *Psychological Reports*, 1978, 42, 1097–1098.
107. KIRTON, M. J. Wilson and Patterson's Conservatism Scale: A shortened alternative form. *British Journal of Social & Clinical Psychology*, 1978, 17, 319–323.
108. KOHN, P. M., & ANNIS, H. M. Personality and social factors in adolescent marijuana use: A path-analytic study. *Journal of Consulting & Clinical Psychology*, 1978, 46, 366–367.
109. VERMA, G. Conservatism and personality factors in a sample of adolescents. *Contemporary Educational Psychology*, 1978, 3, 51–56.
110. BARLING, J., & FINCHAM, F. The effects of alcohol on psychological conservatism. *Journal of Social Psychology*, 1979, 107, 129–130.
111. FEATHER, N. T. Value correlates of conservatism. *Journal of Personality & Social Psychology*, 1979, 37, 1617–1630.

112. FINCHAM, F., & BARLING, J. Moral judgment and psychological conservatism. *Journal of Social Psychology*, 1979, 107, 139-140.
113. FORGAS, J., & MENYHART, J. The perception of political leaders: A multidimensional analysis. *Australian Journal of Psychology*, 1979, 31, 213-223.
114. HEAVEN, P. C. L. The internal consistency of Wilson's Conservatism Scale. *Journal of Social Psychology*, 1979, 109, 143-144.
115. LAPSLEY, D. K., & ENRIGHT, R. D. The effects of social desirability, intelligence and milieu on an American validation of the Conservatism Scale. *Journal of Social Psychology*, 1979, 107, 9-14.
116. SCHNEIDER, J. F., KOHLER, A., & WACHTER, H. Conservatism and cognitive complexity. *Psychological Reports*, 1979, 44, 981-982.
117. FEATHER, N. T. Conservatism, acquiescence, and the effects of sample heterogeneity. *Australian Journal of Psychology*, 1980, 32, 11-16.
118. FORGAS, J. P. Images of crime: A multidimensional analysis of individual differences in crime perception. *International Journal of Psychology*, 1980, 15, 287-299.
119. HOUSTON, L. N., & SPRINGER, S. I. Self-esteem and conservatism among female college students. *Psychological Reports*, 1980, 47, 543-546.
120. MYNHARDT, J. C. Prejudice among Afrikaans-and English-speaking South African students. *Journal of Social Psychology*, 1980, 110, 9-17.
121. MERCER, G. W., & CAIRNS, E. Conservatism and its relationship to general and specific ethnocentrism in Northern Ireland. *British Journal of Social Psychology*, 1981, 20, 13-16.
122. RUSSELL, G. W. Conservatism, birth order, leadership, and the aggression of Canadian ice hockey players. *Perceptual & Motor Skills*, 1981, 53, 3-7.

[2630]
The Wilson Teacher-Appraisal Scale. Ratings by students in grades 7-16; 1948-57; also available as part of *A Self Appraisal Scale for Teachers*; Howard Wilson; A. R. A.*

For additional information and a review by James R. Hayden, see 6:711.

[2631]
Wing Standardised Tests of Musical Intelligence. Ages 8 and over; 1939-61; 8 scores: chord analysis, pitch change, memory, rhythmic accent, harmony, intensity, phrasing, total; H. D. Wing; distributed by NFER-Nelson Publishing Co. [England].*

See T2:217 (14 references); for reviews by William S. Larson and Robert W. Lundin, see 6:354 (6 references); see also 5:254 (4 references); for a review by John McLeish of an earlier edition, see 4:230 (6 references).

REFERENCES

1-6. See 4:230.
7-10. See 5:254.
11-15. See 6:354.
16-29. See T2:217.
30. DYSON, R. S. The relationship between musical abilities and certain personality characteristics in secondary school children: A pilot study. *Council for Research in Music Education. Bulletin*, 1977, 50, 11-13.
31. MARTIN, P. J. Distinguishing school orchestra members. *Council for Research in Music Education. Bulletin*, 1979, 59, 62-67.

[2632]
★**WISC-R Split-Half Short Form.** Ages 6-16; 1980; uses only selected items from 9 of the 12 subtests of the *Wechsler Intelligence Scale for Children-Revised*; 12 scores: verbal (information, similarities, arithmetic, vocabulary, comprehension, total), performance (picture completion, picture arrangement, block design, object assembly, total), total; Kenneth L. Hobby; Western Psychological Services.*

[2633]
★**Wisconsin Card Sorting Test.** Ages 12 and over; 1980-81; WCST; originally designed to assess abstraction abilities; 6 scores: number correct, number of errors, perseverative responses, nonperseverative errors, perseverative errors, number of categories; Robert K. Heaton (manual), David A. Grant, and Esta A. Berg (test); Psychological Assessment Resources, Inc.*

[2634]
Wisconsin Tests of Reading Skill Development: Study Skills. Grades kgn-1, 1-2, 2-3, 3-4, 4-5, 5-6, 6-7; 1970-73; WTRSD:SS; part of the Wisconsin Design for Reading Skill Development; criterion-referenced; 2-14 "single-skill" scores at each of 7 levels; overview and planning guide by Wayne Otto (principal investigator), Eunice Askov, and Robert D. Chester (planning guide); manuals by Deborah M. Stewart, Karlyn Kamm, James Allen, and Diane K. Sals (*c - e*); NCS Interpretive Scoring Systems.*

a) LEVEL A. Grades kgn-1; 2 scores: position of objects, measurement (size); test by Karlyn Kamm, Deborah M. Stewart, and Virginia L. Van Blaricom.
b) LEVEL B. Grades 1-2; 4 scores: picture symbols, picture grids, measurement (distance), graphs (relative amounts); test by Karlyn Kamm, Deborah M. Stewart, and Virginia L. Van Blaricom.
c) LEVEL C. Grades 2-3; 10 scores: nonpictorial symbols, color keys, number-letter grids, measurement (size, distance), graphs (exact amounts, differences), tables (relative amounts, one cell), alphabetizing; test by Karlyn Kamm, Deborah M. Stewart, Virginia L. Van Blaricom, James Allen, and Mary L. Ramberg.
d) LEVEL D. Grades 3-4; 12 scores: point and line symbols, scale (whole units), graphs (differences, approximate amounts), tables (differences), reference (indexes, tables of contents, alphabetizing, guide words, headings and subheadings, selecting sources, facts or opinions); test by Karlyn Kamm, Deborah M. Stewart, Virginia L. Van Blaricom, Evelyn Weible, James Allen, J. Laird Marshall, Mary L. Ramberg, and Diane K. Sals.
e) LEVEL E. Grades 4-5; 14 scores: point-line-area symbols, intermediate directions, scale (multiple whole units), graphs (differences, purpose and summary), tables (multiplicative differences, purpose and summary), reference (indexes, dictionary meanings, cross references, guide words, guide cards, specialized references, fact checking).
f) LEVEL F. Grades 5-6; 12 scores: maps (analysis), map projections, inset maps, different scales, graphs (differences), schedules (relationship), reference (*Subject Index*, dictionary pronunciation, card filing rules, Dewey Decimal System, outlining, catalog cards).
g) LEVEL G. Grades 6-7; 10 scores: maps (synthesis), latitude and longitude, meridians and parallels, scale (fractional units), graphs (multiplicative differences, projecting and relating), schedules (problem solving), references (*Reader's Guide*, card catalogs, outlining).

For additional information and a review by John J. Geyer, see 8:823 (3 references).

REFERENCES

1-3. See 8:823.
4. ASKOV, E. N., KAMM, K., & KLUMB, R. Study skill mastery among elementary school teachers. *Reading Teacher*, 1977, 30, 485-488.

[2635]
Wisconsin Tests of Reading Skill Development: Word Attack. Grades kgn-2, 1, 1-3, 2-4, 3-6; 1970-72; WTRSD:WA; part of the Wisconsin Design for Reading Skill Development; criterion-referenced; 6-16 "single-skill" scores at each of 5 levels; overview and planning guide by Wayne Otto (principal investigator)

and Eunice Askov; tests and manuals by Karlyn Kamm, Pamela J. Miles, Deborah M. Stewart, Virginia L. Van Blaricom (tests), and Margaret L. Harris (tests); NCS Interpretive Scoring Systems.*

a) LEVEL A. Grades kgn–2; "early readiness" level; 6 scores: rhyming words, rhyming phrases, shapes, letters and numbers, words and phrases, initial consonants.

b) TRANSITION LEVEL A-B. Grade 1; "advanced readiness or preprimer" level; selected items from Levels A and B; 7 scores: rhyming words, rhyming phrases, words and phrases, initial consonants, beginning consonants, ending consonants, consonant blends.

c) LEVEL B. Grades 1–3; "primer or first reader" level; 11 scores: beginning consonants, ending consonants, consonant blends, rhyming elements, short vowels, consonant digraphs, compound words, contractions, base words and endings, plurals, possessives.

d) LEVEL C. Grades 2–4; "second reader" level; 16 scores: consonant variants, consonant blends, long vowels, vowel plus r/a plus i/a plus w, diphthongs, long and short oo, middle vowel, 2 vowels separated, 2 vowels together, final vowel, consonant digraphs, base words, plurals, homonyms, synonyms and antonyms, multiple meanings.

e) LEVEL D. Grades 3–6; "third reader" level; 6 scores: 3-letter consonant blends, silent letters, syllabication, accent, unaccented schwa, possessives.

For additional information and reviews by Rebecca C. Barr and Richard Rystrom, see 8:778 (6 references); see also T2:1655 (1 reference).

[2636]

★**WLW Personal Survey, Form 3.** Supervisors and potential supervisors; 1964–72; 25 scores: information (general information, word knowledge, arithmetic, concepts, total), personal (friendliness, aggressiveness, emotional stability, energy, total), interests (social, persuasive, economic-practical, managerial, scientific-theoretical, planning-writing, total), motives (achievement, consideration, independence, ego, total), judgment, consideration, initiative; Robert W. Henderson; William, Lynde & Williams, Inc.* (Publisher informs us that this test is no longer available "for public distribution.")

[2637]

Wonderlic Personnel Selection Procedure. Applicants for employment; 1967–69; WPSP; 8 parts; E. F. Wonderlic & Associates, Inc.*

a) P-1: INTRODUCTORY APPLICATION.
b) P-2: PERSONNEL APPLICATION.
c) P-3: WONDERLIC PERSONNEL TEST, FORM 1.
d) P-4: PERSONNEL INTERVIEWER'S GUIDE.
e) P-5: HEALTH QUESTIONNAIRE.
f) P-6: [WRITTEN REFERENCE REPORTS].
g) P-7: TELEPHONE REFERENCE CHECK.
h) P-8: PRE-EMPLOYMENT SUMMARY.

For additional information, see 7:1075.

[2638]

*****Wonderlic Personnel Test.** Adults; 1939–81; WPT; revision consists of minor word changes in items; (French and Spanish editions available); E. F. Wonderlic; E. F. Wonderlic & Associates, Inc.*

See T2:482 (10 references); for reviews by Robert C. Droege and John P. Foley, Jr., see 7:401 (28 references); for reviews by N. M. Downie and Marvin D. Dunnette, see 6:513 (17 references); see also 5:400 (59 references); for reviews by H. E. Brogden, Charles D. Flory, and Irving Lorge, see 3:269 (7 references); see also 2:1415 (2 references).

REFERENCES

1–2. See 2:1415.
3–9. See 3:269.
10–68. See 5:400.
69–85. See 6:513.
86–113. See 7:401.
114–123. See T2:482.
124. DENNEY, D. R., & RUPERT, P. A. Desensitization and self-control in the treatment of test anxiety. *Journal of Counseling Psychology*, 1977, 24, 272–280.
125. FINGER, R., & GALASSI, J. P. Effects of modifying cognitive versus emotionality responses in the treatment of test anxiety. *Journal of Consulting & Clinical Psychology*, 1977, 45, 280–287.
126. GRIGGS, B. M. A systems approach to the development and evaluation of a minicourse for nurses. *Nursing Research*, 1977, 26, 34–41.
127. JARNECKE, R. W., & CHAMBERS, E. D. MMPI content scales: Dimensional structure, construct validity, and interpretive norms in a psychiatric population. *Journal of Consulting & Clinical Psychology*, 1977, 45, 1126–1131.
128. MOUNT, M. K., MUCHINSKY, P. M., & HAUSER, L. M. The predictive validity of a work sample: A laboratory study. *Personnel Psychology*, 1977, 30, 637–645.
129. OLESKER, W. Physiognomic perception and empathy. *Perceptual & Motor Skills*, 1977, 45, 83–86.
130. DODRILL, C. B. A neuropsychological battery for epilepsy. *Epilepsia*, 1978, 19, 611–623.
131. GOLDFRIED, M. R., LINEHAN, M. M., & SMITH, J. L. Reduction of test anxiety through cognitive restructuring. *Journal of Consulting & Clinical Psychology*, 1978, 46, 32–39.
132. RAPHAEL, D., MOSS, S., & CROSS, W. Budner's intolerance of ambiguity: A note concerning intelligence. *Psychological Reports*, 1978, 43, 624–626.
133. DEFFENBACHER, J. L., MATHIS, H., & MICHAELS, A. C. Two self-control procedures in the reduction of targeted and nontargeted anxieties. *Journal of Counseling Psychology*, 1979, 26, 120–127.
134. HAYES, C. B., & PAGE, W. F. Locus of control and attrition among American high school youth. *Journal of Psychology*, 1979, 101, 189–195.
135. KARMOS, A. H. The development and validation of a nonverbal measure of self-esteem: The sliding person test. *Educational & Psychological Measurement*, 1979, 39, 479–484.
136. KARMOS, A. H., & KARMOS, J. S. Construct validity analyses of a "nonverbal" measure of self-esteem: The sliding person test. *Psychological Reports*, 1979, 44, 895–910.
137. McCORDICK, S. M., KAPLAN, R. M., FINN, M. E., & SMITH, S. H. Cognitive behavior modification and modeling for test anxiety. *Journal of Consulting & Clinical Psychology*, 1979, 47, 419–420.
138. PENK, W. E., CHARLES, H. L., & VAN HOOSE, T. A. Psychological test comparison of day hospital and inpatient treatment. *Journal of Clinical Psychology*, 1979, 35, 837–839.
139. RAPHAEL, D., MOSS, S. W., & ROSSER, M. E. Evidence concerning the construct validity of conceptual level as a personality variable. *Canadian Journal of Behavioral Science*, 1979, 11, 327–339.
140. BARRIOS, B. A., GINTER, E. J., SCALISE, J. J., & MILLER, F. G. Treatment of test anxiety by applied relaxation and cue-controled relaxation. *Psychological Reports*, 1980, 46, 1287–1296.
141. DEFFENBACHER, J. L., & MICHAELS, A. C. Two self-control procedures in the reduction of targeted and nontargeted anxieties – A year later. *Journal of Counseling Psychology*, 1980, 27, 9–15.
142. DEFFENBACHER, J. L., MICHAELS, A. C., DALEY, P. C., & MICHAELS, T. A comparison of homogeneous and heterogeneous anxiety management training. *Journal of Counseling Psychology*, 1980, 27, 630–634.
143. DEFFENBACHER, J. L., MICHAELS, A. C., MICHAELS, T., & DALEY, P. C. Comparison of anxiety management training and self-control desensitization. *Journal of Counseling Psychology*, 1980, 27, 232–239.
144. DODRILL, C. B. Rapid evaluation of intelligence in adults with epilepsy. *Epilepsia*, 1980, 21, 359–367.
145. ILGEN, D. R., & KNOWLTON, W. A., JR. Performance attributional effects on feedback from superiors. *Organizational Behavior & Human Performance*, 1980, 26, 441–456.
146. KNOWLTON, W. A., JR., & MITCHELL, T. R. Effects of causal attributions on a supervisor's evaluation of subordinate performance. *Journal of Applied Psychology*, 1980, 65, 459–466.
147. DODRILL, C. B. An economical method for the evaluation of general intelligence in adults. *Journal of Consulting & Clinical Psychology*, 1981, 49, 668–673.

[2639]

★Woodcock-Johnson Psycho-Educational Battery. Ages 3–80; 1977–78; applications of the battery include individual identification of special problems or disabilities, diagnosis of specific weaknesses that may interfere with related aspects of development, occupational and instructional selection and placement, individual program planning, guidance, prediction and conformation of future performance, evaluation of individual growth, evaluation of programs, research, and psychometric training; 31 scores: 27 subtest scores divided into 3 parts; Part One (cognitive ability), 12 scores: picture vocabulary, spatial relationships, memory for sentences, visual-auditory learning, blending, quantitative concepts, visual matching, antonyms-synonyms, analysis-synthesis, numbers reversed, concept formation, analogies; Part Two (achievement), 10 scores: letter-word identification, word attack, passage comprehension, calculation, applied problems, dictation, proofing, science, social studies, humanities; Part Three (interest level), 5 scores: reading interest, mathematics interest, language interest, physical interest, social interest; plus 4 derived scores referred to as Relative Performance indexes: reading, mathematics, written language, knowledge; Richard W. Woodcock and Mary Bonner Johnson; Teaching Resources Corporation.*

REFERENCES

1. LICHTENSTEIN, R. Comparative validity of two preschool screening tests: Correlational and classification approaches. *Journal of Learning Disabilities*, 1981, 14, 68–72.
2. STREIN, W., & BRANTLEY, J. Woodcock–Johnson Psycho-Educational Battery. *Journal of School Psychology*, 1981, 19, 184–187.
3. YSSELDYKE, J., SHINN, M., & EPPS, S. A comparison of the WISC–R and the Woodcock–Johnson tests of cognitive ability. *Psychology in the Schools*, 1981, 18, 15–19.

[2640]

★Woodcock Language Proficiency Battery. Ages 3 and over; 1980–81; WLPB; represents selected portions of the *Woodcock-Johnson Psycho-Educational Battery*; 8 subtests: oral language (picture vocabulary, antonyms-synonyms, analogies), reading (letter-word identification, word attack, passage comprehension), written language (dictation, proofing); 2 forms; Richard W. Woodcock; Teaching Resources Corporation.*
a) ENGLISH FORM. 1980.
b) SPANISH FORM. 1981.

[2641]

Woodcock Reading Mastery Tests. Grades kgn–12; 1972–73; WRMT; 6 scores (letter identification, word identification, word attack, word comprehension, passage comprehension, total) plus derived scores in these same 6 areas at each of 4 levels (easy reading level [96% mastery], reading grade score [90% mastery], failure reading level [75% mastery], relative mastery of grade level); Richard W. Woodcock; American Guidance Service.*

For additional information, reviews by Carol Anne Dwyer and J. Jaap Tuinman, and excerpted reviews by Alex Bannatyne, Richard L. Allington, Cherry Houck (with Larry A. Harris), and Barton B. Proger, see 8:779 (7 references).

REFERENCES

1–7. See 8:779.
8. MEDWAY, F. J., & BARON, R. M. Locus of control and tutor's instructional style as determinants of cross-age tutoring effectiveness. *Contemporary Educational Psychology*, 1977, 2, 298–310.

9. ALLINGTON, R. L., & FLEMING, J. T. The misreading of high-frequency words. *Journal of Special Education*, 1978, 12, 417–421.
10. BRUININKS, V. L. Actual and perceived peer status of learning-disabled students in mainstream programs. *Journal of Special Education*, 1978, 12, 51–58.
11. BRUININKS, V. L. Peer status and personality characteristics of learning disabled and nondisabled students. *Journal of Learning Disabilities*, 1978, 11, 484–489.
12. LAFFEY, J. L., & KELLY, D. Woodcock Reading Mastery Tests. *Reading Teacher*, 1979, 33, 335–339.
13. ALLINGTON, R. L., & MCGILL-FRANZEN, A. Word identification errors in isolation and in context: Apples vs. oranges. *Reading Teacher*, 1980, 33, 795–800.
14. BLOOM, A., WAGNER, M., RESKIN, L., & BERGMAN, A. A comparison of intellectually delayed and primary reading disabled children on measures of intelligence and achievement. *Journal of Clinical Psychology*, 1980, 36, 788–790.
15. POPE, J., LEHRER, B., & STEVENS, J. A multiphasic reading screening procedure. *Journal of Learning Disabilities*, 1980, 13, 47–51.
16. SANDOVAL, J. Reliability and concurrent validity of Light's Retention Scale. *Psychology in the Schools*, 1980, 17, 442–445.
17. SCHUSTER, D. H., & VINCENT, L. Teaching math and reading with suggestion and music. *Academic Therapy*, 1980, 16, 69–72.
18. BLOOM, A., WAGNER, M., BERGMAN, A., ALTSHULER, L., & RASKIN, L. Relationship between intellectual status and reading skills for developmentally disabled children. *Perceptual & Motor Skills*, 1981, 52, 853–854.
19. BRODER, P. K., DUNIVANT, N., SMITH, E. C., & SUTTON, L. P. Further observations on the link between learning disabilities and juvenile delinquency. *Journal of Educational Psychology*, 1981, 73, 838–850.
20. JANICKE, E. M. Massive oraly decoding. *Academic Therapy*, 1981, 17, 157–161.
21. KATZ, R. B., SHANKWEILER, D., & LIBERMAN, I. Y. Memory for item order and phonetic recoding in the beginning reader. *Journal of Experimental Child Psychology*, 1981, 32, 474–484.
22. POWELL, G., MOORE, D., & CALLAWAY, B. A concurrent validity study of the Woodcock Word Comprehension Test. *Psychology in the Schools*, 1981, 18, 24–27.
23. PUTNAM, L. R. Minnesota Percepto-Diagnostic Test and reading achievement. *Perceptual & Motor Skills*, 1981, 53, 235–238.
24. WALMSLEY, S. A., SCOTT, K. M., & LEHRER, R. Effects of document simplification on the reading comprehension of the elderly. *Journal of Reading Behavior*, 1981, 13, 237–248.

[2642]

★Word and Number Assessment Inventory. High school students and adults; 1976–77; WNAI; 3 scores matched to appropriate career areas: word, number, total; Jean C. Johansson, Charles B. Johansson, and Linda L. Kellogg (inventory); NCS Interpretive Scoring Systems.*

[2643]

Word Dexterity Test. Grades 7–16; 1942–50; Shailer Peterson; the Author.* (In-print status uncertain; no reply from publisher.)

For additional information, see 4:218; see also 3:170 (2 references).

[2644]

Word Discrimination Test. Grades 1–8; 1958; WDT; no manual; Chas. B. Huelsman, Jr.; Miami University Alumni Association.*

For additional information, see 7:736 (2 references).

REFERENCES

1–2. See 7:736.
3. KIRCHMEIMER, J. Auditory and visual factors related to spelling success. *Psychology in the Schools*, 1979, 16, 491–494.

[2645]

Word Fluency. Industrial employees; 1959–61; Raymond J. Corsini and Measurement Research Division, Human Resources Center, University of Chicago; the Center.*

See T2:594 (2 references); for a review by James E. Kennedy, see 6:562.

REFERENCES

1–2. See T2:594.
3. DiSimoni, F. G., Darley, F. L., & Aronson, A. E. Patterns of dysfunction in schizophrenic patients on an aphasia test battery. *Journal of Speech & Hearing Disorders*, 1977, 42, 498–513.

[2646]
Word Intelligibility by Picture Identification. Hearing impaired children ages 5–13; 1971; WIPI; speech discrimination; Mark Ross and Jay Lerman; Stanwix House, Inc.*

For additional information and reviews by Leija V. McReynolds and Robert L. Rosenbaum, see 8:953 (5 references); see also T2:2061 (3 references).

REFERENCES

1–3. See T2:2061.
4–8. See 8:953.
9. Freeman, B. A., & Beasley, D. S. Discrimination of time altered sentential approximations and monosyllables by children with reading problems. *Journal of Speech & Hearing Research*, 1978, 21, 497–506.
10. Glenn, L. E., Nerbonne, G. P., & Tolhurst, G. C. Environmental noise in a residential institution for mentally retarded persons. *American Journal of Mental Deficiency*, 1978, 82, 594–597.
11. Samples, J. M., & Lane, V. W. Language gains in global aphasia over a three-year period: A case study. *Journal of Communication Disorders*, 1980, 13, 49–57.
12. Cherry, R. S. Development of selective auditory attention skills in children. *Perceptual & Motor Skills*, 1981, 52, 379–385.

[2647]
Word Recognition Test. Preschool to age 8.5; 1970; WRT; Clifford Carver; Hodder & Stoughton Educational [England].*

REFERENCES

1. Norton, S. J., Schultz, M. C., Reed, C. M., Braida, L. D., Durlach, N. I., Rabinowitz, W. M., & Chomsky, C. Analytic study of the Tadoma method: Background and preliminary results. *Journal of Speech & Hearing Research*, 1977, 20, 574–595.

[2648]
★**The WORD Test.** Ages 7 and over; 1981; ratings by a trained teacher or other professional; assesses the expressive vocabulary and semantic abilities of children whose language problems affect academic progress and communicative interaction; 7 scores: associations, synonyms, semantic absurdities, antonyms, definitions, multiple definitions, total; Carol Jorgensen, Mark Barrett, Rosemary Huisingh, & Linda Zachman; LinguiSystems, Inc.*

[2649]
Word Understanding. Grades 6–12; 1969; WU; R. Hoepfner, M. Hendricks, and R. H. Silverman; Monitor.*

For additional information and a review by Nikola N. Filby, see 8:82.

[2650]
★**Work Attitudes Questionnaire, Research Version.** Adults; 1980–81; WAQ; 3 scores: psychological health, work commitment, total; Maxene S. Doty and Nancy E. Betz; Marathon Consulting & Press.*

[2651]
★**Work Elements Inventory.** Employees; 1978–81; WEI; 16 scores: setting organizational objectives, financial planning and review, improving work procedures and policies, interdepartmental coordination developing and implementing technical ideas, judgment and decision-making, developing group cooperation and teamwork, coping with difficulties and emergencies, promoting safety attitudes and practices, communications, developing employee potential, supervisory practices, self-development and improvement, personnel practices, promoting community-organization relations, handling outside contacts; Melany E. Baehr, Wallace G. Longergan, and Bruce A. Hunt; Human Resources Center, University of Chicago.*

[2652]
★**Work Environment Scale.** Employees and supervisors; 1974–81; WES; a part of *The Social Climate Scales* (2227); 10 scores: involvement, peer cohesion, supervisor support, autonomy, task orientation, work pressure, clarity, control, innovation, physical comfort; Paul M. Insel and Rudolf H. Moos; Consulting Psychologists Press, Inc.*

For additional information, see 8:713 (3 references). For a review of *The Social Climate Scales*, see 8:681.

REFERENCES

1–3. See 8:713.
4. Finney, J. W., Moos, R. H., & Mewborn, C. R. Post treatment experiences and treatment outcome of alcoholic patients six months and two years after hospitalization. *Journal of Consulting & Clinical Psychology*, 1980, 48, 17–29.
5. Schmitt, N., Colligan, M. J., & Fitzgerald, M. Unexplained physical symptoms in eight organizations: Individual and organizational analyses. *Journal of Occupational Psychology*, 1980, 53, 305–317.

[2653]
Work Information Inventory. Employee groups in industry; 1958; WII; morale; Raymond E. Bernberg; Psychometric Affiliates.*

For additional information and a review by Albert K. Kurtz, see 8:1057.

[2654]
★**Work Interest Index.** Grades 7–12 and college and adults; 1959–65; WII; non-verbal; 14 scores: 12 factor scores (professional and technical, social and verbal, authority and prestige, artistic and interpretative, artistic and stylized, artistic and creative, technical and scientific, clerical and routine, business contact and structured, personal service and persuasive, mechanical and productive, control of massive equipment), flexibility of interest, aspiration level; Melany E. Baehr, Richard Renck, Robert K. Burns, and Robert W. Pranis (manual); Human Resources Center, University of Chicago.*

[2655]
[**Work Motivation**]. Managers, employees; 1967–73; 2 tests, 5 scores for each: basic-creature comfort, safety and order, belonging and affiliation, ego-status, actualization and self-expression; no manual; Jay Hall and Martha Williams (*b*); Teleometrics Int'l.*

a) MANAGEMENT OF MOTIVES INDEX. Managers; 1968–73; MMI; assumptions and practices characterizing attempts to motivate employees.
b) WORK MOTIVATION INVENTORY. Employees; 1967–73; WMI; motivational needs and values.

For additional information, see 8:1189 (3 references).

REFERENCES

1–3. See 8:1189.
4. Ferguson, E. The relationship of work motivation to selected demographic characteristics of black female workers. *Business Education Forum*, 1977, 32, 40.

5. HALL, J., & DONNELL, S. M. Managerial achievement: The personal side of behavior. *Human Relations*, 1979, 32, 77–101.
6. WARD, G. R., PORTER, S., & OMIZO, M. M. Personality characteristics and motivational needs of preservice and inservice teachers: Implications for practice. *Journal of Teaching & Learning*, 1980, 5, 38–47.
7. WENDT, J. D., WARD, G. R., & JACKSON, A. S. Personality determinants of the Herzberg's conceptualization of the maintenance–motivator. *Journal of Teaching & Learning*, 1980, 5, 26–38.

[2656]

Work Reference Check. Job applicants; 1965; information and ratings by former employer; Psychological Publications Press.* (In-print status uncertain; no reply from publisher.)

For additional information, see 7:1076.

[2657]

Work Values Inventory. Grades 7–16 and adults; 1968–70; WVI; 15 scales: altruism, esthetics, creativity, intellectual stimulation, independence, achievement, prestige, management, economic returns, security, surroundings, supervisory relations, associates, variety, way of life; Donald E. Super; Riverside Publishing Co.*

For additional information and an excerpted review by Frederick Brown, see 8:1030 (52 references); see also T2:2221 (12 references); for reviews by Ralph F. Berdie and David V. Tiedeman, and an excerpted review by John W. French, see 7:1042 (33 references).

REFERENCES

1–33. See 7:1042.
34–45. See T2:2221.
46–98. See 8:1030.
99. DIETRICH, M. C. Work values evolution in a baccalaureate student nurse population. *Journal of Vocational Behavior*, 1977, 10, 25–34.
100. GREENHAUS, J. H., & SIMON, W. E. Career salience, work values, and vocational indecision. *Journal of Vocational Behavior*, 1977, 10, 104–110.
101. HAMED, C. A comparison of traditional capstone office occupations courses with intensive office occupations block programs based on selected work values of twelfth grade students in Ohio. *Delta Pi Epsilon Journal*, 1977, 14, 1–6.
102. KUIPER, S. Work values and problem perceptions of young married women in clerical occupations. *Business Education Forum*, 1977, 32, 46.
103. KUIPER, S. Work values and problem perceptions of young married women in clerical occupations. *Journal of Business Education*, 1977, 52, 193.
104. MCCARREY, M. W., EDWARDS, S., & JONES, R. The influence of ethnolinguistic group membership, sex and position level on motivational orientation of Canadian anglophone and francophone employees. *Canadian Journal of Behavioural Science*, 1977, 9, 274–282.
105. WEARNE, T. D., & POWELL, J. C. The differential long-term effects of client-centered, developmental counselling with individuals and group. *Canadian Counsellor*, 1977, 11, 83–92.
106. WOODBURY, R., & PATE, D. H. Vocational and personality dimensions of adjudicated delinquents. *Measurement & Evaluation in Guidance*, 1977, 10, 106–112.
107. DRUMMOND, R. J., MCINTIRE, W. G., & SKAGGS, C. T. The relationship of work values to occupational level in young adult workers. *Journal of Employment Counseling*, 1978, 15, 117–121.
108. HALPIN, G., BROGDON, R. E., & TAYLOR, G. C. Robert revisited: Intra– and interindividual comparisons in Super's Work Values Inventory. *Measurement & Evaluation in Guidance*, 1978, 11, 20–25.
109. KUIPER, S. Work values and problem perceptions of young married women in clerical occupations. *Delta Pi Epsilon Journal*, 1978, 20, 23–39.
110. BLIMLING, G. S., & PAULSEN, F. M. The Educational Developmental Group Enrichment (EDGE) program: A comprehensive model for student development in residence halls. *Journal of the National Association for Women Deans, Administrators & Counselors*, 1979, 42, 24–33.
111. VUNDERINK, P. Identification and comparison of the work values and job perceptions of urban business education students and clerical officer workers. *Business Education Forum*, 1979, 34, 59.
112. BOLTON, B. Second-order dimensions of the Work Values Inventory (WVI). *Journal of Vocational Behavior*, 1980, 17, 33–40.
113. WEARNE, T. D., POWELL, J. C., & REIMER, A. Patterns of work values held by secondary school girls. *Alberta Journal of Educational Research*, 1980, 26, 241–246.
114. SAMPSON, J. P., JR., & LOESCH, L. C. Relationship among work values and job knowledge. *Vocational Guidance Quarterly*, 1981, 29, 229–235.
115. STAATS, S. Work Values Inventory scores from 1970 to 1980. *Perceptual & Motor Skills*, 1981, 53, 113–114.

[2658]

World History/Objective Tests. 1, 2 semesters high school; 1961–70; revision of *Objective Tests in World History* by Earl Bridgewater; 16 tests: 13 unit tests, 2 semester tests, and a final examination; no manual; Perfection Form Co.* (In-print status uncertain; no reply from publisher.)

For additional information concerning the earlier tests, see 6:1007.

[2659]

World Literature Anthology Tests. High school; 1964–70; revision of *Objective Tests in World Anthology* by Dorothy A. Mason; 5 tests; no manual; Perfection Form Co.* (In-print status uncertain; no reply from publisher.)
a) CLASSICAL LITERATURE.
b) EUROPEAN LITERATURE.
c) ORIENTAL LITERATURE.
d) RUSSIAN LITERATURE.
e) FINAL TEST.

[2660]

★**WRITE: Junior and Senior High.** Junior high school, senior high school; 1979–81; "assessment of skills in written composition"; 2 levels; Los Angeles Unified School District; CTB/McGraw-Hill.*

[2661]

★**Writing Proficiency Program.** Grades 6–9, 9–10, 11–13; 1979–81; WPP; "criterion-referenced assessment and instructional system"; 3 levels; Richard M. Bossone; CTB/McGraw-Hill.*
a) WRITING PROFICIENCY PROGRAM/INTERMEDIATE SYSTEM. Grades 6–9; WPP/IS; 21 scores: 15 multiple-choice test objective scores (capitalization, pronouns, adjectives and adverbs, verb tense, quotation and end marks, commas, conjunctions, sentence sequence, topic/supporting sentences, use of transitions, sentence fragments, misplaced modifiers, subject/verb agreement, run-together sentences, total number of objectives with mastery scores), 6 writing exercise scores (holistic and primary-trait scores for narration, description and persuasion exercises).
b) WRITING PROFICIENCY PROGRAM. Grades 9–10, 11–13; WPP; 18 or 19 scores: language expression (sentence fragments, run-together sentences, subject-verb agreement, verb form, pronoun case), punctuation and mechanics, capitalization, spelling, topic sentences, paragraph organization, paragraph coherence, main topics/sub-topics, essay organization, the letter (Test 1 only), total, 4 writing sample scores (holistic and analytical scores for paragraph and essay); 2 levels.

[2662]

Writing Test: McGraw-Hill Basic Skills System. Grades 11–14; 1970; also called *MHBSS Writing Test*; although designed for use with the MHBSS instructional program, the test may be used independently; 4 scores:

language mechanics, sentence patterns, paragraph patterns, total; Alton L. Raygor; McGraw-Hill Book Co., Inc.*

For additional information and a review by Leonard S. Feldt, see 7:214.

REFERENCES

1. WALKER, L. S. University success for Canadian Indians. *Canadian Journal of Behavioural Science*, 1977, 9, 169–175.

[2663]

★**Written Language Syntax Test.** Hearing impaired students primary–grade 12; 1981; WLST; Sharon R. Berry; Gallaudet College Press.*

a) SCREENING LEVEL. Used to determine the appropriate level for administration.

b) LEVEL I. Students with 3 or fewer correct on screening level.

c) LEVEL II. Students with 4–6 items correct on screening level.

d) LEVEL III. Students with 7–10 items correct on screening level.

[2664]

Yarn Dexterity Test. Textile workers and applicants; 1964–65; YDT; Robert L. Brown; Brown & Associates, Inc.* (In-print status uncertain; no reply from publisher.)

For additional information, see 7:1048.

[2665]

Yellow Brick Road. Ages 3–6; 1975; YBR; "a gross screening tool for identifying children with special learning needs"; 4 batteries, 29 scores: 28 scores listed below plus total; Christine Kallstrom; Teaching Resources Corporation.*

a) MOTOR BATTERY. 7 scores: imitation, movement, body parts, spatial relationships, right-left, draw-a-person, total.

b) VISUAL BATTERY. 7 scores: tracking, fusion, visual discrimination, visual memory, visual motor, figure-ground, total.

c) AUDITORY BATTERY. 7 scores: auditory discrimination, how many, copy cat, sequence, automatic associations, guess what I am, total.

d) LANGUAGE BATTERY. 7 scores: motor encoding, vocal encoding, categories, go-togethers, articulation, conversation, total.

For additional information and reviews by Robert P. Anderson and James C. Reed, see 8:451.

REFERENCES

1. FRANCE, G. A., COUCH, J., CAUTHEN, D., CARPENTER, H., JONES, M., JORDON, P., MORGAN, C., LOTTINVILLE, E., & NEPH, L. Yellow Brick Road revisited. *Journal of Consulting & Clinical Psychology*, 1979, 47, 760–761.
2. BROWN, J., SHERRILL, C., & GENCH, B. Effects of an integrated physical education/music program in changing early childhood perceptual–motor performance. *Perceptual & Motor Skills*, 1981, 53, 151–154.

[2666]

Y.E.M.R. Performance Profile for the Young Moderately and Mildly Retarded. Ages 5–9; 1967; 11 scores: social behavior, self-help, safety, communication, motor skills, manipulative skills, perceptual and intellectual development, academics, imagination and creative expression, emotional behavior, total; Alfred J. DiNola, Bernard P. Kaminsky, and Allan E. Sternfeld; Educational Performance Associates, Inc.*

[2667]

Youth Research Survey. Ages 13–19; 1958–71; YRS; revision of *CYR Youth Survey* (CYR is acronym for Church Youth Research) which was a revision of *LYR Youth Inventory* (LYR is acronym for Lutheran Youth Research); for group and individual measurement in religious congregations and high schools; yields 25 profiled scores: concerns (family unity, parental understanding, family pressures, life partner, lack of self-confidence, academic problems, personal faults, classroom relationships, national issues, God relationship), beliefs-values (interest in help, maturity of values, orientation for change, moral responsibility, meaningful life, religious participation, social action, self regard, human relations, God awareness, biblical concepts), perception (youth group vitality, adult caring, family social concerns), frankness plus a computer group report of about 120 pages of narrative statements and percentage responses in 36 areas: general description of your youth (tally, frankness, family, school, leisure), life perspective (world view, self regard), concerns about family (family unity, parental understanding, family pressures), concerns about one-self (lack of self-confidence, academic problems, personal faults, classroom relationships), personal battles (dating and emotions, moral issues, maturity of values, moral responsibility, drug use), feeling for people (national issues, orientation for change, human relations), perception of church (youth group vitality, adult caring, family social concern), religious commitment (God awareness, God relationship, participation in religious activities, biblical concepts, meaningful life, social action, needs of others), interest in help (marriage concerns-life partner, interest in the worship service, focal points for a ministry, interest in help items); Merton P. Strommen and Ram K. Gupta; Search Institute.*

See T2:1029 (1 reference) and P:22 (2 references).

[2668]

ZECO Pure Tone Screening for Children. Ages 3–8; 1972; ZECO; Zenith Hearing Instrument Corporation.* (Availability uncertain; no reply from manufacturer.)

[2669]

Zenith Audiometers. Preschool, grades kgn and over; 1959–73; 3 models; Zenith Hearing Instrument Corporation.* (Availability uncertain; no reply from manufacturer.)

a) ZENITH SPEECH SCREENING AUDIOMETER. Preschool; 1971; for speech tests using programmed cassettes; Model ZA-111.

b) ZENITH PURE TONE SCREENING AUDIOMETER. Grades kgn and over; 1972; for use in schools and industry; for pure tone air conduction testing; optional talkover module; Model ZA-112A.

c) ZENITH DIAGNOSTIC AUDIOMETER. Grades kgn and over; 1961–73; for use in schools, industry, clinics, and physicians' offices; for pure tone air and bone conduction testing with masking; optional speech module for live and recorded testing; Model ZA-113A.

For additional information concerning earlier models, see 6:953. For comments by Louis M. DiCarlo on screening audiometers in general and specific comments on an earlier Zenith portable model and three other portable audiometers, see 6:942.

[2670]
Zimmerman-Sanders Social Studies Test. 1, 2 semesters in grades 7–8; 1962–64; first published 1962–63 in the Every Pupil Scholarship Test series; John J. Zimmerman and M. W. Sanders; Bureau of Educational Measurements.*

For additional information and a review by Mary Friend Adams, see 8:893.

[2671]
★**Zip Scale for Determining Independent Reading Level.** Junior and senior high school; 1979; criterion-referenced test; 3 scores: comprehension (reading, listening), word recognition; Ward Cramer and Suzanne Dorsey; J. Weston Walch.*

[2672]
The Zulliger Individual and Group Test. Ages 3 and over; 1948–69; ZT; formerly called *Z-Test*; Hans Zulliger; English manual edited by Fritz Salomon, translated by Dusya T. Dubrovsky; Hans Huber [Switzerland]. (United States distributor: International Universities Press, Inc.)*

For additional information and excerpted reviews by Margaret Mercer and Bernard I. Murstein, see 7:183 (13 references); for an excerpted review by Boris Semeonoff, see 7:B664.

INDEX OF TITLES

This title index includes a comprehensive listing of tests currently in print and included in this volume as well as out of print (or status unknown) tests which were listed in either The Eighth Mental Measurements Yearbook *or* Tests in Print II. *Numbers without colons refer to in print tests. Numbers with colons refer to out of print tests not listed in this volume; readers interested in these tests are referred to the last volume listing the test. For example, 8:770 refers to test 770 in* The 8th MMY; T2:1354 *refers to test 1354 in* TIP II. *Superseded titles are listed with a cross reference to the present title. Tests which are part of a series are also listed under series titles. All numbers refer to test entries, not to page numbers.*

AAHPER Cooperative Health Education Test, 1
AAHPER Cooperative Physical Education Tests, 2
AAHPER-Kennedy Foundation Special Fitness Test for the Mentally Retarded, 3
AAHPER Sport Skills Tests, 4
AAHPER Youth Fitness Test, 5
AAMD Adaptive Behavior Scale for Children and Adults, 1974 Revision, 6
AAMD-Becker Reading-Free Vocational Interest Inventory, see Reading-Free Vocational Interest Inventory, 1993
AATG National Standardized Testing Program, see National German Examination for High School Students, 1559
ABC Inventory to Determine Kindergarten and School Readiness, 7
A-B-C Vision Test for Ocular Dominance, T2:1905
Abortion Scale, 8
Abstract Reasoning: Differential Aptitude Tests, 9
Abstract Spatial Relations Test, Second Edition, T2:541
AC Test of Creative Ability, 10
Academic Alertness "AA": Individual Placement Series (status unknown), T2:334
Academic Aptitude Test, 11
Academic Aptitude Test: Non-Verbal Intelligence: Acorn National Aptitude Tests, 12
Academic Aptitude Test: Verbal Intelligence: Acorn National Aptitude Tests, 13
Academic Freedom Survey, 14
Academic Proficiency Battery, 15
Academic Promise Tests, T2:1063

Academic Readiness Scale, 16
Academic-Technical Aptitude Tests, 18
Account Clerk Test, T2:2322
A.C.E.R. Advanced Test B40, 19
ACER Advanced Test N, 20
A.C.E.R. Advanced Tests AL and AQ, 21
ACER and University of Melbourne Music Evaluation Kit, 22
A.C.E.R. Arithmetic Tests: Standardized for Use in New Zealand, 23
ACER Checklists for School Beginners, 24
ACER Chemistry Test Item Collection: Year 12 (Chemtic), 25
ACER Class Achievement Test in Mathematics, 26
ACER Early School Series, 27
A.C.E.R. Higher Tests, 28
A.C.E.R. Intermediate Test A, 29
A.C.E.R. Intermediate Tests C and D, 30
A.C.E.R. Junior Non-Verbal Test, 31
A.C.E.R. Junior Test A, 32
ACER Listening Tests: 10-year-olds and 14-year-olds, 33
A.C.E.R. Lower Grades General Ability Scale, Second Edition, 34
A.C.E.R. Lower Grades Reading Test: Level 1, Second Edition, T2:1529
ACER Mathematics Profile Series, 35
ACER Mathematics Tests: AM Series, 36
A.C.E.R. Mechanical Comprehension Test, 37
A.C.E.R. Mechanical Reasoning Test, 38
A.C.E.R. Number Test, 39
ACER Paragraph Reading Test, 40

ACER Physics Unit Tests: Diagnostic Aids, 41
ACER Primary Reading Survey Tests, 42
ACER Short Clerical Test—Form C, 43
A.C.E.R. Silent Reading Tests: Standardized for Use in New Zealand, 44
A.C.E.R. Speed and Accuracy Tests, 45
ACER Spelling Test Years 3–6, 46
ACER Test of Learning Ability, 47
A.C.E.R. Word Knowledge Test—Adult Form B, 48
Achievement Examinations for Secondary Schools: Advanced Algebra, T2:664; Bookkeeping, T2:775; Business Relations and Occupations, T2:779; Chemistry, T2:1834; Elementary Algebra, T2:677; English IX–XII, T2:74; General Mathematics III, T2:617; General Science III, T2:1786; German I and II, T2:268; Latin I and II, T2:294; Modern World History, T2:1997; Physics, T2:1870; Plane Geometry, T2:756; Solid Geometry, T2:758; Spanish I and II, T2:320
Achievement Series: SRA Assessment Survey, see SRA Achievement Series, 2260
Achievement Test—Hebrew Language, 49
Achievement Test in Jewish History, 50
Achievement Test—Jewish Life and Observances, 51
Achievement Test—The State of Israel, 52
Achievement Tests: Grades 1–8, 53
Achievement Tests in Nursing, 54
Achievement Tests in Practical Nursing, 55
Acorn Achievement Tests: Junior High School Mathematics Test, 1230; Primary Reading Test, T2:1578
Acorn National Achievement Tests: Health Education Test, 1066; Social Studies Test, T2:1950; World History Test, T2:2003
Acorn National Aptitude Tests: Academic Aptitude Test: Non-Verbal Intelligence, 12; Academic Aptitude Test: Verbal Intelligence, 13; Clerical Aptitude Test, 464; Inventory of Vocational Interests, 1186; Mechanical Aptitute Test, 1450
ACS Cooperative Examination in Brief Physical Chemistry, T2:1817; Inorganic-Organic-Biological Chemistry (for Paramedical Programs), 8:839
ACS Cooperative Examinations, see ACS Examinations
ACS Examination: Brief Course in Organic Chemistry, 56
ACS Examination in Analytical Chemistry, Graduate Level, 57; Analytical Chemistry (Quantitative Analysis), 58; Biochemistry, 59; Brief Qualitative Analysis, 60; General Chemistry, 61; General Chemistry (Brief Test), 62; General-Organic-Biological Chemistry (for Allied Health Science Programs), 63; Inorganic Chemistry, 64; Inorganic Chemistry, Graduate Level, 65; Instrumental Determinations (Analysis), 66; Organic Chemistry, 67; Organic Chemistry, Graduate Level, 68; Physical Chemistry, 69; Physical Chemistry fo the Life Sciences, 70; Physical Chemistry, Graduate Level, 71; Polymer Chemistry 72; Qualitative Analysis, 73
ACS-NSTA Examination in High School Chemistry, [Advanced Level], 74; [Lower Level], 75
ACT Assessment, see ACT Assessment Program, 76
ACT Assessment Program, 76
ACT Career Planning Program, 77
ACT Evaluation/Survey Service, 78
ACT Guidance Profile, Two-Year College Edition, T2:2167
ACT Mathematics Placement Examination, T2:596
ACT Proficiency Examination in Adult Nursing, 80; Afro-American History, 81; American History, 82; American Literature, 8:62; Anatomy and Physiology, 83; Business Environment and Strategy, 84; Corrective and Remedial Instruction in Reading, 85; Criminal Investigation, 86; Earth Science, 87; Educational Psychology, 88; Freshman English, 89; Fundamentals of Nursing, 90; History of American Education, 91; Introduction to Criminal Justice, 92; Nursing Health Care, 93; Occupational Strategy, Nursing, 94; Philosophy of Education, 8:361; Professional Strategies, Nursing, 95; Psychiatric/Mental Health Nursing, 96; Reading Instruction in the Elementary School, 97; Shakespeare, 98
ACT Proficiency Examination Program, 79
ACT Proficiency Examinations in Accounting, 99; Commonalities in Nursing Care, Areas I and II, 100; Differences in Nursing Care, Areas I and II, 101; Finance, 102; Health, 8:408; Health Restoration, Areas I and II, 103; Health Support, Areas I and II, 104; Management of Human Resources, 105; Marketing, 106; Maternal and Child Nursing, 107; Operations Management, 108
Action-Choice Tests for Competitive Sports Situations, 109
Activities For Assessing Classification Skills, Experimental Edition, 110
Activity Vector Analysis (status unknown), T2:1091
Adaptability Test, 111
Adaptive Functioning Index, 112
Addiction Research Center Inventory, 113
Additional Personality Factor Inventory—2, 114
Aden-Crosthwait Adolescent Psychology Achievement Test, 115
Adjective Checklist, 116
Adjustment and Adaptation Profiles, 117
Adjustment Inventory, 118
Adkins-McBride General Science Test, T2:1777
Administrator Image Questionnaire, 119
Adolescent Alienation Index, 120
Adston Diagnostic Instruments in Elementary School Mathematics: Whole Numbers (status unknown), T2:692
Adult Basic Education Student Survey, T2:2
Adult Basic Learning Examination, 121
Adult Basic Reading Inventory, 8:811
Adult Performance Level Survey, 8:3
Adult Self Expression Scale, 122
Advanced Algebra: Achievement Examinations for Secondary Schools, T2:664
Advanced Mathematics (Including Trigonometry): Minnesota High School Achievement Examinations, 123
Advanced Placement Examination in American History, 125; Biology, 126; Chemistry, 127; English (Composition and Literature), 128; English (Language and Composition), 129; European History, 130; French Language, Level 3, 131; French Literature, Level 3, 132; German, T2:262; German Language, Level 3, 133; German Literature, Level 3, 8:126; History of Art, 134; Latin, Level 3 (Catullus-Horace), 135; Latin, Level 3 (Vergil), 136; Music Listening and Literature, 137; Music Theory, 138; Spanish Language, Level 3, 139; Spanish Literature, Level 3, 140; Studio Art, 141
Advanced Placement Examinations, 124; in Mathematics, 142; in Physics, 143

INDEX OF TITLES

Affect Scale, 144
Affective Domain Descriptor Program, 145
Affective Perception Inventory, 146
African T.A.T., 147
Agribusiness Achievement Test: Content Evaluation Series, 8:319
AH1 Forms X and Y, 148
AH2/AH3, 149
Ahr's Individual Development Survey, 150
Ai3Q: A Measure of Obsessional Personality or Anal Character, 8:494
Albert Mate Selection Check List (status unknown), T2:813
Alberta Essay Scales: Models, 151
Alcadd Test, 152
Algebra, Geometry and Trigonometry Test for Stds 9 and 10, 153
Algebra Readiness Test, T2:665
Algebra Test for Engineering and Science: National Achievement Tests, 154
[Aliferis-Stecklin Music Achievement Tests], 155
Alpha Biographical Inventory, T2:2273
Alphabet Mastery, 156
Alternate Uses, 157
Ambco Audiometers (status unknown), T2:2027
Ambco Speech Test Record (status unknown), T2:2027A
Ambiguous Word Language Dominance Test, Spanish/English, 158
American Automobile Association Driver Testing Apparatus, T2:842
American Council on Education Cumulative Record Folders, T2:1008
American Government: IOX Objectives-Based Tests, 159
American High School Mathematics Examinations, 160
American History-Government-Problems of Democracy: Acorn Achievement Tests, T2:1936
American History: Junior High-Objective, 161; Senior High-Objective, 162
American History Test: National Achievement Tests, T2:1984
American Home Scale, 163
American Institute of Certified Public Accountants Testing Programs, 164
American Literacy Test, 165
American Literature Anthology Tests, 166
American Numerical Test, 167
American Political Behavior Achievement Test, 8:918
American School Achievement Tests: Arithmetic Readiness, 168
American School Achievement Tests, Revised Edition, 169
American School Achievement Tests: Part 4, Social Studies and Science, 170
American School Achievement Tests: Part 1, Reading, Revised Edition, 171
American School Achievement Tests: Part 3, Language and Spelling, Revised Edition, 172
American School Achievement Tests: Part 2, Arithmetic, Revised Edition, 173
American School Intelligence Test, 174
American School Reading Readiness Test, Revised, 175
American School Reading Tests, 176
[American Transit Association Tests], 177
Analysis of Learning Potential, T2:340

Analysis of Readiness Skills: Reading and Mathematics, 178
Analysis of Relationships, 179
Analysis of Skills: Language Arts, 8:41; Mathematics, 8:251; Reading, 8:748
Analytical Survey Test in Computational Arithmetic, 180
Analytical Survey Test in English Fundamentals, T2:53
Animal Crackers: A Test of Motivation to Achieve, 8:497
A/9 Cumulative Record Folder, T2:1007
Ann Arbor Learning Inventory, 181
ANPA Foundation Newspaper Test, 1972 Edition, T2:1735
ANSER System—Aggregate Neurobehavioral Student Health and Educational Review, 182
Anton Brenner Developmental Gestalt Test of School Readiness, 183
Anxiety Scale for the Blind, 184
AO Sight Screener, 185
APELL Test: Assessment Program of Early Learning Levels (status unknown), 8:794
Application Interview Screening Form, 186
Applied Biological and Agribusiness Interest Inventory, 187
Appraisal of Occupational Aptitudes, 8:1032
APT Controlled Interview, T2:2294
APT Dictation Test, T2:2119
APT Manual Dexterity Test, 188
APT Performance Test, T2:332
Aptitude Assessment Battery: Programming, 189
Aptitude Test for Junior Secondary Pupils, T2:1065
Aptitude Tests for Occupations, 190
Aptitude Tests for School Beginners, 191
Aptitudes Associates Test of Sales Aptitude: A Test for Measuring Knowledge of Basic Principles of Selling, 192
A.P.U. Arithmetic Test, 193
A.P.U. Occupational Interests Guide: Intermediate Version, T2:2168
A.P.U. Vocabulary Test, 194
Architectural School Aptitude Test, T2:2359
Arithmetic Computation: Public School Achievement Tests, T2:697
Arithmetic Reasoning: Public School Achievement Tests, T2:698
Arithmetic Reasoning Test: [Personnel Research Institute Clerical Battery], 195
Arithmetic Test (Fundamentals and Reasoning): Municipal Tests: National Achievement Tests, 196
Arithmetic Test: National Achievement Tests, 197
Arithmetic Tests EA2A and EA4, 198
Arithmetical Problems: Test A/68, 199
Arizona Articulation Proficiency Scale: Revised, 200
Arlin-Hills Attitude Surveys, 201
Armed Services Vocational Aptitude Battery, 202
Army Alpha Examination: First Nebraska Revision, T2:341A
Army General Classification Test, First Civilian Edition, T2:342
Art Vocabulary, 203
Arthur Point Scale of Performance Tests, 204
A-S Reaction Study: A Scale for Measuring Ascendance-Submission in Personality, T2:1090
Assessing Reading Difficulties: A diagnostic and remedial approach, 205
Assessment in Mathematics, 206

Assessment in Nursery Education, 207
Assessment of Basic Competencies, 208; Information Processing Module, 209; Language Module, 210; Mathematics Module, 211
Assessment of Career Development, 8:991
Assessment of Children's Language Comprehension, 1973 Revision, 212
Assessment of Coping Style, 213
Assessment of Phonological Processes, 214
Assessment of Qualitative and Structural Dimensions of Object Representations, 215
Assessment of Reading Growth, 216
Assessment of Skills in Computation, 217
Association Adjustment Inventory, 218
Athlete's Affective Response Profile, 219
Athletic Motivation Inventory, 8:409
Atlantic City Eye Test, T2:1907
Attitude-Interest Analysis Test, T2:1101
Attitude Inventory (status unknown), T2:916
Attitude to School Questionnaire, 220
Attitude Toward School, 221
Attitude Toward School K–12, 222
Attitudes Related to Tolerance 9–12, 223
Attitudes to Science Questionnaire, see Science Attitude Questionnaire, 2096
Attitudes Toward Industrialization, T2:1102
Attitudes Toward Mainstreaming Scale, 224
Attitudes Toward Parental Control of Children, 225
Auditory Apperception Test, T2:1446
Auditory Discrimination Test, 226
Auditory Memory Span Test, 227
Auditory Pointing Test, 228
Auditory Sequential Memory Test, 229
Auditory Tests, 230
AULC Interview Rating Form, see Oral Rating Form for Rating Language Proficiency in Speaking and Understanding English, 1738
Austin Spanish Articulation Test, 231
Australian Item Bank, 232
Australian Test for Advanced Music Studies, 233
Autism Screening Instrument for Educational Planning, (First Edition), 234
Automata EDT 1200 Educational Data Terminal (status unknown), T2:1030
Automated Graphogestalt Technique (status unknown), T2:976
Axiometric Test, see Hartman Value Profile, 1062
Ayres Measuring Scale for Handwriting: Gettysburg Edition, T2:908
Ayres Space Test, T2:1104
Babcock Test of Mental Efficiency, T2:1105
BACKS: Basic Achievement of Common Knowledge and Skills (status unknown), 8:422
Baker-Schulberg Community Mental Health Ideology Scale (status unknown), T2:1106
Balthazar Scales of Adaptive Behavior, 235
Baltimore County French Test, 236
Baltimore County Spanish Test, 237
Barber Scales of Self-Regard for Preschool Children, 238
Barclay Classroom Assessment System, 239
Barclay Classroom Climate Inventory, see Barclay Classroom Assessment System, 239
Barclay Early Childhood Skill Assessment Guide, 240
Barclay Learning Needs Assessment Inventory, 241
Barranquilla Rapid Survey Intelligence Test, 8:177

Barrett-Ryan English Test, 242
Barron-Welsh Art Scale: A Portion of the Welsh Figure Preference Test, 243
Barsch Learning Style Inventory, 244
Basic Arithmetic Skill Evaluation, 245
Basic Concept Inventory, Field Research, T2:1697
Basic Economics Test, 246
Basic Educational Skills Inventory, 247; Math, 248; Reading, 249
Basic Educational Skills Test, 250
Basic Fitness Test, T2:917
Basic Inventory of Natural Language, 251
Basic Mathematics Tests, 252
Basic Number Diagnostic Test, 253
Basic Number Screening Test, 254
Basic Proficiency in French Tests, 8:114
Basic Reading Inventory, Second Edition, 255
Basic Reading Rate Scale (status unknown), 8:814
Basic School Skills Inventory, 256
Basic Screen Test-Vision: Measurement of Skill Test 12 (status unknown), T2:1908
Basic Screening and Referral Form for Children With Suspected Learning and Behavioral Disabilities, 257
Basic Sight Word Test, 258
Basic Skills Assessment, 259; Mathematics, 260; Reading, 261; A Writer's Skills, 262; Writing Sample, 263
Basic Skills in Arithmetic Test, 264
Basic Skills Inventory, 265; Language Arts, 266; Mathematics, 267; Reading, 268
Basic Word Vocabulary Test, 269
Bayley Scales of Infant Development, 270
Behavior Analysis Forms for Clinical Intervention, 271
Behavior Rating Instrument for Autistic and Other Atypical Children, 272
Behavior Rating Profile, 273
Behavior Rating Scales, 274
Behavior Status Inventory, 275
Behavioral Academic Self-Esteem, 276
Belmont Measures of Athletic Performance, T2:918
Beltone Audiometers, 277
Belwin-Mills Singing Achievement Test, 8:92
Bem Sex-Role Inventory, 278
Bench Mark Measures, 279
[Bender-Gestalt Test], 280
Bender-Purdue Reflex Test: For Signs of Symmetric Tonic Neck Reflex Immaturity, 281
Bennett Mechanical Comprehension Test, 282
Benton Visual Retention Test, Revised Edition, 283
Ber-Sil Spanish Test, 284
Bernreuter Personality Inventory, see Personality Inventory, 1795
Berry-Talbott Language Test: Comprehension of Grammar, 285
Bessell Measurement of Emotional Maturity Scales, 286
Bible and You (A Test of Factual Knowledge About the Bible), T2:1023
Biblical Survey Test, 287
Bicycle Safety-Performance and Skill Tests, 1962 Revision, T2:843
Biemiller Test of Reading Processes, 288
Bilingual Oral Language Test, 289
Bilingual Syntax Measure, 290
Bilingual Syntax Measure II, 291
Bingham Button Test, 292

INDEX OF TITLES

Binion-Beck Reading Readiness Test for Kindergarten and First Grade, T2:1698
Biographical Index, T2:2274
Biographical Inventory-Creativity, T2:544
Biological Science: Interaction of Experiments and Ideas, Revised Edition (status unknown), T2:1802
Biology: Minnesota High School Achievement Examinations, 293
BIP Bender Test, see Canter Background Interference Procedure for the Bender Gestalt Test, 280h
Bipolar Psychological Inventory, 294
Birth to Three Developmental Scale, 295
BITCH Test (Black Intelligence Test of Cultural Homogeneity), 296
Black History: A Test to Create Awareness and Arouse Interest, 297
Blacky Pictures: A Technique for the Exploration of Personality Dynamics, 298
Blind Learning Aptitude Test, 299
Block-Design Test, see Kohs Block-Design Test, 1265
Bloom Sentence Completion Survey, 300
Blyth Second-Year Algebra Test, Revised Edition, T2:668
Bobbs-Merrill Arithmetic Achievement Tests, 301
Boehm Test of Basic Concepts, 302
Bookkeeping: Achievement Examinations for Secondary Schools, T2:775
Bookkeeping: Minnesota High School Achievement Examinations, 303
Bookkeeping Test: National Business Entrance Tests, 304
Booklet Category Test, 305
Borman-Sanders Elementary Science Test, 306
Borromean Family Index, 307
Boston Diagnostic Aphasia Examination, 308
Botel Reading Inventory, 309
Bowman Chronological Age Calculator, T2:802
Bowman M. A. and I. Q. Kalkulator, T2:803
Bradfield Classroom Interaction Analysis, 310
Brandywine Achievement Test in Geography for Secondary Schools (status unknown), T2:1973
Braverman-Chevigny Auditory Projective Test, T2:1449
Brazelton Behavioral Assessment Scale, see Brazelton Neonatal Assessment Scale, 311
Brazelton Neonatal Assessment Scale, 311
Brenner Gestalt Test, see Anton Brenner Developmental Gestalt Test of School Readiness, 183
Breslich Algebra Survey Test, 312
Brief Survey of Arithmetic Skills, Revised Edition, T2:706
Brigance Diagnostic Inventory of Basic Skills, 313
Brigance Diagnostic Inventory of Early Development, 314
Brigance Diagnostic Inventory of Essential Skills, 315
Brigance K & 1 Screen for Kindergarten and First Grade, 316
Bristol Achievement Tests, 317; English Language, 318; Mathematics, 319; Study Skills, 320
Bristol Social Adjustment Guides, 321
British Ability Scales, 322
Brook Reaction Test, 8:509
Brown-Carlsen Listening Comprehension Test, T2:993
Bruce Vocabulary Inventory, 323
Bruininks-Oseretsky Test of Motor Proficiency, 324
Bryant-Schwan Design Test, Part 1 (status unknown), 8:85

BSCS Achievement Tests, T2:1801
Buckingham Extension of the Ayres Spelling Scale, 325
Buffalo Reading Test for Speed and Comprehension, 326
Burks' Behavior Rating Scale for Organic Brain Dysfunction, 327
Burks' Behavior Rating Scales, 328
Burnett Reading Series: Survey Test, T2:1535
Burnham-Clark-Munsell Color Memory Test, T2:1909
Burt Word Reading Test, New Zealand Revision, 329
Burt Word Reading Test, 1974 Revision, 330
Business English Test: The Daily Vocational Tests, 331
Business Fundamentals and General Information Test: National Business Entrance Tests, 332
Business Judgment Test, Revised, 333
Business Relations and Occupations: Achievement Examinations for Secondary Schools, T2:779
Business Test, 334
Buswell-John Diagnostic Test for Fundamental Processes in Arithmetic, 335
Butler Life Science Concept Test, 336
Buttons: A Projective Test for Pre-Adolescent and Adolescent Boys and Girls, 337
Bzoch-League Receptive-Expressive Emergent Language Scale: For the Measurement of Language Skills in Infancy, 338
C-PAC: Clinical Probes of Articulation Consistency, 339
C-R Opinionaire, 340
C-Scale, see Wilson-Patterson Attitude Inventory, 2629
CAAP Scale, 341
CAHPER Fitness-Performance II Test, 342
Cain-Levine Social Competency Scale, 343
California Achievement Tests, Forms C and D, 344; Language, 8:45; Mathematics, Form C, 345; Reading, Forms C and D, 346; Spelling and Reference Skills, Form C, 347
California Algebra Aptitude Test, T2:671
California Child Q-Set, 348
California Cumulative Record and Health Insert (status unknown), T2:1009
California Life Goals Evaluation Schedules, 349
California Marriage Readiness Evaluation, 350
California Medical Survey, T2:1119
California Occupational Preference System, 351
California Phonics Survey, 352
California Pre-Counseling Self-Analysis Protocol Booklet, T2:2171
California Preschool Social Competency Scale, 353
California Psychological Inventory, 354
[Re California Psychological Inventory] Behaviordyne Psychodiagnostic Laboratory Service, 355
California Q-Set, 356
California Short-Form Test of Mental Maturity, 1963 Revision, 8:179
California Survey Series: Survey of Reading Achievement, T2:1606; Survey Test of Algebraic Aptitude, T2:689
California Test of Mental Maturity, 1963 Revision, T2:349
California Test of Personality, 357
Callahan Anxiety Pictures, 358
Camelot Behavioral Checklist, 359
Canadian Academic Aptitude Test, T2:350
Canadian Achievement Test in English, T2:62; French, T2:242; Mathematics, T2:604; Technical and Commercial Mathematics, T2:605
Canadian Achievement Tests, Form A, 360

Canadian Cognitive Abilities Test, 361
Canadian English Achievement Test, T2:63
Canadian English Language Achievement Test, T2:63A
Canadian Intelligence Test, 1966 Revision, T2:486
Canadian Lorge-Thorndike Intelligence Tests, Multi-Level Edition, 362
Canadian Mathematics Achievement Test, T2:606
Canadian Scholastic Aptitude Test, T2:353
Canadian Test Battery, Grade 10, T2:1046; Grades 8–9, T2:1047
Canadian Tests of Basic Skills, 363
Canfield Time Problems Inventory, 364
CAP Achievement Series, 365
Career Adaptive Behavior Inventory, 366
Career Assessment Inventory, 367
Career Awareness Inventory, 368
Career Counseling Personal Data Form, 369
Career Decision Scale, 370
Career Development Inventory [Consulting Psychologists Press, Inc.], 371
Career Development Inventory [Science Research Associates, Inc.], 372
Career Guidance Inventory, 373
Career Maturity Inventory, 374
Career Planning Program for Grades 8–12, 8:998
Career Skills Assessment Program, 375
Caring Relationship Inventory, 376
Carrow Auditory-Visual Abilities Test, 377
Carrow Elicited Language Inventory, 378
Carver-Darby Chunked Reading Tests (status unknown), T2:1537
Caso Test for Limited English Speaking Students, 379
Cass-Sanders Psychology Test, 380
Cassel Developmental Record, T2:1010
Cassel Group Level of Aspiration Test, T2:1124
Cattell Infant Intelligence Scale, 381
Cattell Intelligence Tests, T2:354
CGA Mental Ability Tests, T2:346
CGP Self-Scoring Placement Tests in English and Mathematics, 382
Change Agent Questionnaire, 383
Chapin Social Insight Test, 384
Characteristics Scale, 385
Chart of Initiative and Independence, 386
Chatterji's Non-Language Preference Record, 387
Checklist/Guide to Selecting a Small Computer, 388
Chemical Operators Selection Test, Revised Edition, 389
Chemistry: Achievement Examinations for Secondary Schools, T2:1834
Chemistry Achievement Test for CHEM Study or Equivalent, T2:1835
Chemistry: Minnesota High School Achievement Examinations, 390
Chicago Non-Verbal Examination, T2:355
Child and Adolescent Adjustment Profile, see CAAP Scale, 341
Child Anxiety Scale, 391
Child Behavior Rating Scale, 392
Child Center Operational Assessment Tool, 393
Child Development Center Q-Sort, 394
Childrens Adaptive Behavior Scale, 395
Children's Apperception Test, 396
Children's Depression Scale, 397
Children's Embedded Figures Test, 398
Children's Hypnotic Susceptibility Scale, 399
Children's Personality Questionnaire, 1975 Edition, 400
ChilDS Test, see Visco Child Development Screening Test, 2559
Christensen-Guilford Fluency Tests, 401
Chriswell Structural Dexterity Test, 402
Chronological Age Computer, 403
C.I.D. Auditory Tests, see Auditory Tests, 230
CIRCUS, 404
Clarke Reading Self-Assessment Survey, 405
Classification and Placement Examination, T2:9
Classification Tasks, Experimental Edition, T2:488
Classification Test Battery, 406
Classroom Atmosphere Questionnaire, 407
Classroom Environment Index, 408
Classroom Environment Scale, 409
Classroom Reading Inventory, Third Edition, 8:749
Cleary-Now Test of Perceptual-Motor Readiness, 410
CLEP General Examinations, 411; English Composition and English Composition Test with Essay, 412; Humanities, 413; Mathematics, 414; Natural Sciences, 415; Social Sciences and History, 416
CLEP Subject Examination in Afro-American History, 417; American Government, 418; American History I: Early Colonizations to 1877, 419; American History II: 1865 to the Present, 420; American Literature, 421; Analysis and Interpretation of Literature, 422; Anatomy, Physiology, Microbiology: North Carolina Nursing Equivalency Examinations, 423; Behavioral Sciences for Nurses: North Carolina Nursing Equivalency Examinations, 424; Calculus with Elementary Functions, 425; Clinical Chemistry, 426; College Algebra, 427; College Algebra-Trigonometry, 428; College Composition, 429; College French Levels 1 and 2, 430; College German, Levels 1 and 2, 431; College Spanish, Levels 1 and 2, 432; Computers and Data Processing, 433; Dental Materials: Dental Auxiliary Education, 434; Educational Psychology, 435; Elementary Computer Programming-Fortran IV, 436; English Literature, 437; Freshman English, 438; Fundamentals of Nursing: North Carolina Nursing Equivalency Examinations, 439; General Biology, 440; General Chemistry, 441; General Psychology, 442; Head, Neck, and Oral Anatomy: Dental Auxiliary Education, 443; Hematology, 444; Human Growth and Development, 445; Immunohematology an Blood Banking, 446; Introduction to Management, 447; Introductory Accounting 448; Introductory Business Law, 449; Introductory Macroeconomics, 450; Introductory Marketing, 451; Introductory Micro- and Macroeconomics, 452; Introductory Microeconomics, 453; Introductory Sociology, 454; Medical-Surgical Nursing: North Carolina Nursing Equivalency Examinations, 455; Microbiology, 456; Money and Banking, 457; Oral Radiography: Dental Auxiliary Education, 458; Statistics, 459; Tooth Morphology and Function: Dental Auxiliary Education, 460; Trigonometry, 461; Western Civilization I: Ancient Near East to 1648, 462; Western Civilization II: 1648 to the Presen 463
Clerical Aptitude Test: Acorn National Aptitude Tests, 464
Clerical Skills Series, 465
Clerical Speed and Accuracy: Differential Aptitude Tests, 466
Clerical Tests, 467
Clerical Tests FG and 2, T2:781A

INDEX OF TITLES

Clerical Tests, Series N, 468
Clerical Tests, Series V, 469
Clerical Worker Examination, 470
Client-Centered Counseling Progress Record (status unknown), T2:1130
Clifton Assessment Procedures for the Elderly, 471
Clinical Analysis Questionnaire, 472
Clinical Behavior Check List and Rating Scale, 473
Clinical Evaluation of Language Functions—Diagnostic Battery, 474
Clinical Evaluation of Language Functions, Elementary and Advanced Screening Tests, 475
Clinical Experience Record for Nursing Students, 476
Closure Flexibility (Concealed Figures), 477
Closure Speed (Gestalt Completion), 478
Cloze Procedure [Ebbinghaus Completion Method] as Applied to Reading, 479
CLS: Classroom Learning Screening, 480
Cluster Analysis of Wechsler/WRAT, 481
Clymer-Barrett Prereading Battery, 482
Cognitive Abilities Test, 483
Cognitive Skills Assessment Battery, Second Edition, 484
Coitometer, 485
College Adjustment and Study Skills Inventory (status unknown), T2:1751
College and University Environment Scales, Second Edition, 486
College Board Achievement Test in American History and Social Studies, 487; Biology, 488; Chemistry, 489; English Composition, 490; European History and World Cultures, 491; French Reading, 492; German Reading, 493; Hebrew, 494; Latin, 495; Literature, 496; Physics, 497; Spanish Reading, 498; Mathematics 499
College Board Admissions Testing Program, 500
College Board Scholastic Aptitude Test and Test of Standard Written English, 501
College Characteristics Index, 502
College English Placement Test, 503
College English Test: National Achievement Tests, 504
College Guidance Program, T2:1049
College Health Knowledge Test, Personal Health, T2:921
College Interest Inventory (status unknown), T2:2174
College Inventory of Academic Adjustment, 505
College Level Examination Program, 506
College Placement Test in American History and Social Studies, 508; Biology, 509; Chemistry, 510; European History and World Cultures, 511; French Listening Comprehension, 512; French Listening-Reading, 513; French Reading 514; German Listening Comprehension, 515; German Listening-Reading, 516; German Reading, 517; Greek Reading, 518; Hebrew Reading, 519; Italian Listening Comprehension, 8:141; Italian Listening-Reading, 520; Italian Reading, 521; Latin Reading, 522; Literature, 523; Physics, 524; Russian Listening Comprehension, 8:148; Russian Listening-Reading, 525; Russian Reading, 526; Spanish Listening Comprehension, 527; Spanish Listening-Reading, 528; Spanish Reading, 529; Spatial Relations, 8:1041
College Placement Tests, 507; in English Composition, 530; in Mathematics, 531
College Qualification Tests, T2:358
College Student Experiences, 532
College Student Questionnaires, 8:524

College Student Satisfaction Questionnaire (status unknown), 8:524A
Colleges of Podiatry Admission Test, T2:2354
Color-matching Aptitude Test, 1978 Edition, 533
Color Pyramid Test, T2:1452
Colorado Braille Battery: Literary Code Tests, T2:769; Nemeth Code Tests, T2:770
Columbia Mental Maturity Scale, Third Edition, 534
Columbus: Picture Analysis of Growth Towards Maturity, 535
Combination Inventory, Form 2, T2:2396
Commerce Reading Comprehension Test, 536
Commercial Tests, 537
Communication Screen, 538
Communication Sensitivity Inventory, 539
Communicative Evaluation Chart From Infancy to Five Years, 540
Community Adaptation Schedule (status unknown), T2:1137
Community Improvement Scale, T2:1138
Community Living Observational System, 541
Community Oriented Programs Environment Scale, 542
Comparative Guidance and Placement Program, 543
Complex Figure Test, 544
Comprehension of Oral Language, 545
Comprehension Test for College of Education Students, 546
Comprehensive Ability Battery, 547
Comprehensive Career Assessment Scale, 8:999
Comprehensive Developmental Evaluation Chart, 548
Comprehensive English Language Test for Speakers of English as a Second Language, 549
Comprehensive Identification Process, 550
Comprehensive Primary Reading Scales, T2:1540
Comprehensive Reading Scales, T2:1541
Comprehensive Teaching and Training Evaluation, T2:856
Comprehensive Tests of Basic Skills, [Forms U & V], 551; Language, T2:68; Mathematics, [Forms U & V], 552; Reading, [Forms U & V], 553; Science and Social Studies, Third Edition, 554; Study Skills, T2:1752
Compton Fabric Preference Test, T2:948
Computation Test A/67, 555
Computer Operator Aptitude Battery, 556
Computer Programmer Aptitude Battery, 557
Comrey Personality Scales, 558
Concept Assessment Kit—Conservation, 559
Concept Attainment Test, 560
Concept Formation: The Assessment and Remediation of Concept Deficit in the Young Child, 561
Concept Mastery Test, T2:359
Concept-Specific Anxiety Scale, 562
Conceptual Systems Test, 563
Concise Word Reading Tests, 564
Concordia Bible Information Inventory, T2:1025
Conference Evaluation, T2:2276
Conference Meeting Rating Scale, T2:2277
Conflict Management Survey, 565
Connolly Occupational Interests Questionnaire, T2:2175
Consequences [National Institute for Personnel Research], T2:552
Consequences [Sheridan Psychological Services, Inc.], 566
Contemporary School Readiness Test (status unknown), T2:1700
Content Evaluation Series: Agribusiness Achievement

Test, 8:319; Language Arts Tests, 1279; Mathematics Test, 1414; Modern Algebra Test, 1524; Modern Economics Test, 1525; Modern Geometry Test, 1526; Office Information and Skills Test, 1675; Science Tests, 2098
Content Inventories: English, Social Studies, Science, 567
Continuing Education Assessment Inventory, 568
Continuous Letter Checking and Continuous Symbol Checking, T2:2278
Cooper-McGuire Diagnostic Word-Analysis Test, 569
Cooperative Academic Ability Test, T2:360
Cooperative Biology Test: Educational Records Bureau Edition, T2:1807
Cooperative Chemistry Test: Educational Records Bureau Edition, T2:1839
Cooperative English Tests, 570; Reading Comprehension, 1991; English Expression, 571
Cooperative French Listening Comprehension Test, T2:248
Cooperative Industrial Arts Tests: Electricity/Electronics, T2:968; General Industrial Arts, T2:970; Woods, T2:975
Cooperative Institutional Research Program, 572
Cooperative Latin Test: Elementary and Advanced Levels, T2:291
Cooperative Literature Tests, T2:132
Cooperative Mathematics Tests: Algebra I and II, 573; Algebra III, 574; Analytic Geometry, 575; Arithmetic, 576; Calculus, 577; Geometry, 578; Structure of the Number System, 579; Trigonometry, 580
Cooperative Physics Test: Educational Records Bureau Edition, T2:1861
Cooperative Preschool Inventory, Revised Edition, 581
Cooperative Primary Tests, 582; Listening, 583; Mathematics, 584; Reading, 585; Word Analysis, 586; Writing Skills, 587
Cooperative Reading Comprehension Test, Form Y, 588; Forms L and M, 589
Cooperative School and College Ability Tests, Series II, 590
Cooperative Science Tests: Advanced General Science, 591; Biology, 592; Chemistry, 593; General Science, 594; Physics, 595
Cooperative Social Studies Tests: American Government, 596; American History, 597; Civics, 598; Modern European History, 599; Problems of Democracy, 600; World History, 601
Cooperative Topical Tests in American History, 602
Coopersmith Self-Esteem Inventories, 603
COPE Coping Operations Preference Enquiry, 890e
COPSystem and COPSystem Inventory, see California Occupational Preference System, 351
Cornell Class-Reasoning Test, 604
Cornell Conditional-Reasoning Test, 605
Cornell Critical Thinking Tests, 606
Cornell Index, T2:1144
Cornell Inventory for Student Appraisal of Teaching and Courses, 607
Cornell Learning and Study Skills Inventory, 608
Cornell Medical Index—Health Questionnaire, 609
Cornell Word Form 2, 610
Correct Spelling, 611
Correctional Institutions Environment Scale, 612
Correctional Policy Inventory: A Survey of Correctional Philosophy and Characteristic Methods of Dealing with Offenders, 613
Corrective Reading Mastery Tests, 614
Cosmetology Student Admissions Examination, 615
Cotswold Junior Ability Tests, 616
Cotswold Junior Arithmetic Ability Test, T2:710
Cotswold Junior English Ability Test, T2:71
Cotswold Measurement of Ability, T2:363; Arithmetic, T2:711; English, T2:72
Cotswold Personality Assessment P.A.1, 617
Counseling Services Assessment Blank, 618
Counselor Rating Scales (Short Form), 619
Course Evaluation Questionnaire, 620
Course-Faculty Instrument, 621
Courtship Analysis, 622
[Cox Mechanical and Manual Tests], 623
CPH Patient Attitude Scale, 624
C.P. 66 Test, T2:347
Crane Oral Dominance Test: Spanish/English, 625
Crary American History Test, Revised Edition, T2:1992
Crawford Psychological Adjustment Scale, 626
Crawford Small Parts Dexterity Test, 627
Creativity Attitude Survey, 628
Creativity Checklist, 629
Creativity Tests for Children, 630
Cree Questionnaire, 631
Crichton Vocabulary Scale, 632
Crissey Dexterity Test, 633
Criterion Reading: Individualized Learning Management System, 634
Criterion Test of Basic Skills, 635
Croft Readiness Assessment in Comprehension Kit, 636
Cross Reference Test, 637
Crowley Occupational Interests Blank, 638
Crown-Crisp Experiential Index, 639
CSMS Number Operations, 640
CSMS Science Reasoning Tasks, 641
CTBS Readiness Test, 642
Cultural Attitude Inventories, 8:532
Cultural Attitude Scales, 8:533
Culture Fair Intelligence Test, 643
Culture-Free Self-Esteem Inventories for Children and Adults, 644
Cumulative Reading Record, 1956 Revision, T2:1659
Current and Past Psychopathology Scales, 645
Current News Test, 646
Curtis Completion Form, 647
Curtis Interest Scale, 648
[Curtis Object Completion and Space Form Tests], 649
Curtis Verbal-Clerical Skills Tests, 650
Cutrona Child Study Profile of Psycho-Educational Abilities, 651
Cutrona Reading Inventory, 652
D-K Scale of Lateral Dominance, 653
Dailey Vocational Tests, 654; Business English Test, 331; Spatial Visualization Test, T2:2270; Technical and Scholastic Test, 2406
[Daily Behavior System], 655
D.A.L.E. System: Developmental Assessment of Life Experiences, 656
Damron Reading/Language Kit, 657
DAT Career Planning Program, 658
Dating Problems Checklist, 659
Dating Scale, 660
Davis Reading Test, T2:1546

INDEX OF TITLES

Decimal Currency Test, T2:760
Decoding Inventory, 661
Decorations, 662
Deductive Reasoning Test, 663
Deep Test of Articulation, 664
Deeside Non-Verbal Reasoning Test: English-Welsh Bilingual Version, T2:367
Deeside Picture Puzzles, T2:368
Defense Mechanism Inventory, 665
Defining Issues Test, 666
Degrees of Reading Power, 667
Del Rio Language Screening Test, 668
Delaware County Silent Reading Test, Second Edition, 669
Delco Readiness Test, T2:1701
Demos D Scale: An Attitude Scale for the Identification of Dropouts, 670
Demos Dropout Scale, see Demos D Scale: An Attitude Scale for the Identification of Dropouts, 670
Dennis Test of Child Development, 671
Dennis Test of Scholastic Aptitude, 672
Dennis Visual Perception Scale, T2:1910
Dental Admission Testing Program, 673
Dental Hygiene Aptitude Testing Program, 674
Denver Articulation Screening Exam, 675
Denver Audiometric Screening Test, 676
Denver Community Mental Health Questionnaire-Revised, 677
Denver Developmental Screening Test, 678
Denver Eye Screening Test, 679
Denver Prescreening Developmental Questionnaire, 680
Denver Public Schools Reading Inventory (status unknown), T2:1621
Depression Adjective Check Lists, 681
Depressive Experience Questionniare, 682
Derogatis Sexual Functioning Inventory, 683
Description of Body Scale, 684
Descriptive Tests of Language Skills, 685
Descriptive Tests of Mathematics Skills, 686
Design for Math, 687
Detroit Adjustment Inventory, T2:1155
Detroit Clerical Aptitudes Examination, 688
Detroit General Aptitudes Examination, 689
Detroit General Intelligence Examination, T2:370
Detroit Mechanical Aptitudes Examination, Revised, 690
Detroit Retail Selling Inventory, T2:2397
Detroit Tests of Learning Aptitude, 691
Developing Cognitive Abilities Test, 692
Developmental Activities Screening Inventory, 693
Developmental Assessment for the Severely Handicapped, 694
Developmental Checklist, 695
Developmental Indicators for the Assessment of Learning, 696
Developmental Potential of Preschool Children, 697
Developmental Profile II, 698
Developmental Task Analysis, 699
Developmental Tasks for Kindergarten Readiness, 700
Developmental Test of Visual-Motor Integration, 701
Developmental Test of Visual Perception, see Marianne Frostig Developmental Test of Visual Perception, Third Edition, 1371
Devereux Adolescent Behavior Rating Scale, 702
Devereux Child Behavior Rating Scale, 703
Devereux Elementary School Behavior Rating Scale, 704

Devereux Test of Extremity Coordination, 705
DF Opinion Survey, 706
D48 Test, 707
Diagnosing Abilities in Math, 708
Diagnosis: An Instructional Aid: Mathematics, Levels A and B, 709
Diagnosis: An Instructional Aid: Reading, 710
Diagnostic Analysis of Reading Errors, 711
Diagnostic Analysis of Reading Tasks, 712
Diagnostic Arithmetic Tests, T2:712
Diagnostic Chart for Fundamental Processes in Arithmetic, 713
Diagnostic Decimal Tests, 714
Diagnostic Examination of Silent Reading Abilities, T2:1622
Diagnostic Fractions Test 3, 715
Diagnostic Math Test (status unknown), 8:304
Diagnostic Mathematics Inventory, 716
Diagnostic Number Tests 1-2, 717
Diagnostic Reading Inventory, 718
Diagnostic Reading Scales, 719
Diagnostic Reading Test: Pupil Progress Series, T2:1625
Diagnostic Reading Tests, 720
Diagnostic Screening Test: Achievement, 721; Language, Second Edition, 722; Math, Third Edition, 723; Reading, Third Edition, 724; Spelling, Third Edition, 725
Diagnostic Skills Battery, 726
Diagnostic Teacher-Rating Scale, 727
Diagnostic Test for Students of English as a Second Language, 728
Diagnostic Test in Basic Algebra, T2:674
Diagnostic Test in Mathematics-Level 1, 8:266
Diagnostic Test of Speechreading, 729
Diagnostic Tests and Self-Helps in Arithmetic, T2:717
Diagnostic Word Patterns Tests, 730
Diebold Personnel Tests, 731
Differential Aptitude Tests (Forms V and W), 732; Abstract Reasoning, 9; Clerical Speed and Accuracy, 466; Language Usage, 1288; Mechanical Reasoning, 1456; Numerical Ability, 1653; Space Relations, 2246; Spelling, 2254; Verbal Reasoning, 2554
Differential Test Battery, 733
Dimensions of Self-Concept, 734
Dimock L Inventory, 735
Diplomacy Test of Empathy, 736
Discharge Readiness Inventory (status unknown), T2:1161
Distar Mastery Tests, 737; Arithmetic I, 738; Arithmetic II, 739; Language I, 740; Language II, 741; Reading I, 742; Reading II, 743
Do I Know How to Apply For a Job?, 744
Dole Vocational Sentence Completion Blank, 745
Domain Phonic Tests, 746
Dominion Table for Converting Mental Age to I.Q., T2:805
Dominion Tests: Group Test of Learning Capacity, T2:387; Group Test of Reading Readiness, T2:1704; Survey Tests of Arithmetic Fundamentals, T2:739
Doppelt Mathematical Reasoning Test, 747
Doren Diagnostic Reading Test of Word Recognition Skills, 1973 Edition, 748
Dos Amigos Verbal Language Scales, 749
Draw-A-Man Test for Indian Children, 750
Draw-A-Person, 751

Draw-A-Person Quality Scale, 752
Drawing: Cooperative Industrial Arts Tests, T2:967
Driscoll Play Kit, T2:1457
Driver Attitude Survey, 753
[Driver Selection Forms and Tests], 754
Driving Skill Exercises, T2:845
Drug Abuse Knowledge Test, 755
Drug Knowledge Inventory, Experimental Edition, T2:923
Drumcondra Attainment Tests, 756
DTLS Logical Relationships Test, 757
DTLS Reading Comprehension Test, 758
DTLS Sentence Structure Test, 759
DTLS Usage Test, 760
DTLS Vocabulary Test, 761
DTMS Arithmetic Skills Test, 762
DTMS Elementary Algebra Test, 763
DTMS Functions and Graphs Test, 764
DTMS Intermediate Algebra Test, 765
Dubins Earth Science Test, T2:1853
Dunning-Abeles Physics Test, T2:1863
Durrell Analysis of Reading Difficulty, Third Edition, 766
Durrell Listening-Reading Series, T2:1660
Durrell-Sullivan Reading Capacity and Achievement Tests, T2:1661
Dvorine Color Vision Test, see Dvorine Pseudo-Isochromatic Plates, 767
Dvorine Pseudo-Isochromatic Plates, 767
Dyadic Parent-Child Interaction Coding System: A Manual, 768
Dynamic Personality Inventory, 769
Dyslexia Schedule, 770
Early Childhood Environment Rating Scale, 771
Early School Personality Questionnaire, 772
Eckstein Audiometers, 773
Economic Geography: Achievement Examinations for Secondary Schools, T2:1974
[Economics/Objective Tests], 774
Edinburgh Articulation Test, see Ingram Edinburgh Articulation Test, 1153
Edinburgh Reading Tests, 775
Education Apperception Test, 776
Educational Goal Attainment Tests, 777
Educational Interest Inventory, Revised Edition, 778
Educational Skills Tests: College Edition, 8:17; English, College Edition, 8:51; Mathematics, College Edition, 8:268
Educational Values Assessment Questionnaire, 779
Edwards Personal Preference Schedule, 780
Edwards Personality Inventory, T2:1165
Effective Study Test, 781
Effectiveness Motivation Scale, 782
Ego Development Scale, 8:543
Ego-Ideal and Conscience Development Test, 783
Ego State Inventory, 784
Ego Strength Q-Sort Test, 785
Eidetic Parents Test, 786
Eight State Questionnaire, 787
Ekwall Reading Inventory, 788
El Circo, 789
El Senoussi Multiphasic Marital Inventory, 8:336
Electrical Sophistication Test, 790
Electricity/Electronics: Cooperative Industrial Arts Tests, T2:968

Elementary Algebra: Achievement Examinations for Secondary Schools, T2:677
Elementary Algebra: Minnesota High School Achievement Examinations, 791
Elementary Rhythm and Pitch Test: For Selecting Band and Orchestra Members in Grades Four to Eight, T2:196
Elementary Science Test: National Achievement Tests, T2:1782
Eliot-Price Perspective Test, 792
Elizur Test of Psycho-Organicity: Children and Adults, 793
Embedded Figures Test, 794
Emo Questionnaire, 795
Emotions Profile Index, 796
Empathy Inventory, 797
Empathy Test, 798
Employee Aptitude Survey, 799
Employee Competency Scale, T2:2297
Employee Evaluation Form for Interviewers, T2:2298
Employee Performance Appraisal, 800
Employee Progress Appraisal Form, 801
[Employee Rating and Development Forms], 802
Emporia American History Test, 803
Emporia Arithmetic Tests, 804
Emporia Biology Test, 805
Emporia Chemistry Test, 806
Emporia Clothing Test, 807
Emporia Elementary Health Test, 808
Emporia First Year Latin Test, 809
Emporia Foods Test, 810
Emporia General Science Test, 811
Emporia High School Health Test, 812
Emporia Industrial Arts Test, 813
Emporia Physics Test, 814
Emporia Reading Test, 815
Emporia Second Year Latin Test, 816
Emporia State Algebra II Test, 817
Endeavor Instructional Rating System, 818
Engineer Performance Description Form, 819
Engineering Aide Test, T2:2341
English Knowledge and Comprehension Test, 820
English Language Achievement Test, see Test A/65, 2415
English Language Skills Assessment in a Reading Context, 821
English Literature Anthology Tests, 822
English IX–XII: Achievement Examinations for Secondary Schools, T2:74
English Picture Vocabulary Test, 823
English Placement Test, 824
English Progress Tests, 825
English Test F3, 826
English Test: Municipal Tests: National Achievement Tests, 827
English Test: National Achievement Tests, 828
English Tests for Outside Reading, 829
English Usage Test for Non-Native Speakers of English, 830
Entrance Examination for Schools of Nursing, 831
Entrance Examination for Schools of Practical/Vocational Nursing, 832
Entrance Level Firefighter, 833
Environmental Language Inventory, 834
Environmental Participation Index, 835

INDEX OF TITLES

Environmental Prelanguage Battery, 836
Environmental Response Inventory, 837
ERB Comprehensive Testing Program II, 838
ERB Modern Arithmetic Test, T2:718
ERB Modern Elementary Algebra Test, T2:165
ERB Modern Mathematics Test, T2:616
ERB Modern Second Year Algebra Test, 839
Erotometer: A Technique for the Measurement of Heterosexual Love, 840
E.S. Survey, 841
Essential Intelligence Test, 842
Essential Mathematics, 843
Essentials of English Tests, Revised Edition, 844
Estes Attitude Scales: Measures of Attitudes Toward School Subjects, 845
ETSA Tests, 846
Evaluation Aptitude Test, 847
Evaluation Disposition Toward the Environment, 848
Evaluation Modality Test, 849
Evaluation Record, T2:2398
Evanston Early Identification Scale, Field Research Edition, 850
Everyday Skills Tests, 851
Examination in Structure (English as a Foreign Language), 8:103
Examining for Aphasia, Revised Edition, 852
Executive Employment Review (status unknown), T2:374
[Executive, Industrial, and Sales Personnel Forms], 853
Executive Profile Survey, 854
Experiential World Inventory, 855
Expressional Growth Through Handwriting Evaluation Scale, 856
Expressive One-Word Picture Vocabulary Test, 857
Eyberg Child Behavior Inventory, 858
Eysenck Personality Inventory, 859
Eysenck Personality Questionnaire, 860
Eysenck-Withers Personality Inventory (For I.Q. 50-80 Range), 861
Facial Interpersonal Perception Inventory, 862
Factorial Interest Blank, 863
Faculty Morale Scale for Institutional Improvement, 864
Fairview Development Scale: For the Infirm Mentally Retarded, 865
Fairview Language Evaluation Scale, 866
Fairview Problem Behavior Record, 867
Fairview Self-Help Scale, 868
Fairview Social Skills Scale: For Mildly and Moderately Retarded, 869
Familism Scale, 870
Family Adjustment Test, 871
Family Environment Scale, 872
Family Pre-Counseling Inventory, 873
Family Relations Indicator, Revised Edition, T2:1459
Family Relations Test, 874
Family Violence Scale, 875
Famous Sayings, 876
Farnsworth Dichotomous Test for Color Blindness: Panel D-15, 877
Farnsworth-Munsell 100-Hue Test for the Examination of Color Discrimination, 878
Farnum Music Test, 879
Farnum String Scale: A Performance Scale for All String Instruments, 880
Fast Tyson Health Knowledge Test, 881
Fatigue Scales Kit, T2:1184
F.A.T.S.A. Test (Flowers Auditory Test of Selective Attention), 882
Fear Survey Schedule, 883
Fels Parent Behavior Rating Scales, 884
Field Work Performance Report, 885
Fiesenheiser Test of Ability to Read Drawings, T2:2416
Figure Classification Test, 886
Figure Reasoning Test: A Non-Verbal Intelligence Test, Second Edition, T2:375
Fire Promotion Tests, 887
Firefighter Test: B-2(m), 888
Fireman Examination, 889
FIRO Awareness Scales, 890
FIRO-B Fundamental Interpersonal Relations Orientation-Behavior, 890a
FIRO-BC, 890b
FIRO-F Fundamental Interpersonal Relations Orientation-Feelings, 890c
First Grade Screening Test, 891
First Year Algebra Test: National Achievement Tests, 892
First Year Arabic Final Examination, 1972 Edition, 893
First Year French Test, 894
First Year Spanish Test, 895
Fisher-Logemann Test of Articulation Competence, 896
Five Task Test: A Performance and Projective Test of Emotionality, Motor Skill and Organic Brain Damage, 897
Flags: A Test of Space Thinking, 898
Flanagan Aptitude Classification Tests, 899
Flanagan Industrial Tests, 900
Flash-X Sight Vocabulary Test, T2:1678
Flexibility Language Dominance Test, Spanish/English, 901
Flint Infant Security Scale, 902
Florida Cumulative Guidance Record, Revised, 903
Florida International Diagnostic-Prescriptive Vocational Competency Profile, 904
Flowers-Costello Tests of Central Auditory Abilities, 905
Fluharty Preschool Speech and Language Screening Test, 906
Ford-Hicks French Grammar Completion Tests, 907
Forer Structured Sentence Completion Test, 908
Forer Vocational Survey, 909
Form Perception Test, T2:2246
Form Relations Group Test, 910
Forms From Diagnostic Methods in Speech Pathology, 911
Forty-Eight Item Counseling Evaluation Test, 912
Fountain Valley Teacher Support System in Mathematics, 913; Reading, 914; Secondary Reading, 915
Four Tone Screening for Older Children and Adults, 916
Franck Drawing Completion Test, 917
Freeman Anxiety Neurosis and Psychosomatic Test, T2:1188
French Comprehension Tests, 918
Frost-Safran School Situations Test, 919
Frost Self Description Questionnaire, 920
Frost Self Description Questionnaire: Extended Scales, 921
Frostig Developmental Test of Visual Perception, see Marianne Frostig Developmental Test of Visual Perception, Third Edition, 1371

Frostig Movement Skills Test Battery, Experimental Edition, 922
Full-Range Picture Vocabulary Test, 923
Fullerton Language Test for Adolescents, Experimental Edition, 924
Functional Communication Profile, 925
Functional Grammar Test, 926
Fundamental Achievement Series, T2:376
Furness Test of Aural Comprehension in Spanish, 927
G-F-W Battery, see Goldman-Fristoe-Woodcock Auditory Skills Test Battery, 961
GAP Reading Comprehension Test, 928
GAPADOL, 929
Gardner Analysis of Personality Survey, 8:564
Garnett College Test in Engineering/Science, 930
Gates Associative Learning Tests, 931
Gates-MacGinitie Reading Tests, 932
Gates-MacGinitie Reading Tests, Canadian Edition, 933
Gates-MacGinitie Reading Tests: Readiness Skills, T2:1702
Gates-MacGinitie Reading Tests: Survey F, 934
Gates-McKillop-Horowitz Reading Diagnostic Tests, Second Edition, 935
Gates-McKillop Reading Diagnostic Tests, see Gates-McKillop-Horowitz Reading Diagnostic Tests, Second Edition, 935
G.C. Anecdotal Record Form, 936
Geist Picture Interest Inventory, 937
Geist Picture Interest Inventory: Deaf Form, T2:2181
General Biology Test: National Achievement Tests, T2:1810
General Chemistry Test: National Achievement Tests, 938
General Clerical Ability Test: ETSA Test 3A, 939
General Clerical Test, 940
General Health Questionnaire, 941
General Industrial Arts: Cooperative Industrial Arts Tests, T2:970
General Mathematics III: Achievement Examinations for Secondary Schools, T2:617
General Mental Ability Test: ETSA Test 1A, 942
General Municipal Employees Performance (Efficiency) Rating System, 943
General Office Clerical Test: National Business Entrance Tests, 944
General Physics Test: National Achievement Tests, 945
General Science Test, 946
General Science Test: National Achievement Tests, 947
General Science III: Achievement Examinations for Secondary Schools, T2:1786
General Test on Traffic and Driving Knowledge, T2:846
General Tests of Language and Arithmetic, T2:14
General Tests of Language and Arithmetic for Students, T2:862
Geography Test: Municipal Tests: National Achievement Tests, T2:1975
Geography Test: National Achievement Tests, T2:1976
Geometry (Including Plane and Solid Geometry): Minnesota High School Achievement Examinations, 948
Geometry Test for Stds 9 and 10, 8:310
George Washington University Series: Interest Inventory for Elementary Grades, 1165; Social Intelligence Test, 2228; Teaching Aptitude Test, 2403; Test for Ability to Sell, 2418
George Washington University Series Nursing Tests, 949
German I and II: Achievement Examinations for Secondary Schools, T2:268
Gerontological Apperception Test, 950
Gesell Developmental Schedules, 1940 Series, T2:497
Gesell Developmental Tests, see Gesell School Readiness Test, 953
Gesell Preschool Test, 952
Gesell School Readiness Test, 953
Getting Along, 954
Gibson Spiral Maze, 955
Gifted and Talented Screening Form, 956
Gilliland Learning Potential Examination (status unknown), T2:380
Gillingham-Childs Phonics Proficiency Scales, 957
Gilmore Oral Reading Test, 958
Gochnour Idiom Screening Test: An English Idiom Comprehension Test for the Deaf, 959
Goldman-Fristoe Test of Articulation, 960
Goldman-Fristoe-Woodcock Auditory Skills Test Battery, 961
Goldman-Fristoe-Woodcock Test of Auditory Discrimination, 962
Goldstein-Scheerer Tests of Abstract and Concrete Thinking, 963
Goodenough-Harris Drawing Test, 964
Gordon Occupational Check List, 965
Gordon Personal Inventory, see Gordon Personal Profile—Inventory, 966
Gordon Personal Profile, see Gordon Personal Profile—Inventory, 966
Gordon Personal Profile-Inventory, 966
Gottesfeld Community Mental Health Critical Issues Test, 967
Gottschaldt Figures [National Institute for Personnel Research], 968
Gottschalk-Gleser Content Analysis Scales, 969
[Government/Objective Tests], 970
Goyer Organization of Ideas Test, 971
Grade Averaging Charts (status unknown), T2:806
Graded Arithmetic-Mathematics Test, 972
Graded Word Reading Test, T2:1680
Graduate Management Admission Test, 973
Graduate Record Examinations Advanced Chemistry Test, 974; Computer Science Test, 975; Economics Test, 976; Education Test, 977; Engineering Test, 978; French Test, 979; (General) Biology Test, 980; Geography Test, 981; Geology Test, 982; German Test, 983; History Test, 984; Literature in English Test, 985; Mathematics Test, 986; Music Test, 987; Philosophy Test, 988; Physics Test, 989; Political Science Test, 990; Psychology Test, 991; Sociology Test, 992; Spanish Test, 993
Graduate Record Examinations: Aptitude and Advanced, 994
Graduate Record Examinations Aptitude Test, 995
Graduate Record Examinations: National Program for Graduate School Selection, see Graduate Record Examinations: Aptitude and Advanced, 994
Graduate School Foreign Language Testing Program, 996
Graduate School Foreign Language Test: French, 997; German, 998; Russian, 999; Spanish, 1000
Grammar and Usage Test Series, 1001
Grammar, Usage, and Structure Test and Vocabulary Test, T2:84

INDEX OF TITLES

Graphoscopic Scale: A Projective Psychodiagnostic Method, 1002
Grason-Stadler Audiometers, 1003
Grassi Basic Cognitive Evaluation, 1004
Grassi Block Substitution Test: For Measuring Organic Brain Pathology, 1005
Graves Design Judgment Test, T2:185
Gravidometer, 1006
Gray Oral Reading Test, 1007
Gray-Votaw-Rogers General Achievement Tests, T2:15
Grayson Perceptualization Test, T2:1197
Gregory Academic Interest Inventory, T2:2183
Gretsch-Tilson Musical Aptitude Test, 1008
Grid Test of Schizophrenic Thought Disorder, 1009
Group Cohesiveness: A Study of Group Morale, 1010
Group Diagnostic Reading Aptitude and Achievement Tests, 1011
Group Diagnostic Spelling Test, 1012
Group Dimensions Descriptions Questionnaire, T2:1200
Group Embedded Figures Test, 1013
Group Encounter Survey, 1014
Group Environment Scale, 1015
Group Inventory for Finding Creative Talent, 1016
Group Inventory For Finding Interests, 1017
Group Literacy Assessment, 1018
Group Mathematics Test, Second Edition, 1019
Group Personality Projective Test, 1020
Group Phonics Analysis, 1021
Group Projection Sketches for the Study of Small Groups, 1022
Group Psychotherapy Suitability Evaluation Scale, 1023
Group Reading Assessment, 1024
Group Reading Test, Second Edition, 1025
Group Test for Indian South Africans, 1026
Group Test of Learning Capacity: Dominion Tests, T2:387
Group Test of Reading Readiness: Dominion Tests, T2:1704
Group Test 20, 1027
Group Test 36, 1028
Group Test 75, 1029
Group Test 80A, 1030
Group Test 81, 1031
Group Test 82, 1032
Group Test 91, 1033
Group Test 95, 1034
Group Tests 61A, 64, and 66A, 1035
Group Tests 70 and 70B, 1036
Group Tests 72 and 73, 1037
Group Tests 90A and 90B, 1038
[Guidance Cumulative Folder and Record Forms], 1039
Guidance Inventory, 1040
Guidance Test Battery for Secondary Pupils (Standard 8), 1041
Guilford-Holley L Inventory, 1042
Guilford-Martin Inventory of Factors GAMIN, Abridged Edition, T2:1205
Guilford-Martin Personnel Inventory, T2:1206
Guilford-Shneidman-Zimmerman Interest Survey, 1043
Guilford-Zimmerman Aptitude Survey, 1044
Guilford-Zimmerman Interest Inventory, 1045
Guilford-Zimmerman Temperament Survey, 1046
Gullo Workshop and Seminar Evaluation, T2:2280
Guy's Colour Vision Test for Young Children, T2:1914
H-T-P: House-Tree-Person Projective Technique, 1047

Hackman-Gaither Vocational Interest Inventory: Standard Edition, 1048
Hahn Self Psychoevaluation Materials, T2:1208
Hahnemann Elementary School Behavior Rating Scale, 1049
Hahnemann High School Behavior Rating Scale, 1050
Hall Occupational Orientation Inventory, 1051
Hall Salespower Inventory (status unknown), T2:2399
Halstead Aphasia Test, 8:963
Halstead-Reitan Neuropsychological Test Battery, 1052
Hand Test, 1053
Hand-Tool Dexterity Test, 1054
Handicap Problems Inventory, 1055
Hanes Sales Selection Inventory, Revised Edition, T2:2400
Hankes Scoring Service (status unknown), T2:1031
Hannaford Industrial Safety Attitude Scales, 1056
Haptic Intelligence Scale for Adult Blind (status unknown), T2:498
Harding Skyscraper, 1057
Harding Stress-Fair Compatibility, 1058
Harrington-O'Shea Career Decision-Making System, 1059
Harris Tests of Lateral Dominance, 1060
Harrison-Stroud Reading Readiness Profiles, 1061
Hartman Value Profile, 1062
Harvard Group Scale of Hypnotic Susceptibility, 1063
Harvard-MLA Tests of Chinese Language Proficiency, T2:225
Hay Aptitude Test Battery, 1064
Health and Safety Education Test: National Achievement Tests, 1065
Health Behavior Inventory, T2:927
Health Education Test: Knowledge and Application: Acorn National Achievement Tests, Revised Edition, 1066
Health Knowledge Test for College Freshmen: National Achievement Tests, 1067
Health Test: National Achievement Tests, 1068
Healy Pictorial Completion Tests, 1069
Hearing Measurement Scale, 1070
[Hearing of Speech Tests], 1071
Height Weight Interpretation Folders, T2:1014
Hellenic Affiliation Scale: An Inventory of Student Behavior and Beliefs for Use by School Personnel, Experimental Form, 1072
Henderson Analysis of Interest, (Second Edition) (status unknown), T2:2188
Henmon-Nelson Tests of Mental Ability, 1073
Henshaw Secondary Mathematics Test, 1074
Hess School Readiness Scale, 1075
Heterosocial Adequacy Test, 1076
HFD Test, T2:1468
Hidden Figures Test, 1077
Hiett Simplified Shorthand Test (Gregg), 1078
Higgins-Wertman Test: Threshold of Visual Closure (status unknown), T2:560
High Level Battery: Test A/75, 1079
High School Characteristics Index, 1080
High School Fundamental Evaluation Test, T2:17
High School Interest Questionnaire, 1081
High School Reading Test: National Achievement Tests, 1082
High School Subject Tests, 1083; Algebra, 1084; American Government, 1085; American History, 1086; Biology, 1087; Chemistry, 1088; Consumer Education,

1089; General Mathematics, 1090; Geometry, 1091; Health, 1092; Language, 1093; Literature and Vocabulary, 1094; Physical Science, 1095; World Geography, 1096; World History, 1097; Writing and Mechanics, 1098
Hill Interaction Matrix, 1099
Hill Performance Test of Selected Positional Concepts, 1100
Hiskey-Nebraska Test of Learning Aptitude, 1101
History and Civics Test: Municipal Tests: National Achievement Tests, T2:1943
Hoffer-Osmond Diagnostic Test, T2:1215
Holborn Reading Scale, 1102
Hollien-Thompson Group Hearing Test, T2:2040
Hollingsworth-Sanders Geography Test, 1103
Hollingsworth-Sanders Intermediate History Test, 1104
Hollingsworth-Sanders Junior High School Literature Test, 1105
Holtzman Inkblot Technique, 1106
[Re Holtzman Inkblot Technique] Computer Scoring Service for the Holtzman Inkblot Technique, T2:1472
Home Index, 1107
Home Observation for Measurement of the Environment, 1108
Hooper Visual Organization Test, 1109
Horn Art Aptitude Inventory, 1110
Hoskins-Sanders Literature Test, 1111
Hospital Adjustment Scale, T2:1217
Hostility and Direction of Hostility Questionnaire: Personality and Personal Illness Questionnaires, 8:579
Houston Test for Language Development (status unknown), T2:2077
How A Child Learns, 1112
How I See Myself Scale, 8:580
How Supervise?, 1113
How to Drive Tests, 8:358
How Well Do You Know Your Interests (status unknown), T2:2189
How Well Do You Know Yourself (status unknown), T2:1220
Howard Ink Blot Test, T2:1473
Howarth Mood Adjective Check List, 1114
Howarth Personality Questionnaire, 1115
Howell Geometry Test, T2:750
Hoyum-Sanders English Tests, 1116
Human Figure Drawing Techniques, 1117
Human Relations Inventory, 1118
Humm-Wadsworth Temperament Scale (status unknown), T2:1222
Hunt-Minnesota Test for Organic Brain Damage, T2:1223
Hunter-Grundin Literacy Profiles, 1119
Hysteriod-Obsessoid Questionnaire: Personality and Personal Illness Questionnaires, T2:1224
I-Am Sentence Completion Test (status unknown), T2:819
IBM 1230 Optical Mark Scoring Reader, T2:1032
IBM 3881 Optical Mark Reader, 1120
ICES: Instructor and Course Evaluation System, 1121
Ideal Leader Behavior Description Questionnaire, 1122
IES Test, 1123
Illinois Algebra Test, T2:680
Illinois Children's Language Assessment Test, 1124
Illinois Course Evaluation Questionnaire, 1125
Illinois Index of Scholastic Aptitude, T2:392
Illinois Ratings of Character in Physical Education, T2:931
Illinois Ratings of Teacher Effectiveness, T2:865
Illinois Teacher Evaluation Questionnaire, 8:374
Illinois Test of Psycholinguistic Abilities, Revised Edition, 1126
[Re Illinois Test of Psycholinguistic Abilities] A Filmed Demonstration of the ITPA, T2:982
Illinois Tests in the Teaching of English, 1127
Ilyin Oral Interview, 1128
Immediate Test: A Quick Verbal Intelligence Test, 1129
Impact Message Inventory: Form II, 1130
In-Basket Test, T2:2450
Incomplete Sentence Test, 1131
Incomplete Sentences Task, 1132
Independent Activities Questionniare, 1133
Independent Living Behavior Checklist, 1134
Indiana-Oregon Music Discrimination Test, 1135
Indiana Physical Fitness Test, 1136
Individual and Family Developmental Review, T2:820
Individual Career Exploration, 1137
Individual Learning Disabilities Classroom Screening Instrument (status unknown), 8:432
Individual Phonics Criterion Test, 1138
Individual Placement Series (status unknown), T2:2108
Individual Pupil Monitoring System—Mathematics, Forms S and T, 1139
Individual Pupil Monitoring System—Reading, 1140
Individual Reading Placement Inventory, Field Research Edition, T2:1163
Individual Reading Test, T2:1557
Individual Scale for Indian South Africans, 1141
Individualized Criterion Referenced Testing: Math, 1142
Individualized Criterion Referenced Testing: Reading, 1143
Industrial Arts Aptitude Battery: Woodworking Test, 1144
Industrial Reading Test, 1145
Industrial Sentence Completion Form, 1146
Infant Rating Scale, 1147
Inferred Self-Concept Scale, 1148
Informal Evaluation of Oral Reading Grade Level, 1149
Informal Reading Assessment Tests, T2:1558
Information Index, T2:2401
Information Test on Drugs and Drug Abuse, 1150
Information Test on Human Reproduction, 1151
Informeter: An International Technique for the Measurement of Political Information, 1152
Ingram Edinburgh Articulation Test, 1153
Initial Placement Inventory, 1154
Initial Survey Test, 8:799
Inpatient Multidimensional Psychiatric Scale, 8:585
Instant Word Recognition Test, 1156
Instant Words Criterion Test, 1157
Institute of Child Study Security Test, T2:1233
Institutional Functioning Inventory, 1158
Institutional Goals Inventory, 1159
Institutional Self-Study Service Survey, College Student Form, T2:1236
Instructional Styles Inventory, 1160
Instrument for Disability Screening, [Developmental Edition], 1161
Integration Level Test Series, 1162
Inter-American Series: Test of Reading and Number,

2455; Tests of General Abiltiy, 2484; Tests of Reading, 2488
Interest Check List, 1979 Edition, 1163
Interest Determination, Exploration and Assessment System, 1164
Interest Inventory for Elementary Grades: George Washington University Series, 1165
Interest Questionnaire for Indian South Africans, 1166
Intermediate Personality Questionnaire for Indian Pupils (Standards 6 to 8), 1167
International Primary Factors Test Battery (status unknown), 8:487
Inter-Person Perception Test, 1168
Interpersonal Behavior Survery, 1169
Interpersonal Check List, 1170
Interpersonal Communication Inventory, 1171
Interpersonal Conflict Scales, 1172
Interpersonal Orientation Scale, T2:1242
Interpersonal Perception Method, T2:1243
Interpersonal Style Inventory, 1173
Inter-Society Color Council Color Aptitude Test, see Color-Matching Aptitude Test, 1978 Edition, 533
Intra- and Interpersonal Relations Scale, 1174
Introducing Career Concepts Inventory, 1175
Intuitive Mechanics (Weights & Pulleys), 1176
Inventory No. 2, 1177
Inventory of Anger Communication, 1178
Inventory of Certain Feelings, 1179
Inventory of College Activities, T2:1244
Inventory of Factors STDCR, T2:1245
Inventory of Individually Perceived Group Cohesiveness, 1180
Inventory of Interests, 1181
Inventory of Primary Skills, 1182
Inventory of Religious Activities and Interests, 1183
Inventory of Self-Hypnosis, 1184
Inventory of Teacher Knowledge of Reading, Revised Edition, 1185
Inventory of Vocational Interests: Acorn National Aptitude Tests, 1186
Inventory-Survey Tests, 1187
Iowa Algebra Aptitude Test, Third Edition, 1188
Iowa Geometry Aptitude Test, Third Edition, 1189
Iowa High School Content Examination, T2:18
Iowa Parent Behavior Inventory, 1190
Iowa Placement Examinations: Chemistry Aptitude, T2:1844; Chemistry Training: Series CT1, Revised, T2:1845; English Aptitude, T2:86; English Training, T2:87; Foreign Language Aptitude, T2:220; French Training, T2:254; Mathematics Aptitude, T2:621; Mathematics Training: Series MT1, Revised, T2:662; Physics Aptitude, T2:1867; Physics Training: Series PT1, Revised, T2:1868; Spanish Training, T2:313
Iowa Silent Reading Tests, 1191
Iowa Spelling Scales, T2:149
Iowa Tests of Basic Skills, Forms 7 and 8, 1192
Iowa Tests of Educational Development, [Seventh Edition], 1193
Iowa Tests of Music Literacy, 1194
IOX Basic Skill System, 1195
IOX Basic Skill Word List, 1196
IOX Objectives-Based Tests: American Government, 159; Language Arts, 1277; Mathematics, 1412; Reading, 1997

IPAT Anxiety Scale, see IPAT Anxiety Scale Questionnaire, 1197
IPAT Anxiety Scale Questionnaire, 1197
IPAT Contact Personality Factor Test, T2:1226
IPAT Depression Scale, 1198
IPAT 8-Parallel-Form Anxiety Battery, T2:1227
IPAT Humor Test of Personality, T2:1228
IPAT Neurotic Personality Factor Test, T2:1229
IPMA Fire Service Tests, 1199
IPMA Police Service Tests, 1200
I.Q. Calculator, T2:807
"Is of Identity" Test, T2:1246
It Scale for Children, 1201
Item Analysis of Slosson Intelligence Test, 1202
Jackson Personality Inventory, 1203
Jackson Vocational Interest Survey, 1204
James Language Dominance Test, 8:167
Jansky Screening Index, 1205
Jenkins Activity Survey, 1206
Jensen Alternation Board, 1207
Jesness Behavior Checklist, 1208
Jesness Inventory, 1209
JEVS Work Sample Evaluation System, 1210
JIIG-CAL Occupational Interests Guide, 1211
Job Activity Preference Questionnaire, 1212
Job Analysis and Interest Measurement, 1213
[Job Application Forms], 1214
Job Attitude Analysis, 1215
Job Attitude Scale, 1216
Job Awareness Inventory, 1217
Job Ideas and Information Generator-Computer Assisted Learning, see JIIG-CAL Occupational Interests Guide, 1211
JOB-O, see Judgement of Occupational Behavior-Orientation, 1227
Job Performance Scale, 1218
Job-Tests Program, 1219
Johnson Basic Sight Vocabulary Test, 1220
Johnson-Kenney Screening Test, 1221
Johnson-O'Connor English Vocabulary Worksamples, T2:167
Johnson-O'Connor Vocabulary Tests, T2:168
Jones-Mohr Listening Test, 1222
Jones Music Recognition Test, T2:200
Jones Personality Rating Scale, 1223
Jordan Left-Right Reversal Test, Second Revised Edition, 1224
Joseph Pre-School and Primary Self-Concept Screening Test, 1225
Journalism Test, 1226
Judgement of Occupational Behavior-Orientation, 1227
Junior Aptitude Tests for Indian South Africans, 1228
Junior College Placement Program, T2:1054
Junior Eysenck Personality Inventory, 1229
Junior High School Mathematics Test: Acorn Achievement Tests, 1230
Junior High School Record, 1231
Junior High School Test of Economics, 1232
Junior Index of Motivation, T2:867
Junior Scholastic Aptitude Test, Revised Edition, T2:394
Jr.-Sr. High School Personality Questionnaire, 1233
Juvenile Justice Policy Inventory, 1234
Ka-Ro Inkblot Test, 1235
Kahn Intelligence Tests, 1236
Kahn Test of Symbol Arrangement, 1237

Kansas Spelling Tests, 1238
Kasanin-Hanfmann Concept Formation Test, 1239
Katz Adjustment Scales, 1240
Katz-Zalk Opinion Questionnaire, 1241
Kaufman Development Scale, 1242
KD Proneness Scale and Check List, T2:1254
Keele Pre-School Assessment Guide, 1243
Kelvin Measurement of Ability in Arithmetic, T2:720
Kelvin Measurement of Ability in Infant Classes, 1244
Kelvin Measurement of Mental Ability, T2:396
Kelvin Measurement of Reading Ability, T2:1561
Kelvin Measurement of Spelling Ability, T2:151
Kendrick Battery for the Detection of Dementia in the Elderly, 1245
Kent Infant Development Scale, 1246
Kent-Rosanoff Free Association Test, 1247
Kent Series of Emergency Scales, T2:503
Kepner Mid-Year Algebra Achievement Tests, 1248
Kerby Learning Modality Test, Revised 1980, 1249
Key Math Diagnostic Arithmetic Test, 1250
Keystone Ready-to-Read Tests, T2:1916
Keystone Tests of Binocular Skill, 1251
[Keystone Visual Screening Tests], 1252
Khatena-Torrance Creative Perception Inventory, 1253
Kilander-Leach Health Knowledge Test, 1254
Kindergarten Auditory Screening Test, 1255
Kindergarten Behavioural Index: A Screening Technique for Reading Readiness, 1256
Kindergarten Evaluation of Learning Potential, T2:1709
Kinetic Family Drawings, 8:601
Kingston Test of Intelligence, T2:397
Kingston Test of Silent Reading, T2:1562
Kit of Factor Referenced Cognitive Tests, 1257
Kit of Reference Tests for Cognitive Factors, 1963 Revision, see Kit of Factor Referenced Cognitive Tests, 1257
Knauber Art Ability Test (status unknown), T2:187
Knauber Art Vocabulary Test (status unknown), T2:188
Knowledge and Attitudes of Drug Usage, 1258
Knowledge of Occupations Test, 1259
Knox's Cube Test, 1260
Knuth Achievement Tests in Music: Recognition of Rhythm and Melody, 1261
Kohlberg's Moral Judgment Interview, 1262
Kohn Problem Checklist, 1263
Kohn Social Competence Scale, 1264
Kohs Block-Design Test, 1265
Kraner Preschool Math Inventory, 1266
Krantz Health Opinion Survey, 1267
K.S.U. Speech Discrimination Test, 1268
Kuder C, see Kuder Preference Record—Vocational, 1271
Kuder General Interest Survey, 1269
Kuder Occupational Interest Survey, 1270
Kuder Preference Record—Personal, T2:1256
Kuder Preference Record—Vocational, 1271
Kuhlmann-Anderson Test, Seventh Edition, 1272
Kuhlmann-Finch Tests, T2:399
Kundu's Neurotic Personality Inventory, 1273
Kupfer-Detre System (status unknown), T2:1258
Kwalwasser-Dykema Music Tests, T2:202
Kwalwasser Music Talent Test, 1274
Kwalwasser-Ruch Test of Musical Accomplishment, 1275
L & L Clerical Tests (status unknown), T2:2133
Lake St. Clair Incident, 1276
Language Arts Diagnostic Probes, T2:89

Language Arts: IOX Objectives-Based Tests, 1277
Language Arts: Minnesota High School Achievement Examinations, 1278
Language Arts Tests: Content Evaluation Series, 1279
Language Assessment Battery, 1280
Language Assessment Scales, 1281
Language Facility Test, 1282
Language Imitation Test, 1283
Language Modalities Test for Aphasia, T2:2079
Language Perception Test, T2:92
Language Proficiency Test, 1284
Language Proficiency Tests, 1285
Language Sampling, Analysis, and Training, Revised Edition, 1286
Language-Structured Auditory Retention Span Test, 1287
Language Usage: Differential Aptitude Tests, 1288
Lankton First-Year Algebra Test, Revised Edition, T2:683
Larsen-Hammill Test of Written Spelling, 8:75
Laterality Preference Schedule, 1289
Latin I and II: Achievement Examinations for Secondary Schools, T2:294
Laurita-Trembley Diagnostic Word Processing Test, 1290
Law Enforcement Perception Questionnaire, 1291
Law School Admission Test, 1292
Lawshe-Kephart Personnel Comparison System, 1293
LD Program that Works, 1294
Leader Behavior Description Questionnaire, 1295
Leader Behavior Description Questionnaire, Form 12, 1296
Leadership Ability Evaluation, 1297
Leadership and Self-Development Scale, 1298
Leadership Evaluation and Development Scale, 1299
Leadership Opinion Questionnaire, 1300
Leadership Practices Inventory, 1301
Leadership Q-Sort Test (A Test of Leadership Values), 1302
Learning Ability Profile, 1303
Learning Disability Rating Procedure, 1304
Learning Efficiency Test, 1305
Learning Methods Test, 1306
Learning Staircase, 1307
Learning Style Identification Scale, 1308
Learning Styles Inventory [Creative Learning Press, Inc.], 1309
Learning Styles Inventory [Humanics Media], 1310
Learning through Listening, 1311
Leavell Hand-Eye Coordinator Tests, 1312
Lee-Clark Reading Test, T2:1563
Lee Test of Algebraic Ability, Revised, 1313
Leeds Scales for the Self-Assessment of Anxiety and Depression, 1314
Leicester Number Test: Basic Number Concepts, 1315
Leisure Activities Blank, 1316
Leisure Interest Inventory, 1317
Leiter Adult Intelligence Scale, 1318
Leiter International Performance Scale, 1319
Level of Aspiration Board, 1320
Lewis Counseling Inventory, 1321
Lexington Developmental Scales, 1322
LIAMA Inventory of Job Attitudes, T2:2402
Library Orientation Test for College Freshmen, T2:1759
Library Skills Test, 1323
Library Tests, 1324
Life Adjustment Inventory, 1325

INDEX OF TITLES

Life Skills, Forms 1 and 2, 1326
Life Style Questionnaire, 1327
Light's Retention Scale, Revised Edition 1981, 1328
Ligondé Equivalence Test, 1329
Lincoln Diagnostic Spelling Tests, 1330
Lincoln-Oseretsky Motor Development Scale, 1331
Lindamood Auditory Conceptualization Test, Revised Edition, 1332
LIPHE Life Interpersonal History Enquiry, 890d
Lippincott Reading Readiness Test (Including Readiness Check List), 1333
Listening Comprehension, 1334
Listening Comprehension Group Tests, 1335
Literature Test: National Achievement Tests, T2:139
Literature Tests/Objective, 1336
Logical Reasoning, 1337
Lollipop Test: A Diagnostic Screening Test of School Readiness, 1338
London House Personnel Selection Inventory, 1339
London Reading Test, 1340
Look at Literature: The NCTE Cooperative Test of Critical Reading and Appreciation, 8:70
Lorge-Thorndike Intelligence Tests, 1341
Lorge-Thorndike Intelligence Tests, College Edition, T2:401
Lorimer Braille Recognition Test: A Test of Ability in Reading Braille Contractions, 1342
Louisville Behavior Checklist, 1343
Love Attitudes Inventory, 1344
LRA Standard Mastery Tasks in Language, 1345
LRS Seriation Test, T2:1710
Luria-Nebraska Neuropsychological Battery, 1346
Lüscher Color Test, 1347
Luther Hospital Sentence Completions, 1348
M-B History Record: Self-Administered Form, 1349
M-Scale: An Inventory of Attitudes Toward Black/White Relations in the United States, 1350
MACC Behavioral Adjustment Scale, Revised 1971, 1351
Machine Calculation Test: National Business Entrance Tests, 1352
Machover Draw-A-Person Test, 1353
Machover Figure Drawing Test, see Machover Draw-A-Person Test, 1353
Macmillan Diagnostic Reading Pack, 1354
Macmillan Reader Placement Test, 1355
Macmillan Reading Readiness Test, Revised Edition, 8:801
MacQuarrie Test for Mechanical Ability, 1356
Maferr Inventory of Feminine Values, 1357
Maferr Inventory of Masculine Values, 1358
Maico Audiometers, 1359
Maico Hearing Impairment Calculator, T2:2044
Maintaining Reading Efficiency Tests, see Reading Efficiency Tests, 1993
Major-Minor-Finder, 1360
Make A Picture Story, 1361
Making Objects, 1362
Male Impotence Test, T2:822
Management Relations Survey, 1363
Management Style Diagnosis Test, Second Edition, 1364
Management Transactions Audit, 1365
Managerial Philosophies Scale, 1366
Managerial Scale for Enterprise Improvement, T2:2456
Managerial Style Questionnaire (status unknown), 8:1182
Manchester Scales of Social Adaptation, 1367

Mandel Social Adjustment Scale, 1368
Manipulative Aptitude Test, 8:1040
Manson Evaluation, 1369
Manual Accuracy and Speed Test, 1370
Marianne Frostig Developmental Test of Visual Perception, Third Edition, 1371
Marital Communication Inventory, 1372
Marital Diagnostic Inventory, T2:824
Marital Pre-Counseling Inventory, 1373
Marital Roles Inventory, T2:825
Marital Satisfaction Inventory, 1374
Marriage Adjustment Form, 1375
Marriage Adjustment Inventory, 1376
Marriage Adjustment Sentence Completion Survey, T2:828
Marriage Analysis, Experimental Edition, 1377
Marriage Counseling Kit, 1378
Marriage Evaluation, 1379
Marriage Expectation Inventories, 1380
Marriage Inventory, 1381
Marriage-Personality Inventory, Educational Research Edition, T2:831
Marriage Prediction Schedule, 1382
Marriage Role Expectation Inventory, 1383
Marriage Scale (For Measuring Compatibility of Interests), 1384
Marriage Skills Analysis (status unknown), 8:348
Martin Performance Appraisal, T2:2307
Martin S-D Inventory, 1385
Martinek-Zaichkowsky Self-Concept Scale for Children, 1386
Maryland Parent Attitude Survey, 1387
Maryland Test Behavior Checklist, see Psychometric Behavior Checklist, 1932
Maslach Burnout Inventory, 1388
Massachusetts Hearing Test (status unknown), T2:2045
Mastery: An Evaluation Tool: Mathematics, 1389
Mastery: An Evaluation Tool: Reading, 1390
Mastery: An Evaluation Tool: Selected Short SOBAR Reading Tests, 1391; Comprehension I, 1392; Comprehension II, 1393; Comprehension III, 1394; Phonic Analysis, 1395; Structural Analysis, 1396; Study Skills, 1397; Vocabulary I, 1398; Vocabulary II, 1399; Vocabulary III, 1400
Mastery: Survival Skills Tests, 1401
Mastery Tests, 1402
Match Problems, 1403
Match Problems V, 1404
MATE Marital Attitudes Evaluation, 890f
Mathematical and Technical Test, T2:2282
Mathematics Anxiety Rating Scale, 1405
Mathematics Attainment Test EF, 1406
Mathematics Attainment Tests C1 and C3, 1407
Mathematics Attainment Tests DE1 and DE2, 1408
Mathematics Attainment Tests (Oral), 1409
Mathematics Attitudes Inventory, 1410
Mathematics Evaluation Procedures K-2, 1411
Mathematics Inventory Tests (status unknown), T2:630
Mathematics: IOX Objectives-Based Tests, 1412
Mathematics: Minnesota High School Achievement Examinations, 1413
Mathematics Test: Content Evaluation Series, 1414
Mathematics Test for Grades Four, Five and Six, 1415
Mathematics Test for Seniors, 1416

Mathematics Test: McGraw-Hill Basic Skills System, 1417
Mathematics Topic Tests: Elementary Level, 1418
Maturity Level for School Entrance and Reading Readiness, T2:1715
Maudsley Personality Inventory, 1419
Maxfield-Buchholz Scale of Social Maturity for Use With Preschool Blind Children, 1420
McCall-Crabbs Standard Test Lessons in Reading, 1421
[McCann Typing Tests], 1422
McCarthy Individualized Diagnostic Reading Inventory, Revised Edition, 1423
McCarthy Scales of Children's Abilities, 1424
McCarthy Screening Test, 1425
McCormick Job Performance Measurement "Rate-$-Scales", 1426
McCullough Word-Analysis Tests, 1427
McGlade Road Test for Use in Driver Licensing, Education and Employment, 1428
McGrath Diagnostic Reading Test, 1429
McGrath Test of Reading Skills, Second Edition, 1430
McGrath's Preliminary Screening Test in Reading, 1431
McGrath's Silent Reading Paragraphs Test, Comprehension, 1432
McGraw-Hill Basic Skills System: Mathematics Test, 1417; Reading Test, 2002; Spelling Test, 2257; Vocabulary Test, 2568; Writing Test, 2662
McGuire-Bumpus Diagnostic Comprehension Test, 1433
McGuire Safe Driver Scale and Interview Guide, T2:2471
McHugh-McParland Reading Readiness Test, 1434
McLeod Phonic Worksheets, 1435
McMenemy Measure of Reading Ability (status unknown), T2:1565
McQuaig Manpower Selection Series (status unknown), T2:2306
Means-Ends Problem-Solving Procedure, 1436
Meares-Sanders Junior High School History Test, 1437
Measure of Arousal Seeking Tendency, 1438
Measure of Child Stimulus Screening and Arousability, 1439
Measure of Individual Differences in Dominance-Submissiveness, 1440
Measurement of Self Concept in Kindergarten Children, 1441
Measurement of Skill: A Battery of Placement Tests for Business, Industrial and Educational Use (status unknown), T2:1080
Measures of Achieving Tendency, 1442
Measures of Affiliative Tendency and Sensitivity to Rejection, 1443
Measures of Individual Differences in Temperament, 1444
Measures of Language Skills for Two- to Seven-Year-Old Children, 1445
Measures of Musical Abilities, 1446
Measures of Occupational Stress, Strain, and Coping, 1447
Measures of Pleasure-, Arousal-, and Dominance–Inducing Qualities of Parental Attitudes, 1448
Measures of Self-Concept K–12, 1449
Mechanical Aptitude Test: Acorn National Aptitude Tests, 1450
Mechanical Comprehension Test, Second Edition, 1451
Mechanical Familiarity Test: ETSA Test 5A, 1452

Mechanical Handyman Test, T2:2418
Mechanical Information Test, 1453
Mechanical Knowledge Test: ETSA Test 6A, 1454
Mechanical Movements: A Test of Mechanical Comprehension, 1455
Mechanical Reasoning: Differential Aptitude Tests, 1456
Medical School Instructor Attitude Inventory, 1457
Medical Sciences Knowledge Profile, 1458
Meeting Street School Screening Test, 1459
Meier Art Tests, 1460
Mellenbruch Mechanical Motivation Test, T2:2257
Melvin-Smith Receptive-Expressive Observation, 1461
Memory-For-Designs, 1462
Memory for Events, 1463
Memory for Meanings, 1464
Menometer, 1465
Menstrual Distress Questionnaire, 1466
Mental Age Calculator, T2:808
Mental Alertness: Tests B/1 and B/2, 1467
Mental Status Schedule, T2:1278
Merit Rating Series, 1468
Merrill-Demos DD Scale: An Attitude Scale for the Identification of Potential or Actual Primary and Secondary Drug Abuse and Delinquent Behavior, 1469
Merrill Language Screening Test, 1470
Merrill-Palmer Scale of Mental Tests, 1471
Mertens Visual Perception Test, 8:437
Meta-Motivation Inventory, 1472
Metals: Cooperative Industrial Arts Tests, T2:971
Metropolitan Achievement Tests, 5th Edition (1978), 1473; Language Instructional Test, 1474; Mathematics Instructional Test, 1475; Reading Instructional Test, 1476; Survey Battery: Mathematics, 1978 Edition, 1477; Survey Battery: Reading, 1978 Edition, 1478
Metropolitan Readiness Tests, 1976 Edition, 1479
MHBSS Mathematics Test, see Mathematics Test: McGraw-Hill Basic Skills System, 1417
MHBSS Reading Test, see Reading Test: McGraw-Hill Basic Skills System, 2002
MHBSS Spelling Test, see Spelling Test: McGraw-Hill Basic Skills System, 2257
MHBSS Study Skills, see Study Skills Test: McGraw-Hill Basic Skills System, 2347
MHBSS Vocabulary Test, see Vocabulary Test: McGraw-Hill Basic Skills System, 2568
MHBSS Writing Test, see Writing Test: McGraw-Hill Basic Skills System, 2662
Michigan Picture Test—Revised, 1480
Michigan Prescriptive Program in English, 1481
Michigan Prescriptive Program in Mathematics, 1482
Michigan Test of Aural Comprehension, 1483
Michigan Test of English Language Proficiency, 1484
Mid-Year Algebra Test, T2:685
Mid-Year Geometry Test, T2:752
Middlesex Hospital Questionnaire, see Crown-Crisp Experiential Index, 639
Mill Hill Vocabulary Scale, 1485
Miller Analogies Test, 1486
Millon Behavioral Health Inventory, 1487
Millon Clinical Multiaxial Inventory, 1488
Milwaukee Academic Interest Inventory, 1489
Miner Sentence Completion Scale, T2:1484
Minimum Essentials for Modern Mathematics, 1490
Minimum Essentials Test, 1491

INDEX OF TITLES

Minnesota Check List for Food Preparation and Serving, Third Edition, T2:951
Minnesota Child Development Inventory, 1492
Minnesota Clerical Test, 1493
Minnesota Counseling Inventory, T2:1280
Minnesota Engineering Analogies Test, 1494
Minnesota High School Achievement Examinations: Advanced Mathematics (Including Trigonometry), 123; Biology, 293; Bookkeeping, 303; Chemistry, 390; Elementary Algebra, 791; Geometry (Including Plane and Solid Geometry), 948; Language Arts, 1278; Mathematics, 1413; Physics, 1816; Science, 2097; Social Studies Grade 10 (American History), 2232; Social Studies Grade 11 (World History), 2233; Social Studies Grade 12 (American Problems), 2234; Social Studies, 2235; Trigonometry, 2525
Minnesota Importance Questionnaire, 1975 Revision, 1495
Minnesota Infant Development Inventory, 1496
Minnesota Job Description Questionnaire, 1497
Minnesota MAST, see Manual Accuracy and Speed Test, 1370
Minnesota Multiphasic Personality Inventory, 1498
[Re Minnesota Multiphasic Personality Inventory] Automated Psychological Assessment, 8:618
[Re Minnesota Multiphasic Personality Inventory] Behaviordyne Psychodiagnostic Laboratory Service, 1499
[Re Minnesota Multiphasic Personality Inventory] Caldwell Report: An MMPI Interpretation, 1500
[Re Minnesota Multiphasic Personality Inventory] MMPI-ICA Computer Report (status unknown), 8:621
[Re Minnesota Multiphasic Personality Inventory] Psychological Assessment Services, 1501
[Re Minnesota Multiphasic Personality Inventory] Roche MMPI Computerized Interpretation Service, 1502
Minnesota Percepto-Diagnostic Test (Revised), 1503
Minnesota Preschool Inventory, 1504
Minnesota Preschool Scale, 1505
Minnesota Rate of Manipulation Test, 1969 Edition, 1506
Minnesota Rating Scale for Personal Qualities and Abilities, T2:1286
Minnesota Reading Examination for College Students, 1507
Minnesota Satisfaction Questionniare, 1508
Minnesota Satisfactoriness Scales, 1509
Minnesota Scholastic Aptitude Test, 1510
Minnesota Spatial Relations Test, Revised Edition, 1511
Minnesota Speed of Reading Test for College Students, 1512
Minnesota Teacher Attitude Inventory, 8:377
Minnesota Test for Differential Diagnosis of Aphasia, 1513
Minnesota Vocational Interest Inventory, T2:2197
Miskimins Self-Goal-Other Discrepancy Scale, 1514
Missouri Children's Picture Series, 1515
Mitchell Vocabulary Test, T2:406
MKM Binocular Preschool Test, 1516
MKM Monocular and Binocular Reading Test, 1517
MKM Picture Arrangement Test, 1518
MLA Cooperative Foreign Language Proficiency Tests: French, T2:255; German, T2:271; Italian, T2:286; Russian, T2:300; Spanish, T2:314
MLA-Cooperative Foreign Language Tests: French, 1519; German, 1520; Italian, 1521; Russian, 1522; Spanish, 1523
Modern Algebra Test: Content Evaluation Series, 1524
Modern Economics Test: Content Evaluation Series, 1525
Modern Geometry Test: Content Evaluation Series, 1526
Modern Language Aptitude Test, 1527
Modern Language Aptitude Test-Elementary, T2:222
Modern Mathematics Supplement to the Canadian Tests of Basic Skills, 8:284
Modern Mathematics Supplement to the Iowa Tests of Basic Skills, T2:639
Modern Photography Comprehension Test, 1528
Modern World History: Achievement Examinations for Secondary Schools, T2:1997
Modified Alpha Examination Form 9, T2:407
Modified Rhyme Hearing Test (status unknown), T2:2046
Modified Sjöstrand Physical Work Capacity Test, T2:936
Monroe Diagnostic Reading Examination for Diagnosis of Special Difficulty in Reading, 1529
Monroe's Standardized Silent Reading Test, 1530
Mood Altering Substances: A Behavior Inventory (status unknown), T2:1288
Mooney Problem Check List, 1950 Revision, 1531
Moore Eye-Hand Coordination and Color-Matching Test, 1532
Moray House Arithmetic Test, T2:722
Moray House English Tests, 1533
Moray House Mathematics Tests, 1534
Moray House Picture Tests, T2:408
Moray House Verbal Reasoning Tests, 1535
Moreton Arithmetic Tests, T2:723
Moreton Mathematics Tests, 1536
Mother-Child Relationship Evaluation, 1537
Motivation Analysis Test, 1538
Motivation and Potential for Adoptive Parenthood Scale, 1539
Motor-Free Visual Perception Test, 1540
Motor Problems Inventory, see Riley Motor Problems Inventory, Revised 1976, 2023
Motorcycle Operator's Test, 8:359
Multi-Aptitude Test, 1541
Multidimensional Assessment of Gains in School, 8:378
Multidimensional Assessment of Philosophy of Education, 1542
Multidimensional Maturity Scale, 1543
Multi-Ethnic Awareness Survey, 1544
Multijurisdictional Police Officer Examination, 1545
Multiphasic Environmental Assessment Procedure, 1546
Multiple Affect Adjective Check List, 1547
Multiple Aptitude Tests, 1959 Edition, T2:1082
Multiple Assessment Programs and Services, 1548
Multiple-Choice Intelligibility Test, T2:2022
Multiple Purpose Self Trainer, 1549
Multivariate Vocational Evaluation System, 1550
Murphy-Durrell Reading Readiness Analysis, 1551
Music Achievement Tests, T2:207
Music Aptitude Test (status unknown), T2:208
Musical Aptitude Profile, 1552
Mutually Responsible Facilitation Inventory, 1553
My Self Checklist, 8:629
My Vocational Situation, 1554
Myers-Briggs Type Indicator, 1555

Nagel Personnel Interviewing and Screening Forms, T2:2309
National Achievement Tests, T2:23; Algebra Test for Engineering and Science, 154; American History Test, T2:1984; Arithmetic Test (Fundamentals and Reasoning): Municipal Tests, 196; Arithmetic Test, 197; College English Test, 504; Elementary Science Test, T2:1782; English Test: Municipal Tests, 827; English Test, 828; First Year Algebra Test, 892; General Biology Test, T2:1810; General Chemistry Test, 938; General Physics Test, 945; General Science Test, 947; Geography Test: Municipal Tests, T2:1975; Geography Test, T2:1976; Health and Safety Education Test, 1065; Health Knowledge Test for College Freshmen, 1067; Health Test, 1068; History and Civics Test: Municipal Tests, T2:1943; Literature Test, T2:139; Plane Geometry, 1837; Plane Trigonometry, 1838; Reading Comprehension Test (Crow, Kuhlmann, and Crow), T2:1586; Reading Comprehension Test (Speer and Smith), T2:1587
National Business Entrance Tests, 1556; Bookkeeping Test, 304; Business Fundamentals and General Information Test, 332; General Office Clerical Test, 944; Machine Calculation Test, 1352; Stenographic Test, 2307; Typewriting Test, 2527
National Educational Development Tests, 1557
National Engineering Aptitude Search Test: The Junior Engineering Technical Society, 1558
National German Examination for High School Students, 1559
National Guidance Testing Program: Series 2, T2:1055
National Institute for Personnel Research Intermediate Battery, 1560
National Institute for Personnel Research Normal Battery, 1561
National Occupational Competency Testing Program, 1562
[National Science Foundation Graduate Fellowship Testing Program], 1563
National Spanish Examination (status unknown), 8:168
National Teacher Examinations, see NTE Programs, 1625
National Teacher Examinations: Common Examinations, see NTE Core Battery, 1624
National Teacher Examinations: Education in an Urban Setting, T2:871
National Teacher Examinations (Specialty Area Tests), see NTE Specialty Area Tests
National Test of Basic Words (status unknown), T2:1667
National Test of Library Skills (status unknown), T2:1762
Nationwide English Composition Examination (status unknown), T2:97
Nationwide English Grammar Examination (status unknown), T2:98
Nationwide English Vocabulary Examination (status unknown), T2:169
Nationwide Library Skills Examination (status unknown), T2:1763
Nationwide Speech Examination (status unknown), T2:2083
Nationwide Spelling Examination (status unknown), T2:154
Naylor-Harwood Adult Intelligence Scale, 1564
N.B. Aptitude Tests (Junior), T2:1083

N.B. Arithmetic Tests, T2:724
N.B. Group Tests, 8:194
N.B. Mathematics Tests, T2:642
N.B. Silent Reading Tests (Beginners): Reading Comprehension Test, T2:1570
N.B. Spelling Tests, 1565
[NCRI Achievement Tests in Hebrew], 1566
NCS Scoring and Reporting Services, T2:1035
NCS Sentry, T2:1036
NCS Student Survey, 8:380
Neale Analysis of Reading Ability, Second Edition, 1567
Nelson Biology Test, Revised Edition, T2:1812
Nelson-Denny Reading Test, Forms E and F, 1568
Nelson Reading Skills Test, Forms 3 and 4, 1569
Nelson Reading Test, Revised Edition, 1570
Netherne Study Difficulties Battery for Student Nurses, T2:2388
Neurological Dysfunctions of Children, 1571
Neuropsychological Questionnaire, 1572
Neuroticism Scale Questionnaire, 1573
New Developmental Reading Tests, T2:1574
New Group Pure Tone Hearing Test (status unknown), T2:2048
New Guinea Performance Scales, 1574
New Iowa Spelling Scale, 1575
New Junior Maudsley Inventory, T2:1296
New Medical College Admission Test, 1576
New Mexico Career Education Test Series, 1577
New Purdue Placement Test in English, T2:99
New South African Group Test, 1578
New Sucher-Allred Reading Placement Inventory, 1579
New Uses, 1580
Newsweek NewsQuiz, 1581
N.I.I.P. Engineering Apprentice Selection Test Battery, 1582
NIIP Group Test 36, 1583
19 Field Interest Inventory, 1584
NLN Achievement Tests for Schools Preparing Registered Nurses, 1585
NLN Aide Selection Test, T2:2384
NLN Practical Nursing Achievement Tests, 1586
NLN Pre-Admission and Classification Examination, T2:2386
NLN Pre-Nursing and Guidance Examination, 1587
NM Concepts of Ecology Test, 1588
NM Consumer Mathematics Test, 1589
NM Consumer Rights and Responsibilities Test, 1590
NOCTI Examination: Air Conditioning and Refrigeration, 1591; Airframe and Power Plant Mechanic, 1592; Architectural Drafting, 1593; Auto Body Repair, 1594; Auto Mechanic, 1595; Cabinet Making and Millwork, 1596; Carpentry, 1597; Civil Technology, 1598; Cosmetology, 1599; Diesel Engine Repair, 1600; Electrical Installation, 1601; Electronics Communications, 1602; Industrial Electrician, 1603; Industrial Electronics, 1604; Machine Drafting, 1605; Machine Trades, 1606; Masonry, 1607; Mechanical Technology, 1608; Plumbing, 1609; Printing, 1610; Quantity Food Preparation, 1611; Sheet Metal, 1612; Small Engine Repair, 1613; Welding, 1614
Non-Language Test of Verbal Intelligence—Form 768, 1615
Non-Readers Intelligence Test, Third Edition, 1616
Non-Verbal Intelligence Scale S.O.N. 2–7, see Snijders-

INDEX OF TITLES

Oomen Non-Verbal Intelligence Scale for Young Children, 2221
Non-Verbal Intelligence Tests for Deaf and Hearing Subjects, 1617
Non-Verbal Reasoning Test, 1618
Nonverbal Test of Cognitive Skills, 1619
Non-Verbal Tests, 1620
Northampton Activity Rating Scale, 1621
Northumberland Mental Tests, T2:416
Northwestern Syntax Screening Test, 1622
Nottingham Number Test, 1623
NTE Core Battery, 1624
NTE Programs, 1625
NTE Specialty Area Tests: Art Education Specialty Area Test, 1626; Audiology Specialty Area Test, 1627; Biology and General Science Specialty Area Test, 1628; Business Education Specialty Area Test, 1629; Chemistry, Physics, and General Science Specialty Area Test, 1630; Early Childhood Education Specialty Area Test, 1631; Education in the Elementary School Specialty Area Test, 1632; Education of the Mentally Retarded Specialty Area Test, 1633; Educational Administration and Supervision Specialty Area Test, 1634; English Language and Literature Specialty Area Test, 1635; French Specialty Area Test, 1636; German Specialty Area Test, 1637; Guidance Counselor Specialty Area Test, 1638; Home Economics Education Specialty Area Test, 1639; Industrial Arts Education Specialty Area Test, 1640; Introduction to the Teaching of Reading Specialty Area Test, 1641; Mathematics Specialty Area Test, 1642; Media Specialist-Library and Audio-Visual Services Specialty Area Test, 1643; Music Education Specialty Area Test, 1644; Physical Education Specialty Area Test, 1645; Reading Specialist Specialty Area Test, 1646; Social Studies Specialty Area Test, 1647; Spanish Specialty Area Test, 1648; Speech-Communication and Theatre Specialty Area Test, 1649; Speech Pathology Specialty Area Test, 1650; Texas Government Specialty Area Test, 1651
Number Test DE, 1652
Numerical Ability: Differential Aptitude Tests, 1653
Nurse Attitudes Inventory, 1654
Nurses' Observation Scale for Inpatient Evaluation, 1655
Nutrition Achievement Tests, 1656
Nutrition Information Test, 1657
Nutrition Knowledge and Interest Questionnaire, 1658
OARS Multidimensional Functional Assessment Questionnaire, 1659
Object Relations Technique, 1660
Object Sorting Scales, 1661
Objective-Analytic (O-A) Anxiety Battery, T2:1300
Objective-Analytic (O-A) Test Battery, 1662
Objective Tests in Constructive English, 1663
Objective Tests in Mathematics: Algebra, T2:687; Arithmetic and Trigonometry, T2:645; Geometry, T2:754; Statistics, T2:1043
Objective Tests in Physics (status unknown), T2:1869
Objective Tests in Punctuation, 1664
Objectives-Referenced Bank of Items and Tests: Mathematics, 1665
Objectives-Referenced Bank of Items and Tests: Reading and Communication Skills, 1666
Observation Test for Policeman, 1667
OC Diagnostic Dictionary Test (status unknown), T2:1764
OC Diagnostic Syllabizing Test (status unknown), T2:1668
Occ-U-Sort, 1668
Occupational Check List, 1669
Occupational Interest Inventory, 1956 Revision, T2:2199
Occupational Interest Survey (With Pictures): Individual Placement Series (status unknown), T2:2200
Occupations and Careers Information BOXSCORE, 8:1015
O'Connor Finger Dexterity Test, 1670
O'Connor Tweezer Dexterity, 1671
O'Connor Wiggly Block, 1672
Offer Self-Image Questionnaire for Adolescents, 1673
Office Arithmetic Test: ETSA Test 2A, 1674
Office Information and Skills Test: Content Evaluation Series, 1675
Office Skills Achievement Test, 1676
Office Skills Tests, 1677
Office Worker Test, T2:2137
Ohio Accounting/Computing Clerk Achievement Test, 1678
Ohio Agricultural Business Achievement Test, 1679
Ohio Agricultural Mechanic Achievement Test, 1680
Ohio Apparel and Accessories Achievement Test, 1681
Ohio Auto Body Mechanic Achievement Test, 1682
Ohio Automotive Mechanics Achievement Test, 1683
Ohio Carpentry Achievement Test, 1684
Ohio Clerk-Stenographer Achievement Test, 1685
Ohio Clerk Typist Achievement Test, 1686
Ohio College Association Rating Scale, T2:1301
Ohio Commercial Art Achievement Test, 1687
Ohio Communication Products Electronics Achievement Test, 1688
Ohio Community and Home Services Achievement Test, 1689
Ohio Construction Electricity Achievement Test, 1690
Ohio Cosmetology Achievement Test, 1691
Ohio Data Processing Achievement Test, 1692
Ohio D.E. Food Service Personnel Achievement Test, 1693
Ohio Dental Assisting Achievement Test, 1694
Ohio Diesel Mechanic Achievement Test, 1695
Ohio Diversified Health Occupations Achievement Test, 1696
Ohio Drafting Achievement Test, 1697
Ohio Fabric Services Achievement Test, 1698
Ohio Farm Management Achievement Test, 1699
Ohio Food Marketing Key Employee Achievement Test, 1700
Ohio General Merchandising Achievement Test, 1701
Ohio General Office Clerk Achievement Test, 1702
Ohio Heating, Air Conditioning, and Refrigeration Achievement Test, 1703
Ohio H.Ec. Food Services Achievement Test, 1704
Ohio Horticulture Achievement Test, 1705
Ohio Industrial Electronics Achievement Test, 1706
Ohio Lithographic Printing Achievement Test, 1707
Ohio Machine Trades Achievement Test, 1708
Ohio Masonry Achievement Test, 1709
Ohio Medical Assisting Achievement Test, 1710
Ohio Nursery School Teacher Aide/Child Care Achievement Test, 1711
Ohio Penal Classification Test, 1712
Ohio Production Agriculture Achievement Test, 1713
Ohio School Library/Media Test, 1714

Ohio Sheet Metal Achievement Test, 1715
Ohio State University Psychological Test, 1716
Ohio State University Test for Identifying Misarticulations, 1717
Ohio Survey Tests (status unknown), T2:1057
Ohio Teaching Record: Anecdotal Observation Form, Second Revised Edition, T2:877
Ohio Tests of Articulation and Perception of Sounds, 1718
Ohio Vocational Education Achievement Test Program, 1719
Ohio Vocational Interest Survey, Second Edition, 1720
Ohio Welding Achievement Test, 1721
Ohio Word Processing Achievement Test, 1722
Ohio Work Values Inventory (status unknown), 8:1017
Ohwaki-Kohs Tactile Block Design Intelligence Test for the Blind, T2:513
OISE Achievement Tests in Silent Reading: Advanced Primary Battery, 8:736
OISE Picture Reasoning Test: Primary, 8:196
Oliphant Auditory Discrimination Memory Test, 1723
Oliphant Auditory Synthesizing Test, 1724
Oliver: Parent-Administered Communication Inventory, 1725
Omnibus Personality Inventory, 1726
One Hole Test, 1727
Ontario School Record System, 1972 Edition, 1728
Open School Evaluation System, 8:389
Opinion, Attitude, and Interest Survey, 1729
Opinions Toward Adolescents, 1730
OpScan Test Scoring and Document Scanning System (status unknown), T2:1037
Optometry College Admission Test, 1731
Oral English/Spanish Proficiency Placement Test, 1732
Oral Language Dominance Measure, 1733
Oral Language Evaluation, 1734
Oral Language Proficiency Measure, 1735
Oral Language Sentence Imitation Diagnostic Inventory—F, 1736
Oral Language Sentence Imitation Screening Test, 1737
Oral Rating Form for Rating Language Proficiency in Speaking and Understanding English, 1738
Oral Reading Criterion Test, 1739
Oral Verbal Intelligence Test, 1740
Oral Word Reading Test, T2:1685
Oral Word-Recognition Test, 1741
Oregon Academic Ranking Test, 1742
Organic Integrity Test, 1743
Organization Health Survey, 1744
Organizational Climate Index, 1745
Organizational Value Dimensions Questionnaire: Business Form, 1746
Orientation and Motivation Inventory, 1747
Orientation Inventory, 1748
Orleans-Hanna Algebra Prognosis Test, 1749
Orleans-Hanna Geometry Prognosis Test, T2:755
O'Rourke Clerical Aptitude Test, Junior Grade, 1750
O'Rourke General Classification Test, Senior Grade, T2:421
O'Rourke Mechanical Aptitude Test, 1751
Orr-Graham Listening Test, T2:995
Ortho-Rater, 1752
"Orton" Intelligence Test, No. 4, 1753
Orzeck Aphasia Evaluation, T2:2085

Oseretsky Tests of Motor Proficiency: A Translation From the Portuguese Adaptation, T2:1898
Otis Employment Tests, T2:423
Otis-Lennon School Ability Test, 1754
Otis Quick-Scoring Mental Ability Tests, T2:425
Otis Self-Administering Tests of Mental Ability, 1755
Ottawa School Behavior Check List (status unknown), 8:637
Otto Pre-Marital Counseling Schedules, 1756
Pacific Design Construction Test, T2:514
Pacific Reasoning Series Tests: Pacific Test Series, T2:427
Pacific Test Series: Pacific Reasoning Series Tests, T2:427; Pacific Tests of English Attainment and Skills, T2:102
Pacific Tests of English Attainment and Skills: Pacific Tests Series, T2:102
Pain Apperception Test, 1757
Pair Attraction Inventory, 1758
PAL-C Scale, 1759
PAL-H Scale, 1760
Parent-Adolescent Communication Inventory, 1761
Parent As A Teacher Inventory, 1762
Parent Opinion Inventory, 1763
Parent Readiness Evaluation of Preschoolers, 1764
PARS Scale, 1765
Partial Index of Modernization: Measurement of Attitudes Toward Morality, 1766
Passalong Test: A Performance Test of Intelligence, T2:515
Patient's Self-History Form, Second Edition, T2:939
Pattern Perception Test, T2:428
Pattern Relations Test, 1767
Patterned Elicitation Syntax Screening Test, 1768
Patterson Test or Study Exercises on the Constitution of the United States, T2:2011
Peabody Individual Achievement Test, 1769
Peabody Mathematics Readiness Test, 1770
Peabody Picture Vocabulary Test-Revised, 1771
Peek-a-Boo Test, 1772
Peer Attitudes Toward the Handicapped Scale, 1773
Pennsylvania Bi-Manual Worksample, 1774
Per-Flu-Dex Tests, 1775
Perception of Values Inventory, 1776
Perceptual Battery, 1777
Perceptual Forms Test (status unknown), T2:1881
Perceptual Maze Test, 1778
Perceptual Motor Test, 1779
Perceptual Speed (Identical Forms), 1780
Performance Alertness "PA" (With Pictures): Individual Placement Series (status unknown), T2:429
Performance Assessment in Reading, 1781
[Performance Review Forms], 1782
Permanent Record Folder, T2:1017
Perrin Motor Coordination Test, T2:1899
Personal Adjustment and Role Skills Scale, see PARS Scale, 1765
Personal Adjustment Index: ETSA Test 8A, 1783
Personal Adjustment Inventory (status unknown), T2:1313
Personal Audit, 1784
Personal Background Inventory, 1785
Personal Career Development Profile, 1786
Personal Data Blank, T2:2311
Personal Distress Inventory and Scales, 1787
Personal History Index, 1788

Personal Orientation Inventory, 1789
Personal Preference Scale, 1790
Personal Questionnaire Rapid Scaling Technique, 1791
Personal Relations Inventory, 1792
Personal Sphere Model, 1793
Personal Values Abstract, 8:642
Personal Values Inventory, 1794
Personality Evaluation Form: A Technique for the Organization and Interpretation of Personality Data, T2:1319
Personality Inventory, 1795
Personality Inventory for Children, 1796
Personality Rating Scale, 1797
Personality Research Form, 1798
Personnel Institute Clerical Tests (status unknown), T2:2139
Personnel Institute Hiring Kit (status unknown), T2:2403
[Personnel Interviewing Forms], 1799
Personnel Performance Problems Inventory, 1800
Personnel Rating Scale, 1801
Personnel Reaction Blank, Revised Edition, 1802
Personnel Relations Survey, 1803
Personnel Research Institute Classification Test, 1804
Personnel Research Institute Clerical Battery, 1805; Arithmetic Reasoning Test, 195; Spelling Test for Clerical Workers, 2256
Personnel Research Institute Factory Series Test, 1806
Personnel Research Institute Test of Shorthand Skills, 1807
Personnel Security Preview, see TA Survey, 2389 and E.S. Survey, 841
Personnel Tests for Industry, 1808
Pertinent Questions, 1809
Philadelphia J.E.V.S. Work Sample Battery, see JEVS Work Sample Evaluation System, 1210
Phillips Occupational Preference Scale, T2:2202
Philo-Phobe, T2:1324
Phoneme Baseline Recording Forms, 1810
Phonetic Reading Chain Oral Reading Diagnostic Decoding Test, 1811
Phonics Criterion Test, 1812
Phonics Knowledge Survey, T2:1637
Phonics Test for Teachers, T2:1669
Phonovisual Diagnostic Tests, [1975 Revision], 1813
Photo Articulation Test, 1814
PHSF Relations Questionnaire, 1815
Physics: Achievement Examinations for Secondary Schools, T2:1870
Physics: Minnesota High School Achievement Examinations, 1816
Physiognomic Cue Test, 1817
Pickford Projective Pictures, T2:1489
Pictographic Self Rating Scale, 1818
Pictorial Interest Inventory, 1819
Pictorial Inventory of Careers, 1820
Pictorial Study of Values: Pictorial Allport-Vernon, 1821
Pictorial Test of Bilingualism and Language Dominance, 1822
Pictorial Test of Intelligence, 1823
Picture Articulation & Language Screening Test, 1824
Picture Identification Test, 1825
Picture Impressions Test, T2:1491
Picture Interest Exploration Survey, 1826
Picture Interest Inventory, T2:2205
Picture Situation Test, 1827
Picture Story Language Test, T2:103
Picture Story Test Blank, 1828
Picture Test A, 1829
Picture World Test, 1830
Piers-Harris Children's Self Concept Scale (The Way I Feel About Myself), 1831
Pill Scale, 1832
Pimsleur French Proficiency Tests, T2:258
Pimsleur German Proficiency Tests, T2:275
Pimsleur Language Aptitude Battery, 1833
Pimsleur Spanish Proficiency Tests, T2:318
Pintner-Cunningham Primary Test, T2:435
Pintner-Manikin Test, 1834
Pintner-Paterson Feature Profile Test, 1835
PIP Development Charts, 1836
Plane Geometry: Achievement Examinations for Secondary Schools, T2:756
Plane Geometry: National Achievement Tests, 1837
Plane Trigonometry: National Achievement Tests, 1838
Planning Career Goals, 1839
Plot Titles, 1840
PMA Readiness Level, 1841
Poetry Test/Objective, 1842
Polarity Scale, Fourth Edition, T2:1327
Police Officer A-1(M), 1843
Police Performance Rating System, 1844
Police Promotion Tests, 1845
Police Sergeant, 1846
Policeman Examination, 1847
Policeman Test, T2:2371
Politte Sentence Completion Test, 1848
Polyfactorial Study of Personality, 1849
Pope Inventory of Basic Reading Skills, 1850
Porch Index of Communicative Ability, 1851
Porch Index of Communicative Ability in Children, 1852
Porteus Maze Test, 1853
Portland Prognostic Test for Mathematics, 1854
Position Analysis Questionnaire, 1855
Possible Jobs, 1856
Potential for Foster Parenthood Scale, 1857
Potter-Nash Aptitude Test for Lumber Inspectors and Other General Personnel Who Handle Lumber, 1858
Power of Influence Test, T2:1329
Power Reading Survey Test, 1859
Practical Articulation Kit, 1860
Practical Dexterity Board (status unknown), T2:2232
Practical Policy Test (status unknown), T2:1330
PRADI Autobiographical Form, 1861
PRADI Draw-A-Person Test, 1862
Pre-Academic Learning Inventory, 1863
Predictive Ability Test, Adult Edition, 1864
Predictive Screening Test of Articulation, 1865
Preference Analysis, T2:2206
Preliminary Scholastic Aptitude Test/National Merit Scholarship Qualifying Test, 1866
Premarital Communication Inventory, 1867
Pre-Marital Counseling Inventory, 1868
Premarital Counseling Kit, 1869
Pre-Reading Assessment Kit, T2:1719
PreReading Expectancy Screening Scales, 1870
Pre-Reading Screening Procedures, 1871
Preschool and Early Primary Skills Survey, Preliminary Edition, 1872
Preschool and Kindergarten Performance Profile, 1873

Preschool Attainment Record, Research Edition, 1874
Preschool Behavior Questionnaire, 1874A
Preschool Embedded Figures Test, 1875
Preschool Language Assessment Instrument, Experimental Edition, 1876
Preschool Language Scale, Revised Edition, 1877
Preschool Screening Instrument, 1878
Preschool Self-Concept Picture Test, 1879
Prescriptive Mathematics Inventory, T2:647
Prescriptive Mathematics Inventory Interim Evaluation Tests, T2:648
Prescriptive Reading Inventory, 1880
Prescriptive Reading Inventory Interim Tests, 1881
Prescriptive Reading Performance Test, 1882
Present State Examination, 1883
Press Test, 1884
[Pressey Classification and Verifying Tests], 1885
Pressey Diagnostic Reading Tests, 1886
Pressey Diagnostic Tests in English Composition, 1887
PRI/Reading Systems, 1888
Primary Academic Sentiment Scale, 1889
[Primary Mathematics Survey Tests], 1890
Primary Measures of Music Audiation, 1891
Primary Mechanical Ability Tests, 1892
Primary Reading Assessment Units, 1893
Primary Reading Profiles, 1894
[Primary Reading Survey Tests], 1895
Primary Reading Test: Acorn Achievement Tests, T2:1578
Primary Self-Concept Inventory, 1896
Primary Social Studies Test, T2:1946
[Primary Survey Tests], 1897
Primary Test of Economic Understanding, 1898
Primary Visual Motor Test, 1899
Principles of Democracy Test, T2:2012
Priority Counseling Survey (status unknown), 8:1020
Pritchard-Fox Phoneme Auditory Discrimination Tests: Test Four, 1900
Problem Check List: Form for Rural Young People, T2:1335
Process Diagnostic, 1901
Process for In-School Screening of Children With Emotional Handicaps, see Process for the Assessment of Effective Student Functioning, 1902
Process for the Assessment of Effective Student Functioning, 1902
Profile of a School, 1903
Profile of Adaptation to Life-Clinical Scale, see PAL-C, 1759
Profile of Adaptation to Life-Holistic Scale, see PAL-H, 1760
Profile of Mood States, 1904
[Profiles from Rensis Likert Associates, Inc.], 1905
Program for Assessing Youth Employment Skills, 1906
Programmer Aptitude/Competence Test System, 1907
Progress Assessment Chart of Social Development, 1908
Progress Evaluation Scales, 1909
Progressive Achievement Tests of Listening Comprehension, 1910
Progressive Achievement Tests of Mathematics, 1911
Progressive Achievement Tests of Reading, 1912
Progressive Achievement Tests of Study Skills, 1913
Progressive Matrices, 1914
Project MEMPHIS Instruments for Individual Program Planning and Evaluation, 1915

Project Talent Test Battery: A National Inventory of Aptitudes and Abilities, T2:1058
Projective Assessment of Aging Method, 1916
Projective Index of Body Awareness, 1917
Proof-Reading Tests of Spelling, 1918
Proverbs Test, 1919
PSB-Aptitude for Practical Nursing Examination, 1920
Pseudo-Isochromatic Plates for Testing Color Perception, 1921
Psychiatric Attitudes Battery, T2:1496
Psychiatric Evaluation Form, 1922
Psychiatric Status Schedules: Subject Form, Second Edition, 1923
Psychodiagnostic Test Report Blank, 1924
Psycho-Educational Battery, 1925
Psychoeducational Evaluation of the Preschool Child: A Manual Utilizing the Haeussermann Approach, 1926
Psychoeducational Inventory of Basic Learning Abilities, 1927
Psychoeducational Profile of Basic Learning Abilities, 1928
Psycho-Epistemological Profile, 1929
Psycholinguistic Rating Scale, 1930
Psychological Audit for Interpersonal Relations, Revised Edition (status unknown), T2:1341
Psychological Resources, T2:1038
Psychological Screening Inventory, 1931
Psychometric Behavior Checklist, 1932
Psychometric Research and Service Chart Showing the Davis Difficulty and Discrimination Indices for Item Analysis, T2:810
Psycho-Somatic Inventory, T2:1344
Psychotic Inpatient Profile, 1933
Psychotic Reaction Profile: An Inventory of Patient Behavior for Use by Hospital Personnel, T2:1346
Public School Achievement Tests, T2:28; Arithmetic Computation, T2:697; Arithmetic Reasoning, T2:698; Reading, T2:1590
Public School Primary Intelligence Test, T2:441
Pupil Behavior Inventory (status unknown), T2:1347
Pupil Rating Scale Revised: Screening for Learning Disabilities, 1934
Pupil Record of Educational Behavior, 1935
Purdue Clerical Adaptability Test, Revised Edition, 1936
Purdue Creativity Test, 1937
Purdue Hand Precision Test, 1938
Purdue High School English Test, 1939
Purdue Industrial Mathematics Test, 1940
Purdue Industrial Supervisors Word-Meaning Test, 1941
Purdue Industrial Training Classification Test, 1942
Purdue Instructor Performance Indicator, 1943
Purdue Interview Aids, 1944
Purdue Master Attitude Scales, 1945
Purdue Mechanical Adaptability Test, 1946
Purdue Non-Language Personnel Test, 1947
Purdue Pegboard, 1948
Purdue Perceptual-Motor Survey, 1949
Purdue Rating Scale for Administrators and Executives, 1950
Purdue Rating Scale for Instruction, 1951
Purdue Reading Test for Industrial Supervisors, 1952
Purdue Student-Teacher Opinionaire, 1953
Purdue Teacher Evaluation Scale, 1954
Purdue Teacher Opinionaire, 1955

INDEX OF TITLES

Purdue Trade Information Test for Sheetmetal Workers, 1956
Purdue Trade Information Test in Carpentry, 1957
Purdue Trade Information Test in Engine Lathe Operation, 1958
Purdue Trade Information Test in Welding, Revised Edition, 1959
Purpose in Life Test, 1960
Q-Tags Test of Personality, 1961
Quality of School Life Scale, 1962
Quantitative Evaluative Device, T2:443
Queensland Test, T2:520
Queensland University Aphasia and Language Test, 1963
Questionnaire Measure of Stimulus Screening and Arousability, 1964
QUESTS: A Life-Choice Inventory, 1965
Quick Language Assessment Inventory, 1966
Quick Neurological Screening Test, Revised Edition, 1967
Quick Screening Scale of Mental Development, 1968
Quick Test, 1969
Quick Word Test, 1970
Quickscreen, 1971
RAD Scales, 1972
Rail-Walking Test, T2:1900
Ransom Program Reading Tests, 8:770
Rapid Exam for Early Referral, 1973
Rapid-Rater (status unknown), T2:811
Rating of Behavior Scale, 1974
Ratio I. Q. Computer, T2:812
RBH Arithmetic Fundamentals Test, 1975
RBH Arithmetic Reasoning Test, 1976
RBH Basic Reading and Word Test, T2:1580
RBH Breadth of Information, T2:2287
RBH Checking Test, T2:2143
RBH Classifying Test, 1977
RBH Individual Background Survey, T2:2314
RBH Number Checking Test, 1978
RBH Scientific Reading Test, 1979
RBH Shop Arithmetic Test, 1980
RBH Spelling Test and Word Meaning Test, T2:106
RBH Test of Chemical Comprehension, 1981
RBH Test of Dictation Speed, 1982
RBH Test of Language Skills, 1983
RBH Test of Learning Ability, 1984
RBH Test of Non-Verbal Reasoning, 1985
RBH Test of Reading Comprehension, 1986
RBH Test of Supervisory Judgment, T2:2458
RBH Test of Typing Speed, 1987
RBH Three-Dimensional Space Test, T2:2264
RBH Two-Dimensional Space Test, T2:2265
RBH Vocabulary Test, T2:171
Reactions to Everyday Situations, 1988
Reader Rater With Self-Scoring Profile (status unknown), T2:1670
Reader's Inventory, T2:1671
Reading Adequacy "READ" Test: Individual Placement Series (status unknown), T2:1741
Reading: Adult Basic Education Student Survey, Parts 1 and 2, T2:1742
Reading and Vocabulary Test for Students of English as a Second Language, 1989
Reading Aptitude Tests, T2:1724
Reading Classification Test, 1990

Reading Comprehension: Canadian English Achievement Test, Part 1, T2:1582
Reading Comprehension: Cooperative English Tests, 1991
Reading Comprehension Test, T2:1584
Reading Comprehension Test DE, 1992
Reading Comprehension Test for Personnel Selection, T2:1743
Reading Comprehension Test: National Achievement Tests (Crow, Kuhlmann, and Crow), T2:1586
Reading Comprehension Test: National Achievement Tests (Speer and Smith), T2:1587
Reading Diagnostic Probes (status unknown), T2:1642
Reading Efficiency Tests, 1993
Reading/Everyday Activities in Life, 1993A
Reading Eye II, 1994
Reading for Understanding Placement Test, 1995
Reading-Free Vocational Interest Inventory, 1996
Reading Inventory Probe 1 (status unknown), T2:1725
Reading: IOX Objectives-Based Tests, 1997
Reading Miscue Inventory, 8:790
Reading Progress Scale (status unknown), 8:740
Reading: Public School Achievement Tests, T2:1590
Reading Readiness Inventory, 1998
Reading Skills Diagnostic Test, 1999
Reading Test AD, 2000
Reading Test (Comprehension and Speed): Municipal Tests: National Achievement Tests, 2001
Reading Test: McGraw-Hill Basic Skills System, 2002
Reading Tests A and BD, 2003
Reading Tests EH 1-3, 2004
Reading Versatility Test, T2:1673
Reasoning Tests for Higher Levels of Intelligence, T2:446
REEL Scale, see Bzoch-League Receptive-Expressive Emergent Language Scale: For the Measurement of Language Skills in Infancy, 338
Rehabilitation Client Rating Scale, 2005
Reicherter-Sanders Typewriting I and II, 2006
Reid Report/Reid Survey, 2007
Relevant Aspects of Potential (status unknown), 8:243
Religion Scale, 2008
Religious Attitudes Inventory, 2009
Remmlein's School Law Test, T2:885
Remote Associates Test, 8:244
Research Personnel Review Form, 2010
Reversal Test, 2011
Revised Behavior Problem Checklist, 2012
Revised Beta Examination, Second Edition, 2013
Revised Developmental Screening Inventory—1980, 2014
Revised Minnesota Paper Form Board Test, 2015
Revised Pre-Reading Screening Procedures, 2016
Revised Southend Attainment Test in Mechanical Arithmetic, T2:730
Revised Token Test, 2017
Reynell Developmental Language Scales (Revised), 2018
Reynell-Zinkin Scales: Developmental Scales for Young Visually Handicapped Children Part 1—Mental Development, 2019
Rhode Island Profile of Early Learning Behavior, 2020
Rhode Island Pupil Identification Scale, see Rhode Island Profile of Early Learning Behavior, 2020
Richardson Emergency Psychodiagnostic Summary, T2:1354

Richmond Tests of Basic Skills, 2021
Riley Articulation and Language Test, Revised, 2022
Riley Motor Problems Inventory, Revised 1976, 2023
Riley Preschool Developmental Screening Inventory, 2024
Ring and Peg Tests of Behavior Development, 2025
Risk-Taking-Attitude-Values Inventory, 2026
Road Test Check List for Passenger Car Drivers, T2:849
Road Test Check List for Testing, Selecting, Rating, and Training Coach Operators, T2:2472
Road Test in Traffic for Testing, Selecting, Rating, and Training Truck Drivers [1955 Revision], T2:2473
Robbins Speech Sound Discrimination and Verbal Imagery Type Test (status unknown), T2:2052
Robinson-Hall Reading Tests, T2:1745
Rock-A-Bye, Baby: A Group Projective Test for Children, 2027
Rockford Infant Developmental Evaluation Scales, 2028
Rohde Sentence Completions Test, T2:1498
Rokeach Value Survey, 2029
Rorschach, 2030
Rosenzweig Picture-Frustration Study, 2031
Rosner Perceptual Survey, Experimental Edition, T2:1884
Ross Test of Higher Cognitive Processes, 2032
Roswell-Chall Auditory Blending Test, 2033
Roswell-Chall Diagnostic Reading Test of Word Analysis Skills, Revised and Extended, 2034
Rothwell-Miller Interest Blank, 2035; [British Edition], 2036
Rotter Incomplete Sentences Blank, 2037
Roughness Discrimination Test, 2038
Rucker-Gable Educational Programming Scale, 2039
Runner Studies of Attitude Patterns: Interview Form (status unknown), T2:1356
[Rush Hughes (PB 50): Phonetically Balanced Lists 5–12], 2040
Russell-Sanders Bookkeeping Test, 2041
Rutgers Drawing Test (status unknown), T2:575
Rutgers Social Attribute Inventory, 2042
Ruth Fry Symbolic Profile, 2043
Ryburn Group Intelligence Tests, T2:448
S-D Proneness Checklist, 2044
S-O Rorschach Test, see Structured-Objective Rorschach Test: Preliminary Edition, 2323
Safran Culture Reduced Intelligence Test, 2045
Safran Student's Interest Inventory, Revised Edition, 2046
St. Lucia Graded Word Reading Test, 2047
St. Lucia Reading Comprehension Test, 2048
Sales Aptitude Tests: ETSA Test 7A, 2049
Sales Attitudes Check List, 2050
Sales Comprehension Test, 2051
Sales Method Index, T2:2407
[Sales Motivation], 2052
Sales Motivation Inventory, Revised, 2053
[Sales Relations], 2054
Sales Sentence Completion Blank, 2055
Sales Style Diagnosis Test, 2056
Sales Transaction Audit, 2057
Salford Sentence Reading Test, 2058
San Francisco Vocational Competency Scale, 2059
Sand: Concepts About Print Test, 2060
Sanders-Buller World History Test, 2061
Sanders-Fletcher Spelling Test, 2062

Sanders-Fletcher Vocabulary Test, 2063
Santostefano Tests of Cognitive Control, 2064
SAQS Chicago Q Sort, 2065
Sare-Sanders American Government Test, T2:2013
Sare-Sanders Constitution Test, 2066
Sare-Sanders Sociology Test, 2067
Scale of Effectiveness Motivation, see Effectiveness Motivation Scale, 782
Scale of Socio-Egocentrism (status unknown), T2:1362
Scale to Measure Attitudes Toward Disabled Persons, 2068
Scales for Appraising High School Homemaking Programs, T2:954
Scales for Rating the Behavioral Characteristics of Superior Students, 2069
SCC Clerical Skills Series, 2070
Scholastic Achievement Test for English Lower Standards 2 and 3, 2071; Lower Standards 9 and 10, 2072
Scholastic Achievement Test in Arithmetic, 2073
Scholastic Achievement Test of English Second Language Standard 1, 2074
Scholastic Achievement Tests for English First Language, 2075
Scholastic Mental Ability Tests, T2:454
Scholastic Proficiency Battery, 2076
Schonell Diagnostic Arithmetic Tests, T2:734
Schonell Diagnostic English Tests, T2:110
Schonell Reading Tests, 2077
School Administration and Supervision, 2078
School Apperception Method, 2079
School Atmosphere Questionnaire, 2080
School Attitude Measure, 2081
School Attitude Survey: Feelings I Have About School, 2082
School Attitude Test, 8:395
School Behavior Checklist, 2083
School Equivalence Test, see Ligondé Equivalence Test, 1329
School/Home Observation and Referral System, 2084
School Interest Inventory, 2085
School Inventory, 2086
School Motivation Analysis Test, 2087
School Personnel Research and Evaluation Services, 2088
School Problem Screening Inventory, Fifth Edition, 2089
School Readiness Checklist, 2090
School Readiness Survey, Second Edition, 2091
School Readiness Test, 8:808
School Survey of Interpersonal Relationships, 2092
School Vision Tester, 2093
School Weekly News Quiz, 2094
Schrammel-Gray High School and College Reading Test, T2:1598
Schubert General Ability Battery, 2095
Science Attitude Questionnaire, 2096
Science: Minnesota High School Achievement Examinations, 2097
Science Research Temperament Scale, T2:1368
Science Tests: Content Evaluation Series, 2098
Scientific Knowledge and Aptitude Test, 2099
SCL-90-R, 2100
Scott Mental Alertness Test, 2101
SCREEN, 2102
Screening Deep Test of Articulation, 2103
Screening Speech Articulation Test, 2104
Screening Test for Auditory Perception, 2105

INDEX OF TITLES

Screening Test for the Assignment of Remedial Treatments, 2106
Screening Test of Academic Readiness, 2107
Screening Test of Adolescent Language, 2108
Screening Test of Spanish Grammar, 2109
Screening Tests for Identifying Children With Specific Language Disability, 2110
SEARCH—A Scanning Instrument for the Identification of Potential Learning Disability, Second Edition, Expanded, 2111
Seashore-Bennett Stenographic Proficiency Test: A Standard Recorded Stenographic Worksample, 2112
Seashore Measures of Musical Talents, 2113
Second Year French Test, 2114
Second Year Spanish Test, 2115
Secondary Level English Proficiency Test, 2116
Secondary School Administration, 2117
Secondary School Admission Test: General School Ability and Reading, 2118
Secondary-School Record, 2119
Secondary School Research Program, 8:396
Secondary School Supervision, 2120
Secretarial Performance Analysis, T2:2149
Security-Insecurity Inventory, 2121
SEED Developmental Profiles, 2122
Seeing Faults, T2:576
Seeing Problems, 2123
Seeing Through Arithmetic Tests, T2:735
Seeking of Noetic Goals Test, 2124
Seguin-Goddard Formboard, 2125
[Selection Interview Forms], 2126
Selection Tests for Office Personnel, T2:2150
Self-Actualization Inventory, 2127
Self-Administered Dependency Questionnaire, 2128
Self Administered Health Questionnaire for Secondary School Students (status unknown), T2:940
Self-Analysis Inventory, T2:1371
Self Appraisal Scale for Teachers, 2129
Self-Concept Adjective Checklist, 2130
Self-Concept and Motivation Inventory: What Face Would You Wear?, 2131
Self-Concept as a Learner Scale, 2132
Self-Description Inventory, 2133
Self Directed Search: A Guide to Educational and Vocational Planning, 2134
Self-Esteem Questionnaire, 2135
Self Explorations Inventory, 2136
Self-Interview Inventory, T2:1375
Self-Motivated Career Planning, 2137
Self Perception Inventory [Psychologists and Educators, Inc.], 2138
Self-Perception Inventory [SOARES Associates], 2139
Self Profile Q-Sort, 2140
Self-Rating Depression Scale, 8:675
Self-Rating Scale for Leadership Qualifications, 2141
Self-Report Inventory, 2142
Self-Scoring Mathematics Placement Tests, 2143
Self-Scoring Placement Tests in English and Mathematics, see CGP Self-Scoring Placement Tests in English and Mathematics, 382
Self-Scoring Reading Placement Test, 2144
Self-Scoring Written English Expression Placement Test, 2145
SELF (Self-concept Evaluation of Location Form), 2146
Self Valuation Test, 2147

Senior Apperception Technique, 2148
Senior Aptitude Tests, 2149
Senior English Test, 2150
Senior High Assessment of Reading Performance, 2151
Senior Mathematics Test, 2152
Senior South African Individual Scale, 2153
Sentence Completion Blank, 2154
Sentence Completion Test, 2155
Sentence Comprehension Test, Experimental Edition, 2156
Sentence Imitation Screening Tests, 2157
Separation Anxiety Test, 2158
Sequenced Inventory of Communication Development, 2159
Sequential Tests of Educational Progress (Original Series): Listening, T2:997; Series II, 2160; English Expression, Series II, 2161; Mathematics, Series II, 2162; Mechanics of Writing, Series II, 2163; Reading, Series II, 2164; Science, Series II, 2165; Social Studies, Series II, 2166
Service for Admission to College and University Testing Program, T2:1060
Seven Squares Technique, T2:1508
Sex Attitudes Survey and Profile, Trial Edition, 2167
Sex Knowledge and Attitude Test, Second Edition, 2168
Sex Knowledge Inventory, 2169
Sexometer, 2170
Sexual Adjustment Inventory, 2171
Sexual Communication Inventory, 2172
Sexual Compatibility Test, 2173
Sexual Concerns Checklist, Experimental Edition, 2174
Sexual Development Scale for Females, T2:839
Shapes Analysis Test, 2175
Sheltered Employment Work Experience Program, 2176
Sheridan Gardiner Test of Visual Acuity, 2177
Sherman Mental Impairment Test, T2:1379
Ship Destination Test, 2178
Shipley-Institute of Living Scale for Measuring Intellectual Impairment, 2179
Short Employment Tests, 2180
Short Form Test of Academic Aptitude, 2181
Short Occupational Knowledge Test for Auto Mechanics, 2182; Bookkeepers, 2183; Carpenters, 2184; Draftsmen, 2185; Electricians, 2186; Machinists, 2187; Office Machine Operators, 2188; Plumbers, 2189; Secretaries, 2190; Tool and Die Makers, 2191; Truck Drivers, 2192; Welders, 2193
Short Tests of Clerical Ability, 2194
Shorthand Aptitude Test, 2195
Shorthand Test: Individual Placement Series (status unknown), T2:2156
Shutt Primary Language Indicator Test, 2196
Siebrecht Attitude Scale, 2197
Silent Reading Diagnostic Tests, T2:1647
Silent Reading Tests, T2:1600
Simile Interpretations, 2198
Similes, 2199
Simons Measurements of Music Listening Skills, 2200
Simplex GNV Intelligence Tests, T2:459
Simplex Group Intelligence Scale, T2:460
Simplex Junior Intelligence Tests, T2:461
Simplified Road Test, T2:851
Single and Double Simultaneous (Face-Hand) Stimulation Test, 2201
Sipay Word Analysis Tests, 2202

Situational Attitude Scale, 2203
Situational Leadership, 2204
Situational Parenting, 2205
Situational Preference Inventory, 2206
Six Inventories to Assess Affective Impact of Basic Skills Instructional Programs, 2207
Sixteen Personality Factor Questionnaire, 2208
Sketches, 2209
Skill in Typing: Measurement of Skill Test 9 (status unknown), T2:2157
Skills and Attributes Inventory, 2210
Skills for Independent Living, 2211
Skills Inventory for Parents, 2212
Skills Monitoring System: Reading, 8:776
Sklar Aphasia Scale, Revised 1973, 2213
Sleight Non-Verbal Intelligence Test, T2:462
Slingerland Screening Tests for Identifying Children with Specific Language Disability, 2214
Sloan Achromatopsia Test, 2215
Slosson Drawing Coordination Test for Children and Adults, 2216
Slosson Intelligence Test, 2217
Slosson Oral Reading Test, 2218
Smedley Hand Dynamometer, 2219
Smith-Johnson Nonverbal Performance Scale, 2220
Snijders-Oomen Non-Verbal Intelligence Scale for Young Children, 2221
Snyder Knuth Music Achievement Test, 2222
SOBER Español, 2223
Social and Prevocational Information Battery, 2224
Social Attitude Scale, 2225
Social Behavior Assessment, 2226
Social Climate Scales, 2227
Social Competence Inventories, T2:1385
Social Intelligence Test: George Washington University Series, 2228
Social Interaction and Creativity in Communication System, 2229
Social Relations Test, 2230
Social Skills for Severely Retarded Adults—An Inventory and Training Program, 2231
Social Studies Grade 10 (American History): Minnesota High School Achievement Examinations, 2232
Social Studies Grade 11 (World History): Minnesota High School Achievement Examinations, 2233
Social Studies Grade 12 (American Problems): Minnesota High School Achievement Examinations, 2234
Social Studies: Minnesota High School Achievement Examinations, 2235
Social Studies Test: Acorn National Achievement Tests, T2:1950
Social Studies Test: National Achievement Tests, T2:1951
Socio-Economic Status Scales, 2236
Socio-Sexual Knowledge & Attitudes Test, 2237
Solid Geometry: Achievement Examinations for Secondary Schools, T2:758
Solid Geometry: National Achievement Tests, 2238
Somatic Inkblot Series, 2239
Sound-Apperception Test, 2240
South African Personality Questionnaire, 2241
South African Picture Analysis Test, 2242
Southend Attainment Test in Mechanical Arithmetic, T2:736
Southend Test of Intelligence, T2:463

Southern California Figure-Ground Visual Perception Test, T2:1928
Southern California Kinesthesia and Tactile Perception Tests, T2:1885
Southern California Motor Accuracy Test, 2243
Southern California Perceptual-Motor Tests, T2:1886
Southern California Sensory Integration Tests, 2244
Southgate Group Reading Tests, 2245
Space Relations: Differential Aptitude Tests, 2246
Spache Binocular Reading Test, 2247
Spanish/English Language Performance Screening, 8:172
Spanish/English Reading Comprehension Test, 2248
Spanish I and II: Achievement Examinations for Secondary Schools, T2:320
SPAR Reading Test, 2249
SPAR Spelling Test, 2250
Spatial Orientation Memory Test, 2251
Spatial Visualization Test: The Dailey Vocational Tests, T2:2270
Specific Language Disability Test, 2252
Speech-Appearance Record, T2:2317
Speech Defect Questionnaire (status unknown), T2:2093
Speech Diagnostic Chart (status unknown), T2:2094
Speed of Color Discrimination Test, T2:1930
Speed Scale for Determining Independent Reading Level, 2253
Spelling: Differential Aptitude Tests, 2254
Spelling Errors Test, 2255
Spelling Test for Clerical Workers: [Personnel Research Institute Clerical Battery], 2256
Spelling Test: McGraw-Hill Basic Skills System, 2257
Spelling Test: National Achievement Tests, 2258
Spellmaster, 2259
Spiral Aftereffect Test (status unknown), T2:1387
Spiral Nines, Sixth Edition, T2:464
SPIRE Individual Reading Evaluation (status unknown), 8:773
Sprigle School Readiness Screening Test (status unknown), T2:1731
SRA Achievement Series, 2260
SRA Arithmetic Index, 2261
SRA Attitude Survey, 2262
SRA Clerical Aptitudes, 2263
SRA Coping Skills: A Survey plus Activities, 2264
SRA High School Placement Test, T2:31
SRA Mechanical Aptitudes, 2265
SRA Nonverbal Form, 2266
SRA Pictorial Reasoning Test, 2267
SRA Placement and Counseling Program, 2268
SRA Primary Mental Abilities, 1962 Edition, 2269
SRA Reading Index, 2270
SRA Reading Record, 2271
SRA Sales Attitudes Check List, 2272
SRA Short Test of Educational Ability, T2:451
SRA Test of Mechanical Concepts, 2273
SRA Typing 5, 2274
SRA Typing Skills, 2275
SRA Verbal Form, 2276
Staff Burnout Scale for Health Professionals, 2277
Staffordshire Arithmetic Test, T2:737
Staffordshire Test of Computation, 1974 Revision, 2278
Stamp Behaviour Study Technique, 2279
Standard Reading Inventory, 2280
Standard Reading Tests, 2281
Standardized Bible Content Tests, 2282

INDEX OF TITLES

Standardized Oral Reading Check Tests, 2283
Standardized Oral Reading Paragraphs Test, 2284
Standardized Road-Map Test of Direction Sense, 2285
Stanford Achievement Test: High School Basic Battery, T2:37; High School English and Spelling Tests, T2:114; High School Mathematics, T2:653; High School Numerical Competence Test, T2:654; High School Reading Test, T2:1602; High School Science Test, T2:1795; High School Social Studies Test, T2:1952
Stanford Achievement Test, 1964 Edition: Social Studies Tests, T2:1953; Spelling and Language Tests, T2:115
Stanford Achievement Test, 1973 Edition, 2286; Mathematics Tests, 1973 Edition, 2287; Reading Tests, 1973 Edition, 2288
Stanford-Binet Intelligence Scale, Third Revision, 2289
[Re Stanford-Binet Intelligence Scale] A Clinical Profile for the Stanford Binet Intelligence Scale (L-M), 2290
Stanford Diagnostic Arithmetic Test, T2:738
Stanford Diagnostic Mathematics Test, 2291
Stanford Diagnostic Reading Test, 1976 Edition, 2292
Stanford Early School Achievement Test, 2293
Stanford Hypnotic Susceptibility Scale, 2294
Stanford Mental Arithmetic Test, 2295
Stanford Modern Mathematics Concepts Test, T2:656
Stanford Multi-Modality Imagery Test, T2:773
Stanford-Ohwaki-Kohs Block Design Intelligence Test for the Blind: American Revision of the Ohwaki-Kohs Test, 2296
Stanford Profile Scales of Hypnotic Susceptibility, Revised Edition, 2297
Stanford TASK, see Stanford Test of Academic Skills, 2298
Stanford Test of Academic Skills, 2298
STARS Test (Short Term Auditory Retrieval and Storage), 2299
State-Trait Anxiety Inventory, 2300
State-Trait Anxiety Inventory for Children, 2301
Statistically Validated Written Tests for Police Officer, 2302
Steenburgen Diagnostic-Prescriptive Math Program, 2303
Steinbach Test of Reading Readiness, T2:1732
Stenographic Aptitude Test, T2:794
Stenographic Dictation Test, 2304
Stenographic Skill-Dictation Test, 2305
Stenographic Skills Test: ETSA Test 4A, 2306
Stenographic Test: National Business Entrance Tests, 2307
Stereopathy-Acquiescence Schedule, T2:1393
Stern Activities Index, 2308
[Stevens-Thurow Personnel Forms], 2309
Steward Basic Factors Inventory (1960 Edition), 2310
Steward Life Insurance Knowledge Test, 2311
Steward Occupational Objectives Inventory, 1957 Edition, 2312
Steward Personal Background Inventory (1960 Revised Edition), 2313
Steward Personnel Tests (Short Form), 1958 Edition, 2314
Stockton Geriatric Rating Scale, T2:1396
Stogdill Behavior Cards: A Test-Interview for Delinquent Children, 2315
Strait Biblical Knowledge Test, 2316
Stromberg Dexterity Test, 2317
Strong-Campbell Interest Inventory, 2318
Stroop Color and Word Test, 2319
Structure of Intellect Learning Abilities Test, 2320
Structure Tests—English Language, 2321
Structured and Scaled Interview to Assess Maladjustment, 2322
Structured Clinical Interview, T2:1398
Structured Doll Play Test (status unknown), T2:1512
Structured-Objective Rorschach Test: Preliminary Edition, 2323
STS Closed High School Placement Tests, 2324
STS Educational Development Series: Scholastic Tests, 2325
STS Junior Inventory, 2326
STS Youth Inventory, 2327
Student Attitude Inventory, 2328
Student Description Form, 2329
Student Development Task Inventory (Revised, Second Edition), 2330
Student Disability Survey, 2331
Student Evaluation Scale, 2332
Student Information Form, 2333
Student Instructional Report, 2334
Student Opinion Inventory, 2335
Student Orientations Survey, 2336
Student Reactions to College, 2337
Student's Rating Scale of an Instructor, 2338
Students Typewriting Tests, 2339
Study Attitudes and Methods Survey, 2340
Study Habits Checklist, T2:1767
Study Habits Evaluation and Instruction Kit, 2341
Study Habits Inventory, Revised Edition, 2342
Study of Choices, T2:1402
Study of Values: A Scale for Measuring the Dominant Interests in Personality, Third Edition, 2343; British Edition, 1965, 2344
Study Performance Test, T2:1769
Study Skills Counseling Evaluation, 2345
Study Skills Surveys, 2346
Study Skills Test: McGraw-Hill Basic Skills System, 2347
Stycar Hearing Tests, 2348
Stycar Language Test, 2349
Stycar Vision Tests, 2350
Style of Mind Inventory: Trait, Value and Belief Patterns in Greek, Roman and Hebrew Perspectives, T2:1405
[Styles of Leadership and Management], 2351
Subsumed Abilities Test, 2352
Sucher-Allred Reading Placement Inventory, see New Sucher-Allred Reading Placement Inventory, 1579
Suinn Test Anxiety Behavior Scale, 2353
Suitability Evaluation Scale, see Group Psychotherapy Suitability Evaluation Scale, 1023
Supervisor's Evaluation of Research Personnel, T2:2392
Supervisory Behavior Description, 2354
Supervisory Index, 2355
Supervisory Inventory on Communication, 2356
Supervisory Inventory on Discipline, 2357
Supervisory Inventory on Grievances, 2358
Supervisory Inventory on Human Relations, 2359
Supervisory Inventory on Labor Relations, 2360
Supervisory Inventory on Safety, 2361
Supervisory Practices Inventory, Form A, 2362
Supervisory Practices Test, Revised, 2363
Survey of Basic Competencies, 2364
Survey of Clerical Skills: Individual Placement Series (status unknown), T2:2161

Survey of College Achievement, T2:40
Survey of Educational Leadership Practices, 2365
Survey of Interpersonal Values, 2366
Survey of Management Perception, 2367
Survey of Object Visualization, 2368
Survey of Organizations, 2369
Survey of Personal Attitude "SPA" (With Pictures): Individual Placement Series (status unknown), T2:1408
Survey of Personal Values, 2370
Survey of Primary Reading Development, 2371
Survey of Reading Achievement: California Survey Series, T2:1606
Survey of School Attitudes, 2372
Survey of Space Relations Ability, 2373
Survey of Study Habits and Attitudes, 2374
Survey Test of Algebraic Aptitude: California Survey Series, T2:689
Survey Test of Vocabulary, 2375
Survey Tests of Arithmetic Fundamentals: Dominion Tests, T2:739
Survey Tests of English Usage, T2:116
Survey Tests of Reading, T2:1607
Surveys of Research Administration and Environment, 2376
Swansea Test of Phonic Skills, Experimental Version, T2:1652
SWCEL-P Oral Placement Test for Adults, 2377
SWCEL-P Test of Oral Language Proficiency, 2378
Sweet Technical Information Test, 2379
Swimming Ability Scales for Boys in Secondary Schools: National Swimming Norms, T2:941
Symbol Digit Modalities Test, 2380
Symbol Elaboration Test, 2381
Symbol Identities, 2382
Symbol Series Test: I.B.P. Edition, 1968, T2:584
Symbolic Play Test, Experimental Edition, 2383
Symonds Picture-Story Test, 2384
Symptom Sign Inventory: Personality and Personal Illness Questionnaire, T2:1410
Syntax One, 2385
Syntax Two, 2386
System of Multicultural Pluralistic Assessment, 2387
Systematic Interview Guides, T2:1411
Szondi Test, 2388
TA Survey, 2389
Tapping Test: A Predictor of Typing and Other Tapping Operations, 2390
TARC Assessment Inventory for Severely Handicapped Children, 2391
Target Behavior, 8:690
Task Assessment For Prescriptive Teaching, 2392
Tasks of Emotional Development Test, 2393
TAV Selection System, 2394
Taylor-Helmstadter Pair Comparison Scale of Aesthetic Judgement, 2395
Taylor-Johnson Temperament Analysis, 2396
Teacher Attitude Inventory, 2397
Teacher Education Examination Program, T2:898; Art Education, T2:191; Biology and General Science, T2:1797; Business Education, T2:797; Chemistry, Physics and General Science, T2:1798; Early Childhood Education, T2:899; Elementary School Education, T2:900; English Language and Literature, T2:117; French, T2:260; General Professional Examinations, T2:41; Home Economics Education, T2:955; Industrial Arts, T2:973; Mathematics, T2:657; Music Education, T2:213; Physical Education, T2:942; Social Studies, T2:1954; Spanish, T2:321
Teacher Evaluation by Objectives, 8:404
Teacher-Image Questionnaire, 2398
Teacher Opinionaire on Democracy, 2399
Teacher Preference Schedule, T2:902
Teacher Self-Rating Inventory, 2400
Teacher's Handbook of Diagnostic Inventories, Second Edition, 2401
Teacher's Handbook of Diagnostic Screening, Second Edition, 2402
Teaching Aptitude Test: George Washington University Series, 2403
Teaching Evaluation Record, T2:905
Teaching Research Motor-Development Scale, 2404
Team Effectiveness Survey, 2405
Tear Ballot for Industry, T2:2289
Technical and Scholastic Test: The Dailey Vocational Tests, 2406
Technical Personnel Recruiting Inventory, 2407
Technical Tests, 2408
Temperament and Values Inventory, 2409
Temperament Comparator, 2410
Temperament Inventory, 2411
Temperament Questionnaire, T2:1414
Templin-Darley Tests of Articulation, 2412
Tennessee Self Concept Scale, 2413
Tests A/8: Arithmetic, 2414
Test A/16 (Mathematical Achievement Test), T2:658
Test A/65, 2415
Test Anxiety Profile, 2416
Test Attitude Inventory, 2417
Test for Ability to Sell: George Washington University Series, 2418
Test for Colour-Blindness, 2419
Test for Developmental Age in Girls, T2:1416
Test for Firefighter B-1(m), 2420
Test for High School Entrants, T2:42
Test for Police Officer A-1, T2:2374
Test of Active Vocabulary, 2421
Test of Adolescent Language, 2422
Test of Adult College Aptitude, 2423
Test of Auditory Comprehension, 2424
Test of Auditory Discrimination, 2425
Test of Aural Perception in English for Japanese Students, 2426
Test of Aural Perception in English for Latin-American Students, 2427
Test of Basic Assumptions, 2428
Test of Behavioral Rigidity, Research Edition, 2429
Test of Children's Learning Ability—Individual Version, 2430
Test of Cognitive Skills, 2431
Test of Competence in Mathematics Level 4–5, 6–7, 8–9, 2432
Test of Concept Utilization, 2433
Test of Consumer Competencies, 2434
Test of Creative Potential, 2435
Test of Early Language Development, 2436
Test of Early Learning Skills, 2437
Test of Early Reading Ability, 2438
Test of Economic Achievement, 2439
Test of Economic Literacy, 2440

INDEX OF TITLES

Test of Economic Understanding, T2:1968
Test of Elementary Economics, Revised Experimental Edition, 8:901
Test of English as a Foreign Language, 2441
Test of English Usage, 2442
Test of Enquiry Skills, 2443
Test of Family Attitudes (status unknown), T2:1518
Test of Family Life Knowledge and Attitudes: Betty Crocker Search for Leadership in Family Living, T2:956
Test of Grammatically Correct Spanish/English, Written and Oral, 2444
Test of Individual Needs in Reading, Seventh Edition (status unknown), T2:1653
Test of Language Development, 2445
Test of Lateral Awareness and Directionality, 2446
Test of Library/Study Skills, 2447
Test of Listening Accuracy in Children, 2448
Test of Minimal Articulation Competence, 2449
Test of Motor Impairment, 2450
Test of Musicality, Fourth Edition, 2451
Test of Nonverbal Auditory Discrimination, 2452
Test of Perceptual Organization, 2453
Test of Performance in Computational Skills, 2454
Test of Phonic Skills, T2:1654
Test of Reading and Number: Inter-American Series, 2455
Test of Reading Comprehension: A Method for Assessing the Understanding of Written Language, 2456
Test of Retail Sales Insight, 2457
Test of Scholastic Abilities, 2458
Test of Science-Related Attitudes, 2459
Test of Social Inferences, 2460
Test of Social Insight, 2461
Test of the Hierarchy of Inductive Knowledge, 2462
Test of Understanding in College Economics, T2:1970
Test of Understanding in Personal Economics, 2463
Test of Work Competency and Stability, 2464
Test of Written English, 2465
Test of Written Language, 2466
Test on the Fundamentals of Hebrew, 2467
Test on Understanding Science, 2467A
Test on Use of the Dictionary, 2468
Test Orientation Procedure, 2469
Testing Academic Achievement, 2470
[Tests A/9 and A/10], 2471
Tests for Auditory Comprehension of Language, 2472
Tests for Everyday Living, 2473
Tests for Venereal Disease Education, T2:943
Tests of Academic Progress, 2474; Composition, T2:119; Literature, T2:143; Mathematics, T2:659; Reading, T2:1608; Science, T2:1799; Social Studies, T2:1955
Tests of Achievement and Proficiency, Form T, 2475
Tests of Achievement in Basic Skills: Mathematics, 2476
Tests of Adult Basic Education, 1976 Edition, 2477
Tests of Arithmetic and Language for Indian South Africans, T2:46
Tests of Basic Experiences 2, 2478; Language, 2479; Mathematics, 2480; Science, 2481; Social Studies, 2482
Tests of English as a Second Language, 2483
Tests of General Ability: Inter-American Series, 2484
Tests of General Ability [Science Research Associates, Inc.], T2:467
Tests of General Educational Development, 2485

Tests of Perception of Scientists and Self, 2486
Tests of Proficiency in English, 2487
Tests of Reading: Inter-American Series, 2488
Tests of Social Intelligence, 2489
Tests of the Physical Science Study Committee, T2:1872
Thackray Reading Readiness Profiles, 2490
Thematic Apperception Test, 2491
Thematic Apperception Test for African Subjects, T2:1520
Themes Concerning Blacks, 2492
Theological School Inventory, 2493
Therapy Attitude Inventory, 2494
Thinking Creatively in Action and Movement, 2495
Thinking Creatively With Sounds and Words, Research Edition, 2496
This I Believe Test, 2497
Thompson Smoking and Tobacco Knowledge Test, 2498
Thorman Family Relations Technique, 8:356
Thorndike Dimensions of Temperament, T2:1422
3-D Test of Visualization Skill, 8:885
Thurstone Employment Tests, T2:2162
Thurstone Interest Schedule, T2:2214
Thurstone Temperament Schedule, 2499
Thurstone Test of Mental Alertness, 2500
Tickmaster, 2501
Time Appreciation Test, 2502
Time Current Affairs Test, 2503
Time Monthly News Quiz, 2504
Time Questionnaire: Assessing Suicide Potential, 2505
Titmus Vision Tester, 2506
T.M.R. Performance Profile for the Severely and Moderately Retarded, 2507
T.M.R. School Competency Scales, 2508
Token Test for Children, 2509
Toledo Chemistry Placement Examination, 2510
Tomkins-Horn Picture Arrangement Test, T2:1522
Tooze Braille Speed Test: A Test of Basic Ability in Reading Braille, 2511
Torrance Tests of Creative Thinking, 2512
Toy World Test, 2513
TRACOR Audiometers, 2514
Trait Evaluation Index, 2515
Trankell's Laterality Tests: A Battery of Diagnostic Tests for the Determination of Degree of Left-Hand Preference and Asymmetry of Motor Skills, T2:1890
Transactional Analysis Life Position Survey, 2516
Transitional Assessment, 2517
Transitional Assessment Modules, see Transitional Assessment, 2517
Traxler High School Reading Test, Revised, 2518
Traxler High School Spelling Test, 2519
Traxler Silent Reading Test, 2520
Tree · Bee Test of Auditory Discrimination, 2521
Tree Test, 2522
Tressler English Minimum Essentials Test, Revised Edition, 2523
Triadal Equated Personality Inventory, 2524
Trigonometry: Minnesota High School Achievement Examinations, 2525
Trigonometry Test for Stds 9 and 10, 8:315
Truck Driver Test, T2:2475
Turse Shorthand Aptitude Test, T2:798
Twitchell-Allen Three-Dimensional Personality Test, 2526
Two-Figure Formboard, T2:590

Typewriting Test: National Business Entrance Tests, 2527
Typing Skill, 2528
Typing Test for Business, 2529
Typing Test: Individual Placement Series (status unknown), T2:2165
Uncritical Inference Test, T2:1774
Undergraduate Assessment Program, 8:480
Understanding Communication (Verbal Comprehension), 2530
Understanding in Science Test, 2531
Uniform Performance Assessment System, 2532
United Students Typewriting Test, Volume 14, 2533
University Residence Environment Scale, 2534
UP Aptitude Test, 8:204
UP Area Tests, 8:36
UP Field Test in Art History, 8:88; Biology, 8:836; Business, 8:330; Chemistry, 8:854; Drama and Theatre, 8:979; Economics, 8:903; Education, 8:406; Engineering, 8:1089; French, 8:125; Geography, 8:905; Geology, 8:856; German, 8:137; History, 8:916; Literature, 8:71; Mathematics, 8:295; Music, 8:100; Philosophy, 8:456; Physical Education, 8:415; Physics, 8:867; Political Science, 8:924; Psychology, 8:462; Scholastic Philosophy, 8:457; Sociology, 8:927; Spanish, 8:173; Speech Pathology and Audiology, 8:931
USES Basic Occupational Literacy Test, 2535
USES Clerical Skills Tests, 2536
USES General Aptitude Test Battery, 2537
USES Interest Inventory, 2538
USES Nonreading Aptitude Test Battery, 1982 Edition, 2539
Uses Test, 2540
Utah Test of Language Development, Revised Edition, 2541
Utility Test, T2:591
VALCAN Vocational Interest Profile (VIP), 2542
VAL-ED Educational Values, 890g
Valett Developmental Survey of Basic Learning Abilities, 2543
Valett Inventory of Critical Thinking Abilities, 2544
Values Inventory, 2545
Values Inventory for Children, 2546
Van Wagenen Analytical Reading Scales, T2:1612
Van Wagenen Reading Readiness Scales, T2:1733
Vane Evaluation of Language Scale, 2547
Vane Kindergarten Test, 2548
Vane-L, see Vane Evaluation of Language Scale, 2547
Vasectomy Scale: Attitudes, 2549
VD Knowledge Test, T2:946
Verbal Auditory Screening for Children, 2550
Verbal Language Developmental Scale, 2551
Verbal Power Test of Concept Equivalence, 2552
Verbal Reasoning, 2553
Verbal Reasoning: Differential Aptitude Tests, 2554
Veterinary Aptitude Test, 2555
Vigotsky Test, see Kasanin-Hanfmann Concept Formation Test, 1239
Vincent Mechanical Diagrams Test, 2556
Vineland Social Maturity Scale, 2557
Violence Scale, 2558
Visco Child Development Screening Test, 2559
Visual Apperception Test '60 (status unknown), T2:1526
Visual Aural Digit Span Test, 2560

Visual Comprehension Test for Detective, T2:2375
Visual Discrimination Test, 2561
Visual Memory Scale, 2562
Visual Memory Test, 2563
Visual Pattern Recognition Test and Diagnostic Schedule, 2564
Visual-Verbal Test: A Measure of Conceptual Thinking, 2565
Visualization Test of Three Dimensional Orthographic Shape, T2:1935
Vocabulary Comprehension Scale, 2566
Vocabulary Survey Test, T2:175
Vocabulary Test for High School Students and College Freshmen, 2567
Vocabulary Test: McGraw-Hill Basic Skills System, 2568
Vocabulary Test: National Achievement Tests, 2569
Vocational Adaptation Rating Scale, 2570
Vocational Apperception Test: Advanced Form, 2571
Vocational Behavior Checklist, 2572
Vocational Exploration and Insight Kit, 2573
Vocational Interest and Sophistication Assessment, 2574
Vocational Interest, Experience, and Skill Assessment, 2575
Vocational Interest Inventory, 2576
Vocational Interest Profile, 2577
Vocational Interest Questionnaire for Pupils in Standards 6-10, 2578
Vocational Opinion Index, 2579
Vocational Planning Inventory, 8:1027
Vocational Preference Index, 2580
Vocational Preference Inventory, Seventh Revision, 2581
Wachs Analysis of Cognitive Structures, 2582
Wahler Physical Symptoms Inventory, 2583
Wahler Self-Description Inventory, 2584
W.A.L. English Comprehension Test, T2:1613
Walker Problem Behavior Identification Checklist, 2585
Walton-Sanders English Test, 2586
Ward Atmosphere Scale, 2587
Ward Behavior Inventory, 2588
Washington Pre-College Test, 2589
Washington Speech Sound Discrimination Test, 2590
Washington University Sentence Completion Test, 8:708
Watkins-Farnum Performance Scale: A Standardized Achievement Test for All Band Instruments, 2591
Watson Diagnostic Mathematics Test: Computation, Fourth Edition, 2592
Watson English Usage and Appreciation Test, Fourth Edition, 2593
Watson-Glaser Critical Thinking Appraisal, 2594
Watson Number-Readiness Test, Fifth Edition, 2595
Watson Reading-Readiness Test, 2596
Weber Advanced Spatial Perception Test, 2597
Wechsler Adult Intelligence Scale-Revised, 2598
[Re Wechsler Adult Intelligence Scale] Rhodes WAIS Scatter Profile, 2599
[Re Wechsler Adult Intelligence Scale] WAIS Mental Description Sheet, 2600
[Re Wechsler Adult Intelligence Scale] WAIS Test Profile, 2601
Wechsler Intelligence Scale for Children-Revised, 2602
[Re Wechsler Intelligence Scale for Children-Revised] WISC-R Profile Form, 2603
[Re Wechsler Intelligence Scale for Children] California Abbreviated WISC, T2:534

INDEX OF TITLES

[Re Wechsler Intelligence Scale for Children] Rhodes WISC Scatter Profile, 2604
[Re Wechsler Intelligence Scale for Children] WISC Test Profile and WISC-R Profile, 2605
Wechsler Intelligence Scales for Children-Revised: For the Deaf, 2606
Wechsler Memory Scale, 2607
Wechsler Preschool and Primary Scale of Intelligence, 2608
[Re Wechsler Preschool and Primary Scale of Intelligence] WPPSI Test Profile, 2609
Weidner-Fensch Speech Screening Test, T2:2099
Weighted-Score Likability Rating Scale (status unknown), T2:1436
Weights and Pulleys: A Test of Intuitive Mechanics, 2610
Weiss Comprehensive Articulation Test, 2611
Weller-Strawser Scales of Adaptive Behavior, 2612
Welsh Figure Preference Test, 2613
Wesman Personnel Classification Test, 2614
Western Aphasia Battery, 2615
Western Personality Inventory, 2616
Western Personnel Tests, 2617
Wetzel Grid Charts, T2:947
What I Like to Do: An Inventory of Students' Interests, 2618
Whisler Strategy Test, 2619
Whitaker Index of Schizophrenic Thinking, 2620
Wide Range Achievement Test, 1978 Edition, 2621
Wide Range Employability Sample Test, 2622
Wide Range Intelligence and Personality Test, 2623
Wide Range Interest-Opinion Test, 2624
Wide Range Vocabulary Test, T2:179
Wide-span Reading Test, 2625
Williams Awareness Sentence Completion, 2626
Williams Intelligence Test for Children With Defective Vision, 2627
Williams Primary Reading Test, T2:1615
Williams Reading Test for Grades 4–9, T2:1616
Willner Instance Similarities Test (status unknown), T2:593
Wilson Driver Selection Test, 2628
Wilson-Patterson Attitude Inventory, 2629
Wilson Teacher-Appraisal Scale, 2630
Wing Standardised Tests of Musical Intelligence, 2631
WISC—R Split-Half Short Form, 2632
Wisconsin Card Sorting Test, 2633
Wisconsin Tests of Reading Skill Development: Study Skills, 2634; Word Attack, 2635
WLW Personal Survey, Form 3, 2636
Wold Digit-Symbol Test, T2:1891
Wold Sentence Copying Test, T2:1892
Wold Visuo-Motor Test, T2:1893
Wonderlic Personnel Selection Procedure, 2637
Wonderlic Personnel Test, 2638
Woodcock-Johnson Psycho-Educational Battery, 2639
Woodcock Language Proficiency Battery, 2640
Woodcock Reading Mastery Tests, 2641
Woods: Cooperative Industrial Arts Tests, T2:975
Word and Number Assessment Inventory, 2642
Word Clue Tests, T2:180
Word Dexterity Test, 2643
Word Discrimination Test, 2644
Word Fluency, 2645
Word Intelligibility by Picture Identification, 2646
Word Recognition Test, 2647
WORD Test, 2648
Word Understanding, 2649
Work Attitudes Questionnaire, Research Version, 2650
Work Elements Inventory, 2651
Work Environment Preference Schedule, 8:712
Work Environment Scale, 2652
Work Information Inventory 2653
Work Interest Index, 2654
[Work Motivation], 2655
Work Reference Check, 2656
Work Values Inventory, 2657
Workshop Evaluation Scale, 8:1058
World History/Objective Tests, 2658
World History Test: Acorn National Achievement Tests, T2:2003
World Literature Anthology Tests, 2659
World of Work Inventory, 8:1031
WPS Supervisor-Executive Tri-Dimensional Evaluation Scales, 8:1188
WRITE: Junior and Senior High, 2660
Writing Proficiency Program, 2661
Writing Skills Test, T2:124
Writing Test: McGraw-Hill Basic Skills System, 2662
Written Language Syntax Test, 2663
Yarn Dexterity Test, 2664
Yellow Brick Road, 2665
Y.E.M.R. Performance Profile for the Young Moderately and Mildly Retarded, 2666
Youth Research Survey, 2667
ZECO Pure Tone Screening for Children, 2668
Zenith Audiometers, 2669
Zimmerman-Sanders Social Studies Test, 2670
Zip Scale for Determining Independent Reading Level, 2671
Zulliger Individual and Group Test, 2672

CLASSIFIED SUBJECT INDEX

This index classifies all tests included in TIP III into seventeen subject categories: Achievement Batteries, Developmental, English, Fine Arts, Foreign Languages, Intelligence and Scholastic Aptitude, Mathematics, Miscellaneous, Multi-Aptitude Batteries, Neuropsychological, Personality, Reading, Science, Sensory-Motor, Social Studies, Speech and Hearing, and Vocations. Each test category appears in alphabetical order. Most categories also include subcategories. Tests are ordered alphabetically within the smallest category. Each test entry includes test title, population for which the test is intended, and the test entry number in TIP III. Where appropriate, a given test may be included in more than one category. Brief suggestions for the use of this index are presented in the Introduction.

ACHIEVEMENT BATTERIES

Academic Proficiency Battery, college entrants, see 15
Adult Basic Learning Examination, adults with achievement levels grades 1–4, 5–8, 9–12, see 121
American School Achievement Tests, Revised Edition, grades 1–9, see 169
Assessment of Basic Competencies, ages 3+–15 years, see 208
Australian Item Bank, grades 8–12, see 232
Basic Educational Skills Inventory, grades kgn–6, see 247
Basic Educational Skills Test, grades 1.5–5, see 250
Basic Skills Assessment, grades 7 and over, see 259
Basic Skills Inventory, grades kgn–12, see 265
Brigance Diagnostic Inventory of Basic Skills, grades kgn–6, see 313
Brigance Diagnostic Inventory of Early Development, ages 0–7, see 314
Brigance Diagnostic Inventory of Essential Skills, grades 4–12, see 315
Brigance K & 1 Screen for Kindergarten and First Grade, grades kgn, 1, see 316
Bristol Achievement Tests, ages 8–0 to 13–11, see 317
California Achievement Tests, Forms C and D, grades kgn to 12–9, see 344
California Achievement Tests: Spelling and Reference Skills, Form C, grades 3–6 to 12–9, see 347
Canadian Achievement Tests, Form A, grades 1.6–12.9, see 360

Canadian Tests of Basic Skills, grades 1.7–8, see 363
CAP Achievement Series, kgn–12.9, see 365
CGP Self-Scoring Placement Tests in English and Mathematics, students entering postsecondary institutions with open-door policies, see 382
CIRCUS, nursery school and kgn entrants, first grade entrants, see 404
CLEP General Examinations, 1–2 years college or equivalent, see 411
CLS: Classroom Learning Screening, grades 1–6, see 480
Cluster Analysis of Wechsler/WRAT, ages 5 and over, see 481
Comprehensive Tests of Basic Skills, [Forms U & V], grades kgn to 12–9, see 551
Cooperative Primary Tests, grades 1.5–3, see 582
Criterion Test of Basic Skills, grades kgn–8, see 635
Diagnostic Screening Test: Achievement, grades kgn–13, see 721
Diagnostic Skills Battery, grades 1–8, see 726
Distar Mastery Tests, preschool–grade 3, see 737
Drumcondra Attainment Tests, grades 2–9, see 756
Educational Goal Attainment Tests, grades 7–12, see 777
El Circo, ages 4–6, see 789
ERB Comprehensive Testing Program II, grades 1–12, see 838
Everyday Skills Tests, grades 6–12, see 851

521

Guidance Test Battery for Secondary Pupils (Standard 8), secondary pupils, see 1041
High Level Battery: Test A/75, adults with at least 12 years of education, see 1079
Iowa Tests of Basic Skills, Forms 7 and 8, grades kgn–9, see 1192
Iowa Tests of Educational Development, [Seventh Edition], grades 9–12, see 1193
IOX Basic Skill System, end of grades 5 or 6 to grade 12, see 1195
Life Skills, Forms 1 and 2, grades 9–12 and adults, see 1326
Ligondé Equivalence Test, adults who left elementary or secondary school 15 to 20 years ago, see 1329
Mastery: Survival Skills Tests, grades 7–12, see 1401
Metropolitan Achievement Tests, 5th Edition (1978), grades kgn–12.9, see 1473
Minimum Essentials Test, grades 8–12 and adults, see 1491
National Educational Development Tests, grades 7–10, see 1557
NTE Core Battery, college seniors and teachers, see 1624
NTE Programs, college seniors and teachers, see 1625
Optometry College Admission Test, optometry college applicants, see 1731
Peabody Individual Achievement Test, grades kgn–12, see 1769
[Primary Survey Tests], grades 2, 3, see 1897
Richmond Tests of Basic Skills, junior school (ages 8–1 to 11–0) and secondary school (ages 11–1 to 14–0), see 2021
Scholastic Proficiency Battery, standards 8–10, see 2076
Sequential Tests of Educational Progress, Series II, grades 4–14, see 2160

SRA Achievement Series, grades kgn–12, see 2260
Standardized Bible Content Tests, bible college, see 2282
Stanford Achievement Test, 1973 Edition, grades 1.5–9.5, see 2286
Stanford Early School Achievement Test, grades kgn–1.8, see 2293
Stanford Test of Academic Skills, grades 8–12 and grade 13 in junior/community college, see 2298
STS Closed High School Placement Tests, grade 9 entrants, see 2324
Survey of Basic Competencies, ages 3–15, see 2364
Task Assessment For Prescriptive Teaching, ages 6 and over, see 2392
Test of Enquiry Skills, junior high school, see 2443
Test of Reading and Number: Inter-American Series, grade 4 entrants, see 2455
Tests of Academic Progress, grades 9–12, see 2474
Tests of Achievement and Proficiency, Form T, grades 9–12, see 2475
Tests of Adult Basic Education, 1976 Edition, adults at reading levels grades 2–9, see 2477
Tests of Basic Experiences 2, prekgn–grade 1, see 2478
Tests of General Educational Development, candidates for high school equivalency certificates, see 2485
Transitional Assessment, students transferring from primary to secondary schools, see 2517
USES Basic Occupational Literacy Test, educationally disadvantaged adults, see 2535
Washington Pre-College Test, college bound high school students, see 2589
Wide Range Achievement Test, 1978 Edition, ages 5–11, 12 and over, see 2621
Word and Number Assessment Inventory, high school students and adults, see 2642

DEVELOPMENTAL

ABC Inventory to Determine Kindergarten and School Readiness, entrants to kgn and grade 1, see 7
Academic Readiness Scale, first grade entrants, see 16
ACER Checklists for School Beginners, age 5, see 24
ACER Early School Series, 5–5½-year old school beginners, see 27
Ahr's Individual Development Survey, grades kgn–1, see 150
Ann Arbor Learning Inventory, grades kgn–4, see 181
Anton Breener Developmental Gestalt Test of School Readiness, ages 5–6, see 183
Assessment in Nursery Education, ages 3–5, see 207
Autism Screening Instrument for Educational Planning, (First Edition), preschool and school aged severely handicapped and autistic, see 234
Barclay Early Childhood Skill Assessment Guide, preschool–grade 1, see 240
Basic School Skills Inventory, ages 4–8, see 256
Bayley Scales of Infant Development, ages 2–30 months, see 270
Birth to Three Developmental Scale, birth to 3 years and older children suspected to fall below the 3-year age level developmentally, see 295
Brazelton Neonatal Assessment Scale, age 3 days to 4 weeks, see 311

Brigance Diagnostic Inventory of Early Development, ages 0–7, see 314
Brigance K & 1 Screen for Kindergarten and First Grade, grades kgn, 1, see 316
CLEP Subject Examination in Human Growth and Development, persons entering college or already in college, see 445
Comprehensive Identification Process, ages 2.5–5.5, see 550
Cooperative Preschool Inventory, Revised Edition, ages 3–6, see 581
Cutrona Child Study Profile of Psycho-Educational Abilities, grades kgn–3 and special education classes, see 651
D.A.L.E. System: Developmental Assessment of Life Experiences, profound to severely mentally retarded, less impaired mental abilities, see 656
Dennis Test of Child Development, grades kgn–1, see 671
Denver Developmental Screening Test, ages 2 weeks to 6 years, see 678
Denver Prescreening Developmental Questionnaire, ages 3 months–6 years, see 680
Developmental Activities Screening Inventory, ages 6–60 months, see 693
Developmental Assessment for the Severely Handi-

capped, individuals functioning within the 0–6 year developmental range, see 694
Developmental Checklist, visually impaired multi-handicapped children ages 1–8, see 695
Developmental Indicators for the Assessment of Learning, ages 2.5–5.5, see 696
Developmental Potential of Preschool Children, handicapped children ages 2–6, see 697
Developmental Profile II, birth to age 9, see 698
Developmental Task Analysis, grades kgn–6, see 699
Developmental Tasks for Kindergarten Readiness, children prior to kindergarten entrance, see 700
Environmental Prelanguage Battery, children with language delays functioning at or below the single-word level, see 836
Evanston Early Identification Scale, Field Research Edition, ages 5–0 to 6–3, see 850
Fairview Development Scale: For the Infirm Mentally Retarded, severely and profoundly mentally retarded, see 865
Fairview Social Skills Scale: For Mildly and Moderately Retarded, mentally retarded, see 869
First Grade Screening Test, first grade entrants, see 891
Gesell Preschool Test, ages 2.5–6, see 952
Gesell School Readiness Test, ages 5–9, see 953
Grassi Basic Cognitive Evaluation, ages 3–9, see 1004
Infant Rating Scale, ages 5, 7, see 1147
Instrument for Disability Screening, [Developmental Edition], primary grade children, see 1161
Inventory of Primary Skills, grades kgn–1, see 1182
Johnson-Kenney Screening Test, ages 5.5–6.5, see 1221
Kaufman Development Scale, birth to age 9 and mentally retarded all ages, see 1242
Keele Pre-School Assessment Guide, children in nursery school, see 1243
Kent Infant Development Scale, ages 2–13 months, see 1246
Learning Staircase, developmental ages 1½–7, see 1307
Lexington Developmental Scales, ages birth–6 years, see 1322
Lollipop Test: A Diagnostic Screening Test of School Readiness, see 1338
Marianne Frostig Developmental Test of Visual Perception, Third Edition, ages 3–8, see 1371
McCarthy Scales of Children's Abilities, ages 2.5–8.5, see 1424
McCarthy Screening Test, ages 4–6.5, see 1425
Meeting Street School Screening Test, grades kgn–1, see 1459
Minnesota Child Development Inventory, ages 1–6, see 1492
Minnesota Infant Development Inventory, birth to 15 months, see 1496
Minnesota Preschool Inventory, ages 3–6, see 1504

PIP Development Charts, mentally handicapped children birth to age 5, see 1836
Pre-Academic Learning Inventory, ages 4.5–6, see 1863
Preschool Attainment Record, Research Edition, ages 6 months to 7 years, see 1874
Preschool Language Assessment Instrument, Experimental Edition, ages 3–6, see 1876
Preschool Language Scale, Revised Edition, ages 2–6, see 1877
Preschool Screening Instrument, ages 4–5, see 1878
Primary Academic Sentiment Scale, ages 4–4 to 7–3, see 1889
Progress Assessment Chart of Social Development, mentally handicapped ages birth–1, 1–7, 6–15, adults, see 1908
Psycho-Educational Battery, grades kgn–6, 7–16 and adults, see 1925
Psychoeducational Evaluation of the Preschool Child: A Manual Utilizing the Haeussermann Approach, preschool children, see 1926
Quickscreen, grades kgn–2, see 1971
Rapid Exam for Early Referral, ages 3–6, see 1973
Revised Developmental Screening Inventory—1980, ages 1–36 months, see 2014
Reynell Developmental Language Scales (Revised), ages 1–7, see 2018
Reynell-Zinkin Scales: Developmental Scales for Young Visually Handicapped Children Part 1—Mental Development, ages 0–5, see 2019
Riley Preschool Developmental Screening Inventory, ages 3–5, see 2024
Ring and Peg Tests of Behavior Development, birth to age 6, see 2025
Rockford Infant Developmental Evaluation Scales, birth to 4 years, see 2028
Santostefano Tests of Cognitive Control, children and adults, see 2064
School Readiness Checklist, ages 5–6, see 2090
School Readiness Survey, Second Edition, ages 4–6, see 2091
SEED Developmental Profiles, birth to 48 months, see 2122
Test of Early Language Development, ages 3–0 to 7–11, see 2436
Test of Early Learning Skills, ages 3.5–5.5, see 2437
Tests of Basic Experiences 2, prekgn–grade 1, see 2478
Uniform Performance Assessment System, all ages with developmental level birth to 6 years, see 2532
Valett Developmental Survey of Basic Learning Abilities, ages 2–7, see 2543
Vane Kindergarten Test, ages 4–6, see 2548
Visco Child Development Screening Test, ages 3–7, see 2559
Wachs Analysis of Cognitive Structures, ages 3–6, see 2582

ENGLISH

ACT Proficiency Examination in Freshman English, college and adults, see 89
Advanced Placement Examination in English (Composition and Literature), high school students desiring credit for college level courses or admission to advanced courses, see 128

Advanced Placement Examination in English (Language and Composition), high school students desiring credit for college level courses or admission to advanced courses, see 129

Alberta Essay Scales: Models, high school English teachers, see 151

Alphabet Mastery, second semester kindergarten to 2.5, second semester kindergarten and over, see 156

Ambiguous Word Language Dominance Test, Spanish/English, bilingual students ages 10 and over, see 158

American School Achievement Tests: Part 3, Language and Spelling, Revised Edition, grades 2–9, see 172

Assessment of Basic Competencies: Language Module, ages 3–15, see 210

Barrett-Ryan English Test, grades 7–13, see 242

Basic Inventory of Natural Language, grades kgn–12, see 251

Basic Skills Assessment: A Writer's Skills, grades 7 and over, see 262

Basic Skills Assessment: Writing Sample, grades 7 and over, see 263

Basic Skills Inventory: Language Arts, grades kgn–12, see 266

Berry-Talbott Language Test: Comprehension of Grammar, ages 5–8, see 285

Bilingual Oral Language Test, grades 7–12, see 289

Bilingual Syntax Measure, bilingual children grades kgn–2, see 290

Bilingual Syntax Measure II, grades 3–12, see 291

Bristol Achievement Tests: English Language, ages 8–0 to 13–11, see 318

Business English Test: The Daily Vocational Tests, grades 8–12 and adults, see 331

Caso Test for Limited English Speaking Students, limited English-speaking students ages 8–12 living in an English-speaking setting, see 379

CGP Self-Scoring Placement Tests in English and Mathematics, students entering postsecondary institutions with open-door policies, see 382

CLEP General Examinations: English Composition and English Composition Test with Essay, 1–2 years or equivalent, see 412

CLEP Subject Examination in College Composition, persons entering college or already in college, see 429

CLEP Subject Examination in Freshman English, persons entering college or already in college, see 438

Clinical Evaluation of Language Functions—Diagnostic Battery, grades kgn–12, see 474

Clinical Evaluation of Language Functions, Elementary and Advanced Screening Tests, grades kgn–12, see 475

College Board Achievement Test in English Composition, candidates for college entrance, see 490

College Board Scholastic Aptitude Test and Test of Standard Written English, candidates for college entrance, see 501

College English Placement Test, college entrants, see 503

College English Test: National Achievement Tests, grades 12–13, see 504

College Placement Test in English Composition, entering college freshmen, see 530

Communication Screen, ages 2–10 to 5–9, see 538

Comprehensive English Language Test for Speakers of English as a Second Language, non-native speakers of English, see 549

Cooperative English Tests, grades 9–14, see 570

Cooperative English Tests: English Expression, grades 9–14, see 571

Cooperative Primary Tests: Writing Skills, grades 2.5–3, see 587

Diagnostic Screening Test: Language, Second Edition, grades 1–12, see 722

Diagnostic Word Patterns Tests, grades 3 and over, see 730

Distar Mastery Tests: Language I, preschool–grade 3, see 740

Distar Mastery Tests: Language II, preschool–grade 3, see 741

Dos Amigos Verbal Language Scales, ages 5–0 to 13–5, see 749

DTLS Sentence Structure Test, beginning students in two- and four-year institutions, see 759

DTLS Usage Test, beginning students in two- and four-year institutions, see 760

English Progress Tests, various ages 7–3 to 15–6, see 825

English Test F3, ages 12–13, see 826

English Test: Municipal Tests: National Achievement Tests, grades 3–8, see 827

English Test: National Achievement Tests, grades 3–12, see 828

Environmental Language Inventory, children with severe delay in expressive language, see 834

Essentials of English Tests, Revised Edition, grades 7–13, see 844

Flexibility Language Dominance Test, Spanish/English, Spanish/English bilingual students ages 10 and over, see 901

Fluharty Preschool Speech and Language Screening Test, ages 2–6, see 906

Fullerton Language Test for Adolescents, Experimental Edition, ages 11–18, see 924

Functional Grammar Test, high school and college, see 926

Gochnour Idiom Screening Test: An English Idiom Comprehension Test for the Deaf, junior high through college level deaf students, see 959

Grammar and Usage Test Series, grades 7–12, see 1001

High School Subject Tests: Language, grades 9–12, see 1093

High School Subject Tests: Writing and Mechanics, grades 9–12, see 1098

Hoyum-Sanders English Tests, 1, 2 semesters in grades 2–8, see 1116

Hunter-Grundin Literacy Profiles, ages 6.5–10.0, see 1119

Illinois Children's Language Assessment Test, ages 3–6, see 1124

Illinois Tests in the Teaching of English, high school English teachers, see 1127

Ilyin Oral Interview, junior high and secondary and adult students, see 1128

Language Arts: IOX Objectives-Based Tests, grades kgn–6, see 1277

Language Arts: Minnesota High School Achievement Examinations, grades 7–12, see 1278

Language Arts Tests: Content Evaluation Series, grades 7–9, see 1279

Language Assessment Battery, grades kgn–12, see 1280

Language Assessment Scales, grades kgn–5, 6–12 and over, see 1281

CLASSIFIED SUBJECT INDEX

Language Facility Test, ages 3 and over, see 1282

Language Imitation Test, severely educational subnormal children ages 5 and over, see 1283

Language Proficiency Test, grades 9 and over, see 1284

Language Sampling, Analysis, and Training, Revised Edition, children with language delay, see 1286

Language Usage: Differential Aptitude Tests, grades 8–12 and adults, see 1288

Learning through Listening, ages 10–11, 13–14, 17–18, see 1311

Listening Comprehension Group Tests, adult education students of English as a second language, see 1335

Measures of Language Skills for Two- to Seven-Year-Old Children, ages 2–7, see 1445

Merrill Language Screening Test, ages 64–85 months, see 1470

Metropolitan Achievement Tests: Language Instructional Test, grades kgn–9.9, see 1474

Michigan Prescriptive Program in English, persons striving to obtain 10th grade equivalency or pass the G.E.D. Tests, see 1481

Moray House English Tests, ages 8.5–14, see 1533

NTE Specialty Area Tests: English Language and Literature Specialty Area Test, college seniors and teachers, see 1635

Objective Tests in Constructive English, grades 7–12, see 1663

Objective Tests in Punctuation, grades 7–12, see 1664

Oral English/Spanish Proficiency Placement Test, ages 4–20, see 1732

Oral Language Dominance Measure, bilingual (Spanish/English) students grades kgn–3, see 1733

Oral Language Evaluation, elementary students, see 1734

Oral Language Proficiency Measure, grades 4–6, see 1735

Oral Language Sentence Imitation Diagnostic Inventory—F, ages 5–7, see 1736

Oral Language Sentence Imitation Screening Test, ages 3–7, see 1737

Patterned Elicitation Syntax Screening Test, ages 3–7.5, see 1768

Pictorial Test of Bilingualism and Language Dominance, grades kgn–2, see 1822

Porch Index of Communicative Ability, aphasic adults, see 1851

Porch Index of Communicative Ability in Children, ages 3–12, see 1852

Practical Articulation Kit, grades 2–12, see 1860

Preschool Language Assessment Instrument, Experimental Edition, ages 3–6, see, 1876

Preschool Language Scale, Revised Edition, ages 2–6, see 1877

Pressey Diagnostic Tests in English Composition, grades 7–12, see 1887

Psycholinguistic Rating Scale, grades kgn–8.9, see 1930

Purdue High School English Test, grades 9–12, see 1939

Queensland University Aphasia and Language Test, ages 2–10, see 1963

Quick Language Assessment Inventory, grades kgn–6, see 1966

RBH Test of Language Skills, business and industry, see 1983

Reynell Developmental Language Scales (Revised), ages 1–7, see 2018

Scholastic Achievement Tests for English First Language, grade 2/sub B, standards 1–6, 9–10, see 2075

Screening Test of Adolescent Language, junior and senior high school, see 2108

Secondary Level English Proficiency Test, students in grades 7–11 whose native language is not English, see 2116

Self-Scoring Written English Expression Placement Test, students entering postsecondary institutions with open-door policies, see 2145

Senior English Test, technical college entrants, see 2150

Sentence Comprehension Test, Experimental Edition, ages 3–5, see 2156

Sentence Imitation Screening Tests, ages 3–6, see 2157

Sequential Tests of Educational Progress: English Expression, Series II, grades 4–14, see 2161

Sequential Tests of Educational Progress: Mechanics of Writing, Series II, grades 4–12, see 2163

Shutt Primary Language Indicator Test, grades kgn–6, see 2196

Spanish/English Reading Comprehension Test, grades 1–12 and adults, see 2248

Structure Tests—English Language, high school and over, see 2321

SWCEL-P Oral Placement Test for Adults, non-English and limited English speaking students, see 2377

SWCEL-P Test of Oral Language Proficiency, non-English and limited English speaking students, see 2378

Syntax One, developmental ages 5 and over, see 2385

Syntax Two, developmental ages 5 and over, see 2386

Test of Adolescent Language, grades 6–12, see 2422

Test of Early Language Development, ages 3–0 to 7–11, see 2436

Test of English Usage, English-speaking high school and college students and adults, see 2442

Test of Grammatically Correct Spanish/English, Written and Oral, grades kgn–4, see 2444

Test of Language Development, ages 4–0 to 12–11, see 2445

Test of Written English, grades 1–6, see 2465

Test of Written Language, grades 3–12, see 2466

Tests of Basic Experiences 2: Language, prekgn–grade 1, see 2479

Tressler English Minimum Essentials Test, Revised Edition, grades 8–12, see 2523

Walton-Sanders English Test, 2 semesters in grades 9–13, see 2586

Watson English Usage and Appreciation Test, Fourth Edition, grades 4–8, see 2593

Woodcock Language Proficiency Battery, ages 3 and over, see 2640

WORD Test, ages 7 and over, see 2648

WRITE: Junior and Senior High, junior and senior high school, see 2660

Writing Proficiency Program, grades 6–13, see 2661

Writing Test: McGraw-Hill Basic Skills System, grades 11–14, see 2662

Written Language Syntax Test, hearing impaired students primary–grade 12, see 2663

LITERATURE

ACT Proficiency Examination in Shakespeare, college and adults, see 98

American Literature Anthology Tests, high school, see 166

CLEP General Examinations: Humanities, 1–2 years or equivalent, see 413
CLEP Subject Examination in American Literature, persons entering college or already in college, see 421
CLEP Subject Examination in Analysis and Interpretation of Literature, persons entering college or already in college, see 422
CLEP Subject Examination in English Literature, persons entering college or already in college, see 437
College Board Achievement Test in Literature, candidates for college entrance, see 496
College Placement Test in Literature, entering college freshmen, see 523
English Literature Anthology Tests, high school, see 822
English Tests for Outside Reading, grades 9–12, see 829
Graduate Record Examinations Advanced Literature in English Test, graduate school candidates, see 985
High School Subject Tests: Literature and Vocabulary, grades 9–12, see 1094
Hollingsworth-Sanders Junior High School Literature Test, 1, 2 semesters in grades 7–8, see 1105
Hoskins-Sanders Literature Test, 1, 2 semesters grades 9–13, see 1111
Literature Tests/Objective, high school, see 1336
NTE Specialty Area Tests: English Language and Literature Specialty Area Test, college seniors and teachers, see 1635
Poetry Test/Objective, grades 7–12, see 1842
World Literature Anthology Tests, high school, see 2659

SPELLING

ACER Spelling Test Years 3–6, school years 3–6, see 46
American School Achievement Tests: Part 3, Language and Spelling, Revised Edition, grades 2–9, see 172
Buckingham Extension of the Ayres Spelling Scale, grades 2–9, see 325
California Achievement Tests: Spelling and Reference Skills, Form C, grades 3–6 to 12–9, see 347
Correct Spelling, grades 10–13, see 611
Diagnostic Screening Test: Spelling, Third Edition, grades 1–12, see 725
Group Diagnostic Spelling Test, grades 9–13, see 1012
Kansas Spelling Tests, 2 semesters in grades 3–8, see 1238
Lincoln Diagnostic Spelling Tests, grades 2–4 or 2–5, 4–8, 8–12 or 9–12, see 1330
N.B. Spelling Tests, "standards 1–10 for English pupils and 3–10 for Afrikaans pupils," see 1565
New Iowa Spelling Scale, grades 2–8, see 1575
Proof-Reading Tests of Spelling, standards 2–4 and Forms 1–2, see 1918
Sanders-Fletcher Spelling Test, 1, 2 semesters in grades 9–13, see 2062
SPAR Spelling Test, ages 7–0 to 15–11, see 2250
Spelling: Differential Aptitude Tests, grades 8–12 and adults, see 2254
Spelling Errors Test, grades 2–8, see 2255
Spelling Test for Clerical Workers: [Personnel Research Institute Clerical Battery], stenographic applicants and high school, see 2256
Spelling Test: McGraw-Hill Basic Skills System, grades 11–14, see 2257
Spelling Test: National Achievement Tests, grades 3–12, see 2258
Spellmaster, grades 1–adult, see 2259
Traxler High School Spelling Test, grades 9–12, see 2519

VOCABULARY

A.C.E.R. Word Knowledge Test—Adult Form B, ages 18 and over, see 48
American Literacy Test, adults, see 165
A.P.U. Vocabulary Test, ages 11–17, see 194
Art Vocabulary, grades 6–12, see 203
Assessment of Basic Competencies: Language Module, ages 3–15, see 210
Basic Word Vocabulary Test, grades 4 and over, see 269
Bruce Vocabulary Inventory, business and industry, see 323
Descriptive Tests of Language Skills, beginning students in two- and four-year institutions, see 685
DTLS Vocabulary Test, beginning students in two- and four-year institutions, see 761
High School Subject Tests: Literature and Vocabulary, grades 9–12, see 1094
Johnson Basic Sight Vocabulary Test, grades 1–2, see 1220
Mastery: An Evaluation Tool: Selected Short SOBAR Reading Tests: Vocabulary I, grades 4–5, see 1398
Mastery: An Evaluation Tool: Selected Short SOBAR Reading Tests: Vocabulary II, grades 4–5, see 1399
Mastery: An Evaluation Tool: Selected Short SOBAR Reading Tests: Vocabulary III, grades 8–9, see 1400
Purdue Industrial Supervisors Word-Meaning Test, supervisors, see 1941
Reading and Vocabulary Test for Students of English as a Second Language, non-native speakers of English, see 1989
Sanders-Fletcher Vocabulary Test, 1, 2 semesters in grades 9–13, see 2063
Survey Test of Vocabulary, grades 3–12, see 2375
Test of Active Vocabulary, grades 9–12, see 2421
Vocabulary Comprehension Scale, ages 2–6, see 2566
Vocabulary Test for High School Students and College Freshmen, grades 9–13, see 2567
Vocabulary Test: McGraw-Hill Basic Skills System, grades 11–14, see 2568
Vocabulary Test: National Achievement Tests, grades 3–12, see 2569
Word Dexterity Test, grades 7–16, see 2643
Word Understanding, grades 6–12, see 2649

FINE ARTS

CLEP General Examinations: Humanities, 1–2 years or equivalent, see 413
Taylor-Helmstadter Pair Comparison Scale of Aesthetic Judgement, ages 4 and over, see 2395

ART

Advanced Placement Examination in History of Art, high school students desiring credit for college level courses and admission to advanced courses, see 134
Advanced Placement Examination in Studio Art, high school students desiring credit for college level courses and admission to advanced courses, see 141
Art Vocabulary, grades 6–12, see 203
Barron-Welsh Art Scale: A Portion of the Welsh Figure Preference Test, ages 6 and over, see 243
Horn Art Aptitude Inventory, grades 12–16 and adults, see 1110
Meier Art Tests, grades 7–16 and adults, see 1460
NTE Specialty Area Tests: Art Education Specialty Area Test, college seniors and teachers, see 1626

MUSIC

ACER and University of Melbourne Music Evaluation Kit, beginning of secondary school, see 22
Advanced Placement Examination in Music Listening and Literature, high school students desiring credit for college level courses and admission to advanced courses, see 137
Advanced Placement Examination in Music Theory, high school students desiring credit for college level courses and admission to advanced courses, see 138
[Aliferis-Stecklin Music Achievement Tests], music students, see 155
Australian Test for Advanced Music Studies, tertiary education entrance level, see 233
Farnum Music Test, grades 4–9, see 879
Farnum String Scale: A Performance Scale for All String Instruments, grades 7–12, see 880
Graduate Record Examinations Advanced Music Test, graduate school candidates, see 987
Gretsch-Tilson Musical Aptitude Test, grades 4–12, see 1008
Indiana-Oregon Music Discrimination Test, grades 5 through graduate school, see 1135
Iowa Tests of Music Literacy, grades 4–12, see 1194
Knuth Achievement Tests in Music: Recognition of Rhythm and Melody, grades 3–12, see 1261
Kwalwasser Music Talent Test, grades 4–16 and adults, see 1274
Kwalwasser-Ruch Test of Musical Accomplishment, grades 4–12, see 1275
Measures of Musical Abilities, ages 7–14, see 1446
Musical Aptitude Profile, grades 4–12, see 1552
NTE Specialty Area Tests: Music Education Specialty Area Test, college seniors and teachers, see 1644
Primary Measures of Music Audiation, grades kgn–3, see 1891
Seashore Measures of Musical Talents, grades 4–16 and adults, see 2113
Simons Measurements of Music Listening Skills, grades kgn–3, see 2200
Snyder Knuth Music Achievement Test, elementary education and music majors, see 2222
Test of Musicality, Fourth Edition, grades 4–12, see 2451
Watkins-Farnum Performance Scale: A Standardized Achievement Test for All Band Instruments, music students, see 2591
Wing Standardised Tests of Musical Intelligence, ages 8 and over, see 2631

FOREIGN LANGUAGES

Graduate School Foreign Language Testing Program, graduate level degree candidates required to demonstrate foreign language reading proficiency, see 996
Modern Language Aptitude Test, grades 9 and over, see 1527
Pimsleur Language Aptitude Battery, grades 6–12, see 1833

ARABIC

First Year Arabic Final Examination, 1972 Edition, 1 year college, see 893

ENGLISH

Comprehensive English Language Test for Speakers of English as a Second Language, non-native speakers of English, see 549
Diagnostic Test for Students of English as a Second Language, applicants from non-English language countries for admission to American colleges, see 728
English Knowledge and Comprehension Test, high school, see 820
English Language Skills Assessment in a Reading Context, beginning to advanced students of English as a second language from upper elementary to college and adult students, see 821
English Placement Test, entrants to courses in English as a second language, see 824
English Usage Test for Non-Native Speakers of English, non-native speakers of English, see 830
Language Proficiency Tests, "Black pupils in forms IV, V," see 1285
Listening Comprehension Group Tests, adult education students of English as a second language, see 1335
Michigan Test of Aural Comprehension, college applicants from non-English language countries, see 1483
Michigan Test of English Language Proficiency, college applicants from non-English language countries, see 1484
Oral Rating Form for Rating Language Proficiency in Speaking and Understanding English, non-native speakers of English, see 1738
Scholastic Achievement Test for English Lower Standards 2 and 3, standards 2, 3, see 2071
Scholastic Achievement Test for English Lower Standards 9 and 10, standards 9, 10, see 2072
Scholastic Achievement Test of English Second Language Standard 1, standard 1, see 2074

Test A/65, matriculants and higher, see 2415
Test of Aural Perception in English for Japanese Students, Japanese students in American colleges, see 2426
Test of Aural Perception in English for Latin-American Students, Latin-American students of English, see 2427
Test of English as a Foreign Language, college and other institutional applicants from non-English language countries, see 2441
Test of English Usage, English-speaking high school and college students and adults, see 2442
Tests of English as a Second Language, for use only in rating English proficiency of proposed participants for AID training programs, see 2483
Tests of Proficiency in English, non-native speakers of English ages 7–11, see 2487

FRENCH

Advanced Placement Examination in French Language, Level 3, high school students desiring credit for college level courses and admission to advanced courses, see 131
Advanced Placement Examination in French Literature, Level 3, high school students desiring credit for college level courses and admission to advanced courses, see 132
Baltimore County French Test, 1 year high school, see 236
CLEP Subject Examination in College French, Levels 1 and 2, persons entering college or already in college, see 430
College Board Achievement Test in French Reading, candidates for college entrance with 2–4 years high school French, see 492
College Placement Test in French Listening Comprehension, entering college freshmen, see 512
College Placement Test in French Listening-Reading, entering college freshmen, see 513
College Placement Test in French Reading, entering college freshmen, see 514
First Year French Test, high school and college, see 894
Ford-Hicks French Grammar Completion Tests, high school, see 907
French Comprehension Tests, grades kgn–5, see 918
Graduate Record Examinations Advanced French Test, graduate school candidates, see 979
Graduate School Foreign Language Test: French, graduate level degree candidates required to demonstrate reading proficiency in French, see 997
MLA-Cooperative Foreign Language Tests: French, 1–2 years high school or 2 semesters college, see 1519
NTE Specialty Area Tests: French Specialty Area Test, college seniors and teachers, see 1636
Second Year French Test, high school and college, see 2114

GERMAN

Advanced Placement Examination in German Language, Level 3, high school students desiring credit for college level courses and admission to advanced courses, see 133
CLEP Subject Examination in College German, Levels 1 and 2, persons entering college or already in college, see 431
College Board Achievement Test in German Reading, candidates for college entrance with 2–4 years high school German, see 493
College Placement Test in German Listening Comprehension, entering college freshmen, see 515
College Placement Test in German Listening-Reading, entering college freshmen, see 516
College Placement Test in German Reading, entering college freshmen, see 517
Graduate Record Examinations Advanced German Test, graduate school candidates, see 983
Graduate School Foreign Language Test: German, graduate level degree candidates required to demonstrate reading proficiency in German, see 998
MLA-Cooperative Foreign Language Tests: German, 1–2 years high school or 2 semesters college, see 1520
National German Examination for High School Students, 2–4 years high school, see 1559
NTE Specialty Area Tests: German Specialty Area Test, college seniors and teachers, see 1637

GREEK

College Placement Test in Greek Reading, entering college freshmen, see 518

HEBREW

Achievement Test—Hebrew Language, grades 5–7, see 49
College Board Achievement Test in Hebrew, candidates for college entrance with 2–4 years high school Hebrew, see 494
College Placement Test in Hebrew Reading, entering college freshmen, see 519
[NCRI Achievement Tests in Hebrew], grades 5–9, see 1566
Test on the Fundamentals of Hebrew, grades 2–7, see 2467

ITALIAN

College Placement Test in Italian Listening-Reading, entering college freshmen, see 520
College Placement Test in Italian Reading, entering college freshmen, see 521
MLA-Cooperative Foreign Language Tests: Italian, 1–2 years high school or 2 semesters college, see 1521

LATIN

Advanced Placement Examination in Latin, Level 3 (Catullus-Horace), high school students desiring credit for college level courses and admission to advanced courses, see 135
Advanced Placement Examination in Latin, Level 3 (Vergil), high school students desiring credit for college level courses and admission to advanced courses, see 136
College Board Achievement Test in Latin, candidates for

CLASSIFIED SUBJECT INDEX

college entrance with 2–4 years high school Latin, see 495
College Placement Test in Latin Reading, entering college freshmen, see 522
Emporia First Year Latin Test, 1 year high school, see 809
Emporia Second Year Latin Test, 2 years high school, see 816

RUSSIAN

College Placement Test in Russian Listening-Reading, entering college freshmen, see 525
College Placement Test in Russian Reading, entering college freshmen, see 526
Graduate School Foreign Language Test: Russian, graduate level degree candidates required to demonstrate reading proficiency in Russian, see 999
MLA-Cooperative Foreign Language Tests: Russian, 1–2 years high school or 2 semesters college, see 1522

SPANISH

Advanced Placement Examination in Spanish Language, Level 3, high school students desiring credit for college level courses and admission to advanced courses, see 139
Advanced Placement Examination in Spanish Literature, Level 3, high school students desiring credit for college level courses and admission to advanced courses, see 140
Ambiguous Word Language Dominance Test, Spanish/English, bilingual students ages 10 and over, see 158
Austin Spanish Articulation Test, ages 3–12, see 231
Baltimore County Spanish Test, 1 year high school, see 237
Ber-Sil Spanish Test, ages 5–17, see 284
Bilingual Oral Language Test, grades 7–12, see 289
Bilingual Syntax Measure, bilingual children grades kgn–2, see 290
Bilingual Syntax Measure II, grades 3–12, see 291
CLEP Subject Examination in College Spanish, Levels 1 and 2, persons entering college or already in college, see 432

College Board Achievement Test in Spanish Reading, candidates for college entrance with 2–4 years high school Spanish, see 498
College Placement Test in Spanish Listening Comprehension, entering college freshmen, see 527
College Placement Test in Spanish Listening-Reading, entering college freshmen, see 528
College Placement Test in Spanish Reading, entering college freshmen, see 529
Crane Oral Dominance Test: Spanish/English, ages 4–8, see 625
Dos Amigos Verbal Language Scales, ages 5–0 to 13–5, see 749
First Year Spanish Test, high school and college, see 895
Furness Test of Aural Comprehension in Spanish, 1–3 years high school or 1–2 years college, see 927
Graduate Record Examinations Advanced Spanish Test, graduate school candidates, see 993
Graduate School Foreign Language Test: Spanish, graduate level degree candidates required to demonstrate reading proficiency in Spanish, see 1000
MLA-Cooperative Foreign Language Tests: Spanish, 1–2 years high school or 2 semesters college, see 1523
NTE Specialty Area Tests: Spanish Specialty Area Test, college seniors and teachers, see 1648
Oral English/Spanish Proficiency Placement Test, ages 4–20, see 1732
Oral Language Dominance Measure, bilingual (Spanish/English) students grades kgn–3, see 1733
Oral Language Proficiency Measure, grades 4–6, see 1735
Pictorial Test of Bilingualism and Language Dominance, grades kgn–2, see 1822
Quick Language Assessment Inventory, grades kgn–6, see 1966
Screening Test of Spanish Grammar, Spanish-speaking children ages 3–6, see 2109
Second Year Spanish Test, high school and college, see 2115
Shutt Primary Language Indicator Test, grades kgn–6, see 2196
SOBER Espanol, grades kgn–3, see 2223
Spanish/English Reading Comprehension Test, grades 1–12 and adults, see 2248
Test of Grammatically Correct Spanish/English, Written and Oral, grades kgn–4, see 2444

INTELLIGENCE AND SCHOLASTIC APTITUDE

GROUP

Abstract Reasoning: Differential Aptitude Tests, grades 8–12 and adults, see 9
Academic Aptitude Test: Non-Verbal Intelligence: Acorn National Aptitude Tests, grades 7–16 and adults, see 12
Academic Aptitude Test: Verbal Intelligence: Acorn National Aptitude Tests, grades 7–16 and adults, see 13
A.C.E.R. Advanced Test B40, ages 13 and over, see 19
ACER Advanced Test N, ages 15 and over, see 20

A.C.E.R. Advanced Tests AL and AQ, college and superior adults, see 21
A.C.E.R. Higher Tests, ages 13 and over, see 28
A.C.E.R. Intermediate Test A, ages 10–0 to 14–0, see 29
A.C.E.R. Intermediate Tests C and D, ages 10–0 to 14–0, see 30
A.C.E.R. Junior Non-Verbal Test, ages 8.5–12.0, see 31
A.C.E.R. Junior Test A, ages 8.5–12.0, see 32
A.C.E.R. Lower Grades General Ability Scale, Second Edition, ages 6–6 to 9–1, see 34
ACER Test of Learning Ability, grades 4, 6, see 47
Activities For Assessing Classification Skills, Experimental

Edition, ages 7–8 and slow learning children, 9–12 and advanced younger children, see 110
Adaptability Test, job applicants, see 111
AH1 Forms X and Y, ages 7–11 for classroom purposes and 5–11 for research, see 148
AH2/AH3, ages 9 and over, see 149
American School Intelligence Test, grades kgn–12, see 174
Analysis of Relationships, grades 12–16 and industry, see 179
BITCH Test (Black Intelligence Test of Cultural Homogeneity), adolescents and adults, see 296
Boehm Test of Basic Concepts, kgn–2, see 302
British Ability Scales, ages 2.5–17, see 322
Business Test, clerical workers, see 334
Canadian Cognitive Abilities Test, grades kgn–9, see 361
Canadian Lorge-Thorndike Intelligence Tests, Multi-Level Edition, grades 3–9, see 362
Cognitive Abilities Test, kgn–12, see 483
College Board Scholastic Aptitude Test and Test of Standard Written English, candidates for college entrance, see 501
Cooperative School and College Ability Tests, Series II, grades 4–14, see 590
Cotswold Junior Ability Tests, ages 8.5–10.5, see 616
Culture Fair Intelligence Test, ages 4–8 and mentally retarded adults, 8–14 and average adults, grades 9–16 and superior adults, see 643
Dennis Test of Scholastic Aptitude, grades 4–8, see 672
Detroit Tests of Learning Aptitude, ages 3 and over, see 691
Developing Cognitive Abilities Test, grades 2–12, see 692
D48 Test, grades 5 and over, see 707
Draw-A-Man Test for Indian Children, ages 6–10, see 750
Essential Intelligence Test, ages 8–12, see 842
Figure Classification Test, applicants for industrial work with 7 to 9 years of schooling, see 886
General Mental Ability Test: ETSA Test 1A, job applicants, see 942
Goodenough-Harris Drawing Test, ages 3–15, see 964
Graduate Record Examinations Aptitude Test, graduate school candidates, see 995
Group Test for Indian South Africans, standards 4–10, see 1026
Group Test 36, ages 10–14, see 1028
Group Test 75, ages 12–13, see 1029
Group Test 91, industrial applicants, see 1033
Group Test 95, ages 14 and over, see 1034
Group Tests 70 and 70B, ages 15 and over, see 1036
Group Tests 72 and 73, industrial applicants, see 1037
Group Tests 90A and 90B, ages 15 and over, see 1038
Harding Skyscraper, ages 17 and over with intelligence level in top 1% of population, see 1057
Henmon-Nelson Tests of Mental Ability, grades kgn–12, see 1073
Hess School Readiness Scale, ages 3.5–7.0, see 1075
Inventory No. 2, ages 16 and over, see 1177
Kelvin Measurement of Ability in Infant Classes, ages 5–8, see 1244
Kuhlmann-Anderson Test, Seventh Edition, grades kgn–12, see 1272
Learning Ability Profile, grades 5–16 and adults, see 1303

Lorge-Thorndike Intelligence Tests, grades kgn–13, see 1341
Mental Alertness: Tests B/1 and B/2, job applicants with 9–11, 12 or more years of education, see 1467
Mill Hill Vocabulary Scale, ages 4 and over, 11–14, 14 and over, see 1485
Miller Analogies Test, candidates for graduate school, see 1486
Moray House Verbal Reasoning Tests, ages 8.5–14.5, 13.5 and over, see 1535
New South African Group Test, ages 8–17, see 1578
NIIP Group Test 36, ages 10–13, see 1583
Non-Language Test of Verbal Intelligence—Form 768, class 8 (ages 11–13), see 1615
Non-Readers Intelligence Test, Third Edition, ages 6–5 to 8–11, see 1616
Non-Verbal Reasoning Test, job applicants and industrial employees, see 1618
Non-Verbal Tests, ages 8 to 15, see 1620
Ohio Penal Classification Test, penal institutions, see 1712
Ohio State University Psychological Test, grades 9–16 and adults, see 1716
Oral Verbal Intelligence Test, ages 7.5–14, see 1740
Oregon Academic Ranking Test, gifted children grades 3–7, see 1742
"Orton" Intelligence Test, No. 4, ages 10–14, see 1753
Otis-Lennon School Ability Test, grades 1–12, see 1754
Otis Self-Administering Tests of Mental Ability, ages 9–14, 12.5 and over, see 1755
Personnel Research Institute Classification Test, adults, see 1804
Personnel Research Institute Factory Series Test, applicants for routine industrial positions, see 1806
Personnel Tests for Industry, trade school and adults, see 1808
Picture Test A, ages 7–0 to 8–1, see 1829
Preliminary Scholastic Aptitude Test/National Merit Scholarship Qualifying Test, grades 10–12, see 1866
Preschool and Early Primary Skills Survey, Preliminary Edition, ages 3–3 to 7–2, see 1872
[Pressey Classification and Verifying Tests], grades 1–12, see 1885
Progressive Matrices, ages 5 and over, see 1914
Proverbs Test, grades 5–16 and adults, see 1919
Purdue Non-Language Personnel Test, business and industry, see 1947
Quick Word Test, grades 4–adults, see 1970
RBH Test of Learning Ability, business and industry, see 1984
RBH Test of Non-Verbal Reasoning, business and industry, see 1985
Revised Beta Examination, Second Edition, ages 16–64, see 2013
Ross Test of Higher Cognitive Processes, grades 4–6, see 2032
Safran Culture Reduced Intelligence Test, grades 1–6, 4 and over, see 2045
Schubert General Ability Battery, grades 12–16 and adults, see 2095
Scott Mental Alertness Test, applicants for office positions, see 2101
Ship Destination Test, grades 9 and over, see 2178
Short Form Test of Academic Aptitude, grades 1.5–12, see 2181
Slosson Intelligence Test, ages 2 weeks and over, see 2217

CLASSIFIED SUBJECT INDEX

SRA Nonverbal Form, ages 12 and over, see 2266
SRA Pictorial Reasoning Test, ages 14 and over, see 2267
SRA Verbal Form, grades 7–16 and adults, see 2276
Test of Adult College Aptitude, evening college entrants, see 2423
Test of Cognitive Skills, grades 2–12, see 2431
Test of Perceptual Organization, normals and psychiatric patients ages 12 and over, see 2453
Test of Scholastic Abilities, ages 9–0 to 14–11, see 2458
Tests of General Ability: Inter-American Series, pre-school–grade 13.5, see 2484
Thurstone Test of Mental Alertness, grades 9–12 and adults, see 2500
Verbal Power Test of Concept Equivalence, ages 14 and over, see 2552
Verbal Reasoning, job applicants and industrial employees, see 2553
Wesman Personnel Classification Test, grades 8–16 and adults, see 2614
Western Personnel Tests, college and adults, see 2617
Wonderlic Personnel Test, adults, see 2638

INDIVIDUAL

Arthur Point Scale of Performance Tests, ages 4.5 or 5.5 to superior adults, see 204
Bayley Scales of Infant Development, ages 2–30 months, see 270
Bingham Button Test, disadvantaged children ages 3–6, see 292
Blind Learning Aptitude Test, blind ages 6–20, see 299
Brazelton Neonatal Assessment Scale, age 3 days to 4 weeks, see 311
Cattell Infant Intelligence Scale, ages 3–30 months, see 381
Cluster Analysis of Wechsler/WRAT, ages 5 and over, see 481
Columbia Mental Maturity Scale, Third Edition, ages 3–6 to 9–11, see 534
Comprehensive Developmental Evaluation Chart, developmental ages birth to 3 years, see 548
Cooperative Preschool Inventory, Revised Edition, ages 3–6, see 581
Crichton Vocabulary Scale, ages 4–11, see 632
Dennis Test of Child Development, grades kgn–1, see 671
Developmental Activities Screening Inventory, ages 6–60 months, see 693
English Picture Vocabulary Test, ages 5–8, 7–11, 11 and over, see 823
Full-Range Picture Vocabulary Test, ages 2 and over, see 923
Hiskey-Nebraska Test of Learning Aptitude, ages 3–17, see 1101
Immediate Test: A Quick Verbal Intelligence Test, adults, see 1129
Individual Scale for Indian South Africans, ages 8–17, see 1141
Infant Rating Scale, ages 5, 7, see 1147
Item Analysis of Slosson Intelligence Test, children and adults, see 1202
Kahn Intelligence Tests, ages 1 month and over (particularly the verbally or culturally handicapped), see 1236
Kaufman Development Scale, birth to age 9 and mentally retarded all ages, see 1242
Leiter Adult Intelligence Scale, adults, see 1318
Leiter International Performance Scale, ages 2–18, see 1319
McCarthy Scales of Children's Abilities, ages 2.5–8.5, see 1424
McCarthy Screening Test, ages 4–6.5, see 1425
Merrill-Palmer Scale of Mental Tests, ages 24–63 months, see 1471
Minnesota Preschool Scale, ages 1.5–6.0, see 1505
Naylor-Harwood Adult Intelligence Scale, ages 18 and over, see 1564
New Guinea Performance Scales, pre-literates ages 17 and over, see 1574
Non-Verbal Intelligence Tests for Deaf and Hearing Subjects, ages 3–16, see 1617
Nonverbal Test of Cognitive Skills, ages 6–13, see 1619
Peabody Picture Vocabulary Test-Revised, ages 2.5–40, see 1771
Pictorial Test of Intelligence, ages 3–8, see 1823
Porteus Maze Test, ages 3 and over, see 1853
Preschool Attainment Record, Research Edition, ages 6 months to 7 years, see 1874
Quick Screening Scale of Mental Development, ages 6 months to 10 years, see 1968
Quick Test, ages 2 and over, see 1969
Ring and Peg Tests of Behavior Development, birth to age 6, see 2025
Senior South African Individual Scale, ages 6–17, see 2153
Smith-Johnson Nonverbal Performance Scale, ages 2–4, see 2220
Snijders-Oomen Non-Verbal Intelligence Scale for Young Children, ages 2.5–7, see 2221
Stanford-Binet Intelligence Scale, Third Revision, ages 2 and over, see 2289
[Re Stanford-Binet Intelligence Scale] A Clinical Profile for the Stanford-Binet Intelligence Scale (L–M), ages 5 and over, see 2290
Stanford-Ohwaki-Kohs Block Design Intelligence Test for the Blind: American Revision of the Ohwaki-Kohs Test, blind and partially sighted ages 16 and over, see 2296
Test of Children's Learning Ability—Individual Version, ages 7–8, see 2430
Token Test for Children, ages 3–12, see 2509
Vane Kindergarten Test, ages 4–6, see 2548
Wechsler Adult Intelligence Scale-Revised, ages 16 and over, see 2598
[Re Wechsler Adult Intelligence Scale] Rhodes WAIS Scatter Profile, ages 16 and over, see 2599
[Re Wechsler Adult Intelligence Scale] WAIS Mental Description Sheet, ages 16 and over, see 2600
[Re Wechsler Adult Intelligence Scale] WAIS Test Profile, ages 16 and over, see 2601
Wechsler Intelligence Scale for Children-Revised, ages 6–16, see 2602
[Re Wechsler Intelligence Scale for Children-Revised] WISC-R Profile Form, ages 6–17, see 2603
[Re Wechsler Intelligence Scale for Children] Rhodes WISC Scatter Profile, ages 5–15, see 2604
[Re Wechsler Intelligence Scale for Children] WISC Test Profile and WISC-R Profile, ages 5–15, see 2605

TESTS IN PRINT III

Wechsler Intelligence Scales for Children-Revised: For the Deaf, ages 6–16, see 2606
Wechsler Preschool and Primary Scale of Intelligence, ages 4–6.5, see 2608
[Re Wechsler Preschool and Primary Scale of Intelligence] WPPSI Test Profile, ages 4–6.5, see 2609
Williams Intelligence Test for Children With Defective Vision, blind and partially sighted ages 5–15, see 2627
WISC-R Split-Half Short Form, ages 6–16, see 2632

SPECIFIC

Alternate Uses, grades 6–16 and adults, see 157
Auditory Sequential Memory Test, ages 5–8, see 229
Benton Visual Retention Test, Revised Edition, ages 8 and over, see 283
Christensen-Guilford Fluency Tests, grades 7–16 and adults, see 401
Closure Flexibility (Concealed Figures), industrial employees, see 477
Closure Speed (Gestalt Completion), industrial employees, see 478
Concept Assessment Kit—Conservation, ages 4–7, see 559
Concept Attainment Test, college and adults, see 560
Concept Formation: The Assessment and Remediation of Concept Deficit in the Young Child, ages 3–8, see 561
Consequences [Sheridan Psychological Services, Inc.], grades 9–16 and adults, see 566
Creativity Attitude Survey, grades 4–6, see 628
Creativity Tests for Children, grades 4–6, see 630
Decorations, grades 9–16 and adults, see 662
Deductive Reasoning Test, candidates for graduate scientists and higher level professional occupations, see 663
Doppelt Mathematical Reasoning Test, grades 16–17 and employees, see 747
DTLS Logical Relationships Test, beginning students in two- and four-year institutions, see 757
Eliot-Price Perspective Test, grades 2 and over, see 792
Evaluation Aptitude Test, candidates for college and graduate school entrance, see 847
Expressive One-Word Picture Vocabulary Test, ages 2–12, see 857
Goldstein-Scheerer Tests of Abstract and Concrete Thinking, brain damaged adults, see 963
Gottschaldt Figures [National Institute for Personnel Research], job applicants with at least 10 years of education, see 968
Goyer Organization of Ideas Test, college and adults, see 971
Healy Pictorial Completion Tests, ages 5 and over, see 1069
Hidden Figures Test, grades 6–16, see 1077
Jensen Alternation Board, ages 5 and over, see 1207
Kasanin-Hanfmann Concept Formation Test, normal and schizophrenic adults, see 1239
Kendrick Battery for the Detection of Dementia in the Elderly, ages 55 and over, see 1245
Kit of Factor Referenced Cognitive Tests, various grades 6–16, see 1257
Knox's Cube Test, ages 3–8, 9 and over, see 1260
Kohs Block-Design Test, mental ages 5–20, see 1265
Language-Structured Auditory Retention Span Test, mental ages 3.7 to adult, see 1287

Learning Efficiency Test, ages 6 and over, see 1305
Logical Reasoning, grades 9–16 and adults, see 1337
Making Objects, grades 9–16 and adults, see 1362
Match Problems, grades 9–16 and adults, see 1403
Match Problems V, grades 9–16, see 1404
Memory for Events, grades 9–13, see 1463
Memory for Meanings, grades 7–16, see 1464
Minnesota Scholastic Aptitude Test, high school and college, see 1510
New Uses, grades 10–16, see 1580
Numerical Ability: Differential Aptitude Tests, grades 8–12 and adults, see 1653
Pattern Relations Test, college graduates, see 1767
Perceptual Speed (Identical Forms), grades 9–16 and industrial employees, see 1780
Pertinent Questions, grades 9–16 and adults, see 1809
Pintner-Manikin Test, ages 2 and over, see 1834
Pintner-Paterson Feature Profile Test, ages 4 and over, see 1835
Plot Titles, grades 9–16, see 1840
Possible Jobs, grades 6–16 and adults, see 1856
Predictive Ability Test, Adult Edition, ages 17 and over, see 1864
Santostefano Tests of Cognitive Control, children and adults, see 2064
Seeing Problems, grades 9–16, see 2123
Seguin-Goddard Formboard, ages 5–14, see 2125
Shipley-Institute of Living Scale for Measuring Intellectual Impairment, adults, see 2179
Simile Interpretations, grades 10–16, see 2198
Similes, grades 4–16, see 2199
Sketches, grades 9 and over, see 2209
Space Relations: Differential Aptitude Tests, grades 8–12 and adults, see 2246
Subsumed Abilities Test, ages 9 and over, see 2352
Survey of Object Visualization, grades 9–16 and adults, see 2368
Survey of Space Relations Ability, grades 9–16 and adults, see 2373
Symbol Identities, grades 10 and over, see 2382
Test of Concept Utilization, ages 4.5–18.5, see 2433
Test of Creative Potential, grades 2–12 and adults, see 2435
Thinking Creatively in Action and Movement, ages 3–8, see 2495
Thinking Creatively With Sounds and Words, Research Edition, grades 3–12, adults, see 2496
Time Appreciation Test, ages 10 and over, see 2502
Torrance Tests of Creative Thinking, kgn through graduate school, see 2512
Verbal Reasoning: Differential Aptitude Tests, grades 8–12 and adults, see 2554
Visual Aural Digit Span Test, ages 5.5–12, see 2560
Visual Memory Test, ages 5–8, see 2563
Visual-Verbal Test: A Measure of Conceptual Thinking, schizophrenic patients, see 2565
Wachs Analysis of Cognitive Structures, ages 3–6, see 2582
Watson-Glaser Critical Thinking Appraisal, grades 9–16 and adults, see 2594
Wechsler Memory Scale, adults, see 2607
Wisconsin Card Sorting Test, ages 12 and over, see 2633
Word Fluency, industrial employees, see 2645

MATHEMATICS

Advanced Mathematics (Including Trigonometry): Minnesota High School Achievement Examinations, high school, see 123

Algebra, Geometry and Trigonometry Test for Stds 9 and 10, standards 9, 10, see 153

American High School Mathematics Examinations, high school students competing for individual and school awards, see 160

Analysis of Readiness Skills: Reading and Mathematics, grades kgn–1, see 178

Assessment in Mathematics, primary and lower secondary school children, see 206

Basic Mathematics Tests, ages 7–0 to 14–6, see 252

Basic Skills Assessment: Mathematics, grades 7 and over, see 260

Basic Skills Inventory: Mathematics, grades kgn–12, see 267

California Achievement Tests: Mathematics, Form C, grades 3–6 to 12–9, see 345

CGP Self-Scoring Placement Tests in English and Mathematics, students entering postsecondary institutions with open-door policies, see 382

CLEP General Examinations: Mathematics, 1–2 years or equivalent, see 414

CLEP Subject Examination in College Algebra-Trigonometry, persons entering college or already in college, see 428

College Board Achievement Tests in Mathematics, candidates for college entrance, see 499

College Placement Tests in Mathematics, entering college freshmen, see 531

Comprehensive Tests of Basic Skills: Mathematics, [Forms U & V], grades kgn to 12–9, see 552

Cooperative Mathematics Tests: Structure of the Number System, grades 7–8, see 579

Cooperative Primary Tests: Mathematics, grades 1.5–3, see 584

Descriptive Tests of Mathematics Skills, beginning students in two- and four-year institutions, see 686

Design for Math, grades kgn–6, 6 and over, see 687

Diagnosing Abilities in Math, slow learning children in math, see 708

Diagnosis: An Instructional Aid: Mathematics, Levels A and B, grades kgn–8, see 709

Distar Mastery Tests: Arithmetic I, preschool–grade 3, see 738

Distar Mastery Tests: Arithmetic II, preschool–grade 3, see 739

DTMS Functions and Graphs Test, beginning students in two- and four-year institutions, see 764

Essential Mathematics, ages 7–14, see 843

Fountain Valley Teacher Support System in Mathematics, grades kgn–8, see 913

Graded Arithmetic-Mathematics Test, ages 6–21, see 972

Graduate Record Examinations Advanced Mathematics Test, graduate school candidates, see 986

Group Mathematics Test, Second Edition, ages 6.5–8.5, see 1019

Henshaw Secondary Mathematics Test, grades 9–10, see 1074

High School Subject Tests: General Mathematics, grades 9–12, see 1090

Individual Pupil Monitoring System—Mathematics, Forms S and T, grades 1–8, see 1139

Individualized Criterion Referenced Testing: Math, grades 1–8, see 1142

Junior High School Mathematics Test: Acorn Achievement Tests, grades 7–9, see 1230

Kraner Preschool Math Inventory, ages 3–0 to 6–6, see 1266

Mastery: An Evaluation Tool: Mathematics, grades kgn–9, see 1389

Mathematics Attainment Test EF, ages 11–0 to 13–0, see 1406

Mathematics Attainment Tests C1 and C3, ages 9–3 to 10–8, see 1407

Mathematics Attainment Tests DE1 and DE2, ages 10–0 to 12–0, see 1408

Mathematics Attainment Tests (Oral), ages 7–0 to 9–8, see 1409

Mathematics Attitudes Inventory, grades 7–12, see 1410

Mathematics: IOX Objectives-Based Tests, grades kgn–9, see 1412

Mathematics: Minnesota High School Achievement Examinations, grades 7–9, see 1413

Mathematics Test: Content Evaluation Series, grades 7–9, see 1414

Mathematics Test for Grades Four, Five and Six, grades 4–6, see 1415

Mathematics Test for Seniors, standards 9, 10, see 1416

Mathematics Test: McGraw-Hill Basic Skills System, grades 11–14, see 1417

Mathematics Topic Tests: Elementary Level, grades 4–9, see 1418

Metropolitan Achievement Tests: Mathematics Instructional Test, grades kgn–9.9, see 1475

Metropolitan Achievement Tests: Survey Battery: Mathematics, 1978 Edition, grades kgn–12.9, see 1477

Michigan Prescriptive Program in Mathematics, persons striving to obtain 10th grade equivalency or pass the G.E.D. test in math, see 1482

Minimum Essentials for Modern Mathematics, grades 6–8, see 1490

Moray House Mathematics Tests, ages 8.5–12, see 1534

Moreton Mathematics Tests, grades 3–7, see 1536

NM Consumer Mathematics Test, grades 9–12, see 1589

NTE Specialty Area Tests: Mathematics Specialty Area Test, college seniors and teachers, see 1642

Objectives-Referenced Bank of Items and Tests: Mathematics, grades kgn–12 and adults, see 1665

Peabody Mathematics Readiness Test, grades kgn–12, see 1770

Portland Prognostic Test for Mathematics, grades 6.9–9.0, see 1854

[Primary Mathematics Survey Tests], grades 2, 3, see 1890

Progressive Achievement Tests of Mathematics, standards 2–4 and Forms I–IV (ages 8–14), see 1911
Purdue Industrial Mathematics Test, adults, see 1940
Self-Scoring Mathematics Placement Tests, students entering postsecondary institutions with open-door policies, see 2143
Senior Mathematics Test, technical college entrants, see 2152
Sequential Tests of Educational Progress: Mathematics, Series II, grades 4–14, see 2162
Stanford Achievement Test, Mathematics Tests, 1973 Edition, grades 1.5–9.5, see 2287
Stanford Diagnostic Mathematics Test, grade 1.5–13, see 2291
Steenburgen Diagnostic-Prescriptive Math Program, grades 1–6, see 2303
Test of Competence in Mathematics Level 4–5, 6–7, 8–9, grades 4–9, see 2432
Tests of Achievement in Basic Skills: Mathematics, preschool–grade 12, see 2476
Watson Diagnostic Mathematics Test: Computation, Fourth Edition, grades 1–10, see 2592

ALGEBRA

Algebra, Geometry and Trigonometry Test for Stds 9 and 10, standards 9, 10, see 153
Algebra Test for Engineering and Science: National Achievement Tests, college entrants, see 154
Breslich Algebra Survey Test, 1, 2 semesters high school, see 312
CLEP Subject Examination in College Algebra, persons entering college or already in college, see 427
CLEP Subject Examination in College Algebra-Trigonometry, persons entering college or already in college, see 428
Cooperative Mathematics Tests: Algebra I and II, grades 8–12, see 573
Cooperative Mathematics Tests: Algebra III, high school and college, see 574
DTMS Elementary Algebra Test, beginning students in two- and four-year institutions, see 763
DTMS Intermediate Algebra Test, beginning students in two- and four-year institutions, see 765
Elementary Algebra: Minnesota High School Achievement Examinations, high school, see 791
Emporia State Algebra II Test, high school, see 817
ERB Modern Second Year Algebra Test, high school, see 839
First Year Algebra Test: National Achievement Tests, 1 year high school, see 892
High School Subject Tests: Algebra, grades 9–12, see 1084
Iowa Algebra Aptitude Test, Third Edition, grade 8, see 1188
Kepner Mid-Year Algebra Achievement Tests, 1 semester high school, see 1248
Lee Test of Algebraic Ability, Revised, grades 7–8, see 1313
Modern Algebra Test: Content Evaluation Series, 1 year high school, see 1524
Orleans-Hanna Algebra Prognosis Test, grades 7–11, see 1749

ARITHMETIC

A.C.E.R. Arithmetic Tests: Standardized for Use in New Zealand, ages 9–12, see 23
ACER Class Achievement Test in Mathematics, grades 4–7, see 26
ACER Mathematics Profile Series, grades 4–10, see 35
ACER Mathematics Tests: AM Series, grades 4–6; see 36
A.C.E.R. Number Test, ages 13.5 and over, see 39
American Numerical Test, adults, see 167
American School Achievement Tests: Arithmetic Readiness, grades kgn–1, see 168
American School Achievement Tests: Part 2, Arithmetic, Revised Edition, grades 2–9, see 173
Analytical Survey Test in Computational Arithmetic, grades 7–12, see 180
A.P.U. Arithmetic Test, ages 11–18, see 193
Arithmetic Reasoning Test: [Personnel Research Institute Clerical Battery], clerical applicants and high school, see 195
Arithmetic Test (Fundamentals and Reasoning): Municipal Tests: National Achievement Tests, grades 3–8, see 196
Arithmetic Test: National Achievement Tests, grades 3–8, see 197
Arithmetic Tests EA2A and EA4, ages 14.5 and over, see 198
Arithmetical Problems: Test A/68, job applicants with at least 10 years of education, see 199
Assessment of Basic Competencies: Mathematics Module, ages 3–15, see 211
Assessment of Skills in Computation, junior high school, see 217
Basic Arithmetic Skill Evaluation, grades 1–10, see 245
Basic Educational Skills Inventory: Math, grades kgn–6, see 248
Basic Number Diagnostic Test, ages 5–7, see 253
Basic Number Screening Test, ages 7–12, see 254
Basic Skills in Arithmetic Test, grades 6–12, see 264
Bobbs-Merrill Arithmetic Achievement Tests, grades 1–9, see 301
Bristol Achievement Tests: Mathematics, ages 8–13, see 319
Buswell-John Diagnostic Test for Fundamental Processes in Arithmetic, pupils doing unsatisfactory work in arithmetic, see 335
Computation Test A/67, job applicants with at least 6 years of education, see 555
Cooperative Mathematics Tests: Arithmetic, grades 7–9, see 576
CSMS Number Operations, ages 11–12, see 640
Diagnostic Chart for Fundamental Processes in Arithmetic, grades 2–8, see 713
Diagnostic Decimal Tests, ages 9–13, see 714
Diagnostic Fractions Test 3, ages 7–11, see 715
Diagnostic Mathematics Inventory, grades 1.5–8.5, see 716
Diagnostic Number Tests 1–2, ages 8–12, see 717
Diagnostic Screening Test: Math, Third Edition, grades 1–12, see 723
DTMS Arithmetic Skills Test, beginning students in two- and four-year institutions, see 762
Emporia Arithmetic Tests, grades 1–8, see 804
Key Math Diagnostic Arithmetic Test, preschool–grade 6, see 1250

Leicester Number Test: Basic Number Concepts, ages 7–1 to 9–0, see 1315
Mathematics Evaluation Procedures K–2, grades kgn–4, see 1411
Nottingham Number Test, ages 9–1 to 11–0, see 1623
Number Test DE, ages 10.5–12.5, see 1652
Office Arithmetic Test: ETSA Test 2A, job applicants, see 1674
RBH Arithmetic Fundamentals Test, business and industry, see 1975
RBH Arithmetic Reasoning Test, business and industry, see 1976
RBH Shop Arithmetic Test, industry, see 1980
Scholastic Achievement Test in Arithmetic, grades 1/substandard A, 2/substandard B, standards 1–4, see 2073
SRA Arithmetic Index, job applicants ages 14 and over with poor educational background, see 2261
Staffordshire Test of Computation, 1974 Revision, ages 7–15, see 2278
Stanford Mental Arithmetic Test, grades 1–6, see 2295
Test of Performance in Computational Skills, grades 9–12, see 2454
Tests A/8: Arithmetic, technical college students and applicants for clerical and trade positions with 8–12 years of education, see 2414
Tests of Basic Experiences 2: Mathematics, prekgn–grade 1, see 2480
Watson Number-Readiness Test, Fifth Edition, grades kgn–1, see 2595

CALCULUS

Advanced Placement Examinations in Mathematics, high school students desiring credit for college level courses and admission to advanced courses, see 142
CLEP Subject Examination in Calculus with Elementary Functions, persons entering college or already in college, see 425
Cooperative Mathematics Tests: Calculus, high school and college, see 577

GEOMETRY

Algebra, Geometry and Trigonometry Test for Stds 9 and 10, standards 9, 10, see 153
Cooperative Mathematics Tests: Analytic Geometry, high school and college, see 575
Cooperative Mathematics Tests: Geometry, grades 10–12, see 578
Geometry (Including Plane and Solid Geometry): Minnesota High School Achievement Examinations, high school, see 948
High School Subject Tests: Geometry, grades 9–12, see 1091
Iowa Geometry Aptitude Test, Third Edition, high school, see 1189
Modern Geometry Test: Content Evaluation Series, grades 10–12, see 1526
Plane Geometry: National Achievement Tests, high school, see 1837
Solid Geometry: National Achievement Tests, high school, see 2238

STATISTICS

CLEP Subject Examination in Statistics, persons entering college or already in college, see 459

TRIGONOMETRY

Algebra, Geometry and Trigonometry Test for Stds 9 and 10, standards 9, 10, see 153
CLEP Subject Examination in College Algebra-Trigonometry, persons entering college or already in college, see 428
CLEP Subject Examination in Trigonometry, persons entering college or already in college, see 461
Cooperative Mathematics Tests: Trigonometry, high school and college, see 580
Plane Trigonometry; National Achievement Tests, grades 10–16, see 1838
Trigonometry: Minnesota High School Achievement Examinations, high school, see 2525

MISCELLANEOUS

ACT Evaluation/Survey Service, junior high school students through adults, see 78
Adaptive Functioning Index, ages 14 and over in rehabilitation or special education settings, see 112
Ahr's Individual Development Survey, grades kgn–1, see 150
Assessment of Basic Competencies: Information Processing Module, ages 3–15, see 209
Behavior Rating Instrument for Autistic and Other Atypical Children, autistic and atypical children, see 272
Career Adaptive Behavior Inventory, disabled students ages 5–15, see 366
Checklist/Guide to Selecting a Small Computer, individuals selecting a small computer for a business, see 388

Child Center Operational Assessment Tool, regular or special classroom students, see 393
Clifton Assessment Procedures for the Elderly, ages 60 and over, see 471
Community Living Observational System, severely and profoundly mentally retarded persons living in group homes, see 541
Community Oriented Programs Environment Scale, patients and staff of community oriented psychiatric facilities, see 542
Counseling Services Assessment Blank, college and adult counseling clients, see 618
Counselor Rating Scales (Short Form), subjects in counseling experiments, see 619
Crane Oral Dominance Test: Spanish/English, ages 4–8, see 625

Educational Goal Attainment Tests, grades 7–12, see 777
Juvenile Justice Policy Inventory, juvenile justice professionals, see 1234
Modern Photography Comprehension Test, photography students, see 1528
Multi-Ethnic Awareness Survey, grades 7–12 and teachers, see 1544
Multiphasic Environmental Assessment Procedure, adults, various settings, see 1546
OARS Multidimensional Functional Assessment Questionnaire, ages 60 and over, see 1659
Organization Health Survey, managers, administrators, and supervisors in government and industry, see 1744
Potential for Foster Parenthood Scale, applicants for foster parenthood, see 1857
[Profiles from Rensis Likert Associates, Inc.], for measurement of groups, not individuals, see 1905
Psycho-Educational Battery, grades kgn–6, 7–16 and adults, see 1925
Skills for Independent Living, educable mentally retarded secondary students and low achieving nonretarded secondary students, see 2211
Skills Inventory for Parents, parents of handicapped or developmentally delayed children, see 2212
Social Climate Scales, members of various groups, see 2227
STS Educational Development Series: Scholastic Tests, grades 2–12, see 2325
System of Multicultural Pluralistic Assessment, ages 5–11, see 2387
Teacher's Handbook of Diagnostic Inventories, Second Edition, grades kgn–8, see 2401
T.M.R. School Competency Scales, trainable mentally retarded ages 5–17, see 2508
Ward Atmosphere Scale, patients and staff of hospital-based psychiatric treatment programs, see 2587
Woodcock-Johnson Psycho-Educational Battery, ages 3–80, see 2639
Work Environment Scale, employees and supervisors, see 2652

BLIND

Anxiety Scale for the Blind, blind and partially sighted ages 13 and over, see 184
Blind Learning Aptitude Test, blind ages 6–20, see 299
Developmental Checklist, visually impaired multi-handicapped children ages 1–8, see 695
Lorimer Braille Recognition Test: A Test of Ability in Reading Braille Contractions, students (ages 7–13) in grade 2 braille, see 1342
Roughness Discrimination Test, blind children in grades kgn–1, see 2038
Stanford-Ohwaki-Kohs Block Design Intelligence Test for the Blind: American Revision of the Ohwaki-Kohs Test, blind and partially sighted ages 16 and over, see 2296
Tooze Braille Speed Test: A Test of Basic Ability in Reading Braille, students (ages 7–13) in grades 1 or 2 braille, see 2511

BUSINESS EDUCATION

Bookkeeping: Minnesota High School Achievement Examinations, high school, see 303
Bookkeeping Test: National Business Entrance Tests, grades 11–16 and adults, see 304
Business English Test: The Daily Vocational Tests, grades 8–12 and adults, see 331
Business Fundamentals and General Information Test: National Business Entrance Tests, grades 11–16 and adults, see 332
Clerical Aptitude Test: Acorn National Aptitude Tests, grades 7–16 and adults, see 464
General Office Clerical Test: National Business Entrance Tests, grades 11–16 and adults, see 944
Hiett Simplified Shorthand Test (Gregg), 1, 2 semesters high school, see 1078
Machine Calculation Test: National Business Entrance Tests, grades 11–16 and adults, see 1352
National Business Entrance Tests, grades 11–16 and adults, see 1556
NTE Specialty Area Tests: Business Education Specialty Area Test, college seniors and teachers, see 1629
Office Information and Skills Test: Content Evaluation Series, grade 12, see 1675
Reicherter-Sanders Typewriting I and II, 1, 2 semesters high school, see 2006
Russell-Sanders Bookkeeping Test, 1, 2 semesters high school, see 2041
Shorthand Aptitude Test, high school, see 2195
SRA Clerical Aptitudes, grades 9–12 and adults, see 2263
Stenographic Test: National Business Entrance Tests, grades 11–16 and adults, see 2307
Tapping Test: A Predictor of Typing and Other Tapping Operations, high school, see 2390
Typewriting Test: National Business Entrance Tests, grades 11–16 and adults, see 2527
United Students Typewriting Test, Volume 14, 1–4 semesters, see 2533

COMPUTATIONAL & TESTING DEVICES

Chronological Age Computer, ages 3–7 to 19–5, see 403
Multiple Purpose Self Trainer, high school and adults, see 1549

COURTSHIP & MARRIAGE

Abortion Scale, older adolescents and adults, see 8
Borromean Family Index, adolescents and adults, see 307
California Marriage Readiness Evaluation, premarital counselees, see 350
Caring Relationship Inventory, premarital and marital counselees, see 376
Coitometer, older adolescents and adults, see 485
Dating Problems Checklist, high school and college, see 659
Dating Scale, adolescents and adults, see 660
Erotometer: A Technique for the Measurement of Heterosexual Love, older adolescents and adults, see 840
Familism Scale, adolescents and adults, see 870

Family Environment Scale, family members, see 872
Family Pre-Counseling Inventory, adolescents and their parents, see 873
Family Violence Scale, adolescents and adults, see 875
Gravidometer, older adolescents and adults, see 1006
Home Observation for Measurement of the Environment, birth to age 3, preschool, see 1108
Marital Pre-Counseling Inventory, married couples beginning counseling, see 1373
Marital Satisfaction Inventory, married couples beginning counseling, see 1374
Marriage Adjustment Form, adults, see 1375
Marriage Adjustment Inventory, marital counselees, see 1376
Marriage Analysis, Experimental Edition, married couples in counseling, see 1377
Marriage Counseling Kit, premarital couples, see 1378
Marriage Evaluation, marital counselees, see 1379
Marriage Expectation Inventories, engaged and married couples, see 1380
Marriage Inventory, married couples in counseling, see 1381
Marriage Prediction Schedule, adults, see 1382
Marriage Role Expectation Inventory, adolescents and adults, see 1383
Marriage Scale (For Measuring Compatibility of Interests), premarital and marital counselees, see 1384
Otto Pre-Marital Counseling Schedules, adult couples, see 1756
Pair Attraction Inventory, college and adults, see 1758
Pill Scale, older adolescents and adults, see 1832
Premarital Communication Inventory, premarital counselees, see 1867
Sex Knowledge and Attitude Test, Second Edition, college and adults, see 2168
Sexometer, adolescents and adults, see 2170
Sexual Adjustment Inventory, adults, see 2171
Sexual Compatibility Test, couples, see 2173
Socio-Sexual Knowledge & Attitudes Test, developmentally disabled ages 18–42 and non-retarded persons of all ages, see 2237
Vasectomy Scale: Attitudes, older adolescents and adults, see 2549

DRIVING & SAFETY EDUCATION

Driver Attitude Survey, drivers, see 753
Hannaford Industrial Safety Attitude Scales, industry, see 1056
McGlade Road Test for Use in Driver Licensing, Education and Employment, prospective drivers, see 1428
Siebrecht Attitude Scale, grades 9–16 and adults, see 2197

EDUCATION

Academic Freedom Survey, college students and faculty, see 14
ACT Proficiency Examination in History of American Education, college and adults, see 91
Administrator Image Questionnaire, administrators, see 119
Attitude to School Questionnaire, grades kgn–2, see 220
Attitude Toward School, elementary, secondary school students, see 221
Attitude Toward School K–12, grades kgn–12, see 222
Classroom Atmosphere Questionnaire, grades 4–9, see 407
Classroom Environment Index, grades 7 through graduate school, see 408
Classroom Environment Scale, students and teachers in grades 7–12, see 409
College and University Environment Scales, Second Edition, college, see 486
College Characteristics Index, grades 13–16, see 502
Cooperative Institutional Research Program, college freshmen, transfer, and part-time students, see 572
Cornell Inventory for Student Appraisal of Teaching and Courses, college teachers, see 607
Course Evaluation Questionnaire, high school and college, see 620
Course-Faculty Instrument, business faculty and courses, see 621
Diagnostic Teacher-Rating Scale, grades 4–12, see 727
Educational Values Assessment Questionnaire, adults, see 779
Endeavor Instructional Rating System, college, see 818
Faculty Morale Scale for Institutional Improvement, college faculty, see 864
Graduate Record Examinations Advanced Education Test, graduate school candidates, see 977
High School Characteristics Index, grades 9–13, see 1080
ICES: Instructor and Course Evaluation System, college students, see 1121
Illinois Course Evaluation Questionnaire, college, see 1125
Institutional Functioning Inventory, college faculty and administrators, see 1158
Institutional Goals Inventory, college faculty and students and other subgroups, see 1159
Inventory of Individually Perceived Group Cohesiveness, group members grades 5 and over, see 1180
Knowledge and Attitudes of Drug Usage, grades 4–12, see 1258
Lake St. Clair Incident, adults, see 1276
Light's Retention Scale, Revised Edition 1981, grades kgn–12, see 1328
Multidimensional Assessment of Philosophy of Education, teachers and prospective teachers, see 1542
NTE Core Battery, college seniors and teachers, see 1624
NTE Programs, college seniors and teachers, see 1625
NTE Specialty Area Tests: Early Childhood Education Specialty Area Test, college seniors and teachers, see 1631
NTE Specialty Area Tests: Education in the Elementary School Specialty Area Test, college seniors and teachers, see 1632
NTE Specialty Area Tests: Education of the Mentally Retarded Specialty Area Test, college seniors and teachers, see 1633
NTE Specialty Area Tests: Educational Administration and Supervision Specialty, college seniors and teachers, see 1634
NTE Specialty Area Tests: Guidance Counselor Specialty Area Test, prospective guidance counselors, see 1638
NTE Specialty Area Tests: Media Specialist-Library and Audio-Visual Services Specialty Area Test, college seniors and teachers, see 1643
Organizational Climate Index, employees, see 1745

Parent Opinion Inventory, parents of school children, see 1763
Pictographic Self Rating Scale, high school and college, see 1818
Profile of a School, students and parents and school personnel, see 1903
Purdue Instructor Performance Indicator, college teachers, see 1943
Purdue Rating Scale for Instruction, college teachers, see 1951
Purdue Student-Teacher Opinionaire, student teachers, see 1953
Purdue Teacher Evaluation Scale, teachers grades 7–12, see 1954
Purdue Teacher Opinionaire, teachers, see 1955
Quality of School Life Scale, grades 4–12, see 1962
School Administration and Supervision, prospective elementary school administrators and supervisors, see 2078
School Atmosphere Questionnaire, grades 7–12, see 2080
School/Home Observation and Referral System, preschool–grade 3, see 2084
School Personnel Research and Evaluation Services, teachers and prospective administrators and supervisors, see 2088
School Survey of Interpersonal Relationships, teachers, see 2092
Secondary School Administration, prospective secondary school administrators, see 2117
Secondary School Supervision, prospective secondary school supervisors, see 2120
Self Appraisal Scale for Teachers, teachers, see 2129
Six Inventories to Assess Affective Impact of Basic Skills Instructional Programs, older primary level and secondary level students, see 2207
Student Information Form, entering college freshmen, see 2333
Student Instructional Report, college teachers, see 2334
Student Opinion Inventory, high school, see 2335
Student Orientations Survey, college students, see 2336
Student Reactions to College, 1 or more semesters of 2- or 4-year college, see 2337
Student's Rating Scale of an Instructor, high school and college, see 2338
Survey of Educational Leadership Practices, teachers and school administrators, see 2365
Survey of School Attitudes, grades 1–8, see 2372
Teacher Attitude Inventory, teachers and prospective teachers, see 2397
Teacher-Image Questionnaire, grades 7–12, see 2398
Teacher Opinionaire on Democracy, teachers, see 2399
Teacher Self-Rating Inventory, teachers, see 2400
Teaching Aptitude Test: George Washington University Series, grades 12–16, see 2403
University Residence Environment Scale, students in university living groups, see 2534
Wilson Teacher-Appraisal Scale, ratings by students in grades 7–16, see 2630

HANDWRITING

Expressional Growth Through Handwriting Evaluation Scale, grades 1 through high school, see 856

HEALTH & PHYSICAL EDUCATION

AAHPER Cooperative Health Education Test, grades 5–9, see 1
AAHPER Cooperative Physical Education Tests, grades 4–12, see 2
AAHPER-Kennedy Foundation Special Fitness Test for the Mentally Retarded, grades 8–18, see 3
AAHPER Sport Skills Tests, ages 10–18, see 4
AAHPER Youth Fitness Test, grades 5–12, see 5
Action-Choice Tests for Competitive Sports Situations, high school and college, see 109
CAHPER Fitness-Performance II Test, ages 7–44, see 342
CLEP Subject Examination in Human Growth and Development, persons entering college or already in college, see 445
Drug Abuse Knowledge Test, grades 10–12, see 755
Emporia Elementary Health Test, 1, 2 semesters in grades 6–8, see 808
Emporia High School Health Test, high school and college, see 812
Fast Tyson Health Knowledge Test, high school and college, see 881
Health and Safety Education Test: National Achievement Tests, grades 3–6, see 1065
Health Education Test: Knowledge and Application: Acorn National Achievement Tests, Revised Edition, grades 7–13, see 1066
Health Knowledge Test for College Freshmen: National Achievement Tests, grade 13, see 1067
Health Test: National Achievement Tests, grades 3–8, see 1068
High School Subject Tests: Health, grades 9–12, see 1092
Indiana Physical Fitness Test, grades 4–12, see 1136
Information Test on Drugs and Drug Abuse, grades 9–16 and adults, see 1150
Information Test on Human Reproduction, grades 9–16 and adults, see 1151
Kilander-Leach Health Knowledge Test, grades 12–16, see 1254
Krantz Health Opinion Survey, college, see 1267
Menometer, adolescents and adults, see 1465
NTE Specialty Area Tests: Physical Education Specialty Area Test, college seniors and teachers, see 1645
Thompson Smoking and Tobacco Knowledge Test, grades 7–16, see 2498

HOME ECONOMICS

Emporia Clothing Test, high school, see 807
Emporia Foods Test, high school, see 810
High School Subject Tests: Consumer Education, grades 9–12, see 1089
NM Consumer Rights and Responsibilities Test, grades 9–12, see 1590
NTE Specialty Area Tests: Home Economics Education Specialty Area Test, college seniors and teachers, see 1639
Nutrition Achievement Tests, grades kgn–6, see 1656
Nutrition Information Test, grades 9–16 and adults, see 1657
Nutrition Knowledge and Interest Questionnaire, grades 9 and above, see 1658

Test of Consumer Competencies, grades 8–12, see 2434
Tests for Everyday Living, junior and senior high school, see 2473

INDUSTRIAL ARTS

Emporia Industrial Arts Test, high school, see 813
Industrial Arts Aptitude Battery: Woodworking Test, grades 7–14, see 1144
NTE Specialty Area Tests: Industrial Arts Education Specialty Area Test, college seniors and teachers, see 1640
Technical and Scholastic Test: The Dailey Vocational Tests, grades 8–12 and adult, see 2406

LEARNING DISABILITIES

ACER Early School Series, 5–5½-year old school beginners, see 27
Auditory Pointing Test, ages 5–10, see 228
Barclay Early Childhood Skill Assessment Guide, preschool–grade 1, see 240
Barclay Learning Needs Assessment Inventory, grades 6–12 and college, see 241
Basic School Skills Inventory, ages 4–8, see 256
Basic Screening and Referral Form for Children With Suspected Learning and Behavioral Disabilities, grades 1–12, see 257
Comprehensive Identification Process, ages 2.5–5.5, see 550
Cutrona Child Study Profile of Psycho-Educational Abilities, grades kgn–3 and special education classes, see 651
Damron Reading/Language Kit, psycholinguistic ages 2–10, see 657
Del Rio Language Screening Test, age 3 to 6–11, see 668
Developmental Indicators for the Assessment of Learning, ages 2.5–5.5, see 696
Developmental Task Analysis, grades kgn–6, see 699
First Grade Screening Test, first grade entrants, see 891
Grassi Basic Cognitive Evaluation, ages 3–9, see 1004
Illinois Test of Psycholinguistic Abilities, Revised Edition, ages 2–10, see 1126
Johnson-Kenney Screening Test, ages 5.5–6.5, see 1221
Kerby Learning Modality Test, Revised 1980, ages 5–11, see 1249
LD Program that Works, learning disabled children, see 1294
Learning Disability Rating Procedure, grades kgn–12, see 1304
Meeting Street School Screening Test, grades kgn–1, see 1459
Melvin-Smith Receptive-Expressive Observation, grades 1–12, see 1461
Pre-Reading Screening Procedures, first grade entrants of average or superior intelligence, see 1871
Project MEMPHIS Instruments for Individual Program Planning and Evaluation, preschool handicapped children, see 1915
Psychoeducational Inventory of Basic Learning Abilities, ages 5–12 with suspected learning disabilities, see 1927
Psychoeducational Profile of Basic Learning Abilities, ages 2–14 with learning disabilities, see 1928
Pupil Record of Educational Behavior, preschool through upper primary levels, see 1935
Queensland University Aphasia and Language Test, ages 2–10, see 1963
Quickscreen, grades kgn–2, see 1971
Revised Token Test, children and adults, see 2017
Rhode Island Profile of Early Learning Behavior, grades kgn–2, see 2020
Rucker-Gable Educational Programming Scale, teachers and administrators, see 2039
School Problem Screening Inventory, Fifth Edition, grades kgn–12, see 2089
SCREEN, grades kgn–3, see 2102
Screening Test for the Assignment of Remedial Treatments, ages 4–6 to 6–5, see 2106
Screening Tests for Identifying Children With Specific Language Disability, grades 1–6, see 2110
SEARCH—A Scanning Instrument for the Identification of Potential Learning Disability, Second Edition, Expanded, children ages 63 to 80 months, see 2111
Slingerland Screening Tests for Identifying Children with Specific Language Disability, grades 1–6, see 2214
Specific Language Disability Test, average to high IQ children in grades 6–8, see 2252
Student Disability Survey, grades 1–9, see 2331
Survey of Basic Competencies, ages 3–15, see 2364
Valett Developmental Survey of Basic Learning Abilities, ages 2–7, see 2543
Visual Discrimination Test, ages 5–8, see 2561
Visual Memory Scale, ages 5–6, see 2562
Visual Memory Test, ages 5–8, see 2563
Yellow Brick Road, ages 3–6, see 2665

LISTENING COMPREHENSION

ACER Listening Tests: 10-year-olds and 14-year-olds, ages 10, 14, see 33
Assessment of Children's Language Comprehension, 1973 Revision, ages 3–7, see 212
Cooperative Primary Tests: Listening, grades 1.5–3, see 583
Jones-Mohr Listening Test, persons in educational and training programs, see 1222
Listening Comprehension, grades 1–3, see 1334
Progressive Achievement Tests of Listening Comprehension, standards 1–4 and Forms I–IV, see 1910
Tests for Auditory Comprehension of Language, ages 3–6, see 2472

PHILOSOPHY

Graduate Record Examinations Advanced Philosophy Test, graduate school candidates, see 988

PSYCHOLOGY

ACT Proficiency Examination in Educational Psychology, college and adults, see 88
Aden-Crosthwait Adolescent Psychology Achievement Test, college, see 115
Cass-Sanders Psychology Test, high school and college, see 380
CLEP Subject Examination in Educational Psychology, persons entering college or already in college, see 435
CLEP Subject Examination in General Psychology, persons entering college or already in college, see 442

Graduate Record Examinations Advanced Psychology Test, graduate school candidates, see 991

RECORD & REPORT FORMS

ANSER System—Aggregate Neurobehavioral Student Health and Educational Review, ages 3–12+, see 182
Behavior Analysis Forms for Clinical Intervention, behavior therapy clients, see 271
Florida Cumulative Guidance Record, Revised, grades 1–12, see 903
G.C. Anecdotal Record Form, teachers' recordings of student actions, see 936
Gifted and Talented Screening Form, grades kgn–9, see 956
[Guidance Cumulative Folder and Record Forms], grades kgn–12, see 1039
Junior High School Record, grades 7–10, see 1231
Ontario School Record System, 1972 Edition, grades kgn–13, see 1728
Psychodiagnostic Test Report Blank, psychologists, see 1924
Secondary-School Record, grades 9–12, see 2119

RELIGIOUS EDUCATION

Achievement Test in Jewish History, junior high school, see 50
Achievement Test—Jewish Life and Observances, grades 5–7, see 51
Achievement Test—The State of Israel, "pupils who have completed an organized course of study on the state of Israel," see 52
Biblical Survey Test, college, see 287
Inventory of Religious Activities and Interests, high school and college students considering church-related occupations and theological school students, see 1183
Partial Index of Modernization: Measurement of Attitudes Toward Morality, children and adults, see 1766
Religion Scale, adolescents and adults, see 2008
Religious Attitudes Inventory, religious counselees, see 2009
Strait Biblical Knowledge Test, grades 9–16 and adults, see 2316
Theological School Inventory, incoming seminary students, see 2493
Youth Research Survey, ages 13–19, see 2667

SCORING MACHINES & SERVICES

IBM 3881 Optical Mark Reader, for reading IBM 3881 answer sheets, see 1120

SOCIOECONOMIC STATUS

American Home Scale, grades 8–16, see 163
Environmental Participation Index, culturally disadvantaged ages 12 and over, see 835
Home Index, grades 4–12, see 1107
Socio-Economic Status Scales, urban students, adults, rural families, see 2236

TEST PROGAMS

ACT Assessment Program, candidates for college entrance, see 76
ACT Proficiency Examination Program, college and adults, see 79
Advanced Placement Examinations, high school students desiring credit for college level courses or admission to advanced courses, see 124
College Board Admissions Testing Program, candidates for college entrance, see 500
College Level Examination Program, persons entering college or already in college, see 506
College Placement Tests, college freshmen, see 507
Comparative Guidance and Placement Program, entrants to postsecondary institutions, see 543
Graduate Record Examinations: Aptitude and Advanced, graduate school candidates, see 994
High School Subject Tests, grades 9–12, see 1083
Multiple Assessment Programs and Services, entering and continuing college students, see 1548
[National Science Foundation Graduate Fellowship Testing Program], applicants for N.S.F. fellowship for graduate study in the sciences, see 1563
Ohio Vocational Education Achievement Test Program, grades 11–12, see 1719
Science: Minnesota High School Achievement Examinations, grades 7–9, see 2097
Secondary School Admission Test: General School Ability and Reading, grades 5–10, see 2118
Testing Academic Achievement, high school graduates and college students, see 2470

MULTI–APTITUDE BATTERIES

Academic Aptitude Test, first-year university, see 11
Academic-Technical Aptitude Tests, "coloured pupils" in standards 6–8, see 18
Aptitude Tests for Occupations, grades 9–13 and adults, see 190
Aptitude Tests for School Beginners, grade 1 entrants, see 191
Armed Services Vocational Aptitude Battery, high school, see 202
Basic Occupational Literacy Test, educationally disadvantaged adults, see 2535

Comprehensive Ability Battery, ages 15 and over, see 547
Detroit General Aptitudes Examination, grades 6–12, see 689
Differential Aptitude Tests (Forms V and W), grades 8–12 and adults, see 732
Differential Test Battery, ages 11 to "tax university level," see 733
Employee Aptitude Survey, ages 16 and over, see 799
ETSA Tests, job applicants, see 846
Flanagan Aptitude Classification Tests, grades 9–12 and adults, see 899

CLASSIFIED SUBJECT INDEX

Guidance Test Battery for Secondary Pupils (Standard 8), secondary pupils, see 1041
Guilford-Zimmerman Aptitude Survey, grades 9–16 and adults, see 1044
Hay Aptitude Test Battery, clerical and plant workers, see 1064
High Level Battery: Test A/75, adults with at least 12 years of education, see 1079
Junior Aptitude Tests for Indian South Africans, standards 6–8, see 1228
Multi-Aptitude Test, college courses in testing, see 1541
National Institute for Personnel Research Intermediate Battery, standards 7–10 and job applicants with 9–12 years of education, see 1560
National Institute for Personnel Research Normal Battery, standards 6–10 and job applicants with 8–11 years of education, see 1561
Senior Aptitude Tests, standards 8–10 and college and adults, see 2149
SRA Primary Mental Abilities, 1962 Edition, grades kgn–12, see 2269
Structure of Intellect Learning Abilities Test, preschool–adults, see 2320
USES Basic Occupational Literacy Test, educationally disadvantaged adults, see 2535
USES General Aptitude Test Battery, grades 9–12 and adults, see 2537
USES Nonreading Aptitude Test Battery, 1982 Edition, disadvantaged grades 9–12 and adults, see 2539
Valett Inventory of Critical Thinking Abilities, ages 4–15, see 2544
Wide Range Intelligence and Personality Test, ages 9.5–54, see 2623

NEUROPSYCHOLOGICAL

Booklet Category Test, adolescents and adults, see 305
Burks' Behavior Rating Scale for Organic Brain Dysfunction, grades kgn–6, see 327
Complex Figure Test, ages 16 and over, see 544
D-K Scale of Lateral Dominance, grades 2–6, see 653
First Grade Screening Test, first grade entrants, see 891
Five Task Test: A Performance and Projective Test of Emotionality, Motor Skill and Organic Brain Damage, ages 8 and over, see 897
Grassi Block Substitution Test: For Measuring Organic Brain Pathology, mental patients, see 1005
Halstead-Reitan Neuropsychological Test Battery, ages 5–8, 9–14, 15 and over, see 1052
Hooper Visual Organization Test, ages 14 and over, see 1109
Luria-Nebrasksa Neuropsychological Battery, ages 15 and over, see 1346
Memory-For-Designs, ages 8.5 and over, see 1462
Neurological Dysfunctions of Children, ages 3–10, see 1571
Neuropsychological Questionnaire, children, adults, see 1572
Object Sorting Scales, ages 16 and over, see 1661
Organic Integrity Test, ages 5 and over, see 1743
Perceptual Maze Test, ages 6–16, and adults, see 1778
Quick Neurological Screening Test, Revised Edition, ages 5 and over, see 1967
Revised Token Test, children and adults, see 2017
Single and Double Simultaneous (Face-Hand) Stimulation Test, ages 18–75, see 2201
Slosson Drawing Coordination Test for Children and Adults, ages 1.5 and over, see 2216
Stroop Color and Word Test, ages 7 and over, see 2319
Symbol Digit Modalities Test, ages 8 and over, see 2380
Test of Lateral Awareness and Directionality, grades 1–12, see 2446
Western Aphasia Battery, adults with language disorders, see 2615

PERSONALITY

AAMD Adaptive Behavior Scale for Children and Adults, 1974 Revision, mentally retarded and emotionally maladjusted ages 3–adults, see 6
Abortion Scale, older adolescents and adults, see 8
ACT Evaluation/Survey Service, junior high school students through adults, see 78
Addiction Research Center Inventory, drug addicts, see 113
Additional Personality Factor Inventory—2, college and adults, see 114
Adjective Checklist, grades 9–16 and adults, see 116
Adjustment and Adaptation Profiles, children and adults in mental health, counseling, or medical service centers, see 117
Adjustment Inventory, grades 9–10, adults, see 118
Adolescent Alienation Index, ages 12–19, see 120
Adult Self Expression Scale, adults, see 122
Affect Scale, college, see 144
Affective Domain Descriptor Program, ages 6–18, see 145
Affective Perception Inventory, grades 1–12, see 146
African T.A.T., urban African adults, see 147
Alcadd Test, adults, see 152
Anxiety Scale for the Blind, blind and partially sighted ages 13 and over, see 184
Arlin-Hills Attitude Surveys, grades kgn–12, see 201
Assessment of Coping Style, grades kgn–12, see 213
Assessment of Qualitative and Structural Dimensions of Object Representations, adolescents and adults (patients and normals), see 215
Association Adjustment Inventory, normal and institutionalized adults, see 218
Athlete's Affective Response Profile, high school and college and adult athletes, see 219
Attitudes Related to Tolerance 9–12, grades 9–12, see 223
Attitudes Toward Mainstreaming Scale, adults, see 224

Attitudes Toward Parental Control of Children, adults, see 225
Autism Screening Instrument for Educational Planning, (First Edition), preschool and school aged severely handicapped and autistic, see 234
Balthazar Scales of Adaptive Behavior, profoundly and severely mentally retarded adults and the younger less retarded, see 235
Barber Scales of Self-Regard for Preschool Children, ages 2–5, see 238
Barclay Classroom Assessment System, grades 3–6, see 239
Barclay Learning Needs Assessment Inventory, grades 6–12 and college, see 241
Barron-Welsh Art Scale: A Portion of the Welsh Figure Preference Test, ages 6 and over, see 243
Barsch Learning Style Inventory, grades 7–12 and college, see 244
Behavior Rating Profile, grades 1–12, see 273
Behavior Rating Scales, grades kgn–8, see 274
Behavior Status Inventory, psychiatric inpatients, see 275
Behavioral Academic Self-Esteem, preschool–grade 8, see 276
Bem Sex-Role Inventory, high school and college and adults, see 278
[Bender-Gestalt Test], ages 4 and over, see 280
Bessell Measurement of Emotional Maturity Scales, ages 5–11, see 286
Bipolar Psychological Inventory, college and adults, see 294
Blacky Pictures: A Technique for the Exploration of Personality Dynamics, ages 5 and over, see 298
Bloom Sentence Completion Survey, students age 6–21, see 300
Bradfield Classroom Interaction Analysis, grades kgn–12, see 310
Bristol Social Adjustment Guides, ages 5–15, see 321
Burks' Behavior Rating Scale for Organic Brain Dysfunction, grades kgn–6, see 327
Burks' Behavior Rating Scales, preschool–8, see 328
Buttons: A Projective Test for Pre-Adolescent and Adolescent Boys and Girls, grades 7–9, see 337
CAAP Scale, children and adolescents seen in mental health centers, see 341
Cain-Levine Social Competency Scale, mentally retarded children ages 5–13, see 343
California Child Q-Set, ratings of children by teachers and counselors, see 348
California Life Goals Evaluation Schedules, ages 15 and over, see 349
California Preschool Social Competency Scale, ages 2.5–5.5, see 353
California Psychological Inventory, ages 13 and over, see 354
[Re California Psychological Inventory] Behaviordyne Psychodiagnostic Laboratory Service, computerized scoring and interpreting service, see 355
California Q-Set, adults, see 356
California Test of Personality, kgn–14 and adults, see 357
Callahan Anxiety Pictures, ages 5–13, see 358
Camelot Behavioral Checklist, mentally retarded, see 359
Canfield Time Problems Inventory, management and administrative personnel, see 364
Career Development Inventory [Consulting Psychologists Press, Inc.], grades 8–12, see 371

Career Skills Assessment Program, high school and college students, see 375
Chapin Social Insight Test, ages 13 and over, see 384
Characteristics Scale, grades kgn–8, see 385
Chart of Initiative and Independence, mentally handicapped adults, see 386
Child Anxiety Scale, grades kgn–5, see 391
Child Behavior Rating Scale, grades kgn–3, see 392
Child Development Center Q-Sort, ages 1.5 to adult, see 394
Childrens Adaptive Behavior Scale, ages 5–10, see 395
Children's Apperception Test, ages 3–10, see 396
Children's Depression Scale, ages 9–16, see 397
Children's Embedded Figures Test, ages 5–12, see 398
Children's Hypnotic Susceptibility Scale, ages 5–16, see 399
Children's Personality Questionnaire, 1975 Edition, ages 8–12, see 400
Clinical Analysis Questionnaire, ages 16 and over, see 472
Clinical Behavior Check List and Rating Scale, clinical clients, see 473
College and University Environment Scales, Second Edition, college, see 486
College Inventory of Academic Adjustment, college, see 505
College Student Experiences, college, see 532
Columbus: Picture Analysis of Growth Towards Maturity, ages 5–20, see 535
Communication Sensitivity Inventory, managers, see 539
Community Oriented Programs Environment Scale, patients and staff of community oriented psychiatric facilities, see 542
Complex Figure Test, ages 16 and over, see 544
Comrey Personality Scales, ages 16 and over, see 558
Concept-Specific Anxiety Scale, college and adults, see 562
Conceptual Systems Test, grades 7 and over, see 563
Continuing Education Assessment Inventory, mentally retarded adolescents and adults, see 568
Coopersmith Self-Esteem Inventories, ages 8–15, 16 and above, see 603
Cornell Medical Index—Health Questionnaire, ages 14 and over, see 609
Cornell Word Form 2, adults, see 610
Correctional Institutions Environment Scale, residents and staff of juvenile and adult correctional facilities, see 612
Cotswold Personality Assessment P.A.1, ages 11–16, see 617
Counseling Services Assessment Blank, college and adult counseling clients, see 618
Counselor Rating Scales (Short Form), subjects in counseling experiments, see 619
Courtship Analysis, dating and engaged couples, see 622
CPH Patient Attitude Scale, mental patients, see 624
C-R Opinionaire, grades 11–16 and adults, see 340
Crawford Psychological Adjustment Scale, psychiatric patients, see 626
Creativity Checklist, grades kgn–graduate school, see 629
Cree Questionnaire, adults, see 631
Crown-Crisp Experiential Index, normal and psychoneurotic adults, see 639
Culture-Free Self-Esteem Inventories for Children and Adults, grades 3–9 and adults, see 644

CLASSIFIED SUBJECT INDEX

Current and Past Psychopathology Scales, psychiatric patients and nonpatients, see 645

Curtis Completion Form, grades 11–16 and adults, see 647

[Daily Behavior System], children and adults with problem behaviors, see 655

Defense Mechanism Inventory, ages 16 and over, see 665

Defining Issues Test, grades 9–12 and college and adults, see 666

Demos D Scale: An Attitude Scale for the Identification of Dropouts, grades 7–12, see 670

Denver Adjective Check Lists, grades 9–16 and adults, see 681

Denver Community Mental Health Questionnaire-Revised, mental health clients, see 677

Depressive Experience Questionnaire, adolescents and adults (patients and normals), see 682

Derogatis Sexual Functioning Inventory, adults, see 683

Description of Body Scale, adolescents and adults, see 684

Devereux Adolescent Behavior Rating Scale, normally and emotionally disturbed children ages 13–18, see 702

Devereux Child Behavior Rating Scale, emotionally disturbed and mentally retarded children ages 8–12, see 703

Devereux Elementary School Behavior Rating Scale, grades kgn–6, see 704

DF Opinion Survey, grades 12–16 and adults, see 706

Dimensions of Self-Concept, grades 4–12, see 734

Dimock L Inventory, high school and adults, see 735

Diplomacy Test of Empathy, business and industry, see 736

Dole Vocational Sentence Completion Blank, grades 7–12, see 745

Draw-A-Person, ages 5 and over, see 751

Draw-A-Person Quality Scale, ages 16–25, see 752

Dyadic Parent-Child Interaction Coding System: A Manual, children ages 2–10 and their parents, see 768

Dynamic Personality Inventory, ages 15 or 17 and over with IQs of 80 and over, see 769

Early Childhood Environment Rating Scale, early childhood settings, see 771

Early School Personality Questionnaire, ages 6–8, see 772

Education Apperception Test, preschool and elementary school, see 776

Edwards Personal Preference Schedule, college and adults, see 780

Effectiveness Motivation Scale, ages 3–5, see 782

Ego-Ideal and Conscience Development Test, ages 12–18, see 783

Ego State Inventory, adolescents and adults, see 784

Ego Strength Q-Sort Test, grades 9–16 and adults, see 785

Eidetic Parents Test, clinical patients and marriage and family counselees, see 786

Eight State Questionnaire, ages 16 and over, see 787

Elizur Test of Psycho-Organicity: Children and Adults, ages 6 and over, 10 and over, see 793

Embedded Figures Test, ages 10 and over, see 794

Emo Questionnaire, adults, see 795

Emotions Profile Index, college and adults, see 796

Empathy Inventory, nursing instructors, see 797

Empathy Test, ages 13 and over, see 798

Environmental Response Inventory, college and adults, see 837

E.S. Survey, job applicants and employees, see 841

Estes Attitude Scales: Measures of Attitudes Toward School Subjects, grades 2–12, see 845

Evaluation Disposition Toward the Environment, high school and college, see 848

Evaluation Modality Test, adults, see 849

Executive Profile Survey, business executives, see 854

Experiential World Inventory, disturbed adolescents and adults, see 855

Eyberg Child Behavior Inventory, ages 2–16, see 858

Eysenck Personality Inventory, grades 9–16 and adults, see 859

Eysenck Personality Questionnaire, ages 7–15, 16 and over, see 860

Eysenck-Withers Personality Inventory (For I.Q. 50–80 Range), institutionalized subnormal adults, see 861

Facial Interpersonal Perception Inventory, ages 5 and over, see 862

Fairview Development Scale: For the Infirm Mentally Retarded, severely and profoundly mentally retarded, see 865

Fairview Problem Behavior Record, mentally retarded, see 867

Fairview Self-Help Scale, mentally retarded, see 868

Fairview Social Skills Scale: For Mildly and Moderately Retarded, mentally retarded, see 869

Family Adjustment Test, ages 12 and over, see 871

Family Relations Test, ages 3–15 and adults, see 874

Famous Sayings, grades 9–16 and business and industry, see 876

Fear Survey Schedule, college and adults, see 883

Fels Parent Behavior Rating Scales, "for the use of the trained home visitor in appraising certain aspects of parent-child relationships", see 884

FIRO Awareness Scales, grades 4–16 and adults, see 890

Five Task Test: A Performance and Projective Test of Emotionality, Motor Skill and Organic Brain Damage, ages 8 and over, see 897

Flint Infant Security Scale, ages 3–24 months, see 902

Forer Structured Sentence Completion Test, ages 10–18 and adults, see 908

Forer Vocational Survey, adolescents and adults, see 909

Forty-Eight Item Counseling Evaluation Test, adolescents and adults, see 912

Franck Drawing Completion Test, ages 6 and over, see 917

Frost-Safran School Situations Test, ages 9–12, see 919

Frost Self Description Questionnaire, ages 8–14, see 920

Frost Self Description Questionnaire: Extended Scales, ages 9–14, see 921

General Health Questionnaire, adolescents and adults, see 941

Gerontological Apperception Test, ages 66 and over, see 950

Getting Along, grades 7–9, see 954

Gibson Spiral Maze, ages 8.5 and over, see 955

Goldstein-Scheerer Tests of Abstract and Concrete Thinking, brain damaged adults, see 963

Gordon Personal Profile-Inventory, grades 9–16 and adults, see 966

Gottesfeld Community Mental Health Critical Issues Test, mental health professionals, see 967

Gottschalk-Gleser Content Analysis Scales, ages 14 and over, see 969

Graphoscopic Scale: A Projective Psychodiagnostic Method, ages 5–16, 15 and over, see 1002

Grassi Block Substitution Test: For Measuring Organic Brain Pathology, mental patients, see 1005
Grid Test of Schizophrenic Thought Disorder, adults, see 1009
Group Cohesiveness: A Study of Group Morale, adults, see 1010
Group Embedded Figures Test, ages 10 and over, see 1013
Group Encounter Survey, group members, see 1014
Group Environment Scale, group members and leaders, see 1015
Group Inventory for Finding Creative Talent, grades kgn–6, see 1016
Group Inventory For Finding Interests, grades 6–12, see 1017
Group Personality Projective Test, ages 11 and over, see 1020
Group Projection Sketches for the Study of Small Groups, ages 16 and over, see 1022
Group Psychotherapy Suitability Evaluation Scale, patients in group therapy, see 1023
Guidance Inventory, high school, see 1040
Guilford-Holley L Inventory, college and adults, see 1042
Guilford-Zimmerman Temperament Survey, grades 12–16 and adults, see 1046
Hahnemann Elementary School Behavior Rating Scale, elementary school students in both regular and open classrooms, see 1049
Hahnemann High School Behavior Rating Scale, grades 7–12, see 1050
Hand Test, ages 6 and over, see 1053
Handicap Problems Inventory, ages 16 and over with physical disabilities, see 1055
Harding Stress-Fair Compatibility Test, adults, see 1058
Hartman Value Profile, ages 12 and over, see 1062
Harvard Group Scale of Hypnotic Susceptibility, college and adults, see 1063
Hellenic Affiliation Scale: An Inventory of Student Behavior and Beliefs for Use by School Personnel, Experimental Form, college, see 1072
Heterosocial Adequacy Test, male college students, see 1076
Hill Interaction Matrix, prospective members and members, leaders of psychotherapy groups, see 1099
Holtzman Inkblot Technique, ages 5 and over, see 1106
Hooper Visual Organization Test, ages 14 and over, see 1109
How A Child Learns, grades 1–8, see 1112
Howarth Mood Adjective Check List, college and adults, see 1114
Howarth Personality Questionnaire, college and adult, see 1115
H-T-P: House-Tree-Person Projective Technique, ages 3 and over, see 1047
Human Figure Drawing Techniques, ages 3 and over, see 1117
Human Relations Inventory, grades 9–16 and adults, see 1118
IES Test, ages 10 and over and latency period girls, see 1123
Impact Message Inventory: Form II, college students and adults, see 1130
Incomplete Sentence Test, employees, college, see 1131

Incomplete Sentences Task, grades 7–12, college-age adolescents, see 1132
Independent Activities Questionniare, high school and college, see 1133
Independent Living Behavior Checklist, behaviorally impaired adults, see 1134
Industrial Sentence Completion Form, employee applicants, see 1146
Inferred Self-Concept Scale, grades 1–6, see 1148
Instructional Styles Inventory, instructors, see 1160
Integration Level Test Series, adults, see 1162
Interest Inventory for Elementary Grades: George Washington University Series, grades 4–6, see 1165
Intermediate Personality Questionnaire for Indian Pupils (Standards 6 to 8), standards 6–8, see 1167
Inter-Person Perception Test, ages 6 and over, see 1168
Interpersonal Behavior Survey, grades 9–16 and adults, see 1169
Interpersonal Check List, adults, see 1170
Interpersonal Communication Inventory, grades 9–16 and over, see 1171
Interpersonal Conflict Scales, adults, see 1172
Interpersonal Style Inventory, high school and college and adults, see 1173
Intra- and Interpersonal Relations Scale, "Bantu pupils in Forms IV and V", see 1174
Inventory of Anger Communication, high school and adults, see 1178
Inventory of Certain Feelings, applicants for employment, see 1179
Inventory of Individually Perceived Group Cohesiveness, group members grades 5 and over, see 1180
Inventory of Self-Hypnosis, college and adults, see 1184
Iowa Parent Behavior Inventory, parents, see 1190
IPAT Anxiety Scale Questionnaire, ages 14 and over, see 1197
IPAT Depression Scale, adults, see 1198
It Scale for Children, ages 5–6, see 1201
Jackson Personality Inventory, grades 10–16 and adults, see 1203
Jenkins Activity Survey, employed adults ages 25–65, see 1206
Jesness Behavior Checklist, ages 10 and over, see 1208
Jesness Inventory, disturbed children and adolescents ages 8–18, adults, see 1209
Jones Personality Rating Scale, grades 9–12 and adults, see 1223
Joseph Pre-School and Primary Self-Concept Screening Test, ages 3–6 to 9–11, see 1225
Junior Eysenck Personality Inventory, ages 7–15, see 1229
Jr.-Sr. High School Personality Questionnaire, ages 12–18, see 1233
Kahn Test of Symbol Arrangement, ages 6 and over, see 1237
Ka-Ro Inkblot Test, ages 3 and over, see 1235
Kasanin-Hanfmann Concept Formation Test, normal and schizophrenic adults, see 1239
Katz Adjustment Scales, normal and mentally disordered adults, see 1240
Katz-Zalk Opinion Questionnaire, grades 1–6, see 1241
Kent-Rosanoff Free Association Test, ages 4 and over, see 1247
Khatena-Torrance Creative Perception Inventory, ages 12 and over, see 1253

CLASSIFIED SUBJECT INDEX

Knowledge and Attitudes of Drug Usage, grades 4–12, see 1258

Kohlberg's Moral Judgment Interview, ages 10 and over, see 1262

Kohn Problem Checklist, children ages 3–6 in preschool programs, see 1263

Kohn Social Competence Scale, children ages 3–6 in half-day, full-day preschool programs, see 1264

Kundu's Neurotic Personality Inventory, adults, see 1273

Lake St. Clair Incident, adults, see 1276

Leadership Ability Evaluation, grades 9–16 and adults, see 1297

Leadership and Self-Development Scale, college, see 1298

Leadership Q-Sort Test (A Test of Leadership Values), adults, see 1302

Learning Style Identification Scale, grades 1–8, see 1308

Learning Styles Inventory [Creative Learning Press, Inc.], grades 4–12 and teachers, see 1309

Learning Styles Inventory [Humanics Media], grades 6 through post-graduate level, see 1310

Leeds Scales for the Self-Assessment of Anxiety and Depression, psychiatric patients, see 1314

Leisure Activities Blank, ages 15 and over, see 1316

Leisure Interest Inventory, high school and college and adults, see 1317

Level of Aspiration Board, mental ages 12.5 and over, see 1320

Lewis Counseling Inventory, adolescents in school, see 1321

Life Adjustment Inventory, high school, see 1325

Life Style Questionnaire, ages 14 and over, see 1327

London House Personnel Selection Inventory, job applicants, see 1339

Louisville Behavior Checklist, ages 4–17, see 1343

Love Attitudes Inventory, grade 12 and college, see 1344

Luscher Color Test, adults, see 1347

MACC Behavioral Adjustment Scale, Revised 1971, psychiatric patients, see 1351

Machover Draw-A-Person Test, ages 2 and over, see 1353

Maferr Inventory of Feminine Values, junior and senior high school, college and adults, see 1357

Maferr Inventory of Masculine Values, junior and senior high school, college and adults, see 1358

Make A Picture Story, ages 6 and over, see 1361

Manchester Scales of Social Adaptation, ages 6–15, see 1367

Mandel Social Adjustment Scale, psychiatric patients and others, see 1368

Manson Evaluation, adults, see 1369

Marital Communication Inventory, adults, see 1372

Marital Pre-Counseling Inventory, married couples beginning counseling, see 1373

Marital Satisfaction Inventory, married couples beginning counseling, see 1374

Marriage Adjustment Form, adults, see 1375

Marriage Adjustment Inventory, marital counselees, see 1376

Marriage Analysis, Experimental Edition, married couples in counseling, see 1377

Marriage Counseling Kit, premarital couples, see 1378

Marriage Evaluation, marital counselees, see 1379

Marriage Expectation Inventories, engaged and married couples, see 1380

Marriage Inventory, married couples in counseling, see 1381

Marriage Prediction Schedule, adults, see 1382

Marriage Role Expectation Inventory, adolescents and adults, see 1383

Marriage Scale (For Measuring Compatibility of Interests), premarital and marital counselees, see 1384

Martin S-D Inventory, clients and patients, see 1385

Martinek-Zaichkowsky Self-Concept Scale for Children, grades 1–8, see 1386

Maryland Parent Attitude Survey, parents, see 1387

Maslach Burnout Inventory, staff members in human service and educational institutions, see 1388

Mathematics Anxiety Rating Scale, grades 7–12, college and adults, see 1405

Mathematics Attitudes Inventory, grades 7–12, see 1410

Maudsley Personality Inventory, college and adults, see 1419

Maxfield-Buchholz Scale of Social Maturity for Use With Preschool Blind Children, infancy–6 years, see 1420

M-B History Record: Self-Administered Form, psychiatric patients and penal groups, see 1349

Means-Ends Problem-Solving Procedure, adults, see 1436

Measure of Arousal Seeking Tendency, college, see 1438

Measure of Child Stimulus Screening and Arousability, ages 3 months to 7 years, see 1439

Measure of Individual Differences in Dominance-Submissiveness, college, see 1440

Measurement of Self Concept in Kindergarten Children, kgn, see 1441

Measures of Achieving Tendency, college, see 1442

Measures of Affiliative Tendency and Sensitivity to Rejection, college students and adults, see 1443

Measures of Individual Differences in Temperament, college students and adults, see 1444

Measures of Occupational Stress, Strain, and Coping, employed adults, see 1447

Measures of Pleasure-, Arousal-, and Dominance-Inducing Qualities of Parental Attitudes, ages 3 months–8 years, see 1448

Measures of Self-Concept K–12, grades kgn–12, see 1449

Memory-For-Designs, ages 8.5 and over, see 1462

Menstrual Distress Questionnaire, adult women, see 1466

Merrill-Demos DD Scale: An Attitude Scale for the Identification of Potential or Actual Primary and Secondary Drug Abuse and Delinquent Behavior, grades 3–9, see 1469

Meta-Motivation Inventory, managers and persons in leadership positions, see 1472

Michigan Picture Test-Revised, ages 8–14, see 1480

Millon Behavioral Health Inventory, physical and behavioral medicine patients ages 17 and over, see 1487

Millon Clinical Multiaxial Inventory, adults receiving psychotherapy or participating in psychological assessment, see 1488

Minnesota Multiphasic Personality Inventory, ages 16 and over, see 1498

[Re Minnesota Multiphasic Personality Inventory] Behaviordyne Psychodiagnostic Laboratory Service, computerized scoring and interpreting for qualified users, see 1499

[Re Minnesota Multiphasic Personality Inventory] Caldwell Report: An MMPI Interpretation, computerized scoring and interpreting for qualified users, see 1500

[Re Minnesota Multiphasic Personality Inventory] Psychological Assessment Services, computerized scoring

and interpreting for qualified professional personnel in correctional and court-related facilities, see 1501
[Re Minnesota Multiphasic Personality Inventory] Roche MMPI Computerized Interpretation Service, computerized scoring and interpreting service for clinical psychologists and physicians in clinical practice and research, see 1502
Miskimins Self-Goal-Other Discrepancy Scale, children and adults, see 1514
Missouri Children's Picture Series, ages 5–16, see 1515
Mooney Problem Check List, 1950 Revision, grades 7–16, adults, see 1531
Mother-Child Relationship Evaluation, mothers, see 1537
Motivation Analysis Test, ages 17 and over, see 1538
Motivation and Potential for Adoptive Parenthood Scale, adults seeking to adopt children, see 1539
M-Scale: An Inventory of Attitudes Toward Black/White Relations in the United States, college and adults, see 1350
Multidimensional Maturity Scale, grades kgn–12, see 1543
Multiple Affect Adjective Check List, grades 8–16 and adults, see 1547
Mutually Responsible Facilitation Inventory, adults, see 1553
Myers-Briggs Type Indicator, grades 9–16 and adults, see 1555
Neuroticism Scale Questionnaire, ages 13 and over, see 1573
Northampton Activity Rating Scale, mental patients, see 1621
Nurse Attitudes Inventory, prospective nursing students, see 1654
Nurses' Observation Scale for Inpatient Evaluation, mental patients, see 1655
Object Relations Technique, ages 11 and over, see 1660
Object Sorting Scales, ages 16 and over, see 1661
Objective-Analytic (O-A) Test Battery, ages 14 and over, see 1662
Offer Self-Image Questionnaire for Adolescents, ages 14–18, see 1673
Omnibus Personality Inventory, college, see 1726
Opinion, Attitude, and Interest Survey, high school seniors and college students, see 1729
Opinions Toward Adolescents, college and adults, see 1730
Organic Integrity Test, ages 5 and over, see 1743
Orientation and Motivation Inventory, grades 11 and 12 and college freshmen and sophomores, see 1747
Orientation Inventory, college and industry, see 1748
Pain Apperception Test, adults, see 1757
PAL-C Scale, counseling, mental health, or medical services clients, see 1759
PAL-H Scale, counseling, mental health, or medical services clients, see 1760
Parent-Adolescent Communication Inventory, ages 13 and over, see 1761
Parent As A Teacher Inventory, mothers and fathers with children ages 3–9, see 1762
PARS Scale, mental patients and clinical clients, see 1765
Partial Index of Modernization: Measurement of Attitudes Toward Morality, children and adults, see 1766
Peer Attitudes Toward the Handicapped Scale, grades 4–8, see 1773

Perception of Values Inventory, grades kgn–3, 4–12 and adults, see 1776
Perceptual Maze Test, ages 6–16, and adults, see 1778
Personal Adjustment Index: ETSA Test 8A, job applicants, see 1783
Personal Audit, grades 9–16 and adults, see 1784
Personal Background Inventory, job applicants, see 1785
Personal Distress Inventory and Scales, psychiatric patients and normal adults, see 1787
Personal Orientation Inventory, grades 9–16 and adults, see 1789
Personal Preference Scale, ages 15 and over, see 1790
Personal Questionnaire Rapid Scaling Technique, adolescents and adults, see 1791
Personal Relations Inventory, high school and over, see 1792
Personal Sphere Model, adolescents and adults, see 1793
Personal Values Inventory, grades 12–13, see 1794
Personality Inventory, grades 9–16 and adults, see 1795
Personality Inventory for Children, ages 3–16, see 1796
Personality Rating Scale, grades 4–12, see 1797
Personality Research Form, grades 7–16 and adults, see 1798
Personnel Performance Problems Inventory, managment and administrative personnel, see 1800
Personnel Reaction Blank, Revised Edition, adults, see 1802
PHSF Relations Questionnaire, standards 6–10 and college and adults, see 1815
Physiognomic Cue Test, college and adults, see 1817
Pictographic Self Rating Scale, high school and college, see 1818
Pictorial Study of Values: Pictorial Allport-Vernon, ages 14 and over, see 1821
Picture Identification Test, high school and college, see 1825
Picture Situation Test, adult males, see 1827
Picture Story Test Blank, clinical clients, see 1828
Picture World Test, ages 6 and over, see 1830
Piers-Harris Children's Self Concept Scale (The Way I Feel About Myself), grades 3–12, see 1831
Politte Sentence Completion Test, grades 1–12, see 1848
Polyfactorial Study of Personality, adults, see 1849
PRADI Autobiographical Form, clinical clients, see 1861
PRADI Draw-A-Person Test, clinical clients, see 1862
Pre-Marital Counseling Inventory, premarital counselees, see 1868
Premarital Counseling Kit, premarital counselees, see 1869
Preschool Behavior Questionnaire, ages 3–6, see 1874A
Preschool Embedded Figures Test, ages 3–5, see 1875
Preschool Self-Concept Picture Test, ages 4–5, see 1879
Present State Examination, adult psychiatric patients, see 1883
Primary Self-Concept Inventory, grades kgn–6, see 1896
Process for the Assessment of Effective Student Functioning, grades kgn–7, see 1902
Profile of Mood States, college and psychiatric outpatients, see 1904
Progress Evaluation Scales, ages 6–17, see 1909
Projective Assessment of Aging Method, elderly, see 1916
Projective Index of Body Awareness, mental patients, see 1917
Psychiatric Evaluation Form, psychiatric patients and nonpatients, see 1922

Psychiatric Status Schedules: Subject Form, Second Edition, psychiatric patients and nonpatients, see 1923
Psycho-Epistemological Profile, college and adults, see 1929
Psychological Screening Inventory, ages 16 and over, see 1931
Psychometric Behavior Checklist, adults, see 1932
Psychotic Inpatient Profile, mental patients, see 1933
Pupil Rating Scale Revised: Screening for Learning Disabilities, ages 5–14, see 1934
Purdue Master Attitude Scales, grades 7–16, see 1945
Purdue Rating Scale for Administrators and Executives, administrators and executives, see 1950
Purpose in Life Test, adults, see 1960
Q-Tags Test of Personality, ages 6 and over, 12 and over, see 1961
Questionnaire Measure of Stimulus Screening and Arousability, college and adults, see 1964
QUESTS: A Life-Choice Inventory, grades 9–12, see 1965
Quick Neurological Screening Test, Revised Edition, ages 5 and over, see 1967
Rating of Behavior Scale, children, adolescents, and adults, see 1974
Reactions to Everyday Situations, ages 16 and over, see 1988
Reid Report/Reid Survey, job applicants, see 2007
Religion Scale, adolescents and adults, see 2008
Religious Attitudes Inventory, religious counselees, see 2009
Revised Behavior Problem Checklist, children ages 5–12 and adolescents, see 2012
Risk-Taking-Attitude-Values Inventory, ages 3 and over, see 2026
Rock-A-Bye, Baby: A Group Projective Test for Children, ages 5–10, see 2027
Rokeach Value Survey, ages 11 and over, see 2029
Rorschach, ages 3 and over, see 2030
Rosenzweig Picture-Frustration Study, ages 4–13, 12–18, 14 and over, see 2031
Rotter Incomplete Sentences Blank, grades 9–16, adults, see 2037
Rucker-Gable Educational Programming Scale, teachers and administrators, see 2039
Rutgers Social Attribute Inventory, adults, see 2042
Ruth Fry Symbolic Profile, ages 14 and over, see 2043
SAQS Chicago Q Sort, college and adults, see 2065
Scale to Measure Attitudes Toward Disabled Persons, disabled and nondisabled adults, see 2068
Scales for Rating the Behavioral Characteristics of Superior Students, developed from research with students grades 4–6, see 2069
School Apperception Method, grades kgn–9, see 2079
School Attitude Measure, grades 4–12, see 2081
School Attitude Survey: Feelings I Have About School, grades 3–6, see 2082
School Behavior Checklist, ages 4–13, see 2083
School Interest Inventory, grades 7–12, see 2085
School Inventory, high school, see 2086
School Motivation Analysis Test, ages 12–17, see 2087
Science Attitude Questionnaire, secondary schools, see 2096
SCL-90-R, psychiatric and medical patients, see 2100
S-D Proneness Checklist, clients and patients, see 2044
Security-Insecurity Inventory, grades 9–16 and adults, see 2121
Seeking of Noetic Goals Test, adolescents and adults, see 2124
Self-Actualization Inventory, managers and students of administration, see 2127
Self-Administered Dependency Questionnaire, ages 8–15, see 2128
Self-Concept Adjective Checklist, grades kgn–8, see 2130
Self-Concept and Motivation Inventory: What Face Would You Wear?, age 4–grade 12, see 2131
Self-Concept as a Learner Scale, grades 4–12, see 2132
Self-Description Inventory, grades 9 and over, see 2133
Self-Esteem Questionnaire, ages 9 and over, see 2135
Self Explorations Inventory, college and adults, see 2136
Self Perception Inventory [Psychologists and Educators, Inc.], ages 12 and over, see 2138
Self-Perception Inventory [SOARES Associates], grades 1–12, high school ages and adults, teachers and student teachers, see 2139
Self Profile Q-Sort, grades 2–8, see 2140
Self-Report Inventory, college, see 2142
SELF (Self-Concept Evaluation of Location Form), adolescents and adults, see 2146
Self Valuation Test, ages 7–15, adults, see 2147
Senior Apperception Technique, ages 65 and over, see 2148
Sentence Completion Blank, college and adults, see 2154
Sentence Completion Test, high school and college, see 2155
Separation Anxiety Test, ages 11–18, see 2158
Sex Attitudes Survey and Profile, Trial Edition, marital and premarital counselees and adult sex education students, see 2167
Sex Knowledge Inventory, students in sex education classes in high school and college and adults, see 2169
Sexual Communication Inventory, premarital and marital conselees, see 2172
Sexual Concerns Checklist, Experimental Edition, junior high and high school, adults, see 2174
Shipley-Institute of Living Scale for Measuring Intellectual Impairment, adults, see 2179
Situational Attitude Scale, college and adults, see 2203
Situational Parenting, parents and their children, see 2205
Situational Preference Inventory, grades 9–16 and adults, see 2206
Sixteen Personality Factor Questionnaire, ages 16 and over, see 2208
Slosson Drawing Coordination Test for Children and Adults, ages 1.5 and over, see 2216
Social Attitude Scale, high school graduates and above, see 2225
Social Behavior Assessment, grades kgn–6, see 2226
Social Climate Scales, members of various groups, see 2227
Social Intelligence Test: George Washington University Series, grades 9–16 and adults, see 2228
Social Interaction and Creativity in Communication System, grades 1 and over, see 2229
Social Relations Test, adult males, see 2230
Social Skills for Severely Retarded Adults—An Inventory and Training Program, severely or profoundly handicapped adolescents and adults, see 2231
Socio-Sexual Knowledge & Attitudes Test, developmental-

ly disabled ages 18–42 and non-retarded persons of all ages, see 2237
Somatic Inkblot Series, ages 3 and over, see 2239
Sound-Apperception Test, ages 16 and over, see 2240
South African Personality Questionnaire, grades 12 and over, see 2241
South African Picture Analysis Test, ages 5–13, see 2242
SRA Coping Skills: A Survey plus Activities, grades 7–adult, see 2264
Staff Burnout Scale for Health Professionals, health professionals, see 2277
Stamp Behaviour Study Technique, ages 3–5, see 2279
Stanford Hypnotic Susceptibility Scale, college and adults, see 2294
Stanford Profile Scales of Hypnotic Susceptibility, Revised Edition, college and adults, see 2297
State-Trait Anxiety Inventory, grades 9–16 and adults, see 2300
State-Trait Anxiety Inventory for Children, ages 4–6, see 2301
Stern Activities Index, grades 7–16 and adults, see 2308
Stogdill Behavior Cards: A Test-Interview for Delinquent Children, delinquents having a reading score 4.5 or higher, see 2315
Stroop Color and Word Test, ages 7 and over, see 2319
Structured and Scaled Interview to Assess Maladjustment, mental patients, see 2322
Structured-Objective Rorschach Test: Preliminary Edition, adults, see 2323
STS Junior Inventory, grades 4–8, see 2326
STS Youth Inventory, grades 7–12, see 2327
Student Attitude Inventory, college, see 2328
Student Description Form, grades 9–12, see 2329
Student Development Task Inventory (Revised, Second Edition), ages 17–23, see 2330
Student Evaluation Scale, grades 1–12, see 2332
Study of Values: A Scale for Measuring the Dominant Interests in Personality, Third Edition, grades 10–16 and adults, see 2343
Study of Values: British Edition, 1965, college and adults, see 2344
Suinn Test Anxiety Behavior Scale, college and adults, see 2353
Survey of Interpersonal Values, grades 9–16 and adults, see 2366
Survey of Personal Values, grades 11–16 and adults, see 2370
Survey of Study Habits and Attitudes, grades 7–14, see 2374
Symbol Elaboration Test, ages 6 and over, see 2381
Symonds Picture-Story Test, grades 7–12, see 2384
Szondi Test, ages 5 and over, see 2388
TA Survey, employee screening, see 2389
TARC Assessment Inventory for Severely Handicapped Children, severely handicapped ages 3–16, see 2391
Tasks of Emotional Development Test, ages 6–18, see 2393
Taylor-Johnson Temperament Analysis, grades 7–16 and adults, see 2396
Temperament and Values Inventory, grades 9 and over, see 2409
Temperament Comparator, managers, supervisors, salesmen, and professionals, see 2410
Temperament Inventory, college and adults, see 2411
Tennessee Self Concept Scale, ages 12 and over, see 2413
Test Anxiety Profile, grades 9–12 and college, see 2416
Test Attitude Inventory, high school and college students, see 2417
Test of Basic Assumptions, adults, see 2428
Test of Behavioral Rigidity, Research Edition, ages 21 and over, see 2429
Test of Science-Related Attitudes, grades 7–10, see 2459
Test of Social Inferences, normals (ages 7–13), mildly retarded (ages 9 and over), moderately retarded (ages 12 and over), see 2460
Test of Social Insight, grades 6–16 and adults, see 2461
Test of the Hierarchy of Inductive Knowledge, educable mentally retarded children ages 9–24, see 2462
Test of Work Competency and Stability, ages 21 and over, see 2464
Tests of Perception of Scientists and Self, grades 9–12, see 2486
Tests of Social Intelligence, high school and adults, see 2489
Thematic Apperception Test, ages 4 and over, see 2491
Themes Concerning Blacks, Blacks ages 4 and over, see 2492
Therapy Attitude Inventory, parents, see 2494
This I Believe Test, grades 10 and over, see 2497
Thurstone Temperament Schedule, grades 9–16 and adults, see 2499
Time Questionnaire: Assessing Suicide Potential, adults, see 2505
T.M.R. Performance Profile for the Severely and Moderately Retarded, ages 4 and over, see 2507
Toy World Test, ages 2 and over, see 2513
Trait Evaluation Index, college and adults, see 2515
Transactional Analysis Life Position Survey, ages 18 and over, see 2516
Tree Test, ages 9 and over, see 2522
Triadal Equated Personality Inventory, adult males, see 2524
Twitchell-Allen Three-Dimensional Personality Test, ages 3 and over (sighted and sightless), see 2526
University Residence Environment Scale, students in university living groups, see 2534
Uses Test, ages 11–13, see 2540
Values Inventory, managers and students of managers, see 2545
Values Inventory for Children, grades 1–7, see 2546
Vasectomy Scale: Attitudes, older adolescents and adults, see 2549
Vineland Social Maturity Scale, birth to maturity, see 2557
Violence Scale, adolescents and adults, see 2558
Visual-Verbal Test: A Measure of Conceptual Thinking, schizophrenic patients, see 2565
Vocational Adaptation Rating Scale, ages 13–50 (mentally retarded individuals), see 2570
Vocational Preference Inventory, Seventh Revision, high school and college and adults, see 2581
Wahler Physical Symptoms Inventory, psychiatric patients and counselees, see 2583
Wahler Self-Description Inventory, grades 7 and over and psychiatric patients, see 2584
Walker Problem Behavior Identification Checklist, grades 4–6, see 2585
Ward Atmosphere Scale, patients and staff of hospital-based psychiatric treatment programs, see 2587
Ward Behavior Inventory, mental patients, see 2588

CLASSIFIED SUBJECT INDEX

Weller-Strawser Scales of Adaptive Behavior, learning disabled students age 6–18, see 2612
Welsh Figure Preference Test, ages 6 and over, see 2613
Western Personality Inventory, adults, see 2616
What I Like to Do: An Inventory of Students' Interests, grades 4–7, see 2618
Whitaker Index of Schizophrenic Thinking, mental patients, see 2620
Wide Range Interest-Opinion Test, grades kgn–12 and adults, see 2624
Williams Awareness Sentence Completion, ages 15 and over, see 2626
Wilson-Patterson Attitude Inventory, ages 14 and over, see 2629
Work Attitudes Questionnaire, Research Version, adults, see 2650
Work Values Inventory, grades 7–16 and adults, see 2657
Y.E.M.R. Performance Profile for the Young Moderately and Mildly Retarded, ages 5–9, see 2666
Youth Research Survey, ages 13–19, see 2667
Zulliger Individual and Group Test, ages 3 and over, see 2672

READING

ACER Paragraph Reading Test, grades 6–8, see 40
ACER Primary Reading Survey Tests, grades 1–6, see 42
ACER Silent Reading Tests: Standardized for Use in New Zealand, ages 9–12, see 44
Achievement Tests: Grades 1–8, grades 1–8, see 53
ACT Proficiency Examination in Corrective and Remedial Instruction in Reading, college and adults, see 85
ACT Proficiency Examination in Reading Instruction in the Elementary School, college and adults, see 97
American School Achievement Tests: Part 1, Reading, Revised Edition, grades 2–9, see 171
American School Reading Tests, grades 10–13, see 176
Assessment of Basic Competencies: Language Module, ages 3–15, see 210
Assessment of Reading Growth, grades 3, 7, and 11, see 216
Basic Educational Skills Inventory: Reading, grades kgn–6, see 249
Basic Reading Inventory, Second Edition, reading level grades kgn–8, see 255
Basic Skills Assessment: Reading, grades 7 and over, see 261
Basic Skills Inventory: Reading, grades kgn–12, see 268
Bench Mark Measures, ungraded, see 279
Biemiller Test of Reading Processes, grades 2–6, see 288
Buffalo Reading Test for Speed and Comprehension, grades 9–16, see 326
Burt Word Reading Test, New Zealand Revision, ages 6–0 to 12–11, see 329
California Achievement Tests: Reading, Forms C and D, grades 3–6 to 12–9, see 346
Clarke Reading Self-Assessment Survey, grades 11–12 and college freshmen, see 405
Cloze Procedure [Ebbinghaus Completion Method] as Applied to Reading, all ages, see 479
Commerce Reading Comprehension Test, grades 12–16 and adults, see 536
Comprehension Test for College of Education Students, training college students and applicants for admission, see 546
Comprehensive Tests of Basic Skills: Reading, [Forms U & V], grades kgn to 12–9, see 553
Cooperative Primary Tests: Reading, grades 1.5–3, see 585
Cooperative Reading Comprehension Test, Form Y, secondary forms 5–6 and university, see 588
Cooperative Reading Comprehension Test, Forms L and M, secondary forms 2–4 (ages 14–16), see 589
Corrective Reading Mastery Tests, students grades 4–12 and adults in the Corrective Reading Program, see 614
Criterion Reading: Individualized Learning Management System, grades kgn–adult basic education, see 634
Damron Reading/Language Kit, psycholinguistic ages 2–10, see 657
Decoding Inventory, grades 1 and over, see 661
Degrees of Reading Power, students grades 3–14, see 667
Delaware County Silent Reading Test, Second Edition, grades 1–8, see 669
Descriptive Tests of Language Skills, beginning students in two- and four-year institutions, see 685
Diagnostic Analysis of Reading Errors, adolescents and adults, see 711
Diagnostic Reading Inventory, students grades 3–12 with reading problems, see 718
Diagnostic Reading Scales, grades 1–7 and poor readers in grades 8–12, see 719
Distar Mastery Tests: Reading I, preschool-grade 3, see 742
Distar Mastery Tests: Reading II, preschool-grade 3, see 743
DTLS Reading Comprehension Test, beginning students in two- and four-year institutions, see 758
Edinburgh Reading Tests, ages 7–0 to 16–0, see 775
Ekwall Reading Inventory, grades kgn–9, see 788
Emporia Reading Tests, grades 1–8, see 815
Fountain Valley Teacher Support System in Reading, grades 1–6, see 914
GAP Reading Comprehension Test, grades 2–7, see 928
GAPADOL, ages 10–16, see 929
Gates Associative Learning Tests, grades 1.5–7.0, see 931
Gates-MacGinitie Reading Tests, grades 1–12, see 932
Gates-MacGinitie Reading Tests, Canadian Edition, grades 1–12, see 933
Gates-MacGinitie Reading Tests: Survey F, grades 10–12, see 934
Gates-McKillop-Horowitz Reading Diagnostic Tests, Second Edition, grades 1–6, see 935
Group Literacy Assessment, end of junior school and beginning of secondary school, see 1018
Group Reading Assessment, end of first year junior school, see 1024
Group Reading Test, Second Edition, ages 6–5 to 12–10, see 1025

High School Reading Test: National Achievement Tests, grades 7–12, see 1082
Informal Evaluation of Oral Reading Grade Level, ages 5–11 and adolescents and adults with reading difficulties, see 1149
Initial Placement Inventory, grades 1–8, see 1154
Instant Word Recognition Test, primary grades and remedial reading situations, see 1156
Instant Words Criterion Test, elementary students, see 1157
Inventory-Survey Tests, grades 4–8, see 1187
Iowa Silent Reading Tests, grades 6–16, see 1191
IOX Basic Skill Word List, grades 1–12, see 1196
Jordan Left-Right Reversal Test, Second Revised Edition, ages 6–12, see 1224
London Reading Test, ages 10–7 to 12–4, see 1340
Macmillan Reader Placement Test, grades 1 and over, see 1355
Mastery: An Evaluation Tool: Selected Short SOBAR Reading Tests, grades 3–9, see 1391
Mastery: An Evaluation Tool: Selected Short SOBAR Reading Tests: Comprehension I, grades 4–5, see 1392
Mastery: An Evaluation Tool: Selected Short SOBAR Reading Tests: Comprehension II, grades 6–7, see 1393
Mastery: An Evaluation Tool: Selected Short SOBAR Reading Tests: Comprehension III, grades 8–9, see 1394
Mastery: An Evaluation Tool: Selected Short SOBAR Reading Tests: Phonic Analysis, grades 3–5, see 1395
Mastery: An Evaluation Tool: Selected Short SOBAR Reading Tests: Structural Analysis, grades 3–9, see 1396
Mastery: An Evaluation Tool: Selected Short SOBAR Reading Tests: Vocabulary I, grades 4–5, see 1398
Mastery: An Evaluation Tool: Selected Short SOBAR Reading Tests: Vocabulary II, grades 4–5, see 1399
Mastery: An Evaluation Tool: Selected Short SOBAR Reading Tests: Vocabulary III, grades 8–9, see 1400
Mastery Tests, reading level grades 1–6, see 1402
McCall-Crabbs Standard Test Lessons in Reading, reading level grades 3–8, see 1421
McGrath Test of Reading Skills, Second Edition, grades 1–13, see 1430
McGrath's Silent Reading Paragraphs Test, Comprehension, grades 1–13, see 1432
McLeod Phonic Worksheets, reading level grade 3.5 and under, see 1435
Metropolitan Achievement Tests: Reading Instructional Test, grades kgn–9.9, see 1476
Metropolitan Achievement Tests: Reading, 1978 Edition, grades kgn–12.9, see 1478
Minnesota Reading Examination for College Students, grades 9–16, see 1507
Monroe's Standardized Silent Reading Test, grades 3–12, see 1530
Nelson-Denny Reading Test, Forms E and F, grades 9–12 and adults, see 1568
Nelson Reading Skills Test, Forms 3 and 4, grades 3.0–9.9, see 1569
Nelson Reading Test, Revised Edition, grades 3–9, see 1570
New Sucher-Allred Reading Placement Inventory, reading level grades 1–9, see 1579
NTE Specialty Area Tests: Introduction to the Teaching of Reading Specialty Area Test, college seniors and teachers, see 1641
NTE Specialty Area Tests: Reading Specialist Specialty Area Test, college seniors and teachers, see 1646
Performance Assessment in Reading, junior high school students, see 1781
Pope Inventory of Basic Reading Skills, reading level grades 4 and less, see 1850
Prescriptive Reading Performance Test, grades 1–12 and adults, see 1882
Pressey Diagnostic Reading Tests, grades 3–9, see 1886
PRI/Reading Systems, grades kgn–9, see 1888
Primary Reading Assessment Units, grades 1–3, see 1893
[Primary Reading Survey Tests], grades 2, 3, see 1895
Progressive Achievement Tests of Reading, standards 2–4 and Forms I–IV, see 1912
RBH Test of Reading Comprehension, business and industry, see 1986
Reading and Vocabulary Test for Students of English as a Second Language, non-native speakers of English, see 1989
Reading Comprehension: Cooperative English Tests, grades 9–14, see 1991
Reading Comprehension Test DE, ages 10–12.5, see 1992
Reading for Understanding Placement Test, grades 3–16, see 1995
Reading Test AD, ages 7–6 to 11–1, see 2000
Reading Test (Comprehension and Speed): Municipal Tests: National Achievement Tests, grades 3–8, see 2001
Reading Test: McGraw-Hill Basic Skills System, grades 11–14, see 2002
Reading Tests A and BD, 2–4 years primary school, see 2003
Reading Tests EH 1–3, first 4 years of secondary school, see 2004
St. Lucia Reading Comprehension Test, grades 2–4, see 2048
Self-Scoring Reading Placement Test, students entering postsecondary institutions with open-door policies, see 2144
Senior High Assessment of Reading Performance, grades 9–12, see 2151
Sequential Tests of Educational Progress: Reading, Series II, grades 4–14, see 2164
Southgate Group Reading Tests, ages 6–8, see 2245
SPAR Reading Test, ages 7–0 to 15–11, see 2249
SRA Reading Record, grades 6–12, see 2271
Stanford Achievement Test, Reading Tests, 1973 Edition, grades 1.5–9.5, see 2288
Survey of Primary Reading Development, grades 1–4, see 2371
Test of Reading Comprehension: A Method for Assessing the Understanding of Written Language, ages 6–6 to 14–6, see 2456
Tests of Reading: Inter-American Series, grades 1–13, see 2488
Traxler High School Reading Test, Revised, grades 10–12, see 2518
Traxler Silent Reading Test, grades 7–10, see 2520
Wide-span Reading Test, ages 7–15, see 2625

DIAGNOSTIC

Assessing Reading Difficulties: A diagnostic and remedial approach, children in primary school and older, see 205
California Phonics Survey, grades 7–12 and college, see 352
Cooperative Primary Tests: Word Analysis, grades 1.5–3, see 586
Cooper-McGuire Diagnostic Word-Analysis Test, grades 1–5 and over, see 569
Diagnosis: An Instructional Aid: Reading, grades 1–6, see 710
Diagnostic Analysis of Reading Tasks, grades 2.5 and below, 2.5 and above, see 712
Diagnostic Reading Tests, grades kgn–13, see 720
Diagnostic Screening Test: Reading, Third Edition, grades 1–12, see 724
Domain Phonic Tests, ages 5–9, see 746
Doren Diagnostic Reading Test of Word Recognition Skills, 1973 Edition, grades 1–4, see 748
Durrell Analysis of Reading Difficulty, Third Edition, grades 1–6, see 766
Fountain Valley Teacher Support System in Secondary Reading, grades 7–12, see 915
Gillingham-Childs Phonics Proficiency Scales, grades 2–8, see 957
Group Diagnostic Reading Aptitude and Achievement Tests, grades 3–9, see 1011
Group Phonics Analysis, reading level grades 1–3, see 1021
Individual Phonics Criterion Test, grades 1–8, see 1138
Individual Pupil Monitoring System—Reading, grades 1–6, see 1140
Individualized Criterion Referenced Testing: Reading, grades kgn–8, see 1143
Laurita-Trembley Diagnostic Word Processing Test, grades 1.9–college, see 1290
LRA Standard Mastery Tasks in Language, grades 1, 2, see 345
Macmillan Diagnostic Reading Pack, reading ages 5–9, see 1354
Mastery: An Evaluation Tool: Reading, grades kgn–9, see 1390
McCarthy Individualized Diagnostic Reading Inventory, Revised Edition, grades kgn–12, see 1423
McCullough Word-Analysis Tests, grades 4–6, see 1427
McGrath Diagnostic Reading Test, grades 1–13, see 1429
McGuire-Bumpus Diagnostic Comprehension Test, reading levels grades 1.5–6, see 1433
Monroe Diagnostic Reading Examination for Diagnosis of Special Difficulty in Reading, grades 1–4, see 1529
Objectives-Referenced Bank of Items and Tests: Reading and Communication Skills, grades kgn–12 and adults, see 1666
Phonetic Reading Chain Oral Reading Diagnostic Decoding Test, students having difficulties in phonics, see 1811
Phonics Criterion Test, reading level grades 1–3, see 1812
Phonovisual Diagnostic Tests [1975 Revision], grades 3–12, see 1813
Power Reading Survey Test, grades 1–12, see 1859
Prescriptive Reading Inventory, grades kgn–6.5, see 1880
Prescriptive Reading Inventory Interim Tests, grades 1.5–6.5, see 1881
Primary Reading Profiles, grades 1–3, see 1894
Reading: IOX Objectives-Based Tests, grades kgn–6, see 1997
Reading Skills Diagnostic Test, grades 2–8, see 1999
Roswell-Chall Diagnostic Reading Test of Word Analysis Skills, Revised and Extended, reading level grades 1–4, see 2034
Sand: Concepts About Print Test, ages 5–0 to 7–0, see 2060
Schonell Reading Tests, ages 5–15, 6–9, 7–11, 9–13, see 2077
Sipay Word Analysis Tests, grades 1–adult, see 2202
Standard Reading Inventory, grades 1–7, see 2280
Standard Reading Tests, reading ages up to 9–0, see 2281
Stanford Diagnostic Reading Test, 1976 Edition, grades 1–6 to 13–0, see 2292
Wisconsin Tests of Reading Skill Development: Word Attack, grades kgn–6, see 2635
Woodcock Reading Mastery Tests, grades kgn–12, see 2641

MISCELLANEOUS

Assessment of Basic Competencies: Information Processing Module, ages 3–15, see 209
Basic Sight Word Test, grades 1–2, see 258
Botel Reading Inventory, grades 1–12, see 309
Dyslexia Schedule, children having reading difficulties and first grade entrants, see 770
Industrial Reading Test, grade 9 and over vocational students and applicants or trainees in technical or vocational training programs, see 1145
Inventory of Teacher Knowledge of Reading, Revised Edition, elementary school teachers and college students, see 1185
Learning Methods Test, grades kgn–3, see 1306
Reading Efficiency Tests, grades 7–16 and adults, see 1993
Reading Eye II, grades 1–16 and adults, see 1994
Roswell-Chall Auditory Blending Test, grades 1–4, see 2033
Speed Scale for Determining Independent Reading Level, grades 1–12, see 2253
Syntax One, developmental ages 5 and over, see 2385
Syntax Two, developmental ages 5 and over, see 2386
Word Discrimination Test, grades 1–8, see 2644
Word Recognition Test, preschool to age 8.5, see 2647
Zip Scale for Determining Independent Reading Level, junior and senior high school, see 2671

ORAL

Burt Word Reading Test, 1974 Revision, ages 5 and over, see 330
Concise Word Reading Tests, ages 7–12, see 564
Cutrona Reading Inventory, grades kgn–12 and adults, see 652
Gilmore Oral Reading Test, grades 1–8, see 958
Gray Oral Reading Test, grades 1–16 and adults, see 1007
Holborn Reading Scale, ages 5.5–11.0, see 1102
McGrath's Preliminary Screening Test in Reading, grades 1–13, see 1431
Neale Analysis of Reading Ability, Second Edition, ages 6–13, see 1567

Oral Reading Criterion Test, grades 1–7, see 1739
Oral Word-Recognition Test, grades 1–13, see 1741
Reading Classification Test, ages 7.5–11.5, see 1990
St. Lucia Graded Word Reading Test, grades 2–7, see 2047
Salford Sentence Reading Test, ages 6–10 to 10–6, see 2058
Slosson Oral Reading Test, grades 1–8 and high school, see 2218
Standardized Oral Reading Check Tests, grades 1–8, see 2283
Standardized Oral Reading Paragraphs Test, grades 1.4–8.0, see 2284

READINESS

ABC Inventory to Determine Kindergarten and School Readiness, entrants to kgn and grade 1, see 7
Academic Readiness Scale, first grade entrants, see 16
American School Reading Readiness Test, Revised, first grade entrants, see 175
Analysis of Readiness Skills: Reading and Mathematics, grades kgn–1, see 178
Anton Brenner Developmental Gestalt Test of School Readiness, ages 5–6, see 183
Clymer-Barrett Prereading Battery, first grade entrants, see 482
Cognitive Skills Assessment Battery, Second Edition, prekgn–kgn, see 484
Croft Readiness Assessment in Comprehension Kit, children from whom diagnostic information in reading readiness is needed, see 636
CTBS Readiness Test, grades kgn–0 to 1–3, see 642
Evanston Early Identification Scale, Field Research Edition, ages 5–0 to 6–3, see 850
Harrison-Stroud Reading Readiness Profiles, grades kgn–1, see 1061
Hess School Readiness Scale, ages 3.5–7.0, see 1075
Inventory of Primary Skills, grades kgn–1, see 1182
Jansky Screening Index, kgn, see 1205
Kindergarten Behavioural Index: A Screening Technique for Reading Readiness, grades kgn–1, see 1256
Lippincott Reading Readiness Test (Including Readiness Check List), grades kgn–1, see 1333
Lollipop Test: A Diagnostic Screening Test of School Readiness, see 1338
McHugh-McParland Reading Readiness Test, grades kgn–1, see 1434
Metropolitan Achievement Tests, 1976 Edition, first half kgn, second half kgn and first grade entrants, see 1479
Murphy-Durrell Reading Readiness Analysis, first grade entrants, see 1551
Parent Readiness Evaluation of Preschoolers, ages 3–9 to 5–8, see 1764
PMA Readiness Level, grades kgn–1, see 1841
PreReading Expectancy Screening Scales, first grade entrants, see 1870
Pre-Reading Screening Procedures, first grade entrants of average or superior intelligence, see 1871
Preschool and Kindergarten Performance Profile, preschool and kgn, see 1873
Primary Academic Sentiment Scale, ages 4–4 to 7–3, see 1889
Reading Readiness Inventory, ages 4–7, see 1998
Reversal Test, grade 1 entrants, see 2011
Revised Pre-Reading Screening Procedures, first grade entrants, see 2016
Riley Preschool Developmental Screening Inventory, ages 3–5, see 2024
School Readiness Checklist, ages 5–6, see 2090
School Readiness Survey, Second Edition, ages 4–6, see 2091
Screening Test of Academic Readiness, ages 4–0 to 6–5, see 2107
Teacher's Handbook of Diagnostic Screening, Second Edition, ages 4, 6 and over, see 2402
Test of Early Reading Ability, ages 3–0 to 7–11, see 2438
Thackray Reading Readiness Profiles, ages 4–8 to 5–8, see 2490
Visual Pattern Recognition Test and Diagnostic Schedule, ages 4–7 to 5–6, see 2564
Watson Reading-Readiness Test, grades kgn–1, see 2596

SPECIAL FIELDS

Content Inventories: English, Social Studies, Science, grades 4–12, see 567
Purdue Reading Test for Industrial Supervisors, supervisors, see 1952
RBH Scientific Reading Test, employees in technical companies, see 1979
Reading/Everyday Activities in Life, ages 10 and over, see 1993A
SRA Reading Index, job applicants ages 14 and over with poor educational background, see 2270
Understanding Communication (Verbal Comprehension), industrial employees at the skilled level or below, see 2530

SPEED

Minnesota Speed of Reading Test for College Students, grades 12–16, see 1512

STUDY SKILLS

Bristol Achievement Tests: Study Skills, ages 8–13, see 320
Cornell Class-Reasoning Test, grades 4–12, see 604
Cornell Conditional-Reasoning Test, grades 4–12, see 605
Cornell Critical Thinking Tests, grades 7–16, see 606
Cornell Learning and Study Skills Inventory, grades 7–16, see 608
Effective Study Test, grades 8–13, see 781
Evaluation Aptitude Test, candidates for college and graduate school entrance, see 847
Library Skills Test, grades 7–12 and college freshmen, see 1323
Library Tests, college, see 1324
Logical Reasoning, grades 9–16 and adults, see 1337
Mastery: An Evaluation Tool: Selected Short SOBAR Reading Tests: Study Skills, grades 4–9, see 1397
Ohio School Library/Media Test, grades 4–12, see 1714
Progressive Achievement Tests of Study Skills, standards 3–4 and Forms I–IV (ages 9–15), see 1913
Study Attitudes and Methods Survey, high school and college, see 2340

CLASSIFIED SUBJECT INDEX

Study Habits Evaluation and Instruction Kit, Forms 4–6 (ages 14–17), see 2341
Study Habits Inventory, Revised Edition, grades 12–16, see 2342
Study Skills Counseling Evaluation, high school and college, see 2345
Study Skills Surveys, grades 9–16, see 2346
Study Skills Test: McGraw-Hill Basic Skills System, grades 11–14, see 2347

Survey of Study Habits and Attitudes, grades 7–14, see 2374
Test of Library/Study Skills, grades 2–12, see 2447
Test on Use of the Dictionary, high school and college, see 2468
Wisconsin Tests of Reading Skill Development: Study Skills, grades kgn–7, see 2634

SCIENCE

American School Achievements Tests: Part 4, Social Studies and Science, Grades 4–9, see 170
Borman-Sanders Elementary Science Test, 1, 2 semesters in grades 5–8, see 306
CLEP General Examinations: Natural Sciences, 1–2 years or equivalent, see 415
Comprehensive Tests of Basic Skills: Science and Social Studies, Third Edition, grades 1–6 to 12–9, see 554
Cooperative Science Tests: Advanced General Science, grades 8–9, see 591
Cooperative Science Tests: General Science, grades 7–9, see 594
CSMS Science Reasoning Tasks, ages 10–16 and older children and adults, see 641
Emporia General Science Test, 1, 2 semesters high school, see 811
General Science Test, matriculants and higher, see 946
General Science Test: National Achievement Tests, grades 7–9, see 947
High School Subject Tests: Physical Science, grades 9–12, see 1095
NTE Specialty Area Tests: Biology and General Science Specialty Area Test, college seniors and teachers, see 1628
NTE Specialty Area Tests: Chemistry, Physics, and General Science Area Test, college seniors and teachers, see 1630
Science: Minnesota High School Achievement Examinations, grades 7–9, see 2097
Science Tests: Content Evaluation Series, grades 8–9, see 2098
Scientific Knowledge and Aptitude Test, high school, see 2099
Sequential Tests of Educational Progress: Science, Series II, grades 4–14, see 2165
Tests of Basic Experiences 2: Science, prekgn–grade 1, see 2481

BIOLOGY

Advanced Placement Examination in Biology, high school students desiring credit for college level courses or admission to advanced courses, see 126
Biology: Minnesota High School Achievement Examinations, high school, see 293
CLEP Subject Examination in General Biology, persons entering college or already in college, see 440
College Board Achievement Test in Biology, candidates for college entrance, see 488

College Placement Test in Biology, entering college freshmen, see 509
Cooperative Science Tests: Biology, grades 10–12, see 592
Emporia Biology Test, 1, 2 semesters high school, see 805
Graduate Record Examinations Advanced (General) Biology Test, graduate school candidates, see 980
High School Subject Tests: Biology, grades 9–12, see 1087
NTE Specialty Area Tests: Biology and General Science Specialty Area Test, college seniors and teachers, see 1628

CHEMISTRY

ACER Chemistry Test Item Collection: Year 12 (Chemtic), grade 12, see 25
ACS Examination: Brief Course in Organic Chemistry, 1 semester college, see 56
ACS Examination in Analytical Chemistry, Graduate Level, entering graduate students, see 57
ACS Examination in Analytical Chemistry (Quantitative Analysis), college, see 58
ACS Examination in Biochemistry, college, see 59
ACS Examination in Brief Qualitative Analysis, college, see 60
ACS Examination in General Chemistry, 1 year college, see 61
ACS Examination in General Chemistry (Brief Test), 1 year college, see 62
ACS Examination in General-Organic-Biological Chemistry (for Allied Health Science Programs), see 63
ACS Examination in Inorganic Chemistry, college juniors and seniors and graduate students, see 64
ACS Examination in Inorganic Chemistry, Graduate Level, graduate level, see 65
ACS Examination in Instrumental Determinations (Analysis), college juniors and seniors, see 66
ACS Examination in Organic Chemistry, 1 year college, see 67
ACS Examination in Organic Chemistry, Graduate level, graduate level, see 68
ACS Examination in Physical Chemistry, 1 year college, see 69
ACS Examination in Physical Chemistry for the Life Sciences, 1 semester college, see 70
ACS Examination in Physical Chemistry, Graduate Level, graduate level, see 71
ACS Examination in Polymer Chemistry, college, see 72
ACS Examination in Qualitative Analysis, college, see 73

ACS-NSTA Examination in High School Chemistry, [Advanced Level], advanced high school classes, see 74
ACS-NSTA Examination in High School Chemistry, [Lower Level], 1 year high school, see 75
Advanced Placement Examination in Chemistry, high school students desiring credit for college level courses or admission to advanced courses, see 127
Chemistry: Minnesota High School Achievement Examinations, high school, see 390
CLEP Subject Examination in General Chemistry, persons entering college or already in college, see 441
College Board Achievement Test in Chemistry, candidates for college entrance, see 489
College Placement Test in Chemistry, entering college freshmen, see 510
Cooperative Science Tests: Chemistry, grades 9–12, see 593
Emporia Chemistry Test, 2 semesters high school, see 806
General Chemistry Test: National Achievement Tests, grades 10–16, see 938
Graduate Record Examinations Advanced Chemistry Test, graduate school candidates, see 974
High School Subject Tests: Chemistry, grades 9–12, see 1088
RBH Test of Chemical Comprehension, employee applicants and applicants for nurses training, see 1981
Toledo Chemistry Placement Examination, college entrants, see 2510

GEOLOGY

Graduate Record Examinations Advanced Geology Test, graduate school candidates, see 982

MISCELLANEOUS

ACT Proficiency Examination in Anatomy and Physiology, college and adults (associate degree), see 83
ACT Proficiency Examination in Earth Science, college and adults, see 87
Butler Life Science Concept Test, grades 1–6, see 336
NM Concepts of Ecology Test, grades 6–12, see 1588
Science Attitude Questionnaire, secondary schools, see 2096
Test on Understanding Science, grades 5–6, junior high school students, high school and college students and adults, see 2467A
Understanding in Science Test, grades 7–9, see 2531

PHYSICS

ACER Physics Unit Tests: Diagnostic Aids, grades 11–12, see 41
Advanced Placement Examinations in Physics, high school students desiring credit for college level courses and admission to advanced courses, see 143
College Board Achievement Test in Physics, candidates for college entrance, see 497
College Placement Test in Physics, entering college freshmen, see 524
Cooperative Science Tests: Physics, grades 10–12, see 595
Emporia Physics Test, 1, 2 semesters high school, see 814
General Physics Test: National Achievement Tests, grades 10–16, see 945
Graduate Record Examinations Advanced Physics Test, graduate school candidates, see 989
Physics: Minnesota High School Achievement Examinations, high school, see 1816

SENSORY–MOTOR

Bender-Purdue Reflex Test: For Signs of Symmetric Tonic Neck Reflex Immaturity, ages 6–12, see 281
Cleary-Now Test of Perceptual-Motor Readiness, grades kgn–1, see 410
Developmental Test of Visual-Motor Integration, ages 2–15, see 701
Frostig Movement Skills Test Battery, Experimental Edition, ages 6–12, see 922
Gibson Spiral Maze, ages 8.5 and over, see 955
Harris Tests of Lateral Dominance, ages 7 and over, see 1060
Hill Performance Test of Selected Positional Concepts, visually impaired children ages 6–10, see 1100
Laterality Preference Schedule, children and adults, see 1289
Leavell Hand-Eye Coordinator Tests, ages 8–14, see 1312
Minnesota Percepto-Diagnostic Test (Revised), ages 5–16, see 1503
MKM Picture Arrangement Test, grades kgn–6, see 1518
Moore Eye-Hand Coordination and Color-Matching Test, ages 2–6, 7 and over, see 1532
Primary Visual Motor Test, ages 4–8, see 1899
Purdue Perceptual-Motor Survey, ages 6–10, see 1949
Southern California Sensory Integration Tests, ages 4–10 with learning problems, see 2244
Spatial Orientation Memory Test, ages 5–9, see 2251
Standardized Road-Map Test of Direction Sense, ages 7–18, see 2285
Symbol Digit Modalities Test, ages 8 and over, see 2380

MOTOR

Bruininks-Oseretsky Test of Motor Proficiency, ages 4–5 to 14–5, see 324
Devereux Test of Extremity Coordination, emotionally handicapped and neurologically impaired ages 4–10, see 705
Lincoln-Oseretsky Motor Development Scale, ages 6–14, see 1331
Manual Accuracy and Speed Test, ages 4 and over, see 1370
Perceptual Motor Test, grades 1–3, see 1779
Riley Motor Problems Inventory, Revised 1976, ages 4–9, see 2023
Smedley Hand Dynamometer, ages 6–18, see 2219

Southern California Motor Accuracy Test, ages 4–7 with nervous system dysfunction, see 2243
Teaching Research Motor-Development Scale, moderately and severely retarded (preschool–grade 12), see 2404
Test of Motor Impairment, ages 5–14, see 2450

VISION

AO Sight Screener, adults, see 185
Carrow Auditory-Visual Abilities Test, ages 4–10, see 377
Color-Matching Aptitude Test, 1978 Edition, adults, see 533
Denver Eye Screening Test, ages 6 months and over, see 679
Dvorine Pseudo-Isochromatic Plates, ages 3 and over, see 767
Farnsworth Dichotomous Test for Color Blindness: Panel D–15, ages 12 and over, see 877
Farnsworth-Munsell 100-Hue Test for the Examination of Color Discrimination, mental ages 12 and over, see 878
Keystone Tests of Binocular Skill, grades 1–5, 8 and over, see 1251
[Keystone Visual Screening Tests], preschool and over, see 1252
Marianne Frostig Developmental Test of Visual Perception, Third Edition, ages 3–8, see 1371
MKM Binocular Preschool Test, preschool, see 1516
MKM Monocular and Binocular Reading Test, grades 1–2, 3 and over, see 1517
Motor-Free Visual Perception Test, ages 4–8, see 1540
Ortho-Rater, adults, see 1752
Peek-a-Boo Test, ages 3–6 and children not yet able to read, see 1772
Pseudo-Isochromatic Plates for Testing Color Perception, ages 7 and over, see 1921
School Vision Tester, grades kgn and over, see 2093
Sheridan Gardiner Test of Visual Acuity, ages 5 and over, see 2177
Sloan Achromatopsia Test, individuals suspected of total color blindness, see 2215
Spache Binocular Reading Test, nonreaders and grade 1, grades 1.5–2, 3 and over, see 2247
Stycar Vision Tests, normal and handicapped children 6 months or over, see 2350
Test for Colour-Blindness, ages 4 and over, see 2419
Titmus Vision Tester, ages 3 and over, see 2506

SOCIAL STUDIES

American School Achievement Tests: Part 4, Social Studies and Science, grades 4–9, see 170
CLEP General Examinations: Social Sciences and History, 1–2 years or equivalent, see 416
College Board Achievement Test in American History and Social Studies, candidates for college entrance, see 487
College Board Achievement Test in European History and World Cultures, candidates for college entrance, see 491
College Placement Test in American History and Social Studies, entering college freshmen, see 508
College Placement Test in European History and World Cultures, entering college freshmen, see 511
Comprehensive Tests of Basic Skills: Science and Social Studies, Third Edition, grades 1–6 to 12–9, see 554
NTE Specialty Area Tests: Social Studies Specialty Area Test, college seniors and teachers, see 1647
Sequential Tests of Educational Progress: Social Studies, Series II, grades 4–14, see 2166
Social Studies: Minnesota High School Achievement Examinations, grades 7–9, see 2235
Tests of Basic Experiences 2: Social Studies, prekgn–grade 1, see 2482
Zimmerman-Sanders Social Studies Test, 2 semesters in grades 7, 8, see 2670

CONTEMPORARY AFFAIRS

Current News Test, grades 9–12, see 646
Newsweek NewsQuiz, grades 9–12, see 1581
School Weekly News Quiz, high school, see 2094
Time Current Affairs Test, grades 9–12 and adults, see 2503
Time Monthly News Quiz, grades 9–12 and adults, see 2504

ECONOMICS

Basic Economics Test, grades 4–6, see 246
CLEP Subject Examination in Introductory Macroeconomics, persons entering college or already in college, see 450
CLEP Subject Examination in Introductory Micro- and Macroeconomics, persons entering college or already in college, see 452
CLEP Subject Examination in Introductory Microeconomics, persons entering college or already in college, see 453
[Economics/Objective Tests], 1 semester high school, see 774
Graduate Record Examinations Advanced Economics Test, graduate school candidates, see 976
Junior High School Test of Economics, grades 7–9, see 1232
Modern Economics Test: Content Evaluation Series, grades 10–12, see 1525
Primary Test of Economic Understanding, grades 2–3, see 1898
Test of Economic Achievement, high school, see 2439
Test of Economic Literacy, grades 11–12, see 2440
Test of Understanding in Personal Economics, high school, see 2463

GEOGRAPHY

Graduate Record Examinations Advanced Geography Test, graduate school candidates, see 981
High School Subject Tests: World Geography, grades 9–12, see 1096
Hollingsworth-Sanders Geography Test, 1, 2 semesters in grades 5–7, see 1103

HISTORY

Achievement Test in Jewish History, junior high school, see 50
ACT Proficiency Examination in Afro-American History, college and adults, see 81
ACT Proficiency Examination in American History, college level and adults, see 82
Advanced Placement Examination in American History, high school students desiring credit for college level courses or admission to advanced courses, see 125
Advanced Placement Examination in European History, high school students desiring credit for college level courses and admission to advanced courses, see 130
Advanced Placement Examination in History of Art, high school students desiring credit for college level courses and admission to advanced couses, see 134
American History: Junior High-Objective, 1, 2 semesters in grades 7–9, see 161
American History: Senior High-Objective, 1, 2 semesters in high school, see 162
Black History: A Test to Create Awareness and Arouse Interest, teachers, see 297
CLEP General Examinations: Social Sciences and History, 1–2 years or equivalent, see 416
CLEP Subject Examination in Afro-American History, persons entering college or already in college, see 417
CLEP Subject Examination in American History I: Early Colonizations to 1877, persons entering college or already in college, see 419
CLEP Subject Examination in American History II: 1865 to the Present, persons entering college or already in college, see 420
CLEP Subject Examination in Western Civilization I: Ancient Near East to 1648, persons entering college or already in college, see 462
CLEP Subject Examination in Western Civilization II: 1648 to the Present, persons entering college or already in college, see 463
College Board Achievement Test in American History and Social Studies, candidates for college entrance, see 487
College Board Achievement Test in European History and World Cultures, candidates for college entrance, see 491
College Placement Test in American History and Social Studies, entering college freshmen, see 508
College Placement Test in European History and World Cultures, entering college freshmen, see 511
Cooperative Social Studies Tests: American History, grades 7–8, 10–12, see 597
Cooperative Social Studies Tests: Modern European History, grades 10–12, see 599
Cooperative Social Studies Tests: World History, grades 10–12, see 601
Cooperative Topical Tests in American History, high school, see 602
Emporia American History Test, 1, 2 semesters high school, see 803
Graduate Record Examinations Advanced History Test, graduate school candidates, see 984
High School Subject Tests: American History, grades 9–12, see 1086
High School Subject Tests: World History, grades 9–12, see 1097
Hollingsworth-Sanders Intermediate History Test, 2 semesters in grades 5–6, see 1104
Meares-Sanders Junior High School History Test, 2 semesters in grades 7–8, see 1437
Sanders-Buller World History Test, 1, 2 semesters high school, see 2061
Social Studies Grade 10 (American History): Minnesota High School Achievement Examinations, grade 10, see 2232
Social Studies Grade 11 (World History): Minnesota High School Achievement Examinations, grade 11, see 2233
World History/Objective Tests, 1, 2 semesters high school, see 2658

POLITICAL SCIENCE

Achievement Test—The State of Israel, "pupils who have completed an organized course of study on the state of Israel," see 52
American Government: IOX Objectives-Based Tests, grades 10–12, see 159
CLEP Subject Examination in American Government, persons entering college or already in college, see 418
Cooperative Social Studies Tests: American Government, grades 10–12, see 596
Cooperative Social Studies Tests: Civics, grades 8–9, see 598
Cooperative Social Studies Tests: Problems of Democracy, grades 10–12, see 600
[Government/Objective Tests], 1 semester in grades 11–12, see 970
Graduate Record Examinations Advanced Political Science Test, graduate school candidates, see 990
High School Subject Tests: American Government, grades 9–12, see 1085
Informeter: An International Technique for the Measurement of Political Information, older adolescents and adults, see 1152
NTE Specialty Area Tests: Texas Government Specialty Area Test, college seniors and teachers, see 1651
Sare-Sanders Constitution Test, high school and college, see 2066
Social Studies Grade 12 (American Problems): Minnesota High School Achievememt Examinations, grade 12, see 2234

SOCIOLOGY

CLEP Subject Examination in Introductory Sociology, persons entering college or already in college, see 454
Graduate Record Examinations Advanced Sociology Test, graduate school candidates, see 992

Sare-Sanders Sociology Test, high school and college, see 2067

SPEECH & HEARING

Diagnostic Test of Speechreading, deaf children ages 4–9, see 729
Ohio Tests of Articulation and Perception of Sounds, ages 5–8, see 1718
Porch Index of Communicative Ability, aphasic adults, see 1851
Porch Index of Communicative Ability in Children, ages 3–12, see 1852
Sequenced Inventory of Communication Development, ages 4 months–4 years, see 2159
Sklar Aphasia Scale, Revised 1973, brain damaged adults, see 2213
Symbolic Play Test, Experimental Edition, ages 1–3, see 2383

HEARING

Auditory Discrimination Test, ages 5–8, see 226
Auditory Memory Span Test, ages 5–8, see 227
Auditory Sequential Memory Test, ages 5–8, see 229
Auditory Tests, grades 2 and over, see 230
Beltone Audiometers, grades kgn and over, see 277
Comprehension of Oral Language, grades kgn–1, see 545
Denver Audiometric Screening Test, ages 3–6, see 676
Eckstein Audiometers, grades kgn and over, see 773
F.A.T.S.A. Test (Flowers Auditory Test of Selective Attention), grades 1–6, see 882
Flowers-Costello Tests of Central Auditory Abilities, grades kgn–6, see 905
Four Tone Screening for Older Children and Adults, ages 8 and over, see 916
Goldman-Fristoe-Woodcock Auditory Skills Test Battery, ages 3 and over, see 961
Goldman-Fristoe-Woodcock Test of Auditory Discrimination, ages 4 and over, see 962
Grason-Stadler Audiometers, ages 6 and over, see 1003
Hearing Measurement Scale, adults, see 1070
[Hearing of Speech Tests], ages 3–12, see 1071
Kindergarten Auditory Screening Test, grades kgn–1, see 1255
K.S.U. Speech Discrimination Test, persons with hearing loss grades 3 and over, see 1268
Language-Structured Auditory Retention Span Test, mental ages 3.7 to adult, see 1287
Lindamood Auditory Conceptualization Test, Revised Edition, preschool children and over, see 1332
Maico Audiometers, grades kgn and older, see 1359
NTE Specialty Area Tests: Audiology Specialty Area Test, college seniors and teachers, see 1627
Oliphant Auditory Discrimination Memory Test, grades 1–8, see 1723
Oliphant Auditory Synthesizing Test, grades 1–8, see 1724
Pritchard-Fox Phoneme Auditory Discrimination Tests: Test Four, grades kgn and over, see 1900

[Rush Hughes (PB 50): Phonetically Balanced Lists 5–12], grades 2 and over, see 2040
Screening Test for Auditory Perception, grades 1–6, see 2105
STARS Test (Short Term Auditory Retrieval and Storage), grades 1–6, see 2299
Stycar Hearing Tests, ages 6 months to 7 years, see 2348
Test of Auditory Comprehension, hearing impaired ages 4–17, see 2424
Test of Auditory Discrimination, grades kgn–6, see 2425
Test of Listening Accuracy in Children, grades kgn–6, see 2448
Test of Nonverbal Auditory Discrimination, grades kgn–3, see 2452
TRACOR Audiometers, grades kgn and over, see 2514
Tree · Bee Test of Auditory Discrimination, ages 3 and over, see 2521
Verbal Auditory Screening for Children, ages 3–6, see 2550
Washington Speech Sound Discrimination Test, ages 3–5, see 2590
Word Intelligibility by Picture Identification, hearing impaired children ages 5–13, see 2646
ZECO Pure Tone Screening for Children, ages 3–8, see 2668
Zenith Audiometers, preschool, grades kgn and over, see 2669

SPEECH

Arizona Articulation Proficiency Scale: Revised, mental ages 2–14 and over, see 200
Assessment of Phonological Processes, ages 2–9, see 214
Boston Diagnostic Aphasia Examination, aphasic patients, see 308
Bzoch-League Receptive-Expressive Emergent Language Scale: For the Measurement of Language Skills in Infancy, birth to age 3, see 338
Carrow Elicited Language Inventory, ages 3–7, see 378
Communicative Evaluation Chart From Infancy to Five Years, infancy to 5 years, see 540
C-PAC: Clinical Probes of Articulation Consistency, ages 5 and over, see 339
Deep Test of Articulation, reading levels grades 2 and under, grade 3 and over, see 664
Denver Articulation Screening Exam, economically disadvantaged ages 2.5–6.0, see 675
Examining for Aphasia, Revised Edition, adolescents and adults, see 852
Fairview Language Evaluation Scale, mentally retarded, see 866
Fisher-Logemann Test of Articulation Competence, preschool to adult, see 896
Fluharty Preschool Speech and Language Screening Test, ages 2–6, see 906

Forms From Diagnostic Methods in Speech Pathology, children and adults with speech problems, see 911
Functional Communication Profile, aphasic adults, see 925
Goldman-Fristoe Test of Articulation, ages 2 and over, see 960
Ingram Edinburgh Articulation Test, ages 3–0 to 6–0, see 1153
Minnesota Test for Differential Diagnosis of Aphasia, adults, see 1513
Northwestern Syntax Screening Test, ages 3–7, see 1622
NTE Specialty Area Tests: Speech-Communication and Theatre Specialty Area Test, college seniors and teachers, see 1649
NTE Specialty Area Tests: Speech Pathology Specialty Area Test, college seniors and teachers, see 1650
Ohio State University Test for Identifying Misarticulations, speech clinicians and senior speech majors, see 1717
Oliver: Parent-Administered Communication Inventory, all ages "who have yet to develop age appropriate communication," see 1725
Phoneme Baseline Recording Forms, grades kgn–6 and mentally retarded and learning disabled children, see 1810
Photo Articulation Test, ages 3–12, see 1814
Picture Articulation & Language Screening Test, grade 1, see 1824
Predictive Screening Test of Articulation, grade 1, see 1865
Riley Articulation and Language Test, Revised, grades kgn–2, see 2022
A Screening Deep Test of Articulation, grades kgn and over, see 2103
Screening Speech Articulation Test, ages 3.5–8.5, see 2104
Stycar Language Test, mental ages 11 months to 6 years, with marked speech and language difficulties, see 2349
Templin-Darley Tests of Articulation, ages 3 and over, see 2412
Test of Minimal Articulation Competence, ages 3 and over, see 2449
Utah Test of Language Development, Revised Edition, ages 1.5 to 14.5, see 2541
Vane Evaluation of Language Scale, ages 2.5–6.5, see 2547
Verbal Language Developmental Scale, birth to age 15, see 2551
Weiss Comprehensive Articulation Test, preschool children and over, see 2611

VOCATIONS

CAREERS & INTERESTS

Career Decision Scale, grades 9–12 and college, see 370
Classification Test Battery, illiterate and semi-literate applicants for unskilled and semiskilled mining jobs, see 406
Dailey Vocational Tests, grades 4–12 and adults, see 654
Do I Know How to Apply For a Job?, job applicants, see 744
ETSA Tests, job applicants, see 846
Flanagan Industrial Tests, business and industry, see 900
JEVS Work Sample Evaluation System, high school and adults, see 1210
Measures of Occupational Stress, Strain, and Coping, employed adults, see 1447
Multivariate Vocational Evaluation System, high school and adults, see 1550
My Vocational Situation, high school and college and adults, see 1554
Ohio Vocational Education Achievement Test Program, grades 11–12, see 1719
Personal History Index, job applicants, see 1788
Position Analysis Questionnaire, business and industry, see 1855
Press Test, industrial employees, see 1884
Steward Basic Factors Inventory (1960 Edition), applicants for sales and office positions, see 2310
Steward Personnel Tests (Short Form), 1958 Edition, applicants for sales and office positions, see 2314
TAV Selection System, adults, see 2394
Wide Range Employability Sample Test, ages 16–54 (normal and handicapped), see 2622

ACT Career Planning Program, grades 8 through 10, see 77
Applied Biological and Agribusiness Interest Inventory, grade 8, see 187
California Occupational Preference System, high school and college, see 351
Career Assessment Inventory, "individuals (grades 8 and over) seeking a career that does not generally require a four-year or advanced college degree," see 367
Career Awareness Inventory, grades 4–8, see 368
Career Development Inventory [Consulting Psychologists Press, Inc.], grades 8–12, see 371
Career Development Inventory [Science Research Associates, Inc.], grades 9–10 and out-of-school youth and adults, see 372
Career Guidance Inventory, grades 7–13 students interested in trades, services, and technologies, see 373
Career Maturity Inventory, grades 6–12, see 374
Career Skills Assessment Program, high school and college students, see 375
Chatterji's Non-Language Preference Record, ages 11–16, see 387
Crowley Occupational Interests Blank, secondary school pupils of average ability or less, see 638
Curtis Interest Scale, grades 9–16 and adults, see 648
DAT Career Planning Program, grades 8–12, see 658
Educational Interest Inventory, Revised Edition, high school and college, see 778
Factorial Interest Blank, ages 11–16, see 863
Geist Picture Interest Inventory, grades 8–16 and adults, see 937

CLASSIFIED SUBJECT INDEX

Gordon Occupational Check List, high school students not planning to enter college, see 965
Guilford-Shneidman-Zimmerman Interest Survey, grades 9–16 and adults, see 1043
Guilford-Zimmerman Interest Inventory, grades 10–16 and adults, see 1045
Hackman-Gaither Vocational Interest Inventory: Standard Edition, grades 9–12 and adults, see 1048
Hall Occupational Orientation Inventory, grades 3–16 and adults, see 1051
Harrington-O'Shea Career Decision-Making System, grades 7–12 and college and adults, see 1059
High School Interest Questionnaire, "coloured pupils" in standards 7–10, see 1081
Individual Career Exploration, grades 8–12, see 1137
Interest Check List, 1979 Edition, grades 9–12 and adults, see 1163
Interest Determination, Exploration and Assessment System, grades 6–12, see 1164
Interest Questionnaire for Indian South Africans, standards 6–10, see 1166
Introducing Career Concepts Inventory, grades 5–9, see 1175
Inventory of Interests, adolescents and adults, see 1181
Inventory of Vocational Interests: Acorn National Aptitude Tests, grades 7–16 and adults, see 1186
Jackson Vocational Interest Survey, high school and over, see 1204
JIIG-CAL Occupational Interests Guide, high school and college students, see 1211
Job Activity Preference Questionnaire, business and industry, see 1212
Job Analysis and Interest Measurement, adults, see 1213
Judgement of Occupational Behavior-Orientation, grades 6–adult, see 1227
Knowledge of Occupations Test, high school, see 1259
Kuder General Interest Survey, grades 6–12, see 1269
Kuder Occupational Interest Survey, grades 11–16 and adults, see 1270
Kuder Preference Record—Vocational, grades 9–16 and adults, see 1271
Major-Minor-Finder, ages 16–adult, see 1360
Milwaukee Academic Interest Inventory, grades 12–14, see 1489
New Mexico Career Education Test Series, grades 9–12, see 1577
Field Interest Inventory, standards 8–10 and college and adults, see 1584
Occupational Check List, ages 15 and over ("above average ability"), see 1669
Occ-U-Sort, grades 7 and over and adults, see 1668
Ohio Vocational Interest Survey, Second Edition, grades 7–college and adults, see 1720
Personal Career Development Profile, ages 16 and over, see 1786
Pictorial Interest Inventory, adult males, see 1819
Pictorial Inventory of Careers, grades 3–14 and disadvantaged adults, see 1820
Picture Interest Exploration Survey, grades 7–12, see 1826
Planning Career Goals, grades 8–12, see 1839
Reading-Free Vocational Interest Inventory, educable mentally retarded at the high school level, see 1996
Rothwell-Miller Interest Blank, ages 13 and over, see 2035

Rothwell-Miller Interest Blank, [British Edition], ages 11 and over, see 2036
Safran Student's Interest Inventory, Revised Edition, grades 8–12, see 2046
Self Directed Search: A Guide to Educational and Vocational Planning, high school and college and adults, see 2134
Self-Motivated Career Planning, high school and college and adults, see 2137
Strong-Campbell Interest Inventory, ages 16 and over, see 2318
USES Interest Inventory, grades 12 and adults, see 2538
VALCAN Vocational Interest Profile (VIP), ages 15 and over, see 2542
Vocational Apperception Test: Advanced Form, college, see 2571
Vocational Exploration and Insight Kit, high school and college and adults, see 2573
Vocational Interest and Sophistication Assessment, retarded adolescents and young adults, see 2574
Vocational Interest, Experience, and Skill Assessment, grades 8–10, grade 11–adult, see 2575
Vocational Interest Inventory, high school, see 2576
Vocational Interest Profile, ages 15 and over, see 2577
Vocational Interest Questionnaire for Pupils in Standards 6–10, pupils in standards 6–10, see 2578
Vocational Preference Index, ages 8 and over, see 2580
Vocational Preference Inventory, Seventh Revision, high school and college and adults, see 2581
Wide Range Interest-Opinion Test, grades kgn–12 and adults, see 2624
Work Interest Index, grades 7–12 and college and adults, see 2654
Work Values Inventory, grades 7–16 and adults, see 2657

CLERICAL

ACER Short Clerical Test—Form C, ages 13 and over, see 43
A.C.E.R. Speed and Accuracy Tests, ages 13.5 and over, see 45
Clerical Skills Series, clerical workers and applicants, see 465
Clerical Speed and Accuracy: Differential Aptitude Tests, grades 8–12, see 466
Clerical Tests, applicants for clerical positions, see 467
Clerical Tests, Series N, applicants for clerical positions not involving frequent use of typewriter or verbal skill, see 468
Clerical Tests, Series V, applicants for typing and stenographic positions, see 469
Clerical Worker Examination, clerical workers, see 470
Commercial Tests, standards 6–8, see 537
Cross Reference Test, clerical job applicants, see 637
Curtis Verbal-Clerical Skills Tests, applicants for clerical positions, see 650
Detroit Clerical Aptitudes Examination, grades 9–12, see 688
General Clerical Ability Test: ETSA Test 3A, job applicants, see 939
General Clerical Test, grades 9–16 and clerical job applicants, see 940
General Office Clerical Test: National Business Entrance Tests, grades 11–16 and adults, see 944

Group Test 20, ages 15 and over, see 1027
Group Tests 61A, 64, and 66A, clerical applicants, see 1035
[McCann Typing Tests], applicants for typing positions, see 1422
Minnesota Clerical Test, grades 8–12 and adults, see 1493
Office Skills Achievement Test, employees, see 1676
Office Skills Tests, applicants for clerical positions, see 1677
Ohio Accounting/Computing Clerk Achievement Test, grades 11–12, see 1678
Ohio Clerk-Stenographer Achievement Test, grades 11–12, see 1685
Ohio Clerk Typist Achievement Test, grades 11–12, see 1686
Ohio General Office Clerk Achievement Test, grades 11–12, see 1702
O'Rourke Clerical Aptitude Test, Junior Grade, applicants for clerical positions, see 1750
[Personnel Research Institute Clerical Battery], applicants for clerical positions, see 1805
Personnel Research Institute Test of Shorthand Skills, stenographers, see 1807
Purdue Clerical Adaptability Test, Revised Edition, applicants for clerical positions, see 1936
RBH Classifying Test, business and industry, see 1977
RBH Number Checking Test, business and industry, see 1978
RBH Test of Dictation Speed, stenographers, see 1982
RBH Test of Typing Speed, applicants for clerical positions, see 1987
SCC Clerical Skills Series, job applicants, see 2070
Seashore-Bennett Stenographic Proficiency Test: A Standard Recorded Stenographic Worksample, adults, see 2112
Short Employment Tests, applicants for clerical positions, see 2180
Short Occupational Knowledge Test for Bookkeepers, job applicants, see 2183
Short Occupational Knowledge Test for Office Machine Operators, job applicants, see 2188
Short Occupational Knowledge Test for Secretaries, job applicants, see 2190
Short Tests of Clerical Ability, applicants for office positions, see 2194
SRA Clerical Aptitudes, grades 9–12 and adults, see 2263
SRA Typing 5, prospective employees, see 2274
SRA Typing Skills, applicants for clerical positions, see 2275
Stenographic Dictation Test, applicants for stenographic positions, see 2304
Stenographic Skill-Dictation Test, applicants for stenographic positions, see 2305
Stenographic Skills Test: ETSA Test 4A, job applicants, see 2306
Students Typewriting Tests, students completing typewriting instruction of 1st, 2nd, 3rd, or 4th semesters, see 2339
Typing Skill, typists, see 2528
Typing Test for Business, applicants for typing positions, see 2529
USES Clerical Skills Tests, applicants for clerical positions, see 2536

MANUAL DEXTERITY

APT Manual Dexterity Test, automobile and truck mechanics' helpers, see 188
Crawford Small Parts Dexterity Test, high school and adults, see 627
Crissey Dexterity Test, job applicants, see 633
Hand-Tool Dexterity Test, adolescents and adults, see 1054
Minnesota Rate of Manipulation Test, 1969 Edition, grade 7 to adults, see 1506
O'Connor Finger Dexterity Test, ages 14 and over, see 1670
O'Connor Tweezer Dexterity, ages 14 and over, see 1671
One Hole Test, job applicants, see 1727
Pennsylvania Bi-Manual Worksample, ages 16 and over, see 1774
Purdue Hand Precision Test, ages 17 and over, see 1938
Purdue Pegboard, grades 9–16 and adults, see 1948
Stromberg Dexterity Test, trade school and adults, see 2317
Yarn Dexterity Test, textile workers and applicants, see 2664

MECHANICAL ABILITY

A.C.E.R. Mechanical Comprehension Test, ages 13.5 and over, see 37
A.C.E.R. Mechanical Reasoning Test, ages 13–9 and over, see 38
Bennett Mechanical Comprehension Test, grades 9–12 and adults, see 282
Chriswell Structural Dexterity Test, grades 7–9, see 402
[Cox Mechanical and Manual Tests], boys ages 10–14 and over, see 623
[Curtis Object Completion and Space Form Tests], applicants for mechanical and technical jobs, see 649
Detroit Mechanical Aptitudes Examination, Revised, grades 7–16, see 690
Flags: A Test of Space Thinking, industrial employees, see 898
Form Relations Group Test, ages 14 and over, see 910
Group Test 80A, ages 15 and over, see 1030
Group Test 81, ages 14 and over, see 1031
Group Test 82, ages 14.5 and over, see 1032
Intuitive Mechanics (Weights & Pulleys), engineering students and industrial workers, see 1176
MacQuarrie Test for Mechanical Ability, grades 7 and over, see 1356
Mechanical Aptitude Test: Acorn National Aptitude Tests, grades 7–16 and adults, see 1450
Mechanical Comprehension Test, Second Edition, male technical apprentices and trainee engineer applicants, see 1451
Mechanical Familiarity Test: ETSA Test 5A, job applicants, see 1452
Mechanical Information Test, ages 15 and over, see 1453
Mechanical Movements: A Test of Mechanical Comprehension, industrial employees, see 1455
Mechanical Reasoning: Differential Aptitude Tests, grades 8–12 and adults, see 1456
Minnesota Spatial Relations Test, Revised Edition, ages 16 and over, see 1511
O'Connor Wiggly Block, ages 16 and over, see 1672

CLASSIFIED SUBJECT INDEX

Ohio Agricultural Mechanic Achievement Test, grades 11–12, see 1680
Ohio Auto Body Mechanic Achievement Test, grades 11–12, see 1682
Ohio Automotive Mechanics Achievement Test, grades 11–12, see 1683
O'Rourke Mechanical Aptitude Test, grades 7–12 and adults, see 1751
Perceptual Battery, job applicants with at least 10 years of education, see 1777
Primary Mechanical Ability Tests, applicants for positions requiring mechanical ability, see 1892
Purdue Mechanical Adaptability Test, males ages 15 and over, see 1946
Revised Minnesota Paper Form Board Test, grades 9–16 and adults, see 2015
Shapes Analysis Test, ages 14 and over, see 2175
Space Relations: Differential Aptitude Tests, grades 8–12 and adults, see 2246
SRA Mechanical Aptitudes, grades 9–12 and adults, see 2265
SRA Test of Mechanical Concepts, high school and adults, see 2273
Vincent Mechanical Diagrams Test, ages 15 and over, see 2556
Weber Advanced Spatial Perception Test, ages 13–17, see 2597
Weights and Pulleys: A Test of Intuitive Mechanics, engineering students and industrial employees, see 2610

MISCELLANEOUS

Business Judgment Test, Revised, adults, see 333
Florida International Diagnostic-Prescriptive Vocational Competency Profile, adolescents and adults (educable and trainable mentally retarded, specific learning disabled, seriously emotionally disturbed, economically disadvantaged), see 904
Forer Vocational Survey, adolescents and adults, see 909
Group Encounter Survey, group members, see 1014
Hay Aptitude Test Battery, clerical and plant workers, see 1064
Job Attitude Analysis, production and clerical workers, see 1215
Job Attitude Scale, adults, see 1216
Job Awareness Inventory, average and special needs students in grades 10–12, see 1217
Job-Tests Program, adults, see 1219
Minnesota Importance Questionnaire, 1975 Revision, vocational counselees, see 1495
Minnesota Job Description Questionnaire, employees and supervisors, see 1497
Minnesota Satisfaction Questionnaire, business and industry, see 1508
Per-Flu-Dex Tests, college and industry, see 1775
Personnel Reaction Blank, Revised Edition, adults, see 1802
Process Diagnostic, group members, see 1901
Program for Assessing Youth Employment Skills, adolescents and young adults with low verbal skills, see 1906
RBH Test of Language Skills, business and industry, see 1983
RBH Test of Learning Ability, business and industry, see 1984
RBH Test of Non-Verbal Reasoning, business and industry, see 1985
RBH Test of Reading Comprehension, business and industry, see 1986
Reid Report/Reid Survey, job applicants, see 2007
Self-Rating Scale for Leadership Qualifications, adults, see 2141
Sheltered Employment Work Experience Program, mentally retarded teenagers and adults, see 2176
Skills and Attributes Inventory, job incumbents and supervisors, see 2210
Social and Prevocational Information Battery, educable mentally retarded grades 7–12, trainable mentally retarded grades 7–12, see 2224
SRA Attitude Survey, employees, see 2262
SRA Placement and Counseling Program, grades 4.5–10.5, see 2268
Survey of Organizations, employees, see 2369
Team Effectiveness Survey, team members, see 2405
Test Orientation Procedure, job applicants and trainees, see 2469
[Tests A/9 and A/10], applicants for technical and apprentice jobs, see 2471
Vocational Adaptation Rating Scale, ages 13–50 (mentally retarded individuals), see 2570
Vocational Behavior Checklist, vocational rehabilitation clients, see 2572
Vocational Opinion Index, disadvantaged trainees in vocational skills programs, see 2579
Whisler Strategy Test, business and industry, see 2619
Work Attitudes Questionnaire, Research Version, adults, see 2650
Work Elements Inventory, employees, see 2651
Work Environment Scale, employees and supervisors, see 2652
Work Information Inventory, employee groups in industry, see 2653

SELECTION & RATING FORMS

Application Interview Screening Form, job applicants, see 186
Career Counseling Personal Data Form, vocational counselees, see 369
Employee Performance Appraisal, business and industry, see 800
Employee Progress Appraisal Form, business and industry, see 801
[Employee Rating and Development Forms], executive, industrial, office, and sales pesonnel, see 802
[Executive, Industrial, and Sales Personnel Forms], applicants for executive, industrial, office, or sales positions, see 853
[Job Application Forms], job applicants and employees, see 1214
Job Performance Scale, employees, see 1218
Lawshe-Kephart Personnel Comparison System, employees, see 1293
McCormick Job Performance Measurement "Rate–$–Scales", employees, see 1426
Merit Rating Series, industry, see 1468
Minnesota Satisfactoriness Scales, employees, see 1509

[Performance Review Forms], employees, managers, see 1782
[Personnel Interviewing Forms], business and industry, see 1799
Personnel Rating Scale, employees, see 1801
Rehabilitation Client Rating Scale, vocational rehabilitation counselees, see 2005
Research Personnel Review Form, research and engineering and scientific firms, see 2010
San Francisco Vocational Competency Scale, mentally retarded adults, see 2059
[Selection Interview Forms], business and industry, see 2126
[Stevens-Thurow Personnel Forms], business and industry, see 2309
Tickmaster, job applicants, see 2501
Wonderlic Personnel Selection Procedure, applicants for employment, see 2637
Work Reference Check, job applicants, see 2656

SPECIFIC VOCATIONS

ACCOUNTING

ACT Proficiency Examinations in Accounting, college and adults, see 99
American Institute of Certified Public Accountants Testing Programs, grades 13–16 and accountants, see 164
CLEP Subject Examination in Introductory Accounting, persons entering college or already in college, see 448

BUSINESS

ACT Proficiency Examination in Business Environment and Strategy, college and adults, see 84
ACT Proficiency Examination in Finance, college and adults, see 102
ACT Proficiency Examinations in Operations Management, college and adults, see 108
ACT Proficiency Examinations in Management of Human Resources, college and adults, see 105
ACT Proficiency Examinations in Marketing, college and adults, see 106
Business Judgment Test, Revised, adults, see 333
Business Test, clerical workers, see 334
CLEP Subject Examination in Introduction to Management, persons entering college or already in college, see 447
CLEP Subject Examination in Introductory Business Law, persons entering college or already in college, see 449
CLEP Subject Examination in Introductory Marketing, persons entering college or already in college, see 451
CLEP Subject Examination in Money and Banking, persons entering college or already in college, see 457
Graduate Management Admission Test, business graduate students, see 973
Ohio Agricultural Business Achievement Test, grades 11–12, see 1679
Ohio General Merchandising Achievement Test, grades 11–12, see 1701
Organizational Value Dimensions Questionnaire: Business Form, adults, see 1746

COMPUTER PROGRAMMING

Aptitude Assessment Battery: Programming, programmers and trainees, see 189
CLEP Subject Examination in Cumputers and Data Processing, persons entering college or already in college, see 433
CLEP Subject Examination in Elementary Computer Programming—Fortran IV, persons entering college or already in college, see 436
Computer Operator Aptitude Battery, experienced operators and trainees, see 556
Computer Programmer Aptitude Battery, applicants for training or employment in computer programmer and systems analysis fields, see 557
Diebold Personnel Tests, programmers and systems analysts for automatic data processing and computing installations, see 731
Graduate Record Examinations Advanced Computer Science Test, graduate school candidates, see 975
Programmer Aptitude/Competence Test System, computer programmers and applicants for programmer training, see 1907

DENTISTRY

CLEP Subject Examination in Dental Materials: Dental Auxiliary Education, dental hygicnists and assistants, see 434
CLEP Subject Examination in Head, Neck, and Oral Anatomy: Dental Auxiliary Education, dental hygienists and assistants, see 443
CLEP Subject Examination in Oral Radiography: Dental Auxiliary Education, dental hygienists and assistants, see 458
CLEP Subject Examination in Tooth Morphology and Function: Dental Auxiliary Education, dental hygienists and assistants, see 460
Dental Admission Testing Program, dental school applicants, see 673
Dental Hygiene Aptitude Testing Program, dental hygiene school applicants, see 674
Ohio Dental Assisting Achievement Test, grades 11–12, see 1694

ENGINEERING

AC Test of Creative Ability, engineers and supervisors, see 10
Engineer Performance Description Form, nonsupervisory college graduate engineers, see 819
Garnett College Test in Engineering Science, 1–2 years technical college, see 930
Graduate Record Examinations Advanced Engineering Test, graduate school candidates, see 978
Minnesota Engineering Analogies Test, candidates for graduate school and industry, see 1494
National Engineering Aptitude Search Test: The Junior Engineering Technical Society, grades 9–12, see 1558
N.I.I.P. Engineering Apprentice Selection Test Battery, engineering apprentices, see 1582
Purdue Creativity Test, applicants for engineering positions, see 1937

CLASSIFIED SUBJECT INDEX

LAW

ACT Proficiency Examination in Criminal Investigation, college and adults, see 86
ACT Proficiency Examination in Introduction to Criminal Justice, college and adults, see 92
Correctional Policy Inventory: A Survey of Correctional Philosophy and Characteristic Methods of Dealing with Offenders, correctional managers, see 613
IPMA Police Service Tests, prospective police service personnel, see 1200
Law Enforcement Perception Questionnaire, law enforcement personnel, see 1291
Law School Admission Test, law school entrants, see 1292
Multijurisdictional Police Officer Examination, prospective police officers, see 1545
Observation Test for Policeman, prospective policemen, see 1667
Police Officer A-1(M), prospective police officers, see 1843
Police Performance Rating System, policemen, see 1844
Police Promotion Tests, prospective policemen promotees, see 1845
Police Sergeant, prospective sergeants, see 1846
Policeman Examination, prospective policemen, see 1847
Statistically Validated Written Tests for Police Officer, prospective police officers, see 2302

MEDICINE

CLEP Subject Examination in Clinical Chemistry, medical technologists, see 426
CLEP Subject Examination in Hematology, medical technologists, see 444
CLEP Subject Examination in Immunohematology and Blood Banking, medical technologists, see 446
CLEP Subject Examination in Microbiology, medical technologists, see 456
Medical School Instructor Attitude Inventory, medical school faculty members, see 1457
Medical Sciences Knowledge Profile, citizens or permanent resident aliens in the United States and Canada, see 1458
New Medical College Admission Test, applicants for admission to member colleges of the Association of American Medical Colleges and to other participating institutions, see 1576
Ohio Medical Assisting Achievement Test, grades 11-12, see 1710
Veterinary Aptitude Tests, veterinary school applicants, see 2555

MISCELLANEOUS

Change Agent Questionnaire, adults, whose work primarily concerns changing behavior of others, see 383
Chemical Operators Selection Test, Revised Edition, chemical operators and applicants, see 389
Cosmetology Student Admissions Examination, prospective cosmetology students, see 615
Entrance Level Firefighter, prospective firefighters, see 833
Field Work Performance Report, occupational therapy students, see 885
Fire Promotion Tests, prospective firemen promotees, see 887
Firefighter Test: B-2(m), prospective firemen, see 888
Fireman Examination, prospective firemen, see 889
General Municipal Employees Performance (Efficiency) Rating System, municipal employees, see 943
IPMA Fire Service Tests, prospective fire service personnel, see 1199
Journalism Test, high school, see 1226
Life Style Questionnaire, ages 14 and over, see 1327
Ohio Apparel and Accessories Achievement Test, grades 11-12, see 1681
Ohio Carpentry Achievement Test, grades 11-12, see 1684
Ohio Commercial Art Achievement Test, grades 11-12, see 1687
Ohio Community and Home Services Achievement Test, grades 11-12, see 1689
Ohio D.E. Food Service Personnel Achievement Test, grades 11-12, see 1693
Ohio Diesel Mechanic Achievement Test, grades 11-12, see 1695
Ohio Diversified Health Occupations Achievement Test, grades 11-12, see 1696
Ohio Farm Management Achievement Test, grades 11-12, see 1699
Ohio Food Marketing Key Employee Achievement Test, grades 11-12, see 1700
Ohio H.Ec. Food Services Achievement Test, grades 11-12, see 1704
Ohio Horticulture Achievement Test, grades 11-12, see 1705
Ohio Nursery School Teacher Aide/Child Care Achievement Test, grades 11-12, see 1711
Ohio Production Agriculture Achievement Test, grades 11-12, see 1713
Ohio Word Processing Achievement Test, grades 11-12, see 1722
Optometry College Admission Test, optometry college applicants, see 1731
Potter-Nash Aptitude Test for Lumber Inspectors and Other General Personnel Who Handle Lumber, employees in woodworking industries, see 1858
Test for Firefighter B-1(m), firemen and prospective firemen, see 2420

NURSING

Achievement Tests in Nursing, students in schools of registered nursing, see 54
Achievement Tests in Practical Nursing, practical nursing students, see 55
ACT Proficiency Examination in Adult Nursing, baccalaureate level nursing students, see 80
ACT Proficiency Examination in Fundamentals of Nursing, college and adults (associate degree), see 90
ACT Proficiency Examination in Nursing Health Care, college and adults, see 93
ACT Proficiency Examination in Occupational Strategy, Nursing, college and adults (associate degree), see 94
ACT Proficiency Examination in Professional Strategies, Nursing, baccalaureate level nursing students, see 95
ACT Proficiency Examination in Psychiatric/Mental

Health Nursing, baccalaureate level nursing students, see 96
ACT Proficiency Examinations in Commonalities in Nursing Care, Areas I and II, college and adults (associate degree), see 100
ACT Proficiency Examinations in Differences in Nursing Care, Areas I and II, college and adults (associate degree), see 101
ACT Proficiency Examinations in Health Restoration, Areas I and II, baccalaureate level nursing students, see 103
ACT Proficiency Examinations in Health Support, Areas I and II, baccalaureate level nursing students, see 104
ACT Proficiency Examinations in Maternal and Child Nursing, college and adults, see 107
CLEP Subject Examination in Anatomy, Physiology, Microbiology: North Carolina Nursing Equivalency Examinations, persons entering college or already in college, see 423
CLEP Subject Examination in Behavioral Sciences for Nurses: North Carolina Nursing Equivalency Examinations, persons entering college or already in college, see 424
CLEP Subject Examination in Fundamentals of Nursing: North Carolina Nursing Equivalency Examinations, persons entering college or already in college, see 439
CLEP Subject Examination in Medical-Surgical Nursing: North Carolina Nursing Equivalency Examinations, persons entering college or already in college, see 455
Clinical Experience Record for Nursing Students, nursing students and nurses, see 476
Empathy Inventory, nursing instructors, see 797
Entrance Examination for Schools of Nursing, applicants to schools of registered nursing, see 831
Entrance Examination for Schools of Practical/Vocational Nursing, applicants to schools of practical nursing, see 832
George Washington University Series Nursing Tests, prospective nurses, see 949
Luther Hospital Sentence Completions, prospective nursing students, see 1348
NLN Achievement Tests for Schools Preparing Registered Nurses, students in state-approved schools preparing registered nurses, see 1585
NLN Practical Nursing Achievement Tests, students in state-approved schools of practical nursing, see 1586
NLN Pre-Nursing and Guidance Examination, applicants for admission to state-approved schools preparing registered nurses, see 1587
Nurse Attitudes Inventory, prospective nursing students, see 1654
PSB-Aptitude for Practical Nursing Examination, applicants for admission to practical nursing schools, see 1920

RESEARCH

Surveys of Research Administration and Environment, research and engineering and scientific firms, see 2376
Technical Personnel Recruiting Inventory, research and engineering and scientific firms, see 2407

SALES (SELLING)

Aptitudes Associates Test of Sales Aptitude: A Test for Measuring Knowledge of Basic Principles of Selling, applicants for sales positions, see 192
Sales Aptitude Tests: ETSA Test 7A, job applicants, see 2049
Sales Attitudes Check List, applicants for sales positions, see 2050
Sales Comprehension Test, applicants for sales positions, see 2051
[Sales Motivation], sales managers, sales people, see 2052
Sales Motivation Inventory, Revised, applicants for sales positions, see 2053
[Sales Relations], sales people, customers, see 2054
Sales Sentence Completion Blank, applicants for sales positions, see 2055
Sales Style Diagnosis Test, salespeople, see 2056
Sales Transaction Audit, salespeople, see 2057
SRA Sales Attitudes Check List, applicants for sales positions, see 2272
Steward Basic Factors Inventory (1960 Edition), applicants for sales and office positions, see 2310
Steward Life Insurance Knowledge Test, applicants for life insurance agent or supervisory positions, see 2311
Steward Occupational Objectives Inventory, 1957 Edition, applicants for supervisory positions in life insurance companies or agencies, see 2312
Steward Personal Background Inventory (1960 Revised Edition), applicants for sales positions, see 2313
Steward Personnel Tests (Short Form), 1958 Edition, applicants for sales and office positions, see 2314
Test for Ability to Sell: George Washington University Series, grades 7–16 and adults, see 2418
Test of Retail Sales Insight, retail clerks and students, see 2457

SKILLED TRADES

Electrical Sophistication Test, job applicants, see 790
Mechanical Knowledge Test: ETSA Test 6A, job applicants, see 1454
National Occupational Competency Testing Program, teachers and prospective teachers in skilled trades, see 1562
NOCTI Examination: Air Conditioning and Refrigeration, teachers and prospective teachers, see 1591
NOCTI Examination: Airframe and Power Plant Mechanics, teachers and prospective teachers, see 1592
NOCTI Examination: Architectural Drafting, teachers and prospective teachers, see 1593
NOCTI Examination: Auto Body Repair, teachers and prospective teachers, see 1594
NOCTI Examination: Auto Mechanic, teachers and prospective teachers, see 1595
NOCTI Examination: Cabinet Making and Millwork, teachers and prospective teachers, see 1596
NOCTI Examination: Carpentry, teachers and prospective teachers, see 1597
NOCTI Examination: Civil Technology, teachers and prospective teachers, see 1598
NOCTI Examination: Cosmetology, teachers and prospective teachers, see 1599

CLASSIFIED SUBJECT INDEX

NOCTI Examination: Diesel Engine Repair, teachers and prospective teachers, see 1600
NOCTI Examination: Electrical Installation, teachers and prospective teachers, see 1601
NOCTI Examination: Electronics Communications, teachers and prospective teachers, see 1602
NOCTI Examination: Industrial Electrician, teachers and prospective teachers, see 1603
NOCTI Examination: Industrial Electronics, teachers and prospective teachers, see 1604
NOCTI Examination: Machine Drafting, teachers and prospective teachers, see 1605
NOCTI Examination: Machine Trades, teachers and prospective teachers, see 1606
NOCTI Examination: Masonry, teachers and prospective teachers, see 1607
NOCTI Examination: Mechanical Technology, teachers and prospective teachers, see 1608
NOCTI Examination: Plumbing, teachers and prospective teachers, see 1609
NOCTI Examination: Printing, teachers and prospective teachers, see 1610
NOCTI Examination: Quantity Food Preparation, teachers and prospective teachers, see 1611
NOCTI Examination: Sheet Metal, teachers and prospective teachers, see 1612
NOCTI Examination: Small Engine Repair, teachers and prospective teachers, see 1613
NOCTI Examination: Welding, teachers and prospective teachers, see 1614
Ohio Communication Products Electronics Achievement Test, grades 11–12, see 1688
Ohio Construction Electricity Achievement Test, grades 11–12, see 1690
Ohio Cosmetology Achievement Test, grades 11–12, see 1691
Ohio Data Processing Achievement Test, grades 11–12, see 1692
Ohio Drafting Achievement Test, grades 11–12, see 1697
Ohio Fabric Services Achievement Test, grades 11–12, see 1698
Ohio Heating, Air Conditioning, and Refrigeration Achievement Test, grades 11–12, see 1703
Ohio Industrial Electronics Achievement Test, grades 11–12, see 1706
Ohio Lithographic Printing Achievement Test, grades 11–12, see 1707
Ohio Machine Trades Achievement Test, grades 11–12, see 1708
Ohio Masonry Achievement Test, grades 11–12, see 1709
Ohio Sheet Metal Achievement Test, grades 11–12, see 1715
Ohio Welding Achievement Test, grades 11–12, see 1721
Purdue Industrial Training Classification Test, grades 9–12 and adults, see 1942
Purdue Interview Aids, applicants for industrial employment, see 1944
Purdue Trade Information Test for Sheetmetal Workers, sheetmetal workers, see 1956
Purdue Trade Information Test in Carpentry, vocational school and adults, see 1957
Purdue Trade Information Test in Engine Lathe Operation, vocational school and adults, see 1958
Purdue Trade Information Test in Welding, Revised Edition, vocational school and adults, see 1959

Short Occupational Knowledge Test for Auto Mechanics, job applicants, see 2182
Short Occupational Knowledge Test for Carpenters, job applicants, see 2184
Short Occupational Knowledge Test for Draftsmen, job applicants, see 2185
Short Occupational Knowledge Test for Electricians, job applicants, see 2186
Short Occupational Knowledge Test for Machinists, job applicants, see 2187
Short Occupational Knowledge Test for Plumbers, job applicants, see 2189
Short Occupational Knowledge Test for Tool and Die Makers, job applicants, see 2191
Short Occupational Knowledge Test for Truck Drivers, job applicants, see 2192
Short Occupational Knowledge Test for Welders, job applicants, see 2193
Sweet Technical Information Test, ages 14–17, see 2379
Technical Tests, standards 6–8 (ages 13–15), see 2408

SUPERVISION

Communication Sensitivity Inventory, managers, see 539
Conflict Management Survey, adults, see 565
How Supervise?, supervisors, see 1113
Ideal Leader Behavior Description Questionnaire, supervisors, see 1122
Leader Behavior Description Questionnaire, supervisors, see 1295
Leader Behavior Description Questionnaire, Form 12, supervisors, see 1296
Leadership Evaluation and Development Scale, prospective supervisors, see 1299
Leadership Opinion Questionnaire, supervisors and prospective supervisors, see 1300
Leadership Practices Inventory, supervisors, see 1301
Management Relations Survey, managers, see 1363
Management Style Diagnosis Test, Second Edition, managers, see 1364
Management Transactions Audit, managers, see 1365
Managerial Philosophies Scale, managers, see 1366
Organization Health Survey, managers, administrators, and supervisors in government and industry, see 1744
Personnel Performance Problems Inventory, management and administrative personnel, see 1800
Personnel Relations Survey, managers, see 1803
RAD Scales, supervisors, see 1972
Situational Leadership, managers, leaders, administrators, supervisors, and staff, see 2204
Steward Occupational Objectives Inventory, 1957 Edition, applicants for supervisory positions in life insurance companies or agencies, see 2312
[Styles of Leadership and Management], managers, see 2351
Supervisory Behavior Description, supervisors, see 2354
Supervisory Index, supervisors, see 2355
Supervisory Inventory on Communication, supervisors and prospective supervisors, see 2356
Supervisory Inventory on Discipline, supervisors, see 2357
Supervisory Inventory on Grievances, supervisors, see 2358
Supervisory Inventory on Human Relations, supervisors and prospective supervisors, see 2359

Supervisory Inventory on Labor Relations, supervisors in unionized firms, see 2360
Supervisory Inventory on Safety, supervisors and prospective supervisors, see 2361
Supervisory Practices Inventory, Form A, managers or administrators, see 2362
Supervisory Practices Test, Revised, supervisors, see 2363
Survey of Management Perception, supervisors, see 2367
WLW Personal Survey, Form 3, supervisors and potential supervisors, see 2636

[Work Motivation], managers, employees, see 2655

TRANSPORTATION

[American Transit Association Tests], transit operating personnel, see 177
[Driver Selection Forms and Tests], truck drivers, see 754
Wilson Driver Selection Test, prospective motor vehicle operators, see 2628

PUBLISHERS DIRECTORY AND INDEX

This directory and index gives the addresses and test entry numbers of all publishers represented in this volume. All foreign tests distributed by United States publishers are listed; however, United States tests distributed by foreign publishers are listed only if the tests have been revised or supplemented for foreign use.

Academic Therapy Publications, 20 Commercial Boulevard, Novato, CA 94947: 228, 244, 250, 280f, 281, 310, 405, 635, 749, 857, 1224, 1284, 1287, 1304, 1305, 1328, 1540, 1863, 1967, 2032, 2105, 2253, 2285, 2303, 2425, 2446, 2465, 2521, 2544, 2612

Addison-Wesley Publishing Co., Inc., 2725 Sand Hill Road, Menlo Park, CA 94025: 1, 2, 259, 260, 261, 262, 263, 404, 570, 571, 573, 574, 575, 576, 577, 578, 579, 580, 581, 582, 583, 584, 585, 586, 587, 590, 591, 592, 593, 594, 595, 596, 597, 598, 599, 600, 601, 602, 789, 1519, 1520, 1521, 1522, 1523, 1991, 2160, 2161, 2162, 2163, 2164, 2165, 2166

Adult Self Expression Scale, P.O. Box 220174, Charlotte, NC 28222: 122

Ahluwalia, S. P., Faculty of Education, University of Saugar, Sagar – 470003, M.P. India: 2397

Allington Corporation, P.O. Box 125, Remington, VA 22734: 1282

Allyn and Bacon, Inc., 470 Atlantic Avenue, Boston, MA 02210: 788, 2401, 2402

Alpha Educational Associates, 122 Deerhurst Park Blvd., Buffalo, NY 14217: 1900

American Alliance for Health, Physical Education, Recreation and Dance, 1900 Association Drive, Reston, VA 22091: 3, 4, 5

American Association of Bible Colleges, P.O. Box 1523, Fayetteville, AR 72701: 2282

American Association of Teachers of German, Inc., 523 Bldg., Suite 201, Rt. 38, Cherry Hill, NJ 08034: 1559

American Association on Mental Deficiency, 5101 Wisconsin Avenue, N.W., Washington, DC 20016: 6a

American College Testing Program, 2201 North Dodge Street, P.O. Box 168, Iowa City, IA 52243: 76, 77, 78, 79, 80, 81, 82, 83, 84, 85, 86, 87, 88, 89, 90, 91, 92, 93, 94, 95, 96, 97, 98, 99, 100, 101, 102, 103, 104, 105, 106, 107, 108, 2575

American Foundation for the Blind, 15 West 16th Street, New York, NY 10011: 184, 1420

American Guidance Service, Publishers' Building, Circle Pines, MN 55014: 123, 293, 303, 324, 390, 403, 748, 791, 844, 891, 948, 960, 961, 962, 1059, 1250, 1278, 1413, 1505, 1506, 1511, 1769, 1771, 1774, 1816, 1874, 2097, 2232, 2233, 2234, 2235, 2525, 2551, 2557, 2641

American Language Institute, Georgetown University, 3605 "O" Street, N.W., Washington, DC 20057: 830, 1738, 1989, 2483

American Occupational Therapy Association, Inc., 1383 Piccard Drive, Rockville, MD 20850: 885

American Optical Corporation, Industrial Safety Division, Southbridge, MA 01550: 185

American Optical Corporation, Instrument Division, Box A, Buffalo, NY 14215: 1921

American Orthopsychiatric Association, Inc., 1775 Broadway, New York, NY 10019: 280a

American Printing House for the Blind, Inc., 1839 Frankfort Avenue, P.O. Box 6085, Louisville, KY 40206: 2038

American Testronics, 209 Holiday Road, Coralville, IA 52241: 365, 692, 1083, 1084, 1085, 1086, 1087, 1088, 1089, 1090, 1091, 1092, 1093, 1094, 1095, 1096, 1097, 1098, 1491, 2081

American Transit Association, 1225 Connecticut Ave., N.W., Washington, DC 20036: 177

Anand Agencies, 1433 A Shukrawar, Poona 2, India: 750

Andrews University Press, Berrien Springs, MI 49104: 2411

Anhinga Press, Route 2, Box 513, Tallahassee, FL 32301: 338

Ann Arbor Publishers, Inc., P.O. Box 7249, Naples, FL 33940: 156, 181, 1481, 1482

A.R.A., Irvine Town Center, Box 4211, Irvine, CA 92716: 2129, 2630

Arden Press, 8331 Alvarado Dr., Huntington Beach, CA 92646: 16, 17, 327, 328, 2082, 2331, 2400

ASIEP Education Co., 3216 NE 27th Ave., Portland, OR 97212: 234

Associated Personnel Technicians, Inc., P.O. Box 1036, Wichita, KS 67201: 188

Associates for Research in Behavior, Inc., The Science Center, 34th & Market Streets, Philadelphia, PA 19104: 2579

Association for the Education and Welfare of the Visually Handicapped, St. John's School House, Hadzor, Nr. Droitwich Spa., Worcestershire WR9 7DR: 1342, 2511

Association of American Medical Colleges, Suite 200, One Dupont Circle, N.W., Washington, DC 20036: 1576

Attwood, Madge, School of Education, University of Michigan, Ann Arbor, MI 48104: 755

Audio-Visual Services, Pennsylvania State University, 6 Willard Bldg., University Park, PA 16802: 2027

Audiotone, 2422 West Holly, Phoenix, AZ 85009: 1268

Australian Council for Educational Research, P.O. Box 210 Hawthorn, Victoria, Australia 3122: 19, 20, 21, 22, 24, 25, 26, 27, 28, 29, 30, 31, 32, 33, 34, 35, 36, 37, 38, 39, 40, 41, 42, 43, 45, 46, 47, 48, 232, 233, 397, 588, 589, 714, 715, 717, 917, 1074, 1256, 1411, 1564, 1620a1, 1661, 1755, 1912, 1963, 2035, 2195, 2279, 2328, 2379, 2443, 2459, 2486, 2531, 2597

Ballen, Roland, P.O. Box 11209, Palo Alto, CA 94306: 2501

Barber Center Press, Inc., 136 East Avenue, Erie, PA 16507: 568, 656, 2176

Bardis, Panos D., University of Toledo, Toledo, OH 43606: 8, 307, 485, 660, 840, 870, 875, 1006, 1152, 1465, 1766, 1832, 2008, 2170, 2549, 2558

Bausch & Lomb, Inc., Rochester, NY 14602: 1752, 2093

Baylor University Press, 5th and Speight, Waco, TX 76703: 287

Bealls (J. & P.) Ltd., Gallowagate, New Castle Upon Tyne, Northumberland, England: 2147

Beatty, James R., College of Business Administration, San Diego State University, San Diego, CA 92182: 1161

Behar, Lenore, State of North Carolina, Dept. of Human Resources, Albemarle Building, 325 No. Salisbury Street, Raleigh, NC 27611: 1874A

Behavior Arts Center, 77 Lyons Place, Westwood, NJ 07675: 1655

Behavior Science Systems, Inc., P.O. Box 1108, Minneapolis, MN 55440: 1492, 1496, 1504

Behaviordyne, Inc., 599 College Avenue, Palo Alto, CA 94306: 355, 1499

Behaviormetrics Publishing Co., Box 1168, Venice, CA 90291: 655

Beltone Electronics Corporation, 4201 West Victoria Street, Chicago, IL 60646: 277

Belwin-Mills Publishing Corporation, 25 Deshon Drive, Melville, NY 11746: 1274

Ber-Sil Co., 3412 Seaglen Drive, Rancho Palos Verdes, CA 90274: 284

Berg, Ian, High Lands Adolescent Unit, Scalebor Park, Burley-in-Wharfedale, Ilkley, Yorkshire LS 29 7 AJ, England: 2128

Berry Language Tests, 4332 Pine Crest Road, Rockford, IL 61107: 285

BFA Educational Media, 2211 Michigan Avenue, Santa Monica, CA 90406: 1859

Bienvenu, Millard J., Sr., Northwestern State University of Louisiana, Department of Sociology & Social Work, Natchitoches, LA 71457: 1171, 1178, 1867

Bingham Button Test, 46211 N. 125th Street East, Lancaster, CA 93534: 292

Blatt, Sidney J., Yale University, School of Medicine, Department of Psychiatry, 25 Park Street, New Haven, CT 06519: 215, 682

B. M. P. (Bilingual Media Productions), Inc., P.O. Box 9337 North Berkeley Station, Berkeley, CA 94709: 289

Bobbs-Merrill Co., Inc., 4300 West 62nd Street, P.O. Box 7080, Indianapolis, IN 46206: 175, 176, 180, 236, 237, 301, 312, 325, 335, 643b, 688, 689, 690, 691, 713, 744, 1233b, 1313, 1330b, 1530, 1885, 1886, 1887, 2283, 2284, 2518, 2519, 2520, 2523, 2567

Bond Publishing Co., 787 Willett Ave., Riverside, RI 02915: 879

Book-Lab, Inc., 1449 Thirty-Seventh Street, Brooklyn, NY 11218: 1149, 1850, 1925

Book Society of Canada Ltd., 4386 Sheppard Ave. East, P.O. Box 200, Agincourt, Ontario M1S 3B6, Canada: 2592, 2593, 2595, 2596

Boston Center for Blind Children, 147 South Huntington Avenue, Boston, MA 02130: 695

Boyle, Barbara S., 944 Bryant Avenue, Chico, CA 95926: 2179

Bradley, Robert H., University of Arkansas at Little Rock, 33rd and University, Little Rock, AR 72204: 1108

Brador Publications, Inc., Education Division, 36 Main Street, Livonia, NY 14487: 1999

Brandon House, Inc., P.O. Box 240, Bronx, NY 10471: 786

Brook Educational Publishing Ltd., Box 1171, Guelph, Ontario, N1H 6N3, Canada: 2450

Brown & Associates, Inc., P.O. Box 5092, Station B, Greenville, SC 29606: 2664

Bruce (Martin M.), Ph.D., Publishers, 50 Larchwood Road, Larchmont, NY 10538: 192, 218, 323, 333, 369, 465, 800, 1146, 1528, 1782, 1799, 1849, 2051, 2053, 2055, 2126, 2352, 2363, 2461, 2515, 2628

Bureau of Educational Measurements, Emporia State University, 1200 Commercial, Emporia, KS 66801: 242, 306, 380, 803, 804, 805, 806, 807, 808, 809, 810, 811, 812, 813, 814, 815, 816, 817, 894, 895, 1078, 1103, 1104, 1105, 1111, 1116, 1144, 1238, 1437, 2006, 2041, 2061, 2062, 2063, 2066, 2067, 2114, 2115, 2316, 2586, 2670

Bureau of Educational Research and Service, The University of Iowa, W325 Seashore Hall, Iowa City, IA 52242: 1188, 1189, 1194, 1248, 1275, 1460, 1575, 2412

Butler, Edward, 1355 Hunter Avenue, Columbus, OH 43201: 1320

Cal-State Bookstore, 25776 Hillary Street, Hayward, CA 94542: 1434

Caldwell, Bettye M., University of Arkansas at Little Rock, 33rd and University, Little Rock, AR 72204: 1108

Caldwell Report, 3122 Santa Monica Boulevard, Santa Monica, CA 90404: 1500

PUBLISHERS DIRECTORY AND INDEX

Cambridge, The Adult Education Co., 888 Seventh Avenue, New York, NY 10019: 1906
Cambridge University Press, 32 East 57th Street, New York, NY 10022: 1262, 1883
Camelot Behavioral Systems, P.O. Box 3447, Lawrence, KS 66044: 359
Canadian Association for Health, Physical Education and Recreation, 333 River Road, Vanier City, Ontario K1L 8B9, Canada: 342
Carney, Weedman and Associates, 3308 Military Drive, Suite 835, San Diego, CA 92110: 684, 862, 1776, 1974, 2026, 2146
Carroll Publications, 463 East Deerfield Road, Mt. Pleasant, MI 48858: 2562
Cash, Thomas F., Psychology Department, Old Dominion University, Norfolk, VA 23508: 619
Cassell, Wilfred A., 1709 Bragaw, Suite B, Anchorage, AK 99504: 1917, 2239
Cedars Press, Inc., P.O. Box 29351, Columbus, OH 43229: 2226
Center for Advanced Study in Theoretical Psychology, University of Alberta, Edmonton, Alberta T6G 2E9, Canada: 1929
Center for Psychological Service, 1511 K Street, NW #430, Washington, DC 20005: 949, 1165, 2228, 2403, 2418
Center for Safety, New York University, New York, NY 10003: 1056, 1428, 2197
Center for the Study of Sex Education in Medicine, 4025 Chestnut Street, Second Floor, Philadelphia, PA 19104: 2168
Centre de Psychologie Appliquee, Department Editions, Square Jouvenet, Paris 16e, France: 2513
CFKR Career Materials, Inc., P.O. Box 4, Belmont, CA 94002: 1227, 1360
Chambers, Jay L., Center for Psychological Services, College of William and Mary, Williamsburg, VA 23185: 1825
Chapman, Brook & Kent, 1215 DeLaVina, Suite F, Santa Barbara, CA 93101: 482, 1220, 1427
Character Research Association, Peace Research Laboratory, 6251 San Bonita, St. Louis, MO 63105: 340, 2399
Chatterji, S., Indian Statistical Institute, 203 Barrackpore Trunk Road, Calcutta – 35, India: 820, 2099
CHECpoint Systems, Inc., 1520 N. Waterman Ave., San Bernardino, CA 92404: 251
Child Center (The), P.O. Box 144, Kentfield, CA 94914: 393
Child Development Resources, P.O. Box 299, Lightfoot, VA 23090: 2212
Chronicle Guidance Publications, Inc., Moravia, NY 13118: 1039
Churchill Livingstone, 23 Ravelston Terrace, Edinburgh EH4 3TL, Scotland; distributed in the U.S. by Churchill Livingstone, Inc., 19 West 44th St., New York, N.Y. 10036: 1153
Ciarlo, James A., University of Denver, Mental Health Systems Evaluation Project, 70 West Sixth Avenue, Denver, CO 80204: 677
Clinical Psychology Publishing Co., Inc., 4 Conant Square, Brandon, VT 05733: 700, 1162, 1349, 1503, 2547, 2548
Coffin Associates, 21 Darling Street, Marblehead, MA 01945: 297, 1544
Colgate University Testing Service, Hamilton, NY 13346: 1794
College Board (The), Box 886, New York, NY 10101: 375, 667
Committee on Diagnostic Reading Tests, Inc., Mountain Home, NC 28758: 720
Communication Research Associates, Inc., P.O. Box 11012, Salt Lake City, UT 84147: 2104, 2157, 2448, 2541
Communication Skill Builders, Inc., 3130 N. Dodge Blvd., P.O. Box 42050, Tucson, AZ 85733: 538, 561, 1768, 1810, 2385, 2386
Consulting Psychologists Press, Inc., 577 College Ave., Palo Alto, CA 94306: 116, 117, 118, 179, 212, 235, 243, 276, 278, 341, 343, 348, 353, 354, 356, 371, 384, 398, 399, 409, 505, 542, 603, 612, 707, 794, 837, 872, 890, 922, 924, 1013, 1015, 1063, 1184, 1208, 1209, 1286, 1316, 1371, 1388, 1554, 1555, 1748, 1756, 1759, 1760, 1765, 1795, 1802, 1851, 1852, 1875, 1928, 2086, 2091, 2121, 2134, 2227, 2290, 2294, 2297, 2300, 2301, 2342, 2417, 2429, 2505, 2508, 2534, 2543, 2573, 2581, 2587, 2601, 2605, 2609, 2613, 2652
Cornell University Medical College, 1300 York Ave., Box 88, New York, NY 10021: 609, 610
Council on Dental Education, American Dental Association, 211 East Chicago Ave., Chicago, IL 60611: 673
Counselor Recordings and Tests, Box 6184 Acklen Station, Nashville, TN 37212: 280h, 1831, 2413
Cox, Charles J., Beufort House, Marlborough Rd., Bowdon, Altrincham, Cheshire WA14 2RW, England: 623
C.P.S., Inc., Box 83, Larchmont, NY 10538: 396, 1924, 2148
Crane Publishing Co., 1301 Hamilton Avenue, P.O. Box 3713, Trenton, NJ 08629: 625
Crawford, Paul L., Department of Psychology, West Virginia State College, Institute, WV 25112: 626
Creative Arts Research Associates, Inc., P.O. Box 117, Monmouth, OR 97361: 1261, 2222
Creative Learning Press, Inc., P.O. Box 320, Mansfield Center, CT 06250: 1309, 2069
Crippled Children and Adults of Rhode Island, Inc., Meeting Street School, 667 Waterman Avenue, East Providence, RI 02914: 1459
Croft, Inc., 4601 York Rd., Baltimore, MD 21212: 569, 636, 1433
CTB/McGraw-Hill, Del Monte Research Park, Monterey, CA 93940: 217, 344, 345, 346, 347, 352, 357, 374, 551, 552, 553, 554, 642, 657, 716, 719, 851, 1356, 1665, 1666, 1781, 1839, 1880, 1881, 1888, 2084, 2151, 2181, 2211, 2224, 2431, 2454, 2477, 2478, 2479, 2480, 2481, 2482, 2660, 2661
Curriculum Associates, Inc., 5 Esquire Road, North Billerica, MA 01862: 313, 314, 315, 316
Cutronics Educational Institute, 128 West 56th Street, Bayonne, NJ 07002: 651, 652
Dartnell Corporation, 4660 Ravenswood Ave., Chicago, IL 60640: 754, 802, 853
Dean, Raymond S., Washington University, School of Medicine, Department of Psychiatry—Neuropsychology Lab, Jewish Hospital, 216 S. Kingshighway, St. Louis, MO 63110: 1289
Delaware County Intermediate Unit, Nicholas A. Spenna-

to, Language Arts Specialist, 6th and Olive Sts., Media, PA 19063: 669
Dent (J. M.) & Sons (Canada) Ltd., 100 Scarsdale Road, Don Mills, Ontario M3B 2R8, Canada: 907
Dennis, William H., Trumbull County Reading Clinic, 255 Bonnie Brae Avenue N.E., Warren, OH 44483: 671, 672
Department of Mental Health Sciences, Hahnemann Medical College and Hospital, 230 North Broad Street, Philadelphia, PA 19102: 1049, 1050, 1436
Department of Photography and Cinema, Ohio State University, 156 West 19th Avenue, Columbus, OH 43210: 1717
Department of Psychological Testing, De Paul University, 25 East Jackson Blvd., Chicago, IL 60604: 536
Department of Psychology, Oklahoma State University, 115 South Murray Hall, Stillwater, OK 74074: 2225
Derogatis, Leonard R., Clinical Psychometric Research, 1228 Wine Spring Lane, Towson, MD 21204: 683, 2100
Developmental Reading Distributors, 1944 Sheridan Ave., Laramie, WY 82070: 1993
Devereux Foundation Press, P.O. Box 400, 19 S. Waterloo Road, Devon, PA 19333: 702, 703, 704, 705
Diagnostic Specialists Inc., 1170 North 660 West, Orem, UT 84057: 294
Dial, Inc., 6 Jennifer Lane, DeKalb, IL 60115: 696
Diebold (John) & Associates, 430 Park Avenue, New York, NY 10022: 731
Dillard, Harry, The Winnetka Public Schools, 1155 Oak Street, Winnetka, IL 60093: 850
Dow Chemical Co., Midland, MI 48640: 389
Drew (Edward) Co., P.O. Box 553, Jacksonville, FL 32201: 903
Duke University Medical Center, Box 3003, Durham, NC 27710: 1659
Eckstein Bros., Inc., 4807 W. 118th Place, Hawthorne, CA 90250: 773
Economy Co., 1901 North Walnut, P.O. Box 25308, Oklahoma City, OK 73125: 1579
EdITS/Educational and Industrial Testing Service, P.O. Box 7234, San Diego, CA 92107: 321a, 351, 376, 558, 559, 681, 859a, 860a, 883, 1229, 1419b, 1547, 1758, 1789, 1904, 1905, 2340, 2476, 2599, 2604
Education Achievement Corporation, P.O. Box 7310, Waco, TX 76710: 1826
Educational Activities, Inc., 1937 Grand Avenue, Baldwin, NY 11510: 1779, 2460, 2559
Educational & Industrial Test Services Ltd., 83 High Street, Hemel Hempstead HP1 3AH, England: 733
Educational Assessment Service, Inc., Route One, Box 139–A, Watertown, WI 53094: 1016, 1017
Educational Development Corporation, 4235 South Memorial, Tulsa, OK 74145: 1142, 1143
Educational Development Laboratories, Inc., 1221 Avenue of the Americas, New York, NY 10020: 1994
Educational Division, Readers Digest, Pleasantville, NY 10570: 245
Educational Evaluation Enterprises, 5 Marsh Street, Bristol 1 Glos., England: 823
Educational Guidance, Inc., P.O. Box 511, Main Post Office, Dearborn, MI 48121: 373, 778
Educational Performance Associates, Inc., 600 Broad Avenue, Ridgefield, NJ 07657: 1873, 2507, 2666
Educational Publications, Dublin, NH 03444: 2421

Educational Records Bureau, Box 619, Rosedale Rd., Princeton, NJ 08541: 838, 839, 1330a
Educational Research Centre, St. Patrick's College, Dublin 9, Ireland: 756
Educational Research Consultants, Inc., 4436 Engle Road, Sacramento, CA 95821: 1461
Educational Resources, 19 Peacedale Grove, Nunawading 3131, Australia: 1990
Educational Skills Development, Inc., 179 East Maxwell Street, Lexington, KY 40508: 240, 241
Educational Testing Service (Berkeley Office), 1947 Center Street, Berkeley, CA 94704: 2371
Educational Testing Service, Princeton, NJ 08540: 124, 125, 126, 127, 128, 129, 130, 131, 132, 133, 134, 135, 136, 137, 138, 139, 140, 141, 142, 143, 382, 411, 412, 413, 414, 415, 416, 417, 418, 419, 420, 421, 422, 423, 424, 425, 426, 427, 428, 429, 430, 431, 432, 433, 434, 435, 436, 437, 438, 439, 440, 441, 442, 443, 444, 445, 446, 447, 448, 449, 450, 451, 452, 453, 454, 455, 456, 457, 458, 459, 460, 461, 462, 463, 486, 487, 488, 489, 490, 491, 492, 493, 494, 495, 496, 497, 498, 499, 500, 501, 506, 507, 508, 509, 510, 511, 512, 513, 514, 515, 516, 517, 518, 519, 520, 521, 522, 523, 524, 525, 526, 527, 528, 529, 530, 531, 543, 685, 686, 757, 758, 759, 760, 761, 762, 763, 764, 765, 973, 974, 975, 976, 977, 978, 979, 980, 981, 982, 983, 984, 985, 986, 987, 988, 989, 990, 991, 992, 993, 994, 995, 996, 997, 998, 999, 1000, 1023, 1077, 1133, 1158, 1159, 1257, 1548, 1563, 1624, 1625, 1626, 1627, 1628, 1629, 1630, 1631, 1632, 1633, 1634, 1635, 1636, 1637, 1638, 1639, 1640, 1641, 1642, 1643, 1644, 1645, 1646, 1647, 1648, 1649, 1650, 1651, 1866, 2078, 2088, 2116, 2117, 2118, 2120, 2143, 2144, 2145, 2334, 2337, 2441, 2470
Educator Feedback Center, Western Michigan University, 12 Bigelow Annex, Kalamazoo, MI 49008: 119, 2398
Educators Assistance Institute, 2500 Colorado Avenue, Santa Monica, CA 90406: 1820
Educators'-Employers' Tests & Services Associates, 120 Detzel Place, Cincinnati, OH 45219: 727, 846, 939, 942, 1452, 1454, 1674, 1783, 1797, 2049, 2306
Educators Publishing Service, Inc., 75 Moulton Street, Cambridge, MA 02138: 182, 279, 540, 730, 770, 957, 1334, 1423, 1435, 1723, 1724, 1871, 2016, 2110, 2202, 2214, 2252
Edwards, Carl N., 61 Winthrop Street, West Newton, MA 02165: 2206
Effective Study Materials, P.O. Box 603, San Marcos, TX 78666: 781, 2346
Eidsmoe, Russell M., Morningside College, Sioux City, IA 51106: 2338
El Paso Public Schools, 6531 Boeing Drive, P.O. Box 20100, El Paso, TX 79998: 1733, 1735
El Paso Rehabilitation Center, 2630 Richmond St., El Paso, TX 79930: 548
Elbern Publications, P.O. Box 09497, Columbus, OH 43209: 1996
Elmore, Patricia B., Guidance & Educational Psychology Department, Southern Illinois University at Carbondale, Carbondale, IL 62901: 274, 385, 1298
EMC Publishing, 180 East Sixth Street, Saint Paul, MN 55101: 1734

PUBLISHERS DIRECTORY AND INDEX

Endeavor Information Systems, Inc., 2407 Prospect Ave., Evanston, IL 60201: 818

English Language Institute, University of Michigan, 2001 NU, Testing and Certification Division, Ann Arbor, MI 48109: 824, 1483, 1484, 2426, 2427

Essay Press, Inc., P.O. Box 2323, La Jolla, CA 92037: 2033, 2034

Evaluation Research Associates, P.O. Box 6503, Teall Station, Syracuse, NY 13217: 408, 502, 1080, 1745, 2308

Evaluation Systems Inc., 640 N. LaSalle Street, Chicago, IL 60610: 1550

Examinations Committee, American Chemical Society, Test Distribution Center, University of South Florida, Chemistry Room 112, Tampa, FL 33620: 56, 57, 58, 59, 60, 61, 62, 63, 64, 65, 66, 67, 68, 69, 70, 71, 72, 73, 74, 75, 2510

Exceptional Resources, Inc., 7701 Cameron Rd., Suite 105, Austin, TX 78766: 694

Eyberg, Sheila M., The Oregon Health Sciences University, School of Medicine, Department of Medical Psychology, 3181 S.W. Sam Jackson Park Road, Portland, OR 97201: 768, 858, 2494

Facilitation House, Box 611-E, Ottawa, IL 61350: 721, 722, 723, 724, 725, 1112, 1553, 2089

Family Life Publications, Inc., P.O. Box 427, Saluda, NC 28773: 622, 659, 1172, 1344, 1372, 1375, 1377, 1379, 1380, 1381, 1382, 1383, 1761, 1869, 2009, 2167, 2169, 2172, 2174

Fast, Charles G., Northeast Missouri State University, Kirksville, MO 63501: 881

Fearon Education, 6 Davis Drive, Belmont, CA 94002: 257, 699, 1182, 1915, 1927

Federation of Societies for Coatings Technology, 1315 Walnut Street, Philadelphia, PA 19107: 533

Fels Research Institute, 800 Livermore Street, Yellow Springs, OH 45387: 884

Follett Publishing Co., 1010 West Washington Boulevard, Chicago, IL 60607: 309, 701, 1255, 2452

Foreworks, Box 9747, North Hollywood, CA 91609: 2424

Foster, Arthur L., 248 Blossom Hill Road, Los Gatos, CA 95030: 2173

Foundation for Research in Mental Health, Box 1483, Wilmington, DE 19809: 653

Free Press, 866 Third Avenue, New York, NY 10022: 2029

Friedman, Myles I., College of Education, University of South Carolina, Columbia, SC 29208: 1864

Gallagher, Ralph, 613 North Mountain Avenue, Bound Brook, NJ 08805: 1040

Gallaudet College Press, Gallaudet College, Kendall Green, Washington, DC 20002: 2663

Garrard Publishing Co., 1607 North Market Street, Champaign, IL 61820: 258

General Educational Development Testing Service of the American Council on Education, One Dupont Circle, Washington, DC 20036: 2485

G. I. A. Publications, Inc., 7404 South Mason Avenue, Chicago, IL 60638: 1891

Gibson (Robert) & Sons, Glasgow, Ltd., 17, Fitzroy Place, Glasgow G3 7BR, Scotland: 616, 617, 1244, 1753

Girona, Ricardo, 428 Columbus Avenue, Sandusky, OH 44870: 144

Gleser, Goldine C., 7110 Medical Sciences Building, ML #59, 231 Bethesda Avenue, Cincinnati, OH 45267: 665

Goodrich, Jerry D., Indiana University, Dept. of Psychiatry, 1100 West Michigan Street, Indianapolis, IN 46223: 1076

Gough, Harrison G., University of California, Berkeley, Institute of Personality Assessment and Research, 3657 Tolman Hall, Berkeley, CA 94720: 1107

Goyer, Robert S., Department of Communication, Arizona State University, Tempe, AZ 85287: 971

Graham-Field, 415 2nd Avenue, New Hyde Park, NY 11040: 2419

Grason-Stadler Co., Inc., Concord, MA 01742: 1003

Grassi (Joseph R.), Inc., 3501 Jackson St. #110, Hollywood, FL 33021: 1004, 1005

Gretsch (Fred) Co., Inc., 1801 Gilbert Avenue, Cincinnati, OH 45202: 1008

Grune & Stratton, Inc., 111 Fifth Avenue, New York, NY 10003: 280b, 280c, 280e, 697, 729, 1480, 1793, 1876, 1899, 1926, 1934, 2030, 2388, 2560, 2615

Guidance Centre, University of Toronto, 252 Bloor Street West, Toronto, Ontario M5S 2Y3, Canada: 288, 902, 936, 1418, 1728, 2432, 2439

Guidance Testing Associates, St. Mary's University, One Camino Santa Maria, San Antonio, TX 78284: 545, 1181, 2455, 2484, 2488

H & H Enterprises, Inc., Box 3342, Lawrence, KS 66044: 2391

Halgren Tests, 873 Persimmon Avenue, Sunnyvale, CA 94087: 2029

Harding, Chris., P.O. Box 271, North Rockhampton, Queensland, 4701, Australia: 1057, 1058

Harrap Ltd., P.O. Box 70, 182 High Holborn, London WC1V 7AX, England: 1102, 1446, 2278, 2289

Hart-Davis Educational Ltd., P.O. Box 9, 29 Frogmore, St. Albans, Herts AL2 2NF, England: 2281

Harvard Personnel Testing, P.O. Box 1104, St. Laurent Station, Montreal, Canada H4L 4W6; distributed in the U.S. by Wolfe Computer Aptitude Testing Co., Box 319, Oradell, NJ 07649: 1303

Harvard University Press, 79 Garden Street, Cambridge, MA 02138: 2491

Harvey, O. J., Dept. of Psychology, University of Colorado, Boulder, CO 80302: 2497

Haskins, Mary Jane, Dept. of Health, Dance, and Women's Physical Education, Lamar University, Beaumont, TX 77710: 109

Haverly Systems, Inc., 78 Broadway, P.O. Box 919, Denville, NJ 07834: 1907

Hayes Educational Tests, 7040 North Portsmouth Ave., Portland, OR 97203: 1490, 1854

Heinemann Educational Books, Inc., 4 Front Street, Exeter, NH 03833: 2060

Heinemann Educational Books Ltd., 26 Kilham Ave., Auckland 9, P.O. Box 36064, New Zealand: 928b, 2060

Heinemann (William) Medical Books, 23 Bedford Square, London WC1B 3HT, England: 311

Heinemann Publishers Australia Pty Ltd., 85 Abinger Street, Box 133, Richmond, 3121 Australia: 928a, 929

Henry, William E., 555 Vermont Street, San Francisco, CA 94107: 1022

Hicks, John S., Special Education Program, Fordham

University, 113 West 60 Street, New York, NY 10023: 2005

Higher Education Research Institute of the University of California, Los Angeles, 924 Westwood Blvd., Suite 837, Los Angeles, CA 90024: 532, 572, 2333

Hill, Wm. Fawcett, 1633 Lynoak Drive, Claremont, CA 91711: 1099

Hiskey, Marshall S., 5640 Baldwin, Lincoln, NE 68507: 1101

Hobsons Press (Cambridge) Ltd. for Careers Research Advisory Centre, Bateman St., Cambridge CB2 1LZ, England: 638, 1669

Hodder & Stoughton Educational, P.O. Box 702, Dunton Green, Sevenoaks, Kent TN13 2YD, England: 193, 194, 253, 254, 321, 330, 471, 639, 775, 859b, 860b, 861, 955, 972, 1018, 1019, 1024, 1025, 1147, 1211, 1315, 1419a, 1533, 1534, 1535, 1616, 1623, 1740, 1836, 1998, 2058, 2245, 2249, 2250, 2490, 2647

Howarth, Edgar, The University of Alberta, Department of Psychology, Edmonton, Alberta T6G 2E9, Canada: 114, 1114, 1115

Huber, Hans, Langgassstrasse 76, 3000 Bern 9, Switzerland: 2030, 2388, 2522, 2672

Hubert, Edwina E., 313 Wellesley S. E., Albuquerque, NM 87106: 1317

Human Resources Center, Albertson, NY 11507: 2068

Human Resources Center, The University of Chicago, 1225 East 60th Street, Chicago, IL 60637: 10, 477, 478, 631, 795, 898, 1176, 1455, 1618, 1780, 1785, 1788, 1884, 2210, 2410, 2530, 2553, 2610, 2645, 2651, 2654

Human Sciences Press, 72 Fifth Avenue, New York, NY 10011: 779, 950, 967, 1817

Human Sciences Research Council, Private Bag X41, 0001 Pretoria, Republic of South Africa: 11, 15, 18, 153, 191, 400, 537, 1026, 1041, 1081, 1141, 1166, 1167, 1174, 1197, 1228, 1233a, 1285, 1416, 1565, 1578, 1584, 1815, 2071, 2072, 2073, 2074, 2075, 2076, 2149, 2153, 2408, 2578

Humanics Ltd., P.O. Box 7447, 1182 West Peachtree Street, Atlanta, GA 30309: 395, 1338

Humanics Media, Box 188, Rochester, MI 48063: 364, 1160, 1276, 1310, 1472, 1800, 2362

Illinois Thinking Project, University of Illinois at Urbana-Champaign, College of Education, Bureau of Educational Research, 188 Education Building, 1310 South Sixth Street, Champaign, IL 61820: 604, 605, 606

Indiana Public Health Foundation, Inc., 1330 West Michigan Street, Indianapolis, IN 46202: 1136

Industrial Psychological Services, Box 9571, Johannesburg, Republic of South Africa: 147, 2230

Industrial Psychology, Inc., 515 Madison Avenue, New York, NY 10022: 1219, 1468, 2208b

Institute for Personality and Ability Testing, Inc., Test Services Division, P.O. Box 188, Champaign, IL 61820: 391, 400, 472, 547, 643a, 772, 787, 854, 1197, 1198, 1233a, 1538, 1573, 1662, 1786, 2087, 2137, 2208

Institute of Psychological Research, Inc., 34 Ovest, rue Fleury Street West, Montreal, Quebec H3L 1S9, Canada: 769, 1329, 1961, 2464

Institute of Rehabilitation Medicine, New York University Medical Center, 400 East 34th Street, New York, NY 10016: 925

Instructional Objectives Exchange, 11411 West Jefferson Blvd., Culver City, CA 90230: 159, 221, 222, 223, 1195, 1196, 1258, 1277, 1412, 1449, 1997, 2207

International Business Machines Corporation, 44 South Broadway, White Plains, NY 10601: 1120

International Personnel Management Association, 1850 K Street, N.W., Suite 870, Washington, DC 20006: 888, 1199, 1200, 1545, 1843, 2070, 2420

International Universities Press, Inc., 315 Fifth Avenue, New York, NY 10016: 2672

Interstate Printers & Publishers, Inc., 19–27 North Jackson Street, Danville, IL 61832: 187, 214, 911, 959, 1124, 1378, 1814, 1860, 2590

Intran Corporation, 4555 West 77th Street, Minneapolis, MN 55435: 265, 266, 267, 268, 2535, 2537, 2538

Iowa State University, North Central 124 Regional Research Project, Ames, IA 50010: 1656

Iowa State University Research Foundation, Inc., Department of Child Development, 101 Child Development Building, Research Laboratories, Ames, IA 50011: 1190

J-K Screening Service, 124 Solano St., San Rafael, CA 94901: 1221

JAIM Research, Inc., 1808 Collingwood Rd., Alexandria, VA 22308: 1213

Jamestown Publishers, P.O. Box 6743, Providence, RI 02940: 216, 269, 1021, 1138, 1156, 1157, 1739, 1812, 2020

Jastak Associates, Inc., 1526 Gilpin Avenue, Wilmington, DE 19806: 481, 711, 2621, 2622, 2623, 2624

Jewish Education Service of North America, Inc., 114 Fifth Avenue, New York, NY 10011: 49, 50, 51, 52, 1566, 2467

Jewish Employment and Vocational Service, Inc., Vocational Research Institute, 1700 Sansom Street, Philadelphia, PA 19103: 1210

Joint Council on Economic Education, 1212 Ave. of the Americas, New York, NY 10036: 246, 1232, 1898, 2440, 2463

Jones Teaching Aids, 3442 Avenue C, Council Bluffs, IA 51501: 1223

Jung (C. G.) Educational Center, 4803 Montrose Blvd., Houston, TX 77006: 2043

Kahn, Marvin W., Department of Psychology, University of Arizona, Tucson, AZ 85721: 624

Kanehara Shuppan Co., Ltd., 31–14, 2 Chome Yushima, Bunkyo-Ku, Tokyo 112, Japan: 2419

Kaneko Shobo Publisher, 3–7, 3–Chome Otsuka, Bunkyo-Ku, Tokyo 112, Japan: 1235

Karger (S.), AG, P.O. Box, CH 4009 Basel, Switzerland: 535

Kaso Industries, Inc., P.O. Box 635, Weston, MA 02193: 379

Katz, Martin M., Clinical Research Branch, National Institute of Mental Health, 5600 Fishers Lane, Rockville, MD 20852: 1240

Keeler Instruments Ltd., Clewer Hill Road, Windsor, Berks, SL4 4AA, England; distributed in the U.S. by Keeler Instruments Inc., 456 Parkway, Lawrence Park Industrial District, Broomall, PA 19008: 2177

Kendall/Hunt Publishing Co., 2460 Kerper Boulevard, Dubuque, IA 52001: 255, 567, 661, 718

Kent Developmental Metrics, 7551 Diagonal Road, Kent, OH 44240: 1246

Keystone Publications, 1657 Broadway, New York, NY 10019: 615

Keystone View, 2212 East 12th Street, Davenport, IA 52803: 1251, 1252, 1312, 1772, 2247

Kiesler, Donald J., 4131 V Town House Rd., Richmond, VA 23228: 1130

Kirkpatrick, Donald L., 1080 Lower Ridgeway, Elm Grove, WI 53122: 2356, 2359, 2361

Klamath Printing Co., 628 Oak Street, Klamath Falls, OR 97601: 2280

Klopfer, L. E., University of Pittsburgh, 816 LRDC Bldg., 3939 O'Hara Street, Pittsburgh, PA 15260: 2467A

Knobloch, Hilda, 230 E. Oglethorpe Ave., Savannah, GA 31401: 2014

Kohn, Martin, The William Alanson White Institute of Psychiatry, Psychoanalysis and Psychology, 20 West 74th Street, New York, NY 10023: 1263, 1264

Krantz, David S., Department of Medical Psychology, Uniformed Services University of the Health Sciences, 4301 Jones Bridge Road, Bethesda, MD 20014: 1267

Kreiger (Robert E.) Publishing Co., Inc., P.O. Box 9542, Melbourne, FL 32901: 2158

Kundu, Ramanath, Department of Psychology, University of Calcutta, 92 Acharya Prafulla Chandra Road, Calcutta – 9, India: 1273

L & T Educational Materials, Inc., P.O. Box 403, Yorktown Heights, NY 10598: 1290

LADOCA Publishing Foundation, University of Colorado Health Sciences Center, John F. Kennedy Child Development Center, 4200 East Ninth Avenue, Denver, CO 80262: 675, 676, 678, 679, 680

Lafayette Instrument Co., P.O. Box 5729, Lafayette, IN 47903: 1207, 1370, 1670, 1671, 1672, 1727, 1938

LaForge, Ralph, 83 Homestead Blvd., Mill Valley, CA 94941: 1170

Landsman, Myril, The Winnetka Public Schools, 1155 Oak Street, Winnetka, IL 60093: 850

Language Research Associates, Inc., 2480 Durango Circle, Palm Springs, CA 92262: 226, 227, 229, 2251, 2561, 2563

Larlin Corporation, P.O. Box 1523, 1119 Cobb Pkwy., South, Marietta, GA 30061: 2447

Las Cruces Public Schools, 301 West Amador Avenue, Las Cruces, NM 88001: 2444

Law School Admission Council, Suite 150, 11 Dupont Circle, NW, Washington, DC 20036: 1292

Lawrence, Trudys, 5916 Del Loma Avenue, San Gabriel, CA 91775: 954

Layton, Wilbur L., 3604 Ross Road, Ames, IA 50010: 1510, 1716

Lea & Febiger, 600 Washington Square, Philadelphia, PA 19106: 308

Leach (Glenn C.), Publisher, Wagner College, Staten Island, NY 10301: 1150, 1151, 1254, 1657

Learnco Inc., 128 High Street, Greenland, NH 03840: 2259

Learning Research Associates, Inc., 1501 Broadway, New York, NY 10036: 1345

Learning Resources Corporation, 8517 Production Avenue, San Diego, CA 92121: 2204, 2205

Leonard (Hal) Publishing Corporation, 960 East Mark St., Winona, MN 55987: 880, 2591

Lewis (H. K.) & Co. Ltd., 136 Gower Street, London WC1E 6BS, England: 632, 1485

Linguametrics Group, P.O. Box 3495, San Rafael, CA 94912: 1281

LinguiSystems, Inc., Suite 806, 1630 Fifth Avenue, Moline, IL 61265: 1736, 1737, 2648

Lippincott (J. B.) Co., East Washington Square, Philadelphia, PA 19105: 311, 1333

London House Management Consultants, Inc., 1550 Northwest Highway, Park Ridge, IL 60068: 1339, 2277

Longman, Inc., 19 West 44th Street, Suite 1012, New York, NY 10036: 1153

Lorr, Maurice, Department of Psychology, The Catholic University of America, Washington, DC 20064: 1173, 1747, 1792

Los Angeles Unified School District, Box 3307, Los Angeles, CA 90051: 734

Lucas Brothers Publishers, 909 Lowry, Columbia, MO 65201: 1185

M.A.A. Committee on High School Contests, Department of Mathematics and Statistics, 917 Oldfather Hall, University of Nebraska, Lincoln, NE 68588: 160

Maas, James B., The Center for Improvement of Undergraduate Education, 115 Rand Hall, Cornell University, Ithaca, NY 14850: 607

Macmillan Education, Registered Office, 4 Little Essex Street, London WC2R 3LF, England: 205, 206, 1311, 1354, 1567

Macmillan Publishing Co., Inc., 866 Third Avenue, New York, NY 10022: 53, 1154, 1355, 1402

Maferr Foundation, Inc., 9 East 81 Street, New York, NY 10028: 1357, 1358

Mafex Associates, Inc., 90 Cherry St., Box 519, Johnstown, PA 15907: 708, 1075, 1217, 1294, 1811, 1872

Maico Hearing Instruments, Inc., 7375 Bush Lake Road, Minneapolis, MN 55435: 1359

Management Research Associates, R.R. 25, Box 225, Terre Haute, IN 47802: 1301, 1549, 2365, 2367

Management Research Institute, Suite 900, 4330 East-West Highway, Washington, DC 20014: 2354

Manasayan, 32 Netaji Subhash Marg, Darya Ganj, New Delhi 110002, India: 387, 2236, 2442

Mandel, Nathan G., Dept. of Corrections, State of Minnesota, St. Paul, MN 55101: 1368

Marathon Consulting & Press, 575 Enfield Road, Columbus, OH 43209: 370, 1447, 2650

Mathis, Harold, 21650 Eleven Mile, Suite 103, Southfield, MI 48076: 835

Matt-Jansky, 120 East 89th Street, New York, NY 10028: 1205

McCann Associates, 2755 Philmont Avenue, Huntington Valley, PA 19006: 470, 833, 887, 889, 943, 1422, 1667, 1844, 1845, 1846, 1847, 2302, 2304

McGrath Publishing Co., P.O. Box 535, Whitmore Lake, MI 48189: 1429, 1430, 1431, 1432, 1741

McGraw-Hill Book Co., Inc., 1221 Avenue of the Americas, New York, NY 10020: 549, 728, 1417, 2002, 2257, 2347, 2568, 2662

McGraw-Hill Ryerson Ltd., 330 Progress Avenue, Scarborough, Ontario M1P 2Z5, Canada: 360

Medical Research Council, The Royal Free Hospital, Department of Psychological Medicine, Pond Street, Hampstead, London NW3 2QG, England: 1778

Mehrabian, Albert, University of California, Department of Psychology, 405 Hilgard Avenue, Los Angeles, CA 90024: 1438, 1439, 1440, 1442, 1443, 1444, 1445, 1448, 1964

Mens Sana Publishing Inc., P.O. Box 2966, Grand Central Station, New York, NY 10017: 855
Merrill (Charles E.) Publishing Co., 1300 Alum Creek Drive, Columbus, OH 43216: 213, 339, 474, 475, 480, 834, 836, 1470, 1619, 1725, 1877, 1949, 1973, 2449, 2532
Meta-Visions, P.O. Box 453, Plymouth, MI 48170: 1472
Miami University Alumni Association, Murstein Alumni Center, Miami University, Oxford, OH 45056: 2644
Middle East Center, University of Utah, Salt Lake City, UT 84112: 893
Midwest Music Tests, Newell H. Long, 1304 East University St., Bloomington, IN 47401: 1135
Mills Center (The), P.O. Box 597, Black Mountain, NC 28711: 1306
Ministry Inventories, P.O. Box 8265, Dallas, TX 75205: 1183, 2493
Minnesota Moral Research Projects, University of Minnesota, Dept. of Social, Psychological, and Philosophical Foundations of Education, 330 Burton Hall, 178 Pillsbury Drive S.E., Minneapolis, MN 55455: 666
Minnesota Research and Evaluation Center, University of Minnesota, c/o Wayne W. Welch, 210 Burton Hall, Minneapolis, MN 55455: 1410
MKM, Inc., 809 Kansas City St., Rapid City, SD 57701: 1516, 1517, 1518
Monitor, P.O. Box 2337, Hollywood, CA 90028: 120, 203, 220, 783, 1168, 1539, 1577, 1588, 1589, 1590, 2435, 2516, 2649
Moore (Joseph E.) and Associates, R.F.D. 12, Box 309, Gainesville, GA 30506: 1532
Moos, Rudolf H., Social Ecology Lab, Stanford University Medical Center, Palo Alto, CA 94304: 1466
Moreno Educational Co., 6837 Elaine Way, San Diego, CA 92120: 1732, 1966, 2248
Morrison, James H., 9804 Hadley Street, Overland Park, KS 66212: 1350, 2428
Morstain, Barry R., College of Urban Affairs and Public Policy, Raub Hall, University of Delaware, Newark, DE 19711: 2336
Munsell Color Co., 2441 North Calvert St., Baltimore, MD 21218: 878, 2215
Nash, N., Great Eastern Lumber Co., Inc., 2315 Broadway, New York, NY 10024: 1858
National Association of Secondary-School Principals, 1904 Association Drive, Reston, VA 22091: 1231, 2119, 2329
National Board of Medical Examiners, Suite 200, One Dupont Circle, N.W., Washington, DC 20036: 1458
National Business Education Association, 1906 Association Drive, Reston, VA 22091: 304, 332, 944, 1352, 1556, 2307, 2339, 2527, 2533
National Council on Crime and Delinquency, Continental Plaza, 411 Hackensack Avenue, Hackensack, NJ 07601: 613, 1234
National Dairy Council, 6300 North River Road, Rosemont, IL 60018: 1656
National Educational Laboratory Publishers, Inc., 813 Airport Boulevard, Austin, TX 78702: 668
National Foremen's Institute, Inc., 24 Rope Ferry Road, Waterford, CT 06385: 801, 2141
National Institute for Personnel Research, P.O. Box 32410, Braamfontein, 2017, South Africa: 199, 406, 555, 560, 663, 886, 946, 968, 1079, 1451, 1467, 1560, 1561, 1767, 1777, 1827, 1988, 2241, 2414, 2415, 2471, 2598
National Institute of Drug Abuse, Addiction Research Center, (Attn: Charles A. Haertzen), c/o Baltimore City Hospital, Bldg. D-5E, 4940 Eastern Avenue, Baltimore, MD 21224: 113
National League for Nursing, Inc., 10 Columbus Circle, New York, NY 10019: 1585, 1586, 1587
National Occupational Competency Testing Institute, 45 Colvin Avenue, Albany, NY 12206: 1562, 1591, 1592, 1593, 1594, 1595, 1596, 1597, 1598, 1599, 1600, 1601, 1602, 1603, 1604, 1605, 1606, 1607, 1608, 1609, 1610, 1611, 1612, 1613, 1614
National Study of School Evaluation, 5201 Leesburg Pike, Falls Church, VA 22041: 1763, 2335
National Textbook Co., 8259 Niles Center Road, Skokie, IL 60076: 927
NCS Interpretive Scoring Systems, P.O. Box 1416, Minneapolis, MN 55440: 367, 687, 1164, 1487, 1488, 1498, 2133, 2409, 2634, 2635, 2642
Nelson Canada, 1120 Birchmont Road, Scarborough, Ontario M1K 5G4, Canada: 361, 362, 363, 933, 2046
Neuropsychology Laboratory, University of Arizona, 1338 East Edison Street, Tucson, AZ 85719: 1052
Nevins (C.H.) Printing Co., 311 Bryn Mawr Island, Bayshore Gardens, Bradenton, FL 33507: 1011
New York Times, 229 West 43rd Street, New York, NY 10036: 2094
New York University, Graduate School of Business Administration, 600 Tisch Hall, Washington Square, New York, NY 10003: 621
New Zealand Council for Educational Research, Education House, 178-182 Willis Street, Wellington 1, New Zealand: 23, 44 329, 1910, 1911, 1912, 1913, 1918, 2134a, 2341, 2458
Newbury House Publishers, Inc., 54 Warehouse Lane, Rowley, MA 01969: 821, 1128, 1335, 2321
Newsweek Educational Division, 444 Madison Avenue, New York, NY 10022: 646, 1581
NFER-Nelson Publishing Co., Darville House, 2 Oxford Road East, Windsor Berkshire SL4 1DF, England: 38, 110, 148, 149, 198, 207, 252, 282, 317, 318, 319, 320, 322, 386, 483b, 546, 557, 640, 641, 782, 825, 826, 843, 863, 874, 910, 930, 940, 941, 972, 1027, 1028, 1029, 1030, 1031, 1032, 1033, 1034, 1035, 1036, 1037, 1038, 1233a, 1243, 1245, 1283, 1321, 1340, 1367, 1406, 1407, 1408, 1409, 1453, 1567, 1582, 1583, 1620, 1652, 1660, 1787, 1791, 1808, 1829, 1992, 2000, 2003, 2004, 2015, 2018, 2019, 2021, 2036, 2096, 2150, 2152, 2156, 2344, 2348, 2349, 2350, 2383, 2430, 2487, 2517, 2556, 2564, 2598, 2602, 2608, 2625, 2627, 2629, 2631
Northwestern State University of Louisiana, P.O. Box 5003, Natchitoches, LA 71457: 2606
Northwestern University Press, 1735 Benson Avenue, Evanston, IL 60201: 1622, 2109
Nursing Research Associates, 3752 Cummings St., Eau Claire, WI 54701: 797, 1348, 1654
OAIS Testing Program, P.O. Box 388, Ann Arbor, MI 48107: 1729
Offer, Daniel, Michael Reese Hospital and Medical Center, 29th Street and Ellis Avenue, Chicago, IL 60616: 1673
Office of Instructional Resources, University of Illinois at Urbana-Champaign, Measurement and Research Divi-

PUBLISHERS DIRECTORY AND INDEX

sion, 307 Engineering Hall, 1308 W. Green, Urbana, IL 61801: 1121, 1125

Office of Self-Instructional Programs, Division of Continuing Education, Western Michigan University, Kalamazoo, MI 49008: 1865

Oliver & Boyd, Robert Stevenson House, 1–3 Baxter's Place, Leith Walk, Edinburgh EH1 3AF, England: 746, 842, 2077

Ontario Institute for Studies in Education, 252 Bloor Street West, Toronto, Ontario M5S 1V6, Canada: 918, 1893

Organizational Tests Ltd., P.O. Box 324, Fredericton, N.B., Canada: 539, 1364, 1744, 2056, 2127, 2545

O'Rourke Publications, Post Office Box 1118, Lake Alfred, FL 33850: 1750, 1751, 2375

PAQ Services, Inc., 1625 North 1000 East, Logan, UT 84321: 1212, 1855

Parauniversity Resources, 640 N.W. 36th Drive, Gainesville, FL 32607: 1542

Parnicky, Joseph J., Nisonger Center, Ohio State University, 1580 Cannon Drive, Columbus, OH 43210: 2574

Peacock (F.E.) Publishers Test Division, 115 N. Prospect Ave., Itasca, IL 60143: 1970

Perceptual Learning Systems, P.O. Box 864, Dearborn, MI 48121: 882, 905, 2299

Perfection Form Co., 1000 North Second Avenue, Logan, IA 51546: 161, 162, 166, 774, 822, 970, 1001, 1324, 1336, 1663, 1664, 1842, 2658, 2659

Perri, Michael G., Medical Center, 1481 West Tenth Street, Indianapolis, IN 46202: 1076

Person-O-Metrics, Inc., 20504 Williamsburg Road, Dearborn Heights, MI 48127: 848, 1965, 2131

Personnel Security Corporation, Oak Brook Executive Plaza, 1301 West 22nd Street, Oak Brook, IL 60521: 841, 2389

Peterson, Shailer, University of Texas Dental School at San Antonio, 7703 Floyd Curl Drive, San Antonio, TX 78284: 2643

Phi Delta Kappa, Inc., Box 789, Bloomington, IN 47402: 777

Phonovisual Products, Inc., 12216 Parklawn Drive, Rockville, MD 20852: 1813

Pilot Books, 347 Fifth Avenue, New York, NY 10016: 388

Priority Innovations, Inc., Post Office Box 792, Skokie, IL 60076: 150, 1543, 1764, 1889, 2106, 2107

PRO-ED, 5341 Industrial Oaks Blvd., Austin, TX 78735: 168, 169, 170, 171, 172, 173, 174, 190, 256, 273, 845, 1007, 1773, 2422, 2436, 2438, 2445, 2456, 2466

Professional Examination Service, 475 Riverside Drive, New York, NY 10115: 2462

Programming Specialists, Inc., P.O. Box 160, Brooklyn, NY 11234: 189

Programs for Education, Inc., 1200 Broadway, New York, NY 10001: 952, 953

Psych/Graphic Publishers, 470 Nautilus St., Suite 303, La Jolla, CA 92037: 286

Psychodiagnostic Test Co., Box 859, East Lansing, MI 48823: 1743

Psychodynamic Instruments, Box 1221, Ann Arbor, MI 48106: 298

Psychoeducational Clinic, University of Calgary, Barry P. Frost, 2920 24th Avenue N.W., Calgary, Alberta T2N 1N4, Canada: 919, 920, 921

Psychological Assessment and Services, Inc., P.O. Box 1031, Iowa City, IA 52244: 1515

Psychological Assessment Resources, Inc., 17408 Gunn Highway, P.O. Box 98, Odessa, FL 33556: 305, 1572, 2633

Psychological Assessment Services, P.O. Box 1400, Tuscaloosa, AL 35401: 1501

Psychological Corporation (The), 757 Third Avenue, New York, NY 10017: 9, 54, 55, 121, 164, 204b, 270, 282, 283, 290, 291, 302, 381, 466, 534, 627, 658, 674, 732, 747, 766, 767, 780, 831, 832, 852, 877, 940, 958, 963, 964, 965, 966, 1054, 1060, 1106, 1113, 1145, 1191, 1206, 1288, 1361, 1424, 1425, 1456, 1473, 1474, 1475, 1476, 1477, 1478, 1479, 1486, 1493, 1494, 1527, 1531, 1541, 1551, 1558, 1653, 1720, 1726, 1731, 1749, 1754, 1833, 1853b, 1853c, 1853d, 1914, 2013, 2015, 2037, 2059, 2112, 2113, 2180, 2246, 2254, 2286, 2287, 2288, 2291, 2292, 2293, 2298, 2317, 2372, 2374, 2387, 2469, 2529, 2554, 2555, 2594, 2598, 2602, 2607, 2608, 2614

Psychological Development Publications, P.O. Box 3198, Aspen, CO 81612: 698

Psychological Publications, Inc., 5300 Hollywood Blvd., Los Angeles, CA 90027: 2396

Psychological Publications Press, 16040 West McNichols Rd., Detroit, MI 48235: 186, 473, 1801, 1828, 1861, 1862, 2136, 2154, 2656

Psychological Research Services, Case Western Reserve University, 11220 Bellflower Road, Mather Memorial Building, Cleveland, OH 44106: 195, 1804, 1805, 1806, 1807, 2256

Psychological Service Center of Philadelphia, Suite 904, 1422 Chestnut Street, Philadelphia, PA 19102: 1048

Psychological Services Bureau, P.O. Box 4, St. Thomas, PA 17252: 1920

Psychological Services, Inc., 3450 Wilshire Blvd., Suite 1200, Los Angeles, CA 90010: 633, 799, 1299, 2368, 2373

Psychological Test Publications, 107, Pilton Street, Barnstaple, Devon., England: 1009, 1314

Psychological Test Specialists, Box 9229, Missoula, MT 59807: 876, 923, 1020, 1123, 1201, 1236, 1237, 1462, 1919, 1969, 2540, 2571

Psychologists and Educators, Inc., Sales Division, 211 West State Street, Jacksonville, IL 62650: 201, 275, 608, 628, 1259, 1384, 1385, 1386, 1730, 1848, 1870, 2044, 2130, 2138, 2140, 2155, 2332, 2453, 2457, 2600, 2603

Psychometric Affiliates, Box 3167, Munster, IN 46321: 12, 13, 14, 115, 154, 163, 165, 167, 196, 197, 336, 464, 504, 637, 648, 649, 650, 736, 785, 790, 798, 827, 828, 847, 849, 864, 871, 892, 926, 938, 945, 947, 1010, 1065, 1066, 1067, 1068, 1082, 1118, 1186, 1215, 1230, 1291, 1302, 1325, 1415, 1450, 1676, 1712, 1775, 1818, 1821, 1837, 1838, 1929, 1960, 1968, 2001, 2025, 2042, 2065, 2124, 2238, 2258, 2524, 2569, 2619, 2653

Psychometric Techniques Associates, c/o A.I.R., 4614 Fifth Ave., Pittsburgh, PA 15213: 476, 2390

Psykologiförlaget AB, Box 461, S–126 04 Hagersten 4, Sweden: 2011

Publications Sales Division, Ohio State University Press, 2070 Neil Avenue, Columbus, OH 43210: 1122, 1295, 1296, 1746, 1972

Publishers Test Service, 2500 Garden Road, Monterey, CA 93940: 6b, 158, 901, 1308, 1571, 1668, 1902, 2473

Pumroy, Donald K., University of Maryland, Division of Human and Community Resources, College of Education, College Park, MD 20742: 1387

Quay, Herbert C., University of Miami, Applied Social Sciences, P.O. Box 248074, Coral Gables, FL 33124: 2012

Random House, Inc., 201 East 50th Street, New York, NY 10022: 634, 1347

Reading Clinic (The), Temple University, 265–66, Philadelphia, PA 19122: 931

Reading Laboratory and Clinic, University of Florida, Gainesville, FL 32601: 1012, 1131, 2255, 2468

Rehabilitation Research and Training Center in Mental Retardation, University of Oregon, College of Education, Clinical Services Building, Eugene, OR 97403: 541

Reid Psychological Systems, 233 North Michigan Avenue, Chicago, IL 60601: 2007

Remediation Associates, Inc., P.O. Box 318, Linden, NJ 07036: 2092

Rensis Likert Associates, Inc., Suite 401 Wolverine Tower, 3001 S. State Street, Ann Arbor, MI 48104: 1903

Research and Development Center for Teacher Education, University of Texas, College of Education, Austin, TX 78712: 2142

Research Assessment and Training Unit, New York State Psychiatric Institute, 722 West 168th St., New York, NY 10032: 645, 1922, 1923

Research Concepts, 1368 East Airport Road, Muskegon, MI 49444: 7, 1062, 1441, 2090

Research Department, Fairview State Hospital, 2501 Harbor Blvd., Costa Mesa, CA 92626: 865, 866, 867, 868, 869

Research Press, 2612 N. Mattis, Champaign, IL 61820: 271, 873, 1373, 1868, 2171, 2231

Research Psychologists Press, Inc., P.O. Box 984, Port Huron, MI 48060: 1203, 1204, 1798, 1931, 2199

Richards, C. Steven, Indiana University, Dept. of Psychiatry, 1100 West Michigan Street, Indianapolis, IN 46223: 1076

Richardson, Bellows, Henry & Co., Inc., 1140 Connecticut Ave., N.W., Washington, DC 20036: 1975, 1976, 1977, 1978, 1979, 1980, 1981, 1982, 1983, 1984, 1985, 1986, 1987

Riverside Publishing Co., 8420 Bryn Mawr Avenue, Chicago, IL 60631: 178, 331, 483, 503, 654, 896, 932, 934, 1061, 1073, 1139, 1140, 1192, 1279, 1280, 1326, 1341, 1414, 1524, 1525, 1526, 1552, 1568, 1569, 1570, 1675, 1823, 1894, 1939, 1526, 1552, 1568, 1569, 1570, 1675, 1823, 1894, 1939, 1962, 2085, 2098, 2289, 2343, 2406, 2474, 2475, 2657

Roche Psychiatric Service Institute, Hoffmann-LaRoche Inc., Nutley, NJ 07110: 1502

Rocky Mountain Behavioral Science Institute, Inc., P.O. Box 1066, Fort Collins, CO 80522: 219, 562, 618, 1405, 1514, 2353, 2416

Rosenzweig, Saul, 8029 Washington Avenue, St. Louis, MO 63114: 2031

Rosinski, Edwin F., School of Medicine, University of California, 1356 Third Avenue, San Francisco, CA 94143: 1457

Rucker-Gable Assoc., Rockridge, Box 97, Storrs, CT 06268: 2039

S-O Publishers, 1822 Old Canyon Drive, Hacienda Heights, CA 91745: 2323

Sachar, Jane, 1700 Main Street, Santa Monica, CA 90406: 2295

Safran, C., Calgary School Board, Calgary, Alberta, Canada: 2045

Saleh, Shoukry D., Chairman, Dept. of Management Services, University of Waterloo, Waterloo, Ontario N2L 3G1, Canada: 1216

Santostefano, Sebastiano, Hall-Mercer Children's Center, 115 Mill Street, Belmont, MA 02178: 2064

Scarborough, Barron B., Florida State University, Tallahassee, FL 32306: 1819

Scherer, Isidor W., 231 Wells Road, Palm Beach, FL 33480: 1621

Scholastic Testing Service, Inc., 480 Meyer Road, P.O. Box 1056, Bensenville, IL 60106: 208, 209, 210, 211, 368, 550, 726, 1051, 1137, 1272, 1323, 1762, 1770, 2028, 2324, 2325, 2326, 2327, 2364, 2392, 2434, 2437, 2495, 2496, 2512

Schubert, Herman J. P., 500 Klein Road, Buffalo, NY 14221: 752, 2095

Science Research Associates, Inc., 155 North Wacker Drive, Chicago, IL 60606: 111, 264, 372, 556, 557, 614, 709, 710, 737, 738, 739, 740, 741, 742, 743, 899, 900, 1175, 1193, 1269, 1270, 1271, 1300, 1389, 1390, 1391, 1392, 1393, 1394, 1395, 1396, 1397, 1398, 1399, 1400, 1401, 1557, 1677, 1784, 1841, 1948, 1995, 2050, 2182, 2183, 2184, 2185, 2186, 2187, 2188, 2189, 2190, 2191, 2192, 2193, 2194, 2223, 2260, 2261, 2262, 2263, 2264, 2265, 2266, 2267, 2268, 2269, 2270, 2271, 2272, 2273, 2274, 2275, 2276, 2355, 2366, 2370, 2499, 2500, 2618

Scott, Foresman & Co., 1900 East Lake Avenue, Glenview, IL 60025: 1187, 1890, 1895, 1897

SCREEN, Inc., P.O. Box 26642, Tucson, AZ 85726: 2102

Search Institute, 122 West Franklin Avenue, Minneapolis, MN 55404: 2667

SEFA (Publications) Ltd., 4, Great William St., Stratford upon Avon, England; distributed in the U.S. by Aux Chandelles Village Press, P.O. Box 398, Bristol, IN 46507: 1908

Sewall Rehabilitation Center, 1360 Vine Street, Denver, CO 80206: 2122

Shepherd (Hilton) Co., Inc., P.O. Box 846, Fort Worth, TX 76101: 1214

Sheridan Psychological Services, Inc., P.O. Box 6101, Orange, CA 92667: 157, 401, 566, 611, 630, 662, 706, 735, 753, 1042, 1043, 1044, 1045, 1046, 1129, 1257c2, 1257d1, 1257o3, 1257q2, 1257r3, 1257x2, 1337, 1362, 1403, 1404, 1463, 1464, 1469, 1580, 1809, 1840, 1856, 2123, 2178, 2198, 2209, 2382, 2489, 2546

Shiawassee County Community Mental Health Services Board, 826 West King Street, P.O. Box 479, Owasso, MI 48867: 1909

Silliman, Henrietta, 404 North Washington, Toulon, IL 61483: 829

Slosson Educational Publications, Inc., P.O. Box 280, East Aurora, NY 14052: 712, 1202, 2216, 2217, 2218, 2580

PUBLISHERS DIRECTORY AND INDEX

SOARES Associates, 111 Teeter Rock Road, Trumbull, CT 06611: 146, 2139

Social Ecology Laboratory, Dept. of Psychiatry at Stanford University Medical Center, 3801 Miranda Avenue, Palo Alto, CA 94304: 1546

Society for New Guinea Psychological Research and Publications, P.O. Box 5008, Boroto, Papua, New Guinea: 1574

SOI Institute, 343 Richmond Street, El Segundo, CA 90245: 2320

Sound Apperception Test Distributor, 3505 Oakdale, Temple, TX 76502: 2240

South, John C., School of Business and Administration, Duquesne University, Pittsburgh, PA 15219: 819

Southern Illinois University Press, P.O. Box 3697, Carbondale, IL 62901: 1127

Southwestern Cooperative Educational Laboratory, 229 Truman N.E., Albuquerque, NM 87108: 2377, 2378

Special Child Publications, 4535 Union Bay Place NE, Seattle, WA 98105: 366, 644

Specialty Case Manufacturing Co., P.O. Box 495, Huntingdon Valley, PA 19006: 2537, 2539

Speech Pathology & Audiology, Pennsylvania State University, 110 Moore Building, University Park, PA 16802: 1071

Springer Publishing Co., Inc., 200 Park Avenue South, New York, NY 10003: 1916, 2079, 2322, 2588

Stanford University Press, Stanford, CA 94305: 2318

Stanwix House, Inc., 3020 Chartiers Avenue, Pittsburgh, PA 15204: 664, 1718, 2103, 2646

Statistical Publishing Society, 204/1 Barrackpore Trunk Road, Calcutta 35, India: 1615

Stein, Morris I., New York University, 6 Washington Place, Seventh Floor, New York, NY 10003: 2010, 2376, 2407

Stevens, Thurow & Associates, Inc., 100 West Monroe Street, Chicago, IL 60603: 467, 468, 469, 1177, 1892, 2309

Steward-Mortensen & Associates, 1080 Medford Road, Pasadena, CA 91107: 2310, 2311, 2312, 2313, 2314

Stoelting Co., 1350 S. Kostner Avenue, Chicago, IL 60623: 204a, 272, 300, 394, 410, 629, 745, 784, 904, 956, 1069, 1100, 1110, 1132, 1180, 1225, 1239, 1242, 1247, 1253, 1260, 1265, 1318, 1319, 1331, 1471, 1529, 1670, 1671, 1672, 1822, 1834, 1835, 1853a, 1878, 2101, 2125, 2200, 2219, 2229, 2237, 2315, 2319

Stogdill, Ralph M., 3658 Olentangy Blvd., Columbus, OH 43214: 225

Stone, LeRoy A., P.O. Box 395, Harpers Ferry, WV 25425: 1072

Stratton-Christian Press, Box 1055, University Place Station, Des Moines, IA 50311: 1226

Student Development Associates, 110 Crestwood Drive, Athens, GA 30605: 2330

Sunset Distributors, Department PM-1, 9200 Sunset, Suite 932, Los Angeles, CA 90069: 358

Swets North America, Inc., P.O. Box 517, Berwyn, PA 19312: 544, 1617, 2242

Swets Test Services, Heereweg 347B, 2161 CA LISSE, The Netherlands: 544, 1617, 2221, 2242

Tabin, Johanna Krout, 162 Park Avenue, Glencoe, IL 60022: 1179, 1790, 2381

TACA Development Fund, University of Missouri, 8001 Natural Bridge, St. Louis, MO 63121: 2423

TAV Selection System, 12807 Arminta St., North Hollywood, CA 91605: 2394

Taylor, Anne P., P.O. Box 603, Corrales, NM 87048: 2395

Teachers College Press, P.O. Box 1540, Hagerstown, MD 21740: 484, 771, 935, 1421, 1658, 2384

Teaching and Testing Resources, P.O. Box 77, Fortitude Valley, Qld. 4006, Australia: 564, 1536, 2047, 2048

Teaching Resources Corporation, 50 Pond Park Road, Hingham, MA 02043: 231, 295, 377, 378, 693, 906, 1266, 1307, 1332, 1896, 2472, 2509, 2566, 2611, 2639, 2640, 2665

Technisonic Studios, Inc., 1201 Brentwood Blvd., St. Louis, MO 63117: 230, 2040

T.E.D. Associates, 42 Lowell Road, Brookline, MA 02146: 2393

Teleometrics Int'l., 1755 Woodstead Court, The Woodlands, TX 77380: 383, 565, 1014, 1363, 1365, 1366, 1803, 1901, 2052, 2054, 2057, 2351, 2405, 2655

Test Agency, Cournswood House, North Dean, High Wycombe, Bucks, England 3384: 1119, 1327, 2175

Test Analysis and Development Corporation, 2400 Park Lane Drive, Boulder, CO 80301: 407, 563, 620, 2080, 2135

Test of Musicality, 2515 Arkansas, Lawrence, KS 66044: 2451

Thomas (Charles C), Publisher, 2600 South First Street, Springfield, IL 62717: 1353, 2404

Thompson, Clem W., Mankato State College, Mankato, MN 56001: 2498

Time, Inc., Time and Life Bldg., Rockefeller Center, New York, NY 10020: 2503, 2504

Titmus Optical Co., Inc., Petersburg, VA 23803: 2506

Touliatos, John, Division of Family and Child Studies, Texas Christian University, Fort Worth, TX 76129: 1857

Tracor, Inc., 6500 Tracor Lane, Austin, TX 78721: 2514

Trademark Design Products, Inc., P.O. Box 2010, Boca Raton, FL 33432: 1426

Twitchell-Allen, Doris, RFD 1, Box 272, Ellsworth, ME 04605: 2526

Union College Character Research Project, 207 State Street, Schenectady, NY 12305: 238

United Cerebral Palsy of the Bluegrass, P.O. Box 8003, 465 Springhill Drive, Lexington, KY 40503: 1322

United States Government Printing Office, U.S. Employment Service, U.S. Department of Labor, Washington, DC 20213: 1163, 2535, 2536, 2537, 2538

US Military Enlistment Processing Command, Dr. William W. Graham, Technical Advisor, Attn: MEPCT-0, Fort Sheridan, IL 60037: 202

University Associates, Inc., P.O. Box 26240, 8517 Production Avenue, San Diego, CA 92126: 1222, 2369

University Book Store, Purdue University, Center for Instructional Services, Engineering Administration Building, West Lafayette, IN 47907: 1055, 1855, 1936, 1937, 1940, 1941, 1942, 1943, 1944, 1945, 1946, 1947, 1950, 1951, 1952, 1953, 1954, 1955, 1956, 1957, 1958, 1959

University Counseling Center, University of Maryland, Shoemaker Hall, College Park, MD 20742: 1932, 2203

University of Alberta, 6-102 Education North, Edmonton, Alberta, Canada T6G 2G5: 151

University of British Columbia Bookstore, Vancouver 8, British Columbia, Canada: 2542, 2577
University of California Press, 2223 Fulton Street, Berkeley, CA 94720: 969
University of Georgia, College of Education, Division for the Education of Exceptional Children, Athens, GA 30602: 224
University of Illinois Press, Box 5081, Station A, Champaign, IL 61820: 299, 1126
University of Maryland, University Counseling Center, College Park, MD 20742: 792
University of Minnesota Press, 2037 University Avenue S.E., Minneapolis, MN 55414: 155, 1498, 1507, 1512, 1513
University of New England, The University of New England Publishing Unit, Armidale, N.S.W. 2351, Australia: 1070
University of Washington Press, Seattle, WA 98105: 2108, 2159
University Park Press, 300 No. Charles St., Baltimore, MD 21201: 2017
University Press of America, P.O. Box 19101, Washington, DC 20036: 1002
Village Book Cellar, 308 West State Street, West Lafayette, IN 47906: 1293
Vocational and Rehabilitation Research Institute, 2500 University Drive N.W., Calgary, Alberta, T2N 1N4, Canada: 112
Vocational Guidance Service, 8845 Sheridan Drive, Williamsville, NY 14221: 402
Vocational Instructional Materials Laboratory, Ohio State University, 112 Townshend Hall, 1885 Neil Avenue, Columbus, OH 43210: 1678, 1679, 1680, 1681, 1682, 1683, 1684, 1685, 1686, 1687, 1688, 1689, 1690, 1691, 1692, 1693, 1694, 1695, 1696, 1697, 1698, 1699, 1700, 1701, 1702, 1703, 1704, 1705, 1706, 1707, 1708, 1709, 1710, 1711, 1713, 1715, 1719, 1721, 1722
Vocational Psychology Research, N620 Elliott Hall, University of Minnesota, 75 East River Road, Minneapolis, MN 55455: 1495, 1497, 1508, 1509
Waetjen, Walter B., Cleveland State University, Cleveland, OH 44115: 2132
Wagner, Mazie Earle, 500 Klein Road, Buffalo, NY 14221: 326
Walch, J. Weston, P.O. Box 658, Portland, ME 04104: 2671
Walker Educational Book Corporation, 720 Fifth Avenue, New York, NY 10019: 2111
WARD Aircraft Printing Co., 707 Phillips Avenue, Toledo, OH 43612: 1714

Warwick Products Co., 7909 Rockside Road, Cleveland, OH 44131: 2537, 2539
Washington Pre-College Testing Program (The), 1400 N.E. Campus Parkway, Room 530, University of Washington, PA-25, Seattle, WA 98195: 2589
Webster Division, McGraw-Hill Book Co., 1221 Avenue of the Americas, New York, NY 10020: 2196
West Virginia Rehabilitation Research and Training Center, No. 1 Dunbar Plaza, Suite E, Dunbar, WV 25064: 1134, 2572
Western Psychological Services, 12031 Wilshire Blvd., Los Angeles, CA 90025: 152, 183, 200, 239, 280d, 280g, 337, 349, 350, 392, 647, 670, 751, 776, 793, 796, 897, 908, 909, 912, 937, 1047, 1053, 1109, 1148, 1169, 1249, 1297, 1343, 1346, 1351, 1369, 1374, 1376, 1489, 1537, 1742, 1757, 1796, 1830, 1882, 1930, 1933, 1971, 2022, 2023, 2024, 2083, 2201, 2213, 2220, 2243, 2244, 2296, 2345, 2380, 2433, 2502, 2552, 2565, 2570, 2576, 2582, 2583, 2584, 2585, 2616, 2617, 2620, 2632
Westwood Press, 770 Broadway, 3rd Floor, New York, NY 10003: 1993A
William, Lynde & Williams, Inc., 401 Painesville Center, 153 E. Erie Street, Painesville, OH 44077: 2636
Williams (Robert L.) & Associates, Inc., Educational & Psychological Services, 6372 Delmar Blvd., St. Louis, MO 63130: 296, 2492, 2626
Winch (B. L.) & Associates, 45 Hitching Post Dr., Bldg. 2, Rolling Hills Estate, CA 90274: 145, 247, 248, 249
Wonderlic (E. F.) & Associates, Inc., P.O. Box 7, Northfield, IL 60093: 334, 1064, 1218, 2305, 2528, 2637, 2638
Woolner, Rosestelle B., 3551 Aurora Circle, Memphis, TN 38111: 1879
Word Making Productions, 70 West Louise Ave., Salt Lake City, UT 84115: 1824
Wyman, Earl J., University of California, Institute of Industrial Relations, Berkeley, CA 94720: 2357, 2358, 2360
Zalk, Sue R., Hunter College of The City University of New York, 695 Park Avenue, New York, NY 10021: 1241
Zaner-Bloser Co., 823 Church St., Homesdale, PA 18431: 856
Zenetron, Inc., 6501 W. Grand Avenue, Chicago, IL 60635: 2550
Zenith Hearing Instrument Corporation, 6501 West Grand Avenue, Chicago, IL 60635: 916, 2668, 2669
Zweig (Richard L.) Associates, Inc., 1711 McGaw Avenue, Irvine, CA 92714: 913, 914, 915

INDEX OF NAMES

This analytical index indicates whether a citation refers to authorship of a test, a test review, an excerpted review, or a reference dealing with a specific test. Numbers refer to test entries, not to pages. The abbreviations and numbers following the names may be interpreted thus: "test, 168" indicates authorship of test 168; "rev, 472" authorship of a review of test 472; "exc, 368" authorship of an excerpted review of test 368; and "ref, 1275(50)," authorship of reference number 50 for test 1275.

Aaron, I. E.: rev, 309, 929, 1859, 1999, 2033, 2034
Aaron, P. G.: ref, 2602(1726)
Abadzi, H.: ref, 1484(14), 2441(38)
Abartis, C.: ref, 1568(140)
Abbas, K. A.: ref, 639(52)
Abbate, M. S.: test, 1718
Abbott, K.: ref, 2029(211)
Abdel–Halim, A. A.: ref, 2300(378)
Abel, G. G.: ref, 859(842)
Abell, E. L.: exc, 344, 2518
Abeloff, M. D.: ref, 2100(4)
Abelsohn, D. S.: ref, 874(47), 2208(1560)
Abidin, R. R.: ref, 932(117), 1831(201), 2286(342)
Abikoff, H.: ref, 2602(1588)
Abraham, T.: ref, 2620(5)
Abrahams, N. M.: ref 2318(1599)
Abrahamson, D. S.: ref, 280(1022, 1099), 363(3), 400(123), 582(3), 751(2), 770(4), 932(54), 1109(17), 1126(648), 1229(78), 1233(211), 2030(4942), 2086(12), 2286(272), 2289(1594, 1696), 2557(209)
Abramowitz, C. V.: ref, 2037(147)
Abramowitz, S. I.: ref, 883(104), 2037(147)
Abrams, A. A.: ref, 1904(76)
Abrams, A. I.: ref, 1473(162, 182), 1479(360), 1914(782, 819), 2608(224)
Abrams, D.: ref, 354(1430), 681(33)
Abrams, D. B.: ref, 883(91, 112), 2300(453, 543)
Abrams, L.: ref, 1498(5310)
Abrams, R.: ref, 2598(1809)
Abrams, R. M.: test, 2259
Abramson, L. M.: ref, 780(1642)
Abramson, L. Y.: ref, 1547(297, 313, 345), 2179(210)
Abramson, P. R.: ref, 780(1642)

Abrass, I.: ref, 859(880), 1789(702)
Abroms, K. I.: ref, 2218(157)
Achorn, E.: ref, 859(772)
Achterberg, G.: ref, 280(1095), 2602(1825), 2621(309)
Ackenstein, G.: ref, 928(5), 2281(3)
Ackerman, A.: ref, 2322(9)
Ackerman, P. T.: ref, 1007(27, 36, 41), 1229(98, 105), 2602(1589, 1885, 2032, 2033, 2152), 2621(219, 329, 394, 395, 431)
Ackles, P.: ref, 1969(98)
Ackrill, P.: ref, 1513(31)
Acredolo, L.: ref, 1771(653)
Acree, N. J.: ref, 1498(5148)
Acuff, F. G.: ref, 1960(73)
Adair, A.: ref, 1831(152), 2621(303)
Adair, F. L.: rev, 1499, 1500, 1501
Adair, N.: test, 7
Adamowicz, J. K.: ref, 732(397), 898(2), 1970(12, 13)
Adams, A. J.: ref, 780(1643)
Adams, C. R.: test, 1784; rev, 659, 1376, 2169
Adams, D.: ref, 2217(118), 2269(445), 2289(1645), 2602(1703)
Adams, D. E.: ref, 116(537)
Adams, D. R.: ref, 354(1544)
Adams, E. F.: ref, 1295(283), 1296(171)
Adams, G. S.: rev, 247, 310, 2488
Adams, H. E.: ref, 681(55), 1498(5373)
Adams, I. G.: ref, 859(933)
Adams, J.: ref, 1771(585)
Adams, K.: ref, 1498(5446), 2598(1583)
Adams, K. M.: ref, 1498(5268), 2598(1675)
Adams, M.: ref, 1126(706), 2598(1641), 2602(1954)
Adams, M. F.: rev, 246, 2670
Adams, M. L.: ref, 2598(1633), 2608(217)

Adams, P. L.: ref, 1498(5564, 5565)
Adams, R. B.: test, 1083, 1093
Adams, R. H.: test, 842
Adams, R. L.: ref, 1922(16), 2598(1294)
Adams, V. M.: ref, 501(863), 1013(76, 85, 108), 1077(64, 65, 66, 75), 1257(142, 143)
Adamson, G.: test, 247, 248, 249, 808, 919; ref, 919(1)
Adcock, C. J.: rev, 900, 1233, 1498, 2178, 2208, 2491
Adcock, S.: ref, 941(23, 34), 1883(33, 69)
Addicott, M. A.: test, 2590
Adebimpe, V. R.: ref, 1498(5404)
Adelaja, O.: ref, 860(87)
Adelman, H.: ref, 280(1027), 344(165), 585(2), 2608(177)
Adelstein, D. M.: ref, 374(205)
Aden, R. C.: test, 115
Ader, D. N.: ref, 1883(87)
Aderman, M.: ref, 1233(227), 1300(122)
Adesso, V.: ref, 859(917), 2300(541)
Adesso, V. J.: ref, 2179(200)
Adey, P.: test, 641
Adi, H.: ref, 2179(232)
Adkins, D. C.: rev, 799, 1352, 2261, 2270
Adkinson, D. R.: test, 1169
Adler, J. M.: ref, 2030(5010), 2491(2048)
Adrian, M.: ref, 2165(26), 2298(1)
Affleck, J. Q.: test, 2532
Agard, F. B.: rev, 927
Agarwal, A.: ref, 2491(2075)
Agor, B. J.: ref, 1128(1)
Agrawal, A.: ref, 2491(2050)
Agren, G.: ref, 1005(26), 1462(155)
Aguanno, J. C.: ref, 621(2, 5)
Ahammer, I. M.: ref, 1203(7)
Ahern, E. H.: ref, 590(385), 2160(71)
Ahlfors, U. G.: ref, 1655(118)
Ahlgren, A.: ref, 354(1431), 1073(119)
Ahluwalia, S. P.: test, 2397
Ahmad, N.: ref, 2121(67)
Ahmann, J. S.: rev, 551, 620, 2474
Ahmed, S. M. S.: ref, 1197(303)
Ahr, A. E.: test, 150, 1764, 2106, 2107
Ahrens, J. B.: test, 369
Ahsen, A.: test, 786
Aickin, M.: ref, 609(201), 1498(5073)
Aiken, M.: test, 1804
Aiken, P. A.: ref, 681(64)
Airasian, P. W.: rev, 247, 582
Aitken, R. C. B.: ref, 859(940), 2208(1676)
Akamatsu, T. J.: ref, 2300(334)
Akers, T. K.: ref, 1498(5035)
Alampur, A. G.: ref, 1883(45)
Albaum, G.: ref, 116(521, 522)
Albert, R. E.: ref, 1498(5328)
Albert, R. S.: ref, 354(1515), 2155(10), 2343(1049), 2581(335)
Albert, S.: ref, 2030(5049)
Alberts, N. F.: test, 15, 1584, 2076, 2149
Albin, J. B.: test, 782
Albright, L. E.: rev, 1495, 1508, 2469, 2617
Alcorn, J. D.: ref, 859(836), 1754(73), 2300(388), 2461(8)
Alden, L.: ref, 1351(25), 1933(18), 2286(322), 2587(36, 37), 2621(362)
Alderman, D. L.: ref, 500(58), 501(876, 918), 1866(37)

Alderson, J. C.: rev, 479
Aldridge, W. S.: ref, 264(2)
Aleamoni, L. M.: test, 1125; rev, 411, 2337; ref, 76(600), 501(813), 590(379)
Alesandrini, K. L.: ref, 2598(1810)
Alexander, A. B.: ref, 2300(566)
Alexander, C. F.: ref, 1191(119)
Alexander, D. G.: ref, 551(18, 29)
Alexander, J. W.: ref, 270(79)
Alexander, K. L.: ref, 501(919), 590(380, 387), 1866(34), 2160(57, 78)
Alexander, R. A.: ref, 794(364), 1013(78, 86, 119), 1053(68)
Alexander, R. S.: ref, 1498(5299)
Alf, E. F.: ref, 195(2), 558(64)
Alford, D. W.: ref, 2621(316)
Algozzine, B.: ref, 551(48), 2602(2112)
Algozzine, R.: ref, 6(50), 1192(181), 2602(1858), 2621(317)
Alheidt, P.: ref, 344(177), 483(32), 2030(5050)
Alichne, M. C.: ref, 501(920), 949(12), 1754(115), 2366(202), 2370(18)
Aliferis, J.: test, 155
Aliotti, N. C.: ref, 280(1051), 1462(125)
Alkalay, I.: ref, 1498(5566)
Alker, H. A.: rev, 1498, 1538, 1794; ref, 116(523), 354(1383, 1432), 2208(1517)
Allain, A. N.: ref, 116(572), 1498(5374, 5375, 5536, 5712, 5713), 1914(788, 789), 2179(219, 220, 248)
Allard, J. M.: test, 2580
Alleman, S. A.: exc, 1899
Allen, A. C.: ref, 2289(1764)
Allen, D. A.: exc, 2163
Allen, D. R.: ref, 1170(231)
Allen, D. V.: ref, 378(17), 1622(53), 1851(35), 2472(28)
Allen, G. J.: ref, 883(89)
Allen, J.: test, 2634
Allen, J. E.: ref, 501(906)
Allen, J. R.: ref, 270(63), 338(8), 1771(543), 2289(1615), 2257(214), 2602(1646), 2608(182)
Allen, L.: ref, 1531(290), 2413(645)
Allen, L. M.: ref, 2289(1721)
Allen, M.: ref, 1473(191), 1479(361)
Allen, M. J.: ref, 794(385), 1257(115)
Allen, R.: ref, 1498(5551)
Allen, R. E.: ref, 1765(7)
Allen, R. H.: ref, 677(1), 1498(5120, 5293, 5405, 5567)
Allen, R. M.: rev, 235, 327; ref, 2602(1590), 2621(220)
Alley, G. R.: ref, 2260(47), 2598(1738), 2602(2060)
Allington, R. L.: exc, 2641; ref, 719(27), 766(21), 958(40), 1007(12), 1769(98), 1771(771), 2641(9, 13)
Allison, E. E.: exc, 2608
Allman, T. W.: ref, 1126(750)
Alloway, W. J.: ref, 2134(122), 2581(332)
Alloy, L. B.: ref, 1547(297, 345)
Allport, G. W.: test, 2343, 2344
Allred, G. H.: ref, 1171(6)
Allred, R. A.: test, 1579
Ally, G.: ref, 859(918)
Almagor, M.: ref, 1498(5755)
Almeida, E.: ref, 1477(15)
Almond, P. J.: test, 234
Alnot, S. D.: test, 1193

INDEX OF NAMES

Alpaugh, P. K.: ref, 243(114), 1257(104), 1403(23), 1404(1), 1580(1), 1840(24), 2598(1295)
Alpern, G. D.: test, 698
Alpert, M.: ref, 280(1131), 2030(5052), 2598(1296, 1680)
Alpiner, J. G.: ref, 2015(213)
Als, H.: ref, 311(20)
Alston, H. L.: ref, 1192(209, 210), 2320(1, 2), 2581(307)
Altekruse, M. K.: ref, 1531(292)
Alterman, A. I.: ref, 1498(5210, 5228), 1969(89), 2179(211)
Altmaier, E. M.: ref, 2300(578), 2374(198)
Altmann, H.: ref, 2413(587)
Altschuld, J. W.: ref, 1719(3), 2181(21)
Altshuler, K. Z.: ref, 1853(274), 2030(4981)
Altshuler, L.: ref, 2602(2160), 2641(18)
Altus, W. D.: rev, 923; exc, 1853
Alvares, K. M.: ref, 1295(286)
Alverman, D. E.: ref, 2292(31)
Alwin, D. F.: ref, 643(133), 1341(177)
Aman, M. G.: ref, 1831(200)
Amanat, E.: ref, 703(7)
Amante, D.: ref, 280(1021), 643(127)
Amatora, M.: test, 727
Amatora, S. M.: test, 1797
Ambron, S. R.: rev, 404
Ambujadevi, K. R.: ref, 270(116)
Amburn, E.: test, 813, 1144
AMEG Commission on Sex Bias in Measurement: ref, 76(585), 1051(13), 1269(25), 1270(74), 1495(78), 1720(32), 2318(1522)
Amenson, C. S.: ref, 681(38), 1498(5304, 5735)
Ament, M. E.: ref, 953(14)
American Association of Teachers of German: test, 1559
American Association of University Professors: test, 864
American Chemical Society: test, 56, 57, 58, 59, 60, 61, 62, 63, 64, 65, 66, 67, 68, 69, 70, 71, 72, 73, 74, 75
American College Testing Program: test, 76, 77, 78, 79, 80, 81, 82, 83, 84, 85, 86, 87, 88, 89, 90, 91, 92, 93, 94, 95, 96, 97, 98, 99, 100, 101, 102, 103, 104, 105, 106, 107, 108, 2575
American Guidance Service: test, 1511
American Institutes for Research: test, 1576, 1839
American Optical Corporation: test, 185, 1921
American Testronics: test, 1084, 1085, 1086, 1087, 1088, 1089, 1090, 1091, 1092, 1094, 1095, 1096, 1097, 1098
Amerikaner, M.: ref, 2343(1042)
Amerman, J. D.: ref, 961(1), 2602(1799), 2608(203)
Amernic, J.: ref, 2134(138, 142)
Amerson, V. M.: rev, 332
Ames, C.: ref, 1192(164, 185), 1831(133, 157)
Ames, L. B.: test, 952, 953; ref, 953(12)
Ames, R.: ref, 818(6), 1192(164)
Ames, S. G.: ref, 2286(270), 2293(8)
Ames, T.: test, 1354
Ames, W. S.: ref, 1126(714, 715)
Amin, M. E.: ref, 1013(62)
Amini, F.: ref, 1170(230)
Amir, Y.: ref, 2269(434), 2413(583)
Ammons, C. H.: test, 1969; exc, 6, 535, 544, 955, 1347, 1424, 1874, 1877, 2243, 2285, 2393, 2608; ref, 1020(20), 1123(59), 1919(41)
Ammons, F.: ref, 2413(691)

Ammons, H. S.: test, 923
Ammons, P.: ref, 2413(691)
Ammons, R. B.: test, 923, 1969, 2571; exc, 6, 535, 544, 1347, 1424, 2393; ref, 1020(20), 1123(59), 1919(41)
Amolsch, T. J.: ref, 2598(1474)
Amos, S. P.: ref, 354(1433), 2030(5051)
Amuso, K. F.: ref, 2179(233), 2300(506), 2587(46)
Anadon, M.: ref, 76(644)
Ananth, J.: ref, 1197(293), 1419(686)
Anastasi, A.: rev, 111, 400, 691, 964, 1044, 1073, 1798, 2269, 2500, 2546, 2623
Anastasiow, M.: ref, 501(788)
Anastasiow, N.: rev, 1282
Anastasiow, N. J.: rev, 1934; ref, 1531(279)
Anchin, J. C.: test, 1130; ref, 1130(1)
Ancoli, S.: ref, 558(52), 780(1644)
Anderegg, T.: ref, 2621(341)
Anderhalter, O. F.: test, 726, 2325; rev, 576, 1477
Anders, T. F.: ref, 270(71), 311(19)
Andersen, M.: ref, 1319(81), 2598(1605)
Andersen, S. M.: ref, 116(623), 157(154)
Andersen, V. R.: test, 2465
Anderson, B.: ref, 280(1159), 2602(2153)
Anderson, B. J.: ref, 1233(221), 2413(637)
Anderson, B. L.: ref, 2537(544), 2607(127)
Anderson, C. C.: ref, 859(840), 1341(165), 2288(81)
Anderson, C. J.: ref, 311(42)
Anderson, C. V.: rev, 2550
Anderson, C. W.: ref, 344(181)
Anderson, D.: ref, 1498(5549), 2179(229)
Anderson, D. E.: ref, 1771(781)
Anderson, D. R.: ref, 559(47)
Anderson, D. S.: test, 2328
Anderson, G. V.: exc, 2613
Anderson, H. L.: ref, 2208(1522)
Anderson, H. N.: ref, 859(933), 2218(147), 2602(1921)
Anderson, H. R.: rev, 487, 508, 803, 2232; ref, 1052(4), 1771(768), 2602(2145), 2621(427)
Anderson, I. H.: rev, 1479
Anderson, J.: test, 929
Anderson, J. D.: ref, 2472(20)
Anderson, J. M.: rev, 2602
Anderson, L. D.: test, 2015
Anderson, L. M.: ref, 344(181), 1473(170), 1478(75), 1479(341, 367)
Anderson, L. T.: ref, 2598(1296)
Anderson, L. W.: ref, 1341(166)
Anderson, M. C.: ref, 1257(116)
Anderson, R.: ref, 2598(1418)
Anderson, R. C.: ref, 1257(116)
Anderson, R. E.: ref, 486(312)
Anderson, R. G.: test, 1272
Anderson, R. L.: ref, 7(6), 701(67), 2218(152)
Anderson, R. M.: test, 540
Anderson, R. P.: rev, 550, 2665
Anderson, S. A.: ref, 1372(11)
Anderson, T. H.: ref, 1257(117)
Anderson, W. P.: ref, 1498(5406)
Anderson, W. R.: ref, 1498(5164, 5493)
Anderson, W. W.: ref, 1579(5)
Andersson, K. E.: rev, 61, 2510; ref, 935(33), 2602(1994), 2621(379)
Andert, J. N.: ref, 280(1062), 2289(1650), 2598(1313, 1419)
Ando, H.: ref, 2602(1859)

Andrade, R. D.: test, 2426
Andre, M. E. D. A.: ref, 1257(117)
Andre, T.: ref, 1257(155)
Andreasen, N. C.: ref, 859(841), 1240(58)
Andreewsky, E.: ref, 1914(881)
Andreoli, K. G.: ref, 2413(692)
Andres, D.: ref, 357(506, 511, 512, 519), 363(7), 1201(75, 77, 78), 2608(180, 193, 214)
Andres, J.: ref, 2602(1689)
Andres, J. R.: ref, 2602(1816)
Andrew, D. M.: test, 1493
Andrew, E. M.: ref, 381(70), 2289(1754)
Andrew, J. M.: ref, 2390(6), 2598(1420), 2602(1727), 2621(274)
Andrew, L. P.: ref, 280(1073), 1126(692), 2602(1740)
Andrews, D. A.: ref, 1498(5088)
Andrews, G.: ref, 911(5), 941(21, 26, 27, 41), 1914(861)
Andrews, J.: ref, 1771(783)
Andrews, J. V.: ref, 2208(1558)
Andrews, L.: ref, 859(925)
Andrews, M.: test, 2430
Andrews, P. M.: ref, 780(1667)
Andrews, R.: ref, 270(114, 129)
Andrews, R. H.: ref, 1498(5679), 1765(13)
Andrews, R. J.: test, 564, 1536, 2047, 2048; ref, 270(148)
Andrews, T. F.: test, 805
Andruss, H. A.: rev, 304
Andry, R. G.: exc, 321
Andy, O. J.: ref, 2607(137)
Angelo, J. K. B.: ref, 1568(141), 2244(38), 2621(380)
Angrist, B.: ref, 113(25)
Angrist, B. M.: ref, 1655(99)
Angstadt, A.: ref, 2602(1860)
Aniloff, L.: ref, 1831(114)
Aniskiewicz, A. S.: ref, 1498(5407)
Annis, D. B.: ref, 2594(200)
Annis, H. M.: ref, 2629(108)
Annis, L.: ref, 1257(118)
Annis, L. F.: ref, 1013(77), 2594(200)
Annis, L. V.: ref, 2557(219)
Anolik, S. A.: ref, 1798(247)
Ansara, A. S.: test, 2110
Ansari, A.: exc, 2236
Ansink, B. J.: ref, 280(1125), 2602(1972)
Ansolabehere, E. M.: ref, 964(484)
Anthony, A.: test, 1153
Anthony, J.: test, 874
Anthony, S. E.: ref, 1789(686)
Anthony, W. Z.: ref, 2598(1676)
Antill, J. K.: ref, 354(1516), 558(71), 1798(248, 272)
Anwar, F.: ref, 534(108, 109)
Apfel, N.: ref, 270(110)
Apfeldorf, M.: ref, 116(574), 1498(5229, 5736)
Apolloni, T.: ref, 2289(1593)
Aponte, C.: ref, 1498(5167)
Apostol, R. A.: ref, 2208(1516)
Appel, P.: ref, 2300(356)
Applebaum, A. S.: ref, 270(75), 678(19), 1771(515), 2602(1591, 1836, 2136)
Appelbaum, M. I.: ref, 1192(217), 2413(647)
Appelyard, R.: ref, 149(9)
Applebarth, D. A.: ref, 681(39)
Appleyard, R.: ref, 972(9)

Apprich, R. V.: ref, 374(217)
April, R. S.: ref, 283(134), 1513(20), 1771(516), 1914(702), 1948(93), 2598(1297)
Aquino, N. S.: ref, 2300(454), 2441(35)
Arad, R.: ref, 2208(1689)
Aram, D. M.: ref, 2286(336)
Aranya, N.: ref, 2134(138, 142)
Arbel, T.: ref, 311(36)
Arbit, J.: ref, 226(182), 280(1063), 1007(40), 1462(127), 1914(873), 2598(1421), 2602(2149), 2607(150, 173), 2621(430)
Archer, R. B.: ref, 2300(379)
Archer, R. P.: ref, 1498(5230, 5375, 5408, 5475, 5536, 5537, 5568, 5712), 2179(220, 233, 248), 2300(455, 457, 505, 506), 2587(46), 2598(1554), 2602(1861)
Arcia, M. A.: ref, 374(219), 501(913), 1473(210), 1478(77), 1754(114)
Arcuri, A. F.: ref, 116(563, 565)
Ardaiolo, F. P.: ref, 1726(367)
Arduino, N. L.: ref, 381(70), 2289(1754)
Arenberg, D.: ref, 283(135, 141), 1046(576, 582, 583), 2598(1422)
Arend, R. A.: ref, 270(90), 883(75)
Argulewicz, E. N.: ref, 2512(609)
Ariagno, R. L.: ref, 1471(54), 2289(1748)
Arick, J. R.: test, 234
Arkin, R. M.: ref, 1547(320)
Arkowitz, H.: ref, 859(911)
Arlin, M.: test, 201; ref, 201(2, 3), 932(70)
Arlt, P. B.: test, 1124
Arman, A.: ref, 643(128)
Armbruster, G.: ref, 1498(5254), 2030(4987)
Armbruster, G. L.: ref, 2030(4988)
Armenakis, A. A.: ref, 116(545, 603), 1508(123)
Armenia, J. W.: test, 687
Armentrout, D. P.: ref, 2413(638)
Armentrout, J. A.: rev, 873; ref, 280(1076), 354(1384), 958(46), 1498(5231), 2602(1761, 1811), 2621(299)
Armstrong, G.: ref, 2512(575), 2598(1361)
Armstrong, H. E.: ref, 609(220)
Armstrong, J. M.: ref, 573(18), 1473(212), 2015(212), 2286(343)
Arndt, S.: ref, 6(82), 1257(119), 2598(1423)
Arndt, W. B.: ref, 1126(646, 662, 675), 1622(30, 31), 1894(3), 2103(6, 8), 2412(34, 36), 2425(1), 2621(221)
Arnold, B. R.: ref, 2300(380)
Arnold, D. L.: rev, 2326
Arnold, G. F.: rev, 1319
Arnold, L.: ref, 1555(324), 2602(2163)
Arnold, L. E.: ref, 280(1064, 1065), 2111(1), 2602(1592), 2621(222)
Arnold, L. S.: ref, 1498(5036, 5689), 1914(862), 2598(1770)
Arnold, M. R.: ref, 290(6)
Arnold, P.: ref, 9(13), 466(3), 1371(262), 2554(13)
Arnold, P. D.: test, 2267
Aron, A.: ref, 354(1557), 653(171)
Aronoff, J.: ref, 354(1558), 780(1707)
Aronow, E.: ref, 1106(359), 2030(5021)
Aronson, A. E.: ref, 2645(3)
Aronson, M.: ref, 1655(99)
Arrindell, W. A.: ref, 883(105), 2100(7)
Arthur, G.: test, 204, 1319
Artley, A. S.: test, 1185

INDEX OF NAMES

Artner, J.: ref, 280(1041), 2289(1622), 2602(1661), 2621(249)
Artwohl, A.: ref, 1498(5409)
Arvey, R. D.: ref, 116(549, 583, 629), 1508(112, 122, 129, 131), 1855(18, 29), 2318(1553, 1574, 1617)
Arzi, Y.: ref, 2269(434), 2413(583)
Asarnow, R. F.: ref, 1436(13), 1498(5654), 1923(19), 2300(468), 2598(1424, 1425, 1426)
Asato, H.: ref, 6(83)
Asbury, C. A.: ref, 1473(144), 1479(324), 1771(586), 2269(447)
Asch, P. A. S.: ref, 2413(631)
Ascough, J. C.: ref, 859(769)
Ash, D. G.: ref, 1498(5271), 2208(1575)
Ash, R. A.: ref, 1855(28)
Ash, T.: ref, 2602(1601, 1602, 2006)
Ashby, S.: ref, 270(93)
Ashcroft, S. C.: ref, 2208(1690)
Ashe, M.: ref, 1754(95), 2621(360)
Ashem, B.: ref, 1424(33)
Asher, S. R.: ref, 2325(2)
Ashford, T. A.: rev, 127
Ashley, L.: ref, 609(199)
Ashman, A. F.: ref, 1462(149), 1853(289), 2491(2076), 2602(1995)
Ashmore, L.: rev, 1723, 2425
Ashmore, L. L.: ref, 212(7), 378(14), 1771(729)
Ashmore, R. J.: ref, 280(1129, 1151), 1473(208), 2602(1996), 2621(381)
Ashour, A.: ref, 1883(88)
Ashton, J.: ref, 270(64), 311(17)
Ashton, R.: ref, 2598(1729)
Askov, E.: test, 2634, 2635
Askov, E. N.: ref, 1955(106, 108, 110, 111, 112), 2634(4)
Asso, D.: ref, 1914(824)
Associates for Research in Behavior, Inc.: test, 2579
Association of American Medical Colleges: test, 1576
Assor, A.: ref, 354(1558), 780(1707)
Astbury, J. A.: ref, 2300(550)
Asthana, H.: ref, 2343(1048)
Astilla, E.: ref, 354(1555), 1077(70, 71, 83), 1754(111, 112, 113)
Astin, A. W.: test, 572, 2333; rev, 506, 2318
Atanasoff, G. E.: ref, 2134(124)
Atchison, M. J.: ref, 932(91)
Athanason, J. A.: ref, 2581(344)
Atkeson, B. M.: ref, 1904(125)
Atkin, R.: ref, 590(368, 369), 2160(49, 50)
Atkins, A.: ref, 2030(4992)
Atkins, A. L.: ref, 665(50), 883(100), 1077(69), 1106(372), 1817(3)
Atkins, H. G.: ref, 283(159, 160), 1498(5762), 1914(891)
Atkinson, B. L.: ref, 6(48)
Atkinson, H.: ref, 1904(76)
Atkinson, J.: test, 746, 1435
Atsaides, J. P.: ref, 1498(5037)
Attarian, P. J.: ref, 2134(103)
Attewell, P. A.: ref, 354(1404), 1106(361), 1853(270), 1904(58, 59)
Attwood, M.: test, 755
Atwell, B.: ref, 2387(6), 2602(2138)
Atwell, C. W.: ref, 270(96), 1331(40)
Au, K. H.: ref, 2608(212)

Audiologic Services and Southwest School for the Hearing Impaired, Office of the Los Angeles County Superintendent of Schools: test, 2424
Auerbach, J.: ref, 270(153), 311(45)
Auerbach, S.: ref, 2300(381)
Auerbach, S. M.: ref, 1498(5251), 1771(524)
Aufseeser, C. L.: ref, 1424(86)
Aughton, M. E.: ref, 1485(77), 1914(833), 2598(1691), 2607(191)
August, G. J.: ref, 1341(167), 1831(115, 134), 2598(1677), 2602(2154), 2608(242), 2621(432)
Auld, F.: ref, 1933(16), 2620(9)
Ault, R. L.: ref, 302(25)
Aurora, R.: ref, 653(167), 2491(2091)
Ausberger, C.: test, 2385, 2386
Auster, M.: ref, 1969(98)
Austin, A.: ref, 346(106)
Austin, J. D.: ref, 501(844, 877)
Austin, J. J.: test, 2090
Austin, M. C.: rev, 1371
Austin, M. F.: ref, 1547(346), 1798(300)
Australian Council for Educational Research: test, 19, 20, 25, 26, 29, 30, 32, 36, 37, 38, 40, 43, 46, 47, 232
Auvenshine, C. D.: test, 355, 1499
Avakian, M.: ref, 1224(7)
Aved, B. M.: ref, 609(215)
Aver, M.: ref, 588(9), 2288(82)
Averbach, S. M.: ref, 1106(357), 2300(335)
Averett, M.: ref, 354(1385), 859(721)
Averill, M.: ref, 1351(202), 1914(896)
Aviezer, Y.: ref, 280(1130), 1272(137)
Avila, L.: ref, 1073(118)
Avila, V.: ref, 251(1), 290(9), 1771(754)
Aviram, O.: ref, 2413(646), 2491(2058)
Avirett, P.: test, 839
Avolio, B. J.: ref, 1013(78, 119), 1053(67)
Awvenshine, A. A.: test, 1322
Ayabe, H. I.: ref, 1484(9), 2260(27)
Ayer, G. W.: rev, 139, 140
Ayers, J. B.: ref, 76(623), 995(131), 1625(104), 2441(30)
Ayers, J. D.: rev, 559, 1329, 2058, 2249, 2250
Ayers, J. L.: ref, 1498(5194, 5309, 5379, 5539), 2598(1659)
Aylward, G. P.: ref, 270(131), 311(34)
Ayrer, J.: ref, 344(137)
Ayres, A. J.: test, 2243, 2244; ref, 905(3, 4, 5), 1126(647, 684), 1771(711), 2218(6, 9), 2244(24, 25, 26, 29), 2289(1651), 2602(1728), 2621(223, 224, 275)
Azen, C. G.: ref, 1126(776), 1371(261), 2289(1779), 2598(1814)
Azen, S. P.: ref, 270(80)
Azuma, H.: ref, 1479(346, 365), 1771(649), 2598(1577, 1724), 2602(1882, 2049)
Baade, L. E.: ref, 1479(373, 377), 2602(2031)
Babad, E. Y.: ref, 116(581), 472(19), 794(411), 964(492), 2602(1593), 2621(225)
Babcock, S. D.: ref, 780(1703)
Baber, W. C.: ref, 1508(130)
Babich, J. M.: ref, 1547(300), 2208(1606)
Babigian, H. M.: ref, 645(12), 1197(286)
Babl, J. D.: ref, 354(1477)
Babladelis, G.: ref, 890(330)
Baca, L.: exc, 668; ref, 6(44), 2387(1)

Bacca, H. R.: ref, 780(1665)
Bachara, G. H.: ref, 1371(256), 2445(5)
Bachman, J. G.: ref, 932(53), 1969(82), 2537(545)
Back, R.: ref, 2602(1594)
Back, R. D.: ref, 2602(1997)
Backer, J. C.: ref, 1479(309), 1896(7)
Backer, T. E.: ref, 558(58, 59)
Backteman, G.: ref, 1937(4)
Bacon, M. L.: ref, 76(586), 1945(65)
Bader, C. A.: ref, 280(1021), 643(127)
Badian, N.: ref, 2602(1595)
Badian, N. A.: ref, 1007(13), 1341(151), 1769(99), 2292(20)
Baehr, G. O.: test, 795
Baehr, M. E.: test, 795, 1785, 1788, 1884, 2210, 2262, 2410, 2651, 2654; ref, 1123(58)
Baekgaard, W.: ref, 1419(676)
Baer, D. M.: ref, 1498(5038)
Baer, P. E.: ref, 1498(5093, 5569)
Baggaley, A.: ref, 977(21), 995(142)
Baggaley, A. R.: test, 1489; rev, 706, 1821; ref, 1489(6)
Bagley, C.: ref, 639(54)
Bagley, C. R.: ref 1831(184)
Bagley, M. T.: test, 1773
Bagnato, S.: ref, 270(159), 678(37), 1420(3)
Bahrke, M.: ref, 859(854), 1904(90)
Bailey, B. E.: ref, 2491(2008)
Bailey, B. S.: ref, 6(51), 2602(1862)
Bailey, J. A.: ref, 374(195)
Bailey, K. G.: ref, 501(790), 1498(5437), 2598(1318, 1555, 1581)
Bailey, L.: ref, 2208(1636, 1696)
Bailey, R. C.: ref, 1351(181)
Bailey, R. L.: ref, 501(785, 814)
Bailey, S.: ref, 1513(32, 33), 1914(874)
Bailis, K. L.: ref, 2300(484)
Bain, J. D.: ref, 1013(72)
Bainton, D.: ref, 925(13), 1513(27)
Bair, R. L.: exc, 1522
Baird, L. L.: rev, 243, 2512
Baird, P.: ref, 1498(5410)
Baither, R.: ref, 1931(54)
Bak, J. S.: ref, 2598(1678), 2607(189)
Bakeman, R.: ref, 270(128, 131), 311(33, 34), 2289(1740)
Baker, A. M.: ref, 398(116), 1341(168), 2286(287)
Baker, B. S.: ref, 1547(298)
Baker, E.: ref, 1515(16)
Baker, G. L.: ref, 2289(1644)
Baker, H.: ref, 2602(1729, 1863)
Baker, H. J.: test, 301, 688, 689, 690, 691
Baker, J.: ref, 1655(83), 1883(28)
Baker, J. A.: ref, 344(170), 551(43)
Baker, J. C.: ref, 116(528)
Baker, J. M.: ref, 1547(253, 325)
Baker, K.: ref, 116(522)
Baker, L.: ref, 859(846), 960(15), 1007(35), 1126(752), 1771(717), 2602(2016), 2608(228), 2621(389)
Baker, L. J.: ref, 280(1096), 1498(5390), 2030(5012), 2289(1692), 2491(2051), 2598(1541), 2602(1847)
Baker, M.: ref, 2030(4982), 2512(583)
Baker, R. D.: ref, 1485(59), 1771(540), 2598(1338)
Baker, R. L.: ref, 1295(294)
Baker, S. D.: ref, 1257(164)

Baker, T. B.: ref, 280(1096), 1498(5390), 2030(5012), 2289(1692), 2491(2051), 2598(1541), 2602(1847)
Baker, W. G.: ref, 349(7)
Baker–Nobles, L.: ref, 1949(59), 2244(34)
Bakewell, W. E.: ref, 1576(211)
Bakow, H. A.: ref, 270(97), 311(29)
Balance, W. D. G.: ref, 1798(242)
Baldauf, R. B.: ref, 932(71, 92, 100), 1484(9, 10, 15), 1912(3), 2048(1), 2260(27)
Baldwin, A. L.: test, 884
Baldwin, A. Y.: ref, 344(135), 2217(107), 2286(271)
Baldwin, R. S.: ref, 932(84, 85), 1013(111), 1570(9)
Baldwin, T. S.: rev, 299, 654, 1562
Baldwin, V. L.: test, 2404
Bali, L. R.: ref, 2322(17)
Balinski, B.: exc, 2289
Balinsky, B.: test, 2126; rev, 909, 1131, 2571
Balka, E. B.: ref, 701(85), 703(10), 704(20), 1126(775), 1331(41), 1473(211), 1923(25), 2293(16), 2602(2146)
Balkin, J.: ref, 2029(195)
Ball, I. L.: test, 1990
Ball, L. R.: test, 354(1455)
Ball, O. E.: ref, 2512(634)
Ball, R. M.: test, 339
Ball, R. S.: rev, 1505; exc, 381
Ballen, R.: test, 2501
Ballenger, J.: ref, 883(110)
Ballenger, J. C.: ref, 1498(5655)
Baller, W. R.: rev, 2326
Ballering, M.: ref, 1192(187), 1473(146), 1754(71), 2286(288)
Ballinger, C. B.: ref, 941(16)
Balloun, K. D.: ref, 1498(5411)
Balow, B.: ref, 270(122, 123), 932(72), 1126(709, 737, 738), 1479(332, 333, 356, 357), 2286(301, 321), 2287(37), 2289(1686, 1732, 1733), 2598(1524), 2602(1947, 1948), 2621(300, 359)
Balow, I. H.: test, 1473, 1474, 1475, 1476, 1477, 1478
Balsley, I. W.: rev, 1807; ref, 1495(84), 2598(1556)
Baltes, P. B.: ref, 653(158, 172), 1257(131, 156), 1914(825), 2300(591)
Balthazar, E. E.: test, 235; ref, 235(11)
Baltimore County French Language Committee: test, 236, 237
Bamber, J. H.: ref, 883(64)
Banas, N.: ref, 691(32, 37, 38), 2602(1596)
Bander, R. S.: ref, 354(1519), 1498(5576), 2300(382, 579)
Badian, N. A.: ref, 2602(2155)
Bandler, W.: ref, 1547(317)
Bandura, A.: ref, 1473(213)
Bangs, T. E.: test, 295, 2566
Banham, K. M.: test, 1968, 2025
Banister, P. A.: ref, 354(1400), 859(738), 2208(1537)
Bank, L.: test, 1442; ref, 1498(5326), 1798(244)
Banks, C.: rev, 632, 1914
Banks, C. E. K.: rev, 1829
Banks, D. L.: ref, 1754(88)
Banks, E. M.: test, 1256
Banks, J. M.: ref, 543(30)
Banks, M. H.: ref, 941(32, 40)
Bankson, N. W.: rev, 1255, 2452
Bannatyne, A.: exc, 338, 748, 962, 1224, 1250, 1459, 1769, 2109, 2641; ref, 2602(1864, 1998)

Bannatyne, M.: exc, 1622
Banner, C. N.: ref, 362(3), 363(10)
Bannister, D.: test, 1009
Banreti–Fuchs, K. M.: ref, 362(1), 363(5)
Baquet, G. M.: ref, 308(12)
Barack, L. I.: ref, 860(103)
Barack, R. C.: ref, 701(56), 1371(251)
Barahol, R. M.: ref, 2217(179)
Barak, A.: ref, 2134(138)
Barash, P.: ref, 113(26), 1904(103)
Barbee, R. A.: ref, 1576(186)
Barber, G. A.: test, 568, 656
Barber, L. W.: test, 238
Barber, P. J.: ref, 859(943)
Barber Center Press, Inc.: test, 2176
Barbieri, R. J.: ref, 280(1176), 751(43)
Barbour, A.: ref, 2289(1694), 2602(1855)
Barbour, J. S.: ref, 2294(123)
Barbre, A. R.: ref, 2318(1555)
Barcher, P. R.: test, 2570; ref, 6(58)
Barcikowski, R.: ref, 1831(120)
Barcikowski, R. S.: ref, 354(1429), 1831(177)
Barclay, A.: exc, 1899; ref, 354(1438), 1874(10), 2217(127), 2608(195)
Barclay, A. G.: rev, 703
Barclay, J. R.: test, 239, 240, 241; ref, 239(13, 14), 1914(826)
Barclay, L. K.: test, 240
Bardis, P. D.: test, 8, 307, 485, 660, 840, 870, 875, 1006, 1152, 1465, 1766, 1832, 2008, 2170, 2549, 2558
Bardo, H.: ref, 1250(22)
Bardon, J. I.: ref, 2557(210)
Bardsley, P.: ref, 354(1518), 859(893), 1547(319)
Barefoot, S.: ref, 691(34), 1126(711), 1462(138), 1914(787)
Barenboim, C.: ref, 1436(17)
Barett, G. V.: ref, 1013(119)
Barg, G. A.: ref, 678(26), 960(11), 1771(655), 2107(9), 2218(143), 2598(1582), 2602(1889), 2608(213)
Bargh, J.: ref, 500(57), 501(917)
Barik, H. C.: test, 918; ref, 361(4), 363(6), 918(2), 1479(336), 1754(82)
Barker, B. M.: ref, 1498(5232), 2300(336)
Barker, D.: test, 1767
Barker, D. G.: ref, 116(550)
Barker, E. T.: ref, 780(1666), 2208(1561)
Barker, H. R.: ref, 1498(5232, 5508), 2300(336)
Barker, J.: test, 679
Barker, L.: ref, 859(846)
Barker, S.: ref, 2134(125)
Barker, T. E.: ref, 280(1019), 751(1), 1498(5029), 2030(4941), 2037(146), 2179(194), 2598(1292), 2607(125)
Barkley, R. A.: ref, 1771(631, 637, 646)
Barling, J.: ref, 1371(259), 1771(638, 639), 2629(110, 112)
Barlow, A.: ref, 1126(746), 2602(1989)
Barlow, D. H.: ref, 859(842), 1904(121)
Barlow, F.: ref, 1655(105)
Barnabas, B.: test, 188
Barnard, B.: test, 825
Barnard, D.: ref, 2598(1637)
Barnard, E. L.: test, 1652, 1992
Barnbind, D. C.: ref, 1171(5)
Barnebey, N.: ref, 2111(1), 2602(1592), 2621(222)

Barnes, D. F.: ref, 1798(228)
Barnes, G. E.: ref, 780(1682), 794(412), 1013(98), 1498(5412, 5570), 1798(249), 2030(5022), 2208(1599), 2491(2053)
Barnes, J.: ref, 551(35)
Barnes, M. R.: ref, 681(30)
Barnett, L. R.: ref, 1798(250)
Barnett, M.: test, 815
Barnett, M. A.: ref, 1477(16), 1754(67), 2260(33)
Barnett, O.: ref, 558(57)
Barnett, W. H.: ref, 780(1666), 2208(1561)
Barnette, J. J.: ref, 1789(649)
Barnette, W. L.: rev, 912
Barnhill, B.: ref, 6(70), 923(83), 1351(33)
Barnlund, D. C.: ref, 890(324)
Barnowe, J. T.: ref, 2318(1575), 2334(20)
Barnstein, P. H.: ref, 1798(196)
Barnwell, A.: ref, 1769(56), 2598(1482)
Barocas, R.: ref, 1771(656), 1853(282), 2602(1890), 2621(332)
Baron, A.: ref, 859(782, 876), 1904(96), 2598(1813)
Baron, J.: ref, 363(2)
Baron, M.: ref, 645(27), 1498(5571)
Baron, M. B.: ref, 1914(806)
Baron, R. M.: ref, 346(102), 2641(8)
Barone, R. J.: ref, 280(1070)
Barr, A. S.: rev, 2403
Barr, H.: ref, 1498(5328)
Barr, R. C.: rev, 719, 1434, 1551, 1997, 2635
Barr, S. Z.: ref, 1555(326)
Barranco, S. F.: ref, 1940(86)
Barratt, E. S.: ref, 1351(199), 2300(580), 2598(1811), 2607(213)
Barredo, V. H.: ref, 354(1492), 1771(660), 1831(170), 1853(283), 2322(12), 2621(339)
Barrera, M.: ref, 883(65, 78), 1498(5413), 2598(1327)
Barrett, C.: ref, 609(216)
Barrett, C. A.: ref, 1771(587)
Barrett, D. E.: ref, 551(15)
Barrett, E. R.: test, 242
Barrett, G. V.: ref, 794(364), 1013(65, 78, 86), 1053(68), 1257(124), 2614(21)
Barrett, J.: test, 161; ref, 1419(670), 1498(5108)
Barrett, J. S.: test, 1327
Barrett, M.: test, 1736, 1737, 2648
Barrett, P.: ref, 226(172), 701(65), 1371(254), 1771(678), 2113(252), 2602(1929)
Barrett, R.: ref, 1969(98)
Barrett, R. S.: rev, 802, 1748
Barrett, T. C.: test, 482; rev, 2371; ref, 2413(584, 585)
Barrios, B. A.: ref, 1547(318), 2300(507), 2353(33), 2598(1679), 2638(140)
Barron, F.: test, 243; rev, 780; ref, 243(122), 653(161)
Barron, J.: ref, 1513(31)
Barron, R. W.: ref, 363(2)
Barroso, F.: ref, 2598(1333)
Barry, K.: ref, 2289(1593)
Barry, N. J.: ref, 1319(71)
Barry, S. M.: ref, 883(72), 1498(5139)
Barsch, J.: test, 244
Barsel–Bowers, G.: ref, 270(120)
Barstow, J.: ref, 2300(508)
Bart, W. M.: ref, 1292(52), 1914(827), 2015(207)
Bartel, A. G.: ref, 1904(101)
Bartel, N. R.: ref, 1126(659), 1622(33)

Barth, J. T.: ref, 2300(598), 2598(1842)
Barthlow, V. L.: ref, 1498(5379, 5539), 2598(1659)
Bartlett, D.: ref, 2100(9)
Bartley, L. S.: ref, 1877(10), 2289(1745)
Bartlung, H. C.: ref, 76(649), 2318(1606)
Bartolucci, G.: ref, 226(159), 1319(80)
Barton, K.: ref, 1233(210), 2269(483)
Barton, R.: ref, 1498(5649)
Bartsch, J. R.: ref, 2030(5023)
Barufald, J. P.: ref, 583(2)
Baruth, L. G.: test, 1259
Basgall, J.: ref, 1547(326), 2300(532)
Bash, I. Y.: ref, 280(1131), 2030(5052), 2598(1680)
Bashaw, W. L.: rev, 1188, 1313, 1749; ref, 344(144), 551(21), 1192(179), 1473(136), 2160(55), 2260(30)
Bashi, J.: ref, 1914(703)
Bashir, A. S.: ref, 270(100)
Bass, A.: ref, 542(23)
Bass, A. R.: rev, 1426, 1855
Bass, B. M.: test, 876, 1748; ref, 1046(579), 1486(179)
Bassett, J. E.: ref, 1371(240), 1498(5039, 5262), 2366(190), 2370(15), 2598(1557)
Bassin, S. L.: ref, 922(9)
Bassler, O. C.: test, 1770
Basso, A.: ref, 1914(875), 2598(1427, 1812)
Bassos, C.: ref, 1498(5040)
Bastian, J.: ref, 932(111), 2491(2085)
Basu, A. K.: ref, 2300(517)
Bate, M.: test, 207
Bate, S. M.: test, 2004
Bateman, N. J.: ref, 226(175), 1126(741), 2244(36)
Bates, E.: ref, 1771(517)
Bates, J. E.: ref, 1798(251)
Batesky, J. A.: ref, 2134(126)
Bath, D.: ref, 2018(18), 2472(29)
Batini, P.: ref, 226(176), 701(71), 1771(709)
Batlis, N. C.: ref, 116(570), 501(815), 1300(119), 2208(1600)
Batshaw, M. L.: ref, 280(1132), 283(154), 2598(1681), 2621(382)
Batson, C. D.: ref, 116(627)
Batt, R.: ref, 6(69)
Batten, D. E.: ref, 859(783)
Battistich, V. A.: ref, 354(1577), 917(77)
Battle, J.: test, 644; ref, 1498(5572), 1914(828), 1948(99), 2077(31), 2602(1869), 2621(318)
Battle, J. J.: ref, 644(1)
Baty, M. L.: ref, 344(171)
Batzel, L. W.: ref, 1498(5573), 2598(1682)
Baucom, D. H.: ref, 116(601), 354(1517, 1530), 681(43, 64), 1498(5414, 5427, 5525, 5614)
Bauer, D.: ref, 2029(217)
Bauer, G. P.: ref, 2300(456)
Bauer, L.: ref, 1831(120)
Bauer, R. H.: ref, 2602(1597)
Bauer, R. M.: ref, 1547(299)
Bauer, S. F.: ref, 280(1167), 751(41), 2030(5088), 2491(2103), 2598(1832)
Bauer, W. D.: ref, 751(28)
Bauernfeind, R. B.: test, 2326
Bauernfeind, R. H.: test, 2325; rev, 169, 1742, 1797, 2260; exc, 351
Baulougouris, J. C.: ref, 859(878)
Baum, A.: test, 1267; ref, 1267(1), 1498(5644)
Baum, D. D.: ref, 2217(138, 139), 2608(208, 209)

Bauman, E.: ref, 1233(230)
Baumann, J. F.: ref, 1473(214)
Bausch & Lomb, Inc.: test, 1752, 2093
Baxter, B.: rev, 1468
Baxter, E. G.: ref, 1914(887), 2300(594)
Baxter, J.: ref, 1914(827), 2015(207)
Bay, K. S.: ref, 681(75), 860(156), 1969(97), 2598(1547)
Bayley, N.: test, 270; rev, 1471, 1505, 2598
Bayton, J. A.: ref, 558(66), 2413(588)
Bayton, J. E.: ref, 780(1706)
Beach, L. R.: ref, 2300(393)
Beadle, K. R.: ref, 212(5), 701(57), 962(27), 964(493), 1126(717), 1771(640), 2289(1697)
Beal, D.: ref, 780(1641), 2491(2006)
Bean, A. G.: ref, 6(76), 354(1521), 501(881)
Bean, K. L.: test, 2240; rev, 2113
Bean, T. W.: ref, 1013(111), 1570(9), 2164(41), 2288(83)
Bear: ref, 1547(247)
Bear, D.: ref, 2598(1717), 2607(199)
Bear, R. M.: rev, 1991
Beard, J. G.: ref, 1839(1)
Beard, M. T.: ref, 1655(88)
Beard, R. W.: ref, 639(40), 859(722)
Beardsworth, T.: ref, 794(443)
Bearison, D. J.: ref, 1341(152)
Bearse, L. N.: ref, 2343(1051)
Beasley, D. S.: ref, 1332(7), 2646(9)
Beatty, J. R.: test, 1161; ref, 1161(1, 2, 3)
Beatty, L. S.: test, 2291
Beatty, M. J.: ref, 2300(383, 509, 581)
Beatty-DeSana, J.: ref, 1771(798), 2159(4), 2472(31)
Beauchamp, D. P.: ref, 2602(1865)
Beaudet, R.: ref, 298(167)
Beaulne, C.: ref, 2318(1614)
Beauvais, L. L.: ref, 1295(305)
Beauvois, M. F.: ref, 2598(1558)
Bebbington, P.: ref, 1883(92, 93)
Becerra-Aldama, J.: ref, 1498(5611)
Becher, R. M.: ref, 1479(310)
Bechtoldt, H.: rev, 732, 1044
Bechtoldt, H. P.: rev, 282, 899, 1219, 2537
Beck, A. T.: ref, 859(950), 1904(117)
Beck, C. K.: ref, 116(602)
Beck, E. A.: ref, 1498(5041)
Beck, E. C.: ref, 1462(117, 151), 2598(1299)
Beck, F. W.: ref, 344(166), 551(36), 1568(131), 1769(67), 2602(1866)
Beck, J.: ref, 2598(1499), 2602(2081)
Beck, M. D.: ref, 116(602), 1473(177, 207), 1478(68), 2372(1)
Beck, M. M.: ref, 2246(25)
Beck, R. W.: ref, 1197(281), 1498(5182), 1547(267)
Beck, S.: ref, 1473(217)
Beck, S. J.: rev, 118, 2030; exc, 298, 356
Beck, T.: ref, 36(1), 42(4)
Beck, Y. M.: test, 2588
Becker, A. D.: ref, 573(17), 578(4)
Becker, A. T.: ref, 1547(312)
Becker, B. J.: ref, 9(17), 76(637), 501(878), 573(14), 1456(17), 2246(30)
Becker, J.: ref, 1547(305)
Becker, J. P.: ref, 1257(120, 153)

INDEX OF NAMES

Becker, L. D.: ref, 1914(739), 2286(270), 2293(8), 2621(276)
Becker, R. E.: ref, 883(71), 1240(49), 1655(119)
Becker, R. L.: test, 1996; ref, 1996(8)
Becker, S.: ref, 354(1386), 1269(26)
Becker, W. C.: rev, 876, 1795
Beckerman, T. M.: ref, 483(19), 1192(195, 196)
Becklund, J. D.: test, 2211
Beckman, L.: ref, 2602(1598)
Beckman, L. J.: ref, 354(1434, 1518), 859(784, 893), 917(74), 1547(278, 319)
Beckwith, L.: ref, 270(108)
Bedeian, A. G.: ref, 116(524, 545, 546, 603)
Bedell, J. A.: ref, 2300(337), 2621(226)
Bedell, J. R.: ref, 2179(233), 2300(457, 506)
Bedell, R. C.: rev, 1531
Bedford, A.: test, 1787; ref, 1419(687), 2208(1562)
Bednar, R. L.: ref, 116(613), 1099(65, 67, 70)
Bedrosian, J. L.: ref, 1622(36), 1771(588), 2289(1652)
Bedrosian, R.: ref, 883(79), 1197(282)
Bedwell, C. H.: ref, 1567(17)
Bee, D. E.: ref, 2602(1836)
Beebe, M. C.: ref, 2602(1818)
Beech, H. R.: rev, 1660; ref, 1904(118)
Beech, R. P.: ref, 2029(203, 229)
Beecher, R.: ref, 2111(2), 2621(306)
Beedle, B.: ref, 5(170)
Beehr, T. A.: ref, 1295(293)
Beeker, C.: ref, 2620(5)
Beelen, L.: ref, 681(75), 860(156)
Beers, M. I.: test, 1770
Beery, K. E.: test, 701
Beggs, D. L.: test, 274, 385, 692
Begle, E. G.: rev, 345, 2287
Behar, L.: test, 1874A; ref, 1050(1)
Behnke, R. R.: ref, 2300(383, 509, 581)
Behr, M. J.: ref, 9(11)
Behrens, L. T.: ref, 361(5), 1533(15)
Beiman, I.: ref, 1547(256, 279), 2300(352, 384, 385)
Beit–Hallahmi, B.: ref, 874(55)
Beitel, P. A.: ref, 325(33), 794(431), 2246(31)
Bejar, I. I.: rev, 290; ref, 501(921), 1798(197), 2335(1)
Bekker, L. D.: ref, 665(44)
Belcastro, F. P.: ref, 780(1683), 2318(1576)
Belfer, M. L.: ref, 751(22), 1831(158)
Belfer, P. L.: ref, 1798(231)
Belford, B.: ref, 2598(1428)
Belgrade, P. S.: test, 1193
Belka, D. E.: ref, 226(170, 177), 280(1100, 1133), 302(35, 37), 1126(718, 748), 1371(252, 257), 1479(342, 362, 376), 1894(4, 6)
Belkin, B.: ref, 2607(190)
Bell, A. E.: ref, 280(1022, 1099), 363(3), 400(123), 582(3), 751(2), 770(4), 932(54), 1109(17), 1126(648), 1229(78), 1233(211), 2030(4942), 2086(12), 2286(272), 2289(1594, 1696), 2557(209)
Bell, C. W.: ref, 1498(5606)
Bell, D. P.: ref, 501(824)
Bell, E. C.: ref, 780(1645)
Bell, E. F.: ref, 678(13)
Bell, H. M.: test, 118, 2086
Bell, J. E.: rev, 396, 871, 874, 1537
Bell, L. W.: ref, 1419(677)
Bell, R. C.: ref, 2602(2156)
Bellack, A. S.: ref, 859(947), 860(123), 2179(254)

Bellak, L.: test, 396, 1924, 2148; exc, 1660
Bellak, S. S.: test, 396, 2148
Bellarosa, A.: ref, 1253(2), 2199(6)
Belleville, R. E.: test, 113
Belleza, T.: ref, 280(1101)
Bellucci, J. T.: ref, 501(920), 949(12), 1754(115), 2366(202), 2370(18)
Belmont, I.: ref, 1473(145)
Belmont, L.: ref, 282(140, 141), 464(2), 1473(145), 1914(704, 705)
Belmore, S. M.: ref, 113(27), 1498(5593), 1904(110), 2179(251)
Beloff, H.: test, 1233
Belsey, E. M.: ref, 639(40), 859(722)
Beltone Electronics Corporation: test, 277
Bem, D. J.: ref, 356(4)
Bem, S. L.: test, 278
Bement, G.: ref, 2621(407)
Ben–Porat, A.: ref, 1300(124)
Ben–Zeev, S.: ref, 1771(519), 1914(706), 2602(1599)
Benbow, C. P.: ref, 501(879, 880, 934)
Bender, D. A.: ref, 1883(70)
Bender, L.: test, 280
Bender, M. L.: test, 281
Bender, N. N.: ref, 1771(518), 2621(276)
Bender, P. R.: ref, 398(100)
Bene, E.: test, 874
Benenson, T. F.: ref, 1576(200)
Benfeldt, F.: ref, 794(400)
Benge, E. J.: test, 2141
Benigas, J. E.: ref, 1372(11)
Benjamin, D.: ref, 1424(89)
Benjamin, L. S.: ref, 890(355), 1498(5589)
Benjamins, D.: ref, 270(77), 678(20), 701(45), 1771(597), 1877(7), 2289(1656), 2557(220)
Bennet, R. W.: ref, 547(5, 6), 732(391, 399), 2537(552)
Bennett, B.: ref, 2300(510)
Bennett, B. B.: ref, 890(325)
Bennett, C.: ref, 859(831)
Bennett, D. E.: exc, 2091
Bennett, F. C.: ref, 270(102, 155), 2289(1698, 1789), 2602(2190)
Bennett, F. W.: ref, 1498(5574)
Bennett, G. K.: test, 9, 282, 466, 732, 1054, 1288, 1456, 1653, 2112, 2180, 2246, 2254, 2469, 2554; rev, 1043
Bennett, J. M.: test, 1568
Bennett, K.: ref, 311(39), 1203(7)
Bennett, N.: ref, 1855(28)
Bennett, T. S.: ref, 701(75), 1771(722), 1796(5), 2217(165), 2602(2021, 2157), 2621(433)
Bennett, V. C.: ref, 2557(210)
Bennett, W. E.: test, 388
Bennett–Levy, J.: ref, 2598(1683)
Bennik, C. D.: ref, 76(615), 794(404), 2598(1522)
Benninga, J. S.: ref, 1754(99)
Benninger, W. B.: ref, 2134(127), 2581(336)
Bennink, C. D.: ref, 1013(79)
Benson, A. L.: ref, 1262(1)
Benson, B. A.: ref, 883(113), 1013(120)
Benson, D. F.: ref, 308(2)
Benson, G. P.: ref, 2288(86)
Benson, J.: ref, 1477(18)
Benson, K.: ref, 2598(1429)
Bental, L. M.: test, 843
Bentin, S.: ref, 2598(1559)

Bentler, P. M.: test, 559; rev, 1170, 1831, 2413; exc, 1473
Bentley, A.: test, 1446
Bentley, C.: ref, 116(611), 2413(679)
Bentley, K.: ref, 381(62)
Bentley, R. R.: test, 1953, 1954, 1955; exc, 1446
Benton, A. L.: test, 283; rev, 280, 1498, 2213, 2216, 2491
Benz, H. E.: rev, 713
Benzies, B.: test, 2505
Berbaum, M. L.: ref, 2289(1741)
Berdie, R. F.: rev, 732, 899, 1271, 2269, 2657
Berenson, B. G.: test, 1932
Berenson, G. S.: ref, 1831(220)
Berent, S.: ref, 1769(50), 2300(598), 2598(1842, 1853), 2602(2197)
Beres, C. A.: ref, 2598(1813)
Berg, A.: ref, 1769(84)
Berg, E. A.: test, 2633
Berg, H. D.: rev, 125, 1647
Berg, I.: test, 2128; ref, 859(785), 1229(84), 2128(8), 2602(1730)
Berg, P. A.: ref, 2598(1298)
Berg, R.: ref, 1346(5)
Berg, R. A.: ref, 1346(2, 4)
Berg–Cross, G.: ref, 860(100), 1537(2), 1798(278), 2602(2039), 2621(397)
Berg–Cross, L.: ref, 860(100), 1537(2), 1798(278), 2602(2039), 2621(397)
Bergan, J. R.: ref, 2608(210)
Berger, A.: rev, 608, 669, 2340, 2371
Berger, C.: ref, 1424(47), 1771(657)
Berger, D. E.: ref, 1257(119), 2598(1423)
Berger, E.: ref, 794(413), 2598(1560)
Berger, G. H.: ref, 1460(49, 53)
Berger, J. C.: ref, 1498(5647)
Berger, K. W.: test, 1268
Berger, M.: rev, 2021
Berger, N. S.: ref, 1192(186), 1754(68)
Berger, R. M.: test, 1403, 1809, 1840
Bergerone, C.: ref, 794(439, 447)
Berglund, M.: ref, 283(136, 142), 627(22), 1265(75, 76), 1462(128), 1914(740)
Bergman, A.: ref, 2602(2003, 2160), 2641(14, 18)
Bergman, H.: ref, 1005(26), 1462(150, 155), 2030(4983)
Bergmann, T. J.: ref, 1508(137)
Bergum, B. O.: ref, 1013(71)
Beringer, M. L.: test, 284
Berk, L. E.: ref, 2512(666)
Berk, R. A.: ref, 270(113), 1007(30), 2289(1709), 2621(335)
Berk, S. N.: ref, 2030(4943)
Berkow, J. W.: ref, 877(20)
Berkowitz, P. H.: test, 337
Berkowitz, R.: ref, 1883(91)
Berler, E. S.: ref, 1126(749), 1473(192), 1771(712), 2602(1999), 2621(383)
Berlin, D. F.: ref, 2269(473), 2602(2000, 2158)
Berlin, L. J.: test, 1876
Berliner, D. C.: ref, 551(27)
Berman, E.: ref, 298(168), 1197(317)
Berman, W.: ref, 1498(5468)
Bernadt, M. W.: ref, 859(894), 883(106)
Bernard, L. C.: ref, 116(547), 354(1559), 384(5), 1046(586), 1498(5737), 2208(1563, 1643), 2318(1607)
Bernard, M. L.: ref, 1271(908)
Bernard, R.: ref, 2602(2166)
Bernardin, H. J.: ref, 2208(1518)
Bernberg, R. E.: test, 1118, 2563
Berndt, D. J.: ref, 1547(280)
Berndt, L.: ref, 1894(5)
Bernreuter, R. G.: test, 1795; rev, 2086
Bernstein, B. L.: ref, 794(414)
Bernstein, I. H.: ref, 1498(5575)
Bernstein, M.: ref, 1073(129)
Berrier, G. D.: ref, 859(941)
Berry, C. A.: ref, 501(924), 1576(220)
Berry, G. L.: ref, 1531(277)
Berry, M. F.: test, 285
Berry, P.: test, 1283; ref, 270(114, 129, 148)
Berry, R.: ref, 1883(51, 73)
Berry, S.: ref, 551(24)
Berry, S. R.: test, 2663
Berryman, C.: test, 224; ref, 224(3)
Berryman, J. D.: test, 224; ref, 224(1, 2, 3)
Bertinetti, J. F.: ref, 2413(586)
Berzins, J. I.: ref, 1798(228, 229, 292)
Bessai, F.: ref, 363(11)
Bessell, H.: test, 286
Besson, J. A. O.: ref, 283(155), 1485(76), 1853(290), 1914(829), 2598(1684)
Best, C. L.: ref, 859(723), 1498(5042), 1904(50), 2300(338)
Best, D. L.: ref, 116(543, 599)
Best, J.: test, 2321
Bestgen, B. J.: ref, 2286(326)
Bethell, M. S.: ref, 1655(123)
Betts, E. A.: rev, 2034, 2164
Betz, N. E.: test, 2650; ref, 76(650), 354(1519), 1498(5576), 2318(1582, 1608), 2134(115), 2300(386, 579)
Betz, W.: rev, 1230
Beukelman, D. R.: ref, 1851(44)
Beukes, D. P. M.: test, 1079
Beutler, L.: ref, 1498(5768), 1923(28)
Beutler, L. E.: ref, 890(342), 1498(5569, 5738), 2300(339)
Beveridge, M.: ref, 381(57), 823(10), 2018(13), 2289(1595), 2557(211, 225)
Beveridge, R.: ref, 653(140)
Bhatara, V.: ref, 280(1065)
Bhattacharyya, A. K.: ref, 2300(517)
Bhogle, S.: ref, 270(116)
Bhrolcháin, M. N.: ref, 1883(39)
Bhushan, V.: ref, 1754(84)
Biaggio, M. K.: ref, 354(1520)
Bialer, I.: ref, 701(85), 703(10), 704(20), 1126(682, 775), 1331(41), 1473(211), 1771(583), 1923(25), 2293(16), 2602(2146)
Bialystok, E.: ref, 1077(54)
Bianchi, G. N.: ref, 859(724)
Bianchi, J. R.: ref, 354(1521), 501(881)
Biderman, M.: ref, 1203(9)
Biderman, M. D.: ref, 2244(35)
Bidus, D. R.: ref, 2318(1547)
Biedermann, L. W.: test, 2268
Bieger, E.: ref, 958(43)
Biemiller, A.: test, 288; ref, 1473(124)

INDEX OF NAMES

Bienvenu, M. J.: test, 1171, 1178, 1372, 1761, 1867, 1869, 2172
Bierenbaum, H.: ref, 1498(5323)
Biersdorf, K. C.: test, 1932
Biersner, R. J.: ref, 932(104), 1914(830), 2300(340), 2607(128)
Bigelow, L. B.: ref, 2598(1372, 1449, 1561)
Biggs, A.: ref, 1771(695)
Biggs, V. E.: ref, 1904(121)
Biglan, A.: ref, 2300(410)
Biller, H. B.: ref, 354(1421), 917(73)
Billig, J. M.: ref, 2587(45)
Billig, M.: ref, 2029(212)
Billings, A.: ref, 1498(5415)
Billingslea, F. Y.: exc, 280
Billmeier, G. J.: ref, 1771(680), 2289(1729), 2602(1938), 2621(353)
Bills, M. A.: rev, 13, 111, 464, 1186
Bilotta, J.: ref, 1817(4)
Bindelglas, P. M.: ref, 2491(2036)
Binder, D. M.: ref, 280(1172), 701(90)
Bingham, G.: ref, 374(196, 212)
Bingham, R.: ref, 2134(123), 2581(333)
Bingham, R. P.: ref, 2134(104), 2581(313)
Bingham, W. C.: rev, 372
Bingham, W. J.: test, 292
Binik, Y. M.: ref, 2030(5040), 2512(656)
Bink, M. P.: ref, 1949(59), 2244(34)
Binyildiz, P.: ref, 643(128)
Birch, L. B.: rev, 363, 823, 2281; exc, 2289
Birch, M. C.: ref, 2602(1793)
Birchmore, D. F.: ref, 1197(300)
Bird, A. C.: ref, 2289(1632)
Bird, A. M.: ref, 1295(284)
Bird, E. I.: ref, 400(127), 1904(120)
Bird, R. C.: ref, 1479(315), 2217(112)
Biren, P. L.: ref, 371(243)
Birenbaum, M.: ref, 1233(226)
Birk, J. M.: ref, 1387(13), 2134(121), 2573(1)
Birley, J. L. T.: ref, 1883(52, 61)
Birnbom, F.: ref, 1240(59)
Birney, R. C.: ref, 157(150)
Birren, J. E.: ref, 243(114), 1257(104), 1403(23), 1404(1), 1580(1), 1840(24), 2598(1295)
Birsh, E.: test, 2121
Birtchnell, J.: ref, 1498(5177, 5416, 5428)
Biscoe, M.: test, 1340
Bishop, D.: ref, 2602(1867), 2608(211)
Bishop, D. V. M.: ref, 860(85), 1567(15), 2602(1868, 2001), 2608(225)
Bishop, E. R.: ref, 1498(5417)
Bishop, G. A.: ref, 1655(75)
Bishop, J. B.: ref, 618(5)
Bishop, M.: ref, 2588(33)
Bishop, S.: ref, 1883(80)
Bistline, J. L.: ref, 2300(511), 2353(34)
Biswas, P. K.: ref, 2300(517)
Bitter, E. J.: ref, 2030(5073)
Bittner, R. H.: rev, 1064, 1293, 1450, 2305
Bixler, H. H.: rev, 2256
Bizman, A.: ref, 1914(831)
Bjerke, T.: ref, 116(599)
Bjerstedt, A.: rev, 780, 2301
Blacha, M. D.: ref, 665(40)
Blache, S.: ref, 200(14)
Blache, S. E.: ref, 896(6), 1814(7)
Blacher–Dixon, J.: ref, 270(88), 1771(589), 2289(1669)
Black, D. B.: rev, 928, 2002
Black, E. L.: test, 546
Black, F. W.: ref, 280(1019, 1057, 1066), 751(1), 1498(5029), 1771(571), 2030(4941), 2037(146), 2179(194), 2598(1292, 1430, 1685), 2602(1699, 1823), 2607(125, 151), 2621(263)
Black, H.: rev, 2163
Black, J. D.: test, 707; rev, 1297, 2366, 2461
Black, J. T.: ref, 1568(150)
Black, L.: ref, 270(103)
Black, R.: ref, 645(17), 1904(74)
Black, R. W.: ref, 2621(370)
Blackburn, G. L.: ref, 1498(5186)
Blackburn, I. M.: ref, 1883(80)
Blackburn, R.: ref, 1498(5418)
Blackman, L. S.: ref, 2289(1746), 2602(2013)
Blackmore, D. E.: ref, 344(190), 1914(890)
Blackstone, E. G.: rev, 2527
Blackwell, B.: ref, 2300(375)
Blackwell, P.: ref, 2445(2)
Blackwell, S.: ref, 859(931), 2300(558)
Blackwell, S. L.: ref, 701(50), 958(44), 2602(1784), 2621(292)
Blager, F. B.: ref, 2015(213)
Blaha, J.: ref, 280(1102), 964(494), 2218(140), 2602(1844, 2140)
Blain, B. B.: ref, 1576(195)
Blaine, J. D.: ref, 890(340)
Blair, E. M.: ref, 2366(196), 2370(17)
Blair, G. E.: ref, 280(1114), 354(1572, 1573), 899(20), 1053(66), 1498(5482, 5483), 1789(730, 731), 1970(16), 2030(5002), 2179(201, 223, 224, 256), 2217(114, 181), 2218(148), 2512(575, 660), 2598(1361)
Blair, M. C.: ref, 116(604)
Blair, M. J.: exc, 870
Blake, A. J. D.: ref, 588(10), 589(2), 1013(99), 2531(2)
Blake, R.: ref, 2318(1577)
Blakemore, C. B.: rev, 280
Blakeney, R. N.: ref, 780(1645)
Blan, J. A.: ref, 859(805)
Blanchard, E. B.: ref, 859(842), 1046(568)
Blanchard, E. G.: ref, 1371(240)
Blanchard, J. S.: ref, 551(49), 1498(5739), 1771(713)
Blanchard, K. H.: test, 2205
Blanchard, S. L.: ref, 2017(4)
Blaney, P. H.: ref, 1498(5340), 1933(17)
Blank, M.: test, 1876
Blank, S. S.: ref, 363(4), 2512(568)
Blanton, W. E.: test, 1859
Blashfield, R. K.: ref, 1498(5577)
Blatchley, M. E.: ref, 501(816)
Blatt, S. J.: test, 215, 682; ref, 682(1), 2030(4944)
Blattstein, A.: ref, 551(60), 1831(198)
Blattstein, D.: ref, 551(60), 1831(198)
Blaylock, R.: test, 812
Blazer, D.: ref, 1498(5578, 5579), 1659(1)
Blazer, D. G.: ref, 1498(5419)
Blazer, J. A.: test, 2600
Blazier, D. C.: test, 1377
Bleda, P. R.: ref, 1296(169), 1547(248), 1948(94)
Bledsoe, J. C.: ref, 1295(285, 289, 296, 297), 1508(113, 121, 130), 2208(1601), 2343(1045), 2413(667)

Blesch, G.: test, 7
Bless, D. M.: ref, 859(768)
Blew, E. O.: ref, 501(921)
Blick, K. A.: ref, 1191(126), 1498(5391), 2300(448)
Bliesmer, E. P.: rev, 1007, 1427; ref, 1191(120)
Bligh, S.: ref, 896(4)
Blimling, G. S.: ref, 76(624, 625), 1726(365), 2134(113), 2318(1578), 2657(110)
Blinkhorn, S.: test, 940
Bliss, L. B.: ref, 1192(228)
Bliss, L. S.: ref, 378(17), 1622(53), 2472(28)
Blitchington, W. P.: test, 2411; ref, 859(900), 1771(590), 2411(1)
Blixt, S.: ref, 1969(118)
Blixt, S. L.: ref, 551(72), 2372(5)
Bloch, D. W.: ref, 2366(196), 2370(17)
Block, J.: test, 348, 356; rev, 860; ref, 348(1, 2), 860(86), 1914(876), 2602(2159)
Block, J. H.: ref, 348(1, 2), 1914(876), 2602(2159)
Block, J. R.: test, 2068
Block, S.: ref, 2300(569)
Block, Z.: ref, 964(480), 2289(1623)
Blockburn, R.: ref, 1498(5420)
Blom, B. E.: ref, 2598(1638)
Blommers, P.: rev, 573, 1642
Blomquist, B. L.: ref, 2029(221)
Blonsky, E. R.: ref, 896(3)
Bloom, A.: ref, 1126(690), 2602(1738, 2003, 2160), 2641(14, 18)
Bloom, A. S.: ref, 280(1090), 701(54), 2289(1596, 1683), 2602(1695, 1807, 2002), 2621(296)
Bloom, B. S.: rev, 506
Bloom, J. R.: ref, 1904(131)
Bloom, L. J.: ref, 1498(5233), 1547(249, 281, 284), 1798(230), 2413(612)
Bloom, R. B.: ref, 666(1), 1831(159)
Bloom, W.: test, 300; ref, 1498(5043)
Bloomer, R. H.: test, 1999
Bloomers, P.: rev, 573, 1642
Bloskovics, M.: ref, 1126(776), 1371(261), 2289(1779), 2598(1814)
Blosser, P.: ref, 1555(313)
Blount, H. C.: test, 1379
Blount, H. P.: ref, 1125(17)
Blowers, E. A.: ref, 691(29), 962(23), 1126(649), 1771(520), 2602(1600)
Blowers, T.: ref, 1914(828), 1948(99)
Bloxom, B.: rev, 890, 1789
Bloxom, B. M.: rev, 2208
Blue, F. R.: ref, 1498(5421)
Blue, L. A.: ref, 1498(5421)
Blues, A. G.: ref, 1726(353)
Blum, G. S.: test, 298; ref, 2294(123)
Blum, I.: ref, 1473(174), 1479(347)
Blum, I. H.: ref, 1479(343)
Blum, L. H.: test, 534
Blum, M. L.: rev, 1163, 1511, 2537
Blum, R. A.: ref, 1479(343)
Blumberg, N. L.: ref, 398(117), 681(53), 794(432), 2300(512), 2598(1686)
Blumberg, S. R.: ref, 883(108), 1498(5623)
Blume, F.: ref, 1726(373)
Blume, H. G.: ref, 1498(5466, 5467)
Blumenthal, R.: ref, 280(1167), 751(41), 2030(5088), 2491(2103), 2598(1832)

Blumetti, A. E.: ref, 2030(4984)
Blunt, P.: ref, 859(786)
Blusewicz, M. J.: ref, 1462(117), 2598(1299)
Blustein, D. L.: ref, 2374(179)
Blyth, D. A.: ref, 1192(208)
Board of Education of the City of New York: test, 1280
Bobbitt, B. L.: ref, 1914(769)
Bobinski, V.: ref, 1960(77)
Bobruff, A.: ref, 1904(123)
Bock, D. G.: ref, 780(1684)
Bodden, J. L.: rev, 351, 367, 1577; ref, 2208(1578)
Bode, K. W.: test, 2273
Body, B.: ref, 1479(360), 2602(1808), 2608(205, 224)
Boegli, R. G.: ref, 2260(34)
Boehm, A. E.: test, 302, 484
Boersma, F. J.: ref, 362(4, 6), 1754(85, 116), 1831(135, 160, 204), 2077(31), 2602(1869), 2621(318)
Bogen, J. E.: ref, 283(158), 1771(773), 1914(878), 2201(1), 2380(6), 2598(1818), 2602(2164)
Bogle, D.: test, 1153
Bogner, C. N.: ref, 1771(521)
Bohanan, A. L.: ref, 1771(755), 2602(2111)
Bohannon, W. E.: ref, 354(1478, 1542, 1543)
Bohn, M. J.: ref, 1498(5422, 5580)
Bohn, S. A.: ref, 354(1524)
Bohning, G.: ref, 691(39), 2218(158)
Boileau, R. A.: ref, 5(165)
Boillat, J.: ref, 280(1116), 1506(75), 2598(1624), 2607(184)
Boland, P.: ref, 683(6)
Bole, R. E.: ref, 1192(249)
Bolen, L. M.: ref, 1424(69), 2512(584)
Boll, T.: ref, 2598(1853)
Boll, T. J.: test, 698; ref, 1769(50), 2300(598), 2598(1842), 2602(2197)
Bollenbacher, J.: rev, 175, 1551; exc, 2567
Boller, F.: ref, 308(3), 1498(5044), 1948(95), 2113(237), 2598(1300), 2607(129)
Bolocofsky, D. N.: ref, 696(5), 1013(100), 1479(378), 2217(183)
Bolstad, O. D.: ref, 932(55), 2585(2)
Bolt, M.: ref, 1960(72), 2029(201)
Bolter, J.: ref, 2598(1815), 2607(214)
Bolton, B.: ref, 400(130), 772(29), 1101(39), 1233(229), 1498(5423), 1960(83), 2029(243), 2030(4947), 2208(1602, 1603, 1604, 1609, 1629, 1644, 1645, 1693), 2413(639), 2491(2096), 2598(1687), 2657(112)
Bolton, B. F.: rev, 1101, 2208
Bolton, N.: ref, 354(1400), 859(738), 1914(778), 1931(45), 2077(29), 2208(1537, 1588)
Bonan, F. P.: test, 839
Bonaporte, B. H.: ref, 2208(1605)
Bonaventura, E.: test, 2020; ref, 2020(7)
Bond, B.: ref, 1351(198)
Bond, G. L.: rev, 766
Bond, J. B.: ref, 1547(250)
Bond, M. R.: ref, 1485(77), 1914(833), 2598(1691), 2607(191)
Bond, N. A.: test, 706
Bond, N. W.: ref, 1460(52)
Bond, P. A.: ref, 1883(40)
Bonge, D.: ref, 2030(5082), 2300(596)
Bonheur, H.: ref, 280(1134), 2030(5053), 2491(2077), 2598(1688)

INDEX OF NAMES

Boniface, D.: ref, 2557(226)
Bonnycastle, D. E.: ref, 1622(38), 1771(599), 2218(10)
Bonsall, M. R.: test, 2618
Bonta, B. W.: ref, 311(21)
Bonta, J. L.: ref, 1347(5)
Bonynge, E. R.: ref, 780(1647), 1498(5045), 1798(198)
Book, R. M.: ref, 280(1135), 1192(229), 2218(159), 2286(327), 2289(1742)
Bookbinder, G. E.: test, 2058
Booker, I. A.: rev, 346, 1191, 1478, 1568
Bookwalter, K. W.: test, 1136
Boone, D. R.: rev, 308, 1851, 2213
Boone, K. E.: ref, 2602(1645), 2621(241)
Booth, J. A. G.: ref, 2537(561)
Booth, J. B.: ref, 639(41)
Booth, L.: ref, 2491(2105)
Booth, R. F.: ref, 195(1, 2), 464(3), 558(64, 73), 1451(1)
Booth, S. B.: ref, 76(638)
Borden, R. J.: ref, 354(1435)
Borders–Patterson, A.: ref, 701(53), 1771(620), 1934(9), 2478(11)
Bordin, E. S.: rev, 1186, 1271, 2318; exc, 218, 780, 1419, 1527, 1849, 2323, 2461, 2623
Boren, R. B.: ref, 2030(5037), 2620(14, 19)
Borengasser, M. A.: ref, 270(150), 698(6)
Borg, S.: ref, 1462(150), 2030(4983)
Borg, W. R.: ref, 553(17)
Borgatta, E. F.: test, 1970
Borgen, F. H.: test, 1497; rev, 323, 778, 2534; exc, 372; ref, 372(3), 2318(1551)
Borgen, W. A.: ref, 2046(2)
Borgers, S. B.: ref, 76(587)
Borgstadt, C.: ref, 2512(635)
Borko, H.: rev, 2515, 2613
Borkovec, T. D.: ref, 883(66)
Borland, C. M.: ref, 2208(1611)
Borling, J.: ref, 1771(602)
Borling, J. E.: ref, 1158(32), 1257(175)
Borman, A.: ref, 618(4)
Borman, I. M.: test, 306
Borman, W. C.: rev, 1299, 1363; ref, 1508(126), 2369(13)
Bornstein, S.: test, 695
Boros, T.: ref, 2030(5065)
Boroskin, A.: test, 865, 866
Borow, H.: test, 505
Borstelmann, L. J.: exc, 951, 953
Borthwick, S. A.: ref, 6(85)
Bortner, M.: rev, 6, 632, 1485, 1914, 2561, 2563
Borys, S. V.: ref, 559(54)
Bosaeus, E.: ref, 280(1067), 283(143), 2602(1731)
Boshes, B.: ref, 896(3)
Boskind–Lodahl, M.: ref, 2208(1564)
Boss, M. W.: ref, 1013(62)
Boss, P. G.: ref, 872(12, 17)
Bossard, M. D.: ref, 2289(1699, 1743), 2621(319, 384)
Bosse, M. A.: ref, 483(25), 2512(610)
Bosse, R.: ref, 859(818), 2208(1587)
Bossone, R. M.: test, 2661
Bost, B. A.: ref, 354(1451)
Bost, L.: ref, 6(84)
Bost, L. W.: ref, 6(67)
Boswell, P. C.: ref, 1488(3), 2300(458)
Botel, M.: test, 309

Bothwell, S.: ref, 2322(8)
Botti, E.: ref, 701(85), 703(10), 704(20), 1126(775), 1331(41), 1473(211), 1923(25), 2293(16), 2602(2146)
Bottoms, S. A. H.: ref, 1498(5482)
Botwinick, J.: ref, 280(1068), 1109(20), 2598(1431, 1462, 1649, 1689, 1690, 1823), 2607(152)
Bouchard, T. J.: rev, 732, 1748, 2208
Boucher, J.: ref, 1771(522), 1914(707)
Bouchier, I. A. D.: ref, 941(37)
Boukydis, C. F. Z.: ref, 311(43)
Boulanger, F. D.: ref, 76(601)
Boulet, D. B.: ref, 558(68)
Bouma, H.: ref, 1060(23)
Bountress, N.: ref, 534(98), 1771(641)
Bountress, N. G.: ref, 226(183), 962(37)
Bourdeau, L.: ref, 404(6)
Bourgeois, A.: ref, 1013(70, 101), 1931(46), 2300(415)
Bourgeois, R. P.: ref, 859(890)
Bourke, R. S.: ref, 270(81), 1993(2), 2285(11), 2289(1662), 2557(221)
Bourke, V. M.: ref, 2598(1661), 2602(1975)
Bourne, E.: ref, 116(525)
Bourne, L. E.: ref, 1498(5524), 2179(206), 2620(5, 11, 15)
Bourque, M. L.: ref, 704(17)
Boutilier, L. R.: ref, 1498(5719)
Bovernali, J. F.: ref, 2029(226)
Bowd, A. D.: ref, 357(503), 398(92), 751(3)
Bowden, C. L.: ref, 1922(16)
Bowders, T.: ref, 6(91)
Bowen, C.: ref, 653(146), 1126(685), 2621(311)
Bowen, D.: ref, 270(100)
Bowen, R.: ref, 1831(165)
Bowen, R. C.: ref, 1498(5046), 2598(1301)
Bowen, W. T.: ref, 1789(653)
Bower, E. M.: test, 1902
Bowers, E. V.: test, 1887
Bowers, J. E.: rev, 501
Bowers, K. S.: ref, 2294(124)
Bowers, M. B.: ref, 1319(72), 2018(7)
Bowers, P.: ref, 566(108), 1063(100), 1655(92, 93), 2294(125)
Bowie, M. D.: ref, 280(1142), 2153(2)
Bowling, E. N.: ref, 2292(21)
Bowlsby, R. A.: ref 1831(185)
Bowman, P. C.: ref, 1771(524)
Bown, O. H.: test, 2142
Boyd, H. F.: test, 213, 1619
Boyd, L.: ref, 1769(56), 2598(1482)
Boyd, L. A.: ref, 6(52)
Boyd, M. A.: ref, 1779(1)
Boyd, R. C.: ref, 1099(66)
Boyd, S. T.: ref, 1498(5609)
Boyd, T. L.: ref, 883(115), 1547(350)
Boydstun, J. A.: ref, 883(101), 1498(5772), 2208(1633)
Boyle, E. S.: ref, 2413(693, 694)
Boyle, G.: ref, 2301(31)
Boyle, P.: ref, 280(1039), 1771(803), 1877(11), 2289(1717), 2602(1657)
Bozarth, J. D.: ref, 995(148)
Brabender, V.: ref, 1568(122)
Brace, D. K.: test, 4
Bracken, B. A.: ref, 220(1), 1424(80), 1771(772)
Brackney, B. E.: ref, 665(48), 1498(5444)

Bradbard, M. R.: ref, 302(40)
Bradfield, R. H.: test, 310
Bradford, E. J. G.: rev, 2179, 2384, 2502
Bradford, J. M.: test, 588
Bradley, F. O.: ref, 2602(2004)
Bradley, G.: ref, 1798(199)
Bradley, L.: test, 205; ref, 2602(2161)
Bradley, L. A.: ref, 1498(5688, 5730), 1798(199, 299), 2030(5079), 2491(2094)
Bradley, M.: ref, 302(40), 941(42)
Bradley, R.: ref, 1108(6), 1126(655), 2208(1565), 2413(613)
Bradley, R. H.: test, 1108; ref, 270(104, 130), 704(21), 1108(2, 3, 4, 5, 7, 8, 9, 12, 13), 1192(166, 190), 2289(1597, 1744)
Bradley, R. W.: ref, 562(8), 2289(1705), 2598(1575)
Bradner, M. N.: ref, 1931(53)
Bradshaw, C.: test, 1340
Bradshaw, J.: ref, 2276(6), 2289(1769)
Bradshaw, J. L.: ref, 1771(681)
Brady, C. A.: ref, 1547(300), 2208(1606)
Brady, G. M.: ref, 1877(9), 2541(9)
Brady, P. J.: ref, 1831(136)
Braff, D.: ref, 1922(15)
Braff, D. L.: ref, 2598(1778, 1816, 1851)
Bragg, M. E.: ref, 1904(119)
Braggio, J. T.: ref, 1126(750), 2602(2005)
Braggio, S. M.: ref, 1126(750), 2602(2005)
Brahen, L. S.: ref, 1498(5047), 2029(196), 2030(4945)
Braida, L. D.: ref, 230(51), 549(1), 2598(1374), 2647(1)
Brainard, C.: ref, 1281(1)
Braito, R.: ref, 116(597)
Branchey, L. B.: ref, 1655(120)
Branchey, M. H.: ref, 1655(86, 89, 120)
Branconnier, R. J.: ref, 280(1023, 1069), 968(2), 1904(65), 2607(130, 153)
Brand, C.: ref, 270(102), 2289(1698)
Brand, L. H.: ref, 1769(94), 2621(415)
Brandenburg, D. C.: test, 1125
Brandenburg-Hruska, N. A.: ref, 859(895), 2300(513)
Brandes, P. J.: ref, 961(7), 1540(21), 1769(100), 1914(877), 2621(434)
Brandt, D.: ref, 2029(195)
Brandt, D. E.: ref, 1209(38)
Brandt, E. N.: ref, 1576(207)
Brannigan, G. G.: ref, 226(166, 180), 280(1070), 534(101, 105), 932(80), 1117(441), 1126(702, 766), 1255(5), 1479(329), 1771(617, 745), 2561(2), 2602(1601, 1602, 1603, 1782, 2006, 2073), 2608(200)
Brannon, R.: ref, 2030(5032)
Bransford, J. D.: ref, 551(59)
Brantley, J.: ref, 2639(2)
Brantley, P. J.: ref, 1498(5537, 5713)
Brasel, K. E.: ref, 2164(39), 2286(273)
Brassell, A.: ref, 551(50)
Braswell, C. E.: ref, 2113(241)
Braswell, J.: rev, 1417, 1589, 2476
Braswell, J. S.: ref, 501(817), 1866(35)
Bratt, H. M.: ref, 479(402), 1265(77)
Bratton, J. C.: ref, 2598(1405)
Brauchi, J. T.: ref, 2620(5)
Braun, C. M. J.: ref, 1347(5)

Braun, J. R.: rev, 670, 1776, 1960, 2138
Braun, N. J.: ref, 28(3), 37(3), 45(5), 1269(27)
Brauzer, B.: ref, 1904(71)
Braverman, B. B.: ref, 346(106)
Bravo, R.: test, 289
Bray, J. H.: ref, 2374(196)
Bray, R.: ref, 590(368, 369), 2160(49, 50)
Brayfield, A. H.: rev, 736, 2355; exc, 1271
Brazelton, T. B.: test, 311; ref, 311(22)
Breaugh, J. A.: ref, 973(32)
Brecht, R. D.: ref, 2602(1788)
Breecher, S. V. A.: test, 2108
Breed, B.: ref, 2217(125), 2621(283)
Breedlove, V.: ref, 2277(4)
Breen, L. J.: ref, 354(1436), 2598(1452), 2602(1741)
Breen, M. J.: ref, 2318(1546)
Breese, F. H.: test, 884
Breidbart, S.: ref, 542(21), 2557(224), 2598(1507)
Breihan, S. K.: ref, 922(9)
Breitenbucher, M.: ref, 1197(306), 1798(277),
Brekke, B.: ref, 964(483), 1341(172), 1371(247), 1479(317, 325), 1540(11), 2217(122, 123)
Brekke, B. W.: ref, 932(69), 1192(184), 2015(206)
Breland, H. M.: ref, 501(786, 845, 912)
Brenden, D. R.: ref, 1125(14)
Brenner, A.: test, 183
Brenner, O. C.: ref, 1798(273)
Brent, D.: ref, 1053(66), 2030(5002), 2602(1826)
Brenza, B. A.: ref, 302(41)
Breslich, E. R.: test, 312
Breslow, R.: ref, 2607(190)
Brett, A.: ref, 1341(169)
Brett, E. M.: ref, 2602(1781), 2608(199)
Breuning, S. E.: ref, 1341(170), 1754(69), 2602(1732)
Brewer, B. R.: ref, 2208(1516)
Brewer, D.: ref, 681(54), 2300(514)
Brewington, A.: rev, 2112, 2307
Brice, R.: ref, 1831(118), 2286(276)
Bricklin, B.: exc, 786
Brickner, A.: rev, 2105, 2448
Bridge, C. A.: ref, 2286(344)
Bridge, G. W. K.: test, 1314
Bridgeman, B.: ref, 344(178), 581(12), 582(6, 7), 1914(741, 832), 2165(25), 2602(2007)
Bridger, W.: ref, 270(61), 2289(1610)
Bridges, A. F.: test, 1067
Bridges, D.: test, 233; ref, 233(1)
Bridgewater, E.: test, 162, 2658
Bridgwater, C. A.: ref, 1831(202)
Briére, E. J.: ref, 1484(11)
Briere, J.: ref, 2602(2228)
Brierley, L. M.: ref, 270(74), 1126(683), 1471(51), 2018(10), 2602(1722)
Brigance, A.: test, 313, 314, 315, 316
Briggs, J. T.: ref, 1077(76)
Briggs, K. C.: test, 1555
Briggs, P. F.: test, 1349, 1370
Briggs, S. R.: ref, 859(896)
Brigman, S. L.: ref, 501(788)
Brill, J. V.: ref, 1128(1)
Brimer, A.: test, 317, 318, 319, 320, 2625
Brimer, M. A.: test, 823, 825; rev, 172, 1533, 1567, 2150
Bringle, R. G.: ref, 2602(2127), 2621(420)

INDEX OF NAMES

Bringmann, W. G.: ref, 1798(242)
Brinich, P. M.: ref, 2289(1780), 2608(226, 243)
Brinker, R. P.: ref, 270(145)
Brinkmann, J. R.: ref, 2413(640)
Brinly, B. L.: ref, 2491(2045)
Brisco, C. M.: ref, 1193(142), 2269(461)
Briscoe, C. D.: ref, 2537(566)
Brisson, M.: ref, 1063(123)
Brittan, E.: ref, 381(63)
Brock, A. M.: ref, 2366(193)
Brock, P. B.: ref, 1371(248)
Brockington, I. F.: ref, 1883(30, 41, 60)
Brockner, J.: ref, 384(8)
Broder, I.: ref, 859(869)
Broder, P. K.: ref, 280(1160), 1250(21), 2602(2162), 2641(19)
Broderick, E. F.: ref, 1498(5048)
Brodman, K.: test, 609
Brodsky, S. L.: rev, 2007
Brody, D. S.: ref, 941(33)
Brody, G. H.: ref, 2602(1677)
Brody, H.: ref, 609(202), 1904(61)
Brody, N.: ref, 270(67)
Brodzinsky, D. M.: ref, 1341(153), 1351(182, 189), 1754(52)
Broen, P. A.: ref, 1771(811), 2412(46)
Broen, W. E.: test, 1796
Broga, M. I.: ref, 1919(38)
Brogden, H. E.: rev, 2638
Brogdon, R. E.: ref, 2657(108)
Bromage, B. K.: ref, 501(895)
Broman, M.: ref, 1948(98)
Broman, S. H.: ref, 2602(1683)
Bromet, E.: ref, 542(19), 872(11)
Brook, J. S.: ref, 354(1560)
Brook, R. C.: ref, 2029(206)
Brooke, R. I.: ref, 1498(5532), 1798(268)
Brookings, J. B.: ref, 1960(83), 2491(2096)
Brooks, C. M.: ref, 1576(216)
Brooks, C. R.: ref, 2030(5024), 2286(328), 2289(1598), 2602(1604, 1870, 2008), 2621(227)
Brooks, D. M.: ref, 551(50)
Brooks, D. N.: ref, 1485(77), 1914(833), 2598(1691), 2607(191)
Brooks, F. R.: ref, 116(582), 1555(325)
Brooks, G. C.: test, 2203
Brooks, G. R.: ref, 2300(515)
Brooks, N.: rev, 236, 728, 894, 979
Brooks, R.: ref, 701(74), 1126(753), 1192(231), 1540(18), 1771(719), 2217(162)
Brookshire, R. H.: ref, 1851(38, 47), 2017(5)
Broomfield, S.: ref, 378(19), 1153(9), 2018(20), 2472(30)
Brophy, J. E.: ref, 344(167, 181), 1473(128, 170), 1479(341)
Brophy, J. T.: ref, 344(182)
Brophy, P. D.: ref, 1771(573)
Brosh, M. C.: ref, 1769(92)
Brosnan, P. G.: ref, 2602(2009)
Brotherton, P. L.: ref, 1904(116)
Broughton, A.: ref, 780(1676)
Brouse, T. R.: ref, 501(827)
Brousseau, K. R.: ref, 1046(575, 587)
Brouwers, E. Y. M.: ref, 2598(1312)
Broverman, D. M.: ref, 794(444), 2598(1817)

Brower, D.: exc, 1235
Brown, A. S.: rev, 69; ref, 283(159, 160), 1498(5762), 1914(891)
Brown, A. W.: rev, 204; ref, 1771(521)
Brown, B. A.: ref, 1769(79), 2621(369)
Brown, B. J.: ref, 1233(218)
Brown, C.: ref, 1567(13), 2077(28)
Brown, C. C.: ref, 1498(5157)
Brown, C. M.: rev, 309, 1813
Brown, C. S.: ref, 308(21)
Brown, D. G.: test, 1201
Brown, D. H.: ref, 553(16)
Brown, D. R.: ref, 1576(198), 1726(363)
Brown, D. S.: ref, 1798(263)
Brown, E. B.: ref, 280(1108), 751(26), 1126(727), 2289(1711), 2602(1899), 2621(337)
Brown, E. L.: ref, 1498(5597)
Brown, E. V.: ref, 964(495)
Brown, F.: exc, 2134, 2657; ref, 280(1045)
Brown, F. G.: rev, 551, 2260; exc, 1270
Brown, G.: ref, 1771(720), 2217(163), 2598(1552)
Brown, G. L.: ref, 1498(5655)
Brown, G. M.: test, 352
Brown, G. S.: ref, 2300(582)
Brown, G. W.: ref, 1883(39)
Brown, H. S.: ref, 2598(1562)
Brown, I. D. R.: ref, 559(51), 653(145), 1771(623), 1914(784)
Brown, J.: ref, 1498(5315), 2300(420), 2665(2)
Brown, J. A.: ref, 2286(269), 2557(242)
Brown, J. B.: ref, 378(12), 501(807), 1498(5234), 2472(18)
Brown, J. F.: ref, 1424(57)
Brown, J. I.: test, 503, 1568
Brown, J. J.: ref, 2208(1519)
Brown, J. S.: ref, 609(198), 1498(5049)
Brown, J. V.: ref, 270(128, 131), 311(33, 34), 2289(1740)
Brown, K. E.: ref, 2218(145), 2602(1911, 2062, 2063)
Brown, L.: ref, 665(44), 1192(208), 2289(1607)
Brown, L. L.: test, 273; ref, 1986(1), 2292(32)
Brown, L. S.: ref, 1498(5325)
Brown, M.: test, 640; ref, 1063(92)
Brown, M. H.: ref, 559(55)
Brown, M. J.: ref, 280(1024), 701(36)
Brown, N. W.: ref, 354(1488), 2029(222)
Brown, P. L.: ref, 1498(5377)
Brown, P. S.: ref, 76(626)
Brown, R.: ref, 2598(1639), 2602(1949)
Brown, R. A.: ref, 2208(1646)
Brown, R. D.: test, 2434
Brown, R. L.: test, 2664
Brown, R. T.: ref, 1771(714), 2602(2010), 2621(385)
Brown, S. D.: ref, 883(107), 1197(304), 2413(668)
Brown, S. E.: ref, 501(846), 1295(285, 289, 296, 297), 1366(1), 1508(113, 121)
Brown, T. C.: ref, 1555(321), 1726(362), 2208(1589), 2318(1560)
Brown, T. J.: ref, 1479(311)
Brown, T. R.: ref, 677(2)
Brown, V. L.: test, 2422, 2456; exc, 2202
Brown, W.: test, 635; ref, 1771(631)
Brown, W. A.: ref, 794(401), 1789(676), 1904(51, 73, 108)
Brown, W. F.: test, 781, 2346, 2374

Brown, W. R.: ref, 1473(203)
Browne, G. W.: ref, 1883(74)
Browne, J. A.: ref, 354(1387), 558(53), 859(725), 1046(569), 1419(669), 1498(5050), 1726(349), 2208(1520)
Browne, T.: ref, 2289(1599), 2602(1605), 2621(228)
Brownell, W. A.: rev, 197, 345, 1625
Browning, R.: ref, 1769(68)
Brownlee, J. R.: ref, 270(158), 2598(1848)
Brownlee, L.: ref, 559(58)
Brownless, V.: test, 2195
Browns, F.: ref, 1622(46), 2218(12)
Broyles, J. W.: ref, 590(389)
Brubaker, P.: ref, 354(1557), 653(171)
Bruce, J. D.: test, 705
Bruce, M. H.: ref, 501(897), 1046(584)
Bruce, M. M.: test, 192, 218, 323, 333, 465, 800, 1146, 1528, 2051, 2053, 2363
Bruch, C. B.: ref, 2512(585, 602)
Bruch, M. A.: ref, 1931(40)
Bruchon–Schweitzer, M.: ref, 859(843), 1046(580), 2208(1607), 2343(1043)
Bruder, G.: ref, 1883(59)
Brueckner, L. J.: rev, 713
Bruhn, J. G.: ref, 1555(314, 315, 332), 1568(123), 1754(70)
Bruininks, R. H.: test, 324; ref, 719(29)
Bruininks, V. L.: ref, 398(112), 691(40), 701(58), 890(331, 332), 962(28), 1126(719), 1192(212), 1250(13, 14), 1769(51), 2269(462), 2641(10, 11)
Brumback, R. A.: ref, 701(73), 1126(751, 788), 1771(715, 809), 1831(186, 218), 1853(299), 2602(2011, 2012, 2216, 2217), 2608(227, 250), 2621(386, 387, 459, 460)
Brumfield, S. M.: ref, 285(2)
Brumwell, M.: ref, 1555(324)
Brun, B.: ref, 794(403)
Brun, J. K.: test, 1656
Brunclik, H. L.: test, 797, 1348, 1654
Bruning, R. H.: ref, 1192(187), 1473(146), 1568(136, 144), 1754(71), 2286(288), 2512(644)
Brunner, R. L.: ref, 270(105), 280(1103), 751(23), 2289(1700), 2557(227), 2602(1871), 2621(320)
Brunnguell, D.: ref, 1798(301), 2179(252)
Brunson, B.: ref, 2217(176), 2598(1786)
Brunt, D.: ref, 2244(39)
Brush, D. H.: ref, 501(847), 2318(1579)
Brusilow, S. W.: ref, 280(1132), 283(154), 2598(1681), 2621(382)
Bruya, L. D.: ref, 1831(116)
Bryan, C.: ref, 6(84)
Bryan, J. E.: test, 2231; rev, 755, 808, 881, 1067, 1254
Bryan, M. M.: rev, 344, 2260, 2286
Bryan, T.: ref, 1473(171), 1771(799), 1831(161), 2621(321)
Bryant, C. K.: ref, 1424(34, 56)
Bryant, L. W.: ref, 590(382), 1585(16), 2160(63)
Bryant, N. D.: rev, 240, 719, 935; ref, 1351(180), 1575(3)
Bryant, P.: ref, 2602(2161)
Bryce, J.: test, 22
Bryden, M. P.: ref, 2246(24), 2285(10)
Bryla, D. A.: ref, 678(24)
Bryntwick, S.: ref, 1197(293), 1419(686)
Bryson, R. A.: ref, 1257(105)

Bubenzer, D. L.: ref, 354(1479), 2208(1608)
Bucci, W.: ref, 2598(1432)
Buchanan, A. D.: rev, 1139
Buchanan, R. G.: test, 2469
Buchholz, S.: test, 1420
Buchsbaum, H. K.: ref, 1351(197), 2300(561), 2594(201)
Buchsbaum, M. S.: ref, 1247(164), 1498(5449, 5581, 5592, 5618), 1531(294), 1771(752), 2030(5055), 2413(670), 2598(1570, 1692, 1696)
Buchtel, H. A.: ref, 2598(1621), 2607(183)
Buchwald, A. M.: ref, 1498(5558)
Buck, C. W.: ref, 1424(82)
Buck, J. A.: ref, 1498(5235)
Buck, J. N.: test, 1047, 2502
Buck, P. S.: ref, 859(726)
Buck, R.: ref, 794(428)
Buckingham, B. R.: test, 325
Buckingham, M. S.: ref, 2168(9)
Buckland, P.: ref, 1754(95), 2621(360)
Buckley, E.: test, 730
Buckley, J. M.: ref, 1555(311)
Buckner, T.: ref, 794(443)
Bucky, S.: ref, 558(72), 1498(5607)
Bucky, S. F.: ref, 558(70), 1498(5557), 2300(502)
Budtz–Olsen, I.: ref, 859(962)
Buel, C. L.: ref, 400(131), 2208(1647)
Bues, H. W.: test, 1945
Buffardi, L.: ref, 1013(102), 2499(82)
Buffington, W. D.: rev, 999
Bugatch, S.: test, 1566
Bugen, L. A.: ref, 890(322)
Bugental, D. B.: ref, 1771(523), 1853(267, 275)
Bugg, P. W.: ref, 2491(2055)
Bugge, I. D.: ref, 1798(196)
Buhler, C.: test, 897, 1830, 2513
Buhmeyer, K. J.: ref, 890(323, 333), 1555(302, 316, 317), 1789(637, 659, 660), 2343(1028, 1037)
Buhrich, N.: ref, 354(1480), 751(24), 917(75), 2598(1563)
Bukstel, L. H.: ref, 392(4)
Buktenica, N. A.: test, 701, 2452; ref, 701(37), 1473(125), 1479(312), 1754(53), 2452(12)
Bull, K. S.: ref, 116(548), 2496(37)
Buller, R.: test, 2061
Bullock, W. B.: test, 181
Bumpas, T. C.: ref, 960(7)
Bumpus, M. J.: test, 636, 1433
Bunce, H.: ref, 1555(314, 315, 332), 1568(123), 1754(70)
Buncic, R. J.: ref, 270(93)
Bunt, M. M.: ref, 76(645)
Buonphane, N.: ref, 1498(5208)
Burack, C. M.: ref, 270(153), 311(45)
Buranen, C.: ref, 1498(5548)
Burch, E. A.: ref, 280(1136)
Burch, R. L.: rev, 345, 1477, 2287
Burchett, K. E.: rev, 203
Burdett, A. D.: test, 2574
Burdg, N. B.: ref, 2602(2078)
Burdick, B. M.: ref, 1498(5582)
Burdick, J. A.: ref, 859(844)
Burdock, E. I.: test, 2588
Burdsal, C.: ref, 400(131), 472(12), 1063(90), 2208(1609, 1647)

INDEX OF NAMES

Bureau of Business Research, Ohio State University: test, 1296
Burg, C.: ref, 1877(10), 2289(1745)
Burgemeister, B. B.: test, 534
Burger, A. L.: ref, 2289(1746), 2602(2013)
Burger, G. K.: ref, 354(1388, 1438, 1481, 1571), 1498(5063), 2208(1525)
Burger, J. M.: ref, 1063(132), 1547(320)
Burgess, A. E.: ref, 1498(5527)
Burgess, E. W.: test, 1375, 1382
Burgess, R. L.: ref, 609(216)
Burgess, T. C.: rev, 1531
Buriel, R.: ref, 398(103), 1473(147), 2598(1433)
Burish, T. G.: ref, 1547(249, 284, 301, 331), 2300(459)
Burke, C. L.: rev, 932
Burke, E. L.: ref, 1170(230)
Burke, H.: ref, 1498(5051)
Burke, H. R.: ref, 1498(5424)
Burke, J.: ref, 964(483), 2217(122)
Burke, J. P.: ref, 1356(98)
Burke, M.: ref, 1073(126), 1919(44), 2208(1638), 2598(1564)
Burke, R. J.: ref, 354(1522), 2208(1648)
Burkhart, B. R.: ref, 76(602), 354(1437), 1498(5236, 5237, 5241, 5448, 5583), 1798(255), 1904(89, 109)
Burkhart, G.: ref, 6(53)
Burks, H. F.: test, 16, 327, 328, 2082, 2331, 2400
Burley, P. M.: ref, 1485(70), 2228(69)
Burnett, K.: ref, 1904(133)
Burnham, R. A.: ref, 1498(5430)
Burnharn, D. K.: ref, 883(82)
Burns, B. J.: ref, 780(1667)
Burns, C. J.: ref, 964(476)
Burns, E.: ref, 1126(650)
Burns, F. M.: test, 1785
Burns, J. K.: ref, 2289(1630), 2602(1673)
Burns, J. W.: ref, 2300(405)
Burns, K. A.: ref, 1771(591), 2214(1)
Burns, R. B.: ref, 551(51), 653(159), 1257(157)
Burns, R. K.: test, 1788, 2262, 2654
Burns, W. J.: ref, 1424(32, 51), 1771(561, 591, 675), 2024(1, 2), 2214(1)
Burr, D. B.: ref, 1126(686, 708)
Burr, E. T.: rev, 2500
Burrow, G. N.: ref, 1576(224)
Burrows, E. H.: ref, 932(73), 962(25), 1771(592), 2293(10), 2472(14)
Burrows, G. D.: ref, 1757(16)
Bursill, A.: exc, 1419
Burson, S. L.: exc, 61
Burstein, A. G.: rev, 2030, 2598, 2602; ref, 1754(105), 1798(252, 260, 274), 2030(5065)
Burstiner, I.: ref, 2512(561)
Burt, C.: test, 329, 330; rev, 2269; exc, 2289
Burt, M. A.: ref, 2602(2014)
Burt, M. K.: test, 290, 291; ref, 1282(2)
Burton, C. A.: ref, 2300(387)
Burton, J. K.: ref, 374(235), 1192(187), 1473(146), 1754(71), 2286(288)
Burton, M. D.: ref, 890(363)
Bus, D. M.: ref, 348(1)
Busby, K.: ref, 1498(5584), 2208(1649), 2300(516)
Busch, N.: ref, 1538(70)
Buse, S. T.: ref, 2289(1608)
Busemeyer, J.: ref, 392(4)

Bush, D.: ref, 1498(5228), 2179(211)
Bush, D. M.: ref, 1192(208)
Bush, M.: ref, 1498(5052), 2598(1302)
Bush, P. G.: ref, 280(1177), 534(111), 823(25), 1153(10), 2018(22), 2281(4), 2602(2229)
Bushnell, J. A.: ref, 859(739), 1197(276)
Buss, A. H.: ref, 859(896)
Buss, D. M.: ref, 354(1523, 1561), 1798(275, 302), 1914(876), 2602(2159)
Busse, T. V.: ref, 1192(188), 1341(171), 1479(326), 2286(289)
Buswell, G. T.: test, 335, 713, 2271
Butcher, H. J.: rev, 590
Butcher, J. N.: rev, 1499, 1500, 1501, 1502; ref, 1498(5032, 5059, 5238, 5755, 5585)
Butkovich, C.: ref, 2621(217)
Butkowsky, I. S.: ref, 653(160), 932(105)
Butkus, M.: ref, 1796(1)
Butler, A. J. P.: ref, 780(1703)
Butler, C.: ref, 2602(1606)
Butler, C. G.: ref, 1473(129), 2286(277)
Butler, D. F.: test, 336
Butler, G. S.: ref, 2557(243)
Butler, K. G.: rev, 961, 1332, 2018, 2541, 2551
Butler, L.: ref, 1831(187)
Butler, M. L.: test, 618
Butler, M. N.: test, 2571
Butler, W. T.: ref, 354(1471), 780(1675), 859(824), 1498(5349), 1576(206)
Butt, D. S.: rev, 1208, 1209
Butt, J. H.: ref, 2300(439, 494)
Buttafuoco, P. M.: ref, 351(5)
Butter, E. J.: ref, 1568(124)
Butter, H. J.: ref, 859(807), 1498(5300)
Butterfield, D. A.: ref, 1295(303), 1296(179)
Butterfield, E. C.: exc, 2623
Butterfield, P.: ref, 270(126), 338(10)
Butters, E.: ref, 116(527)
Butters, N.: ref, 794(374), 2598(1345, 1434), 2607(154)
Butterworth, G.: ref, 2608(176)
Butterworth, G. E.: ref, 2602(1867), 2608(211)
Byck, R.: ref, 113(26), 1904(103)
Bylenga, C.: ref, 732(402)
Bynum, J. E.: ref, 1960(73, 79)
Byrd, S. H.: ref, 2602(1745)
Byrne, B.: ref, 21(4), 2113(250), 2602(2163)
Byrne, D. G.: ref, 859(845), 941(23, 34), 1883(33, 69)
Byrne, M. C.: rev, 960, 1650, 1851; ref, 483(15), 1622(32), 2602(1674)
Byrne, T. P.: ref, 2134(114, 128), 2413(669)
Byrne, W. J.: ref, 953(14)
Byrnes, M. M.: ref, 1754(97), 2181(18), 2218(153)
Byrum, W.: ref, 2030(5075)
Bzoch, K. R.: test, 338
Caban, J. P.: ref, 1257(121)
Cabianca, W. A.: ref, 2353(31)
Cabot, R.: test, 1345
Cabrera, Y. A.: exc, 2223
Cacciola, J.: ref, 1883(89)
Cadieux, R.: ref, 1498(5636)
Cadow, B.: ref, 354(1389), 1498(5053)
Cady, M.: ref, 2621(407)
Caffey, E. M.: ref, 1240(51)
Cagney, M. A.: ref, 2217(108)

Cahen, L. S.: rev, 2324; ref, 551(27)
Cahill, M. C.: ref, 1798(231)
Cain, L. F.: test, 343, 2508
Cain, R. B.: ref, 794(375, 400)
Caine, E. D.: ref, 308(6), 2598(1435)
Cairns, E.: ref, 2269(463), 2629(121)
Cairns, N. U.: ref, 874(50), 1831(162), 2491(2054)
Cairo, P. C.: ref, 2318(1580)
Caldwell, A. B.: test, 1500; ref, 1498(5635, 5636, 5637)
Caldwell, B. M.: test, 581, 1108; ref, 270(104, 130), 704(12, 22), 1108(1, 2, 3, 4, 6, 7, 8, 9, 12, 13), 1126(655), 1351(204), 2289(1597, 1744)
Caldwell, J. R.: rev, 574
Caldwell, M. A.: ref, 2598(1667)
Calef, R. A.: ref, 2289(1600)
Calef, R. S.: ref, 2289(1600)
Calfee, K. H.: rev, 484
Calfee, R. C.: rev, 353
Calhoun, G.: ref, 964(484), 1831(117), 2286(274)
Calhoun, K. S.: ref, 1904(125)
Calhoun, L. G.: ref, 1419(672), 1798(212)
Caliste, E. R.: ref, 552(2), 553(18), 1531(289)
Calkins, V.: ref, 1555(324)
Call, T.: ref, 6(40, 79)
Callahan, C. M.: test, 2069; ref, 2512(562)
Callahan, L. G.: rev, 584, 2478, 2480
Callahan, R.: ref, 1424(61), 1969(108)
Callahan, R. J.: test, 358
Callaway, A. B.: ref, 344(136)
Callaway, B.: ref, 1771(673, 802), 2217(149, 184), 2218(20), 2602(1928, 2199), 2641(22)
Callaway, G.: test, 1340
Callegari, A. I.: ref, 2491(2043)
Callendar, J. C.: ref, 1981(1)
Callis, R.: test, 2298
Calnen, T.: ref, 2602(1603)
Calsyn, D.: ref, 1498(5085, 5086)
Calsyn, D. A.: ref, 472(18, 20), 1013(109, 132), 1498(5054, 5171, 5227, 5307, 5761, 5608), 2179(243), 2598(1453, 1714)
Caltagirone, C.: ref, 1914(711, 756)
Calvanio, R.: ref, 2598(1745), 2607(201)
Calvert, B.: test, 1620
Calvert, E. J.: ref, 2598(1436)
Calvey, H.: ref, 1193(138)
Cambell, K.: ref, 1996(8)
Cameron, J.: ref, 270(85), 2289(1667)
Camfield, C. S.: ref, 270(107), 2289(1701)
Camfield, P. R.: ref, 270(107), 2289(1701)
Camilleri, R.: ref, 1789(679)
Camilli, G.: ref, 1351(202), 1914(896)
Cammock, T.: ref, 2269(463)
Camp, B. W.: ref, 302(26, 27), 1126(651, 652), 2269(435), 2602(1607, 1608), 2621(229, 230, 231)
Camp, C.: ref, 1855(29)
Camp, J.: ref, 995(141)
Campagna, W. D.: ref, 354(1562), 2208(1677)
Campanini, T.: ref, 2598(1621), 2607(183)
Campbell, A.: ref, 859(787), 2208(1566)
Campbell, A. A.: test, 1915
Campbell, A. L.: ref, 283(158), 1771(773), 1914(878), 2201(1), 2380(6), 2598(1818), 2602(2164)
Campbell, B. A.: test, 2182, 2183, 2184, 2185, 2186, 2187, 2188, 2189, 2190, 2191, 2192, 2193, 2261, 2267, 2270, 2276
Campbell, B. K.: ref, 890(324), 1171(5)
Campbell, D.: rev, 152, 1369
Campbell, D. P.: test, 2318; rev, 187, 863, 1015, 1316, 1528; exc, 2318
Campbell, D. T.: rev, 1945
Campbell, E.: test, 1893
Campbell, F. A.: ref, 270(95, 121), 1424(42, 54), 2289(1682, 1730), 2598(1634), 2602(1939)
Campbell, H. G.: ref, 1498(5055)
Campbell, J. A.: rev, 61, 127, 441, 938
Campbell, J. B.: ref, 354(1390), 2208(1521)
Campbell, J. T.: rev, 1113, 1302
Campbell, L.: ref, 609(203), 911(2)
Campbell, M.: ref, 2289(1653), 2608(187)
Campbell, N. J.: ref, 374(220), 2289(1722), 2602(1922)
Campbell, R.: ref, 1922(17)
Campbell, R. L.: ref, 1831(203), 2286(345), 2413(641)
Campbell, R. T.: ref, 1341(156)
Campbell, S. B.: ref, 398(93), 2602(1609), 2608(171)
Campbell, T. F.: ref, 664(10)
Campbell, V. N.: rev, 598
Canadian Association for Health, Physical Education and Recreation: test, 342
Canavan–Gumpert, D.: ref, 2286(275)
Canfield, A. A.: test, 364, 1160, 1276, 1310, 1800, 2362
Canfield, J. S.: test, 1160, 2362
Cangelosi, A.: ref, 1831(188)
Canney, G.: ref, 2292(19)
Canning, P. M.: ref, 1771(716), 2602(2015), 2621(388)
Cannon, R. A.: ref, 953(14)
Cansler, D.: ref, 280(1152), 1498(5703), 2598(1788), 2602(2122)
Canter, A.: test, 280
Canter, F. M.: ref, 1555(331)
Canter, G. J.: ref, 932(91)
Canter, M. A.: ref, 378(13)
Cantor, S.: ref, 325(34), 2602(2055)
Cantrell, R. P.: ref, 1473(126), 1754(54)
Cantwell, D. P.: ref, 280(1120), 859(846), 960(15), 1007(35), 1126(752), 1769(78, 93, 104), 1771(717), 1853(286), 2602(1953, 2016, 2109), 2608(228), 2621(389)
Caparulo, B. K.: ref, 1319(72), 2018(7)
Capitani, E.: ref, 1914(875), 2598(1812)
Caplan, J. R.: ref, 282(146), 1976(1), 1981(3)
Caplan, M. E.: ref, 681(57)
Capone, T.: ref, 1498(5047), 2029(196), 2030(4945)
Caponigro, J. D.: ref, 1769(96), 2286(340), 2621(423)
Capote, B.: ref, 1655(90)
Cappa, S. F.: ref, 1914(794), 2598(1565)
Cappadona, D. L.: ref, 551(37), 2087(24), 2181(15)
Caputo, D. V.: ref, 280(1058), 2602(1708)
Caramazza, A.: ref, 308(15)
Carbonell, J.: ref, 1498(5357)
Card, S. C.: ref, 896(5)
Cardenas, C.: ref, 1789(672)
Cardwell, G. F.: ref, 2030(4993), 2598(1463)
Career Skills Assessment Program of The College Board: test, 375
Carey, B. J.: ref, 1771(613)
Carey, J. C.: ref, 1771(593), 2289(1654)
Carey, M. A.: ref, 374(206), 551(38)
Carey, R. G.: ref, 1940(87)

INDEX OF NAMES

Carifo, J.: ref, 859(729), 1798(200), 2208(1528)
Carkin, S.: ref, 1077(61)
Carl, H.: ref, 1555(338)
Carlen, P. C.: ref, 1052(3)
Carlen, P. L.: ref, 2598(1804)
Carlin, A. S.: ref, 645(13), 1498(5056, 5239, 5268)
Carline, D. E.: test, 815
Carlock, C. J.: ref, 1789(638)
Carlomusto, M.: ref, 2300(362, 423), 2598(1501)
Carlson, D.: exc, 581
Carlson, J. S.: ref, 1914(742, 743, 834), 2621(322)
Carlson, K. A.: rev, 612; ref, 859(768)
Carlson, L.: test, 1287; ref, 2608(244)
Carlson, R.: ref, 1555(333)
Carlson, R. L.: ref, 378(8)
Carlson, R. W.: ref, 1498(5240), 2030(5054)
Carlson, S. B.: ref, 991(16), 995(153), 1257(173)
Carlson, T. R.: rev, 1390, 1986
Carlyn, M.: ref, 1555(303)
Carman, S. M.: ref, 2413(699), 2602(2185)
Carmichael, J. S.: ref, 2587(35)
Carmody, T. P.: ref, 1798(196)
Carney, C. G.: test, 370
Carney, M. L.: ref, 1568(134)
Carney, P.: ref, 76(603)
Carney, R. E.: test, 862, 2026, 2146
Carney, Weedman and Associates: test, 684, 1974
Caron, M.: ref, 1798(290), 2300(556)
Carp, A.: ref, 1498(5740), 2491(2097), 2598(1819)
Carp, F. M.: ref, 1498(5740), 2491(2097), 2598(1819)
Carpenter, D.: ref, 344(150), 2602(2078)
Carpenter, H.: ref, 2665(1)
Carpenter, J. C.: ref, 354(1482), 1498(5506), 1555(304)
Carpenter, L.: ref, 1883(60)
Carpenter, P. J.: ref, 890(335), 1904(66)
Carpenter, R. L.: ref, 212(9), 1126(764), 1622(50), 1771(741), 2472(25), 2557(239)
Carpenter, S.: ref, 344(150)
Carpenter, T. P.: ref, 1077(56)
Carr, A. C.: ref, 280(1104, 1167), 751(25, 41), 2030(5025, 5088), 2491(2103), 2598(1566, 1832)
Carr, D.: test, 548; ref, 2598(1336)
Carr, G. D.: ref, 1555(326)
Carr, G. L.: ref, 1960(75)
Carr-Kaffashan, L.: ref, 2300(460)
Carrell, M. R.: ref, 1508(132)
Carrera, R. N.: ref, 883(81), 1498(5438)
Carriere, R. A.: ref, 344(161)
Carrieri, V. L.: ref, 1904(129)
Carrington, P.: ref, 1197(310), 2300(542)
Carroll, D. J.: test, 775; rev, 1024, 2625
Carroll, J. A.: ref, 1462(139), 1503(65), 1771(642), 2602(1610, 1872), 2621(323)
Carroll, J. B.: test, 1527; rev, 547, 549, 732, 899, 1044, 1126, 1483, 1484, 2269, 2537
Carroll, J. E.: ref, 280(1052), 1771(567)
Carroll, J. F. X.: ref, 1798(303), 2413(614)
Carroll, J. L.: test, 2562; ref, 961(2), 1020(21), 1462(139), 1498(5127), 1503(65), 1771(642), 2208(1567), 2602(1610, 1872), 2621(323)
Carron, A. V.: ref, 890(325, 334)
Carron, T. S.: ref, 1855(24)
Carrow, E.: test, 378, 2472; ref, 2472(9)
Carrow-Woolfolk, E.: test, 377
Carruth, B. R.: ref, 2208(1522)

Carruthers, R. L.: ref, 707(19)
Carry, L. R.: rev, 575; ref, 1257(179)
Carsello, C. J.: ref, 76(627), 2318(1581)
Carskadon, T. G.: ref, 751(20), 1555(305, 318), 2497(41)
Carson, C. C.: ref, 1498(5425)
Carson, T. P.: ref, 681(55)
Carsrud, A. L.: ref, 6(66), 883(92), 1547(302)
Carsrud, K. B.: ref, 6(66), 883(92), 1547(302)
Cartelli, L. M.: ref, 1478(65, 69, 72), 2289(1601, 1751)
Carter, D. E.: ref, 280(1071), 1192(189), 1473(193), 2602(1733)
Carter, H.: ref, 860(116), 1013(80, 103)
Carter, H. D.: rev, 1165, 1186, 1271, 2318, 2518
Carter, J.: ref, 2512(586)
Carter, J. A.: ref, 398(109)
Carter, J. L.: ref, 280(1091), 1007(25), 2216(1), 2217(135), 2621(301)
Carter, M.: ref, 859(944)
Carter, P.: ref, 2269(465, 477)
Carter, R. C.: ref, 1257(138)
Carter, T.: ref, 665(42), 2318(1552)
Cartwright, C. A.: ref, 2039(11)
Cartwright, L. K.: ref, 116(526), 354(1391)
Cartwright, R.: ref, 116(527)
Caruso, A.: ref, 911(4)
Carvajal, T. L.: exc, 231
Carver, C.: test, 2647
Carver, C. S.: ref, 1046(578)
Carver, G.: ref, 2598(1852)
Casale, U.: ref, 1568(138)
Case, H. W.: test, 2373
Casey, J. P.: ref, 1371(248)
Casey, N. A.: ref, 1765(10)
Cash, M.: ref, 354(1572), 1789(730)
Cash, T. F.: test, 619
Cashen, V. M.: test, 2325
Cashman, J. F.: ref, 1295(298), 1296(176)
Caskey, W. E.: ref, 280(1025, 1137), 1754(55, 100)
Caslyn, D.: ref, 1498(5085)
Caso, A.: test, 379
Cason, C. L.: ref, 2300(589)
Caspar, R.: ref, 1498(5276)
Casper, R. C.: ref, 1498(5586), 1673(11)
Cass, D. H.: test, 380
Cassaretto, F. P.: rev, 61
Cassel, R.: test, 608, 2457
Cassel, R. N.: test, 392, 783, 785, 1020, 1297, 1302, 2461
Cassell, W. A.: test, 1917, 2239; ref, 2239(3)
Cassidy, A. M.: ref, 766(22), 932(56), 1479(313)
Cassidy, J.: ref, 1479(363), 2217(160), 2218(13)
Cassisi, J. P.: ref, 780(1703)
Castner, B. M.: rev, 1471
Caston, E. E.: ref, 1798(218)
Catalan, J.: ref, 860(143), 941(42), 2300(534)
Catlin, F. I.: ref, 280(1073), 1126(692), 2602(1740)
Catron, D. W.: ref, 2318(1523), 2598(1437, 1567), 2602(1611)
Catron, S. S.: ref, 2602(1611)
Cattell, A. K. S.: test, 643
Cattell, M. D. L.: test, 1233
Cattell, P.: test, 381; rev, 1272
Cattell, R. B.: test, 400, 547, 643, 772, 787, 1197, 1219,

597

1233, 1538, 1573, 1662, 2087, 2208; rev, 118, 357; ref, 547(7), 732(400), 1233(210), 2269(452)
Catterson, J. H.: test, 766
Cautela, J. R.: test, 271
Cauter, E. V.: ref, 1612(1)
Cauthen, D.: ref, 2665(1)
Cauthen, N.: ref, 2598(1438)
Cauthen, N. R.: ref, 2598(1303, 1439), 2607(131)
Cavior, N.: ref, 1473(215), 1771(774)
Cawley, J. F.: test, 692
Cawley, L. J.: test, 692
Cazden, C. B.: rev, 378, 2293, 2478
Cecconi, C. P.: ref, 1192(165)
Ceci, S. J.: ref, 280(1075), 330(18), 2602(1755)
Cegalis, J. A.: ref, 1498(5057, 5587), 2598(1304, 1693, 1820)
Cei, A.: ref, 794(439, 447)
Celedon, J. M.: ref, 270(132)
Celistino, J. F.: ref, 472(13)
Celliers, C. P.: test, 18
Center for the Study of Aging and Human Development: test, 1659
Center for the Study of Evaluation, UCLA: test, 1390, 1391, 1392, 1393, 1394, 1395, 1396, 1397, 1398, 1399, 1400
Centofanti, C. C.: test, 2201
Centra, J. A.: test, 1158; ref, 995(132, 149), 2334(18)
Central Institute for the Deaf: test, 2040
Cerf, F. A.: ref, 2208(1664)
Ceridono, D.: ref, 794(439)
Cermak, L. S.: ref, 308(13)
Cermak, S. A.: ref, 2218(14), 2244(40), 2602(2017)
Cerniglia, R. P.: ref, 2413(615)
Cerreto, M.: ref, 1498(5165)
Cervantes, H.: ref, 6(44), 2387(1)
Cervenka, E. J.: rev, 1484
Cesari, J.: ref, 374(210)
Chabot, R. J.: ref, 2621(290)
Chacon, C.: ref, 1883(62)
Chadbourn, R. A.: exc, 1188
Chadwick, O.: ref, 1567(19), 2602(2165)
Chakrobarti, P. K.: ref, 859(751)
Chalip, L.: ref, 1013(81)
Chall, J. S.: test, 2033, 2034
Challman, R. C.: rev, 1377, 1383, 1756, 2031
Chalus, G. A.: ref, 1547(282), 2030(4985), 2491(2037)
Chamberlain, C. J.: ref, 1462(133), 2607(161)
Chamberlain, J. C.: test, 11, 1285
Chamberlin, K.: ref, 2300(397)
Chamberlin, R. W.: ref, 1492(9)
Chambers, C. A.: ref, 1883(31)
Chambers, E. D.: ref, 1498(5115), 2638(127)
Chambers, E. G.: rev, 1027, 1030, 1031, 1271, 2373
Chambers, J. A.: ref, 243(122), 653(161)
Chambers, J. L.: test, 1825; ref, 1825(20, 22)
Chambers, R. L.: ref, 794(391), 859(795)
Chambliss, J.: ref, 551(19), 1896(8)
Champagne, D.: ref, 2537(562)
Champion, D. W.: ref, 1473(215), 1771(774)
Champney, H.: test, 884
Champoux, J. E.: ref, 116(619), 1316(4)
Chan, D. W.: ref, 1798(257)
Chan, S. W. C.: ref, 308(19)
Chander, A.: ref, 859(863)
Chandler, D.: ref, 280(1036), 922(6), 2602(1651)
Chandler, E.: ref, 1197(294), 1198(1)
Chandler, L.: ref, 311(16)
Chandler, M.: ref, 1240(60), 2602(1965), 2608(220)
Chandler, T. A.: ref, 2300(461)
Chaney, E. F.: ref, 890(349, 350), 1013(59, 93), 1462(118), 1498(5058, 5171, 5172, 5250, 5325, 5497, 5498, 5499, 5673), 2179(195, 212, 227, 228), 2413(627), 2587(44), 2598(1375, 1513, 1628, 1629)
Chaney, L. A.: ref, 1853(275)
Chang, A.: ref, 1940(85)
Chang, A. F.: ref, 1498(5347)
Chansky, N.: ref, 398(124), 2287(40)
Chansky, N. M.: ref, 501(874), 590(381), 1754(72), 2160(58)
Chapel, J. L.: ref, 2168(10), 2602(1959)
Chapey, R.: ref, 1814(4), 1851(31)
Chapin, F. S.: test, 384
Chaplin, S.: ref, 270(107), 2289(1701)
Chaplin, W.: ref, 1498(5649)
Chapman, C. R.: ref, 2300(350)
Chapman, D. L.: ref, 212(11), 378(5), 1622(37, 54), 1771(775)
Chapman, D. W.: ref, 442(1, 2)
Chapman, J. P.: ref, 1798(232)
Chapman, J. W.: ref, 362(4, 6), 1754(85, 116), 1831(135, 160, 204), 2077(31), 2602(1869), 2621(318)
Chapman, L. H.: rev, 203, 1626
Chapman, L. J.: ref, 1798(232), 2030(5027)
Chapman, M.: ref, 501(787), 794(365)
Chapparo, C. J.: ref, 2244(43)
Charles, H. L.: ref, 283(151), 859(875), 1197(301), 1498(5679), 1765(13), 2638(138)
Charles, R. I.: ref, 1192(230)
Charlop, M.: ref, 1331(40)
Charman, D. K.: ref, 860(117)
Charney, D. S.: ref, 1498(5635, 5636, 5637)
Charney, J.: ref, 2100(12)
Charron, P. A.: ref, 1013(107)
Chase, C. I.: rev, 1126, 2298, 2441, 2474; ref, 483(43), 1192(259)
Chasey, W. C.: ref, 2289(1602)
Chason, L. R.: ref, 501(836), 1498(5358)
Chassin, L.: ref, 1498(5741)
Chatterjea, R. G.: ref, 794(445), 859(942), 2300(517)
Chatterji, S.: test, 387, 820, 1615, 2099; ref, 732(398), 1615(3)
Chattin, C.: ref, 1054(7)
Chattopadhyay, P. K.: ref, 2300(517)
Chaudhry, R.: ref, 1655(121)
Chauncey, H.: rev, 1193
Chavez, E. L.: ref, 280(1138), 964(501), 1771(718), 2598(1694)
Chavis, G. L.: ref, 1077(51)
Chazan, M.: rev, 1229; exc, 1367
Chazan, S.: ref, 2621(346, 404)
Cheadle, A. J.: ref, 1883(32, 44)
Cheap, T. L.: ref, 1557(10)
Chebib, F. S.: ref, 859(844)
Checketts, K. T.: ref, 76(617), 354(1408), 890(328)
Checkley, S. A.: ref, 1883(61, 70)
Cheek, F. E.: ref, 116(528)
Cheek, J. M.: ref, 859(896)
Cheek, M. C.: ref, 958(48), 1575(2)
Cheffers, J. T. F.: ref, 1386(1), 1831(143)

INDEX OF NAMES

Cheloha, R. S.: ref, 1508(133)
Chelune, G. J.: ref, 1498(5284, 5588), 1769(55), 2598(1471, 1568, 1608), 2607(159)
Chemtob, C. M.: ref, 243(120)
Chen, K.: ref, 2208(1523)
Chen, S. T.: ref, 964(478, 496)
Chenery, M. F.: ref, 2300(535)
Cheney, K.: ref, 501(833)
Cheong, G. S. C.: ref, 1831(137)
Cherkes, M.: test, 692
Chermak, G. D.: ref, 691(46), 1126(777)
Chermol, B.: ref, 1789(663)
Chernovetz, M. E. O.: ref, 157(138)
Cherry, F. F.: ref, 1126(653), 2289(1603), 2602(1612)
Cherry, R. S.: ref, 2646(12)
Chesler, D. J.: test, 195, 1804, 1805, 2256
Chester, R. D: ref, 845(6)
Chester, R. D.: test, 2634
Chetham, D.: ref, 2598(1717), 2607(199)
Cheves, R.: test, 1935
Chevron, E.: ref, 682(1)
Chevron, E. S.: test, 215
Chew, A. L.: test, 1338
Chian, J. Y. C.: ref, 859(890)
Chiappetta, E. L.: ref, 732(406)
Chiappone, A. D.: test, 691
Chick, J.: ref, 1485(71)
Chilcutt, J.: ref, 6(48)
Child Center: test, 393
Childs, B.: ref, 1007(18), 2217(116)
Childs, R. de S.: test, 957
Childs, S. B.: test, 957
Chiles, J. A.: ref, 890(355), 1498(5589)
Chinsky, J. M.: ref, 1341(176)
Chirico, B. M.: test, 1130; ref, 1130(1)
Chissom, B. S.: rev, 701, 1371, 2023, 2380; ref, 707(19, 20), 1493(123), 2614(22)
Chisson, B. S.: ref, 6(52)
Chizmar, J. F.: test, 246
Chlebnikow, B.: ref, 1272(131)
Cho, D. W.: ref, 1498(5104, 5105), 1904(97)
Cho, J. H.: ref, 2029(215)
Chodoff, P.: ref, 1419(670), 1498(5108)
Chodos, L.: ref, 719(27), 766(21), 958(40), 1007(12)
Cholet, M. E.: ref, 794(385)
Chomsky, C.: ref, 549(1), 2598(1374), 2647(1)
Choo, K.: ref, 2015(208)
Chowdhury, M. E. H.: ref, 1883(62)
Christ, A.: ref, 958(50), 1126(771), 1769(91), 2034(6), 2602(2101)
Christenfeld, R.: ref, 681(34)
Christensen, C. E.: ref, 1295(290)
Christensen, E. W.: ref, 2413(615)
Christensen, J. E.: ref, 1295(290)
Christensen, M.: ref, 429(3)
Christensen, M. G.: ref, 2491(2055)
Christensen, P. R.: test, 157, 401, 566, 630, 706, 1257, 2178, 2198
Christenson, B.: ref, 5(168)
Christeson, B.: test, 28
Christian, W. L.: ref, 76(602), 354(1437), 1498(5236, 5237, 5241)
Christie, D. J.: ref, 1914(835)
Christie, J. E.: ref, 1883(80)
Christodoulou, G. N.: ref, 283(137), 2598(1305)

Christofferson, H. C.: test, 180
Christoph, P.: ref, 1498(5490)
Christopher, J. R.: ref, 1192(178)
Chriswell, M. I.: test, 402
Chronicle Guidance Publications, Inc.: test, 1039
Chudy, J. F.: ref, 2491(2089)
Chun, K.: ref, 354(1390), 2208(1521)
Church, G. E.: ref, 2300(529)
Cianflone, R.: ref, 501(882), 2217(161)
Ciarlo, J. A.: test, 677; ref, 677(2)
Cicala, G. A.: ref, 859(819), 883(86), 2300(416)
Cicchetti, D.: ref, 270(89), 2289(1678)
Cicciarelli, A. W.: ref, 1851(27)
Cicirelli, V. G.: ref, 950(8)
Ciesla, S. G.: test, 790
Cimbolic, P.: ref, 1498(5574)
Cimini, C.: ref, 280(1143), 2598(1723)
Cinquanta, C. M. D.: ref, 2017(2)
Cionini, L.: ref, 1555(327)
Ciporen, F.: ref, 121(11), 2477(3)
Circo, J.: ref, 121(8), 1007(16), 1271(906), 1853(271), 1914(723), 2537(549), 2598(1360), 2607(141)
Ciula, B. A.: ref, 1969(90, 116), 2598(1440)
Clabby, J. F.: ref, 116(605), 1798(276)
Claghorn, J. L.: ref, 1498(5405, 5567), 1573(40), 1904(78, 94), 2300(481, 482)
Claiborn, C. D.: ref, 1904(68)
Clair, M. S.: ref, 2030(4971), 2121(69)
Clance, P. R.: ref, 964(477), 1117(442)
Clancy, E.: test, 1820
Claridge, G.: ref, 860(101)
Clarizio, H.: ref, 2602(2166)
Clarizio, S.: ref, 678(15), 1319(74), 2289(1631)
Clark, A.: ref, 1341(172), 2217(123)
Clark, A. T.: ref, 559(47)
Clark, C.: ref, 2289(1620), 2598(1319), 2602(1656, 2020), 2607(134)
Clark, C. A.: rev, 1237
Clark, C. G.: ref, 472(16), 2208(1635)
Clark, C. M.: ref, 484(1), 1077(57), 1257(128, 129)
Clark, C. R.: ref, 719(29), 1771(776)
Clark, D. F.: rev, 639, 955; ref, 2208(1524)
Clark, D. L.: ref, 280(1065)
Clark, E.: ref, 1513(32, 33), 1914(874, 879), 2598(1712)
Clark, G. M.: ref, 874(50), 1831(162), 2491(2054)
Clark, G. W.: rev, 1078
Clark, J. L. D.: rev, 824, 2114; exc, 1519, 1520, 1521, 1522, 1523
Clark, J. R.: rev, 312
Clark, K. E.: rev, 1945, 2327
Clark, L.: ref, 2343(1048)
Clark, L. V.: ref, 1914(846)
Clark, M. K.: test, 1355
Clark, M. L.: test, 28, 30, 34, 42, 1912; exc, 1912; ref, 1655(73)
Clark, P.: ref, 1914(795)
Clark, P. M.: rev, 2199, 2496
Clark, S.: ref, 2598(1441)
Clark, S. G.: test, 1190
Clark, S. R.: test, 2071, 2075
Clark, W. W.: test, 357, 2181; rev, 1557
Clarke, A. M.: ref, 2602(1846)
Clarke, F. C.: ref, 2598(1499), 2602(2081)
Clarke, J. H.: test, 405

Clarke, K. M.: ref, 1789(691)
Clarke, S.: test, 1340
Clarke, W. M.: ref, 766(30), 2412(41)
Clarke-Stewart, K. A.: ref, 270(106, 133), 1492(5, 7), 1771(643), 2289(1702, 1747), 2598(1569)
Clarkin, J. E.: ref, 1904(106)
Clarkson, Q. D.: ref, 1498(5055)
Clarren, S. K.: ref, 2289(1703), 2602(1873)
Claudy, J. G.: ref, 1576(201)
Claveaux, R. A.: ref, 1498(5147)
Clavelle, P. R.: ref, 1498(5059)
Clawson, A.: test, 280
Clawson, T.: ref, 995(141)
Clay, M. M.: test, 2060
Clayson, D.: ref, 2512(654)
Clayton, M. R.: ref, 1498(5426)
Clayton, P.: ref, 1498(5144)
Cleary, B.: test, 410
Cleary, P.: ref, 1240(66), 1498(5769)
Cleary, P. A.: ref, 2100(2, 3)
Cleeland, C. S.: ref, 2598(1336)
Cleeton, G. U.: test, 177; rev, 2228
Cleghorn, J. M.: ref, 1498(5654), 1923(19), 2598(1399)
Cleland, J. F.: ref, 859(937), 1197(314), 1498(5717)
Clemans, W. V.: rev, 747, 1991
Clements, P. R.: ref, 6(67, 84)
Cleminshaw, H. K.: ref, 1479(344)
Clendenen, D. M.: rev, 727, 1055, 2318
Cleveland, C.: test, 1380
Cleveland, W. P.: ref, 1498(5651)
Click, M.: ref, 1229(89)
Cliff, N.: ref, 558(54), 2289(1752)
Cliff, S.: test, 548
Clifford, B. R.: ref, 859(788)
Clifford, R. M.: test, 771
Cline, V. B.: rev, 859
Clingman, J.: ref, 1771(533)
Clingman, J. M.: ref, 1771(524), 1798(253)
Cloninger, C. R.: ref, 1771(672), 2208(1672)
Cloninger, R.: ref, 1498(5144)
Clopton, J. R.: rev, 1758, 1867; ref, 1498(5060, 5061, 5242, 5243, 5244, 5427, 5428, 5477, 5758)
Close, D.: test, 541
Close, D. W.: ref, 541(1), 2557(212)
Closs, S. J.: test, 193, 194, 1211
Clover, W. H.: ref, 76(608)
Clum, G. A.: ref, 157(149), 794(427)
Clyman, B.: ref, 859(880), 1789(702)
Clymer, T.: test, 482
Co, M.: ref, 678(26), 960(11), 1771(655), 2107(9), 2218(143), 2598(1582), 2602(1889), 2608(213)
Coan, R. W.: test, 772, 1233; rev, 1106, 1503, 1555, 1726, 1789, 2497
Coates, A.: ref, 1655(123)
Coates, S. W.: test, 1875
Coble, C. B.: ref, 2208(1639)
Coburn, T. G.: ref, 2286(346)
Coché, E.: ref, 1436(12), 2031(458), 2491(2038)
Cochran, D. J.: ref, 76(591)
Cochran, G. M.: ref, 280(1107), 701(61)
Cochran, J. R.: ref 2318(1588)
Cochran, J. W.: ref, 1771(594), 2289(1655), 2607(155)
Cochran, L.: ref, 2208(1685)
Cochran, R.: test, 1958
Cochrane, J.: ref, 941(48), 2208(1694)

Cochrane, R.: ref, 2029(212)
Cochrane, R. G.: test, 1536
Cockerille, C. E.: test, 170
Cocking, R. R.: ref, 1771(651)
Cockshott, C.: ref, 1547(253)
Cody, J. J.: ref, 1969(90), 2598(1440)
Coe, K. J.: ref, 409(12)
Coe, W. C.: ref, 1063(116, 134, 135), 2294(126, 135)
Coetzee, T. M.: test, 191, 2578
Cofer, C. N.: rev, 908, 909, 2037, 2502
Coffer, J. H.: test, 2009
Coffin, G. C.: test, 297, 1544
Coffin, N. S.: test, 1544
Coffing, D. G.: ref, 1257(121)
Coffman, W. E.: rev, 1590, 2434, 2520
Cohen, A.: ref, 354(1392, 1483, 1529)
Cohen, B.: ref, 121(11), 2477(3)
Cohen, B. D.: rev, 795, 1849, 2322, 2620
Cohen, C. R.: test, 2259
Cohen, D.: ref, 401(73), 860(118), 1362(10), 1404(2), 1547(332), 1555(339), 2269(436), 2598(1306, 1695)
Cohen, D. B.: ref, 1419(677)
Cohen, D. J.: ref, 1319(72), 1771(787), 2018(7), 2289(1768), 2393(11), 2598(1782), 2602(2115, 2181), 2608(239)
Cohen, E.: ref, 1347(3)
Cohen, G.: test, 1922, 1923
Cohen, G. H.: ref, 116(572), 1547(264), 1914(789), 2598(1366)
Cohen, H.: test, 2393; ref, 6(38)
Cohen, H. B.: ref, 681(44), 1547(304), 1940(88)
Cohen, I.: ref, 1498(5768), 1923(28)
Cohen, J.: rev, 1197, 2029, 2087, 2515, 2524; ref, 1923(14, 22)
Cohen, L.: ref, 2030(4946)
Cohen, L. K.: ref, 400(137)
Cohen, L. R.: ref, 1425(2)
Cohen, M.: ref, 1555(339), 2598(1429)
Cohen, M. J.: ref, 2300(572), 2598(1801)
Cohen, P. M.: ref, 2244(40)
Cohen, R.: ref, 1771(777), 2213(4), 2621(324)
Cohen, R. B.: ref, 1192(166, 190)
Cohen, R. J.: ref, 2598(1347)
Cohen, R. L.: ref, 2602(1734), 2621(277)
Cohen, R. S.: ref, 1471(54), 2289(1748)
Cohen, S.: test, 289; ref, 226(178, 184)
Cohen, S. A.: rev, 1764, 2252; exc, 2477
Cohen, S. E.: ref, 270(76, 108)
Cohen, S. L.: rev, 2057
Cohen, S. P.: test, 1878
Cohler, B. J.: ref, 381(59), 794(366, 372, 389), 1771(536), 2179(196, 216, 234), 2289(1609, 1749), 2602(1754), 2608(172, 229)
Cohn, S. J.: ref, 9(12), 501(818), 573(13), 1456(15)
Cohn-Jones, L.: ref, 1771(595)
Coie, J. D.: ref, 1498(5030)
Coil, A.: ref, 1191(121), 1568(125)
Coker, G.: ref, 1831(163), 2286(305)
Coker, H.: ref, 1192(167, 201)
Colangelo, N.: ref, 2029(238)
Colarusso, R.: ref, 701(72, 74), 1126(753, 768), 1192(231), 1540(17, 18), 1771(525, 719), 2217(109, 162), 2602(2076)
Colarusso, R. P.: test, 1540; ref, 701(59), 1126(687, 720), 1540(13), 1771(644), 2218(141)

INDEX OF NAMES

Colbert, C.: ref, 964(502), 2512(636)
Colbert, G. A.: ref, 1855(23)
Colby, A.: test, 1262; ref, 1262(2)
Cole, A.: ref, 1498(5770)
Cole, C. S.: ref, 1547(251)
Cole, C. W.: test, 219, 562
Cole, E.: ref, 1831(187)
Cole, J. N.: ref, 1557(6)
Cole, J. O.: ref, 280(1023, 1069), 968(2), 1655(92, 93), 1904(65, 123), 2607(130, 153)
Cole, L.: test, 6
Cole, M.: ref, 280(1116), 1506(75), 2269(470), 2598(1624, 1646), 2607(184)
Cole, N. S.: rev, 368, 1576
Cole, R.: ref, 934(5)
Cole, S.: ref, 398(110), 2602(1791)
Coleman, C. A.: test, 1322
Coleman, J.: ref, 6(64), 609(199), 1908(10)
Coleman, J. M.: ref, 1473(163, 166), 1831(151, 155), 2602(1696, 1697, 1822)
Coleman, M.: ref, 1771(720), 2217(163), 2602(1839)
Coleman, R. M.: ref, 1498(5775, 5742)
Coles, G. S.: ref, 121(9, 11), 2477(3)
Collard, R. R.: rev, 270, 1874
Collart, D. S.: ref, 2289(1608)
The College Board: test, 375, 667
The College Board and Educational Testing Service: test, 124, 125, 126, 127, 128, 129, 130, 131, 132, 133, 134, 135, 136, 137, 138, 139, 140, 141, 142, 143, 382, 411, 412, 413, 414, 415, 416, 417, 418, 419, 420, 421, 422, 423, 424, 425, 426, 427, 428, 429, 430, 431, 432, 433, 434, 435, 436, 437, 438, 439, 440, 441, 442, 443, 444, 445, 446, 447, 448, 449, 450, 451, 452, 453, 454, 455, 456, 457, 458, 459, 460, 461, 462, 463, 487, 488, 489, 490, 491, 492, 493, 494, 495, 496, 497, 498, 499, 500, 501, 506, 507, 508, 509, 510, 511, 512, 513, 514, 515, 516, 517, 518, 519, 520, 521, 522, 523, 524, 525, 526, 527, 528, 529, 530, 531, 543, 685, 686, 757, 758, 759, 760, 761, 762, 763, 764, 765, 1548, 1866, 2143, 2144, 2145, 2470
Collehi, L. F.: ref, 691(41), 1126(721), 2602(1874)
Collette, M. A.: ref, 1007(26), 1060(25), 2621(325)
Collette-Harris, M.: ref, 280(1072), 691(33), 751(11)
Colletti, A. B.: test, 615
Collier, G.: ref, 354(1426), 681(75), 732(395), 794(382), 860(156), 1046(574), 1486(177), 2029(200), 2343(1035), 2607(149)
Colligan, M. J.: ref, 2652(5)
Colligan, R. C.: ref, 1333(2, 3), 1479(314, 345), 1492(4), 1498(5062, 5590), 1934(6, 10), 2286(306), 2621(232, 326)
Collins, B. E.: ref, 1771(707)
Collins, C.: ref, 1568(140)
Collins, F.: ref, 354(1471), 780(1675), 859(824), 1498(5349), 1576(206)
Collins, H.: ref, 1874(10), 2217(127)
Collins, H. A.: ref, 1498(5063, 5429), 2208(1525), 2318(1547)
Collins, J. F.: ref, 681(57), 1765(10)
Collins, J. L.: ref, 542(20), 2208(1690)
Collins, K. W.: ref, 2374(191)
Collins, L.: ref, 1853(275)
Collins, M.: ref, 1851(42)
Collins, M. N.: ref, 1855(24)
Collins, P. J.: ref, 645(14)
Collins, S.: ref, 354(1486), 1498(5440), 1853(275)
Collison, B. B.: exc, 551
Colon, C. J.: ref, 6(64), 1908(10)
Color Test Evaluation Committee, Inter-Society Color Council: test, 533
Colvin, L. M.: ref, 1789(645)
Colwell, L. C.: test, 1776
Colwell, R.: rev, 1135, 1446, 2222
Colwill, J. M.: ref, 1576(205)
Colwill, N. L.: ref, 1576(196)
Comeau, H.: ref, 2512(637)
Comkowycz, S.: ref, 1736(1), 1737(1)
Commey, J. O. O.: ref, 270(109)
Commins, W. D.: rev, 1493, 1945, 2266, 2276
Commission on Testing and Measurement of the American Association of Bible Colleges: test, 2282
Committee on Diagnostic Reading Tests, Inc.: test, 720
Committee on Tests of the Jewish Education Service of North America, Inc.: test, 2467
Compton, J. V.: ref, 354(1425)
Comrey, A. L.: test, 558, 2102; rev, 563, 1538, 1775, 2537; ref, 558(58, 59, 62, 67), 859(866)
Comstock, B. S.: ref, 1498(5093)
Conger, A. J.: ref, 883(103), 2602(1875)
Conger, J. C.: ref, 883(103), 2602(1875)
Conger, R. D.: ref, 609(216)
Conkling, F. R.: test, 1887
Conley, F. K.: ref, 1346(4)
Conley, J. J.: ref, 1498(5591), 2491(2039)
Conn, M. G.: ref, 1498(5521)
Conner, D.: ref, 277(2), 2506(7)
Conner, J. M.: ref, 1875(2), 2608(173)
Conner, R.: ref, 1823(33), 2602(1905)
Conners, C. K.: ref, 962(31), 964(503), 1503(68), 1853(291), 2602(2018), 2621(390)
Connolly, A. J.: test, 1250
Connolly, B.: ref, 381(69), 2289(1750), 2557(235)
Connolly, J.: ref, 1126(755), 1771(725), 2472(22)
Connolly, R.: ref, 1498(5228), 2179(211)
Connor, J. M.: ref, 398(104, 105), 2608(218)
Connor, R.: ref, 1424(67)
Connors, E. T.: ref, 719(32), 766(28), 935(30)
Connors, G.: ref, 1473(131), 1831(121), 2602(1638)
Conrad, A.: ref, 2111(1), 2602(1592), 2621(222)
Conrad, C.: ref, 590(381), 1754(72), 2160(58)
Conrad, H. S.: rev, 2485
Conrad, R.: ref, 1914(708), 2625(1)
Conrad, S. G.: ref, 2413(676)
Conroy, J. W.: ref, 6(38)
Conry, R. F.: ref, 1779(1)
Constantini, E.: ref, 116(606)
Constantino, R. E.: ref, 681(65)
Consulting Psychologists Press: test, 2601, 2605, 2609
Conte, H.: ref, 1531(278), 2366(195)
Conture, E. G.: ref, 911(4)
Conway, B. E.: ref, 1073(129)
Conway, D.: ref, 675(5), 1771(553, 721)
Conway, M.: ref, 2512(652)
Conway, M. T.: ref, 1257(121)
Cook, D. W.: ref, 2300(341)
Cook, J.: rev, 1019, 1315, 1407, 1409
Cook, J. E.: ref, 226(179), 962(32), 2217(164), 2280(11, 13)
Cook, M.: ref, 6(55), 590(380), 1866(34), 2160(57)

Cook, M. A.: ref, 501(919), 590(387), 2160(78)
Cook, R. S.: test, 938, 945
Cook, W. W.: rev, 169, 1625, 2286
Cooke, M.: test, 22
Cooke, T. A.: ref, 2289(1593)
Cooker, H. S.: ref, 1771(613)
Cookson, P. W.: ref, 501(890)
Cooley, E.: ref, 1555(341)
Cooley, N. R.: ref, 2608(230)
Cooley, R. S.: ref, 2413(642)
Cooley, V. C.: test, 1322
Cooley, W. W.: test, 2467A; ref, 553(25), 720(70), 2621(447)
Coolidge, F.: ref, 2598(1404)
Coolidge, F. L.: ref, 1498(5261)
Coombs, C. H.: rev, 1940
Coon, R. C.: ref, 766(33), 1007(37), 2288(89)
Cooney, J. B.: ref, 1498(5669)
Coons, A. E.: test, 1122, 1295, 1296
Coop, R. H.: ref, 1108(5), 1771(687)
Cooper, A.: test, 394; ref, 394(1)
Cooper, B. L.: ref, 1960(73)
Cooper, C.: ref, 1371(262)
Cooper, C. L.: ref, 2208(1526, 1568)
Cooper, H. M.: ref, 1473(127)
Cooper, J. A. D.: ref, 1576(187)
Cooper, J. E.: test, 1883
Cooper, J. F.: ref, 1955(107)
Cooper, J. L.: test, 569
Cooper, L. D.: ref, 1851(32)
Cooper, L. M.: test, 2297
Cooper, S.: ref, 1769(85), 2218(15), 2602(2019), 2621(391)
Cooper, S. F.: ref, 941(17)
Cooper, S. J.: ref, 1655(123)
Cooper, T.: ref, 501(899), 551(58), 553(24), 734(2)
Cooper, T. L.: ref, 551(65)
Cooperman, E. W.: ref, 1013(104), 2554(14)
Coopersmith, S.: test, 276, 603
Copans, S. A.: ref, 311(30)
Copas, J. B.: ref, 1883(77)
Copeland, M. L.: ref, 590(381), 1754(72), 2160(58)
Coppage, K. W.: ref, 1771(645), 2472(16)
Coppage, S. J.: ref, 1257(176)
Coppen, A.: ref, 2588(33)
Corazzini, J. G.: ref, 486(309)
Corbett, J.: ref, 2602(1613)
Corcoran, M. E.: ref, 859(733), 2294(109)
Cordero, L.: ref, 6(57), 2289(1716)
Cordess, C.: ref, 941(43), 1883(81)
Cordoni, B. K.: ref, 484(2), 1769(101), 2621(435)
Corey, S. M.: rev, 1945; exc, 691
Cormack, R. W.: test, 841, 2389
Cornblatt, B.: ref, 1498(5196)
Cornbleth, T.: ref, 2598(1307), 2607(132)
Cornejo, R. J.: test, 2223
Cornelius, E. T.: ref, 1855(24), 2537(563)
Cornelius, S. W.: ref, 653(158), 1257(156), 1914(825)
Cornes, C.: ref, 2300(557)
Cornish, G.: test, 35
Corno, L.: ref, 483(23, 26, 33), 1473(194), 1478(71), 1914(796, 836)
Corotto, L. V.: ref, 1347(8, 9), 1351(31), 2598(1467, 1585)
Corriere, R.: ref, 859(800, 915), 1789(668, 713)

Corrigan, A.: test, 824
Corriveau, D. P.: ref, 1789(716), 1904(51)
Corser, C. M.: ref, 941(22)
Corsini, R.: test, 2065
Corsini, R. J.: test, 1129, 1618, 1884, 1970, 2553, 2645
Corson, J. A.: ref, 2582(14)
Corssen, G.: ref, 1547(312)
Cortner, R. H.: ref, 280(1095), 2602(1825, 2068), 2621(309)
Cory, C. H.: ref, 1257(105)
Cosden, M. A.: ref, 1257(139)
Cosner, T.: ref, 2300(461)
Cosslen, M.: ref, 1257(160)
Costa, A. L.: ref, 1192(191), 1473(148), 2286(290)
Costa, L.: ref, 1883(59)
Costa, P. T.: ref, 609(200), 859(818, 897, 920), 1046(582, 583, 588), 2208(1527, 1587, 1650, 1661), 2318(1524)
Costanzo, P. R.: ref, 1498(5030)
Costello, A. J.: test, 2383
Costello, M. R.: test, 905
Costello, R. M.: ref, 472(13), 1351(26, 32), 1498(5064)
Coster, W.: ref, 2218(14), 2602(2017)
Costiloe, J. P.: ref, 1655(73)
Costin, F.: rev, 2334; ref, 994(55)
Cotten, P. D.: ref, 868(5)
Cottereau, M. J.: ref, 1655(111)
Cottle, W. C.: test, 2085; rev, 2324; ref, 354(1564)
Cotton, C. C.: ref, 1419(701)
Cottrell, A. B.: test, 352
Couch, J.: ref, 2665(1)
Couchman, T.: test, 386
Coughlan, A. K.: ref, 1513(24), 1771(596), 1914(744), 2598(1442)
Coughran, L.: test, 1307
Coulson, J. E.: ref, 344(151), 1191(122)
Coulter, C. L.: ref, 1473(128)
Council on Dental Education, American Dental Association: test, 673
Counts, D. K.: ref, 1754(73), 2300(388)
Couper, J. L.: ref, 2244(44)
Coursey, R. D.: ref, 1247(164), 1498(5592, 5618), 1531(294), 2030(5055), 2413(670), 2598(1570, 1696)
Court, J. H.: ref, 1485(67), 1914(745)
Courtis, S. A.: rev, 1272, 2269
Courtney, D.: ref, 1192(225), 2181(16)
Courtney, P. D.: rev, 2621
Courtois, M. R.: ref, 2300(462), 2417(2)
Coury, V. M.: ref, 1046(568)
Cousino, F.: test, 2090
Cousins, J. B.: ref, 1960(78), 2124(1)
Coutts, L. M.: ref, 559(43)
Covin, T. M.: ref, 1754(74), 1771(526, 527, 544), 2217(110, 111), 2602(1614, 1615, 1616, 1617, 1618, 1619, 1620, 1621, 1647)
Covington, J. E.: ref, 1051(14), 1059(3), 1204(1)
Cowan, J. D.: ref, 113(27), 1498(5593), 1904(110)
Cowan, P. A.: ref, 398(94), 883(83)
Coward, R. T.: ref, 398(113)
Cowgell, V. G.: ref, 1498(5065), 1904(52)
Cowley, L. M.: ref, 1655(104)
Cox, A. R.: test, 279
Cox, D. N.: ref, 354(1447)
Cox, G.: ref, 1498(5030)

INDEX OF NAMES

Cox, G. N.: ref, 2134(122), 2581(332)
Cox, J. W.: test, 623
Cox, M. O.: ref, 1552(73)
Cox, M. V.: ref, 823(11, 15), 1914(709, 746)
Cox, P. W.: ref, 794(377)
Cox, R. C.: rev, 710, 1075; exc, 483, 2107
Cox, R. S.: ref, 2512(563)
Cox, W. M.: ref, 501(819), 1498(5245)
Coxhead, P.: ref, 859(926)
Coyle, J. T.: ref, 1883(78)
Coyle, R. T.: ref, 964(477)
Coyne, J. C.: ref, 872(7), 1547(251)
Coyne, L.: ref, 1498(5595), 2598(1398)
Cozac, C.: ref, 336(11)
Cozac, E.: ref, 336(12), 2602(2089)
Crabbs, M. A.: ref, 2300(518)
Craddick, R. A.: ref, 1183(3)
Craft, D. B.: ref, 2300(465)
Craft, N. P.: ref, 2598(1571), 2602(1876)
Crager, R. L.: test, 2433
Craig, E. M.: ref, 1106(366)
Craig, G.: ref, 354(1441)
Craig, M. J.: ref, 859(847)
Craig, R. J.: ref, 1498(5594), 2598(1572)
Craighead, W. E.: ref, 1547(299, 303)
Craik, K. H.: ref, 116(606), 354(1523, 1561), 1798(275, 302)
Cramer, P.: ref, 665(42), 2318(1552), 2491(2078)
Cramer, S. H.: ref, 732(392), 2134(93)
Cramer, W.: test, 2253, 2671
Crandall, J. E.: ref, 501(883), 859(898), 1547(321), 1789(707), 1960(80), 2029(223)
Crandall, K.: ref, 691(34), 1126(711), 1462(138), 1914(787)
Crandall, K. E.: ref, 1101(40)
Crandall, P. H.: ref, 2598(1384, 1516), 2607(148, 167)
Crandall, R.: rev, 1896, 2135
Crane, B. J.: test, 625
Crane, W. E.: test, 2009
Cranney, A. G.: rev, 781
Cranney, J.: ref, 1063(115)
Cranny, C. J.: rev, 940, 2274
Crano, W. D.: ref, 932(78)
Crary, W. G.: ref, 1498(5066), 2300(342)
Crase, S. J.: test, 1190; ref, 2512(630)
Craven, P. A.: ref, 932(123)
Crawford, A. B.: rev, 1271; exc, 2269
Crawford, D. A.: ref, 1914(710)
Crawford, D. M.: test, 627
Crawford, H. J.: ref, 1063(133), 2294(139), 2297(11)
Crawford, J.: ref, 501(820), 1473(128), 1798(233)
Crawford, J. E.: test, 627
Crawford, J. H.: ref, 1126(722), 2289(1704), 2602(1877)
Crawford, P. L.: test, 626
Crawford, W. R.: rev, 75, 2510
Crealock, C.: ref, 1798(254)
Creamer, M.: ref, 964(485), 1063(94)
Creaser, J.: ref, 354(1466)
Creaser, J. W.: ref, 76(627), 2318(1581)
Creese, I.: ref, 1883(78, 94)
Creson, B.: test, 244
Cresswell, D. L.: ref, 681(66), 1931(56)
Crichton, L.: ref, 1798(301), 2179(252)
Crichton, L. I.: ref, 1866(36)

Criner, J.: test, 310
Crisp, A. H.: test, 639; ref, 639(42, 47, 49, 50, 59), 780(1657), 859(773, 848)
Crissey, O. L.: test, 633
Critchlow, D. E.: test, 749
Critelli, J. W.: ref, 354(1525), 2208(1651)
Crites, J. O.: test, 374; rev, 912, 965, 1729, 2134, 2318; exc, 354, 799, 1073, 1123, 1568, 1573, 1798, 2055, 2394, 2413, 2594
Crnic, K. A.: ref, 392(3), 2602(1735)
Croake, J. W.: ref, 1498(5067)
Crocetti, G.: ref, 1831(209)
Crockenberg, S. B.: ref, 311(44)
Crocker, L.: ref, 1477(18)
Crocker, L. M.: test, 885
Crocker, R. K.: ref, 932(81)
Crockett, A. C.: test, 689, 690
Crockett, D.: ref, 2602(2020)
Crofoot, M. J.: ref, 701(75), 1771(722), 2217(165), 2602(2021)
Croft, A. C.: test, 1913, 2341
Croft, C.: test, 329, 1918, 2458
Croft, L. W.: rev, 505
Croft, S.: ref, 2565(9)
Cromack, T. R.: ref, 398(118)
Cromer, C. C.: ref, 302(25)
Cromwell, L. D.: ref, 270(155), 2289(1789), 2602(2190)
Cromwell, R. L.: ref, 1771(761), 2598(1424)
Cronbach, L. J.: rev, 296, 354, 1165, 1945, 2045, 2366, 2535; ref, 202(9)
Cronin, C. M.: ref, 701(50), 958(44), 2602(1784), 2621(292)
Cronk, C. E.: ref, 270(146), 2557(244)
Cronkite, R. C.: ref, 542(18), 872(13)
Crook, T.: ref, 1240(63), 2598(1697, 1712), 2607(192)
Crook, T. H.: ref, 280(1089), 2598(1515), 2607(166)
Crookes, T. G.: ref, 859(899), 1503(64)
Croon, C. W.: rev, 844, 2485
Cross, D.: test, 811; ref, 1063(97)
Cross, D. G.: ref, 1063(119), 1789(708, 724)
Cross, D. T.: ref, 354(1438, 1481)
Cross, G. M.: ref, 1192(232)
Cross, H.: ref, 1555(339)
Cross, H. J.: ref, 1547(285), 1789(671), 2029(204)
Cross, L. H.: ref, 1192(232), 1498(5068)
Cross, W.: ref, 2638(132)
Cross, W. C.: ref, 2413(598)
Crosson, B.: ref, 308(22), 1851(45)
Crosthwait, C.: test, 115
Croucher, A.: ref, 972(11), 1485(84)
Crouthamel, C. S.: ref, 1923(21)
Crovitz, H. F.: ref, 2598(1573)
Crow, L. D.: test, 938, 945, 947, 1065
Crow, T. A.: ref, 551(25)
Crow, T. J.: ref, 1883(84)
Crowe, M. J.: ref, 1498(5373)
Crowell, D. C.: ref, 2608(212)
Crowell, O.: ref, 354(1472), 859(825)
Crowley, A. D.: test, 638, 1669
Crowley, P. A.: ref, 859(822), 1940(81)
Crowley, T. J.: ref, 1498(5069, 5452), 1923(15, 26), 2598(1592)
Crown, S.: test, 639; ref, 639(43, 48), 769(39, 42)
Crowne, D. P.: rev, 1123, 2429

Crozier, W. R.: ref, 883(114), 2598(1436)
Cruickshank, W. M.: rev, 923, 2557
Cruise, P. D.: ref, 2029(221)
Cruise, R. J.: test, 2411; ref, 859(900), 2029(221), 2411(1)
Crumbaugh, J. C.: test, 1960, 2124; ref, 1960(66, 75)
Crump, W. D.: ref, 1126(703), 1250(15), 1831(180), 2269(459)
Cruz, R.: test, 289
Csapo, M.: ref, 2585(6, 7)
Csaszar, D.: ref, 270(132)
CTB/McGraw–Hill: test, 344, 345, 346, 347, 551, 552, 553, 554, 642, 851, 1665, 1666, 1880, 1881, 1888, 2431, 2477
Cudeck, R.: ref, 2289(1752)
Culatta, B.: ref, 302(30), 701(43), 1126(688), 2244(30), 2608(188)
Culbertson, W. C.: ref, 793(6), 1109(18)
Cull, J. G.: ref, 1771(723)
Cullen, J. K.: ref, 691(44), 766(29), 960(14), 1126(742), 1771(692), 2289(1736)
Cullen, J. L.: ref, 362(6), 1831(204), 1754(116)
Cullen, S. M.: ref, 270(146), 2557(244)
Cullen, T. J.: ref, 1576(209)
Cullinan, T. F.: ref, 1498(5456)
Cullinan, W. L.: ref, 308(21)
Cullison, B. L.: ref, 1126(731), 1771(670)
Culliton, T. E.: rev, 352, 1306
Culp, R.: ref, 270(64), 311(17)
Culp, R. E.: ref, 964(504)
Culton, G. L.: ref, 1851(33)
Culver, C. M.: ref, 2113(238), 2598(1324, 1343), 2621(247)
Cummings, B. S.: test, 159
Cummings, C.: ref, 270(107), 2289(1701)
Cummings, E. M.: ref, 1547(284)
Cummings, J.: ref, 308(16), 1109(21), 1853(292), 2598(1698), 2602(1736), 2607(193), 2621(280)
Cummings, J. A.: ref, 302(38), 344(179), 1192(233), 1473(195), 2292(29)
Cummins, A.: ref, 2217(125), 2621(283)
Cummins, J.: ref, 361(6), 1257(106), 1914(747, 748, 749, 797)
Cummins, J. P.: ref, 2077(32), 2602(2022), 2621(392)
Cummins, M.: ref, 2602(2023), 2608(231)
Cummins, R. A.: ref, 859(962)
Cummins, R. P.: ref, 1568(151)
Cundall, R. L.: ref, 1883(40)
Cundick, B. F.: ref, 1498(5123)
Cuneo, D.: ref, 1969(116)
Cunningham, A. E.: ref, 2286(347), 2621(458)
Cunningham, C. E.: ref, 1771(637, 646)
Cunningham, C. H.: ref, 1192(209), 2208(1594), 2320(1, 2), 2581(307)
Cunningham, J. A.: ref, 1498(5743)
Cunningham, J. D.: ref, 354(1516), 558(71), 1798(248, 272)
Cunningham, J. W.: ref, 1192(192)
Cunningham, M. D.: ref, 766(34), 2015(214), 2621(436)
Cunningham, M. M.: ref, 701(44), 1332(6), 2621(278)
Cunningham, M. R.: ref, 859(727)
Cunningham, P. M.: ref, 1192(192)
Cunningham, T.: ref, 6(45)
Cunningham, W. R.: ref, 1257(122, 177)

Cunnington, B. F.: test, 2496
Curd, D.: ref, 958(41)
Cureton, E. E.: test, 1541; rev, 940, 1064, 1189
Cureton, K. J.: ref, 5(165)
Cureton, L. W.: test, 1541; rev, 1804, 1805
Curnutt, R. H.: ref, 2598(1467, 1585)
Curran, J. D.: ref, 859(733), 1209(35), 2294(109)
Curran, J. P.: test, 787; ref, 859(720), 1789(716)
Curran, S. M.: ref, 116(603)
Curry, D. J.: ref, 76(611)
Curry, E.: ref, 1073(125)
Curry, S. H.: ref, 1883(30)
Curtis, C. J.: ref, 551(39), 701(60)
Curtis, C. K.: ref, 606(17)
Curtis, D.: ref, 1948(100)
Curtis, E. K.: ref, 1576(203)
Curtis, F. D.: rev, 947
Curtis, J.: ref, 2413(587)
Curtis, J. W.: test, 637, 647, 648, 649, 650
Curtis, M. E.: ref, 719(35)
Curtis, W. S.: ref, 381(64), 1387(12), 1877(5), 2289(1658)
Curtiss, G.: ref, 2030(5070)
Curwen, M.: test, 2018
Cutler, A.: test, 1227, 1360
Cutler, N. R.: ref, 681(44), 1547(304), 1940(88)
Cutrona, C. E.: ref, 860(147), 2300(562), 2602(1878), 2621(327)
Cutrona, M. P.: test, 651, 652
Cutting, J.: ref, 1485(68, 72, 73), 1883(42, 64), 2598(1443, 1444), 2607(156, 174, 194, 215)
Cutts, C. C.: exc, 2134; ref, 374(219), 501(913), 1473(210), 1478(77), 1754(114), 2134(90)
Cuyler, R.: ref, 1197(294), 1198(1)
Cysewski, B.: ref, 1498(5172)
Czeisler, C. A.: ref, 1498(5775)
Czeizel, A.: ref, 280(1139), 964(505), 2289(1753)
Dabbert, D.: ref, 2217(125), 2621(283)
Dabbs, J. M.: ref, 1486(176), 2015(208), 2246(22)
Dabiri, C.: ref, 270(83), 311(25), 678(21)
D'Afflitti, J. P.: test, 682
Dagenais, F.: ref, 1300(120, 121), 1726(366, 371, 374)
D'Agostino, R. B.: ref, 1296(169)
Dahl, P. A.: rev, 74, 806
Dahl, T. A.: exc, 302
Dahlem, N. W.: ref, 302(27), 1126(652), 1498(5641), 2602(1608), 2621(231)
Dahlstrom, G.: ref, 1498(5328)
Dahlstrom, W. G.: rev, 218, 795, 1349, 1730; ref, 1498(5273)
Daiger, D.: test, 1554
Dailey, J. T.: test, 331, 654, 1282, 2406; rev, 501, 995, 1486
Dalby, J. T.: ref, 2602(1622), 2621(233)
Dale, F. W.: test, 705
Dale, L. G.: test, 2531
Dale, R. R.: rev, 2000
Dalessio, A.: ref, 2208(1658)
Daley, P. C.: ref, 2300(520, 521), 2638(142, 143)
Dalgleish, B.: ref, 1914(837)
Dallam, J. W.: ref, 76(651)
Dally, P.: ref, 859(908)
Dalpes, D.: ref, 1498(5224)
Dalton, P.: ref, 859(856)
Dalton, S.: ref, 501(788), 1281(2), 2286(270), 2293(8)

INDEX OF NAMES

Dalton, S. L.: ref, 1295(296, 297)
Daly, D. A.: ref, 2621(279)
Daly, J. A.: ref, 354(1439), 412(6), 501(923), 2002(6)
Daly, W. K.: ref, 1498(5549, 5727), 2179(229)
Damarin, F.: rev, 270, 381
Damon, S. G.: ref, 308(8)
Damron, O. R.: test, 657
Damsteegt, D. C.: ref, 76(657), 1405(11), 2300(601)
Dana, R. H.: rev, 2030, 2031, 2381, 2491; ref, 1960(83), 2030(4947, 5082), 2491(2096), 2602(1594, 1997)
Danaher, B. G.: ref, 2598(1357)
Danahy, S.: ref, 794(446), 2413(695)
Daneel, D.: test, 1767
Daneman, D.: ref, 270(134), 2557(236), 2608(232)
Danesereau, D. F.: ref, 2374(191)
Danesino, A.: ref, 2030(5026)
Dang, R.: ref, 2300(371)
Dangel, H.: ref, 1126(687)
D'Angelo, K.: ref, 719(38)
D'Anglejan, A.: exc, 918
Daniels, J.: ref, 2030(5026), 2602(1860)
Daniels, J. C.: test, 2281
Daniloff, R.: ref, 896(2), 960(8), 2412(37)
Daniloff, R. G.: ref, 2412(42)
Danker–Brown, P.: ref, 681(43), 2224(5, 6), 2598(1783)
Danko, G. P.: ref, 859(744), 1547(257)
Dannenburg, M. A.: ref, 2301(26)
Dansky, J. L.: ref, 559(56), 1126(754), 2608(233)
Dappen, L.: ref, 280(1163), 701(86), 2260(49), 2472(27), 2602(1943, 2203), 2608(241, 248), 2621(355, 429, 452)
Daramola, S. F.: ref, 2608(183)
Darden, B. J.: ref, 2413(588)
Darley, F. L.: test, 911, 2412; ref, 1513(26), 1851(22, 30, 37, 39), 2645(3)
Darley, J. G.: rev, 118, 2318
Darnell, M. H.: ref, 1498(5252), 1655(91)
Darnell, R. E.: rev, 281, 1779
Dartnell Corporation: test, 754
Das, H.: ref, 2334(20)
Das, J. P.: ref, 361(6), 932(63), 1126(689), 1257(126), 1341(157, 175), 1462(115, 120, 129, 134, 144, 149), 1567(12), 1853(289), 1914(700, 719, 747, 749, 750, 751, 770, 771, 813), 2077(32), 2269(456, 457), 2491(2076), 2602(1586, 1736, 1995, 2022), 2621(280, 392)
Das, R. S.: test, 2442
Daserg, H.: ref, 639(51)
Dash, J.: ref, 2300(538, 577)
DaSilva, L.: ref, 1883(82)
Dass, J.: rev, 1142
Dastoor, D. P.: ref, 280(1105, 1116), 1506(73, 75), 2598(1574, 1624), 2607(175, 184)
Dates, B. G.: ref, 280(1034, 1035), 2413(593), 2621(246)
Dattore, P. J.: ref, 1498(5595)
Daubney, J. H.: ref, 1053(77), 2030(5056), 2598(1699)
Daughton, D.: ref, 1498(5257, 5606)
Dauphinais, S. M.: ref, 2289(1705), 2598(1575)
Daus, A. T.: ref, 609(207), 1498(5540)
Dauterman, W. L.: test, 2296
Davenport, R. K.: ref, 1192(245)
David, J. L.: ref, 551(26), 932(74)
David, R. M.: ref, 925(13), 1513(27)
Davids, A.: ref, 2602(1648)
Davidshofer, C.: ref, 1789(644)
Davidshofer, C. O.: ref, 618(4)
Davidson, C. W.: ref, 1754(86)
Davidson, D. M.: ref, 1904(133)
Davidson, G.: ref, 252(2), 775(2)
Davidson, J. L.: ref, 2602(1695)
Davidson, P. W.: ref, 270(77), 678(20), 701(45), 1771(597), 1877(7), 2289(1656), 2557(220)
Davidson, W. B.: ref, 1013(63, 64), 1798(234, 235)
Davies, A. D. M.: ref, 1462(156), 1485(87), 1914(880)
Davies, G.: ref, 859(869)
Davies, K.: ref, 1771(800)
Davies, M. G.: ref, 1462(156), 1485(87), 1914(880)
Davies, M. M.: ref, 2581(320)
Davies, P. S.: ref, 1498(5098)
Davis, A. L.: test, 728
Davis, B. G.: ref, 551(52)
Davis, C.: ref, 1948(105)
Davis, C. C.: rev, 429, 490, 530, 1939, 2163, 2586
Davis, D. A.: ref, 1498(5070, 5246)
Davis, D. F.: ref, 2164(40)
Davis, D. J.: ref, 270(131), 311(34)
Davis, D. R.: rev, 852
Davis, E. E.: exc, 1424; ref, 1473(141), 1831(130), 2602(1623, 1696, 1697, 1698)
Davis, F. B.: test, 588; rev, 346, 490, 501, 530, 590, 720, 1191, 1512, 2520; exc, 1191, 1272
Davis, G. A.: test, 1017; ref, 116(548, 589), 1016(1), 2496(37)
Davis, H.: ref, 1624(3), 1625(103)
Davis, J.: test, 2570; ref, 6(58), 859(937), 1197(314), 1498(5717)
Davis, J. K.: ref, 1077(80), 1257(118)
Davis, J. M.: ref, 1498(5276, 5586), 2472(10), 2602(1959)
Davis, J. P.: ref, 1789(679)
Davis, K. E.: ref, 501(807)
Davis, K. L.: ref, 1498(5037)
Davis, L. C.: ref, 890(341)
Davis, L. J.: ref, 2607(165)
Davis, L. L.: ref, 1237(93)
Davis, P. C.: rev, 707, 1318
Davis, R.: ref, 1498(5732)
Davis, R. A.: ref, 2602(1680)
Davis, S.: ref, 1197(294), 1198(1)
Davis, S. A.: ref, 1192(239, 251)
Davis, S. E.: rev, 1818, 2345
Davis, S. F.: ref, 1831(150)
Davis, S. M.: ref, 2472(21)
Davis, S. O.: ref, 1405(4)
Davis, T. M.: ref, 2598(1576)
Davis, W. E.: ref, 283(148), 1073(121), 1498(5096, 5392, 5430), 2380(5), 2598(1484, 1544)
Davison, D. G.: test, 1898
Davison, K.: ref, 2598(1722), 2602(2047)
Davison, M.: ref, 590(368, 369), 2160(49, 50)
Davison, M. L.: ref, 2318(1594), 2581(327)
Dawes, B. E.: ref, 76(651)
Dawes, R. M.: rev, 1015, 2629
Dawis, R. V.: test, 1495, 1497, 1508, 1509; ref, 1495(83, 88), 1497(25, 26), 1855(21), 2113(260), 2318(1594, 1595), 2581(327)
Dawkins, M. P.: ref, 294(13)

Dawley, H. H.: ref, 1498(5431)
Daws, J. T.: ref, 116(599)
Dawson, C.: rev, 831
Dawson, E.: ref, 859(921), 1498(5485, 5658)
Dawson, G.: ref, 2208(1632)
Dawson, G. D.: ref, 2602(2167)
Dawson, J. G.: ref, 1498(5222), 2030(4997, 5023), 2294(131)
Dawson, J. L. M.: ref, 794(367)
Dawson, R. L. T.: ref, 1484(15), 1912(3), 2048(1)
Dawson-Saunders, B.: ref, 1576(217)
Day, B.: ref, 1831(118), 2286(276)
Day, B. D.: ref, 559(59)
Day, H. D.: ref, 1831(179)
Day, M. C.: ref, 1914(898)
Day, T.: ref, 354(1518), 859(893), 1547(319)
Daya, D. K.: ref, 1170(226), 1498(5112), 2491(2013)
Daymont, T. N.: ref, 1073(117)
Dayton, C. M.: ref, 398(122), 551(62), 1013(113)
Dean, C.: ref, 1883(83)
Dean, L. M.: ref, 681(41)
Dean, R. S.: test, 1289; ref, 280(1161, 1162), 1126(778, 779), 1289(1, 2, 3, 4, 5, 6), 1769(39, 40, 69), 2208(1678, 1679), 2602(1624, 1625, 1626, 1627, 1737, 1879, 1880, 2024, 2025, 2168, 2169), 2621(234)
de Andraca, I.: ref, 270(132)
Dearborn, L. W.: rev, 1375, 1382
Deardorff, P. A.: ref, 2300(343)
Deaton, W.: ref, 1798(306)
De Avila, E. A.: test, 1281; ref, 398(115), 1281(3, 4)
Debalssie, R. R.: ref, 2602(1967)
Debbane, E. G.: ref, 354(1413), 1498(5184), 2208(1551)
Debell, S.: ref, 1771(697), 2218(156), 2602(1978)
DeBell, S. M.: ref, 1769(41), 2602(1628), 2621(235)
deBlij, K.: ref, 2491(2079), 2602(2026)
DeBoer, G. E.: ref, 501(922), 1794(21)
DeBonis, J. N.: test, 1383
Debout, J.: ref, 354(1551), 1726(372), 1789(721)
DeBusk, R. F.: ref, 1904(133)
Decker, S. N.: ref, 653(162), 1769(86), 2269(474), 2602(2027)
DeCoster, D. A.: ref, 501(848)
Decuir, A. A.: ref, 2113(241, 251)
Dee, G.: ref, 2491(2036)
Deen, C. C.: test, 1322
Deese, J.: rev, 2374
DeFelice, G.: ref, 1192(163), 1473(123)
Deffenbacher, J. L.: test, 2416; ref, 1197(284, 295), 1486(174), 2300(389, 519, 520, 521), 2353(27), 2638(133, 141, 142, 143)
DeFilippis, N. A.: test, 305; ref, 701(76), 1515(17), 1771(724), 1969(106), 2602(1881, 2028)
DeFiore, R. M.: ref, 2208(1680), 2370(19)
DeFour, D.: ref, 354(1440), 1798(236)
DeFries, J. C.: ref, 643(135, 162), 932(58), 962(24), 1126(658, 691), 1257(123), 1473(130), 1769(43, 52, 86), 2269(437, 474), 2286(278), 2598(1323), 2602(1636, 2027), 2621(236)
De Gaffenreid, H.: ref, 1126(690), 2602(1738)
DeGood, D. E.: ref, 2300(372)
DeGroote, M. V.: ref, 1531(280)
DeHaven, G. E.: test, 705
de Hirsch, K.: test, 1205

Dehlavi, N. S.: ref, 2512(638)
Dehnel, L.: ref, 1498(5178), 1547(266), 2300(366)
DeHorn, A.: ref, 1771(598), 2602(1739)
DeHorn, A. B.: ref, 1796(2)
Deichmann, J.: ref, 643(138), 1341(174), 1726(360)
Deinard, A.: ref, 1197(316), 1798(298), 2179(250)
Deitz, J. C.: ref, 885(2)
De Julio, S.: ref, 859(728)
de Jung, J.: test, 2460
De Karapetian, A.: ref, 780(1651)
Dekirmenjian, H.: ref, 1498(5276), 2602(1959)
de Koninck, J.: ref, 794(396), 1498(5298, 5584), 2208(1649), 2300(516)
DeLacey, P. R.: ref, 1126(654), 1771(528), 2608(174)
De la Fuente, J. R.: ref, 280(1140), 1498(5596), 2030(5057), 2602(2029), 2607(195)
Delahunt, J.: ref, 859(720)
DeLancey, A. L.: ref, 1789(716)
Delaney, R. C.: ref, 2598(1700), 2607(196)
DeLean, G.: ref, 1343(1)
deLemos, H.: ref, 2168(8)
DeLeo, P. J.: ref, 732(409), 1754(106), 2286(337)
Del Gaudio, A. C.: ref, 890(335), 1904(66)
Della-Piana, G. M.: rev, 935
Dell'Orto, V. J.: rev, 983, 998
Delmonte, M. M.: ref, 859(901)
Del Nuovo, A.: ref, 558(70), 1498(5557), 2300(502)
Deloche, G.: ref, 1914(881)
Deloria, D. J.: rev, 16, 183, 2020, 2090
Delp, H. A.: rev, 1318, 2602
Deluty, R. H.: ref, 1831(205)
Delworth, U.: ref, 1726(368)
Demaline, R.: rev, 553, 913
deMann, A. F,: ref, 1573(42)
Demaree, R. G.: rev, 558, 883, 2394
Demask, R. S.: ref, 1498(5338)
Dembo, M. H.: ref, 1831(146), 2413(626)
Dement, W.: ref, 1498(5775)
Dement, W. C.: ref, 1498(5097, 5742)
DeMers, S. T.: ref, 280(1163), 701(86)
De Michele, G.: ref, 2598(1584)
deMille, R.: test, 2489
Deming, A. L.: ref, 1789(709)
Demos, G.: test, 2345
Demos, G. D.: test, 670, 1469
Dempsey, J.: ref, 270(83), 311(25), 678(21)
Dempsey, J. R.: ref, 270(82), 311(24)
Dempsey, R. L.: ref, 1498(5124), 2598(1348)
Denes, F.: ref, 1914(752)
Deniker, P.: ref, 1655(111)
DeNisi, A. S.: ref, 282(142), 799(19), 1295(304), 1296(182), 1370(2), 1808(10), 1855(25), 2016(197), 2537(558)
Denker, E. R.: ref, 1270(75, 77)
Denmark, F. L.: ref, 780(1678)
Dennehy, S. E.: ref, 1424(81)
Denney, D. R.: ref, 1547(326), 2300(532), 2353(25), 2638(124)
Denning, R. K.: ref, 1655(99)
Dennis, W.: test, 2540
Dennis, W. H.: test, 671, 672
Deno, E.: rev, 2106, 2110
Denson, T. A.: ref, 964(489)
Deonauth, J.: ref, 542(21), 2557(224), 2598(1507)
Deo Saran, R. A.: ref, 643(136)

INDEX OF NAMES

D'Eon, J. L.: ref, 1063(101, 126, 128)
DePaulo, J. R.: ref, 1883(78, 94)
De Pauw, K. P.: ref, 2244(31)
Depp, R.: ref, 678(23)
Deptula, M. S.: ref, 2598(1820)
Deputy, P. N.: ref, 200(15)
DeQuattro, V.: ref, 1197(274), 2208(1529)
Derby, D. P.: ref, 2581(330)
Derby, R.: ref, 701(76), 1771(724)
D'ercole, A. J.: ref, 2602(2123)
DeRemer, P.: ref, 698(4)
Deri, S. K.: rev, 2388
de Ridder, J. C.: test, 147, 2230
Derie, F.: ref, 1851(24)
DeRisi, D. T.: ref, 1853(280)
De Risio, C.: ref, 2598(1621), 2607(183)
Derogatis, L. R.: test, 683, 2100; ref, 683(1, 2, 3, 4, 5, 6), 2100(1, 2, 3, 4)
Derouesne, J.: ref, 2598(1558)
Derrick, C.: test, 570, 571, 588, 589, 1991; rev, 172, 242, 413, 503
Derry, P. A.: ref, 2607(216)
Dershowitz, Z.: ref, 794(368)
Derthick, C. H.: test, 1742
Derthick, L. G.: rev, 1625
DeSanctis, M.: ref, 2224(6)
Desberg, P.: ref, 1771(647)
Deschambault, A.: ref, 1063(123)
De Setto, L.: ref, 958(52), 2217(185), 2602(2225)
Desgranges, L.: ref, 2111(1), 2602(1592), 2621(222)
Desi, M.: ref, 1914(881)
Desiderato, O.: ref, 2413(690)
Desiderio, D.: ref, 1498(5047), 2029(196), 2030(4945)
DeSilva, H.: ref, 2300(375)
DeSilva, R. A.: ref, 280(1173), 1498(5765), 1547(354)
DeSilva, W. P.: ref, 479(401), 2598(1308)
Des Lauriers, M.: ref, 1798(306)
Desmond, M. M.: ref, 270(151), 280(1073), 1126(692), 2602(1740)
Desousa, A. L.: ref, 2289(1657)
Detrio, D. M.: ref, 859(769)
Dettmer, P.: ref, 1555(340)
Detzer, E.: ref, 645(13), 1498(5239)
Deutsch, J. E.: ref, 2300(454), 2441(35)
Deutsch, S. E.: ref, 308(23)
Devaney, R.: ref, 606(18)
Devaul, R. A.: ref, 1498(5403)
DeVault, M. V.: rev, 579
De Vault, R. M.: ref, 1668(2), 2581(323)
DeVillafranca, E. F.: rev, 75, 593
Devine, D. A.: ref, 1798(196)
Devine, V. T.: ref, 2179(257)
Devito, P. J.: ref, 932(57)
Devoge, J. T.: ref, 1063(81)
de Vries, M.: ref, 311(23)
DeVries, R.: exc, 559
DeWaard, R. J.: ref, 859(876), 1904(96)
Dewart, H. M.: ref, 1126(723), 1771(648)
DeWeaver, M. J.: ref, 691(42), 719(31)
Dewey, J. C.: rev, 346, 1478
Dewhirst, H. D.: ref, 116(549, 583, 629), 1508(122, 129, 131), 2318(1553, 1574, 1617)
DeWire, H.: test, 2493
Dewitz, P.: ref, 932(122), 2288(76)
Dewolfe, A. S.: ref, 1969(91)
DeWolfe, A. S.: ref, 2598(1777)
Deyarman, R.: ref, 1552(72)
Deyoub, P. L.: ref, 1063(102)
Dharanendraiah, A. S.: ref, 780(1680)
Diack, H.: test, 2281
Diamond, E.: ref, 1831(200)
Diamond, E. E.: test, 372, 2574; rev, 1996, 2478; ref, 76(639), 124(18), 202(10), 344(180), 404(7), 500(56), 506(32), 543(31), 590(386), 732(407), 899(19), 995(150), 1192(234), 1193(143), 1270(80, 85), 1473(196), 1866(38), 2160(72), 2260(45), 2286(329), 2324(4), 2537(564), 2621(393)
Diamond, H.: ref, 859(959)
Diamond, J. J.: ref, 344(137)
Dias, S.: ref, 859(729), 1798(200), 2208(1528)
Diaz, A. P. D. L.: ref, 1493(122)
Diaz-Guerrero, R.: ref, 1106(358), 1798(201), 2602(1629)
DiBenedetto, B.: ref, 958(50), 1126(771), 1769(91), 2034(6), 2602(2101)
DiCarlo, L. M.: rev, 226, 277, 1359, 2669; exc, 852
Dick, M.: ref, 2602(2036)
Dicken, C. F.: rev, 966
Dickey, P. A.: ref, 1197(305)
Dickey, S. E.: test, 1814
Dickhaus, R. C.: ref, 1568(122)
Dickson, D. A.: ref, 859(793, 855)
Dickson, G. S.: rev, 2318
Dickson, W. P.: ref, 1479(346, 365), 1771(649), 2598(1577, 1724), 2602(1882, 2049)
Dickstein, E. B.: ref, 2413(643)
Dickstein, L. S.: ref, 1257(158)
Dickstein, R.: ref, 2602(2090)
DiCuio, R. F.: ref, 2608(183)
Diderichsen, B.: ref, 2602(2045)
Diebold (John) & Associates: test, 731
Diebold, M. H.: ref, 381(64), 1387(12), 1877(5), 2289(1658)
Diederich, P. B.: rev, 1105, 1116
Diekhoff, G.: ref, 2374(191)
Diekhoff, J. S.: rev, 128
Dielman, T. E.: ref, 1233(210)
Diener, E.: ref, 354(1440, 1484), 1798(236), 2491(2056)
Diener, R. G.: ref, 653(156), 1209(40), 2413(664), 2621(368)
Dietch, J.: ref, 1789(661)
Dietrich, D.: ref, 701(68), 2030(5041), 2491(2065), 2602(1958)
Dietrich, M. C.: ref, 282(145), 2015(209), 2317(11), 2657(99)
Dietvorst, T. F.: ref, 1498(5432), 2179(213), 2598(1445, 1578)
Dietz, D.: ref, 751(14)
Dietz, W. H.: ref, 381(70), 2289(1754)
Dietze, D.: ref, 1462(135), 1498(5305), 2179(217)
Diewold, P.: ref, 1883(36)
Diggs, C. C.: ref, 664(14)
DiGuisto, E. L.: ref, 1460(52)
Dikmen, S.: ref, 1498(5071, 5152), 2113(254), 2598(1309, 1310, 1311, 1446, 1701), 2607(197)
Dikmen, S. S.: ref, 2113(243)
Dillard, H.: test, 850
Dillard, J. M.: ref, 374(213, 220), 1478(66), 1831(119)
Dillbeck, M. C.: ref, 2300(344)

Diller, L.: ref, 1547(323)
Dillon, R.: ref, 1319(82), 1914(840), 2621(322)
Dillon, R. F.: ref, 202(12), 1013(121), 1914(798, 838, 839, 882, 883, 884)
DiMatteo, M. R.: ref, 859(905), 1798(279, 280)
Dimock, H. G.: test, 735
Dimond, S. J.: ref, 2598(1312)
Dineen, J. T.: ref, 2598(1642)
Dinero, T. E.: ref, 280(1106), 653(173), 2214(2), 2602(1883)
Dinges, N. G.: ref, 398(106)
Dingwall, J. M.: ref, 2588(32)
Dinham, S. M.: ref, 1576(186)
Dinius, S. H.: ref, 76(628)
Dinning, W. D.: ref, 280(1062), 1498(5072, 5078, 5604), 2289(1650), 2300(345, 346, 522), 2598(1313, 1419), 2620(6, 7, 17)
Dinnsen, D.: ref, 960(20)
DiNola, A. J.: test, 1873, 2507, 2666
Dinsmoor, J. A.: ref, 2602(2194)
Dinur, Y.: ref, 2208(1684)
DiNuzzo, T. M.: ref, 2581(345)
Dipboye, R. L.: rev, 1295, 1296; ref, 116(549, 583), 1508(122, 131), 2318(1553)
Di Pietro, R. J.: ref, 290(7)
Dirks, J.: ref, 2217(166), 2602(2030)
Dirks, J. D.: ref, 1498(5640, 5641)
Dirks, J. F.: ref, 1498(5247, 5433, 5434, 5597)
Dirks, S. J.: ref, 1498(5134)
DiSalvo, V. S.: ref, 664(12)
Disch, J. G.: ref, 2208(1626)
Diseker, R. A.: ref, 1576(218)
DiSessa, T. G.: ref, 270(119), 2289(1724)
Dishner, E. K.: ref, 1013(111), 1570(9)
DiSimoni, F.: test, 2509
DiSimoni, F. G.: ref, 1851(25, 39), 2645(3)
Dispoto, R. G.: ref, 501(884)
Distefano, M. K.: ref, 1547(269), 1808(11), 2598(1382)
DiStefano, P.: ref, 719(36)
Dittes, J. E.: test, 2493
Dittmar, K.: ref, 883(77)
Dittmar, N. D.: ref, 1655(112)
Dittrich, J. E.: ref, 1508(132)
DiVesta, F. J.: ref, 1191(127)
Divgi, D. R.: ref, 1478(78)
Division of Testing and Certification: test, 1484
Dixit, R. C.: ref, 1201(74), 1498(5598)
Dixon, C.: ref, 2413(667)
Dixon, D.: ref, 1771(569), 1823(32)
Dixon, P. N.: ref, 2208(1569, 1570, 1681)
Dixon, P. W.: ref, 590(385), 2160(71)
Dixon, W. J.: ref, 1351(24, 36), 1498(5153, 5759), 2179(203), 2602(1747)
Doan, B. D.: ref, 1099(69), 1923(16), 2208(1628), 2322(14)
Doane, J. A.: ref, 1498(5744, 5745), 2491(2098)
Dobbins, D. A.: ref, 2289(1604), 2602(1630)
Dobias, B.: ref, 280(1124), 2602(1971), 2608(221)
Dobson, B.: test, 824
Dobson, D. J. G.: ref, 2620(16)
Dobson, K. S.: ref, 9(14), 1206(1), 1547(335), 1914(799), 2300(551)
Docherty, J.: ref, 2100(12)
Docter, R.: ref, 588(9), 2288(82)
Docter, R. F.: rev, 1853

Dodd, B. G.: ref, 6(66)
Dodds, J. B.: test, 678
Dodge, J. A.: ref, 859(823), 1547(290)
Dodrill, C. B.: ref, 1498(5248, 5573, 5746), 2113(242, 243), 2390(7), 2598(1447, 1448, 1682, 1702, 1821), 2607(157, 176), 2638(130, 144, 147)
Dods, L. Y.: ref, 1789(662, 687), 2300(390, 445)
Dodson, S.: test, 295
Dodson, W. E.: ref, 1371(253), 1771(661), 2289(1712), 2557(228)
Doebler, L. K.: ref, 501(849), 794(415), 1557(9)
Doehring, D. G.: ref, 1622(38), 1771(599), 2218(7, 10), 2602(1631)
Doehrman, S.: ref, 2598(1673)
Doell, S. R.: ref, 2300(530)
Doenau, S. J.: ref, 30(5)
Doerr, H.: ref, 2015(215), 2602(2207)
Doerr, S. L.: ref, 2512(639)
Dogon, I. L.: ref, 501(927), 673(52), 1779(2)
Doherty, C.: test, 821
Doherty, E. G.: ref, 2587(32)
Doherty, G.: ref, 2353(30)
Doherty, M. E.: ref, 76(608), 2602(2224)
Doherty, P. A.: ref, 2413(616)
Dohner, C. W.: ref, 1576(209)
Dohrenwend, B. P.: ref, 1923(12)
Doi, K.: ref, 780(1664), 2491(2035)
Dokecki, P. R.: ref, 1473(141), 1831(130), 2602(1696, 1697, 1698)
Dolan, A. B.: ref, 270(78), 2608(189)
Dolan, L. J.: test, 2081
Dolan, M. P.: ref, 283(159, 160), 1462(119), 1498(5762), 1655(74), 1914(891), 2598(1314)
Dolby, R. M.: ref, 311(46), 2294(107, 133)
Dolch, E. W.: test, 258
Dolcourt, J. L.: ref, 1108(11), 1969(114), 2621(230)
Dole, A. A.: test, 745; ref, 977(21), 995(142), 1489(6)
Dolinskas, C. A.: ref, 2598(1664)
Dolke, A. M.: ref, 1419(696)
Doll, E. A.: test, 1874, 2557
Doll, R. C.: test, 1325
Doller, J. C.: ref, 1655(106)
Dollimore, J.: ref, 639(56), 859(902), 1883(65)
Dollinger, S. J.: ref, 2608(190)
Dolliver, P.: ref, 2621(349)
Dolliver, R. H.: rev, 1051, 1270, 2318; exc, 2134; ref, 2134(91), 2318(1525, 1550, 1609, 1610)
Dolphin, W. D.: ref, 76(660), 1510(45, 48)
Domangue, J. C.: ref, 1192(245)
Domaracki, J.: ref, 719(27), 766(21), 958(40), 1007(12)
Dombrose, L. A.: test, 1123
Dombrower, E.: ref, 551(40)
Dombrower, J.: ref, 551(40)
Domelsmith, D. E.: ref, 1063(81)
Domino, G.: rev, 1960, 1996, 2441, 2574; ref, 116(529), 157(134), 243(115), 354(1467, 1524), 917(72, 76), 1531(280, 282), 1856(11), 2199(5, 8), 2374(186)
Domitor, P. J.: ref, 794(418), 1106(371), 2300(467)
Donah, C. H.: ref, 280(1106), 2214(2), 2602(1883)
Donahoe, C. P.: ref, 643(139), 1073(120)
Donahue, M.: ref, 1771(799)
Donaldson, G. B.: ref, 878(27)
Donegan, R.: test, 1232
Donlon, T. F.: rev, 2477; ref, 995(151), 1192(213), 1473(172), 2160(64)

INDEX OF NAMES

Donnan, G. A.: ref, 2598(1767), 2607(207)
Donnell, S. M.: ref, 2351(9), 2655(5)
Donnelly, E. F.: ref, 280(1164), 1197(287), 1498(5249, 5599), 2598(1315, 1354, 1372, 1449, 1703, 1704)
Donnelly, E. P.: ref, 2598(1561)
Donoghue, A.: test, 2205
Donoghue, J.: test, 2205
Donovan, C. M.: ref, 678(25)
Donovan, D. M.: ref, 472(14), 665(41), 890(349, 350), 1013(59), 1498(5172, 5250, 5497, 5498, 5673), 2179(227, 228), 2587(44), 2598(1375, 1628, 1629)
Donovan, G.: ref, 1371(249), 1540(12)
Doolen, D. R.: ref, 1576(217)
Doppelt, J. E.: test, 747, 1808, 2469, 2529; rev, 333, 973, 1129, 1300, 1509, 1866, 1941, 1952; ref, 2602(1632)
Dor–Shav, N. K.: ref, 280(1074), 794(386), 1117(440), 2030(4986), 2208(1571), 2598(1450)
Doran, R. L.: ref, 282(145), 2015(209), 2317(11)
d'Orbán, P. T.: ref, 2598(1579)
Doren, M.: test, 748
Dorethy, R.: ref, 357(516), 794(416), 1754(87), 2429(24)
Dorhout, B.: ref, 1498(5033)
Dorle, J.: ref, 1479(333), 2286(285), 2287(37), 2602(1686), 2621(258)
Dorlen, J.: ref, 2621(258)
Dornbush, R. L.: ref, 1904(124)
Dorner, S.: ref, 2602(1781), 2608(199)
Dorr, K. E.: ref, 1498(5631)
Dorsen, M. M.: ref, 270(63), 338(8), 1771(543), 2289(1615), 2557(214), 2602(1646), 2608(182)
Dorsey, G. C.: ref, 2179(257)
Dorsey, S.: test, 2671
Dorus, W.: ref, 645(21)
Dorval, B.: ref, 553(14), 719(30)
Doster, J. T.: ref, 2602(1606)
Doty, M. S.: test, 2650; ref, 2134(115), 2318(1582)
Doty, R. L.: ref, 1466(2)
Dougherty, A. M.: ref, 2581(320)
Doughtie, E. B.: ref, 681(54), 2300(514), 2581(307)
Doughty, P.: test, 2404
Douglas, A. A.: ref, 1436(12)
Douglas, B.: ref, 2217(125), 2621(283)
Douglas, D.: ref, 549(3)
Douglas, J. E.: ref, 823(16), 2018(11), 2289(1659), 2608(191)
Douglas, K.: ref, 1046(576)
Douglas, V.: ref, 964(486), 1853(277)
Douglass, C. B.: ref, 1013(82)
Douglass, F. M.: ref, 859(789), 1498(5435)
Dowd, R.: ref, 2208(1682)
Dowds, B. N.: ref, 1765(11)
Dowling, J. R.: ref, 1229(96), 1535(39)
Downey, R. G.: ref, 76(604), 501(850), 570(328), 1531(285), 1555(322, 329), 2347(4, 6), 2374(188, 194)
Downie, N. M.: rev, 1806, 2638; exc, 2059
Downing, C. J.: ref, 1769(42)
Downing, J.: test, 1998; rev, 2091
Downing, R. W.: ref, 1498(5371, 5530)
Downs, M.: test, 676
Doyle, A.: ref, 270(107), 2289(1701)
Doyle, A. B.: ref, 381(65), 1126(755), 1771(725), 2289(1660), 2472(22), 2551(14)

Doyle, C.: ref, 1547(339)
Doyle, K. O.: rev, 818, 1953; ref, 973(29), 1510(47), 1866(36), 2335(1)
Doyle, R. E.: ref, 1473(173), 2286(307)
Doyle, S. X.: ref, 780(1695)
D'Oyley, V. R.: rev, 2593
Draba, R. E.: ref, 2160(51)
Drabin, I. R.: ref, 1575(3)
Drachman, D.: ref, 941(43), 1883(81)
Drachman, D. A.: ref, 2598(1705)
Drahozal, E. C.: ref, 1569(8)
Drake, B. L.: ref, 2244(41)
Drake, C.: ref, 2218(14), 2602(2017)
Drake, R. M.: rev, 643, 1188, 2013, 2484
Drasgow, J.: test, 2565
Drayton, W.: ref, 1547(322)
Dreese, M.: test, 1165
Dreger, R. M.: rev, 2203, 2300
Dreher, M. J.: ref, 1257(178)
Drennen, W.: ref, 890(343), 1170(233), 1789(663, 690)
Dressel, P. L.: rev, 124, 142, 486, 506, 1158, 2162
Drew (Edward) Co.: test, 903
Drew, F. L.: ref, 1576(203)
Drewes, A. A.: ref, 1771(529)
Drews, J.: ref, 381(71), 2289(1759)
Dreyer, A. S.: ref, 794(428), 1875(6)
Dreyer, D. E.: ref, 1513(25)
Dreyer, J.: ref, 859(880), 1789(702)
Dreyer, P. H.: rev, 872, 873
Drinkard, K.: test, 2618
Driscoll, L. A.: rev, 238, 2566
Droege, R. C.: rev, 900, 2638
Droes, J.: ref, 1922(15)
Droppleman, L. F.: test, 1904
Drory, A.: ref, 1300(124)
Drotar, D.: ref, 1515(18), 2031(459)
Druce, N. R.: ref, 1233(218)
Drucker, S. A.: ref, 1771(529)
Druckman, J. M.: ref, 872(9)
Drues, J.: ref, 1922(6, 7, 9)
Druley, K. A.: ref, 1498(5228), 2179(211)
Drum, P.: rev, 1156
Drum, P. A.: rev, 249
Drummond, J.: ref, 2131(7)
Drummond, R. J.: ref, 328(4), 400(124, 133), 769(43), 772(27), 1013(51), 1754(60), 1831(126), 1934(8), 2131(5), 2260(29), 2657(107)
Drummond, S. S.: ref, 308(24)
Drumwright, A. F.: test, 675
Drury, D. W.: ref, 2160(73)
D'Souza, S. W.: ref, 1153(8), 2018(19)
Dua, J. K.: ref, 883(82)
Dube, G. G.: ref, 2289(1661), 2548(14)
DuBois, J. J.: exc, 1859
DuBois, P. H.: test, 2423; rev, 501, 1189, 1576
DuBois, Y.: ref, 6(84)
DuBois, Y. G.: ref, 6(67)
DuBose, R. F.: test, 693; ref, 270(60), 381(58, 64), 1387(12), 1471(47), 1877(5), 2289(1658)
Dubrovsky, D. T.: test, 2672
Duck, G. A.: ref, 344(161)
Duck, S. W.: ref, 354(1441)
Ducker, D. G.: ref, 1576(189)
Duckett, J.: ref, 6(39)
Duckro, P.: ref, 780(1641), 2491(2006)

Duckro, R.: ref, 780(1641), 2491(2006)
Dudek, S. Z.: ref, 2030(4966)
Dudley, D. L.: ref, 609(201), 1498(5073)
Dudley, G. E.: ref, 665(43)
Dudley, H. K.: ref, 1106(366)
Dudley, J. R.: ref, 501(821), 570(323)
Dudley, P.: test, 1311
Dueck, R.: ref, 325(34)
Duff, T. B.: ref, 1510(42), 2463(6)
Duffelmeyer, F. A.: ref, 932(106), 1568(132)
Duffy, J. R.: ref, 1851(46)
Duffy, K.: ref, 859(728)
Duffy, R. A.: ref, 243(123), 1013(105), 1229(97), 2512(640)
Duffy, R. J.: ref, 1851(46)
Dugdale, A. E.: ref, 280(1036), 922(6), 964(478, 496), 2602(1651)
Duggins, L. A.: rev, 958
Duignan, P.: ref, 2301(25)
Duke, M. P.: ref, 116(566)
Dulay, H. C.: test, 290, 291
Duley, S. M.: ref, 1831(208)
Dulin, K. L.: ref, 845(6)
Dumaret, A.: ref, 2602(1817)
Dumas, R. A.: ref, 1063(93)
Dumbrower, J.: ref, 551(65)
Dumond, D. L.: ref, 1851(26)
Dunbar, P. W.: ref, 1498(5234, 5569)
Dunbar, R. E.: ref, 2343(1051)
Dunbar, S. B.: ref, 1292(55, 56)
Duncan, J.: ref, 794(369)
Duncan, P.: test, 807, 810
Duncan, S.: ref, 1281(3)
Duncan, S. E.: test, 1281; ref, 1281(4)
Duncan-Jones, P.: ref, 941(23, 24, 34), 1883(33, 34, 69)
Duncan-Rose, C.: ref, 1771(647)
Dunckley, R. A.: ref, 1921(39)
Dungan, D. S.: ref, 2491(2100)
Dunham, R. B.: ref, 1855(19), 2537(546)
Dunivant, N.: ref, 280(1160), 751(38), 1250(21), 2602(2162), 2641(19)
Dunkel, H. B.: rev, 493, 495, 515, 517, 522; exc, 1527
Dunkin, M. J.: ref, 30(5)
Dunlap, J. W.: rev, 1473
Dunlap, K.: exc, 767
Dunlap, R.: test, 1952
Dunlap, R. A.: ref, 1655(96)
Dunlap, W. P.: ref, 2602(1884), 2621(328)
Dunleavy, R. A.: ref, 1479(377), 2602(2031)
Dunn, J. A.: rev, 392, 964
Dunn, L. M.: test, 823, 1769, 1771
Dunn, M. S.: test, 1383
Dunn, R. S.: ref, 1754(101)
Dunn, S.: test, 2195
Dunn, S. S.: rev, 707, 1061, 1551
Dunn, T. L.: ref, 639(56), 859(902), 1547(253, 325), 1883(65)
Dunn, V.: test, 1246; ref, 1246(1)
Dunnett, S.: ref, 859(943)
Dunnette, M. D.: test, 1494; rev, 846, 2638; ref, 2180(36)
Dupecher, D. R.: rev, 1519
DuPlessis, J. M.: ref, 400(138)
Dupuis, M. M.: ref, 1955(106, 108, 110, 111, 112)

Dupuy, H. J.: test, 269
DuRapau, V. J.: ref, 1257(179)
Durfee, J. T.: ref, 270(117)
Durham, T.: ref, 2289(1613), 2602(1643)
Durio, H. F.: ref, 157(143), 1362(11), 2199(9)
Durlach, N. I.: ref, 230(51), 549(1), 2598(1374), 2647(1)
Durost, W. N.: rev, 716, 1885, 2484
Durrell, D. D.: test, 766, 1551
Dusewicz, R. A.: test, 653
Dustman, R. E.: ref, 1462(117, 151), 2598(1299)
Dutch, R. D.: rev, 318, 617, 1025
Duthie, R. B.: ref, 116(550)
du Toit, J. P.: test, 1041
du Toit, L.: test, 400
Duvall, S.: ref, 1771(616), 1969(93), 2598(1493)
Duvall, S. W.: ref, 1319(75), 1498(5656), 1969(113), 2598(1451, 1748)
Duyme, M.: ref, 2602(1817)
Dvorak, A.: rev, 1073
Dvorak, B. J.: rev, 2527
Dvorine, I.: test, 767
Dworkin, J. P.: ref, 2103(9)
Dworkin, N. E.: ref, 1769(70), 1771(650)
Dworkin, P. H.: ref, 1424(53)
Dworkin, R. H.: ref, 1498(5074), 1798(237)
Dwyer, C. A.: rev, 2641
Dwyer, E. J.: ref, 719(37), 1478(73), 2218(16)
Dwyer, J. T.: ref, 381(70), 2289(1754)
Dyck, D. G.: ref, 2598(1452), 2602(1741)
Dyckman, J. M.: ref, 883(83, 104)
Dye, C. J.: ref, 2300(583), 2598(1822)
Dye, O. A.: ref, 2598(1580)
Dyer, H. S.: rev, 176, 1473
Dyer, J. W.: ref, 653(150), 2246(27)
Dykes, M. K.: test, 694
Dykman, R. A.: ref, 1007(27, 36, 41), 1229(98, 105), 2602(1589, 1885, 2032, 2033, 2152), 2621(219, 329, 394, 395, 431)
Dykstra, K.: test, 1470
Dykstra, R.: rev, 1479, 1841, 1870
Dyson, R. S.: ref, 1233(212), 2631(30)
Eadie, M. J.: test, 1963
Eads, G. M.: ref, 116(536, 537)
Eagle, N.: rev, 543, 1590, 1712
Eagleeye, D.: ref, 1191(125)
Eames, N.: ref, 681(51), 1498(5562)
Eanet, M. G.: ref, 1568(126)
Eardley, J.: ref, 874(43)
Early, G. H.: ref, 1192(163), 1473(123)
Eash, M. J.: rev, 409
Easley, H.: rev, 1073
Eason, B. J.: ref, 1498(5741)
Eason, G.: ref, 363(14)
Easterday, K. E.: ref, 890(356)
Eastman, B. G.: ref, 653(154)
Eastman, J.: ref, 2289(1605)
Eastman, P. M.: ref, 9(11)
Easton, B.: ref, 2289(1625)
Eaton, E. L.: test, 815; ref, 1126(653), 2289(1603), 2602(1612)
Eaves, L.: ref, 1771(554)
Ebel, R. L.: rev, 1576, 2286; exc, 2440
Ebeling, K. S.: ref, 2512(641)
Eber, H. W.: test, 2208

INDEX OF NAMES

Eberly, C.: ref, 1498(5295)
Eberst, R. M.: ref, 2300(391)
Ebert, J. N.: ref, 2030(4948), 2588(31)
Ebert, M. H.: ref, 308(6), 2598(1435, 1867), 2607(220)
Ebmeier, H.: ref, 2260(38)
Echternacht, G.: ref, 2318(1592)
Eckardt, M. J.: ref, 283(156), 2179(235), 2598(1706)
Eckert, E. D.: ref, 1498(5509, 5586)
Eckstein Bros., Inc.: test, 773
Eddy, S.: ref, 2030(5007), 2598(1520)
Edel, D.: test, 1149
Edelbrock, C.: ref, 1771(600)
Edell, W. S.: ref, 2030(5027)
Edelson, R. I.: ref, 1498(5075), 2587(33)
Edfeldt, A. W.: test, 2011
Edgar, E. B.: test, 2532
Edgar, M.: ref, 1498(5542)
Edinger, J.: ref, 1498(5295)
Edinger, J. D.: ref, 1106(357), 1498(5251, 5436, 5437), 2286(298), 2300(335), 2598(1503, 1581)
Edington, A.: ref, 1419(687)
Edmonds, E. M.: ref, 2300(433)
Edmondson, R. J.: ref, 357(517), 1831(164)
Edmonson, B.: test, 2237, 2460; ref, 2237(1)
Edmonston, W. E.: ref, 1063(82)
Edmunds, G.: ref, 859(730)
Educational Development Corporation: test, 1142, 1143
Educational Records Bureau: test, 838
Educational Research Centre: test, 756
Educational Testing Service: test, 1, 2, 259, 260, 261, 262, 263, 404, 573, 574, 575, 576, 577, 578, 579, 580, 582, 583, 584, 585, 586, 587, 590, 591, 592, 593, 594, 595, 596, 597, 598, 599, 600, 601, 602, 789, 974, 975, 976, 977, 978, 979, 980, 981, 982, 983, 984, 985, 986, 987, 988, 989, 990, 991, 992, 993, 994, 995, 996, 997, 998, 999, 1000, 1077, 1519, 1520, 1521, 1522, 1523, 1545, 1559, 1563, 1624, 1625, 1626, 1627, 1628, 1629, 1630, 1631, 1632, 1633, 1634, 1635, 1636, 1637, 1638, 1639, 1640, 1641, 1642, 1643, 1644, 1645, 1646, 1647, 1648, 1649, 1650, 1651, 1866, 1906, 2078, 2088, 2116, 2117, 2118, 2120, 2160, 2161, 2162, 2163, 2164, 2165, 2166, 2441, 2493
Educator Feedback Center, Western Michigan University: test, 119, 2398
Edwards, A. L.: test, 780; rev, 356, 785
Edwards, B. C.: test, 1334
Edwards, C. D.: test, 2301
Edwards, C. N.: test, 2206
Edwards, D.: ref, 270(119), 2289(1724)
Edwards, D. W.: ref, 677(2)
Edwards, E. M.: ref, 1099(69), 1923(16), 2208(1628), 2322(14)
Edwards, H. P.: ref, 2318(1539)
Edwards, J. R.: ref, 116(607)
Edwards, K. J.: ref, 1099(68)
Edwards, K. R.: ref, 1498(5681), 1948(103)
Edwards, L. L.: ref, 1789(678), 2121(70)
Edwards, N. B.: ref, 2179(210)
Edwards, R.: rev, 826
Edwards, R. C.: ref, 501(789)
Edwards, R. P.: ref, 2602(2134)
Edwards, S.: ref, 2657(104)
Egan, D.: ref, 2602(2224)

Egel, A. L.: ref, 1319(83)
Egeland, B.: exc, 2091; ref, 1197(306, 316), 1798(277, 298, 301), 2179(250, 252), 2289(1666)
Egeland, B. R.: rev, 256, 534; ref, 311(40)
Egelson, R.: ref, 1771(746)
Egelston, R. L.: ref, 1126(762), 2472(23)
Egelston–Dodd, J.: ref, 346(106)
Eggeraat, J. B.: ref, 883(84)
Eggertsen, C.: ref, 2598(1610)
Eggleston, P. J.: ref, 1531(279)
Eglevsky, D. A.: ref, 1498(5081)
Egner, J. R.: ref, 374(197)
Egner, K.: ref, 1771(671), 2621(348)
Egri, G.: ref, 1923(12)
Egry, A. M.: ref, 352(4, 6)
Ehinger, D. M.: ref, 961(7), 1540(21), 1769(100), 1914(877), 2621(434)
Ehman, L. H.: rev, 1232, 1525
Ehrensing, R. H.: ref, 1655(75)
Ehrenstein, W. H.: ref, 1771(777)
Ehrlich, C. H.: ref, 270(126), 338(10)
Ehrlichman, H.: ref, 794(377)
Ehrman, L.: ref, 627(24)
Eich, W. F.: ref, 280(1141), 1969(107), 2217(167)
Eichel, E.: ref, 872(6)
Eichenberger, R. J.: ref, 2512(587)
Eichman, W. J.: rev, 117, 645, 1499, 1502, 1655, 1765, 1904
Eichorn, D. H.: test, 1242, 2548; rev, 897, 2608; ref, 2289(1628)
Eichorn, J.: ref, 2289(1599), 2602(1605), 2621(228)
Eicke, F. J.: ref, 794(415)
Eidelson, R. J.: ref, 780(1696)
Eidsmoe, R. M.: test, 2338
Eiduson, B. T.: ref, 270(79)
Eignor, D. R.: ref, 709(1), 710(1), 716(1), 913(1), 1139(1), 1140(1), 1389(1), 1390(2), 1880(6), 2291(1), 2292(25)
Eimon, M. C.: ref, 2179(214), 2244(32)
Eipper, D. S.: ref, 270(80)
Eisdorfer, C.: ref, 2598(1417, 1695)
Eisenmann, R.: ref, 1498(5600)
Eisenson, J.: test, 852
Eiser, C.: ref, 330(16, 17, 19), 1424(30, 35), 2598(1707), 2602(1633, 1742, 2034), 2608(175)
Eisert, D. C.: ref, 1726(358)
Eisner, H.: test, 1230
Eklund, S. J.: ref, 1531(279)
Ekstrom, R. B.: test, 1077, 1257; ref, 1192(213), 1473(172), 2160(64)
Ekwall, E. E.: test, 788
Elardo, P. T.: ref, 704(12)
Elardo, R.: ref, 270(104), 1108(2, 4, 6, 9), 1126(655)
Elashoff, J. D.: ref, 551(27)
Elbert, M.: ref, 664(11), 960(9, 20), 1771(601, 792)
Eldredge, A. R.: ref, 1473(216), 1831(206)
Eldridge, F. L.: ref, 1498(5097)
Eldridge, M. S.: ref, 1831(120)
Elenewski, J. J.: ref, 1498(5438)
Elfant, I. L.: ref, 1506(71), 2244(27)
Elfenbein, J. L.: ref, 1126(780), 1771(778)
Elgaard, F.: ref, 681(52), 1547(316)
Elgart, B.: ref, 1655(89)
Elgart, D. B.: ref, 932(75)
Elgerot, A.: ref, 1914(753)

Elias, G.: test, 871
Elias, M. F.: ref, 2598(1642)
Elias, S. F.: ref, 2208(1570, 1681), 2598(1783)
Eliot, J.: test, 792; ref, 733(7), 792(1), 1555(306), 1620(21), 1652(1), 2004(1)
Elithorn, A.: test, 1778
Elizur, A.: test, 793
Elizur, D.: ref, 1495(79), 1497(24), 1508(114)
Elkind, D.: ref, 1831(165)
Elkins, J.: test, 1536, 2048; exc, 1912; ref, 1126(663, 693, 781), 2047(1), 2245(1)
Ellenberg, J. H.: ref, 2602(1743), 2621(281)
Ellenberg, L.: ref, 1485(78), 2300(538, 577)
Eller, W.: rev, 1306
Ellerbusch, R. C.: ref, 1798(285)
Ellett, C. D.: ref, 1192(177), 2208(1610, 1652)
Elley, W. B.: test, 1910, 1912; rev, 479
Ellingsen, P.: ref, 1655(107)
Ellington, J. E.: ref, 354(1525), 2208(1651)
Elliot, M.: ref, 1769(102), 2289(1781), 2602(2170), 2621(437)
Elliot, R. N.: ref, 1831(117), 2286(274)
Elliot, W. A.: ref, 283(157), 1914(841)
Elliott, A. G. P.: ref, 2208(1683)
Elliott, C. D.: test, 322
Elliott, D.: ref, 1771(779)
Elliott, D. N.: test, 1951
Elliott, P. A.: ref, 1655(105)
Elliott, R. M.: test, 2015
Ellis, A.: rev, 298, 376, 871, 1047, 1376, 1498, 2169, 2396
Ellis, B. W.: exc, 654
Ellis, C. R.: ref, 1969(118)
Ellis, E. M.: ref, 1904(125)
Ellis, H. C.: ref, 681(70), 1257(139)
Ellis, L. S.: ref, 2413(671)
Ellis, N. C.: ref, 2602(2035)
Ellis, R. A.: ref, 354(1526)
Ellis, W. D.: ref, 1498(5215)
Ellis, W. G.: exc, 503
Ellison, S.: ref, 6(83)
Ellison, T. A.: ref, 409(4)
Ells, P.: ref, 1851(40)
Ellsworth, B. R.: test, 1765; ref, 1765(10)
Ellsworth, R.: ref, 76(603), 1185(8)
Ellsworth, R. B.: test, 117, 341, 1351, 1759, 1760
Ellsworth, S. L.: test, 117, 341, 1759, 1760, 1765
El-Meligi, A. M.: test, 855
Elmore-Nicholas, L.: ref, 1851(47)
Elmore, P. B.: test, 274, 385, 1298; ref, 1257(159), 1298(1, 2), 1498(5601)
Elmore, R. F.: ref, 2208(1610, 1652)
El Paso Public Schools: test, 1733, 1735
Elsasser, T. C.: ref, 2208(1536)
Elsayed, M.: ref, 653(163), 2208(1653)
Elsom, B.: ref, 559(53)
Elstein, M.: ref, 2168(9)
Elsworth, G. R.: ref, 2300(550)
Elton, D.: ref, 1757(16)
Elveback, L. R.: ref, 1498(5211)
Elzey, F. F.: test, 343, 353, 2059, 2508
Emans, R.: ref, 1073(128), 2292(33)
Eme, R.: ref, 2602(1744)
Emerick, L. L.: rev, 1724, 1852
Emery, G. D.: ref, 1904(117)

Emler, N. P.: ref, 1485(69)
Emling, R. C.: ref, 2318(1601)
Emmelkamp, P. M. G.: ref, 883(84)
Emmer, E. T.: ref, 344(167, 182)
Emmerich, W.: ref, 1771(651), 1875(3)
Emmett, W. G.: rev, 1272
Emory, E.: ref, 1883(96), 2621(425)
Enderby, P.: ref, 925(13), 1513(27)
Endicott, J.: test, 645, 1922, 1923; ref, 1923(14, 22)
Endler, N. S.: rev, 2301, 2353; ref, 354(1436)
Endler, P. B.: ref, 2179(214), 2244(32)
Endres, J. M. B.: ref, 2608(195)
Enelow, C. T.: ref, 1655(88)
Engel, D.: ref, 2213(4)
Engel, K. L.: ref, 1498(5747)
Engel, M.: exc, 321; ref, 483(28), 1473(179)
Engel, R.: ref, 1126(776), 1371(261), 2289(1779), 2598(1814)
Engelbrecht, G.: test, 1041
Engelhardt, M. D.: rev, 510
Engelhart, M. D.: rev, 76, 489, 974
Engelman, M. A.: ref, 2512(588)
Engelman, S. R.: ref, 1117(442)
Engelmann, H. O.: test, 849
Engelson, I.: test, 804
Engin, A.: ref, 2602(1837, 1841)
Engin, A. W.: ref, 280(1060), 344(149), 553(16), 704(10), 1503(63)
England, G. W.: test, 1508
Engle, P. L.: ref, 2602(1770)
Engle, R. W.: ref, 1771(789), 2602(2036)
Englehardt, D. M.: ref, 1240(54)
Engleman, S.: test, 614
Engstrand, E.: ref, 1655(107)
Engum, E.: ref, 1346(4)
Enkin, M. W.: ref, 311(39)
Ennis, R. H.: test, 604, 605, 606
Eno, L.: ref, 643(137, 138), 1341(173, 174), 1726(359, 360), 2602(2037), 2621(396)
Enos, M. M.: test, 2081
Enright, R. D.: ref, 1771(726), 1914(809), 2289(1755), 2602(2038), 2629(115)
Entin, E. B.: ref, 1568(133)
Epperson, D. L.: ref, 1269(28)
Epps, S: ref, 2602(2230)
Epps, S.: ref, 2639(3)
Epstein, B.: ref, 1919(45), 2179(241), 2620(18)
Epstein, D. J.: ref, 116(547), 384(5), 2208(1563)
Epstein, H. R.: ref, 6(80), 2598(1802), 2602(2141)
Epstein, J.: ref, 1537(2), 1798(278), 2602(2039), 2621(397)
Epstein, J. L.: test, 1962; ref, 1192(174)
Epstein, M.: ref, 2217(134)
Epstein, M. H.: ref, 1272(131), 2217(118), 2269(445), 2289(1645), 2602(1703)
Epstein, S.: ref, 859(849), 1046(581)
Erber, J. T.: ref, 2300(583), 2598(1822, 1823)
Erdman, J. B.: ref, 1576(210)
Erdmann, A. J.: test, 609
Erdmann, J. B.: ref, 1576(215)
Erdwins, C.: ref, 6(47), 2413(672)
Erdwins, C. J.: ref, 354(1527), 357(524), 780(1697), 2413(673)
Erenkrantz, B. D.: ref, 2343(1051)
Erez, M.: ref, 354(1528), 1295(299), 2581(337)

INDEX OF NAMES

Ericksen, G. L.: rev, 1248, 1413, 1490
Erickson, J. G.: test, 550
Erickson, L. W.: rev, 2006, 2274, 2275, 2527
Erickson, M. T.: ref, 707(22), 2602(1919)
Erickson, R. C.: rev, 1609, 1614; ref, 665(46), 1462(118), 1498(5058, 5076), 2179(195), 2598(1453)
Erickson, R. L.: test, 1865
Ericson, A. T.: test, 806
Eridge, S.: ref, 960(10), 1622(44), 1771(629), 2472(15)
Erikson, C. L.: ref, 2602(1745)
Erlenmeyer-Kimling, L.: ref, 1498(5196)
Erlings, B.: ref, 1552(70)
Erman, M. K.: ref, 2598(1708)
Ernhart, C. B.: ref, 302(28), 581(10), 1424(61, 62), 1771(530), 1874(8), 1969(83, 108), 2551(13)
Ernst, M. L.: ref, 859(798), 1904(72)
Eron, L. D.: rev, 2030, 2491; ref, 1498(5290, 5302, 5602)
Errickson, E.: ref, 1498(5252, 5509), 1655(91)
Erway, E.: ref, 2445(4)
Erwin, C. W.: ref, 1498(5651), 2300(412, 595)
Erwin, T. D.: ref, 501(886), 1568(142), 1726(368)
Eschette, N.: ref, 1046(568)
Escobar, V.: ref, 2289(1605)
Eshbaugh, D. M.: ref, 1498(5253, 5603), 1789(685)
Eskew, R. W.: ref, 2155(13)
Esler, M.: ref, 1197(274), 2208(1529)
Esler, W. K.: ref, 1479(315), 1769(71), 2217(112)
Eson, M. E.: ref, 270(81), 1993(2), 2285(11), 2289(1662), 2557(221)
Espenschade, A.: rev, 324, 1331
Espindola, E.: ref, 1498(5213)
Esposito, R. P.: ref, 1789(664), 2134(92)
Esser, B. F.: rev, 293, 811
Estabrook. W.: ref, 1109(22), 2598(1716)
Estes, J. J.: test, 845
Estes, T. H.: test, 845
Estock, R. E.: ref, 1498(5143)
Etaugh, C.: ref, 1060(28)
Eun, B. S.: ref, 1831(159)
Eurich, A. C.: test, 1507, 1512; rev, 2518
Evaluation Systems, Inc.: test, 1550
Evans, A. S.: test, 1920
Evans, D.: ref, 280(1142), 823(12), 1126(656), 2153(2), 2289(1606)
Evans, D. R.: ref, 1197(277), 1498(5077), 1547(259)
Evans, F. J.: ref, 1063(83, 84, 85, 95, 103), 2294(110, 127)
Evans, G.: ref, 31(5), 1620(22), 1910(3)
Evans, G. W.: ref, 226(178, 184), 409(10)
Evans, J.: test, 635, 2084
Evans, J. G.: ref, 2602(1760, 1792)
Evans, J. R.: ref, 2602(2119)
Evans, M.: ref, 1473(174), 1479(347)
Evans, M. A.: ref, 1914(800), 2286(308)
Evans, M. E.: ref, 1771(626), 1914(786)
Evans, R.: ref, 1498(5078), 2300(346), 2620(7)
Evans, R. G.: ref, 665(47), 1498(5072, 5604), 1969(121), 2300(345, 522), 2598(1709), 2620(6, 17)
Evans, S. H.: ref, 2374(191)
Evans, T.: ref, 2289(1607)
Evans, W. H.: test, 1127
Evasco, K. M.: ref, 2445(3)
Even, A.: rev, 595

Evens, M. G.: ref, 1498(5723), 2413(689)
Evensen, E. P.: ref, 1099(67)
Evered, R. D.: ref, 1555(307)
Everett, M.: ref, 1531(279)
Everitt, B. S.: ref, 2537(565)
Evertson, C. M.: ref, 344(167, 181, 182), 1473(128, 170), 1479(341)
Evesham, M.: ref, 1126(657), 1771(531), 2018(8), 2602(1634)
Ewing, J. H.: ref, 2030(4948), 2588(31)
Exline, R. V.: ref, 501(854), 1498(5445), 2318(1584)
Exner, J. E.: exc, 356; ref, 280(1026), 794(370), 963(128), 1240(50), 1498(5079, 5080, 5254), 2030(4949, 4950, 4951, 4987, 4988, 5018, 5058), 2598(1316, 1317), 2607(133)
Exton, A. H.: test, 1806
Eyberg, S.: test, 858, 2494
Eyberg, S. M.: test, 768; ref, 768(1), 858(1, 2), 2494(1)
Eyde, L. D.: rev, 2194, 2273
Eyman, R. K.: ref, 6(40, 85)
Eyo, I. E.: ref, 2413(696)
Eysenck, H. J.: test, 859, 860, 1419; rev, 639, 1106, 1498, 2030, 2499; ref, 860(87, 88, 89, 90, 104, 115, 119, 124, 137, 142), 1229(101)
Eysenck, M. C.: ref, 860(120)
Eysenck, M. W.: ref, 149(3), 859(907), 860(120)
Eysenck, S.: ref, 860(105, 115)
Eysenck, S. B. G.: test, 859, 860, 861, 1229; ref, 702(2), 859(851), 860(87, 88, 89, 90, 104, 111, 113, 121, 124, 138, 139, 140, 142), 1229(87, 101, 104), 1883(66)
Ezeilo, B.: ref, 1853(276)
Ezrachi, O.: ref, 1547(323)
Faber, R.: ref, 308(25)
Fabes, R. A.: ref, 1969(120), 2598(1824)
Fabian, M. S.: ref, 280(1165), 1462(157), 1914(885), 2179(253), 2598(1825)
Fabre, T.: ref, 280(1080), 1462(136), 2602(1786)
Fabry, J.: ref, 2318(1526, 1577), 2413(586)
Facziende, B.: ref, 1769(67), 2602(1866)
Fadale, L. M.: test, 368
Fagan, T. J.: ref, 1498(5605), 1904(67, 75), 2300(523), 2598(1614)
Faigley, L.: ref, 412(6), 501(923), 2002(6)
Fainsilber, L.: ref, 2512(656)
Fairbairn, V. J.: test, 1988
Fairchild, L.: ref, 794(433)
Fairweather, H.: ref, 2602(1746), 2608(176)
Fakouri, M. E.: ref, 1192(199)
Falbo, T.: ref, 780(1685), 2491(2057)
Falender, C. A.: test, 1439, 1448; ref, 1439(1), 1448(1)
Falgout, J. C.: ref, 1473(161), 1754(80), 2602(1806)
Falk, R.: ref, 1498(5265)
Falloon, I. R. H.: ref, 1883(40)
Falls, H. B.: ref, 5(169)
Fanaroff, A. A.: ref, 270(69), 2289(1629)
Fancher, R. E.: ref, 665(40)
Fandal, A. W.: test, 678
Fanslow, A. M.: test, 1656
Fant, H.: ref, 398(109)
Fantz, R. L.: ref, 270(69), 2289(1629)
Farber, P. D.: ref, 1498(5435)
Farbry, J. E.: ref, 2300(439)
Farel, A. M.: ref, 2478(13), 2608(234)
Farge, E. J.: ref, 2208(1535, 1611)
Farkas, M. S.: ref, 609(221)

Farley, F. H.: ref, 354(1392, 1483, 1529, 1544), 859(734), 1771(727), 2512(589)
Farley, G. K.: ref, 1853(284), 2602(1907)
Farmer, A.: ref, 308(4)
Farnsworth, D.: test, 877, 878
Farnsworth, P. R.: rev, 155, 1274, 1460, 2113, 2451; exc, 1446
Farnum, S. E.: test, 879, 880, 2591
Faroqi, M. A.: exc, 750
Farr, J. L.: ref, 354(1470), 780(1674), 1508(133), 2413(630)
Farr, R.: test, 1191, 1473, 1474, 1475, 1476, 1477, 1478; rev, 482, 1880
Farr, S. D.: exc, 590
Farrah, G. A.: test, 2131
Farran, D. C.: ref, 270(121), 1126(756), 2289(1730), 2598(1634, 1710), 2602(1939, 2040)
Farrell, A. D.: ref, 883(103), 2602(1875)
Farrell, M.: ref, 1789(639)
Farrow, D. L.: ref, 2491(2099)
Faschingbauer, T.: ref, 2300(452)
Faschingbauer, T. R.: ref, 1498(5081, 5255, 5320, 5403)
Fash, D. S.: ref, 1771(780)
Fast, C. G.: test, 881
Faunce, P. S.: ref, 2318(1570)
Fauria, T.: ref, 472(18, 20), 1013(109, 132), 1498(5761), 2179(243)
Fauria, T. M.: ref, 1013(93)
Favero, J.: ref, 551(40, 65)
Fawaz, N.: ref, 280(1102), 964(494), 2218(140)
Fawcett, H. P.: exc, 2594
Fawcus, R.: exc, 1153
Fay, G.: ref, 719(39), 2621(438)
Fay, J. W.: rev, 1261
Fay, W. H.: ref, 1771(781)
Fazio, R. H.: ref, 501(802)
Feather, N. T.: ref, 2029(213, 214, 224, 225, 239), 2629(104, 111, 117)
Feczko, M.: ref, 2030(5070)
Federman, E. J.: test, 1130; ref, 501(790), 1130(1), 2598(1318, 1555)
Fedio, P.: ref, 1498(5038)
Fedirka, P. J.: ref, 1969(91)
Feeney, D. M.: ref, 1257(139)
Fehr, L. A.: ref, 1197(296), 2300(463, 496), 2343(1029, 1044)
Fehrenbach, P. A.: ref, 472(20), 1013(132), 1498(5761)
Fehrer, E.: rev, 1352, 2307
Feier, C. D.: ref, 2598(1711)
Feifel, H.: ref, 2179(236)
Feigenbaum, D.: ref, 280(1117), 345(46), 346(105), 2387(3), 2602(1930)
Feigenbaum, E.: ref, 1922(9)
Feild, H. S.: ref, 1508(123)
Fein, D.: ref, 922(10), 1771(652)
Fein, G. G.: ref, 270(11)
Feinberg, L. B.: ref, 2300(392)
Feinburg, H.: rev, 691
Feindler, E. L.: ref, 2346(1)
Feingold, J.: ref, 2602(1817)
Feinman, J. M.: ref, 1498(5082), 2030(4952)
Feirstein, A.: ref, 2030(4944)
Feitz, R. H.: ref, 1576(194)
Feld, S.: ref, 1192(206, 214), 1473(164, 175)
Feldhusen, J.: test, 1348

Feldhusen, J. F.: test, 797, 1654; ref, 1295(291), 1831(207), 2512(591)
Feldman, A.: ref, 1771(653)
Feldman, D. H.: ref, 2269(444)
Feldman, G.: ref, 695(1)
Feldman, H.: ref, 2300(557, 600)
Feldman, M. J.: test, 2565
Feldman-Summers, S.: ref, 1498(5542)
Feldmann, S.: exc, 748
Feldmann, S. C.: rev, 585, 586, 957; exc, 2202
Feldstein, A. M.: ref, 859(946)
Feldt, L. S.: test, 1193; rev, 438, 570, 1316, 2662; ref, 1193(145)
Felker, D. W.: ref, 1192(164), 1831(115, 136, 157)
Fellner, M. J.: test, 1822
Fellows, B. J.: ref, 964(485), 1063(94)
Feltham, D. W.: test, 2046
Feltz, D. L.: ref, 501(827)
Fennell, R. S.: ref, 653(154)
Fennema, E.: ref, 573(17), 578(4), 732(394), 1970(9, 11), 2246(21, 23), 2474(3)
Fennema, E. H.: ref, 483(18), 2246(26)
Fenton, C. H.: ref, 1931(53)
Fenton, F. R.: ref, 1922(14)
Fenton, G. W.: ref, 639(56), 859(902), 1498(5256), 1883(65), 2598(1454)
Fenwick, P. B. C.: ref, 639(56), 859(902), 1498(5256), 1883(65), 2598(1454)
Feo, A. F.: ref, 1233(231)
Ferguson, B.: ref, 2179(222)
Ferguson, E.: ref, 2655(4)
Ferguson, G. A.: rev, 1716
Ferguson, J. D.: ref, 1063(110)
Ferguson, J. M.: ref, 1940(84)
Ferguson, L. R.: ref, 1170(231)
Ferguson, L. W.: rev, 2180
Ferguson, M. L.: ref, 1547(292)
Ferguson, N.: ref, 2208(1530)
Ferguson, P. A.: ref, 1851(33)
Ferguson, R.: ref, 76(605)
Ferguson, R. L.: ref, 76(606, 618), 1568(130), 2160(62)
Ferguson, W.: ref, 1498(5256), 2598(1454)
Fergusson, D.: ref, 2018(17)
Fergusson, D. M.: ref, 859(724)
Ferjo, N.: ref, 2179(215), 2289(1664), 2598(1457), 2602(1750)
Fermanian, J.: ref, 1655(100)
Fernando, S. J. M.: ref, 639(44)
Ferone, L.: ref, 2621(341)
Ferrara, J.: ref, 2289(1767), 2598(1774), 2602(2103)
Ferrari, M.: ref, 1424(63), 1771(728)
Ferrel, A.: test, 2377
Ferrell, R. B.: ref, 2113(238), 2598(1324)
Ferrell, R. H.: rev, 984
Ferrell, W. L.: ref, 2300(584)
Ferris, S.: ref, 280(1089), 2598(1515, 1697), 2607(166, 192)
Ferris, S. H.: ref, 2289(1653), 2598(1319, 1712), 2607(134), 2608(187)
Ferry, F.: test, 1227, 1360
Feshbach, S.: ref, 280(1027), 585(2), 2602(1878), 2608(177), 2621(327)
Fess, N.: test, 1277
Feuer, V.: ref, 1754(52)
Feuerstein, R.: ref, 707(21), 1853(281), 2269(467)

INDEX OF NAMES

Fever, V.: ref, 1341(153)
Feverstein, M.: ref, 2300(385)
Feverstein, R.: ref, 794(417)
Ficher, I. V.: ref, 1498(5705)
Fidler, M.: test, 317, 320
Fiebert, M. S.: ref, 859(913)
Fiedler, D.: ref, 2300(393)
Fiedler, L.: ref, 116(592)
Fiedler, M. F.: ref, 270(73), 2289(1649), 2602(1720), 2621(272)
Fiedler, N.: ref, 2602(2224)
Field, D.: ref, 1771(532)
Field, J. A.: rev, 125
Field, T.: ref, 270(83), 311(25), 678(21)
Field, T. M.: ref, 270(82, 135), 311(24, 32, 35), 678(31), 2300(524)
Fieldhouse, A. E.: test, 23, 44
Fielding, D.: ref, 859(785), 1229(84), 2128(8), 2602(1730)
Fielding, R.: ref, 1197(307)
Fields, T. A.: ref, 212(7), 378(14), 1771(729)
Fifer, G.: rev, 2162
Figley, C.: ref, 280(1080), 1462(136), 2602(1786)
Figley, C. R.: ref, 2413(685)
Figueroa, R.: test, 6
Figuerres, C.: ref, 1077(80)
Figuerres, C. I.: ref, 1831(136)
Filby, N. N.: rev, 1191, 2649
File, Q. W.: test, 1113
Filley, F. S.: ref, 859(768)
Filsinger, E. E.: ref, 1077(62, 72, 77), 2208(1612)
Filskov, S. B.: ref, 2598(1328, 1609, 1836)
Finch, A. J.: ref, 354(1535), 1498(5322, 5672), 1904(60), 2300(343, 404), 2301(23, 24, 26)
Fincham, F.: ref, 1250(11), 1578(5, 6), 1771(602, 639), 2629(110, 112)
Finchum, K. G.: ref, 780(1686)
Findley, W. G.: rev, 76, 124, 344, 506, 551, 779, 1473, 2260, 2485
Fine, B. J.: ref, 878(31)
Fine, E.: ref, 1197(281), 1498(5182), 1547(267)
Fine, E. W.: ref, 859(889), 1462(140), 1940(83)
Fine, H. J.: ref, 1498(5082), 2030(4952)
Fineberg, B. L.: ref, 280(1107), 701(61)
Finer, N. N.: ref, 701(87), 2289(1782), 2551(16)
Finger, E.: ref, 1473(158), 1754(79)
Finger, J. A.: test, 1794
Finger, R.: ref, 2638(125)
Finitzo-Hieber, T.: ref, 1771(603)
Fink, S. R.: rev, 431
Finkel, P.: ref, 2598(1456)
Finkelstein, N. W.: ref, 701(77), 1126(756), 1771(730), 1934(11), 2478(14)
Finlay-Jones, R. A.: ref, 941(28), 1883(43)
Finlayson, L.: test, 940, 1233
Finlayson, M. A. J.: ref, 2598(1320, 1321)
Finlayson, R. E.: ref, 1498(5484), 2179(225)
Finley, G. E.: ref, 398(94)
Finley, K. H.: ref, 2289(1608)
Finn, M. E.: ref, 2638(137)
Finn, P. A.: test, 1348
Finnerty, R. J.: ref, 1904(55)
Finney, J. C.: test, 355, 1499
Finney, J. W.: ref, 872(14), 2652(4)

Fioravanti, M.: ref, 116(552, 553, 562, 586, 620), 282(144), 501(823), 707(17), 1914(761)
Firestone, G.: test, 1169
Firestone, P.: ref, 964(486), 1853(277)
Firlej, M. D. E.: ref, 1060(26)
Firzhardinge, P. M.: ref, 270(93)
Fisch, H.: ref, 859(903)
Fisch, R. O.: ref, 270(123), 1126(738), 1479(357), 2289(1733), 2602(1948)
Fischer, D. G.: ref, 1497(27), 2160(59), 2269(448), 2537(555)
Fischer, F. W.: ref, 1007(21), 1771(685), 2621(365)
Fischer, J.: ref, 542(22), 1789(640), 2587(43)
Fischoff, S.: ref, 1197(297)
Fish, B.: ref, 280(1028), 953(11), 2030(4953), 2491(2009), 2598(1322), 2602(1635, 1747)
Fish, J. M.: ref, 2598(1713), 2607(198)
Fish, T. A.: ref, 2512(625)
Fishbein, H. D.: ref, 1126(724), 2621(330)
Fishburne, F.: ref, 1346(7)
Fishburne, F. J.: ref, 1346(4), 2300(598), 2598(1839, 1842)
Fishco, D. T.: rev, 1185
Fisher, C. W.: ref, 590(376), 1257(114)
Fisher, D.: ref, 2300(548), 2598(1753)
Fisher, E. P.: ref, 2343(1052)
Fisher, E. S.: ref, 280(1073), 1126(692), 2602(1740)
Fisher, H. B.: test, 896; ref, 896(3, 7)
Fisher, J.: ref, 551(35)
Fisher, J. M.: ref, 2491(2007)
Fisher, L.: ref, 354(1485), 1240(65), 2030(5059), 2413(644)
Fisher, R. L.: ref, 2343(1052)
Fisher, R. S.: ref, 1240(53)
Fisher, S.: rev, 1063, 2297; ref, 157(152), 354(1442), 1106(364, 369, 375), 1904(70), 2300(394, 464)
Fisher, W. D.: rev, 1527
Fishkin, S. M.: ref, 1498(5083), 1547(288), 2620(8, 13)
Fishman, J. A.: rev, 2500
Fishman, R.: ref, 344(137)
Fisk, R. A.: ref, 363(15), 701(88), 1351(200), 2621(439)
Fiske, D. W.: rev, 780
Fitch, M. J.: ref, 270(84)
Fitts, W. H.: test, 2413
Fitzgerald, E. F.: ref, 344(152)
Fitzgerald, I.: ref, 2037(148)
Fitzgerald, J.: ref, 363(14)
Fitzgerald, J. A.: rev, 2258
Fitzgerald, J. M.: ref, 1170(232)
Fitzgerald, M.: ref, 2652(5)
Fitzgerald, T. P.: ref, 344(152)
Fitzhardinge, P. M.: ref, 270(109, 154)
Fitzmaurice, A. M.: test, 692
Fitzner, D. H.: ref, 2395(1)
Fitzpatrick, J. L.: ref, 1193(139), 1473(129), 2286(277, 291)
Fitzpatrick, R.: rev, 323, 465, 2369
Fitzpatrick, T.: ref, 2598(1789)
Fitzsimmons, G.: ref, 2134(116)
Fivars, G.: test, 476, 2390
Fix, A. J.: ref, 1498(5606)
Fix, J. A.: ref, 1498(5257)
Fjeldsted, B.: ref, 325(34)
Flaherty, J. A.: ref, 2587(41)

Flanagan, J. C.: test, 899, 900, 2390; rev, 346, 2165, 2614
Flangan, J. C.: test, 476
Fleck, J. R.: ref, 2208(1674)
Fleischer–Gallagher, A. M.: ref, 691(44), 766(29), 960(14), 1126(742), 1771(692), 2289(1736)
Fleishman, E. A.: test, 1300, 2354
Fleiss, J.: ref, 1883(59)
Fleiss, J. L.: ref, 1923(14)
Fleming, C. M.: test, 616, 617, 1244; rev, 1102
Fleming, J.: ref, 678(34)
Fleming, J. T.: ref, 2641(9)
Fleming, O.: ref, 859(790)
Fleming, W. G.: rev, 1991, 2345
Flessas, A.: ref, 1498(5116)
Fletcher, C.: ref, 2208(1658)
Fletcher, C. M.: ref, 1771(812), 2621(462)
Fletcher, G.: test, 2062, 2063
Fletcher, J. M.: ref, 2598(1455), 2607(158)
Flexer, B. K.: ref, 1013(106), 1473(205)
Flexer, R.: ref, 2224(6)
Flexer, R. J.: ref, 501(822)
Flexer, R.: ref, 2224(6)
Flexer, R. J.: ref, 501(822)
Flexer, R. W.: ref, 2224(5)
Fling, S.: ref, 1771(556)
Flinn, J. M.: ref, 794(422)
Flint, B. M.: test, 902
Flint, D. L.: ref, 353(3)
Flocken, J. M.: ref, 2208(1654)
Floden, R. E.: ref, 551(32), 1192(204), 1473(160), 2286(299)
Flood, J. E.: ref, 1192(193)
Flook, W. M.: ref, 2020(6)
Flora, R. R.: ref, 1761(6), 2413(617)
Flory, C. D.: rev, 1808, 2638
Flournoy, J. E.: ref, 2103(7)
Flowers, A.: test, 882, 905, 2299; ref, 2618(14)
Floyd, C. S.: ref, 1555(315, 332)
Floyd, M.: ref, 202(13)
Fluharty, N. B.: test, 906
Flutcher, W. G. A.: ref, 859(900)
Flynn, L. A.: ref, 344(153), 701(46), 964(487), 1479(327), 1771(604), 2217(124)
Flynn, T. M.: ref, 344(153), 701(46), 964(487), 1479(327), 1771(604), 2217(124)
Foa, E. B.: ref, 1197(288)
Foch, T. T.: ref, 643(135), 932(58), 961(5, 6), 962(24), 1126(658, 691), 1257(123, 161), 1424(66), 1473(130), 1769(43, 52, 88), 2269(437), 2286(278), 2598(1323), 2602(1636, 2051, 2093), 2621(236, 412)
Fodor, E. M.: ref, 2491(2099)
Fogarty, S. J.: ref, 859(891)
Fogel, D. S.: ref, 2029(202)
Fogel, M. L.: ref, 2030(5020, 5048, 5081), 2294(122)
Fogelman, K.: ref, 321(43)
Fogg, C. P.: ref, 501(871)
Foldi, N. S.: ref, 308(15)
Foley, J. J.: rev, 2145, 2163
Foley, J. P.: rev, 853, 1508, 1950, 2272, 2638
Folger, M. K.: ref, 1322(1)
Folkins, C.: ref, 116(621), 1508(115)
Folkins, C. H.: ref, 116(564)
Follman, D. E.: ref, 1371(247), 1479(325)

Folstein, M.: ref, 941(39, 43), 1883(81)
Folstein, M. F.: ref, 941(18, 36)
Fonkalsrud, E. W.: ref, 953(14)
Fontaine, P.: ref, 2300(397)
Fontana, A. F.: ref, 1765(11)
Fontana, M. C.: rev, 896, 1622
Foorman, B. R.: ref, 1875(5)
Foote, B.: ref, 76(640), 501(887)
Foote, J.: ref, 2148(3)
Forbach, G. B.: ref, 1969(121)
Forbes, G. B.: ref, 703(6)
Forbes, J. B.: ref, 1013(65), 1257(124), 2614(21)
Forcucci, R.: ref, 1124(1)
Ford, A. L.: ref, 885(3)
Ford, H. E.: test, 907
Ford, H. T.: ref, 4(5), 1831(217)
Ford, J. D.: ref, 1547(283)
Ford, J. S.: test, 799
Ford, M. A.: ref, 1771(684)
Forehand, R.: ref, 116(632), 932(119), 1473(217), 2300(526)
Foreman, D.: ref, 1771(671), 2621(348)
Foreman, S. T.: ref, 501(849), 1557(9)
Forer, B. R.: test, 908, 909; rev, 218, 1106
Forest, J.: ref, 1789(710, 711, 722)
Forgas, J.: ref, 1960(76), 2629(113)
Forgas, J. P.: ref, 859(904), 2629(118)
Forisha, B. L.: ref, 2512(590)
Forkin, D.: ref, 1170(230)
Forman, B. D.: ref, 116(551, 584)
Forman, D.: test, 2056
Forman, S. G.: ref, 116(551, 584), 704(16), 1192(173, 194), 2269(441, 449), 2300(585)
Formo, A.: ref, 1883(45)
Forness, S. R.: ref, 2289(1706), 2621(331)
Fornoff, F. J.: rev, 61, 64, 74, 75, 2510
Foroughi, D.: ref, 859(859)
Forseth, S. D.: ref, 1473(197), 2286(330), 2512(642)
Forsyth, R.: ref, 76(643), 1192(243), 1193(144, 146)
Forsyth, R. A.: test, 1193; rev, 573, 1414, 1568, 2518; ref, 1192(175, 235), 1405(5)
Forsythe, A. B.: ref, 701(78), 964(506), 1351(27), 1498(5384, 5385)
Fortuna, S.: ref, 2286(348)
Foster, A. L.: test, 2173
Foster, D. J.: ref, 2557(240), 2598(1742), 2602(2065)
Foster, G.: ref, 357(504), 1769(44), 2621(237)
Foster, L. M.: ref, 1013(52)
Foster, P. J.: ref, 354(1563), 1576(219), 2594(204)
Foster, R.: test, 6, 212
Foster, R. W.: test, 359
Foster, S.: ref, 378(11)
Foster, S. F.: ref, 354(1544)
Foster, S. K.: ref, 200(17), 378(15), 1771(737)
Foth, D.: ref, 766(23), 2217(121), 2602(1724)
Fouché, F. A.: test, 15, 1584, 1815, 2076, 2149
Foulds, G.: test, 1787
Foulds, G. A.: exc, 1419
Foulds, M. L.: ref, 1789(641)
Foureman, W. C.: ref, 1498(5748)
Fourie, D. P.: ref, 2294(134)
Fouts, G. T.: ref, 1229(89)
Fowell, N.: ref, 1771(612)
Fowler, B.: ref, 76(607, 641), 1191(123), 1510(44)
Fowler, C. A.: ref, 1771(685), 2621(365)

INDEX OF NAMES

Fowler, H. M.: rev, 590, 1073, 1271
Fowler, P. C.: ref, 872(15), 1479(328), 2260(35)
Fowler, R. D.: test, 1501, 1502; rev, 645, 1883
Fowler, R. L.: ref, 1771(533)
Fowler, S. C.: ref, 2300(531)
Fowler, W.: ref, 338(9)
Fowles, D. C.: ref, 1498(5084)
Fox, B. S.: test, 1900
Fox, C. F.: ref, 2030(5076)
Fox, D. J.: test, 1357, 1358
Fox, E. E.: ref, 1197(319)
Fox, G. L.: ref, 1192(236)
Fox, H. M.: ref, 2030(5049)
Fox, J.: ref, 2607(180)
Fox, J. A.: ref, 1498(5692)
Fox, J. H.: ref, 1771(594), 2289(1655), 2607(155)
Fox, L. H.: rev, 590, 2181, 2431
Fox, R.: ref, 551(60), 1771(731), 1831(198), 2217(168)
Fox, S.: ref, 2208(1684)
Foy, D. W.: ref, 1547(286)
Fozard, J. L.: ref, 2208(1527), 2318(1524)
Fraas, J. W.: ref, 501(888)
Frackenpohl, H.: test, 1994
France, G. A.: ref, 2665(1)
France, N.: test, 2021
Frances, A.: ref, 1904(106)
Frances, R. J.: ref, 558(72), 1498(5607)
Francesco, E.: test, 2552
Francis, H.: exc, 1153
Francis, J. L.: ref, 354(1435)
Francis, K. T.: ref, 1547(347), 2300(586)
Francis, L.: ref, 859(944)
Francis–Williams, J. M.: exc, 2490
Franck, K.: test, 917
Franco, E. A.: ref, 794(371)
Franco, J. N.: ref, 76(652), 2300(395, 465)
Frandsen, H.: ref, 121(13)
Frane, J. W.: ref, 1904(63)
Frane, M.: ref, 1904(63)
Frank, A. C.: rev, 1051, 1489; ref, 590(370), 1726(350), 2318(1527)
Frank, E.: ref, 2300(587)
Frank, G.: ref, 2030(4989, 4990)
Frank, H.: ref, 1914(754), 2318(1554)
Frank, J. D.: test, 2322
Frank, R. A.: ref, 2393(11)
Frank, R. E.: exc, 73
Frank, R. W.: test, 1811
Frankel, A.: ref, 780(1649), 1498(5128), 2208(1543)
Frankel, D. G.: ref, 311(36)
Frankel, F.: ref, 1471(53)
Frankel, Y.: ref, 2413(624)
Frankenburg, W. K.: test, 676, 678, 679, 680
Frankenhaeuser, M.: ref, 2208(1692)
Frankle, A. H.: ref, 354(1443), 1931(42)
Franklin, B. S.: ref, 2512(564)
Franklin, C. C.: ref, 1771(726)
Franklin, J. L.: ref, 1655(112)
Franklin, M. R.: ref, 1831(208)
Franklin, R. D.: test, 1939
Franks, D. D.: ref, 1498(5439)
Fransella, F.: test, 1009
Frantz, T. T.: rev, 778, 1720, 2046
Franzini, L. R.: ref, 559(49), 2289(1663, 1677), 2602(1748)

Fraps, C. L.: ref, 1914(872)
Frary, R. B.: ref, 1498(5068)
Fraser, A. W.: ref, 2491(2084)
Fraser, B. J.: test, 2443, 2459; ref, 2459(1), 2486(1)
Fraser, E. D.: rev, 2289, 2602
Fraser, F. C.: ref, 2289(1616)
Fraser, I.: test, 2021
Fraser, R. T.: ref, 1498(5573), 2598(1682)
Frauenheim, J. G.: ref, 935(27), 1011(4), 2602(1749)
Frazell, K.: ref, 859(948), 1547(348)
Frazelle, J.: ref, 354(1447)
Frazer, D. W.: ref, 6(38)
Freagon, S.: ref, 2218(151), 2289(1731)
Freda, J. S.: ref, 116(595)
Fredericks, H. D.: test, 2404
Fredericks, R. S.: ref, 2598(1456)
Fredericksen, N.: ref, 1257(173)
Frederiksen, N.: rev, 732, 899, 1532, 2199, 2269; ref, 991(15, 16), 995(137, 153)
Fredrick, W. C.: ref, 1192(215)
Fredrickson, L. C.: ref, 2602(1637), 2608(178)
Freed, E. X.: ref, 1904(53)
Freed, F.: ref, 1789(679)
Freedman, A. M.: ref, 1904(124)
Freedman, B. J.: ref, 643(139), 1073(120)
Freedman, M.: test, 1170
Freedman, N.: ref, 2598(1432)
Freedman, R. D.: test, 621; ref, 621(1, 2, 4, 5, 6, 7)
Freeland, C. A. B.: ref, 1798(251)
Freeman, B. A.: ref, 1332(7), 2646(9)
Freeman, B. J.: ref, 1471(53)
Freeman, C.: ref, 1498(5085)
Freeman, C. P. L.: ref, 639(57, 60), 1485(86), 1883(79), 1914(870)
Freeman, C. W.: ref, 1498(5054, 5086, 5171, 5227, 5307, 5608), 2598(1714)
Freeman, D. J.: ref, 551(32), 1192(204), 1473(160), 2286(299)
Freeman, F. N.: test, 856
Freeman, F. S.: rev, 1341, 2327; exc, 302
Freeman, H.: ref, 1883(44)
Freeman, H. L.: ref, 1883(32)
Freeman, J.: ref, 1914(755)
Freeman, L. R.: ref, 212(8)
Freeman, M.: ref, 398(105)
Freeman, N.: ref, 2598(1333)
Freeman, R.: ref, 2208(1583), 2289(1676), 2598(1486)
Freeman, S. J. J.: ref, 941(46, 48), 1883(45), 2208(1687, 1694)
Freeman, W. M.: ref, 701(79), 2243(14)
Freeman–Browne, D. L.: ref, 1883(77)
Freemon, J. E.: ref, 890(364)
Freese, J. J.: ref, 354(1482)
Frei, D.: ref, 1498(5457)
Freidenbergs, I.: ref, 1547(323)
Freides, D.: rev, 120, 2289, 2602
Freilinger, J. J.: rev, 227, 229
Freitag, C. B.: ref, 780(1686), 1498(5179, 5341)
Freitas, J. L.: ref, 2217(170), 2289(1677)
Fremauw, W. J.: ref, 2346(1)
Fremer, J.: exc, 634
Fremont, T.: ref, 280(1157)
Fremont, T. S.: ref, 2602(1845)
French, J. L.: test, 1073, 1823; rev, 581; exc, 2285

French, J. W.: test, 1077, 1257; rev, 351, 630, 706, 1186, 1775, 2435; exc, 2657
French, N. H.: ref, 2602(2178)
French, R. L.: rev, 995, 2581
French, S. J.: rev, 61
Freneau, P. J.: ref, 1170(234)
Frenz, A.: ref, 2030(5086)
Frere, L. J.: ref, 116(620)
Frese, W.: ref, 1754(89, 117)
Fretz, B. R.: ref, 116(604)
Frey, J.: ref, 1940(86)
Frey, M. C.: test, 1083, 1093
Frey, P. W.: test, 818
Frey, S.: ref, 1914(827), 2015(207)
Freyman, L.: test, 1279
Fricke, B. G.: test, 1729; rev, 500, 966, 1068
Friden, T. P.: ref, 1851(42)
Friedenberg, W. P.: ref, 2413(674)
Frieder, I.: ref, 2413(646), 2491(2058)
Friedhoff, A.: ref, 1498(5328)
Friedland, J.: ref, 226(182), 1007(40), 1914(873), 2602(2149), 2621(430)
Friedman, A. F.: ref, 280(1029), 861(5), 2602(1848)
Friedman, C. P.: ref, 1576(211)
Friedman, D.: ref, 378(5), 1622(37)
Friedman, E. G.: ref, 1126(776), 1371(261), 2289(1779), 2598(1814)
Friedman, F.: ref, 501(810), 853, 1013(61, 83), 2512(591)
Friedman, H. S.: ref, 859(905), 1798(279, 280)
Friedman, J.: ref, 859(912)
Friedman, J. B.: ref, 932(59)
Friedman, M. I.: test, 1864
Friedman, M. J.: ref, 2113(238), 2598(1324)
Friedman, P.: ref, 398(107), 1831(152), 2269(451), 2621(303)
Friedman, R.: ref, 701(78), 964(506), 1831(187)
Friedman, W. F.: ref, 270(119), 2289(1724)
Friedmann, J.: ref, 1498(5090), 1904(54)
Friedmeyer, M. H.: ref, 1498(5147), 2179(202)
Friedrich, D.: ref, 1473(176), 1503(66), 1771(654)
Friedrich, W. N.: ref, 1498(5258)
Friel, J.: ref, 226(168, 176), 701(55, 71), 1771(624, 709)
Frieman, M.: ref, 2413(646), 2491(2058)
Friesen, J.: ref, 1498(5656), 1969(113), 2585(7), 2598(1748)
Frieswyk, S.: ref, 2030(4954)
Frieswyk, S. H.: ref, 923(80)
Frieze, I. H.: ref, 2269(475)
Frigan, J. Y.: ref, 859(731)
Frimpter, G. W.: ref, 2289(1734), 2557(231)
Frisbie, D. A.: rev, 124, 506; ref, 507(1)
Frisell, W. R.: exc, 59
Fristoe, M.: test, 960, 961, 962
Frith, C. D.: ref, 860(140), 1883(49, 66)
Frith, G. H.: ref, 2318(1616)
Frith, M.: ref, 1567(20)
Frith, U.: ref, 534(110), 1771(808)
Froehlich, C. P.: rev, 190, 1271, 2537
Froehlich, G. J.: rev, 179, 1193, 2485
Froehlich, L. H.: ref, 2139(3)
Froelich, D. L.: ref, 2300(509)
Froemel, E. C.: ref, 1123(58)
Fröhlich, M.: ref, 1077(54)
Froming, W. J.: ref, 2602(1886)
Fromkin, H. L.: ref, 1798(223)
Fromuth, M. E.: ref, 1498(5583), 1904(109)
Frontz, H. O.: ref, 1508(124)
Fross, K. H.: ref, 1346(3), 1498(5247)
Frost, A. G.: ref, 1077(73)
Frost, B. P.: test, 919, 920, 921; ref, 919(1)
Frost, M.: ref, 2343(1038)
Frost, P. J.: ref, 2318(1575), 2334(20)
Frost, R. O.: ref, 1547(305)
Frost, T.: ref, 890(336)
Frostig, M.: test, 1371
Frugè, E.: ref, 2300(385)
Fruss, K. H.: ref, 1498(5434)
Fry, E.: test, 216, 1021, 1138, 1156, 1157, 1739, 1812
Fry, E. B.: rev, 171; exc, 121
Fry, K. L.: ref, 547(4)
Fry, L. W.: ref, 1508(134)
Fry, M. A.: ref, 7(5), 1126(722), 1479(319), 2269(442), 2286(282), 2289(1704), 2602(1877)
Fry, P. S.: ref, 409(12), 1013(107), 2598(1826)
Fry, R. T.: test, 2043
Fryrear, J. L.: ref, 2413(589)
Fuchs, C. Z.: ref, 1498(5512)
Fuchs, D.: ref, 701(62), 932(72, 93)
Fudala, J. B.: test, 200, 228, 1882, 1971, 2521; ref, 2218(142), 2602(1887)
Fudge, J. W.: ref, 1498(5335, 5507)
Fuerth, J. H.: ref, 701(78), 964(506)
Fuhs, N. N.: ref, 2413(685)
Fuld, P. A.: exc, 1021, 1156, 1739
Fulkerson, F. G.: ref, 1655(73)
Fulkerson, K. F.: ref, 2413(688)
Fulkerson, S. C.: ref, 701(79), 2243(14)
Fuller, A. R.: ref, 859(791)
Fuller, G. B.: test, 1503; ref, 766(31), 1020(21), 1462(139), 1473(176), 1498(5127), 1503(65, 66, 69), 1771(642, 654, 732), 2030(5060), 2208(1567), 2602(1872), 2621(323)
Fuller, P.: ref, 2015(215), 2602(2207)
Fuller, W.: ref, 280(1027), 344(165), 585(2), 2608(177)
Fullerton, A. M.: ref, 2598(1715)
Fulmer, K.: ref, 1969(106), 2602(2028)
Fulton, J. P.: ref, 1576(204)
Funder, D. C.: ref, 356(4)
Funderburk, S. J.: ref, 2179(215), 2289(1664), 2598(1457), 2602(1750)
Funk, L. G.: ref, 1013(110)
Furchtgott, E.: ref, 2598(1768)
Furfey, P. H.: rev, 2557
Furlong, M. J.: ref, 1498(5087), 1771(782), 2621(440)
Furman, W.: ref, 116(561), 1798(239)
Furneaux, W. D.: ref, 2269(450)
Furness, E. L.: test, 927
Furnham, A.: ref, 860(149)
Furr, M. L.: ref, 1126(646, 662), 1622(31), 1894(3), 2412(34), 2621(221)
Furst, E. J.: rev, 169, 2318, 2440; ref, 995(143), 1486(181)
Fusilier, M. R.: ref, 1798(269)
Futcher, W. G. A.: test, 2411; ref, 2411(1)
Fyfe, B.: ref, 890(359), 2168(11)
Gaas, E.: ref, 883(67)
Gabel, D.: ref, 1405(10)

INDEX OF NAMES

Gabel, H.: ref, 1473(131), 1831(121), 2602(1638)
Gable, R. K.: test, 2039; ref, 570(322), 1991(122), 2594(194, 197)
Gabler, E. R.: exc, 357, 1191
Gabriel, K. R.: ref, 1883(58)
Gabrielli, W. F.: ref, 2602(2041, 2192)
Gabrys, J. B.: ref, 859(906), 1229(90, 99, 100), 2602(1639, 1888), 2607(177)
Gacka, R. C.: ref, 891(5, 6)
Gaddis, E.: ref, 270(64), 311(17)
Gadzella, B. M.: ref, 588(7), 1991(123, 124), 2374(174, 175, 178, 189, 192)
Gaensbauer, J. T.: ref, 344(168)
Gaes, G.: ref, 1486(184)
Gaeth, J. H.: ref, 1851(35)
Gaffney, V. T.: ref, 1769(96), 2286(340), 2621(423)
Gage, N. L.: rev, 2286, 2343
Gagne, E D.: ref, 2286(309)
Gaguardi, J. V.: ref, 311(21)
Gaier, E. L.: rev, 1919
Gaines, R.: rev, 2105; ref, 645(22), 1771(534)
Gaines, T.: ref, 1498(5259), 2598(1458)
Gainotti, G.: ref, 1914(711, 756)
Gairola, L.: ref, 1914(773)
Gaiter, J. L.: ref, 270(115)
Gaither, G. H.: ref, 501(901)
Gaither, J. W.: test, 1048
Gajar, A. H.: ref, 2602(2042), 2621(398)
Gal–Choppin, R.: test, 110
Galass, J. P.: ref, 116(533)
Galassi, J. P.: test, 122; ref, 122(1, 2), 859(941), 2300(584), 2638(125)
Galbraith, G. C.: ref, 6(77)
Gale, C. A.: ref, 547(8), 2087(25)
Galizio, M.: ref, 859(782)
Galkowska, M.: ref, 1419(685)
Gall, M. D.: ref, 551(27)
Gallagher, J. J.: ref, 1126(756)
Gallagher, J. M.: ref, 1013(58)
Gallagher, R.: test, 1040
Gallagher, T. M.: ref, 308(24), 1771(535)
Gallaher, A. J.: ref, 308(26)
Gallant, D.: ref, 794(372, 389), 1771(536), 2179(216), 2602(1754)
Gallant, D. H.: ref, 381(59), 794(366), 2179(196, 234), 2289(1609, 1749), 2608(172, 229)
Gallant, D. M.: ref, 1655(81)
Gallimore, R.: ref, 2608(179)
Galloway, G. M.: ref, 1576(205)
Galluzzi, E. G.: ref, 357(505), 1831(122, 189)
Gallwey, J.: ref, 941(42)
Galusha, R.: ref, 2289(1699), 2621(319)
Gambaro, S.: ref, 883(72), 1498(5139)
Gambill, J. D.: ref, 1904(70)
Gamble, L. G.: ref, 934(4)
Gamer, E.: ref, 381(59), 794(366, 372), 1771(536), 2179(196, 234), 2289(1609, 1749), 2608(172, 229)
Gandara, P.: ref, 552(4), 553(21)
Gange, J. J.: ref, 859(850)
Ganley, R.: ref, 2179(257)
Ganong, L.: ref, 1771(720), 2217(163)
Ganster, D. C.: ref, 374(198), 1798(269), 2134(105)
Garabedian, A. A.: ref, 2208(1678, 1679)
Garant, J.: ref, 354(1413), 1498(5184), 2208(1551)
Garber, J.: ref, 2179(210)

Garcia, E.: ref, 1655(122)
Gard, B.: ref, 1498(5167)
Gard, G.: ref, 2602(1961)
Garde, M.: ref, 2413(602, 655)
Gardin, T. H.: ref, 1498(5748)
Gardiner, H.: ref, 1197(274), 2208(1529)
Gardiner, P. A.: test, 2177
Gardiner, W. L.: test, 604, 605
Gardner, D. C.: ref, 374(221)
Gardner, E. F.: test, 121, 2286, 2287, 2288, 2291, 2292, 2293, 2298; rev, 986, 1010, 1073, 1193, 1479, 2164, 2337
Gardner, E. R.: ref, 1655(113)
Gardner, H.: ref, 308(14, 15), 2598(1543)
Gardner, L. I.: ref, 678(26), 960(11), 1771(655), 2107(9), 2218(143), 2598(1582), 2602(1889), 2608(213)
Gardner, M. F.: test, 857
Gardner, R. A.: ref, 678(27), 1331(38), 1948(98), 2602(2171)
Gardner, S.: test, 630, 662, 1362, 2209
Gardos, G.: ref, 1655(92, 93), 1904(70, 123)
Garett, K.: ref, 606(13), 1498(5260)
Garfield, S. L.: ref, 2030(4999)
Garfinkel, A.: rev, 237, 993
Garfinkel, P. E.: ref, 859(945), 941(44), 1498(5749), 2318(1611)
Gargan, M.: ref, 2602(2090)
Gargiulo, R. M.: ref, 1272(130), 1479(380), 2512(579, 653)
Garin, E. H.: ref, 653(154)
Garland, J.: ref, 2374(191)
Garman, D.: ref, 1126(782)
Garman, E. T.: test, 2434
Garman, L. W.: test, 1805
Garner, R. G.: test, 389
Garni, K. F.: ref, 501(851)
Garren, R. B.: ref, 1769(87)
Garrett, E. R.: rev, 664, 2103
Garrett, H. E.: rev, 1272, 2269
Garris, R. P.: ref, 6(70), 923(83), 1351(33)
Garrison, G.: ref, 2566(1)
Garrison, W. M.: ref, 1831(136), 2413(618)
Garrity, L. I.: ref, 678(22), 1492(6), 1771(605), 1914(757)
Garron, D. C.: ref, 1498(5648), 1771(769), 2607(180)
Garson, A.: ref, 2208(1531)
Garvie, G. T.: ref, 890(334)
Garwood, J.: ref, 2030(4991)
Garwood, S. G.: ref, 1531(290), 2413(645)
Gasparikova–Krasnec, M.: ref, 681(59), 1498(5510, 5685)
Gasparrini, W. G.: ref, 1498(5261)
Gasser, B.: ref, 283(148), 1498(5392), 2380(5)
Gast–Rosenberg, I.: ref, 557(8)
Gasta, C.: ref, 116(571)
Gaston, E. T.: test, 2451
Gastorf, J.: ref, 1486(184)
Gatchel, R. J.: ref, 883(67, 93), 1547(252), 2300(471)
Gates, A. I.: test, 934, 935
Gates, B.: ref, 953(14)
Gath, A.: ref, 859(732)
Gatta, L. A.: test, 1083, 1093
Gatto, F.: test, 168
Gauch, R. R.: ref, 2602(1796)

Gaughran, J.: ref, 2030(5090)
Gaulin-Kremer, E.: ref, 678(30), 1771(699), 2131(6), 2557(234)
Gaumont, M.: ref, 1576(196)
Gaunitz, S. C. B.: ref, 1460(49, 53)
Gauquelin, F.: ref, 859(851), 860(121)
Gauquelin, M.: ref, 859(851), 860(121)
Gauron, E. F.: ref, 1789(642)
Gauthier, W. J.: ref, 2413(636)
Gauvain, M.: test, 1546
Gaver, D.: ref, 2260(39)
Gawin, F.: ref, 354(1432)
Gawkoski, R. S.: ref, 501(862)
Gay, E. G.: test, 1495
Gay, M. L.: test, 122; ref, 116(533), 122(1, 2)
Gayle, G. M. H.: ref, 477(27), 2029(240)
Gaynor, J. C.: ref, 501(845)
Gaynor, P.: ref, 2602(1839)
Gayton, W. F.: ref, 1371(240), 1498(5039, 5262), 1798(202), 2366(190), 2370(15), 2598(1557)
Gazet, J.: ref, 639(42)
Gazzaniga, M. S.: ref, 1126(664), 1462(122), 2607(139)
Gdowski, C. L.: ref, 1498(5469), 1796(2, 3)
Gealy, J.: ref, 398(95), 551(16), 582(4)
Gear, G. H.: ref, 2602(1751)
Geddis, D. C.: ref, 874(43)
Geen, R. G.: ref, 859(850)
Geers, A. E.: ref, 378(6)
Geffen, G.: ref, 283(150), 2598(1598), 2607(179)
Geffner, D.: ref, 960(16)
Geffner, D. S.: ref, 212(8)
Geis, L.: ref, 1568(134)
Geisinger, K. F.: ref, 994(58), 1486(188)
Geist, C. R.: ref, 1498(5609)
Geist, H.: test, 937
Gekoski, N.: test, 2055, 2355
Gelabert, T.: ref, 1126(685)
Gelder, M.: ref, 860(143), 2300(534)
Gelenberg, A. J.: ref, 1655(106), 2598(1459)
Gelfand, R.: ref, 1063(107), 2294(130)
Gelineau, E. P.: ref, 1798(304)
Gelink, M.: test, 2180
Gellens, H. K.: ref, 1498(5210), 1969(89)
Geller, A. M.: ref, 2030(4992)
Geller, B.: ref, 2289(1653), 2608(187)
Gelso, C. J.: ref, 1387(13), 2300(401)
Gench, B.: ref, 2665(2)
Gendreau, P.: ref, 354(1486), 1498(5088, 5440)
General Educational Development Testing Service of the American Council on Education: test, 2485
Genesee, F.: ref, 1771(606), 1914(758)
Genn, M. M.: exc, 298, 396
Genthner, R. W.: ref, 860(91)
Gentil, M. L. F.: ref, 2300(466)
Gentile, L. M.: ref, 588(8)
Gentry, J. M.: ref, 2581(338)
Gentry, L.: ref, 1498(5321)
Gentry, W. D.: ref, 1498(5402, 5688), 1757(15), 2300(412)
Genz, J. L.: ref, 780(1703)
Genzel, R.: ref, 1128(1)
George, L. K.: ref, 2208(1572)
George, R.: test, 2418

George, W. C.: ref, 483(27), 501(852), 1192(216), 2286(310)
Georgeff, M.: ref, 31(5), 1620(22), 1910(3)
Gerald, P. S.: ref, 270(100)
Gerard, J.: test, 1284
Gerard, J. A.: ref, 701(80), 1371(258), 1540(19)
Gerber, G. L.: ref, 1498(5263)
Gerberich, J. R.: rev, 169, 242, 844, 1512
Gericke, F. W.: test, 11
Gericke, J. S.: test, 11
Gerken, K. C.: ref, 1319(76), 1424(36), 2289(1665), 2608(192)
Gerken, M. A.: test, 1308
German, S. C.: ref, 354(1564)
Gerner, R.: ref, 1109(22), 2598(1716)
Gerow, J. R.: ref, 1568(143)
Gerry, M. H.: ref, 2317(1537)
Gershen, J. A.: ref, 558(55)
Gershenson, J.: ref, 780(1656), 1498(5183)
Gershon, A.: test, 630, 662, 1362, 1856, 2209
Gershon, S.: ref, 113(25), 280(1089), 1655(99), 2598(1319, 1515), 2607(134, 166)
Gerst, M. S.: test, 2534
Gerstman, L. J.: ref, 2598(1711)
Gertman, D.: ref, 1007(18), 2217(116)
Gerzi, S.: ref, 298(168), 1197(317)
Geschwind, N.: ref, 2598(1717), 2607(199)
Gesell, G. P.: ref, 157(144), 794(419)
Geske, D.: ref, 678(17)
Gessel, J.: test, 716
Getsinger, S. H.: ref, 2537(547)
Getter, H.: ref, 1931(55)
Gettinger, M.: ref, 1192(237), 1351(183), 1575(3), 1754(102), 2260(40), 2286(311), 2602(2043)
Gettys, C.: ref, 157(152)
Gettys, C. F.: ref, 1351(179)
Getz, D. J.: ref, 2621(399)
Geyer, J. J.: rev, 1994, 2251, 2634
Geyer, S.: ref, 1498(5374), 1914(788), 2179(219)
Ghadirian, A.: ref, 859(807), 1498(5300)
Ghiselli, E. E.: test, 179; rev, 1506, 1774
Ghiselli, E. F.: rev, 1948
Ghodsian, M.: ref, 321(37, 43)
Gholson, B.: ref, 2289(1688)
Ghuman, P. A. S.: ref, 794(387, 388), 1914(759), 2602(1752)
Giacobbe, G. A.: ref, 357(510), 2208(1573)
Giambra, L. M.: ref, 283(138), 681(31, 35), 1046(570), 2598(1325)
Giampiccolo, J. S.: test, 865, 869
Giannetti, R. A.: ref, 645(8, 15, 19, 20, 24), 1498(5129, 5264, 5633)
Gibb, C. A.: rev, 1010, 1022, 1297, 1299, 1300, 1302
Gibb, E. G.: test, 1890, 1895, 1897
Gibbons, F. X.: ref, 501(802)
Gibbons, R. D.: ref, 226(189), 1371(264), 1949(61), 2602(2218)
Gibbs, J.: ref, 1262(2)
Gibbs, M.: ref, 1498(5638)
Gibbs, V.: ref, 2286(279), 2288(77)
Gibson, A. J.: test, 1245; ref, 1485(74, 79)
Gibson, D. E.: ref, 2135(3)
Gibson, D. L.: test, 1509
Gibson, H. B.: test, 955; exc, 1853; ref, 859(733), 1038(4), 2294(108, 109), 2344(5, 6)

INDEX OF NAMES

Gibson, J. F.: ref, 1013(102), 2499(82)
Gibson, L. J.: ref, 1424(87), 2608(247)
Gibson, V. L.: ref, 590(385), 2160(71)
Giddan, J. J.: test, 212
Gideon, D. A.: ref, 1498(5124), 2598(1348)
Gideon, W. L.: ref, 1498(5610)
Gidlingham, P.: ref, 860(108)
Gidynski, C. B.: ref, 1883(57), 2322(16)
Gierut, J.: ref, 1771(659)
Giesbrecht, E.: ref, 733(8)
Gifford, K.: ref, 270(159), 678(37), 1420(3)
Gifford, R.: ref, 837(4), 1798(305)
Giffore, R. J.: ref, 2602(1865)
Gift, T. E.: ref, 645(16), 1883(68), 2598(1460, 1721, 1829)
Gigandet, J.: ref, 1498(5404)
Giladi, D.: ref, 859(801), 2353(29)
Gilbert, A. R.: ref, 2499(81)
Gilbert, C.: ref, 2598(1326)
Gilbert, G. S.: ref, 1904(68), 2300(427)
Gilbert, J. G.: ref, 2598(1697), 2607(192)
Gilbert, K. A.: ref, 6(55), 1126(725)
Gilberts, R.: test, 276
Gilbride, T. V.: ref, 1436(15), 1488(1)
Gildemeister, J. E.: ref, 398(107), 2269(451)
Gilgen, A. R.: ref, 76(638), 2029(215)
Gilhooly, K. J.: ref, 632(6), 1485(80)
Gilhooly, M. L. M.: ref, 632(6), 1485(80)
Gill, D. L.: ref, 2300(347, 525)
Gill, R. W. T.: ref, 2208(1613)
Gill, S: ref, 1192(231)
Gill, S.: ref, 701(74), 1126(753), 1540(18), 1771(719), 2217(162)
Gill, S. H.: ref, 1771(525), 2217(109)
Gilleard, C. J.: test, 471; ref, 955(10), 2607(178)
Gillen, C.: ref, 1498(5376), 2029(208)
Giller, B.: ref, 2289(1653)
Gillespie, C.: test, 952, 953; ref, 953(12)
Gillespie, C. R.: ref, 859(907)
Gillespie, F. H.: test, 1945
Gillespie, J.: test, 711
Gillet, J. W.: ref, 932(94)
Gillett, A. N.: test, 801
Gillham, C.: test, 1315
Gillham, W. E. C.: test, 253, 254, 1623
Gillian, J. C.: ref, 2598(1449)
Gilliland, B. E.: ref, 1271(908)
Gilliland, K.: ref, 732(410), 787(6), 859(932), 995(152)
Gilliland, L.: ref, 2598(1406)
Gillin, J. C.: ref, 2491(2087), 2598(1372, 1867), 2602(2077), 2607(220), 2621(408)
Gillingham, A.: test, 957
Gillingham, D. E.: ref, 859(928), 1405(7), 2300(553)
Gillingham, P.: ref, 1498(5272), 2598(1464)
Gillingham, W. H.: ref, 1051(15), 2318(1583)
Gillis, J. S.: test, 391; ref, 966(175), 2208(1614), 2413(674)
Gillis, R. D.: test, 1655
Gillis, W. T.: ref, 2419(101)
Gillooley, W. B.: ref, 932(59)
Gillum, B.: ref, 1498(5476, 5756)
Gillum, R.: ref, 1498(5476, 5611, 5756)
Gillung, T. B.: ref, 2039(10)
Gilmer, J.: ref, 1193(146)
Gilmore, A.: test, 329, 1918, 2458

Gilmore, D. C.: ref, 1295(293)
Gilmore, E. C.: test, 958
Gilmore, G.: exc, 1515
Gilmore, J. V.: test, 958
Gilmour, R.: ref, 2208(1576)
Ginestet, D.: ref, 1655(100)
Gingerich, W.: ref, 1295(301)
Gingrich, P. S.: ref, 1191(125)
Ginot, E.: ref, 665(49)
Ginsberg, A.: ref, 1106(370)
Ginsburg, B. E.: ref, 932(86), 1479(334)
Ginter, E. J.: ref, 1547(318), 2300(507), 2353(33), 2598(1679), 2638(140)
Ginther, J. R.: ref, 1257(125)
Gioielli, M. M. P.: ref, 1106(370)
Giordani, B.: ref, 2300(598), 2598(1842)
Gipps, C.: test, 2430
Girgenti, J. R.: ref, 2301(29)
Girona, R.: test, 144
Gironda, R. J.: ref, 2602(1640)
Gispert, M.: ref, 1498(5265)
Gitlin, C. M.: test, 221
Gittelman-Klein, R.: ref, 2602(1588)
Gitter, G. A.: ref, 1296(169)
Givens, T.: ref, 6(68)
Givner, N.: ref, 1576(202, 212, 213, 222)
Gjerde, P. F.: ref, 1914(876), 2602(2159)
Glaman, G. V.: ref, 719(29)
Glaser, E. M.: test, 2594
Glasgow, R. E.: ref, 883(78), 2598(1327)
Glass, G. V.: rev, 2085, 2288, 2370; ref, 1473(152), 1914(764)
Glass, R.: ref, 1471(53)
Glaubman, H.: ref, 1106(365), 1904(69), 2413(646), 2491(2058), 2602(1798, 1933)
Glaubman, R.: ref, 2512(657, 658)
Glazzard, M.: ref, 932(60)
Glazzard, P.: ref, 932(95)
Gleason, J. B.: ref, 308(17)
Glegg, C. W.: ref, 941(32)
Glen, A. I. M.: ref, 1883(80)
Glen, R. S.: ref, 1655(104)
Glenn, L. E.: ref, 2646(10)
Glenn, R. N.: ref, 1498(5089)
Glennon, J. R.: rev, 1804
Glenwick, D. S.: ref, 1771(656), 1853(282), 2602(1890), 2621(332)
Gleser, G. C.: test, 665, 969, 1909; rev, 566, 855, 1053, 1357, 1922, 1933; ref, 1909(1), 1922(12)
Glick, I. D.: ref, 1498(5733), 1922(6, 7, 8, 9, 15, 19)
Glickman, C. D.: ref, 1914(835)
Globus, G.: ref, 1498(5090), 1904(54)
Glock, M. D.: rev, 167, 1278
Gloss, D. S.: ref, 1670(62)
Glossop, J. A.: ref, 149(9), 972(9)
Glover, J. A.: ref, 178(1), 1568(135, 136, 139, 144, 147), 2286(295), 2512(565, 597, 611, 635, 643, 644)
Gluck, G. A.: ref, 890(344)
Gluck, L.: ref, 270(119), 2289(1724)
Gluckman, S.: ref, 1371(259)
Glueck, B. C.: ref, 1498(5491)
Gnagey, P.: test, 1112
Gnagey, P. A.: test, 721, 722
Gnagey, T.: test, 1112
Gnagey, T. D.: test, 721, 722, 723, 724, 725, 1553, 2089

Gochnour, E. A.: test, 959
Gocka, E. F.: ref, 780(1677)
Godard, D. R.: ref, 1798(303)
Goddard, H. H.: test, 225, 2125
Goddard, P. W. B.: test, 631
Goddard, R. C.: ref, 354(1565), 1789(725)
Godfrey, S.: ref, 860(96)
Godfrey Thomson Unit, University of Edinburgh: test, 775, 1533, 1534, 1535
Goebel, B.: ref, 354(1393), 2208(1532)
Goeman, R. D.: test, 145
Goering, M. L.: ref, 2318(1545)
Goethals, G. R.: ref, 2343(1038)
Goetz, E.: ref, 2046(2)
Goetz, K. M.: ref, 472(16), 2208(1635)
Goff, J. R.: ref, 1052(4), 1771(768), 2300(429), 2301(28), 2602(2145), 2621(427)
Goff, M.: test, 1307
Gogan, J. L.: ref, 2557(240), 2598(1742), 2602(2065)
Goh, D. S.: ref, 859(734), 860(106), 1424(46, 64), 1914(760), 2602(1891, 1892, 2044)
Gökhan, N.: ref, 643(128)
Gold, A.: ref, 1883(49, 84)
Gold, A. M.: ref, 732(390)
Gold, D.: ref, 363(7), 357(506, 511, 512, 519), 630(2), 1201(75, 77, 78), 1424(47), 1771(657), 2479(3), 2480(1), 2608(180, 193, 214)
Gold, K. S.: ref, 2565(9)
Gold, M.: ref, 1192(206, 214), 1473(164, 175)
Gold, P.: ref, 270(111, 112, 113, 147), 1007(28, 29, 30, 42), 2289(1707, 1708, 1709, 1783), 2602(1893, 1894, 2172), 2621(333, 334, 335, 441)
Gold, S.: ref, 859(800), 1789(668)
Gold, S. N.: ref, 1498(5612)
Goldbart, J.: ref, 270(145)
Goldberg, A.: ref, 1498(5755)
Goldberg, D.: test, 941; exc, 1883
Goldberg, D. P.: ref, 859(860)
Goldberg, H. L.: ref, 1904(55)
Goldberg, L.: test, 2546
Goldberg, L. A.: ref, 2607(219)
Goldberg, L. R.: rev, 354, 1203; ref, 354(1394, 1444), 780(1668), 860(150), 1077(63), 1498(5266, 5750), 1798(203), 2208(1655), 2269(464)
Goldberg, R. A.: ref, 1341(154)
Goldberg, R. T.: ref, 2413(650)
Goldberg, S.: ref, 1498(5276)
Goldberg, S. C.: ref, 1498(5586)
Goldberg, W. M.: ref, 1498(5722)
Goldberger, L.: ref, 794(413), 1013(73), 2598(1560)
Golden, C. J.: test, 1346, 2319; ref, 1257(166), 1346(1, 2, 3, 4, 5, 7), 1498(5441, 5466, 5467, 5606), 1769(58), 2208(1574), 2598(1839)
Golden, M.: ref, 270(61), 2289(1610)
Golden, R. R.: ref, 1498(5442, 5613)
Goldenberg, D. S.: test, 696
Goldenberg, E.: ref, 609(220)
Goldenberg, I.: ref, 6(46), 698(3), 1319(77), 1424(37), 2289(1671), 2602(1767)
Goldensohn, E. S.: ref, 280(1077), 283(145), 1007(23), 1914(763), 2598(1477), 2607(160)
Goldenstein, D.: ref, 932(115), 1771(749)
Goldfried, A. P.: ref, 2300(348)
Goldfried, M. R.: ref, 2300(348, 396, 474), 2353(28), 2598(1461), 2638(131)

Golding, E.: ref, 2598(1827)
Golding, S. H.: test, 250
Golding, S. L.: rev, 1931
Goldman, B.: test, 1010
Goldman, B. A.: rev, 1955, 2013
Goldman, B. L.: ref, 794(418), 1106(371), 2300(467)
Goldman, F. W.: ref, 2594(205)
Goldman, G.: ref, 2374(180)
Goldman, J.: ref, 1769(95)
Goldman, J. A.: ref, 1789(726), 2374(182)
Goldman, J. G.: ref, 1471(48), 2608(181)
Goldman, M.: ref, 354(1388), 1485(78), 2594(205)
Goldman, M. S.: ref, 1485(64)
Goldman, R.: test, 960, 961, 962; rev, 2348, 2349
Goldman, R. K.: ref, 751(34)
Goldman, T.: ref, 2602(1711)
Goldschmid, M. L.: test, 559; rev, 483, 2548
Goldsmith, H. H.: ref, 1498(5091)
Goldsmith, L. A.: ref, 1498(5443)
Goldsmith, S.: ref, 1904(92)
Goldson, E.: ref, 270(84)
Goldstein, A.: ref, 1197(288)
Goldstein, A. D.: test, 679
Goldstein, A. G.: ref, 2300(418, 484)
Goldstein, B. J.: ref, 1904(71)
Goldstein, D.: ref, 1771(677), 1914(814), 2289(1666), 2602(2133)
Goldstein, E. G.: ref, 280(1104, 1167), 751(25, 41), 2030(5025, 5088), 2491(2103), 2598(1566, 1832)
Goldstein, G.: ref, 1170(225), 1498(5098, 5110), 2598(1329, 1797)
Goldstein, J. O.: ref, 1789(712)
Goldstein, K.: test, 963
Goldstein, K. M.: ref, 280(1058), 2602(1708)
Goldstein, L.: ref, 1063(118), 2294(136)
Goldstein, M.: ref, 2208(1542)
Goldstein, M. J.: ref, 1498(5744, 5745), 2491(2098, 2104)
Goldstein, S. E.: ref, 1240(59)
Goldstein, S. G.: ref, 118(250), 1498(5226), 2598(1328)
Goldston, J.: ref, 2374(175)
Goldston, J. T.: ref, 588(7), 1991(123, 124), 2374(174, 178, 189)
Goldstone, S.: ref, 280(1030), 2598(1330)
Golin, S.: ref, 1547(322)
Gollin, J. B.: ref, 2218(157)
Golly, K.: ref, 6(54)
Golmon, M. E.: test, 1083, 1093; ref, 501(924), 1576(220)
Golomb, C.: ref, 923(81), 2289(1611)
Golub, S.: ref, 681(67), 1466(3), 2300(588)
Gomes, L. F.: ref, 116(634)
Gomes-Schwartz, B.: ref, 1498(5267)
Gomez, H.: ref, 2602(1785), 2608(201)
Gomez, J.: ref, 859(908)
Goncalves, S.: ref, 6(64), 1908(10)
Gonella, J. S.: ref, 1576(208)
Gonick, P.: ref, 1498(5705)
Gonzales-Singh, E.: ref, 280(1138), 964(501), 1771(718), 2598(1694)
Gonzalez, J.: ref, 1498(5454), 1754(105)
Good, T. L.: ref, 483(19), 1192(168, 195, 196), 2260(38)
Goodacre, E. J.: rev, 320
Goodban, M.: ref, 896(4)

Goodenough, D. R.: ref, 501(810, 853), 1013(61, 83)
Goodenough, F. L.: test, 964, 1505; rev, 1471, 2269
Goodglass, H.: test, 308; ref, 308(7, 9, 17)
Goodman, J. F.: ref, 270(62, 85), 1771(537), 1853(268), 1914(712), 2289(1612, 1667), 2598(1331)
Goodman, J. T.: ref, 1498(5206)
Goodman, K. S.: test, 1890, 1895, 1897
Goodman, N.: ref, 1771(783)
Goodman, Y. M.: ref, 2060(1)
Goodnight, C. J.: rev, 592
Goodrich, J. D.: test, 1076
Goodstein, L. D.: rev, 505, 681, 1013, 1358, 2366
Goodwin, F. K.: ref, 1197(287), 1498(5249, 5655), 2598(1703)
Goodwin, W. L.: rev, 404, 1492; exc, 2085
Goodyear, R. K.: ref, 590(370), 1726(350), 2318(1527)
Goor, A.: ref, 2512(566), 2613(79)
Goosman, E. T.: test, 1377
Gopal, A. K.: ref, 2236(4)
Goplerud, C. P.: ref, 2289(1693), 2602(1853), 2621(314)
Gor, R. E.: ref, 1460(54)
Gordet, R.: test, 394; ref, 394(1)
Gordon, A. D. G.: ref, 2168(9)
Gordon, A. S.: ref, 354(1560)
Gordon, D. A.: ref, 1192(169), 1831(123, 166), 2602(1641)
Gordon, E.: test, 1194, 1552; rev, 2222
Gordon, E. E.: test, 1891; ref, 1891(1)
Gordon, H. C.: rev, 1568
Gordon, H. W.: ref, 2598(1559, 1718)
Gordon, L. B.: ref, 1904(111), 2030(5061), 2491(2080)
Gordon, L. V.: test, 965, 966, 1531, 2366, 2370; rev, 670, 2085, 2310, 2313, 2314; ref, 2366(199, 200)
Gordon, M.: ref, 407(2), 1486(185), 2030(5083)
Gordon, N: ref, 964(507)
Gordon, N. G.: ref, 665(48), 1498(5444), 2602(1895)
Gordon, N. H.: ref, 964(513)
Gordon, R. H.: ref, 2301(24)
Gordon, T. L.: ref, 1576(188)
Gordon, W. A.: ref, 1547(323)
Gordon, W. P.: ref, 308(10)
Gorham, D. R.: test, 1919
Gorman, C. D.: ref, 76(608)
Gormly, J.: ref, 2598(1340)
Gorney, R.: ref, 2029(197)
Gorsuch, R. L.: test, 2300
Gose, A.: ref, 551(53)
Goss, A. E.: ref, 1568(129)
Gossop, M. R.: ref, 860(92, 107, 139)
Goswick, R. A.: ref, 890(364)
Gotlib, I. H.: ref, 1436(13), 2300(468)
Gottesfeld, H.: test, 779, 967
Gottesman, D.: ref, 2300(477)
Gottesman, I. I.: ref, 280(1044), 1498(5091, 5145, 5618), 2179(199), 2598(1359), 2602(1664)
Gottheil, E.: ref, 501(854), 1498(5210, 5445), 1969(89), 2318(1584)
Gotthold, J.: ref, 1515(18), 2031(459)
Gottlieb, B.: ref, 1473(173), 2286(307)
Gottlieb, D. E.: ref, 1771(538)
Gottlieb, H.: ref, 1197(297), 1498(5092), 2318(1528), 2598(1332)
Gottlieb, J.: ref, 1063(98, 125)
Gottlieb, M. I.: ref, 280(1128), 2598(1674), 2602(1857, 1993), 2621(315, 378)
Gottman, J. M.: ref, 1853(284), 2602(1907)
Gottredson, G. D.: ref, 202(6), 2134(96)
Gotts, E. E.: exc, 2393; ref, 2387(4)
Gottschalk, L. A.: test, 969
Gottsleben, R.: test, 1286
Götz, K.: ref, 860(122)
Götz, K. O.: ref, 860(122)
Gough, H.: ref, 116(586)
Gough, H. G.: test, 116, 354, 384, 1107, 1802; rev, 400, 505, 785, 794, 920, 1042, 1821, 2343; ref, 116(530, 531, 552, 553, 562, 585, 620, 622), 282(144), 354(1395, 1396, 1566), 501(823), 707(17), 1419(670), 1493(120), 1498(5108), 1576(189, 190, 191, 192), 1914(761), 2318(1529)
Goujet, M. A.: ref, 1655(100)
Gould, E.: ref, 1498(5733), 1922(8, 19)
Gould, J.: ref, 270(74), 1126(683), 1471(49, 51), 2018(9, 10), 2557(213), 2602(1642, 1722)
Gould, S.: ref, 1547(253), 2491(2081)
Gourlay, N.: test, 825
Gourley, T. J.: ref, 2512(567)
Gouze, K. R.: ref, 2608(235)
Gouze, M.: ref, 1498(5476)
Governali, J. F.: ref, 2029(226)
Gow, L.: ref, 1853(293)
Goyer, R. S.: test, 971
Grabe, M.: ref, 1191(128), 1510(45)
Graber, B.: ref, 1346(3, 5)
Graber, L. W.: ref, 1831(195)
Grace, M. C.: ref, 1922(20)
Gracenin, C. T.: ref, 2280(11)
Gradenigo, G.: ref, 1914(752)
Graduate Management Admission Council: test, 973
Grady, L.: ref, 1736(1), 1737(1)
Graef, R.: test, 1884
Graf, K.: ref, 1498(5093)
Graf, M.: ref, 1547(305)
Graf, M. H.: ref, 280(1166)
Graff, T. T.: ref, 1171(6)
Grah, C. R.: ref, 280(1114), 1498(5483)
Graham, C.: ref, 1063(84), 2294(110)
Graham, C. R.: rev, 290
Graham, F.: ref, 1931(57), 2208(1688)
Graham, F. K.: test, 1462
Graham, F. M.: ref, 2208(1656)
Graham, H. B.: test, 190
Graham, J. R.: ref, 1498(5235, 5426, 5520)
Graham, L. E.: ref, 2300(475)
Graham, P.: ref, 2557(226)
Graham, R. M.: ref, 357(510), 2208(1573)
Graham, S.: ref, 2512(645)
Graham, W. K.: ref, 195(2), 558(64)
Grala, C.: ref, 2030(5062)
Grand, S.: ref, 2598(1333)
Grandy, J.: ref, 501(912)
Granger, R. C.: ref, 1825(21)
Granite, D.: ref, 1128(1)
Grant, A.: exc, 1569, 1570
Grant, B. A.: ref, 354(1486), 1498(5440)
Grant, D. A.: test, 2633
Grant, D. B.: ref, 2602(1781), 2608(199)
Grant, E. A.: ref, 2598(1462)
Grant, G. W. B.: ref, 6(41)

Grant, I.: ref, 280(1053), 1498(5268, 5446), 1503(62), 2598(1583, 1675)
Grant, L.: ref, 1108(11), 1969(114)
Grant, R.: ref, 1567(17)
Grant, T. N.: ref, 1547(346), 1798(300)
Granvold, D. K.: ref, 2300(349)
Graser, E.: test, 1279
Grason–Stadler Co., Inc.: test, 1003
Grasser, B.: ref, 2598(1544)
Grassi, J. R.: test, 1004, 1005; ref, 1004(1), 2289(1710), 2621(336)
Grau, B.: ref, 1197(283)
Graves, D. H.: ref, 932(61)
Graves, M.: ref, 2(2), 1831(140)
Graves, M. F.: ref, 934(7), 1473(206)
Graves, P. L.: ref, 2014(4)
Gray, G.: ref, 859(831, 887)
Gray, J.: test, 548; ref, 1240(64)
Gray, K.: ref, 76(599), 501(812), 551(23), 2340(11)
Gray, M.: ref, 378(19), 1153(9), 2018(20), 2472(30)
Gray, M. W.: ref, 501(933)
Gray, R. F.: ref, 361(7), 363(9)
Gray, R. M.: test, 2336
Gray, S. W.: ref, 270(136), 2217(169), 2289(1756)
Gray, W. S.: test, 1007, 2283, 2284; rev, 1061
Gray–Little, B.: ref, 1192(217), 2413(647)
Graybill, D.: ref, 1473(131), 1831(121, 138), 2602(1638)
Graydon, J.: ref, 2246(32)
Grayson, P.: ref, 116(608)
Graziani, L. J.: ref, 200(18), 1771(788)
Greaner, J.: ref, 2300(569)
Greaser, R. C.: ref, 1555(314), 1568(123), 1754(70)
Greden, J. F.: ref, 2300(397)
Green, A. H.: ref, 645(22)
Green, B. L.: ref, 1922(12, 20)
Green, C.: test, 844
Green, C. J.: test, 1487
Green, D. E.: ref, 859(909, 961)
Green, E.: ref, 308(17)
Green, H. G.: ref, 1126(757, 758)
Green, J.: ref, 2491(2008)
Green, J. E.: ref, 1798(221)
Green, K. D.: ref, 1473(217)
Green, K. E.: ref, 1831(190)
Green, K. F.: ref, 780(1644)
Green, K. R.: ref, 558(52)
Green, L.: ref, 1498(5269)
Green, P.: ref, 344(137), 1567(18), 2598(1719)
Green, P. A.: ref, 2318(1601)
Green, P. C.: ref, 1300(119), 2208(1600)
Green, R. F.: rev, 590, 2484
Green, S. B.: ref, 1498(5616), 1798(255)
Green, S. G.: ref, 995(138), 1295(287)
Greenberg, D. B.: ref, 270(86)
Greenberg, E.: ref, 1106(359)
Greenberg, E. A.: ref, 890(337), 2587(38)
Greenberg, I.: ref, 1498(5186)
Greenberg, J.: ref, 1771(658)
Greenberg, L. S.: ref, 1789(691)
Greenberg, M. A.: ref, 1552(71)
Greenberg, M. T.: ref, 698(5)
Greenberg, R. P.: ref, 116(554), 1106(375), 2030(4984, 4993), 2598(1463)
Greenberg, S.: test, 2462; ref, 2602(2120)

Greene, C. E.: ref, 932(96)
Greene, C. N.: ref, 1296(177)
Greene, E. B.: rev, 333, 2307, 2537
Greene, F.: rev, 1390
Greene, H. A.: test, 1188, 1575; rev, 828, 1887
Greene, J. C.: ref, 1351(192)
Greene, J. F.: test, 1773
Greene, M.: ref, 354(1554), 503(5), 2208(1669), 2491(2092)
Greene, R. L.: ref, 354(1487, 1530), 732(404), 1498(5270, 5388, 5414, 5447, 5614), 2598(1678), 2607(189)
Greene, R. S.: ref, 1053(64)
Greener, J. M.: ref, 1451(2), 1486(182), 1981(2), 1984(6)
Greenfeld, S.: ref, 1508(134), 2491(2072)
Greenfield, D.: ref, 270(94), 1771(801)
Greenhaus, J. H.: ref, 2657(100)
Greenhill, L.: ref, 645(11), 2030(4978), 2598(1412)
Greenlaw, M. J.: ref, 1479(348)
Greenough, T. J.: ref, 1498(5271), 2208(1575)
Greenspan, S.: ref, 1771(674)
Greenstein, J.: ref, 1250(12)
Greenwald, D. P.: ref, 2413(619)
Greenwood, C. R.: ref, 2621(238)
Greer, R. N.: ref, 363(4), 2512(568)
Greeson, L. E.: ref, 1126(783), 2289(1784)
Gregoire, P. A.: ref, 751(6)
Gregory, D.: ref, 121(12), 472(17), 653(166), 1538(71)
Gregory, M. K.: ref, 280(1031), 703(5)
Gregory, R.: ref, 2598(1761)
Gregory, R. J.: ref, 116(555), 354(1445)
Greiffenstein, M.: ref, 2598(1750, 1828)
Greig, M. E.: test, 2325
Greis, A. B.: test, 1322
Gressard, C. F.: ref, 1831(188)
Greyson, B.: ref, 1498(5094)
Gribbin, K.: ref, 401(73), 1362(10), 1404(2), 2269(436, 454, 476), 2429(23, 25), 2598(1306)
Grice, H. H.: test, 1945
Griebstein, M. G.: ref, 859(938), 2300(567)
Gries, K.: rev, 495, 518, 522
Griest, D. L.: ref, 116(632), 932(119), 2300(526)
Grieve, J. H.: ref, 280(1021), 643(127)
Griffere, R. J.: ref, 2602(1951)
Griffeth, P.: ref, 2581(316)
Griffin, C. L.: ref, 1372(11)
Griffin, L. J.: ref, 1341(177)
Griffin, W. B.: test, 1956, 1959
Griffing, P.: ref, 964(508)
Griffith, C. L.: test, 1365, 2054, 2057
Griffith, F.: exc, 1479
Griffith, J. E.: ref, 1498(5367)
Griffith, J. H.: ref, 860(140), 1883(66)
Griffith, J. J.: ref, 2602(2045)
Griffith, P. L.: ref, 1771(733)
Griffiths, J.: ref, 1883(36)
Griffiths, P. D.: test, 1451
Griffiths, R. D. P.: ref, 860(108), 1498(5095, 5272), 2598(1334, 1464)
Griffiths, R. S.: ref, 1884(4)
Griffiths, T. J.: ref, 2300(398, 469)
Griffitt, W.: ref, 780(1653)
Griffore, R. J.: ref, 666(2)
Griggs, B. M.: ref, 1568(114), 2638(126)

INDEX OF NAMES

Grill, J. J.: rev, 696, 1004; ref, 1126(659), 1622(33)
Grimmett, S. A.: ref, 932(107)
Grimsley, G.: test, 799
Grinnell, R. M.: ref, 995(144), 2300(470)
Grisell, J.: ref, 2598(1552)
Grisell, J. L.: ref, 1498(5468)
Grissom, W. M.: ref, 1192(163), 1473(123)
Gritter, G. W.: ref, 1909(1)
Groat, A.: ref, 632(5), 1914(801)
Grobbelaar, P. E.: test, 1815
Grobe, C. H.: ref, 2002(1)
Grobe, S. F.: ref, 2002(1)
Grobman, H.: rev, 600, 2080, 2463, 2467A
Groesch, S. J.: ref, 1498(5096)
Groff, M.: ref, 2602(2054, 2176)
Groff, P.: rev, 1021
Groher, M.: ref, 1851(18), 2607(135)
Gronlund, N. E.: rev, 1473, 2477
Gronwall, D.: ref, 1969(122), 2607(217)
Groom, A.: test, 53
Gross, H.: test, 317, 318, 2625
Gross, K.: ref, 1007(22), 1754(75), 2602(1753)
Gross, M. B.: ref, 2608(194)
Gross, R.: ref, 2413(672)
Gross, R. B.: ref, 354(1421), 917(73)
Gross, R. E.: rev, 416, 602, 2166
Gross, R. H.: ref, 1508(112)
Gross, T. F.: ref, 2300(527)
Gross, Y.: ref, 2413(646), 2491(2058)
Grosscup, S. J.: ref, 1498(5615)
Grossi, D. : ref, 2598(1584, 1844)
Grossman, F. K.: ref, 311(41), 2491(2095)
Grossman, F. M.: ref, 2208(1533)
Grossman, L.: ref, 2598(1720)
Grossnickle, F. E.: rev, 196, 713, 1477
Grotelueschen, A.: exc, 1754
Grotevant, H. D.: ref, 2318(1530, 1557, 1585), 2598(1335)
Grouws, D. A.: ref, 1192(168, 196)
Grove, E.: ref, 76(633)
Grove, W. R.: rev, 204
Grover, P. L.: ref, 2374(181)
Growe, G.: ref, 2289(1687), 2602(1814, 2066), 2608(206)
Growe, G. A.: ref, 2587(34)
Gruba, G. H.: ref, 1498(5525)
Gruber, J. J.: ref, 2621(239)
Gruen, P.: ref, 1655(99)
Gruenau, C.: ref, 2491(2087), 2602(2077), 2621(408)
Grundin, H. U.: test, 1119
Grundvig, J. L.: ref, 1462(133), 2607(161)
Grunebaum, H.: ref, 381(59), 794(389), 2179(216), 2289(1609), 2602(1754)
Grunebaum, H. U.: ref, 2179(234), 2289(1749), 2608(229)
Grunebaum, H. V.: ref, 794(366, 372), 1771(536), 2179(196), 2608(172)
Gruss, L.: ref, 2491(2088)
Gruzelier, J.: ref, 1883(67)
Gruzelier, J. H.: ref, 1883(46), 2598(1465)
Grygier, P.: test, 769
Grygier, T.: ref, 769(46)
Grygier, T. G.: test, 769
Grylls, D. G.: ref, 860(130)
Guay, M.: ref, 2300(510)

Guckes, A. D.: ref, 609(208), 859(792)
Guedry, P.: ref, 344(166), 551(36), 1568(131)
Gueretle, J. L.: ref, 2537(556)
Guerrera, A.: ref, 794(447)
Guertin, W. H.: test, 1542; rev, 849, 1351, 2598; exc, 2242
Guetzkow, H.: test, 1022
Guffey, R. L.: ref, 2134(102), 2581(312)
Gugel, J. F.: ref, 995(139)
Guhr, K. E.: ref, 1498(5148)
Guidance Centre: test, 936
Guidance Testing Associates: test, 545, 1181
Guidry, L.: ref, 1547(264), 2598(1366)
Guidry, L. L.: ref, 2598(1466)
Guidubaldi, J.: ref, 239(12, 15), 1479(344), 1769(54), 2217(126), 2289(1728), 2621(351)
Guiler, W. S.: test, 180; rev, 1330
Guilford, A. M.: ref, 378(18)
Guilford, J. P.: test, 157, 401, 566, 611, 630, 662, 706, 753, 1042, 1043, 1044, 1046, 1257, 1337, 1362, 1403, 1404, 1463, 1464, 1580, 1809, 1840, 1856, 2123, 2178, 2198, 2209, 2382, 2489; rev, 118, 995, 1073, 1197, 1486, 1716; ref, 1046(567)
Guilford, J. S.: test, 1045, 2546; ref, 1046(567)
Guilleminault, C.: ref, 1498(5097)
Guilleminault, C. c.: ref, 1498(5742)
Guinee, V. J.: ref, 1498(5527)
Guion, R. M.: rev, 1508, 1803
Guitart, J.: ref, 477(25)
Gullette, I.: test, 2447
Gullickson, A. R.: rev, 554, 2478, 2481
Gulliksen, H.: rev, 1188, 1749
Gully, K. J.: ref, 6(86)
Gumaer, J.: ref, 2260(41)
Gumnit, R. J.: ref, 1498(5691)
Gundlach, R. H.: ref, 157(144), 794(419)
Gunn, P.: ref, 270(114, 129, 148)
Gunn, R. L.: test, 2617
Gunnoe, C.: ref, 226(172), 701(65), 1371(254), 1771(678), 2113(252), 2602(1929)
Gunzburg, H. C.: test, 1908
Gupta, B. S.: ref, 859(852, 872), 1419(706)
Gupta, M.: ref, 1531(281)
Gupta, P.: ref, 1531(281)
Gupta, R.: ref, 280(1075), 330(18), 2602(1755)
Gupta, R. K.: test, 2667
Gupta, S.: ref, 1201(74)
Gupta, S. C.: ref, 2491(2062)
Gupta, V. G: ref, 1125(17)
Gupta, W.: test, 2546
Gur, R. C.: ref, 859(853, 881), 1044(64), 1547(306)
Guralnick, M. J.: ref, 1771(784)
Gurland, B.: ref, 1883(59)
Gurland, B. J.: test, 2322
Gürses, C.: ref, 643(128)
Gurvitz, M.: test, 2013
Guskey, T. R.: test, 1491; ref, 1192(238, 250), 1272(138), 1479(364)
Gussett, J. C.: ref, 501(889), 506(33)
Gustad, J. W.: exc, 780
Gustafson, L.: ref, 283(144), 1462(130)
Gustafsson, J. E.: ref, 1233(222)
Gutcher, D.: ref, 1562(7), 1591(1), 1593(1), 1595(2), 1601(2), 1610(1)
Gutenberg, R. L.: ref, 1855(29)

Guterman, S. S.: ref, 935(29), 1969(99), 2537(557)
Guthrie, A.: ref, 283(157), 1914(841)
Guthrie, D.: ref, 1471(53), 2289(1706), 2621(331)
Guthrie, G. M.: rev, 783, 784
Guthrie, J. T.: rev, 178; ref, 932(62), 1007(18), 1771(539), 2217(116)
Gutkin, T. B.: ref, 1769(90), 2289(1743), 2602(1756, 1896, 1897, 1943, 2046, 2099, 2173), 2621(355, 384)
Gutmann, D.: ref, 2491(2059)
Gutsch, K. U.: ref, 1373(1), 1758(13), 2602(1656, 1860)
Gutstein, S.: ref, 2300(477)
Guttentag, R. E.: ref, 1192(218)
Gutteridge, D.: ref, 666(8), 2512(665)
Guyot, G. W.: ref, 794(433)
Guze, S.: ref, 1498(5144)
Guze, S. B.: ref, 1771(672)
Guzzetta, J.: test, 605
Gynther, M.: ref, 1498(5031)
Gynther, M. D.: rev, 354, 1498; ref, 76(602), 354(1437), 1498(5236, 5237, 5241, 5273, 5448, 5583, 5616, 5629), 1853(294), 1904(89, 109), 1940(89)
Haack, R.: ref, 2289(1726)
Haagen, C. H.: ref, 354(1556)
Haaland, K. Y.: ref, 2598(1336)
Haase, R. F.: ref, 374(210), 1754(88)
Haboucha, S.: ref, 2208(1684)
Haburton, E.: ref, 2374(176), 2413(590)
Hack, M.: ref, 270(69), 2289(1629)
Hackel, E.: ref, 381(62)
Hacker, B.: ref, 325(32)
Hackett, E.: ref, 1940(86)
Hackett, M. G.: test, 634
Hackman, J. D.: ref, 501(791), 1205(15), 1479(355)
Hackman, R. B.: test, 1048
Hackmann, A.: ref, 1547(258), 2300(355)
Hackney, G. R.: ref, 1498(5617), 1547(324)
Hadar, M.: ref, 2030(5094), 2512(664), 2602(2220)
Haddad, L. B.: ref, 1351(35), 1933(22, 23)
Haddock, M.: ref, 2300(570)
Hadfield, R.: ref, 1547(327)
Hadley, S. T.: test, 846, 939, 942, 1452, 1454, 1674, 1783, 2049, 2306
Hadley, S. W.: ref, 1498(5534)
Hadley, T. J.: ref, 6(70), 923(83), 1351(33)
Haertzen, C. A.: test, 113; ref, 113(24), 354(1446), 1498(5274)
Haeussermann, E.: test, 697
Hafner, J.: ref, 639(53), 883(97)
Hafner, J. L.: ref, 1347(8, 9), 1351(31), 2598(1467, 1585)
Hafner, J. R.: ref, 639(45, 46), 859(735), 883(68, 69)
Hagberg, B.: ref, 283(144), 1462(130)
Hagberg, J. M.: ref, 859(854), 1904(90)
Hageman, C. F.: ref, 2017(1)
Hagen, E.: test, 361, 362, 483, 1341; rev, 488, 509, 2097, 2293
Hagen, J. M.: ref, 1462(152), 2598(1741)
Hagen, R. L.: ref, 2289(1613), 2602(1643)
Hagerman, H.: ref, 551(64), 2218(18)
Hagerman, S. M.: ref, 1789(716)
Hageseth, J. A.: ref, 374(226), 2581(346)
Haggard, E. A.: ref, 2030(4994)

Haggard, M. R.: ref, 2512(592), 2598(1468), 2602(1757)
Haggerty, M. E.: test, 1507
Haggerty, R.: ref, 226(164), 1060(24), 1126(694)
Hagin, R. A.: test, 2111; ref, 2111(2), 2621(306)
Hagiwara, M. P.: rev, 131, 132, 430, 1519
Hahn, M. E.: test, 349; rev, 192, 937
Haier, R. J.: ref, 501(792), 1498(5275, 5449, 5618)
Haight, J. M.: ref, 1233(223)
Haimes, P. E.: test, 702
Haimo, S. F.: ref, 2030(5028), 2598(1586)
Haines, J.: test, 952, 953; ref, 953(12)
Hainsworth, P. K.: test, 1459
Hakel, M. D.: ref, 1855(27)
Hakerem, G.: test, 2588
Hakstian, A. R.: test, 547; rev, 1191, 1833, 2453; ref, 547(5, 6, 7, 8), 681(48), 732(391, 399, 400), 860(128), 1498(5486), 2087(25), 2269(452), 2537(552)
Halberstadt, A. G.: ref, 1831(191)
Halcomb, P. H.: ref, 1498(5379, 5539), 2598(1659)
Hale, R. L.: ref, 321(39, 44, 45), 2012(3), 2217(125), 2602(1758, 1898, 2174, 2175), 2621(282, 283, 442, 443)
Hales, L.: ref, 2581(314)
Haley, H. B.: ref, 1576(193), 2343(1030, 1032), 2366(191, 192)
Haley, J. M.: ref, 2287(41)
Haley, M.: ref, 1789(639)
Halff, N. F.: ref, 507(1)
Halfter, I. T.: test, 536
Halgin. R.: ref, 2598(1337)
Halinski, R. S.: test, 246; ref, 76(598), 411(28)
Hall, A. D.: ref, 1126(750)
Hall, A. E.: rev, 442, 1013
Hall, B. D.: ref, 1771(593), 2289(1654)
Hall, C.: ref, 2300(510)
Hall, C. J.: ref, 794(391), 859(795)
Hall, D. A.: ref, 2607(128)
Hall, E. G.: ref, 2300(528, 529)
Hall, G. E.: ref, 344(138), 1460(50)
Hall, J.: test, 383, 565, 1014, 1363, 1365, 1803, 1901, 2052, 2054, 2057, 2351, 2405, 2655; ref, 2351(9), 2655(5, 6)
Hall, J. A.: ref, 1831(191)
Hall, J. N.: ref, 1485(59), 1771(540), 2598(1338)
Hall, J. R.: ref, 1203(9)
Hall, J. W.: exc, 121
Hall, K.: ref, 280(1101)
Hall, L. C.: ref, 1771(682)
Hall, L. G.: test, 1051
Hall, P.: ref, 1655(123)
Hall, P. K.: ref, 1192(197), 1193(140), 1471(52), 2289(1668), 2557(222), 2602(1759)
Hall, R. C. W.: ref, 1655(113)
Hall, S. M.: ref, 542(23)
Hall, V. C.: exc, 559; ref, 1771(541, 542), 1914(713, 714, 806), 2289(1614)
Hall, W. B.: rev, 798; ref, 116(530, 531), 354(1395, 1396), 1493(120), 1576(190, 191, 192), 2318(1529)
Hall, W. C.: ref, 1473(132), 2594(195)
Hall, W. E.: rev, 2485
Hall, W. M.: ref, 2413(591)
Hallahan, D. P.: ref, 935(33), 1272(139), 2602(1994), 2621(379, 405)

INDEX OF NAMES

Halle, E.: ref, 2100(8)
Haller, A. O.: ref, 1073(125)
Haller, D.: ref, 1498(5146)
Haller, E. J.: ref, 1192(239, 251)
Haller, R.: ref, 1498(5140)
Haller, R. M.: rev, 200, 925, 2022, 2412, 2590
Hallinan, M.: ref, 2343(1050)
Halliwell, M.: test, 1340
Hallock, N.: ref, 270(83), 311(25), 678(21)
Hallock, N. F.: ref, 270(82), 311(24)
Halmi, K. A.: ref, 1498(5276, 5586)
Halperin, K. M.: ref, 1498(5098), 2598(1329)
Halperin, S.: ref, 2300(392)
Halpern, A. S.: test, 2211, 2224, 2473; ref, 2224(3, 4, 7, 9), 2473(1)
Halpern, H.: rev, 925
Halpin, A. W.: test, 1295
Halpin, G.: ref, 76(653), 344(189), 501(925), 2512(569, 599, 612), 2657(108)
Halverson, C. F.: ref, 2286(341)
Hambleton, R. K.: rev, 382, 851; exc, 282; ref, 709(1), 710(1), 716(1), 913(1), 1139(1), 1140(1), 1257(121), 1389(1), 1390(2), 1880(6), 2291(1), 2292(25)
Hamed, C.: ref, 2657(101)
Hamersma, R. J.: ref, 280(1166)
Hamilton, E. W.: rev, 1477
Hamilton, J. E.: ref, 1498(5569)
Hamilton, M.: test, 1314; ref, 283(149), 860(93)
Hamm, H. A.: ref, 2602(1760)
Hamm, N. H.: ref, 1948(100)
Hamm, R. J.: ref, 2491(2010)
Hammack, F. M.: ref, 501(890)
Hammeke, T. A.: test, 1346; ref, 1346(1)
Hammen, C. L.: ref, 681(36)
Hammer, L. Z.: ref, 2029(210)
Hammer, M.: ref, 780(1646)
Hammers, C. P.: ref, 1555(319)
Hammett, V. L.: ref, 734(4), 1192(256)
Hammill, D. D.: test, 256, 273, 1540, 2422, 2436, 2438, 2445, 2456, 2466; ref, 1126(759)
Hammitt, K. B.: ref, 1769(84)
Hammond, D. C.: ref, 1269(28)
Hammond, J. M.: ref, 1831(167, 168, 169), 2585(8, 9, 10)
Hammond, K. R.: ref, 859(903)
Hammond, M. A.: ref, 270(141), 311(38), 1108(10), 2159(3)
Hammond, N.: ref, 2598(1465)
Hammond, N. V.: ref, 1883(46)
Hample, D.: ref, 76(624)
Hampson, J. L.: ref, 1498(5630), 2598(1731)
Hampson, S. E.: ref, 769(40), 859(736), 861(4), 1853(269), 2208(1534, 1576), 2491(2011), 2629(97)
Hampton, J. D.: ref, 1789(692)
Hamrick, K. B.: ref, 1250(17)
Hanawalt, N. G.: rev, 118, 283, 2121
Hanback, J. W.: ref, 1498(5277)
Hancock, K. A.: ref, 1424(36), 2289(1665)
Hand, D. J.: ref, 941(31)
Hand, G. S.: ref, 1576(216)
Hand, H. H.: ref, 1295(294)
Handal, P. J.: ref, 1209(33)
Handler, L.: ref, 354(1397), 1197(275), 2413(592)
Handley, H. M.: ref, 2208(1577)
Handley, S. L.: ref, 1547(253, 325)
Handy, L.: ref, 2208(1583), 2289(1676), 2598(1486)
Hanes, B. F.: ref, 559(45), 2548(12)
Hanewicz, W. B.: ref, 1555(308)
Haney, R.: ref, 344(139), 2347(1)
Hanfmann, E.: test, 1239
Hankins, G.: ref, 357(507), 2585(4)
Hankins, N.: ref, 2602(1838, 1840, 1841, 1977)
Hanlon, M. J.: ref, 1419(677)
Hanlon, T. E.: ref, 1498(5099)
Hanna, C.: test, 668
Hanna, G.: test, 1568, 1569
Hanna, G. S.: test, 1524, 1526, 1749; rev, 851, 1557; exc, 582, 732; ref, 374(192, 199, 200), 1569(7, 8), 1570(11), 2164(42, 43), 2602(2004)
Hanna, L. A.: rev, 1193
Hanna, P. R.: rev, 2286
Hanna, S. A.: test, 893
Hannaford, E. S.: test, 1056
Hannay, H. J.: ref, 2113(258), 2300(405), 2598(1587, 1841)
Hannigan, P. S.: ref, 1789(641)
Hänninen, H.: ref, 2030(4995, 5011), 2598(1469)
Hansburg, H. G.: test, 2158
Hansell, S.: ref, 76(634)
Hansen, C. J.: ref, 1270(79)
Hansen, J.: ref, 1013(122)
Hansen, J. C.: test, 2318; rev, 351; ref, 374(203), 2318(1531, 1532, 1558, 1602), 2413(604, 629)
Hansen, J. D. L.: ref, 280(1142), 2153(2)
Hansen, J. L.: ref, 1479(377)
Hansen, L. M.: ref, 282(143)
Hansen, L. S.: ref, 76(654), 374(227)
Hansen, R.: ref, 2594(203)
Hansen, R. N.: exc, 2134; ref, 2134(91)
Hansen, S. L.: ref, 698(2)
Hansford, B. C.: ref, 859(737)
Hanshaw, J. B.: ref, 678(25)
Hanson, C. J.: ref, 1013(135), 1316(5)
Hanson, G. R.: rev, 973; ref, 76(588, 595, 614), 77(21)
Hanson, W. R.: ref, 1851(27)
Hansson, R. O.: ref, 157(138)
Haramis, S. L.: ref, 1053(78), 2030(5063)
Harbaugh, D.: ref, 1851(36)
Harber, J. R.: ref, 766(32), 1126(726, 760), 1540(14), 1914(762)
Harberg, E.: ref, 859(946)
Harbison, J.: ref, 1209(35)
Harburg, E.: ref, 1197(274), 2208(1529)
Harden, J.: ref, 896(8), 1771(797)
Harder, D.: ref, 1883(76), 2030(5072), 2598(1772)
Harder, D. W.: ref, 1240(57, 60, 65), 1883(38, 68), 2030(5029, 5030), 2491(2060), 2598(1588, 1721, 1829), 2602(1965), 2608(220)
Hardesty, A. S.: test, 2588; ref, 1655(122)
Hardin, V. B.: test, 1185
Harding, C.: test, 1057, 1058
Harding, I. W.: ref, 1568(150)
Harding, P. S.: ref, 2322(11)
Hardman, M. L.: ref, 302(31), 1473(149), 2541(5), 2621(284)
Hardy, B. W.: ref, 157(137), 243(119), 1106(363), 2413(643)
Hardy, C. A.: ref, 1771(790), 2557(245)
Hardy, J. C.: ref, 1771(610), 1851(26), 2412(38)

Hardy, R. C.: ref, 1555(306)
Hardy, R. E.: test, 184; ref, 1771(723)
Hare, B. A.: ref, 226(160), 371(241), 1126(660), 2288(78), 2621(240)
Hare, J.: test, 940
Hare, R. D.: ref, 354(1447), 1498(5343)
Harel, Z.: ref, 398(114)
Hargie, O. D. W.: ref, 859(793, 855)
Hargreaves, D. J.: ref, 2512(570)
Hargreaves, W.: ref, 1498(5733), 1922(19)
Hargreaves, W. A.: ref, 542(23), 1922(6, 7, 9, 15)
Hargreaves-Heap, S.: ref, 2288(87)
Hargrett, N. T.: ref, 442(1, 2)
Haring, N. G.: test, 2532
Harkins, E. B.: ref, 609(209)
Harkins, S. G.: ref, 859(850)
Harkins, S. W.: ref, 2300(350)
Harkulich, J. F.: ref, 280(1108), 751(26), 1126(727), 2289(1711), 2602(1899), 2621(337)
Harlen, W.: test, 317, 320
Harley, C.: ref, 1485(82), 2598(1735)
Harley, E. F.: test, 297
Harley, J. P.: ref, 1498(5152), 2598(1310)
Harlow, S. D.: ref, 964(483), 1479(317), 1540(11), 2217(122)
Harmatz, J. S.: ref, 2491(2017)
Harmer, W. R.: ref, 1769(53), 2621(285)
Harmon, L. W.: rev, 1271, 1357; ref, 1270(81), 2134(129), 2318(1603)
Harmon, M. H.: ref, 354(1531), 780(1698), 1726(369)
Harmon, R. J.: ref, 270(115)
Harmon, T. M.: ref, 681(56), 1498(5619)
Harms, T.: test, 771
Harnett, R. T.: ref, 995(132)
Harney, B. J.: ref, 226(161)
Harnisch, D. L.: ref, 1292(55, 56)
Härnquist, K.: ref, 2269(453)
Harper, A. E.: test, 2442
Harper, D. C.: ref, 1498(5278, 5279, 5693)
Harper, F. B. W.: ref, 1798(204)
Harper, G. F.: ref, 1769(54), 2217(126)
Harper, J. F.: ref, 859(764)
Harper, R. A.: rev, 350, 659, 1377
Harper, R. G.: ref, 116(617), 794(442), 859(939), 2300(575), 2598(1803)
Harper, R. S.: ref, 2598(1852)
Harper, S.: ref, 1904(112)
Harrell, E. H.: ref, 1754(62)
Harrell, T. W.: rev, 1774, 1948
Harrigan, J.: ref, 354(1550)
Harriman, P. L.: rev, 752, 1047, 1201, 1353
Harrington, D. M.: ref, 116(623), 157(154), 681(67), 1466(3), 2300(588)
Harrington, N.: ref, 859(794)
Harrington, S. A.: exc, 2374
Harrington, T. F.: test, 1059; ref, 1059(1, 2), 2581(339)
Harris, A. F.: test, 1212
Harris, A. J.: test, 1060, 1355; rev, 958, 1007, 1427, 2247
Harris, B.: ref, 639(58)
Harris, C. W.: rev, 571
Harris, D. B.: test, 964, 1831; rev, 751, 874, 884, 1515, 1537, 1797, 1899
Harris, D. H.: test, 1937

Harris, D. P.: test, 549, 570, 571, 589, 830, 1738, 1989, 1991, 2483; rev, 429, 490, 2145
Harris, E.: ref, 354(1393), 1498(5404), 2208(1532)
Harris, G.: ref, 639(50), 2353(35)
Harris, J.: ref, 302(33)
Harris, J. A.: ref, 2300(340)
Harris, J. B.: ref, 2374(195)
Harris, J. E.: ref, 2208(1578)
Harris, J. G.: rev, 2323; ref, 1798(281)
Harris, L. A.: rev, 1192, 1427, 2001; exc, 2641
Harris, M. B.: ref, 1668(5)
Harris, M. E.: ref, 354(1487), 732(404), 890(326)
Harris, M. L.: test, 2635
Harris, M. M.: ref, 1734(1), 2155(6)
Harris, P. L.: ref, 2208(1576)
Harris, R.: ref, 2602(1613)
Harris, R. H.: test, 10
Harris, T. L.: rev, 856; ref, 354(1488, 1489), 2208(1631)
Harris, T. O.: ref, 1883(39)
Harris, W. G.: ref, 645(23), 1498(5632), 2179(238)
Harris, W. J.: ref, 328(4), 400(133), 769(43), 772(27), 1934(8)
Harrison, A. M.: ref, 751(22), 1831(158)
Harrison, B.: ref, 859(910)
Harrison, B. T.: ref, 344(169), 501(855)
Harrison, D. F.: ref, 1498(5620)
Harrison, J.: ref, 2512(657, 658)
Harrison, K. A.: ref, 691(36), 1424(45)
Harrison, M. L.: test, 1061
Harrison, M. T.: rev, 2529
Harrison, P. L.: ref, 1424(52, 65, 84), 2289(1725)
Harrison, P. M.: exc, 1153
Harrison, W. H.: ref, 1798(255)
Harrow, M.: ref, 1883(37, 90), 1919(39, 42, 43), 2030(4955), 2598(1339, 1470, 1589)
Harsh, C. M.: rev, 282, 2208, 2368, 2499
Harsh, J. R.: test, 2371
Harshman, H. W.: ref, 701(39), 1371(244)
Hart, D. H.: ref, 280(1087), 1769(62), 2208(1519), 2602(1802, 1936), 2621(295)
Hart, J.: ref, 859(800, 915), 1789(668, 713)
Hart, L. S.: ref, 2208(1615, 1657)
Hart, M. E.: ref, 1013(123), 1576(221)
Hart, R. R.: ref, 2598(1590, 1591)
Hartfield, M. J.: ref, 2300(589)
Harth, R.: ref, 371(242), 1126(661), 2602(1644)
Hartlage, L.: ref, 2602(1944), 2621(356)
Hartlage, L. C.: test, 1870; ref, 751(4), 1170(237), 1498(5450), 2602(1645), 2621(241, 242, 243)
Hartlage, P. L.: ref, 751(4), 2621(242)
Hartley, R. N.: rev, 1143
Hartman, A. D.: test, 2529
Hartman, B.: ref, 2134(112)
Hartman, B. G.: test, 109
Hartman, B. J.: test, 1543
Hartman, E. L.: ref, 2598(1459)
Hartman, L. M.: ref, 1931(50), 2135(2)
Hartman, R. K.: test, 2069
Hartman, R. S.: test, 1062
Hartman, T.: ref, 2581(314)
Hartman, W. T.: ref, 501(824)
Hartmann, E.: ref, 1106(365), 1498(5451), 1655(92, 93), 1904(69)
Hartmann, G. W.: rev, 340, 2399

INDEX OF NAMES

Hartnett, R. T.: test, 1158; rev, 241
Hartson, L. D.: rev, 1716
Hartsough, C. S.: test, 1902; ref, 6(88)
Hartung, G. H.: ref, 2208(1535, 1611)
Hartung, J.: ref, 1106(376)
Harvey, D. W.: ref, 2318(1562)
Harvey, H. L.: ref, 1462(152), 2598(1741)
Harvey, J. B.: test, 2351
Harvey, M. A. S.: ref, 2289(1703), 2602(1873)
Harvey, M. T.: ref, 2598(1573)
Harvey, O. J.: test, 563, 2497; ref, 2497(40)
Harvey, P.: ref, 645(26)
Harvey, R.: ref, 911(5), 941(41)
Harvey, S.: ref, 559(49)
Harvill, L. M.: ref, 2366(203)
Harway, N. I.: ref, 1126(673), 2602(1684)
Harwood, E.: test, 1564
Hasbrouck, J. M.: ref, 962(33)
Hase, H. D.: ref, 891(4)
Hasenpusch, B.: ref, 354(1514), 1498(5559), 1853(288), 2208(1640)
Haskell, D. S.: ref, 1904(70)
Haskell, S. D.: ref, 354(1397), 1197(275), 2413(592)
Haskett, J.: ref, 270(87)
Haskins, M. J.: test, 109
Haskins, R.: ref, 270(88), 2289(1669)
Haslam, M. T.: ref, 1498(5280)
Haslam, R. H. A.: ref, 270(63), 338(8), 1771(543), 2289(1615), 2557(214), 2602(1646), 2608(182)
Haslam, R. W.: ref, 1904(130), 2300(608)
Haspiel, G. S.: test, 1071
Hass, G.: rev, 169
Hassan, R. K.: ref, 2300(564)
Hassanyeh, F.: ref, 2598(1722), 2602(2047)
Hassold, T.: ref, 381(62)
Hastings, A. C.: ref, 116(556), 354(1448), 1498(5281), 2491(2040)
Hastings, C. N.: ref, 1473(220)
Hastings, J. T.: rev, 382, 847, 1866, 2520; exc, 2286
Haswell, K.: ref, 2289(1785)
Hatano, G.: ref, 1771(734)
Hatch, G.: ref, 2602(1620)
Hatch, G. L.: ref, 1771(544), 2602(1621, 1647)
Hatch, J. P.: ref, 883(67, 93), 2300(471)
Hatch, R. S.: rev, 736
Hatch, V.: ref, 1351(181)
Hatcher, C. W.: ref, 2292(23)
Hatcher, E. M.: ref, 859(914), 1498(5634), 1914(845), 2179(239)
Hatcher, R. W.: ref, 354(1427)
Hatfield, F.: test, 2447
Hathaway, C.: ref, 1762(3)
Hathaway, K. M.: ref, 794(424)
Hathaway, S. R.: test, 1498
Hatley, R. V.: ref, 890(338)
Hatten, J. T.: rev, 2472
Hattie, J.: ref, 1789(693, 727), 2512(646)
Hauck, W. E.: ref, 2286(309)
Hauer, A. L.: ref, 280(1076), 2602(1761)
Haugh, O. M.: test, 503, 2474, 2475
Hauri, P.: ref, 1197(318), 1498(5451)
Hausafus, C. O.: test, 1656
Hauser, L. M.: ref, 2638(128)
Hauser, R. M.: ref, 1073(117)
Hautala, L. W.: ref, 1473(150)

Havemeyer, E.: ref, 2598(1505)
Haver, A. L.: ref, 1498(5231)
Haverkamp, A. D.: ref, 270(140), 311(37)
Haverly Systems, Inc.: test, 1907
Havu, G. F.: ref, 1798(202)
Hawkins, D. I.: ref, 2300(417)
Hawkins, D. R.: ref, 354(1510), 609(218)
Hawkins, J. G.: ref, 562(8)
Hawkins, R. C.: ref, 2300(530)
Hawkridge, D. G.: rev, 1669
Hawley, K. E.: ref, 890(345)
Haworth, M. R.: test, 396, 1899, 2027; rev, 1047, 2289; ref, 1899(7)
Hawton, K.: ref, 941(42)
Hay, E. N.: test, 334, 1064, 2305, 2528; rev, 940, 1556, 1936, 2263
Haycraft, J. L.: ref, 2288(86)
Hayden, A. H.: test, 2532
Hayden, B.: ref, 2602(1648)
Hayden, J. R.: rev, 2324, 2338, 2630
Hayden, M. E.: ref, 200(19, 20), 896(9), 960(18, 19), 1319(79), 1814(8), 2412(44, 47)
Hayes, A. E.: ref, 1185(9)
Hayes, C. B.: ref, 2638(134)
Hayes, E.: test, 1490, 1854
Hayes, K. N.: ref, 354(1556)
Hayes, L. A.: ref, 1771(704)
Hayes, S. C.: ref, 681(56), 1498(5619)
Haynes, C. D.: ref, 1498(5124), 2598(1348)
Haynes, J.: ref, 2598(1340)
Haynes, J. M.: test, 2430
Haynes, L. M.: rev, 39
Haynes, M. D.: ref, 378(10)
Haynes, W. O.: ref, 378(10)
Hays, J. R.: ref, 280(1152), 653(164), 872(10), 1498(5703), 1508(127), 1831(174), 2208(1663), 2598(1788), 2602(1649, 1762, 2048, 2122)
Hayslip, B.: ref, 1053(79)
Hayward, K. G.: ref, 1191(120, 127)
Hayward, R. W.: ref, 308(11)
Haywood, K. M.: ref, 1251(2)
Hazelhurst, J. H.: test, 1892
Hazzard, M. E.: ref, 780(1669)
Head, D. N.: ref, 2413(648, 675)
Heald, F. P.: ref, 280(1055, 1112)
Healey, A. F.: ref, 1655(83), 1883(28)
Healy, C. C.: test, 1577; exc, 77; ref, 374(209), 1577(3)
Healy, W.: test, 1069
Heaps, R. A.: ref, 354(1449), 1498(5282)
Hearn, J. C.: ref, 409(5)
Heath, C. P.: ref, 696(5), 1479(378), 2217(183)
Heath, D. H.: ref, 501(793), 1498(5100, 5101, 5102, 5283), 2030(4956, 4957, 4958, 4996)
Heath, R. G.: ref, 1655(76)
Heath, R. L.: ref, 2029(202)
Heathcote, M. E.: ref, 2602(1685)
Heather, N.: ref, 1485(69)
Heaton, K. L.: rev, 1950, 1951
Heaton, R. K.: test, 2633; ref, 1498(5069, 5284, 5285, 5319, 5452), 1769(55), 1923(15), 2113(244), 2598(1409, 1471, 1472, 1504, 1568, 1592, 1608, 1676, 1773), 2607(159)
Heaven, P. C. L.: ref, 2629(114)
Hebben, N. A.: ref, 308(16), 1109(21), 1853(292), 2598(1698), 2607(193)

Hebert, D. J.: ref, 995(145)
Hebert, J.: ref, 1436(15), 1488(1)
Hebron, M. E.: test, 2278
Hecht, L. W.: ref, 1557(8)
Hechtman, L.: ref, 794(420), 2598(1549, 1596), 2602(1851)
Heck, E. J.: ref, 2155(9)
Heckler, V. J.: ref, 1789(643)
Hector, J. H.: ref, 121(13)
Hedge, M. N.: ref, 1771(659, 735)
Hedges, W. D.: test, 1542
Hedlund, J. L.: ref, 1498(5103, 5104, 5105), 1655(77), 1922(10)
Hedrick, D. L.: test, 2159
Heenan, D. K.: rev, 491, 511
Heffler, D.: ref, 1498(5141)
Heft, C. S.: ref, 501(834), 570(326)
Hegarty, S.: test, 2430
Hegarty, S. F.: ref, 2602(1763)
Hegarty, W. H.: ref, 2343(1039)
Hegedus, A.: ref, 2598(1797)
Heidbreder, E.: test, 2015
Heidt, P.: ref, 2300(590)
Heil, J.: ref, 2608(195)
Heilbron, D.: ref, 354(1468), 2318(1561)
Heilbrun, A. B.: test, 116; rev, 275, 647, 780, 784, 966, 1919; ref, 116(532, 557, 558, 559, 587, 609, 624), 354(1490, 1491), 653(151), 1498(5106, 5453), 2491(2012), 2598(1473), 2621(338)
Heilbrun, K. S.: ref, 1498(5106)
Heilman, K. M.: ref, 1498(5261)
Heim, A. W.: test, 148, 149, 2175; rev, 2036; exc, 321, 859; ref, 149(2)
Heimberg, R. G.: ref, 1498(5620)
Heimovics, R. D.: ref, 890(339)
Heinen, J. R. K.: ref, 2621(324)
Heinen, J. S.: ref, 890(345)
Heinichen, F. W. O.: test, 1026, 1141
Heinonen, O. P.: ref, 2289(1641, 1643)
Heinrich, D. L.: ref, 995(146), 2300(472)
Heinrich, R.: ref, 859(880), 1789(702)
Heintzelman, M. E.: ref, 2343(1029)
Heist, P.: test, 1726
Hekmat, H.: ref, 883(70), 1931(41)
Helkala, E.: ref, 1498(5352), 2030(5009), 2598(1525)
Heller, A. S.: ref, 1498(5641)
Heller, M.: ref, 2607(162, 200)
Heller, M. S.: ref, 302(35), 2286(303)
Heller, R. M.: ref, 1233(227)
Helm, W. H.: rev, 1884
Helme, W. H.: rev, 1219
Helmes, E.: ref, 354(1398), 860(141), 1498(5107), 1798(205, 206)
Helms, J. E.: ref, 2581(321)
Helms, S. B.: ref, 1126(735), 2412(40)
Helmstadter, G. C.: rev, 243; exc, 2594
Helps, R.: ref, 859(856)
Helson, R.: ref, 116(610), 354(1399, 1532)
Hemenway, J.: test, 2435
Hemming, H.: ref, 6(55, 87), 1126(725), 2598(1830)
Hemming, J. H.: ref, 859(857)
Hemphill, J. K.: test, 1122, 1295, 1296; rev, 1788, 2366
Hemsley, D. R.: ref, 479(401), 860(155), 1485(81), 2598(1308)
Henchman, J.: test, 825

Hendel, D. D.: test, 1495; ref, 973(29), 1405(4, 8, 9), 1495(80, 81, 85), 2353(36)
Henderson, R. W.: test, 1804, 2636
Henderson, S.: ref, 941(23, 24, 34, 45), 1883(33, 34, 69)
Henderson, S. E.: test, 2450; ref, 534(110)
Hendeson, R. W.: ref, 1424(88)
Hendler, N.: ref, 280(1143), 2598(1723)
Hendrick, S. S.: ref, 1376(1)
Hendricks, M.: test, 203, 2649
Hendrickson, E.: ref, 1914(802), 2598(1593)
Hendrickson, N. J.: ref, 698(2)
Hendrix, J. C.: ref, 76(587)
Hendry, E.: test, 825
Heneman, H. G.: ref, 1508(120)
Heninger, G. R.: ref, 2300(443)
Henington, M.: ref, 1789(728)
Henk, W. A.: ref, 995(154)
Henker, B.: ref, 1771(523, 707), 1853(267)
Henkin, R. I.: ref, 2419(101)
Hennelly, R. A.: ref, 2602(2035)
Hennessy, J. J.: ref, 1904(106)
Henning, M. M.: test, 1303
Henninger, G. R.: ref, 1904(107)
Henrichs, T. F.: ref, 2598(1474)
Henry, D. L.: ref, 1347(4)
Henry, D. R.: ref, 859(868)
Henry, J. A.: ref, 34(2), 42(1), 559(48)
Henry, M.: ref, 2100(6)
Henry, R. M.: ref, 2608(236)
Henry, S. E.: ref, 400(128), 551(41), 552(3), 553(19)
Henry, W. E.: test, 1022; rev, 1480, 2571
Henshaw, J.: test, 1074
Hensley, J. H.: ref, 1789(665)
Heppner, P. P.: ref, 2134(117)
Hepworth, S. J.: ref, 941(35)
Herald, D.: ref, 958(46), 2602(1811), 2621(299)
Herbert, C. H.: test, 251
Herbert, D. A.: ref, 1969(124), 2598(1834)
Herbert, G. R.: ref, 1798(238)
Herbert, T. T.: ref, 354(1533)
Herceg–Baron, R. L.: ref, 1419(692)
Herder, J.: ref, 1498(5178, 5393, 5550, 5728), 1547(266, 296, 314, 343), 2300(366, 449, 500, 573)
Hered, W.: rev, 61, 74, 75, 489, 510
Hereford, S. M.: ref, 501(856), 994(56)
Herjanic, B. M.: ref, 354(1492), 1771(660), 1831(170), 1853(283), 2322(12), 2621(339)
Herjanic, M.: ref, 354(1492), 1771(660), 1831(170), 1853(283), 2322(12), 2621(339)
Herlick, L.: ref, 859(959)
Herman, A.: ref, 374(204, 228)
Herman, C. S.: ref, 270(98), 2289(1690, 1757), 2598(1534), 2602(1828)
Herman, D. O.: rev, 900, 1056, 1259
Herman, H.: exc, 396
Herman, M. W.: ref, 1576(208)
Hermann, B. P.: ref, 1498(5621)
Hermelin, B.: ref, 534(109)
Hernández, O. F.: test, 895, 2115
Hernandez Ch., E.: test, 290, 291
Hernandez–Chavez, E.: ref, 1282(2)
Herrick, V. E.: rev, 169, 1192, 2286
Herrington, S.: ref, 1495(87, 90), 2208(1623, 1686), 2318(1586, 1615), 2491(2061), 2614(24)

Herrman, D. J.: ref, 2208(1536)
Herrmann, W. J.: ref, 899(20), 2512(660)
Herron, E. W.: test, 1106
Herron, J.: ref, 2015(210)
Herron, W. G.: ref, 1883(55)
Hersch, R. G.: ref, 645(17), 1904(74)
Hersen, M.: ref, 859(947), 860(123), 2179(254), 2301(34)
Hersey, P.: test, 2204, 2205
Hershey, C. F.: test, 2390
Hershey, M.: ref, 2512(613)
Herst, J.: test, 2122
Hertel, P. T.: ref, 1257(160)
Hertzka, A. F.: test, 1257, 1337
Hertzog, C.: ref, 2269(454), 2429(23)
Hertzog, M.: ref, 346(106)
Hervis, O.: ref, 1923(29)
Herz, M. I.: ref, 1923(14)
Herzberger, S.: ref, 590(368, 369), 2160(49, 50), 2286(322), 2621(362)
Herzig, S. A.: test, 2571
Herzoff, N.: ref, 2300(475)
Herzog, P. M.: ref, 501(816)
Herzog–Spokane, R.: ref, 2581(349)
Heskin, K. J.: ref, 354(1400), 859(738), 2208(1537)
Hess, A. K.: ref, 1798(207), 2602(1783), 2621(291)
Hess, J. L.: ref, 1498(5336, 5677), 1914(859)
Hess, L. W.: test, 744
Hess, R.: ref, 2472(20)
Hess, R. D.: ref, 1479(346, 365), 1771(649), 2598(1577, 1724), 2602(1882, 2049)
Hess, R. J.: test, 1075
Hess, T. M.: ref, 1192(252)
Hesse, K. A.: test, 254, 1315, 1623
Hesselbrock, V.: ref, 751(33), 2030(5047), 2491(2073), 2598(1807), 2602(1992, 2148)
Hesselbrock, V. M.: ref, 2602(1771)
Hestand, D. A.: test, 145
Hester, S. B.: ref, 2300(531)
Hesterly, O.: ref, 2602(1934)
Heston, L.: ref, 1498(5509)
Hetherington, E. M.: ref, 1771(576)
Hetrick, E. W.: ref, 280(1109), 2602(1900), 2621(340)
Heussenstamm, F. K.: test, 120, 1168
Heverly, M. A.: ref, 226(180), 534(105), 1126(766), 1771(745), 2602(2073)
Hevner, K.: test, 1135
Hewett, B. B.: ref, 113(24), 354(1446), 1498(5274, 5622), 2179(237), 2598(1725), 2621(400)
Hewett, G.: ref, 1192(248), 1479(371), 1754(108), 2269(480)
Hewitson, M.: ref, 1955(109)
Hewitt, E. C.: ref, 859(888), 1063(109), 2598(1654)
Hewson, D. M.: ref, 941(21)
Heykants, J. J. P.: ref, 2588(32)
Hibbard, M.: ref, 1547(323)
Hibbs, B. J.: ref, 1498(5454)
Hibbs, C.: ref, 501(808), 2208(1556), 2581(311)
Hibler, N. S.: ref, 2300(569)
Hick, T. L.: ref, 353(3), 1771(608)
Hickey, R. H.: ref, 1765(10)
Hicks, C.: ref, 1126(761), 1351(193), 2292(30), 2512(647)
Hicks, J. S.: test, 2005
Hicks, M. M.: ref, 995(151)

Hicks, R. A.: ref, 653(140)
Hicks, R. K.: test, 907
Hicks, T. M.: ref, 1960(84)
Hickson, J. F.: ref, 2208(1577)
Hiebert, B.: ref, 1197(319)
Hier, D. B.: ref, 2598(1475), 2602(1764)
Hieronymus, A. N.: test, 363, 1192, 1894, 2021; rev, 121, 2163, 2477; ref, 1341(158), 2328(3)
Hiett, V. C.: test, 1078
Higdon, G.: ref, 2512(573)
Higgins, C. W.: ref, 1498(5176)
Higgins, E. T.: ref, 2269(438)
Higgins, J. P.: ref, 1436(16)
Higgins, J. V.: ref, 381(62)
Higgins, K.: ref, 1009(55)
Higgins, M. J.: exc, 2374
Higgins, R. L.: ref, 859(948), 1547(348)
Higher Education Research Institute: test, 2333
Highland, A. C.: ref, 1197(308)
Highlen, P. S.: ref, 1203(11), 1798(282)
Hilgard, E. R.: test, 2294, 2297; ref, 2294(118), 2297(10, 11)
Hilgard, J. R.: ref, 2297(10)
Hill, A. L.: ref, 2598(1476)
Hill, D. E.: test, 813
Hill, D. M.: ref, 1257(140), 2531(1)
Hill, D. S.: ref, 653(165), 1540(20), 2181(19)
Hill, E. F.: ref, 280(1144), 751(35), 1106(377), 2491(2082), 2598(1726)
Hill, E. W.: test, 1100
Hill, H. E.: test, 113
Hill, J.: ref, 1762(2)
Hill, K. A.: ref, 1460(55), 1969(100), 2208(1616)
Hill, K. D.: ref, 1296(183)
Hill, M.: ref, 794(433)
Hill, P. J.: test, 1772
Hill, S. D.: ref, 280(1057), 1771(571), 2602(1699), 2621(263)
Hill, S. Y.: ref, 280(1061)
Hill, W. F.: test, 1099
Hill, W. H.: rev, 847, 2594
Hillier, V. F.: ref, 1883(41)
Hillingdon Education Authority: test, 2517
Hillman, L. S.: ref, 1371(253), 1771(661), 2289(1712), 2557(228)
Hillman, R. E.: ref, 1371(253), 1771(661), 2289(1712), 2557(228)
Hills, J. R.: rev, 76, 507; exc, 573, 574, 575, 576, 577, 578, 579, 580
Hilpert, P. L.: ref, 2301(32)
Hilton, M. R.: ref, 152(11)
Hilton, S.: ref, 1914(715)
Hilton, T. L.: ref, 590(378), 2160(56)
Hilton Shepherd, Co., Inc.: test, 1214
Hiltzheimer, N. B.: ref, 2260(41)
Hilyer, J. C.: ref, 2413(649)
Himadi, W. G.: ref, 859(911)
Himelstein, P.: rev, 1823, 2217
Himmelhoch, J.: ref, 2300(557, 600)
Himmelhoch, J. M.: ref, 859(947), 2179(254)
Hinckley, E. D.: rev, 2318
Hindley, C. B.: ref, 149(5, 10), 2289(1670, 1713)
Hine, J. R.: test, 1378
Hines, C. B.: ref, 1719(3)
Hines, C. V.: ref, 2181(21)

Hines, D.: ref, 1498(5310)
Hinman, S.: ref, 2030(4947)
Hinrichsen, J. J.: ref, 280(1150), 2491(2079), 2602(2026)
Hinton, J.: ref, 860(109), 2598(1564)
Hinton, R.: ref, 859(911)
Hinzman, J.: ref, 2293(15)
Hird, F.: ref, 1923(18)
Hirsch, C. R.: ref, 573(12), 1193(136)
Hirsch, F. J.: ref, 1969(109), 2602(2050)
Hirsch, S. J.: ref, 1969(109), 2602(2050)
Hirsch, S. R.: ref, 639(56), 859(902), 941(29), 1883(47, 50, 53, 65, 71, 85)
Hirschberg, N.: ref, 1170(238), 1798(283)
Hirschfeld, R.: ref, 1419(688)
Hirschfeld, R. M. A.: ref, 354(1401), 890(327), 1046(589), 1419(703), 1498(5752), 1555(309), 2613(80)
Hirschfield, R. M. A.: ref, 1419(670), 1498(5108)
Hirshoren, A.: ref, 1101(41, 43), 2286(292), 2602(1650, 1769, 1901)
Hisama, T.: ref, 1371(248), 2602(1902)
Hiscock, M.: ref, 1970(14), 2343(1040)
Hiskey, M. S.: test, 1101; rev, 343, 534
Hix, J. A.: ref, 1789(665)
Hjelle, L. A.: ref, 1197(285), 1789(656)
Hlasny, R. G.: ref, 2029(227)
Hlavaty, J. H.: test, 892, 1837, 1838, 2238
Ho, H.: ref, 961(5), 1424(66), 1769(88), 2602(2051)
Ho, H. Z.: ref, 1257(161)
Hoard, J.: rev, 1887
Hobbs, T. R.: ref, 2602(1903)
Hobby, K. L.: test, 1930, 2603, 2632
Ho Beng, T.: ref, 2300(481)
Hobsbaum, A.: test, 2156
Hobson, J. R.: rev, 346, 1478, 1894, 2164, 2269, 2288
Hobson, R. L.: test, 1950
Hocevar, D.: ref, 157(145, 146, 147), 566(109, 110), 2512(614, 615)
Hoch, E. H.: rev, 1602, 1604
Hock, E.: ref, 270(137), 2289(1785)
Hockersmith, V.: ref, 1498(5092), 2318(1528), 2598(1332)
Hockman, B.: test, 1484
Hodapp, A. F.: ref, 1771(736), 2602(2052)
Hodapp, J.: ref, 1771(736), 2602(2052)
Hodges, J.: ref, 1567(14), 2602(1834), 2608(207)
Hodges, J. O.: rev, 246, 1898
Hodgson, J. W.: ref, 501(926), 681(68)
Hodgson, M. L.: ref, 732(392), 2134(93)
Hodgson, R. W.: ref, 1547(254)
Hodinko, B.: ref, 367(1), 377(233), 2581(350)
Hodinko, B. A.: ref, 486(310)
Hodson, B. W.: test, 214
Hoefnagel–Hohle, M.: ref, 1771(628)
Hoehn, M. M.: ref, 1498(509, 5452), 1923(15), 2598(1592)
Hoekstra, R. R.: test, 2231
Hoelter, J. A.: ref, 2300(399)
Hoelter, J. W.: ref, 2300(399)
Hoeltke, G. M.: test, 1308
Hoepfner, R.: test, 203, 220, 611, 1168, 1464, 1580, 2198, 2382, 2435, 2649; exc, 1191, 1424, 2512
Hoeppner, J.: ref, 1498(5647)
Hofeditz, D.: test, 2392

Hoffer, G. L.: ref, 1729(80)
Hoffey, P.: ref, 1754(86)
Hoffman, C.: ref, 794(373), 2598(1341)
Hoffman, D. A.: ref, 1013(66), 1831(139), 2181(13)
Hoffman, G.: ref, 2598(1537)
Hoffman, H.: ref, 780(1647), 1498(5045, 5286), 1798(198), 2598(1548)
Hoffman, H. H.: ref, 1576(216)
Hoffman, J.: ref, 2602(1765)
Hoffman, J. A.: ref, 859(858)
Hoffman, M.: ref, 707(21), 794(417), 1853(281)
Hoffman, M. A.: ref, 2318(1612)
Hoffman, N.: ref, 1498(5585)
Hoffman, N. G.: ref, 1498(5032)
Hoffman, P. R.: ref, 664(9), 960(5)
Hoffman, R. G.: ref, 354(1470), 501(825), 780(1674), 2413(630)
Hoffman, V.: test, 1298; ref, 1298(1, 2)
Hoffmann, C. M.: ref, 2068(88)
Hoffmann, H.: ref, 1789(688)
Hoffmann, N. G.: ref, 2598(1508)
Hoffmann, R. J.: ref, 2286(338)
Hoffmeister, J. K.: test, 407, 563, 620, 2080, 2135
Hofland, B. F.: ref, 653(172), 2300(591)
Hofmann, G.: ref, 1473(203)
Hofmann, R. J.: ref, 280(1032)
Hogaboam, T.: ref, 1473(158), 1754(79)
Hogaboam, T. W.: ref, 1473(151), 1754(76)
Hogan, D. K.: test, 1144
Hogan, H. W.: ref, 1789(666), 2029(228), 2629(98)
Hogan, J. C.: ref, 354(1450)
Hogan, R.: rev, 120, 1233, 1798, 2343; ref, 354(1463, 1570), 384(6), 501(898), 2134(139)
Hogan, R. D.: test, 1144
Hogan, T. P.: test, 1473, 1474, 1475, 1476, 1477, 1478, 2372; rev, 160; ref, 1473(198), 2372(2)
Hogarty, G. E.: ref, 1240(63)
Hogarty, P. S.: ref, 2289(1628)
Hoge, R. D.: ref, 362(2), 363(8), 1894(5)
Hogg, M.: ref, 2029(212)
Hohl, S.: test, 1334
Hohn, L.: ref, 1005(26), 1462(155)
Hohn, R. L.: ref, 1798(306)
Hoiberg, A.: ref, 558(60, 61)
Hojat, M.: ref, 859(859)
Hokanson, J. E.: ref, 883(108), 1498(5353, 5354, 5623), 1547(307)
Hoke, W. E.: ref, 1347(10)
Holcomb, H.: ref, 653(175)
Holcombé, B. M.: ref, 551(18, 29)
Holden, C.: ref, 202(11), 1498(5624), 2387(2), 2598(1727), 2602(1766)
Holden, R. H.: rev, 270
Holden, R. R.: ref, 1798(256)
Hollan, S. D.: ref, 397(1)
Holland, J. E.: ref, 374(188), 2134(95)
Holland, J. L.: test, 1554, 2134, 2573, 2581; exc, 2512; ref, 202(6), 374(188), 2134(94, 95, 96, 120, 140), 2318(1613), 2581(331)
Holland, T. R.: ref, 280(1110), 1498(5109, 5287, 5288, 5455, 5625, 5626, 5627), 2598(1594, 1595, 1728)
Hollandsworth, J. G.: test, 122; ref, 116(533), 122(1, 2), 781(3, 4), 883(94), 1754(73, 104), 2300(388)
Hollar, D. W.: ref, 270(87)
Hollembeak, N.: ref, 2300(351)

INDEX OF NAMES

Hollenback, J.: ref, 732(409), 1754(106), 2286(337)
Hollenback, J. H.: ref, 1508(116)
Hollenbeck, A. R.: ref, 398(106)
Holley, C. D.: ref, 2374(191)
Holley, J. W.: test, 1042
Holley, W. H.: ref, 1508(123)
Hollien, H.: exc, 2412
Hollingsworth, L.: test, 1103, 1104, 1105
Hollingsworth, P. M.: ref, 932(76), 1771(607)
Hollmén, A.: ref, 1498(5352), 2030(5009), 2598(1525)
Hollon, S. D.: ref, 859(950)
Holloway, A. J.: test, 556, 1175
Holm, L.: ref, 1462(150)
Holman, E. R.: ref, 2512(593)
Holmes, A. F.: ref, 995(145)
Holmes, C. B.: ref, 6(69), 1462(137, 147, 159), 1498(5582), 2208(1624, 1627, 1691), 2491(2100)
Holmes, C. M.: ref, 1726(370)
Holmes, C. S.: ref, 1853(297)
Holmes, D. L.: ref, 1007(14), 2621(244)
Holmes, D. R.: ref, 932(97), 1771(662)
Holmes, D. S.: ref, 1351(197), 1498(5411), 1547(249, 291, 342), 2300(435, 561), 2594(201)
Holmes, F. J.: test, 1775
Holmes, R. L.: ref, 1192(257), 2621(449)
Holmstrom, F.: ref, 1576(207)
Holroyd, K. A.: ref, 2300(400), 2353(24)
Holstein, R. B.: ref, 1771(576)
Holt, D. L.: ref, 1851(25)
Holt, M. M.: ref, 2602(1903)
Holt, R. R.: rev, 1022; exc, 396, 2384
Holthouse, N. D.: ref, 1479(323)
Holtzhausen, J. A.: test, 2073
Holtzman, R. N. N.: ref, 280(1077), 283(145), 1007(23), 1914(763), 2598(1477), 2607(160)
Holtzman, W. H.: test, 1106, 2374; rev, 1625
Holyroyd, J.: ref, 6(46), 698(3), 1319(77), 1424(37), 2289(1671), 2602(1767)
Holzer, F.: test, 33
Holzman, P. S.: ref, 2030(5000, 5028), 2598(1489, 1586)
Holzmuller, A.: ref, 116(578)
Hong, B.: ref, 2208(1672)
Hong, K. M.: ref, 354(1493)
Honig, A. S.: ref, 270(92), 1108(1)
Honig, P.: ref, 354(1496)
Honigfeld, G.: test, 1655
Honigmann, I.: test, 2121
Honzik, C. H.: rev, 152, 1369,
Honzik, M. P.: rev, 1236, 1471, 1505; exc, 964; ref, 2289(1608)
Hood, A.: ref, 76(649), 2318(1606)
Hood, A. B.: rev, 2333, 2336
Hood, J.: ref, 1192(220), 1351(185), 1771(664), 2280(12)
Hood, J. E.: rev, 1138, 1870
Hood, R.: ref, 501(802)
Hood, R. W.: ref, 1203(9)
Hood, S. B.: rev, 228, 882; ref, 1192(165)
Hood, V. R.: test, 245
Hook, J. D.: test, 1169
Hooper, A.: ref, 1655(105)
Hooper, F. E.: rev, 61
Hooper, H. E.: test, 1109
Hoops, H. R.: ref, 766(30), 2412(41)

Hoosain, R.: ref, 1914(842)
Hoover, H. D.: test, 1192; ref, 76(643), 1192(243, 244, 247), 1193(144)
Hoover, T.: ref, 2208(1617)
Hoover, T. O.: ref, 1053(65)
Hope, D. J.: ref, 666(6)
Hope, L.: ref, 116(550)
Hopkins, C. R.: ref, 332(2)
Hopkins, D. R.: ref, 4(4)
Hopkins, H. K.: ref, 280(1101)
Hopkins, J.: ref, 794(420), 2598(1596)
Hopkins, K. D.: rev, 269, 483, 2423
Hopper, G.: ref, 2286(280), 2300(518)
Hoppes, E.: ref, 1883(96)
Hops, H.: ref, 2621(238)
Hopwood, J.: ref, 354(1493)
Horan, M.: ref, 2598(1729)
Horan, M. D.: ref, 353(3), 1771(608)
Horenstein, D.: ref, 2413(615)
Hörlén, M.: ref, 283(136), 1265(75)
Horn, A. C.: ref, 1513(31)
Horn, C. C.: test, 1110
Horn, G.: test, 1663, 1664
Horn, J.: ref, 116(627)
Horn, J. L.: test, 1538; rev, 1853; exc, 900, 2267; ref, 643(129), 942(1), 2113(257)
Horn, J. M.: ref, 2208(1557), 2598(1671), 2602(1987)
Horn, P. W.: ref, 280(1115), 1479(350), 2602(1925)
Horn, R. W.: ref, 2598(1573)
Horn, T. D.: rev, 1238, 2062, 2257
Horn, W. R.: ref, 395(1)
Hornbergr, R.: ref, 1498(5505)
Hornbostel, L. K.: ref, 780(1699)
Hornby, P. A.: ref, 962(34), 2602(2053), 2621(401)
Horne, A. M.: ref, 872(8)
Horne, E. P.: ref, 877(19)
Horne, M. D.: ref, 704(13)
Horned, C. M.: ref, 116(534)
Hornstein, D.: ref, 1229(79), 1233(213), 2621(245)
Hornstra, R. K.: ref, 681(32, 41)
Hornsveld, R. H. J.: ref, 883(95)
Horodezky, B.: ref, 2218(144)
Horovitz, J. H.: ref, 1498(5564, 5565)
Horowitz, E. C.: test, 935
Horowitz, F. D.: ref, 270(64), 311(17, 26)
Horst, P. A.: ref, 859(769)
Horstman, D. H.: ref, 681(42), 859(820), 1904(79), 2300(421)
Horstmeier, D. S.: test, 836
Horton, A. M.: ref, 1498(5628)
Horton, C. W.: rev, 126, 488, 509, 980
Horton, J. A.: ref, 2134(102, 123), 2581(312, 333)
Horton, R. L.: ref, 111(26), 116(588), 966(176)
Horton, W. G.: ref, 2598(1627)
Horttonen, L.: ref, 1498(5352), 2030(5009), 2598(1525)
Horvath, T.: ref, 859(912), 1883(48)
Horwitz, B.: ref, 2300(439)
Horwitz, E. A.: ref, 2300(494)
Horwitz, S. H.: ref, 344(192), 551(69)
Hosch, H. M.: ref, 6(54), 1498(5382)
Hosford, R. E.: ref, 1498(5164, 5493)
Hoshko, I. M.: ref, 2218(7), 2602(1631)
Hosie, T. W.: ref, 374(203), 2413(629)
Hoskins, C.: test, 1172

Hoskins, T.: test, 1111
Hoskins, T. A.: ref, 2413(640)
Hosley, D.: ref, 549(4), 2441(32, 36)
Hosseini, A. A.: ref, 501(826)
Hosticka, A.: ref, 1192(253)
Hotchkiss, L.: ref, 1073(125)
Houck, C.: exc, 2641
Houck, D. G.: ref, 551(63), 1126(773), 2289(1774), 2602(2132)
Houck, R. L.: ref, 2030(4997)
Hounshell, P. B.: ref, 2208(1639)
Houpt, J. L.: ref, 1498(5419)
House, E. R.: ref, 1473(152), 1914(764)
House, P. A.: ref, 573(19), 590(388)
House, W. C.: ref, 2228(70)
House, W. J.: ref, 1013(63, 64), 1798(234, 235)
Householder, D. L.: rev, 1597, 1612
Houston, B. K.: ref, 1229(79), 1233(213), 1547(249, 284, 301, 326, 338), 2300(459, 532), 2598(1765), 2621(245)
Houston, L. N.: ref, 501(891), 2629(119)
Houston, N.: ref, 1904(133)
Houston, S.: ref, 2208(1665)
Houston, W. B.: ref, 251(1), 290(9), 1771(754)
Hovanitz, C.: ref, 1498(5448), 1904(89)
Hovanitz, C. A.: ref, 1498(5629), 1853(294)
Hovland, C. I.: rev, 995, 1486, 2594
Hovne, R.: ref, 874(56), 1537(3), 2602(2189)
Howard, D. V.: ref, 1969(110), 2598(1730)
Howard, K. I.: test, 1673
Howard, M. L.: ref, 1063(116), 2294(135)
Howard, M. R.: ref, 200(17), 378(11, 15), 1771(737)
Howard, N. J.: ref, 270(134), 2557(236), 2608(232)
Howard, R. W.: rev, 504
Howard, W. J.: ref, 1197(281), 1498(5182), 1547(267)
Howard-Peebles, P. N.: ref, 960(12), 2541(7), 2598(1597)
Howarth, E.: test, 114, 1114, 1115; rev, 558, 1726; ref, 354(1387), 558(53), 859(725), 1046(569), 1419(669), 1498(5050), 1726(349), 2208(1520)
Howe, T.: ref, 932(77)
Howell, E. R.: ref, 30(6), 929(1), 1620(23)
Howell, F. M.: ref, 1754(89, 117)
Howell, J.: ref, 378(19), 1153(9), 2018(20), 2472(30)
Howell, K. W.: ref, 2621(286)
Howell, R. J.: test, 294; ref, 116(616), 294(12)
Howell, R. T.: ref, 2602(1685)
Howells, K.: ref, 1162(21), 1498(5289)
Howes, C.: ref, 1771(803), 1877(11)
Howes, M. J.: ref, 1547(307)
Howie, D.: rev, 21, 1337
Hoy, R. V.: ref, 2286(309)
Hoyenga, K. B.: ref, 767(43)
Hoyer, W. J.: ref, 609(221), 1914(867), 2598(1781, 1845)
Hoyt, C.: ref, 1498(5253)
Hoyt, C. J.: rev, 1188, 1313, 1716, 1749, 1854
Hoyt, C. N.: ref, 1498(5603)
Hoyt, K. B.: test, 331, 654, 2406; rev, 965, 1045
Hoyum, V. D.: test, 1116
Hresko, W. P.: test, 2436, 2438; ref, 962(29), 1771(663)
Hryhorczuk, L.: ref, 1796(1)
Hsia, Y. E.: ref, 1052(1), 2602(1988), 2621(377)
Hsu, L. K. G.: ref, 639(59), 859(848)

Huba, G. J.: ref, 1798(208, 295)
Hubbard, B.: ref, 354(1404), 401(74), 1106(361), 1460(51), 2598(1344)
Hubbard, D. J.: ref, 1851(23)
Hubbard, H. R.: ref, 2343(1045)
Hubbard, R. B.: ref, 1853(270), 1904(58, 59)
Hubble, L. M.: ref, 2598(1478), 2602(2054, 2176)
Hubble, M. A.: ref, 1013(124), 2300(401, 592)
Huber, C. H.: ref, 1495(86), 1996(7), 2224(8), 2539(9)
Huber, J.: ref, 2512(616)
Hubert, E. E.: test, 1317
Huberty, C. J.: rev, 709, 1417, 1589
Huchcroft, S. A.: ref, 1424(82)
Huddleston, N. J.: ref, 2602(1826)
Hudesman, J.: ref, 883(96)
Hudgin, A. L.: ref, 2243(12)
Hudgins, A. L.: ref, 280(1033), 1540(10)
Hudgins, E. W.: ref, 357(518), 1831(171), 2208(1618)
Hudgins, W.: ref, 2413(627)
Hudson, B. R.: ref, 732(397), 1970(13)
Hudson, G. R.: ref, 1789(670)
Huebner, M. H.: rev, 2107; ref, 2561(2)
Huelsberg, E. L.: test, 156
Huelsman, C. B.: test, 2644
Huesmann, L. R.: ref, 1498(5290, 5302, 5602)
Huestis, R. D.: ref, 280(1064)
Huey, L.: ref, 1106(360), 1247(162), 1498(5114)
Huey, L. Y.: ref, 354(1404), 401(74), 1106(361), 1460(51), 1853(270), 1904(58, 59, 113), 2598(1344, 1737)
Hufano, L.: exc, 1424
Hug, N.: ref, 1874(10), 2217(127)
Huggins, G. R.: ref, 1466(2)
Hughes, D. C.: test, 1911
Hughes, G.: exc, 2223
Hughes, J. M.: ref, 1904(57)
Hughes, L. A.: ref, 1765(11)
Hughes, L. C.: ref, 2289(1674), 2602(1776)
Hughes, L. H.: ref, 2602(2194)
Hughes, R. J.: ref, 1754(56), 1945(66)
Hughes, R. N.: ref, 794(390, 391), 859(739, 795), 1013(67), 1197(276)
Hughson, E. A.: test, 112
Huh, S. J.: ref, 2602(1746)
Huisingh, R.: test, 1736, 1737, 2648
Huk, W.: ref, 1077(79), 1914(886)
Hulfish, S.: ref, 653(141), 1013(68), 2413(620)
Hulin, C. L.: ref, 1295(283)
Hulit, L. M.: ref, 200(17), 378(11, 15), 1771(737)
Hultgen, D. D.: ref, 1183(3)
Hum, A.: ref, 780(1670), 1555(320), 2208(1584)
Human Sciences Research Council: test, 537, 1026, 1565, 1578, 2153, 2408
Hume, N.: ref, 1170(225), 1498(5110)
Humes, M.: ref, 859(746)
Humm, D. G.: rev, 118
Hummel, H.: ref, 859(740), 1046(571)
Hummel-Rossi, B.: ref, 1233(214, 215), 2286(281)
Humphrey, B.: test, 1015
Humphrey, F. J.: ref, 1498(5637)
Humphrey, L. L.: ref, 2374(199)
Humphrey, M.: ref, 860(94), 1240(56)
Humphrey, T.: ref, 962(35)
Humphreys, J. M.: ref, 896(6), 1814(7)
Humphreys, L.: ref, 590(368, 369), 2160(49, 50)

Humphreys, L. G.: rev, 190, 282, 690, 732, 1486, 2537; ref, 590(383), 995(133), 2160(65)
Humphreys, M. S.: ref, 732(410), 859(847, 932)
Humphry, R.: ref, 964(504)
Hundal, P. S.: ref, 643(129), 942(1), 2208(1579), 2236(3), 2491(2041)
Hundleby, J. D.: rev, 1947, 2343; ref, 859(741), 1498(5111), 2208(1538)
Hunley, P. J.: ref, 116(574), 1498(5736)
Hunsicker, A. L.: rev, 152, 1369
Hunsicker, P.: test, 5
Hunt, B. A.: test, 2651
Hunt, D.: ref, 400(132), 1077(74), 1257(146, 162), 2160(59), 2269(448)
Hunt, D. D.: ref, 1498(5630), 2598(1731)
Hunt, E. B.: ref, 1568(146)
Hunt, H. F.: ref, 280(1104, 1167), 751(25, 41), 2030(5025, 5088), 2491(2103), 2598(1566, 1832)
Hunt, J. G.: ref, 1296(170)
Hunt, J. M.: ref, 1771(738), 2289(1758)
Hunt, J. T.: ref, 1101(41), 2286(292), 2602(1650, 1769)
Hunt, J. V.: rev, 698, 902, 1424, 2025, 2217; ref, 270(65), 381(60)
Hunt, R. D.: ref, 308(6), 2598(1435)
Hunt, S. M.: ref, 2294(128)
Hunt, T.: test, 949, 2228, 2403, 2418; rev, 940, 1493
Hunt, T. C.: ref, 620(2)
Hunt, V. V.: ref, 2300(501)
Hunt, W. A.: rev, 2179
Hunter, A. G. W.: ref, 2289(1616)
Hunter, C.: exc, 964
Hunter, G. W.: rev, 947
Hunter, I.: ref, 1347(3)
Hunter, J. A.: ref, 1192(198), 2602(1768)
Hunter, J. E.: ref, 282(146), 557(8), 1976(1), 1981(3)
Hunter, K.: ref, 2598(1613)
Hunter, M. L.: ref, 1498(5148)
Hunter, R.: exc, 1191
Hunter, S. M.: ref, 1831(183, 220)
Hunter-Grundin, E.: test, 1119
Huntley, A.: ref, 1498(5090), 1904(54)
Huntzinger, R. S.: ref, 1498(5731)
Huppertz, J. W.: ref, 1771(541), 1914(713)
Hurlburt, G.: ref, 860(151)
Hurlbut, N. L.: ref, 2269(439)
Hurley, J. D.: ref, 1063(117), 1197(309)
Hurley, O. L.: ref, 1101(41, 43, 44), 2286(292, 312), 2602(1650, 1769, 1901, 1904)
Hurray, J.: ref, 1883(92)
Hurry, J.: ref, 1883(93)
Hurst, J. C.: test, 618
Hurst, M. W.: ref, 354(1568)
Hurvich, M. S.: test, 396
Hurwitz, J. I.: ref, 1170(226), 1498(5112), 2491(2013)
Husa, H. F.: ref, 1789(667)
Husak, W. S.: ref, 1506(74), 1896(12), 2260(42)
Husek, T. R.: exc, 1269
Hushak, L. J.: ref, 346(101), 1479(316)
Hushak, L.J.: ref, 553(13)
Hustak, T. L.: ref, 280(1062), 2289(1650), 2598(1313, 1419)
Hustmyer, F. E.: ref, 673(53), 794(451)
Hutcherson, R.: ref, 302(32), 1771(609)
Hutchings, D. F.: ref, 1547(326), 2300(532)

Hutchings, E. M. J.: test, 775
Hutchings, J. L.: ref, 2300(485)
Hutchings, M. J.: test, 193, 775
Hutchins, D. E.: ref, 1051(16)
Hutchins, T. C.: ref, 1498(5671)
Hutchinson, B.: ref, 378(16), 381(74), 1771(762), 2289(1771)
Hutchinson, J. M.: ref, 200(15)
Hutchinson, K.: ref, 1485(59), 1771(540), 2598(1338)
Hutson, G. S.: ref, 501(914), 2534(15)
Hutt, L. D.: ref, 2030(5075)
Hutt, M. L.: test, 280, 1480; ref, 280(1034, 1035), 2413(593), 2621(246)
Huxley, P. J.: ref, 859(860)
Huynh, H.: ref, 551(54), 1576(193), 2343(1030, 1032), 2366(191, 192)
Hyde, E. M.: ref, 1272(132)
Hyde, M. R.: ref, 308(17)
Hyde, R.: ref, 1655(84)
Hydinger-Macdonald, M.: ref, 1923(26)
Hyer, L.: ref, 1765(10)
Hyland, A. M.: test, 1714
Hyman, C. A.: ref, 2208(1539), 2598(1342)
Hyman, I.: ref, 1531(278)
Hyman, R. B.: ref, 1789(694)
Hymen, S. P.: ref, 2300(402)
Hymowitz, P.: ref, 2491(2083)
Hynan, M.: ref, 1904(112)
Hynd, G. W.: ref, 1424(67), 1473(218), 1823(33), 2602(1905, 2177)
Hynes, K.: ref, 1295(291), 1576(212, 213, 222)
Ibrahim, A.: ref, 860(95), 1498(5113)
Ibrahim, A. S.: ref, 859(861)
Ickes, W.: ref, 1046(578)
Idol-Maestas, L.: ref, 1914(843)
Igi, C. H.: ref, 1356(98)
Iglehart, V. R.: ref, 277(2), 2506(7)
Ignatoff, E.: ref, 270(135), 311(35), 678(31), 2300(524)
Ihalainen, O.: ref, 1498(5352), 2030(5009), 2598(1525)
Ihilevich, D.: test, 665, 1909; ref, 1909(1)
Ikegami, T.: ref, 2030(5031)
Ilg, F. L.: test, 953; ref, 953(12)
Ilgen, D. R.: ref, 1508(116), 2638(145)
Illfelder, J. K.: ref, 2300(533)
Illinois Association of College and Research Libraries: test, 1323
Ilmer, S.: ref, 381(71), 2289(1759)
Ilyin, D.: test, 821, 1128, 1335, 2321
Imada, A. S.: ref, 2208(1658)
Imlach, R.: ref, 1912(4)
Immergluck, L.: rev, 963
Imoda, F.: ref, 1131(1), 2491(2042)
Imperio, A. M.: ref, 1498(5456)
Imus, H. A.: rev, 185, 1752
Ina-Oka, H.: ref, 354(1402)
Inabinette, N.: ref, 794(421)
Inagaki, K.: ref, 1126(728)
Inayatulla, M.: ref, 2602(2055)
Inazu, J. K.: ref, 1192(236)
Inbar, J.: ref, 472(19)
Indiresan, J.: ref, 1295(282, 300)
Industrial Psychology, Inc.: test, 1219
Ingram, C.: ref, 2602(1884), 2621(328)
Ingram, T. T. S.: test, 1153

Ingwell, R. H.: ref, 1498(5198), 2179(207)
Inman, D. J.: ref, 2491(2014)
Inman, V.: ref, 1462(160), 2598(1849)
Innes, J. M.: ref, 1247(161), 2208(1682)
Insel, P. M.: test, 2652
Insler, V.: ref, 859(747)
Institute for Social Research, University of Michigan: test, 2369
Institutional Research Program for Higher Education: test, 2334
Instructional Objectives Exchange: test, 222, 223, 1195, 1196, 1258, 1449
Intagliata, J. C.: ref, 2598(1479)
International Business Machines Corporation: test, 1120
International Personnel Management Association: test, 888, 1199, 1200, 1843, 2420
Iona, M.: rev, 143; ref, 143(6)
Ippel, M. J.: ref, 1013(125), 1077(78)
Irby, D.: ref, 2300(570)
Ireland, J. F.: ref, 653(152), 2602(1906)
Ireland–Galman, M. M.: ref, 2602(2056)
Ireton, H.: test, 1496, 1504
Ireton, H. R.: test, 1492
Ironson, G. H.: ref, 116(589), 2343(1051)
Irvin, F. S.: test, 2155
Irvin, L. K.: test, 2211, 2224, 2473; ref, 2224(3, 4, 7, 9), 2473(1)
Irvine, C.: ref, 973(27), 1486(175)
Irvine, D. J.: ref, 353(3)
Irvine, R. W.: ref, 354(1494)
Irwin, H. J.: ref, 780(1708)
Irwin, J. V.: test, 1322
Irwin, M.: ref, 2602(1770)
Irwin, R. B.: test, 1717, 1718
Irwin, R. J.: ref, 1771(545)
Isakson, R. L.: ref, 76(603)
Isely, C.: ref, 1351(198)
Isett, R.: ref, 6(91)
Isett, R. D.: ref, 6(56)
Ishihara, S.: test, 2419
Islam, M. T.: ref, 2598(1640)
Ismail, A. H.: ref, 653(163), 859(742), 1547(255), 2208(1540, 1559, 1653)
Iso–Ahola, S. E.: ref, 1831(185)
Israel, A. C.: ref, 883(71)
Israel, E.: ref, 1547(256, 279), 2300(352, 384)
Isralsky, M.: ref, 2413(650)
Ito, H. R.: ref, 2621(402, 444)
Itskowitz, R.: ref, 2030(5094), 2512(664), 2602(2220)
Ivancevich, J. M.: ref, 1508(135)
Iverson, D. C.: ref, 609(211)
Ives, J. O.: ref, 2100(9), 2598(1328)
Ives, M.: rev, 2179
Ivey, A. E.: ref, 1789(682)
Ivey, C.: ref, 653(146), 2621(311)
Ivimey, J. K.: ref, 1424(76, 77), 1425(1), 2602(2128), 2621(421)
Ivison, D. J.: ref, 2607(136)
Ivnik, R. J.: ref, 1498(5291), 2113(245, 246), 2598(1480, 1481), 2621(287, 288)
Iwanicki, E. F.: rev, 407, 2398; ref, 344(183), 1192(240), 1473(199), 2160(74), 2260(46)
Iwawaki, S.: ref, 860(142), 1229(101)
Izral, R.: ref, 2602(1744)

Jackoway, M. L.: ref, 1771(715), 2602(2011), 2608(227), 2621(386)
Jackson, A. M.: ref, 1853(284), 2602(1907)
Jackson, A. S.: ref, 2208(1671), 2655(7)
Jackson, B.: ref, 1459(16), 1473(221), 1479(381), 1514(1)
Jackson, D. J.: ref, 374(197)
Jackson, D. N.: test, 1203, 1204, 1798; rev, 796, 1233, 1349, 2489; ref, 354(1398), 1203(8), 1498(5107, 5366), 1798(205, 206, 222, 256, 257, 265, 284, 293)
Jackson, J. C.: ref, 597(2)
Jackson, J. R.: ref, 1576(216)
Jackson, M.: ref, 859(913), 928(5), 2281(3)
Jackson, M. P.: ref, 859(862)
Jackson, P.: test, 1918, 2458
Jackson, P. F.: test, 1913, 2341; ref, 1913(1)
Jackson, P. R.: ref, 941(32, 40)
Jackson, R.: ref, 501(892)
Jackson, R. E.: ref, 793(6), 1109(18)
Jackson, R. L.: ref, 2413(651)
Jackson, R. W.: ref, 1372(10)
Jackson, R. W. B.: rev, 2160
Jackson, S. E.: test, 1388
Jackson, T. T.: ref, 859(750)
Jacob, J.: ref, 270(119), 2289(1724)
Jacob, M.: ref, 2300(587)
Jacob, T.: ref, 2491(2074)
Jacobs, E.: ref, 1007(34), 2608(223)
Jacobs, H. D.: test, 661, 718
Jacobs, K. W.: ref, 859(743), 1193(142), 1347(4), 2269(461)
Jacobs, L.: ref, 1498(5216, 5315, 5395, 5550, 5729), 1547(314), 2179(221), 2300(420, 500), 2598(1545)
Jacobs, P. H.: test, 1127
Jacobsen, G.: ref, 883(110)
Jacobsen, K.: ref, 372(4), 2581(328)
Jacobson, A. F.: ref, 1904(71)
Jacobson, G. R.: ref, 1960(67), 2343(1031)
Jacoby, J.: test, 1366
Jacoby, R. J.: ref, 2598(1732, 1733)
Jaeger, R. M.: rev, 119
Jaffe, E. D.: ref, 874(44)
Jahoda, G.: ref, 398(108)
Jalali, B.: ref, 1831(209)
Jalali, M.: ref, 1831(209)
Jamal, M.: ref, 2318(1575)
James, C. J.: ref, 1527(45)
James, J. F.: ref, 121(12), 472(17), 653(166), 1538(71)
James, L. B.: ref, 200(16), 2103(10)
James, M. A.: ref, 653(142), 2269(455)
James, S.: ref, 609(210), 859(796), 2208(1580)
Jamieson, D. G.: ref, 1257(130), 2015(200)
Jamison, C. B.: rev, 1871, 1949, 2016
Jamison, K. R.: ref, 859(839)
Jamison, R. N.: ref, 1229(91)
Jamison, W.: ref, 559(56), 1013(75), 1257(135)
Janaganathan, P.: ref, 859(754)
Jancey, C.: ref, 1567(15), 2602(1868)
Janda, L. H.: ref, 116(567), 883(77), 1498(5089), 2300(426)
Janes, C. L.: ref, 2602(1771)
Janes, M. D.: ref, 1424(33)
Janicke, E. M.: ref, 720(69), 2641(20)
Janicki, T. C.: ref, 354(1546), 381(75), 1914(817, 892), 2160(66), 2269(479), 2300(555)

INDEX OF NAMES

Janke, R. W.: ref, 2621(403)
Jannoun, L.: ref, 860(143), 2300(534)
Janowsky, D. S.: ref, 354(1404), 401(74), 1106(360, 361), 1247(162), 1460(51), 1498(5114), 1853(270), 1904(58, 59, 76, 113), 2598(1344, 1737)
Jansen, M. A.: ref, 1931(51)
Jansing, C.: exc, 75
Jansky, J.: test, 1205
Janzen, H. L.: ref, 363(15), 701(88), 1351(200), 2621(439)
Jardine, E.: ref, 1209(35)
Jaremko, M. E.: ref, 1547(308, 327, 328), 2300(473, 511), 2353(34)
Jarman, R.: ref, 1462(131), 2602(1772)
Jarman, R. F.: ref, 1462(132, 141, 142), 1914(765, 766, 803, 804, 844), 2319(1), 2602(1773)
Jarnecke, R. W.: ref, 1498(5115), 2638(127)
Jarrett, S.: ref, 1547(322)
Jarvik, L.: ref, 1109(22), 2598(1716)
Jarvik, L. F.: ref, 1498(5326)
Jarvik, M. E.: ref, 1547(340)
Järvinen, H.: ref, 1498(5754), 2030(5087), 2491(2102)
Jarvis, R.: ref, 2218(17)
Jason, L.: ref, 270(66)
Jason, L. A.: ref, 2621(341)
Jastak, J. F.: test, 481, 2621, 2622, 2623, 2624
Jastak, S.: test, 481, 2621
Jastak, S. R.: test, 2624
Jatlow, P.: ref, 113(26), 1904(103)
Javaid, J.: ref, 2602(1959)
Jeanneret, P. R.: test, 1212, 1855
Jedrysek, E.: test, 1926
Jeeves, M. A.: ref, 283(150), 2598(1598), 2607(179)
Jeffers, V.: ref, 2300(530)
Jeffree, D. M.: test, 1836
Jeffrey, G. S.: ref, 859(750)
Jeffrey, H.: ref, 280(1036), 922(6), 2602(1651)
Jeffrey, T. E.: test, 477, 478, 898, 1176, 1455, 1780, 2610
Jeffs, P. M.: test, 2096
Jeguier, J. C.: ref, 342(4)
Jehle, W. O.: ref, 1969(119)
Jehu, D.: ref, 823(13), 1567(8)
Jenden, D. J.: ref, 1351(36)
Jengeleski, J. L.: ref, 501(874)
Jenkins, B. L.: ref, 932(108)
Jenkins, C. D.: test, 1206; ref, 1498(5116)
Jenkins, C. W.: ref, 1498(5124), 2598(1348)
Jenkins, J. R.: ref, 1473(153), 1769(57), 2217(128), 2621(289)
Jenkins, J. S.: ref, 859(760)
Jenkins, J. W.: test, 1620
Jenkins, M. B.: ref, 1769(56), 2598(1482)
Jenks, J.: ref, 1960(77)
Jenkyn, L. R.: ref, 2598(1343), 2621(247)
Jenner, F. A.: ref, 354(1552), 859(934), 2208(1667)
Jennings, J. R.: rev, 37, 38
Jennings, K. D.: ref, 270(115)
Jennings, S. J.: ref, 1798(283)
Jensen, A. R.: rev, 874, 1361, 1419, 2030, 2491; ref, 1351(194), 2286(331)
Jensen, C. M.: ref, 1914(834)
Jensen, H. T.: ref, 1814(5), 2602(1797)
Jensen, L. R.: ref, 344(154), 2512(594), 2602(1774)
Jensen, M.: ref, 1473(177)

Jensen, M. B.: test, 1207
Jensen, S.: ref, 1197(294), 1198(1)
Jepsen, D. A.: ref, 374(222), 1193(147)
Jepson, D. A.: ref, 2139(3)
Jerdonek, C.: ref, 239(11)
Jerse, F. W.: ref, 1192(199)
Jesness, C. F.: test, 1208, 1209; rev, 702, 835
Jessor, R.: rev, 1237
Jeste, D. V.: ref, 280(1164)
Jesudason, V.: ref, 270(116)
Jew, C.: ref, 2598(1529)
Jewish Education Service of North America, Inc.: test, 49, 51, 52
Jewish Employment and Vocational Service, Inc.: test, 1210
Jex, F. B.: rev, 1318
Jex, J. L.: test, 2104, 2448, 2541
Joe, V. C.: ref, 2629(99, 105)
Joensen, E.: ref, 1009(54)
Joesting, J.: ref, 280(1037), 354(1403), 681(69), 964(477), 1547(349), 1904(126), 2300(353, 354), 2602(1652)
Joffe, P. E.: ref, 354(1451)
Johansen, L. J.: ref, 681(63)
Johansson, C. B.: test, 376, 1164, 2133, 2409, 2642
Johansson, J. C.: test, 2642
John, L.: test, 335, 713
Johns, G.: ref, 1296(172)
Johns, J.: exc, 1579
Johns, J. L.: test, 255
Johnsgard, K.: ref, 780(1648), 1498(5117), 2208(1541)
Johnson, A.: ref, 1762(1)
Johnson, A. B.: ref, 2039(11)
Johnson, A. F.: ref, 1126(646, 662, 675), 1622(31), 1894(3), 2103(6, 8), 2412(34, 36), 2425(1), 2621(221)
Johnson, A. H.: ref, 890(323, 333), 1555(302, 317), 1789(637, 660), 2343(1028, 1037)
Johnson, A. P.: rev, 402, 1494
Johnson, B. W.: ref, 483(34), 1831(192)
Johnson, C. A.: ref, 1063(81), 1300(122)
Johnson, C. D.: ref, 932(78)
Johnson, C. H.: ref, 1498(5628)
Johnson, C. W.: ref, 372(11)
Johnson, D.: ref, 270(67), 2598(1734)
Johnson, D. C.: ref, 76(589), 2441(31)
Johnson, D. D.: test, 1220; rev, 1140; ref, 1498(5631)
Johnson, D. G.: ref, 1576(188)
Johnson, D. J.: ref, 2(2), 1831(140)
Johnson, D. L.: test, 629, 956, 1180, 2229; exc, 338; ref, 270(149), 1479(317), 1540(11), 2598(1379)
Johnson, D. S.: ref, 1831(210)
Johnson, D. T.: ref, 1498(5255), 2300(339)
Johnson, D. W.: ref, 666(3), 1498(5118)
Johnson, E.: ref, 2602(1793)
Johnson, E. G.: ref, 1505(13), 1771(546), 1914(715)
Johnson, E. P.: ref, 2300(351)
Johnson, E. S.: ref, 1914(767)
Johnson, F. L.: ref, 1771(739)
Johnson, G.: ref, 1798(274)
Johnson, G. B.: ref, 1789(729)
Johnson, G. E.: ref, 1498(5034), 2598(1293), 2621(218)
Johnson, G. F. S.: ref, 878(28)
Johnson, G. O.: test, 213, 1619

637

Johnson, H. H.: ref, 76(656), 681(72), 1498(5763)
Johnson, J.: ref, 374(211, 223), 872(17), 1771(569), 1823(32), 2618(14)
Johnson, J. A.: ref, 116(625), 354(1567, 1570), 2134(139, 140), 2318(1613)
Johnson, J. D.: ref, 1471(54), 2289(1748)
Johnson, J. E.: ref, 681(45, 72), 1498(5763, 5560)
Johnson, J. H.: ref, 645(6, 7, 8, 9, 15, 19, 20, 23, 24), 1498(5119, 5129, 5130, 5131, 5264, 5292, 5632, 5633), 1547(309), 1931(43, 48, 49), 2179(197, 198, 231, 238), 2620(10)
Johnson, J. I.: ref, 1126(762), 2472(23)
Johnson, J. P.: ref, 1851(19)
Johnson, K. A.: ref, 2598(1321)
Johnson, L.: ref, 1498(5090), 1904(54)
Johnson, L. D.: exc, 56
Johnson, L. S.: ref, 1063(106), 2294(118), 2297(10, 12)
Johnson, M. B.: test, 2639
Johnson, M. S.: rev, 1579
Johnson, N.: ref, 374(211, 223), 1789(695), 2618(14)
Johnson, O.: ref, 1485(82), 2598(1735)
Johnson, P.: ref, 501(791), 2134(125)
Johnson, P. J.: ref, 1257(160)
Johnson, P. O.: rev, 61, 497, 524, 2165
Johnson, R. A.: ref, 357(513, 515, 521, 522), 483(20, 24, 40, 41), 1272(133, 135, 141, 142), 1351(184, 195), 1479(374, 375), 1754(90, 103), 2260(36, 37, 50), 2289(1714, 1760), 2496(35, 38), 2512(571), 2598(1599, 1736), 2602(1908, 2057)
Johnson, R. C.: test, 1221; ref, 859(744), 1547(257)
Johnson, R. E.: test, 2220
Johnson, R. H.: test, 2396; ref, 995(139)
Johnson, R. P.: ref, 372(10)
Johnson, R. T.: rev, 167, 556, 557, 2164
Johnson, R. W.: rev, 658; exc, 2318; ref, 116(582), 1555(325), 1931(43), 2318(1533, 1555, 1556)
Johnson, S.: test, 568; ref, 794(422), 1153(7), 1789(695), 2300(385)
Johnson, S. A.: ref, 1547(279), 2300(384)
Johnson, S. B.: ref, 2353(35)
Johnson, S. C.: ref, 2618(14)
Johnson, S. M.: ref, 932(55), 2343(1051), 2585(2)
Johnson, S. O.: test, 2182, 2183, 2184, 2185, 2186, 2187, 2188, 2189, 2190, 2191, 2192, 2193
Johnson, V. M.: ref, 1371(260), 1769(89), 2289(1761)
Johnson, W.: test, 911
Johnston, C. W.: ref, 1771(785)
Johnston, D. R.: ref, 1771(687)
Johnston, D. W.: ref, 883(109)
Johnston, G. S.: ref, 1508(138)
Johnston, J. A.: rev, 2581; ref, 372(4), 2581(328)
Johnston, J. D.: ref, 501(794), 2474(2)
Johnston, M.: ref, 1547(258), 2300(355)
Johnston, R. P.: ref, 1771(547)
Johnstone, E. C.: ref, 1883(49, 63, 82, 84)
Johnstone, J.: ref, 2015(210)
Joiner, E. G.: ref, 1527(46), 2512(572)
Joint Council on Economic Education: test, 2440, 2463
Jolles, I.: test, 1047
Jones, A.: ref, 823(13), 1567(8)
Jones, B.: ref, 1063(110, 136)
Jones, B. D.: ref, 1099(69), 1923(16), 2208(1628), 2322(14)
Jones, B. M.: ref, 859(914), 1498(5634), 1914(845), 2179(239, 240)

Jones, C.: rev, 2036
Jones, C. O.: ref, 501(795)
Jones, D.: test, 1778; rev, 1009, 1513
Jones, D. L.: rev, 1837
Jones, E. E.: ref, 116(590), 794(392)
Jones, E. S.: rev, 2342
Jones, F. N.: rev, 185, 1252, 1752
Jones, F. R.: ref, 691(45)
Jones, H.: ref, 559(44), 2548(13)
Jones, H. E.: rev, 1531
Jones, H. J.: test, 1223
Jones, I. H.: ref, 1498(5457)
Jones, J. D.: test, 2104, 2157, 2448, 2541; ref, 1568(115), 1831(211)
Jones, J. E.: test, 1222; ref, 1498(5745), 2030(5059), 2491(2015, 2098)
Jones, J. G.: ref, 1498(5345), 2300(432)
Jones, J. J.: ref, 696(5), 1479(378), 2217(183)
Jones, J. R.: ref, 1789(651)
Jones, J. W.: test, 2277; ref, 1339(1, 2), 2277(1, 2, 3, 4, 5)
Jones, L.: ref, 1668(5)
Jones, L. K.: test, 1668; ref, 1668(1, 2, 3, 4), 2300(535), 2581(322, 323)
Jones, L. L.: ref, 1185(9)
Jones, L. V.: ref, 995(130)
Jones, M.: ref, 2665(1)
Jones, M. B.: ref, 1192(219)
Jones, M. G.: ref, 639(49)
Jones, M. K.: ref, 859(914), 1498(5634), 1914(845), 2179(239, 240)
Jones, M. T.: ref, 2620(19)
Jones, N. F.: test, 624; ref, 1498(5247, 5370, 5640, 5642)
Jones, P.: ref, 1485(77), 1498(5306), 1914(833), 2598(1691), 2607(191)
Jones, P. A.: ref, 1013(53)
Jones, R.: ref, 2657(104)
Jones, R. A.: rev, 2324
Jones, R. D.: ref, 1555(328), 2208(1619)
Jones, R. F.: ref, 1576(223)
Jones, R. H.: ref, 1831(166)
Jones, R. K.: ref, 121(12), 472(17), 653(166), 1538(71)
Jones, R. L.: rev, 493, 1637
Jones, R. N.: ref, 2629(99)
Jones, T.: ref, 1498(5321), 2620(12)
Jones, W. H.: ref, 157(138), 890(364), 2413(594)
Jones, W. J.: exc, 844
Jones, W. R.: rev, 1191, 2260
Jongsma, E.: ref, 932(109)
Jongsma, E. A.: ref, 1568(127), 2456(1)
Joost, M. G.: ref, 2602(1909), 2621(342)
Jordaan, J. P.: test, 371
Jordan, A. C.: test, 504
Jordan, B. T.: test, 1224
Jordan, F. L.: test, 2091
Jordan, L. S.: ref, 1771(610), 2412(38)
Jordan, T. E.: ref, 581(10), 1874(8), 2551(13), 2608(196)
Jordon, L.: ref, 1498(5645)
Jordon, L. S.: ref, 962(36), 1101(47), 1126(763), 1622(49), 1771(740), 2472(24), 2602(2058)
Jordon, P.: ref, 2665(1)
Jordon, T. E.: ref, 302(28), 1771(530), 1969(83)
Jordon, V. B.: ref, 2602(2059)

INDEX OF NAMES

Joreskog, K. G.: ref, 501(809, 841)
Jorgensen, C.: test, 1736, 1737, 2648
Jorgensen, G.: test, 2122
Jorgenson, D. O.: ref, 837(3)
Jorgenson, G. W.: ref, 704(7), 1007(15), 1769(45)
Jorm, A. F.: ref, 928(7), 1567(9), 1914(716)
Jorstad, H. L.: rev, 492, 979; ref, 1527(45)
Josefowitz, N.: ref, 2629(106)
Joseph, J.: test, 1225
Joslyn, D.: ref, 1462(133), 2607(161)
Joubert, C. E.: ref, 859(745, 797), 876(30)
Joyce, C. R. B.: ref, 859(903)
Juan, I. R.: ref, 1576(194), 2343(1030, 1032), 2366(191, 192)
Judd, L. L.: ref, 354(1404), 401(74), 1106(360, 361), 1247(162), 1460(51), 1498(5114, 5268), 1853(270), 1904(58, 59, 91, 113), 2598(1344, 1600, 1737)
Judd, T.: ref, 2598(1543)
Judd-Safian Associates: test, 1799
Julius, S.: ref, 1197(274), 2208(1529)
Jung, A. L.: ref, 280(1132), 283(154), 2598(1681), 2621(382)
Jungeblut, A.: ref, 501(929)
Jungwirth, E.: rev, 187
Juni, S.: ref, 665(51), 2030(5032, 5084, 5085, 5086)
Junkala, J.: ref, 701(80), 1371(258), 1540(19)
Junus, F.: ref, 1460(55), 1969(100), 2208(1616)
Juola, J. F.: ref, 1851(34), 2288(90), 2621(290)
Jurenec, G.: ref, 2602(2224)
Jurgensen, C. E.: rev, 2015, 2305, 2363, 2368, 2373, 2527, 2530
Jurko, M. F.: ref, 2607(137)
Jurkovic, G. J.: ref, 354(1495), 1126(695)
Jurs, S.: ref, 404(4)
Justen, J. E.: ref, 371(242), 1126(661), 2602(1644)
Justesen, D. R.: ref, 1498(5524), 2620(5, 15)
Justice, B.: ref, 677(1), 1498(5120, 5293, 5405)
Justman, J.: rev, 173
Jwaideh, A. R.: ref, 2602(2194)
Ka-Ro Research Group: test, 1235
Kaback, M. M.: ref, 1319(78)
Kachanoff, R.: ref, 280(1105), 1506(73), 2598(1574), 2607(175)
Kachel, D. W.: ref, 570(324)
Kaczmarek, M.: ref, 76(652)
Kaestner, E.: ref, 2208(1542), 2300(356)
Kafka, G. F.: ref, 76(620), 2208(1596)
Kafry, D.: ref, 384(4), 1300(115), 1914(738), 2553(1)
Kagan, D. M.: ref, 994(57), 1486(186)
Kagan, J.: ref, 794(393)
Kagan, S.: ref, 398(95, 96), 551(16), 582(4), 794(373), 2491(2101)
Kagel, S. A.: ref, 872(7)
Kagen, E.: ref, 280(1098), 1126(716, 744), 1270(77), 1479(339, 359)
Kagen, J.: ref, 2602(1775)
Kagen, S.: ref, 2598(1341)
Kagitcibasi, C.: ref, 964(497)
Kah, M. W.: ref, 2030(5049)
Kahane, J.: ref, 1960(77)
Kahle, J. B.: ref, 1754(118), 2512(659)
Kahn, A. M.: ref, 780(1700)
Kahn, H.: test, 2574
Kahn, M. W.: test, 624; ref, 653(152), 780(1709), 794(446), 1498(5753), 2148(3), 2413(695, 697), 2602(1906)
Kahn, P.: ref, 2602(2204)
Kahn, R.: ref, 2208(1568)
Kahn, T. C.: test, 1020, 1236, 1237
Kahnweiler, W.: ref, 2134(134)
Kail, R.: ref, 2269(465, 477)
Kail, R. V.: ref, 1473(154), 1754(77)
Kaiser, D. L.: ref, 1477(16), 1754(67), 2260(33)
Kaiser, H. E.: ref, 1192(170), 1831(124)
Kaiser, L.: ref, 2413(634)
Kales, A.: ref, 1498(5635, 5636, 5637)
Kales, J. D.: ref, 1498(5635, 5636, 5637)
Kalhorn, J.: test, 884
Kalin, M.: ref, 859(916), 2300(537)
Kalish, B. I.: test, 272
Kalish, R. A.: ref, 701(72), 1540(17)
Kalk, M.: ref, 1126(767), 2217(171)
Kalla, V.: ref, 1655(117)
Kallas, C.: ref, 1904(112)
Kallman, C.: ref, 932(128), 2602(2221)
Kallstrom, C.: test, 2665
Kalman, K. S.: test, 839
Kaloupek, D. G.: ref, 883(115), 1547(350)
Kaltreider, N. B.: ref, 1904(92)
Kaltsounis, B.: ref, 2512(573, 595, 617, 618)
Kalucy, R. S.: ref, 639(42)
Kameen, M. C.: ref, 2286(269)
Kamhi, A. G.: ref, 1319(85, 86)
Kamil, M. L.: ref, 932(118)
Kaminsky, B. P.: test, 1873, 2507, 2666
Kamm, K.: test, 2634, 2635; ref, 551(28), 2634(4)
Kammeier, M. L.: ref, 1498(5591)
Kammerer, B.: ref, 2289(1717)
Kamons, J.: test, 932, 933
Kamp, D. A.: test, 687
Kamp, J.: ref, 1498(5611, 5756)
Kamphaus, R. W.: ref, 1914(889), 2602(2195)
Kanas, N.: ref, 1922(17)
Kandaswamy, S.: ref, 1126(768), 2602(2076)
Kandefer, C.: ref, 2318(1562)
Kandil, S. A.: ref, 2512(596)
Kandler, H.: ref, 2366(195)
Kane, B. J.: ref, 2260(47), 2598(1738), 2602(2060)
Kane, J.: ref, 1655(116)
Kanekar, S.: ref, 1914(717)
Kangas, J.: ref, 1498(5205)
Kannarkat, J. P.: ref, 558(66)
Kanno, P. H.: ref, 859(821), 1498(5316, 5666)
Kanofsky, D. L.: ref, 270(63), 338(8), 1771(543), 2289(1615), 2557(214), 2602(1646), 2608(182)
Kanoy, K. W.: ref, 483(34), 1831(192)
Kanoy, R. C.: ref, 483(34), 1191(126), 1498(5391), 1831(192), 2300(448)
Kanter, N. J.: ref, 2300(474)
Kantner, J. E.: ref, 1798(285)
Kantor, D. R.: ref, 2602(1895)
Kantor, H. I.: ref, 859(798), 1904(72)
Kantor, N. J.: test, 478, 1780
Kantorowitz, D. A.: ref, 859(799)
Kapes, J. T.: ref, 1719(2), 2581(315)
Kaplan, A. S.: ref, 1498(5566)
Kaplan, E.: test, 308
Kaplan, M. N.: ref, 563(30)
Kaplan, M. S.: exc, 964

Kaplan, R.: ref, 2208(1641)
Kaplan, R. M.: ref, 2638(137)
Kaplan, S. J.: ref, 2598(1780)
Kaplan, S. L.: ref, 354(1496)
Kapoor, T. N.: ref, 859(863)
Kapp, K.: ref, 1831(172), 2602(1910)
Kappes, B. M.: ref, 2208(1620), 2300(536)
Kapur, M.: ref, 283(146), 1077(55)
Kapur, N.: ref, 794(374), 2598(1345)
Kapur, R. L.: ref, 2208(1621)
Karagan, N. J.: ref, 1101(48), 2602(2061)
Karam, E.: ref, 1498(5732)
Karan, D.: ref, 1126(750)
Karasu, T. B.: ref, 1531(278)
Karayanni, M.: ref, 374(224)
Karle, W.: ref, 859(800, 915), 1789(668, 713)
Karlin, R.: ref, 1063(118), 2294(136)
Karlin, R. A.: ref, 1063(104)
Karlsen, B.: test, 121, 2286, 2287, 2288, 2291, 2292
Karmos, A. H.: ref, 1197(298, 299), 1831(173), 2638(135, 136)
Karmos, J. S.: ref, 1197(299), 1250(22), 2638(136)
Karn, H. W.: rev, 802
Karnes, F. A.: ref, 2218(145), 2602(1911, 2062, 2063)
Karnes, L. R.: ref, 1479(349), 1871(3), 2218(146), 2602(1920)
Karnes, W. E.: ref, 1498(5621)
Karni, E.: ref, 2413(624)
Karoly, P.: ref, 872(5), 1498(5121), 1547(261)
Karp, S. A.: test, 398, 794, 1013
Karpf, R. J.: ref, 2460(11)
Karson, M.: ref, 609(222), 1460(56), 2208(1659)
Karweit, N.: ref, 551(66), 552(5)
Kasanin, J.: test, 1239
Kasbohm, M.: ref, 932(72)
Kasdon, L. M.: rev, 256, 957, 2292; exc, 2286
Kase, J. B.: ref, 2301(27)
Kashani, J.: ref, 1209(39), 2598(1651), 2602(1962)
Kashiwagi, K.: ref, 1479(365), 2598(1724), 2602(2049)
Kaskey, M.: ref, 1883(76), 2030(5072), 2598(1772)
Kass, I.: ref, 1498(5257, 5606)
Kass, M.: ref, 1498(5257), 1771(613)
Kass, W.: rev, 1830, 2384
Kassen, A.: ref, 609(229), 1498(5704)
Kassinove, H.: ref, 859(916, 919), 1229(95), 1547(330), 2300(537, 544), 2301(35), 2598(1746)
Kastin, A. J.: ref, 1655(75)
Kaszniak, A. W.: ref, 1771(769), 2607(180)
Kataguchi, Y.: test, 1235
Kates, L.: ref, 272(1)
Katkin, E. S.: rev, 562, 2300
Katkovsky, W.: rev, 1123
Katoff, L.: test, 1246; ref, 678(32), 1246(1), 1874(11), 2014(5), 2551(15), 2557(237)
Katz, A. N.: ref, 116(591), 157(148), 1257(141)
Katz, B.: ref, 2029(203, 229)
Katz, C.: ref, 2029(195)
Katz, E.: test, 1804
Katz, J.: test, 1255
Katz, L.: ref, 551(17)
Katz, L. G.: exc, 404
Katz, M.: rev, 1271; ref, 2030(4977), 2289(1790), 2602(2205)
Katz, M. M.: test, 1240
Katz, M. R.: rev, 374, 2318

Katz, N. W.: ref, 2294(129)
Katz, P. A.: test, 1241
Katz, R.: ref, 1508(117)
Katz, R. B.: ref, 551(67), 2217(180), 2641(21)
Katz–Garris, L.: ref, 6(70), 923(83), 1351(33)
Katzell, R. A.: rev, 627, 846, 940, 1750, 2015, 2051, 2054, 2267
Katzenmeyer, W. G.: ref, 1473(126), 1754(54)
Katzow, J. J.: ref, 1922(7)
Kauffman, C.: ref, 794(389), 2179(216), 2602(1754)
Kauffman, G. B.: exc, 64
Kauffman, J. M.: ref, 1272(131), 1341(168), 2286(287)
Kaufman, A. S.: rev, 292, 534; ref, 1126(696), 1424(31, 38, 39, 65, 68, 75, 84), 1914(889), 2289(1617, 1672, 1673, 1766), 2602(1632, 1653, 1912, 1983, 2100, 2195), 2608(183, 197, 238)
Kaufman, D.: ref, 280(1111), 1462(143), 1473(178), 1914(805)
Kaufman, D. M.: ref, 590(374)
Kaufman, D. W.: ref, 2289(1641, 1643)
Kaufman, H.: test, 1242
Kaufman, H. S.: ref, 371(243)
Kaufman, N. L.: ref, 1424(39, 68), 1473(200), 1479(366), 1914(889), 2602(2195)
Kaufman, P.: ref, 280(1111), 1462(143), 1473(178), 1914(805)
Kauk, R.: test, 1227, 1360
Kaulfers, W. V.: rev, 492, 514, 927, 979
Kausch, D. F.: ref, 1492(8)
Kausler, D. H.: ref, 2598(1635, 1739, 1831)
Kavale, K.: ref, 1101(41, 43), 2286(292), 2602(1650, 1769, 1901)
Kavanagh, J. A.: ref, 1170(240)
Kavanagh, M. J.: rev, 1972, 2354; ref, 354(1568)
Kavanagh, T.: ref, 1419(671, 680), 1498(5122, 5362)
Kavanaugh, P. B.: ref, 1933(16), 2620(9)
Kawa, T.: test, 2096
Kawamura–Reynolds, M.: ref, 2491(2016)
Kawash, G.: ref, 1538(70)
Kay, D. C.: ref, 113(27), 1498(5593), 1904(110)
Kay, E.: ref, 1789(669)
Kay, E. J.: ref, 116(560), 354(1452)
Kay, S. R.: ref, 6(71), 751(36), 964(479), 1655(78, 114), 1969(84, 111), 2557(215, 238), 2598(1601, 1602)
Kay, W. K.: ref, 859(944)
Kaya, E.: exc, 582, 590
Kaye, B. W.: ref, 890(337), 2587(38)
Kaye, D.: ref, 1292(54)
Kaye, D. B.: ref, 1771(542), 1914(714, 806, 867), 2289(1614), 2598(1781)
Kaye, K.: ref, 311(27)
Kaye, W.: ref, 2598(1867), 2607(220)
Kazanas, H. C.: ref, 374(225), 1726(351), 2413(654)
Kazandkian, A.: ref, 392(2)
Kazarian, S. S.: ref, 1197(277), 1547(259)
Kazdin, A. E.: ref, 860(123), 2602(2178)
Kazelskis, R.: ref, 1126(697)
Kazimour, K. K.: ref, 1473(219), 2387(7), 2602(2179)
Kazuk, E.: test, 676
Keane, S. P.: ref, 1498(5638)
Keane, T. M.: ref, 1547(329)
Kear–Colwell, J. J.: ref, 2607(138, 162, 200)
Kearns, P.: ref, 2512(613)
Keating, D. P.: ref, 1914(768, 769, 846), 2228(71)

Keating, T. J.: rev, 1914
Keats, J. A.: rev, 401, 732
Kedward, H. B.: ref, 1883(29)
Keech, V.: ref, 357(504), 1769(44), 2621(237)
Keefe, J. A.: ref, 157(151), 243(124)
Keefe, J. W.: ref, 590(371), 2132(2), 2160(52)
Keegan, D. L.: ref, 1498(5271), 2208(1575)
Keegan, J. F.: ref, 1498(5458, 5469)
Keeler, M. H.: ref, 1498(5459)
Keeley, S. M.: ref, 751(21), 2030(5017)
Keeling, B.: test, 2134; ref, 964(512), 1911(1), 1914(734), 2134(106, 137), 2208(1668), 2217(175)
Keenan, V.: ref, 1126(767), 2217(171)
Kegel–Flom, P.: rev, 1731; ref, 837(2), 2318(1534)
Kehle, T. J.: ref, 239(12, 15), 1769(54), 2217(126), 2289(1728), 2621(351)
Kehoe, P. T.: test, 1744
Keilty, J. W.: test, 2204, 2205
Keir, G. H.: exc, 1229
Keirn, W. C.: ref, 1498(5312)
Keiser, H.: ref, 1771(786)
Keiser, T. W.: ref, 2598(1740)
Keith, R. L.: ref, 1851(39)
Keith, T. Z.: ref, 1424(69)
Kellaghan, T.: rev, 1024, 2021; ref, 643(130), 972(10), 2269(466), 2289(1618)
Kellar, B.: test, 1945
Kellaway, D. S.: ref, 1405(6)
Keller, G. D.: test, 158, 901
Keller, H.: ref, 1914(735), 2512(581)
Keller, H. T.: ref, 1555(334)
Keller, J.: ref, 780(1680)
Keller, J. M.: ref, 2374(182)
Kellerman, H.: test, 796; ref, 796(34), 1758(11)
Kellerman, J.: ref, 2300(538, 577)
Kellett, J.: ref, 859(949)
Kellett, J. M.: ref, 1883(30)
Kelley, C.: ref, 1498(5294)
Kelley, C. K.: ref, 1498(5125, 5126, 5460, 5461, 5462, 5639), 2598(1349)
Kelley, I. B.: test, 1945
Kelley, P. L.: ref, 1789(642)
Kelley, T. L.: rev, 2269
Kelley, V. R.: ref, 1789(642)
Kellman, E.: test, 824
Kellner, R.: ref, 1419(687)
Kellogg, C. E.: test, 2013
Kellogg, L. L.: test, 2642
Kellogg, T. M.: ref, 932(64)
Kellow, W. F.: ref, 1576(208)
Kelly, B.: ref, 1568(138)
Kelly, D.: ref, 2641(12)
Kelly, D. H.: ref, 2288(79), 2412(35)
Kelly, E.: ref, 2366(199)
Kelly, E. L.: rev, 354, 1197, 1547, 1573, 1798
Kelly, F. D.: ref, 2134(114)
Kelly, I. W.: ref, 362(5), 363(13), 1969(117)
Kelly, J. A.: ref, 76(609), 116(561), 1798(239, 240)
Kelly, K.: ref, 1462(161), 2598(1850)
Kelly, M. J.: ref, 1498(5218), 2030(4976)
Kelly, M. P.: ref, 1771(594), 2289(1655), 2607(155)
Kelly, P.: ref, 609(203), 911(2)
Kelly, R. R.: ref, 1473(189), 1771(693, 694), 2286(324)
Kelly, S.: ref, 226(184)
Kelly, T. J.: ref, 2217(139), 2608(209)

Kelly, V.: ref, 2512(567)
Kelly, W. F.: ref, 1883(70)
Kelsey, E.: ref, 2602(2082)
Kelso, G. I.: ref, 202(6), 354(1534), 374(189), 2134(96, 122), 2581(332)
Kelter, S.: ref, 2213(4)
Keltikangas–Järvinen, L.: ref, 1498(5754), 2030(5087), 2491(2102)
Kemp, N. J.: ref, 941(32)
Kemp, T. G.: test, 1012
Kendall, A. J.: ref, 344(146)
Kendall, B. S.: test, 1462
Kendall, J. R.: ref, 1192(220), 1351(185), 1771(664), 2280(12)
Kendall, P. C.: ref, 354(1535, 1536), 1498(5295, 5322, 5585), 1771(548, 665), 1853(285, 295, 298), 1969(85), 2300(343, 381, 403, 404, 475), 2301(24, 26), 2598(1346), 2602(1654)
Kendall, R. E.: ref, 1883(83)
Kendall, W. E.: rev, 2055
Kendel, E. H.: test, 264
Kendell, R. E.: ref, 639(57, 60), 1485(86), 1883(30, 41, 79), 1914(870)
Kender, J. P.: ref, 2288(80)
Kendra, J. M.: ref, 2030(5033)
Kendrick, D.: ref, 1485(79)
Kendrick, D. C.: test, 1245; exc, 1853; ref, 1485(74, 75)
Kenis, I.: ref, 1295(292), 1508(125)
Kennard, D.: ref, 1498(5398, 5463), 2208(1597, 1622), 2598(1551)
Kennedy, E. C.: ref, 1789(643)
Kennedy, J. E.: rev, 1618, 2553, 2645
Kennedy, K. J.: ref, 1969(123)
Kennedy, P.: ref, 1923(18)
Kennedy, S. P.: ref, 1341(155)
Kennell, J.: ref, 212(4), 1622(42), 2598(1521)
Kennelly, K. J.: ref, 2179(247)
Kenney, M.: ref, 2218(8)
Kenney, R. K.: test, 1221
Kenny, D. T.: rev, 396
Kenny, F. T.: ref, 883(85), 1197(289)
Kenny, T. J.: ref, 280(1055, 1112)
Kent, G. H.: test, 1247; exc, 2289
Kent, R. N.: ref, 344(140)
Keogh, B. K.: rev, 484, 1224; ref, 552(4), 553(21)
Keogh, N. J.: ref, 1498(5700)
Kephart, N. C.: test, 1293, 1949; rev, 1371, 2243
Kepner, H. S.: test, 1248; ref, 573(16), 2286(339)
Kerasotes, D.: ref, 653(144)
Kerasotes, D. L.: ref, 1789(692)
Kerber, K. W.: ref, 354(1484), 2491(2056)
Kerby, M. L.: test, 1249
Kerckhoff, A. C.: ref, 1341(156)
Kerlin, M. A.: ref, 2585(3)
Kern, R. M.: ref, 357(507), 2585(4)
Kernaleguen, A.: ref, 1106(374), 2413(676)
Kernberg, O. F.: ref, 280(1104, 1167), 751(25, 41), 2030(5025, 5088), 2491(2103), 2598(1566, 1832)
Kerr, M.: ref, 2598(1639), 2602(1949)
Kerr, W. A.: test, 163, 736, 798; rev, 1986, 2628
Kershner, J. R.: ref, 361(3), 653(3), 934(3), 2621(343)
Kershner, K. M.: test, 653
Kertesz, A.: test, 2615; ref, 308(18), 1914(807, 868), 2015(204), 2598(1603), 2607(181)
Kerzner–Lipsky, D.: ref, 551(37), 2087(24), 2181(15)

Kesselman, G. A.: ref, 2614(23)
Kessen, W.: ref, 1576(224)
Kessler, C.: ref, 1655(81)
Kestenbaum, J. M.: ref, 2030(4998)
Ketcham, B.: ref, 1831(125)
Ketefian, S.: ref, 2594(206)
Ketron, J. L.: ref, 1073(129)
Kettelkamp, G. C.: rev, 493, 517, 1559
Kettering, R.: ref, 665(45)
Kew, C. E.: test, 1023
Keystone View: test, 1251, 1252
Khajavi, A. F.: ref, 1931(41)
Khamnee, A. K.: ref, 1655(123)
Khan, J. A.: ref, 1789(708, 724)
Khan, M. A.: ref, 1197(281), 1498(5182), 1547(267)
Khanna, P.: ref, 1547(334), 2030(5075), 2598(1752)
Khantzian, E. J.: ref, 1923(20)
Khatena, J.: test, 1253, 2496; ref, 1253(1, 2), 2199(6)
Khavari, K. A.: ref, 859(746, 789), 1498(5223, 5224, 5435)
Khayyer, M.: ref, 2602(1913)
Khoka, E. W.: ref, 678(14)
Khouri, P. J.: ref, 1498(5449)
Kibby, M. W.: ref, 932(116), 1007(38), 1771(549, 767), 2218(19), 2289(1619), 2602(1655)
Kicklighter, R. H.: test, 395
Kidd, A. H.: ref, 354(1539), 780(1701)
Kidd, N. V.: ref, 1789(670)
Kidd, R. M.: ref, 780(1701)
Kidd, R. V.: ref, 859(761), 1197(280), 1498(5180)
Kidwell, J. C.: ref, 1557(7), 2217(115), 2602(1667)
Kieffer, D. M.: ref, 1769(58)
Kieffer, L. F.: ref, 2301(22)
Kielhofner, G.: ref, 1356(98)
Kier, R. J.: ref, 1771(550)
Kieren, T. E.: rev, 1418
Kierscht, M. S.: ref, 701(63), 1771(666), 2289(1715)
Kiesler, D. J.: test, 1130; ref, 1130(1)
Kiesling, H.: ref, 344(141)
Kietzman, M. L.: ref, 645(14)
Kihlstrom, J. F.: ref, 1063(85, 95), 1798(237)
Kikel, S.: ref, 2598(1357)
Kikuchi, A.: ref, 2354(34), 2366(194)
Kilander, H. F.: test, 1150, 1151, 1254, 1657
Kilbride, P. L.: ref, 270(138)
Kilgore, J. H.: test, 1898
Killan, J. B.: ref, 2289(1674), 2602(1776)
Killian, G. A.: ref, 270(106), 1492(7), 1771(643), 2289(1702), 2598(1569)
Kilmann, P. R.: ref, 392(4), 400(128), 551(41), 552(3), 553(19), 1547(260), 2413(595)
Kilpatrick, D. G.: ref, 859(723), 1498(5042, 5537), 1904(50, 93, 127), 2100(5, 11), 2300(338, 476, 593)
Kilpatrick, J.: rev, 499, 1524
Kilpatrick-Tabak, B.: ref, 707(18)
Kim, P. Y.: ref, 76(590), 1510(43), 2463(7)
Kim, S. P.: ref, 2598(1347)
Kim, Y.: ref, 308(3), 1498(5044), 1948(95), 2113(237), 2598(1300), 2607(129)
Kim, Y. C.: ref, 590(389)
Kimball, H. C.: ref, 1498(5123)
Kimball, J. G.: ref, 280(1038), 751(5), 1771(551), 2244(28)
Kimball, W. H.: ref, 1547(303)
Kimbarow, M. L.: ref, 2621(279)
Kimbel, P.: ref, 1498(5566)
Kimlicka, T. M.: ref, 1547(285), 1789(671), 2029(204)
Kimmell, G. M.: test, 2105
Kimura, D.: ref, 1513(21)
Kimura, T.: ref, 590(385), 2160(71)
Kinard, E. M.: ref, 1831(193), 2031(460), 2393(12)
Kincaid, J. P.: ref, 934(4)
Kincel, R. L.: ref, 1498(5522)
Kincey, V. A.: ref, 859(860)
Kindelan, K. M.: ref, 2029(216)
Kinder, D. R.: ref, 501(857)
Kinder, E. F.: rev, 2557
King, D. C.: ref, 1300(117)
King, D. E.: test, 2622
King, D. J.: ref, 972(10), 1655(123), 2269(466)
King, D. R.: ref, 328(4), 400(133), 769(43), 772(27), 1934(8)
King, E.: ref, 2413(652)
King, E. H.: ref, 354(1453), 579(2)
King, E. M.: test, 363
King, G. D.: rev, 1498; ref, 354(1430), 681(33), 1498(5124, 5125, 5126, 5294, 5460, 5461, 5462, 5639), 2300(405), 2598(1348, 1349)
King, H. A.: ref, 1351(29)
King, H. F.: ref, 1498(5127)
King, J. E.: test, 1219, 1468, 2266
King, J. W.: test, 1516, 1517, 1518
King, L. L.: ref, 1013(90)
King, M.: ref, 1789(696), 2413(653)
King, M. R.: test, 572, 2333
King, T.: ref, 6(72)
Kingerlee, P. E.: ref, 1655(105)
Kingsbury, G. G.: ref, 2602(2187), 2621(448)
Kingsley, R. F.: ref, 344(158), 2602(1819), 2621(305)
Kingston, A. J.: rev, 720, 934, 1993
Kinicki, A. J.: ref, 1296(174)
Kinjo, K.: ref, 2353(30)
Kinne, R. D.: ref, 2068(87)
Kinney, J. A. S.: ref, 1257(163)
Kinsbourne, M.: ref, 964(509), 2602(1622), 2621(233)
Kinsman, R. A.: ref, 1498(5247, 5370, 5433, 5597, 5640, 5641)
Kinter, M.: ref, 872(17)
Kintisch, L. S.: ref, 501(858)
Kinzer, J. R.: rev, 1356, 1506
Kipp, D. J.: ref, 1789(697)
Kipper, D. A.: ref, 665(49), 859(747, 801), 1237(92), 1914(718), 2353(29)
Kirby, E. A.: ref, 1831(189)
Kirby, J. R.: ref, 932(63), 1257(126), 1341(157, 175), 1462(120, 134), 1914(719, 770, 771), 2269(456, 457)
Kirchmeimer, J.: ref, 691(43), 766(26), 1351(186), 2644(3)
Kirchner, G. L.: ref, 2289(1757)
Kirchner, W. K.: rev, 1300
Kiresuk, T. J.: ref, 677(2)
Kirk, B. A.: rev, 1269, 2318
Kirk, C.: ref, 2602(1914)
Kirk, K. W.: ref, 2318(1555)
Kirk, S. A.: test, 1126; ref, 1126(663, 680, 698)
Kirk, W. D.: test, 1126; ref, 1126(698)
Kirkendall, A.: ref, 1771(616), 1969(93), 2598(1493)
Kirkendall, L. A.: test, 2174
Kirker, W. S.: ref, 1798(219)

INDEX OF NAMES

Kirkham, R. W.: ref, 1419(707)
Kirkland, K.: ref, 781(3, 4), 1754(104)
Kirkpatrick, D. L.: test, 2356, 2358, 2359, 2361
Kirkpatrick, M.: ref, 1106(381), 1117(444), 2602(2180)
Kirnan, J. P.: ref, 994(58), 1486(188)
Kirsch, I.: ref, 1007(18), 2217(116)
Kirschenbaum, D. S.: ref, 1547(261), 2374(199)
Kirton, M.: ref, 157(139), 354(1405, 1407), 794(394), 859(748, 802), 860(110), 2015(202), 2269(458), 2629(101)
Kirton, M. J.: ref, 354(1406), 2629(100, 107)
Kish, G. B.: ref, 780(1649), 1462(152), 1498(5128), 2208(1543), 2598(1741)
Kisker, C. T.: ref, 2289(1693), 2602(1853), 2621(314)
Kissinger, J. F.: ref, 1013(126), 1257(180)
Kitay, P. M.: rev, 280, 751, 1353
Kitchell, M.: ref, 2289(1644, 1693), 2602(1853), 2621(314)
Kitwood, T.: rev, 2029
Kiulighan, D. M.: ref, 374(226), 2581(346)
Kiyak, H. A.: ref, 1671(46)
Kjaerby, O.: ref, 2598(1537)
Kjeldergaard, P. M.: rev, 1726
Klaiber, E. L.: ref, 794(444), 2598(1817)
Klane, L. T.: ref, 1462(161), 2598(1850)
Klapper, Z. S.: test, 1926
Klare, G. R.: ref, 1568(133)
Klarreich, S. H.: ref, 890(365), 2413(698)
Klass, D. B.: ref, 2587(34)
Klassen, D.: ref, 681(32, 61)
Klaus, M.: ref, 212(4), 1622(42), 2598(1521)
Klaus, M. H.: ref, 270(69), 2289(1629)
Klawans, H. L.: ref, 1771(769)
Klebanoff, M. A.: ref, 381(72), 1101(49), 2602(2064)
Kleber, H.: ref, 2100(12)
Kleber, H. D.: ref, 1883(89)
Klee, S. H.: ref, 280(1090), 701(54), 2289(1596, 1683), 2602(1807), 2621(296)
Klee, T. M.: ref, 1622(52)
Kleeck, A. V.: ref, 212(9), 1126(764), 1622(50), 1771(741), 2472(25), 2557(239)
Kleeman, M.: ref, 1498(5092), 2318(1528), 2598(1332)
Kleiger, J. H.: ref, 1498(5433, 5642)
Kleiman, M. B.: ref, 2289(1657)
Klein, A.: ref, 1192(254), 1622(51), 2293(14)
Klein, A. E.: ref, 551(55), 701(47), 2107(6, 7, 8, 10), 2217(129), 2286(293, 294, 313, 314), 2293(9, 11, 12, 13)
Klein, D. F.: ref, 1240(52), 1655(116), 2602(1588)
Klein, F.: ref, 2537(553)
Klein, G. L.: ref, 1498(5244)
Klein, H. M.: ref, 354(1569)
Klein, I.: ref, 280(1097), 1053(72), 2030(5015), 2598(1542)
Klein, J.: ref, 890(346), 1498(5464)
Klein, J. R.: ref, 357(523), 1466(4), 1831(212)
Klein, K. L.: ref, 2318(1535, 1572)
Klein, M. I.: ref, 2413(614)
Klein, N.: ref, 1769(45)
Klein, P. S.: ref, 226(171), 958(49), 1101(45), 1126(729), 1771(667), 2602(1915), 2621(344)
Klein, R. E.: ref, 794(376), 2602(1770)
Klein, R. P.: ref, 270(117, 139), 311(30)
Klein, R. S.: test, 1562

Klein, S. P.: test, 220, 1133, 1577
Kleinke, D. J.: ref, 2286(332)
Kleinman, M.: ref, 1498(5755)
Kleinmuntz, B.: rev, 787, 1502, 2429, 2623
Klerman, G. L.: ref, 1419(670, 675, 684, 688), 1498(5108), 2598(1459)
Klett, C. J.: test, 1655
Kletzing, K.: ref, 2292(28)
Klich, R. J.: ref, 1622(43), 1771(625), 1814(6)
Klimek, R. J.: ref, 367(1), 374(233), 486(310), 2581(350)
Kline, D. W.: ref, 2598(1483)
Kline, G. E.: ref, 720(67)
Kline, M. V.: rev, 2294
Kline, P.: rev, 638, 860, 861; ref, 471(1), 639(55), 769(40, 41, 44, 45), 859(736, 749, 803, 804), 861(4), 1853(269), 2208(1534, 1544, 1581), 2491(2011), 2629(97)
Kline, W. E.: test, 301; rev, 414, 577, 1405
Klinedinst, J. K.: test, 1796
Kling, F.: test, 2493
Kling, J. O.: ref, 1073(121), 2598(1484)
Kling, J. S.: ref, 1498(5473)
Kling, M.: rev, 770, 1143
Klinge, V.: ref, 1771(598), 2598(1604), 2602(1739)
Klingler, D. E.: ref, 645(6, 7, 8, 9, 15, 19, 20, 24), 1498(5119, 5129, 5130, 5131, 5264, 5292, 5633), 2179(197, 198), 2620(10)
Klingner, A.: ref, 280(1105, 1116), 1506(73, 75), 2598(1574, 1624), 2607(175, 184)
Klintberg, I.: ref, 1576(202, 212)
Kljajíc, I.: ref, 283(139), 2598(1350)
Klockars, A. J.: ref, 1798(286)
Klonoff, H.: ref, 2289(1620), 2602(1656, 2020)
Klopfer, F.: ref, 859(750)
Klopfer, L. E.: test, 2467A
Klorman, R.: ref, 2301(32)
Klugh, H. E.: ref, 354(1458)
Klujber, L.: ref, 280(1139), 964(505), 2289(1753)
Klumb, R.: ref, 2634(4)
Knapp, G.: ref, 270(84)
Knapp, L.: test, 351; ref, 351(5, 6), 732(393), 1789(673), 2537(548, 554)
Knapp, R. R.: test, 351, 1419, 2476; rev, 1794; ref, 116(534), 351(5, 6), 732(393), 1758(12), 1789(640, 672, 673), 2537(548, 554)
Kneipp, S. A.: ref, 2579(1)
Knellinger, L. D.: ref, 1071(9)
Knickerbocker, B.: ref, 1789(644)
Knief, L.: ref, 653(142), 2269(455)
Knifong, J. D.: ref, 344(184), 551(56), 1192(241), 1473(201), 2286(333)
Knight, G. P.: ref, 2491(2101)
Knight, J.: test, 233
Knight, R. A.: ref, 963(129), 1919(45), 1933(17), 2179(241), 2620(18)
Knights, A.: ref, 1883(47, 50, 71, 85)
Knights, E. B.: ref, 941(18)
Kniker, C. R.: ref, 570(324)
Knobbe, T.: ref, 6(57), 2289(1716)
Knobloch, H.: test, 2014
Knoche, M.: ref, 28(3), 37(3), 45(5), 1269(27)
Knopf, I. J.: ref, 472(11), 643(132), 1046(572), 1498(5169), 2030(4964), 2208(1549), 2318(1542), 2491(2022), 2598(1373), 2621(255)

643

Knopke, H. J.: ref, 780(1687)
Knost, E. K.: ref, 1073(121), 2598(1484)
Knott, J. R.: ref, 859(805)
Knott, V. J.: ref, 859(864, 865)
Knouse, S. B.: ref, 2413(621)
Knowlton, W. A.: ref, 2638(145, 146)
Knox, A.: exc, 2412
Knox, A. W.: ref, 1851(23, 34)
Knox, B. J.: ref, 178(1), 2286(295), 2512(597)
Knox, D.: test, 1344, 1381
Knox, V. J.: ref, 1063(86)
Knox, W. J.: ref, 2300(539)
Knudson, K. H. M.: ref, 398(96)
Knudson, M. C.: ref, 2497(41)
Knudson, M. L.: ref, 1555(318)
Knudson, R. M.: ref, 483(39), 1013(117), 1257(174), 1914(871)
Knuth, A. S.: test, 2222
Knuth, W. E.: test, 1261
Knutson, J. F.: rev, 2030
Kobal, A.: test, 12, 13, 464, 1186, 1450
Kobasa, S. C.: ref, 1798(258)
Kobasigawa, A.: ref, 559(43)
Kobler, F. J.: ref, 1789(643, 704)
Kobos, J.: ref, 1798(274)
Kobos, J. C.: ref, 1498(5454, 5662, 5696), 1798(252, 260), 2598(1294)
Kobrick, J. L.: ref, 878(31)
Koch, C.: test, 2522
Koch, C. C.: exc, 767
Koch, J. L.: ref, 2369(14)
Kochansky, G. E.: ref, 2491(2017)
Kocsis, J.: ref, 2607(190)
Kodman, F.: ref, 280(1168)
Koebernick, L. F.: ref, 1547(252)
Koegel, R. L.: ref, 1319(83), 1771(815), 2472(33)
Koehler, G.: ref, 780(1702)
Koenig, C. H.: test, 480, 1973
Koenig, C. R.: ref, 2(2), 1831(140)
Koenig, G. R.: ref, 2587(39)
Koenig, K. P.: ref, 859(828)
Koenke, K.: ref, 226(165), 2105(2), 2425(2)
Koepke, T.: ref, 2602(1818)
Koerner, B. L.: ref, 1296(180)
Koff, E.: ref, 280(1039), 751(12), 2289(1717), 2602(1657)
Kogan, K. B.: ref, 1547(287), 1931(47)
Kogan, K. L.: rev, 963, 1239, 2607; ref, 1387(14)
Kogan, W. S.: rev, 1239
Koh, S. D.: ref, 1498(5132, 5296, 5643), 2598(1351)
Kohaut, S. M.: ref, 2366(190), 2370(15)
Kohlbeg, L.: exc, 559
Kohlberg, L.: test, 1262; ref, 1262(2)
Kohler, A.: ref, 2629(116)
Kohlhepp, K. A.: ref, 2155(13)
Kohn, M.: test, 1263, 1264
Kohn, M. L.: ref, 751(13, 15), 794(395, 402)
Kohn, P. M.: ref, 2629(108)
Kohout, L. J.: ref, 1547(317)
Kohs, S. C.: test, 1265
Kohutek, K.: ref, 1498(5399)
Kojima, H.: ref, 2602(1777), 2608(198)
Kok, L. P.: ref, 859(778), 1498(5212)
Kokes, R. F.: ref, 1240(57, 65), 1883(38, 58, 68), 2598(1721, 1829)

Kokosh, J.: ref, 1498(5297)
Kolata, G. B.: ref, 501(893), 1192(242)
Kolbe, L. J.: ref, 609(211)
Kolen, M.: ref, 1193(148)
Kolff, C.: ref, 1831(190)
Koller, H.: ref, 2289(1790), 2602(2205)
Koller, J. R.: ref, 868(4)
Koller, R.: ref, 1498(5092), 2318(1528), 2598(1332)
Kolloff, M. B.: ref, 1831(207)
Kolodny, E. H.: ref, 2289(1679), 2557(223)
Konanc, J.: ref, 1498(5167)
Konanc, J. T.: ref, 2030(5037), 2620(14)
Kondo, C. Y.: ref, 859(805), 1798(241)
Konigsberg, R.: ref, 121(11), 2477(3)
Konstadt, N.: test, 398
Konstantareas, M. M.: ref, 1126(730), 2018(14), 2289(1718)
Koocher, G. P.: ref, 2557(240), 2598(1742), 2602(2065)
Koopman, P. R.: exc, 590
Koops, B.: ref, 270(126), 338(10)
Koorland, M. A.: ref, 2391(1)
Kootz, J. P.: ref, 1771(787), 2602(2181)
Kopel, D.: rev, 2284
Kopell, B. S.: ref, 152(12), 2598(1498)
Kopp, C. B.: ref, 678(14)
Köppen, S.: ref, 2030(4983)
Koppitz, E. M.: test, 280, 2560; ref, 280(1169), 2560(1, 2), 2621(445)
Koran, J. J.: ref, 1257(164, 165)
Koran, M. L.: ref, 1257(164, 165)
Korboot, P. J.: ref, 2598(1352)
Korchin, S. J.: ref, 1419(670), 1498(5108)
Korer, J.: ref, 1883(32)
Kores, J. R.: ref, 1883(44)
Korman, A. K.: rev, 1364, 2351
Korman, M.: ref, 2598(1833), 2621(446)
Korn, J. H.: ref, 2029(236)
Kornblith, S. J.: ref, 1498(5512)
Kornse, D. D.: ref, 200(18), 1771(788)
Korsager, S.: ref, 1319(81), 2598(1605)
Koschier, M.: test, 370
Kosinski, S. C.: ref, 344(170), 551(43)
Kosmoski, G. J.: ref, 1192(200), 1831(141)
Koss, M. P.: ref, 1498(5032)
Kosuth, T.: test, 1820
Kotenko, V.: ref, 1567(18), 2598(1719)
Kotzker, E.: ref, 116(571)
Koulack, D.: ref, 794(396), 1498(5298, 5697)
Koun, S.: ref, 859(943)
Kovacs, M.: ref, 859(950)
Kowalski, J.: ref, 681(72), 1498(5763)
Kowalski, R.: test, 933
Kowalski, R. L.: test, 932
Koziol, S. M.: rev, 1277, 2478, 2479
Kozup, J. M.: ref, 961(3)
Kraaimaat, F. W.: ref, 883(95)
Kraemer, R.: ref, 2208(1642)
Krafchuk, E. E.: ref, 270(97), 311(29)
Kraft, M. A.: test, 177
Krajkovich, J. G.: ref, 551(47), 2181(17)
Kralik, P.: ref, 2300(481)
Krall, V.: ref, 2289(1687), 2602(1814, 2066), 2608(206)
Kramer, F. D.: test, 2516

INDEX OF NAMES

Kramer, J.: ref, 2286(322), 2621(362)
Kramer, J. J.: ref, 1771(789)
Kramer, M.: ref, 1789(715), 2413(678)
Kramer, M. S.: ref, 1424(70), 1771(742)
Kramer, R.: ref, 1424(67), 1823(33), 2602(1905)
Kramer, T. J.: ref, 2208(1680), 2370(19)
Krane, W. R.: ref, 1798(245)
Kraner, R. E.: test, 1266
Krantz, D. S.: test, 1267; ref, 226(178, 184), 1267(1), 1498(5644)
Kranz, P. L.: ref, 2413(699), 2602(2185)
Kraska, M. F.: ref, 374(225)
Krasnoff, A.: ref, 1498(5133)
Krasnoff, A. G.: ref, 116(575)
Kratochwill, T. R.: ref, 273(1), 2602(1677)
Kraude, W. H.: ref, 1498(5759)
Krause, J. B.: ref, 2134(117)
Krauskopf, C. J.: rev, 296, 2318, 2575
Krauss, D. R.: ref, 859(880), 1789(702)
Krauss, H. H.: ref, 1197(292), 1789(689)
Krauss, I. K.: ref, 2269(478)
Krauthamer, C.: ref, 1387(15), 1498(5465), 1537(1)
Krawchick, F. B.: test, 2529
Krefft, K.: ref, 1197(294), 1198(1)
Kregor, E.: ref, 2030(5065)
Kreitler, H.: ref, 1197(320)
Kreitler, S.: ref, 1197(320)
Kress, G. C.: ref, 501(927), 673(52), 1779(2)
Kress, R. A.: rev, 1459, 1871, 2016, 2202
Kreth, E.: ref, 1922(17)
Krichev, A.: rev, 1287; exc, 169, 776, 1224, 1424, 1540; ref, 635(1), 2032(1), 2285(9)
Krickev, A.: exc, 2285
Kricos, P. B.: ref, 302(41)
Kriedt, P. H.: rev, 637, 2194
Krieger, J.: ref, 1063(108), 1789(703)
Krieger, K. M.: ref, 621(6)
Kriel, R. L.: ref, 1769(56), 2598(1482)
Kriewall, M. A.: ref, 501(916)
Krishnappa, U.: ref, 1197(293), 1419(686)
Kristjansson, I.: ref, 860(92)
Kritzinger, L. J. R.: test, 2071, 2072, 2074, 2075
Kroeger, E.: ref, 1914(772)
Kroeker, L.: ref, 116(527)
Kroeker, L. P.: ref, 1896(9)
Krohn, A.: test, 2510
Krohn, E. J.: ref, 678(28), 701(64), 964(498), 1424(48), 2289(1719)
Kroll, B. M.: ref, 76(607, 641), 1191(123), 1510(44)
Kroman, L. J.: ref, 1909(1)
Kronenberger, E. J.: ref, 2598(1571), 2602(1876)
Kronsberg, S.: ref, 1875(6)
Krotinger, H.: ref, 859(870)
Krouse, H. J.: ref, 2037(154)
Krouse, J. H.: ref, 2037(154)
Krout, J.: test, 1790, 2381
Krout, M. H.: test, 1179, 1790
Krug, D. A.: test, 234
Krug, S.: test, 1198
Krug, S. E.: test, 472, 854, 1197, 2087; ref, 472(10), 1233(226), 2208(1582)
Kruger, S. J. P.: test, 153, 1416, 2073
Krugman, M.: rev, 1047, 1480, 1531, 2030; exc, 2289
Krumboltz, J. D.: rev, 1818
Krygier, K. M.: ref, 378(12), 2472(18)

Krynicki, V. E.: ref, 280(1078), 2602(1778, 1916)
Krywaniuk, L. W.: ref, 1462(115), 1914(700), 2319(1), 2602(1586, 1773)
Krznaric, S.: ref, 1498(5163)
Kubey, R. W.: ref, 501(859)
Kucala, T.: ref, 2179(221), 2598(1545)
Kuch, R. J.: ref, 960(13)
Küchmann, D.: test, 641
Kuczaj, S. A.: ref, 1771(668)
Kuder, F.: test, 1271; rev, 1755
Kuder, G. F.: test, 372, 1269, 1270; rev, 689
Kuehner, K. J.: test, 1083, 1093
Kuh, G. D.: ref, 1726(352, 367)
Kuhlenschmidt, S. L.: ref, 859(938), 2300(567)
Kuhlman, T. L.: ref, 751(27)
Kuhlman-Harrison, J.: ref, 372(7)
Kuhlmann, F.: test, 1272
Kuhns, J. W.: test, 1571
Kuiken, D.: ref, 1789(714)
Kuiper, N. A.: ref, 681(37), 1798(219, 259, 267), 2607(216)
Kuiper, S.: ref, 2657(102, 103, 109)
Kuipers, A. C. M.: ref, 883(84)
Kuipers, L.: ref, 1883(91)
Kujoth, R. K.: ref, 1547(262, 263)
Kukuk, S. E.: ref, 353(3)
Kuldau, J. M.: ref, 1498(5134)
Kumar, K.: ref, 1655(115)
Kumar, P.: ref, 1914(773)
Kumar, R.: ref, 860(146)
Kumar, S.: ref, 1462(121)
Kumar, V. K.: ref, 1769(45)
Kunce, J. T.: ref, 1498(5406), 2300(341), 2602(1917)
Kuncel, R. B.: ref, 1798(209, 210)
Kundert, D. K.: ref, 280(1161, 1162), 1126(778, 779), 2602(2168, 2169)
Kundu, R.: test, 1273; ref, 859(751)
Kunze, K. R.: test, 12, 13, 464, 1186, 1450
Kunze, L. H.: test, 228
Kunzelmann, H. P.: test, 480, 1973
Kuo, Y. Y.: ref, 2512(619)
Kuperman, S. K.: ref, 1498(5466, 5467)
Kupfer, D. J.: ref, 1576(203)
Kupietz, S.: ref, 701(85), 703(10), 704(20), 1126(775), 1331(41), 1473(211), 1923(25), 2293(16), 2602(2146)
Kupietz, S. S.: ref, 1769(59), 2034(4)
Kupke, T.: ref, 1498(5470), 2598(1606), 2621(345)
Kupperman, P.: ref, 896(4)
Kuppuswamy, B.: test, 2236
Kurdek, L. A.: ref, 1796(4), 1914(774, 808, 847)
Kurdesk, L. A.: ref, 1914(720)
Kurfman, D. G.: rev, 159, 1103, 1104
Kurland, A. A.: ref, 1498(5099)
Kurlinski, J.: ref, 270(119), 2289(1724)
Kurlychek, R. T.: ref, 1498(5645)
Kurth, R. J.: ref, 2292(27)
Kurtines, W. M.: ref, 354(1454, 1455), 1923(29)
Kurtz, A. K.: rev, 1804, 1805, 2190, 2269, 2355, 2653
Kurtz, R. M.: ref, 2030(4999)
Kurtzman, H.: ref, 131(1)
Kusumo, K. S.: ref, 1485(60)
Kutie, R. C.: ref, 1508(118), 1855(20)
Kvaraceus, W. C.: rev, 2315
Kvashny, A.: ref, 2512(598)

Kwalwasser, J.: test, 1274, 1275
Kwawer, J. S.: ref, 2030(4959, 5034)
Kwiatkowski, J.: ref, 859(768)
Kyle, E. M.: test, 1130; ref, 1130(1)
Kyte, N. S.: ref, 995(144), 2300(470)
LaBarre, R.: ref, 342(4)
Labeck, L.: ref, 1498(5252), 1655(91)
La Berteaux, P. J.: ref, 872(8)
Labouvie–Vief, G.: ref, 2269(439)
Labrentz, E. L.: ref, 1192(163), 1473(123)
Lacefield, W.: ref, 1953(13)
Lachar, D.: test, 1796; ref, 1498(5273, 5299, 5458, 5468, 5469, 5470, 5471, 5472), 1796(1, 2, 3)
Lachman, J. L.: ref, 2598(1607)
Lachman, R.: ref, 2598(1607)
Lachman, S. J.: test, 1861, 2136, 2154
Lachterman, T.: ref, 1424(58), 2602(1960), 2608(219)
Lackey, J. E.: test, 926
Lacks, P. B.: ref, 280(1145)
Lacoursiere, R. B.: ref, 2598(1398)
LaCroix, H.: ref, 2046(2)
Lacy, W. B.: ref, 1726(361)
Ladawan, T.: ref, 1366(1)
Ladd, E. M.: rev, 16
Lader, M.: ref, 2300(466)
Laderberg, C. M.: ref, 226(183), 962(37)
Lado, R.: test, 2426, 2427; rev, 1000, 1523
Lafayette, A. D.: ref, 2602(2142)
Lafayette, R. H.: ref, 1814(5), 2602(1797)
Lafferty, J. C.: test, 1441, 2090
Laffey, J. L.: test, 1859; ref, 2292(21), 2641(12)
Lafky, J. D.: test, 1525
LaForge, R.: test, 1170
Lagotic, D. L.: ref, 309(8)
LaGreca, A. M.: ref, 2030(5064), 2512(648)
Lah, M. I.: ref, 2037(155)
Lahey, B. B.: ref, 719(28), 2602(1606)
Lahmer, V.: ref, 2602(2113)
Lahr, D.: ref, 588(9), 2288(82)
Laing, J.: ref, 1270(78)
Lair, C. V.: ref, 2602(1783), 2621(291)
Laird, J. D.: ref, 794(369)
Laird, J. T.: test, 1503
Laker, D. R.: ref, 1295(283)
Lalani, S.: ref, 883(85), 1197(289)
Lam, C. T.: ref, 1498(5256), 2598(1454)
Lam, D. J.: ref, 2608(179)
Lamarre, P. A.: ref, 302(29)
Lamb, D.: ref, 1547(275), 2300(406)
Lamb, D. H.: ref, 2300(540)
Lamb, M. E.: ref, 1771(810)
Lamb, M. M.: exc, 357
Lamb, P.: ref, 1192(221)
Lamb, R. R.: ref, 76(629, 632, 642)
Lambeet, L.: ref, 321(43)
Lambert, C.: ref, 859(949)
Lambert, M. J.: ref, 1789(674), 2413(622)
Lambert, N.: test, 6
Lambert, N. M.: test, 1902; ref, 6(88), 280(1170), 553(22), 582(5), 2030(5089), 2287(38), 2288(88), 2602(2182)
Lambert, W. E.: ref, 1771(606), 1914(758), 2015(205)
Lamberti, J. W.: ref, 2168(10)
Lamberts, F.: ref, 1622(39), 1771(611), 2159(1)
Lambourne, R. D.: ref, 149(13)

Lambrecht, J. J.: ref, 570(325)
Lamiell–Landy, A.: ref, 1300(116)
Lamke, T. A.: test, 1073; rev, 2162
Lamont, J.: ref, 1197(297)
Lamont, L. M.: ref, 1798(211), 2208(1545)
La Morto–Corse, A.: ref, 1004(1), 2289(1710), 2621(336)
Lamp, R.: ref, 1874(10), 2217(127)
Lamprecht, M. J.: ref, 1769(75), 2602(1941)
Lancaster, D.: ref, 883(77)
Lancaster, D. W.: ref, 116(567)
Lancee, W.: ref, 941(46), 2208(1687)
Land, V. C.: test, 825
Landa, B.: ref, 1424(61, 62), 1969(108)
Landauer, S. P.: ref, 116(532)
Lander, H.: ref, 701(68), 751(33), 2030(5041, 5047), 2491(2065, 2073), 2602(1958, 1992)
Landers, D. M.: ref, 501(827)
Landig, H.: ref, 2289(1675)
Landis, D.: rev, 1949
Landis, R. E.: ref, 606(19), 2594(207)
Landman, J. T.: test, 2473; ref, 2224(9), 2473(1)
Landreneau, E.: ref, 2512(599, 612)
Landrum, G. C.: ref, 883(108), 1498(5623)
Landry, H. A.: rev, 1751
Landsman, M.: test, 850
Landy, F. J.: rev, 565, 1299; ref, 1300(116)
Lane, B.: test, 568
Lane, J. B.: ref, 1498(5472)
Lane, M. K.: ref, 2598(1441)
Lane, M. S.: ref, 1576(194)
Lane, P. J.: ref, 1498(5473)
Lane, S.: test, 1525
Lane, V. W.: ref, 1851(43), 2646(11)
Lang, A. R.: ref, 859(917), 2300(541)
Lang, C.: ref, 1077(79), 1914(886)
Lang, E.: ref, 2030(5007), 2598(1520)
Lang, G.: test, 50
Lang, M.: test, 397
Lang, P. J.: test, 883; ref, 883(90)
Lang, R. J.: ref, 859(752, 806), 1498(5135), 1655(94), 1914(791), 2413(596, 623), 2598(1353, 1485, 1540), 2607(172)
Lang, V. R.: test, 854
Lange, G.: ref, 398(113)
Lange, J. D.: ref, 794(401), 1789(676)
Langendoerfer, S.: ref, 270(140), 311(37)
Langer, G. B.: ref, 354(1577), 917(77)
Langeveld, M. J.: test, 535
Langevin, R.: ref, 2208(1583), 2289(1676), 2598(1486)
Langhorne, J. E.: ref, 280(1113), 2602(1918)
Langley, M. B.: test, 693
Langlie, T. A.: rev, 1716
Langlois, A.: ref, 2017(2)
Langmeyer, D.: ref, 2413(631)
Langmuir, C. R.: test, 1808; rev, 1337, 1530
Langner, H.: ref, 2602(1961)
Langston, J. W.: ref, 1052(4), 1771(768), 2602(2145), 2621(427)
Languis, M. L.: ref, 2269(473), 2602(2000, 2158)
Lannholm, G. V.: rev, 844
Lansdell, H.: ref, 2598(1354)
Lansdown, R.: exc, 2490; ref, 330(16), 1424(30), 2602(1633), 2608(175)
Lansky, L. M.: ref, 501(905)

INDEX OF NAMES

Lansky, S. B.: ref, 874(50), 1831(162), 2491(2054)
Lantz, J. B.: ref, 1498(5723), 2413(689)
Lányi–Englemayer, A.: ref, 280(1139), 964(505), 2289(1753)
Lanyon, B.: test, 1132
Lanyon, R. I.: test, 1931; rev, 384, 542, 859, 1197; ref, 681(66), 1498(5136), 1931(44, 56)
Laosa, L. M.: ref, 398(115, 119), 794(434), 1117(443), 2598(1743), 2602(2067)
Lapidus, D. R.: ref, 794(393), 2602(1775)
Lapidus, L. B.: ref, 559(46), 2030(5093), 2598(1392)
Lapierre, Y. D.: ref, 859(807), 1240(55), 1498(5300), 1655(121)
Lapine, L.: ref, 780(1667)
Lapoint, C.: ref, 308(5), 1126(681), 1513(23), 1622(35)
LaPointe, C.: ref, 691(31)
LaPorte, D. J.: ref, 1419(704), 2179(255)
Lappan, G.: rev, 2291
Lappan, P. A.: rev, 154, 428, 499
Lapsley, D. K.: ref, 1914(809), 2629(115)
Larcen, S. W.: ref, 1341(176)
Largen, J.: ref, 1573(40), 1904(94)
Larned, D. T.: ref, 551(42), 1896(13)
Larner, S.: ref, 1485(61), 2598(1355)
Larocco, J. M.: ref, 932(104), 1914(830)
LaRossa, M. M.: ref, 270(131), 311(34)
Larrabee, P. E.: ref, 691(45)
Larrivee, B.: ref, 704(13, 17)
Larsen, J. A.: ref, 2413(677)
Larsen, S. C.: test, 2422, 2466
Larsen, W. W.: ref, 1914(848)
Larson, B. A.: ref, 701(48), 1949(58), 2217(130)
Larson, C. H.: test, 166, 822
Larson, D. G.: ref, 2030(5092)
Larson, D. W.: ref, 1498(5695)
Larson, G. L.: ref, 280(1025, 1106, 1137), 1754(55, 100), 2214(2), 2602(1883)
Larson, J. C.: ref, 1473(162, 182), 1914(782, 819)
Larson, J. R.: ref, 1295(287)
Larson, P. C.: ref, 2413(693)
Larson, W. S.: rev, 987, 1275, 1644, 2113, 2631
Larsons, P. F.: ref, 1655(75)
LaRusso, L.: ref, 1969(92)
Lasaga, M. I.: ref, 1969(110)
Las Cruces Public Schools: test, 2444
Lasky, E. Z.: ref, 302(41)
Lasky, R.: ref, 794(376)
Latcham, R.: ref, 2598(1487)
Latham, W. L.: ref, 2585(3)
Lathey, J. W.: ref, 235(10)
LaTorre, A.: rev, 2602(2183)
LaTorre, R. A.: ref, 751(6), 794(397, 423), 1498(5474), 2602(2183)
Latta, R. M.: ref, 1510(45)
Latus, G.: ref, 1233(230)
Lau, S.: ref, 818(6), 1077(80)
Laudeman, K. A.: ref, 2581(316)
Lauer, J. B.: ref, 1498(5723), 2413(689)
Lauer, L. W.: test, 2297
Lauerman, R.: ref, 859(917), 2300(541)
Laufer, W. S.: ref, 354(1570), 2581(340)
Laughlin, J. E.: test, 1198; ref, 400(128), 472(10), 551(41), 552(3), 553(19)
Laughlin, J. S.: test, 817
Laughlin, S. A.: ref, 308(10)

Laughren, T. P.: ref, 1904(73)
Laughton, J.: ref, 2512(620)
Laurence, K. M.: ref, 2602(1685)
Laurent, H.: test, 1807
Laurin–Dumas, M. S.: ref, 2537(561)
Laurita, R. E.: test, 1290
Laursen, P.: ref, 2598(1537)
Laval, R. A.: ref, 392(4)
Lavallee, H.: ref, 342(4)
Lave, C.: ref, 2269(470), 2598(1646)
LaVeck, B.: ref, 270(68, 141), 311(38), 1108(10), 2159(3)
LaVeck, G. D.: ref, 270(68, 141), 311(38), 1108(10), 2159(3)
Lavender, A.: ref, 6(55)
Lavender, T.: ref, 6(87), 2598(1830)
LaVigne, G.: ref, 280(1053), 1503(62)
Lavine, S. B.: ref, 1126(699)
LaVoie, A. L.: rev, 1198, 2366
Lavrakas, P. J.: ref, 477(24), 653(153), 1419(689), 2489(8)
Law, J. G.: ref, 1969(124), 2598(1834)
Lawes, J. S.: rev, 1617, 2221
Lawler, A.: ref, 2413(688)
Lawlis, F. G.: ref, 472(13)
Lawlis, G. F.: ref, 280(1095), 1798(260), 2602(1825, 2068), 2621(309)
Lawlor, G.: exc, 302
Lawlor, M.: ref, 2208(1685)
Lawrence, B. E.: ref, 1547(288)
Lawrence, D. M.: ref, 794(435), 1498(5646)
Lawrence, R. E.: ref, 2579(1)
Lawrence, T.: test, 954
Lawriw, I.: ref, 2598(1488)
Law School Admission Services: test, 1292
Lawshe, C. H.: test, 111, 1293, 1936, 1937, 1940, 1942, 1944, 1946; rev, 1054, 1356
Lawson, A. E.: ref, 1013(54)
Lawson, R.: ref, 2029(222)
Lawton, J. T.: ref, 823(14, 17), 1771(612)
Laxar, K.: ref, 1054(7)
Layman, S.: ref, 878(30)
Layne, C.: ref, 859(808, 809, 883, 918), 1498(5301, 5663), 2030(5069)
Layne, F. M.: test, 1863
Layton, T. L.: ref, 1771(669, 790), 2557(245)
Layton, W. L.: test, 1510; rev, 351, 400, 502, 1043, 1080, 1745, 2160, 2308
Lazar, A. L.: ref, 2557(232)
Lazar, B.: ref, 2602(2066)
Lazar, B. S.: ref, 2289(1687), 2602(1814), 2608(206)
Lazar, Z.: ref, 2030(5039)
Lazerwitz, J. L.: ref, 344(168)
Lazzari, R.: ref, 116(552, 553, 562, 586), 282(144), 501(823), 707(17), 1914(761)
Leach, C.: ref, 941(17)
Leach, E. M.: test, 2460
Leach, G. C.: test, 1254
Leach, J. A.: ref, 374(207)
Leader, C.: ref, 859(962)
League, R.: test, 338
Leak, G. K.: ref, 294(14, 15), 354(1537, 1540), 1498(5660)
Leal, L. L.: ref, 1914(887), 2300(594)
Leard, H. M.: ref, 780(1670), 1555(320), 2208(1584)

Leary, T.: test, 1170
Leaske, F.: test, 2090
Leavell, U. W.: test, 1312
Leaverton, D. R.: ref, 2491(2018), 2602(1658), 2621(248)
Leavitt, F.: ref, 1498(5647, 5648)
Leblanc, A. G.: test, 2464
Leblon, J.: test, 894, 2114
Leboeuf, A.: ref, 794(436), 859(753), 2300(357)
Lebron-Rodriguez, D. E.: ref, 357(508), 2217(113), 2602(1659)
LeCann, A. F.: ref, 1655(113)
Lecomte, C.: ref, 794(414)
Ledbetter, E.: test, 2399
Leder, S. B.: ref, 1126(762), 2472(23)
Lederer, H.: rev, 431, 1520
Lederman, E.: ref, 2300(407)
Lederman, R. P.: ref, 2300(407)
Ledford, R. S.: ref, 1347(10)
Ledgerwood, R.: rev, 1473
Ledoux, J. E.: ref, 1126(664), 1462(122), 2607(139)
Lee, A.: ref, 398(109)
Lee, C. A.: ref, 2598(1561)
Lee, C. A. B.: ref, 2491(2055)
Lee, C. C.: ref, 704(18), 1831(194), 2286(334)
Lee, D. C.: ref, 558(68), 966(175), 2208(1614)
Lee, D. M.: test, 1620; ref, 1295(286)
Lee, D. Y.: ref, 6(42), 1754(88), 1771(552)
Lee, F.: test, 1291; ref, 1099(65)
Lee, H. B.: ref, 558(62, 67), 859(866)
Lee, I.: ref, 2300(447)
Lee, J. H.: ref, 1655(86, 89)
Lee, J. M.: test, 1313; rev, 1193
Lee, J. W.: ref, 1955(106, 112)
Lee, L.: test, 1622
Lee, L. L.: ref, 1622(34)
Lee, S. G.: rev, 1347, 2242
Lee, S. S.: ref, 1754(91)
Leeman, M. M.: ref, 878(28)
Leen, D.: ref, 1498(5057), 2598(1304)
Leenaars, A. A.: ref, 1798(242)
Leeper, H. A.: ref, 1771(743), 2598(1744)
Lees-Haley, P. R.: ref, 1170(239)
Lefcourt, H. M.: ref, 1904(128)
Lefever, D. W.: test, 1371, 2260; rev, 344, 977, 1073, 1113, 1219, 1942
Leff, J.: ref, 1883(72, 86, 91)
Leff, J. P.: ref, 1883(35)
Lefkowitz, J.: ref, 2491(2084)
Lefkowitz, M. M.: ref, 964(507, 513), 1498(5290, 5302)
Legaretta, D.: ref, 1914(810)
Legein, C. P.: ref, 1060(23)
Leggett, J.: ref, 1498(5475)
Legutki, G.: ref, 559(58)
Lehman, A. W.: ref, 1498(5319), 2598(1504)
Lehman, E. B.: ref, 357(524)
Lehman, J. D.: ref, 1754(118), 2512(659)
Lehman, L. B.: ref, 1205(15), 1479(355)
Lehman, P. R.: rev, 1135, 1194, 1644
Lehman, R. A. W.: ref, 1498(5284, 5285), 1769(55), 2113(244), 2598(1471, 1472, 1568, 1608, 1676, 1773), 2607(159)
Lehmann, I. J.: rev, 74, 75, 1816, 2324; exc, 591, 592, 593, 594, 595, 2286

Lehmann, P. W.: test, 2421
Lehmkuhl, G.: ref, 2598(1766, 1835)
Lehn, T.: ref, 551(57, 58), 553(23, 24), 734(1, 2)
Lehr, E. R.: ref, 678(26), 960(11), 1771(655), 2107(9), 2218(143), 2598(1582), 2602(1889), 2608(213)
Lehren, P. M.: ref, 2300(408)
Lehrer, B.: ref, 1459(15), 2217(173), 2621(413), 2641(15)
Lehrer, B. E.: ref, 1192(171), 1341(158), 2328(3)
Lehrer, P. M.: ref, 1197(310), 2300(542)
Lehrer, R.: ref, 2641(24)
Lehrl, S.: ref, 1077(79), 1914(886)
Lehtonen, T.: ref, 1498(5754), 2030(5087), 2491(2102)
Lei, H.: ref, 609(228), 1203(12), 1798(296)
Leib, J. P.: ref, 2598(1516), 2607(167)
Leibel, R.: ref, 270(94)
Leibel, R. L.: ref, 1771(801)
Leichtman, S. R.: ref, 707(22, 23), 2602(1919, 2069)
Leichty, J.: ref, 859(844)
Leiderman, D. B.: ref, 1466(1)
Leigh, J.: test, 256
Leigh, J. M.: ref, 859(754)
Leight, K. A.: ref, 681(70)
Leijonquist, H.: ref, 283(136, 142), 627(22), 1265(75, 76), 1462(128), 1914(740)
Leinhardt, G.: ref, 483(13, 28), 553(25), 720(70), 891(7), 1473(133, 179), 1914(721), 2286(335), 2621(447)
Leipciger, M.: ref, 354(1486), 1498(5440)
Leisman, G.: ref, 2602(1779)
Leiter, R. G.: test, 1318, 1319
Leitner, D. W.: ref, 76(646), 354(1526), 685(1)
LeJeune, S. J.: test, 1415
Leland, B.: test, 691
Leland, H.: test, 6, 2460
Leli, D. A.: ref, 2598(1609, 1836)
Lemaire, T. E.: ref, 1498(5758)
LeMay, M.: ref, 2598(1475), 2602(1764)
Lemire, D.: ref, 780(1688)
Lemke, E. A.: ref, 1233(221), 2413(637)
Lemke, S.: test, 1546; ref, 1546(1, 2, 3, 4)
Lempert, H.: ref, 964(509)
Lenk, R. G.: ref, 2179(206), 2620(11)
Lennon, R. T.: test, 1754
Lent, R. W.: ref, 2300(409), 2374(183)
Lentz, T. F.: test, 340, 2399; rev, 1531
Leon, G. R.: ref, 1498(5476, 5611, 5755, 5756)
Leonard, C. V.: ref, 1498(5137)
Leonard, H. S.: ref, 226(180), 534(105), 1126(766), 1771(745), 2602(2073)
Leonard, J. P.: rev, 570
Leonard, L. B.: ref, 378(9), 1126(739), 1322(1), 1622(45, 47), 2472(17), 2541(8)
Leonard, M. D.: ref, 1498(5666)
Leonard, P.: ref, 308(16), 1109(21), 1853(292), 2260(28), 2598(1698), 2607(193)
Leonardson, G. R.: ref, 570(329)
Leonetti, R.: test, 1896
Leong, C. K.: ref, 1126(644, 689, 765), 1462(116, 129, 153), 1567(12), 1914(701, 750, 849)
Lepley, W. M.: test, 1784
Lerer, M. P.: ref, 280(1040, 1041), 2289(1621, 1622), 2598(1356), 2602(1660, 1661), 2621(249)
Lerer, R. J.: ref, 280(1040, 1041), 2289(1621, 1622), 2598(1356), 2602(1660, 1661), 2621(249)

INDEX OF NAMES

Leri, S. M.: ref, 1126(732)
Lerman, J.: test, 2646
Lerner, A.: test, 1376
Lerner, H. D.: ref, 2030(5090)
Lerner, J. V.: ref, 357(509)
Lerner, M.: ref, 1424(86)
Lerner, P.: ref, 1498(5655)
Lerner, R. M.: ref, 357(509)
Lesiak, J.: ref, 483(14), 932(79), 1126(665)
Lesiak, W. J.: test, 700
Leslie, L.: ref, 932(110), 1351(196), 2280(14)
Lesser, R.: ref, 308(8)
Lessig, V. P.: ref, 966(177)
Lester, D.: ref, 116(563, 565), 780(1703), 859(740, 755, 867), 1046(571), 1270(82, 83), 1419(678), 1498(5477, 5494), 1789(645)
Lester, E. H.: ref, 2179(201), 2217(114)
Lester, J. W.: ref, 354(1471), 780(1675), 859(824), 1498(5349), 1576(206)
Leton, D. A.: rev, 653, 701; ref, 1498(5087)
Letourneau, J. E.: ref, 2318(1614)
Lett, W. R.: ref, 2512(577, 600, 621, 633)
Leunes, A.: ref, 118(251), 354(1504), 1013(70), 1931(46), 2300(415)
Leung, A. K. C.: ref, 678(29)
Leung, L. S.: ref, 1498(5190)
Leuva, A.: ref, 1498(5080), 2030(4951), 2598(1317)
Levander, S. E.: ref, 354(1456), 859(810)
Levenson, H.: ref, 1013(101)
Levenson, R. L.: ref, 1424(49, 50), 2289(1720)
Leventhal, B.: ref, 2621(370)
Leventhal, D.: ref, 1498(5357)
Leventhal, D. B.: ref, 2598(1298)
Leventhal, G.: ref, 116(626), 1498(5138)
Leverman, D.: test, 668
Levey, L. M.: ref, 1341(152)
Levi, A.: ref, 1771(541), 1914(713)
Levi, A. M.: ref, 2413(684)
Levi, G.: ref, 534(99)
Levi, M.: ref, 1498(5625, 5626), 2598(1595)
Levin, H.: ref, 2598(1508)
Levin, H. S.: ref, 1771(688), 2598(1509)
Levin, J.: ref, 2029(195), 2413(624)
Levin, J. R.: ref, 2269(439)
Levin, K.: ref, 2598(1717), 2607(199)
Levin, S.: ref, 270(64), 311(17), 958(46), 2602(1811), 2621(299)
Levin, S. M.: ref, 883(72), 1498(5139)
Levine, B. A.: ref, 883(111)
Levine, D. N.: ref, 2598(1745), 2607(201)
Levine, E. L.: ref, 1855(28)
Levine, L.: ref, 1547(323)
Levine, L. Y.: test, 1441
Levine, M. D.: test, 182; ref, 1424(53, 86)
Levine, M. V.: ref, 1473(220)
Levine, P. M.: ref, 1547(341), 2598(1784)
Levine, S.: test, 343, 353, 2059, 2508
Levinson, B. M.: ref, 964(480), 2289(1623)
Levis, D. J.: ref, 883(116), 1547(350)
Levit, M.: test, 2428
Levita, E.: ref, 925(12)
Leviton, A.: ref, 226(172), 701(65), 1371(254), 1771(678), 2113(252), 2602(1929)
Levitt, E. E.: rev, 609, 1503, 2168, 2297; ref, 681(47), 1498(5303)

Levitt, M.: ref, 1498(5571)
Levitt, R.: ref, 2300(546)
Levy, D. L.: ref, 2030(5000), 2598(1489)
Levy, G. W.: ref, 501(831), 1498(5317), 2015(203)
Levy, M. F.: ref, 1495(87, 90), 2208(1623, 1686), 2318(1586, 1615), 2491(2061), 2614(24)
Levy, N. M.: ref, 1498(5515)
Levy, P. M.: rev, 823
Levy, R.: ref, 1914(802), 2598(1593, 1732, 1733)
Levy, R. B.: ref, 1060(28)
Levy, S.: test, 1782; rev, 1468, 2359
Lewandowski, L. A.: ref, 1789(715), 2413(678)
Lewandowski, N. G.: ref, 2602(1662)
Lewandowski, R. C.: ref, 2602(2009)
Lewinsohn, P. M.: ref, 681(38, 46, 62), 1498(5140, 5304, 5478, 5561, 5615, 5649, 5695, 5734, 5735), 2598(1327, 1357)
Lewis, A.: ref, 823(21)
Lewis, C. E.: ref, 751(14), 1462(135), 1498(5305), 2179(217), 2300(410)
Lewis, D.: test, 2113
Lewis, D. C.: ref, 645(17), 1904(74)
Lewis, D. G.: test, 1321
Lewis, G. P.: ref, 1346(1, 4)
Lewis, H. P.: ref, 964(481, 510), 2289(1624, 1762), 2602(2070)
Lewis, J.: ref, 116(611), 483(21), 666(2), 1473(155), 1478(74), 2413(679)
Lewis, J. A.: ref, 1498(5452), 1923(15), 2598(1592)
Lewis, J. D.: ref, 2598(1837)
Lewis, J. F.: test, 2387
Lewis, J. M.: ref, 2491(2104)
Lewis, L. A.: ref, 1013(123), 1576(221)
Lewis, M.: test, 353; ref, 270(72), 794(383), 1771(582), 2598(1410)
Lewis, M. L.: ref, 1233(221), 2413(637)
Lewis, M. S.: ref, 2300(477)
Lewis, N. D. C.: exc, 852
Lewis, P.: ref, 2300(447)
Lewis, R.: ref, 1498(5470), 1771(697), 2218(156), 2598(1606, 1750, 1828), 2602(1978), 2621(345)
Lewis, R. A.: ref, 1170(234)
Lewis, R. D.: rev, 2374
Lewis, R. F.: ref, 2598(1610)
Lewis, R. G.: ref, 1295(301)
Lewis, S. C.: ref, 2160(61)
Lewitter, F. I.: ref, 643(135), 1126(691), 1257(123), 1769(52)
Lewkowicz, N. K.: ref, 1877(8)
Lewnau, L. E.: ref, 2445(4)
Lewy, R.: ref, 964(483), 2217(122)
Leyman, L.: ref, 932(66), 1949(57)
Leynes, C.: ref, 1498(5650)
Lezak, M. D.: exc, 793; ref, 2598(1611)
Leznoff, A.: ref, 859(869)
Lharman, W. T.: ref, 280(1030), 2598(1330)
Li–Repac, D.: ref, 116(612), 354(1538)
Liang, V.: ref, 645(22)
Libb, J. W.: ref, 400(135), 772(30)
Liben, L. S.: ref, 794(398), 1044(61), 1126(743), 1771(696)
Liberman, I. Y.: ref, 551(67), 1007(21), 1771(685), 2217(180), 2621(365), 2641(21)
Libo, L. M.: rev, 639, 967
Lichtenberg, J. W.: ref, 2155(9)

Lichtenstein, R.: ref, 678(35), 696(4), 1771(791), 2289(1786), 2639(1)
Lichter, J. H.: ref, 2602(1920)
Lichter, S. R.: ref, 2491(2059)
Lichtman, M.: test, 1993
Lick, J. R.: ref, 1498(5141)
Lidberg, L.: ref, 354(1456), 859(810)
Lidberg, Y.: ref, 354(1456), 859(810)
Liddell, A.: ref, 859(811)
Lieber, D. J.: ref, 2491(2019)
Lieberman, B. A.: ref, 639(40), 859(722)
Lieberman, M.: ref, 1262(2)
Liebman, R.: ref, 354(1496)
Lief, H. I.: test, 2168; ref, 1547(352)
Liewendahl, K.: ref, 2602(2071)
Life, M. L.: ref, 398(109)
Lifshitz, M.: ref, 280(1042, 1079)
Lifton, W. M.: test, 2325
Liggett, J.: test, 2147; rev, 1030, 1038
Light, H. W.: test, 1328
Lightner, E. S.: ref, 534(103), 1771(621), 2289(1685)
Ligondé, P.: test, 1329
Ligthelm, G. J.: test, 1041
Likert, J. G.: test, 1903, 1905
Likert, R.: test, 1903, 1905, 2015
Liles, B. Z.: ref, 1771(613)
Lilleskov, R. K.: ref, 2289(1634)
Limburg, J.: ref, 859(854), 1904(90)
Lin, K.: ref, 609(217, 224)
Lin, P. C.: ref, 995(133)
Lin, T.: ref, 1655(79)
Lin, Y.: ref, 2598(1612)
Linaweaver, P. G.: ref, 2607(128)
Lincoln, A.: ref, 2621(346, 404)
Lincoln, A. L.: test, 1330
Lincoln, C. A.: ref, 2300(574)
Lincoln, N. B.: ref, 1851(40, 48), 1914(722), 2598(1358), 2602(1663), 2607(140)
Lindamood, C. A.: exc, 1789
Lindamood, C. H.: test, 1332
Lindamood, P. C.: test, 1332
Lindauer, M. S.: ref, 1077(73), 1817(4)
Lindblad, R. A.: ref, 2413(597)
Lindeman, R. H.: test, 371
Linden, J.: exc, 859
Linden, J. D.: ref, 859(726)
Lindenbaum, R. H.: ref, 2602(2213)
Linder, F.: ref, 2029(217)
Linder, L. H.: ref, 883(116), 1498(5757)
Lindgren, S. D.: ref, 701(49), 1101(51), 1771(614), 2012(6), 2602(2206), 2621(453)
Lindheim, E. L.: test, 221
Lindholm, B. W.: test, 1539, 1857; ref, 344(148, 160), 2012(4, 5)
Lindner, R. M.: test, 2013
Lindquist, E. F.: test, 363, 1192, 1193, 2021
Lindquist, M. M.: rev, 1389
Lindsay, G. A.: test, 1147
Lindseth, P.: ref, 2300(530)
Lindsey, A. M.: ref, 1904(129)
Lindsey, C. J.: ref, 1498(5142, 5150)
Lindsey, J. D.: ref, 1769(67), 2318(1616), 2602(1866)
Lindsey, R.: ref, 1547(308), 2300(473)
Lindvall, C. M.: rev, 1193, 2063, 2474
Lindy, J. D.: ref, 1922(20)
Lindzey, G.: test, 2343, 2344
Lindzey, G. E.: test, 1804
Linehan, M. M.: ref, 2300(396), 2353(28), 2598(1461), 2638(131)
Lines, R.: ref, 859(826)
Ling, A. H.: ref, 1622(38), 1771(599), 2218(10)
Lingjaerde, O.: ref, 1655(107)
Lingoes, J. C.: rev, 859, 1419, 1498
Lingwall, J. B.: rev, 228, 1287
Link, R.: test, 2224
Linkowski, P.: ref, 645(18, 25)
Linn, L. S.: ref, 2366(197)
Linn, M. W.: ref, 1240(51), 2587(35), 2598(1613)
Linn, P.: ref, 311(26)
Linn, R. L.: test, 1158; rev, 673, 732; ref, 344(145, 174), 501(809, 841), 551(22, 46), 1292(55, 56), 1473(140, 220), 2160(67), 2260(32, 44)
Linney, J. A.: ref, 2286(322), 2621(362)
Linnoila, M.: ref, 1498(5651), 1655(87), 2300(595)
Linnoila, M. K.: ref, 2300(412)
Linsday, B. A.: test, 403
Lintereur, G. E.: rev, 1593, 1596
Linton, P. H.: ref, 1498(5143)
Lion, L. S.: ref, 2030(5001), 2300(411)
Lipe, L. O.: ref, 398(109)
Lipkin, M.: ref, 354(1485), 2413(644)
Lipkins, R.: ref, 1547(323)
Lipscomb, T. R.: ref, 883(112), 2300(543)
Lipsky, M. J.: ref, 859(919), 1547(330), 2300(544), 2598(1746)
Lira, F. T.: ref, 349(6), 1498(5160, 5605), 1904(60, 67, 75), 2300(523), 2301(23), 2598(1370, 1614)
Lis, D. J.: ref, 1013(60, 84)
Liskin–Gasparro, J. E.: ref, 139(5)
Liskow, B. I.: ref, 1498(5144)
Lisman, S. A.: ref, 1547(329)
List, G.: ref, 2213(2)
Lister, J. A.: ref, 859(940), 2208(1676)
Litcher, J. H.: test, 1542; ref, 1479(349), 1871(3), 2218(146), 2602(1920)
Litrownik, A. J.: ref, 559(49), 2217(170), 2289(1663, 1677), 2602(1748)
Litt, I. F.: ref, 357(523), 1466(4), 1831(212)
Littel, A. S.: ref, 1498(5610)
Littell, W. M.: rev, 704
Little, D. K.: ref, 1498(5191)
Little, R. E.: ref, 2289(1757)
Little, T. L.: test, 1915
Little, V. L.: ref, 1771(548), 1969(85), 2598(1346), 2602(1654)
Litwack, L.: ref, 1931(51)
Litwack, T. R.: ref, 2030(5035)
Liv, W. T.: ref, (609)212
Livingood, A. B.: ref, 270(150), 698(6)
Livingston, J. E.: ref, 681(39)
Livingston, M. K.: ref, 559(49)
Livingston, S. A.: ref, 1013(127), 1168(1)
Livson, N.: ref, 964(481, 510), 2289(1624, 1762), 2602(2070)
Lloreda, P.: ref, 2602(1785), 2608(201)
Lloyd, B.: ref, 2160(54)
Lloyd, B. B.: ref, 2289(1625)
Lloyd, C.: ref, 2300(452)
Lloyd, D. N.: ref, 344(155)
Lloyd, J. K.: ref, 2289(1632)

INDEX OF NAMES

Lloyd, M. C.: test, 1813
Lloyd–Bostock, S. M. A.: ref, 149(11)
Loberg, T.: ref, 1498(5652), 2598(1747), 2607(202)
Lobitz, W. C.: ref, 681(58, 59), 1498(5479, 5684, 5685), 2598(1615)
Lobley, D. M.: ref, 859(833), 2029(207)
Locher, P. J.: ref, 280(1043)
Lochman, J. E.: ref, 2582(18)
Lochner, L. M.: ref, 400(138)
Lockavitch, J.: test, 2446
Lockhart, A. S.: rev, 5
Lockhart, L.: ref, 76(646), 685(1)
Lockhart, W. E.: test, 1481, 1482
Lockheed, M. E.: ref, 1013(55), 1192(213), 1473(172), 2160(64)
Lockwood, J. L.: ref, 1106(378), 2031(461)
Loeb, P.: ref, 542(23)
Loeb, R. C.: ref, 116(560), 354(1452)
Loeffler, D.: ref, 116(592)
Loehlin, J. C.: ref, 2598(1671), 2602(1987)
Loehr, V.: ref, 2180(36)
Loesch, L. C.: ref, 995(136), 1798(226), 2581(317), 2657(114)
Loevinger, J.: rev, 1168; exc, 1798
Loffredo, D. A.: ref, 734(4), 1192(256)
Lofquist, L. H.: test, 1495, 1497, 1508, 1509; ref, 1495(88), 1497(25, 26), 1855(21)
Loftsgard, S. O.: ref, 1498(5258)
Loftus, E. F.: ref, 1547(295)
Logan, P.: ref, 2300(478, 479)
Logemann, J. A.: test, 896; ref, 896(3, 7)
Logue, P.: ref, 2607(182)
Logue, P. E.: ref, 2300(412, 595), 2607(203, 212)
Logue, R. D.: rev, 1622
Lohman, D. F.: ref, 1914(883)
Lohman, T. G.: ref, 5(165, 166)
Lohmann, V. L.: test, 123, 293, 303, 390, 791, 948, 1278, 1413, 1816, 2097, 2232, 2233, 2234, 2235, 2525
Lohnes, P. R.: rev, 367, 1007, 1269, 2164, 2581
Lohr, J. M.: ref, 2300(596)
Loilson, G. S.: ref, 270(151)
Lojk, L.: ref, 860(124)
Lokan, J.: ref, 643(131), 1456(14), 1570(7)
Lokare, V. G.: ref, 152(11)
Loman, W.: test, 2418
Lomax, P. S.: rev, 1556
Lombard, J. W.: rev, 346, 1975, 1976, 1980, 2340
Lombard, T. J.: ref, 226(161), 2602(1780)
Lombardi, T. P.: test, 366
Londerville, S.: ref, 270(152)
London, P.: test, 399
London House Management Consultants, Inc.: test, 1339
Loney, J.: ref, 280(1113), 2602(1918, 1927)
Long, C. G.: ref, 1367(2), 1567(16)
Long, C. J.: ref, 2598(1815), 2607(214)
Long, D.: ref, 280(1143), 2598(1723)
Long, D. A.: test, 1941
Long, F. Y.: ref, 859(778), 1498(5212)
Long, G. L.: ref, 9(15), 1013(87), 2246(28)
Long, G. T.: ref, 1419(672), 1798(212)
Long, J. A.: test, 1872
Long, J. V.: ref, 344(192), 551(69), 932(64)
Long, M.: ref, 1771(566), 2602(1682)
Long, N. H.: test, 1135

Longabaugh, R.: ref, 1922(13), 1923(13)
Longergan, W. G.: test, 2651
Longmaid, W. H.: ref, 932(108)
Longmire, B. J.: test, 830
Longstaff, H. P.: test, 1493
Longstreth, L. E.: ref, 483(22), 1771(615)
Lonowski, D. J.: ref, 1351(29)
Lonski, A. B.: test, 154
Loo, H.: ref, 1655(111)
Loo, R.: ref, 478(7), 794(399), 859(756, 812, 813), 860(116, 125, 126, 127, 136), 1013(56, 69, 80, 97, 103), 2300(413, 414, 478, 479, 480, 504), 2598(1490)
Loonen, M. C. B.: ref, 2602(1716)
Looney, J. G.: ref, 609(212)
Lopata, D. J.: ref, 953(10), 2217(106), 2289(1591)
Loper, A. B.: ref, 1272(139), 2621(405)
Lopez, F. E.: ref, 2614(23)
Lopez, M. A.: ref, 609(223), 2300(545)
Loprete, L. J.: ref, 2602(1603)
Lorber, J.: ref, 2289(1787), 2602(2184)
Lorch, B.: ref, 609(214)
Lord, F. M.: ref, 501(796), 590(372), 995(134), 1754(57), 2160(53)
Lord, R. G.: ref, 1295(288, 306)
Lore, S. W.: test, 176
Lorentz, J. L.: ref, 1192(167, 201)
Lorenz, L.: ref, 1769(72), 2621(347)
Lorge, I.: test, 361, 362, 483, 534, 1341; rev, 688, 689, 690, 1808, 2638
Lorimer, J.: test, 1342, 1567
Lorimer, M. F.: rev, 570
Lorimer, R.: ref, 1498(5405)
Lorimor, R.: ref, 1498(5567)
Lorr, M.: test, 1173, 1747, 1792, 1904, 1933; rev, 855, 1351, 2208; ref, 354(1571), 558(56), 780(1650), 1173(1), 1197(290), 1798(213, 214), 2155(7, 8)
Losak, J.: ref, 506(31)
Los Angeles County Superintendent of Schools Test Development Center: test, 265, 266, 267, 268
Los Angeles Unified School District: test, 217, 2151, 2660
Lose, B. D.: ref, 2217(174), 2602(2104)
Lothstein, L. M.: ref, 1498(5306)
Lott, D. R.: ref, 883(81)
Lottinville, E.: ref, 2665(1)
Lou, H. C.: ref, 381(67)
Loucks, S.: ref, 1754(105), 1798(252, 260, 274), 1904(114), 2030(5065), 2413(680)
Loucks, S. F.: ref, 344(138)
Louis, K. O.: ref, 1126(769)
Louko, L. J.: ref, 664(12)
Louks, J. L.: ref, 1498(5307)
Lounsbury, J. E.: ref, 1051(15), 2318(1583)
Lounsbury, J. W.: ref, 1855(18)
Lounsbury, M. L.: ref, 1798(251)
Louttit, C. M.: rev, 118, 1853, 2557; exc, 381
Lovallo, W.: ref, 859(923)
Lovallo, W. R.: ref, 1498(5083), 1547(288), 2179(206), 2620(8, 11, 13)
Love, C. T.: ref, 704(19)
Love, E.: ref, 2602(1966)
Love, R. J.: ref, 1851(20)
Lovegrove, W.: ref, 1567(13), 2077(28)
Lovekin, A.: ref, 1789(679)

Lovel, B.: ref, 409(10)
Loveland, R. J.: ref, 2582(17)
Lovell, J. E.: ref, 374(198), 2134(105)
Lovell, K.: rev, 319, 823
Lovenberg, W.: ref, 1498(5655)
Lovett, M. W.: ref, 766(27), 1754(92)
Lovibond, S. H.: test, 1661
Lovinger, S. L.: ref, 766(31), 1503(69), 1771(732), 2030(5060)
Lovitt, R.: ref, 2030(5066), 2598(1833), 2621(446)
Low, B. P.: ref, 751(7), 874(46), 1361(64), 2602(1679)
Low, L. Y.: ref, 1877(8)
Low, M. D.: ref, 2289(1620), 2602(1656)
Lowe, B.: ref, 2581(347)
Lowe, J. D.: ref, 1192(198), 1498(5699), 2602(1768)
Lowe, M.: test, 2383
Lowe, R. C.: ref, 1473(215), 1771(774)
Lowe, W. F.: ref, 501(800), 1969(88)
Lowell, W. E.: ref, 1969(112)
Lowery, H. A.: test, 1240
Lowman, J.: ref, 1498(5653)
Lown, B.: ref, 280(1173), 1498(5765), 1547(354)
Lowrance, D.: ref, 2218(147), 2602(1921)
Lowry, L. D.: ref, 1466(2)
Lowry, S.: ref, 2300(602)
Lowy, D.: ref, 2598(1740)
Loyd, B. H.: ref, 76(643), 1192(243, 244, 247), 1193(144)
Loyd, R. R.: ref, 664(10)
Loye, D.: ref, 2029(197)
Lozano, R. A.: ref, 1513(25)
Luber, R. F.: ref, 1170(227)
Lubetsky, M.: ref, 2300(397)
Lubin, A.: rev, 2208, 2388
Lubin, B.: test, 681, 1547; ref, 116(534), 681(34, 40, 41, 47, 54, 57, 61, 74), 890(347), 1547(310), 2300(514), 2598(1491)
Lubinski, R.: ref, 1851(31)
Luborsky, L.: ref, 1498(5490)
Lucas, B. A.: ref, 2602(2004)
Lucas, C. J.: ref, 639(43, 48), 769(39, 42)
Lucas, D.: test, 2430
Lucas, D. G.: test, 1870
Lucas, L. F.: ref, 1789(675)
Lucas, M. J.: ref, 941(36)
Lucas, R. A.: ref, 1498(5721)
Lucas, R. W.: ref, 2134(97)
Lucas, W. A.: ref, 121(10), 2485(130)
Lucca, J. A.: ref, 2557(246)
Luce, S. R.: ref, 363(8), 362(2)
Luciani, J. J.: test, 862
Lucido, D.: ref, 1547(323)
Lucker, G. W.: ref, 1831(195)
Ludlow, C.: ref, 1771(752)
Ludlow, C. L.: ref, 1126(731), 1771(670)
Ludlow, J. R.: ref, 2289(1721)
Ludwig, A. M.: ref, 794(375, 400)
Lueger, R. J.: ref, 2012(2)
Luhey, B. B.: ref, 2602(1606)
Lukasevich, A.: ref, 363(9), 361(7)
Lukin, P. R.: ref, 1208(4)
Lumsden, J.: rev, 30, 1126, 2195
Lund, N. L.: ref, 2413(699), 2602(2185)
Lund, Y.: ref, 1009(54)
Lundberg, I.: ref, 534(100), 1914(850)

Lundberg, P. K.: ref, 609(230), 1948(101)
Lundberg, U.: ref, 860(144)
Lundell, K.: test, 635
Lundin, R. W.: rev, 349, 1552, 2113, 2631
Lundquist, T.: ref, 1053(82)
Lundsteen, S. W.: ref, 1351(187), 2164(44), 2286(315)
Lundstrom, W. J.: ref, 1798(211), 2208(1545)
Lunghi, M. E.: ref, 859(814)
Lunneborg, C. E.: rev, 1158, 1159; ref, 799(20), 1257(107), 1493(121), 1914(775), 2598(1492)
Lunneborg, P. A.: ref, 2576(1)
Lunneborg, P. W.: test, 2576; rev, 2082, 2318; ref, 76(630), 2134(118), 2318(1536, 1537, 1587), 2576(2), 2581(324)
Lunzer, E. A.: test, 1367
Luria, R. E.: ref, 1883(51, 73)
Luria, S. M.: ref, 1257(163)
Lüscher, M.: test, 1347
Luscomb, R. L.: ref, 157(149), 794(427)
Lushene, R.: test, 2300
Lushene, R. E.: test, 2301
Lushene, R. L.: ref, 1798(253)
Lusk, E. J.: ref, 1013(128, 129)
Lustig, D. A.: ref, 2030(5010), 2491(2048)
Lutz, W. C.: test, 1308
Luzzatti, C.: ref, 1914(875), 2598(1812)
Lyall, W. A. L.: ref, 941(48), 2208(1694)
Lyerly, S. B.: test, 1240
Lykken, D. T.: rev, 356, 609, 1198, 1203
Lyle, J. G.: ref, 2607(168)
Lyle, O. E.: ref, 280(1044), 1498(5145), 2179(199), 2598(1359), 2602(1664)
Lyman, H. B.: rev, 1769, 1771, 2598
Lyman, R.: ref, 1498(5437), 2598(1581)
Lyman, R. D.: ref, 2602(2200), 2621(450)
Lynch, B. E.: ref, 859(868)
Lynch, D.: ref, 2030(4998)
Lynch, J.: ref, 2134(130)
Lynch, J. I.: ref, 1319(79)
Lynch, R. M.: ref, 2134(130)
Lynch, T.: test, 1794
Lynch–Sauer, J.: ref, 116(540)
Lyness, K. S.: ref, 2537(563)
Lynn, A. M.: ref, 953(13)
Lynn, M. R.: ref, 1547(298)
Lyon, R.: ref, 226(185), 691(47), 701(89), 1126(784), 1462(158), 1769(103), 1914(888), 2602(2186)
Lyons, A.: ref, 116(560), 354(1452), 1789(669)
Lyons, A. W.: ref, 354(1457)
Lyons, G.: ref, 780(1656), 1498(5183)
Lyons, J.: ref, 1170(238)
Lytle, W. G.: ref, 2289(1722), 2602(1922)
Lytton, H.: rev, 353; ref, 675(5), 1771(553, 554, 721)
M. A. A. Committee on High School Contests: test, 160
Ma, L.: ref, 501(860, 861)
Ma, T.: ref, 280(1143), 2598(1723)
Maas, H. S.: rev, 163
Maas, J. B.: test, 607
Maas, J. W.: ref, 2300(443)
Mabee, W. S.: ref, 1126(700)
Mabry, E.: ref, 859(746)
Mabry, E. A.: ref, 1498(5223, 5224)
Macaitis, L.: test, 2261, 2270, 2276
Macaitis, L. A.: test, 2274
MacAndrew, C.: ref, 1498(5480, 5308)

INDEX OF NAMES

MacBride, A.: ref, 941(46), 2208(1687)
MacCrimmon, D. J.: ref, 1498(5654, 5722), 1923(19), 2598(1399, 1425)
MacDonald, A. J.: ref, 941(37)
Macdonald, H.: ref, 2294(118), 2297(10, 11)
MacDonald, H. M.: ref, 2289(1764)
Macdonald, I.: test, 386
MacDonald, I.: ref, 1914(715)
MacDonald, I. M.: ref, 1655(80)
MacDonald, J.: ref, 1567(11), 2602(1687)
MacDonald, J. D.: test, 834, 836, 1725
MacDonald, M. G.: ref, 1498(5165)
MacDonald, M. L.: ref, 1655(95)
MacFaul, R.: ref, 2602(1781), 2608(199)
MacGinitie, R. K.: test, 932, 933
MacGinitie, W. H.: test, 932, 933, 934
Machock, B. J.: ref, 1272(132)
Machover, K.: test, 1353
Macintyre, M. M. J.: ref, 859(873)
Mack, J. L.: ref, 308(3), 1498(5044), 1948(95), 2113(237), 2598(1300), 2607(129)
Mackay, I. R.: ref, 1914(732)
Mackay, L. D.: test, 2486
Mackay, T.: test, 932, 933
MacKenzie, G. N.: rev, 169
Mackin, R. K.: ref, 76(654), 374(227)
MacKinney, A. C.: rev, 900, 2614
Maclean, A. W.: ref, 149(14)
MacLean, P. R.: test, 1211
MacLean, W. E.: ref, 2602(1641)
MacLeod, C. M.: ref, 1568(146)
MacLeod, P. M.: ref, 681(39)
Maclin, J.: ref, 2602(1990)
MacMillan, J. F.: ref, 1883(84)
Macon, R. S.: ref, 354(1487, 1530), 732(404), 1498(5614)
MacQuarrie, T. W.: test, 1356
MacQueen, A. H.: ref, 344(161)
MacRae, K. D.: ref, 859(763)
MacVane, J. R.: ref, 794(401), 1789(676)
MacWhinney, B.: ref, 2289(1626)
Macy, D. J.: ref, 344(170), 551(43)
Madans, A. B.: test, 2469
Madaus, G. F.: rev, 169; ref, 972(10), 2269(466)
Madden, R.: test, 121, 2286, 2287, 2288, 2291, 2292, 2293, 2298
Maddux, R. E.: ref, 553(20)
Madge, E. M.: test, 400, 1197, 1233
Madigan, R. J.: ref, 1126(666), 1769(46), 1771(555), 2602(1665)
Madison, C. L.: ref, 1771(780)
Madison, J. K.: ref, 2598(1473)
Madison, S. S.: ref, 374(219), 501(913), 1473(210), 1478(77), 1754(114)
Madorsky, A.: ref, 1498(5092), 2318(1528), 2598(1332)
Madrazo–Peterson, R.: ref, 2353(32)
Madsen, H. S.: ref, 1483(1), 1484(13)
Madura, J. A.: ref, 1498(5723), 2413(689)
Maenpaa, J.: ref, 2602(2071)
Maestas, L. C.: ref, 551(68), 1192(255)
Magaro, P.: ref, 1555(327)
Magaro, P. A.: ref, 157(151), 243(124), 794(371), 1077(50)
Magee, P.: ref, 2445(1)
Maggiore, R. P.: ref, 1126(701)
Magill, R. A.: ref, 1506(74), 1896(12), 2260(42)
Magliocca, L. A.: ref, 2478(12)
Magnasco, J.: ref, 1789(639)
Magnusson, D.: ref, 1937(4)
Magoon, J.: exc, 2107
Magoon, T.: ref, 1789(700)
Magoon, T. M.: test, 1932; ref, 2134(99, 101, 110), 2318(1612)
Magrath, K. H.: ref, 883(98)
Magrina, A.: ref, 501(906)
Maguire, G. P.: ref, 859(860)
Maguire, T. O.: ref, 362(6), 1341(165), 1754(116), 1831(160, 204), 2288(81)
Mah, C. D.: ref, 1063(101, 126)
Mahadevan, R.: ref, 280(1124), 2602(1971), 2608(221)
Mahan, J. M.: ref, 1953(12, 13)
Maher, B. A.: ref, 479(403), 1883(87)
Maher, C.: ref, 226(172), 701(65), 1371(254), 1771(678), 2113(252), 2602(1929)
Mahlios, M. C.: ref, 1013(130, 131)
Maholick, L. T.: test, 1960
Mahoney, D.: ref, 1798(289)
Mahoney, E. F.: test, 1826
Mahoney, J.: ref, 2029(230)
Mahoney, N. D.: ref, 2598(1627)
Maico Hearing Instruments, Inc.: test, 1359
Maier, R. A.: ref, 477(24), 653(153), 1419(689), 2489(8)
Main, C. J.: ref, 859(940), 1655(96), 2208(1676)
Main, M.: ref, 270(152)
Mair, W. G. P.: ref, 1914(811)
Maisels, J.: ref, 270(159), 678(37), 1420(3)
Maisto, A. A.: ref, 2602(2072), 2621(406)
Maisto, S. A.: ref, 1547(331), 2179(200)
Majcher, D.: ref, 794(444), 2598(1817)
Majer, K.: test, 1326
Majeres, R. L.: ref, 678(36)
Major, L. F.: ref, 1498(5655)
Majovski, L. V.: ref, 2602(1796)
Makowski, T.: test, 1217
Malaby, J. E.: ref, 2621(252, 349)
Malachowski, N.: ref, 1471(54)
Malacos, J. A.: ref, 2134(126)
Malatesta, C. Z.: ref, 121(8), 1007(16), 1271(906), 1853(271), 1914(723), 2537(549), 2598(1360), 2607(141)
Malcom, P. J.: test, 1308
Malcomesius, N.: test, 2252
Maldonado, A.: test, 668
Maldonado, B. M.: ref, 2413(598)
Malek, V. F.: test, 1083, 1093
Malett, S. D.: ref, 2134(107), 2318(1559, 1569), 2374(199)
Malgady, R. G.: test, 2570; ref, 6(58), 1341(159), 2512(574)
Malik, S. C.: ref, 1655(115)
Maller, J. B.: rev, 2086
Mallinger, M.: ref, 2208(1568)
Mallinson, G.: test, 2325
Mallinson, G. G.: rev, 415, 591, 2165
Mallinson, J.: test, 2325
Mallinson, J. V.: rev, 1588, 1630, 2097, 2098
Malloch, D. C.: ref, 76(655), 501(928)
Mallory, L. H.: ref, 2598(1838)

Malloy, F.: ref, 2598(1840)
Malloy, P. F.: ref, 1346(6)
Malloy, T. E.: ref, 890(357, 358, 359), 1798(303)
Malone, A.: test, 2014
Malone, D. R.: ref, 1555(337), 2534(14)
Maloney, L. J.: ref, 874(49)
Maloney, M. P.: ref, 1319(75), 1498(5656), 1771(616), 1969(93, 113), 2598(1451, 1493, 1748)
Maloney, P.: ref, 1053(73)
Maloy, C. F.: ref, 1331(39), 2602(1816, 1923)
Malpass, R. S.: ref, 59(390)
Malsbary, D. R.: rev, 332, 2194
Maltzman, I.: ref, 1498(5716)
Mamunes, P.: ref, 381(61), 2557(218)
Manchanda, R.: ref, 2491(2062)
Mandal, G.: ref, 2121(68)
Mandel, H. P.: ref, 1498(5553)
Mandel, N. G.: test, 1368
Mandelbrote, B.: ref, 2208(1598), 2598(1553)
Mandelcorn, B.: ref, 2491(2107), 2602(2198)
Mandelkorn, T.: ref, 2208(1664)
Mandell, A.: ref, 1272(140), 2260(48)
Mandell, M. M.: rev, 1113
Mandelzys, N.: ref, 1498(5481), 2598(1616)
Manders, K. R.: ref, 472(13)
Manderscheid, R. W.: ref, 354(1423), 1099(71, 72, 73), 2208(1555, 1593), 2587(39)
Mandeville, K.: test, 897
Mangan, G. L.: ref, 157(140), 477(23), 859(815)
Manganiello, J. A.: ref, 2413(625)
Mangel, M.: ref, 2208(1522)
Mangieri, J. N.: ref, 1568(116)
Manheim, L. A.: ref, 1771(726)
Manka, M.: ref, 701(69), 2602(1964)
Mankin, D.: ref, 116(560), 354(1452), 1789(669)
Mann, K.: ref, 2208(1583), 2289(1676), 2598(1486)
Mann, L.: rev, 1004, 1371, 2543
Mann, M. J.: rev, 2165
Mann, P. H.: test, 2401, 2402
Mann, R.: ref, 2598(1426)
Mann, R. B.: ref, 973(32)
Mannarino, A. P.: ref, 1831(142)
Manni, J.: ref, 701(38), 2289(1638), 2602(1692)
Manni, J. L.: ref, 200(18), 374(229), 732(414), 932(126), 1771(788), 1914(895), 2413(702), 2598(1854), 2621(455)
Manning, C. M.: ref, 157(152)
Manning, D. T.: ref, 2477(2)
Manning, J.: rev, 599, 2061
Manning, J. C.: test, 1890, 1895, 1897
Manning, T. T.: ref, 2155(7, 8)
Manning, W. H.: ref, 664(10, 12, 13)
Mannino, J. P.: test, 656
Manosevitz, M.: ref, 1771(556)
Mans, L.: ref, 270(89), 2289(1678)
Manschreck, T. C.: ref, 479(403), 1883(87)
Mansdorf, I. J.: ref, 1319(73)
Mansfield, R.: ref, 408(182), 502(182), 1080(182), 1745(182)
Manson, M. P.: test, 152, 350, 1369, 1376, 1830, 2616, 2617
Mantz, D.: ref, 2598(1837)
Manual, H. T.: test, 2484
Manuck, S. B.: ref, 2565(9)
Manuel, H.: rev, 1318

Manuel, H. T.: test, 2455, 2488; rev, 728; exc, 1527
Maple, C.: ref, 859(800), 1789(668)
Maples, E. G.: ref, 1193(149), 2260(51)
Maqsud, M.: ref, 1229(102, 103), 1914(724, 851, 852)
Maranto, C. D.: ref, 2113(251)
Marbach, E. S.: ref, 964(511), 1771(744)
Marchese, A. C.: test, 476
Marchner, T. J.: ref, 280(1108), 751(26), 1126(727), 2289(1711), 2602(1899), 2621(337)
Marcia, J. E.: ref, 859(927), 1555(335), 2512(649)
Marco, G. L.: ref, 506(27), 1292(51)
Marcos, L. R.: ref, 2598(1333, 1617)
Marcovitch, P.: ref, 1063(107), 2294(130)
Marcus, A.: ref, 2598(1639), 2602(1949)
Marcus, B. B.: ref, 270(118)
Marcus, J.: ref, 270(153), 311(45)
Marcus, J. L.: ref, 1765(11)
Marcus, M.: ref, 1192(182, 207), 1479(322, 335)
Marcus, R.: ref, 1498(5051)
Mardell, C. D.: test, 696
Marder, S. R.: ref, 1655(124), 2598(1864)
Margalit, C.: ref, 2300(546)
Margarey, C. J.: ref, 1498(5380)
Margolis, A. J.: ref, 1904(92)
Margolis, H.: ref, 226(163, 166, 180), 280(1070), 534(97, 101, 105), 932(80), 1117(441), 1126(667, 702, 766), 1255(4, 5), 1479(329), 1771(557, 617, 745), 2561(2), 2602(1666, 1782, 2006, 2073), 2608(200)
Margolis, R.: ref, 1498(5688)
Margules, P. H.: ref, 280(1021), 643(127)
Margulies, T.: ref, 1498(5732)
Marholin, D.: ref, 2289(1679), 2557(223)
Marinelli, B.: ref, 1771(787), 2602(2181)
Marini, J. L.: ref, 859(830), 1123(60), 1498(5361), 1547(293), 1771(627), 2031(457)
Marion, R. J.: ref, 2300(566)
Mariotto, M. J.: ref, 883(103)
Marjoribanks, K.: ref, 42(2), 149(6, 12), 400(126, 129, 134), 1895(1), 1914(776, 777, 812), 2629(102, 106)
Mark, L. S.: ref, 1771(685), 2621(365)
Markel, D.: ref, 1498(5636)
Markestad, T.: ref, 270(154)
Markiton, R. I.: ref, 960(12), 2541(7), 2598(1597)
Markoff, R. A.: ref, 1498(5328)
Marks, C. J.: ref, 1126(682), 1771(583)
Marks, H. E.: ref, 6(73)
Marks, M. R.: rev, 1556, 1804
Marks, M. W.: ref, 1498(5388)
Marks, P. A.: ref, 1498(5146, 5161)
Markus, H.: ref, 116(535)
Markwardt, F. C.: test, 1769
Marlatt, G. A.: ref, 2179(212)
Marler, M.: ref, 2300(423), 2598(1501)
Marlett, N. J.: test, 112
Marlowe, W.: ref, 1771(671), 2621(348)
Marmorale, A. M.: ref, 280(1045)
Marohn, R. C.: ref, 2030(5070)
Marone, J. G.: ref, 681(40), 2598(1491)
Marowitz, J. W.: ref, 627(24)
Marquardt, T. P.: ref, 664(15), 1513(28)
Marr, M. B.: ref, 932(118)
Marrero, B.: ref, 2602(1826)
Marsden, L. R.: ref, 1197(300)
Marsella, A. J.: ref, 1257(166)

INDEX OF NAMES

Marsh, D. T.: ref, 1436(17)
Marsh, G.: ref, 1771(558, 647)
Marsh, G. E.: ref, 2541(6)
Marsh, G. G.: ref, 2598(1749)
Marsh, H. W.: ref, 501(868, 894), 818(7)
Marsh, L. A.: ref, 354(1525), 2208(1651)
Marsh, N. R.: ref, 794(426, 437)
Marsh, R. W.: ref, 1485(83), 1914(853), 2289(1763), 2602(2074)
Marshall, C. V.: ref, 1473(154), 1754(77)
Marshall, D. D.: ref, 2208(1660)
Marshall, J. L.: test, 2634
Marshall, J. R.: ref, 1419(704), 2179(255)
Marshall, R. C.: ref, 1851(28, 41)
Marshall, R. J.: ref, 1576(204)
Marshall, W.: ref, 2602(1783), 2621(291)
Martelin, T.: ref, 2030(4995), 2598(1469)
Martin, A. D.: ref, 1851(21)
Martin, C. J.: ref, 609(201), 1498(5073)
Martin, D.: ref, 2015(215), 2602(2207)
Martin, D. C.: ref, 2602(2133)
Martin, D. G.: exc, 1106
Martin, D. W.: ref, 1498(5610)
Martin, E. D.: ref, 1498(5635)
Martin, E. M.: ref, 1754(58), 1789(646), 1960(68)
Martin, F.: ref, 2289(1723), 2598(1618), 2602(1924), 2608(215)
Martin, G. T.: ref, 354(1425)
Martin, H. J.: ref, 1498(5690)
Martin, H. P.: ref, 2217(179)
Martin, J.: ref, 270(119), 1478(75), 1479(367), 1914(887), 2289(1724), 2300(594)
Martin, J. D.: ref, 280(1114), 354(1572, 1573), 899(20), 1053(66), 1498(5309, 5482, 5483), 1557(7), 1754(58), 1789(646, 730, 731), 1960(68), 1970(16), 2030(5002), 2179(201, 223, 224, 256), 2217(114, 115, 181), 2218(148), 2512(575, 660), 2598(1361), 2602(1667)
Martin, J. R.: ref, 2179(255)
Martin, K.: ref, 1498(5705)
Martin, M. E.: ref, 1877(9), 2541(9)
Martin, N. G.: ref, 1771(554)
Martin, P. J.: ref, 1135(17), 1229(92), 1233(224), 1498(5142, 5147, 5148, 5149, 5150), 2179(202), 2631(31)
Martin, P. Y.: ref, 1789(638)
Martin, R.: ref, 701(38)
Martin, R. A.: ref, 2602(1793, 2082)
Martin, R. B.: ref, 1719(2), 2581(315)
Martin, R. D.: ref, 932(111), 2491(2085)
Martin, R. L.: ref, 1771(672)
Martin, S.: test, 2332
Martin, W.: ref, 1257(167)
Martin, W. R.: ref, 113(24), 354(1446), 1498(5274, 5622), 2179(237), 2598(1725), 2621(400)
Martin, W. T.: test, 275, 1385, 1730, 2044, 2138, 2332, 2453
Martindale, C.: ref, 1498(5310)
Martinek, T. J.: test, 1386; ref, 1386(1, 3), 1831(143, 196)
Martinetti, R. F.: ref, 1252(89)
Martinez, M. E.: ref, 872(10), 1831(174)
Martinez, R. L.: ref, 354(1539)
Martini, J. L.: ref, 2029(205, 206)
Martois, J.: ref, 344(139), 2347(1)

Martorano, S. C.: ref, 1754(59)
Marullo, S.: ref, 1197(294), 1198(1)
Marusarz, T. Z.: ref, 1498(5643)
Maruta, T.: ref, 1498(5484, 5714), 2179(225, 249)
Maruyama, G.: ref, 2602(2187), 2621(448)
Marvin, R. S.: ref, 698(5)
Marwit, S. J.: ref, 2621(425)
Marx, M. H.: ref, 590(389)
Marx, R. W.: ref, 1077(57), 1257(129), 1831(132, 144, 197), 1914(887), 2160(75), 2300(594)
Marzillier, J. S.: ref, 859(949)
Marzolf, S. S.: rev, 1272
Maschino, P. A.: test, 389
Masek, B. J.: ref, 2300(405)
Mash, E. J.: ref, 2582(11)
Masia, B. B.: rev, 1527
Maslach, C.: test, 1388; ref, 1063(105)
Masling, J.: ref, 665(51), 2030(5032, 5067)
Maslow, A. H.: test, 2121
Maslow, P.: test, 1371
Mason, D. A.: test, 166, 822, 2659
Mason, G. E.: ref, 344(136), 1473(150)
Mason, J.: ref, 1969(97), 2598(1547)
Mason, P.: ref, 559(43)
Massad, C. E.: rev, 1880; ref, 1831(213)
Massad, C. M.: ref, 1831(213)
Massaro, D. W.: ref, 932(98, 112), 1568(145), 2160(76)
Massey, J.: test, 2091
Masson, L. I.: test, 1961
Massong, S. F.: ref, 280(1175), 701(92), 1371(263)
Massong, S. R.: ref, 280(1151), 1473(208)
Mastenbrook, M.: ref, 2300(527)
Masters, L.: ref, 2541(6)
Mastie, M. M.: ref, 2581(318)
Masuda, M.: ref, 609(217, 224)
Matalon, R.: ref, 338(11), 960(17), 1622(55), 1771(794), 2289(1788)
Matarazzo, J. D.: ref, 116(617), 296(9), 609(206), 794(442), 859(939), 1498(5151, 5219), 2030(4960), 2300(575), 2318(1538), 2598(1362, 1414, 1494, 1803)
Matarazzo, R. G.: ref, 2494(1)
Matas, L.: ref, 270(90)
Matefy, R. E.: ref, 1754(78), 1831(145), 2286(296)
Matheny, A. P.: ref, 270(78), 2608(189)
Matheny, P. A.: test, 540
Mathes, E. W.: ref, 2121(70), 1789(677, 678)
Mathew, R. J.: ref, 859(895, 951), 1573(40), 1904(78, 94), 2300(481, 482, 513, 597)
Mathews, M.: ref, 1771(565), 1825(21)
Mathews, N. N.: ref, 1568(146)
Mathews, R. C.: ref, 766(33), 1007(37), 2288(89)
Mathewson, P. D.: ref, 1236(10), 2598(1363)
Mathis, G.: ref, 701(59), 1126(720), 1540(13), 1771(644), 2218(141)
Mathis, H.: test, 835; ref, 2638(133)
Mathis, H. J.: ref, 701(39), 1371(244)
Mathis, R. M.: ref, 1(1)
Matson, J. L.: ref, 6(89), 1197(278)
Matsui, T.: ref, 354(1402), 2354(32, 33, 34), 2366(194)
Mattes, J. A.: ref, 1240(52)
Matteson, R. W.: rev, 2086
Matthews, B. A. J.: ref, 1718(9)
Matthews, C. G.: ref, 1498(5152), 2598(1309, 1310)

Matthews, H. P.: ref, 2412(39), 2557(229), 2598(1619), 2602(1926), 2608(216)
Matthews, J. P.: ref, 2134(122), 2581(332)
Matthews, K. A.: ref, 116(627), 2598(1364), 2602(1668)
Matthews, R. W.: ref, 2598(1833), 2621(446)
Matthews, S. M.: ref, 354(1401), 890(327), 1555(309), 2613(80)
Matthysse, S.: ref, 1655(99)
Mattison, R. E.: ref, 960(15), 1007(35), 1126(752), 1771(717), 2602(2016), 2608(228), 2621(389)
Mattson, R. H.: ref, 2598(1700), 2607(196)
Matturo, M.: ref, 116(626)
Matussek, P.: ref, 1419(705)
Mauer, R. G.: ref, 2602(2075)
Mauger, P. A.: test, 1169
Maughan, M. R. C.: ref, 890(336)
Maultsby, M. C.: ref, 2353(26)
Maune, S.: ref, 1771(786)
Maurer, K. M.: test, 1505
Maurice, W. L.: test, 2171
Mauser, A.: test, 2446
Mauter, M.: ref, 2512(579)
Maver, H.: ref, 1923(21)
Mavissakalian, M.: ref, 639(61), 1904(121)
Mavrogenes, N. A.: ref, 1220(1)
Maxey, E. J.: ref, 76(605)
Maxey, J.: test, 1189
Maxfield, F. N.: rev, 2289; exc, 1073
Maxfield, K. E.: test, 1420
Maxwell, B. A.: ref, 2512(601)
Maxwell, J.: rev, 766; exc, 2289
Maxwell, M.: ref, 1568(128), 1914(865), 2374(184)
Maxwell, M. J.: test, 1932
Maxwell, S.: ref, 964(516), 1424(85), 2602(2196)
Maxwell, S. E.: ref, 995(130), 1855(29), 2374(196)
Maxwell, W. A.: ref, 2300(568), 2353(37)
May, A. E.: ref, 2598(1562)
May, D.: test, 1412
May, D. C.: ref, 964(488, 489)
May, J. G.: ref, 1771(572), 2602(1700), 2621(264)
May, J. R.: ref, 883(73, 74)
May, L. J.: test, 245
May, P. R. A.: ref, 1351(24, 27, 28, 30, 34, 36), 1498(5153, 5384, 5385, 5759), 1655(103, 124), 2179(203), 2598(1864)
May, R. J.: ref, 551(18, 29)
May, W. W.: ref, 2300(367)
Mayeda, T.: ref, 6(79)
Mayer, J.: ref, 645(17), 1904(74)
Mayer, J. H.: ref, 398(112), 691(40), 701(58), 962(28), 1126(719), 1192(212), 2269(462)
Mayer, R. E.: ref, 501(797, 798, 828, 895), 1257(108), 2300(358)
Mayer, R. S.: exc, 404; ref, 404(5)
Mayes, B.: ref, 354(1458)
Mayfield, B.: ref, 483(29), 551(44), 1351(188), 2512(622)
Maynard, A.: ref, 883(93)
Maynard, M.: ref, 2581(325)
Maynard, N.: ref, 872(16)
Maynard, P.: ref, 872(16)
Maynes, J. O.: test, 1734
Maynor, W.: ref, 1192(222)
Mayo, S. T.: rev, 10, 1937, 1979, 2325

Mazer, G. E.: exc, 1538
Mazza, P.: ref, 794(440)
McAdam, J. A.: ref, 1479(338)
McAdams, D. P.: ref, 2491(2086, 2105, 2106)
McAdoo, H.: ref, 1789(664)
McAllister, H. A.: ref, 1498(5657)
McAllister, S.: ref, 1798(253)
McAlpine, P. J.: ref, 2289(1616)
McAndrews, M. P.: ref, 1969(110)
McArthur, C. C.: rev, 2030
McArthur, K.: ref, 823(23)
McArthur, R. G.: ref, 678(29)
McAuley, H.: ref, 941(24), 1883(34)
McAuliffe, S.: ref, 1771(707)
McAvin, M. W.: ref, 2366(200)
McBee, G.: ref, 1498(5405)
McBee, G. W.: ref, 1498(5120, 5293)
McBride, J. F.: test, 775
McBride, J. W.: ref, 732(406)
McBride, R. D.: ref, 1424(87), 2608(247)
McBride, W. A.: ref, 2598(1466)
McCabe, J. J. C.: ref, 859(816)
McCabe, M. S.: ref, 1883(27)
McCabe, O. L.: ref, 1498(5099)
McCaffrey, S. S.: ref, 501(914), 2534(15)
McCaig, R. A.: ref, 1192(172)
McCall, J. N.: rev, 965, 1269; ref, 780(1699)
McCall, R. B.: ref, 2269(440), 2289(1627, 1628), 2598(1365)
McCall, R. J.: test, 536; rev, 2030; exc, 1106
McCall, W. A.: test, 1421; rev, 2342
McCall, W. C.: rev, 1507
McCallister, J. M.: rev, 1507
McCallum, D. I.: ref, 733(7), 1620(21), 1652(1), 2004(1)
McCampbell, E.: test, 305
McCandless, B. R.: rev, 302, 1201, 1968, 1969, 2289, 2602
McCann, D.: ref, 2300(407)
McCann, D. C.: ref, 2602(2188)
McCann Associates: test, 470, 833, 887, 889, 943, 1422, 1667, 1844, 1845, 1846, 1847, 2302, 2304
McCanne, T. R.: ref, 794(424)
McCarley, D. G.: test, 784
McCarrey, M.: ref, 2029(241)
McCarrey, M. W.: ref, 2029(216, 227), 2657(104)
McCarron, L.: ref, 280(1115), 1479(350), 2602(1925)
McCarthy, D.: test, 1424
McCarthy, J. J.: test, 1126; rev, 696, 850, 2039
McCarthy, M.: ref, 2598(1712)
McCarthy, S. V.: ref, 501(896)
McCarthy, W. G.: test, 1423
McCartney, E.: ref, 823(23), 1153(8), 2018(19)
McCarty, D.: ref, 1498(5670)
McCarty, J. J.: test, 165, 167
McCarty, S. M.: ref, 1498(5670), 2607(203, 212)
McCary, J. L.: rev, 1380
McCaughan, L. R.: ref, 1442(1)
McCaughey, M. W.: ref, 2288(90), 2621(290)
McCaughran, D. A.: ref, 2289(1687), 2602(1814), 2608(206)
McCaul, K. D.: ref, 1547(342)
McCaul, R. L.: rev, 1082, 2520
McClain, E.: ref, 354(1459), 780(1671), 2208(1585)

INDEX OF NAMES

McClain, E. W.: ref, 354(1460), 780(1672), 2208(1586)
McClain, N. J.: ref, 1192(163), 1473(123)
McClearn, G. E.: ref, 932(58), 962(24), 1126(658), 1473(130), 1769(43), 2269(437), 2286(278), 2598(1323), 2602(1636), 2621(236)
McClelland, D. C.: ref, 501(843), 2491(2034, 2052)
McClelland, M.: ref, 2300(452)
McClelland, S. E.: ref, 2289(1642)
McClennen, S. E.: test, 2231
McClung, R. M.: test, 2401, 2402
McClure, J.: ref, 1126(767), 2217(171)
McClure, L. F.: ref, 1341(176)
McClure, R. F.: ref, 859(817)
McColgan, E. B.: ref, 2602(1886)
McCollam, J. B.: ref, 1547(331)
McCombs, K.: ref, 2237(1)
McCombs, K. F.: test, 2237
McConaghy, N.: ref, 354(1480), 751(24), 917(75), 2598(1563)
McConkey, K. M.: ref, 1063(97, 115, 119)
McConkey, R.: test, 1836
McConnell, J. W.: test, 1083, 1093
McConnell, T. R.: test, 1726
McCooskey, J. C.: ref, 2208(1552)
McCordick, S. M.: ref, 2638(137)
McCormick, C.: ref, 1007(31)
McCormick, C. C.: ref, 1170(240)
McCormick, D. J.: ref, 2289(1752)
McCormick, D. P.: ref, 280(1046), 896(1), 964(482), 1007(17), 1126(668), 1459(14), 1771(559), 2557(216), 2602(1669), 2621(250)
McCormick, E. J.: test, 1212, 1855; ref, 1855(25), 2537(558)
McCormick, R. R.: test, 1426
McCornack, R. L.: ref, 1077(56)
McCoy, M.: ref, 932(107)
McCracken, R. A.: test, 2280
McCrady, B. S.: ref, 1547(287), 1931(47)
McCrae, R. R.: ref, 609(200), 859(818, 897, 920), 1046(582, 583, 588), 2208(1527, 1587, 1650, 1661), 2318(1524)
McCraw, R. K.: ref, 2030(4961)
McCray, D. S.: ref, 2602(2032), 2621(394)
McCreadie, R. G.: ref, 1655(80, 96), 2588(32)
McCreary, C.: ref, 1498(5155, 5386, 5485)
McCreary, C. P.: ref, 558(55), 859(921), 1498(5154, 5658)
McCreight, K.: ref, 1851(36)
McCroskey, R. L.: ref, 2472(21)
McCubbin, H. I.: ref, 872(16)
McCullers, J. C.: ref, 1969(120), 2598(1824)
McCulloch, R. W.: rev, 2077
McCulloch, T. L.: exc, 381
McCullough, C. M.: test, 844, 1427; rev, 352, 504, 1569, 1570, 2518
McCully, R. S.: ref, 2030(5003, 5068)
McCutchen, M. B.: ref, 1372(11)
McCutcheon, L. E.: ref, 2208(1546)
McDade, C. E.: ref, 76(610)
McDade, H. L.: ref, 378(7)
McDaniel, E. L.: test, 1148
McDaniel, H.: ref, 344(136)
McDaniel, S. H.: ref, 1498(5760), 1923(27)

McDermott, P. A.: ref, 280(1047), 1126(669), 2030(4962), 2491(2020), 2602(1670), 2621(251)
McDevitt, S. C.: ref, 6(43)
McDill, E.: ref, 590(380), 1866(34), 2160(57)
McDonald, A. S.: rev, 1994
McDonald, B. A.: ref, 2374(191)
McDonald, C.: test, 1380
McDonald, D. H.: test, 687
McDonald, E. T.: test, 664, 2103; ref, 2103(12)
McDonald, P. J.: test, 1380
McDonald, R. T.: ref, 501(862)
McDonough, M. M.: test, 1860
McDuffie, T. E.: ref, 501(897), 1046(584)
McElwain, D. W.: rev, 37, 45, 2015, 2373
McErlaine, E.: test, 1893
McEwan, A. W.: ref, 1931(57), 2208(1688)
McFall, R. M.: ref, 643(139), 1073(120)
McFarlain, R. A.: ref, 1547(264), 2598(1366)
McFarlane, A. H.: ref, 2029(231)
McGaghie, W. C.: rev, 620, 2334
McGaughey, K. J.: ref, 1498(5760), 1923(27)
McGaun, J. D.: ref, 1371(250), 1424(40), 2289(1681)
McGauvran, M. E.: test, 1479
McGee, H.: ref, 2602(1841, 1977)
McGee, M. G.: ref, 2587(40)
McGee, R.: ref, 222(1), 1386(2), 1449(1)
McGhie, A.: ref, 149(14)
McGill, J. C.: ref, 1498(5659)
McGill–Franzen, A.: ref, 2641(13)
McGillivray, J.: ref, 1771(751)
McGinn, P. V.: ref, 501(898)
McGinty, R. L.: ref, 1914(725)
McGlade, F. S.: test, 1428
McGlone, J.: ref, 1485(62), 1513(22), 1771(560), 2269(481), 2598(1367, 1495), 2607(142)
McGlynn, F. D.: ref, 1498(5214), 2353(30)
McGonagle, B.: ref, 2602(1671)
McGough, R. L.: ref, 2413(654)
McGovern, T. V.: ref, 374(226), 2581(346)
McGowan, A. S.: ref, 374(190), 2134(98)
McGrath, F.: test, 2121
McGrath, J. E.: test, 1429, 1430, 1431, 1432, 1741
McGrath, M. J.: ref, 1419(677), 1547(332)
McGraw, K. O.: ref, 2598(1838)
McGraw–Hill Book Co., Inc.: test, 1417
McGraw–Hill Ryerson Ltd.: test, 360
McGrew, J. F.: ref, 2598(1369)
McGuinness, B.: ref, 639(50)
McGuinness, J.: ref, 2228(69)
McGuire, B.: ref, 2413(700)
McGuire, C.: rev, 125, 990
McGuire, C. H.: rev, 673, 831, 2440
McGuire, F. L.: ref, 1576(214)
McGuire, J. P.: ref, 294(15), 354(1540), 1498(5660)
McGuire, M. L.: test, 569, 636, 1433
McGurk, B. J.: ref, 860(138), 1498(5311, 5661), 1914(778), 1931(45, 57), 2077(29), 2208(1588, 1688), 2598(1496)
McGurk, R. E.: ref, 1498(5661)
McHugh, G.: test, 622, 659, 2167, 2169
McHugh, T. G.: test, 2167
McHugh, W. J.: test, 1434
McInnis, C. E.: ref, 2318(1540)
McIntire, W. G.: ref, 400(124), 859(776), 1013(51),

1754(60), 1831(126), 2131(5, 7), 2260(29), 2657(107)
McIntosh, J. R.: test, 2542, 2577
McIntyre, C. W.: ref, 701(50), 958(44), 2602(1784), 2621(292)
McIntyre, S. C.: ref, 76(628), 1498(5041)
McIsaac, M. W.: test, 1153
McIver, D.: ref, 2208(1562)
McKay, A.: ref, 2602(1785), 2608(201)
McKay, H.: ref, 2602(1785), 2608(201)
McKay, S. E.: ref, 1346(7), 2598(1839)
McKeachie, W. J.: rev, 607
McKechnie, G. E.: test, 837, 1316
McKee, D. C.: ref, 2620(19)
McKee, J. H.: test, 1939
McKee, M. G.: rev, 780
McKee, P.: test, 1894
McKeever, W. F.: ref, 932(97), 1771(662)
McKelvie, S. J.: ref, 732(401), 1044(62), 2208(1697)
McKenna, G. J.: ref, 1923(20)
McKenna, M. C.: ref, 226(186), 932(120), 1771(796), 2217(182), 2251(2)
McKenna, P.: ref, 1914(779)
McKenzie, R. B.: ref, 506(29)
McKeown, J. M.: ref, 1655(83), 1883(28)
McKeown, J. R.: ref, 1567(17)
McKernan, J.: ref, 2029(232)
McKerracher, D. W.: ref, 860(113)
McKie, D.: exc, 590
McKiernan, J.: ref, 1224(7)
McKillop, A. S.: test, 935
McKim, M. G.: rev, 1478, 2288
McKinley, J. C.: test, 1498
McKinley, K.: ref, 270(159), 678(37), 1420(3)
McKinney, A. W.: ref, 1192(176), 1341(161)
McKinney, J. D.: ref, 1192(173, 194), 2269(441, 449)
McKinney, M. E.: ref, 1547(252)
McKlean, E. K.: ref, 941(31)
McKnight, R. T.: ref, 354(1541), 1063(120)
McLachlan, J. F. C.: ref, 1197(300), 1498(5156)
McLaren, J.: ref, 2289(1790), 2602(2205)
McLaughlin, A. J.: ref, 780(1666), 2208(1561)
McLaughlin, S. P.: ref, 1914(737), 2077(27)
McLaughlin, T. F.: ref, 2621(252, 349, 407)
McLaughlin, T. J.: ref, 2030(5026)
McLead, T. M.: ref, 1126(703), 1250(15), 2269(459)
McLean, A.: ref, 1498(5206)
McLean, G. N.: ref, 332(2), 1508(119), 1509(10), 1510(46)
McLean, J. E.: ref, 374(191), 1831(180)
McLean, L. D.: ref, 1473(152), 1914(764)
McLean, P. D.: ref, 681(48), 860(128), 1498(5486)
McLeish, J.: rev, 1446, 1552, 2113, 2631
McLellan, A. T.: ref, 1419(704), 2179(255)
McLendon, J. C.: rev, 2166
McLeod, D. B.: ref, 501(863), 1013(85, 108), 1077(56, 64, 65, 66, 75, 76), 1257(142, 143)
McLeod, D. G.: ref, 1013(76)
McLeod, J.: test, 746, 770, 928, 929, 1435; rev, 569
McLeod, P. H.: test, 1333
McLeskey, J.: ref, 1771(525), 2217(109)
McLesky, J.: ref, 1126(768), 2602(2076)
McMahon, F. B.: test, 912
McMahon, R. C.: ref, 2602(1917)
McMahon, R. J.: ref, 116(632), 932(119), 2300(526)

McManis, D. L.: ref, 280(1080), 354(1385), 859(721), 1462(136), 1473(142), 1769(48, 64), 2286(286, 302), 2602(1786), 2621(262, 302)
McManus, J.: ref, 2111(1), 2602(1592), 2621(222)
McMichael, P.: ref, 534(104, 106), 2245(2, 3), 2490(5, 6)
McMillan, D. D.: ref, 678(29)
McMillan, M.: ref, 588(8)
McMordie, W. R.: ref, 1655(108)
McMullin, J. A.: ref, 1798(294)
McMurray, J. G.: exc, 1005
McMurry, R. N.: test, 754, 802, 853, 1788, 2266, 2267
McNair, D.: rev, 472
McNair, D. M.: test, 1904, 2584; rev, 681; ref, 1904(70)
McNairy, R. M.: ref, 1498(5149)
McNamara, S. R.: ref, 2218(8)
McNarnee, B. H.: ref, 645(5)
McNaught, P. C.: test, 775
McNees, M. P.: ref, 719(28)
McNeil, J.: test, 1997
McNeil, M. R.: test, 2017; ref, 2017(2)
McNinch, G.: ref, 1479(320)
McNutt, J. C.: ref, 1126(732), 2103(4)
McParland, M.: test, 1434
McPartland, J. M.: test, 1962; ref, 1192(174)
McPhail, I. P.: ref, 1191(124), 2374(185)
McPherson, J. H.: test, 389
McQuary, J. P.: exc, 899
McQuillan, W.: ref, 859(814)
McRae, K. N.: rev, 2086; ref, 280(1022), 363(3), 400(123), 582(3), 751(2), 770(4), 932(54), 1109(17), 1126(648), 1229(78), 1233(211), 2030(4942), 2086(12), 2286(272), 2289(1594), 2557(209)
McReynolds, L. V.: rev, 2590, 2646; ref, 664(11), 960(9), 1771(601, 792)
McReynolds, P.: rev, 1197, 1726, 2087
McRoskey, R. L.: ref, 1622(40)
McSpadden, J. V.: ref, 691(30)
McTeer, J. H.: ref, 597(2)
McWilliams, B. J.: ref, 2412(39), 2557(229), 2598(1619), 2602(1926), 2608(216)
McWilliams, J.: ref, 1498(5157)
McWilliams, J. M.: ref, 1789(666)
McWilliams, L.: test, 567
McWilliams, S. A.: ref, 890(348), 1789(698)
Mead, B. J.: ref, 325(33)
Meade, E. R.: ref, 1771(793)
Meadows, A. W.: rev, 706, 917
Meagher, R. B.: test, 1487
Mealey, J.: ref, 2289(1657)
Mealor, D. J.: ref, 6(74), 343(11), 2512(609)
Meares, R.: ref, 859(912), 1883(48)
Meares, S.: test, 803, 1437
Measurement Research Division, Human Resources Center, University of Chicago: test, 10, 898, 1455, 1618, 2530, 2553, 2610, 2645
Mecham, M. J.: test, 2104, 2157, 2448, 2541, 2551
Mecham, R. C.: test, 1212, 1855
Meck, D. S.: ref, 1013(70), 1931(46, 54), 2300(415)
Meconi, L. J.: ref, 1405(12)
Medlung, J. M.: ref, 2029(241)
Mednick, B.: ref, 1462(123), 2557(217), 2602(1672)
Mednick, S.: ref, 1462(146), 1883(96)

INDEX OF NAMES

Mednick, S. A.: ref, 2602(2041, 2045, 2192)
Medway, F. J.: ref, 346(102), 1771(746), 2641(8)
Meehan, J.: ref, 2031(458)
Meehl, P. E.: rev, 2343; ref, 1498(5442, 5613)
Meeker, M.: test, 2320
Meeker, R.: test, 2320
Megargee, E. I.: rev, 1208, 1547; ref, 1498(5033, 5777)
Meglino, B. M.: ref, 1295(294)
Mehan, H.: ref, 2602(1787)
Mehle, T.: ref, 157(152)
Mehlinger, H. D.: rev, 418, 596, 2166
Mehrabian, A.: test, 1438, 1439, 1440, 1442, 1443, 1444, 1445, 1448, 1964; ref, 859(757, 922), 1438(1), 1439(1, 2), 1443(1), 1444(1), 1448(1), 1798(215, 243, 244, 287), 2300(359, 547)
Mehren, B.: test, 1546
Mehrens, W.: exc, 591, 592, 593, 594, 595, 1313
Mehrens, W. A.: rev, 2063, 2293, 2325; ref, 77(22)
Mehryar, A. H.: ref, 1931(41)
Meier, M. J.: rev, 308, 1778, 2213
Meier, N. C.: test, 1460
Meier, P.: ref, 6(57), 2289(1716)
Meijer, A.: ref, 874(51, 53, 56), 1537(3), 2602(2189)
Meikle, S.: ref, 609(202), 1904(61)
Mein, L.: ref, 76(592), 2300(364)
Meiners, M. L.: ref, 1486(176), 2246(22)
Meir, E. I.: ref, 374(208), 2208(1642)
Meister, B.: test, 181
Meites, K.: ref, 859(923)
Melaney, C.: ref, 2600(1)
Meldman, M. J.: ref, 226(189), 1371(264), 1949(61), 2602(2218)
Meldrum, W. B.: rev, 58, 73
Meleis, A. I.: ref, 1383(7), 1726(371, 374)
Melendez, F.: test, 1572
Melhus, G. E.: ref, 1547(273), 1789(652)
Melican, G. J.: ref, 1193(145)
Melikian, L. H.: ref, 780(1651)
Meline, T.: ref, 1266(1)
Melisaratos, N.: ref, 683(2), 2100(4)
Mellenbruch, P. L.: test, 1215, 1676; rev, 1957, 2180
Mellinger, J.: ref, 2208(1666)
Mellinger, J. C.: ref, 354(1527), 780(1697), 2413(673)
Mellinger, J. J.: test, 631
Mellis, L. P.: ref, 2598(1837)
Mellits, D.: ref, 932(128), 2602(2221)
Mellits, E. D.: ref, 270(63), 338(8), 1771(543), 2289(1615), 2557(214), 2602(1646), 2608(182)
Mellon, P. M.: ref, 732(402), 1508(136)
Mellstrom, M.: ref, 859(819), 883(86), 2300(416)
Melman, B. S.: ref, 1789(731)
Melnick, C. R.: ref, 338(11), 960(17), 1622(55), 1771(794), 2289(1788)
Melnick, J.: ref, 2300(360)
Melnick, M.: ref, 2289(1605)
Melnychuk, D.: ref, 2134(116)
Melton, R. S.: rev, 649, 1137
Meltzer, H.: rev, 2396
Meltzer, L.: ref, 1250(11)
Menasco, M. B.: ref, 76(611), 2300(417)
Mendel, M.: ref, 1771(815), 2472(33)
Mendelsohn, F. S.: ref, 1923(12)
Mendelsohn, G. A.: rev, 1555
Mendelsohn, M.: ref, 6(47)

Mendelson, W.: ref, 2491(2087), 2602(2077), 2621(408)
Mendhiratta, S. S.: ref, 280(1081), 1419(679), 2598(1497)
Mendlewicz, J.: ref, 645(10, 18, 25, 27)
Mendrovski, L.: ref, 311(36)
Mengel, W.: ref, 701(53), 1771(620), 1934(9), 2478(11)
Mengelkoch, R. F.: test, 1957
Menges, R. J.: rev, 1125
Menn, A. Z.: ref, 354(1401), 890(327), 1555(309), 2613(80)
Mensh, I. N.: rev, 283, 1129, 2607; ref, 1498(5154)
Mentink, J.: ref, 1555(321), 1726(362), 2208(1589), 2318(1560)
Menyhart, J.: ref, 1960(76), 2629(113)
Merbaum, M.: ref, 1498(5158)
Mercer, B. J.: ref, 2582(11)
Mercer, G. W.: ref, 2629(121)
Mercer, J. R.: test, 2387
Mercer, M.: exc, 950, 2672
Mercure, R.: ref, 935(28)
Mercurio, R.: ref, 2030(4963), 2208(1547)
Mercy, J. A.: ref, 2602(2124)
Meredith, K.: ref, 549(4), 2441(36)
Merenda, P. F.: test, 2020; exc, 1969, 2286; ref, 2020(7)
Mergargee, E. I.: rev, 1020
Merian, E. M.: ref, 1498(5662)
Merilä, M.: ref, 1498(5352), 2030(5009), 2598(1525)
Merits-Patterson, R.: ref, 1771(795), 2608(245)
Merricks, A. R.: ref, 932(81)
Merrifield, P.: test, 1172; ref, 1233(214)
Merrifield, P. R.: test, 157, 566, 630, 662, 1257, 1362, 1404, 1809, 2123, 2209; rev, 10, 1937; ref, 1233(215), 2286(281)
Merrill, M. A.: test, 2289
Merritt, T. A.: ref, 270(119), 2289(1724)
Merwin, J. C.: test, 2286, 2287, 2288, 2298; rev, 344, 1625, 2621; exc, 573, 574, 575, 576, 577, 578, 579, 580, 654, 732, 1970, 2614
Mery, M.: exc, 559
Merz, W. R.: rev, 1859
Merzbacher, C. F.: ref, 354(1497), 1498(5487), 2598(1620)
Mesnikoff, A.: test, 1922
Messé, L.: ref, 354(1558), 780(1707)
Messer, S. B.: ref, 1351(182, 189), 2602(1790)
Messerly, C. L.: ref, 2286(336)
Messick, S.: ref, 501(929)
Mestre, J. P.: ref, 501(930), 2455(1)
Metcalfe, R. J. A.: ref, 149(7), 157(141)
Métneki, J.: ref, 280(1139), 964(505), 2289(1753)
Metz, D. E.: ref, 896(5), 911(4)
Metzl, M. N.: ref, 270(142)
Metzner, R.: ref, 859(924)
Meuser, D. M.: ref, 2318(1539)
Meuser, P. E.: ref, 2318(1540)
Mevwissen, J.: ref, 701(63), 1771(666), 2289(1715)
Mew, J. R. C.: ref, 2208(1695)
Mewborn, C. R.: ref, 872(14), 2652(4)
Meyer, B.: rev, 1941, 2528
Meyer, D. E.: ref, 2355(4), 2363(7)
Meyer, D. L.: rev, 892
Meyer, E.: ref, 2581(344)
Meyer, J. K.: ref, 683(1, 3, 4, 6), 2100(8)

Meyer, J. P.: ref, 1547(333), 1798(216)
Meyer, M.: ref, 1479(349), 1871(3), 2218(146), 2602(1920)
Meyer, R. A.: ref, 1192(202), 1257(127), 2269(460)
Meyer, R. E.: ref, 645(5)
Meyer, W. J.: ref, 2289(1666), 2598(1539), 2602(2009)
Meyerowitz, B. E.: ref, 2602(2083)
Meyers, C. E.: test, 2618; rev, 235, 2224; ref, 6(90), 1108(14), 1896(14)
Meyers, R. S.: ref, 2286(320)
Mezynski, K.: ref, 577(1)
Mezzich, A. C.: ref, 1498(5488, 5489)
Mezzich, J. E.: ref, 1498(5488, 5489)
Miaoulis, C. N.: ref, 1373(1), 1758(13)
Miceli, G.: ref, 1914(711, 756)
Michael, J. J.: test, 2340; rev, 1279; ref, 551(39), 553(15), 606(14, 18), 701(60), 932(82)
Michael, L. D.: test, 1516, 1517, 1518
Michael, R.: ref, 2301(32)
Michael, W. B.: test, 734, 2340; rev, 899, 1272, 1510; ref, 76(655), 157(147), 202(7), 344(139, 172, 173), 351(6), 354(1499), 501(829, 864, 865, 899, 928), 551(30, 39, 40, 57, 58, 65, 70), 553(15, 23, 24), 566(110), 606(14, 18, 19), 701(60), 732(393), 734(1, 2, 4, 5), 932(82), 995(147), 1013(114), 1192(256), 1570(8), 1765(7), 1789(672), 1831(128, 146), 2002(4), 2208(1626), 2347(1), 2413(626), 2485(131), 2512(615), 2537(548, 554, 566), 2594(207), 2602(2056)
Michaels, A. C.: ref, 1498(5233), 1798(230), 2300(519, 520, 521), 2413(612), 2638(133, 141, 142, 143)
Michaels, L. A.: ref, 1192(175), 1405(5)
Michaels, T.: ref, 2300(520, 521), 2638(142, 143)
Michal, R. D.: ref, 2134(111)
Michal, W. L.: ref, 794(364)
Michalik, M.: ref, 558(70), 1498(5557), 2300(502)
Michals, K. K.: ref, 338(11), 960(17), 1622(55), 1771(794), 2289(1788)
Michaud, A.: ref, 859(772)
Micheels, W. J.: rev, 1958, 2368
Michela, J. L.: ref, 1904(119)
Michell, L.: ref, 149(13)
Michels, P. J.: ref, 1498(5663), 2030(5069)
Michelson, L.: ref, 639(61)
Michielutte, R.: ref, 1576(218)
Michlin, M. L.: ref, 1272(134), 1351(178)
Middents, G. J.: ref, 1498(5159), 1568(117), 2318(1541), 2598(1368)
Middlesworth, K. L.: ref, 1622(41)
Middleton, P.: ref, 354(1461)
Middleton, W.: test, 2418
Middletown, J.: ref, 270(132)
Midgett, J.: ref, 1479(315), 2217(112)
Midlarsky, E.: ref, 1020(22)
Miele, T. A.: ref, 280(1032)
Mielke, D. H.: ref, 1655(81)
Mierzwa, J. A.: ref, 372(8), 2413(682)
Miezitis, S.: ref, 1831(187)
Migliolli, M.: ref, 2598(1621), 2607(183)
Mihalov, T.: ref, 2289(1634)
Mihler, P.: ref, 2018(13)
Miille, M. P. W.: ref, 2602(2108)
Mikkelsen, E. J.: ref, 1771(752), 2491(2087), 2602(2077), 2621(408)
Mikulecky, L.: ref, 2292(22)

Mikulka, P. J.: ref, 116(567, 595)
Milar, C. R.: ref, 1108(11), 1969(114)
Milberg, W.: ref, 2598(1750, 1828)
Milchus, N. J.: test, 848, 1965, 2131
Miles, L. E.: ref, 1498(5742)
Miles, M.: test, 540
Miles, P. J.: test, 2635
Miles, T. R.: rev, 852, 1620
Miley, D. P.: ref, 1904(76)
Milgram, N. A.: ref, 1914(726)
Milgram, R. M.: ref, 1914(726), 2208(1689), 2300(444)
Milholland, J. E.: rev, 411, 643, 1193, 1341, 1754, 2267, 2269
Milich, R. S.: ref, 2602(1927)
Mill, T. W.: ref, 1498(5664)
Millan, D.: ref, 1240(52)
Millard, B. A.: ref, 2300(486)
Millard, J.: ref, 845(8), 1192(224)
Millard, P. H.: ref, 116(628)
Millen, L.: ref, 2413(599)
Miller, A.: ref, 1250(22), 1555(341)
Miller, C.: ref, 6(85)
Miller, D. J.: ref, 2300(418, 485)
Miller, D. R.: test, 2368
Miller, E.: ref, 2512(612)
Miller, F.: test, 1226
Miller, F. G.: ref, 1547(318), 2300(507), 2353(33), 2598(1679), 2638(140)
Miller, G. H.: ref, 1498(5553)
Miller, H. E.: test, 1945
Miller, H. R.: ref, 1498(5533)
Miller, I. W.: ref, 665(53), 681(71), 1077(50)
Miller, J.: ref, 751(15), 794(402)
Miller, J. E.: ref, 2602(1820)
Miller, J. V.: ref, 2372(3)
Miller, J. W.: ref, 226(186), 932(120), 1185(8), 1771(796), 2217(182), 2251(2)
Miller, K.: ref, 751(15), 794(402)
Miller, K. M.: test, 972, 2035, 2036
Miller, L. C.: test, 1343, 2083; rev, 6, 772, 776, 1515
Miller, L. G.: ref, 381(70), 2289(1754)
Miller, L. J.: ref, 2602(2078)
Miller, L. L.: test, 1993
Miller, L. S.: ref, 1473(165)
Miller, M.: ref, 2602(1788, 2079)
Miller, M. F.: ref, 374(201)
Miller, M. J.: ref, 2318(1588), 2598(1840)
Miller, M. M.: test, 809, 816, 894, 895, 2114, 2115
Miller, M. P.: ref, 2300(419)
Miller, N.: ref, 859(916), 2300(537)
Miller, N. J.: ref, 859(919), 1547(330), 2300(544), 2598(1746)
Miller, P. M.: ref, 859(814)
Miller, R.: ref, 707(21), 794(417), 1853(281)
Miller, R. J.: ref, 1013(91), 1257(147)
Miller, R. S.: ref, 1904(128)
Miller, S.: ref, 1508(115), 2598(1389)
Miller, S. H.: ref, 116(564)
Miller, S. M.: ref, 860(129), 2300(483)
Miller, S. R.: ref, 1769(47), 2621(253)
Miller, T. K.: test, 2330
Miller, T. L.: ref, 1769(60), 2621(293)
Miller, T. P.: ref, 2300(419)
Miller, T. W.: ref, 1495(83)

INDEX OF NAMES

Miller, W. C.: ref, 1498(5160, 5459), 2598(1370)
Miller, W. G.: ref, 1257(144)
Miller, W. H.: ref, 932(114), 1498(5312), 1769(73), 2621(350)
Miller, W. R.: ref, 1498(5313), 1547(352), 1798(288), 1904(77, 115), 2598(1751)
Miller, W. S.: test, 1486
Miller–Tiedeman, A.: test, 1137
Millham, J.: ref, 6(48)
Millichap, J. G.: ref, 280(1082), 2602(1789)
Milligan, W. L.: ref, 1498(5314), 2598(1768)
Millikan, J. L.: ref, 501(886), 1568(142)
Millikin, N. L.: ref, 2413(600)
Millman, J.: test, 606; rev, 245, 934
Millon, T.: test, 1487, 1488
Mills, C.: ref, 354(1462, 1463), 384(6), 501(830), 1192(203), 2343(1041)
Mills, C. J.: ref, 354(1478, 1542, 1543)
Mills, R. E.: test, 1306
Mills, R. H.: ref, 308(24), 1851(34)
Milner, K.: ref, 1295(290)
Milner, R.: ref, 311(39)
Milofsky, E.: ref, 501(911), 2598(1795)
Milon, T. A.: ref, 2602(1745)
Milone, M. N.: ref, 2208(1690)
Milstein, R. M.: ref, 1576(224)
Milstein, V.: ref, 2598(1840)
Milton, F.: ref, 639(53), 883(97)
Milton, L. J.: ref, 859(798), 1904(72)
Mindingall, A.: ref, 400(135), 772(30)
Mineo, R. J.: ref, 1771(558)
Miner, A.: test, 2590
Mines, R. A.: ref, 1831(188)
Ministry of Education, Ontario: test, 1728
Mink, I. T.: ref, 6(90), 1108(14), 1896(14)
Minke, K. A.: ref, 280(1072), 691(33), 751(11)
Minnaar, C. L. J.: test, 15
Minnaar, G. G.: test, 1174
Minnesota Employment Stabilization Research Institute: test, 1506
Minnie, R.: test, 11
Minto, J.: ref, 2598(1729)
Minton, M. J.: ref, 932(113)
Mintz, J.: ref, 1498(5490)
Mirabi, M.: ref, 859(951), 1904(78), 2300(597)
Mirabile, C. S.: ref, 1498(5491)
Miranda, S. B.: ref, 270(69), 2289(1629)
Mirin, S. M.: ref, 645(5)
Miron, M.: ref, 1341(160)
Mischel, W.: ref, 1498(5649)
Mishara, B. L.: ref, 1933(19), 2598(1622)
Mishler, C.: ref, 1473(198)
Mishra, A. B.: ref, 732(405), 2598(1632)
Mishra, S. P.: ref, 1424(83), 1914(854), 2602(2080)
Misiak, H.: ref, 2598(1337)
Miskimins, R. W.: test, 1514
Misner, J. E.: ref, 5(165, 166)
Mitchell, C.: ref, 302(25)
Mitchell, C. T.: ref, 2413(677)
Mitchell, J. V.: rev, 486, 1625, 2534; ref, 590(384)
Mitchell, M.: ref, 1117(442)
Mitchell, M. M.: ref, 1371(249), 1540(12)
Mitchell, N. B.: ref, 2598(1369)
Mitchell, R.: ref, 890(342), 1498(5738)
Mitchell, R. B.: ref, 2208(1662)

Mitchell, R. W.: rev, 815
Mitchell, T. R.: ref, 1295(287), 2638(146)
Mitchell, W.: ref, 2413(649)
Mitroff, I. I.: ref, 2037(148)
Mittelmann, B.: test, 610
Mittler, P.: test, 1283, 2156; ref, 381(57), 823(10), 2289(1595), 2557(211, 225)
Mittman, A.: rev, 1415, 1665, 2143, 2162; exc, 1248
Mittman, B.: ref, 1498(5254), 2030(4987)
Mix, B. J.: test, 2391
Miyake, K.: ref, 1771(734)
Miyake, N.: ref, 1479(346), 1771(649), 2598(1577), 2602(1882)
Miyashita, T.: ref, 371(245), 1126(670)
Mize, J. M.: ref, 1771(673), 2218(149), 2602(1928)
Mlott, S. R.: ref, 349(6), 1498(5160), 2598(1370)
Mobley, W. H.: ref, 1295(294)
Modern Language Association of America: test, 1519, 1520, 1521, 1522, 1523
Modisette, B. R.: test, 1956
Modjeski, R. B.: ref, 202(7), 551(30), 1570(8), 2485(131)
Modu, C. C.: ref, 139(5)
Moelis, I.: ref, 1106(369), 2300(464)
Moeller, G.: ref, 1054(7)
Moen, J. L.: ref, 2289(1630), 2602(1673)
Moers, F.: ref, 302(33)
Moeschler, J. B.: ref, 270(155), 2289(1789), 2602(2190)
Moffitt, T. E.: ref, 2602(2191, 2192)
Mohan, J.: ref, 769(44), 859(803, 863)
Mohandas, T.: ref, 1319(78)
Mohr, L.: test, 1222
Mohs, R. C.: ref, 152(12), 2598(1498)
Moir, W. L. N.: ref, 1535(40)
Mojdehi, H.: ref, 2602(1913)
Moldenhauer, D. L.: ref, 932(114)
Moldofsky, H.: ref, 859(869)
Molina, H.: rev, 2472; exc, 2109
Molinari, V.: ref, 1547(334), 2598(1752)
Molla, P. M.: ref, 1831(214)
Mollenkopf, W. G.: test, 2405; rev, 1746
Mollick, L. R.: ref, 2602(1790)
Molloy, G. N.: ref, 1462(144), 1914(813)
Moncrieff, M.: ref, 1498(5492)
Monetti, C.: ref, 2598(1584)
Money, J.: test, 2285; ref, 2598(1499), 2602(2081)
Monica, E. L.: rev, 455
Monroe, L. J.: ref, 1498(5161)
Monroe, M.: test, 1011, 1187, 1529, 1890, 1895, 1897; rev, 766
Monroe, W. S.: test, 1530
Monsalud, A.: ref, 2208(1523)
Monsen, R. B.: ref, 2598(1500)
Monson, L. B.: ref, 1771(674)
Monson, R. R.: ref, 2289(1641, 1643)
Montague, J.: ref, 1771(786)
Montandon, H. E.: ref, 1498(5162)
Montare, A.: ref, 270(61), 2289(1610)
Montare, A. P. S.: test, 777; ref, 777(1)
Montgomery, D.: test, 2564
Montgomery, G. K.: ref, 1547(265)
Montgomery, K.: ref, 2598(1434), 2607(154)
Montgomery, L. E.: ref, 2300(404)
Montgomery, P.: ref, 922(7)

661

Monti, P. M.: ref, 1789(716), 1904(51)
Montuori, J.: test, 2301
Moodie, A. D.: ref, 280(1142), 2153(2)
Moody, A.: ref, 374(234), 2134(143), 2581(351)
Moog, J. S.: ref, 378(6)
Mooney, E.: test, 1165
Mooney, R. L.: test, 1531
Moore, A. M.: ref, 1197(278)
Moore, C.: ref, 860(106), 1914(760)
Moore, C. A.: ref, 501(810, 853), 1013(61, 83)
Moore, C. L.: ref, 1424(32, 51), 1771(561, 675), 2024(1, 2), 2608(202, 246)
Moore, D.: ref, 1479(348), 1771(802), 2217(184), 2218(20), 2602(2199), 2641(22)
Moore, D. G.: test, 2262
Moore, F. B.: ref, 551(31), 1896(10), 2478(9)
Moore, H.: test, 1936
Moore, J. E.: test, 1532; rev, 627, 754, 1936; ref, 1498(5147, 5149, 5150)
Moore, J. L.: ref, 2113(258), 2598(1841)
Moore, J. M.: ref, 270(86)
Moore, J. R.: ref, 1367(2), 1567(16)
Moore, J. W.: ref, 2286(309)
Moore, L. M.: ref, 1295(302)
Moore, M.: ref, 620(3), 794(393), 1125(15), 2602(1775)
Moore, M. E.: ref, 2030(4943)
Moore, M. J.: ref, 1498(5377)
Moore, M. K.: ref, 1771(755), 2602(2111)
Moore, M. W.: ref, 2621(316)
Moore, P.: ref, 1904(123)
Moore, S.: ref, 859(870)
Moore, S. F.: ref, 398(110), 2602(1791)
Moore, T. L.: ref, 374(191)
Moore, W. A.: ref, 398(123)
Moores, B.: ref, 6(41)
Moos, B.: ref, 872(11)
Moos, B. S.: test, 872; ref, 409(7)
Moos, R. H.: test, 409, 542, 612, 872, 1015, 1466, 1546, 2227, 2534, 2587, 2652; ref, 409(5, 6, 7, 8), 542(18, 19), 872(11, 13, 14), 1466(1), 1546(1, 2, 3, 4), 2652(4)
Moracco, J.: ref, 202(13), 392(2)
Moran, J. D.: ref, 1969(120), 2598(1824)
Moran, M.: ref, 1498(5315), 1831(146), 2300(420), 2413(626)
Moran, M. R.: ref, 483(15), 2602(1674)
Moran, P. W.: ref, 1117(441)
Moran, R. T.: ref, 549(2), 2286(297)
Moray House College of Education: test, 775
More, W. W.: test, 1792
Moreau, V. K.: ref, 1754(109), 2412(43)
Moreault, D. M.: ref, 2602(2123)
Moreland, K. L.: ref, 2030(5004)
Moreland, R. L.: ref, 2289(1741)
Morelli, G.: ref, 859(870, 925)
Morency, A.: test, 227, 229, 2561, 2563
Moreno, S.: test, 1732, 1966, 2248
Moretti, V.: ref, 501(902)
Morey, L. C.: ref, 1498(5577)
Morf, M.: ref, 1498(5163)
Morf, M. E.: ref, 1798(245)
Morgan, A. H.: test, 2297; ref, 2294(118), 2297(10)
Morgan, A. M.: ref, 2160(54)
Morgan, A. M. B.: ref, 2602(2193)
Morgan, C.: ref, 2665(1)
Morgan, D.: test, 1340; ref, 1063(118), 2294(136)
Morgan, F. B.: ref, 1192(222)
Morgan, G.: ref, 859(811)
Morgan, G. A.: ref, 270(115)
Morgan, G. A. V.: test, 826; rev, 317, 321, 617, 1192, 1367
Morgan, J. R.: ref, 2301(26)
Morgan, M.: ref, 344(185)
Morgan, M. S.: ref, 76(631), 501(866), 794(425)
Morgan, R. T. T.: ref, 823(13), 1567(8)
Morgan, S.: ref, 381(69), 2289(1750), 2557(235)
Morgan, S. F.: ref, 2113(254), 2598(1701), 2607(197)
Morgan, S. R.: ref, 1126(733)
Morgan, W. A.: ref, 1555(321), 1726(362), 2208(1589), 2318(1560)
Morgan, W. P.: ref, 681(42), 859(820), 1904(79), 2300(421, 430)
Morgan, W. R.: ref, 1341(177)
Morguelan, F. N.: ref, 1765(7)
Moriarity, A. E.: rev, 678
Morine-Dershimer, G.: ref, 1473(156, 202)
Moritz, C.: test, 1238
Morler, M.: ref, 2300(362)
Morley, N. C.: ref, 1904(120)
Morman, R. R.: test, 2394
Morran, D. K.: ref, 2413(681)
Morris, C. D.: ref, 551(59)
Morris, G. B.: ref, 1789(699)
Morris, H. L.: ref, 1126(780), 1771(610, 778), 2412(38)
Morris, J.: ref, 534(110)
Morris, J. D.: ref, 1192(222), 2602(1792, 1793, 2082)
Morris, J. E.: test, 2038; ref, 1372(11)
Morris, J. H.: ref, 354(1464)
Morris, J. J.: ref, 678(15), 1319(74), 2289(1631)
Morris, K.: ref, 2300(339)
Morris, L.: ref, 344(147), 2598(1400), 2602(1705), 2621(265)
Morris, L. M.: ref, 116(555), 354(1445)
Morris, L. W.: ref, 1405(6), 2598(1396)
Morris, M.: test, 1872
Morris, R.: ref, 1498(5259), 2598(1458)
Morris, R. J.: ref, 883(98)
Morris, T. L.: ref, 1013(71)
Morrisby, J. R.: test, 733
Morrison, A.: ref, 348(2)
Morrison, D.: ref, 270(91), 1126(704), 1771(618), 2289(1680)
Morrison, F. C.: test, 1418, 2432
Morrison, F. J.: ref, 794(376)
Morrison, G.: ref, 2621(276)
Morrison, H. L.: ref, 2030(5036)
Morrison, J. H.: test, 1350, 2428
Morrison, K.: ref, 1671(46)
Morrison, L. P.: test, 2396
Morrison, R. E.: ref, 1726(351)
Morrison, R. F.: ref, 372(2), 1960(69), 2276(4), 2370(16)
Morrison, S.: ref, 42(3), 406(1), 1914(783)
Morrison, S. M.: ref, 2512(578)
Morrison, W. L.: test, 2396
Morrissett, I.: rev, 976, 1525
Morrissey, E. F.: ref, 1831(150)
Morrow, B. H.: ref, 704(14), 2286(316)

INDEX OF NAMES

Morrow, G. R.: ref, 890(335), 1904(66)
Morrow, J. R.: ref, 2208(1626, 1637)
Morrow, R.: test, 604, 605
Morse, J. A.: ref, 2512(585, 602)
Morse, R. M.: ref, 1498(5432), 2179(213), 2598(1445, 1578)
Morsink, C.: ref, 2621(254)
Morstain, B.: ref, 2336(7)
Morstain, B. R.: test, 2336; ref, 2334(19), 2336(5, 6)
Morton, N. W.: test, 2013; rev, 282, 1022, 2318
Morton, R. L.: rev, 197
Morton, T. L.: ref, 280(1096), 1498(5390), 2030(5012), 2289(1692), 2491(2051), 2598(1541), 2602(1847)
Morton, V.: ref, 794(435), 1498(5646)
Mos, L. P.: test, 1929
Mosby, R. J.: ref, 704(15), 2286(317)
Moser, H. E.: rev, 168
Moses, J. A.: ref, 354(1535), 1346(1, 4, 5, 7), 2598(1839)
Mosher, D. L.: rev, 376, 1381, 2396; ref, 780(1642)
Mosher, L. R.: ref, 354(1401), 890(327), 1555(309), 2613(80)
Mosier, C. I.: rev, 1113, 1795, 1942
Moskow, I.: test, 1412
Moskowitz, D. S.: ref, 1875(6)
Moss, C. S.: rev, 399, 2294; ref, 1498(5164, 5493)
Moss, D. M.: ref, 2396(42)
Moss, F. A.: test, 2228, 2403, 2418
Moss, M. H.: test, 2478, 2479, 2480, 2481, 2482
Moss, M. K.: ref, 883(75)
Moss, S.: ref, 2638(132)
Moss, S. W.: ref, 2300(489), 2638(139)
Mossholder, K. W.: ref, 116(629), 1948(102), 2318(1617)
Mothersill, K. J.: ref, 1498(5532), 1798(268)
Motowidlo, S. J.: rev, 1365, 2369; ref, 116(630), 354(1498), 1508(126), 2180(36), 2369(13)
Motta, R. W.: ref, 302(39), 1424(78), 2289(1775), 2608(240)
Moughan, J.: ref, 860(91)
Mount, M. K.: ref, 282(143), 2134(108, 109), 2638(128)
Mourad, S.: ref, 2199(7), 2496(34, 36), 2512(607, 627), 2613(82)
Moutoux, A. C.: test, 1942
Mouw, J. T.: test, 692
Mowbray, R. M.: ref, 883(85), 1197(289)
Mowday, R. G.: ref, 1798(225, 261)
Mowry, H. W.: test, 1299
Moyal, B. R.: ref, 1831(127)
Moyer, S. B.: ref, 1007(32), 2598(1623)
Moyes, F. A.: test, 2450
Moyes, I. C. A.: exc, 1883; ref, 1485(74, 75, 79)
Moynihan, C.: test, 1445
Mozdzierz, G. J.: ref, 1498(5665), 2179(242)
Muchinsky, P. M.: ref, 282(143), 2134(108, 109), 2638(128)
Mucklow, B. M.: ref, 116(593)
Mucowski, R. J.: ref, 1798(262)
Muehl, S.: ref, 76(621)
Muelder, W.: ref, 2537(566)
Mueller, C.: ref, 1257(155)
Mueller, J. H.: ref, 2300(361, 362, 418, 422, 423, 462, 484, 485, 548, 549), 2417(2), 2598(1371, 1501, 1753)
Mueller, K. H.: rev, 1274, 2451
Mueller, L.: ref, 1960(67), 2343(1031)
Mueller, L. K.: ref, 2512(603)
Mueller, S. G.: ref, 202(8), 1193(141)
Mueller, T.: ref, 506(30)
Muia, J. A.: ref, 719(32), 766(28), 935(30)
Mukerjee, M.: test, 820, 1615, 2099; ref, 732(398), 1615(3)
Mulac, A.: ref, 2550(12)
Mulcahy, R.: ref, 1914(748, 797)
Mulder, D. W.: ref, 1498(5337)
Mulhall, D. J.: test, 1791
Mulherin, A.: ref, 1547(333)
Mullaney, D.: ref, 1498(5090), 1904(54)
Mullaney, J. A.: ref, 472(15), 859(871), 883(99)
Mullen, J. M.: ref, 1106(366)
Mullen, P. A.: ref, 200(13), 960(6)
Muller, D.: ref, 551(19, 42, 53), 1479(309), 1896(7, 8, 13), 2300(438)
Muller, D. G.: test, 1896
Muller, D. P. R.: ref, 2289(1632)
Müller, H. F.: ref, 280(1105, 1116), 1506(73, 75), 2598(1574, 1624), 2607(175, 184)
Mulligan, G.: ref, 1257(167)
Mulligan, J. C.: ref, 2289(1764)
Mullin, J. P.: ref, 859(854), 1904(90)
Mullinix, S. D.: ref, 859(941)
Mullins, D.: ref, 2208(1663)
Mullis, I. V. S.: rev, 1437, 2166
Mulvaney, D. E.: ref, 2602(2194)
Mumm, M.: test, 1470
Munby, M.: ref, 860(143), 883(109), 2300(534)
Munday, L. A.: rev, 1292
Munford, A. M.: ref, 2602(2083)
Munford, P. R.: ref, 2602(1794, 2083, 2084)
Mungas, D. M.: ref, 1798(263, 264, 307)
Munger, A. M.: rev, 631, 1884
Munjack, D. J.: ref, 859(821), 1498(5316, 5666)
Munjas, B. A.: ref, 1013(126), 1257(180)
Munoz, A.: ref, 2602(2084)
Muñoz, R. F.: ref, 1498(5561)
Munro, M. E.: ref, 780(1684)
Munson, J. M.: ref, 2029(233, 234)
Munz, D. C.: ref, 2208(1680), 2370(19)
Muramoto, O.: ref, 1126(734)
Murawski, B. J.: ref, 280(1173), 1498(5765), 1547(354)
Murchie, D. K.: ref, 2621(409)
Murden, R.: ref, 1576(205)
Murgatroyd, D.: ref, 780(1678)
Murphey, H. A.: ref, 653(157), 2621(372)
Murphy, D. L.: ref, 1197(287), 1247(164), 1498(5249, 5387, 5592, 5599, 5618), 1531(294), 2030(5055), 2413(670), 2598(1570, 1696, 1703)
Murphy, D. P.: ref, 1568(143)
Murphy, E.: ref, 941(28), 1883(43, 74)
Murphy, H.: ref, 2208(1632)
Murphy, H. A.: test, 1551
Murphy, H. D.: exc, 899
Murphy, J.: ref, 270(140, 159), 311(37), 678(37), 1420(3)
Murphy, J. A.: rev, 132, 1636
Murphy, M. J.: ref, 1557(10)

Murphy, P. J.: ref, 766(34), 2015(214), 2300(419), 2621(436)
Murphy, R.: ref, 1754(61)
Murphy, T. J.: ref, 1789(717)
Murranka, P. A.: ref, 1855(26)
Murray, A. D.: ref, 311(46)
Murray, D.: ref, 1904(130), 2300(608)
Murray, D. J.: test, 322
Murray, E.: rev, 877, 878; exc, 767
Murray, E. J.: ref, 794(418), 1106(371), 1488(3), 2300(458, 467)
Murray, G. B.: ref, 2598(1708)
Murray, H. A.: test, 2491
Murray, J. D.: ref, 1771(676)
Murray, J. E.: ref, 751(22), 1831(158)
Murray, M. E.: ref, 701(50, 51), 766(24), 958(44, 45), 1831(147), 2602(1784, 1795), 2621(292, 294)
Murray, P.: ref, 678(30), 1771(699), 2131(6), 2557(234)
Murray, R. B.: ref, 1754(81)
Murray, R. E.: ref, 1486(183)
Murray, R. M.: ref, 1883(52, 61)
Murray, S. G.: ref, 354(1574), 1495(91), 2318(1618)
Murray, T.: ref, 2621(217)
Murray, T. J.: ref, 609(203), 911(2)
Murrell, M. E.: ref, 116(565), 1498(5494)
Murrillo, L. G.: ref, 280(1026), 794(370), 963(128), 1240(50), 1498(5079), 2030(4949), 2598(1316), 2607(133)
Mursell, J. L.: rev, 1261, 1275, 2113
Murstein, B. I.: rev, 396, 1372; exc, 1347, 2672; ref, 1498(5165)
Musatti, T.: ref, 534(99)
Mushak, P.: ref, 1108(11), 1969(114)
Musselwhite, C. R.: ref, 1126(769), 1771(747)
Musun–Baskett, L.: ref, 704(23)
Muthard, J. E.: test, 885
Mutti, M.: test, 1967
Myers, B.: ref, 1771(677), 1914(814)
Myers, C. B.: ref, 1473(132), 2594(195)
Myers, C. T.: rev, 178, 2175
Myers, H.: ref, 2208(1636, 1696)
Myers, I. B.: test, 1555
Myers, J. A.: ref, 2160(60), 2217(131)
Myers, J. K.: ref, 1922(11), 2322(11)
Myers, L. B.: ref, 501(831), 1498(5317), 2015(203)
Myers, M.: ref, 344(191)
Myers, R. A.: test, 371
Myers, S. S.: rev, 2238
Myhill, J.: ref, 1197(290)
Myklebust, H. R.: test, 729, 1934
Mylet, M.: ref, 1498(5495), 2179(226)
Mynhardt, J. C.: ref, 2629(120)
Myrianthopoulos, N. C.: ref, 2289(1703), 2602(1873)
Myrick, R. D.: ref, 2602(2014)
Myrow, D. L.: ref, 1257(145)
Nacev, V.: ref, 1498(5667)
Nachtman, W.: test, 1250
Nadeau, G. G.: ref, 2537(556)
Nadelman, L.: ref, 116(540), 2608(235)
Naditch, M. P.: ref, 1498(5166)
Naeser, M.: ref, 308(19)
Naeser, M. A.: ref, 308(10, 11)
Nafincy, A.: ref, 2598(1754)
Nafziger, D. H.: rev, 1259, 1839

Nagel, D.: ref, 1419(705)
Nagel, K. E.: ref, 1498(5084)
Nagelberg, D. B.: ref, 1498(5668)
Nagle, R. J.: ref, 1479(351), 1754(107), 2286(318), 2602(2036, 2095)
Naglieri, J. A.: ref, 270(156), 964(516), 1424(52, 65, 71, 72, 84, 85), 1914(889), 2289(1725), 2602(2085, 2086, 2087, 2195, 2196), 2621(410, 411)
Nagpal, M.: ref, 859(872)
Nagy, K. A.: ref, 1934(12)
Nagy, V. T.: ref, 2179(236)
Nahas, A. D.: ref, 2602(1916)
Nahinsky, I. D.: ref, 76(631), 501(866), 794(425)
Nahor, A.: ref, 1240(62), 1904(105), 2328(4)
Nairn, A.: ref, 501(900)
Naismith, L. D.: ref, 859(873)
Naitoh, P.: ref, 1498(5090), 1904(54)
Nalachowski, N.: ref, 2289(1748)
Nammalvar, N.: ref, 280(1050), 2607(146)
Nanassy, L. C.: rev, 334, 1952
Nance, A. L.: ref, 308(27), 1851(49)
Nangia, B. S.: ref, 280(1124), 2602(1971), 2608(221)
Naper, J. T.: test, 1175
Napier, J. D.: ref, 606(15)
Napoli, A.: ref, 780(1654)
Nardi, P. M.: ref, 354(1474), 1498(5383)
Naremore, R. C.: ref, 1771(633)
Nasby, W.: ref, 2602(1648)
Nash, M. M.: ref, 1498(5318)
Nash, M. R.: ref, 1063(106), 2297(12)
Nash, N.: test, 1858
Naslund, R. A.: test, 2260
Nason, D. E.: rev, 1220, 2024
Nasrallah, H. A.: ref, 2598(1372, 1449)
Nassi, A. J.: ref, 2037(147)
Natalicio, D. S.: rev, 231, 2109
Nathan, P. E.: ref, 2300(543)
Nathan, R. G.: ref, 681(40), 2598(1491)
Nation, J. E.: ref, 212(11), 1622(54), 1771(775)
Nation, J. R.: ref, 1498(5669)
Nation, R. L.: ref, 311(46)
National Association of Secondary–School Principals: test, 1231, 2119, 2329
National Board of Medical Examiners: test, 1458
National Business Education Association: test, 304, 332, 944, 1352, 1556, 2307, 2339, 2527
National Institute for Personnel Research: test, 199, 406, 555, 946, 968, 1467, 1777, 2414, 2415, 2471
National Institute of Industrial Psychology: test, 198, 910, 1027, 1028, 1029, 1030, 1031, 1032, 1033, 1034, 1035, 1036, 1037, 1038, 1453, 1582, 1583, 2556
National League for Nursing, inc.: test, 1585, 1586, 1587
National Merit Scholarship Corporation: test, 1866
National Occupational Competency Testing Institute: test, 1591, 1592, 1593, 1594, 1595, 1596, 1597, 1598, 1599, 1600, 1601, 1602, 1603, 1604, 1605, 1606, 1607, 1608, 1609, 1610, 1611, 1612, 1613, 1614
National Study of School Evaluation: test, 1763, 2335
Naumann, T. F.: rev, 631, 1520, 1559; ref, 2289(1675)
Navarro, D. J.: ref, 1462(145), 1498(5496)
Navran, L.: ref, 780(1652), 2318(1589)
Naylor, F. D.: ref, 1197(321), 2300(424, 550), 2318(1619)
Naylor, G. F. K.: test, 1564; ref, 2598(1352)

INDEX OF NAMES

Naylor, G. J.: ref, 1883(31)
Ndetei, D. M.: ref, 1883(95)
Neafsey, S.: ref, 2598(1794), 2602(2137)
Neal, W. R.: test, 224; ref, 224(1, 2)
Neale, J. M.: ref, 645(26)
Neale, M. D.: test, 1567; exc, 2289
Nedd, A. N. B.: ref, 794(426, 437), 1013(57)
Nedelsky, L.: rev, 143, 989
Nee, J.: ref, 1923(14, 22)
Nee, L.: ref, 2491(2087), 2602(2077), 2621(408)
Needleman, H. L.: ref, 226(172), 701(65), 1371(254), 1771(678), 2113(252), 2602(1929)
Neel, A. F.: ref, 280(1048), 2491(2021), 2602(1675)
Neely, M. A.: ref, 372(7, 11), 374(192, 199, 200, 214)
Neff, J. M.: ref, 381(72), 1101(49), 2602(2064)
Neidert, G. L.: ref, 113(27), 1498(5593), 1904(110)
Neidhart, H.: ref, 859(737)
Neidt, C. O.: rev, 344, 2118
Neilans, T. H.: ref, 883(71)
Nel, B. F.: test, 2242
Nell, V.: ref, 354(1465)
Nelson–Jones, R.: ref, 859(926)
Nelson, A. R.: test, 2515
Nelson, B. A.: ref, 1077(51)
Nelson, C. H.: rev, 126, 440, 594, 1065; exc, 591, 592, 593, 594, 595
Nelson, C. W.: test, 1301, 1549, 2365, 2367
Nelson, D.: test, 1822; ref, 1771(616), 1789(674), 1969(93), 2413(622), 2598(1493)
Nelson, D. A.: ref, 1557(10), 2598(1585)
Nelson, D. L.: ref, 2300(493), 2417(1)
Nelson, H. E.: ref, 823(22), 2077(33), 2598(1502), 2602(2088)
Nelson, H. L.: ref, 1655(101)
Nelson, J. G.: ref, 354(1544), 1914(844), 2244(43)
Nelson, J. L.: rev, 159, 1647
Nelson, K. B.: ref, 2602(1743), 2621(281)
Nelson, M. J.: test, 1073, 1570
Nelson, N. M.: ref, 311(39)
Nelson, N. W.: ref, 1622(40)
Nelson, P.: ref, 344(165)
Nelson, P. K.: ref, 1013(110)
Nelson, R. B.: ref, 302(38), 344(179), 1192(233), 1473(195), 2292(29)
Nelson, R. O.: ref, 681(56), 883(87), 1498(5619)
Nelson, R. W.: ref, 2598(1610)
Nelson, V. L.: ref, 354(1408), 890(328)
Nelson, W. H.: ref, 2602(2143)
Nelson, W. M.: ref, 1498(5437), 2286(298), 2301(24, 36), 2582(18), 2598(1503, 1581)
Neman, R. S.: ref, 1498(5507)
Nemec, R. E.: ref, 280(1083), 2607(163)
Nemeth, G.: ref, 1498(5522)
Nendlewicz, J.: ref, 1612(1)
Nenty, H. J.: ref, 653(173)
Neph, L.: ref, 2665(1)
Nerbonne, G. P.: ref, 2646(10)
Nerviano, V. J.: ref, 354(1409, 1427), 1498(5670), 2208(1548)
Ness, R. C.: ref, 609(225)
Nesselroade, J. R.: ref, 653(158), 1257(156), 1765(10), 1914(825)
Netley, C.: ref, 2602(1734), 2621(277)
Nettle, M. D.: ref, 883(76), 2300(365)

Neu, R. L.: ref, 678(26), 960(11), 1771(655), 2107(9), 2218(143), 2598(1582), 2602(1889), 2608(213)
Neufeld, J. S.: ref, 363(12), 2602(2089)
Neufeld, R. W. J.: ref, 9(14), 1914(799), 1919(38), 2300(425), 2620(16)
Neufeldt, D. E.: ref, 2208(1624)
Neuger, G. J.: ref, 2300(598), 2598(1842)
Neuman, S. B.: ref, 932(121), 1126(785), 1478(79)
Neuringer, C.: rev, 1385, 2044; ref, 1498(5037, 5060, 5061, 5098)
Nevill, D. D.: ref, 1789(647), 2413(601)
Neville, C. W.: ref, 2300(339)
Neville, D.: ref, 1798(207)
Neville, M. H.: ref, 928(4)
Nevo, B.: ref, 354(1410)
New Mexico State Department of Education: test, 1588, 1589, 1590
New York Times: test, 2094
Newburg, J. E.: test, 669
Newcomb, T.: rev, 1795, 1945
Newcomer, P. L.: test, 2445; rev, 550, 1935; ref, 1126(759), 2445(1)
Newland, G. A.: ref, 2512(661)
Newland, J. K.: ref, 1771(545)
Newland, T. E.: test, 299; rev, 534, 1101, 1823, 2627
Newlon, L. L.: ref, 501(901)
Newman, A.: ref, 2491(2088), 2602(2090)
Newman, A. P.: ref, 1193(137)
Newman, B. H.: rev, 2041
Newman, E. H.: ref, 1969(86), 2607(143)
Newman, F. L.: ref, 677(2)
Newman, J.: rev, 283, 2607
Newman, K.: ref, 195(1), 464(3), 1451(1)
Newman, O. S.: ref, 1498(5319), 2598(1504)
Newman, T. S.: ref, 2607(128)
Newman, W.: ref, 116(560), 354(1452), 1789(669)
Newmark, C. S.: ref, 1498(5167, 5168, 5255, 5320, 5321, 5322, 5671, 5672), 2030(5037), 2620(12, 14, 19)
Newport, K.: ref, 280(1145)
Newson–Smith, J. G. B.: ref, 941(29), 1883(53)
Newsweek Educational Program: test, 646, 1581
Newton, K. R.: rev, 298, 2384
Neyhart, A. E.: test, 754
Neyhart, H. L.: test, 754
Neyhus, A. I.: test, 729
Neyland, D.: ref, 932(73), 962(25), 1771(592), 2293(10), 2472(14)
NFER–Nelson Publishing Co.: test, 252, 1406, 1407, 1408, 1409, 2003, 2150, 2152, 2487, 2517
Nias, D. K. B.: ref, 859(758), 1229(93), 1914(815)
Nibbelink, W. H.: rev, 248, 1415
Nicewander, A.: ref, 157(152)
Nicewander, A. W.: ref, 1351(179)
Nichol, S. S.: ref, 2413(594)
Nicholas, L. E.: ref, 1851(38), 2017(5)
Nicholls, J. G.: ref, 1771(587)
Nichols, M. P.: ref, 472(11), 643(132), 1046(572), 1498(5169, 5323), 2030(4964), 2208(1549), 2300(387), 2318(1542), 2491(2022), 2598(1373), 2621(255)
Nichols, N. J.: ref, 1192(176), 1341(161)
Nichols, P. L.: ref, 280(1118), 751(29), 1126(736), 2602(1946), 2621(358)
Nichols, R. C.: rev, 483, 2453; ref, 354(1416)

Nicholson, C. L.: ref, 1969(87), 2602(1676)
Nicholson, T.: ref, 1912(4)
Nicoll, R. C.: ref, 582(5)
Nidiffer, F. D.: ref, 1531(295)
Nielsen, H. D.: ref, 409(8)
Nielsen, H. H.: ref, 280(1146), 381(73), 751(37), 1505(14), 2602(2091)
Nielsen, J.: ref, 1419(676)
Nielsen, L.: ref, 116(594)
Nielsen, S. L.: ref, 1547(351)
Nielson, E. C.: ref, 354(1408), 890(328)
Nielson, W. R.: ref, 1206(1), 1547(335), 2300(551)
Nieman, L. L.: ref, 501(832), 1527(47)
Nies, A.: ref, 2100(9)
Niesz, N. L.: ref, 1789(648)
Nietzel, M. T.: ref, 1798(250, 292)
Nightingale, M. E.: ref, 859(935), 1063(129)
Nigl, A. J.: ref, 2602(2202), 2621(451)
Nihira, K.: test, 6; ref, 6(90), 1108(14), 1896(14)
Nijs, P.: ref, 1498(5513)
Niles, J. A.: ref, 1769(61)
Nilgram, P.: ref, 1671(46)
Nimnicht, G.: ref, 2602(1808), 2608(205)
Nisbet, J.: rev, 1620
Nisbet, S.: test, 825; rev, 972, 1102
Nitko, A. J.: rev, 551, 914, 1412
Niven, R. G.: ref, 1498(5432), 2598(1578)
Nixon, G. F.: ref, 2300(363)
Noble, E. P.: ref, 1052(2), 2179(244)
Noble, F. C.: ref, 1013(124), 2300(592)
Noble, W. G.: test, 1070
Noddin, E. M.: ref, 1498(5554)
Noerager, J. P.: ref, 2208(1625)
Noeth, R. J.: ref, 76(588), 77(21), 2577(2)
Nogrady, M. E.: test, 2618
Nolan, C. Y.: test, 2038
Nolan, G. A.: ref, 226(179), 962(32), 2217(164), 2280(13)
Nolan, J. D.: ref, 2598(1505)
Nolan, M.: ref, 823(23), 1153(8), 2018(19)
Noland, M.: ref, 2621(239)
Noll, J. D.: ref, 1851(29), 2017(3), 2509(1)
Noll, R. L.: ref, 1789(649)
Noll, V. H.: rev, 165, 336, 1082, 2467A; exc, 302
Noppe, L. D.: ref, 1013(58)
Norbeck, J. S.: ref, 1904(129)
Norcross, C. E.: rev, 2286
Nordland, F.: ref, 1754(118), 2512(659)
Nordquist, T. A.: ref, 2029(235), 2155(11)
Nordstrom, C.: ref, 1192(238), 1272(138), 1479(364)
Norem–Hebeisen, A.: ref, 1498(5118)
Norlin, B.: ref, 2030(4983)
Norman, G. R.: ref, 2029(231)
Norman, R. D.: ref, 780(1689), 2598(1625)
Norman, W. B.: ref, 2598(1590, 1591)
Norman, W. H.: ref, 665(53), 681(71)
Norman, W. T.: rev, 648, 1042, 1498; ref, 2208(1655)
Norrell, C. L.: test, 1822
Norris, A. H.: ref, 1046(588)
Norris, D. A.: ref, 270(63), 338(8), 1771(543), 2289(1615), 2557(214), 2602(1646), 2608(182)
Norris, E.: ref, 1940(86)
Norris, L.: ref, 76(591)
Norris, M.: ref, 896(8), 1771(797)
Norris, R. C.: rev, 1118

Norrish, M.: ref, 860(96), 2602(2023), 2608(231)
Norsworthy, N.: test, 2125
North, A. J.: ref, 2598(1843), 2607(218)
North, B.: ref, 2598(1717), 2607(199)
North, R. D.: rev, 344, 345, 2325, 2500
Northrop, G.: ref, 1498(5647)
North Sydney Region Infants' Mistresses' Council: test, 1411
Norton, J. C.: ref, 280(1084), 609(204), 1462(119), 1498(5170, 5324), 1655(74), 2598(1314, 1506, 1626), 2607(164)
Norton, P. M.: ref, 701(69), 2602(1964)
Norton, S. J.: ref, 549(1), 2598(1374), 2647(1)
Novack, H. S.: test, 2020; ref, 2020(7)
Novaco, R. W.: ref, 2598(1533)
Noval, R.: ref, 1498(5768), 1923(28)
Novar, L.: ref, 2289(1687), 2602(1814), 2608(206)
Novelly, R. A.: ref, 2598(1700), 2607(196)
Now, J.: test, 410
Nowak, M. J.: ref, 1233(231)
Nowick, K. D.: ref, 270(140), 311(37)
Nowicki, S.: ref, 116(566), 501(811), 1831(166), 2300(486)
Noyes, E. S.: rev, 570
Nuell, L. R.: ref, 2413(589)
Numey, O. D.: test, 1965
Nunn, T.: test, 1340
Nunnally, J. C.: rev, 1970
Nurcombe, B.: ref, 1126(654), 1771(528), 2608(174)
Nurminen, M.: ref, 2030(4995), 2598(1469)
Nurnberg, H. G.: ref, 280(1030), 2598(1330)
Nurss, J. R.: test, 1479
Nuttall, D.: test, 2096
Nuttall, E. V.: ref, 1233(225)
Nuttall, R. L.: ref, 1233(225)
Nutting, P. A.: ref, 344(171)
Nyberg, A. M.: test, 151; ref, 151(1)
Nyberg, V. R.: test, 151; ref, 151(1), 344(190), 1914(890)
Nyborg, H.: ref, 1419(676)
Nyfield, G.: test, 38, 149, 282, 940, 1808
Nyman, B.: ref, 2217(176), 2598(1786)
Nymann, C.: test, 548
Nystul, M.: ref, 1789(732)
Nystul, M. S.: ref, 1771(757), 2413(602, 655)
Oakland, J. A.: ref, 1789(679)
Oakland, T.: rev, 922, 961; ref, 226(169), 280(1117), 344(156, 162, 186), 345(46), 346(105), 482(6, 8), 958(47), 1473(157, 169), 1479(330, 340), 1771(636), 2217(132), 2218(11), 2387(3, 5), 2478(10), 2602(1930, 2092)
Oakley, C. A.: rev, 623
Oanh, N. T.: ref, 1831(128)
Oaster, T. R.: ref, 2164(42)
Obenauf, P. A.: ref, 1257(140), 2531(1)
Ober, S. S.: test, 839
Oberklaid, F.: ref, 1424(53, 86)
Obermeier, G. E.: ref, 501(827)
Obitz, F. W.: ref, 890(337), 2587(38)
Obler, L.: ref, 308(16, 17), 1109(21), 1853(292), 2598(1698), 2607(193)
Oboler, L.: ref, 76(600), 501(813), 590(379)
O'Brien, C. P.: ref, 1197(281), 1419(704), 1498(5182), 1547(267, 352), 2179(255)
O'Brien, D. P.: ref, 378(13)

INDEX OF NAMES

O'Brien, G. T.: ref, 883(66)
O'Brien, M.: ref, 200(14)
O'Brien, R. A.: ref, 1875(4)
O'Brien, S. F.: ref, 932(108)
O'Brien, T. C.: rev, 716
Obrist, W. D.: ref, 2598(1664)
Obrzut, A.: ref, 1473(218), 2602(2177)
Obrzut, J. E.: ref, 696(5), 1473(218), 1479(378), 2217(183), 2602(2177)
Obstoj, I.: ref, 1063(87), 2294(111)
Obuchi, K.: ref, 2491(2063)
Ochoa, A. S.: rev, 598, 1898
Ochsner, G. J.: ref, 308(27), 1851(49)
Oclatis, K. A.: ref, 1789(718), 2300(552)
O'Connell, A.: ref, 2598(1502)
O'Connell, A. N.: ref, 354(1545)
O'Connell, E.: test, 2098
O'Connell, E. J.: ref, 308(20), 311(18)
O'Connell, L.: ref, 2289(1687), 2602(1814, 2066), 2608(206)
O'Connell, P. F.: ref, 308(20)
O'Connell, V. I.: ref, 691(46), 1126(777)
O'Conner, J. P.: ref, 1798(213)
O'Conner, K.: ref, 860(145)
O'Conner, P. D.: ref, 1473(180), 2582(12), 2602(1931)
O'Connor, J.: test, 1670, 1671, 1672
O'Connor, J. P.: ref, 558(56), 780(1650), 1173(1)
O'Connor, M.: ref, 953(14)
O'Connor, M. J.: ref, 270(143)
Oczkowski, G.: ref, 794(396), 1498(5298)
Oda, E. A.: exc, 1970
Oddsen, K. T.: exc, 1915
Oddy, M.: ref, 1240(56)
Odell, C. W.: rev, 344, 1473
O'Dell, S. L.: ref, 2598(1627)
Odom, J. V.: ref, 883(87)
O'Donnell, J. M.: ref, 542(20)
O'Donnell, J. P.: ref, 703(8), 1126(706), 1371(250), 1424(40, 73), 2289(1681)
O'Donoghue, P. A.: ref, 2289(1764)
O'Donoghue, P. D.: ref, 678(23)
Oertel, J.: ref, 1498(5522)
Oeschger, D. E.: ref, 76(631), 501(866), 794(425)
Oetting, E. E.: test, 219
Oetting, E. R.: test, 562, 2416
Oettinger, L.: ref, 2602(1796)
O'Farrell, E.: ref, 780(1669)
Offenbach, S. I.: ref, 932(83), 1126(705), 2602(1800)
Offer, D.: test, 1673; ref, 1673(11), 2030(5070)
Office of Instructional Resources, University of Illinois at Urbana–Champaign: test, 1121
Offord, K. P.: ref, 1498(5590)
Ogawa, T.: ref, 2030(5091)
Oglesby, D. M.: ref, 1007(27, 36, 41), 1229(98, 105), 2602(1885, 2033, 2152), 2621(329, 395, 431)
Ogletree, A. M.: ref, 2491(2017)
O'Gorman, J.: ref, 2581(344)
O'Gorman, J. G.: ref, 2491(2023)
O'Grady, D. J.: ref, 270(105), 280(1103), 751(23), 2289(1700), 2557(227), 2602(1871), 2621(320)
O'Grady, K. E.: ref, 116(567, 595), 2300(426)
Ogunlade, J. O.: ref, 1914(780)
O'Haire, T. D.: ref, 859(927), 1555(335), 2512(649)
O'Hara, M. W.: ref, 681(49)
O'Hara, T.: ref, 1257(144)

O'hara–Devereaux, M.: ref, 1555(321), 1726(362), 2208(1589), 2318(1560)
Ohlde, C. D.: ref, 2318(1590), 2413(656)
Ohlson, E. L.: ref, 76(592), 2300(364)
Ohtsuka, Y.: ref, 2354(33, 34), 2366(194)
Ohvall, R. A.: ref, 2318(1555)
Ohwaki, S.: ref, 381(66)
Oikawa, K.: ref, 542(21), 2557(224), 2598(1507)
Okada, M.: ref, 354(1436)
Okasha, A.: ref, 1883(88)
Okasha, M. S.: ref, 1883(50)
O'Keefe, E. J.: ref, 1853(296)
Okoh, N.: ref, 483(35), 2512(650)
Okuna, J. S.: ref, 590(385), 2160(71)
Olczak, P. V.: ref, 1209(36), 1789(726)
Oldridge, O. A.: exc, 2608
Oldroyd, R. J.: ref, 294(12)
O'Leary, D. E.: ref, 890(349), 1498(5497, 5673), 2179(227), 2598(1513)
O'Leary, D. S.: ref, 2300(598), 2598(1842, 1853), 2602(2197)
O'Leary, K. D.: ref, 344(140)
O'Leary, M.: ref, 890(349), 1498(5076, 5085, 5171), 2179(227)
O'Leary, M. R.: ref, 472(14, 18, 20), 665(41, 46), 890(350), 1013(59, 93, 109, 132), 1462(118), 1498(5058, 5086, 5172, 5250, 5325, 5497, 5498, 5499, 5673, 5761), 2179(195, 212, 228, 243), 2413(627), 2587(44), 2598(1375, 1391, 1513, 1628, 1629)
O'Leary, S. G.: ref, 344(142), 1479(318), 2621(256)
O'Leary, V.: test, 613, 1234
Olejnik, A. B.: ref, 666(5)
Olen, L. G.: test, 614
Olesker, W.: ref, 963(130), 1817(1), 2638(129)
Oleski, M. S.: ref, 1197(279)
Olexy, J. E.: test, 705
Olguin, L.: ref, 344(172, 173)
Oliphant, G.: test, 1724
Oliphant, G. G.: test, 1723
Olivas, L.: ref, 1493(124)
Oliver, D. W.: rev, 2166
Oliver, J. E.: test, 373, 778
Oliver, L. W.: ref, 374(193), 1970(10), 2318(1543), 2581(308)
Oliverio, M. E.: rev, 944, 1675, 1936, 2363
Olivier, N. M.: test, 191
Ollendick, D. G.: ref, 483(30), 872(8), 932(99), 2300(487), 2301(33)
Ollendick, T. H.: ref, 883(76), 2300(365), 2301(34), 2602(1932)
Oller, D. K.: ref, 1814(5), 2602(1797)
Oller, J. W.: exc, 290
Ollerenshaw, S. J.: ref, 2300(349)
Ollila, L.: ref, 932(87)
Olofsson, A.: ref, 1914(850)
Olsen, E. J.: ref, 1498(5326)
Olsen, H. D.: ref, 1568(116)
Olsen, L. K.: ref, 1(1)
Olshavsky, J. E.: ref, 2292(28)
Olson, A. T.: ref, 859(928), 1405(7), 2300(553)
Olson, C. J.: rev, 306, 591
Olson, D.: ref, 1498(5691)
Olson, D. R.: ref, 2300(554)
Olson, R. P.: ref, 2179(257)

Olson, T. D.: ref, 1498(5067)
Olsson, N. G.: ref, 1351(199), 2300(580), 2598(1811), 2607(213)
Oltman, P. K.: test, 398, 794, 1013; ref, 501(810, 853), 794(377, 410), 1013(61, 83)
Oltmanns, T. F.: ref, 1498(5327), 1655(97)
O'Malia, L.: ref, 472(16), 2208(1635)
O'Malley, J. E.: ref, 2557(240), 2598(1742), 2602(2065)
O'Malley, P. M.: ref, 932(53), 1969(82), 2537(545)
Omizo, M.: ref, 2208(1637)
Omizo, M. M.: ref, 354(1499), 732(408), 734(3, 4), 995(147), 1192(256), 2208(1626, 1670), 2655(6)
Omran, A. R.: ref, 1498(5328)
Omvig, C. P.: ref, 374(194)
Omwake, K. T.: test, 2228
O'Neil, J. M.: ref, 2134(99, 110, 111, 119), 2318(1591, 1604)
O'Neil, P.: ref, 2300(385)
O'Neil, P. M.: ref, 116(615)
O'Neill, G. P.: ref, 653(143)
O'Neill, J.: ref, 1424(60)
O'Neill, J. M.: ref, 2134(131)
O'Neill, M.: ref, 860(109), 2598(1564)
O'Neill, P.: ref, 398(111), 478(8), 1257(137), 1771(634), 2030(5019)
O'Neill, P. C.: ref, 398(111), 478(8), 1257(137), 1771(634), 2030(5019)
Oon, M. C. H.: ref, 1883(52, 61)
Oosthuizen, S.: test, 1026, 1166, 1167, 1228
Opel, M. R.: ref, 1257(122)
Opolot, J. A.: ref, 859(759), 1914(727), 2491(2024), 2598(1376)
Oppenheimer, K. C.: ref, 2300(576)
O'Pray, R. J.: ref, 2374(193)
Orbach, I.: ref, 2413(646), 2491(2058), 2602(1798, 1933)
Orchik, D. J.: ref, 378(11), 2472(18)
Orcutt, M. A.: ref, 2343(1046), 2581(326)
Ord, I. G.: test, 1574
O'Reilly, C.: ref, 1508(115)
O'Reilly, C. A.: ref, 116(564)
O'Reilly, E.: ref, 859(922), 1439(2), 1798(287), 2300(547)
O'Reilly, M.: ref, 859(903)
O'Reilly, R. P.: ref, 344(143), 2181(10)
Organ, D. W.: ref, 859(952)
Organ, L. M.: test, 2618
Orlando, V. P.: ref, 1191(120, 127)
Orleans, J. B.: test, 1749
Orleans, J. S.: rev, 264, 1068, 1556, 2260, 2275, 2488
Orleans, M.: ref, 270(140), 311(37)
Orley, J.: ref, 1883(54)
Orme-Johnson, D.: ref, 354(1557), 653(171)
Orme-Rogers, C.: ref, 2598(1483)
Ormont, R. J.: ref, 1817(2)
Orne, E. C.: test, 1063
Orne, M. T.: ref, 354(1512)
Ornstein, P.: ref, 152(13), 1109(19), 1904(53), 2179(204)
Ornstein, R.: ref, 2015(210)
Oró-Beutler, M. E.: ref, 890(342)
O'Rourke, L. J.: test, 1750, 1751, 2375
Orpet, R. E.: test, 922
Orr, D. B.: rev, 384, 1568, 1761, 2042

Orr, J.: ref, 2598(1751)
Orr, R.: ref, 1771(716), 2602(2015), 2621(388)
Orr, R. R.: ref, 874(48)
Orraschel, H.: ref, 1462(146)
Orsin, A.: ref, 2598(1584)
Orsini, A.: ref, 2598(1844)
Ortins, J. B.: ref, 1498(5692)
Orton, K. D.: exc, 333
Orvin, G. H.: ref, 1498(5230, 5408), 2598(1554), 2602(1861)
Ory, J. C.: ref, 1798(308)
Osborn, D. K.: ref, 559(55)
Osborn, H. B.: test, 1219
Osborn, R. N.: ref, 1296(170)
Osborne, A.: rev, 1665
Osborne, A. R.: rev, 576
Osborne, D.: ref, 1498(5062, 5173, 5174, 5329, 5330, 5425, 5590), 2607(165)
Osborne, J. W.: ref, 859(953), 1789(733)
Osborne, R. T.: rev, 2602
Osborne, T.: ref, 1568(115)
Osburn, H. G.: ref, 1451(2), 1486(182), 1981(1, 2), 1984(6)
Osburn, W. J.: rev, 197, 935, 1479, 2258
Oscar-Berman, M.: ref, 1914(855, 856), 2598(1755, 1756), 2607(204, 205)
O'Shaughnessy, T. E.: ref, 1531(279)
O'Shea, A. J.: test, 1059; ref, 1059(1, 2), 2581(339)
Oshman, H.: ref, 2030(5083)
Osipow, S. H.: test, 370, 1447
Oskamp, S.: rev, 1020, 2026
Oski, F. A.: ref, 270(92)
Osmon, D.: ref, 1498(5467)
Osmon, D. C.: ref, 1346(1), 1498(5441)
Osmond, H.: test, 855
Osofsky, J. D.: ref, 311(18)
Osser, H.: ref, 2289(1626)
Ost, L.: ref, 883(88)
Oster, G. D.: ref, 2289(1637), 2598(1388, 1637)
Osterlund, B. L.: ref, 501(833)
Ostrand, J.: ref, 354(1466)
Ostroga-Parker, J.: ref, 1884(3)
Ostrov, E.: test, 1673; ref, 1673(11), 2030(5070)
O'Sullivan, M.: test, 2489
Oswald, W. T.: ref, 859(929)
Otis, A. S.: test, 1754
Otis, J. L.: test, 195, 1804, 1805, 1806, 1807, 2256; rev, 1532, 1751
O'Toole, J. J.: ref, 354(1562), 2208(1677)
Otten, M. W.: ref, 590(373), 995(135), 1789(650)
Ottenbacher, K.: ref, 2244(33, 35, 42)
Otterstrom, R.: test, 804
Otteson, J. P.: ref, 477(26), 1063(121), 2251(1), 2598(1757)
Otto, H. A.: test, 1756
Otto, L. B.: ref, 643(133)
Otto, W.: test, 2634, 2635; exc, 748; ref, 2621(254)
Ottomanelli, G.: ref, 1498(5331)
Ottomanelli, G. A.: ref, 1498(5175)
O'Tuama, L. A.: ref, 270(77), 678(20), 701(45), 1771(597), 1877(7), 2289(1656), 2557(220)
Ovcharchyn, C. A.: ref, 76(656)
Overall, J. E.: ref, 1498(5176), 2598(1508, 1509)
Overall, J. U.: ref, 501(868, 894)
Overmann, P. B.: ref, 1319(71)

INDEX OF NAMES

Overton, T. D.: ref, 2318(1593)
Overy, J. M. N.: ref, 2537(562)
Owen, C. F.: ref, 149(5, 10), 2289(1670, 1713)
Owen, D.: ref, 501(853), 1013(83)
Owen, D. R.: ref, 501(810), 1013(61)
Owen, D. W.: ref, 116(523), 354(1383), 2208(1517)
Owen, J. A.: ref, 2602(2005)
Owen, K.: test, 18
Owen, P.: ref, 1498(5399)
Owen, S. V.: ref, 570(322), 1991(122), 2594(194, 197)
Owen, T. R.: test, 607
Owens, A.: ref, 1771(798), 2159(4), 2472(31)
Owens, D. G. C.: ref, 1883(63, 84)
Owens, J.: ref, 1341(153), 1754(52)
Owens, J. G.: ref, 1655(88)
Owens, R.: ref, 1515(18), 2031(459)
Owens, W. A.: test, 282, 2555; rev, 1455, 2435, 2610
Owings, R. A.: ref, 551(59)
Oxman, J.: ref, 1126(730), 2018(14), 2289(1718)
Oxman, T. E.: ref, 2598(1758)
Oyewumi, L. K.: ref, 859(807), 1498(5300)
Ozgoren, F.: ref, 859(946)
Oziel, J. L.: ref, 859(821), 1498(5316)
Ozmon, K. L.: ref, 1371(240), 1498(5262), 1798(202)
Paal, N.: ref, 2602(1934)
Pablo, R. Y.: ref, 1851(24)
Pace, C. R.: test, 486, 532; rev, 409, 543, 1943, 1951, 2336, 2399, 2485
Pachman, J. S.: ref, 1547(286)
Paciello, R. A.: ref, 1498(5664)
Pack, J.: ref, 1547(300), 2208(1606)
Packard, A. G.: rev, 1774, 1948
Packard, V. N.: ref, 964(504)
Packer, J.: ref, 1013(72)
Packett, J. R.: ref, 4(5)
Pacosa, F.: ref, 270(140), 311(37)
Padget, J.: ref, 1969(116)
Padgett, W. B.: ref, 1576(207)
Padian, N. S.: ref, 1419(702)
Padilla, E.: ref, 1498(5155)
Padilla, G. J.: ref, 2602(2056)
Page, E. B.: rev, 128, 129, 1193
Page, R. D.: ref, 280(1085), 1498(5332, 5500), 1765(12), 1914(728), 1940(80), 2179(205, 218), 2413(657), 2598(1377)
Page, W. F.: ref, 2638(134)
Paige, A. B.: ref, 1498(5608), 2598(1714)
Paige, W. D.: ref, 479(404), 934(8)
Painter, M. J.: ref, 678(23), 2289(1764)
Paitich, D.: ref, 2208(1583), 2289(1676), 2598(1486)
Paiva, R. E. A.: ref, 1576(193), 2343(1030, 1032), 2366(191, 192)
Paivio, A.: ref, 2016(199)
Palen, C.: ref, 1622(41)
Paley, A.: ref, 1498(5434)
Palfrey, J. S.: ref, 1424(86)
Palisin, H.: ref, 2289(1765), 2608(237)
Palkes, H.: ref, 2602(1718), 2621(271)
Palladino, J. J.: ref, 354(1467), 1531(282, 283), 2374(186)
Pallan, S.: test, 2122
Pallas, A. M.: ref, 501(919), 590(387), 2160(78)
Pallis, D. J.: ref, 859(760), 1498(5177, 5428)
Pallrand, G. J.: ref, 501(902)
Palmer, A. S.: test, 1484

Palmer, D. J.: ref, 1769(74), 2602(1935)
Palmer, E. A.: ref, 270(159), 678(37), 1420(3)
Palmer, F. B.: ref, 280(1158), 964(515)
Palmer, L. A.: test, 549, 830, 1989, 2483; ref, 2441(33)
Palmer, L. L.: ref, 226(181), 551(20), 1341(162), 1866(32), 2181(11)
Palmer, M.: ref, 551(35)
Palmer, O.: rev, 1110
Palmer, O. E.: rev, 503, 504, 2523
Palmo, A. J.: ref, 374(229), 732(414), 932(126), 1914(895), 2413(702), 2598(1854), 2621(455)
Palormo, J. M.: test, 557, 2194; rev, 800, 2619
Paloutzian, R. F.: ref, 1960(85)
Palow, N. G.: ref, 2103(5)
Paludan, B.: ref, 2598(1537)
Paludi, M. A.: ref, 609(230), 751(16, 28)
Pamment, P.: ref, 859(780)
Panackal, A. A.: ref, 501(834, 903), 570(326)
Panagos, J. L.: ref, 1192(257), 2621(449)
Panagos, J. M.: ref, 960(13), 1622(43), 1771(625), 1814(6)
Panakal, A. A.: ref, 1625(105)
Pandey, J.: ref, 780(1653)
Pandey, R. E.: ref, 2491(2064)
Pandi, G. R.: ref, 1933(20)
Pandina, R. J.: ref, 1831(215)
Pandurangi, A. K.: ref, 2208(1621)
Pane, J. B.: rev, 1521
Panek, P. E.: ref, 6(59), 794(364), 1013(74, 86, 110), 1053(67, 68, 69, 74, 75, 76, 79, 80), 2030(5071), 2289(1726, 1727)
Panels, P. E.: ref, 1914(857)
Pankaskie, M.: exc, 1191
Pannbacker, M.: ref, 1771(743), 2598(1744)
Panto, L. T.: ref, 1498(5333)
Panton, D. B.: ref, 966(177)
Panton, J. H.: ref, 1498(5501, 5502, 5503)
Panunto, B.: ref, 1473(181), 1771(635, 679), 1914(793, 816)
Pany, D.: ref, 1473(153), 1769(57), 2217(128), 2621(289)
Panzarella, R.: ref, 1789(719)
Paolino, T. J.: ref, 1547(287), 1931(47)
Papa, L. L.: ref, 890(360)
Pape, K. E.: ref, 270(93)
Papenfuss, J. F.: test, 2325
Papikh, N.: ref, 1655(90)
Papsdorf, J. D.: ref, 2300(610)
Paradise, C. A.: ref, 2030(4974), 2491(2031)
Paradise, L. V.: ref, 1531(291), 1729(80), 2387(9)
Parameswaran, E. G.: exc, 2236
Parasinis, I.: ref, 9(15), 1013(87), 2246(28)
Paraskevopoulos, J.: ref, 1771(738), 2289(1758)
Pardine, P.: ref, 780(1654)
Pardue, L. H.: ref, 1498(5731)
Pardue, S. F.: ref, 606(16), 1955(113)
Paredes, A.: ref, 1655(73)
Pareek, U.: test, 2236
Parham, I.: ref, 2269(476), 2429(25)
Parham, I. A.: ref, 2269(443)
Parham, J. A. W.: ref, 1555(310), 2002(2)
Paris, S. G.: ref, 344(191)
Parish, T. S.: ref, 116(536, 537), 1831(148, 149), 2208(1620)
Parisi, G.: rev, 993

669

Paritaky, R.: ref, 1789(700)
Park, R.: ref, 280(1086), 701(52), 1007(24)
Park, R. D.: ref, 590(383), 2160(65)
Park, S.: ref, 1655(122)
Parker, C. A.: ref, 230(52)
Parker, E. S.: ref, 1052(2), 2179(244)
Parker, G.: ref, 859(874), 941(19)
Parker, J. C.: ref, 1904(68), 2300(427)
Parker, K. P.: ref, 2300(599)
Parker, M.: ref, 1498(5225), 2029(238), 2300(376)
Parker, N.: ref, 2598(1759)
Parker, T.: ref, 2621(376)
Parkes, K. R.: ref, 1077(81)
Parkes, M.: ref, 1473(134), 1771(562)
Parkman, M. C.: test, 807, 810
Parks, D. H.: ref, 1197(295)
Parks, H.: ref, 76(599), 501(812), 551(23), 2340(11)
Parks, J. C.: ref, 2621(411)
Parks, R.: ref, 1498(5748)
Parnell, M. M.: ref, 961(1), 2602(1799), 2608(203)
Parnes, B.: test, 1263, 1264
Parnicky, J. J.: test, 2574
Parott, R.: ref, 2300(380)
Parr, G. D.: ref, 551(31), 1473(129), 1896(10), 2208(1681), 2286(277), 2478(9)
Parr, V. E.: ref, 226(162)
Parr, W. C.: ref, 1498(5678)
Parra, E. B.: ref, 2608(210)
Parrill, T.: ref, 1498(5080), 2030(4951), 2598(1317)
Parrish, J. M.: ref, 1771(524)
Parsons, C. K.: ref, 590(383), 2160(65)
Parsons, O. A.: ref, 280(1165, 1174), 1462(157, 162), 1914(858, 885), 2179(245, 253), 2598(1760, 1825, 1857), 2607(206)
Parsons, S. L.: ref, 896(6), 1814(7)
Partin, J. C.: ref, 270(105), 280(1103), 751(23), 2289(1700), 2557(227), 2602(1871), 2621(320)
Partin, J. S.: ref, 270(105), 280(1103), 751(23), 2289(1700), 2557(227), 2602(1871), 2621(320)
Pascal, G. R.: test, 280
Pascale, L.: ref, 2322(9)
Pascarella, E. P.: ref, 501(869)
Pascarella, E. T.: ref, 501(904), 2297(8)
Paschal, B. J.: ref, 2512(619)
Pasewark, R. A.: ref, 534(102), 780(1690), 1424(41), 2608(204)
Paskewicz, C. W.: ref, 1479(373)
Pasmore, W. A.: ref, 1300(117)
Pasnak, R.: ref, 357(508), 953(10), 2217(106, 113), 2289(1591), 2602(1659)
Pasnav, R. O.: ref, 859(839)
Pasquali, L.: ref, 2491(2043)
Passafiume, D.: ref, 794(430), 1257(154), 2269(472)
Passini, F. T.: ref, 1498(5178, 5393), 1547(266, 296), 2300(366, 449)
Passino, E. M.: ref, 1855(18)
Passow, A. H.: rev, 2286
Passwater, G. D.: test, 1658
Pasternack, B. S.: ref, 1498(5328)
Patalano, F.: ref, 1498(5334, 5674, 5675)
Patberg, J. P.: ref, 932(122)
Patchen, M.: ref, 1473(203)
Pate, D. H.: ref, 1209(34), 1720(33), 2657(106)
Pate, J. E.: test, 891
Patel, K.: ref, 2208(1550), 2512(576)

Paterson, D. G.: test, 1493, 1835, 2015; rev, 192, 464
Patil, K. D.: ref, 1498(5257)
Patrick, A. W.: ref, 116(538), 780(1655), 2491(2025)
Patrick, J.: ref, 2598(1630)
Patrick, O. L.: ref, 780(1673)
Patsiokas, A. T.: ref, 157(149), 794(427)
Patterson, G. R.: rev, 2602
Patterson, J.: test, 2629
Patterson, L.: ref, 1922(17)
Patterson, T. W.: ref, 2598(1535)
Patterson, V.: ref, 354(1468), 2318(1561)
Pattie, A. H.: test, 471
Pattinson, W.: test, 2278
Pattison, D.: ref, 1771(786)
Patton, J.: ref, 1351(199), 2300(580), 2598(1811), 2607(213)
Patton, J. E.: ref, 932(83), 1126(705), 2602(1800)
Patton, J. F.: ref, 1498(5179)
Patton, M. J.: ref, 1555(312)
Patz, A.: ref, 877(20)
Pauk, W.: test, 608; rev, 2347
Pauker, J. D.: test, 1515; rev, 1573, 1922, 2450, 2464
Paul, B.: ref, 794(445), 859(942)
Paul, G. L.: ref, 1498(5075, 5747), 2587(33)
Paul, J.: ref, 2598(1761)
Paul, O. D.: ref, 890(356)
Paul, V.: ref, 794(444), 2598(1817)
Paul, V. H.: test, 2076
Paulhus, D.: ref, 2294(132)
Paulsen, E. P.: ref, 1052(1), 2602(1988), 2621(377)
Paulsen, F. M.: ref, 76(625), 1726(365), 2134(113), 2318(1578), 2657(110)
Paulsen, K.: ref, 703(8)
Paulsen, K. A.: ref, 1371(250), 1424(40, 73), 2289(1681)
Paulson, L.: test, 1277, 1997
Paulson, M. A.: ref, 2300(429), 2301(28)
Paulus, D.: test, 604, 605
Paunonen, S. V.: ref, 1798(265)
Pautler, C. P.: ref, 283(156), 2179(235), 2598(1706)
Pawlak, A. E.: ref, 1063(101, 126, 128)
Paxton, N.: test, 1277, 1997
Payer, A. F.: ref, 2602(2009)
Paykel, E. S.: ref, 1419(673), 2322(10)
Payne, D. A.: rev, 174; ref, 845(7), 1013(123), 1192(177), 1459(16), 1473(221), 1479(381), 1576(221), 2602(1815, 1950)
Payne, I. R.: test, 294
Payne, L. C.: test, 2555
Payne, M. C.: ref, 1192(245)
Payne, P. A.: ref, 1531(288)
Payne, R.: ref, 408(182), 502(182), 1080(182), 1745(182)
Payne, R. B.: ref, 1257(133, 176)
Payne, R. W.: rev, 963, 1009, 1462, 1661, 2565, 2620
Paynter, E. T.: ref, 960(7)
Peach, R. W.: ref, 308(12)
Peacher, W. G.: rev, 1060
Peacock, A. C.: ref, 1798(284)
Peacock, E. J.: ref, 1789(734), 1960(86)
Peake, T. H.: ref, 1498(5504), 1904(95)
Pearce, B.: test, 1887
Pearce, N. W.: ref, 2300(574)
Pearl, R.: ref, 1473(171), 1771(799), 1831(161), 2621(321)

INDEX OF NAMES

Pearson, D.: ref, 1498(5492)
Pearson, D. R.: ref, 2602(1792)
Pearson, H. A.: ref, 1424(70), 1771(742)
Pearson, L. S.: test, 322
Pearson, P. D.: rev, 724
Pearson, P. R.: ref, 859(944)
Pease, D.: test, 1190
Pease, D. M.: ref, 308(7)
Pease, P. M.: test, 804
Peatling, J. H.: test, 238
Peatman, J. G.: rev, 689
Pechacek, T. F.: ref, 2300(475)
Pechura, C. M.: ref, 2029(230)
Peck, R.: ref, 551(60), 1831(198)
Peckman, P. H.: ref, 1576(209)
Pedersen, H.: ref, 381(67)
Pedersen, R. A.: test, 2275; exc, 118
Pederson, J. A.: ref, 270(133), 2289(1747)
Pedhazur, E. J.: rev, 1953, 2629
Pedrini, B. C.: ref, 76(593, 594, 612)
Pedrini, D. T.: ref, 76(593, 594, 612)
Pedro, J. D.: ref, 573(17), 578(4)
Peeke, H. V.: ref, 2322(17)
Peel, E. A.: rev, 733, 1620
Peet, M.: ref, 1655(123)
Pelavin, S. H.: ref, 551(26), 932(74)
Pelham, W. E.: ref, 1272(136), 1754(93), 2286(319)
Pelled, O.: ref, 2413(646), 2491(2058)
Pellegreno, D.: ref, 1013(88)
Pellegrini, A. D.: ref, 344(192), 551(69), 1479(368)
Pellegrino, J.: ref, 2269(465, 477)
Pelser, A. J. K.: test, 2242
Pena-Ramos, A.: ref, 1498(5505)
Pendergast, K.: test, 1814
Pendergrass, J.: ref, 1914(872)
Pendleton, C. W.: rev, 1595, 1600
Penfield, D. A.: ref, 290(6)
Penick, E. C.: ref, 280(1147), 609(204, 226), 859(822, 930), 1771(750), 1798(241, 289, 291), 1940(81), 2607(208)
Penick, J. E.: ref, 2512(663)
Penick, P. B.: ref, 1126(769), 1771(747)
Penk, M. L.: ref, 751(8), 1498(5707), 2179(208)
Penk, W. E.: ref, 283(151, 159, 160), 859(761, 875), 1197(280, 301), 1498(5180, 5335, 5336, 5506, 5507, 5676, 5677, 5678, 5679, 5694, 5762), 1765(8, 9, 13), 1914(859, 891), 2638(138)
Penman, K. A.: ref, 1192(178)
Penn, R.: ref, 2029(211)
Penna, J. P.: rev, 74, 593
Penner, K. A.: ref, 1771(619)
Penner, W. J.: ref, 2561(2)
Pennington, B. H.: ref, 1498(5508)
Penny, G. D.: ref, 1498(5680)
Penny, R. E.: test, 1785, 2210
Penrose, L. S.: rev, 1498
Pentecoste, J. C.: ref, 501(800), 1969(88)
Pentz, C. A.: ref, 2598(1642)
Peper, R. J.: ref, 1007(14), 2621(244)
Peplau, L. A.: ref, 860(147), 1547(292), 1904(119), 2300(562)
Pepper, S.: ref, 1798(216)
Perachio, J. J.: test, 1768
Perell, I. B. E.: ref, 627(24)

Peresie, H.: ref, 226(172), 701(65), 1371(254), 1771(678), 2113(252), 2602(1929)
Perez, F. M.: ref, 1126(770)
Perez, M. M.: ref, 1883(75)
Perfection Form Co.: test, 774, 970, 1001, 1324, 1336, 1842
Perfetti, C. A.: ref, 1473(151, 158), 1754(76, 79)
Perissaki, C.: ref, 859(878)
Perkins, M. J.: test, 1130; ref, 1130(1)
Perkins, M. L.: ref, 1192(177)
Perkins, W. H.: rev, 2541, 2551
Perl, J.: ref, 859(911)
Perlman, C. L.: test, 1491
Perlman, R.: ref, 1498(5571)
Perlman, T.: ref, 398(93), 794(420), 2598(1549, 1596), 2602(1609, 1851), 2608(171)
Perlo, V. P.: ref, 2598(1475), 2602(1764)
Perman, B. E.: ref, 2077(30), 2598(1510), 2602(1801)
Perney, L. R.: ref, 1272(132)
Peron-Magnan, P.: ref, 1655(100)
Perone, M.: ref, 859(876), 1904(96)
Perovich, G. M.: ref, 372(8), 2413(682)
Perozzi, J. A.: ref, 2109(4), 2472(11)
Perr, I. N.: ref, 1498(5181)
Perri, M. G.: test, 1076
Perrin, D. W.: ref, 374(213), 1478(66), 1831(119)
Perry, C.: ref, 1063(88, 89, 96, 107), 2294(112, 113, 119, 130), 2297(9)
Perry, F.: test, 839
Perry, H. B.: ref, 354(1411)
Perry, J. D.: ref, 2289(1728), 2621(351)
Perry, L.: ref, 2512(578)
Perry, N. W.: ref, 1473(161), 1754(80), 2602(1806)
Perryer, X.: test, 2430
Pershin, P.: ref, 751(19)
Persinger, B. D.: ref, 1462(137, 147, 159), 1969(101), 2208(1627, 1691)
Persky, H.: ref, 1197(281), 1498(5182), 1547(267, 352)
Personnel Research Board, Ohio State University: test, 1122, 1295
Personnel Research & Development Corporation: test, 2272
Pestonjie, D. M.: ref, 2121(67)
Petchers-Cassell, M.: ref, 963(129)
Peter, B.: ref, 280(1094), 794(407), 1771(630), 2602(1824), 2621(308)
Peteroy, E. T.: ref, 1789(701), 1969(115), 2598(1762)
Peters, C. W.: ref, 932(65)
Peters, J. E.: ref, 2602(1589), 2621(219)
Peters, J. W. R.: ref, 1509(11)
Peters, K. L.: ref, 701(87), 2289(1782), 2551(16)
Peters, P. K.: ref, 1498(5337)
Peters, R. A.: ref, 2300(428)
Peters, R. D.: ref, 1771(800)
Peters, R. M.: ref, 995(131), 2441(30)
Peters, S. D.: ref, 681(36)
Peters, W. H.: ref, 1726(353)
Petersen, C.: ref, 1568(139, 147)
Petersen, C. R.: ref, 280(1087), 1769(62), 2602(1802), 2621(295)
Petersen, G. A.: ref, 551(59)
Peterson, A. V.: ref, 1158(30)
Peterson, C. R.: ref, 2602(1936),
Peterson, D. A.: ref, 883(115), 1547(350)
Peterson, D. R.: test, 2012; rev, 1849, 2565

671

Peterson, G. V.: ref, 704(11), 1192(211)
Peterson, H. A.: rev, 664, 675, 1153, 2103; ref, 664(15), 1513(28)
Peterson, J.: test, 1484
Peterson, J. M.: ref, 501(905)
Peterson, L. P.: ref, 1498(5508)
Peterson, M. K.: ref, 960(10), 1622(44), 1771(629), 2472(15)
Peterson, P. J.: ref, 1488(2), 1498(5702), 2598(1787)
Peterson, P. L.: ref, 354(1412, 1500, 1546), 381(75), 1077(57), 1257(128, 129), 1914(817, 892), 2160(66), 2269(479), 2300(488, 555)
Peterson, R.: ref, 1498(5338)
Peterson, R. A.: rev, 1106, 2030; ref, 1498(5132, 5296), 1896(9), 2598(1351)
Peterson, R. E.: test, 1158, 1159
Peterson, S.: test, 2643; rev, 67, 2368
Peterson, W.: ref, 932(69), 964(483), 1192(184), 2217(122)
Peterson, W. J.: ref, 1126(666), 1769(46), 1771(555), 2602(1665)
Pethö, B.: ref, 1419(690), 2030(5038), 2322(13), 2557(230)
Petracca, M.: ref, 1498(5164)
Petrakis, E.: ref, 1013(89, 133, 134, 135), 1316(5)
Petrosko, J. M.: exc, 534
Petrosko, J. Z.: exc, 2602
Petrovich, D. V.: test, 1757
Petrucci, J. A.: ref, 1904(73)
Petrucci, R. J.: ref, 2413(658)
Petrusic, W. M.: ref, 1257(130), 2015(200)
Petry, S.: ref, 551(50)
Pettas, M.: ref, 378(13)
Pettee, J. L.: test, 1994
Petti, T. A.: ref, 2289(1653), 2608(187)
Pettigrew, C. G.: ref, 2294(131)
Pettit, J. M.: ref, 1126(735), 2412(40)
Petty, N. E.: ref, 1754(62)
Petzel, T. P.: ref, 76(656), 681(45, 72), 1498(5339, 5560, 5763)
Peyser, J. M.: ref, 1498(5681), 1948(103)
Peyton, L. J.: ref, 1126(750)
Pfeffer, J.: ref, 973(28)
Pfeiffer, S. I.: ref, 2039(12)
Pfouts, J. H.: ref, 354(1547), 874(54), 2217(172)
Phatak, P.: test, 750
Phelan, G. K.: ref, 116(593)
Phelan, W. J.: ref, 1371(256), 2445(5)
Phelps, M. R.: ref, 1831(150)
Phelps, R. P.: rev, 233, 879, 1644
Philbert, D.: ref, 1547(341), 2598(1784)
Philbrick, J. L.: ref, 1960(82)
Philip, A.: ref, 941(22)
Philip, A. E.: ref, 1655(82, 109)
Philipp, R. L.: ref, 874(48)
Phillips, A. M.: ref, 1919(46), 2179(246), 2598(1763), 2620(20)
Phillips, B. L.: ref, 534(102), 1424(41), 2608(204)
Phillips, D. A.: ref, 1771(748)
Phillips, D. S.: ref, 1851(28, 41)
Phillips, E.: ref, 1508(127)
Phillips, E. L.: ref, 780(1656), 1498(5183)
Phillips, F. L.: ref, 2581(338)
Phillips, J. L.: ref, 235(11)
Phillips, J. S.: ref, 1013(74), 1053(69), 1295(306)

Phillips, T. G.: rev, 497, 524, 814, 945, 989
Phillips, W. M.: ref, 1919(46), 1960(81), 2179(246), 2598(1378, 1763), 2620(20)
Phillipson, H.: test, 1660
Phillipson, O. T.: ref, 1655(83), 1883(28)
Phinney, I. R.: ref, 1498(5696)
Phipps, J.: ref, 308(18)
Piatt, S.: ref, 1883(47)
Piazza, D. M.: ref, 2598(1764)
Piche, G. L.: ref, 1272(134), 1341(178)
Pickard, C. W.: ref, 859(890)
Pickens, R.: ref, 1498(5509)
Pickering, J. W.: ref, 2598(1379)
Pickersgill, M. J.: ref, 1851(48)
Pickett, L.: ref, 354(1388)
Pidgeon, D. A.: test, 1620; rev, 31, 775, 1272, 1341, 1912, 2162
Piedmont, R. L.: ref, 2294(140)
Pierce, J. E.: ref, 270(88), 2289(1669)
Pierce, J. W.: ref, 398(120)
Pierce, K. A.: ref, 374(195)
Pierce, L.: ref, 2289(1607)
Pierce, L. C.: ref, 553(20)
Pierce, R. S.: ref, 308(28)
Pierce, S. J.: ref, 226(159), 1319(80)
Pierce-Jones, J.: rev, 1271, 2042, 2461
Piercy, D. C.: ref, 1498(5519)
Piermarini, T.: ref, 1960(77)
Piers, E. V.: test, 1831; rev, 1771, 1969; ref, 1831(129)
Piersel, W. C.: ref, 302(42), 2602(1677)
Pierson, E.: test, 2493
Pietarila, M.: ref, 1498(5352), 2030(5009), 2598(1525)
Pihl, R. O.: ref, 400(136), 751(40), 1473(134, 209), 1486(187), 1547(336, 344), 1771(562, 766), 1798(217, 290, 297), 1914(860), 1934(12, 13), 2300(556), 2491(2107), 2602(2139, 2150, 2198)
Pikaart, L.: rev, 1526, 2162
Pikulski, J. J.: ref, 1192(219)
Pikunas, J.: test, 1002
Pilch, J.: test, 1566
Pilkington, T. R. E.: ref, 639(42)
Pilkonas, P. A.: ref, 2300(600)
Pilkonis, P. A.: ref, 859(762), 2300(557)
Pill, R.: ref, 6(87), 2598(1830)
Pillay, M.: ref, 780(1657)
Pillemer, D. B.: ref, 1424(44)
Pilliner, A. E. G.: rev, 20, 317, 1740, 2487
Pilon, R. N.: ref, 1931(53)
Pimsleur, P.: test, 1833
Pine, M. A.: ref, 116(568), 1473(159), 1551(35)
Pines, S. F.: ref, 501(931)
Pinneau, S. R.: test, 2289
Pinnel, L. E.: ref, 701(87), 2289(1782)
Pinnell, L. E.: ref, 2551(16)
Pino, C. J.: ref, 780(1704), 890(361), 1498(5682)
Pintilie, D.: test, 940
Pintner, R.: test, 1834, 1835; rev, 1716
Pinto, W.: ref, 678(26), 960(11), 1771(655), 2107(9), 2218(143), 2598(1582), 2602(1889), 2608(213)
Piper, E.: ref, 2289(1600)
Piper, W. E.: ref, 354(1413), 794(423), 1099(69), 1498(5184, 5474), 1923(16), 2208(1551, 1628), 2322(14)
Pirozzolo, F. J.: ref, 1771(785), 2602(1937)
Pirro, E. B.: test, 1380

INDEX OF NAMES

Pishkin, V.: ref, 859(923), 1162(18, 20), 1498(5083), 1547(288), 2179(206), 2620(8, 11, 13)
Pitariu, H.: ref, 354(1575)
Pitcher–Baker, G.: ref, 701(41)
Pittman, N. L.: ref, 1547(311, 337)
Pittman, R. B.: ref, 2621(352)
Pittman, T. S.: ref, 1547(311, 337)
Pittner, M. S.: ref, 1547(338), 2598(1765)
Pizzamiglio, L.: ref, 794(430), 1257(154), 2269(472, 482)
Pizzuti, M.: test, 1810
Plake, B. S.: ref, 76(657), 1192(223, 246, 247), 1405(11), 2300(601, 602)
Planas, M.: ref, 1063(122)
Plankenhorn, A.: ref, 701(74), 1126(753), 1192(231), 1540(18), 1771(719), 2217(162)
Plant, W. T.: ref, 354(1469)
Plante, A. J.: ref, 1473(135), 2484(12), 2488(13)
Planty, E.: test, 2359
Plason, A.: test, 2121
Platman, S. R: ref, 796(35)
Platnick, D. M.: ref, 501(801), 1257(109)
Platt, J. J.: test, 1436
Platt, L. J.: ref, 1914(861)
Platt, S. D.: ref, 1883(71)
Platten, M. R.: ref, 1831(175, 216)
Platzek, D.: test, 2301
Plax, T. G.: ref, 354(1414, 1419, 1501, 1548), 780(1658, 1660, 1691, 1705), 2343(1033, 1034, 1047), 2413(603, 606, 659, 683)
Plembel, D.: ref, 1498(5774)
Plemel, D.: ref, 1073(126), 1498(5394, 5395), 1919(44), 2208(1638), 2598(1546)
Plemons, G.: ref, 1498(5185)
Plemons, J. K.: ref, 1257(131)
Plessas, G. P.: rev, 914, 1330, 2519
Pliske, R.: ref, 2602(2224)
Plomin, R.: ref, 961(5, 6), 1257(161), 1424(66), 1769(88), 2602(2051, 2093), 2621(412)
Plotkin, W. B.: ref, 1498(5764), 2300(603)
Plouffe, L.: ref, 859(877)
Plowman, S. A.: ref, 5(169)
Plude, D. J.: ref, 2598(1845)
Plumlee, L. B.: rev, 123, 791, 1189
Plutchik, R.: test, 796; ref, 796(35), 1531(278), 2366(195)
Poag, J. R.: ref, 116(591), 157(148), 1257(141)
Poborca, B.: ref, 823(24)
Pock, A. C.: ref, 2321(1)
Poddar, M.: ref, 859(852)
Podosin, R. L.: ref, 1126(776), 1371(261), 2289(1779), 2598(1814)
Podraza, B. L.: ref, 1851(22)
Podruch, P. E.: ref, 2289(1633)
Poeck, K.: ref, 2598(1766, 1835)
Poff, M. G.: ref, 2491(2018), 2602(1658), 2621(248)
Pogge, D. L.: ref, 374(218, 232)
Poggio, J. P.: ref, 1798(308), 2318(1526)
Pogrow, S.: ref, 973(30)
Pohl, R. E.: ref, 2289(1679), 2557(223)
Pohlmann, J. T.: ref, 1914(883)
Poitras–Wright, H.: ref, 964(486), 1853(277)
Poizner, S. B.: ref, 1351(179)
Poland, W. D.: ref, 890(354), 1547(315), 1748(57)
Polenz, D.: ref, 1498(5257)

Polit, D. F.: ref, 116(569)
Politte, A. J.: test, 1848, 2130, 2140
Polivy, J.: ref, 681(73), 1547(339, 353), 2300(604)
Polk, C. L. H.: ref, 932(115), 1771(749)
Pollack, D.: ref, 1498(5683)
Pollack, I. W.: ref, 121(9)
Pollack, R. H.: ref, 2598(1369)
Pollak, C. P.: ref, 1498(5775)
Pollak, J. M.: ref, 1789(680)
Pollitt, E.: ref, 270(94), 1771(801)
Pollock, V.: ref, 1904(97)
Polovy, P.: ref, 354(1549)
Pomerantz, A. S.: ref, 1498(5186)
Pomerantz, S.: ref, 2228(70)
Pond, R. E.: test, 1877
Ponsford, J. L.: ref, 2598(1767), 2607(207)
Pontius, A.: ref, 280(1171), 751(42)
Poole, A. D.: ref, 1009(56)
Poole, M.: ref, 2512(633)
Poole, M. E.: ref, 28(4), 31(5), 157(135, 142), 1229(85), 1620(22), 1910(3), 2512(577, 600, 621)
Poole, M. S.: ref, 890(366)
Pooley, R. C.: rev, 128, 129, 490, 530, 570, 985
Pope, J.: ref, 1459(15), 2217(173), 2621(413), 2641(15)
Pope, L.: test, 1850, 1925, 1926
Popham, R. J.: test, 1277
Popham, W. J.: test, 159, 1277, 1412, 1997, 2207
Popkin, M. K.: ref, 1655(113)
Popper, R. W.: ref, 2289(1608)
Porch, B.: ref, 226(185), 691(47), 701(89), 1126(784), 1462(158), 1769(103), 1914(888), 2602(2186)
Porch, B. E.: test, 1851, 1852; ref, 1851(42)
Porter, A. C.: ref, 551(32), 1192(204), 1473(160), 2286(299)
Porter, D.: ref, 501(909, 910)
Porter, G. L.: ref, 280(1172), 701(90)
Porter, J. M.: rev, 1450, 2373
Porter, L. W.: rev, 2310, 2313, 2314; ref, 1798(225, 261)
Porter, R. B.: test, 174, 400
Porter, R. J.: ref, 280(1057), 1771(571), 2602(1699), 2621(263)
Porter, S.: ref, 2208(1670), 2655(6)
Porteus, S. D.: test, 1853; rev, 2013
Posavec, E. J.: ref, 1940(87)
Poser, C. M.: ref, 1498(5681), 1948(103)
Posey, T. B.: ref, 1197(291), 2413(632)
Posluszny, R.: ref, 2269(483)
Posner, B. Z.: ref, 2029(233, 234)
Post, A. L.: ref, 2208(1536)
Post, F.: ref, 1914(802), 2598(1593)
Post, R. D.: ref, 681(58, 59), 1498(5479, 5510, 5684, 5685), 2598(1615)
Post, W. L.: rev, 828
Postuma, R.: ref, 325(34)
Pothier, P.: ref, 270(91), 1126(704), 1771(618), 2289(1680)
Potkin, S.: ref, 2598(1372)
Pottas, A. P. J.: test, 1041
Potter, E. L.: ref, 1125(18)
Potter, L. L.: ref, 2300(418)
Potter, R. E.: ref, 1126(713)
Potter F. T.: test, 1858
Potts, C.: ref, 354(1469)

673

Potts, M.: ref, 932(66), 1949(57)
Poucher, K. E.: rev, 163, 1595, 1613
Pound, R. E.: ref, 1568(127), 2413(604, 628)
Powazek, M.: ref, 1771(680), 2289(1729), 2300(429), 2301(28), 2602(1938), 2621(353)
Powell, B. J.: ref, 280(1147), 609(204, 226), 859(822, 930), 1771(750), 1798(241, 289, 291), 1940(81), 2607(208)
Powell, C. H.: ref, 280(1136)
Powell, D. A.: ref, 2598(1768)
Powell, G.: ref, 1771(802), 2217(184), 2218(20), 2602(2199), 2641(22)
Powell, G. E.: ref, 860(130), 1229(86), 1265(78), 1513(29, 32, 33), 1914(818, 874), 2598(1631, 1683), 2607(185)
Powell, G. N.: ref, 1295(303)
Powell, J. C.: ref, 1919(40), 2657(105, 113)
Powell, R.: ref, 1789(714)
Powell, W. R.: exc, 932
Power, C. N.: ref, 30(4), 1233(216)
Power, D. G.: ref, 2607(203)
Power, P. G.: test, 1554
Power, R. P.: ref, 859(763)
Powers, D. E.: ref, 501(876), 995(155), 1866(37)
Powers, J.: ref, 2491(2106)
Powers, J. E.: ref, 1013(60, 84)
Powers, P. S.: ref, 2301(29)
Powers, R.: ref, 1387(13)
Powers, R. J.: ref, 374(202)
Powers, S. M.: ref, 76(613), 704(8), 2548(11)
Powers, W. A.: ref, 76(613)
Poythress, N. G.: ref, 1498(5340)
Prandoni, J. R.: ref, 280(1088), 2030(5005), 2037(151), 2598(1511)
Pranis, R. W.: test, 2410, 2654
Prasad, M. B.: ref, 2491(2044, 2049)
Prasinos, S.: ref, 243(121), 872(18)
Prasse, D. P.: ref, 1771(772)
Prather, E.: test, 2590
Prather, E. M.: test, 2108, 2159
Pratt, D. F.: ref, 1568(129)
Pratt, T. C.: ref, 2587(35)
Pratt, W. E.: test, 168, 169, 170, 171, 172, 173, 174, 175, 176
Prawat, R.: ref, 559(53)
Prawat, R. S.: ref, 559(44, 45), 653(144), 2218(17), 2548(12, 13)
Prediger, D.: exc, 1577
Prediger, D. J.: ref, 76(588, 595, 614, 629, 632, 642), 77(21), 374(222), 1193(147), 2134(132, 133, 141), 2318(1605), 2577(2)
Preen, B.: exc, 2490
Prentice, N. M.: ref, 1771(556), 2602(2188)
Prentice, W.: ref, 1191(128)
Prentice–Dunn, S.: ref, 2602(2200), 2621(450)
Prescott, G. A.: test, 1473, 1474, 1475, 1476, 1477, 1478
Prescott, T. E.: test, 2017; ref, 2017(2, 4)
Presnall, D.: ref, 6(45)
Press, M.: ref, 958(50), 1126(771), 1769(91), 2034(6), 2602(2101)
Pressey, L. C.: test, 1885, 1886, 1887
Pressey, S. L.: test, 1885, 1886, 1887
Pressley, M.: ref, 666(6)
Pressner, J. A.: ref, 1547(268)
Preston, C.: ref, 860(102), 2343(1036), 2629(103)

Preston, J.: rev, 1961; ref, 2598(1294, 1826), 2602(1803)
Preston, J. C.: ref, 1013(90)
Preston, M. S.: ref, 1007(18), 2217(116)
Preston, R. C.: rev, 169, 2286
Price, D. H.: test, 1940
Price, D. R.: ref, 1969(124), 2598(1834)
Price, F. T.: ref, 2413(652)
Price, G. C.: ref, 1479(365), 2598(1724), 2602(2049)
Price, G. E.: ref, 76(587), 1754(101), 2134(111, 119), 2318(1591)
Price, J.: test, 1953; rev, 552
Price, K. P.: ref, 859(931), 2300(558)
Price, L.: test, 792
Price, L. A.: test, 1257
Price, L. B.: test, 1077
Price, R. A.: ref, 558(63), 860(114), 1914(790)
Price, R. G.: rev, 304, 1629, 2390
Price, T. B.: ref, 344(171)
Price–Williams, D. R.: ref, 157(136), 1771(563)
Prichard, C. L.: ref, 961(3)
Prichard, K. K.: ref, 1771(632), 1969(119), 2602(1842)
Prickett, J.: ref, 559(50)
Priddle, R. L.: ref, 559(51), 653(145), 1771(623), 1914(784)
Priest, H. F.: rev, 863
Priest, S. R.: ref, 2598(1661), 2602(1975)
Prifitera, A.: ref, 1346(8), 2598(1846)
Prigatano, G. P.: ref, 2598(1769), 2607(144)
Prigge, G. R.: ref, 1192(205)
Prillaman, K.: ref, 2030(5037), 2620(14, 19)
Prince, E.: ref, 2300(570)
Prince, J. B.: ref, 1046(587)
Prince, J. S.: test, 2330
Prince, L. M.: ref, 859(905), 1798(280)
Pringle, M. L. K.: rev, 321, 1367, 1829, 2077, 2245, 2281; exc, 964
Prins, D.: ref, 298(167), 2208(1664)
Prinsloo, R. J.: test, 1026, 1141
Prinz, P. N.: ref, 2598(1380), 2607(145)
Prior, J.: ref, 1912(3), 2048(1)
Prior, M.: ref, 1771(751)
Prior, M. R.: ref, 1126(671), 1771(564, 681, 682)
Pristo, L. J.: ref, 2602(1804)
Pritchard, A. S.: test, 1900
Pritchard, D. A.: ref, 1498(5350, 5686, 5687), 2598(1523), 2621(298)
Pritchard, R. D.: ref, 354(1553), 732(409), 1754(106), 2286(337)
Pritchett, E. M.: test, 1250
Prochaska, J. O.: ref, 354(1421), 917(73)
Prociuk, T. J.: ref, 354(1436)
Procopis, P.: ref, 270(157)
Proctor, L. R.: ref, 2030(5000), 2598(1489)
Proctor, S.: ref, 2286(279), 2288(77)
Proger, B. B.: rev, 1997, 2102; exc, 184, 200, 235, 302, 338, 353, 962, 1769, 1877, 1934, 2106, 2110, 2453, 2476, 2478, 2641
Project RHISE, Children's Development Center, Rockford, IL.: test, 2028
Prokop, C.: ref, 2413(594)
Prokop, C. K.: ref, 1498(5187, 5688), 2030(4965), 2598(1381)
Propst, I. K.: ref, 932(71, 92, 100), 1912(3), 2048(1)
Prosen, M.: ref, 1919(42, 43), 2598(1470, 1589)

INDEX OF NAMES

Provost, G. L.: ref, 1013(136)
Pruesse, M. G.: ref, 1498(5689), 1914(862), 2598(1770)
Prusoff, B. A.: ref, 1419(684, 692, 702), 2100(12), 2322(10, 11)
Prutting, C. A.: ref, 1622(36), 1771(588), 2289(1652)
Pruzek, R. M.: ref, 958(52), 2217(185), 2602(2225)
Pryer, M. W.: ref, 1547(269), 1808(11), 2598(1382)
Pryke, M. M.: ref, 859(764)
Pryor, J. B.: ref, 501(802)
Pryor, R. G. L.: ref, 1271(909)
Prytula, R. E.: ref, 1831(150)
Pryzwansky, W. B.: ref, 280(1049), 701(40)
The Psychological Corporation: test, 54, 55, 164, 674, 831, 832, 1425, 1558, 1731, 1808, 2529; ref, 732(389)
Psychological Measurement Division; The Psychological Corporation: test, 1145
Psychological Publications Press: test, 186, 1801, 2656
Psychological Research and Development Institute: test, 473, 1828, 1861, 1862
Psychological Services Bureau: test, 846, 1452, 1454, 1783, 1920, 2049, 2306
Psychometric Affiliates: test, 2524
Puckett, J. M.: ref, 2598(1739, 1831)
Puckett, J. R.: ref, 1831(217)
Pueschel, S. M.: ref, 270(120, 146), 280(1039), 2289(1717), 2557(244), 2602(1657)
Pugh, A. K.: ref, 928(4)
Pugh, J. C.: ref, 1567(10)
Pugh, M.: ref, 890(343), 1170(233), 1789(690)
Pugh, W. M.: ref, 558(61)
Puhan, B. N.: ref, 653(174), 732(405, 413), 1914(893), 2598(1632, 1847)
Pullias, E. V.: rev, 1473
Pullis, J. M.: ref, 1754(94)
Pulos, S.: ref, 2179(232)
Pumfrey, P. D.: test, 1321
Pumroy, D. K.: test, 1387, 1932
Punch, J. L.: ref, 230(52)
Purcell, D.: test, 1412
Purcell, K. M.: ref, 2134(126)
Purdue Research Foundation: test, 1948
Purdy, G.: ref, 381(62)
Purgaire, C.: ref, 1270(83)
Purisch, A. D.: test, 1346; ref, 1346(1)
Pursell, S. A.: ref, 1498(5430)
Purves, A. C.: rev, 172, 1111
Purvis, J. W.: ref, 2300(430)
Putham, L. L.: ref, 1213(27)
Putman, L. L.: ref, 780(1692)
Putnam, B. A.: ref, 374(203), 2413(604, 629)
Putnam, L. L.: ref, 563(32), 890(351), 1300(123), 1798(266)
Putnam, L. R.: ref, 1503(70), 2641(23)
Putnins, A. L.: ref, 1209(41)
Pyrczak, F.: rev, 1192, 1478; ref, 1568(118)
Pysh, F.: ref, 609(202), 675(5), 1771(721), 1904(61)
Quackenbush, R.: ref, 1424(67), 1823(33), 2602(1905)
Qualls, G. S.: ref, 76(623), 1625(104)
Qualls, P. E.: ref, 677(1)
Quarfoth, J.: ref, 2217(166), 2602(2030)
Quarn, K. C.: ref, 482(7)
Quasha, W. H.: test, 2015
Quattrocchi, M.: ref, 2602(2094)
Quattrochi–Tubin, S.: ref, 2277(4)
Quay, H. C.: test, 2012; ref, 704(19)
Quay, L. C.: ref, 1771(565), 1825(21)
Quayhagen, M.: ref, 2269(478)
Queen, L.: ref, 1498(5341)
Queensland Department of Public Instruction: test, 38, 2195
Quenon, B.: ref, 2217(166), 2602(2030)
Quereshi, M. Y.: rev, 558, 732, 1044, 1159, 2269
Query, J. M. N.: ref, 2537(562)
Query, W. T.: ref, 354(1502), 1969(102)
Quesney, L. F.: ref, 1498(5691)
Quick, A. D.: test, 1915
Quigley, H.: test, 1340
Quigley, S. P.: ref, 2164(39), 2286(273)
Quine, M. E.: ref, 960(13)
Quinlan, D.: ref, 1919(39), 2030(4955), 2598(1339, 1734)
Quinlan, D. M.: test, 215, 682; ref, 398(111), 478(8), 682(1), 1257(137), 1771(634), 2030(5019)
Quinn, J. A.: ref, 1934(7)
Quinn, P. O.: ref, 1877(10), 2289(1745)
Quinn, P. T.: ref, 1914(861)
Quinsey, V. L.: ref, 1498(5036, 5689), 1914(862), 2598(1770)
Quinsland, L.: ref, 346(106)
Quintero, E. J.: ref, 2244(40)
Quorn, K. C.: ref, 226(167), 1479(331)
Raasoch, J.: ref, 1655(84)
Rabarilas, A.: ref, 859(954)
Rabavilas, A. D.: ref, 859(878)
Raben, C. S.: ref, 354(1470), 780(1674), 2413(630)
Raber, S. M.: ref, 2602(2201)
Rabetz, M.: test, 1916
Rabin, A. I.: rev, 396, 1361, 2030, 2388, 2602
Rabiner, C. J.: ref, 2598(1670)
Rabinowitz, A.: ref, 2037(149), 2491(2026)
Rabinowitz, F. M.: ref, 2557(243)
Rabinowitz, S.: ref, 1914(781), 2030(5006), 2598(1512)
Rabinowitz, W. M.: ref, 549(1), 2598(1374), 2647(1)
Race, G. S.: ref, 1372(11)
Rachelson, S.: ref, 2160(54)
Rachman, D.: ref, 2134(142)
Radcliffe, J. A.: test, 1538; rev, 780, 966, 1118, 2343
Rader, C. M.: ref, 1498(5188)
Rader, G. E.: ref, 665(44)
Radford, L. M.: ref, 2598(1513)
Radonsky, V. E.: ref, 1555(336)
Radtke, H. L.: ref, 859(935), 1063(129, 136)
Radtke, R. C.: ref, 1192(252)
Radtke–Bodorik, H. L.: ref, 1063(110, 112, 122, 127, 128, 131), 1247(165)
Rae, D.: ref, 2598(1712)
Rae, G.: ref, 1620(19), 2003(1)
Raffeld, P.: test, 2224
Rafferty, J. E.: test, 2037
Ragan, J.: ref, 2300(451)
Ragsdale, R.: ref, 378(12), 2472(18)
Rahaim, S.: ref, 2179(247)
Rahe, R. H.: ref, 609(212)
Rahman, M. A.: ref, 860(111)
Rainer, J. D.: ref, 645(10, 11), 2030(4978), 2598(1412)
Rajic, M.: ref, 342(4)
Rajkumar, S.: ref, 280(1126), 964(499), 2602(1974)
Rakes, T. A.: test, 567

Rakestraw, P.: ref, 2300(570)
Rakow, E. A.: ref, 972(10), 2269(466)
Rallis, K.: ref, 280(1159), 2602(2153)
Ralls, E. M.: ref, 7(5), 1479(319), 2269(442), 2286(282)
Ralph, P. C.: ref, 639(50)
Ralston, A. R.: ref, 1513(31)
Ramanaiah, N.: ref, 609(227), 1257(112)
Ramanaiah, N. V.: ref, 354(1415), 780(1659), 1126(706), 1498(5189, 5190, 5690), 2318(1544), 2598(1633), 2608(217)
Ramani, S. V.: ref, 1498(5691)
Ramaraiah, N. V.: ref, 558(69), 1203(10), 1798(271), 2413(665)
Ramberg, M. L.: test, 2634
Rambo, W. W.: test, 2225
Ramey, C.: ref, 2478(11)
Ramey, C. T.: ref, 270(70, 88, 95, 101, 121, 158), 701(53, 77), 1424(42, 54), 1771(620, 730), 1934(9, 11), 2289(1669, 1682, 1695, 1730), 2478(14), 2598(1634, 1710, 1848), 2602(1939, 2040)
Ramirez, M.: ref, 157(136), 1771(563)
Ramirez, M. P.: ref, 501(906)
Rampp, D. L.: ref, 691(44), 766(29), 960(14), 1126(742), 1771(692), 2289(1736)
Ramsey, P. H.: ref, 1257(132), 2598(1514)
Ramshaw, J. E.: ref, 860(152)
Rand, D.: ref, 2512(616)
Rand, S. W.: ref, 1498(5511)
Rand, Y.: ref, 707(21), 794(417), 1853(281), 2269(467)
Randall, O.: ref, 1197(274), 2208(1529)
Randel, M. A.: ref, 7(5), 1479(319), 2269(442), 2286(282)
Randhawa, B. S.: ref, 400(132), 1257(146), 2160(59), 2269(448)
Randolph, D. L.: ref, 1798(218), 1831(154)
Randolph, G. C.: ref, 1969(116)
Randolph, J. J.: ref, 1969(116)
Randolph, S. R.: ref, 1851(29)
Rank, D.: ref, 1547(289)
Rankin, B.: ref, 354(1471), 780(1675), 859(824), 1498(5349), 1576(206)
Rankin, E. F.: rev, 553, 775, 928, 2288
Rankin, J. L.: ref, 2598(1635)
Rankin, R. J.: ref, 1424(88)
Ransom, G. A.: exc, 891
Rantakylä, S.: ref, 1498(5352), 2030(5009), 2598(1525)
Rao, A. V.: ref, 280(1050), 2607(146)
Rao, D. G.: exc, 2236
Rao, V. A. R.: ref, 2588(33)
Raphael, B.: ref, 941(49)
Raphael, D.: ref, 2300(489, 605), 2638(132, 139)
Rapkin, R. M.: ref, 1904(123)
Rapoport, J. L.: ref, 1771(752), 1877(10), 2289(1745), 2491(2087), 2602(2077), 2621(408)
Rapoport, T.: ref, 2512(566), 2613(79)
Rapp, D. J.: ref, 2243(13), 2602(1805)
Rappaport, E.: ref, 1498(5342), 2300(431, 490, 491)
Rappaport, J.: ref, 2286(322), 2621(362)
Rappaport, M.: ref, 280(1101)
Rappard, P.: ref, 1126(755), 1771(725), 2472(22)
Raps, C. S.: ref, 681(60)
Rarick, G. L.: test, 3; ref, 2289(1604), 2602(1630)

Rasbury, W. C.: ref, 653(154), 1473(161), 1754(80), 2602(1806)
Raschke, H. J.: ref, 1831(176)
Raschke, V. J.: ref, 1831(176)
Rasher, S. P.: ref, 1192(215)
Raskin, A.: ref, 280(1089), 2598(1515), 2607(166)
Raskin, D. C.: ref, 1498(5343)
Raskin, E.: test, 398, 794, 1013; rev, 489, 510; ref, 501(810, 853), 1013(61, 83)
Raskin, L.: ref, 2602(2160), 2641(18)
Raskin, L. M.: ref, 280(1090), 701(41, 54), 2289(1596, 1683), 2602(1695, 1807, 2002), 2621(296)
Raskin, M.: ref, 2322(17)
Raskind, L. T.: ref, 1754(107), 2602(2095)
Rastogi, G. D.: ref, 2300(563)
Ratcliffe, K. J.: ref, 1319(84), 2602(2096)
Ratcliffe, M. W.: ref, 1319(84), 2602(2096)
Ratekin, N.: ref, 934(6), 935(31)
Ratener, P.: ref, 1671(46)
Raths, J.: exc, 404
Rathus, S. A.: ref, 1498(5344, 5692)
Ratusnik, C. M.: ref, 1622(52)
Ratusnik, D. L.: ref, 664(9), 960(5), 1622(52)
Rauchway, A.: ref, 1106(359), 2030(5021)
Raulin, M. L.: ref, 1798(232)
Rausch, R.: ref, 2598(1383, 1384, 1516), 2607(147, 148, 167)
Rauscher, F. P.: ref, 2598(1372)
Rauste–von Wright, M.: ref, 2208(1692)
Ravaris, C. L.: ref, 2100(9)
Raven, J. C.: test, 632, 1485, 1914; exc, 955
Raven, R. J.: ref, 934(5), 1193(138), 1754(81), 2165(26), 2298(1)
Rawling, P.: ref, 2607(168)
Rawlings, E. I.: ref, 1789(642)
Rawlinson, M. E.: ref, 609(198), 1498(5049)
Ray, C.: ref, 116(539), 2300(492)
Ray, J. J.: ref, 1419(691, 697, 698)
Ray, P. B.: ref, 2413(609)
Ray, R. M.: ref, 2598(1455), 2607(158)
Ray, S.: test, 2606
Rayburn, W. G.: ref, 344(169), 501(855)
Raychaudhuri, M.: exc, 786
Rayder, N.: ref, 2602(1808), 2608(205)
Rayder, N. F.: ref, 1473(162, 182), 1479(360), 1914(782, 819), 2608(224)
Raygor, A. L.: test, 2002, 2257, 2347, 2568, 2662; rev, 1993
Raymond, B. A.: ref, 2512(591)
Rayner, K.: ref, 2602(1937)
Rayner, S. A.: rev, 2166
Raynor, A. L.: rev, 1568
Rayson, B.: ref, 2289(1687), 2602(1814, 2066), 2608(206)
Raz, D.: ref, 1498(5193)
Read, M. R.: ref, 280(1147), 609(226), 859(822, 930), 1771(750), 1798(289, 291), 1940(81), 2607(208)
Readance, J. E.: ref, 932(84, 85), 1013(111), 1570(9), 1734(1)
Reading, J. C.: ref, 1940(84)
Reading Clinic (The): test, 931
Reading Support Services Center of the Los Angeles Unified School District: test, 1781
Ream, J. H.: ref, 1236(11)
Rearden, J.: ref, 296(10), 2179(230)

INDEX OF NAMES

Reardon, J. P.: ref, 1547(270), 2413(605)
Reardon, R.: ref, 2134(125, 134)
Reardon, R. C.: ref, 2134(114)
Rearn, J. H.: ref, 2598(1517)
Reberg, B. J.: ref, 2340(12), 2347(5, 7)
Rechter, B.: test, 42, 233
Reckless, J.: ref, 2208(1531)
Reddin, W. G.: test, 539
Reddin, W. J.: test, 1364, 1744, 2056, 2127, 2545
Redding, S.: test, 548
Reddy, W. B.: ref, 2413(631)
Redfering, D. L.: ref, 354(1503), 1197(302), 1498(5345), 2208(1565), 2300(432), 2413(613)
Redfield, D. L.: ref, 1576(198)
Redfield, J.: ref, 2598(1809)
Redican, K. J.: ref, 1(1)
Reeb, R.: ref, 2300(574)
Reed, C. G.: ref, 1771(795), 2608(245)
Reed, C. M.: ref, 230(51), 549(1), 2598(1374), 2647(1)
Reed, D. M.: test, 2168
Reed, G. F.: ref, 2598(1385, 1386)
Reed, H. B. C.: rev, 2244; ref, 381(70), 932(101), 1007(33), 1250(18), 2034(5), 2113(253), 2125(26), 2289(1754), 2602(1940), 2621(354)
Reed, J. C.: rev, 327, 2216, 2285, 2380, 2665; ref, 381(70), 2289(1754)
Reed, M.: ref, 2300(559)
Reed, P. L.: ref, 354(1398), 1498(5107), 1798(206)
Reed, R.: ref, 226(172), 270(146), 701(65), 1371(254), 1498(5268, 5446), 1771(678), 2113(252), 2557(244), 2598(1583, 1675), 2602(1929)
Rees, J. A.: ref, 645(25)
Rees, R.: ref, 1762(4), 2269(450)
Reese, A.: ref, 280(1090), 701(54), 2289(1683), 2602(1807), 2621(296)
Reeve, T. G.: ref, 2208(1675)
Reeves, A. G.: ref, 2598(1343), 2621(247)
Reeves, D.: ref, 357(516), 794(416), 1754(87), 2429(24)
Reeves, R.: test, 1279
Reeves, R. A.: ref, 2300(367, 433)
Reeves, W. H.: ref, 1237(94), 1239(55), 1919(47), 2602(2097)
Reevy, W. R.: rev, 622, 1756
Regan, M. C.: ref, 1726(364)
Regehr, C. N.: ref, 374(228)
Regestein, Q.: ref, 1498(5517)
Regev, E.: ref, 874(55)
Rehak, P. J.: ref, 1547(303)
Rehermann, O.: ref, 794(403)
Rehm, L. P.: ref, 681(49), 1498(5512)
Reich, J. H.: ref, 1919(48)
Reich, P.: ref, 280(1173), 1498(5765), 1547(354)
Reich, T.: ref, 2208(1672)
Reicherter, R. F.: test, 2006
Reichman, W.: ref, 1495(87, 90), 2208(1623, 1686), 2318(1586, 1615), 2491(2061), 2614(24)
Reichmann, B.: ref, 270(64), 311(17)
Reichstein, M. B.: ref, 308(25)
Reichurdt, K. W.: ref, 1007(19), 1503(61)
Reid, D. K.: test, 2436, 2438
Reid, D. M.: ref, 280(1035), 2413(593), 2621(246)
Reid, I.: ref, 972(11), 1485(84)
Reid, J. C.: ref, 1576(195, 205)
Reid, L.: ref, 2472(17)

Reid, N.: test, 329, 1918, 2458
Reid, N. A.: test, 1910, 1911, 1912, 1913, 2341
Reid Psychological Systems: test, 2007
Reid, W. R.: ref, 6(50), 2602(1858), 2621(317)
Reidel, R. G.: ref, 2602(1780)
Reidy, T.: ref, 2491(2027)
Reiff, G. G.: test, 5
Reifsnider, L. C.: ref, 1498(5527)
Reilley, R. R.: ref, 1498(5191, 5706), 2512(601)
Reilly, R.: ref, 2318(1592)
Reilly, T. F.: ref, 1769(97)
Reimer, A.: ref, 2657(113)
Reimherr, F.: ref, 1498(5770)
Reimherr, F. S.: ref, 1331(42)
Reimherr, F. W.: ref, 794(450), 1498(5034, 5776), 1853(300), 2598(1293), 2621(218, 464)
Rein, I.: ref, 1170(228)
Reiner, W. B.: test, 2474
Reinhard, K. E.: ref, 681(60)
Reinhart, J. B.: ref, 664(15), 1513(28)
Reis, M.: ref, 630(2), 1424(47), 1771(657), 2479(3), 2480(1)
Reisboard, R. J.: rev, 1224
Reisman, F. K.: ref, 1479(369), 2512(651)
Reister, B. W.: ref, 2353(26)
Reitan, R. M.: test, 1052; rev, 1109, 1743; ref, 1498(5071), 2598(1311, 1321, 1446, 1643, 1644), 2602(1835, 1956, 1957), 2621(363, 364)
Reiter, S.: ref, 2413(684)
Reitta, S.: ref, 226(185), 691(47), 701(89), 1126(784), 1462(158), 1769(103), 1914(888), 2602(2186)
Reitz, W.: test, 2131
Reitz, W. E.: rev, 337, 2079
Reker, D.: ref, 1904(97)
Reker, G. T.: ref, 859(765), 1789(734), 1960(70, 78, 86), 2124(1)
Rekers, G. A.: ref, 751(7), 874(45, 46), 1201(76), 1361(63, 64), 2602(1678, 1679)
Relinger, H.: ref, 1798(196)
Remer, R.: ref, 2491(2045)
Remmers, H. H.: test, 163, 1055, 1113, 1939, 1943, 1945, 1950, 1951, 2326, 2327; rev, 340, 1066, 1192, 1541
Rempel, A. M.: test, 1955
Renaer, M.: ref, 1498(5513)
Renck, R.: test, 2553, 2654
Renehan, W. T.: test, 42
Renfrow, N. E.: ref, 2208(1604, 1629, 1693)
Renner, J. W.: ref, 2181(20)
Rennick, P.: ref, 2598(1606), 2621(345)
Rennick, P. M.: ref, 1498(5268), 2598(1424, 1650)
Rensis Likert Associates, Inc.: test, 2369
Rentz, R. R.: ref, 344(144), 551(21), 1192(179), 1473(136), 2160(55), 2260(30)
Renzulli, J. S.: test, 1309, 2069; ref, 2512(562)
Resch, R. C.: ref, 2289(1634)
Reschly, D. J.: ref, 1460(50), 1473(183, 219), 1769(75), 2387(7, 8), 2602(1680, 1809, 1941, 1942, 2179)
Research and Evaluation Branch of the Los Angeles Unified School District: test, 2454
Resick, P. A.: ref, 1257(133), 1904(93, 127), 2100(5, 11), 2300(476, 593)
Reskin, L.: ref, 2602(2003), 2641(14)
Resnick, J. H.: ref, 2030(4943)
Resnick, R. J.: ref, 2602(1681)

Resnikoff, M.: rev, 2030
Rest, J. R.: test, 666
Reuter, J.: test, 1246; ref, 678(32), 1246(1), 1874(11), 2014(5), 2551(15), 2557(237)
Reuter, L.: ref, 1874(11)
Reuterfors, D. L.: ref, 2318(1593)
Revelle, W.: ref, 732(410), 859(847, 932, 955), 860(154), 1498(5277)
Reviere, R.: ref, 1197(291), 2413(632)
Revill, S. I.: ref, 859(823), 1547(290)
Reynell, J.: test, 2019
Reynell, J. K.: test, 2018
Reynold, W. M.: ref, 1473(184)
Reynolds, B. J.: ref, 280(1055, 1112)
Reynolds, C. H.: ref, 354(1416)
Reynolds, C. R.: ref, 302(42), 581(14), 701(81), 1424(43, 55, 74, 75, 87), 1473(204), 1479(352, 353, 370), 1769(76, 90), 2260(49), 2289(1743, 1766, 1773), 2300(560), 2472(26, 27), 2478(15), 2602(1943, 1944, 2046, 2098, 2099, 2100, 2173, 2202, 2203), 2608(238, 241, 244, 247, 248), 2621(355, 356, 384, 422, 429, 451, 452)
Reynolds, D. J.: ref, 2030(4948), 2588(31)
Reynolds, M. C.: rev, 958
Reynolds, V. J.: ref, 1771(727)
Reynolds, W. M.: test, 2224; ref, 2218(150), 2224(4), 2598(1518)
Reys, R. E.: ref, 2286(326, 346)
Rezler, A. G.: ref, 1555(311)
Reznikoff, M.: rev, 1020; ref, 2030(5021)
Rhodes, B. L.: test, 1544
Rhodes, B. M. L.: test, 297
Rhodes, F.: test, 2599, 2604
Rhodes, G. S.: exc, 2571
Rhodes, J.: ref, 226(185), 691(47), 701(89), 1126(784), 1462(158), 1769(103), 1914(888), 2602(2186)
Rhodes, J. W.: ref, 2512(662)
Rhodes, L.: ref, 270(65), 381(60)
Rhodes, L. M.: ref, 2587(47)
Rhodes, R. E.: test, 1544
Rhodes, R. J.: ref, 1498(5192, 5345, 5346, 5524), 2620(15)
Rhosenow, D. J.: ref, 665(46)
Ribich, F.: ref, 1257(112)
Ribich, F. D.: ref, 2594(199)
Ribner, S.: ref, 2602(2204)
Ribordy, S. C.: ref, 1351(197), 1498(5617), 1547(324), 1771(760), 2300(561), 2594(201)
Riccomini, A. P.: test, 568
Rice, A. S.: ref, 1498(5192)
Rice, D. R.: ref, 1498(5356), 2491(2047)
Rice, J. A.: rev, 701, 1779
Rice, J. K.: ref, 2318(1545)
Rice, K. M.: ref, 1498(5764), 2300(603)
Rice, M. F.: test, 1491
Rice, W. J.: ref, 2598(1455), 2607(158)
Rice, W. K.: test, 1491
Rich, A.: ref, 344(148, 160)
Rich, C. E.: ref, 1831(177)
Rich, N. S.: ref, 368(2), 1073(122), 2286(300)
Rich, Y.: ref, 874(52), 1914(820)
Richard, G. P.: ref, 1485(70)
Richards, C. S.: test, 1076
Richards, G.: ref, 653(154)
Richards, H.: ref, 1769(50)

Richards, H. C.: test, 845; ref, 932(94), 935(33), 1479(328), 2260(35, 39), 2602(1994), 2621(379)
Richards, J.: ref, 1771(641)
Richards, J. M.: rev, 837, 1576, 2227; ref, 2581(309)
Richards, J. S.: ref, 280(1148), 2598(1771), 2607(209)
Richards, L. G.: ref, 501(801), 1257(109)
Richards, M. A.: ref, 643(134), 966(173), 2594(196)
Richards, P. N.: ref, 2512(564)
Richards, R. A.: rev, 1278, 1635, 1910, 2523
Richards, R. T.: ref, 701(87), 2289(1782), 2551(16)
Richards, W. A.: ref, 1498(5348), 1789(681)
Richards-Munn, B.: ref, 1126(731), 1771(670)
Richardson, A.: ref, 45(4), 968(1), 1257(110), 1462(124), 1485(63), 2015(201)
Richardson, B.: ref, 381(69), 2289(1750), 2557(235)
Richardson, Bellows, Henry & Co., Inc.: test, 1975, 1976, 1977, 1978, 1979, 1980, 1981, 1982, 1983, 1984, 1985, 1986, 1987, 2263, 2265
Richardson, E.: ref, 958(50), 1126(771), 1769(59, 91), 2034(4, 6), 2602(2101)
Richardson, E. H.: ref, 1498(5719)
Richardson, F. C.: ref, 2300(515)
Richardson, G.: ref, 1498(5775)
Richardson, G. T.: test, 572, 2333
Richardson, J. T. E.: ref, 1060(26), 2598(1519)
Richardson, J. W.: ref, 1484(12), 2441(34)
Richardson, K.: ref, 2472(20)
Richardson, L. I.: test, 1770
Richardson, M.: ref, 1655(120)
Richardson, M. W.: test, 2275; rev, 688, 1188
Richardson, P.: ref, 354(1553)
Richardson, P. H.: ref, 1485(81)
Richardson, S.: test, 2344
Richardson, S. A.: ref, 2289(1790), 2602(2205)
Richardson, S. C.: rev, 826
Richardson, W. B.: ref, 1295(291)
Richardt, C.: ref, 665(44), 1009(54)
Richek, M. A.: ref, 482(5), 1126(672), 2563(3)
Richert, A. J.: ref, 665(45)
Richert, M.: ref, 280(1080), 1462(136), 2602(1786)
Richey, M. H.: test, 1932
Richman, C. L.: ref, 780(1685), 2491(2057)
Richman, J. M.: ref, 2534(13)
Richman, L. C.: ref, 1101(42, 46, 48, 50, 51), 1498(5279, 5693), 1771(683), 2012(1, 6), 2602(1810, 1945, 2061, 2102, 2206), 2621(297, 357, 414, 453)
Richman, N.: ref, 609(213)
Richmond, B. O.: test, 395; ref, 6(51, 74), 280(1051), 343(11), 395(1), 1462(125), 1769(63), 1771(566), 2217(133), 2512(609), 2585(5), 2602(1682, 1862)
Richmond, J. B.: ref, 270(100)
Richmond, M. G.: ref, 1479(320)
Richter, D. J.: ref, 1295(293)
Richter, E.: ref, 922(7)
Rickard, R. B.: ref, 2441(37)
Rickards, J. P.: ref, 2292(23)
Rickel, A. V.: ref, 1295(302)
Rickels, K.: ref, 1498(5371, 5530), 2100(1)
Ricker, L. H.: ref, 378(8)
Ricks, J. H.: rev, 334, 372
Riddle, M.: ref, 1853(278)
Rider, B.: ref, 751(17), 1655(98)
Ridgeway, C. L.: ref, 1077(52)
Riding, R. J.: ref, 1229(94), 1567(10)

Ridley, D. R.: ref, 157(150), 243(116, 117), 2613(81)
Ridley, S. E.: ref, 780(1706)
Rie, E. D.: ref, 1192(180), 2289(1635), 2621(257)
Rie, H. E.: ref, 1192(180), 2289(1635), 2621(257)
Rieder, D. O.: ref, 280(1118), 751(29), 1126(736), 2602(1946)
Rieder, R. O.: ref, 1498(5449), 2602(1683), 2621(358)
Riedesel, C. A.: rev, 301, 1477, 2287, 2476
Riedner, E.: ref, 941(39)
Riedsel, C. A.: rev, 552
Riege, W. H.: ref, 1462(160, 161), 2300(572), 2598(1801, 1849, 1850)
Riegler, J.: ref, 2113(255)
Rieman, W.: rev, 58, 73
Rierdan, J.: ref, 751(12), 2030(5007), 2598(1520)
Rietz, E. G.: rev, 75, 390
Rifkin, A.: ref, 1655(116)
Riggio, R. E.: ref, 859(905), 1798(280)
Riggs, N.: ref, 2289(1608)
Riggs, S. T.: ref, 2286(328), 2602(2008)
Rigler, D.: ref, 2300(538, 577)
Rigrodsky, S.: rev, 1513; ref, 1851(32)
Riker, H. C.: ref, 372(10), 1798(270)
Riklan, M.: ref, 1498(5456), 2598(1337)
Riley, C. M. D.: test, 2024
Riley, E. P.: ref, 1904(53)
Riley, G. D.: test, 2022, 2023; ref, 1126(772), 2023(1)
Riley, J.: ref, 653(150), 1126(772), 2023(1), 2246(27)
Rim, Y.: ref, 859(766, 879)
Rimland, B.: ref, 1257(105)
Rimm, D. C.: ref, 883(77)
Rimm, S.: ref, 1016(1)
Rimm, S. B.: test, 1016, 1017
Rimoin, D. L.: ref, 1319(78)
Rinaldi, R. T.: ref, 2478(12)
Rinderer, R. E.: ref, 1719(3), 2181(21)
Rines, A. R.: rev, 439
Ringel, L.: test, 604, 605
Ringel, S. P.: ref, 280(1052), 1771(567)
Ringler, L. H.: ref, 2286(320)
Ringler, N.: ref, 212(4), 1622(42), 2598(1521)
Rinieris, P.: ref, 859(954)
Rinsland, H. D.: rev, 2519
Ripka, G. E.: test, 1675
Risko, V.: test, 2425
Risse, G. L.: ref, 1126(664), 1462(122), 2607(139)
Ritchie, J.: ref, 2301(25)
Ritchie, K.: ref, 941(24), 1883(34)
Ritter, D. P.: ref, 1960(67), 2343(1031)
Ritter, D. R.: ref, 678(16), 1874(9)
Ritterman, S. I.: ref, 378(8), 1771(684)
Rittgarn, G.: ref, 2217(125), 2621(283)
Ritvo, E.: ref, 1471(53)
Ritzen, J. M.: ref, 2288(87)
Ritzler, B.: ref, 1883(76), 2030(5072), 2598(1772)
Ritzler, B. A.: ref, 645(16), 1240(57), 1498(5699), 1883(38, 58, 68), 2030(5008, 5030), 2491(2089), 2598(1387, 1460, 1588, 1721, 1829)
Rivard, E.: ref, 2030(4966)
Rivera–Calimlim, L.: ref, 2598(1372)
Rivers, S. M.: ref, 1063(98, 112, 125)
Riverside Publishing Co.: test, 1139, 1140
Rivlin, H. N.: rev, 977, 1625
Rizvi, S.: ref, 1485(77), 1914(833), 2598(1691), 2607(191)

Rizzo, J. M.: ref, 1969(125)
Rizzo, J. P.: rev, 123
Ro–Trock, G. K.: ref, 1170(229), 1372(9), 1761(5)
Roach, D. A.: ref, 1077(67, 82), 1570(12)
Roach, E. G.: test, 1949
Roan, Y.: ref, 280(1132), 283(154), 2598(1681), 2621(382)
Roark, A. E.: exc, 2374
Robak, O. H.: ref, 1655(107)
Robbins, A. S.: ref, 859(880), 1789(702)
Robbins, B. J.: ref, 1904(116)
Robbins, E. L.: test, 1859
Robbins, J. M.: ref, 1498(5514)
Robbins, P. I.: ref, 2318(1562)
Robbins, R. L.: ref, 1126(673), 2602(1684)
Roberge, J. J.: ref, 932(123), 1013(106), 1473(205)
Roberge, L. P.: ref, 1479(349), 1871(3), 2218(146), 2602(1920)
Robert Gibson & Sons, Glasgow, Ltd.: test, 1753
Roberts, A. D.: ref, 570(322), 1991(122), 2594(194, 197)
Roberts, A. H.: ref, 1853(278)
Roberts, A. O. H.: rev, 282
Roberts, C.: ref, 149(9), 972(9)
Roberts, C. L.: ref, 1170(234)
Roberts, H.: rev, 326, 490, 530, 1082, 1635; ref, 941(31)
Roberts, H. D.: rev, 1191
Roberts, J. R.: test, 1774
Roberts, K.: ref, 1508(115)
Roberts, K. H.: ref, 116(564)
Roberts, R.: ref, 1498(5084)
Roberts, R. N.: ref, 2218(155), 2598(1660)
Roberts, S. H.: ref, 2602(1685)
Roberts, W. R.: ref, 283(159, 160), 1498(5762), 1914(891)
Robertson, C. M.: ref, 701(87), 2289(1782), 2551(16)
Robertson, S. A.: ref, 1960(74), 2208(1590)
Robin, A.: ref, 1883(77)
Robinett, R.: test, 1227, 1360
Robinowitz, R.: ref, 283(159, 160), 1498(5335, 5336, 5507, 5676, 5677, 5678, 5694, 5762), 1765(9), 1914(859, 891)
Robins, L. N.: ref, 280(1061)
Robinson, A.: test, 1238; ref, 2300(375), 2598(1568)
Robinson, A. L.: ref, 2598(1773)
Robinson, B. E.: ref, 116(596)
Robinson, D. S.: ref, 2100(9)
Robinson, E. A.: test, 768; ref, 768(1), 858(2)
Robinson, E. H.: ref, 1769(92)
Robinson, G. E.: rev, 577
Robinson, H. A.: rev, 1478, 1569, 1570, 1646, 2280
Robinson, H. B.: ref, 2289(1642)
Robinson, H. M.: test, 1007; rev, 175, 766, 2093, 2247, 2288
Robinson, J. A.: ref, 76(615), 116(631), 794(404), 1257(181), 2598(1522)
Robinson, J. E.: ref, 224(2)
Robinson, J. F.: ref, 859(873)
Robinson, J. H.: ref, 1771(733)
Robinson, K. M.: ref, 860(146)
Robinson, M. A.: ref, 501(907)
Robinson, R. D.: rev, 608, 1993
Robinson, S. E.: ref, 1013(124), 2300(592)
Robinson, T. N.: ref, 860(131, 153)

Robitaille, D. F.: ref, 590(374)
Robyak, J. E.: ref, 1531(284, 285), 1555(312, 322, 329), 2342(24), 2347(2, 3, 4, 6), 2374(187, 188, 194)
Rochford, J.: ref, 280(1053), 1503(62)
Rock, A. F.: ref, 2100(1)
Rock, D.: ref, 1462(146)
Rock, D. A.: ref, 501(809)
Rock, D. R.: ref, 501(841, 912)
Rock, M. H.: ref, 1013(73)
Rocklin, T.: ref, 859(847, 955), 860(154)
Rodd, W. G.: ref, 2598(1780)
Rodd–Marks, J.: ref, 6(73)
Rodger, A.: rev, 623, 1356, 1450, 1936, 2015, 2265
Rodgers, D. A.: rev, 1498
Rodgers, W. C.: test, 1824
Rodnick, E. H.: ref, 1498(5744, 5745), 2491(2098, 2104)
Rodnight, R.: ref, 1883(52, 61)
Rodrigues, M. C.: test, 178
Rodriguez, R.: ref, 1798(292)
Rodriguez, V. L.: ref, 2598(1576)
Rodriguez–Brown, F. V.: ref, 927(2)
Rodriguez–Giegling, M.: ref, 2300(495)
Rodwell, D. N.: test, 1965
Roe, A.: test, 1137
Roe, A. V.: test, 294
Roe, J. E.: ref, 1099(68)
Roe, K. V.: ref, 280(1054), 1126(674, 707), 1471(50), 1771(568), 2289(1636, 1684)
Roe, M. D.: ref, 311(16)
Roe, W. T.: ref, 1884(4)
Roeder, W. S.: test, 190
Roelfs, P. J.: test, 2337; ref, 995(143), 1486(181)
Roeper, P.: ref, 859(946)
Roessler, R.: ref, 354(1471), 780(1675), 859(824), 1498(5349), 1576(206)
Roettger, D.: test, 845; ref, 845(8), 1192(224)
Roffe, M. W.: ref, 1424(34, 56), 1498(5767), 2413(701)
Rogers, B.: ref, 375(1), 1059(3)
Rogers, B. G.: ref, 1192(248), 1479(371), 1754(108), 2269(480)
Rogers, B. J.: ref, 2300(498)
Rogers, C. A.: rev, 1620
Rogers, C. M.: ref, 1473(163, 167), 1831(131, 151, 156), 2602(1827)
Rogers, D. L.: ref, 280(1149)
Rogers, J.: ref, 941(48), 2208(1694)
Rogers, J. G.: ref, 2598(1539)
Rogers, M.: ref, 1922(17)
Rogers, M. H.: ref, 2030(4948), 2588(31)
Rogers, P.: ref, 2300(452)
Rogers, P. J.: ref, 1498(5403), 1798(267)
Rogers, S.: ref, 118(251), 354(1504), 2217(117)
Rogers, T. B.: ref, 1798(219, 259, 267)
Rogers, T. R.: ref, 116(632)
Rogers, W.: ref, 1054(7)
Roginski, J.: ref, 1771(743), 2598(1744)
Rogol, A.: ref, 2598(1372)
Rohde, M. J.: ref, 681(45)
Rohn, R.: ref, 280(1112)
Rohn, R. D.: ref, 280(1055)
Rohr, A.: ref, 1126(686, 708)
Rohrberg, M. M.: ref, 732(401), 1044(62)
Rohsenow, D. J.: ref, 665(41, 46), 1498(5499)

Rokeach, M.: test, 2029
Roll, S.: ref, 243(121), 1106(378), 2031(461), 2413(599)
Roll, W. G.: ref, 1063(108), 1789(703)
Romaine, M. F.: ref, 270(144)
Romanczyk, R. G.: ref, 1126(749), 1473(192), 1771(712), 2602(1999), 2621(383)
Romano, J. L.: ref, 2353(31)
Romano, J. M.: ref, 1498(5512)
Romano, P.: ref, 1498(5170)
Romberg, T. A.: rev, 580, 584, 1139
Romine, P. G.: ref, 354(1472), 859(825)
Romirowsky, S.: ref, 1197(311), 2031(462)
Ron, M.: ref, 1485(65)
Ronco, B.: ref, 1914(831)
Ronning, R. R.: ref, 1568(139, 147)
Ronshausen, N. L.: ref, 1477(17), 1479(354)
Roodin, P.: ref, 780(1676)
Roodin, P. A.: ref, 1229(88), 2602(1832)
Rooks, Y.: ref, 1424(70), 1771(742)
Roos, N. P.: ref, 1576(196)
Rorensaville, B. J.: ref, 2100(12)
Rorer, L. G.: rev, 116, 2208; ref, 483(39), 1013(117), 1257(174), 1914(871)
Rorie, I. L.: ref, 1185(7)
Rorschach, H.: test, 2030
Rosado, J. W.: ref, 290(6)
Rosanoff, A. J.: test, 1247
Roscioli, D. L.: ref, 1798(303)
Rose, A.: ref, 1237(95)
Rose, D.: ref, 2030(5073)
Rose, G. S.: ref, 116(613), 1099(70)
Rose, R.: ref, 354(1568)
Rose, R. G.: ref, 799(21), 1914(863), 2594(202)
Rose, S. A.: test, 1876
Rosegrant, J.: ref, 1106(379)
Rosén, A.: ref, 354(1417, 1418), 2029(235), 2155(11), 2497(39)
Rosen, A. C.: ref, 751(7), 874(46), 1361(64), 2602(1679)
Rosen, A. J.: ref, 1498(5643), 2598(1700), 2607(196)
Rosen, B.: ref, 1240(52, 54), 2366(198, 201)
Rosen, C. L.: rev, 922, 1540, 2093, 2506
Rosen, E.: rev, 1047; exc, 298
Rosen, G. M.: ref, 883(65, 78)
Rosen, H.: ref, 2607(186)
Rosen, J. B.: ref, 2300(498)
Rosen, L.: ref, 2300(356)
Rosen, M.: rev, 343; ref, 6(43), 1479(333), 2287(37)
Rosen, R. C.: ref, 534(103), 1771(621), 2289(1685)
Rosenbach, J. H.: rev, 590, 2160
Rosenbaum, A. H.: ref, 280(1140), 1498(5596), 2030(5057), 2602(2029), 2607(195)
Rosenbaum, G.: ref, 1485(64, 78), 2598(1552, 1650, 1828)
Rosenbaum, M.: ref, 1498(5193)
Rosenbaum, R. L.: rev, 2547, 2646
Rosenberg, A.: ref, 357(523), 1466(4), 1831(212)
Rosenberg, D.: ref, 1197(306), 1798(277)
Rosenberg, H.: test, 904
Rosenberg, I. K.: ref, 1013(137)
Rosenberg, L.: test, 963
Rosenberg, L. A.: ref, 280(1132), 283(154), 2598(1681), 2602(1603), 2621(382)
Rosenberger, P. B.: ref, 2598(1475), 2602(1764)

INDEX OF NAMES

Rosenblatt, A.: ref, 1498(5686, 5687)
Rosenblatt, A. I.: ref, 1498(5350), 2598(1523), 2621(298)
Rosenbloom, P. C.: rev, 986
Rosenfeld, L. B.: ref, 354(1414, 1419, 1501, 1548), 780(1658, 1660, 1691, 1705), 2343(1033, 1034, 1047), 2413(603, 606, 659, 683)
Rosenfeld, M.: test, 1545
Rosenfield, D.: ref, 1473(188)
Rosenkrantz, A.: ref, 1197(294), 1198(1)
Rosenman, R. H.: test, 1206; ref, 116(627)
Rosenstiel, A. K.: ref, 2607(203)
Rosenthal, D.: ref, 42(3), 406(1), 645(11), 1498(5275), 1914(783), 2030(4978), 2598(1412), 2602(1683)
Rosenthal, D. A.: ref, 859(826), 1914(864), 2512(578, 652)
Rosenthal, G. T.: ref, 766(33), 1007(37), 2288(89)
Rosenthal, L.: ref, 643(139), 1073(120)
Rosenthal, M.: ref, 872(5), 1498(5121)
Rosentretter, G.: ref, 2355(4), 2363(7)
Rosenzweig, P.: test, 668
Rosenzweig, S.: test, 2031; ref, 2031(456)
Roser, N. L.: rev, 585, 719
Rosier, P.: ref, 2288(85)
Rosinski, E. F.: test, 1457
Roskam, K.: ref, 1769(77)
Rosman, B. L.: test, 1263, 1264; ref, 354(1496)
Rosmann, M.: ref, 2300(457)
Rosner, B.: rev, 1939, 1947, 1955
Rosner, J.: rev, 850, 1889; ref, 719(34), 1914(823)
Rosner, R.: ref, 280(1134), 2030(5053), 2491(2077), 2598(1688)
Ross, A. J.: ref, 1513(30)
Ross, A. O.: rev, 1902
Ross, A. W.: ref, 858(1, 2)
Ross, B. E.: ref, 859(741), 1498(5111), 2208(1538)
Ross, C. M.: test, 2032
Ross, C. S.: rev, 196
Ross, C. W.: ref, 2491(2046)
Ross, D.: ref, 1655(116)
Ross, D. L.: ref, 2030(5010), 2491(2048)
Ross, F. E.: ref, 113(27), 1498(5593), 1904(110)
Ross, G. R.: ref, 2300(434)
Ross, H. G.: ref, 354(1550)
Ross, J. D.: test, 228, 2032
Ross, L.: ref, 1077(68)
Ross, M.: test, 2646; ref, 1498(5310)
Ross, M. B.: ref, 780(1646)
Ross, P. F.: rev, 799, 2619
Ross, R. T.: test, 865, 867, 868, 869
Ross, S. A.: ref, 678(29)
Rosser, M. E.: ref, 2300(489), 2638(139)
Rosskopf, M. F.: rev, 1230
Rossman, J. F.: ref, 1568(119), 2286(283)
Rosso, B. R.: ref, 1073(128), 2292(33)
Roswell, F. G.: test, 2033, 2034
Roszkowski, M. J.: ref, 6(60, 75, 76), 2557(241)
Rotatori, A. F.: ref, 1771(731), 1969(94), 2217(134, 168), 2218(151), 2289(1731)
Roth, A.: ref, 681(61)
Roth, A. V.: ref, 681(41, 74)
Roth, D. M.: ref, 1498(5512)
Roth, G.: ref, 201(2), 932(70)
Roth, L.: ref, 121(9)
Roth, R. A.: ref, 2286(284)
Roth, R. M.: test, 1537
Roth, R. S.: ref, 1498(5035, 5771)
Roth, S.: ref, 707(18)
Roth, W. T.: ref, 152(12), 2598(1498)
Rothberg, A. D.: ref, 270(159), 678(37), 1420(3)
Rothberg, D. L.: ref, 2491(2090)
Rothchild, G.: ref, 874(52), 1914(820)
Rothe, H. F.: rev, 2112
Rothen, W.: ref, 1257(171)
Rothenberg, J. J.: ref, 1205(15), 1479(355)
Rothenberg, S.: ref, 1007(22), 1754(75), 2602(1753)
Rothman, E. P.: test, 337
Rothman, S.: ref, 2491(2059)
Rothney, J. W. M.: rev, 1040, 1325, 1720, 2289, 2557, 2618; exc, 2318
Rothpearl, A.: ref, 1197(312)
Rothstein, A. L.: ref, 5(167)
Rothstein, M.: ref, 1798(293)
Rothwell, J. W.: test, 2035, 2036
Rotrosen, J.: ref, 1655(99)
Rotter, J. B.: test, 1320, 2037; rev, 1498, 2491; ref, 2037(155)
Rounds, J. B.: ref, 1405(8, 9), 1495(83, 88), 1497(25, 26), 1855(21), 2318(1594, 1595), 2353(36), 2581(327)
Rounsaville, B. J.: ref, 1419(692), 1883(89)
Rourke, B. P.: ref, 1771(716), 2602(2015), 2621(388)
Rourke, D.: ref, 2598(1552, 1750)
Rourke, D. L.: ref, 311(31)
Rouse, L. O.: ref, 2300(368)
Rouse, M. J.: exc, 964
Rousseau, E. W.: ref, 1831(208)
Routh, D. K.: ref, 1424(57)
Rovezzi-Carroll, S.: ref, 501(908)
Rowan, R. W.: ref, 76(616)
Rowe, H. A. H.: test, 24, 27
Rowe, J.: ref, 2512(579)
Rowell, K.: test, 539, 2127, 2545
Rowen, M. R.: ref, 501(795)
Rowley, P. T.: ref, 354(1485), 2413(644)
Rowson, V. J.: ref, 823(23)
Roy, A.: ref, 860(97, 112, 132), 941(20, 25, 47)
Roy, A. R.: ref, 2300(517)
Roy, R.: ref, 1106(381), 1117(444), 2029(231), 2602(2180)
Roy, W. J.: ref, 890(326)
Royce, J. R.: test, 1929
Royer, H. L.: rev, 303
Royer, P. N.: ref, 1257(111)
Royster, R. F.: test, 177
Rozenfeld, I. H.: ref, 2289(1687), 2602(1814), 2608(206)
Rozier, J. S.: ref, 2602(1826)
Rozsnafszky, J.: ref, 2155(12)
Rubenstein, H.: ref, 200(18), 1771(788), 2288(80)
Rubenstein, J. L.: ref, 1771(803), 1877(11)
Rubenstein, J. S.: ref, 958(46), 2602(1811), 2621(299)
Rubin, D. L.: ref, 1272(134), 1341(178)
Rubin, K. H.: ref, 559(51), 653(145), 1771(622, 623), 1914(784)
Rubin, L.: ref, 1771(529)
Rubin, R. A.: ref, 270(122, 123), 1126(709, 737, 738), 1479(332, 333, 356, 357), 2286(285, 301, 321), 2287(36, 37), 2288(84), 2289(1686, 1732, 1733),

2598(1524), 2602(1686, 1947, 1948, 2187), 2621(258, 300, 359, 448)
Rubin, S.: test, 1335; ref, 2300(606), 2621(324)
Rubin, S. I.: rev, 1219; ref, 230(51)
Rubinstein, D. N.: ref, 1576(203)
Rubinstein, M. R.: ref, 2318(1563)
Rubinstein, R. A.: ref, 794(438)
Rubinton, N.: ref, 374(215)
Ruch, F.: test, 2373
Ruch, F. L.: test, 799; rev, 802, 853, 2418
Ruch, G. M.: test, 1275
Rucker, C. N.: test, 2039; ref, 2039(10)
Rucklos, M. E.: ref, 479(403), 1883(87)
Rudd, N. L.: ref, 2289(1616)
Ruddell, R. B.: ref, 583(1), 585(3), 586(1), 845(9), 1479(358)
Rudel, R. G.: ref, 280(1077), 283(145), 1007(23), 1914(763), 2598(1477), 2607(160)
Ruderman, A.: ref, 1771(538)
Rudestam, K. E.: ref, 883(79), 1197(282)
Rudman, H. C.: test, 2286, 2287, 2288
Rudolf, J. A.: ref, 2289(1661), 2548(14)
Rudolph, L. B.: ref, 1789(731)
Rudorfer, L.: ref, 1240(54)
Rudrud, E.: ref, 2289(1767), 2598(1774), 2602(2103)
Rudy, K. R.: ref, 280(1056), 2181(12), 2621(259)
Rueda, R.: ref, 2109(4), 2472(11)
Ruedisili, C. H.: rev, 1113
Ruff, C. F.: ref, 1498(5194, 5379, 5539), 2598(1659)
Rugel, R. P.: ref, 2602(1812)
Rugen, M. E.: rev, 1066
Ruggieri, V.: ref, 794(439, 440, 447)
Ruhland, D.: ref, 1192(206, 214), 1473(164, 175)
Ruhlen, H.: test, 1887
Rulla, L. M.: ref, 1131(1), 2491(2042)
Rummo, J. H.: ref, 1424(57)
Rummo, N. J.: ref, 1424(57)
Rump, E. E.: ref, 243(118)
Rumsey, J. M.: ref, 2602(1813)
Rundall, T. G.: ref, 2068(86)
Rundell, O. H.: ref, 121(12), 472(17), 653(166), 1538(71)
Ruoff, L. O.: ref, 2015(215), 2602(2207)
Ruoff, P.: ref, 2015(215), 2602(2207)
Rupert, P. A.: ref, 1547(291), 2300(435), 2353(25), 2638(124)
Rupley, W. H.: ref, 1754(63, 64, 95), 2260(31), 2621(360)
Rupp, J. W.: ref, 2491(2018), 2602(1658), 2621(248)
Ruscello, D. M.: ref, 1754(109), 2103(8), 2412(43)
Rusch, R.: ref, 1580(2)
Rush, A. J.: ref, 859(950)
Rush, M. C.: ref, 1013(74), 1053(69), 1295(288, 305, 306)
Rush, W. A.: ref, 1498(5556)
Rushton, J. P.: ref, 859(787), 2208(1566)
Russ, S. W.: ref, 483(36), 1894(7), 2030(5074)
Russakoff, S.: ref, 1498(5220, 5397)
Russell, B.: ref, 1203(11), 1798(282)
Russell, D.: ref, 860(147), 1547(292), 2300(562)
Russell, D. H.: rev, 175, 2283
Russell, E. W.: ref, 1498(5195), 2598(1428, 1636, 1775)
Russell, F. F.: ref, 381(69), 2289(1750), 2557(235)

Russell, G.: ref, 280(1059), 1126(677), 2348(1), 2350(14)
Russell, G. W.: ref, 2629(122)
Russell, H. L.: ref, 280(1091), 1007(25), 2216(1), 2217(135), 2621(301)
Russell, J.: ref, 1914(865)
Russell, J. D.: ref, 501(816)
Russell, J. E. A.: ref, 76(659), 2581(348)
Russell, J. L.: ref, 2029(232)
Russell, M.: ref, 1257(134), 1498(5351)
Russell, R. B.: test, 2041
Russell, R. D.: ref, 1050(2)
Russell, R. K.: ref, 2300(382, 409), 2374(183)
Russell, S.: ref, 1498(5770)
Russell, S. N.: ref, 2602(1884), 2621(328)
Russo, T. J.: ref, 76(617)
Rust, J.: ref, 860(90)
Rust, J. O.: ref, 1473(165), 1498(5680), 2165(25), 2217(174), 2289(1637), 2598(1388, 1637), 2602(2104)
Ruth, L. P.: rev, 421, 490
Ruth, R. A.: rev, 2543
Rutherford, P. K.: ref, 270(131), 311(34)
Rutledge, C. O.: ref, 1498(5069)
Rutman, J. Y.: ref, 2289(1734), 2557(231)
Rutschmann, J.: ref, 1498(5196)
Rutsohn, P.: ref, 1555(323)
Ruttenberg, B. A.: test, 272
Rutter, M.: ref, 859(846), 1567(19), 1914(795), 2602(2165)
Ruttle, K.: ref, 270(118, 136), 2217(169), 2289(1756)
Ryack, B.: ref, 1054(7)
Ryan, C.: ref, 2598(1776)
Ryan, E. B.: ref, 653(177), 932(129), 2218(8)
Ryan, F. L.: ref, 344(157)
Ryan, J.: ref, 2300(369)
Ryan, J. J.: ref, 1346(8), 1498(5197), 2598(1638, 1777, 1846)
Ryan, K. J.: ref, 1498(5517)
Ryan, L. C.: test, 1065
Ryan, T. J.: ref, 404(6), 1498(5116)
Ryan, T. M.: test, 242
Ryan, V. L.: ref, 1771(686)
Ryans, D. G.: rev, 1618, 2499, 2553
Ryba, K. A.: ref, 1914(791), 2598(1540), 2607(172)
Ryback, D.: ref, 1125(19)
Ryback, R. S.: ref, 283(156), 2179(235), 2598(1706)
Ryberg, D. C.: exc, 1833
Rybolt, J. F.: ref, 2286(326)
Rychlak, J. F.: ref, 1341(167), 1498(5198), 1831(134), 2179(207), 2602(1813)
Ryckman, D. B.: ref, 226(187), 398(125), 932(124), 1771(804), 1914(894), 2113(259)
Ryden, E. R.: test, 1818
Ryder, R. J.: ref, 934(7), 1473(206)
Ryder, S.: ref, 2629(99)
Ryhänen, P.: ref, 1498(5352), 2030(5009), 2598(1525)
Ryken, K.: ref, 2294(126)
Ryle, A.: ref, 941(38), 1567(11), 2602(1687)
Rylee, K. E.: ref, 1498(5506)
Ryman, D. H.: ref, 2300(340)
Rypma, C. B.: ref, 859(957, 958)
Rystrom, R.: rev, 2635
Sabatelli, R. M.: ref, 794(428)
Sabatino, D. A.: ref, 226(173), 280(1119), 701(66),

INDEX OF NAMES

961(4), 1255(6), 1371(255), 1540(15), 1769(47, 60), 2472(19), 2621(253, 293)
Sabers, D.: test, 1188, 1189, 1248
Sabers, D. C.: ref, 1473(183), 2602(1942)
Sabers, D. L.: rev, 269, 1478; ref, 1576(198), 1831(208)
Sabine, G.: ref, 501(835)
Sabini, J. P.: ref, 354(1473), 1914(785)
Sabourin, M.: ref, 1063(123)
Sacco, W. P.: ref, 883(108), 1498(5353, 5354, 5623)
Saccuzzo, D. P.: ref, 2598(1389, 1639, 1778, 1816, 1851), 2602(1662, 1949)
Sachar, E. J.: ref, 1655(99)
Sachar, J.: test, 2295; ref, 2295(1)
Sachs, H.: ref, 2602(2066)
Sachs, H. K.: ref, 2289(1687), 2602(1814), 2608(206)
Sackeim, H. A.: ref, 859(853, 881), 1044(64), 1547(306), 2294(132)
Sackett, D. L.: ref, 311(39)
Sacks, H. V.: ref, 149(3)
Sacks, J. G.: ref, 1498(5515)
Sacks, S.: ref, 1343(1)
Sadick, T. L.: ref, 932(86), 1479(334)
Sadowski, C.: ref, 354(1573), 2179(256), 2217(181)
Sadowski, C. J.: ref, 384(7, 9)
Saetveit, J. R.: test, 2113
Saffran, E. M.: ref, 1771(753)
Safi, A.: ref, 558(58)
Safran, C.: test, 919, 2045, 2046
Sagen, H. B.: rev, 543, 1748, 2581
Sahakian, B. J.: ref, 2598(1705)
Saigal, S.: ref, 311(39)
Saigh, P. A.: ref, 1351(201), 2598(1640), 2602(1815, 1950, 2105, 2208)
Sailor, W.: test, 2391
St. Jean, R.: ref, 1063(130, 135), 2294(138)
St. Louis, K. O.: ref, 1126(769), 1771(747)
Sakheim, D. K.: ref, 1904(121)
Saklofske, D. H.: ref, 362(5), 363(13), 702(2), 704(9), 860(113), 1229(80, 81, 87, 104), 1969(117)
Salasnek, S.: ref, 1170(230)
Saleh, S. D.: test, 1216
Salfield, S. A. W.: ref, 2289(1787), 2602(2184)
Salick, M. R.: ref, 2343(1051)
Salih, M. A.: ref, 1883(50)
Salley, R. D.: ref, 2030(5075)
Sallustro, F.: ref, 270(96)
Salmi, I.: test, 2256
Salmon, S. J.: ref, 1851(34)
Salome, R. A.: ref, 794(380), 1257(113)
Salomon, F.: test, 2672
Salomon, G.: ref, 398(97)
Salomone, P. R.: ref, 2581(319)
Sals, D. K.: test, 2634
Salt, P.: ref, 2598(1459)
Salthouse, T. A.: ref, 2598(1526)
Saltoun, J.: ref, 372(9), 2134(135)
Saltz, E.: ref, 1771(569), 1823(32)
Salvendy, G.: test, 1727; ref, 2602(1909), 2621(342)
Salvia, J.: ref, 1192(181), 1769(68)
Salzinger, K.: exc, 969
Salzman, C.: ref, 2491(2017)
Sameroff, A. J.: ref, 270(97), 311(28, 29), 645(12), 1197(286)
Samples, J. M.: ref, 1851(43), 2646(11)
Sampsel, B. D.: ref, 794(448)
Sampson, J. P.: ref, 2581(317), 2657(114)
Samson, W. E.: ref, 1576(209)
Samuel, W.: ref, 2602(1688, 2106)
Samuels, D. D.: ref, 2602(1865, 1951)
Samuels, S. J.: ref, 932(122), 1007(31)
Sanchez, D.: ref, 273(1)
Sanchez, O.: ref, 381(61), 2557(218)
Sanchez, P.: exc, 625
Sanchez, V.: ref, 681(62)
Sanchez, V. C.: ref, 1498(5695)
Sandall, P. H.: test, 863
Sanders, C.: rev, 19, 20, 28
Sanders, J.: test, 264
Sanders, J. J.: ref, 1125(19)
Sanders, J. L.: ref, 1106(362), 1798(220)
Sanders, J. R.: test, 2352
Sanders, L. J.: ref, 2472(13)
Sanders, M. W.: test, 242, 306, 380, 803, 804, 805, 806, 807, 808, 809, 810, 811, 812, 813, 814, 815, 816, 1103, 1104, 1105, 1111, 1116, 1238, 1437, 2006, 2041, 2061, 2062, 2063, 2066, 2067, 2586, 2670
Sanders, S. J.: ref, 157(137), 243(119), 1106(363)
Sanderson, H.: ref, 860(98), 2128(7)
Sandidge, S.: ref, 2286(285), 2602(1686), 2621(258)
Sandilands, M. L.: ref, 1798(294)
Sandman, C. A.: ref, 283(153), 1771(701)
Sandman, P. H.: ref, 1547(248), 1948(94)
Sandman, R. S.: test, 1410; ref, 1410(1)
Sandoval, J.: ref, 344(187), 701(82), 1250(19), 1328(1), 2602(1952, 2107, 2108), 2641(16)
Sandquist, V.: ref, 113(24), 354(1446), 1498(5274)
Sanford, D.: exc, 1347
Sanford, J.: ref, 354(1505), 1419(693)
Sanford, T. R.: ref, 76(596), 501(803)
Sanner, R.: ref, 1769(64), 2286(302), 2621(302)
Sansaricq, C.: ref, 701(69), 2602(1964)
Santa, C. M.: ref, 501(870), 2002(5)
Santisteban, D.: ref, 1923(29)
Santo, Y.: ref, 2413(614)
Santostefano, S.: test, 2064
Sapon, S. M.: test, 1527
Sappenfield, B. R.: rev, 298, 897, 2031
Sappington, A. A.: ref, 1498(5199), 1547(271, 272, 312)
Sappington, J.: ref, 1498(5200)
Sappington, J. T.: ref, 1948(104), 2598(1779)
Sapsford, R. J.: ref, 1498(5355)
Saracho, O.: ref, 398(121), 551(61), 794(441), 1013(112)
Saracho, O. N.: ref, 398(122), 551(62), 1013(113)
Saraf, K.: ref, 1655(116)
Sarason, I. G.: rev, 647; ref, 1547(309, 351), 1931(48, 49)
Sarbin, T. R.: rev, 118
Sare, H.: test, 2067
Sare, H. V.: test, 2066
Sargent, C. L.: ref, 2208(1591)
Sargent, H.: rev, 2030
Sarles, R. M.: ref, 280(1055), 1112)
Sarlin, B.: ref, 645(11), 2030(4978), 2598(1412)
Sarmousakis, G.: exc, 786
Sarno, M. T.: test, 925
Sartorius, N.: test, 1883
Sasek, J.: ref, 280(1029)
Saslow, C.: ref, 2300(559)
Sassenrath, J. M.: ref, 553(20)

Sathananthan, G.: ref, 280(1089), 2598(1319, 1515), 2607(134, 166)
Satin, M.: ref, 681(34)
Satlow, I. D.: rev, 303
Satter, G. A.: rev, 282, 940, 1751, 2263
Satterfield, B. T.: ref, 280(1120), 1769(78, 93, 104), 1853(286), 2602(1953, 2109)
Satterfield, J. H.: ref, 280(1120), 1769(78, 93, 104), 1853(286), 2602(1953, 2109)
Satterly, D. J.: ref, 859(882)
Sattler, J. M.: rev, 923, 1424; ref, 251(1), 290(9), 1331(39), 1771(754, 755), 2602(1689, 1816, 1923, 2110, 2111)
Satz, P.: ref, 226(168, 176), 701(55, 71), 1498(5261), 1771(624, 709), 2598(1404)
Sauers, C. A.: ref, 609(204)
Saunders, A. W.: rev, 1460
Saunders, D. R.: rev, 1046; ref, 2598(1780)
Saunders, G. R.: ref, 1498(5766)
Saunders, J. C.: ref, 551(54)
Saurenman, D. A.: ref, 1013(114)
Sautter, F.: ref, 2512(565)
Sauvé, R.: ref, 1771(553)
Sauve, R. S.: ref, 678(29)
Savage, C.: ref, 1498(5099)
Savage, J. E.: ref, 1831(152), 2621(303)
Savage, R. D.: ref, 2598(1641), 2602(1954)
Savarese, J. M.: ref, 1013(91), 1257(147)
Saville, P.: test, 282, 557, 940, 1233, 2598, 2608
Savitsky, J. C.: ref, 1547(268)
Sawyer, A.: ref, 116(611), 2413(679)
Sawyer, C. E.: ref, 1233(218)
Sawyer, J. C.: ref, 1479(372)
Sawyer, R. N.: ref, 780(1690), 1823(34)
Sawyer, W. E.: ref, 1479(372)
Sax, D.: ref, 2598(1434), 2607(154)
Sax, G.: rev, 915; exc, 1970
Saxe, G. B.: ref, 701(91), 2602(2209)
Saxena, A. K.: ref, 2300(563)
Saxena, B.: ref, 1655(101)
Saxon, S.: ref, 890(340)
Say, M. W.: ref, 1192(210)
Sayeed, O. B.: ref, 2029(242)
Scagliotta, E. G.: test, 1294
Scalise, J. J.: ref, 1547(318), 2300(507), 2353(33), 2598(1679), 2638(140)
Scammell, R. E.: ref, 2598(1312)
Scanlan, T. J.: ref, 2581(341)
Scanlon, D. M.: ref, 958(52), 2217(185), 2602(2225)
Scannell, D. P.: test, 2474, 2475
Scarborough, B. B.: test, 1819
Scarbro, H.: ref, 400(128), 551(41), 552(3), 553(19)
Scardamalia, M.: ref, 2598(1390), 2602(1690)
Scarlett, W. G.: ref, 1771(756)
Scarr, S.: ref, 859(956), 2318(1530), 2598(1335, 1527)
Scates, D. E.: rev, 2342
Schachter, F. F.: test, 394; ref, 394(1)
Schackman, M.: ref, 398(104)
Schadler, M.: ref, 2288(90), 2621(290)
Schaefer, C. E.: test, 628, 2199
Schaefer, W. C.: rev, 2276
Schaeffer, D. S.: ref, 1419(674), 2030(4967)
Schaeffer, R. H.: ref, 76(658), 501(932)
Schaer, B. B.: ref, 76(653), 344(189), 501(925)
Schafer, A. T.: ref, 501(933)

Schafer, R. B.: ref, 116(597)
Schafer, W. D.: ref, 1789(651)
Schaffer, H. G.: ref, 280(1073), 1126(692), 2602(1740)
Schaffran, J. A.: ref, 932(64)
Schaie, J. P.: rev, 950
Schaie, K. W.: test, 2429; rev, 2148; ref, 401(73), 1170(235), 1362(10), 1404(2), 2269(436, 443, 454, 476, 478), 2429(23, 25), 2491(2071), 2598(1306)
Schaller, S.: ref, 1914(866)
Schalling, D.: ref, 354(1456), 859(810)
Schalock, R. L.: ref, 2598(1852)
Schandry, R.: ref, 2300(607)
Schaninger, C. M.: ref, 966(177)
Schapiro, M.: ref, 2602(1857), 2621(315)
Schau, E. J.: ref, 665(41), 2598(1391, 1629)
Schaub, L. H.: ref, 280(1085), 1498(5332, 5500), 1765(12), 1914(728), 1940(80), 2179(205, 218), 2413(657), 2598(1377)
Scheaffe, P.: ref, 1914(715)
Scheel, V.: ref, 6(77)
Scheer, B. R.: ref, 664(13)
Scheer, J.: ref, 1250(22)
Scheerer, M: test, 963
Scheff, B. J.: ref, 1922(13, 18), 1923(13, 24)
Scheiber, S. C.: ref, 1498(5768), 1923(28)
Scheidt, P. C.: ref, 678(24)
Scheier, I. H.: test, 1197, 1573; rev, 1573
Scheier, M. F.: ref, 1046(578)
Schein, J. D.: ref, 272(1), 959(1)
Schein, S.: ref, 558(70), 1498(5557), 2300(502)
Schell, L. M.: test, 1569; ref, 346(107), 1192(225), 2181(16)
Schellman, G. C.: ref, 1498(5039), 2366(190), 2370(15)
Schenck, J. P.: ref, 1562(8)
Schenck, S. J.: ref, 2602(1850), 2621(312)
Schenk, G. E.: ref, 372(4), 2581(328)
Schenkenberg, T.: ref, 1462(117), 2598(1299)
Schepers, J. M.: test, 560; rev, 2242
Scher, L.: ref, 1789(664)
Scher, M.: ref, 751(14), 1462(135), 1498(5305), 2179(217)
Scher, S. S.: ref, 1498(5516)
Scherer, C.: ref, 2208(1630), 2413(660)
Scherer, I. W.: test, 1621
Scherich, H. H.: ref, 1569(7), 1570(11)
Scheuerle, J.: ref, 378(18)
Scheupbach, C. S.: ref, 2598(1453)
Schiappa, O.: ref, 2598(1844)
Schiff, I.: ref, 1498(5517)
Schiff, M.: ref, 2602(1817)
Schild, A. H.: test, 2474, 2475
Schill, T.: ref, 609(227), 1498(5190)
Schiller, A.: test, 1890, 1895, 1897
Schilling, K. M.: ref, 2030(5080)
Schindler, A. W.: rev, 344
Schissel, R. J.: ref, 200(16), 2103(7, 10, 11, 12)
Schleifer, M.: ref, 398(93), 2602(1609), 2608(171)
Schlesinger, L. B.: ref, 2030(5076)
Schlesser, G. E.: test, 1794
Schleuter, S. L.: ref, 1552(72)
Schlosser, L.: ref, 2602(2112)
Schlottmann, R. S.: ref, 2300(456, 554)
Schlundt, D. G.: ref, 643(139), 1073(120)
Schmauch, V. A.: ref, 1622(43), 1771(625), 1814(6)

INDEX OF NAMES

Schmeck, R. R.: ref, 76(633), 1257(112), 1568(148), 2374(196, 197), 2594(199)
Schmeiser, C. B.: ref, 76(606, 618), 1568(130), 2160(62)
Schmid, R. F.: ref, 76(647)
Schmidt, C. W.: ref, 1240(53), 2100(8)
Schmidt, F. L.: rev, 2622; ref, 282(146), 557(8), 995(139), 1976(1), 1981(3)
Schmidt, J. J.: ref, 1555(342)
Schmidt, J. P.: ref, 794(405), 859(827), 860(118), 1106(367), 2300(436)
Schmidt, M. R.: ref, 2413(616)
Schmidt, W. H.: ref, 551(32), 1192(204), 1473(160), 2286(299)
Schmidtke, A.: ref, 1914(866)
Schmiedeck, R. A.: test, 1793
Schmieder, M.: test, 2410
Schmierer, D.: ref, 666(6)
Schmitt, N.: ref, 590(375), 732(402), 1508(136), 2318(1564), 2652(5)
Schmolling, P.: ref, 2598(1392)
Schmuckler, J.: exc, 75
Schnabl-Dickey, E. A.: ref, 1387(11)
Schneidemann, N. V.: exc, 381
Schneider, D.: ref, 1473(173), 2286(307)
Schneider, D. U.: ref, 2607(126)
Schneider, F. W.: ref, 1798(221)
Schneider, J. F.: ref, 2629(116)
Schneider, K. S.: ref, 1046(573)
Schneider, L. A.: ref, 1771(647)
Schneider, L. J.: ref, 2318(1593)
Schneider, L. M.: ref, 483(44)
Schneider, L. S.: ref, 2181(20)
Schneider, M. A.: ref, 280(1121), 2602(1955)
Schneider, M. R.: ref, 344(142), 1479(318), 2621(256)
Schneider, S.: ref, 1498(5356), 2491(2047)
Schneider, S. J.: ref, 1498(5518)
Schneier, C. E.: ref, 354(1506)
Schnell, L. H.: rev, 197
Schnell, R. R.: ref, 270(146), 2557(244)
Schnell, W.: test, 2418
Schnelle, J. F.: ref, 719(28)
Schnidman, R. E.: ref, 859(883)
Schnitzer, B. R.: ref, 2300(437)
Schoen, H. L.: ref, 2286(346)
Schoenfeld, L. S.: ref, 1498(5662, 5696), 1922(16)
Schoenfeldt, L. F.: rev, 633, 1506, 2273; ref, 501(847), 2318(1579)
Schofield, J. W.: ref, 751(18)
Schofield, M.: test, 2267, 2276
Schofield, W.: rev, 283, 2037
Schoicket, S.: ref, 1197(310), 2300(542)
Scholastic Testing Service, Inc.: test, 2324
Schold, S. C.: ref, 280(1052), 1771(567)
Schonell, F. J.: test, 842, 2077
Schooff, K.: ref, 1498(5268, 5468)
Schoolar, J. C.: ref, 1170(229), 1372(9), 1761(5)
Schooler, C.: ref, 751(13, 15), 794(395, 402)
Schooler, D. L.: ref, 7(6), 701(67), 2218(152), 2602(1818)
Schoonover, R. A.: ref, 1765(10)
Schori, T. R.: ref, 2030(4968)
Schottenfeld, S.: ref, 1007(22), 1754(75), 2602(1753)
Schraa, J. C.: ref, 1498(5597)
Schrader, W. B.: rev, 12, 13, 1486, 1494, 2095, 2178

Schraibman, J.: ref, 139(5)
Schrammel, H. E.: test, 242, 1078
Schreiner, D.: ref, 280(1152), 1498(5703), 2598(1788), 2602(1762, 2122)
Schreiner, J.: ref, 627(23), 1948(97), 2598(1528), 2621(304)
Schreiner, R.: test, 1569; ref, 2292(19)
Schreiner, R. L.: rev, 719, 748
Schriesheim, C. A.: ref, 1295(304, 307), 1296(174, 177, 181, 182, 183), 1508(128)
Schriesheim, J. F.: ref, 1296(174, 178)
Schroeder, C. C.: ref, 1015(1), 1555(330, 337), 2534(14)
Schroeder, D.: ref, 280(1029)
Schroeder, D. F.: exc, 2169
Schroeder, D. J.: ref, 1498(5519)
Schroeder, J. E.: ref, 859(828)
Schroeder, J. J.: ref, 1789(704)
Schroeder, L. C.: test, 1421
Schroeder, N.: ref, 551(33), 2512(604)
Schroeder, S. R.: ref, 1108(11), 1969(114)
Schroll, E. F.: ref, 1969(98)
Schroth, M. L.: ref, 396(78), 483(42), 2148(2), 2602(2210, 2211)
Schroth, P.: ref, 1471(53)
Schubert, D. S. P.: test, 326, 2095; ref, 1904(62, 98)
Schubert, H. J. P.: test, 752, 2095
Schubert, W. K.: ref, 270(105), 280(1103), 751(23), 2289(1700), 2557(227), 2602(1871), 2621(320)
Schuck, J.: ref, 1498(5357)
Schuckers, G. H.: ref, 664(9), 960(5)
Schuckit, M. A.: ref, 1498(5325, 5766)
Schueler, H.: rev, 515, 517
Schuell, H.: test, 1513
Schuepfer, T.: ref, 2289(1688)
Schuerger, J. M.: test, 1662; ref, 1233(231)
Schuettler, A. K.: test, 1219
Schuh, A. J.: ref, 799(22), 1046(577, 585)
Schuld, D.: ref, 1498(5217)
Schuler, S.: ref, 542(20)
Schull, C.: ref, 1996(8)
Schulsinger, F.: ref, 1462(146), 1883(96), 2602(2045, 2192)
Schultz, B. B.: ref, 1904(130), 2300(608)
Schultz, C. L.: ref, 1771(757), 1883(55)
Schultz, D. G.: rev, 1676, 1977, 1978, 2265
Schultz, E. W.: ref, 328(4), 769(43), 1934(8)
Schultz, H. A.: rev, 1460, 1626
Schultz, K. J.: ref, 1498(5697)
Schultz, M. C.: ref, 549(1), 2598(1374), 2647(1)
Schultz, N. R.: ref, 1914(867), 2598(1642, 1781)
Schultz, R. A.: ref, 409(11)
Schumm, W. R.: ref, 1372(10, 11), 2413(685)
Schumsky, D.: ref, 1498(5040)
Schunk, D. H.: ref, 1473(213)
Schupbach, R.: rev, 1522
Schur, H. M.: ref, 2289(1634)
Schur, L. M.: test, 1232
Schurr, K. T.: ref, 2512(619)
Schuster, D. H.: test, 753; rev, 2628; ref, 1250(20), 2641(17)
Schut, J.: ref, 116(571), 1904(102)
Schutz, R. E.: rev, 732, 2160, 2269, 2484
Schutz, W. C.: test, 890
Schuyler, B. A.: ref, 1063(134)

Schwab, D. P.: ref, 1508(120)
Schwab, R.: ref, 354(1489)
Schwachman, H.: ref, 2413(650)
Schwam, E.: ref, 534(107)
Schwantes, F. M.: ref, 932(125), 1192(258)
Schwarting, F. G.: ref, 2602(1691), 2621(260)
Schwarting, K. R.: ref, 2602(1691), 2621(260)
Schwartz, A. A.: ref, 226(171), 958(49), 1101(45), 1126(729), 1771(667), 2602(1915), 2621(344)
Schwartz, C. C.: ref, 1922(11)
Schwartz, E.: ref, 2208(1655)
Schwartz, F.: ref, 2030(5039)
Schwartz, H.: ref, 1013(57)
Schwartz, H. L.: ref, 116(587, 609), 354(1491)
Schwartz, H. P.: test, 817
Schwartz, M. F.: ref, 1498(5520)
Schwartz, M. L.: ref, 1498(5333)
Schwartz, M. S.: ref, 1498(5621)
Schwartz, N. H.: ref, 1289(3, 6)
Schwartz, R.: ref, 308(13)
Schwartz, S.: ref, 472(12), 860(133), 1063(90), 1341(154), 1351(190)
Schwartz, S. L.: test, 2355
Schwarz, J. C.: ref, 116(579, 580), 1931(52, 55), 2037(152)
Schwarz, M.: rev, 237
Schwarz, M. R.: ref, 1576(209)
Schwarzmueller, B.: ref, 1771(565)
Schwarzwald, J.: ref, 2413(661)
Schweitzer, J.: ref, 2602(1831)
Schweitzer, P. K.: ref, 1498(5637)
Schwesinger, G. C.: rev, 643, 1853
Schworm, R. W.: ref, 2621(361)
Scida, J.: ref, 751(30)
Science Research Associates, Inc.: test, 710, 737, 738, 739, 740, 741, 742, 743, 1389, 1401, 1677, 2262, 2264
Scissons, E. H.: ref, 354(1507), 780(1693), 2581(329)
Scoles, P. E.: ref, 859(889)
Scollay, R. W.: test, 1712
Scott, C. C.: ref, 1341(166)
Scott, C. S.: rev, 119, 1954
Scott, D. J.: ref, 2029(231)
Scott, I. A.: test, 1347
Scott, J.: ref, 280(1036), 859(788), 922(6), 2602(1651)
Scott, J. C.: ref, 2300(493), 2417(1)
Scott, K. M.: ref, 2641(24)
Scott, L. H.: ref, 964(517)
Scott, N.: ref, 1013(137)
Scott, N. A.: ref, 398(123), 1498(5521, 5698)
Scott, R.: ref, 941(23, 34), 1883(33, 69), 2269(468)
Scott, T. B.: ref, 76(644)
Scott Co.: test, 2101
Scottish Council for Research in Education: test, 329, 330
The Scottish Education Department and The Educational Institute of Scotland: test, 775
Scovern, A. W.: ref, 392(4)
Scroggins, W. F.: ref, 1789(682)
Scroka, R. D.: ref, 1192(245)
Scudder, R. R.: ref, 962(26)
Scull, J. W.: ref, 1769(94), 2621(415)
Scullen, T.: ref, 958(41)
Scyving, J.: ref, 2300(429), 2301(28)
Sczechowicz, E.: ref, 280(1150)
Seager, C. P.: ref, 859(790)

Seagoe, M. V.: rev, 2403
Seagull, E.: ref, 1424(89)
Searfoss, L. W.: test, 661, 718
Searle, M.: ref, 280(1059), 1126(677), 2348(1), 2350(14)
Searleman, A.: ref, 1060(27)
Searles, J.: ref, 859(917), 2300(541)
Searls, E.: ref, 6(91)
Sears, J. D.: ref, 2512(579)
Sears, J. T.: ref, 2512(598)
Seashore, C. E.: test, 2113; rev, 1261
Seashore, H.: test, 2112; rev, 991, 994, 1625, 2160
Seashore, H. G.: test, 9, 466, 732, 1288, 1456, 1653, 2246, 2254, 2554; rev, 177
Seat, P. D.: test, 1796
Seaton, H. W.: ref, 483(16), 1473(137), 1478(67), 1479(321), 1877(6)
Seay, T. A.: ref, 1531(292)
Sechrist, W. C.: ref, 2029(226)
Secord, W.: test, 339, 1470, 2449
Seddon, G. M.: ref, 149(4), 859(767)
Sedlacek, W. E.: test, 2203; ref, 2134(136), 2413(608)
Sedlack, B.: ref, 2218(151), 2289(1731)
Sedlack, R. A.: ref, 709(2)
Seefeldt, C.: ref, 302(36), 1479(379)
Seefeldt, F. M.: ref, 1347(6)
Seegmiller, B. R.: ref, 751(38)
Seeman, A. Z.: ref, 354(1518), 859(893), 1547(319)
Seeman, J.: ref, 2413(642)
Seeman, W.: rev, 1784; ref, 1498(5040)
Seewald, A. M.: ref, 483(28), 1473(179)
Sefer, J. W.: test, 1513
Segal, B.: ref, 1798(208, 295)
Segal, D. S.: ref, 1904(113), 2598(1737)
Segal, S.: ref, 2289(1734), 2557(231)
Segal, Z.: ref, 1486(187), 1547(336), 1914(860)
Segall, S. R.: ref, 665(52)
Segel, D.: rev, 1188, 1272
Segel, R. C.: test, 250
Segger, J. F.: ref, 1789(674), 2413(622)
Seguin, E.: test, 2125
Segura, J. W.: ref, 1498(5425)
Sehgal, M.: ref, 653(155), 860(134), 1573(41)
Seidenberg, M.: ref, 2598(1853), 2602(2197)
Seidl, M.: test, 2561, 2563
Seidman, E.: ref, 2286(322), 2621(362)
Seidner, C. J.: ref, 2160(61)
Seif, B.: ref, 116(633)
Seif, M. N.: ref, 665(50), 883(100), 1077(69), 1106(372), 1817(3)
Seifert, M.: ref, 932(62), 1771(539)
Seifert, R. F.: ref, 558(56), 780(1650), 1173(1), 1798(213, 214)
Seim, N. J.: test, 2052
Seim, R.: ref, 6(53), 1771(595)
Seitz, S.: ref, 678(17)
Selby, J. W.: ref, 1419(672), 1798(212)
Selby, R.: ref, 2598(1668)
Selby, R. B.: ref, 1498(5725)
Selection Consultation Center: test, 2070
Seligman, M. E. P.: ref, 681(60), 1547(313), 2179(210)
Seligman, R.: exc, 2134
Seling, M. J.: ref, 2318(1551)
Sell, D. E.: test, 847, 1712
Sells, C. J.: ref, 270(102), 2289(1698)

Sells, S. B.: rev, 610, 769, 969
Selmar, J. W.: test, 1814
Selover, R. B.: rev, 1493
Seltzer, J.: ref, 932(117), 1831(201), 2286(342)
Selvik, R.: ref, 2491(2105)
Selz, M.: ref, 2598(1643, 1644), 2602(1956, 1957), 2621(363, 364)
Selzer, M. L.: ref, 354(1420)
Selzer, U.: ref, 590(368, 369), 2160(49, 50)
Semel, E. M.: test, 474, 475; ref, 226(188), 308(5), 378(20), 691(31, 48), 1126(681, 786), 1513(23), 1622(35), 1771(805), 2602(2212), 2621(454)
Semenza, C.: ref, 1914(752)
Semeonoff, B.: rev, 2323; exc, 874, 1229, 1969, 2672
Semmel, A.: ref, 1547(313)
Semmel, M. I.: rev, 6
Semyck, R. W.: ref, 1498(5665), 2179(242)
Sen, A.: ref, 859(779), 2030(4973)
Sen, D. M.: ref, 859(747)
Senay, E. C.: ref, 645(21)
Sendbuehler, J. M.: ref, 1498(5522)
Senf, G. M.: test, 2102
Seni, C.: ref, 2374(175)
Seni, C. L.: ref, 1991(124), 2374(189)
Sepie, A. C.: ref, 1911(1)
Sepkoski, C. M.: ref, 1257(122)
Sepos, V.: ref, 1655(121)
Serafetinides, E. A.: ref, 2598(1384), 2607(148)
Serafica, F. C.: ref, 1436(17)
Serafine, M. L.: ref, 559(57), 751(31)
Seraydarian, L.: ref, 1192(188), 1341(171), 1479(326), 2286(289)
Serban, G.: ref, 1883(56, 57), 2322(15, 16)
Serbin, L. A.: ref, 398(104, 105), 1875(2), 2608(173, 218)
Sergent, J.: ref, 2015(205), 2030(5040)
Sergent, M. W.: ref, 2598(1590, 1591)
Serow, R. C.: ref, 1107(12), 2276(5)
Service, J.: ref, 1498(5631)
Servos, A. B.: ref, 678(22), 1492(6), 1771(605), 1914(757)
Seta, J. J.: ref, 2300(564)
Sethi, B. B.: ref, 2491(2062)
Settles, B. H.: ref, 2557(246)
Settles, R. B.: ref, 995(148)
Seville, E. W.: test, 714, 715, 717
Sewell, T.: ref, 701(38), 2289(1638), 2602(1692)
Sewell, T. E.: ref, 374(229), 732(414), 932(126), 1914(895), 2289(1639), 2413(702), 2598(1854), 2608(184), 2621(455)
Sewell, W. H.: ref, 1073(127)
Sexton, L. C.: ref, 962(30), 1540(16), 2260(43), 2269(469)
Seybold, A.: test, 815
Seyfort, B.: ref, 2602(2113)
Seymour, C. M.: ref, 1718(9)
Seymour, P. H. K.: ref, 1535(40)
Seymour, W. D.: test, 1727
Sganga, F. T.: test, 708
Shaak, M.: ref, 1240(62), 1904(105), 2328(4)
Shabad, P.: ref, 701(68), 2030(5041), 2491(2065), 2602(1958)
Shachar, T.: ref, 1914(831)
Shacter, H.: rev, 1325
Shadbolt, D. R.: ref, 149(8), 859(829)

Shade, B. J.: ref, 772(28), 1013(138), 2598(1855)
Shader, R. I.: ref, 2491(2017), 2598(1717), 2607(199)
Shadish, W. R.: ref, 1789(720)
Shaffer, D.: ref, 1567(19), 2602(2165)
Shaffer, G. L.: ref, 346(103)
Shaffer, J. W.: ref, 1240(53), 2318(1565)
Shaffer, L. F.: rev, 357, 647, 1797, 2030; exc, 190, 298, 346, 354, 396, 767, 780, 852, 897, 966, 1046, 1073, 1197, 1219, 1237, 1318, 1318, 1319, 1480, 1830, 1853, 2326, 2343, 2499, 2602, 2618
Shaffer, P.: ref, 501(829, 864, 865, 899), 2002(4)
Shah, R. S.: ref, 678(26), 960(11), 1771(655), 2107(9), 2218(143), 2598(1582), 2602(1889), 2608(213)
Shah, U.: ref, 280(1158), 964(515)
Shaheen, S.: ref, 701(91), 2602(2209)
Shakow, D.: ref, 2030(4969), 2289(1640)
Shalif, I.: ref, 639(51)
Shallice, T.: ref, 308(29), 1771(626, 703, 806), 1914(786), 2077(34), 2598(1856)
Shand, J.: ref, 1197(283)
Shank, S.: rev, 2520
Shanker, P.: ref, 2343(1048)
Shankweiler, D.: ref, 551(67), 1007(21), 1771(685), 2217(180), 2621(365), 2641(21)
Shanmugarn, T. E.: ref, 859(884)
Shannon, A. J.: ref, 1568(149)
Shannon, D.: ref, 2289(1613), 2602(1643)
Shannon, L. R.: ref, 2208(1665)
Shao, D.: ref, 872(16)
Shapiro, A.: ref, 2413(607)
Shapiro, A. K.: ref, 1106(373), 1498(5523), 1904(99), 2598(1645)
Shapiro, B.: ref, 1904(124)
Shapiro, B. P.: ref, 780(1695)
Shapiro, D.: ref, 2294(120)
Shapiro, E.: ref, 645(14), 1106(373), 1498(5523), 1904(99), 2598(1645)
Shapiro, H. M.: ref, 1726(354)
Shapiro, J. P.: ref, 2491(2066)
Shapiro, L. N.: ref, 794(384), 2030(4979), 2598(1415)
Shapiro, M.: ref, 1498(5705)
Shapiro, S.: ref, 2289(1641, 1643)
Shapiro, S. H.: ref, 270(107), 2289(1701)
Shapson, S. M.: ref, 363(14), 398(98)
Sharabany, R.: ref, 874(55)
Sharf, R. S.: ref, 570(327), 618(5), 1729(79), 2318(1566)
Shark, M. L.: ref, 1209(33)
Sharkey, C. T.: ref, 357(520)
Sharkey, K. J.: ref, 2491(2089)
Sharma, S.: ref, 1498(5201), 2300(370, 371)
Sharma, V. K.: ref, 2236(4)
Sharman, R.: ref, 1498(5566)
Sharp, D.: ref, 2269(470), 2598(1646)
Sharp, G. L.: ref, 2300(438)
Sharp, J. D.: test, 782
Sharp, J. R.: ref, 1485(64)
Sharp, L. F.: ref, 501(836), 1498(5358)
Sharp, S.: rev, 638, 769
Sharpe, L.: ref, 1883(59)
Shartle, C. L.: test, 1746
Shasby, G.: ref, 344(158), 2602(1819), 2621(305)
Shaskan, E. G.: ref, 1240(49)
Shatin, L.: ref, 2598(1647)

Shavit, H.: ref, 2030(5094), 2512(664), 2602(2114, 2220)
Shaw, C. K.: ref, 2445(3)
Shaw, G. B.: ref, 859(873),
Shaw, J. B.: ref, 282(142), 799(19), 1013(94), 1370(2), 1808(10), 1855(25), 2016(197), 2537(558)
Shaw, J. H.: test, 1066
Shaw, L.: test, 2230
Shaw, M. E.: rev, 1350, 2203
Shaw, R.: ref, 76(645)
Shawver, L.: ref, 2598(1529)
Shay, C. B.: rev, 915, 2372, 2374
Shay, J. S.: ref, 673(53), 794(451)
Shaycoft, M. F.: rev, 1527, 2324
Shayer, M.: test, 641
Shaywitz, B. A.: ref, 1319(72), 2018(7), 2289(1768), 2598(1782), 2602(2115), 2608(239)
Shaywitz, S. E.: ref, 2289(1768), 2598(1782), 2602(2115), 2608(239)
Shea, D.: ref, 794(444), 2598(1817)
Shea, R. J.: ref, 1831(159)
Sheahan, R. K.: ref, 1914(864)
Shealy, A. E.: ref, 280(1092, 1093), 1498(5359, 5360), 2598(1494, 1530, 1531), 2607(169, 170)
Shealy, R. C.: ref, 1498(5699)
Shean, J. M.: ref, 2512(623)
Sheard, M. H.: ref, 859(830), 1123(60), 1498(5361), 1547(293), 1771(627), 2031(457)
Sheare, J. B.: ref, 1192(181), 1831(153)
Shearer, M. S.: test, 698
Shearer, S. L.: ref, 1498(5771)
Shearn, C. R.: ref, 1919(46), 2179(246), 2598(1763), 2620(20)
Shearn, D. F.: ref, 1831(154)
Sheehan, D. S.: ref, 1192(182, 207, 226), 1479(322, 335)
Sheehan, D. V.: ref, 883(110)
Sheehan, P. W.: ref, 1063(87, 91, 97, 119, 124), 1789(708, 724), 2294(107, 111, 114, 133, 137)
Sheehe, P. R.: ref, 270(103)
Sheeley, E. C.: rev, 882, 962, 1071, 2425
Sheinker, A.: ref, 2512(645)
Shekim, W. O.: ref, 2602(1959)
Sheldon, A. R.: ref, 941(48), 2208(1694)
Sheldon, C. N.: ref, 932(108)
Sheldon, W. D.: rev, 1569, 1570
Shellenberger, S.: ref, 1192(177), 1424(58), 2602(1960), 2608(219)
Shellhaas, M.: test, 6
Shelly, C.: ref, 2598(1797)
Shelton, J.: ref, 2208(1631)
Shelton, J. L.: ref, 1498(5233), 1798(230), 2300(389), 2353(27, 32), 2413(612)
Shelton, R. L.: rev, 960, 962, 1865, 2022; ref, 1126(646, 662, 675), 1622(31), 1894(3), 2103(6, 8), 2412(34, 36), 2425(1), 2621(221)
Shemberg, K. B.: ref, 1498(5668)
Shenfeld, M.: ref, 2030(5067)
Shepard, K. F.: ref, 2343(1050)
Shepard, L.: rev, 2131, 2139; ref, 482(9), 551(45), 1351(202), 1473(185), 1914(896)
Shepard, L. A.: ref, 890(352), 1789(705), 2491(2067)
Shepard, R. J.: ref, 1419(671)
Shepel, L.: ref, 1498(5046), 2598(1301)
Shephard, L.: ref, 1434(1)

Shephard, R. J.: ref, 1419(680), 1498(5122, 5362)
Shephared, R. J.: ref, 342(4)
Sheppard, G. P.: ref, 1655(110)
Sherbenou, R. J.: ref, 1986(1), 2292(32)
Sherick, R. B.: ref, 2602(2178)
Sheridan, E. P.: ref, 1547(273), 1789(652)
Sheridan, J. E.: ref, 1296(173)
Sheridan, M. D.: test, 2177, 2348, 2349, 2350; exc, 1899
Sherk, D.: ref, 1904(128)
Sherman, D.: exc, 960
Sherman, E. E.: test, 1011
Sherman, J.: ref, 483(37), 732(394), 1970(9, 11, 17), 2162(22), 2246(21, 23, 29, 33), 2295(2), 2474(3)
Sherman, J. A.: ref, 483(18, 38), 732(411), 2246(26)
Sherman, J. L.: ref, 1233(226)
Sherman, L. W.: ref, 2286(338)
Sherman, M.: ref, 1009(55)
Sherman, M. F.: ref, 2029(237)
Sherman, N. C.: ref, 2029(237)
Sherrad, D. J.: ref, 1498(5608), 2598(1714)
Sherrard D. J.: ref, 1498(5227)
Sherrets, S.: ref, 2602(1961, 2094)
Sherrill, C.: ref, 2665(2)
Sherrill, J. M.: ref, 590(374)
Sherry, G. S.: ref, 883(111)
Sherwin, N. V.: ref, 2160(61)
Sherwood, J. C.: rev, 422, 530, 571, 2161
Sherwood, R. D.: ref, 1405(10)
Shessel, D.: ref, 701(59), 1126(720), 1540(13), 1771(644), 2218(141)
Shevrin, H.: ref, 794(429), 2030(5042, 5044), 2598(1648, 1653)
Shewan, C. M.: ref, 1914(868)
Shiek, D. A.: ref, 2602(1820)
Shields, P. H.: ref, 719(33)
Shiffler, N.: ref, 116(540)
Shiffner, J.: ref, 2030(5067)
Shigehisa, T.: ref, 859(885)
Shill, M.: ref, 2491(2108)
Shimberg, B.: test, 2327; rev, 654, 937
Shimoni, N.: ref, 2217(136)
Shinall, S. L.: rev, 979, 997
Shine, R. E.: rev, 2448
Shinn, M.: ref, 2602(2230), 2639(3)
Shiomi, K.: ref, 1419(681, 682, 694, 699)
Shipkin, D.: ref, 308(13)
Shipley, R. H.: ref, 2300(439, 494)
Shipley, W. C.: test, 2179; rev, 1914, 2013
Shipman, V. C.: ref, 581(12), 582(6), 1914(741)
Shiran, D.: ref, 374(208)
Shirberg, L. D.: ref, 859(768)
Shirley, J. G.: ref, 1851(35)
Shisslak, C.: ref, 2300(475)
Shneidman, E.: test, 1043
Shneidman, E. S.: test, 1361; exc, 1480
Shneorson, Z.: ref, 2581(337)
Shoaff, J. E.: ref, 280(1114), 1498(5483)
Shoben, E. J.: rev, 1237, 2526
Shoemaker, D. M.: exc, 2181, 2431
Shoemaker, L. M.: exc, 1254
Shoham, M.: ref, 2413(661)
Shohet, J.: test, 711
Sholley, B. K.: ref, 1726(370)
Sholomkas, A. J.: ref, 2100(12)
Sholomkas, D.: ref, 2100(12)

Sholtis, D.: ref, 1754(109), 2412(43)
Shonburn, S.: ref, 378(18)
Shontz, F. C.: ref, 1498(5595)
Shooster, C.: test, 1821
Shor, R. E.: test, 1063, 1184
Shore, J. H.: ref, 1498(5683)
Shore, R. E.: ref, 1498(5328)
Shores, J. H.: rev, 344
Shorr, D. N.: ref, 2289(1642)
Short, M. A.: ref, 2244(35)
Shostrom, E. L.: test, 376, 1758, 1789
Shostrom, F. L.: ref, 1758(12)
Shouval, R.: ref, 2037(149), 2491(2026)
Showstack, J. A.: ref, 1922(6, 7, 9)
Shrago, M.: test, 247, 248, 249
Shriberg, L. D.: rev, 1814, 2022
Shrivastava, G. P.: ref, 2121(66)
Shubsachs, A. P. W.: ref, 1497(25, 26), 1855(21)
Shueler, H.: rev, 493
Shueman, S. A.: ref, 2413(608)
Shuey, I.: ref, 1904(108)
Shuger, D.: ref, 354(1551), 1726(372), 1789(721)
Shull, E. D.: rev, 578
Shulman, R.: ref, 1883(36)
Shum, K.: ref, 1063(86)
Shuman, H. H.: ref, 270(82, 83), 311(24, 25), 678(21)
Shumway, R. J.: ref, 2286(346)
Shurley, J. T.: ref, 1547(288)
Shutt, D. L.: test, 2196
Shweder, R. A.: ref, 1498(5202)
Shymansky, J. A.: ref, 1013(115), 2512(663)
Siberschatz, G.: ref, 1498(5363), 1547(294)
Sica, M. G.: test, 1525
Sicz, G.: ref, 1789(710, 711, 722)
Siddall, J. W.: ref, 1498(5700)
Sideroff, S. I.: ref, 1547(340)
Siders, J.: ref, 551(48)
Siebel, C. E.: ref, 2134(100)
Siebrecht, E. B.: test, 2197
Sieg, D.: ref, 2598(1800)
Siegel, D.: ref, 1948(105)
Siegel, H. B.: ref, 794(378), 2030(4970)
Siegel, J. M.: ref, 1547(295, 309), 1931(48)
Siegel, L.: rev, 1726; exc, 118, 570, 909, 966, 1192, 1460, 1527, 1555, 1726, 2160, 2323, 2326, 2327, 2366
Siegel, L. S.: ref, 270(124, 160), 2018(15, 21), 2289(1735)
Siegenthaler, B. M.: test, 1071; ref, 1071(9)
Siegfried, J. J.: ref, 501(804), 506(28)
Siegler, I. C.: ref, 2598(1649, 1689)
Sielski, K. A.: ref, 2413(694)
Sienko, M. J.: ref, 64(7)
Sieracki, S.: ref, 2208(1666)
Sigel, I. E.: ref, 1771(651)
Sigelman, C. K.: ref, 2224(5, 6), 2581(338), 2598(1783)
Sigg, J. M.: ref, 2512(653)
Sigman, M.: ref, 678(14)
Signorella, M. L.: ref, 1013(75), 1257(135)
Sigueland, M. L.: test, 1459
Sikes, S. M.: ref, 2301(27)
Silance, E. B.: test, 1945
Silberberg, M. C.: ref, 958(42), 1007(20), 1473(138), 2621(261)

Silberberg, N. E.: ref, 958(42), 1007(20), 1473(138), 2621(261)
Silberfarb, P. M.: ref, 1547(341), 1923(21), 2598(1758, 1784)
Silbergeld, S.: ref, 1099(71, 72, 73), 2587(39)
Silberstein, J. A.: ref, 280(1165, 1174), 1462(157, 162), 1914(885), 2179(253), 2598(1825, 1857)
Silbert, A. R.: ref, 270(100)
Silliman, E. R.: ref, 1351(191), 1754(96)
Silliman, H.: test, 829
Sillin, P. C.: ref, 1192(170), 1831(124)
Sills, F. D.: test, 4
Silva, J. A.: ref, 1498(5701)
Silva, J. M.: ref, 1904(130), 2300(608)
Silva, P. A.: ref, 2018(17), 2276(6), 2289(1769)
Silva, S. S.: ref, 378(8)
Silvaroli, N. J.: test, 1734
Silver, A. A.: test, 2111; ref, 2111(2), 2621(306)
Silver, E. A.: ref, 9(16), 1653(14)
Silver, M.: ref, 354(1473), 1914(785)
Silverman, B.: ref, 1192(227)
Silverman, E. M.: ref, 357(514), 1192(183)
Silverman, G.: ref, 860(99)
Silverman, I.: ref, 2602(1695)
Silverman, L. H.: ref, 2030(5010), 2491(2048)
Silverman, R. H.: test, 203, 2649
Silvern, L.: ref, 1771(517)
Silvern, L. E.: ref, 1771(686)
Silverstein, A. B.: rev, 691, 1424, 2608; exc, 235; ref, 559(58), 1126(710), 1769(105), 2289(1706, 1770), 2598(1393, 1785), 2602(1693, 1694, 2116, 2117, 2118), 2608(185), 2621(307, 331, 416)
Silverstein, M. L.: ref, 1883(37, 90), 2598(1650)
Silverstone, E.: ref, 751(12)
Silverstone, T.: ref, 859(894), 883(106)
Silvestri, R.: ref, 116(541), 1655(85)
Simberg, A. L.: test, 10
Simeonsson, R. J.: ref, 1771(589, 674)
Simmonds, V.: test, 148, 149, 2175
Simmons, D. D.: ref, 2029(198)
Simmons, F. B.: ref, 1498(5097)
Simmons, J. Q.: ref, 2598(1794), 2602(2137)
Simmons, R. G.: ref, 1192(208)
Simon, A.: ref, 1914(729, 730, 821), 2077(26), 2289(1791)
Simon, J. L.: ref, 2621(316)
Simon, J. M.: ref, 2602(2119)
Simon, L.: ref, 732(410), 859(932)
Simon, N.: ref, 1419(677)
Simon, P.: ref, 1655(100)
Simon, W. E.: ref, 2657(100)
Simonds, J. F.: ref, 1209(39), 2598(1651), 2602(1962)
Simono, R. B.: ref, 1498(5364), 2208(1632), 2318(1567)
Simons, B.: test, 1764
Simons, E. S.: ref, 1473(139)
Simons, G. M.: test, 2200
Simons, M. R.: ref, 1424(64)
Simons, R. C.: ref, 1576(197)
Simpson, B. K.: test, 1776
Simpson, C.: ref, 582(8)
Simpson, D. A.: ref, 283(150), 2598(1598), 2607(179)
Simpson, G. B.: ref, 1498(5524), 1655(86), 2620(15)
Simpson, J. M.: ref, 1655(89)

Simpson, M.: ref, 1498(5321), 2030(5037), 2620(12, 14, 19)
Simpson, M. A.: ref, 378(7)
Simpson, S.: ref, 280(1130), 1272(137)
Simpson-Housley, P.: ref, 2208(1697)
Sims, A.: ref, 2598(1487)
Sims, C. A.: exc, 1883
Sims, H. P.: ref, 2343(1039)
Sims, J. P.: ref, 2582(18)
Sims, V. M.: rev, 163, 357, 2375, 2621
Sims-Knight, J. E.: ref, 963(129)
Sinclair, J.: ref, 21(4), 2113(250)
Sines, J. O.: test, 1515; rev, 772; ref, 1257(134), 1498(5203, 5351), 2598(1394)
Sines, L. K.: test, 1515; ref, 1498(5525)
Singer, B. A.: ref, 2030(5043)
Singer, D. G.: ref, 404(8), 1771(695, 758)
Singer, H.: rev, 935, 1479, 1551; ref, 1257(178)
Singer, J. H.: ref, 6(49), 2289(1689)
Singer, J. L.: ref, 404(8), 1771(695, 758), 1798(208, 295)
Singer, M. G.: ref, 1771(698), 1969(104), 2602(1979)
Singer, M. T.: ref, 2030(5092)
Singer, R. N.: ref, 1442(1)
Singer, S. M.: ref, 643(135), 932(58), 962(24), 1126(658, 691), 1257(123), 1473(130), 1769(43, 52), 2269(437), 2286(278), 2598(1323), 2602(1636), 2621(236)
Singerman, B.: ref, 941(39)
Singerman, L. J.: ref, 877(20)
Singh, A. K.: ref, 2236(4)
Singh, A. N.: ref, 1655(101)
Singh, B.: ref, 941(49)
Singh, M. P.: ref, 2121(68)
Singh, N.: ref, 678(25)
Singh, S.: ref, 200(19, 20), 653(155, 167), 860(134), 896(9), 960(18, 19), 1419(698), 1573(41), 1814(8), 2208(1579), 2236(3), 2412(44, 47), 2491(2041, 2068, 2091)
Singh, V. K.: ref, 1419(706)
Singleton, C. H.: ref, 1771(547)
Singleton, W.: ref, 859(894), 883(106)
Sinha, B. P.: ref, 2491(2044, 2049)
Sinha, P.: ref, 2029(242)
Sinisterra, L.: ref, 2602(1785), 2608(201)
Sink, C.: ref, 368(3)
Sinkel, P.: ref, 2598(1713), 2607(198)
Sinnette, C. H.: ref, 277(2), 2506(7)
Sinsabaugh, L. L.: ref, 1498(5055)
Siomopoulos, G.: ref, 2598(1347)
Sipay, E. R.: test, 1402, 2202; rev, 1333, 1434, 1999
Sipe, S.: ref, 2602(2072), 2621(406)
Sipprelle, R. C.: ref, 859(769)
Siskind, V.: ref, 2289(1641, 1643)
Sison, G. F. P.: ref, 868(5)
Sitaram, N.: ref, 2598(1867), 2607(220)
Sitarz, A. M.: ref, 2300(343)
Sitton, L. R.: ref, 859(933)
Sitts, B.: test, 809, 816
Skager, R. W.: rev, 502, 1080, 1745, 2308
Skaggs, C. T.: ref, 2657(107)
Skaggs, S.: ref, 2300(530)
Skanes, G. R.: ref, 1914(733)
Skaret, D. J.: ref, 1296(170)
Skeel, D. J.: ref, 2029(199)

Skeen, D. R.: test, 1072
Skeen, P.: ref, 559(55)
Skeeters, D. E.: test, 355, 1499
Skevington, S. M.: ref, 859(770)
Skinner, C.: ref, 378(19), 1153(9), 2018(20), 2472(30)
Skinner, H. A.: ref, 609(228), 1203(12), 1498(5365, 5366), 1798(222, 296, 309, 310), 1914(897), 2598(1858, 1859), 2621(456)
Skinner, J. T.: test, 1734
Sklar, M.: test, 2213
Skolnick, N. J.: ref, 859(886), 1498(5526), 1789(706)
Skonieczka, K.: ref, 2413(621)
Skorka, D.: ref, 1106(376)
Skov, H.: ref, 381(67)
Skurdal, M. A.: test, 1072
Skurnik, L. S.: test, 2096
Skvarcius, R. S.: ref, 1077(56)
Slack, W. V.: ref, 501(909, 910)
Slade, P.: ref, 354(1552), 859(934), 2208(1667)
Slaney, F. M.: ref, 2318(1620)
Slaney, R. B.: ref, 76(659), 2134(124), 2318(1568, 1600, 1620), 2581(319, 342, 343, 348)
Slater, A. M.: ref, 280(1075), 330(18), 2602(1755)
Slater, B. R.: test, 484
Slater, P.: rev, 1186, 1535, 2368; ref, 639(49)
Slaughter, H.: ref, 1762(3, 4)
Slaughter, M. H.: ref, 5(166)
Slavin, R. E.: ref, 551(66), 552(5), 1116(1, 2, 3)
Slavney, P. R.: ref, 1883(78, 94)
Slaymaker, J.: ref, 885(2)
Slaymaker, J. E.: test, 885
Sledge, W. H.: ref, 883(101), 2208(1633)
Sleigh, G.: ref, 2602(2213)
Sletten, I.: ref, 1063(92)
Slinde, J. A.: ref, 344(145, 174), 551(22, 46), 1473(140), 2160(67), 2260(32, 44)
Slingerland, B. H.: test, 1871, 2016, 2110, 2214
Slivnick, P.: test, 14
Sloan, L. L.: test, 2215
Sloan, T. S.: ref, 1726(363)
Sloan, W.: test, 1331; rev, 1101
Slobin, M. S.: test, 1123
Slocumb, P. R.: ref, 6(62), 1424(60)
Slone, D.: ref, 2289(1641, 1643)
Slosson, R. L.: test, 2216, 2217, 2218
Slosson Educational Publications, Inc.: test, 1202
Slotnick, H. B.: ref, 1576(225)
Slough, N. M.: ref, 1387(14)
Slutsky, J. M.: ref, 883(89)
Small, A.: ref, 2413(672)
Small, A. C.: ref, 116(570, 614), 354(1421), 917(73)
Small, A. M.: ref, 2289(1653), 2608(187)
Small, I. F.: ref, 2598(1840)
Small, V.: test, 905
Smallberg, S. A.: ref, 2598(1867), 2607(220)
Smart, R.: ref, 964(512), 2208(1668), 2217(175)
Smart, R. G.: ref, 859(831, 887)
Smart, W. D.: ref, 932(87)
Smead, V.: ref, 483(43), 1192(259)
Smedley, F.: test, 2219
Smeltzer, D. J.: ref, 280(1064), 2111(1), 2602(1592), 2621(222)
Smid, K.: ref, 1257(155)
Smith, A.: test, 2201, 2380; ref, 283(158), 883(72),

INDEX OF NAMES

1498(5139), 1771(773), 1883(52, 93), 1914(878), 2201(1), 2380(6), 2598(1818), 2602(2164)
Smith, A. C.: ref, 2598(1587)
Smith, A. D.: ref, 2598(1395, 1715)
Smith, A. E.: exc, 1754
Smith, A. H. W.: ref, 941(30)
Smith, A. J.: test, 2220
Smith, A. L.: ref, 653(164), 2602(2048)
Smith, A. N.: ref, 1771(759)
Smith, B.: ref, 121(8), 1007(16), 1271(906), 1853(271), 1914(723), 2537(549), 2598(1360), 2607(141)
Smith, B. D.: ref, 352(5), 859(832), 957, 958), 1568(120)
Smith, B. J.: ref, 270(70)
Smith, C.: ref, 116(628), 1106(381), 1117(444), 2602(2180)
Smith, C. A.: ref, 2598(1396)
Smith, C. B.: test, 1859
Smith, C. E.: rev, 1535
Smith, C. F.: ref, 2298(3)
Smith, C. J.: ref, 116(572), 1914(789)
Smith, D.: ref, 883(67)
Smith, D. D.: ref, 859(771), 2300(566)
Smith, D. E.: ref, 609(208), 859(771, 792)
Smith, D. E. P.: test, 1345; rev, 176, 2530
Smith, D. F.: ref, 355, 1499
Smith, D. G.: ref, 501(805), 890(329), 2594(198)
Smith, D. H.: ref, 1405(6)
Smith, D. I.: ref, 1419(707)
Smith, D. U.: ref, 1013(137)
Smith, D. V.: test, 844
Smith, D. W.: ref, 270(98), 2289(1690, 1703), 2598(1534), 2602(1828, 1873)
Smith, E. B.: test, 1813
Smith, E. C.: ref, 280(1160), 1250(21), 2602(2162), 2641(19)
Smith, E. P.: ref, 76(657), 1405(11), 2300(601)
Smith, F. M.: rev, 2260
Smith, F. V.: ref, 354(1400), 859(738), 2208(1537)
Smith, G. A.: ref, 30(6), 929(1), 1620(23)
Smith, G. M.: ref, 501(871)
Smith, H.: ref, 1576(200)
Smith, H. H.: ref, 1498(5285), 2113(244), 2598(1397, 1472)
Smith, H. P.: test, 2474
Smith, I. D.: ref, 2301(30)
Smith, I. L.: test, 2462; ref, 2602(2120)
Smith, I. M.: test, 930, 1620; rev, 643, 649, 898; ref, 733(7), 1620(21), 1652(1), 2004(1)
Smith, J.: test, 1778
Smith, J. C.: ref, 1573(39), 2208(1592), 2300(440), 2413(633)
Smith, J. D.: ref, 280(1122), 1771(570)
Smith, J. E.: ref, 1855(27)
Smith, J. K.: test, 365, 692; ref, 551(47), 2181(17)
Smith, J. L.: ref, 2300(396), 2353(28), 2598(1461), 2638(131)
Smith, J. M.: test, 1345, 1461
Smith, J. P.: rev, 425, 427; ref, 1798(284)
Smith, J. S.: ref, 2629(105)
Smith, J. W.: ref, 1771(673), 2218(149), 2602(1928)
Smith, K. J.: rev, 346, 482, 958, 2283, 2284
Smith, L. H.: test, 1309, 2069
Smith, L. S.: ref, 1289(6), 2598(1397)
Smith, L. T.: ref, 2287(41)

Smith, M.: test, 207; ref, 1771(687), 1914(778), 1931(45), 2077(29), 2208(1588)
Smith, M. D.: ref, 1473(141, 163, 166, 167, 186), 1831(130, 131, 151, 155, 156, 178), 2029(218), 2602(1696, 1697, 1698, 1821, 1822, 1827, 1856, 1963)
Smith, M. E.: ref, 859(768)
Smith, M. F.: ref, 1953(12)
Smith, M. K.: ref, 1473(142), 1769(48), 2286(286), 2621(262)
Smith, M. L.: rev, 368, 2496
Smith, N. L.: rev, 556, 557
Smith, N. M.: ref, 483(31), 2160(68)
Smith, P.: test, 1779; ref, 1351(198), 1555(327)
Smith, P. B.: ref, 890(347), 1547(310)
Smith, P. C.: ref, 2343(1051)
Smith, P. J.: ref, 2581(310)
Smith, P. K.: ref, 581(13), 964(490), 2018(12)
Smith, R. A.: test, 734; ref, 553(15), 606(14), 932(82)
Smith, R. B.: ref, 1498(5527)
Smith, R. E.: ref, 1931(49)
Smith, R. J.: ref, 501(872), 1498(5367)
Smith, R. N.: test, 2542, 2577
Smith, S.: test, 196, 197, 827, 828, 947, 1068, 1082, 2001, 2258, 2569; ref, 2217(176), 2598(1786)
Smith, S. D.: ref, 354(1508), 483(16), 874(50), 1478(67), 1479(321), 1831(162), 1877(6), 2413(662), 2491(2054)
Smith, S. H.: ref, 2638(137)
Smith, S. M.: ref, 280(1123), 1473(187), 1498(5528), 2037(153), 2537(559), 2598(1652), 2621(366)
Smith, T. A.: exc, 1823
Smith, T. P.: ref, 1771(760)
Smith, V.: ref, 392(4)
Smith, W. D.: ref, 354(1508), 2413(662)
Smith, W. E.: ref, 1473(207)
Smith, W. F.: ref, 501(832), 1527(47)
Smith, W. L.: rev, 479
Smith–Burke, M.: ref, 1191(125)
Smith–Burke, M. T.: ref, 2286(320)
Smitheimer, L. S.: ref, 378(13)
Smither, R.: ref, 2134(140), 2300(495), 2318(1613)
Smithers, A. G.: ref, 859(833), 2029(207)
Smock, C. D.: rev, 302; exc, 559
Smokler, I. A.: ref, 794(429), 2030(5042, 5044), 2598(1648, 1653)
Smolen, R. C.: ref, 1969(95)
Smyers, P. L.: ref, 1053(63)
Smyth, T. J. C.: ref, 1568(137)
Snaith, R. P.: test, 1314
Snedden, D.: exc, 204
Snedeker, J. H.: test, 1943
Snelbecker, G. E.: ref, 6(38)
Snell, M. E.: ref, 381(68)
Snibbe, J. R.: ref, 1488(2), 1498(5702), 2598(1787)
Snijder, J. T.: test, 1617
Snijders–Oomen, N.: test, 1617, 2221
Snijders, J. T.: test, 2221
Snodgrass, G.: ref, 374(209)
Snow, C. E.: ref, 1771(628)
Snow, M. E.: ref, 270(133), 2289(1747)
Snowling, M.: ref, 1567(20), 1771(808)
Snowling, M. J.: ref, 1771(807), 2602(2121, 2214)
Snowman, J.: ref, 76(646), 685(1), 1257(144), 1319(82), 1914(840)

Snyder, A. L.: ref, 1197(284)
Snyder, C. R.: ref, 1798(223), 2030(4971), 2121(69)
Snyder, D. K.: test, 1374
Snyder, H. N.: ref, 2269(475)
Snyder, L. S.: ref, 270(99)
Snyder, M. K.: ref, 1769(101), 2621(435)
Snyder, P. J.: ref, 1466(2)
Snyder, P. P.: ref, 280(1175), 701(92), 1371(263)
Snyder, R. A.: ref, 354(1464, 1470), 780(1674), 1295(298), 1296(176), 2413(630)
Snyder, R. T.: ref, 280(1129, 1151, 1175), 701(92), 1371(263), 1473(208), 1831(125), 2602(1996), 2621(381)
Snyder, S. H.: ref, 1883(78, 94)
Snyder, S. S.: ref, 2269(444)
Snyder, V.: ref, 76(646), 685(1)
Snyderman, S. E.: ref, 701(69), 2602(1964)
Soares, A.: ref, 2598(1352)
Soares, A. T.: test, 146, 2139
Soares, L. M.: test, 146, 2139
Sobel, H. J.: ref, 1498(5529), 1904(100)
Sobell, M. B.: ref, 1547(331)
Sobesky, W.: ref, 1771(686)
Sobkow, J.: ref, 2537(555)
Sobkow, J. A.: ref, 1497(27)
Sobleman, S.: ref, 2300(511), 2353(34)
Sobol, E. G.: ref, 1789(683), 2300(441)
Sobol, M. P.: ref, 2602(1622), 2621(233)
Sobotka, K. R.: ref, 280(1057), 1771(571, 572), 2602(1699, 1700, 1823), 2621(263, 264)
Soder, A. L.: test, 1814
Soderstrom, D.: ref, 1960(71)
Soeberg, D.: test, 2371
Soldatos, C. R.: ref, 1498(5635, 5636, 5637)
Söldner, M.: ref, 1419(705)
Solfvin, G. F.: ref, 1063(108), 1789(703)
Solhkhah, N.: ref, 1233(227)
Solla, J.: ref, 398(94)
Sollod, R.: ref, 559(46)
Solly, D. C.: ref, 2602(1701)
Soloff, P. H.: ref, 1904(101)
Solomon, D.: ref, 344(146)
Solomon, E. J.: ref, 1498(5057), 2598(1304)
Solomon, G. F.: ref, 2300(368)
Solomon, I. L.: test, 2079
Solomon, M. J.: ref, 1798(311)
Solomon, R. J.: rev, 2485
Solomon, S.: ref, 1547(342)
Solomon, S. J.: ref, 1229(79), 1233(213), 2621(245)
Solway, K. S.: ref, 280(1152), 872(10), 1498(5703), 1831(174), 2598(1788), 2602(1649, 1762, 2122)
Solyom, L.: ref, 1197(293), 1419(686)
Somers, H.: ref, 1153(7)
Somers, K.: ref, 381(65), 2289(1660), 2551(14)
Somervill, J. W.: ref, 76(638), 1771(573)
Somerville, S. C.: ref, 1914(864)
Sommers, A. F.: ref, 1883(45)
Sommers, J. K.: ref, 374(230)
Sommers, R. K.: rev, 200, 866; ref, 378(4), 911(3), 960(10), 1622(44), 1771(629), 1851(19, 36), 2472(12, 15)
Somwaru, J. P.: test, 208, 209, 210, 211, 2364, 2437
Sonderman, J. C.: ref, 212(6)
Sones, R. A.: test, 776
Sonstegard, M.: ref, 551(64), 2218(18)

Soper, J. C.: test, 2440
Sophn, H. E.: ref, 2598(1789)
SoRelle, E.: test, 287
Sorensen, G.: ref, 2208(1552)
Sorensen, J. P.: ref, 1101(48), 2602(2061)
Sorenson, G.: exc, 374
Sosner, B.: ref, 1488(2), 1498(5702), 2598(1787)
Sostek, A. J.: ref, 1498(5581), 2598(1692)
Sostek, A. M.: rev, 311; ref, 270(71), 311(19)
Sotile, W. M.: ref, 1547(260), 2413(595)
Soto, C.: ref, 2277(5)
Soucar, E.: ref, 6(72)
Souheaver, G. T.: ref, 1498(5197), 2300(369), 2598(1777)
Soule, A. B.: ref, 311(30)
Soule, J. C.: ref, 2131(7)
Sousley, S. A.: ref, 1479(380)
South, J. C.: test, 819; ref, 819(2)
Southern, M. L.: ref, 354(1469)
Southgate, V.: test, 2245
Southwestern Cooperative Educational Laboratory: test, 2377, 2378
Sovchik, R.: ref, 1405(12)
Sowards, S. K.: ref, 280(1107), 701(61)
Sowder, L.: rev, 709, 2291
Soysa, P.: ref, 1914(751)
Spaan, M.: test, 824, 1483, 1484
Space, L. G.: ref, 1771(761)
Spache, G.: test, 1131, 2255; rev, 1330
Spache, G. D.: test, 719, 2247, 2468; rev, 766, 935, 1813, 1994
Spadafore, G. J.: test, 1304
Spadafore, S. J.: test, 1304
Spalding, N. V.: test, 1967
Spaner, S. D.: ref, 302(28), 581(10), 1192(257), 1771(530), 1874(8), 1969(83), 2551(13), 2621(449)
Spaney, E.: rev, 123, 180, 1188, 1749
Spanos, N. P.: ref, 859(888, 935), 1063(98, 101, 109, 110, 111, 112, 113, 122, 125, 126, 127, 128, 129, 131, 136), 1247(165), 2598(1654)
Sparacino, J.: ref, 76(634)
Sparkes, R. S.: ref, 1319(78)
Sparks, S.: ref, 378(16), 381(74), 1771(762), 2289(1771)
Spartanburg, S. C.: ref, 121(10), 2485(130)
Spaulding, G.: test, 588; rev, 2114
Spauling, W.: ref, 1498(5368), 1969(96)
Speakman, H. G. B.: ref, 2068(88)
Spear, P. S.: ref, 2512(641)
Spear, W. E.: ref, 2030(5093)
Spearman, C.: rev, 2269
Spearritt, D.: test, 21, 28, 30, 31, 39, 1755; rev, 1936
Spector, J.: ref, 2491(2038)
Spector, P. B.: ref, 896(5)
Speer, E. V.: ref, 1170(237)
Speer, R. K.: test, 196, 197, 827, 828, 947, 1068, 1082, 2001, 2258, 2569
Speidel, G. E.: ref, 2608(179)
Spellacy, F.: ref, 280(1094), 283(140, 147), 794(379, 406, 407), 1498(5204, 5369), 1771(630), 1853(272, 279), 2113(239, 247), 2598(1532), 2602(1702, 1824), 2621(308)
Spelman, M. S.: ref, 1462(156), 1485(87), 1914(880)
Speltz, M. L.: ref, 890(350), 1498(5498), 2179(228), 2587(44)

INDEX OF NAMES

Spence, C. M.: ref, 1771(759)
Spencer, B.: ref, 1789(674), 2413(622)
Spencer, C. M.: ref, 283(149)
Spencer, D.: rev, 357
Spencer, F.: ref, 1923(29)
Spencer, J.: ref, 2018(13), 2557(225)
Spencer, M.: ref, 1424(89)
Spencer, P. L.: rev, 1477
Spencer, R. E.: test, 1125
Spengler, D. M.: ref, 1498(5054)
Spennato, N. A.: test, 669
Spensley, J.: ref, 116(621)
Sperl, B.: ref, 1020(22)
Spero, A. J.: ref, 280(1071), 1192(189), 2602(1733)
Speroff, B. J.: test, 798
Sperry, R. W.: ref, 627(21), 1356(97), 1506(72), 1774(12), 1914(899), 1948(96), 2317(10)
Spevack, M.: ref, 2512(656)
Speyer, H.: exc, 381
Spiegel, D.: ref, 1904(131)
Spiegel, M. R.: ref, 1351(180)
Spielberg, G.: test, 2146
Spielberger, C. D.: test, 2300, 2301, 2417; rev, 883, 1757; ref, 2300(569), 2301(27)
Spielman, A. J.: ref, 1498(5775)
Spiers, P.: ref, 1798(217)
Spies, C. A.: ref, 2300(461)
Spilsbury, G.: ref, 1257(136), 2113(249)
Spinetta, J. J.: ref, 874(49)
Spinnler, H.: ref, 1914(875), 2598(1812)
Spinweber, C. L.: ref, 1498(5451)
Spirito, A.: ref, 280(1153), 701(83)
Spiro, A.: ref, 653(158), 1257(156), 1914(825)
Spiro, R. J.: ref, 1013(116), 1257(116), 2621(417)
Spitz, H. H.: ref, 559(54), 1754(97), 1853(280), 2181(18), 2218(153)
Spitzer, R. L.: test, 645, 1922, 1923; ref, 1923(22)
Spitzer, S. E.: ref, 1063(93)
Spivack, G.: test, 702, 703, 704, 1049, 1050, 1436; ref, 280(1121), 2602(1955)
Spoelstra, T.: ref, 1013(79)
Spohn, H.: ref, 2491(2083)
Spohn, H. E.: ref, 2598(1398)
Spokane, A. R.: test, 1447; ref, 2134(107), 2318(1559, 1569, 1596, 1597, 1612), 2581(330, 349)
Spolter, B. M.: ref, 780(1677)
Spooncer, F. A.: test, 1018, 1024
Spotts, J.: test, 702, 703
Spotts, L. H.: test, 50
Spratt, K. F.: ref, 1192(235)
Spreat, S.: ref, 6(38, 56, 61, 78)
Sprecher, J. W.: ref, 243(122), 653(161)
Spreen, O.: rev, 1109, 1462; ref, 2602(2113)
Spreng, L.: ref, 354(1426), 732(395), 794(382), 1046(574), 1486(177), 2029(200), 2343(1035), 2607(149)
Spriestersbach, D. C.: test, 911
Spriggs, A. J.: test, 2433
Springer, S. I.: ref, 2629(119)
Springer, S. P.: ref, 1126(664), 1462(122), 2607(139)
Squier, R. W.: ref, 2208(1695)
Squire, L.: ref, 2602(1689)
Squire, L. S.: ref, 2602(1816)
Squyres, E. M.: ref, 2491(2109)

Srivastava, A. K.: ref, 1914(731), 2342(23)
Srole, L.: ref, 609(229), 1498(5704)
Sroufe, L. A.: ref, 270(89, 90, 127), 2289(1678, 1738)
Staats, S.: ref, 2657(115)
Stabler, B.: ref, 2602(2123)
Stace, G.: ref, 859(936), 1197(313), 2300(565)
Stachnik, T. J.: ref, 1576(197)
Stack, W. B.: ref, 707(19)
Staff, P.: ref, 270(144)
Stafford, E. M.: ref, 941(32, 40)
Stafford, J.: exc, 719, 958, 1551, 1579
Stafford, M. L.: test, 2108
Stagg, R.: ref, 1914(732)
Stahmann, R. F.: rev, 376, 2396; exc, 1269, 1270
Stair, L. H.: ref, 2491(2023)
Stake, R. E.: exc, 2286
Staley, J. S.: ref, 1789(674), 2413(622)
Staley, N. K.: ref, 1568(137)
Stallings, M. A.: ref, 1498(5069, 5452), 1923(15), 2598(1592)
Stallings, W. M.: ref, 1125(17)
Stalnaker, J. M.: rev, 571, 2163; exc, 2269
Stam, H. J.: ref, 859(935), 1063(111, 113, 127, 128, 129, 131, 136), 1247(165)
Stamm, J. S.: ref, 226(164), 1060(24), 1126(694)
Stamp, I. M.: test, 2279
Stamp, P.: ref, 354(1509), 2208(1634)
Stamps, L. E.: ref, 1197(296), 2300(463, 496), 2343(1044)
Stanard, S. J.: test, 2273, 2274
Stancik, E. J.: test, 1297
Standifer, C. E.: ref, 1193(149), 2260(51)
Standing, L.: ref, 859(936), 1197(313), 1351(198), 2300(565)
Standley, K.: ref, 311(30)
Staniforth, D.: ref, 1883(67)
Stankov, L.: ref, 354(1422), 1077(58), 1257(136, 168), 2113(248, 249, 256, 257), 2208(1553)
Stanley, F.: ref, 678(24)
Stanley, G.: ref, 30(6), 751(19), 860(152), 929(1), 1620(23)
Stanley, G. E.: ref, 1823(34)
Stanley, G. V.: ref, 1757(16)
Stanley, J. C.: rev, 590, 2165, 2317; exc, 2289; ref, 501(806, 879, 880, 934), 577(1)
Stanley, M.: ref, 1655(99)
Stanley, T. O.: test, 2434; ref, 2434(2)
Stanovich, K. E.: ref, 2286(347), 2621(313, 367, 457, 458)
Stansfield, C.: ref, 1013(122)
Stansfield, C. W.: rev, 895, 1648
Stanton, B.: ref, 1798(252, 260, 274)
Stanton, G. C.: ref, 551(27)
Stanton, H. E.: ref, 2413(663, 686)
Staples, D. J.: ref, 1914(722), 2598(1358), 2602(1663), 2607(140)
Staples, F. R.: ref, 890(341), 1498(5666)
Staples, R. B.: ref, 1498(5705)
Stappenbeck, H.: ref, 1158(31)
Star, B.: ref, 472(16), 2208(1635)
Starck, A.: ref, 2030(4983)
Stark, J.: test, 212; rev, 1153, 1877, 2018; ref, 1914(715)
Stark, R.: ref, 932(128), 2602(2221)
Stark, R. E.: ref, 932(127), 1101(52), 1126(787),

1622(56), 2412(45), 2472(32), 2602(2215), 2608(249)
Stark, R. H.: test, 1849
Stark-Adamec, C.: ref, 1798(297)
Starkey, K. L.: ref, 378(4), 911(3), 2472(12)
Starkman, S.: ref, 2621(217)
Starr, A. S.: rev, 2557
Starr, B. D.: test, 1916, 2079
Starr, R. P.: test, 1421
Starr, S.: ref, 868(5)
Starry, A. R.: test, 1954
Stary, J. E.: ref, 2598(1379)
Staso, W. H.: ref, 2512(624)
Staton, R. D.: ref, 701(73), 1126(751, 788), 1771(809), 1831(186, 218), 1853(299), 2602(2012, 2216, 2217), 2608(250), 2621(387, 459, 460)
Staudenmayer, H.: ref, 1498(5370, 5433)
Stauffacher, R.: ref, 2030(5082)
Stauffer, A. J.: ref, 2293(15)
Stauffer, R. G.: rev, 171, 2371
Stauss, D.: ref, 1547(352)
Stauss, F. F.: ref, 1498(5056, 5239)
Stauss, F. S.: ref, 890(355), 1498(5589)
Stava, L. J.: ref, 1063(137), 1555(343)
Stavig, G. R.: ref, 2537(550)
Stayrook, N. G.: ref, 483(23)
Stayton, S. E.: ref, 381(66), 653(156), 1209(40), 2413(664), 2621(368)
Stecker, V.: exc, 2539
Stecklein, J. E.: test, 155; rev, 2160
Steckol, K. F.: ref, 1126(739), 1622(47), 2541(8)
Stedman, D. J.: ref, 270(88), 701(53), 1771(620), 1934(9), 2289(1669), 2478(11)
Stedman, J. M.: ref, 280(1095), 2602(1825, 2068), 2621(309)
Stedman, M. E.: ref, 2318(1546)
Steel, A. M.: ref, 1567(15), 2602(1868)
Steel, D. H.: ref, 2300(398, 469)
Steele, C. T.: ref, 2621(243)
Steele, G.: ref, 2029(197)
Steele, G. P.: ref, 941(23), 1883(33)
Steele, R. S.: ref, 2491(2028)
Steelman, L. C.: ref, 2602(2124)
Steenburgen, F.: test, 2303
Steer, R. A.: ref, 116(571), 859(889, 959), 1462(140), 1904(102, 117), 1940(82, 83), 2100(6)
Steers, R. M.: ref, 1798(224)
Steeves, L.: ref, 859(953), 1789(733)
Stefan, D.: ref, 1498(5662)
Stefanik, K.: ref, 609(203), 911(2)
Stefanis, C.: ref, 859(878, 954)
Steffe, L. P.: rev, 173, 579
Steffeck, J. C.: ref, 2300(363)
Stefferud, B.: ref, 2029(243)
Steffy, A. R. F.: ref, 2598(1399)
Steffy, R. A.: ref, 1498(5654), 1923(19), 2598(1399)
Stefic, E. C.: test, 1747
Steggles, S.: ref, 1063(112)
Stehbens, J. A.: ref, 2289(1693), 2602(1853), 2621(314)
Stehlens, J. A.: ref, 2289(1644)
Steibe, S. C.: ref, 558(68)
Stein, B. S.: ref, 551(59)
Stein, C. L. E.: ref, 1769(95)
Stein, D. K.: ref, 2300(379)

Stein, G. M.: ref, 226(189), 1371(264), 1949(61), 2602(2218)
Stein, J. M.: rev, 998
Stein, M.: test, 2121
Stein, M. D.: ref, 1515(16)
Stein, M. I.: test, 1817, 2010, 2376, 2407
Stein, M. K.: ref, 1498(5371, 5530)
Stein, M. T.: ref, 2366(201)
Stein, Z.: ref, 282(141), 464(2), 1914(705)
Steinbauer, E.: ref, 302(34), 2286(303)
Steinberg, F. A.: ref, 1498(5531)
Steinbert, E.: test, 712
Steinbock, E.: ref, 2300(410)
Steinbook, R. M.: ref, 1904(71)
Steiner, E.: ref, 1405(12)
Steiner, J.: ref, 1580(2)
Steiner, V. G.: test, 1877
Steinglass, P.: ref, 2100(13)
Steinhauer, J. C.: exc, 2318
Steinhoff, C. R.: test, 1745
Steinkamp, M. W.: ref, 280(1154), 2602(2125), 2621(418)
Steinkellner, L. L.: ref, 2160(51)
Steinlauf, B.: ref, 1436(14), 2300(497)
Steinmann, A. G.: test, 1357, 1358
Steinschneider, A.: ref, 270(103)
Stelmack, R. M.: ref, 859(772, 877, 890)
Stenchever, M.: ref, 2300(570)
Stenn, P. G.: ref, 1498(5532), 1798(268)
Stenner, A. J.: ref, 1473(126), 1754(54)
Stenslie, C. E.: ref, 1498(5771)
Stephan, W. G.: ref, 1473(188)
Stephen, L. S.: ref, 780(1709), 1498(5753), 2413(697)
Stephens, D.: ref, 1050(1)
Stephens, J. H.: ref, 2318(1565)
Stephens, M. I.: ref, 896(2), 960(8), 1969(125), 2412(37, 42)
Stephens, N.: ref, 1831(179)
Stephens, T. M.: test, 2226; ref, 2226(1), 2478(12)
Stephenson, W.: rev, 1046, 1302, 1419, 2065, 2343
Sterling, F. E.: ref, 1351(29)
Sterling, H. M.: test, 1967; ref, 678(18)
Sterling, P. J.: ref, 678(18)
Stern, A.: ref, 2598(1403)
Stern, G. G.: test, 408, 502, 1080, 1745, 2308
Stern, J. A.: ref, 1063(92)
Stern, M. J.: ref, 1240(66), 1498(5769), 2322(9)
Sternberg, L.: ref, 2217(118), 2269(445), 2289(1645), 2602(1703)
Sternberg, R. J.: ref, 653(168), 732(412), 1073(129), 1257(169, 170), 2015(211), 2246(34), 2554(15)
Sterne, A. L.: ref, 1498(5142, 5149, 5150), 2179(202)
Sternfeld, A. E.: test, 1873, 2507, 2666
Sterns, H. L.: ref, 794(364), 1013(78, 86, 119)
Steronko, R. J.: ref, 1498(5372)
Stetson, D.: ref, 1053(81)
Stevens, D. P.: ref, 1914(732)
Stevens, F.: test, 2014
Stevens, F. W.: ref, 2318(1601)
Stevens, G. Z.: test, 187
Stevens, J.: ref, 1459(15), 2217(173), 2621(413), 2641(15)
Stevens, M.: ref, 1883(49)
Stevens, M. R.: ref, 1498(5706)

INDEX OF NAMES

Stevens, Thurow & Associates, Inc.: test, 467, 468, 469, 1177, 2309
Stevenson, D. K.: ref, 1471(54), 2289(1748)
Stevenson, H. W.: ref, 2621(376)
Stevenson, J. F.: ref, 859(834)
Stevenson, L. P.: ref, 2602(2126)
Stevenson, M. B.: ref, 270(125)
Stevenson, M. J.: ref, 1851(36)
Stever, J.: ref, 1109(22), 2598(1716)
Steward, V.: test, 2310, 2311, 2312, 2313, 2314
Stewart, A. J.: ref, 2491(2033, 2034)
Stewart, B. D.: ref, 2300(587)
Stewart, C. A.: ref, 2512(654)
Stewart, D.: ref, 609(220)
Stewart, D. J.: ref, 1831(180)
Stewart, D. M.: test, 2634, 2635
Stewart, D. W.: ref, 344(147), 1126(676), 1538(69), 2208(1554), 2598(1400), 2602(1704, 1705), 2621(265)
Stewart, J.: ref, 344(159), 2602(1817)
Stewart, J. H.: ref, 2598(1860), 2602(2219)
Stewart, J. M.: ref, 1877(9), 2541(9)
Stewart, M.: ref, 1341(154), 1547(322), 2602(1718), 2621(271)
Stewart, M. A.: ref, 2602(2075, 2154), 2608(242), 2621(432)
Stewart, N.: rev, 964, 1353, 2352, 2618
Stewart, R. A.: ref, 860(130), 1229(86)
Stewart, R. A. C.: ref, 860(102), 1229(82), 2343(1036), 2629(103)
Stewart, R. M.: ref, 2289(1679), 2557(223)
Steyaert, J. P.: ref, 2288(86)
Steyn, D. W.: test, 2241
Stick, S.: ref, 2445(3)
Stick, S. L.: ref, 1771(669)
Stickle, F.: ref, 1013(88)
Stickney, S. K.: ref, 1655(113)
Stiefel, D. J.: ref, 2068(87)
Stiggins, R. J.: ref, 76(618), 1568(130), 2160(62)
Stiles, W. B.: ref, 1498(5760), 1923(27)
Stillman, B. W.: test, 957
Stillman, P. L.: ref, 1576(198)
Stilson, D.: ref, 1498(5069)
Stilson, D. W.: ref, 2598(1773)
Stilwell, G. K.: ref, 1498(5211)
Stilwell, S. R.: ref, 2208(1612)
Stilwell, W. E.: ref, 239(13)
Stimmel, B.: ref, 1576(200)
Stimpson, D. V.: ref, 780(1694), 890(336), 1347(7)
Stimpson, M. F.: ref, 780(1694), 1347(7)
Stinard, T. A.: ref, 76(660), 1510(48)
Stiner, A.: ref, 1789(718), 2300(552)
Stipek, D.: ref, 1771(763), 2621(419)
Stipek, D. J.: ref, 1771(810)
Stitt, F. W.: ref, 1904(63)
Stock, W. A.: ref, 76(647), 994(57), 1486(186)
Stocker, M. J.: ref, 283(149)
Stockton, R. A.: ref, 2353(26), 2413(681)
Stocco, J. L.: ref, 2318(1602)
Stodden, R. A.: ref, 2557(232)
Stoffelmayr, B. E.: ref, 1765(14), 1904(122), 2100(10)
Stoffer, G. R.: ref, 501(807)
Stogdill, R. M.: test, 225, 1296, 1746, 1972, 2315
Stokes, E. H.: ref, 1498(5309), 2179(201), 2217(114), 2512(575), 2598(1361), 2602(1826)

Stokols, D.: ref, 226(178, 184), 2598(1533)
Stokols, J.: ref, 2598(1533)
Stoller, J. E.: ref, 1625(106)
Stone, A. R.: test, 2322
Stone, B.: ref, 1914(898)
Stone, B. G.: ref, 2512(655), 2582(16)
Stone, C. P.: test, 2607
Stone, C. R.: rev, 2283, 2284
Stone, E. F.: ref, 1013(92), 1798(225, 261, 269)
Stone, I. R.: exc, 1053
Stone, J. B.: test, 2323
Stone, L.: ref, 1914(715)
Stone, L. A.: test, 1072
Stone, L. J.: rev, 396, 2513
Stone, M.: ref, 2300(529)
Stone, M. H.: test, 1260
Stone, M. K.: ref, 398(118)
Stone, N. W.: ref, 1771(688)
Stone, R.: test, 839
Stone, S.: ref, 2602(1744)
Stone, T. H.: ref, 780(1643)
Stoneburner, R. L.: ref, 212(10), 678(33), 701(84), 1769(79), 1771(764), 2217(177), 2602(1788), 2621(369)
Stonehill, E.: ref, 639(47), 859(773, 848)
Stoner, S.: ref, 1053(70, 74, 82), 2413(634)
Stoner, S. B.: ref, 1914(857)
Stones, C. R.: ref, 1789(723), 1960(82)
Stones, M. J.: ref, 283(152), 859(774, 775), 1462(148), 1503(67), 2598(1655), 2607(187)
Stonnington, H. H.: ref, 1498(5211)
Stoppa, E.: ref, 1914(752)
Storandt, M.: ref, 280(1068), 1109(20), 2598(1401, 1431, 1462, 1690, 1823), 2607(152)
Storer, D.: ref, 941(17)
Storey, A. G.: test, 1961
Storey, R.: ref, 769(41, 45), 859(749, 804), 2208(1544, 1581)
Storms, L.: ref, 1106(360), 1247(162), 1498(5114)
Storms, L. H.: ref, 1247(163)
Storr, M. A.: test, 389
Stotsky, B. A.: ref, 2289(1599), 2602(1605), 2621(228)
Stott, D. H.: test, 321, 782, 2450; ref, 321(38, 40)
Stott, M. W. R.: ref, 1209(36)
Stouffer, G. A. W.: test, 169, 171, 172, 173, 174, 846, 939, 942, 1452, 1454, 1674, 1783, 1872, 1920, 2049, 2306
Stouffer, G. W.: test, 175
Stouffer, S. A.: test, 1557
Stout, J. R.: ref, 2598(1840)
Stracca, M.: ref, 116(553), 282(144), 501(823), 707(17), 1914(761)
Strade, B. W.: test, 2516
Strain, P. S.: ref, 691(30), 1250(12)
Strait, J.: test, 2316
Straley, H. W.: ref, 501(907)
Strand, A. L.: test, 841, 2389
Strand, K. H.: ref, 2300(540)
Strand, L.: ref, 2537(554)
Strang, H. R.: ref, 2165(25)
Strang, L.: ref, 1473(167), 1831(156), 2602(1827)
Strang, R.: rev, 1507, 1512, 2318
Strange, C.: ref, 2300(582)
Strange, W.: ref, 1771(811), 2412(46)
Strassberg, D. S.: ref, 1498(5205, 5770, 5743)

695

Stratford, B.: ref, 1771(690, 699)
Stratta, L.: test, 1311
Stratton, K.: test, 1226
Strauch, A. B.: ref, 2602(1706)
Strauss, B. P. A.: test, 11
Strauss, F. F.: ref, 645(13)
Strauss, H.: ref, 2030(5094), 2512(657, 658, 664), 2602(2220)
Strauss, J. S.: ref, 645(16), 1240(57, 60, 65), 1883(38, 58, 68), 2598(1460, 1721, 1829), 2602(1965), 2608(220)
Strauss, M. E.: ref, 311(31)
Strawser, S.: test, 2612
Streeter, R. E.: ref, 344(143), 2181(10)
Streff, M.: ref, 691(34), 1126(711), 1462(138), 1914(787)
Strein, W.: ref, 2639(2)
Streiner, D. L.: ref, 1498(5206, 5533), 2029(231)
Streissguth, A. P.: ref, 270(98), 2289(1690, 1757), 2598(1534), 2602(1828)
Streitman, J.: ref, 2374(179)
Strichart, S. S.: ref, 691(35), 1126(712), 1224(6), 2602(1966)
Stricker, L. J.: rev, 780, 837, 860, 2410; ref, 1798(257)
Strickland, G. P.: test, 220
Stricklin, A.: ref, 280(1127), 2179(247)
Stricklin, A. B.: ref, 1498(5707)
Striffler, N.: test, 538
Stringer, P.: ref, 639(43, 48), 769(39, 42)
Stringer, S.: ref, 270(135), 311(35), 678(31), 2300(524)
Stringfield, S.: test, 1874
Strite, L. C.: ref, 1498(5092), 2318(1528), 2598(1332)
Strizich, M.: ref, 2587(34)
Strohmer, D. C.: ref, 374(231)
Strohner, H.: ref, 2213(4)
Strom, R.: ref, 1762(1, 2, 3, 4)
Strom, R. D.: test, 1762
Stromberg, E. L.: test, 2317
Strommen, M. P.: test, 2667
Strong, E. K.: test, 2318
Strong, R. W.: test, 206
Strong, S. R.: rev, 658
Strother, C. R.: rev, 852, 963, 1361
Stroud, J. B.: test, 1061, 1894; rev, 1991
Stroup, A. L.: ref, 354(1423), 2208(1555, 1593)
Strowe, L.: test, 824
Strub, R. L.: ref, 280(1066), 2598(1430), 2607(151), 2621(370)
Struening, E. L.: ref, 1106(373), 1498(5523), 1904(99), 1922(14), 2598(1645)
Strümpfer, D. J. W.: ref, 354(1465)
Strupp, H. H.: rev, 1923; ref, 1498(5534, 5708, 5709, 5710, 5711), 1923(23)
Stuart, F.: test, 873, 1868, 2171
Stuart, I. R.: ref, 780(1678)
Stuart, J. E.: test, 1829
Stuart, R. B.: test, 873, 1373, 1868, 2171
Stuck, G. B.: ref, 1108(5), 1473(180, 190), 2582(12, 15), 2602(1931)
Studer, S. E.: test, 815
Stueland, D.: ref, 2208(1657)
Stuit, D. B.: rev, 690, 2015
Stumme, J.: ref, 2269(468)
Stumpf, S. A.: test, 621; ref, 621(1, 2, 3, 4, 5, 6, 7)
Stumphauzer, J. S.: test, 655

Stuntz, J. T.: ref, 953(13)
Sturgeon, D.: ref, 1883(91)
Sturges, P. T.: ref, 2300(442)
Stuss, D. T.: ref, 308(9)
Stutsman, R.: test, 1471
Styfco, S. J.: ref, 1498(5495), 1771(550), 2179(226)
Stylo, D. A.: ref, 1655(107)
Suarez, Y.: ref, 1498(5373)
Subers, D. C.: ref, 2602(1942)
Subkoviak, M. J.: ref, 501(837)
Sucher, F.: test, 1579
Suczek, R.: test, 1170
Suddick, D. E.: ref, 501(935)
Suddick, R. P.: ref, 673(53), 794(451)
Suedfeld, P.: ref, 1547(289)
Suen, H.: ref, 6(59), 1053(76)
Suess, A. R.: rev, 1601, 1603
Suess, W. M.: ref, 2300(566)
Sugarman, A.: ref, 2030(5090)
Sugawara, A. I.: ref, 1771(600)
Sugerman, A. A.: ref, 1655(102)
Sugishita, M.: ref, 1126(734)
Sugita, H.: ref, 1126(734)
Suib, M. R.: ref, 2598(1538)
Suinn, R. M.: test, 1405, 2296, 2353; rev, 2413
Suiter, M. L.: ref, 1126(713)
Suiter, P. A.: test, 2401, 2402
Sullivan, E. T.: test, 2181
Sullivan, J. A.: ref, 780(1679)
Sullivan, J. W.: ref, 311(26)
Sullivan, R. J.: ref, 2372(4)
Suls, J.: ref, 1486(178, 184)
Sultan, F. E.: ref, 1498(5588)
Sultan, S.: ref, 645(22)
Sultmann, W. F.: ref, 1126(781)
Summerlin, M. L.: ref, 1896(11), 2208(1594)
Summers, E. G.: ref, 845(10), 1478(76)
Summers, F.: ref, 1240(61), 1361(65, 66), 1498(5207, 5535), 2491(2029, 2069), 2598(1720)
Sundberg, N. D.: rev, 1148, 1168, 1555, 2079, 2289
Sundell, S.: ref, 1498(5069)
Sunderland, L.: test, 2590
Sung, Y. H.: ref, 2113(260)
Sunshine, P.: ref, 1471(54), 2289(1748)
Super, C. M.: ref, 311(23)
Super, D. D.: rev, 1493
Super, D. E.: test, 371, 658, 2657; rev, 733, 1271, 1839; ref, 372(5)
Supramanium, S.: ref, 639(43, 48), 769(39, 42)
Surma, M. B.: ref, 1825(20)
Surma, M. E.: ref, 1825(22)
Surwit, R. S.: ref, 1931(53)
Sushinsky, L.: ref, 1498(5338)
Sutaria, R.: ref, 1419(696)
Suter, B.: ref, 751(38)
Sutker, L. W.: ref, 2598(1488)
Sutker, P. B.: ref, 116(572, 615), 1498(5230, 5374, 5375, 5536, 5537, 5712, 5713), 1914(789), 2179(219, 220, 248)
Suttell, B. J.: test, 280
Sutter, P.: ref, 6(79)
Sutterer, J. R.: ref, 2374(182)
Sutton, A.: ref, 823(16), 2018(11), 2289(1659), 2608(191)
Sutton, E.: ref, 2413(641)

INDEX OF NAMES

Sutton, J. M.: ref, 859(776)
Sutton, L. P.: ref, 280(1160), 1250(21), 2602(2162), 2641(19)
Sutton, S.: ref, 645(14), 1883(59)
Suydam, M. N.: rev, 804, 1412, 2287
Suzuki, N. S.: ref, 1341(155)
Svanum, S.: ref, 2602(2127), 2621(420)
Sveen, O. B.: ref, 2301(32)
Svendsen, D.: ref, 2598(1790)
Swafford, J. O.: ref, 573(15, 16), 2286(339), 2287(39)
Swain, M.: ref, 361(4), 363(6), 918(2), 1479(336), 1754(82)
Swaminathan, H.: ref, 1257(121)
Swan, M.: ref, 1531(293)
Swann, W. S.: ref, 823(18)
Swanson, B. B.: ref, 1459(16), 1473(221), 1479(381)
Swanson, D. W.: ref, 1498(5484, 5714), 2179(225, 249)
Swanson, E. N.: ref, 2602(1967)
Swanson, G. E.: ref, 1790(10), 2294(121)
Swanson, H. L.: ref, 2602(1707)
Swanson, J. M.: ref, 2602(1622), 2621(233)
Swanson, L.: ref, 226(174), 1351(203), 1754(83, 110), 1769(65), 2160(79), 2218(154), 2602(1829), 2621(310, 371)
Swanson, R. A.: rev, 1591, 1697, 1959, 2193
Swanson, R. M.: rev, 304
Swanson, R. S.: rev, 2184
Swaringer, S.: ref, 878(30)
Swart, D. J.: test, 191, 1141
Swartz, C. P.: ref, 280(1088), 2030(5005), 2037(151), 2598(1511)
Swartz, J. D.: test, 1106; rev, 2491; exc, 1235
Swassing, R.: ref, 2598(1656)
Swearingen, D. J.: ref, 1531(286)
Sweeney, D. R.: ref, 2300(443)
Sweeney, H. W.: ref, 2300(566)
Sweeney, T. J.: ref, 354(1429)
Sweeney, T. M.: ref, 1798(263)
Sweet, J. J.: ref, 1498(5441)
Sweet, R.: test, 2379
Swencionis, C.: ref, 2015(210)
Swendsen, L. A.: ref, 1383(7)
Sweney, A. B.: test, 1538, 2087
Swensen, C. H.: rev, 2065; ref, 2155(13)
Swenson, A.: ref, 338(9)
Swenson, C. H.: ref, 2413(607)
Swensen, W. M.: ref, 1498(5330, 5337, 5432, 5631), 2170(213), 2598(1445, 1578)
Swerdlik, M.: ref, 2602(1830)
Swerdlik, M. E.: ref, 2602(1831, 1968)
Swett, C.: ref, 1904(132)
Swiercinsky, D. P.: ref, 2598(1402, 1535, 1657), 2621(266)
Swift, J. W.: ref, 583(2)
Swift, M.: test, 704, 1049, 1050
Swing, S. R.: ref, 354(1546), 381(75), 1914(892), 2269(479), 2300(555)
Swint, E. B.: ref, 1655(108)
Swinton, S. S.: ref, 995(155)
Swisher, C. N.: ref, 270(77), 678(20), 701(45), 1771(597), 1877(7), 2289(1656), 2557(220)
Swoope, C. C.: ref, 609(208), 859(792)
Sy, M. J.: ref, 2374(177)
Syddall, S.: ref, 581(13), 964(490), 2018(12)
Sydiaha, D.: ref, 859(892)
Sydiaha–Symor, D.: ref, 859(777)
Sykes, E. G.: test, 321
Sylph, J. A.: ref, 1883(29)
Symonds, P. M.: test, 2384; rev, 118, 357, 908, 1784, 2031
Syndulko, K.: ref, 1498(5716)
Syrotuik, J.: ref, 1498(5163)
Szabo, M.: ref, 932(96)
Szapocznik, J.: ref, 1923(29)
Szasz, C. W.: ref, 1479(373, 377)
Szasz, G.: test, 2171
Szeto, J. A.: ref, 1257(113)
Szeto, J. W.: ref, 794(380)
Szoc, R.: ref, 1498(5132), 2598(1351)
Szondi, L.: test, 2388
Szumowski, E. K.: ref, 1492(9)
Szymczuk, M.: ref, 845(8), 932(77), 1192(224)
Tabachnick, B. G.: ref, 2602(1969)
Tabaka–Juedes, E.: test, 561
Taborelli, A.: ref, 2598(1427)
Taft, T. B.: ref, 2246(25)
Tait, P. E.: ref, 2391(1)
Tajima, N.: ref, 1771(734)
Takahashi, K. I.: ref, 401(74), 1460(51), 1853(270), 1904(58), 2598(1344)
Takai, R.: ref, 2134(120), 2581(331)
Talbert, R. L.: ref, 1798(274)
Talbot, D. B.: ref, 2134(121), 2573(1)
Talbott, J. A.: ref, 1498(5376), 2029(208)
Talbott, R.: test, 285
Talkington, J.: ref, 681(46), 1498(5478)
Tallal, P.: ref, 932(127, 128), 1101(52), 1126(787), 1622(56), 2412(45), 2472(32), 2602(2215, 2221), 2608(249)
Talmage, H.: ref, 1479(337)
Taloumis, T.: ref, 1754(98), 2269(471), 2286(323)
Tam, C. I.: ref, 681(75), 860(156), 1969(97), 2598(1547)
Tamez, E. G.: ref, 1498(5377)
Tamkin, A.: ref, 280(1155), 2598(1792)
Tamkin, A. S.: ref, 1498(5538, 5715), 2030(5045, 5077), 2598(1658, 1791)
Tamor, L.: ref, 958(51), 2621(461)
Tan, N.: ref, 2289(1746), 2602(2013)
Tan–Willman, C.: ref, 157(153), 666(7, 8), 2512(665)
Tanck, M. L.: test, 1232
Tannenbaum, A. J.: rev, 643; ref, 2269(467)
Tannenbaum, J.: ref, 1108(1)
Tannenbaum, S. I.: ref, 1498(5116)
Tapasak, R. C.: ref, 1229(88), 2602(1832)
Tapley, S. M.: ref, 2246(24), 2285(10)
Tarana, E.: ref, 1883(58)
Taranta, A.: ref, 1798(279)
Tarlow, S.: ref, 2598(1434), 2607(154)
Tarneus, M.: ref, 534(100)
Tarnopolsky, A.: ref, 941(31)
Tarpey, E. A.: ref, 2374(195)
Tarr, L. H.: ref, 116(573), 1498(5378)
Tarrier, N.: ref, 116(634)
Tarrier, R. B.: test, 1051
Tarsy, D.: ref, 1904(123)
Tartaglia, J. F.: ref, 270(126), 338(10)
Tarter, R. E.: ref, 1498(5208), 2607(126)
Taschow, H. G.: ref, 363(16), 1007(43)
Tatsuoka, M. M.: test, 2208

Taub, H. A.: ref, 720(67)
Taub, H. B.: ref, 280(1058), 2602(1708)
Taub, J. M.: ref, 354(1510), 609(218)
Tauber, R. T.: ref, 2413(621)
Taulbee, E. S.: rev, 2587, 2588; ref, 1498(5547, 5773)
Taunton–Blackwood, A.: ref, 883(93)
Tavakoli, M.: ref, 1547(312)
Tavormina, J.: ref, 1498(5039, 5262), 1798(202)
Taylor, A. M.: ref, 1771(574)
Taylor, A. P.: test, 2395
Taylor, B. M.: ref, 932(102), 1769(61)
Taylor, C. A.: ref, 1798(288), 1904(115)
Taylor, C. B.: ref, 1904(133), 1940(84)
Taylor, C. I.: ref, 1498(5459)
Taylor, E.: ref, 962(31), 964(503), 1503(68), 1853(291), 2602(2018), 2621(390)
Taylor, E. K.: test, 2050, 2272; rev, 799, 1493, 1808, 1984, 1985, 2262, 2552, 2614, 2617
Taylor, E. M.: exc, 951, 953
Taylor, G. A.: ref, 932(98, 112), 1498(5063), 1568(145), 2160(76), 2208(1525), 2318(1547)
Taylor, G. C.: ref, 2657(108)
Taylor, H. E.: ref, 501(795)
Taylor, H. R.: rev, 1163, 2228, 2537
Taylor, I. A.: ref, 1300(118), 1789(684), 2512(605, 608, 625)
Taylor, I. G.: ref, 1153(8), 2018(19)
Taylor, J.: test, 317, 320; ref, 2413(687), 2598(1861), 2602(1833, 2129)
Taylor, J. B.: ref, 1498(5209)
Taylor, J. C.: ref, 1831(148, 149), 2289(1693), 2602(1853), 2621(314)
Taylor, K. F.: ref, 354(1534), 2134(122), 2581(332)
Taylor, L.: ref, 344(165)
Taylor, L. B.: test, 1776
Taylor, L. J.: ref, 398(99), 1126(740), 1914(733), 2602(1709, 1970), 2608(186)
Taylor, L. K.: ref, 551(70), 734(5)
Taylor, L. R.: ref, 1855(22, 23)
Taylor, M. A.: ref, 2598(1809)
Taylor, N.: ref, 1473(174), 1479(347)
Taylor, N. E.: ref, 1479(343)
Taylor, P. A.: exc, 551
Taylor, P. M.: ref, 2289(1764)
Taylor, R. A.: test, 1322
Taylor, R. L.: ref, 6(62), 1424(59, 60, 76, 77), 1425(1), 1771(691), 2602(2128), 2621(421)
Taylor, R. M.: test, 2396
Taylor, R. N.: rev, 1365, 2180
Taylor, S. E.: test, 1994; ref, 1771(538)
Taylor, T. D.: ref, 1831(132)
Taylor, T. R.: test, 886
Taylor, V.: test, 541
Tazuma, L.: ref, 609(217, 224)
Teaching Resources Corporation: test, 231
Teagarden, F. M.: rev, 381, 1471, 1505, 2557
Teagno, L.: ref, 116(614)
Teasdale, G. R.: ref, 1126(714)
Teasdale, J. D.: ref, 859(891)
Tecce, J. J.: ref, 1655(92, 93)
Technisonic Studios, Inc.: test, 230
Tedeschi, J. T.: ref, 2491(2070)
Tedford, W. H.: ref, 157(137), 243(119), 751(8), 1106(363), 2179(208)
Teegarden, L.: rev, 1506, 1511

Teglasi, H.: ref, 751(39)
Tegtmeyer, P. F.: ref, 1498(5587), 2598(1693)
Teichman, M.: ref, 2300(609)
Teichman, Y.: ref, 2300(546)
Tejani, A.: ref, 280(1124), 2602(1971), 2608(221)
Tekieli, M. E.: ref, 961(3)
Teleford, R.: ref, 2598(1536), 2607(171)
Tellegen, A.: test, 1370; rev, 859, 860; ref, 1498(5238)
Teller, H. E.: ref, 2318(1616)
Temple, I. G.: ref, 226(175), 794(381), 1126(741), 2244(36)
Templer, A. J.: test, 1827
Templer, D. I.: ref, 609(207), 1498(5194, 5379, 5539, 5540), 2598(1659)
Templin, M. C.: test, 2412; rev, 1101
Tenenbaum, G.: ref, 2300(444)
Teng, E. L.: ref, 1969(103)
Tennant, C.: ref, 941(21, 26, 27), 1883(92, 93)
Tennyson, C. L.: ref, 1257(171)
Tennyson, R. D.: ref, 1257(171, 172)
Tennyson, W. W.: rev, 1716
Terborg, J. R.: test, 1366; ref, 354(1553)
Terenzini, P. T.: ref, 501(869, 904)
Terestman, N.: ref, 2289(1772)
Terman, L. M.: test, 2289
Terrell, F.: ref, 2413(687), 2598(1861), 2602(1833, 2129)
Terrell, S. L.: ref, 2598(1861), 2602(1833, 2129)
Terry, J. A.: ref, 294(13)
Tervoort, B. T.: ref, 280(1125), 2602(1972)
Tesch, F. E.: ref, 116(598), 890(353)
Teschner, R. V.: exc, 749
Tesiny, E. P.: ref, 964(507, 513)
Teska, J. A.: ref, 212(10), 678(33), 701(84), 1771(764), 2217(177)
Tesolowski, D. G.: test, 904
Tessier, K. E.: ref, 2374(181)
Tessier, L.: ref, 1922(14)
Tetlow, E. W.: ref, 1555(334)
Teu, J. D.: ref, 1351(182)
Tew, B.: ref, 321(41), 2018(16), 2557(233), 2602(1973), 2608(222)
Teyber, E. C.: ref, 859(858)
Thacker, B. T.: ref, 1498(5439)
Thackray, D.: test, 1998, 2490
Thackray, L.: test, 2490
Thalbourne, M. A.: ref, 859(960)
Tharp, R. G.: ref, 2608(179)
Tharp, V. K.: ref, 1498(5716)
Thauberger, P. C.: ref, 859(777, 892, 937), 1197(314), 1498(5717)
Thaxton, A. B.: ref, 5(167)
Thaxton, N. A.: ref, 5(167)
Thayer, P. W.: rev, 1676, 1901, 2180, 2194
Theberge, L.: ref, 1106(374)
Theilgaard, A.: ref, 2598(1537)
Thelen, M. H.: ref, 2300(334), 2608(190)
Thetford, W. N.: rev, 1106
Thexton, J. D.: test, 2439
Thibeault, R. J.: ref, 76(597), 1866(33)
Thiel, G. W.: ref, 6(92), 2289(1773), 2598(1862), 2621(422)
Thiele, C. L.: rev, 345
Thiele, D. A.: ref, 1498(5759)
Thies, A. P.: ref, 1436(16)

Thomae–Forgues, M.: ref, 1576(215, 223)
Thomas, B.: ref, 76(635), 994(54), 2512(626)
Thomas, C. A.: rev, 826
Thomas, C. B.: ref, 2030(4968)
Thomas, C. L.: ref, 76(636)
Thomas, D.: ref, 639(52)
Thomas, D. B.: ref, 311(46)
Thomas, D. M.: test, 1945
Thomas, E. C.: ref, 653(175)
Thomas, E. G.: ref, 374(194)
Thomas, J. C.: ref, 1295(288)
Thomas, J. L.: ref, 2286(304)
Thomas, J. R.: ref, 398(100)
Thomas, L. E.: ref, 2318(1562, 1598)
Thomas, N. G.: ref, 2512(666)
Thomas, P. J.: ref, 707(20), 1493(123), 1771(575), 2602(2130), 2614(22)
Thomas, R. E.: ref, 1484(12), 2441(34)
Thompson, A. J.: ref, 1192(183)
Thompson, A. P.: ref, 2340(12), 2347(5, 7)
Thompson, A. S.: test, 371; rev, 10, 401, 2262; ref, 372(5)
Thompson, B.: ref, 1192(209, 210), 2320(1, 2)
Thompson, C. C.: ref, 2598(1567)
Thompson, C. W.: test, 2498
Thompson, D.: ref, 1562(7), 1591(1), 1593(1), 1595(2), 1601(2), 1610(1), 2602(1793)
Thompson, D. L.: ref, 501(908)
Thompson, D. S.: ref, 547(4)
Thompson, E.: ref, 1052(4), 1771(768), 2602(2145), 2621(427)
Thompson, G.: ref, 270(86)
Thompson, G. R.: test, 1889
Thompson, H. J.: ref, 2218(155), 2598(1660)
Thompson, J.: ref, 1567(19), 2602(2165)
Thompson, J. C.: ref, 859(938), 2300(567)
Thompson, J. E.: ref, 1451(3)
Thompson, J. M.: test, 776
Thompson, K.: ref, 2598(1398)
Thompson, M.: ref, 1197(285), 1789(656)
Thompson, P.: ref, 2512(632), 2602(2224)
Thompson, P. A.: ref, 2300(602)
Thompson, R. J.: ref, 1498(5541), 2289(1646), 2602(2131, 2222)
Thompson, S. B.: ref, 577(2)
Thompson, S. K.: test, 2465
Thompson, T.: ref, 1498(5509)
Thompson, W. D.: ref, 2322(11)
Thompson, W. E.: ref, 1960(79)
Thomsen, J.: ref, 2598(1537)
Thomson, A. J.: ref, 280(1059), 1126(677), 2348(1), 2350(14)
Thomson, E. I. M.: rev, 2077
Thomson, G. H.: rev, 2269
Thomson, L.: ref, 1655(84)
Thomson–Rountree, P.: ref, 704(22, 23), 1351(204)
Thoreson, R. W.: ref, 2300(427)
Thormahlen, P.: test, 2508
Thorndike, R. L.: test, 361, 362, 483, 1341, 2289; rev, 354, 487, 508, 736, 772, 798, 876, 2228, 2298, 2410, 2512, 2621; ref, 2289(1647)
Thorndike, R. M.: rev, 547
Thorne, F. C.: test, 1162; ref, 1162(18, 19, 20)
Thornell, J. G.: ref, 398(101)
Thornton, C. C.: ref, 1498(5210), 1969(89)

Thornton, R. F.: test, 1545
Thornton, S.: ref, 1883(67)
Thorpe, J. S.: test, 1106
Thorpe, L. P.: test, 357, 2260; rev, 2621
Thorson, J. A.: ref, 780(1661)
Thorsteinsson, G.: ref, 1498(5211)
Thorum, A. R.: test, 924
Thouless, R. H.: rev, 2594
Thrash, M. L.: ref, 1940(86)
Thrasher, R.: test, 1483, 1484
Threadgill, J.: ref, 1257(148)
Thronesbery, C.: ref, 2598(1607)
Thumin, F.: ref, 2598(1403)
Thune, E. S.: ref, 1099(71, 72, 73)
Thurber, S.: exc, 2478
Thurlow, M. L.: ref, 1771(574)
Thurman, R. L.: test, 1770; ref, 1192(257), 2621(449)
Thurmond, V. B.: ref, 2292(24)
Thurston, J. R.: test, 797, 1348, 1654
Thurstone, L. L.: test, 477, 478, 898, 1176, 1455, 1780, 2262, 2269, 2276, 2499, 2500, 2610
Thurstone, T. G.: test, 631, 1557, 1841, 1995, 2269, 2276, 2500, 2530
Thvedt, J. E.: test, 1134
Thwing, E.: test, 1496, 1504
Thwing, E. J.: test, 1492
Thyer, B. A.: ref, 2300(610)
Tibbenham, A.: ref, 321(43)
Tichenor, C. C.: ref, 2068(86)
Tickle, L. S.: ref, 1771(711)
Tidwell, R.: test, 2207; ref, 1831(199), 2132(3)
Tiedeman, D. V.: rev, 2118, 2657; exc, 76, 937
Tiegs, E. W.: test, 357, 2181
Tien, H. C.: test, 1743
Tierney, R. J.: ref, 1126(714, 715), 2286(344)
Tiffin, J.: test, 111, 1936, 1938, 1941, 1946, 1947, 1948, 1952, 1956, 1957, 1958, 1959
Tilkian, A.: ref, 1498(5097)
Till, J. A.: rev, 212, 1332
Tillar, T. C.: ref, 1051(16)
Tillman, C. E.: ref, 720(66), 1568(121), 2002(3)
Tillman, M. H.: rev, 299
Tillman, T. W.: ref, 1771(603)
Tilquin, C.: ref, 116(599)
Tilson, L. M.: test, 1008
Time, Inc.: test, 2503, 2504
Timm, S.: ref, 558(72), 1498(5607)
Timmer, T.: ref, 678(36)
Timmins, P.: ref, 1877(10), 2289(1745)
Timmons, J.: ref, 378(17), 2472(28)
Tindall, R. C.: ref, 534(102), 1424(41), 2608(204)
Tinder, P.: ref, 922(10), 1771(652)
Ting, G.: ref, 270(83), 311(25), 678(21)
Tingstrom, D. H.: ref, 1498(5214)
Tinker, M. A.: rev, 766, 767, 1060, 2520; exc, 767
Tinklenberg, J. R.: ref, 152(12), 2598(1498)
Tinsley, D. J.: ref, 1495(82, 89), 1726(355), 2318(1548, 1570), 2537(551)
Tinsley, H. E. A.: test, 1497; ref, 1495(82, 89), 1726(355), 2318(1548), 2413(584, 585, 700), 2537(551)
Tips, M. L.: ref, 1568(127)
Tipton, R. D.: ref, 1063(106), 2297(12)
Tipton, R. M.: ref, 374(226), 2581(346)
Tirre, W. C.: ref, 1013(116), 2621(417)

Tisher, M.: test, 397
Tisher, R. P.: test, 2531
Titmus Optical Co., Inc.: test, 2506
Tittle, C. K.: rev, 483, 1341; exc, 2602; ref, 1270(75, 77)
Tittler, B. I.: ref, 243(121), 872(18)
Tittmar, H. G.: ref, 859(793, 855)
Tivan, T.: ref, 1424(44)
Tizard, B.: ref, 1567(14), 2602(1834), 2608(207)
Tjosvold, D.: ref, 666(3)
Toback, C.: ref, 280(1126), 964(499), 2602(1974)
Tobacyk, J.: ref, 794(449), 2029(219), 2208(1636, 1696)
Tobey, E. A.: ref, 691(44), 766(29), 960(14), 1126(742), 1771(692), 2289(1736)
Tobin, A. R.: test, 2159
Todd, J.: ref, 2598(1404)
Todd, P. B.: ref, 1498(5380)
Todd, R.: ref, 483(21), 1473(155)
Todd, R. M.: ref, 374(235)
Todt, E. H.: ref, 116(616)
Toews, W.: ref, 2160(69)
Togurri, A. G.: ref, 2602(2009)
Tokar, E. B.: ref, 1479(323)
Tokar, J. T.: ref, 780(1677)
Tolbert, E. L.: ref, 2581(345)
Tolhurst, G. C.: ref, 2646(10)
Tollison, C. D.: ref, 1498(5450)
Tolna, J.: ref, 1419(690), 2030(5038), 2322(13), 2557(230)
Tolonen, M.: ref, 2030(4995, 5011), 2598(1469)
Tolor, A.: ref, 280(1176), 751(43)
Tomblin, J. B.: ref, 1192(197), 1193(140), 1471(52), 2289(1668), 2557(222), 2602(1759)
Tomelleri, C. J.: ref, 354(1492), 1771(660), 1831(170), 1853(283), 2322(12), 2621(339)
Tomkiewicz, J.: ref, 1798(273)
Tomkiewicz, S.: ref, 2602(1817)
Tomlinson, C. N.: ref, 2550(12)
Tomlinson-Keasey, C.: ref, 1473(189), 1726(358), 1771(693, 694), 2286(324)
Tompkins, C. A.: ref, 1851(28, 41)
Toner, I. J.: ref, 1771(576)
Toney, D. H.: ref, 251(1), 290(9), 1771(754)
Tonge, W. L.: ref, 941(17)
Tonne, H. A.: rev, 1950
Tooley, M.: ref, 860(96)
Toombs, M. S.: ref, 200(19, 20), 896(9), 960(18, 19), 1814(8), 2412(44, 47)
Toomey, K. E.: ref, 1319(78)
Toone, B. K.: ref, 1485(65)
Toops, H. A.: test, 1510, 1716, 2015
Tooze, F. H. G.: test, 2511
Topetzes, N. J.: ref, 1547(262, 263)
Toplis, J.: exc, 2369
Torch, E. M.: ref, 1498(5417)
Tores, C.: ref, 609(227)
Torgerson, T. L.: rev, 935
Torgesen, J.: ref, 1126(685), 2602(1711)
Torgesen, J. K.: ref, 551(63), 653(146, 157), 1126(773), 2289(1774), 2602(1710, 2132), 2621(267, 311, 372)
Torki, M. A.: ref, 1498(5718)
Toro, M.: test, 1357, 1358
Toronto, A. S.: test, 668, 2109; ref, 290(5)
Torpy, D. M.: ref, 890(362)

Torrance, E. P.: test, 1253, 2495, 2496, 2512; ref, 1479(369), 2199(7), 2289(1792), 2496(34, 36), 2512(584, 586, 596, 606, 607, 627, 634, 651, 667), 2602(2223), 2613(82)
Torrey, E. F.: ref, 2598(1561)
Torshen, K. P.: ref, 1896(9)
Tosi, D. J.: exc, 1789; ref, 1498(5253, 5603), 1547(270), 1789(685), 2413(605)
Toth, J. C.: ref, 1197(315)
Touchette, P. E.: ref, 2289(1679), 2557(223)
Touchton, J. G.: ref, 2134(101)
Touhey, J. C.: ref, 298(166)
Touliatos, J.: test, 1539, 1857; ref, 116(546), 344(148, 160), 2012(4, 5)
Tower, R. B.: ref, 1771(695, 765)
Towne, W. S.: ref, 1126(774), 1462(126), 1498(5381, 5543), 1771(578), 2113(240), 2602(1713, 1714, 2135), 2621(268, 424)
Towner, G.: test, 2570; ref, 6(58)
Townes, B. D.: ref, 719(39), 2598(1661), 2602(1835, 1975, 2133), 2621(438)
Townsend, A.: rev, 171, 1530, 1568, 2288
Townsend, J.: ref, 2602(1770)
Townsend, M. A. R.: ref, 1914(734)
Townsend, N. M.: ref, 2289(1679), 2557(223)
Townsend, P. C.: ref, 2029(209)
Townsend, P. J.: ref, 859(756), 1013(56)
Toyokura, Y.: ref, 1126(734)
Trabue, M. R.: test, 174
Tracey, T. J.: ref, 2134(110, 119, 136), 2318(1591)
Tracor, Inc.: test, 2514
Tracy, D.: ref, 2512(616)
Tracy, D. B.: ref, 2300(351)
Tracy, P.: test, 1893
Trahan, D.: ref, 280(1127)
Tramill, J. K.: ref, 2602(2134)
Tramill, J. L.: ref, 2602(2134)
Transou, D. L.: ref, 2300(433)
Traub, R. E.: ref, 590(376), 1257(114)
Traugh, C.: ref, 1192(253)
Traupmann, K. L.: ref, 2598(1793)
Trause, M. A.: ref, 212(4), 1622(42), 2598(1521)
Trautt, G. M.: ref, 1547(281)
Travers, K. J.: rev, 573
Travers, R. M. W.: rev, 947, 2165
Travis, C. B.: ref, 1789(686)
Travis, F.: ref, 2512(628)
Travis, T. A.: ref, 859(805)
Traxler, A. E.: test, 2518, 2519, 2520, 2567; rev, 1271, 1557, 2288
Traxler, A. J.: ref, 678(28)
Traxlere, A. J.: ref, 701(64), 964(498), 1424(48), 2289(1719)
Traynor, T. D.: ref, 681(35)
Tredoux, M.: test, 191
Treffinger, D.: ref, 2512(616)
Treloar, J. H.: ref, 962(30), 1540(16), 2260(43), 2269(469)
Trembath, R. J.: ref, 589(1)
Trembley, P. W.: test, 1290; ref, 1769(96), 2286(340), 2621(423)
Trent, J. T.: ref, 2300(568), 2353(37)
Trent, P. J.: ref, 2300(454), 2441(35)
Trent, R.: test, 2253
Trentham, L. L.: ref, 2512(629)

INDEX OF NAMES

Trepanier, M. L.: ref, 1126(743), 1771(696)
Treppa, J. A.: ref, 1789(662, 687), 2300(390, 445)
Tressler, J. C.: test, 2523
Trevenen, C.: ref, 325(34)
Trevithick, L.: ref, 1498(5382)
Trickett, E. J.: test, 409; ref, 409(4, 9)
Triggs, F. O.: rev, 2271
Trigos, M. C.: test, 1062
Trimble, C. S.: ref, 551(52)
Trimble, H. C.: rev, 1911, 2287
Trimble, M. R.: ref, 1883(75)
Tripathi, L. B.: ref, 2491(2075)
Tripathi, R. R.: ref, 2491(2050)
Trippett, C. J.: ref, 472(15), 859(871), 883(99)
Trivedi, A.: ref, 1771(577), 2217(119), 2602(1712)
Trivedi, G.: test, 2236
Trojanowicz, R. C.: ref, 1213(26)
Troll, E. W.: ref, 2160(61)
Trontel, E. H.: ref, 1798(263, 307)
Trotman, F. K.: ref, 1473(143), 1754(65)
Troutman, A. P.: test, 709
Troutman, J. G.: ref, 501(838), 2289(1691)
Troyer, M. E.: test, 1066
Truckenmiller, J. L.: ref, 1170(235), 2491(2071)
Trudel, G.: ref, 883(102)
Truex, S.: ref, 719(27), 766(21), 958(40), 1007(12)
Trupin, E.: ref, 719(39), 2621(438)
Trupin, E. W.: ref, 2602(1835, 2133)
Truscott, R. B.: ref, 501(870), 2002(5)
Trussell, R. P.: ref, 2300(446)
Tryniechi, T.: ref, 703(7)
Tryon, G. S.: ref, 1531(283, 287), 2318(1571), 2374(177, 190)
Tryon, R. C.: rev, 2269
Tsai, L.: ref, 2602(2154), 2608(242), 2621(432)
Tsai, M.: ref, 1498(5542)
Tse, P. C.: ref, 283(134), 1513(20), 1771(516), 1914(702), 1948(93), 2598(1297)
Tseng, M. S.: ref, 1498(5215)
Tsoi, W. F.: ref, 859(778), 1498(5212)
Tsu, V.: ref, 872(11)
Tsujimoto, R. N.: ref, 354(1474), 1498(5383), 1789(675)
Tsushima, W. T.: ref, 1126(774), 1462(126), 1498(5381, 5543, 5544), 1771(578), 2113(240), 2598(1405, 1662), 2602(1713, 1714, 2135), 2621(268, 424)
Tuck, B. F.: test, 2134; ref, 2134(106, 137)
Tucker, D. M.: ref, 1498(5035, 5771)
Tucker, G. H.: ref, 2598(1538)
Tucker, G. R.: ref, 1771(606), 1914(758)
Tucker, R. K.: ref, 1192(165)
Tuckman, B. W.: test, 777; rev, 2535, 2539; ref, 777(1)
Tuddenham, R. D.: exc, 321
Tuinman, J. J.: rev, 2253, 2641
Tukko, H.: ref, 2512(608)
Tulchin, S. H.: rev, 2315
Tulchinsky, D.: ref, 1498(5517)
Tull, M. J.: ref, 890(338)
Tullman, G. M.: ref, 2300(498)
Tullman, M. J.: ref, 2300(498)
Tuma, A. H.: ref, 1351(24, 27, 30), 1498(5153, 5384, 5385, 5759), 2179(203)
Tuma, J. M.: ref, 1771(515), 2030(4961), 2602(1591, 1836, 2136)

Tune, L. E.: ref, 1883(78, 94)
Tung, T. M.: ref, 609(212)
Tunkel, L. S.: test, 1562
Tunmer, W. E.: ref, 1771(812), 2621(462)
Tuohino, V.: ref, 1498(5352), 2030(5009), 2598(1525)
Turaids, D.: test, 2251
Turnbull, C. E.: ref, 877(19)
Turnbull, H.: ref, 252(2), 775(2)
Turnbull, M. E.: rev, 236, 894
Turnbull, W. W.: rev, 326, 720, 1191, 1808, 2271
Turner, C. E.: rev, 997, 2114
Turner, D. J.: ref, 681(50)
Turner, F.: ref, 1831(209)
Turner, I. F.: ref, 874(43)
Turner, J.: ref, 859(921), 1046(568), 1498(5386, 5485, 5658)
Turner, P. E.: ref, 2598(1627)
Turner, R. G.: ref, 501(808, 839), 1046(578), 2208(1556, 1557), 2581(311), 2598(1406, 1407)
Turner, R. K.: ref, 823(13), 1567(8)
Turner, R. R.: ref, 1473(168), 1478(70)
Turner, R. W.: ref, 681(50)
Turner, S. M.: ref, 860(123), 2300(587)
Turney, A. H.: rev, 118, 1272
Turns, R.: ref, 883(93)
Turnure, J. E.: ref, 1771(574)
Turpin, G.: ref, 1883(91)
Turpin, W. B.: ref, 6(67)
Turton, L. J.: rev, 866, 896
Tuska, S. A.: test, 476, 2390
Tusnády, G.: ref, 280(1139), 964(505), 1419(690), 2030(5038), 2289(1753), 2322(13), 2557(230)
Tutone, R. M.: ref, 1904(64)
Tuttle, H. G.: ref, 477(25)
Tuttle, M.: ref, 1257(155)
Twa, R. J.: ref, 354(1554), 503(5), 2208(1669), 2491(2092)
Twemilow, S. W.: ref, 1789(653)
Twemlow, S. W.: ref, 1765(10)
Twiggs, D. G.: ref, 6(83)
Twitchell–Allen, D.: test, 2526
Tyack, D.: test, 1286
Tyer, Z. E.: ref, 354(1527), 780(1697), 794(422), 2413(673)
Tyler, L. E.: rev, 477, 478, 648, 794, 994, 1073, 1795
Tyler, N. B.: ref, 1387(14)
Tyler, R. W.: rev, 487, 508, 2166
Tyler, S.: test, 1243
Tyma, S.: test, 824
Tymchuk, A. J.: ref, 2598(1794), 2602(2137)
Tyrer, J. H.: test, 1963
Tyrer, P.: ref, 2300(447)
Tyson, G. A.: ref, 354(1424)
Tyson, H. L.: test, 881
Tzeng, O.: ref, 1319(82), 1914(840)
Tziner, A.: ref, 1495(79), 1497(24), 1508(114)
UBEA Research Foundation: test, 2533
Udall, L.: ref, 357(523), 1466(4), 1831(212)
Uhl, N. P.: test, 1159
Uhlemann, M. R.: ref, 2340(12), 2347(5, 7)
Ulatowska, H. K.: ref, 2598(1843), 2607(218)
Ullagaddi, S.: ref, 780(1680)
Ullman, D. G.: ref, 932(67), 1492(8), 1515(16), 1754(66), 1771(631), 2217(120), 2602(2224), 2621(269)

Ullom, J.: ref, 1498(5031)
Ulmer, G.: test, 1414, 2474, 2475
Ulrich, R. F.: ref, 1240(63)
Umansky, W.: ref, 1425(2)
Umeh, B. J.: ref, 270(133), 2289(1747)
Unares–Orama, N.: ref, 2472(13)
Underwood, L. E.: ref, 2602(2123)
Undheim, J. O.: ref, 653(147)
Ungerer, J.: ref, 113(26), 1904(103)
Ungerleider, J. T.: ref, 751(32), 1170(236), 1498(5545), 2598(1663)
United Cerebral Palsy of the Bluegrass: test, 1322
United States Employment Service: test, 1163, 2535, 2536, 2537, 2538, 2539
US Military Enlistment Processing Command: test, 202
Uno, T.: ref, 2512(579)
Unwin, S. M.: test, 825; ref, 149(2)
Upshall, C. C.: rev, 332, 1940
Upshur, J.: test, 1483, 1484
Urban, M. D.: ref, 2598(1539)
Urban, W. H.: test, 751
Urbanski, C.: ref, 553(22), 2287(38), 2288(88)
Urberg, K.: ref, 2269(439)
Urist, J.: ref, 2030(4972)
Ursano, R. J.: ref, 116(635), 747(5), 751(44), 780(1710), 966(178), 1046(590), 1486(189), 1494(11), 1498(5772), 2030(5095), 2037(156), 2155(14), 2491(2110), 2598(1863)
Ushpiz, V.: ref, 2413(661)
Uttley, D.: ref, 1240(56)
Utz, P.: ref, 2134(112)
Uzzell, B. P.: ref, 2598(1664)
Vacc, N. A.: ref, 2030(4963), 2208(1547), 2387(6), 2602(2138)
Vacca, R. T.: ref, 845(11), 1570(10)
Vaccaro, P.: ref, 2300(398, 469)
Vachon, M. L. S.: ref, 941(48), 2208(1694)
Vadher, A.: ref, 1883(95)
Vahdat, P.: ref, 1498(5621)
Vaida, C.: ref, 2300(574)
Vaidya, S.: ref, 398(124), 2287(40)
Vail, N.: test, 2325
Vaillant, G. E.: ref, 501(911), 941(21), 2491(2093), 2598(1795)
Vaitenas, R.: ref, 780(1662, 1663), 966(174), 2037(150), 2318(1549), 2491(2030)
Vale, D. W.: ref, 1798(270)
Valencia, R. R.: ref, 1424(88), 1914(822)
Valencia, S.: ref, 719(36)
Valenti, J. J.: test, 2365
Valentine, J. D.: ref, 1851(48)
Valentine, L. D.: exc, 1798
Valesio, P.: rev, 521
Valett, R. E.: test, 257, 699, 1182, 1927, 1928, 2290, 2543, 2544; rev, 1764, 2252
Valine, W. J.: ref, 2413(591)
Vallano, T. W.: 1568(124)
Valle, R. S.: ref, 2300(372)
Valliant, P. M.: ref, 2208(1697)
Valmont, W. J.: rev, 2202
Van Blaricom, V. L.: test, 2634, 2635
Van Camp, S. S.: ref, 953(15)
Vance, B.: ref, 2602(2140)
Vance, F. L.: rev, 116, 118, 2327; ref, 2134(107), 2318(1559, 1569)

Vance, H.: ref, 6(63), 1771(632), 1969(118, 119), 2602(1715, 1837, 1839, 1840, 1841, 1842, 1843, 1844, 1845, 1976, 1977, 1979)
Vance, H. B.: ref, 1769(41), 1771(697, 698), 1969(104), 2218(156), 2602(1628, 1838, 1978), 2621(235)
Van Dam–Baggen, R. M. J.: ref, 883(95)
Van Demark, A. A.: ref, 1851(26)
Vandenberg, S. G.: exc, 535; ref, 558(63), 860(114), 1914(790)
van den Hoed, J.: ref, 1498(5742)
VanDercar, D. H.: ref, 2300(569)
Vandergoot, D.: ref, 2579(1)
Vandergriff, A. F.: ref, 2602(1852, 2143)
Vander Kolk, C. J.: ref, 2598(1408)
van der Linde, R. H.: test, 839
Vanderplas, M. A.: ref, 1914(872)
Vanderploeg, A. J.: ref, 202(8), 1193(141)
Van Der Ploeg, H. M.: ref, 2300(499)
Van Der Spuy, H. I. J.: ref, 280(1142), 874(47), 1914(781), 2030(5006), 2153(2), 2208(1560), 2598(1512)
Vander Stoep, L. P.: ref, 270(106), 1492(7), 1771(643), 2289(1702), 2598(1569)
Vandiver, P. L.: ref, 2289(1737), 2602(1980)
Vandiver, S. S.: ref, 2289(1737), 2602(1980)
Van Dongen, H. R.: ref, 2602(1716)
Van Doorninck, W.: ref, 270(140), 311(37)
Van Doorninck, W. J.: ref, 302(27), 1126(652), 2602(1608), 2621(231)
Van Dyke, C.: ref, 113(26), 1904(103)
Van Dyne, W. T.: ref, 751(20), 1063(137), 1555(343)
Vane, J. R.: test, 2547, 2548; ref, 302(39), 1424(78), 2289(1775), 2608(240)
Van Erd, M.: ref, 1547(286)
Van Etten, C.: ref, 922(8), 1250(16)
Van Etten, G.: test, 247, 248, 249
Van Hagen, J.: ref, 2289(1617), 2602(1653)
Van Hecke, G. R.: rev, 69, 71
Van Hemelrijck, T.: ref, 1498(5513)
Van Hoose, T. A.: ref, 283(151), 859(875), 1197(301), 2638(138)
Van Houten, V. W.: ref, 280(1021), 643(127)
Van Kammen, D. P.: ref, 1498(5387)
Van Maanen, J.: ref, 1508(117)
Vannicelli, M.: ref, 751(30), 1240(62), 1904(104, 105), 1922(13, 18), 1923(13, 24), 2328(4)
Vannucci, R. C.: ref, 270(159), 678(37), 1420(3)
Van Ord, A.: ref, 1240(57), 1883(38, 58)
Van Putte, A. W.: ref, 1831(181)
Van Putten, T.: ref, 1351(28, 34, 36), 1655(103, 124), 2598(1864)
Van Riper, C.: test, 1865
Van Roekel, B. H.: rev, 720, 748, 932, 1140, 1430, 2033, 2034, 2292
van Staden, J. D.: test, 1041
Van Steenberg, N.: rev, 1046
Van Steenberg, N. J.: rev, 2499
Van Tuinen, M.: ref, 558(69), 1203(10), 1798(271), 2413(665)
Van Wagenen, M. J.: test, 1505
Varma, P. N.: ref, 280(1124), 2602(1971, 1971), 2608(221)
Varni, J. W.: ref, 874(45), 1201(76), 1361(63), 2602(1678)

INDEX OF NAMES

Varro, L.: ref, 1257(130), 2015(200)
Vasu, E. S.: ref, 1257(159), 1498(5601)
Vaughan, L. J.: test, 2582
Vaughan, M.: ref, 1462(154), 1485(60), 2598(1796)
Vaughan, M. M.: ref, 1446(17), 2512(580)
Vaughn, B.: ref, 1197(316), 1798(298), 2179(250)
Vaughn, B. E.: ref, 311(40)
Vaughn, C.: ref, 1883(72, 86)
Vaught, G. M.: ref, 780(1676), 1229(88), 2602(1832)
Vaux, A.: ref, 1771(707)
Vazquez, N.: ref, 683(1)
Veal, M. C.: ref, 1771(645), 2472(16)
Veal, R.: exc, 503
Vebersax, J. S.: ref, 1498(5679), 1765(13)
Vecchio, R.: ref, 994(55)
Vecchio, R. P.: ref, 1296(184)
Vecchiotti, D. I.: ref, 2029(236)
Vecker, A. E.: ref, 1498(5719)
Veeraraghavan, V.: ref, 859(779), 2030(4973)
Vega, A.: ref, 2598(1797)
Vela, J. E.: ref, 486(311)
Velasco, M. M.: ref, 751(34)
Veldman, D. J.: test, 2142; rev, 557, 1795; ref, 1478(75), 1479(367)
Velecogna, F.: ref, 1555(327)
Velicer, W. F.: ref, 859(834, 929), 2020(6)
Velicher, W. F.: ref, 964(476)
Vellutino, F. R.: rev, 240, 1221; ref, 958(52), 2217(185), 2602(2225)
Velner, I.: ref, 1498(5036)
Veloski, J.: ref, 1576(208)
Venables, P. H.: ref, 859(865)
Veneklasen, J.: ref, 2598(1815), 2607(214)
Venezky, R. L.: ref, 932(98)
Venham, L. L.: ref, 678(30), 1771(699), 2131(6), 2557(234)
Veno, A.: ref, 859(780)
Verbanck, P.: ref, 645(18)
Vereen, D. R.: ref, 1883(87)
Verinis, J. S.: ref, 1498(5213), 2587(41), 2598(1572)
Verma, G.: ref, 1233(219), 2629(109)
Verma, G. K.: ref, 1831(184)
Verma, S. K.: ref, 280(1081), 1419(679), 2598(1497)
Verner, R.: ref, 1825(21)
Vernon, L. N.: test, 1712
Vernon, M. D.: rev, 1567, 2245
Vernon, P. E.: test, 329, 330, 972, 2343, 2344; rev, 357, 733, 1044, 1233, 1419, 2269; exc, 321, 2245; ref, 361(5), 859(752), 1498(5135), 1533(15), 1914(791), 2413(596), 2598(1353, 1540), 2607(172)
Vernon, P. V.: rev, 628
Veroff, A. E.: ref, 2598(1798), 2607(210)
Veronen, L. J.: ref, 1904(93, 127), 2100(5, 11), 2300(476, 593)
Versey, J.: ref, 823(19), 1914(792)
Verster, J. M.: test, 663
Vertommen, H.: ref, 1498(5513)
Vestewig, R. E.: ref, 2030(4974), 2491(2031)
Vestre, N. D.: test, 1933; ref, 1498(5388)
Vexler, E. B.: ref, 1073(118)
Vicencio, A.: ref, 1655(89)
Vicino, F. L.: ref, 1046(579), 1486(179)
Vickers, D. M.: ref, 1970(16), 2179(223, 224), 2218(148)
Vickery, V. L.: rev, 748, 1894

Victor, J. B.: ref, 2286(341)
Vidiloff, J. S.: ref, 1498(5035)
Vidler, D.: ref, 2594(203)
Vidoni, D. O.: ref, 116(542)
Viernstein, M. C.: ref, 501(898)
Vietze, P. M.: ref, 270(118)
Vietzi, P.: ref, 1771(704)
Vig, S.: ref, 2598(1505)
Viglione, D.: ref, 2030(4988)
Vignolo, L. A.: ref, 1914(794), 2598(1427, 1565)
Vila, J.: ref, 1904(118)
Vilkki, J.: ref, 1106(368)
Villiger, J.: ref, 2301(25)
Vincent, D. R.: ref, 551(52)
Vincent, K. R.: ref, 280(1156), 1106(380), 1498(5389, 5546, 5720), 2598(1665, 1666, 1799), 2607(211)
Vincent, L.: ref, 1250(20), 2641(17)
Vincent, L. R.: ref, 1498(5546), 2598(1666)
Viney, L. L.: ref, 969(37), 2602(1846)
Vinokur, A.: ref, 354(1420)
Vinson, B. P.: ref, 1771(619)
Visco, C. R.: test, 2559
Visco, S. J.: test, 2559
Viscusi, D.: ref, 1547(345)
Vishnoi, P. L.: ref, 1498(5598)
Visser, R. S. H.: test, 544
Viteles, M. S.: rev, 177, 1506, 1670, 1671
Viukari, M.: ref, 1655(87)
Vladovic, R.: ref, 551(57, 58), 553(23, 24), 734(1, 2)
Vlett, G. A.: ref, 1063(92)
Vocational Instructional Materials Laboratory, Ohio State University: test, 1678, 1679, 1680, 1681, 1682, 1683, 1684, 1685, 1686, 1687, 1688, 1689, 1690, 1691, 1692, 1693, 1694, 1695, 1696, 1697, 1698, 1699, 1700, 1701, 1702, 1703, 1704, 1705, 1706, 1707, 1708, 1709, 1710, 1711, 1713, 1715, 1719, 1721, 1722
Vockall, E. L.: ref, 1192(200)
Vockell, E.: ref, 1769(72), 2621(347)
Vockell, E. L.: ref, 1831(141)
Voelker, P. H.: test, 688, 689, 690
Vogel, J. M.: ref, 1771(579)
Vogel, P. A.: ref, 354(1511)
Vogel, R. E.: ref, 76(598), 411(28)
Vogel, S. A.: ref, 285(1), 581(11), 932(68), 1126(678), 1771(580)
Vogel, W.: ref, 794(444), 2598(1817)
Vogler, R. E.: ref, 354(1425)
Vogler, W. H.: test, 178
Vogrin, D.: ref, 1229(95), 2301(35)
Vogrin, D. J.: ref, 703(9), 2602(1981)
Vogt, A. T.: ref, 1498(5285, 5452), 1923(15), 2113(244), 2598(1409, 1472, 1592)
Voight, N. L.: ref, 2413(688)
Volavka, J.: ref, 1904(97)
Volle, M.: ref, 342(4)
vonBaeyer, C.: ref, 1547(313)
Von Isser, A.: ref, 704(19), 1126(663, 679, 680)
VonKuster, L. N.: test, 687
Vontver, L.: ref, 2300(570)
von Wright, J.: ref, 2208(1692)
Vorderman, A. L.: ref, 280(1073), 1126(692), 2602(1740)
Vorhaus, P. G.: ref, 2030(4975)
Vorih, L.: ref, 2288(85)

Vorster, J. F.: test, 1416
Vosk, B.: ref, 1473(217)
Voss, H. G.: ref, 10(25), 1914(735), 2512(581)
VosStrache, C.: ref, 1295(295), 1296(175)
Vrana, F.: ref, 751(40), 1473(209), 1771(766), 1934(13), 2602(2139)
Vredenburgh, D. J.: ref, 1296(173)
Vrtunski, B.: ref, 308(3), 1498(5044), 1948(95), 2113(237), 2598(1300), 2607(129)
Vukelich, C.: ref, 766(22), 932(56), 1479(313, 338, 363), 2217(160), 2218(13)
Vunderink, P.: ref, 2657(111)
Vyas, B. K.: ref, 1655(117)
Wachs, H.: test, 2582
Wachs, T. D.: ref, 698(4)
Wachtel, D.: ref, 2300(385)
Wachter, H.: ref, 2629(116)
Waddell, D. D.: ref, 2289(1776)
Wadden, E. P.: ref, 1831(137)
Waddon, T. A.: ref, 1498(5721)
Wade, T. C.: ref, 280(1096), 1498(5390), 2030(5012), 2289(1692), 2491(2051), 2598(1541), 2602(1847)
Wade, T. H.: ref, 1424(36), 2289(1665)
Wadell, D.: test, 1326
Wadkins, J. R. J.: rev, 1524, 1526
Wadsworth, A. P.: ref, 2300(336)
Wadsworth, H. M.: ref, 280(1110), 2598(1594)
Waetjen, W. B.: test, 2132
Wagemans, L.: ref, 1498(5513)
Waggoner, W. H.: exc, 60
Wagman, M.: ref, 1419(683, 695, 700)
Wagner, C.: ref, 1013(101)
Wagner, C. F.: ref, 1053(83), 2030(5016, 5078)
Wagner, D. A.: ref, 398(102)
Wagner, E. E.: test, 1053; ref, 6(59), 280(1097), 501(936), 1053(67, 68, 71, 72, 73, 75, 76, 77, 78, 80, 81, 83), 2030(5013, 5014, 5015, 5016, 5056, 5063, 5071, 5078), 2289(1727), 2594(208), 2598(1542, 1667, 1699)
Wagner, J.: ref, 1498(5092), 2318(1528), 2598(1332)
Wagner, M.: ref, 1126(690), 2602(1738, 2003, 2160), 2641(14, 18)
Wagner, M. E.: test, 326, 752
Wagner, M. K.: ref, 1547(260), 2413(595)
Wagstaff, G. F.: ref, 2294(115)
Wahl, J.: test, 2105
Wahl, O. F.: ref, 2598(1800)
Wahler, H. J.: test, 2583, 2584
Waid, L. R.: ref, 1191(126), 1498(5391), 2179(247), 2300(448)
Waid, W. M.: ref, 354(1512)
Wainwright, S.: ref, 1883(30, 41)
Wait, R. B.: ref, 270(151)
Waite, W. W.: rev, 1944
Waits, C.: ref, 1769(63), 2217(133), 2585(5)
Waits, J. V.: rev, 177
Wakefield, J. A.: ref, 280(1029), 861(5), 1192(209), 2320(1, 2), 2581(307), 2602(1848)
Waksman, S. A.: ref, 1831(182), 2582(13, 17)
Walberg, H. J.: ref, 354(1431), 1073(119), 1192(215, 249), 1479(337)
Walden, J.: ref, 1769(80), 1771(700), 2621(373)
Walderman, R. L.: ref, 1197(300)
Waldman, B.: ref, 1576(199)

Waldman, I. N.: ref, 1498(5249, 5599), 2598(1315, 1703, 1704)
Waldron, G.: ref, 1547(325)
Waldrop, R.: ref, 116(574)
Walker, A. A.: ref, 559(52)
Walker, B.: test, 570, 571, 589, 1991
Walker, B. A.: ref, 609(205), 2179(209)
Walker, B. B.: ref, 283(153), 1771(701)
Walker, C. A.: ref, 280(1177), 534(111), 823(25), 1153(10), 2018(22), 2281(4), 2602(2229)
Walker, D. A.: rev, 2150
Walker, D. F.: ref, 1473(152), 1914(764)
Walker, D. R.: ref, 280(1093), 1498(5360), 2598(1531), 2607(170)
Walker, E.: ref, 1883(96), 2621(425, 463)
Walker, H. M.: test, 2585; ref, 2621(238)
Walker, J.: ref, 859(754), 1883(41)
Walker, J. A.: test, 1472
Walker, J. L.: ref, 2300(571)
Walker, J. T.: ref, 116(575)
Walker, L.: ref, 344(175)
Walker, L. G.: ref, 1933(21)
Walker, L. J. S.: ref, 2300(571)
Walker, L. S.: ref, 2662(1)
Walker, M. V.: test, 1211
Walker, N. W.: ref, 2602(2226)
Walker, R. D.: ref, 472(14), 1013(93), 2598(1628, 1629)
Walker, R. E.: ref, 1789(643)
Walker, R. W.: test, 187; ref, 2318(1589)
Walker, S. A.: ref, 925(14)
Walker, W. E.: ref, 1191(126), 1498(5391), 1547(327), 1726(370), 2300(448)
Walker, W. J.: test, 408
Walkey, F. H.: ref, 859(909, 961)
Walkup, H. R.: ref, 1798(286)
Wall, L. A.: test, 809, 816
Wall, S.: ref, 1914(850)
Wall, S. M.: ref, 2387(9)
Wall, T. D.: ref, 941(32)
Wall, W. D.: rev, 632, 1914
Wallace, B.: ref, 767(43), 1063(99, 114)
Wallace, E. M.: test, 2108
Wallace, F. C.: test, 2403
Wallace, F. R.: ref, 861(5), 2602(1848)
Wallace, I. G.: ref, 2016(198)
Wallace, J.: ref, 1498(5437), 2286(298), 2598(1503, 1581)
Wallace, J. E.: ref, 1498(5722)
Wallace, M.: test, 2137
Wallace, S. R.: rev, 754, 799, 2053
Wallace, W. L.: rev, 76, 179, 501, 506, 1556
Wallach, H. F.: ref, 2300(572), 2598(1801)
Wallach, L.: ref, 553(14), 719(30)
Wallach, M. A.: exc, 2512; ref, 553(14), 719(30)
Wallbrown, F.: ref, 2602(1840, 1841)
Wallbrown, F. H.: ref, 280(1060, 1102, 1157), 344(149), 553(16), 704(10), 923(82), 964(491, 494), 1503(63), 1771(632), 2218(140), 2602(1715, 1842, 1843, 1844, 1845, 1849, 2140)
Wallbrown, J. D.: ref, 280(1060), 344(149), 704(10), 1503(63)
Wallen, A.: ref, 6(60)
Wallen, N. E.: rev, 1073, 1726
Waller, M. R.: ref, 1513(26), 1851(30, 37)

INDEX OF NAMES

Waller, R. W.: ref, 751(21), 2030(5017)
Waller, S.: ref, 609(214)
Wallinga, C. R.: ref, 2512(630)
Wallis, E.: ref, 501(899)
Wallman, L.: ref, 2300(595)
Wallmark, M. M.: ref, 995(151)
Walls, R.: ref, 1498(5214)
Walls, R. T.: test, 1134, 2572; ref, 1498(5215)
Walmsley, S. A.: ref, 2641(24)
Walsh, A. C.: ref, 2600(1)
Walsh, B.: ref, 1063(96), 2294(119)
Walsh, D. B.: ref, 2598(1343), 2621(247)
Walsh, D. M.: ref, 732(403), 859(835)
Walsh, F.: ref, 1361(65, 66), 1498(5207, 5535), 2491(2029, 2069)
Walsh, J. A.: rev, 354, 665, 1405, 2208; ref, 280(1071), 1192(189), 1473(193), 2602(1733)
Walsh, M. D.: ref, 732(403), 794(408, 409), 859(835), 1044(63), 1073(123), 1077(59)
Walsh, R. N.: ref, 859(962)
Walsh, W. B.: rev, 1270; exc, 2581; ref, 2134(100, 102, 104, 123, 127), 2343(1046), 2581(312, 313, 326, 333, 336)
Walter, D. A.: ref, 354(1479), 2208(1608)
Walter, G.: ref, 9(13), 466(3), 691(34), 1126(711), 1456(16), 1462(138), 1914(787), 2554(13)
Walter, G. G.: ref, 346(104)
Walter, H. J.: test, 1136
Walter, L. J.: test, 2404
Walter, T.: ref, 280(1097), 1053(72), 2030(5015), 2598(1542)
Walter, V.: test, 1786, 2137
Walters, G. D.: ref, 2353(38)
Walters, H. A.: ref, 1798(263, 264)
Walters, J.: ref, 1771(702)
Walters, T. J.: ref, 2598(1466)
Walther, R.: test, 1213
Walther, R. H.: ref, 1213(25)
Walton, C. E.: test, 2586
Walton, E. G.: ref, 1050(2)
Waltrip, J. B.: test, 2212
Walzer, S.: ref, 270(100)
Wampler, K. S.: ref, 1498(5723), 2413(689)
Wampler, R. S.: ref, 1498(5723), 2413(689)
Wander, B. D.: ref, 1419(701)
Wandt, E.: rev, 1625
Wang, C. S. Y.: ref, 1073(127)
Wang, P. L.: ref, 1053(63), 2607(219)
Wankel, L. M.: ref, 2300(373)
Wantman, M. J.: rev, 1576
Wapner, W.: ref, 308(14), 2598(1543)
Warburton, D.: ref, 678(13)
Warburton, F. W.: rev, 842
Ward, B. A.: ref, 551(27)
Ward, B. H.: ref, 953(13)
Ward, C. F.: rev, 790, 2186
Ward, D.: ref, 2602(1875)
Ward, E. S.: ref, 860(155)
Ward, G. R.: ref, 1896(11), 2208(1594, 1626, 1637, 1670, 1671), 2655(6, 7)
Ward, H. W.: ref, 609(212)
Ward, J.: ref, 1853(293), 1940(86)
Ward, J. W.: ref, 1498(5726)
Ward, L. C.: ref, 1498(5547, 5724, 5725, 5726, 5773), 2598(1668)
Ward, L. O.: ref, 1914(729, 730, 736, 821), 2077(26), 2289(1791)
Ward, M.: ref, 1498(5770)
Ward, M. F.: ref, 681(50)
Ward, M. N.: test, 1322
Ward, N. J.: ref, 2288(90)
Ward, R.: ref, 354(1499)
Ward, R. H.: ref, 2289(1703), 2602(1873)
Ward, W. C.: rev, 2433, 2622; ref, 991(15, 16), 995(137, 153), 1257(173)
Wardle, M. G.: ref, 1670(62)
Wardrop, J. L.: rev, 1579, 2164; ref, 1473(220)
Ware, E. E.: ref, 1904(128)
Ware, M. E.: ref, 374(216, 217, 218, 232)
Waring, E. M.: ref, 859(945), 941(44), 1498(5749), 2318(1611)
Warnath, C. F.: rev, 660, 786
Warner, R.: ref, 1555(337), 2534(14)
Warren, J. R.: test, 2337
Warren, N. D.: test, 799; rev, 627, 1054, 1774, 1948
Warren, R.: ref, 2300(402)
Warren, R. L.: ref, 308(22), 1851(23, 45)
Warren, S. A.: ref, 6(62), 935(28)
Warrington, E.: ref, 1771(703)
Warrington, E. K.: ref, 823(22), 878(29), 1513(24), 1771(596, 813), 1914(744, 779, 811), 2077(33), 2598(1442, 1865), 2602(2088)
Warrington, W. G.: rev, 75, 574
Warrior–Benjamin, J.: ref, 1478(66), 1831(119)
Warshaw, J. B.: ref, 311(21)
Wartenberg, H.: ref, 313(1)
Washburn, S.: ref, 1922(13), 1923(13)
Washburn, S. L.: ref, 1922(18), 1923(24)
Washington, D. S.: ref, 1771(633)
Washington, E. R.: ref, 859(836), 2461(8)
Washington, L. A.: ref, 1424(70), 1771(742)
Washington Pre–College Testing Program: test, 2589
Wasik, B. H.: ref, 559(59), 2260(34)
Wasik, J. L.: ref, 559(59)
Wasserman, M.: ref, 501(873)
Wasserman, S.: ref, 932(88)
Wasserman, T. H.: ref, 703(9), 2602(1981)
Waterer, B.: ref, 1914(715)
Waterhouse, L.: ref, 922(10), 1485(71), 1771(652)
Waterhouse, S. M. A.: test, 1561, 1988
Waterman, J.: ref, 2217(179)
Waterman, J. M.: ref, 1771(686)
Waterman, L.: ref, 559(43)
Waters, B. K.: ref, 590(377)
Waters, E.: ref, 270(127), 311(40), 2289(1738)
Waters, J. E.: ref, 612(17)
Waterstreet, M. A.: ref, 2289(1673)
Watkins, D.: ref, 354(1555), 859(837), 1077(70, 71, 83), 1754(111, 112, 113), 2336(7)
Watkins, E. J.: ref, 1914(737), 2077(27)
Watkins, E. O.: test, 280; ref, 1424(79)
Watkins, J. G.: test, 2591; rev, 399
Watkins, M.: ref, 1970(15), 2208(1595)
Watkins, M. W.: ref, 2539(10), 2602(1982)
Watkins, R. W.: rev, 1954
Watson, A. S.: ref, 1909(1)
Watson, B.: ref, 226(185), 691(47), 701(89), 922(8), 1126(784), 1250(16), 1462(158), 1769(103), 1914(888), 2602(2186)
Watson, C. G.: ref, 283(148), 1073(126), 1498(5178,

5216, 5217, 5288, 5315, 5392, 5393, 5394, 5395, 5548, 5549, 5550, 5626, 5627, 5727, 5728, 5729, 5774), 1547(266, 296, 314, 343), 1919(44), 2179(221, 229), 2208(1638), 2300(366, 420, 449, 500, 573), 2380(5), 2598(1544, 1545, 1546, 1595, 1728)
Watson, F.: test, 839
Watson, G: test, 2594; rev, 340
Watson, G. M.: test, 2592, 2593, 2595, 2596
Watson, J.: ref, 563(31), 2135(1)
Watson, J. J.: ref, 2491(2045)
Watson, J. S.: ref, 1771(704)
Watson, P. J.: ref, 883(67), 1203(9), 2244(35)
Watson, T. E.: ref, 1823(34)
Watters, R. G.: ref, 1771(814), 2289(1793), 2602(2227)
Watters, W. E.: ref, 1771(814), 2289(1793), 2602(2227)
Watts, A. F.: test, 825, 1102, 2000
Watts, F.: ref, 2537(565)
Watts, K. P.: test, 148, 149, 2175; ref, 149(2)
Waugh, N. C.: ref, 1485(85), 1914(869)
Waugh, R. P.: exc, 1126
Waxer, P. H.: ref, 2300(374)
Waxler, N. E.: ref, 1923(17)
Waxman, H. C.: ref, 1192(249)
Way, J. W.: ref, 551(71), 1831(219)
Wayne, N. M.: ref, 883(77)
Waziri, M.: ref, 1126(780), 1771(778)
Wearing, M. P.: ref, 1424(82)
Wearne, T. D.: ref, 2657(105, 113)
Weaver, D.: ref, 2289(1605)
Weaver, H. M.: ref, 2208(1639)
Weaver, J. F.: rev, 173
Weaver, L. A.: ref, 2598(1328)
Weaver, P. A.: ref, 719(34), 1914(823)
Weaver, W. T.: ref, 76(619), 501(840), 995(140)
Webb, L. J.: ref, 1498(5551)
Webb, N. L.: ref, 1257(149), 2587(35)
Webb, R.: test, 892, 1837, 1838, 2238; ref, 704(22)
Webb, R. C.: ref, 868(4)
Webb, S. C.: test, 1183; ref, 1183(3)
Webb, W. B.: ref, 354(1513), 609(219), 1498(5552)
Webb, W. G.: ref, 1851(20)
Webb, W. W.: test, 891
Webber, L. S.: ref, 1831(183, 220)
Webber, P. L.: test, 2409; ref, 859(956)
Weber, C. R.: ref, 1125(16), 1726(356), 1789(654)
Weber, D. B.: ref, 6(80), 2598(1802), 2602(2141)
Weber, L. J.: ref, 374(206), 551(38), 620(2)
Weber, P. G.: test, 2597
Weber–Olsen, M.: ref, 290(8)
Webster, C. D.: ref, 1126(730), 2018(14), 2289(1718)
Webster, D. W.: ref, 374(205)
Webster, E. G.: ref, 195(2), 558(64)
Webster, H.: test, 1726; rev, 1729, 2121
Webster, J. S.: ref, 1346(6)
Webster, P. S.: ref, 6(81)
Webster, R. E.: test, 1305; ref, 1771(705), 2598(1669), 2602(1850, 2142), 2621(312, 374, 426)
Webster, S.: ref, 860(109)
Webster, W. J.: rev, 597
Wechsler, D.: test, 610, 2598, 2602, 2607, 2608; rev, 1485, 1914, 2013; ref, 2598(1866)
Weckowicz, T. E.: rev, 1904, 1933; ref, 354(1426), 681(75), 732(395), 794(382), 860(156), 1046(574),
1486(177), 1969(97), 2029(200), 2343(1035), 2598(1547), 2607(149), 2621(409)
Wedding, D.: ref, 1498(5544), 2598(1662)
Wediger, T. A.: ref, 1257(174)
Weed, W.: ref, 1424(67)
Weedman, C. W.: test, 2146
Weeks, A.: test, 839
Weeks, D.: ref, 639(57, 60), 1485(86), 1883(79), 1914(870)
Weeks, D. G.: ref, 1904(119), 1914(872)
Weeks, R.: ref, 2598(1312)
Weerts, T. C.: ref, 883(90)
Wegener, J. I.: test, 389
Wegner, D. M.: ref, 1341(163)
Wehler, R.: ref, 1498(5286, 5556), 1789(688), 2598(1548)
Wehner, W. L.: rev, 879, 880
Weible, E.: test, 2634
Weidemann, C. C.: rev, 1189
Weidemann, C. F.: ref, 2030(5035)
Weider, A.: test, 610
Weidner, W. F.: ref, 1851(19)
Weigel, D. J.: ref, 2288(86)
Weigel, R. G.: test, 618; ref, 618(4)
Weight, D. G.: ref, 116(600), 2413(666)
Weijola, M. J.: test, 1469
Weikart, D. P.: rev, 7, 1764
Weikel, W. J.: ref, 995(136), 1798(226)
Weil, E. M.: ref, 1257(170), 2246(34), 2554(15)
Weil, G. R.: test, 2393
Weil, W. B.: ref, 1424(89)
Weiman, A. L.: ref, 2294(132)
Weimer, S. R.: ref, 1498(5396)
Wein, K. S.: ref, 883(87)
Wein, S.: test, 215
Wein, S. J.: ref, 682(1)
Weinberg, J. C.: ref, 1498(5553)
Weinberg, R. A.: ref, 2318(1530), 2598(1335, 1527)
Weinberg, R. S.: ref, 2300(450, 451, 501)
Weinberg, W. A.: ref, 1771(581, 715), 2602(1717, 2011), 2608(227), 2621(270, 386)
Weinberger, D. R.: ref, 1498(5218), 2030(4976), 2598(1704)
Weinberger, L. J.: ref, 1498(5730), 1798(299), 2030(5079), 2491(2094)
Weiner, B.: ref, 2602(1765)
Weiner, F. J.: ref, 2030(4946)
Weiner, I. B.: ref, 2030(5018)
Weiner, M.: ref, 344(176), 543(29), 1191(129), 2030(5066), 2160(70), 2298(2)
Weiner, M. B.: test, 1916
Weiner, S. G.: ref, 2602(1983)
Weiner, Y.: ref, 2318(1535, 1572)
Weingartner, H.: ref, 308(6), 1771(752), 2598(1435, 1867), 2607(220)
Weinhouse, S.: ref, 1555(328), 2208(1619)
Weinman, M.: ref, 859(895), 1498(5567), 2300(482, 513)
Weinman, M. L.: ref, 859(951), 1498(5405), 2300(597)
Weinrach, S. G.: ref, 1270(84)
Weinraub, M.: ref, 794(383), 1771(582), 2598(1410)
Weinrott, M. R.: ref, 2582(14)
Weinstein, L.: ref, 1573(42)
Weinstein, M.: ref, 116(527)
Weinstein, M. A.: test, 1154

INDEX OF NAMES

Weinstein, N. D.: ref, 354(1475), 859(838), 1798(246), 2598(1411)
Weinstein, P.: ref, 1671(46)
Weinstock, A.: ref, 6(64), 1908(10)
Weinstock, G.: test, 1284
Weinstock, R. B.: ref, 269(2)
Weintraub, M.: ref, 270(72)
Weintraub, S.: ref, 308(17), 645(26)
Weintraub, S. A.: rev, 238, 398, 1209
Weir, T.: ref, 354(1522), 2208(1648)
Weisbord, A.: ref, 2029(237)
Weisbrodt, J. A.: test, 1951
Weiser, M. A.: ref, 367(1), 374(233), 2581(350)
Weiskott, G. N.: ref, 2300(382)
Weiskrantz, L.: ref, 1914(811)
Weismer, G.: ref, 960(20)
Weiss, B. L.: ref, 1904(71)
Weiss, C. E.: test, 2611
Weiss, D. J.: test, 1495, 1497, 1508, 1509; rev, 202, 2537, 2623
Weiss, D. S.: ref, 116(622, 636, 637), 354(1566, 1576)
Weiss, G.: ref, 398(93), 794(420), 2598(1549, 1596), 2602(1609, 1851), 2608(171)
Weiss, H. M.: ref, 1013(94), 2354(35)
Weiss, J. L.: ref, 794(366), 2179(196, 234), 2289(1749), 2608(172, 229)
Weiss, K. L.: ref, 1789(655)
Weiss, R. L.: ref, 609(215)
Weiss, R. W.: ref, 1498(5220, 5397)
Weiss, S. C.: ref, 653(169), 964(514), 1853(287)
Weiss, W. V.: ref, 2030(4977)
Weissbach, T. A.: ref, 354(1425)
Weissberg, M.: ref, 1547(274, 275)
Weissenberg, P.: ref, 1077(60)
Weisskopf, B.: ref, 2289(1633)
Weissman, M. M.: ref, 1419(675, 684, 692, 702), 1883(89), 2100(12), 2322(8, 10, 11)
Weisz, J. R.: ref, 398(111), 478(8), 1257(137), 1771(634), 2030(5019), 2289(1648, 1739), 2602(2201)
Weithorn, C. J.: ref, 280(1098), 1126(716, 744), 1479(339, 359)
Weitkamp, L. R.: ref, 1498(5731)
Weitz, H.: rev, 464, 720, 1048, 2390, 2618
Weitzel, W. D.: ref, 354(1409, 1427), 2208(1548)
Weitzenhoffer, A.: exc, 399
Weitzenhoffer, A. M: test, 2294, 2297
Weitzman, E. D.: ref, 1498(5775)
Welch, M.: ref, 400(135), 772(30)
Welch, W. W.: rev, 595, 2165
Weldon, D. E.: ref, 590(390)
Weldon, E.: ref, 1904(106)
Welford, A. T.: rev, 910
Weller, C.: test, 2612
Welling, J. S.: ref, 2463(8)
Welling, M. A.: ref, 1798(229)
Wellisch, D. K.: ref, 751(32), 859(839), 1170(229, 236), 1372(9), 1498(5545), 1761(5), 2598(1663)
Wellisch, J. B.: ref, 344(161)
Wellman, B. L.: rev, 381, 1505
Wellman, M. M.: ref, 1473(191), 1479(361)
Wells, F. L.: rev, 691, 2269, 2289
Wells, K. C.: ref, 116(632), 2300(526)
Wells, M. G.: ref, 704(11), 1192(211)
Wells, R. A.: ref, 1170(227)

Wells, W. D.: test, 2042
Welner, A.: ref, 2602(1718), 2621(271)
Welner, Z.: ref, 2602(1718), 2621(271)
Welsh, G. S.: test, 243, 2613
Welsh, M. C.: ref, 1796(5), 2602(2157), 2621(433)
Wemmer, D.: ref, 280(1064)
Wenar, C.: test, 272; ref, 6(57), 2289(1716, 1785)
Wenberg, R. A.: ref, 859(956)
Wendell, T. A.: ref, 270(84)
Wender, P. H.: ref, 645(11), 794(450), 1331(42), 1498(5034, 5275, 5776), 1853(300), 2030(4978), 2598(1293, 1412), 2621(218, 464)
Wendt, J. C.: ref, 2208(1671), 2655(7)
Wenger, W. K.: ref, 558(65)
Wentland, T. J.: ref, 1126(745)
Wentling, T. L.: rev, 1605, 2185
Wepfer, J. W.: ref, 2602(1934)
Wepman, J. M.: test, 226, 227, 229, 1890, 1895, 1897, 2251, 2561, 2563; rev, 793, 1743, 2110
Werner, E. E.: rev, 678, 1319, 2025
Werner, P. D.: ref, 116(576), 354(1476)
Werner, T. J.: test, 2572
Werry, J. S.: ref, 1831(200)
Wersh, J.: ref, 2602(2228)
Wertheim, E. G.: ref, 973(31), 1292(53), 1486(180)
Werts, C. E.: ref, 501(809, 841, 912), 590(378), 2160(56)
Wertz, R. T.: ref, 1851(42)
Weslander, D.: ref, 1271(907)
Weslander, D. L.: ref, 2581(334)
Wesley, F.: ref, 116(599)
Wesman, A. G.: test, 9, 466, 732, 1288, 1456, 1653, 1808, 2246, 2254, 2554, 2614; rev, 124, 1193, 1292, 1557, 1576
Wessberg, H. W.: ref, 883(103)
Wessels, K.: ref, 2217(166), 2602(2030)
Wessen, A. F.: ref, 1576(204)
Wessler, R.: exc, 1798
West, D.: ref, 2300(587)
West, E. M.: ref, 309(8), 1995(3)
West, J.: ref, 551(64), 2218(18)
West, J. C.: ref, 1798(288), 1904(115)
West, J. H.: ref, 2413(609)
West, J. V.: test, 287
West, K. L.: ref, 1498(5745), 2491(2098)
West, L. J.: rev, 1629, 2527, 2529
West, P.: ref, 280(1061)
West, R.: ref, 280(1068), 1109(20), 2598(1431), 2607(152)
West, R. F.: ref, 2286(347), 2621(313, 458)
Westbrook, B. W.: rev, 373, 965; exc, 1577; ref, 374(219), 375(1), 501(913), 1059(3), 1473(210), 1478(77), 1754(114), 1820(1)
Westby, C. E.: ref, 1771(706), 2512(631)
Westby, G.: rev, 1036, 1660, 1914
Western, J. S.: test, 2328
Western, R. D.: ref, 2298(3)
Western Psychological Services: test, 280
Westling, D. L.: ref, 2391(1)
Westman, A. S.: rev, 2244; ref, 1555(331)
Weston, G. A.: test, 1232
Westover, F. L.: rev, 2488
Wetherby, A. M.: ref, 1771(815), 2472(33)
Wetter, R. E.: ref, 1798(229)
Wetzel, R. D.: ref, 1498(5732), 2208(1672)

Wexler, B. E.: ref, 1904(107)
Wexler, M.: ref, 1498(5066), 2300(342)
Weybrew, B. B.: ref, 1498(5554)
Weyman, A.: ref, 1883(47)
Whalen, C. K.: ref, 1771(523, 707), 1853(267)
Whaley, W. J.: ref, 932(116), 1007(38), 1771(767), 2218(19)
Whalley, L. J.: ref, 1883(80)
Whatley, J. L.: ref, 1063(81)
Wheat, H. G.: rev, 345, 1477
Wheatley, G. H.: ref, 2286(346)
Wheatley, R. D.: ref, 1498(5772)
Wheaton, P. J.: ref, 2602(1852, 2143)
Wheelan, S. A.: ref, 2413(658)
Wheeler, K. J.: ref, 354(1573), 2179(256), 2217(181)
Wheeler, L.: ref, 1769(97)
Wheeler, L. J.: ref, 1771(814), 2289(1793), 2602(2227)
Wheeler, T. J.: ref, 1914(737), 2077(27)
Wheldall, K.: test, 2156; ref, 823(20, 24)
Wherry, K. L.: ref, 2300(549)
Whiddon, M. F.: ref, 2218(155), 2598(1660)
Whisler, L.: test, 1945
Whisler, L. D.: test, 2619
Whissell, C. M.: ref, 859(910)
Whitaker, D. B.: ref, 2208(1673)
Whitaker, L. C.: test, 2620; ref, 2620(5, 13)
White, A.: ref, 2598(1487)
White, A. J.: test, 2069; ref, 501(846)
White, A. L.: ref, 2286(346)
White, A. P.: ref, 149(15), 653(176)
White, B. C.: ref, 2300(574)
White, C.: ref, 1498(5315), 2300(420)
White, C. A.: ref, 2289(1693), 2602(1853), 2621(314)
White, C. L.: ref, 270(119), 2289(1724)
White, D.: ref, 1473(181), 1771(635, 679), 1914(793, 816)
White, D. R.: ref, 1007(34), 2608(223)
White, E.: ref, 559(53)
White, E. M.: rev, 437, 985
White, F.: ref, 1319(79)
White, G. W.: ref, 562(8)
White, H. R.: rev, 280; ref, 1831(215)
White, J. G.: test, 1384
White, J. L.: ref, 1498(5230, 5408), 2598(1554), 2602(1861)
White, K. P.: ref, 1108(5)
White, M.: ref, 226(176), 701(70, 71), 1622(48), 1771(708, 709), 2244(37)
White, M. A.: ref, 1192(237), 1351(183), 1754(102), 2260(40), 2286(311), 2602(2043)
White, M. J.: ref, 1904(60), 2301(23), 2598(1614)
White, M. T.: ref, 479(403)
White, O. R.: test, 2532
White, P.: ref, 2134(125), 2413(589)
White, R. B.: ref, 1498(5555)
White, R. M.: ref, 872(7)
White, R. T.: test, 2486; ref, 589(1)
White, T. H.: ref, 964(500), 1769(81), 2602(1984)
White, V.: exc, 551
White, W. C.: ref, 2208(1558, 1564)
White, W. F.: ref, 2512(593)
White, W. G.: ref, 2602(1985)
Whitehead, A.: ref, 2598(1413)
Whitehead, G. I.: ref, 2300(354)
Whitehead, L.: ref, 321(42)

Whitehead, R. L.: ref, 200(13), 960(6)
Whitehead, W. E.: ref, 2300(375)
Whitehouse, D.: ref, 280(1158), 964(515)
Whiteley, A. M.: ref, 878(29)
Whitely, S. E.: ref, 76(648), 483(44), 732(396), 1257(150), 1341(164), 1510(47)
Whitely, S. J.: ref, 1513(31)
Whitesel, L. S.: ref, 116(577)
Whiteside, M: ref, 2413(610, 611, 635)
Whitford, T. M.: test, 38, 45, 48
Whitla, D. K.: rev, 500
Whitley, J. D.: ref, 964(484)
Whitley, T. W.: ref, 201(3)
Whitman, D.: ref, 2598(1552)
Whitman, M.: ref, 354(1560)
Whitman, R. D.: ref, 1485(64, 78)
Whitmer, C. A.: test, 175; rev, 204
Whitt, J. K.: ref, 2602(2123)
Whittaker, C. A.: ref, 2383(1)
Whittaker, E. M.: ref, 1233(220)
Whittlesey, J. R. B.: test, 1371
Whitworth, R. H.: rev, 2602
Whorton, J.: ref, 551(48)
Whorton, J. E.: ref, 6(50), 2602(1858), 2621(317)
Whyte, L.: ref, 280(1020), 922(5), 1060(22), 1126(645), 1949(56), 2289(1592), 2602(1587, 1719)
Whyte, R.: ref, 1498(5331)
Wicher, D.: ref, 2300(360)
Wick, J. W.: test, 365, 692; ref, 1192(238), 1272(138), 1479(364)
Wicklund, R. A.: ref, 501(802)
Wickramasekera, I. E.: ref, 2294(116)
Widaman, K.: ref, 1073(125)
Widaman, K. F.: ref, 794(448)
Wideman, J. V.: ref, 1267(1)
Wideman, M. V.: test, 1267; ref, 1498(5644)
Widerstrom, A. H.: ref, 501(874)
Widiger, T. A.: ref, 483(39), 1013(117), 1914(871), 2030(5080)
Widmayer, J. D.: test, 2580
Widmayer, S. M.: ref, 270(135), 311(35), 678(31), 2300(524)
Widom, C. S.: ref, 354(1428), 859(781), 860(103), 973(31), 1292(53), 1486(180), 1498(5074, 5221), 1853(273)
Widseth, J. C.: ref, 1498(5070, 5246)
Wiebe, K. F.: ref, 2208(1674)
Wiebe, M. J.: ref, 691(36), 1424(45, 79)
Wiechert, V.: ref, 1498(5047), 2029(196), 2030(4945)
Wiederanders, M. R.: ref, 2497(40)
Wiederholt, J. L.: test, 2422, 2456; rev, 651, 1126
Wiedl, K. H.: ref, 1914(743)
Wiener, F. D.: ref, 2445(4)
Wiener, J.: ref, 2602(2144)
Wiener, Y.: ref, 780(1662, 1663), 966(174), 2037(150), 2318(1549), 2491(2030)
Wiens, A. N.: ref, 116(617), 296(9), 609(206), 794(442), 859(939), 1498(5151, 5219), 2030(4960), 2300(575), 2318(1538), 2598(1362, 1414, 1494, 1803)
Wientge, K. W.: test, 2423
Wierzbicki, M.: ref, 2598(1550)
Wieselberg, N.: ref, 116(621), 883(104)
Wiesner, E.: ref, 883(96)
Wig, N. N.: ref, 280(1081), 1419(679), 2598(1497)

INDEX OF NAMES

Wiggins, J. D.: ref, 374(234), 1271(907), 2134(143), 2581(334, 351)
Wiggins, J. S.: rev, 1247, 1798; ref, 116(578)
Wiggins, R. D.: ref, 941(31)
Wigglesworth, M. J.: ref, 859(832)
Wiig, E. H.: test, 474, 475; ref, 226(188), 308(5), 378(20), 691(31, 48), 1126(681, 786), 1513(23), 1622(35), 1771(805), 2602(2212), 2621(454)
Wijesinghe, O. B. A.: ref, 1485(66)
Wikler, A.: ref, 794(400)
Wikoff, R. L.: ref, 76(620), 1769(66, 82, 83), 2208(1596), 2602(1854, 1986)
Wilchesky, M.: ref, 2582(14)
Wilcocks, A. M.: test, 1560
Wilcox, B. M.: ref, 270(144)
Wilcox, C.: ref, 1914(754), 2318(1554)
Wilcox, H. E.: exc, 58
Wilcox, K.: ref, 2412(42)
Wilcox, K. W.: rev, 1047
Wilcox, L. E.: ref, 354(1536), 1771(665), 1853(285, 295)
Wilcox, M. J.: ref, 378(9), 1622(45)
Wilcox, P.: ref, 1498(5222)
Wilcox, R. D.: ref, 2289(1630), 2602(1673)
Wilcox, W. W.: ref, 558(65)
Wild, C. M.: ref, 794(384), 2030(4979), 2598(1415)
Wilder, D. A.: ref, 1451(3)
Wilder, D. H.: ref, 1531(291), 1729(80)
Wildman, R. C.: ref, 501(842)
Wildman, R. W.: ref, 2598(1416)
Wiles, D. H.: ref, 2588(32)
Wilimas, J.: ref, 1052(4), 1771(768), 2602(2145), 2621(427)
Wilk, S.: ref, 1655(99)
Wilke, D.: test, 2392
Wilkie, F. L.: ref, 2598(1417)
Wilkins, L. E.: ref, 2557(242)
Wilkins, W. E.: ref, 1197(285, 292), 1789(656, 689)
Wilkinson, A.: test, 1311; ref, 2621(376)
Wilkinson, A. C.: ref, 1007(39), 2621(428)
Wilkinson, D. A.: ref, 1052(3), 2598(1804)
Wilkinson, J. C. M.: ref, 639(40), 859(722)
Wilkinson, L.: ref, 270(153), 311(45), 1170(238), 1576(224)
Wilkinson, W. A.: ref, 701(81), 2472(26)
Wilks, L.: ref, 2512(632)
Wilks, S. S.: rev, 1313, 1749
Wilkus, R.J.: ref, 2598(1448)
Will, J. A.: ref, 2318(1525)
Will, R. J.: test, 656
Willerman, L.: ref, 270(73), 354(1569), 2289(1649), 2598(1407, 1671, 1754), 2602(1720, 1987), 2621(272)
Willi, F. J. P.: ref, 1498(5225), 2300(376)
Williams, A. J.: ref, 280(1177), 534(111), 823(25), 1153(10), 2018(22), 2281(4), 2512(577, 600, 621, 633), 2602(2229)
Williams, A. M.: ref, 1126(682), 1771(583)
Williams, B. O.: ref, 925(14)
Williams, C. D.: ref, 1498(5579)
Williams, C. L.: ref, 1498(5588)
Williams, D. G.: ref, 860(148)
Williams, D. M.: ref, 666(4)
Williams, F.: ref, 226(169), 344(162), 482(8), 958(47), 1473(169), 1479(340), 1769(53), 1771(636), 2621(285)
Williams, H. G.: ref, 226(170, 175, 177), 280(1100, 1133), 302(35, 37), 794(381), 1126(718, 741, 748), 1371(252, 257), 1479(342, 362), 1894(4, 6), 2244(36)
Williams, H. L.: test, 782
Williams, H. S.: rev, 37, 38
Williams, J.: ref, 1341(172), 2217(123)
Williams, J. A.: ref, 1319(83)
Williams, J. D.: ref, 932(69), 964(483), 1192(184), 1371(247), 1479(325), 2015(206), 2217(122)
Williams, J. E.: ref, 116(543, 599, 607, 618)
Williams, J. H.: ref, 76(621)
Williams, J. R.: rev, 1902; ref, 1077(53)
Williams, K. B.: ref, 116(618)
Williams, L.: ref, 2300(475)
Williams, L. R.: ref, 1831(175, 216)
Williams, M: test, 2627, 2655; ref, 860(100)
Williams, M. A.: ref, 280(1177), 534(111), 823(25), 1153(10), 2018(22), 2281(4), 2366(196), 2370(17), 2602(2229)
Williams, M. S.: test, 383, 1014, 1803, 2351
Williams, M. T.: test, 1238
Williams, N. H.: ref, 1126(689), 1462(129), 1567(12), 1914(750)
Williams, P.: ref, 2602(2151)
Williams, P. A.: ref, 653(170), 1771(770), 2217(178), 2289(1778), 2598(1808)
Williams, P. R.: ref, 2286(348)
Williams, R. B. J.: ref, 2208(1531)
Williams, R. E.: ref, 400(125), 1233(217), 2512(582)
Williams, R. L.: test, 296, 2492, 2626
Williams, T. A.: ref, 645(6, 7, 8, 9, 15, 19), 1498(5119, 5129, 5130, 5131, 5264, 5292), 2179(197, 198), 2620(10)
Williams, V.: ref, 311(21)
Williams, W. E.: ref, 2413(641)
Williamson, H. J.: test, 1990
Williamson, W. E.: ref, 2286(325), 2621(375)
Willig, S.: test, 538
Willingham, W. W.: rev, 995, 1486
Willis, C. G.: rev, 428, 1059
Willis, K. A.: ref, 1498(5556)
Willis, S. L.: ref, 653(158, 172), 1257(131, 156), 1914(825), 2300(591)
Willis, T. J.: ref, 751(7), 874(46), 1361(64), 2602(1679)
Willits, J. M.: rev, 111
Willmuth, R.: ref, 1655(84)
Willner, A. E.: ref, 2598(1670)
Willoughby, R. H.: ref, 270(77), 678(20), 701(45), 1771(597), 1877(7), 2289(1656), 2557(220)
Willoughby, T. L.: ref, 1568(138)
Willower, D. J.: ref, 1789(649)
Willows, D. M.: ref, 653(148, 149, 160, 177), 932(89, 90, 105, 129)
Wills, I. H.: ref, 691(32, 37, 38), 2602(1596)
Wills, U.: ref, 2602(1729, 1863)
Willson, V. L.: rev, 2165, 2372; ref, 1625(106)
Wilmeth, J. R.: rev, 992, 2067
Wilmot, G.: test, 41
Wilmotte, J.: ref, 645(18)
Wilson, A.: ref, 878(30)
Wilson, A. P.: ref, 76(597), 1866(33)

709

Wilson, A. S.: ref, 1498(5223, 5224)
Wilson, B. J.: ref, 1192(248), 1479(371), 1754(108), 1934(7), 2269(480)
Wilson, C.: ref, 381(62), 859(867)
Wilson, C. L.: test, 2628
Wilson, D.: ref, 202(13)
Wilson, D. G.: ref, 501(936), 2594(208)
Wilson, D. H.: ref, 1126(664), 1462(122), 2607(139)
Wilson, D. M.: ref, 321(38)
Wilson, D. R.: ref, 2602(2200), 2621(450)
Wilson, F. R.: ref, 2602(1968)
Wilson, G. D.: test, 2629
Wilson, G. M.: rev, 1477
Wilson, G. T.: ref, 883(91, 112), 2300(453, 543)
Wilson, H.: test, 2129, 2630; ref, 701(73), 1126(751, 788), 1831(186, 218), 1853(299), 2602(2012, 2217), 2621(387, 460)
Wilson, J. A. R.: ref, 1351(187), 2164(44), 2286(315)
Wilson, J. F.: test, 178
Wilson, J. T.: test, 1542
Wilson, K. L.: ref, 935(32), 1073(124), 1969(105), 2537(560)
Wilson, L.: ref, 2244(43)
Wilson, L. J.: ref, 1531(293)
Wilson, P.: ref, 1498(5331)
Wilson, R.: ref, 2621(376)
Wilson, R. C.: test, 157, 630, 1257
Wilson, R. J.: ref, 859(957, 958)
Wilson, R. S.: ref, 1771(769), 2598(1552), 2602(1721)
Wilson, S.: ref, 486(309), 673(53), 794(451), 1498(5398, 5463), 2208(1597, 1598, 1622), 2598(1551, 1553)
Wilson, S. A.: ref, 2289(1600)
Wilson, S. K.: ref, 354(1512)
Wilson, T. D.: ref, 354(1420)
Wilson, V. E.: ref, 1904(120)
Wilson, W. H.: ref, 1473(165)
Wilson, W. R.: ref, 270(86)
Wilsoncroft, W. E.: ref, 1884(3, 4)
Wilton, K.: ref, 964(512), 2208(1668), 2217(175), 2289(1694), 2602(1855)
Wimmer, D.: ref, 6(65)
Wincze, J. P.: ref, 1904(121)
Windmiller, M.: test, 6
Winefordner, D. W.: test, 1720
Winegardner, J.: ref, 1798(263, 307)
Winer, G.: ref, 2111(1), 2602(1592), 2621(222)
Winer, G. A.: ref, 794(448)
Winer, J.: test, 370
Winer, J. L.: ref, 374(210), 2581(338)
Wines, R.: test, 35
Wing, H. D.: test, 2631; rev, 155, 2113, 2591
Wing, J. K.: test, 1883; exc, 2322; ref, 1883(54)
Wing, L.: ref, 270(74), 1126(683), 1471(51), 2018(10), 2602(1722)
Wingard, J. A.: exc, 1473
Wingate, M. E.: ref, 2491(2032)
Winget, C. N.: test, 969; ref, 1922(12)
Winitz, H.: rev, 1268, 1718
Winkelmayer, R.: ref, 501(854), 1498(5445), 2318(1584)
Winkler, D. R.: ref, 2288(87)
Winkler, S.: ref, 2159(2)
Winne, P. H.: ref, 483(17, 23), 551(27), 1831(132, 144, 197), 2160(75)

Winnick, R. H.: ref, 280(1122)
Winograd, E.: ref, 2300(486)
Winokur, G.: ref, 859(841), 1240(58)
Winsberg, B. G.: ref, 701(85), 703(10), 704(20), 1126(775), 1331(41), 1473(211), 1923(25), 2293(16), 2602(2146)
Winship, G. P.: rev, 2567, 2568
Winstead, D. K.: ref, 1498(5225, 5431), 2300(376)
Winston, R. B.: test, 2330; ref, 501(914), 2534(15)
Winter, D. G.: ref, 501(843), 2491(2033, 2034, 2052)
Winter, R. A.: ref, 1508(138)
Winterbourn, R.: rev, 32, 842
Winters, K.: ref, 645(26)
Winton, M.: ref, 1485(69)
Wintrob, R. M.: ref, 609(225)
Wippman, J.: ref, 270(127), 2289(1738)
Wirt, R. D.: test, 1796; rev, 396, 400, 861, 1229; ref, 354(1493)
Wise, G. W.: ref, 1789(657)
Wise, S.: ref, 311(41), 2491(2095)
Wisely, R.: ref, 2602(1816)
Wiseman, E. E.: rev, 2182
Wiseman, S.: rev, 1193, 2000, 2164, 2278
Wish, E.: ref, 2602(1718), 2621(271)
Wish, J.: ref, 2237(1)
Wish, J. R.: test, 2237
Wisher, R. A.: ref, 202(12), 1914(884)
Wisniewski, A.: ref, 1346(7), 2598(1839)
Wisniewski, A. M.: ref, 1346(4)
Wisniewski, L.: ref, 381(62)
Witelson, S. F.: ref, 2602(1723)
Withers, G. P.: test, 42
Witkin, H. A.: test, 398, 794, 1013; ref, 501(810, 853), 1013(61, 83)
Witmer, J. M.: ref, 1831(120, 177)
Witte, S. P.: ref, 412(6), 501(923), 2002(6)
Witten, G. L.: test, 814
Wittenborn, J. R.: rev, 2030, 2208, 2491
Wittes, J.: ref, 282(141), 464(2), 1914(705)
Wittes, S.: test, 405
Wittig, M. A.: ref, 859(956)
Wittmaier, B. C.: ref, 2208(1536)
Wittman, L. A.: ref, 1655(124), 2598(1864)
Wittmer, J.: test, 2092
Wittstruck, M. L.: ref, 664(10)
Witty, P. A.: rev, 175, 344
Wlinstock, A.: ref, 6(64)
Wodarski, J. S.: ref, 1209(37)
Wods, R. T.: ref, 308(8)
Woehlke, P.: ref, 643(138), 1341(174), 1726(360), 2602(2037), 2621(396)
Wolchik, S. A.: ref, 1904(121)
Wold, D.: ref, 1771(786)
Woldenberg, L.: ref, 859(915), 1789(713)
Wolf, A.: ref, 2292(22)
Wolf, A. S.: ref, 2598(1805)
Wolf, B.: ref, 1052(1), 2557(242), 2602(1988), 2621(377)
Wolf, C.: ref, 1547(323)
Wolf, E.: ref, 794(429), 2030(5042), 2598(1648, 1745), 2607(201)
Wolf, E. G.: test, 272; ref, 272(1)
Wolf, F. M.: ref, 551(72), 2372(5)
Wolf, M. S.: ref, 2587(42)
Wolf, R. M.: rev, 239, 1473

INDEX OF NAMES

Wolf, T. M.: ref, 1831(183, 220)
Wolfaardt, J. B.: test, 1081
Wolfe, J. H.: test, 2318(1573)
Wolfe, J. M.: test, 189
Wolfe, L. K.: ref, 76(650), 2318(1608)
Wolfe, S.: test, 2122
Wolfe, W. G.: ref, 859(750)
Wolff, H.: test, 610
Wolff, H. G.: test, 609
Wolff, J.: ref, 2413(690)
Wolff, P. H.: ref, 270(100), 2602(1595)
Wolff, S.: ref, 1126(746), 1485(71), 2602(1989)
Wolfgang, C. H.: ref, 1479(310)
Wolfinsohn, L.: ref, 883(72), 1498(5139)
Wolfle, L. M.: ref, 590(382), 1585(16), 2160(63)
Wolfson, S. L.: ref, 859(963)
Wolins, L.: rev, 1780
Wolk, R. B.: test, 950
Wolk, R. L.: test, 950
Wolkind, S.: exc, 311; ref, 609(199)
Wolkon, G. H.: ref, 890(341)
Woll, G.: ref, 1771(777)
Woll, S. B.: ref, 1914(872)
Wolleat, P. L.: ref, 573(17), 578(4)
Wollert, R. W.: ref, 1498(5558)
Wollman, W. T.: ref, 1013(54)
Wolpe, J.: test, 883
Woltmann, A. G.: test, 2027; exc, 396, 964, 2037
Womack, S.: ref, 1257(155)
Womer, F.: rev, 344
Womer, F. B.: rev, 169, 174
Wonderlic, E. F.: rev, 464, 688, 940, 1493
Wonderlic (E. F.) & Associates, Inc.: test, 1218, 2637, 2638
Wong, B.: ref, 766(23, 25), 2217(121, 137), 2602(1724)
Wong, C.: ref, 558(59)
Wong, R.: ref, 766(23), 2217(121), 2602(1724)
Wood, C.: ref, 1904(112)
Wood, D.: ref, 558(70), 1498(5557), 2300(502)
Wood, D. A.: ref, 1808(12)
Wood, D. R.: ref, 794(450), 1331(42), 1498(5034, 5776), 1853(300), 2598(1293), 2621(218, 464)
Wood, E. R.: test, 242
Wood, F.: ref, 1655(73)
Wood, G. H.: ref, 354(1455)
Wood, G. S.: ref, 1192(178)
Wood, H. B.: rev, 344, 1473
Wood, J. B.: ref, 1498(5104, 5105)
Wood, K. A.: ref, 861(5), 2602(1848)
Wood, M.: test, 890; ref, 551(19), 1896(8)
Wood, M. H.: test, 1863
Wood, M. M.: ref, 2491(2072)
Wood, N. E.: ref, 751(9), 1371(246), 1771(584), 2621(273)
Wood, R. E.: ref, 2602(1725)
Wood, W. G.: ref, 2598(1642)
Wood, W. W.: ref, 1779(1)
Woodbury, R.: ref, 1209(34), 1720(33), 2657(106)
Woodcock, P. R.: ref, 374(204)
Woodcock, R. W.: test, 961, 962, 2639, 2640, 2641
Wooden, S.: ref, 551(53), 1479(309), 1896(7)
Woodford, P. E.: exc, 625; ref, 2441(33)
Woodman, R. W.: ref, 1798(269)
Woodmansee, J. J.: ref, 780(1681)

Woodruff, R.: ref, 1498(5144)
Woods, B. T.: ref, 2598(1806), 2602(2147)
Woods, D. J.: ref, 1498(5372), 1547(276), 2300(576), 2587(40, 45)
Woods, R. T.: ref, 308(8), 2607(188)
Woodward, H. R.: ref, 384(9)
Woodward, L. G.: test, 2228
Woodward, M.: ref, 2300(578), 2374(198)
Woodward, W. A.: ref, 1498(5336, 5677, 5678, 5694), 1914(859)
Woody, C.: rev, 2375, 2569
Woody, E.: ref, 860(101)
Woody, G.: ref, 1498(5168)
Woody, G. G.: ref, 1498(5672)
Woody, M. M.: ref, 780(1649), 1462(152), 1498(5128), 2208(1543), 2598(1741)
Woolfolk, R. L.: ref, 1197(310), 2300(460, 542)
Woolner, R. B.: test, 1879
Wooster, R. A.: ref, 501(860, 861)
Worcester, D. A.: rev, 1478; exc, 691
Worden, J. W.: ref, 1498(5529), 1904(100)
Worell, L.: ref, 76(609), 1798(227, 240)
Work, B. A.: ref, 2300(407)
Workman, B. L.: ref, 2602(1990)
Workman, E. A.: ref, 2602(1990)
Worland, J.: ref, 701(68), 751(33), 2030(5041, 5046, 5047), 2491(2065, 2073), 2598(1672, 1807), 2602(1958, 1991, 1992, 2148)
Wormack, L.: ref, 501(875, 915), 1013(95, 96, 118), 1257(151, 152), 2160(77)
Wormith, J. S.: ref, 354(1514), 1498(5088, 5559), 1853(288), 2208(1640)
Worms, P. F.: ref, 280(1043)
Worrall, E. P.: ref, 2598(1536), 2607(171)
Worrell, L.: ref, 1798(227)
Worsley, A.: ref, 859(964), 1940(85)
Wortel, L. H.: ref, 973(31), 1292(53), 1486(180)
Worthen, B. R.: rev, 804, 1279
Worthington, E. L.: ref, 2318(1550, 1610)
Wortis, J.: test, 1926
Woudenberg, R. A.: ref, 890(354), 1531(288), 1547(315), 1748(57)
Woychowski, B.: ref, 780(1642)
Wray, R. H.: ref, 1126(714)
Wren, F. L.: rev, 264
Wrenn, C. G.: test, 2342; rev, 2374, 2518
Wright, B. D.: test, 1260
Wright, B. M.: ref, 1765(14), 1904(122), 2100(10)
Wright, D.: ref, 280(1163), 701(81, 86), 2260(49), 2472(26, 27), 2602(1943, 2203), 2608(241, 248), 2621(355, 429, 452)
Wright, D. M.: ref, 1106(369), 2300(464)
Wright, E.: ref, 1162(21), 1498(5289)
Wright, E. N.: test, 361, 362, 2046; ref, 363(14)
Wright, E. W.: ref, 1960(71)
Wright, G. N.: test, 1055
Wright, H.: ref, 1013(128, 129)
Wright, H. W.: ref, 1498(5547, 5773)
Wright, J.: ref, 1798(218)
Wright, M. J.: ref, 581(15), 2289(1777)
Wright, P.: ref, 501(916)
Wright, T.: ref, 1419(678)
Wright, W. J.: rev, 1277, 2161
Wrightson, P.: ref, 1969(122), 2607(217)

Wrightstone, J. W.: test, 12, 13, 464, 1186, 1325, 1450; exc, 690, 2518, 2520
Wrinkle, W. L.: test, 264
Wrobel, T. A.: ref, 1498(5471)
Wu, W.: ref, 239(14), 1914(826)
Wudel, P.: ref, 860(135, 136), 1013(97), 2300(503, 504)
Wulach, J. S.: ref, 2030(4980)
Wulf, K.: ref, 606(13), 1498(5260)
Wulkan, P.: ref, 6(64), 1908(10)
Wurster, S.: ref, 1762(4)
Wyatt, J. W.: ref, 2286(326)
Wyatt, R. J.: ref, 280(1164), 2598(1372, 1449, 1703, 1704)
Wyckoff, W. L.: ref, 1949(60)
Wyke, M. A.: ref, 1914(824)
Wykoff, G. S.: test, 1939
Wylam, H.: test, 641
Wyle, H.: test, 2418
Wylie, J.: ref, 1498(5080), 2030(4950, 4951), 2598(1317)
Wyman, E. J.: test, 2357, 2358, 2360
Wyne, M. D.: ref, 1473(180, 190), 2582(12, 15), 2602(1931)
Wyrick, L.: ref, 2607(182)
Wyrick, L. C.: ref, 1547(277)
Wyrick, R. A.: ref, 1547(277)
Wysocki, A. C.: ref, 751(10)
Wysocki, B. A.: ref, 751(10)
Xelowski, H.: ref, 2300(605)
Yager, J.: ref, 2030(5035)
Yager, T. J.: ref, 1923(12)
Yale, C.: ref, 1351(27, 34, 36), 1498(5384, 5385, 5459)
Yalom, I.: ref, 1904(131)
Yamada, J.: ref, 549(3)
Yamamoto, K.: rev, 628, 630
Yamamura, H.: ref, 1498(5768), 1923(28)
Yamauchi, H.: ref, 780(1664), 2491(2035)
Yanagi, G.: ref, 6(79)
Yangquist, J.: ref, 1424(46), 2602(1892)
Yanico, B.: test, 370
Yanico, B. J.: ref, 2134(144)
Yankofsky, L.: ref, 1486(187), 1547(336), 1914(860)
Yanovski, A.: ref, 2030(5020, 5048, 5081), 2294(122)
Yanuzzi, J. R.: test, 169, 171, 172, 173, 1920
Yap, K. O.: ref, 932(103)
Yarber, W. L.: ref, 2208(1641)
Yarborough, B. H.: ref, 357(513, 515, 521, 522), 483(20, 24, 40, 41), 1272(133, 135, 141, 142), 1479(374, 375), 2260(36, 37, 50)
Yarborough, C.: ref, 794(376)
Yarbrough, C.: ref, 2602(1770)
Yard, G. J.: ref, 1192(257), 2621(449)
Yaroushi, R. A.: ref, 2620(5)
Yarrow, L. J.: ref, 270(115, 139)
Yarworth, J. S.: ref, 2413(636)
Yates, A. J.: rev, 793, 1778, 2179
Yates, C.: ref, 374(211, 223)
Yates, C. E.: ref, 751(7), 874(46), 1361(64), 2602(1679)
Yates, R. A.: ref, 1655(123)
Yawkey, T. D.: ref, 964(511), 1771(744)
Yeakey, C. C.: ref, 1508(138)
Yeates, S. R.: ref, 270(74), 1126(683), 1471(51), 2018(10), 2602(1722)

Yee, A. H.: rev, 2257
Yee, S.: ref, 6(79)
Yekovich, F. R.: ref, 653(150), 2246(27)
Yellin, A. M.: ref, 354(1493)
Yen, F. B.: ref, 1577(3)
Yen, J. K.: ref, 270(81), 1993(2), 2285(11), 2289(1662), 2557(221)
Yen, W. M.: ref, 344(163, 188), 551(34, 73), 2181(14)
Yerxa, E. J.: ref, 2244(43)
Yesavage, J. A.: ref, 1498(5701)
Yeudall, L.: ref, 1914(828), 1948(99)
Yinon, Y.: ref, 1914(831)
Yoch, K.: ref, 501(811)
Yoder, J.: ref, 1547(264), 2598(1366)
Yonge, G.: test, 1726
Yonge, G. D.: ref, 1726(357, 364), 1789(658)
Yongue, I. T.: ref, 374(235)
Yore, L. D.: ref, 226(167), 482(7), 1013(115), 1479(331)
York, R.: ref, 2289(1607)
Yorkston, K. M.: ref, 1851(44)
Yorkston, N.: ref, 1883(67)
Yorkston, N. J.: test, 2322
Yoshimura, I.: ref, 2602(1859)
Yoshioka–Maxwell, B.: ref, 552(4), 553(21)
Yost, M.: ref, 1073(118)
Young, A.: ref, 296(10), 2179(230)
Young, C. D.: ref, 1257(120, 153)
Young, D.: test, 1019, 1025, 1616, 1740, 2249, 2250
Young, E. C.: test, 1768
Young, J. A.: ref, 1547(344)
Young, J. C.: test, 2476
Young, M.: ref, 1914(861), 2208(1675)
Young, R. A.: ref, 372(6), 2029(220)
Young, R. C.: ref, 1498(5733), 1922(15, 19), 1933(20)
Young, R. D.: ref, 1498(5741), 2598(1550)
Young, R. J.: ref, 653(163), 859(742), 1547(255), 2208(1540, 1559, 1653)
Young, R. V.: test, 168, 170, 175
Young, V.: ref, 116(561), 1798(239)
Youngman, M. B.: ref, 252(1), 775(1), 928(6), 1620(20)
Youngren, M. A.: ref, 1498(5734)
Youngsmith, N.: ref, 2289(1687), 2602(1814), 2608(206)
Youniss, R. P.: test, 1173, 1747
Younng, J. H.: test, 2068
Yozawitz, A.: ref, 1883(59)
Ysseldyke, J.: ref, 2602(2230), 2639(3)
Ysseldyke, J. E.: rev, 2331; ref, 701(42), 1622(39), 1769(49, 68), 1771(611), 2269(446)
Yu, H. K.: ref, 2179(231)
Yuen, R. K. W.: ref, 1495(89)
Yufit, R.: test, 2505
Yuker, H. E.: test, 2068
Yule, W.: rev, 2625; exc, 1459; ref, 2221(8)
Yunis, J. J.: ref, 381(61), 2557(218)
Zabel, R. H.: ref, 1771(710)
Zachman, L.: test, 1736, 1737, 2648
Zagar, R.: ref, 226(182), 1914(873), 2602(2149), 2607(173), 2621(430)
Zager, L. D.: ref, 1498(5777)
Zager, R.: ref, 280(1063), 1007(40), 1462(127), 2598(1421), 2607(150)
Zahn, G. L.: ref, 398(95), 551(16), 582(4)

INDEX OF NAMES

Zahn, T. P.: ref, 860(131), 1771(752)
Zahner, L. C.: rev, 2163
Zaichkowsky, L. D.: test, 1386; ref, 1386(1), 1831(143)
Zaidel, D.: ref, 627(21), 1356(97), 1506(72), 1774(12), 1948(96), 2317(10)
Zaidel, D. W.: ref, 1914(899)
Zaidel, E.: ref, 1126(747), 1914(899)
Zais, R. S.: ref, 720(68)
Zajonc, R. B.: ref, 500(57), 501(917)
Zak, I.: ref, 1233(228), 2208(1642)
Zaki, S.: ref, 1883(67)
Zaleski, Z.: ref, 1419(685)
Zalinski, J. S.: ref, 2318(1599)
Zalk, S. R.: test, 1241
Zalma, R.: ref, 1424(39)
Zamansky, H. S.: ref, 2294(117)
Zambianco, D.: ref, 1883(76), 2030(5072), 2598(1772)
Zammarelli, J. E.: ref, 149(15), 653(176)
Zampogna, J.: ref, 477(25)
Zane, T.: test, 1134, 2572
Zangwill, O. L.: rev, 963, 1239
Zanotti, R. J.: ref, 226(179), 962(32), 2217(164), 2280(13)
Zarantonello, M. M.: ref, 1498(5560)
Zarcone, V.: ref, 2598(1429)
Zarcone, V. P.: ref, 1498(5742)
Zarle, T. H.: ref, 1099(66)
Zarski, J. J.: ref, 354(1429, 1479), 2217(164), 2208(1608)
Zax, M.: ref, 645(12), 1197(286)
Zayat, M.: ref, 794(401), 1789(676)
Zedeck, S.: rev, 1495, 1497; ref, 384(4), 1300(115), 1914(738), 2553(1)
Zegans, L. S.: ref, 1229(83)
Zegans, S.: ref, 1229(83)
Zehrbach, R. R.: test, 550
Zeichner, K. M.: ref, 344(164)
Zeiss, A. M.: ref, 1498(5140, 5561)
Zeiss, R. A.: ref, 1498(5140), 2598(1327)
Zeitner, R. M.: ref, 116(600), 2413(666)
Zeitschel, K. A.: ref, 701(72), 1540(17)
Zekulin-Hartley, X. Y.: ref, 2217(186)
Zeldow, P. B.: ref, 116(554)
Zeleznik, C.: ref, 1576(208)
Zelickman, I.: test, 1340
Zella, W. F.: ref, 1341(170), 1754(69), 2602(1732)
Zeltzer, L.: ref, 2300(538, 577)
Zemelman, D.: ref, 890(339)
Zemore, R.: ref, 681(51, 52, 63), 1498(5562), 1547(316)
Zendel, I. H.: ref, 400(136), 2602(2150)
Zenetron, Inc.: test, 2550
Zenith Hearing Instrument Corporation: test, 916, 2668, 2669
Zenner, A. A.: ref, 1771(684)
Zentall, S. S.: ref, 701(56), 1371(251)
Zentall, T. R.: ref, 701(56), 1371(251)
Zenzen, M. J.: ref, 2029(210)
Zeskind, P. S.: ref, 270(101), 2289(1695)
Zetler, A. G.: ref, 76(597), 1866(33)
Zheutlin, S.: ref, 118(250), 1498(5226)
Ziarnik, J.: ref, 2289(1767), 2598(1774), 2602(2103)
Ziarnik, J. P.: ref, 1498(5227)
Zibrin, M.: ref, 344(176), 543(29), 1191(129), 2160(70), 2298(2)

Ziegfeld, E.: rev, 1110, 1460
Ziegler, M. E.: ref, 2598(1673)
Ziegler, R.: ref, 1498(5399)
Zielinski, J. J.: ref, 1498(5563)
Zielony, R. D.: ref, 1919(45), 2179(241), 2620(18)
Ziesat, H. A.: ref, 1498(5400, 5401, 5402), 1757(14, 15), 2607(203, 212)
Zifcak, M.: ref, 2217(187), 2621(465)
Ziff, D.: ref, 1498(5168)
Ziff, D. R.: ref, 1498(5322, 5672)
Zigler, E.: ref, 1498(5495), 1771(550, 748), 2179(226)
Zigler, E. F.: ref, 1771(810)
Zigler-Shini, Z.: ref, 859(747)
Zigmond, N.: ref, 553(25), 720(70), 2621(447)
Zilberg, N. J.: ref, 1170(230)
Zilstorff, K.: ref, 2598(1537)
Zimet, C. N.: ref, 116(544)
Zimet, S. G.: ref, 116(544), 302(27), 1126(652), 1853(284), 2602(1608, 1907), 2621(231)
Zimmer, C.: ref, 357(514)
Zimmer, J. W.: ref, 1568(136, 139, 144), 2512(644)
Zimmer, S. E.: ref, 2246(25)
Zimmerman, A.: ref, 1498(5549, 5727), 2179(229)
Zimmerman, I. L.: test, 1877
Zimmerman, J. C.: ref, 1498(5775)
Zimmerman, J. J.: test, 2670
Zimmerman, R.: test, 695
Zimmerman, R. A.: ref, 2598(1664)
Zimmerman, R. R.: ref, 1969(98)
Zimmerman, W. S.: test, 1043, 1044, 1045, 1046, 1257, 2340; rev, 501, 1866; ref, 76(599), 501(812), 551(23), 1046(567), 2340(11)
Zimmermann, M.: ref, 2374(175)
Zimmermann, M. L.: ref, 588(7), 1991(123, 124), 2374(174, 178, 189)
Zinck, R. A.: ref, 2292(26)
Zingale, S. A.: ref, 1473(166), 1831(155), 2602(1822, 1856)
Zinkin, P.: test, 2019
Zinkus, P. W.: ref, 280(1128), 2598(1674), 2602(1857, 1993), 2621(315, 378)
Zinner, E. G.: test, 2618
Zino, T. C.: ref, 1424(49, 50), 2289(1720)
Zion, T. E.: ref, 280(1073), 1126(692), 2602(1740)
Zirkel, K.: ref, 860(102), 2343(1036), 2629(103)
Ziskind, E.: ref, 609(205), 1498(5716), 2179(209)
Zisook, S.: ref, 1498(5403), 2300(452)
Zitlow, D.: test, 1232
Zlotowitz, H. I.: ref, 1240(53), 2318(1565)
Zmud, R. W.: ref, 116(524)
Zoccolotti, P.: ref, 794(410, 430), 1257(154), 2269(472, 482)
Zohn, C. J.: ref, 1798(196)
Zola-Morgan, S. M.: ref, 1914(855, 856), 2598(1755, 1756), 2607(204, 205)
Zoltan, V.: ref, 1771(615)
Zoppel, C. L.: ref, 116(590)
Zoref, L.: ref, 653(170), 1771(770), 2217(178), 2289(1778), 2598(1808), 2602(2151)
Zoss, S. K.: test, 1169
Zotterman, A.: ref, 2030(4983)
Zubin, J.: test, 2588
Zucea, R.: ref, 2512(567)
Zucker, G.: ref, 1351(199), 2300(580), 2598(1811), 2607(213)

713

Zucker, K. B.: ref, 357(505), 1831(122, 189)
Zucker, R. A.: ref, 354(1577), 917(77)
Zuckerman, C.: ref, 321(45), 2012(3)
Zuckerman, D. M.: ref, 76(622), 1419(702)
Zuckerman, E.: ref, 2491(2074)
Zuckerman, M.: test, 1547; ref, 116(538), 780(1655), 859(819, 886), 860(105, 115), 883(80, 86), 1498(5526), 1789(706), 2300(377, 416), 2491(2025)
Zulliger, H.: test, 2672
Zullo, T. G.: ref, 501(882), 2217(161)
Zultowski, W. H.: ref, 116(549, 583), 1508(122, 131), 2318(1523, 1553)
Zurif, E. B.: ref, 308(15)
Zuroff, D. C.: ref, 116(579, 580), 1931(52), 2037(152)
Zusman, J.: exc, 1883
Zweifler, A.: ref, 1197(274), 2208(1529)
Zweig (Richard L.) Associates, Inc.: test, 913, 914, 915
Zweigenhaft, R. L.: ref, 354(1556)
Zwitman, D. H.: ref, 212(6)
Zytowski, D. G.: rev, 374, 1051, 1183, 2624; ref, 1270(76, 78, 79, 81), 2134(129), 2318(1603)
Zyzanski, S. J.: test, 1206; ref, 1498(5116)